# *Time Series Analysis*

# *Time Series Analysis*

James D. Hamilton

PRINCETON UNIVERSITY PRESS
PRINCETON, NEW JERSEY

Published by Princeton University Press, 41 William St.,
Princeton, New Jersey 08540
In the United Kingdom: Princeton University Press,
Chichester, West Sussex



**Library of Congress Cataloging-in-Publication Data**
Hamilton, James D. (James Douglas), (1954–)
Time series analysis / James D. Hamilton.
p. cm.
Includes bibliographical references and indexes.
ISBN 0-691-04289-6
1. Time-series analysis. I. Title.
QA280.H264 1994
519.5′5—dc20 93-4958
CIP

This book has been composed in Times Roman.

Princeton University Press books are printed on acid-free paper and meet the guidelines for permanence and durability of the Committee on Production Guidelines for Book Longevity of the Council on Library Resources.

Printed in the United States of America

10 9 8 7 6 5 4 3 2

# *Contents*

## 4 *Forecasting* *72*



## 5 *Maximum Likelihood Estimation* *117*

# *Preface*

Much of economics is concerned with modeling dynamics. There has been an explosion of research in this area in the last decade, as "time series econometrics" has practically come to be synonymous with "empirical macroeconomics."

Several texts provide good coverage of the advances in the economic analysis of dynamic systems, while others summarize the earlier literature on statistical inference for time series data. There seemed a use for a text that could integrate the theoretical and empirical issues as well as incorporate the many advances of the last decade, such as the analysis of vector autoregressions, estimation by generalized method of moments, and statistical inference for nonstationary data. This is the goal of *Time Series Analysis*.

A principal anticipated use of the book would be as a textbook for a graduate econometrics course in time series analysis. The book aims for maximum flexibility through what might be described as an integrated modular structure. As an example of this, the first three sections of Chapter 13 on the Kalman filter could be covered right after Chapter 4, if desired. Alternatively, Chapter 13 could be skipped altogether without loss of comprehension. Despite this flexibility, state-space ideas are fully integrated into the text beginning with Chapter 1, where a state-space representation is used (without any jargon or formalism) to introduce the key results concerning difference equations. Thus, when the reader encounters the formal development of the state-space framework and the Kalman filter in Chapter 13, the notation and key ideas should already be quite familiar.

Spectral analysis (Chapter 6) is another topic that could be covered at a point of the reader's choosing or skipped altogether. In this case, the integrated modular structure is achieved by the early introduction and use of autocovariance-generating functions and filters. Wherever possible, results are described in terms of these rather than the spectrum.

Although the book is designed with an econometrics couse in time series methods in mind, the book should be useful for several other purposes. It is completely self-contained, starting from basic principles accessible to first-year graduate students and including an extensive math review appendix. Thus the book would be quite suitable for a first-year graduate course in macroeconomics or dynamic methods that has no econometric content. Such a course might use Chapters 1 and 2, Sections 3.1 through 3.5, and Sections 4.1 and 4.2.

Yet another intended use for the book would be in a conventional econometrics course without an explicit time series focus. The popular econometrics texts do not have much discussion of such topics as numerical methods; asymptotic results for serially dependent, heterogeneously distributed observations; estimation of models with distributed lags; autocorrelation- and heteroskedasticity-consistent standard errors; Bayesian analysis; or generalized method of moments. All of these topics receive extensive treatment in *Time Series Analysis*. Thus, an econometrics course without an explicit focus on time series might make use of Sections 3.1 through 3.5, Chapters 7 through 9, and Chapter 14, and perhaps any of Chapters 5, 11, and 12 as well. Again, the text is self-contained, with a fairly complete discussion of conventional simultaneous equations methods in Chapter 9. Indeed, a very important goal of the text is to develop the parallels between (1) the traditional econometric approach to simultaneous equations and (2) the current popularity of vector autoregressions and generalized method of moments estimation.

Finally, the book attempts to provide a rigorous motivation for the methods and yet still be accessible for researchers with purely applied interests. This is achieved by relegation of many details to mathematical appendixes at the ends of chapters, and by inclusion of numerous examples that illustrate exactly how the theoretical results are used and applied in practice.

The book developed out of my lectures at the University of Virginia. I am grateful first and foremost to my many students over the years whose questions and comments have shaped the course of the manuscript. I also have an enormous debt to numerous colleagues who have kindly offered many useful suggestions, and would like to thank in particular Donald W. K. Andrews, Jushan Bai, Peter Bearse, Stephen R. Blough, John Cochrane, George Davis, Michael Dotsey, John Elder, Robert Engle, T. Wake Epps, Marjorie Flavin, John Geweke, Eric Ghysels, Carlo Giannini, Clive W. J. Granger, Alastair Hall, Bruce E. Hansen, Kevin Hassett, Tomoo Inoue, Ravi Jagannathan, Kenneth F. Kroner, Jaime Marquez, Rocco Mosconi, Masao Ogaki, Adrian Pagan, Peter C. B. Phillips, Peter Rappoport, Glenn Rudebusch, Raul Susmel, Mark Watson, Kenneth D. West, Halbert White, and Jeffrey M. Wooldridge. I would also like to thank Pok-sang Lam and John Rogers for graciously sharing their data. Thanks also go to Keith Sill and Christopher Stomberg for assistance with the figures, to Rita Chen for assistance with the statistical tables in Appendix B, and to Richard Mickey for a superb job of copy editing.

*James D. Hamilton*

# *Time Series Analysis*

# 1

# Difference Equations

## 1.1. *First-Order Difference Equations*

This book is concerned with the dynamic consequences of events over time. Let's say we are studying a variable whose value at date $t$ is denoted $y_t$. Suppose we are given a dynamic equation relating the value $y$ takes on at date $t$ to another variable $w_t$ and to the value $y$ took on in the previous period:

$$y_t = \phi y_{t-1} + w_t. \qquad [1.1.1]$$

Equation [1.1.1] is a *linear first-order difference equation*. A *difference equation* is an expression relating a variable $y_t$ to its previous values. This is a *first-order* difference equation because only the first lag of the variable ($y_{t-1}$) appears in the equation. Note that it expresses $y_t$ as a linear function of $y_{t-1}$ and $w_t$.

An example of [1.1.1] is Goldfeld's (1973) estimated money demand function for the United States. Goldfeld's model related the log of the real money holdings of the public ($m_t$) to the log of aggregate real income ($I_t$), the log of the interest rate on bank accounts ($r_{bt}$), and the log of the interest rate on commercial paper ($r_{ct}$):

$$m_t = 0.27 + 0.72m_{t-1} + 0.19I_t - 0.045r_{bt} - 0.019r_{ct}. \qquad [1.1.2]$$

This is a special case of [1.1.1] with $y_t = m_t$, $\phi = 0.72$, and

$$w_t = 0.27 + 0.19I_t - 0.045r_{bt} - 0.019r_{ct}.$$

For purposes of analyzing the dynamics of such a system, it simplifies the algebra a little to summarize the effects of all the input variables ($I_t$, $r_{bt}$, and $r_{ct}$) in terms of a scalar $w_t$ as here.

In Chapter 3 the input variable $w_t$ will be regarded as a random variable, and the implications of [1.1.1] for the statistical properties of the output series $y_t$ will be explored. In preparation for this discussion, it is necessary first to understand the mechanics of difference equations. For the discussion in Chapters 1 and 2, the values for the input variable $\{w_1, w_2, \ldots\}$ will simply be regarded as a sequence of deterministic numbers. Our goal is to answer the following question: If a dynamic system is described by [1.1.1], what are the effects on $y$ of changes in the value of $w$?

### *Solving a Difference Equation by Recursive Substitution*

The presumption is that the dynamic equation [1.1.1] governs the behavior of $y$ for all dates $t$. Thus, for each date we have an equation relating the value of

$y$ for that date to its previous value and the current value of $w$:

| *Date* | *Equation* | |
|---|---|---|
| 0 | $y_0 = \phi y_{-1} + w_0$ | [1.1.3] |
| 1 | $y_1 = \phi y_0 + w_1$ | [1.1.4] |
| 2 | $y_2 = \phi y_1 + w_2$ | [1.1.5] |
| $\vdots$ | $\vdots$ | |
| $t$ | $y_t = \phi y_{t-1} + w_t.$ | [1.1.6] |

If we know the starting value of $y$ for date $t = -1$ and the value of $w$ for dates $t = 0, 1, 2, \ldots$, then it is possible to simulate this dynamic system to find the value of $y$ for any date. For example, if we know the value of $y$ for $t = -1$ and the value of $w$ for $t = 0$, we can calculate the value of $y$ for $t = 0$ directly from [1.1.3]. Given this value of $y_0$ and the value of $w$ for $t = 1$, we can calculate the value of $y$ for $t = 1$ from [1.1.4]:

$$y_1 = \phi y_0 + w_1 = \phi(\phi y_{-1} + w_0) + w_1,$$

or

$$y_1 = \phi^2 y_{-1} + \phi w_0 + w_1.$$

Given this value of $y_1$ and the value of $w$ for $t = 2$, we can calculate the value of $y$ for $t = 2$ from [1.1.5]:

$$y_2 = \phi y_1 + w_2 = \phi(\phi^2 y_{-1} + \phi w_0 + w_1) + w_2,$$

or

$$y_2 = \phi^3 y_{-1} + \phi^2 w_0 + \phi w_1 + w_2.$$

Continuing recursively in this fashion, the value that $y$ takes on at date $t$ can be described as a function of its initial value $y_{-1}$ and the history of $w$ between date 0 and date $t$:

$$y_t = \phi^{t+1} y_{-1} + \phi^t w_0 + \phi^{t-1} w_1 + \phi^{t-2} w_2 + \cdots + \phi w_{t-1} + w_t. \quad [1.1.7]$$

This procedure is known as solving the difference equation [1.1.1] by *recursive substitution.*

## *Dynamic Multipliers*

Note that [1.1.7] expresses $y_t$ as a linear function of the initial value $y_{-1}$ and the historical values of $w$. This makes it very easy to calculate the effect of $w_0$ on $y_t$. If $w_0$ were to change with $y_{-1}$ and $w_1, w_2, \ldots, w_t$ taken as unaffected, the effect on $y_t$ would be given by

$$\frac{\partial y_t}{\partial w_0} = \phi^t. \quad [1.1.8]$$

Note that the calculations would be exactly the same if the dynamic simulation were started at date $t$ (taking $y_{t-1}$ as given); then $y_{t+j}$ could be described as a function of $y_{t-1}$ and $w_t, w_{t+1}, \ldots, w_{t+j}$:

$$y_{t+j} = \phi^{j+1}y_{t-1} + \phi^j w_t + \phi^{j-1}w_{t+1} + \phi^{j-2}w_{t+2} + \cdots + \phi w_{t+j-1} + w_{t+j}. \qquad [1.1.9]$$

The effect of $w_t$ on $y_{t+j}$ is given by

$$\frac{\partial y_{t+j}}{\partial w_t} = \phi^j. \qquad [1.1.10]$$

Thus the *dynamic multiplier* [1.1.10] depends only on $j$, the length of time separating the disturbance to the input ($w_t$) and the observed value of the output ($y_{t+j}$). The multiplier does not depend on $t$; that is, it does not depend on the dates of the observations themselves. This is true of any linear difference equation.

As an example of calculating a dynamic multiplier, consider again Goldfeld's money demand specification [1.1.2]. Suppose we want to know what will happen to money demand two quarters from now if current income $I_t$ were to increase by one unit today with future income $I_{t+1}$ and $I_{t+2}$ unaffected:

$$\frac{\partial m_{t+2}}{\partial I_t} = \frac{\partial m_{t+2}}{\partial w_t} \times \frac{\partial w_t}{\partial I_t} = \phi^2 \times \frac{\partial w_t}{\partial I_t}.$$

From [1.1.2], a one-unit increase in $I_t$ will increase $w_t$ by 0.19 units, meaning that $\partial w_t/\partial I_t = 0.19$. Since $\phi = 0.72$, we calculate

$$\frac{\partial m_{t+2}}{\partial I_t} = (0.72)^2(0.19) = 0.098.$$

Because $I_t$ is the log of income, an increase in $I_t$ of 0.01 units corresponds to a 1% increase in income. An increase in $m_t$ of $(0.01)\cdot(0.098) \cong 0.001$ corresponds to a 0.1% increase in money holdings. Thus the public would be expected to increase its money holdings by a little less than 0.1% two quarters following a 1% increase in income.

Different values of $\phi$ in [1.1.1] can produce a variety of dynamic responses of $y$ to $w$. If $0 < \phi < 1$, the multiplier $\partial y_{t+j}/\partial w_t$ in [1.1.10] decays geometrically toward zero. Panel (a) of Figure 1.1 plots $\phi^j$ as a function of $j$ for $\phi = 0.8$. If $-1 < \phi < 0$, the multiplier $\partial y_{t+j}/\partial w_t$ will alternate in sign as in panel (b). In this case an increase in $w_t$ will cause $y_t$ to be higher, $y_{t+1}$ to be lower, $y_{t+2}$ to be higher, and so on. Again the absolute value of the effect decays geometrically toward zero. If $\phi > 1$, the dynamic multiplier increases exponentially over time as in panel (c). A given increase in $w_t$ has a larger effect the farther into the future one goes. For $\phi < -1$, the system [1.1.1] exhibits explosive oscillation as in panel (d).

Thus, if $|\phi| < 1$, the system is stable; the consequences of a given change in $w_t$ will eventually die out. If $|\phi| > 1$, the system is explosive. An interesting possibility is the borderline case, $\phi = 1$. In this case, the solution [1.1.9] becomes

$$y_{t+j} = y_{t-1} + w_t + w_{t+1} + w_{t+2} + \cdots + w_{t+j-1} + w_{t+j}. \qquad [1.1.11]$$

Here the output variable $y$ is the sum of the historical inputs $w$. A one-unit increase in $w$ will cause a permanent one-unit increase in $y$:

$$\frac{\partial y_{t+j}}{\partial w_t} = 1 \qquad \text{for } j = 0, 1, \ldots.$$

We might also be interested in the effect of $w$ on the present value of the stream of future realizations of $y$. For a given stream of future values $y_t, y_{t+1},$

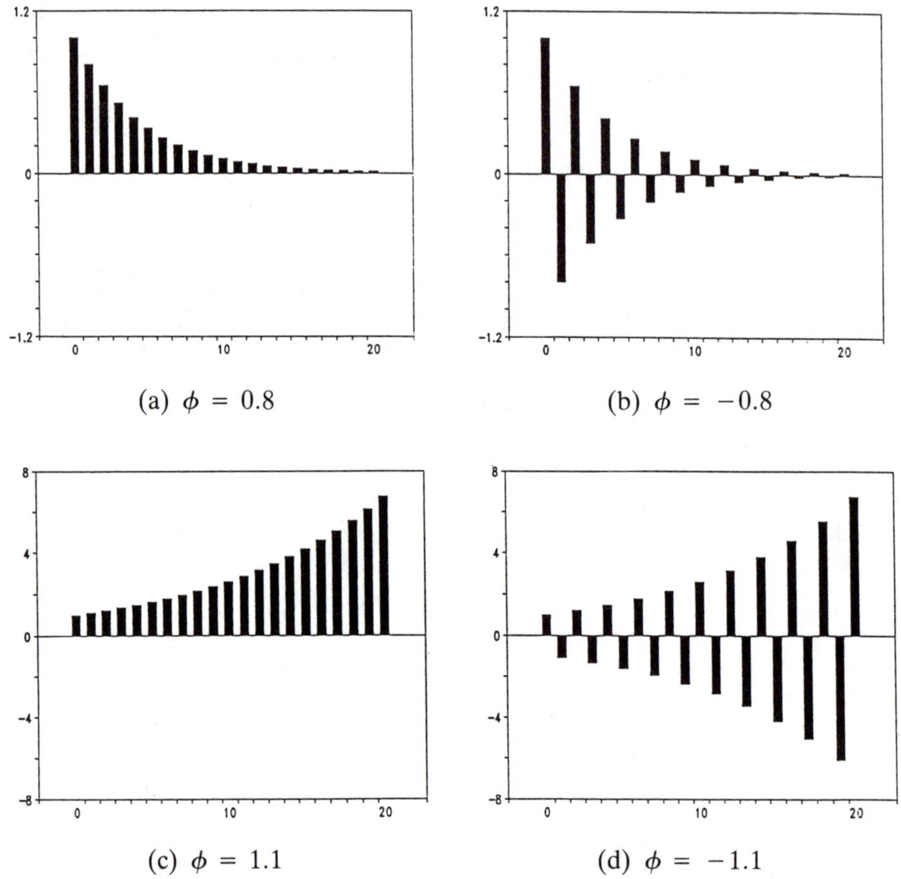


**FIGURE 1.1** Dynamic multiplier for first-order difference equation for different values of $\phi$ (plot of $\partial y_{t+j}/\partial w_t = \phi^j$ as a function of the lag $j$).

$y_{t+2}, \ldots$ and a constant interest rate[1] $r > 0$, the *present value* of the stream at time $t$ is given by

$$y_t + \frac{y_{t+1}}{1 + r} + \frac{y_{t+2}}{(1 + r)^2} + \frac{y_{t+3}}{(1 + r)^3} + \cdots. \qquad [1.1.12]$$

Let $\beta$ denote the discount factor:

$$\beta \equiv 1/(1 + r).$$

Note that $0 < \beta < 1$. Then the present value [1.1.12] can be written as

$$\sum_{j=0}^{\infty} \beta^j y_{t+j}. \qquad [1.1.13]$$

Consider what would happen if there were a one-unit increase in $w_t$ with $w_{t+1}, w_{t+2}, \ldots$ unaffected. The consequences of this change for the present value of $y$ are found by differentiating [1.1.13] with respect to $w_t$ and then using [1.1.10]

[1]The interest rate is measured here as a fraction of 1; thus $r = 0.1$ corresponds to a 10% interest rate.

to evaluate each derivative:

$$\sum_{j=0}^{\infty} \beta^j \frac{\partial y_{t+j}}{\partial w_t} = \sum_{j=0}^{\infty} \beta^j \phi^j = 1/(1 - \beta\phi), \qquad [1.1.14]$$

provided that $|\beta\phi| < 1$.

In calculating the dynamic multipliers [1.1.10] or [1.1.14], we were asking what would happen if $w_t$ were to increase by one unit with $w_{t+1}, w_{t+2}, \ldots, w_{t+j}$ unaffected. We were thus finding the effect of a purely transitory change in $w$. Panel (a) of Figure 1.2 shows the time path of $w$ associated with this question, and panel (b) shows the implied path for $y$. Because the dynamic multiplier [1.1.10] calculates the response of $y$ to a single impulse in $w$, it is also referred to as the *impulse-response function*.

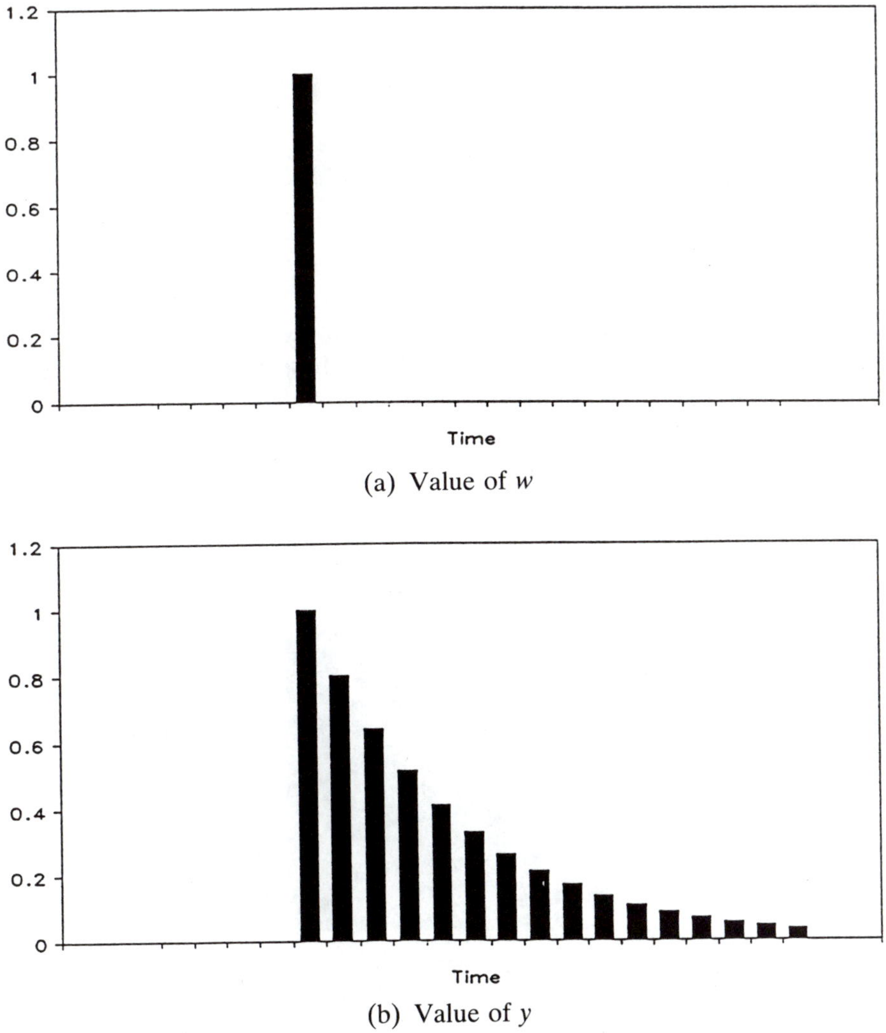


**FIGURE 1.2** Paths of input variable ($w_t$) and output variable ($y_t$) assumed for dynamic multiplier and present-value calculations.

Sometimes we might instead be interested in the consequences of a permanent change in $w$. A permanent change in $w$ means that $w_t, w_{t+1}, \ldots,$ and $w_{t+j}$ would all increase by one unit, as in Figure 1.3. From formula [1.1.10], the effect on $y_{t+j}$ of a permanent change in $w$ beginning in period $t$ is given by

$$\frac{\partial y_{t+j}}{\partial w_t} + \frac{\partial y_{t+j}}{\partial w_{t+1}} + \frac{\partial y_{t+j}}{\partial w_{t+2}} + \cdots + \frac{\partial y_{t+j}}{\partial w_{t+j}} = \phi^j + \phi^{j-1} + \phi^{j-2} + \cdots + \phi + 1.$$

When $|\phi| < 1$, the limit of this expression as $j$ goes to infinity is sometimes described as the "long-run" effect of $w$ on $y$:

$$\begin{aligned}\lim_{j\to\infty}\left[\frac{\partial y_{t+j}}{\partial w_t} + \frac{\partial y_{t+j}}{\partial w_{t+1}} + \frac{\partial y_{t+j}}{\partial w_{t+2}} + \cdots + \frac{\partial y_{t+j}}{\partial w_{t+j}}\right] &= 1 + \phi + \phi^2 + \cdots \\ &= 1/(1 - \phi).\end{aligned} \qquad [1.1.15]$$

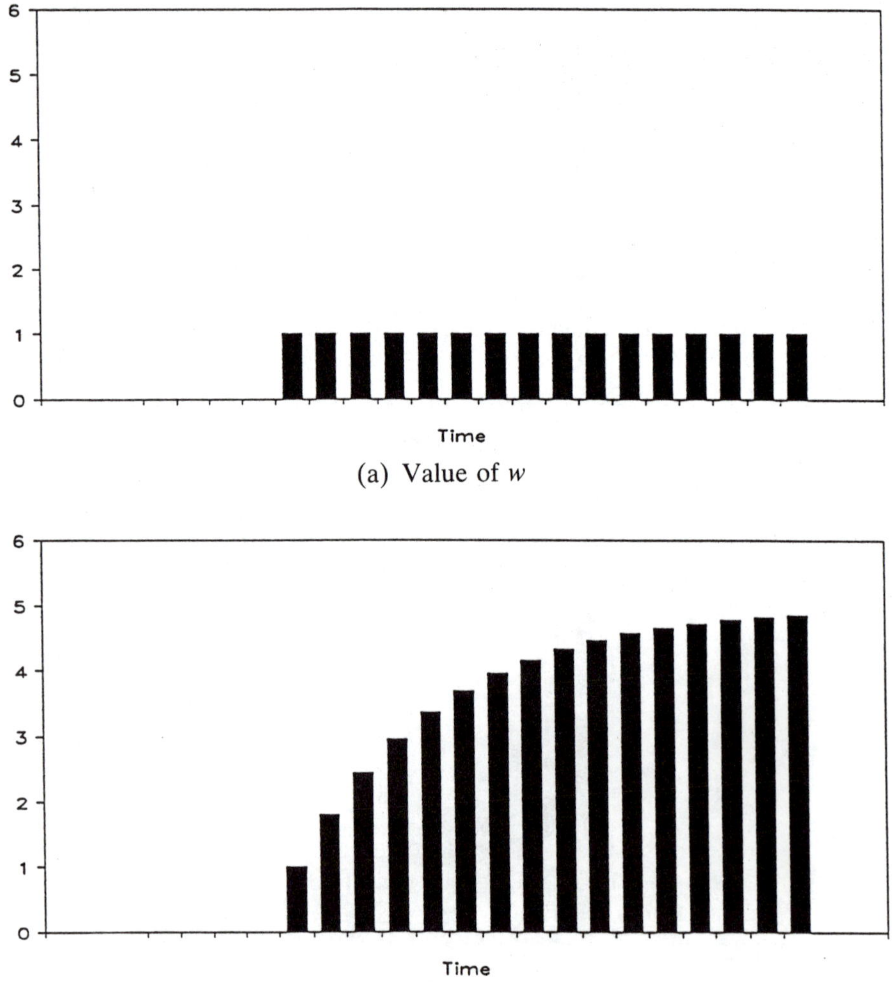


(a) Value of $w$



(b) Value of $y$

**FIGURE 1.3** Paths of input variable ($w_t$) and output variable ($y_t$) assumed for long-run effect calculations.

For example, the long-run income elasticity of money demand in the system [1.1.2] is given by

$$\frac{0.19}{1 - 0.72} = 0.68.$$

A permanent 1% increase in income will eventually lead to a 0.68% increase in money demand.

Another related question concerns the cumulative consequences for $y$ of a one-time change in $w$. Here we consider a transitory disturbance to $w$ as in panel (a) of Figure 1.2, but wish to calculate the sum of the consequences for all future values of $y$. Another way to think of this is as the effect on the present value of $y$ [1.1.13] with the discount rate $\beta = 1$. Setting $\beta = 1$ in [1.1.14] shows this cumulative effect to be equal to

$$\sum_{j=0}^{\infty} \frac{\partial y_{t+j}}{\partial w_t} = 1/(1 - \phi), \qquad [1.1.16]$$

provided that $|\phi| < 1$. Note that the cumulative effect on $y$ of a transitory change in $w$ (expression [1.1.16]) is the same as the long-run effect on $y$ of a permanent change in $w$ (expression [1.1.15]).

## 1.2. *p*th-Order Difference Equations

Let us now generalize the dynamic system [1.1.1] by allowing the value of $y$ at date $t$ to depend on $p$ of its own lags along with the current value of the input variable $w_t$:

$$y_t = \phi_1 y_{t-1} + \phi_2 y_{t-2} + \cdots + \phi_p y_{t-p} + w_t. \qquad [1.2.1]$$

Equation [1.2.1] is a linear $p$th-order difference equation.

It is often convenient to rewrite the $p$th-order difference equation [1.2.1] in the scalar $y_t$ as a first-order difference equation in a vector $\boldsymbol{\xi}_t$. Define the $(p \times 1)$ vector $\boldsymbol{\xi}_t$ by

$$\boldsymbol{\xi}_t \equiv \begin{bmatrix} y_t \\ y_{t-1} \\ y_{t-2} \\ \vdots \\ y_{t-p+1} \end{bmatrix}. \qquad [1.2.2]$$

That is, the first element of the vector $\boldsymbol{\xi}$ at date $t$ is the value $y$ took on at date $t$. The second element of $\boldsymbol{\xi}_t$ is the value $y$ took on at date $t - 1$, and so on. Define the $(p \times p)$ matrix $\mathbf{F}$ by

$$\mathbf{F} \equiv \begin{bmatrix} \phi_1 & \phi_2 & \phi_3 & \cdots & \phi_{p-1} & \phi_p \\ 1 & 0 & 0 & \cdots & 0 & 0 \\ 0 & 1 & 0 & \cdots & 0 & 0 \\ \vdots & \vdots & \vdots & \cdots & \vdots & \vdots \\ 0 & 0 & 0 & \cdots & 1 & 0 \end{bmatrix}. \qquad [1.2.3]$$

For example, for $p = 4$, $\mathbf{F}$ refers to the following $4 \times 4$ matrix:

$$\mathbf{F} = \begin{bmatrix} \phi_1 & \phi_2 & \phi_3 & \phi_4 \\ 1 & 0 & 0 & 0 \\ 0 & 1 & 0 & 0 \\ 0 & 0 & 1 & 0 \end{bmatrix}.$$

For $p = 1$ (the first-order difference equation [1.1.1]), $\mathbf{F}$ is just the scalar $\phi$. Finally, define the $(p \times 1)$ vector $\mathbf{v}_t$ by

$$\mathbf{v}_t \equiv \begin{bmatrix} w_t \\ 0 \\ 0 \\ \vdots \\ 0 \end{bmatrix}. \qquad [1.2.4]$$

Consider the following first-order vector difference equation:

$$\boldsymbol{\xi}_t = \mathbf{F}\boldsymbol{\xi}_{t-1} + \mathbf{v}_t, \qquad [1.2.5]$$

or

$$\begin{bmatrix} y_t \\ y_{t-1} \\ y_{t-2} \\ \vdots \\ y_{t-p+1} \end{bmatrix} = \begin{bmatrix} \phi_1 & \phi_2 & \phi_3 & \cdots & \phi_{p-1} & \phi_p \\ 1 & 0 & 0 & \cdots & 0 & 0 \\ 0 & 1 & 0 & \cdots & 0 & 0 \\ \vdots & \vdots & \vdots & \cdots & \vdots & \vdots \\ 0 & 0 & 0 & \cdots & 1 & 0 \end{bmatrix} \begin{bmatrix} y_{t-1} \\ y_{t-2} \\ y_{t-3} \\ \vdots \\ y_{t-p} \end{bmatrix} + \begin{bmatrix} w_t \\ 0 \\ 0 \\ \vdots \\ 0 \end{bmatrix}.$$

This is a system of $p$ equations. The first equation in this system is identical to equation [1.2.1]. The second equation is simply the identity

$$y_{t-1} = y_{t-1},$$

owing to the fact that the second element of $\boldsymbol{\xi}_t$ is the same as the first element of $\boldsymbol{\xi}_{t-1}$. The third equation in [1.2.5] states that $y_{t-2} = y_{t-2}$; the $p$th equation states that $y_{t-p+1} = y_{t-p+1}$.

Thus, the first-order vector system [1.2.5] is simply an alternative representation of the $p$th-order scalar system [1.2.1]. The advantage of rewriting the $p$th-order system [1.2.1] in the form of a first-order system [1.2.5] is that first-order systems are often easier to work with than $p$th-order systems.

A dynamic multiplier for [1.2.5] can be found in exactly the same way as was done for the first-order scalar system of Section 1.1. If we knew the value of the vector $\boldsymbol{\xi}$ for date $t = -1$ and of $\mathbf{v}$ for date $t = 0$, we could find the value of $\boldsymbol{\xi}$ for date 0 from

$$\boldsymbol{\xi}_0 = \mathbf{F}\boldsymbol{\xi}_{-1} + \mathbf{v}_0.$$

The value of $\boldsymbol{\xi}$ for date 1 is

$$\boldsymbol{\xi}_1 = \mathbf{F}\boldsymbol{\xi}_0 + \mathbf{v}_1 = \mathbf{F}(\mathbf{F}\boldsymbol{\xi}_{-1} + \mathbf{v}_0) + \mathbf{v}_1 = \mathbf{F}^2\boldsymbol{\xi}_{-1} + \mathbf{F}\mathbf{v}_0 + \mathbf{v}_1.$$

Proceeding recursively in this fashion produces a generalization of [1.1.7]:

$$\boldsymbol{\xi}_t = \mathbf{F}^{t+1}\boldsymbol{\xi}_{-1} + \mathbf{F}^t\mathbf{v}_0 + \mathbf{F}^{t-1}\mathbf{v}_1 + \mathbf{F}^{t-2}\mathbf{v}_2 + \cdots + \mathbf{F}\mathbf{v}_{t-1} + \mathbf{v}_t. \qquad [1.2.6]$$

Writing this out in terms of the definitions of $\boldsymbol{\xi}$ and $\mathbf{v}$,

$$\begin{bmatrix} y_t \\ y_{t-1} \\ y_{t-2} \\ \vdots \\ y_{t-p+1} \end{bmatrix} = \mathbf{F}^{t+1} \begin{bmatrix} y_{-1} \\ y_{-2} \\ y_{-3} \\ \vdots \\ y_{-p} \end{bmatrix} + \mathbf{F}^{t} \begin{bmatrix} w_0 \\ 0 \\ 0 \\ \vdots \\ 0 \end{bmatrix} + \mathbf{F}^{t-1} \begin{bmatrix} w_1 \\ 0 \\ 0 \\ \vdots \\ 0 \end{bmatrix} + \cdots + \mathbf{F}^{1} \begin{bmatrix} w_{t-1} \\ 0 \\ 0 \\ \vdots \\ 0 \end{bmatrix} + \begin{bmatrix} w_t \\ 0 \\ 0 \\ \vdots \\ 0 \end{bmatrix}. \qquad [1.2.7]$$

Consider the first equation of this system, which characterizes the value of $y_t$. Let $f_{11}^{(t)}$ denote the (1, 1) element of $\mathbf{F}^t$, $f_{12}^{(t)}$ the (1, 2) element of $\mathbf{F}^t$, and so on. Then the first equation of [1.2.7] states that

$$y_t = f_{11}^{(t+1)}y_{-1} + f_{12}^{(t+1)}y_{-2} + \cdots + f_{1p}^{(t+1)}y_{-p} + f_{11}^{(t)}w_0 + f_{11}^{(t-1)}w_1 + \cdots + f_{11}^{(1)}w_{t-1} + w_t. \qquad [1.2.8]$$

This describes the value of $y$ at date $t$ as a linear function of $p$ initial values of $y$ $(y_{-1}, y_{-2}, \ldots, y_{-p})$ and the history of the input variable $w$ since time 0 $(w_0, w_1, \ldots, w_t)$. Note that whereas only one initial value for $y$ (the value $y_{-1}$) was needed in the case of a first-order difference equation, $p$ initial values for $y$ (the values $y_{-1}, y_{-2}, \ldots, y_{-p}$) are needed in the case of a $p$th-order difference equation.

The obvious generalization of [1.1.9] is

$$\boldsymbol{\xi}_{t+j} = \mathbf{F}^{j+1}\boldsymbol{\xi}_{t-1} + \mathbf{F}^{j}\mathbf{v}_t + \mathbf{F}^{j-1}\mathbf{v}_{t+1} + \mathbf{F}^{j-2}\mathbf{v}_{t+2} + \cdots + \mathbf{F}\mathbf{v}_{t+j-1} + \mathbf{v}_{t+j} \qquad [1.2.9]$$

from which

$$y_{t+j} = f_{11}^{(j+1)}y_{t-1} + f_{12}^{(j+1)}y_{t-2} + \cdots + f_{1p}^{(j+1)}y_{t-p} + f_{11}^{(j)}w_t + f_{11}^{(j-1)}w_{t+1} + f_{11}^{(j-2)}w_{t+2} + \cdots + f_{11}^{(1)}w_{t+j-1} + w_{t+j}. \qquad [1.2.10]$$

Thus, for a $p$th-order difference equation, the dynamic multiplier is given by

$$\frac{\partial y_{t+j}}{\partial w_t} = f_{11}^{(j)} \qquad [1.2.11]$$

where $f_{11}^{(j)}$ denotes the (1, 1) element of $\mathbf{F}^j$. For $j = 1$, this is simply the (1, 1) element of $\mathbf{F}$, or the parameter $\phi_1$. Thus, for any $p$th-order system, the effect on $y_{t+1}$ of a one-unit increase in $w_t$ is given by the coefficient relating $y_t$ to $y_{t-1}$ in equation [1.2.1]:

$$\frac{\partial y_{t+1}}{\partial w_t} = \phi_1.$$

Direct multiplication of [1.2.3] reveals that the (1, 1) element of $\mathbf{F}^2$ is $(\phi_1^2 + \phi_2)$, so

$$\frac{\partial y_{t+2}}{\partial w_t} = \phi_1^2 + \phi_2$$

in a $p$th-order system.

For larger values of $j$, an easy way to obtain a numerical value for the dynamic multiplier $\partial y_{t+j}/\partial w_t$ is to simulate the system. This is done as follows. Set $y_{-1} = y_{-2} = \cdots = y_{-p} = 0$, $w_0 = 1$, and set the value of $w$ for all other dates to 0. Then use [1.2.1] to calculate the value of $y_t$ for $t = 0$ (namely, $y_0 = 1$). Next substitute this value along with $y_{t-1}, y_{t-2}, \ldots, y_{t-p+1}$ back into [1.2.1] to calculate $y_{t+1}$, and continue recursively in this fashion. The value of $y$ at step $t$ gives the effect of a one-unit change in $w_0$ on $y_t$.

Although numerical simulation may be adequate for many circumstances, it is also useful to have a simple analytical characterization of $\partial y_{t+j}/\partial w_t$, which, we know from [1.2.11], is given by the (1, 1) element of $\mathbf{F}^j$. This is fairly easy to obtain in terms of the eigenvalues of the matrix $\mathbf{F}$. Recall that the eigenvalues of a matrix $\mathbf{F}$ are those numbers $\lambda$ for which

$$|\mathbf{F} - \lambda \mathbf{I}_p| = 0. \qquad [1.2.12]$$

For example, for $p = 2$ the eigenvalues are the solutions to

$$\left| \begin{bmatrix} \phi_1 & \phi_2 \\ 1 & 0 \end{bmatrix} - \begin{bmatrix} \lambda & 0 \\ 0 & \lambda \end{bmatrix} \right| = 0$$

or

$$\begin{vmatrix} (\phi_1 - \lambda) & \phi_2 \\ 1 & -\lambda \end{vmatrix} = \lambda^2 - \phi_1 \lambda - \phi_2 = 0. \qquad [1.2.13]$$

The two eigenvalues of $\mathbf{F}$ for a second-order difference equation are thus given by

$$\lambda_1 = \frac{\phi_1 + \sqrt{\phi_1^2 + 4\phi_2}}{2} \qquad [1.2.14]$$

$$\lambda_2 = \frac{\phi_1 - \sqrt{\phi_1^2 + 4\phi_2}}{2}. \qquad [1.2.15]$$

For a general $p$th-order system, the determinant in [1.2.12] is a $p$th-order polynomial in $\lambda$ whose $p$ solutions characterize the $p$ eigenvalues of $\mathbf{F}$. This polynomial turns out to take a very similar form to [1.2.13]. The following result is proved in Appendix 1.A at the end of this chapter.

***Proposition 1.1:*** *The eigenvalues of the matrix* $\mathbf{F}$ *defined in equation [1.2.3] are the values of* $\lambda$ *that satisfy*

$$\lambda^p - \phi_1 \lambda^{p-1} - \phi_2 \lambda^{p-2} - \cdots - \phi_{p-1}\lambda - \phi_p = 0. \qquad [1.2.16]$$

Once we know the eigenvalues, it is straightforward to characterize the dynamic behavior of the system. First we consider the case when the eigenvalues of $\mathbf{F}$ are distinct; for example, we require that $\lambda_1$ and $\lambda_2$ in [1.2.14] and [1.2.15] be different numbers.

## *General Solution of a* pth-*Order Difference Equation with Distinct Eigenvalues*

Recall[2] that if the eigenvalues of a $(p \times p)$ matrix $\mathbf{F}$ are distinct, there exists a nonsingular $(p \times p)$ matrix $\mathbf{T}$ such that

$$\mathbf{F} = \mathbf{T}\mathbf{\Lambda}\mathbf{T}^{-1} \qquad [1.2.17]$$

where $\mathbf{\Lambda}$ is a $(p \times p)$ matrix with the eigenvalues of $\mathbf{F}$ along the principal diagonal and zeros elsewhere:

$$\mathbf{\Lambda} = \begin{bmatrix} \lambda_1 & 0 & 0 & \cdots & 0 \\ 0 & \lambda_2 & 0 & \cdots & 0 \\ \vdots & \vdots & \vdots & \cdots & \vdots \\ 0 & 0 & 0 & \cdots & \lambda_p \end{bmatrix}. \qquad [1.2.18]$$

This enables us to characterize the dynamic multiplier (the (1, 1) element of $\mathbf{F}^j$ in [1.2.11]) very easily. For example, from [1.2.17] we can write $\mathbf{F}^2$ as

$$\begin{aligned} \mathbf{F}^2 &= \mathbf{T}\mathbf{\Lambda}\mathbf{T}^{-1} \times \mathbf{T}\mathbf{\Lambda}\mathbf{T}^{-1} \\ &= \mathbf{T} \times \mathbf{\Lambda} \times (\mathbf{T}^{-1}\mathbf{T}) \times \mathbf{\Lambda} \times \mathbf{T}^{-1} \\ &= \mathbf{T} \times \mathbf{\Lambda} \times \mathbf{I}_p \times \mathbf{\Lambda} \times \mathbf{T}^{-1} \\ &= \mathbf{T}\mathbf{\Lambda}^2\mathbf{T}^{-1}. \end{aligned}$$

The diagonal structure of $\mathbf{\Lambda}$ implies that $\mathbf{\Lambda}^2$ is also a diagonal matrix whose elements are the squares of the eigenvalues of $\mathbf{F}$:

$$\mathbf{\Lambda}^2 = \begin{bmatrix} \lambda_1^2 & 0 & 0 & \cdots & 0 \\ 0 & \lambda_2^2 & 0 & \cdots & 0 \\ \vdots & \vdots & \vdots & \cdots & \vdots \\ 0 & 0 & 0 & \cdots & \lambda_p^2 \end{bmatrix}.$$

More generally, we can characterize $\mathbf{F}^j$ in terms of the eigenvalues of $\mathbf{F}$ as

$$\begin{aligned} \mathbf{F}^j &= \underbrace{\mathbf{T}\mathbf{\Lambda}\mathbf{T}^{-1} \times \mathbf{T}\mathbf{\Lambda}\mathbf{T}^{-1} \times \cdots \times \mathbf{T}\mathbf{\Lambda}\mathbf{T}^{-1}}_{j \text{ terms}} \\ &= \mathbf{T} \times \mathbf{\Lambda} \times (\mathbf{T}^{-1}\mathbf{T}) \times \mathbf{\Lambda} \times (\mathbf{T}^{-1}\mathbf{T}) \times \cdots \times \mathbf{\Lambda} \times \mathbf{T}^{-1}, \end{aligned}$$

which simplifies to

$$\mathbf{F}^j = \mathbf{T}\mathbf{\Lambda}^j\mathbf{T}^{-1} \qquad [1.2.19]$$

where

$$\mathbf{\Lambda}^j = \begin{bmatrix} \lambda_1^j & 0 & 0 & \cdots & 0 \\ 0 & \lambda_2^j & 0 & \cdots & 0 \\ \vdots & \vdots & \vdots & \cdots & \vdots \\ 0 & 0 & 0 & \cdots & \lambda_p^j \end{bmatrix}.$$

[2]See equation [A.4.24] in the Mathematical Review (Appendix A) at the end of the book.

Let $t_{ij}$ denote the row $i$, column $j$ element of $\mathbf{T}$ and let $t^{ij}$ denote the row $i$, column $j$ element of $\mathbf{T}^{-1}$. Equation [1.2.19] written out explicitly becomes

$$\mathbf{F}^j = \begin{bmatrix} t_{11} & t_{12} & \cdots & t_{1p} \\ t_{21} & t_{22} & \cdots & t_{2p} \\ \vdots & \vdots & \cdots & \vdots \\ t_{p1} & t_{p2} & \cdots & t_{pp} \end{bmatrix} \begin{bmatrix} \lambda_1^j & 0 & 0 & \cdots & 0 \\ 0 & \lambda_2^j & 0 & \cdots & 0 \\ \vdots & \vdots & \vdots & \cdots & \vdots \\ 0 & 0 & 0 & \cdots & \lambda_p^j \end{bmatrix} \begin{bmatrix} t^{11} & t^{12} & \cdots & t^{1p} \\ t^{21} & t^{22} & \cdots & t^{2p} \\ \vdots & \vdots & \cdots & \vdots \\ t^{p1} & t^{p2} & \cdots & t^{pp} \end{bmatrix}$$

$$= \begin{bmatrix} t_{11}\lambda_1^j & t_{12}\lambda_2^j & \cdots & t_{1p}\lambda_p^j \\ t_{21}\lambda_1^j & t_{22}\lambda_2^j & \cdots & t_{2p}\lambda_p^j \\ \vdots & \vdots & \cdots & \vdots \\ t_{p1}\lambda_1^j & t_{p2}\lambda_2^j & \cdots & t_{pp}\lambda_p^j \end{bmatrix} \begin{bmatrix} t^{11} & t^{12} & \cdots & t^{1p} \\ t^{21} & t^{22} & \cdots & t^{2p} \\ \vdots & \vdots & \cdots & \vdots \\ t^{p1} & t^{p2} & \cdots & t^{pp} \end{bmatrix}$$

from which the (1, 1) element of $\mathbf{F}^j$ is given by

$$f_{11}^{(j)} = [t_{11}t^{11}]\lambda_1^j + [t_{12}t^{21}]\lambda_2^j + \cdots + [t_{1p}t^{p1}]\lambda_p^j$$

or

$$f_{11}^{(j)} = c_1\lambda_1^j + c_2\lambda_2^j + \cdots + c_p\lambda_p^j \qquad [1.2.20]$$

where

$$c_i = [t_{1i}t^{i1}]. \qquad [1.2.21]$$

Note that the sum of the $c_i$ terms has the following interpretation:

$$c_1 + c_2 + \cdots + c_p = [t_{11}t^{11}] + [t_{12}t^{21}] + \cdots + [t_{1p}t^{p1}], \qquad [1.2.22]$$

which is the (1, 1) element of $\mathbf{T}\cdot\mathbf{T}^{-1}$. Since $\mathbf{T}\cdot\mathbf{T}^{-1}$ is just the $(p \times p)$ identity matrix, [1.2.22] implies that the $c_i$ terms sum to unity:

$$c_1 + c_2 + \cdots + c_p = 1. \qquad [1.2.23]$$

Substituting [1.2.20] into [1.2.11] gives the form of the dynamic multiplier for a $p$th-order difference equation:

$$\frac{\partial y_{t+j}}{\partial w_t} = c_1\lambda_1^j + c_2\lambda_2^j + \cdots + c_p\lambda_p^j. \qquad [1.2.24]$$

Equation [1.2.24] characterizes the dynamic multiplier as a weighted average of each of the $p$ eigenvalues raised to the $j$th power.

The following result provides a closed-form expression for the constants $(c_1, c_2, \ldots, c_p)$.

***Proposition 1.2:*** *If the eigenvalues* $(\lambda_1, \lambda_2, \ldots, \lambda_p)$ *of the matrix* $\mathbf{F}$ *in [1.2.3] are distinct, then the magnitude* $c_i$ *in [1.2.21] can be written*

$$c_i = \frac{\lambda_i^{p-1}}{\prod_{\substack{k=1 \\ k \neq i}}^{p} (\lambda_i - \lambda_k)}. \qquad [1.2.25]$$

To summarize, the $p$th-order difference equation [1.2.1] implies that

$$y_{t+j} = f_{11}^{(j+1)}y_{t-1} + f_{12}^{(j+1)}y_{t-2} + \cdots + f_{1p}^{(j+1)}y_{t-p} + w_{t+j} + \psi_1 w_{t+j-1} + \psi_2 w_{t+j-2} + \cdots + \psi_{j-1}w_{t+1} + \psi_j w_t. \qquad [1.2.26]$$

The dynamic multiplier

$$\frac{\partial y_{t+j}}{\partial w_t} = \psi_j \qquad [1.2.27]$$

is given by the (1, 1) element of $\mathbf{F}^j$:

$$\psi_j = f_{11}^{(j)}. \qquad [1.2.28]$$

A closed-form expression for $\psi_j$ can be obtained by finding the eigenvalues of $\mathbf{F}$, or the values of $\lambda$ satisfying [1.2.16]. Denoting these $p$ values by $(\lambda_1, \lambda_2, \ldots, \lambda_p)$ and assuming them to be distinct, the dynamic multiplier is given by

$$\psi_j = c_1\lambda_1^j + c_2\lambda_2^j + \cdots + c_p\lambda_p^j \qquad [1.2.29]$$

where $(c_1, c_2, \ldots, c_p)$ is a set of constants summing to unity given by expression [1.2.25].

For a first-order system ($p = 1$), this rule would have us solve [1.2.16],

$$\lambda - \phi_1 = 0,$$

which has the single solution

$$\lambda_1 = \phi_1. \qquad [1.2.30]$$

According to [1.2.29], the dynamic multiplier is given by

$$\frac{\partial y_{t+j}}{\partial w_t} = c_1\lambda_1^j. \qquad [1.2.31]$$

From [1.2.23], $c_1 = 1$. Substituting this and [1.2.30] into [1.2.31] gives

$$\frac{\partial y_{t+j}}{\partial w_t} = \phi_1^j,$$

or the same result found in Section 1.1.

For higher-order systems, [1.2.29] allows a variety of more complicated dynamics. Suppose first that all the eigenvalues of $\mathbf{F}$ (or solutions to [1.2.16]) are real. This would be the case, for example, if $p = 2$ and $\phi_1^2 + 4\phi_2 > 0$ in the solutions [1.2.14] and [1.2.15] for the second-order system. If, furthermore, all of the eigenvalues are less than 1 in absolute value, then the system is stable, and its dynamics are represented as a weighted average of decaying exponentials or decaying exponentials oscillating in sign. For example, consider the following second-order difference equation:

$$y_t = 0.6y_{t-1} + 0.2y_{t-2} + w_t.$$

From equations [1.2.14] and [1.2.15], the eigenvalues of this system are given by

$$\lambda_1 = \frac{0.6 + \sqrt{(0.6)^2 + 4(0.2)}}{2} = 0.84$$

$$\lambda_2 = \frac{0.6 - \sqrt{(0.6)^2 + 4(0.2)}}{2} = -0.24.$$

From [1.2.25], we have

$$c_1 = \lambda_1/(\lambda_1 - \lambda_2) = 0.778$$

$$c_2 = \lambda_2/(\lambda_2 - \lambda_1) = 0.222.$$

The dynamic multiplier for this system,

$$\frac{\partial y_{t+j}}{\partial w_t} = c_1\lambda_1^j + c_2\lambda_2^j,$$

is plotted as a function of $j$ in panel (a) of Figure 1.4.[3] Note that as $j$ becomes larger, the pattern is dominated by the larger eigenvalue ($\lambda_1$), approximating a simple geometric decay at rate $\lambda_1$.

If the eigenvalues (the solutions to [1.2.16]) are real but at least one is greater than unity in absolute value, the system is explosive. If $\lambda_1$ denotes the eigenvalue that is largest in absolute value, the dynamic multiplier is eventually dominated by an exponential function of that eigenvalue:

$$\lim_{j\to\infty} \frac{\partial y_{t+j}}{\partial w_t} \cdot \frac{1}{\lambda_1^j} = c_1.$$

Other interesting possibilities arise if some of the eigenvalues are complex. Whenever this is the case, they appear as complex conjugates. For example, if $p = 2$ and $\phi_1^2 + 4\phi_2 < 0$, then the solutions $\lambda_1$ and $\lambda_2$ in [1.2.14] and [1.2.15] are complex conjugates. Suppose that $\lambda_1$ and $\lambda_2$ are complex conjugates, written as

$$\lambda_1 = a + bi \qquad [1.2.32]$$

$$\lambda_2 = a - bi. \qquad [1.2.33]$$

For the $p = 2$ case of [1.2.14] and [1.2.15], we would have

$$a = \phi_1/2 \qquad [1.2.34]$$

$$b = (1/2)\sqrt{-\phi_1^2 - 4\phi_2}. \qquad [1.2.35]$$

Our goal is to characterize the contribution to the dynamic multiplier $c_1\lambda_1^j$ when $\lambda_1$ is a complex number as in [1.2.32]. Recall that to raise a complex number to a power, we rewrite [1.2.32] in polar coordinate form:

$$\lambda_1 = R\cdot[\cos(\theta) + i\cdot\sin(\theta)], \qquad [1.2.36]$$

where $\theta$ and $R$ are defined in terms of $a$ and $b$ by the following equations:

$$R = \sqrt{a^2 + b^2}$$
$$\cos(\theta) = a/R$$
$$\sin(\theta) = b/R.$$

Note that $R$ is equal to the modulus of the complex number $\lambda_1$.

The eigenvalue $\lambda_1$ in [1.2.36] can be written as[4]

$$\lambda_1 = R[e^{i\theta}],$$

and so

$$\lambda_1^j = R^j[e^{i\theta j}] = R^j[\cos(\theta j) + i\cdot\sin(\theta j)]. \qquad [1.2.37]$$

Analogously, if $\lambda_2$ is the complex conjugate of $\lambda_1$, then

$$\lambda_2 = R[\cos(\theta) - i\cdot\sin(\theta)],$$

which can be written[5]

$$\lambda_2 = R[e^{-i\theta}].$$

Thus

$$\lambda_2^j = R^j[e^{-i\theta j}] = R^j[\cos(\theta j) - i\cdot\sin(\theta j)]. \qquad [1.2.38]$$

[3]Again, if one's purpose is solely to generate a numerical plot as in Figure 1.4, the easiest approach is numerical simulation of the system.

[4]See equation [A.3.25] in the Mathematical Review (Appendix A) at the end of the book.

[5]See equation [A.3.26].

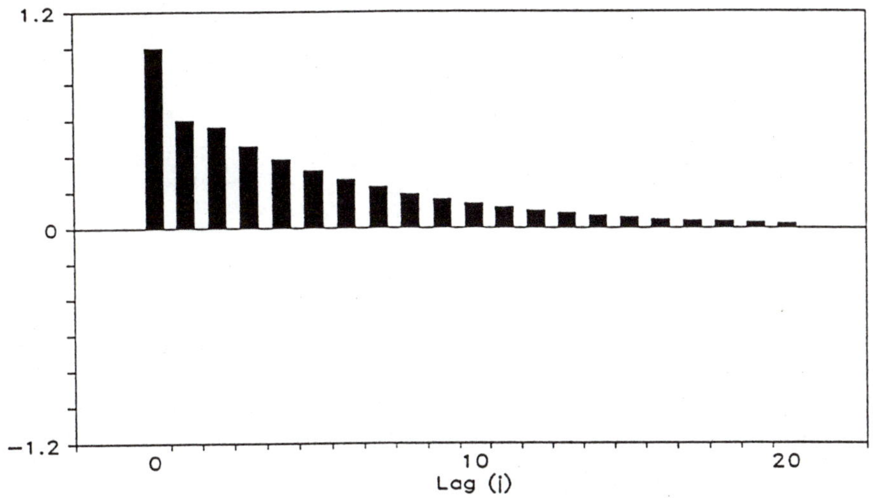


(a) $\phi_1 = 0.6, \phi_2 = 0.2$

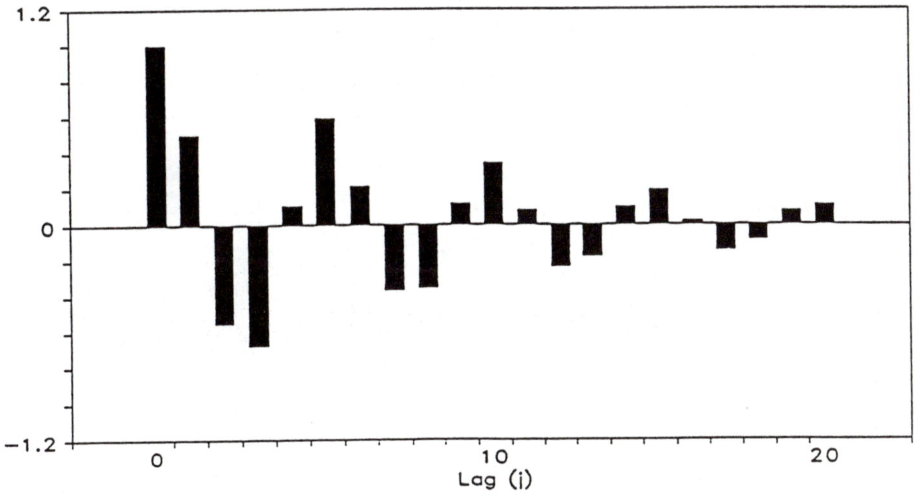


(b) $\phi_1 = 0.5, \phi_2 = -0.8$

**FIGURE 1.4** Dynamic multiplier for second-order difference equation for different values of $\phi_1$ and $\phi_2$ (plot of $\partial y_{t+j}/\partial w_t$ as a function of the lag $j$).

Substituting [1.2.37] and [1.2.38] into [1.2.29] gives the contribution of the complex conjugates to the dynamic multiplier $\partial y_{t+j}/\partial w_t$:

$$\begin{aligned} c_1\lambda_1^j + c_2\lambda_2^j &= c_1R^j[\cos(\theta j) + i\cdot\sin(\theta j)] + c_2R^j[\cos(\theta j) - i\cdot\sin(\theta j)] \\ &= [c_1 + c_2]\cdot R^j\cdot\cos(\theta j) + i\cdot[c_1 - c_2]\cdot R^j\cdot\sin(\theta j). \end{aligned} \qquad [1.2.39]$$

The appearance of the imaginary number $i$ in [1.2.39] may seem a little troubling. After all, this calculation was intended to give the effect of a change in the real-valued variable $w_t$ on the real-valued variable $y_{t+j}$ as predicted by the real-valued system [1.2.1], and it would be odd indeed if the correct answer involved the imaginary number $i$! Fortunately, it turns out from [1.2.25] that if $\lambda_1$ and $\lambda_2$ are complex conjugates, then $c_1$ and $c_2$ are complex conjugates; that is, they can be written as

$$c_1 = \alpha + \beta i$$
$$c_2 = \alpha - \beta i$$

for some real numbers $\alpha$ and $\beta$. Substituting these expressions into [1.2.39] yields

$$\begin{aligned} c_1\lambda_1^j + c_2\lambda_2^j &= [(\alpha + \beta i) + (\alpha - \beta i)]\cdot R^j\cos(\theta j) + i\cdot[(\alpha + \beta i) - (\alpha - \beta i)]\cdot R^j\sin(\theta j) \\ &= [2\alpha]\cdot R^j\cos(\theta j) + i\cdot[2\beta i]\cdot R^j\sin(\theta j) \\ &= 2\alpha R^j\cos(\theta j) - 2\beta R^j\sin(\theta j), \end{aligned}$$

which is strictly real.

Thus, when some of the eigenvalues are complex, they contribute terms proportional to $R^j\cos(\theta j)$ and $R^j\sin(\theta j)$ to the dynamic multiplier $\partial y_{t+j}/\partial w_t$. Note that if $R = 1$—that is, if the complex eigenvalues have unit modulus—the multipliers are periodic sine and cosine functions of $j$. A given increase in $w_t$ increases $y_{t+j}$ for some ranges of $j$ and decreases $y_{t+j}$ over other ranges, with the impulse never dying out as $j \to \infty$. If the complex eigenvalues are less than 1 in modulus ($R < 1$), the impulse again follows a sinusoidal pattern though its amplitude decays at the rate $R^j$. If the complex eigenvalues are greater than 1 in modulus ($R > 1$), the amplitude of the sinusoids explodes at the rate $R^j$.

For an example of dynamic behavior characterized by decaying sinusoids, consider the second-order system

$$y_t = 0.5y_{t-1} - 0.8y_{t-2} + w_t.$$

The eigenvalues for this system are given from [1.2.14] and [1.2.15]:

$$\lambda_1 = \frac{0.5 + \sqrt{(0.5)^2 - 4(0.8)}}{2} = 0.25 + 0.86i$$

$$\lambda_2 = \frac{0.5 - \sqrt{(0.5)^2 - 4(0.8)}}{2} = 0.25 - 0.86i,$$

with modulus

$$R = \sqrt{(0.25)^2 + (0.86)^2} = 0.9.$$

Since $R < 1$, the dynamic multiplier follows a pattern of damped oscillation plotted in panel (b) of Figure 1.4. The frequency[6] of these oscillations is given by the parameter $\theta$ in [1.2.39], which was defined implicitly by

$$\cos(\theta) = a/R = (0.25)/(0.9) = 0.28$$

or

$$\theta = 1.29.$$

The cycles associated with the dynamic multiplier function [1.2.39] thus have a period of

$$\frac{2\pi}{\theta} = \frac{(2)(3.14159)}{1.29} = 4.9;$$

that is, the peaks in the pattern in panel (b) of Figure 1.4 appear about five periods apart.

[6]See Section A.1 of the Mathematical Review (Appendix A) at the end of the book for a discussion of the frequency and period of a sinusoidal function.

## *Solution of a Second-Order Difference Equation with Distinct Eigenvalues*

The second-order difference equation ($p = 2$) comes up sufficiently often that it is useful to summarize the properties of the solution as a general function of $\phi_1$ and $\phi_2$, which we now do.[7]

The eigenvalues $\lambda_1$ and $\lambda_2$ in [1.2.14] and [1.2.15] are complex whenever

$$\phi_1^2 + 4\phi_2 < 0,$$

or whenever $(\phi_1, \phi_2)$ lies below the parabola indicated in Figure 1.5. For the case of complex eigenvalues, the modulus $R$ satisfies

$$R^2 = a^2 + b^2,$$

or, from [1.2.34] and [1.2.35],

$$R^2 = (\phi_1/2)^2 - (\phi_1^2 + 4\phi_2)/4 = -\phi_2.$$

Thus, a system with complex eigenvalues is explosive whenever $\phi_2 < -1$. Also, when the eigenvalues are complex, the frequency of oscillations is given by

$$\theta = \cos^{-1}(a/R) = \cos^{-1}[\phi_1/(2\sqrt{-\phi_2})],$$

where "$\cos^{-1}(x)$" denotes the inverse of the cosine function, or the radian measure of an angle whose cosine is $x$.

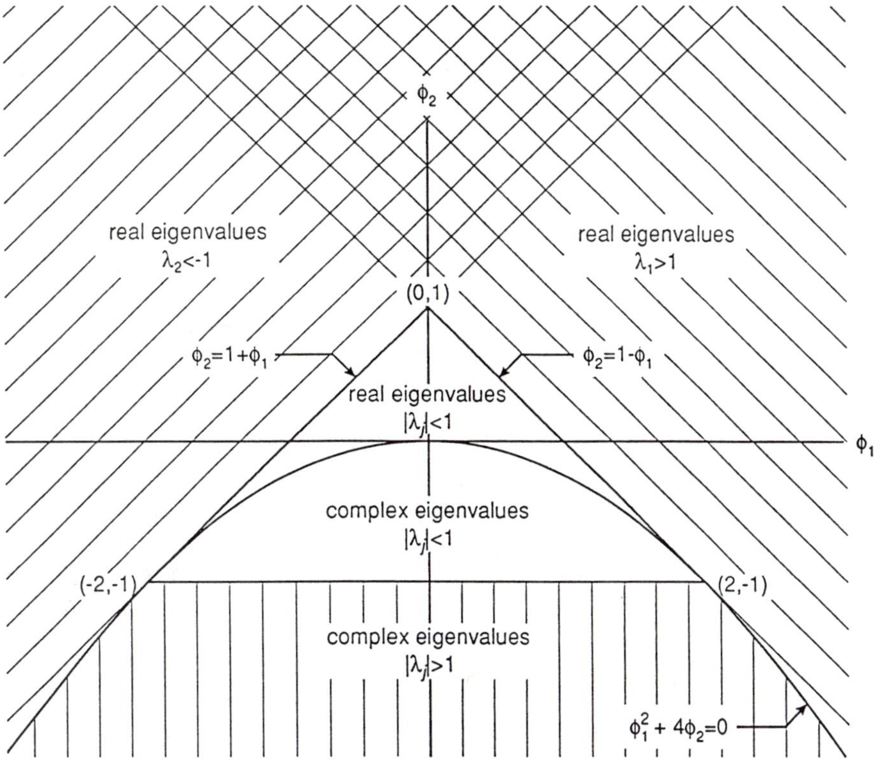


**FIGURE 1.5** Summary of dynamics for a second-order difference equation.

[7]This discussion closely follows Sargent (1987, pp. 188–89).

For the case of real eigenvalues, the arithmetically larger eigenvalue ($\lambda_1$) will be greater than unity whenever

$$\frac{\phi_1 + \sqrt{\phi_1^2 + 4\phi_2}}{2} > 1$$

or

$$\sqrt{\phi_1^2 + 4\phi_2} > 2 - \phi_1.$$

Assuming that $\lambda_1$ is real, the left side of this expression is a positive number and the inequality would be satisfied for any value of $\phi_1 > 2$. If, on the other hand, $\phi_1 < 2$, we can square both sides to conclude that $\lambda_1$ will exceed unity whenever

$$\phi_1^2 + 4\phi_2 > 4 - 4\phi_1 + \phi_1^2$$

or

$$\phi_2 > 1 - \phi_1.$$

Thus, in the real region, $\lambda_1$ will be greater than unity either if $\phi_1 > 2$ or if $(\phi_1, \phi_2)$ lies northeast of the line $\phi_2 = 1 - \phi_1$ in Figure 1.5. Similarly, with real eigenvalues, the arithmetically smaller eigenvalue ($\lambda_2$) will be less than $-1$ whenever

$$\frac{\phi_1 - \sqrt{\phi_1^2 + 4\phi_2}}{2} < -1$$

$$-\sqrt{\phi_1^2 + 4\phi_2} < -2 - \phi_1$$

$$\sqrt{\phi_1^2 + 4\phi_2} > 2 + \phi_1.$$

Again, if $\phi_1 < -2$, this must be satisfied, and in the case when $\phi_1 > -2$, we can square both sides:

$$\phi_1^2 + 4\phi_2 > 4 + 4\phi_1 + \phi_1^2$$

$$\phi_2 > 1 + \phi_1.$$

Thus, in the real region, $\lambda_2$ will be less than $-1$ if either $\phi_1 < -2$ or $(\phi_1, \phi_2)$ lies to the northwest of the line $\phi_2 = 1 + \phi_1$ in Figure 1.5.

The system is thus stable whenever $(\phi_1, \phi_2)$ lies within the triangular region of Figure 1.5.

## *General Solution of a pth-Order Difference Equation with Repeated Eigenvalues*

In the more general case of a difference equation for which $\mathbf{F}$ has repeated eigenvalues and $s < p$ linearly independent eigenvectors, result [1.2.17] is generalized by using the Jordan decomposition,

$$\mathbf{F} = \mathbf{MJM}^{-1} \qquad [1.2.40]$$

where $\mathbf{M}$ is a $(p \times p)$ matrix and $\mathbf{J}$ takes the form

$$\mathbf{J} = \begin{bmatrix} \mathbf{J}_1 & \mathbf{0} & \cdots & \mathbf{0} \\ \mathbf{0} & \mathbf{J}_2 & \cdots & \mathbf{0} \\ \vdots & \vdots & \cdots & \vdots \\ \mathbf{0} & \mathbf{0} & \cdots & \mathbf{J}_s \end{bmatrix}$$

with

$$\mathbf{J}_i = \begin{bmatrix} \lambda_i & 1 & 0 & \cdots & 0 & 0 \\ 0 & \lambda_i & 1 & \cdots & 0 & 0 \\ 0 & 0 & \lambda_i & \cdots & 0 & 0 \\ \vdots & \vdots & \vdots & \cdots & \vdots & \vdots \\ 0 & 0 & 0 & \cdots & \lambda_i & 1 \\ 0 & 0 & 0 & \cdots & 0 & \lambda_i \end{bmatrix} \qquad [1.2.41]$$

for $\lambda_i$ an eigenvalue of $\mathbf{F}$. If [1.2.17] is replaced by [1.2.40], then equation [1.2.19] generalizes to

$$\mathbf{F}^j = \mathbf{M}\mathbf{J}^j\mathbf{M}^{-1} \qquad [1.2.42]$$

where

$$\mathbf{J}^j = \begin{bmatrix} \mathbf{J}_1^j & \mathbf{0} & \cdots & \mathbf{0} \\ \mathbf{0} & \mathbf{J}_2^j & \cdots & \mathbf{0} \\ \vdots & \vdots & \cdots & \vdots \\ \mathbf{0} & \mathbf{0} & \cdots & \mathbf{J}_s^j \end{bmatrix}.$$

Moreover, from [1.2.41], if $\mathbf{J}_i$ is of dimension $(n_i \times n_i)$, then[8]

$$\mathbf{J}_i^j = \begin{bmatrix} \lambda_i^j & \binom{j}{1}\lambda_i^{j-1} & \binom{j}{2}\lambda_i^{j-2} & \cdots & \binom{j}{n_i-1}\lambda_i^{j-n_i+1} \\ 0 & \lambda_i^j & \binom{j}{1}\lambda_i^{j-1} & \cdots & \binom{j}{n_i-2}\lambda_i^{j-n_i+2} \\ \vdots & \vdots & \vdots & \cdots & \vdots \\ 0 & 0 & 0 & \cdots & \lambda_i^j \end{bmatrix} \qquad [1.2.43]$$

where

$$\binom{j}{n} \equiv \begin{cases} \dfrac{j(j-1)(j-2)\cdots(j-n+1)}{n(n-1)\cdots 3\cdot 2\cdot 1} & \text{for } j \geq n \\ 0 & \text{otherwise.} \end{cases}$$

Equation [1.2.43] may be verified by induction by multiplying [1.2.41] by [1.2.43] and noticing that $\binom{j}{n} + \binom{j}{n-1} = \binom{j+1}{n}$.

For example, consider again the second-order difference equation, this time with repeated roots. Then

$$\mathbf{F}^j = \mathbf{M}\begin{bmatrix} \lambda^j & j\lambda^{j-1} \\ 0 & \lambda^j \end{bmatrix}\mathbf{M}^{-1},$$

so that the dynamic multiplier takes the form

$$\frac{\partial y_{t+j}}{\partial w_t} = f_{11}^{(j)} = k_1\lambda^j + k_2 j\lambda^{j-1}.$$

## *Long-Run and Present-Value Calculations*

If the eigenvalues are all less than 1 in modulus, then $\mathbf{F}^j$ in [1.2.9] goes to zero as $j$ becomes large. If all values of $w$ and $y$ are taken to be bounded, we can

[8]This expression is taken from Chiang (1980, p. 444).

think of a "solution" of $y_t$ in terms of the infinite history of $w$,

$$y_t = w_t + \psi_1 w_{t-1} + \psi_2 w_{t-2} + \psi_3 w_{t-3} + \cdots, \qquad [1.2.44]$$

where $\psi_j$ is given by the (1, 1) element of $\mathbf{F}^j$ and takes the particular form of [1.2.29] in the case of distinct eigenvalues.

It is also straightforward to calculate the effect on the present value of $y$ of a transitory increase in $w$. This is simplest to find if we first consider the slightly more general problem of the hypothetical consequences of a change in any element of the vector $\mathbf{v}_t$ on any element of $\boldsymbol{\xi}_{t+j}$ in a general system of the form of [1.2.5]. The answer to this more general problem can be inferred immediately from [1.2.9]:

$$\frac{\partial \boldsymbol{\xi}_{t+j}}{\partial \mathbf{v}_t'} = \mathbf{F}^j. \qquad [1.2.45]$$

The true dynamic multiplier of interest, $\partial y_{t+j}/\partial w_t$, is just the (1, 1) element of the $(p \times p)$ matrix in [1.2.45]. The effect on the present value of $\boldsymbol{\xi}$ of a change in $\mathbf{v}$ is given by

$$\frac{\partial \sum_{j=0}^{\infty} \beta^j \boldsymbol{\xi}_{t+j}}{\partial \mathbf{v}_t'} = \sum_{j=0}^{\infty} \beta^j \mathbf{F}^j = (\mathbf{I}_p - \beta \mathbf{F})^{-1}, \qquad [1.2.46]$$

provided that the eigenvalues of $\mathbf{F}$ are all less than $\beta^{-1}$ in modulus. The effect on the present value of $y$ of a change in $w$,

$$\frac{\partial \sum_{j=0}^{\infty} \beta^j y_{t+j}}{\partial w_t},$$

is thus the (1, 1) element of the $(p \times p)$ matrix in [1.2.46]. This value is given by the following proposition.

***Proposition 1.3:*** *If the eigenvalues of the $(p \times p)$ matrix $\mathbf{F}$ defined in [1.2.3] are all less than $\beta^{-1}$ in modulus, then the matrix $(\mathbf{I}_p - \beta\mathbf{F})^{-1}$ exists and the effect of $w$ on the present value of $y$ is given by its (1, 1) element:*

$$1/(1 - \phi_1\beta - \phi_2\beta^2 - \cdots - \phi_{p-1}\beta^{p-1} - \phi_p\beta^p).$$

Note that Proposition 1.3 includes the earlier result for a first-order system (equation [1.1.14]) as a special case.

The cumulative effect of a one-time change in $w_t$ on $y_t, y_{t+1}, \ldots$ can be considered a special case of Proposition 1.3 with no discounting. Setting $\beta = 1$ in Proposition 1.3 shows that, provided the eigenvalues of $\mathbf{F}$ are all less than 1 in modulus, the cumulative effect of a one-time change in $w$ on $y$ is given by

$$\sum_{j=0}^{\infty} \frac{\partial y_{t+j}}{\partial w_t} = 1/(1 - \phi_1 - \phi_2 - \cdots - \phi_p). \qquad [1.2.47]$$

Notice again that [1.2.47] can alternatively be interpreted as giving the eventual long-run effect on $y$ of a permanent change in $w$:

$$\lim_{j\to\infty} \frac{\partial y_{t+j}}{\partial w_t} + \frac{\partial y_{t+j}}{\partial w_{t+1}} + \frac{\partial y_{t+j}}{\partial w_{t+2}} + \cdots + \frac{\partial y_{t+j}}{\partial w_{t+j}} = 1/(1 - \phi_1 - \phi_2 - \cdots - \phi_p).$$

## APPENDIX 1.A. *Proofs of Chapter 1 Propositions*

■ **Proof of Proposition 1.1.** The eigenvalues of **F** satisfy

$$|\mathbf{F} - \lambda \mathbf{I}_p| = 0. \qquad [1.A.1]$$

For the matrix **F** defined in equation [1.2.3], this determinant would be

$$\left| \begin{bmatrix} \phi_1 & \phi_2 & \phi_3 & \cdots & \phi_{p-1} & \phi_p \\ 1 & 0 & 0 & \cdots & 0 & 0 \\ 0 & 1 & 0 & \cdots & 0 & 0 \\ \vdots & \vdots & \vdots & \cdots & \vdots & \vdots \\ 0 & 0 & 0 & \cdots & 1 & 0 \end{bmatrix} - \begin{bmatrix} \lambda & 0 & 0 & \cdots & 0 & 0 \\ 0 & \lambda & 0 & \cdots & 0 & 0 \\ 0 & 0 & \lambda & \cdots & 0 & 0 \\ \vdots & \vdots & \vdots & \cdots & \vdots & \vdots \\ 0 & 0 & 0 & \cdots & 0 & \lambda \end{bmatrix} \right|$$

$$= \begin{vmatrix} (\phi_1 - \lambda) & \phi_2 & \phi_3 & \cdots & \phi_{p-1} & \phi_p \\ 1 & -\lambda & 0 & \cdots & 0 & 0 \\ 0 & 1 & -\lambda & \cdots & 0 & 0 \\ \vdots & \vdots & \vdots & \cdots & \vdots & \vdots \\ 0 & 0 & 0 & \cdots & 1 & -\lambda \end{vmatrix}. \qquad [1.A.2]$$

Recall that if we multiply a column of a matrix by a constant and add the result to another column, the determinant of the matrix is unchanged. If we multiply the $p$th column of the matrix in [1.A.2] by $(1/\lambda)$ and add the result to the $(p - 1)$th column, the result is a matrix with the same determinant as that in [1.A.2]:

$$|\mathbf{F} - \lambda \mathbf{I}_p| = \begin{vmatrix} \phi_1 - \lambda & \phi_2 & \phi_3 & \cdots & \phi_{p-2} & \phi_{p-1} + (\phi_p/\lambda) & \phi_p \\ 1 & -\lambda & 0 & \cdots & 0 & 0 & 0 \\ 0 & 1 & -\lambda & \cdots & 0 & 0 & 0 \\ \vdots & \vdots & \vdots & \cdots & \vdots & \vdots & \vdots \\ 0 & 0 & 0 & \cdots & 1 & -\lambda & 0 \\ 0 & 0 & 0 & \cdots & 0 & 0 & -\lambda \end{vmatrix}.$$

Next, multiply the $(p - 1)$th column by $(1/\lambda)$ and add the result to the $(p - 2)$th column:

$$|\mathbf{F} - \lambda \mathbf{I}_p|$$

$$= \begin{vmatrix} \phi_1 - \lambda & \phi_2 & \phi_3 & \cdots & \phi_{p-2} + \phi_{p-1}/\lambda + \phi_p/\lambda^2 & \phi_{p-1} + \phi_p/\lambda & \phi_p \\ 1 & -\lambda & 0 & \cdots & 0 & 0 & 0 \\ 0 & 1 & -\lambda & \cdots & 0 & 0 & 0 \\ \vdots & \vdots & \vdots & \cdots & \vdots & \vdots & \vdots \\ 0 & 0 & 0 & \cdots & 0 & -\lambda & 0 \\ 0 & 0 & 0 & \cdots & 0 & 0 & -\lambda \end{vmatrix}.$$

Continuing in this fashion shows [1.A.1] to be equivalent to the determinant of the following upper triangular matrix:

$$|\mathbf{F} - \lambda \mathbf{I}_p|$$

$$= \begin{vmatrix} \phi_1 - \lambda + \phi_2/\lambda + \phi_3/\lambda^2 + \cdots + \phi_p/\lambda^{p-1} & \phi_2 + \phi_3/\lambda + \phi_4/\lambda^2 + \cdots + \phi_p/\lambda^{p-2} & \cdots & \phi_{p-1} + \phi_p/\lambda & \phi_p \\ 0 & -\lambda & \cdots & 0 & 0 \\ 0 & 0 & \cdots & 0 & 0 \\ \vdots & \vdots & \cdots & \vdots & \vdots \\ 0 & 0 & \cdots & -\lambda & 0 \\ 0 & 0 & \cdots & 0 & -\lambda \end{vmatrix}.$$

But the determinant of an upper triangular matrix is simply the product of the terms along the principal diagonal:

$$\begin{aligned} |\mathbf{F} - \lambda \mathbf{I}_p| &= [\phi_1 - \lambda + \phi_2/\lambda + \phi_3/\lambda^2 + \cdots + \phi_p/\lambda^{p-1}] \cdot [-\lambda]^{p-1} \\ &= (-1)^p \cdot [\lambda^p - \phi_1\lambda^{p-1} - \phi_2\lambda^{p-2} - \cdots - \phi_p]. \end{aligned} \qquad [1.A.3]$$

The eigenvalues of $\mathbf{F}$ are thus the values of $\lambda$ for which [1.A.3] is zero, or for which

$$\lambda^p - \phi_1\lambda^{p-1} - \phi_2\lambda^{p-2} - \cdots - \phi_p = 0,$$

as asserted in Proposition 1.1. ■

■ **Proof of Proposition 1.2.** Assuming that the eigenvalues $(\lambda_1, \lambda_2, \ldots, \lambda_p)$ are distinct, the matrix $\mathbf{T}$ in equation [1.2.17] can be constructed from the eigenvectors of $\mathbf{F}$. Let $\mathbf{t}_i$ denote the following $(p \times 1)$ vector,

$$\mathbf{t}_i = \begin{bmatrix} \lambda_i^{p-1} \\ \lambda_i^{p-2} \\ \lambda_i^{p-3} \\ \vdots \\ \lambda_i^1 \\ 1 \end{bmatrix}, \qquad [1.A.4]$$

where $\lambda_i$ denotes the $i$th eigenvalue of $\mathbf{F}$. Notice

$$\mathbf{F}\mathbf{t}_i = \begin{bmatrix} \phi_1 & \phi_2 & \phi_3 & \cdots & \phi_{p-1} & \phi_p \\ 1 & 0 & 0 & \cdots & 0 & 0 \\ 0 & 1 & 0 & \cdots & 0 & 0 \\ \vdots & \vdots & \vdots & \cdots & \vdots & \vdots \\ 0 & 0 & 0 & \cdots & 1 & 0 \end{bmatrix} \begin{bmatrix} \lambda_i^{p-1} \\ \lambda_i^{p-2} \\ \lambda_i^{p-3} \\ \vdots \\ \lambda_i^1 \\ 1 \end{bmatrix}$$

$$= \begin{bmatrix} \phi_1\lambda_i^{p-1} + \phi_2\lambda_i^{p-2} + \phi_3\lambda_i^{p-3} + \cdots + \phi_{p-1}\lambda_i + \phi_p \\ \lambda_i^{p-1} \\ \lambda_i^{p-2} \\ \vdots \\ \lambda_i^2 \\ \lambda_i \end{bmatrix}. \qquad [1.A.5]$$

Since $\lambda_i$ is an eigenvalue of $\mathbf{F}$, it satisfies [1.2.16]:

$$\lambda_i^p - \phi_1\lambda_i^{p-1} - \phi_2\lambda_i^{p-2} - \cdots - \phi_{p-1}\lambda_i - \phi_p = 0. \qquad [1.A.6]$$

Substituting [1.A.6] into [1.A.5] reveals

$$\mathbf{F}\mathbf{t}_i = \begin{bmatrix} \lambda_i^p \\ \lambda_i^{p-1} \\ \lambda_i^{p-2} \\ \vdots \\ \lambda_i^2 \\ \lambda_i \end{bmatrix} = \lambda_i \begin{bmatrix} \lambda_i^{p-1} \\ \lambda_i^{p-2} \\ \lambda_i^{p-3} \\ \vdots \\ \lambda_i^1 \\ 1 \end{bmatrix}$$

or

$$\mathbf{F}\mathbf{t}_i = \lambda_i\mathbf{t}_i. \qquad [1.A.7]$$

Thus $\mathbf{t}_i$ is an eigenvector of $\mathbf{F}$ associated with the eigenvalue $\lambda_i$.

We can calculate the matrix $\mathbf{T}$ by combining the eigenvectors $(\mathbf{t}_1, \mathbf{t}_2, \ldots, \mathbf{t}_p)$ into a $(p \times p)$ matrix

$$\mathbf{T} = [\mathbf{t}_1 \quad \mathbf{t}_2 \quad \cdots \quad \mathbf{t}_p]. \qquad [1.A.8]$$

To calculate the particular values for $c_i$ in equation [1.2.21], recall that $\mathbf{T}^{-1}$ is characterized by

$$\mathbf{T}\mathbf{T}^{-1} = \mathbf{I}_p, \qquad [1.A.9]$$

where $\mathbf{T}$ is given by [1.A.4] and [1.A.8]. Writing out the first column of the matrix system of equations [1.A.9] explicitly, we have

$$\begin{bmatrix} \lambda_1^{p-1} & \lambda_2^{p-1} & \cdots & \lambda_p^{p-1} \\ \lambda_1^{p-2} & \lambda_2^{p-2} & \cdots & \lambda_p^{p-2} \\ \lambda_1^{p-3} & \lambda_2^{p-3} & \cdots & \lambda_p^{p-3} \\ \vdots & \vdots & \cdots & \vdots \\ \lambda_1^1 & \lambda_2^1 & \cdots & \lambda_p^1 \\ 1 & 1 & \cdots & 1 \end{bmatrix} \begin{bmatrix} t^{11} \\ t^{21} \\ t^{31} \\ \vdots \\ t^{p-1,1} \\ t^{p1} \end{bmatrix} = \begin{bmatrix} 1 \\ 0 \\ 0 \\ \vdots \\ 0 \\ 0 \end{bmatrix}.$$

This gives a system of $p$ linear equations in the $p$ unknowns $(t^{11}, t^{21}, \ldots, t^{p1})$. Provided that the $\lambda_i$ are all distinct, the solution can be shown to be[9]

$$\begin{aligned} t^{11} &= \frac{1}{(\lambda_1 - \lambda_2)(\lambda_1 - \lambda_3) \cdots (\lambda_1 - \lambda_p)} \\ t^{21} &= \frac{1}{(\lambda_2 - \lambda_1)(\lambda_2 - \lambda_3) \cdots (\lambda_2 - \lambda_p)} \\ &\vdots \\ t^{p1} &= \frac{1}{(\lambda_p - \lambda_1)(\lambda_p - \lambda_2) \cdots (\lambda_p - \lambda_{p-1})}. \end{aligned}$$

Substituting these values into [1.2.21] gives equation [1.2.25]. ■

■ **Proof of Proposition 1.3.** The first claim in this proposition is that if the eigenvalues of $\mathbf{F}$ are less than $\beta^{-1}$ in modulus, then the inverse of $(\mathbf{I}_p - \beta\mathbf{F})$ exists. Suppose the inverse of $(\mathbf{I}_p - \beta\mathbf{F})$ did not exist. Then the determinant $|\mathbf{I}_p - \beta\mathbf{F}|$ would have to be zero. But

$$|\mathbf{I}_p - \beta\mathbf{F}| = |-\beta \cdot [\mathbf{F} - \beta^{-1}\mathbf{I}_p]| = (-\beta)^p|\mathbf{F} - \beta^{-1}\mathbf{I}_p|,$$

so that $|\mathbf{F} - \beta^{-1}\mathbf{I}_p|$ would have to be zero whenever the inverse of $(\mathbf{I}_p - \beta\mathbf{F})$ fails to exist. But this would mean that $\beta^{-1}$ is an eigenvalue of $\mathbf{F}$, which is ruled out by the assumption that all eigenvalues of $\mathbf{F}$ are strictly less than $\beta^{-1}$ in modulus. Thus, the matrix $\mathbf{I}_p - \beta\mathbf{F}$ must be nonsingular.

Since $[\mathbf{I}_p - \beta\mathbf{F}]^{-1}$ exists, it satisfies the equation

$$[\mathbf{I}_p - \beta\mathbf{F}]^{-1}[\mathbf{I}_p - \beta\mathbf{F}] = \mathbf{I}_p. \qquad [1.A.10]$$

Let $x_{ij}$ denote the row $i$, column $j$ element of $[\mathbf{I}_p - \beta\mathbf{F}]^{-1}$, and write [1.A.10] as

$$\begin{bmatrix} x_{11} & x_{12} & \cdots & x_{1p} \\ x_{21} & x_{22} & \cdots & x_{2p} \\ \vdots & \vdots & \cdots & \vdots \\ x_{p1} & x_{p2} & \cdots & x_{pp} \end{bmatrix} \begin{bmatrix} 1 - \beta\phi_1 & -\beta\phi_2 & \cdots & -\beta\phi_{p-1} & -\beta\phi_p \\ -\beta & 1 & \cdots & 0 & 0 \\ \vdots & \vdots & \cdots & \vdots & \vdots \\ 0 & 0 & \cdots & -\beta & 1 \end{bmatrix} \qquad [1.A.11]$$

$$= \begin{bmatrix} 1 & 0 & \cdots & 0 \\ 0 & 1 & \cdots & 0 \\ \vdots & \vdots & \cdots & \vdots \\ 0 & 0 & \cdots & 1 \end{bmatrix}.$$

The task is then to find the (1, 1) element of $[\mathbf{I}_p - \beta\mathbf{F}]^{-1}$, that is, to find the value of $x_{11}$. To do this we need only consider the first row of equations in [1.A.11]:

$$[x_{11} \ \ x_{12} \ \ \cdots \ \ x_{1p}] \begin{bmatrix} 1 - \beta\phi_1 & -\beta\phi_2 & \cdots & -\beta\phi_{p-1} & -\beta\phi_p \\ -\beta & 1 & \cdots & 0 & 0 \\ \vdots & \vdots & \cdots & \vdots & \vdots \\ 0 & 0 & \cdots & -\beta & 1 \end{bmatrix}$$

$$= [1 \ \ 0 \ \ \cdots \ \ 0 \ \ 0]. \qquad [1.A.12]$$

[9]See Lemma 2 of Chiang (1980, p. 144).

Consider postmultiplying this system of equations by a matrix with 1s along the principal diagonal, $\beta$ in the row $p$, column $p - 1$ position, and 0s elsewhere:

$$\begin{bmatrix} 1 & 0 & \cdots & 0 & 0 \\ 0 & 1 & \cdots & 0 & 0 \\ \vdots & \vdots & \cdots & \vdots & \vdots \\ 0 & 0 & \cdots & \beta & 1 \end{bmatrix}.$$

The effect of this operation is to multiply the $p$th column of a matrix by $\beta$ and add the result to the $(p - 1)$th column:

$$[x_{11} \quad x_{12} \cdots x_{1p}] \begin{bmatrix} 1 - \beta\phi_1 & -\beta\phi_2 & \cdots & -\beta\phi_{p-1} - \beta^2\phi_p & -\beta\phi_p \\ -\beta & 1 & \cdots & 0 & 0 \\ \vdots & \vdots & \cdots & \vdots & \vdots \\ 0 & 0 & \cdots & 0 & 1 \end{bmatrix} = [1 \quad 0 \cdots 0 \quad 0].$$

Next multiply the $(p - 1)$th column by $\beta$ and add the result to the $(p - 2)$th column. Proceeding in this fashion, we arrive at

$$[x_{11} \quad x_{12} \quad \cdots \quad x_{1p}] \times$$

$$\begin{bmatrix} 1 - \beta\phi_1 - \beta^2\phi_2 - \cdots - \beta^{p-1}\phi_{p-1} - \beta^p\phi_p & -\beta\phi_2 - \beta^2\phi_3 - \cdots - \beta^{p-1}\phi_p & \cdots & -\beta\phi_{p-1} - \beta^2\phi_p & -\beta\phi_p \\ 0 & 1 & \cdots & 0 & 0 \\ \vdots & \vdots & \cdots & \vdots & \vdots \\ 0 & 0 & \cdots & 0 & 1 \end{bmatrix}$$

$$= [1 \quad 0 \quad \cdots \quad 0 \quad 0]. \qquad [1.A.13]$$

The first equation in [1.A.13] states that

$$x_{11} \cdot (1 - \beta\phi_1 - \beta^2\phi_2 - \cdots - \beta^{p-1}\phi_{p-1} - \beta^p\phi_p) = 1$$

or

$$x_{11} = 1/(1 - \beta\phi_1 - \beta^2\phi_2 - \cdots - \beta^p\phi_p),$$

as claimed in Proposition 1.3. ■

## *Chapter 1 References*


Chiang, Chin Long. 1980. *An Introduction to Stochastic Processes and Their Applications.* Huntington, N.Y.: Krieger.

Goldfeld, Stephen M. 1973. "The Demand for Money Revisited," *Brookings Papers on Economic Activity* 3:577–638.

Sargent, Thomas J. 1987. *Macroeconomic Theory*, 2d ed. Boston: Academic Press.

# 2 Lag Operators

## 2.1. *Introduction*

The previous chapter analyzed the dynamics of linear difference equations using matrix algebra. This chapter develops some of the same results using time series operators. We begin with some introductory remarks on some useful time series operators.

A time series is a collection of observations indexed by the date of each observation. Usually we have collected data beginning at some particular date (say, $t = 1$) and ending at another (say, $t = T$):

$$(y_1, y_2, \ldots, y_T).$$

We often imagine that we could have obtained earlier observations $(y_0, y_{-1}, y_{-2}, \ldots)$ or later observations $(y_{T+1}, y_{T+2}, \ldots)$ had the process been observed for more time. The observed sample $(y_1, y_2, \ldots, y_T)$ could then be viewed as a finite segment of a doubly infinite sequence, denoted $\{y_t\}_{t=-\infty}^{\infty}$:

$$\{y_t\}_{t=-\infty}^{\infty} = \{\ldots, y_{-1}, y_0, \underbrace{y_1, y_2, \ldots, y_T}_{\text{observed sample}}, y_{T+1}, y_{T+2}, \ldots\}.$$

Typically, a time series $\{y_t\}_{t=-\infty}^{\infty}$ is identified by describing the $t$th element. For example, a *time trend* is a series whose value at date $t$ is simply the date of the observation:

$$y_t = t.$$

We could also consider a time series in which each element is equal to a constant $c$, regardless of the date of the observation $t$:

$$y_t = c.$$

Another important time series is a *Gaussian white noise process*, denoted

$$y_t = \varepsilon_t,$$

where $\{\varepsilon_t\}_{t=-\infty}^{\infty}$ is a sequence of independent random variables each of which has a $N(0, \sigma^2)$ distribution.

We are used to thinking of a function such as $y = f(x)$ or $y = g(x, w)$ as an operation that accepts as input a number $(x)$ or group of numbers $(x, w)$ and produces the output $(y)$. A time series *operator* transforms one time series or group of time series into a new time series. It accepts as input a sequence such as $\{x_t\}_{t=-\infty}^{\infty}$ or a group of sequences such as $(\{x_t\}_{t=-\infty}^{\infty}, \{w_t\}_{t=-\infty}^{\infty})$ and has as output a new sequence $\{y_t\}_{t=-\infty}^{\infty}$. Again, the operator is summarized by describing the value of a typical element of $\{y_t\}_{t=-\infty}^{\infty}$ in terms of the corresponding elements of $\{x_t\}_{t=-\infty}^{\infty}$.

An example of a time series operator is the multiplication operator, represented as

$$y_t = \beta x_t. \qquad [2.1.1]$$

Although it is written exactly the same way as simple scalar multiplication, equation [2.1.1] is actually shorthand for an infinite sequence of multiplications, one for each date $t$. The operator multiplies the value $x$ takes on at any date $t$ by some constant $\beta$ to generate the value of $y$ for that date.

Another example of a time series operator is the addition operator:

$$y_t = x_t + w_t.$$

Here the value of $y$ at any date $t$ is the sum of the values that $x$ and $w$ take on for that date.

Since the multiplication or addition operators amount to element-by-element multiplication or addition, they obey all the standard rules of algebra. For example, if we multiply each observation of $\{x_t\}_{t=-\infty}^{\infty}$ by $\beta$ and each observation of $\{w_t\}_{t=-\infty}^{\infty}$ by $\beta$ and add the results,

$$\beta x_t + \beta w_t,$$

the outcome is the same as if we had first added $\{x_t\}_{t=-\infty}^{\infty}$ to $\{w_t\}_{t=-\infty}^{\infty}$ and then multiplied each element of the resulting series by $\beta$:

$$\beta(x_t + w_t).$$

A highly useful operator is the lag operator. Suppose that we start with a sequence $\{x_t\}_{t=-\infty}^{\infty}$ and generate a new sequence $\{y_t\}_{t=-\infty}^{\infty}$, where the value of $y$ for date $t$ is equal to the value $x$ took on at date $t - 1$:

$$y_t = x_{t-1}. \qquad [2.1.2]$$

This is described as applying the *lag operator* to $\{x_t\}_{t=-\infty}^{\infty}$. The operation is represented by the symbol $L$:

$$Lx_t \equiv x_{t-1}. \qquad [2.1.3]$$

Consider the result of applying the lag operator twice to a series:

$$L(Lx_t) = L(x_{t-1}) = x_{t-2}.$$

Such a double application of the lag operator is indicated by "$L^2$":

$$L^2 x_t = x_{t-2}.$$

In general, for any integer $k$,

$$L^k x_t = x_{t-k}. \qquad [2.1.4]$$

Notice that if we first apply the multiplication operator and then the lag operator, as in

$$x_t \rightarrow \beta x_t \rightarrow \beta x_{t-1},$$

the result will be exactly the same as if we had applied the lag operator first and then the multiplication operator:

$$x_t \rightarrow x_{t-1} \rightarrow \beta x_{t-1}.$$

Thus the lag operator and multiplication operator are commutative:

$$L(\beta x_t) = \beta \cdot L x_t.$$

Similarly, if we first add two series and then apply the lag operator to the result,

$$(x_t, w_t) \to x_t + w_t \to x_{t-1} + w_{t-1},$$

the result is the same as if we had applied the lag operator before adding:

$$(x_t, w_t) \to (x_{t-1}, w_{t-1}) \to x_{t-1} + w_{t-1}.$$

Thus, the lag operator is distributive over the addition operator:

$$L(x_t + w_t) = Lx_t + Lw_t.$$

We thus see that the lag operator follows exactly the same algebraic rules as the multiplication operator. For this reason, it is tempting to use the expression "multiply $y_t$ by $L$" rather than "operate on $\{y_t\}_{t=-\infty}^{\infty}$ by $L$." Although the latter expression is technically more correct, this text will often use the former shorthand expression to facilitate the exposition.

Faced with a time series defined in terms of compound operators, we are free to use the standard commutative, associative, and distributive algebraic laws for multiplication and addition to express the compound operator in an alternative form. For example, the process defined by

$$y_t = (a + bL)Lx_t$$

is exactly the same as

$$y_t = (aL + bL^2)x_t = ax_{t-1} + bx_{t-2}.$$

To take another example,

$$\begin{aligned}(1 - \lambda_1 L)(1 - \lambda_2 L)x_t &= (1 - \lambda_1 L - \lambda_2 L + \lambda_1\lambda_2 L^2)x_t \\ &= (1 - [\lambda_1 + \lambda_2]L + \lambda_1\lambda_2 L^2)x_t \\ &= x_t - (\lambda_1 + \lambda_2)x_{t-1} + (\lambda_1\lambda_2)x_{t-2}.\end{aligned} \qquad [2.1.5]$$

An expression such as $(aL + bL^2)$ is referred to as a *polynomial in the lag operator*. It is algebraically similar to a simple polynomial $(az + bz^2)$ where $z$ is a scalar. The difference is that the simple polynomial $(az + bz^2)$ refers to a particular number, whereas a polynomial in the lag operator $(aL + bL^2)$ refers to an operator that would be applied to one time series $\{x_t\}_{t=-\infty}^{\infty}$ to produce a new time series $\{y_t\}_{t=-\infty}^{\infty}$.

Notice that if $\{x_t\}_{t=-\infty}^{\infty}$ is just a series of constants,

$$x_t = c \qquad \text{for all } t,$$

then the lag operator applied to $x_t$ produces the same series of constants:

$$Lx_t = x_{t-1} = c.$$

Thus, for example,

$$(\alpha L + \beta L^2 + \gamma L^3)c = (\alpha + \beta + \gamma) \cdot c. \qquad [2.1.6]$$

## 2.2. *First-Order Difference Equations*

Let us now return to the first-order difference equation analyzed in Section 1.1:

$$y_t = \phi y_{t-1} + w_t. \qquad [2.2.1]$$

Equation [2.2.1] can be rewritten using the lag operator [2.1.3] as

$$y_t = \phi L y_t + w_t.$$

This equation, in turn, can be rearranged using standard algebra,

$$y_t - \phi L y_t = w_t,$$

or

$$(1 - \phi L)y_t = w_t. \qquad [2.2.2]$$

Next consider "multiplying" both sides of [2.2.2] by the following operator:

$$(1 + \phi L + \phi^2 L^2 + \phi^3 L^3 + \cdots + \phi^t L^t). \qquad [2.2.3]$$

The result would be

$$\begin{aligned}(1 + \phi L &+ \phi^2 L^2 + \phi^3 L^3 + \cdots + \phi^t L^t)(1 - \phi L)y_t \\ &= (1 + \phi L + \phi^2 L^2 + \phi^3 L^3 + \cdots + \phi^t L^t)w_t.\end{aligned} \qquad [2.2.4]$$

Expanding out the compound operator on the left side of [2.2.4] results in

$$\begin{aligned}(1 + \phi L &+ \phi^2 L^2 + \phi^3 L^3 + \cdots + \phi^t L^t)(1 - \phi L) \\ &= (1 + \phi L + \phi^2 L^2 + \phi^3 L^3 + \cdots + \phi^t L^t) \\ &\quad - (1 + \phi L + \phi^2 L^2 + \phi^3 L^3 + \cdots + \phi^t L^t)\phi L \\ &= (1 + \phi L + \phi^2 L^2 + \phi^3 L^3 + \cdots + \phi^t L^t) \\ &\quad - (\phi L + \phi^2 L^2 + \phi^3 L^3 + \cdots + \phi^t L^t + \phi^{t+1} L^{t+1}) \\ &= (1 - \phi^{t+1} L^{t+1}).\end{aligned} \qquad [2.2.5]$$

Substituting [2.2.5] into [2.2.4] yields

$$(1 - \phi^{t+1} L^{t+1})y_t = (1 + \phi L + \phi^2 L^2 + \phi^3 L^3 + \cdots + \phi^t L^t)w_t. \qquad [2.2.6]$$

Writing [2.2.6] out explicitly using [2.1.4] produces

$$y_t - \phi^{t+1} y_{t-(t+1)} = w_t + \phi w_{t-1} + \phi^2 w_{t-2} + \phi^3 w_{t-3} + \cdots + \phi^t w_{t-t}$$

or

$$y_t = \phi^{t+1} y_{-1} + w_t + \phi w_{t-1} + \phi^2 w_{t-2} + \phi^3 w_{t-3} + \cdots + \phi^t w_0. \qquad [2.2.7]$$

Notice that equation [2.2.7] is identical to equation [1.1.7]. Applying the operator [2.2.3] is performing exactly the same set of recursive substitutions that were employed in the previous chapter to arrive at [1.1.7].

It is interesting to reflect on the nature of the operator [2.2.3] as $t$ becomes large. We saw in [2.2.5] that

$$(1 + \phi L + \phi^2 L^2 + \phi^3 L^3 + \cdots + \phi^t L^t)(1 - \phi L)y_t = y_t - \phi^{t+1} y_{-1}.$$

That is, $(1 + \phi L + \phi^2 L^2 + \phi^3 L^3 + \cdots + \phi^t L^t)(1 - \phi L)y_t$ differs from $y_t$ by the term $\phi^{t+1} y_{-1}$. If $|\phi| < 1$ and if $y_{-1}$ is a finite number, this residual $\phi^{t+1} y_{-1}$ will become negligible as $t$ becomes large:

$$(1 + \phi L + \phi^2 L^2 + \phi^3 L^3 + \cdots + \phi^t L^t)(1 - \phi L)y_t \cong y_t \qquad \text{for } t \text{ large}.$$

A sequence $\{y_t\}_{t=-\infty}^{\infty}$ is said to be *bounded* if there exists a finite number $\bar{y}$ such that

$$|y_t| < \bar{y} \qquad \text{for all } t.$$

Thus, when $|\phi| < 1$ and when we are considering applying an operator to a bounded sequence, we can think of

$$(1 + \phi L + \phi^2 L^2 + \phi^3 L^3 + \cdots + \phi^j L^j)$$

as approximating the inverse of the operator $(1 - \phi L)$, with this approximation made arbitrarily accurate by choosing $j$ sufficiently large:

$$(1 - \phi L)^{-1} = \lim_{j\to\infty} (1 + \phi L + \phi^2 L^2 + \phi^3 L^3 + \cdots + \phi^j L^j). \quad [2.2.8]$$

This operator $(1 - \phi L)^{-1}$ has the property

$$(1 - \phi L)^{-1}(1 - \phi L) = 1,$$

where "1" denotes the identity operator:

$$1 y_t = y_t.$$

The following chapter discusses stochastic sequences rather than the deterministic sequences studied here. There we will speak of mean square convergence and stationary stochastic processes in place of limits of bounded deterministic sequences, though the practical meaning of [2.2.8] will be little changed.

Provided that $|\phi| < 1$ and we restrict ourselves to bounded sequences or stationary stochastic processes, both sides of [2.2.2] can be "divided" by $(1 - \phi L)$ to obtain

$$y_t = (1 - \phi L)^{-1} w_t$$

or

$$y_t = w_t + \phi w_{t-1} + \phi^2 w_{t-2} + \phi^3 w_{t-3} + \cdots. \quad [2.2.9]$$

It should be emphasized that if we were not restricted to considering bounded sequences or stationary stochastic processes $\{w_t\}_{t=-\infty}^{\infty}$ and $\{y_t\}_{t=-\infty}^{\infty}$, then expression [2.2.9] would not be a necessary implication of [2.2.1]. Equation [2.2.9] is consistent with [2.2.1], but adding a term $a_o \phi^t$,

$$y_t = a_o \phi^t + w_t + \phi w_{t-1} + \phi^2 w_{t-2} + \phi^3 w_{t-3} + \cdots, \quad [2.2.10]$$

produces another series consistent with [2.2.1] for any constant $a_o$. To verify that [2.2.10] is consistent with [2.2.1], multiply [2.2.10] by $(1 - \phi L)$:

$$\begin{aligned}(1 - \phi L)y_t &= (1 - \phi L)a_o \phi^t + (1 - \phi L)(1 - \phi L)^{-1} w_t \\ &= a_o \phi^t - \phi \cdot a_o \phi^{t-1} + w_t \\ &= w_t,\end{aligned}$$

so that [2.2.10] is consistent with [2.2.1] for any constant $a_o$.

Although any process of the form of [2.2.10] is consistent with the difference equation [2.2.1], notice that since $|\phi| < 1$,

$$|a_o \phi^t| \to \infty \quad \text{as} \quad t \to -\infty.$$

Thus, even if $\{w_t\}_{t=-\infty}^{\infty}$ is a bounded sequence, the solution $\{y_t\}_{t=-\infty}^{\infty}$ given by [2.2.10] is unbounded unless $a_o = 0$ in [2.2.10]. Thus, there was a particular reason for defining the operator [2.2.8] to be the inverse of $(1 - \phi L)$—namely, $(1 - \phi L)^{-1}$ defined in [2.2.8] is the unique operator satisfying

$$(1 - \phi L)^{-1}(1 - \phi L) = 1$$

that maps a bounded sequence $\{w_t\}_{t=-\infty}^{\infty}$ into a bounded sequence $\{y_t\}_{t=-\infty}^{\infty}$.

The nature of $(1 - \phi L)^{-1}$ when $|\phi| \geq 1$ will be discussed in Section 2.5.

## 2.3. *Second-Order Difference Equations*

Consider next a second-order difference equation:

$$y_t = \phi_1 y_{t-1} + \phi_2 y_{t-2} + w_t. \quad [2.3.1]$$

Rewriting this in lag operator form produces

$$(1 - \phi_1 L - \phi_2 L^2)y_t = w_t. \qquad [2.3.2]$$

The left side of [2.3.2] contains a second-order polynomial in the lag operator $L$. Suppose we factor this polynomial, that is, find numbers $\lambda_1$ and $\lambda_2$ such that

$$(1 - \phi_1 L - \phi_2 L^2) = (1 - \lambda_1 L)(1 - \lambda_2 L) = (1 - [\lambda_1 + \lambda_2]L + \lambda_1\lambda_2 L^2). \qquad [2.3.3]$$

This is just the operation in [2.1.5] in reverse. Given values for $\phi_1$ and $\phi_2$, we seek numbers $\lambda_1$ and $\lambda_2$ with the properties that

$$\lambda_1 + \lambda_2 = \phi_1$$

and

$$\lambda_1\lambda_2 = -\phi_2.$$

For example, if $\phi_1 = 0.6$ and $\phi_2 = -0.08$, then we should choose $\lambda_1 = 0.4$ and $\lambda_2 = 0.2$:

$$(1 - 0.6L + 0.08L^2) = (1 - 0.4L)(1 - 0.2L). \qquad [2.3.4]$$

It is easy enough to see that these values of $\lambda_1$ and $\lambda_2$ work for this numerical example, but how are $\lambda_1$ and $\lambda_2$ found in general? The task is to choose $\lambda_1$ and $\lambda_2$ so as to make sure that the operator on the right side of [2.3.3] is identical to that on the left side. This will be true whenever the following represent the identical functions of $z$:

$$(1 - \phi_1 z - \phi_2 z^2) = (1 - \lambda_1 z)(1 - \lambda_2 z). \qquad [2.3.5]$$

This equation simply replaces the lag operator $L$ in [2.3.3] with a scalar $z$. What is the point of doing so? With [2.3.5], we can now ask, For what values of $z$ is the right side of [2.3.5] equal to zero? The answer is, if either $z = \lambda_1^{-1}$ or $z = \lambda_2^{-1}$, then the right side of [2.3.5] would be zero. It would not have made sense to ask an analogous question of [2.3.3]—$L$ denotes a particular operator, not a number, and $L = \lambda_1^{-1}$ is not a sensible statement.

Why should we care that the right side of [2.3.5] is zero if $z = \lambda_1^{-1}$ or if $z = \lambda_2^{-1}$? Recall that the goal was to choose $\lambda_1$ and $\lambda_2$ so that the two sides of [2.3.5] represented the identical polynomial in $z$. This means that for any particular value $z$ the two functions must produce the same number. If we find a value of $z$ that sets the right side to zero, that same value of $z$ must set the left side to zero as well. But the values of $z$ that set the left side to zero,

$$(1 - \phi_1 z - \phi_2 z^2) = 0, \qquad [2.3.6]$$

are given by the quadratic formula:

$$z_1 = \frac{\phi_1 - \sqrt{\phi_1^2 + 4\phi_2}}{-2\phi_2} \qquad [2.3.7]$$

$$z_2 = \frac{\phi_1 + \sqrt{\phi_1^2 + 4\phi_2}}{-2\phi_2}. \qquad [2.3.8]$$

Setting $z = z_1$ or $z_2$ makes the left side of [2.3.5] zero, while $z = \lambda_1^{-1}$ or $\lambda_2^{-1}$ sets the right side of [2.3.5] to zero. Thus

$$\lambda_1^{-1} = z_1 \qquad [2.3.9]$$

$$\lambda_2^{-1} = z_2. \qquad [2.3.10]$$

Returning to the numerical example [2.3.4] in which $\phi_1 = 0.6$ and $\phi_2 = -0.08$, we would calculate

$$z_1 = \frac{0.6 - \sqrt{(0.6)^2 - 4(0.08)}}{2(0.08)} = 2.5$$

$$z_2 = \frac{0.6 + \sqrt{(0.6)^2 - 4(0.08)}}{2(0.08)} = 5.0,$$

and so

$$\lambda_1 = 1/(2.5) = 0.4$$

$$\lambda_2 = 1/(5.0) = 0.2,$$

as was found in [2.3.4].

When $\phi_1^2 + 4\phi_2 < 0$, the values $z_1$ and $z_2$ are complex conjugates, and their reciprocals $\lambda_1$ and $\lambda_2$ can be found by first writing the complex number in polar coordinate form. Specifically, write

$$z_1 = a + bi$$

as

$$z_1 = R\cdot[\cos(\theta) + i\cdot\sin(\theta)] = R\cdot e^{i\theta}.$$

Then

$$z_1^{-1} = R^{-1}\cdot e^{-i\theta} = R^{-1}\cdot[\cos(\theta) - i\cdot\sin(\theta)].$$

Actually, there is a more direct method for calculating the values of $\lambda_1$ and $\lambda_2$ from $\phi_1$ and $\phi_2$. Divide both sides of [2.3.5] by $z^2$:

$$(z^{-2} - \phi_1 z^{-1} - \phi_2) = (z^{-1} - \lambda_1)(z^{-1} - \lambda_2) \qquad [2.3.11]$$

and define $\lambda$ to be the variable $z^{-1}$:

$$\lambda \equiv z^{-1}. \qquad [2.3.12]$$

Substituting [2.3.12] into [2.3.11] produces

$$(\lambda^2 - \phi_1\lambda - \phi_2) = (\lambda - \lambda_1)(\lambda - \lambda_2). \qquad [2.3.13]$$

Again, [2.3.13] must hold for all values of $\lambda$ in order for the two sides of [2.3.5] to represent the same polynomial. The values of $\lambda$ that set the right side to zero are $\lambda = \lambda_1$ and $\lambda = \lambda_2$. These same values must set the left side of [2.3.13] to zero as well:

$$(\lambda^2 - \phi_1\lambda - \phi_2) = 0. \qquad [2.3.14]$$

Thus, to calculate the values of $\lambda_1$ and $\lambda_2$ that factor the polynomial in [2.3.3], we can find the roots of [2.3.14] directly from the quadratic formula:

$$\lambda_1 = \frac{\phi_1 + \sqrt{\phi_1^2 + 4\phi_2}}{2} \qquad [2.3.15]$$

$$\lambda_2 = \frac{\phi_1 - \sqrt{\phi_1^2 + 4\phi_2}}{2}. \qquad [2.3.16]$$

For the example of [2.3.4], we would thus calculate

$$\lambda_1 = \frac{0.6 + \sqrt{(0.6)^2 - 4(0.08)}}{2} = 0.4$$

$$\lambda_2 = \frac{0.6 - \sqrt{(0.6)^2 - 4(0.08)}}{2} = 0.2.$$

It is instructive to compare these results with those in Chapter 1. There the dynamics of the second-order difference equation [2.3.1] were summarized by calculating the eigenvalues of the matrix $\mathbf{F}$ given by

$$\mathbf{F} = \begin{bmatrix} \phi_1 & \phi_2 \\ 1 & 0 \end{bmatrix}. \qquad [2.3.17]$$

The eigenvalues of $\mathbf{F}$ were seen to be the two values of $\lambda$ that satisfy equation [1.2.13]:

$$(\lambda^2 - \phi_1\lambda - \phi_2) = 0.$$

But this is the same calculation as in [2.3.14]. This finding is summarized in the following proposition.

***Proposition 2.1:*** *Factoring the polynomial* $(1 - \phi_1 L - \phi_2 L^2)$ *as*

$$(1 - \phi_1 L - \phi_2 L^2) = (1 - \lambda_1 L)(1 - \lambda_2 L) \qquad [2.3.18]$$

*is the same calculation as finding the eigenvalues of the matrix* $\mathbf{F}$ *in [2.3.17]. The eigenvalues* $\lambda_1$ *and* $\lambda_2$ *of* $\mathbf{F}$ *are the same as the parameters* $\lambda_1$ *and* $\lambda_2$ *in [2.3.18], and are given by equations [2.3.15] and [2.3.16].*

The correspondence between calculating the eigenvalues of a matrix and factoring a polynomial in the lag operator is very instructive. However, it introduces one minor source of possible semantic confusion about which we have to be careful. Recall from Chapter 1 that the system [2.3.1] is stable if both $\lambda_1$ and $\lambda_2$ are less than 1 in modulus and explosive if either $\lambda_1$ or $\lambda_2$ is greater than 1 in modulus. Sometimes this is described as the requirement that the roots of

$$(\lambda^2 - \phi_1\lambda - \phi_2) = 0 \qquad [2.3.19]$$

lie inside the unit circle. The possible confusion is that it is often convenient to work directly with the polynomial in the form in which it appears in [2.3.2],

$$(1 - \phi_1 z - \phi_2 z^2) = 0, \qquad [2.3.20]$$

whose roots, we have seen, are the reciprocals of those of [2.3.19]. Thus, we could say with equal accuracy that "the difference equation [2.3.1] is stable whenever the roots of [2.3.19] lie *inside* the unit circle" or that "the difference equation [2.3.1] is stable whenever the roots of [2.3.20] lie *outside* the unit circle." The two statements mean exactly the same thing. Some scholars refer simply to the "roots of the difference equation [2.3.1]," though this raises the possibility of confusion between [2.3.19] and [2.3.20]. This book will follow the convention of using the term "eigenvalues" to refer to the roots of [2.3.19]. Wherever the term "roots" is used, we will indicate explicitly the equation whose roots are being described.

From here on in this section, it is assumed that the second-order difference equation is stable, with the eigenvalues $\lambda_1$ and $\lambda_2$ distinct and both inside the unit circle. Where this is the case, the inverses

$$(1 - \lambda_1 L)^{-1} = 1 + \lambda_1^1 L + \lambda_1^2 L^2 + \lambda_1^3 L^3 + \cdots$$
$$(1 - \lambda_2 L)^{-1} = 1 + \lambda_2^1 L + \lambda_2^2 L^2 + \lambda_2^3 L^3 + \cdots$$

are well defined for bounded sequences. Write [2.3.2] in factored form:

$$(1 - \lambda_1 L)(1 - \lambda_2 L)y_t = w_t$$

and operate on both sides by $(1 - \lambda_1 L)^{-1}(1 - \lambda_2 L)^{-1}$:

$$y_t = (1 - \lambda_1 L)^{-1}(1 - \lambda_2 L)^{-1} w_t. \qquad [2.3.21]$$

Following Sargent (1987, p. 184), when $\lambda_1 \neq \lambda_2$, we can use the following operator:

$$(\lambda_1 - \lambda_2)^{-1}\left\{\frac{\lambda_1}{1 - \lambda_1 L} - \frac{\lambda_2}{1 - \lambda_2 L}\right\}. \qquad [2.3.22]$$

Notice that this is simply another way of writing the operator in [2.3.21]:

$$\begin{aligned}(\lambda_1 - \lambda_2)^{-1}&\left\{\frac{\lambda_1}{1 - \lambda_1 L} - \frac{\lambda_2}{1 - \lambda_2 L}\right\} \\ &= (\lambda_1 - \lambda_2)^{-1}\left\{\frac{\lambda_1(1 - \lambda_2 L) - \lambda_2(1 - \lambda_1 L)}{(1 - \lambda_1 L)\cdot(1 - \lambda_2 L)}\right\} \\ &= \frac{1}{(1 - \lambda_1 L)\cdot(1 - \lambda_2 L)}.\end{aligned}$$

Thus, [2.3.21] can be written as

$$\begin{aligned}y_t &= (\lambda_1 - \lambda_2)^{-1}\left\{\frac{\lambda_1}{1 - \lambda_1 L} - \frac{\lambda_2}{1 - \lambda_2 L}\right\}w_t \\ &= \left\{\frac{\lambda_1}{\lambda_1 - \lambda_2}[1 + \lambda_1 L + \lambda_1^2 L^2 + \lambda_1^3 L^3 + \cdots] \right. \\ &\quad \left. - \frac{\lambda_2}{\lambda_1 - \lambda_2}[1 + \lambda_2 L + \lambda_2^2 L^2 + \lambda_2^3 L^3 + \cdots]\right\}w_t\end{aligned}$$

or

$$\begin{aligned}y_t = [c_1 + c_2]w_t + [c_1\lambda_1 + c_2\lambda_2]w_{t-1} + [c_1\lambda_1^2 + c_2\lambda_2^2]w_{t-2} \\ + [c_1\lambda_1^3 + c_2\lambda_2^3]w_{t-3} + \cdots,\end{aligned} \qquad [2.3.23]$$

where

$$c_1 = \lambda_1/(\lambda_1 - \lambda_2) \qquad [2.3.24]$$

$$c_2 = -\lambda_2/(\lambda_1 - \lambda_2). \qquad [2.3.25]$$

From [2.3.23] the dynamic multiplier can be read off directly as

$$\frac{\partial y_{t+j}}{\partial w_t} = c_1\lambda_1^j + c_2\lambda_2^j,$$

the same result arrived at in equations [1.2.24] and [1.2.25].

## 2.4. *p*th-Order Difference Equations

These techniques generalize in a straightforward way to a $p$th-order difference equation of the form

$$y_t = \phi_1 y_{t-1} + \phi_2 y_{t-2} + \cdots + \phi_p y_{t-p} + w_t. \qquad [2.4.1]$$

Write [2.4.1] in terms of lag operators as

$$(1 - \phi_1 L - \phi_2 L^2 - \cdots - \phi_p L^p)y_t = w_t. \qquad [2.4.2]$$

Factor the operator on the left side of [2.4.2] as

$$(1 - \phi_1 L - \phi_2 L^2 - \cdots - \phi_p L^p) = (1 - \lambda_1 L)(1 - \lambda_2 L)\cdots(1 - \lambda_p L). \qquad [2.4.3]$$

This is the same as finding the values of $(\lambda_1, \lambda_2, \ldots, \lambda_p)$ such that the following polynomials are the same for all $z$:

$$(1 - \phi_1 z - \phi_2 z^2 - \cdots - \phi_p z^p) = (1 - \lambda_1 z)(1 - \lambda_2 z)\cdots(1 - \lambda_p z).$$

As in the second-order system, we multiply both sides of this equation by $z^{-p}$ and define $\lambda \equiv z^{-1}$:

$$(\lambda^p - \phi_1\lambda^{p-1} - \phi_2\lambda^{p-2} - \cdots - \phi_{p-1}\lambda - \phi_p) = (\lambda - \lambda_1)(\lambda - \lambda_2) \cdots (\lambda - \lambda_p). \quad [2.4.4]$$

Clearly, setting $\lambda = \lambda_i$ for $i = 1, 2, \ldots,$ or $p$ causes the right side of [2.4.4] to equal zero. Thus the values $(\lambda_1, \lambda_2, \ldots, \lambda_p)$ must be the numbers that set the left side of expression [2.4.4] to zero as well:

$$\lambda^p - \phi_1\lambda^{p-1} - \phi_2\lambda^{p-2} - \cdots - \phi_{p-1}\lambda - \phi_p = 0. \quad [2.4.5]$$

This expression again is identical to that given in Proposition 1.1, which characterized the eigenvalues $(\lambda_1, \lambda_2, \ldots, \lambda_p)$ of the matrix $\mathbf{F}$ defined in equation [1.2.3]. Thus, Proposition 2.1 readily generalizes.

***Proposition 2.2:*** *Factoring a pth-order polynomial in the lag operator,*

$$(1 - \phi_1 L - \phi_2 L^2 - \cdots - \phi_p L^p) = (1 - \lambda_1 L)(1 - \lambda_2 L) \cdots (1 - \lambda_p L),$$

*is the same calculation as finding the eigenvalues of the matrix* $\mathbf{F}$ *defined in [1.2.3]. The eigenvalues* $(\lambda_1, \lambda_2, \ldots, \lambda_p)$ *of* $\mathbf{F}$ *are the same as the parameters* $(\lambda_1, \lambda_2, \ldots, \lambda_p)$ *in [2.4.3] and are given by the solutions to equation [2.4.5].*

The difference equation [2.4.1] is stable if the eigenvalues (the roots of [2.4.5]) lie inside the unit circle, or equivalently if the roots of

$$1 - \phi_1 z - \phi_2 z^2 - \cdots - \phi_p z^p = 0 \quad [2.4.6]$$

lie outside the unit circle.

Assuming that the eigenvalues are inside the unit circle and that we are restricting ourselves to considering bounded sequences, the inverses $(1 - \lambda_1 L)^{-1}$, $(1 - \lambda_2 L)^{-1}, \ldots, (1 - \lambda_p L)^{-1}$ all exist, permitting the difference equation

$$(1 - \lambda_1 L)(1 - \lambda_2 L) \cdots (1 - \lambda_p L)y_t = w_t$$

to be written as

$$y_t = (1 - \lambda_1 L)^{-1}(1 - \lambda_2 L)^{-1} \cdots (1 - \lambda_p L)^{-1} w_t. \quad [2.4.7]$$

Provided further that the eigenvalues $(\lambda_1, \lambda_2, \ldots, \lambda_p)$ are all distinct, the polynomial associated with the operator on the right side of [2.4.7] can again be expanded with partial fractions:

$$\frac{1}{(1 - \lambda_1 z)(1 - \lambda_2 z) \cdots (1 - \lambda_p z)} = \frac{c_1}{(1 - \lambda_1 z)} + \frac{c_2}{(1 - \lambda_2 z)} + \cdots + \frac{c_p}{(1 - \lambda_p z)}. \quad [2.4.8]$$

Following Sargent (1987, pp. 192–93), the values of $(c_1, c_2, \ldots, c_p)$ that make [2.4.8] true can be found by multiplying both sides by $(1 - \lambda_1 z)(1 - \lambda_2 z) \cdots (1 - \lambda_p z)$:

$$\begin{aligned} 1 = {} & c_1(1 - \lambda_2 z)(1 - \lambda_3 z) \cdots (1 - \lambda_p z) \\ & + c_2(1 - \lambda_1 z)(1 - \lambda_3 z) \cdots (1 - \lambda_p z) + \cdots \\ & + c_p(1 - \lambda_1 z)(1 - \lambda_2 z) \cdots (1 - \lambda_{p-1} z). \end{aligned} \quad [2.4.9]$$

Equation [2.4.9] has to hold for all values of $z$. Since it is a $(p - 1)$th-order polynomial, if $(c_1, c_2, \ldots, c_p)$ are chosen so that [2.4.9] holds for $p$ particular distinct values of $z$, then [2.4.9] must hold for all $z$. To ensure that [2.4.9] holds at $z = \lambda_1^{-1}$ requires that

$$1 = c_1(1 - \lambda_2\lambda_1^{-1})(1 - \lambda_3\lambda_1^{-1}) \cdots (1 - \lambda_p\lambda_1^{-1})$$

or

$$c_1 = \frac{\lambda_1^{p-1}}{(\lambda_1 - \lambda_2)(\lambda_1 - \lambda_3) \cdots (\lambda_1 - \lambda_p)}. \qquad [2.4.10]$$

For [2.4.9] to hold for $z = \lambda_2^{-1}, \lambda_3^{-1}, \ldots, \lambda_p^{-1}$ requires

$$c_2 = \frac{\lambda_2^{p-1}}{(\lambda_2 - \lambda_1)(\lambda_2 - \lambda_3) \cdots (\lambda_2 - \lambda_p)} \qquad [2.4.11]$$

$$\vdots$$

$$c_p = \frac{\lambda_p^{p-1}}{(\lambda_p - \lambda_1)(\lambda_p - \lambda_2) \cdots (\lambda_p - \lambda_{p-1})}. \qquad [2.4.12]$$

Note again that these are identical to expression [1.2.25] in Chapter 1. Recall from the discussion there that $c_1 + c_2 + \cdots + c_p = 1$.

To conclude, [2.4.7] can be written

$$\begin{aligned} y_t &= \frac{c_1}{(1 - \lambda_1 L)} w_t + \frac{c_2}{(1 - \lambda_2 L)} w_t + \cdots + \frac{c_p}{(1 - \lambda_p L)} w_t \\ &= c_1(1 + \lambda_1 L + \lambda_1^2 L^2 + \lambda_1^3 L^3 + \cdots)w_t + c_2(1 + \lambda_2 L + \lambda_2^2 L^2 + \lambda_2^3 L^3 + \cdots)w_t \\ &\quad + \cdots + c_p(1 + \lambda_p L + \lambda_p^2 L^2 + \lambda_p^3 L^3 + \cdots)w_t \end{aligned}$$

or

$$\begin{aligned} y_t = {} & [c_1 + c_2 + \cdots + c_p]w_t + [c_1\lambda_1 + c_2\lambda_2 + \cdots + c_p\lambda_p]w_{t-1} \\ & + [c_1\lambda_1^2 + c_2\lambda_2^2 + \cdots + c_p\lambda_p^2]w_{t-2} \\ & + [c_1\lambda_1^3 + c_2\lambda_2^3 + \cdots + c_p\lambda_p^3]w_{t-3} + \cdots \end{aligned} \qquad [2.4.13]$$

where $(c_1, c_2, \ldots, c_p)$ are given by equations [2.4.10] through [2.4.12]. Again, the dynamic multiplier can be read directly off [2.4.13]:

$$\frac{\partial y_{t+j}}{\partial w_t} = [c_1\lambda_1^j + c_2\lambda_2^j + \cdots + c_p\lambda_p^j], \qquad [2.4.14]$$

reproducing the result from Chapter 1.

There is a very convenient way to calculate the effect of $w$ on the present value of $y$ using the lag operator representation. Write [2.4.13] as

$$y_t = \psi_0 w_t + \psi_1 w_{t-1} + \psi_2 w_{t-2} + \psi_3 w_{t-3} + \cdots \qquad [2.4.15]$$

where

$$\psi_j = [c_1\lambda_1^j + c_2\lambda_2^j + \cdots + c_p\lambda_p^j]. \qquad [2.4.16]$$

Next rewrite [2.4.15] in lag operator notation as

$$y_t = \psi(L)w_t, \qquad [2.4.17]$$

where $\psi(L)$ denotes an infinite-order polynomial in the lag operator:

$$\psi(L) = \psi_0 + \psi_1 L + \psi_2 L^2 + \psi_3 L^3 + \cdots.$$

Notice that $\psi_j$ is the dynamic multiplier [2.4.14]. The effect of $w_t$ on the present value of $y$ is given by

$$\frac{\partial \sum_{j=0}^{\infty} \beta^j y_{t+j}}{\partial w_t} = \sum_{j=0}^{\infty} \beta^j \frac{\partial y_{t+j}}{\partial w_t} = \sum_{j=0}^{\infty} \beta^j \psi_j. \qquad [2.4.18]$$

Thinking of $\psi(z)$ as a polynomial in a real number $z$,

$$\psi(z) = \psi_0 + \psi_1 z + \psi_2 z^2 + \psi_3 z^3 + \cdots,$$

it appears that the multiplier [2.4.18] is simply this polynomial evaluated at $z = \beta$:

$$\frac{\partial \sum_{j=0}^{\infty} \beta^j y_{t+j}}{\partial w_t} = \psi(\beta) = \psi_0 + \psi_1 \beta + \psi_2 \beta^2 + \psi_3 \beta^3 + \cdots. \qquad [2.4.19]$$

But comparing [2.4.17] with [2.4.7], it is apparent that

$$\psi(L) = [(1 - \lambda_1 L)(1 - \lambda_2 L) \cdots (1 - \lambda_p L)]^{-1},$$

and from [2.4.3] this means that

$$\psi(L) = [1 - \phi_1 L - \phi_2 L^2 - \cdots - \phi_p L^p]^{-1}.$$

We conclude that

$$\psi(z) = [1 - \phi_1 z - \phi_2 z^2 - \cdots - \phi_p z^p]^{-1}$$

for any value of $z$, so, in particular,

$$\psi(\beta) = [1 - \phi_1 \beta - \phi_2 \beta^2 - \cdots - \phi_p \beta^p]^{-1}. \qquad [2.4.20]$$

Substituting [2.4.20] into [2.4.19] reveals that

$$\frac{\partial \sum_{j=0}^{\infty} \beta^j y_{t+j}}{\partial w_t} = \frac{1}{1 - \phi_1 \beta - \phi_2 \beta^2 - \cdots - \phi_p \beta^p}, \qquad [2.4.21]$$

reproducing the claim in Proposition 1.3. Again, the long-run multiplier obtains as the special case of [2.4.21] with $\beta = 1$:

$$\lim_{j \to \infty} \left[ \frac{\partial y_{t+j}}{\partial w_t} + \frac{\partial y_{t+j}}{\partial w_{t+1}} + \cdots + \frac{\partial y_{t+j}}{\partial w_{t+j}} \right] = \frac{1}{1 - \phi_1 - \phi_2 - \cdots - \phi_p}.$$

## 2.5. *Initial Conditions and Unbounded Sequences*

Section 1.2 analyzed the following problem. Given a $p$th-order difference equation

$$y_t = \phi_1 y_{t-1} + \phi_2 y_{t-2} + \cdots + \phi_p y_{t-p} + w_t, \qquad [2.5.1]$$

$p$ initial values of $y$,

$$y_{-1}, y_{-2}, \ldots, y_{-p}, \qquad [2.5.2]$$

and a sequence of values for the input variable $w$,

$$\{w_0, w_1, \ldots, w_t\}, \qquad [2.5.3]$$

we sought to calculate the sequence of values for the output variable $y$:

$$\{y_0, y_1, \ldots, y_t\}.$$

Certainly there are systems where the question is posed in precisely this form. We may know the equation of motion for the system [2.5.1] and its current state [2.5.2] and wish to characterize the values that $\{y_0, y_1, \ldots, y_t\}$ might take on for different specifications of $\{w_0, w_1, \ldots, w_t\}$.

However, there are many examples in economics and finance in which a theory specifies just the equation of motion [2.5.1] and a sequence of driving variables [2.5.3]. Clearly, these two pieces of information alone are insufficient to determine the sequence $\{y_0, y_1, \ldots, y_t\}$, and some additional theory beyond that contained in the difference equation [2.5.1] is needed to describe fully the dependence of $y$ on $w$. These additional restrictions can be of interest in their own right and also help give some insight into some of the technical details of manipulating difference equations. For these reasons, this section discusses in some depth an example of the role of initial conditions and their implications for solving difference equations.

Let $P_t$ denote the price of a stock and $D_t$ its dividend payment. If an investor buys the stock at date $t$ and sells it at $t + 1$, the investor will earn a yield of $D_t/P_t$ from the dividend and a yield of $(P_{t+1} - P_t)/P_t$ in capital gains. The investor's total return $(r_{t+1})$ is thus

$$r_{t+1} = (P_{t+1} - P_t)/P_t + D_t/P_t.$$

A very simple model of the stock market posits that the return investors earn on stocks is constant across time periods:

$$r = (P_{t+1} - P_t)/P_t + D_t/P_t \qquad r > 0. \tag{2.5.4}$$

Equation [2.5.4] may seem too simplistic to be of much practical interest; it assumes among other things that investors have perfect foresight about future stock prices and dividends. However, a slightly more realistic model in which *expected* stock returns are constant involves a very similar set of technical issues. The advantage of the perfect-foresight model [2.5.4] is that it can be discussed using the tools already in hand to gain some further insight into using lag operators to solve difference equations.

Multiply [2.5.4] by $P_t$ to arrive at

$$rP_t = P_{t+1} - P_t + D_t$$

or

$$P_{t+1} = (1 + r)P_t - D_t. \tag{2.5.5}$$

Equation [2.5.5] will be recognized as a first-order difference equation of the form of [1.1.1] with $y_t = P_{t+1}$, $\phi = (1 + r)$, and $w_t = -D_t$. From [1.1.7], we know that [2.5.5] implies that

$$\begin{aligned} P_{t+1} = (1 + r)^{t+1}P_0 - (1 + r)^tD_0 - (1 + r)^{t-1}D_1 - (1 + r)^{t-2}D_2 \\ - \cdots - (1 + r)D_{t-1} - D_t. \end{aligned} \tag{2.5.6}$$

If the sequence $\{D_0, D_1, \ldots, D_t\}$ *and* the value of $P_0$ were given, then [2.5.6] could determine the values of $\{P_1, P_2, \ldots, P_{t+1}\}$. But if only the values $\{D_0, D_1, \ldots, D_t\}$ are given, then equation [2.5.6] would not be enough to pin down $\{P_1, P_2, \ldots, P_{t+1}\}$. There are an infinite number of possible sequences $\{P_1, P_2, \ldots, P_{t+1}\}$ consistent with [2.5.5] and with a given $\{D_0, D_1, \ldots, D_t\}$. This infinite number of possibilities is indexed by the initial value $P_0$.

A further simplifying assumption helps clarify the nature of these different paths for $\{P_1, P_2, \ldots, P_{t+1}\}$. Suppose that dividends are constant over time:

$$D_t = D \qquad \text{for all } t.$$

Then [2.5.6] becomes

$$\begin{aligned} P_{t+1} &= (1 + r)^{t+1}P_0 - [(1 + r)^t + (1 + r)^{t-1} \\ &\quad + \cdots + (1 + r) + 1]D \\ &= (1 + r)^{t+1}P_0 - \frac{1 - (1 + r)^{t+1}}{1 - (1 + r)} D \\ &= (1 + r)^{t+1}[P_0 - (D/r)] + (D/r). \end{aligned} \qquad [2.5.7]$$

Consider first the solution in which $P_0 = D/r$. If the initial stock price should happen to take this value, then [2.5.7] implies that

$$P_t = D/r \qquad [2.5.8]$$

for all $t$. In this solution, dividends are constant at $D$ and the stock price is constant at $D/r$. With no change in stock prices, investors never have any capital gains or losses, and their return is solely the dividend yield $D/P = r$. In a world with no changes in dividends this seems to be a sensible expression of the theory represented by [2.5.4]. Equation [2.5.8] is sometimes described as the "market fundamentals" solution to [2.5.4] for the case of constant dividends.

However, even with constant dividends, equation [2.5.8] is not the only result consistent with [2.5.4]. Suppose that the initial price exceeded $D/r$:

$$P_0 > D/r.$$

Investors seem to be valuing the stock beyond the potential of its constant dividend stream. From [2.5.7] this could be consistent with the asset pricing theory [2.5.4] provided that $P_1$ exceeds $D/r$ by an even larger amount. As long as investors all believe that prices will continue to rise over time, each will earn the required return $r$ from the realized capital gain and [2.5.4] will be satisfied. This scenario has reminded many economists of a speculative bubble in stock prices.

If such bubbles are to be ruled out, additional knowledge about the process for $\{P_t\}_{t=-\infty}^{\infty}$ is required beyond that contained in the theory of [2.5.4]. For example, we might argue that finite world resources put an upper limit on feasible stock prices, as in

$$|P_t| < \bar{P} \qquad \text{for all } t. \qquad [2.5.9]$$

Then the only sequence for $\{P_t\}_{t=-\infty}^{\infty}$ consistent with both [2.5.4] and [2.5.9] would be the market fundamentals solution [2.5.8].

Let us now relax the assumption that dividends are constant and replace it with the assumption that $\{D_t\}_{t=-\infty}^{\infty}$ is a bounded sequence. What path for $\{P_t\}_{t=-\infty}^{\infty}$ in [2.5.6] is consistent with [2.5.9] in this case? The answer can be found by returning to the difference equation [2.5.5]. We arrived at the form [2.5.6] by recursively substituting this equation backward. That is, we used the fact that [2.5.5] held for dates $t, t - 1, t - 2, \ldots, 0$ and recursively substituted to arrive at [2.5.6] as a logical implication of [2.5.5]. Equation [2.5.5] could equally well be solved recursively *forward*. To do so, equation [2.5.5] is written as

$$P_t = \frac{1}{1 + r}[P_{t+1} + D_t]. \qquad [2.5.10]$$

An analogous equation must hold for date $t + 1$:

$$P_{t+1} = \frac{1}{1+r}[P_{t+2} + D_{t+1}]. \tag{2.5.11}$$

Substitute [2.5.11] into [2.5.10] to deduce

$$\begin{aligned} P_t &= \frac{1}{1+r}\left[\frac{1}{1+r}[P_{t+2} + D_{t+1}] + D_t\right] \\ &= \left[\frac{1}{1+r}\right]^2 P_{t+2} + \left[\frac{1}{1+r}\right]^2 D_{t+1} + \left[\frac{1}{1+r}\right] D_t. \end{aligned} \tag{2.5.12}$$

Using [2.5.10] for date $t + 2$,

$$P_{t+2} = \frac{1}{1+r}[P_{t+3} + D_{t+2}],$$

and substituting into [2.5.12] gives

$$P_t = \left[\frac{1}{1+r}\right]^3 P_{t+3} + \left[\frac{1}{1+r}\right]^3 D_{t+2} + \left[\frac{1}{1+r}\right]^2 D_{t+1} + \left[\frac{1}{1+r}\right] D_t.$$

Continuing in this fashion $T$ periods into the future produces

$$\begin{aligned} P_t = {} & \left[\frac{1}{1+r}\right]^T P_{t+T} + \left[\frac{1}{1+r}\right]^T D_{t+T-1} + \left[\frac{1}{1+r}\right]^{T-1} D_{t+T-2} \\ & + \cdots + \left[\frac{1}{1+r}\right]^2 D_{t+1} + \left[\frac{1}{1+r}\right] D_t. \end{aligned} \tag{2.5.13}$$

If the sequence $\{P_t\}_{t=-\infty}^{\infty}$ is to satisfy [2.5.9], then

$$\lim_{T\to\infty} \left[\frac{1}{1+r}\right]^T P_{t+T} = 0.$$

If $\{D_t\}_{t=-\infty}^{\infty}$ is likewise a bounded sequence, then the following limit exists:

$$\lim_{T\to\infty} \sum_{j=0}^{T} \left[\frac{1}{1+r}\right]^{j+1} D_{t+j}.$$

Thus, if $\{P_t\}_{t=-\infty}^{\infty}$ is to be a bounded sequence, then we can take the limit of [2.5.13] as $T \to \infty$ to conclude

$$P_t = \sum_{j=0}^{\infty} \left[\frac{1}{1+r}\right]^{j+1} D_{t+j}, \tag{2.5.14}$$

which is referred to as the "market fundamentals" solution of [2.5.5] for the general case of time-varying dividends. Notice that [2.5.14] produces [2.5.8] as a special case when $D_t = D$ for all $t$.

Describing the value of a variable at time $t$ as a function of future realizations of another variable as in [2.5.14] may seem an artifact of assuming a perfect-foresight model of stock prices. However, an analogous set of operations turns out to be appropriate in a system similar to [2.5.4] in which expected returns are constant.[1] In such systems [2.5.14] generalizes to

$$P_t = \sum_{j=0}^{\infty} \left[\frac{1}{1+r}\right]^{j+1} E_t D_{t+j},$$

[1]See Sargent (1987) and Whiteman (1983) for an introduction to the manipulation of difference equations involving expectations.

where $E_t$ denotes an expectation of an unknown future quantity based on information available to investors at date $t$.

Expression [2.5.14] determines the particular value for the initial price $P_0$ that is consistent with the boundedness condition [2.5.9]. Setting $t = 0$ in [2.5.14] and substituting into [2.5.6] produces

$$\begin{aligned} P_{t+1} &= (1+r)^{t+1}\left\{\left[\frac{1}{1+r}\right]D_0 + \left[\frac{1}{1+r}\right]^2 D_1 + \left[\frac{1}{1+r}\right]^3 D_2 \right. \\ &\quad \left. + \cdots + \left[\frac{1}{1+r}\right]^{t+1} D_t + \left[\frac{1}{1+r}\right]^{t+2} D_{t+1} + \cdots \right\} - (1+r)^t D_0 \\ &\quad - (1+r)^{t-1}D_1 - (1+r)^{t-2}D_2 - \cdots - (1+r)D_{t-1} - D_t \\ &= \left[\frac{1}{1+r}\right]D_{t+1} + \left[\frac{1}{1+r}\right]^2 D_{t+2} + \left[\frac{1}{1+r}\right]^3 D_{t+3} + \cdots. \end{aligned}$$

Thus, setting the initial condition $P_0$ to satisfy [2.5.14] is sufficient to ensure that it holds for all $t$. Choosing $P_0$ equal to any other value would cause the consequences of each period's dividends to accumulate over time so as to lead to a violation of [2.5.9] eventually.

It is useful to discuss these same calculations from the perspective of lag operators. In Section 2.2 the recursive substitution backward that led from [2.5.5] to [2.5.6] was represented by writing [2.5.5] in terms of lag operators as

$$[1 - (1+r)L]P_{t+1} = -D_t \qquad [2.5.15]$$

and multiplying both sides of [2.5.15] by the following operator:

$$[1 + (1+r)L + (1+r)^2L^2 + \cdots + (1+r)^tL^t]. \qquad [2.5.16]$$

If $(1 + r)$ were less than unity, it would be natural to consider the limit of [2.5.16] as $t \to \infty$:

$$[1 - (1+r)L]^{-1} = 1 + (1+r)L + (1+r)^2L^2 + \cdots.$$

In the case of the theory of stock returns discussed here, however, $r > 0$ and this operator is not defined. In this case, a lag operator representation can be sought for the recursive substitution forward that led from [2.5.5] to [2.5.13]. This is accomplished using the inverse of the lag operator,

$$L^{-1}w_t = w_{t+1},$$

which extends result [2.1.4] to negative values of $k$. Note that $L^{-1}$ is indeed the inverse of the operator $L$:

$$L^{-1}(Lw_t) = L^{-1}w_{t-1} = w_t.$$

In general,

$$L^{-k}L^j = L^{j-k},$$

with $L^0$ defined as the identity operator:

$$L^0w_t \equiv w_t.$$

Now consider multiplying [2.5.15] by

$$[1 + (1 + r)^{-1}L^{-1} + (1 + r)^{-2}L^{-2} + \cdots + (1 + r)^{-(T-1)}L^{-(T-1)}] \times [-(1 + r)^{-1}L^{-1}] \quad [2.5.17]$$

to obtain

$$\begin{aligned}&[1 + (1 + r)^{-1}L^{-1} + (1 + r)^{-2}L^{-2} + \cdots + (1 + r)^{-(T-1)}L^{-(T-1)}] \\ &\times [1 - (1 + r)^{-1}L^{-1}]P_{t+1} \\ &= [1 + (1 + r)^{-1}L^{-1} + (1 + r)^{-2}L^{-2} + \cdots \\ &\quad + (1 + r)^{-(T-1)}L^{-(T-1)}] \times (1 + r)^{-1}D_{t+1}\end{aligned}$$

or

$$\begin{aligned}[1 - (1 + r)^{-T}L^{-T}]P_{t+1} &= \left[\frac{1}{1 + r}\right]D_{t+1} + \left[\frac{1}{1 + r}\right]^2 D_{t+2} \\ &\quad + \left[\frac{1}{1 + r}\right]^3 D_{t+3} + \cdots + \left[\frac{1}{1 + r}\right]^T D_{t+T},\end{aligned}$$

which is identical to [2.5.13] with $t$ in [2.5.13] replaced with $t + 1$.

When $r > 0$ and $\{P_t\}_{t=-\infty}^{\infty}$ is a bounded sequence, the left side of the preceding equation will approach $P_{t+1}$ as $T$ becomes large. Thus, when $r > 0$ and $\{P_t\}_{t=-\infty}^{\infty}$ and $\{D_t\}_{t=-\infty}^{\infty}$ are bounded sequences, the limit of the operator in [2.5.17] exists and could be viewed as the inverse of the operator on the left side of [2.5.15]:

$$\begin{aligned}[1 - (1 + r)L]^{-1} &= -(1 + r)^{-1}L^{-1} \\ &\quad \times [1 + (1 + r)^{-1}L^{-1} + (1 + r)^{-2}L^{-2} + \cdots].\end{aligned}$$

Applying this limiting operator to [2.5.15] amounts to solving the difference equation forward as in [2.5.14] and selecting the market fundamentals solution among the set of possible time paths for $\{P_t\}_{t=-\infty}^{\infty}$ given a particular time path for dividends $\{D_t\}_{t=-\infty}^{\infty}$.

Thus, given a first-order difference equation of the form

$$(1 - \phi L)y_t = w_t, \quad [2.5.18]$$

Sargent's (1987) advice was to solve the equation "backward" when $|\phi| < 1$ by multiplying by

$$[1 - \phi L]^{-1} = [1 + \phi L + \phi^2L^2 + \phi^3L^3 + \cdots] \quad [2.5.19]$$

and to solve the equation "forward" when $|\phi| > 1$ by multiplying by

$$\begin{aligned}[1 - \phi L]^{-1} &= \frac{-\phi^{-1}L^{-1}}{1 - \phi^{-1}L^{-1}} \\ &= -\phi^{-1}L^{-1}[1 + \phi^{-1}L^{-1} + \phi^{-2}L^{-2} + \phi^{-3}L^{-3} + \cdots].\end{aligned} \quad [2.5.20]$$

Defining the inverse of $[1 - \phi L]$ in this way amounts to selecting an operator $[1 - \phi L]^{-1}$ with the properties that

$$[1 - \phi L]^{-1} \times [1 - \phi L] = 1 \qquad \text{(the identity operator)}$$

and that, when it is applied to a bounded sequence $\{w_t\}_{t=-\infty}^{\infty}$,

$$[1 - \phi L]^{-1}w_t,$$

the result is another bounded sequence.

The conclusion from this discussion is that in applying an operator such as $[1 - \phi L]^{-1}$, we are implicitly imposing a boundedness assumption that rules out phenomena such as the speculative bubbles of equation [2.5.7] a priori. Where that is our intention, so much the better, though we should not apply the rules [2.5.19] or [2.5.20] without some reflection on their economic content.

## *Chapter 2 References*

Sargent, Thomas J. 1987. *Macroeconomic Theory*, 2d ed. Boston: Academic Press.

Whiteman, Charles H. 1983. *Linear Rational Expectations Models: A User's Guide*. Minneapolis: University of Minnesota Press.

# 3 Stationary ARMA Processes

This chapter introduces univariate *ARMA* processes, which provide a very useful class of models for describing the dynamics of an individual time series. The chapter begins with definitions of some of the key concepts used in time series analysis. Sections 3.2 through 3.5 then investigate the properties of various *ARMA* processes. Section 3.6 introduces the autocovariance-generating function, which is useful for analyzing the consequences of combining different time series and for an understanding of the population spectrum. The chapter concludes with a discussion of invertibility (Section 3.7), which can be important for selecting the *ARMA* representation of an observed time series that is appropriate given the uses to be made of the model.

## 3.1. *Expectations, Stationarity, and Ergodicity*

### *Expectations and Stochastic Processes*

Suppose we have observed a sample of size $T$ of some random variable $Y_t$:

$$\{y_1, y_2, \ldots, y_T\}. \tag{3.1.1}$$

For example, consider a collection of $T$ independent and identically distributed (i.i.d.) variables $\varepsilon_t$,

$$\{\varepsilon_1, \varepsilon_2, \ldots, \varepsilon_T\}, \tag{3.1.2}$$

with

$$\varepsilon_t \sim N(0, \sigma^2).$$

This is referred to as a sample of size $T$ from a *Gaussian white noise* process.

The observed sample [3.1.1] represents $T$ particular numbers, but this set of $T$ numbers is only one possible outcome of the underlying stochastic process that generated the data. Indeed, even if we were to imagine having observed the process for an infinite period of time, arriving at the sequence

$$\{y_t\}_{t=-\infty}^{\infty} = \{\ldots, y_{-1}, y_0, y_1, y_2, \ldots, y_T, y_{T+1}, y_{T+2}, \ldots\},$$

the infinite sequence $\{y_t\}_{t=-\infty}^{\infty}$ would still be viewed as a single realization from a time series process. For example, we might set one computer to work generating an infinite sequence of i.i.d. $N(0, \sigma^2)$ variates, $\{\varepsilon_t^{(1)}\}_{t=-\infty}^{\infty}$, and a second computer generating a separate sequence, $\{\varepsilon_t^{(2)}\}_{t=-\infty}^{\infty}$. We would then view these as two independent realizations of a Gaussian white noise process.

Imagine a battery of $I$ such computers generating sequences $\{y_t^{(1)}\}_{t=-\infty}^{\infty}$, $\{y_t^{(2)}\}_{t=-\infty}^{\infty}$, . . . , $\{y_t^{(I)}\}_{t=-\infty}^{\infty}$, and consider selecting the observation associated with date $t$ from each sequence:

$$\{y_t^{(1)}, y_t^{(2)}, \ldots, y_t^{(I)}\}.$$

This would be described as a sample of $I$ realizations of the random variable $Y_t$. This random variable has some density, denoted $f_{Y_t}(y_t)$, which is called the *unconditional density* of $Y_t$. For example, for the Gaussian white noise process, this density is given by

$$f_{Y_t}(y_t) = \frac{1}{\sqrt{2\pi}\sigma} \exp\left[\frac{-y_t^2}{2\sigma^2}\right].$$

The *expectation* of the $t$th observation of a time series refers to the mean of this probability distribution, provided it exists:

$$E(Y_t) \equiv \int_{-\infty}^{\infty} y_t f_{Y_t}(y_t)\, dy_t. \qquad [3.1.3]$$

We might view this as the probability limit of the ensemble average:

$$E(Y_t) = \operatorname*{plim}_{I\to\infty} (1/I) \sum_{i=1}^{I} Y_t^{(i)}. \qquad [3.1.4]$$

For example, if $\{Y_t\}_{t=-\infty}^{\infty}$ represents the sum of a constant $\mu$ plus a Gaussian white noise process $\{\varepsilon_t\}_{t=-\infty}^{\infty}$,

$$Y_t = \mu + \varepsilon_t, \qquad [3.1.5]$$

then its mean is

$$E(Y_t) = \mu + E(\varepsilon_t) = \mu. \qquad [3.1.6]$$

If $Y_t$ is a time trend plus Gaussian white noise,

$$Y_t = \beta t + \varepsilon_t, \qquad [3.1.7]$$

then its mean is

$$E(Y_t) = \beta t. \qquad [3.1.8]$$

Sometimes for emphasis the expectation $E(Y_t)$ is called the *unconditional mean* of $Y_t$. The unconditional mean is denoted $\mu_t$:

$$E(Y_t) = \mu_t.$$

Note that this notation allows the general possibility that the mean can be a function of the date of the observation $t$. For the process [3.1.7] involving the time trend, the mean [3.1.8] is a function of time, whereas for the constant plus Gaussian white noise, the mean [3.1.6] is not a function of time.

The *variance* of the random variable $Y_t$ (denoted $\gamma_{0t}$) is similarly defined as

$$\gamma_{0t} \equiv E(Y_t - \mu_t)^2 = \int_{-\infty}^{\infty} (y_t - \mu_t)^2 f_{Y_t}(y_t)\, dy_t. \qquad [3.1.9]$$

For example, for the process [3.1.7], the variance is

$$\gamma_{0t} = E(Y_t - \beta t)^2 = E(\varepsilon_t^2) = \sigma^2.$$

## *Autocovariance*

Given a particular realization such as $\{y_t^{(1)}\}_{t=-\infty}^{\infty}$ on a time series process, consider constructing a vector $\mathbf{x}_t^{(1)}$ associated with date $t$. This vector consists of the $[j + 1]$ most recent observations on $y$ as of date $t$ for that realization:

$$\mathbf{x}_t^{(1)} \equiv \begin{bmatrix} y_t^{(1)} \\ y_{t-1}^{(1)} \\ \vdots \\ y_{t-j}^{(1)} \end{bmatrix}.$$

We think of each realization $\{y_t\}_{t=-\infty}^{\infty}$ as generating one particular value of the vector $\mathbf{x}_t$ and want to calculate the probability distribution of this vector $\mathbf{x}_t^{(i)}$ across realizations $i$. This distribution is called the *joint distribution* of $(Y_t, Y_{t-1}, \ldots, Y_{t-j})$. From this distribution we can calculate the $j$th *autocovariance* of $Y_t$ (denoted $\gamma_{jt}$):

$$\begin{aligned} \gamma_{jt} &= \int_{-\infty}^{\infty}\int_{-\infty}^{\infty}\cdots\int_{-\infty}^{\infty}(y_t - \mu_t)(y_{t-j} - \mu_{t-j}) \\ &\quad \times f_{Y_t,Y_{t-1},\ldots,Y_{t-j}}(y_t, y_{t-1}, \ldots, y_{t-j})\, dy_t\, dy_{t-1} \cdots dy_{t-j} \qquad [3.1.10] \\ &= E(Y_t - \mu_t)(Y_{t-j} - \mu_{t-j}). \end{aligned}$$

Note that [3.1.10] has the form of a covariance between two variables $X$ and $Y$:

$$\text{Cov}(X, Y) = E(X - \mu_X)(Y - \mu_Y).$$

Thus [3.1.10] could be described as the covariance of $Y_t$ with its own lagged value; hence, the term "autocovariance." Notice further from [3.1.10] that the 0th autocovariance is just the variance of $Y_t$, as anticipated by the notation $\gamma_{0t}$ in [3.1.9].

The autocovariance $\gamma_{jt}$ can be viewed as the $(1, j + 1)$ element of the variance-covariance matrix of the vector $\mathbf{x}_t$. For this reason, the autocovariances are described as the second moments of the process for $Y_t$.

Again it may be helpful to think of the $j$th autocovariance as the probability limit of an ensemble average:

$$\gamma_{jt} = \operatorname*{plim}_{I\to\infty} (1/I) \sum_{i=1}^{I} [Y_t^{(i)} - \mu_t] \cdot [Y_{t-j}^{(i)} - \mu_{t-j}]. \qquad [3.1.11]$$

As an example of calculating autocovariances, note that for the process in [3.1.5] the autocovariances are all zero for $j \neq 0$:

$$\gamma_{jt} = E(Y_t - \mu)(Y_{t-j} - \mu) = E(\varepsilon_t\varepsilon_{t-j}) = 0 \qquad \text{for } j \neq 0.$$

## *Stationarity*

If neither the mean $\mu_t$ nor the autocovariances $\gamma_{jt}$ depend on the date $t$, then the process for $Y_t$ is said to be *covariance-stationary* or *weakly stationary*:

$$\begin{aligned} E(Y_t) &= \mu && \text{for all } t \\ E(Y_t - \mu)(Y_{t-j} - \mu) &= \gamma_j && \text{for all } t \text{ and any } j. \end{aligned}$$

For example, the process in [3.1.5] is covariance-stationary:

$$E(Y_t) = \mu$$

$$E(Y_t - \mu)(Y_{t-j} - \mu) = \begin{cases} \sigma^2 & \text{for } j = 0 \\ 0 & \text{for } j \neq 0. \end{cases}$$

By contrast, the process of [3.1.7] is not covariance-stationary, because its mean, $\beta t$, is a function of time.

Notice that if a process is covariance-stationary, the covariance between $Y_t$ and $Y_{t-j}$ depends only on $j$, the length of time separating the observations, and not on $t$, the date of the observation. It follows that for a covariance-stationary process, $\gamma_j$ and $\gamma_{-j}$ would represent the same magnitude. To see this, recall the definition

$$\gamma_j = E(Y_t - \mu)(Y_{t-j} - \mu). \qquad [3.1.12]$$

If the process is covariance-stationary, then this magnitude is the same for any value of $t$ we might have chosen; for example, we can replace $t$ with $t + j$:

$$\gamma_j = E(Y_{t+j} - \mu)(Y_{[t+j]-j} - \mu) = E(Y_{t+j} - \mu)(Y_t - \mu) = E(Y_t - \mu)(Y_{t+j} - \mu).$$

But referring again to the definition [3.1.12], this last expression is just the definition of $\gamma_{-j}$. Thus, for any covariance-stationary process,

$$\gamma_j = \gamma_{-j} \qquad \text{for all integers } j. \qquad [3.1.13]$$

A different concept is that of *strict stationarity*. A process is said to be strictly stationary if, for any values of $j_1, j_2, \ldots, j_n$, the joint distribution of $(Y_t, Y_{t+j_1}, Y_{t+j_2}, \ldots, Y_{t+j_n})$ depends only on the intervals separating the dates $(j_1, j_2, \ldots, j_n)$ and not on the date itself $(t)$. Notice that if a process is strictly stationary with finite second moments, then it must be covariance-stationary—if the densities over which we are integrating in [3.1.3] and [3.1.10] do not depend on time, then the moments $\mu_t$ and $\gamma_{jt}$ will not depend on time. However, it is possible to imagine a process that is covariance-stationary but not strictly stationary; the mean and autocovariances could not be functions of time, but perhaps higher moments such as $E(Y_t^3)$ are.

In this text the term "stationary" by itself is taken to mean "covariance-stationary."

A process $\{Y_t\}$ is said to be *Gaussian* if the joint density

$$f_{Y_t, Y_{t+j_1}, \ldots, Y_{t+j_n}}(y_t, y_{t+j_1}, \ldots, y_{t+j_n})$$

is Gaussian for any $j_1, j_2, \ldots, j_n$. Since the mean and variance are all that are needed to parameterize a multivariate Gaussian distribution completely, a covariance-stationary Gaussian process is strictly stationary.

## *Ergodicity*

We have viewed expectations of a time series in terms of ensemble averages such as [3.1.4] and [3.1.11]. These definitions may seem a bit contrived, since usually all one has available is a single realization of size $T$ from the process, which we earlier denoted $\{y_1^{(1)}, y_2^{(1)}, \ldots, y_T^{(1)}\}$. From these observations we would calculate the sample mean $\bar{y}$. This, of course, is not an ensemble average but rather a time average:

$$\bar{y} \equiv (1/T) \sum_{t=1}^{T} y_t^{(1)}. \qquad [3.1.14]$$

Whether time averages such as [3.1.14] eventually converge to the ensemble concept $E(Y_t)$ for a stationary process has to do with *ergodicity*. A covariance-stationary process is said to be *ergodic for the mean* if [3.1.14] converges in probability to $E(Y_t)$ as $T \to \infty$.[1] A process will be ergodic for the mean provided that the autocovariance $\gamma_j$ goes to zero sufficiently quickly as $j$ becomes large. In Chapter 7 we will see that if the autocovariances for a covariance-stationary process satisfy

$$\sum_{j=0}^{\infty} |\gamma_j| < \infty, \qquad [3.1.15]$$

then $\{Y_t\}$ is ergodic for the mean.

Similarly, a covariance-stationary process is said to be ergodic for second moments if

$$[1/(T-j)] \sum_{t=j+1}^{T} (Y_t - \mu)(Y_{t-j} - \mu) \xrightarrow{p} \gamma_j$$

for all $j$. Sufficient conditions for second-moment ergodicity will be presented in Chapter 7. In the special case where $\{Y_t\}$ is a stationary Gaussian process, condition [3.1.15] is sufficient to ensure ergodicity for all moments.

For many applications, stationarity and ergodicity turn out to amount to the same requirements. For purposes of clarifying the concepts of stationarity and ergodicity, however, it may be helpful to consider an example of a process that is stationary but not ergodic. Suppose the mean $\mu^{(i)}$ for the $i$th realization $\{y_t^{(i)}\}_{t=-\infty}^{\infty}$ is generated from a $N(0, \lambda^2)$ distribution, say

$$Y_t^{(i)} = \mu^{(i)} + \varepsilon_t. \qquad [3.1.16]$$

Here $\{\varepsilon_t\}$ is a Gaussian white noise process with mean zero and variance $\sigma^2$ that is independent of $\mu^{(i)}$. Notice that

$$\mu_t = E(\mu^{(i)}) + E(\varepsilon_t) = 0.$$

Also,

$$\gamma_{0t} = E(\mu^{(i)} + \varepsilon_t)^2 = \lambda^2 + \sigma^2$$

and

$$\gamma_{jt} = E(\mu^{(i)} + \varepsilon_t)(\mu^{(i)} + \varepsilon_{t-j}) = \lambda^2 \qquad \text{for } j \neq 0.$$

Thus the process of [3.1.16] is covariance-stationary. It does not satisfy the sufficient condition [3.1.15] for ergodicity for the mean, however, and indeed, the time average

$$(1/T) \sum_{t=1}^{T} Y_t^{(i)} = (1/T) \sum_{t=1}^{T} (\mu^{(i)} + \varepsilon_t) = \mu^{(i)} + (1/T) \sum_{t=1}^{T} \varepsilon_t$$

converges to $\mu^{(i)}$ rather than to zero, the mean of $Y_t$.

## 3.2. *White Noise*

The basic building block for all the processes considered in this chapter is a sequence $\{\varepsilon_t\}_{t=-\infty}^{\infty}$ whose elements have mean zero and variance $\sigma^2$,

$$E(\varepsilon_t) = 0 \qquad [3.2.1]$$

$$E(\varepsilon_t^2) = \sigma^2, \qquad [3.2.2]$$

and for which the $\varepsilon$'s are uncorrelated across time:

[1]Often "ergodicity" is used in a more general sense; see Anderson and Moore (1979, p. 319) or Hannan (1970, pp. 201–20).

$$E(\varepsilon_t\varepsilon_\tau) = 0 \qquad \text{for } t \neq \tau. \qquad [3.2.3]$$

A process satisfying [3.2.1] through [3.2.3] is described as a *white noise process*.

We shall on occasion wish to replace [3.2.3] with the slightly stronger condition that the $\varepsilon$'s are independent across time:

$$\varepsilon_t,\ \varepsilon_\tau \text{ independent for } t \neq \tau. \qquad [3.2.4]$$

Notice that [3.2.4] implies [3.2.3] but [3.2.3] does not imply [3.2.4]. A process satisfying [3.2.1] through [3.2.4] is called an *independent white noise process*.

Finally, if [3.2.1] through [3.2.4] hold along with

$$\varepsilon_t \sim N(0, \sigma^2), \qquad [3.2.5]$$

then we have the *Gaussian white noise process*.

## 3.3. *Moving Average Processes*

### *The First-Order Moving Average Process*

Let $\{\varepsilon_t\}$ be white noise as in [3.2.1] through [3.2.3], and consider the process

$$Y_t = \mu + \varepsilon_t + \theta\varepsilon_{t-1}, \qquad [3.3.1]$$

where $\mu$ and $\theta$ could be any constants. This time series is called a *first-order moving average process*, denoted $MA(1)$. The term "moving average" comes from the fact that $Y_t$ is constructed from a weighted sum, akin to an average, of the two most recent values of $\varepsilon$.

The expectation of $Y_t$ is given by

$$E(Y_t) = E(\mu + \varepsilon_t + \theta\varepsilon_{t-1}) = \mu + E(\varepsilon_t) + \theta\cdot E(\varepsilon_{t-1}) = \mu. \qquad [3.3.2]$$

We used the symbol $\mu$ for the constant term in [3.3.1] in anticipation of the result that this constant term turns out to be the mean of the process.

The variance of $Y_t$ is

$$\begin{aligned} E(Y_t - \mu)^2 &= E(\varepsilon_t + \theta\varepsilon_{t-1})^2 \\ &= E(\varepsilon_t^2 + 2\theta\varepsilon_t\varepsilon_{t-1} + \theta^2\varepsilon_{t-1}^2) \\ &= \sigma^2 + 0 + \theta^2\sigma^2 \\ &= (1 + \theta^2)\sigma^2. \end{aligned} \qquad [3.3.3]$$

The first autocovariance is

$$\begin{aligned} E(Y_t - \mu)(Y_{t-1} - \mu) &= E(\varepsilon_t + \theta\varepsilon_{t-1})(\varepsilon_{t-1} + \theta\varepsilon_{t-2}) \\ &= E(\varepsilon_t\varepsilon_{t-1} + \theta\varepsilon_{t-1}^2 + \theta\varepsilon_t\varepsilon_{t-2} + \theta^2\varepsilon_{t-1}\varepsilon_{t-2}) \\ &= 0 + \theta\sigma^2 + 0 + 0. \end{aligned} \qquad [3.3.4]$$

Higher autocovariances are all zero:

$$E(Y_t - \mu)(Y_{t-j} - \mu) = E(\varepsilon_t + \theta\varepsilon_{t-1})(\varepsilon_{t-j} + \theta\varepsilon_{t-j-1}) = 0 \qquad \text{for } j > 1. \qquad [3.3.5]$$

Since the mean and autocovariances are not functions of time, an $MA(1)$ process is covariance-stationary regardless of the value of $\theta$. Furthermore, [3.1.15] is clearly satisfied:

$$\sum_{j=0}^{\infty} |\gamma_j| = (1 + \theta^2)\sigma^2 + |\theta\sigma^2|.$$

Thus, if $\{\varepsilon_t\}$ is Gaussian white noise, then the $MA(1)$ process [3.3.1] is ergodic for all moments.

The $j$th *autocorrelation* of a covariance-stationary process (denoted $\rho_j$) is defined as its $j$th autocovariance divided by the variance:

$$\rho_j \equiv \gamma_j/\gamma_0. \qquad [3.3.6]$$

Again the terminology arises from the fact that $\rho_j$ is the correlation between $Y_t$ and $Y_{t-j}$:

$$\text{Corr}(Y_t, Y_{t-j}) = \frac{\text{Cov}(Y_t, Y_{t-j})}{\sqrt{\text{Var}(Y_t)}\sqrt{\text{Var}(Y_{t-j})}} = \frac{\gamma_j}{\sqrt{\gamma_0}\sqrt{\gamma_0}} = \rho_j.$$

Since $\rho_j$ is a correlation, $|\rho_j| \le 1$ for all $j$, by the Cauchy-Schwarz inequality. Notice also that the 0th autocorrelation $\rho_0$ is equal to unity for any covariance-stationary process by definition.

From [3.3.3] and [3.3.4], the first autocorrelation for an $MA(1)$ process is given by

$$\rho_1 = \frac{\theta\sigma^2}{(1 + \theta^2)\sigma^2} = \frac{\theta}{(1 + \theta^2)}. \qquad [3.3.7]$$

Higher autocorrelations are all zero.

The autocorrelation $\rho_j$ can be plotted as a function of $j$ as in Figure 3.1. Panel (a) shows the autocorrelation function for white noise, while panel (b) gives the autocorrelation function for the $MA(1)$ process:

$$Y_t = \varepsilon_t + 0.8\varepsilon_{t-1}.$$

For different specifications of $\theta$ we would obtain different values for the first autocorrelation $\rho_1$ in [3.3.7]. Positive values of $\theta$ induce positive autocorrelation in the series. In this case, an unusually large value of $Y_t$ is likely to be followed by a larger-than-average value for $Y_{t+1}$, just as a smaller-than-average $Y_t$ may well be followed by a smaller-than-average $Y_{t+1}$. By contrast, negative values of $\theta$ imply negative autocorrelation—a large $Y_t$ might be expected to be followed by a small value for $Y_{t+1}$.

The values for $\rho_1$ implied by different specifications of $\theta$ are plotted in Figure 3.2. Notice that the largest possible value for $\rho_1$ is 0.5; this occurs if $\theta = 1$. The smallest value for $\rho_1$ is $-0.5$, which occurs if $\theta = -1$. For any value of $\rho_1$ between $-0.5$ and 0.5, there are two different values of $\theta$ that could produce that autocorrelation. This is because the value of $\theta/(1 + \theta^2)$ is unchanged if $\theta$ is replaced by $1/\theta$:

$$\rho_1 = \frac{(1/\theta)}{1 + (1/\theta)^2} = \frac{\theta^2 \cdot (1/\theta)}{\theta^2[1 + (1/\theta)^2]} = \frac{\theta}{\theta^2 + 1}.$$

For example, the processes

$$Y_t = \varepsilon_t + 0.5\varepsilon_{t-1}$$

and

$$Y_t = \varepsilon_t + 2\varepsilon_{t-1}$$

would have the same autocorrelation function:

$$\rho_1 = \frac{2}{(1 + 2^2)} = \frac{0.5}{(1 + 0.5^2)} = 0.4.$$

We will have more to say about the relation between two $MA(1)$ processes that share the same autocorrelation function in Section 3.7.

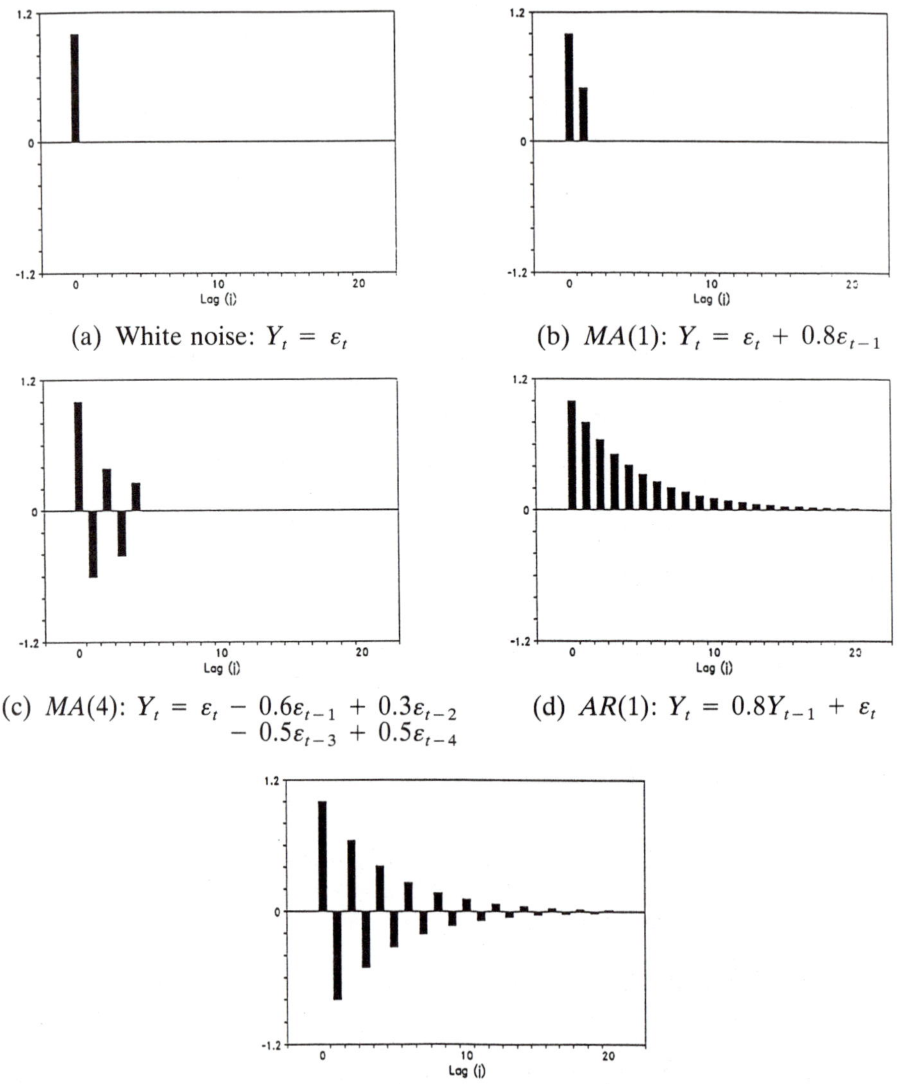


(a) White noise: $Y_t = \varepsilon_t$

(b) $MA(1)$: $Y_t = \varepsilon_t + 0.8\varepsilon_{t-1}$

(c) $MA(4)$: $Y_t = \varepsilon_t - 0.6\varepsilon_{t-1} + 0.3\varepsilon_{t-2} - 0.5\varepsilon_{t-3} + 0.5\varepsilon_{t-4}$

(d) $AR(1)$: $Y_t = 0.8Y_{t-1} + \varepsilon_t$

(e) $AR(1)$: $Y_t = -0.8Y_{t-1} + \varepsilon_t$

**FIGURE 3.1** Autocorrelation functions for assorted *ARMA* processes.

## *The* q*th-Order Moving Average Process*

A *qth-order moving average process*, denoted $MA(q)$, is characterized by

$$Y_t = \mu + \varepsilon_t + \theta_1\varepsilon_{t-1} + \theta_2\varepsilon_{t-2} + \cdots + \theta_q\varepsilon_{t-q}, \qquad [3.3.8]$$

where $\{\varepsilon_t\}$ satisfies [3.2.1] through [3.2.3] and $(\theta_1, \theta_2, \ldots, \theta_q)$ could be any real numbers. The mean of [3.3.8] is again given by $\mu$:

$$E(Y_t) = \mu + E(\varepsilon_t) + \theta_1 \cdot E(\varepsilon_{t-1}) + \theta_2 \cdot E(\varepsilon_{t-2}) + \cdots + \theta_q \cdot E(\varepsilon_{t-q}) = \mu.$$

The variance of an $MA(q)$ process is

$$\gamma_0 = E(Y_t - \mu)^2 = E(\varepsilon_t + \theta_1\varepsilon_{t-1} + \theta_2\varepsilon_{t-2} + \cdots + \theta_q\varepsilon_{t-q})^2. \qquad [3.3.9]$$

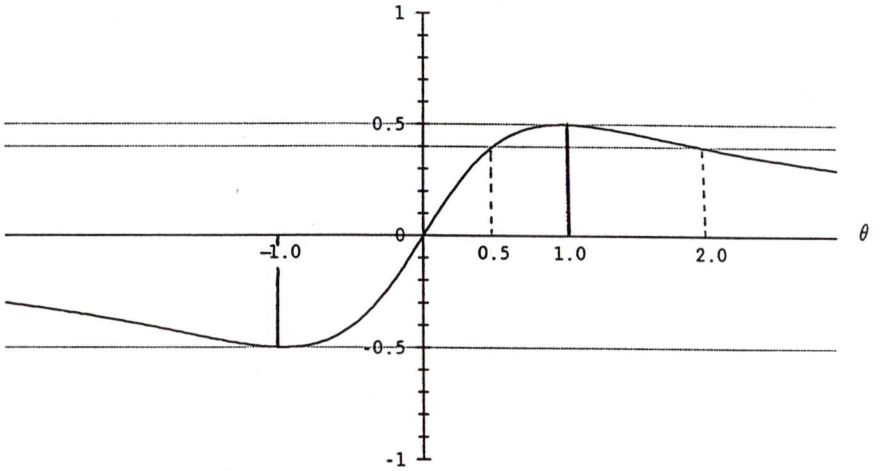


**FIGURE 3.2** The first autocorrelation ($\rho_1$) for an $MA(1)$ process possible for different values of $\theta$.

Since the $\varepsilon$'s are uncorrelated, the variance [3.3.9] is[2]

$$\gamma_0 = \sigma^2 + \theta_1^2\sigma^2 + \theta_2^2\sigma^2 + \cdots + \theta_q^2\sigma^2 = (1 + \theta_1^2 + \theta_2^2 + \cdots + \theta_q^2)\sigma^2. \quad [3.3.10]$$

For $j = 1, 2, \ldots, q$,

$$\begin{aligned} \gamma_j &= E[(\varepsilon_t + \theta_1\varepsilon_{t-1} + \theta_2\varepsilon_{t-2} + \cdots + \theta_q\varepsilon_{t-q}) \\ &\quad \times (\varepsilon_{t-j} + \theta_1\varepsilon_{t-j-1} + \theta_2\varepsilon_{t-j-2} + \cdots + \theta_q\varepsilon_{t-j-q})] \\ &= E[\theta_j\varepsilon_{t-j}^2 + \theta_{j+1}\theta_1\varepsilon_{t-j-1}^2 + \theta_{j+2}\theta_2\varepsilon_{t-j-2}^2 + \cdots + \theta_q\theta_{q-j}\varepsilon_{t-q}^2]. \end{aligned} \quad [3.3.11]$$

Terms involving $\varepsilon$'s at different dates have been dropped because their product has expectation zero, and $\theta_0$ is defined to be unity. For $j > q$, there are no $\varepsilon$'s with common dates in the definition of $\gamma_j$, and so the expectation is zero. Thus,

$$\gamma_j = \begin{cases} [\theta_j + \theta_{j+1}\theta_1 + \theta_{j+2}\theta_2 + \cdots + \theta_q\theta_{q-j}]\cdot\sigma^2 & \text{for } j = 1, 2, \ldots, q \\ 0 & \text{for } j > q. \end{cases} \quad [3.3.12]$$

For example, for an $MA(2)$ process,

$$\begin{aligned} \gamma_0 &= [1 + \theta_1^2 + \theta_2^2]\cdot\sigma^2 \\ \gamma_1 &= [\theta_1 + \theta_2\theta_1]\cdot\sigma^2 \\ \gamma_2 &= [\theta_2]\cdot\sigma^2 \\ \gamma_3 &= \gamma_4 = \cdots = 0. \end{aligned}$$

For any values of $(\theta_1, \theta_2, \ldots, \theta_q)$, the $MA(q)$ process is thus covariance-stationary. Condition [3.1.15] is satisfied, so for Gaussian $\varepsilon_t$ the $MA(q)$ process is also ergodic for all moments. The autocorrelation function is zero after $q$ lags, as in panel (c) of Figure 3.1.

### *The Infinite-Order Moving Average Process*

The $MA(q)$ process can be written

$$Y_t = \mu + \sum_{j=0}^{q} \theta_j\varepsilon_{t-j}$$

[2]See equation [A.5.18] in Appendix A at the end of the book.

with $\theta_0 \equiv 1$. Consider the process that results as $q \to \infty$:

$$Y_t = \mu + \sum_{j=0}^{\infty} \psi_j \varepsilon_{t-j} = \mu + \psi_0 \varepsilon_t + \psi_1 \varepsilon_{t-1} + \psi_2 \varepsilon_{t-2} + \cdots. \qquad [3.3.13]$$

This could be described as an $MA(\infty)$ process. To preserve notational flexibility later, we will use $\psi$'s for the coefficients of an infinite-order moving average process and $\theta$'s for the coefficients of a finite-order moving average process.

Appendix 3.A to this chapter shows that the infinite sequence in [3.3.13] generates a well defined covariance-stationary process provided that

$$\sum_{j=0}^{\infty} \psi_j^2 < \infty. \qquad [3.3.14]$$

It is often convenient to work with a slightly stronger condition than [3.3.14]:

$$\sum_{j=0}^{\infty} |\psi_j| < \infty. \qquad [3.3.15]$$

A sequence of numbers $\{\psi_j\}_{j=0}^{\infty}$ satisfying [3.3.14] is said to be *square summable*, whereas a sequence satisfying [3.3.15] is said to be *absolutely summable*. Absolute summability implies square-summability, but the converse does not hold—there are examples of square-summable sequences that are not absolutely summable (again, see Appendix 3.A).

The mean and autocovariances of an $MA(\infty)$ process with absolutely summable coefficients can be calculated from a simple extrapolation of the results for an $MA(q)$ process:[3]

$$E(Y_t) = \lim_{T\to\infty} E(\mu + \psi_0 \varepsilon_t + \psi_1 \varepsilon_{t-1} + \psi_2 \varepsilon_{t-2} + \cdots + \psi_T \varepsilon_{t-T}) \qquad [3.3.16]$$
$$= \mu$$

$$\begin{aligned} \gamma_0 &= E(Y_t - \mu)^2 \\ &= \lim_{T\to\infty} E(\psi_0 \varepsilon_t + \psi_1 \varepsilon_{t-1} + \psi_2 \varepsilon_{t-2} + \cdots + \psi_T \varepsilon_{t-T})^2 \\ &= \lim_{T\to\infty} (\psi_0^2 + \psi_1^2 + \psi_2^2 + \cdots + \psi_T^2)\cdot\sigma^2 \end{aligned} \qquad [3.3.17]$$

$$\begin{aligned} \gamma_j &= E(Y_t - \mu)(Y_{t-j} - \mu) \\ &= \sigma^2(\psi_j\psi_0 + \psi_{j+1}\psi_1 + \psi_{j+2}\psi_2 + \psi_{j+3}\psi_3 + \cdots). \end{aligned} \qquad [3.3.18]$$

Moreover, an $MA(\infty)$ process with absolutely summable coefficients has absolutely summable autocovariances:

$$\sum_{j=0}^{\infty} |\gamma_j| < \infty. \qquad [3.3.19]$$

Hence, an $MA(\infty)$ process satisfying [3.3.15] is ergodic for the mean (see Appendix 3.A). If the $\varepsilon$'s are Gaussian, then the process is ergodic for all moments.

[3]Absolute summability of $\{\psi_j\}_{j=0}^{\infty}$ and existence of the second moment $E(\varepsilon_t^2)$ are sufficient conditions to permit interchanging the order of integration and summation. Specifically, if $\{X_T\}_{T=1}^{\infty}$ is a sequence of random variables such that

$$\sum_{T=1}^{\infty} E|X_T| < \infty,$$

then

$$E\left\{\sum_{T=1}^{\infty} X_T\right\} = \sum_{T=1}^{\infty} E(X_T).$$

See Rao (1973, p. 111).

## 3.4. *Autoregressive Processes*

### *The First-Order Autoregressive Process*

A *first-order autoregression*, denoted $AR(1)$, satisfies the following difference equation:

$$Y_t = c + \phi Y_{t-1} + \varepsilon_t. \qquad [3.4.1]$$

Again, $\{\varepsilon_t\}$ is a white noise sequence satisfying [3.2.1] through [3.2.3]. Notice that [3.4.1] takes the form of the first-order difference equation [1.1.1] or [2.2.1] in which the input variable $w_t$ is given by $w_t = c + \varepsilon_t$. We know from the analysis of first-order difference equations that if $|\phi| \geq 1$, the consequences of the $\varepsilon$'s for $Y$ accumulate rather than die out over time. It is thus perhaps not surprising that when $|\phi| \geq 1$, there does not exist a covariance-stationary process for $Y_t$ with finite variance that satisfies [3.4.1]. In the case when $|\phi| < 1$, there is a covariance-stationary process for $Y_t$ satisfying [3.4.1]. It is given by the stable solution to [3.4.1] characterized in [2.2.9]:

$$\begin{aligned} Y_t &= (c + \varepsilon_t) + \phi\cdot(c + \varepsilon_{t-1}) + \phi^2\cdot(c + \varepsilon_{t-2}) + \phi^3\cdot(c + \varepsilon_{t-3}) + \cdots \\ &= [c/(1 - \phi)] + \varepsilon_t + \phi\varepsilon_{t-1} + \phi^2\varepsilon_{t-2} + \phi^3\varepsilon_{t-3} + \cdots. \end{aligned} \qquad [3.4.2]$$

This can be viewed as an $MA(\infty)$ process as in [3.3.13] with $\psi_j$ given by $\phi^j$. When $|\phi| < 1$, condition [3.3.15] is satisfied:

$$\sum_{j=0}^{\infty} |\psi_j| = \sum_{j=0}^{\infty} |\phi|^j,$$

which equals $1/(1 - |\phi|)$ provided that $|\phi| < 1$. The remainder of this discussion of first-order autoregressive processes assumes that $|\phi| < 1$. This ensures that the $MA(\infty)$ representation exists and can be manipulated in the obvious way, and that the $AR(1)$ process is ergodic for the mean.

Taking expectations of [3.4.2], we see that

$$E(Y_t) = [c/(1 - \phi)] + 0 + 0 + \cdots,$$

so that the mean of a stationary $AR(1)$ process is

$$\mu = c/(1 - \phi). \qquad [3.4.3]$$

The variance is

$$\begin{aligned} \gamma_0 &= E(Y_t - \mu)^2 \\ &= E(\varepsilon_t + \phi\varepsilon_{t-1} + \phi^2\varepsilon_{t-2} + \phi^3\varepsilon_{t-3} + \cdots)^2 \\ &= (1 + \phi^2 + \phi^4 + \phi^6 + \cdots)\cdot\sigma^2 \\ &= \sigma^2/(1 - \phi^2), \end{aligned} \qquad [3.4.4]$$

while the $j$th autocovariance is

$$\begin{aligned} \gamma_j &= E(Y_t - \mu)(Y_{t-j} - \mu) \\ &= E[\varepsilon_t + \phi\varepsilon_{t-1} + \phi^2\varepsilon_{t-2} + \cdots + \phi^j\varepsilon_{t-j} + \phi^{j+1}\varepsilon_{t-j-1} \\ &\qquad + \phi^{j+2}\varepsilon_{t-j-2} + \cdots] \times [\varepsilon_{t-j} + \phi\varepsilon_{t-j-1} + \phi^2\varepsilon_{t-j-2} + \cdots] \\ &= [\phi^j + \phi^{j+2} + \phi^{j+4} + \cdots]\cdot\sigma^2 \\ &= \phi^j[1 + \phi^2 + \phi^4 + \cdots]\cdot\sigma^2 \\ &= [\phi^j/(1 - \phi^2)]\cdot\sigma^2. \end{aligned} \qquad [3.4.5]$$

It follows from [3.4.4] and [3.4.5] that the autocorrelation function,

$$\rho_j = \gamma_j/\gamma_0 = \phi^j, \qquad [3.4.6]$$

follows a pattern of geometric decay as in panel (d) of Figure 3.1. Indeed, the autocorrelation function [3.4.6] for a stationary $AR(1)$ process is identical to the dynamic multiplier or impulse-response function [1.1.10]; the effect of a one-unit increase in $\varepsilon_t$ on $Y_{t+j}$ is equal to the correlation between $Y_t$ and $Y_{t+j}$. A positive value of $\phi$, like a positive value of $\theta$ for an $MA(1)$ process, implies positive correlation between $Y_t$ and $Y_{t+1}$. A negative value of $\phi$ implies negative first-order but positive second-order autocorrelation, as in panel (e) of Figure 3.1.

Figure 3.3 shows the effect on the appearance of the time series $\{y_t\}$ of varying the parameter $\phi$. The panels show realizations of the process in [3.4.1] with $c = 0$ and $\varepsilon_t \sim N(0, 1)$ for different values of the autoregressive parameter $\phi$. Panel (a) displays white noise ($\phi = 0$). A series with no autocorrelation looks choppy and patternless to the eye; the value of one observation gives no information about the value of the next observation. For $\phi = 0.5$ (panel (b)), the series seems smoother, with observations above or below the mean often appearing in clusters of modest duration. For $\phi = 0.9$ (panel (c)), departures from the mean can be quite prolonged; strong shocks take considerable time to die out.

The moments for a stationary $AR(1)$ were derived above by viewing it as an $MA(\infty)$ process. A second way to arrive at the same results is to assume that the process is covariance-stationary and calculate the moments directly from the difference equation [3.4.1]. Taking expectations of both sides of [3.4.1],

$$E(Y_t) = c + \phi \cdot E(Y_{t-1}) + E(\varepsilon_t). \qquad [3.4.7]$$

Assuming that the process is covariance-stationary,

$$E(Y_t) = E(Y_{t-1}) = \mu. \qquad [3.4.8]$$

Substituting [3.4.8] into [3.4.7],

$$\mu = c + \phi\mu + 0$$

or

$$\mu = c/(1 - \phi), \qquad [3.4.9]$$

reproducing the earlier result [3.4.3].

Notice that formula [3.4.9] is clearly not generating a sensible statement if $|\phi| \geq 1$. For example, if $c > 0$ and $\phi > 1$, then $Y_t$ in [3.4.1] is equal to a positive constant plus a positive number times its lagged value plus a mean-zero random variable. Yet [3.4.9] seems to assert that $Y_t$ would be negative on average for such a process! The reason that formula [3.4.9] is not valid when $|\phi| \geq 1$ is that we assumed in [3.4.8] that $Y_t$ is covariance-stationary, an assumption which is not correct when $|\phi| \geq 1$.

To find the second moments of $Y_t$ in an analogous manner, use [3.4.3] to rewrite [3.4.1] as

$$Y_t = \mu(1 - \phi) + \phi Y_{t-1} + \varepsilon_t$$

or

$$(Y_t - \mu) = \phi(Y_{t-1} - \mu) + \varepsilon_t. \qquad [3.4.10]$$

Now square both sides of [3.4.10] and take expectations:

$$E(Y_t - \mu)^2 = \phi^2 E(Y_{t-1} - \mu)^2 + 2\phi E[(Y_{t-1} - \mu)\varepsilon_t] + E(\varepsilon_t^2). \qquad [3.4.11]$$

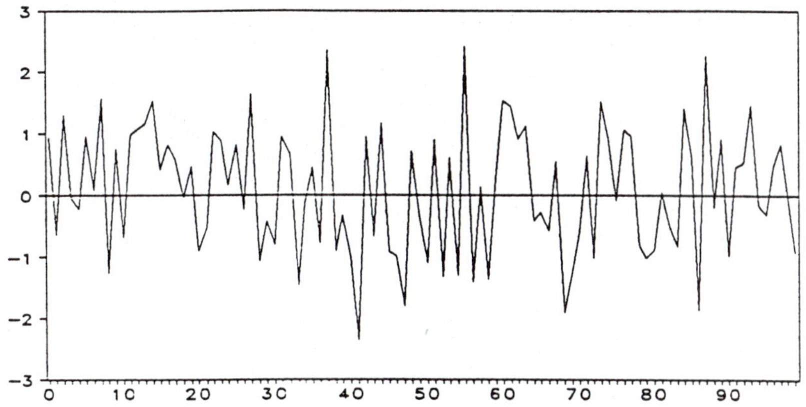


(a) $\phi = 0$ (white noise)

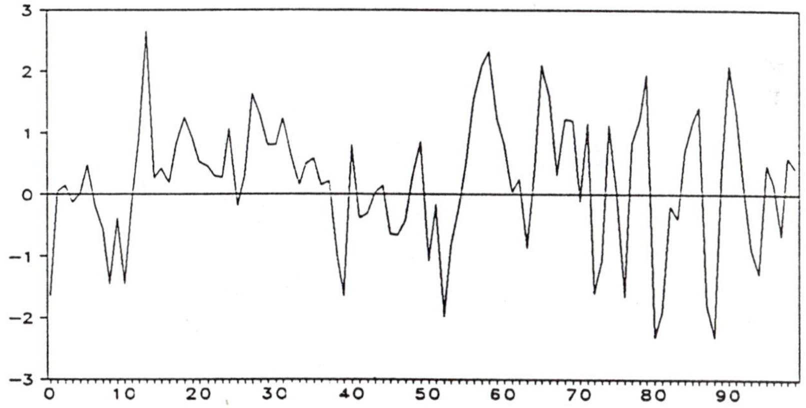


(b) $\phi = 0.5$

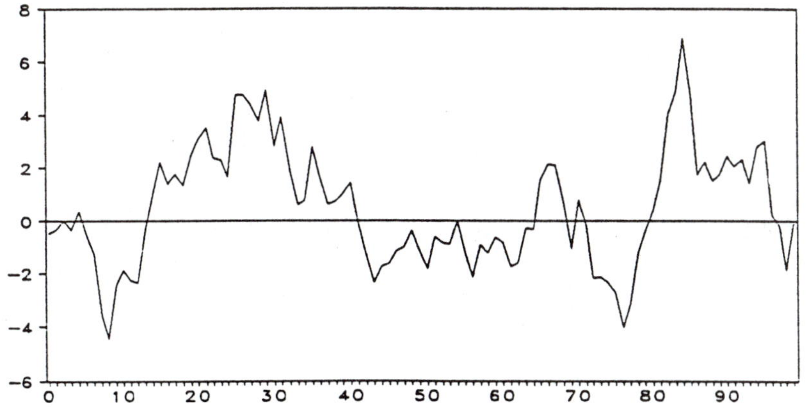


(c) $\phi = 0.9$

**FIGURE 3.3** Realizations of an $AR(1)$ process, $Y_t = \phi Y_{t-1} + \varepsilon_t$, for alternative values of $\phi$.

Recall from [3.4.2] that $(Y_{t-1} - \mu)$ is a linear function of $\varepsilon_{t-1}, \varepsilon_{t-2}, \ldots$:

$$(Y_{t-1} - \mu) = \varepsilon_{t-1} + \phi\varepsilon_{t-2} + \phi^2\varepsilon_{t-3} + \cdots.$$

But $\varepsilon_t$ is uncorrelated with $\varepsilon_{t-1}, \varepsilon_{t-2}, \ldots$, so $\varepsilon_t$ must be uncorrelated with $(Y_{t-1} - \mu)$. Thus the middle term on the right side of [3.4.11] is zero:

$$E[(Y_{t-1} - \mu)\varepsilon_t] = 0. \qquad [3.4.12]$$

Again, assuming covariance-stationarity, we have

$$E(Y_t - \mu)^2 = E(Y_{t-1} - \mu)^2 = \gamma_0. \qquad [3.4.13]$$

Substituting [3.4.13] and [3.4.12] into [3.4.11],

$$\gamma_0 = \phi^2\gamma_0 + 0 + \sigma^2$$

or

$$\gamma_0 = \sigma^2/(1 - \phi^2),$$

reproducing [3.4.4].

Similarly, we could multiply [3.4.10] by $(Y_{t-j} - \mu)$ and take expectations:

$$\begin{aligned} E[(Y_t - \mu)(Y_{t-j} - \mu)] \\ = \phi \cdot E[(Y_{t-1} - \mu)(Y_{t-j} - \mu)] + E[\varepsilon_t(Y_{t-j} - \mu)]. \end{aligned} \qquad [3.4.14]$$

But the term $(Y_{t-j} - \mu)$ will be a linear function of $\varepsilon_{t-j}, \varepsilon_{t-j-1}, \varepsilon_{t-j-2}, \ldots$, which, for $j > 0$, will be uncorrelated with $\varepsilon_t$. Thus, for $j > 0$, the last term on the right side in [3.4.14] is zero. Notice, moreover, that the expression appearing in the first term on the right side of [3.4.14],

$$E[(Y_{t-1} - \mu)(Y_{t-j} - \mu)],$$

is the autocovariance of observations on $Y$ separated by $j - 1$ periods:

$$E[(Y_{t-1} - \mu)(Y_{[t-1]-[j-1]} - \mu)] = \gamma_{j-1}.$$

Thus, for $j > 0$, [3.4.14] becomes

$$\gamma_j = \phi\gamma_{j-1}. \qquad [3.4.15]$$

Equation [3.4.15] takes the form of a first-order difference equation,

$$y_t = \phi y_{t-1} + w_t,$$

in which the autocovariance $\gamma$ takes the place of the variable $y$ and in which the subscript $j$ (which indexes the order of the autocovariance) replaces $t$ (which indexes time). The input $w_t$ in [3.4.15] is identically equal to zero. It is easy to see that the difference equation [3.4.15] has the solution

$$\gamma_j = \phi^j\gamma_0,$$

which reproduces [3.4.6]. We now see why the impulse-response function and autocorrelation function for an $AR(1)$ process coincide—they both represent the solution to a first-order difference equation with autoregressive parameter $\phi$, an initial value of unity, and no subsequent shocks.

### *The Second-Order Autoregressive Process*

A *second-order autoregression*, denoted $AR(2)$, satisfies

$$Y_t = c + \phi_1 Y_{t-1} + \phi_2 Y_{t-2} + \varepsilon_t, \qquad [3.4.16]$$

or, in lag operator notation,

$$(1 - \phi_1 L - \phi_2 L^2)Y_t = c + \varepsilon_t. \qquad [3.4.17]$$

The difference equation [3.4.16] is stable provided that the roots of

$$(1 - \phi_1 z - \phi_2 z^2) = 0 \qquad [3.4.18]$$

lie outside the unit circle. When this condition is satisfied, the $AR(2)$ process turns out to be covariance-stationary, and the inverse of the autoregressive operator in [3.4.17] is given by

$$\psi(L) = (1 - \phi_1 L - \phi_2 L^2)^{-1} = \psi_0 + \psi_1 L + \psi_2 L^2 + \psi_3 L^3 + \cdots. \qquad [3.4.19]$$

Recalling [1.2.44], the value of $\psi_j$ can be found from the (1, 1) element of the matrix $\mathbf{F}$ raised to the $j$th power, as in expression [1.2.28]. Where the roots of [3.4.18] are distinct, a closed-form expression for $\psi_j$ is given by [1.2.29] and [1.2.25]. Exercise 3.3 at the end of this chapter discusses alternative algorithms for calculating $\psi_j$.

Multiplying both sides of [3.4.17] by $\psi(L)$ gives

$$Y_t = \psi(L)c + \psi(L)\varepsilon_t. \qquad [3.4.20]$$

It is straightforward to show that

$$\psi(L)c = c/(1 - \phi_1 - \phi_2) \qquad [3.4.21]$$

and

$$\sum_{j=0}^{\infty} |\psi_j| < \infty; \qquad [3.4.22]$$

the reader is invited to prove these claims in Exercises 3.4 and 3.5. Since [3.4.20] is an absolutely summable $MA(\infty)$ process, its mean is given by the constant term:

$$\mu = c/(1 - \phi_1 - \phi_2). \qquad [3.4.23]$$

An alternative method for calculating the mean is to assume that the process is covariance-stationary and take expectations of [3.4.16] directly:

$$E(Y_t) = c + \phi_1 E(Y_{t-1}) + \phi_2 E(Y_{t-2}) + E(\varepsilon_t),$$

implying

$$\mu = c + \phi_1 \mu + \phi_2 \mu + 0,$$

reproducing [3.4.23].

To find second moments, write [3.4.16] as

$$Y_t = \mu \cdot (1 - \phi_1 - \phi_2) + \phi_1 Y_{t-1} + \phi_2 Y_{t-2} + \varepsilon_t$$

or

$$(Y_t - \mu) = \phi_1(Y_{t-1} - \mu) + \phi_2(Y_{t-2} - \mu) + \varepsilon_t. \qquad [3.4.24]$$

Multiplying both sides of [3.4.24] by $(Y_{t-j} - \mu)$ and taking expectations produces

$$\gamma_j = \phi_1 \gamma_{j-1} + \phi_2 \gamma_{j-2} \qquad \text{for } j = 1, 2, \ldots. \qquad [3.4.25]$$

Thus, the autocovariances follow the same second-order difference equation as does the process for $Y_t$, with the difference equation for $\gamma_j$ indexed by the lag $j$. The autocovariances therefore behave just as the solutions to the second-order difference equation analyzed in Section 1.2. An $AR(2)$ process is covariance-stationary provided that $\phi_1$ and $\phi_2$ lie within the triangular region of Figure 1.5.

When $\phi_1$ and $\phi_2$ lie within the triangular region but above the parabola in that figure, the autocovariance function $\gamma_j$ is the sum of two decaying exponential functions of $j$. When $\phi_1$ and $\phi_2$ fall within the triangular region but below the parabola, $\gamma_j$ is a damped sinusoidal function.

The autocorrelations are found by dividing both sides of [3.4.25] by $\gamma_0$:

$$\rho_j = \phi_1\rho_{j-1} + \phi_2\rho_{j-2} \qquad \text{for } j = 1, 2, \ldots . \tag{3.4.26}$$

In particular, setting $j = 1$ produces

$$\rho_1 = \phi_1 + \phi_2\rho_1$$

or

$$\rho_1 = \phi_1/(1 - \phi_2). \tag{3.4.27}$$

For $j = 2$,

$$\rho_2 = \phi_1\rho_1 + \phi_2. \tag{3.4.28}$$

The variance of a covariance-stationary second-order autoregression can be found by multiplying both sides of [3.4.24] by $(Y_t - \mu)$ and taking expectations:

$$\begin{aligned} E(Y_t - \mu)^2 = {} & \phi_1 \cdot E(Y_{t-1} - \mu)(Y_t - \mu) + \phi_2 \cdot E(Y_{t-2} - \mu)(Y_t - \mu) \\ & + E(\varepsilon_t)(Y_t - \mu), \end{aligned}$$

or

$$\gamma_0 = \phi_1\gamma_1 + \phi_2\gamma_2 + \sigma^2. \tag{3.4.29}$$

The last term $(\sigma^2)$ in [3.4.29] comes from noticing that

$$\begin{aligned} E(\varepsilon_t)(Y_t - \mu) &= E(\varepsilon_t)[\phi_1(Y_{t-1} - \mu) + \phi_2(Y_{t-2} - \mu) + \varepsilon_t] \\ &= \phi_1 \cdot 0 + \phi_2 \cdot 0 + \sigma^2. \end{aligned}$$

Equation [3.4.29] can be written

$$\gamma_0 = \phi_1\rho_1\gamma_0 + \phi_2\rho_2\gamma_0 + \sigma^2. \tag{3.4.30}$$

Substituting [3.4.27] and [3.4.28] into [3.4.30] gives

$$\gamma_0 = \left[\frac{\phi_1^2}{(1 - \phi_2)} + \frac{\phi_2\phi_1^2}{(1 - \phi_2)} + \phi_2^2\right]\gamma_0 + \sigma^2$$

or

$$\gamma_0 = \frac{(1 - \phi_2)\sigma^2}{(1 + \phi_2)[(1 - \phi_2)^2 - \phi_1^2]}.$$

## *The* pth-*Order Autoregressive Process*

A *pth-order autoregression*, denoted $AR(p)$, satisfies

$$Y_t = c + \phi_1 Y_{t-1} + \phi_2 Y_{t-2} + \cdots + \phi_p Y_{t-p} + \varepsilon_t. \tag{3.4.31}$$

Provided that the roots of

$$1 - \phi_1 z - \phi_2 z^2 - \cdots - \phi_p z^p = 0 \tag{3.4.32}$$

all lie outside the unit circle, it is straightforward to verify that a covariance-stationary representation of the form

$$Y_t = \mu + \psi(L)\varepsilon_t \tag{3.4.33}$$

exists where

$$\psi(L) = (1 - \phi_1 L - \phi_2 L^2 - \cdots - \phi_p L^p)^{-1}$$

and $\Sigma_{j=0}^{\infty} |\psi_j| < \infty$. Assuming that the stationarity condition is satisfied, one way to find the mean is to take expectations of [3.4.31]:

$$\mu = c + \phi_1 \mu + \phi_2 \mu + \cdots + \phi_p \mu,$$

or

$$\mu = c/(1 - \phi_1 - \phi_2 - \cdots - \phi_p). \qquad [3.4.34]$$

Using [3.4.34], equation [3.4.31] can be written

$$\begin{aligned} Y_t - \mu = \phi_1(Y_{t-1} - \mu) + \phi_2(Y_{t-2} - \mu) + \cdots \\ + \phi_p(Y_{t-p} - \mu) + \varepsilon_t. \end{aligned} \qquad [3.4.35]$$

Autocovariances are found by multiplying both sides of [3.4.35] by $(Y_{t-j} - \mu)$ and taking expectations:

$$\gamma_j = \begin{cases} \phi_1 \gamma_{j-1} + \phi_2 \gamma_{j-2} + \cdots + \phi_p \gamma_{j-p} & \text{for } j = 1, 2, \ldots \\ \phi_1 \gamma_1 + \phi_2 \gamma_2 + \cdots + \phi_p \gamma_p + \sigma^2 & \text{for } j = 0. \end{cases} \qquad [3.4.36]$$

Using the fact that $\gamma_{-j} = \gamma_j$, the system of equations in [3.4.36] for $j = 0, 1, \ldots, p$ can be solved for $\gamma_0, \gamma_1, \ldots, \gamma_p$ as functions of $\sigma^2, \phi_1, \phi_2, \ldots, \phi_p$. It can be shown[4] that the $(p \times 1)$ vector $(\gamma_0, \gamma_1, \ldots, \gamma_{p-1})'$ is given by the first $p$ elements of the first column of the $(p^2 \times p^2)$ matrix $\sigma^2[\mathbf{I}_{p^2} - (\mathbf{F} \otimes \mathbf{F})]^{-1}$ where $\mathbf{F}$ is the $(p \times p)$ matrix defined in equation [1.2.3] and $\otimes$ indicates the Kronecker product.

Dividing [3.4.36] by $\gamma_0$ produces the *Yule-Walker equations*:

$$\rho_j = \phi_1 \rho_{j-1} + \phi_2 \rho_{j-2} + \cdots + \phi_p \rho_{j-p} \qquad \text{for } j = 1, 2, \ldots. \qquad [3.4.37]$$

Thus, the autocovariances and autocorrelations follow the same $p$th-order difference equation as does the process itself [3.4.31]. For distinct roots, their solutions take the form

$$\gamma_j = g_1 \lambda_1^j + g_2 \lambda_2^j + \cdots + g_p \lambda_p^j, \qquad [3.4.38]$$

where the eigenvalues $(\lambda_1, \ldots, \lambda_p)$ are the solutions to

$$\lambda^p - \phi_1 \lambda^{p-1} - \phi_2 \lambda^{p-2} - \cdots - \phi_p = 0.$$

## 3.5. *Mixed Autoregressive Moving Average Processes*

An *ARMA*$(p, q)$ *process* includes both autoregressive and moving average terms:

$$\begin{aligned} Y_t = c + \phi_1 Y_{t-1} + \phi_2 Y_{t-2} + \cdots + \phi_p Y_{t-p} + \varepsilon_t + \theta_1 \varepsilon_{t-1} \\ + \theta_2 \varepsilon_{t-2} + \cdots + \theta_q \varepsilon_{t-q}, \end{aligned} \qquad [3.5.1]$$

or, in lag operator form,

$$\begin{aligned} (1 - \phi_1 L - \phi_2 L^2 - \cdots - \phi_p L^p) Y_t \\ = c + (1 + \theta_1 L + \theta_2 L^2 + \cdots + \theta_q L^q) \varepsilon_t. \end{aligned} \qquad [3.5.2]$$

Provided that the roots of

$$1 - \phi_1 z - \phi_2 z^2 - \cdots - \phi_p z^p = 0 \qquad [3.5.3]$$

[4]The reader will be invited to prove this in Exercise 10.1 in Chapter 10.

lie outside the unit circle, both sides of [3.5.2] can be divided by $(1 - \phi_1 L - \phi_2 L^2 - \cdots - \phi_p L^p)$ to obtain

$$Y_t = \mu + \psi(L)\varepsilon_t$$

where

$$\psi(L) = \frac{(1 + \theta_1 L + \theta_2 L^2 + \cdots + \theta_q L^q)}{(1 - \phi_1 L - \phi_2 L^2 - \cdots - \phi_p L^p)}$$

$$\sum_{j=0}^{\infty} |\psi_j| < \infty$$

$$\mu = c/(1 - \phi_1 - \phi_2 - \cdots - \phi_p).$$

Thus, stationarity of an *ARMA* process depends entirely on the autoregressive parameters $(\phi_1, \phi_2, \ldots, \phi_p)$ and not on the moving average parameters $(\theta_1, \theta_2, \ldots, \theta_q)$.

It is often convenient to write the *ARMA* process [3.5.1] in terms of deviations from the mean:

$$\begin{aligned} Y_t - \mu = {} & \phi_1(Y_{t-1} - \mu) + \phi_2(Y_{t-2} - \mu) + \cdots \\ & + \phi_p(Y_{t-p} - \mu) + \varepsilon_t + \theta_1\varepsilon_{t-1} + \theta_2\varepsilon_{t-2} + \cdots + \theta_q\varepsilon_{t-q}. \end{aligned} \qquad [3.5.4]$$

Autocovariances are found by multiplying both sides of [3.5.4] by $(Y_{t-j} - \mu)$ and taking expectations. For $j > q$, the resulting equations take the form

$$\gamma_j = \phi_1\gamma_{j-1} + \phi_2\gamma_{j-2} + \cdots + \phi_p\gamma_{j-p} \qquad \text{for } j = q+1, q+2, \ldots. \qquad [3.5.5]$$

Thus, after $q$ lags the autocovariance function $\gamma_j$ (and the autocorrelation function $\rho_j$) follow the $p$th-order difference equation governed by the autoregressive parameters.

Note that [3.5.5] does not hold for $j \leq q$, owing to correlation between $\theta_j\varepsilon_{t-j}$ and $Y_{t-j}$. Hence, an $ARMA(p, q)$ process will have more complicated autocovariances for lags 1 through $q$ than would the corresponding $AR(p)$ process. For $j > q$ with distinct autoregressive roots, the autocovariances will be given by

$$\gamma_j = h_1\lambda_1^j + h_2\lambda_2^j + \cdots + h_p\lambda_p^j. \qquad [3.5.6]$$

This takes the same form as the autocovariances for an $AR(p)$ process [3.4.38], though because the initial conditions $(\gamma_0, \gamma_1, \ldots, \gamma_q)$ differ for the *ARMA* and *AR* processes, the parameters $h_k$ in [3.5.6] will not be the same as the parameters $g_k$ in [3.4.38].

There is a potential for redundant parameterization with *ARMA* processes. Consider, for example, a simple white noise process,

$$Y_t = \varepsilon_t. \qquad [3.5.7]$$

Suppose both sides of [3.5.7] are multiplied by $(1 - \rho L)$:

$$(1 - \rho L)Y_t = (1 - \rho L)\varepsilon_t. \qquad [3.5.8]$$

Clearly, if [3.5.7] is a valid representation, then so is [3.5.8] for any value of $\rho$. Thus, [3.5.8] might be described as an $ARMA(1, 1)$ process, with $\phi_1 = \rho$ and $\theta_1 = -\rho$. It is important to avoid such a parameterization. Since any value of $\rho$ in [3.5.8] describes the data equally well, we will obviously get into trouble trying to estimate the parameter $\rho$ in [3.5.8] by maximum likelihood. Moreover, theoretical manipulations based on a representation such as [3.5.8] may overlook key cancellations. If we are using an $ARMA(1, 1)$ model in which $\theta_1$ is close to $-\phi_1$, then the data might better be modeled as simple white noise.

A related overparameterization can arise with an $ARMA(p, q)$ model. Consider factoring the lag polynomial operators in [3.5.2] as in [2.4.3]:

$$(1 - \lambda_1 L)(1 - \lambda_2 L) \cdots (1 - \lambda_p L)(Y_t - \mu) \\ = (1 - \eta_1 L)(1 - \eta_2 L) \cdots (1 - \eta_q L)\varepsilon_t. \qquad [3.5.9]$$

We assume that $|\lambda_i| < 1$ for all $i$, so that the process is covariance-stationary. If the autoregressive operator $(1 - \phi_1 L - \phi_2 L^2 - \cdots - \phi_p L^p)$ and the moving average operator $(1 + \theta_1 L + \theta_2 L^2 + \cdots + \theta_q L^q)$ have any roots in common, say, $\lambda_i = \eta_j$ for some $i$ and $j$, then both sides of [3.5.9] can be divided by $(1 - \lambda_i L)$:

$$\prod_{\substack{k=1 \\ k \neq i}}^{p} (1 - \lambda_k L)(Y_t - \mu) = \prod_{\substack{k=1 \\ k \neq j}}^{q} (1 - \eta_k L)\varepsilon_t,$$

or

$$(1 - \phi_1^* L - \phi_2^* L^2 - \cdots - \phi_{p-1}^* L^{p-1})(Y_t - \mu) \\ = (1 + \theta_1^* L + \theta_2^* L^2 + \cdots + \theta_{q-1}^* L^{q-1})\varepsilon_t, \qquad [3.5.10]$$

where

$$(1 - \phi_1^* L - \phi_2^* L^2 - \cdots - \phi_{p-1}^* L^{p-1}) \\ \equiv (1 - \lambda_1 L)(1 - \lambda_2 L) \cdots (1 - \lambda_{i-1} L)(1 - \lambda_{i+1} L) \cdots (1 - \lambda_p L)$$

$$(1 + \theta_1^* L + \theta_2^* L^2 + \cdots + \theta_{q-1}^* L^{q-1}) \\ \equiv (1 - \eta_1 L)(1 - \eta_2 L) \cdots (1 - \eta_{j-1} L)(1 - \eta_{j+1} L) \cdots (1 - \eta_q L).$$

The stationary $ARMA(p, q)$ process satisfying [3.5.2] is clearly identical to the stationary $ARMA(p - 1, q - 1)$ process satisfying [3.5.10].

## 3.6. *The Autocovariance-Generating Function*

For each of the covariance-stationary processes for $Y_t$ considered so far, we calculated the sequence of autocovariances $\{\gamma_j\}_{j=-\infty}^{\infty}$. If this sequence is absolutely summable, then one way of summarizing the autocovariances is through a scalar-valued function called the *autocovariance-generating function*:

$$g_Y(z) = \sum_{j=-\infty}^{\infty} \gamma_j z^j. \qquad [3.6.1]$$

This function is constructed by taking the $j$th autocovariance and multiplying it by some number $z$ raised to the $j$th power, and then summing over all the possible values of $j$. The argument of this function ($z$) is taken to be a complex scalar.

Of particular interest as an argument for the autocovariance-generating function is any value of $z$ that lies on the complex unit circle,

$$z = \cos(\omega) - i\sin(\omega) = e^{-i\omega},$$

where $i = \sqrt{-1}$ and $\omega$ is the radian angle that $z$ makes with the real axis. If the autocovariance-generating function is evaluated at $z = e^{-i\omega}$ and divided by $2\pi$, the resulting function of $\omega$,

$$s_Y(\omega) = \frac{1}{2\pi} g_Y(e^{-i\omega}) = \frac{1}{2\pi} \sum_{j=-\infty}^{\infty} \gamma_j e^{-i\omega j},$$

is called the *population spectrum* of $Y$. The population spectrum will be discussed in detail in Chapter 6. There it will be shown that for a process with absolutely summable autocovariances, the function $s_Y(\omega)$ exists and can be used to calculate all of the autocovariances. This means that if two different processes share the same autocovariance-generating function, then the two processes exhibit the identical sequence of autocovariances.

As an example of calculating an autocovariance-generating function, consider the $MA(1)$ process. From equations [3.3.3] to [3.3.5], its autocovariance-generating function is

$$g_Y(z) = [\theta\sigma^2]z^{-1} + [(1 + \theta^2)\sigma^2]z^0 + [\theta\sigma^2]z^1 = \sigma^2 \cdot [\theta z^{-1} + (1 + \theta^2) + \theta z].$$

Notice that this expression could alternatively be written

$$g_Y(z) = \sigma^2(1 + \theta z)(1 + \theta z^{-1}). \tag{3.6.2}$$

The form of expression [3.6.2] suggests that for the $MA(q)$ process,

$$Y_t = \mu + (1 + \theta_1 L + \theta_2 L^2 + \cdots + \theta_q L^q)\varepsilon_t,$$

the autocovariance-generating function might be calculated as

$$\begin{aligned} g_Y(z) = \sigma^2(1 + \theta_1 z + \theta_2 z^2 + \cdots + \theta_q z^q) \\ \times (1 + \theta_1 z^{-1} + \theta_2 z^{-2} + \cdots + \theta_q z^{-q}). \end{aligned} \tag{3.6.3}$$

This conjecture can be verified by carrying out the multiplication in [3.6.3] and collecting terms by powers of $z$:

$$\begin{aligned} &(1 + \theta_1 z + \theta_2 z^2 + \cdots + \theta_q z^q) \times (1 + \theta_1 z^{-1} + \theta_2 z^{-2} + \cdots + \theta_q z^{-q}) \\ &= (\theta_q)z^q + (\theta_{q-1} + \theta_q\theta_1)z^{(q-1)} + (\theta_{q-2} + \theta_{q-1}\theta_1 + \theta_q\theta_2)z^{(q-2)} \\ &\quad + \cdots + (\theta_1 + \theta_2\theta_1 + \theta_3\theta_2 + \cdots + \theta_q\theta_{q-1})z^1 \\ &\quad + (1 + \theta_1^2 + \theta_2^2 + \cdots + \theta_q^2)z^0 \\ &\quad + (\theta_1 + \theta_2\theta_1 + \theta_3\theta_2 + \cdots + \theta_q\theta_{q-1})z^{-1} + \cdots + (\theta_q)z^{-q}. \end{aligned} \tag{3.6.4}$$

Comparison of [3.6.4] with [3.3.10] or [3.3.12] confirms that the coefficient on $z^j$ in [3.6.3] is indeed the $j$th autocovariance.

This method for finding $g_Y(z)$ extends to the $MA(\infty)$ case. If

$$Y_t = \mu + \psi(L)\varepsilon_t \tag{3.6.5}$$

with

$$\psi(L) = \psi_0 + \psi_1 L + \psi_2 L^2 + \cdots \tag{3.6.6}$$

and

$$\sum_{j=0}^{\infty} |\psi_j| < \infty, \tag{3.6.7}$$

then

$$g_Y(z) = \sigma^2\psi(z)\psi(z^{-1}). \tag{3.6.8}$$

For example, the stationary $AR(1)$ process can be written as

$$Y_t - \mu = (1 - \phi L)^{-1}\varepsilon_t,$$

which is in the form of [3.6.5] with $\psi(L) = 1/(1 - \phi L)$. The autocovariance-generating function for an $AR(1)$ process could therefore be calculated from

$$g_Y(z) = \frac{\sigma^2}{(1 - \phi z)(1 - \phi z^{-1})}. \tag{3.6.9}$$

To verify this claim directly, expand out the terms in [3.6.9]:

$$\frac{\sigma^2}{(1 - \phi z)(1 - \phi z^{-1})} = \sigma^2(1 + \phi z + \phi^2 z^2 + \phi^3 z^3 + \cdots) \times (1 + \phi z^{-1} + \phi^2 z^{-2} + \phi^3 z^{-3} + \cdots),$$

from which the coefficient on $z^j$ is

$$\sigma^2(\phi^j + \phi^{j+1}\phi + \phi^{j+2}\phi^2 + \cdots) = \sigma^2\phi^j/(1 - \phi^2).$$

This indeed yields the $j$th autocovariance as earlier calculated in equation [3.4.5].

The autocovariance-generating function for a stationary $ARMA(p, q)$ process can be written

$$g_Y(z) = \frac{\sigma^2(1 + \theta_1 z + \theta_2 z^2 + \cdots + \theta_q z^q)(1 + \theta_1 z^{-1} + \theta_2 z^{-2} + \cdots + \theta_q z^{-q})}{(1 - \phi_1 z - \phi_2 z^2 - \cdots - \phi_p z^p)(1 - \phi_1 z^{-1} - \phi_2 z^{-2} - \cdots - \phi_p z^{-p})}. \quad [3.6.10]$$

## *Filters*

Sometimes the data are *filtered*, or treated in a particular way before they are analyzed, and we would like to summarize the effects of this treatment on the autocovariances. This calculation is particularly simple using the autocovariance-generating function. For example, suppose that the original data $Y_t$ were generated from an $MA(1)$ process,

$$Y_t = (1 + \theta L)\varepsilon_t, \quad [3.6.11]$$

with autocovariance-generating function given by [3.6.2]. Let's say that the data as actually analyzed, $X_t$, represent the change in $Y_t$ over its value the previous period:

$$X_t = Y_t - Y_{t-1} = (1 - L)Y_t. \quad [3.6.12]$$

Substituting [3.6.11] into [3.6.12], the observed data can be characterized as the following $MA(2)$ process,

$$X_t = (1 - L)(1 + \theta L)\varepsilon_t = [1 + (\theta - 1)L - \theta L^2]\varepsilon_t \equiv [1 + \theta_1 L + \theta_2 L^2]\varepsilon_t, \quad [3.6.13]$$

with $\theta_1 \equiv (\theta - 1)$ and $\theta_2 \equiv -\theta$. The autocovariance-generating function of the observed data $X_t$ can be calculated by direct application of [3.6.3]:

$$g_X(z) = \sigma^2(1 + \theta_1 z + \theta_2 z^2)(1 + \theta_1 z^{-1} + \theta_2 z^{-2}). \quad [3.6.14]$$

It is often instructive, however, to keep the polynomial $(1 + \theta_1 z + \theta_2 z^2)$ in its factored form of the first line of [3.6.13],

$$(1 + \theta_1 z + \theta_2 z^2) = (1 - z)(1 + \theta z),$$

in which case [3.6.14] could be written

$$\begin{aligned} g_X(z) &= \sigma^2(1 - z)(1 + \theta z)(1 - z^{-1})(1 + \theta z^{-1}) \\ &= (1 - z)(1 - z^{-1}) \cdot g_Y(z). \end{aligned} \quad [3.6.15]$$

Of course, [3.6.14] and [3.6.15] represent the identical function of $z$, and which way we choose to write it is simply a matter of convenience. Applying the filter

$(1 - L)$ to $Y_t$ thus results in multiplying its autocovariance-generating function by $(1 - z)(1 - z^{-1})$.

This principle readily generalizes. Suppose that the original data series $\{Y_t\}$ satisfies [3.6.5] through [3.6.7]. Let's say the data are filtered according to

$$X_t = h(L)Y_t \qquad [3.6.16]$$

with

$$h(L) = \sum_{j=-\infty}^{\infty} h_j L^j$$

$$\sum_{j=-\infty}^{\infty} |h_j| < \infty.$$

Substituting [3.6.5] into [3.6.16], the observed data $X_t$ are then generated by

$$X_t = h(1)\mu + h(L)\psi(L)\varepsilon_t \equiv \mu^* + \psi^*(L)\varepsilon_t,$$

where $\mu^* \equiv h(1)\mu$ and $\psi^*(L) \equiv h(L)\psi(L)$. The sequence of coefficients associated with the compound operator $\{\psi_j^*\}_{j=-\infty}^{\infty}$ turns out to be absolutely summable,[5] and the autocovariance-generating function of $X_t$ can accordingly be calculated as

$$g_X(z) = \sigma^2\psi^*(z)\psi^*(z^{-1}) = \sigma^2 h(z)\psi(z)\psi(z^{-1})h(z^{-1}) = h(z)h(z^{-1})g_Y(z). \qquad [3.6.17]$$

Applying the filter $h(L)$ to a series thus results in multiplying its autocovariance-generating function by $h(z)h(z^{-1})$.

## 3.7. *Invertibility*

### *Invertibility for the* MA*(1) Process*

Consider an $MA(1)$ process,

$$Y_t - \mu = (1 + \theta L)\varepsilon_t, \qquad [3.7.1]$$

with

$$E(\varepsilon_t\varepsilon_\tau) = \begin{cases} \sigma^2 & \text{for } t = \tau \\ 0 & \text{otherwise.} \end{cases}$$

[5]Specifically,

$$\begin{aligned}\psi^*(z) &= \left(\sum_{j=-\infty}^{\infty} h_j z^j\right)\left(\sum_{k=0}^{\infty} \psi_k z^k\right) \\ &= (\cdots + h_{-j}z^{-j} + h_{-j+1}z^{-j+1} + \cdots + h_{-1}z^{-1} + h_0 z^0 + h_1 z^1 + \cdots \\ &\qquad + h_j z^j + h_{j+1}z^{j+1} + \cdots)(\psi_0 z^0 + \psi_1 z^1 + \psi_2 z^2 + \cdots),\end{aligned}$$

from which the coefficient on $z^j$ is

$$\psi_j^* = h_j\psi_0 + h_{j-1}\psi_1 + h_{j-2}\psi_2 + \cdots = \sum_{v=0}^{\infty} h_{j-v}\psi_v.$$

Then

$$\sum_{j=-\infty}^{\infty} |\psi_j^*| = \sum_{j=-\infty}^{\infty} \left|\sum_{v=0}^{\infty} h_{j-v}\psi_v\right| \le \sum_{j=-\infty}^{\infty}\sum_{v=0}^{\infty} |h_{j-v}\psi_v| = \sum_{v=0}^{\infty} |\psi_v| \sum_{j=-\infty}^{\infty} |h_{j-v}| = \sum_{v=0}^{\infty} |\psi_v| \sum_{j=-\infty}^{\infty} |h_j| < \infty.$$

Provided that $|\theta| < 1$, both sides of [3.7.1] can be multiplied by $(1 + \theta L)^{-1}$ to obtain[6]

$$(1 - \theta L + \theta^2 L^2 - \theta^3 L^3 + \cdots)(Y_t - \mu) = \varepsilon_t, \qquad [3.7.2]$$

which could be viewed as an $AR(\infty)$ representation. If a moving average representation such as [3.7.1] can be rewritten as an $AR(\infty)$ representation such as [3.7.2] simply by inverting the moving average operator $(1 + \theta L)$, then the moving average representation is said to be *invertible*. For an $MA(1)$ process, invertibility requires $|\theta| < 1$; if $|\theta| \geq 1$, then the infinite sequence in [3.7.2] would not be well defined.

Let us investigate what invertibility means in terms of the first and second moments of the process. Recall that the $MA(1)$ process [3.7.1] has mean $\mu$ and autocovariance-generating function

$$g_Y(z) = \sigma^2(1 + \theta z)(1 + \theta z^{-1}). \qquad [3.7.3]$$

Now consider a seemingly different $MA(1)$ process,

$$\tilde{Y}_t - \mu = (1 + \tilde{\theta} L)\tilde{\varepsilon}_t, \qquad [3.7.4]$$

with

$$E(\tilde{\varepsilon}_t \tilde{\varepsilon}_\tau) = \begin{cases} \tilde{\sigma}^2 & \text{for } t = \tau \\ 0 & \text{otherwise.} \end{cases}$$

Note that $\tilde{Y}_t$ has the same mean ($\mu$) as $Y_t$. Its autocovariance-generating function is

$$\begin{aligned} g_{\tilde{Y}}(z) &= \tilde{\sigma}^2(1 + \tilde{\theta} z)(1 + \tilde{\theta} z^{-1}) \\ &= \tilde{\sigma}^2\{(\tilde{\theta}^{-1} z^{-1} + 1)(\tilde{\theta} z)\}\{(\tilde{\theta}^{-1} z + 1)(\tilde{\theta} z^{-1})\} \qquad [3.7.5] \\ &= (\tilde{\sigma}^2 \tilde{\theta}^2)(1 + \tilde{\theta}^{-1} z)(1 + \tilde{\theta}^{-1} z^{-1}). \end{aligned}$$

Suppose that the parameters of [3.7.4], $(\tilde{\theta}, \tilde{\sigma}^2)$, are related to those of [3.7.1] by the following equations:

$$\theta = \tilde{\theta}^{-1} \qquad [3.7.6]$$

$$\sigma^2 = \tilde{\theta}^2 \tilde{\sigma}^2. \qquad [3.7.7]$$

Then the autocovariance-generating functions [3.7.3] and [3.7.5] would be the same, meaning that $Y_t$ and $\tilde{Y}_t$ would have identical first and second moments.

Notice from [3.7.6] that if $|\theta| < 1$, then $|\tilde{\theta}| > 1$. In other words, for any invertible $MA(1)$ representation [3.7.1], we have found a noninvertible $MA(1)$ representation [3.7.4] with the same first and second moments as the invertible representation. Conversely, given any noninvertible representation with $|\tilde{\theta}| > 1$, there exists an invertible representation with $\theta = (1/\tilde{\theta})$ that has the same first and second moments as the noninvertible representation. In the borderline case where $\theta = \pm 1$, there is only one representation of the process, and it is noninvertible.

Not only do the invertible and noninvertible representations share the same moments, either representation [3.7.1] or [3.7.4] could be used as an equally valid description of any given $MA(1)$ process! Suppose a computer generated an infinite sequence of $\tilde{Y}$'s according to [3.7.4] with $\tilde{\theta} > 1$. Thus we know for a fact that the data were generated from an $MA(1)$ process expressed in terms of a noninvertible representation. In what sense could these same data be associated with an invertible $MA(1)$ representation?

[6]Note from [2.2.8] that

$$(1 + \theta L)^{-1} = [1 - (-\theta)L]^{-1} = 1 + (-\theta)L + (-\theta)^2 L^2 + (-\theta)^3 L^3 + \cdots.$$

Imagine calculating a series $\{\varepsilon_t\}_{t=-\infty}^{\infty}$ defined by

$$\begin{aligned}\varepsilon_t &\equiv (1 + \theta L)^{-1}(\tilde{Y}_t - \mu) \\ &= (\tilde{Y}_t - \mu) - \theta(\tilde{Y}_{t-1} - \mu) + \theta^2(\tilde{Y}_{t-2} - \mu) - \theta^3(\tilde{Y}_{t-3} - \mu) + \cdots,\end{aligned} \qquad [3.7.8]$$

where $\theta = (1/\tilde{\theta})$ is the moving average parameter associated with the invertible $MA(1)$ representation that shares the same moments as [3.7.4]. Note that since $|\theta| < 1$, this produces a well-defined, mean square convergent series $\{\varepsilon_t\}$.

Furthermore, the sequence $\{\varepsilon_t\}$ so generated is white noise. The simplest way to verify this is to calculate the autocovariance-generating function of $\varepsilon_t$ and confirm that the coefficient on $z^j$ (the $j$th autocovariance) is equal to zero for any $j \neq 0$. From [3.7.8] and [3.6.17], the autocovariance-generating function for $\varepsilon_t$ is given by

$$g_\varepsilon(z) = (1 + \theta z)^{-1}(1 + \theta z^{-1})^{-1} g_{\tilde{Y}}(z). \qquad [3.7.9]$$

Substituting [3.7.5] into [3.7.9],

$$\begin{aligned}g_\varepsilon(z) &= (1 + \theta z)^{-1}(1 + \theta z^{-1})^{-1}(\tilde{\sigma}^2\tilde{\theta}^2)(1 + \tilde{\theta}^{-1}z)(1 + \tilde{\theta}^{-1}z^{-1}) \\ &= \tilde{\sigma}^2\tilde{\theta}^2,\end{aligned} \qquad [3.7.10]$$

where the last equality follows from the fact that $\tilde{\theta}^{-1} = \theta$. Since the autocovariance-generating function is a constant, it follows that $\varepsilon_t$ is a white noise process with variance $\tilde{\theta}^2\tilde{\sigma}^2$.

Multiplying both sides of [3.7.8] by $(1 + \theta L)$,

$$\tilde{Y}_t - \mu = (1 + \theta L)\varepsilon_t$$

is a perfectly valid invertible $MA(1)$ representation of data that were actually generated from the noninvertible representation [3.7.4].

The converse proposition is also true—suppose that the data were really generated from [3.7.1] with $|\theta| < 1$, an invertible representation. Then there exists a noninvertible representation with $\tilde{\theta} = 1/\theta$ that describes these data with equal validity. To characterize this noninvertible representation, consider the operator proposed in [2.5.20] as the appropriate inverse of $(1 + \tilde{\theta}L)$:

$$\begin{aligned}&(\tilde{\theta})^{-1}L^{-1}[1 - (\tilde{\theta}^{-1})L^{-1} + (\tilde{\theta}^{-2})L^{-2} - (\tilde{\theta}^{-3})L^{-3} + \cdots] \\ &= \theta L^{-1}[1 - \theta L^{-1} + \theta^2 L^{-2} - \theta^3 L^{-3} + \cdots].\end{aligned}$$

Define $\tilde{\varepsilon}_t$ to be the series that results from applying this operator to $(Y_t - \mu)$,

$$\tilde{\varepsilon}_t \equiv \theta(Y_{t+1} - \mu) - \theta^2(Y_{t+2} - \mu) + \theta^3(Y_{t+3} - \mu) - \cdots, \qquad [3.7.11]$$

noting that this series converges for $|\theta| < 1$. Again this series is white noise:

$$\begin{aligned}g_{\tilde{\varepsilon}}(z) &= \{\theta z^{-1}[1 - \theta z^{-1} + \theta^2 z^{-2} - \theta^3 z^{-3} + \cdots]\} \\ &\quad \times \{\theta z[1 - \theta z^1 + \theta^2 z^2 - \theta^3 z^3 + \cdots]\}\sigma^2(1 + \theta z)(1 + \theta z^{-1}) \\ &= \theta^2\sigma^2.\end{aligned}$$

The coefficient on $z^j$ is zero for $j \neq 0$, so $\tilde{\varepsilon}_t$ is white noise as claimed. Furthermore, by construction,

$$Y_t - \mu = (1 + \tilde{\theta}L)\tilde{\varepsilon}_t,$$

so that we have found a noninvertible $MA(1)$ representation of data that were actually generated by the invertible $MA(1)$ representation [3.7.1].

Either the invertible or the noninvertible representation could characterize any given data equally well, though there is a practical reason for preferring the invertible representation. To find the value of $\varepsilon$ for date $t$ associated with the invertible representation as in [3.7.8], we need to know current and past values of $Y$. By contrast, to find the value of $\tilde{\varepsilon}$ for date $t$ associated with the noninvertible representation as in [3.7.11], we need to use all of the future values of $Y$! If the intention is to calculate the current value of $\varepsilon_t$ using real-world data, it will be feasible only to work with the invertible representation. Also, as will be noted in Chapters 4 and 5, some convenient algorithms for estimating parameters and forecasting are valid only if the invertible representation is used.

The value of $\varepsilon_t$ associated with the invertible representation is sometimes called the *fundamental innovation* for $Y_t$. For the borderline case when $|\theta| = 1$, the process is noninvertible, but the innovation $\varepsilon_t$ for such a process will still be described as the fundamental innovation for $Y_t$.

## *Invertibility for the* MA(q) *Process*

Consider now the $MA(q)$ process,

$$(Y_t - \mu) = (1 + \theta_1 L + \theta_2 L^2 + \cdots + \theta_q L^q)\varepsilon_t \tag{3.7.12}$$

$$E(\varepsilon_t \varepsilon_\tau) = \begin{cases} \sigma^2 & \text{for } t = \tau \\ 0 & \text{otherwise.} \end{cases}$$

Provided that the roots of

$$(1 + \theta_1 z + \theta_2 z^2 + \cdots + \theta_q z^q) = 0 \tag{3.7.13}$$

lie outside the unit circle, [3.7.12] can be written as an $AR(\infty)$ simply by inverting the $MA$ operator,

$$(1 + \eta_1 L + \eta_2 L^2 + \eta_3 L^3 + \cdots)(Y_t - \mu) = \varepsilon_t,$$

where

$$(1 + \eta_1 L + \eta_2 L^2 + \eta_3 L^3 + \cdots) = (1 + \theta_1 L + \theta_2 L^2 + \cdots + \theta_q L^q)^{-1}.$$

Where this is the case, the $MA(q)$ representation [3.7.12] is invertible.

Factor the moving average operator as

$$(1 + \theta_1 L + \theta_2 L^2 + \cdots + \theta_q L^q) = (1 - \lambda_1 L)(1 - \lambda_2 L)\cdots(1 - \lambda_q L). \tag{3.7.14}$$

If $|\lambda_i| < 1$ for all $i$, then the roots of [3.7.13] are all outside the unit circle and the representation [3.7.12] is invertible. If instead some of the $\lambda_i$ are outside (but not on) the unit circle, Hansen and Sargent (1981, p. 102) suggested the following procedure for finding an invertible representation. The autocovariance-generating function of $Y_t$ can be written

$$\begin{aligned} g_Y(z) = \sigma^2 \cdot \{(1 - \lambda_1 z)(1 - \lambda_2 z) \cdots (1 - \lambda_q z)\} \\ \times \{(1 - \lambda_1 z^{-1})(1 - \lambda_2 z^{-1}) \cdots (1 - \lambda_q z^{-1})\}. \end{aligned} \tag{3.7.15}$$

Order the $\lambda$'s so that $(\lambda_1, \lambda_2, \ldots, \lambda_n)$ are inside the unit circle and $(\lambda_{n+1}, \lambda_{n+2}, \ldots, \lambda_q)$ are outside the unit circle. Suppose $\sigma^2$ in [3.7.15] is replaced by $\sigma^2 \cdot \lambda_{n+1}^2 \cdot \lambda_{n+2}^2 \cdots \lambda_q^2$; since complex $\lambda_i$ appear as conjugate pairs, this is a positive real number. Suppose further that $(\lambda_{n+1}, \lambda_{n+2}, \ldots, \lambda_q)$ are replaced with their reciprocals, $(\lambda_{n+1}^{-1}, \lambda_{n+2}^{-1}, \ldots, \lambda_q^{-1})$. The resulting function would be

$$\sigma^2\lambda_{n+1}^2\lambda_{n+2}^2 \cdots \lambda_q^2\left\{\prod_{i=1}^{n}(1 - \lambda_i z)\right\}\left\{\prod_{i=n+1}^{q}(1 - \lambda_i^{-1}z)\right\}$$

$$\times\left\{\prod_{i=1}^{n}(1 - \lambda_i z^{-1})\right\}\left\{\prod_{i=n+1}^{q}(1 - \lambda_i^{-1}z^{-1})\right\}$$

$$= \sigma^2\left\{\prod_{i=1}^{n}(1 - \lambda_i z)\right\}\left\{\prod_{i=n+1}^{q}[(\lambda_i z^{-1})(1 - \lambda_i^{-1}z)]\right\}$$

$$\times\left\{\prod_{i=1}^{n}(1 - \lambda_i z^{-1})\right\}\left\{\prod_{i=n+1}^{q}[(\lambda_i z)(1 - \lambda_i^{-1}z^{-1})]\right\}$$

$$= \sigma^2\left\{\prod_{i=1}^{n}(1 - \lambda_i z)\right\}\left\{\prod_{i=n+1}^{q}(\lambda_i z^{-1} - 1)\right\}$$

$$\times\left\{\prod_{i=1}^{n}(1 - \lambda_i z^{-1})\right\}\left\{\prod_{i=n+1}^{q}(\lambda_i z - 1)\right\}$$

$$= \sigma^2\left\{\prod_{i=1}^{q}(1 - \lambda_i z)\right\}\left\{\prod_{i=1}^{q}(1 - \lambda_i z^{-1})\right\},$$

which is identical to [3.7.15].

The implication is as follows. Suppose a noninvertible representation for an $MA(q)$ process is written in the form

$$Y_t = \mu + \prod_{i=1}^{q}(1 - \lambda_i L)\tilde{\varepsilon}_t, \qquad [3.7.16]$$

where

$$|\lambda_i| < 1 \qquad \text{for } i = 1, 2, \ldots, n$$
$$|\lambda_i| > 1 \qquad \text{for } i = n + 1, n + 2, \ldots, q$$

and

$$E(\tilde{\varepsilon}_t\tilde{\varepsilon}_\tau) = \begin{cases} \tilde{\sigma}^2 & \text{for } t = \tau \\ 0 & \text{otherwise.} \end{cases}$$

Then the invertible representation is given by

$$Y_t = \mu + \left\{\prod_{i=1}^{n}(1 - \lambda_i L)\right\}\left\{\prod_{i=n+1}^{q}(1 - \lambda_i^{-1}L)\right\}\varepsilon_t, \qquad [3.7.17]$$

where

$$E(\varepsilon_t\varepsilon_\tau) = \begin{cases} \tilde{\sigma}^2\lambda_{n+1}^2\lambda_{n+2}^2 \cdots \lambda_q^2 & \text{for } t = \tau \\ 0 & \text{otherwise.} \end{cases}$$

Then [3.7.16] and [3.7.17] have the identical autocovariance-generating function, though only [3.7.17] satisfies the invertibility condition.

From the structure of the preceding argument, it is clear that there are a number of alternative $MA(q)$ representations of the data $Y_t$ associated with all the possible "flips" between $\lambda_i$ and $\lambda_i^{-1}$. Only one of these has all of the $\lambda_i$ on or inside the unit circle. The innovations associated with this representation are said to be the fundamental innovations for $Y_t$.

## APPENDIX 3.A. *Convergence Results for Infinite-Order Moving Average Processes*

This appendix proves the statements made in the text about convergence for the $MA(\infty)$ process [3.3.13].

First we show that absolute summability of the moving average coefficients implies square-summability. Suppose that $\{\psi_j\}_{j=0}^{\infty}$ is absolutely summable. Then there exists an $N < \infty$ such that $|\psi_j| < 1$ for all $j \geq N$, implying $\psi_j^2 < |\psi_j|$ for all $j \geq N$. Then

$$\sum_{j=0}^{\infty} \psi_j^2 = \sum_{j=0}^{N-1} \psi_j^2 + \sum_{j=N}^{\infty} \psi_j^2 < \sum_{j=0}^{N-1} \psi_j^2 + \sum_{j=N}^{\infty} |\psi_j|.$$

But $\Sigma_{j=0}^{N-1} \psi_j^2$ is finite, since $N$ is finite, and $\Sigma_{j=N}^{\infty} |\psi_j|$ is finite, since $\{\psi_j\}$ is absolutely summable. Hence $\Sigma_{j=0}^{\infty} \psi_j^2 < \infty$, establishing that [3.3.15] implies [3.3.14].

Next we show that square-summability does not imply absolute summability. For an example of a series that is square-summable but not absolutely summable, consider $\psi_j = 1/j$ for $j = 1, 2, \ldots$. Notice that $1/j > 1/x$ for all $x > j$, meaning that

$$1/j > \int_j^{j+1} (1/x)\, dx$$

and so

$$\sum_{j=1}^{N} 1/j > \int_1^{N+1} (1/x)\, dx = \log(N + 1) - \log(1) = \log(N + 1),$$

which diverges to $\infty$ as $N \to \infty$. Hence $\{\psi_j\}_{j=1}^{\infty}$ is not absolutely summable. It is, however, square-summable, since $1/j^2 < 1/x^2$ for all $x < j$, meaning that

$$1/j^2 < \int_{j-1}^{j} (1/x^2)\, dx$$

and so

$$\sum_{j=1}^{N} 1/j^2 < 1 + \int_1^N (1/x^2)\, dx = 1 + (-1/x)|_{x=1}^{N} = 2 - (1/N),$$

which converges to 2 as $N \to \infty$. Hence $\{\psi_j\}_{j=1}^{\infty}$ is square-summable.

Next we show that square-summability of the moving average coefficients implies that the $MA(\infty)$ representation in [3.3.13] generates a mean square convergent random variable. First recall what is meant by convergence of a deterministic sum such as $\Sigma_{j=0}^{\infty} a_j$ where $\{a_j\}$ is just a sequence of numbers. One criterion for determining whether $\Sigma_{j=0}^{T} a_j$ converges to some finite number as $T \to \infty$ is the *Cauchy criterion*. The Cauchy criterion states that $\Sigma_{j=0}^{\infty} a_j$ converges if and only if, for any $\varepsilon > 0$, there exists a suitably large integer $N$ such that, for any integer $M > N$,

$$\left| \sum_{j=0}^{M} a_j - \sum_{j=0}^{N} a_j \right| < \varepsilon.$$

In words, once we have summed $N$ terms, calculating the sum out to a larger number $M$ does not change the total by any more than an arbitrarily small number $\varepsilon$.

For a stochastic process such as [3.3.13], the comparable question is whether $\Sigma_{j=0}^{T} \psi_j \varepsilon_{t-j}$ converges in mean square to some random variable $Y_t$ as $T \to \infty$. In this case the Cauchy criterion states that $\Sigma_{j=0}^{\infty} \psi_j \varepsilon_{t-j}$ converges if and only if, for any $\varepsilon > 0$, there exists a suitably large integer $N$ such that for any integer $M > N$

$$E\left[ \sum_{j=0}^{M} \psi_j \varepsilon_{t-j} - \sum_{j=0}^{N} \psi_j \varepsilon_{t-j} \right]^2 < \varepsilon. \qquad [3.A.1]$$

In words, once $N$ terms have been summed, the difference between that sum and the one obtained from summing to $M$ is a random variable whose mean and variance are both arbitrarily close to zero.

Now, the left side of [3.A.1] is simply

$$E[\psi_M\varepsilon_{t-M} + \psi_{M-1}\varepsilon_{t-M+1} + \cdots + \psi_{N+1}\varepsilon_{t-N-1}]^2$$
$$= (\psi_M^2 + \psi_{M-1}^2 + \cdots + \psi_{N+1}^2) \cdot \sigma^2 \qquad [3.A.2]$$
$$= \left[\sum_{j=0}^{M} \psi_j^2 - \sum_{j=0}^{N} \psi_j^2\right] \cdot \sigma^2.$$

But if $\Sigma_{j=0}^{\infty} \psi_j^2$ converges as required by [3.3.14], then by the Cauchy criterion the right side of [3.A.2] may be made as small as desired by choice of a suitably large $N$. Thus the infinite series in [3.3.13] converges in mean square provided that [3.3.14] is satisfied.

Finally, we show that absolute summability of the moving average coefficients implies that the process is ergodic for the mean. Write [3.3.18] as

$$\gamma_j = \sigma^2 \sum_{k=0}^{\infty} \psi_{j+k}\psi_k.$$

Then

$$|\gamma_j| = \sigma^2 \left|\sum_{k=0}^{\infty} \psi_{j+k}\psi_k\right|.$$

A key property of the absolute value operator is that

$$|a + b + c| \leq |a| + |b| + |c|.$$

Hence

$$|\gamma_j| \leq \sigma^2 \sum_{k=0}^{\infty} |\psi_{j+k}\psi_k|$$

and

$$\sum_{j=0}^{\infty} |\gamma_j| \leq \sigma^2 \sum_{j=0}^{\infty}\sum_{k=0}^{\infty} |\psi_{j+k}\psi_k| = \sigma^2 \sum_{j=0}^{\infty}\sum_{k=0}^{\infty} |\psi_{j+k}| \cdot |\psi_k| = \sigma^2 \sum_{k=0}^{\infty} |\psi_k| \sum_{j=0}^{\infty} |\psi_{j+k}|.$$

But there exists an $M < \infty$ such that $\Sigma_{j=0}^{\infty} |\psi_j| < M$, and therefore $\Sigma_{j=0}^{\infty} |\psi_{j+k}| < M$ for $k = 0, 1, 2, \ldots$, meaning that

$$\sum_{j=0}^{\infty} |\gamma_j| < \sigma^2 \sum_{k=0}^{\infty} |\psi_k| \cdot M < \sigma^2 M^2 < \infty.$$

Hence [3.1.15] holds and the process is ergodic for the mean.

## *Chapter 3 Exercises*

3.1. Is the following $MA(2)$ process covariance-stationary?

$$Y_t = (1 + 2.4L + 0.8L^2)\varepsilon_t$$
$$E(\varepsilon_t\varepsilon_\tau) = \begin{cases} 1 & \text{for } t = \tau \\ 0 & \text{otherwise.} \end{cases}$$

If so, calculate its autocovariances.

3.2. Is the following $AR(2)$ process covariance-stationary?

$$(1 - 1.1L + 0.18L^2)Y_t = \varepsilon_t$$
$$E(\varepsilon_t\varepsilon_\tau) = \begin{cases} 1 & \text{for } t = \tau \\ 0 & \text{otherwise.} \end{cases}$$

If so, calculate its autocovariances.

3.3. A covariance-stationary $AR(p)$ process,

$$(1 - \phi_1 L - \phi_2 L^2 - \cdots - \phi_p L^p)(Y_t - \mu) = \varepsilon_t,$$

has an $MA(\infty)$ representation given by

$$(Y_t - \mu) = \psi(L)\varepsilon_t$$

with

$$\psi(L) = 1/[1 - \phi_1 L - \phi_2 L^2 - \cdots - \phi_p L^p]$$

or

$$[1 - \phi_1 L - \phi_2 L^2 - \cdots - \phi_p L^p]\,[\psi_0 + \psi_1 L + \psi_2 L^2 + \cdots] = 1.$$

In order for this equation to be true, the implied coefficient on $L^0$ must be unity and the coefficients on $L^1$, $L^2$, $L^3$, . . . must be zero. Write out these conditions explicitly and show that they imply a recursive algorithm for generating the $MA(\infty)$ weights $\psi_0$, $\psi_1$, . . . . Show that this recursion is algebraically equivalent to setting $\psi_j$ equal to the (1, 1) element of the matrix **F** raised to the $j$th power as in equation [1.2.28].

3.4. Derive [3.4.21].

3.5. Verify [3.4.22].

3.6. Suggest a recursive algorithm for calculating the $AR(\infty)$ weights,

$$(1 + \eta_1 L + \eta_2 L^2 + \cdots)(Y_t - \mu) = \varepsilon_t$$

associated with an invertible $MA(q)$ process,

$$(Y_t - \mu) = (1 + \theta_1 L + \theta_2 L^2 + \cdots + \theta_q L^q)\varepsilon_t.$$

Give a closed-form expression for $\eta_j$ as a function of the roots of

$$(1 + \theta_1 z + \theta_2 z^2 + \cdots + \theta_q z^q) = 0,$$

assuming that these roots are all distinct.

3.7. Repeat Exercise 3.6 for a noninvertible $MA(q)$ process. (HINT: Recall equation [3.7.17].)

3.8. Show that the $MA(2)$ process in Exercise 3.1 is not invertible. Find the invertible representation for the process. Calculate the autocovariances of the invertible representation using equation [3.3.12] and verify that these are the same as obtained in Exercise 3.1.

## *Chapter 3 References*


Anderson, Brian D. O., and John B. Moore. 1979. *Optimal Filtering*. Englewood Cliffs, N.J.: Prentice-Hall.

Hannan, E. J. 1970. *Multiple Time Series*. New York: Wiley.

Hansen, Lars P., and Thomas J. Sargent. 1981. "Formulating and Estimating Dynamic Linear Rational Expectations Models," in Robert E. Lucas, Jr., and Thomas J. Sargent, eds., *Rational Expectations and Econometric Practice*, Vol. I. Minneapolis: University of Minnesota Press.

Rao, C. Radhakrishna. 1973. *Linear Statistical Inference and Its Applications*, 2d ed. New York: Wiley.

Sargent, Thomas J. 1987. *Macroeconomic Theory*, 2d ed. Boston: Academic Press.

# 4 Forecasting

This chapter discusses how to forecast time series. Section 4.1 reviews the theory of forecasting and introduces the idea of a linear projection, which is a forecast formed from a linear function of past observations. Section 4.2 describes the forecasts one would use for *ARMA* models if an infinite number of past observations were available. These results are useful in theoretical manipulations and in understanding the formulas in Section 4.3 for approximate optimal forecasts when only a finite number of observations are available.

Section 4.4 describes how to achieve a triangular factorization and Cholesky factorization of a variance-covariance matrix. These results are used in that section to calculate exact optimal forecasts based on a finite number of observations. They will also be used in Chapter 11 to interpret vector autoregressions, in Chapter 13 to derive the Kalman filter, and in a number of other theoretical calculations and numerical methods appearing throughout the text. The triangular factorization is used to derive a formula for updating a forecast in Section 4.5 and to establish in Section 4.6 that for Gaussian processes the linear projection is better than any nonlinear forecast.

Section 4.7 analyzes what kind of process results when two different *ARMA* processes are added together. Section 4.8 states Wold's decomposition, which provides a basis for using an $MA(\infty)$ representation to characterize the linear forecast rule for any covariance-stationary process. The section also describes a popular empirical approach for finding a reasonable approximation to this representation that was developed by Box and Jenkins (1976).

## 4.1. *Principles of Forecasting*

### *Forecasts Based on Conditional Expectation*

Suppose we are interested in forecasting the value of a variable $Y_{t+1}$ based on a set of variables $\mathbf{X}_t$ observed at date $t$. For example, we might want to forecast $Y_{t+1}$ based on its $m$ most recent values. In this case, $\mathbf{X}_t$ would consist of a constant plus $Y_t, Y_{t-1}, \ldots,$ and $Y_{t-m+1}$.

Let $Y^*_{t+1|t}$ denote a forecast of $Y_{t+1}$ based on $\mathbf{X}_t$. To evaluate the usefulness of this forecast, we need to specify a *loss function*, or a summary of how concerned we are if our forecast is off by a particular amount. Very convenient results are obtained from assuming a quadratic loss function. A quadratic loss function means choosing the forecast $Y^*_{t+1|t}$ so as to minimize

$$E(Y_{t+1} - Y^*_{t+1|t})^2. \qquad [4.1.1]$$

Expression [4.1.1] is known as the *mean squared error* associated with the forecast $Y^*_{t+1|t}$, denoted

$$MSE(Y^*_{t+1|t}) \equiv E(Y_{t+1} - Y^*_{t+1|t})^2.$$

The forecast with the smallest mean squared error turns out to be the expectation of $Y_{t+1}$ conditional on $\mathbf{X}_t$:

$$Y^*_{t+1|t} = E(Y_{t+1}|\mathbf{X}_t). \qquad [4.1.2]$$

To verify this claim, consider basing $Y^*_{t+1|t}$ on any function $g(\mathbf{X}_t)$ other than the conditional expectation,

$$Y^*_{t+1|t} = g(\mathbf{X}_t). \qquad [4.1.3]$$

For this candidate forecasting rule, the $MSE$ would be

$$\begin{aligned} E[Y_{t+1} - g(\mathbf{X}_t)]^2 &= E[Y_{t+1} - E(Y_{t+1}|\mathbf{X}_t) + E(Y_{t+1}|\mathbf{X}_t) - g(\mathbf{X}_t)]^2 \\ &= E[Y_{t+1} - E(Y_{t+1}|\mathbf{X}_t)]^2 \\ &\quad + 2E\{[Y_{t+1} - E(Y_{t+1}|\mathbf{X}_t)][E(Y_{t+1}|\mathbf{X}_t) - g(\mathbf{X}_t)]\} \\ &\quad + E\{[E(Y_{t+1}|\mathbf{X}_t) - g(\mathbf{X}_t)]^2\}. \end{aligned} \qquad [4.1.4]$$

Write the middle term on the right side of [4.1.4] as

$$2E[\eta_{t+1}], \qquad [4.1.5]$$

where

$$\eta_{t+1} \equiv \{[Y_{t+1} - E(Y_{t+1}|\mathbf{X}_t)][E(Y_{t+1}|\mathbf{X}_t) - g(\mathbf{X}_t)]\}.$$

Consider first the expectation of $\eta_{t+1}$ conditional on $\mathbf{X}_t$. Conditional on $\mathbf{X}_t$, the terms $E(Y_{t+1}|\mathbf{X}_t)$ and $g(\mathbf{X}_t)$ are known constants and can be factored out of this expectation:[1]

$$\begin{aligned} E[\eta_{t+1}|\mathbf{X}_t] &= [E(Y_{t+1}|\mathbf{X}_t) - g(\mathbf{X}_t)] \times E([Y_{t+1} - E(Y_{t+1}|\mathbf{X}_t)]|\mathbf{X}_t) \\ &= [E(Y_{t+1}|\mathbf{X}_t) - g(\mathbf{X}_t)] \times 0 \\ &= 0. \end{aligned}$$

By a straightforward application of the law of iterated expectations, equation [A.5.10], it follows that

$$E[\eta_{t+1}] = E_{\mathbf{X}_t}(E[\eta_{t+1}|\mathbf{X}_t]) = 0.$$

Substituting this back into [4.1.4] gives

$$E[Y_{t+1} - g(\mathbf{X}_t)]^2 = E[Y_{t+1} - E(Y_{t+1}|\mathbf{X}_t)]^2 + E([E(Y_{t+1}|\mathbf{X}_t) - g(\mathbf{X}_t)]^2). \qquad [4.1.6]$$

The second term on the right side of [4.1.6] cannot be made smaller than zero, and the first term does not depend on $g(\mathbf{X}_t)$. The function $g(\mathbf{X}_t)$ that makes the mean squared error [4.1.6] as small as possible is the function that sets the second term in [4.1.6] to zero:

$$E(Y_{t+1}|\mathbf{X}_t) = g(\mathbf{X}_t). \qquad [4.1.7]$$

Thus the forecast $g(\mathbf{X}_t)$ that minimizes the mean squared error is the conditional expectation $E(Y_{t+1}|\mathbf{X}_t)$, as claimed.

The $MSE$ of this optimal forecast is

$$E[Y_{t+1} - g(\mathbf{X}_t)]^2 = E[Y_{t+1} - E(Y_{t+1}|\mathbf{X}_t)]^2. \qquad [4.1.8]$$

[1]The conditional expectation $E(Y_{t+1}|\mathbf{X}_t)$ represents the conditional population moment of the random variable $Y_{t+1}$ and is not a function of the random variable $Y_{t+1}$ itself. For example, if $Y_{t+1}|\mathbf{X}_t \sim N(\boldsymbol{\alpha}'\mathbf{X}_t, \boldsymbol{\Omega})$, then $E(Y_{t+1}|\mathbf{X}_t) = \boldsymbol{\alpha}'\mathbf{X}_t$, which does not depend on $Y_{t+1}$.

## *Forecasts Based on Linear Projection*

We now restrict the class of forecasts considered by requiring the forecast $Y^*_{t+1|t}$ to be a linear function of $\mathbf{X}_t$:

$$Y^*_{t+1|t} = \boldsymbol{\alpha}'\mathbf{X}_t. \qquad [4.1.9]$$

Suppose we were to find a value for $\boldsymbol{\alpha}$ such that the forecast error $(Y_{t+1} - \boldsymbol{\alpha}'\mathbf{X}_t)$ is uncorrelated with $\mathbf{X}_t$:

$$E[(Y_{t+1} - \boldsymbol{\alpha}'\mathbf{X}_t)\mathbf{X}_t'] = \mathbf{0}'. \qquad [4.1.10]$$

If [4.1.10] holds, then the forecast $\boldsymbol{\alpha}'\mathbf{X}_t$ is called the *linear projection* of $Y_{t+1}$ on $\mathbf{X}_t$.

The linear projection turns out to produce the smallest mean squared error among the class of linear forecasting rules. The proof of this claim closely parallels the demonstration of the optimality of the conditional expectation among the set of all possible forecasts. Let $\mathbf{g}'\mathbf{X}_t$ denote any arbitrary linear forecasting rule. Note that its *MSE* is

$$\begin{aligned} &E[Y_{t+1} - \mathbf{g}'\mathbf{X}_t]^2 \\ &\quad = E[Y_{t+1} - \boldsymbol{\alpha}'\mathbf{X}_t + \boldsymbol{\alpha}'\mathbf{X}_t - \mathbf{g}'\mathbf{X}_t]^2 \\ &\quad = E[Y_{t+1} - \boldsymbol{\alpha}'\mathbf{X}_t]^2 + 2E\{[Y_{t+1} - \boldsymbol{\alpha}'\mathbf{X}_t][\boldsymbol{\alpha}'\mathbf{X}_t - \mathbf{g}'\mathbf{X}_t]\} \\ &\qquad + E[\boldsymbol{\alpha}'\mathbf{X}_t - \mathbf{g}'\mathbf{X}_t]^2. \end{aligned} \qquad [4.1.11]$$

As in the case of [4.1.4], the middle term on the right side of [4.1.11] is zero:

$$E([Y_{t+1} - \boldsymbol{\alpha}'\mathbf{X}_t][\boldsymbol{\alpha}'\mathbf{X}_t - \mathbf{g}'\mathbf{X}_t]) = (E[Y_{t+1} - \boldsymbol{\alpha}'\mathbf{X}_t]\mathbf{X}_t')[\boldsymbol{\alpha} - \mathbf{g}] = \mathbf{0}'[\boldsymbol{\alpha} - \mathbf{g}],$$

by virtue of [4.1.10]. Thus [4.1.11] simplifies to

$$E[Y_{t+1} - \mathbf{g}'\mathbf{X}_t]^2 = E[Y_{t+1} - \boldsymbol{\alpha}'\mathbf{X}_t]^2 + E[\boldsymbol{\alpha}'\mathbf{X}_t - \mathbf{g}'\mathbf{X}_t]^2. \qquad [4.1.12]$$

The optimal linear forecast $\mathbf{g}'\mathbf{X}_t$ is the value that sets the second term in [4.1.12] equal to zero:

$$\mathbf{g}'\mathbf{X}_t = \boldsymbol{\alpha}'\mathbf{X}_t,$$

where $\boldsymbol{\alpha}'\mathbf{X}_t$ satisfies [4.1.10].

For $\boldsymbol{\alpha}'\mathbf{X}_t$ satisfying [4.1.10], we will use the notation

$$\hat{P}(Y_{t+1}|\mathbf{X}_t) = \boldsymbol{\alpha}'\mathbf{X}_t,$$

or sometimes simply

$$\hat{Y}_{t+1|t} = \boldsymbol{\alpha}'\mathbf{X}_t,$$

to indicate the linear projection of $Y_{t+1}$ on $\mathbf{X}_t$. Notice that

$$MSE[\hat{P}(Y_{t+1}|\mathbf{X}_t)] \geq MSE[E(Y_{t+1}|\mathbf{X}_t)],$$

since the conditional expectation offers the best possible forecast.

For most applications a constant term will be included in the projection. We will use the symbol $\hat{E}$ to indicate a linear projection on a vector of random variables $\mathbf{X}_t$ along with a constant term:

$$\hat{E}(Y_{t+1}|\mathbf{X}_t) \equiv \hat{P}(Y_{t+1}|1, \mathbf{X}_t).$$

## *Properties of Linear Projection*

It is straightforward to use [4.1.10] to calculate the projection coefficient $\boldsymbol{\alpha}$ in terms of the moments of $Y_{t+1}$ and $\mathbf{X}_t$:

$$E(Y_{t+1}\mathbf{X}_t') = \boldsymbol{\alpha}'E(\mathbf{X}_t\mathbf{X}_t'),$$

or

$$\boldsymbol{\alpha}' = E(Y_{t+1}\mathbf{X}_t')[E(\mathbf{X}_t\mathbf{X}_t')]^{-1}, \qquad [4.1.13]$$

assuming that $E(\mathbf{X}_t\mathbf{X}_t')$ is a nonsingular matrix. When $E(\mathbf{X}_t\mathbf{X}_t')$ is singular, the coefficient vector $\boldsymbol{\alpha}$ is not uniquely determined by [4.1.10], though the product of this vector with the explanatory variables, $\boldsymbol{\alpha}'\mathbf{X}_t$, is uniquely determined by [4.1.10].[2]

The *MSE* associated with a linear projection is given by

$$E(Y_{t+1} - \boldsymbol{\alpha}'\mathbf{X}_t)^2 = E(Y_{t+1})^2 - 2E(\boldsymbol{\alpha}'\mathbf{X}_tY_{t+1}) + E(\boldsymbol{\alpha}'\mathbf{X}_t\mathbf{X}_t'\boldsymbol{\alpha}). \qquad [4.1.14]$$

Substituting [4.1.13] into [4.1.14] produces

$$\begin{aligned} E(Y_{t+1} - \boldsymbol{\alpha}'\mathbf{X}_t)^2 &= E(Y_{t+1})^2 - 2E(Y_{t+1}\mathbf{X}_t')[E(\mathbf{X}_t\mathbf{X}_t')]^{-1}E(\mathbf{X}_tY_{t+1}) \\ &\quad + E(Y_{t+1}\mathbf{X}_t')[E(\mathbf{X}_t\mathbf{X}_t')]^{-1} \\ &\qquad \times E(\mathbf{X}_t\mathbf{X}_t')[E(\mathbf{X}_t\mathbf{X}_t')]^{-1}E(\mathbf{X}_tY_{t+1}) \\ &= E(Y_{t+1})^2 - E(Y_{t+1}\mathbf{X}_t')[E(\mathbf{X}_t\mathbf{X}_t')]^{-1}E(\mathbf{X}_tY_{t+1}). \end{aligned} \qquad [4.1.15]$$

Notice that if $\mathbf{X}_t$ includes a constant term, then the projection of $(aY_{t+1}+b)$ on $\mathbf{X}_t$ (where $a$ and $b$ are deterministic constants) is equal to

$$\hat{P}[(aY_{t+1} + b)|\mathbf{X}_t] = a\cdot\hat{P}(Y_{t+1}|\mathbf{X}_t) + b.$$

To see this, observe that $a\cdot\hat{P}(Y_{t+1}|\mathbf{X}_t) + b$ is a linear function of $\mathbf{X}_t$. Moreover, the forecast error,

$$[aY_{t+1} + b] - [a\cdot\hat{P}(Y_{t+1}|\mathbf{X}_t) + b] = a[Y_{t+1} - \hat{P}(Y_{t+1}|\mathbf{X}_t)],$$

is uncorrelated with $\mathbf{X}_t$, as required of a linear projection.

## *Linear Projection and Ordinary Least Squares Regression*

Linear projection is closely related to ordinary least squares regression. This subsection discusses the relationship between the two concepts.

A linear regression model relates an observation on $y_{t+1}$ to $\mathbf{x}_t$:

$$y_{t+1} = \boldsymbol{\beta}'\mathbf{x}_t + u_t. \qquad [4.1.16]$$

Given a sample of $T$ observations on $y$ and $\mathbf{x}$, the sample sum of squared residuals is defined as

$$\sum_{t=1}^{T} (y_{t+1} - \boldsymbol{\beta}'\mathbf{x}_t)^2. \qquad [4.1.17]$$

The value of $\boldsymbol{\beta}$ that minimizes [4.1.17], denoted $\mathbf{b}$, is the *ordinary least squares* (*OLS*) estimate of $\boldsymbol{\beta}$. The formula for $\mathbf{b}$ turns out to be

$$\mathbf{b} = \left[\sum_{t=1}^{T} \mathbf{x}_t\mathbf{x}_t'\right]^{-1}\left[\sum_{t=1}^{T} \mathbf{x}_ty_{t+1}\right], \qquad [4.1.18]$$

[2]If $E(\mathbf{X}_t\mathbf{X}_t')$ is singular, there exists a nonzero vector $\mathbf{c}$ such that $\mathbf{c}'\cdot E(\mathbf{X}_t\mathbf{X}_t')\cdot\mathbf{c} = E(\mathbf{c}'\mathbf{X}_t)^2 = 0$, so that some linear combination $\mathbf{c}'\mathbf{X}_t$ is equal to zero for all realizations. For example, if $\mathbf{X}_t$ consists of two random variables, the second variable must be a rescaled version of the first: $X_{2t} = c\cdot X_{1t}$. One could simply drop the redundant variables from such a system and calculate the linear projection of $Y_{t+1}$ on $\mathbf{X}_t^*$, where $\mathbf{X}_t^*$ is a vector consisting of the nonredundant elements of $\mathbf{X}_t$. This linear projection $\boldsymbol{\alpha}^{*\prime}\mathbf{X}_t^*$ can be uniquely calculated from [4.1.13] with $\mathbf{X}_t$ in [4.1.13] replaced by $\mathbf{X}_t^*$. Any linear combination of the original variables $\boldsymbol{\alpha}'\mathbf{X}_t$ satisfying [4.1.10] represents this same random variable; that is, $\boldsymbol{\alpha}'\mathbf{X}_t = \boldsymbol{\alpha}^{*\prime}\mathbf{X}_t^*$ for all values of $\boldsymbol{\alpha}$ consistent with [4.1.10].

which equivalently can be written

$$\mathbf{b} = \left[(1/T)\sum_{t=1}^{T}\mathbf{x}_t\mathbf{x}_t'\right]^{-1}\left[(1/T)\sum_{t=1}^{T}\mathbf{x}_t y_{t+1}\right]. \qquad [4.1.19]$$

Comparing the *OLS* coefficient estimate $\mathbf{b}$ in equation [4.1.19] with the linear projection coefficient $\boldsymbol{\alpha}$ in equation [4.1.13], we see that $\mathbf{b}$ is constructed from the sample moments $(1/T)\Sigma_{t=1}^{T}\mathbf{x}_t\mathbf{x}_t'$ and $(1/T)\Sigma_{t=1}^{T}\mathbf{x}_t y_{t+1}$ while $\boldsymbol{\alpha}$ is constructed from population moments $E(\mathbf{X}_t\mathbf{X}_t')$ and $E(\mathbf{X}_t Y_{t+1})$. Thus *OLS* regression is a summary of the particular sample observations $(\mathbf{x}_1, \mathbf{x}_2, \ldots, \mathbf{x}_T)$ and $(y_2, y_3, \ldots, y_{T+1})$, whereas linear projection is a summary of the population characteristics of the stochastic process $\{\mathbf{X}_t, Y_{t+1}\}_{t=-\infty}^{\infty}$.

Although linear projection describes population moments and ordinary least squares describes sample moments, there is a formal mathematical sense in which the two operations are the same. Appendix 4.A to this chapter discusses this parallel and shows how the formulas for an *OLS* regression can be viewed as a special case of the formulas for a linear projection.

Notice that if the stochastic process $\{\mathbf{X}_t, Y_{t+1}\}$ is covariance-stationary and ergodic for second moments, then the sample moments will converge to the population moments as the sample size $T$ goes to infinity:

$$(1/T)\sum_{t=1}^{T}\mathbf{X}_t\mathbf{X}_t' \xrightarrow{p} E(\mathbf{X}_t\mathbf{X}_t')$$

$$(1/T)\sum_{t=1}^{T}\mathbf{X}_t Y_{t+1} \xrightarrow{p} E(\mathbf{X}_t Y_{t+1}),$$

implying

$$\mathbf{b} \xrightarrow{p} \boldsymbol{\alpha}. \qquad [4.1.20]$$

Thus *OLS* regression of $y_{t+1}$ on $\mathbf{x}_t$ yields a consistent estimate of the linear projection coefficient. Note that this result requires only that the process be ergodic for second moments. By contrast, structural econometric analysis requires much stronger assumptions about the relation between $\mathbf{X}$ and $Y$. The difference arises because structural analysis seeks the *effect* of $\mathbf{X}$ on $Y$. In structural analysis, changes in $\mathbf{X}$ are associated with a particular structural event such as a change in Federal Reserve policy, and the objective is to evaluate the consequences for $Y$. Where that is the objective, it is very important to consider the nature of the correlation between $\mathbf{X}$ and $Y$ before relying on *OLS* estimates. In the case of linear projection, however, the only concern is forecasting, for which it does not matter whether it is $\mathbf{X}$ that causes $Y$ or $Y$ that causes $\mathbf{X}$. Their observed historical comovements (as summarized by $E(\mathbf{X}_t Y_{t+1})$) are all that is needed for calculating a forecast. Result [4.1.20] shows that ordinary least squares regression provides a sound basis for forecasting under very mild assumptions.

One possible violation of these assumptions should nevertheless be noted. Result [4.1.20] was derived by assuming a covariance-stationary, ergodic process. However, the moments of the data may have changed over time in fundamental ways, or the future environment may be different from that in the past. Where this is the case, ordinary least squares may be undesirable, and better forecasts can emerge from careful structural analysis.

### *Forecasting Vectors*

The preceding results can be extended to forecast an $(n \times 1)$ vector $\mathbf{Y}_{t+1}$ on the basis of a linear function of an $(m \times 1)$ vector $\mathbf{X}_t$:

$$\hat{P}(\mathbf{Y}_{t+1}|\mathbf{X}_t) = \boldsymbol{\alpha}'\mathbf{X}_t \equiv \hat{\mathbf{Y}}_{t+1|t}. \qquad [4.1.21]$$

Then $\boldsymbol{\alpha}'$ would denote an $(n \times m)$ matrix of projection coefficients satisfying

$$E[(\mathbf{Y}_{t+1} - \boldsymbol{\alpha}'\mathbf{X}_t)\mathbf{X}_t'] = \mathbf{0}; \qquad [4.1.22]$$

that is, each of the $n$ elements of $(\mathbf{Y}_{t+1} - \hat{\mathbf{Y}}_{t+1|t})$ is uncorrelated with each of the $m$ elements of $\mathbf{X}_t$. Accordingly, the $j$th element of the vector $\hat{\mathbf{Y}}_{t+1|t}$ gives the minimum *MSE* forecast of the scalar $Y_{j,t+1}$. Moreover, to forecast any linear combination of the elements of $\mathbf{Y}_{t+1}$, say, $z_{t+1} = \mathbf{h}'\mathbf{Y}_{t+1}$, the minimum *MSE* forecast of $z_{t+1}$ requires $(z_{t+1} - \hat{z}_{t+1|t})$ to be uncorrelated with $\mathbf{X}_t$. But since each of the elements of $(\mathbf{Y}_{t+1} - \hat{\mathbf{Y}}_{t+1|t})$ is uncorrelated with $\mathbf{X}_t$, clearly $\mathbf{h}'(\mathbf{Y}_{t+1} - \hat{\mathbf{Y}}_{t+1|t})$ is also uncorrelated with $\mathbf{X}_t$. Thus when $\hat{\mathbf{Y}}_{t+1|t}$ satisfies [4.1.22], then $\mathbf{h}'\hat{\mathbf{Y}}_{t+1|t}$ is the minimum *MSE* forecast of $\mathbf{h}'\mathbf{Y}_{t+1}$ for any value of $\mathbf{h}$.

From [4.1.22], the matrix of projection coefficients is given by

$$\boldsymbol{\alpha}' = [E(\mathbf{Y}_{t+1}\mathbf{X}_t')]\cdot[E(\mathbf{X}_t\mathbf{X}_t')]^{-1}. \qquad [4.1.23]$$

The matrix generalization of the formula for the mean squared error [4.1.15] is

$$\begin{aligned} MSE(\boldsymbol{\alpha}'\mathbf{X}_t) &\equiv E\{[\mathbf{Y}_{t+1} - \boldsymbol{\alpha}'\mathbf{X}_t]\cdot[\mathbf{Y}_{t+1} - \boldsymbol{\alpha}'\mathbf{X}_t]'\} \\ &= E(\mathbf{Y}_{t+1}\mathbf{Y}_{t+1}') - [E(\mathbf{Y}_{t+1}\mathbf{X}_t')]\cdot[E(\mathbf{X}_t'\mathbf{X}_t)]^{-1}\cdot[E(\mathbf{X}_t\mathbf{Y}_{t+1}')]. \end{aligned} \qquad [4.1.24]$$

## 4.2. *Forecasts Based on an Infinite Number of Observations*

### *Forecasting Based on Lagged ε's*

Consider a process with an $MA(\infty)$ representation

$$(Y_t - \mu) = \psi(L)\varepsilon_t \qquad [4.2.1]$$

with $\varepsilon_t$ white noise and

$$\begin{aligned} \psi(L) &\equiv \sum_{j=0}^{\infty} \psi_j L^j \\ \psi_0 &= 1 \\ \sum_{j=0}^{\infty} |\psi_j| &< \infty. \end{aligned} \qquad [4.2.2]$$

Suppose that we have an infinite number of observations on $\varepsilon$ through date $t$, $\{\varepsilon_t, \varepsilon_{t-1}, \varepsilon_{t-2}, \ldots\}$, and further know the values of $\mu$ and $\{\psi_1, \psi_2, \ldots\}$. Say we want to forecast the value of $Y_{t+s}$, that is, the value that $Y$ will take on $s$ periods from now. Note that [4.2.1] implies

$$\begin{aligned} Y_{t+s} = \mu &+ \varepsilon_{t+s} + \psi_1\varepsilon_{t+s-1} + \cdots + \psi_{s-1}\varepsilon_{t+1} + \psi_s\varepsilon_t \\ &+ \psi_{s+1}\varepsilon_{t-1} + \cdots. \end{aligned} \qquad [4.2.3]$$

The optimal linear forecast takes the form

$$\hat{E}[Y_{t+s}|\varepsilon_t, \varepsilon_{t-1}, \ldots] = \mu + \psi_s\varepsilon_t + \psi_{s+1}\varepsilon_{t-1} + \psi_{s+2}\varepsilon_{t-2} + \cdots. \qquad [4.2.4]$$

That is, the unknown future $\varepsilon$'s are set to their expected value of zero. The error associated with this forecast is

$$Y_{t+s} - \hat{E}[Y_{t+s}|\varepsilon_t, \varepsilon_{t-1}, \ldots] = \varepsilon_{t+s} + \psi_1\varepsilon_{t+s-1} + \cdots + \psi_{s-1}\varepsilon_{t+1}. \quad [4.2.5]$$

In order for [4.2.4] to be the optimal linear forecast, condition [4.1.10] requires the forecast error to have mean zero and to be uncorrelated with $\varepsilon_t, \varepsilon_{t-1}, \ldots$. It is readily confirmed that the error in [4.2.5] has these properties, so [4.2.4] must indeed be the linear projection, as claimed. The mean squared error associated with this forecast is

$$E(Y_{t+s} - \hat{E}[Y_{t+s}|\varepsilon_t, \varepsilon_{t-1}, \ldots])^2 = (1 + \psi_1^2 + \psi_2^2 + \cdots + \psi_{s-1}^2)\sigma^2. \quad [4.2.6]$$

For example, for an $MA(q)$ process,

$$\psi(L) = 1 + \theta_1 L + \theta_2 L^2 + \cdots + \theta_q L^q,$$

the optimal linear forecast is

$$\hat{E}[Y_{t+s}|\varepsilon_t, \varepsilon_{t-1}, \ldots] \quad [4.2.7]$$
$$= \begin{cases} \mu + \theta_s\varepsilon_t + \theta_{s+1}\varepsilon_{t-1} + \cdots + \theta_q\varepsilon_{t-q+s} & \text{for } s = 1, 2, \ldots, q \\ \mu & \text{for } s = q+1, q+2, \ldots. \end{cases}$$

The $MSE$ is

$$\begin{cases} \sigma^2 & \text{for } s = 1 \\ (1 + \theta_1^2 + \theta_2^2 + \cdots + \theta_{s-1}^2)\sigma^2 & \text{for } s = 2, 3, \ldots, q \\ (1 + \theta_1^2 + \theta_2^2 + \cdots + \theta_q^2)\sigma^2 & \text{for } s = q+1, q+2, \ldots. \end{cases}$$

The $MSE$ increases with the forecast horizon $s$ up until $s = q$. If we try to forecast an $MA(q)$ farther than $q$ periods into the future, the forecast is simply the unconditional mean of the series ($E(Y_t) = \mu$) and the $MSE$ is the unconditional variance of the series ($\text{Var}(Y_t) = (1 + \theta_1^2 + \theta_2^2 + \cdots + \theta_q^2)\sigma^2$).

These properties also characterize the $MA(\infty)$ case as the forecast horizon $s$ goes to infinity. It is straightforward to establish from [4.2.2] that as $s \to \infty$, the forecast in [4.2.4] converges in mean square to $\mu$, the unconditional mean. The $MSE$ [4.2.6] likewise converges to $\sigma^2 \sum_{j=0}^{\infty}\psi_j^2$, which is the unconditional variance of the $MA(\infty)$ process [4.2.1].

A compact lag operator expression for the forecast in [4.2.4] is sometimes used. Consider taking the polynomial $\psi(L)$ and dividing by $L^s$:

$$\frac{\psi(L)}{L^s} = L^{-s} + \psi_1 L^{1-s} + \psi_2 L^{2-s} + \cdots + \psi_{s-1}L^{-1} + \psi_s L^0$$
$$+ \psi_{s+1}L^1 + \psi_{s+2}L^2 + \cdots.$$

The *annihilation operator*[3] (indicated by $[\cdot]_+$) replaces negative powers of $L$ by zero; for example,

$$\left[\frac{\psi(L)}{L^s}\right]_+ = \psi_s + \psi_{s+1}L^1 + \psi_{s+2}L^2 + \cdots. \quad [4.2.8]$$

Comparing [4.2.8] with [4.2.4], the optimal forecast could be written in lag operator notation as

$$\hat{E}[Y_{t+s}|\varepsilon_t, \varepsilon_{t-1}, \ldots] = \mu + \left[\frac{\psi(L)}{L^s}\right]_+ \varepsilon_t. \quad [4.2.9]$$

[3]This discussion of forecasting based on the annihilation operator is similar to that in Sargent (1987).

## *Forecasting Based on Lagged Y's*

The previous forecasts were based on the assumption that $\varepsilon_t$ is observed directly. In the usual forecasting situation, we actually have observations on lagged $Y$'s, not lagged $\varepsilon$'s. Suppose that the process [4.2.1] has an $AR(\infty)$ representation given by

$$\eta(L)(Y_t - \mu) = \varepsilon_t, \tag{4.2.10}$$

where $\eta(L) \equiv \Sigma_{j=0}^{\infty}\eta_j L^j$, $\eta_0 = 1$, and $\Sigma_{j=0}^{\infty}|\eta_j| < \infty$. Suppose further that the $AR$ polynomial $\eta(L)$ and the $MA$ polynomial $\psi(L)$ are related by

$$\eta(L) = [\psi(L)]^{-1}. \tag{4.2.11}$$

A covariance-stationary $AR(p)$ model of the form

$$(1 - \phi_1 L - \phi_2 L^2 - \cdots - \phi_p L^p)(Y_t - \mu) = \varepsilon_t, \tag{4.2.12}$$

or, more compactly,

$$\phi(L)(Y_t - \mu) = \varepsilon_t,$$

clearly satisfies these requirements, with $\eta(L) = \phi(L)$ and $\psi(L) = [\phi(L)]^{-1}$. An $MA(q)$ process

$$Y_t - \mu = (1 + \theta_1 L + \theta_2 L^2 + \cdots + \theta_q L^q)\varepsilon_t \tag{4.2.13}$$

or

$$Y_t - \mu = \theta(L)\varepsilon_t$$

is also of this form, with $\psi(L) = \theta(L)$ and $\eta(L) = [\theta(L)]^{-1}$, provided that [4.2.13] is based on the invertible representation. With a noninvertible $MA(q)$, the roots must first be flipped as described in Section 3.7 before applying the formulas given in this section. An $ARMA(p, q)$ also satisfies [4.2.10] and [4.2.11] with $\psi(L) = \theta(L)/\phi(L)$, provided that the autoregressive operator $\phi(L)$ satisfies the stationarity condition (roots of $\phi(z) = 0$ lie outside the unit circle) and that the moving average operator $\theta(L)$ satisfies the invertibility condition (roots of $\theta(z) = 0$ lie outside the unit circle).

Where the restrictions associated with [4.2.10] and [4.2.11] are satisfied, observations on $\{Y_t, Y_{t-1}, \ldots\}$ will be sufficient to construct $\{\varepsilon_t, \varepsilon_{t-1}, \ldots\}$. For example, for an $AR(1)$ process [4.2.10] would be

$$(1 - \phi L)(Y_t - \mu) = \varepsilon_t. \tag{4.2.14}$$

Thus, given $\phi$ and $\mu$ and observation of $Y_t$ and $Y_{t-1}$, the value of $\varepsilon_t$ can be constructed from

$$\varepsilon_t = (Y_t - \mu) - \phi(Y_{t-1} - \mu).$$

For an $MA(1)$ process written in invertible form, [4.2.10] would be

$$(1 + \theta L)^{-1}(Y_t - \mu) = \varepsilon_t.$$

Given an infinite number of observations on $Y$, we could construct $\varepsilon$ from

$$\begin{aligned}\varepsilon_t = (Y_t - \mu) - \theta(Y_{t-1} - \mu) + \theta^2(Y_{t-2} - \mu)\\ - \theta^3(Y_{t-3} - \mu) + \cdots.\end{aligned} \tag{4.2.15}$$

Under these conditions, [4.2.10] can be substituted into [4.2.9] to obtain the forecast of $Y_{t+s}$ as a function of lagged $Y$'s:

$$\hat{E}[Y_{t+s}|Y_t, Y_{t-1}, \ldots] = \mu + \left[\frac{\psi(L)}{L^s}\right]_+ \eta(L)(Y_t - \mu);$$

or, using [4.2.11],

$$\hat{E}[Y_{t+s}|Y_t, Y_{t-1}, \ldots] = \mu + \left[\frac{\psi(L)}{L^s}\right]_+ \frac{1}{\psi(L)}(Y_t - \mu). \qquad [4.2.16]$$

Equation [4.2.16] is known as the *Wiener-Kolmogorov prediction formula*. Several examples of using this forecasting rule follow.

## *Forecasting an* AR*(1) Process*

For the covariance-stationary $AR(1)$ process [4.2.14], we have

$$\psi(L) = 1/(1 - \phi L) = 1 + \phi L + \phi^2 L^2 + \phi^3 L^3 + \cdots \qquad [4.2.17]$$

and

$$\left[\frac{\psi(L)}{L^s}\right]_+ = \phi^s + \phi^{s+1}L^1 + \phi^{s+2}L^2 + \cdots = \phi^s/(1 - \phi L). \qquad [4.2.18]$$

Substituting [4.2.18] into [4.2.16] yields the optimal linear $s$-period-ahead forecast for a stationary $AR(1)$ process:

$$\begin{aligned} \hat{E}[Y_{t+s}|Y_t, Y_{t-1}, \ldots] &= \mu + \frac{\phi^s}{1 - \phi L}(1 - \phi L)(Y_t - \mu) \\ &= \mu + \phi^s(Y_t - \mu). \end{aligned} \qquad [4.2.19]$$

The forecast decays geometrically from $(Y_t - \mu)$ toward $\mu$ as the forecast horizon $s$ increases. From [4.2.17], the moving average weight $\psi_j$ is given by $\phi^j$, so from [4.2.6], the mean squared $s$-period-ahead forecast error is

$$[1 + \phi^2 + \phi^4 + \cdots + \phi^{2(s-1)}]\sigma^2.$$

Notice that this grows with $s$ and asymptotically approaches $\sigma^2/(1 - \phi^2)$, the unconditional variance of $Y$.

## *Forecasting an* AR(p) *Process*

Next consider forecasting the stationary $AR(p)$ process [4.2.12]. The Wiener-Kolmogorov formula in [4.2.16] essentially expresses the value of $(Y_{t+s} - \mu)$ in terms of initial values $\{(Y_t - \mu), (Y_{t-1} - \mu), \ldots\}$ and subsequent values of $\{\varepsilon_{t+1}, \varepsilon_{t+2}, \ldots, \varepsilon_{t+s}\}$ and then drops the terms involving future $\varepsilon$'s. An expression of this form was provided by equation [1.2.26], which described the value of a variable subject to a $p$th-order difference equation in terms of initial conditions and subsequent shocks:

$$\begin{aligned} Y_{t+s} - \mu = f_{11}^{(s)}(Y_t - \mu) + f_{12}^{(s)}(Y_{t-1} - \mu) + \cdots + f_{1p}^{(s)}(Y_{t-p+1} - \mu) \\ + \varepsilon_{t+s} + \psi_1\varepsilon_{t+s-1} + \psi_2\varepsilon_{t+s-2} + \cdots + \psi_{s-1}\varepsilon_{t+1}, \end{aligned} \qquad [4.2.20]$$

where

$$\psi_j = f_{11}^{(j)}. \qquad [4.2.21]$$

Recall that $f_{11}^{(j)}$ denotes the (1, 1) element of $\mathbf{F}^j$, $f_{12}^{(j)}$ denotes the (1, 2) element of $\mathbf{F}^j$, and so on, where $\mathbf{F}$ is the following $(p \times p)$ matrix:

$$\mathbf{F} \equiv \begin{bmatrix} \phi_1 & \phi_2 & \phi_3 & \cdots & \phi_{p-1} & \phi_p \\ 1 & 0 & 0 & \cdots & 0 & 0 \\ 0 & 1 & 0 & \cdots & 0 & 0 \\ \vdots & \vdots & \vdots & \cdots & \vdots & \vdots \\ 0 & 0 & 0 & \cdots & 1 & 0 \end{bmatrix}.$$

The optimal $s$-period-ahead forecast is thus

$$\begin{aligned} \hat{Y}_{t+s|t} = \mu &+ f_{11}^{(s)}(Y_t - \mu) + f_{12}^{(s)}(Y_{t-1} - \mu) + \cdots \\ &+ f_{1p}^{(s)}(Y_{t-p+1} - \mu). \end{aligned} \qquad [4.2.22]$$

Notice that for any forecast horizon $s$ the optimal forecast is a constant plus a linear function of $\{Y_t, Y_{t-1}, \ldots, Y_{t-p+1}\}$. The associated forecast error is

$$Y_{t+s} - \hat{Y}_{t+s|t} = \varepsilon_{t+s} + \psi_1\varepsilon_{t+s-1} + \psi_2\varepsilon_{t+s-2} + \cdots + \psi_{s-1}\varepsilon_{t+1}. \qquad [4.2.23]$$

The easiest way to calculate the forecast in [4.2.22] is through a simple recursion. This recursion can be deduced independently from a principle known as the *law of iterated projections*, which will be proved formally in Section 4.5. Suppose that at date $t$ we wanted to make a one-period-ahead forecast of $Y_{t+1}$. The optimal forecast is clearly

$$\begin{aligned} (\hat{Y}_{t+1|t} - \mu) = \phi_1(Y_t - \mu) &+ \phi_2(Y_{t-1} - \mu) + \cdots \\ &+ \phi_p(Y_{t-p+1} - \mu). \end{aligned} \qquad [4.2.24]$$

Consider next a two-period-ahead forecast. Suppose that at date $t + 1$ we were to make a one-period-ahead forecast of $Y_{t+2}$. Replacing $t$ with $t + 1$ in [4.2.24] gives the optimal forecast as

$$\begin{aligned} (\hat{Y}_{t+2|t+1} - \mu) = \phi_1(Y_{t+1} - \mu) &+ \phi_2(Y_t - \mu) + \cdots \\ &+ \phi_p(Y_{t-p+2} - \mu). \end{aligned} \qquad [4.2.25]$$

The law of iterated projections asserts that if this date $t + 1$ forecast of $Y_{t+2}$ is projected on date $t$ information, the result is the date $t$ forecast of $Y_{t+2}$. At date $t$ the values $Y_t, Y_{t-1}, \ldots, Y_{t-p+2}$ in [4.2.25] are known. Thus,

$$\begin{aligned} (\hat{Y}_{t+2|t} - \mu) = \phi_1(\hat{Y}_{t+1|t} - \mu) &+ \phi_2(Y_t - \mu) + \cdots \\ &+ \phi_p(Y_{t-p+2} - \mu). \end{aligned} \qquad [4.2.26]$$

Substituting [4.2.24] into [4.2.26] then yields the two-period-ahead forecast for an $AR(p)$ process:

$$\begin{aligned} (\hat{Y}_{t+2|t} - \mu) &= \phi_1[\phi_1(Y_t - \mu) + \phi_2(Y_{t-1} - \mu) + \cdots + \phi_p(Y_{t-p+1} - \mu)] \\ &\quad + \phi_2(Y_t - \mu) + \phi_3(Y_{t-1} - \mu) + \cdots + \phi_p(Y_{t-p+2} - \mu) \\ &= (\phi_1^2 + \phi_2)(Y_t - \mu) + (\phi_1\phi_2 + \phi_3)(Y_{t-1} - \mu) + \cdots \\ &\quad + (\phi_1\phi_{p-1} + \phi_p)(Y_{t-p+2} - \mu) + \phi_1\phi_p(Y_{t-p+1} - \mu). \end{aligned}$$

The $s$-period-ahead forecasts of an $AR(p)$ process can be obtained by iterating on

$$\begin{aligned} (\hat{Y}_{t+j|t} - \mu) = \phi_1(\hat{Y}_{t+j-1|t} - \mu) &+ \phi_2(\hat{Y}_{t+j-2|t} - \mu) + \cdots \\ &+ \phi_p(\hat{Y}_{t+j-p|t} - \mu) \end{aligned} \qquad [4.2.27]$$

for $j = 1, 2, \ldots, s$ where

$$\hat{Y}_{\tau|t} = Y_\tau \qquad \text{for } \tau \leq t.$$

### *Forecasting an* MA*(1) Process*

Next consider an invertible $MA(1)$ representation,

$$Y_t - \mu = (1 + \theta L)\varepsilon_t \qquad [4.2.28]$$

with $|\theta| < 1$. Replacing $\psi(L)$ in the Wiener-Kolmogorov formula [4.2.16] with $(1 + \theta L)$ gives

$$\hat{Y}_{t+s|t} = \mu + \left[\frac{1 + \theta L}{L^s}\right]_+ \frac{1}{1 + \theta L}(Y_t - \mu). \qquad [4.2.29]$$

To forecast an $MA(1)$ process one period into the future ($s = 1$),

$$\left[\frac{1 + \theta L}{L^1}\right]_+ = \theta,$$

and so

$$\begin{aligned}\hat{Y}_{t+1|t} &= \mu + \frac{\theta}{1 + \theta L}(Y_t - \mu) \\ &= \mu + \theta(Y_t - \mu) - \theta^2(Y_{t-1} - \mu) + \theta^3(Y_{t-2} - \mu) - \cdots.\end{aligned} \qquad [4.2.30]$$

It is sometimes useful to write [4.2.28] as

$$\varepsilon_t = \frac{1}{1 + \theta L}(Y_t - \mu)$$

and view $\varepsilon_t$ as the outcome of an infinite recursion,

$$\hat{\varepsilon}_t = (Y_t - \mu) - \theta\hat{\varepsilon}_{t-1}. \qquad [4.2.31]$$

The one-period-ahead forecast [4.2.30] could then be written as

$$\hat{Y}_{t+1|t} = \mu + \theta\hat{\varepsilon}_t. \qquad [4.2.32]$$

Equation [4.2.31] is in fact an exact characterization of $\varepsilon_t$, deduced from simple rearrangement of [4.2.28]. The "hat" notation ($\hat{\varepsilon}_t$) is introduced at this point in anticipation of the approximations to $\varepsilon_t$ that will be introduced in the following section and substituted into [4.2.31] and [4.2.32].

To forecast an $MA(1)$ process for $s = 2, 3, \ldots$ periods into the future,

$$\left[\frac{1 + \theta L}{L^s}\right]_+ = 0 \qquad \text{for } s = 2, 3, \ldots;$$

and so, from [4.2.29],

$$\hat{Y}_{t+s|t} = \mu \qquad \text{for } s = 2, 3, \ldots. \qquad [4.2.33]$$

### *Forecasting an* MA(q) *Process*

For an invertible $MA(q)$ process,

$$(Y_t - \mu) = (1 + \theta_1 L + \theta_2 L^2 + \cdots + \theta_q L^q)\varepsilon_t,$$

the forecast [4.2.16] becomes

$$\hat{Y}_{t+s|t} = \mu + \left[\frac{1 + \theta_1 L + \theta_2 L^2 + \cdots + \theta_q L^q}{L^s}\right]_+ \times \frac{1}{1 + \theta_1 L + \theta_2 L^2 + \cdots + \theta_q L^q}(Y_t - \mu). \quad [4.2.34]$$

Now

$$\left[\frac{1 + \theta_1 L + \theta_2 L^2 + \cdots + \theta_q L^q}{L^s}\right]_+ = \begin{cases} \theta_s + \theta_{s+1} L + \theta_{s+2} L^2 + \cdots + \theta_q L^{q-s} & \text{for } s = 1, 2, \ldots, q \\ 0 & \text{for } s = q+1, q+2, \ldots. \end{cases}$$

Thus, for horizons of $s = 1, 2, \ldots, q$, the forecast is given by

$$\hat{Y}_{t+s|t} = \mu + (\theta_s + \theta_{s+1} L + \theta_{s+2} L^2 + \cdots + \theta_q L^{q-s})\hat{\varepsilon}_t, \quad [4.2.35]$$

where $\hat{\varepsilon}_t$ can be characterized by the recursion

$$\hat{\varepsilon}_t = (Y_t - \mu) - \theta_1 \hat{\varepsilon}_{t-1} - \theta_2 \hat{\varepsilon}_{t-2} - \cdots - \theta_q \hat{\varepsilon}_{t-q}. \quad [4.2.36]$$

A forecast farther than $q$ periods into the future is simply the unconditional mean $\mu$.

### *Forecasting an* ARMA*(1, 1) Process*

For an *ARMA*(1, 1) process

$$(1 - \phi L)(Y_t - \mu) = (1 + \theta L)\varepsilon_t$$

that is stationary ($|\phi| < 1$) and invertible ($|\theta| < 1$),

$$\hat{Y}_{t+s|t} = \mu + \left[\frac{1 + \theta L}{(1 - \phi L)L^s}\right]_+ \frac{1 - \phi L}{1 + \theta L}(Y_t - \mu). \quad [4.2.37]$$

Here

$$\begin{aligned} \left[\frac{1 + \theta L}{(1 - \phi L)L^s}\right]_+ &= \left[\frac{(1 + \phi L + \phi^2 L^2 + \cdots)}{L^s} + \frac{\theta L(1 + \phi L + \phi^2 L^2 + \cdots)}{L^s}\right]_+ \\ &= (\phi^s + \phi^{s+1} L + \phi^{s+2} L^2 + \cdots) + \theta(\phi^{s-1} + \phi^s L + \phi^{s+1} L^2 + \cdots) \\ &= (\phi^s + \theta\phi^{s-1})(1 + \phi L + \phi^2 L^2 + \cdots) \\ &= \frac{\phi^s + \theta\phi^{s-1}}{1 - \phi L}. \end{aligned} \quad [4.2.38]$$

Substituting [4.2.38] into [4.2.37] gives

$$\begin{aligned} \hat{Y}_{t+s|t} &= \mu + \left[\frac{\phi^s + \theta\phi^{s-1}}{1 - \phi L}\right]\frac{1 - \phi L}{1 + \theta L}(Y_t - \mu) \\ &= \mu + \frac{\phi^s + \theta\phi^{s-1}}{1 + \theta L}(Y_t - \mu). \end{aligned} \quad [4.2.39]$$

Note that for $s = 2, 3, \ldots$, the forecast [4.2.39] obeys the recursion

$$(\hat{Y}_{t+s|t} - \mu) = \phi(\hat{Y}_{t+s-1|t} - \mu).$$

Thus, beyond one period, the forecast decays geometrically at the rate $\phi$ toward the unconditional mean $\mu$. The one-period-ahead forecast ($s = 1$) is given by

$$\hat{Y}_{t+1|t} = \mu + \frac{\phi + \theta}{1 + \theta L}(Y_t - \mu). \qquad [4.2.40]$$

This can equivalently be written

$$(\hat{Y}_{t+1|t} - \mu) = \frac{\phi(1 + \theta L) + \theta(1 - \phi L)}{1 + \theta L}(Y_t - \mu) = \phi(Y_t - \mu) + \theta\hat{\varepsilon}_t \qquad [4.2.41]$$

where

$$\hat{\varepsilon}_t = \frac{(1 - \phi L)}{(1 + \theta L)}(Y_t - \mu)$$

or

$$\hat{\varepsilon}_t = (Y_t - \mu) - \phi(Y_{t-1} - \mu) - \theta\hat{\varepsilon}_{t-1} = Y_t - \hat{Y}_{t|t-1}. \qquad [4.2.42]$$

## *Forecasting an* ARMA(p, q) *Process*

Finally, consider forecasting a stationary and invertible $ARMA(p, q)$ process:

$$(1 - \phi_1 L - \phi_2 L^2 - \cdots - \phi_p L^p)(Y_t - \mu) = (1 + \theta_1 L + \theta_2 L^2 + \cdots + \theta_q L^q)\varepsilon_t.$$

The natural generalizations of [4.2.41] and [4.2.42] are

$$\begin{aligned}(\hat{Y}_{t+1|t} - \mu) = {} & \phi_1(Y_t - \mu) + \phi_2(Y_{t-1} - \mu) + \cdots \\ & + \phi_p(Y_{t-p+1} - \mu) + \theta_1\hat{\varepsilon}_t + \theta_2\hat{\varepsilon}_{t-1} + \cdots + \theta_q\hat{\varepsilon}_{t-q+1},\end{aligned} \qquad [4.2.43]$$

with $\{\hat{\varepsilon}_t\}$ generated recursively from

$$\hat{\varepsilon}_t = Y_t - \hat{Y}_{t|t-1}. \qquad [4.2.44]$$

The $s$-period-ahead forecasts would be

$$(\hat{Y}_{t+s|t} - \mu) \qquad [4.2.45]$$

$$= \begin{cases} \phi_1(\hat{Y}_{t+s-1|t} - \mu) + \phi_2(\hat{Y}_{t+s-2|t} - \mu) + \cdots + \phi_p(\hat{Y}_{t+s-p|t} - \mu) \\ \quad + \theta_s\hat{\varepsilon}_t + \theta_{s+1}\hat{\varepsilon}_{t-1} + \cdots + \theta_q\hat{\varepsilon}_{t+s-q} \qquad \text{for } s = 1, 2, \ldots, q \\ \phi_1(\hat{Y}_{t+s-1|t} - \mu) + \phi_2(\hat{Y}_{t+s-2|t} - \mu) + \cdots + \phi_p(\hat{Y}_{t+s-p|t} - \mu) \\ \qquad\qquad\qquad\qquad\qquad\qquad \text{for } s = q + 1, q + 2, \ldots, \end{cases}$$

where

$$\hat{Y}_{\tau|t} = Y_\tau \qquad \text{for } \tau \leq t.$$

Thus for a forecast horizon $s$ greater than the moving average order $q$, the forecasts follow a $p$th-order difference equation governed solely by the autoregressive parameters.

## 4.3. *Forecasts Based on a Finite Number of Observations*

The formulas in the preceding section assumed that we had an infinite number of past observations on $Y$, $\{Y_t, Y_{t-1}, \ldots\}$, and knew with certainty population parameters such as $\mu$, $\phi$, and $\theta$. This section continues to assume that population parameters are known with certainty, but develops forecasts based on a finite number of observations $\{Y_t, Y_{t-1}, \ldots, Y_{t-m+1}\}$.

For forecasting an $AR(p)$ process, an optimal $s$-period-ahead linear forecast based on an infinite number of observations $\{Y_t, Y_{t-1}, \ldots\}$ in fact makes use of only the $p$ most recent values $\{Y_t, Y_{t-1}, \ldots, Y_{t-p+1}\}$. For an $MA$ or $ARMA$ process, however, we would in principle require all of the historical values of $Y$ in order to implement the formulas of the preceding section.

### *Approximations to Optimal Forecasts*

One approach to forecasting based on a finite number of observations is to act as if presample $\varepsilon$'s were all equal to zero. The idea is thus to use the approximation

$$\begin{aligned}&\hat{E}(Y_{t+s}|Y_t, Y_{t-1}, \ldots)\\ &\qquad \cong \hat{E}(Y_{t+s}|Y_t, Y_{t-1}, \ldots, Y_{t-m+1}, \varepsilon_{t-m} = 0, \varepsilon_{t-m-1} = 0, \ldots).\end{aligned} \quad [4.3.1]$$

For example, consider forecasting an $MA(q)$ process. The recursion [4.2.36] can be started by setting

$$\hat{\varepsilon}_{t-m} = \hat{\varepsilon}_{t-m-1} = \cdots = \hat{\varepsilon}_{t-m-q+1} = 0 \quad [4.3.2]$$

and then iterating on [4.2.36] to generate $\hat{\varepsilon}_{t-m+1}, \hat{\varepsilon}_{t-m+2}, \ldots, \hat{\varepsilon}_t$. These calculations produce

$$\begin{aligned}\hat{\varepsilon}_{t-m+1} &= (Y_{t-m+1} - \mu),\\ \hat{\varepsilon}_{t-m+2} &= (Y_{t-m+2} - \mu) - \theta_1\hat{\varepsilon}_{t-m+1},\\ \hat{\varepsilon}_{t-m+3} &= (Y_{t-m+3} - \mu) - \theta_1\hat{\varepsilon}_{t-m+2} - \theta_2\hat{\varepsilon}_{t-m+1},\end{aligned}$$

and so on. The resulting values for $(\hat{\varepsilon}_t, \hat{\varepsilon}_{t-1}, \ldots, \hat{\varepsilon}_{t-q+s})$ are then substituted directly into [4.2.35] to produce the forecast [4.3.1]. For example, for $s = q = 1$, the forecast would be

$$\begin{aligned}\hat{Y}_{t+1|t} = \mu &+ \theta(Y_t - \mu) - \theta^2(Y_{t-1} - \mu)\\ &+ \theta^3(Y_{t-2} - \mu) - \cdots + (-1)^{m-1}\theta^m(Y_{t-m+1} - \mu),\end{aligned} \quad [4.3.3]$$

which is to be used as an approximation to the $AR(\infty)$ forecast,

$$\mu + \theta(Y_t - \mu) - \theta^2(Y_{t-1} - \mu) + \theta^3(Y_{t-2} - \mu) - \cdots. \quad [4.3.4]$$

For $m$ large and $|\theta|$ small, this clearly gives an excellent approximation. For $|\theta|$ closer to unity, the approximation may be poorer. Note that if the moving average operator is noninvertible, the forecast [4.3.1] is inappropriate and should not be used.

## *Exact Finite-Sample Forecasts*

An alternative approach is to calculate the exact projection of $Y_{t+1}$ on its $m$ most recent values. Let

$$\mathbf{X}_t \equiv \begin{bmatrix} 1 \\ Y_t \\ Y_{t-1} \\ \vdots \\ Y_{t-m+1} \end{bmatrix}.$$

We thus seek a linear forecast of the form

$$\boldsymbol{\alpha}^{(m)\prime}\mathbf{X}_t = \alpha_0^{(m)} + \alpha_1^{(m)}Y_t + \alpha_2^{(m)}Y_{t-1} + \cdots + \alpha_m^{(m)}Y_{t-m+1}. \qquad [4.3.5]$$

The coefficient relating $Y_{t+1}$ to $Y_t$ in a projection of $Y_{t+1}$ on the $m$ most recent values of $Y$ is denoted $\alpha_1^{(m)}$ in [4.3.5]. This will in general be different from the coefficient relating $Y_{t+1}$ to $Y_t$ in a projection of $Y_{t+1}$ on the $m + 1$ most recent values of $Y$; the latter coefficient would be denoted $\alpha_1^{(m+1)}$.

If $Y_t$ is covariance-stationary, then $E(Y_tY_{t-j}) = \gamma_j + \mu^2$. Setting $\mathbf{X}_t = (1, Y_t, Y_{t-1}, \ldots, Y_{t-m+1})'$ in [4.1.13] implies

$$\begin{aligned}\boldsymbol{\alpha}^{(m)\prime} &\equiv [\alpha_0^{(m)} \quad \alpha_1^{(m)} \quad \alpha_2^{(m)} \quad \cdots \quad \alpha_m^{(m)}] \\ &= [\mu \quad (\gamma_1 + \mu^2) \quad (\gamma_2 + \mu^2) \quad \cdots \quad (\gamma_m + \mu^2)] \\ &\quad \times \begin{bmatrix} 1 & \mu & \mu & \cdots & \mu \\ \mu & \gamma_0 + \mu^2 & \gamma_1 + \mu^2 & \cdots & \gamma_{m-1} + \mu^2 \\ \mu & \gamma_1 + \mu^2 & \gamma_0 + \mu^2 & \cdots & \gamma_{m-2} + \mu^2 \\ \vdots & \vdots & \vdots & \cdots & \vdots \\ \mu & \gamma_{m-1} + \mu^2 & \gamma_{m-2} + \mu^2 & \cdots & \gamma_0 + \mu^2 \end{bmatrix}^{-1}. \end{aligned} \qquad [4.3.6]$$

When a constant term is included in $\mathbf{X}_t$, it is more convenient to express variables in deviations from the mean. Then we could calculate the projection of $(Y_{t+1} - \mu)$ on $\mathbf{X}_t = [(Y_t - \mu), (Y_{t-1} - \mu), \ldots, (Y_{t-m+1} - \mu)]'$:

$$\begin{aligned}\hat{Y}_{t+1|t} - \mu = \alpha_1^{(m)}(Y_t - \mu) &+ \alpha_2^{(m)}(Y_{t-1} - \mu) + \cdots \\ &+ \alpha_m^{(m)}(Y_{t-m+1} - \mu).\end{aligned} \qquad [4.3.7]$$

For this definition of $\mathbf{X}_t$ the coefficients can be calculated directly from [4.1.13] to be

$$\begin{bmatrix} \alpha_1^{(m)} \\ \alpha_2^{(m)} \\ \vdots \\ \alpha_m^{(m)} \end{bmatrix} = \begin{bmatrix} \gamma_0 & \gamma_1 & \cdots & \gamma_{m-1} \\ \gamma_1 & \gamma_0 & \cdots & \gamma_{m-2} \\ \vdots & \vdots & \cdots & \vdots \\ \gamma_{m-1} & \gamma_{m-2} & \cdots & \gamma_0 \end{bmatrix}^{-1} \begin{bmatrix} \gamma_1 \\ \gamma_2 \\ \vdots \\ \gamma_m \end{bmatrix}. \qquad [4.3.8]$$

We will demonstrate in Section 4.5 that the coefficients $(\alpha_1^{(m)}, \alpha_2^{(m)}, \ldots, \alpha_m^{(m)})$ in equations [4.3.8] and [4.3.6] are identical. This is analogous to a familiar result for ordinary least squares regression—slope coefficients would be unchanged if all variables are expressed in deviations from their sample means and the constant term is dropped from the regression.

To generate an $s$-period-ahead forecast $\hat{Y}_{t+s|t}$, we would use

$$\hat{Y}_{t+s|t} = \mu + \alpha_1^{(m,s)}(Y_t - \mu) + \alpha_2^{(m,s)}(Y_{t-1} - \mu) + \cdots + \alpha_m^{(m,s)}(Y_{t-m+1} - \mu),$$

where

$$\begin{bmatrix} \alpha_1^{(m,s)} \\ \alpha_2^{(m,s)} \\ \vdots \\ \alpha_m^{(m,s)} \end{bmatrix} = \begin{bmatrix} \gamma_0 & \gamma_1 & \cdots & \gamma_{m-1} \\ \gamma_1 & \gamma_0 & \cdots & \gamma_{m-2} \\ \vdots & \vdots & \cdots & \vdots \\ \gamma_{m-1} & \gamma_{m-2} & \cdots & \gamma_0 \end{bmatrix}^{-1} \begin{bmatrix} \gamma_s \\ \gamma_{s+1} \\ \vdots \\ \gamma_{s+m-1} \end{bmatrix}. \qquad [4.3.9]$$

Using expressions such as [4.3.8] requires inverting an $(m \times m)$ matrix. Several algorithms can be used to evaluate [4.3.8] using relatively simple calculations. One approach is based on the Kalman filter discussed in Chapter 13, which can generate exact finite-sample forecasts for a broad class of processes including any *ARMA* specification. A second approach is based on triangular factorization of the matrix in [4.3.8]. This second approach is developed in the next two sections. This approach will prove helpful for the immediate question of calculating finite-sample forecasts and is also a useful device for establishing a number of later results.

## 4.4. *The Triangular Factorization of a Positive Definite Symmetric Matrix*

Any positive definite symmetric $(n \times n)$ matrix $\mathbf{\Omega}$ has a unique representation of the form

$$\mathbf{\Omega} = \mathbf{ADA}', \qquad [4.4.1]$$

where $\mathbf{A}$ is a lower triangular matrix with 1s along the principal diagonal,

$$\mathbf{A} = \begin{bmatrix} 1 & 0 & 0 & \cdots & 0 \\ a_{21} & 1 & 0 & \cdots & 0 \\ a_{31} & a_{32} & 1 & \cdots & 0 \\ \vdots & \vdots & \vdots & \cdots & \vdots \\ a_{n1} & a_{n2} & a_{n3} & \cdots & 1 \end{bmatrix},$$

and $\mathbf{D}$ is a diagonal matrix,

$$\mathbf{D} = \begin{bmatrix} d_{11} & 0 & 0 & \cdots & 0 \\ 0 & d_{22} & 0 & \cdots & 0 \\ 0 & 0 & d_{33} & \cdots & 0 \\ \vdots & \vdots & \vdots & \cdots & \vdots \\ 0 & 0 & 0 & \cdots & d_{nn} \end{bmatrix},$$

where $d_{ii} > 0$ for all $i$. This is known as the *triangular factorization* of $\mathbf{\Omega}$.

To see how the triangular factorization can be calculated, consider

$$\boldsymbol{\Omega} = \begin{bmatrix} \Omega_{11} & \Omega_{12} & \Omega_{13} & \cdots & \Omega_{1n} \\ \Omega_{21} & \Omega_{22} & \Omega_{23} & \cdots & \Omega_{2n} \\ \Omega_{31} & \Omega_{32} & \Omega_{33} & \cdots & \Omega_{3n} \\ \vdots & \vdots & \vdots & \cdots & \vdots \\ \Omega_{n1} & \Omega_{n2} & \Omega_{n3} & \cdots & \Omega_{nn} \end{bmatrix}. \qquad [4.4.2]$$

We assume that $\boldsymbol{\Omega}$ is positive definite, meaning that $\mathbf{x}'\boldsymbol{\Omega}\mathbf{x} > 0$ for any nonzero $(n \times 1)$ vector $\mathbf{x}$. We also assume that $\boldsymbol{\Omega}$ is symmetric, so that $\Omega_{ij} = \Omega_{ji}$.

The matrix $\boldsymbol{\Omega}$ can be transformed into a matrix with zero in the (2, 1) position by multiplying the first row of $\boldsymbol{\Omega}$ by $\Omega_{21}\Omega_{11}^{-1}$ and subtracting the resulting row from the second. A zero can be put in the (3, 1) position by multiplying the first row by $\Omega_{31}\Omega_{11}^{-1}$ and subtracting the resulting row from the third. We proceed in this fashion down the first column. This set of operations can be summarized as pre-multiplying $\boldsymbol{\Omega}$ by the following matrix:

$$\mathbf{E}_1 = \begin{bmatrix} 1 & 0 & 0 & \cdots & 0 \\ -\Omega_{21}\Omega_{11}^{-1} & 1 & 0 & \cdots & 0 \\ -\Omega_{31}\Omega_{11}^{-1} & 0 & 1 & \cdots & 0 \\ \vdots & \vdots & \vdots & \cdots & \vdots \\ -\Omega_{n1}\Omega_{11}^{-1} & 0 & 0 & \cdots & 1 \end{bmatrix}. \qquad [4.4.3]$$

This matrix always exists, provided that $\Omega_{11} \neq 0$. This is ensured in the present case, because $\Omega_{11}$ is equal to $\mathbf{e}_1'\boldsymbol{\Omega}\mathbf{e}_1$, where $\mathbf{e}_1' = [1 \quad 0 \quad 0 \cdots 0]$. Since $\boldsymbol{\Omega}$ is positive definite, $\mathbf{e}_1'\boldsymbol{\Omega}\mathbf{e}_1$ must be greater than zero.

When $\boldsymbol{\Omega}$ is premultiplied by $\mathbf{E}_1$ and postmultiplied by $\mathbf{E}_1'$ the result is

$$\mathbf{E}_1\boldsymbol{\Omega}\mathbf{E}_1' = \mathbf{H}, \qquad [4.4.4]$$

where

$$\mathbf{H} = \begin{bmatrix} h_{11} & 0 & 0 & \cdots & 0 \\ 0 & h_{22} & h_{23} & \cdots & h_{2n} \\ 0 & h_{32} & h_{33} & \cdots & h_{3n} \\ \vdots & \vdots & \vdots & \cdots & \vdots \\ 0 & h_{n2} & h_{n3} & \cdots & h_{nn} \end{bmatrix} \qquad [4.4.5]$$

$$= \begin{bmatrix} \Omega_{11} & 0 & 0 & \cdots & 0 \\ 0 & \Omega_{22} - \Omega_{21}\Omega_{11}^{-1}\Omega_{12} & \Omega_{23} - \Omega_{21}\Omega_{11}^{-1}\Omega_{13} & \cdots & \Omega_{2n} - \Omega_{21}\Omega_{11}^{-1}\Omega_{1n} \\ 0 & \Omega_{32} - \Omega_{31}\Omega_{11}^{-1}\Omega_{12} & \Omega_{33} - \Omega_{31}\Omega_{11}^{-1}\Omega_{13} & \cdots & \Omega_{3n} - \Omega_{31}\Omega_{11}^{-1}\Omega_{1n} \\ \vdots & \vdots & \vdots & \cdots & \vdots \\ 0 & \Omega_{n2} - \Omega_{n1}\Omega_{11}^{-1}\Omega_{12} & \Omega_{n3} - \Omega_{n1}\Omega_{11}^{-1}\Omega_{13} & \cdots & \Omega_{nn} - \Omega_{n1}\Omega_{11}^{-1}\Omega_{1n} \end{bmatrix}.$$

We next proceed in exactly the same way with the second column of $\mathbf{H}$. The approach now will be to multiply the second row of $\mathbf{H}$ by $h_{32}h_{22}^{-1}$ and subtract the result from the third row. Similarly, we multiply the second row of $\mathbf{H}$ by $h_{42}h_{22}^{-1}$ and subtract the result from the fourth row, and so on down through the second column of $\mathbf{H}$. These operations can be represented as premultiplying $\mathbf{H}$ by the following matrix:

$$\mathbf{E}_2 = \begin{bmatrix} 1 & 0 & 0 & \cdots & 0 \\ 0 & 1 & 0 & \cdots & 0 \\ 0 & -h_{32}h_{22}^{-1} & 1 & \cdots & 0 \\ \vdots & \vdots & \vdots & \cdots & \vdots \\ 0 & -h_{n2}h_{22}^{-1} & 0 & \cdots & 1 \end{bmatrix}. \qquad [4.4.6]$$

This matrix always exists provided that $h_{22} \neq 0$. But $h_{22}$ can be calculated as $h_{22} = \mathbf{e}_2'\mathbf{H}\mathbf{e}_2$, where $\mathbf{e}_2' = [0 \quad 1 \quad 0 \cdots 0]$. Moreover, $\mathbf{H} = \mathbf{E}_1\mathbf{\Omega}\mathbf{E}_1'$, where $\mathbf{\Omega}$ is positive definite and $\mathbf{E}_1$ is given by [4.4.3]. Since $\mathbf{E}_1$ is lower triangular, its determinant is the product of terms along the principal diagonal, which are all unity. Thus $\mathbf{E}_1$ is nonsingular, meaning that $\mathbf{H} = \mathbf{E}_1\mathbf{\Omega}\mathbf{E}_1'$ is positive definite and so $h_{22} = \mathbf{e}_2'\mathbf{H}\mathbf{e}_2$ must be strictly positive. Thus the matrix in [4.4.6] can always be calculated.

If $\mathbf{H}$ is premultiplied by the matrix in [4.4.6] and postmultiplied by the transpose, the result is

$$\mathbf{E}_2\mathbf{H}\mathbf{E}_2' = \mathbf{K},$$

where

$$\mathbf{K} = \begin{bmatrix} h_{11} & 0 & 0 & \cdots & 0 \\ 0 & h_{22} & 0 & \cdots & 0 \\ 0 & 0 & h_{33} - h_{32}h_{22}^{-1}h_{23} & \cdots & h_{3n} - h_{32}h_{22}^{-1}h_{2n} \\ \vdots & \vdots & \vdots & \cdots & \vdots \\ 0 & 0 & h_{n3} - h_{n2}h_{22}^{-1}h_{23} & \cdots & h_{nn} - h_{n2}h_{22}^{-1}h_{2n} \end{bmatrix}.$$

Again, since $\mathbf{H}$ is positive definite and since $\mathbf{E}_2$ is nonsingular, $\mathbf{K}$ is positive definite and in particular $k_{33}$ is positive. Proceeding through each of the columns with the same approach, we see that for any positive definite symmetric matrix $\mathbf{\Omega}$ there exist matrices $\mathbf{E}_1, \mathbf{E}_2, \ldots, \mathbf{E}_{n-1}$ such that

$$\mathbf{E}_{n-1} \cdots \mathbf{E}_2\mathbf{E}_1\mathbf{\Omega}\mathbf{E}_1'\mathbf{E}_2' \cdots \mathbf{E}_{n-1}' = \mathbf{D}, \qquad [4.4.7]$$

where

$$\mathbf{D} = \begin{bmatrix} \Omega_{11} & 0 & 0 & \cdots & 0 \\ 0 & \Omega_{22} - \Omega_{21}\Omega_{11}^{-1}\Omega_{12} & 0 & \cdots & 0 \\ 0 & 0 & h_{33} - h_{32}h_{22}^{-1}h_{23} & \cdots & 0 \\ \vdots & \vdots & \vdots & \cdots & \vdots \\ 0 & 0 & 0 & \cdots & c_{nn} - c_{n,n-1}c_{n-1,n-1}^{-1}c_{n-1,n} \end{bmatrix},$$

with all the diagonal entries of $\mathbf{D}$ strictly positive. The matrices $\mathbf{E}_1$ and $\mathbf{E}_2$ in [4.4.7] are given by [4.4.3] and [4.4.6]. In general, $\mathbf{E}_j$ is a matrix with nonzero values in the $j$th column below the principal diagonal, 1s along the principal diagonal, and zeros everywhere else.

Thus each $\mathbf{E}_j$ is lower triangular with unit determinant. Hence $\mathbf{E}_j^{-1}$ exists, and the following matrix exists:

$$\mathbf{A} = (\mathbf{E}_{n-1} \cdots \mathbf{E}_2\mathbf{E}_1)^{-1} = \mathbf{E}_1^{-1}\mathbf{E}_2^{-1} \cdots \mathbf{E}_{n-1}^{-1}. \qquad [4.4.8]$$

If [4.4.7] is premultiplied by $\mathbf{A}$ and postmultiplied by $\mathbf{A}'$, the result is

$$\mathbf{\Omega} = \mathbf{ADA}'. \qquad [4.4.9]$$

Recall that $\mathbf{E}_1$ represents the operation of multiplying the first row of $\mathbf{\Omega}$ by certain numbers and subtracting the results from each of the subsequent rows. Its inverse $\mathbf{E}_1^{-1}$ undoes this operation, which would be achieved by multiplying the first row by these same numbers and *adding* the results to the subsequent rows. Thus

$$\mathbf{E}_1^{-1} = \begin{bmatrix} 1 & 0 & 0 & \cdots & 0 \\ \Omega_{21}\Omega_{11}^{-1} & 1 & 0 & \cdots & 0 \\ \Omega_{31}\Omega_{11}^{-1} & 0 & 1 & \cdots & 0 \\ \vdots & \vdots & \vdots & \cdots & \vdots \\ \Omega_{n1}\Omega_{11}^{-1} & 0 & 0 & \cdots & 1 \end{bmatrix}, \qquad [4.4.10]$$

as may be verified directly by multiplying [4.4.3] by [4.4.10] to obtain the identity matrix. Similarly,

$$\mathbf{E}_2^{-1} = \begin{bmatrix} 1 & 0 & 0 & \cdots & 0 \\ 0 & 1 & 0 & \cdots & 0 \\ 0 & h_{32}h_{22}^{-1} & 1 & \cdots & 0 \\ \vdots & \vdots & \vdots & \cdots & \vdots \\ 0 & h_{n2}h_{22}^{-1} & 0 & \cdots & 1 \end{bmatrix},$$

and so on. Because of this special structure, the series of multiplications in [4.4.8] turns out to be trivial to carry out:

$$\mathbf{A} = \begin{bmatrix} 1 & 0 & 0 & \cdots & 0 \\ \Omega_{21}\Omega_{11}^{-1} & 1 & 0 & \cdots & 0 \\ \Omega_{31}\Omega_{11}^{-1} & h_{32}h_{22}^{-1} & 1 & \cdots & 0 \\ \vdots & \vdots & \vdots & \cdots & \vdots \\ \Omega_{n1}\Omega_{11}^{-1} & h_{n2}h_{22}^{-1} & k_{n3}k_{33}^{-1} & \cdots & 1 \end{bmatrix}. \qquad [4.4.11]$$

That is, the $j$th column of $\mathbf{A}$ is just the $j$th column of $\mathbf{E}_j^{-1}$.

We should emphasize that the simplicity of carrying out these matrix multiplications is due not just to the special structure of the $\mathbf{E}_j^{-1}$ matrices but also to the order in which they are multiplied. For example, $\mathbf{A}^{-1} = \mathbf{E}_{n-1}\mathbf{E}_{n-2} \cdots \mathbf{E}_1$ cannot be calculated simply by using the $j$th column of $\mathbf{E}_j$ for the $j$th column of $\mathbf{A}^{-1}$.

Since the matrix $\mathbf{A}$ in [4.4.11] is lower triangular with 1s along the principal diagonal, expression [4.4.9] is the triangular factorization of $\mathbf{\Omega}$.

For illustration, the triangular factorization $\mathbf{\Omega} = \mathbf{ADA}'$ of a $(2 \times 2)$ matrix is

$$\begin{bmatrix} \Omega_{11} & \Omega_{12} \\ \Omega_{21} & \Omega_{22} \end{bmatrix} = \begin{bmatrix} 1 & 0 \\ \Omega_{21}\Omega_{11}^{-1} & 1 \end{bmatrix} \times \begin{bmatrix} \Omega_{11} & 0 \\ 0 & \Omega_{22} - \Omega_{21}\Omega_{11}^{-1}\Omega_{12} \end{bmatrix} \begin{bmatrix} 1 & \Omega_{11}^{-1}\Omega_{12} \\ 0 & 1 \end{bmatrix}, \qquad [4.4.12]$$

while that of a $(3 \times 3)$ matrix is

$$\begin{bmatrix} \Omega_{11} & \Omega_{12} & \Omega_{13} \\ \Omega_{21} & \Omega_{22} & \Omega_{23} \\ \Omega_{31} & \Omega_{32} & \Omega_{33} \end{bmatrix} = \begin{bmatrix} 1 & 0 & 0 \\ \Omega_{21}\Omega_{11}^{-1} & 1 & 0 \\ \Omega_{31}\Omega_{11}^{-1} & h_{32}h_{22}^{-1} & 1 \end{bmatrix} \times \begin{bmatrix} \Omega_{11} & 0 & 0 \\ 0 & h_{22} & 0 \\ 0 & 0 & h_{33} - h_{32}h_{22}^{-1}h_{23} \end{bmatrix} \begin{bmatrix} 1 & \Omega_{11}^{-1}\Omega_{12} & \Omega_{11}^{-1}\Omega_{13} \\ 0 & 1 & h_{22}^{-1}h_{23} \\ 0 & 0 & 1 \end{bmatrix}, \tag{4.4.13}$$

where $h_{22} = (\Omega_{22} - \Omega_{21}\Omega_{11}^{-1}\Omega_{12})$, $h_{33} = (\Omega_{33} - \Omega_{31}\Omega_{11}^{-1}\Omega_{13})$, and $h_{23} = h_{32} = (\Omega_{23} - \Omega_{21}\Omega_{11}^{-1}\Omega_{13})$.

## *Uniqueness of the Triangular Factorization*

We next establish that the triangular factorization is unique. Suppose that

$$\mathbf{\Omega} = \mathbf{A}_1\mathbf{D}_1\mathbf{A}_1' = \mathbf{A}_2\mathbf{D}_2\mathbf{A}_2', \tag{4.4.14}$$

where $\mathbf{A}_1$ and $\mathbf{A}_2$ are both lower triangular with 1s along the principal diagonal and $\mathbf{D}_1$ and $\mathbf{D}_2$ are both diagonal with positive entries along the principal diagonal. Then all the matrices have inverses. Premultiplying [4.4.14] by $\mathbf{D}_1^{-1}\mathbf{A}_1^{-1}$ and postmultiplying by $[\mathbf{A}_2']^{-1}$ yields

$$\mathbf{A}_1'[\mathbf{A}_2']^{-1} = \mathbf{D}_1^{-1}\mathbf{A}_1^{-1}\mathbf{A}_2\mathbf{D}_2. \tag{4.4.15}$$

Since $\mathbf{A}_2'$ is upper triangular with 1s along the principal diagonal, $[\mathbf{A}_2']^{-1}$ must likewise be upper triangular with 1s along the principal diagonal. Since $\mathbf{A}_1'$ is also of this form, the left side of [4.4.15] is upper triangular with 1s along the principal diagonal. By similar reasoning, the right side of [4.4.15] must be lower triangular. The only way an upper triangular matrix can equal a lower triangular matrix is if all the off-diagonal terms are zero. Moreover, since the diagonal entries on the left side of [4.4.15] are all unity, this matrix must be the identity matrix:

$$\mathbf{A}_1'[\mathbf{A}_2']^{-1} = \mathbf{I}_n.$$

Postmultiplication by $\mathbf{A}_2'$ establishes that $\mathbf{A}_1' = \mathbf{A}_2'$. Premultiplying [4.4.14] by $\mathbf{A}^{-1}$ and postmultiplying by $[\mathbf{A}']^{-1}$ then yields $\mathbf{D}_1 = \mathbf{D}_2$.

## *The Cholesky Factorization*

A closely related factorization of a symmetric positive definite matrix $\mathbf{\Omega}$ is obtained as follows. Define $\mathbf{D}^{1/2}$ to be the $(n \times n)$ diagonal matrix whose diagonal entries are the square roots of the corresponding elements of the matrix $\mathbf{D}$ in the triangular factorization:

$$\mathbf{D}^{1/2} = \begin{bmatrix} \sqrt{d_{11}} & 0 & 0 & \cdots & 0 \\ 0 & \sqrt{d_{22}} & 0 & \cdots & 0 \\ 0 & 0 & \sqrt{d_{33}} & \cdots & 0 \\ \vdots & \vdots & \vdots & \cdots & \vdots \\ 0 & 0 & 0 & \cdots & \sqrt{d_{nn}} \end{bmatrix}.$$

Since the matrix $\mathbf{D}$ is unique and has strictly positive diagonal entries, the matrix $\mathbf{D}^{1/2}$ exists and is unique. Then the triangular factorization can be written

$$\mathbf{\Omega} = \mathbf{A}\mathbf{D}^{1/2}\mathbf{D}^{1/2}\mathbf{A}' = \mathbf{A}\mathbf{D}^{1/2}(\mathbf{A}\mathbf{D}^{1/2})'$$

or

$$\boldsymbol{\Omega} = \mathbf{PP}', \tag{4.4.16}$$

where

$$\mathbf{P} \equiv \mathbf{AD}^{1/2}$$

$$= \begin{bmatrix} 1 & 0 & 0 & \cdots & 0 \\ a_{21} & 1 & 0 & \cdots & 0 \\ a_{31} & a_{32} & 1 & \cdots & 0 \\ \vdots & \vdots & \vdots & \cdots & \vdots \\ a_{n1} & a_{n2} & a_{n3} & \cdots & 1 \end{bmatrix} \begin{bmatrix} \sqrt{d_{11}} & 0 & 0 & \cdots & 0 \\ 0 & \sqrt{d_{22}} & 0 & \cdots & 0 \\ 0 & 0 & \sqrt{d_{33}} & \cdots & 0 \\ \vdots & \vdots & \vdots & \cdots & \vdots \\ 0 & 0 & 0 & \cdots & \sqrt{d_{nn}} \end{bmatrix}$$

$$= \begin{bmatrix} \sqrt{d_{11}} & 0 & 0 & \cdots & 0 \\ a_{21}\sqrt{d_{11}} & \sqrt{d_{22}} & 0 & \cdots & 0 \\ a_{31}\sqrt{d_{11}} & a_{32}\sqrt{d_{22}} & \sqrt{d_{33}} & \cdots & 0 \\ \vdots & \vdots & \vdots & \cdots & \vdots \\ a_{n1}\sqrt{d_{11}} & a_{n2}\sqrt{d_{22}} & a_{n3}\sqrt{d_{33}} & \cdots & \sqrt{d_{nn}} \end{bmatrix}.$$

Expression [4.4.16] is known as the *Cholesky factorization* of $\boldsymbol{\Omega}$. Note that $\mathbf{P}$, like $\mathbf{A}$, is lower triangular, though whereas $\mathbf{A}$ has 1s along the principal diagonal, the Cholesky factor has the square roots of the elements of $\mathbf{D}$ along the principal diagonal.

## 4.5. *Updating a Linear Projection*

### *Triangular Factorization of a Second-Moment Matrix and Linear Projection*

Let $\mathbf{Y} = (Y_1, Y_2, \ldots, Y_n)'$ be an $(n \times 1)$ vector of random variables whose second-moment matrix is given by

$$\boldsymbol{\Omega} = E(\mathbf{YY}'). \tag{4.5.1}$$

Let $\boldsymbol{\Omega} = \mathbf{ADA}'$ be the triangular factorization of $\boldsymbol{\Omega}$, and define

$$\tilde{\mathbf{Y}} \equiv \mathbf{A}^{-1}\mathbf{Y}. \tag{4.5.2}$$

The second-moment matrix of these transformed variables is given by

$$E(\tilde{\mathbf{Y}}\tilde{\mathbf{Y}}') = E(\mathbf{A}^{-1}\mathbf{YY}'[\mathbf{A}']^{-1}) = \mathbf{A}^{-1}E(\mathbf{YY}')[\mathbf{A}']^{-1}. \tag{4.5.3}$$

Substituting [4.5.1] into [4.5.3], the second-moment matrix of $\tilde{\mathbf{Y}}$ is seen to be diagonal:

$$E(\tilde{\mathbf{Y}}\tilde{\mathbf{Y}}') = \mathbf{A}^{-1}\boldsymbol{\Omega}[\mathbf{A}']^{-1} = \mathbf{A}^{-1}\mathbf{ADA}'[\mathbf{A}']^{-1} = \mathbf{D}. \tag{4.5.4}$$

That is,

$$E(\tilde{Y}_i\tilde{Y}_j) = \begin{cases} d_{ii} & \text{for } i = j \\ 0 & \text{for } i \neq j. \end{cases} \tag{4.5.5}$$

Thus the $\tilde{Y}$'s form a series of random variables that are uncorrelated with one another.[4] To see the implication of this, premultiply [4.5.2] by $\mathbf{A}$:

$$\mathbf{A}\tilde{\mathbf{Y}} = \mathbf{Y}. \tag{4.5.6}$$

[4] We will use "$Y_i$ and $Y_j$ are uncorrelated" to mean "$E(Y_iY_j) = 0$." The terminology will be correct if $Y_i$ and $Y_j$ have zero means or if a constant term is included in the linear projection.

Expression [4.4.11] can be used to write out [4.5.6] explicitly as

$$\begin{bmatrix} 1 & 0 & 0 & \cdots & 0 \\ \Omega_{21}\Omega_{11}^{-1} & 1 & 0 & \cdots & 0 \\ \Omega_{31}\Omega_{11}^{-1} & h_{32}h_{22}^{-1} & 1 & \cdots & 0 \\ \vdots & \vdots & \vdots & \cdots & \vdots \\ \Omega_{n1}\Omega_{11}^{-1} & h_{n2}h_{22}^{-1} & k_{n3}k_{33}^{-1} & \cdots & 1 \end{bmatrix} \begin{bmatrix} \tilde{Y}_1 \\ \tilde{Y}_2 \\ \tilde{Y}_3 \\ \vdots \\ \tilde{Y}_n \end{bmatrix} = \begin{bmatrix} Y_1 \\ Y_2 \\ Y_3 \\ \vdots \\ Y_n \end{bmatrix}. \qquad [4.5.7]$$

The first equation in [4.5.7] states that

$$\tilde{Y}_1 = Y_1, \qquad [4.5.8]$$

so the first elements of the vectors $\mathbf{Y}$ and $\tilde{\mathbf{Y}}$ represent the same random variable.

The second equation in [4.5.7] asserts that

$$\Omega_{21}\Omega_{11}^{-1}\tilde{Y}_1 + \tilde{Y}_2 = Y_2,$$

or, using [4.5.8],

$$\tilde{Y}_2 = Y_2 - \Omega_{21}\Omega_{11}^{-1}Y_1 \equiv Y_2 - \alpha Y_1, \qquad [4.5.9]$$

where we have defined $\alpha \equiv \Omega_{21}\Omega_{11}^{-1}$. The fact that $\tilde{Y}_2$ is uncorrelated with $\tilde{Y}_1$ implies

$$E(\tilde{Y}_2\tilde{Y}_1) = E[(Y_2 - \alpha Y_1)Y_1] = 0. \qquad [4.5.10]$$

But, recalling [4.1.10], the value of $\alpha$ that satisfies [4.5.10] is defined as the coefficient of the linear projection of $Y_2$ on $Y_1$. Thus the triangular factorization of $\mathbf{\Omega}$ can be used to infer that the coefficient of a linear projection of $Y_2$ on $Y_1$ is given by $\alpha = \Omega_{21}\Omega_{11}^{-1}$, confirming the earlier result [4.1.13]. In general, the row $i$, column 1 entry of $\mathbf{A}$ is $\Omega_{i1}\Omega_{11}^{-1}$, which is the coefficient from a linear projection of $Y_i$ on $Y_1$.

Since $\tilde{Y}_2$ has the interpretation as the residual from a projection of $Y_2$ on $Y_1$, from [4.5.5] $d_{22}$ gives the *MSE* of this projection:

$$E(\tilde{Y}_2^2) = d_{22} = \Omega_{22} - \Omega_{21}\Omega_{11}^{-1}\Omega_{12}.$$

This confirms the formula for the *MSE* of a linear projection derived earlier (equation [4.1.15]).

The third equation in [4.5.7] states that

$$\Omega_{31}\Omega_{11}^{-1}\tilde{Y}_1 + h_{32}h_{22}^{-1}\tilde{Y}_2 + \tilde{Y}_3 = Y_3.$$

Substituting in from [4.5.8] and [4.5.9] and rearranging,

$$\tilde{Y}_3 = Y_3 - \Omega_{31}\Omega_{11}^{-1}Y_1 - h_{32}h_{22}^{-1}(Y_2 - \Omega_{21}\Omega_{11}^{-1}Y_1). \qquad [4.5.11]$$

Thus $\tilde{Y}_3$ is the residual from subtracting a particular linear combination of $Y_1$ and $Y_2$ from $Y_3$. From [4.5.5], this residual is uncorrelated with either $\tilde{Y}_1$ or $\tilde{Y}_2$:

$$E[Y_3 - \Omega_{31}\Omega_{11}^{-1}Y_1 - h_{32}h_{22}^{-1}(Y_2 - \Omega_{21}\Omega_{11}^{-1}Y_1)]\tilde{Y}_j = 0 \qquad \text{for } j = 1 \text{ or } 2.$$

Thus this residual is uncorrelated with either $Y_1$ or $Y_2$, meaning that $\tilde{Y}_3$ has the interpretation as the residual from a linear projection of $Y_3$ on $Y_1$ and $Y_2$. According to [4.5.11], the linear projection is given by

$$\hat{P}(Y_3|Y_2,Y_1) = \Omega_{31}\Omega_{11}^{-1}Y_1 + h_{32}h_{22}^{-1}(Y_2 - \Omega_{21}\Omega_{11}^{-1}Y_1). \qquad [4.5.12]$$

The *MSE* of the linear projection is the variance of $\tilde{Y}_3$, which from [4.5.5] is given by $d_{33}$:

$$E[Y_3 - \hat{P}(Y_3|Y_2,Y_1)]^2 = h_{33} - h_{32}h_{22}^{-1}h_{23}. \qquad [4.5.13]$$

Expression [4.5.12] gives a convenient formula for updating a linear projection. Suppose we are interested in forecasting the value of $Y_3$. Let $Y_1$ be some initial information on which this forecast might be based. A forecast of $Y_3$ on the basis of $Y_1$ alone takes the form

$$\hat{P}(Y_3|Y_1) = \Omega_{31}\Omega_{11}^{-1}Y_1.$$

Let $Y_2$ represent some new information with which we could update this forecast. If we were asked to guess the magnitude of this second variable on the basis of $Y_1$ alone, the answer would be

$$\hat{P}(Y_2|Y_1) = \Omega_{21}\Omega_{11}^{-1}Y_1.$$

Equation [4.5.12] states that

$$\hat{P}(Y_3|Y_2,Y_1) = \hat{P}(Y_3|Y_1) + h_{32}h_{22}^{-1}[Y_2 - \hat{P}(Y_2|Y_1)]. \quad [4.5.14]$$

We can thus optimally update the initial forecast $\hat{P}(Y_3|Y_1)$ by adding to it a multiple $(h_{32}h_{22}^{-1})$ of the unanticipated component of the new information $[Y_2 - \hat{P}(Y_2|Y_1)]$. This multiple $(h_{32}h_{22}^{-1})$ can also be interpreted as the coefficient on $Y_2$ in a linear projection of $Y_3$ on $Y_2$ and $Y_1$.

To understand the nature of the multiplier $(h_{32}h_{22}^{-1})$, define the $(n \times 1)$ vector $\tilde{\mathbf{Y}}(1)$ by

$$\tilde{\mathbf{Y}}(1) \equiv \mathbf{E}_1\mathbf{Y}, \quad [4.5.15]$$

where $\mathbf{E}_1$ is the matrix given in [4.4.3]. Notice that the second-moment matrix of $\tilde{\mathbf{Y}}(1)$ is given by

$$E\{\tilde{\mathbf{Y}}(1)[\tilde{\mathbf{Y}}(1)]'\} = E\{\mathbf{E}_1\mathbf{Y}\mathbf{Y}'\mathbf{E}_1'\} = \mathbf{E}_1\boldsymbol{\Omega}\mathbf{E}_1'.$$

But from [4.4.4] this is just the matrix $\mathbf{H}$. Thus $\mathbf{H}$ has the interpretation as the second-moment matrix of $\tilde{\mathbf{Y}}(1)$. Substituting [4.4.3] into [4.5.15],

$$\tilde{\mathbf{Y}}(1) = \begin{bmatrix} Y_1 \\ Y_2 - \Omega_{21}\Omega_{11}^{-1}Y_1 \\ Y_3 - \Omega_{31}\Omega_{11}^{-1}Y_1 \\ \vdots \\ Y_n - \Omega_{n1}\Omega_{11}^{-1}Y_1 \end{bmatrix}.$$

The first element of $\tilde{\mathbf{Y}}(1)$ is thus just $Y_1$ itself, while the $i$th element of $\tilde{\mathbf{Y}}(1)$ for $i = 2, 3, \ldots, n$ is the residual from a projection of $Y_i$ on $Y_1$. The matrix $\mathbf{H}$ is thus the second-moment matrix of the residuals from projections of each of the variables on $Y_1$. In particular, $h_{22}$ is the *MSE* from a projection of $Y_2$ on $Y_1$:

$$h_{22} = E[Y_2 - \hat{P}(Y_2|Y_1)]^2,$$

while $h_{32}$ is the expected product of this error with the error from a projection of $Y_3$ on $Y_1$:

$$h_{32} = E\{[Y_3 - \hat{P}(Y_3|Y_1)][Y_2 - \hat{P}(Y_2|Y_1)]\}.$$

Thus equation [4.5.14] states that a linear projection can be updated using the following formula:

$$\begin{aligned} \hat{P}(Y_3|Y_2,Y_1) = \hat{P}(Y_3|Y_1) & \\ + \{E[Y_3 - \hat{P}(Y_3|Y_1)][Y_2 - \hat{P}(Y_2|Y_1)]\} & \quad [4.5.16] \\ \times \{E[Y_2 - \hat{P}(Y_2|Y_1)]^2\}^{-1} \times [Y_2 - \hat{P}(Y_2|Y_1)]. & \end{aligned}$$

For example, suppose that $Y_1$ is a constant term, so that $\hat{P}(Y_2|Y_1)$ is just $\mu_2$, the mean of $Y_2$, while $\hat{P}(Y_3|Y_1) = \mu_3$. Equation [4.5.16] then states that

$$\hat{P}(Y_3|Y_2,1) = \mu_3 + \text{Cov}(Y_3, Y_2)\cdot[\text{Var}(Y_2)]^{-1}\cdot(Y_2 - \mu_2).$$

The *MSE* associated with this updated linear projection can also be calculated from the triangular factorization. From [4.5.5], the *MSE* from a linear projection of $Y_3$ on $Y_2$ and $Y_1$ can be calculated from

$$\begin{aligned} E[Y_3 - \hat{P}(Y_3|Y_2,Y_1)]^2 &= E(\tilde{Y}_3^2) \\ &= d_{33} \\ &= h_{33} - h_{32}h_{22}^{-1}h_{23}. \end{aligned}$$

In general, for $i > 2$, the coefficient on $Y_2$ in a linear projection of $Y_i$ on $Y_2$ and $Y_1$ is given by the $i$th element of the second column of the matrix $\mathbf{A}$. For any $i > j$, the coefficients on $Y_j$ in a linear projection of $Y_i$ on $Y_j, Y_{j-1}, \ldots, Y_1$ is given by the row $i$, column $j$ element of $\mathbf{A}$. The magnitude $d_{ii}$ gives the *MSE* for a linear projection of $Y_i$ on $Y_{i-1}, Y_{i-2}, \ldots, Y_1$.

### *Application: Exact Finite-Sample Forecasts for an* MA*(1) Process*

As an example of applying these results, suppose that $Y_t$ follows an $MA(1)$ process:

$$Y_t = \mu + \varepsilon_t + \theta\varepsilon_{t-1},$$

where $\varepsilon_t$ is a white noise process with variance $\sigma^2$ and $\theta$ is unrestricted. Suppose we want to forecast the value of $Y_n$ on the basis of the previous $n - 1$ values ($Y_1, Y_2, \ldots, Y_{n-1}$). Let

$$\mathbf{Y}' \equiv [(Y_1 - \mu) \quad (Y_2 - \mu) \quad \cdots \quad (Y_{n-1} - \mu) \quad (Y_n - \mu)],$$

and let $\mathbf{\Omega}$ denote the $(n \times n)$ variance-covariance matrix of $\mathbf{Y}$:

$$\mathbf{\Omega} = E(\mathbf{YY}') = \sigma^2 \begin{bmatrix} 1+\theta^2 & \theta & 0 & \cdots & 0 \\ \theta & 1+\theta^2 & \theta & \cdots & 0 \\ 0 & \theta & 1+\theta^2 & \cdots & 0 \\ \vdots & \vdots & \vdots & \cdots & \vdots \\ 0 & 0 & 0 & \cdots & 1+\theta^2 \end{bmatrix}. \qquad [4.5.17]$$

Appendix 4.B to this chapter shows that the triangular factorization of $\mathbf{\Omega}$ is

$$\mathbf{A} = \qquad [4.5.18]$$

$$\begin{bmatrix} 1 & 0 & 0 & \cdots & 0 & 0 \\ \dfrac{\theta}{1+\theta^2} & 1 & 0 & \cdots & 0 & 0 \\ 0 & \dfrac{\theta(1+\theta^2)}{1+\theta^2+\theta^4} & 1 & \cdots & 0 & 0 \\ \vdots & \vdots & \vdots & \cdots & \vdots & \vdots \\ 0 & 0 & 0 & \cdots & \dfrac{\theta[1+\theta^2+\theta^4+\cdots+\theta^{2(n-2)}]}{1+\theta^2+\theta^4+\cdots+\theta^{2(n-1)}} & 1 \end{bmatrix}$$

$$\mathbf{D} = \sigma^2 \begin{bmatrix} 1+\theta^2 & 0 & 0 & \cdots & 0 \\ 0 & \dfrac{1+\theta^2+\theta^4}{1+\theta^2} & 0 & \cdots & 0 \\ 0 & 0 & \dfrac{1+\theta^2+\theta^4+\theta^6}{1+\theta^2+\theta^4} & \cdots & 0 \\ \vdots & \vdots & \vdots & \cdots & \vdots \\ 0 & 0 & 0 & \cdots & \dfrac{1+\theta^2+\theta^4+\cdots+\theta^{2n}}{1+\theta^2+\theta^4+\cdots+\theta^{2(n-1)}} \end{bmatrix}. \qquad [4.5.19]$$

To use the triangular factorization to calculate exact finite-sample forecasts, recall that $\tilde{Y}_i$, the $i$th element of $\tilde{\mathbf{Y}} = \mathbf{A}^{-1}\mathbf{Y}$, has the interpretation as the residual from a linear projection of $Y_i$ on a constant and its previous values:

$$\tilde{Y}_i = Y_i - \hat{E}(Y_i|Y_{i-1}, Y_{i-2}, \ldots, Y_1).$$

The system of equations $\mathbf{A}\tilde{\mathbf{Y}} = \mathbf{Y}$ can be written out explicitly as

$$\begin{aligned} \tilde{Y}_1 &= Y_1 - \mu \\ \frac{\theta}{1+\theta^2}\tilde{Y}_1 + \tilde{Y}_2 &= Y_2 - \mu \\ \frac{\theta(1+\theta^2)}{1+\theta^2+\theta^4}\tilde{Y}_2 + \tilde{Y}_3 &= Y_3 - \mu \\ &\vdots \\ \frac{\theta[1+\theta^2+\theta^4+\cdots+\theta^{2(n-2)}]}{1+\theta^2+\theta^4+\cdots+\theta^{2(n-1)}}\tilde{Y}_{n-1} + \tilde{Y}_n &= Y_n - \mu. \end{aligned}$$

Solving the last equation for $\tilde{Y}_n$,

$$\begin{aligned} Y_n - \hat{E}(Y_n|Y_{n-1}, Y_{n-2}, \ldots, Y_1) &= Y_n - \mu \\ &\quad - \frac{\theta[1+\theta^2+\theta^4+\cdots+\theta^{2(n-2)}]}{1+\theta^2+\theta^4+\cdots+\theta^{2(n-1)}}[Y_{n-1} - \hat{E}(Y_{n-1}|Y_{n-2}, Y_{n-3}, \ldots, Y_1)], \end{aligned}$$

implying

$$\begin{aligned} \hat{E}(Y_n|Y_{n-1}, Y_{n-2}, \ldots, Y_1) &= \mu \\ &\quad + \frac{\theta[1+\theta^2+\theta^4+\cdots+\theta^{2(n-2)}]}{1+\theta^2+\theta^4+\cdots+\theta^{2(n-1)}}[Y_{n-1} - \hat{E}(Y_{n-1}|Y_{n-2}, Y_{n-3}, \ldots, Y_1)]. \end{aligned} \qquad [4.5.20]$$

The *MSE* of this forecast is given by $d_{nn}$:

$$MSE[\hat{E}(Y_n|Y_{n-1}, Y_{n-2}, \ldots, Y_1)] = \sigma^2 \frac{1+\theta^2+\theta^4+\cdots+\theta^{2n}}{1+\theta^2+\theta^4+\cdots+\theta^{2(n-1)}}. \qquad [4.5.21]$$

It is interesting to note the behavior of this optimal forecast as the number of observations ($n$) becomes large. First, suppose that the moving average representation is invertible ($|\theta| < 1$). In this case, as $n \to \infty$, the coefficient in [4.5.20] tends to $\theta$:

$$\frac{\theta[1+\theta^2+\theta^4+\cdots+\theta^{2(n-2)}]}{1+\theta^2+\theta^4+\cdots+\theta^{2(n-1)}} \to \theta,$$

while the *MSE* [4.5.21] tends to $\sigma^2$, the variance of the fundamental innovation. Thus the optimal forecast for a finite number of observations [4.5.20] eventually tends toward the forecast rule used for an infinite number of observations [4.2.32].

Alternatively, the calculations that produced [4.5.20] are equally valid for a noninvertible representation with $|\theta| > 1$. In this case the coefficient in [4.5.20] tends toward $\theta^{-1}$:

$$\begin{aligned}\frac{\theta[1 + \theta^2 + \theta^4 + \cdots + \theta^{2(n-2)}]}{1 + \theta^2 + \theta^4 + \cdots + \theta^{2(n-1)}} &= \frac{\theta[1 - \theta^{2(n-1)}]/(1 - \theta^2)}{(1 - \theta^{2n})/(1 - \theta^2)} \\ &= \frac{\theta(\theta^{-2n} - \theta^{-2})}{\theta^{-2n} - 1} \\ &\to \frac{\theta(-\theta^{-2})}{-1} \\ &= \theta^{-1}.\end{aligned}$$

Thus, the coefficient in [4.5.20] tends to $\theta^{-1}$ in this case, which is the moving average coefficient associated with the invertible representation. The *MSE* [4.5.21] tends to $\sigma^2\theta^2$:

$$\sigma^2 \frac{[1 - \theta^{2(n+1)}]/(1 - \theta^2)}{(1 - \theta^{2n})/(1 - \theta^2)} \to \sigma^2\theta^2,$$

which will be recognized from [3.7.7] as the variance of the innovation associated with the fundamental representation.

This observation explains the use of the expression "fundamental" in this context. The fundamental innovation $\varepsilon_t$ has the property that

$$Y_t - \hat{E}(Y_t|Y_{t-1}, Y_{t-2}, \ldots, Y_{t-m}) \overset{m.s.}{\to} \varepsilon_t \qquad [4.5.22]$$

as $m \to \infty$ where $\overset{m.s.}{\to}$ denotes mean square convergence. Thus when $|\theta| > 1$, the coefficient $\theta$ in the approximation in [4.3.3] should be replaced by $\theta^{-1}$. When this is done, expression [4.3.3] will approach the correct forecast as $m \to \infty$.

It is also instructive to consider the borderline case $\theta = 1$. The optimal finite-sample forecast for an $MA(1)$ process with $\theta = 1$ is seen from [4.5.20] to be given by

$$\hat{E}(Y_n|Y_{n-1}, Y_{n-2}, \ldots, Y_1) = \mu + \frac{n-1}{n}[Y_{n-1} - \hat{E}(Y_{n-1}|Y_{n-2}, Y_{n-3}, \ldots, Y_1)],$$

which, after recursive substitution, becomes

$$\begin{aligned}&\hat{E}(Y_n|Y_{n-1}, Y_{n-2}, \ldots, Y_1) \\ &\quad = \mu + \frac{n-1}{n}(Y_{n-1} - \mu) - \frac{n-2}{n}(Y_{n-2} - \mu) \\ &\quad\quad + \frac{n-3}{n}(Y_{n-3} - \mu) - \cdots + (-1)^n \frac{1}{n}(Y_1 - \mu).\end{aligned} \qquad [4.5.23]$$

The *MSE* of this forecast is given by [4.5.21]:

$$\sigma^2(n + 1)/n \to \sigma^2.$$

Thus the variance of the forecast error again tends toward that of $\varepsilon_t$. Hence the innovation $\varepsilon_t$ is again fundamental for this case in the sense of [4.5.22]. Note the contrast between the optimal forecast [4.5.23] and a forecast based on a naive application of [4.3.3],

$$\begin{aligned}&\mu + (Y_{n-1} - \mu) - (Y_{n-2} - \mu) + (Y_{n-3} - \mu) \\ &\qquad - \cdots + (-1)^n(Y_1 - \mu).\end{aligned} \qquad [4.5.24]$$

The approximation [4.3.3] was derived under the assumption that the moving average representation was invertible, and the borderline case $\theta = 1$ is not invertible. For this reason [4.5.24] does not converge to the optimal forecast [4.5.23] as $n$ grows large. When $\theta = 1$, $Y_t = \mu + \varepsilon_t + \varepsilon_{t-1}$ and [4.5.24] can be written as

$$\mu + (\varepsilon_{n-1} + \varepsilon_{n-2}) - (\varepsilon_{n-2} + \varepsilon_{n-3}) + (\varepsilon_{n-3} + \varepsilon_{n-4}) - \cdots + (-1)^n(\varepsilon_1 + \varepsilon_0) = \mu + \varepsilon_{n-1} + (-1)^n\varepsilon_0.$$

The difference between this and $Y_n$, the value being forecast, is $\varepsilon_n - (-1)^n\varepsilon_0$, which has *MSE* $2\sigma^2$ for all $n$. Thus, whereas [4.5.23] converges to the optimal forecast as $n \to \infty$, [4.5.24] does not.

## *Block Triangular Factorization*

Suppose we have observations on two sets of variables. The first set of variables is collected in an $(n_1 \times 1)$ vector $\mathbf{Y}_1$ and the second set in an $(n_2 \times 1)$ vector $\mathbf{Y}_2$. Their second-moment matrix can be written in partitioned form as

$$\mathbf{\Omega} \equiv \begin{bmatrix} E(\mathbf{Y}_1\mathbf{Y}_1') & E(\mathbf{Y}_1\mathbf{Y}_2') \\ E(\mathbf{Y}_2\mathbf{Y}_1') & E(\mathbf{Y}_2\mathbf{Y}_2') \end{bmatrix} = \begin{bmatrix} \mathbf{\Omega}_{11} & \mathbf{\Omega}_{12} \\ \mathbf{\Omega}_{21} & \mathbf{\Omega}_{22} \end{bmatrix},$$

where $\mathbf{\Omega}_{11}$ is an $(n_1 \times n_1)$ matrix, $\mathbf{\Omega}_{22}$ is an $(n_2 \times n_2)$ matrix, and the $(n_1 \times n_2)$ matrix $\mathbf{\Omega}_{12}$ is the transpose of the $(n_2 \times n_1)$ matrix $\mathbf{\Omega}_{21}$.

We can put zeros in the lower left $(n_2 \times n_1)$ block of $\mathbf{\Omega}$ by premultiplying $\mathbf{\Omega}$ by the following matrix:

$$\overline{\mathbf{E}}_1 = \begin{bmatrix} \mathbf{I}_{n_1} & \mathbf{0} \\ -\mathbf{\Omega}_{21}\mathbf{\Omega}_{11}^{-1} & \mathbf{I}_{n_2} \end{bmatrix}.$$

If $\mathbf{\Omega}$ is premultiplied by $\overline{\mathbf{E}}_1$ and postmultiplied by $\overline{\mathbf{E}}_1'$, the result is

$$\begin{bmatrix} \mathbf{I}_{n_1} & \mathbf{0} \\ -\mathbf{\Omega}_{21}\mathbf{\Omega}_{11}^{-1} & \mathbf{I}_{n_2} \end{bmatrix} \begin{bmatrix} \mathbf{\Omega}_{11} & \mathbf{\Omega}_{12} \\ \mathbf{\Omega}_{21} & \mathbf{\Omega}_{22} \end{bmatrix} \begin{bmatrix} \mathbf{I}_{n_1} & -\mathbf{\Omega}_{11}^{-1}\mathbf{\Omega}_{12} \\ \mathbf{0} & \mathbf{I}_{n_2} \end{bmatrix} = \begin{bmatrix} \mathbf{\Omega}_{11} & \mathbf{0} \\ \mathbf{0} & \mathbf{\Omega}_{22} - \mathbf{\Omega}_{21}\mathbf{\Omega}_{11}^{-1}\mathbf{\Omega}_{12} \end{bmatrix}. \qquad [4.5.25]$$

Define

$$\overline{\mathbf{A}} \equiv \overline{\mathbf{E}}_1^{-1} = \begin{bmatrix} \mathbf{I}_{n_1} & \mathbf{0} \\ \mathbf{\Omega}_{21}\mathbf{\Omega}_{11}^{-1} & \mathbf{I}_{n_2} \end{bmatrix}.$$

If [4.5.25] is premultiplied by $\overline{\mathbf{A}}$ and postmultiplied by $\overline{\mathbf{A}}'$, the result is

$$\begin{aligned} \begin{bmatrix} \mathbf{\Omega}_{11} & \mathbf{\Omega}_{12} \\ \mathbf{\Omega}_{21} & \mathbf{\Omega}_{22} \end{bmatrix} &= \begin{bmatrix} \mathbf{I}_{n_1} & \mathbf{0} \\ \mathbf{\Omega}_{21}\mathbf{\Omega}_{11}^{-1} & \mathbf{I}_{n_2} \end{bmatrix} \\ &\quad \times \begin{bmatrix} \mathbf{\Omega}_{11} & \mathbf{0} \\ \mathbf{0} & \mathbf{\Omega}_{22} - \mathbf{\Omega}_{21}\mathbf{\Omega}_{11}^{-1}\mathbf{\Omega}_{12} \end{bmatrix} \begin{bmatrix} \mathbf{I}_{n_1} & \mathbf{\Omega}_{11}^{-1}\mathbf{\Omega}_{12} \\ \mathbf{0} & \mathbf{I}_{n_2} \end{bmatrix} \\ &= \overline{\mathbf{A}}\overline{\mathbf{D}}\overline{\mathbf{A}}'. \end{aligned} \qquad [4.5.26]$$

This is similar to the triangular factorization $\mathbf{\Omega} = \mathbf{ADA}'$, except that $\overline{\mathbf{D}}$ is a block-diagonal matrix rather than a truly diagonal matrix:

$$\overline{\mathbf{D}} = \begin{bmatrix} \mathbf{\Omega}_{11} & \mathbf{0} \\ \mathbf{0} & \mathbf{\Omega}_{22} - \mathbf{\Omega}_{21}\mathbf{\Omega}_{11}^{-1}\mathbf{\Omega}_{12} \end{bmatrix}.$$

As in the earlier case, $\bar{\mathbf{D}}$ can be interpreted as the second-moment matrix of the vector $\tilde{\mathbf{Y}} = \bar{\mathbf{A}}^{-1}\mathbf{Y}$,

$$\begin{bmatrix} \tilde{\mathbf{Y}}_1 \\ \tilde{\mathbf{Y}}_2 \end{bmatrix} = \begin{bmatrix} \mathbf{I}_{n_1} & \mathbf{0} \\ -\mathbf{\Omega}_{21}\mathbf{\Omega}_{11}^{-1} & \mathbf{I}_{n_2} \end{bmatrix} \begin{bmatrix} \mathbf{Y}_1 \\ \mathbf{Y}_2 \end{bmatrix};$$

that is, $\tilde{\mathbf{Y}}_1 = \mathbf{Y}_1$ and $\tilde{\mathbf{Y}}_2 = \mathbf{Y}_2 - \mathbf{\Omega}_{21}\mathbf{\Omega}_{11}^{-1}\mathbf{Y}_1$. The $i$th element of $\tilde{\mathbf{Y}}_2$ is given by $Y_{2i}$ minus a linear combination of the elements of $\mathbf{Y}_1$. The block-diagonality of $\bar{\mathbf{D}}$ implies that the product of any element of $\tilde{\mathbf{Y}}_2$ with any element of $\mathbf{Y}_1$ has expectation zero. Thus $\mathbf{\Omega}_{21}\mathbf{\Omega}_{11}^{-1}$ gives the matrix of coefficients associated with the linear projection of the vector $\mathbf{Y}_2$ on the vector $\mathbf{Y}_1$,

$$\hat{P}(\mathbf{Y}_2|\mathbf{Y}_1) = \mathbf{\Omega}_{21}\mathbf{\Omega}_{11}^{-1}\mathbf{Y}_1, \tag{4.5.27}$$

as claimed in [4.1.23]. The *MSE* matrix associated with this linear projection is

$$\begin{aligned} E\{[\mathbf{Y}_2 - \hat{P}(\mathbf{Y}_2|\mathbf{Y}_1)][\mathbf{Y}_2 - \hat{P}(\mathbf{Y}_2|\mathbf{Y}_1)]'\} &= E(\tilde{\mathbf{Y}}_2\tilde{\mathbf{Y}}_2') \\ &= \bar{\mathbf{D}}_{22} \\ &= \mathbf{\Omega}_{22} - \mathbf{\Omega}_{21}\mathbf{\Omega}_{11}^{-1}\mathbf{\Omega}_{12}, \end{aligned} \tag{4.5.28}$$

as claimed in [4.1.24].

The calculations for a $(3 \times 3)$ matrix similarly extend to a $(3 \times 3)$ block matrix without complications. Let $\mathbf{Y}_1$, $\mathbf{Y}_2$, and $\mathbf{Y}_3$ be $(n_1 \times 1)$, $(n_2 \times 1)$, and $(n_3 \times 1)$ vectors. A block-triangular factorization of their second-moment matrix is obtained from a simple generalization of equation [4.4.13]:

$$\begin{aligned} \begin{bmatrix} \mathbf{\Omega}_{11} & \mathbf{\Omega}_{12} & \mathbf{\Omega}_{13} \\ \mathbf{\Omega}_{21} & \mathbf{\Omega}_{22} & \mathbf{\Omega}_{23} \\ \mathbf{\Omega}_{31} & \mathbf{\Omega}_{32} & \mathbf{\Omega}_{33} \end{bmatrix} &= \begin{bmatrix} \mathbf{I}_{n_1} & \mathbf{0} & \mathbf{0} \\ \mathbf{\Omega}_{21}\mathbf{\Omega}_{11}^{-1} & \mathbf{I}_{n_2} & \mathbf{0} \\ \mathbf{\Omega}_{31}\mathbf{\Omega}_{11}^{-1} & \mathbf{H}_{32}\mathbf{H}_{22}^{-1} & \mathbf{I}_{n_3} \end{bmatrix} \\ &\times \begin{bmatrix} \mathbf{\Omega}_{11} & \mathbf{0} & \mathbf{0} \\ \mathbf{0} & \mathbf{H}_{22} & \mathbf{0} \\ \mathbf{0} & \mathbf{0} & \mathbf{H}_{33} - \mathbf{H}_{32}\mathbf{H}_{22}^{-1}\mathbf{H}_{23} \end{bmatrix} \begin{bmatrix} \mathbf{I}_{n_1} & \mathbf{\Omega}_{11}^{-1}\mathbf{\Omega}_{12} & \mathbf{\Omega}_{11}^{-1}\mathbf{\Omega}_{13} \\ \mathbf{0} & \mathbf{I}_{n_2} & \mathbf{H}_{22}^{-1}\mathbf{H}_{23} \\ \mathbf{0} & \mathbf{0} & \mathbf{I}_{n_3} \end{bmatrix} \end{aligned} \tag{4.5.29}$$

where $\mathbf{H}_{22} = (\mathbf{\Omega}_{22} - \mathbf{\Omega}_{21}\mathbf{\Omega}_{11}^{-1}\mathbf{\Omega}_{12})$, $\mathbf{H}_{33} = (\mathbf{\Omega}_{33} - \mathbf{\Omega}_{31}\mathbf{\Omega}_{11}^{-1}\mathbf{\Omega}_{13})$, and $\mathbf{H}_{23} = \mathbf{H}_{32}' = (\mathbf{\Omega}_{23} - \mathbf{\Omega}_{21}\mathbf{\Omega}_{11}^{-1}\mathbf{\Omega}_{13})$.

This allows us to generalize the earlier result [4.5.12] on updating a linear projection. The optimal forecast of $\mathbf{Y}_3$ conditional on $\mathbf{Y}_2$ and $\mathbf{Y}_1$ can be read off the last block row of $\bar{\mathbf{A}}$:

$$\begin{aligned} \hat{P}(\mathbf{Y}_3|\mathbf{Y}_2,\mathbf{Y}_1) &= \mathbf{\Omega}_{31}\mathbf{\Omega}_{11}^{-1}\mathbf{Y}_1 + \mathbf{H}_{32}\mathbf{H}_{22}^{-1}(\mathbf{Y}_2 - \mathbf{\Omega}_{21}\mathbf{\Omega}_{11}^{-1}\mathbf{Y}_1) \\ &= \hat{P}(\mathbf{Y}_3|\mathbf{Y}_1) + \mathbf{H}_{32}\mathbf{H}_{22}^{-1}[\mathbf{Y}_2 - \hat{P}(\mathbf{Y}_2|\mathbf{Y}_1)], \end{aligned} \tag{4.5.30}$$

where

$$\begin{aligned} \mathbf{H}_{22} &= E\{[\mathbf{Y}_2 - \hat{P}(\mathbf{Y}_2|\mathbf{Y}_1)][\mathbf{Y}_2 - \hat{P}(\mathbf{Y}_2|\mathbf{Y}_1)]'\} \\ \mathbf{H}_{32} &= E\{[\mathbf{Y}_3 - \hat{P}(\mathbf{Y}_3|\mathbf{Y}_1)][\mathbf{Y}_2 - \hat{P}(\mathbf{Y}_2|\mathbf{Y}_1)]'\}. \end{aligned}$$

The *MSE* of this forecast is the matrix generalization of [4.5.13],

$$E\{[\mathbf{Y}_3 - \hat{P}(\mathbf{Y}_3|\mathbf{Y}_2,\mathbf{Y}_1)][\mathbf{Y}_3 - \hat{P}(\mathbf{Y}_3|\mathbf{Y}_2,\mathbf{Y}_1)]'\} = \mathbf{H}_{33} - \mathbf{H}_{32}\mathbf{H}_{22}^{-1}\mathbf{H}_{23}, \tag{4.5.31}$$

where

$$\mathbf{H}_{33} = E\{[\mathbf{Y}_3 - \hat{P}(\mathbf{Y}_3|\mathbf{Y}_1)][\mathbf{Y}_3 - \hat{P}(\mathbf{Y}_3|\mathbf{Y}_1)]'\}.$$

### *Law of Iterated Projections*

Another useful result, the law of iterated projections, can be inferred immediately from [4.5.30]. What happens if the projection $\hat{P}(\mathbf{Y}_3|\mathbf{Y}_2,\mathbf{Y}_1)$ is itself projected on $\mathbf{Y}_1$? The *law of iterated projections* says that this projection is equal to the simple projection of $\mathbf{Y}_3$ on $\mathbf{Y}_1$:

$$\hat{P}[\hat{P}(\mathbf{Y}_3|\mathbf{Y}_2,\mathbf{Y}_1)|\mathbf{Y}_1] = \hat{P}(\mathbf{Y}_3|\mathbf{Y}_1). \tag{4.5.32}$$

To verify this claim, we need to show that the difference between $\hat{P}(\mathbf{Y}_3|\mathbf{Y}_2,\mathbf{Y}_1)$ and $\hat{P}(\mathbf{Y}_3|\mathbf{Y}_1)$ is uncorrelated with $\mathbf{Y}_1$. But from [4.5.30], this difference is given by

$$\hat{P}(\mathbf{Y}_3|\mathbf{Y}_2,\mathbf{Y}_1) - \hat{P}(\mathbf{Y}_3|\mathbf{Y}_1) = \mathbf{H}_{32}\mathbf{H}_{22}^{-1}[\mathbf{Y}_2 - \hat{P}(\mathbf{Y}_2|\mathbf{Y}_1)],$$

which indeed is uncorrelated with $\mathbf{Y}_1$ by the definition of the linear projection $\hat{P}(\mathbf{Y}_2|\mathbf{Y}_1)$.

## 4.6. *Optimal Forecasts for Gaussian Processes*

The forecasting rules developed in this chapter are optimal within the class of linear functions of the variables on which the forecast is based. For Gaussian processes, we can make the stronger claim that as long as a constant term is included among the variables on which the forecast is based, the optimal unrestricted forecast turns out to have a linear form and thus is given by the linear projection.

To verify this, let $\mathbf{Y}_1$ be an $(n_1 \times 1)$ vector with mean $\boldsymbol{\mu}_1$, and $\mathbf{Y}_2$ an $(n_2 \times 1)$ vector with mean $\boldsymbol{\mu}_2$, where the variance-covariance matrix is given by

$$\begin{bmatrix} E(\mathbf{Y}_1 - \boldsymbol{\mu}_1)(\mathbf{Y}_1 - \boldsymbol{\mu}_1)' & E(\mathbf{Y}_1 - \boldsymbol{\mu}_1)(\mathbf{Y}_2 - \boldsymbol{\mu}_2)' \\ E(\mathbf{Y}_2 - \boldsymbol{\mu}_2)(\mathbf{Y}_1 - \boldsymbol{\mu}_1)' & E(\mathbf{Y}_2 - \boldsymbol{\mu}_2)(\mathbf{Y}_2 - \boldsymbol{\mu}_2)' \end{bmatrix} = \begin{bmatrix} \boldsymbol{\Omega}_{11} & \boldsymbol{\Omega}_{12} \\ \boldsymbol{\Omega}_{21} & \boldsymbol{\Omega}_{22} \end{bmatrix}.$$

If $\mathbf{Y}_1$ and $\mathbf{Y}_2$ are Gaussian, then the joint probability density is

$$f_{\mathbf{Y}_1,\mathbf{Y}_2}(\mathbf{y}_1, \mathbf{y}_2) = \frac{1}{(2\pi)^{(n_1+n_2)/2}} \begin{vmatrix} \boldsymbol{\Omega}_{11} & \boldsymbol{\Omega}_{12} \\ \boldsymbol{\Omega}_{21} & \boldsymbol{\Omega}_{22} \end{vmatrix}^{-1/2} \times \exp\left\{ -\frac{1}{2}[(\mathbf{y}_1 - \boldsymbol{\mu}_1)' \; (\mathbf{y}_2 - \boldsymbol{\mu}_2)'] \begin{bmatrix} \boldsymbol{\Omega}_{11} & \boldsymbol{\Omega}_{12} \\ \boldsymbol{\Omega}_{21} & \boldsymbol{\Omega}_{22} \end{bmatrix}^{-1} \begin{bmatrix} \mathbf{y}_1 - \boldsymbol{\mu}_1 \\ \mathbf{y}_2 - \boldsymbol{\mu}_2 \end{bmatrix} \right\}. \tag{4.6.1}$$

The inverse of $\boldsymbol{\Omega}$ is readily found by inverting [4.5.26]:

$$\begin{aligned} \boldsymbol{\Omega}^{-1} &= [\bar{\mathbf{A}}\bar{\mathbf{D}}\bar{\mathbf{A}}']^{-1} \\ &= [\bar{\mathbf{A}}']^{-1}\bar{\mathbf{D}}^{-1}\bar{\mathbf{A}}^{-1} \\ &= \begin{bmatrix} \mathbf{I}_{n_1} & -\boldsymbol{\Omega}_{11}^{-1}\boldsymbol{\Omega}_{12} \\ \mathbf{0} & \mathbf{I}_{n_2} \end{bmatrix} \begin{bmatrix} \boldsymbol{\Omega}_{11}^{-1} & \mathbf{0} \\ \mathbf{0} & (\boldsymbol{\Omega}_{22} - \boldsymbol{\Omega}_{21}\boldsymbol{\Omega}_{11}^{-1}\boldsymbol{\Omega}_{12})^{-1} \end{bmatrix} \\ &\quad \times \begin{bmatrix} \mathbf{I}_{n_1} & \mathbf{0} \\ -\boldsymbol{\Omega}_{21}\boldsymbol{\Omega}_{11}^{-1} & \mathbf{I}_{n_2} \end{bmatrix}. \end{aligned} \tag{4.6.2}$$

Likewise, the determinant of $\boldsymbol{\Omega}$ can be found by taking the determinant of [4.5.26]:

$$|\boldsymbol{\Omega}| = |\bar{\mathbf{A}}| \cdot |\bar{\mathbf{D}}| \cdot |\bar{\mathbf{A}}'|.$$

But $\bar{\mathbf{A}}$ is a lower triangular matrix. Its determinant is therefore given by the product of terms along the principal diagonal, all of which are unity. Hence $|\bar{\mathbf{A}}| = 1$ and $|\boldsymbol{\Omega}| = |\bar{\mathbf{D}}|$:[5]

$$\begin{vmatrix} \boldsymbol{\Omega}_{11} & \boldsymbol{\Omega}_{12} \\ \boldsymbol{\Omega}_{21} & \boldsymbol{\Omega}_{22} \end{vmatrix} = \begin{vmatrix} \boldsymbol{\Omega}_{11} & \mathbf{0} \\ \mathbf{0} & \boldsymbol{\Omega}_{22} - \boldsymbol{\Omega}_{21}\boldsymbol{\Omega}_{11}^{-1}\boldsymbol{\Omega}_{12} \end{vmatrix} = |\boldsymbol{\Omega}_{11}| \cdot |\boldsymbol{\Omega}_{22} - \boldsymbol{\Omega}_{21}\boldsymbol{\Omega}_{11}^{-1}\boldsymbol{\Omega}_{12}|. \qquad [4.6.3]$$

Substituting [4.6.2] and [4.6.3] into [4.6.1], the joint density can be written

$$\begin{aligned} & f_{\mathbf{Y}_1,\mathbf{Y}_2}(\mathbf{y}_1, \mathbf{y}_2) \\ &= \frac{1}{(2\pi)^{(n_1+n_2)/2}} |\boldsymbol{\Omega}_{11}|^{-1/2} \cdot |\boldsymbol{\Omega}_{22} - \boldsymbol{\Omega}_{21}\boldsymbol{\Omega}_{11}^{-1}\boldsymbol{\Omega}_{12}|^{-1/2} \\ &\quad \times \exp\left\{ -\frac{1}{2} [(\mathbf{y}_1 - \boldsymbol{\mu}_1)' \ (\mathbf{y}_2 - \boldsymbol{\mu}_2)'] \begin{bmatrix} \mathbf{I}_{n_1} & -\boldsymbol{\Omega}_{11}^{-1}\boldsymbol{\Omega}_{12} \\ \mathbf{0} & \mathbf{I}_{n_2} \end{bmatrix} \right. \\ &\quad \left. \times \begin{bmatrix} \boldsymbol{\Omega}_{11}^{-1} & \mathbf{0} \\ \mathbf{0} & (\boldsymbol{\Omega}_{22} - \boldsymbol{\Omega}_{21}\boldsymbol{\Omega}_{11}^{-1}\boldsymbol{\Omega}_{12})^{-1} \end{bmatrix} \begin{bmatrix} \mathbf{I}_{n_1} & \mathbf{0} \\ -\boldsymbol{\Omega}_{21}\boldsymbol{\Omega}_{11}^{-1} & \mathbf{I}_{n_2} \end{bmatrix} \begin{bmatrix} \mathbf{y}_1 - \boldsymbol{\mu}_1 \\ \mathbf{y}_2 - \boldsymbol{\mu}_2 \end{bmatrix} \right\} \\ &= \frac{1}{(2\pi)^{(n_1+n_2)/2}} |\boldsymbol{\Omega}_{11}|^{-1/2} \cdot |\boldsymbol{\Omega}_{22} - \boldsymbol{\Omega}_{21}\boldsymbol{\Omega}_{11}^{-1}\boldsymbol{\Omega}_{12}|^{-1/2} \\ &\quad \times \exp\left\{ -\frac{1}{2} [(\mathbf{y}_1 - \boldsymbol{\mu}_1)' \ (\mathbf{y}_2 - \mathbf{m})'] \right. \qquad [4.6.4] \\ &\quad \left. \times \begin{bmatrix} \boldsymbol{\Omega}_{11}^{-1} & \mathbf{0} \\ \mathbf{0} & (\boldsymbol{\Omega}_{22} - \boldsymbol{\Omega}_{21}\boldsymbol{\Omega}_{11}^{-1}\boldsymbol{\Omega}_{12})^{-1} \end{bmatrix} \begin{bmatrix} \mathbf{y}_1 - \boldsymbol{\mu}_1 \\ \mathbf{y}_2 - \mathbf{m} \end{bmatrix} \right\} \\ &= \frac{1}{(2\pi)^{(n_1+n_2)/2}} |\boldsymbol{\Omega}_{11}|^{-1/2} \cdot |\boldsymbol{\Omega}_{22} - \boldsymbol{\Omega}_{21}\boldsymbol{\Omega}_{11}^{-1}\boldsymbol{\Omega}_{12}|^{-1/2} \\ &\quad \times \exp\left\{ -\frac{1}{2} (\mathbf{y}_1 - \boldsymbol{\mu}_1)'\boldsymbol{\Omega}_{11}^{-1}(\mathbf{y}_1 - \boldsymbol{\mu}_1) \right. \\ &\quad \left. - \frac{1}{2} (\mathbf{y}_2 - \mathbf{m})'(\boldsymbol{\Omega}_{22} - \boldsymbol{\Omega}_{21}\boldsymbol{\Omega}_{11}^{-1}\boldsymbol{\Omega}_{12})^{-1}(\mathbf{y}_2 - \mathbf{m}) \right\}, \end{aligned}$$

where

$$\mathbf{m} \equiv \boldsymbol{\mu}_2 + \boldsymbol{\Omega}_{21}\boldsymbol{\Omega}_{11}^{-1}(\mathbf{y}_1 - \boldsymbol{\mu}_1). \qquad [4.6.5]$$

The conditional density of $\mathbf{Y}_2$ given $\mathbf{Y}_1$ is found by dividing the joint density [4.6.4] by the marginal density:

$$f_{\mathbf{Y}_1}(\mathbf{y}_1) = \frac{1}{(2\pi)^{n_1/2}} |\boldsymbol{\Omega}_{11}|^{-1/2} \exp\left[ -\frac{1}{2} (\mathbf{y}_1 - \boldsymbol{\mu}_1)'\boldsymbol{\Omega}_{11}^{-1}(\mathbf{y}_1 - \boldsymbol{\mu}_1) \right].$$

[5]Write $\boldsymbol{\Omega}_{11}$ in Jordan form as $\mathbf{M}_1\mathbf{J}_1\mathbf{M}_1^{-1}$, where $\mathbf{J}_1$ is upper triangular with eigenvalues of $\boldsymbol{\Omega}_{11}$ along the principal diagonal. Write $\boldsymbol{\Omega}_{22} - \boldsymbol{\Omega}_{21}\boldsymbol{\Omega}_{11}^{-1}\boldsymbol{\Omega}_{12}$ as $\mathbf{M}_2\mathbf{J}_2\mathbf{M}_2^{-1}$. Then $\boldsymbol{\Omega} = \mathbf{MJM}^{-1}$, where

$$\mathbf{M} = \begin{bmatrix} \mathbf{M}_1 & \mathbf{0} \\ \mathbf{0} & \mathbf{M}_2 \end{bmatrix} \qquad \mathbf{J} = \begin{bmatrix} \mathbf{J}_1 & \mathbf{0} \\ \mathbf{0} & \mathbf{J}_2 \end{bmatrix}.$$

Thus $\boldsymbol{\Omega}$ has the same determinant as $\mathbf{J}$. Because $\mathbf{J}$ is upper triangular, its determinant is the product of terms along the principal diagonal, or $|\mathbf{J}| = |\mathbf{J}_1| \cdot |\mathbf{J}_2|$. Hence $|\boldsymbol{\Omega}| = |\boldsymbol{\Omega}_{11}| \cdot |\boldsymbol{\Omega}_{22} - \boldsymbol{\Omega}_{21}\boldsymbol{\Omega}_{11}^{-1}\boldsymbol{\Omega}_{12}|$.

The result of this division is

$$
\begin{aligned}
f_{\mathbf{Y}_2|\mathbf{Y}_1}(\mathbf{y}_2|\mathbf{y}_1) &= \frac{f_{\mathbf{Y}_1,\mathbf{Y}_2}(\mathbf{y}_1, \mathbf{y}_2)}{f_{\mathbf{Y}_1}(\mathbf{y}_1)} \\
&= \frac{1}{(2\pi)^{n_2/2}} |\mathbf{H}|^{-1/2} \exp\left[ -\frac{1}{2}(\mathbf{y}_2 - \mathbf{m})'\mathbf{H}^{-1}(\mathbf{y}_2 - \mathbf{m}) \right],
\end{aligned}
$$

where

$$\mathbf{H} \equiv \mathbf{\Omega}_{22} - \mathbf{\Omega}_{21}\mathbf{\Omega}_{11}^{-1}\mathbf{\Omega}_{12}. \tag{4.6.6}$$

In other words,

$$
\begin{aligned}
\mathbf{Y}_2|\mathbf{Y}_1 &\sim N(\mathbf{m}, \mathbf{H}) \\
&\sim N\Big( [\boldsymbol{\mu}_2 + \mathbf{\Omega}_{21}\mathbf{\Omega}_{11}^{-1}(\mathbf{y}_1 - \boldsymbol{\mu}_1)], [\mathbf{\Omega}_{22} - \mathbf{\Omega}_{21}\mathbf{\Omega}_{11}^{-1}\mathbf{\Omega}_{12}] \Big).
\end{aligned} \tag{4.6.7}
$$

We saw in Section 4.1 that the optimal unrestricted forecast is given by the conditional expectation. For a Gaussian process, the optimal forecast is thus

$$E(\mathbf{Y}_2|\mathbf{Y}_1) = \boldsymbol{\mu}_2 + \mathbf{\Omega}_{21}\mathbf{\Omega}_{11}^{-1}(\mathbf{y}_1 - \boldsymbol{\mu}_1).$$

On the other hand, for any distribution, the linear projection of the vector $\mathbf{Y}_2$ on a vector $\mathbf{Y}_1$ and a constant term is given by

$$\hat{E}(\mathbf{Y}_2|\mathbf{Y}_1) = \boldsymbol{\mu}_2 + \mathbf{\Omega}_{21}\mathbf{\Omega}_{11}^{-1}(\mathbf{y}_1 - \boldsymbol{\mu}_1).$$

Hence, for a Gaussian process, the linear projection gives the unrestricted optimal forecast.

## 4.7. *Sums of* ARMA *Processes*

This section explores the nature of series that result from adding two different *ARMA* processes together, beginning with an instructive example.

### *Sum of an* MA*(1) Process Plus White Noise*

Suppose that a series $X_t$ follows a zero-mean $MA(1)$ process:

$$X_t = u_t + \delta u_{t-1}, \tag{4.7.1}$$

where $u_t$ is white noise:

$$E(u_t u_{t-j}) = \begin{cases} \sigma_u^2 & \text{for } j = 0 \\ 0 & \text{otherwise.} \end{cases}$$

The autocovariances of $X_t$ are thus

$$E(X_t X_{t-j}) = \begin{cases} (1 + \delta^2)\sigma_u^2 & \text{for } j = 0 \\ \delta\sigma_u^2 & \text{for } j = \pm 1 \\ 0 & \text{otherwise.} \end{cases} \tag{4.7.2}$$

Let $v_t$ indicate a separate white noise series:

$$E(v_t v_{t-j}) = \begin{cases} \sigma_v^2 & \text{for } j = 0 \\ 0 & \text{otherwise.} \end{cases} \tag{4.7.3}$$

Suppose, furthermore, that $v$ and $u$ are uncorrelated at all leads and lags:

$$E(u_t v_{t-j}) = 0 \qquad \text{for all } j,$$

implying

$$E(X_t v_{t-j}) = 0 \qquad \text{for all } j. \qquad [4.7.4]$$

Let an observed series $Y_t$ represent the sum of the $MA(1)$ and the white noise process:

$$\begin{aligned} Y_t &= X_t + v_t \\ &= u_t + \delta u_{t-1} + v_t. \end{aligned} \qquad [4.7.5]$$

The question now posed is, What are the time series properties of $Y$?

Clearly, $Y_t$ has mean zero, and its autocovariances can be deduced from [4.7.2] through [4.7.4]:

$$\begin{aligned} E(Y_t Y_{t-j}) &= E(X_t + v_t)(X_{t-j} + v_{t-j}) \\ &= E(X_t X_{t-j}) + E(v_t v_{t-j}) \\ &= \begin{cases} (1 + \delta^2)\sigma_u^2 + \sigma_v^2 & \text{for } j = 0 \\ \delta\sigma_u^2 & \text{for } j = \pm 1 \\ 0 & \text{otherwise.} \end{cases} \end{aligned} \qquad [4.7.6]$$

Thus, the sum $X_t + v_t$ is covariance-stationary, and its autocovariances are zero beyond one lag, as are those for an $MA(1)$. We might naturally then ask whether there exists a zero-mean $MA(1)$ representation for $Y$,

$$Y_t = \varepsilon_t + \theta\varepsilon_{t-1}, \qquad [4.7.7]$$

with

$$E(\varepsilon_t \varepsilon_{t-j}) = \begin{cases} \sigma^2 & \text{for } j = 0 \\ 0 & \text{otherwise,} \end{cases}$$

whose autocovariances match those implied by [4.7.6]. The autocovariances of [4.7.7] would be given by

$$E(Y_t Y_{t-j}) = \begin{cases} (1 + \theta^2)\sigma^2 & \text{for } j = 0 \\ \theta\sigma^2 & \text{for } j = \pm 1 \\ 0 & \text{otherwise.} \end{cases}$$

In order to be consistent with [4.7.6], it would have to be the case that

$$(1 + \theta^2)\sigma^2 = (1 + \delta^2)\sigma_u^2 + \sigma_v^2 \qquad [4.7.8]$$

and

$$\theta\sigma^2 = \delta\sigma_u^2. \qquad [4.7.9]$$

Equation [4.7.9] can be solved for $\sigma^2$,

$$\sigma^2 = \delta\sigma_u^2/\theta, \qquad [4.7.10]$$

and then substituted into [4.7.8] to deduce

$$\begin{aligned} (1 + \theta^2)(\delta\sigma_u^2/\theta) &= (1 + \delta^2)\sigma_u^2 + \sigma_v^2 \\ (1 + \theta^2)\delta &= [(1 + \delta^2) + (\sigma_v^2/\sigma_u^2)]\theta \\ \delta\theta^2 - [(1 + \delta^2) + (\sigma_v^2/\sigma_u^2)]\theta + \delta &= 0. \end{aligned} \qquad [4.7.11]$$

For given values of $\delta$, $\sigma_u^2$, and $\sigma_v^2$, two values of $\theta$ that satisfy [4.7.11] can be found from the quadratic formula:

$$\theta = \frac{[(1 + \delta^2) + (\sigma_v^2/\sigma_u^2)] \pm \sqrt{[(1 + \delta^2) + (\sigma_v^2/\sigma_u^2)]^2 - 4\delta^2}}{2\delta}. \qquad [4.7.12]$$

If $\sigma_v^2$ were equal to zero, the quadratic equation in [4.7.11] would just be

$$\delta\theta^2 - (1 + \delta^2)\theta + \delta = \delta(\theta - \delta)(\theta - \delta^{-1}) = 0, \qquad [4.7.13]$$

whose solutions are $\theta = \delta$ and $\tilde{\theta} = \delta^{-1}$, the moving average parameter for $X_t$ from the invertible and noninvertible representations, respectively. Figure 4.1 graphs equations [4.7.11] and [4.7.13] as functions of $\theta$ assuming positive autocorrelation for $X_t$ ($\delta > 0$). For $\theta > 0$ and $\sigma_v^2 > 0$, equation [4.7.11] is everywhere lower than [4.7.13] by the amount $(\sigma_v^2/\sigma_u^2)\theta$, implying that [4.7.11] has two real solutions for $\theta$, an invertible solution $\theta^*$ satisfying

$$0 < |\theta^*| < |\delta|, \qquad [4.7.14]$$

and a noninvertible solution $\tilde{\theta}^*$ characterized by

$$1 < |\delta^{-1}| < |\tilde{\theta}^*|.$$

Taking the values associated with the invertible representation $(\theta^*, \sigma^{*2})$, let us consider whether [4.7.7] could indeed characterize the data $\{Y_t\}$ generated by [4.7.5]. This would require

$$(1 + \theta^* L)\varepsilon_t = (1 + \delta L)u_t + v_t, \qquad [4.7.15]$$

or

$$\begin{aligned} \varepsilon_t &= (1 + \theta^* L)^{-1}[(1 + \delta L)u_t + v_t] \\ &= (u_t - \theta^* u_{t-1} + \theta^{*2} u_{t-2} - \theta^{*3} u_{t-3} + \cdots) \\ &\quad + \delta(u_{t-1} - \theta^* u_{t-2} + \theta^{*2} u_{t-3} - \theta^{*3} u_{t-4} + \cdots) \\ &\quad + (v_t - \theta^* v_{t-1} + \theta^{*2} v_{t-2} - \theta^{*3} v_{t-3} + \cdots). \end{aligned} \qquad [4.7.16]$$

The series $\varepsilon_t$ defined in [4.7.16] is a distributed lag on past values of $u$ and $v$, so it might seem to possess a rich autocorrelation structure. In fact, it turns out to be

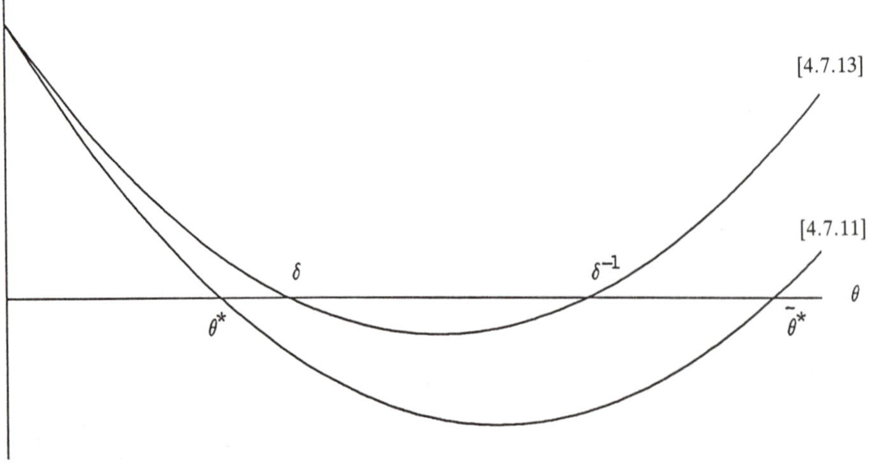


**FIGURE 4.1** Graphs of equations [4.7.13] and [4.7.11].

white noise! To see this, note from [4.7.6] that the autocovariance-generating function of $Y$ can be written

$$g_Y(z) = (1 + \delta z)\sigma_u^2(1 + \delta z^{-1}) + \sigma_v^2, \qquad [4.7.17]$$

so that the autocovariance-generating function of $\varepsilon_t = (1 + \theta^* L)^{-1} Y_t$ is

$$g_\varepsilon(z) = \frac{(1 + \delta z)\sigma_u^2(1 + \delta z^{-1}) + \sigma_v^2}{(1 + \theta^* z)(1 + \theta^* z^{-1})}. \qquad [4.7.18]$$

But $\theta^*$ and $\sigma^{*2}$ were chosen so as to make the autocovariance-generating function of $(1 + \theta^* L)\varepsilon_t$, namely,

$$(1 + \theta^* z)\sigma^{*2}(1 + \theta^* z^{-1}),$$

identical to the right side of [4.7.17]. Thus, [4.7.18] is simply equal to

$$g_\varepsilon(z) = \sigma^{*2},$$

a white noise series.

To summarize, adding an $MA(1)$ process to a white noise series with which it is uncorrelated at all leads and lags produces a new $MA(1)$ process characterized by [4.7.7].

Note that the series $\varepsilon_t$ in [4.7.16] could not be forecast as a linear function of lagged $\varepsilon$ or of lagged $Y$. Clearly, $\varepsilon$ could be forecast, however, on the basis of lagged $u$ or lagged $v$. The histories $\{u_t\}$ and $\{v_t\}$ contain more information than $\{\varepsilon_t\}$ or $\{Y_t\}$. The optimal forecast of $Y_{t+1}$ on the basis of $\{Y_t, Y_{t-1}, \ldots\}$ would be

$$\hat{E}(Y_{t+1}|Y_t, Y_{t-1}, \ldots) = \theta^* \varepsilon_t$$

with associated mean squared error $\sigma^{*2}$. By contrast, the optimal linear forecast of $Y_{t+1}$ on the basis of $\{u_t, u_{t-1}, \ldots, v_t, v_{t-1}, \ldots\}$ would be

$$\hat{E}(Y_{t+1}|u_t, u_{t-1}, \ldots, v_t, v_{t-1}, \ldots) = \delta u_t$$

with associated mean squared error $\sigma_u^2 + \sigma_v^2$. Recalling from [4.7.14] that $|\theta^*| < |\delta|$, it appears from [4.7.9] that $(\theta^{*2})\sigma^{*2} < \delta^2\sigma_u^2$, meaning from [4.7.8] that $\sigma^2 > \sigma_u^2 + \sigma_v^2$. In other words, past values of $Y$ contain less information than past values of $u$ and $v$.

This example can be useful for thinking about the consequences of differing information sets. One can always make a sensible forecast on the basis of what one knows, $\{Y_t, Y_{t-1}, \ldots\}$, though usually there is other information that could have helped more. An important feature of such settings is that even though $\varepsilon_t$, $u_t$, and $v_t$ are all white noise, there are complicated correlations between these white noise series.

Another point worth noting is that all that can be estimated on the basis of $\{Y_t\}$ are the two parameters $\theta^*$ and $\sigma^{*2}$, whereas the true "structural" model [4.7.5] has three parameters ($\delta$, $\sigma_u^2$, and $\sigma_v^2$). Thus the parameters of the structural model are *unidentified* in the sense in which econometricians use this term—there exists a family of alternative configurations of $\delta$, $\sigma_u^2$, and $\sigma_v^2$ with $|\delta| < 1$ that would produce the identical value for the likelihood function of the observed data $\{Y_t\}$.

The processes that were added together for this example both had mean zero. Adding constant terms to the processes will not change the results in any interesting way—if $X_t$ is an $MA(1)$ process with mean $\mu_X$ and if $v_t$ is white noise plus a constant $\mu_v$, then $X_t + v_t$ will be an $MA(1)$ process with mean given by $\mu_X + \mu_v$. Thus, nothing is lost by restricting the subsequent discussion to sums of zero-mean processes.

## *Adding Two Moving Average Processes*

Suppose next that $X_t$ is a zero-mean $MA(q_1)$ process:

$$X_t = (1 + \delta_1 L + \delta_2 L^2 + \cdots + \delta_{q_1} L^{q_1})u_t \equiv \delta(L)u_t,$$

with

$$E(u_t u_{t-j}) = \begin{cases} \sigma_u^2 & \text{for } j = 0 \\ 0 & \text{otherwise.} \end{cases}$$

Let $W_t$ be a zero-mean $MA(q_2)$ process:

$$W_t = (1 + \kappa_1 L + \kappa_2 L^2 + \cdots + \kappa_{q_2} L^{q_2})v_t \equiv \kappa(L)v_t,$$

with

$$E(v_t v_{t-j}) = \begin{cases} \sigma_v^2 & \text{for } j = 0 \\ 0 & \text{otherwise.} \end{cases}$$

Thus, $X$ has autocovariances $\gamma_0^X, \gamma_1^X, \ldots, \gamma_{q_1}^X$ of the form of [3.3.12] while $W$ has autocovariances $\gamma_0^W, \gamma_1^W, \ldots, \gamma_{q_2}^W$ of the same basic structure. Assume that $X$ and $W$ are uncorrelated with each other at all leads and lags:

$$E(X_t W_{t-j}) = 0 \qquad \text{for all } j;$$

and suppose we observe

$$Y_t = X_t + W_t.$$

Define $q$ to be the larger of $q_1$ or $q_2$:

$$q \equiv \max\{q_1, q_2\}.$$

Then the $j$th autocovariance of $Y$ is given by

$$\begin{aligned} E(Y_t Y_{t-j}) &= E(X_t + W_t)(X_{t-j} + W_{t-j}) \\ &= E(X_t X_{t-j}) + E(W_t W_{t-j}) \\ &= \begin{cases} \gamma_j^X + \gamma_j^W & \text{for } j = 0, \pm 1, \pm 2, \ldots, \pm q \\ 0 & \text{otherwise.} \end{cases} \end{aligned}$$

Thus the autocovariances are zero beyond $q$ lags, suggesting that $Y_t$ might be represented as an $MA(q)$ process.

What more would we need to show to be fully convinced that $Y_t$ is indeed an $MA(q)$ process? This question can be posed in terms of autocovariance-generating functions. Since

$$\gamma_j^Y = \gamma_j^X + \gamma_j^W,$$

it follows that

$$\sum_{j=-\infty}^{\infty} \gamma_j^Y z^j = \sum_{j=-\infty}^{\infty} \gamma_j^X z^j + \sum_{j=-\infty}^{\infty} \gamma_j^W z^j.$$

But these are just the definitions of the respective autocovariance-generating functions,

$$g_Y(z) = g_X(z) + g_W(z). \qquad [4.7.19]$$

Equation [4.7.19] is a quite general result—if one adds together two covariance-stationary processes that are uncorrelated with each other at all leads and lags, the autocovariance-generating function of the sum is the sum of the autocovariance-generating functions of the individual series.

If $Y_t$ is to be expressed as an $MA(q)$ process,

$$Y_t = (1 + \theta_1 L + \theta_2 L^2 + \cdots + \theta_q L^q)\varepsilon_t \equiv \theta(L)\varepsilon_t$$

with

$$E(\varepsilon_t \varepsilon_{t-j}) = \begin{cases} \sigma^2 & \text{for } j = 0 \\ 0 & \text{otherwise,} \end{cases}$$

then its autocovariance-generating function would be

$$g_Y(z) = \theta(z)\theta(z^{-1})\sigma^2.$$

The question is thus whether there always exist values of $(\theta_1, \theta_2, \ldots, \theta_q, \sigma^2)$ such that [4.7.19] is satisfied:

$$\theta(z)\theta(z^{-1})\sigma^2 = \delta(z)\delta(z^{-1})\sigma_u^2 + \kappa(z)\kappa(z^{-1})\sigma_v^2. \qquad [4.7.20]$$

It turns out that there do. Thus, the conjecture turns out to be correct that if two moving average processes that are uncorrelated with each other at all leads and lags are added together, the result is a new moving average process whose order is the larger of the order of the original two series:

$$MA(q_1) + MA(q_2) = MA(\max\{q_1, q_2\}). \qquad [4.7.21]$$

A proof of this assertion, along with a constructive algorithm for achieving the factorization in [4.7.20], will be provided in Chapter 13.

### *Adding Two Autoregressive Processes*

Suppose now that $X_t$ and $W_t$ are two $AR(1)$ processes:

$$(1 - \pi L)X_t = u_t \qquad [4.7.22]$$

$$(1 - \rho L)W_t = v_t, \qquad [4.7.23]$$

where $u_t$ and $v_t$ are each white noise with $u_t$ uncorrelated with $v_\tau$ for all $t$ and $\tau$. Again suppose that we observe

$$Y_t = X_t + W_t$$

and want to forecast $Y_{t+1}$ on the basis of its own lagged values.

If, by chance, $X$ and $W$ share the same autoregressive parameter, or

$$\pi = \rho,$$

then [4.7.22] could simply be added directly to [4.7.23] to deduce

$$(1 - \pi L)X_t + (1 - \pi L)W_t = u_t + v_t$$

or

$$(1 - \pi L)(X_t + W_t) = u_t + v_t.$$

But the sum $u_t + v_t$ is white noise (as a special case of result [4.7.21]), meaning that $Y_t$ has an $AR(1)$ representation

$$(1 - \pi L)Y_t = \varepsilon_t.$$

In the more likely case that the autoregressive parameters $\pi$ and $\rho$ are different, then [4.7.22] can be multiplied by $(1 - \rho L)$:

$$(1 - \rho L)(1 - \pi L)X_t = (1 - \rho L)u_t; \qquad [4.7.24]$$

and similarly, [4.7.23] could be multiplied by $(1 - \pi L)$:

$$(1 - \pi L)(1 - \rho L)W_t = (1 - \pi L)v_t. \qquad [4.7.25]$$

Adding [4.7.24] to [4.7.25] produces

$$(1 - \rho L)(1 - \pi L)(X_t + W_t) = (1 - \rho L)u_t + (1 - \pi L)v_t. \qquad [4.7.26]$$

From [4.7.21], the right side of [4.7.26] has an $MA(1)$ representation. Thus, we could write

$$(1 - \phi_1 L - \phi_2 L^2)Y_t = (1 + \theta L)\varepsilon_t,$$

where

$$(1 - \phi_1 L - \phi_2 L^2) = (1 - \rho L)(1 - \pi L)$$

and

$$(1 + \theta L)\varepsilon_t = (1 - \rho L)u_t + (1 - \pi L)v_t.$$

In other words,

$$AR(1) + AR(1) = ARMA(2, 1). \qquad [4.7.27]$$

In general, adding an $AR(p_1)$ process

$$\pi(L)X_t = u_t,$$

to an $AR(p_2)$ process with which it is uncorrelated at all leads and lags,

$$\rho(L)W_t = v_t,$$

produces an $ARMA(p_1 + p_2, \max\{p_1, p_2\})$ process,

$$\phi(L)Y_t = \theta(L)\varepsilon_t,$$

where

$$\phi(L) = \pi(L)\rho(L)$$

and

$$\theta(L)\varepsilon_t = \rho(L)u_t + \pi(L)v_t.$$

## 4.8. *Wold's Decomposition and the Box-Jenkins Modeling Philosophy*

### *Wold's Decomposition*

All of the covariance-stationary processes considered in Chapter 3 can be written in the form

$$Y_t = \mu + \sum_{j=0}^{\infty} \psi_j \varepsilon_{t-j}, \qquad [4.8.1]$$

where $\varepsilon_t$ is the white noise error one would make in forecasting $Y_t$ as a linear function of lagged $Y$ and where $\sum_{j=0}^{\infty}\psi_j^2 < \infty$ with $\psi_0 = 1$.

One might think that we were able to write all these processes in the form of [4.8.1] because the discussion was restricted to a convenient class of models. However, the following result establishes that the representation [4.8.1] is in fact fundamental for any covariance-stationary time series.

***Proposition 4.1:*** *(Wold's decomposition). Any zero-mean covariance-stationary process $Y_t$ can be represented in the form*

$$Y_t = \sum_{j=0}^{\infty} \psi_j \varepsilon_{t-j} + \kappa_t, \qquad [4.8.2]$$

*where $\psi_0 = 1$ and $\Sigma_{j=0}^{\infty}\psi_j^2 < \infty$. The term $\varepsilon_t$ is white noise and represents the error made in forecasting $Y_t$ on the basis of a linear function of lagged $Y$:*

$$\varepsilon_t \equiv Y_t - \hat{E}(Y_t|Y_{t-1}, Y_{t-2}, \ldots). \qquad [4.8.3]$$

*The value of $\kappa_t$ is uncorrelated with $\varepsilon_{t-j}$ for any $j$, though $\kappa_t$ can be predicted arbitrarily well from a linear function of past values of $Y$:*

$$\kappa_t = \hat{E}(\kappa_t|Y_{t-1}, Y_{t-2}, \ldots).$$

The term $\kappa_t$ is called the *linearly deterministic* component of $Y_t$, while $\Sigma_{j=0}^{\infty}\psi_j\varepsilon_{t-j}$ is called the *linearly indeterministic* component. If $\kappa_t \equiv 0$, then the process is called *purely linearly indeterministic*.

This proposition was first proved by Wold (1938).[6] The proposition relies on stable second moments of $Y$ but makes no use of higher moments. It thus describes only optimal linear forecasts of $Y$.

Finding the Wold representation in principle requires fitting an infinite number of parameters $(\psi_1, \psi_2, \ldots)$ to the data. With a finite number of observations on $(Y_1, Y_2, \ldots, Y_T)$, this will never be possible. As a practical matter, we therefore need to make some additional assumptions about the nature of $(\psi_1, \psi_2, \ldots)$. A typical assumption in Chapter 3 was that $\psi(L)$ can be expressed as the ratio of two finite-order polynomials:

$$\sum_{j=0}^{\infty} \psi_j L^j = \frac{\theta(L)}{\phi(L)} \equiv \frac{1 + \theta_1 L + \theta_2 L^2 + \cdots + \theta_q L^q}{1 - \phi_1 L - \phi_2 L^2 - \cdots - \phi_p L^p}. \qquad [4.8.4]$$

Another approach, based on the presumed "smoothness" of the population spectrum, will be explored in Chapter 6.

## *The Box-Jenkins Modeling Philosophy*

Many forecasters are persuaded of the benefits of parsimony, or using as few parameters as possible. Box and Jenkins (1976) have been influential advocates of this view. They noted that in practice, analysts end up replacing the true operators $\theta(L)$ and $\phi(L)$ with estimates $\hat{\theta}(L)$ and $\hat{\phi}(L)$ based on the data. The more parameters to estimate, the more room there is to go wrong.

Although complicated models can track the data very well over the historical period for which parameters are estimated, they often perform poorly when used for out-of-sample forecasting. For example, the 1960s saw the development of a number of large macroeconometric models purporting to describe the economy using hundreds of macroeconomic variables and equations. Part of the disillusionment with such efforts was the discovery that univariate *ARMA* models with small values of $p$ or $q$ often produced better forecasts than the big models (see for example Nelson, 1972).[7] As we shall see in later chapters, large size alone was hardly the only liability of these large-scale macroeconometric models. Even so, the claim that simpler models provide more robust forecasts has a great many believers across disciplines.

[6] See Sargent (1987, pp. 286–90) for a nice sketch of the intuition behind this result.

[7] For more recent pessimistic evidence about current large-scale models, see Ashley (1988).

The approach to forecasting advocated by Box and Jenkins can be broken down into four steps:

(1) Transform the data, if necessary, so that the assumption of covariance-stationarity is a reasonable one.
(2) Make an initial guess of small values for $p$ and $q$ for an $ARMA(p, q)$ model that might describe the transformed series.
(3) Estimate the parameters in $\phi(L)$ and $\theta(L)$.
(4) Perform diagnostic analysis to confirm that the model is indeed consistent with the observed features of the data.

The first step, selecting a suitable transformation of the data, is discussed in Chapter 15. For now we merely remark that for economic series that grow over time, many researchers use the change in the natural logarithm of the raw data. For example, if $X_t$ is the level of real GNP in year $t$, then

$$Y_t = \log X_t - \log X_{t-1} \qquad [4.8.5]$$

might be the variable that an $ARMA$ model purports to describe.

The third and fourth steps, estimation and diagnostic testing, will be discussed in Chapters 5 and 14. Analysis of seasonal dynamics can also be an important part of step 2 of the procedure; this is briefly discussed in Section 6.4. The remainder of this section is devoted to an exposition of the second step in the Box-Jenkins procedure on nonseasonal data, namely, selecting candidate values for $p$ and $q$.[8]

## *Sample Autocorrelations*

An important part of this selection procedure is to form an estimate $\hat{\rho}_j$ of the population autocorrelation $\rho_j$. Recall that $\rho_j$ was defined as

$$\rho_j \equiv \gamma_j/\gamma_0$$

where

$$\gamma_j = E(Y_t - \mu)(Y_{t-j} - \mu).$$

A natural estimate of the population autocorrelation $\rho_j$ is provided by the corresponding sample moments:

$$\hat{\rho}_j = \hat{\gamma}_j/\hat{\gamma}_0,$$

where

$$\hat{\gamma}_j = \frac{1}{T}\sum_{t=j+1}^{T}(y_t - \bar{y})(y_{t-j} - \bar{y}) \qquad \text{for } j = 0, 1, 2, \ldots, T-1 \qquad [4.8.6]$$

$$\bar{y} = \frac{1}{T}\sum_{t=1}^{T} y_t. \qquad [4.8.7]$$

Note that even though only $T - j$ observations are used to construct $\hat{\gamma}_j$, the denominator in [4.8.6] is $T$ rather than $T - j$. Thus, for large $j$, expression [4.8.6] shrinks the estimates toward zero, as indeed the population autocovariances go to zero as $j \to \infty$, assuming covariance-stationarity. Also, the full sample of observations is used to construct $\bar{y}$.

[8]Box and Jenkins refer to this step as "identification" of the appropriate model. We avoid Box and Jenkins's terminology, because "identification" has a quite different meaning for econometricians.

Recall that if the data really follow an $MA(q)$ process, then $\rho_j$ will be zero for $j > q$. By contrast, if the data follow an $AR(p)$ process, then $\rho_j$ will gradually decay toward zero as a mixture of exponentials or damped sinusoids. One guide for distinguishing between $MA$ and $AR$ representations, then, would be the decay properties of $\rho_j$. Often, we are interested in a quick assessment of whether $\rho_j = 0$ for $j = q + 1, q + 2, \ldots$. If the data were really generated by a Gaussian $MA(q)$ process, then the variance of the estimate $\hat{\rho}_j$ could be approximated by[9]

$$\text{Var}(\hat{\rho}_j) \cong \frac{1}{T}\left\{1 + 2\sum_{i=1}^{q} \rho_i^2\right\} \qquad \text{for } j = q + 1, q + 2, \ldots. \qquad [4.8.8]$$

Thus, in particular, if we suspect that the data were generated by Gaussian white noise, then $\hat{\rho}_j$ for any $j \neq 0$ should lie between $\pm 2/\sqrt{T}$ about 95% of the time.

In general, if there is autocorrelation in the process that generated the original data $\{Y_t\}$, then the estimate $\hat{\rho}_j$ will be correlated with $\hat{\rho}_i$ for $i \neq j$.[10] Thus patterns in the estimated $\hat{\rho}_j$ may represent sampling error rather than patterns in the true $\rho_j$.

## *Partial Autocorrelation*

Another useful measure is the *partial autocorrelation*. The $m$th population partial autocorrelation (denoted $\alpha_m^{(m)}$) is defined as the last coefficient in a linear projection of $Y$ on its $m$ most recent values (equation [4.3.7]):

$$\hat{Y}_{t+1|t} - \mu = \alpha_1^{(m)}(Y_t - \mu) + \alpha_2^{(m)}(Y_{t-1} - \mu) + \cdots + \alpha_m^{(m)}(Y_{t-m+1} - \mu).$$

We saw in equation [4.3.8] that the vector $\boldsymbol{\alpha}^{(m)}$ can be calculated from

$$\begin{bmatrix} \alpha_1^{(m)} \\ \alpha_2^{(m)} \\ \vdots \\ \alpha_m^{(m)} \end{bmatrix} = \begin{bmatrix} \gamma_0 & \gamma_1 & \cdots & \gamma_{m-1} \\ \gamma_1 & \gamma_0 & \cdots & \gamma_{m-2} \\ \vdots & \vdots & \cdots & \vdots \\ \gamma_{m-1} & \gamma_{m-2} & \cdots & \gamma_0 \end{bmatrix}^{-1} \begin{bmatrix} \gamma_1 \\ \gamma_2 \\ \vdots \\ \gamma_m \end{bmatrix}.$$

Recall that if the data were really generated by an $AR(p)$ process, only the $p$ most recent values of $Y$ would be useful for forecasting. In this case, the projection coefficients on $Y$'s more than $p$ periods in the past are equal to zero:

$$\alpha_m^{(m)} = 0 \qquad \text{for } m = p + 1, p + 2, \ldots.$$

By contrast, if the data really were generated by an $MA(q)$ process with $q \geq 1$, then the partial autocorrelation $\alpha_m^{(m)}$ asymptotically approaches zero instead of cutting off abruptly.

A natural estimate of the $m$th partial autocorrelation is the last coefficient in an $OLS$ regression of $y$ on a constant and its $m$ most recent values:

$$y_{t+1} = \hat{c} + \hat{\alpha}_1^{(m)} y_t + \hat{\alpha}_2^{(m)} y_{t-1} + \cdots + \hat{\alpha}_m^{(m)} y_{t-m+1} + \hat{e}_t,$$

where $\hat{e}_t$ denotes the $OLS$ regression residual. If the data were really generated by an $AR(p)$ process, then the sample estimate ($\hat{\alpha}_m^{(m)}$) would have a variance around the true value (0) that could be approximated by[11]

$$\text{Var}(\hat{\alpha}_m^{(m)}) \cong 1/T \qquad \text{for } m = p + 1, p + 2, \ldots.$$

[9]See Box and Jenkins (1976, p. 35).

[10]Again, see Box and Jenkins (1976, p. 35).

[11]Box and Jenkins (1976, p. 65).

Moreover, if the data were really generated by an $AR(p)$ process, then $\hat{\alpha}_i^{(i)}$ and $\hat{\alpha}_j^{(j)}$ would be asymptotically independent for $i, j > p$.

### *Example 4.1*

We illustrate the Box-Jenkins approach with seasonally adjusted quarterly data on U.S. real GNP from 1947 through 1988. The raw data $(x_t)$ were converted to log changes $(y_t)$ as in [4.8.5]. Panel (a) of Figure 4.2 plots the sample autocorrelations of $y$ ($\hat{\rho}_j$ for $j = 0, 1, \ldots, 20$), while panel (b) displays the sample partial autocorrelations ($\hat{\alpha}_m^{(m)}$ for $m = 0, 1, \ldots, 20$). Ninety-five percent confidence bands ($\pm 2/\sqrt{T}$) are plotted on both panels; for panel (a), these are appropriate under the null hypothesis that the data are really white noise, whereas for panel (b) these are appropriate if the data are really generated by an $AR(p)$ process for $p$ less than $m$.

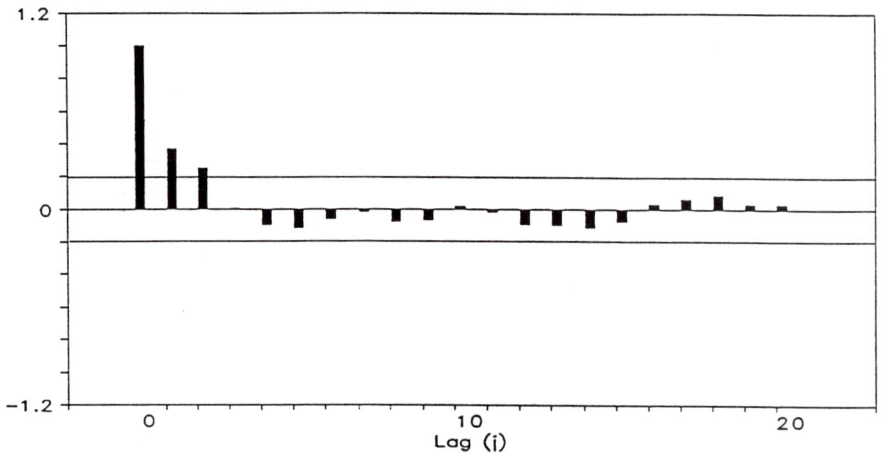


(a) Sample autocorrelations

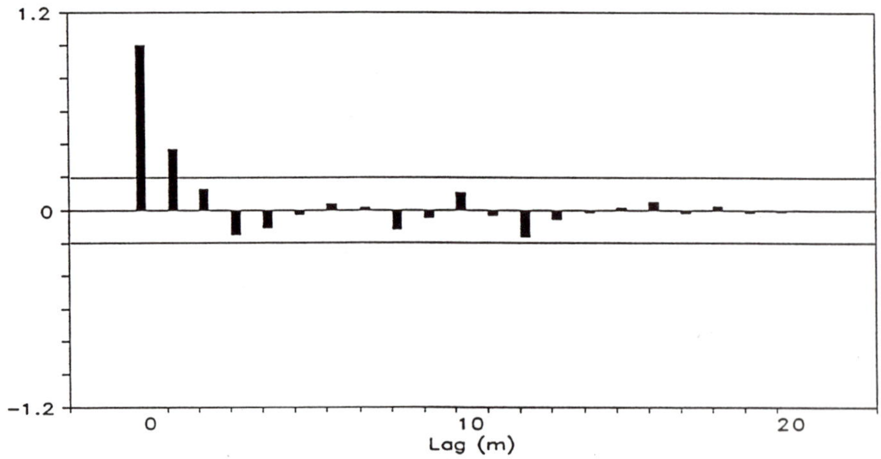


(b) Sample partial autocorrelations

**FIGURE 4.2** Sample autocorrelations and partial autocorrelations for U.S. quarterly real GNP growth, 1947:II to 1988:IV. Ninety-five percent confidence intervals are plotted as $\pm 2/\sqrt{T}$.

The first two autocorrelations appear nonzero, suggesting that $q = 2$ would be needed to describe these data as coming from a moving average process. On the other hand, the pattern of autocorrelations appears consistent with the simple geometric decay of an $AR(1)$ process,

$$\rho_j = \phi^j$$

with $\phi \cong 0.4$. The partial autocorrelation could also be viewed as dying out after one lag, also consistent with the $AR(1)$ hypothesis. Thus, one's initial guess for a parsimonious model might be that GNP growth follows an $AR(1)$ process, with $MA(2)$ as another possibility to be considered.

## APPENDIX 4.A. *Parallel Between* OLS *Regression and Linear Projection*

This appendix discusses the parallel between ordinary least squares regression and linear projection. This parallel is developed by introducing an artificial random variable specifically constructed so as to have population moments identical to the sample moments of a particular sample. Say that in some particular sample on which we intend to perform *OLS* we have observed $T$ particular values for the explanatory vector, denoted $\mathbf{x}_1, \mathbf{x}_2, \ldots, \mathbf{x}_T$. Consider an artificial discrete-valued random variable $\boldsymbol{\xi}$ that can take on only one of these particular $T$ values, each with probability $(1/T)$:

$$\begin{aligned} P\{\boldsymbol{\xi} &= \mathbf{x}_1\} = 1/T \\ P\{\boldsymbol{\xi} &= \mathbf{x}_2\} = 1/T \\ &\vdots \\ P\{\boldsymbol{\xi} &= \mathbf{x}_T\} = 1/T. \end{aligned}$$

Thus $\boldsymbol{\xi}$ is an artificially constructed random variable whose population probability distribution is given by the empirical distribution function of $\mathbf{x}_t$. The population mean of the random variable $\boldsymbol{\xi}$ is

$$E(\boldsymbol{\xi}) = \sum_{t=1}^{T} \mathbf{x}_t \cdot P\{\boldsymbol{\xi} = \mathbf{x}_t\} = \frac{1}{T}\sum_{t=1}^{T} \mathbf{x}_t.$$

Thus, the population mean of $\boldsymbol{\xi}$ equals the observed sample mean of the truc random variable $\mathbf{X}_t$. The population second moment of $\boldsymbol{\xi}$ is

$$E(\boldsymbol{\xi}\boldsymbol{\xi}') = \frac{1}{T}\sum_{t=1}^{T} \mathbf{x}_t\mathbf{x}_t', \qquad [4.A.1]$$

which is the sample second moment of $(\mathbf{x}_1, \mathbf{x}_2, \ldots, \mathbf{x}_T)$.

We can similarly construct a second artificial variable $\omega$ that can take on one of the discrete values $(y_2, y_3, \ldots, y_{T+1})$. Suppose that the joint distribution of $\omega$ and $\boldsymbol{\xi}$ is given by

$$P\{\boldsymbol{\xi} = \mathbf{x}_t, \omega = y_{t+1}\} = 1/T \qquad \text{for } t = 1, 2, \ldots, T.$$

Then

$$E(\boldsymbol{\xi}\omega) = \frac{1}{T}\sum_{t=1}^{T} \mathbf{x}_t y_{t+1}. \qquad [4.A.2]$$

The coefficient for a linear projection of $\omega$ on $\boldsymbol{\xi}$ is the value of $\boldsymbol{\alpha}$ that minimizes

$$E(\omega - \boldsymbol{\alpha}'\boldsymbol{\xi})^2 = \frac{1}{T}\sum_{t=1}^{T} (y_{t+1} - \boldsymbol{\alpha}'\mathbf{x}_t)^2. \qquad [4.A.3]$$

This is algebraically the same problem as choosing $\boldsymbol{\beta}$ so as to minimize [4.1.17]. Thus, ordinary least squares regression (choosing $\boldsymbol{\beta}$ so as to minimize [4.1.17]) can be viewed as a special case of linear projection (choosing $\boldsymbol{\alpha}$ so as to minimize [4.A.3]). The value of $\boldsymbol{\alpha}$

that minimizes [4.A.3] can be found from substituting the expressions for the population moments of the artificial random variables (equations [4.A.1] and [4.A.2]) into the formula for a linear projection (equation [4.1.13]):

$$\boldsymbol{\alpha} = [E(\boldsymbol{\xi}\boldsymbol{\xi}')]^{-1}E(\boldsymbol{\xi}\omega) = \left[\frac{1}{T}\sum_{t=1}^{T}\mathbf{x}_t\mathbf{x}_t'\right]^{-1}\left[\frac{1}{T}\sum_{t=1}^{T}\mathbf{x}_t y_{t+1}\right].$$

Thus the formula for the *OLS* estimate $\mathbf{b}$ in [4.1.18] can be obtained as a special case of the formula for the linear projection coefficient $\boldsymbol{\alpha}$ in [4.1.13].

Because linear projections and *OLS* regressions share the same mathematical structure, statements about one have a parallel in the other. This can be a useful device for remembering results or confirming algebra. For example, the statement about population moments,

$$E(Y^2) = \mathrm{Var}(Y) + [E(Y)]^2, \qquad [4.A.4]$$

has the sample analog

$$\frac{1}{T}\sum_{t=1}^{T} y_t^2 = \frac{1}{T}\sum_{t=1}^{T}(y_t - \bar{y})^2 + (\bar{y})^2 \qquad [4.A.5]$$

with $\bar{y} = (1/T)\Sigma_{t=1}^{T} y_t$.

As a second example, suppose that we estimate a series of $n$ *OLS* regressions, with $y_{it}$ the dependent variable for the $i$th regression and $\mathbf{x}_t$ a $(k \times 1)$ vector of explanatory variables common to each regression. Let $\mathbf{y}_t \equiv (y_{1t}, y_{2t}, \ldots, y_{nt})'$ and write the regression model as

$$\mathbf{y}_t = \boldsymbol{\Pi}'\mathbf{x}_t + \mathbf{u}_t$$

for $\boldsymbol{\Pi}'$ an $(n \times k)$ matrix of regression coefficients. Then the sample variance-covariance matrix of the *OLS* residuals can be inferred from [4.1.24]:

$$\frac{1}{T}\sum_{t=1}^{T}\hat{\mathbf{u}}_t\hat{\mathbf{u}}_t' = \left[\frac{1}{T}\sum_{t=1}^{T}\mathbf{y}_t\mathbf{y}_t'\right] - \left[\frac{1}{T}\sum_{t=1}^{T}\mathbf{y}_t\mathbf{x}_t'\right]\left[\frac{1}{T}\sum_{t=1}^{T}\mathbf{x}_t\mathbf{x}_t'\right]^{-1}\left[\frac{1}{T}\sum_{t=1}^{T}\mathbf{x}_t\mathbf{y}_t'\right], \qquad [4.A.6]$$

where $\hat{\mathbf{u}}_t = \mathbf{y}_t - \hat{\boldsymbol{\Pi}}'\mathbf{x}_t$ and the $i$th row of $\hat{\boldsymbol{\Pi}}'$ is given by

$$\hat{\boldsymbol{\pi}}_i' = \left\{\left[\frac{1}{T}\sum_{t=1}^{T}\mathbf{x}_t\mathbf{x}_t'\right]^{-1}\left[\frac{1}{T}\sum_{t=1}^{T}\mathbf{x}_t y_{it}\right]\right\}'.$$

## APPENDIX 4.B. *Triangular Factorization of the Covariance Matrix for an* MA(*1*) *Process*

This appendix establishes that the triangular factorization of $\boldsymbol{\Omega}$ in [4.5.17] is given by [4.5.18] and [4.5.19].

The magnitude $\sigma^2$ is simply a constant term that will end up multiplying every term in the $\mathbf{D}$ matrix. Recognizing this, we can initially solve the factorization assuming that $\sigma^2 = 1$, and then multiply the resulting $\mathbf{D}$ matrix by $\sigma^2$ to obtain the result for the general case. The (1, 1) element of $\mathbf{D}$ (ignoring the factor $\sigma^2$) is given by the (1, 1) element of $\boldsymbol{\Omega}$: $d_{11} = (1 + \theta^2)$. To put a zero in the (2, 1) position of $\boldsymbol{\Omega}$, we multiply the first row of $\boldsymbol{\Omega}$ by $\theta/(1 + \theta^2)$ and subtract the result from the second; hence, $a_{21} = \theta/(1 + \theta^2)$. This operation changes the (2, 2) element of $\boldsymbol{\Omega}$ to

$$d_{22} = (1 + \theta^2) - \frac{\theta^2}{1 + \theta^2} = \frac{(1 + \theta^2)^2 - \theta^2}{1 + \theta^2} = \frac{1 + \theta^2 + \theta^4}{1 + \theta^2}.$$

To put a zero in the (3, 2) element of $\boldsymbol{\Omega}$, the second row of the new matrix must be multiplied by $\theta/d_{22}$ and then subtracted from the third row; hence,

$$a_{32} = \theta/d_{22} = \frac{\theta(1 + \theta^2)}{1 + \theta^2 + \theta^4}.$$

This changes the (3, 3) element to

$$\begin{aligned} d_{33} &= (1 + \theta^2) - \frac{\theta^2(1 + \theta^2)}{1 + \theta^2 + \theta^4} \\ &= \frac{(1 + \theta^2)(1 + \theta^2 + \theta^4) - \theta^2(1 + \theta^2)}{1 + \theta^2 + \theta^4} \\ &= \frac{(1 + \theta^2 + \theta^4) + \theta^2(1 + \theta^2 + \theta^4) - \theta^2(1 + \theta^2)}{1 + \theta^2 + \theta^4} \\ &= \frac{1 + \theta^2 + \theta^4 + \theta^6}{1 + \theta^2 + \theta^4}. \end{aligned}$$

In general, for the $i$th row,

$$d_{ii} = \frac{1 + \theta^2 + \theta^4 + \cdots + \theta^{2i}}{1 + \theta^2 + \theta^4 + \cdots + \theta^{2(i-1)}}.$$

To put a zero in the $(i + 1, i)$ position, multiply by

$$a_{i+1,i} = \theta/d_{ii} = \frac{\theta[1 + \theta^2 + \theta^4 + \cdots + \theta^{2(i-1)}]}{1 + \theta^2 + \theta^4 + \cdots + \theta^{2i}}$$

and subtract from the $(i + 1)$th row, producing

$$\begin{aligned} d_{i+1,i+1} &= (1 + \theta^2) - \frac{\theta^2[1 + \theta^2 + \theta^4 + \cdots + \theta^{2(i-1)}]}{1 + \theta^2 + \theta^4 + \cdots + \theta^{2i}} \\ &= \frac{(1 + \theta^2 + \theta^4 + \cdots + \theta^{2i}) + \theta^2(1 + \theta^2 + \theta^4 + \cdots + \theta^{2i})}{1 + \theta^2 + \theta^4 + \cdots + \theta^{2i}} \\ &\quad - \frac{\theta^2[1 + \theta^2 + \theta^4 + \cdots + \theta^{2(i-1)}]}{1 + \theta^2 + \theta^4 + \cdots + \theta^{2i}} \\ &= \frac{1 + \theta^2 + \theta^4 + \cdots + \theta^{2(i+1)}}{1 + \theta^2 + \theta^4 + \cdots + \theta^{2i}}. \end{aligned}$$

## *Chapter 4 Exercises*

4.1. Use formula [4.3.6] to show that for a covariance-stationary process, the projection of $Y_{t+1}$ on a constant and $Y_t$ is given by

$$\hat{E}(Y_{t+1}|Y_t) = (1 - \rho_1)\mu + \rho_1 Y_t$$

where $\mu = E(Y_t)$ and $\rho_1 = \gamma_1/\gamma_0$.

(a) Show that for the $AR(1)$ process, this reproduces equation [4.2.19] for $s = 1$.

(b) Show that for the $MA(1)$ process, this reproduces equation [4.5.20] for $n = 2$.

(c) Show that for an $AR(2)$ process, the implied forecast is

$$\mu + [\phi_1/(1 - \phi_2)](Y_t - \mu).$$

Is the error associated with this forecast correlated with $Y_t$? Is it correlated with $Y_{t-1}$?

4.2. Verify equation [4.3.3].

4.3. Find the triangular factorization of the following matrix:

$$\begin{bmatrix} 1 & -2 & 3 \\ -2 & 6 & -4 \\ 3 & -4 & 12 \end{bmatrix}.$$

4.4. Can the coefficient on $Y_2$ from a linear projection of $Y_4$ on $Y_3$, $Y_2$, and $Y_1$ be found from the (4, 2) element of the matrix $\mathbf{A}$ from the triangular factorization of $\mathbf{\Omega} = E(\mathbf{YY}')$?

4.5. Suppose that $X_t$ follows an $AR(p)$ process and $v_t$ is a white noise process that is uncorrelated with $X_{t-j}$ for all $j$. Show that the sum

$$Y_t = X_t + v_t$$

follows an $ARMA(p, p)$ process.

4.6. Generalize Exercise 4.5 to deduce that if one adds together an $AR(p)$ process with an $MA(q)$ process and if these two processes are uncorrelated with each other at all leads and lags, then the result is an $ARMA(p, p + q)$ process.

## Chapter 4 References


Ashley, Richard. 1988. "On the Relative Worth of Recent Macroeconomic Forecasts." *International Journal of Forecasting* 4:363–76.

Box, George E. P., and Gwilym M. Jenkins. 1976. *Time Series Analysis: Forecasting and Control*, rev. ed. San Francisco: Holden-Day.

Nelson, Charles R. 1972. "The Prediction Performance of the F.R.B.–M.I.T.–PENN Model of the U.S. Economy." *American Economic Review* 62:902–17.

Sargent, Thomas J. 1987. *Macroeconomic Theory*, 2d ed. Boston: Academic Press.

Wold, Herman. 1938 (2d ed. 1954). *A Study in the Analysis of Stationary Time Series.* Uppsala, Sweden: Almqvist and Wiksell.

# 5 Maximum Likelihood Estimation

## 5.1. *Introduction*

Consider an *ARMA* model of the form

$$Y_t = c + \phi_1 Y_{t-1} + \phi_2 Y_{t-2} + \cdots + \phi_p Y_{t-p} + \varepsilon_t + \theta_1 \varepsilon_{t-1} + \theta_2 \varepsilon_{t-2} + \cdots + \theta_q \varepsilon_{t-q}, \qquad [5.1.1]$$

with $\varepsilon_t$ white noise:

$$E(\varepsilon_t) = 0 \qquad [5.1.2]$$

$$E(\varepsilon_t \varepsilon_\tau) = \begin{cases} \sigma^2 & \text{for } t = \tau \\ 0 & \text{otherwise.} \end{cases} \qquad [5.1.3]$$

The previous chapters assumed that the population parameters $(c, \phi_1, \ldots, \phi_p, \theta_1, \ldots, \theta_q, \sigma^2)$ were known and showed how population moments such as $E(Y_t Y_{t-j})$ and linear forecasts $\hat{E}(Y_{t+s}|Y_t, Y_{t-1}, \ldots)$ could be calculated as functions of these population parameters. This chapter explores how to estimate the values of $(c, \phi_1, \ldots, \phi_p, \theta_1, \ldots, \theta_q, \sigma^2)$ on the basis of observations on $Y$.

The primary principle on which estimation will be based is *maximum likelihood*. Let $\boldsymbol{\theta} \equiv (c, \phi_1, \ldots, \phi_p, \theta_1, \ldots, \theta_q, \sigma^2)'$ denote the vector of population parameters. Suppose we have observed a sample of size $T$ $(y_1, y_2, \ldots, y_T)$. The approach will be to calculate the probability density

$$f_{Y_T, Y_{T-1}, \ldots, Y_1}(y_T, y_{T-1}, \ldots, y_1; \boldsymbol{\theta}), \qquad [5.1.4]$$

which might loosely be viewed as the probability of having observed this particular sample. The maximum likelihood estimate (*MLE*) of $\boldsymbol{\theta}$ is the value for which this sample is most likely to have been observed; that is, it is the value of $\boldsymbol{\theta}$ that maximizes [5.1.4].

This approach requires specifying a particular distribution for the white noise process $\varepsilon_t$. Typically we will assume that $\varepsilon_t$ is Gaussian white noise:

$$\varepsilon_t \sim \text{i.i.d. } N(0, \sigma^2). \qquad [5.1.5]$$

Although this assumption is strong, the estimates of $\boldsymbol{\theta}$ that result from it will often turn out to be sensible for non-Gaussian processes as well.

Finding maximum likelihood estimates conceptually involves two steps. First, the likelihood function [5.1.4] must be calculated. Second, values of $\boldsymbol{\theta}$ must be found that maximize this function. This chapter is organized around these two steps. Sections 5.2 through 5.6 show how to calculate the likelihood function for different Gaussian *ARMA* specifications, while subsequent sections review general techniques for numerical optimization.

## 5.2. *The Likelihood Function for a Gaussian* AR*(1) Process*

### *Evaluating the Likelihood Function*

A Gaussian $AR(1)$ process takes the form

$$Y_t = c + \phi Y_{t-1} + \varepsilon_t, \qquad [5.2.1]$$

with $\varepsilon_t \sim$ i.i.d. $N(0, \sigma^2)$. For this case, the vector of population parameters to be estimated consists of $\boldsymbol{\theta} \equiv (c, \phi, \sigma^2)'$.

Consider the probability distribution of $Y_1$, the first observation in the sample. From equations [3.4.3] and [3.4.4] this is a random variable with mean

$$E(Y_1) = \mu = c/(1 - \phi)$$

and variance

$$E(Y_1 - \mu)^2 = \sigma^2/(1 - \phi^2).$$

Since $\{\varepsilon_t\}_{t=-\infty}^{\infty}$ is Gaussian, $Y_1$ is also Gaussian. Hence, the density of the first observation takes the form

$$\begin{aligned} f_{Y_1}(y_1; \boldsymbol{\theta}) &= f_{Y_1}(y_1; c, \phi, \sigma^2) \\ &= \frac{1}{\sqrt{2\pi}\sqrt{\sigma^2/(1 - \phi^2)}} \exp\left[\frac{-\{y_1 - [c/(1 - \phi)]\}^2}{2\sigma^2/(1 - \phi^2)}\right]. \end{aligned} \qquad [5.2.2]$$

Next consider the distribution of the second observation $Y_2$ conditional on observing $Y_1 = y_1$. From [5.2.1],

$$Y_2 = c + \phi Y_1 + \varepsilon_2. \qquad [5.2.3]$$

Conditioning on $Y_1 = y_1$ means treating the random variable $Y_1$ as if it were the deterministic constant $y_1$. For this case, [5.2.3] gives $Y_2$ as the constant $(c + \phi y_1)$ plus the $N(0, \sigma^2)$ variable $\varepsilon_2$. Hence,

$$(Y_2 | Y_1 = y_1) \sim N((c + \phi y_1), \sigma^2),$$

meaning

$$f_{Y_2|Y_1}(y_2|y_1; \boldsymbol{\theta}) = \frac{1}{\sqrt{2\pi\sigma^2}} \exp\left[\frac{-(y_2 - c - \phi y_1)^2}{2\sigma^2}\right]. \qquad [5.2.4]$$

The joint density of observations 1 and 2 is then just the product of [5.2.4] and [5.2.2]:

$$f_{Y_2,Y_1}(y_2, y_1; \boldsymbol{\theta}) = f_{Y_2|Y_1}(y_2|y_1; \boldsymbol{\theta}) \cdot f_{Y_1}(y_1; \boldsymbol{\theta}).$$

Similarly, the distribution of the third observation conditional on the first two is

$$f_{Y_3|Y_2,Y_1}(y_3|y_2, y_1; \boldsymbol{\theta}) = \frac{1}{\sqrt{2\pi\sigma^2}} \exp\left[\frac{-(y_3 - c - \phi y_2)^2}{2\sigma^2}\right],$$

from which

$$f_{Y_3,Y_2,Y_1}(y_3, y_2, y_1; \boldsymbol{\theta}) = f_{Y_3|Y_2,Y_1}(y_3|y_2, y_1; \boldsymbol{\theta}) \cdot f_{Y_2,Y_1}(y_2, y_1; \boldsymbol{\theta}).$$

In general, the values of $Y_1, Y_2, \ldots, Y_{t-1}$ matter for $Y_t$ only through the value of $Y_{t-1}$, and the density of observation $t$ conditional on the preceding $t - 1$ observations is given by

$$\begin{aligned} &f_{Y_t|Y_{t-1},Y_{t-2},\ldots,Y_1}(y_t|y_{t-1}, y_{t-2}, \ldots, y_1; \boldsymbol{\theta}) \\ &\qquad = f_{Y_t|Y_{t-1}}(y_t|y_{t-1}; \boldsymbol{\theta}) \\ &\qquad = \frac{1}{\sqrt{2\pi\sigma^2}} \exp\left[\frac{-(y_t - c - \phi y_{t-1})^2}{2\sigma^2}\right]. \end{aligned} \qquad [5.2.5]$$

The joint density of the first $t$ observations is then

$$f_{Y_t,Y_{t-1},\ldots,Y_1}(y_t, y_{t-1}, \ldots, y_1; \boldsymbol{\theta}) = f_{Y_t|Y_{t-1}}(y_t|y_{t-1}; \boldsymbol{\theta}) \cdot f_{Y_{t-1},Y_{t-2},\ldots,Y_1}(y_{t-1}, y_{t-2}, \ldots, y_1; \boldsymbol{\theta}). \quad [5.2.6]$$

The likelihood of the complete sample can thus be calculated as

$$f_{Y_T,Y_{T-1},\ldots,Y_1}(y_T, y_{T-1}, \ldots, y_1; \boldsymbol{\theta}) = f_{Y_1}(y_1; \boldsymbol{\theta}) \cdot \prod_{t=2}^{T} f_{Y_t|Y_{t-1}}(y_t|y_{t-1}; \boldsymbol{\theta}). \quad [5.2.7]$$

The log likelihood function (denoted $\mathcal{L}(\boldsymbol{\theta})$) can be found by taking logs of [5.2.7]:

$$\mathcal{L}(\boldsymbol{\theta}) = \log f_{Y_1}(y_1; \boldsymbol{\theta}) + \sum_{t=2}^{T} \log f_{Y_t|Y_{t-1}}(y_t|y_{t-1}; \boldsymbol{\theta}). \quad [5.2.8]$$

Clearly, the value of $\boldsymbol{\theta}$ that maximizes [5.2.8] is identical to the value that maximizes [5.2.7]. However, Section 5.8 presents a number of useful results that can be calculated as a by-product of the maximization if one always poses the problem as maximization of the log likelihood function [5.2.8] rather than the likelihood function [5.2.7].

Substituting [5.2.2] and [5.2.5] into [5.2.8], the log likelihood for a sample of size $T$ from a Gaussian $AR(1)$ process is seen to be

$$\begin{aligned}\mathcal{L}(\boldsymbol{\theta}) = & -\tfrac{1}{2}\log(2\pi) - \tfrac{1}{2}\log[\sigma^2/(1 - \phi^2)] \\ & - \frac{\{y_1 - [c/(1 - \phi)]\}^2}{2\sigma^2/(1 - \phi^2)} - [(T - 1)/2]\log(2\pi) \\ & - [(T - 1)/2]\log(\sigma^2) - \sum_{t=2}^{T}\left[\frac{(y_t - c - \phi y_{t-1})^2}{2\sigma^2}\right].\end{aligned} \quad [5.2.9]$$

## *An Alternative Expression for the Likelihood Function*

A different description of the likelihood function for a sample of size $T$ from a Gaussian $AR(1)$ process is sometimes useful. Collect the full set of observations in a $(T \times 1)$ vector,

$$\underset{(T\times 1)}{\mathbf{y}} \equiv (y_1, y_2, \ldots, y_T)'.$$

This vector could be viewed as a single realization from a $T$-dimensional Gaussian distribution. The mean of this $(T \times 1)$ vector is

$$\begin{bmatrix} E(Y_1) \\ E(Y_2) \\ \vdots \\ E(Y_T) \end{bmatrix} = \begin{bmatrix} \mu \\ \mu \\ \vdots \\ \mu \end{bmatrix}, \quad [5.2.10]$$

where, as before, $\mu = c/(1 - \phi)$. In vector form, [5.2.10] could be written

$$E(\mathbf{Y}) = \boldsymbol{\mu},$$

where $\boldsymbol{\mu}$ denotes the $(T \times 1)$ vector on the right side of [5.2.10]. The variance-covariance matrix of $\mathbf{Y}$ is given by

$$E[(\mathbf{Y} - \boldsymbol{\mu})(\mathbf{Y} - \boldsymbol{\mu})'] = \boldsymbol{\Omega}, \quad [5.2.11]$$

where

$$\mathbf{\Omega} = \begin{bmatrix} E(Y_1 - \mu)^2 & E(Y_1 - \mu)(Y_2 - \mu) & \cdots & E(Y_1 - \mu)(Y_T - \mu) \\ E(Y_2 - \mu)(Y_1 - \mu) & E(Y_2 - \mu)^2 & \cdots & E(Y_2 - \mu)(Y_T - \mu) \\ \vdots & \vdots & \cdots & \vdots \\ E(Y_T - \mu)(Y_1 - \mu) & E(Y_T - \mu)(Y_2 - \mu) & \cdots & E(Y_T - \mu)^2 \end{bmatrix}. \qquad [5.2.12]$$

The elements of this matrix correspond to autocovariances of $Y$. Recall that the $j$th autocovariance for an $AR(1)$ process is given by

$$E(Y_t - \mu)(Y_{t-j} - \mu) = \sigma^2\phi^j/(1 - \phi^2). \qquad [5.2.13]$$

Hence, [5.2.12] can be written as

$$\mathbf{\Omega} = \sigma^2\mathbf{V}, \qquad [5.2.14]$$

where

$$\mathbf{V} = \frac{1}{1 - \phi^2}\begin{bmatrix} 1 & \phi & \phi^2 & \cdots & \phi^{T-1} \\ \phi & 1 & \phi & \cdots & \phi^{T-2} \\ \phi^2 & \phi & 1 & \cdots & \phi^{T-3} \\ \vdots & \vdots & \vdots & \cdots & \vdots \\ \phi^{T-1} & \phi^{T-2} & \phi^{T-3} & \cdots & 1 \end{bmatrix}. \qquad [5.2.15]$$

Viewing the observed sample $\mathbf{y}$ as a single draw from a $N(\boldsymbol{\mu}, \mathbf{\Omega})$ distribution, the sample likelihood could be written down immediately from the formula for the multivariate Gaussian density:

$$f_{\mathbf{Y}}(\mathbf{y}; \boldsymbol{\theta}) = (2\pi)^{-T/2}\, |\mathbf{\Omega}^{-1}|^{1/2} \exp[-\tfrac{1}{2}(\mathbf{y} - \boldsymbol{\mu})'\mathbf{\Omega}^{-1}(\mathbf{y} - \boldsymbol{\mu})], \qquad [5.2.16]$$

with log likelihood

$$\mathcal{L}(\boldsymbol{\theta}) = (-T/2)\log(2\pi) + \tfrac{1}{2}\log|\mathbf{\Omega}^{-1}| - \tfrac{1}{2}(\mathbf{y} - \boldsymbol{\mu})'\mathbf{\Omega}^{-1}(\mathbf{y} - \boldsymbol{\mu}). \qquad [5.2.17]$$

Evidently, [5.2.17] and [5.2.9] must represent the identical function of $(y_1, y_2, \ldots, y_T)$. To verify that this is indeed the case, define

$$\underset{(T\times T)}{\mathbf{L}} \equiv \begin{bmatrix} \sqrt{1 - \phi^2} & 0 & 0 & \cdots & 0 & 0 \\ -\phi & 1 & 0 & \cdots & 0 & 0 \\ 0 & -\phi & 1 & \cdots & 0 & 0 \\ \vdots & \vdots & \vdots & \cdots & \vdots & \vdots \\ 0 & 0 & 0 & \cdots & -\phi & 1 \end{bmatrix}. \qquad [5.2.18]$$

It is straightforward to show that[1]

$$\mathbf{L}'\mathbf{L} = \mathbf{V}^{-1}, \qquad [5.2.19]$$

[1]By direct multiplication, one calculates

$$\mathbf{LV} = \frac{1}{1 - \phi^2}\begin{bmatrix} \sqrt{1 - \phi^2} & \phi\sqrt{1 - \phi^2} & \phi^2\sqrt{1 - \phi^2} & \cdots & \phi^{T-1}\sqrt{1 - \phi^2} \\ 0 & (1 - \phi^2) & \phi(1 - \phi^2) & \cdots & \phi^{T-2}(1 - \phi^2) \\ 0 & 0 & (1 - \phi^2) & \cdots & \phi^{T-3}(1 - \phi^2) \\ \vdots & \vdots & \vdots & \cdots & \vdots \\ 0 & 0 & 0 & \cdots & (1 - \phi^2) \end{bmatrix},$$

and premultiplying this by $\mathbf{L}'$ produces the $(T \times T)$ identity matrix. Thus, $\mathbf{L}'\mathbf{LV} = \mathbf{I}_T$, confirming [5.2.19].

implying from [5.2.14] that

$$\mathbf{\Omega}^{-1} = \sigma^{-2}\mathbf{L}'\mathbf{L}. \qquad [5.2.20]$$

Substituting [5.2.20] into [5.2.17] results in

$$\mathcal{L}(\boldsymbol{\theta}) = (-T/2)\log(2\pi) + \tfrac{1}{2}\log|\sigma^{-2}\mathbf{L}'\mathbf{L}| - \tfrac{1}{2}(\mathbf{y} - \boldsymbol{\mu})'\sigma^{-2}\mathbf{L}'\mathbf{L}(\mathbf{y} - \boldsymbol{\mu}). \qquad [5.2.21]$$

Define the $(T \times 1)$ vector $\tilde{\mathbf{y}}$ to be

$$\begin{aligned}
\tilde{\mathbf{y}} &\equiv \mathbf{L}(\mathbf{y} - \boldsymbol{\mu}) \\
&= \begin{bmatrix} \sqrt{1-\phi^2} & 0 & 0 & \cdots & 0 & 0 \\ -\phi & 1 & 0 & \cdots & 0 & 0 \\ 0 & -\phi & 1 & \cdots & 0 & 0 \\ \vdots & \vdots & \vdots & \cdots & \vdots & \vdots \\ 0 & 0 & 0 & \cdots & -\phi & 1 \end{bmatrix} \begin{bmatrix} y_1 - \mu \\ y_2 - \mu \\ y_3 - \mu \\ \vdots \\ y_T - \mu \end{bmatrix} \qquad [5.2.22] \\
&= \begin{bmatrix} \sqrt{1-\phi^2}\,(y_1 - \mu) \\ (y_2 - \mu) - \phi(y_1 - \mu) \\ (y_3 - \mu) - \phi(y_2 - \mu) \\ \vdots \\ (y_T - \mu) - \phi(y_{T-1} - \mu) \end{bmatrix}.
\end{aligned}$$

Substituting $\mu = c/(1 - \phi)$, this becomes

$$\tilde{\mathbf{y}} = \begin{bmatrix} \sqrt{1-\phi^2}\,[y_1 - c/(1-\phi)] \\ y_2 - c - \phi y_1 \\ y_3 - c - \phi y_2 \\ \vdots \\ y_T - c - \phi y_{T-1} \end{bmatrix}.$$

The last term in [5.2.21] can thus be written

$$\begin{aligned}
\tfrac{1}{2}(\mathbf{y} - \boldsymbol{\mu})'\sigma^{-2}\mathbf{L}'\mathbf{L}(\mathbf{y} - \boldsymbol{\mu}) &= [1/(2\sigma^2)]\tilde{\mathbf{y}}'\tilde{\mathbf{y}} \\
&= [1/(2\sigma^2)](1 - \phi^2)[y_1 - c/(1-\phi)]^2 \qquad [5.2.23] \\
&\quad + [1/(2\sigma^2)]\sum_{t=2}^{T}(y_t - c - \phi y_{t-1})^2.
\end{aligned}$$

The middle term in [5.2.21] is similarly

$$\begin{aligned}
\tfrac{1}{2}\log|\sigma^{-2}\mathbf{L}'\mathbf{L}| &= \tfrac{1}{2}\log\{\sigma^{-2T}\cdot|\mathbf{L}'\mathbf{L}|\} \\
&= -\tfrac{1}{2}\log\sigma^{2T} + \tfrac{1}{2}\log|\mathbf{L}'\mathbf{L}| \qquad [5.2.24] \\
&= (-T/2)\log\sigma^2 + \log|\mathbf{L}|,
\end{aligned}$$

where use has been made of equations [A.4.8], [A.4.9], and [A.4.11] in the Mathematical Review (Appendix A) at the end of the book. Moreover, since $\mathbf{L}$ is lower triangular, its determinant is given by the product of the terms along the principal diagonal: $|\mathbf{L}| = \sqrt{1-\phi^2}$. Thus, [5.2.24] states that

$$\tfrac{1}{2}\log|\sigma^{-2}\mathbf{L}'\mathbf{L}| = (-T/2)\log\sigma^2 + \tfrac{1}{2}\log(1 - \phi^2). \qquad [5.2.25]$$

Substituting [5.2.23] and [5.2.25] into [5.2.21] reproduces [5.2.9]. Thus, equations [5.2.17] and [5.2.9] are just two different expressions for the same magnitude, as claimed. Either expression accurately describes the log likelihood function.

Expression [5.2.17] requires inverting a $(T \times T)$ matrix, whereas [5.2.9] does not. Thus, expression [5.2.9] is clearly to be preferred for computations. It avoids inverting a $(T \times T)$ matrix by writing $Y_t$ as the sum of a forecast $(c + \phi Y_{t-1})$ and a forecast error $(\varepsilon_t)$. The forecast error is independent from previous observations by construction, so the log of its density is simply added to the log likelihood of the preceding observations. This approach is known as a *prediction-error decomposition* of the likelihood function.

### *Exact Maximum Likelihood Estimates for the Gaussian* AR*(1) Process*

The *MLE* $\hat{\boldsymbol{\theta}}$ is the value for which [5.2.9] is maximized. In principle, this requires differentiating [5.2.9] and setting the result equal to zero. In practice, when an attempt is made to carry this out, the result is a system of nonlinear equations in $\boldsymbol{\theta}$ and $(y_1, y_2, \ldots, y_T)$ for which there is no simple solution for $\boldsymbol{\theta}$ in terms of $(y_1, y_2, \ldots, y_T)$. Maximization of [5.2.9] thus requires iterative or numerical procedures described in Section 5.7.

### *Conditional Maximum Likelihood Estimates*

An alternative to numerical maximization of the exact likelihood function is to regard the value of $y_1$ as deterministic and maximize the likelihood conditioned on the first observation,

$$f_{Y_T,Y_{T-1},\ldots,Y_2|Y_1}(y_T, y_{T-1}, \ldots, y_2|y_1; \boldsymbol{\theta}) = \prod_{t=2}^{T} f_{Y_t|Y_{t-1}}(y_t|y_{t-1}; \boldsymbol{\theta}), \qquad [5.2.26]$$

the objective then being to maximize

$$\begin{aligned} &\log f_{Y_T,Y_{T-1},\ldots,Y_2|Y_1}(y_T, y_{T-1}, \ldots, y_2|y_1; \boldsymbol{\theta}) \\ &\quad = -[(T-1)/2]\log(2\pi) - [(T-1)/2]\log(\sigma^2) \qquad [5.2.27] \\ &\quad\quad - \sum_{t=2}^{T}\left[\frac{(y_t - c - \phi y_{t-1})^2}{2\sigma^2}\right]. \end{aligned}$$

Maximization of [5.2.27] with respect to $c$ and $\phi$ is equivalent to minimization of

$$\sum_{t=2}^{T}(y_t - c - \phi y_{t-1})^2, \qquad [5.2.28]$$

which is achieved by an ordinary least squares (*OLS*) regression of $y_t$ on a constant and its own lagged value. The conditional maximum likelihood estimates of $c$ and $\phi$ are therefore given by

$$\begin{bmatrix} \hat{c} \\ \hat{\phi} \end{bmatrix} = \begin{bmatrix} T-1 & \Sigma y_{t-1} \\ \Sigma y_{t-1} & \Sigma y_{t-1}^2 \end{bmatrix}^{-1} \begin{bmatrix} \Sigma y_t \\ \Sigma y_{t-1}y_t \end{bmatrix},$$

where $\Sigma$ denotes summation over $t = 2, 3, \ldots, T$.

The conditional maximum likelihood estimate of the innovation variance is found by differentiating [5.2.27] with respect to $\sigma^2$ and setting the result equal to zero:

$$\frac{-(T-1)}{2\sigma^2} + \sum_{t=2}^{T}\left[\frac{(y_t - c - \phi y_{t-1})^2}{2\sigma^4}\right] = 0,$$

or

$$\hat{\sigma}^2 = \sum_{t=2}^{T} \left[ \frac{(y_t - \hat{c} - \hat{\phi} y_{t-1})^2}{T - 1} \right].$$

In other words, the conditional *MLE* is the average squared residual from the *OLS* regression [5.2.28].

In contrast to exact maximum likelihood estimates, the conditional maximum likelihood estimates are thus trivial to compute. Moreover, if the sample size $T$ is sufficiently large, the first observation makes a negligible contribution to the total likelihood. The exact *MLE* and conditional *MLE* turn out to have the same large-sample distribution, provided that $|\phi| < 1$. And when $|\phi| > 1$, the conditional *MLE* continues to provide consistent estimates, whereas maximization of [5.2.9] does not. This is because [5.2.9] is derived from [5.2.2], which does not accurately describe the density of $Y_1$ when $|\phi| > 1$. For these reasons, in most applications the parameters of an autoregression are estimated by *OLS* (conditional maximum likelihood) rather than exact maximum likelihood.

## 5.3. *The Likelihood Function for a Gaussian* AR(p) *Process*

This section discusses a Gaussian $AR(p)$ process,

$$Y_t = c + \phi_1 Y_{t-1} + \phi_2 Y_{t-2} + \cdots + \phi_p Y_{t-p} + \varepsilon_t, \qquad [5.3.1]$$

with $\varepsilon_t \sim$ i.i.d. $N(0, \sigma^2)$. In this case, the vector of population parameters to be estimated is $\boldsymbol{\theta} = (c, \phi_1, \phi_2, \ldots, \phi_p, \sigma^2)'$.

### *Evaluating the Likelihood Function*

A combination of the two methods described for the $AR(1)$ case is used to calculate the likelihood function for a sample of size $T$ for an $AR(p)$ process. The first $p$ observations in the sample $(y_1, y_2, \ldots, y_p)$ are collected in a $(p \times 1)$ vector $\mathbf{y}_p$, which is viewed as the realization of a $p$-dimensional Gaussian variable. The mean of this vector is $\boldsymbol{\mu}_p$, which denotes a $(p \times 1)$ vector each of whose elements is given by

$$\mu = c/(1 - \phi_1 - \phi_2 - \cdots - \phi_p). \qquad [5.3.2]$$

Let $\sigma^2 \mathbf{V}_p$ denote the $(p \times p)$ variance-covariance matrix of $(Y_1, Y_2, \ldots, Y_p)$:

$$\sigma^2 \mathbf{V}_p = \begin{bmatrix} E(Y_1 - \mu)^2 & E(Y_1 - \mu)(Y_2 - \mu) & \cdots & E(Y_1 - \mu)(Y_p - \mu) \\ E(Y_2 - \mu)(Y_1 - \mu) & E(Y_2 - \mu)^2 & \cdots & E(Y_2 - \mu)(Y_p - \mu) \\ \vdots & \vdots & \cdots & \vdots \\ E(Y_p - \mu)(Y_1 - \mu) & E(Y_p - \mu)(Y_2 - \mu) & \cdots & E(Y_p - \mu)^2 \end{bmatrix}. \qquad [5.3.3]$$

For example, for a first-order autoregression ($p = 1$), $\mathbf{V}_p$ is the scalar $1/(1 - \phi^2)$. For a general $p$th-order autoregression,

$$\sigma^2 \mathbf{V}_p = \begin{bmatrix} \gamma_0 & \gamma_1 & \gamma_2 & \cdots & \gamma_{p-1} \\ \gamma_1 & \gamma_0 & \gamma_1 & \cdots & \gamma_{p-2} \\ \gamma_2 & \gamma_1 & \gamma_0 & \cdots & \gamma_{p-3} \\ \vdots & \vdots & \vdots & \cdots & \vdots \\ \gamma_{p-1} & \gamma_{p-2} & \gamma_{p-3} & \cdots & \gamma_0 \end{bmatrix},$$

where $\gamma_j$, the $j$th autocovariance for an $AR(p)$ process, can be calculated using the methods in Chapter 3. The density of the first $p$ observations is then that of a $N(\boldsymbol{\mu}_p, \sigma^2\mathbf{V}_p)$ variable:

$$
\begin{aligned}
&f_{Y_p,Y_{p-1},\ldots,Y_1}(y_p, y_{p-1}, \ldots, y_1; \boldsymbol{\theta}) \\
&\quad = (2\pi)^{-p/2}|\sigma^{-2}\mathbf{V}_p^{-1}|^{1/2} \exp\left[-\frac{1}{2\sigma^2}(\mathbf{y}_p - \boldsymbol{\mu}_p)'\mathbf{V}_p^{-1}(\mathbf{y}_p - \boldsymbol{\mu}_p)\right] \\
&\quad = (2\pi)^{-p/2}(\sigma^{-2})^{p/2}|\mathbf{V}_p^{-1}|^{1/2} \exp\left[-\frac{1}{2\sigma^2}(\mathbf{y}_p - \boldsymbol{\mu}_p)'\mathbf{V}_p^{-1}(\mathbf{y}_p - \boldsymbol{\mu}_p)\right],
\end{aligned} \tag{5.3.4}
$$

where use has been made of result [A.4.8].

For the remaining observations in the sample, $(y_{p+1}, y_{p+2}, \ldots, y_T)$, the prediction-error decomposition can be used. Conditional on the first $t - 1$ observations, the $t$th observation is Gaussian with mean

$$c + \phi_1 y_{t-1} + \phi_2 y_{t-2} + \cdots + \phi_p y_{t-p}$$

and variance $\sigma^2$. Only the $p$ most recent observations matter for this distribution. Hence, for $t > p$,

$$
\begin{aligned}
&f_{Y_t|Y_{t-1},Y_{t-2},\ldots,Y_1}(y_t|y_{t-1}, y_{t-2}, \ldots, y_1; \boldsymbol{\theta}) \\
&\quad = f_{Y_t|Y_{t-1},Y_{t-2},\ldots,Y_{t-p}}(y_t|y_{t-1}, y_{t-2}, \ldots, y_{t-p}; \boldsymbol{\theta}) \\
&\quad = \frac{1}{\sqrt{2\pi\sigma^2}} \exp\left[\frac{-(y_t - c - \phi_1 y_{t-1} - \phi_2 y_{t-2} - \cdots - \phi_p y_{t-p})^2}{2\sigma^2}\right].
\end{aligned}
$$

The likelihood function for the complete sample is then

$$
\begin{aligned}
&f_{Y_T,Y_{T-1},\ldots,Y_1}(y_T, y_{T-1}, \ldots, y_1; \boldsymbol{\theta}) \\
&\quad = f_{Y_p,Y_{p-1},\ldots,Y_1}(y_p, y_{p-1}, \ldots, y_1; \boldsymbol{\theta}) \\
&\quad\quad \times \prod_{t=p+1}^{T} f_{Y_t|Y_{t-1},Y_{t-2},\ldots,Y_{t-p}}(y_t|y_{t-1}, y_{t-2}, \ldots, y_{t-p}; \boldsymbol{\theta}),
\end{aligned} \tag{5.3.5}
$$

and the log likelihood is therefore

$$
\begin{aligned}
\mathcal{L}(\boldsymbol{\theta}) &= \log f_{Y_T,Y_{T-1},\ldots,Y_1}(y_T, y_{T-1}, \ldots, y_1; \boldsymbol{\theta}) \\
&= -\frac{p}{2}\log(2\pi) - \frac{p}{2}\log(\sigma^2) + \frac{1}{2}\log|\mathbf{V}_p^{-1}| \\
&\quad - \frac{1}{2\sigma^2}(\mathbf{y}_p - \boldsymbol{\mu}_p)'\mathbf{V}_p^{-1}(\mathbf{y}_p - \boldsymbol{\mu}_p) \\
&\quad - \frac{T-p}{2}\log(2\pi) - \frac{T-p}{2}\log(\sigma^2) \\
&\quad - \sum_{t=p+1}^{T} \frac{(y_t - c - \phi_1 y_{t-1} - \phi_2 y_{t-2} - \cdots - \phi_p y_{t-p})^2}{2\sigma^2} \qquad [5.3.6] \\
&= -\frac{T}{2}\log(2\pi) - \frac{T}{2}\log(\sigma^2) + \frac{1}{2}\log|\mathbf{V}_p^{-1}| \\
&\quad - \frac{1}{2\sigma^2}(\mathbf{y}_p - \boldsymbol{\mu}_p)'\mathbf{V}_p^{-1}(\mathbf{y}_p - \boldsymbol{\mu}_p) \\
&\quad - \sum_{t=p+1}^{T} \frac{(y_t - c - \phi_1 y_{t-1} - \phi_2 y_{t-2} - \cdots - \phi_p y_{t-p})^2}{2\sigma^2}.
\end{aligned}
$$

Evaluation of [5.3.6] requires inverting the $(p \times p)$ matrix $\mathbf{V}_p$. Denote the row $i$, column $j$ element of $\mathbf{V}_p^{-1}$ by $v^{ij}(p)$. Galbraith and Galbraith (1974, equation

16, p. 70) showed that

$$v^{ij}(p) = \left[\sum_{k=0}^{i-1} \phi_k\phi_{k+j-i} - \sum_{k=p+1-j}^{p+i-j} \phi_k\phi_{k+j-i}\right] \quad \text{for } 1 \le i \le j \le p, \qquad [5.3.7]$$

where $\phi_0 \equiv -1$. Values of $v^{ij}(p)$ for $i > j$ can be inferred from the fact that $\mathbf{V}_p^{-1}$ is symmetric ($v^{ij}(p) = v^{ji}(p)$). For example, for an $AR(1)$ process, $\mathbf{V}_p^{-1}$ is a scalar whose value is found by taking $i = j = p = 1$:

$$\mathbf{V}_1^{-1} = \left[\sum_{k=0}^{0} \phi_k\phi_k - \sum_{k=1}^{1} \phi_k\phi_k\right] = (\phi_0^2 - \phi_1^2) = (1 - \phi^2).$$

Thus $\sigma^2\mathbf{V}_1 = \sigma^2/(1 - \phi^2)$, which indeed reproduces the formula for the variance of an $AR(1)$ process. For $p = 2$, equation [5.3.7] implies

$$\mathbf{V}_2^{-1} = \begin{bmatrix} (1 - \phi_2^2) & -(\phi_1 + \phi_1\phi_2) \\ -(\phi_1 + \phi_1\phi_2) & (1 - \phi_2^2) \end{bmatrix},$$

from which one readily calculates

$$|\mathbf{V}_2^{-1}| = \left|(1 + \phi_2)\begin{bmatrix} (1 - \phi_2) & -\phi_1 \\ -\phi_1 & (1 - \phi_2) \end{bmatrix}\right| = (1 + \phi_2)^2[(1 - \phi_2)^2 - \phi_1^2]$$

and

$$\begin{aligned}
&(\mathbf{y}_2 - \boldsymbol{\mu}_2)'\mathbf{V}_2^{-1}(\mathbf{y}_2 - \boldsymbol{\mu}_2) \\
&\qquad = [(y_1 - \mu) \quad (y_2 - \mu)](1 + \phi_2)\begin{bmatrix} (1 - \phi_2) & -\phi_1 \\ -\phi_1 & (1 - \phi_2) \end{bmatrix}\begin{bmatrix} (y_1 - \mu) \\ (y_2 - \mu) \end{bmatrix} \\
&\qquad = (1 + \phi_2) \times \{(1 - \phi_2)(y_1 - \mu)^2 \\
&\qquad\quad - 2\phi_1(y_1 - \mu)(y_2 - \mu) + (1 - \phi_2)(y_2 - \mu)^2\}.
\end{aligned}$$

The exact log likelihood for a Gaussian $AR(2)$ process is thus given by

$$\begin{aligned}
\mathcal{L}(\boldsymbol{\theta}) = &-\frac{T}{2}\log(2\pi) - \frac{T}{2}\log(\sigma^2) + \frac{1}{2}\log\{(1 + \phi_2)^2[(1 - \phi_2)^2 - \phi_1^2]\} \\
&- \left\{\frac{1 + \phi_2}{2\sigma^2}\right\} \times \{(1 - \phi_2)(y_1 - \mu)^2 \\
&\quad - 2\phi_1(y_1 - \mu)(y_2 - \mu) + (1 - \phi_2)(y_2 - \mu)^2\} \\
&- \sum_{t=3}^{T} \frac{(y_t - c - \phi_1 y_{t-1} - \phi_2 y_{t-2})^2}{2\sigma^2},
\end{aligned} \qquad [5.3.8]$$

where $\mu = c/(1 - \phi_1 - \phi_2)$.

### *Conditional Maximum Likelihood Estimates*

Maximization of the exact log likelihood for an $AR(p)$ process [5.3.6] must be accomplished numerically. In contrast, the log of the likelihood conditional on the first $p$ observations assumes the simple form

$$\begin{aligned}
&\log f_{Y_T, Y_{T-1}, \ldots, Y_{p+1} | Y_p, \ldots, Y_1}(y_T, y_{T-1}, \ldots, y_{p+1} | y_p, \ldots, y_1; \boldsymbol{\theta}) \\
&\quad = -\frac{T - p}{2}\log(2\pi) - \frac{T - p}{2}\log(\sigma^2) \\
&\quad\quad - \sum_{t=p+1}^{T} \frac{(y_t - c - \phi_1 y_{t-1} - \phi_2 y_{t-2} - \cdots - \phi_p y_{t-p})^2}{2\sigma^2}.
\end{aligned} \qquad [5.3.9]$$

The values of $c, \phi_1, \phi_2, \ldots, \phi_p$ that maximize [5.3.9] are the same as those that minimize

$$\sum_{t=p+1}^{T} (y_t - c - \phi_1 y_{t-1} - \phi_2 y_{t-2} - \cdots - \phi_p y_{t-p})^2. \qquad [5.3.10]$$

Thus, the conditional maximum likelihood estimates of these parameters can be obtained from an *OLS* regression of $y_t$ on a constant and $p$ of its own lagged values. The conditional maximum likelihood estimate of $\sigma^2$ turns out to be the average squared residual from this regression:

$$\hat{\sigma}^2 = \frac{1}{T-p} \sum_{t=p+1}^{T} (y_t - \hat{c} - \hat{\phi}_1 y_{t-1} - \hat{\phi}_2 y_{t-2} - \cdots - \hat{\phi}_p y_{t-p})^2.$$

The exact maximum likelihood estimates and the conditional maximum likelihood estimates again have the same large-sample distribution.

## *Maximum Likelihood Estimation for Non-Gaussian Time Series*

We noted in Chapter 4 that an *OLS* regression of a variable on a constant and $p$ of its lags would yield a consistent estimate of the coefficients of the linear projection,

$$\hat{E}(Y_t | Y_{t-1}, Y_{t-2}, \ldots, Y_{t-p}),$$

provided that the process is ergodic for second moments. This *OLS* regression also maximizes the Gaussian conditional log likelihood [5.3.9]. Thus, even if the process is non-Gaussian, if we mistakenly form a Gaussian log likelihood function and maximize it, the resulting estimates $(\hat{c}, \hat{\phi}_1, \hat{\phi}_2, \ldots, \hat{\phi}_p)$ will provide consistent estimates of the population parameters in [5.3.1].

An estimate that maximizes a misspecified likelihood function (for example, an *MLE* calculated under the assumption of a Gaussian process when the true data are non-Gaussian) is known as a *quasi-maximum likelihood estimate*. Sometimes, as turns out to be the case here, quasi-maximum likelihood estimation provides consistent estimates of the population parameters of interest. However, standard errors for the estimated coefficients that are calculated under the Gaussianity assumption need not be correct if the true data are non-Gaussian.[2]

Alternatively, if the raw data are non-Gaussian, sometimes a simple transformation such as taking logs will produce a Gaussian time series. For a positive random variable $Y_t$, Box and Cox (1964) proposed the general class of transformations

$$Y_t^{(\lambda)} = \begin{cases} \dfrac{Y_t^{\lambda} - 1}{\lambda} & \text{for } \lambda \neq 0 \\ \log Y_t & \text{for } \lambda = 0. \end{cases}$$

One approach is to pick a particular value of $\lambda$ and maximize the likelihood function for $Y_t^{(\lambda)}$ under the assumption that $Y_t^{(\lambda)}$ is a Gaussian *ARMA* process. The value of $\lambda$ that is associated with the highest value of the maximized likelihood is taken as the best transformation. However, Nelson and Granger (1979) reported discouraging results from this method in practice.

[2]These points were first raised by White (1982) and are discussed further in Sections 5.8 and 14.4.

Li and McLeod (1988) and Janacek and Swift (1990) described approaches to maximum likelihood estimation for some non-Gaussian *ARMA* models. Martin (1981) discussed robust time series estimation for contaminated data.

## 5.4. *The Likelihood Function for a Gaussian* MA*(1) Process*

### *Conditional Likelihood Function*

Calculation of the likelihood function for an autoregression turned out to be much simpler if we conditioned on initial values for the $Y$'s. Similarly, calculation of the likelihood function for a moving average process is simpler if we condition on initial values for the $\varepsilon$'s.

Consider the Gaussian $MA(1)$ process

$$Y_t = \mu + \varepsilon_t + \theta\varepsilon_{t-1} \qquad [5.4.1]$$

with $\varepsilon_t \sim$ i.i.d. $N(0, \sigma^2)$. Let $\boldsymbol{\theta} = (\mu, \theta, \sigma^2)'$ denote the population parameters to be estimated. If the value of $\varepsilon_{t-1}$ were known with certainty, then

$$Y_t|\varepsilon_{t-1} \sim N((\mu + \theta\varepsilon_{t-1}), \sigma^2)$$

or

$$f_{Y_t|\varepsilon_{t-1}}(y_t|\varepsilon_{t-1}; \boldsymbol{\theta}) = \frac{1}{\sqrt{2\pi\sigma^2}} \exp\left[\frac{-(y_t - \mu - \theta\varepsilon_{t-1})^2}{2\sigma^2}\right]. \qquad [5.4.2]$$

Suppose that we knew for certain that $\varepsilon_0 = 0$. Then

$$(Y_1|\varepsilon_0 = 0) \sim N(\mu, \sigma^2).$$

Moreover, given observation of $y_1$, the value of $\varepsilon_1$ is then known with certainty as well:

$$\varepsilon_1 = y_1 - \mu,$$

allowing application of [5.4.2] again:

$$f_{Y_2|Y_1,\varepsilon_0=0}(y_2|y_1, \varepsilon_0 = 0; \boldsymbol{\theta}) = \frac{1}{\sqrt{2\pi\sigma^2}} \exp\left[\frac{-(y_2 - \mu - \theta\varepsilon_1)^2}{2\sigma^2}\right].$$

Since $\varepsilon_1$ is known with certainty, $\varepsilon_2$ can be calculated from

$$\varepsilon_2 = y_2 - \mu - \theta\varepsilon_1.$$

Proceeding in this fashion, it is clear that given knowledge that $\varepsilon_0 = 0$, the full sequence $\{\varepsilon_1, \varepsilon_2, \ldots, \varepsilon_T\}$ can be calculated from $\{y_1, y_2, \ldots, y_T\}$ by iterating on

$$\varepsilon_t = y_t - \mu - \theta\varepsilon_{t-1} \qquad [5.4.3]$$

for $t = 1, 2, \ldots, T$, starting from $\varepsilon_0 = 0$. The conditional density of the $t$th observation can then be calculated from [5.4.2] as

$$\begin{aligned} &f_{Y_t|Y_{t-1},Y_{t-2},\ldots,Y_1,\varepsilon_0=0}(y_t|y_{t-1}, y_{t-2}, \ldots, y_1, \varepsilon_0 = 0; \boldsymbol{\theta}) \\ &\quad = f_{Y_t|\varepsilon_{t-1}}(y_t|\varepsilon_{t-1}; \boldsymbol{\theta}) \qquad [5.4.4] \\ &\quad = \frac{1}{\sqrt{2\pi\sigma^2}} \exp\left[\frac{-\varepsilon_t^2}{2\sigma^2}\right]. \end{aligned}$$

The sample likelihood would then be the product of these individual densities:

$$f_{Y_T,Y_{T-1},\ldots,Y_1|\varepsilon_0=0}(y_T, y_{T-1}, \ldots, y_1|\varepsilon_0 = 0; \boldsymbol{\theta})$$

$$= f_{Y_1|\varepsilon_0=0}(y_1|\varepsilon_0 = 0; \boldsymbol{\theta}) \prod_{t=2}^{T} f_{Y_t|Y_{t-1},Y_{t-2},\ldots,Y_1,\varepsilon_0=0}(y_t|y_{t-1}, y_{t-2}, \ldots, y_1, \varepsilon_0 = 0; \boldsymbol{\theta}).$$

The conditional log likelihood is

$$\begin{aligned} \mathcal{L}(\boldsymbol{\theta}) &= \log f_{Y_T,Y_{T-1},\ldots,Y_1|\varepsilon_0=0}(y_T, y_{T-1}, \ldots, y_1|\varepsilon_0 = 0; \boldsymbol{\theta}) \\ &= -\frac{T}{2}\log(2\pi) - \frac{T}{2}\log(\sigma^2) - \sum_{t=1}^{T}\frac{\varepsilon_t^2}{2\sigma^2}. \end{aligned} \quad [5.4.5]$$

For a particular numerical value of $\boldsymbol{\theta}$, we thus calculate the sequence of $\varepsilon$'s implied by the data from [5.4.3]. The conditional log likelihood [5.4.5] is then a function of the sum of squares of these $\varepsilon$'s. Although it is simple to program this iteration by computer, the log likelihood is a fairly complicated nonlinear function of $\mu$ and $\theta$, so that an analytical expression for the maximum likelihood estimates of $\mu$ and $\theta$ is not readily calculated. Hence, even the conditional maximum likelihood estimates for an $MA(1)$ process must be found by numerical optimization.

Iteration on [5.4.3] from an arbitrary starting value of $\varepsilon_0$ will result in

$$\begin{aligned} \varepsilon_t = (y_t - \mu) - \theta(y_{t-1} - \mu) + \theta^2(y_{t-2} - \mu) - \cdots \\ + (-1)^{t-1}\theta^{t-1}(y_1 - \mu) + (-1)^t\theta^t\varepsilon_0. \end{aligned}$$

If $|\theta|$ is substantially less than unity, the effect of imposing $\varepsilon_0 = 0$ will quickly die out and the conditional likelihood [5.4.4] will give a good approximation to the unconditional likelihood for a reasonably large sample size. By contrast, if $|\theta| > 1$, the consequences of imposing $\varepsilon_0 = 0$ accumulate over time. The conditional approach is not reasonable in such a case. If numerical optimization of [5.4.5] results in a value of $\theta$ that exceeds 1 in absolute value, the results must be discarded. The numerical optimization should be attempted again with the reciprocal of $\hat{\theta}$ used as a starting value for the numerical search procedure.

### *Exact Likelihood Function*

Two convenient algorithms are available for calculating the exact likelihood function for a Gaussian $MA(1)$ process. One approach is to use the Kalman filter discussed in Chapter 13. A second approach uses the triangular factorization of the variance-covariance matrix. The second approach is described here.

As in Section 5.2, the observations on $y$ can be collected in a $(T \times 1)$ vector $\mathbf{y} \equiv (y_1, y_2, \ldots, y_T)'$ with mean $\boldsymbol{\mu} \equiv (\mu, \mu, \ldots, \mu)'$ and $(T \times T)$ variance-covariance matrix

$$\boldsymbol{\Omega} = E(\mathbf{Y} - \boldsymbol{\mu})(\mathbf{Y} - \boldsymbol{\mu})'.$$

The variance-covariance matrix for $T$ consecutive draws from an $MA(1)$ process is

$$\boldsymbol{\Omega} = \sigma^2 \begin{bmatrix} (1+\theta^2) & \theta & 0 & \cdots & 0 \\ \theta & (1+\theta^2) & \theta & \cdots & 0 \\ 0 & \theta & (1+\theta^2) & \cdots & 0 \\ \vdots & \vdots & \vdots & \cdots & \vdots \\ 0 & 0 & 0 & \cdots & (1+\theta^2) \end{bmatrix}.$$

The likelihood function is then

$$f_{\mathbf{Y}}(\mathbf{y}; \boldsymbol{\theta}) = (2\pi)^{-T/2}|\boldsymbol{\Omega}|^{-1/2}\exp[-\tfrac{1}{2}(\mathbf{y} - \boldsymbol{\mu})'\boldsymbol{\Omega}^{-1}(\mathbf{y} - \boldsymbol{\mu})]. \quad [5.4.6]$$

A prediction-error decomposition of the likelihood is provided from the triangular factorization of $\mathbf{\Omega}$,

$$\mathbf{\Omega} = \mathbf{ADA}', \qquad [5.4.7]$$

where $\mathbf{A}$ is the lower triangular matrix given in [4.5.18] and $\mathbf{D}$ is the diagonal matrix in [4.5.19]. Substituting [5.4.7] into [5.4.6] gives

$$f_{\mathbf{Y}}(\mathbf{y};\,\boldsymbol{\theta}) = (2\pi)^{-T/2}|\mathbf{ADA}'|^{-1/2} \times \exp[-\tfrac{1}{2}(\mathbf{y} - \boldsymbol{\mu})'[\mathbf{A}']^{-1}\mathbf{D}^{-1}\mathbf{A}^{-1}(\mathbf{y} - \boldsymbol{\mu})]. \qquad [5.4.8]$$

But $\mathbf{A}$ is a lower triangular matrix with 1s along the principal diagonal. Hence, $|\mathbf{A}| = 1$ and

$$|\mathbf{ADA}'| = |\mathbf{A}|\cdot|\mathbf{D}|\cdot|\mathbf{A}'| = |\mathbf{D}|.$$

Further defining

$$\tilde{\mathbf{y}} \equiv \mathbf{A}^{-1}(\mathbf{y} - \boldsymbol{\mu}), \qquad [5.4.9]$$

the likelihood [5.4.8] can be written

$$f_{\mathbf{Y}}(\mathbf{y};\,\boldsymbol{\theta}) = (2\pi)^{-T/2}\,|\mathbf{D}|^{-1/2}\exp[-\tfrac{1}{2}\tilde{\mathbf{y}}'\mathbf{D}^{-1}\tilde{\mathbf{y}}]. \qquad [5.4.10]$$

Notice that [5.4.9] implies

$$\mathbf{A}\tilde{\mathbf{y}} = \mathbf{y} - \boldsymbol{\mu}.$$

The first row of this system states that $\tilde{y}_1 = y_1 - \mu$, while the $t$th row implies that

$$\tilde{y}_t = y_t - \mu - \frac{\theta[1 + \theta^2 + \theta^4 + \cdots + \theta^{2(t-2)}]}{1 + \theta^2 + \theta^4 + \cdots + \theta^{2(t-1)}}\,\tilde{y}_{t-1}. \qquad [5.4.11]$$

The vector $\tilde{\mathbf{y}}$ can thus be calculated by iterating on [5.4.11] for $t = 2, 3, \ldots, T$ starting from $\tilde{y}_1 = y_1 - \mu$. The variable $\tilde{y}_t$ has the interpretation as the residual from a linear projection of $y_t$ on a constant and $y_{t-1}, y_{t-2}, \ldots, y_1$, while the $t$th diagonal element of $\mathbf{D}$ gives the $MSE$ of this linear projection:

$$d_{tt} = E(\tilde{Y}_t^2) = \sigma^2\,\frac{1 + \theta^2 + \theta^4 + \cdots + \theta^{2t}}{1 + \theta^2 + \theta^4 + \cdots + \theta^{2(t-1)}}. \qquad [5.4.12]$$

Since $\mathbf{D}$ is diagonal, its determinant is the product of the terms along the principal diagonal,

$$|\mathbf{D}| = \prod_{t=1}^{T} d_{tt}, \qquad [5.4.13]$$

while the inverse of $\mathbf{D}$ is obtained by taking reciprocals of the terms along the principal diagonal. Hence,

$$\tilde{\mathbf{y}}'\mathbf{D}^{-1}\tilde{\mathbf{y}} = \sum_{t=1}^{T}\frac{\tilde{y}_t^2}{d_{tt}}. \qquad [5.4.14]$$

Substituting [5.4.13] and [5.4.14] into [5.4.10], the likelihood function is

$$f_{\mathbf{Y}}(\mathbf{y};\,\boldsymbol{\theta}) = (2\pi)^{-T/2}\left[\prod_{t=1}^{T} d_{tt}\right]^{-1/2}\exp\left[-\frac{1}{2}\sum_{t=1}^{T}\frac{\tilde{y}_t^2}{d_{tt}}\right]. \qquad [5.4.15]$$

The exact log likelihood for a Gaussian $MA(1)$ process is therefore

$$\mathcal{L}(\boldsymbol{\theta}) = \log f_{\mathbf{Y}}(\mathbf{y};\,\boldsymbol{\theta}) = -\frac{T}{2}\log(2\pi) - \frac{1}{2}\sum_{t=1}^{T}\log(d_{tt}) - \frac{1}{2}\sum_{t=1}^{T}\frac{\tilde{y}_t^2}{d_{tt}}. \qquad [5.4.16]$$

Given numerical values for $\mu$, $\theta$, and $\sigma^2$, the sequence $\tilde{y}_t$ is calculated by iterating on [5.4.11] starting with $\tilde{y}_1 = y_1 - \mu$, while $d_{tt}$ is given by [5.4.12].

In contrast to the conditional log likelihood function [5.4.5], expression [5.4.16] will be valid regardless of whether $\theta$ is associated with an invertible $MA(1)$ representation. The value of [5.4.16] at $\theta = \tilde{\theta}$, $\sigma^2 = \tilde{\sigma}^2$ will be identical to its value at $\theta = \tilde{\theta}^{-1}$, $\sigma^2 = \tilde{\theta}^2\tilde{\sigma}^2$; see Exercise 5.1.

## 5.5. *The Likelihood Function for a Gaussian* MA(q) *Process*

### *Conditional Likelihood Function*

For the $MA(q)$ process,

$$Y_t = \mu + \varepsilon_t + \theta_1 \varepsilon_{t-1} + \theta_2 \varepsilon_{t-2} + \cdots + \theta_q \varepsilon_{t-q}, \qquad [5.5.1]$$

a simple approach is to condition on the assumption that the first $q$ values for $\varepsilon$ were all zero:

$$\varepsilon_0 = \varepsilon_{-1} = \cdots = \varepsilon_{-q+1} = 0. \qquad [5.5.2]$$

From these starting values we can iterate on

$$\varepsilon_t = y_t - \mu - \theta_1 \varepsilon_{t-1} - \theta_2 \varepsilon_{t-2} - \cdots - \theta_q \varepsilon_{t-q} \qquad [5.5.3]$$

for $t = 1, 2, \ldots, T$. Let $\boldsymbol{\varepsilon}_0$ denote the $(q \times 1)$ vector $(\varepsilon_0, \varepsilon_{-1}, \ldots, \varepsilon_{-q+1})'$. The conditional log likelihood is then

$$\begin{aligned} \mathcal{L}(\boldsymbol{\theta}) &= \log f_{Y_T, Y_{T-1}, \ldots, Y_1 | \boldsymbol{\varepsilon}_0 = \mathbf{0}}(y_T, y_{T-1}, \ldots, y_1 | \boldsymbol{\varepsilon}_0 = \mathbf{0}; \boldsymbol{\theta}) \\ &= -\frac{T}{2}\log(2\pi) - \frac{T}{2}\log(\sigma^2) - \sum_{t=1}^{T} \frac{\varepsilon_t^2}{2\sigma^2}, \end{aligned} \qquad [5.5.4]$$

where $\boldsymbol{\theta} = (\mu, \theta_1, \theta_2, \ldots, \theta_q, \sigma^2)'$. Again, expression [5.5.4] is useful only if all values of $z$ for which

$$1 + \theta_1 z + \theta_2 z^2 + \cdots + \theta_q z^q = 0$$

lie outside the unit circle.

### *Exact Likelihood Function*

The exact likelihood function is given by

$$f_{\mathbf{Y}}(\mathbf{y}; \boldsymbol{\theta}) = (2\pi)^{-T/2} |\boldsymbol{\Omega}|^{-1/2} \exp[-\tfrac{1}{2}(\mathbf{y} - \boldsymbol{\mu})' \boldsymbol{\Omega}^{-1} (\mathbf{y} - \boldsymbol{\mu})], \qquad [5.5.5]$$

where as before $\mathbf{y} \equiv (y_1, y_2, \ldots, y_T)'$ and $\boldsymbol{\mu} \equiv (\mu, \mu, \ldots, \mu)'$. Here $\boldsymbol{\Omega}$ represents the variance-covariance matrix of $T$ consecutive draws from an $MA(q)$ process:

$\boldsymbol{\Omega} =$

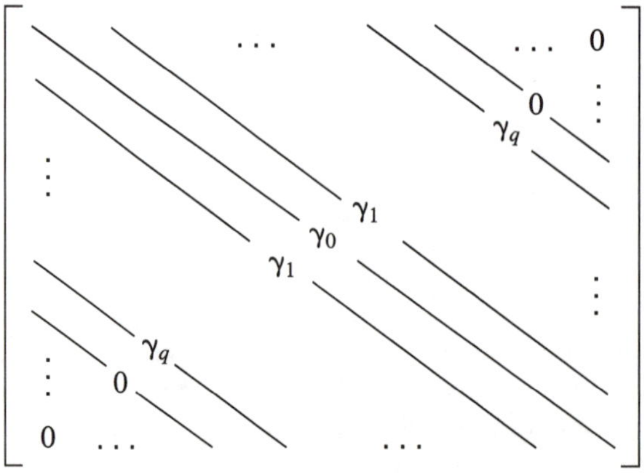


. [5.5.6]

The row $i$, column $j$ element of $\mathbf{\Omega}$ is given by $\gamma_{|i-j|}$, where $\gamma_k$ is the $k$th autocovariance of an $MA(q)$ process:

$$\gamma_k = \begin{cases} \sigma^2(\theta_k + \theta_{k+1}\theta_1 + \theta_{k+2}\theta_2 + \cdots + \theta_q\theta_{q-k}) & \text{for } k = 0, 1, \ldots, q \\ 0 & \text{for } k > q, \end{cases} \tag{5.5.7}$$

where $\theta_0 \equiv 1$. Again, the exact likelihood function [5.5.5] can be evaluated using either the Kalman filter of Chapter 13 or the triangular factorization of $\mathbf{\Omega}$,

$$\mathbf{\Omega} = \mathbf{ADA}', \tag{5.5.8}$$

where $\mathbf{A}$ is the lower triangular matrix given by [4.4.11] and $\mathbf{D}$ is the diagonal matrix given by [4.4.7]. Note that the band structure of $\mathbf{\Omega}$ in [5.5.6] makes $\mathbf{A}$ and $\mathbf{D}$ simple to calculate. After the first $(q + 1)$ rows, all the subsequent entries in the first column of $\mathbf{\Omega}$ are already zero, so no multiple of the first row need be added to make these zero. Hence, $a_{i1} = 0$ for $i > q + 1$. Similarly, beyond the first $(q + 2)$ rows of the second column, no multiple of the second row need be added to make these entries zero, meaning that $a_{i2} = 0$ for $i > q + 2$. Thus $\mathbf{A}$ is a lower triangular band matrix with $a_{ij} = 0$ for $i > q + j$:

$$\mathbf{A} = \begin{bmatrix} 1 & 0 & 0 & \cdots & 0 & 0 \\ a_{21} & 1 & 0 & \cdots & 0 & 0 \\ a_{31} & a_{32} & 1 & \cdots & 0 & 0 \\ \vdots & \vdots & \vdots & \cdots & \vdots & \vdots \\ a_{q+1,1} & a_{q+1,2} & a_{q+1,3} & \cdots & 0 & 0 \\ 0 & a_{q+2,2} & a_{q+2,3} & \cdots & 0 & 0 \\ \vdots & \vdots & \vdots & \cdots & \vdots & \vdots \\ 0 & 0 & 0 & \cdots & a_{T,T-1} & 1 \end{bmatrix}.$$

A computer can be programmed to calculate these matrices quickly for a given numerical value for $\boldsymbol{\theta}$.

Substituting [5.5.8] into [5.5.5], the exact likelihood function for a Gaussian $MA(q)$ process can be written as in [5.4.10]:

$$f_{\mathbf{Y}}(\mathbf{y}; \boldsymbol{\theta}) = (2\pi)^{-T/2}|\mathbf{D}|^{-1/2} \exp[-\tfrac{1}{2}\tilde{\mathbf{y}}'\mathbf{D}^{-1}\tilde{\mathbf{y}}]$$

where

$$\mathbf{A}\tilde{\mathbf{y}} = \mathbf{y} - \boldsymbol{\mu}. \tag{5.5.9}$$

The elements of $\tilde{\mathbf{y}}$ can be calculated recursively by working down the rows of [5.5.9]:

$$\begin{aligned} \tilde{y}_1 &= y_1 - \mu \\ \tilde{y}_2 &= (y_2 - \mu) - a_{21}\tilde{y}_1 \\ \tilde{y}_3 &= (y_3 - \mu) - a_{32}\tilde{y}_2 - a_{31}\tilde{y}_1 \\ &\vdots \\ \tilde{y}_t &= (y_t - \mu) - a_{t,t-1}\tilde{y}_{t-1} - a_{t,t-2}\tilde{y}_{t-2} - \cdots - a_{t,t-q}\tilde{y}_{t-q}. \end{aligned}$$

The exact log likelihood function can then be calculated as in [5.4.16]:

$$\mathcal{L}(\boldsymbol{\theta}) = \log f_{\mathbf{Y}}(\mathbf{y}; \boldsymbol{\theta}) = -\frac{T}{2}\log(2\pi) - \frac{1}{2}\sum_{t=1}^{T}\log(d_{tt}) - \frac{1}{2}\sum_{t=1}^{T}\frac{\tilde{y}_t^2}{d_{tt}}. \tag{5.5.10}$$

## 5.6. *The Likelihood Function for a Gaussian ARMA(p, q) Process*

### *Conditional Likelihood Function*

A Gaussian $ARMA(p, q)$ process takes the form

$$\begin{aligned} Y_t = c + \phi_1 Y_{t-1} + \phi_2 Y_{t-2} + \cdots + \phi_p Y_{t-p} + \varepsilon_t \\ + \theta_1 \varepsilon_{t-1} + \theta_2 \varepsilon_{t-2} + \cdots + \theta_q \varepsilon_{t-q}, \end{aligned} \qquad [5.6.1]$$

where $\varepsilon_t \sim$ i.i.d. $N(0, \sigma^2)$. The goal is to estimate the vector of population parameters $\boldsymbol{\theta} = (c, \phi_1, \phi_2, \ldots, \phi_p, \theta_1, \theta_2, \ldots, \theta_q, \sigma^2)'$.

The approximation to the likelihood function for an autoregression conditioned on initial values of the $y$'s. The approximation to the likelihood function for a moving average process conditioned on initial values of the $\varepsilon$'s. A common approximation to the likelihood function for an $ARMA(p, q)$ process conditions on both $y$'s and $\varepsilon$'s.

Taking initial values for $\mathbf{y}_0 \equiv (y_0, y_{-1}, \ldots, y_{-p+1})'$ and $\boldsymbol{\varepsilon}_0 \equiv (\varepsilon_0, \varepsilon_{-1}, \ldots, \varepsilon_{-q+1})'$ as given, the sequence $\{\varepsilon_1, \varepsilon_2, \ldots, \varepsilon_T\}$ can be calculated from $\{y_1, y_2, \ldots, y_T\}$ by iterating on

$$\begin{aligned} \varepsilon_t = y_t - c - \phi_1 y_{t-1} - \phi_2 y_{t-2} - \cdots - \phi_p y_{t-p} \\ - \theta_1 \varepsilon_{t-1} - \theta_2 \varepsilon_{t-2} - \cdots - \theta_q \varepsilon_{t-q} \end{aligned} \qquad [5.6.2]$$

for $t = 1, 2, \ldots, T$. The conditional log likelihood is then

$$\begin{aligned} \mathcal{L}(\boldsymbol{\theta}) &= \log f_{Y_T, Y_{T-1}, \ldots, Y_1 | \mathbf{Y}_0, \boldsymbol{\varepsilon}_0}(y_T, y_{T-1}, \ldots, y_1 | \mathbf{y}_0, \boldsymbol{\varepsilon}_0; \boldsymbol{\theta}) \\ &= -\frac{T}{2}\log(2\pi) - \frac{T}{2}\log(\sigma^2) - \sum_{t=1}^{T} \frac{\varepsilon_t^2}{2\sigma^2}. \end{aligned} \qquad [5.6.3]$$

One option is to set initial $y$'s and $\varepsilon$'s equal to their expected values. That is, set $y_s = c/(1 - \phi_1 - \phi_2 - \cdots - \phi_p)$ for $s = 0, -1, \ldots, -p + 1$ and set $\varepsilon_s = 0$ for $s = 0, -1, \ldots, -q + 1$, and then proceed with the iteration in [5.6.2] for $t = 1, 2, \ldots, T$. Alternatively, Box and Jenkins (1976, p. 211) recommended setting $\varepsilon$'s to zero but $y$'s equal to their actual values. Thus, iteration on [5.6.2] is started at date $t = p + 1$ with $y_1, y_2, \ldots, y_p$ set to the observed values and

$$\varepsilon_p = \varepsilon_{p-1} = \cdots = \varepsilon_{p-q+1} = 0.$$

Then the conditional likelihood calculated is

$$\begin{aligned} &\log f(y_T, \ldots, y_{p+1} | y_p, \ldots, y_1, \varepsilon_p = 0, \ldots, \varepsilon_{p-q+1} = 0) \\ &\qquad = -\frac{T-p}{2}\log(2\pi) - \frac{T-p}{2}\log(\sigma^2) - \sum_{t=p+1}^{T} \frac{\varepsilon_t^2}{2\sigma^2}. \end{aligned}$$

As in the case for the moving average processes, these approximations should be used only if all values of $z$ satisfying

$$1 + \theta_1 z + \theta_2 z^2 + \cdots + \theta_q z^q = 0$$

lie outside the unit circle.

### *Alternative Algorithms*

The simplest approach to calculating the exact likelihood function for a Gaussian *ARMA* process is to use the Kalman filter described in Chapter 13. For more details on exact and approximate maximum likelihood estimation of *ARMA* models, see Galbraith and Galbraith (1974), Box and Jenkins (1976, Chapter 6), Hannan and Rissanen (1982), and Koreisha and Pukkila (1989).

## 5.7. *Numerical Optimization*

Previous sections of this chapter have shown how to calculate the log likelihood function

$$\mathcal{L}(\boldsymbol{\theta}) = \log f_{Y_T,Y_{T-1},\ldots,Y_1}(y_T, y_{T-1}, \ldots, y_1; \boldsymbol{\theta}) \qquad [5.7.1]$$

for various specifications of the process thought to have generated the observed data $y_1, y_2, \ldots, y_T$. Given the observed data, the formulas given could be used to calculate the value of $\mathcal{L}(\boldsymbol{\theta})$ for any given numerical value of $\boldsymbol{\theta}$.

This section discusses how to find the value of $\hat{\boldsymbol{\theta}}$ that maximizes $\mathcal{L}(\boldsymbol{\theta})$ given no more knowledge than this ability to calculate the value of $\mathcal{L}(\boldsymbol{\theta})$ for any particular value of $\boldsymbol{\theta}$. The general approach is to write a procedure that enables a computer to calculate the numerical value of $\mathcal{L}(\boldsymbol{\theta})$ for any particular numerical values for $\boldsymbol{\theta}$ and the observed data $y_1, y_2, \ldots, y_T$. We can think of this procedure as a "black box" that enables us to guess some value of $\boldsymbol{\theta}$ and see what the resulting value of $\mathcal{L}(\boldsymbol{\theta})$ would be:

| ***Input*** | | ***Procedure*** | | ***Output*** |
|---|---|---|---|---|
| values of $y_1, y_2, \ldots, y_T$ and $\boldsymbol{\theta}$ | → | calculates $\mathcal{L}(\boldsymbol{\theta})$ | → | value of $\mathcal{L}(\boldsymbol{\theta})$ . |

The idea will be to make a series of different guesses for $\boldsymbol{\theta}$, compare the value of $\mathcal{L}(\boldsymbol{\theta})$ for each guess, and try to infer from these values for $\mathcal{L}(\boldsymbol{\theta})$ the value $\hat{\boldsymbol{\theta}}$ for which $\mathcal{L}(\boldsymbol{\theta})$ is largest. Such methods are described as *numerical maximization*.

### *Grid Search*

The simplest approach to numerical maximization is known as the *grid search* method. To illustrate this approach, suppose we have data generated by an $AR(1)$ process, for which the log likelihood was seen to be given by [5.2.9]. To keep the example very simple, it is assumed to be known that the mean of the process is zero ($c = 0$) and that the innovations have unit variance ($\sigma^2 = 1$). Thus the only unknown parameter is the autoregressive coefficient $\phi$, and [5.2.9] simplifies to

$$\begin{aligned}\mathcal{L}(\phi) = &-\frac{T}{2}\log(2\pi) + \frac{1}{2}\log(1 - \phi^2) \\ &- \frac{1}{2}(1 - \phi^2)y_1^2 - \frac{1}{2}\sum_{t=2}^{T}(y_t - \phi y_{t-1})^2.\end{aligned} \qquad [5.7.2]$$

Suppose that the observed sample consists of the following $T = 5$ observations:

$$y_1 = 0.8 \qquad y_2 = 0.2 \qquad y_3 = -1.2 \qquad y_4 = -0.4 \qquad y_5 = 0.0.$$

If we make an arbitrary guess as to the value of $\phi$, say, $\phi = 0.0$, and plug this guess into expression [5.7.2], we calculate that $\mathcal{L}(\phi) = -5.73$ at $\phi = 0.0$. Trying another guess ($\phi = 0.1$), we calculate $\mathcal{L}(\phi) = -5.71$ at $\phi = 0.1$—the log likelihood is higher at $\phi = 0.1$ than at $\phi = 0.0$. Continuing in this fashion, we could calculate the value of $\mathcal{L}(\phi)$ for every value of $\phi$ between $-0.9$ and $+0.9$ in increments of

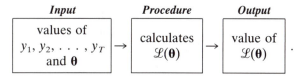

0.1. The results are reported in Figure 5.1. It appears from these calculations that the log likelihood function $\mathcal{L}(\phi)$ is nicely behaved with a unique maximum at some value of $\phi$ between 0.1 and 0.3. We could then focus on this subregion of the parameter space and evaluate $\mathcal{L}(\phi)$ at a finer grid, calculating the value of $\mathcal{L}(\phi)$ for all values of $\phi$ between 0.1 and 0.3 in increments of 0.02. Proceeding in this fashion, it should be possible to get arbitrarily close to the value of $\phi$ that maximizes $\mathcal{L}(\phi)$ by making the grid finer and finer.

Note that this procedure does not find the *exact MLE* $\hat{\phi}$, but instead approximates it with any accuracy desired. In general, this will be the case with any numerical maximization algorithm. To use these algorithms we therefore have to specify a *convergence criterion*, or some way of deciding when we are close enough to the true maximum. For example, suppose we want an estimate $\hat{\phi}$ that differs from the true *MLE* by no more than $\pm 0.0001$. Then we would continue refining the grid until the increments are in steps of 0.0001, and the best estimate among the elements of that grid would be the numerical *MLE* of $\phi$.

For the simple $AR(1)$ example in Figure 5.1, the log likelihood function is *unimodal*—there is a unique value $\boldsymbol{\theta}$ for which $\partial\mathcal{L}(\boldsymbol{\theta})/\partial\boldsymbol{\theta} = \mathbf{0}$. For a general numerical maximization problem, this need not be the case. For example, suppose that we are interested in estimating a scalar parameter $\theta$ for which the log likelihood function is as displayed in Figure 5.2. The value $\theta = -0.6$ is a *local maximum*, meaning that the likelihood function is higher there than for any other $\theta$ in a neighborhood around $\theta = -0.6$. However, the *global maximum* occurs around $\theta = 0.2$. The grid search method should work well for a unimodal likelihood as long as $\mathcal{L}(\boldsymbol{\theta})$ is continuous. When there are multiple local maxima, the grid must be sufficiently fine to reveal all of the local "hills" on the likelihood surface.

### *Steepest Ascent*

Grid search can be a very good method when there is a single unknown parameter to estimate. However, it quickly becomes intractable when the number of elements of $\boldsymbol{\theta}$ becomes large. An alternative numerical method that often suc-

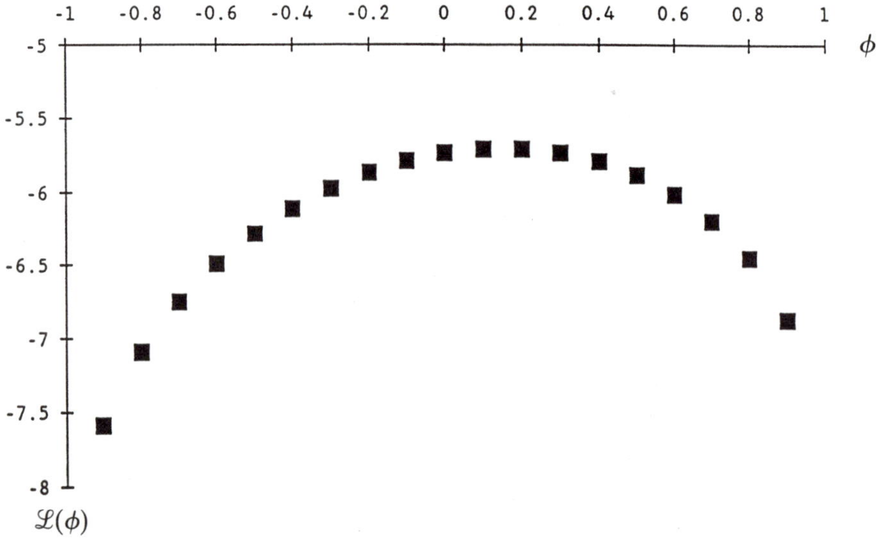


**FIGURE 5.1** Log likelihood for an $AR(1)$ process for various guesses of $\phi$.

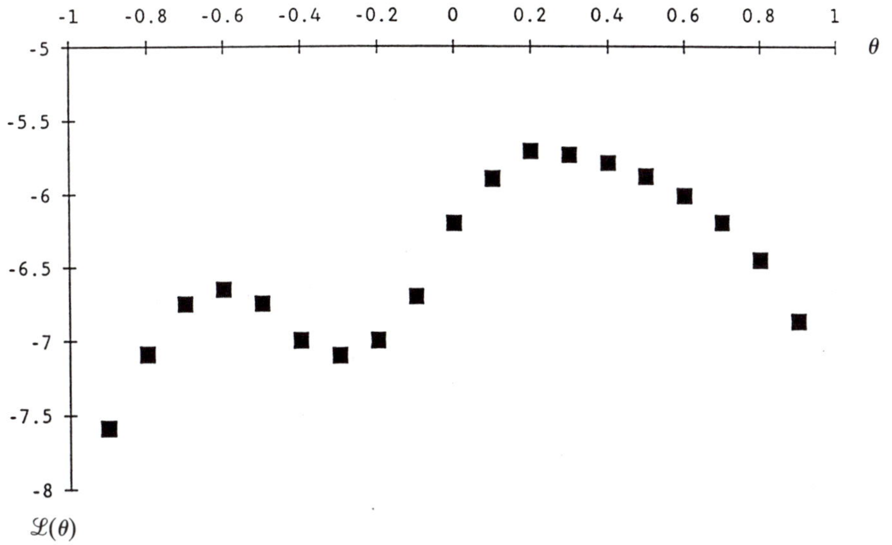


**FIGURE 5.2** Bimodal log likelihood function.

ceeds in maximizing a continuously differentiable function of a large number of parameters is known as *steepest ascent.*

To understand this approach, let us temporarily disregard the "black box" nature of the investigation and instead examine how we would proceed analytically with a particular maximization problem. Suppose we have an initial estimate of the parameter vector, denoted $\boldsymbol{\theta}^{(0)}$, and wish to come up with a better estimate $\boldsymbol{\theta}^{(1)}$. Imagine that we are constrained to choose $\boldsymbol{\theta}^{(1)}$ so that the squared distance between $\boldsymbol{\theta}^{(0)}$ and $\boldsymbol{\theta}^{(1)}$ is some fixed number $k$:

$$\{\boldsymbol{\theta}^{(1)} - \boldsymbol{\theta}^{(0)}\}'\{\boldsymbol{\theta}^{(1)} - \boldsymbol{\theta}^{(0)}\} = k.$$

The optimal value to choose for $\boldsymbol{\theta}^{(1)}$ would then be the solution to the following constrained maximization problem:

$$\max_{\boldsymbol{\theta}^{(1)}} \mathcal{L}(\boldsymbol{\theta}^{(1)}) \qquad \text{subject to} \quad \{\boldsymbol{\theta}^{(1)} - \boldsymbol{\theta}^{(0)}\}'\{\boldsymbol{\theta}^{(1)} - \boldsymbol{\theta}^{(0)}\} = k.$$

To characterize the solution to this problem,[3] form the Lagrangean,

$$J(\boldsymbol{\theta}^{(1)}) = \mathcal{L}(\boldsymbol{\theta}^{(1)}) + \lambda[k - \{\boldsymbol{\theta}^{(1)} - \boldsymbol{\theta}^{(0)}\}'\{\boldsymbol{\theta}^{(1)} - \boldsymbol{\theta}^{(0)}\}], \tag{5.7.3}$$

where $\lambda$ denotes a Lagrange multiplier. Differentiating [5.7.3] with respect to $\boldsymbol{\theta}^{(1)}$ and setting the result equal to zero yields

$$\left.\frac{\partial \mathcal{L}(\boldsymbol{\theta})}{\partial \boldsymbol{\theta}}\right|_{\boldsymbol{\theta}=\boldsymbol{\theta}^{(1)}} - (2\lambda)\{\boldsymbol{\theta}^{(1)} - \boldsymbol{\theta}^{(0)}\} = \mathbf{0}. \tag{5.7.4}$$

Let $\mathbf{g}(\boldsymbol{\theta})$ denote the gradient vector of the log likelihood function:

$$\mathbf{g}(\boldsymbol{\theta}) \equiv \frac{\partial \mathcal{L}(\boldsymbol{\theta})}{\partial \boldsymbol{\theta}}.$$

If there are $a$ elements of $\boldsymbol{\theta}$, then $\mathbf{g}(\boldsymbol{\theta})$ is an $(a \times 1)$ vector whose $i$th element represents the derivative of the log likelihood with respect to the $i$th element of $\boldsymbol{\theta}$.

[3]See Chiang (1974) for an introduction to the use of Lagrange multipliers for solving a constrained optimization problem.

Using this notation, expression [5.7.4] can be written as

$$\boldsymbol{\theta}^{(1)} - \boldsymbol{\theta}^{(0)} = [1/(2\lambda)] \cdot \mathbf{g}(\boldsymbol{\theta}^{(1)}). \qquad [5.7.5]$$

Expression [5.7.5] asserts that if we are allowed to change $\boldsymbol{\theta}$ by only a fixed amount, the biggest increase in the log likelihood function will be achieved if the change in $\boldsymbol{\theta}$ (the magnitude $\boldsymbol{\theta}^{(1)} - \boldsymbol{\theta}^{(0)}$) is chosen to be a constant $1/(2\lambda)$ times the gradient vector $\mathbf{g}(\boldsymbol{\theta}^{(1)})$. If we are contemplating a very small step (so that $k$ is near zero), the value $\mathbf{g}(\boldsymbol{\theta}^{(1)})$ will approach $\mathbf{g}(\boldsymbol{\theta}^{(0)})$. In other words, the gradient vector $\mathbf{g}(\boldsymbol{\theta}^{(0)})$ gives the direction in which the log likelihood function increases most steeply from $\boldsymbol{\theta}^{(0)}$.

For illustration, suppose that $a = 2$ and let the log likelihood be

$$\mathcal{L}(\boldsymbol{\theta}) = -1.5\theta_1^2 - 2\theta_2^2. \qquad [5.7.6]$$

We can easily see analytically for this example that the *MLE* is given by $\hat{\boldsymbol{\theta}} = (0, 0)'$. Let us nevertheless use this example to illustrate how the method of steepest ascent works. The elements of the gradient vector are

$$\frac{\partial \mathcal{L}(\boldsymbol{\theta})}{\partial \theta_1} = -3\theta_1 \qquad \frac{\partial \mathcal{L}(\boldsymbol{\theta})}{\partial \theta_2} = -4\theta_2. \qquad [5.7.7]$$

Suppose that the initial guess is $\boldsymbol{\theta}^{(0)} = (-1, 1)'$. Then

$$\left.\frac{\partial \mathcal{L}(\boldsymbol{\theta})}{\partial \theta_1}\right|_{\boldsymbol{\theta}=\boldsymbol{\theta}^{(0)}} = 3 \qquad \left.\frac{\partial \mathcal{L}(\boldsymbol{\theta})}{\partial \theta_2}\right|_{\boldsymbol{\theta}=\boldsymbol{\theta}^{(0)}} = -4.$$

An increase in $\theta_1$ would increase the likelihood, while an increase in $\theta_2$ would decrease the likelihood. The gradient vector evaluated at $\boldsymbol{\theta}^{(0)}$ is

$$\mathbf{g}(\boldsymbol{\theta}^{(0)}) = \begin{bmatrix} 3 \\ -4 \end{bmatrix},$$

so that the optimal step $\boldsymbol{\theta}^{(1)} - \boldsymbol{\theta}^{(0)}$ should be proportional to $(3, -4)'$. For example, with $k = 1$ we would choose

$$\theta_1^{(1)} - \theta_1^{(0)} = \tfrac{3}{5}$$
$$\theta_2^{(1)} - \theta_2^{(0)} = -\tfrac{4}{5};$$

that is, the new guesses would be $\theta_1^{(1)} = -0.4$ and $\theta_2^{(1)} = 0.2$. To increase the likelihood by the greatest amount, we want to increase $\theta_1$ and decrease $\theta_2$ relative to their values at the initial guess $\boldsymbol{\theta}^{(0)}$. Since a one-unit change in $\theta_2$ has a bigger effect on $\mathcal{L}(\boldsymbol{\theta})$ than would a one-unit change in $\theta_1$, the change in $\theta_2$ is larger in absolute value than the change in $\theta_1$.

Let us now return to the black box perspective, where the only capability we have is to calculate the value of $\mathcal{L}(\boldsymbol{\theta})$ for a specified numerical value of $\boldsymbol{\theta}$. We might start with an arbitrary initial guess for the value of $\boldsymbol{\theta}$, denoted $\boldsymbol{\theta}^{(0)}$. Suppose we then calculate the value of the gradient vector at $\boldsymbol{\theta}^{(0)}$:

$$\mathbf{g}(\boldsymbol{\theta}^{(0)}) = \left.\frac{\partial \mathcal{L}(\boldsymbol{\theta})}{\partial \boldsymbol{\theta}}\right|_{\boldsymbol{\theta}=\boldsymbol{\theta}^{(0)}}. \qquad [5.7.8]$$

This gradient could in principle be calculated analytically, by differentiating the general expression for $\mathcal{L}(\boldsymbol{\theta})$ with respect to $\boldsymbol{\theta}$ and writing a computer procedure to calculate each element of $\mathbf{g}(\boldsymbol{\theta})$ given the data and a numerical value for $\boldsymbol{\theta}$. For example, expression [5.7.7] could be used to calculate $\mathbf{g}(\boldsymbol{\theta})$ for any particular value of $\boldsymbol{\theta}$. Alternatively, if it is too hard to differentiate $\mathcal{L}(\boldsymbol{\theta})$ analytically, we can always get a numerical approximation to the gradient by seeing how $\mathscr{L}(\boldsymbol{\theta})$ changes for a small change in each element of $\boldsymbol{\theta}$. In particular, the $i$th element of $\mathbf{g}(\boldsymbol{\theta}^{(0)})$ might be approximated by

$$
\begin{aligned}
g_i(\boldsymbol{\theta}^{(0)}) \cong \frac{1}{\Delta}\{&\mathscr{L}(\theta_1^{(0)}, \theta_2^{(0)}, \ldots, \theta_{i-1}^{(0)}, \theta_i^{(0)} + \Delta, \theta_{i+1}^{(0)}, \theta_{i+2}^{(0)}, \ldots, \theta_a^{(0)}) \\
&- \mathscr{L}(\theta_1^{(0)}, \theta_2^{(0)}, \ldots, \theta_{i-1}^{(0)}, \theta_i^{(0)}, \theta_{i+1}^{(0)}, \theta_{i+2}^{(0)}, \ldots, \theta_a^{(0)})\},
\end{aligned}
\qquad [5.7.9]
$$

where $\Delta$ represents some arbitrarily chosen small scalar such as $\Delta = 10^{-6}$. By numerically calculating the value of $\mathscr{L}(\boldsymbol{\theta})$ at $\boldsymbol{\theta}^{(0)}$ and at $a$ different values of $\boldsymbol{\theta}$ corresponding to small changes in each of the individual elements of $\boldsymbol{\theta}^{(0)}$, an estimate of the full vector $\mathbf{g}(\boldsymbol{\theta}^{(0)})$ can be uncovered.

Result [5.7.5] suggests that we should change the value of $\boldsymbol{\theta}$ in the direction of the gradient, choosing

$$\boldsymbol{\theta}^{(1)} - \boldsymbol{\theta}^{(0)} = s \cdot \mathbf{g}(\boldsymbol{\theta}^{(0)})$$

for some positive scalar $s$. A suitable choice for $s$ could be found by an adaptation of the grid search method. For example, we might calculate the value of $\mathscr{L}\{\boldsymbol{\theta}^{(0)} + s \cdot \mathbf{g}(\boldsymbol{\theta}^{(0)})\}$ for $s = \frac{1}{16}, \frac{1}{8}, \frac{1}{4}, \frac{1}{2}, 1, 2, 4, 8$, and 16 and choose as the new estimate $\boldsymbol{\theta}^{(1)}$ the value of $\boldsymbol{\theta}^{(0)} + s \cdot \mathbf{g}(\boldsymbol{\theta}^{(0)})$ for which $\mathscr{L}(\boldsymbol{\theta})$ is largest. Smaller or larger values of $s$ could also be explored if the maximum appears to be at one of the extremes. If none of the values of $s$ improves the likelihood, then a very small value for $s$ such as the value $\Delta = 10^{-6}$ used to approximate the derivative should be tried.

We can then repeat the process, taking $\boldsymbol{\theta}^{(1)} = \boldsymbol{\theta}^{(0)} + s \cdot \mathbf{g}(\boldsymbol{\theta}^{(0)})$ as the starting point, evaluating the gradient at the new location $\mathbf{g}(\boldsymbol{\theta}^{(1)})$, and generating a new estimate $\boldsymbol{\theta}^{(2)}$ according to

$$\boldsymbol{\theta}^{(2)} = \boldsymbol{\theta}^{(1)} + s \cdot \mathbf{g}(\boldsymbol{\theta}^{(1)})$$

for the best choice of $s$. The process is iterated, calculating

$$\boldsymbol{\theta}^{(m+1)} = \boldsymbol{\theta}^{(m)} + s \cdot \mathbf{g}(\boldsymbol{\theta}^{(m)})$$

for $m = 0, 1, 2, \ldots$ until some convergence criterion is satisfied, such as that the gradient vector $\mathbf{g}(\boldsymbol{\theta}^{(m)})$ is within some specified tolerance of zero, the distance between $\boldsymbol{\theta}^{(m+1)}$ and $\boldsymbol{\theta}^{(m)}$ is less than some specified threshold, or the change between $\mathscr{L}(\boldsymbol{\theta}^{(m+1)})$ and $\mathscr{L}(\boldsymbol{\theta}^{(m)})$ is smaller than some desired amount.

Figure 5.3 illustrates the method of steepest ascent when $\boldsymbol{\theta}$ contains $a = 2$ elements. The figure displays contour lines for the log likelihood $\mathscr{L}(\boldsymbol{\theta})$; along a given contour, the log likelihood $\mathscr{L}(\boldsymbol{\theta})$ is constant. If the iteration is started at the initial guess $\boldsymbol{\theta}^{(0)}$, the gradient $\mathbf{g}(\boldsymbol{\theta}^{(0)})$ describes the direction of steepest ascent. Finding the optimal step in that direction produces the new estimate $\boldsymbol{\theta}^{(1)}$. The gradient at that point $\mathbf{g}(\boldsymbol{\theta}^{(1)})$ then determines a new search direction on which a new estimate $\boldsymbol{\theta}^{(2)}$ is based, until the top of the hill is reached.

Figure 5.3 also illustrates a multivariate generalization of the problem with multiple local maxima seen earlier in Figure 5.2. The procedure should converge to a local maximum, which in this case is different from the global maximum $\boldsymbol{\theta}^*$. In Figure 5.3, it appears that if $\boldsymbol{\theta}^{(0)*}$ were used to begin the iteration in place of $\boldsymbol{\theta}^{(0)}$, the procedure would converge to the true global maximum $\boldsymbol{\theta}^*$. In practice, the only way to ensure that a global maximum is found is to begin the iteration from a number of different starting values for $\boldsymbol{\theta}^{(0)}$ and to continue the sequence from each starting value until the top of the hill associated with that starting value is discovered.

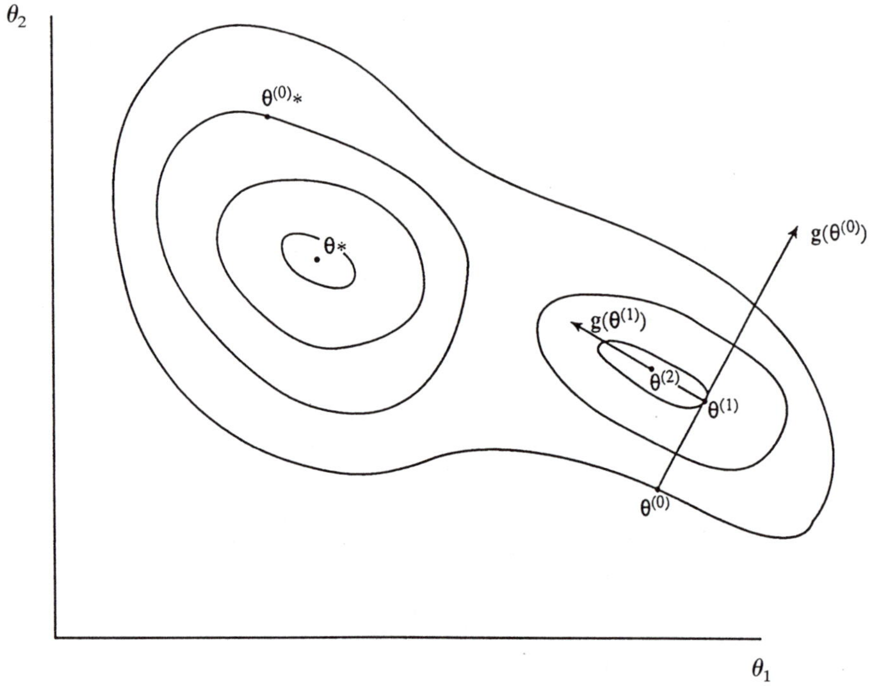


**FIGURE 5.3** Likelihood contours and maximization by steepest ascent.

## *Newton-Raphson*

One drawback to the steepest-ascent method is that it may require a very large number of iterations to close in on the local maximum. An alternative method known as *Newton-Raphson* often converges more quickly provided that (1) second derivatives of the log likelihood function $\mathscr{L}(\boldsymbol{\theta})$ exist and (2) the function $\mathscr{L}(\boldsymbol{\theta})$ is concave, meaning that $-1$ times the matrix of second derivatives is everywhere positive definite.

Suppose that $\boldsymbol{\theta}$ is an $(a \times 1)$ vector of parameters to be estimated. Let $\mathbf{g}(\boldsymbol{\theta}^{(0)})$ denote the gradient vector of the log likelihood function at $\boldsymbol{\theta}^{(0)}$:

$$\underset{(a\times 1)}{\mathbf{g}(\boldsymbol{\theta}^{(0)})} = \left.\frac{\partial \mathscr{L}(\boldsymbol{\theta})}{\partial \boldsymbol{\theta}}\right|_{\boldsymbol{\theta}=\boldsymbol{\theta}^{(0)}};$$

and let $\mathbf{H}(\boldsymbol{\theta}^{(0)})$ denote $-1$ times the matrix of second derivatives of the log likelihood function:

$$\underset{(a\times a)}{\mathbf{H}(\boldsymbol{\theta}^{(0)})} = -\left.\frac{\partial^2 \mathscr{L}(\boldsymbol{\theta})}{\partial \boldsymbol{\theta}\, \partial \boldsymbol{\theta}'}\right|_{\boldsymbol{\theta}=\boldsymbol{\theta}^{(0)}}.$$

Consider approximating $\mathscr{L}(\boldsymbol{\theta})$ with a second-order Taylor series around $\boldsymbol{\theta}^{(0)}$:

$$\mathscr{L}(\boldsymbol{\theta}) \cong \mathscr{L}(\boldsymbol{\theta}^{(0)}) + [\mathbf{g}(\boldsymbol{\theta}^{(0)})]'[\boldsymbol{\theta} - \boldsymbol{\theta}^{(0)}] - \tfrac{1}{2}[\boldsymbol{\theta} - \boldsymbol{\theta}^{(0)}]'\mathbf{H}(\boldsymbol{\theta}^{(0)})[\boldsymbol{\theta} - \boldsymbol{\theta}^{(0)}]. \qquad [5.7.10]$$

The idea behind the Newton-Raphson method is to choose $\boldsymbol{\theta}$ so as to maximize [5.7.10]. Setting the derivative of [5.7.10] with respect to $\boldsymbol{\theta}$ equal to zero results in

$$\mathbf{g}(\boldsymbol{\theta}^{(0)}) - \mathbf{H}(\boldsymbol{\theta}^{(0)})[\boldsymbol{\theta} - \boldsymbol{\theta}^{(0)}] = \mathbf{0}. \qquad [5.7.11]$$

Let $\boldsymbol{\theta}^{(0)}$ denote an initial guess as to the value of $\boldsymbol{\theta}$. One can calculate the derivative of the log likelihood at that initial guess ($\mathbf{g}(\boldsymbol{\theta}^{(0)})$) either analytically, as in [5.7.7], or numerically, as in [5.7.9]. One can also use analytical or numerical methods to calculate the negative of the matrix of second derivatives at the initial guess ($\mathbf{H}(\boldsymbol{\theta}^{(0)})$). Expression [5.7.11] suggests that an improved estimate of $\boldsymbol{\theta}$ (denoted $\boldsymbol{\theta}^{(1)}$) would satisfy

$$\mathbf{g}(\boldsymbol{\theta}^{(0)}) = \mathbf{H}(\boldsymbol{\theta}^{(0)})[\boldsymbol{\theta}^{(1)} - \boldsymbol{\theta}^{(0)}]$$

or

$$\boldsymbol{\theta}^{(1)} - \boldsymbol{\theta}^{(0)} = [\mathbf{H}(\boldsymbol{\theta}^{(0)})]^{-1}\mathbf{g}(\boldsymbol{\theta}^{(0)}). \qquad [5.7.12]$$

One could next calculate the gradient and Hessian at $\boldsymbol{\theta}^{(1)}$ and use these to find a new estimate $\boldsymbol{\theta}^{(2)}$ and continue iterating in this fashion. The $m$th step in the iteration updates the estimate of $\boldsymbol{\theta}$ by using the formula

$$\boldsymbol{\theta}^{(m+1)} = \boldsymbol{\theta}^{(m)} + [\mathbf{H}(\boldsymbol{\theta}^{(m)})]^{-1}\mathbf{g}(\boldsymbol{\theta}^{(m)}). \qquad [5.7.13]$$

If the log likelihood function happens to be a perfect quadratic function, then [5.7.10] holds exactly and [5.7.12] will generate the exact *MLE* in a single step:

$$\boldsymbol{\theta}^{(1)} = \hat{\boldsymbol{\theta}}_{MLE}.$$

If the quadratic approximation is reasonably good, Newton-Raphson should converge to the local maximum more quickly than the steepest-ascent method. However, if the likelihood function is not concave, Newton-Raphson behaves quite poorly. Thus, steepest ascent is often slower to converge but sometimes proves to be more robust compared with Newton-Raphson.

Since [5.7.10] is usually only an approximation to the true log likelihood function, the iteration on [5.7.13] is often modified as follows. Expression [5.7.13] is taken to suggest the search direction. The value of the log likelihood function at several points in that direction is then calculated, and the best value determines the length of the step. This strategy calls for replacing [5.7.13] by

$$\boldsymbol{\theta}^{(m+1)} = \boldsymbol{\theta}^{(m)} + s[\mathbf{H}(\boldsymbol{\theta}^{(m)})]^{-1}\mathbf{g}(\boldsymbol{\theta}^{(m)}), \qquad [5.7.14]$$

where $s$ is a scalar controlling the step length. One calculates $\boldsymbol{\theta}^{(m+1)}$ and the associated value for the log likelihood $\mathscr{L}(\boldsymbol{\theta}^{(m+1)})$ for various values of $s$ in [5.7.14] and chooses as the estimate $\boldsymbol{\theta}^{(m+1)}$ the value that produces the biggest value for the log likelihood.

### *Davidon-Fletcher-Powell*

If $\boldsymbol{\theta}$ contains $a$ unknown parameters, then the symmetric matrix $\mathbf{H}(\boldsymbol{\theta})$ has $a(a + 1)/2$ separate elements. Calculating all these elements can be extremely time-consuming if $a$ is large. An alternative approach reasons as follows. The matrix of second derivatives ($-\mathbf{H}(\boldsymbol{\theta})$) corresponds to the first derivatives of the gradient vector ($\mathbf{g}(\boldsymbol{\theta})$), which tell us how $\mathbf{g}(\boldsymbol{\theta})$ changes as $\boldsymbol{\theta}$ changes. We get some independent information about this by comparing $\mathbf{g}(\boldsymbol{\theta}^{(1)}) - \mathbf{g}(\boldsymbol{\theta}^{(0)})$ with $\boldsymbol{\theta}^{(1)} - \boldsymbol{\theta}^{(0)}$. This is not enough information by itself to estimate $\mathbf{H}(\boldsymbol{\theta})$, but it is information that could be used to update an initial guess about the value of $\mathbf{H}(\boldsymbol{\theta})$. Thus, rather than evaluate $\mathbf{H}(\boldsymbol{\theta})$ directly at each iteration, the idea will be to start with an initial guess about $\mathbf{H}(\boldsymbol{\theta})$ and update the guess solely on the basis of how much $\mathbf{g}(\boldsymbol{\theta})$ changes between iterations, given the magnitude of the change in $\boldsymbol{\theta}$. Such methods are sometimes described as *modified Newton-Raphson*.

One of the most popular modified Newton-Raphson methods was proposed by Davidon (1959) and Fletcher and Powell (1963). Since it is $\mathbf{H}^{-1}$ rather than $\mathbf{H}$

itself that appears in the updating formula [5.7.14], the Davidon-Fletcher-Powell algorithm updates an estimate of $\mathbf{H}^{-1}$ at each step on the basis of the size of the change in $\mathbf{g}(\boldsymbol{\theta})$ relative to the change in $\boldsymbol{\theta}$. Specifically, let $\boldsymbol{\theta}^{(m)}$ denote an estimate of $\boldsymbol{\theta}$ that has been calculated at the $m$th iteration, and let $\mathbf{A}^{(m)}$ denote an estimate of $[\mathbf{H}(\boldsymbol{\theta}^{(m)})]^{-1}$. The new estimate $\boldsymbol{\theta}^{(m+1)}$ is given by

$$\boldsymbol{\theta}^{(m+1)} = \boldsymbol{\theta}^{(m)} + s\mathbf{A}^{(m)}\mathbf{g}(\boldsymbol{\theta}^{(m)}) \qquad [5.7.15]$$

for $s$ the positive scalar that maximizes $\mathscr{L}\{\boldsymbol{\theta}^{(m)} + s\mathbf{A}^{(m)}\mathbf{g}(\boldsymbol{\theta}^{(m)})\}$. Once $\boldsymbol{\theta}^{(m+1)}$ and the gradient at $\boldsymbol{\theta}^{(m+1)}$ have been calculated, a new estimate $\mathbf{A}^{(m+1)}$ is found from

$$\begin{aligned}\mathbf{A}^{(m+1)} = \mathbf{A}^{(m)} &- \frac{\mathbf{A}^{(m)}(\Delta\mathbf{g}^{(m+1)})(\Delta\mathbf{g}^{(m+1)})'\mathbf{A}^{(m)}}{(\Delta\mathbf{g}^{(m+1)})'\mathbf{A}^{(m)}(\Delta\mathbf{g}^{(m+1)})} \\ &- \frac{(\Delta\boldsymbol{\theta}^{(m+1)})(\Delta\boldsymbol{\theta}^{(m+1)})'}{(\Delta\mathbf{g}^{(m+1)})'(\Delta\boldsymbol{\theta}^{(m+1)})}\end{aligned} \qquad [5.7.16]$$

where

$$\begin{aligned}\Delta\boldsymbol{\theta}^{(m+1)} &\equiv \boldsymbol{\theta}^{(m+1)} - \boldsymbol{\theta}^{(m)} \\ \Delta\mathbf{g}^{(m+1)} &\equiv \mathbf{g}(\boldsymbol{\theta}^{(m+1)}) - \mathbf{g}(\boldsymbol{\theta}^{(m)}).\end{aligned}$$

In what sense should $\mathbf{A}^{(m+1)}$ as calculated from [5.7.16] be regarded as an estimate of the inverse of $\mathbf{H}(\boldsymbol{\theta}^{(m+1)})$? Consider first the case when $\boldsymbol{\theta}$ is a scalar ($a = 1$). Then [5.7.16] simplifies to

$$\begin{aligned}A^{(m+1)} &= A^{(m)} - \frac{(A^{(m)})^2(\Delta g^{(m+1)})^2}{(\Delta g^{(m+1)})^2(A^{(m)})} - \frac{(\Delta\theta^{(m+1)})^2}{(\Delta g^{(m+1)})(\Delta\theta^{(m+1)})} \\ &= A^{(m)} - A^{(m)} - \frac{\Delta\theta^{(m+1)}}{\Delta g^{(m+1)}} \\ &= -\frac{\Delta\theta^{(m+1)}}{\Delta g^{(m+1)}}.\end{aligned}$$

In this case,

$$[A^{(m+1)}]^{-1} = -\frac{\Delta g^{(m+1)}}{\Delta\theta^{(m+1)}},$$

which is the natural discrete approximation to

$$H(\theta^{(m+1)}) = -\left.\frac{\partial^2\mathscr{L}}{\partial\theta^2}\right|_{\theta=\theta^{(m+1)}} = -\left.\frac{\partial g}{\partial\theta}\right|_{\theta=\theta^{(m+1)}}.$$

More generally (for $a > 1$), an estimate of the derivative of $\mathbf{g}(\cdot)$ should be related to the observed change in $\mathbf{g}(\cdot)$ according to

$$\mathbf{g}(\boldsymbol{\theta}^{(m+1)}) \cong \mathbf{g}(\boldsymbol{\theta}^{(m)}) + \left.\frac{\partial\mathbf{g}}{\partial\boldsymbol{\theta}'}\right|_{\boldsymbol{\theta}=\boldsymbol{\theta}^{(m+1)}} [\boldsymbol{\theta}^{(m+1)} - \boldsymbol{\theta}^{(m)}].$$

That is,

$$\mathbf{g}(\boldsymbol{\theta}^{(m+1)}) \cong \mathbf{g}(\boldsymbol{\theta}^{(m)}) - \mathbf{H}(\boldsymbol{\theta}^{(m+1)})[\boldsymbol{\theta}^{(m+1)} - \boldsymbol{\theta}^{(m)}]$$

or

$$\Delta\boldsymbol{\theta}^{(m+1)} \cong -[\mathbf{H}(\boldsymbol{\theta}^{(m+1)})]^{-1}\,\Delta\mathbf{g}^{(m+1)}.$$

Hence an estimate $\mathbf{A}^{(m+1)}$ of $[\mathbf{H}(\boldsymbol{\theta}^{(m+1)})]^{-1}$ should satisfy

$$\mathbf{A}^{(m+1)}\,\Delta\mathbf{g}^{(m+1)} = -\Delta\boldsymbol{\theta}^{(m+1)}. \qquad [5.7.17]$$

Postmultiplication of [5.7.16] by $\Delta\mathbf{g}^{(m+1)}$ confirms that [5.7.17] is indeed satisfied by the Davidon-Fletcher-Powell estimate $\mathbf{A}^{(m+1)}$:

$$\begin{aligned}\mathbf{A}^{(m+1)}\,\Delta\mathbf{g}^{(m+1)} &= \mathbf{A}^{(m)}\,\Delta\mathbf{g}^{(m+1)} \\ &\quad - \frac{\mathbf{A}^{(m)}(\Delta\mathbf{g}^{(m+1)})(\Delta\mathbf{g}^{(m+1)})'\mathbf{A}^{(m)}(\Delta\mathbf{g}^{(m+1)})}{(\Delta\mathbf{g}^{(m+1)})'\mathbf{A}^{(m)}(\Delta\mathbf{g}^{(m+1)})} \\ &\quad - \frac{(\Delta\boldsymbol{\theta}^{(m+1)})(\Delta\boldsymbol{\theta}^{(m+1)})'(\Delta\mathbf{g}^{(m+1)})}{(\Delta\mathbf{g}^{(m+1)})'(\Delta\boldsymbol{\theta}^{(m+1)})} \\ &= \mathbf{A}^{(m)}\,\Delta\mathbf{g}^{(m+1)} - \mathbf{A}^{(m)}\,\Delta\mathbf{g}^{(m+1)} - \Delta\boldsymbol{\theta}^{(m+1)} \\ &= -\Delta\boldsymbol{\theta}^{(m+1)}.\end{aligned}$$

Thus, calculation of [5.7.16] produces an estimate of $[\mathbf{H}(\boldsymbol{\theta}^{(m+1)})]^{-1}$ that is consistent with the magnitude of the observed change between $\mathbf{g}(\boldsymbol{\theta}^{(m+1)})$ and $\mathbf{g}(\boldsymbol{\theta}^{(m)})$ given the size of the change between $\boldsymbol{\theta}^{(m+1)}$ and $\boldsymbol{\theta}^{(m)}$.

The following proposition (proved in Appendix 5.A at the end of the chapter) establishes some further useful properties of the updating formula [5.7.16].

***Proposition 5.1:*** *(Fletcher and Powell (1963)). Consider* $\mathcal{L}(\boldsymbol{\theta})$, *where* $\mathcal{L}: \mathbb{R}^a \to \mathbb{R}^1$ *has continuous first derivatives denoted*

$$\underset{(a\times 1)}{\mathbf{g}(\boldsymbol{\theta}^{(m)})} = \left.\frac{\partial\mathcal{L}(\boldsymbol{\theta})}{\partial\boldsymbol{\theta}}\right|_{\boldsymbol{\theta}=\boldsymbol{\theta}^{(m)}}.$$

*Suppose that some element of* $\mathbf{g}(\boldsymbol{\theta}^{(m)})$ *is nonzero, and let* $\mathbf{A}^{(m)}$ *be a positive definite symmetric* $(a \times a)$ *matrix. Then the following hold.*

(*a*) *There exists a scalar* $s > 0$ *such that* $\mathcal{L}(\boldsymbol{\theta}^{(m+1)}) > \mathcal{L}(\boldsymbol{\theta}^{(m)})$ *for*

$$\boldsymbol{\theta}^{(m+1)} = \boldsymbol{\theta}^{(m)} + s\mathbf{A}^{(m)}\mathbf{g}(\boldsymbol{\theta}^{(m)}). \qquad [5.7.18]$$

(*b*) *If* $s$ *in* [5.7.18] *is chosen so as to maximize* $\mathcal{L}(\boldsymbol{\theta}^{(m+1)})$, *then the first-order conditions for an interior maximum imply that*

$$[\mathbf{g}(\boldsymbol{\theta}^{(m+1)})]'[\boldsymbol{\theta}^{(m+1)} - \boldsymbol{\theta}^{(m)}] = 0. \qquad [5.7.19]$$

(*c*) *Provided that* [5.7.19] *holds and that some element of* $\mathbf{g}(\boldsymbol{\theta}^{(m+1)}) - \mathbf{g}(\boldsymbol{\theta}^{(m)})$ *is nonzero, then* $\mathbf{A}^{(m+1)}$ *described by* [5.7.16] *is a positive definite symmetric matrix.*

Result (a) establishes that as long as we are not already at an optimum ($\mathbf{g}(\boldsymbol{\theta}^{(m)}) \neq \mathbf{0}$), there exists a step in the direction suggested by the algorithm that will increase the likelihood further, provided that $\mathbf{A}^{(m)}$ is a positive definite matrix. Result (c) establishes that provided that the iteration is begun with $\mathbf{A}^{(0)}$ a positive definite matrix, then the sequence of matrices $\{\mathbf{A}^{(m)}\}_{m=1}^{N}$ should all be positive definite, meaning that each step of the iteration should increase the likelihood function. A standard procedure is to start the iteration with $\mathbf{A}^{(0)} = \mathbf{I}_a$, the $(a \times a)$ identity matrix.

If the function $\mathcal{L}(\boldsymbol{\theta})$ is exactly quadratic, so that

$$\mathcal{L}(\boldsymbol{\theta}) = \mathcal{L}(\boldsymbol{\theta}^{(0)}) + \mathbf{g}'[\boldsymbol{\theta} - \boldsymbol{\theta}^{(0)}] - \tfrac{1}{2}[\boldsymbol{\theta} - \boldsymbol{\theta}^{(0)}]'\mathbf{H}[\boldsymbol{\theta} - \boldsymbol{\theta}^{(0)}],$$

with $\mathbf{H}$ positive definite, then Fletcher and Powell (1963) showed that iteration on [5.7.15] and [5.7.16] will converge to the true global maximum in $a$ steps:

$$\boldsymbol{\theta}^{(a)} = \hat{\boldsymbol{\theta}}_{MLE} = \boldsymbol{\theta}^{(0)} + \mathbf{H}^{-1}\mathbf{g};$$

and the weighting matrix will converge to the inverse of $-1$ times the matrix of second derivatives:

$$\mathbf{A}^{(a)} = \mathbf{H}^{-1}.$$

More generally, if $\mathscr{L}(\boldsymbol{\theta})$ is well approximated by a quadratic function, then the Davidon-Fletcher-Powell search procedure should approach the global maximum more quickly than the steepest-ascent method,

$$\boldsymbol{\theta}^{(N)} \cong \hat{\boldsymbol{\theta}}_{MLE}$$

for large $N$, while $\mathbf{A}^{(m)}$ should converge to the negative of the matrix of second derivatives of the log likelihood function:

$$\mathbf{A}^{(N)} \cong -\left[\left.\frac{\partial^2 \mathscr{L}(\boldsymbol{\theta})}{\partial \boldsymbol{\theta}\, \partial \boldsymbol{\theta}'}\right|_{\boldsymbol{\theta}=\hat{\boldsymbol{\theta}}_{MLE}}\right]^{-1}. \qquad [5.7.20]$$

In practice, however, the approximation in [5.7.20] can be somewhat poor, and it is better to evaluate the matrix of second derivatives numerically for purposes of calculating standard errors, as discussed in Section 5.8.

If the function $\mathscr{L}(\boldsymbol{\theta})$ is not globally concave or if the starting value $\boldsymbol{\theta}^{(0)}$ is far from the true maximum, the Davidon-Fletcher-Powell procedure can do very badly. If problems are encountered, it often helps to try a different starting value $\boldsymbol{\theta}^{(0)}$, to rescale the data or parameters so that the elements of $\boldsymbol{\theta}$ are in comparable units, or to rescale the initial matrix $\mathbf{A}^{(0)}$—for example, by setting

$$\mathbf{A}^{(0)} = (1 \times 10^{-4})\mathbf{I}_a.$$

### *Other Numerical Optimization Methods*

A variety of other modified Newton-Raphson methods are available, which use alternative techniques for updating an estimate of $\mathbf{H}(\boldsymbol{\theta}^{(m)})$ or its inverse. Two of the more popular methods are those of Broyden (1965, 1967) and Berndt, Hall, Hall, and Hausman (1974). Surveys of these and a variety of other approaches are provided by Judge, Griffiths, Hill, and Lee (1980, pp. 719–72) and Quandt (1983).

Obviously, these same methods can be used to minimize a function $Q(\boldsymbol{\theta})$ with respect to $\boldsymbol{\theta}$. We simply multiply the objective function by $-1$ and then maximize the function $-Q(\boldsymbol{\theta})$.

## 5.8. *Statistical Inference with Maximum Likelihood Estimation*

The previous section discussed ways to find the maximum likelihood estimate $\hat{\boldsymbol{\theta}}$ given only the numerical ability to evaluate the log likelihood function $\mathscr{L}(\boldsymbol{\theta})$. This section summarizes general approaches that can be used to test a hypothesis about $\boldsymbol{\theta}$. The section merely summarizes a number of useful results without providing any proofs. We will return to these issues in more depth in Chapter 14, where the statistical foundation behind many of these claims will be developed.

Before detailing these results, however, it is worth calling attention to two of the key assumptions behind the formulas presented in this section. First, it is assumed that the observed data are strictly stationary. Second, it is assumed that neither the estimate $\hat{\boldsymbol{\theta}}$ nor the true value $\boldsymbol{\theta}_0$ falls on a boundary of the allowable parameter space. For example, suppose that the first element of $\boldsymbol{\theta}$ is a parameter corresponding to the probability of a particular event, which must be between 0 and 1. If the event did not occur in the sample, the maximum likelihood estimate of the probability might be zero. This is an example where the estimate $\hat{\boldsymbol{\theta}}$ falls on the boundary of the allowable parameter space, in which case the formulas presented in this section will not be valid.

## *Asymptotic Standard Errors for Maximum Likelihood Estimates*

If the sample size $T$ is sufficiently large, it often turns out that the distribution of the maximum likelihood estimate $\hat{\boldsymbol{\theta}}$ can be well approximated by the following distribution:

$$\hat{\boldsymbol{\theta}} \approx N(\boldsymbol{\theta}_0, T^{-1}\mathcal{I}^{-1}), \tag{5.8.1}$$

where $\boldsymbol{\theta}_0$ denotes the true parameter vector. The matrix $\mathcal{I}$ is known as the *information matrix* and can be estimated in either of two ways.

The *second-derivative estimate* of the information matrix is

$$\hat{\mathcal{I}}_{2D} = -T^{-1} \left. \frac{\partial^2 \mathcal{L}(\boldsymbol{\theta})}{\partial \boldsymbol{\theta}\, \partial \boldsymbol{\theta}'} \right|_{\boldsymbol{\theta}=\hat{\boldsymbol{\theta}}}. \tag{5.8.2}$$

Here $\mathcal{L}(\boldsymbol{\theta})$ denotes the log likelihood:

$$\mathcal{L}(\boldsymbol{\theta}) = \sum_{t=1}^{T} \log f_{Y_t|\mathcal{Y}_{t-1}}(y_t|\mathcal{Y}_{t-1}; \boldsymbol{\theta});$$

and $\mathcal{Y}_t$ denotes the history of observations on $y$ obtained through date $t$. The matrix of second derivatives of the log likelihood is often calculated numerically. Substituting [5.8.2] into [5.8.1], the terms involving the sample size $T$ cancel out so that the variance-covariance matrix of $\hat{\boldsymbol{\theta}}$ can be approximated by

$$E(\hat{\boldsymbol{\theta}} - \boldsymbol{\theta}_0)(\hat{\boldsymbol{\theta}} - \boldsymbol{\theta}_0)' \cong \left[ - \left. \frac{\partial^2 \mathcal{L}(\boldsymbol{\theta})}{\partial \boldsymbol{\theta}\, \partial \boldsymbol{\theta}'} \right|_{\boldsymbol{\theta}=\hat{\boldsymbol{\theta}}} \right]^{-1}. \tag{5.8.3}$$

A second estimate of the information matrix $\mathcal{I}$ in [5.8.1] is called the *outer-product estimate*:

$$\hat{\mathcal{I}}_{OP} = T^{-1} \sum_{t=1}^{T} [\mathbf{h}(\hat{\boldsymbol{\theta}}, \mathcal{Y}_t)] \cdot [\mathbf{h}(\hat{\boldsymbol{\theta}}, \mathcal{Y}_t)]'. \tag{5.8.4}$$

Here $\mathbf{h}(\hat{\boldsymbol{\theta}}, \mathcal{Y}_t)$ denotes the $(a \times 1)$ vector of derivatives of the log of the conditional density of the $t$th observation with respect to the $a$ elements of the parameter vector $\boldsymbol{\theta}$, with this derivative evaluated at the maximum likelihood estimate $\hat{\boldsymbol{\theta}}$:

$$\mathbf{h}(\hat{\boldsymbol{\theta}}, \mathcal{Y}_t) = \left. \frac{\partial \log f(y_t|y_{t-1}, y_{t-2}, \ldots; \boldsymbol{\theta})}{\partial \boldsymbol{\theta}} \right|_{\boldsymbol{\theta}=\hat{\boldsymbol{\theta}}}.$$

In this case, the variance-covariance matrix of $\hat{\boldsymbol{\theta}}$ is approximated by

$$E(\hat{\boldsymbol{\theta}} - \boldsymbol{\theta}_0)(\hat{\boldsymbol{\theta}} - \boldsymbol{\theta}_0)' \cong \left[ \sum_{t=1}^{T} [\mathbf{h}(\hat{\boldsymbol{\theta}}, \mathcal{Y}_t)] \cdot [\mathbf{h}(\hat{\boldsymbol{\theta}}, \mathcal{Y}_t)]' \right]^{-1}.$$

As an illustration of how such approximations can be used, suppose that the log likelihood is given by expression [5.7.6]. For this case, one can see analytically that

$$\frac{\partial^2 \mathcal{L}(\boldsymbol{\theta})}{\partial \boldsymbol{\theta}\, \partial \boldsymbol{\theta}'} = \begin{bmatrix} -3 & 0 \\ 0 & -4 \end{bmatrix},$$

and so result [5.8.3] suggests that the variance of the maximum likelihood estimate $\hat{\theta}_2$ can be approximated by $\frac{1}{4}$. The *MLE* for this example was $\hat{\theta}_2 = 0$. Thus an approximate 95% confidence interval for $\theta_2$ is given by

$$0 \pm 2\sqrt{\tfrac{1}{4}} = \pm 1.$$

Note that unless the off-diagonal elements of $\hat{\mathcal{J}}$ are zero, in general one needs to calculate all the elements of the matrix $\hat{\mathcal{J}}$ and invert this full matrix in order to obtain a standard error for any given parameter.

Which estimate of the information matrix, $\hat{\mathcal{J}}_{2D}$ or $\hat{\mathcal{J}}_{OP}$, is it better to use in practice? Expression [5.8.1] is only an approximation to the true distribution of $\hat{\boldsymbol{\theta}}$, and $\hat{\mathcal{J}}_{2D}$ and $\hat{\mathcal{J}}_{OP}$ are in turn only approximations to the true value of $\mathcal{J}$. The theory that justifies these approximations does not give any clear guidance to which is better to use, and typically, researchers rely on whichever estimate of the information matrix is easiest to calculate. If the two estimates differ a great deal, this may mean that the model is misspecified. White (1982) developed a general test of model specification based on this idea. One option for constructing standard errors when the two estimates differ significantly is to use the "quasi-maximum likelihood" standard errors discussed at the end of this section.

## *Likelihood Ratio Test*

Another popular approach to testing hypotheses about parameters that are estimated by maximum likelihood is the *likelihood ratio test*. Suppose a null hypothesis implies a set of $m$ different restrictions on the value of the $(a \times 1)$ parameter vector $\boldsymbol{\theta}$. First, we maximize the likelihood function ignoring these restrictions to obtain the unrestricted maximum likelihood estimate $\hat{\boldsymbol{\theta}}$. Next, we find an estimate $\tilde{\boldsymbol{\theta}}$ that makes the likelihood as large as possible while still satisfying all the restrictions. In practice, this is usually achieved by defining a new $[(a - m) \times 1]$ vector $\boldsymbol{\lambda}$ in terms of which all of the elements of $\boldsymbol{\theta}$ can be expressed when the restrictions are satisfied. For example, if the restriction is that the last $m$ elements of $\boldsymbol{\theta}$ are zero, then $\boldsymbol{\lambda}$ consists of the first $a - m$ elements of $\boldsymbol{\theta}$. Let $\mathcal{L}(\hat{\boldsymbol{\theta}})$ denote the value of the log likelihood function at the unrestricted estimate, and let $\mathcal{L}(\tilde{\boldsymbol{\theta}})$ denote the value of the log likelihood function at the restricted estimate. Clearly $\mathcal{L}(\hat{\boldsymbol{\theta}}) > \mathcal{L}(\tilde{\boldsymbol{\theta}})$, and it often proves to be the case that

$$2[\mathcal{L}(\hat{\boldsymbol{\theta}}) - \mathcal{L}(\tilde{\boldsymbol{\theta}})] \approx \chi^2(m). \qquad [5.8.5]$$

For example, suppose that $a = 2$ and we are interested in testing the hypothesis that $\theta_2 = \theta_1 + 1$. Under this null hypothesis the vector $(\theta_1, \theta_2)'$ can be written as $(\lambda, \lambda + 1)'$, where $\lambda = \theta_1$. Suppose that the log likelihood is given by expression [5.7.6]. One can find the restricted *MLE* by replacing $\theta_2$ by $\theta_1 + 1$ and maximizing the resulting expression with respect to $\theta_1$:

$$\tilde{\mathcal{L}}(\theta_1) = -1.5\theta_1^2 - 2(\theta_1 + 1)^2.$$

The first-order condition for maximization of $\tilde{\mathcal{L}}(\theta_1)$ is

$$-3\theta_1 - 4(\theta_1 + 1) = 0,$$

or $\theta_1 = -\frac{4}{7}$. The restricted *MLE* is thus $\tilde{\boldsymbol{\theta}} = (-\frac{4}{7}, \frac{3}{7})'$, and the maximum value attained for the log likelihood while satisfying the restriction is

$$\begin{aligned}\mathcal{L}(\tilde{\boldsymbol{\theta}}) &= (-\tfrac{3}{2})(-\tfrac{4}{7})^2 - (\tfrac{4}{2})(\tfrac{3}{7})^2 \\ &= -\{(3 \cdot 4)/(2 \cdot 7 \cdot 7)\}\{4 + 3\} \\ &= -\tfrac{6}{7}.\end{aligned}$$

The unrestricted *MLE* is $\hat{\boldsymbol{\theta}} = \mathbf{0}$, at which $\mathcal{L}(\hat{\boldsymbol{\theta}}) = 0$. Hence, [5.8.5] would be

$$2[\mathcal{L}(\hat{\boldsymbol{\theta}}) - \mathcal{L}(\tilde{\boldsymbol{\theta}})] = \tfrac{12}{7} = 1.71.$$

The test here involves a single restriction, so $m = 1$. From Table B.2 in Appendix B, the probability that a $\chi^2(1)$ variable exceeds 3.84 is 0.05. Since $1.71 < 3.84$, we accept the null hypothesis that $\theta_2 = \theta_1 + 1$ at the 5% significance level.

## *Lagrange Multiplier Test*

In order to use the standard errors from [5.8.2] or [5.8.4] to test a hypothesis about $\boldsymbol{\theta}$, we need only to find the unrestricted *MLE* $\hat{\boldsymbol{\theta}}$. In order to use the likelihood ratio test [5.8.5], it is necessary to find both the unrestricted *MLE* $\hat{\boldsymbol{\theta}}$ and the restricted *MLE* $\tilde{\boldsymbol{\theta}}$. The *Lagrange multiplier test* provides a third principle with which to test a null hypothesis that requires only the restricted *MLE* $\tilde{\boldsymbol{\theta}}$. This test is useful when it is easier to calculate the restricted estimate $\tilde{\boldsymbol{\theta}}$ than the unrestricted estimate $\hat{\boldsymbol{\theta}}$.

Let $\boldsymbol{\theta}$ be an $(a \times 1)$ vector of parameters, and let $\tilde{\boldsymbol{\theta}}$ be an estimate of $\boldsymbol{\theta}$ that maximizes the log likelihood subject to a set of $m$ restrictions on $\boldsymbol{\theta}$. Let $f(y_t|y_{t-1}, y_{t-2}, \ldots; \boldsymbol{\theta})$ be the conditional density of the $t$th observation, and let $\mathbf{h}(\tilde{\boldsymbol{\theta}}, \mathcal{Y}_t)$ denote the $(a \times 1)$ vector of derivatives of the log of this conditional density evaluated at the restricted estimate $\tilde{\boldsymbol{\theta}}$:

$$\mathbf{h}(\tilde{\boldsymbol{\theta}}, \mathcal{Y}_t) = \left. \frac{\partial \log f(y_t|y_{t-1}, y_{t-2}, \ldots; \boldsymbol{\theta})}{\partial \boldsymbol{\theta}} \right|_{\boldsymbol{\theta} = \tilde{\boldsymbol{\theta}}}.$$

The Lagrange multiplier test of the null hypothesis that the restrictions are true is given by the following statistic:

$$T^{-1} \left[ \sum_{t=1}^{T} \mathbf{h}(\tilde{\boldsymbol{\theta}}, \mathcal{Y}_t) \right]' \mathcal{J}^{-1} \left[ \sum_{t=1}^{T} \mathbf{h}(\tilde{\boldsymbol{\theta}}, \mathcal{Y}_t) \right]. \qquad [5.8.6]$$

If the null hypothesis is true, then for large $T$ this should approximately have a $\chi^2(m)$ distribution. The information matrix $\mathcal{J}$ can again be estimated as in [5.8.2] or [5.8.4] with $\hat{\boldsymbol{\theta}}$ replaced by $\tilde{\boldsymbol{\theta}}$.

## *Quasi-Maximum Likelihood Standard Errors*

It was mentioned earlier in this section that if the data were really generated from the assumed density and the sample size is sufficiently large, the second-derivative estimate $\hat{\mathcal{J}}_{2D}$ and the outer-product estimate $\hat{\mathcal{J}}_{OP}$ of the information matrix should be reasonably close to each other. However, maximum likelihood estimation may still be a reasonable way to estimate parameters even if the data were not generated by the assumed density. For example, we noted in Section 5.2 that the conditional *MLE* for a Gaussian *AR*(1) process is obtained from an *OLS* regression of $y_t$ on $y_{t-1}$. This *OLS* regression is often a very sensible way to estimate parameters of an *AR*(1) process even if the true innovations $\varepsilon_t$ are not i.i.d. Gaussian. Although maximum likelihood may be yielding a reasonable estimate of $\boldsymbol{\theta}$, when the innovations are not i.i.d. Gaussian, the standard errors proposed in [5.8.2] or [5.8.4] may no longer be valid. An approximate variance-covariance matrix for $\hat{\boldsymbol{\theta}}$ that is sometimes valid even if the probability density is misspecified is given by

$$E(\hat{\boldsymbol{\theta}} - \boldsymbol{\theta}_0)(\hat{\boldsymbol{\theta}} - \boldsymbol{\theta}_0)' \cong T^{-1}\{\mathcal{J}_{2D}\mathcal{J}_{OP}^{-1}\mathcal{J}_{2D}\}^{-1}. \qquad [5.8.7]$$

This variance-covariance matrix was proposed by White (1982), who described this approach as *quasi-maximum likelihood estimation*.

## 5.9. *Inequality Constraints*

### *A Common Pitfall with Numerical Maximization*

Suppose we were to apply one of the methods discussed in Section 5.7 such as steepest ascent to the $AR(1)$ likelihood [5.7.2]. We start with an arbitrary initial guess, say, $\phi = 0.1$. We calculate the gradient at this point, and find that it is positive. The computer is then programmed to try to improve this estimate by evaluating the log likelihood at points described by $\phi^{(1)} = \phi^{(0)} + s \cdot g(\phi^{(0)})$ for various values of $s$, seeing what works best. But if the computer were to try a value for $s$ such that $\phi^{(1)} = \phi^{(0)} + s \cdot g(\phi^{(0)}) = 1.1$, calculation of [5.7.2] would involve finding the log of $(1 - 1.1^2) = -0.21$. Attempting to calculate the log of a negative number would typically be a fatal execution error, causing the search procedure to crash.

Often such problems can be avoided by using modified Newton-Raphson procedures, provided that the initial estimate $\boldsymbol{\theta}^{(0)}$ is chosen wisely and provided that the initial search area is kept fairly small. The latter might be accomplished by setting the initial weighting matrix $\mathbf{A}^{(0)}$ in [5.7.15] and [5.7.16] equal to a small multiple of the identity matrix, such as $\mathbf{A}^{(0)} = (1 \times 10^{-4}) \cdot \mathbf{I}_a$. In later iterations, the algorithm should use the shape of the likelihood function in the vicinity of the maximum to keep the search conservative. However, if the true $MLE$ is close to one of the boundaries (for example, if $\hat{\phi}_{MLE} = 0.998$ in the $AR(1)$ example), it will be virtually impossible to keep a numerical algorithm from exploring what happens when $\phi$ is greater than unity, which would induce a fatal crash.

### *Solving the Problem by Reparameterizing the Likelihood Function*

One simple way to ensure that a numerical search always stays within certain specified boundaries is to reparameterize the likelihood function in terms of an $(a \times 1)$ vector $\boldsymbol{\lambda}$ for which $\boldsymbol{\theta} = \mathbf{g}(\boldsymbol{\lambda})$, where the function $\mathbf{g}: \mathbb{R}^a \rightarrow \mathbb{R}^a$ incorporates the desired restrictions. The scheme is then as follows:

| ***Input*** | | ***Procedure*** | | ***Output*** |
|---|---|---|---|---|
| values of $y_1, y_2, \ldots, y_T$ and $\boldsymbol{\lambda}$ | $\rightarrow$ | set $\boldsymbol{\theta} = \mathbf{g}(\boldsymbol{\lambda})$; calculate $\mathcal{L}(\boldsymbol{\theta})$ | $\rightarrow$ | value of $\mathcal{L}(\mathbf{g}(\boldsymbol{\lambda}))$ . |

For example, to ensure that $\phi$ is always between $\pm 1$, we could take

$$\phi = g(\lambda) = \frac{\lambda}{1 + |\lambda|}. \qquad [5.9.1]$$

The goal is to find the value of $\lambda$ that produces the biggest value for the log likelihood. We start with an initial guess such as $\lambda = 3$. The procedure to evaluate the log likelihood function first calculates

$$\phi = 3/(1 + 3) = 0.75$$

and then finds the value for the log likelihood associated with this value of $\phi$ from [5.7.2]. No matter what value for $\lambda$ the computer guesses, the value of $\phi$ in [5.9.1] will always be less than 1 in absolute value and the likelihood function will be well defined. Once we have found the value of $\hat{\lambda}$ that maximizes the likelihood function, the maximum likelihood estimate of $\phi$ is then given by

$$\hat{\phi} = \frac{\hat{\lambda}}{1 + |\hat{\lambda}|}.$$

This technique of reparameterizing the likelihood function so that estimates always satisfy any necessary constraints is often very easy to implement. However, one note of caution should be mentioned. If a standard error is calculated from the matrix of second derivatives of the log likelihood as in [5.8.3], this represents the standard error of $\hat{\lambda}$, not the standard error of $\hat{\phi}$. To obtain a standard error for $\hat{\phi}$, the best approach is first to parameterize the likelihood function in terms of $\lambda$ to find the *MLE*, and then to reparameterize in terms of $\phi$ to calculate the matrix of second derivatives evaluated at $\hat{\phi}$ to get the final standard error for $\hat{\phi}$. Alternatively, one can calculate an approximation to the standard error for $\hat{\phi}$ from the standard error for $\hat{\lambda}$, based on the formula for a Wald test of a nonlinear hypothesis described in Chapter 14.

## *Parameterizations for a Variance-Covariance Matrix*

Another common restriction one needs to impose is that a variance parameter $\sigma^2$ be positive. An obvious way to achieve this is to parameterize the likelihood in terms of $\lambda$ which represents $\pm 1$ times the standard deviation. The procedure to evaluate the log likelihood then begins by squaring this parameter $\lambda$:

$$\sigma^2 = \lambda^2;$$

and if the standard deviation $\sigma$ is itself called, it is calculated as

$$\sigma = \sqrt{\lambda^2}.$$

More generally, let $\mathbf{\Omega}$ denote an $(n \times n)$ variance-covariance matrix:

$$\mathbf{\Omega} = \begin{bmatrix} \sigma_{11} & \sigma_{12} & \cdots & \sigma_{1n} \\ \sigma_{21} & \sigma_{22} & \cdots & \sigma_{2n} \\ \vdots & \vdots & \cdots & \vdots \\ \sigma_{n1} & \sigma_{n2} & \cdots & \sigma_{nn} \end{bmatrix}.$$

Here one needs to impose the condition that $\mathbf{\Omega}$ is positive definite and symmetric. The best approach is to parameterize $\mathbf{\Omega}$ in terms of the $n(n + 1)/2$ distinct elements of the Cholesky decomposition of $\mathbf{\Omega}$:

$$\mathbf{\Omega} = \mathbf{PP}', \qquad [5.9.2]$$

where

$$\mathbf{P} = \begin{bmatrix} \lambda_{11} & 0 & 0 & \cdots & 0 \\ \lambda_{21} & \lambda_{22} & 0 & \cdots & 0 \\ \vdots & \vdots & \vdots & \cdots & \vdots \\ \lambda_{n1} & \lambda_{n2} & \lambda_{n3} & \cdots & \lambda_{nn} \end{bmatrix}.$$

No matter what values the computer guesses for $\lambda_{11}, \lambda_{21}, \ldots, \lambda_{nn}$, the matrix $\mathbf{\Omega}$ calculated from [5.9.2] will be symmetric and positive semidefinite.

### *Parameterizations for Probabilities*

Sometimes some of the unknown parameters are probabilities $p_1, p_2, \ldots, p_K$ which must satisfy the restrictions

$$0 \leq p_i \leq 1 \quad \text{for } i = 1, 2, \ldots, K$$
$$p_1 + p_2 + \cdots + p_K = 1.$$

In this case, one approach is to parameterize the probabilities in terms of $\lambda_1, \lambda_2, \ldots, \lambda_{K-1}$, where

$$p_i = \lambda_i^2/(1 + \lambda_1^2 + \lambda_2^2 + \cdots + \lambda_{K-1}^2) \quad \text{for } i = 1, 2, \ldots, K-1$$
$$p_K = 1/(1 + \lambda_1^2 + \lambda_2^2 + \cdots + \lambda_{K-1}^2).$$

### *More General Inequality Constraints*

For more complicated inequality constraints that do not admit a simple reparameterization, an approach that sometimes works is to put a branching statement in the procedure to evaluate the log likelihood function. The procedure first checks whether the constraint is satisfied. If it is, then the likelihood function is evaluated in the usual way. If it is not, then the procedure returns a large negative number in place of the value of the log likelihood function. Sometimes such an approach will allow an *MLE* satisfying the specified conditions to be found with simple numerical search procedures.

If these measures prove inadequate, more complicated algorithms are available. Judge, Griffiths, Hill, and Lee (1980, pp. 747–49) described some of the possible approaches.

## APPENDIX 5.A. *Proofs of Chapter 5 Propositions*

■ **Proof of Proposition 5.1.**

(a) By Taylor's theorem,

$$\mathcal{L}(\boldsymbol{\theta}^{(m+1)}) = \mathcal{L}(\boldsymbol{\theta}^{(m)}) + [\mathbf{g}(\boldsymbol{\theta}^{(m)})]'[\boldsymbol{\theta}^{(m+1)} - \boldsymbol{\theta}^{(m)}] + R_1(\boldsymbol{\theta}^{(m)}, \boldsymbol{\theta}^{(m+1)}). \quad [5.A.1]$$

Substituting [5.7.18] into [5.A.1],

$$\mathcal{L}(\boldsymbol{\theta}^{(m+1)}) - \mathcal{L}(\boldsymbol{\theta}^{(m)}) = [\mathbf{g}(\boldsymbol{\theta}^{(m)})]'s\mathbf{A}^{(m)}\mathbf{g}(\boldsymbol{\theta}^{(m)}) + R_1(\boldsymbol{\theta}^{(m)}, \boldsymbol{\theta}^{(m+1)}). \quad [5.A.2]$$

Since $\mathbf{A}^{(m)}$ is positive definite and since $\mathbf{g}(\boldsymbol{\theta}^{(m)}) \neq \mathbf{0}$, expression [5.A.2] establishes that

$$\mathcal{L}(\boldsymbol{\theta}^{(m+1)}) - \mathcal{L}(\boldsymbol{\theta}^{(m)}) = s\kappa(\boldsymbol{\theta}^{(m)}) + R_1(\boldsymbol{\theta}^{(m)}, \boldsymbol{\theta}^{(m+1)}),$$

where $\kappa(\boldsymbol{\theta}^{(m)}) > 0$. Moreover, $s^{-1} \cdot R_1(\boldsymbol{\theta}^{(m)}, \boldsymbol{\theta}^{(m+1)}) \to 0$ as $s \to 0$. Hence, there exists an $s$ such that $\mathcal{L}(\boldsymbol{\theta}^{(m+1)}) - \mathcal{L}(\boldsymbol{\theta}^{(m)}) > 0$, as claimed.

(b) Direct differentiation reveals

$$\begin{aligned}\frac{\partial \mathcal{L}(\boldsymbol{\theta}^{(m+1)})}{\partial s} &= \frac{\partial \mathcal{L}}{\partial \theta_1}\frac{\partial \theta_1}{\partial s} + \frac{\partial \mathcal{L}}{\partial \theta_2}\frac{\partial \theta_2}{\partial s} + \cdots + \frac{\partial \mathcal{L}}{\partial \theta_a}\frac{\partial \theta_a}{\partial s} \\ &= [\mathbf{g}(\boldsymbol{\theta}^{(m+1)})]' \frac{\partial \boldsymbol{\theta}^{(m+1)}}{\partial s} \\ &= [\mathbf{g}(\boldsymbol{\theta}^{(m+1)})]'\mathbf{A}^{(m)}\mathbf{g}(\boldsymbol{\theta}^{(m)}),\end{aligned} \quad [5.A.3]$$

with the last line following from [5.7.18]. The first-order conditions set [5.A.3] equal to zero, which implies

$$0 = [\mathbf{g}(\boldsymbol{\theta}^{(m+1)})]'s\mathbf{A}^{(m)}\mathbf{g}(\boldsymbol{\theta}^{(m)}) = [\mathbf{g}(\boldsymbol{\theta}^{(m+1)})]'[\boldsymbol{\theta}^{(m+1)} - \boldsymbol{\theta}^{(m)}],$$

with the last line again following from [5.7.18]. This establishes the claim in [5.7.19].

(c) Let $\mathbf{y}$ be any $(a \times 1)$ nonzero vector. The task is to show that $\mathbf{y}'\mathbf{A}^{(m+1)}\mathbf{y} > 0$. Observe from [5.7.16] that

$$\mathbf{y}'\mathbf{A}^{(m+1)}\mathbf{y} = \mathbf{y}'\mathbf{A}^{(m)}\mathbf{y} - \frac{\mathbf{y}'\mathbf{A}^{(m)}(\Delta\mathbf{g}^{(m+1)})(\Delta\mathbf{g}^{(m+1)})'\mathbf{A}^{(m)}\mathbf{y}}{(\Delta\mathbf{g}^{(m+1)})'\mathbf{A}^{(m)}(\Delta\mathbf{g}^{(m+1)})} - \frac{\mathbf{y}'(\Delta\boldsymbol{\theta}^{(m+1)})(\Delta\boldsymbol{\theta}^{(m+1)})'\mathbf{y}}{(\Delta\mathbf{g}^{(m+1)})'(\Delta\boldsymbol{\theta}^{(m+1)})}. \qquad [5.A.4]$$

Since $\mathbf{A}^{(m)}$ is positive definite, there exists a nonsingular matrix $\mathbf{P}$ such that

$$\mathbf{A}^{(m)} = \mathbf{PP}'.$$

Define

$$\mathbf{y}^* \equiv \mathbf{P}'\mathbf{y}$$
$$\mathbf{x}^* \equiv \mathbf{P}'\Delta\mathbf{g}^{(m+1)}.$$

Then [5.A.4] can be written as

$$\begin{aligned}\mathbf{y}'\mathbf{A}^{(m+1)}\mathbf{y} &= \mathbf{y}'\mathbf{PP}'\mathbf{y} - \frac{\mathbf{y}'\mathbf{PP}'(\Delta\mathbf{g}^{(m+1)})(\Delta\mathbf{g}^{(m+1)})'\mathbf{PP}'\mathbf{y}}{(\Delta\mathbf{g}^{(m+1)})'\mathbf{PP}'(\Delta\mathbf{g}^{(m+1)})} \\ &\quad - \frac{\mathbf{y}'(\Delta\boldsymbol{\theta}^{(m+1)})(\Delta\boldsymbol{\theta}^{(m+1)})'\mathbf{y}}{(\Delta\mathbf{g}^{(m+1)})'(\Delta\boldsymbol{\theta}^{(m+1)})} \\ &= \mathbf{y}^{*\prime}\mathbf{y}^* - \frac{(\mathbf{y}^{*\prime}\mathbf{x}^*)(\mathbf{x}^{*\prime}\mathbf{y}^*)}{\mathbf{x}^{*\prime}\mathbf{x}^*} - \frac{\mathbf{y}'(\Delta\boldsymbol{\theta}^{(m+1)})(\Delta\boldsymbol{\theta}^{(m+1)})'\mathbf{y}}{(\Delta\mathbf{g}^{(m+1)})'(\Delta\boldsymbol{\theta}^{(m+1)})}.\end{aligned} \qquad [5.A.5]$$

Recalling equation [4.A.6], the first two terms in the last line of [5.A.5] represent the sum of squared residuals from an *OLS* regression of $\mathbf{y}^*$ on $\mathbf{x}^*$. This cannot be negative,

$$\mathbf{y}^{*\prime}\mathbf{y}^* - \frac{(\mathbf{y}^{*\prime}\mathbf{x}^*)(\mathbf{x}^{*\prime}\mathbf{y}^*)}{\mathbf{x}^{*\prime}\mathbf{x}^*} \geq 0; \qquad [5.A.6]$$

it would equal zero only if the *OLS* regression has a perfect fit, or if $\mathbf{y}^* = \beta\mathbf{x}^*$ or $\mathbf{P}'\mathbf{y} = \beta\mathbf{P}'\Delta\mathbf{g}^{(m+1)}$ for some $\beta$. Since $\mathbf{P}$ is nonsingular, expression [5.A.6] would only be zero if $\mathbf{y} = \beta\Delta\mathbf{g}^{(m+1)}$ for some $\beta$. Consider two cases.

**Case 1.** There is no $\beta$ such that $\mathbf{y} = \beta\Delta\mathbf{g}^{(m+1)}$. In this case, the inequality [5.A.6] is strict and [5.A.5] implies

$$\mathbf{y}'\mathbf{A}^{(m+1)}\mathbf{y} > -\frac{[\mathbf{y}'\Delta\boldsymbol{\theta}^{(m+1)}]^2}{(\Delta\mathbf{g}^{(m+1)})'(\Delta\boldsymbol{\theta}^{(m+1)})}.$$

Since $[\mathbf{y}'\Delta\boldsymbol{\theta}^{(m+1)}]^2 \geq 0$, it follows that $\mathbf{y}'\mathbf{A}^{(m+1)}\mathbf{y} > 0$, provided that

$$(\Delta\mathbf{g}^{(m+1)})'(\Delta\boldsymbol{\theta}^{(m+1)}) < 0. \qquad [5.A.7]$$

But, from [5.7.19],

$$\begin{aligned}(\Delta\mathbf{g}^{(m+1)})'(\Delta\boldsymbol{\theta}^{(m+1)}) &= [\mathbf{g}(\boldsymbol{\theta}^{(m+1)}) - \mathbf{g}(\boldsymbol{\theta}^{(m)})]'(\Delta\boldsymbol{\theta}^{(m+1)}) \\ &= -\mathbf{g}(\boldsymbol{\theta}^{(m)})'(\Delta\boldsymbol{\theta}^{(m+1)}) \\ &= -\mathbf{g}(\boldsymbol{\theta}^{(m)})'s\mathbf{A}^{(m)}\mathbf{g}(\boldsymbol{\theta}^{(m)}),\end{aligned} \qquad [5.A.8]$$

with the last line following from [5.7.18]. But the final term in [5.A.8] must be negative, by virtue of the facts that $\mathbf{A}^{(m)}$ is positive definite, $s > 0$, and $\mathbf{g}(\boldsymbol{\theta}^{(m)}) \neq \mathbf{0}$. Hence, [5.A.7] holds, meaning that $\mathbf{A}^{(m+1)}$ is positive definite for this case.

**Case 2.** There exists a $\beta$ such that $\mathbf{y} = \beta\Delta\mathbf{g}^{(m+1)}$. In this case, [5.A.6] is zero, so that [5.A.5] becomes

$$\begin{aligned}\mathbf{y}'\mathbf{A}^{(m+1)}\mathbf{y} &= -\frac{\mathbf{y}'(\Delta\boldsymbol{\theta}^{(m+1)})(\Delta\boldsymbol{\theta}^{(m+1)})'\mathbf{y}}{(\Delta\mathbf{g}^{(m+1)})'(\Delta\boldsymbol{\theta}^{(m+1)})} \\ &= -\frac{\beta(\Delta\mathbf{g}^{(m+1)})'(\Delta\boldsymbol{\theta}^{(m+1)})(\Delta\boldsymbol{\theta}^{(m+1)})'\beta(\Delta\mathbf{g}^{(m+1)})}{(\Delta\mathbf{g}^{(m+1)})'(\Delta\boldsymbol{\theta}^{(m+1)})} \\ &= -\beta^2(\Delta\mathbf{g}^{(m+1)})'(\Delta\boldsymbol{\theta}^{(m+1)}) = \beta^2\mathbf{g}(\boldsymbol{\theta}^{(m)})'s\mathbf{A}^{(m)}\mathbf{g}(\boldsymbol{\theta}^{(m)}) > 0,\end{aligned}$$

as in [5.A.8]. ■

## Chapter 5 Exercises

5.1. Show that the value of [5.4.16] at $\theta = \tilde{\theta}$, $\sigma^2 = \tilde{\sigma}^2$ is identical to its value at $\theta = \tilde{\theta}^{-1}$, $\sigma^2 = \tilde{\theta}^2\tilde{\sigma}^2$.

5.2. Verify that expression [5.7.12] calculates the maximum of [5.7.6] in a single step from the initial estimate $\boldsymbol{\theta}^{(0)} = (-1, 1)'$.

5.3. Let $(y_1, y_2, \ldots, y_T)$ be a sample of size $T$ drawn from an i.i.d. $N(\mu, \sigma^2)$ distribution.

(a) Show that the maximum likelihood estimates are given by

$$\hat{\mu} = T^{-1}\sum_{t=1}^{T} y_t$$

$$\hat{\sigma}^2 = T^{-1}\sum_{t=1}^{T} (y_t - \hat{\mu})^2.$$

(b) Show that the matrix $\hat{\mathcal{J}}_{2D}$ in [5.8.2] is

$$\hat{\mathcal{J}}_{2D} = \begin{bmatrix} 1/\hat{\sigma}^2 & 0 \\ 0 & 1/(2\hat{\sigma}^4) \end{bmatrix}.$$

(c) Show that for this example result [5.8.1] suggests

$$\begin{bmatrix} \hat{\mu} \\ \hat{\sigma}^2 \end{bmatrix} \approx N\left(\begin{bmatrix} \mu \\ \sigma^2 \end{bmatrix}, \begin{bmatrix} \hat{\sigma}^2/T & 0 \\ 0 & 2\hat{\sigma}^4/T \end{bmatrix}\right).$$

## Chapter 5 References


Anderson, Brian D. O., and John B. Moore. 1979. *Optimal Filtering*. Englewood Cliffs, N.J.: Prentice-Hall.

Berndt, E. K., B. H. Hall, R. E. Hall, and J. A. Hausman. 1974. "Estimation and Inference in Nonlinear Structural Models." *Annals of Economic and Social Measurement* 3:653–65.

Box, George E. P., and D. R. Cox. 1964. "An Analysis of Transformations." *Journal of the Royal Statistical Society* Series B, 26:211–52.

——— and Gwilym M. Jenkins. 1976. *Time Series Analysis: Forecasting and Control*, rev. ed. San Francisco: Holden-Day.

Broyden, C. G. 1965. "A Class of Methods for Solving Nonlinear Simultaneous Equations." *Mathematics of Computation* 19:577–93.

———. 1967. "Quasi-Newton Methods and Their Application to Function Minimization." *Mathematics of Computation* 21:368–81.

Chiang, Alpha C. 1974. *Fundamental Methods of Mathematical Economics*, 2d ed. New York: McGraw-Hill.

Davidon, W. C. 1959. "Variable Metric Method of Minimization." A.E.C. Research and Development Report ANL-5990 (rev.).

Fletcher, R., and M. J. D. Powell. 1963. "A Rapidly Convergent Descent Method for Minimization." *Computer Journal* 6:163–68.

Galbraith, R. F., and J. I. Galbraith. 1974. "On the Inverses of Some Patterned Matrices Arising in the Theory of Stationary Time Series." *Journal of Applied Probability* 11:63–71.

Hannan, E., and J. Rissanen. 1982. "Recursive Estimation of Mixed Autoregressive–Moving Average Order." *Biometrika* 69:81–94.

Janacek, G. J., and A. L. Swift. 1990. "A Class of Models for Non-Normal Time Series." *Journal of Time Series Analysis* 11:19–31.

Judge, George G., William E. Griffiths, R. Carter Hill, and Tsoung-Chao Lee. 1980. *The Theory and Practice of Econometrics*. New York: Wiley.

Koreisha, Sergio, and Tarmo Pukkila. 1989. "Fast Linear Estimation Methods for Vector Autoregressive Moving-Average Models." *Journal of Time Series Analysis* 10:325–39.

Li, W. K., and A. I. McLeod. 1988. "ARMA Modelling with Non-Gaussian Innovations." *Journal of Time Series Analysis* 9:155–68.

Martin, R. D. 1981. "Robust Methods for Time Series," in D. F. Findley, ed., *Applied Time Series*, Vol. II. New York: Academic Press.

Nelson, Harold L., and C. W. J. Granger. 1979. "Experience with Using the Box-Cox Transformation When Forecasting Economic Time Series." *Journal of Econometrics* 10:57–69.

Quandt, Richard E. 1983. "Computational Problems and Methods," in Zvi Griliches and Michael D. Intriligator, eds., *Handbook of Econometrics*, Vol. 1. Amsterdam: North-Holland.

White, Halbert. 1982. "Maximum Likelihood Estimation of Misspecified Models." *Econometrica* 50:1–25.

# 6 Spectral Analysis

Up to this point in the book, the value of a variable $Y_t$ at date $t$ has typically been described in terms of a sequence of innovations $\{\varepsilon_t\}_{t=-\infty}^{\infty}$ in models of the form

$$Y_t = \mu + \sum_{j=0}^{\infty} \psi_j \varepsilon_{t-j}.$$

The focus has been on the implications of such a representation for the covariance between $Y_t$ and $Y_\tau$ at distinct dates $t$ and $\tau$. This is known as analyzing the properties of $\{Y_t\}_{t=-\infty}^{\infty}$ in the *time domain*.

This chapter instead describes the value of $Y_t$ as a weighted sum of periodic functions of the form $\cos(\omega t)$ and $\sin(\omega t)$, where $\omega$ denotes a particular frequency:

$$Y_t = \mu + \int_0^\pi \alpha(\omega)\cdot\cos(\omega t)\, d\omega + \int_0^\pi \delta(\omega)\cdot\sin(\omega t)\, d\omega.$$

The goal will be to determine how important cycles of different frequencies are in accounting for the behavior of $Y$. This is known as *frequency-domain* or *spectral* analysis. As we will see, the two kinds of analysis are not mutually exclusive. Any covariance-stationary process has both a time-domain representation and a frequency-domain representation, and any feature of the data that can be described by one representation can equally well be described by the other representation. For some features, the time-domain description may be simpler, while for other features the frequency-domain description may be simpler.

Section 6.1 describes the properties of the population spectrum and introduces the spectral representation theorem, which can be viewed as a frequency-domain version of Wold's theorem. Section 6.2 introduces the sample analog of the population spectrum and uses an *OLS* regression framework to motivate the spectral representation theorem and to explain the sense in which the spectrum identifies the contributions to the variance of the observed data of periodic components with different cycles. Section 6.3 discusses strategies for estimating the population spectrum. Section 6.4 provides an example of applying spectral techniques and discusses some of the ways they can be used in practice. More detailed discussions of spectral analysis are provided by Anderson (1971), Bloomfield (1976), and Fuller (1976).

## 6.1. *The Population Spectrum*

### *The Population Spectrum and Its Properties*

Let $\{Y_t\}_{t=-\infty}^{\infty}$ be a covariance-stationary process with mean $E(Y_t) = \mu$ and $j$th autocovariance

$$E(Y_t - \mu)(Y_{t-j} - \mu) = \gamma_j.$$

Assuming that these autocovariances are absolutely summable, the autocovariance-generating function is given by

$$g_Y(z) \equiv \sum_{j=-\infty}^{\infty} \gamma_j z^j, \qquad [6.1.1]$$

where $z$ denotes a complex scalar. If [6.1.1] is divided by $2\pi$ and evaluated at some $z$ represented by $z = e^{-i\omega}$ for $i = \sqrt{-1}$ and $\omega$ a real scalar, the result is called the population spectrum of $Y$:

$$s_Y(\omega) = \frac{1}{2\pi} g_Y(e^{-i\omega}) = \frac{1}{2\pi} \sum_{j=-\infty}^{\infty} \gamma_j e^{-i\omega j}. \qquad [6.1.2]$$

Note that the spectrum is a function of $\omega$: given any particular value of $\omega$ and a sequence of autocovariances $\{\gamma_j\}_{j=-\infty}^{\infty}$, we could in principle calculate the value of $s_Y(\omega)$.

De Moivre's theorem allows us to write $e^{-i\omega j}$ as

$$e^{-i\omega j} = \cos(\omega j) - i{\cdot}\sin(\omega j). \qquad [6.1.3]$$

Substituting [6.1.3] into [6.1.2], it appears that the spectrum can equivalently be written

$$s_Y(\omega) = \frac{1}{2\pi} \sum_{j=-\infty}^{\infty} \gamma_j[\cos(\omega j) - i{\cdot}\sin(\omega j)]. \qquad [6.1.4]$$

Note that for a covariance-stationary process, $\gamma_j = \gamma_{-j}$. Hence, [6.1.4] implies

$$\begin{aligned} s_Y(\omega) &= \frac{1}{2\pi}\gamma_0[\cos(0) - i{\cdot}\sin(0)] \\ &\quad + \frac{1}{2\pi}\left\{\sum_{j=1}^{\infty} \gamma_j[\cos(\omega j) + \cos(-\omega j) - i{\cdot}\sin(\omega j) - i{\cdot}\sin(-\omega j)]\right\}. \end{aligned} \qquad [6.1.5]$$

Next, we make use of the following results from trigonometry:[1]

$$\begin{aligned} \cos(0) &= 1 \\ \sin(0) &= 0 \\ \sin(-\theta) &= -\sin(\theta) \\ \cos(-\theta) &= \cos(\theta). \end{aligned}$$

Using these relations, [6.1.5] simplifies to

$$s_Y(\omega) = \frac{1}{2\pi}\left\{\gamma_0 + 2\sum_{j=1}^{\infty} \gamma_j \cos(\omega j)\right\}. \qquad [6.1.6]$$

Assuming that the sequence of autocovariances $\{\gamma_j\}_{j=-\infty}^{\infty}$ is absolutely summable, expression [6.1.6] implies that the population spectrum exists and that $s_Y(\omega)$ is a continuous, real-valued function of $\omega$. It is possible to go a bit further and show that if the $\gamma_j$'s represent autocovariances of a covariance-stationary process, then $s_Y(\omega)$ will be nonnegative for all $\omega$.[2] Since $\cos(\omega j) = \cos(-\omega j)$ for any $\omega$, the spectrum is symmetric around $\omega = 0$. Finally, since $\cos[(\omega + 2\pi k){\cdot}j] = \cos(\omega j)$ for any integers $k$ and $j$, it follows from [6.1.6] that $s_Y(\omega + 2\pi k) = s_Y(\omega)$ for any integer $k$. Hence, the spectrum is a periodic function of $\omega$. If we know the value of $s_Y(\omega)$ for all $\omega$ between 0 and $\pi$, we can infer the value of $s_Y(\omega)$ for any $\omega$.

[1]These are reviewed in Section A.1 of the Mathematical Review (Appendix A) at the end of the book.

[2]See, for example, Fuller (1976, p. 110).

### *Calculating the Population Spectrum for Various Processes*

Let $Y_t$ follow an $MA(\infty)$ process:

$$Y_t = \mu + \psi(L)\varepsilon_t, \qquad [6.1.7]$$

where

$$\psi(L) = \sum_{j=0}^{\infty} \psi_j L^j$$

$$\sum_{j=0}^{\infty} |\psi_j| < \infty$$

$$E(\varepsilon_t \varepsilon_\tau) = \begin{cases} \sigma^2 & \text{for } t = \tau \\ 0 & \text{otherwise.} \end{cases}$$

Recall from expression [3.6.8] that the autocovariance-generating function for $Y$ is given by

$$g_Y(z) = \sigma^2 \psi(z)\psi(z^{-1}).$$

Hence, from [6.1.2], the population spectrum for an $MA(\infty)$ process is given by

$$s_Y(\omega) = (2\pi)^{-1} \cdot \sigma^2 \psi(e^{-i\omega})\psi(e^{i\omega}). \qquad [6.1.8]$$

For example, for a white noise process, $\psi(z) = 1$ and the population spectrum is a constant for all $\omega$:

$$s_Y(\omega) = \sigma^2/2\pi. \qquad [6.1.9]$$

Next, consider an $MA(1)$ process:

$$Y_t = \varepsilon_t + \theta\varepsilon_{t-1}.$$

Here, $\psi(z) = 1 + \theta z$ and the population spectrum is

$$\begin{aligned} s_Y(\omega) &= (2\pi)^{-1} \cdot \sigma^2 (1 + \theta e^{-i\omega})(1 + \theta e^{i\omega}) \\ &= (2\pi)^{-1} \cdot \sigma^2 (1 + \theta e^{-i\omega} + \theta e^{i\omega} + \theta^2). \end{aligned} \qquad [6.1.10]$$

But notice that

$$e^{-i\omega} + e^{i\omega} = \cos(\omega) - i \cdot \sin(\omega) + \cos(\omega) + i \cdot \sin(\omega) = 2 \cdot \cos(\omega), \qquad [6.1.11]$$

so that [6.1.10] becomes

$$s_Y(\omega) = (2\pi)^{-1} \cdot \sigma^2 [1 + \theta^2 + 2\theta \cdot \cos(\omega)]. \qquad [6.1.12]$$

Recall that $\cos(\omega)$ goes from 1 to $-1$ as $\omega$ goes from 0 to $\pi$. Hence, when $\theta > 0$, the spectrum $s_Y(\omega)$ is a monotonically decreasing function of $\omega$ for $\omega$ in $[0, \pi]$, whereas when $\theta < 0$, the spectrum is monotonically increasing.

For an $AR(1)$ process

$$Y_t = c + \phi Y_{t-1} + \varepsilon_t,$$

we have $\psi(z) = 1/(1 - \phi z)$ as long as $|\phi| < 1$. Thus, the spectrum is

$$\begin{aligned} s_Y(\omega) &= \frac{1}{2\pi} \frac{\sigma^2}{(1 - \phi e^{-i\omega})(1 - \phi e^{i\omega})} \\ &= \frac{1}{2\pi} \frac{\sigma^2}{(1 - \phi e^{-i\omega} - \phi e^{i\omega} + \phi^2)} \\ &= \frac{1}{2\pi} \frac{\sigma^2}{[1 + \phi^2 - 2\phi \cdot \cos(\omega)]}. \end{aligned} \qquad [6.1.13]$$

When $\phi > 0$, the denominator is monotonically increasing in $\omega$ over $[0, \pi]$, meaning that $s_Y(\omega)$ is monotonically decreasing. When $\phi < 0$, the spectrum $s_Y(\omega)$ is a monotonically increasing function of $\omega$.

In general, for an $ARMA(p, q)$ process

$$Y_t = c + \phi_1 Y_{t-1} + \phi_2 Y_{t-2} + \cdots + \phi_p Y_{t-p} + \varepsilon_t + \theta_1 \varepsilon_{t-1} + \theta_2 \varepsilon_{t-2} + \cdots + \theta_q \varepsilon_{t-q},$$

the population spectrum is given by

$$s_Y(\omega) = \frac{\sigma^2}{2\pi} \frac{(1 + \theta_1 e^{-i\omega} + \theta_2 e^{-i2\omega} + \cdots + \theta_q e^{-iq\omega})}{(1 - \phi_1 e^{-i\omega} - \phi_2 e^{-i2\omega} - \cdots - \phi_p e^{-ip\omega})} \times \frac{(1 + \theta_1 e^{i\omega} + \theta_2 e^{i2\omega} + \cdots + \theta_q e^{iq\omega})}{(1 - \phi_1 e^{i\omega} - \phi_2 e^{i2\omega} - \cdots - \phi_p e^{ip\omega})}. \qquad [6.1.14]$$

If the moving average and autoregressive polynomials are factored as follows:

$$1 + \theta_1 z + \theta_2 z^2 + \cdots + \theta_q z^q = (1 - \eta_1 z)(1 - \eta_2 z) \cdots (1 - \eta_q z)$$
$$1 - \phi_1 z - \phi_2 z^2 - \cdots - \phi_p z^p = (1 - \lambda_1 z)(1 - \lambda_2 z) \cdots (1 - \lambda_p z),$$

then the spectral density in [6.1.14] can be written

$$s_Y(\omega) = \frac{\sigma^2 \prod_{j=1}^{q} [1 + \eta_j^2 - 2\eta_j \cdot \cos(\omega)]}{2\pi \prod_{j=1}^{p} [1 + \lambda_j^2 - 2\lambda_j \cdot \cos(\omega)]}.$$

## *Calculating the Autocovariances from the Population Spectrum*

If we know the sequence of autocovariances $\{\gamma_j\}_{j=-\infty}^{\infty}$, in principle we can calculate the value of $s_Y(\omega)$ for any $\omega$ from [6.1.2] or [6.1.6]. The converse is also true: if we know the value of $s_Y(\omega)$ for all $\omega$ in $[0, \pi]$, we can calculate the value of the $k$th autocovariance $\gamma_k$ for any given $k$. This means that the population spectrum $s_Y(\omega)$ and the sequence of autocovariances contain exactly the same information—neither one can tell us anything about the process that is not possible to infer from the other.

The following proposition (proved in Appendix 6.A at the end of this chapter) provides a formula for calculating any autocovariance from the population spectrum.

***Proposition 6.1:*** *Let $\{\gamma_j\}_{j=-\infty}^{\infty}$ be an absolutely summable sequence of autocovariances, and define $s_Y(\omega)$ as in [6.1.2]. Then*

$$\int_{-\pi}^{\pi} s_Y(\omega) e^{i\omega k}\, d\omega = \gamma_k. \qquad [6.1.15]$$

*Result [6.1.15] can equivalently be written as*

$$\int_{-\pi}^{\pi} s_Y(\omega) \cos(\omega k)\, d\omega = \gamma_k. \qquad [6.1.16]$$

## *Interpreting the Population Spectrum*

The following result obtains as a special case of Proposition 6.1 by setting $k = 0$:

$$\int_{-\pi}^{\pi} s_Y(\omega)\, d\omega = \gamma_0. \qquad [6.1.17]$$

In other words, the area under the population spectrum between $\pm\pi$ gives $\gamma_0$, the variance of $Y_t$.

More generally—since $s_Y(\omega)$ is nonnegative—if we were to calculate

$$\int_{-\omega_1}^{\omega_1} s_Y(\omega)\, d\omega$$

for any $\omega_1$ between 0 and $\pi$, the result would be a positive number that we could interpret as the portion of the variance of $Y_t$ that is associated with frequencies $\omega$ that are less than $\omega_1$ in absolute value. Recalling that $s_Y(\omega)$ is symmetric, the claim is that

$$2 \cdot \int_{0}^{\omega_1} s_Y(\omega)\, d\omega \qquad [6.1.18]$$

represents the portion of the variance of $Y$ that could be attributed to periodic random components with frequency less than or equal to $\omega_1$.

What does it mean to attribute a certain portion of the variance of $Y$ to cycles with frequency less than or equal to $\omega_1$? To explore this question, let us consider the following rather special stochastic process. Suppose that the value of $Y$ at date $t$ is determined by

$$Y_t = \sum_{j=1}^{M} [\alpha_j \cdot \cos(\omega_j t) + \delta_j \cdot \sin(\omega_j t)]. \qquad [6.1.19]$$

Here, $\alpha_j$ and $\delta_j$ are zero-mean random variables, meaning that $E(Y_t) = 0$ for all $t$. The sequences $\{\alpha_j\}_{j=1}^{M}$ and $\{\delta_j\}_{j=1}^{M}$ are serially uncorrelated and mutually uncorrelated:

$$E(\alpha_j \alpha_k) = \begin{cases} \sigma_j^2 & \text{for } j = k \\ 0 & \text{for } j \neq k \end{cases}$$

$$E(\delta_j \delta_k) = \begin{cases} \sigma_j^2 & \text{for } j = k \\ 0 & \text{for } j \neq k \end{cases}$$

$$E(\alpha_j \delta_k) = 0 \qquad \text{for all } j \text{ and } k.$$

The variance of $Y_t$ is then

$$\begin{aligned} E(Y_t^2) &= \sum_{j=1}^{M} \Big[ E(\alpha_j^2) \cdot \cos^2(\omega_j t) + E(\delta_j^2) \cdot \sin^2(\omega_j t) \Big] \\ &= \sum_{j=1}^{M} \sigma_j^2 \Big[ \cos^2(\omega_j t) + \sin^2(\omega_j t) \Big] \qquad [6.1.20] \\ &= \sum_{j=1}^{M} \sigma_j^2, \end{aligned}$$

with the last line following from equation [A.1.12]. Thus, for this process, the portion of the variance of $Y$ that is due to cycles of frequency $\omega_j$ is given by $\sigma_j^2$.

If the frequencies are ordered $0 < \omega_1 < \omega_2 < \cdots < \omega_M < \pi$, the portion of the variance of $Y$ that is due to cycles of frequency less than or equal to $\omega_j$ is given by $\sigma_1^2 + \sigma_2^2 + \cdots + \sigma_j^2$.

The $k$th autocovariance of $Y$ is

$$\begin{aligned} E(Y_t Y_{t-k}) &= \sum_{j=1}^{M} \{E(\alpha_j^2)\cdot\cos(\omega_j t)\cdot\cos[\omega_j(t-k)] \\ &\quad + E(\delta_j^2)\cdot\sin(\omega_j t)\cdot\sin[\omega_j(t-k)]\} \\ &= \sum_{j=1}^{M} \sigma_j^2\{\cos(\omega_j t)\cdot\cos[\omega_j(t-k)] \\ &\quad + \sin(\omega_j t)\cdot\sin[\omega_j(t-k)]\}. \end{aligned} \qquad [6.1.21]$$

Recall the trigonometric identity[3]

$$\cos(A - B) = \cos(A)\cdot\cos(B) + \sin(A)\cdot\sin(B). \qquad [6.1.22]$$

For $A = \omega_j t$ and $B = \omega_j(t - k)$, we have $A - B = \omega_j k$, so that [6.1.21] becomes

$$E(Y_t Y_{t-k}) = \sum_{j=1}^{M} \sigma_j^2\cdot\cos(\omega_j k). \qquad [6.1.23]$$

Since the mean and the autocovariances of $Y$ are not functions of time, the process described by [6.1.19] is covariance-stationary, although [6.1.23] implies that the sequence of autocovariances $\{\gamma_k\}_{k=0}^{\infty}$ is not absolutely summable.

We were able to attribute a certain portion of the variance of $Y_t$ to cycles of less than a given frequency for the process in [6.1.19] because that is a rather special covariance-stationary process. However, there is a general result known as the *spectral representation theorem* which says that any covariance-stationary process $Y_t$ can be expressed in terms of a generalization of [6.1.19]. For any fixed frequency $\omega$ in $[0, \pi]$, we define random variables $\alpha(\omega)$ and $\delta(\omega)$ and propose to write a stationary process with absolutely summable autocovariances in the form

$$Y_t = \mu + \int_0^{\pi} [\alpha(\omega)\cdot\cos(\omega t) + \delta(\omega)\cdot\sin(\omega t)]\, d\omega.$$

The random processes represented by $\alpha(\cdot)$ and $\delta(\cdot)$ have zero mean and the further properties that for any frequencies $0 < \omega_1 < \omega_2 < \omega_3 < \omega_4 < \pi$, the variable $\int_{\omega_1}^{\omega_2} \alpha(\omega)\, d\omega$ is uncorrelated with $\int_{\omega_3}^{\omega_4} \alpha(\omega)\, d\omega$ and the variable $\int_{\omega_1}^{\omega_2} \delta(\omega)\, d\omega$ is uncorrelated with $\int_{\omega_3}^{\omega_4} \delta(\omega)\, d\omega$, while for any $0 < \omega_1 < \omega_2 < \pi$ and $0 < \omega_3 < \omega_4 < \pi$, the variable $\int_{\omega_1}^{\omega_2} \alpha(\omega)\, d\omega$ is uncorrelated with $\int_{\omega_3}^{\omega_4} \delta(\omega)\, d\omega$. For such a process, one can calculate the portion of the variance of $Y_t$ that is due to cycles with frequency less than or equal to some specified value $\omega_1$ through a generalization of the procedure used to analyze [6.1.19]. Moreover, this magnitude turns out to be given by the expression in [6.1.18].

We shall not attempt a proof of the spectral representation theorem here; for details the reader is referred to Cramér and Leadbetter (1967, pp. 128–38). Instead, the next section provides a formal derivation of a finite-sample version of these results, showing the sense in which the sample analog of [6.1.18] gives the portion of the sample variance of an observed series that can be attributed to cycles with frequencies less than or equal to $\omega_1$.

[3]See, for example, Thomas (1972, p. 176).

## 6.2. The Sample Periodogram

For a covariance-stationary process $Y_t$ with absolutely summable autocovariances, we have defined the value of the population spectrum at frequency $\omega$ to be

$$s_Y(\omega) = \frac{1}{2\pi}\sum_{j=-\infty}^{\infty} \gamma_j e^{-i\omega j}, \tag{6.2.1}$$

where

$$\gamma_j \equiv E(Y_t - \mu)(Y_{t-j} - \mu)$$

and $\mu = E(Y_t)$. Note that the population spectrum is expressed in terms of $\{\gamma_j\}_{j=0}^{\infty}$, which represents population second moments.

Given an observed sample of $T$ observations denoted $y_1, y_2, \ldots, y_T$, we can calculate up to $T - 1$ sample autocovariances from the formulas

$$\hat{\gamma}_j = \begin{cases} T^{-1} \sum_{t=j+1}^{T} (y_t - \bar{y})(y_{t-j} - \bar{y}) & \text{for } j = 0, 1, 2, \ldots, T-1 \\ \hat{\gamma}_{-j} & \text{for } j = -1, -2, \ldots, -T+1, \end{cases} \tag{6.2.2}$$

where $\bar{y}$ is the sample mean:

$$\bar{y} = T^{-1}\sum_{t=1}^{T} y_t. \tag{6.2.3}$$

For any given $\omega$ we can then construct the sample analog of [6.2.1], which is known as the *sample periodogram*:

$$\hat{s}_y(\omega) = \frac{1}{2\pi}\sum_{j=-T+1}^{T-1} \hat{\gamma}_j e^{-i\omega j}. \tag{6.2.4}$$

As in [6.1.6], the sample periodogram can equivalently be expressed as

$$\hat{s}_y(\omega) = \frac{1}{2\pi}\left[\hat{\gamma}_0 + 2\sum_{j=1}^{T-1} \hat{\gamma}_j \cos(\omega j)\right]. \tag{6.2.5}$$

The same calculations that led to [6.1.17] can be used to show that the area under the periodogram is the sample variance of $y$:

$$\int_{-\pi}^{\pi} \hat{s}_y(\omega)\, d\omega = \hat{\gamma}_0.$$

Like the population spectrum, the sample periodogram is symmetric around $\omega = 0$, so that we could equivalently write

$$\hat{\gamma}_0 = 2\int_0^{\pi} \hat{s}_y(\omega)\, d\omega.$$

There also turns out to be a sample analog to the spectral representation theorem, which we now develop. In particular, we will see that given any $T$ observations on a process $(y_1, y_2, \ldots, y_T)$, there exist frequencies $\omega_1, \omega_2, \ldots, \omega_M$ and coefficients $\hat{\mu}, \hat{\alpha}_1, \hat{\alpha}_2, \ldots, \hat{\alpha}_M, \hat{\delta}_1, \hat{\delta}_2, \ldots, \hat{\delta}_M$ such that the value for $y$ at date $t$ can be expressed as

$$y_t = \hat{\mu} + \sum_{j=1}^{M} \{\hat{\alpha}_j \cdot \cos[\omega_j(t-1)] + \hat{\delta}_j \cdot \sin[\omega_j(t-1)]\}, \tag{6.2.6}$$

where the variable $\hat{\alpha}_j \cdot \cos[\omega_j(t-1)]$ is orthogonal in the sample to $\hat{\alpha}_k \cdot \cos[\omega_k(t-1)]$ for $j \neq k$, the variable $\hat{\delta}_j \cdot \sin[\omega_j(t-1)]$ is orthogonal to $\hat{\delta}_k \cdot \sin[\omega_k(t-1)]$ for $j \neq k$, and the variable $\hat{\alpha}_j \cdot \cos[\omega_j(t-1)]$ is orthogonal to $\hat{\delta}_k \cdot \sin[\omega_k(t-1)]$ for all $j$ and $k$. The sample variance of $y$ is $T^{-1}\Sigma_{t=1}^{T}(y_t - \bar{y})^2$, and the portion of this variance that can be attributed to cycles with frequency $\omega_j$ can be inferred from the sample periodogram $\hat{s}_y(\omega_j)$.

We will develop this claim for the case when the sample size $T$ is an odd number. In this case $y_t$ will be expressed in terms of periodic functions with $M \equiv (T-1)/2$ different frequencies in [6.2.6]. The frequencies $\omega_1, \omega_2, \ldots, \omega_M$ are specified as follows:

$$\begin{aligned} \omega_1 &= 2\pi/T \\ \omega_2 &= 4\pi/T \\ &\vdots \\ \omega_M &= 2M\pi/T. \end{aligned} \qquad [6.2.7]$$

Thus, the highest frequency considered is

$$\omega_M = \frac{2(T-1)\pi}{2T} < \pi.$$

Consider an *OLS* regression of the value of $y_t$ on a constant and on the various cosine and sine terms,

$$y_t = \mu + \sum_{j=1}^{M} \{\alpha_j \cdot \cos[\omega_j(t-1)] + \delta_j \cdot \sin[\omega_j(t-1)]\} + u_t.$$

This can be viewed as a standard regression model of the form

$$y_t = \boldsymbol{\beta}'\mathbf{x}_t + u_t, \qquad [6.2.8]$$

where

$$\mathbf{x}_t = \begin{bmatrix} 1 & \cos[\omega_1(t-1)] & \sin[\omega_1(t-1)] & \cos[\omega_2(t-1)] & \sin[\omega_2(t-1)] \\ & & \cdots \cos[\omega_M(t-1)] & \sin[\omega_M(t-1)] \end{bmatrix}' \qquad [6.2.9]$$

$$\boldsymbol{\beta}' = [\mu \quad \alpha_1 \quad \delta_1 \quad \alpha_2 \quad \delta_2 \quad \cdots \quad \alpha_M \quad \delta_M]. \qquad [6.2.10]$$

Note that $\mathbf{x}_t$ has $(2M+1) = T$ elements, so that there are as many explanatory variables as observations. We will show that the elements of $\mathbf{x}_t$ are linearly independent, meaning that an *OLS* regression of $y_t$ on $\mathbf{x}_t$ yields a perfect fit. Thus, the fitted values for this regression are of the form of [6.2.6] with no error term $u_t$. Moreover, the coefficients of this regression have the property that $\frac{1}{2}(\hat{\alpha}_j^2 + \hat{\delta}_j^2)$ represents the portion of the sample variance of $y$ that can be attributed to cycles with frequency $\omega_j$. This magnitude $\frac{1}{2}(\hat{\alpha}_j^2 + \hat{\delta}_j^2)$ further turns out to be proportional to the sample periodogram evaluated at $\omega_j$. In other words, any observed series $y_1, y_2, \ldots, y_T$ can be expressed in terms of periodic functions as in [6.2.6], and the portion of the sample variance that is due to cycles with frequency $\omega_j$ can be found from the sample periodogram. These points are established formally in the following proposition, which is proved in Appendix 6.A at the end of this chapter.

***Proposition 6.2:*** *Let $T$ denote an odd integer and let $M \equiv (T - 1)/2$. Let $\omega_j = 2\pi j/T$ for $j = 1, 2, \ldots, M$, and let $\mathbf{x}_t$ be the $(T \times 1)$ vector in [6.2.9]. Then*

$$\sum_{t=1}^{T} \mathbf{x}_t\mathbf{x}_t' = \begin{bmatrix} T & \mathbf{0}' \\ \mathbf{0} & (T/2)\cdot\mathbf{I}_{T-1} \end{bmatrix}. \qquad [6.2.11]$$

*Furthermore, let $\{y_1, y_2, \ldots, y_T\}$ be any $T$ numbers. Then the following are true:*

*(a) The value of $y_t$ can be expressed as*

$$y_t = \hat{\mu} + \sum_{j=1}^{M} \{\hat{\alpha}_j\cdot\cos[\omega_j(t - 1)] + \hat{\delta}_j\cdot\sin[\omega_j(t - 1)]\},$$

*with $\hat{\mu} = \bar{y}$ (the sample mean from [6.2.3]) and*

$$\hat{\alpha}_j = (2/T) \sum_{t=1}^{T} y_t\cdot\cos[\omega_j(t - 1)] \quad \text{for } j = 1, 2, \ldots, M \qquad [6.2.12]$$

$$\hat{\delta}_j = (2/T) \sum_{t=1}^{T} y_t\cdot\sin[\omega_j(t - 1)] \quad \text{for } j = 1, 2, \ldots, M. \qquad [6.2.13]$$

*(b) The sample variance of $y_t$ can be expressed as*

$$(1/T) \sum_{t=1}^{T} (y_t - \bar{y})^2 = (1/2) \sum_{j=1}^{M} (\hat{\alpha}_j^2 + \hat{\delta}_j^2), \qquad [6.2.14]$$

*and the portion of the sample variance of $y$ that can be attributed to cycles of frequency $\omega_j$ is given by $\frac{1}{2}(\hat{\alpha}_j^2 + \hat{\delta}_j^2)$.*

*(c) The portion of the sample variance of $y$ that can be attributed to cycles of frequency $\omega_j$ can equivalently be expressed as*

$$(1/2)(\hat{\alpha}_j^2 + \hat{\delta}_j^2) = (4\pi/T)\cdot\hat{s}_y(\omega_j), \qquad [6.2.15]$$

*where $\hat{s}_y(\omega_j)$ is the sample periodogram at frequency $\omega_j$.*

Result [6.2.11] establishes that $\Sigma_{t=1}^{T}\mathbf{x}_t\mathbf{x}_t'$ is a diagonal matrix, meaning that the explanatory variables contained in $\mathbf{x}_t$ are mutually orthogonal. The proposition asserts that any observed time series $(y_1, y_2, \ldots, y_T)$ with $T$ odd can be written as a constant plus a weighted sum of $(T - 1)$ periodic functions with $(T - 1)/2$ different frequencies; a related result can also be developed when $T$ is an even integer. Hence, the proposition gives a finite-sample analog of the spectral representation theorem. The proposition further shows that the sample periodogram captures the portion of the sample variance of $y$ that can be attributed to cycles of different frequencies.

Note that the frequencies $\omega_j$ in terms of which the variance of $y$ is explained all lie in $[0, \pi]$. Why aren't negative frequencies $\omega < 0$ employed as well? Suppose that the data were actually generated by a special case of the process in [6.1.19],

$$Y_t = \alpha\cdot\cos(-\omega t) + \delta\cdot\sin(-\omega t), \qquad [6.2.16]$$

where $-\omega < 0$ represents some particular negative frequency and where $\alpha$ and $\delta$ are zero-mean random variables. Since $\cos(-\omega t) = \cos(\omega t)$ and $\sin(-\omega t) = -\sin(\omega t)$, the process [6.2.16] can equivalently be written

$$Y_t = \alpha\cdot\cos(\omega t) - \delta\cdot\sin(\omega t). \qquad [6.2.17]$$

Thus there is no way of using observed data on $y$ to decide whether the data are generated by a cycle with frequency $-\omega$ as in [6.2.16] or by a cycle with frequency

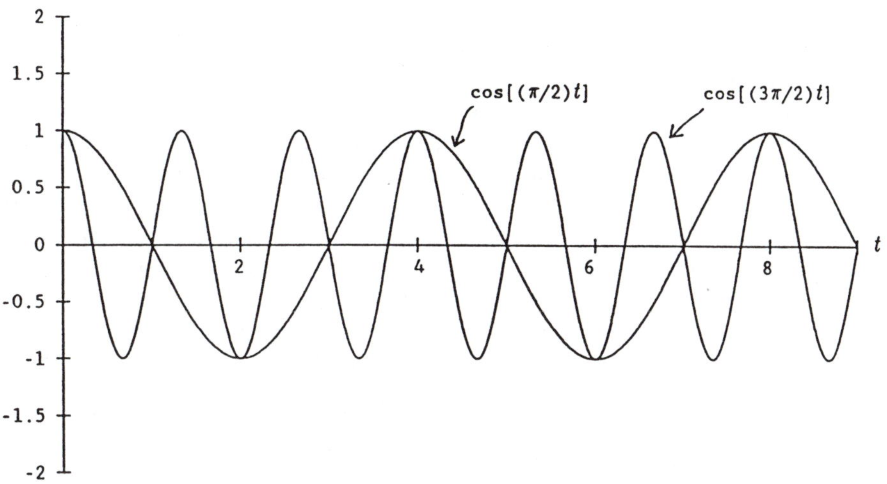


**FIGURE 6.1** Aliasing: plots of $\cos[(\pi/2)t]$ and $\cos[(3\pi/2)t]$ as functions of $t$.

$+\omega$ as in [6.2.17]. It is simply a matter of convention that we choose to focus only on positive frequencies.

Why is $\omega = \pi$ the largest frequency considered? Suppose the data were generated from a periodic function with frequency $\omega > \pi$, say, $\omega = 3\pi/2$ for illustration:

$$Y_t = \alpha \cdot \cos[(3\pi/2)t] + \delta \cdot \sin[(3\pi/2)t]. \qquad [6.2.18]$$

Again, the properties of the sine and cosine function imply that [6.2.18] is equivalent to

$$Y_t = \alpha \cdot \cos[(-\pi/2)t] + \delta \cdot \sin[(-\pi/2)t]. \qquad [6.2.19]$$

Thus, by the previous argument, a representation with cycles of frequency $(3\pi/2)$ is observationally indistinguishable from one with cycles of frequency $(\pi/2)$.

To summarize, if the data-generating process actually includes cycles with negative frequencies or with frequencies greater than $\pi$, these will be imputed to cycles with frequencies between 0 and $\pi$. This is known as *aliasing*.

Another way to think about aliasing is as follows. Recall that the value of the function $\cos(\omega t)$ repeats itself every $2\pi/\omega$ periods, so that a frequency of $\omega$ is associated with a period of $2\pi/\omega$.[4] We have argued that the highest-frequency cycle that one can observe is $\omega = \pi$. Another way to express this conclusion is that the shortest-period cycle that one can observe is one that repeats itself every $2\pi/\pi = 2$ periods. If $\omega = 3\pi/2$, the cycle repeats itself every $\frac{4}{3}$ periods. But if the data are observed only at integer dates, the sampled data will exhibit cycles that are repeated every four periods, corresponding to the frequency $\omega = \pi/2$. This is illustrated in Figure 6.1, which plots $\cos[(\pi/2)t]$ and $\cos[(3\pi/2)t]$ as functions of $t$. When sampled at integer values of $t$, these two functions appear identical. Even though the function $\cos[(3\pi/2)t]$ repeats itself every time that $t$ increases by $\frac{4}{3}$, one would have to observe $y_t$ at four distinct dates $(y_t, y_{t+1}, y_{t+2}, y_{t+3})$ before one would see the value of $\cos[(3\pi/2)t]$ repeat itself for an integer value of $t$.

[4]See Section A.1 of the Mathematical Review (Appendix A) at the end of the book for a further discussion of this point.

Note that in a particular finite sample, the lowest frequency used to account for variation in $y$ is $\omega_1 = 2\pi/T$, which corresponds to a period of $T$. If a cycle takes longer than $T$ periods to repeat itself, there is not much that one could infer about it if one has only $T$ observations available.

Result (c) of Proposition 6.2 indicates that the portion of the sample variance of $y$ that can be attributed to cycles of frequency $\omega_j$ is proportional to the sample periodogram evaluated at $\omega_j$, with $4\pi/T$ the constant of proportionality. Thus, the proposition develops the formal basis for the claim that the sample periodogram reflects the portion of the sample variance of $y$ that can be attributed to cycles of various frequencies.

Why is the constant of proportionality in [6.2.15] equal to $4\pi/T$? The population spectrum $s_Y(\omega)$ could be evaluated at any $\omega$ in the continuous set of points between 0 and $\pi$. In this respect it is much like a probability density $f_X(x)$, where $X$ is a continuous random variable. Although we might loosely think of the value of $f_X(x)$ as the "probability" that $X = x$, it is more accurate to say that the integral $\int_{x_1}^{x_2} f_X(x)\,dx$ represents the probability that $X$ takes on a value between $x_1$ and $x_2$. As $x_2 - x_1$ becomes smaller, the probability that $X$ will be observed to lie between $x_1$ and $x_2$ becomes smaller, and the probability that $X$ would take on precisely the value $x$ is effectively equal to zero. In just the same way, although we can loosely think of the value of $s_Y(\omega)$ as the contribution that cycles with frequency $\omega$ make to the variance of $Y$, it is more accurate to say that the integral

$$\int_{-\omega_1}^{\omega_1} s_Y(\omega)\,d\omega = \int_0^{\omega_1} 2s_Y(\omega)\,d\omega$$

represents the contribution that cycles of frequency less than or equal to $\omega_1$ make to the variance of $Y$, and that $\int_{\omega_1}^{\omega_2} 2s_Y(\omega)\,d\omega$ represents the contribution that cycles with frequencies between $\omega_1$ and $\omega_2$ make to the variance of $Y$. Assuming that $s_Y(\omega)$ is continuous, the contribution that a cycle of any particular frequency $\omega$ makes is technically zero.

Although the population spectrum $s_Y(\omega)$ is defined at any $\omega$ in $[0, \pi]$, the representation in [6.2.6] attributes all of the sample variance of $y$ to the particular frequencies $\omega_1, \omega_2, \ldots, \omega_M$. Any variation in $Y$ that is in reality due to cycles with frequencies other than these $M$ particular values is attributed by [6.2.6] to one of these $M$ frequencies. If we are thinking of the regression in [6.2.6] as telling us something about the population spectrum, we should interpret $\frac{1}{2}(\hat{\alpha}_j^2 + \hat{\delta}_j^2)$ not as the portion of the variance of $Y$ that is due to cycles with frequency exactly equal to $\omega_j$, but rather as the portion of the variance of $Y$ that is due to cycles with frequency near $\omega_j$. Thus [6.2.15] is not an estimate of the height of the population spectrum, but an estimate of the area under the population spectrum.

This is illustrated in Figure 6.2. Suppose we thought of $\frac{1}{2}(\hat{\alpha}_j^2 + \hat{\delta}_j^2)$ as an estimate of the portion of the variance of $Y$ that is due to cycles with frequency between $\omega_{j-1}$ and $\omega_j$, that is, an estimate of 2 times the area under $s_Y(\omega)$ between $\omega_{j-1}$ and $\omega_j$. Since $\omega_j = 2\pi j/T$, the difference $\omega_j - \omega_{j-1}$ is equal to $2\pi/T$. If $\hat{s}_y(\omega_j)$ is an estimate of $s_Y(\omega_j)$, then the area under $s_Y(\omega)$ between $\omega_{j-1}$ and $\omega_j$ could be approximately estimated by the area of a rectangle with width $2\pi/T$ and height $\hat{s}_y(\omega_j)$. The area of such a rectangle is $(2\pi/T)\cdot\hat{s}_j(\omega_j)$. Since $\frac{1}{2}(\hat{\alpha}_j^2 + \hat{\delta}_j^2)$ is an estimate of 2 times the area under $s_Y(\omega)$ between $\omega_{j-1}$ and $\omega_j$, we have $\frac{1}{2}(\hat{\alpha}_j^2 + \hat{\delta}_j^2) = (4\pi/T)\cdot\hat{s}_y(\omega_j)$, as claimed in equation [6.2.15].

Proposition 6.2 also provides a convenient formula for calculating the value of the sample periodogram at frequency $\omega_j = 2\pi j/T$ for $j = 1, 2, \ldots, (T - 1)/2$,

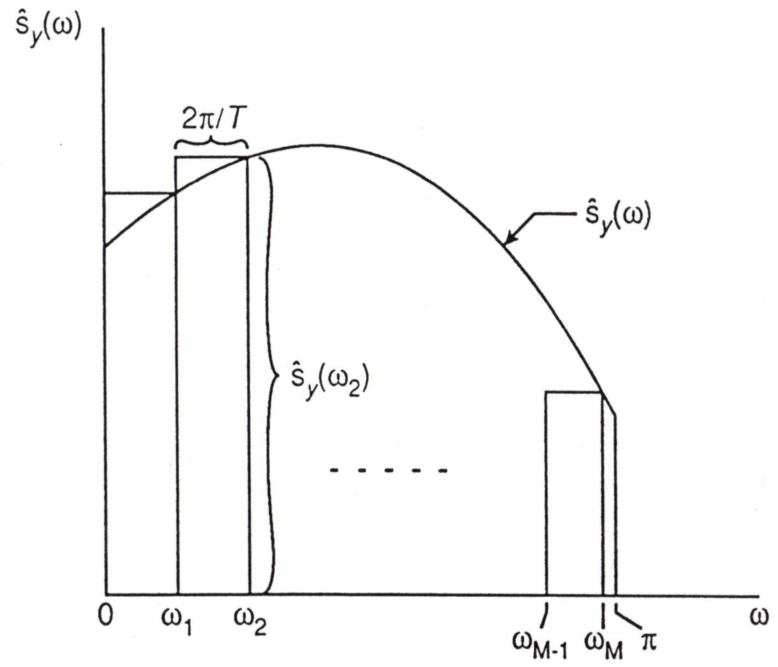


**FIGURE 6.2** The area under the sample periodogram and the portion of the variance of $y$ attributable to cycles of different frequencies.

namely,

$$\hat{s}_y(\omega_j) = [T/(8\pi)](\hat{\alpha}_j^2 + \hat{\delta}_j^2),$$

where

$$\hat{\alpha}_j = (2/T) \sum_{t=1}^{T} y_t \cdot \cos[\omega_j(t - 1)]$$

$$\hat{\delta}_j = (2/T) \sum_{t=1}^{T} y_t \cdot \sin[\omega_j(t - 1)].$$

That is,

$$\hat{s}_y(\omega_j) = \frac{1}{2\pi T}\left\{\left[\sum_{t=1}^{T} y_t \cdot \cos[\omega_j(t - 1)]\right]^2 + \left[\sum_{t=1}^{T} y_t \cdot \sin[\omega_j(t - 1)]\right]^2\right\}.$$

## 6.3. *Estimating the Population Spectrum*

Section 6.1 introduced the population spectrum $s_Y(\omega)$, which indicates the portion of the population variance of $Y$ that can be attributed to cycles of frequency $\omega$. This section addresses the following question: Given an observed sample $\{y_1, y_2, \ldots, y_T\}$, how might $s_Y(\omega)$ be estimated?

### *Large-Sample Properties of the Sample Periodogram*

One obvious approach would be to estimate the population spectrum $s_Y(\omega)$ by the sample periodogram $\hat{s}_y(\omega)$. However, this approach turns out to have some serious limitations. Suppose that

$$Y_t = \sum_{j=0}^{\infty} \psi_j \varepsilon_{t-j},$$

where $\{\psi_j\}_{j=0}^{\infty}$ is absolutely summable and where $\{\varepsilon_t\}_{t=-\infty}^{\infty}$ is an i.i.d. sequence with $E(\varepsilon_t) = 0$ and $E(\varepsilon_t^2) = \sigma^2$. Let $s_Y(\omega)$ be the population spectrum defined in [6.1.2], and suppose that $s_Y(\omega) > 0$ for all $\omega$. Let $\hat{s}_y(\omega)$ be the sample periodogram defined in [6.2.4]. Fuller (1976, p. 280) showed that for $\omega \neq 0$ and a sufficiently large sample size $T$, twice the ratio of the sample periodogram to the population spectrum has approximately the following distribution:

$$\frac{2 \cdot \hat{s}_y(\omega)}{s_Y(\omega)} \approx \chi^2(2). \qquad [6.3.1]$$

Moreover, if $\lambda \neq \omega$, the quantity

$$\frac{2 \cdot \hat{s}_y(\lambda)}{s_Y(\lambda)} \qquad [6.3.2]$$

also has an approximate $\chi^2(2)$ distribution, with the variable in [6.3.1] approximately independent of that in [6.3.2].

Since a $\chi^2(2)$ variable has a mean of 2, result [6.3.1] suggests that

$$E\left[\frac{2 \cdot \hat{s}_y(\omega)}{s_Y(\omega)}\right] \cong 2,$$

or since $s_Y(\omega)$ is a population magnitude rather than a random variable,

$$E[\hat{s}_y(\omega)] \cong s_Y(\omega).$$

Thus, if the sample size is sufficiently large, the sample periodogram affords an approximately unbiased estimate of the population spectrum.

Note from Table B.2 that 95% of the time, a $\chi^2(2)$ variable will fall between 0.05 and 7.4. Thus, from [6.3.1], $\hat{s}_y(\omega)$ is unlikely to be as small as 0.025 times the true value of $s_Y(\omega)$, and $\hat{s}_y(\omega)$ is unlikely to be any larger than 3.7 times as big as $s_Y(\omega)$. Given such a large confidence interval, we would have to say that $\hat{s}_y(\omega)$ is not an altogether satisfactory estimate of $s_Y(\omega)$.

Another feature of result [6.3.1] is that the estimate $\hat{s}_y(\omega)$ is not getting any more accurate as the sample size $T$ increases. Typically, one expects an econometric estimate to get better and better as the sample size grows. For example, the variance for the sample autocorrelation coefficient $\hat{\rho}_j$ given in [4.8.8] goes to zero as $T \to \infty$, so that given a sufficiently large sample, we would be able to infer the true value of $\rho_j$ with virtual certainty. The estimate $\hat{s}_y(\omega)$ defined in [6.2.4] does not have this property, because we have tried to estimate as many parameters ($\gamma_0, \gamma_1, \ldots, \gamma_{T-1}$) as we had observations ($y_1, y_2, \ldots, y_T$).

## *Parametric Estimates of the Population Spectrum*

Suppose we believe that the data could be represented with an *ARMA*$(p, q)$ model,

$$Y_t = \mu + \phi_1 Y_{t-1} + \phi_2 Y_{t-2} + \cdots + \phi_p Y_{t-p} + \varepsilon_t + \theta_1 \varepsilon_{t-1} + \theta_2 \varepsilon_{t-2} + \cdots + \theta_q \varepsilon_{t-q}, \qquad [6.3.3]$$

where $\varepsilon_t$ is white noise with variance $\sigma^2$. Then an excellent approach to estimating the population spectrum is first to estimate the parameters $\mu, \phi_1, \ldots, \phi_p, \theta_1,$

$\ldots, \theta_q$ and $\sigma^2$ by maximum likelihood as described in the previous chapter. The maximum likelihood estimates $(\hat{\phi}_1, \ldots, \hat{\phi}_p, \hat{\theta}_1, \ldots, \hat{\theta}_q, \hat{\sigma}^2)$ could then be plugged into a formula such as [6.1.14] to estimate the population spectrum $s_Y(\omega)$ at any frequency $\omega$. If the model is correctly specified, the maximum likelihood estimates $(\hat{\phi}_1, \ldots, \hat{\phi}_p, \hat{\theta}_1, \ldots, \hat{\theta}_q, \hat{\sigma}^2)$ will get closer and closer to the true values as the sample size grows; hence, the resulting estimate of the population spectrum should have this same property.

Even if the model is incorrectly specified, if the autocovariances of the true process are reasonably close to those for an $ARMA(p, q)$ specification, this procedure should provide a useful estimate of the population spectrum.

## *Nonparametric Estimates of the Population Spectrum*

The assumption in [6.3.3] is that $Y_t$ can be reasonably approximated by an $ARMA(p, q)$ process with $p$ and $q$ small. An alternative assumption is that $s_Y(\omega)$ will be close to $s_Y(\lambda)$ when $\omega$ is close to $\lambda$. This assumption forms the basis for another class of estimates of the population spectrum known as *nonparametric* or *kernel estimates*.

If $s_Y(\omega)$ is close to $s_Y(\lambda)$ when $\omega$ is close to $\lambda$, this suggests that $s_Y(\omega)$ might be estimated with a weighted average of the values of $\hat{s}_y(\lambda)$ for values of $\lambda$ in a neighborhood around $\omega$, where the weights depend on the distance between $\omega$ and $\lambda$. Let $\hat{s}_Y(\omega)$ denote such an estimate of $s_Y(\omega)$ and let $\omega_j = 2\pi j/T$. The suggestion is to take

$$\hat{s}_Y(\omega_j) = \sum_{m=-h}^{h} \kappa(\omega_{j+m}, \omega_j) \cdot \hat{s}_y(\omega_{j+m}). \qquad [6.3.4]$$

Here, $h$ is a *bandwidth* parameter indicating how many different frequencies $\{\omega_{j\pm1}, \omega_{j\pm2}, \ldots, \omega_{j\pm h}\}$ are viewed as useful for estimating $s_Y(\omega_j)$. The *kernel* $\kappa(\omega_{j+m}, \omega_j)$ indicates how much weight each frequency is to be given. The kernel weights sum to unity:

$$\sum_{m=-h}^{h} \kappa(\omega_{j+m}, \omega_j) = 1.$$

One approach is to take $\kappa(\omega_{j+m}, \omega_j)$ to be proportional to $h + 1 - |m|$. One can show that[5]

$$\sum_{m=-h}^{h} [h + 1 - |m|] = (h + 1)^2.$$

Hence, in order to satisfy the property that the weights sum to unity, the proposed kernel is

$$\kappa(\omega_{j+m}, \omega_j) = \frac{h + 1 - |m|}{(h + 1)^2} \qquad [6.3.5]$$

[5]Notice that

$$\begin{aligned}\sum_{m=-h}^{h} [h + 1 - |m|] &= \sum_{m=-h}^{h} (h + 1) - \sum_{m=-h}^{h} |m| \\ &= (h + 1) \sum_{m=-h}^{h} 1 - 2\sum_{s=0}^{h} s \\ &= (2h + 1)(h + 1) - 2h(h + 1)/2 \\ &= (h + 1)^2.\end{aligned}$$

and the estimator [6.3.4] becomes

$$\hat{s}_Y(\omega_j) = \sum_{m=-h}^{h} \left[\frac{h + 1 - |m|}{(h + 1)^2}\right] \hat{s}_y(\omega_{j+m}). \quad [6.3.6]$$

For example, for $h = 2$, this is

$$\hat{s}_Y(\omega_j) = \tfrac{1}{9}\hat{s}_y(\omega_{j-2}) + \tfrac{2}{9}\hat{s}_y(\omega_{j-1}) + \tfrac{3}{9}\hat{s}_y(\omega_j) + \tfrac{2}{9}\hat{s}_y(\omega_{j+1}) + \tfrac{1}{9}\hat{s}_y(\omega_{j+2}).$$

Recall from [6.3.1] and [6.3.2] that the estimates $\hat{s}_y(\omega)$ and $\hat{s}_y(\lambda)$ are approximately independent in large samples for $\omega \neq \lambda$. Because the kernel estimate averages over a number of different frequencies, it should give a much better estimate than does the periodogram.

Averaging $\hat{s}_y(\omega)$ over different frequencies can equivalently be represented as multiplying the $j$th sample autocovariance $\hat{\gamma}_j$ for $j > 0$ in the formula for the sample periodogram [6.2.5] by a weight $\kappa_j^*$. For example, consider an estimate of the spectrum at frequency $\omega$ that is obtained by taking a simple average of the value of $\hat{s}_y(\lambda)$ for $\lambda$ between $\omega - \nu$ and $\omega + \nu$:

$$\hat{s}_Y(\omega) = (2\nu)^{-1} \int_{\omega-\nu}^{\omega+\nu} \hat{s}_y(\lambda)\, d\lambda. \quad [6.3.7]$$

Substituting [6.2.5] into [6.3.7], such an estimate could equivalently be expressed as

$$\begin{aligned} \hat{s}_Y(\omega) &= (4\nu\pi)^{-1} \int_{\omega-\nu}^{\omega+\nu} \left[\hat{\gamma}_0 + 2\sum_{j=1}^{T-1} \hat{\gamma}_j \cos(\lambda j)\right] d\lambda \\ &= (4\nu\pi)^{-1}(2\nu)\hat{\gamma}_0 + (2\nu\pi)^{-1} \sum_{j=1}^{T-1} \hat{\gamma}_j (1/j)\cdot\big[\sin(\lambda j)\big]_{\lambda=\omega-\nu}^{\omega+\nu} \\ &= (2\pi)^{-1}\hat{\gamma}_0 + (2\nu\pi)^{-1} \sum_{j=1}^{T-1} \hat{\gamma}_j(1/j)\cdot\{\sin[(\omega + \nu)j] - \sin[(\omega - \nu)j]\}. \end{aligned} \quad [6.3.8]$$

Using the trigonometric identity[6]

$$\sin(A + B) - \sin(A - B) = 2\cdot\cos(A)\cdot\sin(B), \quad [6.3.9]$$

expression [6.3.8] can be written

$$\begin{aligned} \hat{s}_Y(\omega) &= (2\pi)^{-1}\hat{\gamma}_0 + (2\nu\pi)^{-1} \sum_{j=1}^{T-1} \hat{\gamma}_j (1/j)\cdot[2\cdot\cos(\omega j)\cdot\sin(\nu j)] \\ &= (2\pi)^{-1}\left\{\hat{\gamma}_0 + 2\sum_{j=1}^{T-1}\left[\frac{\sin(\nu j)}{\nu j}\right]\hat{\gamma}_j \cos(\omega j)\right\}. \end{aligned} \quad [6.3.10]$$

Notice that expression [6.3.10] is of the following form:

$$\hat{s}_Y(\omega) = (2\pi)^{-1}\left\{\hat{\gamma}_0 + 2\sum_{j=1}^{T-1} \kappa_j^* \hat{\gamma}_j \cos(\omega j)\right\}, \quad [6.3.11]$$

where

$$\kappa_j^* = \left[\frac{\sin(\nu j)}{\nu j}\right]. \quad [6.3.12]$$

The sample periodogram can be regarded as a special case of [6.3.11] when $\kappa_j^* = 1$. Expression [6.3.12] cannot exceed 1 in absolute value, and so the estimate [6.3.11] essentially downweights $\hat{\gamma}_j$ relative to the sample periodogram.

[6]See, for example, Thomas (1972, pp. 174–75).

Recall that $\sin(\pi j) = 0$ for any integer $j$. Hence, if $\nu = \pi$, then $\kappa_j^* = 0$ for all $j$ and [6.3.11] becomes

$$\hat{s}_Y(\omega) = (2\pi)^{-1}\hat{\gamma}_0. \qquad [6.3.13]$$

In this case, all autocovariances other than $\hat{\gamma}_0$ would be shrunk to zero. When $\nu = \pi$, the estimate [6.3.7] is an unweighted average of $\hat{s}_y(\lambda)$ over all possible values of $\lambda$, and the resulting estimate would be the flat spectrum for a white noise process.

Specification of a kernel function $\kappa(\omega_{j+m}, \omega_j)$ in [6.3.4] can equivalently be described in terms of a weighting sequence $\{\kappa_j^*\}_{j=1}^{T-1}$ in [6.3.11]. Because they are just two different representations for the same idea, the weight $\kappa_j^*$ is also sometimes called a kernel. Smaller values of $\kappa_j^*$ impose more smoothness on the spectrum. Smoothing schemes may be chosen either because they provide a convenient specification for $\kappa(\omega_{j+m}, \omega_j)$ or because they provide a convenient specification for $\kappa_j^*$.

One popular estimate of the spectrum employs the modified *Bartlett kernel*, which is given by

$$\kappa_j^* = \begin{cases} 1 - \dfrac{j}{q+1} & \text{for } j = 1, 2, \ldots, q \\ 0 & \text{for } j > q. \end{cases} \qquad [6.3.14]$$

The Bartlett estimate of the spectrum is thus

$$\hat{s}_Y(\omega) = (2\pi)^{-1}\left\{\hat{\gamma}_0 + 2\sum_{j=1}^{q}[1 - j/(q+1)]\hat{\gamma}_j\cos(\omega j)\right\}. \qquad [6.3.15]$$

Autocovariances $\gamma_j$ for $j > q$ are treated as if they were zero, or as if $Y_t$ followed an $MA(q)$ process. For $j \leq q$, the estimated autocovariances $\hat{\gamma}_j$ are shrunk toward zero, with the shrinkage greater the larger the value of $j$.

How is one to choose the bandwidth parameter $h$ in [6.3.6] or $q$ in [6.3.15]? The periodogram itself is asymptotically unbiased but has a large variance. If one constructs an estimate based on averaging the periodogram at different frequencies, this reduces the variance but introduces some bias. The severity of the bias depends on the steepness of the population spectrum and the size of the bandwidth. One practical guide is to plot an estimate of the spectrum using several different bandwidths and rely on subjective judgment to choose the bandwidth that produces the most plausible estimate.

## 6.4. *Uses of Spectral Analysis*

We illustrate some of the uses of spectral analysis with data on manufacturing production in the United States. The data are plotted in Figure 6.3. The series is the Federal Reserve Board's seasonally unadjusted monthly index from January 1947 to November 1989. Economic recessions in 1949, 1954, 1958, 1960, 1970, 1974, 1980, and 1982 appear as roughly year-long episodes of falling production. There are also strong seasonal patterns in this series; for example, production almost always declines in July and recovers in August.

The sample periodogram for the raw data is plotted in Figure 6.4, which displays $\hat{s}_y(\omega_j)$ as a function of $j$ where $\omega_j = 2\pi j/T$. The contribution to the sample variance of the lowest-frequency components ($j$ near zero) is several orders of magnitude larger than the contributions of economic recessions or the seasonal factors. This is due to the clear upward trend of the series in Figure 6.3. Let $y_t$

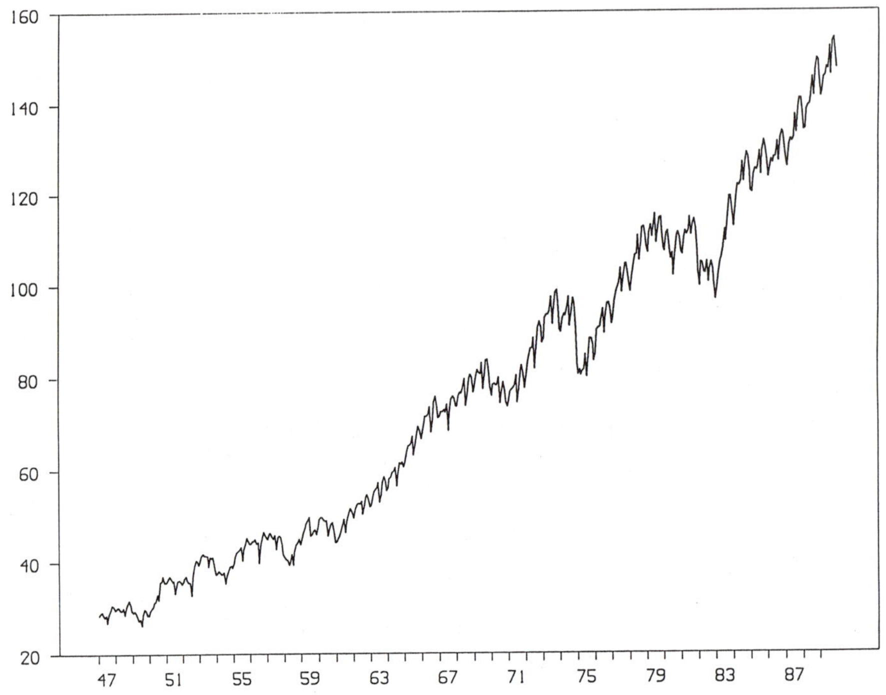


**FIGURE 6.3** Federal Reserve Board's seasonally unadjusted index of industrial production for U.S. manufacturing, monthly 1947:1 to 1989:11.

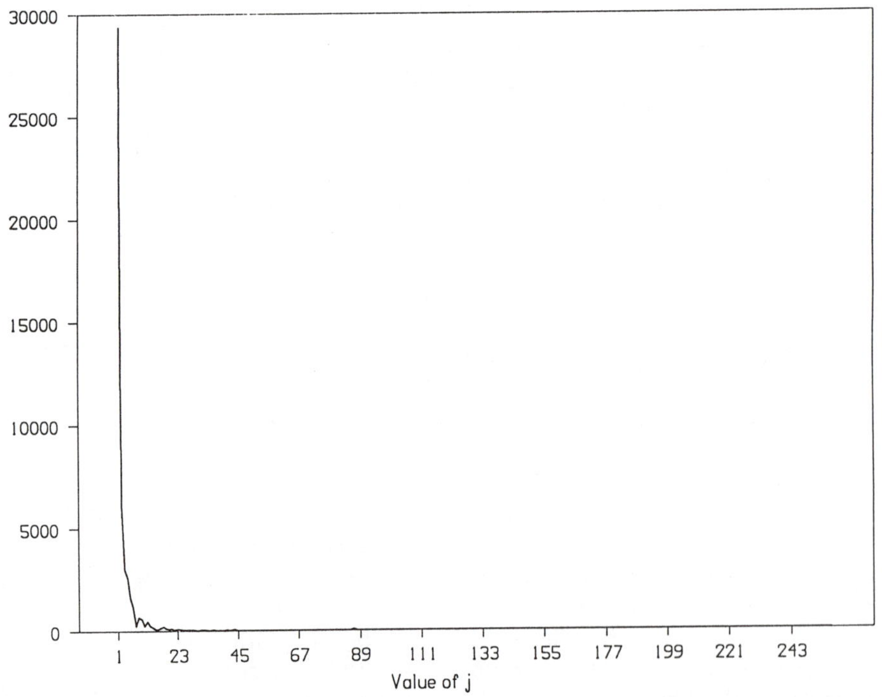


**FIGURE 6.4** Sample periodogram for the data plotted in Figure 6.3. The figure plots $\hat{s}_y(\omega_j)$ as a function of $j$, where $\omega_j = 2\pi j/T$.

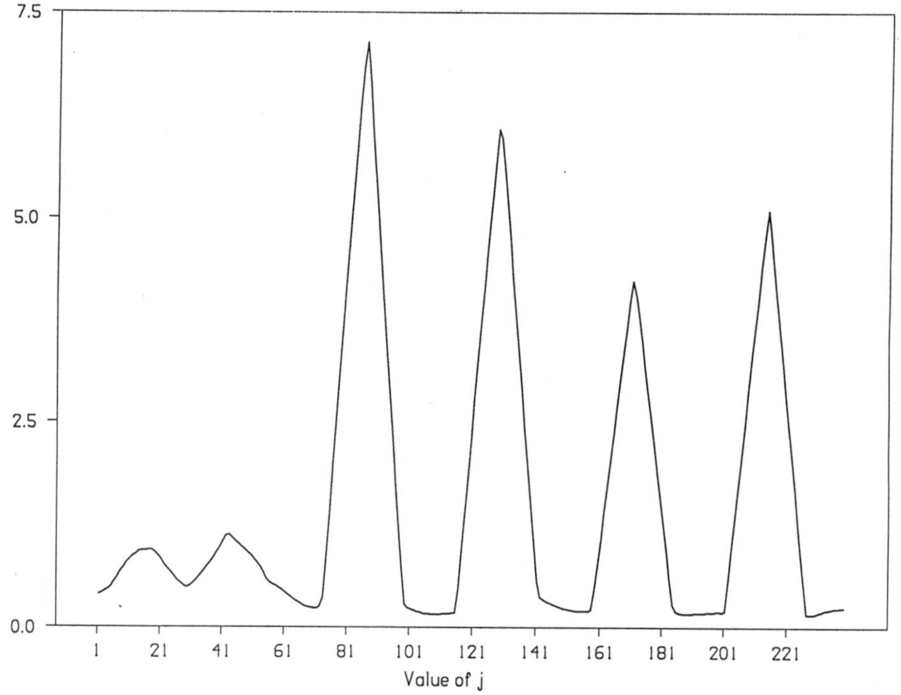


**FIGURE 6.5** Estimate of the spectrum for monthly growth rate of industrial production, or spectrum of 100 times the first difference of the log of the series in Figure 6.3.

represent the series plotted in Figure 6.3. If one were trying to describe this with a sine function

$$y_t = \delta \cdot \sin(\omega t),$$

the presumption would have to be that $\omega$ is so small that even at date $t = T$ the magnitude $\omega T$ would still be less than $\pi/2$. Figure 6.4 thus indicates that the trend or low-frequency components are by far the most important determinants of the sample variance of $y$.

The definition of the population spectrum in equation [6.1.2] assumed that the process is covariance-stationary, which is not a good assumption for the data in Figure 6.3. We might instead try to analyze the monthly growth rate defined by

$$x_t = 100 \cdot [\log(y_t) - \log(y_{t-1})]. \qquad [6.4.1]$$

Figure 6.5 plots the estimate of the population spectrum of $X$ as described in equation [6.3.6] with $h = 12$.

In interpreting a plot such as Figure 6.5 it is often more convenient to think in terms of the period of a cyclic function rather than its frequency. Recall that if the frequency of a cycle is $\omega$, the period of the cycle is $2\pi/\omega$. Thus, a frequency of $\omega_j = 2\pi j/T$ corresponds to a period of $2\pi/\omega_j = T/j$. The sample size is $T = 513$ observations, and the first peak in Figure 6.5 occurs around $j = 18$. This corresponds to a cycle with a period of $513/18 = 28.5$ months, or about $2\frac{1}{2}$ years. Given the dates of the economic recessions noted previously, this is sometimes described as a "business cycle frequency," and the area under this hill might be viewed as telling us how much of the variability in monthly growth rates is due to economic recessions.

The second peak in Figure 6.5 occurs at $j = 44$ and corresponds to a period of $513/44 = 11.7$ months. This is natural to view as a 12-month cycle associated with seasonal effects. The four subsequent peaks correspond to cycles with periods of 6, 4, 3, and 2.4 months, respectively, and again seem likely to be picking up seasonal and calendar effects.

Since manufacturing typically falls temporarily in July, the growth rate is negative in July and positive in August. This induces negative first-order serial correlation to the series in [6.4.1] and a variety of calendar patterns for $x_t$ that may account for the high-frequency peaks in Figure 6.5. An alternative strategy for detrending would use year-to-year growth rates, or the percentage change between $y_t$ and its value for the corresponding month in the previous year:

$$w_t = 100\cdot[\log(y_t) - \log(y_{t-12})]. \qquad [6.4.2]$$

The estimate of the sample spectrum for this series is plotted in Figure 6.6. When the data are detrended in this way, virtually all the variance that remains is attributed to components associated with the business cycle frequencies.

## *Filters*

Apart from the scale parameter, the monthly growth rate $x_t$ in [6.4.1] is obtained from $\log(y_t)$ by applying the filter

$$x_t = (1 - L)\log(y_t), \qquad [6.4.3]$$

where $L$ is the lag operator. To discuss such transformations in general terms, let $Y_t$ be any covariance-stationary series with absolutely summable autocovariances.

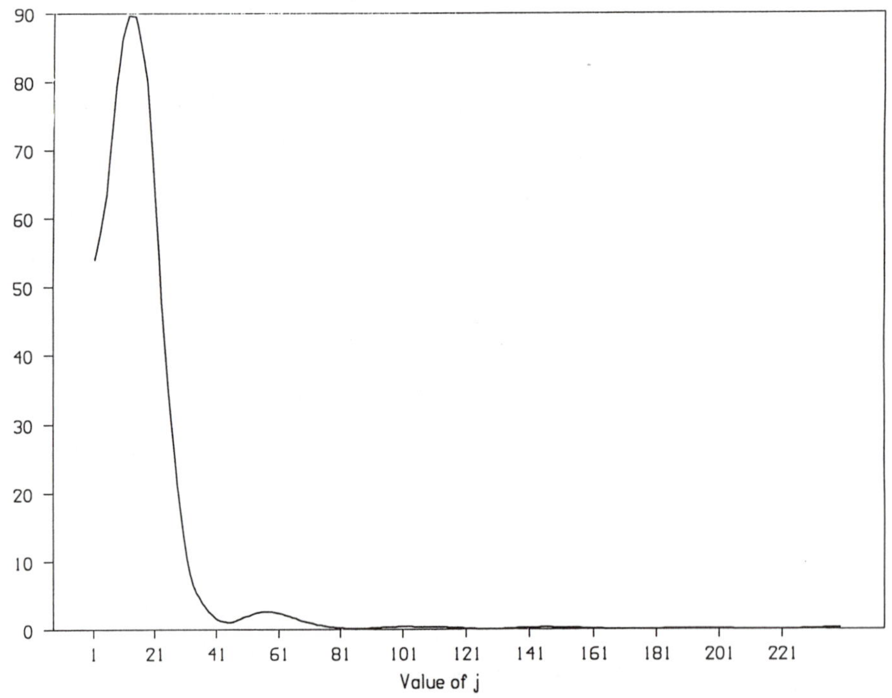


**FIGURE 6.6** Estimate of the spectrum for year-to-year growth rate of monthly industrial production, or spectrum of 100 times the seasonal difference of the log of the series in Figure 6.3.

Denote the autocovariance-generating function of $Y$ by $g_Y(z)$, and denote the population spectrum of $Y$ by $s_Y(\omega)$. Recall that

$$s_Y(\omega) = (2\pi)^{-1} g_Y(e^{-i\omega}). \qquad [6.4.4]$$

Suppose we transform $Y$ according to

$$X_t = h(L)Y_t,$$

where

$$h(L) = \sum_{j=-\infty}^{\infty} h_j L^j$$

and

$$\sum_{j=-\infty}^{\infty} |h_j| < \infty.$$

Recall from equation [3.6.17] that the autocovariance-generating function of $X$ can be calculated from the autocovariance-generating function of $Y$ using the formula

$$g_X(z) = h(z)h(z^{-1})g_Y(z). \qquad [6.4.5]$$

The population spectrum of $X$ is thus

$$s_X(\omega) = (2\pi)^{-1} g_X(e^{-i\omega}) = (2\pi)^{-1} h(e^{-i\omega})h(e^{i\omega})g_Y(e^{-i\omega}). \qquad [6.4.6]$$

Substituting [6.4.4] into [6.4.6] reveals that the population spectrum of $X$ is related to the population spectrum of $Y$ according to

$$s_X(\omega) = h(e^{-i\omega})h(e^{i\omega})s_Y(\omega). \qquad [6.4.7]$$

Operating on a series $Y_t$ with the filter $h(L)$ has the effect of multiplying the spectrum by the function $h(e^{-i\omega})h(e^{i\omega})$.

For the difference operator in [6.4.3], the filter is $h(L) = 1 - L$ and the function $h(e^{-i\omega})h(e^{i\omega})$ would be

$$\begin{aligned} h(e^{-i\omega})h(e^{i\omega}) &= (1 - e^{-i\omega})(1 - e^{i\omega}) \\ &= 1 - e^{-i\omega} - e^{i\omega} + 1 \\ &= 2 - 2\cdot\cos(\omega), \end{aligned} \qquad [6.4.8]$$

where the last line follows from [6.1.11]. If $X_t = (1 - L)Y_t$, then, to find the value of the population spectrum of $X$ at any frequency $\omega$, we first find the value of the population spectrum of $Y$ at $\omega$ and then multiply by $2 - 2\cdot\cos(\omega)$. For example, the spectrum at frequency $\omega = 0$ is multiplied by zero, the spectrum at frequency $\omega = \pi/2$ is multiplied by 2, and the spectrum at frequency $\omega = \pi$ is multiplied by 4. Differencing the data removes the low-frequency components and accentuates the high-frequency components.

Of course, this calculation assumes that the original process $Y_t$ is covariance-stationary, so that $s_Y(\omega)$ exists. If the original process is nonstationary, as appears to be the case in Figure 6.3, the differenced data $(1 - L)Y_t$ in general would not have a population spectrum that is zero at frequency zero.

The seasonal difference filter used in [6.4.2] is $h(L) = 1 - L^{12}$, for which

$$\begin{aligned} h(e^{-i\omega})h(e^{i\omega}) &= (1 - e^{-12i\omega})(1 - e^{12i\omega}) \\ &= 1 - e^{-12i\omega} - e^{12i\omega} + 1 \\ &= 2 - 2\cdot\cos(12\omega). \end{aligned}$$

This function is equal to zero when $12\omega = 0, 2\pi, 4\pi, 6\pi, 8\pi, 10\pi$, or $12\pi$; that is, it is zero at frequencies $\omega = 0, 2\pi/12, 4\pi/12, 6\pi/12, 8\pi/12, 10\pi/12$, and $\pi$. Thus, seasonally differencing not only eliminates the low-frequency ($\omega = 0$) components of a stationary process, but further eliminates any contribution from cycles with periods of 12, 6, 4, 3, 2.4, or 2 months.

### *Composite Stochastic Processes*

Let $X_t$ be covariance-stationary with absolutely summable autocovariances, autocovariance-generating function $g_X(z)$, and population spectrum $s_X(\omega)$. Let $W_t$ be a different covariance-stationary series with absolutely summable autocovariances, autocovariance-generating function $g_W(z)$, and population spectrum $s_W(\omega)$, where $X_t$ is uncorrelated with $W_\tau$ for all $t$ and $\tau$. Suppose we observe the sum of these two processes,

$$Y_t = X_t + W_t.$$

Recall from [4.7.19] that the autocovariance-generating function of the sum is the sum of the autocovariance-generating functions:

$$g_Y(z) = g_X(z) + g_W(z).$$

It follows from [6.1.2] that the spectrum of the sum is the sum of the spectra:

$$s_Y(\omega) = s_X(\omega) + s_W(\omega). \qquad [6.4.9]$$

For example, if a white noise series $W_t$ with variance $\sigma^2$ is added to a series $X_t$ and if $X_t$ is uncorrelated with $W_\tau$ for all $t$ and $\tau$, the effect is to shift the population spectrum everywhere up by the constant $\sigma^2/(2\pi)$. More generally, if $X$ has a peak in its spectrum at frequency $\omega_1$ and if $W$ has a peak in its spectrum at $\omega_2$, then typically the sum $X + W$ will have peaks at both $\omega_1$ and $\omega_2$.

As another example, suppose that

$$Y_t = c + \sum_{j=-\infty}^{\infty} h_j X_{t-j} + \varepsilon_t,$$

where $X_t$ is covariance-stationary with absolutely summable autocovariances and spectrum $s_X(\omega)$. Suppose that the sequence $\{h_j\}_{j=-\infty}^{\infty}$ is absolutely summable and that $\varepsilon_t$ is a white noise process with variance $\sigma^2$ where $\varepsilon$ is uncorrelated with $X$ at all leads and lags. It follows from [6.4.7] that the random variable $\Sigma_{j=-\infty}^{\infty} h_j X_{t-j}$ has spectrum $h(e^{-i\omega})h(e^{i\omega})s_X(\omega)$, and so, from [6.4.9], the spectrum of $Y$ is

$$s_Y(\omega) = h(e^{-i\omega})h(e^{i\omega})s_X(\omega) + \sigma^2/(2\pi).$$

## APPENDIX 6.A. *Proofs of Chapter 6 Propositions*

■ **Proof of Proposition 6.1.** Notice that

$$\begin{aligned}\int_{-\pi}^{\pi} s_Y(\omega)e^{i\omega k}\,d\omega &= \frac{1}{2\pi}\int_{-\pi}^{\pi}\sum_{j=-\infty}^{\infty}\gamma_j e^{-i\omega j}e^{i\omega k}\,d\omega \\ &= \frac{1}{2\pi}\sum_{j=-\infty}^{\infty}\gamma_j\int_{-\pi}^{\pi} e^{i\omega(k-j)}\,d\omega \\ &= \frac{1}{2\pi}\sum_{j=-\infty}^{\infty}\gamma_j\int_{-\pi}^{\pi}\{\cos[\omega(k-j)] + i\cdot\sin[\omega(k-j)]\}\,d\omega.\end{aligned} \qquad [6.A.1]$$

Consider the integral in [6.A.1]. For $k = j$, this would be

$$\int_{-\pi}^{\pi} \{\cos[\omega(k - j)] + i\cdot\sin[\omega(k - j)]\}\,d\omega = \int_{-\pi}^{\pi} \{\cos(0) + i\cdot\sin(0)\}\,d\omega$$
$$= \int_{-\pi}^{\pi} d\omega \qquad [6.A.2]$$
$$= 2\pi.$$

For $k \neq j$, the integral in [6.A.1] would be

$$\int_{-\pi}^{\pi} \{\cos[\omega(k - j)] + i\cdot\sin[\omega(k - j)]\}\,d\omega$$
$$= \left.\frac{\sin[\omega(k - j)]}{k - j}\right|_{\omega=-\pi}^{\pi} - i\cdot\left.\frac{\cos[\omega(k - j)]}{k - j}\right|_{\omega=-\pi}^{\pi} \qquad [6.A.3]$$
$$= (k - j)^{-1}\{\sin[\pi(k - j)] - \sin[-\pi(k - j)]$$
$$- i\cdot\cos[\pi(k - j)] + i\cdot\cos[-\pi(k - j)]\}.$$

But the difference between the frequencies $\pi(k - j)$ and $-\pi(k - j)$ is $2\pi(k - j)$, which is an integer multiple of $2\pi$. Since the sine and cosine functions are periodic, the magnitude in [6.A.3] is zero. Hence, only the term for $j = k$ in the sum in [6.A.1] is nonzero, and using [6.A.2], this sum is seen to be

$$\int_{-\pi}^{\pi} s_Y(\omega)e^{i\omega k}\,d\omega = \frac{1}{2\pi}\gamma_k \int_{-\pi}^{\pi} [\cos(0) + i\cdot\sin(0)]\,d\omega = \gamma_k,$$

as claimed in [6.1.15].

To derive [6.1.16], notice that since $s_Y(\omega)$ is symmetric around $\omega = 0$,

$$\int_{-\pi}^{\pi} s_Y(\omega)e^{i\omega k}\,d\omega = \int_{-\pi}^{0} s_Y(\omega)e^{i\omega k}\,d\omega + \int_{0}^{\pi} s_Y(\omega)e^{i\omega k}\,d\omega$$
$$= \int_{0}^{\pi} s_Y(-\omega)e^{-i\omega k}\,d\omega + \int_{0}^{\pi} s_Y(\omega)e^{i\omega k}\,d\omega$$
$$= \int_{0}^{\pi} s_Y(\omega)(e^{-i\omega k} + e^{i\omega k})\,d\omega$$
$$= \int_{0}^{\pi} s_Y(\omega)\cdot 2\cdot\cos(\omega k)\,d\omega,$$

where the last line follows from [6.1.11]. Again appealing to the symmetry of $s_Y(\omega)$,

$$\int_{0}^{\pi} s_Y(\omega)\cdot 2\cdot\cos(\omega k)\,d\omega = \int_{-\pi}^{\pi} s_Y(\omega)\cos(\omega k)\,d\omega,$$

so that

$$\int_{-\pi}^{\pi} s_Y(\omega)e^{i\omega k}\,d\omega = \int_{-\pi}^{\pi} s_Y(\omega)\cos(\omega k)\,d\omega,$$

as claimed. ■

■ **Derivation of Equation [6.2.11] in Proposition 6.2.** We begin by establishing the following result:

$$\sum_{t=1}^{T} \exp[i(2\pi s/T)(t - 1)] = \begin{cases} T & \text{for } s = 0 \\ 0 & \text{for } s = \pm 1, \pm 2, \ldots, \pm(T - 1). \end{cases} \qquad [6.A.4]$$

That [6.A.4] holds for $s = 0$ is an immediate consequence of the fact that $\exp(0) = 1$. To see that it holds for the other cases in [6.A.4], define

$$z \equiv \exp[i(2\pi s/T)]. \qquad [6.A.5]$$

Then the expression to be evaluated in [6.A.4] can be written

$$\sum_{t=1}^{T} \exp[i(2\pi s/T)(t - 1)] = \sum_{t=1}^{T} z^{(t-1)}. \qquad [6.A.6]$$

We now show that for any $N$,

$$\sum_{t=1}^{N} z^{(t-1)} = \frac{1 - z^N}{1 - z}, \qquad [6.A.7]$$

provided that $z \neq 1$, which is the case whenever $0 < |s| < T$. Expression [6.A.7] can be verified by induction. Clearly, it holds for $N = 1$, for then

$$\sum_{t=1}^{N} z^{(t-1)} = z^{(0)} = 1.$$

Given that [6.A.7] holds for $N$, we see that

$$\begin{aligned}\sum_{t=1}^{N+1} z^{(t-1)} &= \sum_{t=1}^{N} z^{(t-1)} + z^N \\ &= \frac{1 - z^N}{1 - z} + z^N \\ &= \frac{1 - z^N + z^N(1 - z)}{1 - z} \\ &= \frac{1 - z^{N+1}}{1 - z},\end{aligned}$$

as claimed in [6.A.7].

Setting $N = T$ in [6.A.7] and substituting the result into [6.A.6], we see that

$$\sum_{t=1}^{T} \exp[i(2\pi s/T)(t - 1)] = \frac{1 - z^T}{1 - z} \qquad [6.A.8]$$

for $0 < |s| < T$. But it follows from the definition of $z$ in [6.A.5] that

$$\begin{aligned} z^T &= \exp[i(2\pi s/T)\cdot T] \\ &= \exp[i(2\pi s)] \\ &= \cos(2\pi s) + i\cdot\sin(2\pi s) \\ &= 1 \qquad \text{for } s = \pm 1, \pm 2, \ldots, \pm(T - 1). \end{aligned} \qquad [6.A.9]$$

Substituting [6.A.9] into [6.A.8] produces

$$\sum_{t=1}^{T} \exp[i(2\pi s/T)(t - 1)] = 0 \qquad \text{for } s = \pm 1, \pm 2, \ldots, \pm(T - 1),$$

as claimed in [6.A.4].

To see how [6.A.4] can be used to deduce expression [6.2.11], notice that the first column of $\Sigma_{t=1}^{T}\mathbf{x}_t\mathbf{x}_t'$ is given by

$$\begin{bmatrix} T \\ \sum \cos[\omega_1(t - 1)] \\ \sum \sin[\omega_1(t - 1)] \\ \vdots \\ \sum \cos[\omega_M(t - 1)] \\ \sum \sin[\omega_M(t - 1)] \end{bmatrix}, \qquad [6.A.10]$$

where $\Sigma$ indicates summation over $t$ from 1 to $T$. The first row of $\Sigma_{t=1}^{T}\mathbf{x}_t\mathbf{x}_t'$ is the transpose of [6.A.10]. To show that all the terms in [6.A.10] other than the first element are zero, we must show that

$$\sum_{t=1}^{T} \cos[\omega_j(t - 1)] = 0 \qquad \text{for } j = 1, 2, \ldots, M \qquad [6.A.11]$$

and

$$\sum_{t=1}^{T} \sin[\omega_j(t - 1)] = 0 \qquad \text{for } j = 1, 2, \ldots, M \qquad [6.A.12]$$

for $\omega_j$ the frequencies specified in [6.2.7]. But [6.A.4] establishes that

$$\begin{aligned} 0 &= \sum_{t=1}^{T} \exp[i(2\pi j/T)(t - 1)] \\ &= \sum_{t=1}^{T} \cos[(2\pi j/T)(t - 1)] + i\cdot\sum_{t=1}^{T} \sin[(2\pi j/T)(t - 1)] \end{aligned} \qquad [6.A.13]$$

for $j = 1, 2, \ldots, M$. For [6.A.13] to equal zero, both the real and the imaginary component must equal zero. Since $\omega_j = 2\pi j/T$, results [6.A.11] and [6.A.12] follow immediately from [6.A.13].

Result [6.A.4] can also be used to calculate the other elements of $\Sigma_{t=1}^{T}\mathbf{x}_t\mathbf{x}_t'$. To see how, note that

$$\begin{aligned} \frac{1}{2}[e^{i\theta} + e^{-i\theta}] &= \frac{1}{2}[\cos(\theta) + i\cdot\sin(\theta) + \cos(\theta) - i\cdot\sin(\theta)] \\ &= \cos(\theta) \end{aligned} \qquad [6.A.14]$$

and similarly

$$\begin{aligned} \frac{1}{2i}[e^{i\theta} - e^{-i\theta}] &= \frac{1}{2i}\{\cos(\theta) + i\cdot\sin(\theta) - [\cos(\theta) - i\cdot\sin(\theta)]\} \\ &= \sin(\theta). \end{aligned} \qquad [6.A.15]$$

Thus, for example, the elements of $\Sigma_{t=1}^{T}\mathbf{x}_t\mathbf{x}_t'$ corresponding to products of the cosine terms can be calculated as

$$\begin{aligned} &\sum_{t=1}^{T} \cos[\omega_j(t - 1)]\cdot\cos[\omega_k(t - 1)] \\ &\quad = \frac{1}{4}\sum_{t=1}^{T} \{\exp[i\omega_j(t - 1)] + \exp[-i\omega_j(t - 1)]\} \\ &\qquad \times \{\exp[i\omega_k(t - 1)] + \exp[-i\omega_k(t - 1)]\} \\ &\quad = \frac{1}{4}\sum_{t=1}^{T} \{\exp[i(\omega_j + \omega_k)(t - 1)] + \exp[i(-\omega_j + \omega_k)(t - 1)] \\ &\qquad + \exp[i(\omega_j - \omega_k)(t - 1)] + \exp[i(-\omega_j - \omega_k)(t - 1)]\} \\ &\quad = \frac{1}{4}\sum_{t=1}^{T} \{\exp[i(2\pi/T)(j + k)(t - 1)] + \exp[i(2\pi/T)(k - j)(t - 1)] \\ &\qquad + \exp[i(2\pi/T)(j - k)(t - 1)] + \exp[i(2\pi/T)(-j - k)(t - 1)]\}. \end{aligned} \qquad [6.A.16]$$

For any $j = 1, 2, \ldots, M$ and any $k = 1, 2, \ldots, M$ where $k \neq j$, expression [6.A.16] is zero by virtue of [6.A.4]. For $k = j$, the first and last sums in the last line of [6.A.16] are zero, so that the total is equal to

$$(1/4)\sum_{t=1}^{T} (1 + 1) = T/2.$$

Similarly, elements of $\Sigma_{t=1}^T \mathbf{x}_t\mathbf{x}_t'$ corresponding to cross products of the sine terms can be found from

$$\sum_{t=1}^{T} \sin[\omega_j(t-1)]\cdot\sin[\omega_k(t-1)]$$

$$= -\frac{1}{4}\sum_{t=1}^{T} \{\exp[i\omega_j(t-1)] - \exp[-i\omega_j(t-1)]\}$$

$$\times \{\exp[i\omega_k(t-1)] - \exp[-i\omega_k(t-1)]\}$$

$$= -\frac{1}{4}\sum_{t=1}^{T} \{\exp[i(2\pi/T)(j+k)(t-1)] - \exp[i(2\pi/T)(k-j)(t-1)]$$

$$- \exp[i(2\pi/T)(j-k)(t-1)] + \exp[i(2\pi/T)(-j-k)(t-1)]\}$$

$$= \begin{cases} T/2 & \text{for } j = k \\ 0 & \text{otherwise.} \end{cases}$$

Finally, elements of $\Sigma_{t=1}^T \mathbf{x}_t\mathbf{x}_t'$ corresponding to cross products of the sine and cosine terms are given by

$$\sum_{t=1}^{T} \cos[\omega_j(t-1)]\cdot\sin[\omega_k(t-1)]$$

$$= \frac{1}{4i}\sum_{t=1}^{T} \{\exp[i\omega_j(t-1)] + \exp[-i\omega_j(t-1)]\}$$

$$\times \{\exp[i\omega_k(t-1)] - \exp[-i\omega_k(t-1)]\}$$

$$= \frac{1}{4i}\sum_{t=1}^{T} \{\exp[i(2\pi/T)(j+k)(t-1)] + \exp[i(2\pi/T)(k-j)(t-1)]$$

$$- \exp[i(2\pi/T)(j-k)(t-1)] - \exp[i(2\pi/T)(-j-k)(t-1)]\},$$

which equals zero for all $j$ and $k$. This completes the derivation of [6.2.11]. ■

■ **Proof of Proposition 6.2(a).** Let $\mathbf{b}$ denote the estimate of $\boldsymbol{\beta}$ based on *OLS* estimation of the regression in [6.2.8]:

$$\mathbf{b} = \left\{\sum_{t=1}^{T} \mathbf{x}_t\mathbf{x}_t'\right\}^{-1}\left\{\sum_{t=1}^{T} \mathbf{x}_t y_t\right\}$$

$$= \begin{bmatrix} T & \mathbf{0}' \\ \mathbf{0} & (T/2)\cdot\mathbf{I}_{T-1} \end{bmatrix}^{-1}\left\{\sum_{t=1}^{T} \mathbf{x}_t y_t\right\} \qquad [6.A.17]$$

$$= \begin{bmatrix} T^{-1} & \mathbf{0}' \\ \mathbf{0} & (2/T)\cdot\mathbf{I}_{T-1} \end{bmatrix}\left\{\sum_{t=1}^{T} \mathbf{x}_t y_t\right\}.$$

But the definition of $\mathbf{x}_t$ in [6.2.9] implies that

$$\sum_{t=1}^{T} \mathbf{x}_t y_t = \Big[\sum y_t \quad \sum y_t\cdot\cos[\omega_1(t-1)] \quad \sum y_t\cdot\sin[\omega_1(t-1)]$$

$$\sum y_t\cdot\cos[\omega_2(t-1)] \quad \sum y_t\cdot\sin[\omega_2(t-1)] \quad \cdots \qquad [6.A.18]$$

$$\sum y_t\cdot\cos[\omega_M(t-1)] \quad \sum y_t\cdot\sin[\omega_M(t-1)]\Big]',$$

where $\Sigma$ again denotes summation over $t$ from 1 to $T$. Substituting [6.A.18] into [6.A.17] produces result (a) of Proposition 6.2. ■

■ **Proof of Proposition 6.2(b).** Recall from expression [4.A.6] that the residual sum of squares associated with *OLS* estimation of [6.2.8] is

$$\sum_{t=1}^{T} \hat{u}_t^2 = \sum_{t=1}^{T} y_t^2 - \left[\sum_{t=1}^{T} y_t\mathbf{x}_t'\right]\left[\sum_{t=1}^{T} \mathbf{x}_t\mathbf{x}_t'\right]^{-1}\left[\sum_{t=1}^{T} \mathbf{x}_t y_t\right]. \qquad [6.A.19]$$

Since there are as many explanatory variables as observations and since the explanatory variables are linearly independent, the *OLS* residuals $\hat{u}_t$ are all zero. Hence, [6.A.19] implies that

$$\sum_{t=1}^{T} y_t^2 = \left[\sum_{t=1}^{T} y_t \mathbf{x}_t'\right]\left[\sum_{t=1}^{T} \mathbf{x}_t \mathbf{x}_t'\right]^{-1}\left[\sum_{t=1}^{T} \mathbf{x}_t y_t\right]. \qquad [6.A.20]$$

But [6.A.17] allows us to write

$$\sum_{t=1}^{T} \mathbf{x}_t y_t = \begin{bmatrix} T & \mathbf{0}' \\ \mathbf{0} & (T/2)\cdot\mathbf{I}_{T-1} \end{bmatrix}\mathbf{b}. \qquad [6.A.21]$$

Substituting [6.A.21] and [6.2.11] into [6.A.20] establishes that

$$\begin{aligned} \sum_{t=1}^{T} y_t^2 &= \mathbf{b}'\begin{bmatrix} T & \mathbf{0}' \\ \mathbf{0} & (T/2)\cdot\mathbf{I}_{T-1} \end{bmatrix}\begin{bmatrix} T & \mathbf{0}' \\ \mathbf{0} & (T/2)\cdot\mathbf{I}_{T-1} \end{bmatrix}^{-1}\begin{bmatrix} T & \mathbf{0}' \\ \mathbf{0} & (T/2)\cdot\mathbf{I}_{T-1} \end{bmatrix}\mathbf{b} \\ &= \mathbf{b}'\begin{bmatrix} T & \mathbf{0}' \\ \mathbf{0} & (T/2)\cdot\mathbf{I}_{T-1} \end{bmatrix}\mathbf{b} \\ &= T\cdot\hat{\mu}^2 + (T/2)\sum_{j=1}^{M}(\hat{\alpha}_j^2 + \hat{\delta}_j^2) \end{aligned}$$

so that

$$(1/T)\sum_{t=1}^{T} y_t^2 = \hat{\mu}^2 + (1/2)\sum_{j=1}^{M}(\hat{\alpha}_j^2 + \hat{\delta}_j^2). \qquad [6.A.22]$$

Finally, observe from [4.A.5] and the fact that $\hat{\mu} = \bar{y}$ that

$$(1/T)\sum_{t=1}^{T} y_t^2 - \hat{\mu}^2 = (1/T)\sum_{t=1}^{T}(y_t - \bar{y})^2,$$

allowing [6.A.22] to be written as

$$(1/T)\sum_{t=1}^{T}(y_t - \bar{y})^2 = (1/2)\sum_{j=1}^{M}(\hat{\alpha}_j^2 + \hat{\delta}_j^2),$$

as claimed in [6.2.14]. Since the regressors are all orthogonal, the term $\frac{1}{2}(\hat{\alpha}_j^2 + \hat{\delta}_j^2)$ can be interpreted as the portion of the sample variance that can be attributed to the regressors $\cos[\omega_j(t-1)]$ and $\sin[\omega_j(t-1)]$. ■

■ **Proof of Proposition 6.2(c).** Notice that

$$(\hat{\alpha}_j^2 + \hat{\delta}_j^2) = (\hat{\alpha}_j + i\cdot\hat{\delta}_j)(\hat{\alpha}_j - i\cdot\hat{\delta}_j). \qquad [6.A.23]$$

But from result (a) of Proposition 6.2,

$$\hat{\alpha}_j = (2/T)\sum_{t=1}^{T} y_t\cdot\cos[\omega_j(t-1)] = (2/T)\sum_{t=1}^{T}(y_t - \bar{y})\cdot\cos[\omega_j(t-1)], \qquad [6.A.24]$$

where the second equality follows from [6.A.11]. Similarly,

$$\hat{\delta}_j = (2/T)\sum_{t=1}^{T}(y_t - \bar{y})\cdot\sin[\omega_j(t-1)]. \qquad [6.A.25]$$

It follows from [6.A.24] and [6.A.25] that

$$\begin{aligned} \hat{\alpha}_j + i\cdot\hat{\delta}_j &= (2/T)\left\{\sum_{t=1}^{T}(y_t - \bar{y})\cdot\cos[\omega_j(t-1)] \right. \\ &\qquad \left. + i\cdot\sum_{t=1}^{T}(y_t - \bar{y})\cdot\sin[\omega_j(t-1)]\right\} \qquad [6.A.26] \\ &= (2/T)\sum_{t=1}^{T}(y_t - \bar{y})\cdot\exp[i\omega_j(t-1)]. \end{aligned}$$

Similarly,

$$\hat{\alpha}_j - i\cdot\hat{\delta}_j = (2/T) \sum_{\tau=1}^{T} (y_\tau - \bar{y})\cdot\exp[-i\omega_j(\tau - 1)]. \qquad [6.A.27]$$

Substituting [6.A.26] and [6.A.27] into [6.A.23] produces

$$\begin{aligned}
\hat{\alpha}_j^2 + \hat{\delta}_j^2 &= (4/T^2)\left\{\sum_{t=1}^{T} (y_t - \bar{y})\cdot\exp[i\omega_j(t - 1)]\right\} \\
&\quad \times \left\{\sum_{\tau=1}^{T} (y_\tau - \bar{y})\cdot\exp[-i\omega_j(\tau - 1)]\right\} \\
&= (4/T^2) \sum_{t=1}^{T}\sum_{\tau=1}^{T} (y_t - \bar{y})(y_\tau - \bar{y})\cdot\exp[i\omega_j(t - \tau)] \\
&= (4/T^2)\left\{\sum_{t=1}^{T} (y_t - \bar{y})^2 + \sum_{t=1}^{T-1} (y_t - \bar{y})(y_{t+1} - \bar{y})\cdot\exp[-i\omega_j]\right. \\
&\quad + \sum_{t=2}^{T} (y_t - \bar{y})(y_{t-1} - \bar{y})\cdot\exp[i\omega_j] \\
&\quad + \sum_{t=1}^{T-2} (y_t - \bar{y})(y_{t+2} - \bar{y})\cdot\exp[-2i\omega_j] \\
&\quad + \sum_{t=3}^{T} (y_t - \bar{y})(y_{t-2} - \bar{y})\cdot\exp[2i\omega_j] + \cdots \qquad [6.A.28] \\
&\quad + (y_1 - \bar{y})(y_T - \bar{y})\cdot\exp[-(T - 1)i\omega_j] \\
&\quad \left. + (y_T - \bar{y})(y_1 - \bar{y})\cdot\exp[(T - 1)i\omega_j]\right\} \\
&= (4/T)\left\{\hat{\gamma}_0 + \hat{\gamma}_1\cdot\exp[-i\omega_j] + \hat{\gamma}_{-1}\cdot\exp[i\omega_j]\right. \\
&\quad + \hat{\gamma}_2\cdot\exp[-2i\omega_j] + \hat{\gamma}_{-2}\cdot\exp[2i\omega_j] + \cdots \\
&\quad \left. + \hat{\gamma}_{T-1}\cdot\exp[-(T - 1)i\omega_j] + \hat{\gamma}_{-T+1}\cdot\exp[(T - 1)i\omega_j]\right\} \\
&= (4/T)(2\pi)\hat{s}_y(\omega_j),
\end{aligned}$$

from which equation [6.2.15] follows. ■

## Chapter 6 Exercises

6.1. Derive [6.1.12] directly from expression [6.1.6] and the formulas for the autocovariances of an $MA(1)$ process.

6.2. Integrate [6.1.9] and [6.1.12] to confirm independently that [6.1.17] holds for white noise and an $MA(1)$ process.

## Chapter 6 References


Anderson, T. W. 1971. *The Statistical Analysis of Time Series.* New York: Wiley.

Bloomfield, Peter. 1976. *Fourier Analysis of Time Series: An Introduction.* New York: Wiley.

Cramér, Harald, and M. R. Leadbetter. 1967. *Stationary and Related Stochastic Processes*. New York: Wiley.

Fuller, Wayne A. 1976. *Introduction to Statistical Time Series*. New York: Wiley.

Thomas, George B., Jr. 1972. *Calculus and Analytic Geometry*, alternate ed. Reading, Mass.: Addison-Wesley.

# 7 Asymptotic Distribution Theory

Suppose a sample of $T$ observations $(y_1, y_2, \ldots, y_T)$ has been used to construct $\hat{\boldsymbol{\theta}}$, an estimate of the vector of population parameters. For example, the parameter vector $\boldsymbol{\theta} = (c, \phi_1, \phi_2, \ldots, \phi_p, \sigma^2)'$ for an $AR(p)$ process might have been estimated from an $OLS$ regression of $y_t$ on lagged $y$'s. We would like to know how far this estimate $\hat{\boldsymbol{\theta}}$ is likely to be from the true value $\boldsymbol{\theta}$ and how to test a hypothesis about the true value based on the observed sample of $y$'s.

Much of the distribution theory used to answer these questions is *asymptotic*: that is, it describes the properties of estimators as the sample size ($T$) goes to infinity. This chapter develops the basic asymptotic results that will be used in subsequent chapters. The first section summarizes the key tools of asymptotic analysis and presents limit theorems for the sample mean of a sequence of i.i.d. random variables. Section 7.2 develops limit theorems for serially dependent variables with time-varying marginal distributions.

## 7.1. *Review of Asymptotic Distribution Theory*

### *Limits of Deterministic Sequences*

Let $\{c_T\}_{T=1}^{\infty}$ denote a sequence of deterministic numbers. The sequence is said to *converge* to $c$ if for any $\varepsilon > 0$, there exists an $N$ such that $|c_T - c| < \varepsilon$ whenever $T \geq N$; in other words, $c_T$ will be as close as desired to $c$ so long as $T$ is sufficiently large. This is indicated as

$$\lim_{T\to\infty} c_T = c, \qquad [7.1.1]$$

or, equivalently,

$$c_T \to c.$$

For example, $c_T = 1/T$ denotes the sequence $\{1, \frac{1}{2}, \frac{1}{3}, \ldots\}$, for which

$$\lim_{T\to\infty} c_T = 0.$$

A sequence of deterministic $(m \times n)$ matrices $\{\mathbf{C}_T\}_{T=1}^{\infty}$ converges to $\mathbf{C}$ if each element of $\mathbf{C}_T$ converges to the corresponding element of $\mathbf{C}$.

## *Convergence in Probability*

Consider a sequence of scalar random variables, $\{X_T\}_{T=1}^{\infty}$. The sequence is said to *converge in probability* to $c$ if for every $\varepsilon > 0$ and every $\delta > 0$ there exists a value $N$ such that, for all $T \geq N$,

$$P\{|X_T - c| > \delta\} < \varepsilon. \qquad [7.1.2]$$

In words, if we go far enough along in the sequence, the probability that $X_T$ differs from $c$ by more than $\delta$ can be made arbitrarily small for any $\delta$.

When [7.1.2] is satisfied, the number $c$ is called the *probability limit*, or *plim*, of the sequence $\{X_T\}$. This is indicated as

$$\text{plim } X_T = c,$$

or, equivalently,

$$X_T \xrightarrow{p} c.$$

Recall that if $\{c_T\}_{T=1}^{\infty}$ is a deterministic sequence converging to $c$, then there exists an $N$ such that $|c_T - c| < \delta$ for all $T \geq N$. Then $P\{|c_T - c| > \delta\} = 0$ for all $T \geq N$. Thus, if a deterministic sequence converges to $c$, then we could also say that $c_T \xrightarrow{p} c$.

A sequence of $(m \times n)$ matrices of random variables $\{\mathbf{X}_T\}$ converges in probability to the $(m \times n)$ matrix $\mathbf{C}$ if each element of $\mathbf{X}_T$ converges in probability to the corresponding element of $\mathbf{C}$.

More generally, if $\{\mathbf{X}_T\}$ and $\{\mathbf{Y}_T\}$ are sequences of $(m \times n)$ matrices, we will use the notation

$$\mathbf{X}_T \xrightarrow{p} \mathbf{Y}_T$$

to indicate that the difference between the two sequences converges in probability to zero:

$$\mathbf{X}_T - \mathbf{Y}_T \xrightarrow{p} \mathbf{0}.$$

An example of a sequence of random variables of interest is the following. Suppose we have a sample of $T$ observations on a random variable $\{Y_1, Y_2, \ldots, Y_T\}$. Consider the sample mean,

$$\bar{Y}_T \equiv (1/T) \sum_{t=1}^{T} Y_t, \qquad [7.1.3]$$

as an estimator of the population mean,

$$\hat{\mu}_T = \bar{Y}_T.$$

We append the subscript $T$ to this estimator to emphasize that it describes the mean of a sample of size $T$. The primary focus will be on the behavior of this estimator as $T$ grows large. Thus, we will be interested in the properties of the sequence $\{\hat{\mu}_T\}_{T=1}^{\infty}$.

When the plim of a sequence of estimators (such as $\{\hat{\mu}_T\}_{T=1}^{\infty}$) is equal to the true population parameter (in this case, $\mu$), the estimator is said to be *consistent*. If an estimator is consistent, then there exists a sufficiently large sample such that we can be assured with very high probability that the estimate will be within any desired tolerance band around the true value.

The following result is quite helpful in finding plims; a proof of this and some of the other propositions of this chapter are provided in Appendix 7.A at the end of the chapter.

***Proposition 7.1:*** *Let* $\{\mathbf{X}_T\}$ *denote a sequence of* $(n \times 1)$ *random vectors with plim* $\mathbf{c}$, *and let* $\mathbf{g}(\mathbf{c})$ *be a vector-valued function,* $\mathbf{g}: \mathbb{R}^n \rightarrow \mathbb{R}^m$, *where* $\mathbf{g}(\cdot)$ *is continuous at* $\mathbf{c}$ *and does not depend on T. Then* $\mathbf{g}(\mathbf{X}_T) \xrightarrow{p} \mathbf{g}(\mathbf{c})$.

The basic idea behind this proposition is that, since $\mathbf{g}(\cdot)$ is continuous, $\mathbf{g}(\mathbf{X}_T)$ will be close to $\mathbf{g}(\mathbf{c})$ provided that $\mathbf{X}_T$ is close to $\mathbf{c}$. By choosing a sufficiently large value of $T$, the probability that $\mathbf{X}_T$ is close to $\mathbf{c}$ (and thus that $\mathbf{g}(\mathbf{X}_T)$ is close to $\mathbf{g}(\mathbf{c})$) can be brought as near to unity as desired.

Note that $\mathbf{g}(\mathbf{X}_T)$ depends on the *value* of $\mathbf{X}_T$ but cannot depend on the index $T$ itself. Thus, $g(X_T, T) = T \cdot X_T^2$ is not a function covered by Proposition 7.1.

***Example 7.1***

If $X_{1T} \xrightarrow{p} c_1$ and $X_{2T} \xrightarrow{p} c_2$, then $(X_{1T} + X_{2T}) \xrightarrow{p} (c_1 + c_2)$. This follows immediately, since $g(X_{1T}, X_{2T}) \equiv (X_{1T} + X_{2T})$ is a continuous function of $(X_{1T}, X_{2T})$.

***Example 7.2***

Let $\{\mathbf{X}_{1T}\}$ denote a sequence of $(n \times n)$ random matrices with $\mathbf{X}_{1T} \xrightarrow{p} \mathbf{C}_1$, a nonsingular matrix. Let $\mathbf{X}_{2T}$ denote a sequence of $(n \times 1)$ random vectors with $\mathbf{X}_{2T} \xrightarrow{p} \mathbf{c}_2$. Then $[\mathbf{X}_{1T}]^{-1}\mathbf{X}_{2T} \xrightarrow{p} [\mathbf{C}_1]^{-1}\mathbf{c}_2$. To see this, note that the elements of the matrix $[\mathbf{X}_{1T}]^{-1}$ are continuous functions of the elements of $\mathbf{X}_{1T}$ at $\mathbf{X}_{1T} = \mathbf{C}_1$, since $[\mathbf{C}_1]^{-1}$ exists. Thus, $[\mathbf{X}_{1T}]^{-1} \xrightarrow{p} [\mathbf{C}_1]^{-1}$. Similarly, the elements of $[\mathbf{X}_{1T}]^{-1}\mathbf{X}_{2T}$ are sums of products of elements of $[\mathbf{X}_{1T}]^{-1}$ with those of $\mathbf{X}_{2T}$. Since each sum is again a continuous function of $\mathbf{X}_{1T}$ and $\mathbf{X}_{2T}$,

$$\text{plim } [\mathbf{X}_{1T}]^{-1}\mathbf{X}_{2T} = [\text{plim } \mathbf{X}_{1T}]^{-1} \text{ plim } \mathbf{X}_{2T} = [\mathbf{C}_1]^{-1}\mathbf{c}_2.$$

Proposition 7.1 also holds if some of the elements of $\mathbf{X}_T$ are deterministic with conventional limits as in expression [7.1.1]. Specifically, let $\mathbf{X}_T' = (\mathbf{X}_{1T}', \mathbf{c}_{2T}')$, where $\mathbf{X}_{1T}$ is a stochastic $(n_1 \times 1)$ vector and $\mathbf{c}_{2T}$ is a deterministic $(n_2 \times 1)$ vector. If plim $\mathbf{X}_{1T} = \mathbf{c}_1$ and $\lim_{T\to\infty} \mathbf{c}_{2T} = \mathbf{c}_2$, then $\mathbf{g}(\mathbf{X}_{1T}, \mathbf{c}_{2T}) \xrightarrow{p} \mathbf{g}(\mathbf{c}_1, \mathbf{c}_2)$. (See Exercise 7.1.)

***Example 7.3***

Consider an alternative estimator of the mean given by $\bar{Y}_T^* \equiv [1/(T-1)] \times \Sigma_{t=1}^T Y_t$. This can be written as $c_{1T}\bar{Y}_T$, where $c_{1T} \equiv [T/(T-1)]$ and $\bar{Y}_T \equiv (1/T)\Sigma_{t=1}^T Y_t$. Under general conditions detailed in Section 7.2, the sample mean is a consistent estimator of the population mean, implying that $\bar{Y}_T \xrightarrow{p} \mu$. It is also easy to verify that $c_{1T} \rightarrow 1$. Since $c_{1T}\bar{Y}_T$ is a continuous function of $c_{1T}$ and $\bar{Y}_T$, it follows that $c_{1T}\bar{Y}_T \xrightarrow{p} 1 \cdot \mu = \mu$. Thus, $\bar{Y}_T^*$, like $\bar{Y}_T$, is a consistent estimator of $\mu$.

## *Convergence in Mean Square and Chebyshev's Inequality*

A stronger condition than convergence in probability is *mean square convergence*. The random sequence $\{X_T\}$ is said to converge in mean square to $c$, indicated as

$$X_T \xrightarrow{m.s.} c,$$

if for every $\varepsilon > 0$ there exists a value $N$ such that, for all $T \geq N$,

$$E(X_T - c)^2 < \varepsilon. \quad [7.1.4]$$

Another useful result is the following.

***Proposition 7.2:*** (*Generalized Chebyshev's inequality*). *Let $X$ be a random variable with $E(|X|^r)$ finite for some $r > 0$. Then, for any $\delta > 0$ and any value of $c$,*

$$P\{|X - c| > \delta\} \leq \frac{E|X - c|^r}{\delta^r}. \quad [7.1.5]$$

An implication of Chebyshev's inequality is that if $X_T \xrightarrow{m.s.} c$, then $X_T \xrightarrow{p} c$. To see this, note that if $X_T \xrightarrow{m.s.} c$, then for any $\varepsilon > 0$ and $\delta > 0$ there exists an $N$ such that $E(X_T - c)^2 < \delta^2\varepsilon$ for all $T \geq N$. This would ensure that

$$\frac{E(X_T - c)^2}{\delta^2} < \varepsilon$$

for all $T \geq N$. From Chebyshev's inequality, this also implies

$$P\{|X_T - c| > \delta\} < \varepsilon$$

for all $T \geq N$, or that $X_T \xrightarrow{p} c$.

## *Law of Large Numbers for Independent and Identically Distributed Variables*

Let us now consider the behavior of the sample mean $\bar{Y}_T = (1/T)\Sigma_{t=1}^T Y_t$ where $\{Y_t\}$ is i.i.d. with mean $\mu$ and variance $\sigma^2$. For this case, $\bar{Y}_T$ has expectation $\mu$ and variance

$$E(\bar{Y}_T - \mu)^2 = (1/T^2)\,\text{Var}\left(\sum_{t=1}^T Y_t\right) = (1/T^2)\sum_{t=1}^T \text{Var}(Y_t) = \sigma^2/T.$$

Since $\sigma^2/T \to 0$ as $T \to \infty$, this means that $\bar{Y}_T \xrightarrow{m.s.} \mu$, implying also that $\bar{Y}_T \xrightarrow{p} \mu$.

Figure 7.1 graphs an example of the density of the sample mean $f_{\bar{Y}_T}(\bar{y}_T)$ for three different values of $T$. As $T$ becomes large, the density becomes increasingly concentrated in a spike centered at $\mu$.

The result that the sample mean is a consistent estimate of the population mean is known as the *law of large numbers*.[1] It was proved here for the special case of i.i.d. variables with finite variance. In fact, it turns out also to be true of any sequence of i.i.d. variables with finite mean $\mu$.[2] Section 7.2 explores some of the circumstances under which it also holds for serially dependent variables with time-varying marginal distributions.

## *Convergence in Distribution*

Let $\{X_T\}_{T=1}^{\infty}$ be a sequence of random variables, and let $F_{X_T}(x)$ denote the cumulative distribution function of $X_T$. Suppose that there exists a cumulative distribution function $F_X(x)$ such that

$$\lim_{T\to\infty} F_{X_T}(x) = F_X(x)$$

[1]This is often described as the weak law of large numbers. An analogous result known as the strong law of large numbers refers to almost sure convergence rather than convergence in probability of the sample mean.

[2]This is known as *Khinchine's theorem*. See, for example, Rao (1973, p. 112).

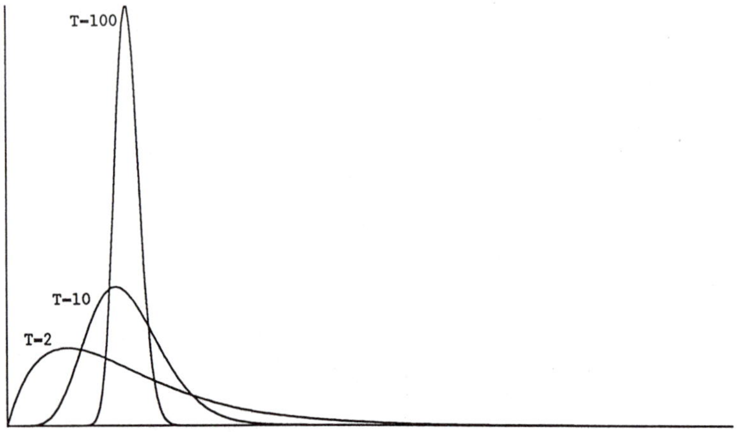


**FIGURE 7.1** Density of the sample mean for a sample of size $T$.

at any value $x$ at which $F_X(\cdot)$ is continuous. Then $X_T$ is said to *converge in distribution* (or in law) to $X$, denoted

$$X_T \xrightarrow{L} X.$$

When $F_X(x)$ is of a common form, such as the cumulative distribution function for a $N(\mu, \sigma^2)$ variable, we will equivalently write

$$X_T \xrightarrow{L} N(\mu, \sigma^2).$$

The definitions are unchanged if the scalar $X_T$ is replaced with an $(n \times 1)$ vector $\mathbf{X}_T$. A simple way to verify convergence in distribution of a vector is the following.[3] If the scalar $(\lambda_1 X_{1T} + \lambda_2 X_{2T} + \cdots + \lambda_n X_{nT})$ converges in distribution to $(\lambda_1 X_1 + \lambda_2 X_2 + \cdots + \lambda_n X_n)$ for any real values of $(\lambda_1, \lambda_2, \ldots, \lambda_n)$, then the vector $\mathbf{X}_T \equiv (X_{1T}, X_{2T}, \ldots, X_{nT})'$ converges in distribution to the vector $\mathbf{X} \equiv (X_1, X_2, \ldots, X_n)'$.

The following results are useful in determining limiting distributions.[4]

***Proposition 7.3:***

(*a*) *Let* $\{\mathbf{Y}_T\}$ *be a sequence of* $(n \times 1)$ *random vectors with* $\mathbf{Y}_T \xrightarrow{L} \mathbf{Y}$. *Suppose that* $\{\mathbf{X}_T\}$ *is a sequence of* $(n \times 1)$ *random vectors such that* $(\mathbf{X}_T - \mathbf{Y}_T) \xrightarrow{p} \mathbf{0}$. *Then* $\mathbf{X}_T \xrightarrow{L} \mathbf{Y}$; *that is,* $\mathbf{X}_T$ *and* $\mathbf{Y}_T$ *have the same limiting distribution.*

(*b*) *Let* $\{\mathbf{X}_T\}$ *be a sequence of random* $(n \times 1)$ *vectors with* $\mathbf{X}_T \xrightarrow{p} \mathbf{c}$, *and let* $\{\mathbf{Y}_T\}$ *be a sequence of random* $(n \times 1)$ *vectors with* $\mathbf{Y}_T \xrightarrow{L} \mathbf{Y}$. *Then the sequence constructed from the sum* $\{\mathbf{X}_T + \mathbf{Y}_T\}$ *converges in distribution to* $\mathbf{c} + \mathbf{Y}$ *and the sequence constructed from the product* $\{\mathbf{X}_T'\mathbf{Y}_T\}$ *converges in distribution to* $\mathbf{c}'\mathbf{Y}$.

(*c*) *Let* $\{\mathbf{X}_T\}$ *be a sequence of random* $(n \times 1)$ *vectors with* $\mathbf{X}_T \xrightarrow{L} \mathbf{X}$, *and let* $\mathbf{g}(\mathbf{X})$, $\mathbf{g}: \mathbb{R}^n \rightarrow \mathbb{R}^m$ *be a continuous function (not dependent on* $T$*). Then the sequence of random variables* $\{\mathbf{g}(\mathbf{X}_T)\}$ *converges in distribution to* $\mathbf{g}(\mathbf{X})$.

[3] This is known as the Cramér-Wold theorem. See Rao (1973, p. 123).

[4] See Rao (1973, pp. 122–24).

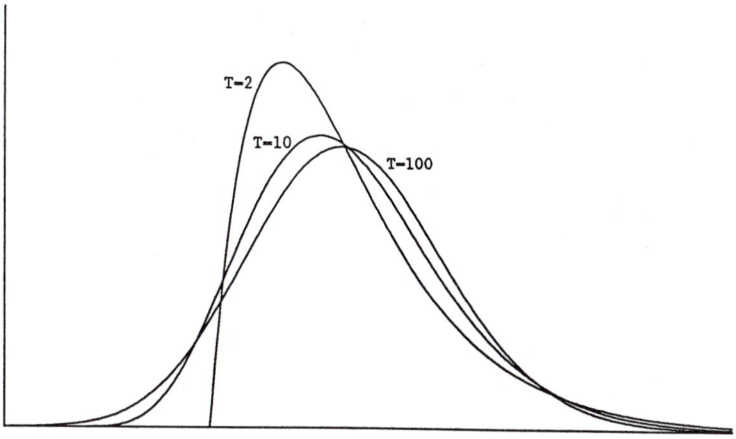


**FIGURE 7.2** Density of $\sqrt{T}(\bar{Y}_T - \mu)$.

***Example 7.4***

Suppose that $X_T \xrightarrow{p} c$ and $Y_T \xrightarrow{L} Y$, where $Y \sim N(\mu, \sigma^2)$. Then, by Proposition 7.3(b), the sequence $X_T Y_T$ has the same limiting probability law as that of $c$ times a $N(\mu, \sigma^2)$ variable. In other words, $X_T Y_T \xrightarrow{L} N(c\mu, c^2\sigma^2)$.

***Example 7.5***

Generalizing the previous result, let $\{\mathbf{X}_T\}$ be a sequence of random $(m \times n)$ matrices and $\{\mathbf{Y}_T\}$ a sequence of random $(n \times 1)$ vectors with $\mathbf{X}_T \xrightarrow{p} \mathbf{C}$ and $\mathbf{Y}_T \xrightarrow{L} \mathbf{Y}$, with $\mathbf{Y} \sim N(\boldsymbol{\mu}, \boldsymbol{\Omega})$. Then the limiting distribution of $\mathbf{X}_T\mathbf{Y}_T$ is the same as that of $\mathbf{CY}$; that is, $\mathbf{X}_T\mathbf{Y}_T \xrightarrow{L} N(\mathbf{C}\boldsymbol{\mu}, \mathbf{C}\boldsymbol{\Omega}\mathbf{C}')$.

***Example 7.6***

Suppose that $X_T \xrightarrow{L} N(0, 1)$. Then Proposition 7.3(c) implies that the square of $X_T$ asymptotically behaves as the square of a $N(0, 1)$ variable: $X_T^2 \xrightarrow{L} \chi^2(1)$.

## *Central Limit Theorem*

We have seen that the sample mean $\bar{Y}_T$ for an i.i.d. sequence has a degenerate probability density as $T \to \infty$, collapsing toward a point mass at $\mu$ as the sample size grows. For statistical inference we would like to describe the distribution of $\bar{Y}_T$ in more detail. For this purpose, note that the random variable $\sqrt{T}(\bar{Y}_T - \mu)$ has mean zero and variance given by $(\sqrt{T})^2 \operatorname{Var}(\bar{Y}_T) = \sigma^2$ for all $T$, and thus, in contrast to $\bar{Y}_T$, the random variable $\sqrt{T}(\bar{Y}_T - \mu)$ might be expected to converge to a nondegenerate random variable as $T$ goes to infinity.

The *central limit theorem* is the result that, as $T$ increases, the sequence $\sqrt{T}(\bar{Y}_T - \mu)$ converges in distribution to a Gaussian random variable. The most familiar, albeit restrictive, version of the central limit theorem establishes that if $Y_t$ is i.i.d. with mean $\mu$ and variance $\sigma^2$, then[5]

$$\sqrt{T}(\bar{Y}_T - \mu) \xrightarrow{L} N(0, \sigma^2). \qquad [7.1.6]$$

Result [7.1.6] also holds under much more general conditions, some of which are explored in the next section.

Figure 7.2 graphs an example of the density of $\sqrt{T}(\bar{Y}_T - \mu)$ for three different

[5]See, for example, White (1984, pp. 108–9).

values of $T$. Each of these densities has mean zero and variance $\sigma^2$. As $T$ becomes large, the density converges to that of a $N(0, \sigma^2)$ variable.

A final useful result is the following.

***Proposition 7.4:*** *Let* $\{\mathbf{X}_t\}$ *be a sequence of random* $(n \times 1)$ *vectors such that* $\sqrt{T}(\mathbf{X}_T - \mathbf{c}) \xrightarrow{L} \mathbf{X}$, *and let* $\mathbf{g}: \mathbb{R}^n \to \mathbb{R}^m$ *have continuous first derivatives with* $\mathbf{G}$ *denoting the* $(m \times n)$ *matrix of derivatives evaluated at* $\mathbf{c}$:

$$\mathbf{G} \equiv \left.\frac{\partial \mathbf{g}}{\partial \mathbf{x}'}\right|_{\mathbf{x}=\mathbf{c}}.$$

*Then* $\sqrt{T}[\mathbf{g}(\mathbf{X}_T) - \mathbf{g}(\mathbf{c})] \xrightarrow{L} \mathbf{G}\mathbf{X}$.

***Example 7.7***

Let $\{Y_1, Y_2, \ldots, Y_T\}$ be an i.i.d. sample of size $T$ drawn from a distribution with mean $\mu \neq 0$ and variance $\sigma^2$. Consider the distribution of the reciprocal of the sample mean, $S_T = 1/\bar{Y}_T$, where $\bar{Y}_T \equiv (1/T)\Sigma_{t=1}^T Y_t$. We know from the central limit theorem that $\sqrt{T}(\bar{Y}_T - \mu) \xrightarrow{L} Y$, where $Y \sim N(0, \sigma^2)$. Also, $g(y) = 1/y$ is continuous at $y = \mu$. Let $G \equiv (\partial g/\partial y)|_{y=\mu} = (-1/\mu^2)$. Then $\sqrt{T}[S_T - (1/\mu)] \xrightarrow{L} G \cdot Y$; in other words, $\sqrt{T}[S_T - (1/\mu)] \xrightarrow{L} N(0, \sigma^2/\mu^4)$.

## 7.2. Limit Theorems for Serially Dependent Observations

The previous section stated the law of large numbers and central limit theorem for independent and identically distributed random variables with finite second moments. This section develops analogous results for heterogeneously distributed variables with various forms of serial dependence. We first develop a law of large numbers for a general covariance-stationary process.

### Law of Large Numbers for a Covariance-Stationary Process

Let $(Y_1, Y_2, \ldots, Y_T)$ represent a sample of size $T$ from a covariance-stationary process with

$$E(Y_t) = \mu \quad \text{for all } t \qquad [7.2.1]$$

$$E(Y_t - \mu)(Y_{t-j} - \mu) = \gamma_j \quad \text{for all } t \qquad [7.2.2]$$

$$\sum_{j=0}^{\infty} |\gamma_j| < \infty. \qquad [7.2.3]$$

Consider the properties of the sample mean,

$$\bar{Y}_T = (1/T) \sum_{t=1}^{T} Y_t. \qquad [7.2.4]$$

Taking expectations of [7.2.4] reveals that the sample mean provides an unbiased estimate of the population mean,

$$E(\bar{Y}_T) = \mu,$$

while the variance of the sample mean is

$$
\begin{aligned}
E(\bar{Y}_T - \mu)^2 \\
&= E\left[(1/T)\sum_{t=1}^{T}(Y_t - \mu)\right]^2 \\
&= (1/T^2)E\{[(Y_1 - \mu) + (Y_2 - \mu) + \cdots + (Y_T - \mu)] \\
&\quad \times [(Y_1 - \mu) + (Y_2 - \mu) + \cdots + (Y_T - \mu)]\} \\
&= (1/T^2)E\{(Y_1 - \mu)[(Y_1 - \mu) + (Y_2 - \mu) + \cdots + (Y_T - \mu)] \\
&\quad + (Y_2 - \mu)[(Y_1 - \mu) + (Y_2 - \mu) + \cdots + (Y_T - \mu)] \\
&\quad + (Y_3 - \mu)[(Y_1 - \mu) + (Y_2 - \mu) + \cdots + (Y_T - \mu)] \\
&\quad + \cdots + (Y_T - \mu)[(Y_1 - \mu) + (Y_2 - \mu) + \cdots + (Y_T - \mu)]\} \\
&= (1/T^2)\ \{[\gamma_0 + \gamma_1 + \gamma_2 + \gamma_3 + \cdots + \gamma_{T-1}] \\
&\quad + [\gamma_1 + \gamma_0 + \gamma_1 + \gamma_2 + \cdots + \gamma_{T-2}] \\
&\quad + [\gamma_2 + \gamma_1 + \gamma_0 + \gamma_1 + \cdots + \gamma_{T-3}] \\
&\quad + \cdots + [\gamma_{T-1} + \gamma_{T-2} + \gamma_{T-3} + \cdots + \gamma_0]\}.
\end{aligned}
$$

Thus,

$$
\begin{aligned}
E(\bar{Y}_T - \mu)^2 = (1/T^2)\{&T\gamma_0 + 2(T-1)\gamma_1 \\
&+ 2(T-2)\gamma_2 + 2(T-3)\gamma_3 + \cdots + 2\gamma_{T-1}\}
\end{aligned}
$$

or

$$
\begin{aligned}
E(\bar{Y}_T - \mu)^2 = (1/T)\{&\gamma_0 + [(T-1)/T](2\gamma_1) + [(T-2)/T](2\gamma_2) \\
&+ [(T-3)/T](2\gamma_3) + \cdots + [1/T](2\gamma_{T-1})\}.
\end{aligned}
\qquad [7.2.5]
$$

It is easy to see that this expression goes to zero as the sample size grows—that is, that $\bar{Y}_T \overset{m.s.}{\rightarrow} \mu$:

$$
\begin{aligned}
T\cdot E(\bar{Y}_T - \mu)^2 &= |\gamma_0 + [(T-1)/T](2\gamma_1) + [(T-2)/T](2\gamma_2) \\
&\quad + [(T-3)/T](2\gamma_3) + \cdots + [1/T](2\gamma_{T-1})| \\
&\le \{|\gamma_0| + [(T-1)/T]\cdot 2|\gamma_1| + [(T-2)/T]\cdot 2|\gamma_2| \\
&\quad + [(T-3)/T]\cdot 2|\gamma_3| + \cdots + [1/T]\cdot 2|\gamma_{T-1}|\} \\
&\le \{|\gamma_0| + 2|\gamma_1| + 2|\gamma_2| + 2|\gamma_3| + \cdots\}.
\end{aligned}
\qquad [7.2.6]
$$

Hence, $T\cdot E(\bar{Y}_T - \mu)^2 < \infty$, by [7.2.3], and so $E(\bar{Y}_T - \mu)^2 \rightarrow 0$, as claimed.

It is also of interest to calculate the limiting value of $T\cdot E(\bar{Y}_T - \mu)^2$. Result [7.2.5] expresses this variance for finite $T$ as a weighted average of the first $T-1$ autocovariances $\gamma_j$. For large $j$, these autocovariances approach zero and will not affect the sum. For small $j$, the autocovariances are given a weight that approaches unity as the sample size grows. Thus, we might guess that

$$
\lim_{T\rightarrow\infty} T\cdot E(\bar{Y}_T - \mu)^2 = \sum_{j=-\infty}^{\infty}\gamma_j = \gamma_0 + 2\gamma_1 + 2\gamma_2 + 2\gamma_3 + \cdots. \qquad [7.2.7]
$$

This conjecture is indeed correct. To verify this, note that the assumption [7.2.3] means that for any $\varepsilon > 0$ there exists a $q$ such that

$$
2|\gamma_{q+1}| + 2|\gamma_{q+2}| + 2|\gamma_{q+3}| + \cdots < \varepsilon/2.
$$

Now

$$\left|\sum_{j=-\infty}^{\infty} \gamma_j - T \cdot E(\overline{Y}_T - \mu)^2\right|$$

$$\begin{aligned} &= |\{\gamma_0 + 2\gamma_1 + 2\gamma_2 + 2\gamma_3 + \cdots\} \\ &\quad - \{\gamma_0 + [(T-1)/T] \cdot 2\gamma_1 + [(T-2)/T] \cdot 2\gamma_2 \\ &\quad + [(T-3)/T] \cdot 2\gamma_3 + \cdots + [1/T] \cdot 2\gamma_{T-1}\}| \\ &\le (1/T) \cdot 2|\gamma_1| + (2/T) \cdot 2|\gamma_2| + (3/T) \cdot 2|\gamma_3| + \cdots \\ &\quad + (q/T) \cdot 2|\gamma_q| + 2|\gamma_{q+1}| + 2|\gamma_{q+2}| + 2|\gamma_{q+3}| + \cdots \\ &\le (1/T) \cdot 2|\gamma_1| + (2/T) \cdot 2|\gamma_2| + (3/T) \cdot 2|\gamma_3| + \cdots \\ &\quad + (q/T) \cdot 2|\gamma_q| + \varepsilon/2. \end{aligned}$$

Moreover, for this given $q$, we can find an $N$ such that

$$(1/T) \cdot 2|\gamma_1| + (2/T) \cdot 2|\gamma_2| + (3/T) \cdot 2|\gamma_3| + \cdots + (q/T) \cdot 2|\gamma_q| < \varepsilon/2$$

for all $T \ge N$, ensuring that

$$\left|\sum_{j=-\infty}^{\infty} \gamma_j - T \cdot E(\overline{Y}_T - \mu)^2\right| < \varepsilon,$$

as was to be shown.

These results can be summarized as follows.

***Proposition 7.5:*** *Let $Y_t$ be a covariance-stationary process with moments given by [7.2.1] and [7.2.2] and with absolutely summable autocovariances as in [7.2.3]. Then the sample mean [7.2.4] satisfies*

(a) $\overline{Y}_T \xrightarrow{m.s.} \mu$

(b) $\lim_{T \to \infty} \{T \cdot E(\overline{Y}_T - \mu)^2\} = \sum_{j=-\infty}^{\infty} \gamma_j.$

Recall from Chapter 3 that condition [7.2.3] is satisfied for any covariance-stationary $ARMA(p, q)$ process,

$$(1 - \phi_1 L - \phi_2 L^2 - \cdots - \phi_p L^p)Y_t = \mu + (1 + \theta_1 L + \theta_2 L^2 + \cdots + \theta_q L^q)\varepsilon_t,$$

with roots of $(1 - \phi_1 z - \phi_2 z^2 - \cdots - \phi_p z^p) = 0$ outside the unit circle.

Alternative expressions for the variance in result (b) of Proposition 7.5 are sometimes used. Recall that the autocovariance-generating function for $Y_t$ is defined as

$$g_Y(z) = \sum_{j=-\infty}^{\infty} \gamma_j z^j,$$

while the spectrum is given by

$$s_Y(\omega) = \frac{1}{2\pi} g_Y(e^{-i\omega}).$$

Thus, result (b) could equivalently be described as the autocovariance-generating function evaluated at $z = 1$,

$$\sum_{j=-\infty}^{\infty} \gamma_j = g_Y(1),$$

or as $2\pi$ times the spectrum at frequency $\omega = 0$,

$$\sum_{j=-\infty}^{\infty} \gamma_j = 2\pi s_Y(0),$$

the last result coming from the fact that $e^0 = 1$. For example, consider the $MA(\infty)$ process

$$Y_t = \mu + \sum_{j=0}^{\infty} \psi_j \varepsilon_{t-j} \equiv \mu + \psi(L)\varepsilon_t$$

with $E(\varepsilon_t \varepsilon_\tau) = \sigma^2$ if $t = \tau$ and 0 otherwise and with $\Sigma_{j=0}^{\infty}|\psi_j| < \infty$. Recall that its autocovariance-generating function is given by

$$g_Y(z) = \psi(z)\sigma^2\psi(z^{-1}).$$

Evaluating this at $z = 1$,

$$\sum_{j=-\infty}^{\infty} \gamma_j = \psi(1)\sigma^2\psi(1) = \sigma^2[1 + \psi_1 + \psi_2 + \psi_3 + \cdots]^2. \qquad [7.2.8]$$

## *Martingale Difference Sequence*

Some very useful limit theorems pertain to *martingale difference sequences*. Let $\{Y_t\}_{t=1}^{\infty}$ denote a sequence of random scalars with $E(Y_t) = 0$ for all $t$.[6] Let $\Omega_t$ denote information available at date $t$, where this information includes current and lagged values of $Y$.[7] For example, we might have

$$\Omega_t = \{Y_t, Y_{t-1}, \ldots, Y_1, X_t, X_{t-1}, \ldots, X_1\},$$

where $X_t$ is a second random variable. If

$$E(Y_t|\Omega_{t-1}) = 0 \qquad \text{for } t = 2, 3, \ldots, \qquad [7.2.9]$$

then $\{Y_t\}$ is said to be a *martingale difference sequence* with respect to $\{\Omega_t\}$.

Where no information set is specified, $\Omega_t$ is presumed to consist solely of current and lagged values of $Y$:

$$\Omega_t = \{Y_t, Y_{t-1}, \ldots, Y_1\}.$$

Thus, if a sequence of scalars $\{Y_t\}_{t=1}^{\infty}$ satisfied $E(Y_t) = 0$ for all $t$ and

$$E(Y_t|Y_{t-1}, Y_{t-2}, \ldots, Y_1) = 0, \qquad [7.2.10]$$

for $t = 2, 3, \ldots$, then we will say simply that $\{Y_t\}$ is a martingale difference sequence. Note that [7.2.10] is implied by [7.2.9] by the law of iterated expectations.

A sequence of $(n \times 1)$ vectors $\{\mathbf{Y}_t\}_{t=1}^{\infty}$ satisfying $E(\mathbf{Y}_t) = \mathbf{0}$ and $E(\mathbf{Y}_t|\mathbf{Y}_{t-1}, \mathbf{Y}_{t-2}, \ldots, \mathbf{Y}_1) = \mathbf{0}$ is said to form a *vector martingale difference sequence*.

[6] Wherever an expectation is indicated, it is taken as implicit that the integral exists, that is, that $E|Y_t|$ is finite.

[7] More formally, $\{\Omega_t\}_{t=1}^{\infty}$ denotes an increasing sequence of $\sigma$-fields ($\Omega_{t-1} \subset \Omega_t$) with $Y_t$ measurable with respect to $\Omega_t$. See, for example, White (1984, p. 56).

Note that condition [7.2.10] is stronger than the condition that $Y_t$ is serially uncorrelated. A serially uncorrelated sequence cannot be forecast on the basis of a linear function of its past values. No function of past values, linear or nonlinear, can forecast a martingale difference sequence. While stronger than absence of serial correlation, the martingale difference condition is weaker than independence, since it does not rule out the possibility that higher moments such as $E(Y_t^2|Y_{t-1}, Y_{t-2}, \ldots, Y_1)$ might depend on past $Y$'s.

### *Example 7.8*

If $\varepsilon_t \sim$ i.i.d. $N(0, \sigma^2)$, then $Y_t = \varepsilon_t\varepsilon_{t-1}$ is a martingale difference sequence but not serially independent.

## $L^1$-*Mixingales*

A more general class of processes known as *$L^1$-mixingales* was introduced by Andrews (1988). Consider a sequence of random variables $\{Y_t\}_{t=1}^{\infty}$ with $E(Y_t) = 0$ for $t = 1, 2, \ldots$. Let $\Omega_t$ denote information available at time $t$, as before, where $\Omega_t$ includes current and lagged values of $Y$. Suppose that we can find sequences of nonnegative deterministic constants $\{c_t\}_{t=1}^{\infty}$ and $\{\xi_m\}_{m=0}^{\infty}$ such that $\lim_{m\to\infty} \xi_m = 0$ and

$$E\left|E(Y_t|\Omega_{t-m})\right| \leq c_t\xi_m \qquad [7.2.11]$$

for all $t \geq 1$ and all $m \geq 0$. Then $\{Y_t\}$ is said to follow an $L^1$-mixingale with respect to $\{\Omega_t\}$.

Thus, a zero-mean process for which the $m$-period-ahead forecast $E(Y_t|\Omega_{t-m})$ converges (in absolute expected value) to the unconditional mean of zero is described as an $L^1$-mixingale.

### *Example 7.9*

Let $\{Y_t\}$ be a martingale difference sequence. Let $c_t = E|Y_t|$, and choose $\xi_0 = 1$ and $\xi_m = 0$ for $m = 1, 2, \ldots$. Then [7.2.11] is satisfied for $\Omega_t = \{Y_t, Y_{t-1}, \ldots, Y_1\}$, so that $\{Y_t\}$ could be described as an $L^1$-mixingale sequence.

### *Example 7.10*

Let $Y_t = \Sigma_{j=0}^{\infty}\psi_j\varepsilon_{t-j}$, where $\Sigma_{j=0}^{\infty}|\psi_j| < \infty$ and $\{\varepsilon_t\}$ is a martingale difference sequence with $E|\varepsilon_t| < M$ for all $t$ for some $M < \infty$. Then $\{Y_t\}$ is an $L^1$-mixingale with respect to $\Omega_t = \{\varepsilon_t, \varepsilon_{t-1}, \ldots\}$. To see this, notice that

$$E\left|E(Y_t|\varepsilon_{t-m}, \varepsilon_{t-m-1}, \ldots)\right| = E\left|\sum_{j=m}^{\infty} \psi_j\varepsilon_{t-j}\right| \leq E\left\{\sum_{j=m}^{\infty} |\psi_j\varepsilon_{t-j}|\right\}.$$

Since $\{\psi_j\}_{j=0}^{\infty}$ is absolutely summable and $E|\varepsilon_{t-j}| < M$, we can interchange the order of expectation and summation:

$$E\left\{\sum_{j=m}^{\infty} |\psi_j\varepsilon_{t-j}|\right\} = \sum_{j=m}^{\infty} |\psi_j|\cdot E|\varepsilon_{t-j}| \leq \sum_{j=m}^{\infty} |\psi_j|\cdot M.$$

Then [7.2.11] is satisfied with $c_t = M$ and $\xi_m = \Sigma_{j=m}^{\infty}|\psi_j|$. Moreover, $\lim_{m\to\infty} \xi_m = 0$, because of absolute summability of $\{\psi_j\}_{j=0}^{\infty}$. Hence, $\{Y_t\}$ is an $L^1$-mixingale.

## *Law of Large Numbers For* $L^1$*-Mixingales*

Andrews (1988) derived the following law of large numbers for $L^1$-mixingales.[8]

***Proposition 7.6:*** *Let $\{Y_t\}$ be an $L^1$-mixingale. If (a) $\{Y_t\}$ is uniformly integrable and (b) there exists a choice for $\{c_t\}$ such that*

$$\lim_{T\to\infty} (1/T)\sum_{t=1}^{T} c_t < \infty,$$

*then $(1/T)\Sigma_{t=1}^{T} Y_t \xrightarrow{p} 0$.*

To apply this result, we need to verify that a sequence is uniformly integrable. A sequence $\{Y_t\}$ is said to be *uniformly integrable* if for every $\varepsilon > 0$ there exists a number $c > 0$ such that

$$E(|Y_t|\cdot\delta_{[|Y_t|\geq c]}) < \varepsilon \qquad [7.2.12]$$

for all $t$, where $\delta_{[|Y_t|\geq c]} = 1$ if $|Y_t| \geq c$ and 0 otherwise. The following proposition gives sufficient conditions for uniform integrability.

***Proposition 7.7:*** *(a) Suppose there exist an $r > 1$ and an $M' < \infty$ such that $E(|Y_t|^r) < M'$ for all $t$. Then $\{Y_t\}$ is uniformly integrable. (b) Suppose there exist an $r > 1$ and an $M' < \infty$ such that $E(|X_t|^r) < M'$ for all $t$. If $Y_t = \Sigma_{j=-\infty}^{\infty} h_j X_{t-j}$ with $\Sigma_{j=-\infty}^{\infty} |h_j| < \infty$, then $\{Y_t\}$ is uniformly integrable.*

Condition (a) requires us to find a moment higher than the first that exists. Typically, we would use $r = 2$. However, even if a variable has infinite variance, it can still be uniformly integrable as long as $E|Y_t|^r$ exists for some $r$ between 1 and 2.

### *Example 7.11*

Let $\bar{Y}_T$ be the sample mean from a martingale difference sequence, $\bar{Y}_T = (1/T)\Sigma_{t=1}^{T} Y_t$ with $E|Y_t|^r < M'$ for some $r > 1$ and $M' < \infty$. Note that this also implies that there exists an $M < \infty$ such that $E|Y_t| < M$. From Proposition 7.7(a), $\{Y_t\}$ is uniformly integrable. Moreover, from Example 7.9, $\{Y_t\}$ can be viewed as an $L^1$-mixingale with $c_t = M$. Thus, $\lim_{T\to\infty} (1/T)\Sigma_{t=1}^{T} c_t = M < \infty$, and so, from Proposition 7.6, $\bar{Y}_T \xrightarrow{p} 0$.

### *Example 7.12*

Let $Y_t = \Sigma_{j=0}^{\infty} \psi_j \varepsilon_{t-j}$, where $\Sigma_{j=0}^{\infty} |\psi_j| < \infty$ and $\{\varepsilon_t\}$ is a martingale difference sequence with $E|\varepsilon_t|^r < M' < \infty$ for some $r > 1$ and some $M' < \infty$. Then, from Proposition 7.7(b), $\{Y_t\}$ is uniformly integrable. Moreover, from Example 7.10, $\{Y_t\}$ is an $L^1$-mixingale with $c_t = M$, where $M$ represents the largest value of $E|\varepsilon_t|$ for any $t$. Then $\lim_{T\to\infty} (1/T)\Sigma_{t=1}^{T} c_t = M < \infty$, establishing again that $\bar{Y}_T \xrightarrow{p} 0$.

Proposition 7.6 can also be applied to a double-indexed array $\{Y_{t,T}\}$; that is, each sample size $T$ can be associated with a different sequence $\{Y_{1,T}, Y_{2,T}, \ldots, Y_{T,T}\}$. The array is said to be an $L^1$-mixingale with respect to an information set $\Omega_{t,T}$ that includes $\{Y_{1,T}, Y_{2,T}, \ldots, Y_{T,T}\}$ if there exist nonnegative constants $\xi_m$ and $c_{t,T}$ such that $\lim_{m\to\infty} \xi_m = 0$ and

$$E|E(Y_{t,T}|\Omega_{t-m,T})| \leq c_{t,T}\xi_m$$

[8] Andrews replaced part (b) of the proposition with the weaker condition $\overline{\lim}_{T\to\infty} (1/T)\, \Sigma_{t=1}^{T} c_t < \infty$. See Royden (1968, p. 36) on the relation between "lim" and "$\overline{\lim}$."

for all $m \geq 0$, $T \geq 1$, and $t = 1, 2, \ldots, T$. If the array is uniformly integrable with $\lim_{T\to\infty} (1/T)\Sigma_{t=1}^{T} c_{t,T} < \infty$, then $(1/T)\Sigma_{t=1}^{T} Y_{t,T} \xrightarrow{p} 0$.

***Example 7.13***

Let $\{\varepsilon_t\}_{t=1}^{\infty}$ be a martingale difference sequence with $E|\varepsilon_t|^r < M'$ for some $r > 1$ and $M' < \infty$, and define $Y_{t,T} \equiv (t/T)\varepsilon_t$. Then the array $\{Y_{t,T}\}$ is a uniformly integrable $L^1$-mixingale with $c_{t,T} = M$, where $M$ denotes the maximal value for $E|\varepsilon_t|$, $\xi_0 = 1$, and $\xi_m = 0$ for $m > 0$. Hence, $(1/T)\Sigma_{t=1}^{T}(t/T)\varepsilon_t \xrightarrow{p} 0$.

## *Consistent Estimation of Second Moments*

Next consider the conditions under which

$$(1/T) \sum_{t=1}^{T} Y_t Y_{t-k} \xrightarrow{p} E(Y_t Y_{t-k})$$

(for notational simplicity, we assume here that the sample consists of $T + k$ observations on $Y$). Suppose that $Y_t = \Sigma_{j=0}^{\infty}\psi_j\varepsilon_{t-j}$, where $\Sigma_{j=0}^{\infty}|\psi_j| < \infty$ and $\{\varepsilon_t\}$ is an i.i.d. sequence with $E|\varepsilon_t|^r < \infty$ for some $r > 2$. Note that the population second moment can be written[9]

$$\begin{aligned} E(Y_t Y_{t-k}) &= E\left(\sum_{u=0}^{\infty} \psi_u \varepsilon_{t-u}\right)\left(\sum_{v=0}^{\infty} \psi_v \varepsilon_{t-k-v}\right) \\ &= E\left(\sum_{u=0}^{\infty}\sum_{v=0}^{\infty} \psi_u\psi_v \varepsilon_{t-u}\varepsilon_{t-k-v}\right) \\ &= \sum_{u=0}^{\infty}\sum_{v=0}^{\infty} \psi_u\psi_v E(\varepsilon_{t-u}\varepsilon_{t-k-v}). \end{aligned} \qquad [7.2.13]$$

Define $X_{t,k}$ to be the following random variable:

$$\begin{aligned} X_{t,k} &\equiv Y_t Y_{t-k} - E(Y_t Y_{t-k}) \\ &= \left(\sum_{u=0}^{\infty}\sum_{v=0}^{\infty} \psi_u\psi_v \varepsilon_{t-u}\varepsilon_{t-k-v}\right) - \left(\sum_{u=0}^{\infty}\sum_{v=0}^{\infty} \psi_u\psi_v E(\varepsilon_{t-u}\varepsilon_{t-k-v})\right) \\ &= \sum_{u=0}^{\infty}\sum_{v=0}^{\infty} \psi_u\psi_v [\varepsilon_{t-u}\varepsilon_{t-k-v} - E(\varepsilon_{t-u}\varepsilon_{t-k-v})]. \end{aligned}$$

Consider a forecast of $X_{t,k}$ on the basis of $\Omega_{t-m} \equiv \{\varepsilon_{t-m}, \varepsilon_{t-m-1}, \ldots\}$ for $m > k$:

$$E(X_{t,k}|\Omega_{t-m}) = \sum_{u=m}^{\infty}\sum_{v=m-k}^{\infty} \psi_u\psi_v [\varepsilon_{t-u}\varepsilon_{t-k-v} - E(\varepsilon_{t-u}\varepsilon_{t-k-v})].$$

[9]Notice that

$$\sum_{u=0}^{\infty}\sum_{v=0}^{\infty} |\psi_u\psi_v| = \sum_{u=0}^{\infty} |\psi_u| \sum_{v=0}^{\infty} |\psi_v| < \infty$$

and $E|\varepsilon_{t-u}\varepsilon_{t-k-v}| < \infty$, permitting us to move the expectation operator inside the summation signs in the last line of [7.2.13].

The expected absolute value of this forecast is bounded by

$$\begin{aligned}
E\left|E(X_{t,k}|\Omega_{t-m})\right| &= E\left|\sum_{u=m}^{\infty}\sum_{v=m-k}^{\infty}\psi_u\psi_v[\varepsilon_{t-u}\varepsilon_{t-k-v} - E(\varepsilon_{t-u}\varepsilon_{t-k-v})]\right| \\
&\le E\left(\sum_{u=m}^{\infty}\sum_{v=m-k}^{\infty}|\psi_u\psi_v|\cdot|\varepsilon_{t-u}\varepsilon_{t-k-v} - E(\varepsilon_{t-u}\varepsilon_{t-k-v})|\right) \\
&\le \sum_{u=m}^{\infty}\sum_{v=m-k}^{\infty}|\psi_u\psi_v|\cdot M
\end{aligned}$$

for some $M < \infty$. Define

$$\xi_m \equiv \sum_{u=m}^{\infty}\sum_{v=m-k}^{\infty}|\psi_u\psi_v| = \sum_{u=m}^{\infty}|\psi_u|\sum_{v=m-k}^{\infty}|\psi_v|.$$

Since $\{\psi_j\}_{j=0}^{\infty}$ is absolutely summable, $\lim_{m\to\infty}\Sigma_{u=m}^{\infty}|\psi_u| = 0$ and $\lim_{m\to\infty}\xi_m = 0$. It follows that $X_{t,k}$ is an $L^1$-mixingale with respect to $\Omega_t$ with coefficient $c_t = M$. Moreover, $X_{t,k}$ is uniformly integrable, from a simple adaptation of the argument in Proposition 7.7(b) (see Exercise 7.5). Hence,

$$(1/T)\sum_{t=1}^{T}X_{t,k} = (1/T)\sum_{t=1}^{T}[Y_tY_{t-k} - E(Y_tY_{t-k})] \xrightarrow{p} 0,$$

from which

$$(1/T)\sum_{t=1}^{T}Y_tY_{t-k} \xrightarrow{p} E(Y_tY_{t-k}). \qquad [7.2.14]$$

It is straightforward to deduce from [7.2.14] that the $j$th sample autocovariance for a sample of size $T$ gives a consistent estimate of the population autocovariance,

$$(1/T)\sum_{t=k+1}^{T}(Y_t - \bar{Y}_T)(Y_{t-k} - \bar{Y}_T) \xrightarrow{p} E(Y_t - \mu)(Y_{t-k} - \mu), \qquad [7.2.15]$$

where $\bar{Y}_T = (1/T)\Sigma_{t=1}^{T}Y_t$; see Exercise 7.6.

### *Central Limit Theorem for a Martingale Difference Sequence*

Next we consider the asymptotic distribution of $\sqrt{T}$ times the sample mean. The following version of the central limit theorem can often be applied.

***Proposition 7.8:*** *(White, 1984, Corollary 5.25, p. 130). Let $\{Y_t\}_{t=1}^{\infty}$ be a scalar martingale difference sequence with $\bar{Y}_T = (1/T)\Sigma_{t=1}^{T}Y_t$. Suppose that (a) $E(Y_t^2) = \sigma_t^2 > 0$ with $(1/T)\Sigma_{t=1}^{T}\sigma_t^2 \to \sigma^2 > 0$, (b) $E|Y_t|^r < \infty$ for some $r > 2$ and all t, and (c) $(1/T)\Sigma_{t=1}^{T}Y_t^2 \xrightarrow{p} \sigma^2$. Then $\sqrt{T}\,\bar{Y}_T \xrightarrow{L} N(0, \sigma^2)$.*

Again, Proposition 7.8 can be extended to arrays $\{Y_{t,T}\}$ as follows. Let $\{Y_{t,T}\}_{t=1}^{T}$ be a martingale difference sequence with $E(Y_{t,T}^2) = \sigma_{t,T}^2 > 0$. Let $\{Y_{t,T+1}\}_{t=1}^{T+1}$ be a potentially different martingale difference sequence with $E(Y_{t,T+1}^2) = \sigma_{t,T+1}^2 > 0$. If (a) $(1/T)\Sigma_{t=1}^{T}\sigma_{t,T}^2 \to \sigma^2$, (b) $E|Y_{t,T}|^r < \infty$ for some $r > 2$ and all $t$ and $T$, and (c) $(1/T)\Sigma_{t=1}^{T}Y_{t,T}^2 \xrightarrow{p} \sigma^2$, then $\sqrt{T}\,\bar{Y}_T \xrightarrow{L} N(0, \sigma^2)$.

Proposition 7.8 also readily generalizes to vector martingale difference sequences.

***Proposition 7.9:*** *Let $\{\mathbf{Y}_t\}_{t=1}^{\infty}$ be an n-dimensional vector martingale difference sequence with $\bar{\mathbf{Y}}_T = (1/T)\Sigma_{t=1}^{T}\mathbf{Y}_t$. Suppose that (a) $E(\mathbf{Y}_t\mathbf{Y}_t') = \mathbf{\Omega}_t$, a positive definite matrix with $(1/T)\Sigma_{t=1}^{T}\mathbf{\Omega}_t \to \mathbf{\Omega}$, a positive definite matrix; (b) $E(Y_{it}Y_{jt}Y_{lt}Y_{mt}) < \infty$ for all t and all i, j, l, and m (including $i = j = l = m$), where $Y_{it}$ is the ith element of the vector $\mathbf{Y}_t$; and (c) $(1/T)\Sigma_{t=1}^{T}\mathbf{Y}_t\mathbf{Y}_t' \xrightarrow{p} \mathbf{\Omega}$. Then $\sqrt{T}\,\bar{\mathbf{Y}}_T \xrightarrow{L} N(\mathbf{0}, \mathbf{\Omega})$.*

Again, Proposition 7.9 holds for arrays $\{\mathbf{Y}_{t,T}\}_{t=1}^{T}$ satisfying the stated conditions.

To apply Proposition 7.9, we will often need to assume that a certain process has finite fourth moments. The following result can be useful for this purpose.

***Proposition 7.10:*** *Let $X_t$ be a strictly stationary stochastic process with $E(X_t^4) = \mu_4 < \infty$. Let $Y_t = \Sigma_{j=0}^{\infty}h_jX_{t-j}$, where $\Sigma_{j=0}^{\infty}|h_j| < \infty$. Then $Y_t$ is a strictly stationary stochastic process with $E|Y_tY_sY_uY_v| < \infty$ for all t, s, u, and v.*

### *Example 7.14*

Let $Y_t = \phi_1Y_{t-1} + \phi_2Y_{t-2} + \cdots + \phi_pY_{t-p} + \varepsilon_t$, where $\{\varepsilon_t\}$ is an i.i.d. sequence and where roots of $(1 - \phi_1z - \phi_2z^2 - \cdots - \phi_pz^p) = 0$ lie outside the unit circle. We saw in Chapter 3 that $Y_t$ can be written as $\Sigma_{j=0}^{\infty}\psi_j\varepsilon_{t-j}$ with $\Sigma_{j=0}^{\infty}|\psi_j| < \infty$. Proposition 7.10 states that if $\varepsilon_t$ has finite fourth moments, then so does $Y_t$.

### *Example 7.15*

Let $Y_t = \Sigma_{j=0}^{\infty}\psi_j\varepsilon_{t-j}$ with $\Sigma_{j=0}^{\infty}|\psi_j| < \infty$ and $\varepsilon_t$ i.i.d. with $E(\varepsilon_t) = 0$, $E(\varepsilon_t^2) = \sigma^2$, and $E(\varepsilon_t^4) < \infty$. Consider the random variable $X_t$ defined by $X_t \equiv \varepsilon_tY_{t-k}$ for $k > 0$. Then $X_t$ is a martingale difference sequence with variance $E(X_t^2) = \sigma^2\cdot E(Y_t^2)$ and with fourth moment $E(\varepsilon_t^4)\cdot E(Y_t^4) < \infty$, by Example 7.14. Hence, if we can show that

$$(1/T)\sum_{t=1}^{T} X_t^2 \xrightarrow{p} E(X_t^2), \qquad [7.2.16]$$

then Proposition 7.8 can be applied to deduce that

$$(1/\sqrt{T})\sum_{t=1}^{T} X_t \xrightarrow{L} N\Big(0,\ E(X_t^2)\Big)$$

or

$$(1/\sqrt{T})\sum_{t=1}^{T} \varepsilon_tY_{t-k} \xrightarrow{L} N\Big(0,\ \sigma^2\cdot E(Y_t^2)\Big). \qquad [7.2.17]$$

To verify [7.2.16], notice that

$$\begin{aligned}(1/T)\sum_{t=1}^{T} X_t^2 &= (1/T)\sum_{t=1}^{T} \varepsilon_t^2Y_{t-k}^2 \\ &= (1/T)\sum_{t=1}^{T}(\varepsilon_t^2 - \sigma^2)Y_{t-k}^2 + (1/T)\sum_{t=1}^{T}\sigma^2Y_{t-k}^2.\end{aligned} \qquad [7.2.18]$$

But $(\varepsilon_t^2 - \sigma^2)Y_{t-k}^2$ is a martingale difference sequence with finite second moment, so, from Example 7.11,

$$(1/T)\sum_{t=1}^{T}(\varepsilon_t^2 - \sigma^2)Y_{t-k}^2 \xrightarrow{p} 0.$$

It further follows from result [7.2.14] that

$$(1/T)\sum_{t=1}^{T}\sigma^2 Y_{t-k}^2 \xrightarrow{p} \sigma^2\cdot E(Y_t^2).$$

Thus, [7.2.18] implies

$$(1/T)\sum_{t=1}^{T} X_t^2 \xrightarrow{p} \sigma^2\cdot E(Y_t^2),$$

as claimed in [7.2.16].

## *Central Limit Theorem for Stationary Stochastic Processes*

We now present a central limit theorem for a serially correlated sequence. Recall from Proposition 7.5 that the sample mean has asymptotic variance given by $(1/T)\Sigma_{j=-\infty}^{\infty}\gamma_j$. Thus, we would expect the central limit theorem to take the form $\sqrt{T}(\bar{Y}_T - \mu) \xrightarrow{L} N(0, \Sigma_{j=-\infty}^{\infty}\gamma_j)$. The next proposition gives a result of this type.

***Proposition 7.11:*** *(Anderson, 1971, p. 429). Let*

$$Y_t = \mu + \sum_{j=0}^{\infty}\psi_j\varepsilon_{t-j},$$

*where $\{\varepsilon_t\}$ is a sequence of i.i.d. random variables with $E(\varepsilon_t^2) < \infty$ and $\Sigma_{j=0}^{\infty}|\psi_j| < \infty$. Then*

$$\sqrt{T}(\bar{Y}_T - \mu) \xrightarrow{L} N(0, \sum_{j=-\infty}^{\infty}\gamma_j). \qquad [7.2.19]$$

A version of [7.2.19] can also be developed for $\{\varepsilon_t\}$ a martingale difference sequence satisfying certain restrictions; see Phillips and Solo (1992).

## APPENDIX 7.A. *Proofs of Chapter 7 Propositions*

■ **Proof of Proposition 7.1.** Let $g_j(\mathbf{c})$ denote the $j$th element of $\mathbf{g}(\mathbf{c})$, $g_j$: $\mathbb{R}^n \to \mathbb{R}^1$. We need to show that for any $\delta > 0$ and $\varepsilon > 0$ there exists an $N$ such that for all $T \geq N$,

$$P\{|g_j(\mathbf{X}_T) - g_j(\mathbf{c})| > \delta\} < \varepsilon. \qquad [7.A.1]$$

Continuity of $g_j(\cdot)$ implies that there exists an $\eta$ such that $|g_j(\mathbf{X}_T) - g_j(\mathbf{c})| > \delta$ only if

$$[(X_{1T} - c_1)^2 + (X_{2T} - c_2)^2 + \cdots + (X_{nT} - c_n)^2] > \eta^2. \qquad [7.A.2]$$

This would be the case only if $(X_{iT} - c_i)^2 > \eta^2/n$ for some $i$. But from the fact that plim $X_{iT} = c_i$, for any $i$ and specified values of $\varepsilon$ and $\eta$ we can find a value of $N$ such that

$$P\{|X_{iT} - c_i| > \eta/\sqrt{n}\} < \varepsilon/n$$

for all $T \geq N$.

Recall the elementary addition rule for the probability of any events $A$ and $B$,

$$P\{A \text{ or } B\} \leq P\{A\} + P\{B\},$$

from which it follows that

$$P\{(|X_{1T} - c_1| > \eta/\sqrt{n}) \text{ or } (|X_{2T} - c_2| > \eta/\sqrt{n}) \text{ or } \cdots \text{ or } (|X_{nT} - c_n| > \eta/\sqrt{n})\}$$
$$< (\varepsilon/n) + (\varepsilon/n) + \cdots + (\varepsilon/n).$$

Hence,

$$P\{[(X_{1T} - c_1)^2 + (X_{2T} - c_2)^2 + \cdots + (X_{nT} - c_n)^2] > \eta^2\} < \varepsilon$$

for all $T \geq N$. Since [7.A.2] was a necessary condition for $|g_j(\mathbf{X}_T) - g_j(\mathbf{c})|$ to be greater than $\delta$, it follows that the probability that $|g_j(\mathbf{X}_T) - g_j(\mathbf{c})|$ is greater than $\delta$ is less than $\varepsilon$, which was to be shown. ■

■ **Proof of Proposition 7.2.** Let $S$ denote the set of all $x$ such that $|x - c| > \delta$, and let $\tilde{S}$ denote its complement (all $x$ such that $|x - c| \leq \delta$). Then, for $f_X(x)$ the density of $x$,

$$\begin{aligned} E|X - c|^r &= \int |x - c|^r f_X(x)\, dx \\ &= \int_S |x - c|^r f_X(x)\, dx + \int_{\tilde{S}} |x - c|^r f_X(x)\, dx \\ &\geq \int_S |x - c|^r f_X(x)\, dx \\ &\geq \int_S \delta^r f_X(x)\, dx \\ &= \delta^r P\{|X - c| > \delta\}, \end{aligned}$$

so that

$$E|X - c|^r \geq \delta^r P\{|X - c| > \delta\},$$

as claimed. ■

■ **Proof of Proposition 7.4.** Consider any real $(m \times 1)$ vector $\boldsymbol{\lambda}$, and form the function $h\colon \mathbb{R}^n \to \mathbb{R}^1$ defined by $h(\mathbf{x}) \equiv \boldsymbol{\lambda}'\mathbf{g}(\mathbf{x})$, noting that $h(\cdot)$ is differentiable. The *mean-value theorem* states that for a differentiable function $h(\cdot)$, there exists an $(n \times 1)$ vector $\mathbf{c}_T$ between $\mathbf{X}_T$ and $\mathbf{c}$ such that[10]

$$h(\mathbf{X}_T) - h(\mathbf{c}) = \left.\frac{\partial h(\mathbf{x})}{\partial \mathbf{x}'}\right|_{\mathbf{x}=\mathbf{c}_T} \times (\mathbf{X}_T - \mathbf{c})$$

and therefore

$$\sqrt{T}\,[h(\mathbf{X}_T) - h(\mathbf{c})] = \left.\frac{\partial h(\mathbf{x})}{\partial \mathbf{x}'}\right|_{\mathbf{x}=\mathbf{c}_T} \times \sqrt{T}(\mathbf{X}_T - \mathbf{c}). \qquad [7.A.3]$$

Since $\mathbf{c}_T$ is between $\mathbf{X}_T$ and $\mathbf{c}$ and since $\mathbf{X}_T \xrightarrow{p} \mathbf{c}$, we know that $\mathbf{c}_T \xrightarrow{p} \mathbf{c}$. Moreover, the derivative $\partial h(\mathbf{x})/\partial \mathbf{x}'$ is itself a continuous function of $\mathbf{x}$. Thus, from Proposition 7.1,

$$\left.\frac{\partial h(\mathbf{x})}{\partial \mathbf{x}'}\right|_{\mathbf{x}=\mathbf{c}_T} \xrightarrow{p} \left.\frac{\partial h(\mathbf{x})}{\partial \mathbf{x}'}\right|_{\mathbf{x}=\mathbf{c}}.$$

Given that $\sqrt{T}(\mathbf{X}_T - \mathbf{c}) \xrightarrow{L} \mathbf{X}$, Proposition 7.3(b) applied to expression [7.A.3] gives

$$\sqrt{T}\,[h(\mathbf{X}_T) - h(\mathbf{c})] \xrightarrow{L} \left.\frac{\partial h(\mathbf{x})}{\partial \mathbf{x}'}\right|_{\mathbf{x}=\mathbf{c}} \mathbf{X},$$

or, in terms of the original function $\mathbf{g}(\cdot)$,

$$\boldsymbol{\lambda}'\{\sqrt{T}\,[\mathbf{g}(\mathbf{X}_T) - \mathbf{g}(\mathbf{c})]\} \xrightarrow{L} \boldsymbol{\lambda}' \left.\frac{\partial \mathbf{g}(\mathbf{x})}{\partial \mathbf{x}'}\right|_{\mathbf{x}=\mathbf{c}} \mathbf{X}.$$

Since this is true for any $\boldsymbol{\lambda}$, we conclude that

$$\sqrt{T}\,[\mathbf{g}(\mathbf{X}_T) - \mathbf{g}(\mathbf{c})] \xrightarrow{L} \left.\frac{\partial \mathbf{g}(\mathbf{x})}{\partial \mathbf{x}'}\right|_{\mathbf{x}=\mathbf{c}} \mathbf{X},$$

as claimed. ■

[10]That is, for any given $\mathbf{X}_T$ there exists a scalar $\mu_T$ with $0 \leq \mu_T \leq 1$ such that $\mathbf{c}_T = \mu_T \mathbf{X}_T + (1 - \mu_T)\mathbf{c}$. See, for example, Marsden (1974, pp. 174–75).

■ **Proof of Proposition 7.7.** Part (a) is established as in Andrews (1988, p. 463) using *Hölder's inequality* (see, for example, White, 1984, p. 30), which states that for $r > 1$, if $E[|Y|^r] < \infty$ and $E[|W|^{r/(r-1)}] < \infty$, then

$$E|YW| \leq \{E[|Y|^r]\}^{1/r} \times \{E[|W|^{r/(r-1)}]\}^{(r-1)/r}.$$

This implies that

$$E(|Y_t|\cdot\delta_{[|Y_t|\geq c]}) \leq \{E[|Y_t|^r]\}^{1/r} \times \{E[(\delta_{[|Y_t|\geq c]})^{r/(r-1)}]\}^{(r-1)/r}. \qquad [7.A.4]$$

Since $\delta_{[|Y_t|\geq c]}$ is either 0 or 1, it follows that

$$(\delta_{[|Y_t|\geq c]})^{r/(r-1)} = \delta_{[|Y_t|\geq c]}$$

and so

$$E[(\delta_{[|Y_t|\geq c]})^{r/(r-1)}] = E[\delta_{[|Y_t|\geq c]}] = \int_{|Y_t|\geq c} 1\cdot f_{Y_t}(y_t)\, dy_t = P\{|Y_t| \geq c\} \leq \frac{E|Y_t|}{c}, \qquad [7.A.5]$$

where the last result follows from Chebyshev's inequality. Substituting [7.A.5] into [7.A.4],

$$E(|Y_t|\cdot\delta_{[|Y_t|\geq c]}) \leq \{E[|Y_t|^r]\}^{1/r} \times \left\{\frac{E|Y_t|}{c}\right\}^{(r-1)/r}. \qquad [7.A.6]$$

Recall that $E[|Y_t|^r] < M'$ for all $t$, implying that there also exists an $M < \infty$ such that $E|Y_t| < M$ for all $t$. Hence,

$$E(|Y_t|\cdot\delta_{[|Y_t|\geq c]}) \leq (M')^{1/r} \times (M/c)^{(r-1)/r}.$$

This expression can be made as small as desired by choosing $c$ sufficiently large. Thus condition [7.2.12] holds, ensuring that $\{Y_t]$ is uniformly integrable.

To establish (b), notice that

$$E(|Y_t|\cdot\delta_{[|Y_t|\geq c]}) = E\left|\sum_{j=-\infty}^{\infty} h_j X_{t-j}\cdot\delta_{[|Y_t|\geq c]}\right| \leq E\left\{\sum_{j=-\infty}^{\infty} |h_j|\cdot|X_{t-j}|\cdot\delta_{[|Y_t|\geq c]}\right\}. \qquad [7.A.7]$$

Since $E[|X_{t-j}|^r] < M'$ and since $\delta_{[|Y_t|\geq c]} \leq 1$, it follows that $E\{|X_{t-j}|\cdot\delta_{[|Y_t|\geq c]}\}$ is bounded. Since $\{h_j\}_{j=-\infty}^{\infty}$ is absolutely summable, we can bring the expectation operator inside the summation in the last expression of [7.A.7] to deduce that

$$\begin{aligned} E\left\{\sum_{j=-\infty}^{\infty} |h_j|\cdot|X_{t-j}|\cdot\delta_{[|Y_t|\geq c]}\right\} &= \sum_{j=-\infty}^{\infty} |h_j|\cdot E\{|X_{t-j}|\cdot\delta_{[|Y_t|\geq c]}\} \\ &\leq \sum_{j=-\infty}^{\infty} |h_j|\cdot\{E[|X_{t-j}|^r]\}^{1/r} \times \left\{\frac{E|Y_t|}{c}\right\}^{(r-1)/r}, \end{aligned}$$

where the last inequality follows from the same arguments as in [7.A.6]. Hence, [7.A.7] becomes

$$E(|Y_t|\cdot\delta_{[|Y_t|\geq c]}) \leq \sum_{j=-\infty}^{\infty} |h_j| \times (M')^{1/r} \times \left\{\frac{E|Y_t|}{c}\right\}^{(r-1)/r}. \qquad [7.A.8]$$

But certainly, $E|Y_t|$ is bounded:

$$E|Y_t| = E\left|\sum_{j=-\infty}^{\infty} h_j X_{t-j}\right| \leq \sum_{j=-\infty}^{\infty} |h_j|\cdot E|X_{t-j}| = K < \infty.$$

Thus, from [7.A.8],

$$E(|Y_t|\cdot\delta_{[|Y_t|\geq c]}) \leq (M')^{1/r}(K/c)^{(r-1)/r} \sum_{j=-\infty}^{\infty} |h_j|. \qquad [7.A.9]$$

Since $\Sigma_{j=-\infty}^{\infty}|h_j|$ is finite, [7.A.9] can again be made as small as desired by choosing $c$ sufficiently large. ■

■ **Proof of Proposition 7.9.** Consider $Y_t \equiv \boldsymbol{\lambda}'\mathbf{Y}_t$ for $\boldsymbol{\lambda}$ any real $(n \times 1)$ vector. Then $Y_t$ is a martingale difference sequence. We next verify that each of the conditions of Proposition

7.8 is satisfied. (a) $E(Y_t^2) = \boldsymbol{\lambda}'\boldsymbol{\Omega}_t\boldsymbol{\lambda} \equiv \sigma_t^2 > 0$, by positive definiteness of $\boldsymbol{\Omega}_t$. Likewise,

$$(1/T)\sum_{t=1}^{T}\sigma_t^2 = \boldsymbol{\lambda}'(1/T)\sum_{t=1}^{T}\boldsymbol{\Omega}_t\boldsymbol{\lambda} \to \boldsymbol{\lambda}'\boldsymbol{\Omega}\boldsymbol{\lambda} \equiv \sigma^2,$$

with $\sigma^2 > 0$, by positive definiteness of $\boldsymbol{\Omega}$. (b) $E(Y_t^4)$ is a finite sum of terms of the form $\lambda_i\lambda_j\lambda_l\lambda_m E(Y_{it}Y_{jt}Y_{lt}Y_{mt})$ and so is bounded for all $t$ by condition (b) of Proposition 7.9; hence, $Y_t$ satisfies condition (b) of Proposition 7.8 for $r = 4$. (c) Define $S_T \equiv (1/T) \times \Sigma_{t=1}^{T} Y_t^2$ and $\mathbf{S}_T \equiv (1/T)\Sigma_{t=1}^{T}\mathbf{Y}_t\mathbf{Y}_t'$, noticing that $S_T = \boldsymbol{\lambda}'\mathbf{S}_T\boldsymbol{\lambda}$. Since $S_T$ is a continuous function of $\mathbf{S}_T$, we know that plim $S_T = \boldsymbol{\lambda}'\boldsymbol{\Omega}\boldsymbol{\lambda} \equiv \sigma^2$, where $\boldsymbol{\Omega}$ is given as the plim of $\mathbf{S}_T$. Thus $Y_t$ satisfies conditions (a) through (c) of Proposition 7.8, and so $\sqrt{T}\,\bar{Y}_T \xrightarrow{L} N(0, \sigma^2)$, or $\sqrt{T}\,\bar{Y}_T \xrightarrow{L} \boldsymbol{\lambda}'\mathbf{Y}$, where $\mathbf{Y} \sim (\mathbf{0}, \boldsymbol{\Omega})$. Since this is true for any $\boldsymbol{\lambda}$, this confirms the claim that $\sqrt{T}\,\bar{\mathbf{Y}}_T \xrightarrow{L} N(\mathbf{0}, \boldsymbol{\Omega})$. ■

■ **Proof of Proposition 7.10.** Let $Y \equiv X_tX_s$ and $W \equiv X_uX_v$. Then Hölder's inequality implies that for $r > 1$,

$$E|X_tX_sX_uX_v| \le \{E|X_tX_s|^r\}^{1/r} \times \{E|X_uX_v|^{r/(r-1)}\}^{(r-1)/r}.$$

For $r = 2$, this means

$$E|X_tX_sX_uX_v| \le \{E(X_tX_s)^2\}^{1/2} \times \{E(X_uX_v)^2\}^{1/2} \le \max\{E(X_tX_s)^2, E(X_uX_v)^2\}.$$

A second application of Hölder's inequality with $Y \equiv X_t^2$ and $W \equiv X_s^2$ reveals that

$$E(X_tX_s)^2 = E(X_t^2X_s^2) \le \{E(X_t^2)^r\}^{1/r} \times \{E(X_s^2)^{r/(r-1)}\}^{(r-1)/r}.$$

Again for $r = 2$, this implies from the strict stationarity of $\{X_t\}$ that

$$E(X_tX_s)^2 \le E(X_t^4).$$

Hence, if $\{X_t\}$ is strictly stationary with finite fourth moment, then

$$E|X_tX_sX_uX_v| \le E(X_t^4) = \mu_4$$

for all $t$, $s$, $u$, and $v$.

Observe further that

$$\begin{aligned} E|Y_tY_sY_uY_v| &= E\left|\sum_{i=0}^{\infty} h_iX_{t-i}\sum_{j=0}^{\infty} h_jX_{s-j}\sum_{l=0}^{\infty} h_lX_{u-l}\sum_{m=0}^{\infty} h_mX_{v-m}\right| \\ &= E\left|\sum_{i=0}^{\infty}\sum_{j=0}^{\infty}\sum_{l=0}^{\infty}\sum_{m=0}^{\infty} h_ih_jh_lh_mX_{t-i}X_{s-j}X_{u-l}X_{v-m}\right| \\ &\le E\left\{\sum_{i=0}^{\infty}\sum_{j=0}^{\infty}\sum_{l=0}^{\infty}\sum_{m=0}^{\infty} |h_ih_jh_lh_m|\cdot|X_{t-i}X_{s-j}X_{u-l}X_{v-m}|\right\}. \end{aligned}$$

But

$$\begin{aligned} \sum_{i=0}^{\infty}\sum_{j=0}^{\infty}\sum_{l=0}^{\infty}\sum_{m=0}^{\infty} |h_ih_jh_lh_m| &= \sum_{i=0}^{\infty}|h_i|\sum_{j=0}^{\infty}|h_j|\sum_{l=0}^{\infty}|h_l|\sum_{m=0}^{\infty}|h_m| \\ &< \infty \end{aligned}$$

and

$$E|X_{t-i}X_{s-j}X_{u-l}X_{v-m}| < \mu_4$$

for any value of any of the indices. Hence,

$$\begin{aligned} E|Y_tY_sY_uY_v| &< \sum_{i=0}^{\infty}\sum_{j=0}^{\infty}\sum_{l=0}^{\infty}\sum_{m=0}^{\infty} |h_ih_jh_lh_m|\cdot\mu_4 \\ &< \infty. \end{aligned}$$ ■

## *Chapter 7 Exercises*

7.1. Let $\{X_T\}$ denote a sequence of random scalars with plim $X_T = \xi$. Let $\{c_T\}$ denote a sequence of deterministic scalars with $\lim_{T\to\infty} c_T = c$. Let $g$: $\mathbb{R}^2 \to \mathbb{R}^1$ be continuous at $(\xi, c)$. Show that $g(X_T, c_T) \xrightarrow{p} g(\xi, c)$.

7.2. Let $Y_t = 0.8Y_{t-1} + \varepsilon_t$ with $E(\varepsilon_t \varepsilon_\tau) = 1$ for $t = \tau$ and zero otherwise.

(a) Calculate $\lim_{T\to\infty} T\cdot\text{Var}(\bar{Y}_T)$.

(b) How large a sample would we need in order to have 95% confidence that $\bar{Y}_T$ differed from the true value zero by no more than 0.1?

7.3. Does a martingale difference sequence have to be covariance-stationary?

7.4. Let $Y_t = \Sigma_{j=0}^{\infty}\psi_j\varepsilon_{t-j}$, where $\Sigma_{j=0}^{\infty}|\psi_j| < \infty$ and $\{\varepsilon_t\}$ is a martingale difference sequence with $E(\varepsilon_t^2) = \sigma^2$. Is $Y_t$ covariance-stationary?

7.5. Define $X_{t,k} \equiv \Sigma_{u=0}^{\infty}\Sigma_{v=0}^{\infty}\psi_u\psi_v[\varepsilon_{t-u}\varepsilon_{t-k-v} - E(\varepsilon_{t-u}\varepsilon_{t-k-v})]$, where $\varepsilon_t$ is an i.i.d. sequence with $E|\varepsilon_t|^r < M''$ for some $r > 2$ and $M'' < \infty$ with $\Sigma_{j=0}^{\infty}|\psi_j| < \infty$. Show that $X_{t,k}$ is uniformly integrable.

7.6. Derive result [7.2.15].

7.7. Let $Y_t$ follow an $ARMA(p, q)$ process,

$$(1 - \phi_1 L - \phi_2 L^2 - \cdots - \phi_p L^p)(Y_t - \mu) = (1 + \theta_1 L + \theta_2 L^2 + \cdots + \theta_q L^q)\varepsilon_t,$$

with roots of $(1 - \phi_1 z - \phi_2 z^2 - \cdots - \phi_p z^p) = 0$ and $(1 + \theta_1 z + \theta_2 z^2 + \cdots + \theta_q z^q) = 0$ outside the unit circle. Suppose $\varepsilon_t$ has mean zero and is independent of $\varepsilon_\tau$ for $t \neq \tau$ with $E(\varepsilon_t^2) = \sigma^2$ and $E(\varepsilon_t^4) < \infty$ for all $t$. Prove the following:

(a) $(1/T)\sum_{t=1}^{T} Y_t \xrightarrow{p} \mu$

(b) $[1/(T-k)]\sum_{t=k+1}^{T} Y_t Y_{t-k} \xrightarrow{p} E(Y_t Y_{t-k})$.

## Chapter 7 References


Anderson, T. W. 1971. *The Statistical Analysis of Time Series*. New York: Wiley.

Andrews, Donald W. K. 1988. "Laws of Large Numbers for Dependent Non-Identically Distributed Random Variables." *Econometric Theory* 4:458–67.

Hoel, Paul G., Sidney C. Port, and Charles J. Stone. 1971. *Introduction to Probability Theory*. Boston: Houghton Mifflin.

Marsden, Jerrold E. 1974. *Elementary Classical Analysis*. San Francisco: Freeman.

Phillips, Peter C. B., and Victor Solo. 1992. "Asymptotics for Linear Processes." *Annals of Statistics* 20:971–1001.

Rao, C. Radhakrishna. 1973. *Linear Statistical Inference and Its Applications*, 2d ed. New York: Wiley.

Royden, H. L. 1968. *Real Analysis*, 2d ed. New York: Macmillan.

Theil, Henri. 1971. *Principles of Econometrics*. New York: Wiley.

White, Halbert. 1984. *Asymptotic Theory for Econometricians*. Orlando, Fla.: Academic Press.

# 8 Linear Regression Models

We have seen that one convenient way to estimate the parameters of an autoregression is with ordinary least squares regression, an estimation technique that is also useful for a number of other models. This chapter reviews the properties of linear regression. Section 8.1 analyzes the simplest case, in which the explanatory variables are nonrandom and the disturbances are i.i.d. Gaussian. Section 8.2 develops analogous results for ordinary least squares estimation of more general models such as autoregressions and regressions in which the disturbances are non-Gaussian, heteroskedastic, or autocorrelated. Linear regression models can also be estimated by generalized least squares, which is described in Section 8.3.

## 8.1. *Review of Ordinary Least Squares with Deterministic Regressors and i.i.d. Gaussian Disturbances*

Suppose that a scalar $y_t$ is related to a $(k \times 1)$ vector $\mathbf{x}_t$ and a disturbance term $u_t$ according to the regression model

$$y_t = \mathbf{x}_t'\boldsymbol{\beta} + u_t. \qquad [8.1.1]$$

This relation could be used to describe either the random variables or their realization. In discussing regression models, it proves cumbersome to distinguish notationally between random variables and their realization, and standard practice is to use small letters for either.

This section reviews estimation and hypothesis tests about $\boldsymbol{\beta}$ under the assumptions that $\mathbf{x}_t$ is deterministic and $u_t$ is i.i.d. Gaussian. The next sections discuss regression under more general assumptions. First, however, we summarize the mechanics of linear regression and present some formulas that hold regardless of statistical assumptions.

### *The Algebra of Linear Regression*

Given an observed sample $(y_1, y_2, \ldots, y_T)$, the *ordinary least squares* (*OLS*) estimate of $\boldsymbol{\beta}$ (denoted $\mathbf{b}$) is the value of $\boldsymbol{\beta}$ that minimizes the residual sum of squares (*RSS*):

$$RSS \equiv \sum_{t=1}^{T} (y_t - \mathbf{x}_t'\boldsymbol{\beta})^2. \qquad [8.1.2]$$

We saw in Appendix 4.A to Chapter 4 that the *OLS* estimate is given by

$$\mathbf{b} = \left[\sum_{t=1}^{T} (\mathbf{x}_t\mathbf{x}_t')\right]^{-1}\left[\sum_{t=1}^{T} (\mathbf{x}_t y_t)\right], \tag{8.1.3}$$

assuming that the $(k \times k)$ matrix $\Sigma_{t=1}^{T}(\mathbf{x}_t\mathbf{x}_t')$ is nonsingular. The *OLS* sample residual for observation $t$ is

$$\hat{u}_t \equiv y_t - \mathbf{x}_t'\mathbf{b}. \tag{8.1.4}$$

Often the model in [8.1.1] is written in matrix notation as

$$\mathbf{y} = \mathbf{X}\boldsymbol{\beta} + \mathbf{u}, \tag{8.1.5}$$

where

$$\underset{(T\times 1)}{\mathbf{y}} \equiv \begin{bmatrix} y_1 \\ y_2 \\ \vdots \\ y_T \end{bmatrix} \qquad \underset{(T\times k)}{\mathbf{X}} \equiv \begin{bmatrix} \mathbf{x}_1' \\ \mathbf{x}_2' \\ \vdots \\ \mathbf{x}_T' \end{bmatrix} \qquad \underset{(T\times 1)}{\mathbf{u}} \equiv \begin{bmatrix} u_1 \\ u_2 \\ \vdots \\ u_T \end{bmatrix}.$$

Then the *OLS* estimate in [8.1.3] can be written as

$$\begin{aligned} \mathbf{b} &= \left\{ [\mathbf{x}_1 \quad \mathbf{x}_2 \cdots \mathbf{x}_T] \begin{bmatrix} \mathbf{x}_1' \\ \mathbf{x}_2' \\ \vdots \\ \mathbf{x}_T' \end{bmatrix} \right\}^{-1} \left\{ [\mathbf{x}_1 \quad \mathbf{x}_2 \cdots \mathbf{x}_T] \begin{bmatrix} y_1 \\ y_2 \\ \vdots \\ y_T \end{bmatrix} \right\} \\ &= (\mathbf{X}'\mathbf{X})^{-1}\mathbf{X}'\mathbf{y}. \end{aligned} \tag{8.1.6}$$

Similarly, the vector of *OLS* sample residuals [8.1.4] can be written as

$$\hat{\mathbf{u}} = \mathbf{y} - \mathbf{X}\mathbf{b} = \mathbf{y} - \mathbf{X}(\mathbf{X}'\mathbf{X})^{-1}\mathbf{X}'\mathbf{y} = [\mathbf{I}_T - \mathbf{X}(\mathbf{X}'\mathbf{X})^{-1}\mathbf{X}']\mathbf{y} = \mathbf{M}_\mathbf{X}\mathbf{y}, \tag{8.1.7}$$

where $\mathbf{M}_\mathbf{X}$ is defined as the following $(T \times T)$ matrix:

$$\mathbf{M}_\mathbf{X} \equiv \mathbf{I}_T - \mathbf{X}(\mathbf{X}'\mathbf{X})^{-1}\mathbf{X}'. \tag{8.1.8}$$

One can readily verify that $\mathbf{M}_\mathbf{X}$ is symmetric:

$$\mathbf{M}_\mathbf{X} = \mathbf{M}_\mathbf{X}';$$

idempotent:

$$\mathbf{M}_\mathbf{X}\mathbf{M}_\mathbf{X} = \mathbf{M}_\mathbf{X};$$

and orthogonal to the columns of $\mathbf{X}$:

$$\mathbf{M}_\mathbf{X}\mathbf{X} = \mathbf{0}. \tag{8.1.9}$$

Thus, from [8.1.7], the *OLS* sample residuals are orthogonal to the explanatory variables in $\mathbf{X}$:

$$\hat{\mathbf{u}}'\mathbf{X} = \mathbf{y}'\mathbf{M}_\mathbf{X}'\mathbf{X} = \mathbf{0}'. \tag{8.1.10}$$

The *OLS* sample residual $(\hat{u}_t)$ should be distinguished from the population residual $(u_t)$. The sample residual is constructed from the sample estimate $\mathbf{b}$ $(\hat{u}_t = y_t - \mathbf{x}_t'\mathbf{b})$, whereas the population residual is a hypothetical construct based on the true population value $\boldsymbol{\beta}$ $(u_t = y_t - \mathbf{x}_t'\boldsymbol{\beta})$. The relation between the sample and population residuals can be found by substituting [8.1.5] into [8.1.7]:

$$\hat{\mathbf{u}} = \mathbf{M_X}(\mathbf{X}\boldsymbol{\beta} + \mathbf{u}) = \mathbf{M_X u}. \qquad [8.1.11]$$

The difference between the *OLS* estimate **b** and the true population parameter **β** is found by substituting [8.1.5] into [8.1.6]:

$$\mathbf{b} = (\mathbf{X'X})^{-1}\mathbf{X'}[\mathbf{X}\boldsymbol{\beta} + \mathbf{u}] = \boldsymbol{\beta} + (\mathbf{X'X})^{-1}\mathbf{X'u}. \qquad [8.1.12]$$

The fit of an *OLS* regression is sometimes described in terms of the sample multiple correlation coefficient, or $R^2$. The *uncentered* $R^2$ (denoted $R_u^2$) is defined as the sum of squares of the fitted values ($\mathbf{x}_t'\mathbf{b}$) of the regression as a fraction of the sum of squares of $y$:

$$R_u^2 \equiv \frac{\sum_{t=1}^{T} (\mathbf{b}'\mathbf{x}_t\mathbf{x}_t'\mathbf{b})}{\sum_{t=1}^{T} y_t^2} = \frac{\mathbf{b'X'Xb}}{\mathbf{y'y}} = \frac{\mathbf{y'X(X'X)^{-1}X'y}}{\mathbf{y'y}}. \qquad [8.1.13]$$

If the only explanatory variable in the regression were a constant term ($\mathbf{x}_t = 1$), then the fitted value for each observation would just be the sample mean $\bar{y}$ and the sum of squares of the fitted values would be $T\bar{y}^2$. This sum of squares is often compared with the sum of squares when a vector of variables $\mathbf{x}_t$ is included in the regression. The *centered* $R^2$ (denoted $R_c^2$) is defined as

$$R_c^2 \equiv \frac{\mathbf{y'X(X'X)^{-1}X'y} - T\bar{y}^2}{\mathbf{y'y} - T\bar{y}^2}. \qquad [8.1.14]$$

Most regression software packages report the centered $R^2$ rather than the uncentered $R^2$. If the regression includes a constant term, then $R_c^2$ must be between zero and unity. However, if the regression does not include a constant term, then $R_c^2$ can be negative.

## *The Classical Regression Assumptions*

Statistical inference requires assumptions about the properties of the explanatory variables $\mathbf{x}_t$ and the population residuals $u_t$. The simplest case to analyze is the following.

***Assumption 8.1:*** (*a*) $\mathbf{x}_t$ *is a vector of deterministic variables (for example,* $\mathbf{x}_t$ *might include a constant term and deterministic functions of t); (b)* $u_t$ *is i.i.d. with mean* 0 *and variance* $\sigma^2$*; (c)* $u_t$ *is Gaussian.*

To highlight the role of each of these assumptions, we first note the implications of Assumption 8.1(a) and (b) alone and then comment on the added implications that follow from (c).

## *Properties of the Estimated* OLS *Coefficient Vector Under Assumption 8.1(a) and (b)*

In vector form, Assumption 8.1(b) could be written $E(\mathbf{u}) = \mathbf{0}$ and $E(\mathbf{uu}') = \sigma^2\mathbf{I}_T$.

Taking expectations of [8.1.12] and using these conditions establishes that **b** is unbiased,

$$E(\mathbf{b}) = \boldsymbol{\beta} + (\mathbf{X'X})^{-1}\mathbf{X'}[E(\mathbf{u})] = \boldsymbol{\beta}, \qquad [8.1.15]$$

with variance-covariance matrix given by

$$\begin{aligned}E[(\mathbf{b}-\boldsymbol{\beta})(\mathbf{b}-\boldsymbol{\beta})'] &= E[(\mathbf{X}'\mathbf{X})^{-1}\mathbf{X}'\mathbf{u}\mathbf{u}'\mathbf{X}(\mathbf{X}'\mathbf{X})^{-1}] \\ &= (\mathbf{X}'\mathbf{X})^{-1}\mathbf{X}'[E(\mathbf{u}\mathbf{u}')]\mathbf{X}(\mathbf{X}'\mathbf{X})^{-1} \\ &= \sigma^2(\mathbf{X}'\mathbf{X})^{-1}\mathbf{X}'\mathbf{X}(\mathbf{X}'\mathbf{X})^{-1} \\ &= \sigma^2(\mathbf{X}'\mathbf{X})^{-1}.\end{aligned} \qquad [8.1.16]$$

The *OLS* coefficient estimate **b** is unbiased and is a linear function of **y**. The *Gauss-Markov theorem* states that the variance-covariance matrix of any alternative estimator of $\boldsymbol{\beta}$, if that estimator is also unbiased and a linear function of **y**, differs from the variance-covariance matrix of **b** by a positive semidefinite matrix.[1] This means that an inference based on **b** about any linear combination of the elements of $\boldsymbol{\beta}$ will have a smaller variance than the corresponding inference based on any alternative linear unbiased estimator. The Gauss-Markov theorem thus establishes the optimality of the *OLS* estimate within a certain limited class.

## *Properties of the Estimated Coefficient Vector Under Assumption 8.1(a) Through (c)*

When **u** is Gaussian, [8.1.12] implies that **b** is Gaussian. Hence, the preceding results imply

$$\mathbf{b} \sim N(\boldsymbol{\beta}, \sigma^2(\mathbf{X}'\mathbf{X})^{-1}). \qquad [8.1.17]$$

It can further be shown that under Assumption 8.1(a) through (c), no unbiased estimator of $\boldsymbol{\beta}$ is more efficient than the *OLS* estimator **b**.[2] Thus, with Gaussian residuals, the *OLS* estimator is optimal.

## *Properties of Estimated Residual Variance Under Assumption 8.1(a) and (b)*

The *OLS* estimate of the variance of the disturbances $\sigma^2$ is

$$s^2 = RSS/(T-k) = \hat{\mathbf{u}}'\hat{\mathbf{u}}/(T-k) = \mathbf{u}'\mathbf{M}_\mathbf{X}'\mathbf{M}_\mathbf{X}\mathbf{u}/(T-k) \qquad [8.1.18]$$

for $\mathbf{M}_\mathbf{X}$ the matrix in [8.1.8]. Recalling that $\mathbf{M}_\mathbf{X}$ is symmetric and idempotent, [8.1.18] becomes

$$s^2 = \mathbf{u}'\mathbf{M}_\mathbf{X}\mathbf{u}/(T-k). \qquad [8.1.19]$$

Also, since $\mathbf{M}_\mathbf{X}$ is symmetric, there exists a $(T \times T)$ matrix **P** such that[3]

$$\mathbf{M}_\mathbf{X} = \mathbf{P}\boldsymbol{\Lambda}\mathbf{P}' \qquad [8.1.20]$$

and

$$\mathbf{P}'\mathbf{P} = \mathbf{I}_T, \qquad [8.1.21]$$

where $\boldsymbol{\Lambda}$ is a $(T \times T)$ matrix with the eigenvalues of $\mathbf{M}_\mathbf{X}$ along the principal diagonal and zeros elsewhere. Note from [8.1.9] that $\mathbf{M}_\mathbf{X}\mathbf{v} = \mathbf{0}$ if **v** should be given by one of the $k$ columns of **X**. Assuming that the columns of **X** are linearly independent, the $k$ columns of **X** thus represent $k$ different eigenvectors of $\mathbf{M}_\mathbf{X}$ each associated

[1]See, for example, Theil (1971, pp. 119–20).

[2]See, for example, Theil (1971, pp. 390–91).

[3]See, for example, O'Nan (1976, p. 296).

with an eigenvalue equal to zero. Also from [8.1.8], $\mathbf{M_X v} = \mathbf{v}$ for any vector $\mathbf{v}$ that is orthogonal to the columns of $\mathbf{X}$ (that is, any vector $\mathbf{v}$ such that $\mathbf{X}'\mathbf{v} = \mathbf{0}$); $(T - k)$ such vectors that are linearly independent can be found, associated with $(T - k)$ eigenvalues equal to unity. Thus, $\mathbf{\Lambda}$ contains $k$ zeros and $(T - k)$ 1s along its principal diagonal. Notice from [8.1.20] that

$$\begin{aligned} \mathbf{u}'\mathbf{M_X u} &= \mathbf{u}'\mathbf{P\Lambda P}'\mathbf{u} \\ &= (\mathbf{P}'\mathbf{u})'\mathbf{\Lambda}(\mathbf{P}'\mathbf{u}) \\ &= \mathbf{w}'\mathbf{\Lambda w} \\ &= w_1^2\lambda_1 + w_2^2\lambda_2 + \cdots + w_T^2\lambda_T, \end{aligned} \qquad [8.1.22]$$

where

$$\mathbf{w} \equiv \mathbf{P}'\mathbf{u}.$$

Furthermore,

$$E(\mathbf{ww}') = E(\mathbf{P}'\mathbf{uu}'\mathbf{P}) = \mathbf{P}'E(\mathbf{uu}')\mathbf{P} = \sigma^2\mathbf{P}'\mathbf{P} = \sigma^2\mathbf{I}_T.$$

Thus, the elements of $\mathbf{w}$ are uncorrelated, with mean zero and variance $\sigma^2$. Since $k$ of the $\lambda$'s are zero and the remaining $T - k$ are unity, [8.1.22] becomes

$$\mathbf{u}'\mathbf{M_X u} = w_1^2 + w_2^2 + \cdots + w_{T-k}^2. \qquad [8.1.23]$$

Furthermore, each $w_t^2$ has expectation $\sigma^2$, so that

$$E(\mathbf{u}'\mathbf{M_X u}) = (T - k)\sigma^2,$$

and from [8.1.19], $s^2$ gives an unbiased estimate of $\sigma^2$:

$$E(s^2) = \sigma^2.$$

## *Properties of Estimated Residual Variance Under Assumption 8.1(a) Through (c)*

When $u_t$ is Gaussian, $w_t$ is also Gaussian and expression [8.1.23] is the sum of squares of $(T - k)$ independent $N(0, \sigma^2)$ variables. Thus,

$$RSS/\sigma^2 = \mathbf{u}'\mathbf{M_X u}/\sigma^2 \sim \chi^2(T - k). \qquad [8.1.24]$$

Again, it is possible to show that under Assumption 8.1(a) through (c), no other unbiased estimator of $\sigma^2$ has a smaller variance than does $s^2$.[4]

Notice also from [8.1.11] and [8.1.12] that $\mathbf{b}$ and $\hat{\mathbf{u}}$ are uncorrelated:

$$E[\hat{\mathbf{u}}(\mathbf{b} - \boldsymbol{\beta})'] = E[\mathbf{M_X uu}'\mathbf{X}(\mathbf{X}'\mathbf{X})^{-1}] = \sigma^2\mathbf{M_X X}(\mathbf{X}'\mathbf{X})^{-1} = \mathbf{0}. \qquad [8.1.25]$$

Under Assumption 8.1(a) through (c), both $\mathbf{b}$ and $\hat{\mathbf{u}}$ are Gaussian, so that absence of correlation implies that $\mathbf{b}$ and $\hat{\mathbf{u}}$ are independent. This means that $\mathbf{b}$ and $s^2$ are independent.

## t *Tests About* $\boldsymbol{\beta}$ *Under Assumption 8.1(a) Through (c)*

Suppose that we wish to test the null hypothesis that $\beta_i$, the $i$th element of $\boldsymbol{\beta}$, is equal to some particular value $\beta_i^0$. The *OLS* $t$ statistic for testing this null hypothesis is given by

$$t = \frac{(b_i - \beta_i^0)}{\hat{\sigma}_{b_i}} = \frac{(b_i - \beta_i^0)}{s(\xi^{ii})^{1/2}}, \qquad [8.1.26]$$

[4]See Rao (1973, p. 319).

where $\xi^{ii}$ denotes the row $i$, column $i$ element of $(\mathbf{X}'\mathbf{X})^{-1}$ and $\hat{\sigma}_{b_i} \equiv \sqrt{s^2\xi^{ii}}$ is the standard error of the *OLS* estimate of the $i$th coefficient. The magnitude in [8.1.26] has an exact $t$ distribution with $T - k$ degrees of freedom so long as $\mathbf{x}_t$ is deterministic and $u_t$ is i.i.d. Gaussian. To verify this claim, note from [8.1.17] that under the null hypothesis, $b_i \sim N(\beta_i^0, \sigma^2\xi^{ii})$, meaning that $(b_i - \beta_i^0)/\sqrt{\sigma^2\xi^{ii}} \sim N(0, 1)$. Thus, if [8.1.26] is written as

$$t = \frac{(b_i - \beta_i^0)/\sqrt{\sigma^2\xi^{ii}}}{\sqrt{s^2/\sigma^2}},$$

the numerator is $N(0, 1)$ while from [8.1.24] the denominator is the square root of a $\chi^2(T - k)$ variable divided by its degrees of freedom. Recalling [8.1.25], the numerator and denominator are independent, confirming the exact $t$ distribution claimed for [8.1.26].

## F Tests About $\boldsymbol{\beta}$ Under Assumption 8.1(a) Through (c)

More generally, suppose we want a joint test of $m$ different linear restrictions about $\boldsymbol{\beta}$, as represented by

$$H_0\colon \mathbf{R}\boldsymbol{\beta} = \mathbf{r}. \qquad [8.1.27]$$

Here $\mathbf{R}$ is a known $(m \times k)$ matrix representing the particular linear combinations of $\boldsymbol{\beta}$ about which we entertain hypotheses and $\mathbf{r}$ is a known $(m \times 1)$ vector of the values that we believe these linear combinations take on. For example, to represent the simple hypothesis $\beta_i = \beta_i^0$ used previously, we would have $m = 1$, $\mathbf{R}$ a $(1 \times k)$ vector with unity in the $i$th position and zeros elsewhere, and $\mathbf{r}$ the scalar $\beta_i^0$. As a second example, consider a regression with $k = 4$ explanatory variables and the joint hypothesis that $\beta_1 + \beta_2 = 1$ and $\beta_3 = \beta_4$. In this case, $m = 2$ and

$$\mathbf{R} = \begin{bmatrix} 1 & 1 & 0 & 0 \\ 0 & 0 & 1 & -1 \end{bmatrix} \qquad \mathbf{r} = \begin{bmatrix} 1 \\ 0 \end{bmatrix}. \qquad [8.1.28]$$

Notice from [8.1.17] that under $H_0$,

$$\mathbf{R}\mathbf{b} \sim N(\mathbf{r}, \sigma^2\mathbf{R}(\mathbf{X}'\mathbf{X})^{-1}\mathbf{R}'). \qquad [8.1.29]$$

A *Wald test* of $H_0$ is based on the following result.

***Proposition 8.1:*** *Consider an $(n \times 1)$ vector $\mathbf{z} \sim N(\mathbf{0}, \boldsymbol{\Omega})$ with $\boldsymbol{\Omega}$ nonsingular. Then $\mathbf{z}'\boldsymbol{\Omega}^{-1}\mathbf{z} \sim \chi^2(n)$.*

For the scalar case $(n = 1)$, observe that if $z \sim N(0, \sigma^2)$, then $(z/\sigma) \sim N(0, 1)$ and $z^2/\sigma^2 \sim \chi^2(1)$, as asserted by the proposition.

To verify Proposition 8.1 for the vector case, since $\boldsymbol{\Omega}$ is symmetric, there exists a matrix $\mathbf{P}$, as in [8.1.20] and [8.1.21], such that $\boldsymbol{\Omega} = \mathbf{P}\boldsymbol{\Lambda}\mathbf{P}'$ and $\mathbf{P}'\mathbf{P} = \mathbf{I}_n$ with $\boldsymbol{\Lambda}$ containing the eigenvalues of $\boldsymbol{\Omega}$. Since $\boldsymbol{\Omega}$ is positive definite, the diagonal elements of $\boldsymbol{\Lambda}$ are positive. Then

$$\begin{aligned}
\mathbf{z}'\boldsymbol{\Omega}^{-1}\mathbf{z} &= \mathbf{z}'(\mathbf{P}\boldsymbol{\Lambda}\mathbf{P}')^{-1}\mathbf{z} \\
&= \mathbf{z}'[\mathbf{P}']^{-1}\boldsymbol{\Lambda}^{-1}\mathbf{P}^{-1}\mathbf{z} \\
&= [\mathbf{P}^{-1}\mathbf{z}]'\boldsymbol{\Lambda}^{-1}\mathbf{P}^{-1}\mathbf{z} \\
&= \mathbf{w}'\boldsymbol{\Lambda}^{-1}\mathbf{w} \qquad [8.1.30] \\
&= \sum_{i=1}^{n} w_i^2/\lambda_i,
\end{aligned}$$

where $\mathbf{w} \equiv \mathbf{P}^{-1}\mathbf{z}$. Notice that $\mathbf{w}$ is Gaussian with mean zero and variance

$$E(\mathbf{ww'}) = E(\mathbf{P}^{-1}\mathbf{zz'}[\mathbf{P'}]^{-1}) = \mathbf{P}^{-1}\mathbf{\Omega}[\mathbf{P'}]^{-1} = \mathbf{P}^{-1}\mathbf{P\Lambda P'}[\mathbf{P'}]^{-1} = \mathbf{\Lambda}.$$

Thus [8.1.30] is the sum of squares of $n$ independent Normal variables, each divided by its variance $\lambda_i$. It accordingly has a $\chi^2(n)$ distribution, as claimed.

Applying Proposition 8.1 directly to [8.1.29], under $H_0$,

$$(\mathbf{Rb} - \mathbf{r})'[\sigma^2\mathbf{R}(\mathbf{X'X})^{-1}\mathbf{R'}]^{-1}(\mathbf{Rb} - \mathbf{r}) \sim \chi^2(m). \qquad [8.1.31]$$

Replacing $\sigma^2$ with the estimate $s^2$ and dividing by the number of restrictions gives the Wald form of the *OLS F* test of a linear hypothesis:

$$F = (\mathbf{Rb} - \mathbf{r})'[s^2\mathbf{R}(\mathbf{X'X})^{-1}\mathbf{R'}]^{-1}(\mathbf{Rb} - \mathbf{r})/m. \qquad [8.1.32]$$

Note that [8.1.32] can be written

$$F = \frac{(\mathbf{Rb} - \mathbf{r})'[\sigma^2\mathbf{R}(\mathbf{X'X})^{-1}\mathbf{R'}]^{-1}(\mathbf{Rb} - \mathbf{r})/m}{[RSS/(T - k)]/\sigma^2}.$$

The numerator is a $\chi^2(m)$ variable divided by its degrees of freedom, while the denominator is a $\chi^2(T - k)$ variable divided by its degrees of freedom. Again, since $\mathbf{b}$ and $\hat{\mathbf{u}}$ are independent, the numerator and denominator are independent of each other. Hence, [8.1.32] has an exact $F(m, T - k)$ distribution under $H_0$ when $\mathbf{x}_t$ is nonstochastic and $u_t$ is i.i.d. Gaussian.

Notice that the $t$ test of the simple hypothesis $\beta_i = \beta_i^0$ is a special case of the general formula [8.1.32], for which

$$F = (b_i - \beta_i^0)[s^2\xi^{ii}]^{-1}(b_i - \beta_i^0). \qquad [8.1.33]$$

This is the square of the $t$ statistic in [8.1.26]. Since an $F(1, T - k)$ variable is just the square of a $t(T - k)$ variable, the identical answer results from (1) calculating [8.1.26] and using $t$ tables to find the probability of so large an absolute value for a $t(T - k)$ variable, or (2) calculating [8.1.33] and using $F$ tables to find the probability of so large a value for an $F(1, T - k)$ variable.

## *A Convenient Alternative Expression for the* F *Test*

It is often straightforward to estimate the model in [8.1.1] subject to the restrictions in [8.1.27]. For example, to impose a constraint $\beta_1 = \beta_1^0$ on the first element of $\boldsymbol{\beta}$, we could just do an ordinary least squares regression of $y_t - \beta_1^0 x_{1t}$ on $x_{2t}, x_{3t}, \ldots, x_{kt}$. The resulting estimates $b_2^*, b_3^*, \ldots, b_k^*$ minimize $\Sigma_{t=1}^T [(y_t - \beta_1^0 x_{1t}) - b_2^* x_{2t} - b_3^* x_{3t} - \cdots - b_k^* x_{kt}]^2$ with respect to $b_2^*, b_3^*, \ldots, b_k^*$ and thus minimize the residual sum of squares [8.1.2] subject to the constraint that $\beta_1 = \beta_1^0$. Alternatively, to impose the constraint in [8.1.28], we could regress $y_t - x_{2t}$ on $(x_{1t} - x_{2t})$ and $(x_{3t} + x_{4t})$:

$$y_t - x_{2t} = \beta_1(x_{1t} - x_{2t}) + \beta_3(x_{3t} + x_{4t}) + u_t.$$

The *OLS* estimates $b_1^*$ and $b_3^*$ minimize

$$\begin{aligned}\sum_{t=1}^T &[(y_t - x_{2t}) - b_1^*(x_{1t} - x_{2t}) - b_3^*(x_{3t} + x_{4t})]^2 \\ &= \sum_{t=1}^T [y_t - b_1^* x_{1t} - (1 - b_1^*)x_{2t} - b_3^* x_{3t} - b_3^* x_{4t}]^2\end{aligned} \qquad [8.1.34]$$

and thus minimize [8.1.2] subject to [8.1.28].

Whenever the constraints in [8.1.27] can be imposed through a simple *OLS* regression on transformed variables, there is an easy way to calculate the $F$ statistic

[8.1.32] just by comparing the residual sum of squares for the constrained and unconstrained regressions. The following result is established in Appendix 8.A at the end of this chapter.

***Proposition 8.2:*** *Let* $\mathbf{b}$ *denote the unconstrained OLS estimate [8.1.6] and let* $RSS_1$ *be the residual sum of squares resulting from using this estimate:*

$$RSS_1 = \sum_{t=1}^{T} (y_t - \mathbf{x}_t'\mathbf{b})^2. \qquad [8.1.35]$$

*Let* $\mathbf{b}^*$ *denote the constrained OLS estimate and* $RSS_0$ *the residual sum of squares from the constrained OLS estimation:*

$$RSS_0 = \sum_{t=1}^{T} (y_t - \mathbf{x}_t'\mathbf{b}^*)^2. \qquad [8.1.36]$$

*Then the Wald form of the OLS F test of a linear hypothesis [8.1.32] can equivalently be calculated as*

$$F = \frac{(RSS_0 - RSS_1)/m}{RSS_1/(T - k)}. \qquad [8.1.37]$$

Expressions [8.1.37] and [8.1.32] will generate exactly the same number, regardless of whether the null hypothesis and the model are valid or not.

For example, suppose the sample size is $T = 50$ observations and the null hypothesis is $\beta_3 = \beta_4 = 0$ in an $OLS$ regression with $k = 4$ explanatory variables. First regress $y_t$ on $x_{1t}, x_{2t}, x_{3t}, x_{4t}$ and call the residual sum of squares from this regression $RSS_1$. Next, regress $y_t$ on just $x_{1t}$ and $x_{2t}$ and call the residual sum of squares from this restricted regression $RSS_0$. If

$$\frac{(RSS_0 - RSS_1)/2}{RSS_1/(50 - 4)}$$

is greater than 3.20 (the 5% critical value for an $F(2, 46)$ random variable), then the null hypothesis should be rejected.

## 8.2. *Ordinary Least Squares Under More General Conditions*

The previous section analyzed the regression model

$$y_t = \mathbf{x}_t'\boldsymbol{\beta} + u_t$$

under the maintained Assumption 8.1 ($\mathbf{x}_t$ is deterministic and $u_t$ is i.i.d. Gaussian). We will hereafter refer to this assumption as "case 1." This section generalizes this assumption to describe specifications likely to arise in time series analysis. Some of the key results are summarized in Table 8.1.

### *Case 2. Error Term i.i.d. Gaussian and Independent of Explanatory Variables*

Consider the case in which $\mathbf{X}$ is stochastic but completely independent of $\mathbf{u}$.

***Assumption 8.2:***[5] *(a)* $\mathbf{x}_t$ *stochastic and independent of* $u_s$ *for all* $t, s$; *(b)* $u_t \sim$ *i.i.d.* $N(0, \sigma^2)$.

[5] This could be replaced with the assumption $\mathbf{u}|\mathbf{X} \sim N(\mathbf{0}, \sigma^2\mathbf{I}_T)$ with all the results to follow unchanged.

Many of the results for deterministic regressors continue to apply for this case. For example, taking expectations of [8.1.12] and exploiting the independence assumption,

$$E(\mathbf{b}) = \boldsymbol{\beta} + \{E[(\mathbf{X}'\mathbf{X})^{-1}\mathbf{X}']\}\{E(\mathbf{u})\} = \boldsymbol{\beta}, \qquad [8.2.1]$$

so that the *OLS* coefficient remains unbiased.

The distribution of test statistics for this case can be found by a two-step procedure. The first step evaluates the distribution conditional on $\mathbf{X}$; that is, it treats $\mathbf{X}$ as deterministic just as in the earlier analysis. The second step multiplies by the density of $\mathbf{X}$ and integrates over $\mathbf{X}$ to find the true unconditional distribution. For example, [8.1.17] implies that

$$\mathbf{b}|\mathbf{X} \sim N(\boldsymbol{\beta}, \sigma^2(\mathbf{X}'\mathbf{X})^{-1}). \qquad [8.2.2]$$

If this density is multiplied by the density of $\mathbf{X}$ and integrated over $\mathbf{X}$, the result is no longer a Gaussian distribution; thus, $\mathbf{b}$ is non-Gaussian under Assumption 8.2. On the other hand, [8.1.24] implies that

$$RSS|\mathbf{X} \sim \sigma^2 \cdot \chi^2(T - k).$$

But this density is the same for all $\mathbf{X}$. Thus, when we multiply the density of $RSS|\mathbf{X}$ by the density of $\mathbf{X}$ and integrate, we will get exactly the same density. Hence, [8.1.24] continues to give the correct unconditional distribution for Assumption 8.2.

The same is true for the $t$ and $F$ statistics in [8.1.26] and [8.1.32]. Conditional on $\mathbf{X}$, $(b_i - \beta_i^0)/[\sigma(\xi^{ii})^{1/2}] \sim N(0, 1)$ and $s/\sigma$ is the square root of an independent $[1/(T - k)]\cdot\chi^2(T - k)$ variable. Hence, conditional on $\mathbf{X}$, the statistic in [8.1.26] has a $t(T - k)$ distribution. Since this is true for any $\mathbf{X}$, when we multiply by the density of $\mathbf{X}$ and integrate over $\mathbf{X}$ we obtain the same distribution.

## *Case 3. Error Term i.i.d. Non-Gaussian and Independent of Explanatory Variables*

Next consider the following specification.

***Assumption 8.3:*** *(a) $\mathbf{x}_t$ stochastic and independent of $u_s$ for all $t$, $s$; (b) $u_t$ non-Gaussian but i.i.d. with mean zero, variance $\sigma^2$, and $E(u_t^4) = \mu_4 < \infty$; (c) $E(\mathbf{x}_t\mathbf{x}_t') = \mathbf{Q}_t$, a positive definite matrix with $(1/T)\Sigma_{t=1}^T \mathbf{Q}_t \to \mathbf{Q}$, a positive definite matrix; (d) $E(x_{it}x_{jt}x_{lt}x_{mt}) < \infty$ for all $i$, $j$, $l$, $m$, and $t$; (e) $(1/T)\Sigma_{t=1}^T(\mathbf{x}_t\mathbf{x}_t') \xrightarrow{p} \mathbf{Q}$.*

Since result [8.2.1] required only the independence assumption, $\mathbf{b}$ continues to be unbiased in this case. However, for hypothesis tests, the small-sample distributions of $s^2$ and the $t$ and $F$ statistics are no longer the same as when the population residuals are Gaussian. To justify the usual *OLS* inference rules, we have to appeal to asymptotic results, for which purpose Assumption 8.3 includes conditions (c) through (e). To understand these conditions, note that if $\mathbf{x}_t$ is covariance-stationary, then $E(\mathbf{x}_t\mathbf{x}_t')$ does not depend on $t$. Then $\mathbf{Q}_t = \mathbf{Q}$ for all $t$ and condition (e) simply requires that $\mathbf{x}_t$ be ergodic for second moments. Assumption 8.3 also allows more general processes in that $E(\mathbf{x}_t\mathbf{x}_t')$ might be different for different $t$, so long as the limit of $(1/T)\Sigma_{t=1}^T E(\mathbf{x}_t\mathbf{x}_t')$ can be consistently estimated by $(1/T)\Sigma_{t=1}^T(\mathbf{x}_t\mathbf{x}_t')$.

**TABLE 8.1**
**Properties of *OLS* Estimates and Test Statistics Under Various Assumptions**

| | *Coefficient* $\mathbf{b}$ | *Variance* $s^2$ | *t statistic* | *F statistic* |
|---|---|---|---|---|
| *Case 1* | unbiased<br>$\mathbf{b} \sim N\big(\boldsymbol{\beta}, \sigma^2(\mathbf{X}'\mathbf{X})^{-1}\big)$ | unbiased<br>$(T - k)s^2/\sigma^2 \sim \chi^2(T - k)$ | exact $t(T - k)$ | exact $F(m, T - k)$ |
| *Case 2* | unbiased<br>non-Gaussian | unbiased<br>$(T - k)s^2/\sigma^2 \sim \chi^2(T - k)$ | exact $t(T - k)$ | exact $F(m, T - k)$ |
| *Case 3* | unbiased<br>$\sqrt{T}(\mathbf{b}_T - \boldsymbol{\beta}) \xrightarrow{L} N(\mathbf{0}, \sigma^2\mathbf{Q}^{-1})$ | unbiased<br>$\sqrt{T}(s_T^2 - \sigma^2) \xrightarrow{L} N(0, \mu_4 - \sigma^4)$ | $t_T \xrightarrow{L} N(0, 1)$ | $mF_T \xrightarrow{L} \chi^2(m)$ |
| *Case 4* | biased<br>$\sqrt{T}(\mathbf{b}_T - \boldsymbol{\beta}) \xrightarrow{L} N(\mathbf{0}, \sigma^2\mathbf{Q}^{-1})$ | biased<br>$\sqrt{T}(s_T^2 - \sigma^2) \xrightarrow{L} N(0, \mu_4 - \sigma^4)$ | $t_T \xrightarrow{L} N(0, 1)$ | $mF_T \xrightarrow{L} \chi^2(m)$ |

Regression model is $\mathbf{y} = \mathbf{X}\boldsymbol{\beta} + \mathbf{u}$, $\mathbf{b}$ is given by [8.1.6], $s^2$ by [8.1.18], $t$ statistic by [8.1.26], and $F$ statistic by [8.1.32]; $\mu_4$ denotes $E(u_t^4)$.
*Case 1*: $\mathbf{X}$ nonstochastic, $\mathbf{u} \sim N(\mathbf{0}, \sigma^2\mathbf{I}_T)$.
*Case 2*: $\mathbf{X}$ stochastic, $\mathbf{u} \sim N(\mathbf{0}, \sigma^2\mathbf{I}_T)$, $\mathbf{X}$ independent of $\mathbf{u}$.
*Case 3*: $\mathbf{X}$ stochastic, $\mathbf{u} \sim$ non-Gaussian $(\mathbf{0}, \sigma^2\mathbf{I}_T)$, $\mathbf{X}$ independent of $\mathbf{u}$, $T^{-1}\Sigma\mathbf{x}_t\mathbf{x}_t' \xrightarrow{p} \mathbf{Q}$.
*Case 4*: Stationary autoregression with independent errors, $\mathbf{Q}$ given by [8.2.27].

To describe the asymptotic results, we denote the *OLS* estimator [8.1.3] by $\mathbf{b}_T$ to emphasize that it is based on a sample of size $T$. Our interest is in the behavior of $\mathbf{b}_T$ as $T$ becomes large. We first establish that the *OLS* coefficient estimator is consistent under Assumption 8.3, that is, that $\mathbf{b}_T \xrightarrow{p} \boldsymbol{\beta}$.

Note that [8.1.12] implies

$$\begin{aligned}\mathbf{b}_T - \boldsymbol{\beta} &= \left[\sum_{t=1}^{T} \mathbf{x}_t\mathbf{x}_t'\right]^{-1}\left[\sum_{t=1}^{T} \mathbf{x}_t u_t\right] \\ &= \left[(1/T)\sum_{t=1}^{T} \mathbf{x}_t\mathbf{x}_t'\right]^{-1}\left[(1/T)\sum_{t=1}^{T} \mathbf{x}_t u_t\right].\end{aligned} \qquad [8.2.3]$$

Consider the first term in [8.2.3]. Assumption 8.3(e) and Proposition 7.1 imply that

$$\left[(1/T)\sum_{t=1}^{T} \mathbf{x}_t\mathbf{x}_t'\right]^{-1} \xrightarrow{p} \mathbf{Q}^{-1}. \qquad [8.2.4]$$

Considering next the second term in [8.2.3], notice that $\mathbf{x}_t u_t$ is a martingale difference sequence with variance-covariance matrix given by

$$E(\mathbf{x}_t u_t \mathbf{x}_t' u_t) = \{E(\mathbf{x}_t\mathbf{x}_t')\}\cdot\sigma^2,$$

which is finite. Thus, from Example 7.11,

$$\left[(1/T)\sum_{t=1}^{T} \mathbf{x}_t u_t\right] \xrightarrow{p} \mathbf{0}. \qquad [8.2.5]$$

Applying Example 7.2 to [8.2.3] through [8.2.5],

$$\mathbf{b}_T - \boldsymbol{\beta} \xrightarrow{p} \mathbf{Q}^{-1}\cdot\mathbf{0} = \mathbf{0},$$

verifying that the *OLS* estimator is consistent.

Next turn to the asymptotic distribution of $\mathbf{b}$. Notice from [8.2.3] that

$$\sqrt{T}(\mathbf{b}_T - \boldsymbol{\beta}) = \left[(1/T)\sum_{t=1}^{T} \mathbf{x}_t\mathbf{x}_t'\right]^{-1}\left[(1/\sqrt{T})\sum_{t=1}^{T} \mathbf{x}_t u_t\right]. \qquad [8.2.6]$$

We saw in [8.2.4] that the first term converges in probability to $\mathbf{Q}^{-1}$. The second term is $\sqrt{T}$ times the sample mean of $\mathbf{x}_t u_t$, where $\mathbf{x}_t u_t$ is a martingale difference sequence with variance $\sigma^2\cdot E(\mathbf{x}_t\mathbf{x}_t') = \sigma^2\mathbf{Q}_t$ and $(1/T)\Sigma_{t=1}^{\infty}\sigma^2\mathbf{Q}_t \rightarrow \sigma^2\mathbf{Q}$. Notice that under Assumption 8.3 we can apply Proposition 7.9:

$$\left[(1/\sqrt{T})\sum_{t=1}^{T} \mathbf{x}_t u_t\right] \xrightarrow{L} N(\mathbf{0}, \sigma^2\mathbf{Q}). \qquad [8.2.7]$$

Combining [8.2.6], [8.2.4], and [8.2.7], we see as in Example 7.5 that

$$\sqrt{T}(\mathbf{b}_T - \boldsymbol{\beta}) \xrightarrow{L} N(\mathbf{0}, [\mathbf{Q}^{-1}\cdot(\sigma^2\mathbf{Q})\cdot\mathbf{Q}^{-1}]) = N(\mathbf{0}, \sigma^2\mathbf{Q}^{-1}). \qquad [8.2.8]$$

In other words, we can act as if

$$\mathbf{b}_T \approx N(\boldsymbol{\beta}, \sigma^2\mathbf{Q}^{-1}/T), \qquad [8.2.9]$$

where the symbol $\approx$ means "is approximately distributed." Recalling Assumption 8.3(e), in large samples $\mathbf{Q}$ should be close to $(1/T)\Sigma_{t=1}^{T}\mathbf{x}_t\mathbf{x}_t'$. Thus $\mathbf{Q}^{-1}/T$ should be close to $[\Sigma_{t=1}^{T}\mathbf{x}_t\mathbf{x}_t']^{-1} = (\mathbf{X}_T'\mathbf{X}_T)^{-1}$ for $\mathbf{X}_T$ the same $(T \times k)$ matrix that was represented in [8.1.5] simply by $\mathbf{X}$ (again, the subscript $T$ is added at this point to emphasize that the dimensions of this matrix depend on $T$). Thus, [8.2.9] can be approximated by

$$\mathbf{b}_T \approx N(\boldsymbol{\beta}, \sigma^2(\mathbf{X}_T'\mathbf{X}_T)^{-1}).$$

This, of course, is the same result obtained in [8.1.17], which assumed Gaussian disturbances. With non-Gaussian disturbances the distribution is not exact, but provides an increasingly good approximation as the sample size grows.

Next, consider consistency of the variance estimate $s_T^2$. Notice that the population residual sum of squares can be written

$$\begin{aligned}(\mathbf{y}_T - \mathbf{X}_T\boldsymbol{\beta})'(\mathbf{y}_T - \mathbf{X}_T\boldsymbol{\beta})\\ &= (\mathbf{y}_T - \mathbf{X}_T\mathbf{b}_T + \mathbf{X}_T\mathbf{b}_T - \mathbf{X}_T\boldsymbol{\beta})'(\mathbf{y}_T - \mathbf{X}_T\mathbf{b}_T + \mathbf{X}_T\mathbf{b}_T - \mathbf{X}_T\boldsymbol{\beta}) \\ &= (\mathbf{y}_T - \mathbf{X}_T\mathbf{b}_T)'(\mathbf{y}_T - \mathbf{X}_T\mathbf{b}_T) + (\mathbf{X}_T\mathbf{b}_T - \mathbf{X}_T\boldsymbol{\beta})'(\mathbf{X}_T\mathbf{b}_T - \mathbf{X}_T\boldsymbol{\beta}),\end{aligned} \qquad [8.2.10]$$

where cross-product terms have vanished, since

$$(\mathbf{y}_T - \mathbf{X}_T\mathbf{b}_T)'\mathbf{X}_T(\mathbf{b}_T - \boldsymbol{\beta}) = 0,$$

by the *OLS* orthogonality condition [8.1.10]. Dividing [8.2.10] by $T$,

$$\begin{aligned}(1/T)(\mathbf{y}_T - \mathbf{X}_T\boldsymbol{\beta})'(\mathbf{y}_T - \mathbf{X}_T\boldsymbol{\beta})\\ &= (1/T)(\mathbf{y}_T - \mathbf{X}_T\mathbf{b}_T)'(\mathbf{y}_T - \mathbf{X}_T\mathbf{b}_T) + (1/T)(\mathbf{b}_T - \boldsymbol{\beta})'\mathbf{X}_T'\mathbf{X}_T(\mathbf{b}_T - \boldsymbol{\beta}),\end{aligned}$$

or

$$\begin{aligned}(1/T)(\mathbf{y}_T - \mathbf{X}_T\mathbf{b}_T)'(\mathbf{y}_T - \mathbf{X}_T\mathbf{b}_T)\\ &= (1/T)(\mathbf{u}_T'\mathbf{u}_T) - (\mathbf{b}_T - \boldsymbol{\beta})'(\mathbf{X}_T'\mathbf{X}_T/T)(\mathbf{b}_T - \boldsymbol{\beta}).\end{aligned} \qquad [8.2.11]$$

Now, $(1/T)(\mathbf{u}_T'\mathbf{u}_T) = (1/T)\Sigma_{t=1}^T u_t^2$, where $\{u_t^2\}$ is an i.i.d. sequence with mean $\sigma^2$. Thus, by the law of large numbers,

$$(1/T)(\mathbf{u}_T'\mathbf{u}_T) \xrightarrow{p} \sigma^2.$$

For the second term in [8.2.11], we have $(\mathbf{X}_T'\mathbf{X}_T/T) \xrightarrow{p} \mathbf{Q}$ and $(\mathbf{b}_T - \boldsymbol{\beta}) \xrightarrow{p} \mathbf{0}$, and so, from Proposition 7.1,

$$(\mathbf{b}_T - \boldsymbol{\beta})'(\mathbf{X}_T'\mathbf{X}_T/T)(\mathbf{b}_T - \boldsymbol{\beta}) \xrightarrow{p} \mathbf{0}'\mathbf{Q}\mathbf{0} = 0.$$

Substituting these results into [8.2.11],

$$(1/T)(\mathbf{y}_T - \mathbf{X}_T\mathbf{b}_T)'(\mathbf{y}_T - \mathbf{X}_T\mathbf{b}_T) \xrightarrow{p} \sigma^2. \qquad [8.2.12]$$

Now, [8.2.12] describes an estimate of the variance, which we denote $\hat{\sigma}_T^2$:

$$\hat{\sigma}_T^2 \equiv (1/T)(\mathbf{y}_T - \mathbf{X}_T\mathbf{b}_T)'(\mathbf{y}_T - \mathbf{X}_T\mathbf{b}_T). \qquad [8.2.13]$$

The *OLS* estimator given in [8.1.18],

$$s_T^2 = [1/(T - k)](\mathbf{y}_T - \mathbf{X}_T\mathbf{b}_T)'(\mathbf{y}_T - \mathbf{X}_T\mathbf{b}_T), \qquad [8.2.14]$$

differs from $\hat{\sigma}_T^2$ by a term that vanishes as $T \rightarrow \infty$,

$$s_T^2 = a_T \cdot \hat{\sigma}_T^2,$$

where $a_T \equiv [T/(T - k)]$ with $\lim_{T\rightarrow\infty} a_T = 1$. Hence, from Proposition 7.1,

$$\text{plim } s_T^2 = 1 \cdot \sigma^2,$$

establishing consistency of $s_T^2$.

To find the asymptotic distribution of $s_T^2$, consider first $\sqrt{T}(\hat{\sigma}_T^2 - \sigma^2)$. From [8.2.11], this equals

$$\begin{aligned}\sqrt{T}(\hat{\sigma}_T^2 - \sigma^2) = (1/\sqrt{T})(\mathbf{u}_T'\mathbf{u}_T) - \sqrt{T}\sigma^2 \\ - \sqrt{T}(\mathbf{b}_T - \boldsymbol{\beta})'(\mathbf{X}_T'\mathbf{X}_T/T)(\mathbf{b}_T - \boldsymbol{\beta}).\end{aligned} \qquad [8.2.15]$$

But

$$(1/\sqrt{T})(\mathbf{u}_T'\mathbf{u}_T) - \sqrt{T}\sigma^2 = (1/\sqrt{T})\sum_{t=1}^{T}(u_t^2 - \sigma^2),$$

where $\{u_t^2 - \sigma^2\}$ is a sequence of i.i.d. variables with mean zero and variance $E(u_t^2 - \sigma^2)^2 = E(u_t^4) - 2\sigma^2 E(u_t^2) + \sigma^4 = \mu_4 - \sigma^4$. Hence, by the central limit theorem,

$$(1/\sqrt{T})(\mathbf{u}_T'\mathbf{u}_T) - \sqrt{T}\sigma^2 \xrightarrow{L} N(0, (\mu_4 - \sigma^4)). \qquad [8.2.16]$$

For the last term in [8.2.15], we have $\sqrt{T}(\mathbf{b}_T - \boldsymbol{\beta}) \xrightarrow{L} N(\mathbf{0}, \sigma^2\mathbf{Q}^{-1})$, $(\mathbf{X}_T'\mathbf{X}_T/T) \xrightarrow{p} \mathbf{Q}$, and $(\mathbf{b}_T - \boldsymbol{\beta}) \xrightarrow{p} \mathbf{0}$. Hence,

$$\sqrt{T}(\mathbf{b}_T - \boldsymbol{\beta})'(\mathbf{X}_T'\mathbf{X}_T/T)(\mathbf{b}_T - \boldsymbol{\beta}) \xrightarrow{p} 0. \qquad [8.2.17]$$

Putting [8.2.16] and [8.2.17] into [8.2.15], we conclude

$$\sqrt{T}(\hat{\sigma}_T^2 - \sigma^2) \xrightarrow{L} N(0, (\mu_4 - \sigma^4)). \qquad [8.2.18]$$

To see that $s_T^2$ has this same limiting distribution, notice that

$$\begin{aligned}\sqrt{T}(s_T^2 - \sigma^2) - \sqrt{T}(\hat{\sigma}_T^2 - \sigma^2) &= \sqrt{T}\{[T/(T - k)]\hat{\sigma}_T^2 - \hat{\sigma}_T^2\} \\ &= [(k\sqrt{T})/(T - k)]\hat{\sigma}_T^2.\end{aligned}$$

But $\lim_{T\to\infty} [(k\sqrt{T})/(T - k)] = 0$, establishing that

$$\sqrt{T}(s_T^2 - \sigma^2) - \sqrt{T}(\hat{\sigma}_T^2 - \sigma^2) \xrightarrow{p} 0\cdot\sigma^2 = 0$$

and hence, from Proposition 7.3(a),

$$\sqrt{T}(s_T^2 - \sigma^2) \xrightarrow{L} N(0, (\mu_4 - \sigma^4)). \qquad [8.2.19]$$

Notice that if we are relying on asymptotic justifications for test statistics, theory offers us no guidance for choosing between $s^2$ and $\hat{\sigma}^2$ as estimates of $\sigma^2$, since they have the same limiting distribution.

Next consider the asymptotic distribution of the *OLS* $t$ test of the null hypothesis $\beta_i = \beta_i^0$,

$$t_T = \frac{(b_{iT} - \beta_i^0)}{s_T\sqrt{\xi_T^{ii}}} = \frac{\sqrt{T}(b_{iT} - \beta_i^0)}{s_T\sqrt{T\xi_T^{ii}}}, \qquad [8.2.20]$$

where $\xi_T^{ii}$ denotes the row $i$, column $i$ element of $(\mathbf{X}_T'\mathbf{X}_T)^{-1}$. We have seen that $\sqrt{T}(b_{i,T} - \beta^0) \xrightarrow{L} N(0, \sigma^2 q^{ii})$, where $q^{ii}$ denotes the row $i$, column $i$ element of $\mathbf{Q}^{-1}$. Similarly, $T\xi_T^{ii}$ is the row $i$, column $i$ element of $(\mathbf{X}_T'\mathbf{X}_T/T)^{-1}$ and converges in probability to $q^{ii}$. Also, $s_T \xrightarrow{p} \sigma$. Hence, the $t$ statistic [8.2.20] has a limiting distribution that is the same as a $N(0, \sigma^2 q^{ii})$ variable divided by $\sqrt{\sigma^2 q^{ii}}$; that is,

$$t_T \xrightarrow{L} N(0, 1). \qquad [8.2.21]$$

Now, under the more restrictive conditions of Assumption 8.2, we saw that $t_T$ would have a $t$ distribution with $(T - k)$ degrees of freedom. Recall that a $t$ variable with $N$ degrees of freedom has the distribution of the ratio of a $N(0, 1)$ variable to the square root of $(1/N)$ times an independent $\chi^2(N)$ variable. But a $\chi^2(N)$ variable in turn is the sum of $N$ squares of independent $N(0, 1)$ variables.

Thus, letting $Z$ denote a $N(0, 1)$ variable, a $t$ variable with $N$ degrees of freedom has the same distribution as

$$t_N = \frac{Z}{\{(Z_1^2 + Z_2^2 + \cdots + Z_N^2)/N\}^{1/2}}.$$

By the law of large numbers,

$$(Z_1^2 + Z_2^2 + \cdots + Z_N^2)/N \xrightarrow{p} E(Z_t^2) = 1,$$

and so $t_N \xrightarrow{L} N(0, 1)$. Hence, the critical value for a $t$ variable with $N$ degrees of freedom will be arbitrarily close to that for a $N(0, 1)$ variable as $N$ becomes large. Even though the statistic calculated in [8.2.20] does not have an exact $t(T - k)$ distribution under Assumption 8.3, if we treat it as if it did, then we will not be far wrong if our sample is sufficiently large.

The same is true of [8.1.32], the $F$ test of $m$ different restrictions:

$$\begin{aligned} F_T &= (\mathbf{R}\mathbf{b}_T - \mathbf{r})'[s_T^2\mathbf{R}(\mathbf{X}_T'\mathbf{X}_T)^{-1}\mathbf{R}']^{-1}(\mathbf{R}\mathbf{b}_T - \mathbf{r})/m \\ &= \sqrt{T}(\mathbf{R}\mathbf{b}_T - \mathbf{r})'[s_T^2\mathbf{R}(\mathbf{X}_T'\mathbf{X}_T/T)^{-1}\mathbf{R}']^{-1}\sqrt{T}(\mathbf{R}\mathbf{b}_T - \mathbf{r})/m. \end{aligned} \qquad [8.2.22]$$

Here $s_T^2 \xrightarrow{p} \sigma^2$, $\mathbf{X}_T'\mathbf{X}_T/T \xrightarrow{p} \mathbf{Q}$, and, under the null hypothesis,

$$\begin{aligned} \sqrt{T}(\mathbf{R}\mathbf{b}_T - \mathbf{r}) &= [\mathbf{R}\sqrt{T}(\mathbf{b}_T - \boldsymbol{\beta})] \\ &\xrightarrow{L} N(\mathbf{0}, \sigma^2\mathbf{R}\mathbf{Q}^{-1}\mathbf{R}'). \end{aligned}$$

Hence, under the null hypothesis,

$$m \cdot F_T \xrightarrow{p} [\mathbf{R}\sqrt{T}(\mathbf{b}_T - \boldsymbol{\beta})]'[\sigma^2\mathbf{R}\mathbf{Q}^{-1}\mathbf{R}']^{-1}[\mathbf{R}\sqrt{T}(\mathbf{b}_T - \boldsymbol{\beta})].$$

This is a quadratic function of a Normal vector of the type described by Proposition 8.1, from which

$$m \cdot F_T \xrightarrow{L} \chi^2(m).$$

Thus an asymptotic inference can be based on the approximation

$$(\mathbf{R}\mathbf{b}_T - \mathbf{r})'[s_T^2\mathbf{R}(\mathbf{X}_T'\mathbf{X}_T)^{-1}\mathbf{R}']^{-1}(\mathbf{R}\mathbf{b}_T - \mathbf{r}) \approx \chi^2(m). \qquad [8.2.23]$$

This is known as the *Wald form* of the *OLS* $\chi^2$ test.

As in the case of the $t$ and limiting Normal distributions, viewing [8.2.23] as $\chi^2(m)$ and viewing [8.2.22] as $F(m, T - k)$ asymptotically amount to the same test. Recall that an $F(m, N)$ variable is a ratio of a $\chi^2(m)$ variable to an independent $\chi^2(N)$ variable, each divided by its degrees of freedom. Thus, if $Z_i$ denotes a $N(0, 1)$ variable and $X$ a $\chi^2(m)$ variable,

$$F_{m,N} = \frac{X/m}{(Z_1^2 + Z_2^2 + \cdots + Z_N^2)/N}.$$

For the denominator,

$$(Z_1^2 + Z_2^2 + \cdots + Z_N^2)/N \xrightarrow{p} E(Z_t^2) = 1,$$

implying

$$F_{m,N} \underset{N\to\infty}{\xrightarrow{L}} X/m.$$

Hence, comparing [8.2.23] with a $\chi^2(m)$ critical value or comparing [8.2.22] with an $F(m, T - k)$ critical value will result in the identical test for sufficiently large $T$ (see Exercise 8.2).

For a given sample of size $T$, the small-sample distribution (the $t$ or $F$ distribution) implies wider confidence intervals than the large-sample distribution (the

Normal or $\chi^2$ distribution). Even when the justification for using the $t$ or $F$ distribution is only asymptotic, many researchers prefer to use the $t$ or $F$ tables rather than the Normal or $\chi^2$ tables on the grounds that the former are more conservative and may represent a better approximation to the true small-sample distribution.

If we are relying only on the asymptotic distribution, the Wald test statistic [8.2.23] can be generalized to allow a test of a nonlinear set of restrictions on $\boldsymbol{\beta}$. Consider a null hypothesis consisting of $m$ separate nonlinear restrictions of the form $\mathbf{g}(\boldsymbol{\beta}) = \mathbf{0}$ where $\mathbf{g}: \mathbb{R}^k \to \mathbb{R}^m$ and $\mathbf{g}(\cdot)$ has continuous first derivatives. Result [8.2.8] and Proposition 7.4 imply that

$$\sqrt{T}[\mathbf{g}(\mathbf{b}_T) - \mathbf{g}(\boldsymbol{\beta}_0)] \xrightarrow{L} \left[\left.\frac{\partial \mathbf{g}}{\partial \boldsymbol{\beta}'}\right|_{\boldsymbol{\beta}=\boldsymbol{\beta}_0}\right]\mathbf{z},$$

where $\mathbf{z} \sim N(\mathbf{0}, \sigma^2\mathbf{Q}^{-1})$ and

$$\left.\frac{\partial \mathbf{g}}{\partial \boldsymbol{\beta}'}\right|_{\boldsymbol{\beta}=\boldsymbol{\beta}_0}$$

denotes the $(m \times k)$ matrix of derivatives of $\mathbf{g}(\cdot)$ with respect to $\boldsymbol{\beta}$, evaluated at the true value $\boldsymbol{\beta}_0$. Under the null hypothesis that $\mathbf{g}(\boldsymbol{\beta}_0) = \mathbf{0}$, it follows from Proposition 8.1 that

$$\{\sqrt{T}\cdot\mathbf{g}(\mathbf{b}_T)\}' \left\{\left[\left.\frac{\partial \mathbf{g}}{\partial \boldsymbol{\beta}'}\right|_{\boldsymbol{\beta}=\boldsymbol{\beta}_0}\right]\sigma^2\mathbf{Q}^{-1}\left[\left.\frac{\partial \mathbf{g}}{\partial \boldsymbol{\beta}'}\right|_{\boldsymbol{\beta}=\boldsymbol{\beta}_0}\right]'\right\}^{-1} \{\sqrt{T}\cdot\mathbf{g}(\mathbf{b}_T)\} \xrightarrow{L} \chi^2(m).$$

Recall that $\mathbf{Q}$ is the plim of $(1/T)(\mathbf{X}_T'\mathbf{X}_T)$. Since $\partial\mathbf{g}/\partial\boldsymbol{\beta}'$ is continuous and since $\mathbf{b}_T \xrightarrow{p} \boldsymbol{\beta}_0$, it follows from Proposition 7.1 that

$$\left[\left.\frac{\partial \mathbf{g}}{\partial \boldsymbol{\beta}'}\right|_{\boldsymbol{\beta}=\mathbf{b}_T}\right] \xrightarrow{p} \left[\left.\frac{\partial \mathbf{g}}{\partial \boldsymbol{\beta}'}\right|_{\boldsymbol{\beta}=\boldsymbol{\beta}_0}\right].$$

Hence a set of $m$ nonlinear restrictions about $\boldsymbol{\beta}$ of the form $\mathbf{g}(\boldsymbol{\beta}) = \mathbf{0}$ can be tested with the statistic

$$\{\mathbf{g}(\mathbf{b}_T)\}' \left\{\left[\left.\frac{\partial \mathbf{g}}{\partial \boldsymbol{\beta}'}\right|_{\boldsymbol{\beta}=\mathbf{b}_T}\right]s_T^2(\mathbf{X}_T'\mathbf{X}_T)^{-1}\left[\left.\frac{\partial \mathbf{g}}{\partial \boldsymbol{\beta}'}\right|_{\boldsymbol{\beta}=\mathbf{b}_T}\right]'\right\}^{-1} \{\mathbf{g}(\mathbf{b}_T)\} \xrightarrow{L} \chi^2(m).$$

Note that the Wald test for linear restrictions [8.2.23] can be obtained as a special case of this more general formula by setting $\mathbf{g}(\boldsymbol{\beta}) = \mathbf{R}\boldsymbol{\beta} - \mathbf{r}$.

One disadvantage of the Wald test for nonlinear restrictions is that the answer one obtains can be different depending on how the restrictions $\mathbf{g}(\boldsymbol{\beta}) = \mathbf{0}$ are parameterized. For example, the hypotheses $\beta_1 = \beta_2$ and $\beta_1/\beta_2 = 1$ are equivalent, and asymptotically a Wald test based on either parameterization should give the same answer. However, in a particular finite sample the answers could be quite different. In effect, the nonlinear Wald test approximates the restriction $\mathbf{g}(\mathbf{b}_T) = \mathbf{0}$ by the linear restriction

$$\mathbf{g}(\boldsymbol{\beta}_0) + \left[\left.\frac{\partial \mathbf{g}}{\partial \boldsymbol{\beta}'}\right|_{\boldsymbol{\beta}=\boldsymbol{\beta}_0}\right](\mathbf{b}_T - \boldsymbol{\beta}_0) = \mathbf{0}.$$

Some care must be taken to ensure that this linearization is reasonable over the range of plausible values for $\boldsymbol{\beta}$. See Gregory and Veall (1985), Lafontaine and White (1986), and Phillips and Park (1988) for further discussion.

### *Case 4. Estimating Parameters for an Autoregression*

Consider now estimation of the parameters of a $p$th-order autoregression by *OLS*.

***Assumption 8.4:*** *The regression model is*

$$y_t = c + \phi_1 y_{t-1} + \phi_2 y_{t-2} + \cdots + \phi_p y_{t-p} + \varepsilon_t, \qquad [8.2.24]$$

*with roots of* $(1 - \phi_1 z - \phi_2 z^2 - \cdots - \phi_p z^p) = 0$ *outside the unit circle and with* $\{\varepsilon_t\}$ *an i.i.d. sequence with mean zero, variance* $\sigma^2$*, and finite fourth moment* $\mu_4$.

An autoregression has the form of the standard regression model $y_t = \mathbf{x}_t'\boldsymbol{\beta} + u_t$ with $\mathbf{x}_t' = (1, y_{t-1}, y_{t-2}, \ldots, y_{t-p})$ and $u_t = \varepsilon_t$. Note, however, that an autoregression cannot satisfy condition (a) of Assumption 8.2 or 8.3. Even though $u_t$ is independent of $\mathbf{x}_t$ under Assumption 8.4, it will not be the case that $u_t$ is independent of $\mathbf{x}_{t+1}$. Without this independence, none of the small-sample results for case 1 applies. Specifically, even if $\varepsilon_t$ is Gaussian, the *OLS* coefficient $\mathbf{b}$ gives a biased estimate of $\boldsymbol{\beta}$ for an autoregression, and the standard $t$ and $F$ statistics can only be justified asymptotically.

However, the asymptotic results for case 4 are the same as for case 3 and are derived in essentially the same way. To adapt the earlier notation, suppose that the sample consists of $T + p$ observations on $y_t$, numbered $(y_{-p+1}, y_{-p+2}, \ldots, y_0, y_1, \ldots, y_T)$; *OLS* estimation will thus use observations 1 through $T$. Then, as in [8.2.6],

$$\sqrt{T}(\mathbf{b}_T - \boldsymbol{\beta}) = \left[(1/T)\sum_{t=1}^{T}\mathbf{x}_t\mathbf{x}_t'\right]^{-1}\left[(1/\sqrt{T})\sum_{t=1}^{T}\mathbf{x}_t u_t\right]. \qquad [8.2.25]$$

The first term in [8.2.25] is

$$\left[(1/T)\sum_{t=1}^{T}\mathbf{x}_t\mathbf{x}_t'\right]^{-1}$$

$$= \begin{bmatrix} 1 & T^{-1}\Sigma y_{t-1} & T^{-1}\Sigma y_{t-2} & \cdots & T^{-1}\Sigma y_{t-p} \\ T^{-1}\Sigma y_{t-1} & T^{-1}\Sigma y_{t-1}^2 & T^{-1}\Sigma y_{t-1}y_{t-2} & \cdots & T^{-1}\Sigma y_{t-1}y_{t-p} \\ T^{-1}\Sigma y_{t-2} & T^{-1}\Sigma y_{t-2}y_{t-1} & T^{-1}\Sigma y_{t-2}^2 & \cdots & T^{-1}\Sigma y_{t-2}y_{t-p} \\ \vdots & \vdots & \vdots & \cdots & \vdots \\ T^{-1}\Sigma y_{t-p} & T^{-1}\Sigma y_{t-p}y_{t-1} & T^{-1}\Sigma y_{t-p}y_{t-2} & \cdots & T^{-1}\Sigma y_{t-p}^2 \end{bmatrix}^{-1},$$

where $\Sigma$ denotes summation over $t = 1$ to $T$. The elements in the first row or column are of the form $T^{-1}\Sigma y_{t-j}$ and converge in probability to $\mu = E(y_t)$, by Proposition 7.5. Other elements are of the form $T^{-1}\Sigma y_{t-i}y_{t-j}$, which, from [7.2.14], converges in probability to

$$E(y_{t-i}y_{t-j}) = \gamma_{|i-j|} + \mu^2.$$

Hence

$$\left[(1/T)\sum_{t=1}^{T}\mathbf{x}_t\mathbf{x}_t'\right]^{-1} \xrightarrow{p} \mathbf{Q}^{-1} \qquad [8.2.26]$$

where

$$\mathbf{Q} \equiv \begin{bmatrix} 1 & \mu & \mu & \cdots & \mu \\ \mu & \gamma_0 + \mu^2 & \gamma_1 + \mu^2 & \cdots & \gamma_{p-1} + \mu^2 \\ \mu & \gamma_1 + \mu^2 & \gamma_0 + \mu^2 & \cdots & \gamma_{p-2} + \mu^2 \\ \vdots & \vdots & \vdots & \cdots & \vdots \\ \mu & \gamma_{p-1} + \mu^2 & \gamma_{p-2} + \mu^2 & \cdots & \gamma_0 + \mu^2 \end{bmatrix}. \qquad [8.2.27]$$

For the second term in [8.2.25], observe that $\mathbf{x}_t u_t$ is a martingale difference sequence with positive definite variance-covariance matrix given by

$$E(\mathbf{x}_t u_t u_t \mathbf{x}_t') = E(u_t^2) \cdot E(\mathbf{x}_t \mathbf{x}_t') = \sigma^2 \mathbf{Q}.$$

Using an argument similar to that in Example 7.15, it can be shown that

$$\left[(1/\sqrt{T}) \sum_{t=1}^{T} \mathbf{x}_t u_t\right] \xrightarrow{L} N(\mathbf{0}, \sigma^2 \mathbf{Q}) \qquad [8.2.28]$$

(see Exercise 8.3). Substituting [8.2.26] and [8.2.28] into [8.2.25],

$$\sqrt{T}(\mathbf{b}_T - \boldsymbol{\beta}) \xrightarrow{L} N(\mathbf{0}, \sigma^2 \mathbf{Q}^{-1}). \qquad [8.2.29]$$

It is straightforward to verify further that $\mathbf{b}_T$ and $s_T^2$ are consistent for this case. From [8.2.26], the asymptotic variance-covariance matrix of $\sqrt{T}(\mathbf{b}_T - \boldsymbol{\beta})$ can be estimated consistently by $s_T^2(\mathbf{X}_T'\mathbf{X}_T/T)^{-1}$, meaning that standard $t$ and $F$ statistics that treat $\mathbf{b}_T$ as if it were $N(\boldsymbol{\beta}, s_T^2(\mathbf{X}_T'\mathbf{X}_T)^{-1})$ will yield asymptotically valid tests of hypotheses about the coefficients of an autoregression.

As a special case of [8.2.29], consider *OLS* estimation of a first-order autoregression,

$$y_t = \phi y_{t-1} + \varepsilon_t,$$

with $|\phi| < 1$. Then $\mathbf{Q}$ is the scalar $E(y_{t-1}^2) = \gamma_0$, the variance of an $AR(1)$ process. We saw in Chapter 3 that this is given by $\sigma^2/(1 - \phi^2)$. Hence, for $\hat{\phi}$ the *OLS* coefficient,

$$\hat{\phi}_T = \frac{\sum_{t=1}^{T} y_{t-1} y_t}{\sum_{t=1}^{T} y_{t-1}^2},$$

result [8.2.29] implies that

$$\sqrt{T}(\hat{\phi}_T - \phi) \xrightarrow{L} N(0, \sigma^2 \cdot [\sigma^2/(1 - \phi^2)]^{-1}) = N(0, 1 - \phi^2). \qquad [8.2.30]$$

If more precise results than the asymptotic approximation in equation [8.2.29] are desired, the exact small-sample distribution of $\hat{\phi}_T$ can be calculated in either of two ways. If the errors in the autoregression [8.2.24] are $N(0, \sigma^2)$, then for any specified numerical value for $\phi_1, \phi_2, \ldots, \phi_p$ and $c$ the exact small-sample distribution can be calculated using numerical routines developed by Imhof (1961); for illustrations of this method, see Evans and Savin (1981) and Flavin (1983). An alternative is to approximate the small-sample distribution by *Monte Carlo* methods. Here the idea is to use a computer to generate pseudo-random variables $\varepsilon_1, \ldots, \varepsilon_T$, each distributed $N(0, \sigma^2)$ from numerical algorithms such as that described in Kinderman and Ramage (1976). For fixed starting values $y_{-p+1}, \ldots, y_1$, the values for $y_1, y_2, \ldots, y_T$ can then be calculated by iterating on [8.2.24].[6] One then estimates the parameters of [8.2.24] with an *OLS* regression on this artificial sample. A new sample is generated for which a new *OLS* regression is estimated. By performing, say, 10,000 such regressions, an estimate of the exact small-sample distribution of the *OLS* estimates can be obtained.

For the case of a first-order autoregression, it is known from such calculations that $\hat{\phi}_T$ is downward-biased in small samples, with the bias becoming more severe as $\phi$ approaches unity. For example, for a sample of size $T = 25$ generated by [8.2.24] with $p = 1$, $c = 0$, and $\phi = 1$, the estimate $\hat{\phi}_T$ based on *OLS* estimation of [8.2.24] (with a constant term included) will be less than the true value of 1 in 95% of the samples, and will even fall below 0.6 in 10% of the samples.[7]

### *Case 5. Errors Gaussian with Known Variance-Covariance Matrix*

Next consider the following case.

***Assumption 8.5:*** *(a)* $\mathbf{x}_t$ *stochastic; (b) conditional on the full matrix* $\mathbf{X}$*, the vector* $\mathbf{u}$ *is* $N(\mathbf{0}, \sigma^2\mathbf{V})$*; (c)* $\mathbf{V}$ *is a known positive definite matrix.*

When the errors for different dates have different variances but are uncorrelated with each other (that is, $\mathbf{V}$ is diagonal), then the errors are said to exhibit *heteroskedasticity*. For $\mathbf{V}$ nondiagonal, the errors are said to be *autocorrelated.* Writing the variance-covariance matrix as the product of some scalar $\sigma^2$ and a matrix $\mathbf{V}$ is a convention that will help simplify the algebra and interpretation for some examples of heteroskedasticity and autocorrelation. Note again that Assumption 8.5(b) could not hold for an autoregression, since conditional on $\mathbf{x}_{t+1} = (1, y_t, y_{t-1}, \ldots, y_{t-p+1})'$ and $\mathbf{x}_t$, the value of $u_t$ is known with certainty.

Recall from [8.1.12] that

$$(\mathbf{b} - \boldsymbol{\beta}) = (\mathbf{X}'\mathbf{X})^{-1}\mathbf{X}'\mathbf{u}.$$

Taking expectations conditional on $\mathbf{X}$,

$$E[(\mathbf{b} - \boldsymbol{\beta})|\mathbf{X}] = (\mathbf{X}'\mathbf{X})^{-1}\mathbf{X}'\cdot E(\mathbf{u}) = \mathbf{0},$$

and by the law of iterated expectations,

$$E(\mathbf{b} - \boldsymbol{\beta}) = E_{\mathbf{X}}\{E[(\mathbf{b} - \boldsymbol{\beta})|\mathbf{X}]\} = \mathbf{0}.$$

Hence, the *OLS* coefficient estimate is unbiased.

The variance of $\mathbf{b}$ conditional on $\mathbf{X}$ is

$$\begin{aligned} E\{[(\mathbf{b} - \boldsymbol{\beta})(\mathbf{b} - \boldsymbol{\beta})']|\mathbf{X}\} &= E\{[(\mathbf{X}'\mathbf{X})^{-1}\mathbf{X}'\mathbf{u}\mathbf{u}'\mathbf{X}(\mathbf{X}'\mathbf{X})^{-1}]|\mathbf{X}\} \\ &= \sigma^2(\mathbf{X}'\mathbf{X})^{-1}\mathbf{X}'\mathbf{V}\mathbf{X}(\mathbf{X}'\mathbf{X})^{-1}. \end{aligned} \qquad [8.2.31]$$

Thus, conditional on $\mathbf{X}$,

$$\mathbf{b}|\mathbf{X} \sim N\left(\boldsymbol{\beta}, \sigma^2(\mathbf{X}'\mathbf{X})^{-1}\mathbf{X}'\mathbf{V}\mathbf{X}(\mathbf{X}'\mathbf{X})^{-1}\right).$$

[6]Alternatively, one can generate the initial values for $y$ with a draw from the appropriate unconditional distribution. Specifically, generate a $(p \times 1)$ vector $\mathbf{v} \sim N(\mathbf{0}, \mathbf{I}_p)$ and set $(y_{-p+1}, \ldots, y_0)' = \mu\cdot\mathbf{1} + \mathbf{P}\cdot\mathbf{v}$, where $\mu = c/(1 - \phi_1 - \phi_2 - \cdots - \phi_p)$, $\mathbf{1}$ denotes a $(p \times 1)$ vector of 1s, and $\mathbf{P}$ is the Cholesky factor such that $\mathbf{P}\cdot\mathbf{P}' = \boldsymbol{\Gamma}$ for $\boldsymbol{\Gamma}$ the $(p \times p)$ matrix whose columns stacked in a $(p^2 \times 1)$ vector comprise the first column of the matrix $\sigma^2[\mathbf{I}_{p^2} - (\mathbf{F} \otimes \mathbf{F})]^{-1}$, where $\mathbf{F}$ is the $(p \times p)$ matrix defined in equation [1.2.3] in Chapter 1.

[7]These values can be inferred from Table B.5.

Unless $\mathbf{V} = \mathbf{I}_T$, this is not the same variance matrix as in [8.1.17], so that the *OLS* $t$ statistic [8.1.26] does not have the interpretation as a Gaussian variable divided by an estimate of its standard deviation. Thus [8.1.26] will not have a $t(T - k)$ distribution in small samples, nor will it even asymptotically be $N(0, 1)$. A valid test of the hypothesis that $\beta_i = \beta_i^0$ for case 5 would be based not on [8.1.26] but rather on

$$t^* = \frac{(b_i - \beta_i^0)}{s\sqrt{d_{ii}}}, \qquad [8.2.32]$$

where $d_{ii}$ denotes the row $i$, column $i$ element of $(\mathbf{X}'\mathbf{X})^{-1}\mathbf{X}'\mathbf{V}\mathbf{X}(\mathbf{X}'\mathbf{X})^{-1}$. This statistic will be asymptotically $N(0, 1)$.

Although one could form an inference based on [8.2.32], in this case in which $\mathbf{V}$ is known, a superior estimator and test procedure are described in Section 8.3. First, however, we consider a more general case in which $\mathbf{V}$ is of unknown form.

### *Case 6. Errors Serially Uncorrelated but with General Heteroskedasticity*

It may be possible to design asymptotically valid tests even in the presence of heteroskedasticity of a completely unknown form. This point was first observed by Eicker (1967) and White (1980) and extended to time series regressions by Hansen (1982) and Nicholls and Pagan (1983).

***Assumption 8.6:*** *(a) $\mathbf{x}_t$ stochastic, including perhaps lagged values of $y$; (b) $\mathbf{x}_t u_t$ is a martingale difference sequence; (c) $E(u_t^2\mathbf{x}_t\mathbf{x}_t') = \mathbf{\Omega}_t$, a positive definite matrix, with $(1/T)\Sigma_{t=1}^T\mathbf{\Omega}_t$ converging to the positive definite matrix $\mathbf{\Omega}$ and $(1/T)\Sigma_{t=1}^T u_t^2\mathbf{x}_t\mathbf{x}_t' \xrightarrow{p} \mathbf{\Omega}$; (d) $E(u_t^4 x_{it}x_{jt}x_{lt}x_{mt}) < \infty$ for all $i$, $j$, $l$, $m$, and $t$; (e) plims of $(1/T)\Sigma_{t=1}^T u_t x_{it}\mathbf{x}_t\mathbf{x}_t'$ and $(1/T)\Sigma_{t=1}^T x_{it}x_{jt}\mathbf{x}_t\mathbf{x}_t'$ exist and are finite for all $i$ and $j$ and $(1/T)\Sigma_{t=1}^T\mathbf{x}_t\mathbf{x}_t' \xrightarrow{p} \mathbf{Q}$, a nonsingular matrix.*

Assumption 8.6(b) requires $u_t$ to be uncorrelated with its own lagged values and with current and lagged values of $\mathbf{x}$. Although the errors are presumed to be serially uncorrelated, Assumption 8.6(c) allows a broad class of conditional heteroskedasticity for the errors. As an example of such heteroskedasticity, consider a regression with a single i.i.d. explanatory variable $x_t$ with $E(x_t^2) = \mu_2$ and $E(x_t^4) = \mu_4$. Suppose that the variance of the residual for date $t$ is given by $E(u_t^2|x_t) = a + bx_t^2$. Then $E(u_t^2x_t^2) = E_x[E(u_t^2|x_t)\cdot x_t^2] = E_x[(a + bx_t^2)\cdot x_t^2] = a\mu_2 + b\mu_4$. Thus, $\Omega_t = a\mu_2 + b\mu_4 = \Omega$ for all $t$. By the law of large numbers, $(1/T)\Sigma_{t=1}^T u_t^2x_t^2$ will converge to the population moment $\Omega$. Assumption 8.6(c) allows more general conditional heteroskedasticity in that $E(u_t^2x_t^2)$ might be a function of $t$, provided that the time average of $(u_t^2x_t^2)$ converges. Assumption 8.6(d) and (e) impose bounds on higher moments of $\mathbf{x}$ and $u$.

Consistency of $\mathbf{b}$ is established using the same arguments as in case 3. The asymptotic variance is found from writing

$$\sqrt{T}(\mathbf{b}_T - \boldsymbol{\beta}) = \left[(1/T)\sum_{t=1}^T \mathbf{x}_t\mathbf{x}_t'\right]^{-1}\left[(1/\sqrt{T})\sum_{t=1}^T \mathbf{x}_t u_t\right].$$

Assumption 8.6(e) ensures that

$$\left[(1/T)\sum_{t=1}^T \mathbf{x}_t\mathbf{x}_t'\right]^{-1} \xrightarrow{p} \mathbf{Q}^{-1}$$

for some nonsingular matrix $\mathbf{Q}$. Similarly, $\mathbf{x}_t u_t$ satisfies the conditions of Proposition 7.9, from which

$$\left[(1/\sqrt{T})\sum_{t=1}^{T}\mathbf{x}_t u_t\right] \xrightarrow{L} N(\mathbf{0}, \mathbf{\Omega}).$$

The asymptotic distribution of the *OLS* estimate is thus given by

$$\sqrt{T}(\mathbf{b}_T - \boldsymbol{\beta}) \xrightarrow{L} N(\mathbf{0}, \mathbf{Q}^{-1}\mathbf{\Omega}\mathbf{Q}^{-1}). \qquad [8.2.33]$$

White's proposal was to estimate the asymptotic variance matrix consistently by substituting $\hat{\mathbf{Q}}_T = (1/T)\Sigma_{t=1}^{T}\mathbf{x}_t\mathbf{x}_t'$ and $\hat{\mathbf{\Omega}}_T = (1/T)\Sigma_{t=1}^{T}\hat{u}_t^2\mathbf{x}_t\mathbf{x}_t'$ into [8.2.33], where $\hat{u}_t$ denotes the *OLS* residual [8.1.4]. The following result is established in Appendix 8.A to this chapter.

***Proposition 8.3:*** *With heteroskedasticity of unknown form satisfying Assumption 8.6, the asymptotic variance-covariance matrix of the OLS coefficient vector can be consistently estimated by*

$$\hat{\mathbf{Q}}_T^{-1}\hat{\mathbf{\Omega}}_T\hat{\mathbf{Q}}_T^{-1} \xrightarrow{p} \mathbf{Q}^{-1}\mathbf{\Omega}\mathbf{Q}^{-1}. \qquad [8.2.34]$$

Recalling [8.2.33], the *OLS* estimate $\mathbf{b}_T$ can be treated as if

$$\mathbf{b}_T \approx N(\boldsymbol{\beta}, \hat{\mathbf{V}}_T/T)$$

where

$$\begin{aligned}\hat{\mathbf{V}}_T &= \hat{\mathbf{Q}}_T^{-1}\hat{\mathbf{\Omega}}_T\hat{\mathbf{Q}}_T^{-1}\\ &= (\mathbf{X}_T'\mathbf{X}_T/T)^{-1}\left[(1/T)\sum_{t=1}^{T}\hat{u}_t^2\mathbf{x}_t\mathbf{x}_t'\right](\mathbf{X}_T'\mathbf{X}_T/T)^{-1} \qquad [8.2.35]\\ &= T\cdot(\mathbf{X}_T'\mathbf{X}_T)^{-1}\left[\sum_{t=1}^{T}\hat{u}_t^2\mathbf{x}_t\mathbf{x}_t'\right](\mathbf{X}_T'\mathbf{X}_t)^{-1}.\end{aligned}$$

The square root of the row $i$, column $i$ element of $\hat{\mathbf{V}}_T/T$ is known as a *heteroskedasticity-consistent standard error* for the *OLS* estimate $b_i$. We can, of course, also use $(\hat{\mathbf{V}}_T/T)$ to test a joint hypothesis of the form $\mathbf{R}\boldsymbol{\beta} = \mathbf{r}$, where $\mathbf{R}$ is an $(m \times k)$ matrix summarizing $m$ separate hypotheses about $\boldsymbol{\beta}$. Specifically,

$$(\mathbf{R}\mathbf{b}_T - \mathbf{r})'[\mathbf{R}(\hat{\mathbf{V}}_T/T)\mathbf{R}']^{-1}(\mathbf{R}\mathbf{b}_T - \mathbf{r}) \qquad [8.2.36]$$

has the same asymptotic distribution as

$$[\sqrt{T}(\mathbf{R}\mathbf{b}_T - \mathbf{r})]'(\mathbf{R}\mathbf{Q}^{-1}\mathbf{\Omega}\mathbf{Q}^{-1}\mathbf{R}')^{-1}[\sqrt{T}(\mathbf{R}\mathbf{b}_T - \mathbf{r})],$$

which, from [8.2.33], is a quadratic form of an asymptotically Normal $(m \times 1)$ vector $\sqrt{T}(\mathbf{R}\mathbf{b}_T - \mathbf{r})$ with weighting matrix the inverse of its variance-covariance matrix, $(\mathbf{R}\mathbf{Q}^{-1}\mathbf{\Omega}\mathbf{Q}^{-1}\mathbf{R}')$. Hence, [8.2.36] has an asymptotic $\chi^2$ distribution with $m$ degrees of freedom.

It is also possible to develop an estimate of the asymptotic variance-covariance matrix of $\mathbf{b}_T$ that is robust with respect to both heteroskedasticity and autocorrelation:

$$\begin{aligned}&(\hat{\mathbf{V}}_T/T)\\ &= (\mathbf{X}_T'\mathbf{X}_T)^{-1}\left[\sum_{t=1}^{T}\hat{u}_t^2\mathbf{x}_t\mathbf{x}_t'\right.\\ &\quad\left. + \sum_{v=1}^{q}\left[1 - \frac{v}{q+1}\right]\sum_{t=v+1}^{T}(\mathbf{x}_t\hat{u}_t\hat{u}_{t-v}\mathbf{x}_{t-v}' + \mathbf{x}_{t-v}\hat{u}_{t-v}\hat{u}_t\mathbf{x}_t')\right](\mathbf{X}_T'\mathbf{X}_T)^{-1}.\end{aligned}$$

Here $q$ is a parameter representing the number of autocorrelations used to approximate the dynamics for $u_t$. The square root of the row $i$, column $i$ element of $(\hat{\mathbf{V}}_T/T)$ is known as the Newey-West (1987) heteroskedasticity- and autocorrelation-consistent standard error for the *OLS* estimator. The basis for this expression and alternative ways to calculate heteroskedasticity- and autocorrelation-consistent standard errors will be discussed in Chapter 10.

## 8.3. *Generalized Least Squares*

The previous section evaluated *OLS* estimation under a variety of assumptions, including $E(\mathbf{uu}') \neq \sigma^2\mathbf{I}_T$. Although *OLS* can be used in this last case, generalized least squares (*GLS*) is usually preferred.

### GLS *with Known Covariance Matrix*

Let us reconsider data generated according to Assumption 8.5, under which $\mathbf{u}|\mathbf{X} \sim N(\mathbf{0}, \sigma^2\mathbf{V})$ with $\mathbf{V}$ a known $(T \times T)$ matrix. Since $\mathbf{V}$ is symmetric and positive definite, there exists a nonsingular $(T \times T)$ matrix $\mathbf{L}$ such that[8]

$$\mathbf{V}^{-1} = \mathbf{L}'\mathbf{L}. \qquad [8.3.1]$$

Imagine transforming the population residuals $\mathbf{u}$ by $\mathbf{L}$:

$$\underset{(T\times 1)}{\tilde{\mathbf{u}}} \equiv \mathbf{Lu}.$$

This would generate a new set of residuals $\tilde{\mathbf{u}}$ with mean $\mathbf{0}$ and variance conditional on $\mathbf{X}$ given by

$$E(\tilde{\mathbf{u}}\tilde{\mathbf{u}}'|\mathbf{X}) = \mathbf{L}\cdot E(\mathbf{uu}'|\mathbf{X})\mathbf{L}' = \mathbf{L}\sigma^2\mathbf{VL}'.$$

But $\mathbf{V} = [\mathbf{V}^{-1}]^{-1} = [\mathbf{L}'\mathbf{L}]^{-1}$, meaning

$$E(\tilde{\mathbf{u}}\tilde{\mathbf{u}}'|\mathbf{X}) = \sigma^2\mathbf{L}[\mathbf{L}'\mathbf{L}]^{-1}\mathbf{L}' = \sigma^2\mathbf{I}_T. \qquad [8.3.2]$$

We can thus take the matrix equation that characterizes the basic regression model,

$$\mathbf{y} = \mathbf{X}\boldsymbol{\beta} + \mathbf{u},$$

and premultiply both sides by $\mathbf{L}$:

$$\mathbf{Ly} = \mathbf{LX}\boldsymbol{\beta} + \mathbf{Lu},$$

to produce a new regression model

$$\tilde{\mathbf{y}} = \tilde{\mathbf{X}}\boldsymbol{\beta} + \tilde{\mathbf{u}}, \qquad [8.3.3]$$

where

$$\tilde{\mathbf{y}} \equiv \mathbf{Ly} \qquad \tilde{\mathbf{X}} \equiv \mathbf{LX} \qquad \tilde{\mathbf{u}} \equiv \mathbf{Lu} \qquad [8.3.4]$$

with $\tilde{\mathbf{u}}|\mathbf{X} \sim N(\mathbf{0}, \sigma^2\mathbf{I}_T)$. Hence, the transformed model [8.3.3] satisfies Assumption 8.2, meaning that all the results for that case apply to [8.3.3]. Specifically, the estimator

$$\tilde{\mathbf{b}} = (\tilde{\mathbf{X}}'\tilde{\mathbf{X}})^{-1}\tilde{\mathbf{X}}'\tilde{\mathbf{y}} = (\mathbf{X}'\mathbf{L}'\mathbf{LX})^{-1}\mathbf{X}'\mathbf{L}'\mathbf{Ly} = (\mathbf{X}'\mathbf{V}^{-1}\mathbf{X})^{-1}\mathbf{X}'\mathbf{V}^{-1}\mathbf{y} \qquad [8.3.5]$$

[8]We know that there exists a nonsingular matrix $\mathbf{P}$ such that $\mathbf{V} = \mathbf{PP}'$ and so $\mathbf{V}^{-1} = [\mathbf{P}']^{-1}\mathbf{P}^{-1}$. Take $\mathbf{L} = \mathbf{P}^{-1}$ to deduce [8.3.1].

is Gaussian with mean $\boldsymbol{\beta}$ and variance $\sigma^2(\tilde{\mathbf{X}}'\tilde{\mathbf{X}})^{-1} = \sigma^2(\mathbf{X}'\mathbf{V}^{-1}\mathbf{X})^{-1}$ conditional on $\mathbf{X}$ and is the minimum-variance unbiased estimator conditional on $\mathbf{X}$. The estimator [8.3.5] is known as the *generalized least squares* (*GLS*) estimator. Similarly,

$$\tilde{s}^2 = [1/(T - k)] \sum_{t=1}^{T} (\tilde{y}_t - \tilde{\mathbf{x}}_t'\tilde{\mathbf{b}})^2 \qquad [8.3.6]$$

has an exact $[\sigma^2/(T - k)]\cdot\chi^2(T - K)$ distribution under Assumption 8.5, while

$$(\mathbf{R}\tilde{\mathbf{b}} - \mathbf{r})'[\tilde{s}^2\mathbf{R}(\mathbf{X}'\mathbf{V}^{-1}\mathbf{X})^{-1}\mathbf{R}']^{-1}(\mathbf{R}\tilde{\mathbf{b}} - \mathbf{r})/m$$

has an exact $F(m, T - k)$ distribution under the null hypothesis $\mathbf{R}\boldsymbol{\beta} = \mathbf{r}$.

We now discuss several examples to make these ideas concrete.

## *Heteroskedasticity*

A simple case to analyze is one for which the variance of $u_t$ is presumed to be proportional to the square of one of the explanatory variables for that equation, say, $x_{1t}^2$:

$$E(\mathbf{uu}'|\mathbf{X}) = \sigma^2 \begin{bmatrix} x_{11}^2 & 0 & \cdots & 0 \\ 0 & x_{12}^2 & \cdots & 0 \\ \vdots & \vdots & \cdots & \vdots \\ 0 & 0 & \cdots & x_{1T}^2 \end{bmatrix} = \sigma^2\mathbf{V}.$$

Then it is easy to see that

$$\mathbf{L} = \begin{bmatrix} 1/|x_{11}| & 0 & \cdots & 0 \\ 0 & 1/|x_{12}| & \cdots & 0 \\ \vdots & \vdots & \cdots & \vdots \\ 0 & 0 & \cdots & 1/|x_{1T}| \end{bmatrix}$$

satisfies conditions [8.3.1] and [8.3.2]. Hence, if we regress $y_t/|x_{1t}|$ on $\mathbf{x}_t/|x_{1t}|$, all the standard *OLS* output from the regression will be valid.

## *Autocorrelation*

As a second example, consider

$$u_t = \rho u_{t-1} + \varepsilon_t, \qquad [8.3.7]$$

where $|\rho| < 1$ and $\varepsilon_t$ is Gaussian white noise with variance $\sigma^2$. Then

$$E(\mathbf{uu}'|\mathbf{X}) = \frac{\sigma^2}{1 - \rho^2} \begin{bmatrix} 1 & \rho & \rho^2 & \cdots & \rho^{T-1} \\ \rho & 1 & \rho & \cdots & \rho^{T-2} \\ \vdots & \vdots & \vdots & \cdots & \vdots \\ \rho^{T-1} & \rho^{T-2} & \rho^{T-3} & \cdots & 1 \end{bmatrix} = \sigma^2\mathbf{V}. \qquad [8.3.8]$$

Notice from expression [5.2.18] that the matrix

$$\mathbf{L} = \begin{bmatrix} \sqrt{1-\rho^2} & 0 & 0 & \cdots & 0 & 0 \\ -\rho & 1 & 0 & \cdots & 0 & 0 \\ 0 & -\rho & 1 & \cdots & 0 & 0 \\ \vdots & \vdots & \vdots & \cdots & \vdots & \vdots \\ 0 & 0 & 0 & \cdots & -\rho & 1 \end{bmatrix} \qquad [8.3.9]$$

satisfies [8.3.1]. The *GLS* estimates are found from an *OLS* regression of $\tilde{\mathbf{y}} = \mathbf{Ly}$ on $\tilde{\mathbf{X}} = \mathbf{LX}$; that is, regress $y_1\sqrt{1-\rho^2}$ on $x_1\sqrt{1-\rho^2}$ and $y_t - \rho y_{t-1}$ on $\mathbf{x}_t - \rho\mathbf{x}_{t-1}$ for $t = 2, 3, \ldots, T$.

## GLS *and Maximum Likelihood Estimation*

Assumption 8.5 asserts that $\mathbf{y}|\mathbf{X} \sim N(\mathbf{X\beta}, \sigma^2\mathbf{V})$. Hence, the log of the likelihood of $\mathbf{y}$ conditioned on $\mathbf{X}$ is given by

$$(-T/2)\log(2\pi) - (1/2)\log|\sigma^2\mathbf{V}| - (1/2)(\mathbf{y} - \mathbf{X\beta})'(\sigma^2\mathbf{V})^{-1}(\mathbf{y} - \mathbf{X\beta}). \qquad [8.3.10]$$

Notice that [8.3.1] can be used to write the last term in [8.3.10] as

$$\begin{aligned} -(1/2)(\mathbf{y} - \mathbf{X\beta})'(\sigma^2\mathbf{V})^{-1}(\mathbf{y} - \mathbf{X\beta}) & \\ &= -[1/(2\sigma^2)](\mathbf{y} - \mathbf{X\beta})'(\mathbf{L}'\mathbf{L})(\mathbf{y} - \mathbf{X\beta}) \\ &= -[1/(2\sigma^2)](\mathbf{Ly} - \mathbf{LX\beta})'(\mathbf{Ly} - \mathbf{LX\beta}) \\ &= -[1/(2\sigma^2)](\tilde{\mathbf{y}} - \tilde{\mathbf{X}}\boldsymbol{\beta})'(\tilde{\mathbf{y}} - \tilde{\mathbf{X}}\boldsymbol{\beta}). \end{aligned} \qquad [8.3.11]$$

Similarly, the middle term in [8.3.10] can be written as in [5.2.24]:

$$-(1/2)\log|\sigma^2\mathbf{V}| = -(T/2)\log(\sigma^2) + \log|\det(\mathbf{L})|, \qquad [8.3.12]$$

where $|\det(\mathbf{L})|$ denotes the absolute value of the determinant of $\mathbf{L}$. Substituting [8.3.11] and [8.3.12] into [8.3.10], the conditional log likelihood can be written as

$$\begin{aligned} -(T/2)\log(2\pi) - (T/2)\log(\sigma^2) + \log|\det(\mathbf{L})| & \\ - [1/(2\sigma^2)](\tilde{\mathbf{y}} - \tilde{\mathbf{X}}\boldsymbol{\beta})'(\tilde{\mathbf{y}} - \tilde{\mathbf{X}}\boldsymbol{\beta}). & \end{aligned} \qquad [8.3.13]$$

Thus, the log likelihood is maximized with respect to $\boldsymbol{\beta}$ by an *OLS* regression of $\tilde{\mathbf{y}}$ on $\tilde{\mathbf{X}}$,[9] meaning that the *GLS* estimate [8.3.5] is also the maximum likelihood estimate under Assumption 8.5.

The *GLS* estimate $\tilde{\mathbf{b}}$ is still likely to be reasonable even if the residuals $\mathbf{u}$ are non-Gaussian. Specifically, the residuals of the transformed regression [8.3.3] have mean $\mathbf{0}$ and variance $\sigma^2\mathbf{I}_T$, and so this regression satisfies the conditions of the Gauss-Markov theorem—even if the residuals are non-Gaussian, $\tilde{\mathbf{b}}$ will have minimum variance (conditional on $\mathbf{X}$) among the class of all unbiased estimators that are linear functions of $\mathbf{y}$. Hence, maximization of [8.3.13], or quasi-maximum likelihood estimation, may offer a useful estimating principle even for non-Gaussian $\mathbf{u}$.

## GLS *When the Variance Matrix of Residuals Must Be Estimated from the Data*

Up to this point we have been assuming that the elements of $\mathbf{V}$ are known a priori. More commonly, $\mathbf{V}$ is posited to be of a particular form $\mathbf{V}(\boldsymbol{\theta})$, where $\boldsymbol{\theta}$ is a

[9]This assumes that the parameters of $\mathbf{L}$ do not involve $\boldsymbol{\beta}$, as is implied by Assumption 8.5.

vector of parameters that must be estimated from the data. For example, with first-order serial correlation of residuals as in [8.3.7], $\mathbf{V}$ is the matrix in [8.3.8] and $\boldsymbol{\theta}$ is the scalar $\rho$. As a second example, we might postulate that the variance of observation $t$ depends on the explanatory variables according to

$$E(u_t^2|\mathbf{x}_t) = \sigma^2(1 + \alpha_1 x_{1t}^2 + \alpha_2 x_{2t}^2),$$

in which case $\boldsymbol{\theta} = (\alpha_1, \alpha_2)'$.

Our task is then to estimate $\boldsymbol{\theta}$ and $\boldsymbol{\beta}$ jointly from the data. One approach is to use as estimates the values of $\boldsymbol{\theta}$ and $\boldsymbol{\beta}$ that maximize [8.3.13]. Since one can always form [8.3.13] and maximize it numerically, this approach has the appeal of offering a single rule to follow whenever $E(\mathbf{uu}'|\mathbf{X})$ is not of the simple form $\sigma^2\mathbf{I}_T$. However, other, simpler estimators can also have desirable properties.

It often turns out to be the case that

$$\sqrt{T}(\mathbf{X}_T'[\mathbf{V}_T(\hat{\boldsymbol{\theta}}_T)]^{-1}\mathbf{X}_T)^{-1}(\mathbf{X}_T'[\mathbf{V}_T(\hat{\boldsymbol{\theta}}_T)]^{-1}\mathbf{y}_T)$$
$$\xrightarrow{p} \sqrt{T}(\mathbf{X}_T'[\mathbf{V}_T(\boldsymbol{\theta}_0)]^{-1}\mathbf{X}_T)^{-1}(\mathbf{X}_T'[\mathbf{V}_T(\boldsymbol{\theta}_0)]^{-1}\mathbf{y}_T),$$

where $\mathbf{V}_T(\boldsymbol{\theta}_0)$ denotes the true variance of errors and $\hat{\boldsymbol{\theta}}_T$ is any consistent estimate of $\boldsymbol{\theta}$. Moreover, a consistent estimate of $\boldsymbol{\theta}$ can often be obtained from a simple analysis of *OLS* residuals. Thus, an estimate coming from a few simple *OLS* and *GLS* regressions can have the same asymptotic distribution as the maximum likelihood estimator. Since regressions are much easier to implement than numerical maximization, the simpler estimates are often used.

## *Estimation with First-Order Autocorrelation of Regression Residuals and No Lagged Endogenous Variables*

We illustrate these issues by considering a regression whose residuals follow the *AR*(1) process [8.3.7]. For now we maintain the assumption that $\mathbf{u}|\mathbf{X}$ has mean zero and variance $\sigma^2\mathbf{V}(\rho)$, noting that this rules out lagged endogenous variables; that is, we assume that $\mathbf{x}_t$ is uncorrelated with $u_{t-s}$. The following subsection comments on the importance of this assumption. Recalling that the determinant of a lower triangular matrix is just the product of the terms on the principal diagonal, we see from [8.3.9] that $\det(\mathbf{L}) = \sqrt{1-\rho^2}$. Thus, the log likelihood [8.3.13] for this case is

$$\begin{aligned} -(T/2)\log(2\pi) &- (T/2)\log(\sigma^2) + (1/2)\log(1-\rho^2) \\ &- [(1-\rho^2)/(2\sigma^2)](y_1 - \mathbf{x}_1'\boldsymbol{\beta})^2 \\ &- [1/(2\sigma^2)]\sum_{t=2}^{T}[(y_t - \mathbf{x}_t'\boldsymbol{\beta}) - \rho(y_{t-1} - \mathbf{x}_{t-1}'\boldsymbol{\beta})]^2. \end{aligned} \qquad [8.3.14]$$

One approach, then, is to maximize [8.3.14] numerically with respect to $\boldsymbol{\beta}$, $\rho$, and $\sigma^2$. The reader may recognize [8.3.14] as the exact log likelihood function for an *AR*(1) process (equation [5.2.9]) with $(y_t - \mu)$ replaced by $(y_t - \mathbf{x}_t'\boldsymbol{\beta})$.

Just as in the *AR*(1) case, simpler estimates (with the same asymptotic distribution) are obtained if we condition on the first observation, seeking to maximize

$$\begin{aligned} -[(T-1)/2]\log(2\pi) &- [(T-1)/2]\log(\sigma^2) \\ &- [1/(2\sigma^2)]\sum_{t=2}^{T}[(y_t - \mathbf{x}_t'\boldsymbol{\beta}) - \rho(y_{t-1} - \mathbf{x}_{t-1}'\boldsymbol{\beta})]^2. \end{aligned} \qquad [8.3.15]$$

If we knew the value of $\rho$, then the value of $\boldsymbol{\beta}$ that maximizes [8.3.15] could be found by an *OLS* regression of $(y_t - \rho y_{t-1})$ on $(\mathbf{x}_t - \rho\mathbf{x}_{t-1})$ for $t = 2, 3, \ldots,$

$T$ (call this regression A). Conversely, if we knew the value of $\boldsymbol{\beta}$, then the value of $\rho$ that maximizes [8.3.15] would be found by an *OLS* regression of $(y_t - \mathbf{x}_t'\boldsymbol{\beta})$ on $(y_{t-1} - \mathbf{x}_{t-1}'\boldsymbol{\beta})$ for $t = 2, 3, \ldots, T$ (call this regression B). We can thus start with an initial guess for $\rho$ (often $\rho = 0$), and perform regression A to get an initial estimate of $\boldsymbol{\beta}$. For $\rho = 0$, this initial estimate of $\boldsymbol{\beta}$ would just be the *OLS* estimate $\mathbf{b}$. This estimate of $\boldsymbol{\beta}$ can be used in regression B to get an updated estimate of $\rho$, for example, by regressing the *OLS* residual $\hat{u}_t = y_t - \mathbf{x}_t'\mathbf{b}$ on its own lagged value. This new estimate of $\rho$ can be used to repeat the two regressions. Zigzagging back and forth between A and B is known as the *iterated Cochrane-Orcutt* method and will converge to a local maximum of [8.3.15].

Alternatively, consider the estimate of $\rho$ that results from the first iteration alone,

$$\hat{\rho} = \frac{(1/T)\sum_{t=1}^{T} \hat{u}_{t-1}\hat{u}_t}{(1/T)\sum_{t=1}^{T} \hat{u}_{t-1}^2}, \qquad [8.3.16]$$

where $\hat{u}_t = y_t - \mathbf{x}_t'\mathbf{b}$ and $\mathbf{b}$ is the *OLS* estimate of $\boldsymbol{\beta}$. To simplify expressions, we have renormalized the number of observations in the original sample to $T + 1$, denoted $y_0, y_1, \ldots, y_T$, so that $T$ observations are used in the conditional maximum likelihood estimation. Notice that

$$\hat{u}_t = (y_t - \boldsymbol{\beta}'\mathbf{x}_t + \boldsymbol{\beta}'\mathbf{x}_t - \mathbf{b}'\mathbf{x}_t) = u_t + (\boldsymbol{\beta} - \mathbf{b})'\mathbf{x}_t,$$

allowing the numerator of [8.3.16] to be written

$$\begin{aligned}
&(1/T)\sum_{t=1}^{T} \hat{u}_t\hat{u}_{t-1} \\
&\quad = (1/T)\sum_{t=1}^{T} [u_t + (\boldsymbol{\beta} - \mathbf{b})'\mathbf{x}_t][u_{t-1} + (\boldsymbol{\beta} - \mathbf{b})'\mathbf{x}_{t-1}] \\
&\quad = (1/T)\sum_{t=1}^{T} (u_t u_{t-1}) + (\boldsymbol{\beta} - \mathbf{b})'(1/T)\sum_{t=1}^{T} (u_t\mathbf{x}_{t-1} + u_{t-1}\mathbf{x}_t) \\
&\qquad + (\boldsymbol{\beta} - \mathbf{b})'\left[(1/T)\sum_{t=1}^{T} \mathbf{x}_t\mathbf{x}_{t-1}'\right](\boldsymbol{\beta} - \mathbf{b}).
\end{aligned} \qquad [8.3.17]$$

As long as $\mathbf{b}$ is a consistent estimate of $\boldsymbol{\beta}$ and boundedness conditions ensure that plims of $(1/T)\Sigma_{t=1}^{T} u_t\mathbf{x}_{t-1}$, $(1/T)\Sigma_{t=1}^{T} u_{t-1}\mathbf{x}_t$, and $(1/T)\Sigma_{t=1}^{T}\mathbf{x}_t\mathbf{x}_{t-1}'$ exist, then

$$\begin{aligned}
(1/T)\sum_{t=1}^{T} \hat{u}_t\hat{u}_{t-1} &\xrightarrow{p} (1/T)\sum_{t=1}^{T} u_t u_{t-1} \\
&= (1/T)\sum_{t=1}^{T} (\varepsilon_t + \rho u_{t-1})u_{t-1} \\
&\xrightarrow{p} \rho\cdot\text{Var}(u).
\end{aligned} \qquad [8.3.18]$$

Similar analysis establishes that the denominator of [8.3.16] converges in probability to $\text{Var}(u)$, so that $\hat{\rho} \xrightarrow{p} \rho$.

If $u_t$ is uncorrelated with $\mathbf{x}_s$ for $s = t - 1$, $t$, and $t + 1$, one can make the stronger claim that an estimate of $\rho$ based on an autoregression of the *OLS* residuals $\hat{u}_t$ (expression [8.3.16]) has the same asymptotic distribution as an estimate of $\rho$ based on the true population residuals $u_t$. Specifically, if $\text{plim}[(1/T)\Sigma_{t=1}^{T} u_t\mathbf{x}_{t-1}] =$

$\text{plim}[(1/T)\Sigma_{t=1}^{T} u_{t-1}\mathbf{x}_t] = \mathbf{0}$, then multiplying [8.3.17] by $\sqrt{T}$, we find

$$
\begin{aligned}
&(1/\sqrt{T}) \sum_{t=1}^{T} \hat{u}_t \hat{u}_{t-1} \\
&\quad = (1/\sqrt{T}) \sum_{t=1}^{T} (u_t u_{t-1}) + \sqrt{T}(\boldsymbol{\beta} - \mathbf{b})'(1/T) \sum_{t=1}^{T} (u_t \mathbf{x}_{t-1} + u_{t-1}\mathbf{x}_t) \\
&\qquad + \sqrt{T}(\boldsymbol{\beta} - \mathbf{b})' \left[ (1/T) \sum_{t=1}^{T} \mathbf{x}_t \mathbf{x}_{t-1}' \right] (\boldsymbol{\beta} - \mathbf{b}) \\
&\quad \xrightarrow{p} (1/\sqrt{T}) \sum_{t=1}^{T} (u_t u_{t-1}) + \sqrt{T}(\boldsymbol{\beta} - \mathbf{b})'\mathbf{0} \\
&\qquad + \sqrt{T}(\boldsymbol{\beta} - \mathbf{b})' \,\text{plim} \left[ (1/T) \sum_{t=1}^{T} \mathbf{x}_t \mathbf{x}_{t-1}' \right] \mathbf{0} \\
&\quad = (1/\sqrt{T}) \sum_{t=1}^{T} (u_t u_{t-1}).
\end{aligned}
\tag{8.3.19}
$$

Hence,

$$
\sqrt{T} \left[ \frac{(1/T) \sum_{t=1}^{T} \hat{u}_{t-1} \hat{u}_t}{(1/T) \sum_{t=1}^{T} \hat{u}_{t-1}^2} \right] \xrightarrow{p} \sqrt{T} \left[ \frac{(1/T) \sum_{t=1}^{T} u_{t-1} u_t}{(1/T) \sum_{t=1}^{T} u_{t-1}^2} \right]. \tag{8.3.20}
$$

The *OLS* estimate of $\rho$ based on the population residuals would have an asymptotic distribution given by [8.2.30]:

$$
\sqrt{T} \left[ \frac{(1/T) \sum_{t=1}^{T} \hat{u}_{t-1} \hat{u}_t}{(1/T) \sum_{t=1}^{T} \hat{u}_{t-1}^2} - \rho \right] \xrightarrow{L} N(0, (1 - \rho^2)). \tag{8.3.21}
$$

Result [8.3.20] implies that an estimate of $\rho$ has the same asymptotic distribution when based on any consistent estimate of $\boldsymbol{\beta}$. If the Cochrane-Orcutt iterations are stopped after just one evaluation of $\hat{\rho}$, the resulting estimate of $\rho$ has the same asymptotic distribution as the estimate of $\rho$ emerging from any subsequent step of the iteration.

The same also turns out to be true of the *GLS* estimate $\tilde{\mathbf{b}}$.

***Proposition 8.4:*** *Suppose that Assumption 8.5(a) and (b) holds with* $\mathbf{V}$ *given by [8.3.8] and* $|\rho| < 1$. *Suppose in addition that* $(1/T)\Sigma_{t=1}^{T} \mathbf{x}_t u_s \xrightarrow{p} \mathbf{0}$ *for all s and that* $(1/T)\Sigma_{t=1}^{T} \mathbf{x}_t \mathbf{x}_t'$ *and* $(1/T)\Sigma_{t=1}^{T} \mathbf{x}_t \mathbf{x}_{t-1}'$ *have finite plims. Then the GLS estimate* $\tilde{\mathbf{b}}$ *constructed from* $\mathbf{V}(\hat{\rho})$ *for* $\hat{\rho}$ *given by [8.3.16] has the same asymptotic distribution as* $\tilde{\mathbf{b}}$ *constructed from* $\mathbf{V}(\rho)$ *for the true value of* $\rho$.

## *Serial Correlation with Lagged Endogenous Variables*

An *endogenous variable* is a variable that is correlated with the regression error term $u_t$. Many of the preceding results about serially correlated errors no longer hold if the regression contains lagged endogenous variables. For example, consider estimation of

$$y_t = \beta y_{t-1} + \gamma x_t + u_t, \qquad [8.3.22]$$

where $u_t$ follows an $AR(1)$ process as in [8.3.7]. Since (1) $u_t$ is correlated with $u_{t-1}$ and (2) $u_{t-1}$ is correlated with $y_{t-1}$, it follows that $u_t$ is correlated with the explanatory variable $y_{t-1}$. Accordingly, it is not the case that $\text{plim}[(1/T)\Sigma_{t=1}^T \mathbf{x}_t u_t] = \mathbf{0}$, the key condition required for consistency of the $OLS$ estimator $\mathbf{b}$. Hence, $\hat{\rho}$ in [8.3.16] is not a consistent estimate of $\rho$.

If one nevertheless iterates on the Cochrane-Orcutt procedure, then the algorithm will converge to a *local* maximum of [8.3.15]. However, the resulting $GLS$ estimate $\tilde{\mathbf{b}}$ need not be a consistent estimate of $\boldsymbol{\beta}$. Notwithstanding, the *global* maximum of [8.3.15] should provide a consistent estimate of $\boldsymbol{\beta}$. By experimenting with start-up values for iterated Cochrane-Orcutt other than $\rho = 0$, one should find this global maximum.[10]

A simple estimate of $\rho$ that is consistent in the presence of lagged endogenous variables was suggested by Durbin (1960). Multiplying [8.3.22] by $(1 - \rho L)$ gives

$$y_t = (\rho + \beta)y_{t-1} - \rho\beta y_{t-2} + \gamma x_t - \rho\gamma x_{t-1} + \varepsilon_t. \qquad [8.3.23]$$

This is a restricted version of the regression model

$$y_t = \alpha_1 y_{t-1} + \alpha_2 y_{t-2} + \alpha_3 x_t + \alpha_4 x_{t-1} + \varepsilon_t, \qquad [8.3.24]$$

where the four regression coefficients $(\alpha_1, \alpha_2, \alpha_3, \alpha_4)$ are restricted to be nonlinear functions of three underlying parameters $(\rho, \beta, \gamma)$. Minimization of the sum of squared $\varepsilon$'s in [8.3.23] is equivalent to maximum likelihood estimation conditioning on the first two observations. Moreover, the error term in equation [8.3.24] is uncorrelated with the explanatory variables, and so the $\alpha$'s can be estimated consistently by $OLS$ estimation of [8.3.24]. Then $-\hat{\alpha}_4/\hat{\alpha}_3$ provides a consistent estimate of $\rho$ despite the presence of lagged endogenous variables in [8.3.24].

Even if consistent estimates of $\rho$ and $\boldsymbol{\beta}$ are obtained, Durbin (1970) emphasized that with lagged endogenous variables it will still not be the case that an estimate of $\rho$ based on $(y_t - \mathbf{x}_t'\hat{\boldsymbol{\beta}})$ has the same asymptotic distribution as an estimate based on $(y_t - \mathbf{x}_t'\boldsymbol{\beta})$. To see this, note that if $\mathbf{x}_t$ contains lagged endogenous variables, then [8.3.19] would no longer be valid. If $\mathbf{x}_t$ includes $y_{t-1}$, for example, then $\mathbf{x}_t$ and $u_{t-1}$ will be correlated and $\text{plim}[(1/T)\Sigma_{t=1}^T u_{t-1}\mathbf{x}_t] \neq \mathbf{0}$, as was assumed in arriving at [8.3.19]. Hence, [8.3.20] will not hold when $\mathbf{x}_t$ includes lagged endogenous variables. Again, an all-purpose procedure that will work is to maximize the log likelihood function [8.3.15] numerically.

## *Higher-Order Serial Correlation*[11]

Consider next the case when the distribution of $\mathbf{u}|\mathbf{X}$ can be described by a $p$th-order autoregression,

$$u_t = \rho_1 u_{t-1} + \rho_2 u_{t-2} + \cdots + \rho_p u_{t-p} + \varepsilon_t.$$

[10] See Betancourt and Kelejian (1981).

[11] This discussion is based on Harvey (1981, pp. 204–6).

The log likelihood conditional on $\mathbf{X}$ for this case becomes

$$
\begin{aligned}
-(T/2)\log(2\pi) &- (T/2)\log(\sigma^2) - (1/2)\log|\mathbf{V}_p| \\
&- [1/(2\sigma^2)](\mathbf{y}_p - \mathbf{X}_p\boldsymbol{\beta})'\mathbf{V}_p^{-1}(\mathbf{y}_p - \mathbf{X}_p\boldsymbol{\beta}) \\
&- [1/(2\sigma^2)]\sum_{t=p+1}^{T}\Bigl[(y_t - \mathbf{x}_t'\boldsymbol{\beta}) - \rho_1(y_{t-1} - \mathbf{x}_{t-1}'\boldsymbol{\beta}) \\
&\qquad - \rho_2(y_{t-2} - \mathbf{x}_{t-2}'\boldsymbol{\beta}) - \cdots - \rho_p(y_{t-p} - \mathbf{x}_{t-p}'\boldsymbol{\beta})\Bigr]^2,
\end{aligned}
\qquad [8.3.25]
$$

where the $(p \times 1)$ vector $\mathbf{y}_p$ denotes the first $p$ observations on $y$, $\mathbf{X}_p$ is the $(p \times k)$ matrix of explanatory variables associated with these first $p$ observations, and $\sigma^2\mathbf{V}_p$ is the $(p \times p)$ variance-covariance matrix of $(\mathbf{y}_p|\mathbf{X}_p)$. The row $i$, column $j$ element of $\sigma^2\mathbf{V}_p$ is given by $\gamma_{|i-j|}$ for $\gamma_k$ the $k$th autocovariance of an $AR(p)$ process with autoregressive parameters $\rho_1, \rho_2, \ldots, \rho_p$ and innovation variance $\sigma^2$. Letting $\mathbf{L}_p$ denote a $(p \times p)$ matrix such that $\mathbf{L}_p'\mathbf{L}_p = \mathbf{V}_p^{-1}$, $GLS$ can be obtained by regressing $\tilde{\mathbf{y}}_p = \mathbf{L}_p\mathbf{y}_p$ on $\tilde{\mathbf{X}}_p = \mathbf{L}_p\mathbf{X}_p$ and $\tilde{y}_t = y_t - \rho_1 y_{t-1} - \rho_2 y_{t-2} - \cdots - \rho_p y_{t-p}$ on $\tilde{\mathbf{x}}_t = \mathbf{x}_t - \rho_1\mathbf{x}_{t-1} - \rho_2\mathbf{x}_{t-2} - \cdots - \rho_p\mathbf{x}_{t-p}$ for $t = p + 1, p + 2, \ldots, T$. Equation [8.3.14] is a special case of [8.3.25] with $p = 1$, $\mathbf{V}_p = 1/(1 - \rho^2)$, and $\mathbf{L}_p = \sqrt{1 - \rho^2}$.

If we are willing to condition on the first $p$ observations, the task is to choose $\boldsymbol{\beta}$ and $\rho_1, \rho_2, \ldots, \rho_p$ so as to minimize

$$
\sum_{t=p+1}^{T}\Bigl[(y_t - \mathbf{x}_t'\boldsymbol{\beta}) - \rho_1(y_{t-1} - \mathbf{x}_{t-1}'\boldsymbol{\beta}) - \rho_2(y_{t-2} - \mathbf{x}_{t-2}'\boldsymbol{\beta}) - \cdots - \rho_p(y_{t-p} - \mathbf{x}_{t-p}'\boldsymbol{\beta})\Bigr]^2.
$$

Again, in the absence of lagged endogenous variables we can iterate as in Cochrane-Orcutt, first taking the $\rho_i$'s as given and regressing $\tilde{y}_t$ on $\tilde{\mathbf{x}}_t$, and then taking $\boldsymbol{\beta}$ as given and regressing $\hat{u}_t$ on $\hat{u}_{t-1}, \hat{u}_{t-2}, \ldots, \hat{u}_{t-p}$.

Any covariance-stationary process for the errors can always be approximated by a finite autoregression, provided that the order of the approximating autoregression ($p$) is sufficiently large. Amemiya (1973) demonstrated that by letting $p$ go to infinity at a slower rate than the sample size $T$, this iterated $GLS$ estimate will have the same asymptotic distribution as would the $GLS$ estimate for the case when $\mathbf{V}$ is known. Alternatively, if theory implies an $ARMA(p, q)$ structure for the errors with $p$ and $q$ known, one can find exact or approximate maximum likelihood estimates by adapting the methods in Chapter 5, replacing $\mu$ in the expressions in Chapter 5 with $\mathbf{x}_t'\boldsymbol{\beta}$.

## *Further Remarks on Heteroskedasticity*

Heteroskedasticity can arise from a variety of sources, and the solution depends on the nature of the problem identified. Using logs rather than levels of variables, allowing the explanatory variables to enter nonlinearly in the regression equation, or adding previously omitted explanatory variables to the regression may all be helpful. Judge, Griffiths, Hill, and Lee (1980) discussed a variety of solutions when the heteroskedasticity is thought to be related to the explanatory variables. In time series regressions, the explanatory variables themselves exhibit dynamic behavior, and such specifications then imply a dynamic structure for the conditional variance. An example of such a model is the autoregressive conditional heteroskedasticity specification of Engle (1982). Dynamic models of heteroskedasticity will be discussed in Chapter 21.

## APPENDIX 8.A. *Proofs of Chapter 8 Propositions*

■ **Proof of Proposition 8.2.** The restricted estimate $\mathbf{b}^*$ that minimizes [8.1.2] subject to [8.1.27] can be calculated using the Lagrangean:

$$J = (1/2)\sum_{t=1}^{T}(y_t - \mathbf{x}_t'\boldsymbol{\beta})^2 + \boldsymbol{\lambda}'(\mathbf{R}\boldsymbol{\beta} - \mathbf{r}). \qquad [8.A.1]$$

Here $\boldsymbol{\lambda}$ denotes an $(m \times 1)$ vector of Lagrange multipliers; $\lambda_i$ is associated with the constraint represented by the $i$th row of $\mathbf{R}\boldsymbol{\beta} = \mathbf{r}$. The term $\frac{1}{2}$ is a normalizing constant to simplify the expressions that follow. The constrained minimum is found by setting the derivative of [8.A.1] with respect to $\boldsymbol{\beta}$ equal to zero:[12]

$$\begin{aligned}\frac{\partial J}{\partial \boldsymbol{\beta}'} &= (1/2)\sum_{t=1}^{T} 2(y_t - \mathbf{x}_t'\boldsymbol{\beta})\frac{\partial(y_t - \mathbf{x}_t'\boldsymbol{\beta})}{\partial \boldsymbol{\beta}'} + \boldsymbol{\lambda}'\mathbf{R}\\ &= -\sum_{t=1}^{T}(y_t - \boldsymbol{\beta}'\mathbf{x}_t)\mathbf{x}_t' + \boldsymbol{\lambda}'\mathbf{R} = \mathbf{0}',\end{aligned}$$

or

$$\mathbf{b}^{*\prime}\sum_{t=1}^{T}\mathbf{x}_t\mathbf{x}_t' = \sum_{t=1}^{T} y_t\mathbf{x}_t' - \boldsymbol{\lambda}'\mathbf{R}.$$

Taking transposes,

$$\left[\sum_{t=1}^{T}\mathbf{x}_t\mathbf{x}_t'\right]\mathbf{b}^* = \sum_{t=1}^{T}\mathbf{x}_t y_t - \mathbf{R}'\boldsymbol{\lambda}$$

$$\begin{aligned}\mathbf{b}^* &= \left[\sum_{t=1}^{T}\mathbf{x}_t\mathbf{x}_t'\right]^{-1}\left[\sum_{t=1}^{T}\mathbf{x}_t y_t\right] - \left[\sum_{t=1}^{T}\mathbf{x}_t\mathbf{x}_t'\right]^{-1}\mathbf{R}'\boldsymbol{\lambda} \qquad [8.A.2]\\ &= \mathbf{b} - (\mathbf{X}'\mathbf{X})^{-1}\mathbf{R}'\boldsymbol{\lambda},\end{aligned}$$

where $\mathbf{b}$ denotes the unrestricted *OLS* estimate. Premultiplying [8.A.2] by $\mathbf{R}$ (and recalling that $\mathbf{b}^*$ satisfies $\mathbf{R}\mathbf{b}^* = \mathbf{r}$),

$$\mathbf{R}\mathbf{b} - \mathbf{r} = \mathbf{R}(\mathbf{X}'\mathbf{X})^{-1}\mathbf{R}'\boldsymbol{\lambda}$$

or

$$\boldsymbol{\lambda} = [\mathbf{R}(\mathbf{X}'\mathbf{X})^{-1}\mathbf{R}']^{-1}(\mathbf{R}\mathbf{b} - \mathbf{r}). \qquad [8.A.3]$$

Substituting [8.A.3] into [8.A.2],

$$\mathbf{b} - \mathbf{b}^* = (\mathbf{X}'\mathbf{X})^{-1}\mathbf{R}'[\mathbf{R}(\mathbf{X}'\mathbf{X})^{-1}\mathbf{R}']^{-1}(\mathbf{R}\mathbf{b} - \mathbf{r}). \qquad [8.A.4]$$

Notice from [8.A.4] that

$$\begin{aligned}(\mathbf{b} - \mathbf{b}^*)'(\mathbf{X}'\mathbf{X})(\mathbf{b} - \mathbf{b}^*) &= \{(\mathbf{R}\mathbf{b} - \mathbf{r})'[\mathbf{R}(\mathbf{X}'\mathbf{X})^{-1}\mathbf{R}']^{-1}\mathbf{R}(\mathbf{X}'\mathbf{X})^{-1}\}(\mathbf{X}'\mathbf{X})\\ &\quad \times \{(\mathbf{X}'\mathbf{X})^{-1}\mathbf{R}'[\mathbf{R}(\mathbf{X}'\mathbf{X})^{-1}\mathbf{R}']^{-1}(\mathbf{R}\mathbf{b} - \mathbf{r})\}\\ &= (\mathbf{R}\mathbf{b} - \mathbf{r})'[\mathbf{R}(\mathbf{X}'\mathbf{X})^{-1}\mathbf{R}']^{-1}[\mathbf{R}(\mathbf{X}'\mathbf{X})^{-1}\mathbf{R}'] \qquad [8.A.5]\\ &\quad \times [\mathbf{R}(\mathbf{X}'\mathbf{X})^{-1}\mathbf{R}']^{-1}(\mathbf{R}\mathbf{b} - \mathbf{r})\\ &= (\mathbf{R}\mathbf{b} - \mathbf{r})'[\mathbf{R}(\mathbf{X}'\mathbf{X})^{-1}\mathbf{R}']^{-1}(\mathbf{R}\mathbf{b} - \mathbf{r}).\end{aligned}$$

Thus, the magnitude in [8.1.32] is numerically identical to

$$F = \frac{(\mathbf{b} - \mathbf{b}^*)'\mathbf{X}'\mathbf{X}(\mathbf{b} - \mathbf{b}^*)/m}{s^2} = \frac{(\mathbf{b} - \mathbf{b}^*)'\mathbf{X}'\mathbf{X}(\mathbf{b} - \mathbf{b}^*)/m}{RSS_1/(T - k)}.$$

Comparing this with [8.1.37], we will have completed the demonstration of the equivalence of [8.1.32] with [8.1.37] if it is the case that

$$RSS_0 - RSS_1 = (\mathbf{b} - \mathbf{b}^*)'(\mathbf{X}'\mathbf{X})(\mathbf{b} - \mathbf{b}^*). \qquad [8.A.6]$$

[12] We have used the fact that $\partial\mathbf{x}_t'\boldsymbol{\beta}/\partial\boldsymbol{\beta}' = \mathbf{x}_t'$. See the Mathematical Review (Appendix A) at the end of the book on the use of derivatives with respect to vectors.

Now, notice that

$$\begin{aligned} RSS_0 &= (\mathbf{y} - \mathbf{Xb}^*)'(\mathbf{y} - \mathbf{Xb}^*) \\ &= (\mathbf{y} - \mathbf{Xb} + \mathbf{Xb} - \mathbf{Xb}^*)'(\mathbf{y} - \mathbf{Xb} + \mathbf{Xb} - \mathbf{Xb}^*) \\ &= (\mathbf{y} - \mathbf{Xb})'(\mathbf{y} - \mathbf{Xb}) + (\mathbf{b} - \mathbf{b}^*)'\mathbf{X}'\mathbf{X}(\mathbf{b} - \mathbf{b}^*), \end{aligned} \qquad [8.A.7]$$

where the cross-product term has vanished, since $(\mathbf{y} - \mathbf{Xb})'\mathbf{X} = \mathbf{0}$ by the least squares property [8.1.10]. Equation [8.A.7] states that

$$RSS_0 = RSS_1 + (\mathbf{b} - \mathbf{b}^*)'\mathbf{X}'\mathbf{X}(\mathbf{b} - \mathbf{b}^*), \qquad [8.A.8]$$

confirming [8.A.6]. ■

■ **Proof of Proposition 8.3.** Assumption 8.6(e) guarantees that $\hat{\mathbf{Q}}_T \xrightarrow{p} \mathbf{Q}$, so the issue is whether $\hat{\mathbf{\Omega}}_T$ gives a consistent estimate of $\mathbf{\Omega}$. Define $\mathbf{\Omega}_T^* \equiv (1/T)\Sigma_{t=1}^T u_t^2\mathbf{x}_t\mathbf{x}_t'$, noting that $\mathbf{\Omega}_T^*$ converges in probability to $\mathbf{\Omega}$ by Assumption 8.6(c). Thus, if we can show that $\hat{\mathbf{\Omega}}_T - \mathbf{\Omega}_T^* \xrightarrow{p} \mathbf{0}$, then $\hat{\mathbf{\Omega}}_T \xrightarrow{p} \mathbf{\Omega}$. Now,

$$\hat{\mathbf{\Omega}}_T - \mathbf{\Omega}_T^* = (1/T)\sum_{t=1}^T (\hat{u}_t^2 - u_t^2)\mathbf{x}_t\mathbf{x}_t'. \qquad [8.A.9]$$

But

$$\begin{aligned} (\hat{u}_t^2 - u_t^2) &= (\hat{u}_t + u_t)(\hat{u}_t - u_t) \\ &= [(y_t - \mathbf{b}_T'\mathbf{x}_t) + (y_t - \boldsymbol{\beta}'\mathbf{x}_t)][(y_t - \mathbf{b}_T'\mathbf{x}_t) - (y_t - \boldsymbol{\beta}'\mathbf{x}_t)] \\ &= [2(y_t - \boldsymbol{\beta}'\mathbf{x}_t) - (\mathbf{b}_T - \boldsymbol{\beta})'\mathbf{x}_t][-(\mathbf{b}_T - \boldsymbol{\beta})'\mathbf{x}_t] \\ &= -2u_t(\mathbf{b}_T - \boldsymbol{\beta})'\mathbf{x}_t + [(\mathbf{b}_T - \boldsymbol{\beta})'\mathbf{x}_t]^2, \end{aligned}$$

allowing [8.A.9] to be written as

$$\hat{\mathbf{\Omega}}_T - \mathbf{\Omega}_T^* = (-2/T)\sum_{t=1}^T u_t(\mathbf{b}_T - \boldsymbol{\beta})'\mathbf{x}_t(\mathbf{x}_t\mathbf{x}_t') + (1/T)\sum_{t=1}^T [(\mathbf{b}_T - \boldsymbol{\beta})'\mathbf{x}_t]^2(\mathbf{x}_t\mathbf{x}_t'). \qquad [8.A.10]$$

The first term in [8.A.10] can be written

$$(-2/T)\sum_{t=1}^T u_t(\mathbf{b}_T - \boldsymbol{\beta})'\mathbf{x}_t(\mathbf{x}_t\mathbf{x}_t') = -2\sum_{i=1}^k (b_{iT} - \beta_i)\left[(1/T)\sum_{t=1}^T u_t x_{it}(\mathbf{x}_t\mathbf{x}_t')\right]. \qquad [8.A.11]$$

The second term in [8.A.11] has a finite plim by Assumption 8.6(e), and $(b_{iT} - \beta_i) \xrightarrow{p} 0$ for each $i$. Hence, the probability limit of [8.A.11] is zero.

Turning next to the second term in [8.A.10],

$$(1/T)\sum_{t=1}^T [(\mathbf{b}_T - \boldsymbol{\beta})'\mathbf{x}_t]^2(\mathbf{x}_t\mathbf{x}_t') = \sum_{i=1}^k\sum_{j=1}^k (b_{iT} - \beta_i)(b_{jT} - \beta_j)\left[(1/T)\sum_{t=1}^T x_{it}x_{jt}(\mathbf{x}_t\mathbf{x}_t')\right],$$

which again has plim zero. Hence, from [8.A.10],

$$\hat{\mathbf{\Omega}}_T - \mathbf{\Omega}_T^* \xrightarrow{p} \mathbf{0}. \quad ■$$

■ **Proof of Proposition 8.4.** Recall from [8.2.6] that

$$\begin{aligned} \sqrt{T}(\tilde{\mathbf{b}}_T - \boldsymbol{\beta}) &= \left[(1/T)\sum_{t=1}^T \tilde{\mathbf{x}}_t\tilde{\mathbf{x}}_t'\right]^{-1}\left[(1/\sqrt{T})\sum_{t=1}^T \tilde{\mathbf{x}}_t\tilde{u}_t\right] \\ &= \left[(1/T)\sum_{t=1}^T (\mathbf{x}_t - \hat{\rho}\mathbf{x}_{t-1})(\mathbf{x}_t - \hat{\rho}\mathbf{x}_{t-1})'\right]^{-1} \\ &\quad \times \left[(1/\sqrt{T})\sum_{t=1}^T (\mathbf{x}_t - \hat{\rho}\mathbf{x}_{t-1})(u_t - \hat{\rho}u_{t-1})\right]. \end{aligned} \qquad [8.A.12]$$

We will now show that $[(1/T)\Sigma_{t=1}^T(\mathbf{x}_t - \hat{\rho}\mathbf{x}_{t-1})(\mathbf{x}_t - \hat{\rho}\mathbf{x}_{t-1})']$ has the same plim as $[(1/T)\Sigma_{t=1}^T(\mathbf{x}_t - \rho\mathbf{x}_{t-1})(\mathbf{x}_t - \rho\mathbf{x}_{t-1})']$ and that $[(1/\sqrt{T})\Sigma_{t=1}^T(\mathbf{x}_t - \hat{\rho}\mathbf{x}_{t-1})(u_t - \hat{\rho}u_{t-1})]$ has the same asymptotic distribution as $[(1/\sqrt{T})\Sigma_{t=1}^T(\mathbf{x}_t - \rho\mathbf{x}_{t-1})(u_t - \rho u_{t-1})]$.

Consider the first term in [8.A.12]:

$$(1/T)\sum_{t=1}^{T}(\mathbf{x}_t - \hat{\rho}\mathbf{x}_{t-1})(\mathbf{x}_t - \hat{\rho}\mathbf{x}_{t-1})'$$

$$\begin{aligned}
&= (1/T)\sum_{t=1}^{T}[\mathbf{x}_t - \rho\mathbf{x}_{t-1} + (\rho - \hat{\rho})\mathbf{x}_{t-1}][\mathbf{x}_t - \rho\mathbf{x}_{t-1} + (\rho - \hat{\rho})\mathbf{x}_{t-1}]' \\
&= (1/T)\sum_{t=1}^{T}(\mathbf{x}_t - \rho\mathbf{x}_{t-1})(\mathbf{x}_t - \rho\mathbf{x}_{t-1})' \\
&\quad + (\rho - \hat{\rho})\cdot(1/T)\sum_{t=1}^{T}(\mathbf{x}_t - \rho\mathbf{x}_{t-1})\mathbf{x}_{t-1}' \\
&\quad + (\rho - \hat{\rho})\cdot(1/T)\sum_{t=1}^{T}\mathbf{x}_{t-1}(\mathbf{x}_t - \rho\mathbf{x}_{t-1})' \\
&\quad + (\rho - \hat{\rho})^2\cdot(1/T)\sum_{t=1}^{T}\mathbf{x}_{t-1}\mathbf{x}_{t-1}'.
\end{aligned} \qquad [8.A.13]$$

But $(\rho - \hat{\rho}) \xrightarrow{p} 0$, and the plims of $(1/T)\Sigma_{t=1}^{T}\mathbf{x}_{t-1}\mathbf{x}_{t-1}'$ and $(1/T)\Sigma_{t=1}^{T}\mathbf{x}_t\mathbf{x}_{t-1}'$ are assumed to exist. Hence [8.A.13] has the same plim as $(1/T)\Sigma_{t=1}^{T}(\mathbf{x}_t - \rho\mathbf{x}_{t-1})(\mathbf{x}_t - \rho\mathbf{x}_{t-1})'$.

Consider next the second term in [8.A.12]:

$$(1/\sqrt{T})\sum_{t=1}^{T}(\mathbf{x}_t - \hat{\rho}\mathbf{x}_{t-1})(u_t - \hat{\rho}u_{t-1})$$

$$\begin{aligned}
&= (1/\sqrt{T})\sum_{t=1}^{T}[\mathbf{x}_t - \rho\mathbf{x}_{t-1} + (\rho - \hat{\rho})\mathbf{x}_{t-1}][u_t - \rho u_{t-1} + (\rho - \hat{\rho})u_{t-1}] \qquad [8.A.14] \\
&= (1/\sqrt{T})\sum_{t=1}^{T}(\mathbf{x}_t - \rho\mathbf{x}_{t-1})(u_t - \rho u_{t-1}) \\
&\quad + \sqrt{T}(\rho - \hat{\rho})\cdot\left[(1/T)\sum_{t=1}^{T}\mathbf{x}_{t-1}(u_t - \rho u_{t-1})\right] \\
&\quad + \sqrt{T}(\rho - \hat{\rho})\cdot\left[(1/T)\sum_{t=1}^{T}(\mathbf{x}_t - \rho\mathbf{x}_{t-1})u_{t-1}\right] \\
&\quad + \sqrt{T}(\rho - \hat{\rho})^2\cdot\left[(1/T)\sum_{t=1}^{T}\mathbf{x}_{t-1}u_{t-1}\right].
\end{aligned}$$

But [8.3.21] established that $\sqrt{T}(\rho - \hat{\rho})$ converges in distribution to a stable random variable. Since $\text{plim}[(1/T)\Sigma_{t=1}^{T}\mathbf{x}_t u_s] = \mathbf{0}$, the last three terms in [8.A.14] vanish asymptotically. Hence,

$$(1/\sqrt{T})\sum_{t=1}^{T}(\mathbf{x}_t - \hat{\rho}\mathbf{x}_{t-1})(u_t - \hat{\rho}u_{t-1}) \xrightarrow{p} (1/\sqrt{T})\sum_{t=1}^{T}(\mathbf{x}_t - \rho\mathbf{x}_{t-1})(u_t - \rho u_{t-1}),$$

which was to be shown.

## *Chapter 8 Exercises*

8.1. Show that the uncentered $R_u^2$ [8.1.13] can equivalently be written as

$$R_u^2 = 1 - \left[\left(\sum_{t=1}^{T}\hat{u}_t^2\right) \div \left(\sum_{t=1}^{T}y_t^2\right)\right]$$

for $\hat{u}_t$ the *OLS* sample residual [8.1.4]. Show that the centered $R_c^2$ can be written as

$$R_c^2 = 1 - \left[\left(\sum_{t=1}^{T}\hat{u}_t^2\right) \div \left(\sum_{t=1}^{T}(y_t - \bar{y})^2\right)\right].$$

8.2. Consider a null hypothesis $H_0$ involving $m = 2$ linear restrictions on $\boldsymbol{\beta}$. How large a sample size $T$ is needed before the 5% critical value based on the Wald form of the *OLS* $F$ test of $H_0$ is within 1% of the critical value of the Wald form of the *OLS* $\chi^2$ test of $H_0$?

8.3. Derive result [8.2.28].

8.4. Consider a covariance-stationary process given by

$$y_t = \mu + \sum_{j=0}^{\infty} \psi_j \varepsilon_{t-j},$$

where $\{\varepsilon_t\}$ is an i.i.d. sequence with mean zero, variance $\sigma^2$, and finite fourth moment and where $\Sigma_{j=0}^{\infty} |\psi_j| < \infty$. Consider estimating a $p$th-order autoregression by *OLS*:

$$y_t = c + \phi_1 y_{t-1} + \phi_2 y_{t-2} + \cdots + \phi_p y_{t-p} + u_t.$$

Show that the *OLS* coefficients give consistent estimates of the population parameters that characterize the linear projection of $y_t$ on a constant and $p$ of its lags—that is, the coefficients give consistent estimates of the parameters $c, \phi_1, \ldots, \phi_p$ defined by

$$\hat{E}(y_t | y_{t-1}, y_{t-2}, \ldots, y_{t-p}) = c + \phi_1 y_{t-1} + \phi_2 y_{t-2} + \cdots + \phi_p y_{t-p}$$

(HINT: Recall that $c, \phi_1, \ldots, \phi_p$ are characterized by equation [4.3.6]).

## *Chapter 8 References*


Amemiya, Takeshi. 1973. "Generalized Least Squares with an Estimated Autocovariance Matrix." *Econometrica* 41:723–32.

Anderson, T. W. 1971. *The Statistical Analysis of Time Series*. New York: Wiley.

Betancourt, Roger, and Harry Kelejian. 1981. "Lagged Endogenous Variables and the Cochrane-Orcutt Procedure." *Econometrica* 49:1073–78.

Brillinger, David R. 1981. *Time Series: Data Anaysis and Theory*, expanded ed. San Francisco: Holden-Day.

Durbin, James. 1960. "Estimation of Parameters in Time-Series Regression Models." *Journal of the Royal Statistical Society* Series B, 22:139–53.

———. 1970. "Testing for Serial Correlation in Least-Squares Regression When Some of the Regressors Are Lagged Dependent Variables." *Econometrica* 38:410–21.

Eicker, F. 1967. "Limit Theorems for Regressions with Unequal and Dependent Errors." *Proceedings of the Fifth Berkeley Symposium on Mathematical Statistics and Probability*, Vol. 1, pp. 59–62. Berkeley: University of California Press.

Engle, Robert F. 1982. "Autoregressive Conditional Heteroscedasticity with Estimates of the Variance of United Kingdom Inflation." *Econometrica* 50:987–1007.

Evans, G. B. A., and N. E. Savin. 1981. "Testing for Unit Roots: 1. *Econometrica* 49:753–79.

Flavin, Marjorie A. 1983. "Excess Volatility in the Financial Markets: A Reassessment of the Empirical Evidence." *Journal of Political Economy* 91:929–56.

Gregory, Allan W., and Michael R. Veall. 1985. "Formulating Wald Tests of Nonlinear Restrictions." *Econometrica* 53:1465–68.

Hansen, Lars P. 1982. "Large Sample Properties of Generalized Method of Moments Estimators." *Econometrica* 50:1029–54.

Harvey, A. C. 1981. *The Econometric Analysis of Time Series*. New York: Wiley.

Hausman, Jerry A., and William E. Taylor. 1983. "Identification in Linear Simultaneous Equations Models with Covariance Restrictions: An Instrumental Variables Interpretation." *Econometrica* 51:1527–49.

Imhof, J. P. 1961. "Computing the Distribution of Quadratic Forms in Normal Variables." *Biometrika* 48:419–26.

Judge, George G., William E. Griffiths, R. Carter Hill, and Tsoung-Chao Lee. 1980. *The Theory and Practice of Econometrics*. New York: Wiley.

Kinderman, A. J., and J. G. Ramage. 1976. "Computer Generation of Normal Random Variables." *Journal of the American Statistical Association* 71:893–96.

Lafontaine, Francine, and Kenneth J. White. 1986. "Obtaining Any Wald Statistic You Want." *Economics Letters* 21:35–40.

Maddala, G. S. 1977. *Econometrics*. New York: McGraw-Hill.

Newey, Whitney K., and Kenneth D. West. 1987. "A Simple Positive Semi-Definite, Heteroskedasticity and Autocorrelation Consistent Covariance Matrix." *Econometrica* 55:703–8.

Nicholls, D. F., and A. R. Pagan. 1983. "Heteroscedasticity in Models with Lagged Dependent Variables." *Econometrica* 51:1233–42.

O'Nan, Michael. 1976. *Linear Algebra*, 2d ed. New York: Harcourt Brace Jovanovich.

Phillips, P. C. B., and Joon Y. Park. 1988. "On the Formulation of Wald Tests of Nonlinear Restrictions." *Econometrica* 56:1065–83.

Rao, C. Radhakrishna. 1973. *Linear Statistical Inference and Its Applications*, 2d ed. New York: Wiley.

Theil, Henri. 1971. *Principles of Econometrics*. New York: Wiley.

White, Halbert. 1980. "A Heteroskedasticity-Consistent Covariance Matrix Estimator and a Direct Test for Heteroskedasticity." *Econometrica* 48:817–38.

———. 1984. *Asymptotic Theory for Econometricians*. Orlando, Fla.: Academic Press.

# 9 Linear Systems of Simultaneous Equations

The previous chapter described a number of possible departures from the ideal regression model arising from errors that are non-Gaussian, heteroskedastic, or autocorrelated. We saw that while these factors can make a difference for the small-sample validity of $t$ and $F$ tests, under any of Assumptions 8.1 through 8.6, the $OLS$ estimator $\mathbf{b}_T$ is either unbiased or consistent. This is because all these cases retained the crucial assumption that $u_t$, the error term for observation $t$, is uncorrelated with $\mathbf{x}_t$, the explanatory variables for that observation. Unfortunately, this critical assumption is unlikely to be satisfied in many important applications.

Section 9.1 discusses why this assumption often fails to hold, by examining a concrete example of *simultaneous equations bias*. Subsequent sections discuss a variety of techniques for dealing with this problem. These results will be used in the structural interpretation of vector autoregressions in Chapter 11 and for understanding generalized method of moments estimation in Chapter 14.

## 9.1. *Simultaneous Equations Bias*

To illustrate the difficulties with endogenous regressors, consider an investigation of the public's demand for oranges. Let $p_t$ denote the log of the price of oranges in a particular year and $q_t^d$ the log of the quantity the public is willing to buy. To keep the example very simple, suppose that price and quantity are covariance-stationary and that each is measured as deviations from its population mean. The demand curve is presumed to take the form

$$q_t^d = \beta p_t + \varepsilon_t^d, \qquad [9.1.1]$$

with $\beta < 0$; a higher price reduces the quantity that the public is willing to buy. Here $\varepsilon_t^d$ represents factors that influence demand other than price. These are assumed to be independent and identically distributed with mean zero and variance $\sigma_d^2$.

The price also influences the supply of oranges brought to the market,

$$q_t^s = \gamma p_t + \varepsilon_t^s, \qquad [9.1.2]$$

where $\gamma > 0$ and $\varepsilon_t^s$ represents factors that influence supply other than price. These omitted factors are again assumed to be i.i.d. with mean zero and variance $\sigma_s^2$, with the supply disturbance $\varepsilon_t^s$ uncorrelated with the demand disturbance $\varepsilon_t^d$.

Equation [9.1.1] describes the behavior of buyers of oranges, and equation [9.1.2] describes the behavior of sellers. Market equilibrium requires $q_t^d = q_t^s$, or

$$\beta p_t + \varepsilon_t^d = \gamma p_t + \varepsilon_t^s.$$

Rearranging,

$$p_t = \frac{\varepsilon_t^d - \varepsilon_t^s}{\gamma - \beta}. \qquad [9.1.3]$$

Substituting this back into [9.1.2],

$$q_t = \gamma \frac{\varepsilon_t^d - \varepsilon_t^s}{\gamma - \beta} + \varepsilon_t^s = \frac{\gamma}{\gamma - \beta}\varepsilon_t^d - \frac{\beta}{\gamma - \beta}\varepsilon_t^s. \qquad [9.1.4]$$

Consider the consequences of trying to estimate [9.1.1] by *OLS*. A regression of quantity on price will produce the estimate

$$b_T = \frac{(1/T)\sum_{t=1}^T p_t q_t}{(1/T)\sum_{t=1}^T p_t^2}. \qquad [9.1.5]$$

Substituting [9.1.3] and [9.1.4] into the numerator in [9.1.5] results in

$$\begin{aligned}\frac{1}{T}\sum_{t=1}^T p_t q_t &= \frac{1}{T}\sum_{t=1}^T \left[\frac{1}{\gamma - \beta}\varepsilon_t^d - \frac{1}{\gamma - \beta}\varepsilon_t^s\right]\left[\frac{\gamma}{\gamma - \beta}\varepsilon_t^d - \frac{\beta}{\gamma - \beta}\varepsilon_t^s\right] \\ &= \frac{1}{T}\sum_{t=1}^T \left[\frac{\gamma}{(\gamma - \beta)^2}(\varepsilon_t^d)^2 + \frac{\beta}{(\gamma - \beta)^2}(\varepsilon_t^s)^2 - \frac{\gamma + \beta}{(\gamma - \beta)^2}\varepsilon_t^d\varepsilon_t^s\right] \\ &\xrightarrow{p} \frac{\gamma\sigma_d^2 + \beta\sigma_s^2}{(\gamma - \beta)^2}.\end{aligned}$$

Similarly, for the denominator,

$$\frac{1}{T}\sum_{t=1}^T p_t^2 = \frac{1}{T}\sum_{t=1}^T \left[\frac{1}{\gamma - \beta}\varepsilon_t^d - \frac{1}{\gamma - \beta}\varepsilon_t^s\right]^2 \xrightarrow{p} \frac{\sigma_d^2 + \sigma_s^2}{(\gamma - \beta)^2}.$$

Hence,

$$b_T \xrightarrow{p} \left[\frac{\sigma_d^2 + \sigma_s^2}{(\gamma - \beta)^2}\right]^{-1}\left[\frac{\gamma\sigma_d^2 + \beta\sigma_s^2}{(\gamma - \beta)^2}\right] = \frac{\gamma\sigma_d^2 + \beta\sigma_s^2}{\sigma_d^2 + \sigma_s^2}. \qquad [9.1.6]$$

*OLS* regression thus gives not the demand elasticity $\beta$ but rather an average of $\beta$ and the supply elasticity $\gamma$, with weights depending on the sizes of the variances $\sigma_d^2$ and $\sigma_s^2$. If the error in the demand curve is negligible ($\sigma_d^2 \to 0$) or if the error term in the supply curve has a big enough variance ($\sigma_s^2 \to \infty$), then [9.1.6] indicates that *OLS* would give a consistent estimate of the demand elasticity $\beta$. On the other hand, if $\sigma_d^2 \to \infty$ or $\sigma_s^2 \to 0$, then *OLS* gives a consistent estimate of the supply elasticity $\gamma$. In the cases in between, one economist might believe the regression was estimating the demand curve [9.1.1] and a second economist might perform the same regression calling it the supply curve [9.1.2]. The actual *OLS* estimates would represent a mixture of both. This phenomenon is known as *simultaneous equations bias*.

Figure 9.1 depicts the problem graphically.[1] At any date in the sample, there is some demand curve (determined by the value of $\varepsilon_t^d$) and a supply curve (determined by $\varepsilon_t^s$), with the observation on $(p_t, q_t)$ given by the intersection of these two curves. For example, date 1 may have been associated with a small negative shock to demand, producing the curve $D_1$, and a large positive shock to supply, producing $S_1$. The date 1 observation will then be $(p_1, q_1)$. Date 2 might have seen

[1]Economists usually display these figures with the axes reversed from those displayed in Figure 9.1.

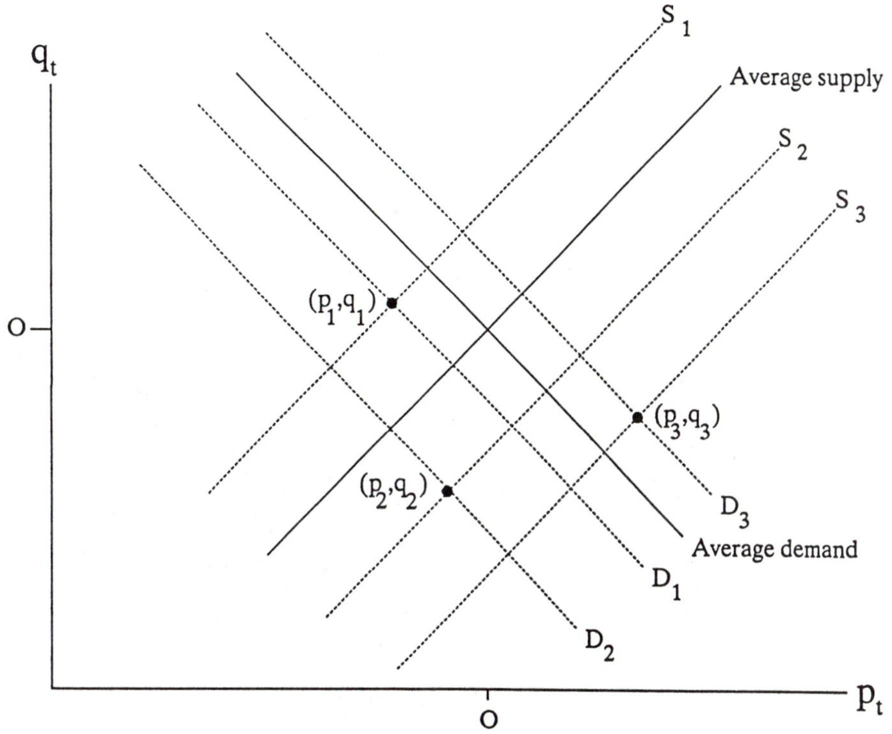


**FIGURE 9.1** Observations on price and quantity implied by disturbances to both supply functions and demand functions.

a bigger negative shock to demand and a negative shock to supply, while date 3 as drawn reflects a modest positive shock to demand and a large negative shock to supply. *OLS* tries to fit a line through the scatter of points $\{p_t, q_t\}_{t=1}^{T}$.

If the shocks are known to be due to the supply curve and not the demand curve, then the scatter of points will trace out the demand curve, as in Figure 9.2. If the shocks are due to the demand curve rather than the supply curve, the scatter will trace out the supply curve, as in Figure 9.3.

The problem of simultaneous equations bias is extremely widespread in the social sciences. It is rare that the relation that we would like to estimate is the only possible reason why there might be a correlation among a group of variables.

## *Consistent Estimation of the Demand Elasticity*

The above analysis suggests that consistent estimates of the demand elasticity might be obtained if we could find a variable that shifts the supply curve but not the demand curve. For example, let $w_t$ represent the number of days of below-freezing temperatures in Florida during year $t$. Recalling that the supply disturbance $\varepsilon_t^s$ was defined as factors influencing supply other than price, $w_t$ seems likely to be an important component of $\varepsilon_t^s$. Define $h$ to be the coefficient from a linear projection of $\varepsilon_t^s$ on $w_t$, and write

$$\varepsilon_t^s = hw_t + u_t^s. \tag{9.1.7}$$

Thus, $u_t^s$ is uncorrelated with $w_t$, by the definition of $h$. Although Florida weather is likely to influence the supply of oranges, it is natural to assume that weather

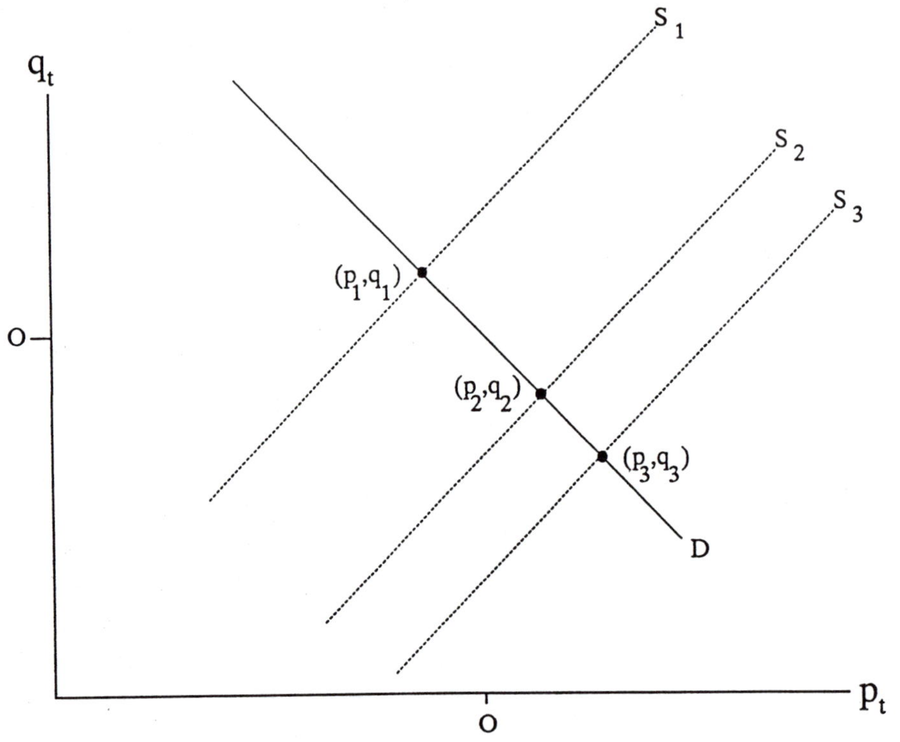


**FIGURE 9.2** Observations on price and quantity implied by disturbances to supply function only.

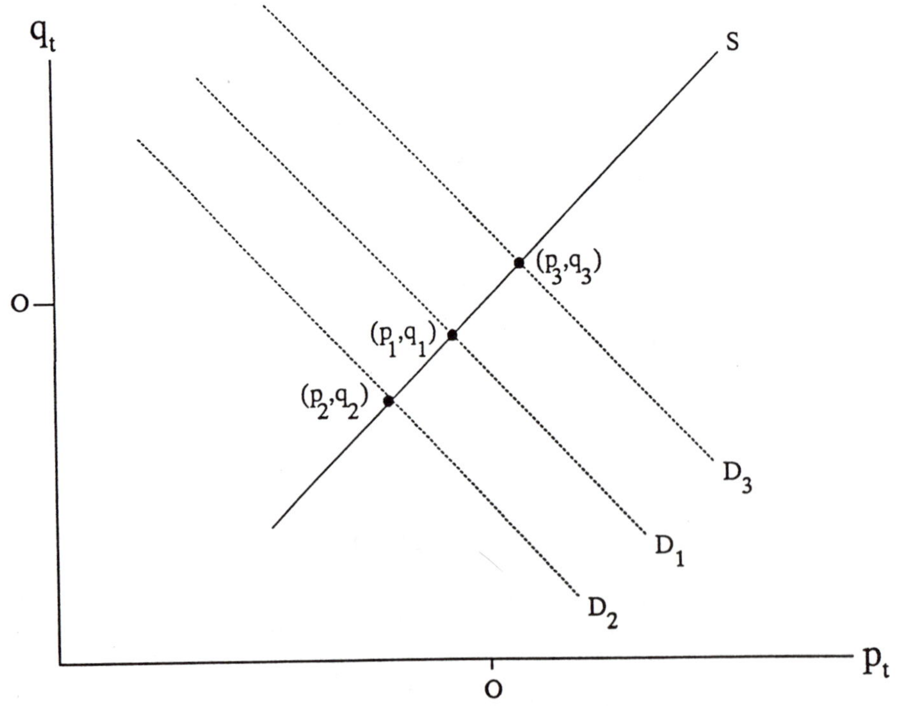


**FIGURE 9.3** Observations on price and quantity implied by disturbances to demand function only.

matters for the public's demand for oranges only through its effect on the price. Under this assumption, both $w_t$ and $u_t^s$ are uncorrelated with $\varepsilon_t^d$. Changes in price that can be attributed to the weather represent supply shifts and not demand shifts.

Define $p_t^*$ to be the linear projection of $p_t$ on $w_t$. Substituting [9.1.7] into [9.1.3],

$$p_t = \frac{\varepsilon_t^d - hw_t - u_t^s}{\gamma - \beta}, \qquad [9.1.8]$$

and thus

$$p_t^* = \frac{-h}{\gamma - \beta} w_t, \qquad [9.1.9]$$

since $\varepsilon_t^d$ and $u_t^s$ are uncorrelated with $w_t$. Equation [9.1.8] can thus be written

$$p_t = p_t^* + \frac{\varepsilon_t^d - u_t^s}{\gamma - \beta},$$

and substituting this into [9.1.1],

$$q_t = \beta\left\{p_t^* + \frac{\varepsilon_t^d - u_t^s}{\gamma - \beta}\right\} + \varepsilon_t^d = \beta p_t^* + v_t, \qquad [9.1.10]$$

where

$$v_t \equiv \frac{-\beta u_t^s}{\gamma - \beta} + \frac{\gamma \varepsilon_t^d}{\gamma - \beta}.$$

Since $u_t^s$ and $\varepsilon_t^d$ are both uncorrelated with $w_t$, it follows that $v_t$ is uncorrelated with $p_t^*$. Hence, if [9.1.10] were estimated by ordinary least squares, the result would be a consistent estimate of $\beta$:

$$\begin{aligned} \hat{\beta}_T^* &= \frac{(1/T)\sum_{t=1}^T p_t^* q_t}{(1/T)\sum_{t=1}^T [p_t^*]^2} \\ &= \frac{(1/T)\sum_{t=1}^T p_t^*(\beta p_t^* + v_t)}{(1/T)\sum_{t=1}^T [p_t^*]^2} \\ &= \beta + \frac{(1/T)\sum_{t=1}^T p_t^* v_t}{(1/T)\sum_{t=1}^T [p_t^*]^2} \\ &\xrightarrow{p} \beta. \end{aligned} \qquad [9.1.11]$$

The suggestion is thus to regress quantity on that component of price that is induced by the weather, that is, regress quantity on the linear projection of price on the weather.

In practice, we will not know the values of the population parameters $h$, $\gamma$, and $\beta$ necessary to construct $p_t^*$ in [9.1.9]. However, the linear projection $p_t^*$ can be consistently estimated by the fitted value for observation $t$ from an *OLS* regression of $p$ on $w$,

$$\hat{p}_t = \hat{\delta}_T w_t, \qquad [9.1.12]$$

where

$$\hat{\delta}_T = \frac{(1/T)\sum_{t=1}^{T} w_t p_t}{(1/T)\sum_{t=1}^{T} w_t^2}.$$

The estimator [9.1.11] with $p_t^*$ replaced by $\hat{p}_t$ is known as the *two-stage least squares* (*2SLS*) coefficient estimator:

$$\hat{\beta}_{2SLS} = \frac{(1/T)\sum_{t=1}^{T} \hat{p}_t q_t}{(1/T)\sum_{t=1}^{T} [\hat{p}_t]^2}. \qquad [9.1.13]$$

Like $\hat{\beta}_T^*$, the 2*SLS* estimator is consistent, as will be shown in the following section.

## 9.2. *Instrumental Variables and Two-Stage Least Squares*

### *General Description of Two-Stage Least Squares*

A generalization of the previous example is as follows. Suppose the objective is to estimate the vector $\boldsymbol{\beta}$ in the regression model

$$y_t = \boldsymbol{\beta}'\mathbf{z}_t + u_t, \qquad [9.2.1]$$

where $\mathbf{z}_t$ is a $(k \times 1)$ vector of explanatory variables. Some subset $n \leq k$ of the variables in $\mathbf{z}_t$ are thought to be endogenous, that is, correlated with $u_t$. The remaining $k - n$ variables in $\mathbf{z}_t$ are said to be *predetermined*, meaning that they are uncorrelated with $u_t$. Estimation of $\boldsymbol{\beta}$ requires variables known as *instruments*. To be a valid instrument, a variable must be correlated with an endogenous explanatory variable in $\mathbf{z}_t$ but uncorrelated with the regression disturbance $u_t$. In the supply-and-demand example, the weather variable $w_t$ served as an instrument for price. At least one valid instrument must be found for each endogenous explanatory variable.

Collect the predetermined explanatory variables together with the instruments in an $(r \times 1)$ vector $\mathbf{x}_t$. For example, to estimate the demand curve, there were no predetermined explanatory variables in equation [9.1.1] and only a single instrument; hence, $r = 1$, and $\mathbf{x}_t$ would be the scalar $w_t$. As a second example, suppose that the equation to be estimated is

$$y_t = \beta_1 + \beta_2 z_{2t} + \beta_3 z_{3t} + \beta_4 z_{4t} + \beta_5 z_{5t} + u_t.$$

In this example, $z_{4t}$ and $z_{5t}$ are endogenous (meaning that they are correlated with $u_t$), $z_{2t}$ and $z_{3t}$ are predetermined (uncorrelated with $u_t$), and $\xi_{1t}$, $\xi_{2t}$, and $\xi_{3t}$ are valid instruments (correlated with $z_{4t}$ and $z_{5t}$ but uncorrelated with $u_t$). Then $r = 6$ and $\mathbf{x}_t' = (1, z_{2t}, z_{3t}, \xi_{1t}, \xi_{2t}, \xi_{3t})$. The requirement that there be at least as many instruments as endogenous explanatory variables implies that $r \geq k$.

Consider an *OLS* regression of $z_{it}$ (the *i*th explanatory variable in [9.2.1]) on $\mathbf{x}_t$:

$$z_{it} = \boldsymbol{\delta}_i'\mathbf{x}_t + e_{it}. \qquad [9.2.2]$$

The fitted values for the regression are given by

$$\hat{z}_{it} = \hat{\boldsymbol{\delta}}_i'\mathbf{x}_t, \qquad [9.2.3]$$

where

$$\hat{\boldsymbol{\delta}}_i = \left[\sum_{t=1}^{T} \mathbf{x}_t\mathbf{x}_t'\right]^{-1}\left[\sum_{t=1}^{T} \mathbf{x}_t z_{it}\right].$$

If $z_{it}$ is one of the predetermined variables, then $z_{it}$ is one of the elements of $\mathbf{x}_t$ and equation [9.2.3] simplifies to

$$\hat{z}_{it} = z_{it}.$$

This is because when the dependent variable ($z_{it}$) is included in the regressors ($\mathbf{x}_t$), a unit coefficient on $z_{it}$ and zero coefficients on the other variables produce a perfect fit and thus minimize the residual sum of squares.

Collect the equations in [9.2.3] for $i = 1, 2, \ldots, k$ in a $(k \times 1)$ vector equation

$$\hat{\mathbf{z}}_t = \hat{\boldsymbol{\delta}}'\mathbf{x}_t, \qquad [9.2.4]$$

where the $(k \times r)$ matrix $\hat{\boldsymbol{\delta}}'$ is given by

$$\hat{\boldsymbol{\delta}}' = \begin{bmatrix} \hat{\boldsymbol{\delta}}_1' \\ \hat{\boldsymbol{\delta}}_2' \\ \vdots \\ \hat{\boldsymbol{\delta}}_k' \end{bmatrix} = \left[\sum_{t=1}^{T} \mathbf{z}_t\mathbf{x}_t'\right]\left[\sum_{t=1}^{T} \mathbf{x}_t\mathbf{x}_t'\right]^{-1}. \qquad [9.2.5]$$

The *two-stage least squares* (*2SLS*) estimate of $\boldsymbol{\beta}$ is found from an *OLS* regression of $y_t$ on $\hat{\mathbf{z}}_t$:

$$\hat{\boldsymbol{\beta}}_{2SLS} = \left[\sum_{t=1}^{T} \hat{\mathbf{z}}_t\hat{\mathbf{z}}_t'\right]^{-1}\left[\sum_{t=1}^{T} \hat{\mathbf{z}}_t y_t\right]. \qquad [9.2.6]$$

An alternative way of writing [9.2.6] is sometimes useful. Let $\hat{e}_{it}$ denote the sample residual from *OLS* estimation of [9.2.2]; that is, let

$$z_{it} = \hat{\boldsymbol{\delta}}_i'\mathbf{x}_t + \hat{e}_{it} = \hat{z}_{it} + \hat{e}_{it}. \qquad [9.2.7]$$

*OLS* causes this residual to be orthogonal to $\mathbf{x}_t$:

$$\sum_{t=1}^{T} \mathbf{x}_t\hat{e}_{it} = \mathbf{0},$$

meaning that the residual is orthogonal to $\hat{z}_{jt}$:

$$\sum_{t=1}^{T} \hat{z}_{jt}\hat{e}_{it} = \hat{\boldsymbol{\delta}}_j' \sum_{t=1}^{T} \mathbf{x}_t\hat{e}_{it} = 0.$$

Hence, if [9.2.7] is multiplied by $\hat{z}_{jt}$ and summed over $t$, the result is

$$\sum_{t=1}^{T} \hat{z}_{jt}z_{it} = \sum_{t=1}^{T} \hat{z}_{jt}(\hat{z}_{it} + \hat{e}_{it}) = \sum_{t=1}^{T} \hat{z}_{jt}\hat{z}_{it}$$

for all $i$ and $j$. This means that

$$\sum_{t=1}^{T} \hat{\mathbf{z}}_t\mathbf{z}_t' = \sum_{t=1}^{T} \hat{\mathbf{z}}_t\hat{\mathbf{z}}_t',$$

so that the *2SLS* estimator [9.2.6] can equivalently be written as

$$\hat{\boldsymbol{\beta}}_{2SLS} = \left[\sum_{t=1}^{T} \hat{\mathbf{z}}_t\mathbf{z}_t'\right]^{-1}\left[\sum_{t=1}^{T} \hat{\mathbf{z}}_t y_t\right]. \qquad [9.2.8]$$

## *Consistency of 2SLS Estimator*

Substituting [9.2.1] into [9.2.8],

$$\begin{aligned}\hat{\boldsymbol{\beta}}_{2SLS,T} &= \left[\sum_{t=1}^{T} \hat{\mathbf{z}}_t \mathbf{z}_t'\right]^{-1} \left[\sum_{t=1}^{T} \hat{\mathbf{z}}_t (\mathbf{z}_t'\boldsymbol{\beta} + u_t)\right] \\ &= \boldsymbol{\beta} + \left[\sum_{t=1}^{T} \hat{\mathbf{z}}_t \mathbf{z}_t'\right]^{-1} \left[\sum_{t=1}^{T} \hat{\mathbf{z}}_t u_t\right],\end{aligned} \qquad [9.2.9]$$

where the subscript $T$ has been added to keep explicit track of the sample size $T$ on which estimation is based. It follows from [9.2.9] that

$$\hat{\boldsymbol{\beta}}_{2SLS,T} - \boldsymbol{\beta} = \left[(1/T) \sum_{t=1}^{T} \hat{\mathbf{z}}_t \mathbf{z}_t'\right]^{-1} \left[(1/T) \sum_{t=1}^{T} \hat{\mathbf{z}}_t u_t\right]. \qquad [9.2.10]$$

Consistency of the 2*SLS* estimator can then be shown as follows. First note from [9.2.4] and [9.2.5] that

$$\begin{aligned}(1/T) \sum_{t=1}^{T} \hat{\mathbf{z}}_t \mathbf{z}_t' &= \hat{\boldsymbol{\delta}}_T' (1/T) \sum_{t=1}^{T} \mathbf{x}_t \mathbf{z}_t' \\ &= \left[(1/T) \sum_{t=1}^{T} \mathbf{z}_t \mathbf{x}_t'\right] \left[(1/T) \sum_{t=1}^{T} \mathbf{x}_t \mathbf{x}_t'\right]^{-1} \left[(1/T) \sum_{t=1}^{T} \mathbf{x}_t \mathbf{z}_t'\right].\end{aligned} \qquad [9.2.11]$$

Assuming that the process $(\mathbf{z}_t, \mathbf{x}_t)$ is covariance-stationary and ergodic for second moments,

$$(1/T) \sum_{t=1}^{T} \hat{\mathbf{z}}_t \mathbf{z}_t' \xrightarrow{p} \mathbf{Q}, \qquad [9.2.12]$$

where

$$\mathbf{Q} = [E(\mathbf{z}_t \mathbf{x}_t')][E(\mathbf{x}_t \mathbf{x}_t')]^{-1}[E(\mathbf{x}_t \mathbf{z}_t')]. \qquad [9.2.13]$$

Turning next to the second term in [9.2.10],

$$\left[(1/T) \sum_{t=1}^{T} \hat{\mathbf{z}}_t u_t\right] = \hat{\boldsymbol{\delta}}_T' (1/T) \sum_{t=1}^{T} \mathbf{x}_t u_t.$$

Again, ergodicity for second moments implies from [9.2.5] that

$$\hat{\boldsymbol{\delta}}_T' \xrightarrow{p} [E(\mathbf{z}_t \mathbf{x}_t')][E(\mathbf{x}_t \mathbf{x}_t')]^{-1}, \qquad [9.2.14]$$

while the law of large numbers will typically ensure that

$$(1/T) \sum_{t=1}^{T} \mathbf{x}_t u_t \xrightarrow{p} E(\mathbf{x}_t u_t) = \mathbf{0},$$

under the assumed absence of correlation between $\mathbf{x}_t$ and $u_t$. Hence,

$$\left[(1/T) \sum_{t=1}^{T} \hat{\mathbf{z}}_t u_t\right] \xrightarrow{p} \mathbf{0}. \qquad [9.2.15]$$

Substituting [9.2.12] and [9.2.15] into [9.2.10], it follows that

$$\hat{\boldsymbol{\beta}}_{2SLS,T} - \boldsymbol{\beta} \xrightarrow{p} \mathbf{Q}^{-1} \cdot \mathbf{0} = \mathbf{0}.$$

Hence, the $2SLS$ estimator is consistent as long as the matrix $\mathbf{Q}$ in [9.2.13] is nonsingular.

Notice that if none of the predetermined variables is correlated with $z_{it}$, then the $i$th row of $E(\mathbf{z}_t\mathbf{x}_t')$ contains all zeros and the corresponding row of $\mathbf{Q}$ in [9.2.13] contains all zeros, in which case $2SLS$ is not consistent. Alternatively, if $z_{it}$ is correlated with $\mathbf{x}_t$ only through, say, the first element $x_{1t}$ and $z_{jt}$ is also correlated with $\mathbf{x}_t$ only through $x_{1t}$, then subtracting some multiple of the $i$th row of $\mathbf{Q}$ from the $j$th row produces a row of zeros, and $\mathbf{Q}$ again is not invertible. In general, consistency of the $2SLS$ estimator requires the rows of $E(\mathbf{z}_t\mathbf{x}_t')$ to be linearly independent. This essentially amounts to the requirement that there be a way of assigning instruments to endogenous variables such that each endogenous variable has an instrument associated with it, with no instrument counted twice for this purpose.

## *Asymptotic Distribution of 2SLS Estimator*

Equation [9.2.10] implies that

$$\sqrt{T}(\hat{\boldsymbol{\beta}}_{2SLS,T} - \boldsymbol{\beta}) = \left[(1/T)\sum_{t=1}^{T}\hat{\mathbf{z}}_t\mathbf{z}_t'\right]^{-1}\left[(1/\sqrt{T})\sum_{t=1}^{T}\hat{\mathbf{z}}_t u_t\right], \qquad [9.2.16]$$

where

$$\left[(1/\sqrt{T})\sum_{t=1}^{T}\hat{\mathbf{z}}_t u_t\right] = \hat{\boldsymbol{\delta}}_T'\,(1/\sqrt{T})\sum_{t=1}^{T}\mathbf{x}_t u_t.$$

Hence, from [9.2.12] and [9.2.14],

$$\sqrt{T}(\hat{\boldsymbol{\beta}}_{2SLS,T} - \boldsymbol{\beta}) \xrightarrow{p} \mathbf{Q}^{-1}\cdot[E(\mathbf{z}_t\mathbf{x}_t')][E(\mathbf{x}_t\mathbf{x}_t')]^{-1}\left((1/\sqrt{T})\sum_{t=1}^{T}\mathbf{x}_t u_t\right). \qquad [9.2.17]$$

Suppose that $\mathbf{x}_t$ is covariance-stationary and that $\{u_t\}$ is an i.i.d. sequence with mean zero and variance $\sigma^2$ with $u_t$ independent of $\mathbf{x}_s$ for all $s \leq t$. Then $\{\mathbf{x}_t u_t\}$ is a martingale difference sequence with variance-covariance matrix given by $\sigma^2\cdot E(\mathbf{x}_t\mathbf{x}_t')$. If $u_t$ and $\mathbf{x}_t$ have finite fourth moments, then we can expect from Proposition 7.9 that

$$\left((1/\sqrt{T})\sum_{t=1}^{T}\mathbf{x}_t u_t\right) \xrightarrow{L} N(\mathbf{0}, \sigma^2\cdot E(\mathbf{x}_t\mathbf{x}_t')). \qquad [9.2.18]$$

Thus, [9.2.17] implies that

$$\sqrt{T}(\hat{\boldsymbol{\beta}}_{2SLS,T} - \boldsymbol{\beta}) \xrightarrow{L} N(\mathbf{0}, \mathbf{V}), \qquad [9.2.19]$$

where

$$\begin{aligned}\mathbf{V} &= \mathbf{Q}^{-1}[E(\mathbf{z}_t\mathbf{x}_t')][E(\mathbf{x}_t\mathbf{x}_t')]^{-1}[\sigma^2\cdot E(\mathbf{x}_t\mathbf{x}_t')][E(\mathbf{x}_t\mathbf{x}_t')]^{-1}[E(\mathbf{x}_t\mathbf{z}_t')]\mathbf{Q}^{-1}\\ &= \sigma^2\mathbf{Q}^{-1}\cdot\mathbf{Q}\cdot\mathbf{Q}^{-1}\\ &= \sigma^2\mathbf{Q}^{-1}\end{aligned} \qquad [9.2.20]$$

for $\mathbf{Q}$ given in [9.2.13]. Hence,

$$\hat{\boldsymbol{\beta}}_{2SLS,T} \approx N(\boldsymbol{\beta}, (1/T)\sigma^2\mathbf{Q}^{-1}). \qquad [9.2.21]$$

Since $\hat{\boldsymbol{\beta}}_{2SLS}$ is a consistent estimate of $\boldsymbol{\beta}$, clearly a consistent estimate of the population residual for observation $t$ is afforded by

$$\hat{u}_{t,T} \equiv y_t - \mathbf{z}_t'\hat{\boldsymbol{\beta}}_{2SLS,T} \xrightarrow{p} u_t. \qquad [9.2.22]$$

Similarly, it is straightforward to show that $\sigma^2$ can be consistently estimated by

$$\hat{\sigma}_T^2 = (1/T)\sum_{t=1}^{T}(y_t - \mathbf{z}_t'\hat{\boldsymbol{\beta}}_{2SLS,T})^2 \qquad [9.2.23]$$

(see Exercise 9.1). Note well that although $\hat{\boldsymbol{\beta}}_{2SLS}$ can be calculated from an *OLS* regression of $y_t$ on $\hat{\mathbf{z}}_t$, the estimates $\hat{u}_t$ and $\hat{\sigma}^2$ in [9.2.22] and [9.2.23] are not based on the residuals from this regression:

$$\hat{u}_t \neq y_t - \hat{\mathbf{z}}_t'\hat{\boldsymbol{\beta}}_{2SLS}$$

$$\hat{\sigma}^2 \neq (1/T)\sum_{t=1}^{T}(y_t - \hat{\mathbf{z}}_t'\hat{\boldsymbol{\beta}}_{2SLS})^2.$$

The correct estimates [9.2.22] and [9.2.23] use the actual explanatory variables $\mathbf{z}_t$ rather than the fitted values $\hat{\mathbf{z}}_t$.

A consistent estimate of $\mathbf{Q}$ is provided by [9.2.11]:

$$\begin{aligned}\hat{\mathbf{Q}}_T &= (1/T)\sum_{t=1}^{T}\hat{\mathbf{z}}_t\hat{\mathbf{z}}_t' \\ &= \left[(1/T)\sum_{t=1}^{T}\mathbf{z}_t\mathbf{x}_t'\right]\left[(1/T)\sum_{t=1}^{T}\mathbf{x}_t\mathbf{x}_t'\right]^{-1}\left[(1/T)\sum_{t=1}^{T}\mathbf{x}_t\mathbf{z}_t'\right].\end{aligned} \qquad [9.2.24]$$

Substituting [9.2.23] and [9.2.24] into [9.2.21], the estimated variance-covariance matrix of the 2*SLS* estimator is

$$\begin{aligned}\hat{\mathbf{V}}_T/T &= \hat{\sigma}_T^2\cdot(1/T)\cdot\left[(1/T)\sum_{t=1}^{T}\hat{\mathbf{z}}_t\hat{\mathbf{z}}_t'\right]^{-1} \\ &= \hat{\sigma}_T^2\cdot\left\{\left[\sum_{t=1}^{T}\mathbf{z}_t\mathbf{x}_t'\right]\left[\sum_{t=1}^{T}\mathbf{x}_t\mathbf{x}_t'\right]^{-1}\left[\sum_{t=1}^{T}\mathbf{x}_t\mathbf{z}_t'\right]\right\}^{-1}.\end{aligned} \qquad [9.2.25]$$

A test of the null hypothesis $\mathbf{R}\boldsymbol{\beta} = \mathbf{r}$ can thus be based on

$$(\mathbf{R}\hat{\boldsymbol{\beta}}_{2SLS,T} - \mathbf{r})'[\mathbf{R}(\hat{\mathbf{V}}_T/T)\mathbf{R}']^{-1}(\mathbf{R}\hat{\boldsymbol{\beta}}_{2SLS,T} - \mathbf{r}), \qquad [9.2.26]$$

which, under the null hypothesis, has an asymptotic distribution that is $\chi^2$ with degrees of freedom given by $m$, where $m$ represents the number of restrictions or the number of rows of $\mathbf{R}$.

Heteroskedasticity- and autocorrelation-consistent standard errors for 2*SLS* estimation will be discussed in Chapter 14.

## *Instrumental Variable Estimation*

Substituting [9.2.4] and [9.2.5] into [9.2.8], the 2*SLS* estimator can be written as

$$\begin{aligned}\hat{\boldsymbol{\beta}}_{2SLS} &= \left[\sum_{t=1}^{T}\hat{\boldsymbol{\delta}}'\mathbf{x}_t\mathbf{z}_t'\right]^{-1}\left[\sum_{t=1}^{T}\hat{\boldsymbol{\delta}}'\mathbf{x}_t y_t\right] \\ &= \left\{\left[\sum_{t=1}^{T}\mathbf{z}_t\mathbf{x}_t'\right]\left[\sum_{t=1}^{T}\mathbf{x}_t\mathbf{x}_t'\right]^{-1}\left[\sum_{t=1}^{T}\mathbf{x}_t\mathbf{z}_t'\right]\right\}^{-1}\left\{\left[\sum_{t=1}^{T}\mathbf{z}_t\mathbf{x}_t'\right]\left[\sum_{t=1}^{T}\mathbf{x}_t\mathbf{x}_t'\right]^{-1}\left[\sum_{t=1}^{T}\mathbf{x}_t y_t\right]\right\}.\end{aligned}$$

[9.2.27]

Consider the special case in which the number of instruments is exactly equal to the number of endogenous explanatory variables, so that $r = k$, as was the case for estimation of the demand curve in Section 9.1. Then $\Sigma_{t=1}^{T}\mathbf{z}_t\mathbf{x}_t'$ is a $(k \times k)$ matrix and [9.2.27] becomes

$$\begin{aligned}\hat{\boldsymbol{\beta}}_{IV} &= \left\{\left[\sum_{t=1}^{T}\mathbf{x}_t\mathbf{z}_t'\right]^{-1}\left[\sum_{t=1}^{T}\mathbf{x}_t\mathbf{x}_t'\right]\left[\sum_{t=1}^{T}\mathbf{z}_t\mathbf{x}_t'\right]^{-1}\right\} \\ &\quad\times\left\{\left[\sum_{t=1}^{T}\mathbf{z}_t\mathbf{x}_t'\right]\left[\sum_{t=1}^{T}\mathbf{x}_t\mathbf{x}_t'\right]^{-1}\left[\sum_{t=1}^{T}\mathbf{x}_t y_t\right]\right\} \qquad [9.2.28] \\ &= \left[\sum_{t=1}^{T}\mathbf{x}_t\mathbf{z}_t'\right]^{-1}\left[\sum_{t=1}^{T}\mathbf{x}_t y_t\right].\end{aligned}$$

Expression [9.2.28] is known as the *instrumental variable* (*IV*) estimator.

A key property of the *IV* estimator can be seen by premultiplying both sides of [9.2.28] by $\Sigma_{t=1}^{T}\mathbf{x}_t\mathbf{z}_t'$:

$$\sum_{t=1}^{T}\mathbf{x}_t\mathbf{z}_t'\hat{\boldsymbol{\beta}}_{IV} = \sum_{t=1}^{T}\mathbf{x}_t y_t,$$

implying that

$$\sum_{t=1}^{T}\mathbf{x}_t(y_t - \mathbf{z}_t'\hat{\boldsymbol{\beta}}_{IV}) = \mathbf{0}. \qquad [9.2.29]$$

Thus, the *IV* sample residual $(y_t - \mathbf{z}_t'\hat{\boldsymbol{\beta}}_{IV})$ has the property that it is orthogonal to the instruments $\mathbf{x}_t$, in contrast to the *OLS* sample residual $(y_t - \mathbf{z}_t'\mathbf{b})$, which is orthogonal to the explanatory variables $\mathbf{z}_t$. The *IV* estimator is preferred to *OLS* because the population residual of the equation we are trying to estimate $(u_t)$ is correlated with $\mathbf{z}_t$ but uncorrelated with $\mathbf{x}_t$.

Since the *IV* estimator is a special case of *2SLS*, it shares the consistency property of the *2SLS* estimator. Its estimated variance with i.i.d. residuals can be calculated from [9.2.25]:

$$\hat{\sigma}_T^2\left[\sum_{t=1}^{T}\mathbf{x}_t\mathbf{z}_t'\right]^{-1}\left[\sum_{t=1}^{T}\mathbf{x}_t\mathbf{x}_t'\right]\left[\sum_{t=1}^{T}\mathbf{z}_t\mathbf{x}_t'\right]^{-1}. \qquad [9.2.30]$$

## 9.3. *Identification*

We noted in the supply-and-demand example in Section 9.1 that the demand elasticity $\beta$ could not be estimated consistently by an *OLS* regression of quantity on price. Indeed, in the absence of a valid instrument such as $w_t$, the demand elasticity cannot be estimated by any method! To see this, recall that the system as written in [9.1.1] and [9.1.2] implied the expressions [9.1.4] and [9.1.3]:

$$\begin{aligned}q_t &= \frac{\gamma}{\gamma - \beta}\varepsilon_t^d - \frac{\beta}{\gamma - \beta}\varepsilon_t^s \\ p_t &= \frac{\varepsilon_t^d - \varepsilon_t^s}{\gamma - \beta}.\end{aligned}$$

If $\varepsilon_t^d$ and $\varepsilon_t^s$ are i.i.d. Gaussian, then these equations imply that the vector $(q_t, p_t)'$ is Gaussian with mean zero and variance-covariance matrix

$$\mathbf{\Omega} \equiv [1/(\gamma - \beta)^2] \cdot \begin{bmatrix} \gamma^2\sigma_d^2 + \beta^2\sigma_s^2 & \gamma\sigma_d^2 + \beta\sigma_s^2 \\ \gamma\sigma_d^2 + \beta\sigma_s^2 & \sigma_d^2 + \sigma_s^2 \end{bmatrix}.$$

This matrix is completely described by three magnitudes, these being the variances of $q$ and $p$ along with their covariance. Given a large enough sample, the values of these three magnitudes can be inferred with considerable confidence, but that is all that can be inferred, because these magnitudes can completely specify the process that generated the data under the maintained assumption of zero-mean i.i.d. Gaussian observations. There is no way to uncover the four parameters of the structural model $(\beta, \gamma, \sigma_d^2, \sigma_s^2)$ from these three magnitudes. For example, the values $(\beta, \gamma, \sigma_d^2, \sigma_s^2) = (1, 2, 3, 4)$ imply exactly the same observable properties for the data as would $(\beta, \gamma, \sigma_d^2, \sigma_s^2) = (2, 1, 4, 3)$.

If two different values for a parameter vector $\boldsymbol{\theta}$ imply the same probability distribution for the observed data, then the vector $\boldsymbol{\theta}$ is said to be *unidentified*.

When a third Gaussian white noise variable $w_t$ is added to the set of observations, three additional magnitudes are available to characterize the process for observables, these being the variance of $w$, the covariance between $w$ and $p$, and the covariance between $w$ and $q$. If the new variable $w$ enters both the demand and the supply equation, then three new parameters would be required to estimate the structural model—the parameter that summarizes the effect of $w$ on demand, the parameter that summarizes its effect on supply, and the variance of $w$. With three more estimable magnitudes but three more parameters to estimate, we would be stuck with the same problem, having no basis for estimation of $\beta$.

Consistent estimation of the demand elasticity was achieved by using two-stage least squares because it was assumed that $w$ appeared in the supply equation but was excluded from the demand equation. This is known as achieving identification through *exclusion restrictions*.

We showed in Section 9.2 that the parameters of an equation could be estimated (and thus must be identified) if (1) the number of instruments for that equation is at least as great as the number of endogenous explanatory variables for that equation and (2) the rows of $E(\mathbf{z}_t\mathbf{x}_t')$ are linearly independent. The first condition is known as the *order* condition for identification, and the second is known as the *rank* condition.

The rank condition for identification can be summarized more explicitly by specifying a complete system of equations for all of the endogenous variables. Let $\mathbf{y}_t$ denote an $(n \times 1)$ vector containing all of the endogenous variables in the system, and let $\mathbf{x}_t$ denote an $(m \times 1)$ vector containing all of the predetermined variables. Suppose that the system consists of $n$ equations written as

$$\mathbf{B}\mathbf{y}_t + \mathbf{\Gamma}\mathbf{x}_t = \mathbf{u}_t, \qquad [9.3.1]$$

where $\mathbf{B}$ and $\mathbf{\Gamma}$ are $(n \times n)$ and $(n \times m)$ matrices of coefficients, respectively, and $\mathbf{u}_t$ is an $(n \times 1)$ vector of disturbances. The statement that $\mathbf{x}_t$ is predetermined is taken to mean that $E(\mathbf{x}_t\mathbf{u}_t') = \mathbf{0}$. For example, the demand and supply equations considered in Section 9.1 were

$$q_t = \beta p_t + u_t^d \qquad \text{(demand)} \qquad [9.3.2]$$

$$q_t = \gamma p_t + h w_t + u_t^s \qquad \text{(supply)}. \qquad [9.3.3]$$

For this system, there are $n = 2$ endogenous variables, with $\mathbf{y}_t = (q_t, p_t)'$; and $m = 1$ predetermined variable, so that $\mathbf{x}_t = w_t$. This system can be written in the form of [9.3.1] as

$$\begin{bmatrix} 1 & -\beta \\ 1 & -\gamma \end{bmatrix} \begin{bmatrix} q_t \\ p_t \end{bmatrix} + \begin{bmatrix} 0 \\ -h \end{bmatrix} w_t = \begin{bmatrix} u_t^d \\ u_t^s \end{bmatrix}. \qquad [9.3.4]$$

Suppose we are interested in the equation represented by the first row of the vector system of equations in [9.3.1]. Let $y_{0t}$ be the dependent variable in the first equation, and let $\mathbf{y}_{1t}$ denote an $(n_1 \times 1)$ vector consisting of those endogenous variables that appear in the first equation as explanatory variables. Similarly, let $\mathbf{x}_{1t}$ denote an $(m_1 \times 1)$ vector consisting of those predetermined variables that appear in the first equation as explanatory variables. Then the first equation in the system is

$$y_{0t} + \mathbf{B}_{01}\mathbf{y}_{1t} + \mathbf{\Gamma}_{01}\mathbf{x}_{1t} = u_{0t},$$

where $\mathbf{B}_{01}$ is a $(1 \times n_1)$ vector and $\mathbf{\Gamma}_{01}$ is a $(1 \times m_1)$ vector. Let $\mathbf{y}_{2t}$ denote an $(n_2 \times 1)$ vector consisting of those endogenous variables that do not appear in the first equation; thus, $\mathbf{y}_t' = (y_{0t}, \mathbf{y}_{1t}', \mathbf{y}_{2t}')$ and $1 + n_1 + n_2 = n$. Similarly, let $\mathbf{x}_{2t}$ denote an $(m_2 \times 1)$ vector consisting of those predetermined variables that do not appear in the first equation, so that $\mathbf{x}_t' = (\mathbf{x}_{1t}', \mathbf{x}_{2t}')$ and $m_1 + m_2 = m$. Then the system in [9.3.1] can be written in partitioned form as

$$\begin{bmatrix} 1 & \mathbf{B}_{01} & \mathbf{0}' \\ \mathbf{B}_{10} & \mathbf{B}_{11} & \mathbf{B}_{12} \\ \mathbf{B}_{20} & \mathbf{B}_{21} & \mathbf{B}_{22} \end{bmatrix} \begin{bmatrix} y_{0t} \\ \mathbf{y}_{1t} \\ \mathbf{y}_{2t} \end{bmatrix} + \begin{bmatrix} \mathbf{\Gamma}_{01} & \mathbf{0}' \\ \mathbf{\Gamma}_{11} & \mathbf{\Gamma}_{12} \\ \mathbf{\Gamma}_{21} & \mathbf{\Gamma}_{22} \end{bmatrix} \begin{bmatrix} \mathbf{x}_{1t} \\ \mathbf{x}_{2t} \end{bmatrix} = \begin{bmatrix} u_{0t} \\ \mathbf{u}_{1t} \\ \mathbf{u}_{2t} \end{bmatrix}. \qquad [9.3.5]$$

Here, for example, $\mathbf{B}_{12}$ is an $(n_1 \times n_2)$ matrix consisting of rows 2 through $(n_1 + 1)$ and columns $(n_1 + 2)$ through $n$ of the matrix $\mathbf{B}$.

An alternative useful representation of the system is obtained by moving $\mathbf{\Gamma x}_t$ to the right side of [9.3.1] and premultiplying both sides by $\mathbf{B}^{-1}$:

$$\mathbf{y}_t = -\mathbf{B}^{-1}\mathbf{\Gamma}\mathbf{x}_t + \mathbf{B}^{-1}\mathbf{u}_t = \mathbf{\Pi}'\mathbf{x}_t + \mathbf{v}_t, \qquad [9.3.6]$$

where

$$\mathbf{\Pi}' = -\mathbf{B}^{-1}\mathbf{\Gamma} \qquad [9.3.7]$$

$$\mathbf{v}_t = \mathbf{B}^{-1}\mathbf{u}_t. \qquad [9.3.8]$$

Expression [9.3.6] is known as the *reduced-form* representation of the structural system [9.3.1]. In the reduced-form representation, each endogenous variable is expressed solely as a function of predetermined variables. For the example of [9.3.4], the reduced form is

$$\begin{aligned} \begin{bmatrix} q_t \\ p_t \end{bmatrix} &= -\begin{bmatrix} 1 & -\beta \\ 1 & -\gamma \end{bmatrix}^{-1} \begin{bmatrix} 0 \\ -h \end{bmatrix} w_t + \begin{bmatrix} 1 & -\beta \\ 1 & -\gamma \end{bmatrix}^{-1} \begin{bmatrix} u_t^d \\ u_t^s \end{bmatrix} \\ &= [1/(\beta - \gamma)] \begin{bmatrix} -\gamma & \beta \\ -1 & 1 \end{bmatrix} \begin{bmatrix} 0 \\ h \end{bmatrix} w_t \\ &\quad + [1/(\beta - \gamma)] \begin{bmatrix} -\gamma & \beta \\ -1 & 1 \end{bmatrix} \begin{bmatrix} u_t^d \\ u_t^s \end{bmatrix} \\ &= [1/(\beta - \gamma)] \begin{bmatrix} \beta h \\ h \end{bmatrix} w_t + [1/(\beta - \gamma)] \begin{bmatrix} -\gamma u_t^d + \beta u_t^s \\ -u_t^d + u_t^s \end{bmatrix}. \end{aligned} \qquad [9.3.9]$$

The reduced form for a general system can be written in partitioned form as

$$\begin{bmatrix} y_{0t} \\ \mathbf{y}_{1t} \\ \mathbf{y}_{2t} \end{bmatrix} = \begin{bmatrix} \mathbf{\Pi}_{01} & \mathbf{\Pi}_{02} \\ \mathbf{\Pi}_{11} & \mathbf{\Pi}_{12} \\ \mathbf{\Pi}_{21} & \mathbf{\Pi}_{22} \end{bmatrix} \begin{bmatrix} \mathbf{x}_{1t} \\ \mathbf{x}_{2t} \end{bmatrix} + \begin{bmatrix} v_{0t} \\ \mathbf{v}_{1t} \\ \mathbf{v}_{2t} \end{bmatrix}, \qquad [9.3.10]$$

where, for example, $\mathbf{\Pi}_{12}$ denotes an $(n_1 \times m_2)$ matrix consisting of rows 2 through $(n_1 + 1)$ and columns $(m_1 + 1)$ through $m$ of the matrix $\mathbf{\Pi}'$.

To apply the rank condition for identification of the first equation stated earlier, we would form the matrix of cross products between the explanatory variables in the first equation ($\mathbf{x}_{1t}$ and $\mathbf{y}_{1t}$) and the predetermined variables for the whole system ($\mathbf{x}_{1t}$ and $\mathbf{x}_{2t}$):

$$\mathbf{M} = \begin{bmatrix} E(\mathbf{x}_{1t}\mathbf{x}'_{1t}) & E(\mathbf{x}_{1t}\mathbf{x}'_{2t}) \\ E(\mathbf{y}_{1t}\mathbf{x}'_{1t}) & E(\mathbf{y}_{1t}\mathbf{x}'_{2t}) \end{bmatrix}. \qquad [9.3.11]$$

In the earlier notation, the explanatory variables for the first equation consist of $\mathbf{z}_t = (\mathbf{x}'_{1t}, \mathbf{y}'_{1t})'$, while the predetermined variables for the system as a whole consist of $\mathbf{x}_t = (\mathbf{x}'_{1t}, \mathbf{x}'_{2t})'$. Thus, the rank condition, which required the rows of $E(\mathbf{z}_t\mathbf{x}'_t)$ to be linearly independent, amounts to the requirement that the rows of the $[(m_1 + n_1) \times m]$ matrix $\mathbf{M}$ in [9.3.11] be linearly independent. The rank condition can equivalently be stated in terms of the structural parameter matrices $\mathbf{B}$ and $\mathbf{\Gamma}$ or the reduced-form parameter matrix $\mathbf{\Pi}$. The following proposition is adapted from Fisher (1966) and is proved in Appendix 9.A at the end of this chapter.

***Proposition 9.1:*** *If the matrix* $\mathbf{B}$ *in* [9.3.1] *and the matrix of second moments of the predetermined variables* $E(\mathbf{x}_t\mathbf{x}'_t)$ *are both nonsingular, then the following conditions are equivalent:*

(*a*) *The rows of the* $[(m_1 + n_1) \times m]$ *matrix* $\mathbf{M}$ *in* [9.3.11] *are linearly independent.*

(*b*) *The rows of the* $[(n_1 + n_2) \times (m_2 + n_2)]$ *matrix*

$$\begin{bmatrix} \mathbf{\Gamma}_{12} & \mathbf{B}_{12} \\ \mathbf{\Gamma}_{22} & \mathbf{B}_{22} \end{bmatrix} \qquad [9.3.12]$$

*are linearly independent.*

(*c*) *The rows of the* $(n_1 \times m_2)$ *matrix* $\mathbf{\Pi}_{12}$ *are linearly independent.*

For example, for the system in [9.3.4], no endogenous variables are excluded from the first equation, and so $y_{0t} = q_t$, $\mathbf{y}_{1t} = p_t$, and $\mathbf{y}_{2t}$ contains no elements. No predetermined variables appear in the first equation, and so $\mathbf{x}_{1t}$ contains no elements and $\mathbf{x}_{2t} = w_t$. The matrix in [9.3.12] is then just given by the parameter $\mathbf{\Gamma}_{12}$. This represents the coefficient on $\mathbf{x}_{2t}$ in the equation describing $\mathbf{y}_{1t}$ and is equal to the scalar parameter $-h$. Result (b) of Proposition 9.1 thus states that the first equation is identified provided that $h \neq 0$. The value of $\mathbf{\Pi}_{12}$ can be read directly off the coefficient on $w_t$ in the second row of [9.3.9] and turns out to be given by $h/(\beta - \gamma)$. Since $\mathbf{B}$ is assumed to be nonsingular, $(\beta - \gamma)$ is nonzero, and so $\mathbf{\Gamma}_{12}$ is zero if and only if $\mathbf{\Pi}_{12}$ is zero.

## *Achieving Identification Through Covariance Restrictions*

Another way in which parameters can be identified is through restrictions on the covariances of the errors of the structural equations. For example, consider again the supply and demand model, [9.3.2] and [9.3.3]. We saw that the demand elasticity $\beta$ was identified by the exclusion of $w_t$ from the demand equation. Consider now estimation of the supply elasticity $\gamma$.

Suppose first that we somehow knew the value of the demand elasticity $\beta$ with certainty. Then the error in the demand equation could be constructed from

$$u_t^d = q_t - \beta p_t.$$

Notice that $u_t^d$ would then be a valid instrument for the supply equation [9.3.3], since $u_t^d$ is correlated with the endogenous explanatory variable for that equation ($p_t$) but $u_t^d$ is uncorrelated with the error for that equation ($u_t^s$). Since $w_t$ is also uncorrelated with the error $u_t^s$, it follows that the parameters of the supply equation could be estimated consistently by instrumental variable estimation with $\mathbf{x}_t = (u_t^d, w_t)'$:

$$\begin{bmatrix} \hat{\gamma}_T^* \\ \hat{h}_T^* \end{bmatrix} = \begin{bmatrix} \Sigma u_t^d p_t & \Sigma u_t^d w_t \\ \Sigma w_t p_t & \Sigma w_t^2 \end{bmatrix}^{-1} \begin{bmatrix} \Sigma u_t^d q_t \\ \Sigma w_t q_t \end{bmatrix} \xrightarrow{p} \begin{bmatrix} \gamma \\ h \end{bmatrix}, \qquad [9.3.13]$$

where $\Sigma$ indicates summation over $t = 1, 2, \ldots, T$.

Although in practice we do not know the true value of $\beta$, it can be estimated consistently by *IV* estimation of [9.3.2] with $w_t$ as an instrument:

$$\hat{\beta} = (\Sigma w_t p_t)^{-1}(\Sigma w_t q_t).$$

Then the residual $u_t^d$ can be estimated consistently with $\hat{u}_t^d = q_t - \hat{\beta} p_t$. Consider, therefore, the estimator [9.3.13] with the population residual $u_t^d$ replaced by the *IV* sample residual:

$$\begin{bmatrix} \hat{\gamma}_T \\ \hat{h}_T \end{bmatrix} = \begin{bmatrix} \Sigma \hat{u}_t^d p_t & \Sigma \hat{u}_t^d w_t \\ \Sigma w_t p_t & \Sigma w_t^2 \end{bmatrix}^{-1} \begin{bmatrix} \Sigma \hat{u}_t^d q_t \\ \Sigma w_t q_t \end{bmatrix}. \qquad [9.3.14]$$

It is straightforward to use the fact that $\hat{\beta} \xrightarrow{p} \beta$ to deduce that the difference between the estimators in [9.3.14] and [9.3.13] converges in probability to zero. Hence, the estimator [9.3.14] is also consistent.

Two assumptions allowed the parameters of the supply equation ($\gamma$ and $h$) to be estimated. First, an exclusion restriction allowed $\beta$ to be estimated consistently. Second, a restriction on the covariance between $u_t^d$ and $u_t^s$ was necessary. If $u_t^d$ were correlated with $u_t^s$, then $u_t^d$ would not be a valid instrument for the supply equation and the estimator [9.3.13] would not be consistent.

### *Other Approaches to Identification*

A good deal more can be said about identification. For example, parameters can also be identified through the imposition of certain restrictions on parameters such as $\beta_1 + \beta_2 = 1$. Useful references include Fisher (1966), Rothenberg (1971), and Hausman and Taylor (1983).

## 9.4. *Full-Information Maximum Likelihood Estimation*

Up to this point we have considered estimation of a single equation of the form $y_t = \boldsymbol{\beta}'\mathbf{z}_t + u_t$. A more general approach is to specify a similar equation for every endogenous variable in the system, calculate the joint density of the vector of all of the endogenous variables conditional on the predetermined variables, and maximize the joint likelihood function. This is known as *full-information maximum likelihood* estimation, or *FIML*.

For illustration, suppose in [9.3.1] that the $(n \times 1)$ vector of structural disturbances $\mathbf{u}_t$ for date $t$ is distributed $N(\mathbf{0}, \mathbf{D})$. Assume, further, that $\mathbf{u}_t$ is independent of $\mathbf{u}_\tau$ for $t \neq \tau$ and that $\mathbf{u}_t$ is independent of $\mathbf{x}_\tau$ for all $t$ and $\tau$. Then the reduced-form disturbance $\mathbf{v}_t = \mathbf{B}^{-1}\mathbf{u}_t$ is distributed $N(\mathbf{0}, \mathbf{B}^{-1}\mathbf{D}(\mathbf{B}^{-1})')$, and the reduced-form representation [9.3.6] implies that

$$\mathbf{y}_t|\mathbf{x}_t \sim N\left(\mathbf{\Pi}'\mathbf{x}_t, \mathbf{B}^{-1}\mathbf{D}(\mathbf{B}^{-1})'\right) = N\left(-\mathbf{B}^{-1}\mathbf{\Gamma}\mathbf{x}_t, \mathbf{B}^{-1}\mathbf{D}(\mathbf{B}^{-1})'\right).$$

The conditional log likelihood can then be found from

$$\begin{aligned}\mathcal{L}(\mathbf{B}, \mathbf{\Gamma}, \mathbf{D}) &\\ &= \sum_{t=1}^{T} \log f(\mathbf{y}_t|\mathbf{x}_t; \mathbf{B}, \mathbf{\Gamma}, \mathbf{D}) \\ &= -(Tn/2)\log(2\pi) - (T/2)\log\left|\mathbf{B}^{-1}\mathbf{D}(\mathbf{B}^{-1})'\right| \\ &\quad - (1/2)\sum_{t=1}^{T} [\mathbf{y}_t + \mathbf{B}^{-1}\mathbf{\Gamma}\mathbf{x}_t]'[\mathbf{B}^{-1}\mathbf{D}(\mathbf{B}^{-1})']^{-1}[\mathbf{y}_t + \mathbf{B}^{-1}\mathbf{\Gamma}\mathbf{x}_t].\end{aligned} \qquad [9.4.1]$$

But

$$\begin{aligned}&[\mathbf{y}_t + \mathbf{B}^{-1}\mathbf{\Gamma}\mathbf{x}_t]'[\mathbf{B}^{-1}\mathbf{D}(\mathbf{B}^{-1})']^{-1}[\mathbf{y}_t + \mathbf{B}^{-1}\mathbf{\Gamma}\mathbf{x}_t] \\ &\qquad = [\mathbf{y}_t + \mathbf{B}^{-1}\mathbf{\Gamma}\mathbf{x}_t]'[\mathbf{B}'\mathbf{D}^{-1}\mathbf{B}][\mathbf{y}_t + \mathbf{B}^{-1}\mathbf{\Gamma}\mathbf{x}_t] \\ &\qquad = [\mathbf{B}(\mathbf{y}_t + \mathbf{B}^{-1}\mathbf{\Gamma}\mathbf{x}_t)]'\mathbf{D}^{-1}[\mathbf{B}(\mathbf{y}_t + \mathbf{B}^{-1}\mathbf{\Gamma}\mathbf{x}_t)] \\ &\qquad = [\mathbf{B}\mathbf{y}_t + \mathbf{\Gamma}\mathbf{x}_t]'\mathbf{D}^{-1}[\mathbf{B}\mathbf{y}_t + \mathbf{\Gamma}\mathbf{x}_t].\end{aligned} \qquad [9.4.2]$$

Furthermore,

$$\begin{aligned}\left|\mathbf{B}^{-1}\mathbf{D}(\mathbf{B}^{-1})'\right| &= |\mathbf{B}^{-1}|\cdot|\mathbf{D}|\cdot|\mathbf{B}^{-1}| \\ &= |\mathbf{D}|/|\mathbf{B}|^2.\end{aligned} \qquad [9.4.3]$$

Substituting [9.4.2] and [9.4.3] into [9.4.1],

$$\begin{aligned}\mathcal{L}(\mathbf{B}, \mathbf{\Gamma}, \mathbf{D}) &= -(Tn/2)\log(2\pi) + (T/2)\log|\mathbf{B}|^2 \\ &\quad - (T/2)\log|\mathbf{D}| - (1/2)\sum_{t=1}^{T} [\mathbf{B}\mathbf{y}_t + \mathbf{\Gamma}\mathbf{x}_t]'\mathbf{D}^{-1}[\mathbf{B}\mathbf{y}_t + \mathbf{\Gamma}\mathbf{x}_t].\end{aligned} \qquad [9.4.4]$$

The *FIML* estimates are then the values of $\mathbf{B}$, $\mathbf{\Gamma}$, and $\mathbf{D}$ for which [9.4.4] is maximized.

For example, for the system of [9.3.4], the *FIML* estimates of $\beta$, $\gamma$, $h$, $\sigma_d^2$, and $\sigma_s^2$ are found by maximizing

$$\begin{aligned}\mathcal{L}(\beta, \gamma, h, \sigma_d^2, \sigma_s^2) &\\ &= -T\log(2\pi) + \frac{T}{2}\log\begin{vmatrix}1 & -\beta \\ 1 & -\gamma\end{vmatrix}^2 - \frac{T}{2}\log\begin{vmatrix}\sigma_d^2 & 0 \\ 0 & \sigma_s^2\end{vmatrix} \\ &\quad - \frac{1}{2}\sum_{t=1}^{T}\left\{[q_t - \beta p_t \quad q_t - \gamma p_t - hw_t]\begin{bmatrix}\sigma_d^2 & 0 \\ 0 & \sigma_s^2\end{bmatrix}^{-1}\begin{bmatrix}q_t - \beta p_t \\ q_t - \gamma p_t - hw_t\end{bmatrix}\right\} \\ &= -T\log(2\pi) + T\log(\gamma - \beta) - (T/2)\log(\sigma_d^2) \\ &\quad - (T/2)\log(\sigma_s^2) - (1/2)\sum_{t=1}^{T}(q_t - \beta p_t)^2/\sigma_d^2 \\ &\quad - (1/2)\sum_{t=1}^{T}(q_t - \gamma p_t - hw_t)^2/\sigma_s^2.\end{aligned} \qquad [9.4.5]$$

The first-order conditions for maximization are

$$\frac{\partial \mathcal{L}}{\partial \beta} = -\frac{T}{\gamma - \beta} + \frac{\sum_{t=1}^{T} (q_t - \beta p_t)p_t}{\sigma_d^2} = 0 \qquad [9.4.6]$$

$$\frac{\partial \mathcal{L}}{\partial \gamma} = \frac{T}{\gamma - \beta} + \frac{\sum_{t=1}^{T} (q_t - \gamma p_t - hw_t)p_t}{\sigma_s^2} = 0 \qquad [9.4.7]$$

$$\frac{\partial \mathcal{L}}{\partial h} = \frac{\sum_{t=1}^{T} (q_t - \gamma p_t - hw_t)w_t}{\sigma_s^2} = 0 \qquad [9.4.8]$$

$$\frac{\partial \mathcal{L}}{\partial \sigma_d^2} = -\frac{T}{2\sigma_d^2} + \frac{\sum_{t=1}^{T} (q_t - \beta p_t)^2}{2\sigma_d^4} = 0 \qquad [9.4.9]$$

$$\frac{\partial \mathcal{L}}{\partial \sigma_s^2} = -\frac{T}{2\sigma_s^2} + \frac{\sum_{t=1}^{T} (q_t - \gamma p_t - hw_t)^2}{2\sigma_s^4} = 0. \qquad [9.4.10]$$

The last two equations characterize the maximum likelihood estimates of the variances as the average squared residuals:

$$\hat{\sigma}_d^2 = (1/T) \sum_{t=1}^{T} (q_t - \hat{\beta} p_t)^2 \qquad [9.4.11]$$

$$\hat{\sigma}_s^2 = (1/T) \sum_{t=1}^{T} (q_t - \hat{\gamma} p_t - \hat{h} w_t)^2. \qquad [9.4.12]$$

Multiplying equation [9.4.7] by $(\beta - \gamma)/T$ results in

$$\begin{aligned} 0 &= -1 + \sum_{t=1}^{T} (q_t - \gamma p_t - hw_t)(\beta p_t - \gamma p_t)/(T\sigma_s^2) \\ &= -1 + \sum_{t=1}^{T} (q_t - \gamma p_t - hw_t)(\beta p_t - q_t + q_t - \gamma p_t)/(T\sigma_s^2). \end{aligned} \qquad [9.4.13]$$

If [9.4.8] is multiplied by $h/T$ and subtracted from [9.4.13], the result is

$$\begin{aligned} 0 &= -1 + \sum_{t=1}^{T} (q_t - \gamma p_t - hw_t)(\beta p_t - q_t + q_t - \gamma p_t - hw_t)/(T\sigma_s^2) \\ &= -1 + \sum_{t=1}^{T} (q_t - \gamma p_t - hw_t)(\beta p_t - q_t)/(T\sigma_s^2) \\ &\quad + \sum_{t=1}^{T} (q_t - \gamma p_t - hw_t)^2/(T\sigma_s^2) \\ &= -1 - \sum_{t=1}^{T} (q_t - \gamma p_t - hw_t)(q_t - \beta p_t)/(T\sigma_s^2) + 1, \end{aligned}$$

by virtue of [9.4.12]. Hence, the *MLE*s satisfy

$$\sum_{t=1}^{T} (q_t - \hat{\gamma} p_t - \hat{h} w_t)(q_t - \hat{\beta} p_t) = 0. \qquad [9.4.14]$$

Similarly, multiplying [9.4.6] by $(\gamma - \beta)/T$,

$$0 = -1 + \sum_{t=1}^{T} (q_t - \beta p_t)(\gamma p_t - q_t + q_t - \beta p_t)/(T\sigma_d^2)$$

$$= -1 - \sum_{t=1}^{T} (q_t - \beta p_t)(q_t - \gamma p_t)/(T\sigma_d^2) + \sum_{t=1}^{T} (q_t - \beta p_t)^2/(T\sigma_d^2).$$

Using [9.4.11],

$$\sum_{t=1}^{T} (q_t - \hat{\beta} p_t)(q_t - \hat{\gamma} p_t) = 0. \qquad [9.4.15]$$

Subtracting [9.4.14] from [9.4.15],

$$0 = \sum_{t=1}^{T} (q_t - \hat{\beta} p_t)[(q_t - \hat{\gamma} p_t) - (q_t - \hat{\gamma} p_t - \hat{h} w_t)] = \hat{h} \sum_{t=1}^{T} (q_t - \hat{\beta} p_t) w_t.$$

Assuming that $\hat{h} \neq 0$, the *FIML* estimate of $\beta$ thus satisfies

$$\sum_{t=1}^{T} (q_t - \hat{\beta} p_t) w_t = 0;$$

that is, the demand elasticity is chosen so as to make the estimated residual for the demand equation orthogonal to $w_t$. Hence, the instrumental variable estimator $\hat{\beta}_{IV}$ turns out also to be the *FIML* estimator. Equations [9.4.8] and [9.4.14] assert that the parameters for the supply equation ($\gamma$ and $h$) are chosen so as to make the residual for that equation orthogonal to $w_t$ and to the demand residual $\hat{u}_t^d = q_t - \hat{\beta} p_t$. Hence, the *FIML* estimates for these parameters are the same as the instrumental-variable estimates suggested in [9.3.14].

For this example, two-stage least squares, instrumental variable estimation, and full-information maximum likelihood all produced the identical estimates. This is because the model is *just identified*. A model is said to be just identified if for any admissible value for the parameters of the reduced-form representation there exists a unique value for the structural parameters that implies those reduced-form parameters. A model is said to be *overidentified* if some admissible values for the reduced-form parameters are ruled out by the structural restrictions. In an overidentified model, *IV*, *2SLS*, and *FIML* estimation are not equivalent, and *FIML* typically produces the most efficient estimates.

For a general overidentified simultaneous equation system with no restrictions on the variance-covariance matrix, the *FIML* estimates can be calculated by iterating on a procedure known as *three-stage least squares*; see, for example, Maddala (1977, pp. 482–90). Rothenberg and Ruud (1990) discussed *FIML* estimation in the presence of covariance restrictions. *FIML* estimation of dynamic time series models will be discussed further in Chapter 11.

## 9.5 *Estimation Based on the Reduced Form*

If a system is just identified as in [9.3.2] and [9.3.3] with $u_t^d$ uncorrelated with $u_t^s$, one approach is to maximize the likelihood function with respect to the reduced-form parameters. The values of the structural parameters associated with these values for the reduced-form parameters are the same as the *FIML* estimates in a just-identified model.

The log likelihood [9.4.1] can be expressed in terms of the reduced-form parameters $\mathbf{\Pi}$ and $\mathbf{\Omega}$ as

$$\begin{aligned}\mathcal{L}(\mathbf{\Pi}, \mathbf{\Omega}) &= \sum_{t=1}^{T} \log f(\mathbf{y}_t|\mathbf{x}_t; \mathbf{\Pi}, \mathbf{\Omega}) \\ &= -(Tn/2)\log(2\pi) - (T/2)\log|\mathbf{\Omega}| \\ &\quad - (1/2)\sum_{t=1}^{T} [\mathbf{y}_t - \mathbf{\Pi}'\mathbf{x}_t]'\mathbf{\Omega}^{-1}[\mathbf{y}_t - \mathbf{\Pi}'\mathbf{x}_t],\end{aligned} \qquad [9.5.1]$$

where $\mathbf{\Omega} = E(\mathbf{v}_t\mathbf{v}_t') = \mathbf{B}^{-1}\mathbf{D}(\mathbf{B}^{-1})'$. The value of $\mathbf{\Pi}$ that maximizes [9.5.1] will be shown in Chapter 11 to be given by

$$\hat{\mathbf{\Pi}}' = \left[\sum_{t=1}^{T} \mathbf{y}_t\mathbf{x}_t'\right]\left[\sum_{t=1}^{T} \mathbf{x}_t\mathbf{x}_t'\right]^{-1};$$

in other words, the $i$th row of $\hat{\mathbf{\Pi}}'$ is obtained from an *OLS* regression of the $i$th endogenous variable on all of the predetermined variables:

$$\hat{\boldsymbol{\pi}}_i' = \left[\sum_{t=1}^{T} y_{it}\mathbf{x}_t'\right]\left[\sum_{t=1}^{T} \mathbf{x}_t\mathbf{x}_t'\right]^{-1}.$$

The *MLE* of $\mathbf{\Omega}$ turns out to be

$$\hat{\mathbf{\Omega}} = (1/T)\left[\sum_{t=1}^{T} (\mathbf{y}_t - \hat{\mathbf{\Pi}}'\mathbf{x}_t)(\mathbf{y}_t - \hat{\mathbf{\Pi}}'\mathbf{x}_t)'\right].$$

For a just-identified model, the *FIML* estimates are the values of $(\mathbf{B}, \mathbf{\Gamma}, \mathbf{D})$ for which $\hat{\mathbf{\Pi}}' = -\mathbf{B}^{-1}\mathbf{\Gamma}$ and $\hat{\mathbf{\Omega}} = \mathbf{B}^{-1}\mathbf{D}(\mathbf{B}^{-1})'$.

We now show that the estimates of $\mathbf{B}$, $\mathbf{\Gamma}$, and $\mathbf{D}$ inferred in this fashion from the reduced-form parameters for the just-identified supply-and-demand example are the same as the *FIML* estimates. The estimate $\hat{\pi}_1$ is found by *OLS* regression of $q_t$ on $w_t$, while $\hat{\pi}_2$ is the coefficient from an *OLS* regression of $p_t$ on $w_t$. These estimates satisfy

$$\sum_{t=1}^{T} (q_t - \hat{\pi}_1 w_t)w_t = 0 \qquad [9.5.2]$$

$$\sum_{t=1}^{T} (p_t - \hat{\pi}_2 w_t)w_t = 0 \qquad [9.5.3]$$

and

$$\begin{bmatrix}\hat{\Omega}_{11} & \hat{\Omega}_{12} \\ \hat{\Omega}_{21} & \hat{\Omega}_{22}\end{bmatrix} = (1/T)\begin{bmatrix}\Sigma(q_t - \hat{\pi}_1 w_t)^2 & \Sigma(q_t - \hat{\pi}_1 w_t)(p_t - \hat{\pi}_2 w_t) \\ \Sigma(p_t - \hat{\pi}_2 w_t)(q_t - \hat{\pi}_1 w_t) & \Sigma(p_t - \hat{\pi}_2 w_t)^2\end{bmatrix}. \qquad [9.5.4]$$

The structural estimates satisfy $\mathbf{B}\hat{\mathbf{\Pi}}' = -\mathbf{\Gamma}$ or

$$\begin{bmatrix}1 & -\beta \\ 1 & -\gamma\end{bmatrix}\begin{bmatrix}\hat{\pi}_1 \\ \hat{\pi}_2\end{bmatrix} = \begin{bmatrix}0 \\ h\end{bmatrix}. \qquad [9.5.5]$$

Multiplying [9.5.3] by $\beta$ and subtracting the result from [9.5.2] produces

$$\begin{aligned} 0 &= \sum_{t=1}^{T} (q_t - \hat{\pi}_1 w_t - \beta p_t + \beta \hat{\pi}_2 w_t) w_t \\ &= \sum_{t=1}^{T} (q_t - \beta p_t) w_t - \sum_{t=1}^{T} (\hat{\pi}_1 - \beta \hat{\pi}_2) w_t^2 \\ &= \sum_{t=1}^{T} (q_t - \beta p_t) w_t, \end{aligned}$$

by virtue of the first row of [9.5.5]. Thus, the estimate of $\beta$ inferred from the reduced-form parameters is the same as the *IV* or *FIML* estimate derived earlier. Similarly, multiplying [9.5.3] by $\gamma$ and subtracting the result from [9.5.2] gives

$$\begin{aligned} 0 &= \sum_{t=1}^{T} (q_t - \hat{\pi}_1 w_t - \gamma p_t + \gamma \hat{\pi}_2 w_t) w_t \\ &= \sum_{t=1}^{T} [q_t - \gamma p_t - (\hat{\pi}_1 - \gamma \hat{\pi}_2) w_t] w_t \\ &= \sum_{t=1}^{T} [q_t - \gamma p_t - h w_t] w_t, \end{aligned}$$

by virtue of the second row of [9.5.5], reproducing the first-order condition [9.4.8] for *FIML*. Finally, we need to solve $\mathbf{D} = \mathbf{B}\hat{\mathbf{\Omega}}\mathbf{B}'$ for $\mathbf{D}$ and $\gamma$ (the remaining element of $\mathbf{B}$). These equations are

$$\begin{aligned} &\begin{bmatrix} \sigma_d^2 & 0 \\ 0 & \sigma_s^2 \end{bmatrix} \\ &= \begin{bmatrix} 1 & -\beta \\ 1 & -\gamma \end{bmatrix} \begin{bmatrix} \hat{\Omega}_{11} & \hat{\Omega}_{12} \\ \hat{\Omega}_{21} & \hat{\Omega}_{22} \end{bmatrix} \begin{bmatrix} 1 & 1 \\ -\beta & -\gamma \end{bmatrix} \\ &= \frac{1}{T} \sum_{t=1}^{T} \left\{ \begin{bmatrix} 1 & -\beta \\ 1 & -\gamma \end{bmatrix} \begin{bmatrix} q_t - \hat{\pi}_1 w_t \\ p_t - \hat{\pi}_2 w_t \end{bmatrix} [q_t - \hat{\pi}_1 w_t \quad p_t - \hat{\pi}_2 w_t] \begin{bmatrix} 1 & 1 \\ -\beta & -\gamma \end{bmatrix} \right\} \\ &= \frac{1}{T} \sum_{t=1}^{T} \left\{ \begin{bmatrix} q_t - \beta p_t - (\hat{\pi}_1 - \beta \hat{\pi}_2) w_t \\ q_t - \gamma p_t - (\hat{\pi}_1 - \gamma \hat{\pi}_2) w_t \end{bmatrix} \begin{bmatrix} q_t - \beta p_t - (\hat{\pi}_1 - \beta \hat{\pi}_2) w_t \\ q_t - \gamma p_t - (\hat{\pi}_1 - \gamma \hat{\pi}_2) w_t \end{bmatrix}' \right\} \\ &= \frac{1}{T} \sum_{t=1}^{T} \left\{ \begin{bmatrix} q_t - \beta p_t \\ q_t - \gamma p_t - h w_t \end{bmatrix} [q_t - \beta p_t \quad q_t - \gamma p_t - h w_t] \right\}. \end{aligned}$$

The diagonal elements of this matrix system of equations reproduce the earlier formulas for the *FIML* estimates of the variance parameters, while the off-diagonal element reproduces the result [9.4.14].

## 9.6. *Overview of Simultaneous Equations Bias*

The problem of simultaneous equations bias is extremely widespread in the social sciences. It is rare that the relation that we are interested in estimating is the only possible reason why the dependent and explanatory variables might be correlated. For example, consider trying to estimate the effect of military service on an individual's subsequent income. This parameter cannot be estimated by a regression of income on a measure of military service and other observed variables. The error term in such a regression represents other characteristics of the individual that influence income, and these omitted factors are also likely to have influenced the individual's military participation. As another example, consider trying to estimate the success of long prison sentences in deterring crime. This cannot be estimated by regressing the crime rate in a state on the average prison term in that state, because some states may have adopted stiffer prison sentences in response to higher crime. The error term in the regression, which represents other factors that influence crime, is thus likely also to be correlated with the explanatory variable. Regardless of whether the researcher is interested in the factors that determine military service or prison terms or has any theory about them, simultaneous equations bias must be recognized and dealt with.

Furthermore, it is not enough to find an instrument $\mathbf{x}_t$ that is uncorrelated with the residual $u_t$. In order to satisfy the rank condition, the instrument $\mathbf{x}_t$ must be correlated with the endogenous explanatory variables $\mathbf{z}_t$. The calculations by Nelson and Startz (1990) suggest that very poor estimates can result if $\mathbf{x}_t$ is only weakly correlated with $\mathbf{z}_t$.

Finding valid instruments is often extremely difficult and requires careful thought and a bit of good luck. For the question about military service, Angrist (1990) found an ingenious instrument for military service based on the institutional details of the draft in the United States during the Vietnam War. The likelihood that an individual was drafted into military service was determined by a lottery based on birthdays. Thus, an individual's birthday during the year would be correlated with military service but presumably uncorrelated with other factors influencing income. Unfortunately, it is unusual to be able to find such a compelling instrument for many questions that one would like to ask of the data.

## APPENDIX 9.A. *Proofs of Chapter 9 Proposition*

■ **Proof of Proposition 9.1.** We first show that (a) implies (c). The middle block of [9.3.10] states that

$$\mathbf{y}_{1t} = \mathbf{\Pi}_{11}\mathbf{x}_{1t} + \mathbf{\Pi}_{12}\mathbf{x}_{2t} + \mathbf{v}_{1t}.$$

Hence,

$$\begin{aligned} \mathbf{M} &= E\left\{\begin{bmatrix} \mathbf{x}_{1t} \\ \mathbf{y}_{1t} \end{bmatrix} [\mathbf{x}'_{1t} \quad \mathbf{x}'_{2t}]\right\} \\ &= E\left\{\begin{bmatrix} \mathbf{I}_{m_1} & \mathbf{0} \\ \mathbf{\Pi}_{11} & \mathbf{\Pi}_{12} \end{bmatrix}\begin{bmatrix} \mathbf{x}_{1t} \\ \mathbf{x}_{2t} \end{bmatrix}[\mathbf{x}'_{1t} \quad \mathbf{x}'_{2t}] + \begin{bmatrix} \mathbf{0} \\ \mathbf{v}_{1t} \end{bmatrix}[\mathbf{x}'_{1t} \quad \mathbf{x}'_{2t}]\right\} \\ &= \begin{bmatrix} \mathbf{I}_{m_1} & \mathbf{0} \\ \mathbf{\Pi}_{11} & \mathbf{\Pi}_{12} \end{bmatrix} E(\mathbf{x}_t\mathbf{x}'_t), \end{aligned} \qquad [9.A.1]$$

since $\mathbf{x}_t$ is uncorrelated with $\mathbf{u}_t$ and thus uncorrelated with $\mathbf{v}_t$.

Suppose that the rows of $\mathbf{M}$ are linearly independent. This means that $[\boldsymbol{\lambda}' \quad \boldsymbol{\mu}']\mathbf{M} \neq \mathbf{0}'$ for any $(m_1 \times 1)$ vector $\boldsymbol{\lambda}$ and any $(n_1 \times 1)$ vector $\boldsymbol{\mu}$ that are not both zero. In particular, $[-\boldsymbol{\mu}'\mathbf{\Pi}_{11} \quad \boldsymbol{\mu}']\mathbf{M} \neq \mathbf{0}'$. But from the right side of [9.A.1], this implies that

$$[-\boldsymbol{\mu}'\mathbf{\Pi}_{11} \quad \boldsymbol{\mu}']\begin{bmatrix} \mathbf{I}_{m_1} & \mathbf{0} \\ \mathbf{\Pi}_{11} & \mathbf{\Pi}_{12} \end{bmatrix} E(\mathbf{x}_t\mathbf{x}'_t) = [\mathbf{0}' \quad \boldsymbol{\mu}'\mathbf{\Pi}_{12}]E(\mathbf{x}_t\mathbf{x}'_t) \neq \mathbf{0}'$$

for any nonzero $(n_1 \times 1)$ vector $\boldsymbol{\mu}$. But this could be true only if $\boldsymbol{\mu}'\mathbf{\Pi}_{12} \neq \mathbf{0}'$. Hence, if the rows of $\mathbf{M}$ are linearly independent, then the rows of $\mathbf{\Pi}_{12}$ are also linearly independent.

To prove that (c) implies (a), premultiply both sides of [9.A.1] by any nonzero vector $[\boldsymbol{\lambda}' \quad \boldsymbol{\mu}']$. The right side becomes

$$[\boldsymbol{\lambda}' \quad \boldsymbol{\mu}']\begin{bmatrix} \mathbf{I}_{m_1} & \mathbf{0} \\ \boldsymbol{\Pi}_{11} & \boldsymbol{\Pi}_{12} \end{bmatrix} E(\mathbf{x}_t\mathbf{x}_t') = [(\boldsymbol{\lambda}' + \boldsymbol{\mu}'\boldsymbol{\Pi}_{11}) \quad \boldsymbol{\mu}'\boldsymbol{\Pi}_{12}]E(\mathbf{x}_t\mathbf{x}_t') \equiv \boldsymbol{\eta}'E(\mathbf{x}_t\mathbf{x}_t'),$$

where $\boldsymbol{\eta}' \equiv [(\boldsymbol{\lambda}' + \boldsymbol{\mu}'\boldsymbol{\Pi}_{11}) \quad \boldsymbol{\mu}'\boldsymbol{\Pi}_{12}]$. If the rows of $\boldsymbol{\Pi}_{12}$ are linearly independent, then $\boldsymbol{\eta}'$ cannot be the zero vector unless both $\boldsymbol{\mu}$ and $\boldsymbol{\lambda}$ are zero. To see this, note that if $\boldsymbol{\mu}$ is nonzero, then $\boldsymbol{\mu}'\boldsymbol{\Pi}_{12}$ cannot be the zero vector, while if $\boldsymbol{\mu} = \mathbf{0}$, then $\boldsymbol{\eta}$ will be zero only if $\boldsymbol{\lambda}$ is also the zero vector. Furthermore, since $E(\mathbf{x}_t\mathbf{x}_t')$ is nonsingular, a nonzero $\boldsymbol{\eta}$ means that $\boldsymbol{\eta}'E(\mathbf{x}_t\mathbf{x}_t')$ cannot be the zero vector. Thus, if the right side of [9.A.1] is premultiplied by any nonzero vector $(\boldsymbol{\lambda}', \boldsymbol{\mu}')$, the result is not zero. The same must be true of the left side: $[\boldsymbol{\lambda}' \quad \boldsymbol{\mu}']\mathbf{M} \neq \mathbf{0}'$ for any nonzero $(\boldsymbol{\lambda}', \boldsymbol{\mu}')$, establishing that linear independence of the rows of $\boldsymbol{\Pi}_{12}$ implies linear independence of the rows of $\mathbf{M}$.

To see that (b) implies (c), write [9.3.7] as

$$\begin{bmatrix} \boldsymbol{\Pi}_{01} & \boldsymbol{\Pi}_{02} \\ \boldsymbol{\Pi}_{11} & \boldsymbol{\Pi}_{12} \\ \boldsymbol{\Pi}_{21} & \boldsymbol{\Pi}_{22} \end{bmatrix} = -\mathbf{B}^{-1}\begin{bmatrix} \boldsymbol{\Gamma}_{01} & \mathbf{0}' \\ \boldsymbol{\Gamma}_{11} & \boldsymbol{\Gamma}_{12} \\ \boldsymbol{\Gamma}_{21} & \boldsymbol{\Gamma}_{22} \end{bmatrix}. \qquad [9.A.2]$$

We also have the identity

$$\begin{bmatrix} 1 & \mathbf{0}' & \mathbf{0}' \\ \mathbf{0} & \mathbf{I}_{n_1} & \mathbf{0} \\ \mathbf{0} & \mathbf{0} & \mathbf{I}_{n_2} \end{bmatrix} = \mathbf{B}^{-1}\begin{bmatrix} 1 & \mathbf{B}_{01} & \mathbf{0}' \\ \mathbf{B}_{10} & \mathbf{B}_{11} & \mathbf{B}_{12} \\ \mathbf{B}_{20} & \mathbf{B}_{21} & \mathbf{B}_{22} \end{bmatrix}. \qquad [9.A.3]$$

The system of equations represented by the second block column of [9.A.2] and the third block column of [9.A.3] can be collected as

$$\begin{bmatrix} \boldsymbol{\Pi}_{02} & \mathbf{0}' \\ \boldsymbol{\Pi}_{12} & \mathbf{0} \\ \boldsymbol{\Pi}_{22} & \mathbf{I}_{n_2} \end{bmatrix} = \mathbf{B}^{-1}\begin{bmatrix} \mathbf{0}' & \mathbf{0}' \\ -\boldsymbol{\Gamma}_{12} & \mathbf{B}_{12} \\ -\boldsymbol{\Gamma}_{22} & \mathbf{B}_{22} \end{bmatrix}. \qquad [9.A.4]$$

If both sides of [9.A.4] are premultiplied by the row vector $[0 \quad \boldsymbol{\mu}_1' \quad \mathbf{0}']$ where $\boldsymbol{\mu}_1$ is any $(n_1 \times 1)$ vector, the result is

$$\begin{aligned} [\boldsymbol{\mu}_1'\boldsymbol{\Pi}_{12} \quad \mathbf{0}'] &= [0 \quad \boldsymbol{\mu}_1' \quad \mathbf{0}']\mathbf{B}^{-1}\begin{bmatrix} \mathbf{0}' & \mathbf{0}' \\ -\boldsymbol{\Gamma}_{12} & \mathbf{B}_{12} \\ -\boldsymbol{\Gamma}_{22} & \mathbf{B}_{22} \end{bmatrix} \\ &= [\lambda_0 \quad \boldsymbol{\lambda}_1' \quad \boldsymbol{\lambda}_2']\begin{bmatrix} \mathbf{0}' & \mathbf{0}' \\ -\boldsymbol{\Gamma}_{12} & \mathbf{B}_{12} \\ -\boldsymbol{\Gamma}_{22} & \mathbf{B}_{22} \end{bmatrix} \\ &= [\boldsymbol{\lambda}_1' \quad \boldsymbol{\lambda}_2']\begin{bmatrix} -\boldsymbol{\Gamma}_{12} & \mathbf{B}_{12} \\ -\boldsymbol{\Gamma}_{22} & \mathbf{B}_{22} \end{bmatrix}, \end{aligned} \qquad [9.A.5]$$

where

$$[\lambda_0 \quad \boldsymbol{\lambda}_1' \quad \boldsymbol{\lambda}_2'] \equiv [0 \quad \boldsymbol{\mu}_1' \quad \mathbf{0}']\mathbf{B}^{-1},$$

implying

$$[0 \quad \boldsymbol{\mu}_1' \quad \mathbf{0}'] = [\lambda_0 \quad \boldsymbol{\lambda}_1' \quad \boldsymbol{\lambda}_2']\mathbf{B}. \qquad [9.A.6]$$

Suppose that the rows of the matrix $\left[\begin{smallmatrix} \boldsymbol{\Gamma}_{12} & \mathbf{B}_{12} \\ \boldsymbol{\Gamma}_{22} & \mathbf{B}_{22} \end{smallmatrix}\right]$ are linearly independent. Then the only values for $\boldsymbol{\lambda}_1$ and $\boldsymbol{\lambda}_2$ for which the right side of [9.A.5] can be zero are $\boldsymbol{\lambda}_1 = \mathbf{0}$ and $\boldsymbol{\lambda}_2 = \mathbf{0}$. Substituting these values into [9.A.6], the only value of $\boldsymbol{\mu}_1$ for which the left side of [9.A.5] can be zero must satisfy

$$\begin{aligned} [0 \quad \boldsymbol{\mu}_1' \quad \mathbf{0}'] &= [\lambda_0 \quad \mathbf{0}' \quad \mathbf{0}']\mathbf{B} \\ &= [\lambda_0 \quad \lambda_0\mathbf{B}_{01} \quad \mathbf{0}']. \end{aligned}$$

Matching the first elements in these vectors implies $\lambda_0 = 0$, and thus matching the second elements requires $\boldsymbol{\mu}_1 = \mathbf{0}$. Thus, if condition (b) is satisfied, then the only value of $\boldsymbol{\mu}_1$ for which the left side of [9.A.5] can be zero is $\boldsymbol{\mu}_1 = \mathbf{0}$, establishing that the rows of $\boldsymbol{\Pi}_{12}$ are linearly independent. Hence, condition (c) is satisfied whenever (b) holds.

Conversely, to see that (c) implies (b), let $\boldsymbol{\lambda}_1$ and $\boldsymbol{\lambda}_2$ denote any $(n_1 \times 1)$ and $(n_2 \times 1)$ vectors, and premultiply both sides of [9.A.4] by the row vector $[0 \quad \boldsymbol{\lambda}_1' \quad \boldsymbol{\lambda}_2']\mathbf{B}$:

$$[0 \quad \boldsymbol{\lambda}_1' \quad \boldsymbol{\lambda}_2']\mathbf{B}\begin{bmatrix} \boldsymbol{\Pi}_{02} & \mathbf{0}' \\ \boldsymbol{\Pi}_{12} & \mathbf{0} \\ \boldsymbol{\Pi}_{22} & \mathbf{I}_{n_2} \end{bmatrix} = [0 \quad \boldsymbol{\lambda}_1' \quad \boldsymbol{\lambda}_2']\begin{bmatrix} \mathbf{0}' & \mathbf{0}' \\ -\boldsymbol{\Gamma}_{12} & \mathbf{B}_{12} \\ -\boldsymbol{\Gamma}_{22} & \mathbf{B}_{22} \end{bmatrix}$$

or

$$[\mu_0 \quad \boldsymbol{\mu}_1' \quad \boldsymbol{\mu}_2']\begin{bmatrix} \boldsymbol{\Pi}_{02} & \mathbf{0}' \\ \boldsymbol{\Pi}_{12} & \mathbf{0} \\ \boldsymbol{\Pi}_{22} & \mathbf{I}_{n_2} \end{bmatrix} = [\boldsymbol{\lambda}_1' \quad \boldsymbol{\lambda}_2']\begin{bmatrix} -\boldsymbol{\Gamma}_{12} & \mathbf{B}_{12} \\ -\boldsymbol{\Gamma}_{22} & \mathbf{B}_{22} \end{bmatrix} \qquad [9.A.7]$$

where

$$[\mu_0 \quad \boldsymbol{\mu}_1' \quad \boldsymbol{\mu}_2'] \equiv [0 \quad \boldsymbol{\lambda}_1' \quad \boldsymbol{\lambda}_2']\mathbf{B}. \qquad [9.A.8]$$

Premultiplying both sides of equation [9.A.4] by $\mathbf{B}$ implies that

$$\begin{bmatrix} 1 & \mathbf{B}_{01} & \mathbf{0}' \\ \mathbf{B}_{10} & \mathbf{B}_{11} & \mathbf{B}_{12} \\ \mathbf{B}_{20} & \mathbf{B}_{21} & \mathbf{B}_{22} \end{bmatrix}\begin{bmatrix} \boldsymbol{\Pi}_{02} & \mathbf{0}' \\ \boldsymbol{\Pi}_{12} & \mathbf{0} \\ \boldsymbol{\Pi}_{22} & \mathbf{I}_{n_2} \end{bmatrix} = \begin{bmatrix} \mathbf{0}' & \mathbf{0}' \\ -\boldsymbol{\Gamma}_{12} & \mathbf{B}_{12} \\ -\boldsymbol{\Gamma}_{22} & \mathbf{B}_{22} \end{bmatrix}.$$

The upper left element of this matrix system asserts that

$$\boldsymbol{\Pi}_{02} + \mathbf{B}_{01}\boldsymbol{\Pi}_{12} = \mathbf{0}'. \qquad [9.A.9]$$

Substituting [9.A.9] into [9.A.7],

$$[\mu_0 \quad \boldsymbol{\mu}_1' \quad \boldsymbol{\mu}_2']\begin{bmatrix} -\mathbf{B}_{01}\boldsymbol{\Pi}_{12} & \mathbf{0}' \\ \boldsymbol{\Pi}_{12} & \mathbf{0} \\ \boldsymbol{\Pi}_{22} & \mathbf{I}_{n_2} \end{bmatrix} = [\boldsymbol{\lambda}_1' \quad \boldsymbol{\lambda}_2']\begin{bmatrix} -\boldsymbol{\Gamma}_{12} & \mathbf{B}_{12} \\ -\boldsymbol{\Gamma}_{22} & \mathbf{B}_{22} \end{bmatrix}. \qquad [9.A.10]$$

In order for the left side of [9.A.10] to be zero, it must be the case that $\boldsymbol{\mu}_2 = \mathbf{0}$ and that

$$-\mu_0\mathbf{B}_{01}\boldsymbol{\Pi}_{12} + \boldsymbol{\mu}_1'\boldsymbol{\Pi}_{12} = (\boldsymbol{\mu}_1' - \mu_0\mathbf{B}_{01})\boldsymbol{\Pi}_{12} = \mathbf{0}'. \qquad [9.A.11]$$

But if the rows of $\boldsymbol{\Pi}_{12}$ are linearly independent, [9.A.11] can be zero only if

$$\boldsymbol{\mu}_1' = \mu_0\mathbf{B}_{01}. \qquad [9.A.12]$$

Substituting these results into [9.A.8], it follows that [9.A.10] can be zero only if

$$\begin{aligned} [0 \quad \boldsymbol{\lambda}_1' \quad \boldsymbol{\lambda}_2']\mathbf{B} &= [\mu_0 \quad \mu_0\mathbf{B}_{01} \quad \mathbf{0}'] \\ &= [\mu_0 \quad \mathbf{0}' \quad \mathbf{0}']\begin{bmatrix} 1 & \mathbf{B}_{01} & \mathbf{0}' \\ \mathbf{B}_{10} & \mathbf{B}_{11} & \mathbf{B}_{12} \\ \mathbf{B}_{20} & \mathbf{B}_{21} & \mathbf{B}_{22} \end{bmatrix} \\ &= [\mu_0 \quad \mathbf{0}' \quad \mathbf{0}']\mathbf{B}. \end{aligned} \qquad [9.A.13]$$

Since $\mathbf{B}$ is nonsingular, both sides of [9.A.13] can be postmultiplied by $\mathbf{B}^{-1}$ to deduce that [9.A.10] can be zero only if

$$[0 \quad \boldsymbol{\lambda}_1' \quad \boldsymbol{\lambda}_2'] = [\mu_0 \quad \mathbf{0}' \quad \mathbf{0}'].$$

Thus, the right side of [9.A.10] can be zero only if $\boldsymbol{\lambda}_1$ and $\boldsymbol{\lambda}_2$ are both zero, establishing that the rows of the matrix in [9.3.12] must be linearly independent. ■

## *Chapter 9 Exercise*

9.1. Verify that [9.2.23] gives a consistent estimate of $\sigma^2$.

## *Chapter 9 References*


Angrist, Joshua D. 1990. "Lifetime Earnings and the Vietnam Era Draft Lottery: Evidence from Social Security Administration Records." *American Economic Review* 80:313–36. Errata, 1990, 80:1284–86.

Fisher, Franklin M. 1966. *The Identification Problem in Econometrics*. New York: McGraw-Hill.

Hausman, Jerry A., and William E. Taylor. 1983. "Identification in Linear Simultaneous Equations Models with Covariance Restrictions: An Instrumental Variables Interpretation." *Econometrica* 51:1527–49.

Maddala, G. S. 1977. *Econometrics*. New York: McGraw-Hill.

Nelson, Charles R., and Richard Startz. 1990. "Some Further Results on the Exact Small Sample Properties of the Instrumental Variable Estimator." *Econometrica* 58:967–76.

Rothenberg, Thomas J. 1971. "Identification in Parametric Models." *Econometrica* 39:577–91.

——— and Paul A. Ruud. 1990. "Simultaneous Equations with Covariance Restrictions." *Journal of Econometrics* 44:25–39.

# 10 Covariance-Stationary Vector Processes

This is the first of two chapters introducing vector time series. Chapter 10 is devoted to the theory of multivariate dynamic systems, while Chapter 11 focuses on empirical issues of estimating and interpreting vector autoregressions. Only the first section of Chapter 10 is necessary for understanding the material in Chapter 11.

Section 10.1 introduces some of the key ideas in vector time series analysis. Section 10.2 develops some convergence results that are useful for deriving the asymptotic properties of certain statistics and for characterizing the consequences of multivariate filters. Section 10.3 introduces the autocovariance-generating function for vector processes, which is used to analyze the multivariate spectrum in Section 10.4. Section 10.5 develops a multivariate generalization of Proposition 7.5, describing the asymptotic properties of the sample mean of a serially correlated vector process. These last results are useful for deriving autocorrelation- and heteroskedasticity-consistent estimators for *OLS*, for understanding the properties of generalized method of moments estimators discussed in Chapter 14, and for deriving some of the tests for unit roots discussed in Chapter 17.

## 10.1. *Introduction to Vector Autoregressions*

Chapter 3 proposed modeling a scalar time series $y_t$ in terms of an autoregression:

$$y_t = c + \phi_1 y_{t-1} + \phi_2 y_{t-2} + \cdots + \phi_p y_{t-p} + \varepsilon_t, \qquad [10.1.1]$$

where

$$E(\varepsilon_t) = 0 \qquad [10.1.2]$$

$$E(\varepsilon_t \varepsilon_\tau) = \begin{cases} \sigma^2 & \text{for } t = \tau \\ 0 & \text{otherwise.} \end{cases} \qquad [10.1.3]$$

Note that we will continue to use the convention introduced in Chapter 8 of using lowercase letters to denote either a random variable or its realization. This chapter describes the dynamic interactions among a set of variables collected in an $(n \times 1)$ vector $\mathbf{y}_t$. For example, the first element of $\mathbf{y}_t$ (denoted $y_{1t}$) might represent the level of GNP in year $t$, the second element ($y_{2t}$) the interest rate paid on Treasury bills in year $t$, and so on. A *pth-order vector autoregression*, denoted *VAR*($p$), is a vector generalization of [10.1.1] through [10.1.3]:

$$\mathbf{y}_t = \mathbf{c} + \mathbf{\Phi}_1 \mathbf{y}_{t-1} + \mathbf{\Phi}_2 \mathbf{y}_{t-2} + \cdots + \mathbf{\Phi}_p \mathbf{y}_{t-p} + \boldsymbol{\varepsilon}_t. \qquad [10.1.4]$$

Here $\mathbf{c}$ denotes an $(n \times 1)$ vector of constants and $\mathbf{\Phi}_j$ an $(n \times n)$ matrix of autoregressive coefficients for $j = 1, 2, \ldots, p$. The $(n \times 1)$ vector $\boldsymbol{\varepsilon}_t$ is a vector generalization of white noise:

$$E(\boldsymbol{\varepsilon}_t) = \mathbf{0} \qquad [10.1.5]$$

$$E(\boldsymbol{\varepsilon}_t\boldsymbol{\varepsilon}_\tau') = \begin{cases} \boldsymbol{\Omega} & \text{for } t = \tau \\ \mathbf{0} & \text{otherwise,} \end{cases} \qquad [10.1.6]$$

with $\boldsymbol{\Omega}$ an $(n \times n)$ symmetric positive definite matrix.

Let $c_i$ denote the $i$th element of the vector $\mathbf{c}$ and let $\phi_{ij}^{(1)}$ denote the row $i$, column $j$ element of the matrix $\boldsymbol{\Phi}_1$. Then the first row of the vector system in [10.1.4] specifies that

$$\begin{aligned} y_{1t} = c_1 &+ \phi_{11}^{(1)}y_{1,t-1} + \phi_{12}^{(1)}y_{2,t-1} + \cdots + \phi_{1n}^{(1)}y_{n,t-1} \\ &+ \phi_{11}^{(2)}y_{1,t-2} + \phi_{12}^{(2)}y_{2,t-2} + \cdots + \phi_{1n}^{(2)}y_{n,t-2} \\ &+ \cdots + \phi_{11}^{(p)}y_{1,t-p} + \phi_{12}^{(p)}y_{2,t-p} + \cdots + \phi_{1n}^{(p)}y_{n,t-p} + \varepsilon_{1t}. \end{aligned} \qquad [10.1.7]$$

Thus, a vector autoregression is a system in which each variable is regressed on a constant and $p$ of its own lags as well as on $p$ lags of each of the other variables in the *VAR*. Note that each regression has the same explanatory variables.

Using lag operator notation, [10.1.4] can be written in the form

$$[\mathbf{I}_n - \boldsymbol{\Phi}_1 L - \boldsymbol{\Phi}_2 L^2 - \cdots - \boldsymbol{\Phi}_p L^p]\mathbf{y}_t = \mathbf{c} + \boldsymbol{\varepsilon}_t$$

or

$$\boldsymbol{\Phi}(L)\mathbf{y}_t = \mathbf{c} + \boldsymbol{\varepsilon}_t.$$

Here $\boldsymbol{\Phi}(L)$ indicates an $(n \times n)$ matrix polynomial in the lag operator $L$. The row $i$, column $j$ element of $\boldsymbol{\Phi}(L)$ is a scalar polynomial in $L$:

$$\boldsymbol{\Phi}(L) = [\delta_{ij} - \phi_{ij}^{(1)}L^1 - \phi_{ij}^{(2)}L^2 - \cdots - \phi_{ij}^{(p)}L^p],$$

where $\delta_{ij}$ is unity if $i = j$ and zero otherwise.

A vector process $\mathbf{y}_t$ is said to be covariance-stationary if its first and second moments ($E[\mathbf{y}_t]$ and $E[\mathbf{y}_t\mathbf{y}_{t-j}']$, respectively) are independent of the date $t$. If the process is covariance-stationary, we can take expectations of both sides of [10.1.4] to calculate the mean $\boldsymbol{\mu}$ of the process:

$$\boldsymbol{\mu} = \mathbf{c} + \boldsymbol{\Phi}_1\boldsymbol{\mu} + \boldsymbol{\Phi}_2\boldsymbol{\mu} + \cdots + \boldsymbol{\Phi}_p\boldsymbol{\mu},$$

or

$$\boldsymbol{\mu} = (\mathbf{I}_n - \boldsymbol{\Phi}_1 - \boldsymbol{\Phi}_2 - \cdots - \boldsymbol{\Phi}_p)^{-1}\mathbf{c}.$$

Equation [10.1.4] can then be written in terms of deviations from the mean as

$$\begin{aligned} (\mathbf{y}_t - \boldsymbol{\mu}) &= \boldsymbol{\Phi}_1(\mathbf{y}_{t-1} - \boldsymbol{\mu}) \\ &\quad + \boldsymbol{\Phi}_2(\mathbf{y}_{t-2} - \boldsymbol{\mu}) + \cdots + \boldsymbol{\Phi}_p(\mathbf{y}_{t-p} - \boldsymbol{\mu}) + \boldsymbol{\varepsilon}_t. \end{aligned} \qquad [10.1.8]$$

## *Rewriting a* VAR(p) *as a* VAR(*1*)

As in the case of the univariate $AR(p)$ process, it is helpful to rewrite [10.1.8] in terms of a $VAR(1)$ process. Toward this end, define

$$\underset{(np \times 1)}{\boldsymbol{\xi}_t} \equiv \begin{bmatrix} \mathbf{y}_t - \boldsymbol{\mu} \\ \mathbf{y}_{t-1} - \boldsymbol{\mu} \\ \vdots \\ \mathbf{y}_{t-p+1} - \boldsymbol{\mu} \end{bmatrix} \qquad [10.1.9]$$

$$\underset{(np \times np)}{\mathbf{F}} \equiv \begin{bmatrix} \boldsymbol{\Phi}_1 & \boldsymbol{\Phi}_2 & \boldsymbol{\Phi}_3 & \cdots & \boldsymbol{\Phi}_{p-1} & \boldsymbol{\Phi}_p \\ \mathbf{I}_n & \mathbf{0} & \mathbf{0} & \cdots & \mathbf{0} & \mathbf{0} \\ \mathbf{0} & \mathbf{I}_n & \mathbf{0} & \cdots & \mathbf{0} & \mathbf{0} \\ \vdots & \vdots & \vdots & \cdots & \vdots & \vdots \\ \mathbf{0} & \mathbf{0} & \mathbf{0} & \cdots & \mathbf{I}_n & \mathbf{0} \end{bmatrix} \qquad [10.1.10]$$

$$\underset{(np \times 1)}{\mathbf{v}_t} \equiv \begin{bmatrix} \boldsymbol{\varepsilon}_t \\ \mathbf{0} \\ \vdots \\ \mathbf{0} \end{bmatrix}.$$

The $VAR(p)$ in [10.1.8] can then be rewritten as the following $VAR(1)$:

$$\boldsymbol{\xi}_t = \mathbf{F}\boldsymbol{\xi}_{t-1} + \mathbf{v}_t, \qquad [10.1.11]$$

where

$$E(\mathbf{v}_t\mathbf{v}_\tau') = \begin{cases} \mathbf{Q} & \text{for } t = \tau \\ \mathbf{0} & \text{otherwise} \end{cases}$$

and

$$\underset{(np \times np)}{\mathbf{Q}} \equiv \begin{bmatrix} \boldsymbol{\Omega} & \mathbf{0} & \cdots & \mathbf{0} \\ \mathbf{0} & \mathbf{0} & \cdots & \mathbf{0} \\ \vdots & \vdots & \cdots & \vdots \\ \mathbf{0} & \mathbf{0} & \cdots & \mathbf{0} \end{bmatrix}.$$

## *Conditions for Stationarity*

Equation [10.1.11] implies that

$$\boldsymbol{\xi}_{t+s} = \mathbf{v}_{t+s} + \mathbf{F}\mathbf{v}_{t+s-1} + \mathbf{F}^2\mathbf{v}_{t+s-2} + \cdots + \mathbf{F}^{s-1}\mathbf{v}_{t+1} + \mathbf{F}^s\boldsymbol{\xi}_t. \qquad [10.1.12]$$

In order for the process to be covariance-stationary, the consequences of any given $\boldsymbol{\varepsilon}_t$ must eventually die out. If the eigenvalues of $\mathbf{F}$ all lie inside the unit circle, then the *VAR* turns out to be covariance-stationary.

The following result generalizes Proposition 1.1 from Chapter 1 (for a proof see Appendix 10.A at the end of this chapter).

***Proposition 10.1:*** *The eigenvalues of the matrix* $\mathbf{F}$ *in [10.1.10] satisfy*

$$|\mathbf{I}_n\lambda^p - \boldsymbol{\Phi}_1\lambda^{p-1} - \boldsymbol{\Phi}_2\lambda^{p-2} - \cdots - \boldsymbol{\Phi}_p| = 0. \qquad [10.1.13]$$

Hence, a $VAR(p)$ is covariance-stationary as long as $|\lambda| < 1$ for all values of $\lambda$ satisfying [10.1.13]. Equivalently, the *VAR* is covariance-stationary if all values of $z$ satisfying

$$|\mathbf{I}_n - \boldsymbol{\Phi}_1 z - \boldsymbol{\Phi}_2 z^2 - \cdots - \boldsymbol{\Phi}_p z^p| = 0$$

lie outside the unit circle.

### *Vector* MA(∞) *Representation*

The first $n$ rows of the vector system represented in [10.1.12] constitute a vector generalization of equation [4.2.20]:

$$\begin{aligned}\mathbf{y}_{t+s} &= \boldsymbol{\mu} + \boldsymbol{\varepsilon}_{t+s} + \boldsymbol{\Psi}_1\boldsymbol{\varepsilon}_{t+s-1} + \boldsymbol{\Psi}_2\boldsymbol{\varepsilon}_{t+s-2} + \cdots + \boldsymbol{\Psi}_{s-1}\boldsymbol{\varepsilon}_{t+1} \\ &\quad + \mathbf{F}_{11}^{(s)}(\mathbf{y}_t - \boldsymbol{\mu}) + \mathbf{F}_{12}^{(s)}(\mathbf{y}_{t-1} - \boldsymbol{\mu}) + \cdots + \mathbf{F}_{1p}^{(s)}(\mathbf{y}_{t-p+1} - \boldsymbol{\mu}).\end{aligned} \qquad [10.1.14]$$

Here $\boldsymbol{\Psi}_j = \mathbf{F}_{11}^{(j)}$ and $\mathbf{F}_{11}^{(j)}$ denotes the upper left block of $\mathbf{F}^j$, where $\mathbf{F}^j$ is the matrix $\mathbf{F}$ raised to the $j$th power—that is, the $(n \times n)$ matrix $\mathbf{F}_{11}^{(j)}$ indicates rows 1 through $n$ and columns 1 through $n$ of the $(np \times np)$ matrix $\mathbf{F}^j$. Similarly, $\mathbf{F}_{12}^{(j)}$ denotes the block of $\mathbf{F}^j$ consisting of rows 1 through $n$ and columns $(n + 1)$ through $2n$, while $\mathbf{F}_{1p}^{(j)}$ denotes rows 1 through $n$ and columns $[n(p - 1) + 1]$ through $np$ of $\mathbf{F}^j$.

If the eigenvalues of $\mathbf{F}$ all lie inside the unit circle, then $\mathbf{F}^s \rightarrow \mathbf{0}$ as $s \rightarrow \infty$ and $\mathbf{y}_t$ can be expressed as a convergent sum of the history of $\boldsymbol{\varepsilon}$:

$$\mathbf{y}_t = \boldsymbol{\mu} + \boldsymbol{\varepsilon}_t + \boldsymbol{\Psi}_1\boldsymbol{\varepsilon}_{t-1} + \boldsymbol{\Psi}_2\boldsymbol{\varepsilon}_{t-2} + \boldsymbol{\Psi}_3\boldsymbol{\varepsilon}_{t-3} + \cdots \equiv \boldsymbol{\mu} + \boldsymbol{\Psi}(L)\boldsymbol{\varepsilon}_t, \qquad [10.1.15]$$

which is a vector $MA(\infty)$ representation.

Note that $\mathbf{y}_{t-j}$ is a linear function of $\boldsymbol{\varepsilon}_{t-j}, \boldsymbol{\varepsilon}_{t-j-1}, \ldots$, each of which is uncorrelated with $\boldsymbol{\varepsilon}_{t+1}$ for $j = 0, 1, \ldots$. It follows that $\boldsymbol{\varepsilon}_{t+1}$ is uncorrelated with $\mathbf{y}_{t-j}$ for any $j \geq 0$. Thus, the linear forecast of $\mathbf{y}_{t+1}$ on the basis of $\mathbf{y}_t, \mathbf{y}_{t-1}, \ldots$ is given by

$$\hat{\mathbf{y}}_{t+1|t} = \boldsymbol{\mu} + \boldsymbol{\Phi}_1(\mathbf{y}_t - \boldsymbol{\mu}) + \boldsymbol{\Phi}_2(\mathbf{y}_{t-1} - \boldsymbol{\mu}) + \cdots + \boldsymbol{\Phi}_p(\mathbf{y}_{t-p+1} - \boldsymbol{\mu}),$$

and $\boldsymbol{\varepsilon}_{t+1}$ can be interpreted as the fundamental innovation for $\mathbf{y}_{t+1}$, that is, the error in forecasting $\mathbf{y}_{t+1}$ on the basis of a linear function of a constant and $\mathbf{y}_t, \mathbf{y}_{t-1}, \ldots$. More generally, it follows from [10.1.14] that a forecast of $\mathbf{y}_{t+s}$ on the basis of $\mathbf{y}_t, \mathbf{y}_{t-1}, \ldots$ will take the form

$$\begin{aligned}\hat{\mathbf{y}}_{t+s|t} &= \boldsymbol{\mu} + \mathbf{F}_{11}^{(s)}(\mathbf{y}_t - \boldsymbol{\mu}) + \mathbf{F}_{12}^{(s)}(\mathbf{y}_{t-1} - \boldsymbol{\mu}) \\ &\quad + \cdots + \mathbf{F}_{1p}^{(s)}(\mathbf{y}_{t-p+1} - \boldsymbol{\mu}).\end{aligned} \qquad [10.1.16]$$

The moving average matrices $\boldsymbol{\Psi}_j$ could equivalently be calculated as follows. The operators $\boldsymbol{\Phi}(L)$ and $\boldsymbol{\Psi}(L)$ are related by

$$\boldsymbol{\Psi}(L) = [\boldsymbol{\Phi}(L)]^{-1},$$

requiring

$$[\mathbf{I}_n - \boldsymbol{\Phi}_1 L - \boldsymbol{\Phi}_2 L^2 - \cdots - \boldsymbol{\Phi}_p L^p][\mathbf{I}_n + \boldsymbol{\Psi}_1 L + \boldsymbol{\Psi}_2 L^2 + \cdots] = \mathbf{I}_n.$$

Setting the coefficient on $L^1$ equal to the zero matrix, as in Exercise 3.3 of Chapter 3, produces

$$\boldsymbol{\Psi}_1 - \boldsymbol{\Phi}_1 = \mathbf{0}. \qquad [10.1.17]$$

Similarly, setting the coefficient on $L^2$ equal to zero gives

$$\boldsymbol{\Psi}_2 = \boldsymbol{\Phi}_1\boldsymbol{\Psi}_1 + \boldsymbol{\Phi}_2, \qquad [10.1.18]$$

and in general for $L^s$,

$$\boldsymbol{\Psi}_s = \boldsymbol{\Phi}_1\boldsymbol{\Psi}_{s-1} + \boldsymbol{\Phi}_2\boldsymbol{\Psi}_{s-2} + \cdots + \boldsymbol{\Phi}_p\boldsymbol{\Psi}_{s-p} \quad \text{for } s = 1, 2, \ldots, \qquad [10.1.19]$$

with $\boldsymbol{\Psi}_0 = \mathbf{I}_n$ and $\boldsymbol{\Psi}_s = \mathbf{0}$ for $s < 0$.

Note that the innovation in the $MA(\infty)$ representation [10.1.15] is $\boldsymbol{\varepsilon}_t$, the fundamental innovation for $\mathbf{y}$. There are alternative moving average representations based on vector white noise processes other than $\boldsymbol{\varepsilon}_t$. Let $\mathbf{H}$ denote a nonsingular

$(n \times n)$ matrix, and define

$$\mathbf{u}_t \equiv \mathbf{H}\boldsymbol{\varepsilon}_t. \qquad [10.1.20]$$

Then certainly $\mathbf{u}_t$ is white noise. Moreover, from [10.1.15] we could write

$$\begin{aligned} \mathbf{y}_t &= \boldsymbol{\mu} + \mathbf{H}^{-1}\mathbf{H}\boldsymbol{\varepsilon}_t + \boldsymbol{\Psi}_1\mathbf{H}^{-1}\mathbf{H}\boldsymbol{\varepsilon}_{t-1} + \boldsymbol{\Psi}_2\mathbf{H}^{-1}\mathbf{H}\boldsymbol{\varepsilon}_{t-2} \\ &\quad + \boldsymbol{\Psi}_3\mathbf{H}^{-1}\mathbf{H}\boldsymbol{\varepsilon}_{t-3} + \cdots \qquad [10.1.21] \\ &= \boldsymbol{\mu} + \mathbf{J}_0\mathbf{u}_t + \mathbf{J}_1\mathbf{u}_{t-1} + \mathbf{J}_2\mathbf{u}_{t-2} + \mathbf{J}_3\mathbf{u}_{t-3} + \cdots, \end{aligned}$$

where

$$\mathbf{J}_s \equiv \boldsymbol{\Psi}_s\mathbf{H}^{-1}.$$

For example, $\mathbf{H}$ could be any matrix that diagonalizes $\boldsymbol{\Omega}$, the variance-covariance matrix of $\boldsymbol{\varepsilon}_t$:

$$\mathbf{H}\boldsymbol{\Omega}\mathbf{H}' = \mathbf{D},$$

with $\mathbf{D}$ a diagonal matrix. For such a choice of $\mathbf{H}$, the elements of $\mathbf{u}_t$ are uncorrelated with one another:

$$E(\mathbf{u}_t\mathbf{u}_t') = E(\mathbf{H}\boldsymbol{\varepsilon}_t\boldsymbol{\varepsilon}_t'\mathbf{H}') = \mathbf{D}.$$

Thus, it is always possible to write a stationary $VAR(p)$ process as a convergent infinite moving average of a white noise vector $\mathbf{u}_t$ whose elements are mutually uncorrelated.

There is one important difference between the $MA(\infty)$ representations [10.1.15] and [10.1.21], however. In [10.1.15], the leading $MA$ parameter matrix ($\boldsymbol{\Psi}_0$) is the identity matrix, whereas in [10.1.21] the leading $MA$ parameter matrix ($\mathbf{J}_0$) is not the identity matrix. To obtain the $MA$ representation for the fundamental innovations, we must impose the normalization $\boldsymbol{\Psi}_0 = \mathbf{I}_n$.

### *Assumptions Implicit in a* VAR

For a covariance-stationary process, the parameters $\mathbf{c}$ and $\boldsymbol{\Phi}_1, \ldots, \boldsymbol{\Phi}_p$ in equation [10.1.4] could be defined as the coefficients of the projection of $\mathbf{y}_t$ on a constant and $\mathbf{y}_{t-1}, \ldots, \mathbf{y}_{t-p}$. Thus, $\boldsymbol{\varepsilon}_t$ is uncorrelated with $\mathbf{y}_{t-1}, \ldots, \mathbf{y}_{t-p}$ by the definition of $\boldsymbol{\Phi}_1, \ldots, \boldsymbol{\Phi}_p$. The parameters of a vector autoregression can accordingly be estimated consistently with $n$ $OLS$ regressions of the form of [10.1.7]. The additional assumption implicit in a $VAR$ is that the $\boldsymbol{\varepsilon}_t$ defined by this projection is further uncorrelated with $\mathbf{y}_{t-p-1}, \mathbf{y}_{t-p-2}, \ldots$. The assumption that $\mathbf{y}_t$ follows a vector autoregression is basically the assumption that $p$ lags are sufficient to summarize all of the dynamic correlations between elements of $\mathbf{y}$.

## 10.2. *Autocovariances and Convergence Results for Vector Processes*

### *The* j*th Autocovariance Matrix*

For a covariance-stationary $n$-dimensional vector process, the $j$th autocovariance is defined to be the following $(n \times n)$ matrix:

$$\boldsymbol{\Gamma}_j = E[(\mathbf{y}_t - \boldsymbol{\mu})(\mathbf{y}_{t-j} - \boldsymbol{\mu})']. \qquad [10.2.1]$$

Note that although $\gamma_j = \gamma_{-j}$ for a scalar process, the same is not true of a vector process:

$$\Gamma_j \neq \Gamma_{-j}.$$

For example, the (1, 2) element of $\Gamma_j$ gives the covariance between $y_{1t}$ and $y_{2,t-j}$. The (1, 2) element of $\Gamma_{-j}$ gives the covariance between $y_{1t}$ and $y_{2,t+j}$. There is no reason that these should be related—the response of $y_1$ to previous movements in $y_2$ could be completely different from the response of $y_2$ to previous movements in $y_1$.

Instead, the correct relation is

$$\Gamma_j' = \Gamma_{-j}. \qquad [10.2.2]$$

To derive [10.2.2], notice that covariance-stationarity would mean that $t$ in [10.2.1] could be replaced with $t + j$:

$$\Gamma_j = E[(\mathbf{y}_{t+j} - \boldsymbol{\mu})(\mathbf{y}_{(t+j)-j} - \boldsymbol{\mu})'] = E[(\mathbf{y}_{t+j} - \boldsymbol{\mu})(\mathbf{y}_t - \boldsymbol{\mu})'].$$

Taking transposes,

$$\Gamma_j' = E[(\mathbf{y}_t - \boldsymbol{\mu})(\mathbf{y}_{t+j} - \boldsymbol{\mu})'] = \Gamma_{-j},$$

as claimed.

## *Vector* MA(q) *Process*

A *vector moving average process* of order $q$ takes the form

$$\mathbf{y}_t = \boldsymbol{\mu} + \boldsymbol{\varepsilon}_t + \boldsymbol{\Theta}_1\boldsymbol{\varepsilon}_{t-1} + \boldsymbol{\Theta}_2\boldsymbol{\varepsilon}_{t-2} + \cdots + \boldsymbol{\Theta}_q\boldsymbol{\varepsilon}_{t-q}, \qquad [10.2.3]$$

where $\boldsymbol{\varepsilon}_t$ is a vector white noise process satisfying [10.1.5] and [10.1.6] and $\boldsymbol{\Theta}_j$ denotes an $(n \times n)$ matrix of *MA* coefficients for $j = 1, 2, \ldots, q$. The mean of $\mathbf{y}_t$ is $\boldsymbol{\mu}$, and the variance is

$$\begin{aligned}\Gamma_0 &= E[(\mathbf{y}_t - \boldsymbol{\mu})(\mathbf{y}_t - \boldsymbol{\mu})'] \\ &= E[\boldsymbol{\varepsilon}_t\boldsymbol{\varepsilon}_t'] + \boldsymbol{\Theta}_1 E[\boldsymbol{\varepsilon}_{t-1}\boldsymbol{\varepsilon}_{t-1}']\boldsymbol{\Theta}_1' + \boldsymbol{\Theta}_2 E[\boldsymbol{\varepsilon}_{t-2}\boldsymbol{\varepsilon}_{t-2}']\boldsymbol{\Theta}_2' \\ &\quad + \cdots + \boldsymbol{\Theta}_q E[\boldsymbol{\varepsilon}_{t-q}\boldsymbol{\varepsilon}_{t-q}']\boldsymbol{\Theta}_q' \\ &= \boldsymbol{\Omega} + \boldsymbol{\Theta}_1\boldsymbol{\Omega}\boldsymbol{\Theta}_1' + \boldsymbol{\Theta}_2\boldsymbol{\Omega}\boldsymbol{\Theta}_2' + \cdots + \boldsymbol{\Theta}_q\boldsymbol{\Omega}\boldsymbol{\Theta}_q',\end{aligned} \qquad [10.2.4]$$

with autocovariances

$$\Gamma_j = \begin{cases} \boldsymbol{\Theta}_j\boldsymbol{\Omega} + \boldsymbol{\Theta}_{j+1}\boldsymbol{\Omega}\boldsymbol{\Theta}_1' + \boldsymbol{\Theta}_{j+2}\boldsymbol{\Omega}\boldsymbol{\Theta}_2' + \cdots + \boldsymbol{\Theta}_q\boldsymbol{\Omega}\boldsymbol{\Theta}_{q-j}' & \text{for } j = 1, 2, \ldots, q \\ \boldsymbol{\Omega}\boldsymbol{\Theta}_{-j}' + \boldsymbol{\Theta}_1\boldsymbol{\Omega}\boldsymbol{\Theta}_{-j+1}' + \boldsymbol{\Theta}_2\boldsymbol{\Omega}\boldsymbol{\Theta}_{-j+2}' + \cdots + \boldsymbol{\Theta}_{q+j}\boldsymbol{\Omega}\boldsymbol{\Theta}_q' & \text{for } j = -1, -2, \ldots, -q \\ \mathbf{0} & \text{for } |j| > q, \end{cases} \qquad [10.2.5]$$

where $\boldsymbol{\Theta}_0 = \mathbf{I}_n$. Thus, any vector $MA(q)$ process is covariance-stationary.

## *Vector* MA($\infty$) *Process*

The vector $MA(\infty)$ process is written

$$\mathbf{y}_t = \boldsymbol{\mu} + \boldsymbol{\varepsilon}_t + \boldsymbol{\Psi}_1\boldsymbol{\varepsilon}_{t-1} + \boldsymbol{\Psi}_2\boldsymbol{\varepsilon}_{t-2} + \cdots \qquad [10.2.6]$$

for $\boldsymbol{\varepsilon}_t$ again satisfying [10.1.5] and [10.1.6].

A sequence of scalars $\{h_s\}_{s=-\infty}^{\infty}$ was said to be absolutely summable if $\sum_{s=-\infty}^{\infty} |h_s| < \infty$. For $\mathbf{H}_s$ an $(n \times m)$ matrix, the sequence of matrices $\{\mathbf{H}_s\}_{s=-\infty}^{\infty}$ is absolutely summable if each of its elements forms an absolutely summable scalar sequence. For example, if $\psi_{ij}^{(s)}$ denotes the row $i$, column $j$ element of the moving average parameter matrix $\mathbf{\Psi}_s$ associated with lag $s$, then the sequence $\{\mathbf{\Psi}_s\}_{s=0}^{\infty}$ is absolutely summable if

$$\sum_{s=0}^{\infty} |\psi_{ij}^{(s)}| < \infty \qquad \text{for } i = 1, 2, \ldots, n \text{ and } j = 1, 2, \ldots, n. \qquad [10.2.7]$$

Many of the results for scalar $MA(\infty)$ processes with absolutely summable coefficients go through for vector processes as well. This is summarized by the following theorem, proved in Appendix 10.A to this chapter.

***Proposition 10.2:*** *Let $\mathbf{y}_t$ be an $(n \times 1)$ vector satisfying*

$$\mathbf{y}_t = \boldsymbol{\mu} + \sum_{k=0}^{\infty} \mathbf{\Psi}_k \boldsymbol{\varepsilon}_{t-k},$$

*where $\boldsymbol{\varepsilon}_t$ is vector white noise satisfying [10.1.5] and [10.1.6] and $\{\mathbf{\Psi}_k\}_{k=0}^{\infty}$ is absolutely summable. Let $y_{it}$ denote the ith element of $\mathbf{y}_t$, and let $\mu_i$ denote the ith element of $\boldsymbol{\mu}$. Then*

(*a*) *the autocovariance between the ith variable at time t and the jth variable s periods earlier, $E(y_{it} - \mu_i)(y_{j,t-s} - \mu_j)$, exists and is given by the row i, column j element of*

$$\mathbf{\Gamma}_s = \sum_{v=0}^{\infty} \mathbf{\Psi}_{s+v} \mathbf{\Omega} \mathbf{\Psi}_v' \qquad \textit{for } s = 0, 1, 2, \ldots;$$

(*b*) *the sequence of matrices $\{\mathbf{\Gamma}_s\}_{s=0}^{\infty}$ is absolutely summable.*

*If, furthermore, $\{\boldsymbol{\varepsilon}_t\}_{t=-\infty}^{\infty}$ is an i.i.d. sequence with $E|\varepsilon_{i_1,t}\varepsilon_{i_2,t}\varepsilon_{i_3,t}\varepsilon_{i_4,t}| < \infty$ for $i_1, i_2, i_3, i_4 = 1, 2, \ldots, n$, then also,*

(*c*) *$E|y_{i_1,t_1}y_{i_2,t_2}y_{i_3,t_3}y_{i_4,t_4}| < \infty$ for $i_1, i_2, i_3, i_4 = 1, 2, \ldots, n$ and for all $t_1, t_2, t_3, t_4$;*

(*d*) *$(1/T)\sum_{t=1}^{T} y_{it}y_{j,t-s} \xrightarrow{p} E(y_{it}y_{j,t-s})$ for $i, j = 1, 2, \ldots, n$ and for all s.*

Result (a) implies that the second moments of an $MA(\infty)$ vector process with absolutely summable coefficients can be found by taking the limit of [10.2.5] as $q \to \infty$. Result (b) is a convergence condition on these moments that will turn out to ensure that the vector process is ergodic for the mean (see Proposition 10.5 later in this chapter). Result (c) says that $\mathbf{y}_t$ has bounded fourth moments, while result (d) establishes that $\mathbf{y}_t$ is ergodic for second moments.

Note that the vector $MA(\infty)$ representation of a stationary vector autoregression calculated from [10.1.4] satisfies the absolute summability condition. To see this, recall from [10.1.14] that $\mathbf{\Psi}_s$ is a block of the matrix $\mathbf{F}^s$. If $\mathbf{F}$ has $np$ distinct eigenvalues $(\lambda_1, \lambda_2, \ldots, \lambda_{np})$, then any element of $\mathbf{\Psi}_s$ can be written as a weighted average of these eigenvalues as in equation [1.2.20];

$$\psi_{ij}^{(s)} = c_1(i, j) \cdot \lambda_1^s + c_2(i, j) \cdot \lambda_2^s + \cdots + c_{np}(i, j) \cdot \lambda_{np}^s,$$

where $c_v(i, j)$ denotes a constant that depends on $v$, $i$, and $j$ but not $s$. Absolute summability [10.2.7] then follows from the same arguments as in Exercise 3.5.

## *Multivariate Filters*

Suppose that the $(n \times 1)$ vector $\mathbf{y}_t$ follows an $MA(\infty)$ process:

$$\mathbf{y}_t = \boldsymbol{\mu}_Y + \boldsymbol{\Psi}(L)\boldsymbol{\varepsilon}_t, \qquad [10.2.8]$$

with $\{\boldsymbol{\Psi}_k\}_{k=0}^{\infty}$ absolutely summable. Let $\{\mathbf{H}_k\}_{k=-\infty}^{\infty}$ be an absolutely summable sequence of $(r \times n)$ matrices and suppose that an $(r \times 1)$ vector $\mathbf{x}_t$ is related to $\mathbf{y}_t$ according to

$$\mathbf{x}_t = \mathbf{H}(L)\mathbf{y}_t = \sum_{k=-\infty}^{\infty} \mathbf{H}_k \mathbf{y}_{t-k}. \qquad [10.2.9]$$

That is,

$$\begin{aligned} \mathbf{x}_t &= \mathbf{H}(L)[\boldsymbol{\mu}_Y + \boldsymbol{\Psi}(L)\boldsymbol{\varepsilon}_t] \\ &= \mathbf{H}(1)\boldsymbol{\mu}_Y + \mathbf{H}(L)\boldsymbol{\Psi}(L)\boldsymbol{\varepsilon}_t \qquad [10.2.10] \\ &= \boldsymbol{\mu}_X + \mathbf{B}(L)\boldsymbol{\varepsilon}_t, \end{aligned}$$

where $\boldsymbol{\mu}_X \equiv \mathbf{H}(1)\boldsymbol{\mu}_Y$ and $\mathbf{B}(L)$ is the compound operator given by

$$\mathbf{B}(L) = \sum_{k=-\infty}^{\infty} \mathbf{B}_k L^k = \mathbf{H}(L)\boldsymbol{\Psi}(L). \qquad [10.2.11]$$

The following proposition establishes that $\mathbf{x}_t$ follows an absolutely summable two-sided $MA(\infty)$ process.

***Proposition 10.3:*** *Let $\{\boldsymbol{\Psi}_k\}_{k=0}^{\infty}$ be an absolutely summable sequence of $(n \times n)$ matrices and let $\{\mathbf{H}_k\}_{k=-\infty}^{\infty}$ be an absolutely summable sequence of $(r \times n)$ matrices. Then the sequence of matrices $\{\mathbf{B}_k\}_{k=-\infty}^{\infty}$ associated with the operator $\mathbf{B}(L) = \mathbf{H}(L)\boldsymbol{\Psi}(L)$ is absolutely summable.*

If $\{\boldsymbol{\varepsilon}_t\}$ in [10.2.8] is i.i.d. with finite fourth moments, then $\{\mathbf{x}_t\}$ in [10.2.9] has finite fourth moments and is ergodic for second moments.

## *Vector Autoregression*

Next we derive expressions for the second moments for $\mathbf{y}_t$ following a $VAR(p)$. Let $\boldsymbol{\xi}_t$ be as defined in equation [10.1.9]. Assuming that $\boldsymbol{\xi}$ and $\mathbf{y}$ are covariance-stationary, let $\boldsymbol{\Sigma}$ denote the variance of $\boldsymbol{\xi}$,

$$\begin{aligned} \boldsymbol{\Sigma} &= E(\boldsymbol{\xi}_t\boldsymbol{\xi}_t') \\ &= E\left\{\begin{bmatrix} \mathbf{y}_t - \boldsymbol{\mu} \\ \mathbf{y}_{t-1} - \boldsymbol{\mu} \\ \vdots \\ \mathbf{y}_{t-p+1} - \boldsymbol{\mu} \end{bmatrix} \right. \\ &\qquad \left. \times \left[(\mathbf{y}_t - \boldsymbol{\mu})' \quad (\mathbf{y}_{t-1} - \boldsymbol{\mu})' \quad \cdots \quad (\mathbf{y}_{t-p+1} - \boldsymbol{\mu})'\right]\right\} \\ &= \begin{bmatrix} \boldsymbol{\Gamma}_0 & \boldsymbol{\Gamma}_1 & \cdots & \boldsymbol{\Gamma}_{p-1} \\ \boldsymbol{\Gamma}_1' & \boldsymbol{\Gamma}_0 & \cdots & \boldsymbol{\Gamma}_{p-2} \\ \vdots & \vdots & \cdots & \vdots \\ \boldsymbol{\Gamma}_{p-1}' & \boldsymbol{\Gamma}_{p-2}' & \cdots & \boldsymbol{\Gamma}_0 \end{bmatrix}, \end{aligned} \qquad [10.2.12]$$

where $\mathbf{\Gamma}_j$ denotes the $j$th autocovariance of the original process $\mathbf{y}$. Postmultiplying [10.1.11] by its own transpose and taking expectations gives

$$E[\boldsymbol{\xi}_t\boldsymbol{\xi}_t'] = E[(\mathbf{F}\boldsymbol{\xi}_{t-1} + \mathbf{v}_t)(\mathbf{F}\boldsymbol{\xi}_{t-1} + \mathbf{v}_t)'] = \mathbf{F}E(\boldsymbol{\xi}_{t-1}\boldsymbol{\xi}_{t-1}')\mathbf{F}' + E(\mathbf{v}_t\mathbf{v}_t'),$$

or

$$\boldsymbol{\Sigma} = \mathbf{F}\boldsymbol{\Sigma}\mathbf{F}' + \mathbf{Q}. \qquad [10.2.13]$$

A closed-form solution to [10.2.13] can be obtained in terms of the *vec* operator. If $\mathbf{A}$ is an $(m \times n)$ matrix, then $\text{vec}(\mathbf{A})$ is an $(mn \times 1)$ column vector, obtained by stacking the columns of $\mathbf{A}$, one below the other, with the columns ordered from left to right. For example, if

$$\mathbf{A} = \begin{bmatrix} a_{11} & a_{12} \\ a_{21} & a_{22} \\ a_{31} & a_{32} \end{bmatrix},$$

then

$$\text{vec}(\mathbf{A}) = \begin{bmatrix} a_{11} \\ a_{21} \\ a_{31} \\ a_{12} \\ a_{22} \\ a_{32} \end{bmatrix}. \qquad [10.2.14]$$

Appendix 10.A establishes the following useful result.

***Proposition 10.4:*** *Let* $\mathbf{A}$, $\mathbf{B}$, *and* $\mathbf{C}$ *be matrices whose dimensions are such that the product* $\mathbf{ABC}$ *exists. Then*

$$\text{vec}(\mathbf{ABC}) = (\mathbf{C}' \otimes \mathbf{A}) \cdot \text{vec}(\mathbf{B}) \qquad [10.2.15]$$

*where the symbol* $\otimes$ *denotes the Kronecker product.*

Thus, if the vec operator is applied to both sides of [10.2.13], the result is

$$\text{vec}(\boldsymbol{\Sigma}) = (\mathbf{F} \otimes \mathbf{F}) \cdot \text{vec}(\boldsymbol{\Sigma}) + \text{vec}(\mathbf{Q}) = \boldsymbol{\mathcal{A}}\, \text{vec}(\boldsymbol{\Sigma}) + \text{vec}(\mathbf{Q}), \qquad [10.2.16]$$

where

$$\boldsymbol{\mathcal{A}} \equiv (\mathbf{F} \otimes \mathbf{F}). \qquad [10.2.17]$$

Let $r = np$, so that $\mathbf{F}$ is an $(r \times r)$ matrix and $\boldsymbol{\mathcal{A}}$ is an $(r^2 \times r^2)$ matrix. Equation [10.2.16] has the solution

$$\text{vec}(\boldsymbol{\Sigma}) = [\mathbf{I}_{r^2} - \boldsymbol{\mathcal{A}}]^{-1}\, \text{vec}(\mathbf{Q}), \qquad [10.2.18]$$

provided that the matrix $[\mathbf{I}_{r^2} - \boldsymbol{\mathcal{A}}]$ is nonsingular. This will be true as long as unity is not an eigenvalue of $\boldsymbol{\mathcal{A}}$. But recall that the eigenvalues of $\mathbf{F} \otimes \mathbf{F}$ are all of the form $\lambda_i\lambda_j$, where $\lambda_i$ and $\lambda_j$ are eigenvalues of $\mathbf{F}$. Since $|\lambda_i| < 1$ for all $i$, it follows that all eigenvalues of $\boldsymbol{\mathcal{A}}$ are inside the unit circle, meaning that $[\mathbf{I}_{r^2} - \boldsymbol{\mathcal{A}}]$ is indeed nonsingular.

The first $p$ autocovariance matrices of a $VAR(p)$ process can be calculated by substituting [10.2.12] into [10.2.18]:

$$\text{vec}\begin{bmatrix} \mathbf{\Gamma}_0 & \mathbf{\Gamma}_1 & \cdots & \mathbf{\Gamma}_{p-1} \\ \mathbf{\Gamma}_1' & \mathbf{\Gamma}_0 & \cdots & \mathbf{\Gamma}_{p-2} \\ \vdots & \vdots & \cdots & \vdots \\ \mathbf{\Gamma}_{p-1}' & \mathbf{\Gamma}_{p-2}' & \cdots & \mathbf{\Gamma}_0 \end{bmatrix} = [\mathbf{I}_{r^2} - \mathcal{A}]^{-1}\,\text{vec}(\mathbf{Q}). \qquad [10.2.19]$$

The $j$th autocovariance of $\boldsymbol{\xi}$ (denoted $\mathbf{\Sigma}_j$) can be found by postmultiplying [10.1.11] by $\boldsymbol{\xi}_{t-j}'$ and taking expectations:

$$E(\boldsymbol{\xi}_t\boldsymbol{\xi}_{t-j}') = \mathbf{F}\cdot E(\boldsymbol{\xi}_{t-1}\boldsymbol{\xi}_{t-j}') + E(\mathbf{v}_t\boldsymbol{\xi}_{t-j}').$$

Thus,

$$\mathbf{\Sigma}_j = \mathbf{F}\mathbf{\Sigma}_{j-1} \qquad \text{for } j = 1, 2, \ldots, \qquad [10.2.20]$$

or

$$\mathbf{\Sigma}_j = \mathbf{F}^j\mathbf{\Sigma} \qquad \text{for } j = 1, 2, \ldots. \qquad [10.2.21]$$

The $j$th autocovariance $\mathbf{\Gamma}_j$ of the original process $\mathbf{y}_t$ is given by the first $n$ rows and $n$ columns of [10.2.20]:

$$\mathbf{\Gamma}_j = \mathbf{\Phi}_1\mathbf{\Gamma}_{j-1} + \mathbf{\Phi}_2\mathbf{\Gamma}_{j-2} + \cdots + \mathbf{\Phi}_p\mathbf{\Gamma}_{j-p} \qquad \text{for } j = p, p+1, p+2, \ldots. \qquad [10.2.22]$$

## 10.3. *The Autocovariance-Generating Function for Vector Processes*

### *Definition of Autocovariance-Generating Function for Vector Processes*

Recall that for a covariance-stationary univariate process $y_t$ with absolutely summable autocovariances, the (scalar-valued) autocovariance-generating function $g_Y(z)$ is defined as

$$g_Y(z) \equiv \sum_{j=-\infty}^{\infty} \gamma_j z^j$$

with

$$\gamma_j \equiv E[(y_t - \mu)(y_{t-j} - \mu)]$$

and $z$ a complex scalar. For a covariance-stationary vector process $\mathbf{y}_t$ with an absolutely summable sequence of autocovariance matrices, the analogous matrix-valued autocovariance-generating function $\mathbf{G_Y}(z)$ is defined as

$$\mathbf{G_Y}(z) \equiv \sum_{j=-\infty}^{\infty} \mathbf{\Gamma}_j z^j, \qquad [10.3.1]$$

where

$$\mathbf{\Gamma}_j \equiv E[(\mathbf{y}_t - \boldsymbol{\mu})(\mathbf{y}_{t-j} - \boldsymbol{\mu})']$$

and $z$ is again a complex scalar.

### *Autocovariance-Generating Function for a Vector Moving Average Process*

For example, for the vector white noise process $\boldsymbol{\varepsilon}_t$ characterized by [10.1.5] and [10.1.6], the autocovariance-generating function is

$$\mathbf{G}_{\boldsymbol{\varepsilon}}(z) = \boldsymbol{\Omega}. \qquad [10.3.2]$$

For the vector $MA(q)$ process of [10.2.3], the univariate expression [3.6.3] for the autocovariance-generating function generalizes to

$$\begin{aligned} \mathbf{G}_{\mathbf{Y}}(z) = (\mathbf{I}_n + \boldsymbol{\Theta}_1 z + \boldsymbol{\Theta}_2 z^2 + \cdots + \boldsymbol{\Theta}_q z^q)\boldsymbol{\Omega} \\ \times (\mathbf{I}_n + \boldsymbol{\Theta}_1' z^{-1} + \boldsymbol{\Theta}_2' z^{-2} + \cdots + \boldsymbol{\Theta}_q' z^{-q}). \end{aligned} \qquad [10.3.3]$$

This can be verified by noting that the coefficient on $z^j$ in [10.3.3] is equal to $\boldsymbol{\Gamma}_j$ as given in [10.2.5].

For an $MA(\infty)$ process of the form

$$\mathbf{y}_t = \boldsymbol{\mu} + \boldsymbol{\Psi}_0\boldsymbol{\varepsilon}_t + \boldsymbol{\Psi}_1\boldsymbol{\varepsilon}_{t-1} + \boldsymbol{\Psi}_2\boldsymbol{\varepsilon}_{t-2} + \cdots = \boldsymbol{\mu} + \boldsymbol{\Psi}(L)\boldsymbol{\varepsilon}_t,$$

with $\{\boldsymbol{\Psi}_k\}_{k=0}^{\infty}$ absolutely summable, [10.3.3] generalizes to

$$\mathbf{G}_{\mathbf{Y}}(z) = [\boldsymbol{\Psi}(z)]\boldsymbol{\Omega}[\boldsymbol{\Psi}(z^{-1})]'. \qquad [10.3.4]$$

### *Autocovariance-Generating Function for a Vector Autoregression*

Consider the $VAR(1)$ process $\boldsymbol{\xi}_t = \mathbf{F}\boldsymbol{\xi}_{t-1} + \mathbf{v}_t$ with eigenvalues of $\mathbf{F}$ inside the unit circle and with $\boldsymbol{\xi}_t$ an $(r \times 1)$ vector and $E(\mathbf{v}_t\mathbf{v}_t') = \mathbf{Q}$. Equation [10.3.4] implies that the autocovariance-generating function can be expressed as

$$\begin{aligned} \mathbf{G}_{\boldsymbol{\xi}}(z) &= [\mathbf{I}_r - \mathbf{F}z]^{-1}\mathbf{Q}[\mathbf{I}_r - \mathbf{F}'z^{-1}]^{-1} \\ &= [\mathbf{I}_r + \mathbf{F}z + \mathbf{F}^2z^2 + \mathbf{F}^3z^3 + \cdots]\mathbf{Q} \\ &\quad \times [\mathbf{I}_r + (\mathbf{F}')z^{-1} + (\mathbf{F}')^2z^{-2} + (\mathbf{F}')^3z^{-3} + \cdots]. \end{aligned} \qquad [10.3.5]$$

### *Transformations of Vector Processes*

The autocovariance-generating function of the sum of two univariate processes that are uncorrelated with each other is equal to the sum of their individual autocovariance-generating functions (equation [4.7.19]). This result readily generalizes to the vector case:

$$\begin{aligned} \mathbf{G}_{\mathbf{X}+\mathbf{W}}(z) &= \sum_{j=-\infty}^{\infty} E[(\mathbf{x}_t + \mathbf{w}_t - \boldsymbol{\mu}_{\mathbf{X}} - \boldsymbol{\mu}_{\mathbf{W}}) \\ &\qquad \times (\mathbf{x}_{t-j} + \mathbf{w}_{t-j} - \boldsymbol{\mu}_{\mathbf{X}} - \boldsymbol{\mu}_{\mathbf{W}})']z^j \\ &= \sum_{j=-\infty}^{\infty} E[(\mathbf{x}_t - \boldsymbol{\mu}_{\mathbf{X}})(\mathbf{x}_{t-j} - \boldsymbol{\mu}_{\mathbf{X}})'z^j] \\ &\quad + \sum_{j=-\infty}^{\infty} E[(\mathbf{w}_t - \boldsymbol{\mu}_{\mathbf{W}})(\mathbf{w}_{t-j} - \boldsymbol{\mu}_{\mathbf{W}})'z^j] \\ &= \mathbf{G}_{\mathbf{X}}(z) + \mathbf{G}_{\mathbf{W}}(z). \end{aligned}$$

Note also that if an $(r \times 1)$ vector $\boldsymbol{\xi}_t$ is premultiplied by a nonstochastic $(n \times r)$ matrix $\mathbf{H}'$, the effect is to premultiply the autocovariance by $\mathbf{H}'$ and postmultiply by $\mathbf{H}$:

$$E[(\mathbf{H}'\boldsymbol{\xi}_t - \mathbf{H}'\boldsymbol{\mu}_\xi)(\mathbf{H}'\boldsymbol{\xi}_{t-j} - \mathbf{H}'\boldsymbol{\mu}_\xi)'] = \mathbf{H}'E[(\boldsymbol{\xi}_t - \boldsymbol{\mu}_\xi)(\boldsymbol{\xi}_{t-j} - \boldsymbol{\mu}_\xi)']\mathbf{H},$$

implying

$$\mathbf{G}_{\mathbf{H}'\xi}(z) = \mathbf{H}'\mathbf{G}_\xi(z)\mathbf{H}.$$

Putting these results together, consider $\boldsymbol{\xi}_t$ the $r$-dimensional $VAR(1)$ process $\boldsymbol{\xi}_t = \mathbf{F}\boldsymbol{\xi}_{t-1} + \mathbf{v}_t$ and a new process $\mathbf{u}_t$ given by $\mathbf{u}_t = \mathbf{H}'\boldsymbol{\xi}_t + \mathbf{w}_t$ with $\mathbf{w}_t$ a white noise process that is uncorrelated with $\boldsymbol{\xi}_{t-j}$ for all $j$. Then

$$\mathbf{G}_\mathrm{U}(z) = \mathbf{H}'\mathbf{G}_\xi(z)\mathbf{H} + \mathbf{G}_\mathrm{W}(z),$$

or, if $\mathbf{R}$ is the variance of $\mathbf{w}_t$,

$$\mathbf{G}_\mathrm{U}(z) = \mathbf{H}'[\mathbf{I}_r - \mathbf{F}z]^{-1}\mathbf{Q}[\mathbf{I}_r - \mathbf{F}'z^{-1}]^{-1}\mathbf{H} + \mathbf{R}. \qquad [10.3.6]$$

More generally, consider an $(n \times 1)$ vector $\mathbf{y}_t$ characterized by

$$\mathbf{y}_t = \boldsymbol{\mu}_\mathrm{Y} + \boldsymbol{\Psi}(L)\boldsymbol{\varepsilon}_t,$$

where $\boldsymbol{\varepsilon}_t$ is a white noise process with variance-covariance matrix given by $\boldsymbol{\Omega}$ and where $\boldsymbol{\Psi}(L) = \Sigma_{k=0}^{\infty}\boldsymbol{\Psi}_k L^k$ with $\{\boldsymbol{\Psi}_k\}_{k=0}^{\infty}$ absolutely summable. Thus, the autocovariance-generating function for $\mathbf{y}$ is

$$\mathbf{G}_\mathrm{Y}(z) = \boldsymbol{\Psi}(z)\boldsymbol{\Omega}[\boldsymbol{\Psi}(z^{-1})]'. \qquad [10.3.7]$$

Let $\{\mathbf{H}_k\}_{k=-\infty}^{\infty}$ be an absolutely summable sequence of $(r \times n)$ matrices, and suppose that an $(r \times 1)$ vector $\mathbf{x}_t$ is constructed from $\mathbf{y}_t$ according to

$$\mathbf{x}_t = \mathbf{H}(L)\mathbf{y}_t = \sum_{k=-\infty}^{\infty} \mathbf{H}_k\mathbf{y}_{t-k} = \boldsymbol{\mu}_\mathrm{X} + \mathbf{B}(L)\boldsymbol{\varepsilon}_t,$$

where $\boldsymbol{\mu}_\mathrm{X} = \mathbf{H}(1)\boldsymbol{\mu}_\mathrm{Y}$ and $\mathbf{B}(L) = \mathbf{H}(L)\boldsymbol{\Psi}(L)$ as in [10.2.10] and [10.2.11]. Then the autocovariance-generating function for $\mathbf{x}$ can be found from

$$\mathbf{G}_\mathrm{X}(z) = \mathbf{B}(z)\boldsymbol{\Omega}[\mathbf{B}(z^{-1})]' = [\mathbf{H}(z)\boldsymbol{\Psi}(z)]\boldsymbol{\Omega}[\boldsymbol{\Psi}(z^{-1})]'[\mathbf{H}(z^{-1})]'. \qquad [10.3.8]$$

Comparing [10.3.8] with [10.3.7], the effect of applying the filter $\mathbf{H}(L)$ to $\mathbf{y}_t$ is to premultiply the autocovariance-generating function by $\mathbf{H}(z)$ and to postmultiply by the transpose of $\mathbf{H}(z^{-1})$:

$$\mathbf{G}_\mathrm{X}(z) = [\mathbf{H}(z)]\mathbf{G}_\mathrm{Y}(z)[\mathbf{H}(z^{-1})]'. \qquad [10.3.9]$$

## 10.4. *The Spectrum for Vector Processes*

Let $\mathbf{y}_t$ be an $(n \times 1)$ vector with mean $E(\mathbf{y}_t) = \boldsymbol{\mu}$ and $k$th autocovariance matrix

$$E[(\mathbf{y}_t - \boldsymbol{\mu})(\mathbf{y}_{t-k} - \boldsymbol{\mu})'] = \boldsymbol{\Gamma}_k. \qquad [10.4.1]$$

If $\{\boldsymbol{\Gamma}_k\}_{k=-\infty}^{\infty}$ is absolutely summable and if $z$ is a complex scalar, the autocovariance-generating function of $\mathbf{y}$ is given by

$$\mathbf{G}_\mathrm{Y}(z) = \sum_{k=-\infty}^{\infty} \boldsymbol{\Gamma}_k z^k. \qquad [10.4.2]$$

The function $\mathbf{G_Y}(z)$ associates an $(n \times n)$ matrix of complex numbers with the complex scalar $z$. If [10.4.2] is divided by $2\pi$ and evaluated at $z = e^{-i\omega}$, where $\omega$ is a real scalar and $i = \sqrt{-1}$, the result is the *population spectrum* of the vector $\mathbf{y}$:

$$\mathbf{s_Y}(\omega) = (2\pi)^{-1}\mathbf{G_Y}(e^{-i\omega}) = (2\pi)^{-1} \sum_{k=-\infty}^{\infty} \mathbf{\Gamma}_k e^{-i\omega k}. \qquad [10.4.3]$$

The population spectrum associates an $(n \times n)$ matrix of complex numbers with the real scalar $\omega$.

Identical calculations to those used to establish Proposition 6.1 indicate that when any element of $\mathbf{s_Y}(\omega)$ is multiplied by $e^{i\omega k}$ and the resulting function of $\omega$ is integrated from $-\pi$ to $\pi$, the result is the corresponding element of the $k$th autocovariance matrix of $\mathbf{y}$:

$$\int_{-\pi}^{\pi} \mathbf{s_Y}(\omega)e^{i\omega k}\, d\omega = \mathbf{\Gamma}_k. \qquad [10.4.4]$$

Thus, as in the univariate case, the sequence of autocovariances $\{\mathbf{\Gamma}_k\}_{k=-\infty}^{\infty}$ and the function represented by the population spectrum $\mathbf{s_Y}(\omega)$ contain the identical information.

As a special case, when $k = 0$, equation [10.4.4] implies

$$\int_{-\pi}^{\pi} \mathbf{s_Y}(\omega)\, d\omega = \mathbf{\Gamma}_0. \qquad [10.4.5]$$

In other words, the area under the population spectrum is the unconditional variance-covariance matrix of $\mathbf{y}$.

The $j$th diagonal element of $\mathbf{\Gamma}_k$ is $E(y_{jt} - \mu_j)(y_{j,t-k} - \mu_j)$, the $k$th autocovariance of $y_{jt}$. Thus, the $j$th diagonal element of the multivariate spectrum $\mathbf{s_Y}(\omega)$ is just the univariate spectrum of the scalar $y_{jt}$. It follows from the properties of the univariate spectrum discussed in Chapter 6 that the diagonal elements of $\mathbf{s_Y}(\omega)$ are real-valued and nonnegative for all $\omega$. However, the same is not true of the off-diagonal elements of $\mathbf{s_Y}(\omega)$—in general, the off-diagonal elements of $\mathbf{s_Y}(\omega)$ will be complex numbers.

To gain further understanding of the multivariate spectrum, we concentrate on the case of $n = 2$ variables, denoted

$$\mathbf{y}_t = \begin{bmatrix} X_t \\ Y_t \end{bmatrix}.$$

The $k$th autocovariance matrix is then

$$\begin{aligned} \mathbf{\Gamma}_k &= E\begin{bmatrix} (X_t - \mu_X)(X_{t-k} - \mu_X) & (X_t - \mu_X)(Y_{t-k} - \mu_Y) \\ (Y_t - \mu_Y)(X_{t-k} - \mu_X) & (Y_t - \mu_Y)(Y_{t-k} - \mu_Y) \end{bmatrix} \\ &\equiv \begin{bmatrix} \gamma_{XX}^{(k)} & \gamma_{XY}^{(k)} \\ \gamma_{YX}^{(k)} & \gamma_{YY}^{(k)} \end{bmatrix}. \end{aligned} \qquad [10.4.6]$$

Recall from [10.2.2] that $\mathbf{\Gamma}_k' = \mathbf{\Gamma}_{-k}$. Hence,

$$\gamma_{XX}^{(k)} = \gamma_{XX}^{(-k)} \qquad [10.4.7]$$

$$\gamma_{YY}^{(k)} = \gamma_{YY}^{(-k)} \qquad [10.4.8]$$

$$\gamma_{XY}^{(k)} = \gamma_{YX}^{(-k)}. \qquad [10.4.9]$$

For this $n = 2$ case, the population spectrum [10.4.3] would be

$$\mathbf{s_Y}(\omega)$$
$$= \frac{1}{2\pi}\begin{bmatrix} \sum_{k=-\infty}^{\infty} \gamma_{XX}^{(k)} e^{-i\omega k} & \sum_{k=-\infty}^{\infty} \gamma_{XY}^{(k)} e^{-i\omega k} \\ \sum_{k=-\infty}^{\infty} \gamma_{YX}^{(k)} e^{-i\omega k} & \sum_{k=-\infty}^{\infty} \gamma_{YY}^{(k)} e^{-i\omega k} \end{bmatrix}$$

$$= \frac{1}{2\pi}\begin{bmatrix} \sum_{k=-\infty}^{\infty} \gamma_{XX}^{(k)}\{\cos(\omega k) - i\cdot\sin(\omega k)\} & \sum_{k=-\infty}^{\infty} \gamma_{XY}^{(k)}\{\cos(\omega k) - i\cdot\sin(\omega k)\} \\ \sum_{k=-\infty}^{\infty} \gamma_{YX}^{(k)}\{\cos(\omega k) - i\cdot\sin(\omega k)\} & \sum_{k=-\infty}^{\infty} \gamma_{YY}^{(k)}\{\cos(\omega k) - i\cdot\sin(\omega k)\} \end{bmatrix}. \qquad [10.4.10]$$

Using [10.4.7] and [10.4.8] along with the facts that $\sin(-\omega k) = -\sin(\omega k)$ and $\sin(0) = 0$, the imaginary components disappear from the diagonal terms:

$$\mathbf{s_Y}(\omega)$$
$$= \frac{1}{2\pi}\begin{bmatrix} \sum_{k=-\infty}^{\infty} \gamma_{XX}^{(k)} \cos(\omega k) & \sum_{k=-\infty}^{\infty} \gamma_{XY}^{(k)}\{\cos(\omega k) - i\cdot\sin(\omega k)\} \\ \sum_{k=-\infty}^{\infty} \gamma_{YX}^{(k)}\{\cos(\omega k) - i\cdot\sin(\omega k)\} & \sum_{k=-\infty}^{\infty} \gamma_{YY}^{(k)} \cos(\omega k) \end{bmatrix}. \qquad [10.4.11]$$

However, since in general $\gamma_{XY}^{(k)} \neq \gamma_{XY}^{(-k)}$, the off-diagonal elements are typically complex numbers.

## *The Cross Spectrum, Cospectrum, and Quadrature Spectrum*

The lower left element of the matrix in [10.4.11] is known as the *population cross spectrum* from $X$ to $Y$:

$$s_{YX}(\omega) = (2\pi)^{-1} \sum_{k=-\infty}^{\infty} \gamma_{YX}^{(k)}\{\cos(\omega k) - i\cdot\sin(\omega k)\}. \qquad [10.4.12]$$

The cross spectrum can be written in terms of its real and imaginary components as

$$s_{YX}(\omega) = c_{YX}(\omega) + i\cdot q_{YX}(\omega). \qquad [10.4.13]$$

The real component of the cross spectrum is known as the *cospectrum* between $X$ and $Y$:

$$c_{YX}(\omega) = (2\pi)^{-1} \sum_{k=-\infty}^{\infty} \gamma_{YX}^{(k)} \cos(\omega k). \qquad [10.4.14]$$

One can verify from [10.4.9] and the fact that $\cos(-\omega k) = \cos(\omega k)$ that

$$c_{YX}(\omega) = c_{XY}(\omega). \qquad [10.4.15]$$

The imaginary component of the cross spectrum is known as the *quadrature spectrum* from $X$ to $Y$:

$$q_{YX}(\omega) = -(2\pi)^{-1} \sum_{k=-\infty}^{\infty} \gamma_{YX}^{(k)} \sin(\omega k). \qquad [10.4.16]$$

One can verify from [10.4.9] and the fact that $\sin(-\omega k) = -\sin(\omega k)$ that the quadrature spectrum from $Y$ to $X$ is the negative of the quadrature spectrum from $X$ to $Y$:

$$q_{YX}(\omega) = -q_{XY}(\omega).$$

Recalling [10.4.13], these results imply that the off-diagonal elements of $\mathbf{s}_{\mathbf{Y}}(\omega)$ are complex conjugates of each other; in general, the row $j$, column $m$ element of $\mathbf{s}_{\mathbf{Y}}(\omega)$ is the complex conjugate of the row $m$, column $j$ element of $\mathbf{s}_{\mathbf{Y}}(\omega)$.

Note that both $c_{YX}(\omega)$ and $q_{YX}(\omega)$ are real-valued periodic functions of $\omega$:

$$c_{YX}(\omega + 2\pi j) = c_{YX}(\omega) \qquad \text{for } j = \pm 1, \pm 2, \ldots$$
$$q_{YX}(\omega + 2\pi j) = q_{YX}(\omega) \qquad \text{for } j = \pm 1, \pm 2, \ldots.$$

It further follows from [10.4.14] that

$$c_{YX}(-\omega) = c_{YX}(\omega),$$

while [10.4.16] implies that

$$q_{YX}(-\omega) = -q_{YX}(\omega). \qquad [10.4.17]$$

Hence, the cospectrum and quadrature spectrum are fully specified by the values they assume as $\omega$ ranges between 0 and $\pi$.

Result [10.4.5] implies that the cross spectrum integrates to the unconditional covariance between $X$ and $Y$:

$$\int_{-\pi}^{\pi} s_{YX}(\omega)\, d\omega = E(Y_t - \mu_Y)(X_t - \mu_X).$$

Observe from [10.4.17] that the quadrature spectrum integrates to zero:

$$\int_{-\pi}^{\pi} q_{YX}(\omega)\, d\omega = 0.$$

Hence, the covariance between $X$ and $Y$ can be calculated from the area under the cospectrum between $X$ and $Y$:

$$\int_{-\pi}^{\pi} c_{YX}(\omega)\, d\omega = E(Y_t - \mu_Y)(X_t - \mu_X). \qquad [10.4.18]$$

The cospectrum between $X$ and $Y$ at frequency $\omega$ can thus be interpreted as the portion of the covariance between $X$ and $Y$ that is attributable to cycles with frequency $\omega$. Since the covariance can be positive or negative, the cospectrum can be positive or negative, and indeed, $c_{YX}(\omega)$ may be positive over some frequencies and negative over others.

### *The Sample Multivariate Periodogram*

To gain further understanding of the cospectrum and the quadrature spectrum, let $y_1, y_2, \ldots, y_T$ and $x_1, x_2, \ldots, x_T$ denote samples of $T$ observations on the two variables. If for illustration $T$ is odd, Proposition 6.2 indicates that the value of $y_t$ can be expressed as

$$y_t = \bar{y} + \sum_{j=1}^{M} \{\hat{\alpha}_j \cdot \cos[\omega_j(t - 1)] + \hat{\delta}_j \cdot \sin[\omega_j(t - 1)]\}, \qquad [10.4.19]$$

where $\bar{y}$ is the sample mean of $y$, $M = (T - 1)/2$, $\omega_j = 2\pi j/T$, and

$$\hat{\alpha}_j = (2/T) \sum_{t=1}^{T} y_t \cdot \cos[\omega_j(t - 1)] \qquad [10.4.20]$$

$$\hat{\delta}_j = (2/T) \sum_{t=1}^{T} y_t \cdot \sin[\omega_j(t - 1)]. \qquad [10.4.21]$$

An analogous representation for $x_t$ is

$$x_t = \bar{x} + \sum_{j=1}^{M} \{\hat{a}_j \cdot \cos[\omega_j(t - 1)] + \hat{d}_j \cdot \sin[\omega_j(t - 1)]\} \qquad [10.4.22]$$

$$\hat{a}_j = (2/T) \sum_{t=1}^{T} x_t \cdot \cos[\omega_j(t - 1)] \qquad [10.4.23]$$

$$\hat{d}_j = (2/T) \sum_{t=1}^{T} x_t \cdot \sin[\omega_j(t - 1)]. \qquad [10.4.24]$$

Recall from [6.2.11] that the periodic regressors in [10.4.19] all have sample mean zero and are mutually orthogonal, while

$$\sum_{t=1}^{T} \cos^2[\omega_j(t - 1)] = \sum_{t=1}^{T} \sin^2[\omega_j(t - 1)] = T/2. \qquad [10.4.25]$$

Consider the sample covariance between $x$ and $y$:

$$T^{-1} \sum_{t=1}^{T} (y_t - \bar{y})(x_t - \bar{x}). \qquad [10.4.26]$$

Substituting [10.4.19] and [10.4.22] into [10.4.26] and exploiting the mutual orthogonality of the periodic regressors reveal that

$$\begin{aligned} T^{-1} &\sum_{t=1}^{T} (y_t - \bar{y})(x_t - \bar{x}) \\ &= T^{-1} \sum_{t=1}^{T} \left\{ \sum_{j=1}^{M} \{\hat{\alpha}_j \cdot \cos[\omega_j(t - 1)] + \hat{\delta}_j \cdot \sin[\omega_j(t - 1)]\} \right. \\ &\qquad \left. \times \sum_{j=1}^{M} \{\hat{a}_j \cdot \cos[\omega_j(t - 1)] + \hat{d}_j \cdot \sin[\omega_j(t - 1)]\} \right\} \qquad [10.4.27] \\ &= T^{-1} \sum_{t=1}^{T} \left\{ \sum_{j=1}^{M} \{\hat{\alpha}_j \hat{a}_j \cdot \cos^2[\omega_j(t - 1)] + \hat{\delta}_j \hat{d}_j \cdot \sin^2[\omega_j(t - 1)]\} \right\} \\ &= (1/2) \sum_{j=1}^{M} (\hat{\alpha}_j \hat{a}_j + \hat{\delta}_j \hat{d}_j). \end{aligned}$$

Hence, the portion of the sample covariance between $x$ and $y$ that is due to their common dependence on cycles of frequency $\omega_j$ is given by

$$(1/2)(\hat{\alpha}_j \hat{a}_j + \hat{\delta}_j \hat{d}_j). \qquad [10.4.28]$$

This magnitude can be related to the sample analog of the cospectrum with calculations similar to those used to establish result (c) of Proposition 6.2. Recall that since

$$\sum_{t=1}^{T} \cos[\omega_j(t-1)] = 0,$$

the magnitude $\hat{\alpha}_j$ in [10.4.20] can alternatively be expressed as

$$\hat{\alpha}_j = (2/T) \sum_{t=1}^{T} (y_t - \bar{y}) \cdot \cos[\omega_j(t-1)].$$

Thus,

$$\begin{aligned}
&(\hat{a}_j + i \cdot \hat{d}_j)(\hat{\alpha}_j - i \cdot \hat{\delta}_j) \\
&= (4/T^2) \left\{ \sum_{t=1}^{T} (x_t - \bar{x}) \cdot \cos[\omega_j(t-1)] + i \cdot \sum_{t=1}^{T} (x_t - \bar{x}) \cdot \sin[\omega_j(t-1)] \right\} \\
&\quad \times \left\{ \sum_{\tau=1}^{T} (y_\tau - \bar{y}) \cdot \cos[\omega_j(\tau-1)] - i \cdot \sum_{\tau=1}^{T} (y_\tau - \bar{y}) \cdot \sin[\omega_j(\tau-1)] \right\} \\
&= (4/T^2) \left\{ \sum_{t=1}^{T} (x_t - \bar{x}) \cdot \exp[i \cdot \omega_j(t-1)] \right\} \left\{ \sum_{t=\tau}^{T} (y_\tau - \bar{y}) \cdot \exp[-i \cdot \omega_j(\tau-1)] \right\} \\
&= (4/T^2) \left\{ \sum_{t=1}^{T} (x_t - \bar{x})(y_t - \bar{y}) + \sum_{t=1}^{T-1} (x_t - \bar{x})(y_{t+1} - \bar{y}) \cdot \exp[-i\omega_j] \right. \\
&\quad + \sum_{t=2}^{T} (x_t - \bar{x})(y_{t-1} - \bar{y}) \cdot \exp[i\omega_j] + \sum_{t=1}^{T-2} (x_t - \bar{x})(y_{t+2} - \bar{y}) \cdot \exp[-2i\omega_j] \\
&\quad + \sum_{t=3}^{T} (x_t - \bar{x})(y_{t-2} - \bar{y}) \cdot \exp[2i\omega_j] + \cdots + (x_1 - \bar{x})(y_T - \bar{y}) \cdot \exp[-(T-1)i\omega_j] \\
&\quad \left. + (x_T - \bar{x})(y_1 - \bar{y}) \cdot \exp[(T-1)i\omega_j] \right\} \\
&= (4/T) \left\{ \hat{\gamma}_{yx}^{(0)} + \hat{\gamma}_{yx}^{(1)} \cdot \exp[-i\omega_j] + \hat{\gamma}_{yx}^{(-1)} \cdot \exp[i\omega_j] \right. \\
&\quad + \hat{\gamma}_{yx}^{(2)} \cdot \exp[-2i\omega_j] + \hat{\gamma}_{yx}^{(-2)} \cdot \exp[2i\omega_j] + \cdots \\
&\quad \left. + \hat{\gamma}_{yx}^{(T-1)} \cdot \exp[-(T-1)i\omega_j] + \hat{\gamma}_{yx}^{(-T+1)} \cdot \exp[(T-1)i\omega_j] \right\},
\end{aligned} \qquad [10.4.29]$$

where $\hat{\gamma}_{yx}^{(k)}$ is the sample covariance between the value of $y$ and the value that $x$ assumed $k$ periods earlier:

$$\hat{\gamma}_{yx}^{(k)} = \begin{cases} (1/T) \sum_{t=1}^{T-k} (x_t - \bar{x})(y_{t+k} - \bar{y}) & \text{for } k = 0, 1, 2, \ldots, T-1 \\ (1/T) \sum_{t=-k+1}^{T} (x_t - \bar{x})(y_{t+k} - \bar{y}) & \text{for } k = -1, -2, \ldots, -T+1. \end{cases}$$

[10.4.30]

Result [10.4.29] implies that

$$\tfrac{1}{2}(\hat{a}_j + i\cdot\hat{d}_j)(\hat{\alpha}_j - i\cdot\hat{\delta}_j) = (2/T)\sum_{k=-T+1}^{T-1} \hat{\gamma}_{yx}^{(k)}\cdot\exp[-ki\omega_j] = (4\pi/T)\cdot\hat{s}_{yx}(\omega_j), \qquad [10.4.31]$$

where $\hat{s}_{yx}(\omega_j)$ is the *sample cross periodogram* from $x$ to $y$ at frequency $\omega_j$, or the lower left element of the *sample multivariate periodogram*:

$$\hat{\mathbf{s}}_y(\omega) = (2\pi)^{-1}\begin{bmatrix} \sum_{k=-T+1}^{T-1} \hat{\gamma}_{xx}^{(k)}e^{-i\omega k} & \sum_{k=-T+1}^{T-1} \hat{\gamma}_{xy}^{(k)}e^{-i\omega k} \\ \sum_{k=-T+1}^{T-1} \hat{\gamma}_{yx}^{(k)}e^{-i\omega k} & \sum_{k=-T+1}^{T-1} \hat{\gamma}_{yy}^{(k)}e^{-i\omega k} \end{bmatrix} = \begin{bmatrix} \hat{s}_{xx}(\omega) & \hat{s}_{xy}(\omega) \\ \hat{s}_{yx}(\omega) & \hat{s}_{yy}(\omega) \end{bmatrix}.$$

Expression [10.4.31] states that the sample cross periodogram from $x$ to $y$ at frequency $\omega_j$ can be expressed as

$$\begin{aligned}\hat{s}_{yx}(\omega_j) &= [T/(8\pi)]\cdot(\hat{a}_j + i\cdot\hat{d}_j)(\hat{\alpha}_j - i\cdot\hat{\delta}_j) \\ &= [T/(8\pi)]\cdot(\hat{a}_j\hat{\alpha}_j + \hat{d}_j\hat{\delta}_j) + i\cdot[T/(8\pi)]\cdot(\hat{d}_j\hat{\alpha}_j - \hat{a}_j\hat{\delta}_j).\end{aligned}$$

The real component is the sample analog of the cospectrum, while the imaginary component is the sample analog of the quadrature spectrum:

$$\hat{s}_{yx}(\omega_j) = \hat{c}_{yx}(\omega_j) + i\cdot\hat{q}_{yx}(\omega_j), \qquad [10.4.32]$$

where

$$\hat{c}_{yx}(\omega_j) = [T/(8\pi)]\cdot(\hat{a}_j\hat{\alpha}_j + \hat{d}_j\hat{\delta}_j) \qquad [10.4.33]$$

$$\hat{q}_{yx}(\omega_j) = [T/(8\pi)]\cdot(\hat{d}_j\hat{\alpha}_j - \hat{a}_j\hat{\delta}_j). \qquad [10.4.34]$$

Comparing [10.4.33] with [10.4.28], the sample cospectrum evaluated at $\omega_j$ is proportional to the portion of the sample covariance between $y$ and $x$ that is attributable to cycles with frequency $\omega_j$. The population cospectrum admits an analogous interpretation as the portion of the population covariance between $Y$ and $X$ attributable to cycles with frequency $\omega$ based on a multivariate version of the spectral representation theorem.

What interpretation are we to attach to the quadrature spectrum? Consider using the weights in [10.4.22] to construct a new series $x_t^*$ by shifting the phase of each of the periodic functions by a quarter cycle:

$$x_t^* = \bar{x} + \sum_{j=1}^{M}\{\hat{a}_j\cdot\cos[\omega_j(t-1) + (\pi/2)] + \hat{d}_j\cdot\sin[\omega_j(t-1) + (\pi/2)]\}. \qquad [10.4.35]$$

The variable $x_t^*$ is driven by the same cycles as $x_t$, except that at date $t = 1$ each cycle is one-quarter of the way through rather than just beginning as in the case of $x_t$.

Since $\sin[\theta + (\pi/2)] = \cos(\theta)$ and since $\cos[\theta + (\pi/2)] = -\sin(\theta)$, the variable $x_t^*$ can alternatively be described as

$$x_t^* = \bar{x} + \sum_{j=1}^{M}\{\hat{d}_j\cdot\cos[\omega_j(t-1)] - \hat{a}_j\cdot\sin[\omega_j(t-1)]\}. \qquad [10.4.36]$$

As in [10.4.27], the sample covariance between $y_t$ and $x_t^*$ is found to be

$$T^{-1} \sum_{t=1}^{T} (y_t - \bar{y})(x_t^* - \bar{x}) = (1/2) \sum_{j=1}^{M} (\hat{\alpha}_j \hat{d}_j - \hat{\delta}_j \hat{a}_j).$$

Comparing this with [10.4.34], the sample quadrature spectrum from $x$ to $y$ at frequency $\omega_j$ is proportional to the portion of the sample covariance between $x^*$ and $y$ that is due to cycles of frequency $\omega_j$. Cycles of frequency $\omega_j$ may be quite important for both $x$ and $y$ individually (as reflected by large values for $\hat{s}_{xx}(\omega)$ and $\hat{s}_{yy}(\omega)$) yet fail to produce much contemporaneous covariance between the variables because at any given date the two series are in a different phase of the cycle. For example, the variable $x$ may respond to an economic recession sooner than $y$. The quadrature spectrum looks for evidence of such out-of-phase cycles.

## *Coherence, Phase, and Gain*

The *population coherence* between $X$ and $Y$ is a measure of the degree to which $X$ and $Y$ are jointly influenced by cycles of frequency $\omega$. This measure combines the inferences of the cospectrum and the quadrature spectrum, and is defined as[1]

$$h_{YX}(\omega) = \frac{[c_{YX}(\omega)]^2 + [q_{YX}(\omega)]^2}{s_{YY}(\omega)s_{XX}(\omega)},$$

assuming that $s_{YY}(\omega)$ and $s_{XX}(\omega)$ are nonzero. If $s_{YY}(\omega)$ or $s_{XX}(\omega)$ is zero, the coherence is defined to be zero. It can be shown that $0 \leq h_{YX}(\omega) \leq 1$ for all $\omega$ as long as $X$ and $Y$ are covariance-stationary with absolutely summable autocovariance matrices.[2] If $h_{YX}(\omega)$ is large, this indicates that $Y$ and $X$ have important cycles of frequency $\omega$ in common.

The cospectrum and quadrature spectrum can alternatively be described in polar coordinate form. In this notation, the population cross spectrum from $X$ to $Y$ is written as

$$s_{YX}(\omega) = c_{YX}(\omega) + i \cdot q_{YX}(\omega) = R(\omega) \cdot \exp[i \cdot \theta(\omega)], \qquad [10.4.37]$$

where

$$R(\omega) = \{[c_{YX}(\omega)]^2 + [q_{YX}(\omega)]^2\}^{1/2} \qquad [10.4.38]$$

and $\theta(\omega)$ represents the radian angle satisfying

$$\frac{\sin[\theta(\omega)]}{\cos[\theta(\omega)]} = \frac{q_{YX}(\omega)}{c_{YX}(\omega)}. \qquad [10.4.39]$$

The function $R(\omega)$ is sometimes described as the *gain* while $\theta(\omega)$ is called the *phase*.[3]

[1] The coherence is sometimes alternatively defined as the square root of this magnitude. The sample coherence based on the unsmoothed periodogram is identically equal to 1.

[2] See, for example, Fuller (1976, p. 156).

[3] The gain is sometimes alternatively defined as $R(\omega)/s_{XX}(\omega)$.

## *The Population Spectrum for Vector* MA *and* AR *Processes*

Let $\mathbf{y}_t$ be a vector $MA(\infty)$ process with absolutely summable moving average coefficients:

$$\mathbf{y}_t = \boldsymbol{\mu} + \boldsymbol{\Psi}(L)\boldsymbol{\varepsilon}_t,$$

where

$$E(\boldsymbol{\varepsilon}_t\boldsymbol{\varepsilon}_\tau') = \begin{cases} \boldsymbol{\Omega} & \text{for } t = \tau \\ \mathbf{0} & \text{otherwise.} \end{cases}$$

Substituting [10.3.4] into [10.4.3] reveals that the population spectrum for $\mathbf{y}_t$ can be calculated as

$$\mathbf{s}_{\mathbf{Y}}(\omega) = (2\pi)^{-1}[\boldsymbol{\Psi}(e^{-i\omega})]\boldsymbol{\Omega}[\boldsymbol{\Psi}(e^{i\omega})]'. \qquad [10.4.40]$$

For example, the population spectrum for a stationary $VAR(p)$ as written in [10.1.4] is

$$\begin{aligned} \mathbf{s}_{\mathbf{Y}}(\omega) = (2\pi)^{-1}\{\mathbf{I}_n - \boldsymbol{\Phi}_1 e^{-i\omega} - \boldsymbol{\Phi}_2 e^{-2i\omega} - \cdots - \boldsymbol{\Phi}_p e^{-pi\omega}\}^{-1}\boldsymbol{\Omega} \\ \times \{\mathbf{I}_n - \boldsymbol{\Phi}_1' e^{i\omega} - \boldsymbol{\Phi}_2' e^{2i\omega} - \cdots - \boldsymbol{\Phi}_p' e^{pi\omega}\}^{-1}. \end{aligned} \qquad [10.4.41]$$

## *Estimating the Population Spectrum*

If an observed time series $\mathbf{y}_1, \mathbf{y}_2, \ldots, \mathbf{y}_T$ can be reasonably described by a $p$th-order vector autoregression, one good approach to estimating the population spectrum is to estimate the parameters of the vector autoregression [10.1.4] by *OLS* and then substitute these parameter estimates into equation [10.4.41].

Alternatively, the sample cross periodogram from $x$ to $y$ at frequency $\omega_j = 2\pi j/T$ can be calculated from [10.4.32] to [10.4.34], where $\hat{\alpha}_j$, $\hat{\delta}_j$, $\hat{a}_j$, and $\hat{d}_j$ are as defined in [10.4.20] through [10.4.24]. One would want to smooth these to obtain a more useful estimate of the population cross spectrum. For example, one reasonable estimate of the population cospectrum between $X$ and $Y$ at frequency $\omega_j$ would be

$$\hat{c}_{YX}(\omega_j) = \sum_{m=-h}^{h} \left\{\frac{h + 1 - |m|}{(h + 1)^2}\right\} \hat{c}_{yx}(\omega_{j+m}),$$

where $\hat{c}_{yx}(\omega_{j+m})$ denotes the estimate in [10.4.33] evaluated at frequency $\omega_{j+m} = 2\pi(j + m)/T$ and $h$ is a bandwidth parameter reflecting how many different frequencies are to be used in estimating the cospectrum at frequency $\omega_j$.

Another approach is to express the smoothing in terms of weighting coefficients $\kappa_k^*$ to be applied to $\hat{\boldsymbol{\Gamma}}_k$ when the population autocovariances in expression [10.4.3] are replaced by sample autocovariances. Such an estimate would take the form

$$\hat{\mathbf{s}}_{\mathbf{Y}}(\omega) = (2\pi)^{-1}\left\{\hat{\boldsymbol{\Gamma}}_0 + \sum_{k=1}^{T-1} \kappa_k^*[\hat{\boldsymbol{\Gamma}}_k e^{-i\omega k} + \hat{\boldsymbol{\Gamma}}_k' e^{i\omega k}]\right\}$$

where

$$\hat{\Gamma}_k = T^{-1} \sum_{t=k+1}^{T} (\mathbf{y}_t - \bar{\mathbf{y}})(\mathbf{y}_{t-k} - \bar{\mathbf{y}})'$$

$$\bar{\mathbf{y}} = T^{-1} \sum_{t=1}^{T} \mathbf{y}_t.$$

For example, the modified Bartlett estimate of the multivariate spectrum is

$$\hat{\mathbf{s}}_{\mathbf{Y}}(\omega) = (2\pi)^{-1} \left\{ \hat{\Gamma}_0 + \sum_{k=1}^{q} \left[ 1 - \frac{k}{q+1} \right] [\hat{\Gamma}_k e^{-i\omega k} + \hat{\Gamma}_k' e^{i\omega k}] \right\}. \quad [10.4.42]$$

## *Filters*

Let $\mathbf{x}_t$ be an $r$-dimensional covariance-stationary process with absolutely summable autocovariances and with $(r \times r)$ population spectrum denoted $\mathbf{s}_{\mathbf{X}}(\omega)$. Let $\{\mathbf{H}_k\}_{k=-\infty}^{\infty}$ be an absolutely summable sequence of $(n \times r)$ matrices, and let $\mathbf{y}_t$ denote the $n$-dimensional vector process given by

$$\mathbf{y}_t = \mathbf{H}(L)\mathbf{x}_t = \sum_{k=-\infty}^{\infty} \mathbf{H}_k \mathbf{x}_{t-k}.$$

It follows from [10.3.9] that the population spectrum of $\mathbf{y}$ (denoted $\mathbf{s}_{\mathbf{Y}}(\omega)$) is related to that of $\mathbf{x}$ according to

$$\underset{(n \times n)}{\mathbf{s}_{\mathbf{Y}}(\omega)} = \underset{(n \times r)}{[\mathbf{H}(e^{-i\omega})]} \underset{(r \times r)}{\mathbf{s}_{\mathbf{X}}(\omega)} \underset{(r \times n)}{[\mathbf{H}(e^{i\omega})]'}. \quad [10.4.43]$$

As a special case of this result, let $X_t$ be a univariate stationary stochastic process with continuous spectrum $s_X(\omega)$, and let $u_t$ be a second univariate stationary stochastic process with continuous spectrum $s_U(\omega)$, where $X_t$ and $u_\tau$ are uncorrelated for all $t$ and $\tau$. Thus, the population spectrum of the vector $\mathbf{x}_t \equiv (X_t, u_t)'$ is given by

$$\mathbf{s}_{\mathbf{X}}(\omega) = \begin{bmatrix} s_{XX}(\omega) & 0 \\ 0 & s_{UU}(\omega) \end{bmatrix}.$$

Define a new series $Y_t$ according to

$$Y_t = \sum_{k=-\infty}^{\infty} h_k X_{t-k} + u_t \equiv h(L)X_t + u_t, \quad [10.4.44]$$

where $\{h_k\}_{k=-\infty}^{\infty}$ is absolutely summable. Note that the vector $\mathbf{y}_t \equiv (X_t, Y_t)'$ is obtained from the original vector $\mathbf{x}_t$ by the filter

$$\mathbf{y}_t = \mathbf{H}(L)\mathbf{x}_t,$$

where

$$\mathbf{H}(L) = \begin{bmatrix} 1 & 0 \\ h(L) & 1 \end{bmatrix}.$$

It follows from [10.4.43] that the spectrum of $\mathbf{y}$ is given by

$$\mathbf{s_Y}(\omega) = \begin{bmatrix} 1 & 0 \\ h(e^{-i\omega}) & 1 \end{bmatrix} \begin{bmatrix} s_{XX}(\omega) & 0 \\ 0 & s_{UU}(\omega) \end{bmatrix} \begin{bmatrix} 1 & h(e^{i\omega}) \\ 0 & 1 \end{bmatrix}$$
$$= \begin{bmatrix} s_{XX}(\omega) & s_{XX}(\omega)h(e^{i\omega}) \\ h(e^{-i\omega})s_{XX}(\omega) & h(e^{-i\omega})s_{XX}(\omega)h(e^{i\omega}) + s_{UU}(\omega) \end{bmatrix}, \qquad [10.4.45]$$

where

$$h(e^{-i\omega}) = \sum_{k=-\infty}^{\infty} h_k e^{-i\omega k}. \qquad [10.4.46]$$

The lower left element of the matrix in [10.4.45] indicates that when $Y_t$ and $X_t$ are related according to [10.4.44], the cross spectrum from $X$ to $Y$ can be calculated by multiplying [10.4.46] by the spectrum of $X$.

We can also imagine going through these steps in reverse order. Specifically, suppose we are given an observed vector $\mathbf{y}_t = (X_t, Y_t)'$ with absolutely summable autocovariance matrices and with population spectrum given by

$$\mathbf{s_Y}(\omega) = \begin{bmatrix} s_{XX}(\omega) & s_{XY}(\omega) \\ s_{YX}(\omega) & s_{YY}(\omega) \end{bmatrix}. \qquad [10.4.47]$$

Then the linear projection of $Y_t$ on $\{X_{t-k}\}_{k=-\infty}^{\infty}$ exists and is of the form of [10.4.44], where $u_t$ would now be regarded as the population residual associated with the linear projection. The sequence of linear projection coefficients $\{h_k\}_{k=-\infty}^{\infty}$ can be summarized in terms of the function of $\omega$ given in [10.4.46]. Comparing the lower left elements of [10.4.47] and [10.4.45], this function must satisfy

$$h(e^{-i\omega})s_{XX}(\omega) = s_{YX}(\omega).$$

In other words, the function $h(e^{-i\omega})$ can be calculated from

$$h(e^{-i\omega}) = \frac{s_{YX}(\omega)}{s_{XX}(\omega)}, \qquad [10.4.48]$$

assuming that $s_{XX}(\omega)$ is not zero. When $s_{XX}(\omega) = 0$, we set $h(e^{-i\omega}) = 0$. This magnitude, the ratio of the cross spectrum from $X$ to $Y$ to the spectrum of $X$, is known as the *transfer function* from $X$ to $Y$.

The principles underlying [10.4.4] can further be used to uncover individual transfer function coefficients:

$$h_k = (2\pi)^{-1} \int_{-\pi}^{\pi} h(e^{-i\omega})e^{i\omega k}\, d\omega.$$

In other words, given an observed vector $(X_t, Y_t)'$ with absolutely summable autocovariance matrices and thus with continuous population spectrum of the form of [10.4.47], the coefficient on $X_{t-k}$ in the population linear projection of $Y_t$ on $\{X_{t-k}\}_{k=-\infty}^{\infty}$ can be calculated from

$$h_k = (2\pi)^{-1} \int_{-\pi}^{\pi} \frac{s_{YX}(\omega)}{s_{XX}(\omega)} e^{i\omega k}\, d\omega. \qquad [10.4.49]$$

## 10.5. The Sample Mean of a Vector Process

### Variance of the Sample Mean

Suppose we have a sample of size $T$, $\{\mathbf{y}_1, \mathbf{y}_2, \ldots, \mathbf{y}_T\}$, drawn from an $n$-dimensional covariance-stationary process with

$$E(\mathbf{y}_t) = \boldsymbol{\mu} \qquad [10.5.1]$$

$$E[(\mathbf{y}_t - \boldsymbol{\mu})(\mathbf{y}_{t-j} - \boldsymbol{\mu})'] = \boldsymbol{\Gamma}_j. \qquad [10.5.2]$$

Consider the properties of the sample mean,

$$\bar{\mathbf{y}}_T = (1/T)\sum_{t=1}^{T} \mathbf{y}_t. \qquad [10.5.3]$$

As in the discussion in Section 7.2 of the sample mean of a scalar process, it is clear that $E(\bar{\mathbf{y}}_T) = \boldsymbol{\mu}$ and

$$\begin{aligned}
&E[(\bar{\mathbf{y}}_T - \boldsymbol{\mu})(\bar{\mathbf{y}}_T - \boldsymbol{\mu})'] \\
&\quad = (1/T^2)E\{(\mathbf{y}_1 - \boldsymbol{\mu})[(\mathbf{y}_1 - \boldsymbol{\mu})' + (\mathbf{y}_2 - \boldsymbol{\mu})' + \cdots + (\mathbf{y}_T - \boldsymbol{\mu})'] \\
&\qquad + (\mathbf{y}_2 - \boldsymbol{\mu})[(\mathbf{y}_1 - \boldsymbol{\mu})' + (\mathbf{y}_2 - \boldsymbol{\mu})' + \cdots + (\mathbf{y}_T - \boldsymbol{\mu})'] \\
&\qquad + (\mathbf{y}_3 - \boldsymbol{\mu})[(\mathbf{y}_1 - \boldsymbol{\mu})' + (\mathbf{y}_2 - \boldsymbol{\mu})' + \cdots + (\mathbf{y}_T - \boldsymbol{\mu})'] \\
&\qquad + \cdots + (\mathbf{y}_T - \boldsymbol{\mu})[(\mathbf{y}_1 - \boldsymbol{\mu})' + (\mathbf{y}_2 - \boldsymbol{\mu})' + \cdots + (\mathbf{y}_T - \boldsymbol{\mu})']\} \\
&\quad = (1/T^2)\{[\boldsymbol{\Gamma}_0 + \boldsymbol{\Gamma}_{-1} + \cdots + \boldsymbol{\Gamma}_{-(T-1)}] \qquad [10.5.4] \\
&\qquad + [\boldsymbol{\Gamma}_1 + \boldsymbol{\Gamma}_0 + \boldsymbol{\Gamma}_{-1} + \cdots + \boldsymbol{\Gamma}_{-(T-2)}] \\
&\qquad + [\boldsymbol{\Gamma}_2 + \boldsymbol{\Gamma}_1 + \boldsymbol{\Gamma}_0 + \boldsymbol{\Gamma}_{-1} + \cdots + \boldsymbol{\Gamma}_{-(T-3)}] \\
&\qquad + \cdots + [\boldsymbol{\Gamma}_{T-1} + \boldsymbol{\Gamma}_{T-2} + \boldsymbol{\Gamma}_{T-3} + \cdots + \boldsymbol{\Gamma}_0]\} \\
&\quad = (1/T^2)\{T\boldsymbol{\Gamma}_0 + (T-1)\boldsymbol{\Gamma}_1 + (T-2)\boldsymbol{\Gamma}_2 + \cdots + \boldsymbol{\Gamma}_{T-1} \\
&\qquad + (T-1)\boldsymbol{\Gamma}_{-1} + (T-2)\boldsymbol{\Gamma}_{-2} + \cdots + \boldsymbol{\Gamma}_{-(T-1)}\}.
\end{aligned}$$

Thus,

$$\begin{aligned}
&T \cdot E[(\bar{\mathbf{y}}_T - \boldsymbol{\mu})(\bar{\mathbf{y}}_T - \boldsymbol{\mu})'] \\
&\quad = \boldsymbol{\Gamma}_0 + [(T-1)/T]\boldsymbol{\Gamma}_1 + [(T-2)/T]\boldsymbol{\Gamma}_2 + \cdots \qquad [10.5.5] \\
&\qquad + [1/T]\boldsymbol{\Gamma}_{T-1} + [(T-1)/T]\boldsymbol{\Gamma}_{-1} + [(T-2)/T]\boldsymbol{\Gamma}_{-2} \\
&\qquad + \cdots + [1/T]\boldsymbol{\Gamma}_{-(T-1)}.
\end{aligned}$$

As in the univariate case, the weights on $\boldsymbol{\Gamma}_k$ for $|k|$ small go to unity as $T \to \infty$, and higher autocovariances go to zero for a covariance-stationary process. Hence, we have the following generalization of Proposition 7.5.

***Proposition 10.5:*** *Let $\mathbf{y}_t$ be a covariance-stationary process with moments given by [10.5.1] and [10.5.2] and with absolutely summable autocovariances. Then the sample mean [10.5.3] satisfies*

*(a)* $\bar{\mathbf{y}}_T \xrightarrow{p} \boldsymbol{\mu}$

*(b)* $\lim_{T\to\infty} \{T \cdot E[(\bar{\mathbf{y}}_T - \boldsymbol{\mu})(\bar{\mathbf{y}}_T - \boldsymbol{\mu})']\} = \sum_{\nu=-\infty}^{\infty} \boldsymbol{\Gamma}_\nu.$

The proof of Proposition 10.5 is virtually identical to that of Proposition 7.5. Consider the following $(n \times n)$ matrix:

$$\sum_{v=-\infty}^{\infty} \mathbf{\Gamma}_v - T \cdot E[(\bar{\mathbf{y}}_T - \boldsymbol{\mu})(\bar{\mathbf{y}}_T - \boldsymbol{\mu})'] = \sum_{|v| \geq T} \mathbf{\Gamma}_v + \sum_{v=-(T-1)}^{T-1} (|v|/T)\mathbf{\Gamma}_v, \qquad [10.5.6]$$

where the equality follows from [10.5.5]. Let $\gamma_{ij}^{(v)}$ denote the row $i$, column $j$ element of $\mathbf{\Gamma}_v$. The row $i$, column $j$ element of the matrix in [10.5.6] can then be written

$$\sum_{|v| \geq T} \gamma_{ij}^{(v)} + \sum_{v=-(T-1)}^{T-1} (|v|/T)\gamma_{ij}^{(v)}.$$

Absolutely summability of $\{\mathbf{\Gamma}_v\}_{v=-\infty}^{\infty}$ implies that for any $\varepsilon > 0$ there exists a $q$ such that

$$\sum_{|v| > q} |\gamma_{ij}^{(v)}| < \varepsilon/2.$$

Thus,

$$\left| \sum_{|v| \geq T} \gamma_{ij}^{(v)} + \sum_{v=-(T-1)}^{T-1} (|v|/T)\gamma_{ij}^{(v)} \right| < \varepsilon/2 + \sum_{v=-q}^{q} (|v|/T)|\gamma_{ij}^{(v)}|.$$

This sum can be made less than $\varepsilon$ by choosing $T$ sufficiently large. This establishes claim (b) of Proposition 10.5. From this result, $E(\bar{y}_{i,T} - \mu_i)^2 \to 0$ for each $i$, implying that $\bar{y}_{i,T} \xrightarrow{p} \mu_i$.

## *Consistent Estimation of* T *Times the Variance of the Sample Mean*

Hypothesis tests about the sample mean require an estimate of the matrix in result (b) of Proposition 10.5. Let $\mathbf{S}$ represent this matrix:

$$\mathbf{S} \equiv \lim_{T \to \infty} T \cdot E[(\bar{\mathbf{y}}_T - \boldsymbol{\mu})(\bar{\mathbf{y}}_T - \boldsymbol{\mu})']. \qquad [10.5.7]$$

If the data were generated by a vector $MA(q)$ process, then result (b) would imply

$$\mathbf{S} = \sum_{v=-q}^{q} \mathbf{\Gamma}_v. \qquad [10.5.8]$$

A natural estimate then is

$$\hat{\mathbf{S}} = \hat{\mathbf{\Gamma}}_0 + \sum_{v=1}^{q} (\hat{\mathbf{\Gamma}}_v + \hat{\mathbf{\Gamma}}_v'), \qquad [10.5.9]$$

where

$$\hat{\mathbf{\Gamma}}_v = (1/T) \sum_{t=v+1}^{T} (\mathbf{y}_t - \bar{\mathbf{y}})(\mathbf{y}_{t-v} - \bar{\mathbf{y}})'. \qquad [10.5.10]$$

As long as $\mathbf{y}_t$ is ergodic for second moments, [10.5.9] gives a consistent estimate of [10.5.8]. Indeed, Hansen (1982) and White (1984, Chapter 6) noted that [10.5.9] gives a consistent estimate of the asymptotic variance of the sample mean for a broad class of processes exhibiting time-dependent heteroskedasticity and autocorrelation. To see why, note that for a process satisfying $E(\mathbf{y}_t) = \boldsymbol{\mu}$ with time-varying second moments, the variance of the sample mean is given by

$$
\begin{aligned}
E[(\bar{\mathbf{y}}_T - \boldsymbol{\mu})(\bar{\mathbf{y}}_T - \boldsymbol{\mu})'] \\
&= E\left[(1/T)\sum_{t=1}^{T}(\mathbf{y}_t - \boldsymbol{\mu})\right]\left[(1/T)\sum_{s=1}^{T}(\mathbf{y}_s - \boldsymbol{\mu})\right]' \\
&= (1/T^2)\sum_{t=1}^{T}\sum_{s=1}^{T} E[(\mathbf{y}_t - \boldsymbol{\mu})(\mathbf{y}_s - \boldsymbol{\mu})'].
\end{aligned}
\qquad [10.5.11]
$$

Suppose, first, that $E[(\mathbf{y}_t - \boldsymbol{\mu})(\mathbf{y}_s - \boldsymbol{\mu})'] = \mathbf{0}$ for $|t - s| > q$, as was the case for the vector $MA(q)$ process, though we generalize from the $MA(q)$ process to allow $E[(\mathbf{y}_t - \boldsymbol{\mu})(\mathbf{y}_s - \boldsymbol{\mu})']$ to be a function of $t$ for $|t - s| \leq q$. Then [10.5.11] implies

$$
\begin{aligned}
&T \cdot E[(\bar{\mathbf{y}}_T - \boldsymbol{\mu})(\bar{\mathbf{y}}_T - \boldsymbol{\mu})'] \\
&\quad = (1/T)\sum_{t=1}^{T} E[(\mathbf{y}_t - \boldsymbol{\mu})(\mathbf{y}_t - \boldsymbol{\mu})'] \\
&\qquad + (1/T)\sum_{t=2}^{T} \{E[(\mathbf{y}_t - \boldsymbol{\mu})(\mathbf{y}_{t-1} - \boldsymbol{\mu})'] + E[(\mathbf{y}_{t-1} - \boldsymbol{\mu})(\mathbf{y}_t - \boldsymbol{\mu})']\} \\
&\qquad + (1/T)\sum_{t=3}^{T} \{E[(\mathbf{y}_t - \boldsymbol{\mu})(\mathbf{y}_{t-2} - \boldsymbol{\mu})'] + E[(\mathbf{y}_{t-2} - \boldsymbol{\mu})(\mathbf{y}_t - \boldsymbol{\mu})']\} + \cdots \\
&\qquad + (1/T)\sum_{t=q+1}^{T} \{E[(\mathbf{y}_t - \boldsymbol{\mu})(\mathbf{y}_{t-q} - \boldsymbol{\mu})'] + E[(\mathbf{y}_{t-q} - \boldsymbol{\mu})(\mathbf{y}_t - \boldsymbol{\mu})']\}.
\end{aligned}
\qquad [10.5.12]
$$

The estimate [10.5.9] replaces

$$
(1/T)\sum_{t=v+1}^{T} E[(\mathbf{y}_t - \boldsymbol{\mu})(\mathbf{y}_{t-v} - \boldsymbol{\mu})'] \qquad [10.5.13]
$$

in [10.5.12] with

$$
(1/T)\sum_{t=v+1}^{T} (\mathbf{y}_t - \bar{\mathbf{y}}_T)(\mathbf{y}_{t-v} - \bar{\mathbf{y}}_T)', \qquad [10.5.14]
$$

and thus [10.5.9] provides a consistent estimate of the limit of [10.5.12] whenever [10.5.14] converges in probability to [10.5.13]. Hence, the estimator proposed in [10.5.9] can give a consistent estimate of $T$ times the variance of the sample mean in the presence of both heteroskedasticity and autocorrelation up through order $q$.

More generally, even if $E[(\mathbf{y}_t - \boldsymbol{\mu})(\mathbf{y}_s - \boldsymbol{\mu})']$ is nonzero for all $t$ and $s$, as long as this matrix goes to zero sufficiently quickly as $|t - s| \to \infty$, then there is still a sense in which $\hat{\mathbf{S}}_T$ in [10.5.9] can provide a consistent estimate of $\mathbf{S}$. Specifically, if, as the sample size $T$ grows, a larger number of sample autocovariances $q$ is used to form the estimate, then $\hat{\mathbf{S}}_T \xrightarrow{p} \mathbf{S}$ (see White, 1984, p. 155).

## *The Newey-West Estimator*

Although [10.5.9] gives a consistent estimate of $\mathbf{S}$, it has the drawback that [10.5.9] need not be positive semidefinite in small samples. If $\hat{\mathbf{S}}$ is not positive semidefinite, then some linear combination of the elements of $\mathbf{y}$ is asserted to have a negative variance, a considerable handicap in forming a hypothesis test!

Newey and West (1987) suggested the alternative estimate

$$
\tilde{\mathbf{S}} = \hat{\boldsymbol{\Gamma}}_0 + \sum_{v=1}^{q}\left[1 - \frac{v}{q+1}\right](\hat{\boldsymbol{\Gamma}}_v + \hat{\boldsymbol{\Gamma}}_v'), \qquad [10.5.15]
$$

where $\hat{\Gamma}_v$ is given by [10.5.10]. For example, for $q = 2$,

$$\tilde{S} = \hat{\Gamma}_0 + \tfrac{2}{3}(\hat{\Gamma}_1 + \hat{\Gamma}_1') + \tfrac{1}{3}(\hat{\Gamma}_2 + \hat{\Gamma}_2').$$

Newey and West showed that $\tilde{S}$ is positive semidefinite by construction and has the same consistency properties that were noted for $\hat{S}$, namely, that if $q$ and $T$ both go to infinity with $q/T^{1/4} \to 0$, then $\tilde{S}_T \xrightarrow{p} S$.

### *Application: Autocorrelation- and Heteroskedasticity-Consistent Standard Errors for Linear Regressions*

As an application of using the Newey-West weighting, consider the linear regression model

$$y_t = \mathbf{x}_t'\boldsymbol{\beta} + u_t$$

for $\mathbf{x}_t$ a $(k \times 1)$ vector of explanatory variables. Recall from equation [8.2.6] that the deviation of the *OLS* estimate $\mathbf{b}_T$ from the true value $\boldsymbol{\beta}$ satisfies

$$\sqrt{T}(\mathbf{b}_T - \boldsymbol{\beta}) = \left[(1/T)\sum_{t=1}^{T} \mathbf{x}_t\mathbf{x}_t'\right]^{-1}\left[(1/\sqrt{T})\sum_{t=1}^{T} \mathbf{x}_t u_t\right]. \qquad [10.5.16]$$

In calculating the asymptotic distribution of the *OLS* estimate $\mathbf{b}_T$, we usually assume that the first term in [10.5.16] converges in probability to $\mathbf{Q}^{-1}$:

$$\left[(1/T)\sum_{t=1}^{T} \mathbf{x}_t\mathbf{x}_t'\right]^{-1} \xrightarrow{p} \mathbf{Q}^{-1}. \qquad [10.5.17]$$

The second term in [10.5.16] can be viewed as $\sqrt{T}$ times the sample mean of the $(k \times 1)$ vector $\mathbf{x}_t u_t$:

$$\begin{aligned}\left[(1/\sqrt{T})\sum_{t=1}^{T} \mathbf{x}_t u_t\right] &= (\sqrt{T})(1/T)\sum_{t=1}^{T} \mathbf{y}_t, \\ &= \sqrt{T}\cdot\bar{\mathbf{y}}_T,\end{aligned} \qquad [10.5.18]$$

where $\mathbf{y}_t \equiv \mathbf{x}_t u_t$. Provided that $E(u_t|\mathbf{x}_t) = 0$, the vector $\mathbf{y}_t$ has mean zero. We can allow for conditional heteroskedasticity, autocorrelation, and time variation in the second moments of $\mathbf{y}_t$, as long as

$$\mathbf{S} \equiv \lim_{T\to\infty} T\cdot E(\bar{\mathbf{y}}_T\bar{\mathbf{y}}_T')$$

exists. Under general conditions,[4] it then turns out that

$$\left[(1/\sqrt{T})\sum_{t=1}^{T} \mathbf{x}_t u_t\right] = \sqrt{T}\cdot\bar{\mathbf{y}}_T \xrightarrow{L} N(\mathbf{0}, \mathbf{S}).$$

Substituting this and [10.5.17] into [10.5.16],

$$\sqrt{T}(\mathbf{b}_T - \boldsymbol{\beta}) \xrightarrow{L} N(\mathbf{0}, \mathbf{Q}^{-1}\mathbf{S}\mathbf{Q}^{-1}). \qquad [10.5.19]$$

In light of the foregoing discussion, we might hope to estimate $\mathbf{S}$ by

$$\hat{\mathbf{S}}_T = \hat{\Gamma}_{0,T} + \sum_{v=1}^{q}\left[1 - \frac{v}{q+1}\right](\hat{\Gamma}_{v,T} + \hat{\Gamma}_{v,T}'). \qquad [10.5.20]$$

[4]See, for example, White (1984, p. 119).

Here,

$$\hat{\Gamma}_{v,T} = (1/T) \sum_{t=v+1}^{T} (\mathbf{x}_t \hat{u}_{t,T} \hat{u}_{t-v,T} \mathbf{x}'_{t-v}),$$

$\hat{u}_{t,T}$ is the *OLS* residual for date $t$ in a sample of size $T$ ($\hat{u}_{t,T} = y_t - \mathbf{x}'_t \mathbf{b}_T$), and $q$ is a lag length beyond which we are willing to assume that the correlation between $\mathbf{x}_t u_t$ and $\mathbf{x}_{t-v} u_{t-v}$ is essentially zero. Clearly, $\mathbf{Q}$ is consistently estimated by $\hat{\mathbf{Q}}_T = (1/T)\Sigma_{t=1}^{T} \mathbf{x}_t \mathbf{x}'_t$. Substituting $\hat{\mathbf{Q}}_T$ and $\hat{\mathbf{S}}_T$ into [10.5.19], the suggestion is to treat the *OLS* estimate $\mathbf{b}_T$ as if

$$\mathbf{b}_T \approx N(\boldsymbol{\beta}, (\hat{\mathbf{V}}_T/T))$$

where

$$\begin{aligned}
\hat{\mathbf{V}}_T &= \hat{\mathbf{Q}}_T^{-1} \hat{\mathbf{S}}_T \hat{\mathbf{Q}}_T^{-1} \\
&= \left[(1/T) \sum_{t=1}^{T} \mathbf{x}_t \mathbf{x}'_t\right]^{-1} (1/T) \left[\sum_{t=1}^{T} \hat{u}_t^2 \mathbf{x}_t \mathbf{x}'_t \right. \\
&\quad \left. + \sum_{v=1}^{q} \left[1 - \frac{v}{q+1}\right] \sum_{t=v+1}^{T} (\mathbf{x}_t \hat{u}_t \hat{u}_{t-v} \mathbf{x}'_{t-v} + \mathbf{x}_{t-v} \hat{u}_{t-v} \hat{u}_t \mathbf{x}'_t)\right] \\
&\quad \times \left[(1/T) \sum_{t=1}^{T} \mathbf{x}_t \mathbf{x}'_t\right]^{-1},
\end{aligned}$$

that is, the variance of $\mathbf{b}_T$ is approximated by

$$\begin{aligned}
&(\hat{\mathbf{V}}_T/T) \\
&= \left[\sum_{t=1}^{T} \mathbf{x}_t \mathbf{x}'_t\right]^{-1} \left[\sum_{t=1}^{T} \hat{u}_t^2 \mathbf{x}_t \mathbf{x}'_t \right. \\
&\quad \left. + \sum_{v=1}^{q} \left[1 - \frac{v}{q+1}\right] \sum_{t=v+1}^{T} (\mathbf{x}_t \hat{u}_t \hat{u}_{t-v} \mathbf{x}'_{t-v} + \mathbf{x}_{t-v} \hat{u}_{t-v} \hat{u}_t \mathbf{x}'_t)\right] \left[\sum_{t=1}^{T} \mathbf{x}_t \mathbf{x}'_t\right]^{-1}
\end{aligned} \qquad [10.5.21]$$

where $\hat{u}_t$ is the *OLS* sample residual. The square root of the row $i$, column $i$ element of $\hat{\mathbf{V}}_T/T$ is known as a *heteroskedasticity- and autocorrelation-consistent standard error* for the $i$th element of the estimated *OLS* coefficient vector. The hope is that standard errors based on [10.5.21] will be robust to a variety of forms of heteroskedasticity and autocorrelation of the residuals $u_t$ of the regression.

## *Spectral-Based Estimators*

A number of alternative estimates of $\mathbf{S}$ in [10.5.7] have been suggested in the literature. Notice that as in the univariate case discussed in Section 7.2, if $\mathbf{y}_t$ is covariance-stationary, then $\mathbf{S}$ has the interpretation as the autocovariance-generating function $\mathbf{G_Y}(z) = \Sigma_{v=-\infty}^{\infty} \boldsymbol{\Gamma}_v z^v$ evaluated at $z = 1$, or, equivalently, as $2\pi$ times the population spectrum at frequency zero:

$$\mathbf{S} = \sum_{v=-\infty}^{\infty} \boldsymbol{\Gamma}_v = 2\pi \mathbf{s_Y}(0).$$

Indeed, the Newey-West estimator [10.5.15] is numerically identical to $2\pi$ times the Bartlett estimate of the multivariate spectrum described in [10.4.42] evaluated at frequency $\omega = 0$. Gallant (1987, p. 533) proposed a similar estimator based on a Parzen kernel,

$$\hat{\mathbf{S}} = \hat{\boldsymbol{\Gamma}}_0 + \sum_{v=1}^{q} k[v/(q+1)](\hat{\boldsymbol{\Gamma}}_v + \hat{\boldsymbol{\Gamma}}'_v),$$

where

$$k(z) = \begin{cases} 1 - 6z^2 + 6z^3 & \text{for } 0 \le z \le \frac{1}{2} \\ 2(1 - z)^3 & \text{for } \frac{1}{2} \le z \le 1 \\ 0 & \text{otherwise.} \end{cases}$$

For example, for $q = 2$, we have

$$\hat{\mathbf{S}} = \hat{\mathbf{\Gamma}}_0 + \tfrac{5}{9}(\hat{\mathbf{\Gamma}}_1 + \hat{\mathbf{\Gamma}}_1') + \tfrac{2}{27}(\hat{\mathbf{\Gamma}}_2 + \hat{\mathbf{\Gamma}}_2').$$

Andrews (1991) examined a number of alternative estimators and found the best results for a quadratic spectral kernel:

$$k(z) = \frac{3}{(6\pi z/5)^2}\left[\frac{\sin(6\pi z/5)}{6\pi z/5} - \cos(6\pi z/5)\right].$$

In contrast to the Newey-West and Gallant estimators, Andrews's suggestion makes use of all $T - 1$ estimated autocovariance estimators:

$$\hat{\mathbf{S}} = \frac{T}{T - k}\left[\hat{\mathbf{\Gamma}}_0 + \sum_{v=1}^{T-1} k\left(\frac{v}{q + 1}\right)(\hat{\mathbf{\Gamma}}_v + \hat{\mathbf{\Gamma}}_v')\right]. \qquad [10.5.22]$$

Even though [10.5.22] makes use of all computed autocovariances, there is still a bandwidth parameter $q$ to be chosen for constructing the kernel. For example, for $q = 2$,

$$\hat{\mathbf{\Gamma}}_0 + \sum_{v=1}^{T-1} k(v/3)(\hat{\mathbf{\Gamma}}_v + \hat{\mathbf{\Gamma}}_v') = \hat{\mathbf{\Gamma}}_0 + 0.85(\hat{\mathbf{\Gamma}}_1 + \hat{\mathbf{\Gamma}}_1') + 0.50(\hat{\mathbf{\Gamma}}_2 + \hat{\mathbf{\Gamma}}_2') + 0.14(\hat{\mathbf{\Gamma}}_3 + \hat{\mathbf{\Gamma}}_3') + \cdots.$$

Andrews recommended multiplying the estimate by $T/(T - k)$, where $\mathbf{y}_t = \mathbf{x}_t\hat{u}_t$ for $\hat{u}_t$ the sample *OLS* residual from a regression with $k$ explanatory variables. Andrews (1991) and Newey and West (1992) also offered some guidance for choosing an optimal value of the lag truncation or bandwidth parameter $q$ for each of the estimators of $\mathbf{S}$ that have been discussed here.

The estimators that have been described will work best when $\mathbf{y}_t$ has a finite moving average representation. Andrews and Monahan (1992) suggested an alternative approach to estimating $\mathbf{S}$ that also takes advantage of any autoregressive structure to the errors. Let $\mathbf{y}_t$ be a zero-mean vector, and let $\mathbf{S}$ be the asymptotic variance of the sample mean of $\mathbf{y}$. For example, if we want to calculate heteroskedasticity- and autocorrelation-consistent standard errors for *OLS* estimation, $\mathbf{y}_t$ would correspond to $\mathbf{x}_t\hat{u}_t$ where $\mathbf{x}_t$ is the vector of explanatory variables for the regression and $\hat{u}_t$ is the *OLS* residual. The first step in estimating $\mathbf{S}$ is to fit a low-order *VAR* for $\mathbf{y}_t$,

$$\mathbf{y}_t = \mathbf{\Phi}_1\mathbf{y}_{t-1} + \mathbf{\Phi}_2\mathbf{y}_{t-2} + \cdots + \mathbf{\Phi}_p\mathbf{y}_{t-p} + \mathbf{v}_t, \qquad [10.5.23]$$

where $\mathbf{v}_t$ is presumed to have some residual autocorrelation not entirely captured by the *VAR*. Note that since $\mathbf{y}_t$ has mean zero, no constant term is included in [10.5.23]. The $i$th row represented in [10.5.23] can be estimated by an *OLS* regression of the $i$th element of $\mathbf{y}_t$ on $p$ lags of all the elements of $\mathbf{y}$, though if any eigenvalue of $|\mathbf{I}_n\lambda^p - \hat{\mathbf{\Phi}}_1\lambda^{p-1} - \hat{\mathbf{\Phi}}_2\lambda^{p-2} - \cdots - \hat{\mathbf{\Phi}}_p| = 0$ is too close to the unit circle (say, greater than 0.97 in modulus), Andrews and Monahan (1992, p. 957) recommended altering the *OLS* estimates so as to reduce the largest eigenvalue.

The second step in the Andrews and Monahan procedure is to calculate an estimate $\mathbf{S}^*$ using one of the methods described previously based on the fitted residuals $\hat{\mathbf{v}}_t$ from [10.5.23]. For example,

$$\hat{\mathbf{S}}_T^* = \hat{\mathbf{\Gamma}}_0^* + \sum_{v=1}^{q}\left[1 - \frac{v}{q+1}\right](\hat{\mathbf{\Gamma}}_v^* + \hat{\mathbf{\Gamma}}_v^{*\prime}), \qquad [10.5.24]$$

where

$$\hat{\mathbf{\Gamma}}_v^* = (1/T)\sum_{t=v+1}^{T} \hat{\mathbf{v}}_t \hat{\mathbf{v}}_{t-v}'$$

and where $q$ is a parameter representing the maximal order of autocorrelation assumed for $\mathbf{v}_t$. The matrix $\hat{\mathbf{S}}_T^*$ will be recognized as an estimate of $2\pi \cdot \mathbf{s}_{\mathbf{V}}(0)$, where $\mathbf{s}_{\mathbf{V}}(\omega)$ is the spectral density of $\mathbf{v}$:

$$\mathbf{s}_{\mathbf{V}}(\omega) = (2\pi)^{-1} \sum_{v=-\infty}^{\infty} \{E(\mathbf{v}_t \mathbf{v}_{t-v}')\} e^{-i\omega v}.$$

Notice that the original series $\mathbf{y}_t$ can be obtained from $\mathbf{v}_t$ by applying the following filter:

$$\mathbf{y}_t = [\mathbf{I}_n - \mathbf{\Phi}_1 L - \mathbf{\Phi}_2 L^2 - \cdots - \mathbf{\Phi}_p L^p]^{-1}\mathbf{v}_t.$$

Thus, from [10.4.43], the spectral density of $\mathbf{y}$ is related to the spectral density of $\mathbf{v}$ according to

$$\begin{aligned}\mathbf{s}_{\mathbf{Y}}(\omega) = {} & \{[\mathbf{I}_n - \mathbf{\Phi}_1 e^{-i\omega} - \mathbf{\Phi}_2 e^{-2i\omega} - \cdots - \mathbf{\Phi}_p e^{-pi\omega}]\}^{-1} \mathbf{s}_{\mathbf{V}}(\omega) \\ & \times \{[\mathbf{I}_n - \mathbf{\Phi}_1 e^{i\omega} - \mathbf{\Phi}_2 e^{2i\omega} - \cdots - \mathbf{\Phi}_p e^{pi\omega}]'\}^{-1}.\end{aligned}$$

Hence, an estimate of $2\pi$ times the spectral density of $\mathbf{y}$ at frequency zero is given by

$$\begin{aligned}\hat{\mathbf{S}}_T = {} & \{[\mathbf{I}_n - \hat{\mathbf{\Phi}}_1 - \hat{\mathbf{\Phi}}_2 - \cdots - \hat{\mathbf{\Phi}}_p]\}^{-1}\hat{\mathbf{S}}_T^* \\ & \times \{[\mathbf{I}_n - \hat{\mathbf{\Phi}}_1 - \hat{\mathbf{\Phi}}_2 - \cdots - \hat{\mathbf{\Phi}}_p]'\}^{-1},\end{aligned} \qquad [10.5.25]$$

where $\hat{\mathbf{S}}_T^*$ is calculated from [10.5.24]. The matrix $\hat{\mathbf{S}}_T$ in [10.5.25] is the Andrews-Monahan (1992) estimate of $\mathbf{S}$, where

$$\mathbf{S} = \lim_{T\to\infty} T \cdot E(\bar{\mathbf{y}}_T \bar{\mathbf{y}}_T').$$

## APPENDIX 10.A. *Proofs of Chapter 10 Propositions*

■ **Proof of Proposition 10.1.** The eigenvalues of $\mathbf{F}$ are the values of $\lambda$ for which the following determinant is zero:

$$\begin{vmatrix} (\mathbf{\Phi}_1 - \lambda \mathbf{I}_n) & \mathbf{\Phi}_2 & \mathbf{\Phi}_3 & \cdots & \mathbf{\Phi}_{p-1} & \mathbf{\Phi}_p \\ \mathbf{I}_n & -\lambda\mathbf{I}_n & \mathbf{0} & \cdots & \mathbf{0} & \mathbf{0} \\ \mathbf{0} & \mathbf{I}_n & -\lambda\mathbf{I}_n & \cdots & \mathbf{0} & \mathbf{0} \\ \vdots & \vdots & \vdots & \cdots & \vdots & \vdots \\ \mathbf{0} & \mathbf{0} & \mathbf{0} & \cdots & \mathbf{I}_n & -\lambda\mathbf{I}_n \end{vmatrix}. \qquad [10.A.1]$$

Multiply each of the final block of $n$ columns by $(1/\lambda)$ and add to the previous block. Multiply each of the $n$ columns of this resulting next-to-final block by $(1/\lambda)$ and add the result to the third-to-last block of columns. Proceeding in this manner reveals [10.A.1] to be the same as

$$\begin{vmatrix} \mathbf{X}_1 & \mathbf{X}_2 \\ \mathbf{0} & -\lambda\mathbf{I}_{n(p-1)} \end{vmatrix}, \qquad [10.A.2]$$

where $\mathbf{X}_1$ denotes the following $(n \times n)$ matrix:

$$\mathbf{X}_1 \equiv (\mathbf{\Phi}_1 - \lambda\mathbf{I}_n) + (\mathbf{\Phi}_2/\lambda) + (\mathbf{\Phi}_3/\lambda^2) + \cdots + (\mathbf{\Phi}_p/\lambda^{p-1})$$

and $\mathbf{X}_2$ is a related $[n \times n(p-1)]$ matrix. Let $\mathbf{S}$ denote the following $(np \times np)$ matrix:

$$\mathbf{S} \equiv \begin{bmatrix} \mathbf{0} & \mathbf{I}_{n(p-1)} \\ \mathbf{I}_n & \mathbf{0} \end{bmatrix},$$

and note that its inverse is given by

$$\mathbf{S}^{-1} = \begin{bmatrix} \mathbf{0} & \mathbf{I}_n \\ \mathbf{I}_{n(p-1)} & \mathbf{0} \end{bmatrix},$$

as may be verified by direct multiplication. Premultiplying a matrix by $\mathbf{S}$ and postmultiplying by $\mathbf{S}^{-1}$ will not change the determinant. Thus, [10.A.2] is equal to

$$\left| \begin{bmatrix} \mathbf{0} & \mathbf{I}_{n(p-1)} \\ \mathbf{I}_n & \mathbf{0} \end{bmatrix} \begin{bmatrix} \mathbf{X}_1 & \mathbf{X}_2 \\ \mathbf{0} & -\lambda \mathbf{I}_{n(p-1)} \end{bmatrix} \begin{bmatrix} \mathbf{0} & \mathbf{I}_n \\ \mathbf{I}_{n(p-1)} & \mathbf{0} \end{bmatrix} \right| = \begin{vmatrix} -\lambda \mathbf{I}_{n(p-1)} & \mathbf{0} \\ \mathbf{X}_2 & \mathbf{X}_1 \end{vmatrix}. \qquad [10.A.3]$$

Applying the formula for calculating a determinant [A.4.5] recursively, [10.A.3] is equal to

$$\begin{aligned} (-\lambda)^{n(p-1)}|\mathbf{X}_1| &= (-\lambda)^{n(p-1)}|\mathbf{\Phi}_1 - \lambda \mathbf{I}_n + (\mathbf{\Phi}_2/\lambda) + (\mathbf{\Phi}_3/\lambda^2) + \cdots + (\mathbf{\Phi}_p/\lambda^{p-1})| \\ &= (-1)^{np}|\mathbf{I}_n\lambda^p - \mathbf{\Phi}_1\lambda^{p-1} - \mathbf{\Phi}_2\lambda^{p-2} - \cdots - \mathbf{\Phi}_p|. \end{aligned}$$

Setting this to zero produces equation [10.1.13]. ■

■ **Proof of Proposition 10.2.** It is helpful to define $z_t(i, l)$ to be the component of $y_{it}$ that reflects the cumulative effects of the $l$th element of $\boldsymbol{\varepsilon}$:

$$z_t(i, l) = \psi_{il}^{(0)}\varepsilon_{lt} + \psi_{il}^{(1)}\varepsilon_{l,t-1} + \psi_{il}^{(2)}\varepsilon_{l,t-2} + \cdots = \sum_{v=0}^{\infty} \psi_{il}^{(v)}\varepsilon_{l,t-v}, \qquad [10.A.4]$$

where $\psi_{il}^{(v)}$ denotes the row $i$, column $l$ element of the matrix $\mathbf{\Psi}_v$. The actual value of the $i$th variable $y_{it}$ is the sum of the contributions of each of the $l = 1, 2, \ldots, n$ components of $\boldsymbol{\varepsilon}$:

$$y_{it} = \mu_i + \sum_{l=1}^{n} z_t(i, l). \qquad [10.A.5]$$

The results of Proposition 10.2 are all established by first demonstrating absolute summability of the moments of $z_t(i, l)$ and then observing that the moments of $\mathbf{y}_t$ are obtained from finite sums of these expressions based on $z_t(i, l)$.

**Proof of (a).** Consider the random variable $z_t(i, l) \cdot z_{t-s}(j, m)$, where $i, l, j$, and $m$ represent arbitrary indices between 1 and $n$ and where $s$ is the order of the autocovariance of $\mathbf{y}$ that is being calculated. Note from [10.A.4] that

$$\begin{aligned} E\{z_t(i, l) \cdot z_{t-s}(j, m)\} &= E\left\{\left[\sum_{r=0}^{\infty} \psi_{il}^{(r)}\varepsilon_{l,t-r}\right] \times \left[\sum_{v=0}^{\infty} \psi_{jm}^{(v)}\varepsilon_{m,t-s-v}\right]\right\} \\ &= \sum_{r=0}^{\infty}\sum_{v=0}^{\infty} \{\psi_{il}^{(r)}\psi_{jm}^{(v)}\} \cdot E\{\varepsilon_{l,t-r}\varepsilon_{m,t-s-v}\}. \end{aligned} \qquad [10.A.6]$$

The expectation operator can be moved inside the summation here because

$$\sum_{r=0}^{\infty}\sum_{v=0}^{\infty} |\psi_{il}^{(r)}\psi_{jm}^{(v)}| = \sum_{r=0}^{\infty}\sum_{v=0}^{\infty} |\psi_{il}^{(r)}| \cdot |\psi_{jm}^{(v)}| = \left\{\sum_{r=0}^{\infty} |\psi_{il}^{(r)}|\right\} \times \left\{\sum_{v=0}^{\infty} |\psi_{jm}^{(v)}|\right\} < \infty.$$

Now, the product of $\varepsilon$'s in the final term in [10.A.6] can have nonzero expectation only if the $\varepsilon$'s have the same date, that is, if $r = s + v$. Thus, although [10.A.6] involves a sum over an infinite number of values of $r$, only the value at $r = s + v$ contributes to this sum:

$$E\{z_t(i, l) \cdot z_{t-s}(j, m)\} = \sum_{v=0}^{\infty} \{\psi_{il}^{(s+v)}\psi_{jm}^{(v)}\} \cdot E\{\varepsilon_{l,t-s-v}\varepsilon_{m,t-s-v}\} = \sum_{v=0}^{\infty} \psi_{il}^{(s+v)}\psi_{jm}^{(v)}\sigma_{lm}, \qquad [10.A.7]$$

where $\sigma_{lm}$ represents the covariance between $\varepsilon_{lt}$ and $\varepsilon_{mt}$ and is given by the row $l$, column $m$ element of $\mathbf{\Omega}$.

The row $i$, column $j$ element of $\mathbf{\Gamma}_s$ gives the value of

$$\gamma_{ij}^{(s)} = E(y_{it} - \mu_i)(y_{j,t-s} - \mu_j).$$

Using [10.A.5] and [10.A.7], this can be expressed as

$$\begin{aligned}
E(y_{it} - \mu_i)(y_{j,t-s} - \mu_j) &= E\left\{\left[\sum_{l=1}^{n} z_t(i, l)\right]\left[\sum_{m=1}^{n} z_{t-s}(j, m)\right]\right\} \\
&= \sum_{l=1}^{n} \sum_{m=1}^{n} E\{z_t(i, l) \cdot z_{t-s}(j, m)\} \\
&= \sum_{l=1}^{n} \sum_{m=1}^{n} \sum_{v=0}^{\infty} \psi_{il}^{(s+v)} \psi_{jm}^{(v)} \sigma_{lm} \\
&= \sum_{v=0}^{\infty} \sum_{l=1}^{n} \sum_{m=1}^{n} \psi_{il}^{(s+v)} \psi_{jm}^{(v)} \sigma_{lm}.
\end{aligned} \qquad [10.A.8]$$

But $\Sigma_{l=1}^{n} \Sigma_{m=1}^{n} \psi_{il}^{(s+v)} \psi_{jm}^{(v)} \sigma_{lm}$ is the row $i$, column $j$ element of $\mathbf{\Psi}_{v+s}\mathbf{\Omega}\mathbf{\Psi}_v'$. Thus, [10.A.8] states that the row $i$, column $j$ element of $\mathbf{\Gamma}_s$ is given by the row $i$, column $j$ element of $\Sigma_{v=0}^{\infty} \mathbf{\Psi}_{v+s}\mathbf{\Omega}\mathbf{\Psi}_v'$, as asserted in part (a).

**Proof of (b).** Define $h_s(\cdot)$ to be the moment in [10.A.7]:

$$h_s(i, j, l, m) \equiv E\{z_t(i, l) \cdot z_{t-s}(j, m)\} = \sum_{v=0}^{\infty} \psi_{il}^{(s+v)} \psi_{jm}^{(v)} \sigma_{lm};$$

and notice that the sequence $\{h_s(\cdot)\}_{s=0}^{\infty}$ is absolutely summable:

$$\begin{aligned}
\sum_{s=0}^{\infty} |h_s(i, j, l, m)| &\le \sum_{s=0}^{\infty} \sum_{v=0}^{\infty} |\psi_{il}^{(s+v)}| \cdot |\psi_{jm}^{(v)}| \cdot |\sigma_{lm}| \\
&= |\sigma_{lm}| \sum_{v=0}^{\infty} |\psi_{jm}^{(v)}| \sum_{s=0}^{\infty} |\psi_{il}^{(s+v)}| \\
&\le |\sigma_{lm}| \sum_{v=0}^{\infty} |\psi_{jm}^{(v)}| \sum_{s=0}^{\infty} |\psi_{il}^{(s)}| \\
&< \infty.
\end{aligned} \qquad [10.A.9]$$

Furthermore, the row $i$, column $j$ element of $\mathbf{\Gamma}_s$ was seen in [10.A.8] to be given by

$$\gamma_{ij}^{(s)} = \sum_{l=1}^{n} \sum_{m=1}^{n} h_s(i, j, l, m).$$

Hence,

$$\sum_{s=0}^{\infty} |\gamma_{ij}^{(s)}| \le \sum_{s=0}^{\infty} \sum_{l=1}^{n} \sum_{m=1}^{n} |h_s(i, j, l, m)| = \sum_{l=1}^{n} \sum_{m=1}^{n} \sum_{s=0}^{\infty} |h_s(i, j, l, m)|. \qquad [10.A.10]$$

From [10.A.9], there exists an $M < \infty$ such that

$$\sum_{s=0}^{\infty} |h_s(i, j, l, m)| < M$$

for any value of $i$, $j$, $l$, or $m$. Hence, [10.A.10] implies

$$\sum_{s=0}^{\infty} |\gamma_{ij}^{(s)}| < \sum_{l=1}^{n} \sum_{m=1}^{n} M = n^2 M < \infty,$$

confirming that the row $i$, column $j$ element of $\{\mathbf{\Gamma}_s\}_{s=0}^{\infty}$ is absolutely summable, as claimed by part (b).

**Proof of (c).** Essentially the identical algebra as in the proof of Proposition 7.10 establishes that

$$
\begin{aligned}
E|z_{t_1}(i_1, l_1)\cdot z_{t_2}(i_2, l_2)\cdot z_{t_3}(i_3, l_3)\cdot z_{t_4}(i_4, l_4)| \\
&= E\left|\left\{\sum_{v_1=0}^{\infty} \psi_{i_1,l_1}^{(v_1)}\varepsilon_{l_1,t_1-v_1}\right\}\cdot\left\{\sum_{v_2=0}^{\infty} \psi_{i_2,l_2}^{(v_2)}\varepsilon_{l_2,t_2-v_2}\right\}\right. \\
&\quad \left.\cdot\left\{\sum_{v_3=0}^{\infty} \psi_{i_3,l_3}^{(v_3)}\varepsilon_{l_3,t_3-v_3}\right\}\cdot\left\{\sum_{v_4=0}^{\infty} \psi_{i_4,l_4}^{(v_4)}\varepsilon_{l_4,t_4-v_4}\right\}\right| \qquad [10.A.11] \\
&\le \sum_{v_1=0}^{\infty}\sum_{v_2=0}^{\infty}\sum_{v_3=0}^{\infty}\sum_{v_4=0}^{\infty} |\psi_{i_1,l_1}^{(v_1)}\psi_{i_2,l_2}^{(v_2)}\psi_{i_3,l_3}^{(v_3)}\psi_{i_4,l_4}^{(v_4)}| \\
&\quad \times E|\varepsilon_{l_1,t_1-v_1}\varepsilon_{l_2,t_2-v_2}\varepsilon_{l_3,t_3-v_3}\varepsilon_{l_4,t_4-v_4}| \\
&< \infty.
\end{aligned}
$$

Now,

$$
\begin{aligned}
E|y_{i_1,t_1}y_{i_2,t_2}y_{i_3,t_3}y_{i_4,t_4}| &= E\left|\mu_{i_1} + \sum_{l_1=1}^{n} z_{t_1}(i_1, l_1)\right|\cdot\left|\mu_{i_2} + \sum_{l_2=1}^{n} z_{t_2}(i_2, l_2)\right| \\
&\quad \cdot\left|\mu_{i_3} + \sum_{l_3=1}^{n} z_{t_3}(i_3, l_3)\right|\cdot\left|\mu_{i_4} + \sum_{l_4=1}^{n} z_{t_4}(i_4, l_4)\right| \\
&\le E\left\{|\mu_{i_1}| + \sum_{l_1=1}^{n} |z_{t_1}(i_1, l_1)|\right\}\cdot\left\{|\mu_{i_2}| + \sum_{l_2=1}^{n} |z_{t_2}(i_2, l_2)|\right\} \\
&\quad \cdot\left\{|\mu_{i_3}| + \sum_{l_3=1}^{n} |z_{t_3}(i_3, l_3)|\right\}\cdot\left\{|\mu_{i_4}| + \sum_{l_4=1}^{n} |z_{t_4}(i_4, l_4)|\right\}.
\end{aligned}
$$

But this is a finite sum involving terms of the form of [10.A.11]—which were seen to be finite—along with terms involving first through third moments of $z$, which must also be finite.

**Proof of (d).** Notice that

$$
z_t(i, l)\cdot z_{t-s}(j, m) = \sum_{r=0}^{\infty}\sum_{v=0}^{\infty} \psi_{il}^{(r)}\psi_{jm}^{(v)}\varepsilon_{l,t-r}\varepsilon_{m,t-s-v}.
$$

The same argument leading to [7.2.14] can be used to establish that

$$
(1/T)\sum_{t=1}^{T} z_t(i, l)\cdot z_{t-s}(j, m) \xrightarrow{p} E\{z_t(i, l)\cdot z_{t-s}(j, m)\}. \qquad [10.A.12]
$$

To see that [10.A.12] implies ergodicity for the second moments of $\mathbf{y}$, notice from [10.A.5] that

$$
\begin{aligned}
(1/T)\sum_{t=1}^{T} y_{it}y_{j,t-s} &= (1/T)\sum_{t=1}^{T}\left[\mu_i + \sum_{l=1}^{n} z_t(i, l)\right]\left[\mu_j + \sum_{m=1}^{n} z_{t-s}(j, m)\right] \\
&= \mu_i\mu_j + \mu_i\sum_{m=1}^{n}\left[(1/T)\sum_{t=1}^{T} z_{t-s}(j, m)\right] + \mu_j\sum_{l=1}^{n}\left[(1/T)\sum_{t=1}^{T} z_t(i, l)\right] \\
&\quad + \sum_{l=1}^{n}\sum_{m=1}^{n}\left[(1/T)\sum_{t=1}^{T} z_t(i, l)z_{t-s}(j, m)\right] \\
&\xrightarrow{p} \mu_i\mu_j + \mu_i\sum_{m=1}^{n} E[z_{t-s}(j, m)] + \mu_j\sum_{l=1}^{n} E[z_t(i, l)] \\
&\quad + \sum_{l=1}^{n}\sum_{m=1}^{n} E[z_t(i, l)z_{t-s}(j, m)] \\
&= E\left\{\left[\mu_i + \sum_{l=1}^{n} z_t(i, l)\right]\left[\mu_j + \sum_{m=1}^{n} z_{t-s}(j, m)\right]\right\} \\
&= E[y_{it}y_{j,t-s}],
\end{aligned}
$$

as claimed. ∎

■ **Proof of Proposition 10.3.** Writing out [10.2.11] explicitly,

$$\begin{aligned}\mathbf{H}(L)\mathbf{\Psi}(L) &= (\cdots + \mathbf{H}_{-1}L^{-1} + \mathbf{H}_0L^0 + \mathbf{H}_1L^1 + \cdots)\\ &\quad\times(\mathbf{\Psi}_0L^0 + \mathbf{\Psi}_1L^1 + \mathbf{\Psi}_2L^2 + \cdots),\end{aligned}$$

from which the coefficient on $L^k$ is

$$\mathbf{B}_k = \mathbf{H}_k\mathbf{\Psi}_0 + \mathbf{H}_{k-1}\mathbf{\Psi}_1 + \mathbf{H}_{k-2}\mathbf{\Psi}_2 + \cdots. \qquad [10.A.13]$$

Let $b_{ij}^{(k)}$ denote the row $i$, column $j$ element of $\mathbf{B}_k$, and let $h_{ij}^{(k)}$ and $\psi_{ij}^{(k)}$ denote the row $i$, column $j$ elements of $\mathbf{H}_k$ and $\mathbf{\Psi}_k$, respectively. Then the row $i$, column $j$ element of the matrix equation [10.A.13] states that

$$b_{ij}^{(k)} = \sum_{m=1}^{n} h_{im}^{(k)}\psi_{mj}^{(0)} + \sum_{m=1}^{n} h_{im}^{(k-1)}\psi_{mj}^{(1)} + \sum_{m=1}^{n} h_{im}^{(k-2)}\psi_{mj}^{(2)} + \cdots = \sum_{v=0}^{\infty}\sum_{m=1}^{n} h_{im}^{(k-v)}\psi_{mj}^{(v)}.$$

Thus,

$$\begin{aligned}\sum_{k=-\infty}^{\infty} |b_{ij}^{(k)}| &= \sum_{k=-\infty}^{\infty}\left|\sum_{v=0}^{\infty}\sum_{m=1}^{n} h_{im}^{(k-v)}\psi_{mj}^{(v)}\right|\\ &\le \sum_{k=-\infty}^{\infty}\sum_{v=0}^{\infty}\sum_{m=1}^{n} |h_{im}^{(k-v)}\psi_{mj}^{(v)}| \qquad [10.A.14]\\ &= \sum_{m=1}^{n}\sum_{v=0}^{\infty}|\psi_{mj}^{(v)}|\sum_{k=-\infty}^{\infty}|h_{im}^{(k-v)}|.\end{aligned}$$

But since $\{\mathbf{H}_k\}_{k=-\infty}^{\infty}$ and $\{\mathbf{\Psi}_k\}_{k=-\infty}^{\infty}$ are absolutely summable,

$$\sum_{k=-\infty}^{\infty}|h_{im}^{(k-v)}| < M_1 < \infty$$

$$\sum_{v=0}^{\infty}|\psi_{mj}^{(v)}| < M_2 < \infty.$$

Thus, [10.A.14] becomes

$$\sum_{k=-\infty}^{\infty}|b_{ij}^{(k)}| < \sum_{m=1}^{n} M_1M_2 < \infty. \quad ■$$

■ **Proof of Proposition 10.4.** Let $\mathbf{A}$ be $(m \times n)$, $\mathbf{B}$ be $(n \times r)$, and $\mathbf{C}$ be $(r \times q)$. Let the $(n \times 1)$ vector $\mathbf{b}_i$ denote the $i$th column of $\mathbf{B}$, and let $c_{ij}$ denote the row $i$, column $j$ element of $\mathbf{C}$. Then

$$\begin{aligned}\mathbf{ABC} &= \mathbf{A}[\mathbf{b}_1 \;\; \mathbf{b}_2 \;\cdots\; \mathbf{b}_r]\begin{bmatrix} c_{11} & c_{12} & \cdots & c_{1q}\\ c_{21} & c_{22} & \cdots & c_{2q}\\ \vdots & \vdots & \cdots & \vdots\\ c_{r1} & c_{r2} & \cdots & c_{rq}\end{bmatrix}\\ &= [\{\mathbf{Ab}_1c_{11} + \mathbf{Ab}_2c_{21} + \cdots + \mathbf{Ab}_rc_{r1}\}\\ &\qquad \{\mathbf{Ab}_1c_{12} + \mathbf{Ab}_2c_{22} + \cdots + \mathbf{Ab}_rc_{r2}\}\cdots\\ &\qquad\quad \{\mathbf{Ab}_1c_{1q} + \mathbf{Ab}_2c_{2q} + \cdots + \mathbf{Ab}_rc_{rq}\}]\\ &= [\{c_{11}\mathbf{Ab}_1 + c_{21}\mathbf{Ab}_2 + \cdots + c_{r1}\mathbf{Ab}_r\}\\ &\qquad \{c_{12}\mathbf{Ab}_1 + c_{22}\mathbf{Ab}_2 + \cdots + c_{r2}\mathbf{Ab}_r\}\cdots\\ &\qquad\quad \{c_{1q}\mathbf{Ab}_1 + c_{2q}\mathbf{Ab}_2 + \cdots + c_{rq}\mathbf{Ab}_r\}].\end{aligned}$$

Applying the vec operator gives

$$\begin{aligned}\operatorname{vec}(\mathbf{ABC}) &= \begin{bmatrix} c_{11}\mathbf{Ab}_1 + c_{21}\mathbf{Ab}_2 + \cdots + c_{r1}\mathbf{Ab}_r\\ c_{12}\mathbf{Ab}_1 + c_{22}\mathbf{Ab}_2 + \cdots + c_{r2}\mathbf{Ab}_r\\ \vdots\\ c_{1q}\mathbf{Ab}_1 + c_{2q}\mathbf{Ab}_2 + \cdots + c_{rq}\mathbf{Ab}_r\end{bmatrix}\\ &= \begin{bmatrix} c_{11}\mathbf{A} & c_{21}\mathbf{A} & \cdots & c_{r1}\mathbf{A}\\ c_{12}\mathbf{A} & c_{22}\mathbf{A} & \cdots & c_{r2}\mathbf{A}\\ \vdots & \vdots & \cdots & \vdots\\ c_{1q}\mathbf{A} & c_{2q}\mathbf{A} & \cdots & c_{rq}\mathbf{A}\end{bmatrix}\begin{bmatrix}\mathbf{b}_1\\ \mathbf{b}_2\\ \vdots\\ \mathbf{b}_r\end{bmatrix}\\ &= (\mathbf{C}' \otimes \mathbf{A})\cdot\operatorname{vec}(\mathbf{B}). \quad ■\end{aligned}$$

## Chapter 10 Exercises

10.1. Consider a scalar $AR(p)$ process ($n = 1$). Deduce from equation [10.2.19] that the $(p \times 1)$ vector consisting of the variance and first $(p - 1)$ autocovariances,

$$\begin{bmatrix} \gamma_0 \\ \gamma_1 \\ \gamma_2 \\ \vdots \\ \gamma_{p-1} \end{bmatrix},$$

can be calculated from the first $p$ elements in the first column of the $(p^2 \times p^2)$ matrix $\sigma^2[\mathbf{I}_{p^2} - (\mathbf{F} \otimes \mathbf{F})]^{-1}$ for $\mathbf{F}$ the $(p \times p)$ matrix defined in equation [1.2.3] in Chapter 1.

10.2. Let $\mathbf{y}_t = (X_t, Y_t)'$ be given by

$$X_t = \varepsilon_t + \theta\varepsilon_{t-1}$$
$$Y_t = h_1 X_{t-1} + u_t,$$

where $(\varepsilon_t, u_t)'$ is vector white noise with contemporaneous variance-covariance matrix given by

$$\begin{bmatrix} E(\varepsilon_t^2) & E(\varepsilon_t u_t) \\ E(u_t\varepsilon_t) & E(u_t^2) \end{bmatrix} = \begin{bmatrix} \sigma_\varepsilon^2 & 0 \\ 0 & \sigma_u^2 \end{bmatrix}.$$

(a) Calculate the autocovariance matrices $\{\mathbf{\Gamma}_k\}_{k=-\infty}^{\infty}$ for this process.

(b) Use equation [10.4.3] to calculate the population spectrum. Find the cospectrum between $X$ and $Y$ and the quadrature spectrum from $X$ to $Y$.

(c) Verify that your answer to part (b) could equivalently be calculated from expression [10.4.45].

(d) Verify by integrating your answer to part (b) that [10.4.49] holds; that is, show that

$$(2\pi)^{-1} \int_{-\pi}^{\pi} \frac{s_{YX}(\omega)}{s_{XX}(\omega)} e^{i\omega k}\, d\omega = \begin{cases} h_1 & \text{for } k = 1 \\ 0 & \text{for other integer } k. \end{cases}$$

## Chapter 10 References


Andrews, Donald W. K. 1991. "Heteroskedasticity and Autocorrelation Consistent Covariance Matrix Estimation." *Econometrica* 59:817–58.

——— and J. Christopher Monahan. 1992. "An Improved Heteroskedasticity and Autocorrelation Consistent Covariance Matrix Estimator." *Econometrica* 60:953–66.

Fuller, Wayne A. 1976. *Introduction to Statistical Time Series.* New York: Wiley.

Gallant, A. Ronald. 1987. *Nonlinear Statistical Models.* New York: Wiley.

Hansen, Lars P. 1982. "Large Sample Properties of Generalized Method of Moments Estimators." *Econometrica* 50:1029–54.

Newey, Whitney K., and Kenneth D. West. 1987. "A Simple Positive Semi-Definite, Heteroskedasticity and Autocorrelation Consistent Covariance Matrix." *Econometrica* 55: 703–8.

——— and ———. 1992. "Automatic Lag Selection in Covariance Matrix Estimation." University of Wisconsin, Madison, Mimeo.

Sims, Christopher A. 1980. "Macroeconomics and Reality." *Econometrica* 48:1–48.

White, Halbert. 1984. *Asymptotic Theory for Econometricians.* Orlando, Fla.: Academic Press.

# 11

# *Vector Autoregressions*

The previous chapter introduced some basic tools for describing vector time series processes. This chapter looks in greater depth at vector autoregressions, which are particularly convenient for estimation and forecasting. Their popularity for analyzing the dynamics of economic systems is due to Sims's (1980) influential work. The chapter begins with a discussion of maximum likelihood estimation and hypothesis testing. Section 11.2 examines a concept of causation in bivariate systems proposed by Granger (1969). Section 11.3 generalizes the discussion of Granger causality to multivariate systems and examines estimation of restricted vector autoregressions. Sections 11.4 and 11.5 introduce impulse-response functions and variance decompositions, which are used to summarize the dynamic relations between the variables in a vector autoregression. Section 11.6 reviews how such summaries can be used to evaluate structural hypotheses. Section 11.7 develops formulas needed to calculate standard errors for impulse-response functions.

## 11.1. *Maximum Likelihood Estimation and Hypothesis Testing for an Unrestricted Vector Autoregression*

### *The Conditional Likelihood Function for a Vector Autoregression*

Let $\mathbf{y}_t$ denote an $(n \times 1)$ vector containing the values that $n$ variables assume at date $t$. The dynamics of $\mathbf{y}_t$ are presumed to be governed by a $p$th-order Gaussian vector autoregression,

$$\mathbf{y}_t = \mathbf{c} + \mathbf{\Phi}_1\mathbf{y}_{t-1} + \mathbf{\Phi}_2\mathbf{y}_{t-2} + \cdots + \mathbf{\Phi}_p\mathbf{y}_{t-p} + \boldsymbol{\varepsilon}_t, \qquad [11.1.1]$$

with $\boldsymbol{\varepsilon}_t \sim$ i.i.d. $N(\mathbf{0}, \mathbf{\Omega})$.

Suppose we have observed each of these $n$ variables for $(T + p)$ time periods. As in the scalar autoregression, the simplest approach is to condition on the first $p$ observations (denoted $\mathbf{y}_{-p+1}, \mathbf{y}_{-p+2}, \ldots, \mathbf{y}_0$) and to base estimation on the last $T$ observations (denoted $\mathbf{y}_1, \mathbf{y}_2, \ldots, \mathbf{y}_T$). The objective then is to form the conditional likelihood

$$f_{\mathbf{Y}_T,\mathbf{Y}_{T-1},\ldots,\mathbf{Y}_1|\mathbf{Y}_0,\mathbf{Y}_{-1},\ldots,\mathbf{Y}_{-p+1}}(\mathbf{y}_T, \mathbf{y}_{T-1}, \ldots, \mathbf{y}_1|\mathbf{y}_0, \mathbf{y}_{-1}, \ldots, \mathbf{y}_{-p+1}; \boldsymbol{\theta}) \qquad [11.1.2]$$

and maximize with respect to $\boldsymbol{\theta}$, where $\boldsymbol{\theta}$ is a vector that contains the elements of $\mathbf{c}, \mathbf{\Phi}_1, \mathbf{\Phi}_2, \ldots, \mathbf{\Phi}_p$, and $\mathbf{\Omega}$. Vector autoregressions are invariably estimated on the basis of the conditional likelihood function [11.1.2] rather than the full-sample unconditional likelihood. For brevity, we will hereafter refer to [11.1.2] simply as the "likelihood function" and the value of $\boldsymbol{\theta}$ that maximizes [11.1.2] as the "maximum likelihood estimate."

The likelihood function is calculated in the same way as for a scalar autoregression. Conditional on the values of $\mathbf{y}$ observed through date $t - 1$, the value of $\mathbf{y}$ for date $t$ is equal to a constant,

$$\mathbf{c} + \boldsymbol{\Phi}_1\mathbf{y}_{t-1} + \boldsymbol{\Phi}_2\mathbf{y}_{t-2} + \cdots + \boldsymbol{\Phi}_p\mathbf{y}_{t-p}, \qquad [11.1.3]$$

plus a $N(\mathbf{0}, \boldsymbol{\Omega})$ variable. Thus,

$$\mathbf{y}_t | \mathbf{y}_{t-1}, \mathbf{y}_{t-2}, \ldots, \mathbf{y}_{-p+1} \sim N\Big((\mathbf{c} + \boldsymbol{\Phi}_1\mathbf{y}_{t-1} + \boldsymbol{\Phi}_2\mathbf{y}_{t-2} + \cdots + \boldsymbol{\Phi}_p\mathbf{y}_{t-p}), \boldsymbol{\Omega}\Big). \qquad [11.1.4]$$

It will be convenient to use a more compact expression for the conditional mean [11.1.3]. Let $\mathbf{x}_t$ denote a vector containing a constant term and $p$ lags of each of the elements of $\mathbf{y}$:

$$\mathbf{x}_t \equiv \begin{bmatrix} 1 \\ \mathbf{y}_{t-1} \\ \mathbf{y}_{t-2} \\ \vdots \\ \mathbf{y}_{t-p} \end{bmatrix}. \qquad [11.1.5]$$

Thus, $\mathbf{x}_t$ is an $[(np + 1) \times 1]$ vector. Let $\boldsymbol{\Pi}'$ denote the following $[n \times (np + 1)]$ matrix:

$$\boldsymbol{\Pi}' \equiv [\mathbf{c} \quad \boldsymbol{\Phi}_1 \quad \boldsymbol{\Phi}_2 \quad \cdots \quad \boldsymbol{\Phi}_p]. \qquad [11.1.6]$$

Then the conditional mean [11.1.3] is equal to $\boldsymbol{\Pi}'\mathbf{x}_t$. The $j$th row of $\boldsymbol{\Pi}'$ contains the parameters of the $j$th equation in the *VAR*. Using this notation, [11.1.4] can be written more compactly as

$$\mathbf{y}_t | \mathbf{y}_{t-1}, \mathbf{y}_{t-2}, \ldots, \mathbf{y}_{-p+1} \sim N(\boldsymbol{\Pi}'\mathbf{x}_t, \boldsymbol{\Omega}). \qquad [11.1.7]$$

Thus, the conditional density of the $t$th observation is

$$\begin{aligned} &f_{\mathbf{Y}_t|\mathbf{Y}_{t-1},\mathbf{Y}_{t-2},\ldots,\mathbf{Y}_{-p+1}}(\mathbf{y}_t | \mathbf{y}_{t-1}, \mathbf{y}_{t-2}, \ldots, \mathbf{y}_{-p+1}; \boldsymbol{\theta}) \\ &\quad = (2\pi)^{-n/2}|\boldsymbol{\Omega}^{-1}|^{1/2} \exp[(-1/2)(\mathbf{y}_t - \boldsymbol{\Pi}'\mathbf{x}_t)'\boldsymbol{\Omega}^{-1}(\mathbf{y}_t - \boldsymbol{\Pi}'\mathbf{x}_t)]. \end{aligned} \qquad [11.1.8]$$

The joint density of observations 1 through $t$ conditioned on $\mathbf{y}_0, \mathbf{y}_{-1}, \ldots, \mathbf{y}_{-p+1}$ satisfies

$$\begin{aligned} &f_{\mathbf{Y}_t,\mathbf{Y}_{t-1},\ldots,\mathbf{Y}_1|\mathbf{Y}_0,\mathbf{Y}_{-1},\ldots,\mathbf{Y}_{-p+1}}(\mathbf{y}_t, \mathbf{y}_{t-1}, \ldots, \mathbf{y}_1 | \mathbf{y}_0, \mathbf{y}_{-1}, \ldots, \mathbf{y}_{-p+1}; \boldsymbol{\theta}) \\ &\quad = f_{\mathbf{Y}_{t-1},\ldots,\mathbf{Y}_1|\mathbf{Y}_0,\mathbf{Y}_{-1},\ldots,\mathbf{Y}_{-p+1}}(\mathbf{y}_{t-1}, \ldots, \mathbf{y}_1 | \mathbf{y}_0, \mathbf{y}_{-1}, \ldots, \mathbf{y}_{-p+1}; \boldsymbol{\theta}) \\ &\quad \times f_{\mathbf{Y}_t|\mathbf{Y}_{t-1},\mathbf{Y}_{t-2},\ldots,\mathbf{Y}_{-p+1}}(\mathbf{y}_t | \mathbf{y}_{t-1}, \mathbf{y}_{t-2}, \ldots, \mathbf{y}_{-p+1}; \boldsymbol{\theta}). \end{aligned}$$

Applying this formula recursively, the likelihood for the full sample $\mathbf{y}_T, \mathbf{y}_{T-1}, \ldots, \mathbf{y}_1$ conditioned on $\mathbf{y}_0, \mathbf{y}_{-1}, \ldots, \mathbf{y}_{-p+1}$ is the product of the individual conditional densities:

$$\begin{aligned} &f_{\mathbf{Y}_T,\mathbf{Y}_{T-1},\ldots,\mathbf{Y}_1|\mathbf{Y}_0,\mathbf{Y}_{-1},\ldots,\mathbf{Y}_{-p+1}}(\mathbf{y}_T, \mathbf{y}_{T-1}, \ldots, \mathbf{y}_1 | \mathbf{y}_0, \mathbf{y}_{-1}, \ldots, \mathbf{y}_{-p+1}; \boldsymbol{\theta}) \\ &\quad = \prod_{t=1}^{T} f_{\mathbf{Y}_t|\mathbf{Y}_{t-1},\mathbf{Y}_{t-2},\ldots,\mathbf{Y}_{-p+1}}(\mathbf{y}_t | \mathbf{y}_{t-1}, \mathbf{y}_{t-2}, \ldots, \mathbf{y}_{-p+1}; \boldsymbol{\theta}). \end{aligned} \qquad [11.1.9]$$

The sample log likelihood is found by substituting [11.1.8] into [11.1.9] and taking logs:

$$\begin{aligned}\mathcal{L}(\boldsymbol{\theta}) &= \sum_{t=1}^{T} \log f_{\mathbf{Y}_t|\mathbf{Y}_{t-1},\mathbf{Y}_{t-2},\ldots,\mathbf{Y}_{-p+1}}(\mathbf{y}_t|\mathbf{y}_{t-1},\mathbf{y}_{t-2},\ldots,\mathbf{y}_{-p+1};\boldsymbol{\theta}) \\ &= -(Tn/2)\log(2\pi) + (T/2)\log|\boldsymbol{\Omega}^{-1}| \\ &\quad - (1/2)\sum_{t=1}^{T}\left[(\mathbf{y}_t - \boldsymbol{\Pi}'\mathbf{x}_t)'\boldsymbol{\Omega}^{-1}(\mathbf{y}_t - \boldsymbol{\Pi}'\mathbf{x}_t)\right].\end{aligned} \tag{11.1.10}$$

## *Maximum Likelihood Estimate of* $\boldsymbol{\Pi}$

Consider first the *MLE* of $\boldsymbol{\Pi}$, which contains the constant term $\mathbf{c}$ and autoregressive coefficients $\boldsymbol{\Phi}_j$. This turns out to be given by

$$\underset{[n\times(np+1)]}{\hat{\boldsymbol{\Pi}}'} = \left[\sum_{t=1}^{T}\mathbf{y}_t\mathbf{x}_t'\right]\left[\sum_{t=1}^{T}\mathbf{x}_t\mathbf{x}_t'\right]^{-1}, \tag{11.1.11}$$

which can be viewed as the sample analog of the population linear projection of $\mathbf{y}_t$ on a constant and $\mathbf{x}_t$ (equation [4.1.23]). The $j$th row of $\hat{\boldsymbol{\Pi}}'$ is

$$\underset{[1\times(np+1)]}{\hat{\boldsymbol{\pi}}_j'} = \left[\sum_{t=1}^{T}y_{jt}\mathbf{x}_t'\right]\left[\sum_{t=1}^{T}\mathbf{x}_t\mathbf{x}_t'\right]^{-1}, \tag{11.1.12}$$

which is just the estimated coefficient vector from an *OLS* regression of $y_{jt}$ on $\mathbf{x}_t$. Thus, maximum likelihood estimates of the coefficients for the $j$th equation of a *VAR* are found by an *OLS* regression of $y_{jt}$ on a constant term and $p$ lags of all of the variables in the system.

To verify [11.1.11], write the sum appearing in the last term in [11.1.10] as

$$\begin{aligned}&\sum_{t=1}^{T}\left[(\mathbf{y}_t - \boldsymbol{\Pi}'\mathbf{x}_t)'\boldsymbol{\Omega}^{-1}(\mathbf{y}_t - \boldsymbol{\Pi}'\mathbf{x}_t)\right] \\ &= \sum_{t=1}^{T}\left[(\mathbf{y}_t - \hat{\boldsymbol{\Pi}}'\mathbf{x}_t + \hat{\boldsymbol{\Pi}}'\mathbf{x}_t - \boldsymbol{\Pi}'\mathbf{x}_t)'\boldsymbol{\Omega}^{-1}(\mathbf{y}_t - \hat{\boldsymbol{\Pi}}'\mathbf{x}_t + \hat{\boldsymbol{\Pi}}'\mathbf{x}_t - \boldsymbol{\Pi}'\mathbf{x}_t)\right] \\ &= \sum_{t=1}^{T}\left[[\hat{\boldsymbol{\varepsilon}}_t + (\hat{\boldsymbol{\Pi}} - \boldsymbol{\Pi})'\mathbf{x}_t]'\boldsymbol{\Omega}^{-1}[\hat{\boldsymbol{\varepsilon}}_t + (\hat{\boldsymbol{\Pi}} - \boldsymbol{\Pi})'\mathbf{x}_t]\right],\end{aligned} \tag{11.1.13}$$

where the $j$th element of the $(n \times 1)$ vector $\hat{\boldsymbol{\varepsilon}}_t$ is the sample residual for observation $t$ from an *OLS* regression of $y_{jt}$ on $\mathbf{x}_t$:

$$\hat{\boldsymbol{\varepsilon}}_t \equiv \mathbf{y}_t - \hat{\boldsymbol{\Pi}}'\mathbf{x}_t. \tag{11.1.14}$$

Expression [11.1.13] can be expanded as

$$\begin{aligned}&\sum_{t=1}^{T}\left[(\mathbf{y}_t - \boldsymbol{\Pi}'\mathbf{x}_t)'\boldsymbol{\Omega}^{-1}(\mathbf{y}_t - \boldsymbol{\Pi}'\mathbf{x}_t)\right] \\ &= \sum_{t=1}^{T}\hat{\boldsymbol{\varepsilon}}_t'\boldsymbol{\Omega}^{-1}\hat{\boldsymbol{\varepsilon}}_t + 2\sum_{t=1}^{T}\hat{\boldsymbol{\varepsilon}}_t'\boldsymbol{\Omega}^{-1}(\hat{\boldsymbol{\Pi}} - \boldsymbol{\Pi})'\mathbf{x}_t \\ &\quad + \sum_{t=1}^{T}\mathbf{x}_t'(\hat{\boldsymbol{\Pi}} - \boldsymbol{\Pi})\boldsymbol{\Omega}^{-1}(\hat{\boldsymbol{\Pi}} - \boldsymbol{\Pi})'\mathbf{x}_t.\end{aligned} \tag{11.1.15}$$

Consider the middle term in [11.1.15]. Since this is a scalar, it is unchanged by applying the "trace" operator:

$$\sum_{t=1}^{T} \hat{\varepsilon}_t'\boldsymbol{\Omega}^{-1}(\hat{\boldsymbol{\Pi}} - \boldsymbol{\Pi})'\mathbf{x}_t = \text{trace}\left[\sum_{t=1}^{T} \hat{\varepsilon}_t'\boldsymbol{\Omega}^{-1}(\hat{\boldsymbol{\Pi}} - \boldsymbol{\Pi})'\mathbf{x}_t\right]$$
$$= \text{trace}\left[\sum_{t=1}^{T} \boldsymbol{\Omega}^{-1}(\hat{\boldsymbol{\Pi}} - \boldsymbol{\Pi})'\mathbf{x}_t\hat{\varepsilon}_t'\right] \qquad [11.1.16]$$
$$= \text{trace}\left[\boldsymbol{\Omega}^{-1}(\hat{\boldsymbol{\Pi}} - \boldsymbol{\Pi})' \sum_{t=1}^{T} \mathbf{x}_t\hat{\varepsilon}_t'\right].$$

But the sample residuals from an *OLS* regression are by construction orthogonal to the explanatory variables, meaning that $\Sigma_{t=1}^{T} \mathbf{x}_t\hat{\varepsilon}_{jt} = \mathbf{0}$ for all $j$ and so $\Sigma_{t=1}^{T} \mathbf{x}_t\hat{\varepsilon}_t' = \mathbf{0}$. Hence, [11.1.16] is identically zero, and [11.1.15] simplifies to

$$\sum_{t=1}^{T} \left[(\mathbf{y}_t - \boldsymbol{\Pi}'\mathbf{x}_t)'\boldsymbol{\Omega}^{-1}(\mathbf{y}_t - \boldsymbol{\Pi}'\mathbf{x}_t)\right]$$
$$= \sum_{t=1}^{T} \hat{\varepsilon}_t'\boldsymbol{\Omega}^{-1}\hat{\varepsilon}_t + \sum_{t=1}^{T} \mathbf{x}_t'(\hat{\boldsymbol{\Pi}} - \boldsymbol{\Pi})\boldsymbol{\Omega}^{-1}(\hat{\boldsymbol{\Pi}} - \boldsymbol{\Pi})'\mathbf{x}_t. \qquad [11.1.17]$$

Since $\boldsymbol{\Omega}$ is a positive definite matrix, $\boldsymbol{\Omega}^{-1}$ is as well.[1] Thus, defining the $(n \times 1)$ vector $\mathbf{x}_t^*$ as

$$\mathbf{x}_t^* \equiv (\hat{\boldsymbol{\Pi}} - \boldsymbol{\Pi})'\mathbf{x}_t,$$

the last term in [11.1.17] takes the form

$$\sum_{t=1}^{T} \mathbf{x}_t'(\hat{\boldsymbol{\Pi}} - \boldsymbol{\Pi})\boldsymbol{\Omega}^{-1}(\hat{\boldsymbol{\Pi}} - \boldsymbol{\Pi})'\mathbf{x}_t = \sum_{t=1}^{T} [\mathbf{x}_t^*]'\boldsymbol{\Omega}^{-1}\mathbf{x}_t^*.$$

This is positive for any sequence $\{\mathbf{x}_t^*\}_{t=1}^{T}$ other than $\mathbf{x}_t^* = \mathbf{0}$ for all $t$. Thus, the smallest value that [11.1.17] can take on is achieved when $\mathbf{x}_t^* = \mathbf{0}$, or when $\boldsymbol{\Pi} = \hat{\boldsymbol{\Pi}}$. Since [11.1.17] is minimized by setting $\boldsymbol{\Pi} = \hat{\boldsymbol{\Pi}}$, it follows that [11.1.10] is maximized by setting $\boldsymbol{\Pi} = \hat{\boldsymbol{\Pi}}$, establishing the claim that *OLS* regressions provide the maximum likelihood estimates of the coefficients of a vector autoregression.

## *Some Useful Results on Matrix Derivatives*

The next task is to calculate the maximum likelihood estimate of $\boldsymbol{\Omega}$. Here two results from matrix calculus will prove helpful. The first result concerns the derivative of a quadratic form in a matrix. Let $a_{ij}$ denote the row $i$, column $j$ element of an $(n \times n)$ matrix $\mathbf{A}$. Suppose that the matrix $\mathbf{A}$ is nonsymmetric and unrestricted (that is, the value of $a_{ij}$ is unrelated to the value of $a_{kl}$ when either $i \neq k$ or $j \neq l$). Consider a quadratic form $\mathbf{x}'\mathbf{A}\mathbf{x}$ for $\mathbf{x}$ an $(n \times 1)$ vector. The quadratic form can be written out explicitly as

$$\mathbf{x}'\mathbf{A}\mathbf{x} = \sum_{i=1}^{n} \sum_{j=1}^{n} x_i a_{ij} x_j, \qquad [11.1.18]$$

from which

$$\frac{\partial \mathbf{x}'\mathbf{A}\mathbf{x}}{\partial a_{ij}} = x_i x_j. \qquad [11.1.19]$$

[1]This follows immediately from the fact that $\boldsymbol{\Omega}^{-1}$ can be written as $\mathbf{L}'\mathbf{L}$ for $\mathbf{L}$ a nonsingular matrix as in [8.3.1].

Collecting these $n^2$ different derivatives into an $(n \times n)$ matrix, equation [11.1.19] can conveniently be expressed in matrix form as

$$\frac{\partial \mathbf{x}'\mathbf{A}\mathbf{x}}{\partial \mathbf{A}} = \mathbf{x}\mathbf{x}'. \qquad [11.1.20]$$

The second result concerns the derivative of the determinant of a matrix. Let $\mathbf{A}$ be a nonsymmetric unrestricted $(n \times n)$ matrix with positive determinant. Then

$$\frac{\partial \log|\mathbf{A}|}{\partial a_{ij}} = a^{ji}, \qquad [11.1.21]$$

where $a^{ji}$ denotes the row $j$, column $i$ element of $\mathbf{A}^{-1}$. In matrix form,

$$\frac{\partial \log|\mathbf{A}|}{\partial \mathbf{A}} = (\mathbf{A}')^{-1}. \qquad [11.1.22]$$

To derive [11.1.22], recall the formula for the determinant of $\mathbf{A}$ (equation [A.4.10] in the Mathematical Review, Appendix A, at the end of the book):

$$|\mathbf{A}| = \sum_{j=1}^{n} (-1)^{i+j} a_{ij} |\mathbf{A}_{ij}|, \qquad [11.1.23]$$

where $\mathbf{A}_{ij}$ denotes the $(n - 1) \times (n - 1)$ matrix formed by deleting row $i$ and column $j$ from $\mathbf{A}$. The derivative of [11.1.23] with respect to $a_{ij}$ is

$$\frac{\partial |\mathbf{A}|}{\partial a_{ij}} = (-1)^{i+j} |\mathbf{A}_{ij}|, \qquad [11.1.24]$$

since the parameter $a_{ij}$ does not appear in the matrix $\mathbf{A}_{ij}$. It follows that

$$\frac{\partial \log|\mathbf{A}|}{\partial a_{ij}} = (1/|\mathbf{A}|) \cdot (-1)^{i+j} |\mathbf{A}_{ij}|,$$

which will be recognized from equation [A.4.12] as the row $j$, column $i$ element of $\mathbf{A}^{-1}$, as claimed in equation [11.1.22].

## *The Maximum Likelihood Estimate of* $\boldsymbol{\Omega}$

We now apply these results to find the *MLE* of $\boldsymbol{\Omega}$. When evaluated at the *MLE* $\hat{\boldsymbol{\Pi}}$, the log likelihood [11.1.10] is

$$\begin{aligned} \mathcal{L}(\boldsymbol{\Omega}, \hat{\boldsymbol{\Pi}}) = &-(Tn/2) \log(2\pi) + (T/2) \log|\boldsymbol{\Omega}^{-1}| \\ &- (1/2) \sum_{t=1}^{T} \hat{\boldsymbol{\varepsilon}}_t' \boldsymbol{\Omega}^{-1} \hat{\boldsymbol{\varepsilon}}_t. \end{aligned} \qquad [11.1.25]$$

Our objective is to find a symmetric positive definite matrix $\boldsymbol{\Omega}$ for which this is as large as possible. It is instructive to consider first maximizing [11.1.25] by choosing $\boldsymbol{\Omega}$ to be any unrestricted $(n \times n)$ matrix. For that purpose we can just differentiate [11.1.25] with respect to the elements of $\boldsymbol{\Omega}^{-1}$ using formulas [11.1.20] and [11.1.22]:

$$\begin{aligned} \frac{\partial \mathcal{L}(\boldsymbol{\Omega}, \hat{\boldsymbol{\Pi}})}{\partial \boldsymbol{\Omega}^{-1}} &= (T/2) \frac{\partial \log|\boldsymbol{\Omega}^{-1}|}{\partial \boldsymbol{\Omega}^{-1}} - (1/2) \sum_{t=1}^{T} \frac{\partial \hat{\boldsymbol{\varepsilon}}_t' \boldsymbol{\Omega}^{-1} \hat{\boldsymbol{\varepsilon}}_t}{\partial \boldsymbol{\Omega}^{-1}} \\ &= (T/2)\boldsymbol{\Omega}' - (1/2) \sum_{t=1}^{T} \hat{\boldsymbol{\varepsilon}}_t \hat{\boldsymbol{\varepsilon}}_t'. \end{aligned} \qquad [11.1.26]$$

The likelihood is maximized when this derivative is set to zero, or when

$$\boldsymbol{\Omega}' = (1/T) \sum_{t=1}^{T} \hat{\boldsymbol{\varepsilon}}_t \hat{\boldsymbol{\varepsilon}}_t'. \qquad [11.1.27]$$

The matrix $\boldsymbol{\Omega}$ that satisfies [11.1.27] maximizes the likelihood among the class of all unrestricted $(n \times n)$ matrices. Note, however, that the optimal unrestricted value for $\boldsymbol{\Omega}$ that is specified by [11.1.27] turns out to be symmetric and positive definite. The *MLE*, or the value of $\boldsymbol{\Omega}$ that maximizes the likelihood among the class of all symmetric positive definite matrices, is thus also given by [11.1.27]:

$$\hat{\boldsymbol{\Omega}} = (1/T) \sum_{t=1}^{T} \hat{\boldsymbol{\varepsilon}}_t \hat{\boldsymbol{\varepsilon}}_t'. \qquad [11.1.28]$$

The row $i$, column $i$ element of $\hat{\boldsymbol{\Omega}}$ is given by

$$\hat{\sigma}_i^2 = (1/T) \sum_{t=1}^{T} \hat{\varepsilon}_{it}^2, \qquad [11.1.29]$$

which is just the average squared residual from a regression of the $i$th variable in the *VAR* on a constant term and $p$ lags of all the variables. The row $i$, column $j$ element of $\hat{\boldsymbol{\Omega}}$ is

$$\hat{\sigma}_{ij} = (1/T) \sum_{t=1}^{T} \hat{\varepsilon}_{it} \hat{\varepsilon}_{jt}, \qquad [11.1.30]$$

which is the average product of the *OLS* residual for variable $i$ and the *OLS* residual for variable $j$.

## *Likelihood Ratio Tests*

To perform a likelihood ratio test, we need to calculate the maximum value achieved for [11.1.25]. Thus, consider

$$\begin{aligned} \mathcal{L}(\hat{\boldsymbol{\Omega}}, \hat{\boldsymbol{\Pi}}) = &-(Tn/2) \log(2\pi) + (T/2) \log|\hat{\boldsymbol{\Omega}}^{-1}| \\ &- (1/2) \sum_{t=1}^{T} \hat{\boldsymbol{\varepsilon}}_t' \hat{\boldsymbol{\Omega}}^{-1} \hat{\boldsymbol{\varepsilon}}_t \end{aligned} \qquad [11.1.31]$$

for $\hat{\boldsymbol{\Omega}}$ given by [11.1.28]. The last term in [11.1.31] is

$$\begin{aligned} (1/2) \sum_{t=1}^{T} \hat{\boldsymbol{\varepsilon}}_t' \hat{\boldsymbol{\Omega}}^{-1} \hat{\boldsymbol{\varepsilon}}_t &= (1/2) \operatorname{trace}\left[\sum_{t=1}^{T} \hat{\boldsymbol{\varepsilon}}_t' \hat{\boldsymbol{\Omega}}^{-1} \hat{\boldsymbol{\varepsilon}}_t\right] \\ &= (1/2) \operatorname{trace}\left[\sum_{t=1}^{T} \hat{\boldsymbol{\Omega}}^{-1} \hat{\boldsymbol{\varepsilon}}_t \hat{\boldsymbol{\varepsilon}}_t'\right] \\ &= (1/2) \operatorname{trace}[\hat{\boldsymbol{\Omega}}^{-1}(T\hat{\boldsymbol{\Omega}})] \\ &= (1/2) \operatorname{trace}(T \cdot \mathbf{I}_n) \\ &= Tn/2. \end{aligned}$$

Substituting this into [11.1.31] produces

$$\mathcal{L}(\hat{\boldsymbol{\Omega}}, \hat{\boldsymbol{\Pi}}) = -(Tn/2) \log(2\pi) + (T/2) \log|\hat{\boldsymbol{\Omega}}^{-1}| - (Tn/2). \qquad [11.1.32]$$

This makes likelihood ratio tests particularly simple to perform. Suppose we want to test the null hypothesis that a set of variables was generated from a Gaussian *VAR* with $p_0$ lags against the alternative specification of $p_1 > p_0$ lags. To estimate the system under the null hypothesis, we perform a set of $n$ *OLS* regressions of each variable in the system on a constant term and on $p_0$ lags of all the variables in the system. Let $\hat{\boldsymbol{\Omega}}_0 = (1/T)\sum_{t=1}^{T} \hat{\boldsymbol{\varepsilon}}_t(p_0)[\hat{\boldsymbol{\varepsilon}}_t(p_0)]'$ be the variance-covariance matrix of the residuals from these regressions. The maximum value for the log likelihood under $H_0$ is then

$$\mathcal{L}_0^* = -(Tn/2)\log(2\pi) + (T/2)\log|\hat{\boldsymbol{\Omega}}_0^{-1}| - (Tn/2).$$

Similarly, the system is estimated under the alternative hypothesis by *OLS* regressions that include $p_1$ lags of all the variables. The maximized log likelihood under the alternative is

$$\mathcal{L}_1^* = -(Tn/2)\log(2\pi) + (T/2)\log|\hat{\boldsymbol{\Omega}}_1^{-1}| - (Tn/2),$$

where $\hat{\boldsymbol{\Omega}}_1$ is the variance-covariance matrix of the residuals from this second set of regressions. Twice the log likelihood ratio is then

$$\begin{aligned} 2(\mathcal{L}_1^* - \mathcal{L}_0^*) &= 2\{(T/2)\log|\hat{\boldsymbol{\Omega}}_1^{-1}| - (T/2)\log|\hat{\boldsymbol{\Omega}}_0^{-1}|\} \\ &= T\log(1/|\hat{\boldsymbol{\Omega}}_1|) - T\log(1/|\hat{\boldsymbol{\Omega}}_0|) \\ &= -T\log|\hat{\boldsymbol{\Omega}}_1| + T\log|\hat{\boldsymbol{\Omega}}_0| \\ &= T\{\log|\hat{\boldsymbol{\Omega}}_0| - \log|\hat{\boldsymbol{\Omega}}_1|\}. \end{aligned} \qquad [11.1.33]$$

Under the null hypothesis, this asymptotically has a $\chi^2$ distribution with degrees of freedom equal to the number of restrictions imposed under $H_0$. Each equation in the specification restricted by $H_0$ has $(p_1 - p_0)$ fewer lags on each of $n$ variables compared with $H_1$; thus, $H_0$ imposes $n(p_1 - p_0)$ restrictions on each equation. Since there are $n$ such equations, $H_0$ imposes $n^2(p_1 - p_0)$ restrictions. Thus, the magnitude calculated in [11.1.33] is asymptotically $\chi^2$ with $n^2(p_1 - p_0)$ degrees of freedom.

For example, suppose a bivariate *VAR* is estimated with three and four lags ($n = 2$, $p_0 = 3$, $p_1 = 4$). Say that the original sample contains 50 observations on each variable (denoted $\mathbf{y}_{-3}, \mathbf{y}_{-2}, \ldots, \mathbf{y}_{46}$) and that observations 1 through 46 were used to estimate both the three- and four-lag specifications so that $T = 46$. Let $\hat{\varepsilon}_{it}(p_0)$ be the sample residual for observation $t$ from an *OLS* regression of $y_{it}$ on a constant, three lags of $y_{1t}$, and three lags of $y_{2t}$. Suppose that $(1/T)\sum_{t=1}^T[\hat{\varepsilon}_{1t}(p_0)]^2 = 2.0$, $(1/T)\sum_{t=1}^T[\hat{\varepsilon}_{2t}(p_0)]^2 = 2.5$, and $(1/T)\sum_{t=1}^T\hat{\varepsilon}_{1t}(p_0)\hat{\varepsilon}_{2t}(p_0) = 1.0$. Then

$$\hat{\boldsymbol{\Omega}}_0 = \begin{bmatrix} 2.0 & 1.0 \\ 1.0 & 2.5 \end{bmatrix}$$

and $\log|\hat{\boldsymbol{\Omega}}_0| = \log 4 = 1.386$. Suppose that when a fourth lag is added to each regression, the residual covariance matrix is reduced to

$$\hat{\boldsymbol{\Omega}}_1 = \begin{bmatrix} 1.8 & 0.9 \\ 0.9 & 2.2 \end{bmatrix},$$

for which $\log|\hat{\boldsymbol{\Omega}}_1| = 1.147$. Then

$$2(\mathcal{L}_1^* - \mathcal{L}_0^*) = 46(1.386 - 1.147) = 10.99.$$

The degrees of freedom for this test are $2^2(4 - 3) = 4$. Since $10.99 > 9.49$ (the 5% critical value for a $\chi^2(4)$ variable), the null hypothesis is rejected. The dynamics are not completely captured by a three-lag *VAR*, and a four-lag specification seems preferable.

Sims (1980, p. 17) suggested a modification to the likelihood ratio test to take into account small-sample bias. He recommended replacing [11.1.33] by

$$(T - k)\{\log|\hat{\boldsymbol{\Omega}}_0| - \log|\hat{\boldsymbol{\Omega}}_1|\}, \qquad [11.1.34]$$

where $k = 1 + np_1$ is the number of parameters estimated per equation. The adjusted test has the same asymptotic distribution as [11.1.33] but is less likely to reject the null hypothesis in small samples. For the present example, this test statistic would be

$$(46 - 9)(1.386 - 1.147) = 8.84,$$

and the earlier conclusion would be reversed ($H_0$ would be accepted).

## *Asymptotic Distribution of* $\hat{\mathbf{\Pi}}$

The maximum likelihood estimates $\hat{\mathbf{\Pi}}$ and $\hat{\mathbf{\Omega}}$ will give consistent estimates of the population parameters even if the true innovations are non-Gaussian. Standard errors for $\hat{\mathbf{\Pi}}$ can be based on the usual *OLS* formulas, as the following proposition demonstrates.

***Proposition 11.1:*** *Let*

$$\mathbf{y}_t = \mathbf{c} + \mathbf{\Phi}_1\mathbf{y}_{t-1} + \mathbf{\Phi}_2\mathbf{y}_{t-2} + \cdots + \mathbf{\Phi}_p\mathbf{y}_{t-p} + \boldsymbol{\varepsilon}_t,$$

*where* $\boldsymbol{\varepsilon}_t$ *is independent and identically distributed with mean* $\mathbf{0}$, *variance* $\mathbf{\Omega}$, *and* $E(\varepsilon_{it}\varepsilon_{jt}\varepsilon_{lt}\varepsilon_{mt}) < \infty$ *for all i, j, l, and m and where roots of*

$$|\mathbf{I}_n - \mathbf{\Phi}_1 z - \mathbf{\Phi}_2 z^2 - \cdots - \mathbf{\Phi}_p z^p| = 0 \qquad [11.1.35]$$

*lie outside the unit circle. Let* $k \equiv np + 1$, *and let* $\mathbf{x}_t'$ *be the* $(1 \times k)$ *vector*

$$\mathbf{x}_t' \equiv [1 \quad \mathbf{y}_{t-1}' \quad \mathbf{y}_{t-2}' \quad \cdots \quad \mathbf{y}_{t-p}'].$$

*Let* $\hat{\boldsymbol{\pi}}_T = \operatorname{vec}(\hat{\mathbf{\Pi}}_T)$ *denote the* $(nk \times 1)$ *vector of coefficients resulting from OLS regressions of each of the elements of* $\mathbf{y}_t$ *on* $\mathbf{x}_t$ *for a sample of size T:*

$$\hat{\boldsymbol{\pi}}_T = \begin{bmatrix} \hat{\boldsymbol{\pi}}_{1,T} \\ \hat{\boldsymbol{\pi}}_{2,T} \\ \vdots \\ \hat{\boldsymbol{\pi}}_{n,T} \end{bmatrix},$$

*where*

$$\hat{\boldsymbol{\pi}}_{i,T} = \left[\sum_{t=1}^{T} \mathbf{x}_t\mathbf{x}_t'\right]^{-1}\left[\sum_{t=1}^{T} \mathbf{x}_t y_{it}\right];$$

*and let* $\boldsymbol{\pi}$ *denote the* $(nk \times 1)$ *vector of corresponding population coefficients. Finally, let*

$$\hat{\mathbf{\Omega}}_T = (1/T)\sum_{t=1}^{T} \hat{\boldsymbol{\varepsilon}}_t\hat{\boldsymbol{\varepsilon}}_t',$$

*where*

$$\hat{\boldsymbol{\varepsilon}}_t' = [\hat{\varepsilon}_{1t} \quad \hat{\varepsilon}_{2t} \quad \cdots \quad \hat{\varepsilon}_{nt}]$$

$$\hat{\varepsilon}_{it} = y_{it} - \mathbf{x}_t'\hat{\boldsymbol{\pi}}_{i,T}.$$

*Then*

(*a*) $(1/T)\sum_{t=1}^{T} \mathbf{x}_t\mathbf{x}_t' \xrightarrow{p} \mathbf{Q}$ *where* $\mathbf{Q} = E(\mathbf{x}_t\mathbf{x}_t')$;

(*b*) $\hat{\boldsymbol{\pi}}_T \xrightarrow{p} \boldsymbol{\pi}$;

(c) $\hat{\mathbf{\Omega}}_T \xrightarrow{p} \mathbf{\Omega}$;

(d) $\sqrt{T}(\hat{\boldsymbol{\pi}}_T - \boldsymbol{\pi}) \xrightarrow{L} N(\mathbf{0}, (\mathbf{\Omega} \otimes \mathbf{Q}^{-1}))$, *where* $\otimes$ *denotes the Kronecker product.*

A proof of this proposition is provided in Appendix 11.A to this chapter.

If we are interested only in $\hat{\boldsymbol{\pi}}_{i,T}$, the coefficients of the $i$th regression in the *VAR*, result (d) implies that

$$\sqrt{T}(\hat{\boldsymbol{\pi}}_{i,T} - \boldsymbol{\pi}_i) \xrightarrow{L} N(\mathbf{0}, \sigma_i^2 \mathbf{Q}^{-1}), \qquad [11.1.36]$$

where $\sigma_i^2 = E(\varepsilon_{it}^2)$ is the variance of the innovation of the $i$th equation in the *VAR*. But $\sigma_i^2$ is estimated consistently by $\hat{\sigma}_i^2 = (1/T)\sum_{t=1}^T \hat{\varepsilon}_{it}^2$, the average squared residual from *OLS* estimation of this equation. Similarly, $\mathbf{Q}^{-1}$ is estimated consistently by $[(1/T)\sum_{t=1}^T \mathbf{x}_t\mathbf{x}_t']^{-1}$. Hence, [11.1.36] invites us to treat $\hat{\boldsymbol{\pi}}_i$ approximately as

$$\hat{\boldsymbol{\pi}}_i \approx N\left(\boldsymbol{\pi}_i, \hat{\sigma}_i^2 \left[\sum_{t=1}^T \mathbf{x}_t\mathbf{x}_t'\right]^{-1}\right). \qquad [11.1.37]$$

But this is the standard *OLS* formula for coefficient variances with $s_i^2 = [1/(T - k)] \sum_{t=1}^T \hat{\varepsilon}_{it}^2$ in the standard formula replaced by the maximum likelihood estimate $\hat{\sigma}_i^2$ in [11.1.37]. Clearly, $s_i^2$ and $\hat{\sigma}_i^2$ are asymptotically equivalent, though following Sims's argument in [11.1.34], the larger (and thus more conservative) standard errors resulting from the *OLS* formulas might be preferred. Hence, Proposition 11.1 establishes that the standard *OLS* $t$ and $F$ statistics applied to the coefficients of any single equation in the *VAR* are asymptotically valid and can be evaluated in the usual way.

A more general hypothesis of the form $\mathbf{R}\boldsymbol{\pi} = \mathbf{r}$ involving coefficients across different equations of the *VAR* can be tested using a generalization of the Wald form of the *OLS* $\chi^2$ test (expression [8.2.23]). Result (d) of Proposition 11.1 establishes that

$$\sqrt{T}(\mathbf{R}\hat{\boldsymbol{\pi}}_T - \mathbf{r}) \xrightarrow{L} N\left(\mathbf{0}, \mathbf{R}(\mathbf{\Omega} \otimes \mathbf{Q}^{-1})\mathbf{R}'\right).$$

In the light of results (a) and (c), the asymptotic distribution could equivalently be described as

$$\sqrt{T}(\mathbf{R}\hat{\boldsymbol{\pi}}_T - \mathbf{r}) \xrightarrow{p} N\left(\mathbf{0}, \mathbf{R}(\hat{\mathbf{\Omega}}_T \otimes \mathbf{Q}_T^{-1})\mathbf{R}'\right),$$

where $\hat{\mathbf{\Omega}}_T = (1/T)\sum_{t=1}^T \hat{\boldsymbol{\varepsilon}}_t\hat{\boldsymbol{\varepsilon}}_t'$ and $\mathbf{Q}_T = (1/T)\sum_{t=1}^T \mathbf{x}_t\mathbf{x}_t'$. Hence, the following statistic has an asymptotic $\chi^2$ distribution:

$$\begin{aligned}
\chi^2(m) &= T(\mathbf{R}\hat{\boldsymbol{\pi}}_T - \mathbf{r})'\left(\mathbf{R}(\hat{\mathbf{\Omega}}_T \otimes \mathbf{Q}_T^{-1})\mathbf{R}'\right)^{-1}(\mathbf{R}\hat{\boldsymbol{\pi}}_T - \mathbf{r}) \\
&= (\mathbf{R}\hat{\boldsymbol{\pi}}_T - \mathbf{r})'\left(\mathbf{R}[\hat{\mathbf{\Omega}}_T \otimes (T\mathbf{Q}_T)^{-1}]\mathbf{R}'\right)^{-1}(\mathbf{R}\hat{\boldsymbol{\pi}}_T - \mathbf{r}) \\
&= (\mathbf{R}\hat{\boldsymbol{\pi}}_T - \mathbf{r})'\left\{\mathbf{R}\left[\hat{\mathbf{\Omega}}_T \otimes \left(\sum_{t=1}^T \mathbf{x}_t\mathbf{x}_t'\right)^{-1}\right]\mathbf{R}'\right\}^{-1}(\mathbf{R}\hat{\boldsymbol{\pi}}_T - \mathbf{r}).
\end{aligned} \qquad [11.1.38]$$

The degrees of freedom for this statistic are given by the number of rows of $\mathbf{R}$, or the number of restrictions tested.

For example, suppose we wanted to test the hypothesis that the constant term in the first equation in the *VAR* ($c_1$) is equal to the constant term in the second equation ($c_2$). Then $\mathbf{R}$ is a $(1 \times nk)$ vector with unity in the first position, $-1$ in the $(k + 1)$th position, and zeros elsewhere:

$$\mathbf{R} = [1 \quad 0 \quad 0 \quad \cdots \quad 0 \quad -1 \quad 0 \quad 0 \quad \cdots \quad 0].$$

To apply result [11.1.38], it is convenient to write $\mathbf{R}$ in Kronecker product form as

$$\mathbf{R} = \mathbf{R}_n \otimes \mathbf{R}_k, \qquad [11.1.39]$$

where $\mathbf{R}_n$ selects the equations that are involved and $\mathbf{R}_k$ selects the coefficients. For this example,

$$\underset{(1\times n)}{\mathbf{R}_n} = [1 \quad -1 \quad 0 \quad 0 \quad \cdots \quad 0]$$
$$\underset{(1\times k)}{\mathbf{R}_k} = [1 \quad 0 \quad 0 \quad 0 \quad \cdots \quad 0].$$

We then calculate

$$\begin{aligned}\mathbf{R}\left[\hat{\mathbf{\Omega}} \otimes \left(\sum_{t=1}^{T} \mathbf{x}_t\mathbf{x}_t'\right)^{-1}\right]\mathbf{R}' &= (\mathbf{R}_n \otimes \mathbf{R}_k)\left[\hat{\mathbf{\Omega}} \otimes \left(\sum_{t=1}^{T} \mathbf{x}_t\mathbf{x}_t'\right)^{-1}\right](\mathbf{R}_n' \otimes \mathbf{R}_k') \\ &= (\mathbf{R}_n\hat{\mathbf{\Omega}}\mathbf{R}_n') \otimes \left[\mathbf{R}_k\left(\sum_{t=1}^{T} \mathbf{x}_t\mathbf{x}_t'\right)^{-1}\mathbf{R}_k'\right] \\ &= (\hat{\sigma}_1^2 - 2\hat{\sigma}_{12} + \hat{\sigma}_2^2) \otimes \xi^{11},\end{aligned}$$

where $\hat{\sigma}_{12}$ is the covariance between $\hat{\varepsilon}_{1t}$ and $\hat{\varepsilon}_{2t}$ and $\xi^{11}$ is the (1, 1) element of $(\Sigma_{t=1}^{T} \mathbf{x}_t\mathbf{x}_t')^{-1}$. Since $\xi^{11}$ is a scalar, the foregoing Kronecker product is a simple multiplication. The test statistic [11.1.38] is then

$$\chi^2(1) = \frac{(\hat{c}_1 - \hat{c}_2)^2}{(\hat{\sigma}_1^2 - 2\hat{\sigma}_{12} + \hat{\sigma}_2^2)\xi^{11}}.$$

## *Asymptotic Distribution of* $\hat{\mathbf{\Omega}}$

In considering the asymptotic distribution of the estimates of variances and covariances, notice that since $\mathbf{\Omega}$ is symmetric, some of its elements are redundant. Recall that the "vec" operator transforms an $(n \times n)$ matrix into an $(n^2 \times 1)$ vector by stacking the columns. For example,

$$\text{vec}\begin{bmatrix} \sigma_{11} & \sigma_{12} & \sigma_{13} \\ \sigma_{21} & \sigma_{22} & \sigma_{23} \\ \sigma_{31} & \sigma_{32} & \sigma_{33} \end{bmatrix} = \begin{bmatrix} \sigma_{11} \\ \sigma_{21} \\ \sigma_{31} \\ \sigma_{12} \\ \sigma_{22} \\ \sigma_{32} \\ \sigma_{13} \\ \sigma_{23} \\ \sigma_{33} \end{bmatrix}. \qquad [11.1.40]$$

An analogous "vech" operator transforms an $(n \times n)$ matrix into an $([n(n + 1)/2] \times 1)$ vector by vertically stacking those elements on or below the principal diagonal. For example,

$$\text{vech}\begin{bmatrix} \sigma_{11} & \sigma_{12} & \sigma_{13} \\ \sigma_{21} & \sigma_{22} & \sigma_{23} \\ \sigma_{31} & \sigma_{32} & \sigma_{33} \end{bmatrix} = \begin{bmatrix} \sigma_{11} \\ \sigma_{21} \\ \sigma_{31} \\ \sigma_{22} \\ \sigma_{32} \\ \sigma_{33} \end{bmatrix}. \qquad [11.1.41]$$

***Proposition 11.2:*** *Let*

$$\mathbf{y}_t = \mathbf{c} + \mathbf{\Phi}_1\mathbf{y}_{t-1} + \mathbf{\Phi}_2\mathbf{y}_{t-2} + \cdots + \mathbf{\Phi}_p\mathbf{y}_{t-p} + \boldsymbol{\varepsilon}_t,$$

*where $\boldsymbol{\varepsilon}_t \sim$ i.i.d. $N(\mathbf{0}, \mathbf{\Omega})$ and where roots of*

$$|\mathbf{I}_n - \mathbf{\Phi}_1 z - \mathbf{\Phi}_2 z^2 - \cdots - \mathbf{\Phi}_p z^p| = 0$$

*lie outside the unit circle. Let $\hat{\boldsymbol{\pi}}_T$, $\hat{\mathbf{\Omega}}_T$, and $\mathbf{Q}$ be as defined in Proposition 11.1. Then*

$$\begin{bmatrix} \sqrt{T}[\hat{\boldsymbol{\pi}}_T - \boldsymbol{\pi}] \\ \sqrt{T}[\text{vech}(\hat{\mathbf{\Omega}}_T) - \text{vech}(\mathbf{\Omega})] \end{bmatrix} \xrightarrow{L} N\left(\begin{bmatrix} \mathbf{0} \\ \mathbf{0} \end{bmatrix}, \begin{bmatrix} (\mathbf{\Omega} \otimes \mathbf{Q}^{-1}) & \mathbf{0} \\ \mathbf{0} & \mathbf{\Sigma}_{22} \end{bmatrix}\right).$$

*Let $\sigma_{ij}$ denote the row i, column j element of $\mathbf{\Omega}$; for example, $\sigma_{11}$ is the variance of $\varepsilon_{1t}$. Then the element of $\mathbf{\Sigma}_{22}$ corresponding to the covariance between $\hat{\sigma}_{ij}$ and $\hat{\sigma}_{lm}$ is given by $(\sigma_{il}\sigma_{jm} + \sigma_{im}\sigma_{jl})$ for all $i, j, l, m = 1, 2, \ldots, n$, including $i = j = l = m$.*

For example, for $n = 2$, Proposition 11.2 implies that

$$\sqrt{T}\begin{bmatrix} \hat{\sigma}_{11.T} - \sigma_{11} \\ \hat{\sigma}_{12.T} - \sigma_{12} \\ \hat{\sigma}_{22.T} - \sigma_{22} \end{bmatrix} \xrightarrow{L} N\left(\begin{bmatrix} 0 \\ 0 \\ 0 \end{bmatrix}, \begin{bmatrix} 2\sigma_{11}^2 & 2\sigma_{11}\sigma_{12} & 2\sigma_{12}^2 \\ 2\sigma_{11}\sigma_{12} & \sigma_{11}\sigma_{22} + \sigma_{12}^2 & 2\sigma_{12}\sigma_{22} \\ 2\sigma_{12}^2 & 2\sigma_{12}\sigma_{22} & 2\sigma_{22}^2 \end{bmatrix}\right). \qquad [11.1.42]$$

Thus, a Wald test of the null hypothesis that there is no covariance between $\varepsilon_{1t}$ and $\varepsilon_{2t}$ is given by

$$\frac{\sqrt{T}\hat{\sigma}_{12}}{(\hat{\sigma}_{11}\hat{\sigma}_{22} + \hat{\sigma}_{12}^2)^{1/2}} \approx N(0, 1).$$

A Wald test of the null hypothesis that $\varepsilon_{1t}$ and $\varepsilon_{2t}$ have the same variance is given by

$$\frac{T(\hat{\sigma}_{11} - \hat{\sigma}_{22})^2}{2\hat{\sigma}_{11}^2 - 4\hat{\sigma}_{12}^2 + 2\hat{\sigma}_{22}^2} \approx \chi^2(1),$$

where $\hat{\sigma}_{11}^2$ denotes the square of the estimated variance of the innovation for the first equation.

The matrix $\mathbf{\Sigma}_{22}$ in Proposition 11.2 can be expressed more compactly using the *duplication matrix*. Notice that since $\mathbf{\Omega}$ is symmetric, the $n^2$ elements of vec($\mathbf{\Omega}$) in [11.1.40] are simple duplications of the $n(n + 1)/2$ elements of vech($\mathbf{\Omega}$) in [11.1.41]. There exists a unique $[n^2 \times n(n + 1)/2]$ matrix $\mathbf{D}_n$ that transforms vech($\mathbf{\Omega}$) into vec($\mathbf{\Omega}$), that is, a unique matrix satisfying

$$\mathbf{D}_n \text{ vech}(\mathbf{\Omega}) = \text{vec}(\mathbf{\Omega}). \qquad [11.1.43]$$

For example, for $n = 2$, equation [11.1.43] is

$$\begin{bmatrix} 1 & 0 & 0 \\ 0 & 1 & 0 \\ 0 & 1 & 0 \\ 0 & 0 & 1 \end{bmatrix} \begin{bmatrix} \sigma_{11} \\ \sigma_{21} \\ \sigma_{22} \end{bmatrix} = \begin{bmatrix} \sigma_{11} \\ \sigma_{21} \\ \sigma_{12} \\ \sigma_{22} \end{bmatrix}. \qquad [11.1.44]$$

Further, define $\mathbf{D}_n^+$ to be the following $[n(n+1)/2 \times n^2]$ matrix:[2]

$$\mathbf{D}_n^+ \equiv (\mathbf{D}_n'\mathbf{D}_n)^{-1}\mathbf{D}_n'. \qquad [11.1.45]$$

Notice that $\mathbf{D}_n^+\mathbf{D}_n = \mathbf{I}_{n(n+1)/2}$. Thus, premultiplying both sides of [11.1.43] by $\mathbf{D}_n^+$ reveals $\mathbf{D}_n^+$ to be a matrix that transforms $\text{vec}(\boldsymbol{\Omega})$ into $\text{vech}(\boldsymbol{\Omega})$ for symmetric $\boldsymbol{\Omega}$:

$$\text{vech}(\boldsymbol{\Omega}) = \mathbf{D}_n^+ \, \text{vec}(\boldsymbol{\Omega}). \qquad [11.1.46]$$

For example, for $n = 2$, equation [11.1.46] is

$$\begin{bmatrix} \sigma_{11} \\ \sigma_{21} \\ \sigma_{22} \end{bmatrix} = \begin{bmatrix} 1 & 0 & 0 & 0 \\ 0 & \frac{1}{2} & \frac{1}{2} & 0 \\ 0 & 0 & 0 & 1 \end{bmatrix} \begin{bmatrix} \sigma_{11} \\ \sigma_{21} \\ \sigma_{12} \\ \sigma_{22} \end{bmatrix}. \qquad [11.1.47]$$

It turns out that the matrix $\boldsymbol{\Sigma}_{22}$ described in Proposition 11.2 can be written as[3]

$$\boldsymbol{\Sigma}_{22} = 2\mathbf{D}_n^+(\boldsymbol{\Omega} \otimes \boldsymbol{\Omega})(\mathbf{D}_n^+)'. \qquad [11.1.48]$$

For example, for $n = 2$, expression [11.1.48] becomes

$$2\mathbf{D}_2^+(\boldsymbol{\Omega} \otimes \boldsymbol{\Omega})(\mathbf{D}_2^+)' = 2\begin{bmatrix} 1 & 0 & 0 & 0 \\ 0 & \frac{1}{2} & \frac{1}{2} & 0 \\ 0 & 0 & 0 & 1 \end{bmatrix}$$

$$\times \begin{bmatrix} \sigma_{11}\sigma_{11} & \sigma_{11}\sigma_{12} & \sigma_{12}\sigma_{11} & \sigma_{12}\sigma_{12} \\ \sigma_{11}\sigma_{21} & \sigma_{11}\sigma_{22} & \sigma_{12}\sigma_{21} & \sigma_{12}\sigma_{22} \\ \sigma_{21}\sigma_{11} & \sigma_{21}\sigma_{12} & \sigma_{22}\sigma_{11} & \sigma_{22}\sigma_{12} \\ \sigma_{21}\sigma_{21} & \sigma_{21}\sigma_{22} & \sigma_{22}\sigma_{21} & \sigma_{22}\sigma_{22} \end{bmatrix} \begin{bmatrix} 1 & 0 & 0 \\ 0 & \frac{1}{2} & 0 \\ 0 & \frac{1}{2} & 0 \\ 0 & 0 & 1 \end{bmatrix}$$

$$= \begin{bmatrix} 2\sigma_{11}^2 & 2\sigma_{11}\sigma_{12} & 2\sigma_{12}^2 \\ 2\sigma_{11}\sigma_{12} & \sigma_{11}\sigma_{22} + \sigma_{12}^2 & 2\sigma_{12}\sigma_{22} \\ 2\sigma_{12}^2 & 2\sigma_{12}\sigma_{22} & 2\sigma_{22}^2 \end{bmatrix},$$

which reproduces [11.1.42].

## 11.2. *Bivariate Granger Causality Tests*

One of the key questions that can be addressed with vector autoregressions is how useful some variables are for forecasting others. This section discusses a particular summary of the forecasting relation between two variables proposed by Granger (1969) and popularized by Sims (1972). A more general discussion of a related question in larger vector systems is provided in the following section.

[2]It can be shown that $(\mathbf{D}_n'\mathbf{D}_n)$ is nonsingular. For more details, see Magnus and Neudecker (1988, pp. 48–49).

[3]Magnus and Neudecker (1988, p. 318) derived this expression directly from the information matrix.

## *Definition of Bivariate Granger Causality*

The question investigated in this section is whether a scalar $y$ can help forecast another scalar $x$. If it cannot, then we say that $y$ does not Granger-cause $x$. More formally, *$y$ fails to Granger-cause $x$* if for all $s > 0$ the mean squared error of a forecast of $x_{t+s}$ based on $(x_t, x_{t-1}, \ldots)$ is the same as the $MSE$ of a forecast of $x_{t+s}$ that uses both $(x_t, x_{t-1}, \ldots)$ and $(y_t, y_{t-1}, \ldots)$. If we restrict ourselves to linear functions, $y$ fails to Granger-cause $x$ if

$$MSE[\hat{E}(x_{t+s}|x_t, x_{t-1}, \ldots)] = MSE[\hat{E}(x_{t+s}|x_t, x_{t-1}, \ldots, y_t, y_{t-1}, \ldots)]. \quad [11.2.1]$$

Equivalently, we say that $x$ *is exogenous in the time series sense with respect to* $y$ if [11.2.1] holds. Yet a third expression meaning the same thing is that *$y$ is not linearly informative about future $x$*.

Granger's reason for proposing this definition was that if an event $Y$ is the cause of another event $X$, then the event $Y$ should precede the event $X$. Although one might agree with this position philosophically, there can be serious obstacles to practical implementation of this idea using aggregate time series data, as will be seen in the examples considered later in this section. First, however, we explore the mechanical implications of Granger causality for the time series representation of a bivariate system.

## *Alternative Implications of Granger Causality*

In a bivariate $VAR$ describing $x$ and $y$, $y$ does not Granger-cause $x$ if the coefficient matrices $\mathbf{\Phi}_j$ are lower triangular for all $j$:

$$\begin{bmatrix} x_t \\ y_t \end{bmatrix} = \begin{bmatrix} c_1 \\ c_2 \end{bmatrix} + \begin{bmatrix} \phi_{11}^{(1)} & 0 \\ \phi_{21}^{(1)} & \phi_{22}^{(1)} \end{bmatrix} \begin{bmatrix} x_{t-1} \\ y_{t-1} \end{bmatrix} + \begin{bmatrix} \phi_{11}^{(2)} & 0 \\ \phi_{21}^{(2)} & \phi_{22}^{(2)} \end{bmatrix} \begin{bmatrix} x_{t-2} \\ y_{t-2} \end{bmatrix} + \cdots + \begin{bmatrix} \phi_{11}^{(p)} & 0 \\ \phi_{21}^{(p)} & \phi_{22}^{(p)} \end{bmatrix} \begin{bmatrix} x_{t-p} \\ y_{t-p} \end{bmatrix} + \begin{bmatrix} \varepsilon_{1t} \\ \varepsilon_{2t} \end{bmatrix}. \quad [11.2.2]$$

From the first row of this system, the optimal one-period-ahead forecast of $x$ depends only on its own lagged values and not on lagged $y$:

$$\hat{E}(x_{t+1}|x_t, x_{t-1}, \ldots, y_t, y_{t-1}, \ldots) = c_1 + \phi_{11}^{(1)}x_t + \phi_{11}^{(2)}x_{t-1} + \cdots + \phi_{11}^{(p)}x_{t-p+1}. \quad [11.2.3]$$

Furthermore, the value of $x_{t+2}$ from [11.2.2] is given by

$$x_{t+2} = c_1 + \phi_{11}^{(1)}x_{t+1} + \phi_{11}^{(2)}x_t + \cdots + \phi_{11}^{(p)}x_{t-p+2} + \varepsilon_{1,t+2}.$$

Recalling [11.2.3] and the law of iterated projections, it is clear that the date $t$ forecast of this magnitude on the basis of $(x_t, x_{t-1}, \ldots, y_t, y_{t-1}, \ldots)$ also depends only on $(x_t, x_{t-1}, \ldots, x_{t-p+1})$. By induction, the same is true of an $s$-period-ahead forecast. Thus, for the bivariate $VAR$, $y$ does not Granger-cause $x$ if $\mathbf{\Phi}_j$ is lower triangular for all $j$, as claimed.

Recall from equation [10.1.19] that

$$\mathbf{\Psi}_s = \mathbf{\Phi}_1\mathbf{\Psi}_{s-1} + \mathbf{\Phi}_2\mathbf{\Psi}_{s-2} + \cdots + \mathbf{\Phi}_p\mathbf{\Psi}_{s-p} \qquad \text{for } s = 1, 2, \ldots,$$

with $\mathbf{\Psi}_0$ the identity matrix and $\mathbf{\Psi}_s = \mathbf{0}$ for $s < 0$. This expression implies that if

$\mathbf{\Phi}_j$ is lower triangular for all $j$, then the moving average matrices $\mathbf{\Psi}_s$ for the fundamental representation will be lower triangular for all $s$. Thus, if $y$ fails to Granger-cause $x$, then the $MA(\infty)$ representation can be written

$$\begin{bmatrix} x_t \\ y_t \end{bmatrix} = \begin{bmatrix} \mu_1 \\ \mu_2 \end{bmatrix} + \begin{bmatrix} \psi_{11}(L) & 0 \\ \psi_{21}(L) & \psi_{22}(L) \end{bmatrix} \begin{bmatrix} \varepsilon_{1t} \\ \varepsilon_{2t} \end{bmatrix}, \qquad [11.2.4]$$

where

$$\psi_{ij}(L) = \psi_{ij}^{(0)} + \psi_{ij}^{(1)}L^1 + \psi_{ij}^{(2)}L^2 + \psi_{ij}^{(3)}L^3 + \cdots$$

with $\psi_{11}^{(0)} = \psi_{22}^{(0)} = 1$ and $\psi_{21}^{(0)} = 0$.

Another implication of Granger causality was stressed by Sims (1972).

***Proposition 11.3:*** *Consider a linear projection of $y_t$ on past, present, and future $x$'s,*

$$y_t = c + \sum_{j=0}^{\infty} b_j x_{t-j} + \sum_{j=1}^{\infty} d_j x_{t+j} + \eta_t, \qquad [11.2.5]$$

*where $b_j$ and $d_j$ are defined as population projection coefficients, that is, the values for which*

$$E(\eta_t x_\tau) = 0 \qquad \text{for all } t \text{ and } \tau.$$

*Then $y$ fails to Granger-cause $x$ if and only if $d_j = 0$ for $j = 1, 2, \ldots$.*

## Econometric Tests for Granger Causality

Econometric tests of whether a particular observed series $y$ Granger-causes $x$ can be based on any of the three implications [11.2.2], [11.2.4], or [11.2.5]. The simplest and probably best approach uses the autoregressive specification [11.2.2]. To implement this test, we assume a particular autoregressive lag length $p$ and estimate

$$\begin{aligned} x_t = c_1 + \alpha_1 x_{t-1} + \alpha_2 x_{t-2} + \cdots + \alpha_p x_{t-p} + \beta_1 y_{t-1} \\ + \beta_2 y_{t-2} + \cdots + \beta_p y_{t-p} + u_t \end{aligned} \qquad [11.2.6]$$

by $OLS$. We then conduct an $F$ test of the null hypothesis

$$H_0\!: \beta_1 = \beta_2 = \cdots = \beta_p = 0. \qquad [11.2.7]$$

Recalling Proposition 8.2, one way to implement this test is to calculate the sum of squared residuals from [11.2.6],[4]

$$RSS_1 = \sum_{t=1}^{T} \hat{u}_t^2,$$

and compare this with the sum of squared residuals of a univariate autoregression for $x_t$,

$$RSS_0 = \sum_{t=1}^{T} \hat{e}_t^2,$$

[4]Note that in order for $t$ to run from 1 to $T$ as indicated, we actually need $T + p$ observations on $x$ and $y$, namely, $x_{-p+1}, x_{-p+2}, \ldots, x_T$ and $y_{-p+1}, y_{-p+2}, \ldots, y_T$.

where

$$x_t = c_0 + \gamma_1 x_{t-1} + \gamma_2 x_{t-2} + \cdots + \gamma_p x_{t-p} + e_t \qquad [11.2.8]$$

is also estimated by *OLS*. If

$$S_1 \equiv \frac{(RSS_0 - RSS_1)/p}{RSS_1/(T - 2p - 1)} \qquad [11.2.9]$$

is greater than the 5% critical value for an $F(p, T - 2p - 1)$ distribution, then we reject the null hypothesis that $y$ does not Granger-cause $x$; that is, if $S_1$ is sufficiently large, we conclude that $y$ does Granger-cause $x$.

The test statistic [11.2.9] would have an exact $F$ distribution for a regression with fixed regressors and Gaussian disturbances. With lagged dependent variables as in the Granger-causality regressions, however, the test is valid only asymptotically. An asymptotically equivalent test is given by

$$S_2 \equiv \frac{T(RSS_0 - RSS_1)}{RSS_1}. \qquad [11.2.10]$$

We would reject the null hypothesis that $y$ does not Granger-cause $x$ if $S_2$ is greater than the 5% critical values for a $\chi^2(p)$ variable.

An alternative approach is to base the test on the Sims form [11.2.5] instead of the Granger form [11.2.2]. A problem with the Sims form is that the error term $\eta_t$ is in general autocorrelated. Thus, a standard $F$ test of the hypothesis that $d_j = 0$ for all $j$ in [11.2.5] will not give the correct answer. One option is to use autocorrelation-consistent standard errors for the *OLS* estimates as described in Section 10.5. A second option is to use a generalized least squares transformation. A third option, suggested by Geweke, Meese, and Dent (1983), is as follows. Suppose the error term $\eta_t$ in [11.2.5] has Wold representation $\eta_t = \psi_{22}(L)v_{2t}$. Multiplying both sides of [11.2.5] by $h(L) \equiv [\psi_{22}(L)]^{-1}$ produces

$$y_t = c_2 - \sum_{j=1}^{\infty} h_j y_{t-j} + \sum_{j=0}^{\infty} b_j^* x_{t-j} + \sum_{j=1}^{\infty} d_j^* x_{t+j} + v_{2t}. \qquad [11.2.11]$$

The error term in [11.2.11] is white noise and uncorrelated with any of the explanatory variables. Moreover, $d_j^* = 0$ for all $j$ if and only if $d_j = 0$ for all $j$. Thus, by truncating the infinite sums in [11.2.11] at some finite value, we can test the null hypothesis that $y$ does not Granger-cause $x$ with an $F$ test of $d_1^* = d_2^* = \cdots = d_p^* = 0$.

A variety of other Granger-causality tests have been proposed; see Pierce and Haugh (1977) and Geweke, Meese, and Dent (1983) for selective surveys. Bouissou, Laffont, and Vuong (1986) discussed tests using discrete-valued panel data. The Monte Carlo simulations of Geweke, Meese, and Dent suggest that the simplest and most straightforward test—namely, that based on [11.2.10]—may well be the best.

The results of any empirical test for Granger causality can be surprisingly sensitive to the choice of lag length ($p$) or the methods used to deal with potential nonstationarity of the series. For demonstrations of the practical relevance of such issues, see Feige and Pearce (1979), Christiano and Ljungqvist (1988), and Stock and Watson (1989).

### *Interpreting Granger-Causality Tests*

How is "Granger causality" related to the standard meaning of "causality"? We explore this question with several examples.

### *Example 11.1—Granger-Causality Tests and Forward-Looking Behavior*

The first example uses a modification of the model of stock prices described in Chapter 2. If an investor buys one share of a stock for the price $P_t$ at date $t$, then at $t + 1$ the investor will receive $D_{t+1}$ in dividends and be able to sell the stock for $P_{t+1}$. The ex post rate of return from the stock (denoted $r_{t+1}$) is defined by

$$(1 + r_{t+1})P_t \equiv P_{t+1} + D_{t+1}. \qquad [11.2.12]$$

A simple model of stock prices holds that the expected rate of return for the stock is a constant $r$ at all dates:[5]

$$(1 + r)P_t = E_t[P_{t+1} + D_{t+1}]. \qquad [11.2.13]$$

Here $E_t$ denotes an expectation conditional on all information available to stock market participants at time $t$. The logic behind [11.2.13] is that if investors had information at time $t$ leading them to anticipate a higher-than-normal return to stocks, they would want to buy more stocks at date $t$. Such purchases would drive $P_t$ up until [11.2.13] was satisfied. This view is sometimes called the *efficient markets hypothesis*.

As noted in the discussion of equation [2.5.15] in Chapter 2, equation [11.2.13] along with a boundedness condition implies

$$P_t = E_t \sum_{j=1}^{\infty} \left[\frac{1}{1 + r}\right]^j D_{t+j}. \qquad [11.2.14]$$

Thus, according to the theory, the stock price incorporates the market's best forecast of the present value of future dividends. If this forecast is based on more information than past dividends alone, then stock prices will Granger-cause dividends as investors try to anticipate movements in dividends.

For a simple illustration of this point, suppose that

$$D_t = d + u_t + \delta u_{t-1} + v_t, \qquad [11.2.15]$$

where $u_t$ and $v_t$ are independent Gaussian white noise series and $d$ is the mean dividend. Suppose that investors at time $t$ know the values of $\{u_t, u_{t-1}, \ldots\}$ and $\{v_t, v_{t-1}, \ldots\}$. The forecast of $D_{t+j}$ based on this information is given by

$$E_t(D_{t+j}) = \begin{cases} d + \delta u_t & \text{for } j = 1 \\ d & \text{for } j = 2, 3, \ldots. \end{cases} \qquad [11.2.16]$$

Substituting [11.2.16] into [11.2.14], the stock price would be given by

$$P_t = d/r + \delta u_t/(1 + r). \qquad [11.2.17]$$

[5]A related model was proposed by Lucas (1978):

$$U'(C_t)P_t = E_t\{\beta U'(C_{t+1})(P_{t+1} + D_{t+1})\},$$

with $U'(C_t)$ the marginal utility of consumption at date $t$. If we define $\tilde{P}_t$ to be the marginal-utility-weighted stock price $\tilde{P}_t \equiv U'(C_t)P_t$ and $\tilde{D}_t$ the marginal-utility-weighted dividend, then this becomes

$$\beta^{-1}\tilde{P}_t = E_t\{\tilde{P}_{t+1} + \tilde{D}_{t+1}\},$$

which is the same basic form as [11.2.13]. With risk-neutral investors, $U'(C_t)$ is a constant and the two formulations are identical. The risk-neutral version gained early support from the empirical evidence in Fama (1965).

Thus, for this example, the stock price is white noise and could not be forecast on the basis of lagged stock prices or dividends.[6] No series should Granger-cause stock prices.

On the other hand, notice from [11.2.17] that the value of $u_{t-1}$ can be uncovered from the lagged stock price:

$$\delta u_{t-1} = (1 + r)P_{t-1} - (1 + r)d/r.$$

Recall from Section 4.7 that $u_{t-1}$ contains additional information about $D_t$ beyond that contained in $\{D_{t-1}, D_{t-2}, \ldots\}$. Thus, stock prices Granger-cause dividends, though dividends fail to Granger-cause stock prices. The bivariate *VAR* takes the form

$$\begin{bmatrix} P_t \\ D_t \end{bmatrix} = \begin{bmatrix} d/r \\ -d/r \end{bmatrix} + \begin{bmatrix} 0 & 0 \\ 1 + r & 0 \end{bmatrix} \begin{bmatrix} P_{t-1} \\ D_{t-1} \end{bmatrix} + \begin{bmatrix} \delta u_t/(1 + r) \\ u_t + v_t \end{bmatrix}.$$

Hence, in this model, Granger causation runs in the opposite direction from the true causation. Dividends fail to "Granger-cause" prices, even though investors' perceptions of dividends are the sole determinant of stock prices. On the other hand, prices do "Granger-cause" dividends, even though the market's evaluation of the stock in reality has no effect on the dividend process.

In general, time series that reflect forward-looking behavior, such as stock prices and interest rates, are often found to be excellent predictors of many key economic time series. This clearly does not mean that these series *cause* GNP or inflation to move up or down. Instead, the values of these series reflect the market's best information as to where GNP or inflation might be headed. Granger-causality tests for such series may be useful for assessing the efficient markets view or investigating whether markets are concerned with or are able to forecast GNP or inflation, but should not be used to infer a direction of causation.

There nevertheless are circumstances in which Granger causality may offer useful evidence about the direction of true causation. As an illustration of this theme, consider trying to measure the effects of oil price increases on the economy.

***Example 11.2—Testing for Strict Econometric Exogeneity***[7]

All but one of the economic recessions in the United States since World War II have been preceded by a sharp increase in the price of crude petroleum. Does this mean that oil shocks are a cause of recessions?

One possibility is that the correlation is a fluke—it happened just by chance that oil shocks and recessions appeared at similar times, even though the actual processes that generated the two series are unrelated. We can investigate this possibility by testing the null hypothesis that oil prices do not Granger-cause GNP. This hypothesis is rejected by the data—oil prices help predict the value of GNP, and their contribution to prediction is statistically significant. This argues against viewing the correlation as simply a coincidence.

To place a causal interpretation on this correlation, one must establish that oil price increases were not reflecting some other macroeconomic influence that was the true cause of the recessions. The major oil price increases have

[6]This result is due to the particular specification of the time series properties assumed for dividends. A completely general result is that the excess return series defined by $P_{t+1} + D_{t+1} - (1 + r)P_t$ (which for this example would equal $\delta u_{t+1}/(1 + r) + u_{t+1} + v_{t+1}$) should be unforecastable. The example in the text provides a simpler illustration of the general issues.

[7]This discussion is based on Hamilton (1983, 1985).

been associated with clear historical events such as the Suez crisis of 1956–57, the Arab-Israeli war of 1973–74, the Iranian revolution of 1978–79, the start of the Iran-Iraq war in 1980, and Iraq's invasion of Kuwait in 1990. One could take the view that these events were caused by forces entirely outside the U.S. economy and were essentially unpredictable. If this view is correct, then the historical correlation between oil prices and GNP could be given a causal interpretation. The view has the refutable implication that no series should Granger-cause oil prices. Empirically, one indeed finds very few macroeconomic series that help predict the timing of these oil shocks.

The theme of these two examples is that Granger-causality tests can be a useful tool for testing hypotheses that can be framed as statements about the predictability of a particular series. On the other hand, one may be skeptical about their utility as a general diagnostic for establishing the direction of causation between two arbitrary series. For this reason, it seems best to describe these as tests of whether $y$ helps forecast $x$ rather than tests of whether $y$ causes $x$. The tests may have implications for the latter question, but only in conjunction with other assumptions.

Up to this point we have been discussing two variables, $x$ and $y$, in isolation from any others. Suppose there are other variables that interact with $x$ or $y$ as well. How does this affect the forecasting relationship between $x$ and $y$?

### *Example 11.3—Role of Omitted Information*

Consider the following three-variable system:

$$\begin{bmatrix} y_{1t} \\ y_{2t} \\ y_{3t} \end{bmatrix} = \begin{bmatrix} 1 + \delta L & L & 0 \\ 0 & 1 & 0 \\ 0 & L & 1 \end{bmatrix} \begin{bmatrix} \varepsilon_{1t} \\ \varepsilon_{2t} \\ \varepsilon_{3t} \end{bmatrix},$$

with

$$E(\boldsymbol{\varepsilon}_t \boldsymbol{\varepsilon}_s') = \begin{cases} \begin{bmatrix} \sigma_1^2 & 0 & 0 \\ 0 & \sigma_2^2 & 0 \\ 0 & 0 & \sigma_3^2 \end{bmatrix} & \text{for } t = s \\ \mathbf{0} & \text{otherwise.} \end{cases}$$

Thus, $y_3$ can offer no improvement in a forecast of either $y_1$ or $y_2$ beyond that achieved using lagged $y_1$ and $y_2$.

Let us now examine the bivariate Granger-causality relation between $y_1$ and $y_3$. First, consider the process for $y_1$:

$$y_{1t} = \varepsilon_{1t} + \delta\varepsilon_{1,t-1} + \varepsilon_{2,t-1}.$$

Notice that $y_1$ is the sum of an $MA(1)$ process $(\varepsilon_{1t} + \delta\varepsilon_{1,t-1})$ and an uncorrelated white noise process $(\varepsilon_{2,t-1})$. We know from equation [4.7.15] that the univariate representation for $y_1$ is an $MA(1)$ process:

$$y_{1t} = u_t + \theta u_{t-1}.$$

From [4.7.16], the univariate forecast error $u_t$ can be expressed as

$$\begin{aligned} u_t = {} & (\varepsilon_{1t} - \theta\varepsilon_{1,t-1} + \theta^2\varepsilon_{1,t-2} - \theta^3\varepsilon_{1,t-3} + \cdots) \\ & + \delta(\varepsilon_{1,t-1} - \theta\varepsilon_{1,t-2} + \theta^2\varepsilon_{1,t-3} - \theta^3\varepsilon_{1,t-4} + \cdots) \\ & + (\varepsilon_{2,t-1} - \theta\varepsilon_{2,t-2} + \theta^2\varepsilon_{2,t-3} - \theta^3\varepsilon_{2,t-4} + \cdots). \end{aligned}$$

The univariate forecast error $u_t$ is, of course, uncorrelated with its own lagged values. Notice, however, that it is correlated with $y_{3,t-1}$:

$$E(u_t)(y_{3,t-1}) = E(u_t)(\varepsilon_{3,t-1} + \varepsilon_{2,t-2}) = -\theta\sigma_2^2.$$

Thus, lagged $y_3$ could help improve a forecast of $y_1$ that had been based on lagged values of $y_1$ alone, meaning that $y_3$ Granger-causes $y_1$ in a bivariate system. The reason is that lagged $y_3$ is correlated with the omitted variable $y_2$, which is also helpful in forecasting $y_1$.[8]

## 11.3. *Maximum Likelihood Estimation of Restricted Vector Autoregressions*

Section 11.1 discussed maximum likelihood estimation and hypothesis testing on unrestricted vector autoregressions. In these systems each equation in the *VAR* had the same explanatory variables, namely, a constant term and lags of all the variables in the system. We showed how to calculate a Wald test of linear constraints but did not discuss estimation of the system subject to the constraints. This section examines estimation of a restricted *VAR*.

### *Granger Causality in a Multivariate Context*

As an example of a restricted system that we might be interested in estimating, consider a vector generalization of the issues explored in the previous section. Suppose that the variables of a *VAR* are categorized into two groups, as represented by the $(n_1 \times 1)$ vector $\mathbf{y}_{1t}$ and the $(n_2 \times 1)$ vector $\mathbf{y}_{2t}$. The *VAR* may then be written

$$\mathbf{y}_{1t} = \mathbf{c}_1 + \mathbf{A}_1'\mathbf{x}_{1t} + \mathbf{A}_2'\mathbf{x}_{2t} + \boldsymbol{\varepsilon}_{1t} \qquad [11.3.1]$$

$$\mathbf{y}_{2t} = \mathbf{c}_2 + \mathbf{B}_1'\mathbf{x}_{1t} + \mathbf{B}_2'\mathbf{x}_{2t} + \boldsymbol{\varepsilon}_{2t}. \qquad [11.3.2]$$

Here $\mathbf{x}_{1t}$ is an $(n_1 p \times 1)$ vector containing lags of $\mathbf{y}_{1t}$, and the $(n_2 p \times 1)$ vector $\mathbf{x}_{2t}$ contains lags of $\mathbf{y}_{2t}$:

$$\mathbf{x}_{1t} \equiv \begin{bmatrix} \mathbf{y}_{1,t-1} \\ \mathbf{y}_{1,t-2} \\ \vdots \\ \mathbf{y}_{1,t-p} \end{bmatrix} \qquad \mathbf{x}_{2t} \equiv \begin{bmatrix} \mathbf{y}_{2,t-1} \\ \mathbf{y}_{2,t-2} \\ \vdots \\ \mathbf{y}_{2,t-p} \end{bmatrix}.$$

The $(n_1 \times 1)$ and $(n_2 \times 1)$ vectors $\mathbf{c}_1$ and $\mathbf{c}_2$ contain the constant terms of the *VAR*, while the matrices $\mathbf{A}_1$, $\mathbf{A}_2$, $\mathbf{B}_1$, and $\mathbf{B}_2$ contain the autoregressive coefficients.

The group of variables represented by $\mathbf{y}_1$ is said to be *block-exogenous in the time series sense* with respect to the variables in $\mathbf{y}_2$ if the elements in $\mathbf{y}_2$ are of no help in improving a forecast of any variable contained in $\mathbf{y}_1$ that is based on lagged values of all the elements of $\mathbf{y}_1$ alone. In the system of [11.3.1] and [11.3.2], $\mathbf{y}_1$ is block-exogenous when $\mathbf{A}_2 = \mathbf{0}$. To discuss estimation of the system subject to this constraint, we first note an alternative form in which the unrestricted likelihood can be calculated and maximized.

[8]The reader may note that for this example the correlation between $y_{1t}$ and $y_{3,t-1}$ is zero. However, there are nonzero correlations between (1) $y_{1t}$ and $y_{1,t-1}$ and (2) $y_{1,t-1}$ and $y_{3,t-1}$, and these account for the contribution of $y_{3,t-1}$ to a forecast of $y_{1t}$ that already includes $y_{1,t-1}$.

## An Alternative Expression for the Likelihood Function

Section 11.1 calculated the log likelihood function for a *VAR* using the prediction-error decomposition

$$\mathcal{L}(\boldsymbol{\theta}) = \sum_{t=1}^{T} \log f_{\mathbf{Y}_t|\mathbf{X}_t}(\mathbf{y}_t|\mathbf{x}_t; \boldsymbol{\theta}), \qquad [11.3.3]$$

where $\mathbf{y}_t' = (\mathbf{y}_{1t}', \mathbf{y}_{2t}')$, $\mathbf{x}_t' = (\mathbf{y}_{t-1}', \mathbf{y}_{t-2}', \ldots, \mathbf{y}_{t-p}')$, and

$$\begin{aligned} \log f_{\mathbf{Y}_t|\mathbf{X}_t}&(\mathbf{y}_t|\mathbf{x}_t; \boldsymbol{\theta}) \\ &= -\frac{n_1 + n_2}{2}\log(2\pi) - \tfrac{1}{2}\log\begin{vmatrix} \boldsymbol{\Omega}_{11} & \boldsymbol{\Omega}_{12} \\ \boldsymbol{\Omega}_{21} & \boldsymbol{\Omega}_{22} \end{vmatrix} \\ &\quad - \tfrac{1}{2}[(\mathbf{y}_{1t} - \mathbf{c}_1 - \mathbf{A}_1'\mathbf{x}_{1t} - \mathbf{A}_2'\mathbf{x}_{2t})' \quad (\mathbf{y}_{2t} - \mathbf{c}_2 - \mathbf{B}_1'\mathbf{x}_{1t} - \mathbf{B}_2'\mathbf{x}_{2t})'] \\ &\quad \times \begin{bmatrix} \boldsymbol{\Omega}_{11} & \boldsymbol{\Omega}_{12} \\ \boldsymbol{\Omega}_{21} & \boldsymbol{\Omega}_{22} \end{bmatrix}^{-1} \begin{bmatrix} \mathbf{y}_{1t} - \mathbf{c}_1 - \mathbf{A}_1'\mathbf{x}_{1t} - \mathbf{A}_2'\mathbf{x}_{2t} \\ \mathbf{y}_{2t} - \mathbf{c}_2 - \mathbf{B}_1'\mathbf{x}_{1t} - \mathbf{B}_2'\mathbf{x}_{2t} \end{bmatrix}. \end{aligned} \qquad [11.3.4]$$

Alternatively, the joint density in [11.3.4] could be written as the product of a marginal density of $\mathbf{y}_{1t}$ with the conditional density of $\mathbf{y}_{2t}$ given $\mathbf{y}_{1t}$:

$$f_{\mathbf{Y}_t|\mathbf{X}_t}(\mathbf{y}_t|\mathbf{x}_t; \boldsymbol{\theta}) = f_{\mathbf{Y}_{1t}|\mathbf{X}_t}(\mathbf{y}_{1t}|\mathbf{x}_t; \boldsymbol{\theta}) \cdot f_{\mathbf{Y}_{2t}|\mathbf{Y}_{1t},\mathbf{X}_t}(\mathbf{y}_{2t}|\mathbf{y}_{1t}, \mathbf{x}_t; \boldsymbol{\theta}). \qquad [11.3.5]$$

Conditional on $\mathbf{x}_t$, the density of $\mathbf{y}_{1t}$ is

$$\begin{aligned} f_{\mathbf{Y}_{1t}|\mathbf{X}_t}(\mathbf{y}_{1t}|\mathbf{x}_t; \boldsymbol{\theta}) = (2\pi)^{-n_1/2}|\boldsymbol{\Omega}_{11}|^{-1/2} \\ \times \exp[-\tfrac{1}{2}(\mathbf{y}_{1t} - \mathbf{c}_1 - \mathbf{A}_1'\mathbf{x}_{1t} - \mathbf{A}_2'\mathbf{x}_{2t})'\boldsymbol{\Omega}_{11}^{-1} \\ \times (\mathbf{y}_{1t} - \mathbf{c}_1 - \mathbf{A}_1'\mathbf{x}_{1t} - \mathbf{A}_2'\mathbf{x}_{2t})], \end{aligned} \qquad [11.3.6]$$

while the conditional density of $\mathbf{y}_{2t}$ given $\mathbf{y}_{1t}$ and $\mathbf{x}_t$ is also Gaussian:

$$\begin{aligned} f_{\mathbf{Y}_{2t}|\mathbf{Y}_{1t},\mathbf{X}_t}(\mathbf{y}_{2t}|\mathbf{y}_{1t}, \mathbf{x}_t; \boldsymbol{\theta}) = (2\pi)^{-n_2/2}|\mathbf{H}|^{-1/2} \\ \times \exp[-\tfrac{1}{2}(\mathbf{y}_{2t} - \mathbf{m}_{2t})'\mathbf{H}^{-1}(\mathbf{y}_{2t} - \mathbf{m}_{2t})]. \end{aligned} \qquad [11.3.7]$$

The parameters of this conditional distribution can be calculated using the results from Section 4.6. The conditional variance is given by equation [4.6.6]:

$$\mathbf{H} = \boldsymbol{\Omega}_{22} - \boldsymbol{\Omega}_{21}\boldsymbol{\Omega}_{11}^{-1}\boldsymbol{\Omega}_{12};$$

while the conditional mean ($\mathbf{m}_{2t}$) can be calculated from [4.6.5]:

$$\mathbf{m}_{2t} = E(\mathbf{y}_{2t}|\mathbf{x}_t) + \boldsymbol{\Omega}_{21}\boldsymbol{\Omega}_{11}^{-1}[\mathbf{y}_{1t} - E(\mathbf{y}_{1t}|\mathbf{x}_t)]. \qquad [11.3.8]$$

Notice from [11.3.1] that

$$E(\mathbf{y}_{1t}|\mathbf{x}_t) = \mathbf{c}_1 + \mathbf{A}_1'\mathbf{x}_{1t} + \mathbf{A}_2'\mathbf{x}_{2t},$$

while from [11.3.2],

$$E(\mathbf{y}_{2t}|\mathbf{x}_t) = \mathbf{c}_2 + \mathbf{B}_1'\mathbf{x}_{1t} + \mathbf{B}_2'\mathbf{x}_{2t}.$$

Substituting these expressions into [11.3.8],

$$\begin{aligned} \mathbf{m}_{2t} &= (\mathbf{c}_2 + \mathbf{B}_1'\mathbf{x}_{1t} + \mathbf{B}_2'\mathbf{x}_{2t}) + \boldsymbol{\Omega}_{21}\boldsymbol{\Omega}_{11}^{-1}[\mathbf{y}_{1t} - (\mathbf{c}_1 + \mathbf{A}_1'\mathbf{x}_{1t} + \mathbf{A}_2'\mathbf{x}_{2t})] \\ &= \mathbf{d} + \mathbf{D}_0'\mathbf{y}_{1t} + \mathbf{D}_1'\mathbf{x}_{1t} + \mathbf{D}_2'\mathbf{x}_{2t}, \end{aligned}$$

where

$$\mathbf{d} = \mathbf{c}_2 - \boldsymbol{\Omega}_{21}\boldsymbol{\Omega}_{11}^{-1}\mathbf{c}_1 \qquad [11.3.9]$$

$$\mathbf{D}_0' = \boldsymbol{\Omega}_{21}\boldsymbol{\Omega}_{11}^{-1} \qquad [11.3.10]$$

$$\mathbf{D}_1' = \mathbf{B}_1' - \boldsymbol{\Omega}_{21}\boldsymbol{\Omega}_{11}^{-1}\mathbf{A}_1' \qquad [11.3.11]$$

$$\mathbf{D}_2' = \mathbf{B}_2' - \boldsymbol{\Omega}_{21}\boldsymbol{\Omega}_{11}^{-1}\mathbf{A}_2'. \qquad [11.3.12]$$

The log of the joint density in [11.3.4] can thus equivalently be calculated as the sum of the logs of the marginal density [11.3.6] and the conditional density [11.3.7]:

$$\log f_{\mathbf{Y}_t|\mathbf{X}_t}(\mathbf{y}_t|\mathbf{x}_t;\boldsymbol{\theta}) = \ell_{1t} + \ell_{2t}, \qquad [11.3.13]$$

where

$$\begin{aligned}\ell_{1t} &= (-n_1/2)\log(2\pi) - \tfrac{1}{2}\log|\boldsymbol{\Omega}_{11}| \\ &\quad - \tfrac{1}{2}[(\mathbf{y}_{1t} - \mathbf{c}_1 - \mathbf{A}_1'\mathbf{x}_{1t} - \mathbf{A}_2'\mathbf{x}_{2t})'\boldsymbol{\Omega}_{11}^{-1}(\mathbf{y}_{1t} - \mathbf{c}_1 - \mathbf{A}_1'\mathbf{x}_{1t} - \mathbf{A}_2'\mathbf{x}_{2t})] \qquad [11.3.14]\end{aligned}$$

$$\begin{aligned}\ell_{2t} &= (-n_2/2)\log(2\pi) - \tfrac{1}{2}\log|\mathbf{H}| \\ &\quad - \tfrac{1}{2}[(\mathbf{y}_{2t} - \mathbf{d} - \mathbf{D}_0'\mathbf{y}_{1t} - \mathbf{D}_1'\mathbf{x}_{1t} - \mathbf{D}_2'\mathbf{x}_{2t})'\mathbf{H}^{-1} \qquad [11.3.15] \\ &\quad \times (\mathbf{y}_{2t} - \mathbf{d} - \mathbf{D}_0'\mathbf{y}_{1t} - \mathbf{D}_1'\mathbf{x}_{1t} - \mathbf{D}_2'\mathbf{x}_{2t})].\end{aligned}$$

The sample log likelihood would then be expressed as

$$\mathcal{L}(\boldsymbol{\theta}) = \sum_{t=1}^{T}\ell_{1t} + \sum_{t=1}^{T}\ell_{2t}. \qquad [11.3.16]$$

Equations [11.3.4] and [11.3.13] are two different expressions for the same magnitude. As long as the parameters in the second representation are related to those of the first as in [11.3.9] through [11.3.12], either calculation would produce the identical value for the likelihood. If [11.3.3] is maximized by choice of ($\mathbf{c}_1$, $\mathbf{A}_1$, $\mathbf{A}_2$, $\mathbf{c}_2$, $\mathbf{B}_1$, $\mathbf{B}_2$, $\boldsymbol{\Omega}_{11}$, $\boldsymbol{\Omega}_{12}$, $\boldsymbol{\Omega}_{22}$), the same value for the likelihood will be achieved as by maximizing [11.3.16] by choice of ($\mathbf{c}_1$, $\mathbf{A}_1$, $\mathbf{A}_2$, $\mathbf{d}$, $\mathbf{D}_0$, $\mathbf{D}_1$, $\mathbf{D}_2$, $\boldsymbol{\Omega}_{11}$, $\mathbf{H}$).

The second maximization is as easy to achieve as the first. Since the parameters ($\mathbf{c}_1$, $\mathbf{A}_1$, $\mathbf{A}_2$) appear in [11.3.16] only through $\Sigma_{t=1}^{T}\ell_{1t}$, the *MLE*s of these parameters can be found by *OLS* regressions of the elements of $\mathbf{y}_{1t}$ on a constant and lagged values of $\mathbf{y}_1$ and $\mathbf{y}_2$, that is, by *OLS* estimation of

$$\mathbf{y}_{1t} = \mathbf{c}_1 + \mathbf{A}_1'\mathbf{x}_{1t} + \mathbf{A}_2'\mathbf{x}_{2t} + \boldsymbol{\varepsilon}_{1t}. \qquad [11.3.17]$$

The *MLE* of $\boldsymbol{\Omega}_{11}$ is the sample variance-covariance matrix of the residuals from these regressions, $\hat{\boldsymbol{\Omega}}_{11} = (1/T)\Sigma_{t=1}^{T}\hat{\boldsymbol{\varepsilon}}_{1t}\hat{\boldsymbol{\varepsilon}}_{1t}'$. Similarly, the parameters ($\mathbf{d}$, $\mathbf{D}_0$, $\mathbf{D}_1$, $\mathbf{D}_2$) appear in [11.3.16] only through $\Sigma_{t=1}^{T}\ell_{2t}$, and so their *MLE*s are obtained from *OLS* regressions of the elements of $\mathbf{y}_{2t}$ on a constant, current and lagged values of $\mathbf{y}_1$, and lagged values of $\mathbf{y}_2$:

$$\mathbf{y}_{2t} = \mathbf{d} + \mathbf{D}_0'\mathbf{y}_{1t} + \mathbf{D}_1'\mathbf{x}_{1t} + \mathbf{D}_2'\mathbf{x}_{2t} + \mathbf{v}_{2t}. \qquad [11.3.18]$$

The *MLE* of $\mathbf{H}$ is the sample variance-covariance matrix of the residuals from this second set of regressions, $\hat{\mathbf{H}} = (1/T)\Sigma_{t=1}^{T}\hat{\mathbf{v}}_{2t}\hat{\mathbf{v}}_{2t}'$.

Note that the population residuals associated with the second set of regressions, $\mathbf{v}_{2t}$, are uncorrelated with the population residuals of the first regressions. This is because $\mathbf{v}_{2t} = \mathbf{y}_{2t} - E(\mathbf{y}_{2t}|\mathbf{y}_{1t}, \mathbf{x}_t)$ is uncorrelated by construction with $\mathbf{y}_{1t}$ and $\mathbf{x}_t$, whereas $\boldsymbol{\varepsilon}_{1t}$ is a linear function of $\mathbf{y}_{1t}$ and $\mathbf{x}_t$. Similarly, the *OLS* sample residuals associated with the second regressions,

$$\hat{\mathbf{v}}_{2t} \equiv \mathbf{y}_{2t} - \hat{\mathbf{d}} - \hat{\mathbf{D}}_0'\mathbf{y}_{1t} - \hat{\mathbf{D}}_1'\mathbf{x}_{1t} - \hat{\mathbf{D}}_2'\mathbf{x}_{2t},$$

are orthogonal by construction to $\mathbf{y}_{1t}$, a constant term, and $\mathbf{x}_t$. Since the *OLS* sample residuals associated with the first regressions, $\hat{\boldsymbol{\varepsilon}}_{1t}$, are linear functions of these same elements, $\hat{\mathbf{v}}_{2t}$ is orthogonal by construction to $\hat{\boldsymbol{\varepsilon}}_{1t}$.

### *Maximum Likelihood Estimation of a* VAR *Characterized by Block Exogeneity*

Now consider maximum likelihood estimation of the system subject to the constraint that $\mathbf{A}_2 = \mathbf{0}$. Suppose we view ($\mathbf{d}$, $\mathbf{D}_0$, $\mathbf{D}_1$, $\mathbf{D}_2$, $\mathbf{H}$) rather than ($\mathbf{c}_2$, $\mathbf{B}_1$,

$\mathbf{B}_2, \boldsymbol{\Omega}_{21}, \boldsymbol{\Omega}_{22})$ as the parameters of interest for the second equation and take our objective to be to choose values for $(\mathbf{c}_1, \mathbf{A}_1, \boldsymbol{\Omega}_{11}, \mathbf{d}, \mathbf{D}_0, \mathbf{D}_1, \mathbf{D}_2, \mathbf{H})$ so as to maximize the likelihood function. For this parameterization, the value of $\mathbf{A}_2$ does not affect the value of $\ell_{2t}$ in [11.3.15]. Thus, the full-information maximum likelihood estimates of $\mathbf{c}_1$, $\mathbf{A}_1$, and $\boldsymbol{\Omega}_{11}$ can be based solely on a restricted version of the regressions in [11.3.17],

$$\mathbf{y}_{1t} = \mathbf{c}_1 + \mathbf{A}_1'\mathbf{x}_{1t} + \boldsymbol{\varepsilon}_{1t}. \tag{11.3.19}$$

Let $\hat{\mathbf{c}}_1(0), \hat{\mathbf{A}}_1(0), \hat{\boldsymbol{\Omega}}_{11}(0)$ denote the estimates from these restricted regressions. The maximum likelihood estimates of the other parameters of the system $(\mathbf{d}, \mathbf{D}_0, \mathbf{D}_1, \mathbf{D}_2, \mathbf{H})$ continue to be given by unrestricted *OLS* estimation of [11.3.18], with estimates denoted $(\hat{\mathbf{d}}, \hat{\mathbf{D}}_0, \hat{\mathbf{D}}_1, \hat{\mathbf{D}}_2, \hat{\mathbf{H}})$.

The maximum value achieved for the log likelihood function can be found by applying [11.1.32] to [11.3.13]:

$$\begin{aligned}\mathscr{L}[\hat{\boldsymbol{\theta}}(0)] &= \sum_{t=1}^{T} \ell_{1t}[\hat{\mathbf{c}}_1(0), \hat{\mathbf{A}}_1(0), \hat{\boldsymbol{\Omega}}_{11}(0)] + \sum_{t=1}^{T} \ell_{2t}[\hat{\mathbf{d}}, \hat{\mathbf{D}}_0, \hat{\mathbf{D}}_1, \hat{\mathbf{D}}_2, \hat{\mathbf{H}}] \\ &= [-(Tn_1/2)\log(2\pi) + (T/2)\log|\hat{\boldsymbol{\Omega}}_{11}^{-1}(0)| - (Tn_1/2)] \\ &\quad + [-(Tn_2/2)\log(2\pi) + (T/2)\log|\hat{\mathbf{H}}^{-1}| - (Tn_2/2)].\end{aligned} \tag{11.3.20}$$

By contrast, when the system is estimated with no constraints on $\mathbf{A}_2$, the value achieved for the log likelihood is

$$\begin{aligned}\mathscr{L}(\hat{\boldsymbol{\theta}}) &= \sum_{t=1}^{T} \ell_{1t}[\hat{\mathbf{c}}_1, \hat{\mathbf{A}}_1, \hat{\mathbf{A}}_2, \hat{\boldsymbol{\Omega}}_{11}] + \sum_{t=1}^{T} \ell_{2t}[\hat{\mathbf{d}}, \hat{\mathbf{D}}_0, \hat{\mathbf{D}}_1, \hat{\mathbf{D}}_2, \hat{\mathbf{H}}] \\ &= [-(Tn_1/2)\log(2\pi) + (T/2)\log|\hat{\boldsymbol{\Omega}}_{11}^{-1}| - (Tn_1/2)] \\ &\quad + [-(Tn_2/2)\log(2\pi) + (T/2)\log|\hat{\mathbf{H}}^{-1}| - (Tn_2/2)],\end{aligned} \tag{11.3.21}$$

where $(\hat{\mathbf{c}}_1, \hat{\mathbf{A}}_1, \hat{\mathbf{A}}_2, \hat{\boldsymbol{\Omega}}_{11})$ denote estimates based on *OLS* estimation of [11.3.17]. A likelihood ratio test of the null hypothesis that $\mathbf{A}_2 = \mathbf{0}$ can thus be based on

$$\begin{aligned}2\{\mathscr{L}[\hat{\boldsymbol{\theta}}] - \mathscr{L}[\hat{\boldsymbol{\theta}}(0)]\} &= T\{\log|\hat{\boldsymbol{\Omega}}_{11}^{-1}| - \log|\hat{\boldsymbol{\Omega}}_{11}^{-1}(0)|\} \\ &= T\{\log|\hat{\boldsymbol{\Omega}}_{11}(0)| - \log|\hat{\boldsymbol{\Omega}}_{11}|\}.\end{aligned} \tag{11.3.22}$$

This will have an asymptotic $\chi^2$ distribution with degrees of freedom equal to the number of restrictions. Since $\mathbf{A}_2$ is an $(n_1 \times n_2 p)$ matrix, the number of restrictions is $n_1 n_2 p$.

Thus, to test the null hypothesis that the $n_1$ variables represented by $\mathbf{y}_1$ are block-exogenous with respect to the $n_2$ variables represented by $\mathbf{y}_2$, perform *OLS* regressions of each of the elements of $\mathbf{y}_1$ on a constant, $p$ lags of all of the elements of $\mathbf{y}_1$, and $p$ lags of all of the elements of $\mathbf{y}_2$. Let $\hat{\boldsymbol{\varepsilon}}_{1t}$ denote the $(n_1 \times 1)$ vector of sample residuals for date $t$ from these regressions and $\hat{\boldsymbol{\Omega}}_{11}$ their variance-covariance matrix $(\hat{\boldsymbol{\Omega}}_{11} = (1/T)\Sigma_{t=1}^{T} \hat{\boldsymbol{\varepsilon}}_{1t}\hat{\boldsymbol{\varepsilon}}_{1t}')$. Next perform *OLS* regressions of each of the elements of $\mathbf{y}_1$ on a constant and $p$ lags of all the elements of $\mathbf{y}_1$. Let $\hat{\boldsymbol{\varepsilon}}_{1t}(0)$ denote the $(n_1 \times 1)$ vector of sample residuals from this second set of regressions and $\hat{\boldsymbol{\Omega}}_{11}(0)$ their variance-covariance matrix $(\hat{\boldsymbol{\Omega}}_{11}(0) = (1/T)\Sigma_{t=1}^{T} [\hat{\boldsymbol{\varepsilon}}_{1t}(0)][\hat{\boldsymbol{\varepsilon}}_{1t}(0)]')$. If

$$T\{\log|\hat{\boldsymbol{\Omega}}_{11}(0)| - \log|\hat{\boldsymbol{\Omega}}_{11}|\}$$

is greater than the 5% critical value for a $\chi^2(n_1 n_2 p)$ variable, then the null hypothesis is rejected, and the conclusion is that some of the elements of $\mathbf{y}_2$ are helpful in forecasting $\mathbf{y}_1$.

Thus, if our interest is in estimation of the parameters $(\mathbf{c}_1, \mathbf{A}_1, \boldsymbol{\Omega}_{11}, \mathbf{d}, \mathbf{D}_0, \mathbf{D}_1, \mathbf{D}_2, \mathbf{H})$ or testing a hypothesis about block exogeneity, all that is necessary is $OLS$ regression on the affected equations. Suppose, however, that we wanted full-information maximum likelihood estimates of the parameters of the likelihood as originally parameterized $(\mathbf{c}_1, \mathbf{A}_1, \mathbf{\Omega}_{11}, \mathbf{c}_2, \mathbf{B}_1, \mathbf{B}_2, \mathbf{\Omega}_{21}, \mathbf{\Omega}_{22})$. For the parameters of the first block of equations $(\mathbf{c}_1, \mathbf{A}_1, \mathbf{\Omega}_{11})$, the $MLE$s continue to be given by $OLS$ estimation of [11.3.19]. The parameters of the second block can be found from the $OLS$ estimates by inverting equations [11.3.9] through [11.3.12]:[9]

$$\begin{aligned}
\hat{\mathbf{\Omega}}_{21}(0) &= \hat{\mathbf{D}}_0'[\hat{\mathbf{\Omega}}_{11}(0)] \\
\hat{\mathbf{c}}_2(0) &= \hat{\mathbf{d}} + [\hat{\mathbf{\Omega}}_{21}(0)][\hat{\mathbf{\Omega}}_{11}(0)]^{-1}[\hat{\mathbf{c}}_1(0)] \\
[\hat{\mathbf{B}}_1(0)]' &= \hat{\mathbf{D}}_1' + [\hat{\mathbf{\Omega}}_{21}(0)][\hat{\mathbf{\Omega}}_{11}(0)]^{-1}[\hat{\mathbf{A}}_1(0)]' \\
[\hat{\mathbf{B}}_2(0)]' &= \hat{\mathbf{D}}_2' \\
\hat{\mathbf{\Omega}}_{22}(0) &= \hat{\mathbf{H}} + [\hat{\mathbf{\Omega}}_{21}(0)][\hat{\mathbf{\Omega}}_{11}(0)]^{-1}[\hat{\mathbf{\Omega}}_{12}(0)].
\end{aligned}$$

Thus, the maximum likelihood estimates for the original parameterization of [11.3.2] are found from these equations by combining the $OLS$ estimates from [11.3.19] and [11.3.18].

## *Geweke's Measure of Linear Dependence*

The previous subsection modeled the relation between an $(n_1 \times 1)$ vector $\mathbf{y}_{1t}$ and an $(n_2 \times 1)$ vector $\mathbf{y}_{2t}$ in terms of the $p$th-order $VAR$ [11.3.1] and [11.3.2], where the innovations have a variance-covariance matrix given by

$$E\begin{bmatrix} \boldsymbol{\varepsilon}_{1t}\boldsymbol{\varepsilon}_{1t}' & \boldsymbol{\varepsilon}_{1t}\boldsymbol{\varepsilon}_{2t}' \\ \boldsymbol{\varepsilon}_{2t}\boldsymbol{\varepsilon}_{1t}' & \boldsymbol{\varepsilon}_{2t}\boldsymbol{\varepsilon}_{2t}' \end{bmatrix} = \begin{bmatrix} \mathbf{\Omega}_{11} & \mathbf{\Omega}_{12} \\ \mathbf{\Omega}_{21} & \mathbf{\Omega}_{22} \end{bmatrix}.$$

To test the null hypothesis that $\mathbf{y}_1$ is block exogenous with respect to $\mathbf{y}_2$, we proposed calculating the statistic in [11.3.22],

$$T\{\log|\hat{\mathbf{\Omega}}_{11}(0)| - \log|\hat{\mathbf{\Omega}}_{11}|\} \approx \chi^2(n_1 n_2 p), \qquad [11.3.23]$$

where $\hat{\mathbf{\Omega}}_{11}$ is the variance-covariance matrix of the residuals from $OLS$ estimation of [11.3.1] and $\hat{\mathbf{\Omega}}_{11}(0)$ is the variance-covariance matrix of the residuals from $OLS$ estimation of [11.3.1] when lagged values of $\mathbf{y}_2$ are omitted from the regression (that is, when $\mathbf{A}_2 = \mathbf{0}$ in [11.3.1]).

Clearly, to test the parallel null hypothesis that $\mathbf{y}_2$ is block-exogenous with respect to $\mathbf{y}_1$, we would calculate

$$T\{\log|\hat{\mathbf{\Omega}}_{22}(0)| - \log|\hat{\mathbf{\Omega}}_{22}|\} \approx \chi^2(n_2 n_1 p), \qquad [11.3.24]$$

where $\hat{\mathbf{\Omega}}_{22}$ is the variance-covariance matrix of the residuals from $OLS$ estimation of [11.3.2] and $\hat{\mathbf{\Omega}}_{22}(0)$ is the variance-covariance matrix of the residuals from $OLS$ estimation of [11.3.2] when lagged values of $\mathbf{y}_1$ are omitted from the regression (that is, when $\mathbf{B}_1 = \mathbf{0}$ in [11.3.2]).

Finally, consider maximum likelihood estimation of the $VAR$ subject to the restriction that there is no relation whatsoever between $\mathbf{y}_1$ and $\mathbf{y}_2$, that is, subject

[9] To confirm that the resulting estimate $\hat{\mathbf{\Omega}}(0)$ is symmeteric and positive definite, notice that

$$\hat{\mathbf{\Omega}}_{22}(0) = \hat{\mathbf{H}} + \hat{\mathbf{D}}_0'[\hat{\mathbf{\Omega}}_{11}(0)]\hat{\mathbf{D}}_0$$

and so

$$\begin{bmatrix} \hat{\mathbf{\Omega}}_{11}(0) & \hat{\mathbf{\Omega}}_{12}(0) \\ \hat{\mathbf{\Omega}}_{21}(0) & \hat{\mathbf{\Omega}}_{22}(0) \end{bmatrix} = \begin{bmatrix} \mathbf{I}_{n_1} & \mathbf{0} \\ \hat{\mathbf{D}}_0' & \mathbf{I}_{n_2} \end{bmatrix} \begin{bmatrix} \hat{\mathbf{\Omega}}_{11}(0) & \mathbf{0} \\ \mathbf{0} & \hat{\mathbf{H}} \end{bmatrix} \begin{bmatrix} \mathbf{I}_{n_1} & \hat{\mathbf{D}}_0 \\ \mathbf{0} & \mathbf{I}_{n_2} \end{bmatrix}.$$

to the restrictions that $\mathbf{A}_2 = \mathbf{0}$, $\mathbf{B}_1 = \mathbf{0}$, and $\mathbf{\Omega}_{21} = \mathbf{0}$. For this most restricted specification, the log likelihood becomes

$$\begin{aligned}\mathcal{L}(\boldsymbol{\theta}) = \sum_{t=1}^{T} \Big\{ & -(n_1/2)\log(2\pi) - (1/2)\log|\mathbf{\Omega}_{11}| \\ & - (1/2)(\mathbf{y}_{1t} - \mathbf{c}_1 - \mathbf{A}_1'\mathbf{x}_{1t})'\mathbf{\Omega}_{11}^{-1}(\mathbf{y}_{1t} - \mathbf{c}_1 - \mathbf{A}_1'\mathbf{x}_{1t})\Big\} \\ + \sum_{t=1}^{T} \Big\{ & -(n_2/2)\log(2\pi) - (1/2)\log|\mathbf{\Omega}_{22}| \\ & - (1/2)(\mathbf{y}_{2t} - \mathbf{c}_2 - \mathbf{B}_2'\mathbf{x}_{2t})'\mathbf{\Omega}_{22}^{-1}(\mathbf{y}_{2t} - \mathbf{c}_2 - \mathbf{B}_2'\mathbf{x}_{2t})\Big\}\end{aligned}$$

and the maximized value is

$$\begin{aligned}\mathcal{L}(\hat{\boldsymbol{\theta}}(0)) = & \{-(Tn_1/2)\log(2\pi) - (T/2)\log|\hat{\mathbf{\Omega}}_{11}(0)| - (Tn_1/2)\} \\ & + \{-(Tn_2/2)\log(2\pi) - (T/2)\log|\hat{\mathbf{\Omega}}_{22}(0)| - (Tn_2/2)\}.\end{aligned}$$

A likelihood ratio test of the null hypothesis of no relation at all between $\mathbf{y}_1$ and $\mathbf{y}_2$ is thus given by

$$\begin{aligned}& 2\{\mathcal{L}(\hat{\boldsymbol{\theta}}) - \mathcal{L}(\hat{\boldsymbol{\theta}}(0))\} \\ & \quad = T\left\{\log|\hat{\mathbf{\Omega}}_{11}(0)| + \log|\hat{\mathbf{\Omega}}_{22}(0)| - \log\begin{vmatrix}\hat{\mathbf{\Omega}}_{11} & \hat{\mathbf{\Omega}}_{12} \\ \hat{\mathbf{\Omega}}_{21} & \hat{\mathbf{\Omega}}_{22}\end{vmatrix}\right\},\end{aligned} \qquad [11.3.25]$$

where $\hat{\mathbf{\Omega}}_{12}$ is the covariance matrix between the residuals from unrestricted *OLS* estimation of [11.3.1] and [11.3.2]. This null hypothesis imposed the $(n_1 n_2 p)$ restrictions that $\mathbf{A}_2 = \mathbf{0}$, the $(n_2 n_1 p)$ restrictions that $\mathbf{B}_1 = \mathbf{0}$, and the $(n_2 n_1)$ restrictions that $\mathbf{\Omega}_{21} = \mathbf{0}$. Hence, the statistic in [11.3.25] has a $\chi^2$ distribution with $(n_1 n_2) \times (2p + 1)$ degrees of freedom.

Geweke (1982) proposed $(1/T)$ times the magnitude in [11.3.25] as a measure of the degree of linear dependence between $\mathbf{y}_1$ and $\mathbf{y}_2$. Note that [11.3.25] can be expressed as the sum of three terms:

$$\begin{aligned}& T\left\{\log|\hat{\mathbf{\Omega}}_{11}(0)| + \log|\hat{\mathbf{\Omega}}_{22}(0)| - \log\begin{vmatrix}\hat{\mathbf{\Omega}}_{11} & \hat{\mathbf{\Omega}}_{12} \\ \hat{\mathbf{\Omega}}_{21} & \hat{\mathbf{\Omega}}_{22}\end{vmatrix}\right\} \\ & \quad = T\{\log|\hat{\mathbf{\Omega}}_{11}(0)| - \log|\hat{\mathbf{\Omega}}_{11}|\} + T\{\log|\hat{\mathbf{\Omega}}_{22}(0)| - \log|\hat{\mathbf{\Omega}}_{22}|\} \\ & \qquad + T\left\{\log|\hat{\mathbf{\Omega}}_{11}| + \log|\hat{\mathbf{\Omega}}_{22}| - \log\begin{vmatrix}\hat{\mathbf{\Omega}}_{11} & \hat{\mathbf{\Omega}}_{12} \\ \hat{\mathbf{\Omega}}_{21} & \hat{\mathbf{\Omega}}_{22}\end{vmatrix}\right\}.\end{aligned} \qquad [11.3.26]$$

The first of these three terms, $T\{\log|\hat{\mathbf{\Omega}}_{11}(0)| - \log|\hat{\mathbf{\Omega}}_{11}|\}$, is a measure of the strength of the linear feedback from $\mathbf{y}_2$ to $\mathbf{y}_1$ and is the $\chi^2(n_1 n_2 p)$ statistic calculated in [11.3.23]. The second term, $T\{\log|\hat{\mathbf{\Omega}}_{22}(0)| - \log|\hat{\mathbf{\Omega}}_{22}|\}$, is an analogous measure of the strength of linear feedback from $\mathbf{y}_1$ to $\mathbf{y}_2$ and is the $\chi^2(n_2 n_1 p)$ statistic in [11.3.24]. The third term,

$$T\left\{\log|\hat{\mathbf{\Omega}}_{11}| + \log|\hat{\mathbf{\Omega}}_{22}| - \log\begin{vmatrix}\hat{\mathbf{\Omega}}_{11} & \hat{\mathbf{\Omega}}_{12} \\ \hat{\mathbf{\Omega}}_{21} & \hat{\mathbf{\Omega}}_{22}\end{vmatrix}\right\},$$

is a measure of instantaneous feedback. This corresponds to a likelihood ratio test of the null hypothesis that $\mathbf{\Omega}_{21} = \mathbf{0}$ with $\mathbf{A}_2$ and $\mathbf{B}_1$ unrestricted and has a $\chi^2(n_1 n_2)$ distribution under the null.

Thus, [11.3.26] can be used to summarize the strength of any linear relation between $\mathbf{y}_1$ and $\mathbf{y}_2$ and identify the source of that relation. Geweke showed how these measures can be further decomposed by frequency.

### *Maximum Likelihood Estimation Under General Coefficient Constraints*

We now discuss maximum likelihood estimation of a vector autoregression in which there are constraints that cannot be expressed in a block-recursive form as in the previous example. A *VAR* subject to general exclusion restrictions can be viewed as a system of "seemingly unrelated regressions" as originally analyzed by Zellner (1962).

Let $\mathbf{x}_{1t}$ be a $(k_1 \times 1)$ vector containing a constant term and lags of the variables that appear in the first equation of the *VAR*:

$$y_{1t} = \mathbf{x}_{1t}'\boldsymbol{\beta}_1 + \varepsilon_{1t}.$$

Similarly, let $\mathbf{x}_{2t}$ denote a $(k_2 \times 1)$ vector containing the explanatory variables for the second equation and $\mathbf{x}_{nt}$ a $(k_n \times 1)$ vector containing the variables for the last equation. Hence, the *VAR* consists of the system of equations

$$\begin{aligned} y_{1t} &= \mathbf{x}_{1t}'\boldsymbol{\beta}_1 + \varepsilon_{1t} \\ y_{2t} &= \mathbf{x}_{2t}'\boldsymbol{\beta}_2 + \varepsilon_{2t} \\ &\vdots \\ y_{nt} &= \mathbf{x}_{nt}'\boldsymbol{\beta}_n + \varepsilon_{nt}. \end{aligned} \qquad [11.3.27]$$

Let $k = k_1 + k_2 + \cdots + k_n$ denote the total number of coefficients to be estimated, and collect these in a $(k \times 1)$ vector:

$$\boldsymbol{\beta} = \begin{bmatrix} \boldsymbol{\beta}_1 \\ \boldsymbol{\beta}_2 \\ \vdots \\ \boldsymbol{\beta}_n \end{bmatrix}.$$

Then the system of equations in [11.3.27] can be written in vector form as

$$\mathbf{y}_t = \mathcal{X}_t'\boldsymbol{\beta} + \boldsymbol{\varepsilon}_t, \qquad [11.3.28]$$

where $\mathcal{X}_t'$ is the following $(n \times k)$ matrix:

$$\mathcal{X}_t' \equiv \begin{bmatrix} \mathscr{x}_{1t}' \\ \mathscr{x}_{2t}' \\ \vdots \\ \mathscr{x}_{nt}' \end{bmatrix} \equiv \begin{bmatrix} \mathbf{x}_{1t}' & \mathbf{0}' & \cdots & \mathbf{0}' \\ \mathbf{0}' & \mathbf{x}_{2t}' & \cdots & \mathbf{0}' \\ \vdots & \vdots & \cdots & \vdots \\ \mathbf{0}' & \mathbf{0}' & \cdots & \mathbf{x}_{nt}' \end{bmatrix}.$$

Thus, $\mathscr{x}_{it}'$ is defined as a $(1 \times k)$ vector containing the $k_i$ explanatory variables for equation $i$, with zeros added so as to be conformable with the $(k \times 1)$ vector $\boldsymbol{\beta}$.

The goal is to choose $\boldsymbol{\beta}$ and $\boldsymbol{\Omega}$ so as to maximize the log likelihood function

$$\begin{aligned} \mathcal{L}(\boldsymbol{\beta}, \boldsymbol{\Omega}) = &- (Tn/2)\log(2\pi) + (T/2)\log|\boldsymbol{\Omega}^{-1}| \\ &- (1/2)\sum_{t=1}^{T} (\mathbf{y}_t - \mathcal{X}_t'\boldsymbol{\beta})'\boldsymbol{\Omega}^{-1}(\mathbf{y}_t - \mathcal{X}_t'\boldsymbol{\beta}). \end{aligned} \qquad [11.3.29]$$

This calls for choosing $\boldsymbol{\beta}$ so as to minimize

$$\sum_{t=1}^{T} (\mathbf{y}_t - \mathcal{X}_t'\boldsymbol{\beta})'\boldsymbol{\Omega}^{-1}(\mathbf{y}_t - \mathcal{X}_t'\boldsymbol{\beta}). \qquad [11.3.30]$$

If $\boldsymbol{\Omega}^{-1}$ is written as $\mathbf{L}'\mathbf{L}$, this becomes

$$\sum_{t=1}^{T} (\mathbf{y}_t - \mathcal{X}_t'\boldsymbol{\beta})'\boldsymbol{\Omega}^{-1}(\mathbf{y}_t - \mathcal{X}_t'\boldsymbol{\beta}) = \sum_{t=1}^{T} (\mathbf{L}\mathbf{y}_t - \mathbf{L}\mathcal{X}_t'\boldsymbol{\beta})'(\mathbf{L}\mathbf{y}_t - \mathbf{L}\mathcal{X}_t'\boldsymbol{\beta}) = \sum_{t=1}^{T} (\tilde{\mathbf{y}}_t - \tilde{\mathcal{X}}_t'\boldsymbol{\beta})'(\tilde{\mathbf{y}}_t - \tilde{\mathcal{X}}_t'\boldsymbol{\beta}), \quad [11.3.31]$$

where $\tilde{\mathbf{y}}_t \equiv \mathbf{L}\mathbf{y}_t$ and

$$\tilde{\mathcal{X}}_t' \equiv \mathbf{L}\mathcal{X}_t' \equiv \begin{bmatrix} \tilde{x}_{1t}' \\ \tilde{x}_{2t}' \\ \vdots \\ \tilde{x}_{nt}' \end{bmatrix}.$$

But [11.3.31] is simply

$$\sum_{t=1}^{T} (\tilde{\mathbf{y}}_t - \tilde{\mathcal{X}}_t'\boldsymbol{\beta})'(\tilde{\mathbf{y}}_t - \tilde{\mathcal{X}}_t'\boldsymbol{\beta})$$

$$= \sum_{t=1}^{T} \begin{bmatrix} \tilde{y}_{1t} - \tilde{x}_{1t}'\boldsymbol{\beta} \\ \tilde{y}_{2t} - \tilde{x}_{2t}'\boldsymbol{\beta} \\ \vdots \\ \tilde{y}_{nt} - \tilde{x}_{nt}'\boldsymbol{\beta} \end{bmatrix}' \begin{bmatrix} \tilde{y}_{1t} - \tilde{x}_{1t}'\boldsymbol{\beta} \\ \tilde{y}_{2t} - \tilde{x}_{2t}'\boldsymbol{\beta} \\ \vdots \\ \tilde{y}_{nt} - \tilde{x}_{nt}'\boldsymbol{\beta} \end{bmatrix}$$

$$= \sum_{t=1}^{T} [(\tilde{y}_{1t} - \tilde{x}_{1t}'\boldsymbol{\beta})^2 + (\tilde{y}_{2t} - \tilde{x}_{2t}'\boldsymbol{\beta})^2 + \cdots + (\tilde{y}_{nt} - \tilde{x}_{nt}'\boldsymbol{\beta})^2],$$

which is minimized by an *OLS* regression of $\tilde{y}_{it}$ on $\tilde{x}_{it}$, pooling all the equations $(i = 1, 2, \ldots, n)$ into one big regression. Thus, the maximum likelihood estimate is given by

$$\hat{\boldsymbol{\beta}} = \left\{\sum_{t=1}^{T} [(\tilde{x}_{1t}\tilde{x}_{1t}') + (\tilde{x}_{2t}\tilde{x}_{2t}') + \cdots + (\tilde{x}_{nt}\tilde{x}_{nt}')]\right\}^{-1} \times \left\{\sum_{t=1}^{T} [(\tilde{x}_{1t}\tilde{y}_{1t}) + (\tilde{x}_{2t}\tilde{y}_{2t}) + \cdots + (\tilde{x}_{nt}\tilde{y}_{nt})]\right\}. \quad [11.3.32]$$

Noting that the variance of the residual of this pooled regression is unity by construction,[10] the asymptotic variance-covariance matrix of $\hat{\boldsymbol{\beta}}$ can be calculated from

$$E(\hat{\boldsymbol{\beta}} - \boldsymbol{\beta})(\hat{\boldsymbol{\beta}} - \boldsymbol{\beta})' \cong \left\{\sum_{t=1}^{T} [(\tilde{x}_{1t}\tilde{x}_{1t}') + (\tilde{x}_{2t}\tilde{x}_{2t}') + \cdots + (\tilde{x}_{nt}\tilde{x}_{nt}')]\right\}^{-1}.$$

Construction of the variables $\tilde{y}_{it}$ and $\tilde{x}_{it}$ to use in this pooled *OLS* regression requires knowledge of $\mathbf{L}$ and hence $\boldsymbol{\Omega}$. The parameters in $\boldsymbol{\beta}$ and $\boldsymbol{\Omega}$ can be estimated jointly by maximum likelihood through the following iterative procedure. From $n$ *OLS* regressions of $y_{it}$ on $\mathbf{x}_{it}$, form an initial estimate of the coefficient vector

[10]That is,

$$E(\tilde{\mathbf{y}}_t - \tilde{\mathcal{X}}_t'\boldsymbol{\beta})(\tilde{\mathbf{y}}_t - \tilde{\mathcal{X}}_t'\boldsymbol{\beta})' = \mathbf{L}\boldsymbol{\Omega}\mathbf{L}' = \mathbf{L}(\mathbf{L}'\mathbf{L})^{-1}\mathbf{L}' = \mathbf{I}_n.$$

$\hat{\boldsymbol\beta}(0) = (\mathbf{b}_1' \quad \mathbf{b}_2' \quad \cdots \quad \mathbf{b}_n')'$. Use this to form an initial estimate of the variance matrix,

$$\hat{\boldsymbol\Omega}(0) = (1/T) \sum_{t=1}^{T} [\mathbf{y}_t - \mathcal{X}_t'\hat{\boldsymbol\beta}(0)][\mathbf{y}_t - \mathcal{X}_t'\hat{\boldsymbol\beta}(0)]'.$$

Find a matrix $\hat{\mathbf{L}}(0)$ such that $[\hat{\mathbf{L}}(0)']\hat{\mathbf{L}}(0) = [\hat{\boldsymbol\Omega}(0)]^{-1}$, say, by Cholesky factorization, and form $\tilde{\mathbf{y}}_t(0) = \hat{\mathbf{L}}(0)\mathbf{y}_t$ and $\tilde{\mathcal{X}}_t'(0) = \hat{\mathbf{L}}(0)\mathcal{X}_t'$. A pooled *OLS* regression of $\tilde{\mathbf{y}}_{it}(0)$ on $\tilde{\boldsymbol{x}}_{it}(0)$ combining $i = 1, 2, \ldots, n$ then yields the new estimate $\hat{\boldsymbol\beta}(1)$, from which $\hat{\boldsymbol\Omega}(1) = (1/T)\Sigma_{t=1}^{T}[\mathbf{y}_t - \mathcal{X}_t'\hat{\boldsymbol\beta}(1)][\mathbf{y}_t - \mathcal{X}_t'\hat{\boldsymbol\beta}(1)]'$. Iterating in this manner will produce the maximum likelihood estimates $(\hat{\boldsymbol\beta}, \hat{\boldsymbol\Omega})$, though the estimate after just one iteration has the same asymptotic distribution as the final *MLE* (see Magnus, 1978).

An alternative expression for the *MLE* in [11.3.32] is sometimes used. Notice that

$$\begin{aligned}
&[(\tilde{\boldsymbol{x}}_{1t}\tilde{\boldsymbol{x}}_{1t}') + (\tilde{\boldsymbol{x}}_{2t}\tilde{\boldsymbol{x}}_{2t}') + \cdots + (\tilde{\boldsymbol{x}}_{nt}\tilde{\boldsymbol{x}}_{nt}')] \\
&= [\tilde{\boldsymbol{x}}_{1t} \quad \tilde{\boldsymbol{x}}_{2t} \quad \cdots \quad \tilde{\boldsymbol{x}}_{nt}] \begin{bmatrix} \tilde{\boldsymbol{x}}_{1t}' \\ \tilde{\boldsymbol{x}}_{2t}' \\ \vdots \\ \tilde{\boldsymbol{x}}_{nt}' \end{bmatrix} \\
&= \tilde{\mathcal{X}}_t\tilde{\mathcal{X}}_t' \\
&= \mathcal{X}_t\mathbf{L}'\mathbf{L}\mathcal{X}_t' \\
&= \begin{bmatrix} \mathbf{x}_{1t} & \mathbf{0} & \cdots & \mathbf{0} \\ \mathbf{0} & \mathbf{x}_{2t} & \cdots & \mathbf{0} \\ \vdots & \vdots & \cdots & \vdots \\ \mathbf{0} & \mathbf{0} & \cdots & \mathbf{x}_{nt} \end{bmatrix} \begin{bmatrix} \sigma^{11} & \sigma^{12} & \cdots & \sigma^{1n} \\ \sigma^{21} & \sigma^{22} & \cdots & \sigma^{2n} \\ \vdots & \vdots & \cdots & \vdots \\ \sigma^{n1} & \sigma^{n2} & \cdots & \sigma^{nn} \end{bmatrix} \begin{bmatrix} \mathbf{x}_{1t}' & \mathbf{0}' & \cdots & \mathbf{0}' \\ \mathbf{0}' & \mathbf{x}_{2t}' & \cdots & \mathbf{0}' \\ \vdots & \vdots & \cdots & \vdots \\ \mathbf{0}' & \mathbf{0}' & \cdots & \mathbf{x}_{nt}' \end{bmatrix} \qquad [11.3.33] \\
&= \begin{bmatrix} \sigma^{11}\mathbf{x}_{1t}\mathbf{x}_{1t}' & \sigma^{12}\mathbf{x}_{1t}\mathbf{x}_{2t}' & \cdots & \sigma^{1n}\mathbf{x}_{1t}\mathbf{x}_{nt}' \\ \sigma^{21}\mathbf{x}_{2t}\mathbf{x}_{1t}' & \sigma^{22}\mathbf{x}_{2t}\mathbf{x}_{2t}' & \cdots & \sigma^{2n}\mathbf{x}_{2t}\mathbf{x}_{nt}' \\ \vdots & \vdots & \cdots & \vdots \\ \sigma^{n1}\mathbf{x}_{nt}\mathbf{x}_{1t}' & \sigma^{n2}\mathbf{x}_{nt}\mathbf{x}_{2t}' & \cdots & \sigma^{nn}\mathbf{x}_{nt}\mathbf{x}_{nt}' \end{bmatrix},
\end{aligned}$$

where $\sigma^{ij}$ denotes the row $i$, column $j$ element of $\boldsymbol\Omega^{-1}$. Similarly,

$$\begin{aligned}
&[(\tilde{\boldsymbol{x}}_{1t}\tilde{y}_{1t}) + (\tilde{\boldsymbol{x}}_{2t}\tilde{y}_{2t}) + \cdots + (\tilde{\boldsymbol{x}}_{nt}\tilde{y}_{nt})] \\
&= [\tilde{\boldsymbol{x}}_{1t} \quad \tilde{\boldsymbol{x}}_{2t} \quad \cdots \quad \tilde{\boldsymbol{x}}_{nt}] \begin{bmatrix} \tilde{y}_{1t} \\ \tilde{y}_{2t} \\ \vdots \\ \tilde{y}_{nt} \end{bmatrix} \\
&= \mathcal{X}_t\mathbf{L}'\mathbf{L}\mathbf{y}_t \\
&= \begin{bmatrix} \mathbf{x}_{1t} & \mathbf{0} & \cdots & \mathbf{0} \\ \mathbf{0} & \mathbf{x}_{2t} & \cdots & \mathbf{0} \\ \vdots & \vdots & \cdots & \vdots \\ \mathbf{0} & \mathbf{0} & \cdots & \mathbf{x}_{nt} \end{bmatrix} \begin{bmatrix} \sigma^{11} & \sigma^{12} & \cdots & \sigma^{1n} \\ \sigma^{21} & \sigma^{22} & \cdots & \sigma^{2n} \\ \vdots & \vdots & \cdots & \vdots \\ \sigma^{n1} & \sigma^{n2} & \cdots & \sigma^{nn} \end{bmatrix} \begin{bmatrix} y_{1t} \\ y_{2t} \\ \vdots \\ y_{nt} \end{bmatrix} \qquad [11.3.34] \\
&= \begin{bmatrix} \sigma^{11}\mathbf{x}_{1t}y_{1t} + \sigma^{12}\mathbf{x}_{1t}y_{2t} + \cdots + \sigma^{1n}\mathbf{x}_{1t}y_{nt} \\ \sigma^{21}\mathbf{x}_{2t}y_{1t} + \sigma^{22}\mathbf{x}_{2t}y_{2t} + \cdots + \sigma^{2n}\mathbf{x}_{2t}y_{nt} \\ \vdots \\ \sigma^{n1}\mathbf{x}_{nt}y_{1t} + \sigma^{n2}\mathbf{x}_{nt}y_{2t} + \cdots + \sigma^{nn}\mathbf{x}_{nt}y_{nt} \end{bmatrix}.
\end{aligned}$$

Substituting [11.3.33] and [11.3.34] into [11.3.32], the *MLE* satisfies

$$\hat{\boldsymbol\beta} = \begin{bmatrix} \sigma^{11}\Sigma\mathbf{x}_{1t}\mathbf{x}'_{1t} & \sigma^{12}\Sigma\mathbf{x}_{1t}\mathbf{x}'_{2t} & \cdots & \sigma^{1n}\Sigma\mathbf{x}_{1t}\mathbf{x}'_{nt} \\ \sigma^{21}\Sigma\mathbf{x}_{2t}\mathbf{x}'_{1t} & \sigma^{22}\Sigma\mathbf{x}_{2t}\mathbf{x}'_{2t} & \cdots & \sigma^{2n}\Sigma\mathbf{x}_{2t}\mathbf{x}'_{nt} \\ \vdots & \vdots & \cdots & \vdots \\ \sigma^{n1}\Sigma\mathbf{x}_{nt}\mathbf{x}'_{1t} & \sigma^{n2}\Sigma\mathbf{x}_{nt}\mathbf{x}'_{2t} & \cdots & \sigma^{nn}\Sigma\mathbf{x}_{nt}\mathbf{x}'_{nt} \end{bmatrix}^{-1} \times \begin{bmatrix} \Sigma(\sigma^{11}\mathbf{x}_{1t}y_{1t} + \sigma^{12}\mathbf{x}_{1t}y_{2t} + \cdots + \sigma^{1n}\mathbf{x}_{1t}y_{nt}) \\ \Sigma(\sigma^{21}\mathbf{x}_{2t}y_{1t} + \sigma^{22}\mathbf{x}_{2t}y_{2t} + \cdots + \sigma^{2n}\mathbf{x}_{2t}y_{nt}) \\ \vdots \\ \Sigma(\sigma^{n1}\mathbf{x}_{nt}y_{1t} + \sigma^{n2}\mathbf{x}_{nt}y_{2t} + \cdots + \sigma^{nn}\mathbf{x}_{nt}y_{nt}) \end{bmatrix}, \qquad [11.3.35]$$

where $\Sigma$ denotes summation over $t = 1, 2, \ldots, T$.

The result from Section 11.1 was that when there are no restrictions on the *VAR*, maximum likelihood estimation is achieved by *OLS* equation by equation. This result can be seen as a special case of [11.3.35] by setting $\mathbf{x}_{1t} = \mathbf{x}_{2t} = \cdots = \mathbf{x}_{nt}$, for then [11.3.35] becomes

$$\begin{aligned} \hat{\boldsymbol\beta} &= [\boldsymbol\Omega^{-1} \otimes (\Sigma\mathbf{x}_t\mathbf{x}'_t)]^{-1}\Sigma[(\boldsymbol\Omega^{-1}\mathbf{y}_t) \otimes \mathbf{x}_t] \\ &= [\boldsymbol\Omega \otimes (\Sigma\mathbf{x}_t\mathbf{x}'_t)^{-1}]\Sigma[(\boldsymbol\Omega^{-1}\mathbf{y}_t) \otimes \mathbf{x}_t] \\ &= [\mathbf{I}_n \otimes (\Sigma\mathbf{x}_t\mathbf{x}'_t)^{-1}]\Sigma[\mathbf{y}_t \otimes \mathbf{x}_t] \\ &= \begin{bmatrix} (\Sigma\mathbf{x}_t\mathbf{x}'_t)^{-1} & \mathbf{0} & \cdots & \mathbf{0} \\ \mathbf{0} & (\Sigma\mathbf{x}_t\mathbf{x}'_t)^{-1} & \cdots & \mathbf{0} \\ \vdots & \vdots & \cdots & \vdots \\ \mathbf{0} & \mathbf{0} & \cdots & (\Sigma\mathbf{x}_t\mathbf{x}'_t)^{-1} \end{bmatrix} \begin{bmatrix} \Sigma y_{1t}\mathbf{x}_t \\ \Sigma y_{2t}\mathbf{x}_t \\ \vdots \\ \Sigma y_{nt}\mathbf{x}_t \end{bmatrix} \\ &= \begin{bmatrix} \mathbf{b}_1 \\ \mathbf{b}_2 \\ \vdots \\ \mathbf{b}_n \end{bmatrix}, \end{aligned}$$

as shown directly in Section 11.1.

Maximum likelihood estimation with constraints on both the coefficients and the variance-covariance matrix was discussed by Magnus (1978).

## 11.4. *The Impulse-Response Function*

In equation [10.1.15] a *VAR* was written in vector $MA(\infty)$ form as

$$\mathbf{y}_t = \boldsymbol\mu + \boldsymbol\varepsilon_t + \boldsymbol\Psi_1\boldsymbol\varepsilon_{t-1} + \boldsymbol\Psi_2\boldsymbol\varepsilon_{t-2} + \cdots. \qquad [11.4.1]$$

Thus, the matrix $\boldsymbol\Psi_s$ has the interpretation

$$\frac{\partial\mathbf{y}_{t+s}}{\partial\boldsymbol\varepsilon'_t} = \boldsymbol\Psi_s; \qquad [11.4.2]$$

that is, the row $i$, column $j$ element of $\boldsymbol\Psi_s$ identifies the consequences of a one-unit increase in the $j$th variable's innovation at date $t$ ($\varepsilon_{jt}$) for the value of the $i$th variable at time $t + s$ ($y_{i,t+s}$), holding all other innovations at all dates constant.

If we were told that the first element of $\boldsymbol\varepsilon_t$ changed by $\delta_1$ at the same time that the second element changed by $\delta_2$, . . . , and the $n$th element by $\delta_n$, then the combined effect of these changes on the value of the vector $\mathbf{y}_{t+s}$ would be given by

$$\Delta \mathbf{y}_{t+s} = \frac{\partial \mathbf{y}_{t+s}}{\partial \varepsilon_{1t}} \delta_1 + \frac{\partial \mathbf{y}_{t+s}}{\partial \varepsilon_{2t}} \delta_2 + \cdots + \frac{\partial \mathbf{y}_{t+s}}{\partial \varepsilon_{nt}} \delta_n = \mathbf{\Psi}_s \boldsymbol{\delta}, \qquad [11.4.3]$$

where $\boldsymbol{\delta} = (\delta_1, \delta_2, \ldots, \delta_n)'$.

Several analytic characterizations of $\mathbf{\Psi}_s$ were given in Section 10.1. A simple way to find these dynamic multipliers numerically is by simulation. To implement the simulation, set $\mathbf{y}_{t-1} = \mathbf{y}_{t-2} = \cdots = \mathbf{y}_{t-p} = \mathbf{0}$. Set $\varepsilon_{jt} = 1$ and all other elements of $\boldsymbol{\varepsilon}_t$ to zero, and simulate the system [11.1.1] for dates $t, t+1, t+2, \ldots$, with $\mathbf{c}$ and $\boldsymbol{\varepsilon}_{t+1}, \boldsymbol{\varepsilon}_{t+2}, \ldots$ all zero. The value of the vector $\mathbf{y}_{t+s}$ at date $t+s$ of this simulation corresponds to the $j$th column of the matrix $\mathbf{\Psi}_s$. By doing a separate simulation for impulses to each of the innovations ($j = 1, 2, \ldots, n$), all of the columns of $\mathbf{\Psi}_s$ can be calculated.

A plot of the row $i$, column $j$ element of $\mathbf{\Psi}_s$,

$$\frac{\partial y_{i,t+s}}{\partial \varepsilon_{jt}}, \qquad [11.4.4]$$

as a function of $s$ is called the *impulse-response function*. It describes the response of $y_{i,t+s}$ to a one-time impulse in $y_{jt}$ with all other variables dated $t$ or earlier held constant.

Is there a sense in which this multiplier can be viewed as measuring the causal effect of $y_j$ on $y_i$? The discussion of Granger-causality tests suggests that we should be wary of such a claim. We are on surer ground with an atheoretical *VAR* if we confine ourselves to statements about forecasts. Consider, therefore, the following question. Let

$$\mathbf{x}'_{t-1} = (\mathbf{y}'_{t-1}, \mathbf{y}'_{t-2}, \ldots, \mathbf{y}'_{t-p})$$

denote the information received about the system as of date $t-1$. Suppose we are then told that the date $t$ value of the first variable in the autoregression, $y_{1t}$, was higher than expected, so that $\varepsilon_{1t}$ is positive. How does this cause us to revise our forecast of $y_{i,t+s}$? In other words, what is

$$\frac{\partial \hat{E}(y_{i,t+s} | y_{1t}, \mathbf{x}_{t-1})}{\partial y_{1t}}? \qquad [11.4.5]$$

The answer to this question is given by [11.4.4] with $j = 1$ only in the special case when $E(\boldsymbol{\varepsilon}_t \boldsymbol{\varepsilon}'_t) = \mathbf{\Omega}$ is a diagonal matrix. In the more general case when the elements of $\boldsymbol{\varepsilon}_t$ are contemporaneously correlated with one another, the fact that $\varepsilon_{1t}$ is positive gives us some useful new information about the values of $\varepsilon_{2t}, \ldots, \varepsilon_{nt}$. This information has further implications for the value of $y_{i,t+s}$. To summarize these implications, we need to calculate the vector

$$\frac{\partial \hat{E}(\boldsymbol{\varepsilon}_t | y_{1t}, \mathbf{x}_{t-1})}{\partial y_{1t}}$$

and then use [11.4.3] to calculate the effect of this change in all the elements of $\boldsymbol{\varepsilon}_t$ on the value of $y_{i,t+s}$.

Yet another magnitude we might propose to measure is the forecast revision resulting from new information about, say, the second variable, $y_{2t}$, beyond that contained in the first variable, $y_{1t}$. Thus, we might calculate

$$\frac{\partial \hat{E}(y_{i,t+s} | y_{2t}, y_{1t}, \mathbf{x}_{t-1})}{\partial y_{2t}}. \qquad [11.4.6]$$

Similarly, for the variable designated number 3, we might seek

$$\frac{\partial \hat{E}(y_{i,t+s} | y_{3t}, y_{2t}, y_{1t}, \mathbf{x}_{t-1})}{\partial y_{3t}}, \qquad [11.4.7]$$

and for variable $n$,

$$\frac{\partial \hat{E}(y_{i,t+s} | y_{nt}, y_{n-1,t}, \ldots, y_{1t}, \mathbf{x}_{t-1})}{\partial y_{nt}}. \qquad [11.4.8]$$

This last magnitude corresponds to the effect of $\varepsilon_{nt}$ with $\varepsilon_{1t}, \ldots, \varepsilon_{n-1,t}$ constant and is given simply by the row $i$, column $n$ element of $\mathbf{\Psi}_s$.

The recursive information ordering in [11.4.5] through [11.4.8] is quite commonly used. For this ordering, the indicated multipliers can be calculated from the moving average coefficients ($\mathbf{\Psi}_s$) and the variance-covariance matrix of $\boldsymbol{\varepsilon}_t$ ($\mathbf{\Omega}$) by a simple algorithm. Recall from Section 4.4 that for any real symmetric positive definite matrix $\mathbf{\Omega}$, there exists a unique lower triangular matrix $\mathbf{A}$ with 1s along the principal diagonal and a unique diagonal matrix $\mathbf{D}$ with positive entries along the principal diagonal such that

$$\mathbf{\Omega} = \mathbf{ADA}'. \qquad [11.4.9]$$

Using this matrix $\mathbf{A}$ we can construct an $(n \times 1)$ vector $\mathbf{u}_t$ from

$$\mathbf{u}_t \equiv \mathbf{A}^{-1}\boldsymbol{\varepsilon}_t. \qquad [11.4.10]$$

Notice that since $\boldsymbol{\varepsilon}_t$ is uncorrelated with its own lags or with lagged values of $\mathbf{y}$, it follows that $\mathbf{u}_t$ is also uncorrelated with its own lags or with lagged values of $\mathbf{y}$. The elements of $\mathbf{u}_t$ are furthermore uncorrelated with each other:

$$\begin{aligned} E(\mathbf{u}_t\mathbf{u}_t') &= [\mathbf{A}^{-1}]E(\boldsymbol{\varepsilon}_t\boldsymbol{\varepsilon}_t')[\mathbf{A}^{-1}]' \\ &= [\mathbf{A}^{-1}]\mathbf{\Omega}[\mathbf{A}']^{-1} \\ &= [\mathbf{A}^{-1}]\mathbf{ADA}'[\mathbf{A}']^{-1} \\ &= \mathbf{D}. \end{aligned} \qquad [11.4.11]$$

But $\mathbf{D}$ is a diagonal matrix, verifying that the elements of $\mathbf{u}_t$ are mutually uncorrelated. The $(j, j)$ element of $\mathbf{D}$ gives the variance of $u_{jt}$.

If both sides of [11.4.10] are premultiplied by $\mathbf{A}$, the result is

$$\mathbf{Au}_t = \boldsymbol{\varepsilon}_t. \qquad [11.4.12]$$

Writing out the equations represented by [11.4.12] explicitly,

$$\begin{bmatrix} 1 & 0 & 0 & \cdots & 0 \\ a_{21} & 1 & 0 & \cdots & 0 \\ a_{31} & a_{32} & 1 & \cdots & 0 \\ \vdots & \vdots & \vdots & \cdots & \vdots \\ a_{n1} & a_{n2} & a_{n3} & \cdots & 1 \end{bmatrix} \begin{bmatrix} u_{1t} \\ u_{2t} \\ u_{3t} \\ \vdots \\ u_{nt} \end{bmatrix} = \begin{bmatrix} \varepsilon_{1t} \\ \varepsilon_{2t} \\ \varepsilon_{3t} \\ \vdots \\ \varepsilon_{nt} \end{bmatrix}. \qquad [11.4.13]$$

Thus, $u_{1t}$ is simply $\varepsilon_{1t}$. The $j$th row of [11.4.13] states that

$$u_{jt} = \varepsilon_{jt} - a_{j1}u_{1t} - a_{j2}u_{2t} - \cdots - a_{j,j-1}u_{j-1,t}.$$

But since $u_{jt}$ is uncorrelated with $u_{1t}, u_{2t}, \ldots, u_{j-1,t}$, it follows that $u_{jt}$ has the interpretation as the residual from a projection of $\varepsilon_{jt}$ on $u_{1t}, u_{2t}, \ldots, u_{j-1,t}$:

$$\hat{E}(\varepsilon_{jt} | u_{1t}, u_{2t}, \ldots, u_{j-1,t}) = a_{j1}u_{1t} + a_{j2}u_{2t} + \cdots + a_{j,j-1}u_{j-1,t}. \qquad [11.4.14]$$

The fact that the $u_{jt}$ are uncorrelated further implies that the coefficient on $u_{1t}$ in a projection of $\varepsilon_{jt}$ on $(u_{1t}, u_{2t}, \ldots, u_{j-1,t})$ is the same as the coefficient on

$u_{1t}$ in a projection of $\varepsilon_{jt}$ on $u_{1t}$ alone:

$$\hat{E}(\varepsilon_{jt}|u_{1t}) = a_{j1}u_{1t}. \qquad [11.4.15]$$

Recalling from [11.4.13] that $\varepsilon_{1t} = u_{1t}$, we see that new information about the value of $\varepsilon_{1t}$ would cause us to revise our forecast of $\varepsilon_{jt}$ by the amount

$$\frac{\partial \hat{E}(\varepsilon_{jt}|\varepsilon_{1t})}{\partial \varepsilon_{1t}} = \frac{\partial \hat{E}(\varepsilon_{jt}|u_{1t})}{\partial u_{1t}} = a_{j1}. \qquad [11.4.16]$$

Now $\varepsilon_{1t}$ has the interpretation as $y_{1t} - \hat{E}(y_{1t}|\mathbf{x}_{t-1})$ and $\varepsilon_{jt}$ has the interpretation as $y_{jt} - \hat{E}(y_{jt}|\mathbf{x}_{t-1})$. From the formula for updating a linear projection [4.5.14], the coefficient on $y_{1t}$ in a linear projection of $y_{jt}$ on $y_{1t}$ and $\mathbf{x}_{t-1}$ is the same as the coefficient on $\varepsilon_{1t}$ in a linear projection of $\varepsilon_{jt}$ on $\varepsilon_{1t}$.[11] Hence,

$$\frac{\partial \hat{E}(\varepsilon_{jt}|y_{1t}, \mathbf{x}_{t-1})}{\partial y_{1t}} = a_{j1}. \qquad [11.4.17]$$

Combining these equations for $j = 1, 2, \ldots, n$ into a vector,

$$\frac{\partial \hat{E}(\boldsymbol{\varepsilon}_t|y_{1t}, \mathbf{x}_{t-1})}{\partial y_{1t}} = \mathbf{a}_1, \qquad [11.4.18]$$

where $\mathbf{a}_1$ denotes the first column of $\mathbf{A}$:

$$\mathbf{a}_1 \equiv \begin{bmatrix} 1 \\ a_{21} \\ a_{31} \\ \vdots \\ a_{n1} \end{bmatrix}.$$

Substituting [11.4.18] into [11.4.3], the consequences for $\mathbf{y}_{t+s}$ of new information about $y_{1t}$ beyond that contained in $\mathbf{x}_{t-1}$ are given by

$$\frac{\partial \hat{E}(\mathbf{y}_{t+s}|y_{1t}, \mathbf{x}_{t-1})}{\partial y_{1t}} = \boldsymbol{\Psi}_s\mathbf{a}_1.$$

Similarly, the variable $u_{2t}$ represents the new information in $y_{2t}$ beyond that contained in $(y_{1t}, \mathbf{x}_{t-1})$. This information would, of course, not cause us to change our assessment of $\varepsilon_{1t}$ (which we know with certainty from $y_{1t}$ and $\mathbf{x}_{t-1}$), but from [11.4.14] would cause us to revise our estimate of $\varepsilon_{jt}$ for $j = 2, 3, \ldots, n$ by

$$\frac{\partial \hat{E}(\varepsilon_{jt}|u_{2t}, u_{1t})}{\partial u_{2t}} = a_{j2}.$$

Substituting this into [11.4.3], we conclude that

$$\frac{\partial \hat{E}(\mathbf{y}_{t+s}|y_{2t}, y_{1t}, \mathbf{x}_{t-1})}{\partial y_{2t}} = \boldsymbol{\Psi}_s\mathbf{a}_2,$$

[11]That is

$$\begin{aligned}\hat{E}(y_{jt}|y_{1t}, \mathbf{x}_{t-1}) &= \hat{E}(y_{jt}|\mathbf{x}_{t-1}) \\ &\quad + \text{Cov}\{[y_{jt} - \hat{E}(y_{jt}|\mathbf{x}_{t-1})], [y_{1t} - \hat{E}(y_{1t}|\mathbf{x}_{t-1})]\} \\ &\quad \times \{\text{Var}[y_{1t} - \hat{E}(y_{1t}|\mathbf{x}_{t-1})]\}^{-1}[y_{1t} - \hat{E}(y_{1t}|\mathbf{x}_{t-1})] \\ &= \hat{E}(y_{jt}|\mathbf{x}_{t-1}) + \text{Cov}(\varepsilon_{jt}, \varepsilon_{1t})\cdot\{\text{Var}(\varepsilon_{1t})\}^{-1}\cdot\varepsilon_{1t}.\end{aligned}$$

where

$$\mathbf{a}_2 = \begin{bmatrix} 0 \\ 1 \\ a_{32} \\ a_{42} \\ \vdots \\ a_{n2} \end{bmatrix}.$$

In general,

$$\frac{\partial \hat{E}(\mathbf{y}_{t+s} | y_{jt}, y_{j-1,t}, \ldots, y_{1t}, \mathbf{x}_{t-1})}{\partial y_{jt}} = \boldsymbol{\Psi}_s \mathbf{a}_j, \qquad [11.4.19]$$

where $\mathbf{a}_j$ denotes the $j$th column of the matrix $\mathbf{A}$ defined in [11.4.9].

The magnitude in [11.4.19] is a population moment, constructed from the population parameters $\boldsymbol{\Psi}_s$ and $\boldsymbol{\Omega}$ using [11.4.9]. For a given observed sample of size $T$, we would estimate the autoregressive coefficients $\hat{\boldsymbol{\Phi}}_1, \ldots, \hat{\boldsymbol{\Phi}}_p$ by *OLS* and construct $\hat{\boldsymbol{\Psi}}_s$ by simulating the estimated system. *OLS* estimation would also provide the estimate $\hat{\boldsymbol{\Omega}} = (1/T)\sum_{t=1}^{T} \hat{\boldsymbol{\varepsilon}}_t \hat{\boldsymbol{\varepsilon}}_t'$, where the $i$th element of $\hat{\boldsymbol{\varepsilon}}_t$ is the *OLS* sample residual for the $i$th equation in the *VAR* for date $t$. Matrices $\hat{\mathbf{A}}$ and $\hat{\mathbf{D}}$ satisfying $\hat{\boldsymbol{\Omega}} = \hat{\mathbf{A}}\hat{\mathbf{D}}\hat{\mathbf{A}}'$ could then be constructed from $\hat{\boldsymbol{\Omega}}$ using the algorithm described in Section 4.4. Notice that the elements of the vector $\hat{\mathbf{u}}_t = \hat{\mathbf{A}}^{-1}\hat{\boldsymbol{\varepsilon}}_t$ are then mutually orthogonal by construction:

$$(1/T)\sum_{t=1}^{T} \hat{\mathbf{u}}_t \hat{\mathbf{u}}_t' = (1/T)\sum_{t=1}^{T} \hat{\mathbf{A}}^{-1}\hat{\boldsymbol{\varepsilon}}_t \hat{\boldsymbol{\varepsilon}}_t'(\hat{\mathbf{A}}^{-1})' = \hat{\mathbf{A}}^{-1}\hat{\boldsymbol{\Omega}}(\hat{\mathbf{A}}^{-1})' = \hat{\mathbf{D}}.$$

The sample estimate of [11.4.19] is then

$$\hat{\boldsymbol{\Psi}}_s \hat{\mathbf{a}}_j, \qquad [11.4.20]$$

where $\hat{\mathbf{a}}_j$ denotes the $j$th column of the matrix $\hat{\mathbf{A}}$.

A plot of [11.4.20] as a function of $s$ is known as an *orthogonalized impulse-response function*. It is based on decomposing the original *VAR* innovations $(\varepsilon_{1t}, \ldots, \varepsilon_{nt})$ into a set of uncorrelated components $(u_{1t}, \ldots, u_{nt})$ and calculating the consequences for $\mathbf{y}_{t+s}$ of a unit impulse in $u_{jt}$. These multipliers describe how new information about $y_{jt}$ causes us to revise our forecast of $\mathbf{y}_{t+s}$, though the implicit definition of "new" information is different for each variable $j$.

What is the rationale for treating each variable differently? Clearly, if the *VAR* is being used as a purely atheoretical summary of the dynamics of a group of variables, there can be none—we could just as easily have labeled the second variable $y_{1t}$ and the first variable $y_{2t}$, in which case we would have obtained different dynamic multipliers. By choosing a particular recursive ordering of the variables, the researcher is implicitly asking a set of questions about forecasting of the form of [11.4.5] through [11.4.8]. Whether we should orthogonalize in this way and how the variables should be ordered would seem to depend on why we want to ask such questions about forecasting in the first place. We will explore this issue in more depth in Section 11.6.

Before leaving the recursive orthogonalization, we note another popular form in which it is implemented and reported. Recall that $\mathbf{D}$ is a diagonal matrix whose $(j, j)$ element is the variance of $u_{jt}$. Let $\mathbf{D}^{1/2}$ denote the diagonal matrix whose $(j, j)$ element is the standard deviation of $u_{jt}$. Note that [11.4.9] could be written as

$$\boldsymbol{\Omega} = \mathbf{A}\mathbf{D}^{1/2}\mathbf{D}^{1/2}\mathbf{A}' = \mathbf{P}\mathbf{P}', \qquad [11.4.21]$$

where

$$\mathbf{P} \equiv \mathbf{A}\mathbf{D}^{1/2}.$$

Expression [11.4.21] is the *Cholesky decomposition* of the matrix $\mathbf{\Omega}$. Note that, like $\mathbf{A}$, the $(n \times n)$ matrix $\mathbf{P}$ is lower triangular, though whereas $\mathbf{A}$ has 1s along its principal diagonal, $\mathbf{P}$ has the standard deviation of $\mathbf{u}_t$ along its principal diagonal.

In place of $\mathbf{u}_t$ defined in [11.4.10], some researchers use

$$\mathbf{v}_t \equiv \mathbf{P}^{-1}\boldsymbol{\varepsilon}_t = \mathbf{D}^{-1/2}\mathbf{A}^{-1}\boldsymbol{\varepsilon}_t = \mathbf{D}^{-1/2}\mathbf{u}_t.$$

Thus, $v_{jt}$ is just $u_{jt}$ divided by its standard deviation $\sqrt{d_{jj}}$. A one-unit increase in $v_{jt}$ is the same as a one-standard-deviation increase in $u_{jt}$.

In place of the dynamic multiplier $\partial y_{i,t+s}/\partial u_{jt}$, these researchers then report $\partial y_{i,t+s}/\partial v_{jt}$. The relation between these multipliers is clearly

$$\frac{\partial \mathbf{y}_{t+s}}{\partial v_{jt}} = \frac{\partial \mathbf{y}_{t+s}}{\partial u_{jt}}\sqrt{d_{jj}} = \mathbf{\Psi}_s\mathbf{a}_j\sqrt{d_{jj}}.$$

But $\mathbf{a}_j\sqrt{d_{jj}}$ is just the $j$th column of $\mathbf{AD}^{1/2}$, which is the $j$th column of the Cholesky factor matrix $\mathbf{P}$. Denoting the $j$th column of $\mathbf{P}$ by $\mathbf{p}_j$, we have

$$\frac{\partial \mathbf{y}_{t+s}}{\partial v_{jt}} = \mathbf{\Psi}_s\mathbf{p}_j. \qquad [11.4.22]$$

Expression [11.4.22] is just [11.4.19] multiplied by the constant $\sqrt{\text{Var}(u_{jt})}$. Expression [11.4.19] gives the consequences of a one-unit increase in $y_{jt}$, where the units are those in which $y_{jt}$ itself is measured. Expression [11.4.22] gives the consequences if $y_{jt}$ were to increase by $\sqrt{\text{Var}(u_{jt})}$ units.

## 11.5. *Variance Decomposition*

Equations [10.1.14] and [10.1.16] identify the error in forecasting a *VAR* $s$ periods into the future as

$$\mathbf{y}_{t+s} - \hat{\mathbf{y}}_{t+s|t} = \boldsymbol{\varepsilon}_{t+s} + \mathbf{\Psi}_1\boldsymbol{\varepsilon}_{t+s-1} + \mathbf{\Psi}_2\boldsymbol{\varepsilon}_{t+s-2} + \cdots + \mathbf{\Psi}_{s-1}\boldsymbol{\varepsilon}_{t+1}. \qquad [11.5.1]$$

The mean squared error of this $s$-period-ahead forecast is thus

$$\begin{aligned} MSE(\hat{\mathbf{y}}_{t+s|t}) &= E[(\mathbf{y}_{t+s} - \hat{\mathbf{y}}_{t+s|t})(\mathbf{y}_{t+s} - \hat{\mathbf{y}}_{t+s|t})'] \\ &= \mathbf{\Omega} + \mathbf{\Psi}_1\mathbf{\Omega}\mathbf{\Psi}_1' + \mathbf{\Psi}_2\mathbf{\Omega}\mathbf{\Psi}_2' + \cdots + \mathbf{\Psi}_{s-1}\mathbf{\Omega}\mathbf{\Psi}_{s-1}', \end{aligned} \qquad [11.5.2]$$

where

$$\mathbf{\Omega} = E(\boldsymbol{\varepsilon}_t\boldsymbol{\varepsilon}_t'). \qquad [11.5.3]$$

Let us now consider how each of the orthogonalized disturbances $(u_{1t}, \ldots, u_{nt})$ contributes to this *MSE*. Write [11.4.12] as

$$\boldsymbol{\varepsilon}_t = \mathbf{A}\mathbf{u}_t = \mathbf{a}_1u_{1t} + \mathbf{a}_2u_{2t} + \cdots + \mathbf{a}_nu_{nt}, \qquad [11.5.4]$$

where, as before, $\mathbf{a}_j$ denotes the $j$th column of the matrix $\mathbf{A}$ given in [11.4.9]. Recalling that the $u_{jt}$'s are uncorrelated, postmultiplying equation [11.5.4] by its transpose and taking expectations produces

$$\begin{aligned} \mathbf{\Omega} &= E(\boldsymbol{\varepsilon}_t\boldsymbol{\varepsilon}_t') \\ &= \mathbf{a}_1\mathbf{a}_1'\cdot\text{Var}(u_{1t}) + \mathbf{a}_2\mathbf{a}_2'\cdot\text{Var}(u_{2t}) + \cdots + \mathbf{a}_n\mathbf{a}_n'\cdot\text{Var}(u_{nt}), \end{aligned} \qquad [11.5.5]$$

where $\text{Var}(u_{jt})$ is the row $j$, column $j$ element of the matrix $\mathbf{D}$ in [11.4.9]. Substituting [11.5.5] into [11.5.2], the *MSE* of the $s$-period-ahead forecast can be written as the sum of $n$ terms, one arising from each of the disturbances $u_{jt}$:

$$\begin{aligned} MSE(\hat{\mathbf{y}}_{t+s|t}) = \sum_{j=1}^{n} \{&\text{Var}(u_{jt})\cdot[\mathbf{a}_j\mathbf{a}_j' + \mathbf{\Psi}_1\mathbf{a}_j\mathbf{a}_j'\mathbf{\Psi}_1' \\ &+ \mathbf{\Psi}_2\mathbf{a}_j\mathbf{a}_j'\mathbf{\Psi}_2' + \cdots + \mathbf{\Psi}_{s-1}\mathbf{a}_j\mathbf{a}_j'\mathbf{\Psi}_{s-1}']\}. \end{aligned} \qquad [11.5.6]$$

With this expression, we can calculate the contribution of the $j$th orthogonalized innovation to the $MSE$ of the $s$-period-ahead forecast:

$$\text{Var}(u_{jt})\cdot[\mathbf{a}_j\mathbf{a}_j' + \boldsymbol{\Psi}_1\mathbf{a}_j\mathbf{a}_j'\boldsymbol{\Psi}_1' + \boldsymbol{\Psi}_2\mathbf{a}_j\mathbf{a}_j'\boldsymbol{\Psi}_2' + \cdots + \boldsymbol{\Psi}_{s-1}\mathbf{a}_j\mathbf{a}_j'\boldsymbol{\Psi}_{s-1}'].$$

Again, this magnitude in general depends on the ordering of the variables.

As $s \rightarrow \infty$ for a covariance-stationary $VAR$, $MSE(\hat{\mathbf{y}}_{t+s|t}) \rightarrow \boldsymbol{\Gamma}_0$, the unconditional variance of the vector $\mathbf{y}_t$. Thus, [11.5.6] permits calculation of the portion of the total variance of $y_i$ that is due to the disturbance $u_j$ by letting $s$ become suitably large.

Alternatively, recalling that $\mathbf{a}_j\cdot\sqrt{\text{Var}(u_{jt})}$ is equal to $\mathbf{p}_j$, the $j$th column of the Cholesky factor $\mathbf{P}$, result [11.5.6] can equivalently be written as

$$\begin{aligned} MSE(\hat{\mathbf{y}}_{t+s|t}) = \sum_{j=1}^{n} [&\mathbf{p}_j\mathbf{p}_j' + \boldsymbol{\Psi}_1\mathbf{p}_j\mathbf{p}_j'\boldsymbol{\Psi}_1' + \boldsymbol{\Psi}_2\mathbf{p}_j\mathbf{p}_j'\boldsymbol{\Psi}_2' \\ &+ \cdots + \boldsymbol{\Psi}_{s-1}\mathbf{p}_j\mathbf{p}_j'\boldsymbol{\Psi}_{s-1}']. \end{aligned} \qquad [11.5.7]$$

## 11.6. *Vector Autoregressions and Structural Econometric Models*

### *Pitfalls in Estimating Dynamic Structural Models*

The vector autoregression was introduced in Section 10.1 as a statistical description of the dynamic interrelations between $n$ different variables contained in the vector $\mathbf{y}_t$. This description made no use of prior theoretical ideas about how these variables are expected to be related, and therefore cannot be used to test our theories or interpret the data in terms of economic principles. This section explores the relation between $VAR$s and structural econometric models.

Suppose that we would like to estimate a money demand function that expresses the public's willingness to hold cash as a function of the level of income and interest rates. The following specification was used by some early researchers:

$$M_t - P_t = \beta_0 + \beta_1 Y_t + \beta_2 I_t + \beta_3(M_{t-1} - P_{t-1}) + v_t^D. \qquad [11.6.1]$$

Here, $M_t$ is the log of the nominal money balances held by the public at date $t$, $P_t$ is the log of the aggregate price level, $Y_t$ is the log of real GNP, and $I_t$ is a nominal interest rate. The parameters $\beta_1$ and $\beta_2$ represent the effect of income and interest rates on desired cash holdings. Part of the adjustment in money balances to a change in income is thought to take place immediately, with further adjustments coming in subsequent periods. The parameter $\beta_3$ characterizes this partial adjustment. The disturbance $v_t^D$ represents factors other than income and interest rates that influence money demand.

It was once common practice to estimate such a money demand equation with Cochrane-Orcutt adjustment for first-order serial correlation. The implicit assumption behind this procedure is that

$$v_t^D = \rho v_{t-1}^D + u_t^D, \qquad [11.6.2]$$

where $u_t^D$ is white noise. Write equation [11.6.2] as $(1 - \rho L)v_t^D = u_t^D$ and multiply both sides of [11.6.1] by $(1 - \rho L)$:

$$\begin{aligned} M_t - P_t = (1 - \rho)\beta_0 &+ \beta_1 Y_t - \beta_1\rho Y_{t-1} + \beta_2 I_t - \beta_2\rho I_{t-1} \\ &+ (\beta_3 + \rho)(M_{t-1} - P_{t-1}) - \beta_3\rho(M_{t-2} - P_{t-2}) + u_t^D. \end{aligned} \qquad [11.6.3]$$

Equation [11.6.3] is a restricted version of

$$\begin{aligned} M_t - P_t = \alpha_0 + \alpha_1 Y_t + \alpha_2 Y_{t-1} + \alpha_3 I_t + \alpha_4 I_{t-1} \\ + \alpha_5(M_{t-1} - P_{t-1}) + \alpha_6(M_{t-2} - P_{t-2}) + u_t^D, \end{aligned} \qquad [11.6.4]$$

where the seven parameters $(\alpha_0, \alpha_1, \ldots, \alpha_6)$ are restricted in [11.6.3] to be nonlinear functions of the underlying five parameters $(\rho, \beta_0, \beta_1, \beta_2, \beta_3)$. The assumption of [11.6.2] can thus be tested by comparing the fit of [11.6.3] with that from unconstrained estimation of [11.6.4].

By definition, $v_t^D$ represents factors influencing money demand for which the researcher has no explicit theory. It therefore seems odd to place great confidence in a detailed specification of its dynamics such as [11.6.2] without testing this assumption against the data. For example, there do not seem to be clear theoretical grounds for ruling out a specification such as

$$v_t^D = \rho_1 v_{t-1}^D + \rho_2 v_{t-2}^D + u_t^D,$$

or, for that matter, a specification in which $v_t^D$ is correlated with lagged values of $Y$ or $I$.

Equation [11.6.1] further assumes that the dynamic multiplier relating money demand to income is proportional to that relating money demand to the interest rate:

$$\frac{\partial(M_{t+s} - P_{t+s})}{\partial Y_t} = \beta_1 \beta_3^s$$

$$\frac{\partial(M_{t+s} - P_{t+s})}{\partial I_t} = \beta_2 \beta_3^s.$$

Again, it seems a good idea to test this assumption before imposing it, by comparing the fit of [11.6.1] with that of a more general dynamic model. Finally, inflation may have effects on money demand that are not captured by nominal interest rates. The specification in [11.6.1] incorporates very strong assumptions about the way nominal money demand responds to the price level.

To summarize, a specification such as [11.6.1] and [11.6.2] implicitly imposes many restrictions on dynamics for which there is little or no justification on the basis of economic theory. Before relying on the inferences of [11.6.1] and [11.6.2], it seems a good idea to test that model against a more general specification such as

$$\begin{aligned} M_t = k_1 &+ \beta_{12}^{(0)} P_t + \beta_{13}^{(0)} Y_t + \beta_{14}^{(0)} I_t \\ &+ \beta_{11}^{(1)} M_{t-1} + \beta_{12}^{(1)} P_{t-1} + \beta_{13}^{(1)} Y_{t-1} + \beta_{14}^{(1)} I_{t-1} \\ &+ \beta_{11}^{(2)} M_{t-2} + \beta_{12}^{(2)} P_{t-2} + \beta_{13}^{(2)} Y_{t-2} + \beta_{14}^{(2)} I_{t-2} + \cdots \\ &+ \beta_{11}^{(p)} M_{t-p} + \beta_{12}^{(p)} P_{t-p} + \beta_{13}^{(p)} Y_{t-p} + \beta_{14}^{(p)} I_{t-p} + u_t^D. \end{aligned} \qquad [11.6.5]$$

Like equation [11.6.1], the specification in [11.6.5] is regarded as a structural money demand equation; $\beta_{13}^{(0)}$ and $\beta_{14}^{(0)}$ are interpreted as the effects of current income and the interest rate on desired money holdings, and $u_t^D$ represents factors influencing money demand other than inflation, income, and interest rates. Compared with [11.6.1], the specification in [11.6.5] generalizes the dynamic behavior for the error term $v_t^D$, the partial adjustment process, and the influence of the price level on desired money holdings.

Although [11.6.5] relaxes many of the dubious restrictions on the dynamics implied by [11.6.1], it is still not possible to estimate [11.6.5] by *OLS*, because of simultaneous equations bias. *OLS* estimation of [11.6.5] will summarize the correlation between money, the price level, income, and the interest rate. The public's money demand adjustments are one reason these variables will be correlated, but not the only one. For example, each period, the central bank may be adjusting the interest rate $I_t$ to a level consistent with its policy objectives, which may depend on current and lagged values of income, the interest rate, the price level, and the money supply:

$$\begin{aligned} I_t = k_4 &+ \beta_{41}^{(0)} M_t + \beta_{42}^{(0)} P_t + \beta_{43}^{(0)} Y_t \\ &+ \beta_{41}^{(1)} M_{t-1} + \beta_{42}^{(1)} P_{t-1} + \beta_{43}^{(1)} Y_{t-1} + \beta_{44}^{(1)} I_{t-1} \\ &+ \beta_{41}^{(2)} M_{t-2} + \beta_{42}^{(2)} P_{t-2} + \beta_{43}^{(2)} Y_{t-2} + \beta_{44}^{(2)} I_{t-2} + \cdots \\ &+ \beta_{41}^{(p)} M_{t-p} + \beta_{42}^{(p)} P_{t-p} + \beta_{43}^{(p)} Y_{t-p} + \beta_{44}^{(p)} I_{t-p} + u_t^C. \end{aligned} \qquad [11.6.6]$$

Here, for example, $\beta_{42}^{(0)}$ captures the effect of the current price level on the interest rate that the central bank tries to achieve. The disturbance $u_t^C$ captures changes in policy that cannot be described as a deterministic function of current and lagged money, the price level, income, and the interest rate. If the money demand disturbance $u_t^D$ is unusually large, this will make $M_t$ unusually large. If $\beta_{41}^{(0)} > 0$, this would cause $I_t$ to be unusually large as well, in which case $u_t^D$ would be positively correlated with the explanatory variable $I_t$ in equation [11.6.5]. Thus, [11.6.5] cannot be estimated by *OLS*.

Nor is central bank policy and endogeneity of $I_t$ the only reason to be concerned about simultaneous equations bias. Money demand disturbances and changes in central bank policy also have effects on aggregate output and the price level, so that $Y_t$ and $P_t$ in [11.6.5] are endogenous as well. An aggregate demand equation, for example, might be postulated that relates the level of output to the money supply, price level, and interest rate:

$$\begin{aligned} Y_t = k_3 &+ \beta_{31}^{(0)} M_t + \beta_{32}^{(0)} P_t + \beta_{34}^{(0)} I_t \\ &+ \beta_{31}^{(1)} M_{t-1} + \beta_{32}^{(1)} P_{t-1} + \beta_{33}^{(1)} Y_{t-1} + \beta_{34}^{(1)} I_{t-1} \\ &+ \beta_{31}^{(2)} M_{t-2} + \beta_{32}^{(2)} P_{t-2} + \beta_{33}^{(2)} Y_{t-2} + \beta_{34}^{(2)} I_{t-2} + \cdots \\ &+ \beta_{31}^{(p)} M_{t-p} + \beta_{32}^{(p)} P_{t-p} + \beta_{33}^{(p)} Y_{t-p} + \beta_{34}^{(p)} I_{t-p} + u_t^A, \end{aligned} \qquad [11.6.7]$$

with $u_t^A$ representing other factors influencing aggregate demand. Similarly, an aggregate supply curve might relate the aggregate price level to the other variables being studied. The logical conclusion of such reasoning is that *all* of the date $t$ explanatory variables in [11.6.5] should be treated as endogenous.

### *Relation Between Dynamic Structural Models and Vector Autoregressions*

The system of equations [11.6.5] through [11.6.7] (along with an analogous aggregate supply equation describing $P_t$) can be collected and written in vector form as

$$\mathbf{B}_0 \mathbf{y}_t = \mathbf{k} + \mathbf{B}_1 \mathbf{y}_{t-1} + \mathbf{B}_2 \mathbf{y}_{t-2} + \cdots + \mathbf{B}_p \mathbf{y}_{t-p} + \mathbf{u}_t, \qquad [11.6.8]$$

where

$$\mathbf{y}_t = (M_t, P_t, Y_t, I_t)'$$

$$\mathbf{u}_t = (u_t^D, u_t^S, u_t^A, u_t^C)'$$

$$\mathbf{B}_0 = \begin{bmatrix} 1 & -\beta_{12}^{(0)} & -\beta_{13}^{(0)} & -\beta_{14}^{(0)} \\ -\beta_{21}^{(0)} & 1 & -\beta_{23}^{(0)} & -\beta_{24}^{(0)} \\ -\beta_{31}^{(0)} & -\beta_{32}^{(0)} & 1 & -\beta_{34}^{(0)} \\ -\beta_{41}^{(0)} & -\beta_{42}^{(0)} & -\beta_{43}^{(0)} & 1 \end{bmatrix}$$

$$\mathbf{k} = (k_1, k_2, k_3, k_4)'$$

and $\mathbf{B}_s$ is a $(4 \times 4)$ matrix whose row $i$, column $j$ element is given by $\beta_{ij}^{(s)}$ for $s = 1, 2, \ldots, p$. A large class of structural models for an $(n \times 1)$ vector $\mathbf{y}_t$ can be written in the form of [11.6.8].

Generalizing the argument in [11.6.3], it is assumed that a sufficient number of lags of $p$ are included and the matrices $\mathbf{B}_s$ are defined so that $\mathbf{u}_t$ is vector white noise. If instead, say, $\mathbf{u}_t$ followed an $r$th-order *VAR*, with

$$\mathbf{u}_t = \mathbf{F}_1\mathbf{u}_{t-1} + \mathbf{F}_2\mathbf{u}_{t-2} + \cdots + \mathbf{F}_r\mathbf{u}_{t-r} + \mathbf{e}_t,$$

then we could premultiply [11.6.8] by $(\mathbf{I}_n - \mathbf{F}_1 L^1 - \mathbf{F}_2 L^2 - \cdots - \mathbf{F}_r L^r)$ to arrive at a system of the same basic form as [11.6.8] with $p$ replaced by $(p + r)$ and with $\mathbf{u}_t$ replaced by the white noise disturbance $\mathbf{e}_t$.

If each side of [11.6.8] is premultiplied by $\mathbf{B}_0^{-1}$, the result is

$$\mathbf{y}_t = \mathbf{c} + \mathbf{\Phi}_1\mathbf{y}_{t-1} + \mathbf{\Phi}_2\mathbf{y}_{t-2} + \cdots + \mathbf{\Phi}_p\mathbf{y}_{t-p} + \boldsymbol{\varepsilon}_t, \qquad [11.6.9]$$

where

$$\mathbf{c} = \mathbf{B}_0^{-1}\mathbf{k} \qquad [11.6.10]$$

$$\mathbf{\Phi}_s = \mathbf{B}_0^{-1}\mathbf{B}_s \quad \text{for } s = 1, 2, \ldots, p \qquad [11.6.11]$$

$$\boldsymbol{\varepsilon}_t = \mathbf{B}_0^{-1}\mathbf{u}_t. \qquad [11.6.12]$$

Assuming that [11.6.8] is parameterized sufficiently richly that $\mathbf{u}_t$ is vector white noise, then $\boldsymbol{\varepsilon}_t$ will also be vector white noise and [11.6.9] will be recognized as the vector autoregressive representation for the dynamic structural system [11.6.8]. Thus, a *VAR* can be viewed as the reduced form of a general dynamic structural model.

## *Interpreting Impulse-Response Functions*

In Section 11.4 we calculated the impulse-response function

$$\frac{\partial \mathbf{y}_{t+s}}{\partial \varepsilon_{jt}}. \qquad [11.6.13]$$

This magnitude describes the effect of an innovation in the $j$th variable on future values of each of the variables in the system. According to [11.6.12], the *VAR* innovation $\varepsilon_{jt}$ is a linear combination of the structural disturbances $\mathbf{u}_t$. For example, it might turn out that

$$\varepsilon_{1t} = 0.3u_t^D - 0.6u_t^S + 0.1u_t^A - 0.5u_t^C.$$

In this case, if the cash held by the public is larger than would have been forecast using the *VAR* ($\varepsilon_{1t}$ is positive), this might be because the public's demand for cash is higher than is normally associated with the current level of income and interest rate (that is, $u_t^D$ is positive). Alternatively, $\varepsilon_{1t}$ might be positive because the central bank has chosen to ease credit ($u_t^C$ is negative), or a variety of other factors. In general, $\varepsilon_{1t}$ represents a combination of all the different influences that matter for any variables in the economy. Viewed this way, it is not clear why the magnitude [11.6.13] is of particular interest.

By contrast, if we were able to calculate

$$\frac{\partial \mathbf{y}_{t+s}}{\partial u_t^C}, \qquad [11.6.14]$$

this would be of considerable interest. Expression [11.6.14] identifies the dynamic consequences for the economy if the central bank were to tighten credit more than usual and is a key magnitude for describing the effects of monetary policy on the economy.

Section 11.4 also discussed calculation of an orthogonalized impulse-response function. For $\mathbf{\Omega} = E(\boldsymbol{\varepsilon}_t\boldsymbol{\varepsilon}_t')$, we found a lower triangular matrix $\mathbf{A}$ and a diagonal matrix $\mathbf{D}$ such that $\mathbf{\Omega} = \mathbf{ADA}'$. We then constructed the vector $\mathbf{A}^{-1}\boldsymbol{\varepsilon}_t$ and calculated the consequences of changes in each element of this vector for future values of $\mathbf{y}$.

Recall from [11.6.12] that the structural disturbances $\mathbf{u}_t$ are related to the *VAR* innovations $\boldsymbol{\varepsilon}_t$ by

$$\mathbf{u}_t = \mathbf{B}_0\boldsymbol{\varepsilon}_t. \qquad [11.6.15]$$

Suppose that it happened to be the case that the matrix of structural parameters $\mathbf{B}_0$ was exactly equal to the matrix $\mathbf{A}^{-1}$. Then the orthogonalized innovations would coincide with the true structural disturbances:

$$\mathbf{u}_t = \mathbf{B}_0\boldsymbol{\varepsilon}_t = \mathbf{A}^{-1}\boldsymbol{\varepsilon}_t. \qquad [11.6.16]$$

In this case, the method described in Section 11.4 could be used to find the answers to important questions such as [11.6.14].

Is there any reason to hope that $\mathbf{B}_0$ and $\mathbf{A}^{-1}$ would be the same matrix? Since $\mathbf{A}$ is lower triangular, this clearly requires $\mathbf{B}_0$ to be lower triangular. In the example [11.6.8], this would require that the current values of $P$, $Y$, and $I$ do not influence money demand, that the current value of $M$ but not that of $Y$ or $I$ enters into the aggregate supply curve, and so on. Such assumptions are rather unusual, though there may be another way to order the variables such that a recursive structure is more palatable. For example, a Keynesian might argue that prices respond to other economic variables only with a lag, so that the coefficients on current variables in the aggregate supply equation are all zero. Perhaps money and interest rates influence aggregate demand only with a lag, so that their current values are excluded from the aggregate demand equation. One might try to argue further that the interest rate affects desired money holdings only with a lag as well. Because most central banks monitor current economic conditions quite carefully, perhaps all the current values should be included in the equation for $I_t$. These assumptions suggest ordering the variables as $\mathbf{y}_t = (P_t, Y_t, M_t, I_t)'$, for which the structural model would be

$$\begin{bmatrix} P_t \\ Y_t \\ M_t \\ I_t \end{bmatrix} = \begin{bmatrix} k_1 \\ k_2 \\ k_3 \\ k_4 \end{bmatrix} + \begin{bmatrix} 0 & 0 & 0 & 0 \\ \beta_{21}^{(0)} & 0 & 0 & 0 \\ \beta_{31}^{(0)} & \beta_{32}^{(0)} & 0 & 0 \\ \beta_{41}^{(0)} & \beta_{42}^{(0)} & \beta_{43}^{(0)} & 0 \end{bmatrix} \begin{bmatrix} P_t \\ Y_t \\ M_t \\ I_t \end{bmatrix}$$

$$+ \begin{bmatrix} \beta_{11}^{(1)} & \beta_{12}^{(1)} & \beta_{13}^{(1)} & \beta_{14}^{(1)} \\ \beta_{21}^{(1)} & \beta_{22}^{(1)} & \beta_{23}^{(1)} & \beta_{24}^{(1)} \\ \beta_{31}^{(1)} & \beta_{32}^{(1)} & \beta_{33}^{(1)} & \beta_{34}^{(1)} \\ \beta_{41}^{(1)} & \beta_{42}^{(1)} & \beta_{43}^{(1)} & \beta_{44}^{(1)} \end{bmatrix} \begin{bmatrix} P_{t-1} \\ Y_{t-1} \\ M_{t-1} \\ I_{t-1} \end{bmatrix} + \cdots \qquad [11.6.17]$$

$$+ \begin{bmatrix} \beta_{11}^{(p)} & \beta_{12}^{(p)} & \beta_{13}^{(p)} & \beta_{14}^{(p)} \\ \beta_{21}^{(p)} & \beta_{22}^{(p)} & \beta_{23}^{(p)} & \beta_{24}^{(p)} \\ \beta_{31}^{(p)} & \beta_{32}^{(p)} & \beta_{33}^{(p)} & \beta_{34}^{(p)} \\ \beta_{41}^{(p)} & \beta_{42}^{(p)} & \beta_{43}^{(p)} & \beta_{44}^{(p)} \end{bmatrix} \begin{bmatrix} P_{t-p} \\ Y_{t-p} \\ M_{t-p} \\ I_{t-p} \end{bmatrix} + \begin{bmatrix} u_t^S \\ u_t^A \\ u_t^D \\ u_t^C \end{bmatrix}.$$

Suppose there exists such an ordering of the variables for which $\mathbf{B}_0$ is lower triangular. Write the dynamic structural model [11.6.8] as

$$\mathbf{B}_0\mathbf{y}_t = -\mathbf{\Gamma}\mathbf{x}_t + \mathbf{u}_t, \qquad [11.6.18]$$

where

$$\underset{[n\times(np+1)]}{-\mathbf{\Gamma}} \equiv [\mathbf{k} \quad \mathbf{B}_1 \quad \mathbf{B}_2 \quad \cdots \quad \mathbf{B}_p]$$

$$\underset{[(np+1)\times 1]}{\mathbf{x}_t} \equiv \begin{bmatrix} 1 \\ \mathbf{y}_{t-1} \\ \mathbf{y}_{t-2} \\ \vdots \\ \mathbf{y}_{t-p} \end{bmatrix}.$$

Suppose, furthermore, that the disturbances in the structural equations are serially uncorrelated and uncorrelated with each other:

$$E(\mathbf{u}_t\mathbf{u}_\tau') = \begin{cases} \mathbf{D} & \text{for } t = \tau \\ \mathbf{0} & \text{otherwise,} \end{cases} \qquad [11.6.19]$$

where $\mathbf{D}$ is a diagonal matrix. The *VAR* is the reduced form of the dynamic structural model [11.6.18] and can be written as

$$\mathbf{y}_t = \mathbf{\Pi}'\mathbf{x}_t + \boldsymbol{\varepsilon}_t, \qquad [11.6.20]$$

where

$$\mathbf{\Pi}' = -\mathbf{B}_0^{-1}\mathbf{\Gamma} \qquad [11.6.21]$$

$$\boldsymbol{\varepsilon}_t = \mathbf{B}_0^{-1}\mathbf{u}_t. \qquad [11.6.22]$$

Letting $\mathbf{\Omega}$ denote the variance-covariance matrix of $\boldsymbol{\varepsilon}_t$, [11.6.22] implies

$$\mathbf{\Omega} = E(\boldsymbol{\varepsilon}_t\boldsymbol{\varepsilon}_t') = \mathbf{B}_0^{-1}E(\mathbf{u}_t\mathbf{u}_t')(\mathbf{B}_0^{-1})' = \mathbf{B}_0^{-1}\mathbf{D}(\mathbf{B}_0^{-1})'. \qquad [11.6.23]$$

Note that if the only restrictions on the dynamic structural model are that $\mathbf{B}_0$ is lower triangular with unit coefficients along the principal diagonal and that $\mathbf{D}$ is diagonal, then the structural model is just identified. To see this, note that these restrictions imply that $\mathbf{B}_0^{-1}$ must also be lower triangular with unit coefficients along the principal diagonal. Recall from Section 4.4 that given any positive definite symmetric matrix $\mathbf{\Omega}$, there exist a unique lower triangular matrix $\mathbf{A}$ with 1s along the principal diagonal and a diagonal matrix $\mathbf{D}$ with positive entries along the principal diagonal such that $\mathbf{\Omega} = \mathbf{ADA}'$. Thus, unique values $\mathbf{B}_0^{-1}$ and $\mathbf{D}$ of the required form can always be found that satisfy [11.6.23]. Moreover, any $\mathbf{B}_0$ matrix of this form is nonsingular, so that $\mathbf{\Gamma}$ in [11.6.21] can be calculated uniquely from $\mathbf{B}_0$ and $\mathbf{\Pi}$ as $\mathbf{\Gamma} = -\mathbf{B}_0\mathbf{\Pi}'$. Thus, given any allowable values for the reduced-form parameters ($\mathbf{\Pi}$ and $\mathbf{\Omega}$), there exist unique values for the structural parameters ($\mathbf{B}_0$, $\mathbf{\Gamma}$, and $\mathbf{D}$) of the specified form, establishing that the structural model is just identified.

Since the model is just identified, full-information maximum likelihood (*FIML*) estimates of ($\mathbf{B}_0$, $\mathbf{\Gamma}$, and $\mathbf{D}$) can be obtained by first maximizing the likelihood function with respect to the reduced-form parameters ($\mathbf{\Pi}$ and $\mathbf{\Omega}$) and then using the unique mapping from reduced-form parameters to find the structural parameters. The maximum likelihood estimates of $\mathbf{\Pi}$ are found from *OLS* regressions of the elements of $\mathbf{y}_t$ on $\mathbf{x}_t$, and the *MLE* of $\mathbf{\Omega}$ is obtained from the variance-covariance matrix of the residuals from these regressions. The estimates $\hat{\mathbf{B}}_0^{-1}$ and $\hat{\mathbf{D}}$ are then found from the triangular factorization of $\hat{\mathbf{\Omega}}$. This, however, is precisely the procedure described in calculating the orthogonalized innovations in Section 11.4. The estimate $\hat{\mathbf{A}}$ described there is thus the same as the *FIML* estimate of $\mathbf{B}_0^{-1}$. The vector of orthogonalized residuals $\mathbf{u}_t = \mathbf{A}^{-1}\boldsymbol{\varepsilon}_t$ would correspond to the vector of structural disturbances, and the orthogonalized impulse-response coefficients would give the dynamic consequences of the structural events represented by $\mathbf{u}_t$, provided that the structural model is lower triangular as in [11.6.17].

## *Nonrecursive Structural* VAR*s*

Even if the structural model cannot be written in lower triangular form, it may be possible to give a structural interpretation to a *VAR* using a similar idea to that in equation [11.6.23]. Specifically, a structural model specifies a set of restrictions on $\mathbf{B}_0$ and $\mathbf{D}$, and we can try to find values satisfying these restrictions such that $\mathbf{B}_0^{-1}\mathbf{D}(\mathbf{B}_0^{-1})' = \mathbf{\Omega}$. This point was developed by Bernanke (1986), Blanchard and Watson (1986), and Sims (1986).

For illustration, consider again the model of supply and demand discussed in equations [9.3.2] and [9.3.3]. In that specification, quantity ($q_t$) and price ($p_t$) were endogeneous variables and weather ($w_t$) was exogenous, and it was assumed that both disturbances were i.i.d. The structural *VAR* approach to this model would allow quite general dynamics by adding $p$ lags of all three variables to equations [9.3.2] and [9.3.3], as well as adding a third equation to describe the dynamic behavior of weather. Weather presumably does not depend on the behavior of the market, so the third equation would for this example just be a univariate autoregression. The model would then be

$$\begin{aligned} q_t = \beta p_t &+ \beta_{11}^{(1)}q_{t-1} + \beta_{12}^{(1)}p_{t-1} + \beta_{13}^{(1)}w_{t-1} \\ &+ \beta_{11}^{(2)}q_{t-2} + \beta_{12}^{(2)}p_{t-2} + \beta_{13}^{(2)}w_{t-2} + \cdots \\ &+ \beta_{11}^{(p)}q_{t-p} + \beta_{12}^{(p)}p_{t-p} + \beta_{13}^{(p)}w_{t-p} + u_t^d \end{aligned} \qquad [11.6.24]$$

$$\begin{aligned} q_t = \gamma p_t + h w_t &+ \beta_{21}^{(1)} q_{t-1} + \beta_{22}^{(1)} p_{t-1} + \beta_{23}^{(1)} w_{t-1} \\ &+ \beta_{21}^{(2)} q_{t-2} + \beta_{22}^{(2)} p_{t-2} + \beta_{23}^{(2)} w_{t-2} + \cdots \\ &+ \beta_{21}^{(p)} q_{t-p} + \beta_{22}^{(p)} p_{t-p} + \beta_{23}^{(p)} w_{t-p} + u_t^s \end{aligned} \qquad [11.6.25]$$

$$w_t = \beta_{33}^{(1)} w_{t-1} + \beta_{33}^{(2)} w_{t-2} + \cdots + \beta_{33}^{(p)} w_{t-p} + u_t^w. \qquad [11.6.26]$$

We could then take $(u_t^d, u_t^s, u_t^w)'$ to be a white noise vector with diagonal variance-covariance matrix given by $\mathbf{D}$. This is an example of a structural model [11.6.18] in which

$$\mathbf{B}_0 = \begin{bmatrix} 1 & -\beta & 0 \\ 1 & -\gamma & -h \\ 0 & 0 & 1 \end{bmatrix}. \qquad [11.6.27]$$

There is no way to order the variables so as to make the matrix $\mathbf{B}_0$ lower triangular. However, equation [11.6.22] indicates that the structural disturbances $\mathbf{u}_t$ are related to the *VAR* residuals $\boldsymbol{\varepsilon}_t$ by $\boldsymbol{\varepsilon}_t = \mathbf{B}_0^{-1}\mathbf{u}_t$. Thus, if $\mathbf{B}_0$ is estimated by maximum likelihood, then the impulse-response functions could be calculated as in Section 11.4 with $\mathbf{A}$ replaced by $\mathbf{B}_0^{-1}$, and the results would give the effects of each of the structural disturbances on subsequent values of variables of the system. Specifically,

$$\frac{\partial \boldsymbol{\varepsilon}_t}{\partial \mathbf{u}_t'} = \mathbf{B}_0^{-1},$$

so that the effect on $\boldsymbol{\varepsilon}_t$ of the $j$th structural disturbance $u_{jt}$ is given by $\mathbf{b}^j$, the $j$th column of $\mathbf{B}_0^{-1}$. Thus, we would calculate

$$\frac{\partial \mathbf{y}_{t+s}}{\partial u_{jt}} = \frac{\partial \mathbf{y}_{t+s}}{\partial \boldsymbol{\varepsilon}_t'} \frac{\partial \boldsymbol{\varepsilon}_t}{\partial u_{jt}} = \boldsymbol{\Psi}_s \mathbf{b}^j$$

for $\boldsymbol{\Psi}_s$ the $(n \times n)$ matrix of coefficients for the $s$th lag of the $MA(\infty)$ representation [11.4.1].

## FIML *Estimation of a Structural* VAR *with Unrestricted Dynamics*

*FIML* estimation is particularly simple if there are no restrictions on the coefficients $\boldsymbol{\Gamma}$ on lagged variables in [11.6.18]. For example, this would require including lagged values of $p_{t-j}$ and $q_{t-j}$ in the weather equation [11.6.26]. Using [11.6.23], the log likelihood function for the system [11.6.18] can be written as

$$\begin{aligned} \mathscr{L}(\mathbf{B}_0, \mathbf{D}, \boldsymbol{\Pi}) = &-(Tn/2)\log(2\pi) - (T/2)\log|\mathbf{B}_0^{-1}\mathbf{D}(\mathbf{B}_0^{-1})'| \\ &- (1/2)\sum_{t=1}^{T} [\mathbf{y}_t - \boldsymbol{\Pi}'\mathbf{x}_t]'[\mathbf{B}_0^{-1}\mathbf{D}(\mathbf{B}_0^{-1})']^{-1}[\mathbf{y}_t - \boldsymbol{\Pi}'\mathbf{x}_t]. \end{aligned} \qquad [11.6.28]$$

If there are no restrictions on lagged dynamics, this is maximized with respect to $\boldsymbol{\Pi}$ by *OLS* regression of $\mathbf{y}_t$ on $\mathbf{x}_t$. Substituting this estimate into [11.6.28] as in

[11.1.25] produces

$$\mathscr{L}(\mathbf{B}_0, \mathbf{D}, \hat{\mathbf{\Pi}}) = -(Tn/2)\log(2\pi) - (T/2)\log|\mathbf{B}_0^{-1}\mathbf{D}(\mathbf{B}_0^{-1})'| - (1/2)\sum_{t=1}^{T}\hat{\boldsymbol{\varepsilon}}_t'[\mathbf{B}_0^{-1}\mathbf{D}(\mathbf{B}_0^{-1})']^{-1}\hat{\boldsymbol{\varepsilon}}_t. \qquad [11.6.29]$$

But

$$\begin{aligned}\sum_{t=1}^{T}\hat{\boldsymbol{\varepsilon}}_t'[\mathbf{B}_0^{-1}\mathbf{D}(\mathbf{B}_0^{-1})']^{-1}\hat{\boldsymbol{\varepsilon}}_t &= \sum_{t=1}^{T}\text{trace}\{\hat{\boldsymbol{\varepsilon}}_t'[\mathbf{B}_0^{-1}\mathbf{D}(\mathbf{B}_0^{-1})']^{-1}\hat{\boldsymbol{\varepsilon}}_t\} \\ &= \sum_{t=1}^{T}\text{trace}\{[\mathbf{B}_0^{-1}\mathbf{D}(\mathbf{B}_0^{-1})']^{-1}\hat{\boldsymbol{\varepsilon}}_t\hat{\boldsymbol{\varepsilon}}_t'\} \\ &= \text{trace}\{[\mathbf{B}_0^{-1}\mathbf{D}(\mathbf{B}_0^{-1})']^{-1}T\cdot\hat{\mathbf{\Omega}}\} \\ &= T \times \text{trace}\{[\mathbf{B}_0^{-1}\mathbf{D}(\mathbf{B}_0^{-1})']^{-1}\hat{\mathbf{\Omega}}\} \\ &= T \times \text{trace}\{(\mathbf{B}_0'\mathbf{D}^{-1}\mathbf{B}_0)\hat{\mathbf{\Omega}}\}.\end{aligned} \qquad [11.6.30]$$

Furthermore,

$$\log|\mathbf{B}_0^{-1}\mathbf{D}(\mathbf{B}_0^{-1})'| = \log\{|\mathbf{B}_0^{-1}|\cdot|\mathbf{D}|\cdot|\mathbf{B}_0^{-1}|\} = -\log|\mathbf{B}_0|^2 + \log|\mathbf{D}|. \qquad [11.6.31]$$

Substituting [11.6.31] and [11.6.30] into [11.6.29], *FIML* estimates of the structural parameters are found by choosing $\mathbf{B}_0$ and $\mathbf{D}$ so as to maximize

$$\mathscr{L}(\mathbf{B}_0, \mathbf{D}, \hat{\mathbf{\Pi}}) = -(Tn/2)\log(2\pi) + (T/2)\log|\mathbf{B}_0|^2 - (T/2)\log|\mathbf{D}| - (T/2)\,\text{trace}\{(\mathbf{B}_0'\mathbf{D}^{-1}\mathbf{B}_0)\hat{\mathbf{\Omega}}\}. \qquad [11.6.32]$$

Using calculations similar to those used to analyze [11.1.25], one can show that if there exist unique matrices $\mathbf{B}_0$ and $\mathbf{D}$ of the required form satisfying $\mathbf{B}_0^{-1}\mathbf{D}(\mathbf{B}_0^{-1})' = \mathbf{\Omega}$, then maximization of [11.6.32] will produce estimates $\hat{\mathbf{B}}_0$ and $\hat{\mathbf{D}}$ satisfying

$$\hat{\mathbf{B}}_0^{-1}\hat{\mathbf{D}}(\hat{\mathbf{B}}_0^{-1})' = \hat{\mathbf{\Omega}}. \qquad [11.6.33]$$

This is a nonlinear system of equations, and numerical maximization of [11.6.32] offers a convenient general approach to finding a solution to this system of equations.

## *Identification of Structural* VAR*s*

The existence of a unique maximum of [11.6.32] requires both an order condition and a rank condition for identification. The order condition is that $\mathbf{B}_0$ and $\mathbf{D}$ have no more unknown parameters than $\mathbf{\Omega}$. Since $\mathbf{\Omega}$ is symmetric, it can be summarized by $n(n + 1)/2$ distinct values. If $\mathbf{D}$ is diagonal, it requires $n$ parameters, meaning that $\mathbf{B}_0$ can have no more than $n(n - 1)/2$ free parameters. For the supply-and-demand example of [11.6.24] through [11.6.26], $n = 3$, and the matrix $\mathbf{B}_0$ in [11.6.27] has $3(3 - 1)/2 = 3$ free parameters ($\beta$, $\gamma$, and $h$). Thus, that example satisfies the order condition for identification.

Even if the order condition is satisfied, the model may still not be identified. For example, suppose that

$$\mathbf{B}_0 = \begin{bmatrix} 1 & -\beta & 0 \\ 1 & -\gamma & 0 \\ 0 & 0 & 1 \end{bmatrix}.$$

Even though this specification satisfies the order condition, it fails the rank condition, since the value of the likelihood function will be unchanged if $\beta$ and $\gamma$ are switched along with $\sigma_d^2$ and $\sigma_s^2$.

To characterize the rank condition, suppose that there are $n_B$ elements of $\mathbf{B}_0$ that must be estimated; collect these in an $(n_B \times 1)$ vector $\boldsymbol{\theta}_B$. The identifying assumptions can be represented as a known $(n^2 \times n_B)$ matrix $\mathbf{S}_B$ and a known $(n^2 \times 1)$ vector $\mathbf{s}_B$ for which

$$\text{vec}(\mathbf{B}_0) = \mathbf{S}_B\boldsymbol{\theta}_B + \mathbf{s}_B. \qquad [11.6.34]$$

For example, for the dynamic model of supply and demand represented by [11.6.27],

$$\text{vec}(\mathbf{B}_0) = \begin{bmatrix} 1 \\ 1 \\ 0 \\ -\beta \\ -\gamma \\ 0 \\ 0 \\ -h \\ 1 \end{bmatrix} \qquad \boldsymbol{\theta}_B = \begin{bmatrix} \beta \\ \gamma \\ h \end{bmatrix}$$

$$\mathbf{S}_B = \begin{bmatrix} 0 & 0 & 0 \\ 0 & 0 & 0 \\ 0 & 0 & 0 \\ -1 & 0 & 0 \\ 0 & -1 & 0 \\ 0 & 0 & 0 \\ 0 & 0 & 0 \\ 0 & 0 & -1 \\ 0 & 0 & 0 \end{bmatrix} \qquad \mathbf{s}_B = \begin{bmatrix} 1 \\ 1 \\ 0 \\ 0 \\ 0 \\ 0 \\ 0 \\ 0 \\ 1 \end{bmatrix}.$$

Similarly, collect the unknown elements of $\mathbf{D}$ in an $(n_D \times 1)$ vector $\boldsymbol{\theta}_D$, with

$$\text{vec}(\mathbf{D}) = \mathbf{S}_D\boldsymbol{\theta}_D + \mathbf{s}_D \qquad [11.6.35]$$

for $\mathbf{S}_D$ an $(n^2 \times n_D)$ matrix and $\mathbf{s}_D$ an $(n^2 \times 1)$ vector. For the supply-and-demand example,

$$\text{vec}(\mathbf{D}) = \begin{bmatrix} \sigma_d^2 \\ 0 \\ 0 \\ 0 \\ \sigma_s^2 \\ 0 \\ 0 \\ 0 \\ \sigma_w^2 \end{bmatrix} \qquad \boldsymbol{\theta}_D = \begin{bmatrix} \sigma_d^2 \\ \sigma_s^2 \\ \sigma_w^2 \end{bmatrix}$$

$$\mathbf{S}_D = \begin{bmatrix} 1 & 0 & 0 \\ 0 & 0 & 0 \\ 0 & 0 & 0 \\ 0 & 0 & 0 \\ 0 & 1 & 0 \\ 0 & 0 & 0 \\ 0 & 0 & 0 \\ 0 & 0 & 0 \\ 0 & 0 & 1 \end{bmatrix} \qquad \mathbf{s}_D = \begin{bmatrix} 0 \\ 0 \\ 0 \\ 0 \\ 0 \\ 0 \\ 0 \\ 0 \\ 0 \end{bmatrix}.$$

Since [11.6.33] is an equation relating two symmetric matrices, there are $n^* \equiv n(n + 1)/2$ separate conditions, represented by

$$\text{vech}(\boldsymbol{\Omega}) = \text{vech}\Big( [\mathbf{B}_0(\boldsymbol{\theta}_B)]^{-1}[\mathbf{D}(\boldsymbol{\theta}_D)]\{[\mathbf{B}_0(\boldsymbol{\theta}_B)]^{-1}\}' \Big). \qquad [11.6.36]$$

Denote the right side of [11.6.36] by $\mathbf{f}(\boldsymbol{\theta}_B, \boldsymbol{\theta}_D)$, where $\mathbf{f}\colon (\mathbb{R}^{n_B} \times \mathbb{R}^{n_D}) \rightarrow \mathbb{R}^{n^*}$:

$$\text{vech}(\boldsymbol{\Omega}) = \mathbf{f}(\boldsymbol{\theta}_B, \boldsymbol{\theta}_D). \qquad [11.6.37]$$

Appendix 11.B shows that the $[n^* \times (n_B + n_D)]$ matrix of derivatives of this function is given by

$$\begin{aligned} \mathbf{J} &= \begin{bmatrix} \dfrac{\partial\, \text{vech}(\boldsymbol{\Omega})}{\partial \boldsymbol{\theta}_B'} & \dfrac{\partial\, \text{vech}(\boldsymbol{\Omega})}{\partial \boldsymbol{\theta}_D'} \end{bmatrix} \\ &= \Big[ [-2\mathbf{D}_n^+(\boldsymbol{\Omega} \otimes \mathbf{B}_0^{-1})\mathbf{S}_B] \quad \mathbf{D}_n^+[(\mathbf{B}_0^{-1}) \otimes (\mathbf{B}_0^{-1})]\mathbf{S}_D \Big], \end{aligned} \qquad [11.6.38]$$

where $\mathbf{D}_n^+$ is the $(n^* \times n^2)$ matrix defined in [11.1.45].

Suppose that the columns of the matrix in [11.6.38] were linearly dependent; that is, suppose there exists a nonzero $[(n_B + n_D) \times 1]$ vector $\boldsymbol{\lambda}$ such that $\mathbf{J}\boldsymbol{\lambda} = \mathbf{0}$. This would mean that if a small multiple of $\boldsymbol{\lambda}$ were added to $(\boldsymbol{\theta}_B', \boldsymbol{\theta}_D')'$, the model would imply the same probability distribution for the data. We would have no basis for distinguishing between these alternative values for $(\boldsymbol{\theta}_B', \boldsymbol{\theta}_D')$, meaning that the model would be unidentified.

Thus, the rank condition for identification of a structural *VAR* requires that the $(n_B + n_D)$ columns of the matrix $\mathbf{J}$ in [11.6.38] be linearly independent.[12] The order condition is that the number of rows of $\mathbf{J}$ $(n^* = n(n + 1)/2)$ be at least as great as the number of columns.

To check this condition in practice, the simplest approach is usually to make a guess as to the values of the structural parameters and check $\mathbf{J}$ numerically. Giannini (1992) derived an alternative expression for the rank condition and provided computer software for checking it numerically.

## *Structural* VAR *with Restrictions on* $\boldsymbol{\Pi}$

The supply-and-demand example of [11.6.24] to [11.6.26] did not satisfy the assumptions behind the derivation of [11.6.32], because [11.6.26] imposed the restriction that lagged values of $p$ and $q$ did not belong in the weather equation. Where such restrictions are imposed, it is no longer that case that the *FIML* estimates of $\boldsymbol{\Pi}$ are obtained by *OLS*, and system parameters would have to be estimated as described in Section 11.3. As an alternative, *OLS* estimation of [11.6.24] through [11.6.26] would still give consistent estimates of $\boldsymbol{\Pi}$, and the variance-covariance matrix of the residuals from these regressions would provide a consistent estimate $\hat{\boldsymbol{\Omega}}$. One could still use this estimate in [11.6.32], and the resulting maximization problem would give reasonable estimates of $\mathbf{B}_0$ and $\mathbf{D}$.

## *Structural* VARs *and Forward-Looking Behavior*

The supply-and-demand example assumed that lagged values of price and quantity did not appear in the equation for weather. The spirit of *VAR*s is that

[12]This condition characterizes *local* identification; it may be that even if a model satisfies both the rank and the order condition, there are two noncontiguous values of $(\boldsymbol{\theta}_B', \boldsymbol{\theta}_D')$ for which the likelihood has the same value for all realizations of the data. See Rothenberg (1971, Theorem 6, p. 585).

such assumptions ought to be tested before being imposed. What should we conclude if, contrary to our prior expectations, the price of oranges turned out to Granger-cause the weather in Florida? It certainly cannot be that the price is a cause of the weather. Instead, such a finding would suggest forward-looking behavior on the part of buyers or sellers of oranges; for example, it may be that if buyers anticipate bad weather in the future, they bid up the price of oranges today. If this should prove to be the case, the identifying assumption in [11.6.24] that demand depends on the weather only through its effect on the current price needs to be reexamined. Proper modeling of forward-looking behavior can provide an alternative way to identify *VAR*s, as explored by Flavin (1981), Hansen and Sargent (1981), and Keating (1990), among others.

## *Other Approaches to Identifying Structural* VAR*s*

Identification was discussed in previous subsections primarily in terms of exclusion restrictions on the matrix of structural coefficients $\mathbf{B}_0$. Blanchard and Diamond (1989, 1990) used a priori assumptions about the signs of structural parameters to identify a range of values of $\mathbf{B}_0$ consistent with the data. Shapiro and Watson (1988) and Blanchard and Quah (1989) used assumptions about long-run multipliers to achieve identification.

## *A Critique of Structural* VAR*s*

Structural *VAR*s have appeal for two different kinds of inquiry. The first potential user is someone who is primarily interested in estimating a structural equation such as the money demand function in [11.6.1]. If a model imposes restrictions on the dynamics of the relationship, it seems good practice to test these restrictions against a more general specification such as [11.6.5] before relying on the restricted model for inference. Furthermore, in order to estimate the dynamic consequences of, say, income on money demand, we have to take into account the fact that, historically, when income goes up, this has typically been associated with future changes in income and interest rates. What time path for these explanatory variables should be assumed in order to assess the consequences for money demand at time $t + s$ of a change in income at time $t$? A *VAR* offers a framework for posing this question—we use the time path that would historically be predicted for those variables following an unanticipated change in income.

A second potential user is someone who is interested in summarizing the dynamics of a vector $\mathbf{y}_t$ while imposing as few restrictions as possible. Insofar as this summary includes calculation of impulse-response functions, we need some motivation for what the statictics mean. Suppose we find that there is a temporary rise in income following an innovation in money. One is tempted to interpret this finding as suggesting that expansionary monetary policy has a positive but temporary effect on output. However, such an interpretation implicitly assumes that the orthogonalized "money innovation" is the same as the disturbance term in a description of central bank policy. Insofar as impulse-response functions are used to make statements that are structural in nature, it seems reasonable to try to use an orthogonalization that represents our understanding of these relationships as well as possible. This point has been forcefully argued by Cooley and LeRoy (1985), Leamer (1985), Bernanke (1986), and Blanchard (1989), among others.

Even so, it must be recognized that convincing identifying assumptions are hard to come by. For example, the ordering in [11.6.17] is clearly somewhat arbitrary, and the exclusion restrictions are difficult to defend. Indeed, if there were compelling identifying assumptions for such a system, the fierce debates among macroeconomists would have been settled long ago! Simultaneous equations bias is very pervasive in the social sciences, and drawing structural inferences from observed correlations must always proceed with great care. We surely cannot always expect to find credible identifying assumptions to enable us to identify the causal relations among any arbitrary set of $n$ variables on which we have data.

## 11.7. *Standard Errors for Impulse-Response Functions*

### *Standard Errors for Nonorthogonalized Impulse-Response Function Based on Analytical Derivatives*

Section 11.4 discussed how $\boldsymbol{\Psi}_s$, the matrix of impulse-response coefficients at lag $s$, would be constructed from knowledge of the autoregressive coefficients. In practice, the autoregressive coefficients are not known with certainty but must be estimated by *OLS* regressions. When the estimated values of the autoregressive coefficients are used to calculate $\boldsymbol{\Psi}_s$, it is useful to report the implied standard errors for the estimates $\hat{\boldsymbol{\Psi}}_s$.[13]

Adopting the notation from Proposition 11.1, let $k = np + 1$ denote the number of coefficients in each equation of the *VAR* and let $\boldsymbol{\pi} \equiv \text{vec}(\boldsymbol{\Pi})$ denote the $(nk \times 1)$ vector of parameters for all the equations; the first $k$ elements of $\boldsymbol{\pi}$ give the constant term and autoregressive coefficients for the first equation, the next $k$ elements of $\boldsymbol{\pi}$ give the parameters for the second equation, and so on. Let $\boldsymbol{\psi}_s \equiv \text{vec}(\boldsymbol{\Psi}_s')$ denote the $(n^2 \times 1)$ vector of moving average coefficients associated with lag $s$. The first $n$ elements of $\boldsymbol{\psi}_s$ are given by the first row of $\boldsymbol{\Psi}_s$ and identify the response of $y_{1,t+s}$ to $\boldsymbol{\varepsilon}_t$. The next $n$ elements of $\boldsymbol{\psi}_s$ are given by the second row of $\boldsymbol{\Psi}_s$ and identify the response of $y_{2,t+s}$ to $\boldsymbol{\varepsilon}_t$, and so on. Given the values of the autoregressive coefficients in $\boldsymbol{\pi}$, the *VAR* can be simulated to calculate $\boldsymbol{\psi}_s$. Thus, $\boldsymbol{\psi}_s$ could be regarded as a nonlinear function of $\boldsymbol{\pi}$, represented by the function $\boldsymbol{\psi}_s(\boldsymbol{\pi})$, $\boldsymbol{\psi}_s\colon \mathbb{R}^{nk} \to \mathbb{R}^{n^2}$.

The impulse-response coefficients are estimated by replacing $\boldsymbol{\pi}$ with the *OLS* estimates $\hat{\boldsymbol{\pi}}_T$, generating the estimate $\hat{\boldsymbol{\psi}}_{s,T} = \boldsymbol{\psi}_s(\hat{\boldsymbol{\pi}}_T)$. Recall that under the conditions of Proposition 11.1, $\sqrt{T}(\hat{\boldsymbol{\pi}}_T - \boldsymbol{\pi}) \xrightarrow{L} \mathbf{X}$, where

$$\mathbf{X} \sim N\left(\mathbf{0}, (\boldsymbol{\Omega} \otimes \mathbf{Q}^{-1})\right). \qquad [11.7.1]$$

Standard errors for $\hat{\boldsymbol{\psi}}_s$ can then be calculated by applying Proposition 7.4:

$$\sqrt{T}(\hat{\boldsymbol{\psi}}_{s,T} - \boldsymbol{\psi}_s) \xrightarrow{L} \mathbf{G}_s\mathbf{X},$$

where

$$\underset{(n^2 \times nk)}{\mathbf{G}_s} = \frac{\partial \boldsymbol{\psi}_s(\boldsymbol{\pi})}{\partial \boldsymbol{\pi}'}. \qquad [11.7.2]$$

That is,

$$\sqrt{T}(\hat{\boldsymbol{\psi}}_{s,T} - \boldsymbol{\psi}_s) \xrightarrow{L} N\left(\mathbf{0}, \mathbf{G}_s(\boldsymbol{\Omega} \otimes \mathbf{Q}^{-1})\mathbf{G}_s'\right). \qquad [11.7.3]$$

Standard errors for an estimated impulse-response coefficient are given by the

[13]Calculations related to those developed in this section appeared in Baillie (1987), Lütkepohl (1989, 1990), and Giannini (1992). Giannini provided computer software for calculating some of these magnitudes.

square root of the associated diagonal element of $(1/T)\hat{\mathbf{G}}_{s,T}(\hat{\mathbf{\Omega}}_T \otimes \hat{\mathbf{Q}}_T^{-1})\hat{\mathbf{G}}'_{s,T}$, where

$$\hat{\mathbf{G}}_{s,T} = \left.\frac{\partial \boldsymbol{\psi}_s(\boldsymbol{\pi})}{\partial \boldsymbol{\pi}'}\right|_{\boldsymbol{\pi}=\hat{\boldsymbol{\pi}}_T}$$

$$\hat{\mathbf{Q}}_T = (1/T)\sum_{t=1}^{T} \mathbf{x}_t\mathbf{x}_t',$$

with $\mathbf{x}_t$ and $\hat{\mathbf{\Omega}}_T$ as defined in Proposition 11.1.

To apply this result, we need an expression for the matrix $\mathbf{G}_s$ in [11.7.2]. Appendix 11.B to this chapter establishes that the sequence $\{\mathbf{G}_s\}_{s=1}^{m}$ can be calculated by iterating on

$$\begin{aligned}\mathbf{G}_s = [\mathbf{I}_n \otimes (\mathbf{0}_{n1} \quad \mathbf{\Psi}'_{s-1} \quad \mathbf{\Psi}'_{s-2} \quad \cdots \quad \mathbf{\Psi}'_{s-p})] + (\mathbf{\Phi}_1 \otimes \mathbf{I}_n)\mathbf{G}_{s-1} \\ + (\mathbf{\Phi}_2 \otimes \mathbf{I}_n)\mathbf{G}_{s-2} + \cdots + (\mathbf{\Phi}_p \otimes \mathbf{I}_n)\mathbf{G}_{s-p}.\end{aligned} \quad [11.7.4]$$

Here $\mathbf{0}_{n1}$ denotes an $(n \times 1)$ vector of zeros. The iteration is initialized by setting $\mathbf{G}_0 = \mathbf{G}_{-1} = \cdots = \mathbf{G}_{-p+1} = \mathbf{0}_{n^2,nk}$. It is also understood that $\mathbf{\Psi}_0 = \mathbf{I}_n$ and $\mathbf{\Psi}_s = \mathbf{0}_{nn}$ for $s < 0$. Thus, for example,

$$\mathbf{G}_1 = [\mathbf{I}_n \otimes (\mathbf{0}_{n1} \quad \mathbf{I}_n \quad \mathbf{0}_{nn} \quad \cdots \quad \mathbf{0}_{nn})]$$

$$\mathbf{G}_2 = [\mathbf{I}_n \otimes (\mathbf{0}_{n1} \quad \mathbf{\Psi}'_1 \quad \mathbf{I}_n \quad \cdots \quad \mathbf{0}_{nn})] + (\mathbf{\Phi}_1 \otimes \mathbf{I}_n)\mathbf{G}_1.$$

A closed-form solution for [11.7.4] is given by

$$\mathbf{G}_s = \sum_{i=1}^{s} [\mathbf{\Psi}_{i-1} \otimes (\mathbf{0}_{n1} \quad \mathbf{\Psi}'_{s-i} \quad \mathbf{\Psi}'_{s-i-1} \quad \cdots \quad \mathbf{\Psi}'_{s-i-p+1})]. \quad [11.7.5]$$

### *Alternative Approaches to Calculating Standard Errors for Nonorthogonalized Impulse-Response Function*

The matrix of derivatives $\mathbf{G}_s$ can alternatively be calculated numerically as follows. First we use the *OLS* estimates $\hat{\boldsymbol{\pi}}$ to calculate $\boldsymbol{\psi}_s(\hat{\boldsymbol{\pi}})$ for $s = 1, 2, \ldots, m$. We then increase the value of the $i$th element of $\boldsymbol{\pi}$ by some small amount $\Delta$, holding all other elements constant, and evaluate $\boldsymbol{\psi}_s(\hat{\boldsymbol{\pi}} + \mathbf{e}_i\Delta)$ for $s = 1, 2, \ldots, m$, where $\mathbf{e}_i$ denotes the $i$th column of $\mathbf{I}_{nk}$. Then the $(n^2 \times 1)$ vector

$$\frac{\boldsymbol{\psi}_s(\hat{\boldsymbol{\pi}} + \mathbf{e}_i\Delta) - \boldsymbol{\psi}_s(\hat{\boldsymbol{\pi}})}{\Delta}$$

gives an estimate of the $i$th column of $\mathbf{G}_s$. By conducting separate evaluations of the sequence $\boldsymbol{\psi}_s(\hat{\boldsymbol{\pi}} + \mathbf{e}_i\Delta)$ for each $i = 1, 2, \ldots, nk$, all of the columns of $\mathbf{G}_s$ can be filled in.

Monte Carlo methods can also be used to infer the distribution of $\boldsymbol{\psi}_s(\hat{\boldsymbol{\pi}})$. Here we would randomly generate an $(nk \times 1)$ vector drawn from a $N(\hat{\boldsymbol{\pi}}, (1/T)(\hat{\mathbf{\Omega}} \otimes \hat{\mathbf{Q}}^{-1}))$ distribution. Denote this vector by $\boldsymbol{\pi}^{(1)}$, and calculate $\boldsymbol{\psi}_s(\boldsymbol{\pi}^{(1)})$. Draw a second vector $\boldsymbol{\pi}^{(2)}$ from the same distribution and calculate $\boldsymbol{\psi}_s(\boldsymbol{\pi}^{(2)})$. Repeat this for, say, 10,000 separate simulations. If 9500 of these simulations result in a value of the first element of $\boldsymbol{\psi}_s$ that is between $\underline{\psi}_{s1}$ and $\overline{\psi}_{s1}$, then $(\underline{\psi}_{s1}, \overline{\psi}_{s1})$ can be used as a 95% confidence interval for the first element of $\hat{\boldsymbol{\psi}}_s$.

Runkle (1987) employed a related approach based on *bootstrapping*. The idea behind bootstrapping is to obtain an estimate of the small-sample distribution of $\hat{\boldsymbol{\pi}}$ without assuming that the innovations $\boldsymbol{\varepsilon}_t$ are Gaussian. To implement this procedure, first estimate the *VAR* and save the coefficient estimates $\hat{\boldsymbol{\pi}}$ and the fitted residuals $\{\hat{\boldsymbol{\varepsilon}}_1, \hat{\boldsymbol{\varepsilon}}_2, \ldots, \hat{\boldsymbol{\varepsilon}}_T\}$. Then consider an artificial random variable $\mathbf{u}$ that has probability $(1/T)$ of taking on each of the particular values $\{\hat{\boldsymbol{\varepsilon}}_1, \hat{\boldsymbol{\varepsilon}}_2, \ldots, \hat{\boldsymbol{\varepsilon}}_T\}$. The hope is that the distribution of $\mathbf{u}$ is similar to the distribution of the true population $\boldsymbol{\varepsilon}$'s. Then take a random draw from this distribution (denoted $\mathbf{u}_1^{(1)}$), and use this to construct the first innovation in an artificial sample; that is, set

$$\mathbf{y}_1^{(1)} = \hat{\mathbf{c}} + \hat{\mathbf{\Phi}}_1\mathbf{y}_0 + \hat{\mathbf{\Phi}}_2\mathbf{y}_{-1} + \cdots + \hat{\mathbf{\Phi}}_p\mathbf{y}_{-p+1} + \mathbf{u}_1^{(1)},$$

where $\mathbf{y}_0, \mathbf{y}_{-1}, \ldots,$ and $\mathbf{y}_{-p+1}$ denote the presample values of $\mathbf{y}$ that were actually observed in the historical data. Taking a second draw $\mathbf{u}_2^{(1)}$, generate

$$\mathbf{y}_2^{(1)} = \hat{\mathbf{c}} + \hat{\mathbf{\Phi}}_1\mathbf{y}_1^{(1)} + \hat{\mathbf{\Phi}}_2\mathbf{y}_0 + \cdots + \hat{\mathbf{\Phi}}_p\mathbf{y}_{-p+2} + \mathbf{u}_2^{(1)}.$$

Note that this second draw is with replacement; that is, there is a $(1/T)$ chance that $\mathbf{u}_1^{(1)}$ is exactly the same as $\mathbf{u}_2^{(1)}$. Proceeding in this fashion, a full sample $\{\mathbf{y}_1^{(1)}, \mathbf{y}_2^{(1)}, \ldots, \mathbf{y}_T^{(1)}\}$ can be generated. A *VAR* can be fitted by *OLS* to these simulated data (again taking presample values of $\mathbf{y}$ as their historical values), producing an estimate $\hat{\boldsymbol{\pi}}^{(1)}$. From this estimate, the magnitude $\boldsymbol{\psi}_s(\hat{\boldsymbol{\pi}}^{(1)})$ can be calculated. Next, generate a second set of $T$ draws from the distribution of $\mathbf{u}$, denoted $\{\mathbf{u}_1^{(2)}, \mathbf{u}_2^{(2)}, \ldots, \mathbf{u}_T^{(2)}\}$, fit $\hat{\boldsymbol{\pi}}^{(2)}$ to these data by *OLS*, and calculate $\boldsymbol{\psi}_s(\hat{\boldsymbol{\pi}}^{(2)})$. A series of 10,000 such simulations could be undertaken, and a 95% confidence interval for $\psi_{s1}(\hat{\boldsymbol{\pi}})$ is then inferred from the range that includes 95% of the values for $\psi_{s1}(\hat{\boldsymbol{\pi}}^{(i)})$.

## *Standard Errors for Parameters of a Structural* VAR

Recall from Proposition 11.2 and equation [11.1.48] that if the innovations are Gaussian,

$$\sqrt{T}[\text{vech}(\hat{\mathbf{\Omega}}_T) - \text{vech}(\mathbf{\Omega})] \xrightarrow{L} N\left(\mathbf{0},\, 2\mathbf{D}_n^+(\mathbf{\Omega}\otimes\mathbf{\Omega})(\mathbf{D}_n^+)'\right).$$

The estimates of the parameters of a structural *VAR* ($\hat{\mathbf{B}}_0$ and $\hat{\mathbf{D}}$) are determined as implicit functions of $\hat{\mathbf{\Omega}}$ from

$$\hat{\mathbf{\Omega}} = \hat{\mathbf{B}}_0^{-1}\hat{\mathbf{D}}(\hat{\mathbf{B}}_0^{-1})'. \tag{11.7.6}$$

As in equation [11.6.34], the unknown elements of $\mathbf{B}_0$ are summarized by an $(n_B \times 1)$ vector $\boldsymbol{\theta}_B$ with $\text{vec}(\mathbf{B}_0) = \mathbf{S}_B\boldsymbol{\theta}_B + \mathbf{s}_B$. Similarly, as in [11.6.35], it is assumed that $\text{vec}(\mathbf{D}) = \mathbf{S}_D\boldsymbol{\theta}_D + \mathbf{s}_D$ for $\boldsymbol{\theta}_D$ an $(n_D \times 1)$ vector. It then follows from Proposition 7.4 that

$$\sqrt{T}(\hat{\boldsymbol{\theta}}_{B,T} - \boldsymbol{\theta}_B) \xrightarrow{L} N\left(\mathbf{0},\, 2\mathbf{G}_B\mathbf{D}_n^+(\mathbf{\Omega}\otimes\mathbf{\Omega})(\mathbf{D}_n^+)'\mathbf{G}_B'\right) \tag{11.7.7}$$

$$\sqrt{T}(\hat{\boldsymbol{\theta}}_{D,T} - \boldsymbol{\theta}_D) \xrightarrow{L} N\left(\mathbf{0},\, 2\mathbf{G}_D\mathbf{D}_n^+(\mathbf{\Omega}\otimes\mathbf{\Omega})(\mathbf{D}_n^+)'\mathbf{G}_D'\right), \tag{11.7.8}$$

where

$$\underset{(n_B\times n^*)}{\mathbf{G}_B} = \frac{\partial\boldsymbol{\theta}_B}{\partial[\text{vech}(\mathbf{\Omega})]'} \tag{11.7.9}$$

$$\underset{(n_D\times n^*)}{\mathbf{G}_D} = \frac{\partial\boldsymbol{\theta}_D}{\partial[\text{vech}(\mathbf{\Omega})]'} \tag{11.7.10}$$

and $n^* \equiv n(n + 1)/2$.

Equation [11.6.38] gave an expression for the $[n^* \times (n_B + n_D)]$ matrix:

$$\mathbf{J} = \begin{bmatrix} \dfrac{\partial\,\text{vech}(\mathbf{\Omega})}{\partial\boldsymbol{\theta}_B'} & \dfrac{\partial\,\text{vech}(\mathbf{\Omega})}{\partial\boldsymbol{\theta}_D'} \end{bmatrix}.$$

We noted there that if the model is to be identified, the columns of this matrix must be linearly independent. In the just-identified case, $n^* = (n_B + n_D)$ and $\mathbf{J}^{-1}$

exists, from which

$$\begin{bmatrix} \mathbf{G}_B \\ \mathbf{G}_D \end{bmatrix} = \mathbf{J}^{-1}. \qquad [11.7.11]$$

## *Standard Errors for Orthogonalized Impulse-Response Functions*

Section 11.6 described calculation of the following $(n \times n)$ matrix:

$$\mathbf{H}_s = \mathbf{\Psi}_s\mathbf{B}_0^{-1}. \qquad [11.7.12]$$

The row $i$, column $j$ element of this matrix measures the effect of the $j$th structural disturbance $(u_{jt})$ on the $i$th variable in the system $(y_{i,t+s})$ after a lag of $s$ periods. Collect these magnitudes in an $(n^2 \times 1)$ vector $\mathbf{h}_s \equiv \text{vec}(\mathbf{H}_s')$. Thus, the first $n$ elements of $\mathbf{h}_s$ give the effect of $\mathbf{u}_t$ on $y_{1,t+s}$, the next $n$ elements give the effect of $\mathbf{u}_t$ on $y_{2,t+s}$, and so on.

Since $\hat{\mathbf{\Psi}}_s$ is a function of $\hat{\boldsymbol{\pi}}$ and since $\hat{\mathbf{B}}_0$ is a function of vech$(\hat{\mathbf{\Omega}})$, the distributions of both the autoregressive coefficients and the variances affect the asymptotic distribution of $\hat{\mathbf{h}}_s$. It follows from Proposition 11.2 that with Gaussian innovations,

$$\begin{aligned} &\sqrt{T}(\hat{\mathbf{h}}_{s,T} - \mathbf{h}_s) \\ &\xrightarrow{L} N\left(\mathbf{0}, [\mathbf{\Xi}_\pi \quad \mathbf{\Xi}_\sigma]\begin{bmatrix} \mathbf{\Omega} \otimes \mathbf{Q}^{-1} & \mathbf{0} \\ \mathbf{0} & 2\mathbf{D}_n^+(\mathbf{\Omega} \otimes \mathbf{\Omega})(\mathbf{D}_n^+)' \end{bmatrix}\begin{bmatrix} \mathbf{\Xi}_\pi' \\ \mathbf{\Xi}_\sigma' \end{bmatrix}\right) \qquad [11.7.13] \\ &\sim N\left(\mathbf{0}, [\mathbf{\Xi}_\pi(\mathbf{\Omega} \otimes \mathbf{Q}^{-1})\mathbf{\Xi}_\pi' + 2\mathbf{\Xi}_\sigma\mathbf{D}_n^+(\mathbf{\Omega} \otimes \mathbf{\Omega})(\mathbf{D}_n^+)'\mathbf{\Xi}_\sigma']\right), \end{aligned}$$

where Appendix 11.B demonstrates that

$$\mathbf{\Xi}_\pi = \partial\mathbf{h}_s/\partial\boldsymbol{\pi}' = [\mathbf{I}_n \otimes (\mathbf{B}_0')^{-1}]\mathbf{G}_s \qquad [11.7.14]$$

$$\mathbf{\Xi}_\sigma = \frac{\partial\mathbf{h}_s}{\partial[\text{vech}(\mathbf{\Omega})]'} = -[\mathbf{H}_s \otimes (\mathbf{B}_0')^{-1}]\mathbf{S}_{B'}\mathbf{G}_B. \qquad [11.7.15]$$

Here $\mathbf{G}_s$ is the matrix given in [11.7.5], $\mathbf{G}_B$ is the matrix given in [11.7.11], and $\mathbf{S}_{B'}$ is an $(n^2 \times n_B)$ matrix that takes the elements of $\boldsymbol{\theta}_B$ and puts them in the corresponding position to construct vec$(\mathbf{B}_0')$:

$$\text{vec}(\mathbf{B}_0') = \mathbf{S}_{B'}\boldsymbol{\theta}_B + \mathbf{s}_{B'}.$$

For the supply-and-demand examples of [11.6.24] to [11.6.26],

$$\mathbf{S}_{B'} = \begin{bmatrix} 0 & 0 & 0 \\ -1 & 0 & 0 \\ 0 & 0 & 0 \\ 0 & 0 & 0 \\ 0 & -1 & 0 \\ 0 & 0 & -1 \\ 0 & 0 & 0 \\ 0 & 0 & 0 \\ 0 & 0 & 0 \end{bmatrix}.$$

## *Practical Experience with Standard Errors*

In practice, the standard errors for dynamic inferences based on *VAR*s often turn out to be disappointingly large (see Runkle, 1987, and Lütkepohl, 1990).

Although a *VAR* imposes few restrictions on the dynamics, the cost of this generality is that the inferences drawn are not too precise. To gain more precision, it is necessary to impose further restrictions. One approach is to fit the multivariate dynamics using a restricted model with far fewer parameters, provided that the data allow us to accept the restrictions. A second approach is to place greater reliance on prior expectations about the system dynamics. This second approach is explored in the next chapter.

## APPENDIX 11.A. *Proofs of Chapter 11 Propositions*

■ **Proof of Proposition 11.1.** The condition on the roots of [11.1.35] ensures that the $MA(\infty)$ representation is absolutely summable. Thus $\mathbf{y}_t$ is ergodic for first moments, from Propositions 10.2(b) and 10.5(a), and is also ergodic for second moments, from Proposition 10.2(d). This establishes result 11.1(a).

The proofs of results (b) and (c) are virtually identical to those for a single *OLS* regression with stochastic regressors (results [8.2.5] and [8.2.12]).

To verify result (d), notice that

$$\sqrt{T}(\hat{\boldsymbol{\pi}}_{i,T} - \boldsymbol{\pi}_i) = \left[(1/T)\sum_{t=1}^{T}\mathbf{x}_t\mathbf{x}_t'\right]^{-1}\left[(1/\sqrt{T})\sum_{t=1}^{T}\mathbf{x}_t\varepsilon_{it}\right]$$

and so

$$\sqrt{T}(\hat{\boldsymbol{\pi}}_T - \boldsymbol{\pi}) = \begin{bmatrix} \mathbf{Q}_T^{-1}(1/\sqrt{T})\sum_{t=1}^{T}\mathbf{x}_t\varepsilon_{1t} \\ \mathbf{Q}_T^{-1}(1/\sqrt{T})\sum_{t=1}^{T}\mathbf{x}_t\varepsilon_{2t} \\ \vdots \\ \mathbf{Q}_T^{-1}(1/\sqrt{T})\sum_{t=1}^{T}\mathbf{x}_t\varepsilon_{nt} \end{bmatrix}, \qquad [11.A.1]$$

where

$$\mathbf{Q}_T \equiv \left[(1/T)\sum_{t=1}^{T}\mathbf{x}_t\mathbf{x}_t'\right].$$

Define $\boldsymbol{\xi}_t$ to be the following $(nk \times 1)$ vector:

$$\boldsymbol{\xi}_t \equiv \begin{bmatrix} \mathbf{x}_t\varepsilon_{1t} \\ \mathbf{x}_t\varepsilon_{2t} \\ \vdots \\ \mathbf{x}_t\varepsilon_{nt} \end{bmatrix}.$$

Notice that $\boldsymbol{\xi}_t$ is a martingale difference sequence with finite fourth moments and variance

$$\begin{aligned} E(\boldsymbol{\xi}_t\boldsymbol{\xi}_t') &= \begin{bmatrix} E(\mathbf{x}_t\mathbf{x}_t')\cdot E(\varepsilon_{1t}^2) & E(\mathbf{x}_t\mathbf{x}_t')\cdot E(\varepsilon_{1t}\varepsilon_{2t}) & \cdots & E(\mathbf{x}_t\mathbf{x}_t')\cdot E(\varepsilon_{1t}\varepsilon_{nt}) \\ E(\mathbf{x}_t\mathbf{x}_t')\cdot E(\varepsilon_{2t}\varepsilon_{1t}) & E(\mathbf{x}_t\mathbf{x}_t')\cdot E(\varepsilon_{2t}^2) & \cdots & E(\mathbf{x}_t\mathbf{x}_t')\cdot E(\varepsilon_{2t}\varepsilon_{nt}) \\ \vdots & \vdots & \cdots & \vdots \\ E(\mathbf{x}_t\mathbf{x}_t')\cdot E(\varepsilon_{nt}\varepsilon_{1t}) & E(\mathbf{x}_t\mathbf{x}_t')\cdot E(\varepsilon_{nt}\varepsilon_{2t}) & \cdots & E(\mathbf{x}_t\mathbf{x}_t')\cdot E(\varepsilon_{nt}^2) \end{bmatrix} \\ &= \begin{bmatrix} E(\varepsilon_{1t}^2) & E(\varepsilon_{1t}\varepsilon_{2t}) & \cdots & E(\varepsilon_{1t}\varepsilon_{nt}) \\ E(\varepsilon_{2t}\varepsilon_{1t}) & E(\varepsilon_{2t}^2) & \cdots & E(\varepsilon_{2t}\varepsilon_{nt}) \\ \vdots & \vdots & \cdots & \vdots \\ E(\varepsilon_{nt}\varepsilon_{1t}) & E(\varepsilon_{nt}\varepsilon_{2t}) & \cdots & E(\varepsilon_{nt}^2) \end{bmatrix} \otimes E(\mathbf{x}_t\mathbf{x}_t') \\ &= \boldsymbol{\Omega} \otimes \mathbf{Q}. \end{aligned}$$

It can further be shown that

$$(1/T)\sum_{t=1}^{T}\boldsymbol{\xi}_t\boldsymbol{\xi}_t' \xrightarrow{p} \boldsymbol{\Omega} \otimes \mathbf{Q} \qquad [11.A.2]$$

(see Exercise 11.1). It follows from Proposition 7.9 that

$$(1/\sqrt{T})\sum_{t=1}^{T}\boldsymbol{\xi}_t \xrightarrow{L} N\Big(\mathbf{0},\,(\boldsymbol{\Omega}\otimes\mathbf{Q})\Big). \qquad [11.A.3]$$

Now, expression [11.A.1] can be written

$$\sqrt{T}(\hat{\boldsymbol{\pi}}_T-\boldsymbol{\pi}) = \begin{bmatrix}\mathbf{Q}_T^{-1} & \mathbf{0} & \cdots & \mathbf{0}\\ \mathbf{0} & \mathbf{Q}_T^{-1} & \cdots & \mathbf{0}\\ \vdots & \vdots & \cdots & \vdots\\ \mathbf{0} & \mathbf{0} & \cdots & \mathbf{Q}_T^{-1}\end{bmatrix}\begin{bmatrix}(1/\sqrt{T})\sum_{t=1}^{T}\mathbf{x}_t\varepsilon_{1t}\\ (1/\sqrt{T})\sum_{t=1}^{T}\mathbf{x}_t\varepsilon_{2t}\\ \vdots\\ (1/\sqrt{T})\sum_{t=1}^{T}\mathbf{x}_t\varepsilon_{nt}\end{bmatrix}$$

$$= (\mathbf{I}_n\otimes\mathbf{Q}_T^{-1})(1/\sqrt{T})\sum_{t=1}^{T}\boldsymbol{\xi}_t.$$

But result (a) implies that $\mathbf{Q}_T^{-1}\xrightarrow{p}\mathbf{Q}^{-1}$. Thus,

$$\sqrt{T}(\hat{\boldsymbol{\pi}}_T-\boldsymbol{\pi}) \xrightarrow{p} (\mathbf{I}_n\otimes\mathbf{Q}^{-1})(1/\sqrt{T})\sum_{t=1}^{T}\boldsymbol{\xi}_t. \qquad [11.A.4]$$

But from [11.A.3], this has a distribution that is Gaussian with mean $\mathbf{0}$ and variance

$$(\mathbf{I}_n\otimes\mathbf{Q}^{-1})(\boldsymbol{\Omega}\otimes\mathbf{Q})(\mathbf{I}_n\otimes\mathbf{Q}^{-1}) = (\mathbf{I}_n\boldsymbol{\Omega}\mathbf{I}_n)\otimes(\mathbf{Q}^{-1}\mathbf{Q}\mathbf{Q}^{-1}) = \boldsymbol{\Omega}\otimes\mathbf{Q}^{-1},$$

as claimed. ■

■ **Proof of Proposition 11.2.** Define $\hat{\boldsymbol{\Omega}}_T^*\equiv(1/T)\Sigma_{t=1}^{T}\boldsymbol{\varepsilon}_t\boldsymbol{\varepsilon}_t'$ to be the estimate of $\boldsymbol{\Omega}$ based on the true residuals. We first note that $\hat{\boldsymbol{\Omega}}_T$ has the same asymptotic distribution as $\hat{\boldsymbol{\Omega}}_T^*$. To see this, observe that

$$\begin{aligned}\hat{\boldsymbol{\Omega}}_T^* &= (1/T)\sum_{t=1}^{T}(\mathbf{y}_t-\boldsymbol{\Pi}'\mathbf{x}_t)(\mathbf{y}_t-\boldsymbol{\Pi}'\mathbf{x}_t)'\\ &= (1/T)\sum_{t=1}^{T}[\mathbf{y}_t-\hat{\boldsymbol{\Pi}}_T'\mathbf{x}_t+(\hat{\boldsymbol{\Pi}}_T-\boldsymbol{\Pi})'\mathbf{x}_t][\mathbf{y}_t-\hat{\boldsymbol{\Pi}}_T'\mathbf{x}_t+(\hat{\boldsymbol{\Pi}}_T-\boldsymbol{\Pi})'\mathbf{x}_t]'\\ &= (1/T)\sum_{t=1}^{T}(\mathbf{y}_t-\hat{\boldsymbol{\Pi}}_T'\mathbf{x}_t)(\mathbf{y}_t-\hat{\boldsymbol{\Pi}}_T'\mathbf{x}_t)' \qquad [11.A.5]\\ &\quad+(\hat{\boldsymbol{\Pi}}_T-\boldsymbol{\Pi})'(1/T)\sum_{t=1}^{T}\mathbf{x}_t\mathbf{x}_t'(\hat{\boldsymbol{\Pi}}_T-\boldsymbol{\Pi})\\ &= \hat{\boldsymbol{\Omega}}_T+(\hat{\boldsymbol{\Pi}}_T-\boldsymbol{\Pi})'(1/T)\sum_{t=1}^{T}\mathbf{x}_t\mathbf{x}_t'(\hat{\boldsymbol{\Pi}}_T-\boldsymbol{\Pi}),\end{aligned}$$

where cross-product terms were dropped in the third equality on the right in the light of the *OLS* orthogonality condition $(1/T)\Sigma_{t=1}^{T}(\mathbf{y}_t-\hat{\boldsymbol{\Pi}}_T'\mathbf{x}_t)\mathbf{x}_t'=\mathbf{0}$. Equation [11.A.5] implies that

$$\sqrt{T}(\hat{\boldsymbol{\Omega}}_T^*-\hat{\boldsymbol{\Omega}}_T) = (\hat{\boldsymbol{\Pi}}_T-\boldsymbol{\Pi})'(1/T)\sum_{t=1}^{T}\mathbf{x}_t\mathbf{x}_t'[\sqrt{T}(\hat{\boldsymbol{\Pi}}_T-\boldsymbol{\Pi})].$$

But Proposition 11.1 established that $(\hat{\boldsymbol{\Pi}}_T-\boldsymbol{\Pi})'\xrightarrow{p}\mathbf{0}$, $(1/T)\Sigma_{t=1}^{T}\mathbf{x}_t\mathbf{x}_t'\xrightarrow{p}\mathbf{Q}$, and $\sqrt{T}(\hat{\boldsymbol{\Pi}}_T-\boldsymbol{\Pi})$ converges in distribution. Thus, from Proposition 7.3, $\sqrt{T}(\hat{\boldsymbol{\Omega}}_T^*-\hat{\boldsymbol{\Omega}}_T)\xrightarrow{p}\mathbf{0}$ meaning that $\sqrt{T}(\hat{\boldsymbol{\Omega}}_T^*-\boldsymbol{\Omega})\xrightarrow{p}\sqrt{T}(\hat{\boldsymbol{\Omega}}_T-\boldsymbol{\Omega})$.

Recalling [11.A.4],

$$\begin{bmatrix}\sqrt{T}[\hat{\boldsymbol{\pi}}_T-\boldsymbol{\pi}]\\ \sqrt{T}[\mathrm{vech}(\hat{\boldsymbol{\Omega}}_T)-\mathrm{vech}(\boldsymbol{\Omega})]\end{bmatrix}\xrightarrow{p}\begin{bmatrix}(\mathbf{I}_n\otimes\mathbf{Q}^{-1})(1/\sqrt{T})\sum_{t=1}^{T}\boldsymbol{\xi}_t\\ (1/\sqrt{T})\sum_{t=1}^{T}\boldsymbol{\lambda}_t\end{bmatrix}, \qquad [11.A.6]$$

where $\boldsymbol{\xi}_t = \boldsymbol{\varepsilon}_t \otimes \mathbf{x}_t$ and

$$\boldsymbol{\lambda}_t \equiv \text{vech}\begin{bmatrix} \varepsilon_{1t}^2 - \sigma_{11} & \varepsilon_{1t}\varepsilon_{2t} - \sigma_{12} & \cdots & \varepsilon_{1t}\varepsilon_{nt} - \sigma_{1n} \\ \varepsilon_{2t}\varepsilon_{1t} - \sigma_{21} & \varepsilon_{2t}^2 - \sigma_{22} & \cdots & \varepsilon_{2t}\varepsilon_{nt} - \sigma_{2n} \\ \vdots & \vdots & \cdots & \vdots \\ \varepsilon_{nt}\varepsilon_{1t} - \sigma_{n1} & \varepsilon_{nt}\varepsilon_{2t} - \sigma_{n2} & \cdots & \varepsilon_{nt}^2 - \sigma_{nn} \end{bmatrix}.$$

It is straightforward to show that $(\boldsymbol{\xi}_t', \boldsymbol{\lambda}_t')'$ is a martingale difference sequence that satisfies the conditions of Proposition 7.9, from which

$$\begin{bmatrix} (1/\sqrt{T}) \sum_{t=1}^{T} \boldsymbol{\xi}_t \\ (1/\sqrt{T}) \sum_{t=1}^{T} \boldsymbol{\lambda}_t \end{bmatrix} \xrightarrow{L} N\left(\begin{bmatrix} \mathbf{0} \\ \mathbf{0} \end{bmatrix}, \begin{bmatrix} \boldsymbol{\Sigma}_{11} & \boldsymbol{\Sigma}_{12} \\ \boldsymbol{\Sigma}_{21} & \boldsymbol{\Sigma}_{22} \end{bmatrix}\right), \tag{11.A.7}$$

where

$$\begin{bmatrix} \boldsymbol{\Sigma}_{11} & \boldsymbol{\Sigma}_{12} \\ \boldsymbol{\Sigma}_{21} & \boldsymbol{\Sigma}_{22} \end{bmatrix} = \begin{bmatrix} E(\boldsymbol{\xi}_t\boldsymbol{\xi}_t') & E(\boldsymbol{\xi}_t\boldsymbol{\lambda}_t') \\ E(\boldsymbol{\lambda}_t\boldsymbol{\xi}_t') & E(\boldsymbol{\lambda}_t\boldsymbol{\lambda}_t') \end{bmatrix}.$$

Recall from the proof of Proposition 11.1 that

$$\boldsymbol{\Sigma}_{11} = E(\boldsymbol{\xi}_t\boldsymbol{\xi}_t') = \boldsymbol{\Omega} \otimes \mathbf{Q}.$$

A typical element of $\boldsymbol{\Sigma}_{12}$ is of the form

$$E(\mathbf{x}_t\varepsilon_{lt})(\varepsilon_{it}\varepsilon_{jt} - \sigma_{ij}) = E(\mathbf{x}_t) \cdot E(\varepsilon_{lt}\varepsilon_{it}\varepsilon_{jt}) - \sigma_{ij} \cdot E(\mathbf{x}_t) \cdot E(\varepsilon_{lt}),$$

which equals zero for all $i$, $j$, and $l$. Hence, [11.A.7] becomes

$$\begin{bmatrix} (1/\sqrt{T}) \sum_{t=1}^{T} \boldsymbol{\xi}_t \\ (1/\sqrt{T}) \sum_{t=1}^{T} \boldsymbol{\lambda}_t \end{bmatrix} \xrightarrow{L} N\left(\begin{bmatrix} \mathbf{0} \\ \mathbf{0} \end{bmatrix}, \begin{bmatrix} \boldsymbol{\Omega} \otimes \mathbf{Q} & \mathbf{0} \\ \mathbf{0} & \boldsymbol{\Sigma}_{22} \end{bmatrix}\right),$$

and so, from [11.A.6],

$$\begin{bmatrix} \sqrt{T}[\hat{\boldsymbol{\pi}}_T - \boldsymbol{\pi}] \\ \sqrt{T}[\text{vech}(\hat{\boldsymbol{\Omega}}_T) - \text{vech}(\boldsymbol{\Omega})] \end{bmatrix} \xrightarrow{L} N\left(\begin{bmatrix} \mathbf{0} \\ \mathbf{0} \end{bmatrix}, \begin{bmatrix} \boldsymbol{\Omega} \otimes \mathbf{Q}^{-1} & \mathbf{0} \\ \mathbf{0} & \boldsymbol{\Sigma}_{22} \end{bmatrix}\right).$$

Hence, Proposition 11.2 will be established if we can show that $E(\boldsymbol{\lambda}_t\boldsymbol{\lambda}_t')$ is given by the matrix $\boldsymbol{\Sigma}_{22}$ described in the proposition; that is, we must show that

$$E(\varepsilon_{it}\varepsilon_{jt} - \sigma_{ij})(\varepsilon_{lt}\varepsilon_{mt} - \sigma_{lm}) = \sigma_{il}\sigma_{jm} + \sigma_{im}\sigma_{jl} \tag{11.A.8}$$

for all $i$, $j$, $l$, and $m$.

To derive [11.A.8], let $\boldsymbol{\Omega} = \mathbf{PP}'$ denote the Cholesky decomposition of $\boldsymbol{\Omega}$, and define

$$\mathbf{v}_t \equiv \mathbf{P}^{-1}\boldsymbol{\varepsilon}_t. \tag{11.A.9}$$

Then $E(\mathbf{v}_t\mathbf{v}_t') = \mathbf{P}^{-1}\boldsymbol{\Omega}(\mathbf{P}^{-1})' = \mathbf{I}_n$. Thus, $v_{it}$ is Gaussian with zero mean, unit variance, and fourth moment given by $E(v_{it}^4) = 3$. Moreover, $v_{it}$ is independent of $v_{jt}$ for $i \neq j$.

Equation [11.A.9] implies

$$\boldsymbol{\varepsilon}_t = \mathbf{P}\mathbf{v}_t. \tag{11.A.10}$$

Let $p_{ij}$ denote the row $i$, column $j$ element of $\mathbf{P}$. Then the $i$th row of [11.A.10] states that

$$\varepsilon_{it} = p_{i1}v_{1t} + p_{i2}v_{2t} + \cdots + p_{in}v_{nt} \tag{11.A.11}$$

and

$$\varepsilon_{it}\varepsilon_{jt} = (p_{i1}v_{1t} + p_{i2}v_{2t} + \cdots + p_{in}v_{nt}) \times (p_{j1}v_{1t} + p_{j2}v_{2t} + \cdots + p_{jn}v_{nt}). \tag{11.A.12}$$

Second moments of $\boldsymbol{\varepsilon}_t$ can be found by taking expectations of [11.A.12], recalling that $E(v_{it}v_{jt}) = 1$ if $i = j$ and is zero otherwise:

$$E(\varepsilon_{it}\varepsilon_{jt}) = p_{i1}p_{j1} + p_{i2}p_{j2} + \cdots + p_{in}p_{jn}. \tag{11.A.13}$$

Similarly, fourth moments can be found from

$$
\begin{aligned}
E(\varepsilon_{it}\varepsilon_{jt}\varepsilon_{lt}\varepsilon_{mt}) &= E[(p_{i1}v_{1t} + p_{i2}v_{2t} + \cdots + p_{in}v_{nt})(p_{j1}v_{1t} + p_{j2}v_{2t} + \cdots + p_{jn}v_{nt}) \\
&\quad \times (p_{l1}v_{1t} + p_{l2}v_{2t} + \cdots + p_{ln}v_{nt})(p_{m1}v_{1t} + p_{m2}v_{2t} + \cdots + p_{mn}v_{nt})] \\
&= [3(p_{i1}p_{j1}p_{l1}p_{m1} + p_{i2}p_{j2}p_{l2}p_{m2} + \cdots + p_{in}p_{jn}p_{ln}p_{mn})] \\
&\quad + [(p_{i1}p_{j1})(p_{l2}p_{m2} + p_{l3}p_{m3} + \cdots + p_{ln}p_{mn}) \\
&\quad\quad + (p_{i2}p_{j2})(p_{l1}p_{m1} + p_{l3}p_{m3} + \cdots + p_{ln}p_{mn}) + \cdots \\
&\quad\quad + (p_{in}p_{jn})(p_{l1}p_{m1} + p_{l2}p_{m2} + \cdots + p_{l,n-1}p_{m,n-1})] \\
&\quad + [(p_{i1}p_{l1})(p_{j2}p_{m2} + p_{j3}p_{m3} + \cdots + p_{jn}p_{mn}) \\
&\quad\quad + (p_{i2}p_{l2})(p_{j1}p_{m1} + p_{j3}p_{m3} + \cdots + p_{jn}p_{mn}) + \cdots \\
&\quad\quad + (p_{in}p_{ln})(p_{j1}p_{m1} + p_{j2}p_{m2} + \cdots + p_{j,n-1}p_{m,n-1})] \\
&\quad + [(p_{i1}p_{m1})(p_{j2}p_{l2} + p_{j3}p_{l3} + \cdots + p_{jn}p_{ln}) \\
&\quad\quad + (p_{i2}p_{m2})(p_{j1}p_{l1} + p_{j3}p_{l3} + \cdots + p_{jn}p_{ln}) + \cdots \\
&\quad\quad + (p_{in}p_{mn})(p_{j1}p_{l1} + p_{j2}p_{l2} + \cdots + p_{j,n-1}p_{l,n-1})] \\
&= [(p_{i1}p_{j1} + p_{i2}p_{j2} + \cdots + p_{in}p_{jn})(p_{l1}p_{m1} + p_{l2}p_{m2} + \cdots + p_{ln}p_{mn})] \\
&\quad + [(p_{i1}p_{l1} + p_{i2}p_{l2} + \cdots + p_{in}p_{ln})(p_{j1}p_{m1} + p_{j2}p_{m2} + \cdots + p_{jn}p_{mn})] \\
&\quad + [(p_{i1}p_{m1} + p_{i2}p_{m2} + \cdots + p_{in}p_{mn})(p_{j1}p_{l1} + p_{j2}p_{l2} + \cdots + p_{jn}p_{ln})] \\
&= \sigma_{ij}\sigma_{lm} + \sigma_{il}\sigma_{jm} + \sigma_{im}\sigma_{jl},
\end{aligned} \tag{11.A.14}
$$

where the last line follows from [11.A.13]. Then

$$E[(\varepsilon_{it}\varepsilon_{jt} - \sigma_{ij})(\varepsilon_{lt}\varepsilon_{mt} - \sigma_{lm})] = E(\varepsilon_{it}\varepsilon_{jt}\varepsilon_{lt}\varepsilon_{mt}) - \sigma_{ij}\sigma_{lm} = \sigma_{il}\sigma_{jm} + \sigma_{im}\sigma_{jl},$$

as claimed in [11.A.8]. ■

■ **Proof of Proposition 11.3.** First suppose that $y$ fails to Granger-cause $x$, so that the process can be written as in [11.2.4]. Define $v_{2t}$ to be the residual from a projection of $\varepsilon_{2t}$ on $\varepsilon_{1t}$, with $b_0$ defined to be the projection coefficient:

$$v_{2t} \equiv \varepsilon_{2t} - b_0\varepsilon_{1t}.$$

Thus, $v_{2t}$ and $\varepsilon_{1t}$ are uncorrelated, and, recalling that $\boldsymbol{\varepsilon}_t$ is white noise, $v_{2t}$ must be uncorrelated with $\varepsilon_{1\tau}$ for all $t \neq \tau$ as well. From the first row of [11.2.4], this means that $v_{2t}$ and $x_\tau$ are uncorrelated for all $t$ and $\tau$. With this definition of $v_{2t}$, the second row of [11.2.4] can be written as

$$y_t = \mu_2 + \psi_{21}(L)\varepsilon_{1t} + \psi_{22}(L)[v_{2t} + b_0\varepsilon_{1t}]. \tag{11.A.15}$$

Furthermore, from the first row of [11.2.4],

$$\varepsilon_{1t} = [\psi_{11}(L)]^{-1}(x_t - \mu_1). \tag{11.A.16}$$

Substituting [11.A.16] into [11.A.15] gives

$$y_t = c + b(L)x_t + \eta_t, \tag{11.A.17}$$

where we have defined $b(L) \equiv \{[\psi_{21}(L) + b_0\psi_{22}(L)][\psi_{11}(L)]^{-1}\}$, $c \equiv \mu_2 - b(1)\mu_1$, and $\eta_t \equiv \psi_{22}(L)v_{2t}$. But $\eta_t$, being constructed from $v_{2t}$, is uncorrelated with $x_\tau$ for all $\tau$. Furthermore, only current and lagged values of $x$, as summarized by the operator $b(L)$, appear in equation [11.A.17]. We have thus shown that if [11.2.4] holds, then $d_j = 0$ for all $j$ in [11.2.5].

To prove the converse, suppose that $d_j = 0$ for all $j$ in [11.2.5]. Let

$$x_t = \mu_1 + \psi_{11}(L)\varepsilon_{1t} \tag{11.A.18}$$

denote the univariate Wold representation for $x_t$; thus, $\psi_{11}^{(0)} = 1$. We will be using notation consistent with the form of [11.2.4] in anticipation of the final answer that will be derived; for now, the reader should view [11.A.18] as a new definition of $\psi_{11}(L)$ in terms of the univariate Wold representation for $x$. There also exists a univariate Wold representation for the error term in [11.2.5], denoted

$$\eta_t = \psi_{22}(L)v_{2t}, \qquad [11.A.19]$$

with $\psi_{22}^{(0)} = 1$. Notice that $\eta_t$ as defined in [11.2.5] is uncorrected with $x_s$ for all $t$ and $s$. It follows that $v_{2t}$ is uncorrelated with $x_\tau$ or $\varepsilon_{1\tau}$ for all $t$ and $\tau$.

Substituting [11.A.18] and [11.A.19] into [11.2.5],

$$y_t = c + b(1)\mu_1 + b(L)\psi_{11}(L)\varepsilon_{1t} + \psi_{22}(L)v_{2t}. \qquad [11.A.20]$$

Define

$$\varepsilon_{2t} \equiv v_{2t} + b_0\varepsilon_{1t} \qquad [11.A.21]$$

for $b_0$ the coefficient on $L^0$ of $b(L)$ and

$$\mu_2 \equiv c + b(1)\mu_1. \qquad [11.A.22]$$

Observe that $(\varepsilon_{1t}, \varepsilon_{2t})'$ is vector white noise. Substituting [11.A.21] and [11.A.22] into [11.A.20] produces

$$y_t = \mu_2 + [b(L)\psi_{11}(L) - b_0\psi_{22}(L)]\varepsilon_{1t} + \psi_{22}(L)\varepsilon_{2t}. \qquad [11.A.23]$$

Finally, define

$$\psi_{21}(L) \equiv [b(L)\psi_{11}(L) - b_0\psi_{22}(L)],$$

noting that $\psi_{21}^{(0)} = 0$. Then, substituting this into [11.A.23] produces

$$y_t = \mu_2 + \psi_{21}(L)\varepsilon_{1t} + \psi_{22}(L)\varepsilon_{2t}.$$

This combined with [11.A.18] completes the demonstration that [11.2.5] implies [11.2.4]. ■

## APPENDIX 11.B. *Calculation of Analytic Derivatives*

This appendix calculates the derivatives reported in Sections 11.6 and 11.7.

■ **Derivation of [11.6.38].** Let the scalar $\xi$ represent some particular element of $\boldsymbol{\theta}_B$ or $\boldsymbol{\theta}_D$, and let $\partial\boldsymbol{\Omega}/\partial\xi$ denote the $(n^2 \times n^2)$ matrix that results when each element of $\boldsymbol{\Omega}$ is differentiated with respect to $\xi$. Thus, differentiating [11.6.33] with respect to $\xi$ results in

$$\partial\boldsymbol{\Omega}/\partial\xi = (\partial\mathbf{B}_0^{-1}/\partial\xi)\mathbf{D}(\mathbf{B}_0^{-1})' + \mathbf{B}_0^{-1}(\partial\mathbf{D}/\partial\xi)(\mathbf{B}_0^{-1})' + (\mathbf{B}_0^{-1})\mathbf{D}[\partial(\mathbf{B}_0^{-1})'/\partial\xi]. \qquad [11.B.1]$$

Define

$$\boldsymbol{\chi} \equiv (\partial\mathbf{B}_0^{-1}/\partial\xi)\mathbf{D}(\mathbf{B}_0^{-1})' \qquad [11.B.2]$$

and notice that

$$\boldsymbol{\chi}' = (\mathbf{B}_0^{-1})\mathbf{D}[\partial(\mathbf{B}_0^{-1})'/\partial\xi],$$

since $\mathbf{D}$ is a variance-covariance matrix and must therefore be symmetric. Thus, [11.B.1] can be written

$$\partial\boldsymbol{\Omega}/\partial\xi = \boldsymbol{\chi} + \mathbf{B}_0^{-1}(\partial\mathbf{D}/\partial\xi)(\mathbf{B}_0^{-1})' + \boldsymbol{\chi}'. \qquad [11.B.3]$$

Recall from Proposition 10.4 that

$$\text{vec}(\mathbf{ABC}) = (\mathbf{C}' \otimes \mathbf{A})\cdot\text{vec}(\mathbf{B}). \qquad [11.B.4]$$

Thus, if the vec operator is applied to [11.B.3], the result is

$$\frac{\partial\, \text{vec}(\boldsymbol{\Omega})}{\partial\xi} = \text{vec}(\boldsymbol{\chi} + \boldsymbol{\chi}') + [(\mathbf{B}_0^{-1}) \otimes (\mathbf{B}_0^{-1})]\,\text{vec}(\partial\mathbf{D}/\partial\xi). \qquad [11.B.5]$$

Let $\mathbf{D}_n$ denote the $(n^2 \times n^*)$ duplication matrix introduced in [11.1.43]. Notice that for any $(n \times n)$ matrix $\boldsymbol{\chi}$, the elements of $\mathbf{D}_n' \operatorname{vec}(\boldsymbol{\chi})$ are of the form $\chi_{ii}$ for diagonal elements of $\boldsymbol{\chi}$ and of the form $(\chi_{ij} + \chi_{ji})$ for off-diagonal elements. Hence, $\mathbf{D}_n' \operatorname{vec}(\boldsymbol{\chi}) = \mathbf{D}_n' \operatorname{vec}(\boldsymbol{\chi}')$. If [11.B.5] is premultiplied by $\mathbf{D}_n^+ = (\mathbf{D}_n'\mathbf{D}_n)^{-1}\mathbf{D}_n'$, the result is thus

$$\frac{\partial \operatorname{vech}(\boldsymbol{\Omega})}{\partial \xi} = 2\mathbf{D}_n^+ \operatorname{vec}(\boldsymbol{\chi}) + \mathbf{D}_n^+[(\mathbf{B}_0^{-1}) \otimes (\mathbf{B}_0^{-1})] \operatorname{vec}(\partial \mathbf{D}/\partial \xi), \qquad [11.B.6]$$

since from [11.1.46] $\mathbf{D}_n^+ \operatorname{vec}(\boldsymbol{\Omega}) = \operatorname{vech}(\boldsymbol{\Omega})$.

Differentiating the identity $\mathbf{B}_0^{-1}\mathbf{B}_0 = \mathbf{I}_n$ with respect to $\xi$ produces

$$(\partial \mathbf{B}_0^{-1}/\partial \xi)\mathbf{B}_0 + \mathbf{B}_0^{-1}(\partial \mathbf{B}_0/\partial \xi) = \mathbf{0}_{nn}$$

or

$$\partial \mathbf{B}_0^{-1}/\partial \xi = -\mathbf{B}_0^{-1}(\partial \mathbf{B}_0/\partial \xi)\mathbf{B}_0^{-1}. \qquad [11.B.7]$$

Thus, [11.B.2] can be written

$$\boldsymbol{\chi} = -\mathbf{B}_0^{-1}(\partial \mathbf{B}_0/\partial \xi)\mathbf{B}_0^{-1}\mathbf{D}(\mathbf{B}_0^{-1})' = -\mathbf{B}_0^{-1}(\partial \mathbf{B}_0/\partial \xi)\boldsymbol{\Omega}.$$

Applying the vec operator as in [11.B.4] results in

$$\operatorname{vec}(\boldsymbol{\chi}) = -(\boldsymbol{\Omega} \otimes \mathbf{B}_0^{-1}) \frac{\partial \operatorname{vec}(\mathbf{B}_0)}{\partial \xi}.$$

Substituting this expression into [11.B.6] gives

$$\begin{aligned}\frac{\partial \operatorname{vech}(\boldsymbol{\Omega})}{\partial \xi} &= -2\mathbf{D}_n^+(\boldsymbol{\Omega} \otimes \mathbf{B}_0^{-1}) \frac{\partial \operatorname{vec}(\mathbf{B}_0)}{\partial \xi} + \mathbf{D}_n^+[(\mathbf{B}_0^{-1}) \otimes (\mathbf{B}_0^{-1})] \frac{\partial \operatorname{vec}(\mathbf{D})}{\partial \xi} \\ &= -2\mathbf{D}_n^+(\boldsymbol{\Omega} \otimes \mathbf{B}_0^{-1})\mathbf{S}_B \frac{\partial \boldsymbol{\theta}_B}{\partial \xi} + \mathbf{D}_n^+[(\mathbf{B}_0^{-1}) \otimes (\mathbf{B}_0^{-1})]\mathbf{S}_D \frac{\partial \boldsymbol{\theta}_D}{\partial \xi}.\end{aligned} \qquad [11.B.8]$$

Expression [11.B.8] is an $(n^* \times 1)$ vector that gives the effect of a change in some element of $\boldsymbol{\theta}_B$ or $\boldsymbol{\theta}_D$ on each of the $n^*$ elements of $\operatorname{vech}(\boldsymbol{\Omega})$. If $\xi$ corresponds to the first element of $\boldsymbol{\theta}_B$, then $\partial \boldsymbol{\theta}_B/\partial \xi = \mathbf{e}_1$, the first column of the $(n_B \times n_B)$ identity matrix, and $\partial \boldsymbol{\theta}_D/\partial \xi = \mathbf{0}$. If $\xi$ corresponds to the second element of $\boldsymbol{\theta}_B$, then $\partial \boldsymbol{\theta}_B/\partial \xi = \mathbf{e}_2$. If we stack the vectors in [11.B.8] associated with $\xi = \theta_{B,1}, \xi = \theta_{B,2}, \ldots, \xi = \theta_{B,n_B}$ side by side, the result is

$$\begin{bmatrix} \dfrac{\partial \operatorname{vech}(\boldsymbol{\Omega})}{\partial \theta_{B,1}} & \dfrac{\partial \operatorname{vech}(\boldsymbol{\Omega})}{\partial \theta_{B,2}} & \cdots & \dfrac{\partial \operatorname{vech}(\boldsymbol{\Omega})}{\partial \theta_{B,n_B}} \end{bmatrix} = [-2\mathbf{D}_n^+(\boldsymbol{\Omega} \otimes \mathbf{B}_0^{-1})\mathbf{S}_B][\mathbf{e}_1 \quad \mathbf{e}_2 \quad \cdots \quad \mathbf{e}_{n_B}]. \qquad [11.B.9]$$

That is,

$$\frac{\partial \operatorname{vech}(\boldsymbol{\Omega})}{\partial \boldsymbol{\theta}_B'} = [-2\mathbf{D}_n^+(\boldsymbol{\Omega} \otimes \mathbf{B}_0^{-1})\mathbf{S}_B]. \qquad [11.B.10]$$

Similarly, letting the scalar $\xi$ in [11.B.8] correspond to each of the elements of $\boldsymbol{\theta}_D$ in succession and stacking the resulting columns horizontally results in

$$\frac{\partial \operatorname{vech}(\boldsymbol{\Omega})}{\partial \boldsymbol{\theta}_D'} = \mathbf{D}_n^+[(\mathbf{B}_0^{-1}) \otimes (\mathbf{B}_0^{-1})]\mathbf{S}_D. \qquad [11.B.11]$$

Equation [11.6.38] then follows immediately from [11.B.10] and [11.B.11]. ■

■ **Derivation of [11.7.4].** Recall from equation [10.1.19] that

$$\boldsymbol{\Psi}_s = \boldsymbol{\Phi}_1\boldsymbol{\Psi}_{s-1} + \boldsymbol{\Phi}_2\boldsymbol{\Psi}_{s-2} + \cdots + \boldsymbol{\Phi}_p\boldsymbol{\Psi}_{s-p}. \qquad [11.B.12]$$

Taking transposes,

$$\boldsymbol{\Psi}_s' = \boldsymbol{\Psi}_{s-1}'\boldsymbol{\Phi}_1' + \boldsymbol{\Psi}_{s-2}'\boldsymbol{\Phi}_2' + \cdots + \boldsymbol{\Psi}_{s-p}'\boldsymbol{\Phi}_p'. \qquad [11.B.13]$$

Let the scalar $\xi$ denote some particular element of $\boldsymbol{\pi}$, and differentiate [11.B.13] with respect to $\xi$:

$$\begin{aligned}
\frac{\partial \boldsymbol{\Psi}_s'}{\partial \xi} &= \boldsymbol{\Psi}_{s-1}' \frac{\partial \boldsymbol{\Phi}_1'}{\partial \xi} + \boldsymbol{\Psi}_{s-2}' \frac{\partial \boldsymbol{\Phi}_2'}{\partial \xi} + \cdots + \boldsymbol{\Psi}_{s-p}' \frac{\partial \boldsymbol{\Phi}_p'}{\partial \xi} \\
&\quad + \frac{\partial \boldsymbol{\Psi}_{s-1}'}{\partial \xi} \boldsymbol{\Phi}_1' + \frac{\partial \boldsymbol{\Psi}_{s-2}'}{\partial \xi} \boldsymbol{\Phi}_2' + \cdots + \frac{\partial \boldsymbol{\Psi}_{s-p}'}{\partial \xi} \boldsymbol{\Phi}_p' \\
&= [\mathbf{0}_{n1} \quad \boldsymbol{\Psi}_{s-1}' \quad \boldsymbol{\Psi}_{s-2}' \quad \cdots \quad \boldsymbol{\Psi}_{s-p}'] \begin{bmatrix} \partial \mathbf{c}'/\partial \xi \\ \partial \boldsymbol{\Phi}_1'/\partial \xi \\ \partial \boldsymbol{\Phi}_2'/\partial \xi \\ \vdots \\ \partial \boldsymbol{\Phi}_p'/\partial \xi \end{bmatrix} \\
&\quad + \frac{\partial \boldsymbol{\Psi}_{s-1}'}{\partial \xi} \boldsymbol{\Phi}_1' + \frac{\partial \boldsymbol{\Psi}_{s-2}'}{\partial \xi} \boldsymbol{\Phi}_2' + \cdots + \frac{\partial \boldsymbol{\Psi}_{s-p}'}{\partial \xi} \boldsymbol{\Phi}_p' \\
&= [\mathbf{0}_{n1} \quad \boldsymbol{\Psi}_{s-1}' \quad \boldsymbol{\Psi}_{s-2}' \quad \cdots \quad \boldsymbol{\Psi}_{s-p}'] \frac{\partial \boldsymbol{\Pi}}{\partial \xi} \\
&\quad + \frac{\partial \boldsymbol{\Psi}_{s-1}'}{\partial \xi} \boldsymbol{\Phi}_1' + \frac{\partial \boldsymbol{\Psi}_{s-2}'}{\partial \xi} \boldsymbol{\Phi}_2' + \cdots + \frac{\partial \boldsymbol{\Psi}_{s-p}'}{\partial \xi} \boldsymbol{\Phi}_p'.
\end{aligned} \tag{11.B.14}$$

Recall result [11.B.4], and note the special case when $\mathbf{A}$ is the $(n \times n)$ identity matrix, $\mathbf{B}$ is an $(n \times r)$ matrix, and $\mathbf{C}$ is an $(r \times q)$ matrix:

$$\text{vec}(\mathbf{BC}) = (\mathbf{C}' \otimes \mathbf{I}_n)\, \text{vec}(\mathbf{B}). \tag{11.B.15}$$

For example,

$$\text{vec}\left(\frac{\partial \boldsymbol{\Psi}_{s-1}'}{\partial \xi} \boldsymbol{\Phi}_1'\right) = (\boldsymbol{\Phi}_1 \otimes \mathbf{I}_n)\, \text{vec}\left(\frac{\partial \boldsymbol{\Psi}_{s-1}'}{\partial \xi}\right) = (\boldsymbol{\Phi}_1 \otimes \mathbf{I}_n)\left(\frac{\partial \boldsymbol{\psi}_{s-1}}{\partial \xi}\right). \tag{11.B.16}$$

Another implication of [11.B.4] can be obtained by letting $\mathbf{A}$ be an $(m \times q)$ matrix, $\mathbf{B}$ a $(q \times n)$ matrix, and $\mathbf{C}$ the $(n \times n)$ identity matrix:

$$\text{vec}(\mathbf{AB}) = (\mathbf{I}_n \otimes \mathbf{A})\, \text{vec}(\mathbf{B}). \tag{11.B.17}$$

For example,

$$\begin{aligned}
&\text{vec}\left([\mathbf{0}_{n1} \quad \boldsymbol{\Psi}_{s-1}' \quad \boldsymbol{\Psi}_{s-2}' \quad \cdots \quad \boldsymbol{\Psi}_{s-p}'] \frac{\partial \boldsymbol{\Pi}}{\partial \xi}\right) \\
&= [\mathbf{I}_n \otimes (\mathbf{0}_{n1} \quad \boldsymbol{\Psi}_{s-1}' \quad \boldsymbol{\Psi}_{s-2}' \quad \cdots \quad \boldsymbol{\Psi}_{s-p}')] \left(\frac{\partial\, \text{vec}(\boldsymbol{\Pi})}{\partial \xi}\right) \\
&= [\mathbf{I}_n \otimes (\mathbf{0}_{n1} \quad \boldsymbol{\Psi}_{s-1}' \quad \boldsymbol{\Psi}_{s-2}' \quad \cdots \quad \boldsymbol{\Psi}_{s-p}')] \left(\frac{\partial \boldsymbol{\pi}}{\partial \xi}\right).
\end{aligned} \tag{11.B.18}$$

Applying the vec operator to [11.B.14] and using [11.B.18] and [11.B.16] gives

$$\begin{aligned}
\frac{\partial \boldsymbol{\psi}_s}{\partial \xi} &= [\mathbf{I}_n \otimes (\mathbf{0}_{n1} \quad \boldsymbol{\Psi}_{s-1}' \quad \boldsymbol{\Psi}_{s-2}' \quad \cdots \quad \boldsymbol{\Psi}_{s-p}')] \left(\frac{\partial \boldsymbol{\pi}}{\partial \xi}\right) \\
&\quad + (\boldsymbol{\Phi}_1 \otimes \mathbf{I}_n)\left(\frac{\partial \boldsymbol{\psi}_{s-1}}{\partial \xi}\right) + (\boldsymbol{\Phi}_2 \otimes \mathbf{I}_n)\left(\frac{\partial \boldsymbol{\psi}_{s-2}}{\partial \xi}\right) \\
&\quad + \cdots + (\boldsymbol{\Phi}_p \otimes \mathbf{I}_n)\left(\frac{\partial \boldsymbol{\psi}_{s-p}}{\partial \xi}\right).
\end{aligned} \tag{11.B.19}$$

Letting $\xi$ successively represent each of the elements of $\boldsymbol{\pi}$ and stacking the resulting equations horizontally as in [11.B.9] results in

$$\frac{\partial \boldsymbol{\psi}_s}{\partial \boldsymbol{\pi}'} = [\mathbf{I}_n \otimes (\mathbf{0}_{n1} \quad \boldsymbol{\Psi}'_{s-1} \quad \boldsymbol{\Psi}'_{s-2} \quad \cdots \quad \boldsymbol{\Psi}'_{s-p})] + (\boldsymbol{\Phi}_1 \otimes \mathbf{I}_n)\left[\frac{\partial \boldsymbol{\psi}_{s-1}}{\partial \boldsymbol{\pi}'}\right] + \cdots + (\boldsymbol{\Phi}_p \otimes \mathbf{I}_n)\left[\frac{\partial \boldsymbol{\psi}_{s-p}}{\partial \boldsymbol{\pi}'}\right],$$

as claimed in [11.7.4]. ■

■ **Derivation of [11.7.5].** Here the task is to verify that if $\mathbf{G}_s$ is given by [11.7.5], then [11.7.4] holds:

$$\mathbf{G}_s = [\mathbf{I}_n \otimes (\mathbf{0}_{n1} \quad \boldsymbol{\Psi}'_{s-1} \quad \boldsymbol{\Psi}'_{s-2} \quad \cdots \quad \boldsymbol{\Psi}'_{s-p})] + \sum_{k=1}^{p} (\boldsymbol{\Phi}_k \otimes \mathbf{I}_n)\mathbf{G}_{s-k}. \qquad [11.B.20]$$

Notice that for $\mathbf{G}_s$ given by [11.7.5],

$$\begin{aligned}
&\sum_{k=1}^{p} (\boldsymbol{\Phi}_k \otimes \mathbf{I}_n)\mathbf{G}_{s-k} \\
&= \sum_{k=1}^{p} (\boldsymbol{\Phi}_k \otimes \mathbf{I}_n) \sum_{i=1}^{s-k} [\boldsymbol{\Psi}_{i-1} \otimes (\mathbf{0}_{n1} \quad \boldsymbol{\Psi}'_{s-k-i} \quad \boldsymbol{\Psi}'_{s-k-i-1} \quad \cdots \quad \boldsymbol{\Psi}'_{s-k-i-p+1})] \\
&= \sum_{k=1}^{p} \sum_{i=1}^{s-k} [\boldsymbol{\Phi}_k\boldsymbol{\Psi}_{i-1} \otimes (\mathbf{0}_{n1} \quad \boldsymbol{\Psi}'_{s-k-i} \quad \boldsymbol{\Psi}'_{s-k-i-1} \quad \cdots \quad \boldsymbol{\Psi}'_{s-k-i-p+1})].
\end{aligned}$$

For any given value for $k$ and $i$, define $v \equiv k + i$. When $i = 1$, then $v = k + 1$; when $i = 2$, then $v = k + 2$; and so on:

$$\sum_{k=1}^{p} (\boldsymbol{\Phi}_k \otimes \mathbf{I}_n)\mathbf{G}_{s-k} = \sum_{k=1}^{p} \sum_{v=k+1}^{s} [\boldsymbol{\Phi}_k\boldsymbol{\Psi}_{v-k-1} \otimes (\mathbf{0}_{n1} \quad \boldsymbol{\Psi}'_{s-v} \quad \boldsymbol{\Psi}'_{s-v-1} \quad \cdots \quad \boldsymbol{\Psi}'_{s-v-p+1})].$$

Recalling further that $\boldsymbol{\Psi}_{v-k-1} = \mathbf{0}$ for $v = 2, 3, \ldots, k$, we could equally well write

$$\begin{aligned}
&\sum_{k=1}^{p} (\boldsymbol{\Phi}_k \otimes \mathbf{I}_n)\mathbf{G}_{s-k} \\
&= \sum_{k=1}^{p} \sum_{v=2}^{s} [\boldsymbol{\Phi}_k\boldsymbol{\Psi}_{v-k-1} \otimes (\mathbf{0}_{n1} \quad \boldsymbol{\Psi}'_{s-v} \quad \boldsymbol{\Psi}'_{s-v-1} \quad \cdots \quad \boldsymbol{\Psi}'_{s-v-p+1})] \\
&= \sum_{v=2}^{s} \sum_{k=1}^{p} [\boldsymbol{\Phi}_k\boldsymbol{\Psi}_{v-k-1} \otimes (\mathbf{0}_{n1} \quad \boldsymbol{\Psi}'_{s-v} \quad \boldsymbol{\Psi}'_{s-v-1} \quad \cdots \quad \boldsymbol{\Psi}'_{s-v-p+1})] \\
&= \sum_{v=2}^{s} \left[\left(\sum_{k=1}^{p} \boldsymbol{\Phi}_k\boldsymbol{\Psi}_{v-k-1}\right) \otimes (\mathbf{0}_{n1} \quad \boldsymbol{\Psi}'_{s-v} \quad \boldsymbol{\Psi}'_{s-v-1} \quad \cdots \quad \boldsymbol{\Psi}'_{s-v-p+1})\right] \\
&= \sum_{v=2}^{s} [\boldsymbol{\Psi}_{v-1} \otimes (\mathbf{0}_{n1} \quad \boldsymbol{\Psi}'_{s-v} \quad \boldsymbol{\Psi}'_{s-v-1} \quad \cdots \quad \boldsymbol{\Psi}'_{s-v-p+1})],
\end{aligned} \qquad [11.B.21]$$

by virtue of [11.B.12]. If the first term on the right side of [11.B.20] is added to [11.B.21], the result is

$$\begin{aligned}
&[\mathbf{I}_n \otimes (\mathbf{0}_{n1} \quad \boldsymbol{\Psi}'_{s-1} \quad \boldsymbol{\Psi}'_{s-2} \quad \cdots \quad \boldsymbol{\Psi}'_{s-p})] + \sum_{k=1}^{p} (\boldsymbol{\Phi}_k \otimes \mathbf{I}_n)\mathbf{G}_{s-k} \\
&= [\mathbf{I}_n \otimes (\mathbf{0}_{n1} \quad \boldsymbol{\Psi}'_{s-1} \quad \boldsymbol{\Psi}'_{s-2} \quad \cdots \quad \boldsymbol{\Psi}'_{s-p}) \\
&\quad + \sum_{v=2}^{s} [\boldsymbol{\Psi}_{v-1} \otimes (\mathbf{0}_{n1} \quad \boldsymbol{\Psi}'_{s-v} \quad \boldsymbol{\Psi}'_{s-v-1} \quad \cdots \quad \boldsymbol{\Psi}'_{s-v-p+1})] \\
&= \sum_{v=1}^{s} [\boldsymbol{\Psi}_{v-1} \otimes (\mathbf{0}_{n1} \quad \boldsymbol{\Psi}'_{s-v} \quad \boldsymbol{\Psi}'_{s-v-1} \quad \cdots \quad \boldsymbol{\Psi}'_{s-v-p+1})],
\end{aligned}$$

which is indeed the expression for $\mathbf{G}_s$ given in [11.7.5]. ■

■ **Derivation of [11.7.14] and [11.7.15].** Postmultiplying [11.7.12] by $\mathbf{B}_0$ and transposing results in

$$\mathbf{B}_0'\mathbf{H}_s' = \boldsymbol{\Psi}_s'. \qquad [11.B.22]$$

Let the scalar $\xi$ denote some element of $\boldsymbol{\pi}$ or $\boldsymbol{\Omega}$, and differentiate [11.B.22] with respect to $\xi$:

$$(\partial \mathbf{B}_0'/\partial \xi)\mathbf{H}_s' + \mathbf{B}_0'(\partial \mathbf{H}_s'/\partial \xi) = \partial \boldsymbol{\Psi}_s'/\partial \xi. \qquad [11.B.23]$$

Applying the vec operator to [11.B.23] and using [11.B.15] and [11.B.17],

$$(\mathbf{H}_s \otimes \mathbf{I}_n)(\partial\, \mathrm{vec}(\mathbf{B}_0')/\partial\xi) + (\mathbf{I}_n \otimes \mathbf{B}_0')(\partial\, \mathrm{vec}(\mathbf{H}_s')/\partial\xi) = \partial\, \mathrm{vec}(\mathbf{\Psi}_s')/\partial\xi,$$

implying that

$$\begin{aligned}\partial\mathbf{h}_s/\partial\xi &= -(\mathbf{I}_n \otimes \mathbf{B}_0')^{-1}(\mathbf{H}_s \otimes \mathbf{I}_n)(\partial\, \mathrm{vec}(\mathbf{B}_0')/\partial\xi) + (\mathbf{I}_n \otimes \mathbf{B}_0')^{-1}\, \partial\boldsymbol{\psi}_s/\partial\xi \\ &= -[\mathbf{H}_s \otimes (\mathbf{B}_0')^{-1}](\partial\, \mathrm{vec}(\mathbf{B}_0')/\partial\xi) + [\mathbf{I}_n \otimes (\mathbf{B}_0')^{-1}]\, \partial\boldsymbol{\psi}_s/\partial\xi.\end{aligned} \qquad [11.B.24]$$

Noticing that $\mathbf{B}_0'$ does not depend on $\boldsymbol{\pi}$, if [11.B.24] is stacked horizontally for $\xi = \pi_1, \pi_2, \ldots, \pi_{nk}$, the result is

$$\partial\mathbf{h}_s/\partial\boldsymbol{\pi}' = [\mathbf{I}_n \otimes (\mathbf{B}_0')^{-1}]\, \partial\boldsymbol{\psi}_s/\partial\boldsymbol{\pi}',$$

as claimed in [11.7.14]. Similarly, if $\xi$ is an element of $\mathbf{\Omega}$, then $\xi$ has no effect on $\mathbf{\Psi}_s$, and its influence on $\mathbf{B}_0'$ is given by

$$\frac{\partial\, \mathrm{vec}(\mathbf{B}_0')}{\partial\xi} = \mathbf{S}_{B'}\frac{\partial\boldsymbol{\theta}_B}{\partial\xi}.$$

Stacking [11.B.24] horizontally with $\xi$ representing each of the elements of vech($\mathbf{\Omega}$) thus produces

$$\frac{\partial\mathbf{h}_s}{\partial[\mathrm{vech}(\mathbf{\Omega})]'} = -[\mathbf{H}_s \otimes (\mathbf{B}_0')^{-1}]\mathbf{S}_{B'}\frac{\partial\boldsymbol{\theta}_B}{\partial[\mathrm{vech}(\mathbf{\Omega})]'},$$

as claimed in [11.7.15]. ■

## *Chapter 11 Exercises*

11.1. Verify result [11.A.2].

11.2. Consider the following three-variable *VAR*:

$$\begin{aligned} y_{1t} &= \alpha y_{1,t-1} + \beta y_{2,t-1} + \varepsilon_{1t} \\ y_{2t} &= \gamma y_{1,t-1} + \varepsilon_{2t} \\ y_{3t} &= \xi y_{1,t-1} + \zeta y_{2,t-1} + \eta y_{3,t-1} + \varepsilon_{3t}. \end{aligned}$$

(a) Is $y_{1t}$ block-exogenous with respect to the vector $(y_{2t}, y_{3t})'$?
(b) Is the vector $(y_{1t}, y_{2t})$ block-exogenous with respect to $y_{3t}$?
(c) Is $y_{3t}$ block-exogenous with respect to the vector $(y_{1t}, y_{2t})'$?

11.3. Consider the following bivariate *VAR*:

$$\begin{aligned} y_{1t} &= \alpha_1 y_{1,t-1} + \alpha_2 y_{1,t-2} + \cdots + \alpha_p y_{1,t-p} \\ &\quad + \beta_1 y_{2,t-1} + \beta_2 y_{2,t-2} + \cdots + \beta_p y_{2,t-p} + \varepsilon_{1t} \\ y_{2t} &= \gamma_1 y_{1,t-1} + \gamma_2 y_{1,t-2} + \cdots + \gamma_p y_{1,t-p} \\ &\quad + \delta_1 y_{2,t-1} + \delta_2 y_{2,t-2} + \cdots + \delta_p y_{2,t-p} + \varepsilon_{2t} \end{aligned}$$

$$E(\boldsymbol{\varepsilon}_t\boldsymbol{\varepsilon}_\tau') = \begin{cases} \begin{bmatrix} \Omega_{11} & \Omega_{12} \\ \Omega_{21} & \Omega_{22} \end{bmatrix} & \text{for } t = \tau \\ \mathbf{0} & \text{otherwise.} \end{cases}$$

Use the results of Section 11.3 to write this in the form

$$\begin{aligned} y_{1t} &= \zeta_1 y_{1,t-1} + \zeta_2 y_{1,t-2} + \cdots + \zeta_p y_{1,t-p} \\ &\quad + \eta_1 y_{2,t-1} + \eta_2 y_{2,t-2} + \cdots + \eta_p y_{2,t-p} + u_{1t} \\ y_{2t} &= \lambda_0 y_{1t} + \lambda_1 y_{1,t-1} + \lambda_2 y_{1,t-2} + \cdots + \lambda_p y_{1,t-p} \\ &\quad + \xi_1 y_{2,t-1} + \xi_2 y_{2,t-2} + \cdots + \xi_p y_{2,t-p} + u_{2t}, \end{aligned}$$

where

$$E(\mathbf{u}_t\mathbf{u}_\tau') = \begin{cases} \begin{bmatrix} \sigma_1^2 & 0 \\ 0 & \sigma_2^2 \end{bmatrix} & \text{for } t = \tau \\ \mathbf{0} & \text{otherwise.} \end{cases}$$

What is the relation between the parameters of the first representation ($\alpha_j, \beta_j, \gamma_j, \delta_j, \Omega_{il}$) and those of the second representation ($\zeta_j, \eta_j, \lambda_j, \xi_j, \sigma_i^2$)? What is the relation between $\boldsymbol{\varepsilon}_t$ and $\mathbf{u}_t$?

11.4. Write the result for Exercise 11.3 as

$$\begin{bmatrix} 1 - \zeta(L) & -\eta(L) \\ -\lambda_0 - \lambda(L) & 1 - \xi(L) \end{bmatrix} \begin{bmatrix} y_{1t} \\ y_{2t} \end{bmatrix} = \begin{bmatrix} u_{1t} \\ u_{2t} \end{bmatrix}$$

or

$$\mathbf{A}(L)\mathbf{y}_t = \mathbf{u}_t.$$

Premultiply this system by the adjoint of $\mathbf{A}(L)$,

$$\mathbf{A}^*(L) \equiv \begin{bmatrix} 1 - \xi(L) & \eta(L) \\ \lambda_0 + \lambda(L) & 1 - \zeta(L) \end{bmatrix},$$

to deduce that $y_{1t}$ and $y_{2t}$ each admit a univariate $ARMA(2p, p)$ representation. Show how the argument generalizes to establish that if the $(n \times 1)$ vector $\mathbf{y}_t$ follows a $p$th-order autoregression, then each individual element $y_{it}$ follows an $ARMA[np, (n - 1)p]$ process. (See Zellner and Palm, 1974).

11.5. Consider the following bivariate $VAR$:

$$y_{1t} = 0.3y_{1,t-1} + 0.8y_{2,t-1} + \varepsilon_{1t}$$
$$y_{2t} = 0.9y_{1,t-1} + 0.4y_{2,t-1} + \varepsilon_{2t},$$

with $E(\varepsilon_{1t}\varepsilon_{1\tau}) = 1$ for $t = \tau$ and 0 otherwise, $E(\varepsilon_{2t}\varepsilon_{2\tau}) = 2$ for $t = \tau$ and 0 otherwise, and $E(\varepsilon_{1t}\varepsilon_{2\tau}) = 0$ for all $t$ and $\tau$.

(a) Is this system covariance-stationary?

(b) Calculate $\mathbf{\Psi}_s = \partial \mathbf{y}_{t+s}/\partial \boldsymbol{\varepsilon}_t'$ for $s = 0$, 1, and 2. What is the limit as $s \to \infty$?

(c) Calculate the fraction of the $MSE$ of the two-period-ahead forecast error for variable 1,

$$E[y_{1,t+2} - \hat{E}(y_{1,t+2}|y_t, y_{t-1}, \ldots)]^2,$$

that is due to $\varepsilon_{1,t+1}$ and $\varepsilon_{1,t+2}$.

## Chapter 11 References


Ashley, Richard. 1988. "On the Relative Worth of Recent Macroeconomic Forecasts." *International Journal of Forecasting* 4:363–76.

Baillie, Richard T. 1987. "Inference in Dynamic Models Containing 'Surprise' Variables." *Journal of Econometrics* 35:101–17.

Bernanke, Ben. 1986. "Alternative Explanations of the Money-Income Correlation." *Carnegie-Rochester Conference Series on Public Policy* 25:49–100.

Blanchard, Olivier. 1989. "A Traditional Interpretation of Macroeconomic Fluctuations." *American Economic Review* 79:1146–64.

——— and Peter Diamond. 1989. "The Beveridge Curve." *Brookings Papers on Economic Activity* I:1989, 1–60.

——— and ———. 1990. "The Cyclical Behavior of the Gross Flows of U.S. Workers." *Brookings Papers on Economic Activity* II:1990, 85–155.

——— and Danny Quah. 1989. "The Dynamic Effects of Aggregate Demand and Aggregate Supply Disturbances." *American Economic Review* 79:655–73.

——— and Mark Watson. 1986. "Are Business Cycles All Alike?" in Robert J. Gordon, ed., *The American Business Cycle*. Chicago: University of Chicago Press.

Bouissou, M. B., J. J. Laffont, and Q. H. Vuong. 1986. "Tests of Noncausality under Markov Assumptions for Qualitative Panel Data." *Econometrica* 54:395–414.

Christiano, Lawrence J., and Lars Ljungqvist. 1988. "Money Does Granger-Cause Output in the Bivariate Money-Output Relation." *Journal of Monetary Economics* 22:217–35.

Cooley, Thomas F., and Stephen F. LeRoy. 1985. "Atheoretical Macroeconometrics: A Critique." *Journal of Monetary Economics* 16:283–308.

Fama, Eugene F. 1965. "The Behavior of Stock Market Prices." *Journal of Business* 38:34–105.

Feige, Edgar L., and Douglas K. Pearce. 1979. "The Casual Causal Relationship between Money and Income: Some Caveats for Time Series Analysis." *Review of Economics and Statistics* 61:521–33.

Flavin, Marjorie A. 1981. "The Adjustment of Consumption to Changing Expectations about Future Income." *Journal of Political Economy* 89:974–1009.

Geweke, John. 1982. "Measurement of Linear Dependence and Feedback between Multiple Time Series." *Journal of the American Statistical Association* 77:304–13.

———, Richard Meese, and Warren Dent. 1983. "Comparing Alternative Tests of Causality in Temporal Systems: Analytic Results and Experimental Evidence." *Journal of Econometrics* 21:161–94.

Giannini, Carlo. 1992. *Topics in Structural VAR Econometrics*. New York: Springer-Verlag.

Granger, C. W. J. 1969. "Investigating Causal Relations by Econometric Models and Cross-Spectral Methods." *Econometrica* 37:424–38.

Hamilton, James D. 1983. "Oil and the Macroeconomy since World War II." *Journal of Political Economy* 91:228–48.

———. 1985. "Historical Causes of Postwar Oil Shocks and Recessions." *Energy Journal* 6:97–116.

Hansen, Lars P., and Thomas J. Sargent. 1981. "Formulating and Estimating Dynamic Linear Rational Expectations Models," in Robert E. Lucas, Jr., and Thomas J. Sargent, eds., *Rational Expectations and Econometric Practice*, Vol. I. Minneapolis: University of Minnesota Press.

Keating, John W. 1990. "Identifying VAR Models under Rational Expectations." *Journal of Monetary Economics* 25:453–76.

Leamer, Edward. 1985. "Vector Autoregressions for Causal Inference?" *Carnegie-Rochester Conference Series on Public Policy* 22:255–303.

Lucas, Robert E., Jr. 1978. "Asset Prices in an Exchange Economy." *Econometrica* 46:1429–45.

Lütkepohl, Helmut. 1989. "A Note on the Asymptotic Distribution of Impulse Response Functions of Estimated VAR Models with Orthogonal Residuals." *Journal of Econometrics* 42:371–76.

———. 1990. "Asymptotic Distributions of Impulse Response Functions and Forecast Error Variance Decompositions of Vector Autoregressive Models." *Review of Economics and Statistics* 72:116–25.

Magnus, Jan R. 1978. "Maximum Likelihood Estimation of the GLS Model with Unknown Parameters in the Disturbance Covariance Matrix." *Journal of Econometrics* 7:281–312.

——— and Heinz Neudecker. 1988. *Matrix Differential Calculus with Applications in Statistics and Econometrics*. New York: Wiley.

Pierce, David A., and Larry D. Haugh. 1977. "Causality in Temporal Systems: Characterization and a Survey." *Journal of Econometrics* 5:265–93.

Rothenberg, Thomas J. 1971. "Identification in Parametric Models." *Econometrica* 39:577–91.

———. 1973. *Efficient Estimation with a Priori Information*. New Haven, Conn.: Yale University Press.

Runkle, David E. 1987. "Vector Autoregressions and Reality." *Journal of Business and Economic Statistics* 5:437–42.

Shapiro, Matthew D., and Mark W. Watson. 1988. "Sources of Business Cycle Fluctuations," in Stanley Fischer, ed., *NBER Macroeconomics Annual 1988*. Cambridge, Mass.: MIT Press.

Sims, Christopher A. 1972. "Money, Income and Causality." *American Economic Review* 62:540–52.

———. 1980. "Macroeconomics and Reality." *Econometrica* 48:1–48.

———. 1986. "Are Forecasting Models Usable for Policy Analysis?" *Quarterly Review of the Federal Reserve Bank of Minneapolis* (Winter), 2–16.

Stock, James H., and Mark W. Watson. 1989. "Interpreting the Evidence on Money-Income Causality." *Journal of Econometrics* 40:161–81.

Theil, Henri. 1971. *Principles of Econometrics*. New York: Wiley.

Zellner, Arnold. 1962. "An Efficient Method of Estimating Seemingly Unrelated Regressions and Tests for Aggregation Bias." *Journal of the American Statistical Association* 57:348–68.

——— and Franz Palm. 1974. "Time Series Analysis and Simultaneous Equation Econometric Models." *Journal of Econometrics* 2:17–54.

# 12 Bayesian Analysis

The previous chapter noted that because so many parameters are estimated in a vector autoregression, the standard errors for inferences can be large. The estimates can be improved if the analyst has any information about the parameters beyond that contained in the sample. Bayesian estimation provides a convenient framework for incorporating prior information with as much weight as the analyst feels it merits.

Section 12.1 introduces the basic principles underlying Bayesian analysis and uses them to analyze a standard regression model or univariate autoregression. Vector autoregressions are discussed in Section 12.2. For the specifications in Sections 12.1 and 12.2, the Bayesian estimators can be found analytically. Numerical methods that can be used to analyze more general statistical problems from a Bayesian framework are reviewed in Section 12.3.

## 12.1. *Introduction to Bayesian Analysis*

Let $\boldsymbol{\theta}$ be an $(a \times 1)$ vector of parameters to be estimated from a sample of observations. For example, if $y_t \sim$ i.i.d. $N(\mu, \sigma^2)$, then $\boldsymbol{\theta} = (\mu, \sigma^2)'$ is to be estimated on the basis of $\mathbf{y} \equiv (y_1, y_2, \ldots, y_T)'$. Much of the discussion up to this point in the text has been based on the *classical* statistical perspective that there exists some true value of $\boldsymbol{\theta}$. This true value is regarded as an unknown but fixed number. An estimator $\hat{\boldsymbol{\theta}}$ is constructed from the data, and $\hat{\boldsymbol{\theta}}$ is therefore a random variable. In classical statistics, the mean and plim of the random variable $\hat{\boldsymbol{\theta}}$ are compared with the true value $\boldsymbol{\theta}$. The efficiency of the estimator is judged by the mean squared error of the random variable, $E(\hat{\boldsymbol{\theta}} - \boldsymbol{\theta})(\hat{\boldsymbol{\theta}} - \boldsymbol{\theta})'$. A popular classical estimator is the value $\hat{\boldsymbol{\theta}}$ that maximizes the sample likelihood, which for this example would be

$$f(\mathbf{y}; \boldsymbol{\theta}) = \prod_{t=1}^{T} \frac{1}{\sqrt{2\pi\sigma^2}} \exp\left[\frac{-(y_t - \mu)^2}{2\sigma^2}\right]. \qquad [12.1.1]$$

In Bayesian statistics, by contrast, $\boldsymbol{\theta}$ itself is regarded as a random variable. All inference about $\boldsymbol{\theta}$ takes the form of statements of probability, such as "there is only a 0.05 probability that $\theta_1$ is greater than zero." The view is that the analyst will always have some uncertainty about $\boldsymbol{\theta}$, and the goal of statistical analysis is to describe this uncertainty in terms of a probability distribution. Any information the analyst had about $\boldsymbol{\theta}$ before observing the data is represented by a *prior density*

$f(\boldsymbol{\theta})$.[1] Probability statements that the analyst might have made about $\boldsymbol{\theta}$ before observing the data can be expressed as integrals of $f(\boldsymbol{\theta})$; for example, the previous statement would be expressed as $\int_0^\infty f(\theta_1)\, d\theta_1 = 0.05$ where $f(\theta_1) = \int_{-\infty}^{\infty} \int_{-\infty}^{\infty} \cdots \int_{-\infty}^{\infty} f(\boldsymbol{\theta})\, d\theta_2\, d\theta_3 \cdots d\theta_a$. The sample likelihood [12.1.1] is viewed as the density of $\mathbf{y}$ conditional on the value of the random variable $\boldsymbol{\theta}$, denoted $f(\mathbf{y}|\boldsymbol{\theta})$. The product of the prior density and the sample likelihood gives the joint density of $\mathbf{y}$ and $\boldsymbol{\theta}$:

$$f(\mathbf{y}, \boldsymbol{\theta}) = f(\mathbf{y}|\boldsymbol{\theta}) \cdot f(\boldsymbol{\theta}). \qquad [12.1.2]$$

Probability statements that would be made about $\boldsymbol{\theta}$ after the data $\mathbf{y}$ have been observed are based on the *posterior density* of $\boldsymbol{\theta}$, which is given by

$$f(\boldsymbol{\theta}|\mathbf{y}) = \frac{f(\mathbf{y}, \boldsymbol{\theta})}{f(\mathbf{y})}. \qquad [12.1.3]$$

Recalling [12.1.2] and the fact that $f(\mathbf{y}) = \int_{-\infty}^{\infty} f(\mathbf{y}, \boldsymbol{\theta})\, d\boldsymbol{\theta}$, equation [12.1.3] can be written as

$$f(\boldsymbol{\theta}|\mathbf{y}) = \frac{f(\mathbf{y}|\boldsymbol{\theta}) \cdot f(\boldsymbol{\theta})}{\displaystyle\int_{-\infty}^{\infty} f(\mathbf{y}|\boldsymbol{\theta}) \cdot f(\boldsymbol{\theta})\, d\boldsymbol{\theta}}, \qquad [12.1.4]$$

which is known as *Bayes's law*. In practice, the posterior density can sometimes be found simply by rearranging the elements in [12.1.2] as

$$f(\mathbf{y}, \boldsymbol{\theta}) = f(\boldsymbol{\theta}|\mathbf{y}) \cdot f(\mathbf{y}),$$

where $f(\mathbf{y})$ is a density that does not involve $\boldsymbol{\theta}$; the other factor, $f(\boldsymbol{\theta}|\mathbf{y})$, is then the posterior density.

### *Estimating the Mean of a Gaussian Distribution with Known Variance*

To illustrate the Bayesian approach, let $y_t \sim$ i.i.d. $N(\mu, \sigma^2)$ as before and write the sample likelihood [12.1.1] as

$$f(\mathbf{y}|\mu; \sigma^2) = \frac{1}{(2\pi\sigma^2)^{T/2}} \exp\left\{\left[-\frac{1}{2\sigma^2}\right](\mathbf{y} - \mu\cdot\mathbf{1})'(\mathbf{y} - \mu\cdot\mathbf{1})\right\}, \qquad [12.1.5]$$

where $\mathbf{1}$ denotes a $(T \times 1)$ vector of 1s. Here $\mu$ is regarded as a random variable. To keep the example simple, we will assume that the variance $\sigma^2$ is known with certainty. Suppose that prior information about $\mu$ is represented by the prior distribution $\mu \sim N(m, \sigma^2/\nu)$:

$$f(\mu; \sigma^2) = \frac{1}{(2\pi\sigma^2/\nu)^{1/2}} \exp\left[\frac{-(\mu - m)^2}{2\sigma^2/\nu}\right]. \qquad [12.1.6]$$

Here $m$ and $\nu$ are parameters that describe the nature and quality of prior information about $\mu$. The parameter $m$ can be interpreted as the estimate of $\mu$ the analyst would have made before observing $\mathbf{y}$, with $\sigma^2/\nu$ the *MSE* of this estimate. Expressing this *MSE* as a multiple $(1/\nu)$ of the variance of the distribution for $y_t$ turns out to simplify some of the expressions that follow. Greater confidence in the prior information would be represented by larger values of $\nu$.

[1]Throughout this chapter we will omit the subscript that indicates the random variable whose density is being described; for example, $f_{\boldsymbol{\Theta}}(\boldsymbol{\theta})$ will simply be denoted $f(\boldsymbol{\theta})$. The random variable whose density is being described should always be clear from the context and the argument of $f(\cdot)$.

To make the idea of a prior distribution more concrete, suppose that before observing $\mathbf{y}$ the analyst had earlier obtained a sample of $N$ separate observations $\{z_i, i = 1, 2, \ldots, N\}$ from the $N(\mu, \sigma^2)$ distribution. It would then be natural to take $m$ to be the mean of this earlier sample ($m = \bar{z} = (1/N)\Sigma_{i=1}^N z_i$) and $\sigma^2/\nu$ to be the variance of $\bar{z}$, that is, to take $\nu = N$. The larger this earlier sample ($N$), the greater the confidence in the prior information.

The posterior distribution for $\mu$ after observing the sample $\mathbf{y}$ is described by the following proposition.

***Proposition 12.1:*** *The product of [12.1.5] and [12.1.6] can be written in the form* $f(\mu|\mathbf{y}; \sigma^2)\cdot f(\mathbf{y}; \sigma^2)$, *where*

$$f(\mu|\mathbf{y}; \sigma^2) = \frac{1}{[2\pi\sigma^2/(\nu + T)]^{1/2}} \exp\left[\frac{-(\mu - m^*)^2}{2\sigma^2/(\nu + T)}\right] \quad [12.1.7]$$

$$f(\mathbf{y}; \sigma^2) = \frac{1}{(2\pi\sigma^2)^{T/2}} |\mathbf{I}_T + \mathbf{1}\cdot\mathbf{1}'/\nu|^{-1/2}$$
$$\times \exp\left\{[-1/(2\sigma^2)](\mathbf{y} - m\cdot\mathbf{1})'(\mathbf{I}_T + \mathbf{1}\cdot\mathbf{1}'/\nu)^{-1}(\mathbf{y} - m\cdot\mathbf{1})\right\} \quad [12.1.8]$$

$$m^* = \left(\frac{\nu}{\nu + T}\right)m + \left(\frac{T}{\nu + T}\right)\bar{y} \quad [12.1.9]$$
$$\bar{y} = (1/T)\sum_{t=1}^{T} y_t.$$

*In other words, the distribution of* $\mu$ *conditional on the data* $(y_1, y_2, \ldots, y_T)$ *is* $N(m^*, \sigma^2/(\nu + T))$, *while the marginal distribution of* $\mathbf{y}$ *is* $N(m\cdot\mathbf{1}, \sigma^2(\mathbf{I}_T + \mathbf{1}\cdot\mathbf{1}'/\nu))$.

With a quadratic loss function, the Bayesian estimate of $\mu$ is the value $\hat{\mu}$ that minimizes $E(\mu - \hat{\mu})^2$. Although this is the same expression as the classical *MSE*, its interpretation is different. From the Bayesian perspective, $\mu$ is a random variable with respect to whose distribution the expectation is taken, and $\hat{\mu}$ is a candidate value for the estimate. The optimal value for $\hat{\mu}$ is the mean of the posterior distribution described in Proposition 12.1:

$$\hat{\mu} = \left(\frac{\nu}{\nu + T}\right)m + \left(\frac{T}{\nu + T}\right)\bar{y}.$$

This is a weighted average of the estimate the classical statistician would use ($\bar{y}$) and an estimate based on prior information alone ($m$). Larger values of $\nu$ correspond to greater confidence in prior information, and this would make the Bayesian estimate closer to $m$. On the other hand, as $\nu$ approaches zero, the Bayesian estimate approaches the classical estimate $\bar{y}$. The limit of [12.1.6] as $\nu \to 0$ is known as a *diffuse* or *improper prior* density. In this case, the quality of prior information is so poor that prior information is completely disregarded in forming the estimate $\hat{\mu}$.

The uncertainty associated with the posterior estimate $\hat{\mu}$ is described by the variance of the posterior distribution. To use the data to evaluate the plausibility of the claim that $\mu_0 < \mu < \mu_1$, we simply calculate the probability $\int_{\mu_0}^{\mu_1} f(\mu|\mathbf{y}; \sigma^2)\, d\mu$. For example, the Bayesian would assert that the probability that $\mu$ is within the range $\hat{\mu} \pm 2\sigma/\sqrt{\nu + T}$ is 0.95.

## *Estimating the Coefficients of a Regression Model with Known Variance*

Next, consider the linear regression model

$$y_t = \mathbf{x}_t'\boldsymbol{\beta} + u_t,$$

where $u_t \sim$ i.i.d. $N(0, \sigma^2)$, $\mathbf{x}_t$ is a $(k \times 1)$ vector of exogenous explanatory variables, and $\boldsymbol{\beta}$ is a $(k \times 1)$ vector of coefficients. Let

$$\underset{(T\times 1)}{\mathbf{y}} = \begin{bmatrix} y_1 \\ y_2 \\ \vdots \\ y_T \end{bmatrix} \qquad \underset{(T\times k)}{\mathbf{X}} = \begin{bmatrix} \mathbf{x}_1' \\ \mathbf{x}_2' \\ \vdots \\ \mathbf{x}_T' \end{bmatrix}.$$

Treating $\boldsymbol{\beta}$ as random but $\sigma^2$ as known, we have the likelihood

$$\begin{aligned} f(\mathbf{y}|\boldsymbol{\beta}, \mathbf{X}; \sigma^2) &= \prod_{t=1}^{T} \frac{1}{(2\pi\sigma^2)^{1/2}} \exp\left\{\left[-\frac{1}{2\sigma^2}\right](y_t - \mathbf{x}_t'\boldsymbol{\beta})^2\right\} \\ &= \frac{1}{(2\pi\sigma^2)^{T/2}} \exp\left\{\left[-\frac{1}{2\sigma^2}\right](\mathbf{y} - \mathbf{X}\boldsymbol{\beta})'(\mathbf{y} - \mathbf{X}\boldsymbol{\beta})\right\}. \end{aligned} \qquad [12.1.10]$$

Suppose that prior information about $\boldsymbol{\beta}$ is represented by a $N(\mathbf{m}, \sigma^2\mathbf{M})$ distribution:

$$f(\boldsymbol{\beta}; \sigma^2) = \frac{1}{(2\pi\sigma^2)^{k/2}} |\mathbf{M}|^{-1/2} \exp\left\{\left[-\frac{1}{2\sigma^2}\right](\boldsymbol{\beta} - \mathbf{m})'\mathbf{M}^{-1}(\boldsymbol{\beta} - \mathbf{m})\right\}. \qquad [12.1.11]$$

Thus, prior to observation of the sample, the analyst's best guess as to the value of $\boldsymbol{\beta}$ is represented by the $(k \times 1)$ vector $\mathbf{m}$, and the confidence in this guess is summarized by the $(k \times k)$ matrix $\sigma^2\mathbf{M}$; less confidence is represented by larger diagonal elements of $\mathbf{M}$. Knowledge about the exogenous variables $\mathbf{X}$ is presumed to have no effect on the prior distribution, so that [12.1.11] also describes $f(\boldsymbol{\beta}|\mathbf{X}; \sigma^2)$.

Proposition 12.1 generalizes as follows.

***Proposition 12.2:*** *The product of [12.1.10] and [12.1.11] can be written in the form* $f(\boldsymbol{\beta}|\mathbf{y}, \mathbf{X}; \sigma^2)\cdot f(\mathbf{y}|\mathbf{X}; \sigma^2)$, *where*

$$\begin{aligned} f(\boldsymbol{\beta}|\mathbf{y}, \mathbf{X}; \sigma^2) &= \frac{1}{(2\pi\sigma^2)^{k/2}} |\mathbf{M}^{-1} + \mathbf{X}'\mathbf{X}|^{1/2} \\ &\quad \times \exp\left\{[-1/(2\sigma^2)](\boldsymbol{\beta} - \mathbf{m}^*)'(\mathbf{M}^{-1} + \mathbf{X}'\mathbf{X})(\boldsymbol{\beta} - \mathbf{m}^*)\right\} \end{aligned} \qquad [12.1.12]$$

$$\begin{aligned} f(\mathbf{y}|\mathbf{X}; \sigma^2) &= \frac{1}{(2\pi\sigma^2)^{T/2}} |\mathbf{I}_T + \mathbf{X}\mathbf{M}\mathbf{X}'|^{-1/2} \\ &\quad \times \exp\left\{[-1/(2\sigma^2)](\mathbf{y} - \mathbf{X}\mathbf{m})'(\mathbf{I}_T + \mathbf{X}\mathbf{M}\mathbf{X}')^{-1}(\mathbf{y} - \mathbf{X}\mathbf{m})\right\} \end{aligned} \qquad [12.1.13]$$

$$\mathbf{m}^* = (\mathbf{M}^{-1} + \mathbf{X}'\mathbf{X})^{-1}(\mathbf{M}^{-1}\mathbf{m} + \mathbf{X}'\mathbf{y}). \qquad [12.1.14]$$

*In other words, the distribution of* $\boldsymbol{\beta}$ *conditional on the observed data is* $N\big(\mathbf{m}^*, \sigma^2(\mathbf{M}^{-1} + \mathbf{X}'\mathbf{X})^{-1}\big)$ *and the marginal distribution of* $\mathbf{y}$ *given* $\mathbf{X}$ *is* $N\big(\mathbf{X}\mathbf{m}, \sigma^2(\mathbf{I}_T + \mathbf{X}\mathbf{M}\mathbf{X}')\big)$.

Poor prior information about $\boldsymbol{\beta}$ corresponds to a large variance $\mathbf{M}$, or equivalently a small value for $\mathbf{M}^{-1}$. The diffuse prior distribution for this problem is often represented by the limit as $\mathbf{M}^{-1} \rightarrow \mathbf{0}$, for which the posterior mean [12.1.14] becomes $\mathbf{m}^* = (\mathbf{X}'\mathbf{X})^{-1}\mathbf{X}'\mathbf{y}$, the *OLS* estimator. The variance of the posterior distribution becomes $\sigma^2(\mathbf{X}'\mathbf{X})^{-1}$. Thus, classical regression inference is reproduced as a special case of Bayesian inference with a diffuse prior distribution. At the other extreme, if $\mathbf{X}'\mathbf{X} = \mathbf{0}$, the sample contains no information about $\boldsymbol{\beta}$ and the posterior distribution is $N(\mathbf{m}, \sigma^2\mathbf{M})$, the same as the prior distribution.

If the analyst's prior expectation is that all coefficients are zero ($\mathbf{m} = \mathbf{0}$) and this claim is made with the same confidence for each coefficient ($\mathbf{M}^{-1} = \lambda \cdot \mathbf{I}_k$ for some $\lambda > 0$), then the Bayesian estimator [12.1.14] is

$$\mathbf{m}^* = (\lambda \cdot \mathbf{I}_k + \mathbf{X}'\mathbf{X})^{-1}\mathbf{X}'\mathbf{y}, \qquad [12.1.15]$$

which is the *ridge regression* estimator proposed by Hoerl and Kennard (1970). The effect of ridge regression is to shrink the parameter estimates toward zero.

## *Bayesian Estimation of a Regression Model with Unknown Variance*

Propositions 12.1 and 12.2 assumed that the residual variance $\sigma^2$ was known with certainty. Usually, both $\sigma^2$ and $\boldsymbol{\beta}$ would be regarded as random variables, and Bayesian analysis requires a prior distribution for $\sigma^2$. A convenient prior distribution for this application is provided by the gamma distribution. Let $\{Z_i\}_{i=1}^N$ be a sequence of i.i.d. $N(0, \tau^2)$ variables. Then $W = \Sigma_{i=1}^N Z_i^2$ is said to have a gamma distribution with $N$ degrees of freedom and scale parameter $\lambda$, indicated $W \sim \Gamma(N, \lambda)$, where $\lambda = 1/\tau^2$. Thus, $W$ has the distribution of $\tau^2$ times a $\chi^2(N)$ variable. The mean of $W$ is given by

$$E(W) = N \cdot E(Z_i^2) = N\tau^2 = N/\lambda, \qquad [12.1.16]$$

and the variance is

$$\begin{aligned} E(W^2) - [E(W)]^2 &= N \cdot \{E(Z_i^4) - [E(Z_i^2)]^2\} \\ &= N \cdot (3\tau^4 - \tau^4) = 2N\tau^4 = 2N/\lambda^2. \end{aligned} \qquad [12.1.17]$$

The density of $W$ takes the form

$$f(w) = \frac{(\lambda/2)^{N/2} w^{[(N/2)-1]} \exp[-\lambda w/2]}{\Gamma(N/2)}, \qquad [12.1.18]$$

where $\Gamma(\cdot)$ denotes the gamma function. If $N$ is an even integer, then

$$\Gamma(N/2) = 1 \cdot 2 \cdot 3 \cdots [(N/2) - 1],$$

with $\Gamma(2/2) = 1$; whereas if $N$ is an odd integer, then

$$\Gamma(N/2) = \sqrt{\pi} \cdot \tfrac{1}{2} \cdot \tfrac{3}{2} \cdot \tfrac{5}{2} \cdots [(N/2) - 1],$$

with $\Gamma(\frac{1}{2}) = \sqrt{\pi}$.

Following DeGroot (1970) and Leamer (1978), it is convenient to describe the prior distribution not in terms of the variance $\sigma^2$ but rather in terms of the reciprocal of the variance, $\sigma^{-2}$, which is known as the *precision*. Thus, suppose that the prior distribution is specified as $\sigma^{-2} \sim \Gamma(N, \lambda)$, where $N$ and $\lambda$ are parameters that describe the analyst's prior information:

$$f(\sigma^{-2}|\mathbf{X}) = \frac{(\lambda/2)^{N/2} \sigma^{-2[(N/2)-1]} \exp[-\lambda\sigma^{-2}/2]}{\Gamma(N/2)}. \qquad [12.1.19]$$

Recalling [12.1.16], the ratio $N/\lambda$ is the value expected for $\sigma^{-2}$ on the basis of prior information. As we will see shortly in Proposition 12.3, if the prior information is based on an earlier sample of observations $\{z_1, z_2, \ldots, z_N\}$, the parameter $N$ turns out to describe the size of this earlier sample and $\lambda$ is the earlier sample's sum of squared residuals. For a given ratio of $N/\lambda$, larger values for $N$ imply greater confidence in the prior information.

The prior distribution of $\boldsymbol{\beta}$ conditional on the value for $\sigma^{-2}$ is the same as in [12.1.11]:

$$f(\boldsymbol{\beta}|\sigma^{-2}, \mathbf{X}) = \frac{1}{(2\pi\sigma^2)^{k/2}}|\mathbf{M}|^{-1/2} \times \exp\left\{\left[-\frac{1}{2\sigma^2}\right](\boldsymbol{\beta} - \mathbf{m})'\mathbf{M}^{-1}(\boldsymbol{\beta} - \mathbf{m})\right\}. \quad [12.1.20]$$

Thus, $f(\boldsymbol{\beta}, \sigma^{-2}|\mathbf{X})$, the joint prior density for $\boldsymbol{\beta}$ and $\sigma^{-2}$, is given by the product of [12.1.19] and [12.1.20]. The posterior distribution $f(\boldsymbol{\beta}, \sigma^{-2}|\mathbf{y}, \mathbf{X})$ is described by the following proposition.

***Proposition 12.3:*** *Let the prior density $f(\boldsymbol{\beta}, \sigma^{-2}|\mathbf{X})$ be given by the product of [12.1.19] and [12.1.20], and let the sample likelihood be*

$$f(\mathbf{y}|\boldsymbol{\beta}, \sigma^{-2}, \mathbf{X}) = \frac{1}{(2\pi\sigma^2)^{T/2}}\exp\left\{\left[-\frac{1}{2\sigma^2}\right](\mathbf{y} - \mathbf{X}\boldsymbol{\beta})'(\mathbf{y} - \mathbf{X}\boldsymbol{\beta})\right\}. \quad [12.1.21]$$

*Then the following hold:*

(*a*) *The joint posterior density of $\boldsymbol{\beta}$ and $\sigma^{-2}$ is given by*

$$f(\boldsymbol{\beta}, \sigma^{-2}|\mathbf{y}, \mathbf{X}) = f(\boldsymbol{\beta}|\sigma^{-2}, \mathbf{y}, \mathbf{X})\cdot f(\sigma^{-2}|\mathbf{y}, \mathbf{X}), \quad [12.1.22]$$

*where the posterior distribution of $\boldsymbol{\beta}$ conditional on $\sigma^{-2}$ is $N(\mathbf{m}^*, \sigma^2\mathbf{M}^*)$:*

$$f(\boldsymbol{\beta}|\sigma^{-2}, \mathbf{y}, \mathbf{X}) = \frac{1}{(2\pi\sigma^2)^{k/2}}|\mathbf{M}^*|^{-1/2}\exp\left\{\left[-\frac{1}{2\sigma^2}\right](\boldsymbol{\beta} - \mathbf{m}^*)'(\mathbf{M}^*)^{-1}(\boldsymbol{\beta} - \mathbf{m}^*)\right\}, \quad [12.1.23]$$

*with*

$$\mathbf{m}^* = (\mathbf{M}^{-1} + \mathbf{X}'\mathbf{X})^{-1}(\mathbf{M}^{-1}\mathbf{m} + \mathbf{X}'\mathbf{y}) \quad [12.1.24]$$

$$\mathbf{M}^* = (\mathbf{M}^{-1} + \mathbf{X}'\mathbf{X})^{-1}. \quad [12.1.25]$$

*Furthermore, the marginal posterior distribution of $\sigma^{-2}$ is $\Gamma(N^*, \lambda^*)$:*

$$f(\sigma^{-2}|\mathbf{y}, \mathbf{X}) = \frac{\sigma^{-2[(N^*/2)-1]}(\lambda^*/2)^{N^*/2}}{\Gamma(N^*/2)}\exp[-\lambda^*\sigma^{-2}/2], \quad [12.1.26]$$

*with*

$$N^* = N + T \quad [12.1.27]$$

$$\lambda^* = \lambda + (\mathbf{y} - \mathbf{X}\mathbf{b})'(\mathbf{y} - \mathbf{X}\mathbf{b}) + (\mathbf{b} - \mathbf{m})'\mathbf{M}^{-1}(\mathbf{X}'\mathbf{X} + \mathbf{M}^{-1})^{-1}\mathbf{X}'\mathbf{X}(\mathbf{b} - \mathbf{m}) \quad [12.1.28]$$

*for $\mathbf{b} = (\mathbf{X}'\mathbf{X})^{-1}\mathbf{X}'\mathbf{y}$ the OLS estimator.*

(*b*) *The marginal posterior distribution for $\boldsymbol{\beta}$ is a k-dimensional t distribution with $N^*$ degrees of freedom, mean $\mathbf{m}^*$, and scale matrix $(\lambda^*/N^*)\cdot\mathbf{M}^*$:*

$$f(\boldsymbol{\beta}|\mathbf{y}, \mathbf{X})$$

$$= \left\{ \frac{\Gamma[(k + N^*)/2]}{(\pi N^*)^{k/2}\Gamma(N^*/2)} |(\lambda^*/N^*)\mathbf{M}^*|^{-1/2} \right. \qquad [12.1.29]$$

$$\left. \times [1 + (1/N^*)(\boldsymbol{\beta} - \mathbf{m}^*)'[(\lambda^*/N^*)\mathbf{M}^*]^{-1}(\boldsymbol{\beta} - \mathbf{m}^*)]^{-(k+N^*)/2} \right\}.$$

(c) *Let* $\mathbf{R}$ *be a known* $(m \times k)$ *matrix with linearly independent rows, and define*

$$Q \equiv \frac{[\mathbf{R}(\boldsymbol{\beta} - \mathbf{m}^*)]'[\mathbf{R}(\mathbf{M}^{-1} + \mathbf{X}'\mathbf{X})^{-1}\mathbf{R}']^{-1}\cdot[\mathbf{R}(\boldsymbol{\beta} - \mathbf{m}^*)]/m}{\lambda^*/N^*}. \qquad [12.1.30]$$

*Then* $Q$ *has a marginal posterior distribution that is* $F(m, N^*)$:

$$f(q|\mathbf{y}, \mathbf{X}) = \frac{m^{m/2}(N^*)^{N^*/2}\Gamma[(N^* + m)/2]q^{[(m/2)-1]}}{\Gamma(m/2)\Gamma(N^*/2)(N^* + mq)^{[(N^*+m)/2]}}. \qquad [12.1.31]$$

Recalling [12.1.16], result (a) implies that the Bayesian estimate of the precision is

$$E(\sigma^{-2}|\mathbf{y}, \mathbf{X}) = N^*/\lambda^*. \qquad [12.1.32]$$

Diffuse prior information is sometimes represented as $N = \lambda = 0$ and $\mathbf{M}^{-1} = \mathbf{0}$. Substituting these values into [12.1.27] and [12.1.28] implies that $N^* = T$ and $\lambda^* = (\mathbf{y} - \mathbf{X}\mathbf{b})'(\mathbf{y} - \mathbf{X}\mathbf{b})$. For these values, the posterior mean [12.1.32] would be

$$E(\sigma^{-2}|\mathbf{y}, \mathbf{X}) = T/(\mathbf{y} - \mathbf{X}\mathbf{b})'(\mathbf{y} - \mathbf{X}\mathbf{b}),$$

which is the maximum likelihood estimate of $\sigma^{-2}$. This is the basis for the earlier claim that the parameter $N$ for the prior distribution might be viewed as the number of presample observations on which the prior information is based and that $\lambda$ might be viewed as the sum of squared residuals for these observations.

Result (b) implies that the Bayesian estimate of the coefficient vector is

$$E(\boldsymbol{\beta}|\mathbf{y}, \mathbf{X}) = \mathbf{m}^* = (\mathbf{M}^{-1} + \mathbf{X}'\mathbf{X})^{-1}(\mathbf{M}^{-1}\mathbf{m} + \mathbf{X}'\mathbf{y}), \qquad [12.1.33]$$

which is identical to the estimate derived in Proposition 12.2 for the case where $\sigma^2$ is known. Again, for diffuse prior information, $\mathbf{m}^* = \mathbf{b}$, the *OLS* estimate.

Result (c) describes the Bayesian perspective on a hypothesis about the value of $\mathbf{R}\boldsymbol{\beta}$, where the matrix $\mathbf{R}$ characterizes which linear combinations of the elements of $\boldsymbol{\beta}$ are of interest. A classical statistician would test the hypothesis that $\mathbf{R}\boldsymbol{\beta} = \mathbf{r}$ by calculating an *OLS F* statistic,

$$\frac{(\mathbf{R}\mathbf{b} - \mathbf{r})'[\mathbf{R}(\mathbf{X}'\mathbf{X})^{-1}\mathbf{R}']^{-1}(\mathbf{R}\mathbf{b} - \mathbf{r})/m}{s^2},$$

and evaluating the probability that an $F(m, T - k)$ variable could equal or exceed this magnitude. This represents the probability that the estimated value of $\mathbf{R}\mathbf{b}$ could be as far as it is observed to be from $\mathbf{r}$ given that the true value of $\boldsymbol{\beta}$ satisfies $\mathbf{R}\boldsymbol{\beta} = \mathbf{r}$. By contrast, a Bayesian regards $\mathbf{R}\boldsymbol{\beta}$ as a random variable, the distribution for which is described in result (c). According to [12.1.30], the probability that $\mathbf{R}\boldsymbol{\beta}$ would equal $\mathbf{r}$ is related to the probability that an $F(m, N^*)$ variable would assume the value

$$\frac{(\mathbf{r} - \mathbf{R}\mathbf{m}^*)'[\mathbf{R}(\mathbf{M}^{-1} + \mathbf{X}'\mathbf{X})^{-1}\mathbf{R}']^{-1}(\mathbf{r} - \mathbf{R}\mathbf{m}^*)/m}{\lambda^*/N^*}.$$

The probability that an $F(m, N^*)$ variable could exceed this magnitude represents the probability that the random variable $\mathbf{R\beta}$ might be as far from the posterior mean $\mathbf{Rm}^*$ as is represented by the point $\mathbf{R\beta} = \mathbf{r}$. In the case of a diffuse prior distribution, the preceding expression simplifies to

$$\frac{(\mathbf{r} - \mathbf{Rb})'[\mathbf{R}(\mathbf{X}'\mathbf{X})^{-1}\mathbf{R}']^{-1}(\mathbf{r} - \mathbf{Rb})/m}{(\mathbf{y} - \mathbf{Xb})'(\mathbf{y} - \mathbf{Xb})/T},$$

which is to be compared in this case with an $F(m, T)$ distribution. Recalling that

$$s^2 = (\mathbf{y} - \mathbf{Xb})'(\mathbf{y} - \mathbf{Xb})/(T - k),$$

it appears that, apart from a minor difference in the denominator degrees of freedom, the classical statistician and the Bayesian with a diffuse prior distribution would essentially be calculating the identical test statistic and comparing it with the same critical value in evaluating the plausibility of the hypothesis represented by $\mathbf{R\beta} = \mathbf{r}$.

## *Bayesian Analysis of Regressions with Lagged Dependent Variables*

In describing the sample likelihood (expression [12.1.10] or [12.1.21]), the assumption was made that the vector of explanatory variables $\mathbf{x}_t$ was strictly exogenous. If $\mathbf{x}_t$ contains lagged values of $y$, then as long as we are willing to treat presample values of $y$ as deterministic, the algebra goes through exactly the same. The only changes needed are some slight adjustments in notation and in the description of the results. For example, consider a $p$th-order autoregression with $\mathbf{x}_t = (1, y_{t-1}, y_{t-2}, \ldots, y_{t-p})'$. In this case, the expression on the right side of [12.1.21] describes the likelihood of $(y_1, y_2, \ldots, y_T)$ conditional on $y_0, y_{-1}, \ldots, y_{-p+1}$; that is, it describes $f(\mathbf{y}|\boldsymbol{\beta}, \sigma^{-2}, \mathbf{x}_1)$. The prior distributions [12.1.19] and [12.1.20] are then presumed to describe $f(\sigma^{-2}|\mathbf{x}_1)$ and $f(\boldsymbol{\beta}|\sigma^{-2}, \mathbf{x}_1)$, and the posterior distributions are all as stated in Proposition 12.3.

Note in particular that results (b) and (c) of Proposition 12.3 describe the exact small-sample posterior distributions, even when $\mathbf{x}_t$ contains lagged dependent variables. By contrast, a classical statistician would consider the usual $t$ and $F$ tests to be valid only asymptotically.

## *Calculation of the Posterior Distribution Using a* GLS *Regression*

It is sometimes convenient to describe the prior information in terms of certain linear combinations of coefficients, such as

$$\mathbf{R\beta}|\sigma^{-2} \sim N(\mathbf{r}, \sigma^2\mathbf{V}). \qquad [12.1.34]$$

Here $\mathbf{R}$ denotes a known nonsingular $(k \times k)$ matrix whose rows represent linear combinations of $\boldsymbol{\beta}$ in terms of which it is convenient to describe the analyst's prior information. For example, if the prior expectation is that $\beta_1 = \beta_2$, then the first row of $\mathbf{R}$ could be $(1, -1, 0, \ldots, 0)$ and the first element of $\mathbf{r}$ would be zero. The (1, 1) element of $\mathbf{V}$ reflects the uncertainty of this prior information. If $\boldsymbol{\beta} \sim N(\mathbf{m}, \sigma^2\mathbf{M})$, then $\mathbf{R\beta} \sim N(\mathbf{Rm}, \sigma^2\mathbf{RMR}')$. Thus, the relation between the parameters for the prior distribution as expressed in [12.1.34] ($\mathbf{R}$, $\mathbf{r}$, and $\mathbf{V}$) and the parameters for the prior distribution as expressed in [12.1.20] ($\mathbf{m}$ and $\mathbf{M}$) is given by

$$\mathbf{r} = \mathbf{Rm} \qquad [12.1.35]$$

$$\mathbf{V} = \mathbf{RMR}'. \qquad [12.1.36]$$

Equation [12.1.36] implies

$$\mathbf{V}^{-1} = (\mathbf{R}')^{-1}\mathbf{M}^{-1}\mathbf{R}^{-1}. \qquad [12.1.37]$$

If equation [12.1.37] is premultiplied by $\mathbf{R}'$ and postmultiplied by $\mathbf{R}$, the result is

$$\mathbf{R}'\mathbf{V}^{-1}\mathbf{R} = \mathbf{M}^{-1}. \qquad [12.1.38]$$

Using equations [12.1.35] and [12.1.38], the posterior mean [12.1.33] can be rewritten as

$$\mathbf{m}^* = (\mathbf{R}'\mathbf{V}^{-1}\mathbf{R} + \mathbf{X}'\mathbf{X})^{-1}(\mathbf{R}'\mathbf{V}^{-1}\mathbf{r} + \mathbf{X}'\mathbf{y}). \qquad [12.1.39]$$

To obtain another perspective on [12.1.39], notice that the prior distribution [12.1.34] can be written

$$\mathbf{r} = \mathbf{R}\boldsymbol{\beta} + \boldsymbol{\varepsilon}, \qquad [12.1.40]$$

where $\boldsymbol{\varepsilon} \sim N(\mathbf{0}, \sigma^2\mathbf{V})$. This is of the same form as the observation equations of the regression model,

$$\mathbf{y} = \mathbf{X}\boldsymbol{\beta} + \mathbf{u} \qquad [12.1.41]$$

with $\mathbf{u} \sim N(\mathbf{0}, \sigma^2\mathbf{I}_T)$. The mixed estimation strategy described by Theil (1971, pp. 347–49) thus regards the prior information as a set of $k$ additional observations, with $r_i$ treated as if it were another observation on $y_t$ and the $i$th row of $\mathbf{R}$ corresponding to its vector of explanatory variables $\mathbf{x}_t'$. Specifically, equations [12.1.40] and [12.1.41] are stacked to form the system

$$\mathbf{y}^* = \mathbf{X}^*\boldsymbol{\beta} + \mathbf{u}^*, \qquad [12.1.42]$$

where

$$\underset{(T+k)\times 1}{\mathbf{y}^*} = \begin{bmatrix} \mathbf{r} \\ \mathbf{y} \end{bmatrix} \qquad \underset{(T+k)\times k}{\mathbf{X}^*} = \begin{bmatrix} \mathbf{R} \\ \mathbf{X} \end{bmatrix}$$

$$E(\mathbf{u}^*\mathbf{u}^{*\prime}) = \sigma^2\mathbf{V}^* = \sigma^2\begin{bmatrix} \mathbf{V} & \mathbf{0} \\ \mathbf{0} & \mathbf{I}_T \end{bmatrix}.$$

The $GLS$ estimator for the stacked system is

$$\begin{aligned} \tilde{\mathbf{b}} &= [\mathbf{X}^{*\prime}(\mathbf{V}^*)^{-1}\mathbf{X}^*]^{-1}[\mathbf{X}^{*\prime}(\mathbf{V}^*)^{-1}\mathbf{y}^*] \\ &= \left\{[\mathbf{R}' \quad \mathbf{X}']\begin{bmatrix} \mathbf{V}^{-1} & \mathbf{0} \\ \mathbf{0} & \mathbf{I}_T \end{bmatrix}\begin{bmatrix} \mathbf{R} \\ \mathbf{X} \end{bmatrix}\right\}^{-1} \times \left\{[\mathbf{R}' \quad \mathbf{X}']\begin{bmatrix} \mathbf{V}^{-1} & \mathbf{0} \\ \mathbf{0} & \mathbf{I}_T \end{bmatrix}\begin{bmatrix} \mathbf{r} \\ \mathbf{y} \end{bmatrix}\right\} \\ &= (\mathbf{R}'\mathbf{V}^{-1}\mathbf{R} + \mathbf{X}'\mathbf{X})^{-1}(\mathbf{R}'\mathbf{V}^{-1}\mathbf{r} + \mathbf{X}'\mathbf{y}). \end{aligned}$$

Thus the posterior mean [12.1.39] can be calculated by $GLS$ estimation of [12.1.42]. For known $\sigma^2$, the usual formula for the variance of the $GLS$ estimator,

$$\sigma^2[\mathbf{X}^{*\prime}(\mathbf{V}^*)^{-1}\mathbf{X}^*]^{-1} = \sigma^2(\mathbf{R}'\mathbf{V}^{-1}\mathbf{R} + \mathbf{X}'\mathbf{X})^{-1},$$

gives a correct calculation of the variance of the Bayesian posterior distribution, $\sigma^2(\mathbf{M}^{-1} + \mathbf{X}'\mathbf{X})^{-1}$.

The foregoing discussion assumed that $\mathbf{R}$ was a nonsingular $(k \times k)$ matrix. On some occasions the analyst might have valuable information about some linear combinations of coefficients but not others. Thus, suppose that the prior distribution

[12.1.34] is written as

$$\begin{bmatrix}\mathbf{R}_1\\ \mathbf{R}_2\end{bmatrix}\boldsymbol{\beta} \sim N\left(\begin{bmatrix}\mathbf{r}_1\\ \mathbf{r}_2\end{bmatrix}, \sigma^2\begin{bmatrix}\mathbf{V}_1 & \mathbf{0}\\ \mathbf{0} & \mathbf{V}_2\end{bmatrix}\right),$$

where $\mathbf{R}_1$ is an $(m \times k)$ matrix consisting of those linear combinations for which the prior information is good and $\mathbf{R}_2$ is a $[(k - m) \times k]$ matrix of the remaining linear combinations. Then diffuse prior information about those linear combinations described by $\mathbf{R}_2$ could be represented by the limit as $\mathbf{V}_2^{-1} \to \mathbf{0}$, for which

$$\mathbf{R}'\mathbf{V}^{-1} = [\mathbf{R}_1' \quad \mathbf{R}_2']\begin{bmatrix}\mathbf{V}_1^{-1} & \mathbf{0}\\ \mathbf{0} & \mathbf{V}_2^{-1}\end{bmatrix} \to [\mathbf{R}_1'\mathbf{V}_1^{-1} \quad \mathbf{0}].$$

The Bayesian estimate [12.1.39] then becomes

$$(\mathbf{R}_1'\mathbf{V}_1^{-1}\mathbf{R}_1 + \mathbf{X}'\mathbf{X})^{-1}(\mathbf{R}_1'\mathbf{V}_1^{-1}\mathbf{r}_1 + \mathbf{X}'\mathbf{y}),$$

which can be calculated from *GLS* estimation of a $[(T + m) \times 1]$ system of the form of [12.1.42] in which only the linear combinations for which there is useful prior information are added as observations.

## 12.2. *Bayesian Analysis of Vector Autoregressions*

### *Litterman's Prior Distribution for Estimation of an Equation of a* VAR

This section discusses prior information that might help improve the estimates of a single equation of a *VAR*. Much of the early econometric research with dynamic relations was concerned with estimation of distributed lag relations of the form

$$y_t = c + \omega_0 x_t + \omega_1 x_{t-1} + \cdots + \omega_p x_{t-p} + u_t. \qquad [12.2.1]$$

For this specification, $\omega_s$ has the interpretation as $\partial y_t/\partial x_{t-s}$, and some have argued that this should be a smooth function of $s$; see Almon (1965) and Shiller (1973) for examples. Whatever the merit of this view, it is hard to justify imposing a smoothness condition on the sequences $\{\omega_s\}_{s=1}^p$ or $\{\phi_s\}_{s=1}^p$ in a model with autoregressive terms such as

$$\begin{aligned} y_t = c &+ \phi_1 y_{t-1} + \phi_2 y_{t-2} + \cdots + \phi_p y_{t-p}\\ &+ \omega_0 x_t + \omega_1 x_{t-1} + \cdots + \omega_p x_{t-p} + u_t, \end{aligned}$$

since here the dynamic multiplier $\partial y_t/\partial x_{t-s}$ is a complicated nonlinear function of the $\phi$'s and $\omega$'s.

Litterman (1986) suggested an alternative representation of prior information based on the belief that the change in the series is impossible to forecast:

$$y_t - y_{t-1} = c + \varepsilon_t, \qquad [12.2.2]$$

where $\varepsilon_t$ is uncorrelated with lagged values of any variable. Economic theory predicts such behavior for many time series. For example, suppose that $y_t$ is the log of the real price of some asset at time $t$, that is, the price adjusted for inflation. Then $y_t - y_{t-1}$ is approximately the real rate of return from buying the asset at $t - 1$ and selling it at $t$. In an extension of Fama's (1965) efficient markets argument described in Section 11.2, speculators would have bought more of the asset at time $t - 1$ if they had expected unusually high returns, driving $y_{t-1}$ up in relation to the anticipated value of $y_t$. The time path for $\{y_t\}$ that results from such speculation would exhibit price changes that are unforecastable. Thus, we might expect the real prices of items such as stocks, real estate, or precious metals to satisfy [12.2.2]. Hall (1978) argued that the level of spending by consumers should also satisfy [12.2.2], while Barro (1979) and Mankiw (1987) developed related arguments for the taxes levied and new money issued by the government. Changes in foreign exchange rates are argued by many to be unpredictable as well; see the evidence reviewed in Diebold and Nason (1990).

Write the $i$th equation in a *VAR* as

$$\begin{aligned} y_{it} = c_i &+ \phi_{i1}^{(1)} y_{1,t-1} + \phi_{i2}^{(1)} y_{2,t-1} + \cdots + \phi_{in}^{(1)} y_{n,t-1} \\ &+ \phi_{i1}^{(2)} y_{1,t-2} + \phi_{i2}^{(2)} y_{2,t-2} + \cdots + \phi_{in}^{(2)} y_{n,t-2} + \cdots \\ &+ \phi_{i1}^{(p)} y_{1,t-p} + \phi_{i2}^{(p)} y_{2,t-p} + \cdots + \phi_{in}^{(p)} y_{n,t-p} + \varepsilon_{it}, \end{aligned} \qquad [12.2.3]$$

where $\phi_{ij}^{(s)}$ gives the coefficient relating $y_{it}$ to $y_{j,t-s}$. The restriction [12.2.2] requires $\phi_{ii}^{(1)} = 1$ and all other $\phi_{ij}^{(s)} = 0$. These values (0 or 1) then characterize the mean of the prior distribution for the coefficients. Litterman used a diffuse prior distribution for the constant term $c_i$.

Litterman took the variance-covariance matrix for the prior distribution to be diagonal, with $\gamma$ denoting the standard deviation of the prior distribution for $\phi_{ii}^{(1)}$:

$$\phi_{ii}^{(1)} \sim N(1, \gamma^2).$$

Although each equation $i = 1, 2, \ldots, n$ of the *VAR* is estimated separately, typically the same number $\gamma$ is used for each $i$. A smaller value for $\gamma$ represents greater confidence in the prior information and will force the parameter estimates to be closer to the values predicted in [12.2.2]. A value of $\gamma = 0.20$ means that, before seeing the data, the analyst had 95% confidence that $\phi_{ii}^{(1)}$ is no smaller than 0.60 and no larger than 1.40.

The coefficients relating $y_{it}$ to further lags are predicted to be zero, and Litterman argued that the analyst should have more confidence in this prediction the greater the lag. He therefore suggested taking $\phi_{ii}^{(2)} \sim N(0, (\gamma/2)^2)$, $\phi_{ii}^{(3)} \sim N(0, (\gamma/3)^2), \ldots$, and $\phi_{ii}^{(p)} \sim N(0, (\gamma/p)^2)$, tightening the prior distribution with a harmonic series for the standard deviation as the lag increases.

Note that the coefficients $\phi_{ii}^{(s)}$ are scale-invariant; if each value of $y_{it}$ is multiplied by 100, the values of $\phi_{ii}^{(s)}$ will be the same. The same is not true of $\phi_{ij}^{(s)}$ for $i \neq j$; if series $i$ is multiplied by 100 but series $j$ is not, then $\phi_{ij}^{(s)}$ will be multiplied by 100. Thus, in calculating the weight to be given the prior information about $\phi_{ij}^{(s)}$, an adjustment for the units in which the data are measured is necessary. Litterman proposed using the following standard deviation of the prior distribution for $\phi_{ij}^{(s)}$:

$$\frac{w \cdot \gamma \cdot \hat{\tau}_i}{s \cdot \hat{\tau}_j}. \qquad [12.2.4]$$

Here $(\hat{\tau}_i/\hat{\tau}_j)$ is a correction for the scale of series $i$ compared with series $j$. Litterman suggested that $\hat{\tau}_i$ could be estimated from the standard deviation of the residuals from an *OLS* regression of $y_{it}$ on a constant and on $p$ of its own lagged values. Apart from this scale correction, [12.2.4] simply multiplies $\gamma/s$ (which was the standard deviation for the prior distribution for $\phi_{ii}^{(s)}$) by a parameter $w$. Common experience with many time series is that the own lagged values $y_{i,t-s}$ are likely to be of more help in forecasting $y_{it}$ than will be values of other variables $y_{j,t-s}$. Hence we should have more confidence in the prior belief that $\phi_{ij}^{(s)} = 0$ than the prior belief that $\phi_{ii}^{(s)} = 0$, suggesting a value for $w$ that is less than 1. Doan (1990) recommended a value of $w = 0.5$ in concert with $\gamma = 0.20$.

Several cautions in employing this prior distribution should be noted. First, for some series the natural prior expectation might be that the series is white noise rather than an autoregression with unit coefficient. For example, if $y_{it}$ is a series such as the *change* in stock prices, then the mean of $\phi_{ii}^{(1)}$ should be 0 rather than 1. Second, many economic series display seasonal behavior. In such cases, $\phi_{ij}^{(s)}$ is likely to be nonzero for $s = 12$ and 24 with monthly data, for example. Litterman's prior distribution is not well suited for seasonal data, and some researchers suggest using seasonally adjusted data or including seasonal dummy variables in the regression before employing this prior distribution. Finally, the prior distribution is not well suited for systems that exhibit cointegration, a topic discussed in detail in Chapter 19.

### *Full-Information Bayesian Estimation of a* VAR

Litterman's approach to Bayesian estimation of a *VAR* considered a single equation in isolation. It is possible to analyze all of the equations in a *VAR* together in a Bayesian framework, though the analytical results are somewhat more complicated than for the single-equation case; see Zellner (1971, Chapter 8) and Rothenberg (1973, pp. 139–44) for discussion.

## 12.3. *Numerical Bayesian Methods*

In the previous examples, the class of densities used to represent the prior information was carefully chosen in order to obtain a simple analytical characterization for the posterior distribution. For many specifications of interest, however, it may be impossible to find such a class, or the density that best reflects the analyst's prior information may not be possible to represent with this class. It is therefore useful to have computer-based methods to calculate or approximate posterior moments for a quite general class of problems.

### *Approximating the Posterior Mean by the Posterior Mode*

One option is to use the mode rather than the mean of the posterior distribution, that is, to take the Bayesian estimate $\hat{\boldsymbol{\theta}}$ to be the value that maximizes $f(\boldsymbol{\theta}|\mathbf{y})$. For symmetric unimodal distributions, the mean and the mode will be the same, as turned out to be the case for the coefficient vector $\boldsymbol{\beta}$ in Proposition 12.2. Where the mean and mode differ, with a quadratic loss function the mode is a suboptimal estimator, though typically the posterior mode will approach the posterior mean as the sample size grows (see DeGroot, 1970, p. 236).

Recall from [12.1.2] and [12.1.3] that the posterior density is given by

$$f(\boldsymbol{\theta}|\mathbf{y}) = \frac{f(\mathbf{y}|\boldsymbol{\theta})\cdot f(\boldsymbol{\theta})}{f(\mathbf{y})}, \qquad [12.3.1]$$

and therefore the log of the posterior density is

$$\log f(\boldsymbol{\theta}|\mathbf{y}) = \log f(\mathbf{y}|\boldsymbol{\theta}) + \log f(\boldsymbol{\theta}) - \log f(\mathbf{y}). \qquad [12.3.2]$$

Note that if the goal is to maximize [12.3.2] with respect to $\boldsymbol{\theta}$, it is not necessary to calculate $f(\mathbf{y})$, since this does not depend on $\boldsymbol{\theta}$. The posterior mode can thus be found by maximizing

$$\log f(\boldsymbol{\theta}, \mathbf{y}) = \log f(\mathbf{y}|\boldsymbol{\theta}) + \log f(\boldsymbol{\theta}). \qquad [12.3.3]$$

To evaluate [12.3.2], we need only to be able to calculate the likelihood function $f(\mathbf{y}|\boldsymbol{\theta})$ and the density that describes the prior information, $f(\boldsymbol{\theta})$. Expression [12.3.2] can be maximized by numerical methods, and often the same particular algorithms that maximize the log likelihood will also maximize [12.3.2]. For example, the log likelihood for a Gaussian regression model such as [12.1.21] can be maximized by a *GLS* regression, just as the posterior mode [12.1.39] can be calculated with a *GLS* regression.

### *Tierney and Kadane's Approximation for Posterior Moments*

Alternatively, Tierney and Kadane (1986) noted that the curvature of the likelihood surface can be used to estimate the distance of the posterior mode from the posterior mean. Suppose that the objective is to calculate

$$E[g(\boldsymbol{\theta})|\mathbf{y}] = \int_{-\infty}^{\infty} g(\boldsymbol{\theta})\cdot f(\boldsymbol{\theta}|\mathbf{y})\, d\boldsymbol{\theta}, \qquad [12.3.4]$$

where $\boldsymbol{\theta}$ is an $(a \times 1)$ vector of parameters and $g\colon \mathbb{R}^a \to \mathbb{R}^1$ is a function of interest. For example, if $g(\boldsymbol{\theta}) = \theta_1$, then [12.3.4] is the posterior mean of the first parameter, while $g(\boldsymbol{\theta}) = \theta_1^2$ gives the second moment. Expression [12.3.1] can be used to write [12.3.4] as

$$E[g(\boldsymbol{\theta})|\mathbf{y}] = \frac{\int_{-\infty}^{\infty} g(\boldsymbol{\theta})\cdot f(\mathbf{y}|\boldsymbol{\theta})\cdot f(\boldsymbol{\theta})\, d\boldsymbol{\theta}}{f(\mathbf{y})} = \frac{\int_{-\infty}^{\infty} g(\boldsymbol{\theta})\cdot f(\mathbf{y}|\boldsymbol{\theta})\cdot f(\boldsymbol{\theta})\, d\boldsymbol{\theta}}{\int_{-\infty}^{\infty} f(\mathbf{y}|\boldsymbol{\theta})\cdot f(\boldsymbol{\theta})\, d\boldsymbol{\theta}}. \qquad [12.3.5]$$

Define

$$h(\boldsymbol{\theta}) \equiv (1/T) \log\{g(\boldsymbol{\theta})\cdot f(\mathbf{y}|\boldsymbol{\theta})\cdot f(\boldsymbol{\theta})\} \qquad [12.3.6]$$

and

$$k(\boldsymbol{\theta}) \equiv (1/T) \log\{f(\mathbf{y}|\boldsymbol{\theta})\cdot f(\boldsymbol{\theta})\}. \qquad [12.3.7]$$

This allows [12.3.5] to be written

$$E[g(\boldsymbol{\theta})|\mathbf{y}] = \frac{\int_{-\infty}^{\infty} \exp[T\cdot h(\boldsymbol{\theta})]\, d\boldsymbol{\theta}}{\int_{-\infty}^{\infty} \exp[T\cdot k(\boldsymbol{\theta})]\, d\boldsymbol{\theta}}. \qquad [12.3.8]$$

Let $\boldsymbol{\theta}^*$ be the value that maximizes [12.3.6], and consider a second-order Taylor series approximation to $h(\boldsymbol{\theta})$ around $\boldsymbol{\theta}^*$:

$$\begin{aligned} h(\boldsymbol{\theta}) \cong h(\boldsymbol{\theta}^*) &+ \left.\frac{\partial h(\boldsymbol{\theta})}{\partial \boldsymbol{\theta}'}\right|_{\boldsymbol{\theta}=\boldsymbol{\theta}^*} \cdot (\boldsymbol{\theta} - \boldsymbol{\theta}^*) \\ &+ \frac{1}{2}(\boldsymbol{\theta} - \boldsymbol{\theta}^*)' \left\{\left.\frac{\partial^2 h(\boldsymbol{\theta})}{\partial \boldsymbol{\theta}\, \partial \boldsymbol{\theta}'}\right|_{\boldsymbol{\theta}=\boldsymbol{\theta}^*}\right\} (\boldsymbol{\theta} - \boldsymbol{\theta}^*). \end{aligned} \qquad [12.3.9]$$

Assuming that $\boldsymbol{\theta}^*$ is an interior optimum of $h(\cdot)$, the first derivative $[\partial h(\boldsymbol{\theta})/\partial\boldsymbol{\theta}']|_{\boldsymbol{\theta}=\boldsymbol{\theta}^*}$ is $\mathbf{0}$. Then [12.3.9] could be expressed as

$$h(\boldsymbol{\theta}) \cong h(\boldsymbol{\theta}^*) - (1/2)(\boldsymbol{\theta} - \boldsymbol{\theta}^*)'(\boldsymbol{\Sigma}^*)^{-1}(\boldsymbol{\theta} - \boldsymbol{\theta}^*), \qquad [12.3.10]$$

where

$$\boldsymbol{\Sigma}^* \equiv -\left[\left.\frac{\partial^2 h(\boldsymbol{\theta})}{\partial\boldsymbol{\theta}\,\partial\boldsymbol{\theta}'}\right|_{\boldsymbol{\theta}=\boldsymbol{\theta}^*}\right]^{-1}. \qquad [12.3.11]$$

When [12.3.10] is substituted into the numerator of [12.3.8], the result is

$$\begin{aligned}
&\int_{-\infty}^{\infty} \exp[T\cdot h(\boldsymbol{\theta})]\,d\boldsymbol{\theta} \\
&\cong \int_{-\infty}^{\infty} \exp\left\{T\cdot h(\boldsymbol{\theta}^*) - (T/2)(\boldsymbol{\theta} - \boldsymbol{\theta}^*)'(\boldsymbol{\Sigma}^*)^{-1}(\boldsymbol{\theta} - \boldsymbol{\theta}^*)\right\} d\boldsymbol{\theta} \\
&= \exp[T\cdot h(\boldsymbol{\theta}^*)] \int_{-\infty}^{\infty} \exp\left\{(-T/2)(\boldsymbol{\theta} - \boldsymbol{\theta}^*)'(\boldsymbol{\Sigma}^*)^{-1}(\boldsymbol{\theta} - \boldsymbol{\theta}^*)\right\} d\boldsymbol{\theta} \\
&= \exp[T\cdot h(\boldsymbol{\theta}^*)]\,(2\pi)^{a/2}|\boldsymbol{\Sigma}^*/T|^{1/2} \\
&\quad\times \int_{-\infty}^{\infty} \frac{1}{(2\pi)^{a/2}|\boldsymbol{\Sigma}^*/T|^{1/2}} \exp\left\{-\frac{1}{2}(\boldsymbol{\theta} - \boldsymbol{\theta}^*)'(\boldsymbol{\Sigma}^*/T)^{-1}(\boldsymbol{\theta} - \boldsymbol{\theta}^*)\right\} d\boldsymbol{\theta} \\
&= \exp[T\cdot h(\boldsymbol{\theta}^*)]\,(2\pi)^{a/2}|\boldsymbol{\Sigma}^*/T|^{1/2}.
\end{aligned} \qquad [12.3.12]$$

The last equality follows because the expression being integrated is a $N(\boldsymbol{\theta}^*, \boldsymbol{\Sigma}^*/T)$ density and therefore integrates to unity.

Similarly, the function $k(\boldsymbol{\theta})$ can be approximated with an expansion around the posterior mode $\hat{\boldsymbol{\theta}}$,

$$k(\boldsymbol{\theta}) \cong k(\hat{\boldsymbol{\theta}}) - \frac{1}{2}(\boldsymbol{\theta} - \hat{\boldsymbol{\theta}})'\hat{\boldsymbol{\Sigma}}^{-1}(\boldsymbol{\theta} - \hat{\boldsymbol{\theta}}),$$

where $\hat{\boldsymbol{\theta}}$ maximizes [12.3.7] and

$$\hat{\boldsymbol{\Sigma}} \equiv -\left[\left.\frac{\partial^2 k(\boldsymbol{\theta})}{\partial\boldsymbol{\theta}\,\partial\boldsymbol{\theta}'}\right|_{\boldsymbol{\theta}=\hat{\boldsymbol{\theta}}}\right]^{-1}. \qquad [12.3.13]$$

The denominator in [12.3.8] is then approximated by

$$\int_{-\infty}^{\infty} \exp[T\cdot k(\boldsymbol{\theta})]\,d\boldsymbol{\theta} \cong \exp[T\cdot k(\hat{\boldsymbol{\theta}})]\,(2\pi)^{a/2}|\hat{\boldsymbol{\Sigma}}/T|^{1/2}. \qquad [12.3.14]$$

Tierney and Kadane's approximation is obtained by substituting [12.3.12] and [12.3.14] into [12.3.8]:

$$\begin{aligned}
E[g(\boldsymbol{\theta})|\mathbf{y}] &\cong \frac{\exp[T\cdot h(\boldsymbol{\theta}^*)]\,(2\pi)^{a/2}|\boldsymbol{\Sigma}^*/T|^{1/2}}{\exp[T\cdot k(\hat{\boldsymbol{\theta}})]\,(2\pi)^{a/2}|\hat{\boldsymbol{\Sigma}}/T|^{1/2}} \\
&= \frac{|\boldsymbol{\Sigma}^*|^{1/2}}{|\hat{\boldsymbol{\Sigma}}|^{1/2}} \exp\{T\cdot[h(\boldsymbol{\theta}^*) - k(\hat{\boldsymbol{\theta}})]\}.
\end{aligned} \qquad [12.3.15]$$

To calculate this approximation to the posterior mean of $g(\boldsymbol{\theta})$, we first find the value $\boldsymbol{\theta}^*$ that maximizes $(1/T)\cdot\{\log g(\boldsymbol{\theta}) + \log f(\mathbf{y}|\boldsymbol{\theta}) + \log f(\boldsymbol{\theta})\}$. Then $h(\boldsymbol{\theta}^*)$ in [12.3.15] is the maximum value attained for this function and $\boldsymbol{\Sigma}^*$ is the negative of the inverse of the matrix of second derivatives of this function. Next we find the value $\hat{\boldsymbol{\theta}}$ that maximizes $(1/T)\cdot\{\log f(\mathbf{y}|\boldsymbol{\theta}) + \log f(\boldsymbol{\theta})\}$, with $k(\hat{\boldsymbol{\theta}})$ the maximum value attained and $\hat{\boldsymbol{\Sigma}}$ the negative of the inverse of the matrix of second derivatives.

The required maximization and second derivatives could be calculated analytically or numerically. Substituting the resulting values into [12.3.15] gives the Bayesian posterior estimate of $g(\boldsymbol{\theta})$.

### Monte Carlo Estimation of Posterior Moments

Posterior moments can alternatively be estimated using the Monte Carlo approach suggested by Hammersley and Handscomb (1964, Section 5.4) and Kloek and van Dijk (1978). Again, the objective is taken to be calculation of the posterior mean of $g(\boldsymbol{\theta})$. Let $I(\boldsymbol{\theta})$ be some density function defined on $\boldsymbol{\theta}$ with $I(\boldsymbol{\theta}) > 0$ for all $\boldsymbol{\theta}$. Then [12.3.5] can be written

$$E[g(\boldsymbol{\theta})|\mathbf{y}] = \frac{\int_{-\infty}^{\infty} g(\boldsymbol{\theta}) \cdot f(\mathbf{y}|\boldsymbol{\theta}) \cdot f(\boldsymbol{\theta})\, d\boldsymbol{\theta}}{\int_{-\infty}^{\infty} f(\mathbf{y}|\boldsymbol{\theta}) \cdot f(\boldsymbol{\theta})\, d\boldsymbol{\theta}} = \frac{\int_{-\infty}^{\infty} \{g(\boldsymbol{\theta}) \cdot f(\mathbf{y}|\boldsymbol{\theta}) \cdot f(\boldsymbol{\theta})/I(\boldsymbol{\theta})\} I(\boldsymbol{\theta})\, d\boldsymbol{\theta}}{\int_{-\infty}^{\infty} \{f(\mathbf{y}|\boldsymbol{\theta}) \cdot f(\boldsymbol{\theta})/I(\boldsymbol{\theta})\} I(\boldsymbol{\theta})\, d\boldsymbol{\theta}}. \qquad [12.3.16]$$

The numerator in [12.3.16] can be interpreted as the expectation of the random variable $\{g(\boldsymbol{\theta}) \cdot f(\mathbf{y}|\boldsymbol{\theta}) \cdot f(\boldsymbol{\theta})/I(\boldsymbol{\theta})\}$, where this expectation is taken with respect to the distribution implied by the density $I(\boldsymbol{\theta})$. If $I(\boldsymbol{\theta})$ is a known density such as multivariate Gaussian, it may be simple to generate $N$ separate Monte Carlo draws from this distribution, denoted $\{\boldsymbol{\theta}^{(1)}, \boldsymbol{\theta}^{(2)}, \ldots, \boldsymbol{\theta}^{(N)}\}$. We can then calculate the average realized value of the random variable across these Monte Carlo draws:

$$\sum_{i=1}^{N} (1/N) \cdot \{g(\boldsymbol{\theta}^{(i)}) \cdot f(\mathbf{y}|\boldsymbol{\theta}^{(i)}) \cdot f(\boldsymbol{\theta}^{(i)})/I(\boldsymbol{\theta}^{(i)})\}. \qquad [12.3.17]$$

From the law of large numbers, as $N \to \infty$, this will yield a consistent estimate of

$$E_{I(\boldsymbol{\theta})}\{g(\boldsymbol{\theta}) \cdot f(\mathbf{y}|\boldsymbol{\theta}) \cdot f(\boldsymbol{\theta})/I(\boldsymbol{\theta})\} = \int_{-\infty}^{\infty} \{g(\boldsymbol{\theta}) \cdot f(\mathbf{y}|\boldsymbol{\theta}) \cdot f(\boldsymbol{\theta})/I(\boldsymbol{\theta})\} I(\boldsymbol{\theta})\, d\boldsymbol{\theta}, \qquad [12.3.18]$$

provided that the integral in [12.3.18] exists. The denominator of [12.3.16] is similarly estimated from

$$\sum_{i=1}^{N} (1/N) \cdot \{f(\mathbf{y}|\boldsymbol{\theta}^{(i)}) \cdot f(\boldsymbol{\theta}^{(i)})/I(\boldsymbol{\theta}^{(i)})\}.$$

The integral in [12.3.18] need not exist if the importance density $I(\boldsymbol{\theta})$ goes to zero in the tails faster than the sample likelihood $f(\mathbf{y}|\boldsymbol{\theta})$. Even if [12.3.18] does exist, the Monte Carlo average [12.3.17] may give a poor estimate of [12.3.18] for moderate $N$ if $I(\boldsymbol{\theta})$ is poorly chosen. Geweke (1989) provided advice on specifying $I(\boldsymbol{\theta})$. If the set of allowable values for $\boldsymbol{\theta}$ forms a compact set, then letting $I(\boldsymbol{\theta})$ be the density for the asymptotic distribution of the maximum likelihood estimator is usually a good approach.

A nice illustration of the versatility of Bayesian Monte Carlo methods for analyzing dynamic models is provided by Geweke (1988a). This approach was extended to multivariate dynamic systems in Geweke (1988b).

## APPENDIX 12.A. *Proofs of Chapter 12 Propositions*

■ **Proof of Proposition 12.1.** Note that the product of [12.1.5] and [12.1.6] can be written

$$f(\mathbf{y}, \mu; \sigma^2) = \frac{1}{(2\pi)^{(T+1)/2}} |\mathbf{\Sigma}|^{-1/2} \exp\left\{-\frac{1}{2} \boldsymbol{\alpha}'\mathbf{\Sigma}^{-1}\boldsymbol{\alpha}\right\}, \qquad [12.A.1]$$

where

$$\underset{(T+1)\times 1}{\boldsymbol{\alpha}} \equiv \begin{bmatrix} \mu - m \\ \mathbf{y} - \mu\cdot\mathbf{1} \end{bmatrix} \qquad [12.A.2]$$

$$\underset{(T+1)\times(T+1)}{\mathbf{\Sigma}} \equiv \begin{bmatrix} \sigma^2/\nu & \mathbf{0}' \\ \mathbf{0} & \sigma^2\mathbf{I}_T \end{bmatrix}. \qquad [12.A.3]$$

The goal is to rearrange $\boldsymbol{\alpha}$ so that $\mu$ appears only in the first element. Define

$$\underset{(T+1)\times(T+1)}{\mathbf{A}} \equiv \begin{bmatrix} \nu/(\nu + T) & -\mathbf{1}'/(\nu + T) \\ \mathbf{1} & \mathbf{I}_T \end{bmatrix}. \qquad [12.A.4]$$

Since $\mathbf{1}'\mathbf{1} = T$ and $\mathbf{1}'\mathbf{y} = T\bar{y}$, we have

$$\begin{aligned} \mathbf{A}\boldsymbol{\alpha} &= \begin{bmatrix} [\nu/(\nu + T)](\mu - m) - \mathbf{1}'\mathbf{y}/(\nu + T) + [T/(\nu + T)]\mu \\ \mathbf{y} - m\cdot\mathbf{1} \end{bmatrix} \\ &= \begin{bmatrix} \mu - m^* \\ \mathbf{y} - m\cdot\mathbf{1} \end{bmatrix} \\ &\equiv \boldsymbol{\alpha}^* \end{aligned} \qquad [12.A.5]$$

and

$$\begin{aligned} \mathbf{A\Sigma A}' &= \sigma^2 \begin{bmatrix} 1/(\nu + T) & -\mathbf{1}'/(\nu + T) \\ 1/\nu & \mathbf{I}_T \end{bmatrix} \begin{bmatrix} \nu/(\nu + T) & \mathbf{1}' \\ -\mathbf{1}/(\nu + T) & \mathbf{I}_T \end{bmatrix} \\ &= \begin{bmatrix} \sigma^2/(\nu + T) & \mathbf{0}' \\ \mathbf{0} & \sigma^2(\mathbf{I}_T + \mathbf{1}\cdot\mathbf{1}'/\nu) \end{bmatrix} \\ &\equiv \mathbf{\Sigma}^*. \end{aligned} \qquad [12.A.6]$$

Thus,

$$\boldsymbol{\alpha}'\mathbf{\Sigma}^{-1}\boldsymbol{\alpha} = \boldsymbol{\alpha}'\mathbf{A}'(\mathbf{A}')^{-1}\mathbf{\Sigma}^{-1}\mathbf{A}^{-1}\mathbf{A}\boldsymbol{\alpha} = (\mathbf{A}\boldsymbol{\alpha})'(\mathbf{A\Sigma A}')^{-1}(\mathbf{A}\boldsymbol{\alpha}) = \boldsymbol{\alpha}^{*\prime}(\mathbf{\Sigma}^*)^{-1}\boldsymbol{\alpha}^*. \qquad [12.A.7]$$

Moreover, observe that $\mathbf{A}$ can be expressed as

$$\mathbf{A} = \begin{bmatrix} 1 & -\mathbf{1}'/(\nu + T) \\ \mathbf{0} & \mathbf{I}_T \end{bmatrix} \begin{bmatrix} 1 & \mathbf{0}' \\ \mathbf{1} & \mathbf{I}_T \end{bmatrix}.$$

Each of these triangular matrices has 1s along the principal diagonal and so has unit determinant, implying that $|\mathbf{A}| = 1$. Hence,

$$|\mathbf{\Sigma}^*| = |\mathbf{A}|\cdot|\mathbf{\Sigma}|\cdot|\mathbf{A}'| = |\mathbf{\Sigma}|. \qquad [12.A.8]$$

Substituting [12.A.5] through [12.A.8] into [12.A.1] gives

$$\begin{aligned} &f(\mathbf{y}, \mu; \sigma^2) \\ &= \frac{1}{(2\pi)^{(T+1)/2}} |\mathbf{\Sigma}^*|^{-1/2} \exp\left\{-\frac{1}{2}\boldsymbol{\alpha}^{*\prime}(\mathbf{\Sigma}^*)^{-1}\boldsymbol{\alpha}^*\right\} \\ &= \frac{1}{(2\pi)^{(T+1)/2}} \begin{vmatrix} \sigma^2/(\nu + T) & \mathbf{0}' \\ \mathbf{0} & \sigma^2(\mathbf{I}_T + \mathbf{1}\cdot\mathbf{1}'/\nu) \end{vmatrix}^{-1/2} \\ &\quad\times \exp\left\{-\frac{1}{2} \begin{bmatrix} \mu - m^* \\ \mathbf{y} - m\cdot\mathbf{1} \end{bmatrix}' \begin{bmatrix} \sigma^2/(\nu + T) & \mathbf{0}' \\ \mathbf{0} & \sigma^2(\mathbf{I}_T + \mathbf{1}\cdot\mathbf{1}'/\nu) \end{bmatrix}^{-1} \right. \\ &\quad\times \left. \begin{bmatrix} \mu - m^* \\ \mathbf{y} - m\cdot\mathbf{1} \end{bmatrix} \right\} \end{aligned} \qquad [12.A.9]$$

$$= \frac{1}{(2\pi)^{(T+1)/2}} \left[\frac{\sigma^2}{\nu + T}\right]^{-1/2} \cdot \left|\sigma^2(\mathbf{I}_T + \mathbf{1}\cdot\mathbf{1}'/\nu)\right|^{-1/2}$$

$$\times \exp\left\{\frac{-(\mu - m^*)^2}{2\sigma^2/(\nu + T)} - \frac{(\mathbf{y} - m\cdot\mathbf{1})'(\mathbf{I}_T + \mathbf{1}\cdot\mathbf{1}'/\nu)^{-1}(\mathbf{y} - m\cdot\mathbf{1})}{2\sigma^2}\right\},$$

from which the factorization in Proposition 12.1 follows immediately. ■

■ **Proof of Proposition 12.2.** The product of [12.1.10] and [12.1.11] can be written as

$$f(\mathbf{y}, \boldsymbol{\beta}|\mathbf{X}; \sigma^2) = \frac{1}{(2\pi)^{(T+k)/2}} |\boldsymbol{\Sigma}|^{-1/2} \exp\left\{-\frac{1}{2}\boldsymbol{\alpha}'\boldsymbol{\Sigma}^{-1}\boldsymbol{\alpha}\right\}$$

with

$$\underset{(T+k)\times 1}{\boldsymbol{\alpha}} \equiv \begin{bmatrix} \boldsymbol{\beta} - \mathbf{m} \\ \mathbf{y} - \mathbf{X}\boldsymbol{\beta} \end{bmatrix}$$

$$\underset{(T+k)\times(T+k)}{\boldsymbol{\Sigma}} \equiv \begin{bmatrix} \sigma^2\mathbf{M} & \mathbf{0} \\ \mathbf{0} & \sigma^2\mathbf{I}_T \end{bmatrix}.$$

As in the proof of Proposition 12.1, define

$$\underset{(T+k)\times(T+k)}{\mathbf{A}} = \begin{bmatrix} \mathbf{I}_k & -(\mathbf{M}^{-1} + \mathbf{X}'\mathbf{X})^{-1}\mathbf{X}' \\ \mathbf{0} & \mathbf{I}_T \end{bmatrix} \begin{bmatrix} \mathbf{I}_k & \mathbf{0} \\ \mathbf{X} & \mathbf{I}_T \end{bmatrix}$$

$$= \begin{bmatrix} (\mathbf{M}^{-1} + \mathbf{X}'\mathbf{X})^{-1}\mathbf{M}^{-1} & -(\mathbf{M}^{-1} + \mathbf{X}'\mathbf{X})^{-1}\mathbf{X}' \\ \mathbf{X} & \mathbf{I}_T \end{bmatrix}.$$

Thus, $\mathbf{A}$ has unit determinant and

$$\mathbf{A}\boldsymbol{\alpha} = \begin{bmatrix} \boldsymbol{\beta} - \mathbf{m}^* \\ \mathbf{y} - \mathbf{X}\mathbf{m} \end{bmatrix}$$

with

$$\mathbf{A}\boldsymbol{\Sigma}\mathbf{A}' = \begin{bmatrix} \sigma^2(\mathbf{M}^{-1} + \mathbf{X}'\mathbf{X})^{-1} & \mathbf{0} \\ \mathbf{0} & \sigma^2(\mathbf{I}_T + \mathbf{X}\mathbf{M}\mathbf{X}') \end{bmatrix}.$$

Thus, as in equation [12.A.9],

$$f(\mathbf{y}, \boldsymbol{\beta}|\mathbf{X}; \sigma^2) = \frac{1}{(2\pi)^{(T+k)/2}} \begin{vmatrix} \sigma^2(\mathbf{M}^{-1} + \mathbf{X}'\mathbf{X})^{-1} & \mathbf{0} \\ \mathbf{0} & \sigma^2(\mathbf{I}_T + \mathbf{X}\mathbf{M}\mathbf{X}') \end{vmatrix}^{-1/2}$$

$$\times \exp\left\{-\frac{1}{2}\begin{bmatrix} \boldsymbol{\beta} - \mathbf{m}^* \\ \mathbf{y} - \mathbf{X}\mathbf{m} \end{bmatrix}' \begin{bmatrix} \sigma^2(\mathbf{M}^{-1} + \mathbf{X}'\mathbf{X})^{-1} & \mathbf{0} \\ \mathbf{0} & \sigma^2(\mathbf{I}_T + \mathbf{X}\mathbf{M}\mathbf{X}') \end{bmatrix}^{-1} \begin{bmatrix} \boldsymbol{\beta} - \mathbf{m}^* \\ \mathbf{y} - \mathbf{X}\mathbf{m} \end{bmatrix}\right\}. \quad ■$$

■ **Proof of Proposition 12.3(a).** We have that

$$f(\mathbf{y}, \boldsymbol{\beta}, \sigma^{-2}|\mathbf{X}) = f(\mathbf{y}|\boldsymbol{\beta}, \sigma^{-2}, \mathbf{X})\cdot f(\boldsymbol{\beta}|\sigma^{-2}, \mathbf{X})\cdot f(\sigma^{-2}|\mathbf{X}). \qquad [12.A.10]$$

The first two terms on the right side are identical to [12.1.10] and [12.1.11]. Thus, Proposition 12.2 can be used to write [12.A.10] as

$$f(\mathbf{y}, \boldsymbol{\beta}, \sigma^{-2}|\mathbf{X})$$

$$= \left\{\frac{1}{(2\pi\sigma^2)^{k/2}} |\mathbf{M}^*|^{-1/2} \exp\left\{\left[-\frac{1}{2\sigma^2}\right](\boldsymbol{\beta} - \mathbf{m}^*)'(\mathbf{M}^*)^{-1}(\boldsymbol{\beta} - \mathbf{m}^*)\right\}\right\}$$

$$\times \left\{\frac{1}{(2\pi\sigma^2)^{T/2}} |\mathbf{I}_T + \mathbf{X}\mathbf{M}\mathbf{X}'|^{-1/2} \right. \qquad [12.A.11]$$

$$\left. \times \exp\left\{[-1/(2\sigma^2)](\mathbf{y} - \mathbf{X}\mathbf{m})'(\mathbf{I}_T + \mathbf{X}\mathbf{M}\mathbf{X}')^{-1}(\mathbf{y} - \mathbf{X}\mathbf{m})\right\}\right\}$$

$$\times \left\{\frac{(\lambda/2)^{N/2}\sigma^{-2[(N/2)-1]} \exp[-\lambda\sigma^{-2}/2]}{\Gamma(N/2)}\right\}.$$

Define

$$\lambda^* \equiv \lambda + (\mathbf{y} - \mathbf{Xm})'(\mathbf{I}_T + \mathbf{XMX}')^{-1}(\mathbf{y} - \mathbf{Xm}); \qquad [12.A.12]$$

we will show later that this is the same as the value $\lambda^*$ described in the proposition. For $N^* \equiv N + T$, the density [12.A.11] can be written as

$$\begin{aligned} &f(\mathbf{y}, \boldsymbol{\beta}, \sigma^{-2}|\mathbf{X}) \\ &= \left\{\frac{1}{(2\pi\sigma^2)^{k/2}}|\mathbf{M}^*|^{-1/2}\exp\left\{\left[-\frac{1}{2\sigma^2}\right](\boldsymbol{\beta} - \mathbf{m}^*)'(\mathbf{M}^*)^{-1}(\boldsymbol{\beta} - \mathbf{m}^*)\right\}\right\} \\ &\times \left\{\frac{\sigma^{-2[(N^*/2)-1]}(\lambda/2)^{N/2}}{(2\pi)^{T/2}\Gamma(N/2)}|\mathbf{I}_T + \mathbf{XMX}'|^{-1/2}\exp\left[-\frac{\lambda^*\sigma^{-2}}{2}\right]\right\} \\ &= \left\{\frac{1}{(2\pi\sigma^2)^{k/2}}|\mathbf{M}^*|^{-1/2}\exp\left\{\left[-\frac{1}{2\sigma^2}\right](\boldsymbol{\beta} - \mathbf{m}^*)'(\mathbf{M}^*)^{-1}(\boldsymbol{\beta} - \mathbf{m}^*)\right\}\right\} \qquad [12.A.13] \\ &\times \left\{\frac{\sigma^{-2[(N^*/2)-1]}(\lambda^*/2)^{N^*/2}}{\Gamma(N^*/2)}\exp\left[-\frac{\lambda^*\sigma^{-2}}{2}\right]\right\} \\ &\times \left\{\frac{\Gamma(N^*/2)(\lambda/2)^{N/2}}{(2\pi)^{T/2}\Gamma(N/2)(\lambda^*/2)^{N^*/2}}|\mathbf{I}_T + \mathbf{XMX}'|^{-1/2}\right\}. \end{aligned}$$

The second term does not involve $\boldsymbol{\beta}$, and the third term does not involve $\boldsymbol{\beta}$ or $\sigma^{-2}$. Thus, [12.A.13] provides the factorization

$$f(\mathbf{y}, \boldsymbol{\beta}, \sigma^{-2}|\mathbf{X}) = \{f(\boldsymbol{\beta}|\sigma^{-2}, \mathbf{y}, \mathbf{X})\}\cdot\{f(\sigma^{-2}|\mathbf{y}, \mathbf{X})\}\cdot\{f(\mathbf{y}|\mathbf{X})\},$$

where $f(\boldsymbol{\beta}|\sigma^{-2}, \mathbf{y}, \mathbf{X})$ is a $N(\mathbf{m}^*, \sigma^2\mathbf{M}^*)$ density, $f(\sigma^{-2}|\mathbf{y}, \mathbf{X})$ is a $\Gamma(N^*, \lambda^*)$ density, and $f(\mathbf{y}|\mathbf{X})$ can be written as

$$\begin{aligned} f(\mathbf{y}|\mathbf{X}) &= \left\{\frac{\Gamma(N^*/2)(\lambda/2)^{N/2}}{(2\pi)^{T/2}\Gamma(N/2)(\lambda^*/2)^{N^*/2}}|\mathbf{I}_T + \mathbf{XMX}'|^{-1/2}\right\} \\ &= \left\{\frac{\Gamma[(N + T)/2]\lambda^{N/2}|\mathbf{I}_T + \mathbf{XMX}'|^{-1/2}}{\pi^{T/2}\Gamma(N/2)\{\lambda + (\mathbf{y} - \mathbf{Xm})'(\mathbf{I}_T + \mathbf{XMX}')^{-1}(\mathbf{y} - \mathbf{Xm})\}^{(N+T)/2}}\right\} \\ &= c\cdot\{1 + (1/N)(\mathbf{y} - \mathbf{Xm})'[(\lambda/N)(\mathbf{I}_T + \mathbf{XMX}')]^{-1}(\mathbf{y} - \mathbf{Xm})\}^{-(N+T)/2}, \end{aligned}$$

where

$$c = \frac{\Gamma[(N + T)/2](1/N)^{T/2}|(\lambda/N)(\mathbf{I}_T + \mathbf{XMX}')|^{-1/2}}{\pi^{T/2}\Gamma(N/2)}.$$

Thus, $f(\mathbf{y}|\mathbf{X})$ is a $T$-dimensional Student's $t$ density with $N$ degrees of freedom, mean $\mathbf{Xm}$, and scale matrix $(\lambda/N)(\mathbf{I}_T + \mathbf{XM'X}')$. Hence, the distributions of $(\boldsymbol{\beta}|\sigma^{-2}, \mathbf{y}, \mathbf{X})$ and $(\sigma^{-2}|\mathbf{y}, \mathbf{X})$ are as claimed in Proposition 12.3, provided that the magnitude $\lambda^*$ defined in [12.A.12] is the same as the expression in [12.1.28]. To verify that this is indeed the case, notice that

$$(\mathbf{I}_T + \mathbf{XMX}')^{-1} = \mathbf{I}_T - \mathbf{X}(\mathbf{X}'\mathbf{X} + \mathbf{M}^{-1})^{-1}\mathbf{X}', \qquad [12.A.14]$$

as can be verified by premultiplying [12.A.14] by $(\mathbf{I}_T + \mathbf{XMX}')$:

$$\begin{aligned} &(\mathbf{I}_T + \mathbf{XMX}')[\mathbf{I}_T - \mathbf{X}(\mathbf{X}'\mathbf{X} + \mathbf{M}^{-1})^{-1}\mathbf{X}'] \\ &= \mathbf{I}_T + \mathbf{XMX}' - \mathbf{X}(\mathbf{X}'\mathbf{X} + \mathbf{M}^{-1})^{-1}\mathbf{X}' - \mathbf{XM}(\mathbf{X}'\mathbf{X})(\mathbf{X}'\mathbf{X} + \mathbf{M}^{-1})^{-1}\mathbf{X}' \\ &= \mathbf{I}_T + \mathbf{X}\left\{\mathbf{M}(\mathbf{X}'\mathbf{X} + \mathbf{M}^{-1}) - \mathbf{I}_k - \mathbf{M}(\mathbf{X}'\mathbf{X})\right\}(\mathbf{X}'\mathbf{X} + \mathbf{M}^{-1})^{-1}\mathbf{X}' \\ &= \mathbf{I}_T. \end{aligned}$$

Using [12.A.14], we see that

$$\begin{aligned} &(\mathbf{y} - \mathbf{Xm})'(\mathbf{I}_T + \mathbf{XMX}')^{-1}(\mathbf{y} - \mathbf{Xm}) \\ &= (\mathbf{y} - \mathbf{Xm})'[\mathbf{I}_T - \mathbf{X}(\mathbf{X}'\mathbf{X} + \mathbf{M}^{-1})^{-1}\mathbf{X}'](\mathbf{y} - \mathbf{Xm}) \\ &= (\mathbf{y} - \mathbf{Xb} + \mathbf{Xb} - \mathbf{Xm})'[\mathbf{I}_T - \mathbf{X}(\mathbf{X}'\mathbf{X} + \mathbf{M}^{-1})^{-1}\mathbf{X}'](\mathbf{y} - \mathbf{Xb} + \mathbf{Xb} - \mathbf{Xm}) \\ &= (\mathbf{y} - \mathbf{Xb})'(\mathbf{y} - \mathbf{Xb}) + (\mathbf{b} - \mathbf{m})'\mathbf{X}'[\mathbf{I}_T - \mathbf{X}(\mathbf{X}'\mathbf{X} + \mathbf{M}^{-1})^{-1}\mathbf{X}']\mathbf{X}(\mathbf{b} - \mathbf{m}), \end{aligned} \qquad [12.A.15]$$

where cross-product terms have disappeared because of the *OLS* orthogonality condition $(\mathbf{y} - \mathbf{Xb})'\mathbf{X} = \mathbf{0}'$. Furthermore,

$$\begin{aligned}\mathbf{X}'[\mathbf{I}_T - \mathbf{X}(\mathbf{X}'\mathbf{X} + \mathbf{M}^{-1})^{-1}\mathbf{X}']\mathbf{X} \\ &= [\mathbf{I}_k - (\mathbf{X}'\mathbf{X})(\mathbf{X}'\mathbf{X} + \mathbf{M}^{-1})^{-1}]\mathbf{X}'\mathbf{X} \\ &= [(\mathbf{X}'\mathbf{X} + \mathbf{M}^{-1})(\mathbf{X}'\mathbf{X} + \mathbf{M}^{-1})^{-1} - (\mathbf{X}'\mathbf{X})(\mathbf{X}'\mathbf{X} + \mathbf{M}^{-1})^{-1}]\mathbf{X}'\mathbf{X} \\ &= \mathbf{M}^{-1}(\mathbf{X}'\mathbf{X} + \mathbf{M}^{-1})^{-1}\mathbf{X}'\mathbf{X}.\end{aligned}$$

This allows [12.A.15] to be written as

$$\begin{aligned}(\mathbf{y} - \mathbf{Xm})'(\mathbf{I}_T + \mathbf{XMX}')^{-1}(\mathbf{y} - \mathbf{Xm}) \\ &= (\mathbf{y} - \mathbf{Xb})'(\mathbf{y} - \mathbf{Xb}) + (\mathbf{b} - \mathbf{m})'\mathbf{M}^{-1}(\mathbf{X}'\mathbf{X} + \mathbf{M}^{-1})^{-1}\mathbf{X}'\mathbf{X}(\mathbf{b} - \mathbf{m}),\end{aligned}$$

establishing the equivalence of [12.A.12] and [12.1.28].

**Proof of (b).** The joint posterior density of $\boldsymbol{\beta}$ and $\sigma^{-2}$ is given by

$$\begin{aligned}f(\boldsymbol{\beta}, \sigma^{-2}|\mathbf{y}, \mathbf{X}) \\ &= f(\boldsymbol{\beta}|\sigma^{-2}, \mathbf{y}, \mathbf{X})\cdot f(\sigma^{-2}|\mathbf{y}, \mathbf{X}) \\ &= \left\{\frac{1}{(2\pi\sigma^2)^{k/2}}|\mathbf{M}^*|^{-1/2}\exp\left\{\left[-\frac{1}{2\sigma^2}\right](\boldsymbol{\beta} - \mathbf{m}^*)'(\mathbf{M}^*)^{-1}(\boldsymbol{\beta} - \mathbf{m}^*)\right\}\right\} \\ &\quad\times\left\{\frac{\sigma^{-2[(N^*/2)-1]}(\lambda^*/2)^{N^*/2}}{\Gamma(N^*/2)}\exp[-\lambda^*\sigma^{-2}/2]\right\} \\ &= \left(\frac{\sigma^{-2\{[(k+N^*)/2]-1\}}}{\Gamma[(k+N^*)/2]}\times\left\{\frac{\lambda^*}{2}\cdot[1 + (\boldsymbol{\beta} - \mathbf{m}^*)'(\lambda^*\mathbf{M}^*)^{-1}(\boldsymbol{\beta} - \mathbf{m}^*)]\right\}^{(k+N^*)/2}\right. \\ &\quad\left.\times\exp\left\{-\frac{\lambda^*}{2}\cdot[1 + (\boldsymbol{\beta} - \mathbf{m}^*)'(\lambda^*\mathbf{M}^*)^{-1}(\boldsymbol{\beta} - \mathbf{m}^*)]\sigma^{-2}\right\}\right) \\ &\quad\times\left\{\frac{\Gamma[(k+N^*)/2]}{(\lambda^*)^{k/2}\pi^{k/2}\Gamma(N^*/2)}|\mathbf{M}^*|^{-1/2}[1 + (\boldsymbol{\beta} - \mathbf{m}^*)'(\lambda^*\mathbf{M}^*)^{-1}(\boldsymbol{\beta} - \mathbf{m}^*)]^{-(k+N^*)/2}\right\} \\ &= \{f(\sigma^{-2}|\boldsymbol{\beta}, \mathbf{y}, \mathbf{X})\}\cdot\{f(\boldsymbol{\beta}|\mathbf{y}, \mathbf{X})\},\end{aligned}$$

where $f(\sigma^{-2}|\boldsymbol{\beta}, \mathbf{y}, \mathbf{X})$ will be recognized as a $\Gamma\big((k + N^*), \lambda^*[1 + (\boldsymbol{\beta} - \mathbf{m}^*)'(\lambda^*\mathbf{M}^*)^{-1} \times (\boldsymbol{\beta} - \mathbf{m}^*)]\big)$ density, while $f(\boldsymbol{\beta}|\mathbf{y}, \mathbf{X})$ can be written as

$$\begin{aligned}f(\boldsymbol{\beta}|\mathbf{y}, \mathbf{X}) = &\left\{\frac{\Gamma[(k+N^*)/2]}{(N^*)^{k/2}\pi^{k/2}\Gamma(N^*/2)}|(\lambda^*/N^*)\mathbf{M}^*|^{-1/2}\right. \\ &\left.\times[1 + (1/N^*)(\boldsymbol{\beta} - \mathbf{m}^*)'[(\lambda^*/N^*)\mathbf{M}^*]^{-1}(\boldsymbol{\beta} - \mathbf{m}^*)]^{-(k+N^*)/2}\right\},\end{aligned}$$

which is a $k$-dimensional $t$ density with $N^*$ degrees of freedom, mean $\mathbf{m}^*$, and scale matrix $(\lambda^*/N^*)\mathbf{M}^*$.

**Proof of (c).** Notice that conditional on $\mathbf{y}$, $\mathbf{X}$, and $\sigma^2$, the variable

$$Z \equiv [\mathbf{R}(\boldsymbol{\beta} - \mathbf{m}^*)]'[\sigma^2\mathbf{R}(\mathbf{M}^{-1} + \mathbf{X}'\mathbf{X})^{-1}\mathbf{R}']^{-1}\cdot[\mathbf{R}(\boldsymbol{\beta} - \mathbf{m}^*)]$$

is distributed $\chi^2(m)$, from Proposition 8.1. The variable $Q$ in [12.1.30] is equal to $Z\cdot\sigma^2N^*/(m\lambda^*)$, and so conditional on $\mathbf{y}$, $\mathbf{X}$, and $\sigma^2$, the variable $Q$ is distributed $\Gamma\big(m, (m\lambda^*)/(\sigma^2N^*)\big)$:

$$f(q|\sigma^{-2}, \mathbf{y}, \mathbf{X}) = \frac{[m\lambda^*/(2\sigma^2N^*)]^{m/2}q^{[(m/2)-1]}\exp[-m\lambda^*q/(2\sigma^2N^*)]}{\Gamma(m/2)}. \qquad [12.A.16]$$

The joint posterior density of $q$ and $\sigma^{-2}$ is

$$
\begin{aligned}
f(q, \sigma^{-2}|\mathbf{y}, \mathbf{X}) &= f(q|\sigma^{-2}, \mathbf{y}, \mathbf{X}) \cdot f(\sigma^{-2}|\mathbf{y}, \mathbf{X}) \\
&= \left\{ \frac{[m\lambda^*/(2\sigma^2 N^*)]^{m/2} q^{[(m/2)-1]} \exp[-m\lambda^* q/(2\sigma^2 N^*)]}{\Gamma(m/2)} \right\} \\
&\quad \times \left\{ \frac{\sigma^{-2[(N^*/2)-1]}(\lambda^*/2)^{N^*/2}}{\Gamma(N^*/2)} \exp[-\lambda^*\sigma^{-2}/2] \right\} \\
&= \left\{ \frac{\{(N^* + mq)\cdot[\lambda^*/(2N^*)]\}^{[(N^*+m)/2]}}{\Gamma[(N^* + m)/2]} \right. \\
&\quad \left. \times\ \sigma^{-2\{[(m+N^*)/2]-1\}} \exp[-(N^* + mq)(\lambda^*/N^*)\sigma^{-2}/2] \right\} \\
&\quad \times \left\{ \frac{m^{m/2}(N^*)^{N^*/2}\Gamma[(N^* + m)/2] q^{[(m/2)-1]}}{\Gamma(m/2)\Gamma(N^*/2)(N^* + mq)^{[(N^*+m)/2]}} \right\} \\
&= \{f(\sigma^{-2}|q, \mathbf{y}, \mathbf{X})\} \cdot \{f(q|\mathbf{y}, \mathbf{X})\},
\end{aligned}
\qquad [12.A.17]
$$

where $f(\sigma^{-2}|q, \mathbf{y}, \mathbf{X})$ is a $\Gamma\big((m + N^*), (N^* + mq)(\lambda^*/N^*)\big)$ density and $f(q|\mathbf{y}, \mathbf{X})$ is an $F(m, N^*)$ density. ■

## *Chapter 12 Exercise*

12.1. Deduce Proposition 12.1 as a special case of Proposition 12.2.

## *Chapter 12 References*


Almon, Shirley. 1965. "The Distributed Lag between Capital Appropriations and Expenditures." *Econometrica* 33:178–96.

Barro, Robert J. 1979. "On the Determination of the Public Debt." *Journal of Political Economy* 87:940–71.

DeGroot, Morris H. 1970. *Optimal Statistical Decisions*. New York: McGraw-Hill.

Diebold, Francis X., and James A. Nason. 1990. "Nonparametric Exchange Rate Prediction?" *Journal of International Economics* 28:315–32.

Doan, Thomas A. 1990. *RATS User's Manual*. VAR Econometrics, Suite 612, 1800 Sherman Ave., Evanston, IL 60201.

Fama, Eugene F. 1965. "The Behavior of Stock Market Prices." *Journal of Business* 38:34–105.

Geweke, John. 1988a. "The Secular and Cyclical Behavior of Real GDP in 19 OECD Countries, 1957–1983." *Journal of Business and Economic Statistics* 6:479–86.

———. 1988b. "Antithetic Acceleration of Monte Carlo Integration in Bayesian Inference." *Journal of Econometrics* 38:73–89.

———. 1989. "Bayesian Inference in Econometric Models Using Monte Carlo Integration." *Econometrica* 57:1317–39.

Hall, Robert E. 1978. "Stochastic Implications of the Life Cycle–Permanent Income Hypothesis: Theory and Evidence." *Journal of Political Economy* 86:971–87.

Hammersley, J. M., and D. C. Handscomb. 1964. *Monte Carlo Methods*, 1st ed. London: Methuen.

Hoerl, A. E., and R. W. Kennard. 1970. "Ridge Regression: Biased Estimation for Nonorthogonal Problems." *Technometrics* 12:55–82.

Kloek, T., and H. K. van Dijk. 1978. "Bayesian Estimates of Equation System Parameters: An Application of Integration by Monte Carlo." *Econometrica* 46:1–19.

Leamer, Edward E. 1978. *Specification Searches: Ad Hoc Inference with Nonexperimental Data*. New York: Wiley.

Litterman, Robert B. 1986. "Forecasting with Bayesian Vector Autoregressions—Five Years of Experience." *Journal of Business and Economic Statistics* 4:25–38.

Mankiw, N. Gregory. 1987. "The Optimal Collection of Seigniorage: Theory and Evidence." *Journal of Monetary Economics* 20:327–41.

Rothenberg, Thomas J. 1973. *Efficient Estimation with A Priori Information*. New Haven, Conn.: Yale University Press.

Shiller, Robert J. 1973. "A Distributed Lag Estimator Derived from Smoothness Priors." *Econometrica* 41:775–88.

Theil, Henri. 1971. *Principles of Econometrics*. New York: Wiley.

Tierney, Luke, and Joseph B. Kadane. 1986. "Accurate Approximations for Posterior Moments and Marginal Densities." *Journal of the American Statistical Association* 81:82–86.

Zellner, Arnold. 1971. *An Introduction to Bayesian Inference in Econometrics*. New York: Wiley.

# 13 The Kalman Filter

This chapter introduces some very useful tools named for the contributions of R. E. Kalman (1960, 1963). The idea is to express a dynamic system in a particular form called the *state-space representation*. The Kalman filter is an algorithm for sequentially updating a linear projection for the system. Among other benefits, this algorithm provides a way to calculate exact finite-sample forecasts and the exact likelihood function for Gaussian *ARMA* processes, to factor matrix autocovariance-generating functions or spectral densities, and to estimate vector autoregressions with coefficients that change over time.

Section 13.1 describes how a dynamic system can be written in a form that can be analyzed using the Kalman filter. The filter itself is derived in Section 13.2, and its use in forecasting is described in Section 13.3. Section 13.4 explains how to estimate the population parameters by maximum likelihood. Section 13.5 analyzes the properties of the Kalman filter as the sample size grows, and explains how the Kalman filter is related in the limit to the Wold representation and factoring an autocovariance-generating function. Section 13.6 develops a smoothing algorithm, which is a way to use all the information in the sample to form the best inference about the unobserved state of the process at any historical date. Section 13.7 describes standard errors for smoothed inferences and forecasts. The use of the Kalman filter for estimating systems with time-varying parameters is investigated in Section 13.8.

## 13.1. *The State-Space Representation of a Dynamic System*

### *Maintained Assumptions*

Let $\mathbf{y}_t$ denote an $(n \times 1)$ vector of variables observed at date $t$. A rich class of dynamic models for $\mathbf{y}_t$ can be described in terms of a possibly unobserved $(r \times 1)$ vector $\boldsymbol{\xi}_t$ known as the *state vector*. The *state-space representation* of the dynamics of $\mathbf{y}$ is given by the following system of equations:

$$\boldsymbol{\xi}_{t+1} = \mathbf{F}\boldsymbol{\xi}_t + \mathbf{v}_{t+1} \qquad [13.1.1]$$

$$\mathbf{y}_t = \mathbf{A}'\mathbf{x}_t + \mathbf{H}'\boldsymbol{\xi}_t + \mathbf{w}_t, \qquad [13.1.2]$$

where $\mathbf{F}$, $\mathbf{A}'$, and $\mathbf{H}'$ are matrices of parameters of dimension $(r \times r)$, $(n \times k)$, and $(n \times r)$, respectively, and $\mathbf{x}_t$ is a $(k \times 1)$ vector of exogenous or predetermined variables. Equation [13.1.1] is known as the *state equation*, and [13.1.2] is known as the *observation equation*. The $(r \times 1)$ vector $\mathbf{v}_t$ and the $(n \times 1)$ vector $\mathbf{w}_t$ are vector white noise:

$$E(\mathbf{v}_t\mathbf{v}_\tau') = \begin{cases} \mathbf{Q} & \text{for } t = \tau \\ \mathbf{0} & \text{otherwise} \end{cases} \qquad [13.1.3]$$

$$E(\mathbf{w}_t\mathbf{w}_\tau') = \begin{cases} \mathbf{R} & \text{for } t = \tau \\ \mathbf{0} & \text{otherwise,} \end{cases} \qquad [13.1.4]$$

where $\mathbf{Q}$ and $\mathbf{R}$ are $(r \times r)$ and $(n \times n)$ matrices, respectively. The disturbances $\mathbf{v}_t$ and $\mathbf{w}_t$ are assumed to be uncorrelated at all lags:

$$E(\mathbf{v}_t\mathbf{w}_\tau') = \mathbf{0} \qquad \text{for all } t \text{ and } \tau. \qquad [13.1.5]$$

The statement that $\mathbf{x}_t$ is predetermined or exogenous means that $\mathbf{x}_t$ provides no information about $\boldsymbol{\xi}_{t+s}$ or $\mathbf{w}_{t+s}$ for $s = 0, 1, 2, \ldots$ beyond that contained in $\mathbf{y}_{t-1}, \mathbf{y}_{t-2}, \ldots, \mathbf{y}_1$. Thus, for example, $\mathbf{x}_t$ could include lagged values of $\mathbf{y}$ or variables that are uncorrelated with $\boldsymbol{\xi}_\tau$ and $\mathbf{w}_\tau$ for all $\tau$.

The system of [13.1.1] through [13.1.5] is typically used to describe a finite series of observations $\{\mathbf{y}_1, \mathbf{y}_2, \ldots, \mathbf{y}_T\}$ for which assumptions about the initial value of the state vector $\boldsymbol{\xi}_1$ are needed. We assume that $\boldsymbol{\xi}_1$ is uncorrelated with any realizations of $\mathbf{v}_t$ or $\mathbf{w}_t$:

$$E(\mathbf{v}_t\boldsymbol{\xi}_1') = \mathbf{0} \qquad \text{for } t = 1, 2, \ldots, T \qquad [13.1.6]$$

$$E(\mathbf{w}_t\boldsymbol{\xi}_1') = \mathbf{0} \qquad \text{for } t = 1, 2, \ldots, T. \qquad [13.1.7]$$

The state equation [13.1.1] implies that $\boldsymbol{\xi}_t$ can be written as a linear function of $(\boldsymbol{\xi}_1, \mathbf{v}_2, \mathbf{v}_3, \ldots, \mathbf{v}_t)$:

$$\boldsymbol{\xi}_t = \mathbf{v}_t + \mathbf{F}\mathbf{v}_{t-1} + \mathbf{F}^2\mathbf{v}_{t-2} + \cdots + \mathbf{F}^{t-2}\mathbf{v}_2 + \mathbf{F}^{t-1}\boldsymbol{\xi}_1 \qquad [13.1.8]$$
$$\text{for } t = 2, 3, \ldots, T.$$

Thus, [13.1.6] and [13.1.3] imply that $\mathbf{v}_t$ is uncorrelated with lagged values of $\boldsymbol{\xi}$:

$$E(\mathbf{v}_t\boldsymbol{\xi}_\tau') = \mathbf{0} \qquad \text{for } \tau = t-1, t-2, \ldots, 1. \qquad [13.1.9]$$

Similarly,

$$E(\mathbf{w}_t\boldsymbol{\xi}_\tau') = \mathbf{0} \qquad \text{for } \tau = 1, 2, \ldots, T \qquad [13.1.10]$$

$$\begin{aligned} E(\mathbf{w}_t\mathbf{y}_\tau') &= E[\mathbf{w}_t(\mathbf{A}'\mathbf{x}_\tau + \mathbf{H}'\boldsymbol{\xi}_\tau + \mathbf{w}_\tau)'] \\ &= \mathbf{0} \qquad \text{for } \tau = t-1, t-2, \ldots, 1 \end{aligned} \qquad [13.1.11]$$

$$E(\mathbf{v}_t\mathbf{y}_\tau') = \mathbf{0} \qquad \text{for } \tau = t-1, t-2, \ldots, 1. \qquad [13.1.12]$$

The system of [13.1.1] through [13.1.7] is quite flexible, though it is straightforward to generalize the results further to systems in which $\mathbf{v}_t$ is correlated with $\mathbf{w}_t$.[1] The various parameter matrices ($\mathbf{F}$, $\mathbf{Q}$, $\mathbf{A}$, $\mathbf{H}$, or $\mathbf{R}$) could be functions of time, as will be discussed in Section 13.8. The presentation will be clearest, however, if we focus on the basic form in [13.1.1] through [13.1.7].

[1]See, for example, Anderson and Moore (1979, pp. 105–8).

### *Examples of State-Space Representations*

Consider a univariate $AR(p)$ process,

$$y_{t+1} - \mu = \phi_1(y_t - \mu) + \phi_2(y_{t-1} - \mu) + \cdots + \phi_p(y_{t-p+1} - \mu) + \varepsilon_{t+1}, \qquad [13.1.13]$$

$$E(\varepsilon_t\varepsilon_\tau) = \begin{cases} \sigma^2 & \text{for } t = \tau \\ 0 & \text{otherwise.} \end{cases}$$

This could be written in state-space form as follows:

***State Equation*** $(r = p)$:

$$\begin{bmatrix} y_{t+1} - \mu \\ y_t - \mu \\ \vdots \\ y_{t-p+2} - \mu \end{bmatrix} = \begin{bmatrix} \phi_1 & \phi_2 & \cdots & \phi_{p-1} & \phi_p \\ 1 & 0 & \cdots & 0 & 0 \\ 0 & 1 & \cdots & 0 & 0 \\ \vdots & \vdots & \cdots & \vdots & \vdots \\ 0 & 0 & \cdots & 1 & 0 \end{bmatrix} \begin{bmatrix} y_t - \mu \\ y_{t-1} - \mu \\ \vdots \\ y_{t-p+1} - \mu \end{bmatrix} + \begin{bmatrix} \varepsilon_{t+1} \\ 0 \\ \vdots \\ 0 \end{bmatrix} \qquad [13.1.14]$$

***Observation Equation*** $(n = 1)$:

$$y_t = \mu + [1 \quad 0 \quad \cdots \quad 0] \begin{bmatrix} y_t - \mu \\ y_{t-1} - \mu \\ \vdots \\ y_{t-p+1} - \mu \end{bmatrix}. \qquad [13.1.15]$$

That is, we would specify

$$\boldsymbol{\xi}_t = \begin{bmatrix} y_t - \mu \\ y_{t-1} - \mu \\ \vdots \\ y_{t-p+1} - \mu \end{bmatrix} \qquad \mathbf{F} = \begin{bmatrix} \phi_1 & \phi_2 & \cdots & \phi_{p-1} & \phi_p \\ 1 & 0 & \cdots & 0 & 0 \\ 0 & 1 & \cdots & 0 & 0 \\ \vdots & \vdots & \cdots & \vdots & \vdots \\ 0 & 0 & \cdots & 1 & 0 \end{bmatrix}$$

$$\mathbf{v}_{t+1} = \begin{bmatrix} \varepsilon_{t+1} \\ 0 \\ \vdots \\ 0 \end{bmatrix} \qquad \mathbf{Q} = \begin{bmatrix} \sigma^2 & 0 & \cdots & 0 \\ 0 & 0 & \cdots & 0 \\ \vdots & \vdots & \cdots & \vdots \\ 0 & 0 & \cdots & 0 \end{bmatrix}$$

$$\mathbf{y}_t = y_t \qquad \mathbf{A}' = \mu \qquad \mathbf{x}_t = 1$$

$$\mathbf{H}' = [1 \quad 0 \quad \cdots \quad 0] \qquad \mathbf{w}_t = 0 \qquad \mathbf{R} = 0.$$

Note that the state equation here is simply the first-order vector difference equation introduced in equation [1.2.5]; $\mathbf{F}$ is the same matrix appearing in equation [1.2.3]. The observation equation here is a trivial identity. Thus, we have already seen that the state-space representation [13.1.14] and [13.1.15] is just another way of summarizing the $AR(p)$ process [13.1.13]. The reason for rewriting an $AR(p)$ process in such a form was to obtain a convenient summary of the system's dynamics, and this is the basic reason to be interested in the state-space representation of any system. The analysis of a vector autoregression using equation [10.1.11] employed a similar state-space representation.

As another example, consider a univariate $MA(1)$ process,

$$y_t = \mu + \varepsilon_t + \theta\varepsilon_{t-1}. \qquad [13.1.16]$$

This could be written in state-space form as follows:

***State Equation*** ($r = 2$):

$$\begin{bmatrix} \varepsilon_{t+1} \\ \varepsilon_t \end{bmatrix} = \begin{bmatrix} 0 & 0 \\ 1 & 0 \end{bmatrix} \begin{bmatrix} \varepsilon_t \\ \varepsilon_{t-1} \end{bmatrix} + \begin{bmatrix} \varepsilon_{t+1} \\ 0 \end{bmatrix} \qquad [13.1.17]$$

***Observation Equation*** ($n = 1$):

$$y_t = \mu + [1 \quad \theta] \begin{bmatrix} \varepsilon_t \\ \varepsilon_{t-1} \end{bmatrix}; \qquad [13.1.18]$$

that is,

$$\boldsymbol{\xi}_t = \begin{bmatrix} \varepsilon_t \\ \varepsilon_{t-1} \end{bmatrix} \qquad \mathbf{F} = \begin{bmatrix} 0 & 0 \\ 1 & 0 \end{bmatrix} \qquad \mathbf{v}_{t+1} = \begin{bmatrix} \varepsilon_{t+1} \\ 0 \end{bmatrix}$$

$$\mathbf{Q} = \begin{bmatrix} \sigma^2 & 0 \\ 0 & 0 \end{bmatrix} \qquad \mathbf{y}_t = y_t \qquad \mathbf{A}' = \mu \qquad \mathbf{x}_t = 1$$

$$\mathbf{H}' = [1 \quad \theta] \qquad \mathbf{w}_t = 0 \qquad \mathbf{R} = 0.$$

There are many ways to write a given system in state-space form. For example, the $MA(1)$ process [13.1.16] can also be represented in this way:

***State Equation*** ($r = 2$):

$$\begin{bmatrix} \varepsilon_{t+1} + \theta\varepsilon_t \\ \theta\varepsilon_{t+1} \end{bmatrix} = \begin{bmatrix} 0 & 1 \\ 0 & 0 \end{bmatrix} \begin{bmatrix} \varepsilon_t + \theta\varepsilon_{t-1} \\ \theta\varepsilon_t \end{bmatrix} + \begin{bmatrix} \varepsilon_{t+1} \\ \theta\varepsilon_{t+1} \end{bmatrix} \qquad [13.1.19]$$

***Observation Equation*** ($n = 1$):

$$y_t = \mu + [1 \quad 0] \begin{bmatrix} \varepsilon_t + \theta\varepsilon_{t-1} \\ \theta\varepsilon_t \end{bmatrix}. \qquad [13.1.20]$$

Note that the original $MA(1)$ representation of [13.1.16], the first state-space representation of [13.1.17] and [13.1.18], and the second state-space representation of [13.1.19] and [13.1.20] all characterize the same process. We will obtain the identical forecasts of the process or value for the likelihood function from any of the three representations and can feel free to work with whichever is most convenient.

More generally, a univariate $ARMA(p, q)$ process can be written in state-space form by defining $r \equiv \max\{p, q + 1\}$:

$$\begin{aligned} y_t - \mu = {} & \phi_1(y_{t-1} - \mu) + \phi_2(y_{t-2} - \mu) + \cdots + \phi_r(y_{t-r} - \mu) \\ & + \varepsilon_t + \theta_1\varepsilon_{t-1} + \theta_2\varepsilon_{t-2} + \cdots + \theta_{r-1}\varepsilon_{t-r+1}, \end{aligned} \qquad [13.1.21]$$

where we interpret $\phi_j = 0$ for $j > p$ and $\theta_j = 0$ for $j > q$. Consider the following state-space representation;

***State Equation*** ($r = \max\{p, q + 1\}$):

$$\boldsymbol{\xi}_{t+1} = \begin{bmatrix} \phi_1 & \phi_2 & \cdots & \phi_{r-1} & \phi_r \\ 1 & 0 & \cdots & 0 & 0 \\ 0 & 1 & \cdots & 0 & 0 \\ \vdots & \vdots & \cdots & \vdots & \vdots \\ 0 & 0 & \cdots & 1 & 0 \end{bmatrix} \boldsymbol{\xi}_t + \begin{bmatrix} \varepsilon_{t+1} \\ 0 \\ \vdots \\ 0 \end{bmatrix} \qquad [13.1.22]$$

***Observation Equation*** ($n = 1$):

$$y_t = \mu + [1 \quad \theta_1 \quad \theta_2 \quad \cdots \quad \theta_{r-1}]\boldsymbol{\xi}_t. \qquad [13.1.23]$$

To verify that [13.1.22] and [13.1.23] describe the same process as [13.1.21], let $\xi_{jt}$ denote the $j$th element of $\boldsymbol{\xi}_t$. Thus, the second row of the state equation asserts that

$$\xi_{2,t+1} = \xi_{1t}.$$

The third row asserts that

$$\xi_{3,t+1} = \xi_{2t} = \xi_{1,t-1},$$

and in general the $j$th row implies that

$$\xi_{j,t+1} = L^{j-1}\xi_{1,t+1}.$$

Thus, the first row of the state equation implies that

$$\xi_{1,t+1} = (\phi_1 + \phi_2 L + \phi_3 L^2 + \cdots + \phi_r L^{r-1})\xi_{1t} + \varepsilon_{t+1}$$

or

$$(1 - \phi_1 L - \phi_2 L^2 - \cdots - \phi_r L^r)\xi_{1,t+1} = \varepsilon_{t+1}. \qquad [13.1.24]$$

The observation equation states that

$$y_t = \mu + (1 + \theta_1 L + \theta_2 L^2 + \cdots + \theta_{r-1}L^{r-1})\xi_{1t}. \qquad [13.1.25]$$

Multiplying [13.1.25] by $(1 - \phi_1 L - \phi_2 L^2 - \cdots - \phi_r L^r)$ and using [13.1.24] gives

$$(1 - \phi_1 L - \phi_2 L^2 - \cdots - \phi_r L^r)(y_t - \mu) = (1 + \theta_1 L + \theta_2 L^2 + \cdots + \theta_{r-1}L^{r-1})\varepsilon_t,$$

which indeed reproduces [13.1.21].

The state-space form can also be very convenient for modeling sums of stochastic processes or the consequences of measurement error. For example, Fama and Gibbons (1982) wanted to study the behavior of the ex ante real interest rate (the nominal interest rate $i_t$ minus the expected inflation rate $\pi_t^e$). This variable is unobserved, because the econometrician does not have data on the rate of inflation anticipated by the bond market. Thus, the state variable for this application was the scalar $\xi_t = i_t - \pi_t^e - \mu$, where $\mu$ denotes the average ex ante real interest rate. Fama and Gibbons assumed that the ex ante real rate follows an $AR(1)$ process:

$$\xi_{t+1} = \phi\xi_t + v_{t+1}. \qquad [13.1.26]$$

The econometrician has observations on the ex post real rate (the nominal interest rate $i_t$ minus actual inflation $\pi_t$), which can be written as

$$i_t - \pi_t = (i_t - \pi_t^e) + (\pi_t^e - \pi_t) = \mu + \xi_t + w_t, \qquad [13.1.27]$$

where $w_t \equiv (\pi_t^e - \pi_t)$ is the error that people make in forecasting inflation. If people form these forecasts optimally, then $w_t$ should be uncorrelated with its own lagged values or with the ex ante real interest rate. Thus, [13.1.26] and [13.1.27] are the state equation and observation equation for a state-space model with $r = n = 1$, $\mathbf{F} = \phi$, $y_t = i_t - \pi_t$, $\mathbf{A}'\mathbf{x}_t = \mu$, $\mathbf{H} = 1$, and $w_t = (\pi_t^e - \pi_t)$.

In another interesting application of the state-space framework, Stock and Watson (1991) postulated the existence of an unobserved scalar $C_t$ that represents the state of the business cycle. A set of $n$ different observed macroeconomic variables $(y_{1t}, y_{2t}, \ldots, y_{nt})$ are each assumed to be influenced by the business cycle and also to have an idiosyncratic component (denoted $\chi_{it}$) that is unrelated to movements in $y_{jt}$ for $i \neq j$. If the business cycle and each of the idiosyncratic components could be described by univariate $AR(1)$ processes, then the $[(n + 1) \times 1]$ state vector would be

$$\boldsymbol{\xi}_t = \begin{bmatrix} C_t \\ \chi_{1t} \\ \chi_{2t} \\ \vdots \\ \chi_{nt} \end{bmatrix} \qquad [13.1.28]$$

with state equation

$$\begin{bmatrix} C_{t+1} \\ \chi_{1,t+1} \\ \chi_{2,t+1} \\ \vdots \\ \chi_{n,t+1} \end{bmatrix} = \begin{bmatrix} \phi_C & 0 & 0 & \cdots & 0 \\ 0 & \phi_1 & 0 & \cdots & 0 \\ 0 & 0 & \phi_2 & \cdots & 0 \\ \vdots & \vdots & \vdots & \cdots & \vdots \\ 0 & 0 & 0 & \cdots & \phi_n \end{bmatrix} \begin{bmatrix} C_t \\ \chi_{1t} \\ \chi_{2t} \\ \vdots \\ \chi_{nt} \end{bmatrix} + \begin{bmatrix} v_{C,t+1} \\ v_{1,t+1} \\ v_{2,t+1} \\ \vdots \\ v_{n,t+1} \end{bmatrix} \qquad [13.1.29]$$

and observation equation

$$\begin{bmatrix} y_{1t} \\ y_{2t} \\ \vdots \\ y_{nt} \end{bmatrix} = \begin{bmatrix} \mu_1 \\ \mu_2 \\ \vdots \\ \mu_n \end{bmatrix} + \begin{bmatrix} \gamma_1 & 1 & 0 & \cdots & 0 \\ \gamma_2 & 0 & 1 & \cdots & 0 \\ \vdots & \vdots & \vdots & \cdots & \vdots \\ \gamma_n & 0 & 0 & \cdots & 1 \end{bmatrix} \begin{bmatrix} C_t \\ \chi_{1t} \\ \chi_{2t} \\ \vdots \\ \chi_{nt} \end{bmatrix}. \qquad [13.1.30]$$

Thus, $\gamma_i$ is a parameter that describes the sensitivity of the $i$th series to the business cycle. To allow for $p$th-order dynamics, Stock and Watson replaced $C_t$ and $\chi_{it}$ in [13.1.28] with the $(p \times 1)$ vectors $(C_t, C_{t-1}, \ldots, C_{t-p+1})'$ and $(\chi_{it}, \chi_{i,t-1}, \ldots, \chi_{i,t-p+1})'$ so that $\boldsymbol{\xi}_t$ is an $[(n+1)p \times 1]$ vector. The scalars $\phi_i$ in [13.1.29] are then replaced by $(p \times p)$ matrices $\mathbf{F}_i$ with the structure of the matrix $\mathbf{F}$ in [13.1.14], and $[n \times (p-1)]$ blocks of zeros are added between the columns of $\mathbf{H}'$ in the observation equation [13.1.30].

## 13.2. *Derivation of the Kalman Filter*

### *Overview of the Kalman Filter*

Consider the general state-space system [13.1.1] through [13.1.7], whose key equations are reproduced here for convenience:

$$\underset{(r\times 1)}{\boldsymbol{\xi}_{t+1}} = \underset{(r\times r)(r\times 1)}{\mathbf{F}\cdot\boldsymbol{\xi}_t} + \underset{(r\times 1)}{\mathbf{v}_{t+1}} \qquad [13.2.1]$$

$$\underset{(n\times 1)}{\mathbf{y}_t} = \underset{(n\times k)(k\times 1)}{\mathbf{A}'\cdot\mathbf{x}_t} + \underset{(n\times r)(r\times 1)}{\mathbf{H}'\cdot\boldsymbol{\xi}_t} + \underset{(n\times 1)}{\mathbf{w}_t} \qquad [13.2.2]$$

$$E(\mathbf{v}_t\mathbf{v}_\tau') = \begin{cases} \underset{(r\times r)}{\mathbf{Q}} & \text{for } t = \tau \\ \mathbf{0} & \text{otherwise} \end{cases} \qquad [13.2.3]$$

$$E(\mathbf{w}_t\mathbf{w}_\tau') = \begin{cases} \underset{(n\times n)}{\mathbf{R}} & \text{for } t = \tau \\ \mathbf{0} & \text{otherwise.} \end{cases} \qquad [13.2.4]$$

The analyst is presumed to have observed $\mathbf{y}_1, \mathbf{y}_2, \ldots, \mathbf{y}_T, \mathbf{x}_1, \mathbf{x}_2, \ldots, \mathbf{x}_T$. One of the ultimate objectives may be to estimate the values of any unknown parameters in the system on the basis of these observations. For now, however, we will assume that the particular numerical values of $\mathbf{F}$, $\mathbf{Q}$, $\mathbf{A}$, $\mathbf{H}$, and $\mathbf{R}$ are known with certainty; Section 13.4 will give details on how these parameters can be estimated from the data.

There are many uses of the Kalman filter. It is motivated here as an algorithm for calculating linear least squares forecasts of the state vector on the basis of data observed through date $t$,

$$\hat{\boldsymbol{\xi}}_{t+1|t} \equiv \hat{E}(\boldsymbol{\xi}_{t+1}|\boldsymbol{\mathcal{Y}}_t),$$

where

$$\boldsymbol{\mathcal{Y}}_t \equiv (\mathbf{y}_t', \mathbf{y}_{t-1}', \ldots, \mathbf{y}_1', \mathbf{x}_t', \mathbf{x}_{t-1}', \ldots, \mathbf{x}_1')' \qquad [13.2.5]$$

and $\hat{E}(\boldsymbol{\xi}_{t+1}|\boldsymbol{\mathcal{Y}}_t)$ denotes the linear projection of $\boldsymbol{\xi}_{t+1}$ on $\boldsymbol{\mathcal{Y}}_t$ and a constant. The Kalman filter calculates these forecasts recursively, generating $\hat{\boldsymbol{\xi}}_{1|0}, \hat{\boldsymbol{\xi}}_{2|1}, \ldots,$

$\hat{\boldsymbol{\xi}}_{T|T-1}$ in succession. Associated with each of these forecasts is a mean squared error ($MSE$) matrix, represented by the following $(r \times r)$ matrix:

$$\mathbf{P}_{t+1|t} \equiv E[(\boldsymbol{\xi}_{t+1} - \hat{\boldsymbol{\xi}}_{t+1|t})(\boldsymbol{\xi}_{t+1} - \hat{\boldsymbol{\xi}}_{t+1|t})']. \qquad [13.2.6]$$

## *Starting the Recursion*

The recursion begins with $\hat{\boldsymbol{\xi}}_{1|0}$, which denotes a forecast of $\boldsymbol{\xi}_1$ based on no observations of $\mathbf{y}$ or $\mathbf{x}$. This is just the unconditional mean of $\boldsymbol{\xi}_1$,

$$\hat{\boldsymbol{\xi}}_{1|0} = E(\boldsymbol{\xi}_1),$$

with associated $MSE$

$$\mathbf{P}_{1|0} = E\{[\boldsymbol{\xi}_1 - E(\boldsymbol{\xi}_1)][\boldsymbol{\xi}_1 - E(\boldsymbol{\xi}_1)]'\}.$$

For example, for the state-space representation of the $MA(1)$ system given in [13.1.17] and [13.1.18], the state vector was

$$\boldsymbol{\xi}_t = \begin{bmatrix} \varepsilon_t \\ \varepsilon_{t-1} \end{bmatrix},$$

for which

$$\hat{\boldsymbol{\xi}}_{1|0} = E\begin{bmatrix} \varepsilon_1 \\ \varepsilon_0 \end{bmatrix} = \begin{bmatrix} 0 \\ 0 \end{bmatrix} \qquad [13.2.7]$$

$$\mathbf{P}_{1|0} = E\left(\begin{bmatrix} \varepsilon_1 \\ \varepsilon_0 \end{bmatrix} [\varepsilon_1 \quad \varepsilon_0]\right) = \begin{bmatrix} \sigma^2 & 0 \\ 0 & \sigma^2 \end{bmatrix}, \qquad [13.2.8]$$

where $\sigma^2 = E(\varepsilon_t^2)$.

More generally, if eigenvalues of $\mathbf{F}$ are all inside the unit circle, then the process for $\boldsymbol{\xi}_t$ in [13.2.1] is covariance-stationary. The unconditional mean of $\boldsymbol{\xi}_t$ can be found by taking expectations of both sides of [13.2.1], producing

$$E(\boldsymbol{\xi}_{t+1}) = \mathbf{F}\cdot E(\boldsymbol{\xi}_t),$$

or, since $\boldsymbol{\xi}_t$ is covariance-stationary,

$$(\mathbf{I}_r - \mathbf{F})\cdot E(\boldsymbol{\xi}_t) = \mathbf{0}.$$

Since unity is not an eigenvalue of $\mathbf{F}$, the matrix $(\mathbf{I}_r - \mathbf{F})$ is nonsingular, and this equation has the unique solution $E(\boldsymbol{\xi}_t) = \mathbf{0}$. The unconditional variance of $\boldsymbol{\xi}$ can similarly be found by postmultiplying [13.2.1] by its transpose and taking expectations:

$$E(\boldsymbol{\xi}_{t+1}\boldsymbol{\xi}'_{t+1}) = E[(\mathbf{F}\boldsymbol{\xi}_t + \mathbf{v}_{t+1})(\boldsymbol{\xi}'_t\mathbf{F}' + \mathbf{v}'_{t+1})] = \mathbf{F}\cdot E(\boldsymbol{\xi}_t\boldsymbol{\xi}'_t)\cdot\mathbf{F}' + E(\mathbf{v}_{t+1}\mathbf{v}'_{t+1}).$$

Cross-product terms have disappeared in light of [13.1.9]. Letting $\boldsymbol{\Sigma}$ denote the variance-covariance matrix of $\boldsymbol{\xi}$, this equation implies

$$\boldsymbol{\Sigma} = \mathbf{F}\boldsymbol{\Sigma}\mathbf{F}' + \mathbf{Q},$$

whose solution was seen in [10.2.18] to be given by

$$\text{vec}(\boldsymbol{\Sigma}) = [\mathbf{I}_{r^2} - (\mathbf{F} \otimes \mathbf{F})]^{-1}\cdot\text{vec}(\mathbf{Q}).$$

Thus, in general, provided that the eigenvalues of $\mathbf{F}$ are inside the unit circle, the Kalman filter iterations can be started with $\hat{\boldsymbol{\xi}}_{1|0} = \mathbf{0}$ and $\mathbf{P}_{1|0}$ the $(r \times r)$ matrix whose elements expressed as a column vector are given by

$$\text{vec}(\mathbf{P}_{1|0}) = [\mathbf{I}_{r^2} - (\mathbf{F} \otimes \mathbf{F})]^{-1}\cdot\text{vec}(\mathbf{Q}).$$

If instead some eigenvalues of $\mathbf{F}$ are on or outside the unit circle, or if the initial state $\boldsymbol{\xi}_1$ is not regarded as an arbitrary draw from the process implied by [13.2.1], then $\hat{\boldsymbol{\xi}}_{1|0}$ can be replaced with the analyst's best guess as to the initial value of $\boldsymbol{\xi}_1$, where $\mathbf{P}_{1|0}$ is a positive definite matrix summarizing the confidence in this guess. Larger values for the diagonal elements of $\mathbf{P}_{1|0}$ register greater uncertainty about the true value of $\boldsymbol{\xi}_1$.

## *Forecasting* $\mathbf{y}_t$

Given starting values $\hat{\boldsymbol{\xi}}_{1|0}$ and $\mathbf{P}_{1|0}$, the next step is to calculate analogous magnitudes for the following date, $\hat{\boldsymbol{\xi}}_{2|1}$ and $\mathbf{P}_{2|1}$. The calculations for $t = 2, 3, \ldots, T$ all have the same basic form, so we will describe them in general terms for step $t$; given $\hat{\boldsymbol{\xi}}_{t|t-1}$ and $\mathbf{P}_{t|t-1}$, the goal is to calculate $\hat{\boldsymbol{\xi}}_{t+1|t}$ and $\mathbf{P}_{t+1|t}$.

First note that since we have assumed that $\mathbf{x}_t$ contains no information about $\boldsymbol{\xi}_t$ beyond that contained in $\mathcal{Y}_{t-1}$,

$$\hat{E}(\boldsymbol{\xi}_t|\mathbf{x}_t, \mathcal{Y}_{t-1}) = \hat{E}(\boldsymbol{\xi}_t|\mathcal{Y}_{t-1}) = \hat{\boldsymbol{\xi}}_{t|t-1}.$$

Next consider forecasting the value of $\mathbf{y}_t$:

$$\hat{\mathbf{y}}_{t|t-1} \equiv \hat{E}(\mathbf{y}_t|\mathbf{x}_t, \mathcal{Y}_{t-1}).$$

Notice from [13.2.2] that

$$\hat{E}(\mathbf{y}_t|\mathbf{x}_t, \boldsymbol{\xi}_t) = \mathbf{A}'\mathbf{x}_t + \mathbf{H}'\boldsymbol{\xi}_t,$$

and so, from the law of iterated projections,

$$\hat{\mathbf{y}}_{t|t-1} = \mathbf{A}'\mathbf{x}_t + \mathbf{H}'\cdot\hat{E}(\boldsymbol{\xi}_t|\mathbf{x}_t, \mathcal{Y}_{t-1}) = \mathbf{A}'\mathbf{x}_t + \mathbf{H}'\hat{\boldsymbol{\xi}}_{t|t-1}. \qquad [13.2.9]$$

From [13.2.2], the error of this forecast is

$$\mathbf{y}_t - \hat{\mathbf{y}}_{t|t-1} = \mathbf{A}'\mathbf{x}_t + \mathbf{H}'\boldsymbol{\xi}_t + \mathbf{w}_t - \mathbf{A}'\mathbf{x}_t - \mathbf{H}'\hat{\boldsymbol{\xi}}_{t|t-1} = \mathbf{H}'(\boldsymbol{\xi}_t - \hat{\boldsymbol{\xi}}_{t|t-1}) + \mathbf{w}_t$$

with *MSE*

$$\begin{aligned} &E[(\mathbf{y}_t - \hat{\mathbf{y}}_{t|t-1})(\mathbf{y}_t - \hat{\mathbf{y}}_{t|t-1})'] \\ &\qquad = E[\mathbf{H}'(\boldsymbol{\xi}_t - \hat{\boldsymbol{\xi}}_{t|t-1})(\boldsymbol{\xi}_t - \hat{\boldsymbol{\xi}}_{t|t-1})'\mathbf{H}] + E[\mathbf{w}_t\mathbf{w}_t']. \end{aligned} \qquad [13.2.10]$$

Cross-product terms have disappeared, since

$$E[\mathbf{w}_t(\boldsymbol{\xi}_t - \hat{\boldsymbol{\xi}}_{t|t-1})'] = \mathbf{0}. \qquad [13.2.11]$$

To justify [13.2.11], recall from [13.1.10] that $\mathbf{w}_t$ is uncorrelated with $\boldsymbol{\xi}_t$. Furthermore, since $\hat{\boldsymbol{\xi}}_{t|t-1}$ is a linear function of $\mathcal{Y}_{t-1}$, by [13.1.11] it too must be uncorrelated with $\mathbf{w}_t$.

Using [13.2.4] and [13.2.6], equation [13.2.10] can be written

$$E[(\mathbf{y}_t - \hat{\mathbf{y}}_{t|t-1})(\mathbf{y}_t - \hat{\mathbf{y}}_{t|t-1})'] = \mathbf{H}'\mathbf{P}_{t|t-1}\mathbf{H} + \mathbf{R}. \qquad [13.2.12]$$

## *Updating the Inference About* $\boldsymbol{\xi}_t$

Next the inference about the current value of $\boldsymbol{\xi}_t$ is updated on the basis of the observation of $\mathbf{y}_t$ to produce

$$\hat{\boldsymbol{\xi}}_{t|t} = \hat{E}(\boldsymbol{\xi}_t|\mathbf{y}_t, \mathbf{x}_t, \mathcal{Y}_{t-1}) = \hat{E}(\boldsymbol{\xi}_t|\mathcal{Y}_t).$$

This can be evaluated using the formula for updating a linear projection, equation [4.5.30]:[2]

$$\begin{aligned} \hat{\boldsymbol{\xi}}_{t|t} = \hat{\boldsymbol{\xi}}_{t|t-1} &+ \{E[(\boldsymbol{\xi}_t - \hat{\boldsymbol{\xi}}_{t|t-1})(\mathbf{y}_t - \hat{\mathbf{y}}_{t|t-1})']\} \\ &\times \{E[(\mathbf{y}_t - \hat{\mathbf{y}}_{t|t-1})(\mathbf{y}_t - \hat{\mathbf{y}}_{t|t-1})']\}^{-1} \times (\mathbf{y}_t - \hat{\mathbf{y}}_{t|t-1}). \end{aligned} \qquad [13.2.13]$$

[2]Here $\boldsymbol{\xi}_t$ corresponds to $\mathbf{Y}_3$, $\mathbf{y}_t$ corresponds to $\mathbf{Y}_2$, and $(\mathbf{x}_t', \mathcal{Y}_{t-1}')'$ corresponds to $\mathbf{Y}_1$ in equation [4.5.30].

But

$$\begin{aligned} &E\{(\xi_t - \hat{\xi}_{t|t-1})(\mathbf{y}_t - \hat{\mathbf{y}}_{t|t-1})'\} \\ &\quad = E\{[\xi_t - \hat{\xi}_{t|t-1}][\mathbf{H}'(\xi_t - \hat{\xi}_{t|t-1}) + \mathbf{w}_t]'\} \\ &\quad = E[(\xi_t - \hat{\xi}_{t|t-1})(\xi_t - \hat{\xi}_{t|t-1})'\mathbf{H}] \\ &\quad = \mathbf{P}_{t|t-1}\mathbf{H} \end{aligned} \qquad [13.2.14]$$

by virtue of [13.2.11] and [13.2.6]. Substituting [13.2.14], [13.2.12], and [13.2.9] into [13.2.13] gives

$$\hat{\xi}_{t|t} = \hat{\xi}_{t|t-1} + \mathbf{P}_{t|t-1}\mathbf{H}(\mathbf{H}'\mathbf{P}_{t|t-1}\mathbf{H} + \mathbf{R})^{-1}(\mathbf{y}_t - \mathbf{A}'\mathbf{x}_t - \mathbf{H}'\hat{\xi}_{t|t-1}). \qquad [13.2.15]$$

The *MSE* associated with this updated projection, which is denoted $\mathbf{P}_{t|t}$, can be found from [4.5.31]:

$$\begin{aligned} \mathbf{P}_{t|t} &\equiv E[(\xi_t - \hat{\xi}_{t|t})(\xi_t - \hat{\xi}_{t|t})'] \\ &= E[(\xi_t - \hat{\xi}_{t|t-1})(\xi_t - \hat{\xi}_{t|t-1})'] \\ &\quad - \{E[(\xi_t - \hat{\xi}_{t|t-1})(\mathbf{y}_t - \hat{\mathbf{y}}_{t|t-1})']\} \\ &\quad \times \{E[(\mathbf{y}_t - \hat{\mathbf{y}}_{t|t-1})(\mathbf{y}_t - \hat{\mathbf{y}}_{t|t-1})']\}^{-1} \\ &\quad \times \{E[(\mathbf{y}_t - \hat{\mathbf{y}}_{t|t-1})(\xi_t - \hat{\xi}_{t|t-1})']\} \\ &= \mathbf{P}_{t|t-1} - \mathbf{P}_{t|t-1}\mathbf{H}(\mathbf{H}'\mathbf{P}_{t|t-1}\mathbf{H} + \mathbf{R})^{-1}\mathbf{H}'\mathbf{P}_{t|t-1}. \end{aligned} \qquad [13.2.16]$$

### *Producing a Forecast of* $\xi_{t+1}$

Next, the state equation [13.2.1] is used to forecast $\xi_{t+1}$:

$$\begin{aligned} \hat{\xi}_{t+1|t} &= \hat{E}(\xi_{t+1}|\mathcal{Y}_t) \\ &= \mathbf{F}\cdot\hat{E}(\xi_t|\mathcal{Y}_t) + \hat{E}(\mathbf{v}_{t+1}|\mathcal{Y}_t) \\ &= \mathbf{F}\hat{\xi}_{t|t} + \mathbf{0}. \end{aligned} \qquad [13.2.17]$$

Substituting [13.2.15] into [13.2.17],

$$\begin{aligned} \hat{\xi}_{t+1|t} &= \mathbf{F}\hat{\xi}_{t|t-1} \\ &\quad + \mathbf{F}\mathbf{P}_{t|t-1}\mathbf{H}(\mathbf{H}'\mathbf{P}_{t|t-1}\mathbf{H} + \mathbf{R})^{-1}(\mathbf{y}_t - \mathbf{A}'\mathbf{x}_t - \mathbf{H}'\hat{\xi}_{t|t-1}). \end{aligned} \qquad [13.2.18]$$

The coefficient matrix in [13.2.18] is known as the *gain matrix* and is denoted $\mathbf{K}_t$:

$$\mathbf{K}_t \equiv \mathbf{F}\mathbf{P}_{t|t-1}\mathbf{H}(\mathbf{H}'\mathbf{P}_{t|t-1}\mathbf{H} + \mathbf{R})^{-1}, \qquad [13.2.19]$$

allowing [13.2.18] to be written

$$\hat{\xi}_{t+1|t} = \mathbf{F}\hat{\xi}_{t|t-1} + \mathbf{K}_t(\mathbf{y}_t - \mathbf{A}'\mathbf{x}_t - \mathbf{H}'\hat{\xi}_{t|t-1}). \qquad [13.2.20]$$

The *MSE* of this forecast can be found from [13.2.17] and the state equation [13.2.1]:

$$\begin{aligned} \mathbf{P}_{t+1|t} &= E[(\xi_{t+1} - \hat{\xi}_{t+1|t})(\xi_{t+1} - \hat{\xi}_{t+1|t})'] \\ &= E[(\mathbf{F}\xi_t + \mathbf{v}_{t+1} - \mathbf{F}\hat{\xi}_{t|t})(\mathbf{F}\xi_t + \mathbf{v}_{t+1} - \mathbf{F}\hat{\xi}_{t|t})'] \\ &= \mathbf{F}\cdot E[(\xi_t - \hat{\xi}_{t|t})(\xi_t - \hat{\xi}_{t|t})']\cdot\mathbf{F}' + E[\mathbf{v}_{t+1}\mathbf{v}_{t+1}'] \\ &= \mathbf{F}\mathbf{P}_{t|t}\mathbf{F}' + \mathbf{Q}, \end{aligned} \qquad [13.2.21]$$

with cross-product terms again clearly zero. Substituting [13.2.16] into [13.2.21] produces

$$\mathbf{P}_{t+1|t} = \mathbf{F}[\mathbf{P}_{t|t-1} - \mathbf{P}_{t|t-1}\mathbf{H}(\mathbf{H}'\mathbf{P}_{t|t-1}\mathbf{H} + \mathbf{R})^{-1}\mathbf{H}'\mathbf{P}_{t|t-1}]\mathbf{F}' + \mathbf{Q}. \qquad [13.2.22]$$

*Summary and Remarks*

To summarize, the Kalman filter is started with the unconditional mean and variance of $\boldsymbol{\xi}_1$:

$$\hat{\boldsymbol{\xi}}_{1|0} = E(\boldsymbol{\xi}_1)$$
$$\mathbf{P}_{1|0} = E\{[\boldsymbol{\xi}_1 - E(\boldsymbol{\xi}_1)][\boldsymbol{\xi}_1 - E(\boldsymbol{\xi}_1)]'\}.$$

Typically, these are given by $\hat{\boldsymbol{\xi}}_{1|0} = \mathbf{0}$ and $\text{vec}(\mathbf{P}_{1|0}) = [\mathbf{I}_{r^2} - (\mathbf{F} \otimes \mathbf{F})]^{-1} \cdot \text{vec}(\mathbf{Q})$. We then iterate on

$$\hat{\boldsymbol{\xi}}_{t+1|t} = \mathbf{F}\hat{\boldsymbol{\xi}}_{t|t-1} + \mathbf{F}\mathbf{P}_{t|t-1}\mathbf{H}(\mathbf{H}'\mathbf{P}_{t|t-1}\mathbf{H} + \mathbf{R})^{-1}(\mathbf{y}_t - \mathbf{A}'\mathbf{x}_t - \mathbf{H}'\hat{\boldsymbol{\xi}}_{t|t-1}) \qquad [13.2.23]$$

and [13.2.22] for $t = 1, 2, \ldots, T$. The value $\hat{\boldsymbol{\xi}}_{t+1|t}$ denotes the best forecast of $\boldsymbol{\xi}_{t+1}$ based on a constant and a linear function of $(\mathbf{y}_t, \mathbf{y}_{t-1}, \ldots, \mathbf{y}_1, \mathbf{x}_t, \mathbf{x}_{t-1}, \ldots, \mathbf{x}_1)$. The matrix $\mathbf{P}_{t+1|t}$ gives the *MSE* of this forecast. The forecast of $\mathbf{y}_{t+1}$ is given by

$$\hat{\mathbf{y}}_{t+1|t} \equiv \hat{E}(\mathbf{y}_{t+1}|\mathbf{x}_{t+1}, \mathcal{Y}_t) = \mathbf{A}'\mathbf{x}_{t+1} + \mathbf{H}'\hat{\boldsymbol{\xi}}_{t+1|t} \qquad [13.2.24]$$

with associated *MSE*

$$E[(\mathbf{y}_{t+1} - \hat{\mathbf{y}}_{t+1|t})(\mathbf{y}_{t+1} - \hat{\mathbf{y}}_{t+1|t})'] = \mathbf{H}'\mathbf{P}_{t+1|t}\mathbf{H} + \mathbf{R}. \qquad [13.2.25]$$

It is worth noting that the recursion in [13.2.22] could be calculated without ever evaluating [13.2.23]. The values for $\mathbf{P}_{t|t-1}$ in [13.2.22] and $\mathbf{K}_t$ in [13.2.19] are not functions of the data, but instead are determined entirely by the population parameters of the process.

An alternative way of writing the recursion for $\mathbf{P}_{t+1|t}$ is sometimes useful. Subtracting the Kalman updating equation [13.2.20] from the state equation [13.2.1] produces

$$\boldsymbol{\xi}_{t+1} - \hat{\boldsymbol{\xi}}_{t+1|t} = \mathbf{F}(\boldsymbol{\xi}_t - \hat{\boldsymbol{\xi}}_{t|t-1}) - \mathbf{K}_t(\mathbf{y}_t - \mathbf{A}'\mathbf{x}_t - \mathbf{H}'\hat{\boldsymbol{\xi}}_{t|t-1}) + \mathbf{v}_{t+1}. \qquad [13.2.26]$$

Further substituting the observation equation [13.2.2] into [13.2.26] results in

$$\boldsymbol{\xi}_{t+1} - \hat{\boldsymbol{\xi}}_{t+1|t} = (\mathbf{F} - \mathbf{K}_t\mathbf{H}')(\boldsymbol{\xi}_t - \hat{\boldsymbol{\xi}}_{t|t-1}) - \mathbf{K}_t\mathbf{w}_t + \mathbf{v}_{t+1}. \qquad [13.2.27]$$

Postmultiplying [13.2.27] by its transpose and taking expectations,

$$E[(\boldsymbol{\xi}_{t+1} - \hat{\boldsymbol{\xi}}_{t+1|t})(\boldsymbol{\xi}_{t+1} - \hat{\boldsymbol{\xi}}_{t+1|t})'] = (\mathbf{F} - \mathbf{K}_t\mathbf{H}')E[(\boldsymbol{\xi}_t - \hat{\boldsymbol{\xi}}_{t|t-1})(\boldsymbol{\xi}_t - \hat{\boldsymbol{\xi}}_{t|t-1})'](\mathbf{F}' - \mathbf{H}\mathbf{K}_t') + \mathbf{K}_t\mathbf{R}\mathbf{K}_t' + \mathbf{Q};$$

or, recalling the definition of $\mathbf{P}_{t+1|t}$ in equation [13.2.6],

$$\mathbf{P}_{t+1|t} = (\mathbf{F} - \mathbf{K}_t\mathbf{H}')\mathbf{P}_{t|t-1}(\mathbf{F}' - \mathbf{H}\mathbf{K}_t') + \mathbf{K}_t\mathbf{R}\mathbf{K}_t' + \mathbf{Q}. \qquad [13.2.28]$$

Equation [13.2.28] along with the definition of $\mathbf{K}_t$ in [13.2.19] will produce the same sequence generated by equation [13.2.22].

## 13.3. *Forecasts Based on the State-Space Representation*

The Kalman filter computations in [13.2.22] through [13.2.25] are normally calculated by computer, using the known numerical values of **F**, **Q**, **A**, **H**, and **R** along with the actual data. To help make the ideas more concrete, however, we now explore analytically the outcome of these calculations for a simple example.

### *Example—Using the Kalman Filter to Find Exact Finite-Sample Forecasts for an* MA(*1*) *Process*

Consider again a state-space representation for the $MA(1)$ process:

***State Equation*** ($r = 2$):

$$\begin{bmatrix} \varepsilon_{t+1} \\ \varepsilon_t \end{bmatrix} = \begin{bmatrix} 0 & 0 \\ 1 & 0 \end{bmatrix} \begin{bmatrix} \varepsilon_t \\ \varepsilon_{t-1} \end{bmatrix} + \begin{bmatrix} \varepsilon_{t+1} \\ 0 \end{bmatrix} \qquad [13.3.1]$$

***Observation Equation*** ($n = 1$):

$$y_t = \mu + [1 \quad \theta] \begin{bmatrix} \varepsilon_t \\ \varepsilon_{t-1} \end{bmatrix} \qquad [13.3.2]$$

$$\boldsymbol{\xi}_t = \begin{bmatrix} \varepsilon_t \\ \varepsilon_{t-1} \end{bmatrix} \qquad [13.3.3]$$

$$\mathbf{F} = \begin{bmatrix} 0 & 0 \\ 1 & 0 \end{bmatrix} \qquad [13.3.4]$$

$$\mathbf{v}_{t+1} = \begin{bmatrix} \varepsilon_{t+1} \\ 0 \end{bmatrix} \qquad [13.3.5]$$

$$\mathbf{Q} = \begin{bmatrix} \sigma^2 & 0 \\ 0 & 0 \end{bmatrix} \qquad [13.3.6]$$

$$\mathbf{y}_t = y_t \qquad [13.3.7]$$

$$\mathbf{A}' = \mu \qquad [13.3.8]$$

$$\mathbf{x}_t = 1 \qquad [13.3.9]$$

$$\mathbf{H}' = [1 \quad \theta] \qquad [13.3.10]$$

$$\mathbf{w}_t = 0 \qquad [13.3.11]$$

$$\mathbf{R} = 0. \qquad [13.3.12]$$

The starting values for the filter were described in [13.2.7] and [13.2.8]:

$$\hat{\boldsymbol{\xi}}_{1|0} = \begin{bmatrix} 0 \\ 0 \end{bmatrix}$$

$$\mathbf{P}_{1|0} = \begin{bmatrix} \sigma^2 & 0 \\ 0 & \sigma^2 \end{bmatrix}.$$

Thus, from [13.2.24], the period 1 forecast is

$$\hat{y}_{1|0} = \mu + \mathbf{H}'\hat{\boldsymbol{\xi}}_{1|0} = \mu,$$

with $MSE$ given by [13.2.25]:

$$E(y_1 - \hat{y}_{1|0})^2 = \mathbf{H}'\mathbf{P}_{1|0}\mathbf{H} + \mathbf{R} = [1 \quad \theta] \begin{bmatrix} \sigma^2 & 0 \\ 0 & \sigma^2 \end{bmatrix} \begin{bmatrix} 1 \\ \theta \end{bmatrix} + 0 = \sigma^2(1 + \theta^2).$$

These, of course, are just the unconditional mean and variance of $y$.

To see the structure of the recursion for $t = 2, 3, \ldots, T$, consider the basic form of the updating equation [13.2.23]. Notice that since the first row of $\mathbf{F}$ consists entirely of zeros, the first element of the vector $\hat{\boldsymbol{\xi}}_{t+1|t}$ will always equal zero, for all $t$. We see why if we recall the meaning of the state vector in [13.3.3]:

$$\hat{\boldsymbol{\xi}}_{t+1|t} = \begin{bmatrix} \hat{\varepsilon}_{t+1|t} \\ \hat{\varepsilon}_{t|t} \end{bmatrix}. \qquad [13.3.13]$$

Naturally, the forecast of the future white noise, $\hat{\varepsilon}_{t+1|t}$, is always zero. The forecast of $y_{t+1}$ is given by [13.2.24]:

$$\hat{y}_{t+1|t} = \mu + \begin{bmatrix} 1 & \theta \end{bmatrix} \begin{bmatrix} \hat{\varepsilon}_{t+1|t} \\ \hat{\varepsilon}_{t|t} \end{bmatrix} = \mu + \theta\hat{\varepsilon}_{t|t}. \qquad [13.3.14]$$

The Kalman filter updating equation for the *MSE*, equation [13.2.21], for this example becomes

$$\mathbf{P}_{t+1|t} = \mathbf{F}\mathbf{P}_{t|t}\mathbf{F}' + \mathbf{Q} = \begin{bmatrix} 0 & 0 \\ 1 & 0 \end{bmatrix} \mathbf{P}_{t|t} \begin{bmatrix} 0 & 1 \\ 0 & 0 \end{bmatrix} + \begin{bmatrix} \sigma^2 & 0 \\ 0 & 0 \end{bmatrix}. \qquad [13.3.15]$$

Thus, $\mathbf{P}_{t+1|t}$ is a diagonal matrix of the form

$$\mathbf{P}_{t+1|t} = \begin{bmatrix} \sigma^2 & 0 \\ 0 & p_{t+1} \end{bmatrix}, \qquad [13.3.16]$$

where the (2, 2) element of $\mathbf{P}_{t+1|t}$ (which we have denoted by $p_{t+1}$) is the same as the (1, 1) element of $\mathbf{P}_{t|t}$. Recalling [13.2.6] and [13.3.13], this term has the interpretation as the *MSE* of $\hat{\varepsilon}_{t|t}$:

$$p_{t+1} = E(\varepsilon_t - \hat{\varepsilon}_{t|t})^2. \qquad [13.3.17]$$

The (1, 1) element of $\mathbf{P}_{t+1|t}$ has the interpretation as the *MSE* of $\hat{\varepsilon}_{t+1|t}$. We have seen that this forecast is always zero, and its *MSE* in [13.3.16] is $\sigma^2$ for all $t$. The fact that $\mathbf{P}_{t+1|t}$ is a diagonal matrix means that the forecast error $(\varepsilon_{t+1} - \hat{\varepsilon}_{t+1|t})$ is uncorrelated with $(\varepsilon_t - \hat{\varepsilon}_{t|t})$.

The *MSE* of the forecast of $y_{t+1}$ is given by [13.2.25]:

$$\begin{aligned} E(y_{t+1} - \hat{y}_{t+1|t})^2 &= \mathbf{H}'\mathbf{P}_{t+1|t}\mathbf{H} + \mathbf{R} \\ &= \begin{bmatrix} 1 & \theta \end{bmatrix} \begin{bmatrix} \sigma^2 & 0 \\ 0 & p_{t+1} \end{bmatrix} \begin{bmatrix} 1 \\ \theta \end{bmatrix} + 0 \qquad [13.3.18] \\ &= \sigma^2 + \theta^2 p_{t+1}. \end{aligned}$$

Again, the intuition can be seen from the nature of the forecast in [13.3.14]:

$$\begin{aligned} E(y_{t+1} - \hat{y}_{t+1|t})^2 &= E[(\mu + \varepsilon_{t+1} + \theta\varepsilon_t) - (\mu + \theta\hat{\varepsilon}_{t|t})]^2 \\ &= E(\varepsilon_{t+1}^2) + \theta^2 E(\varepsilon_t - \hat{\varepsilon}_{t|t})^2, \end{aligned}$$

which, from [13.3.17], reproduces [13.3.18].

From [13.2.23], the series for $\hat{\varepsilon}_{t|t}$ is generated recursively from

$$\begin{aligned} \begin{bmatrix} 0 \\ \hat{\varepsilon}_{t|t} \end{bmatrix} &= \begin{bmatrix} 0 & 0 \\ 1 & 0 \end{bmatrix} \begin{bmatrix} 0 \\ \hat{\varepsilon}_{t-1|t-1} \end{bmatrix} \\ &+ \begin{bmatrix} 0 & 0 \\ 1 & 0 \end{bmatrix} \begin{bmatrix} \sigma^2 & 0 \\ 0 & p_t \end{bmatrix} \begin{bmatrix} 1 \\ \theta \end{bmatrix} \{1/[\sigma^2 + \theta^2 p_t]\} \cdot \{y_t - \mu - \theta\hat{\varepsilon}_{t-1|t-1}\} \end{aligned}$$

or

$$\hat{\varepsilon}_{t|t} = \{\sigma^2/[\sigma^2 + \theta^2 p_t]\} \cdot \{y_t - \mu - \theta\hat{\varepsilon}_{t-1|t-1}\} \qquad [13.3.19]$$

starting from the initial value $\hat{\varepsilon}_{0|0} = 0$. Note that the value for $\hat{\varepsilon}_{t|t}$ differs from the approximation suggested in equations [4.2.36] and [4.3.2],

$$\hat{\varepsilon}_t = y_t - \mu - \theta\hat{\varepsilon}_{t-1} \qquad \hat{\varepsilon}_0 = 0,$$

in that [13.3.19] shrinks the inference $\hat{\varepsilon}_t$ toward zero to take account of the nonzero variance $p_t$ of $\hat{\varepsilon}_{t-1|t-1}$ around the true value $\varepsilon_{t-1}$.

The gain matrix $\mathbf{K}_t$ in equation [13.2.19] is given by

$$\mathbf{K}_t = \begin{bmatrix} 0 & 0 \\ 1 & 0 \end{bmatrix} \begin{bmatrix} \sigma^2 & 0 \\ 0 & p_t \end{bmatrix} \begin{bmatrix} 1 \\ \theta \end{bmatrix} \left( \frac{1}{\sigma^2 + \theta^2 p_t} \right) = \begin{bmatrix} 0 \\ \sigma^2/[\sigma^2 + \theta^2 p_t] \end{bmatrix}. \qquad [13.3.20]$$

Finally, notice from [13.2.16] that

$$\mathbf{P}_{t|t} = \begin{bmatrix} \sigma^2 & 0 \\ 0 & p_t \end{bmatrix} - \left(\frac{1}{\sigma^2 + \theta^2 p_t}\right)\begin{bmatrix} \sigma^2 & 0 \\ 0 & p_t \end{bmatrix}\begin{bmatrix} 1 \\ \theta \end{bmatrix}[1 \quad \theta]\begin{bmatrix} \sigma^2 & 0 \\ 0 & p_t \end{bmatrix}.$$

The (1, 1) element of $\mathbf{P}_{t|t}$ (which we saw equals $p_{t+1}$) is thus given by

$$p_{t+1} = \sigma^2 - \{1/[\sigma^2 + \theta^2 p_t]\}\cdot\sigma^4 = \frac{\sigma^2\theta^2 p_t}{\sigma^2 + \theta^2 p_t}. \quad [13.3.21]$$

The recursion in [13.3.21] is started with $p_1 = \sigma^2$ and thus has the solution

$$p_{t+1} = \frac{\sigma^2\theta^{2t}}{1 + \theta^2 + \theta^4 + \cdots + \theta^{2t}}. \quad [13.3.22]$$

It is interesting to note what happens to the filter as $t$ becomes large. First consider the case when $|\theta| \leq 1$. Then, from [13.3.22],

$$\lim_{t\to\infty} p_{t+1} = 0,$$

and so, from [13.3.17],

$$\hat{\varepsilon}_{t|t} \xrightarrow{p} \varepsilon_t.$$

Thus, given a sufficient number of observations on $y$, the Kalman filter inference $\hat{\varepsilon}_{t|t}$ converges to the true value $\varepsilon_t$, and the forecast [13.3.14] converges to that of the Wold representation for the process. The Kalman gain in [13.3.20] converges to $(0, 1)'$.

Alternatively, consider the case when $|\theta| > 1$. From [13.3.22], we have

$$p_{t+1} = \frac{\sigma^2\theta^{2t}(1 - \theta^2)}{1 - \theta^{2(t+1)}} = \frac{\sigma^2(1 - \theta^2)}{\theta^{-2t} - \theta^2}$$

and

$$\lim_{t\to\infty} p_{t+1} = \frac{\sigma^2(1 - \theta^2)}{-\theta^2} > 0.$$

No matter how many observations are obtained, it will not be possible to know with certainty the value of the nonfundamental innovation $\varepsilon_t$ associated with date $t$ on the basis of $(y_t, y_{t-1}, \ldots, y_1)$. The gain is given by

$$\frac{\sigma^2}{\sigma^2 + \theta^2 p_t} \to \frac{\sigma^2}{\sigma^2 - \sigma^2(1 - \theta^2)} = \frac{1}{\theta^2},$$

and the recursion [13.3.19] approaches

$$\hat{\varepsilon}_{t|t} = (1/\theta^2)\cdot(y_t - \mu - \theta\hat{\varepsilon}_{t-1|t-1})$$

or

$$\theta\hat{\varepsilon}_{t|t} = (1/\theta)\cdot(y_t - \mu - \theta\hat{\varepsilon}_{t-1|t-1}).$$

Recalling [13.3.14], we thus have

$$\hat{y}_{t+1|t} - \mu = (1/\theta)\cdot[(y_t - \mu) - (\hat{y}_{t|t-1} - \mu)]$$

or

$$\hat{y}_{t+1|t} - \mu = (1/\theta)\cdot(y_t - \mu) - (1/\theta)^2\cdot(y_{t-1} - \mu) + (1/\theta)^3\cdot(y_{t-2} - \mu) - \cdots,$$

which again is the $AR(\infty)$ forecast associated with the invertible $MA(1)$ representation. Indeed, the forecasts of the Kalman filter with $\theta$ replaced by $\theta^{-1}$ and $\sigma^2$ replaced by $\theta^2\sigma^2$ will be identical for any $t$; see Exercise 13.5.

## *Calculating* s*-Period-Ahead Forecasts with the Kalman Filter*

The forecast of $\mathbf{y}_t$ calculated in [13.2.24] is an exact finite-sample forecast of $\mathbf{y}_t$ on the basis of $\mathbf{x}_t$ and $\mathcal{Y}_{t-1} \equiv (\mathbf{y}'_{t-1}, \mathbf{y}'_{t-2}, \ldots, \mathbf{y}'_1, \mathbf{x}'_{t-1}, \mathbf{x}'_{t-2}, \ldots, \mathbf{x}'_1)'$. If $\mathbf{x}_t$

is deterministic, it is also easy to use the Kalman filter to calculate exact finite-sample $s$-period-ahead forecasts.

The state equation [13.2.1] can be solved by recursive substitution to yield

$$\boldsymbol{\xi}_{t+s} = \mathbf{F}^s\boldsymbol{\xi}_t + \mathbf{F}^{s-1}\mathbf{v}_{t+1} + \mathbf{F}^{s-2}\mathbf{v}_{t+2} + \cdots + \mathbf{F}^1\mathbf{v}_{t+s-1} + \mathbf{v}_{t+s} \qquad [13.3.23]$$
$$\text{for } s = 1, 2, \ldots .$$

The projection of $\boldsymbol{\xi}_{t+s}$ on $\boldsymbol{\xi}_t$ and $\mathcal{Y}_t$ is given by

$$\hat{E}(\boldsymbol{\xi}_{t+s}|\boldsymbol{\xi}_t, \mathcal{Y}_t) = \mathbf{F}^s\boldsymbol{\xi}_t. \qquad [13.3.24]$$

From the law of iterated projections,

$$\hat{\boldsymbol{\xi}}_{t+s|t} \equiv \hat{E}(\boldsymbol{\xi}_{t+s}|\mathcal{Y}_t) = \mathbf{F}^s\hat{\boldsymbol{\xi}}_{t|t}. \qquad [13.3.25]$$

Thus, from [13.3.23] the $s$-period-ahead forecast error for the state vector is

$$\begin{aligned}\boldsymbol{\xi}_{t+s} - \hat{\boldsymbol{\xi}}_{t+s|t} = \mathbf{F}^s(\boldsymbol{\xi}_t - \hat{\boldsymbol{\xi}}_{t|t}) + \mathbf{F}^{s-1}\mathbf{v}_{t+1} + \mathbf{F}^{s-2}\mathbf{v}_{t+2} \\ + \cdots + \mathbf{F}^1\mathbf{v}_{t+s-1} + \mathbf{v}_{t+s}\end{aligned} \qquad [13.3.26]$$

with $MSE$

$$\begin{aligned}\mathbf{P}_{t+s|t} = \mathbf{F}^s\mathbf{P}_{t|t}(\mathbf{F}')^s + \mathbf{F}^{s-1}\mathbf{Q}(\mathbf{F}')^{s-1} + \mathbf{F}^{s-2}\mathbf{Q}(\mathbf{F}')^{s-2} \\ + \cdots + \mathbf{FQF}' + \mathbf{Q}.\end{aligned} \qquad [13.3.27]$$

To forecast the observed vector $\mathbf{y}_{t+s}$, recall from the observation equation that

$$\mathbf{y}_{t+s} = \mathbf{A}'\mathbf{x}_{t+s} + \mathbf{H}'\boldsymbol{\xi}_{t+s} + \mathbf{w}_{t+s}. \qquad [13.3.28]$$

There are advantages if the state vector is defined in such a way that $\mathbf{x}_t$ is deterministic, so that the dynamics of any exogenous variables can be represented through $\boldsymbol{\xi}_t$. If $\mathbf{x}_t$ is deterministic, the $s$-period-ahead forecast of $\mathbf{y}$ is

$$\hat{\mathbf{y}}_{t+s|t} \equiv \hat{E}(\mathbf{y}_{t+s}|\mathcal{Y}_t) = \mathbf{A}'\mathbf{x}_{t+s} + \mathbf{H}'\hat{\boldsymbol{\xi}}_{t+s|t}. \qquad [13.3.29]$$

The forecast error is

$$\begin{aligned}\mathbf{y}_{t+s} - \hat{\mathbf{y}}_{t+s|t} &= (\mathbf{A}'\mathbf{x}_{t+s} + \mathbf{H}'\boldsymbol{\xi}_{t+s} + \mathbf{w}_{t+s}) - (\mathbf{A}'\mathbf{x}_{t+s} + \mathbf{H}'\hat{\boldsymbol{\xi}}_{t+s|t}) \\ &= \mathbf{H}'(\boldsymbol{\xi}_{t+s} - \hat{\boldsymbol{\xi}}_{t+s|t}) + \mathbf{w}_{t+s}\end{aligned}$$

with $MSE$

$$E[(\mathbf{y}_{t+s} - \hat{\mathbf{y}}_{t+s|t})(\mathbf{y}_{t+s} - \hat{\mathbf{y}}_{t+s|t})'] = \mathbf{H}'\mathbf{P}_{t+s|t}\mathbf{H} + \mathbf{R}. \qquad [13.3.30]$$

## 13.4. *Maximum Likelihood Estimation of Parameters*

### *Using the Kalman Filter to Evaluate the Likelihood Function*

The Kalman filter was motivated in Section 13.2 in terms of linear projections. The forecasts $\hat{\boldsymbol{\xi}}_{t|t-1}$ and $\hat{\mathbf{y}}_{t|t-1}$ are thus optimal within the set of forecasts that are linear in $(\mathbf{x}_t, \mathcal{Y}_{t-1})$, where $\mathcal{Y}_{t-1} \equiv (\mathbf{y}'_{t-1}, \mathbf{y}'_{t-2}, \ldots, \mathbf{y}'_1, \mathbf{x}'_{t-1}, \mathbf{x}'_{t-2}, \ldots, \mathbf{x}'_1)'$. If the initial state $\boldsymbol{\xi}_1$ and the innovations $\{\mathbf{w}_t, \mathbf{v}_t\}_{t=1}^T$ are multivariate Gaussian, then we can make the stronger claim that the forecasts $\hat{\boldsymbol{\xi}}_{t|t-1}$ and $\hat{\mathbf{y}}_{t|t-1}$ calculated by the Kalman filter are optimal among any functions of $(\mathbf{x}_t, \mathcal{Y}_{t-1})$. Moreover, if $\boldsymbol{\xi}_1$ and $\{\mathbf{w}_t, \mathbf{v}_t\}_{t=1}^T$ are Gaussian, then the distribution of $\mathbf{y}_t$ conditional on $(\mathbf{x}_t, \mathcal{Y}_{t-1})$ is Gaussian with mean given by [13.2.24] and variance given by [13.2.25]:

$$\mathbf{y}_t|\mathbf{x}_t, \mathcal{Y}_{t-1} \sim N\big((\mathbf{A}'\mathbf{x}_t + \mathbf{H}'\hat{\boldsymbol{\xi}}_{t|t-1}), (\mathbf{H}'\mathbf{P}_{t|t-1}\mathbf{H} + \mathbf{R})\big);$$

that is,

$$\begin{aligned}&f_{\mathbf{Y}_t|\mathbf{X}_t,\mathcal{Y}_{t-1}}(\mathbf{y}_t|\mathbf{x}_t, \mathcal{Y}_{t-1}) \\ &\quad = (2\pi)^{-n/2}|\mathbf{H}'\mathbf{P}_{t|t-1}\mathbf{H} + \mathbf{R}|^{-1/2} \\ &\quad\quad \times \exp\{-\tfrac{1}{2}(\mathbf{y}_t - \mathbf{A}'\mathbf{x}_t - \mathbf{H}'\hat{\boldsymbol{\xi}}_{t|t-1})'(\mathbf{H}'\mathbf{P}_{t|t-1}\mathbf{H} + \mathbf{R})^{-1} \\ &\quad\quad \times (\mathbf{y}_t - \mathbf{A}'\mathbf{x}_t - \mathbf{H}'\hat{\boldsymbol{\xi}}_{t|t-1})\} \qquad \text{for } t = 1, 2, \ldots, T.\end{aligned} \qquad [13.4.1]$$

From [13.4.1], it is a simple matter to construct the sample log likelihood,

$$\sum_{t=1}^{T} \log f_{\mathbf{Y}_t|\mathbf{X}_t,\mathcal{Y}_{t-1}}(\mathbf{y}_t|\mathbf{x}_t, \mathcal{Y}_{t-1}). \qquad [13.4.2]$$

Expression [13.4.2] can then be maximized numerically with respect to the unknown parameters in the matrices **F**, **Q**, **A**, **H**, and **R**; see Burmeister and Wall (1982) for an illustrative application.

As stressed by Harvey and Phillips (1979), this representation of the likelihood is particularly convenient for estimating regressions involving moving average terms. Moreover, [13.4.2] gives the exact log likelihood function, regardless of whether the moving average representation is invertible.

As an illustrative example, suppose we wanted to estimate a bivariate regression model whose equations were

$$y_{1t} = \mathbf{a}_1'\mathbf{x}_t + u_{1t}$$

$$y_{2t} = \mathbf{a}_2'\mathbf{x}_t + u_{2t},$$

where $\mathbf{x}_t$ is a $(k \times 1)$ vector of exogenous explanatory variables and $\mathbf{a}_1$ and $\mathbf{a}_2$ are $(k \times 1)$ vectors of coefficients; if the two regressions have different explanatory variables, the variables from both regressions are included in $\mathbf{x}_t$ with zeros appropriately imposed on $\mathbf{a}_1$ and $\mathbf{a}_2$. Suppose that the disturbance vector follows a bivariate $MA(1)$ process:

$$\begin{bmatrix} u_{1t} \\ u_{2t} \end{bmatrix} = \begin{bmatrix} \varepsilon_{1t} \\ \varepsilon_{2t} \end{bmatrix} + \begin{bmatrix} \theta_{11} & \theta_{12} \\ \theta_{21} & \theta_{22} \end{bmatrix} \begin{bmatrix} \varepsilon_{1,t-1} \\ \varepsilon_{2,t-1} \end{bmatrix},$$

with $(\varepsilon_{1t}, \varepsilon_{2t})' \sim$ i.i.d. $N(\mathbf{0}, \boldsymbol{\Omega})$. This model can be written in state-space form by defining

$$\boldsymbol{\xi}_t = \begin{bmatrix} \varepsilon_{1t} \\ \varepsilon_{2t} \\ \varepsilon_{1,t-1} \\ \varepsilon_{2,t-1} \end{bmatrix} \qquad \mathbf{F} = \begin{bmatrix} 0 & 0 & 0 & 0 \\ 0 & 0 & 0 & 0 \\ 1 & 0 & 0 & 0 \\ 0 & 1 & 0 & 0 \end{bmatrix} \qquad \mathbf{v}_{t+1} = \begin{bmatrix} \varepsilon_{1,t+1} \\ \varepsilon_{2,t+1} \\ 0 \\ 0 \end{bmatrix}$$

$$\mathbf{Q} = \begin{bmatrix} \sigma_{11} & \sigma_{12} & 0 & 0 \\ \sigma_{21} & \sigma_{22} & 0 & 0 \\ 0 & 0 & 0 & 0 \\ 0 & 0 & 0 & 0 \end{bmatrix} \qquad \mathbf{A}' = \begin{bmatrix} \mathbf{a}_1' \\ \mathbf{a}_2' \end{bmatrix}$$

$$\mathbf{H}' = \begin{bmatrix} 1 & 0 & \theta_{11} & \theta_{12} \\ 0 & 1 & \theta_{21} & \theta_{22} \end{bmatrix} \qquad \mathbf{R} = \mathbf{0},$$

where $\sigma_{ij} = E(\varepsilon_{it}\varepsilon_{jt})$. The Kalman filter iteration is started from

$$\hat{\boldsymbol{\xi}}_{1|0} = \begin{bmatrix} 0 \\ 0 \\ 0 \\ 0 \end{bmatrix} \qquad \mathbf{P}_{1|0} = \begin{bmatrix} \sigma_{11} & \sigma_{12} & 0 & 0 \\ \sigma_{21} & \sigma_{22} & 0 & 0 \\ 0 & 0 & \sigma_{11} & \sigma_{12} \\ 0 & 0 & \sigma_{21} & \sigma_{22} \end{bmatrix}.$$

Maximization of [13.4.2] is started by making an initial guess as to the numerical values of the unknown parameters. One obvious way to do this is to regress $y_{1t}$ on the elements of $\mathbf{x}_t$ that appear in the first equation to get an initial guess for $\mathbf{a}_1$. A similar $OLS$ regression for $y_2$ yields a guess for $\mathbf{a}_2$. Setting $\theta_{11} = \theta_{12} = \theta_{21} = \theta_{22} = 0$ initially, a first guess for $\boldsymbol{\Omega}$ could be the estimated variance-covariance matrix of the residuals from these two $OLS$ regressions. For these initial numerical values for the population parameters, we could construct **F**, **Q**, **A**, **H**, and **R** from the expressions just given and iterate on [13.2.22] through [13.2.25] for $t = 1, 2, \ldots, T - 1$. The sequences $\{\hat{\boldsymbol{\xi}}_{t|t-1}\}_{t=1}^{T}$ and $\{\mathbf{P}_{t|t-1}\}_{t=1}^{T}$ resulting from these iterations could then be used in [13.4.1] and [13.4.2] to calculate the value for the log likelihood function that results from these initial parameter values. The numerical optimization methods described in Section 5.7 can then be employed to make better guesses as to the value of the unknown parameters until [13.4.2] is maximized. As noted in Section 5.9, the numerical search will be better behaved if $\mathbf{\Omega}$ is parameterized in terms of its Cholesky factorization.

As a second example, consider a scalar Gaussian $ARMA(1, 1)$ process,

$$y_t - \mu = \phi(y_{t-1} - \mu) + \varepsilon_t + \theta\varepsilon_{t-1},$$

with $\varepsilon_t \sim$ i.i.d. $N(0, \sigma^2)$. This can be written in state-space form as in [13.1.22] and [13.1.23] with $r = 2$ and

$$\mathbf{F} = \begin{bmatrix} \phi & 0 \\ 1 & 0 \end{bmatrix} \qquad \mathbf{v}_{t+1} = \begin{bmatrix} \varepsilon_{t+1} \\ 0 \end{bmatrix} \qquad \mathbf{Q} = \begin{bmatrix} \sigma^2 & 0 \\ 0 & 0 \end{bmatrix}$$

$$\mathbf{A}' = \mu \qquad \mathbf{x}_t = 1 \qquad \mathbf{H}' = [1 \quad \theta] \qquad \mathbf{R} = 0$$

$$\hat{\boldsymbol{\xi}}_{1|0} = \begin{bmatrix} 0 \\ 0 \end{bmatrix} \qquad \mathbf{P}_{1|0} = \begin{bmatrix} \sigma^2/(1 - \phi^2) & \phi\sigma^2/(1 - \phi^2) \\ \phi\sigma^2/(1 - \phi^2) & \sigma^2/(1 - \phi^2) \end{bmatrix}.$$

This value for $\mathbf{P}_{1|0}$ was obtained by recognizing that the state equation [13.1.22] describes the behavior of $\boldsymbol{\xi}_t = (z_t, z_{t-1}, \ldots, z_{t-r+1})'$, where $z_t = \phi_1 z_{t-1} + \phi_2 z_{t-2} + \cdots + \phi_r z_{t-r} + \varepsilon_t$ follows an $AR(r)$ process. For this example, $r = 2$, so that $\mathbf{P}_{1|0}$ is the variance-covariance matrix of two consecutive draws from an $AR(2)$ process with parameters $\phi_1 = \phi$ and $\phi_2 = 0$. The expressions just given for $\mathbf{F}$, $\mathbf{Q}$, $\mathbf{A}$, $\mathbf{H}$, and $\mathbf{R}$ are then used in the Kalman filter iterations. Thus, expression [13.4.2] allows easy computation of the exact likelihood function for an $ARMA(p, q)$ process. This computation is valid regardless of whether the moving average parameters satisfy the invertibility condition. Similarly, expression [13.3.29] gives the exact finite-sample $s$-period-ahead forecast for the process and [13.3.30] its $MSE$, again regardless of whether the invertible representation is used.

Typically, numerical search procedures for maximizing [13.4.2] require the derivatives of the log likelihood. These can be calculated numerically or analytically. To characterize the analytical derivatives of [13.4.2], collect the unknown parameters to be estimated in a vector $\boldsymbol{\theta}$, and write $\mathbf{F}(\boldsymbol{\theta})$, $\mathbf{Q}(\boldsymbol{\theta})$, $\mathbf{A}(\boldsymbol{\theta})$, $\mathbf{H}(\boldsymbol{\theta})$, and $\mathbf{R}(\boldsymbol{\theta})$. Implicitly, then, $\hat{\boldsymbol{\xi}}_{t|t-1}(\boldsymbol{\theta})$ and $\mathbf{P}_{t|t-1}(\boldsymbol{\theta})$ will be functions of $\boldsymbol{\theta}$ as well, and the derivative of the log of [13.4.1] with respect to the $i$th element of $\boldsymbol{\theta}$ will involve $\partial\hat{\boldsymbol{\xi}}_{t|t-1}(\boldsymbol{\theta})/\partial\theta_i$ and $\partial\mathbf{P}_{t|t-1}(\boldsymbol{\theta})/\partial\theta_i$. These derivatives can also be generated recursively by differentiating the Kalman filter recursion, [13.2.22] and [13.2.23], with respect to $\theta_i$; see Caines (1988, pp. 585–86) for illustration.

For many state-space models, the $EM$ algorithm of Dempster, Laird, and Rubin (1977) offers a particularly convenient means for maximizing [13.4.2], as developed by Shumway and Stoffer (1982) and Watson and Engle (1983).

## *Identification*

Although the state-space representation gives a very convenient way to calculate the exact likelihood function, a word of caution should be given. In the absence of restrictions on $\mathbf{F}$, $\mathbf{Q}$, $\mathbf{A}$, $\mathbf{H}$, and $\mathbf{R}$, the parameters of the state-space representation are unidentified—more than one set of values for the parameters can give rise to the identical value of the likelihood function, and the data give us no guide for choosing among these. A trivial example is the following system:

***State Equation*** $(r = 2)$:

$$\boldsymbol{\xi}_{t+1} = \begin{bmatrix} \varepsilon_{1,t+1} \\ \varepsilon_{2,t+1} \end{bmatrix} \qquad [13.4.3]$$

***Observation Equation*** $(n = 1)$:

$$y_t = \varepsilon_{1t} + \varepsilon_{2t}. \qquad [13.4.4]$$

Here, $\mathbf{F} = \mathbf{0}$, $\mathbf{Q} = \begin{bmatrix} \sigma_1^2 & 0 \\ 0 & \sigma_2^2 \end{bmatrix}$, $\mathbf{A}' = 0$, $\mathbf{H}' = [1 \quad 1]$, and $\mathbf{R} = 0$. This model asserts that $y_t$ is white noise, with mean zero and variance given by $(\sigma_1^2 + \sigma_2^2)$. The reader is invited to confirm in Exercise 13.4 that the log of the likelihood function from [13.4.1] and [13.4.2] simplifies to

$$\begin{aligned} &\log f_{\mathbf{Y}_T, \mathbf{Y}_{T-1}, \ldots, \mathbf{Y}_1}(\mathbf{y}_T, \mathbf{y}_{T-1}, \ldots, \mathbf{y}_1) \\ &\quad = -(T/2)\log(2\pi) - (T/2)\log(\sigma_1^2 + \sigma_2^2) - \sum_{t=1}^{T} y_t^2/[2(\sigma_1^2 + \sigma_2^2)]. \end{aligned} \qquad [13.4.5]$$

Clearly, any values for $\sigma_1^2$ and $\sigma_2^2$ that sum to a given constant will produce the identical value for the likelihood function.

The $MA(1)$ process explored in Section 13.3 provides a second example of an unidentified state-space representation. As the reader may verify in Exercise 13.5, the identical value for the log likelihood function [13.4.2] would result if $\theta$ is replaced by $\theta^{-1}$ and $\sigma^2$ by $\theta^2\sigma^2$.

These two examples illustrate two basic forms in which absence of identification can occur. Following Rothenberg (1971), a model is said to be *globally identified* at a particular parameter value $\boldsymbol{\theta}_0$ if for any value of $\boldsymbol{\theta}$ there exists a possible realization $\mathcal{Y}_T$ for which the value of the likelihood at $\boldsymbol{\theta}$ is different from the value of the likelihood at $\boldsymbol{\theta}_0$. A model is said to be *locally identified* at $\boldsymbol{\theta}_0$ if there exists a $\delta > 0$ such that for any value of $\boldsymbol{\theta}$ satisfying $(\boldsymbol{\theta} - \boldsymbol{\theta}_0)'(\boldsymbol{\theta} - \boldsymbol{\theta}_0) < \delta$, there exists a possible realization of $\mathcal{Y}_T$ for which the value of the likelihood at $\boldsymbol{\theta}$ is different from the value of the likelihood at $\boldsymbol{\theta}_0$. Thus, global identification implies local identification. The first example, [13.4.3] and [13.4.4], is neither globally nor locally identified, while the $MA(1)$ example is locally identified but globally unidentified.

Local identification is much easier to test for than global identification. Rothenberg (1971) showed that a model is locally identified at $\boldsymbol{\theta}_0$ if and only if the information matrix is nonsingular in a neighborhood around $\boldsymbol{\theta}_0$. Thus, a common symptom of trying to estimate an unidentified model is difficulty with inverting the matrix of second derivatives of the log likelihood function. One approach to checking for local identification is to translate the state-space representation back into a vector $ARMA$ model and check for satisfaction of the conditions in Hannan (1971); see Hamilton (1985) for an example of this approach. A second approach is to work directly with the state-space representation, as is done in Gevers and Wertz (1984) and Wall (1987). For an illustration of the second approach, see Burmeister, Wall, and Hamilton (1986).

## *Asymptotic Properties of Maximum Likelihood Estimates*

If certain regularity conditions are satisfied, then Caines (1988, Chapter 7) showed that the maximum likelihood estimate $\hat{\boldsymbol{\theta}}_T$ based on a sample of size $T$ is consistent and asymptotically normal. These conditions include the following: (1) the model must be identified; (2) eigenvalues of $\mathbf{F}$ are all inside the unit circle; (3)

apart from a constant term, the variables $\mathbf{x}_t$ behave asymptotically like a full-rank linearly indeterministic covariance-stationary process; and (4) the true value of $\boldsymbol{\theta}$ does not fall on a boundary of the allowable parameter space. Pagan (1980, Theorem 4) and Ghosh (1989) examined special cases of state-space models for which

$$\sqrt{T}\mathcal{J}_{2D,T}^{1/2}(\hat{\boldsymbol{\theta}}_T - \boldsymbol{\theta}_0) \xrightarrow{L} N(\mathbf{0}, \mathbf{I}_a), \qquad [13.4.6]$$

where $a$ is the number of elements of $\boldsymbol{\theta}$ and $\mathcal{J}_{2D,T}$ is the $(a \times a)$ information matrix for a sample of size $T$ as calculated from second derivatives of the log likelihood function:

$$\mathcal{J}_{2D,T} = -\frac{1}{T}E\left(\sum_{t=1}^{T} \frac{\partial^2 \log f(\mathbf{y}_t|\mathbf{x}_t, \mathcal{Y}_{t-1}; \boldsymbol{\theta})}{\partial\boldsymbol{\theta}\,\partial\boldsymbol{\theta}'}\bigg|_{\boldsymbol{\theta}=\boldsymbol{\theta}_0}\right). \qquad [13.4.7]$$

A common practice is to assume that the limit of $\mathcal{J}_{2D,T}$ as $T \to \infty$ is the same as the plim of

$$\hat{\mathcal{J}}_{2D,T} = -\frac{1}{T}\sum_{t=1}^{T} \frac{\partial^2 \log f(\mathbf{y}_t|\mathbf{x}_t, \mathcal{Y}_{t-1}; \boldsymbol{\theta})}{\partial\boldsymbol{\theta}\,\partial\boldsymbol{\theta}'}\bigg|_{\boldsymbol{\theta}=\hat{\boldsymbol{\theta}}_T}, \qquad [13.4.8]$$

which can be calculated analytically or numerically by differentiating [13.4.2]. Reported standard errors for $\hat{\boldsymbol{\theta}}_T$ are then square roots of diagonal elements of $(1/T)(\hat{\mathcal{J}}_{2D,T})^{-1}$.

### *Quasi-Maximum Likelihood Estimation*

Even if the disturbances $\mathbf{v}_t$ and $\mathbf{w}_t$ are non-Gaussian, the Kalman filter can still be used to calculate the linear projection of $\mathbf{y}_{t+s}$ on past observables. Moreover, we can form the function [13.4.2] and maximize it with respect to $\boldsymbol{\theta}$ even for non-Gaussian systems. This procedure will still yield consistent and asymptotically Normal estimates of the elements of $\mathbf{F}$, $\mathbf{Q}$, $\mathbf{A}$, $\mathbf{H}$, and $\mathbf{R}$, with the variance-covariance matrix constructed as described in equation [5.8.7]. Watson (1989, Theorem 2) presented conditions under which the quasi-maximum likelihood estimates satisfy

$$\sqrt{T}(\hat{\boldsymbol{\theta}}_T - \boldsymbol{\theta}_0) \xrightarrow{L} N(\mathbf{0}, [\mathcal{J}_{2D}\mathcal{J}_{OP}^{-1}\mathcal{J}_{2D}]^{-1}), \qquad [13.4.9]$$

where $\mathcal{J}_{2D}$ is the plim of [13.4.8] when evaluated at the true value $\boldsymbol{\theta}_0$ and $\mathcal{J}_{OP}$ is the outer-product estimate of the information matrix,

$$\mathcal{J}_{OP} = \text{plim } (1/T) \sum_{t=1}^{T} [\mathbf{h}(\boldsymbol{\theta}_0, \mathcal{Y}_t)][\mathbf{h}(\boldsymbol{\theta}_0, \mathcal{Y}_t)]',$$

where

$$\mathbf{h}(\boldsymbol{\theta}_0, \mathcal{Y}_t) \equiv \frac{\partial \log f(\mathbf{y}_t|\mathbf{x}_t, \mathcal{Y}_{t-1}; \boldsymbol{\theta})}{\partial\boldsymbol{\theta}}\bigg|_{\boldsymbol{\theta}=\boldsymbol{\theta}_0}.$$

## 13.5. *The Steady-State Kalman Filter*

### *Convergence Properties of the Kalman Filter*

Section 13.3 applied the Kalman filter to an $MA(1)$ process and found that when $|\theta| \leq 1$,

$$\lim_{t\to\infty} \mathbf{P}_{t+1|t} = \begin{bmatrix} \sigma^2 & 0 \\ 0 & 0 \end{bmatrix}$$

$$\lim_{t\to\infty} \mathbf{K}_t = \begin{bmatrix} 0 \\ 1 \end{bmatrix},$$

whereas when $|\theta| > 1$,

$$\lim_{t\to\infty} \mathbf{P}_{t+1|t} = \begin{bmatrix} \sigma^2 & 0 \\ 0 & \sigma^2(\theta^2 - 1)/\theta^2 \end{bmatrix}$$

$$\lim_{t\to\infty} \mathbf{K}_t = \begin{bmatrix} 0 \\ 1/\theta^2 \end{bmatrix}.$$

It turns out to be a property of a broad class of state-space models that the sequences $\{\mathbf{P}_{t+1|t}\}_{t=1}^{T}$ and $\{\mathbf{K}_t\}_{t=1}^{T}$ converge to fixed matrices, as the following proposition shows.

***Proposition 13.1:*** *Let* $\mathbf{F}$ *be an* $(r \times r)$ *matrix whose eigenvalues are all inside the unit circle, let* $\mathbf{H}'$ *denote an arbitrary* $(n \times r)$ *matrix, and let* $\mathbf{Q}$ *and* $\mathbf{R}$ *be positive semidefinite symmetric* $(r \times r)$ *and* $(n \times n)$ *matrices, respectively. Let* $\{\mathbf{P}_{t+1|t}\}_{t=1}^{T}$ *be the sequence of MSE matrices calculated by the Kalman filter,*

$$\mathbf{P}_{t+1|t} = \mathbf{F}[\mathbf{P}_{t|t-1} - \mathbf{P}_{t|t-1}\mathbf{H}(\mathbf{H}'\mathbf{P}_{t|t-1}\mathbf{H} + \mathbf{R})^{-1}\mathbf{H}'\mathbf{P}_{t|t-1}]\mathbf{F}' + \mathbf{Q}, \qquad [13.5.1]$$

*where iteration on [13.5.1] is initialized by letting* $\mathbf{P}_{1|0}$ *be the positive semidefinite* $(r \times r)$ *matrix satisfying*

$$\text{vec}(\mathbf{P}_{1|0}) = [\mathbf{I}_{r^2} - (\mathbf{F} \otimes \mathbf{F})]^{-1} \cdot \text{vec}(\mathbf{Q}). \qquad [13.5.2]$$

*Then* $\{\mathbf{P}_{t+1|t}\}_{t=1}^{T}$ *is a monotonically nonincreasing sequence and converges as* $T \to \infty$ *to a steady-state matrix* $\mathbf{P}$ *satisfying*

$$\mathbf{P} = \mathbf{F}[\mathbf{P} - \mathbf{P}\mathbf{H}(\mathbf{H}'\mathbf{P}\mathbf{H} + \mathbf{R})^{-1}\mathbf{H}'\mathbf{P}]\mathbf{F}' + \mathbf{Q}. \qquad [13.5.3]$$

*Moreover, the steady-state value for the Kalman gain matrix, defined by*

$$\mathbf{K} \equiv \mathbf{F}\mathbf{P}\mathbf{H}(\mathbf{H}'\mathbf{P}\mathbf{H} + \mathbf{R})^{-1}, \qquad [13.5.4]$$

*has the property that the eigenvalues of* $(\mathbf{F} - \mathbf{K}\mathbf{H}')$ *all lie on or inside the unit circle.*

The claim in Proposition 13.1 that $\mathbf{P}_{t+1|t} \leq \mathbf{P}_{t|t-1}$ means that for any real $(r \times 1)$ vector $\mathbf{h}$, the scalar inequality $\mathbf{h}'\mathbf{P}_{t+1|t}\mathbf{h} \leq \mathbf{h}'\mathbf{P}_{t|t-1}\mathbf{h}$ holds.

Proposition 13.1 assumes that the Kalman filter is started with $\mathbf{P}_{1|0}$ equal to the unconditional variance-covariance matrix of the state vector $\boldsymbol{\xi}_t$. Although the sequence $\{\mathbf{P}_{t+1|t}\}$ converges to a matrix $\mathbf{P}$, the solution to [13.5.3] need not be unique; a different starting value for $\mathbf{P}_{1|0}$ might produce a sequence that converges to a different matrix $\mathbf{P}$ satisfying [13.5.3]. Under the slightly stronger assumption that either $\mathbf{Q}$ or $\mathbf{R}$ is strictly positive definite, then iteration on [13.5.1] will converge to a unique solution to [13.5.3], where the starting value for the iteration $\mathbf{P}_{1|0}$ can be any positive semidefinite symmetric matrix.

***Proposition 13.2:*** *Let* $\mathbf{F}$ *be an* $(r \times r)$ *matrix whose eigenvalues are all inside the unit circle, let* $\mathbf{H}'$ *denote an arbitrary* $(n \times r)$ *matrix, and let* $\mathbf{Q}$ *and* $\mathbf{R}$ *be positive semidefinite symmetric* $(r \times r)$ *and* $(n \times n)$ *matrices, respectively, with either* $\mathbf{Q}$ *or* $\mathbf{R}$ *strictly positive definite. Then the sequence of Kalman MSE matrices* $\{\mathbf{P}_{t+1|t}\}_{t=1}^{T}$ *determined by [13.5.1] converges to a unique positive semidefinite steady-state matrix* $\mathbf{P}$ *satisfying [13.5.3], where the value of* $\mathbf{P}$ *is the same for any positive semidefinite symmetric starting value for* $\mathbf{P}_{1|0}$*. Moreover, the steady-state value for the Kalman gain matrix* $\mathbf{K}$ *in [13.5.4] has the property that the eigenvalues of* $(\mathbf{F} - \mathbf{K}\mathbf{H}')$ *are all strictly inside the unit circle.*

We next discuss the relevance of the results in Propositions 13.1 and 13.2 concerning the eigenvalues of $(\mathbf{F} - \mathbf{K}\mathbf{H}')$.

### *Using the Kalman Filter to Find the Wold Representation and Factor an Autocovariance-Generating Function*

Consider a system in which the explanatory variables ($\mathbf{x}_t$) consist solely of a constant term. Without loss of generality, we simplify the notation by assuming that $\mathbf{A}'\mathbf{x}_t \equiv \mathbf{0}$. For such systems, the Kalman filter forecast of the state vector can be written as in [13.2.20]:

$$\hat{\boldsymbol{\xi}}_{t+1|t} = \mathbf{F}\hat{\boldsymbol{\xi}}_{t|t-1} + \mathbf{K}_t(\mathbf{y}_t - \mathbf{H}'\hat{\boldsymbol{\xi}}_{t|t-1}). \qquad [13.5.5]$$

The linear projection of $\mathbf{y}_{t+1}$ on the observed finite sample of its own lagged values is then calculated from

$$\hat{\mathbf{y}}_{t+1|t} = \hat{E}(\mathbf{y}_{t+1}|\mathbf{y}_t, \mathbf{y}_{t-1}, \ldots, \mathbf{y}_1) = \mathbf{H}'\hat{\boldsymbol{\xi}}_{t+1|t}, \qquad [13.5.6]$$

with *MSE* given by [13.2.25]:

$$E[(\mathbf{y}_{t+1} - \hat{\mathbf{y}}_{t+1|t})(\mathbf{y}_{t+1} - \hat{\mathbf{y}}_{t+1|t})'] = \mathbf{H}'\mathbf{P}_{t+1|t}\mathbf{H} + \mathbf{R}. \qquad [13.5.7]$$

Consider the result from applying the Kalman filter to a covariance-stationary process that started up at a time arbitrarily distant in the past. From Proposition 13.1, the difference equation [13.5.5] will converge to

$$\hat{\boldsymbol{\xi}}_{t+1|t} = \mathbf{F}\hat{\boldsymbol{\xi}}_{t|t-1} + \mathbf{K}(\mathbf{y}_t - \mathbf{H}'\hat{\boldsymbol{\xi}}_{t|t-1}), \qquad [13.5.8]$$

with $\mathbf{K}$ given by [13.5.4]. The forecast [13.5.6] will approach the forecast of $\mathbf{y}_{t+1}$ based on the infinite history of its own lagged values:

$$\hat{E}(\mathbf{y}_{t+1}|\mathbf{y}_t, \mathbf{y}_{t-1}, \ldots) = \mathbf{H}'\hat{\boldsymbol{\xi}}_{t+1|t}. \qquad [13.5.9]$$

The *MSE* of this forecast is given by the limiting value of [13.5.7],

$$\begin{aligned} E\{[\mathbf{y}_{t+1} - \hat{E}(\mathbf{y}_{t+1}|\mathbf{y}_t, \mathbf{y}_{t-1}, \ldots)][\mathbf{y}_{t+1} - \hat{E}(\mathbf{y}_{t+1}|\mathbf{y}_t, \mathbf{y}_{t-1}, \ldots)]'\} \\ = \mathbf{H}'\mathbf{P}\mathbf{H} + \mathbf{R}, \end{aligned} \qquad [13.5.10]$$

where $\mathbf{P}$ is given by [13.5.3].

Equation [13.5.8] can be written

$$\hat{\boldsymbol{\xi}}_{t+1|t} = (\mathbf{F} - \mathbf{K}\mathbf{H}')L\hat{\boldsymbol{\xi}}_{t+1|t} + \mathbf{K}\mathbf{y}_t \qquad [13.5.11]$$

for $L$ the lag operator. Provided that the eigenvalues of $(\mathbf{F} - \mathbf{K}\mathbf{H}')$ are all inside the unit circle, [13.5.11] can be expressed as

$$\begin{aligned} \hat{\boldsymbol{\xi}}_{t+1|t} &= [\mathbf{I}_r - (\mathbf{F} - \mathbf{K}\mathbf{H}')L]^{-1}\mathbf{K}\mathbf{y}_t \\ &= [\mathbf{I}_r + (\mathbf{F} - \mathbf{K}\mathbf{H}')L + (\mathbf{F} - \mathbf{K}\mathbf{H}')^2L^2 + (\mathbf{F} - \mathbf{K}\mathbf{H}')^3L^3 + \cdots]\mathbf{K}\mathbf{y}_t. \end{aligned} \qquad [13.5.12]$$

Substituting [13.5.12] into [13.5.9] gives a steady-state rule for forecasting $\mathbf{y}_{t+1}$ as a linear function of its lagged values:

$$\hat{E}(\mathbf{y}_{t+1}|\mathbf{y}_t, \mathbf{y}_{t-1}, \ldots) = \mathbf{H}'[\mathbf{I}_r - (\mathbf{F} - \mathbf{K}\mathbf{H}')L]^{-1}\mathbf{K}\mathbf{y}_t. \qquad [13.5.13]$$

Expression [13.5.13] implies a $VAR(\infty)$ representation for $\mathbf{y}_t$ of the form

$$\mathbf{y}_{t+1} = \mathbf{H}'[\mathbf{I}_r - (\mathbf{F} - \mathbf{K}\mathbf{H}')L]^{-1}\mathbf{K}\mathbf{y}_t + \boldsymbol{\varepsilon}_{t+1}, \qquad [13.5.14]$$

where

$$\boldsymbol{\varepsilon}_{t+1} \equiv \mathbf{y}_{t+1} - \hat{E}(\mathbf{y}_{t+1}|\mathbf{y}_t, \mathbf{y}_{t-1}, \ldots). \qquad [13.5.15]$$

Thus, $\boldsymbol{\varepsilon}_{t+1}$ is the fundamental innovation for $\mathbf{y}_{t+1}$. Since $\boldsymbol{\varepsilon}_{t+1}$ is uncorrelated with $\mathbf{y}_{t-j}$ for any $j \geq 0$, it is also uncorrelated with $\boldsymbol{\varepsilon}_{t-j} = \mathbf{y}_{t-j} - \hat{E}(\mathbf{y}_{t-j}|\mathbf{y}_{t-j-1}, \mathbf{y}_{t-j-2}, \ldots)$ for any $j \geq 0$. The variance-covariance matrix of $\boldsymbol{\varepsilon}_{t+1}$ can be calculated using [13.5.15] and [13.5.10]):

$$\begin{aligned} E(\boldsymbol{\varepsilon}_{t+1}\boldsymbol{\varepsilon}'_{t+1}) &= E\{[\mathbf{y}_{t+1} - \hat{E}(\mathbf{y}_{t+1}|\mathbf{y}_t, \mathbf{y}_{t-1}, \ldots)] \\ &\qquad \times [\mathbf{y}_{t+1} - \hat{E}(\mathbf{y}_{t+1}|\mathbf{y}_t, \mathbf{y}_{t-1}, \ldots)]'\} \\ &= \mathbf{H}'\mathbf{P}\mathbf{H} + \mathbf{R}. \end{aligned} \qquad [13.5.16]$$

Note that [13.5.14] can be written as

$$\{\mathbf{I}_n - \mathbf{H}'[\mathbf{I}_r - (\mathbf{F} - \mathbf{KH}')L]^{-1}\mathbf{K}L\}\mathbf{y}_{t+1} = \boldsymbol{\varepsilon}_{t+1}. \qquad [13.5.17]$$

The following result helps to rewrite the $VAR(\infty)$ representation [13.5.17] in the Wold $MA(\infty)$ form.

***Proposition 13.3:*** *Let* $\mathbf{F}$, $\mathbf{H}'$, *and* $\mathbf{K}$ *be matrices of dimension* $(r \times r)$, $(n \times r)$, *and* $(r \times n)$, *respectively, such that eigenvalues of* $\mathbf{F}$ *and of* $(\mathbf{F} - \mathbf{KH}')$ *are all inside the unit circle, and let* $z$ *be a scalar on the complex unit circle. Then*

$$\{\mathbf{I}_n + \mathbf{H}'(\mathbf{I}_r - \mathbf{F}z)^{-1}\mathbf{K}z\}\{\mathbf{I}_n - \mathbf{H}'[\mathbf{I}_r - (\mathbf{F} - \mathbf{KH}')z]^{-1}\mathbf{K}z\} = \mathbf{I}_n.$$

Applying Proposition 13.3, if both sides of [13.5.17] are premultiplied by $(\mathbf{I}_n + \mathbf{H}'(\mathbf{I}_r - \mathbf{F}L)^{-1}\mathbf{K}L)$, the result is the Wold representation for $\mathbf{y}$:

$$\mathbf{y}_{t+1} = \{\mathbf{I}_n + \mathbf{H}'(\mathbf{I}_r - \mathbf{F}L)^{-1}\mathbf{K}L\}\boldsymbol{\varepsilon}_{t+1}. \qquad [13.5.18]$$

To summarize, the Wold representation can be found by iterating on [13.5.1] until convergence. The steady-state value for $\mathbf{P}$ is then used to construct $\mathbf{K}$ in [13.5.4]. If the eigenvalues of $(\mathbf{F} - \mathbf{KH}')$ are all inside the unit circle, then the Wold representation is given by [13.5.18].

The task of finding the Wold representation is sometimes alternatively posed as the question of factoring the autocovariance-generating function of $\mathbf{y}$. Applying result [10.3.7] to [13.5.16] and [13.5.18], we would anticipate that the autocovariance-generating function of $\mathbf{y}$ can be written in the form

$$\begin{aligned}\mathbf{G_Y}(z) = {} & \{\mathbf{I}_n + \mathbf{H}'(\mathbf{I}_r - \mathbf{F}z)^{-1}\mathbf{K}z\}\{\mathbf{H}'\mathbf{PH} + \mathbf{R}\} \\ & \times \{\mathbf{I}_n + \mathbf{K}'(\mathbf{I}_r - \mathbf{F}'z^{-1})^{-1}\mathbf{H}z^{-1}\}.\end{aligned} \qquad [13.5.19]$$

Compare [13.5.19] with the autocovariance-generating function that we would have written down directly from the structure of the state-space model. From [10.3.5], the autocovariance-generating function of $\boldsymbol{\xi}$ is given by

$$\mathbf{G}_{\boldsymbol{\xi}}(z) = [\mathbf{I}_r - \mathbf{F}z]^{-1}\mathbf{Q}[\mathbf{I}_r - \mathbf{F}'z^{-1}]^{-1},$$

while from [10.3.6] the autocovariance-generating function of $\mathbf{y}_t = \mathbf{H}'\boldsymbol{\xi}_t + \mathbf{w}_t$ is

$$\mathbf{G_Y}(z) = \mathbf{H}'[\mathbf{I}_r - \mathbf{F}z]^{-1}\mathbf{Q}[\mathbf{I}_r - \mathbf{F}'z^{-1}]^{-1}\mathbf{H} + \mathbf{R}. \qquad [13.5.20]$$

Comparing [13.5.19] with [13.5.20] suggests that the limiting values for the Kalman gain and $MSE$ matrices $\mathbf{K}$ and $\mathbf{P}$ can be used to factor an autocovariance-generating function. The following proposition gives a formal statement of this result.

***Proposition 13.4:*** *Let* $\mathbf{F}$ *denote an* $(r \times r)$ *matrix whose eigenvalues are all inside the unit circle; let* $\mathbf{Q}$ *and* $\mathbf{R}$ *denote symmetric positive semidefinite matrices of dimension* $(r \times r)$ *and* $(n \times n)$, *respectively; and let* $\mathbf{H}'$ *denote an arbitrary* $(n \times r)$ *matrix. Let* $\mathbf{P}$ *be a positive semidefinite matrix satisfying [13.5.3] and let* $\mathbf{K}$ *be given by [13.5.4]. Suppose that eigenvalues of* $(\mathbf{F} - \mathbf{KH}')$ *are all inside the unit circle. Then*

$$\begin{aligned}&\mathbf{H}'[\mathbf{I}_r - \mathbf{F}z]^{-1}\mathbf{Q}[\mathbf{I}_r - \mathbf{F}'z^{-1}]^{-1}\mathbf{H} + \mathbf{R} \\ &\quad = \{\mathbf{I}_n + \mathbf{H}'(\mathbf{I}_r - \mathbf{F}z)^{-1}\mathbf{K}z\}\{\mathbf{H}'\mathbf{PH} + \mathbf{R}\}\{\mathbf{I}_n + \mathbf{K}'(\mathbf{I}_r - \mathbf{F}'z^{-1})^{-1}\mathbf{H}z^{-1}\}.\end{aligned} \qquad [13.5.21]$$

A direct demonstration of this claim is provided in Appendix 13.A at the end of this chapter.

As an example of using these results, consider observations on a univariate $AR(1)$ process subject to white noise measurement error, such as the state-space system of [13.1.26] and [13.1.27] with $\mu = 0$. For this system, $\mathbf{F} = \phi$, $\mathbf{Q} = \sigma_V^2$, $\mathbf{A} = \mathbf{0}$, $\mathbf{H} = 1$, and $\mathbf{R} = \sigma_W^2$. The conditions of Proposition 13.2 are satisfied as long as $|\phi| < 1$, establishing that $|F - KH| = |\phi - K| < 1$. From equation

[13.5.14], the $AR(\infty)$ representation for this process can be found from

$$y_{t+1} = [1 - (\phi - K)L]^{-1}Ky_t + \varepsilon_{t+1},$$

which can be written

$$[1 - (\phi - K)L]y_{t+1} = Ky_t + [1 - (\phi - K)L]\varepsilon_{t+1}$$

or

$$y_{t+1} = \phi y_t + \varepsilon_{t+1} - (\phi - K)\varepsilon_t. \qquad [13.5.22]$$

This is an $ARMA(1, 1)$ process with $AR$ parameter given by $\phi$ and $MA$ parameter given by $-(\phi - K)$. The variance of the innovation for this process can be calculated from [13.5.16]:

$$E(\varepsilon_{t+1}^2) = \sigma_W^2 + P. \qquad [13.5.23]$$

The value of $P$ can be found by iterating on [13.5.1]:

$$\begin{aligned} P_{t+1|t} &= \phi^2[P_{t|t-1} - P_{t|t-1}^2/(\sigma_W^2 + P_{t|t-1})] + \sigma_V^2 \\ &= \phi^2 P_{t|t-1}\sigma_W^2/(\sigma_W^2 + P_{t|t-1}) + \sigma_V^2, \end{aligned} \qquad [13.5.24]$$

starting from $P_{1|0} = \sigma_V^2/(1 - \phi^2)$, until convergence. The steady-state Kalman gain is given by [13.5.4]:

$$K = \phi P/(\sigma_W^2 + P). \qquad [13.5.25]$$

As a second example, consider adding an $MA(q_1)$ process to an $MA(q_2)$ process with which the first process is uncorrelated at all leads and lags. This could be represented in state-space form as follows:

***State Equation*** $(r = q_1 + q_2 + 2)$:

$$\begin{bmatrix} u_{t+1} \\ u_t \\ \vdots \\ u_{t-q_1+1} \\ v_{t+1} \\ v_t \\ \vdots \\ v_{t-q_2+1} \end{bmatrix} = \underset{(q_1+q_2+2)\times(q_1+q_2+2)}{\begin{bmatrix} \mathbf{0}' & 0 & \mathbf{0}' & 0 \\ \mathbf{I}_{q_1} & \mathbf{0} & \mathbf{0} & \mathbf{0} \\ \mathbf{0}' & 0 & \mathbf{0}' & 0 \\ \mathbf{0} & \mathbf{0} & \mathbf{I}_{q_2} & \mathbf{0} \end{bmatrix}} \begin{bmatrix} u_t \\ u_{t-1} \\ \vdots \\ u_{t-q_1} \\ v_t \\ v_{t-1} \\ \vdots \\ v_{t-q_2} \end{bmatrix} + \begin{bmatrix} u_{t+1} \\ 0 \\ \vdots \\ 0 \\ v_{t+1} \\ 0 \\ \vdots \\ 0 \end{bmatrix} \qquad [13.5.26]$$

***Observation Equation*** $(n = 1)$:

$$y_t = [1 \quad \delta_1 \quad \delta_2 \quad \cdots \quad \delta_{q_1} \quad 1 \quad \kappa_1 \quad \kappa_2 \quad \cdots \quad \kappa_{q_2}] \begin{bmatrix} u_t \\ u_{t-1} \\ \vdots \\ u_{t-q_1} \\ v_t \\ v_{t-1} \\ \vdots \\ v_{t-q_2} \end{bmatrix}. \qquad [13.5.27]$$

Note that all eigenvalues of $\mathbf{F}$ are equal to zero. Write equation [13.5.18] in the form

$$\begin{aligned} \mathbf{y}_{t+1} &= \{\mathbf{I}_n + \mathbf{H}'(\mathbf{I}_r - \mathbf{F}L)^{-1}\mathbf{K}L\}\varepsilon_{t+1} \\ &= \{\mathbf{I}_n + \mathbf{H}'(\mathbf{I}_r + \mathbf{F}L + \mathbf{F}^2L^2 + \mathbf{F}^3L^3 + \cdots)\mathbf{K}L\}\varepsilon_{t+1}. \end{aligned} \qquad [13.5.28]$$

Let $q \equiv \max\{q_1, q_2\}$, and notice from the structure of $\mathbf{F}$ that $\mathbf{F}^{q+j} = \mathbf{0}$ for $j = 1, 2, \ldots$. Furthermore, from [13.5.4], $\mathbf{F}^q\mathbf{K} = \mathbf{F}^{q+1}\mathbf{PH}(\mathbf{H}'\mathbf{PH} + \mathbf{R})^{-1} = \mathbf{0}$. Thus

[13.5.28] takes the form

$$y_{t+1} = \{1 + \mathbf{H}'(\mathbf{I}_r + \mathbf{F}L + \mathbf{F}^2L^2 + \mathbf{F}^3L^3 + \cdots + \mathbf{F}^{q-1}L^{q-1})\mathbf{K}L\}\varepsilon_{t+1} \qquad [13.5.29]$$
$$= \{1 + \theta_1 L + \theta_2 L^2 + \cdots + \theta_q L^q\}\varepsilon_{t+1},$$

where

$$\theta_j = \mathbf{H}'\mathbf{F}^{j-1}\mathbf{K} \qquad \text{for } j = 1, 2, \ldots, q.$$

This provides a constructive demonstration of the claim that an $MA(q_1)$ process plus an $MA(q_2)$ process with which it is uncorrelated can be described as an $MA(\max\{q_1, q_2\})$ process.

The Kalman filter thus provides a general algorithm for finding the Wold representation or factoring an autocovariance-generating function—we simply iterate on [13.5.1] until convergence, and then use the steady-state gain from [13.5.4] either in [13.5.14] (for the $AR(\infty)$ form) or in [13.5.18] (for the $MA(\infty)$ form).

Although the convergent values provide the Wold representation, for any finite $t$ the Kalman filter forecasts have the advantage of calculating the exact optimal forecast of $\mathbf{y}_{t+1}$ based on a linear function of $\{\mathbf{y}_t, \mathbf{y}_{t-1}, \ldots, \mathbf{y}_1\}$.

## 13.6. *Smoothing*

The Kalman filter was motivated in Section 13.2 as an algorithm for calculating a forecast of the state vector $\boldsymbol{\xi}_t$ as a linear function of previous observations,

$$\hat{\boldsymbol{\xi}}_{t|t-1} \equiv \hat{E}(\boldsymbol{\xi}_t|\mathcal{Y}_{t-1}), \qquad [13.6.1]$$

where $\mathcal{Y}_{t-1} \equiv (\mathbf{y}'_{t-1}, \mathbf{y}'_{t-2}, \ldots, \mathbf{y}'_1, \mathbf{x}'_{t-1}, \mathbf{x}'_{t-2}, \ldots, \mathbf{x}_1)'$. The matrix $\mathbf{P}_{t|t-1}$ represented the MSE of this forecast:

$$\mathbf{P}_{t|t-1} \equiv E[(\boldsymbol{\xi}_t - \hat{\boldsymbol{\xi}}_{t|t-1})(\boldsymbol{\xi}_t - \hat{\boldsymbol{\xi}}_{t|t-1})']. \qquad [13.6.2]$$

For many uses of the Kalman filter these are the natural magnitudes of interest. In some settings, however, the state vector $\boldsymbol{\xi}_t$ is given a structural interpretation, in which case the value of this unobserved variable might be of interest for its own sake. For example, in the model of the business cycle by Stock and Watson, it would be helpful to know the state of the business cycle at any historical date $t$. A goal might then be to form an inference about the value of $\boldsymbol{\xi}_t$ based on the full set of data collected, including observations on $\mathbf{y}_t, \mathbf{y}_{t+1}, \ldots, \mathbf{y}_T, \mathbf{x}_t, \mathbf{x}_{t+1}, \ldots, \mathbf{x}_T$. Such an inference is called the *smoothed* estimate of $\boldsymbol{\xi}_t$, denoted

$$\hat{\boldsymbol{\xi}}_{t|T} \equiv \hat{E}(\boldsymbol{\xi}_t|\mathcal{Y}_T). \qquad [13.6.3]$$

For example, data on GNP from 1954 through 1990 might be used to estimate the value that $\boldsymbol{\xi}$ took on in 1960. The *MSE* of this smoothed estimate is denoted

$$\mathbf{P}_{t|T} \equiv E[(\boldsymbol{\xi}_t - \hat{\boldsymbol{\xi}}_{t|T})(\boldsymbol{\xi}_t - \hat{\boldsymbol{\xi}}_{t|T})']. \qquad [13.6.4]$$

In general, $\mathbf{P}_{t|\tau}$ denotes the *MSE* of an estimate of $\boldsymbol{\xi}_t$ that is based on observations of $\mathbf{y}$ and $\mathbf{x}$ through date $\tau$.

For the reader's convenience, we reproduce here the key equations for the Kalman filter:

$$\hat{\boldsymbol{\xi}}_{t|t} = \hat{\boldsymbol{\xi}}_{t|t-1} + \mathbf{P}_{t|t-1}\mathbf{H}(\mathbf{H}'\mathbf{P}_{t|t-1}\mathbf{H} + \mathbf{R})^{-1}(\mathbf{y}_t - \mathbf{A}'\mathbf{x}_t - \mathbf{H}'\hat{\boldsymbol{\xi}}_{t|t-1}) \qquad [13.6.5]$$

$$\hat{\boldsymbol{\xi}}_{t+1|t} = \mathbf{F}\hat{\boldsymbol{\xi}}_{t|t} \qquad [13.6.6]$$

$$\mathbf{P}_{t|t} = \mathbf{P}_{t|t-1} - \mathbf{P}_{t|t-1}\mathbf{H}(\mathbf{H}'\mathbf{P}_{t|t-1}\mathbf{H} + \mathbf{R})^{-1}\mathbf{H}'\mathbf{P}_{t|t-1} \qquad [13.6.7]$$

$$\mathbf{P}_{t+1|t} = \mathbf{F}\mathbf{P}_{t|t}\mathbf{F}' + \mathbf{Q}. \qquad [13.6.8]$$

Consider the estimate of $\boldsymbol{\xi}_t$ based on observations through date $t$, $\hat{\boldsymbol{\xi}}_{t|t}$. Suppose we were subsequently told the true value of $\boldsymbol{\xi}_{t+1}$. From the formula for updating a linear projection, equation [4.5.30], the new estimate of $\boldsymbol{\xi}_t$ could be expressed as[3]

$$\begin{aligned}\hat{E}(\boldsymbol{\xi}_t|\boldsymbol{\xi}_{t+1}, \boldsymbol{\mathcal{Y}}_t) = \hat{\boldsymbol{\xi}}_{t|t} &+ \{E[(\boldsymbol{\xi}_t - \hat{\boldsymbol{\xi}}_{t|t})(\boldsymbol{\xi}_{t+1} - \hat{\boldsymbol{\xi}}_{t+1|t})']\} \\ &\times \{E[(\boldsymbol{\xi}_{t+1} - \hat{\boldsymbol{\xi}}_{t+1|t})(\boldsymbol{\xi}_{t+1} - \hat{\boldsymbol{\xi}}_{t+1|t})']\}^{-1} \\ &\times (\boldsymbol{\xi}_{t+1} - \hat{\boldsymbol{\xi}}_{t+1|t}).\end{aligned} \qquad [13.6.9]$$

The first term in the product on the right side of [13.6.9] can be written

$$E[(\boldsymbol{\xi}_t - \hat{\boldsymbol{\xi}}_{t|t})(\boldsymbol{\xi}_{t+1} - \hat{\boldsymbol{\xi}}_{t+1|t})'] = E[(\boldsymbol{\xi}_t - \hat{\boldsymbol{\xi}}_{t|t})(\mathbf{F}\boldsymbol{\xi}_t + \mathbf{v}_{t+1} - \mathbf{F}\hat{\boldsymbol{\xi}}_{t|t})'],$$

by virtue of [13.2.1] and [13.6.6]. Furthermore, $\mathbf{v}_{t+1}$ is uncorrelated with $\boldsymbol{\xi}_t$ and $\hat{\boldsymbol{\xi}}_{t|t}$. Thus,

$$E[(\boldsymbol{\xi}_t - \hat{\boldsymbol{\xi}}_{t|t})(\boldsymbol{\xi}_{t+1} - \hat{\boldsymbol{\xi}}_{t+1|t})'] = E[(\boldsymbol{\xi}_t - \hat{\boldsymbol{\xi}}_{t|t})(\boldsymbol{\xi}_t - \hat{\boldsymbol{\xi}}_{t|t})'\mathbf{F}'] = \mathbf{P}_{t|t}\mathbf{F}'. \qquad [13.6.10]$$

Substituting [13.6.10] and the definition of $\mathbf{P}_{t+1|t}$ into [13.6.9] produces

$$\hat{E}(\boldsymbol{\xi}_t|\boldsymbol{\xi}_{t+1}, \boldsymbol{\mathcal{Y}}_t) = \hat{\boldsymbol{\xi}}_{t|t} + \mathbf{P}_{t|t}\mathbf{F}'\mathbf{P}_{t+1|t}^{-1}(\boldsymbol{\xi}_{t+1} - \hat{\boldsymbol{\xi}}_{t+1|t}).$$

Defining

$$\mathbf{J}_t \equiv \mathbf{P}_{t|t}\mathbf{F}'\mathbf{P}_{t+1|t}^{-1}, \qquad [13.6.11]$$

we have

$$\hat{E}(\boldsymbol{\xi}_t|\boldsymbol{\xi}_{t+1}, \boldsymbol{\mathcal{Y}}_t) = \hat{\boldsymbol{\xi}}_{t|t} + \mathbf{J}_t(\boldsymbol{\xi}_{t+1} - \hat{\boldsymbol{\xi}}_{t+1|t}). \qquad [13.6.12]$$

Now, the linear projection in [13.6.12] turns out to be the same as

$$\hat{E}(\boldsymbol{\xi}_t|\boldsymbol{\xi}_{t+1}, \boldsymbol{\mathcal{Y}}_T); \qquad [13.6.13]$$

that is, knowledge of $\mathbf{y}_{t+j}$ or $\mathbf{x}_{t+j}$ for $j > 0$ would be of no added value if we already knew the value of $\boldsymbol{\xi}_{t+1}$. To see this, note that $\mathbf{y}_{t+j}$ can be written as

$$\mathbf{y}_{t+j} = \mathbf{A}'\mathbf{x}_{t+j} + \mathbf{H}'(\mathbf{F}^{j-1}\boldsymbol{\xi}_{t+1} + \mathbf{F}^{j-2}\mathbf{v}_{t+2} + \mathbf{F}^{j-3}\mathbf{v}_{t+3} + \cdots + \mathbf{v}_{t+j}) + \mathbf{w}_{t+j}.$$

But the error

$$\boldsymbol{\xi}_t - \hat{E}(\boldsymbol{\xi}_t|\boldsymbol{\xi}_{t+1}, \boldsymbol{\mathcal{Y}}_t) \qquad [13.6.14]$$

is uncorrelated with $\boldsymbol{\xi}_{t+1}$, by the definition of a linear projection, and uncorrelated with $\mathbf{x}_{t+j}, \mathbf{w}_{t+j}, \mathbf{v}_{t+j}, \mathbf{v}_{t+j-1}, \ldots, \mathbf{v}_{t+2}$ under the maintained assumptions. Thus, the error [13.6.14] is uncorrelated with $\mathbf{y}_{t+j}$ or $\mathbf{x}_{t+j}$ for $j > 0$, meaning that [13.6.13] and [13.6.12] are the same, as claimed:

$$\hat{E}(\boldsymbol{\xi}_t|\boldsymbol{\xi}_{t+1}, \boldsymbol{\mathcal{Y}}_T) = \hat{\boldsymbol{\xi}}_{t|t} + \mathbf{J}_t(\boldsymbol{\xi}_{t+1} - \hat{\boldsymbol{\xi}}_{t+1|t}). \qquad [13.6.15]$$

It follows from the law of iterated projections that the smoothed estimate, $\hat{E}(\boldsymbol{\xi}_t|\boldsymbol{\mathcal{Y}}_T)$, can be obtained by projecting [13.6.15] on $\boldsymbol{\mathcal{Y}}_T$. In calculating this projection, we need to think carefully about the nature of the magnitudes in [13.6.15]. The first term, $\hat{\boldsymbol{\xi}}_{t|t}$, indicates a particular *exact* linear function of $\boldsymbol{\mathcal{Y}}_t$; the coefficients of this function are constructed from population moments, and these coefficients should be viewed as deterministic constants from the point of view of performing a subsequent projection. The projection of $\hat{\boldsymbol{\xi}}_{t|t}$ on $\boldsymbol{\mathcal{Y}}_T$ is thus still $\hat{\boldsymbol{\xi}}_{t|t}$, this same

[3] Here, $\mathbf{Y}_3 = \boldsymbol{\xi}_t$, $\mathbf{Y}_2 = \boldsymbol{\xi}_{t+1}$, and $\mathbf{Y}_1 = \boldsymbol{\mathcal{Y}}_t$.

linear function of $\mathcal{Y}_t$—we can't improve on a perfect fit![4] The term $\mathbf{J}_t$ in [13.6.11] is also a function of population moments, and so is again treated as deterministic for purposes of any linear projection. The term $\hat{\boldsymbol{\xi}}_{t+1|t}$ is another exact linear function of $\mathcal{Y}_t$. Thus, projecting [13.6.15] on $\mathcal{Y}_T$ turns out to be trivial:

$$\hat{E}(\boldsymbol{\xi}_t|\mathcal{Y}_T) = \hat{\boldsymbol{\xi}}_{t|t} + \mathbf{J}_t[\hat{E}(\boldsymbol{\xi}_{t+1}|\mathcal{Y}_T) - \hat{\boldsymbol{\xi}}_{t+1|t}],$$

or

$$\hat{\boldsymbol{\xi}}_{t|T} = \hat{\boldsymbol{\xi}}_{t|t} + \mathbf{J}_t(\hat{\boldsymbol{\xi}}_{t+1|T} - \hat{\boldsymbol{\xi}}_{t+1|t}). \qquad [13.6.16]$$

Thus, the sequence of smoothed estimates $\{\hat{\boldsymbol{\xi}}_{t|T}\}_{t=1}^{T}$ is calculated as follows. First, the Kalman filter, [13.6.5] to [13.6.8], is calculated and the sequences $\{\hat{\boldsymbol{\xi}}_{t|t}\}_{t=1}^{T}$, $\{\hat{\boldsymbol{\xi}}_{t+1|t}\}_{t=0}^{T-1}$, $\{\mathbf{P}_{t|t}\}_{t=1}^{T}$, and $\{\mathbf{P}_{t+1|t}\}_{t=0}^{T-1}$ are stored. The smoothed estimate for the final date in the sample, $\hat{\boldsymbol{\xi}}_{T|T}$, is just the last entry in $\{\hat{\boldsymbol{\xi}}_{t|t}\}_{t=1}^{T}$. Next, [13.6.11] is used to generate $\{\mathbf{J}_t\}_{t=1}^{T-1}$. From this, [13.6.16] is used for $t = T - 1$ to calculate

$$\hat{\boldsymbol{\xi}}_{T-1|T} = \hat{\boldsymbol{\xi}}_{T-1|T-1} + \mathbf{J}_{T-1}(\hat{\boldsymbol{\xi}}_{T|T} - \hat{\boldsymbol{\xi}}_{T|T-1}).$$

Now that $\hat{\boldsymbol{\xi}}_{T-1|T}$ has been calculated, [13.6.16] can be used for $t = T - 2$ to evaluate

$$\hat{\boldsymbol{\xi}}_{T-2|T} = \hat{\boldsymbol{\xi}}_{T-2|T-2} + \mathbf{J}_{T-2}(\hat{\boldsymbol{\xi}}_{T-1|T} - \hat{\boldsymbol{\xi}}_{T-1|T-2}).$$

Proceeding backward through the sample in this fashion permits calculation of the full set of smoothed estimates, $\{\hat{\boldsymbol{\xi}}_{t|T}\}_{t=1}^{T}$.

Next, consider the mean squared error associated with the smoothed estimate. Subtracting both sides of [13.6.16] from $\boldsymbol{\xi}_t$ produces

$$\boldsymbol{\xi}_t - \hat{\boldsymbol{\xi}}_{t|T} = \boldsymbol{\xi}_t - \hat{\boldsymbol{\xi}}_{t|t} - \mathbf{J}_t\hat{\boldsymbol{\xi}}_{t+1|T} + \mathbf{J}_t\hat{\boldsymbol{\xi}}_{t+1|t}$$

or

$$\boldsymbol{\xi}_t - \hat{\boldsymbol{\xi}}_{t|T} + \mathbf{J}_t\hat{\boldsymbol{\xi}}_{t+1|T} = \boldsymbol{\xi}_t - \hat{\boldsymbol{\xi}}_{t|t} + \mathbf{J}_t\hat{\boldsymbol{\xi}}_{t+1|t}.$$

Multiplying this equation by its transpose and taking expectations,

$$\begin{aligned} E[(\boldsymbol{\xi}_t - \hat{\boldsymbol{\xi}}_{t|T})(\boldsymbol{\xi}_t - \hat{\boldsymbol{\xi}}_{t|T})'] &+ \mathbf{J}_t E[(\hat{\boldsymbol{\xi}}_{t+1|T}\hat{\boldsymbol{\xi}}'_{t+1|T})]\mathbf{J}'_t \\ &= E[(\boldsymbol{\xi}_t - \hat{\boldsymbol{\xi}}_{t|t})(\boldsymbol{\xi}_t - \hat{\boldsymbol{\xi}}_{t|t})'] + \mathbf{J}_t E[(\hat{\boldsymbol{\xi}}_{t+1|t}\hat{\boldsymbol{\xi}}'_{t+1|t})]\mathbf{J}'_t. \end{aligned} \qquad [13.6.17]$$

The cross-product terms have disappeared from the left side because $\hat{\boldsymbol{\xi}}_{t+1|T}$ is a linear function of $\mathcal{Y}_T$ and so is uncorrelated with the projection error $\boldsymbol{\xi}_t - \hat{\boldsymbol{\xi}}_{t|T}$. Similarly, on the right side, $\hat{\boldsymbol{\xi}}_{t+1|t}$ is uncorrelated with $\boldsymbol{\xi}_t - \hat{\boldsymbol{\xi}}_{t|t}$.

Equation [13.6.17] states that

$$\mathbf{P}_{t|T} = \mathbf{P}_{t|t} + \mathbf{J}_t\{-E[(\hat{\boldsymbol{\xi}}_{t+1|T}\hat{\boldsymbol{\xi}}'_{t+1|T})] + E[(\hat{\boldsymbol{\xi}}_{t+1|t}\hat{\boldsymbol{\xi}}'_{t+1|t})]\}\mathbf{J}'_t. \qquad [13.6.18]$$

[4]The law of iterated projections states that

$$\hat{E}(\boldsymbol{\xi}_t|\mathcal{Y}_t) = \hat{E}[\hat{E}(\boldsymbol{\xi}_t|\mathcal{Y}_T)|\mathcal{Y}_t].$$

The law of iterated projections thus allows us to go from a larger information set to a smaller. Of course, the same operation does not work in reverse:

$$\hat{E}(\boldsymbol{\xi}_t|\mathcal{Y}_T) \neq \hat{E}[\hat{E}(\boldsymbol{\xi}_t|\mathcal{Y}_t)|\mathcal{Y}_T].$$

We cannot go from a smaller information set to a larger.

An example may clarify this point. Let $y_t$ be an i.i.d. zero-mean sequence with

$$\xi_t = \mu + y_{t+1}.$$

Then

$$\hat{E}(\xi_t|y_t) = \mu$$

and

$$\hat{E}[\hat{E}(\xi_t|y_t)|y_t, y_{t+1}] = \hat{E}[\mu|y_t, y_{t+1}] = \mu.$$

The bracketed term in [13.6.18] can be expressed as

$$\begin{aligned}
&-E[(\hat{\xi}_{t+1|T}\hat{\xi}'_{t+1|T})] + E[(\hat{\xi}_{t+1|t}\hat{\xi}'_{t+1|t})] \\
&\quad = \{E[(\xi_{t+1}\xi'_{t+1})] - E[(\hat{\xi}_{t+1|T}\hat{\xi}'_{t+1|T})]\} - \{E[(\xi_{t+1}\xi'_{t+1})] - E[(\hat{\xi}_{t+1|t}\hat{\xi}'_{t+1|t})]\} \\
&\quad = \{E[(\xi_{t+1} - \hat{\xi}_{t+1|T})(\xi_{t+1} - \hat{\xi}_{t+1|T})']\} - \{E[(\xi_{t+1} - \hat{\xi}_{t+1|t})(\xi_{t+1} - \hat{\xi}_{t+1|t})']\} \\
&\quad = \mathbf{P}_{t+1|T} - \mathbf{P}_{t+1|t}.
\end{aligned} \qquad [13.6.19]$$

The second-to-last equality used the fact that

$$\begin{aligned}
E[\xi_{t+1}\hat{\xi}'_{t+1|T}] &= E[(\xi_{t+1} - \hat{\xi}_{t+1|T} + \hat{\xi}_{t+1|T})\hat{\xi}'_{t+1|T}] \\
&= E[(\xi_{t+1} - \hat{\xi}_{t+1|T})\hat{\xi}'_{t+1|T}] + E[\hat{\xi}_{t+1|T}\hat{\xi}'_{t+1|T}] \\
&= E[\hat{\xi}_{t+1|T}\hat{\xi}'_{t+1|T}],
\end{aligned}$$

since the projection error $(\xi_{t+1} - \hat{\xi}_{t+1|T})$ is uncorrelated with $\hat{\xi}_{t+1|T}$. Similarly, $E(\xi_{t+1}\hat{\xi}'_{t+1|t}) = E(\hat{\xi}_{t+1|t}\hat{\xi}'_{t+1|t})$. Substituting [13.6.19] into [13.6.18] establishes that the smoothed estimate $\hat{\xi}_{t|T}$ has *MSE* given by

$$\mathbf{P}_{t|T} = \mathbf{P}_{t|t} + \mathbf{J}_t(\mathbf{P}_{t+1|T} - \mathbf{P}_{t+1|t})\mathbf{J}'_t. \qquad [13.6.20]$$

Again, this sequence is generated by moving through the sample backward starting with $t = T - 1$.

## 13.7. *Statistical Inference with the Kalman Filter*

The calculation of the mean squared error

$$\mathbf{P}_{\tau|t} = E[(\xi_\tau - \hat{\xi}_{\tau|t})(\xi_\tau - \hat{\xi}_{\tau|t})']$$

described earlier assumed that the parameters of the matrices **F**, **Q**, **A**, **H**, and **R** were known with certainty. Section 13.4 showed how these parameters could be estimated from the data by maximum likelihood. There would then be some sampling uncertainty about the true values of these parameters, and the calculation of $\mathbf{P}_{\tau|t}$ would need to be modified to obtain the true mean squared errors of the smoothed estimates and forecasts.[5]

Suppose the unknown parameters are collected in a vector $\boldsymbol{\theta}$. For any given value of $\boldsymbol{\theta}$, the matrices $\mathbf{F}(\boldsymbol{\theta})$, $\mathbf{Q}(\boldsymbol{\theta})$, $\mathbf{A}(\boldsymbol{\theta})$, $\mathbf{H}(\boldsymbol{\theta})$, and $\mathbf{R}(\boldsymbol{\theta})$ could be used to construct $\hat{\xi}_{\tau|T}(\boldsymbol{\theta})$ and $\mathbf{P}_{\tau|T}(\boldsymbol{\theta})$ in the formulas presented earlier; for $\tau \le T$, these are the smoothed estimate and *MSE* given in [13.6.16] and [13.6.20], respectively; while for $\tau > T$, these are the forecast and its *MSE* in [13.3.25] and [13.3.27]. Let $\mathcal{Y}_T \equiv (\mathbf{y}'_T, \mathbf{y}'_{T-1}, \ldots, \mathbf{y}'_1, \mathbf{x}'_T, \mathbf{x}'_{T-1}, \ldots, \mathbf{x}'_1)'$ denote the observed data, and let $\boldsymbol{\theta}_0$ denote the true value of $\boldsymbol{\theta}$. The earlier derivations assumed that the true value of $\boldsymbol{\theta}$ was used to construct $\hat{\xi}_{\tau|T}(\boldsymbol{\theta}_0)$ and $\mathbf{P}_{\tau|T}(\boldsymbol{\theta}_0)$.

Recall that the formulas for updating a linear projection and its *MSE*, [4.5.30] and [4.5.31], yield the conditional mean and conditional *MSE* when applied to Gaussian vectors; see equation [4.6.7]. Thus, if $\{\mathbf{v}_t\}$, $\{\mathbf{w}_t\}$, and $\xi_1$ are truly Gaussian, then the linear projection $\hat{\xi}_{\tau|T}(\boldsymbol{\theta}_0)$ has the interpretation as the expectation of $\xi_\tau$ conditional on the data,

$$\hat{\xi}_{\tau|T}(\boldsymbol{\theta}_0) = E(\xi_\tau|\mathcal{Y}_T); \qquad [13.7.1]$$

while $\mathbf{P}_{\tau|T}(\boldsymbol{\theta}_0)$ can be described as the conditional *MSE*:

$$\mathbf{P}_{\tau|T}(\boldsymbol{\theta}_0) = E\{[\xi_\tau - \hat{\xi}_{\tau|T}(\boldsymbol{\theta}_0)][\xi_\tau - \hat{\xi}_{\tau|T}(\boldsymbol{\theta}_0)]'|\mathcal{Y}_T\}. \qquad [13.7.2]$$

Let $\hat{\boldsymbol{\theta}}$ denote an estimate of $\boldsymbol{\theta}$ based on $\mathcal{Y}_T$, and let $\hat{\xi}_{\tau|T}(\hat{\boldsymbol{\theta}})$ denote the estimate that results from using $\hat{\boldsymbol{\theta}}$ to construct the smoothed inference or forecast in [13.6.16]

[5]This discussion is based on Hamilton (1986).

or [13.3.25]. The conditional mean squared error of this estimate is

$$\begin{aligned} E\{[\boldsymbol{\xi}_\tau - \hat{\boldsymbol{\xi}}_{\tau|T}(\hat{\boldsymbol{\theta}})][\boldsymbol{\xi}_\tau - \hat{\boldsymbol{\xi}}_{\tau|T}(\hat{\boldsymbol{\theta}})]'|\mathcal{Y}_T\} \\ = E\{[\boldsymbol{\xi}_\tau - \hat{\boldsymbol{\xi}}_{\tau|T}(\boldsymbol{\theta}_0) + \hat{\boldsymbol{\xi}}_{\tau|T}(\boldsymbol{\theta}_0) - \hat{\boldsymbol{\xi}}_{\tau|T}(\hat{\boldsymbol{\theta}})] \\ \times [\boldsymbol{\xi}_\tau - \hat{\boldsymbol{\xi}}_{\tau|T}(\boldsymbol{\theta}_0) + \hat{\boldsymbol{\xi}}_{\tau|T}(\boldsymbol{\theta}_0) - \hat{\boldsymbol{\xi}}_{\tau|T}(\hat{\boldsymbol{\theta}})]'|\mathcal{Y}_T\} \\ = E\{[\boldsymbol{\xi}_\tau - \hat{\boldsymbol{\xi}}_{\tau|T}(\boldsymbol{\theta}_0)][\boldsymbol{\xi}_\tau - \hat{\boldsymbol{\xi}}_{\tau|T}(\boldsymbol{\theta}_0)]'|\mathcal{Y}_T\} \\ + E\{[\hat{\boldsymbol{\xi}}_{\tau|T}(\boldsymbol{\theta}_0) - \hat{\boldsymbol{\xi}}_{\tau|T}(\hat{\boldsymbol{\theta}})][\hat{\boldsymbol{\xi}}_{\tau|T}(\boldsymbol{\theta}_0) - \hat{\boldsymbol{\xi}}_{\tau|T}(\hat{\boldsymbol{\theta}})]'|\mathcal{Y}_T\}. \end{aligned} \qquad [13.7.3]$$

Cross-product terms have disappeared from [13.7.3], since

$$\begin{aligned} E\{[\hat{\boldsymbol{\xi}}_{\tau|T}(\boldsymbol{\theta}_0) - \hat{\boldsymbol{\xi}}_{\tau|T}(\hat{\boldsymbol{\theta}})][\boldsymbol{\xi}_\tau - \hat{\boldsymbol{\xi}}_{\tau|T}(\boldsymbol{\theta}_0)]'|\mathcal{Y}_T\} \\ = [\hat{\boldsymbol{\xi}}_{\tau|T}(\boldsymbol{\theta}_0) - \hat{\boldsymbol{\xi}}_{\tau|T}(\hat{\boldsymbol{\theta}})] \times E\{[\boldsymbol{\xi}_\tau - \hat{\boldsymbol{\xi}}_{\tau|T}(\boldsymbol{\theta}_0)]'|\mathcal{Y}_T\} \\ = [\hat{\boldsymbol{\xi}}_{\tau|T}(\boldsymbol{\theta}_0) - \hat{\boldsymbol{\xi}}_{\tau|T}(\hat{\boldsymbol{\theta}})] \times \mathbf{0}'. \end{aligned}$$

The first equality follows because $\hat{\boldsymbol{\xi}}_{\tau|T}(\boldsymbol{\theta}_0)$ and $\hat{\boldsymbol{\xi}}_{\tau|T}(\hat{\boldsymbol{\theta}})$ are known nonstochastic functions of $\mathcal{Y}_T$, and the second equality is implied by [13.7.1]. Substituting [13.7.2] into [13.7.3] results in

$$\begin{aligned} E\{[\boldsymbol{\xi}_\tau - \hat{\boldsymbol{\xi}}_{\tau|T}(\hat{\boldsymbol{\theta}})][\boldsymbol{\xi}_\tau - \hat{\boldsymbol{\xi}}_{\tau|T}(\hat{\boldsymbol{\theta}})]'|\mathcal{Y}_T\} \\ = \mathbf{P}_{\tau|T}(\boldsymbol{\theta}_0) + E\{[\hat{\boldsymbol{\xi}}_{\tau|T}(\boldsymbol{\theta}_0) - \hat{\boldsymbol{\xi}}_{\tau|T}(\hat{\boldsymbol{\theta}})][\hat{\boldsymbol{\xi}}_{\tau|T}(\boldsymbol{\theta}_0) - \hat{\boldsymbol{\xi}}_{\tau|T}(\hat{\boldsymbol{\theta}})]'|\mathcal{Y}_T\}. \end{aligned} \qquad [13.7.4]$$

Equation [13.7.4] decomposes the mean squared error into two components. The first component, $\mathbf{P}_{\tau|T}(\boldsymbol{\theta}_0)$, might be described as the "filter uncertainty." This is the term calculated from the smoothing iteration [13.6.20] or forecast *MSE* [13.3.27] and represents uncertainty about $\boldsymbol{\xi}_\tau$ that would be present even if the true value $\boldsymbol{\theta}_0$ were known with certainty. The second term in [13.7.4],

$$E\{[\hat{\boldsymbol{\xi}}_{\tau|T}(\boldsymbol{\theta}_0) - \hat{\boldsymbol{\xi}}_{\tau|T}(\hat{\boldsymbol{\theta}})][\hat{\boldsymbol{\xi}}_{\tau|T}(\boldsymbol{\theta}_0) - \hat{\boldsymbol{\xi}}_{\tau|T}(\hat{\boldsymbol{\theta}})]'\},$$

might be called "parameter uncertainty." It reflects the fact that in a typical sample, $\hat{\boldsymbol{\theta}}$ will differ from the true value $\boldsymbol{\theta}_0$.

A simple way to estimate the size of each source of uncertainty is by Monte Carlo integration. Suppose we adopt the Bayesian perspective that $\boldsymbol{\theta}$ itself is a random variable. From this perspective, [13.7.4] describes the *MSE* conditional on $\boldsymbol{\theta} = \boldsymbol{\theta}_0$. Suppose that the posterior distribution of $\boldsymbol{\theta}$ conditional on the data $\mathcal{Y}_T$ is known; the asymptotic distribution for the *MLE* in [13.4.6] suggests that $\boldsymbol{\theta}|\mathcal{Y}_T$ might be regarded as approximately distributed $N(\hat{\boldsymbol{\theta}}, (1/T)\cdot\mathcal{I}^{-1})$, where $\hat{\boldsymbol{\theta}}$ denotes the *MLE*. We might then generate a large number of values of $\boldsymbol{\theta}$, say, $\boldsymbol{\theta}^{(1)}, \boldsymbol{\theta}^{(2)}, \ldots, \boldsymbol{\theta}^{(2000)}$, drawn from a $N(\hat{\boldsymbol{\theta}}, (1/T)\cdot\mathcal{I}^{-1})$ distribution. For each draw $(j)$, we could calculate the smoothed estimate or forecast $\hat{\boldsymbol{\xi}}_{\tau|T}(\boldsymbol{\theta}^{(j)})$. The deviations of these estimates across Monte Carlo draws from the estimate $\hat{\boldsymbol{\xi}}_{\tau|T}(\hat{\boldsymbol{\theta}})$ can be used to describe how sensitive the estimate $\hat{\boldsymbol{\xi}}_{\tau|T}(\hat{\boldsymbol{\theta}})$ is to parameter uncertainty about $\boldsymbol{\theta}$:

$$\frac{1}{2000}\sum_{j=1}^{2000} [\hat{\boldsymbol{\xi}}_{\tau|T}(\boldsymbol{\theta}^{(j)}) - \hat{\boldsymbol{\xi}}_{\tau|T}(\hat{\boldsymbol{\theta}})][\hat{\boldsymbol{\xi}}_{\tau|T}(\boldsymbol{\theta}^{(j)}) - \hat{\boldsymbol{\xi}}_{\tau|T}(\hat{\boldsymbol{\theta}})]'. \qquad [13.7.5]$$

This affords an estimate of

$$E\{[\hat{\boldsymbol{\xi}}_{\tau|T}(\boldsymbol{\theta}) - \hat{\boldsymbol{\xi}}_{\tau|T}(\hat{\boldsymbol{\theta}})][\hat{\boldsymbol{\xi}}_{\tau|T}(\boldsymbol{\theta}) - \hat{\boldsymbol{\xi}}_{\tau|T}(\hat{\boldsymbol{\theta}})]'|\mathcal{Y}_T\},$$

where this expectation is understood to be with respect to the distribution of $\boldsymbol{\theta}$ conditional on $\mathcal{Y}_T$.

For each Monte Carlo realization $\boldsymbol{\theta}^{(j)}$, we can also calculate $\mathbf{P}_{\tau|T}(\boldsymbol{\theta}^{(j)})$ from [13.6.20] or [13.3.27]. Its average value across Monte Carlo draws,

$$\frac{1}{2000}\sum_{j=1}^{2000} \mathbf{P}_{\tau|T}(\boldsymbol{\theta}^{(j)}), \qquad [13.7.6]$$

provides an estimate of the filter uncertainty in [13.7.4],

$$E[\mathbf{P}_{\tau|T}(\boldsymbol{\theta})|\mathcal{Y}_T].$$

Again, this expectation is with respect to the distribution of $\boldsymbol{\theta}|\mathcal{Y}_T$.

The sum of [13.7.5] and [13.7.6] is then proposed as an *MSE* for the estimate $\hat{\boldsymbol{\xi}}_{\tau|T}(\hat{\boldsymbol{\theta}})$ around the true value $\boldsymbol{\xi}_\tau$.

## 13.8. *Time-Varying Parameters*

### *State-Space Model with Stochastically Varying Coefficients*

Up to this point we have been assuming that the matrices **F**, **Q**, **A**, **H**, and **R** were all constant. The Kalman filter can also be adapted for more general state-space models in which the values of these matrices depend on the exogenous or lagged dependent variables included in the vector $\mathbf{x}_t$. Consider

$$\boldsymbol{\xi}_{t+1} = \mathbf{F}(\mathbf{x}_t)\boldsymbol{\xi}_t + \mathbf{v}_{t+1} \qquad [13.8.1]$$

$$\mathbf{y}_t = \mathbf{a}(\mathbf{x}_t) + [\mathbf{H}(\mathbf{x}_t)]'\boldsymbol{\xi}_t + \mathbf{w}_t. \qquad [13.8.2]$$

Here $\mathbf{F}(\mathbf{x}_t)$ denotes an $(r \times r)$ matrix whose elements are functions of $\mathbf{x}_t$; $\mathbf{a}(\mathbf{x}_t)$ similarly describes an $(n \times 1)$ vector-valued function, and $\mathbf{H}(\mathbf{x}_t)$ an $(r \times n)$ matrix-valued function. It is assumed that conditional on $\mathbf{x}_t$ and on data observed through date $t-1$, denoted

$$\mathcal{Y}_{t-1} \equiv (\mathbf{y}'_{t-1}, \mathbf{y}'_{t-2}, \ldots, \mathbf{y}'_1, \mathbf{x}'_{t-1}, \mathbf{x}'_{t-2}, \ldots, \mathbf{x}'_1)',$$

the vector $(\mathbf{v}'_{t+1}, \mathbf{w}'_t)'$ has the Gaussian distribution

$$\left[\begin{matrix}\mathbf{v}_{t+1}\\ \mathbf{w}_t\end{matrix}\middle|\, \mathbf{x}_t, \mathcal{Y}_{t-1}\right] \sim N\left(\begin{bmatrix}\mathbf{0}\\ \mathbf{0}\end{bmatrix}, \begin{bmatrix}\mathbf{Q}(\mathbf{x}_t) & \mathbf{0}\\ \mathbf{0} & \mathbf{R}(\mathbf{x}_t)\end{bmatrix}\right). \qquad [13.8.3]$$

Note that although [13.8.1] to [13.8.3] generalize the earlier framework by allowing for stochastically varying parameters, it is more restrictive in that a Gaussian distribution is assumed in [13.8.3]; the role of the Gaussian requirement will be explained shortly.

Suppose it is taken as given that $\boldsymbol{\xi}_t|\mathcal{Y}_{t-1} \sim N(\hat{\boldsymbol{\xi}}_{t|t-1}, \mathbf{P}_{t|t-1})$. Assuming as before that $\mathbf{x}_t$ contains only strictly exogenous variables or lagged values of $\mathbf{y}$, this also describes the distribution of $\boldsymbol{\xi}_t|\mathbf{x}_t, \mathcal{Y}_{t-1}$. It follows from the assumptions in [13.8.1] to [13.8.3] that

$$\left[\begin{matrix}\boldsymbol{\xi}_t\\ \mathbf{y}_t\end{matrix}\middle|\, \mathbf{x}_t, \mathcal{Y}_{t-1}\right]$$
$$\sim N\left(\begin{bmatrix}\hat{\boldsymbol{\xi}}_{t|t-1}\\ \mathbf{a}(\mathbf{x}_t) + [\mathbf{H}(\mathbf{x}_t)]'\hat{\boldsymbol{\xi}}_{t|t-1}\end{bmatrix}, \begin{bmatrix}\mathbf{P}_{t|t-1} & \mathbf{P}_{t|t-1}\mathbf{H}(\mathbf{x}_t)\\ \mathbf{H}'(\mathbf{x}_t)\mathbf{P}_{t|t-1} & [\mathbf{H}(\mathbf{x}_t)]'\mathbf{P}_{t|t-1}\mathbf{H}(\mathbf{x}_t) + \mathbf{R}(\mathbf{x}_t)\end{bmatrix}\right). \qquad [13.8.4]$$

Conditional on $\mathbf{x}_t$, the terms $\mathbf{a}(\mathbf{x}_t)$, $\mathbf{H}(\mathbf{x}_t)$, and $\mathbf{R}(\mathbf{x}_t)$ can all be treated as deterministic. Thus, the formula for the conditional distribution of Gaussian vectors [4.6.7] can be used to deduce that[6]

$$\boldsymbol{\xi}_t|\mathbf{y}_t, \mathbf{x}_t, \mathcal{Y}_{t-1} \equiv \boldsymbol{\xi}_t|\mathcal{Y}_t \sim N(\hat{\boldsymbol{\xi}}_{t|t}, \mathbf{P}_{t|t}), \qquad [13.8.5]$$

[6]Here $\mathbf{Y}_1 = \mathbf{y}_t$, $\mathbf{Y}_2 = \boldsymbol{\xi}_t$, $\boldsymbol{\mu}_1 = \mathbf{a}(\mathbf{x}_t) + [\mathbf{H}(\mathbf{x}_t)]'\hat{\boldsymbol{\xi}}_{t|t-1}$, $\boldsymbol{\mu}_2 = \hat{\boldsymbol{\xi}}_{t|t-1}$, $\boldsymbol{\Omega}_{11} = \{[\mathbf{H}(\mathbf{x}_t)]'\mathbf{P}_{t|t-1}\mathbf{H}(\mathbf{x}_t) + \mathbf{R}(\mathbf{x}_t)\}$, $\boldsymbol{\Omega}_{22} = \mathbf{P}_{t|t-1}$, and $\boldsymbol{\Omega}_{21} = \mathbf{P}_{t|t-1}\mathbf{H}(\mathbf{x}_t)$.

where

$$\hat{\boldsymbol{\xi}}_{t|t} = \hat{\boldsymbol{\xi}}_{t|t-1} + \Big\{\mathbf{P}_{t|t-1}\mathbf{H}(\mathbf{x}_t)[[\mathbf{H}(\mathbf{x}_t)]'\mathbf{P}_{t|t-1}\mathbf{H}(\mathbf{x}_t) + \mathbf{R}(\mathbf{x}_t)]^{-1} \times [\mathbf{y}_t - \mathbf{a}(\mathbf{x}_t) - [\mathbf{H}(\mathbf{x}_t)]'\hat{\boldsymbol{\xi}}_{t|t-1}]\Big\} \qquad [13.8.6]$$

$$\mathbf{P}_{t|t} = \mathbf{P}_{t|t-1} - \Big\{\mathbf{P}_{t|t-1}\mathbf{H}(\mathbf{x}_t) \times [[\mathbf{H}(\mathbf{x}_t)]'\mathbf{P}_{t|t-1}\mathbf{H}(\mathbf{x}_t) + \mathbf{R}(\mathbf{x}_t)]^{-1}[\mathbf{H}(\mathbf{x}_t)]'\mathbf{P}_{t|t-1}\Big\}. \qquad [13.8.7]$$

It then follows from [13.8.1] and [13.8.3] that $\boldsymbol{\xi}_{t+1}|\mathcal{Y}_t \sim N(\hat{\boldsymbol{\xi}}_{t+1|t}, \mathbf{P}_{t+1|t})$, where

$$\hat{\boldsymbol{\xi}}_{t+1|t} = \mathbf{F}(\mathbf{x}_t)\hat{\boldsymbol{\xi}}_{t|t} \qquad [13.8.8]$$

$$\mathbf{P}_{t+1|t} = \mathbf{F}(\mathbf{x}_t)\mathbf{P}_{t|t}[\mathbf{F}(\mathbf{x}_t)]' + \mathbf{Q}(\mathbf{x}_t). \qquad [13.8.9]$$

Equations [13.8.6] through [13.8.9] are just the Kalman filter equations [13.2.15], [13.2.16], [13.2.17], and [13.2.21] with the parameter matrices **F**, **Q**, **A**, **H**, and **R** replaced by their time-varying analogs. Thus, as long as we are willing to treat the initial state $\boldsymbol{\xi}_1$ as $N(\hat{\boldsymbol{\xi}}_{1|0}, \mathbf{P}_{1|0})$, the Kalman filter iterations go through the same as before. The obvious generalization of [13.4.1] can continue to be used to evaluate the likelihood function.

Note, however, that unlike the constant-parameter case, the inference [13.8.6] is a nonlinear function of $\mathbf{x}_t$. This means that although [13.8.6] gives the optimal inference if the disturbances and initial state are Gaussian, it cannot be interpreted as the linear projection of $\boldsymbol{\xi}_t$ on $\mathcal{Y}_t$ with non-Gaussian disturbances.

### *Linear Regression Models with Time-Varying Coefficients*

One important application of the state-space model with stochastically varying parameters is a regression in which the coefficient vector changes over time. Consider

$$y_t = \mathbf{x}_t'\boldsymbol{\beta}_t + w_t, \qquad [13.8.10]$$

where $\mathbf{x}_t$ is a $(k \times 1)$ vector that can include lagged values of $y$ or variables that are independent of the regression disturbance $w_\tau$ for all $\tau$. The parameters of the coefficient vector are presumed to evolve over time according to

$$(\boldsymbol{\beta}_{t+1} - \bar{\boldsymbol{\beta}}) = \mathbf{F}(\boldsymbol{\beta}_t - \bar{\boldsymbol{\beta}}) + \mathbf{v}_{t+1}. \qquad [13.8.11]$$

If the eigenvalues of the $(k \times k)$ matrix **F** are all inside the unit circle, then $\bar{\boldsymbol{\beta}}$ has the interpretation as the average or steady-state value for the coefficient vector. If it is further assumed that

$$\left[\begin{array}{c} \mathbf{v}_{t+1} \\ w_t \end{array}\middle| \mathbf{x}_t, \mathcal{Y}_{t-1}\right] \sim N\left(\begin{bmatrix} \mathbf{0} \\ 0 \end{bmatrix}, \begin{bmatrix} \mathbf{Q} & \mathbf{0} \\ \mathbf{0}' & \sigma^2 \end{bmatrix}\right), \qquad [13.8.12]$$

then [13.8.10] to [13.8.12] will be recognized as a state-space model of the form of [13.8.1] to [13.8.3] with state vector $\boldsymbol{\xi}_t = \boldsymbol{\beta}_t - \bar{\boldsymbol{\beta}}$. The regression in [13.8.10] can be written as

$$y_t = \mathbf{x}_t'\bar{\boldsymbol{\beta}} + \mathbf{x}_t'\boldsymbol{\xi}_t + w_t, \qquad [13.8.13]$$

which is an observation equation of the form of [13.8.2] with $\mathbf{a}(\mathbf{x}_t) = \mathbf{x}_t'\bar{\boldsymbol{\beta}}$, $\mathbf{H}(\mathbf{x}_t) = \mathbf{x}_t$, and $\mathbf{R}(\mathbf{x}_t) = \sigma^2$. These values are then used in the Kalman filter iterations [13.8.6] to [13.8.9]. A one-period-ahead forecast for [13.8.10] can be calculated from [13.8.4] as

$$E(y_t|\mathbf{x}_t, \mathcal{Y}_{t-1}) = \mathbf{x}_t'\bar{\boldsymbol{\beta}} + \mathbf{x}_t'\hat{\boldsymbol{\xi}}_{t|t-1},$$

where $\{\hat{\xi}_{t|t-1}\}_{t=1}^{T}$ is calculated from [13.8.6] and [13.8.8]. The *MSE* of this forecast can also be inferred from [13.8.4]:

$$E[(y_t - \mathbf{x}_t'\bar{\boldsymbol{\beta}} - \mathbf{x}_t'\hat{\xi}_{t|t-1})^2|\mathbf{x}_t, \mathcal{Y}_{t-1}] = \mathbf{x}_t'\mathbf{P}_{t|t-1}\mathbf{x}_t + \sigma^2,$$

where $\{\mathbf{P}_{t|t-1}\}_{t=1}^{T}$ is calculated from [13.8.7] and [13.8.9]. The sample log likelihood is therefore

$$\sum_{t=1}^{T} \log f(y_t|\mathbf{x}_t, \mathcal{Y}_{t-1}) = -(T/2)\log(2\pi) - (1/2)\sum_{t=1}^{T}\log(\mathbf{x}_t'\mathbf{P}_{t|t-1}\mathbf{x}_t + \sigma^2)$$
$$- (1/2)\sum_{t=1}^{T}(y_t - \mathbf{x}_t'\bar{\boldsymbol{\beta}} - \mathbf{x}_t'\hat{\xi}_{t|t-1})^2/(\mathbf{x}_t'\mathbf{P}_{t|t-1}\mathbf{x}_t + \sigma^2).$$

The specification in [13.8.11] can easily be generalized to allow for a $p$th-order *VAR* for the coefficient vector $\boldsymbol{\beta}_t$ by defining $\xi_t' \equiv [(\boldsymbol{\beta}_t - \bar{\boldsymbol{\beta}})', (\boldsymbol{\beta}_{t-1} - \bar{\boldsymbol{\beta}})', \ldots, (\boldsymbol{\beta}_{t-p+1} - \bar{\boldsymbol{\beta}})']$ and replacing [13.8.11] with

$$\xi_{t+1} = \begin{bmatrix} \boldsymbol{\Phi}_1 & \boldsymbol{\Phi}_2 & \cdots & \boldsymbol{\Phi}_{p-1} & \boldsymbol{\Phi}_p \\ \mathbf{I}_k & \mathbf{0} & \cdots & \mathbf{0} & \mathbf{0} \\ \mathbf{0} & \mathbf{I}_k & \cdots & \mathbf{0} & \mathbf{0} \\ \vdots & \vdots & \cdots & \vdots & \vdots \\ \mathbf{0} & \mathbf{0} & \cdots & \mathbf{I}_k & \mathbf{0} \end{bmatrix} \xi_t + \begin{bmatrix} \mathbf{v}_{t+1} \\ \mathbf{0} \\ \mathbf{0} \\ \vdots \\ \mathbf{0} \end{bmatrix}.$$

## *Estimation of a* VAR *with Time-Varying Coefficients*

Section 12.2 described Litterman's approach to Bayesian estimation of an equation of a vector autoregression with constant but unknown coefficients. A related approach to estimating a *VAR* with time-varying coefficients was developed by Doan, Litterman, and Sims (1984). Although efficiency might be improved by estimating all the equations of the *VAR* jointly, their proposal was to infer the parameters for each equation in isolation from the others.

Suppose for illustration that equation [13.8.10] describes the first equation from a *VAR*, so that the dependent variable ($y_t$) is $y_{1t}$ and the $(k \times 1)$ vector of explanatory variables is $\mathbf{x}_t = (1, \mathbf{y}_{t-1}', \mathbf{y}_{t-2}', \ldots, \mathbf{y}_{t-p}')'$, where $\mathbf{y}_t = (y_{1t}, y_{2t}, \ldots, y_{nt})'$ and $k = np + 1$. The coefficient vector is

$$\boldsymbol{\beta}_t = (c_{1,t}, \phi_{11,t}^{(1)}, \phi_{12,t}^{(1)}, \ldots, \phi_{1n,t}^{(1)}, \phi_{11,t}^{(2)}, \phi_{12,t}^{(2)}, \ldots, \phi_{1n,t}^{(2)}, \ldots,$$
$$\phi_{11,t}^{(p)}, \phi_{12,t}^{(p)}, \ldots, \phi_{1n,t}^{(p)})',$$

where $\phi_{1j,t}^{(s)}$ is the coefficient relating $y_{1t}$ to $y_{j,t-s}$. This coefficient is allowed to be different for each date $t$ in the sample.

Doan, Litterman, and Sims specified a Bayesian prior distribution for the initial value of the coefficient vector at date 1:

$$\boldsymbol{\beta}_1 \sim N(\bar{\boldsymbol{\beta}}, \mathbf{P}_{1|0}). \qquad [13.8.14]$$

The prior distribution is independent across coefficients, so that $\mathbf{P}_{1|0}$ is a diagonal matrix. The mean of the prior distribution, $\bar{\boldsymbol{\beta}}$, is that used by Litterman (1986) for a constant-coefficient *VAR*. This prior distribution holds that changes in $y_{1t}$ are probably difficult to forecast, so that the coefficient on $y_{1,t-1}$ is likely to be near unity and all other coefficients are expected to be near zero:

$$\bar{\boldsymbol{\beta}} = (0, 1, 0, 0, \ldots, 0)'. \qquad [13.8.15]$$

As in Section 12.2, let $\gamma$ characterize the analyst's confidence in the prediction that $\phi_{11,1}^{(1)}$ is near unity:

$$\phi_{11,1}^{(1)} \sim N(1, \gamma^2).$$

Smaller values of $\gamma$ imply more confidence in the prior conviction that $\phi_{11,1}^{(1)}$ is near unity.

The coefficient $\phi_{11,1}^{(s)}$ relates the value of variable 1 at date 1 to its own value

$s$ periods earlier. Doan, Litterman, and Sims had more confidence in the prior conviction that $\phi_{11.1}^{(s)}$ is zero the greater the lag, or the larger the value of $s$. They represented this with a harmonic series for the variance,

$$\phi_{11.1}^{(s)} \sim N(0, \gamma^2/s) \qquad \text{for } s = 2, 3, \ldots, p.$$

The prior distribution for the coefficient relating variable 1 to lags of other variables was taken to be

$$\phi_{1j.1}^{(s)} \sim N\left(0, \frac{w^2 \cdot \gamma^2 \cdot \hat{\tau}_1^2}{s \cdot \hat{\tau}_j^2}\right) \qquad \begin{array}{l} j = 2, 3, \ldots, n \\ s = 1, 2, \ldots, p \end{array}. \qquad [13.8.16]$$

As in expression [12.2.4], this includes a correction $(\hat{\tau}_1^2/\hat{\tau}_j^2)$ for the scale of $y_{1t}$ relative to $y_{jt}$, where $\hat{\tau}_j^2$ is the estimated variance of the residuals for a univariate fixed-coefficient $AR(p)$ process fitted to series $j$. The variance in [13.8.16] also includes a factor $w^2 < 1$ representing the prior expectation that lagged values of $y_j$ for $j \neq 1$ are less likely to be of help in forecasting $y_1$ than would be the lagged values of $y_1$ itself; hence, a tighter prior is used to set coefficients on $y_j$ to zero.

Finally, let $g$ describe the variance of the prior distribution for the constant term:

$$c_{1.1} \sim N(0, g \cdot \hat{\tau}_1^2).$$

To summarize, the matrix $\mathbf{P}_{1|0}$ is specified to be

$$\mathbf{P}_{1|0} = \begin{bmatrix} g \cdot \hat{\tau}_1^2 & \mathbf{0}' \\ \mathbf{0} & (\mathbf{B} \otimes \mathbf{C}) \end{bmatrix}, \qquad [13.8.17]$$

where

$$\underset{(p \times p)}{\mathbf{B}} = \begin{bmatrix} \gamma^2 & 0 & 0 & \cdots & 0 \\ 0 & \gamma^2/2 & 0 & \cdots & 0 \\ 0 & 0 & \gamma^2/3 & \cdots & 0 \\ \vdots & \vdots & \vdots & \cdots & \vdots \\ 0 & 0 & 0 & \cdots & \gamma^2/p \end{bmatrix}$$

$$\underset{(n \times n)}{\mathbf{C}} = \begin{bmatrix} 1 & 0 & 0 & \cdots & 0 \\ 0 & w^2\hat{\tau}_1^2/\hat{\tau}_2^2 & 0 & \cdots & 0 \\ 0 & 0 & w^2\hat{\tau}_1^2/\hat{\tau}_3^2 & \cdots & 0 \\ \vdots & \vdots & \vdots & \cdots & \vdots \\ 0 & 0 & 0 & \cdots & w^2\hat{\tau}_1^2/\hat{\tau}_n^2 \end{bmatrix}.$$

For typical economic time series, Doan, Litterman, and Sims recommended using $\gamma^2 = 0.07$, $w^2 = 1/74$, and $g = 630$. This last value ensures that very little weight is given to the prior expectation that the constant term is zero.

Each of the coefficients in the $VAR$ is then presumed to evolve over time according to a first-order autoregression:

$$\boldsymbol{\beta}_{t+1} = \pi_8 \cdot \boldsymbol{\beta}_t + (1 - \pi_8) \cdot \bar{\boldsymbol{\beta}} + \mathbf{v}_{t+1}. \qquad [13.8.18]$$

Thus, the same scalar $\pi_8$ is used to describe a univariate $AR(1)$ process for each element of $\boldsymbol{\beta}_t$; Doan, Litterman, and Sims recommended a value of $\pi_8 = 0.999$. The disturbance $\mathbf{v}_t$ is assumed to have a diagonal variance-covariance matrix:

$$E(\mathbf{v}_t\mathbf{v}_t') = \mathbf{Q}. \qquad [13.8.19]$$

For all coefficients except the constant term, the variance of the $i$th element of $\mathbf{v}_t$ was assumed to be proportional to the corresponding element of $\mathbf{P}_{1|0}$. Thus, for $i = 2, 3, \ldots, k$, the row $i$, column $i$ element of $\mathbf{Q}$ is taken to be $\pi_7$ times the row $i$, column $i$ element of $\mathbf{P}_{1|0}$. The (1, 1) element of $\mathbf{Q}$ is taken to be $\pi_7$ times the (2, 2) element of $\mathbf{P}_{1|0}$. This adjustment is used because the (1, 1) element of $\mathbf{P}_{1|0}$ represents an effectively infinite variance corresponding to prior ignorance about the value for the constant term. Doan, Litterman, and Sims recommended $\pi_7 = 10^{-7}$ as a suitable value for the constant of proportionality.

Equation [13.8.18] can be viewed as a state equation of the form

$$\boldsymbol{\xi}_{t+1} = \mathbf{F}\boldsymbol{\xi}_t + \mathbf{v}_{t+1}, \qquad [13.8.20]$$

where the state vector is given by $\boldsymbol{\xi}_t = (\boldsymbol{\beta}_t - \bar{\boldsymbol{\beta}})$ and $\mathbf{F} = \pi_8 \cdot \mathbf{I}_k$. The observation equation is

$$y_{1t} = \mathbf{x}_t'\bar{\boldsymbol{\beta}} + \mathbf{x}_t'\boldsymbol{\xi}_t + w_{1t}. \qquad [13.8.21]$$

The one parameter yet to be specified is the variance of $w_{1t}$, the residual in the *VAR*. Doan, Litterman, and Sims suggested taking this to be 0.9 times $\hat{\tau}_1^2$.

Thus, the sequence of estimated state vectors $\{\hat{\boldsymbol{\xi}}_{t|t}\}_{t=1}^T$ is found by iterating on [13.8.6] through [13.8.9] starting from $\hat{\boldsymbol{\xi}}_{1|0} = \mathbf{0}$ and $\mathbf{P}_{1|0}$ given by [13.8.17], with $\mathbf{F}(\mathbf{x}_t) = \pi_8 \cdot \mathbf{I}_k$, $\mathbf{Q}(\mathbf{x}_t) = \pi_7 \cdot \mathbf{P}_{1|0}$, $\mathbf{a}(\mathbf{x}_t) = \mathbf{x}_t'\bar{\boldsymbol{\beta}}$ with $\bar{\boldsymbol{\beta}}$ given by [13.8.15], $\mathbf{H}(\mathbf{x}_t) = \mathbf{x}_t$, and $\mathbf{R}(\mathbf{x}_t) = 0.9 \cdot \hat{\tau}_1^2$. The estimated coefficient vector is then $\hat{\boldsymbol{\beta}}_{t|t} = \bar{\boldsymbol{\beta}} + \hat{\boldsymbol{\xi}}_{t|t}$. Optimal one-period-ahead forecasts are given by $\hat{y}_{1,t+1|t} = \mathbf{x}_t'\hat{\boldsymbol{\beta}}_{t|t}$.

Optimal $s$-period-ahead forecasts are difficult to calculate. However, Doan, Litterman, and Sims suggested a simple approximation. The approximation takes the optimal one-period-ahead forecasts for each of the $n$ variables in the *VAR*, $\hat{\mathbf{y}}_{t+1|t}$, and then treats these forecasts as if they were actual observations on $\mathbf{y}_{t+1}$. Then $E(\mathbf{y}_{t+2}|\mathbf{y}_t, \mathbf{y}_{t-1}, \ldots, \mathbf{y}_1)$ is approximated by $E(\mathbf{y}_{t+2}|\mathbf{y}_{t+1}, \mathbf{y}_t, \ldots, \mathbf{y}_1)$ evaluated at $\mathbf{y}_{t+1} = E(\mathbf{y}_{t+1}|\mathbf{y}_t, \mathbf{y}_{t-1}, \ldots, \mathbf{y}_1)$. The law of iterated expectations does not apply here, since $E(\mathbf{y}_{t+2}|\mathbf{y}_{t+1}, \mathbf{y}_t, \ldots, \mathbf{y}_1)$ is a nonlinear function of $\mathbf{y}_{t+1}$. However, Doan, Litterman, and Sims argued that this simple approach gives a good approximation to the optimal forecast.

## APPENDIX 13.A. *Proofs of Chapter 13 Propositions*

■ **Proof of Proposition 13.1.**[7] Recall that $\mathbf{P}_{t+1|t}$ has the interpretation as the *MSE* of the linear projection of $\boldsymbol{\xi}_{t+1}$ on $\mathcal{Y}_t \equiv (\mathbf{y}_t', \mathbf{y}_{t-1}', \ldots, \mathbf{y}_1', \mathbf{x}_t', \mathbf{x}_{t-1}', \ldots, \mathbf{x}_1')'$,

$$\mathbf{P}_{t+1|t} = MSE[\hat{E}(\boldsymbol{\xi}_{t+1}|\mathcal{Y}_t)]. \qquad [13.A.1]$$

Suppose for some reason we instead tried to forecast $\boldsymbol{\xi}_{t+1}$ using only observations 2, 3, . . . , $t$, discarding the observation for date $t = 1$. Thus, define $\mathcal{Y}_t^* \equiv (\mathbf{y}_t', \mathbf{y}_{t-1}', \ldots, \mathbf{y}_2', \mathbf{x}_t', \mathbf{x}_{t-1}', \ldots, \mathbf{x}_2')'$, and let

$$\mathbf{P}_{t+1|t}^* \equiv MSE[\hat{E}(\boldsymbol{\xi}_{t+1}|\mathcal{Y}_t^*)]. \qquad [13.A.2]$$

Then clearly, [13.A.2] cannot be smaller than [13.A.1], since the linear projection $\hat{E}(\boldsymbol{\xi}_{t+1}|\mathcal{Y}_t)$ made optimal use of $\mathcal{Y}_t^*$ along with the added information in $(\mathbf{y}_1', \mathbf{x}_1')'$. Specifically, if $\mathbf{h}$ is any $(r \times 1)$ vector, the linear projection of $z_{t+1} \equiv \mathbf{h}'\boldsymbol{\xi}_{t+1}$ on $\mathcal{Y}_t$ has *MSE* given by

$$\begin{aligned} E[z_{t+1} - \hat{E}(z_{t+1}|\mathcal{Y}_t)]^2 &= E[\mathbf{h}'\boldsymbol{\xi}_{t+1} - \mathbf{h}' \cdot \hat{E}(\boldsymbol{\xi}_{t+1}|\mathcal{Y}_t)]^2 \\ &= \mathbf{h}' \cdot E\{[\boldsymbol{\xi}_{t+1} - \hat{E}(\boldsymbol{\xi}_{t+1}|\mathcal{Y}_t)][\boldsymbol{\xi}_{t+1} - \hat{E}(\boldsymbol{\xi}_{t+1}|\mathcal{Y}_t)]'\} \cdot \mathbf{h} \\ &= \mathbf{h}'\mathbf{P}_{t+1|t}\mathbf{h}. \end{aligned}$$

Similarly, the linear projection of $z_{t+1}$ on $\mathcal{Y}_t^*$ has *MSE* $\mathbf{h}'\mathbf{P}_{t+1|t}^*\mathbf{h}$, with

$$\mathbf{h}'\mathbf{P}_{t+1|t}\mathbf{h} \le \mathbf{h}'\mathbf{P}_{t+1|t}^*\mathbf{h}. \qquad [13.A.3]$$

But for a system of the form of [13.2.1] and [13.2.2] with eigenvalues of $\mathbf{F}$ inside the unit circle and time-invariant coefficients, it will be the case that

$$\begin{aligned} &MSE[\hat{E}(\boldsymbol{\xi}_{t+1}|\mathbf{y}_t, \mathbf{y}_{t-1}, \ldots, \mathbf{y}_2, \mathbf{x}_t, \mathbf{x}_{t-1}, \ldots, \mathbf{x}_2)] \\ &\qquad = MSE[\hat{E}(\boldsymbol{\xi}_t|\mathbf{y}_{t-1}, \mathbf{y}_{t-2}, \ldots, \mathbf{y}_1, \mathbf{x}_{t-1}, \mathbf{x}_{t-2}, \ldots, \mathbf{x}_1)], \end{aligned}$$

that is,

$$\mathbf{P}_{t+1|t}^* = \mathbf{P}_{t|t-1}.$$

Hence, [13.A.3] implies that

$$\mathbf{h}'\mathbf{P}_{t+1|t}\mathbf{h} \le \mathbf{h}'\mathbf{P}_{t|t-1}\mathbf{h}$$

[7] The arguments in the proofs of Propositions 13.1 and 13.2 are adapted from Anderson and Moore (1979, pp. 76–82).

for any $(r \times 1)$ vector $\mathbf{h}$. The sequence of scalars $\{\mathbf{h}'\mathbf{P}_{t+1|t}\mathbf{h}\}_{t=1}^{T}$ is thus monotonically nonincreasing and is bounded below by zero. It therefore converges to some fixed nonnegative value. Since this is true for any $(r \times 1)$ vector $\mathbf{h}$ and since the matrix $\mathbf{P}_{t+1|t}$ is symmetric, it follows that the sequence $\{\mathbf{P}_{t+1|t}\}_{t=1}^{T}$ converges to some fixed positive semidefinite matrix $\mathbf{P}$.

To verify the claims about the eigenvalues of the matrix $(\mathbf{F} - \mathbf{KH}')$, note that if $\mathbf{P}$ is a fixed point of [13.5.3], then it must also be a fixed point of the equivalent difference equation [13.2.28]:

$$\mathbf{P} = (\mathbf{F} - \mathbf{KH}')\mathbf{P}(\mathbf{F} - \mathbf{KH}')' + \mathbf{KRK}' + \mathbf{Q}. \qquad [13.A.4]$$

Let $\mathbf{x}$ denote an eigenvector of $(\mathbf{F} - \mathbf{KH}')'$ and $\lambda$ its eigenvalue:

$$(\mathbf{F} - \mathbf{KH}')'\mathbf{x} = \lambda\mathbf{x}. \qquad [13.A.5]$$

Although $\mathbf{F}$, $\mathbf{K}$, and $\mathbf{H}$ are all real, the eigenvalue $\lambda$ and eigenvector $\mathbf{x}$ could be complex. If $\mathbf{x}^{H}$ denotes the conjugate transpose of $\mathbf{x}$, then

$$\begin{aligned}\mathbf{x}^{H}(\mathbf{F} - \mathbf{KH}')\mathbf{P}(\mathbf{F} - \mathbf{KH}')'\mathbf{x} &= [(\mathbf{F} - \mathbf{KH}')'\mathbf{x}]^{H}\mathbf{P}[(\mathbf{F} - \mathbf{KH}')'\mathbf{x}] \\ &= [\lambda\mathbf{x}]^{H}\mathbf{P}[\lambda\mathbf{x}] \\ &= |\lambda|^{2}\mathbf{x}^{H}\mathbf{P}\mathbf{x}.\end{aligned}$$

Thus, if [13.A.4] is premultiplied by $\mathbf{x}^{H}$ and postmultiplied by $\mathbf{x}$, the result is

$$\mathbf{x}^{H}\mathbf{P}\mathbf{x} = |\lambda|^{2}\mathbf{x}^{H}\mathbf{P}\mathbf{x} + \mathbf{x}^{H}(\mathbf{KRK}' + \mathbf{Q})\mathbf{x},$$

or

$$(1 - |\lambda|^{2})\mathbf{x}^{H}\mathbf{P}\mathbf{x} = \mathbf{x}^{H}(\mathbf{KRK}' + \mathbf{Q})\mathbf{x}. \qquad [13.A.6]$$

Now, $(\mathbf{KRK}' + \mathbf{Q})$ is positive semidefinite, so the right side of [13.A.6] is nonnegative. Likewise, $\mathbf{P}$ is positive semidefinite, so $\mathbf{x}^{H}\mathbf{P}\mathbf{x}$ is nonnegative. Expression [13.A.6] then requires $|\lambda| \leq 1$, meaning that any eigenvalue of $(\mathbf{F} - \mathbf{KH}')$ must be on or inside the unit circle, as claimed. ■

■ **Proof of Proposition 13.2.** First we establish the final claim of the proposition, concerning the eigenvalues of $(\mathbf{F} - \mathbf{KH}')$. Let $\mathbf{P}$ denote any positive semidefinite matrix that satisfies [13.A.4], and let $\mathbf{K}$ be given by [13.5.4]. Notice that if $\mathbf{Q}$ is positive definite, then the right side of [13.A.6] is strictly positive for any nonzero $\mathbf{x}$, meaning from the left side of [13.A.6] that any eigenvalue $\lambda$ of $(\mathbf{F} - \mathbf{KH}')$ is strictly inside the unit circle. Alternatively, if $\mathbf{R}$ is positive definite, then the only way that the right side of [13.A.6] could fail to be strictly positive would be if $\mathbf{K}'\mathbf{x} = \mathbf{0}$. But from [13.A.5], this would imply that $\mathbf{F}'\mathbf{x} = \lambda\mathbf{x}$, that is, that $\mathbf{x}$ is an eigenvector and $\lambda$ is an eigenvalue of $\mathbf{F}'$. This, in turn, means that $\lambda$ is an eigenvalue of $\mathbf{F}$, in which case $|\lambda| < 1$, by the assumption of stability of $\mathbf{F}$. Thus, there cannot be an eigenvector $\mathbf{x}$ of $(\mathbf{F} - \mathbf{KH}')'$ associated with an eigenvalue whose modulus is greater than or equal to unity if $\mathbf{R}$ is positive definite.

Turning next to the rest of Proposition 13.2, let $\{\mathbf{P}_{t+1|t}\}$ denote the sequence that results from iterating on [13.5.1] starting from an arbitrary positive semidefinite initial value $\mathbf{P}_{1|0}$. We will show that there exist two other sequences of matrices, to be denoted $\{\underset{\sim}{\mathbf{P}}_{t+1|t}\}$ and $\{\tilde{\mathbf{P}}_{t+1|t}\}$, such that

$$\underset{\sim}{\mathbf{P}}_{t+1|t} \leq \mathbf{P}_{t+1|t} \leq \tilde{\mathbf{P}}_{t+1|t} \qquad \text{for all } t,$$

where

$$\lim_{t\to\infty} \underset{\sim}{\mathbf{P}}_{t+1|t} = \lim \tilde{\mathbf{P}}_{t+1|t} = \mathbf{P}$$

and where $\mathbf{P}$ does not depend on $\mathbf{P}_{1|0}$. The conclusion will then be that $\{\mathbf{P}_{t+1|t}\}$ converges to $\mathbf{P}$ regardless of the value of $\mathbf{P}_{1|0}$.

To construct the matrix $\underset{\sim}{\mathbf{P}}_{t+1|t}$ that is to be offered as a lower bound on $\mathbf{P}_{t+1|t}$, consider the sequence $\{\underset{\sim}{\mathbf{P}}_{t+1|t}\}$ that results from iterating on [13.5.1] starting from the initial value $\underset{\sim}{\mathbf{P}}_{1|0} = \mathbf{0}$. This would correspond to treating the intial state $\boldsymbol{\xi}_1$ as if known with certainty:

$$\underset{\sim}{\mathbf{P}}_{t+1|t} = MSE[\hat{E}(\boldsymbol{\xi}_{t+1}|\mathcal{Y}_t, \boldsymbol{\xi}_1)]. \qquad [13.A.7]$$

Note that $\mathbf{y}_1$ and $\mathbf{x}_1$ are correlated with $\boldsymbol{\xi}_{t+1}$ for $t = 1, 2, \ldots$ only through the value of $\boldsymbol{\xi}_1$, which means that we could equally well write

$$\underset{\sim}{\mathbf{P}}_{t+1|t} = MSE[\hat{E}(\boldsymbol{\xi}_{t+1}|\mathcal{Y}_t^{*}, \boldsymbol{\xi}_1)], \qquad [13.A.8]$$

where $\mathcal{Y}_t^{*} \equiv (\mathbf{y}_t', \mathbf{y}_{t-1}', \ldots, \mathbf{y}_2', \mathbf{x}_t', \mathbf{x}_{t-1}', \ldots, \mathbf{x}_2')'$. Added knowledge about $\boldsymbol{\xi}_2$ could not hurt the forecast:

$$MSE[\hat{E}(\boldsymbol{\xi}_{t+1}|\mathcal{Y}_t^{*}, \boldsymbol{\xi}_2, \boldsymbol{\xi}_1)] \leq MSE[\hat{E}(\boldsymbol{\xi}_{t+1}|\mathcal{Y}_t^{*}, \boldsymbol{\xi}_1)], \qquad [13.A.9]$$

and indeed, $\boldsymbol{\xi}_1$ is correlated with $\boldsymbol{\xi}_{t+1}$ for $t = 2, 3, \ldots$ only through the value of $\boldsymbol{\xi}_2$:

$$MSE[\hat{E}(\boldsymbol{\xi}_{t+1}|\mathcal{Y}_t^*, \boldsymbol{\xi}_2, \boldsymbol{\xi}_1)] = MSE[\hat{E}(\boldsymbol{\xi}_{t+1}|\mathcal{Y}_t^*, \boldsymbol{\xi}_2)]. \qquad [13.A.10]$$

Because coefficients are time-invariant,

$$MSE[\hat{E}(\boldsymbol{\xi}_{t+1}|\mathcal{Y}_t^*, \boldsymbol{\xi}_2)] = MSE[\hat{E}(\boldsymbol{\xi}_t|\mathcal{Y}_{t-1}, \boldsymbol{\xi}_1)] = \underset{\sim}{\mathbf{P}}_{t|t-1}. \qquad [13.A.11]$$

Thus, [13.A.10] and [13.A.11] establish that the left side of [13.A.9] is the same as $\underset{\sim}{\mathbf{P}}_{t|t-1}$, while from [13.A.8] the right side of [13.A.9] is the same as $\underset{\sim}{\mathbf{P}}_{t+1|t}$. Thus, [13.A.9] states that

$$\underset{\sim}{\mathbf{P}}_{t|t-1} \leq \underset{\sim}{\mathbf{P}}_{t+1|t},$$

so that $\{\underset{\sim}{\mathbf{P}}_{t+1|t}\}$ is a monotonically nondecreasing sequence; the farther in the past is the perfect information about $\boldsymbol{\xi}_1$, the less value it is for forecasting $\boldsymbol{\xi}_{t+1}$.

Furthermore, a forecast based on perfect information about $\boldsymbol{\xi}_1$, for which $\underset{\sim}{\mathbf{P}}_{t+1|t}$ gives the $MSE$, must be better than one based on imperfect information about $\boldsymbol{\xi}_1$, for which $\mathbf{P}_{t+1|t}$ gives the $MSE$:

$$\underset{\sim}{\mathbf{P}}_{t+1|t} \leq \mathbf{P}_{t+1|t} \qquad \text{for all } t.$$

Thus, $\underset{\sim}{\mathbf{P}}_{t+1|t}$ puts a lower bound on $\mathbf{P}_{t+1|t}$, as claimed. Moreover, since the sequence $\{\underset{\sim}{\mathbf{P}}_{t+1|t}\}$ is monotonically nondecreasing and bounded from above, it converges to a fixed value $\mathbf{P}$ satisfying [13.5.3] and [13.A.4].

To construct an upper bound on $\mathbf{P}_{t+1|t}$, consider a sequence $\{\tilde{\mathbf{P}}_{t+1|t}\}$ that begins with $\tilde{\mathbf{P}}_{1|0} = \mathbf{P}_{1|0}$, the same starting value that was used to construct $\{\mathbf{P}_{t+1|t}\}$. Recall that $\mathbf{P}_{t+1|t}$ gave the $MSE$ of the sequence $\hat{\boldsymbol{\xi}}_{t+1|t}$ described in equation [13.2.20]:

$$\hat{\boldsymbol{\xi}}_{t+1|t} = \mathbf{F}\hat{\boldsymbol{\xi}}_{t|t-1} + \mathbf{K}_t(\mathbf{y}_t - \mathbf{A}'\mathbf{x}_t - \mathbf{H}'\hat{\boldsymbol{\xi}}_{t|t-1}).$$

Imagine instead using a sequence of suboptimal inferences $\{\tilde{\boldsymbol{\xi}}_{t+1|t}\}$defined by the recursion

$$\tilde{\boldsymbol{\xi}}_{t+1|t} = \mathbf{F}\tilde{\boldsymbol{\xi}}_{t|t-1} + \mathbf{K}(\mathbf{y}_t - \mathbf{A}'\mathbf{x}_t - \mathbf{H}'\tilde{\boldsymbol{\xi}}_{t|t-1}), \qquad [13.A.12]$$

where $\mathbf{K}$ is the value calculated from [13.5.4] in which the steady-state value for $\mathbf{P}$ is taken to be the limit of the sequence $\{\underset{\sim}{\mathbf{P}}_{t+1|t}\}$. Note that the magnitude $\tilde{\boldsymbol{\xi}}_{t+1|t}$ so defined is a linear function of $\mathcal{Y}_t$ and so must have a greater $MSE$ than the optimal inference $\hat{\boldsymbol{\xi}}_{t+1|t}$:

$$\tilde{\mathbf{P}}_{t+1|t} \equiv E[(\boldsymbol{\xi}_{t+1} - \tilde{\boldsymbol{\xi}}_{t+1|t})(\boldsymbol{\xi}_{t+1} - \tilde{\boldsymbol{\xi}}_{t+1|t})'] \geq \mathbf{P}_{t+1|t}.$$

Thus, we have established that

$$\underset{\sim}{\mathbf{P}}_{t+1|t} \leq \mathbf{P}_{t+1|t} \leq \tilde{\mathbf{P}}_{t+1|t}$$

and that $\underset{\sim}{\mathbf{P}}_{t+1|t} \to \mathbf{P}$. The proof will be complete if we can further show that $\tilde{\mathbf{P}}_{t+1|t} \to \mathbf{P}$. Parallel calculations to those leading to [13.2.28] reveal that

$$\tilde{\mathbf{P}}_{t+1|t} = (\mathbf{F} - \mathbf{K}\mathbf{H}')\tilde{\mathbf{P}}_{t|t-1}(\mathbf{F} - \mathbf{K}\mathbf{H}')' + \mathbf{K}\mathbf{R}\mathbf{K}' + \mathbf{Q}. \qquad [13.A.13]$$

Apply the vec operator to both sides of [13.A.13] and recall Proposition 10.4:

$$\operatorname{vec}(\tilde{\mathbf{P}}_{t+1|t}) = \mathcal{B}\operatorname{vec}(\tilde{\mathbf{P}}_{t|t-1}) + c = [\mathbf{I}_{r^2} + \mathcal{B} + \mathcal{B}^2 + \cdots + \mathcal{B}^{t-1}]c + \mathcal{B}^t \operatorname{vec}(\tilde{\mathbf{P}}_{1|0}),$$

where

$$\mathcal{B} \equiv (\mathbf{F} - \mathbf{K}\mathbf{H}') \otimes (\mathbf{F} - \mathbf{K}\mathbf{H}')$$
$$c \equiv \operatorname{vec}(\mathbf{K}\mathbf{R}\mathbf{K}' + \mathbf{Q}).$$

Recall further that since either $\mathbf{R}$ or $\mathbf{Q}$ is positive definite, the value of $\mathbf{K}$ has the property that all eigenvalues of $(\mathbf{F} - \mathbf{K}\mathbf{H}')$ are strictly less than unity in modulus. Thus, all eigenvalues of $\mathcal{B}$ are also strictly less than unity in modulus, implying that

$$\lim_{t\to\infty} \operatorname{vec}(\tilde{\mathbf{P}}_{t+1|t}) = (\mathbf{I}_{r^2} - \mathcal{B})^{-1}c,$$

the same value regardless of the starting value for $\tilde{\mathbf{P}}_{1|0}$. In particular, if the iteration on [13.A.13] is started with $\tilde{\mathbf{P}}_{1|0} = \mathbf{P}$, this being a fixed point of the iteration, the result would be $\tilde{\mathbf{P}}_{t+1|t} = \mathbf{P}$ for all $t$. Thus,

$$\lim_{t\to\infty} \tilde{\mathbf{P}}_{t+1|t} = \mathbf{P},$$

regardless of the value of $\tilde{\mathbf{P}}_{1|0} = \mathbf{P}_{1|0}$ from which the iteration for $\tilde{\mathbf{P}}_{t+1|t}$ is started. ■

■ **Proof of Proposition 13.3.** Observe that

$$\begin{aligned}
&\{\mathbf{I}_n + \mathbf{H}'(\mathbf{I}_r - \mathbf{F}z)^{-1}\mathbf{K}z\}\{\mathbf{I}_n - \mathbf{H}'[\mathbf{I}_r - (\mathbf{F} - \mathbf{K}\mathbf{H}')z]^{-1}\mathbf{K}z\}\\
&\quad = \mathbf{I}_n - \mathbf{H}'[\mathbf{I}_r - (\mathbf{F} - \mathbf{K}\mathbf{H}')z]^{-1}\mathbf{K}z + \mathbf{H}'(\mathbf{I}_r - \mathbf{F}z)^{-1}\mathbf{K}z\\
&\qquad - \{\mathbf{H}'(\mathbf{I}_r - \mathbf{F}z)^{-1}\mathbf{K}z\}\{\mathbf{H}'[\mathbf{I}_r - (\mathbf{F} - \mathbf{K}\mathbf{H}')z]^{-1}\mathbf{K}z\} \qquad [13.A.14]\\
&\quad = \mathbf{I}_n + \mathbf{H}'\Big\{-[\mathbf{I}_r - (\mathbf{F} - \mathbf{K}\mathbf{H}')z]^{-1} + [\mathbf{I}_r - \mathbf{F}z]^{-1}\\
&\qquad - [\mathbf{I}_r - \mathbf{F}z]^{-1}\mathbf{K}\mathbf{H}'z[\mathbf{I}_r - (\mathbf{F} - \mathbf{K}\mathbf{H}')z]^{-1}\Big\}\mathbf{K}z.
\end{aligned}$$

The term in curly braces in the last line of [13.A.14] is indeed zero, as may be verified by taking the identity

$$-[\mathbf{I}_r - \mathbf{F}z] + [\mathbf{I}_r - (\mathbf{F} - \mathbf{K}\mathbf{H}')z] - \mathbf{K}\mathbf{H}'z = \mathbf{0}$$

and premultiplying by $[\mathbf{I}_r - \mathbf{F}z]^{-1}$ and postmultiplying by $[\mathbf{I}_r - (\mathbf{F} - \mathbf{K}\mathbf{H}')z]^{-1}$:

$$\begin{aligned}
&-[\mathbf{I}_r - (\mathbf{F} - \mathbf{K}\mathbf{H}')z]^{-1} + [\mathbf{I}_r - \mathbf{F}z]^{-1}\\
&\quad - [\mathbf{I}_r - \mathbf{F}z]^{-1}\mathbf{K}\mathbf{H}'z[\mathbf{I}_r - (\mathbf{F} - \mathbf{K}\mathbf{H}')z]^{-1} = \mathbf{0}. \quad ■
\end{aligned} \qquad [13.A.15]$$

■ **Proof of Proposition 13.4.** Notice that

$$\begin{aligned}
&\{\mathbf{I}_n + \mathbf{H}'(\mathbf{I}_r - \mathbf{F}z)^{-1}\mathbf{K}z\}\{\mathbf{H}'\mathbf{P}\mathbf{H} + \mathbf{R}\}\{\mathbf{I}_n + \mathbf{K}'(\mathbf{I}_r - \mathbf{F}'z^{-1})^{-1}\mathbf{H}z^{-1}\}\\
&\quad = \{\mathbf{H}'\mathbf{P}\mathbf{H} + \mathbf{R}\} + \mathbf{H}'(\mathbf{I}_r - \mathbf{F}z)^{-1}\mathbf{K}\{\mathbf{H}'\mathbf{P}\mathbf{H} + \mathbf{R}\}z \qquad [13.A.16]\\
&\qquad + \{\mathbf{H}'\mathbf{P}\mathbf{H} + \mathbf{R}\}\mathbf{K}'(\mathbf{I}_r - \mathbf{F}'z^{-1})^{-1}\mathbf{H}z^{-1}\\
&\qquad + \mathbf{H}'(\mathbf{I}_r - \mathbf{F}z)^{-1}\mathbf{K}\{\mathbf{H}'\mathbf{P}\mathbf{H} + \mathbf{R}\}\mathbf{K}'(\mathbf{I}_r - \mathbf{F}'z^{-1})^{-1}\mathbf{H}.
\end{aligned}$$

Now [13.5.4] requires that

$$\mathbf{K}\{\mathbf{H}'\mathbf{P}\mathbf{H} + \mathbf{R}\} = \mathbf{F}\mathbf{P}\mathbf{H} \qquad [13.A.17]$$

$$\{\mathbf{H}'\mathbf{P}\mathbf{H} + \mathbf{R}\}\mathbf{K}' = \mathbf{H}'\mathbf{P}\mathbf{F}' \qquad [13.A.18]$$

$$\begin{aligned}
\mathbf{K}\{\mathbf{H}'\mathbf{P}\mathbf{H} + \mathbf{R}\}\mathbf{K}' &= \mathbf{F}\mathbf{P}\mathbf{H}\{\mathbf{H}'\mathbf{P}\mathbf{H} + \mathbf{R}\}^{-1}\mathbf{H}'\mathbf{P}\mathbf{F}'\\
&= \mathbf{F}\mathbf{P}\mathbf{F}' - \mathbf{P} + \mathbf{Q},
\end{aligned} \qquad [13.A.19]$$

with the last equality following from [13.5.3]. Substituting [13.A.17] through [13.A.19] into [13.A.16] results in

$$\begin{aligned}
&\{\mathbf{I}_n + \mathbf{H}'(\mathbf{I}_r - \mathbf{F}z)^{-1}\mathbf{K}z\}\{\mathbf{H}'\mathbf{P}\mathbf{H} + \mathbf{R}\}\{\mathbf{I}_n + \mathbf{K}'(\mathbf{I}_r - \mathbf{F}'z^{-1})^{-1}\mathbf{H}z^{-1}\}\\
&\quad = \{\mathbf{H}'\mathbf{P}\mathbf{H} + \mathbf{R}\} + \mathbf{H}'(\mathbf{I}_r - \mathbf{F}z)^{-1}\mathbf{F}\mathbf{P}\mathbf{H}z + \mathbf{H}'\mathbf{P}\mathbf{F}'(\mathbf{I}_r - \mathbf{F}'z^{-1})^{-1}\mathbf{H}z^{-1}\\
&\qquad + \mathbf{H}'(\mathbf{I}_r - \mathbf{F}z)^{-1}\{\mathbf{F}\mathbf{P}\mathbf{F}' - \mathbf{P} + \mathbf{Q}\}(\mathbf{I}_r - \mathbf{F}'z^{-1})^{-1}\mathbf{H} \qquad [13.A.20]\\
&\quad = \mathbf{R} + \mathbf{H}'\Big\{\mathbf{P} + (\mathbf{I}_r - \mathbf{F}z)^{-1}\mathbf{F}\mathbf{P}z + \mathbf{P}\mathbf{F}'(\mathbf{I}_r - \mathbf{F}'z^{-1})^{-1}z^{-1}\\
&\qquad + (\mathbf{I}_r - \mathbf{F}z)^{-1}\{\mathbf{F}\mathbf{P}\mathbf{F}' - \mathbf{P} + \mathbf{Q}\}(\mathbf{I}_r - \mathbf{F}'z^{-1})^{-1}\Big\}\mathbf{H}.
\end{aligned}$$

The result in Proposition 13.4 follows provided that

$$\begin{aligned}
&\mathbf{P} + (\mathbf{I}_r - \mathbf{F}z)^{-1}\mathbf{F}\mathbf{P}z + \mathbf{P}\mathbf{F}'(\mathbf{I}_r - \mathbf{F}'z^{-1})^{-1}z^{-1} \qquad [13.A.21]\\
&\qquad + (\mathbf{I}_r - \mathbf{F}z)^{-1}\{\mathbf{F}\mathbf{P}\mathbf{F}' - \mathbf{P}\}(\mathbf{I}_r - \mathbf{F}'z^{-1})^{-1} = \mathbf{0}.
\end{aligned}$$

To verify that [13.A.21] is true, start from the identity

$$\begin{aligned}
&(\mathbf{I}_r - \mathbf{F}z)\mathbf{P}(\mathbf{I}_r - \mathbf{F}'z^{-1}) + \mathbf{F}\mathbf{P}z(\mathbf{I}_r - \mathbf{F}'z^{-1}) \qquad [13.A.22]\\
&\qquad + (\mathbf{I}_r - \mathbf{F}z)\mathbf{P}\mathbf{F}'z^{-1} + \mathbf{F}\mathbf{P}\mathbf{F}' - \mathbf{P} = \mathbf{0}.
\end{aligned}$$

Premultiplying [13.A.22] by $(\mathbf{I}_r - \mathbf{F}z)^{-1}$ and postmultiplying by $(\mathbf{I}_r - \mathbf{F}'z^{-1})^{-1}$ confirms [13.A.21]. Substituting [13.A.21] into [13.A.20] produces the claim in Proposition 13.4. ■

## *Chapter 13 Exercises*

13.1. Suppose we have a noisy indicator $y$ on an underlying unobserved random variable $\xi$:

$$y = \xi + \varepsilon.$$

Suppose moreover that the measurement error ($\varepsilon$) is $N(0, \tau^2)$, while the true value $\xi$ is $N(\mu, \sigma^2)$, with $\varepsilon$ uncorrelated with $\xi$. Show that the optimal estimate of $\xi$ is given by

$$E(\xi | y) = \mu + \frac{\sigma^2}{\tau^2 + \sigma^2}(y - \mu)$$

with associated $MSE$

$$E[\xi - E(\xi | y)]^2 = \frac{\sigma^2\tau^2}{\tau^2 + \sigma^2}.$$

Discuss the intuition for these results as $\tau^2 \to \infty$ and $\tau^2 \to 0$.

13.2. Deduce the state-space representation for an $AR(p)$ model in [13.1.14] and [13.1.15] and the state-space representation for an $MA(1)$ model given in [13.1.17] and [13.1.18] as special cases of that for the $ARMA(r, r - 1)$ model of [13.1.22] and [13.1.23].

13.3. Is the following a valid state-space representation of an $MA(1)$ process?

***State Equation:***

$$\begin{bmatrix} \varepsilon_{t+1} \\ \varepsilon_t \end{bmatrix} = \begin{bmatrix} 0 & 0 \\ 0 & 0 \end{bmatrix}\begin{bmatrix} \varepsilon_t \\ \varepsilon_{t-1} \end{bmatrix} + \begin{bmatrix} \varepsilon_{t+1} \\ \varepsilon_t \end{bmatrix}$$

***Observation Equation:***

$$y_t - \mu = [1 \quad \theta]\begin{bmatrix} \varepsilon_t \\ \varepsilon_{t-1} \end{bmatrix}$$

13.4. Derive equation [13.4.5] as a special case of [13.4.1] and [13.4.2] for the model specified in [13.4.3] and [13.4.4] by analysis of the Kalman filter recursion for this case.

13.5. Consider a particular $MA(1)$ representation of the form of [13.3.1] through [13.3.12] parameterized by $(\theta, \sigma^2)$ with $|\theta| < 1$. The noninvertible representation for the same process is parameterized by $(\tilde{\theta}, \tilde{\sigma}^2)$ with $\tilde{\theta} = 1/\theta$ and $\tilde{\sigma}^2 = \theta^2\sigma^2$. The forecast generated by the Kalman filter using the noninvertible representation satisfies

$$\hat{y}_{t+1|t} = \mathbf{A}'\mathbf{x}_{t+1} + \tilde{\mathbf{H}}'\hat{\boldsymbol{\xi}}_{t+1|t} = \mu + \tilde{\theta}\tilde{\varepsilon}_{t|t},$$

where $\tilde{\varepsilon}_{t|t} = \{\tilde{\sigma}^2/[\tilde{\sigma}^2 + \tilde{\theta}^2\tilde{p}_t]\}\cdot\{y_t - \mu - \tilde{\theta}\tilde{\varepsilon}_{t-1|t-1}\}$. The $MSE$ of this forecast is

$$E(y_{t+1} - \hat{y}_{t+1|t})^2 = \tilde{\mathbf{H}}'\tilde{\mathbf{P}}_{t+1|t}\tilde{\mathbf{H}} + \tilde{\mathbf{R}} = \tilde{\sigma}^2 + \tilde{\theta}^2\tilde{p}_{t+1},$$

where $\tilde{p}_{t+1} = (\tilde{\sigma}^2\tilde{\theta}^{2t})/(1 + \tilde{\theta}^2 + \tilde{\theta}^4 + \cdots + \tilde{\theta}^{2t})$. Show that this forecast and $MSE$ are identical to those for the process as parameterized using the invertible representation $(\theta, \sigma^2)$. Deduce that the likelihood function given by [13.4.1] and [13.4.2] takes on the same value at $(\theta, \sigma^2)$ as it does at $(\tilde{\theta}, \tilde{\sigma}^2)$.

13.6. Show that $\varepsilon_t$ in equation [13.5.22] is fundamental for $y_t$. What principle of the Kalman filter ensures that this will be the case? Show that the first autocovariance of the implied $MA(1)$ error process is given by

$$-(\phi - K)E(\varepsilon_t^2) = -\phi\sigma_W^2$$

while the variance is

$$[1 + (\phi - K)^2]E(\varepsilon_t^2) = (1 + \phi^2)\sigma_W^2 + \sigma_V^2.$$

Derive these expressions independently, using the approach to sums of $ARMA$ processes in Section 4.7.

13.7. Consider again the invertible $MA(1)$ of equations [13.3.1] to [13.3.12]. We found that the steady-state value of $\mathbf{P}_{t|t-1}$ is given by

$$\mathbf{P} = \begin{bmatrix} \sigma^2 & 0 \\ 0 & 0 \end{bmatrix}.$$

From this, deduce that the steady-state value of $\mathbf{P}_{t|t+s} = \mathbf{0}$ for $s = 0, 1, 2, \ldots$. Give the intuition for this result.

## *Chapter 13 References*


Anderson, Brian D. O., and John B. Moore. 1979. *Optimal Filtering*. Englewood Cliffs, N.J.: Prentice-Hall.

Burmeister, Edwin, and Kent D. Wall. 1982. "Kalman Filtering Estimation of Unobserved Rational Expectations with an Application to the German Hyperinflation." *Journal of Econometrics* 20:255–84.

———, ———, and James D. Hamilton. 1986. "Estimation of Unobserved Expected Monthly Inflation Using Kalman Filtering." *Journal of Business and Economic Statistics* 4:147–60.

Caines, Peter E. 1988. *Linear Stochastic Systems*. New York: Wiley.

Dempster, A. P., N. M. Laird, and D. B. Rubin. 1977. "Maximum Likelihood from Incomplete Data via the EM Algorithm." *Journal of the Royal Statistical Society* Series B, 39:1–38.

Doan, Thomas, Robert B. Litterman, and Christopher A. Sims. 1984. "Forecasting and Conditional Projection Using Realistic Prior Distributions." *Econometric Reviews* 3:1–100.

Fama, Eugene F., and Michael R. Gibbons. 1982. "Inflation, Real Returns, and Capital Investment." *Journal of Monetary Economics* 9:297–323.

Gevers, M., and V. Wertz. 1984. "Uniquely Identifiable State-Space and ARMA Parameterizations for Multivariable Linear Systems." *Automatica* 20:333–47.

Ghosh, Damayanti. 1989. "Maximum Likelihood Estimation of the Dynamic Shock-Error Model." *Journal of Econometrics* 41:121–43.

Hamilton, James D. 1985. "Uncovering Financial Market Expectations of Inflation." *Journal of Political Economy* 93:1224–41.

———. 1986. "A Standard Error for the Estimated State Vector of a State-Space Model." *Journal of Econometrics* 33:387–97.

Hannan, E. J. 1971. "The Identification Problem for Multiple Equation Systems with Moving Average Errors." *Econometrica* 39:751–65.

Harvey, Andrew, and G. D. A. Phillips. 1979. "Maximum Likelihood Estimation of Regression Models with Autoregressive–Moving Average Disturbances." *Biometrika* 66:49–58.

Kalman, R. E. 1960. "A New Approach to Linear Filtering and Prediction Problems." *Journal of Basic Engineering, Transactions of the ASME* Series D, 82:35–45.

———. 1963. "New Methods in Wiener Filtering Theory," in John L. Bogdanoff and Frank Kozin, eds., *Proceedings of the First Symposium of Engineering Applications of Random Function Theory and Probability*, 270–388. New York: Wiley.

Litterman, Robert B. 1986. "Forecasting with Bayesian Vector Autoregressions—Five Years of Experience." *Journal of Business and Economic Statistics* 4:25–38.

Meinhold, Richard J., and Nozer D. Singpurwalla. 1983. "Understanding the Kalman Filter." *American Statistician* 37:123–27.

Nicholls, D. F., and A. R. Pagan. 1985. "Varying Coefficient Regression," in E. J. Hannan, P. R. Krishnaiah, and M. M. Rao, eds., *Handbook of Statistics*, Vol. 5. Amsterdam: North-Holland.

Pagan, Adrian. 1980. "Some Identification and Estimation Results for Regression Models with Stochastically Varying Coefficients." *Journal of Econometrics* 13:341–63.

Rothenberg, Thomas J. 1971. "Identification in Parametric Models." *Econometrica* 39:577–91.

Shumway, R. H., and D. S. Stoffer. 1982. "An Approach to Time Series Smoothing and Forecasting Using the EM Algorithm." *Journal of Time Series Analysis* 3:253–64.

Sims, Christopher A. 1982. "Policy Analysis with Econometric Models." *Brookings Papers on Economic Activity* 1:107–52.

Stock, James H., and Mark W. Watson. 1991. "A Probability Model of the Coincident Economic Indicators," in Kajal Lahiri and Geoffrey H. Moore, eds., *Leading Economic Indicators: New Approaches and Forecasting Records*. Cambridge, England: Cambridge University Press.

Tanaka, Katsuto. 1983. "Non-Normality of the Lagrange Multiplier Statistic for Testing the Constancy of Regression Coefficients." *Econometrica* 51:1577–82.

Wall, Kent D. 1987. "Identification Theory for Varying Coefficient Regression Models." *Journal of Time Series Analysis* 8:359–71.

Watson, Mark W. 1989. "Recursive Solution Methods for Dynamic Linear Rational Expectations Models." *Journal of Econometrics* 41:65–89.

——— and Robert F. Engle. 1983. "Alternative Algorithms for the Estimation of Dynamic Factor, MIMIC, and Varying Coefficient Regression Models." *Journal of Econometrics* 23:385–400.

White, Halbert. 1982. "Maximum Likelihood Estimation of Misspecified Models." *Econometrica* 50:1–25.

# 14 Generalized Method of Moments

Suppose we have a set of observations on a variable $y_t$ whose probability law depends on an unknown vector of parameters $\boldsymbol{\theta}$. One general approach to estimating $\boldsymbol{\theta}$ is based on the principle of maximum likelihood—we choose as the estimate $\hat{\boldsymbol{\theta}}$ the value for which the data would be most likely to have been observed. A drawback of this approach is that it requires us to specify the form of the likelihood function.

This chapter explores an alternative principle for parameter estimation known as *generalized method of moments* (*GMM*). Although versions of this approach have been used for a long time, the general statement of *GMM* on which this chapter is based was only recently developed by Hansen (1982). The key advantage of *GMM* is that it requires specification only of certain moment conditions rather than the full density. This can also be a drawback, in that *GMM* often does not make efficient use of all the information in the sample.

Section 14.1 introduces the ideas behind *GMM* estimation and derives some of the key results. Section 14.2 shows how various other estimators can be viewed as special cases of *GMM*, including ordinary least squares, instrumental variable estimation, two-stage least squares, estimators for systems of nonlinear simultaneous equations, and estimators for dynamic rational expectations models. Extensions and further discussion are provided in Section 14.3. In many cases, even maximum likelihood estimation can be viewed as a special case of *GMM*. Section 14.4 explores this analogy and uses it to derive some general asymptotic properties of maximum likelihood and quasi-maximum likelihood estimation.

## 14.1. *Estimation by the Generalized Method of Moments*

### *Classical Method of Moments*

It will be helpful to introduce the ideas behind *GMM* with a concrete example. Consider a random variable $Y_t$ drawn from a standard $t$ distribution with $\nu$ degrees of freedom, so that its density is

$$f_{Y_t}(y_t; \nu) = \frac{\Gamma[(\nu + 1)/2]}{(\pi\nu)^{1/2}\Gamma(\nu/2)} [1 + (y_t^2/\nu)]^{-(\nu+1)/2}, \qquad [14.1.1]$$

where $\Gamma(\cdot)$ is the gamma function. Suppose we have an i.i.d. sample of size $T$ ($y_1, y_2, \ldots, y_T$) and want to estimate the degrees of freedom parameter $\nu$. One approach is to estimate $\nu$ by maximum likelihood. This approach calculates the sample log likelihood

$$\mathcal{L}(\nu) = \sum_{t=1}^{T} \log f_{Y_t}(y_t; \nu)$$

and chooses as the estimate $\hat{\nu}$ the value for which $\mathcal{L}(\nu)$ is largest.

An alternative principle on which estimation of $\nu$ might be based reasons as follows. Provided that $\nu > 2$, a standard $t$ variable has population mean zero and variance given by

$$\mu_2 \equiv E(Y_t^2) = \nu/(\nu - 2). \qquad [14.1.2]$$

As the degrees of freedom parameter ($\nu$) goes to infinity, the variance [14.1.2] approaches unity and the density [14.1.1] approaches that of a standard $N(0, 1)$ variable. Let $\hat{\mu}_{2,T}$ denote the average squared value of $y$ observed in the actual sample:

$$\hat{\mu}_{2,T} \equiv (1/T) \sum_{t=1}^{T} y_t^2. \qquad [14.1.3]$$

For large $T$, the sample moment ($\hat{\mu}_{2,T}$) should be close to the population moment ($\mu_2$):

$$\hat{\mu}_{2,T} \xrightarrow{p} \mu_2.$$

Recalling [14.1.2], this suggests that a consistent estimate of $\nu$ can be obtained by finding a solution to

$$\nu/(\nu - 2) = \hat{\mu}_{2,T} \qquad [14.1.4]$$

or

$$\hat{\nu}_T = \frac{2 \cdot \hat{\mu}_{2,T}}{\hat{\mu}_{2,T} - 1}. \qquad [14.1.5]$$

This estimate exists provided that $\hat{\mu}_{2,T} > 1$, that is, provided that the sample seems to exhibit more variability than the $N(0, 1)$ distribution. If we instead observed $\hat{\mu}_{2,T} \leq 1$, the estimate of the degrees of freedom would be infinity—a $N(0, 1)$ distribution fits the sample second moment better than any member of the $t$ family.

The estimator derived from [14.1.4] is known as a *classical method of moments* estimator. A general description of this approach is as follows. Given an unknown $(a \times 1)$ vector of parameters $\boldsymbol{\theta}$ that characterizes the density of an observed variable $y_t$, suppose that $a$ distinct population moments of the random variable can be calculated as functions of $\boldsymbol{\theta}$, such as

$$E(Y_t^i) = \mu_i(\boldsymbol{\theta}) \qquad \text{for } i = i_1, i_2, \ldots, i_a. \qquad [14.1.6]$$

The classical method of moments estimate of $\boldsymbol{\theta}$ is the value $\hat{\boldsymbol{\theta}}_T$ for which these population moments are equated to the observed sample moments; that is, $\hat{\boldsymbol{\theta}}_T$ is the value for which

$$\mu_i(\hat{\boldsymbol{\theta}}_T) = (1/T) \sum_{t=1}^{T} y_t^i \qquad \text{for } i = i_1, i_2, \ldots, i_a.$$

An early example of this approach was provided by Pearson (1894).

## *Generalized Method of Moments*

In the example of the $t$ distribution just discussed, a single sample moment ($\hat{\mu}_{2,T}$) was used to estimate a single population parameter ($\nu$). We might also have made use of other moments. For example, if $\nu > 4$, the population fourth moment of a standard $t$ variable is

$$\mu_4 \equiv E(Y_t^4) = \frac{3\nu^2}{(\nu - 2)(\nu - 4)},$$

and we might expect this to be close to the sample fourth moment,

$$\hat{\mu}_{4,T} \equiv (1/T) \sum_{t=1}^{T} y_t^4.$$

We cannot choose the single parameter $\nu$ so as to match both the sample second moment and the sample fourth moment. However, we might try to choose $\nu$ so as to be as close as possible to both, by minimizing a criterion function such as

$$Q(\nu; y_T, y_{T-1}, \ldots, y_1) \equiv \mathbf{g}'\mathbf{W}\mathbf{g}, \tag{14.1.7}$$

where

$$\mathbf{g} \equiv \begin{bmatrix} \left\{\hat{\mu}_{2,T} - \dfrac{\nu}{\nu - 2}\right\} \\ \left\{\hat{\mu}_{4,T} - \dfrac{3\nu^2}{(\nu - 2)(\nu - 4)}\right\} \end{bmatrix}. \tag{14.1.8}$$

Here $\mathbf{W}$ is a $(2 \times 2)$ positive definite symmetric weighting matrix reflecting the importance given to matching each of the moments. The larger is the (1, 1) element of $\mathbf{W}$, the greater is the importance of being as close as possible to satisfying [14.1.4].

An estimate based on minimization of an expression such as [14.1.7] was called a "minimum chi-square" estimator by Cramér (1946, p. 425), Ferguson (1958), and Rothenberg (1973) and a "minimum distance estimator" by Malinvaud (1970). Hansen (1982) provided the most general characterization of this approach and derived the asymptotic properties for serially dependent processes. Most of the results reported in this section were developed by Hansen (1982), who described this as estimation by the "generalized method of moments."

Hansen's formulation of the estimation problem is as follows. Let $\mathbf{w}_t$ be an $(h \times 1)$ vector of variables that are observed at date $t$, let $\boldsymbol{\theta}$ denote an unknown $(a \times 1)$ vector of coefficients, and let $\mathbf{h}(\boldsymbol{\theta}, \mathbf{w}_t)$ be an $(r \times 1)$ vector-valued function, $\mathbf{h}: (\mathbb{R}^a \times \mathbb{R}^h) \rightarrow \mathbb{R}^r$. Since $\mathbf{w}_t$ is a random variable, so is $\mathbf{h}(\boldsymbol{\theta}, \mathbf{w}_t)$. Let $\boldsymbol{\theta}_0$ denote the true value of $\boldsymbol{\theta}$, and suppose this true value is characterized by the property that

$$E\{\mathbf{h}(\boldsymbol{\theta}_0, \mathbf{w}_t)\} = \mathbf{0}. \tag{14.1.9}$$

The $r$ rows of the vector equation [14.1.9] are sometimes described as *orthogonality conditions*. Let $\mathcal{Y}_T \equiv (\mathbf{w}'_T, \mathbf{w}'_{T-1}, \ldots, \mathbf{w}'_1)'$ be a $(Th \times 1)$ vector containing all the observations in a sample of size $T$, and let the $(r \times 1)$ vector-valued function $\mathbf{g}(\boldsymbol{\theta}; \mathcal{Y}_T)$ denote the sample average of $\mathbf{h}(\boldsymbol{\theta}, \mathbf{w}_t)$:

$$\mathbf{g}(\boldsymbol{\theta}; \mathcal{Y}_T) \equiv (1/T) \sum_{t=1}^{T} \mathbf{h}(\boldsymbol{\theta}, \mathbf{w}_t). \tag{14.1.10}$$

Notice that $\mathbf{g}: \mathbb{R}^a \rightarrow \mathbb{R}^r$. The idea behind *GMM* is to choose $\boldsymbol{\theta}$ so as to make the sample moment $\mathbf{g}(\boldsymbol{\theta}; \mathcal{Y}_T)$ as close as possible to the population moment of zero; that is, the *GMM* estimator $\hat{\boldsymbol{\theta}}_T$ is the value of $\boldsymbol{\theta}$ that minimizes the scalar

$$Q(\boldsymbol{\theta}; \mathcal{Y}_T) = [\mathbf{g}(\boldsymbol{\theta}; \mathcal{Y}_T)]'\mathbf{W}_T[\mathbf{g}(\boldsymbol{\theta}; \mathcal{Y}_T)], \tag{14.1.11}$$

where $\{\mathbf{W}_T\}_{T=1}^{\infty}$ is a sequence of $(r \times r)$ positive definite weighting matrices which may be a function of the data $\mathcal{Y}_T$. Often, this minimization is achieved numerically using the methods described in Section 5.7.

The classical method of moments estimator of $\nu$ given in [14.1.5] is a special case of this formulation with $\mathbf{w}_t = y_t$, $\boldsymbol{\theta} = \nu$, $\mathbf{W}_T = 1$, and

$$h(\boldsymbol{\theta}, \mathbf{w}_t) = y_t^2 - \nu/(\nu - 2)$$

$$g(\boldsymbol{\theta}; \mathcal{Y}_T) = (1/T) \sum_{t=1}^{T} y_t^2 - \nu/(\nu - 2).$$

Here, $r = a = 1$ and the objective function [14.1.11] becomes

$$Q(\boldsymbol{\theta}; \mathcal{Y}_T) = \left\{(1/T) \sum_{t=1}^{T} y_t^2 - \nu/(\nu - 2)\right\}^2.$$

The smallest value that can be achieved for $Q(\cdot)$ is zero, which obtains when $\nu$ is the magnitude given in [14.1.5].

The estimate of $\nu$ obtained by minimizing [14.1.7] is also a *GMM* estimator with $r = 2$ and

$$\mathbf{h}(\boldsymbol{\theta}, \mathbf{w}_t) = \begin{bmatrix} \left\{y_t^2 - \dfrac{\nu}{\nu - 2}\right\} \\ \left\{y_t^4 - \dfrac{3\nu^2}{(\nu - 2)(\nu - 4)}\right\} \end{bmatrix}.$$

Here, $\mathbf{g}(\boldsymbol{\theta}; \mathcal{Y}_T)$ and $\mathbf{W}_T$ would be as described in [14.1.7] and [14.1.8].

A variety of other estimators can also be viewed as examples of *GMM*, including ordinary least squares, instrumental variable estimation, two-stage least squares, nonlinear simultaneous equations estimators, estimators for dynamic rational expectations models, and in many cases even maximum likelihood. These applications will be discussed in Sections 14.2 through 14.4.

If the number of parameters to be estimated ($a$) is the same as the number of orthogonality conditions ($r$), then typically the objective function [14.1.11] will be minimized by setting

$$\mathbf{g}(\hat{\boldsymbol{\theta}}_T; \mathcal{Y}_T) = \mathbf{0}. \qquad [14.1.12]$$

If $a = r$, then the *GMM* estimator is the value $\hat{\boldsymbol{\theta}}_T$ that satisfies these $r$ equations. If instead there are more orthogonality conditions than parameters to estimate ($r > a$), then [14.1.12] will not hold exactly. How close the $i$th element of $\mathbf{g}(\hat{\boldsymbol{\theta}}_T; \mathcal{Y}_T)$ is to zero depends on how much weight the $i$th orthogonality condition is given by the weighting matrix $\mathbf{W}_T$.

For any value of $\boldsymbol{\theta}$, the magnitude of the $(r \times 1)$ vector $\mathbf{g}(\boldsymbol{\theta}; \mathcal{Y}_T)$ is the sample mean of $T$ realizations of the $(r \times 1)$ random vector $\mathbf{h}(\boldsymbol{\theta}, \mathbf{w}_t)$. If $\mathbf{w}_t$ is strictly stationary and $\mathbf{h}(\cdot)$ is continuous, then it is reasonable to expect the law of large numbers to hold:

$$\mathbf{g}(\boldsymbol{\theta}; \mathcal{Y}_T) \xrightarrow{p} E\{\mathbf{h}(\boldsymbol{\theta}, \mathbf{w}_t)\}.$$

The expression $E\{\mathbf{h}(\boldsymbol{\theta}, \mathbf{w}_t)\}$ denotes a population magnitude that depends on the value of $\boldsymbol{\theta}$ and on the probability law of $\mathbf{w}_t$. Suppose that this function is continuous in $\boldsymbol{\theta}$ and that $\boldsymbol{\theta}_0$ is the only value of $\boldsymbol{\theta}$ that satisfies [14.1.9]. Then, under fairly general stationarity, continuity, and moment conditions, the value of $\hat{\boldsymbol{\theta}}_T$ that minimizes [14.1.11] offers a consistent estimate of $\boldsymbol{\theta}_0$; see Hansen (1982), Gallant and White (1988), and Andrews and Fair (1988) for details.

## *Optimal Weighting Matrix*

Suppose that when evaluated at the true value $\boldsymbol{\theta}_0$, the process $\{\mathbf{h}(\boldsymbol{\theta}_0, \mathbf{w}_t)\}_{t=-\infty}^{\infty}$ is strictly stationary with mean zero and $v$th autocovariance matrix given by

$$\boldsymbol{\Gamma}_v = E\{[\mathbf{h}(\boldsymbol{\theta}_0, \mathbf{w}_t)][\mathbf{h}(\boldsymbol{\theta}_0, \mathbf{w}_{t-v})]'\}. \qquad [14.1.13]$$

Assuming that these autocovariances are absolutely summable, define

$$\mathbf{S} \equiv \sum_{v=-\infty}^{\infty} \boldsymbol{\Gamma}_v. \qquad [14.1.14]$$

Recall from the discussion in Section 10.5 that $\mathbf{S}$ is the asymptotic variance of the sample mean of $\mathbf{h}(\boldsymbol{\theta}_0, \mathbf{w}_t)$:

$$\mathbf{S} = \lim_{T\to\infty} T\cdot E\{[\mathbf{g}(\boldsymbol{\theta}_0; \mathcal{Y}_T)][\mathbf{g}(\boldsymbol{\theta}_0; \mathcal{Y}_T)]'\}.$$

The optimal value for the weighting matrix $\mathbf{W}_T$ in [14.1.11] turns out to be given by $\mathbf{S}^{-1}$, the inverse of the asymptotic variance matrix. That is, the minimum asymptotic variance for the *GMM* estimator $\hat{\boldsymbol{\theta}}_T$ is obtained when $\hat{\boldsymbol{\theta}}_T$ is chosen to minimize

$$Q(\boldsymbol{\theta}; \mathcal{Y}_T) = [\mathbf{g}(\boldsymbol{\theta}; \mathcal{Y}_T)]'\mathbf{S}^{-1}[\mathbf{g}(\boldsymbol{\theta}; \mathcal{Y}_T)]. \qquad [14.1.15]$$

To see the intuition behind this claim, consider a simple linear model in which we have $r$ different observations $(y_1, y_2, \ldots, y_r)$ with a different population mean for each observation $(\mu_1, \mu_2, \ldots, \mu_r)$. For example, $y_1$ might denote the sample mean in a sample of $T_1$ observations on some variable, $y_2$ the sample mean from a second sample, and so on. In the absence of restrictions, the estimates would simply be $\hat{\mu}_i = y_i$ for $i = 1, 2, \ldots, r$. In the presence of linear restrictions across the $\mu$'s, the best estimates that are linear functions of the $y$'s would be obtained by generalized least squares. Recall that the *GLS* estimate of $\boldsymbol{\mu}$ is the value that minimizes

$$(\mathbf{y} - \boldsymbol{\mu})'\boldsymbol{\Omega}^{-1}(\mathbf{y} - \boldsymbol{\mu}), \qquad [14.1.16]$$

where $\mathbf{y} = (y_1, y_2, \ldots, y_r)'$, $\boldsymbol{\mu} = (\mu_1, \mu_2, \ldots, \mu_r)'$, and $\boldsymbol{\Omega}$ is the variance-covariance matrix of $\mathbf{y} - \boldsymbol{\mu}$:

$$\boldsymbol{\Omega} = E[(\mathbf{y} - \boldsymbol{\mu})(\mathbf{y} - \boldsymbol{\mu})'].$$

The optimal weighting matrix to use with the quadratic form in [14.1.16] is given by $\boldsymbol{\Omega}^{-1}$. Just as $\boldsymbol{\Omega}$ in [14.1.16] is the variance of $(\mathbf{y} - \boldsymbol{\mu})$, so $\mathbf{S}$ in [14.1.15] is the asymptotic variance of $\sqrt{T}\cdot\mathbf{g}(\cdot)$.

If the vector process $\{\mathbf{h}(\boldsymbol{\theta}_0, \mathbf{w}_t)\}_{t=-\infty}^{\infty}$ were serially uncorrelated, then the matrix $\mathbf{S}$ could be consistently estimated by

$$\mathbf{S}_T^* = (1/T)\sum_{t=1}^{T}[\mathbf{h}(\boldsymbol{\theta}_0, \mathbf{w}_t)][\mathbf{h}(\boldsymbol{\theta}_0, \mathbf{w}_t)]'. \qquad [14.1.17]$$

Calculating this magnitude requires knowledge of $\boldsymbol{\theta}_0$, though it often also turns out that

$$\hat{\mathbf{S}}_T \equiv (1/T)\sum_{t=1}^{T}[\mathbf{h}(\hat{\boldsymbol{\theta}}_T, \mathbf{w}_t)][\mathbf{h}(\hat{\boldsymbol{\theta}}_T, \mathbf{w}_t)]' \xrightarrow{p} \mathbf{S} \qquad [14.1.18]$$

for $\hat{\boldsymbol{\theta}}_T$ any consistent estimate of $\boldsymbol{\theta}_0$, assuming that $\mathbf{h}(\boldsymbol{\theta}_0, \mathbf{w}_t)$ is serially uncorrelated.

Note that this description of the optimal weighting matrix is somewhat circular—before we can estimate $\boldsymbol{\theta}$, we need an estimate of the matrix $\mathbf{S}$, and before we can estimate the matrix $\mathbf{S}$, we need an estimate of $\boldsymbol{\theta}$. The practical procedure used in *GMM* is as follows. An initial estimate $\hat{\boldsymbol{\theta}}_T^{(0)}$ is obtained by minimizing [14.1.11] with an arbitrary weighting matrix such as $\mathbf{W}_T = \mathbf{I}_r$. This estimate of $\boldsymbol{\theta}$ is then used in [14.1.18] to produce an initial estimate $\hat{\mathbf{S}}_T^{(0)}$. Expression [14.1.11] is then minimized with $\mathbf{W}_T = [\hat{\mathbf{S}}_T^{(0)}]^{-1}$ to arrive at a new *GMM* estimate $\hat{\boldsymbol{\theta}}_T^{(1)}$. This process can be iterated until $\hat{\boldsymbol{\theta}}_T^{(j)} \cong \hat{\boldsymbol{\theta}}_T^{(j+1)}$, though the estimate based on a single iteration $\hat{\boldsymbol{\theta}}_T^{(1)}$ has the same asymptotic distribution as that based on an arbitrarily large number of iterations. Iterating nevertheless offers the practical advantage that the resulting estimates are invariant with respect to the scale of the data and to the initial weighting matrix for $\mathbf{W}_T$.

On the other hand, if the vector process $\{\mathbf{h}(\boldsymbol{\theta}_0, \mathbf{w}_t)\}_{t=-\infty}^{\infty}$ is serially correlated, the Newey-West (1987) estimate of $\mathbf{S}$ could be used:

$$\hat{\mathbf{S}}_T = \hat{\boldsymbol{\Gamma}}_{0,T} + \sum_{v=1}^{q} \{1 - [v/(q + 1)]\}(\hat{\boldsymbol{\Gamma}}_{v,T} + \hat{\boldsymbol{\Gamma}}'_{v,T}), \qquad [14.1.19]$$

where

$$\hat{\boldsymbol{\Gamma}}_{v,T} = (1/T) \sum_{t=v+1}^{T} [\mathbf{h}(\hat{\boldsymbol{\theta}}, \mathbf{w}_t)][\mathbf{h}(\hat{\boldsymbol{\theta}}, \mathbf{w}_{t-v})]', \qquad [14.1.20]$$

with $\hat{\boldsymbol{\theta}}$ again an initial consistent estimate of $\boldsymbol{\theta}_0$. Alternatively, the estimators proposed by Gallant (1987), Andrews (1991), or Andrews and Monahan (1992) that were discussed in Section 10.5 could also be applied in this context.

### *Asymptotic Distribution of the* GMM *Estimates*

Let $\hat{\boldsymbol{\theta}}_T$ be the value that minimizes

$$[\mathbf{g}(\boldsymbol{\theta}; \mathcal{Y}_T)]'\hat{\mathbf{S}}_T^{-1}[\mathbf{g}(\boldsymbol{\theta}; \mathcal{Y}_T)], \qquad [14.1.21]$$

with $\hat{\mathbf{S}}_T$ regarded as fixed with respect to $\boldsymbol{\theta}$ and $\hat{\mathbf{S}}_T \xrightarrow{p} \mathbf{S}$. Assuming an interior optimum, this minimization is achieved by setting the derivative of [14.1.21] with respect to $\boldsymbol{\theta}$ to zero. Thus, the *GMM* estimate $\hat{\boldsymbol{\theta}}_T$ is typically a solution to the following system of nonlinear equations:

$$\underbrace{\left\{\left.\frac{\partial \mathbf{g}(\boldsymbol{\theta}; \mathcal{Y}_T)}{\partial \boldsymbol{\theta}'}\right|_{\boldsymbol{\theta}=\hat{\boldsymbol{\theta}}_T}\right\}'}_{(a\times r)} \times \underbrace{\hat{\mathbf{S}}_T^{-1}}_{(r\times r)} \times \underbrace{[\mathbf{g}(\hat{\boldsymbol{\theta}}_T; \mathcal{Y}_T)]}_{(r\times 1)} = \underbrace{\mathbf{0}}_{(a\times 1)}. \qquad [14.1.22]$$

Here $[\partial \mathbf{g}(\boldsymbol{\theta}; \mathcal{Y}_T)/\partial \boldsymbol{\theta}']|_{\boldsymbol{\theta}=\hat{\boldsymbol{\theta}}_T}$ denotes the $(r \times a)$ matrix of derivatives of the function $\mathbf{g}(\boldsymbol{\theta}; \mathcal{Y}_T)$, where these derivatives are evaluated at the *GMM* estimate $\hat{\boldsymbol{\theta}}_T$.

Since $\mathbf{g}(\boldsymbol{\theta}_0; \mathcal{Y}_T)$ is the sample mean of a process whose population mean is zero, $\mathbf{g}(\cdot)$ should satisfy the central limit theorem given conditions such as strict stationarity of $\mathbf{w}_t$, continuity of $\mathbf{h}(\boldsymbol{\theta}, \mathbf{w}_t)$, and restrictions on higher moments. Thus, in many instances it should be the case that

$$\sqrt{T}\cdot\mathbf{g}(\boldsymbol{\theta}_0; \mathcal{Y}_T) \xrightarrow{L} N(\mathbf{0}, \mathbf{S}).$$

Not much more than this is needed to conclude that the *GMM* estimator $\hat{\boldsymbol{\theta}}_T$ is asymptotically Gaussian and to calculate its asymptotic variance. The following proposition, adapted from Hansen (1982), is proved in Appendix 14.A at the end of this chapter.

***Proposition 14.1:*** *Let* $\mathbf{g}(\boldsymbol{\theta}; \mathcal{Y}_T)$ *be differentiable in* $\boldsymbol{\theta}$ *for all* $\mathcal{Y}_T$, *and let* $\hat{\boldsymbol{\theta}}_T$ *be the GMM estimator satisfying* [14.1.22] *with* $r \geq a$. *Let* $\{\hat{\mathbf{S}}_T\}_{T=1}^{\infty}$ *be a sequence of positive definite* $(r \times r)$ *matrices such that* $\hat{\mathbf{S}}_T \xrightarrow{p} \mathbf{S}$, *with* $\mathbf{S}$ *positive definite. Suppose, further, that the following hold:*

*(a)* $\hat{\boldsymbol{\theta}}_T \xrightarrow{p} \boldsymbol{\theta}_0$;
*(b)* $\sqrt{T}\cdot\mathbf{g}(\boldsymbol{\theta}_0; \mathcal{Y}_T) \xrightarrow{L} N(\mathbf{0}, \mathbf{S})$; *and*
*(c) for any sequence* $\{\boldsymbol{\theta}_T^*\}_{T=1}^{\infty}$ *satisfying* $\boldsymbol{\theta}_T^* \xrightarrow{p} \boldsymbol{\theta}_0$, *it is the case that*

$$\text{plim}\left\{\left.\frac{\partial \mathbf{g}(\boldsymbol{\theta}; \mathcal{Y}_T)}{\partial \boldsymbol{\theta}'}\right|_{\boldsymbol{\theta}=\boldsymbol{\theta}_T^*}\right\} = \text{plim}\left\{\left.\frac{\partial \mathbf{g}(\boldsymbol{\theta}; \mathcal{Y}_T)}{\partial \boldsymbol{\theta}'}\right|_{\boldsymbol{\theta}=\boldsymbol{\theta}_0}\right\} \equiv \underset{(r\times a)}{\mathbf{D}'}, \qquad [14.1.23]$$

*with the columns of* $\mathbf{D}'$ *linearly independent.*
*Then*

$$\sqrt{T}(\hat{\boldsymbol{\theta}}_T - \boldsymbol{\theta}_0) \xrightarrow{L} N(\mathbf{0}, \mathbf{V}), \qquad [14.1.24]$$

*where*

$$\mathbf{V} = \{\mathbf{D}\mathbf{S}^{-1}\mathbf{D}'\}^{-1}.$$

Proposition 14.1 implies that we can treat $\hat{\boldsymbol{\theta}}_T$ approximately as

$$\hat{\boldsymbol{\theta}}_T \approx N(\boldsymbol{\theta}_0, \hat{\mathbf{V}}_T/T), \qquad [14.1.25]$$

where

$$\hat{\mathbf{V}}_T = \{\hat{\mathbf{D}}_T\hat{\mathbf{S}}_T^{-1}\hat{\mathbf{D}}_T'\}^{-1}.$$

The estimate $\hat{\mathbf{S}}_T$ can be constructed as in [14.1.18] or [14.1.19], while

$$\underset{(r\times a)}{\hat{\mathbf{D}}_T'} = \left.\frac{\partial \mathbf{g}(\boldsymbol{\theta}; \mathcal{Y}_T)}{\partial \boldsymbol{\theta}'}\right|_{\boldsymbol{\theta}=\hat{\boldsymbol{\theta}}_T}.$$

### *Testing the Overidentifying Restrictions*

When the number of orthogonality conditions exceeds the number of parameters to be estimated ($r > a$), the model is overidentified, in that more orthogonality conditions were used than are needed to estimate $\boldsymbol{\theta}$. In this case, Hansen (1982) suggested a test of whether all of the sample moments represented by $\mathbf{g}(\hat{\boldsymbol{\theta}}_T; \mathcal{Y}_T)$ are as close to zero as would be expected if the corresponding population moments $E\{\mathbf{h}(\boldsymbol{\theta}_0, \mathbf{w}_t)\}$ were truly zero.

From Proposition 8.1 and condition (b) in Proposition 14.1, notice that if the population orthogonality conditions in [14.1.9] were all true, then

$$[\sqrt{T}\cdot\mathbf{g}(\boldsymbol{\theta}_0; \mathcal{Y}_T)]'\mathbf{S}^{-1}[\sqrt{T}\cdot\mathbf{g}(\boldsymbol{\theta}_0; \mathcal{Y}_T)] \xrightarrow{L} \chi^2(r). \qquad [14.1.26]$$

In [14.1.26], the sample moment function $\mathbf{g}(\boldsymbol{\theta}; \mathcal{Y}_T)$ is evaluated at the true value of $\boldsymbol{\theta}_0$. One's first guess might be that condition [14.1.26] also holds when [14.1.26] is evaluated at the *GMM* estimate $\hat{\boldsymbol{\theta}}_T$. However, this is not the case. The reason is that [14.1.22] implies that $a$ different linear combinations of the $(r \times 1)$ vector $\mathbf{g}(\hat{\boldsymbol{\theta}}_T; \mathcal{Y}_T)$ are identically zero, these being the $a$ linear combinations obtained when $\mathbf{g}(\hat{\boldsymbol{\theta}}_T; \mathcal{Y}_T)$ is premultiplied by the $(a \times r)$ matrix

$$\left\{\left.\frac{\partial \mathbf{g}(\boldsymbol{\theta}; \mathcal{Y}_T)}{\partial \boldsymbol{\theta}'}\right|_{\boldsymbol{\theta}=\hat{\boldsymbol{\theta}}_T}\right\}' \times \hat{\mathbf{S}}_T^{-1}.$$

For example, when $a = r$, *all* linear combinations of $\mathbf{g}(\hat{\boldsymbol{\theta}}_T; \mathcal{Y}_T)$ are identically zero, and if $\boldsymbol{\theta}_0$ were replaced by $\hat{\boldsymbol{\theta}}_T$, the magnitude in [14.1.26] would simply equal zero in all samples.

Since the vector $\mathbf{g}(\hat{\boldsymbol{\theta}}_T; \mathcal{Y}_T)$ contains $(r - a)$ nondegenerate random variables, it turns out that a correct test of the overidentifying restrictions for the case when $r > a$ can be based on the fact that

$$[\sqrt{T}\cdot\mathbf{g}(\hat{\boldsymbol{\theta}}_T; \mathcal{Y}_T)]'\hat{\mathbf{S}}_T^{-1}[\sqrt{T}\cdot\mathbf{g}(\hat{\boldsymbol{\theta}}_T; \mathcal{Y}_T)] \xrightarrow{L} \chi^2(r - a). \qquad [14.1.27]$$

Moreover, this test statistic is trivial to calculate, for it is simply the sample size $T$ times the value attained for the objective function [14.1.21] at the *GMM* estimate $\hat{\boldsymbol{\theta}}_T$.

Unfortunately, Hansen's $\chi^2$ test based on [14.1.27] can easily fail to detect a misspecified model (Newey, 1985). It is therefore often advisable to supplement this test with others described in Section 14.3.

## 14.2. *Examples*

This section shows how properties of a variety of different estimators can be obtained as special cases of Hansen's results for generalized method of moments estimation. To facilitate this discussion, we first summarize the results of the preceding section.

## *Summary of* GMM

The statistical model is assumed to imply a set of $r$ orthogonality conditions of the form

$$\underset{(r\times 1)}{E\{\mathbf{h}(\boldsymbol{\theta}_0, \mathbf{w}_t)\}} = \underset{(r\times 1)}{\mathbf{0}}, \tag{14.2.1}$$

where $\mathbf{w}_t$ is a strictly stationary vector of variables observed at date $t$, $\boldsymbol{\theta}_0$ is the true value of an unknown $(a \times 1)$ vector of parameters, and $\mathbf{h}(\cdot)$ is a differentiable $r$-dimensional vector-valued function with $r \geq a$. The *GMM* estimate $\hat{\boldsymbol{\theta}}_T$ is the value of $\boldsymbol{\theta}$ that minimizes

$$\underset{(1\times r)}{[\mathbf{g}(\boldsymbol{\theta}; \mathcal{Y}_T)]'}\underset{(r\times r)}{\hat{\mathbf{S}}_T^{-1}}\underset{(r\times 1)}{[\mathbf{g}(\boldsymbol{\theta}; \mathcal{Y}_T)]}, \tag{14.2.2}$$

where

$$\underset{(r\times 1)}{\mathbf{g}(\boldsymbol{\theta}; \mathcal{Y}_T)} \equiv (1/T) \sum_{t=1}^{T} \underset{(r\times 1)}{\mathbf{h}(\boldsymbol{\theta}, \mathbf{w}_t)} \tag{14.2.3}$$

and $\hat{\mathbf{S}}_T$ is an estimate of[1]

$$\underset{(r\times r)}{\mathbf{S}} = \lim_{T\to\infty} (1/T) \sum_{t=1}^{T} \sum_{v=-\infty}^{\infty} E\{\underset{(r\times 1)}{[\mathbf{h}(\boldsymbol{\theta}_0, \mathbf{w}_t)]}\underset{(1\times r)}{[\mathbf{h}(\boldsymbol{\theta}_0, \mathbf{w}_{t-v})]'}\}. \tag{14.2.4}$$

The *GMM* estimate can be treated as if

$$\underset{(a\times 1)}{\hat{\boldsymbol{\theta}}_T} \approx N(\underset{(a\times 1)}{\boldsymbol{\theta}_0}, \underset{(a\times a)}{\hat{\mathbf{V}}_T/T}), \tag{14.2.5}$$

where

$$\underset{(a\times a)}{\hat{\mathbf{V}}_T} = \{\underset{(a\times r)}{\hat{\mathbf{D}}_T} \cdot \underset{(r\times r)}{\hat{\mathbf{S}}_T^{-1}} \cdot \underset{(r\times a)}{\hat{\mathbf{D}}_T'}\}^{-1} \tag{14.2.6}$$

and

$$\underset{(r\times a)}{\hat{\mathbf{D}}_T'} = \left.\frac{\partial \mathbf{g}(\boldsymbol{\theta}; \mathcal{Y}_T)}{\partial \boldsymbol{\theta}'}\right|_{\boldsymbol{\theta}=\hat{\boldsymbol{\theta}}_T}. \tag{14.2.7}$$

We now explore how these results would be applied in various special cases.

## *Ordinary Least Squares*

Consider the standard linear regression model,

$$y_t = \mathbf{x}_t'\boldsymbol{\beta} + u_t, \tag{14.2.8}$$

for $\mathbf{x}_t$ a $(k \times 1)$ vector of explanatory variables. The critical assumption needed to justify *OLS* regression is that the regression residual $u_t$ is uncorrelated with the explanatory variables:

$$E(\mathbf{x}_t u_t) = \mathbf{0}. \tag{14.2.9}$$

[1]Under strict stationarity, the magnitude

$$E\{[\mathbf{h}(\boldsymbol{\theta}_0, \mathbf{w}_t)][\mathbf{h}(\boldsymbol{\theta}_0, \mathbf{w}_{t-v})]'\} = \boldsymbol{\Gamma}_v$$

does not depend on $t$. The expression in the text is more general than necessary under the stated assumptions. This expression is appropriate for a characterization of *GMM* that does not assume strict stationarity. The expression in the text is also helpful in suggesting estimates of $\mathbf{S}$ that can be used in various special cases described later in this section.

In other words, the true value $\boldsymbol{\beta}_0$ is assumed to satisfy the condition

$$E[\mathbf{x}_t(y_t - \mathbf{x}_t'\boldsymbol{\beta}_0)] = \mathbf{0}. \tag{14.2.10}$$

Expression [14.2.10] describes $k$ orthogonality conditions of the form of [14.2.1], in which $\mathbf{w}_t = (y_t, \mathbf{x}_t')'$, $\boldsymbol{\theta} = \boldsymbol{\beta}$, and

$$\mathbf{h}(\boldsymbol{\theta}, \mathbf{w}_t) = \mathbf{x}_t(y_t - \mathbf{x}_t'\boldsymbol{\beta}). \tag{14.2.11}$$

The number of orthogonality conditions is the same as the number of unknown parameters in $\boldsymbol{\beta}$, so that $r = a = k$. Hence, the standard regression model could be viewed as a just-identified *GMM* specification. Since it is just identified, the *GMM* estimate of $\boldsymbol{\beta}$ is the value that sets the sample average value for [14.2.11] equal to zero:

$$\mathbf{0} = \mathbf{g}(\hat{\boldsymbol{\theta}}_T; \mathcal{Y}_T) = (1/T)\sum_{t=1}^{T} \mathbf{x}_t(y_t - \mathbf{x}_t'\hat{\boldsymbol{\beta}}_T). \tag{14.2.12}$$

Rearranging [14.2.12] results in

$$\sum_{t=1}^{T} \mathbf{x}_t y_t = \left\{\sum_{t=1}^{T} \mathbf{x}_t\mathbf{x}_t'\right\}\hat{\boldsymbol{\beta}}_T$$

or

$$\hat{\boldsymbol{\beta}}_T = \left\{\sum_{t=1}^{T} \mathbf{x}_t\mathbf{x}_t'\right\}^{-1}\left\{\sum_{t=1}^{T} \mathbf{x}_t y_t\right\}, \tag{14.2.13}$$

which is the usual *OLS* estimator. Hence, *OLS* is a special case of *GMM*.

Note that in deriving the *GMM* estimator in [14.2.13] we assumed that the residual $u_t$ was uncorrelated with the explanatory variables, but we did not make any other assumptions about heteroskedasticity or serial correlation of the residuals. In the presence of heteroskedasticity or serial correlation, *OLS* is not as efficient as *GLS*. Because *GMM* uses the *OLS* estimate even in the presence of heteroskedasticity or serial correlation, *GMM* in general is not efficient. However, recall from Section 8.2 that one can still use *OLS* in the presence of heteroskedasticity or serial correlation. As long as condition [14.2.9] is satisfied, *OLS* yields a consistent estimate of $\boldsymbol{\beta}$, though the formulas for standard errors have to be adjusted to take account of the heteroskedasticity or autocorrelation.

The *GMM* expression for the variance of $\hat{\boldsymbol{\beta}}_T$ is given by [14.2.6]. Differentiating [14.2.11], we see that

$$\begin{aligned}\hat{\mathbf{D}}_T' &= \left.\frac{\partial \mathbf{g}(\boldsymbol{\theta}; \mathcal{Y}_T)}{\partial \boldsymbol{\theta}'}\right|_{\boldsymbol{\theta}=\hat{\boldsymbol{\theta}}_T} \\ &= (1/T)\sum_{t=1}^{T} \left.\frac{\partial \mathbf{x}_t(y_t - \mathbf{x}_t'\boldsymbol{\beta})}{\partial \boldsymbol{\beta}'}\right|_{\boldsymbol{\beta}=\hat{\boldsymbol{\beta}}_T} \\ &= -(1/T)\sum_{t=1}^{T} \mathbf{x}_t\mathbf{x}_t'.\end{aligned} \tag{14.2.14}$$

Substituting [14.2.11] into [14.2.4] results in

$$\mathbf{S} = \lim_{T\to\infty} (1/T)\sum_{t=1}^{T}\sum_{v=-\infty}^{\infty} E\{u_t u_{t-v}\mathbf{x}_t\mathbf{x}_{t-v}'\}. \tag{14.2.15}$$

Suppose that $u_t$ is regarded as conditionally homoskedastic and serially uncorrelated:

$$E\{u_t u_{t-v}\mathbf{x}_t\mathbf{x}_{t-v}'\} = \begin{cases}\sigma^2 E(\mathbf{x}_t\mathbf{x}_t') & \text{for } v = 0 \\ \mathbf{0} & \text{for } v \neq 0.\end{cases}$$

In this case the matrix in [14.2.15] should be consistently estimated by

$$\hat{\mathbf{S}}_T = \hat{\sigma}_T^2 \, (1/T) \sum_{t=1}^{T} \mathbf{x}_t\mathbf{x}_t', \qquad [14.2.16]$$

where

$$\hat{\sigma}_T^2 = (1/T) \sum_{t=1}^{T} \hat{u}_t^2$$

for $\hat{u}_t \equiv y_t - \mathbf{x}_t'\hat{\boldsymbol{\beta}}_T$ the *OLS* residual. Substituting [14.2.14] and [14.2.16] into [14.2.6] produces a variance-covariance matrix for the *OLS* estimate $\hat{\boldsymbol{\beta}}_T$ of

$$\begin{aligned}(1/T)\hat{\mathbf{V}}_T &= (1/T)\left\{(1/T)\sum_{t=1}^{T}\mathbf{x}_t\mathbf{x}_t'\left[\hat{\sigma}_T^2(1/T)\sum_{t=1}^{T}\mathbf{x}_t\mathbf{x}_t'\right]^{-1}(1/T)\sum_{t=1}^{T}\mathbf{x}_t\mathbf{x}_t'\right\}^{-1} \\ &= \hat{\sigma}_T^2\left[\sum_{t=1}^{T}\mathbf{x}_t\mathbf{x}_t'\right]^{-1}.\end{aligned}$$

Apart from the estimate of $\sigma^2$, this is the usual expression for the variance of the *OLS* estimator under these conditions.

On the other hand, suppose that $u_t$ is conditionally heteroskedastic and serially correlated. In this case, the estimate of $\mathbf{S}$ proposed in [14.1.19] would be

$$\hat{\mathbf{S}}_T = \hat{\boldsymbol{\Gamma}}_{0,T} + \sum_{v=1}^{q} \{1 - [v/(q + 1)]\}(\hat{\boldsymbol{\Gamma}}_{v,T} + \hat{\boldsymbol{\Gamma}}_{v,T}'),$$

where

$$\hat{\boldsymbol{\Gamma}}_{v,T} = (1/T) \sum_{t=v+1}^{T} \hat{u}_t\hat{u}_{t-v}\mathbf{x}_t\mathbf{x}_{t-v}'.$$

Under these assumptions, the *GMM* approximation for the variance-covariance matrix of $\hat{\boldsymbol{\beta}}_T$ would be

$$\begin{aligned}E[(\hat{\boldsymbol{\beta}}_T - \boldsymbol{\beta})(\hat{\boldsymbol{\beta}}_T - \boldsymbol{\beta})'] &\cong (1/T)\left\{(1/T)\sum_{t=1}^{T}\mathbf{x}_t\mathbf{x}_t'\,\hat{\mathbf{S}}_T^{-1}\,(1/T)\sum_{t=1}^{T}\mathbf{x}_t\mathbf{x}_t'\right\}^{-1} \\ &= T\left[\sum_{t=1}^{T}\mathbf{x}_t\mathbf{x}_t'\right]^{-1}\hat{\mathbf{S}}_T\left[\sum_{t=1}^{T}\mathbf{x}_t\mathbf{x}_t'\right]^{-1},\end{aligned}$$

which is the expression derived earlier in equation [10.5.21]. White's (1980) heteroskedasticity-consistent standard errors in [8.2.35] are obtained as a special case when $q = 0$.

## *Instrumental Variable Estimation*

Consider again a linear model

$$y_t = \mathbf{z}_t'\boldsymbol{\beta} + u_t, \qquad [14.2.17]$$

where $\mathbf{z}_t$ is a $(k \times 1)$ vector of explanatory variables. Suppose now that some of the explanatory variables are endogenous, so that $E(\mathbf{z}_t u_t) \neq \mathbf{0}$. Let $\mathbf{x}_t$ be an $(r \times 1)$ vector of predetermined explanatory variables that are correlated with $\mathbf{z}_t$ but uncorrelated with $u_t$:

$$E(\mathbf{x}_t u_t) = \mathbf{0}.$$

The $r$ orthogonality conditions are now

$$E[\mathbf{x}_t(y_t - \mathbf{z}_t'\boldsymbol{\beta}_0)] = \mathbf{0}. \qquad [14.2.18]$$

This again will be recognized as a special case of the *GMM* framework in which $\mathbf{w}_t = (y_t, \mathbf{z}_t', \mathbf{x}_t')'$, $\boldsymbol{\theta} = \boldsymbol{\beta}$, $a = k$, and

$$\mathbf{h}(\boldsymbol{\theta}, \mathbf{w}_t) = \mathbf{x}_t(y_t - \mathbf{z}_t'\boldsymbol{\beta}). \qquad [14.2.19]$$

Suppose that the number of parameters to be estimated equals the number of orthogonality conditions ($a = k = r$). Then the model is just identified, and the *GMM* estimator satisfies

$$\mathbf{0} = \mathbf{g}(\hat{\boldsymbol{\theta}}_T; \mathcal{Y}_T) = (1/T) \sum_{t=1}^{T} \mathbf{x}_t(y_t - \mathbf{z}_t'\hat{\boldsymbol{\beta}}_T) \qquad [14.2.20]$$

or

$$\hat{\boldsymbol{\beta}}_T = \left\{\sum_{t=1}^{T} \mathbf{x}_t\mathbf{z}_t'\right\}^{-1}\left\{\sum_{t=1}^{T} \mathbf{x}_t y_t\right\},$$

which is the usual instrumental variable estimator for this model. To calculate the standard errors implied by Hansen's (1982) general results, we differentiate [14.2.19] to find

$$\begin{aligned}\hat{\mathbf{D}}_T' &= \left.\frac{\partial \mathbf{g}(\boldsymbol{\theta}; \mathcal{Y}_T)}{\partial \boldsymbol{\theta}'}\right|_{\boldsymbol{\theta}=\hat{\boldsymbol{\theta}}_T} \\ &= (1/T) \sum_{t=1}^{T} \left.\frac{\partial \mathbf{x}_t(y_t - \mathbf{z}_t'\boldsymbol{\beta})}{\partial \boldsymbol{\beta}'}\right|_{\boldsymbol{\beta}=\hat{\boldsymbol{\beta}}_T} \\ &= -(1/T) \sum_{t=1}^{T} \mathbf{x}_t\mathbf{z}_t'.\end{aligned} \qquad [14.2.21]$$

The requirement in Proposition 14.1 that the plim of this matrix have linearly independent columns is the same condition that was needed to establish consistency of the *IV* estimator in Chapter 9, namely, the condition that the rows of $E(\mathbf{z}_t\mathbf{x}_t')$ be linearly independent. The *GMM* variance for $\hat{\boldsymbol{\beta}}_T$ is seen from [14.2.6] to be

$$(1/T)\hat{\mathbf{V}}_T = (1/T)\left\{\left[(1/T) \sum_{t=1}^{T} \mathbf{z}_t\mathbf{x}_t'\right]\hat{\mathbf{S}}_T^{-1}\left[(1/T) \sum_{t=1}^{T} \mathbf{x}_t\mathbf{z}_t'\right]\right\}^{-1}, \qquad [14.2.22]$$

where $\hat{\mathbf{S}}_T$ is an estimate of

$$\mathbf{S} = \lim_{T\to\infty} (1/T) \sum_{t=1}^{T} \sum_{v=-\infty}^{\infty} E\{u_t u_{t-v}\mathbf{x}_t\mathbf{x}_{t-v}'\}. \qquad [14.2.23]$$

If the regression residuals $\{u_t\}$ are serially uncorrelated and homoskedastic with variance $\sigma^2$, the natural estimate of $\mathbf{S}$ is

$$\hat{\mathbf{S}}_T = \hat{\sigma}_T^2 \cdot (1/T) \sum_{t=1}^{T} \mathbf{x}_t\mathbf{x}_t' \qquad [14.2.24]$$

for $\hat{\sigma}_T^2 = (1/T)\sum_{t=1}^{T}(y_t - \mathbf{z}_t'\hat{\boldsymbol{\beta}}_T)^2$. Substituting this estimate into [14.2.22] yields

$$\begin{aligned}E[(\hat{\boldsymbol{\beta}}_T - \boldsymbol{\beta})(\hat{\boldsymbol{\beta}}_T - \boldsymbol{\beta})'] &\cong \hat{\sigma}_T^2\left\{\left[\sum_{t=1}^{T} \mathbf{z}_t\mathbf{x}_t'\right]\left[\sum_{t=1}^{T} \mathbf{x}_t\mathbf{x}_t'\right]^{-1}\left[\sum_{t=1}^{T} \mathbf{x}_t\mathbf{z}_t'\right]\right\}^{-1} \\ &= \hat{\sigma}_T^2\left[\sum_{t=1}^{T} \mathbf{x}_t\mathbf{z}_t'\right]^{-1}\left[\sum_{t=1}^{T} \mathbf{x}_t\mathbf{x}_t'\right]\left[\sum_{t=1}^{T} \mathbf{z}_t\mathbf{x}_t'\right]^{-1},\end{aligned}$$

the same result derived earlier in [9.2.30]. On the other hand, a heteroskedasticity- and autocorrelation-consistent variance-covariance matrix for *IV* estimation is given by

$$E[(\hat{\boldsymbol{\beta}}_T - \boldsymbol{\beta})(\hat{\boldsymbol{\beta}}_T - \boldsymbol{\beta})'] \cong T\left[\sum_{t=1}^{T} \mathbf{x}_t\mathbf{z}_t'\right]^{-1}\hat{\mathbf{S}}_T\left[\sum_{t=1}^{T} \mathbf{z}_t\mathbf{x}_t'\right]^{-1}, \qquad [14.2.25]$$

where

$$\hat{\mathbf{S}}_T = \hat{\boldsymbol{\Gamma}}_{0,T} + \sum_{v=1}^{q} \{1 - [v/(q+1)]\}(\hat{\boldsymbol{\Gamma}}_{v,T} + \hat{\boldsymbol{\Gamma}}'_{v,T}), \qquad [14.2.26]$$

$$\hat{\boldsymbol{\Gamma}}_{v,T} = (1/T) \sum_{t=v+1}^{T} \hat{u}_t \hat{u}_{t-v} \mathbf{x}_t \mathbf{x}'_{t-v}$$

$$\hat{u}_t = y_t - \mathbf{z}'_t \hat{\boldsymbol{\beta}}_T.$$

## *Two-Stage Least Squares*

Consider again the linear model of [14.2.17] and [14.2.18], but suppose now that the number of valid instruments $r$ exceeds the number of explanatory variables $k$. For this overidentified model, *GMM* will no longer set all the sample orthogonality conditions to zero as in [14.2.20], but instead will be the solution to [14.1.22],

$$\begin{aligned} \mathbf{0} &= \left\{ \frac{\partial \mathbf{g}(\boldsymbol{\theta}; \mathcal{Y}_T)}{\partial \boldsymbol{\theta}'} \bigg|_{\boldsymbol{\theta} = \hat{\boldsymbol{\theta}}_T} \right\}' \times \hat{\mathbf{S}}_T^{-1} \times [\mathbf{g}(\hat{\boldsymbol{\theta}}_T; \mathcal{Y}_T)] \\ &= \left\{ -(1/T) \sum_{t=1}^{T} \mathbf{z}_t \mathbf{x}'_t \right\} \hat{\mathbf{S}}_T^{-1} \left\{ (1/T) \sum_{t=1}^{T} \mathbf{x}_t (y_t - \mathbf{z}'_t \hat{\boldsymbol{\beta}}_T) \right\}, \end{aligned} \qquad [14.2.27]$$

with the last line following from [14.2.21] and [14.2.20]. Again, if $u_t$ is serially uncorrelated and homoskedastic with variance $\sigma^2$, a natural estimate of $\mathbf{S}$ is given by [14.2.24]. Using this estimate, [14.2.27] becomes

$$(1/\hat{\sigma}_T^2) \times \left\{ \sum_{t=1}^{T} \mathbf{z}_t \mathbf{x}'_t \right\} \left\{ \sum_{t=1}^{T} \mathbf{x}_t \mathbf{x}'_t \right\}^{-1} \left\{ \sum_{t=1}^{T} \mathbf{x}_t (y_t - \mathbf{z}'_t \hat{\boldsymbol{\beta}}_T) \right\} = \mathbf{0}. \qquad [14.2.28]$$

As in expression [9.2.5], define

$$\hat{\boldsymbol{\delta}}' \equiv \left\{ \sum_{t=1}^{T} \mathbf{z}_t \mathbf{x}'_t \right\} \left\{ \sum_{t=1}^{T} \mathbf{x}_t \mathbf{x}'_t \right\}^{-1}.$$

Thus, $\hat{\boldsymbol{\delta}}'$ is a $(k \times r)$ matrix whose $i$th row represents the coefficients from an *OLS* regression of $z_{it}$ on $\mathbf{x}_t$. Let

$$\hat{\mathbf{z}}_t \equiv \hat{\boldsymbol{\delta}}' \mathbf{x}_t$$

be the $(k \times 1)$ vector of fitted values from these regressions of $\mathbf{z}_t$ on $\mathbf{x}_t$. Then [14.2.28] implies that

$$\sum_{t=1}^{T} \hat{\mathbf{z}}_t (y_t - \mathbf{z}'_t \hat{\boldsymbol{\beta}}_T) = \mathbf{0}$$

or

$$\hat{\boldsymbol{\beta}}_T = \left\{ \sum_{t=1}^{T} \hat{\mathbf{z}}_t \mathbf{z}'_t \right\}^{-1} \left\{ \sum_{t=1}^{T} \hat{\mathbf{z}}_t y_t \right\}.$$

Thus, the *GMM* estimator for this case is simply the two-stage least squares estimator as written in [9.2.8]. The variance given in [14.2.6] would be

$$\begin{aligned} (1/T)\hat{\mathbf{V}}_T &= (1/T) \left\{ \left[ (1/T) \sum_{t=1}^{T} \mathbf{z}_t \mathbf{x}'_t \right] \hat{\mathbf{S}}_T^{-1} \left[ (1/T) \sum_{t=1}^{T} \mathbf{x}_t \mathbf{z}'_t \right] \right\}^{-1} \\ &= \hat{\sigma}_T^2 \left\{ \left[ \sum_{t=1}^{T} \mathbf{z}_t \mathbf{x}'_t \right] \left[ \sum_{t=1}^{T} \mathbf{x}_t \mathbf{x}'_t \right]^{-1} \left[ \sum_{t=1}^{T} \mathbf{x}_t \mathbf{z}'_t \right] \right\}^{-1}, \end{aligned}$$

as earlier derived in expression [9.2.25]. A test of the overidentifying assumptions embodied in the model in [14.2.17] and [14.2.18] is given by

$$T[\mathbf{g}(\hat{\boldsymbol{\theta}}_T; \mathcal{Y}_T)]'\hat{\mathbf{S}}_T^{-1}[\mathbf{g}(\hat{\boldsymbol{\theta}}_T; \mathcal{Y}_T)]$$
$$= T\left\{(1/T)\sum_{t=1}^{T}\mathbf{x}_t(y_t - \mathbf{z}_t'\hat{\boldsymbol{\beta}}_T)\right\}'\left\{\hat{\sigma}_T^2\cdot(1/T)\sum_{t=1}^{T}\mathbf{x}_t\mathbf{x}_t'\right\}^{-1}$$
$$\times\left\{(1/T)\sum_{t=1}^{T}\mathbf{x}_t(y_t - \mathbf{z}_t'\hat{\boldsymbol{\beta}}_T)\right\}$$
$$= \hat{\sigma}_T^{-2}\left\{\sum_{t=1}^{T}\hat{u}_t\mathbf{x}_t'\right\}\left\{\sum_{t=1}^{T}\mathbf{x}_t\mathbf{x}_t'\right\}^{-1}\left\{\sum_{t=1}^{T}\mathbf{x}_t\hat{u}_t\right\}.$$

This magnitude will have an asymptotic $\chi^2$ distribution with $(r - k)$ degrees of freedom if the model is correctly specified.

Alternatively, to allow for heteroskedasticity and autocorrelation for the residuals $u_t$, the estimate $\hat{\mathbf{S}}_T$ in [14.2.24] would be replaced by [14.2.26]. Recall the first-order condition [14.2.27]:

$$\left\{(1/T)\sum_{t=1}^{T}\mathbf{z}_t\mathbf{x}_t'\right\}\hat{\mathbf{S}}_T^{-1}\left\{(1/T)\sum_{t=1}^{T}\mathbf{x}_t(y_t - \mathbf{z}_t'\hat{\boldsymbol{\beta}}_T)\right\} = \mathbf{0}. \qquad [14.2.29]$$

If we now define

$$\tilde{\mathbf{z}}_t \equiv \hat{\boldsymbol{\delta}}'\mathbf{x}_t$$
$$\hat{\boldsymbol{\delta}}' \equiv \left\{(1/T)\sum_{t=1}^{T}\mathbf{z}_t\mathbf{x}_t'\right\}\hat{\mathbf{S}}_T^{-1},$$

then [14.2.29] implies that the *GMM* estimator for this case is given by

$$\hat{\boldsymbol{\beta}}_T = \left\{\sum_{t=1}^{T}\tilde{\mathbf{z}}_t\mathbf{z}_t'\right\}^{-1}\left\{\sum_{t=1}^{T}\tilde{\mathbf{z}}_t y_t\right\}.$$

This characterization of $\hat{\boldsymbol{\beta}}_T$ is circular—in order to calculate $\hat{\boldsymbol{\beta}}_T$, we need to know $\tilde{\mathbf{z}}_t$ and thus $\hat{\mathbf{S}}_T$, whereas to construct $\hat{\mathbf{S}}_T$ from [14.2.26] we first need to know $\hat{\boldsymbol{\beta}}_T$. The solution is first to estimate $\boldsymbol{\beta}$ using a suboptimal weighting matrix such as $\hat{\mathbf{S}}_T = (1/T)\Sigma_{t=1}^{T}\mathbf{x}_t\mathbf{x}_t'$, and then to use this estimate of $\mathbf{S}$ to reestimate $\boldsymbol{\beta}$. The asymptotic variance of the *GMM* estimator is given by

$$E[(\hat{\boldsymbol{\beta}}_T - \boldsymbol{\beta})(\hat{\boldsymbol{\beta}}_T - \boldsymbol{\beta})'] \cong T\left\{\left[\sum_{t=1}^{T}\mathbf{z}_t\mathbf{x}_t'\right]\hat{\mathbf{S}}_T^{-1}\left[\sum_{t=1}^{T}\mathbf{x}_t\mathbf{z}_t'\right]\right\}^{-1}.$$

## *Nonlinear Systems of Simultaneous Equations*

Hansen's (1982) *GMM* also provides a convenient framework for estimating the nonlinear systems of simultaneous equations analyzed by Amemiya (1974), Jorgenson and Laffont (1974), and Gallant (1977). Suppose that the goal is to estimate a system of $n$ nonlinear equations of the form

$$\mathbf{y}_t = \mathbf{f}(\boldsymbol{\theta}, \mathbf{z}_t) + \mathbf{u}_t$$

for $\mathbf{z}_t$ a $(k \times 1)$ vector of explanatory variables and $\boldsymbol{\theta}$ an $(a \times 1)$ vector of unknown parameters. Let $\mathbf{x}_{it}$ denote a vector of instruments that are uncorrelated with the $i$th element of $\mathbf{u}_t$. The $r$ orthogonality conditions for this model are

$$\mathbf{h}(\boldsymbol{\theta}, \mathbf{w}_t) = \begin{bmatrix} [y_{1t} - f_1(\boldsymbol{\theta}, \mathbf{z}_t)]\mathbf{x}_{1t} \\ [y_{2t} - f_2(\boldsymbol{\theta}, \mathbf{z}_t)]\mathbf{x}_{2t} \\ \vdots \\ [y_{nt} - f_n(\boldsymbol{\theta}, \mathbf{z}_t)]\mathbf{x}_{nt} \end{bmatrix},$$

where $f_i(\boldsymbol{\theta}, \mathbf{z}_t)$ denotes the $i$th element of $\mathbf{f}(\boldsymbol{\theta}, \mathbf{z}_t)$ and $\mathbf{w}_t \equiv (\mathbf{y}_t', \mathbf{z}_t', \mathbf{x}_t')'$. The *GMM* estimate of $\boldsymbol{\theta}$ is the value that minimizes

$$Q(\boldsymbol{\theta}; \mathcal{Y}_T) = \left[(1/T) \sum_{t=1}^{T} \mathbf{h}(\boldsymbol{\theta}, \mathbf{w}_t)\right]' \hat{\mathbf{S}}_T^{-1} \left[(1/T) \sum_{t=1}^{T} \mathbf{h}(\boldsymbol{\theta}, \mathbf{w}_t)\right], \qquad [14.2.30]$$

where an estimate of $\mathbf{S}$ that could be used with heteroskedasticity and serial correlation of $u_t$ is given by

$$\hat{\mathbf{S}}_T = \hat{\boldsymbol{\Gamma}}_{0,T} + \sum_{v=1}^{q} \{1 - [v/(q+1)]\}(\hat{\boldsymbol{\Gamma}}_{v,T} + \hat{\boldsymbol{\Gamma}}_{v,T}')$$

$$\hat{\boldsymbol{\Gamma}}_{v,T} = (1/T) \sum_{t=v+1}^{T} [\mathbf{h}(\hat{\boldsymbol{\theta}}, \mathbf{w}_t)][\mathbf{h}(\hat{\boldsymbol{\theta}}, \mathbf{w}_{t-v})]'.$$

Minimization of [14.2.30] can be achieved numerically. Again, in order to evaluate [14.2.30], we first need an initial estimate of $\mathbf{S}$. One approach is to first minimize [14.2.30] with $\mathbf{S}_T = \mathbf{I}_r$, use the resulting estimate $\hat{\boldsymbol{\theta}}$ to construct a better estimate of $\mathbf{S}_T$, and recalculate $\hat{\boldsymbol{\theta}}$; the procedure can be iterated further, if desired. Identification requires an order condition ($r \geq a$) and the rank condition that the columns of the plim of $\hat{\mathbf{D}}_T'$ be linearly independent, where

$$\hat{\mathbf{D}}_T' = (1/T) \sum_{t=1}^{T} \left. \frac{\partial \mathbf{h}(\boldsymbol{\theta}, \mathbf{w}_t)}{\partial \boldsymbol{\theta}'} \right|_{\boldsymbol{\theta} = \hat{\boldsymbol{\theta}}_T}.$$

Standard errors for $\hat{\boldsymbol{\theta}}_T$ are then readily calculated from [14.2.5] and [14.2.6].

## *Estimation of Dynamic Rational Expectation Models*

People's behavior is often influenced by their expectations about the future. Unfortunately, we typically do not have direct observations on these expectations. However, it is still possible to estimate and test behavioral models if people's expectations are formed rationally in the sense that the errors they make in forecasting are uncorrelated with information they had available at the time of the forecast. As long as the econometrician observes a subset of the information people have actually used, the rational expectations hypothesis suggests orthogonality conditions that can be used in the *GMM* framework.

For illustration, we consider the study of portfolio decisions by Hansen and Singleton (1982). Let $c_t$ denote the overall level of spending on consumption goods by a particular stockholder during period $t$. The satisfaction or utility that the stockholder receives from this spending is represented by a function $u(c_t)$, where it is assumed that

$$\frac{\partial u(c_t)}{\partial c_t} > 0 \qquad \frac{\partial^2 u(c_t)}{\partial c_t^2} < 0.$$

The stockholder is presumed to want to maximize

$$\sum_{\tau=0}^{\infty} \beta^{\tau} E\{u(c_{t+\tau}) | \mathbf{x}_t^*\}, \qquad [14.2.31]$$

where $\mathbf{x}_t^*$ is a vector representing all the information available to the stockholder at date $t$ and $\beta$ is a parameter satisfying $0 < \beta < 1$. Smaller values of $\beta$ mean that the stockholder places a smaller weight on future events. At date $t$, the stockholder contemplates purchasing any of $m$ different assets, where a dollar invested in asset $i$ at date $t$ will yield a gross return of $(1 + r_{i,t+1})$ at date $t+1$; in general this rate of return is not known for certain at date $t$. Assuming that the stockholder takes a position in each of these $m$ assets, the stockholder's optimal portfolio will satisfy

$$u'(c_t) = \beta E\{(1 + r_{i,t+1})u'(c_{t+1}) | \mathbf{x}_t^*\} \qquad \text{for } i = 1, 2, \ldots, m, \qquad [14.2.32]$$

where $u'(c_t) \equiv \partial u / \partial c_t$. To see the intuition behind this claim, suppose that condition [14.2.32] failed to hold. Say, for example, that the left side were smaller than the right. Suppose the stockholder were to save one more dollar at date $t$ and invest the dollar in asset $i$, using the returns to boost period $t + 1$ consumption. Following this strategy would cause consumption at date $t$ to fall by one dollar (reducing [14.2.31] by an amount given by the left side of [14.2.32]), while consumption at date $t + 1$ would rise by $(1 + r_{i,t+1})$ dollars (increasing [14.2.31] by an amount given by the right side of [14.2.32]). If the left side of [14.2.32] were less than the right side of [14.2.32], then the stockholder's objective [14.2.31] would be improved under this change. Only when [14.2.32] is satisfied is the stockholder as well off as possible.[2]

Suppose that the utility function is parameterized as

$$u(c_t) = \begin{cases} \dfrac{c_t^{1-\gamma}}{1 - \gamma} & \text{for } \gamma > 0 \text{ and } \gamma \neq 1 \\ \log c_t & \text{for } \gamma = 1. \end{cases}$$

The parameter $\gamma$ is known as the *coefficient of relative risk aversion*, which for this class of utility functions is a constant. For this function, [14.2.32] becomes

$$c_t^{-\gamma} = \beta E\{(1 + r_{i,t+1})c_{t+1}^{-\gamma} | \mathbf{x}_t^*\}. \qquad [14.2.33]$$

Dividing both sides of [14.2.33] by $c_t^{-\gamma}$ results in

$$1 = \beta E\{(1 + r_{i,t+1})(c_{t+1}/c_t)^{-\gamma} | \mathbf{x}_t^*\}, \qquad [14.2.34]$$

where $c_t$ could be moved inside the conditional expectation operator, since it represents a decision based solely on the information contained in $\mathbf{x}_t^*$. Expression [14.2.34] requires that the random variable described by

$$1 - \beta\{(1 + r_{i,t+1})(c_{t+1}/c_t)^{-\gamma}\} \qquad [14.2.35]$$

be uncorrelated with any variable contained in the information set $\mathbf{x}_t^*$ for any asset $i$ that the stockholder holds. It should therefore be the case that

$$E\{[1 - \beta\{(1 + r_{i,t+1})(c_{t+1}/c_t)^{-\gamma}\}]\mathbf{x}_t\} = \mathbf{0}, \qquad [14.2.36]$$

where $\mathbf{x}_t$ is any subset of the stockholder's information set $\mathbf{x}_t^*$ that the econometrician is also able to observe.

Let $\boldsymbol{\theta} \equiv (\beta, \gamma)'$ denote the unknown parameters that are to be estimated, and let $\mathbf{w}_t \equiv (r_{1,t+1}, r_{2,t+1}, \ldots, r_{m,t+1}, c_{t+1}/c_t, \mathbf{x}_t')'$ denote the vector of variables that are observed by the econometrician for date $t$. Stacking the equations in [14.2.36] for $i = 1, 2, \ldots, m$ produces a set of $r$ orthogonality conditions that can be used to estimate $\boldsymbol{\theta}$:

$$\underset{(r\times 1)}{\mathbf{h}(\boldsymbol{\theta}, \mathbf{w}_t)} = \begin{bmatrix} [1 - \beta\{(1 + r_{1,t+1})(c_{t+1}/c_t)^{-\gamma}\}]\mathbf{x}_t \\ [1 - \beta\{(1 + r_{2,t+1})(c_{t+1}/c_t)^{-\gamma}\}]\mathbf{x}_t \\ \vdots \\ [1 - \beta\{(1 + r_{m,t+1})(c_{t+1}/c_t)^{-\gamma}\}]\mathbf{x}_t \end{bmatrix}. \qquad [14.2.37]$$

The sample average value of $\mathbf{h}(\boldsymbol{\theta}, \mathbf{w}_t)$ is

$$\mathbf{g}(\boldsymbol{\theta}; \mathcal{Y}_T) \equiv (1/T) \sum_{t=1}^{T} \mathbf{h}(\boldsymbol{\theta}, \mathbf{w}_t),$$

and the *GMM* objective function is

$$Q(\boldsymbol{\theta}) = [\mathbf{g}(\boldsymbol{\theta}; \mathcal{Y}_T)]'\hat{\mathbf{S}}_T^{-1}[\mathbf{g}(\boldsymbol{\theta}; \mathcal{Y}_T)]. \qquad [14.2.38]$$

This expression can then be minimized numerically with respect to $\boldsymbol{\theta}$.

According to the theory, the magnitude in [14.2.35] should be uncorrelated with any information the stockholder has available at time $t$, which would include

[2]For further details, see Sargent (1987).

lagged values of [14.2.35]. Hence, the vector in [14.2.37] should be uncorrelated with its own lagged values, suggesting that $\mathbf{S}$ can be consistently estimated by

$$\hat{\mathbf{S}}_T = (1/T) \sum_{t=1}^{T} \{[\mathbf{h}(\hat{\boldsymbol{\theta}}, \mathbf{w}_t)][\mathbf{h}(\hat{\boldsymbol{\theta}}, \mathbf{w}_t)]'\},$$

where $\hat{\boldsymbol{\theta}}$ is an initial consistent estimate. This initial estimate $\hat{\boldsymbol{\theta}}$ could be obtained by minimizing [14.2.38] with $\hat{\mathbf{S}}_T = \mathbf{I}_r$.

Hansen and Singleton (1982) estimated such a model using real consumption expenditures for the aggregate United States divided by the U.S. population as their measure of $c_t$. For $r_{1t}$, they used the inflation-adjusted return that an investor would earn if one dollar was invested in every stock listed on the New York Stock Exchange, while $r_{2t}$ was a value-weighted inflation-adjusted return corresponding to the return an investor would earn if the investor owned the entire stock of each company listed on the exchange. Hansen and Singleton's instruments consisted of a constant term, lagged consumption growth rates, and lagged rates of return:

$$\mathbf{x}_t = (1, c_t/c_{t-1}, c_{t-1}/c_{t-2}, \ldots, c_{t-\ell+1}/c_{t-\ell}, r_{1t}, r_{1,t-1}, \ldots,$$
$$r_{1,t-\ell+1}, r_{2,t}, r_{2,t-1}, \ldots, r_{2,t-\ell+1})'.$$

When $\ell$ lags are used, there are $3\ell + 1$ elements in $\mathbf{x}_t$, and thus $r = 2(3\ell + 1)$ separate orthogonality conditions are represented by [14.2.37]. Since $a = 2$ parameters are estimated, the $\chi^2$ statistic in [14.1.27] has $6\ell$ degrees of freedom.

## 14.3. *Extensions*

### GMM *with Nonstationary Data*

The maintained assumption throughout this chapter has been that the $(h \times 1)$ vector of observed variables $\mathbf{w}_t$ is strictly stationary. Even if the raw data appear to be trending over time, sometimes the model can be transformed or reparameterized so that stationarity of the transformed system is a reasonable assumption. For example, the consumption series $\{c_t\}$ used in Hansen and Singleton's study (1982) is increasing over time. However, it was possible to write the equation to be estimated [14.2.36] in such a form that only the consumption growth rate $(c_{t+1}/c_t)$ appeared, for which the stationarity assumption is much more plausible. Alternatively, suppose that some of the elements of the observed vector $\mathbf{w}_t$ are presumed to grow deterministically over time according to

$$\mathbf{w}_t = \boldsymbol{\alpha} + \boldsymbol{\delta} \cdot t + \mathbf{w}_t^*, \qquad [14.3.1]$$

where $\boldsymbol{\alpha}$ and $\boldsymbol{\delta}$ are $(h \times 1)$ vectors of constants and $\mathbf{w}_t^*$ is strictly stationary with mean zero. Suppose that the orthogonality conditions can be expressed in terms of $\mathbf{w}_t^*$ as

$$E\{\mathbf{f}(\boldsymbol{\theta}_0, \mathbf{w}_t^*)\} = \mathbf{0}.$$

Then Ogaki (1993) recommended jointly estimating $\boldsymbol{\theta}$, $\boldsymbol{\alpha}$ and $\boldsymbol{\delta}$ using

$$\mathbf{h}(\boldsymbol{\theta}, \mathbf{w}_t) = \begin{bmatrix} \mathbf{w}_t - \boldsymbol{\alpha} - \boldsymbol{\delta} t \\ \mathbf{f}(\boldsymbol{\theta}, \mathbf{w}_t - \boldsymbol{\alpha} - \boldsymbol{\delta} t) \end{bmatrix}$$

to construct the moment condition in [14.2.3].

### *Testing for Structural Stability*

Suppose we want to test the hypothesis that the $(a \times 1)$ parameter vector $\boldsymbol{\theta}$ that characterizes the first $T_0$ observations in the sample is different from the value that characterizes the last $T - T_0$ observations, where $T_0$ is a known change point. One approach is to obtain an estimate $\hat{\boldsymbol{\theta}}_{1,T_0}$ based solely on the first $T_0$ observations, minimizing

$$Q(\boldsymbol{\theta}_1; \mathbf{w}_{T_0}, \mathbf{w}_{T_0-1}, \ldots, \mathbf{w}_1) = \left[(1/T_0)\sum_{t=1}^{T_0}\mathbf{h}(\boldsymbol{\theta}_1, \mathbf{w}_t)\right]'\hat{\mathbf{S}}_{1,T_0}^{-1}\left[(1/T_0)\sum_{t=1}^{T_0}\mathbf{h}(\boldsymbol{\theta}_1, \mathbf{w}_t)\right], \qquad [14.3.2]$$

where, for example, if $\{\mathbf{h}(\boldsymbol{\theta}_0, \mathbf{w}_t)\}$ is serially uncorrelated,

$$\hat{\mathbf{S}}_{1,T_0} = (1/T_0)\sum_{t=1}^{T_0}[\mathbf{h}(\hat{\boldsymbol{\theta}}_{1,T_0}, \mathbf{w}_t)][\mathbf{h}(\hat{\boldsymbol{\theta}}_{1,T_0}, \mathbf{w}_t)]'.$$

Proposition 14.1 implies that

$$\sqrt{T_0}(\hat{\boldsymbol{\theta}}_{1,T_0} - \boldsymbol{\theta}_1) \xrightarrow{L} N(\mathbf{0}, \mathbf{V}_1) \qquad [14.3.3]$$

as $T_0 \to \infty$, where $\mathbf{V}_1$ can be estimated from

$$\hat{\mathbf{V}}_{1,T_0} = \{\hat{\mathbf{D}}_{1,T_0}\hat{\mathbf{S}}_{1,T_0}^{-1}\hat{\mathbf{D}}'_{1,T_0}\}^{-1}$$

for

$$\hat{\mathbf{D}}'_{1,T_0} \equiv (1/T_0)\sum_{t=1}^{T_0}\left.\frac{\partial\mathbf{h}(\boldsymbol{\theta}_1, \mathbf{w}_t)}{\partial\boldsymbol{\theta}'_1}\right|_{\boldsymbol{\theta}_1=\hat{\boldsymbol{\theta}}_{1,T_0}}.$$

Similarly, a separate estimate $\hat{\boldsymbol{\theta}}_{2,T-T_0}$ can be based on the last $T - T_0$ observations, with analogous measures $\hat{\mathbf{S}}_{2,T-T_0}$, $\hat{\mathbf{V}}_{2,T-T_0}$, $\hat{\mathbf{D}}_{2,T-T_0}$, and

$$\sqrt{T - T_0}(\hat{\boldsymbol{\theta}}_{2,T-T_0} - \boldsymbol{\theta}_2) \xrightarrow{L} N(\mathbf{0}, \mathbf{V}_2) \qquad [14.3.4]$$

as $T - T_0 \to \infty$. Let $\pi \equiv T_0/T$ denote the fraction of observations contained in the first subsample. Then [14.3.3] and [14.3.4] state that

$$\sqrt{T}(\hat{\boldsymbol{\theta}}_{1,T_0} - \boldsymbol{\theta}_1) \xrightarrow{L} N(\mathbf{0}, \mathbf{V}_1/\pi)$$
$$\sqrt{T}(\hat{\boldsymbol{\theta}}_{2,T-T_0} - \boldsymbol{\theta}_2) \xrightarrow{L} N(\mathbf{0}, \mathbf{V}_2/(1 - \pi))$$

as $T \to \infty$. Andrews and Fair (1988) suggested using a Wald test of the null hypothesis that $\boldsymbol{\theta}_1 = \boldsymbol{\theta}_2$, exploiting the fact that under the stationarity conditions needed to justify Proposition 14.1, $\hat{\boldsymbol{\theta}}_1$ is asymptotically independent of $\hat{\boldsymbol{\theta}}_2$:

$$\lambda_T = T(\hat{\boldsymbol{\theta}}_{1,T_0} - \hat{\boldsymbol{\theta}}_{2,T-T_0})' \times \{\pi^{-1}\cdot\hat{\mathbf{V}}_{1,T_0} + (1 - \pi)^{-1}\cdot\hat{\mathbf{V}}_{2,T-T_0}\}^{-1}(\hat{\boldsymbol{\theta}}_{1,T_0} - \hat{\boldsymbol{\theta}}_{2,T-T_0}).$$

Then $\lambda_T \xrightarrow{L} \chi^2(a)$ under the null hypothesis that $\boldsymbol{\theta}_1 = \boldsymbol{\theta}_2$.

One can further test for structural change at a variety of different possible dates, repeating the foregoing test for all $T_0$ between, say, $0.15T$ and $0.85T$ and choosing the largest value for the resulting test statistic $\lambda_T$. Andrews (1993) described the asymptotic distribution of such a test.

Another simple test associates separate moment conditions with the observations before and after $T_0$ and uses the $\chi^2$ test suggested in [14.1.27] to test the validity of the separate sets of conditions. Specifically, let

$$d_{1t} = \begin{cases} 1 & \text{for } t \leq T_0 \\ 0 & \text{for } t > T_0. \end{cases}$$

If $\mathbf{h}(\boldsymbol{\theta}, \mathbf{w}_t)$ is an $(r \times 1)$ vector whose population mean is zero at $\boldsymbol{\theta}_0$, define

$$\underset{(2r\times 1)}{\mathbf{h}^*(\boldsymbol{\theta}, \mathbf{w}_t, d_{1t})} \equiv \begin{bmatrix} \mathbf{h}(\boldsymbol{\theta}, \mathbf{w}_t)\cdot d_{1t} \\ \mathbf{h}(\boldsymbol{\theta}, \mathbf{w}_t)\cdot(1 - d_{1t}) \end{bmatrix}.$$

The $a$ elements of $\boldsymbol{\theta}$ can then be estimated by using the $2r$ orthogonality conditions given by $E\{\mathbf{h}^*(\boldsymbol{\theta}_0, \mathbf{w}_t, d_{1t})\} = \mathbf{0}$ for $t = 1, 2, \ldots, T$, by simply replacing $\mathbf{h}(\boldsymbol{\theta}, \mathbf{w}_t)$

in [14.2.3] with $\mathbf{h}^*(\boldsymbol{\theta}, \mathbf{w}_t, d_{1t})$ and minimizing [14.2.2] in the usual way. Hansen's $\chi^2$ test statistic described in [14.1.27] based on the $\mathbf{h}^*(\cdot)$ moment conditions could then be compared with a $\chi^2(2r - a)$ critical value to provide a test of the hypothesis that $\boldsymbol{\theta}_1 = \boldsymbol{\theta}_2$.

A number of other tests for structural change have been proposed by Andrews and Fair (1988) and Ghysels and Hall (1990a, b).

## GMM *and Econometric Identification*

For the portfolio decision model [14.2.34], it was argued that any variable would be valid to include in the instrument vector $\mathbf{x}_t$, as long as that variable was known to investors at date $t$ and their expectations were formed rationally. Essentially, [14.2.34] represents an asset demand curve. In the light of the discussion of simultaneous equations bias in Section 9.1, one might be troubled by the claim that it is possible to estimate a demand curve without needing to think about the way that variables may affect the demand and supply of assets in different ways.

As stressed by Garber and King (1984), the portfolio choice model avoids simultaneous equations bias because it postulates that equation [14.2.32] holds *exactly*, with no error term. The model as written claims that if the econometrician had the same information $\mathbf{x}_t^*$ used by investors, then investors' behavior could be predicted with an $R^2$ of unity. If there were no error term in the demand for oranges equation [9.1.1], or if the error in the demand for oranges equation were negligible compared with the error term in the supply equation, then we would not have had to worry about simultaneous equations bias in that example, either.

It is hard to take seriously the suggestion that the observed data are exactly described by [14.2.32] with no error. There are substantial difficulties in measuring aggregate consumption, population, and rates of return on assets. Even if these aggregates could in some sense be measured perfectly, it is questionable whether they are the appropriate values to be using to test a theory about individual investor preferences. And even if we had available a perfect measure of the consumption of an individual investor, the notion that the investor's utility could be represented by a function of this precise parametric form with $\gamma$ constant across time is surely hard to defend.

Once we acknowledge that an error term reasonably ought to be included in [14.2.32], then it is no longer satisfactory to say that any variable dated $t$ or earlier is a valid instrument. The difficulties with estimation are compounded by the nonlinearity of the equations of interest. If one wants to take seriously the possibility of an error term in [14.2.32] and its correlation with other variables, the best approach currently available appears to be to linearize the dynamic rational expectations model. Any variable uncorrelated with both the forecast error people make and the specification error in the model could then be used as a valid instrument for traditional instrumental variable estimation; see Sill (1992) for an illustration of this approach.

## *Optimal Choice of Instruments*

If one does subscribe to the view that any variable dated $t$ or earlier is a valid instrument for estimation of [14.2.32], this suggests a virtually infinite set of possible variables that could be used. One's first thought might be that, the more orthogonality conditions used, the better the resulting estimates might be. However, Monte Carlo simulations by Tauchen (1986) and Kocherlakota (1990) strongly suggest that one should be quite parsimonious in the selection of $\mathbf{x}_t$. Nelson and

Startz (1990) in particular stress that in the linear simultaneous equations model $y_t = \mathbf{z}_t'\boldsymbol{\beta} + u_t$, a good instrument not only must be uncorrelated with $u_t$, but must also be strongly correlated with $\mathbf{z}_t$. See Bates and White (1988), Hall (1993), and Gallant and Tauchen (1992) for further discussion on instrument selection.

## 14.4. GMM *and Maximum Likelihood Estimation*

In many cases the maximum likelihood estimate of $\boldsymbol{\theta}$ can also be viewed as a *GMM* estimate. This section explores this analogy and shows how asymptotic properties of maximum likelihood estimation and quasi-maximum likelihood can be obtained from the previous general results about *GMM* estimation.

### *The Score and Its Population Properties*

Let $\mathbf{y}_t$ denote an $(n \times 1)$ vector of variables observed at date $t$, and let $\mathcal{Y}_t \equiv (\mathbf{y}_t', \mathbf{y}_{t-1}', \ldots, \mathbf{y}_1')'$ denote the full set of data observed through date $t$. Suppose that the conditional density of the $t$th observation is given by

$$f(\mathbf{y}_t|\mathcal{Y}_{t-1}; \boldsymbol{\theta}). \qquad [14.4.1]$$

Since [14.4.1] is a density, it must integrate to unity:

$$\int_{\mathcal{A}} f(\mathbf{y}_t|\mathcal{Y}_{t-1}; \boldsymbol{\theta})\, d\mathbf{y}_t = 1, \qquad [14.4.2]$$

where $\mathcal{A}$ denotes the set of possible values that $\mathbf{y}_t$ could take on and $\int d\mathbf{y}_t$ denotes multiple integration:

$$\int h(\mathbf{y}_t)\, d\mathbf{y}_t \equiv \int \int \cdots \int h(y_{1t}, y_{2t}, \ldots, y_{nt})\, dy_{1t}\, dy_{2t} \cdots dy_{nt}.$$

Since [14.4.2] holds for all admissible values of $\boldsymbol{\theta}$, we can differentiate both sides with respect to $\boldsymbol{\theta}$ to conclude that

$$\int_{\mathcal{A}} \frac{\partial f(\mathbf{y}_t|\mathcal{Y}_{t-1}; \boldsymbol{\theta})}{\partial \boldsymbol{\theta}}\, d\mathbf{y}_t = \mathbf{0}. \qquad [14.4.3]$$

The conditions under which the order of differentiation and integration can be reversed as assumed in arriving at [14.4.3] and the equations to follow are known as "regularity conditions" and are detailed in Cramér (1946). Assuming that these hold, we can multiply and divide the integrand in [14.4.3] by the conditional density of $\mathbf{y}_t$:

$$\int_{\mathcal{A}} \frac{\partial f(\mathbf{y}_t|\mathcal{Y}_{t-1}; \boldsymbol{\theta})}{\partial \boldsymbol{\theta}} \frac{1}{f(\mathbf{y}_t|\mathcal{Y}_{t-1}; \boldsymbol{\theta})} f(\mathbf{y}_t|\mathcal{Y}_{t-1}; \boldsymbol{\theta})\, d\mathbf{y}_t = \mathbf{0},$$

or

$$\int_{\mathcal{A}} \frac{\partial \log f(\mathbf{y}_t|\mathcal{Y}_{t-1}; \boldsymbol{\theta})}{\partial \boldsymbol{\theta}} f(\mathbf{y}_t|\mathcal{Y}_{t-1}; \boldsymbol{\theta})\, d\mathbf{y}_t = \mathbf{0}. \qquad [14.4.4]$$

Let $\mathbf{h}(\boldsymbol{\theta}, \mathcal{Y}_t)$ denote the derivative of the log of the conditional density of the $t$th observation:

$$\mathbf{h}(\boldsymbol{\theta}, \mathcal{Y}_t) = \frac{\partial \log f(\mathbf{y}_t|\mathcal{Y}_{t-1}; \boldsymbol{\theta})}{\partial \boldsymbol{\theta}}. \qquad [14.4.5]$$

If there are $a$ elements in $\boldsymbol{\theta}$, then [14.4.5] describes an $(a \times 1)$ vector for each date $t$ that is known as the *score* of the $t$th observation. Since the score is a function of $\mathcal{Y}_t$, it is a random variable. Moreover, substitution of [14.4.5] into [14.4.4] reveals that

$$\int_{\mathcal{A}} \mathbf{h}(\boldsymbol{\theta}, \mathcal{Y}_t) f(\mathbf{y}_t | \mathcal{Y}_{t-1}; \boldsymbol{\theta})\, d\mathbf{y}_t = \mathbf{0}. \qquad [14.4.6]$$

Equation [14.4.6] indicates that if the data were really generated by the density [14.4.1], then the expected value of the score conditional on information observed through date $t - 1$ should be zero:

$$E\{\mathbf{h}(\boldsymbol{\theta}, \mathcal{Y}_t) | \mathcal{Y}_{t-1}\} = \mathbf{0}. \qquad [14.4.7]$$

In other words, the score vectors $\{\mathbf{h}(\boldsymbol{\theta}, \mathcal{Y}_t)\}_{t=1}^{\infty}$ should form a martingale difference sequence. This observation prompted White (1987) to suggest a general specification test for models estimated by maximum likelihood based on whether the sample scores appear to be serially correlated. Expression [14.4.7] further implies that the score has unconditional expectation of zero, provided that the unconditional first moment exists:

$$E\{\mathbf{h}(\boldsymbol{\theta}, \mathcal{Y}_t)\} = \mathbf{0}. \qquad [14.4.8]$$

## *Maximum Likelihood and* GMM

Expression [14.4.8] can be viewed as a set of $a$ orthogonality conditions that could be used to estimate the $a$ unknown elements of $\boldsymbol{\theta}$. The *GMM* principle suggests using as an estimate of $\boldsymbol{\theta}$ the solution to

$$\mathbf{0} = (1/T) \sum_{t=1}^{T} \mathbf{h}(\boldsymbol{\theta}, \mathcal{Y}_t). \qquad [14.4.9]$$

But this is also the characterization of the maximum likelihood estimate, which is based on maximization of

$$\mathcal{L}(\boldsymbol{\theta}) = \sum_{t=1}^{T} \log f(\mathbf{y}_t | \mathcal{Y}_{t-1}; \boldsymbol{\theta}),$$

the first-order conditions for which are

$$\sum_{t=1}^{T} \frac{\partial \log f(\mathbf{y}_t | \mathcal{Y}_{t-1}; \boldsymbol{\theta})}{\partial \boldsymbol{\theta}} = \mathbf{0}, \qquad [14.4.10]$$

assuming an interior maximum. Recalling [14.4.5], observe that [14.4.10] and [14.4.9] are identical conditions—the *MLE* is the same as the *GMM* estimator based on the orthogonality conditions in [14.4.8].

The *GMM* formula [14.2.6] suggests that the variance-covariance matrix of the *MLE* can be approximated by

$$E[(\hat{\boldsymbol{\theta}}_T - \boldsymbol{\theta}_0)(\hat{\boldsymbol{\theta}}_T - \boldsymbol{\theta}_0)'] \cong (1/T)\{\hat{\mathbf{D}}_T \hat{\mathbf{S}}_T^{-1} \hat{\mathbf{D}}_T'\}^{-1}, \qquad [14.4.11]$$

where

$$\begin{aligned} \underset{(a \times a)}{\hat{\mathbf{D}}_T'} &= \left.\frac{\partial \mathbf{g}(\boldsymbol{\theta}; \mathcal{Y}_T)}{\partial \boldsymbol{\theta}'}\right|_{\boldsymbol{\theta} = \hat{\boldsymbol{\theta}}_T} \\ &= (1/T) \sum_{t=1}^{T} \left.\frac{\partial \mathbf{h}(\boldsymbol{\theta}, \mathcal{Y}_t)}{\partial \boldsymbol{\theta}'}\right|_{\boldsymbol{\theta} = \hat{\boldsymbol{\theta}}_T} \qquad [14.4.12] \\ &= (1/T) \sum_{t=1}^{T} \left.\frac{\partial^2 \log f(\mathbf{y}_t | \mathcal{Y}_{t-1}; \boldsymbol{\theta})}{\partial \boldsymbol{\theta}\, \partial \boldsymbol{\theta}'}\right|_{\boldsymbol{\theta} = \hat{\boldsymbol{\theta}}_T}. \end{aligned}$$

Moreover, the observation in [14.4.7] that the scores are serially uncorrelated suggests estimating $\mathbf{S}$ by

$$\hat{\mathbf{S}}_T = (1/T)\sum_{t=1}^{T}[\mathbf{h}(\hat{\boldsymbol{\theta}}, \mathcal{Y}_t)][\mathbf{h}(\hat{\boldsymbol{\theta}}, \mathcal{Y}_t)]'. \qquad [14.4.13]$$

## *The Information Matrix Equality*

Expression [14.4.12] will be recognized as $-1$ times the second derivative estimate of the information matrix. Similarly, expression [14.4.13] is the outer-product estimate of the information matrix. That these two expressions are indeed estimating the same matrix if the model is correctly specified can be seen from calculations similar to those that produced [14.4.6]. Differentiating both sides of [14.4.6] with respect to $\boldsymbol{\theta}'$ reveals that

$$\begin{aligned}\mathbf{0} &= \int_{\mathcal{A}} \frac{\partial \mathbf{h}(\boldsymbol{\theta}, \mathcal{Y}_t)}{\partial \boldsymbol{\theta}'} f(\mathbf{y}_t|\mathcal{Y}_{t-1}; \boldsymbol{\theta})\, d\mathbf{y}_t + \int_{\mathcal{A}} \mathbf{h}(\boldsymbol{\theta}, \mathcal{Y}_t) \frac{\partial f(\mathbf{y}_t|\mathcal{Y}_{t-1}; \boldsymbol{\theta})}{\partial \boldsymbol{\theta}'}\, d\mathbf{y}_t \\ &= \int_{\mathcal{A}} \frac{\partial \mathbf{h}(\boldsymbol{\theta}, \mathcal{Y}_t)}{\partial \boldsymbol{\theta}'} f(\mathbf{y}_t|\mathcal{Y}_{t-1}; \boldsymbol{\theta})\, d\mathbf{y}_t \\ &\quad + \int_{\mathcal{A}} \mathbf{h}(\boldsymbol{\theta}, \mathcal{Y}_t) \frac{\partial \log f(\mathbf{y}_t|\mathcal{Y}_{t-1}; \boldsymbol{\theta})}{\partial \boldsymbol{\theta}'} f(\mathbf{y}_t|\mathcal{Y}_{t-1}; \boldsymbol{\theta})\, d\mathbf{y}_t\end{aligned}$$

or

$$\int_{\mathcal{A}} [\mathbf{h}(\boldsymbol{\theta}, \mathcal{Y}_t)][\mathbf{h}(\boldsymbol{\theta}, \mathcal{Y}_t)]' f(\mathbf{y}_t|\mathcal{Y}_{t-1}; \boldsymbol{\theta})\, d\mathbf{y}_t = -\int_{\mathcal{A}} \frac{\partial \mathbf{h}(\boldsymbol{\theta}, \mathcal{Y}_t)}{\partial \boldsymbol{\theta}'} f(\mathbf{y}_t|\mathcal{Y}_{t-1}; \boldsymbol{\theta})\, d\mathbf{y}_t.$$

This equation implies that if the model is correctly specified, the expected value of the outer product of the vector of first derivatives of the log likelihood is equal to the negative of the expected value of the matrix of second derivatives:

$$\begin{aligned}&E\left\{\left[\frac{\partial \log f(\mathbf{y}_t|\mathcal{Y}_{t-1}; \boldsymbol{\theta})}{\partial \boldsymbol{\theta}}\right]\left[\frac{\partial \log f(\mathbf{y}_t|\mathcal{Y}_{t-1}; \boldsymbol{\theta})}{\partial \boldsymbol{\theta}'}\right]\middle|\, \mathcal{Y}_{t-1}\right\} \\ &\quad = -E\left\{\frac{\partial^2 \log f(\mathbf{y}_t|\mathcal{Y}_{t-1}; \boldsymbol{\theta})}{\partial \boldsymbol{\theta}\, \partial \boldsymbol{\theta}'}\middle|\, \mathcal{Y}_{t-1}\right\} \qquad [14.4.14] \\ &\quad \equiv \mathcal{I}_t.\end{aligned}$$

Expression [14.4.14] is known as the *information matrix equality*. Assuming that $(1/T)\sum_{t=1}^{T}\mathcal{I}_t \xrightarrow{p} \mathcal{I}$, a positive definite matrix, we can reasonably expect that for many models, the estimate $\hat{\mathbf{S}}_T$ in [14.4.13] converges in probability to the information matrix $\mathcal{I}$ and the estimate $\hat{\mathbf{D}}_T'$ in [14.4.12] converges in probability to $-\mathcal{I}$. Thus, result [14.4.11] suggests that if the data are stationary and the estimates do not fall on the boundaries of the allowable parameter space, it will often be the case that

$$\sqrt{T}(\hat{\boldsymbol{\theta}}_T - \boldsymbol{\theta}_0) \xrightarrow{L} N(\mathbf{0}, \mathcal{I}^{-1}), \qquad [14.4.15]$$

where the information matrix $\mathcal{I}$ can be estimated consistently from either $-\hat{\mathbf{D}}_T'$ in [14.4.12] or $\hat{\mathbf{S}}_T$ in [14.4.13].

In small samples, the estimates $-\hat{\mathbf{D}}_T'$ and $\hat{\mathbf{S}}_T$ will differ, though if they differ too greatly this suggests that the model may be misspecified. White (1982) developed an alternative specification test based on comparing these two magnitudes.

## *The Wald Test for Maximum Likelihood Estimates*

Result [14.4.15] suggests a general approach to testing hypotheses about the value of a parameter vector $\boldsymbol{\theta}$ that has been estimated by maximum likelihood.

Consider a null hypothesis involving $m$ restrictions on $\boldsymbol{\theta}$ represented as $\mathbf{g}(\boldsymbol{\theta}) = \mathbf{0}$ where $\mathbf{g}: \mathbb{R}^a \rightarrow \mathbb{R}^m$ is a known differentiable function. The Wald test of this hypothesis is given by

$$\underset{(1\times m)}{T[\mathbf{g}(\hat{\boldsymbol{\theta}}_T)]'}\left\{\underset{(m\times a)}{\left[\left.\frac{\partial \mathbf{g}(\boldsymbol{\theta})}{\partial \boldsymbol{\theta}'}\right|_{\boldsymbol{\theta}=\hat{\boldsymbol{\theta}}_T}\right]}\underset{(a\times a)}{\hat{\mathcal{J}}_T^{-1}}\underset{(a\times m)}{\left[\left.\frac{\partial \mathbf{g}(\boldsymbol{\theta})}{\partial \boldsymbol{\theta}'}\right|_{\boldsymbol{\theta}=\hat{\boldsymbol{\theta}}_T}\right]'}\right\}^{-1}\underset{(m\times 1)}{[\mathbf{g}(\hat{\boldsymbol{\theta}}_T)]}, \qquad [14.4.16]$$

which converges in distribution to a $\chi^2(m)$ variable under the null hypothesis. Again, the estimate of the information matrix $\hat{\mathcal{J}}_T$ could be based on either $-\hat{\mathbf{D}}_T'$ in [14.4.12] or $\hat{\mathbf{S}}_T$ in [14.4.13].

## *The Lagrange Multiplier Test*

We have seen that if the model is correctly specified, the scores $\{\mathbf{h}(\boldsymbol{\theta}_0, \mathcal{Y}_t)\}_{t=1}^{\infty}$ often form a martingale difference sequence. Expression [14.4.14] indicates that the conditional variance-covariance matrix of the $t$th score is given by $\mathcal{J}_t$. Hence, typically,

$$T\left[(1/T)\sum_{t=1}^{T}\mathbf{h}(\boldsymbol{\theta}_0, \mathcal{Y}_t)\right]'\hat{\mathcal{J}}_T^{-1}\left[(1/T)\sum_{t=1}^{T}\mathbf{h}(\boldsymbol{\theta}_0, \mathcal{Y}_t)\right] \xrightarrow{L} \chi^2(a). \qquad [14.4.17]$$

Expression [14.4.17] does not hold when $\boldsymbol{\theta}_0$ is replaced by $\hat{\boldsymbol{\theta}}_T$, since, from [14.4.9], this would cause [14.4.17] to be identically zero.

Suppose, however, that the likelihood function is maximized subject to $m$ constraints on $\boldsymbol{\theta}$, and let $\tilde{\boldsymbol{\theta}}_T$ denote the restricted estimate of $\boldsymbol{\theta}$. Then, as in the *GMM* test for overidentifying restrictions [14.1.27], we would expect that

$$T\left[(1/T)\sum_{t=1}^{T}\mathbf{h}(\tilde{\boldsymbol{\theta}}_T, \mathcal{Y}_t)\right]'\hat{\mathcal{J}}_T^{-1}\left[(1/T)\sum_{t=1}^{T}\mathbf{h}(\tilde{\boldsymbol{\theta}}_T, \mathcal{Y}_t)\right] \xrightarrow{L} \chi^2(m). \qquad [14.4.18]$$

The magnitude in [14.4.18] was called the *efficient score* statistic by Rao (1948) and the *Lagrange multiplier test* by Aitchison and Silvey (1958). It provides an extremely useful class of diagnostic tests, enabling one to estimate a restricted model and test it against a more general specification without having to estimate the more general model. Breusch and Pagan (1980), Engle (1984), and Godfrey (1988) illustrated applications of the usefulness of the Lagrange multiplier principle.

## *Quasi-Maximum Likelihood Estimation*

Even if the data were not generated by the density $f(\mathbf{y}_t|\mathcal{Y}_{t-1}; \boldsymbol{\theta})$, the orthogonality conditions [14.4.8] might still provide a useful description of the parameter vector of interest. For example, suppose that we incorrectly specified that a scalar series $y_t$ came from a Gaussian $AR(1)$ process:

$$\log f(y_t|\mathcal{Y}_{t-1}; \boldsymbol{\theta}) = -\tfrac{1}{2}\log(2\pi) - \tfrac{1}{2}\log(\sigma^2) - (y_t - \phi y_{t-1})^2/(2\sigma^2),$$

with $\boldsymbol{\theta} \equiv (\phi, \sigma^2)'$. The score vector is then

$$\mathbf{h}(\boldsymbol{\theta}, \mathcal{Y}_t) = \begin{bmatrix} (y_t - \phi y_{t-1})y_{t-1}/\sigma^2 \\ -1/(2\sigma^2) + (y_t - \phi y_{t-1})^2/(2\sigma^4) \end{bmatrix},$$

which has expectation zero whenever

$$E[(y_t - \phi y_{t-1})y_{t-1}] = 0 \qquad [14.4.19]$$

$$E[(y_t - \phi y_{t-1})^2] = \sigma^2. \qquad [14.4.20]$$

The value of the parameter $\phi$ that satisfies [14.4.19] corresponds to the coefficient of a linear projection of $y_t$ on $y_{t-1}$ regardless of the time series process followed by $y_t$, while $\sigma^2$ in [14.4.20] is a general characterization of the mean squared error of this linear projection. Hence, the moment conditions in [14.4.8] hold for a broad class of possible processes, and the estimates obtained by maximizing a Gaussian likelihood function (that is, the values satisfying [14.4.9]) should give reasonable estimates of the linear projection coefficient and its mean squared error for a fairly general class of possible data-generating mechanisms.

However, if the data were not generated by a Gaussian $AR(1)$ process, then the information matrix equality no longer need hold. As long as the score vector is serially uncorrelated, the variance-covariance matrix of the resulting estimates could be obtained from [14.4.11]. Proceeding in this fashion—maximizing the likelihood function in the usual way, but using [14.4.11] rather than [14.4.15] to calculate standard errors—was first proposed by White (1982), who described this approach as *quasi-maximum likelihood estimation*.[3]

## APPENDIX 14.A. *Proof of Chapter 14 Proposition*

■ **Proof of Proposition 14.1.** Let $g_i(\boldsymbol{\theta}; \mathcal{Y}_T)$ denote the $i$th element of $\mathbf{g}(\boldsymbol{\theta}; \mathcal{Y}_T)$, so that $g_i\colon \mathbb{R}^a \to \mathbb{R}^1$. By the mean-value theorem,

$$g_i(\hat{\boldsymbol{\theta}}_T; \mathcal{Y}_T) = g_i(\boldsymbol{\theta}_0; \mathcal{Y}_T) + [\mathbf{d}_i(\boldsymbol{\theta}^*_{i,T}; \mathcal{Y}_T)]'(\hat{\boldsymbol{\theta}}_T - \boldsymbol{\theta}_0), \qquad [14.A.1]$$

where

$$\underset{(a\times 1)}{\mathbf{d}_i(\boldsymbol{\theta}^*_{i,T}; \mathcal{Y}_T)} = \left.\frac{\partial g_i(\boldsymbol{\theta}; \mathcal{Y}_T)}{\partial \boldsymbol{\theta}}\right|_{\boldsymbol{\theta}=\boldsymbol{\theta}^*_{i,T}}$$

for some $\boldsymbol{\theta}^*_{i,T}$ between $\boldsymbol{\theta}_0$ and $\hat{\boldsymbol{\theta}}_T$; notice that $\mathbf{d}_i\colon \mathbb{R}^a \to \mathbb{R}^a$. Define

$$\underset{(r\times a)}{\mathbf{D}'_T} \equiv \begin{bmatrix} [\mathbf{d}_1(\boldsymbol{\theta}^*_{1,T}; \mathcal{Y}_T)]' \\ [\mathbf{d}_2(\boldsymbol{\theta}^*_{2,T}; \mathcal{Y}_T)]' \\ \vdots \\ [\mathbf{d}_r(\boldsymbol{\theta}^*_{r,T}; \mathcal{Y}_T)]' \end{bmatrix}. \qquad [14.A.2]$$

Stacking the equations in [14.A.1] in an $(r \times 1)$ vector produces

$$\mathbf{g}(\hat{\boldsymbol{\theta}}_T; \mathcal{Y}_T) = \mathbf{g}(\boldsymbol{\theta}_0; \mathcal{Y}_T) + \mathbf{D}'_T(\hat{\boldsymbol{\theta}}_T - \boldsymbol{\theta}_0). \qquad [14.A.3]$$

If both sides of [14.A.3] are premultiplied by the $(a \times r)$ matrix

$$\left\{\left.\frac{\partial \mathbf{g}(\boldsymbol{\theta}; \mathcal{Y}_T)}{\partial \boldsymbol{\theta}'}\right|_{\boldsymbol{\theta}=\hat{\boldsymbol{\theta}}_T}\right\}' \times \hat{\mathbf{S}}_T^{-1},$$

the result is

$$\begin{aligned} &\left\{\left.\frac{\partial \mathbf{g}(\boldsymbol{\theta}; \mathcal{Y}_T)}{\partial \boldsymbol{\theta}'}\right|_{\boldsymbol{\theta}=\hat{\boldsymbol{\theta}}_T}\right\}' \times \hat{\mathbf{S}}_T^{-1} \times [\mathbf{g}(\hat{\boldsymbol{\theta}}_T; \mathcal{Y}_T)] \\ &= \left\{\left.\frac{\partial \mathbf{g}(\boldsymbol{\theta}; \mathcal{Y}_T)}{\partial \boldsymbol{\theta}'}\right|_{\boldsymbol{\theta}=\hat{\boldsymbol{\theta}}_T}\right\}' \times \hat{\mathbf{S}}_T^{-1} \times [\mathbf{g}(\boldsymbol{\theta}_0; \mathcal{Y}_T)] \qquad [14.A.4] \\ &\quad + \left\{\left.\frac{\partial \mathbf{g}(\boldsymbol{\theta}; \mathcal{Y}_T)}{\partial \boldsymbol{\theta}'}\right|_{\boldsymbol{\theta}=\hat{\boldsymbol{\theta}}_T}\right\}' \times \hat{\mathbf{S}}_T^{-1} \times \mathbf{D}'_T(\hat{\boldsymbol{\theta}}_T - \boldsymbol{\theta}_0). \end{aligned}$$

[3]For further discussion, see Gourieroux, Monfort, and Trognon (1984), Gallant and White (1988), and Wooldridge (1991a, b).

But equation [14.1.22] implies that the left side of [14.A.4] is zero, so that

$$(\hat{\boldsymbol{\theta}}_T - \boldsymbol{\theta}_0) = -\left[\left\{\left.\frac{\partial \mathbf{g}(\boldsymbol{\theta}; \mathcal{Y}_T)}{\partial \boldsymbol{\theta}'}\right|_{\boldsymbol{\theta}=\hat{\boldsymbol{\theta}}_T}\right\}' \times \hat{\mathbf{S}}_T^{-1} \times \mathbf{D}_T'\right]^{-1} \times \left\{\left.\frac{\partial \mathbf{g}(\boldsymbol{\theta}; \mathcal{Y}_T)}{\partial \boldsymbol{\theta}'}\right|_{\boldsymbol{\theta}=\hat{\boldsymbol{\theta}}_T}\right\}' \times \hat{\mathbf{S}}_T^{-1} \times [\mathbf{g}(\boldsymbol{\theta}_0; \mathcal{Y}_T)]. \quad [14.A.5]$$

Now, $\boldsymbol{\theta}_{i,T}^*$ in [14.A.1] is between $\boldsymbol{\theta}_0$ and $\hat{\boldsymbol{\theta}}_T$, so that $\boldsymbol{\theta}_{i,T}^* \xrightarrow{p} \boldsymbol{\theta}_0$ for each $i$. Thus, condition (c) ensures that each row of $\mathbf{D}_T'$ converges in probability to the corresponding row of $\mathbf{D}'$. Then [14.A.5] implies that

$$\sqrt{T}(\hat{\boldsymbol{\theta}}_T - \boldsymbol{\theta}_0) \xrightarrow{p} -\{\mathbf{D}\mathbf{S}^{-1}\mathbf{D}'\}^{-1} \times \{\mathbf{D}\mathbf{S}^{-1}\sqrt{T}\cdot \mathbf{g}(\boldsymbol{\theta}_0; \mathcal{Y}_T)\}. \quad [14.A.6]$$

Define

$$\mathbf{C} \equiv -\{\mathbf{D}\mathbf{S}^{-1}\mathbf{D}'\}^{-1} \times \mathbf{D}\mathbf{S}^{-1},$$

so that [14.A.6] becomes

$$\sqrt{T}(\hat{\boldsymbol{\theta}}_T - \boldsymbol{\theta}_0) \xrightarrow{p} \mathbf{C}\sqrt{T}\cdot \mathbf{g}(\boldsymbol{\theta}_0; \mathcal{Y}_T).$$

Recall from condition (b) of the proposition that

$$\sqrt{T}\cdot \mathbf{g}(\boldsymbol{\theta}_0; \mathcal{Y}_T) \xrightarrow{L} N(\mathbf{0}, \mathbf{S}).$$

It follows as in Example 7.5 of Chapter 7 that

$$\sqrt{T}(\hat{\boldsymbol{\theta}}_T - \boldsymbol{\theta}_0) \xrightarrow{L} N(\mathbf{0}, \mathbf{V}), \quad [14.A.7]$$

where

$$\mathbf{V} = \mathbf{C}\mathbf{S}\mathbf{C}' = \{\mathbf{D}\mathbf{S}^{-1}\mathbf{D}'\}^{-1}\mathbf{D}\mathbf{S}^{-1} \times \mathbf{S} \times \mathbf{S}^{-1}\mathbf{D}'\{\mathbf{D}\mathbf{S}^{-1}\mathbf{D}'\}^{-1} = \{\mathbf{D}\mathbf{S}^{-1}\mathbf{D}'\}^{-1},$$

as claimed. ■

## *Chapter 14 Exercise*

14.1. Consider the Gaussian linear regression model,

$$y_t = \mathbf{x}_t'\boldsymbol{\beta} + u_t,$$

with $u_t \sim$ i.i.d. $N(0, \sigma^2)$ and $u_t$ independent of $\mathbf{x}_\tau$ for all $t$ and $\tau$. Define $\boldsymbol{\theta} \equiv (\boldsymbol{\beta}', \sigma^2)'$. The log of the likelihood of $(y_1, y_2, \ldots, y_T)$ conditional on $(\mathbf{x}_1, \mathbf{x}_2, \ldots, \mathbf{x}_T)$ is given by

$$\mathcal{L}(\boldsymbol{\theta}) = -(T/2)\log(2\pi) - (T/2)\log(\sigma^2) - \sum_{t=1}^{T}(y_t - \mathbf{x}_t'\boldsymbol{\beta})^2/(2\sigma^2).$$

(a) Show that the estimate $\hat{\mathbf{D}}_T'$ in [14.4.12] is given by

$$\hat{\mathbf{D}}_T' = \begin{bmatrix} -\frac{1}{T}\sum_{t=1}^{T}\mathbf{x}_t\mathbf{x}_t'/\hat{\sigma}_T^2 & \mathbf{0} \\ \mathbf{0}' & \frac{1}{T}\sum_{t=1}^{T}\left\{\frac{1}{2\hat{\sigma}_T^4} - \frac{\hat{u}_t^2}{\hat{\sigma}_T^6}\right\} \end{bmatrix},$$

where $\hat{u}_t \equiv (y_t - \mathbf{x}_t'\hat{\boldsymbol{\beta}}_T)$ and $\hat{\boldsymbol{\beta}}_T$ and $\hat{\sigma}_T^2$ denote the maximum likelihood estimates.

(b) Show that the estimate $\hat{\mathbf{S}}_T$ in [14.4.13] is given by

$$\hat{\mathbf{S}}_T = \begin{bmatrix} \frac{1}{T}\sum_{t=1}^{T}\hat{u}_t^2\mathbf{x}_t\mathbf{x}_t'/\hat{\sigma}_T^4 & \frac{1}{T}\sum_{t=1}^{T}\left\{\frac{\hat{u}_t^3\mathbf{x}_t}{2\hat{\sigma}_T^6}\right\} \\ \frac{1}{T}\sum_{t=1}^{T}\left\{\frac{\hat{u}_t^3\mathbf{x}_t'}{2\hat{\sigma}_T^6}\right\} & \frac{1}{T}\sum_{t=1}^{T}\left\{\frac{\hat{u}_t^2}{2\hat{\sigma}_T^4} - \frac{1}{2\hat{\sigma}_T^2}\right\}^2 \end{bmatrix}.$$

(c) Show that $\text{plim}(\hat{\mathbf{S}}_T) = -\text{plim}(\hat{\mathbf{D}}_T) = \mathcal{I}$, where

$$\mathcal{I} = \begin{bmatrix} \mathbf{Q}/\sigma^2 & \mathbf{0} \\ \mathbf{0}' & 1/(2\sigma^4) \end{bmatrix}$$

for $\mathbf{Q} = \text{plim}(1/T)\sum_{t=1}^{T}\mathbf{x}_t\mathbf{x}_t'$.

(d) Consider a set of $m$ linear restrictions on $\boldsymbol{\beta}$ of the form $\mathbf{R}\boldsymbol{\beta} = \mathbf{r}$ for $\mathbf{R}$ a known $(m \times k)$ matrix and $\mathbf{r}$ a known $(m \times 1)$ vector. Show that for $\hat{\mathcal{J}}_T = -\hat{\mathbf{D}}_T$, the Wald test statistic given in [14.4.16] is identical to the Wald form of the $OLS$ $\chi^2$ test in [8.2.23] with the $OLS$ estimate of the variance $s_T^2$ in [8.2.23] replaced by the $MLE$ $\hat{\sigma}_T^2$.

(e) Show that when the lower left and upper right blocks of $\hat{\mathbf{S}}_T$ are set to their plim of zero, then the quasi-maximum likelihood Wald test of $\mathbf{R}\boldsymbol{\beta} = \mathbf{r}$ is identical to the heteroskedasticity-consistent form of the $OLS$ $\chi^2$ test given in [8.2.36].

## *Chapter 14 References*


Aitchison, J., and S. D. Silvey. 1958. "Maximum Likelihood Estimation of Parameters Subject to Restraints." *Annals of Mathematical Statistics* 29:813–28.

Amemiya, Takeshi. 1974. "The Nonlinear Two-Stage Least-Squares Estimator." *Journal of Econometrics* 2:105–10.

Andrews, Donald W. K. 1991. "Heteroskedasticity and Autocorrelation Consistent Covariance Matrix Estimation." *Econometrica* 59:817–58.

———. 1993. "Tests for Parameter Instability and Structural Change with Unknown Change Point." *Econometrica* 61:821–56.

——— and Ray C. Fair. 1988. "Inference in Nonlinear Econometric Models with Structural Change." *Review of Economic Studies* 55:615–40.

——— and J. Christopher Monahan. 1992. "An Improved Heteroskedasticity and Autocorrelation Consistent Covariance Matrix Estimator." *Econometrica* 60:953–66.

Bates, Charles, and Halbert White. 1988. "Efficient Instrumental Variables Estimation of Systems of Implicit Heterogeneous Nonlinear Dynamic Equations with Nonspherical Errors," in William A. Barnett, Ernst R. Berndt, and Halbert White, eds., *Dynamic Econometric Modeling*. Cambridge, England: Cambridge University Press.

Breusch, T. S., and A. R. Pagan. 1980. "The Lagrange Multiplier Test and Its Applications to Model Specification in Econometrics." *Review of Economic Studies* 47:239–53.

Cramér, H. 1946. *Mathematical Methods of Statistics.* Princeton, N.J.: Princeton University Press.

Engle, Robert F. 1984. "Wald, Likelihood Ratio, and Lagrange Multiplier Tests in Econometrics," in Zvi Griliches and Michael D. Intriligator, eds., *Handbook of Econometrics*, Vol. 2. Amsterdam: North-Holland.

Ferguson, T. S. 1958. "A Method of Generating Best Asymptotically Normal Estimates with Application to the Estimation of Bacterial Densities." *Annals of Mathematical Statistics* 29:1046–62.

Gallant, A. Ronald. 1977. "Three-Stage Least-Squares Estimation for a System of Simultaneous, Nonlinear, Implicit Equations." *Journal of Econometrics* 5:71–88.

———. 1987. *Nonlinear Statistical Models.* New York: Wiley.

——— and George Tauchen. 1992. "Which Moments to Match?" Duke University. Mimeo.

——— and Halbert White. 1988. *A Unified Theory of Estimation and Inference for Nonlinear Dynamic Models*. Oxford: Blackwell.

Garber, Peter M., and Robert G. King. 1984. "Deep Structural Excavation? A Critique of Euler Equation Methods." University of Rochester. Mimeo.

Ghysels, Eric, and Alastair Hall. 1990a. "A Test for Structural Stability of Euler Conditions Parameters Estimated via the Generalized Method of Moments Estimator." *International Economic Review* 31:355–64.

——— and ———. 1990b. "Are Consumption-Based Intertemporal Capital Asset Pricing Models Structural?" *Journal of Econometrics* 45:121–39.

Godfrey, L. G. 1988. *Misspecification Tests in Econometrics: The Lagrange Multiplier Principle and Other Approaches*. Cambridge, England: Cambridge University Press.

Gourieroux, C., A. Monfort, and A. Trognon. 1984. "Pseudo Maximum Likelihood Methods: Theory." *Econometrica* 52:681–700.

Hall, Alastair. 1993. "Some Aspects of Generalized Method of Moments Estimation," in C. R. Rao, G. S. Maddala, and H. D. Vinod, eds., *Handbook of Statistics*, Vol. 11, *Econometrics*. Amsterdam: North-Holland.

Hansen, Lars P. 1982. "Large Sample Properties of Generalized Method of Moments Estimators." *Econometrica* 50:1029–54.

——— and Kenneth J. Singleton. 1982. "Generalized Instrumental Variables Estimation of Nonlinear Rational Expectations Models." *Econometrica* 50:1269–86. Errata: *Econometrica* 52:267–68.

Jorgenson, D. W., and J. Laffont. 1974. "Efficient Estimation of Nonlinear Simultaneous Equations with Additive Disturbances." *Annals of Economic and Social Measurement* 3:615–40.

Kocherlakota, Narayana R. 1990. "On Tests of Representative Consumer Asset Pricing Models." *Journal of Monetary Economics* 26:285–304.

Malinvaud, E. 1970. *Statistical Methods of Econometrics*. Amsterdam: North-Holland.

Nelson, Charles R., and Richard Startz. 1990. "Some Further Results on the Exact Small Sample Properties of the Instrumental Variable Estimator." *Econometrica* 58:967–76.

Newey, Whitney K. 1985. "Generalized Method of Moments Specification Testing." *Journal of Econometrics* 29:229–56.

——— and Kenneth D. West. 1987. "A Simple Positive Semi-Definite, Heteroskedasticity and Autocorrelation Consistent Covariance Matrix." *Econometrica* 55:703–8.

Ogaki, Masao. 1993. "Generalized Method of Moments: Econometric Applications," in G. S. Maddala, C. R. Rao, and H. D. Vinod, eds., *Handbook of Statistics*, Vol. 11, *Econometrics*. Amsterdam: North-Holland.

Pearson, Karl. 1894. "Contribution to the Mathematical Theory of Evolution." *Philosophical Transactions of the Royal Society of London*, Series A 185:71–110.

Rao, C. R. 1948. "Large Sample Tests of Statistical Hypotheses Concerning Several Parameters with Application to Problems of Estimation." *Proceedings of the Cambridge Philosophical Society* 44:50–57.

Rothenberg, Thomas J. 1973. *Efficient Estimation with A Priori Information*. New Haven, Conn.: Yale University Press.

Sargent, Thomas J. 1987. *Dynamic Macroeconomic Theory*. Cambridge, Mass.: Harvard University Press.

Sill, Keith. 1992. *Money in the Cash-in-Advance Model: An Empirical Implementation*. Unpublished Ph.D. dissertation, University of Virginia.

Tauchen, George. 1986. "Statistical Properties of Generalized Method-of-Moments Estimators of Structural Parameters Obtained from Financial Market Data." *Journal of Business and Economic Statistics* 4:397–416.

White, Halbert. 1980. "A Heteroskedasticity-Consistent Covariance Matrix Estimator and a Direct Test for Heteroskedasticity." *Econometrica* 48:817–38.

———. 1982. "Maximum Likelihood Estimation of Misspecified Models." *Econometrica* 50:1–25.

———. 1987. "Specification Testing in Dynamic Models," in Truman F. Bewley, ed., *Advances in Econometrics, Fifth World Congress*, Vol. II. Cambridge, England: Cambridge University Press.

Wooldridge, Jeffrey M. 1991a. "On the Application of Robust, Regression-Based Diagnostics to Models of Conditional Means and Conditional Variances." *Journal of Econometrics* 47:5–46.

———. 1991b. "Specification Testing and Quasi-Maximum Likelihood Estimation." *Journal of Econometrics* 48:29–55.

# 15 Models of Nonstationary Time Series

Up to this point our analysis has typically been confined to stationary processes. This chapter introduces several approaches to modeling nonstationary time series and analyzes the dynamic properties of different models of nonstationarity. Consequences of nonstationarity for statistical inference are investigated in subsequent chapters.

## 15.1. *Introduction*

Chapters 3 and 4 discussed univariate time series models that can be written in the form

$$y_t = \mu + \varepsilon_t + \psi_1\varepsilon_{t-1} + \psi_2\varepsilon_{t-2} + \cdots = \mu + \psi(L)\varepsilon_t, \qquad [15.1.1]$$

where $\Sigma_{j=0}^{\infty}|\psi_j| < \infty$, roots of $\psi(z) = 0$ are outside the unit circle, and $\{\varepsilon_t\}$ is a white noise sequence with mean zero and variance $\sigma^2$. Two features of such processes merit repeating here. First, the unconditional expectation of the variable is a constant, independent of the date of the observation:

$$E(y_t) = \mu.$$

Second, as one tries to forecast the series farther into the future, the forecast $\hat{y}_{t+s|t} \equiv \hat{E}(y_{t+s}|y_t, y_{t-1}, \ldots)$ converges to the unconditional mean:

$$\lim_{s\to\infty} \hat{y}_{t+s|t} = \mu.$$

These can be quite unappealing assumptions for many of the economic and financial time series encountered in practice. For example, Figure 15.1 plots the level of nominal gross national product for the United States since World War II. There is no doubt that this series has trended upward over time, and this upward trend should be incorporated in any forecasts of this series.

There are two popular approaches to describing such trends. The first is to include a *deterministic time trend*:

$$y_t = \alpha + \delta t + \psi(L)\varepsilon_t. \qquad [15.1.2]$$

Thus, the mean $\mu$ of the stationary[1] process [15.1.1] is replaced by a linear function of the date $t$. Such a process is sometimes described as *trend-stationary*, because if one subtracts the trend $\alpha + \delta t$ from [15.1.2], the result is a stationary process.

The second specification is a *unit root* process,

$$(1 - L)y_t = \delta + \psi(L)\varepsilon_t, \qquad [15.1.3]$$

[1]Recall that "stationary" is taken to mean "covariance-stationary."

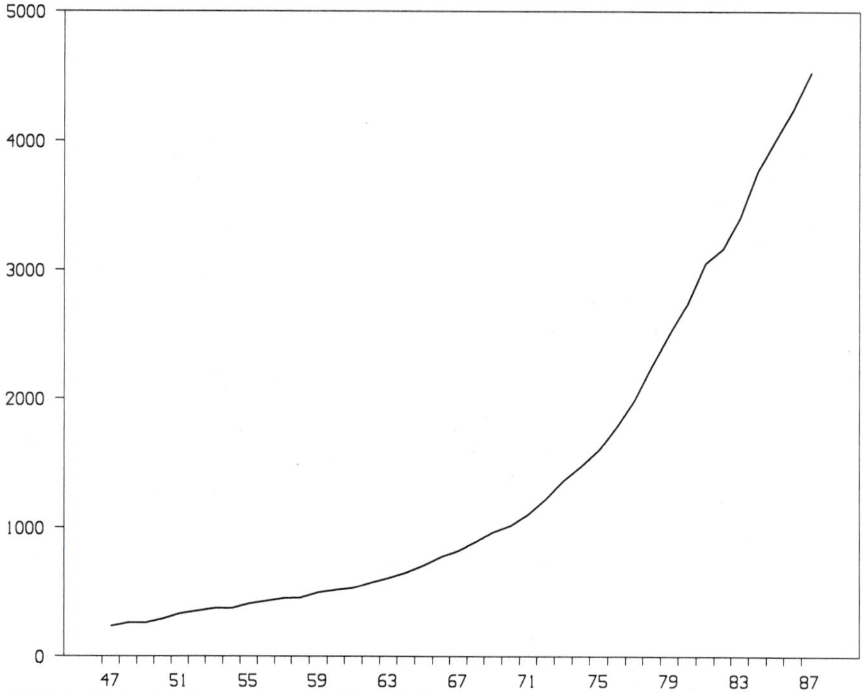

**FIGURE 15.1** U.S. nominal GNP, 1947–87.

where $\psi(1) \neq 0$. For a unit root process, a stationary representation of the form of [15.1.1] describes changes in the series. For reasons that will become clear shortly, the mean of $(1 - L)y_t$ is denoted $\delta$ rather than $\mu$.

The *first-difference* operator $(1 - L)$ will come up sufficiently often that a special symbol (the Greek letter $\Delta$) is reserved for it:

$$\Delta y_t \equiv y_t - y_{t-1}.$$

The prototypical example of a unit root process is obtained by setting $\psi(L)$ equal to 1 in [15.1.3]:

$$y_t = y_{t-1} + \delta + \varepsilon_t. \qquad [15.1.4]$$

This process is known as a *random walk with drift* $\delta$.

In the definition of the unit root process in [15.1.3], it was assumed that $\psi(1)$ is nonzero, where $\psi(1)$ denotes the polynomial

$$\psi(z) = 1 + \psi_1 z^1 + \psi_2 z^2 + \cdots$$

evaluated at $z = 1$. To see why such a restriction must be part of the definition of a unit root process, suppose that the original series $y_t$ is in fact stationary with a representation of the form

$$y_t = \mu + \chi(L)\varepsilon_t.$$

If such a stationary series is differenced, the result is

$$(1 - L)y_t = (1 - L)\chi(L)\varepsilon_t \equiv \psi(L)\varepsilon_t,$$

where $\psi(L) \equiv (1 - L)\chi(L)$. This representation is in the form of [15.1.3]—if the original series $y_t$ is stationary, then so is $\Delta y_t$. However, the moving average operator $\psi(L)$ that characterizes $\Delta y_t$ has the property that $\psi(1) = (1 - 1)\cdot\chi(1) = 0$. When we stipulated that $\psi(1) \neq 0$ in [15.1.3], we were thus ruling out the possibility that the original series $y_t$ is stationary.

It is sometimes convenient to work with a slightly different representation of the unit root process [15.1.3]. Consider the following specification:

$$y_t = \alpha + \delta t + u_t, \qquad [15.1.5]$$

where $u_t$ follows a zero-mean *ARMA* process:

$$\begin{aligned}(1 - \phi_1 L - \phi_2 L^2 - \cdots - \phi_p L^p)u_t \\ = (1 + \theta_1 L + \theta_2 L^2 + \cdots + \theta_q L^q)\varepsilon_t\end{aligned} \qquad [15.1.6]$$

and where the moving average operator $(1 + \theta_1 L + \theta_2 L^2 + \cdots + \theta_q L^q)$ is invertible. Suppose that the autoregressive operator in [15.1.6] is factored as in equation [2.4.3]:

$$(1 - \phi_1 L - \phi_2 L^2 - \cdots - \phi_p L^p) = (1 - \lambda_1 L)(1 - \lambda_2 L) \cdots (1 - \lambda_p L).$$

If all of the eigenvalues $\lambda_1, \lambda_2, \ldots, \lambda_p$ are inside the unit circle, then [15.1.6] can be expressed as

$$u_t = \frac{1 + \theta_1 L + \theta_2 L^2 + \cdots + \theta_q L^q}{(1 - \lambda_1 L)(1 - \lambda_2 L) \cdots (1 - \lambda_p L)} \varepsilon_t \equiv \psi(L)\varepsilon_t,$$

with $\Sigma_{j=0}^{\infty}|\psi_j| < \infty$ and roots of $\psi(z) = 0$ outside the unit circle. Thus, when $|\lambda_i| < 1$ for all $i$, the process [15.1.5] would just be a special case of the trend-stationary process of [15.1.2].

Suppose instead that $\lambda_1 = 1$ and $|\lambda_i| < 1$ for $i = 2, 3, \ldots, p$. Then [15.1.6] would state that

$$\begin{aligned}(1 - L)(1 - \lambda_2 L)(1 - \lambda_3 L) \cdots (1 - \lambda_p L)u_t \\ = (1 + \theta_1 L + \theta_2 L^2 + \cdots + \theta_q L^q)\varepsilon_t,\end{aligned} \qquad [15.1.7]$$

implying that

$$(1 - L)u_t = \frac{1 + \theta_1 L + \theta_2 L^2 + \cdots + \theta_q L^q}{(1 - \lambda_2 L)(1 - \lambda_3 L) \cdots (1 - \lambda_p L)} \varepsilon_t \equiv \psi^*(L)\varepsilon_t,$$

with $\Sigma_{j=0}^{\infty}|\psi_j^*| < \infty$ and roots of $\psi^*(z) = 0$ outside the unit circle. Thus, if [15.1.5] is first-differenced, the result is

$$(1 - L)y_t = (1 - L)\alpha + [\delta t - \delta(t - 1)] + (1 - L)u_t = 0 + \delta + \psi^*(L)\varepsilon_t,$$

which is of the form of the unit root process [15.1.3].

The representation in [15.1.5] explains the use of the term "unit root process." One of the roots or eigenvalues $(\lambda_1)$ of the autoregressive polynomial in [15.1.6] is unity, and all other eigenvalues are inside the unit circle.

Another expression that is sometimes used is that the process [15.1.3] is *integrated* of order 1. This is indicated as $y_t \sim I(1)$. The term "integrated" comes from calculus; if $dy/dt = x$, then $y$ is the integral of $x$. In discrete time series, if $\Delta y_t = x_t$, then $y$ might also be viewed as the integral, or sum over $t$, of $x$.

If a process written in the form of [15.1.5] and [15.1.6] has two eigenvalues $\lambda_1$ and $\lambda_2$ that are both equal to unity with the others all inside the unit circle, then second differences of the data have to be taken before arriving at a stationary time series:

$$(1 - L)^2 y_t = \kappa + \psi(L)\varepsilon_t.$$

Such a process is said to be integrated of order 2, denoted $y_t \sim I(2)$.

A general process written in the form of [15.1.5] and [15.1.6] is called an *autoregressive integrated moving average process*, denoted $ARIMA(p, d, q)$. The first parameter $(p)$ refers to the number of autoregressive lags (not counting the unit roots), the second parameter $(d)$ refers to the order of integration, and the third parameter $(q)$ gives the number of moving average lags. Taking $d$th differences of an $ARIMA(p, d, q)$ produces a stationary $ARMA(p, q)$ process.

## 15.2. *Why Linear Time Trends and Unit Roots?*

One might wonder why, for the trend-stationary specification [15.1.2], the trend is specified to be a linear function of time ($\delta t$) rather than a quadratic function ($\delta t + \gamma t^2$) or exponential ($e^{\delta t}$). Indeed, the GNP series in Figure 15.1, like many economic and financial time series, seems better characterized by an exponential trend than a linear trend. An exponential trend exhibits constant proportional growth; that is, if

$$y_t = e^{\delta t}, \qquad [15.2.1]$$

then $dy/dt = \delta \cdot y_t$. Proportional growth in the population would arise if the number of children born were a constant fraction of the current population. Proportional growth in prices (or constant inflation) would arise if the government were trying to collect a constant level of real revenues from printing money. Such stories are often an appealing starting point for thinking about the sources of time trends, and exponential growth is often confirmed by the visual appearance of the series as in Figure 15.1. For this reason, many economists simply assume that growth is of the exponential form.

Notice that if we take the natural log of the exponential trend [15.2.1], the result is a linear trend,

$$\log(y_t) = \delta t.$$

Thus, it is common to take logs of the data before attempting to describe them with the model in [15.1.2].

Similar arguments suggest taking natural logs before applying [15.1.3]. For small changes, the first difference of the log of a variable is approximately the same as the percentage change in the variable:

$$\begin{aligned}(1 - L)\log(y_t) &= \log(y_t/y_{t-1}) \\ &= \log\{1 + [(y_t - y_{t-1})/y_{t-1}]\} \\ &\cong (y_t - y_{t-1})/y_{t-1},\end{aligned}$$

where we have used the fact that for $x$ close to zero, $\log(1 + x) \cong x$.[2] Thus, if the logs of a variable are specified to follow a unit root process, the assumption is that the rate of growth of the series is a stationary stochastic process. The same arguments used to justify taking logs before applying [15.1.2] also suggest taking logs before applying [15.1.3].

Often the units are slightly more convenient if $\log(y_t)$ is multiplied by 100. Then changes are measured directly in units of percentage change. For example, if $(1 - L)[100 \times \log(y_t)] = 1.0$, then $y_t$ is 1% higher than $y_{t-1}$.

## 15.3. *Comparison of Trend-Stationary and Unit Root Processes*

This section compares a trend-stationary process [15.1.2] with a unit root process [15.1.3] in terms of forecasts of the series, variance of the forecast error, dynamic multipliers, and transformations needed to achieve stationarity.

[2]See result [A.3.36] in the Mathematical Review (Appendix A) at the end of the book.

## *Comparison of Forecasts*

To forecast a trend-stationary process [15.1.2], the known deterministic component ($\alpha + \delta t$) is simply added to the forecast of the stationary stochastic component:

$$\hat{y}_{t+s|t} = \alpha + \delta(t + s) + \psi_s \varepsilon_t + \psi_{s+1}\varepsilon_{t-1} + \psi_{s+2}\varepsilon_{t-2} + \cdots. \qquad [15.3.1]$$

Here $\hat{y}_{t+s|t}$ denotes the linear projection of $y_{t+s}$ on a constant and $y_t, y_{t-1}, \ldots$. Note that for nonstationary processes, we will follow the convention that the "constant" term in a linear projection, in this case $\alpha + \delta(t + s)$, can be different for each date $t + s$. As the forecast horizon ($s$) grows large, absolute summability of $\{\psi_j\}$ implies that this forecast converges in mean square to the time trend:

$$E[\hat{y}_{t+s|t} - \alpha - \delta(t + s)]^2 \to 0 \qquad \text{as} \quad s \to \infty.$$

To forecast the unit root process [15.1.3], recall that the change $\Delta y_t$ is a stationary process that can be forecast using the standard formula:

$$\begin{aligned} \Delta\hat{y}_{t+s|t} &\equiv \hat{E}[(y_{t+s} - y_{t+s-1})|y_t, y_{t-1}, \ldots] \\ &= \delta + \psi_s\varepsilon_t + \psi_{s+1}\varepsilon_{t-1} + \psi_{s+2}\varepsilon_{t-2} + \cdots. \end{aligned} \qquad [15.3.2]$$

The level of the variable at date $t + s$ is simply the sum of the changes between $t$ and $t + s$:

$$\begin{aligned} y_{t+s} &= (y_{t+s} - y_{t+s-1}) + (y_{t+s-1} - y_{t+s-2}) + \cdots \\ &\quad + (y_{t+1} - y_t) + y_t \\ &= \Delta y_{t+s} + \Delta y_{t+s-1} + \cdots + \Delta y_{t+1} + y_t. \end{aligned} \qquad [15.3.3]$$

Taking the linear projection of [15.3.3] on a constant and $y_t, y_{t-1}, \ldots$ and substituting from [15.3.2] gives

$$\begin{aligned} \hat{y}_{t+s|t} &= \Delta\hat{y}_{t+s|t} + \Delta\hat{y}_{t+s-1|t} + \cdots + \Delta\hat{y}_{t+1|t} + y_t \\ &= \{\delta + \psi_s\varepsilon_t + \psi_{s+1}\varepsilon_{t-1} + \psi_{s+2}\varepsilon_{t-2} + \cdots\} \\ &\quad + \{\delta + \psi_{s-1}\varepsilon_t + \psi_s\varepsilon_{t-1} + \psi_{s+1}\varepsilon_{t-2} + \cdots\} \\ &\quad + \cdots + \{\delta + \psi_1\varepsilon_t + \psi_2\varepsilon_{t-1} + \psi_3\varepsilon_{t-2} + \cdots\} + y_t \end{aligned}$$

or

$$\begin{aligned} \hat{y}_{t+s|t} &= s\delta + y_t + (\psi_s + \psi_{s-1} + \cdots + \psi_1)\varepsilon_t \\ &\quad + (\psi_{s+1} + \psi_s + \cdots + \psi_2)\varepsilon_{t-1} + \cdots. \end{aligned} \qquad [15.3.4]$$

Further insight into the forecast of a unit root process is obtained by analyzing some special cases. Consider first the random walk with drift [15.1.4], in which $\psi_1 = \psi_2 = \cdots = 0$. Then [15.3.4] becomes

$$\hat{y}_{t+s|t} = s\delta + y_t.$$

A random walk with drift $\delta$ is expected to grow at the constant rate of $\delta$ per period from whatever its current value $y_t$ happens to be.

Consider next an *ARIMA*(0, 1, 1) specification ($\psi_1 = \theta$, $\psi_2 = \psi_3 = \cdots = 0$). Then

$$\hat{y}_{t+s|t} = s\delta + y_t + \theta\varepsilon_t. \qquad [15.3.5]$$

Here, the current level of the series $y_t$ along with the current innovation $\varepsilon_t$ again defines a base from which the variable is expected to grow at the constant rate $\delta$.

Notice that $\varepsilon_t$ is the one-period-ahead forecast error:

$$\varepsilon_t = y_t - \hat{y}_{t|t-1}.$$

It follows from [15.3.5] that for $\delta = 0$ and $s = 1$,

$$\hat{y}_{t+1|t} = y_t + \theta(y_t - \hat{y}_{t|t-1}) \qquad [15.3.6]$$

or

$$\hat{y}_{t+1|t} = (1 + \theta)y_t - \theta\hat{y}_{t|t-1}. \qquad [15.3.7]$$

Equation [15.3.7] takes the form of a simple first-order difference equation, relating $\hat{y}_{t+1|t}$ to its own lagged value and to the input variable $(1 + \theta)y_t$. Provided that $|\theta| < 1$, expression [15.3.7] can be written using result [2.2.9] as

$$\begin{aligned}\hat{y}_{t+1|t} &= [(1 + \theta)y_t] + (-\theta)[(1 + \theta)y_{t-1}] \\ &\quad + (-\theta)^2[(1 + \theta)y_{t-2}] + (-\theta)^3[(1 + \theta)y_{t-3}] + \cdots \qquad [15.3.8] \\ &= (1 + \theta)\sum_{j=0}^{\infty}(-\theta)^j y_{t-j}.\end{aligned}$$

Expression [15.3.7] is sometimes described as *adaptive expectations*, and its implication [15.3.8] is referred to as *exponential smoothing*; typical applications assume that $-1 < \theta < 0$. Letting $y_t$ denote income, Friedman (1957) used exponential smoothing to construct one of his measures of *permanent income*. Muth (1960) noted that adaptive expectations or exponential smoothing corresponds to a rational forecast of future income only if $y_t$ follows an $ARIMA(0, 1, 1)$ process and the smoothing weight $(-\theta)$ is chosen to equal the negative of the moving average coefficient of the differenced data $(\theta)$.

For an $ARIMA(0, 1, q)$ process, the value of $y_t$ and the $q$ most recent values of $\varepsilon_t$ influence the forecasts $\hat{y}_{t+1|t}, \hat{y}_{t+2|t}, \ldots, \hat{y}_{t+q|t}$, but thereafter the series is expected to grow at the rate $\delta$. For an $ARIMA(p, 1, q)$, the forecast growth rate asymptotically approaches $\delta$.

Thus, the parameter $\delta$ in the unit root process [15.1.3] plays a similar role to that of $\delta$ in the deterministic time trend [15.1.2]. With either specification, the forecast $\hat{y}_{t+s|t}$ in [15.3.1] or [15.3.4] converges to a linear function of the forecast horizon $s$ with slope $\delta$; see Figure 15.2. The key difference is in the intercept of the line. For a trend-stationary process, the forecast converges to a line whose intercept is the same regardless of the value of $y_t$. By contrast, the intercept of the limiting forecast for a unit root process is continually changing with each new observation on $y$.

## *Comparison of Forecast Errors*

The trend-stationary and unit root specifications are also very different in their implications for the variance of the forecast error. For the trend-stationary process [15.1.2], the $s$-period-ahead forecast error is

$$\begin{aligned}y_{t+s} - \hat{y}_{t+s|t} &= \{\alpha + \delta(t + s) + \varepsilon_{t+s} + \psi_1\varepsilon_{t+s-1} + \psi_2\varepsilon_{t+s-2} + \cdots \\ &\quad + \psi_{s-1}\varepsilon_{t+1} + \psi_s\varepsilon_t + \psi_{s+1}\varepsilon_{t-1} + \cdots\} \\ &\quad - \{\alpha + \delta(t + s) + \psi_s\varepsilon_t + \psi_{s+1}\varepsilon_{t-1} + \psi_{s+2}\varepsilon_{t-2} + \cdots\} \\ &= \varepsilon_{t+s} + \psi_1\varepsilon_{t+s-1} + \psi_2\varepsilon_{t+s-2} + \cdots + \psi_{s-1}\varepsilon_{t+1}.\end{aligned}$$

The mean squared error ($MSE$) of this forecast is

$$E[y_{t+s} - \hat{y}_{t+s|t}]^2 = \{1 + \psi_1^2 + \psi_2^2 + \cdots + \psi_{s-1}^2\}\sigma^2.$$

The $MSE$ increases with the forecasting horizon $s$, though as $s$ becomes large, the added uncertainty from forecasting farther into the future becomes negligible:

$$\lim_{s\to\infty} E[y_{t+s} - \hat{y}_{t+s|t}]^2 = \{1 + \psi_1^2 + \psi_2^2 + \cdots\}\sigma^2.$$

Note that the limiting $MSE$ is just the unconditional variance of the stationary component $\psi(L)\varepsilon_t$.

By contrast, for the unit root process [15.1.3], the $s$-period-ahead forecast error is

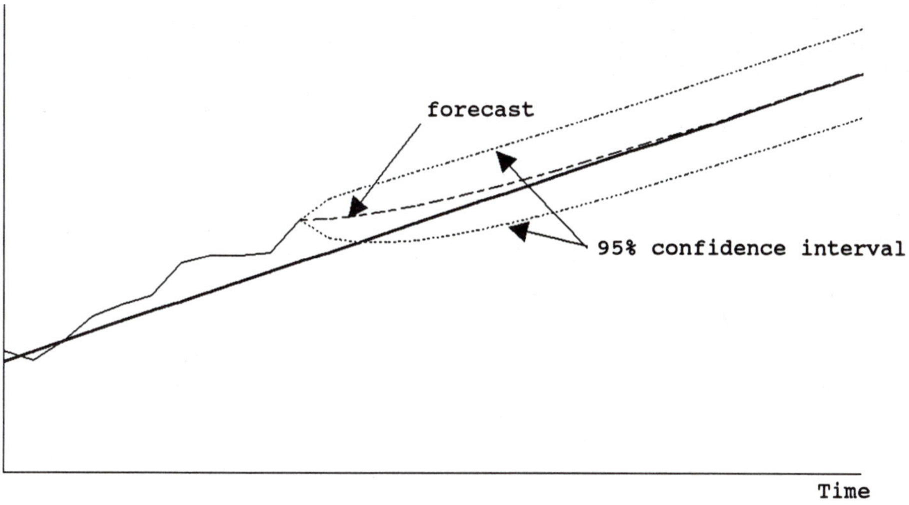


(a) Trend-stationary process

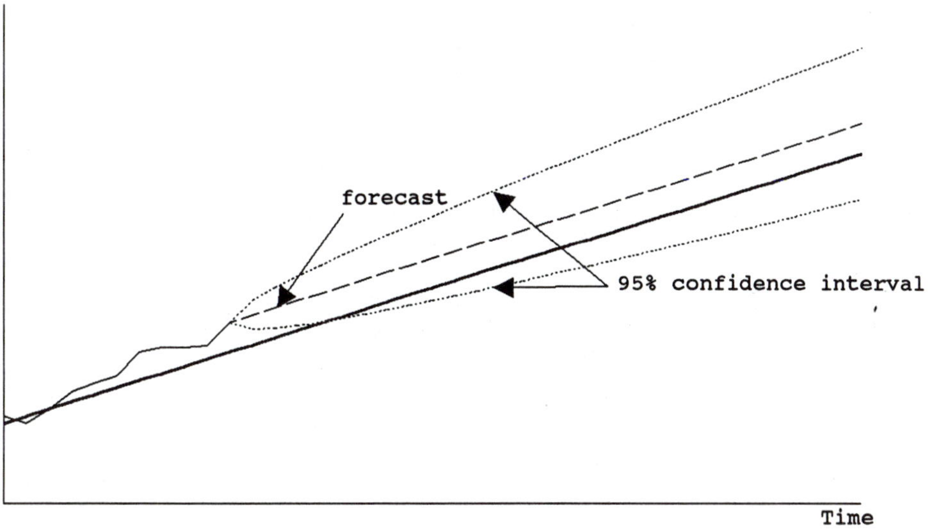


(b) Unit root process

**FIGURE 15.2** Forecasts and 95% confidence intervals.

$$\begin{aligned}
y_{t+s} - \hat{y}_{t+s|t} &= \{\Delta y_{t+s} + \Delta y_{t+s-1} + \cdots + \Delta y_{t+1} + y_t\} \\
&\quad - \{\Delta \hat{y}_{t+s|t} + \Delta \hat{y}_{t+s-1|t} + \cdots + \Delta \hat{y}_{t+1|t} + y_t\} \\
&= \{\varepsilon_{t+s} + \psi_1 \varepsilon_{t+s-1} + \cdots + \psi_{s-1}\varepsilon_{t+1}\} \\
&\quad + \{\varepsilon_{t+s-1} + \psi_1 \varepsilon_{t+s-2} + \cdots + \psi_{s-2}\varepsilon_{t+1}\} + \cdots + \{\varepsilon_{t+1}\} \\
&= \varepsilon_{t+s} + \{1 + \psi_1\}\varepsilon_{t+s-1} + \{1 + \psi_1 + \psi_2\}\varepsilon_{t+s-2} + \cdots \\
&\quad + \{1 + \psi_1 + \psi_2 + \cdots + \psi_{s-1}\}\varepsilon_{t+1},
\end{aligned}$$

with *MSE*

$$\begin{aligned}
E[y_{t+s} - \hat{y}_{t+s|t}]^2 &= \{1 + (1 + \psi_1)^2 + (1 + \psi_1 + \psi_2)^2 + \cdots \\
&\quad + (1 + \psi_1 + \psi_2 + \cdots + \psi_{s-1})^2\}\sigma^2.
\end{aligned}$$

The *MSE* again increases with the length of the forecasting horizon $s$, though in contrast to the trend-stationary case, the *MSE* does not converge to any fixed value as $s$ goes to infinity. Instead, it asymptotically approaches a linear function of $s$ with slope $(1 + \psi_1 + \psi_2 + \cdots)^2\sigma^2$. For example, for an $ARIMA(0, 1, 1)$ process,

$$E[y_{t+s} - \hat{y}_{t+s|t}]^2 = \{1 + (s - 1)(1 + \theta)^2\}\sigma^2. \qquad [15.3.9]$$

To summarize, for a trend-stationary process the *MSE* reaches a finite bound as the forecast horizon becomes large, whereas for a unit root process the *MSE* eventually grows linearly with the forecast horizon. This result is again illustrated in Figure 15.2.

Note that since the *MSE* grows linearly with the forecast horizon $s$, the standard deviation of the forecast error grows with the square root of $s$. On the other hand, if $\delta > 0$, then the forecast itself grows linearly in $s$. Thus, a 95% confidence interval for $y_{t+s}$ expands more slowly than the level of the series, meaning that data from a unit root process with positive drift are certain to exhibit an upward trend if observed for a sufficiently long period. In this sense the trend introduced by a nonzero drift $\delta$ asymptotically dominates the increasing variability arising over time due to the unit root component. This result is very important for understanding the asymptotic statistical results to be presented in Chapters 17 and 18.

Figure 15.3 plots realizations of a Gaussian random walk without drift and with drift. The random walk without drift, shown in panel (a), shows no tendency to return to its starting value or any unconditional mean. The random walk with drift, shown in panel (b), shows no tendency to return to a fixed deterministic trend line, though the series is asymptotically dominated by the positive drift term.

### *Comparison of Dynamic Multipliers*

Another difference between trend-stationary and unit root processes is the persistence of innovations. Consider the consequences for $y_{t+s}$ if $\varepsilon_t$ were to increase by one unit with $\varepsilon$'s for all other dates unaffected. For the trend-stationary process [15.1.2], this dynamic multiplier is given by

$$\frac{\partial y_{t+s}}{\partial \varepsilon_t} = \psi_s.$$

For a trend-stationary process, then, the effect of any stochastic disturbance eventually wears off:

$$\lim_{s\to\infty} \frac{\partial y_{t+s}}{\partial \varepsilon_t} = 0.$$

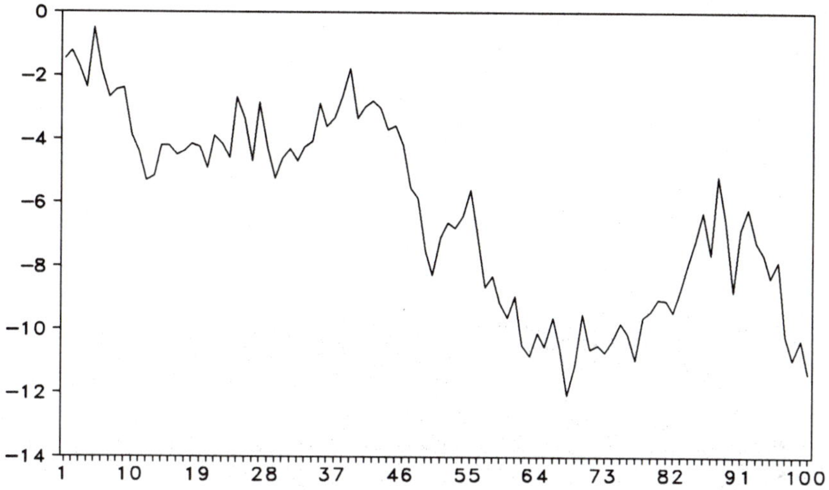


(a) Random walk without drift

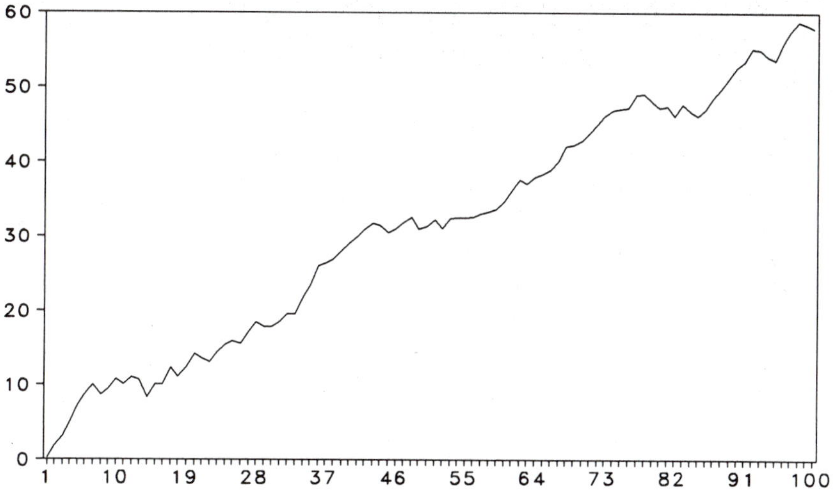


(b) Random walk with drift

**FIGURE 15.3** Sample realizations from Gaussian unit root processes.

By contrast, for a unit root process, the effect of $\varepsilon_t$ on $y_{t+s}$ is seen from [15.3.4] to be[3]

$$\frac{\partial y_{t+s}}{\partial \varepsilon_t} = \frac{\partial y_t}{\partial \varepsilon_t} + \psi_s + \psi_{s-1} + \cdots + \psi_1 = 1 + \psi_1 + \psi_2 + \cdots + \psi_s.$$

An innovation $\varepsilon_t$ has a permanent effect on the level of $y$ that is captured by

$$\lim_{s\to\infty} \frac{\partial y_{t+s}}{\partial \varepsilon_t} = 1 + \psi_1 + \psi_2 + \cdots = \psi(1). \qquad [15.3.10]$$

[3]This, of course, contrasts with the multiplier that describes the effect of $\varepsilon_t$ on the *change* between $y_{t+s}$ and $y_{t+s-1}$, which is given by

$$\frac{\partial \Delta y_{t+s}}{\partial \varepsilon_t} = \psi_s.$$

As an illustration of calculating such a multiplier, the following *ARIMA*(4, 1, 0) model was estimated for $y_t$ equal to 100 times the log of quarterly U.S. real GNP ($t$ = 1952:II to 1984:IV):

$$\Delta y_t = 0.555 + 0.312\,\Delta y_{t-1} + 0.122\,\Delta y_{t-2} - 0.116\,\Delta y_{t-3} - 0.081\,\Delta y_{t-4} + \varepsilon_t.$$

For this specification, the permanent effect of a one-unit change in $\varepsilon_t$ on the level of real GNP is estimated to be

$$\psi(1) = 1/\phi(1) = 1/(1 - 0.312 - 0.122 + 0.116 + 0.081) = 1.31.$$

### *Transformations to Achieve Stationarity*

A final difference between trend-stationary and unit root processes that deserves comment is the transformation of the data needed to generate a stationary time series. If the process is really trend stationary as in [15.1.2], the appropriate treatment is to subtract $\delta t$ from $y_t$ to produce a stationary representation of the form of [15.1.1]. By contrast, if the data were really generated by the unit root process [15.1.3], subtracting $\delta t$ from $y_t$ would succeed in removing the time-dependence of the mean but not the variance. For example, if the data were generated by [15.1.4], the random walk with drift, then

$$y_t - \delta t = y_0 + (\varepsilon_1 + \varepsilon_2 + \cdots + \varepsilon_t) \equiv y_0 + u_t.$$

The variance of the residual $u_t$ is $t\sigma^2$; it grows with the date of the observation. Thus, subtracting a time trend from a unit root process is not sufficient to produce a stationary time series.

The correct treatment for a unit root process is to difference the series, and for this reason a process described by [15.1.3] is sometimes called a *difference-stationary* process. Note, however, that if one were to try to difference a trend-stationary process [15.1.2], the result would be

$$\Delta y_t = \delta + (1 - L)\psi(L)\varepsilon_t.$$

This is a stationary time series, but a unit root has been introduced into the moving average representation. Thus, the result would be a noninvertible process subject to the potential difficulties discussed in Chapters 3 through 5.

## 15.4. *The Meaning of Tests for Unit Roots*

Knowing whether nonstationarity in the data is due to a deterministic time trend or a unit root would seem to be a very important question. For example, macroeconomists are very interested in knowing whether economic recessions have permanent consequences for the level of future GNP, or instead represent temporary downturns with the lost output eventually made up during the recovery. Nelson and Plosser (1982) argued that many economic series are better characterized by unit roots than by deterministic time trends. A number of economists have tried to measure the size of the permanent consequences by estimating $\psi(1)$ for various time series representations of GNP growth.[4]

Although it might be very interesting to know whether a time series has a unit root, several recent papers have argued that the question is inherently un-

[4] See, for example, Watson (1986), Clark (1987), Campbell and Mankiw (1987a, b), Cochrane (1988), Gagnon (1988), Stock and Watson (1988), Durlauf (1989), and Hamilton (1989).

answerable on the basis of a finite sample of observations.[5] The argument takes the form of two observations.

The first observation is that for any unit root process there exists a stationary process that will be impossible to distinguish from the unit root representation for any given sample size $T$. Such a stationary process is found easily enough by setting one of the eigenvalues close to but not quite equal to unity. For example, suppose the sample consists of $T = 10{,}000$ observations that were really generated by a driftless random walk:

$$y_t = y_{t-1} + \varepsilon_t \qquad \textit{true model} \text{ (unit root).} \qquad [15.4.1]$$

Consider trying to distinguish this from the following stationary process:

$$y_t = \phi y_{t-1} + \varepsilon_t \qquad |\phi| < 1 \qquad \textit{false model} \text{ (stationary).} \qquad [15.4.2]$$

The $s$-period-ahead forecast of [15.4.1] is

$$\hat{y}_{t+s|t} = y_t \qquad [15.4.3]$$

with $MSE$

$$E(y_{t+s} - \hat{y}_{t+s|t})^2 = s\sigma^2. \qquad [15.4.4]$$

The corresponding forecast of [15.4.2] is

$$\hat{y}_{t+s|t} = \phi^s y_t \qquad [15.4.5]$$

with $MSE$

$$E(y_{t+s} - \hat{y}_{t+s|t})^2 = (1 + \phi^2 + \phi^4 + \cdots + \phi^{2(s-1)})\cdot\sigma^2. \qquad [15.4.6]$$

Clearly there exists a value of $\phi$ sufficiently close to unity such that the observable implications of the stationary representation ([15.4.5] and [15.4.6]) are arbitrarily close to those of the unit root process ([15.4.3] and [15.4.4]) in a sample of size 10,000.

More formally, the conditional likelihood function for a Gaussian process characterized by [15.1.7] is continuous in the parameter $\lambda_1$. Hence, given any fixed sample size $T$, any small numbers $\eta$ and $\varepsilon$, and any unit root specification with $\lambda_1 = 1$, there exists a stationary specification with $\lambda_1 < 1$ with the property that the probability is less than $\varepsilon$ that one would observe a sample of size $T$ for which the value of the likelihood implied by the unit root representation differs by more than $\eta$ from the value of the likelihood implied by the stationary representation.

The converse proposition is also true—for any stationary process and a given sample size $T$, there exists a unit root process that will be impossible to distinguish from the stationary representation. Again, consider a simple example. Suppose the true process is white noise:

$$y_t = \varepsilon_t \qquad \textit{true model} \text{ (stationary).} \qquad [15.4.7]$$

Consider trying to distinguish this from

$$(1 - L)y_t = (1 + \theta L)\varepsilon_t \qquad |\theta| < 1 \qquad \textit{false model} \text{ (unit root)} \qquad [15.4.8]$$
$$y_0 = \varepsilon_0 = 0.$$

The $s$-period-ahead forecast of [15.4.7] is

$$\hat{y}_{t+s|t} = 0$$

with $MSE$

$$E(y_{t+s} - \hat{y}_{t+s|t})^2 = \sigma^2.$$

[5]See Blough (1992a, b), Cochrane (1991), Christiano and Eichenbaum (1990), Stock (1990), and Sims (1989). The sharpest statement of this view, and the perspective on which the remarks in the text are based, is that of Blough.

The forecast of [15.4.8] is obtained from [15.3.5]:

$$\begin{aligned}\hat{y}_{t+s|t} &= y_t + \theta\varepsilon_t \\ &= \{\Delta y_t + \Delta y_{t-1} + \cdots + \Delta y_2 + y_1\} + \theta\varepsilon_t \\ &= \{(\varepsilon_t + \theta\varepsilon_{t-1}) + (\varepsilon_{t-1} + \theta\varepsilon_{t-2}) + \cdots + (\varepsilon_2 + \theta\varepsilon_1) + (\varepsilon_1)\} + \theta\varepsilon_t \\ &= (1 + \theta)\{\varepsilon_t + \varepsilon_{t-1} + \cdots + \varepsilon_1\}.\end{aligned}$$

From [15.3.9], the *MSE* of the $s$-period-ahead forecast is

$$E(y_{t+s} - \hat{y}_{t+s|t})^2 = \{1 + (s - 1)(1 + \theta)^2\}\sigma^2.$$

Again, clearly, given any fixed sample size $T$, there exists a value of $\theta$ sufficiently close to $-1$ that the unit root process [15.4.8] will have virtually the identical observable implications to those of the stationary process [15.4.7].

Unit root and stationary processes differ in their implications at infinite time horizons, but for any given finite number of observations on the time series, there is a representative from either class of models that could account for all the observed features of the data. We therefore need to be careful with our choice of wording—testing whether a particular time series "contains a unit root," or testing whether innovations "have a permanent effect on the level of the series," however interesting, is simply impossible to do.

Another way to express this is as follows. For a unit root process given by [15.1.3], the autocovariance-generating function of $(1 - L)y_t$ is

$$g_{\Delta Y}(z) = \psi(z)\sigma^2\psi(z^{-1}).$$

The autocovariance-generating function evaluated at $z = 1$ is then

$$g_{\Delta Y}(1) = [\psi(1)]^2\sigma^2. \qquad [15.4.9]$$

Recalling that the population spectrum of $\Delta y$ at frequency $\omega$ is defined by

$$s_{\Delta Y}(\omega) = \frac{1}{2\pi} g_{\Delta Y}(e^{-i\omega}),$$

expression [15.4.9] can alternatively be described as $2\pi$ times the spectrum at frequency zero:

$$s_{\Delta Y}(0) = \frac{1}{2\pi}[\psi(1)]^2\sigma^2.$$

By contrast, if the true process is the trend-stationary specification [15.1.2], the autocovariance-generating function of $\Delta y$ can be calculated from [3.6.15] as

$$g_{\Delta Y}(z) = (1 - z)\psi(z)\sigma^2\psi(z^{-1})(1 - z^{-1}),$$

which evaluated at $z = 1$ is zero. Thus, if the true process is trend-stationary, the population spectrum of $\Delta y$ at frequency zero is zero, whereas if the true process is characterized by a unit root, the population spectrum of $\Delta y$ at frequency zero is positive.

The question of whether $y_t$ follows a unit root process can thus equivalently be expressed as a question of whether the population spectrum of $\Delta y$ at frequency zero is zero. However, there is no information in a sample of size $T$ about cycles with period greater than $T$, just as there is no information in a sample of size $T$ about the dynamic multiplier for a horizon $s > T$.

These observations notwithstanding, there are several closely related and very interesting questions that are answerable. Given enough data, we certainly can ask whether innovations have a significant effect on the level of the series over a specified finite horizon. For a fixed time horizon (say, $s = 3$ years), there exists a sample size (say, the half century of observations since World War II) such that we can meaningfully inquire whether $\partial y_{t+s}/\partial \varepsilon_t$ is close to zero. We cannot tell whether the data were really generated by [15.4.1] or a close relative of the form of [15.4.2], but we can measure whether innovations have much persistence over a fixed interval (as in [15.4.1] or [15.4.2]) or very little persistence over that interval (as in [15.4.7] or [15.4.8]).

We can also arrive at a testable hypothesis if we are willing to restrict further the class of processes considered. Suppose the dynamics of a given sample $\{y_1, \ldots, y_T\}$ are to be modeled using an autoregression of fixed, known order $p$. For example, suppose we are committed to using an $AR(1)$ process:

$$y_t = \phi y_{t-1} + \varepsilon_t. \qquad [15.4.10]$$

Within this class of models, the restriction

$$H_0\colon \phi = 1$$

is certainly testable. While it is true that there exist local alternatives (such as $\phi = 0.99999$) against which a test would have essentially no power, this is true of most hypothesis tests. There are also alternatives (such as $\phi = 0.3$) that would lead to certain rejection of $H_0$ given enough observations. The hypothesis "$\{y_t\}$ is an $AR(1)$ process with a unit root" is potentially refutable; the hypothesis "$\{y_t\}$ is a general unit root process of the form [15.1.3]" is not.

There may be good reasons to restrict ourselves to consider only low-order autoregressive representations. Parsimonious models often perform best, and autoregressions are much easier to estimate and forecast than moving average processes, particularly moving average processes with a root near unity.

If we are indeed committed to describing the data with a low-order autoregression, knowing whether the further restriction of a unit root should be imposed can clearly be important for two reasons. The first involves a familiar trade-off between efficiency and consistency. If a restriction (in this case, a unit root) is true, more efficient estimates result from imposing it. Estimates of the other coefficients and dynamic multipliers will be more accurate, and forecasts will be better. If the restriction is false, the estimates are unreliable no matter how large the sample. Researchers differ in their advice on how to deal with this trade-off. One practical guide is to estimate the model both with and without the unit root imposed. If the key inferences are similar, so much the better. If the inferences differ, some attempt at explaining the conflicting findings (as in Christiano and Ljungqvist, 1988, or Stock and Watson, 1989) may be desirable.

In addition to the familiar trade-off between efficiency and consistency, the decision whether or not to impose unit roots on an autoregression also raises issues involving the asymptotic distribution theory one uses to test hypotheses about the process. This issue is explored in detail in later chapters.

## 15.5. *Other Approaches to Trended Time Series*

Although most of the analysis of nonstationarity in this book will be devoted to unit roots and time trends, this section briefly discusses two alternative approaches to modeling nonstationarity: fractionally integrated processes and processes with occasional, discrete shifts in the time trend.

## *Fractional Integration*

Recall that an integrated process of order $d$ can be represented in the form

$$(1 - L)^d y_t = \psi(L)\varepsilon_t, \quad [15.5.1]$$

with $\sum_{j=0}^{\infty} |\psi_j| < \infty$. The normal assumption is that $d = 1$, or that the first difference of the series is stationary. Occasionally one finds a series for which $d = 2$ might be a better choice.

Granger and Joyeux (1980) and Hosking (1981) suggested that noninteger values of $d$ in [15.5.1] might also be useful. To understand the meaning of [15.5.1] for noninteger $d$, consider the $MA(\infty)$ representation implied by [15.5.1]. It will be shown shortly that the inverse of the operator $(1 - L)^d$ exists provided that $d < \frac{1}{2}$. Multiplying both sides of [15.5.1] by $(1 - L)^{-d}$ results in

$$y_t = (1 - L)^{-d}\psi(L)\varepsilon_t. \quad [15.5.2]$$

For $z$ a scalar, define the function

$$f(z) \equiv (1 - z)^{-d}.$$

This function has derivatives given by

$$\begin{aligned}
\frac{\partial f}{\partial z} &= d\cdot(1 - z)^{-d-1} \\
\frac{\partial^2 f}{\partial z^2} &= (d + 1)\cdot d\cdot(1 - z)^{-d-2} \\
\frac{\partial^3 f}{\partial z^3} &= (d + 2)\cdot(d + 1)\cdot d\cdot(1 - z)^{-d-3} \\
&\vdots \\
\frac{\partial^j f}{\partial z^j} &= (d + j - 1)\cdot(d + j - 2)\cdots(d + 1)\cdot d\cdot(1 - z)^{-d-j}.
\end{aligned}$$

A power series expansion for $f(z)$ around $z = 0$ is thus given by

$$\begin{aligned}
(1 - z)^{-d} &= f(0) + \left.\frac{\partial f}{\partial z}\right|_{z=0}\cdot z + \left.\frac{1}{2!}\frac{\partial^2 f}{\partial z^2}\right|_{z=0}\cdot z^2 + \left.\frac{1}{3!}\frac{\partial^3 f}{\partial z^3}\right|_{z=0}\cdot z^3 + \cdots \\
&= 1 + dz + (1/2!)(d + 1)dz^2 + (1/3!)(d + 2)(d + 1)dz^3 + \cdots.
\end{aligned}$$

This suggests that the operator $(1 - L)^{-d}$ might be represented by the filter

$$\begin{aligned}
(1 - L)^{-d} &= 1 + dL + (1/2!)(d + 1)dL^2 \\
&\quad + (1/3!)(d + 2)(d + 1)dL^3 + \cdots \qquad [15.5.3] \\
&= \sum_{j=0}^{\infty} h_j L^j,
\end{aligned}$$

where $h_0 \equiv 1$ and

$$h_j \equiv (1/j!)(d + j - 1)(d + j - 2)(d + j - 3)\cdots(d + 1)(d). \quad [15.5.4]$$

Appendix 15.A to this chapter establishes that if $d < 1$, $h_j$ can be approximated for large $j$ by

$$h_j \cong (j + 1)^{d-1}. \quad [15.5.5]$$

Thus, the time series model

$$y_t = (1 - L)^{-d}\varepsilon_t = h_0\varepsilon_t + h_1\varepsilon_{t-1} + h_2\varepsilon_{t-2} + \cdots \qquad [15.5.6]$$

describes an $MA(\infty)$ representation in which the impulse-response coefficient $h_j$ behaves for large $j$ like $(j + 1)^{d-1}$. For comparison, recall that the impulse-response coefficient associated with the $AR(1)$ process $y_t = (1 - \phi L)^{-1}\varepsilon_t$ is given by $\phi^j$. The impulse-response coefficients for a stationary $ARMA$ process decay geometrically, in contrast to the slower decay implied by [15.5.5]. Because of this slower rate of decay, Granger and Joyeux proposed the fractionally integrated process as an approach to modeling long memories in a time series.

In a finite sample, this long memory could be approximated arbitrarily well with a suitably large-order $ARMA$ representation. The goal of the fractional-difference specification is to capture parsimoniously long-run multipliers that decay very slowly.

The sequence of limiting moving average coefficients $\{h_j\}_{j=0}^{\infty}$ given in [15.5.4] can be shown to be square-summable provided that $d < \frac{1}{2}$:[6]

$$\sum_{j=0}^{\infty} h_j^2 < \infty \qquad \text{for } d < \tfrac{1}{2}.$$

Thus, [15.5.6] defines a covariance-stationary process provided that $d < \frac{1}{2}$. If $d > \frac{1}{2}$, the proposal is to difference the process before describing it by [15.5.2]. For example, if $d = 0.7$, the process of [15.5.1] implies

$$(1 - L)^{-0.3}(1 - L)y_t = \psi(L)\varepsilon_t;$$

that is, $\Delta y_t$ is fractionally integrated with parameter $d = -0.3 < \frac{1}{2}$.

Conditions under which fractional integration could arise from aggregation of other processes were described by Granger (1980). Geweke and Porter-Hudak (1983) and Sowell (1992) proposed techniques for estimating $d$. Diebold and Rudebusch (1989) analyzed GNP data and the persistence of business cycle fluctuations using this approach, while Lo (1991) provided an interesting investigation of the persistence of movements in stock prices.

## *Occasional Breaks in Trend*

According to the unit root specification [15.1.3], events are occurring all the time that permanently affect the course of $y$. Perron (1989) and Rappoport and Reichlin (1989) have argued that economic events that have large permanent effects

[6]Reasoning as in Appendix 3.A to Chapter 3.

$$\begin{aligned}\sum_{j=0}^{N-1} (j + 1)^{2(d-1)} &= \sum_{j=1}^{N} j^{2(d-1)} \\ &< 1 + \int_1^N x^{2(d-1)}\,dx \\ &= 1 + [1/(2d - 1)]x^{2d-1}\big|_{x=1}^{N} \\ &= 1 + [1/(2d - 1)]\cdot[N^{2d-1} - 1],\end{aligned}$$

which converges to $1 - [1/(2d - 1)]$ as $N \to \infty$, provided that $d < \frac{1}{2}$.

are relatively rare. The idea can be illustrated with the following model, in which $y_t$ is stationary around a trend with a single break:

$$y_t = \begin{cases} \alpha_1 + \delta t + \varepsilon_t & \text{for } t < T_0 \\ \alpha_2 + \delta t + \varepsilon_t & \text{for } t \geq T_0. \end{cases} \qquad [15.5.7]$$

The finding is that such series would appear to exhibit unit root nonstationarity on the basis of the tests to be discussed in Chapter 17.

Another way of thinking about the process in [15.5.7] is as follows:

$$\Delta y_t = \xi_t + \delta + \varepsilon_t - \varepsilon_{t-1}, \qquad [15.5.8]$$

where $\xi_t = (\alpha_2 - \alpha_1)$ when $t = T_0$ and is zero otherwise. Suppose $\xi_t$ is viewed as a random variable with some probability distribution—say,

$$\xi_t = \begin{cases} \alpha_2 - \alpha_1 & \text{with probability } p \\ 0 & \text{with probability } 1 - p. \end{cases}$$

Evidently, $p$ must be quite small to represent the idea that this is a relatively rare event. Equation [15.5.8] could then be rewritten as

$$\Delta y_t = \mu + \eta_t, \qquad [15.5.9]$$

where

$$\mu = p(\alpha_2 - \alpha_1) + \delta$$
$$\eta_t = \xi_t - p(\alpha_2 - \alpha_1) + \varepsilon_t - \varepsilon_{t-1}.$$

But $\eta_t$ is the sum of a zero-mean white noise process $[\xi_t - p(\alpha_2 - \alpha_1)]$ and an independent $MA(1)$ process $[\varepsilon_t - \varepsilon_{t-1}]$. Therefore, an $MA(1)$ representation for $\eta_t$ exists. From this perspective, [15.5.9] could be viewed as an $ARIMA(0, 1, 1)$ process,

$$\Delta y_t = \mu + v_t + \theta v_{t-1},$$

with a non-Gaussian distribution for the innovations $v_t$:

$$v_t = y_t - \hat{E}(y_t | y_{t-1}, y_{t-2}, \ldots).$$

The optimal linear forecasting rule,

$$\hat{E}(y_{t+s} | y_t, y_{t-1}, \ldots) = \mu s + y_t + \theta v_t,$$

puts a nonvanishing weight on each date's innovation. This weight does not disappear as $s \to \infty$, because each period essentially provides a new observation on the variable $\xi_t$ and the realization of $\xi_t$ has permanent consequences for the level of the series. From this perspective, a time series satisfying [15.5.7] could be described as a unit root process with non-Gaussian innovations.

Lam (1990) estimated a model closely related to [15.5.7] where shifts in the slope of the trend line were assumed to follow a Markov chain and where U.S. real GNP was allowed to follow a stationary third-order autoregression around this trend. Results of his maximum likelihood estimation are reported in Figure 15.4. These findings are very interesting for the question of the long-run consequences of economic recessions. According to this specification, events that permanently changed the level of GNP coincided with the recessions of 1957, 1973, and 1980.

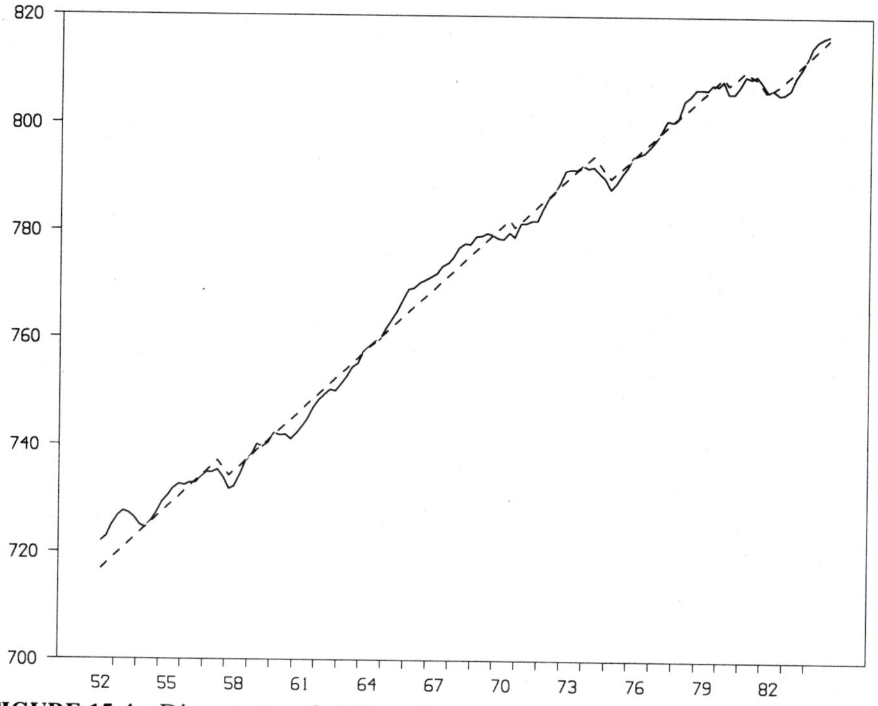


**FIGURE 15.4** Discrete trend shifts estimated for U.S. real GNP, 1952–84 (Lam, 1990).

## APPENDIX 15.A. *Derivation of Selected Equations for Chapter 15*

■ **Derivation of Equation [15.5.5].** Write [15.5.4] as

$$\begin{aligned}
h_j &\equiv (1/j!)(d+j-1)(d+j-2)(d+j-3)\cdots(d+1)(d)\\
&= \left[\frac{d+j-1}{j}\right]\left[\frac{d+j-2}{j-1}\right]\left[\frac{d+j-3}{j-2}\right]\cdots\left[\frac{d+1}{2}\right]\left[\frac{d}{1}\right]\\
&= \left[\frac{j+d-1}{j}\right]\left[\frac{j-1+d-1}{j-1}\right]\left[\frac{j-2+d-1}{j-2}\right]\times\cdots\\
&\quad\times\left[\frac{j-(j-2)+d-1}{j-(j-2)}\right]\left[\frac{j-(j-1)+d-1}{j-(j-1)}\right] \qquad [15.A.1]\\
&= \left[1+\frac{d-1}{j}\right]\left[1+\frac{d-1}{j-1}\right]\left[1+\frac{d-1}{j-2}\right]\times\cdots\\
&\quad\times\left[1+\frac{d-1}{j-(j-2)}\right]\left[1+\frac{d-1}{j-(j-1)}\right].
\end{aligned}$$

For large $j$, we have the approximation

$$\left[1+\frac{d-1}{j}\right]\cong\left[1+\frac{1}{j}\right]^{d-1}. \qquad [15.A.2]$$

To justify this formally, consider the function $g(x)\equiv(1+x)^{d-1}$. Taylor's theorem states that

$$\begin{aligned}
(1+x)^{d-1} &= g(0)+\left.\frac{\partial g}{\partial x}\right|_{x=0}\cdot x+\frac{1}{2}\left.\frac{\partial^2 g}{\partial x^2}\right|_{x=\delta}\cdot x^2 \qquad [15.A.3]\\
&= 1+(d-1)x+\frac{1}{2}(d-1)(d-2)(1+\delta)^{d-3}x^2
\end{aligned}$$

for some $\delta$ between zero and $x$. For $x > -1$ and $d < 1$, equation [15.A.3] implies that

$$(1 + x)^{d-1} \geq 1 + (d - 1)x.$$

Letting $x = 1/j$ gives

$$1 + \frac{d-1}{j} \leq \left[1 + \frac{1}{j}\right]^{d-1} = \left[\frac{j+1}{j}\right]^{d-1} \qquad [15.A.4]$$

for all $j > 0$ and $d < 1$, with the approximation [15.A.2] improving as $j \rightarrow \infty$. Substituting [15.A.4] into [15.A.1] implies that

$$h_j \cong \left[\frac{j+1}{j}\right]^{d-1}\left[\frac{j}{j-1}\right]^{d-1}\left[\frac{j-1}{j-2}\right]^{d-1} \cdots \left[\frac{3}{2}\right]^{d-1}\left[\frac{2}{1}\right]^{d-1} = (j+1)^{d-1}. \qquad [15.A.5]$$

■

## Chapter 15 References


Blough, Stephen R. 1992a. "The Relationship between Power and Level for Generic Unit Root Tests in Finite Samples." *Journal of Applied Econometrics* 7:295–308.

———. 1992b. "Near Observational Equivalence of Unit Root and Stationary Processes: Theory and Implications." Johns Hopkins University. Mimeo.

Box, G. E. P., and Gwilym M. Jenkins. 1976. *Time Series Analysis: Forecasting and Control*, rev. ed. San Francisco: Holden-Day.

Campbell, John Y., and N. Gregory Mankiw. 1987a. "Permanent and Transitory Components in Macroeconomic Fluctuations." *American Economic Review Papers and Proceedings* 77:111–17.

——— and ———. 1987b. "Are Output Fluctuations Transitory?" *Quarterly Journal of Economics* 102:857–80.

Christiano, Lawrence J., and Martin Eichenbaum. 1990. "Unit Roots in Real GNP: Do We Know and Do We Care?" in Allan H. Meltzer, ed., *Unit Roots, Investment Measures, and Other Essays*, 7–61. Carnegie-Rochester Conference Series on Public Policy, Vol. 32. Amsterdam: North-Holland.

——— and Lars Ljungqvist. 1988. "Money Does Granger-Cause Output in the Bivariate Money-Output Relation." *Journal of Monetary Economics* 22:217–35.

Clark, Peter K. 1987. "The Cyclical Component of U.S. Economic Activity." *Quarterly Journal of Economics* 102:797–814.

Cochrane, John H. 1988. "How Big Is the Random Walk in GNP?" *Journal of Political Economy* 96:893–920.

———. 1991. "A Critique of the Application of Unit Root Tests." *Journal of Economic Dynamics and Control* 15:275–84.

Diebold, Francis X., and Glenn D. Rudebusch. 1989. "Long Memory and Persistence in Aggregate Output." *Journal of Monetary Economics* 24:189–209.

Durlauf, Steven N. 1989. "Output Persistence, Economic Structure, and Choice of Stabilization Policy." *Brookings Papers on Economic Activity* 2:1989, 69–116.

Friedman, Milton. 1957. *A Theory of the Consumption Function*. Princeton, N.J.: Princeton University Press.

Gagnon, Joseph E. 1988. "Short-Run Models and Long-Run Forecasts: A Note on the Permanence of Output Fluctuations." *Quarterly Journal of Economics* 103:415–24.

Geweke, John, and Susan Porter-Hudak. 1983. "The Estimation and Application of Long Memory Time Series Models." *Journal of Time Series Analysis* 4:221–38.

Granger, C. W. J. 1980. "Long Memory Relationships and the Aggregation of Dynamic Models." *Journal of Econometrics* 14:227–38.

——— and Roselyne Joyeux. 1980. "An Introduction to Long-Memory Time Series Models and Fractional Differencing." *Journal of Time Series Analysis* 1:15–29.

Hamilton, James D. 1989. "A New Approach to the Economic Analysis of Nonstationary Time Series and the Business Cycle." *Econometrica* 57:357–84.

Hosking, J. R. M. 1981. "Fractional Differencing." *Biometrika* 68:165–76.

Lam, Pok-sang. 1990. "The Hamilton Model with a General Autoregressive Component: Estimation and Comparison with Other Models of Economic Time Series." *Journal of Monetary Economics* 26:409–32.

Lo, Andrew W. 1991. "Long-Term Memory in Stock Market Prices." *Econometrica* 59:1279–1313.

Muth, John F. 1960. "Optimal Properties of Exponentially Weighted Forecasts." *Journal of the American Statistical Association* 55:299–306.

Nelson, Charles R., and Charles I. Plosser. 1982. "Trends and Random Walks in Macroeconomic Time Series: Some Evidence and Implications." *Journal of Monetary Economics* 10:139–62.

Perron, Pierre. 1989. "The Great Crash, the Oil Price Shock, and the Unit Root Hypothesis." *Econometrica* 57:1361–1401.

Rappoport, Peter, and Lucrezia Reichlin. 1989. "Segmented Trends and Nonstationary Time Series." *Economic Journal* supplement 99:168–77.

Sims, Christopher A. 1989. "Modeling Trends." Yale University. Mimeo.

Sowell, Fallaw. 1992. "Maximum Likelihood Estimation of Stationary Univariate Fractionally Integrated Time Series Models." *Journal of Econometrics* 53:165–88.

Stock, James H. 1990. "'Unit Roots in Real GNP: Do We Know and Do We Care?' A Comment," in Allan H. Meltzer, ed., *Unit Roots, Investment Measures, and Other Essays*, 63–82. Carnegie-Rochester Conference Series on Public Policy, Vol. 32. Amsterdam: North-Holland.

——— and Mark W. Watson. 1988. "Variable Trends in Economic Time Series." *Journal of Economic Perspectives* vol. 2, no. 3, 147–74.

——— and ———. 1989. "Interpreting the Evidence on Money-Income Causality." *Journal of Econometrics* 40:161–81.

Watson, Mark W. 1986. "Univariate Detrending Methods with Stochastic Trends." *Journal of Monetary Economics* 18:49–75.

# 16 Processes with Deterministic Time Trends

The coefficients of regression models involving unit roots or deterministic time trends are typically estimated by ordinary least squares. However, the asymptotic distributions of the coefficient estimates cannot be calculated in the same way as are those for regression models involving stationary variables. Among other difficulties, the estimates of different parameters will in general have different asymptotic rates of convergence. This chapter introduces the idea of different rates of convergence and develops a general approach to obtaining asymptotic distributions suggested by Sims, Stock, and Watson (1990).[1] This chapter deals exclusively with processes involving deterministic time trends but no unit roots. One of the results for such processes will be that the usual *OLS* $t$ and $F$ statistics, calculated in the usual way, have the same asymptotic distributions as they do for stationary regressions. Although the limiting distributions are standard, the techniques used to verify these limiting distributions are different from those used in Chapter 8. These techniques will also be used to develop the asymptotic distributions for processes including unit roots in Chapters 17 and 18.

This chapter begins with the simplest example of i.i.d. innovations around a deterministic time trend. Section 16.1 derives the asymptotic distributions of the coefficient estimates for this model and illustrates a rescaling of variables that is necessary to accommodate different asymptotic rates of convergence. Section 16.2 shows that despite the different asymptotic rates of convergence, the standard *OLS* $t$ and $F$ statistics have the usual limiting distributions for this model. Section 16.3 develops analogous results for a covariance-stationary autoregression around a deterministic time trend. That section also introduces the Sims, Stock, and Watson technique of transforming the regression model into a canonical form for which the asymptotic distribution is simpler to describe.

## 16.1. *Asymptotic Distribution of* OLS *Estimates of the Simple Time Trend Model*

This section considers *OLS* estimation of the parameters of a simple time trend,

$$y_t = \alpha + \delta t + \varepsilon_t, \qquad [16.1.1]$$

for $\varepsilon_t$ a white noise process. If $\varepsilon_t \sim N(0, \sigma^2)$, then the model [16.1.1] satisfies the classical regression assumptions[2] and the standard *OLS* $t$ or $F$ statistics in equations

[1]A simpler version of this theme appeared in the analysis of a univariate process with unit roots by Fuller (1976).

[2]See Assumption 8.1 in Chapter 8.

[8.1.26] and [8.1.32] would have exact small-sample $t$ or $F$ distributions. On the other hand, if $\varepsilon_t$ is non-Gaussian, then a slightly different technique for finding the asymptotic distributions of the *OLS* estimates of $\alpha$ and $\delta$ would have to be used from that employed for stationary regressions in Chapter 8. This chapter introduces this technique, which will prove useful not only for studying time trends but also for analyzing estimators for a variety of nonstationary processes in Chapters 17 and 18.[3]

Recall the approach used to find asymptotic distributions for regressions with stationary explanatory variables in Chapter 8. Write [16.1.1] in the form of the standard regression model,

$$y_t = \mathbf{x}_t'\boldsymbol{\beta} + \varepsilon_t, \tag{16.1.2}$$

where

$$\underset{(1\times 2)}{\mathbf{x}_t'} \equiv [1 \quad t] \tag{16.1.3}$$

$$\underset{(2\times 1)}{\boldsymbol{\beta}} \equiv \begin{bmatrix} \alpha \\ \delta \end{bmatrix}. \tag{16.1.4}$$

Let $\mathbf{b}_T$ denote the *OLS* estimate of $\boldsymbol{\beta}$ based on a sample of size $T$:

$$\mathbf{b}_T \equiv \begin{bmatrix} \hat{\alpha}_T \\ \hat{\delta}_T \end{bmatrix} = \left[\sum_{t=1}^{T} \mathbf{x}_t\mathbf{x}_t'\right]^{-1}\left[\sum_{t=1}^{T} \mathbf{x}_t y_t\right]. \tag{16.1.5}$$

Recall from equation [8.2.3] that the deviation of the *OLS* estimate from the true value can be expressed as

$$(\mathbf{b}_T - \boldsymbol{\beta}) = \left[\sum_{t=1}^{T} \mathbf{x}_t\mathbf{x}_t'\right]^{-1}\left[\sum_{t=1}^{T} \mathbf{x}_t \varepsilon_t\right]. \tag{16.1.6}$$

To find the limiting distribution for a regression with stationary explanatory variables, the approach in Chapter 8 was to multiply [16.1.6] by $\sqrt{T}$, resulting in

$$\sqrt{T}(\mathbf{b}_T - \boldsymbol{\beta}) = \left[(1/T)\sum_{t=1}^{T} \mathbf{x}_t\mathbf{x}_t'\right]^{-1}\left[(1/\sqrt{T})\sum_{t=1}^{T} \mathbf{x}_t \varepsilon_t\right]. \tag{16.1.7}$$

The usual assumption was that $(1/T)\Sigma_{t=1}^{T}\mathbf{x}_t\mathbf{x}_t'$ converged in probability to a nonsingular matrix $\mathbf{Q}$ while $(1/\sqrt{T})\Sigma_{t=1}^{T}\mathbf{x}_t\varepsilon_t$ converged in distribution to a $N(\mathbf{0}, \sigma^2\mathbf{Q})$ random variable, implying that $\sqrt{T}(\mathbf{b}_T - \boldsymbol{\beta}) \xrightarrow{L} N(\mathbf{0}, \sigma^2\mathbf{Q}^{-1})$.

To see why this same argument cannot be used for a deterministic time trend, note that for $\mathbf{x}_t$ and $\boldsymbol{\beta}$ given in equations [16.1.3] and [16.1.4], expression [16.1.6] would be

$$\begin{bmatrix} \hat{\alpha}_T - \alpha \\ \hat{\delta}_T - \delta \end{bmatrix} = \begin{bmatrix} \Sigma 1 & \Sigma t \\ \Sigma t & \Sigma t^2 \end{bmatrix}^{-1} \begin{bmatrix} \Sigma \varepsilon_t \\ \Sigma t\varepsilon_t \end{bmatrix}, \tag{16.1.8}$$

[3]The general approach in these chapters follows Sims, Stock, and Watson (1990).

where $\Sigma$ denotes summation for $t = 1$ through $T$. It is straightforward to show by induction that[4]

$$\sum_{t=1}^{T} t = T(T+1)/2 \qquad [16.1.9]$$

$$\sum_{t=1}^{T} t^2 = T(T+1)(2T+1)/6. \qquad [16.1.10]$$

Thus, the leading term in $\Sigma_{t=1}^{T} t$ is $T^2/2$; that is,

$$(1/T^2)\sum_{t=1}^{T} t = (1/T^2)[(T^2/2) + (T/2)] = 1/2 + 1/(2T) \rightarrow 1/2. \qquad [16.1.11]$$

Similarly, the leading term in $\Sigma_{t=1}^{T} t^2$ is $T^3/3$:

$$\begin{aligned}(1/T^3)\sum_{t=1}^{T} t^2 &= (1/T^3)[(2T^3/6) + (3T^2/6) + T/6] \\ &= 1/3 + 1/(2T) + 1/(6T^2) \\ &\rightarrow 1/3.\end{aligned} \qquad [16.1.12]$$

For future reference, we note here the general pattern—the leading term in $\Sigma_{t=1}^{T} t^v$ is $T^{v+1}/(v+1)$:

$$(1/T^{v+1})\sum_{t=1}^{T} t^v \rightarrow 1/(v+1). \qquad [16.1.13]$$

To verify [16.1.13], note that

$$(1/T^{v+1})\sum_{t=1}^{T} t^v = (1/T)\sum_{t=1}^{T} (t/T)^v. \qquad [16.1.14]$$

The right side of [16.1.14] can be viewed as an approximation to the area under the curve

$$f(r) = r^v$$

for $r$ between zero and unity. To see this, notice that $(1/T)\cdot(t/T)^v$ represents the area of a rectangle with width $(1/T)$ and height $r^v$ evaluated at $r = t/T$ (see Figure 16.1). Thus, [16.1.14] is the sum of the area of these rectangles evaluated

[4] Clearly, [16.1.9] and [16.1.10] hold for $T = 1$. Given that [16.1.9] holds for $T$,

$$\sum_{t=1}^{T+1} t = \sum_{t=1}^{T} t + (T+1) = T(T+1)/2 + (T+1) = (T+1)[(T/2) + 1] = (T+1)(T+2)/2,$$

establishing that [16.1.9] holds for $T + 1$. Similarly, given that [16.1.10] holds for $T$,

$$\begin{aligned}\sum_{t=1}^{T+1} t^2 &= T(T+1)(2T+1)/6 + (T+1)^2 \\ &= (T+1)\{[T(2T+1)/6] + (T+1)\} \\ &= (T+1)(2T^2 + 7T + 6)/6 \\ &= (T+1)(T+2)[2(T+1) + 1]/6,\end{aligned}$$

establishing that [16.1.10] holds for $T + 1$.

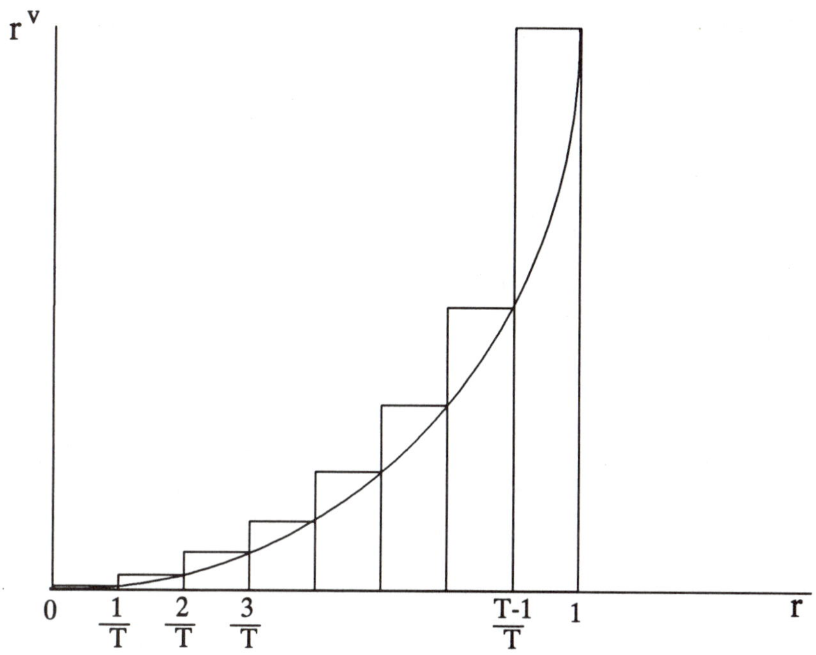


**FIGURE 16.1** Demonstration that $(1/T)\,\Sigma_{t=1}^{T}(t/T)^{\nu} \rightarrow \int_0^1 r^{\nu}\,dr = 1/(\nu + 1)$.

at $r = 1/T, 2/T, \ldots, 1$. As $T \rightarrow \infty$, this sum converges to the area under the curve $f(r)$:

$$(1/T)\sum_{t=1}^{T}(t/T)^{\nu} \rightarrow \int_0^1 r^{\nu}\,dr = r^{\nu+1}/(\nu+1)\big|_{r=0}^{1} = 1/(\nu+1). \qquad [16.1.15]$$

For $\mathbf{x}_t$ given in [16.1.3], results [16.1.9] and [16.1.10] imply that

$$\sum_{t=1}^{T}\mathbf{x}_t\mathbf{x}_t' = \begin{bmatrix} \Sigma 1 & \Sigma t \\ \Sigma t & \Sigma t^2 \end{bmatrix} = \begin{bmatrix} T & T(T+1)/2 \\ T(T+1)/2 & T(T+1)(2T+1)/6 \end{bmatrix}. \qquad [16.1.16]$$

In contrast to the usual result for stationary regressions, for the matrix in [16.1.16], $(1/T)\,\Sigma_{t=1}^{T}\mathbf{x}_t\mathbf{x}_t'$ diverges. To obtain a convergent matrix, [16.1.16] would have to be divided by $T^3$ rather than $T$:

$$T^{-3}\sum_{t=1}^{T}\mathbf{x}_t\mathbf{x}_t' \rightarrow \begin{bmatrix} 0 & 0 \\ 0 & \frac{1}{3} \end{bmatrix}.$$

Unfortunately, this limiting matrix cannot be inverted, as $(1/T)\,\Sigma_{t=1}^{T}\mathbf{x}_t\mathbf{x}_t'$ can be in the usual case. Hence, a different approach from that in the stationary case will be needed to calculate the asymptotic distribution of $\mathbf{b}_T$.

It turns out that the *OLS* estimates $\hat{\alpha}_T$ and $\hat{\delta}_T$ have different asymptotic rates of convergence. To arrive at nondegenerate limiting distributions, $\hat{\alpha}_T$ is multiplied by $\sqrt{T}$, whereas $\hat{\delta}_T$ must be multiplied by $T^{3/2}$! We can think of this adjustment as premultiplying [16.1.6] or [16.1.8] by the matrix

$$\mathbf{Y}_T \equiv \begin{bmatrix} \sqrt{T} & 0 \\ 0 & T^{3/2} \end{bmatrix}, \qquad [16.1.17]$$

resulting in

$$\begin{bmatrix} \sqrt{T}(\hat{\alpha}_T - \alpha) \\ T^{3/2}(\hat{\delta}_T - \delta) \end{bmatrix} = \mathbf{Y}_T \left[ \sum_{t=1}^{T} \mathbf{x}_t \mathbf{x}_t' \right]^{-1} \left[ \sum_{t=1}^{T} \mathbf{x}_t \varepsilon_t \right]$$

$$= \mathbf{Y}_T \left[ \sum_{t=1}^{T} \mathbf{x}_t \mathbf{x}_t' \right]^{-1} \mathbf{Y}_T \mathbf{Y}_T^{-1} \left[ \sum_{t=1}^{T} \mathbf{x}_t \varepsilon_t \right] \qquad [16.1.18]$$

$$= \left\{ \mathbf{Y}_T^{-1} \left[ \sum_{t=1}^{T} \mathbf{x}_t \mathbf{x}_t' \right] \mathbf{Y}_T^{-1} \right\}^{-1} \left\{ \mathbf{Y}_T^{-1} \left[ \sum_{t=1}^{T} \mathbf{x}_t \varepsilon_t \right] \right\}.$$

Consider the first term in the last expression of [16.1.18]. Substituting from [16.1.17] and [16.1.16],

$$\left\{ \mathbf{Y}_T^{-1} \left[ \sum_{t=1}^{T} \mathbf{x}_t \mathbf{x}_t' \right] \mathbf{Y}_T^{-1} \right\} = \left\{ \begin{bmatrix} T^{-1/2} & 0 \\ 0 & T^{-3/2} \end{bmatrix} \begin{bmatrix} \Sigma 1 & \Sigma t \\ \Sigma t & \Sigma t^2 \end{bmatrix} \begin{bmatrix} T^{-1/2} & 0 \\ 0 & T^{-3/2} \end{bmatrix} \right\}$$

$$= \begin{bmatrix} T^{-1}\Sigma 1 & T^{-2}\Sigma t \\ T^{-2}\Sigma t & T^{-3}\Sigma t^2 \end{bmatrix}.$$

Thus, it follows from [16.1.11] and [16.1.12] that

$$\left\{ \mathbf{Y}_T^{-1} \left[ \sum_{t=1}^{T} \mathbf{x}_t \mathbf{x}_t' \right] \mathbf{Y}_T^{-1} \right\} \to \mathbf{Q}, \qquad [16.1.19]$$

where

$$\mathbf{Q} \equiv \begin{bmatrix} 1 & \frac{1}{2} \\ \frac{1}{2} & \frac{1}{3} \end{bmatrix}. \qquad [16.1.20]$$

Turning next to the second term in [16.1.18],

$$\mathbf{Y}_T^{-1} \left[ \sum_{t=1}^{T} \mathbf{x}_t \varepsilon_t \right] = \begin{bmatrix} T^{-1/2} & 0 \\ 0 & T^{-3/2} \end{bmatrix} \begin{bmatrix} \Sigma \varepsilon_t \\ \Sigma t \varepsilon_t \end{bmatrix} = \begin{bmatrix} (1/\sqrt{T})\Sigma \varepsilon_t \\ (1/\sqrt{T})\Sigma (t/T)\varepsilon_t \end{bmatrix}. \qquad [16.1.21]$$

Under standard assumptions about $\varepsilon_t$, this vector will be asymptotically Gaussian. For example, suppose that $\varepsilon_t$ is i.i.d. with mean zero, variance $\sigma^2$, and finite fourth moment. Then the first element of the vector in [16.1.21] satisfies

$$(1/\sqrt{T}) \sum_{t=1}^{T} \varepsilon_t \xrightarrow{L} N(0, \sigma^2),$$

by the central limit theorem.

For the second element of the vector in [16.1.21], observe that $\{(t/T)\varepsilon_t\}$ is a martingale difference sequence that satisfies the conditions of Proposition 7.8. Specifically, its variance is

$$\sigma_t^2 = E[(t/T)\varepsilon_t]^2 = \sigma^2 \cdot (t^2/T^2),$$

where

$$(1/T) \sum_{t=1}^{T} \sigma_t^2 = \sigma^2 (1/T^3) \sum_{t=1}^{T} t^2 \to \sigma^2/3.$$

Furthermore, $(1/T)\sum_{t=1}^{T}[(t/T)\varepsilon_t]^2 \xrightarrow{p} \sigma^2/3$. To verify this last claim, notice that

$$
\begin{aligned}
&E\left((1/T)\sum_{t=1}^{T}[(t/T)\varepsilon_t]^2 - (1/T)\sum_{t=1}^{T}\sigma_t^2\right)^2 \\
&= E\left((1/T)\sum_{t=1}^{T}[(t/T)\varepsilon_t]^2 - (1/T)\sum_{t=1}^{T}(t/T)^2\sigma^2\right)^2 \\
&= E\left((1/T)\sum_{t=1}^{T}(t/T)^2(\varepsilon_t^2 - \sigma^2)\right)^2 \\
&= (1/T)^2\sum_{t=1}^{T}(t/T)^4 E(\varepsilon_t^2 - \sigma^2)^2.
\end{aligned}
\qquad [16.1.22]
$$

But from [16.1.13], $T$ times the magnitude in [16.1.22] converges to

$$(1/T)\sum_{t=1}^{T}(t/T)^4 E(\varepsilon_t^2 - \sigma^2)^2 \to (1/5)\cdot E(\varepsilon_t^2 - \sigma^2)^2,$$

meaning that [16.1.22] itself converges to zero:

$$(1/T)\sum_{t=1}^{T}[(t/T)\varepsilon_t]^2 - (1/T)\sum_{t=1}^{T}\sigma_t^2 \xrightarrow{m.s.} 0.$$

But this implies that

$$(1/T)\sum_{t=1}^{T}[(t/T)\varepsilon_t]^2 \xrightarrow{p} \sigma^2/3,$$

as claimed. Hence, from Proposition 7.8, $(1/\sqrt{T})\sum_{t=1}^{T}(t/T)\varepsilon_t$ satisfies the central limit theorem:

$$(1/\sqrt{T})\sum_{t=1}^{T}(t/T)\varepsilon_t \xrightarrow{L} N(0, \sigma^2/3).$$

Finally, consider the joint distribution of the two elements in the $(2 \times 1)$ vector described by [16.1.21]. Any linear combination of these elements takes the form

$$(1/\sqrt{T})\sum_{t=1}^{T}[\lambda_1 + \lambda_2(t/T)]\varepsilon_t.$$

Then $[\lambda_1 + \lambda_2(t/T)]\varepsilon_t$ is also a martingale difference sequence with positive variance[5] given by $\sigma^2[\lambda_1^2 + 2\lambda_1\lambda_2(t/T) + \lambda_2^2(t/T)^2]$ satisfying

$$
\begin{aligned}
(1/T)\sum_{t=1}^{T}\sigma^2[\lambda_1^2 + 2\lambda_1\lambda_2(t/T) + \lambda_2^2(t/T)^2] &\to \sigma^2[\lambda_1^2 + 2\lambda_1\lambda_2(\tfrac{1}{2}) + \lambda_2^2(\tfrac{1}{3})] \\
&= \sigma^2\boldsymbol{\lambda}'\mathbf{Q}\boldsymbol{\lambda}
\end{aligned}
$$

for $\boldsymbol{\lambda} \equiv (\lambda_1, \lambda_2)'$ and $\mathbf{Q}$ the matrix in [16.1.20]. Furthermore,

$$(1/T)\sum_{t=1}^{T}[\lambda_1 + \lambda_2(t/T)]^2\varepsilon_t^2 \xrightarrow{p} \sigma^2\boldsymbol{\lambda}'\mathbf{Q}\boldsymbol{\lambda}; \qquad [16.1.23]$$

see Exercise 16.1. Thus any linear combination of the two elements in the vector in [16.1.21] is asymptotically Gaussian, implying a limiting bivariate Gaussian dis-

[5]More accurately, a given nonzero $\lambda_1$ and $\lambda_2$ will produce a zero variance for $[\lambda_1 + \lambda_2(t/T)]\varepsilon_t$ for at most a single value of $t$, which does not affect the validity of the asymptotic claim.

tribution:

$$\begin{bmatrix} (1/\sqrt{T})\Sigma\varepsilon_t \\ (1/\sqrt{T})\Sigma(t/T)\varepsilon_t \end{bmatrix} \xrightarrow{L} N(\mathbf{0}, \sigma^2\mathbf{Q}). \qquad [16.1.24]$$

From [16.1.19] and [16.1.24], the asymptotic distribution of [16.1.18] can be calculated as in Example 7.5 of Chapter 7:

$$\begin{bmatrix} \sqrt{T}(\hat{\alpha}_T - \alpha) \\ T^{3/2}(\hat{\delta}_T - \delta) \end{bmatrix} \xrightarrow{L} N(\mathbf{0}, [\mathbf{Q}^{-1}\cdot\sigma^2\mathbf{Q}\cdot\mathbf{Q}^{-1}]) = N(\mathbf{0}, \sigma^2\mathbf{Q}^{-1}). \qquad [16.1.25]$$

These results can be summarized as follows.

***Proposition 16.1:*** *Let $y_t$ be generated according to the simple deterministic time trend [16.1.1] where $\varepsilon_t$ is i.i.d. with $E(\varepsilon_t^2) = \sigma^2$ and $E(\varepsilon_t^4) < \infty$. Then*

$$\begin{bmatrix} \sqrt{T}(\hat{\alpha}_T - \alpha) \\ T^{3/2}(\hat{\delta}_T - \delta) \end{bmatrix} \xrightarrow{L} N\left(\begin{bmatrix} 0 \\ 0 \end{bmatrix}, \sigma^2\begin{bmatrix} 1 & \frac{1}{2} \\ \frac{1}{2} & \frac{1}{3} \end{bmatrix}^{-1}\right). \qquad [16.1.26]$$

Note that the resulting estimate of the coefficient on the time trend ($\hat{\delta}_T$) is *superconsistent*—not only does $\hat{\delta}_T \xrightarrow{p} \delta$, but even when multiplied by $T$, we still have

$$T(\hat{\delta}_T - \delta) \xrightarrow{p} 0; \qquad [16.1.27]$$

see Exercise 16.2.

Different rates of convergence are sometimes described in terms of *order in probability*. A sequence of random variables $\{X_T\}_{T=1}^{\infty}$ is said to be $O_p(T^{-1/2})$ if for every $\varepsilon > 0$, there exists an $M > 0$ such that

$$P\{|X_T| > M/\sqrt{T}\} < \varepsilon \qquad [16.1.28]$$

for all $T$; in other words, the random variable $\sqrt{T}\cdot X_T$ is almost certain to fall within $\pm M$ for any $T$. Most of the estimators encountered for stationary time series are $O_p(T^{-1/2})$. For example, suppose that $X_T$ represents the mean of a sample of size $T$,

$$X_T = (1/T)\sum_{t=1}^{T} y_t,$$

where $\{y_t\}$ is i.i.d. with mean zero and variance $\sigma^2$. Then the variance of $X_T$ is $\sigma^2/T$. But Chebyshev's inequality implies that

$$P\{|X_T| > M/\sqrt{T}\} \leq \frac{\sigma^2/T}{M^2/T} = (\sigma/M)^2$$

for any $M$. By choosing $M$ so that $(\sigma/M)^2 < \varepsilon$, condition [16.1.28] is guaranteed. Since the standard deviation of the estimator is $\sigma/\sqrt{T}$, by choosing $M$ to be a suitable multiple of $\sigma$, the band $X_T \pm M/\sqrt{T}$ can include as much of the density as desired.

As another example, the estimator $\hat{\alpha}_T$ in [16.1.26] would also be said to be $O_p(T^{-1/2})$. Since $\sqrt{T}$ times $(\hat{\alpha}_T - \alpha)$ is asymptotically Gaussian, there exists a band $\pm M/\sqrt{T}$ around $\hat{\alpha}_T$ that contains as much of the probability distribution as desired.

In general, a sequence of random variables $\{X_T\}_{T=1}^{\infty}$ is said to be $O_p(T^{-k})$ if for every $\varepsilon > 0$ there exists an $M > 0$ such that

$$P\{|X_T| > M/(T^k)\} < \varepsilon. \qquad [16.1.29]$$

Thus, for example, the estimator $\hat{\delta}_T$ in [16.1.26] is $O_p(T^{-3/2})$, since there exists a band $\pm M$ around $T^{3/2}(\hat{\delta}_T - \delta)$ that contains as much of the probability distribution as desired.

## 16.2. *Hypothesis Testing for the Simple Time Trend Model*

If the innovations $\varepsilon_t$ for the simple time trend [16.1.1] are Gaussian, then the *OLS* estimates $\hat{\alpha}_T$ and $\hat{\delta}_T$ are Gaussian and the usual *OLS* $t$ and $F$ tests have exact small-sample $t$ and $F$ distributions for all sample sizes $T$. Thus, despite the fact that $\hat{\alpha}_T$ and $\hat{\delta}_T$ have different asymptotic rates of convergence, the standard errors $\hat{\sigma}_{\hat{\alpha}_T}$ and $\hat{\sigma}_{\hat{\delta}_T}$ evidently have offsetting asymptotic behavior so that the statistics such as $(\hat{\delta}_T - \delta_0)/\hat{\sigma}_{\hat{\delta}_T}$ are asymptotically $N(0, 1)$ when the innovations are Gaussian. We might thus conjecture that the usual $t$ and $F$ tests are asymptotically valid for non-Gaussian innovations as well. This conjecture is indeed correct, as we now verify.

First consider the *OLS* $t$ test of the null hypothesis $\alpha = \alpha_0$, which can be written as

$$t_T = \frac{\hat{\alpha}_T - \alpha_0}{\left\{s_T^2[1 \quad 0](\mathbf{X}_T'\mathbf{X}_T)^{-1}\begin{bmatrix}1\\0\end{bmatrix}\right\}^{1/2}}. \qquad [16.2.1]$$

Here $s_T^2$ denotes the *OLS* estimate of $\sigma^2$:

$$s_T^2 = [1/(T-2)]\sum_{t=1}^{T}(y_t - \hat{\alpha}_T - \hat{\delta}_T t)^2; \qquad [16.2.2]$$

and $(\mathbf{X}_T'\mathbf{X}_T) = \Sigma_{t=1}^{T}\mathbf{x}_t\mathbf{x}_t'$ denotes the matrix in equation [16.1.16]. The numerator and denominator of [16.2.1] can further be multiplied by $\sqrt{T}$, resulting in

$$t_T = \frac{\sqrt{T}(\hat{\alpha}_T - \alpha_0)}{\left\{s_T^2[\sqrt{T} \quad 0](\mathbf{X}_T'\mathbf{X}_T)^{-1}\begin{bmatrix}\sqrt{T}\\0\end{bmatrix}\right\}^{1/2}}. \qquad [16.2.3]$$

Note further from [16.1.17] that

$$[\sqrt{T} \quad 0] = [1 \quad 0]\mathbf{Y}_T. \qquad [16.2.4]$$

Substituting [16.2.4] into [16.2.3],

$$t_T = \frac{\sqrt{T}(\hat{\alpha}_T - \alpha_0)}{\left\{s_T^2[1 \quad 0]\mathbf{Y}_T(\mathbf{X}_T'\mathbf{X}_T)^{-1}\mathbf{Y}_T\begin{bmatrix}1\\0\end{bmatrix}\right\}^{1/2}}. \qquad [16.2.5]$$

But recall from [16.1.19] that

$$\mathbf{Y}_T(\mathbf{X}_T'\mathbf{X}_T)^{-1}\mathbf{Y}_T = [\mathbf{Y}_T^{-1}(\mathbf{X}_T'\mathbf{X}_T)\mathbf{Y}_T^{-1}]^{-1} \to \mathbf{Q}^{-1}. \qquad [16.2.6]$$

It is straightforward to show that $s_T^2 \xrightarrow{p} \sigma^2$. Recall further that $\sqrt{T}(\hat{\alpha}_T - \alpha_0) \xrightarrow{L} N(0, \sigma^2 q^{11})$ for $q^{11}$ the (1, 1) element of $\mathbf{Q}^{-1}$. Hence, from [16.2.5],

$$t_T \xrightarrow{p} \frac{\sqrt{T}(\hat{\alpha}_T - \alpha_0)}{\left\{\sigma^2[1 \quad 0]\mathbf{Q}^{-1}\begin{bmatrix}1\\0\end{bmatrix}\right\}^{1/2}} = \frac{\sqrt{T}(\hat{\alpha}_T - \alpha_0)}{\sigma\sqrt{q^{11}}}. \qquad [16.2.7]$$

But this is an asymptotically Gaussian variable divided by the square root of its variance, and so asymptotically it has a $N(0, 1)$ distribution. Thus, the usual *OLS* $t$ test of $\alpha = \alpha_0$ will give an asymptotically valid inference.

Similarly, consider the usual *OLS* $t$ test of $\delta = \delta_0$:

$$t_T = \frac{\hat{\delta}_T - \delta_0}{\left\{s_T^2[0 \quad 1](\mathbf{X}_T'\mathbf{X}_T)^{-1}\begin{bmatrix}0\\1\end{bmatrix}\right\}^{1/2}}.$$

Multiplying numerator and denominator by $T^{3/2}$,

$$t_T = \frac{T^{3/2}(\hat{\delta}_T - \delta_0)}{\left\{s_T^2[0 \quad T^{3/2}](\mathbf{X}_T'\mathbf{X}_T)^{-1}\begin{bmatrix} 0 \\ T^{3/2} \end{bmatrix}\right\}^{1/2}}$$

$$= \frac{T^{3/2}(\hat{\delta}_T - \delta_0)}{\left\{s_T^2[0 \quad 1]\mathbf{Y}_T(\mathbf{X}_T'\mathbf{X}_T)^{-1}\mathbf{Y}_T\begin{bmatrix} 0 \\ 1 \end{bmatrix}\right\}^{1/2}}$$

$$\xrightarrow{p} \frac{T^{3/2}(\hat{\delta}_T - \delta_0)}{\sigma\sqrt{q^{22}}},$$

which again is asymptotically a $N(0, 1)$ variable. Thus, although $\hat{\alpha}_T$ and $\hat{\delta}_T$ converge at different rates, the corresponding standard errors $\hat{\sigma}_{\hat{\alpha}_T}$ and $\hat{\sigma}_{\hat{\delta}_T}$ also incorporate different orders of $T$, with the result that the usual *OLS* $t$ tests are asymptotically valid.

It is interesting also to consider a test of a single hypothesis involving both $\alpha$ and $\delta$,

$$H_0: r_1\alpha + r_2\delta = r,$$

where $r_1$, $r_2$, and $r$ are parameters that describe the hypothesis. A $t$ test of $H_0$ can be obtained from the square root of the *OLS F* test (expression [8.1.32]):[6]

$$t_T = \frac{(r_1\hat{\alpha}_T + r_2\hat{\delta}_T - r)}{\left\{s_T^2[r_1 \quad r_2](\mathbf{X}_T'\mathbf{X}_T)^{-1}\begin{bmatrix} r_1 \\ r_2 \end{bmatrix}\right\}^{1/2}}.$$

In this case we multiply numerator and denominator by $\sqrt{T}$, the slower rate of convergence among the two estimators $\hat{\alpha}_T$ and $\hat{\delta}_T$:

$$t_T = \frac{\sqrt{T}(r_1\hat{\alpha}_T + r_2\hat{\delta}_T - r)}{\left\{s_T^2\sqrt{T}[r_1 \quad r_2](\mathbf{X}_T'\mathbf{X}_T)^{-1}\begin{bmatrix} r_1 \\ r_2 \end{bmatrix}\sqrt{T}\right\}^{1/2}}$$

$$= \frac{\sqrt{T}(r_1\hat{\alpha}_T + r_2\hat{\delta}_T - r)}{\left\{s_T^2\sqrt{T}[r_1 \quad r_2]\mathbf{Y}_T^{-1}\mathbf{Y}_T(\mathbf{X}_T'\mathbf{X}_T)^{-1}\mathbf{Y}_T\mathbf{Y}_T^{-1}\begin{bmatrix} r_1 \\ r_2 \end{bmatrix}\sqrt{T}\right\}^{1/2}}$$

$$= \frac{\sqrt{T}(r_1\hat{\alpha}_T + r_2\hat{\delta}_T - r)}{\{s_T^2\mathbf{r}_T'[\mathbf{Y}_T(\mathbf{X}_T'\mathbf{X}_T)^{-1}\mathbf{Y}_T]\mathbf{r}_T\}^{1/2}},$$

where

$$\mathbf{r}_T \equiv \mathbf{Y}_T^{-1}\begin{bmatrix} r_1 \\ r_2 \end{bmatrix}\sqrt{T} = \begin{bmatrix} r_1 \\ r_2/T \end{bmatrix} \to \begin{bmatrix} r_1 \\ 0 \end{bmatrix}. \qquad [16.2.8]$$

Similarly, recall from [16.1.27] that $\hat{\delta}_T$ is superconsistent, implying that

$$\sqrt{T}(r_1\hat{\alpha}_T + r_2\hat{\delta}_T - r) \xrightarrow{p} \sqrt{T}(r_1\hat{\alpha}_T + r_2\delta - r), \qquad [16.2.9]$$

[6]With a single linear restriction as here, $m = 1$ and expression [8.1.32] describes an $F(1, T - k)$ variable when the innovations are Gaussian. But an $F(1, T - k)$ variable is the square of a $t(T - k)$ variable. The test is described here in terms of a $t$ test rather than an $F$ test in order to facilitate comparison with the earlier results in this section.

where $\delta$ is the true population value for the time trend parameter. Again applying [16.2.6], it follows that

$$t_T \xrightarrow{p} \frac{\sqrt{T}(r_1\hat{\alpha}_T + r_2\delta - r)}{\left\{\sigma^2[r_1 \quad 0]\mathbf{Q}^{-1}\begin{bmatrix} r_1 \\ 0 \end{bmatrix}\right\}^{1/2}} = \frac{\sqrt{T}(r_1\hat{\alpha}_T + r_2\delta - r)}{\{r_1^2\sigma^2q^{11}\}^{1/2}}. \quad [16.2.10]$$

But notice that

$$\begin{aligned}\sqrt{T}(r_1\hat{\alpha}_T + r_2\delta - r) &= \sqrt{T}[r_1(\hat{\alpha}_T - \alpha) + r_1\alpha + r_2\delta - r] \\ &= \sqrt{T}[r_1(\hat{\alpha}_T - \alpha)]\end{aligned}$$

under the null hypothesis. Hence, under the null,

$$t_T \xrightarrow{p} \frac{\sqrt{T}[r_1(\hat{\alpha}_T - \alpha)]}{\{r_1^2\sigma^2q^{11}\}^{1/2}} = \frac{\sqrt{T}(\hat{\alpha}_T - \alpha)}{\{\sigma^2q^{11}\}^{1/2}},$$

which asymptotically has a $N(0, 1)$ distribution. Thus, again, the usual *OLS* $t$ test of $H_0$ is valid asymptotically.

This last example illustrates the following general principle: A test involving a single restriction across parameters with different rates of convergence is dominated asymptotically by the parameters with the slowest rates of convergence. This means that a test involving both $\alpha$ and $\delta$ that employs the estimated value of $\delta$ would have the same asymptotic properties under the null as a test that employs the true value of $\delta$.

Finally, consider a joint test of separate hypotheses about $\alpha$ and $\delta$,

$$H_0: \begin{bmatrix} \alpha \\ \delta \end{bmatrix} = \begin{bmatrix} \alpha_0 \\ \delta_0 \end{bmatrix},$$

or, in vector form,

$$\boldsymbol{\beta} = \boldsymbol{\beta}_0.$$

The Wald form of the *OLS* $\chi^2$ test of $H_0$ is found from [8.2.23] by taking $\mathbf{R} = \mathbf{I}_2$:

$$\begin{aligned}\chi_T^2 &= (\mathbf{b}_T - \boldsymbol{\beta}_0)'[s_T^2(\mathbf{X}_T'\mathbf{X}_T)^{-1}]^{-1}(\mathbf{b}_T - \boldsymbol{\beta}_0) \\ &= (\mathbf{b}_T - \boldsymbol{\beta}_0)'\mathbf{Y}_T[\mathbf{Y}_T s_T^2(\mathbf{X}_T'\mathbf{X}_T)^{-1}\mathbf{Y}_T]^{-1}\mathbf{Y}_T(\mathbf{b}_T - \boldsymbol{\beta}_0) \\ &\xrightarrow{p} [\mathbf{Y}_T(\mathbf{b}_T - \boldsymbol{\beta}_0)]'[\sigma^2\mathbf{Q}^{-1}]^{-1}[\mathbf{Y}_T(\mathbf{b}_T - \boldsymbol{\beta}_0)].\end{aligned}$$

Recalling [16.1.25], this is a quadratic form in a two-dimensional Gaussian vector of the sort considered in Proposition 8.1, from which

$$\chi_T^2 \xrightarrow{L} \chi^2(2).$$

Thus, again, the usual *OLS* test is asymptotically valid.

## 16.3. *Asymptotic Inference for an Autoregressive Process Around a Deterministic Time Trend*

The same principles can be used to study a general autoregressive process around a deterministic time trend:

$$y_t = \alpha + \delta t + \phi_1 y_{t-1} + \phi_2 y_{t-2} + \cdots + \phi_p y_{t-p} + \varepsilon_t. \quad [16.3.1]$$

It is assumed throughout this section that $\varepsilon_t$ is i.i.d. with mean zero, variance $\sigma^2$, and finite fourth moment, and that roots of

$$1 - \phi_1 z - \phi_2 z^2 - \cdots - \phi_p z^p = 0$$

lie outside the unit circle. Consider a sample of $T + p$ observations on $y$, $\{y_{-p+1}, y_{-p+2}, \ldots, y_T\}$, and let $\hat{\alpha}_T, \hat{\delta}_T, \hat{\phi}_{1,T}, \ldots, \hat{\phi}_{p,T}$ denote coefficient estimates based on ordinary least squares estimation of [16.3.1] for $t = 1, 2, \ldots, T$.

## *A Useful Transformation of the Regressors*

Define

$$\delta^* \equiv \frac{\delta}{1 - \phi_1 - \phi_2 - \cdots - \phi_p}$$

$$\alpha^* \equiv \frac{\alpha}{1 - \phi_1 - \phi_2 - \cdots - \phi_p} - \frac{(\phi_1 + 2\phi_2 + \cdots + p\phi_p)\delta^*}{1 - \phi_1 - \phi_2 - \cdots - \phi_p}.$$

Multiplying these equations by $(1 - \phi_1 - \phi_2 - \cdots - \phi_p)$ and substituting the resulting expressions for $\alpha$ and $\delta$ into [16.3.1] produces

$$\begin{aligned} y_t = {} & (1 - \phi_1 - \phi_2 - \cdots - \phi_p)\alpha^* + (\phi_1 + 2\phi_2 + \cdots + p\phi_p)\delta^* \\ & + (1 - \phi_1 - \phi_2 - \cdots - \phi_p)\delta^* t + \phi_1 y_{t-1} + \phi_2 y_{t-2} \\ & + \cdots + \phi_p y_{t-p} + \varepsilon_t \end{aligned} \qquad [16.3.2]$$

or

$$y_t = \alpha^* + \delta^* t + \phi_1^* y_{t-1}^* + \phi_2^* y_{t-2}^* + \cdots + \phi_p^* y_{t-p}^* + \varepsilon_t, \qquad [16.3.3]$$

where

$$\phi_j^* \equiv \phi_j \qquad \text{for } j = 1, 2, \ldots, p$$

and

$$y_{t-j}^* \equiv y_{t-j} - \alpha^* - \delta^*(t - j) \qquad \text{for } j = 1, 2, \ldots, p. \qquad [16.3.4]$$

The idea of transforming the regression into a form such as [16.3.3] is due to Sims, Stock, and Watson (1990).[7] The objective is to rewrite the regressors of [16.3.1] in terms of zero-mean covariance-stationary random variables (the terms $y_{t-j}^*$ for $j = 1, 2, \ldots, p$), a constant term, and a time trend. Transforming the regressors in this way isolates components of the *OLS* coefficient vector with different rates of convergence and provides a general technique for finding the asymptotic distribution of regressions involving nonstationary variables. A general result is that, if such a transformed equation were estimated by *OLS*, the coefficients on zero-mean covariance-stationary random variables (in this case, $\hat{\phi}_{1,T}^*, \hat{\phi}_{2,T}^*, \ldots, \hat{\phi}_{p,T}^*$) would converge at rate $\sqrt{T}$ to a Gaussian distribution. The coefficients $\hat{\alpha}_T^*$ and $\hat{\delta}_T^*$ from *OLS* estimation of [16.3.3] turn out to behave asymptotically exactly like $\hat{\alpha}_T$ and $\hat{\delta}_T$ for the simple time trend model analyzed in Section 16.1 and are asymptotically independent of the $\hat{\phi}^*$'s.

It is helpful to describe this transformation in more general notation that will also apply to more complicated models in the chapters that follow. The original regression model [16.3.1] can be written

$$y_t = \mathbf{x}_t'\boldsymbol{\beta} + \varepsilon_t, \qquad [16.3.5]$$

[7] A simpler version of this theme appeared in the analysis of a univariate process with unit roots by Fuller (1976).

where

$$\underset{(p+2)\times 1}{\mathbf{x}_t} \equiv \begin{bmatrix} y_{t-1} \\ y_{t-2} \\ \vdots \\ y_{t-p} \\ 1 \\ t \end{bmatrix} \qquad \underset{(p+2)\times 1}{\boldsymbol{\beta}} \equiv \begin{bmatrix} \phi_1 \\ \phi_2 \\ \vdots \\ \phi_p \\ \alpha \\ \delta \end{bmatrix} \qquad [16.3.6]$$

The algebraic transformation in arriving at [16.3.3] could then be described as rewriting [16.3.5] in the form

$$y_t = \mathbf{x}_t'\mathbf{G}'[\mathbf{G}']^{-1}\boldsymbol{\beta} + \varepsilon_t = [\mathbf{x}_t^*]'\boldsymbol{\beta}^* + \varepsilon_t, \qquad [16.3.7]$$

where

$$\underset{(p+2)\times(p+2)}{\mathbf{G}'} \equiv \begin{bmatrix} 1 & 0 & \cdots & 0 & 0 & 0 \\ 0 & 1 & \cdots & 0 & 0 & 0 \\ \vdots & \vdots & \cdots & \vdots & \vdots & \vdots \\ 0 & 0 & \cdots & 1 & 0 & 0 \\ -\alpha^* + \delta^* & -\alpha^* + 2\delta^* & \cdots & -\alpha^* + p\delta^* & 1 & 0 \\ -\delta^* & -\delta^* & \cdots & -\delta^* & 0 & 1 \end{bmatrix} \qquad [16.3.8]$$

$$\underset{(p+2)\times(p+2)}{[\mathbf{G}']^{-1}} = \begin{bmatrix} 1 & 0 & \cdots & 0 & 0 & 0 \\ 0 & 1 & \cdots & 0 & 0 & 0 \\ \vdots & \vdots & \cdots & \vdots & \vdots & \vdots \\ 0 & 0 & \cdots & 1 & 0 & 0 \\ \alpha^* - \delta^* & \alpha^* - 2\delta^* & \cdots & \alpha^* - p\delta^* & 1 & 0 \\ \delta^* & \delta^* & \cdots & \delta^* & 0 & 1 \end{bmatrix}$$

$$\mathbf{x}_t^* \equiv \mathbf{G}\mathbf{x}_t = \begin{bmatrix} y_{t-1}^* \\ y_{t-2}^* \\ \vdots \\ y_{t-p}^* \\ 1 \\ t \end{bmatrix} \qquad [16.3.9]$$

$$\boldsymbol{\beta}^* \equiv [\mathbf{G}']^{-1}\boldsymbol{\beta} = \begin{bmatrix} \phi_1^* \\ \phi_2^* \\ \vdots \\ \phi_p^* \\ \alpha^* \\ \delta^* \end{bmatrix} \qquad [16.3.10]$$

The system of [16.3.7] is just an algebraically equivalent representation of the regression model [16.3.5]. Notice that the estimate of $\boldsymbol{\beta}^*$ based on an *OLS* regression of $y_t$ on $\mathbf{x}_t^*$ is given by

$$\begin{aligned} \mathbf{b}^* &= \left[\sum_{t=1}^T \mathbf{x}_t^*[\mathbf{x}_t^*]'\right]^{-1}\left[\sum_{t=1}^T \mathbf{x}_t^* y_t\right] \\ &= \left[\mathbf{G}\left(\sum_{t=1}^T \mathbf{x}_t\mathbf{x}_t'\right)\mathbf{G}'\right]^{-1}\mathbf{G}\left(\sum_{t=1}^T \mathbf{x}_t y_t\right) \\ &= [\mathbf{G}']^{-1}\left(\sum_{t=1}^T \mathbf{x}_t\mathbf{x}_t'\right)^{-1}\mathbf{G}^{-1}\mathbf{G}\left(\sum_{t=1}^T \mathbf{x}_t y_t\right) \\ &= [\mathbf{G}']^{-1}\left(\sum_{t=1}^T \mathbf{x}_t\mathbf{x}_t'\right)^{-1}\left(\sum_{t=1}^T \mathbf{x}_t y_t\right) \\ &= [\mathbf{G}']^{-1}\mathbf{b}, \end{aligned} \qquad [16.3.11]$$

where $\mathbf{b}$ denotes the estimated coefficient vector from an *OLS* regression of $y_t$ on $\mathbf{x}_t$. Thus, the coefficient estimate for the transformed regression ($\mathbf{b}^*$) is a simple linear transformation of the coefficient estimate for the original system ($\mathbf{b}$). The fitted value for date $t$ associated with the transformed regression is

$$[\mathbf{x}_t^*]'\mathbf{b}^* = [\mathbf{G}\mathbf{x}_t]'[\mathbf{G}']^{-1}\mathbf{b} = \mathbf{x}_t'\mathbf{b}.$$

Thus, the fitted values for the transformed regression are numerically identical to the fitted values from the original regression.

Of course, given data only on $\{y_t\}$, we could not actually estimate the transformed regression by *OLS*, because construction of $\mathbf{x}_t^*$ from $\mathbf{x}_t$ requires knowledge of the true values of the parameters $\alpha$ and $\delta$. It is nevertheless helpful to summarize the properties of hypothetical *OLS* estimation of [16.3.7], because [16.3.7] is easier to analyze than [16.3.5]. Moreover, once we find the asymptotic distribution of $\mathbf{b}^*$, the asymptotic distribution of $\mathbf{b}$ can be inferred by inverting [16.3.11]:

$$\mathbf{b} = \mathbf{G}'\mathbf{b}^*. \qquad [16.3.12]$$

## *The Asymptotic Distribution of* OLS *Estimates for the Transformed Regression*

Appendix 16.A to this chapter demonstrates that

$$\mathbf{Y}_T(\mathbf{b}_T^* - \boldsymbol{\beta}^*) \xrightarrow{L} N(\mathbf{0}, \sigma^2[\mathbf{Q}^*]^{-1}), \qquad [16.3.13]$$

where

$$\underset{(p+2)\times(p+2)}{\mathbf{Y}_T} = \begin{bmatrix} \sqrt{T} & 0 & 0 & \cdots & 0 & 0 & 0 \\ 0 & \sqrt{T} & 0 & \cdots & 0 & 0 & 0 \\ \vdots & \vdots & \vdots & \cdots & \vdots & \vdots & \vdots \\ 0 & 0 & 0 & \cdots & \sqrt{T} & 0 & 0 \\ 0 & 0 & 0 & \cdots & 0 & \sqrt{T} & 0 \\ 0 & 0 & 0 & \cdots & 0 & 0 & T^{3/2} \end{bmatrix} \qquad [16.3.14]$$

$$\underset{(p+2)\times(p+2)}{\mathbf{Q}^*} = \begin{bmatrix} \gamma_0^* & \gamma_1^* & \gamma_2^* & \cdots & \gamma_{p-1}^* & 0 & 0 \\ \gamma_1^* & \gamma_0^* & \gamma_1^* & \cdots & \gamma_{p-2}^* & 0 & 0 \\ \vdots & \vdots & \vdots & \cdots & \vdots & \vdots & \vdots \\ \gamma_{p-1}^* & \gamma_{p-2}^* & \gamma_{p-3}^* & \cdots & \gamma_0^* & 0 & 0 \\ 0 & 0 & 0 & \cdots & 0 & 1 & \frac{1}{2} \\ 0 & 0 & 0 & \cdots & 0 & \frac{1}{2} & \frac{1}{3} \end{bmatrix} \qquad [16.3.15]$$

for $\gamma_j^* \equiv E(y_t^* y_{t-j}^*)$. In other words, the *OLS* estimate $\mathbf{b}^*$ is asymptotically Gaussian, with the coefficient on the time trend ($\hat{\delta}^*$) converging at rate $T^{3/2}$ and all other coefficients converging at rate $\sqrt{T}$. The earlier result [16.1.26] is a special case of [16.3.13] with $p = 0$.

## *The Asymptotic Distribution of* OLS *Estimates for the Original Regression*

What does this result imply about the asymptotic distribution of $\mathbf{b}$, the estimated coefficient vector for the *OLS* regression that is actually estimated? Writing out [16.3.12] explicitly using [16.3.8], we have

$$\begin{bmatrix} \hat{\phi}_1 \\ \hat{\phi}_2 \\ \vdots \\ \hat{\phi}_p \\ \hat{\alpha} \\ \hat{\delta} \end{bmatrix} = \begin{bmatrix} 1 & 0 & \cdots & 0 & 0 & 0 \\ 0 & 1 & \cdots & 0 & 0 & 0 \\ \vdots & \vdots & \cdots & \vdots & \vdots & \vdots \\ 0 & 0 & \cdots & 1 & 0 & 0 \\ -\alpha^* + \delta^* & -\alpha^* + 2\delta^* & \cdots & -\alpha^* + p\delta^* & 1 & 0 \\ -\delta^* & -\delta^* & \cdots & -\delta^* & 0 & 1 \end{bmatrix} \begin{bmatrix} \hat{\phi}_1^* \\ \hat{\phi}_2^* \\ \vdots \\ \hat{\phi}_p^* \\ \hat{\alpha}^* \\ \hat{\delta}^* \end{bmatrix}. \quad [16.3.16]$$

The $OLS$ estimates $\hat{\phi}_j$ of the untransformed regression are identical to the corresponding coefficients of the transformed regression $\hat{\phi}_j^*$, so the asymptotic distribution of $\hat{\phi}_j$ is given immediately by [16.3.13]. The estimate $\hat{\alpha}_T$ is a linear combination of variables that converge to a Gaussian distribution at rate $\sqrt{T}$, and so $\hat{\alpha}_T$ behaves the same way. Specifically, $\hat{\alpha}_T = \mathbf{g}'_\alpha \mathbf{b}_T^*$, where

$$\mathbf{g}'_\alpha \equiv [-\alpha^* + \delta^* \quad -\alpha^* + 2\delta^* \quad \cdots \quad -\alpha^* + p\delta^* \quad 1 \quad 0],$$

and so, from [16.3.13],

$$\sqrt{T}(\hat{\alpha}_T - \alpha) \xrightarrow{L} N(0, \sigma^2 \mathbf{g}'_\alpha [\mathbf{Q}^*]^{-1} \mathbf{g}_\alpha). \quad [16.3.17]$$

Finally, the estimate $\hat{\delta}_T$ is a linear combination of variables converging at different rates:

$$\hat{\delta}_T = \mathbf{g}'_\delta \mathbf{b}_T^* + \hat{\delta}_T^*,$$

where

$$\mathbf{g}'_\delta \equiv [-\delta^* \quad -\delta^* \quad \cdots \quad -\delta^* \quad 0 \quad 0].$$

Its asymptotic distribution is governed by the variables with the slowest rate of convergence:

$$\begin{aligned} \sqrt{T}(\hat{\delta}_T - \delta) &= \sqrt{T}(\hat{\delta}_T^* + \mathbf{g}'_\delta \mathbf{b}_T^* - \delta^* - \mathbf{g}'_\delta \boldsymbol{\beta}^*) \\ &\xrightarrow{p} \sqrt{T}(\delta^* + \mathbf{g}'_\delta \mathbf{b}_T^* - \delta^* - \mathbf{g}'_\delta \boldsymbol{\beta}^*) \\ &= \mathbf{g}'_\delta \sqrt{T}(\mathbf{b}_T^* - \boldsymbol{\beta}^*) \\ &\xrightarrow{L} N(0, \sigma^2 \mathbf{g}'_\delta [\mathbf{Q}^*]^{-1} \mathbf{g}_\delta). \end{aligned}$$

Thus, each of the elements of $\mathbf{b}_T$ individually is asymptotically Gaussian and $O_p(T^{-1/2})$. The asymptotic distribution of the full vector $\sqrt{T}(\mathbf{b}_T - \boldsymbol{\beta})$ is multivariate Gaussian, though with a singular variance-covariance matrix. Specifically, the particular linear combination of the elements of $\mathbf{b}_T$ that recovers $\hat{\delta}_T^*$, the time trend coefficient of the hypothetical regression,

$$\hat{\delta}_T^* = -\mathbf{g}'_\delta \mathbf{b}_T^* + \hat{\delta}_T = \delta^* \hat{\phi}_{1,T} + \delta^* \hat{\phi}_{2,T} + \cdots + \delta^* \hat{\phi}_{p,T} + \hat{\delta}_T,$$

converges to a point mass around $\delta^*$ even when scaled by $\sqrt{T}$:

$$\sqrt{T}(\hat{\delta}_T^* - \delta^*) \xrightarrow{p} 0.$$

However, [16.3.13] establishes that

$$T^{3/2}(\hat{\delta}_T^* - \delta^*) \xrightarrow{L} N\big(0, \sigma^2 (q^*)^{p+2,p+2}\big)$$

for $(q^*)^{p+2,p+2}$ the bottom right element of $[\mathbf{Q}^*]^{-1}$.

## *Hypothesis Tests*

The preceding analysis described the asymptotic distribution of $\mathbf{b}$ in terms of the properties of the transformed regression estimates $\mathbf{b}^*$. This might seem to imply that knowledge of the transformation matrix $\mathbf{G}$ in [16.3.8] is necessary in order to conduct hypothesis tests. Fortunately, this is not the case. The results of Section 16.2 turn out to apply equally well to the general model [16.3.1]—the usual $t$ and $F$ tests about $\boldsymbol{\beta}$ calculated in the usual way on the untransformed system are all asymptotically valid.

Consider the following null hypothesis about the parameters of the untransformed system:

$$H_0\colon \mathbf{R}\boldsymbol{\beta} = \mathbf{r}. \tag{16.3.18}$$

Here $\mathbf{R}$ is a known $[m \times (p + 2)]$ matrix, $\mathbf{r}$ is a known $(m \times 1)$ vector, and $m$ is the number of restrictions. The Wald form of the $OLS$ $\chi^2$ test of $H_0$ (expression [8.2.23]) is

$$\chi_T^2 = (\mathbf{R}\mathbf{b}_T - \mathbf{r})'\left[s_T^2\mathbf{R}\left(\sum_{t=1}^{T} \mathbf{x}_t\mathbf{x}_t'\right)^{-1}\mathbf{R}'\right]^{-1}(\mathbf{R}\mathbf{b}_T - \mathbf{r}). \tag{16.3.19}$$

Here $\mathbf{b}_T$ is the $OLS$ estimate of $\boldsymbol{\beta}$ based on observation of $\{y_{-p+1}, y_{-p+2}, \ldots, y_0, y_1, \ldots, y_T\}$ and $s_T^2 = [1/(T - p - 2)]\,\Sigma_{t=1}^{T}(y_t - \mathbf{x}_t'\mathbf{b}_T)^2$.

Under the null hypothesis [16.3.18], expression [16.3.19] can be rewritten

$$\begin{aligned}\chi_T^2 &= [\mathbf{R}(\mathbf{b}_T - \boldsymbol{\beta})]'\left[s_T^2\mathbf{R}\left(\sum_{t=1}^{T} \mathbf{x}_t\mathbf{x}_t'\right)^{-1}\mathbf{R}'\right]^{-1}[\mathbf{R}(\mathbf{b}_T - \boldsymbol{\beta})]\\ &= [\mathbf{R}\mathbf{G}'(\mathbf{G}')^{-1}(\mathbf{b}_T - \boldsymbol{\beta})]'\\ &\quad\times\left[s_T^2\mathbf{R}\mathbf{G}'(\mathbf{G}')^{-1}\left(\sum_{t=1}^{T} \mathbf{x}_t\mathbf{x}_t'\right)^{-1}(\mathbf{G})^{-1}\mathbf{G}\mathbf{R}'\right]^{-1}[\mathbf{R}\mathbf{G}'(\mathbf{G}')^{-1}(\mathbf{b}_T - \boldsymbol{\beta})].\end{aligned} \tag{16.3.20}$$

Notice that

$$(\mathbf{G}')^{-1}\left(\sum_{t=1}^{T} \mathbf{x}_t\mathbf{x}_t'\right)^{-1}(\mathbf{G})^{-1} = \left[\mathbf{G}\left(\sum_{t=1}^{T} \mathbf{x}_t\mathbf{x}_t'\right)\mathbf{G}'\right]^{-1} = \left(\sum_{t=1}^{T} \mathbf{x}_t^*[\mathbf{x}_t^*]'\right)^{-1}$$

for $\mathbf{x}_t^*$ given by [16.3.9]. Similarly, from [16.3.10] and [16.3.11],

$$(\mathbf{b}_T^* - \boldsymbol{\beta}^*) = (\mathbf{G}')^{-1}(\mathbf{b}_T - \boldsymbol{\beta}).$$

Defining

$$\mathbf{R}^* \equiv \mathbf{R}\mathbf{G}',$$

expression [16.3.20] can be written

$$\begin{aligned}\chi_T^2 &= [\mathbf{R}^*(\mathbf{b}_T^* - \boldsymbol{\beta}^*)]'\left[s_T^2\mathbf{R}^*\left(\sum_{t=1}^{T} \mathbf{x}_t^*[\mathbf{x}_t^*]'\right)^{-1}[\mathbf{R}^*]'\right]^{-1}\\ &\quad\times[\mathbf{R}^*(\mathbf{b}_T^* - \boldsymbol{\beta}^*)].\end{aligned} \tag{16.3.21}$$

Expression [16.3.21] will be recognized as the $\chi^2$ test that would be calculated if we had estimated the transformed system and wanted to test the hypothesis that $\mathbf{R}^*\boldsymbol{\beta}^* = \mathbf{r}$ (recall that the fitted values for the transformed and untransformed regressions are identical, so that $s_T^2$ will be the same value for either representation). Observe that the transformed regression does not actually have to be estimated in order to calculate this statistic, since [16.3.21] is numerically identical to the $\chi^2$ statistic [16.3.20] that is calculated from the untransformed system in the usual way. Nevertheless, expression [16.3.21] gives us another way of thinking about the distribution of the statistic as actually calculated in [16.3.20].

Expression [16.3.21] can be further rewritten as

$$\begin{aligned}\chi_T^2 &= [\mathbf{R}^*\mathbf{Y}_T^{-1}\mathbf{Y}_T(\mathbf{b}_T^* - \boldsymbol{\beta}^*)]' \\ &\times \left[s_T^2\mathbf{R}^*\mathbf{Y}_T^{-1}\mathbf{Y}_T\left(\sum_{t=1}^{T}\mathbf{x}_t^*[\mathbf{x}_t^*]'\right)^{-1}\mathbf{Y}_T\mathbf{Y}_T^{-1}[\mathbf{R}^*]'\right]^{-1} \\ &\times [\mathbf{R}^*\mathbf{Y}_T^{-1}\mathbf{Y}_T(\mathbf{b}_T^* - \boldsymbol{\beta}^*)]\end{aligned} \qquad [16.3.22]$$

for $\mathbf{Y}_T$ the matrix in [16.3.14]. Recall the insight from Section 16.2 that hypothesis tests involving coefficients with different rates of convergence will be dominated by the variables with the slowest rate of convergence. This means that some of the elements of $\mathbf{R}^*$ may be irrelevant asymptotically, so that [16.3.22] has the same asymptotic distribution as a simpler expression. To describe this expression, consider two possibilities.

### *Case 1. Each of the* m *Hypotheses Represented by* $\mathbf{R}^*\boldsymbol{\beta}^* = \mathbf{r}$ *Involves a Parameter that Converges at Rate* $\sqrt{T}$

Of course, we could trivially rewrite any system of restrictions so as to involve $O_p(T^{-1/2})$ parameters in every equation. For example, the null hypothesis

$$H_0\colon \phi_2^* = 0, \qquad \delta^* = 0 \qquad [16.3.23]$$

could be rewritten as

$$H_0\colon \phi_2^* = 0, \qquad \delta^* = \phi_2^*, \qquad [16.3.24]$$

which seems to include $\phi_2^*$ in each restriction. For purposes of *implementing* a test of $H_0$, it does not matter which representation of $H_0$ is used, since either will produce the identical value for the test statistic.[8] For purposes of *analyzing the properties* of the test, we distinguish a hypothesis such as [16.3.23] from a hypothesis involving only $\phi_2^*$ and $\phi_3^*$. For this distinction to be meaningful, we will assume that $H_0$ would be written in the form of [16.3.23] rather than [16.3.24].

[8]More generally, let $\mathbf{H}$ be any nonsingular $(m \times m)$ matrix. Then the null hypothesis $\mathbf{R}\boldsymbol{\beta} = \mathbf{r}$ can equivalently be written as $\dot{\mathbf{R}}\boldsymbol{\beta} = \dot{\mathbf{r}}$, where $\dot{\mathbf{R}} \equiv \mathbf{HR}$ and $\dot{\mathbf{r}} \equiv \mathbf{Hr}$. The $\chi^2$ statistic constructed from the second parameterization is

$$\begin{aligned}\chi^2 &= (\dot{\mathbf{R}}\mathbf{b} - \dot{\mathbf{r}})'\left[s_T^2\dot{\mathbf{R}}\left(\sum_{t=1}^{T}\mathbf{x}_t\mathbf{x}_t'\right)^{-1}\dot{\mathbf{R}}'\right]^{-1}(\dot{\mathbf{R}}\mathbf{b} - \dot{\mathbf{r}}) \\ &= (\mathbf{Rb} - \mathbf{r})'\mathbf{H}'[\mathbf{H}']^{-1}\left[s_T^2\mathbf{R}\left(\sum_{t=1}^{T}\mathbf{x}_t\mathbf{x}_t'\right)^{-1}\mathbf{R}'\right]^{-1}\mathbf{H}^{-1}\mathbf{H}(\mathbf{Rb} - \mathbf{r}) \\ &= (\mathbf{Rb} - \mathbf{r})'\left[s_T^2\mathbf{R}\left(\sum_{t=1}^{T}\mathbf{x}_t\mathbf{x}_t'\right)^{-1}\mathbf{R}'\right]^{-1}(\mathbf{Rb} - \mathbf{r}),\end{aligned}$$

which is identical to the $\chi^2$ statistic constructed from the first parameterization. The representation [16.3.24] is an example of such a transformation of [16.3.23], with

$$\mathbf{H} = \begin{bmatrix} 1 & 0 \\ -1 & 1 \end{bmatrix}.$$

In general terms, this means that $\mathbf{R}^*$ is "upper triangular."[9] "Case 1" describes the situation in which the first $p + 1$ elements of the last row of $\mathbf{R}^*$ are not all zero.

For case 1, even though some of the hypotheses may involve $\hat{\delta}_T^*$, a test of the null hypothesis will be asymptotically equivalent to a test that treated $\delta^*$ as if known with certainty. This is a consequence of $\hat{\delta}_T^*$ being superconsistent. To develop this result rigorously, notice that

$$\mathbf{R}^*\mathbf{Y}_T^{-1} = \begin{bmatrix} r_{11}^*/\sqrt{T} & r_{12}^*/\sqrt{T} & \cdots & r_{1,p+1}^*/\sqrt{T} & r_{1,p+2}^*/T^{3/2} \\ r_{21}^*/\sqrt{T} & r_{22}^*/\sqrt{T} & \cdots & r_{2,p+1}^*/\sqrt{T} & r_{2,p+2}^*/T^{3/2} \\ \vdots & \vdots & \cdots & \vdots & \vdots \\ r_{m1}^*/\sqrt{T} & r_{m2}^*/\sqrt{T} & \cdots & r_{m,p+1}^*/\sqrt{T} & r_{m,p+2}^*/T^{3/2} \end{bmatrix},$$

and define

$$\underset{(m \times m)}{\tilde{\mathbf{Y}}_T} \equiv \sqrt{T}\mathbf{I}_m$$

$$\tilde{\mathbf{R}}_T^* \equiv \begin{bmatrix} r_{11}^* & r_{12}^* & \cdots & r_{1,p+1}^* & r_{1,p+2}^*/T \\ r_{21}^* & r_{22}^* & \cdots & r_{2,p+1}^* & r_{2,p+2}^*/T \\ \vdots & \vdots & \cdots & \vdots & \vdots \\ r_{m1}^* & r_{m2}^* & \cdots & r_{m,p+1}^* & r_{m,p+2}^*/T \end{bmatrix}.$$

These matrices were chosen so that

$$\mathbf{R}^*\mathbf{Y}_T^{-1} = \tilde{\mathbf{Y}}_T^{-1}\tilde{\mathbf{R}}_T^*. \qquad [16.3.25]$$

The matrix $\tilde{\mathbf{R}}_T^*$ has the further property that

$$\tilde{\mathbf{R}}_T^* \to \tilde{\mathbf{R}}^*, \qquad [16.3.26]$$

where $\tilde{\mathbf{R}}^*$ involves only those restrictions that affect the asymptotic distribution:

$$\tilde{\mathbf{R}}^* = \begin{bmatrix} r_{11}^* & r_{12}^* & \cdots & r_{1,p+1}^* & 0 \\ r_{21}^* & r_{22}^* & \cdots & r_{2,p+1}^* & 0 \\ \vdots & \vdots & \cdots & \vdots & \vdots \\ r_{m1}^* & r_{m2}^* & \cdots & r_{m,p+1}^* & 0 \end{bmatrix}.$$

[9] "Upper triangular" means that if the set of restrictions in $H_0$ involves parameters $\beta_{i_1}^*, \beta_{i_2}^*, \ldots, \beta_{i_n}^*$ with $i_1 < i_2 < \cdots < i_n$, then elements of $\mathbf{R}^*$ in rows 2 through $m$ and columns 1 through $i_1$ are all zero. This is simply a normalization—any hypothesis $\mathbf{R}^*\boldsymbol{\beta}^* = \mathbf{r}$ can be written in such a form by selecting a restriction involving $\beta_{i_1}^*$ to be the first row of $\mathbf{R}^*$ and then multiplying the first row of this system of equations by a suitable constant and subtracting it from each of the following rows. If the system of restrictions represented by rows 2 through $m$ of the resulting matrix involves parameters $\beta_{j_1}^*, \beta_{j_2}^*, \ldots, \beta_{j_l}^*$ with $j_1 < j_2 < \cdots < j_l$, then it is assumed that the elements in rows 3 through $m$ and columns 1 through $j_1$ are all zero. An example of an upper triangular system is

$$\mathbf{R}^* = \begin{bmatrix} 0 & r_{1,i_1}^* & r_{1,i_2}^* & 0 & \cdots & 0 & r_{1,i_n}^* \\ 0 & 0 & 0 & r_{2,j_1}^* & \cdots & r_{2,j_l}^* & 0 \\ \vdots & \vdots & \vdots & \vdots & \cdots & \vdots & \vdots \\ 0 & 0 & 0 & 0 & \cdots & r_{m,k_z-1}^* & r_{m,k_z}^* \end{bmatrix}.$$

Substituting [16.3.25] into [16.3.22],

$$\chi_T^2 = [\tilde{\mathbf{Y}}_T^{-1}\tilde{\mathbf{R}}_T^*\mathbf{Y}_T(\mathbf{b}_T^* - \boldsymbol{\beta}^*)]'$$

$$\times \left[s_T^2\tilde{\mathbf{Y}}_T^{-1}\tilde{\mathbf{R}}_T^*\mathbf{Y}_T\left(\sum_{t=1}^T \mathbf{x}_t^*[\mathbf{x}_t^*]'\right)^{-1}\mathbf{Y}_T[\tilde{\mathbf{Y}}_T^{-1}\tilde{\mathbf{R}}_T^*]'\right]^{-1}[\tilde{\mathbf{Y}}_T^{-1}\tilde{\mathbf{R}}_T^*\mathbf{Y}_T(\mathbf{b}_T^* - \boldsymbol{\beta}^*)]$$

$$= [\tilde{\mathbf{R}}_T^*\mathbf{Y}_T(\mathbf{b}_T^* - \boldsymbol{\beta}^*)]'\tilde{\mathbf{Y}}_T^{-1}$$

$$\times \tilde{\mathbf{Y}}_T\left[s_T^2\tilde{\mathbf{R}}_T^*\mathbf{Y}_T\left(\sum_{t=1}^T \mathbf{x}_t^*[\mathbf{x}_t^*]'\right)^{-1}\mathbf{Y}_T[\tilde{\mathbf{R}}_T^*]'\right]^{-1}\tilde{\mathbf{Y}}_T\tilde{\mathbf{Y}}_T^{-1}[\tilde{\mathbf{R}}_T^*\mathbf{Y}_T(\mathbf{b}_T^* - \boldsymbol{\beta}^*)]$$

$$= [\tilde{\mathbf{R}}_T^*\mathbf{Y}_T(\mathbf{b}_T^* - \boldsymbol{\beta}^*)]'$$

$$\times \left[s_T^2\tilde{\mathbf{R}}_T^*\mathbf{Y}_T\left(\sum_{t=1}^T \mathbf{x}_t^*[\mathbf{x}_t^*]'\right)^{-1}\mathbf{Y}_T[\tilde{\mathbf{R}}_T^*]'\right]^{-1}[\tilde{\mathbf{R}}_T^*\mathbf{Y}_T(\mathbf{b}_T^* - \boldsymbol{\beta}^*)]$$

$$\xrightarrow{p} [\tilde{\mathbf{R}}^*\mathbf{Y}_T(\mathbf{b}_T^* - \boldsymbol{\beta}^*)]'[\sigma^2\tilde{\mathbf{R}}^*[\mathbf{Q}^*]^{-1}[\tilde{\mathbf{R}}^*]']^{-1}[\tilde{\mathbf{R}}^*\mathbf{Y}_T(\mathbf{b}_T^* - \boldsymbol{\beta}^*)] \qquad [16.3.27]$$

by virtue of [16.3.26] and [16.A.4].

Now [16.3.13] implies that

$$\tilde{\mathbf{R}}^*\mathbf{Y}_T(\mathbf{b}_T^* - \boldsymbol{\beta}^*) \xrightarrow{L} N(\mathbf{0}, \tilde{\mathbf{R}}^*\sigma^2[\mathbf{Q}^*]^{-1}[\tilde{\mathbf{R}}^*]'),$$

and so [16.3.27] is a quadratic form in an asymptotically Gaussian variable of the kind covered in Proposition 8.1. It is therefore asymptotically $\chi^2(m)$. Since [16.3.27] is numerically identical to [16.3.19], the Wald form of the *OLS* $\chi^2$ test, calculated in the usual way from the untransformed regression [16.3.1], has the usual $\chi^2(m)$ distribution.

### *Case 2. One of the Hypotheses Involves Only the Time Trend Parameter* $\delta^*$

Again assuming for purposes of discussion that $\mathbf{R}^*$ is upper triangular, for case 2 the hypothesis about $\delta^*$ will be the sole entry in the $m$th row of $\mathbf{R}^*$:

$$\mathbf{R}^* = \begin{bmatrix} r_{11}^* & r_{12}^* & \cdots & r_{1,p+1}^* & r_{1,p+2}^* \\ r_{21}^* & r_{22}^* & \cdots & r_{2,p+1}^* & r_{2,p+2}^* \\ \vdots & \vdots & \cdots & \vdots & \vdots \\ r_{m-1,1}^* & r_{m-1,2}^* & \cdots & r_{m-1,p+1}^* & r_{m-1,p+2}^* \\ 0 & 0 & \cdots & 0 & r_{m,p+2}^* \end{bmatrix}.$$

For this case, define

$$\underset{(m\times m)}{\tilde{\mathbf{Y}}_T} \equiv \begin{bmatrix} \sqrt{T} & 0 & \cdots & 0 & 0 \\ 0 & \sqrt{T} & \cdots & 0 & 0 \\ \vdots & \vdots & \cdots & \vdots & \vdots \\ 0 & 0 & \cdots & \sqrt{T} & 0 \\ 0 & 0 & \cdots & 0 & T^{3/2} \end{bmatrix}$$

and

$$\tilde{\mathbf{R}}_T^* \equiv \begin{bmatrix} r_{11}^* & r_{12}^* & \cdots & r_{1,p+1}^* & r_{1,p+2}^*/T \\ r_{21}^* & r_{22}^* & \cdots & r_{2,p+1}^* & r_{2,p+2}^*/T \\ \vdots & \vdots & \cdots & \vdots & \vdots \\ r_{m-1,1}^* & r_{m-1,2}^* & \cdots & r_{m-1,p+1}^* & r_{m-1,p+2}^*/T \\ 0 & 0 & \cdots & 0 & r_{m,p+2}^* \end{bmatrix}.$$

Notice that these matrices again satisfy [16.3.25] and [16.3.26] with

$$\tilde{\mathbf{R}}^* = \begin{bmatrix} r_{11}^* & r_{12}^* & \cdots & r_{1,p+1}^* & 0 \\ r_{21}^* & r_{22}^* & \cdots & r_{2,p+1}^* & 0 \\ \vdots & \vdots & \cdots & \vdots & \vdots \\ r_{m-1,1}^* & r_{m-1,2}^* & \cdots & r_{m-1,p+1}^* & 0 \\ 0 & 0 & \cdots & 0 & r_{m,p+2}^* \end{bmatrix}.$$

The analysis of [16.3.27] thus goes through for this case as well with no change.

### *Summary*

Any standard *OLS* $\chi^2$ test of the null hypothesis $\mathbf{R}\boldsymbol{\beta} = \mathbf{r}$ for the regression model [16.3.1] can be calculated and interpreted in the usual way. The test is asymptotically valid for any hypothesis about any subset of the parameters in $\boldsymbol{\beta}$. The elements of $\mathbf{R}$ do not have to be ordered or expressed in any particular form for this to be true.

## APPENDIX 16.A. *Derivation of Selected Equations for Chapter 16*

■ **Derivation of [16.3.13].** As in [16.1.6],

$$\mathbf{b}_T^* - \boldsymbol{\beta}^* = \left[\sum_{t=1}^{T} \mathbf{x}_t^*[\mathbf{x}_t^*]'\right]^{-1}\left[\sum_{t=1}^{T} \mathbf{x}_t^*\varepsilon_t\right], \qquad [16.A.1]$$

since the population residuals $\varepsilon_t$ are identical for the transformed and untransformed representations. As in [16.1.18], premultiply by $\mathbf{Y}_T$ to write

$$\mathbf{Y}_T(\mathbf{b}_T^* - \boldsymbol{\beta}^*) = \left\{\mathbf{Y}_T^{-1}\sum_{t=1}^{T} \mathbf{x}_t^*[\mathbf{x}_t^*]'\mathbf{Y}_T^{-1}\right\}^{-1}\left\{\mathbf{Y}_T^{-1}\sum_{t=1}^{T}\mathbf{x}_t^*\varepsilon_t\right\}. \qquad [16.A.2]$$

From [16.3.9],

$$\sum_{t=1}^{T} \mathbf{x}_t^*[\mathbf{x}_t^*]' = \begin{bmatrix} \Sigma(y_{t-1}^*)^2 & \Sigma y_{t-1}^* y_{t-2}^* & \cdots & \Sigma y_{t-1}^* y_{t-p}^* & \Sigma y_{t-1}^* & \Sigma t y_{t-1}^* \\ \Sigma y_{t-2}^* y_{t-1}^* & \Sigma(y_{t-2}^*)^2 & \cdots & \Sigma y_{t-2}^* y_{t-p}^* & \Sigma y_{t-2}^* & \Sigma t y_{t-2}^* \\ \vdots & \vdots & \cdots & \vdots & \vdots & \vdots \\ \Sigma y_{t-p}^* y_{t-1}^* & \Sigma y_{t-p}^* y_{t-2}^* & \cdots & \Sigma(y_{t-p}^*)^2 & \Sigma y_{t-p}^* & \Sigma t y_{t-p}^* \\ \Sigma y_{t-1}^* & \Sigma y_{t-2}^* & \cdots & \Sigma y_{t-p}^* & \Sigma 1 & \Sigma t \\ \Sigma t y_{t-1}^* & \Sigma t y_{t-2}^* & \cdots & \Sigma t y_{t-p}^* & \Sigma t & \Sigma t^2 \end{bmatrix}$$

and

$$\mathbf{Y}_T^{-1}\sum_{t=1}^{T} \mathbf{x}_t^*[\mathbf{x}_t^*]'\mathbf{Y}_T^{-1}$$

$$= \begin{bmatrix} T^{-1}\Sigma(y_{t-1}^*)^2 & T^{-1}\Sigma y_{t-1}^* y_{t-2}^* & \cdots & T^{-1}\Sigma y_{t-1}^* y_{t-p}^* & T^{-1}\Sigma y_{t-1}^* & T^{-2}\Sigma t y_{t-1}^* \\ T^{-1}\Sigma y_{t-2}^* y_{t-1}^* & T^{-1}\Sigma(y_{t-2}^*)^2 & \cdots & T^{-1}\Sigma y_{t-2}^* y_{t-p}^* & T^{-1}\Sigma y_{t-2}^* & T^{-2}\Sigma t y_{t-2}^* \\ \vdots & \vdots & \cdots & \vdots & \vdots & \vdots \\ T^{-1}\Sigma y_{t-p}^* y_{t-1}^* & T^{-1}\Sigma y_{t-p}^* y_{t-2}^* & \cdots & T^{-1}\Sigma(y_{t-p}^*)^2 & T^{-1}\Sigma y_{t-p}^* & T^{-2}\Sigma t y_{t-p}^* \\ T^{-1}\Sigma y_{t-1}^* & T^{-1}\Sigma y_{t-2}^* & \cdots & T^{-1}\Sigma y_{t-p}^* & T^{-1}\cdot T & T^{-2}\cdot\Sigma t \\ T^{-2}\Sigma t y_{t-1}^* & T^{-2}\Sigma t y_{t-2}^* & \cdots & T^{-2}\Sigma t y_{t-p}^* & T^{-2}\cdot\Sigma t & T^{-3}\cdot\Sigma t^2 \end{bmatrix}.$$

[16.A.3]

For the first $p$ rows and columns, the row $i$, column $j$ element of this matrix is

$$T^{-1}\sum_{t=1}^{T} y_{t-i}^{*}y_{t-j}^{*}.$$

But $y_t^*$ follows a zero-mean stationary $AR(p)$ process satisfying the conditions of Exercise 7.7. Thus, these terms converge in probability to $\gamma_{|i-j|}^{*}$. The first $p$ elements of row $p + 1$ (or the first $p$ elements of column $p + 1$) are of the form

$$T^{-1}\sum_{t=1}^{T} y_{t-i}^{*},$$

which converge in probability to zero. The first $p$ elements of row $p + 2$ (or the first $p$ elements of column $p + 2$) are of the form

$$T^{-1}\sum_{t=1}^{T} (t/T)y_{t-i}^{*},$$

which can be shown to converge in probability to zero with a ready adaptation of the techniques in Chapter 7 (see Exercise 16.3). Finally, the $(2 \times 2)$ matrix in the bottom right corner of [16.A.3] converges to

$$\begin{bmatrix} 1 & \frac{1}{2} \\ \frac{1}{2} & \frac{1}{3} \end{bmatrix}.$$

Thus

$$\mathbf{Y}_T^{-1}\sum_{t=1}^{T} \mathbf{x}_t^{*}[\mathbf{x}_t^{*}]'\mathbf{Y}_T^{-1} \xrightarrow{p} \mathbf{Q}^{*} \qquad [16.A.4]$$

for $\mathbf{Q}^*$ the matrix in [16.3.15].

Turning next to the second term in [16.A.2],

$$\mathbf{Y}_T^{-1}\sum_{t=1}^{T} \mathbf{x}_t^{*}\varepsilon_t = \begin{bmatrix} T^{-1/2}\Sigma y_{t-1}^{*}\varepsilon_t \\ T^{-1/2}\Sigma y_{t-2}^{*}\varepsilon_t \\ \vdots \\ T^{-1/2}\Sigma y_{t-p}^{*}\varepsilon_t \\ T^{-1/2}\Sigma\varepsilon_t \\ T^{-1/2}\Sigma(t/T)\varepsilon_t \end{bmatrix} = T^{-1/2}\sum_{t=1}^{T} \boldsymbol{\xi}_t, \qquad [16.A.5]$$

where

$$\boldsymbol{\xi}_t \equiv \begin{bmatrix} y_{t-1}^{*}\varepsilon_t \\ y_{t-2}^{*}\varepsilon_t \\ \vdots \\ y_{t-p}^{*}\varepsilon_t \\ \varepsilon_t \\ (t/T)\varepsilon_t \end{bmatrix}.$$

But $\boldsymbol{\xi}_t$ is a martingale difference sequence with variance

$$E(\boldsymbol{\xi}_t\boldsymbol{\xi}_t') = \sigma^2\mathbf{Q}_t^{*},$$

where

$$\mathbf{Q}_t^{*} = \begin{bmatrix} \gamma_0^{*} & \gamma_1^{*} & \gamma_2^{*} & \cdots & \gamma_{p-1}^{*} & 0 & 0 \\ \gamma_1^{*} & \gamma_0^{*} & \gamma_1^{*} & \cdots & \gamma_{p-2}^{*} & 0 & 0 \\ \vdots & \vdots & \vdots & \cdots & \vdots & \vdots & \vdots \\ \gamma_{p-1}^{*} & \gamma_{p-2}^{*} & \gamma_{p-3}^{*} & \cdots & \gamma_0^{*} & 0 & 0 \\ 0 & 0 & 0 & \cdots & 0 & 1 & t/T \\ 0 & 0 & 0 & \cdots & 0 & t/T & t^2/T^2 \end{bmatrix}$$

and

$$(1/T)\sum_{t=1}^{T}\mathbf{Q}_t^* \rightarrow \mathbf{Q}^*.$$

Applying the arguments used in Exercise 8.3 and in [16.1.24], it can be shown that

$$\mathbf{Y}_T^{-1}\sum_{t=1}^{T}\mathbf{x}_t^*\varepsilon_t \xrightarrow{L} N(\mathbf{0}, \sigma^2\mathbf{Q}^*). \qquad [16.A.6]$$

It follows from [16.A.4], [16.A.6], and [16.A.2] that

$$\mathbf{Y}_T(\mathbf{b}_T^* - \boldsymbol{\beta}^*) \xrightarrow{L} N(\mathbf{0}, [\mathbf{Q}^*]^{-1}\sigma^2\mathbf{Q}^*[\mathbf{Q}^*]^{-1}) = N(\mathbf{0}, \sigma^2[\mathbf{Q}^*]^{-1}),$$

as claimed in [16.3.13]. ■

## Chapter 16 Exercises

16.1. Verify result [16.1.23].

16.2. Verify expression [16.1.27].

16.3. Let $y_t$ be covariance-stationary with mean zero and absolutely summable autocovariances:

$$\sum_{j=-\infty}^{\infty}|\gamma_j| < \infty$$

for $\gamma_j = E(y_t y_{t-j})$. Adapting the argument in expression [7.2.6], show that

$$T^{-1}\sum_{t=1}^{T}(t/T)y_t \xrightarrow{m.s.} 0.$$

## Chapter 16 References


Fuller, Wayne A. 1976. *Introduction to Statistical Time Series*. New York: Wiley.

Sims, Christopher A., James H. Stock, and Mark W. Watson. 1990. "Inference in Linear Time Series Models with Some Unit Roots." *Econometrica* 58:113–44.

# 17 Univariate Processes with Unit Roots

This chapter discusses statistical inference for univariate processes containing a unit root. Section 17.1 gives a brief explanation of why the asymptotic distributions and rates of convergence for the estimated coefficients of unit root processes differ from those for stationary processes. The asymptotic distributions for unit root processes can be described in terms of functionals on Brownian motion. The basic idea behind Brownian motion is introduced in Section 17.2. The technical tools used to establish that the asymptotic distributions of certain statistics involving unit root processes can be represented in terms of such functionals are developed in Section 17.3, though it is not necessary to master these tools in order to read Sections 17.4 through 17.9. Section 17.4 derives the asymptotic distribution of the estimated coefficient for a first-order autoregression when the true process is a random walk. This distribution turns out to depend on whether a constant or time trend is included in the estimated regression and whether the true random walk is characterized by nonzero drift.

Section 17.5 extends the results of Section 17.3 to cover unit root processes whose differences exhibit general serial correlation. These results can be used to develop two different classes of tests for unit roots. One approach, due to Phillips and Perron (1988), adjusts the statistics calculated from a simple first-order autoregression to account for serial correlation of the differenced data. The second approach, due to Dickey and Fuller (1979), adds lags to the autoregression. These approaches are reviewed in Sections 17.6 and 17.7, respectively. Section 17.7 further derives the properties of all of the estimated coefficients for a $p$th-order autoregression when one of the roots is unity.

Readers interested solely in how these results are applied in practice may want to begin with the summaries in Table 17.2 or Table 17.3 and with the empirical applications described in Examples 17.6 through 17.9.

## 17.1. *Introduction*

Consider *OLS* estimation of a Gaussian $AR(1)$ process,

$$y_t = \rho y_{t-1} + u_t, \qquad [17.1.1]$$

where $u_t \sim$ i.i.d. $N(0, \sigma^2)$, and $y_0 = 0$. The *OLS* estimate of $\rho$ is given by

$$\hat{\rho}_T = \frac{\sum_{t=1}^{T} y_{t-1}y_t}{\sum_{t=1}^{T} y_{t-1}^2}. \qquad [17.1.2]$$

We saw in Chapter 8 that if the true value of $\rho$ is less than 1 in absolute value, then

$$\sqrt{T}(\hat{\rho}_T - \rho) \xrightarrow{L} N(0, (1 - \rho^2)). \quad [17.1.3]$$

If [17.1.3] were also valid for the case when $\rho = 1$, it would seem to claim that $\sqrt{T}(\hat{\rho}_T - \rho)$ has zero variance, or that the distribution collapses to a point mass at zero:

$$\sqrt{T}(\hat{\rho}_T - 1) \xrightarrow{p} 0. \quad [17.1.4]$$

As we shall see shortly, [17.1.4] is indeed a valid statement for unit root processes, but it obviously is not very helpful for hypothesis tests. To obtain a nondegenerate asymptotic distribution for $\hat{\rho}_T$ in the unit root case, it turns out that we have to multiply $\hat{\rho}_T$ by $T$ rather than by $\sqrt{T}$. Thus, the unit root coefficient converges at a faster rate ($T$) than a coefficient for a stationary regression (which converges at $\sqrt{T}$), but at a slower rate than the coefficient on a time trend in the regressions analyzed in the previous chapter (which converged at $T^{3/2}$).

To get a better sense of why scaling by $T$ is necessary when the true value of $\rho$ is unity, recall that the difference between the estimate $\hat{\rho}_T$ and the true value can be expressed as in equation [8.2.3]:[1]

$$(\hat{\rho}_T - 1) = \frac{\sum_{t=1}^{T} y_{t-1}u_t}{\sum_{t=1}^{T} y_{t-1}^2}, \quad [17.1.5]$$

so that

$$T(\hat{\rho}_T - 1) = \frac{(1/T)\sum_{t=1}^{T} y_{t-1}u_t}{(1/T^2)\sum_{t=1}^{T} y_{t-1}^2}. \quad [17.1.6]$$

Consider first the numerator in [17.1.6]. When the true value of $\rho$ is unity, equation [17.1.1] describes a random walk with

$$y_t = u_t + u_{t-1} + \cdots + u_1, \quad [17.1.7]$$

since $y_0 = 0$. It follows from [17.1.7] that

$$y_t \sim N(0, \sigma^2 t). \quad [17.1.8]$$

Note further that for a random walk,

$$y_t^2 = (y_{t-1} + u_t)^2 = y_{t-1}^2 + 2y_{t-1}u_t + u_t^2,$$

implying that

$$y_{t-1}u_t = (1/2)\{y_t^2 - y_{t-1}^2 - u_t^2\}. \quad [17.1.9]$$

If [17.1.9] is summed over $t = 1, 2, \ldots, T$, the result is

$$\sum_{t=1}^{T} y_{t-1}u_t = (1/2)\{y_T^2 - y_0^2\} - (1/2)\sum_{t=1}^{T} u_t^2. \quad [17.1.10]$$

Recalling that $y_0 = 0$, equation [17.1.10] establishes that

$$(1/T)\sum_{t=1}^{T} y_{t-1}u_t = (1/2)\cdot(1/T)y_T^2 - (1/2)\cdot(1/T)\sum_{t=1}^{T} u_t^2, \quad [17.1.11]$$

[1]This discussion is based on Fuller (1976, p. 369).

and if each side of [17.1.11] is divided by $\sigma^2$, the result is

$$\left(\frac{1}{\sigma^2 T}\right) \sum_{t=1}^{T} y_{t-1}u_t = \left(\frac{1}{2}\right)\left(\frac{y_T}{\sigma\sqrt{T}}\right)^2 - \left(\frac{1}{2\sigma^2}\right)\left(\frac{1}{T}\right)\cdot \sum_{t=1}^{T} u_t^2. \qquad [17.1.12]$$

But [17.1.8] implies that $y_T/(\sigma\sqrt{T})$ is a $N(0, 1)$ variable, so that its square is $\chi^2(1)$:

$$[y_T/(\sigma\sqrt{T})]^2 \sim \chi^2(1). \qquad [17.1.13]$$

Also, $\Sigma_{t=1}^{T} u_t^2$ is the sum of $T$ i.i.d. random variables, each with mean $\sigma^2$, and so, by the law of large numbers,

$$(1/T)\cdot \sum_{t=1}^{T} u_t^2 \xrightarrow{p} \sigma^2. \qquad [17.1.14]$$

Using [17.1.13] and [17.1.14], it follows from [17.1.12] that

$$[1/(\sigma^2 T)] \sum_{t=1}^{T} y_{t-1}u_t \xrightarrow{L} (1/2)\cdot(X - 1), \qquad [17.1.15]$$

where $X \sim \chi^2(1)$.

Turning next to the denominator of [17.1.6], consider

$$\sum_{t=1}^{T} y_{t-1}^2. \qquad [17.1.16]$$

Recall from [17.1.8] that $y_{t-1} \sim N(0, \sigma^2(t-1))$, so $E(y_{t-1}^2) = \sigma^2(t-1)$. Consider the mean of [17.1.16],

$$E\left[\sum_{t=1}^{T} y_{t-1}^2\right] = \sigma^2 \sum_{t=1}^{T} (t - 1) = \sigma^2(T - 1)T/2.$$

In order to construct a random variable that could have a convergent distribution, the quantity in [17.1.16] will have to be divided by $T^2$, as was done in the denominator of [17.1.6].

To summarize, if the true process is a random walk, then the deviation of the *OLS* estimate from the true value $(\hat{\rho}_T - 1)$ must be multiplied by $T$ rather than $\sqrt{T}$ to obtain a variable with a useful asymptotic distribution. Moreover, this asymptotic distribution is not the usual Gaussian distribution but instead is a ratio involving a $\chi^2(1)$ variable in the numerator and a separate, nonstandard distribution in the denominator.

The asymptotic distribution of $T(\hat{\rho}_T - 1)$ will be fully characterized in Section 17.4. In preparation for this, the idea of Brownian motion is introduced in Section 17.2, followed by a discussion of the functional central limit theorem in Section 17.3.

## 17.2. *Brownian Motion*

Consider a random walk,

$$y_t = y_{t-1} + \varepsilon_t, \qquad [17.2.1]$$

in which the innovations are standard Normal variables:

$$\varepsilon_t \sim \text{i.i.d } N(0, 1).$$

If the process is started with $y_0 = 0$, then it follows as in [17.1.7] and [17.1.8] that

$$y_t = \varepsilon_1 + \varepsilon_2 + \cdots + \varepsilon_t$$
$$y_t \sim N(0, t).$$

Moreover, the change in the value of $y$ between dates $t$ and $s$,

$$y_s - y_t = \varepsilon_{t+1} + \varepsilon_{t+2} + \cdots + \varepsilon_s,$$

is itself $N(0, (s - t))$ and is independent of the change between dates $r$ and $q$ for any dates $t < s < r < q$.

Consider the change between $y_{t-1}$ and $y_t$. This innovation $\varepsilon_t$ was taken to be $N(0, 1)$. Suppose we view $\varepsilon_t$ as the sum of two independent Gaussian variables:

$$\varepsilon_t = e_{1t} + e_{2t},$$

with $e_{it} \sim$ i.i.d. $N(0, \frac{1}{2})$. We might then associate $e_{1t}$ with the change between $y_{t-1}$ and the value of $y$ at some interim point (say, $y_{t-(1/2)}$),

$$y_{t-(1/2)} - y_{t-1} = e_{1t}, \qquad [17.2.2]$$

and $e_{2t}$ with the change between $y_{t-(1/2)}$ and $y_t$:

$$y_t - y_{t-(1/2)} = e_{2t}. \qquad [17.2.3]$$

Sampled at integer dates $t = 1, 2, \ldots$, the process of [17.2.2] and [17.2.3] will have exactly the same properties as [17.2.1], since

$$y_t - y_{t-1} = e_{1t} + e_{2t} \sim \text{i.i.d. } N(0, 1).$$

In addition, the process of [17.2.2] and [17.2.3] is defined also at the noninteger dates $\{t + \frac{1}{2}\}_{t=0}^{\infty}$ and retains the property for both integer and noninteger dates that $y_s - y_t \sim N(0, s - t)$ with $y_s - y_t$ independent of the change over any other nonoverlapping interval.

By the same reasoning, we could imagine partitioning the change between $t - 1$ and $t$ into $N$ separate subperiods:

$$y_t - y_{t-1} = e_{1t} + e_{2t} + \cdots + e_{Nt},$$

with $e_{it} \sim$ i.i.d. $N(0, 1/N)$. The result would be a process with all the same properties as [17.2.1], defined at a finer and finer grid of dates as we increase $N$. The limit as $N \to \infty$ is a *continuous-time* process known as *standard Brownian motion*. The value of this process at date $t$ is denoted $W(t)$.[2] A continuous-time process is a random variable that takes on a value for any nonnegative real number $t$, as distinct from a discrete-time process, which is only defined at integer values of $t$. To emphasize the distinction, we will put the date in parentheses when describing the value of a continuous-time variable at date $t$ (as in $W(t)$) and use subscripts for a discrete-time variable (as in $y_t$). A discrete-time process was represented as a countable sequence of random variables, denoted $\{y_t\}_{t=1}^{\infty}$. A realization of a continuous-time process can be viewed as a stochastic function, denoted $W(\cdot)$, where $W\colon t \in [0, \infty) \to \mathbb{R}^1$.

A particular realization of Brownian motion turns out to be a continuous function of $t$. To see why it would be continuous, recall that the change between $t$ and $t + \Delta$ is distributed $N(0, \Delta)$. Such a change is essentially certain to be arbitrarily small as the interval $\Delta$ goes to zero.

***Definition:*** *Standard Brownian motion $W(\cdot)$ is a continuous-time stochastic process, associating each date $t \in [0, 1]$ with the scalar $W(t)$ such that:*

(*a*) $W(0) = 0$;

[2]Brownian motion is sometimes also referred to as a *Wiener process*.

(*b*) *For any dates* $0 \leq t_1 < t_2 < \cdots < t_k \leq 1$, *the changes* $[W(t_2) - W(t_1)]$, $[W(t_3) - W(t_2)], \ldots, [W(t_k) - W(t_{k-1})]$ *are independent multivariate Gaussian with* $[W(s) - W(t)] \sim N(0, s - t)$;

(*c*) *For any given realization,* $W(t)$ *is continuous in* $t$ *with probability 1.*

There are advantages to restricting the analysis to dates $t$ within a closed interval. All of the results in this text relate to the behavior of Brownian motion for dates within the unit interval ($t \in [0, 1]$), and in anticipation of this we have simply defined $W(\cdot)$ to be a function mapping $t \in [0, 1]$ into $\mathbb{R}^1$.

Other continuous-time processes can be generated from standard Brownian motion. For example, the process

$$Z(t) = \sigma \cdot W(t)$$

has independent increments and is distributed $N(0, \sigma^2 t)$ across realizations. Such a process is described as *Brownian motion with variance* $\sigma^2$. Thus, standard Brownian motion could also be described as Brownian motion with unit variance.

As another example,

$$Z(t) = [W(t)]^2 \qquad [17.2.4]$$

would be distributed as $t$ times a $\chi^2(1)$ variable across realizations.

Although $W(t)$ is continuous in $t$, it cannot be differentiated using standard calculus; the direction of change at $t$ is likely to be completely different from that at $t + \Delta$, no matter how small we make $\Delta$.[3]

## 17.3. *The Functional Central Limit Theorem*

One of the uses of Brownian motion is to permit more general statements of the central limit theorem than those in Chapter 7. Recall the simplest version of the central limit theorem: if $u_t \sim$ i.i.d. with mean zero and variance $\sigma^2$, then the sample mean $\bar{u}_T \equiv (1/T)\Sigma_{t=1}^{T} u_t$ satisfies

$$\sqrt{T}\bar{u}_T \xrightarrow{L} N(0, \sigma^2).$$

Consider now an estimator based on the following principle: When given a sample of size $T$, we calculate the mean of the first half of the sample and throw out the rest of the observations:

$$\bar{u}_{[T/2]^*} = (1/[T/2]^*) \sum_{t=1}^{[T/2]^*} u_t.$$

Here $[T/2]^*$ denotes the largest integer that is less than or equal to $T/2$; that is, $[T/2]^* = T/2$ for $T$ even and $[T/2]^* = (T - 1)/2$ for $T$ odd. This strange estimator would also satisfy the central limit theorem:

$$\sqrt{[T/2]^*}\,\bar{u}_{[T/2]^*} \xrightarrow[T\to\infty]{L} N(0, \sigma^2). \qquad [17.3.1]$$

Moreover, this estimator would be independent of an estimator that uses only the second half of the sample.

More generally, we can construct a variable $X_T(r)$ from the sample mean of

[3]For an introduction to differentiation and integration of Brownian motion, see Malliaris and Brock (1982, Chapter 2).

the first $r$th fraction of observations, $r \in [0, 1]$, defined by

$$X_T(r) \equiv (1/T) \sum_{t=1}^{[Tr]^*} u_t. \qquad [17.3.2]$$

For any given realization, $X_T(r)$ is a step function in $r$, with

$$X_T(r) = \begin{cases} 0 & \text{for } 0 \le r < 1/T \\ u_1/T & \text{for } 1/T \le r < 2/T \\ (u_1 + u_2)/T & \text{for } 2/T \le r < 3/T \\ \vdots & \\ (u_1 + u_2 + \cdots + u_T)/T & \text{for } r = 1. \end{cases} \qquad [17.3.3]$$

Then

$$\sqrt{T} \cdot X_T(r) = (1/\sqrt{T}) \sum_{t=1}^{[Tr]^*} u_t = (\sqrt{[Tr]^*}/\sqrt{T})(1/\sqrt{[Tr]^*}) \sum_{t=1}^{[Tr]^*} u_t. \qquad [17.3.4]$$

But

$$(1/\sqrt{[Tr]^*}) \sum_{t=1}^{[Tr]^*} u_t \xrightarrow{L} N(0, \sigma^2),$$

by the central limit theorem as in [17.3.1], while $(\sqrt{[Tr]^*}/\sqrt{T}) \rightarrow \sqrt{r}$. Hence, the asymptotic distribution of $\sqrt{T} \cdot X_T(r)$ in [17.3.4] is that of $\sqrt{r}$ times a $N(0, \sigma^2)$ random variable, or

$$\sqrt{T} \cdot X_T(r) \xrightarrow{L} N(0, r\sigma^2)$$

and

$$\sqrt{T} \cdot [X_T(r)/\sigma] \xrightarrow{L} N(0, r). \qquad [17.3.5]$$

If we were similarly to consider the behavior of a sample mean based on observations $[Tr_1]^*$ through $[Tr_2]^*$ for $r_2 > r_1$, we would conclude that this too is asymptotically Normal,

$$\sqrt{T} \cdot [X_T(r_2) - X_T(r_1)]/\sigma \xrightarrow{L} N(0, r_2 - r_1),$$

and is independent of the estimator in [17.3.5], provided that $r < r_1$. It thus should not be surprising that the sequence of stochastic functions $\{\sqrt{T} \cdot X_T(\cdot)/\sigma\}_{T=1}^{\infty}$ has an asymptotic probability law that is described by standard Brownian motion $W(\cdot)$:

$$\sqrt{T} \cdot X_T(\cdot)/\sigma \xrightarrow{L} W(\cdot). \qquad [17.3.6]$$

Note the difference between the claims in [17.3.5] and [17.3.6]. The expression $X_T(\cdot)$ denotes a random function while $X_T(r)$ denotes the value that function assumes at date $r$; thus, $X_T(\cdot)$ is a function, while $X_T(r)$ is a random variable.

Result [17.3.6] is known as the *functional central limit theorem*. The derivation here assumed that $u_t$ was i.i.d. A more general statement will be provided in Section 17.5.

Evaluated at $r = 1$, the function $X_T(r)$ in [17.3.2] is just the sample mean:

$$X_T(1) = (1/T) \sum_{t=1}^{T} u_t.$$

Thus, when the functions in [17.3.6] are evaluated at $r = 1$, the conventional central limit theorem [7.1.6] obtains as a special case of [17.3.6]:

$$\sqrt{T} X_T(1)/\sigma = [1/(\sigma\sqrt{T})] \sum_{t=1}^{T} u_t \xrightarrow{L} W(1) \sim N(0, 1). \qquad [17.3.7]$$

We earlier defined convergence in law for random variables, and now we need to extend the definition to cover random functions. Let $S(\cdot)$ represent a continuous-time stochastic process with $S(r)$ representing its value at some date $r$ for $r \in [0, 1]$. Suppose, further, that for any given realization, $S(\cdot)$ is a continuous function of $r$ with probability 1. For $\{S_T(\cdot)\}_{T=1}^{\infty}$ a sequence of such continuous functions, we say that $S_T(\cdot) \xrightarrow{L} S(\cdot)$ if all of the following hold:[4]

(a) For any finite collection of $k$ particular dates,

$$0 \leq r_1 < r_2 < \cdots < r_k \leq 1,$$

the sequence of $k$-dimensional random vectors $\{\mathbf{y}_T\}_{T=1}^{\infty}$ converges in distribution to the vector $\mathbf{y}$, where

$$\mathbf{y}_T \equiv \begin{bmatrix} S_T(r_1) \\ S_T(r_2) \\ \vdots \\ S_T(r_k) \end{bmatrix} \qquad \mathbf{y} \equiv \begin{bmatrix} S(r_1) \\ S(r_2) \\ \vdots \\ S(r_k) \end{bmatrix};$$

(b) For each $\varepsilon > 0$, the probability that $S_T(r_1)$ differs from $S_T(r_2)$ for any dates $r_1$ and $r_2$ within $\delta$ of each other goes to zero uniformly in $T$ as $\delta \to 0$;
(c) $P\{|S_T(0)| > \lambda\} \to 0$ uniformly in $T$ as $\lambda \to \infty$.

This definition applies to sequences of continuous functions, though the function in [17.3.2] is a discontinuous step function. Fortunately, the discontinuities occur at a countable set of points. Formally, $S_T(\cdot)$ can be replaced with a similar continuous function, interpolating between the steps (as in Hall and Heyde, 1980). Alternatively, the definition of convergence of random functions can be generalized to allow for discontinuities of the type in [17.3.2] (as in Chapter 3 of Billingsley, 1968).

It will also be helpful to extend the earlier definition of convergence in probability to sequences of random functions. Let $\{S_T(\cdot)\}_{T=1}^{\infty}$ and $\{V_T(\cdot)\}_{T=1}^{\infty}$ denote sequences of random continuous functions with $S_T$: $r \in [0, 1] \to \mathbb{R}^1$ and $V_T$: $r \in [0, 1] \to \mathbb{R}^1$. Let the scalar $Y_T$ represent the largest amount by which $S_T(r)$ differs from $V_T(r)$ for any $r$:

$$Y_T \equiv \sup_{r \in [0,1]} |S_T(r) - V_T(r)|.$$

Thus, $\{Y_T\}_{T=1}^{\infty}$ is a sequence of random variables, and we could talk about its probability limit using the standard definition given in [7.1.2]. If the sequence of scalars $\{Y_T\}_{T=1}^{\infty}$ converges in probability to zero, then we say that the sequence of functions $S_T(\cdot)$ converges in probability to $V_T(\cdot)$. That is, the expression

$$S_T(\cdot) \xrightarrow{p} V_T(\cdot)$$

is interpreted to mean that

$$\sup_{r \in [0,1]} |S_T(r) - V_T(r)| \xrightarrow{p} 0.$$

With this definition, result (a) of Proposition 7.3 can be generalized to apply

[4]The sequence of probability measures induced by $\{S_T(\cdot)\}_{T=1}^{\infty}$ weakly converges (in the sense of Billingsley, 1968) to the probability measure induced by $S(\cdot)$ if and only if conditions (a) through (c) hold; see Theorem A.2, p. 275, in Hall and Heyde (1980).

to sequences of functions. Specifically, if $\{S_T(\cdot)\}_{T=1}^{\infty}$ and $\{V_T(\cdot)\}_{T=1}^{\infty}$ are sequences of continuous functions with $V_T(\cdot) \xrightarrow{p} S_T(\cdot)$ and $S_T(\cdot) \xrightarrow{L} S(\cdot)$ for $S(\cdot)$ a continuous function, then $V_T(\cdot) \xrightarrow{L} S(\cdot)$; see, for example, Stinchcombe and White (1993).

### *Example 17.1*

Let $\{x_T\}_{T=1}^{\infty}$ be a sequence of random scalars with $x_T \xrightarrow{p} 0$, and let $\{S_T(\cdot)\}_{T=1}^{\infty}$ be a sequence of random continuous functions, $S_T$: $r \in [0, 1] \rightarrow \mathbb{R}^1$ with $S_T(\cdot) \xrightarrow{L} S(\cdot)$. Then the sequence of functions $\{V_T(\cdot)\}_{T=1}^{\infty}$ defined by $V_T(r) \equiv S_T(r) + x_T$ has the property that $V_T(\cdot) \xrightarrow{L} S(\cdot)$. To see this, note that $V_T(r) - S_T(r) = x_T$ for all $r$, so that

$$\sup_{r\in[0,1]} |S_T(r) - V_T(r)| = |x_T|,$$

which converges in probability to zero. Hence, $V_T(\cdot) \xrightarrow{p} S_T(\cdot)$, and therefore $V_T(\cdot) \xrightarrow{L} S(\cdot)$.

### *Example 17.2*

Let $\eta_t$ be a strictly stationary time series with finite fourth moment, and let $S_T(r) = (1/\sqrt{T}) \cdot \eta_{[Tr]^*}$. Then $S_T(\cdot) \xrightarrow{p} 0$. To see this, note that

$$\begin{aligned}
P\left\{\sup_{r\in[0,1]} |S_T(r)| > \delta\right\} \\
&= P\{[|(1/\sqrt{T})\cdot \eta_1| > \delta] \quad \text{or} \quad [|(1/\sqrt{T})\cdot \eta_2| > \delta] \quad \text{or} \quad \cdots \\
&\qquad \text{or} \quad [|(1/\sqrt{T})\cdot \eta_T| > \delta]\} \\
&\leq T\cdot P\{|(1/\sqrt{T})\cdot \eta_t| > \delta]\} \\
&\leq T\cdot \frac{E\{(1/\sqrt{T})\cdot \eta_t\}^4}{\delta^4} \\
&= \frac{E(\eta_t^4)}{T\delta^4},
\end{aligned}$$

where the next-to-last line follows from Chebyshev's inequality. Since $E(\eta_t^4)$ is finite, this probability goes to zero as $T \rightarrow \infty$, establishing that $S_T(\cdot) \xrightarrow{p} 0$, as claimed.

## *Continuous Mapping Theorem*

In Chapter 7 we saw that if $\{x_T\}_{T=1}^{\infty}$ is a sequence of random variables with $x_T \xrightarrow{L} x$ and if $g$: $\mathbb{R}^1 \rightarrow \mathbb{R}^1$ is a continuous function, then $g(x_T) \xrightarrow{L} g(x)$. A similar result holds for sequences of random functions. Here, the analog to the function $g(\cdot)$ is a continuous *functional*, which could associate a real random variable $y$ with the stochastic function $S(\cdot)$. For example, $y = \int_0^1 S(r)\, dr$ and $y = \int_0^1 [S(r)]^2\, dr$ represent continuous functionals.[5] The *continuous mapping theorem*[6] states that if $S_T(\cdot) \xrightarrow{L} S(\cdot)$ and $g(\cdot)$ is a continuous functional, then $g(S_T(\cdot)) \xrightarrow{L} g(S(\cdot))$.

[5]Continuity of a functional $g(\cdot)$ in this context means that for any $\varepsilon > 0$, there exists a $\delta > 0$ such that if $h(r)$ and $k(r)$ are any continuous bounded functions on $[0, 1]$, $h$: $[0, 1] \rightarrow \mathbb{R}^1$ and $k$: $[0, 1] \rightarrow \mathbb{R}^1$, such that $|h(r) - k(r)| < \delta$ for all $r \in [0, 1]$, then

$$|g[h(\cdot)] - g[k(\cdot)]| < \varepsilon.$$

[6]See, for example, Theorem A.3 on p. 276 in Hall and Heyde (1980).

The continuous mapping theorem also applies to a continuous functional $g(\cdot)$ that maps a continuous bounded function on [0, 1] into another continuous bounded function on [0, 1]. For example, the function whose value at $r$ is a positive constant $\sigma$ times $h(r)$ represents the result of applying the continuous functional $g[h(\cdot)] \equiv \sigma \cdot h(\cdot)$ to $h(\cdot)$.[7] Thus, it follows from [17.3.6] that

$$\sqrt{T} \cdot X_T(\cdot) \xrightarrow{L} \sigma \cdot W(\cdot). \qquad [17.3.8]$$

Recalling that $W(r) \sim N(0, r)$, result [17.3.8] implies that $\sqrt{T} \cdot X_T(r) \approx N(0, \sigma^2 r)$.

As another example, consider the function $S_T(\cdot)$ whose value at $r$ is given by

$$S_T(r) \equiv [\sqrt{T} \cdot X_T(r)]^2. \qquad [17.3.9]$$

Since $\sqrt{T} \cdot X_T(\cdot) \xrightarrow{L} \sigma \cdot W(\cdot)$, it follows that

$$S_T(\cdot) \xrightarrow{L} \sigma^2[W(\cdot)]^2. \qquad [17.3.10]$$

In other words, if the value $W(r)$ from a realization of standard Brownian motion at every date $r$ is squared and then multiplied by $\sigma^2$, the resulting continuous-time process would follow essentially the same probability law as does the continuous-time process defined by $S_T(r)$ in [17.3.9] for $T$ sufficiently large.

## *Applications to Unit Root Processes*

The use of the functional central limit theorem to calculate the asymptotic distribution of statistics constructed from unit root processes was pioneered by Phillips (1986, 1987).[8] The simplest illustration of Phillips's approach is provided by a random walk,

$$y_t = y_{t-1} + u_t, \qquad [17.3.11]$$

where $\{u_t\}$ is an i.i.d. sequence with mean zero and variance $\sigma^2$. If $y_0 = 0$, then [17.3.11] implies that

$$y_t = u_1 + u_2 + \cdots + u_t. \qquad [17.3.12]$$

Equation [17.3.12] can be used to express the stochastic function $X_T(r)$ defined in [17.3.3] as

$$X_T(r) = \begin{cases} 0 & \text{for } 0 \le r < 1/T \\ y_1/T & \text{for } 1/T \le r < 2/T \\ y_2/T & \text{for } 2/T \le r < 3/T \\ \vdots & \\ y_T/T & \text{for } r = 1. \end{cases} \qquad [17.3.13]$$

Figure 17.1 plots $X_T(r)$ as a function of $r$. Note that the area under this step function

[7]Here continuity of the functional $g(\cdot)$ means that for any $\varepsilon > 0$, there exists a $\delta > 0$ such that if $h(r)$ and $k(r)$ are any continuous bounded functions on [0, 1], $h$: $[0, 1] \rightarrow \mathbb{R}^1$ and $k$: $[0, 1] \rightarrow \mathbb{R}^1$, such that $|h(r) - k(r)| < \delta$ for all $r \in [0, 1]$, then

$$|g[h(r)] - g[k(r)]| < \varepsilon$$

for all $r \in [0, 1]$.

[8]Result [17.4.7] in the next section for the case with i.i.d. errors was first derived by White (1958). Phillips (1986, 1987) developed the general derivation presented here based on the functional central limit theorem and the continuous mapping theorem. Other important contributions include Dickey and Fuller (1979), Chan and Wei (1988), Park and Phillips (1988, 1989), Sims, Stock, and Watson (1990), and Phillips and Solo (1992).

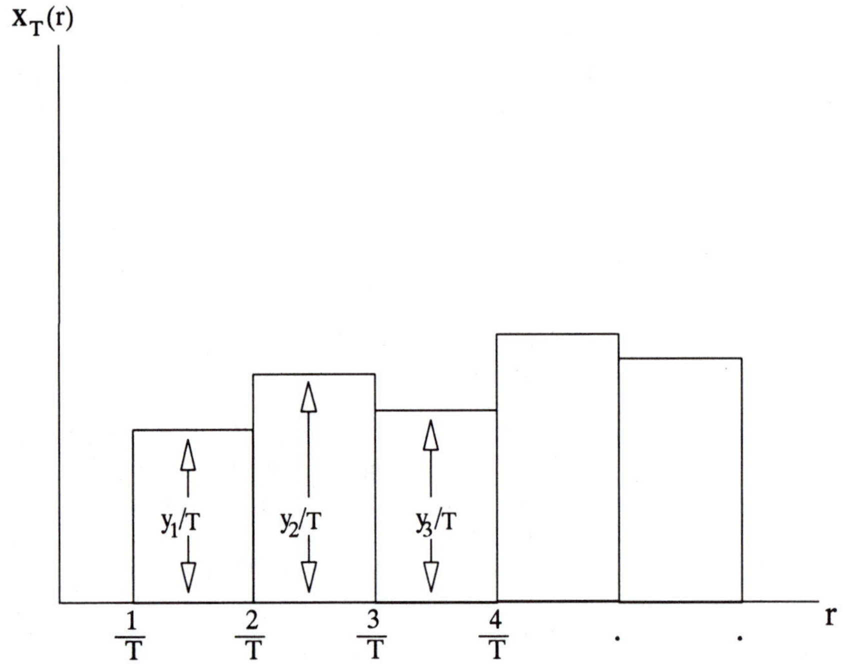


**FIGURE 17.1** Plot of $X_T(r)$ as a function of $r$.

is the sum of $T$ rectangles. The $t$th rectangle has width $1/T$ and height $y_{t-1}/T$, and therefore has area $y_{t-1}/T^2$. The integral of $X_T(r)$ is thus equivalent to

$$\int_0^1 X_T(r)\,dr = y_1/T^2 + y_2/T^2 + \cdots + y_{T-1}/T^2. \qquad [17.3.14]$$

Multiplying both sides of [17.3.14] by $\sqrt{T}$ establishes that

$$\int_0^1 \sqrt{T}\cdot X_T(r)\,dr = T^{-3/2}\sum_{t=1}^{T} y_{t-1}. \qquad [17.3.15]$$

But we know from [17.3.8] and the continuous mapping theorem that as $T \to \infty$,

$$\int_0^1 \sqrt{T}\cdot X_T(r)\,dr \xrightarrow{L} \sigma\cdot\int_0^1 W(r)\,dr,$$

implying from [17.3.15] that

$$T^{-3/2}\sum_{t=1}^{T} y_{t-1} \xrightarrow{L} \sigma\cdot\int_0^1 W(r)\,dr. \qquad [17.3.16]$$

It is also instructive to derive [17.3.16] from first principles. From [17.3.12], we can write

$$\begin{aligned} T^{-3/2}\sum_{t=1}^{T} y_{t-1} &= T^{-3/2}[u_1 + (u_1 + u_2) + (u_1 + u_2 + u_3) + \cdots \\ &\quad + (u_1 + u_2 + u_3 + \cdots + u_{T-1})] \\ &= T^{-3/2}[(T-1)u_1 + (T-2)u_2 + (T-3)u_3 + \cdots \\ &\quad + [T-(T-1)]u_{T-1}] \\ &= T^{-3/2}\sum_{t=1}^{T}(T-t)u_t \\ &= T^{-1/2}\sum_{t=1}^{T} u_t - T^{-3/2}\sum_{t=1}^{T} tu_t. \end{aligned} \qquad [17.3.17]$$

Recall from [16.1.24] that

$$\begin{bmatrix} T^{-1/2}\sum_{t=1}^{T} u_t \\ T^{-3/2}\sum_{t=1}^{T} tu_t \end{bmatrix} \xrightarrow{L} N\left(\begin{bmatrix} 0 \\ 0 \end{bmatrix}, \sigma^2\begin{bmatrix} 1 & \frac{1}{2} \\ \frac{1}{2} & \frac{1}{3} \end{bmatrix}\right). \qquad [17.3.18]$$

Thus, [17.3.17] implies that $T^{-3/2}\sum_{t=1}^{T} y_{t-1}$ is asymptotically Gaussian with mean zero and variance equal to

$$\sigma^2\{1 - 2\cdot(1/2) + 1/3\} = \sigma^2/3.$$

Evidently, $\sigma\cdot\int_0^1 W(r)\,dr$ in [17.3.16] describes a random variable that has a $N(0, \sigma^2/3)$ distribution.

Thus, if $y_t$ is a driftless random walk, the sample mean $T^{-1}\Sigma_{t=1}^{T} y_t$ diverges but $T^{-3/2}\Sigma_{t=1}^{T} y_t$ converges to a Gaussian random variable whose distribution can be described as the integral of the realization of Brownian motion with variance $\sigma^2$.

Expression [17.3.17] also gives us a way to describe the asymptotic distribution of $T^{-3/2}\Sigma_{t=1}^{T} tu_t$ in terms of functionals on Brownian motion:

$$\begin{aligned} T^{-3/2}\sum_{t=1}^{T} tu_t &= T^{-1/2}\sum_{t=1}^{T} u_t - T^{-3/2}\sum_{t=1}^{T} y_{t-1} \\ &\xrightarrow{L} \sigma\cdot W(1) - \sigma\cdot\int_0^1 W(r)\,dr, \end{aligned} \qquad [17.3.19]$$

with the last line following from [17.3.7] and [17.3.16]. Recalling [17.3.18], the random variable on the right side of [17.3.19] evidently has a $N(0, \sigma^2/3)$ distribution.

A similar argument to that in [17.3.15] can be used to describe the asymptotic distribution of the sum of squares of a random walk. The statistic $S_T(r)$ defined in [17.3.9],

$$S_T(r) \equiv T\cdot[X_T(r)]^2, \qquad [17.3.20]$$

can be written using [17.3.13] as

$$S_T(r) = \begin{cases} 0 & \text{for } 0 \le r < 1/T \\ y_1^2/T & \text{for } 1/T \le r < 2/T \\ y_2^2/T & \text{for } 2/T \le r < 3/T \\ \vdots & \\ y_T^2/T & \text{for } r = 1. \end{cases} \qquad [17.3.21]$$

It follows that

$$\int_0^1 S_T(r)\,dr = y_1^2/T^2 + y_2^2/T^2 + \cdots + y_{T-1}^2/T^2.$$

Thus, from [17.3.10] and the continuous mapping theorem,

$$T^{-2}\sum_{t=1}^{T} y_{t-1}^2 \xrightarrow{L} \sigma^2\cdot\int_0^1 [W(r)]^2\,dr. \qquad [17.3.22]$$

Two other useful results are

$$T^{-5/2}\sum_{t=1}^{T} ty_{t-1} = T^{-3/2}\sum_{t=1}^{T} (t/T)y_{t-1} \xrightarrow{L} \sigma\cdot\int_0^1 rW(r)\,dr \qquad [17.3.23]$$

for $r = t/T$ and

$$T^{-3}\sum_{t=1}^{T} ty_{t-1}^2 = T^{-2}\sum_{t=1}^{T}(t/T)y_{t-1}^2 \xrightarrow{L} \sigma^2\cdot\int_0^1 r\cdot[W(r)]^2\,dr. \quad [17.3.24]$$

As yet another useful application, consider the statistic in [17.1.11]:

$$T^{-1}\sum_{t=1}^{T} y_{t-1}u_t = (1/2)\cdot(1/T)y_T^2 - (1/2)\cdot(1/T)\sum_{t=1}^{T}u_t^2.$$

Recalling [17.3.21], this can be written

$$T^{-1}\sum_{t=1}^{T} y_{t-1}u_t = (1/2)S_T(1) - (1/2)(1/T)\sum_{t=1}^{T}u_t^2. \quad [17.3.25]$$

But $(1/T)\Sigma_{t=1}^{T}u_t^2 \xrightarrow{p} \sigma^2$, by the law of large numbers, and $S_T(1) \xrightarrow{L} \sigma^2[W(1)]^2$, by [17.3.10]. It thus follows from [17.3.25] that

$$T^{-1}\sum_{t=1}^{T} y_{t-1}u_t \xrightarrow{L} (1/2)\sigma^2[W(1)]^2 - (1/2)\sigma^2. \quad [17.3.26]$$

Recall that $W(1)$, the value of standard Brownian motion at date $r = 1$, has a $N(0, 1)$ distribution, meaning that $[W(1)]^2$ has a $\chi^2(1)$ distribution. Result [17.3.26] is therefore just another way to express the earlier result [17.1.15] using a functional on Brownian motion instead of the $\chi^2$ distribution.

## 17.4. *Asymptotic Properties of a First-Order Autoregression when the True Coefficient Is Unity*

We are now in a position to calculate the asymptotic distribution of some simple regressions involving unit roots. For convenience, the results from Section 17.3 are collected in the form of a proposition.

***Proposition 17.1:*** *Suppose that $\xi_t$ follows a random walk without drift,*

$$\xi_t = \xi_{t-1} + u_t,$$

*where $\xi_0 = 0$ and $\{u_t\}$ is an i.i.d. sequence with mean zero and variance $\sigma^2$. Then*

(*a*) $T^{-1/2}\sum_{t=1}^{T} u_t \xrightarrow{L} \sigma\cdot W(1)$ [17.3.7];

(*b*) $T^{-1}\sum_{t=1}^{T} \xi_{t-1}u_t \xrightarrow{L} (1/2)\sigma^2\{[W(1)]^2 - 1\}$ [17.3.26];

(*c*) $T^{-3/2}\sum_{t=1}^{T} tu_t \xrightarrow{L} \sigma\cdot W(1) - \sigma\cdot\int_0^1 W(r)\,dr$ [17.3.19];

(*d*) $T^{-3/2}\sum_{t=1}^{T} \xi_{t-1} \xrightarrow{L} \sigma\cdot\int_0^1 W(r)\,dr$ [17.3.16];

(*e*) $T^{-2}\sum_{t=1}^{T} \xi_{t-1}^2 \xrightarrow{L} \sigma^2\cdot\int_0^1 [W(r)]^2\,dr$ [17.3.22];

(*f*) $T^{-5/2}\sum_{t=1}^{T} t\xi_{t-1} \xrightarrow{L} \sigma\cdot\int_0^1 rW(r)\,dr$ [17.3.23];

(*g*) $T^{-3}\sum_{t=1}^{T} t\xi_{t-1}^2 \xrightarrow{L} \sigma^2\cdot\int_0^1 r\cdot[W(r)]^2\,dr$ [17.3.24];

(*h*) $T^{-(v+1)}\sum_{t=1}^{T} t^v \to 1/(v+1)$ *for* $v = 0, 1, \ldots$ [16.1.15].

The expressions in brackets indicate where the stated result was earlier derived. Though the earlier derivations assumed that the initial value $\xi_0$ was equal to zero, the same results are obtained when $\xi_0$ is any fixed value or drawn from a specified distribution as in Phillips (1987).

The asymptotic distributions in Proposition 17.1 are all written in terms of functionals on standard Brownian motion, denoted $W(r)$. Note that this is the *same* Brownian motion $W(r)$ in each result (a) through (g), so that in general the magnitudes in Proposition 17.1 are all correlated. If we are not interested in capturing these correlations, then there are simpler ways to describe the asymptotic distributions. For example, we have seen that (a) is just a $N(0, \sigma^2)$ distribution, (b) is $(1/2)\sigma^2 \cdot [\chi^2(1) - 1]$, and (c) and (d) are $N(0, \sigma^2/3)$. Exercise 17.1 gives an example of one approach to calculating the covariances among random variables described by these functionals on Brownian motion.

Proposition 17.1 can be used to calculate the asymptotic distributions of statistics from a number of simple regressions involving unit roots. This section discusses several key cases.

### *Case 1. No Constant Term or Time Trend in the Regression; True Process Is a Random Walk*

Consider first *OLS* estimation of $\rho$ based on an $AR(1)$ regression,

$$y_t = \rho y_{t-1} + u_t, \qquad [17.4.1]$$

where $u_t$ is i.i.d. with mean zero and variance $\sigma^2$. We are interested in the properties of the *OLS* estimate

$$\hat{\rho}_T = \frac{\sum_{t=1}^{T} y_{t-1} y_t}{\sum_{t=1}^{T} y_{t-1}^2} \qquad [17.4.2]$$

when the true value of $\rho$ is unity. From [17.1.6], the deviation of the *OLS* estimate from the true value is characterized by

$$T(\hat{\rho}_T - 1) = \frac{T^{-1} \sum_{t=1}^{T} y_{t-1} u_t}{T^{-2} \sum_{t=1}^{T} y_{t-1}^2}. \qquad [17.4.3]$$

If the true value of $\rho$ is unity, then

$$y_t = y_0 + u_1 + u_2 + \cdots + u_t. \qquad [17.4.4]$$

Apart from the initial term $y_0$ (which does not affect any of the asymptotic distributions), the variable $y_t$ is the same as the quantity labeled $\xi_t$ in Proposition 17.1. From result (b) of that proposition,

$$T^{-1} \sum_{t=1}^{T} y_{t-1} u_t \xrightarrow{L} (1/2)\sigma^2\{[W(1)]^2 - 1\}, \qquad [17.4.5]$$

while from result (e),

$$T^{-2} \sum_{t=1}^{T} y_{t-1}^2 \xrightarrow{L} \sigma^2 \cdot \int_0^1 [W(r)]^2\, dr. \qquad [17.4.6]$$

Since [17.4.3] is a continuous function of [17.4.5] and [17.4.6], it follows from Proposition 7.3(c) that under the null hypothesis that $\rho = 1$, the *OLS* estimate

$\hat{\rho}_T$ is characterized by

$$T(\hat{\rho}_T - 1) \xrightarrow{L} \frac{(1/2)\{[W(1)]^2 - 1\}}{\int_0^1 [W(r)]^2\, dr}. \qquad [17.4.7]$$

Recall that $[W(1)]^2$ is a $\chi^2(1)$ variable. The probability that a $\chi^2(1)$ variable is less than unity is 0.68, and since the denominator of [17.4.7] must be positive, the probability that $\hat{\rho}_T - 1$ is negative approaches 0.68 as $T$ becomes large. In other words, in two-thirds of the samples generated by a random walk, the estimate $\hat{\rho}_T$ will be less than the true value of unity. Moreover, in those samples for which $[W(1)]^2$ is large, the denominator of [17.4.7] will be large as well. The result is that the limiting distribution of $T(\hat{\rho}_T - 1)$ is skewed to the left.

Recall that in the stationary case when $|\rho| < 1$, the estimate $\hat{\rho}_T$ is downward-biased in small samples. Even so, in the stationary case the limiting distribution of $\sqrt{T}(\hat{\rho}_T - \rho)$ is symmetric around zero. By contrast, when the true value of $\rho$ is unity, even the limiting distribution of $T(\hat{\rho}_T - 1)$ is asymmetric, with negative values twice as likely as positive values.

In practice, critical values for the random variable in [17.4.7] are found by calculating the exact small-sample distribution of $T(\hat{\rho}_T - 1)$ for given $T$, assuming that the innovations $\{u_t\}$ are Gaussian. This can be done either by Monte Carlo, as in the critical values reported in Fuller (1976), or by using exact numerical procedures described in Evans and Savin (1981). Sample percentiles for $T(\hat{\rho}_T - 1)$ are reported in the section labeled Case 1 in Table B.5 of Appendix B. For finite $T$, these are exact only under the assumption of Gaussian innovations. As $T$ becomes large, these values also describe the asymptotic distribution for non-Gaussian innovations.

It follows from [17.4.7] that $\hat{\rho}_T$ is a superconsistent estimate of the true value ($\rho = 1$). This is easily seen by dividing [17.4.3] by $\sqrt{T}$:

$$\sqrt{T}(\hat{\rho}_T - 1) = \frac{T^{-3/2} \sum_{t=1}^{T} y_{t-1} u_t}{T^{-2} \sum_{t=1}^{T} y_{t-1}^2}. \qquad [17.4.8]$$

From Proposition 17.1(b), the numerator in [17.4.8] converges to $T^{-1/2}(1/2)\sigma^2$ times $(X - 1)$, where $X$ is a $\chi^2(1)$ random variable. Since a $\chi^2(1)$ variable has finite variance, the variance of the numerator in [17.4.8] is of order $1/T$, meaning that the numerator converges in probability to zero. Hence,

$$\sqrt{T}(\hat{\rho}_T - 1) \xrightarrow{p} 0.$$

Result [17.4.7] allows the point estimate $\hat{\rho}_T$ to be used by itself to test the null hypothesis of a unit root, without needing to calculate its standard error. Another popular statistic for testing the null hypothesis that $\rho = 1$ is based on the usual *OLS* $t$ test of this hypothesis,

$$t_T = \frac{(\hat{\rho}_T - 1)}{\hat{\sigma}_{\hat{\rho}_T}} = \frac{(\hat{\rho}_T - 1)}{\left\{s_T^2 \div \sum_{t=1}^{T} y_{t-1}^2\right\}^{1/2}}, \qquad [17.4.9]$$

where $\hat{\sigma}_{\hat{\rho}_T}$ is the usual *OLS* standard error for the estimated coefficient,

$$\hat{\sigma}_{\hat{\rho}_T} = \left\{s_T^2 \div \sum_{t=1}^{T} y_{t-1}^2\right\}^{1/2},$$

and $s_T^2$ denotes the *OLS* estimate of the residual variance:

$$s_T^2 = \sum_{t=1}^{T} (y_t - \hat{\rho}_T y_{t-1})^2/(T - 1).$$

Although the $t$ statistic [17.4.9] is calculated in the usual way, it does not have a limiting Gaussian distribution when the true process is characterized by $\rho = 1$. To find the appropriate limiting distribution, note that [17.4.9] can equivalently be expressed as

$$t_T = T(\hat{\rho}_T - 1)\left\{T^{-2} \sum_{t=1}^{T} y_{t-1}^2\right\}^{1/2} \div \{s_T^2\}^{1/2}, \qquad [17.4.10]$$

or, substituting from [17.4.3],

$$t_T = \frac{T^{-1} \sum_{t=1}^{T} y_{t-1}u_t}{\left\{T^{-2} \sum_{t=1}^{T} y_{t-1}^2\right\}^{1/2} \{s_T^2\}^{1/2}}. \qquad [17.4.11]$$

As in Section 8.2, consistency of $\hat{\rho}_T$ implies $s_T^2 \xrightarrow{p} \sigma^2$. It follows from [17.4.5] and [17.4.6] that as $T \to \infty$,

$$t_T \xrightarrow{L} \frac{(1/2)\sigma^2\{[W(1)]^2 - 1\}}{\left\{\sigma^2 \int_0^1 [W(r)]^2\, dr\right\}^{1/2} \{\sigma^2\}^{1/2}} = \frac{(1/2)\{[W(1)]^2 - 1\}}{\left\{\int_0^1 [W(r)]^2\, dr\right\}^{1/2}}. \qquad [17.4.12]$$

Statistical tables for the distribution of [17.4.11] for various sample sizes $T$ are reported in the section labeled Case 1 in Table B.6; again, the small-sample results assume Gaussian innovations.

### *Example 17.3*

The following $AR(1)$ process for the nominal three-month U.S. Treasury bill rate was fitted by *OLS* regression to quarterly data, $t$ = 1947:II to 1989:I:

$$i_t = \underset{(0.010592)}{0.99694}\, i_{t-1}, \qquad [17.4.13]$$

with the standard error of $\hat{\rho}$ in parentheses. Here $T = 168$ and

$$T(\hat{\rho} - 1) = (168)(0.99694 - 1) = -0.51.$$

The distribution of this statistic was calculated in [17.4.7] under the assumption that the true value of $\rho$ is unity. The null hypothesis is therefore that $\rho = 1$, and the alternative is that $\rho < 1$. From Table B.5, in a sample of this size, 95% of the time when there really is a unit root, the statistic $T(\hat{\rho} - 1)$ will be above $-7.9$. The observed value ($-0.51$) is well above this, and so the null hypothesis is accepted at the 5% level and we should conclude that these data might well be described by a random walk.

In order to have rejected the null hypothesis for a sample of this size, the estimated autoregressive coefficient $\hat{\rho}$ would have to be less than 0.95:

$$168(0.95 - 1) = -8.4.$$

The *OLS* $t$ test of $H_0$: $\rho = 1$ is

$$t = (0.99694 - 1)/0.010592 = -0.29.$$

This is well above the 5% critical value from Table B.6 of $-1.95$, so the null hypothesis that the Treasury bill rate follows a random walk is also accepted by this test.

The test statistics [17.4.7] and [17.4.12] are examples of the *Dickey-Fuller test* for unit roots, named for the general battery of tests proposed by Dickey and Fuller (1979).

### *Case 2. Constant Term but No Time Trend Included in the Regression; True Process Is a Random Walk*

For case 2, we continue to assume, as in case 1, that the data are generated by a random walk:

$$y_t = y_{t-1} + u_t,$$

with $u_t$ i.i.d. with mean zero and variance $\sigma^2$. Although the true model is the same as in case 1, suppose now that a constant term is included in the $AR(1)$ specification that is to be estimated by $OLS$:

$$y_t = \alpha + \rho y_{t-1} + u_t. \qquad [17.4.14]$$

The task now is to describe the properties of the $OLS$ estimates,

$$\begin{bmatrix} \hat{\alpha}_T \\ \hat{\rho}_T \end{bmatrix} = \begin{bmatrix} T & \Sigma y_{t-1} \\ \Sigma y_{t-1} & \Sigma y_{t-1}^2 \end{bmatrix}^{-1} \begin{bmatrix} \Sigma y_t \\ \Sigma y_{t-1} y_t \end{bmatrix}, \qquad [17.4.15]$$

under the null hypothesis that $\alpha = 0$ and $\rho = 1$ (here $\Sigma$ indicates summation over $t = 1, 2, \ldots, T$). Recall the familiar characterization in [8.2.3] of the deviation of an estimated $OLS$ coefficient vector ($\mathbf{b}_T$) from the true value ($\boldsymbol{\beta}$),

$$\mathbf{b}_T - \boldsymbol{\beta} = \left[\sum_{t=1}^{T} \mathbf{x}_t \mathbf{x}_t'\right]^{-1} \left[\sum_{t=1}^{T} \mathbf{x}_t u_t\right], \qquad [17.4.16]$$

or, in this case,

$$\begin{bmatrix} \hat{\alpha}_T \\ \hat{\rho}_T - 1 \end{bmatrix} = \begin{bmatrix} T & \Sigma y_{t-1} \\ \Sigma y_{t-1} & \Sigma y_{t-1}^2 \end{bmatrix}^{-1} \begin{bmatrix} \Sigma u_t \\ \Sigma y_{t-1} u_t \end{bmatrix}. \qquad [17.4.17]$$

As in case 1, $y_t$ has the same properties as the variable $\xi_t$ described in Proposition 17.1 under the maintained hypothesis. Thus, result (d) of that proposition establishes that the sum $\Sigma y_{t-1}$ must be divided by $T^{3/2}$ before obtaining a random variable that converges in distribution:

$$T^{-3/2} \Sigma y_{t-1} \xrightarrow{L} \sigma \cdot \int_0^1 W(r)\, dr. \qquad [17.4.18]$$

In other words,

$$\Sigma y_{t-1} = O_p(T^{3/2}).$$

Similarly, results [17.4.5] and [17.4.6] establish that

$$\Sigma y_{t-1} u_t = O_p(T)$$
$$\Sigma y_{t-1}^2 = O_p(T^2),$$

and from Proposition 17.1(a),

$$\Sigma u_t = O_p(T^{1/2}).$$

Thus, the order in probability of the individual terms in [17.4.17] is as follows:

$$\begin{bmatrix} \hat{\alpha}_T \\ \hat{\rho}_T - 1 \end{bmatrix} = \begin{bmatrix} O_p(T) & O_p(T^{3/2}) \\ O_p(T^{3/2}) & O_p(T^2) \end{bmatrix}^{-1} \begin{bmatrix} O_p(T^{1/2}) \\ O_p(T) \end{bmatrix}. \qquad [17.4.19]$$

It is clear from [17.4.19] that the estimates $\hat{\alpha}_T$ and $\hat{\rho}_T$ have different rates of convergence, and as in the previous chapter, a scaling matrix $\mathbf{Y}_T$ is helpful in describing their limiting distributions. Recall from [16.1.18] that this rescaling is achieved by premultiplying [17.4.16] by $\mathbf{Y}_T$ and writing the result as

$$\begin{aligned} \mathbf{Y}_T(\mathbf{b}_T - \boldsymbol{\beta}) &= \mathbf{Y}_T\left[\sum_{t=1}^{T} \mathbf{x}_t\mathbf{x}_t'\right]^{-1} \mathbf{Y}_T\mathbf{Y}_T^{-1}\left[\sum_{t=1}^{T} \mathbf{x}_t u_t\right] \\ &= \left\{\mathbf{Y}_T^{-1}\left[\sum_{t=1}^{T} \mathbf{x}_t\mathbf{x}_t'\right]\mathbf{Y}_T^{-1}\right\}^{-1} \left\{\mathbf{Y}_T^{-1}\left[\sum_{t=1}^{T} \mathbf{x}_t u_t\right]\right\}. \end{aligned} \qquad [17.4.20]$$

From [17.4.19], for this application $\mathbf{Y}_T$ should be specified to be the following matrix:

$$\mathbf{Y}_T \equiv \begin{bmatrix} T^{1/2} & 0 \\ 0 & T \end{bmatrix}, \qquad [17.4.21]$$

for which [17.4.20] becomes

$$\begin{aligned} \begin{bmatrix} T^{1/2} & 0 \\ 0 & T \end{bmatrix} \begin{bmatrix} \hat{\alpha}_T \\ \hat{\rho}_T - 1 \end{bmatrix} &= \left\{\begin{bmatrix} T^{-1/2} & 0 \\ 0 & T^{-1} \end{bmatrix} \begin{bmatrix} T & \Sigma y_{t-1} \\ \Sigma y_{t-1} & \Sigma y_{t-1}^2 \end{bmatrix} \begin{bmatrix} T^{-1/2} & 0 \\ 0 & T^{-1} \end{bmatrix}\right\}^{-1} \\ &\quad \times \left\{\begin{bmatrix} T^{-1/2} & 0 \\ 0 & T^{-1} \end{bmatrix} \begin{bmatrix} \Sigma u_t \\ \Sigma y_{t-1}u_t \end{bmatrix}\right\} \end{aligned}$$

or

$$\begin{bmatrix} T^{1/2}\hat{\alpha}_T \\ T(\hat{\rho}_T - 1) \end{bmatrix} = \begin{bmatrix} 1 & T^{-3/2}\Sigma y_{t-1} \\ T^{-3/2}\Sigma y_{t-1} & T^{-2}\Sigma y_{t-1}^2 \end{bmatrix}^{-1} \begin{bmatrix} T^{-1/2}\Sigma u_t \\ T^{-1}\Sigma y_{t-1}u_t \end{bmatrix}. \qquad [17.4.22]$$

Consider the first term on the right side of [17.4.22]. Results [17.4.6] and [17.4.18] establish that

$$\begin{aligned} &\begin{bmatrix} 1 & T^{-3/2}\Sigma y_{t-1} \\ T^{-3/2}\Sigma y_{t-1} & T^{-2}\Sigma y_{t-1}^2 \end{bmatrix} \\ &\xrightarrow{L} \begin{bmatrix} 1 & \sigma\cdot\int W(r)\,dr \\ \sigma\cdot\int W(r)\,dr & \sigma^2\cdot\int [W(r)]^2\,dr \end{bmatrix} \\ &= \begin{bmatrix} 1 & 0 \\ 0 & \sigma \end{bmatrix} \begin{bmatrix} 1 & \int W(r)\,dr \\ \int W(r)\,dr & \int [W(r)]^2\,dr \end{bmatrix} \begin{bmatrix} 1 & 0 \\ 0 & \sigma \end{bmatrix}, \end{aligned} \qquad [17.4.23]$$

where the integral sign denotes integration over $r$ from 0 to 1. Similarly, result (a) of Proposition 17.1 along with [17.4.5] determines the asymptotic distribution of the second term in [17.4.22]:

$$\begin{bmatrix} T^{-1/2}\Sigma u_t \\ T^{-1}\Sigma y_{t-1}u_t \end{bmatrix} \xrightarrow{L} \begin{bmatrix} \sigma \cdot W(1) \\ (1/2)\sigma^2\{[W(1)]^2 - 1\} \end{bmatrix} = \sigma \begin{bmatrix} 1 & 0 \\ 0 & \sigma \end{bmatrix} \begin{bmatrix} W(1) \\ (1/2)\{[W(1)]^2 - 1\} \end{bmatrix}. \qquad [17.4.24]$$

Substituting [17.4.23] and [17.4.24] into [17.4.22] establishes

$$\begin{bmatrix} T^{1/2}\hat{\alpha}_T \\ T(\hat{\rho}_T - 1) \end{bmatrix} \xrightarrow{L} \sigma \cdot \begin{bmatrix} 1 & 0 \\ 0 & \sigma \end{bmatrix}^{-1} \begin{bmatrix} 1 & \int W(r)\,dr \\ \int W(r)\,dr & \int [W(r)]^2\,dr \end{bmatrix}^{-1}$$

$$\times \begin{bmatrix} 1 & 0 \\ 0 & \sigma \end{bmatrix}^{-1} \begin{bmatrix} 1 & 0 \\ 0 & \sigma \end{bmatrix} \begin{bmatrix} W(1) \\ (1/2)\{[W(1)]^2 - 1\} \end{bmatrix}$$

$$= \begin{bmatrix} \sigma & 0 \\ 0 & 1 \end{bmatrix} \begin{bmatrix} 1 & \int W(r)\,dr \\ \int W(r)\,dr & \int [W(r)]^2\,dr \end{bmatrix}^{-1} \qquad [17.4.25]$$

$$\times \begin{bmatrix} W(1) \\ (1/2)\{[W(1)]^2 - 1\} \end{bmatrix}.$$

Notice that

$$\begin{bmatrix} 1 & \int W(r)\,dr \\ \int W(r)\,dr & \int [W(r)]^2\,dr \end{bmatrix}^{-1} = \Delta^{-1} \begin{bmatrix} \int [W(r)]^2\,dr & -\int W(r)\,dr \\ -\int W(r)\,dr & 1 \end{bmatrix}, \qquad [17.4.26]$$

where

$$\Delta \equiv \int [W(r)]^2\,dr - \left[\int W(r)\,dr\right]^2. \qquad [17.4.27]$$

Thus, the second element in the vector expression in [17.4.25] states that

$$T(\hat{\rho}_T - 1) \xrightarrow{L} \frac{\tfrac{1}{2}\{[W(1)]^2 - 1\} - W(1)\cdot\int W(r)\,dr}{\int [W(r)]^2\,dr - \left[\int W(r)\,dr\right]^2}. \qquad [17.4.28]$$

Neither estimate $\hat{\alpha}_T$ nor $\hat{\rho}_T$ has a limiting Gaussian distribution. Moreover, the asymptotic distribution of the estimate of $\rho$ in [17.4.28] is not the same as the asymptotic distribution in [17.4.7]—when a constant term is included in the distribution, a different table of critical values must be used.

The second section of Table B.5 records percentiles for the distribution of $T(\hat{\rho}_T - 1)$ for case 2. As in case 1, the calculations assume Gaussian innovations, though as $T$ becomes large, these are valid for non-Gaussian innovations as well.

Notice that this distribution is even more strongly skewed than that for case 1, so that when a constant term is included in the regression, the estimated coefficient on $y_{t-1}$ must be farther from unity in order to reject the null hypothesis of a unit root. Indeed, for $T > 25$, 95% of the time the estimated value $\hat{\rho}_T$ will be less than unity. For example, if the estimated value $\hat{\rho}_T$ is 0.999 in a sample of size $T = 100$, the null hypothesis of $\rho = 1$ would be rejected in favor of the alternative that $\rho > 1$! If the true value of $\rho$ is unity, we would not expect to obtain an estimate as large as 0.999.

Dickey and Fuller also proposed an alternative test based on the *OLS t* test of the null hypothesis that $\rho = 1$:

$$t_T = \frac{\hat{\rho}_T - 1}{\hat{\sigma}_{\hat{\rho}_T}}, \qquad [17.4.29]$$

where

$$\hat{\sigma}^2_{\hat{\rho}_T} = s_T^2 [0 \quad 1] \begin{bmatrix} T & \Sigma y_{t-1} \\ \Sigma y_{t-1} & \Sigma y_{t-1}^2 \end{bmatrix}^{-1} \begin{bmatrix} 0 \\ 1 \end{bmatrix} \qquad [17.4.30]$$

$$s_T^2 = (T-2)^{-1} \sum_{t=1}^{T} (y_t - \hat{\alpha}_T - \hat{\rho}_T y_{t-1})^2.$$

Notice that if both sides of [17.4.30] are multiplied by $T^2$, the result can be written as

$$\begin{aligned} T^2 \cdot \hat{\sigma}^2_{\hat{\rho}_T} &= s_T^2 [0 \quad T] \begin{bmatrix} T & \Sigma y_{t-1} \\ \Sigma y_{t-1} & \Sigma y_{t-1}^2 \end{bmatrix}^{-1} \begin{bmatrix} 0 \\ T \end{bmatrix} \\ &= s_T^2 [0 \quad 1] \mathbf{Y}_T \begin{bmatrix} T & \Sigma y_{t-1} \\ \Sigma y_{t-1} & \Sigma y_{t-1}^2 \end{bmatrix}^{-1} \mathbf{Y}_T \begin{bmatrix} 0 \\ 1 \end{bmatrix} \end{aligned} \qquad [17.4.31]$$

for $\mathbf{Y}_T$ the matrix in [17.4.21]. Recall from [17.4.23] that

$$\begin{aligned} &\mathbf{Y}_T \begin{bmatrix} T & \Sigma y_{t-1} \\ \Sigma y_{t-1} & \Sigma y_{t-1}^2 \end{bmatrix}^{-1} \mathbf{Y}_T \\ &= \left\{ \mathbf{Y}_T^{-1} \begin{bmatrix} T & \Sigma y_{t-1} \\ \Sigma y_{t-1} & \Sigma y_{t-1}^2 \end{bmatrix} \mathbf{Y}_T^{-1} \right\}^{-1} \\ &= \begin{bmatrix} 1 & T^{-3/2} \Sigma y_{t-1} \\ T^{-3/2} \Sigma y_{t-1} & T^{-2} \Sigma y_{t-1}^2 \end{bmatrix}^{-1} \\ &\xrightarrow{L} \begin{bmatrix} 1 & 0 \\ 0 & \sigma \end{bmatrix}^{-1} \begin{bmatrix} 1 & \int W(r)\,dr \\ \int W(r)\,dr & \int [W(r)]^2\,dr \end{bmatrix}^{-1} \begin{bmatrix} 1 & 0 \\ 0 & \sigma \end{bmatrix}^{-1}. \end{aligned} \qquad [17.4.32]$$

Thus, from [17.4.31],

$$T^2 \cdot \hat{\sigma}^2_{\hat{\rho}_T} \xrightarrow{p} s_T^2 [0 \quad \sigma^{-1}] \begin{bmatrix} 1 & \int W(r)\,dr \\ \int W(r)\,dr & \int [W(r)]^2\,dr \end{bmatrix}^{-1} \begin{bmatrix} 0 \\ \sigma^{-1} \end{bmatrix}. \qquad [17.4.33]$$

It is also easy to show that

$$s_T^2 \xrightarrow{p} \sigma^2, \qquad [17.4.34]$$

from which [17.4.33] becomes

$$T^2 \cdot \hat{\sigma}^2_{\hat{\rho}_T} \xrightarrow{L} [0 \quad 1] \begin{bmatrix} 1 & \int W(r)\, dr \\ \int W(r)\, dr & \int [W(r)]^2\, dr \end{bmatrix}^{-1} \begin{bmatrix} 0 \\ 1 \end{bmatrix}$$
$$= \frac{1}{\int [W(r)]^2\, dr - \left[\int W(r)\, dr\right]^2}. \qquad [17.4.35]$$

Thus, the asymptotic distribution of the *OLS t* test in [17.4.29] is

$$t_T = \frac{T(\hat{\rho}_T - 1)}{\{T^2 \cdot \hat{\sigma}^2_{\hat{\rho}_T}\}^{1/2}} \xrightarrow{p} T(\hat{\rho}_T - 1) \times \left\{\int [W(r)]^2\, dr - \left[\int W(r)\, dr\right]^2\right\}^{1/2}$$
$$\xrightarrow{L} \frac{\tfrac{1}{2}\{[W(1)]^2 - 1\} - W(1)\cdot \int W(r)\, dr}{\left\{\int [W(r)]^2\, dr - \left[\int W(r)\, dr\right]^2\right\}^{1/2}}. \qquad [17.4.36]$$

Sample percentiles for the *OLS t* test of $\rho = 1$ are reported for case 2 in the second section of Table B.6. As $T$ grows large, these approach the distribution in the last line of [17.4.36].

***Example 17.4***

When a constant term is included in the estimated autoregression for the interest rate data from Example 17.3, the result is

$$i_t = \underset{(0.112)}{0.211} + \underset{(0.019133)}{0.96691}\, i_{t-1}, \qquad [17.4.37]$$

with standard errors reported in parentheses. The Dickey-Fuller test based on the estimated value of $\rho$ for this specification is

$$T(\hat{\rho} - 1) = (168)(0.96691 - 1) = -5.56.$$

From Table B.5, the 5% critical value is found by interpolation to be $-13.8$. Since $-5.56 > -13.8$, the null hypothesis of a unit root ($\rho = 1$) is accepted at the 5% level based on the Dickey-Fuller $\hat{\rho}$ test. The *OLS t* statistic is

$$(0.96691 - 1)/0.019133 = -1.73,$$

which from Table B.6 is to be compared with $-2.89$. Since $-1.73 > -2.89$, the null hypothesis of a unit root is again accepted.

These statistics test the null hypothesis that $\rho = 1$. However, a maintained assumption on which the derivation of [17.4.25] was based is that the true value of $\alpha$ is zero. Thus, it might seem more natural to test for a unit root in this specification by testing the joint hypothesis that $\alpha = 0$ and $\rho = 1$. Dickey and Fuller (1981) used Monte Carlo to calculate the distribution of the Wald form of the *OLS F* test of this hypothesis (expression [8.1.32] or [8.1.37]). Their values are reported under the heading Case 2 in Table B.7.

***Example 17.5***

The *OLS* Wald *F* statistic for testing the joint hypothesis that $\alpha = 0$ and $\rho = 1$ for the regression in [17.4.37] is 1.81. Under the classical regression assumptions, this would have an $F(2, 166)$ distribution. In this case, however, the usual statistic is to be compared with the values under Case 2 in Table B.7, for which the 5% critical value is found by interpolation to be 4.67. Since 1.81 $< 4.67$, the joint null hypothesis that $\alpha = 0$ and $\rho = 1$ is accepted at the 5% level.

### *Case 3. Constant Term but No Time Trend Included in the Regression; True Process Is Random Walk with Drift*

In case 3, the same regression [17.4.14] is estimated as in case 2, though now it is supposed that the true process is a random walk with drift:

$$y_t = \alpha + y_{t-1} + u_t, \qquad [17.4.38]$$

where the true value of $\alpha$ is not zero. Although this might seem like a minor change, it has a radical effect on the asymptotic distribution of $\hat{\alpha}$ and $\hat{\rho}$. To see why, note that [17.4.38] implies that

$$y_t = y_0 + \alpha t + (u_1 + u_2 + \cdots + u_t) = y_0 + \alpha t + \xi_t, \qquad [17.4.39]$$

where

$$\xi_t \equiv u_1 + u_2 + \cdots + u_t \qquad \text{for } t = 1, 2, \ldots, T$$

with $\xi_0 \equiv 0$.

Consider the behavior of the sum

$$\sum_{t=1}^{T} y_{t-1} = \sum_{t=1}^{T} [y_0 + \alpha(t-1) + \xi_{t-1}]. \qquad [17.4.40]$$

The first term in [17.4.40] is just $Ty_0$, and if this is divided by $T$, the result will be a fixed value. The second term, $\Sigma\alpha(t-1)$, must be divided by $T^2$ in order to converge:

$$T^{-2} \sum_{t=1}^{T} \alpha(t-1) \rightarrow \alpha/2,$$

by virtue of Proposition 17.1(h). The third term converges when divided by $T^{3/2}$:

$$T^{-3/2} \sum_{t=1}^{T} \xi_{t-1} \xrightarrow{L} \sigma \cdot \int_0^1 W(r)\, dr,$$

from Proposition 17.1(d). The order in probability of the three individual terms in [17.4.40] is thus

$$\sum_{t=1}^{T} y_{t-1} = \underbrace{\sum_{t=1}^{T} y_0}_{O_p(T)} + \underbrace{\sum_{t=1}^{T} \alpha(t-1)}_{O_p(T^2)} + \underbrace{\sum_{t=1}^{T} \xi_{t-1}}_{O_p(T^{3/2})}.$$

The time trend $\alpha(t-1)$ asymptotically dominates the other two components:

$$\begin{aligned} T^{-2} \sum_{t=1}^{T} y_{t-1} &= T^{-1}y_0 + T^{-2} \sum_{t=1}^{T} \alpha(t-1) + T^{-1/2}\left\{T^{-3/2} \sum_{t=1}^{T} \xi_{t-1}\right\} \\ &\xrightarrow{p} 0 + \alpha/2 + 0. \end{aligned} \qquad [17.4.41]$$

Similarly, we have that

$$\sum_{t=1}^{T} y_{t-1}^2 = \sum_{t=1}^{T} [y_0 + \alpha(t-1) + \xi_{t-1}]^2$$

$$= \underbrace{\sum_{t=1}^{T} y_0^2}_{O_p(T)} + \underbrace{\sum_{t=1}^{T} \alpha^2(t-1)^2}_{O_p(T^3)} + \underbrace{\sum_{t=1}^{T} \xi_{t-1}^2}_{O_p(T^2)}$$

$$+ \underbrace{\sum_{t=1}^{T} 2y_0\alpha(t-1)}_{O_p(T^2)} + \underbrace{\sum_{t=1}^{T} 2y_0\xi_{t-1}}_{O_p(T^{3/2})} + \underbrace{\sum_{t=1}^{T} 2\alpha(t-1)\xi_{t-1}}_{O_p(T^{5/2})}.$$

When divided by $T^3$, the only term that does not vanish asymptotically is that due to the time trend $\alpha^2(t-1)^2$:

$$T^{-3} \sum_{t=1}^{T} y_{t-1}^2 \xrightarrow{p} \alpha^2/3. \qquad [17.4.42]$$

Finally, observe that

$$\sum_{t=1}^{T} y_{t-1}u_t = \sum_{t=1}^{T} [y_0 + \alpha(t-1) + \xi_{t-1}]u_t$$

$$= \underbrace{y_0 \sum_{t=1}^{T} u_t}_{O_p(T^{1/2})} + \underbrace{\sum_{t=1}^{T} \alpha(t-1)u_t}_{O_p(T^{3/2})} + \underbrace{\sum_{t=1}^{T} \xi_{t-1}u_t}_{O_p(T)},$$

from which

$$T^{-3/2} \sum_{t=1}^{T} y_{t-1}u_t \xrightarrow{p} T^{-3/2} \sum_{t=1}^{T} \alpha(t-1)u_t. \qquad [17.4.43]$$

Results [17.4.41] through [17.4.43] imply that when the true process is a random walk with drift, the estimated $OLS$ coefficients in [17.4.15] satisfy

$$\begin{bmatrix} \hat{\alpha}_T - \alpha \\ \hat{\rho}_T - 1 \end{bmatrix} = \begin{bmatrix} O_p(T) & O_p(T^2) \\ O_p(T^2) & O_p(T^3) \end{bmatrix}^{-1} \begin{bmatrix} O_p(T^{1/2}) \\ O_p(T^{3/2}) \end{bmatrix}.$$

Thus, for this case, the Sims, Stock, and Watson scaling matrix would be

$$\mathbf{Y}_T \equiv \begin{bmatrix} T^{1/2} & 0 \\ 0 & T^{3/2} \end{bmatrix},$$

for which [17.4.20] becomes

$$\begin{bmatrix} T^{1/2} & 0 \\ 0 & T^{3/2} \end{bmatrix} \begin{bmatrix} \hat{\alpha}_T - \alpha \\ \hat{\rho}_T - 1 \end{bmatrix}$$

$$= \left\{ \begin{bmatrix} T^{-1/2} & 0 \\ 0 & T^{-3/2} \end{bmatrix} \begin{bmatrix} T & \Sigma y_{t-1} \\ \Sigma y_{t-1} & \Sigma y_{t-1}^2 \end{bmatrix} \begin{bmatrix} T^{-1/2} & 0 \\ 0 & T^{-3/2} \end{bmatrix} \right\}^{-1}$$

$$\times \left\{ \begin{bmatrix} T^{-1/2} & 0 \\ 0 & T^{-3/2} \end{bmatrix} \begin{bmatrix} \Sigma u_t \\ \Sigma y_{t-1}u_t \end{bmatrix} \right\}$$

or

$$\begin{bmatrix} T^{1/2}(\hat{\alpha}_T - \alpha) \\ T^{3/2}(\hat{\rho}_T - 1) \end{bmatrix} = \begin{bmatrix} 1 & T^{-2}\Sigma y_{t-1} \\ T^{-2}\Sigma y_{t-1} & T^{-3}\Sigma y_{t-1}^2 \end{bmatrix}^{-1} \begin{bmatrix} T^{-1/2}\Sigma u_t \\ T^{-3/2}\Sigma y_{t-1}u_t \end{bmatrix}. \qquad [17.4.44]$$

From [17.4.41] and [17.4.42], the first term in [17.4.44] converges to

$$\begin{bmatrix} 1 & T^{-2}\Sigma y_{t-1} \\ T^{-2}\Sigma y_{t-1} & T^{-3}\Sigma y_{t-1}^2 \end{bmatrix} \xrightarrow{p} \begin{bmatrix} 1 & \alpha/2 \\ \alpha/2 & \alpha^2/3 \end{bmatrix} \equiv \mathbf{Q}. \qquad [17.4.45]$$

From [17.4.43] and [17.3.18], the second term in [17.4.44] satisfies

$$\begin{aligned} \begin{bmatrix} T^{-1/2}\Sigma u_t \\ T^{-3/2}\Sigma y_{t-1}u_t \end{bmatrix} &\xrightarrow{p} \begin{bmatrix} T^{-1/2}\Sigma u_t \\ T^{-3/2}\Sigma \alpha(t-1)u_t \end{bmatrix} \\ &\xrightarrow{L} N\left(\begin{bmatrix} 0 \\ 0 \end{bmatrix}, \sigma^2\begin{bmatrix} 1 & \alpha/2 \\ \alpha/2 & \alpha^2/3 \end{bmatrix}\right) \\ &= N(\mathbf{0}, \sigma^2\mathbf{Q}). \end{aligned} \qquad [17.4.46]$$

Combining [17.4.44] through [17.4.46], it follows that

$$\begin{bmatrix} T^{1/2}(\hat{\alpha}_T - \alpha) \\ T^{3/2}(\hat{\rho}_T - 1) \end{bmatrix} \xrightarrow{L} N(\mathbf{0}, \mathbf{Q}^{-1}\cdot\sigma^2\mathbf{Q}\cdot\mathbf{Q}^{-1}) = N(\mathbf{0}, \sigma^2\mathbf{Q}^{-1}). \qquad [17.4.47]$$

Thus, for case 3, both estimated coefficients are asymptotically Gaussian. In fact, the asymptotic properties of $\hat{\alpha}_T$ and $\hat{\rho}_T$ are exactly the same as those for $\hat{\alpha}_T$ and $\hat{\delta}_T$ in the deterministic time trend regression analyzed in Chapter 16. The reason for this correspondence is very simple: the regressor $y_{t-1}$ is asymptotically dominated by the time trend $\alpha\cdot(t-1)$. In large samples, it is as if the explanatory variable $y_{t-1}$ were replaced by the time trend $\alpha\cdot(t-1)$. Recalling the analysis of Section 16.2, it follows that for case 3, the standard *OLS* $t$ and $F$ statistics can be calculated in the usual way and compared with the standard tables (Tables B.3 and B.4, respectively).

### *Case 4. Constant Term and Time Trend Included in the Regression; True Process Is Random Walk With or Without Drift*

Suppose, as in the previous case, that the true model is

$$y_t = \alpha + y_{t-1} + u_t,$$

where $u_t$ is i.i.d. with mean zero and variance $\sigma^2$. For this case, the true value of $\alpha$ turns out not to matter for the asymptotic distribution. In contrast to the previous case, we now assume that a time trend is included in the regression that is actually estimated by *OLS*:

$$y_t = \alpha + \rho y_{t-1} + \delta t + u_t. \qquad [17.4.48]$$

If $\alpha \neq 0$, $y_{t-1}$ would be asymptotically equivalent to a time trend. Since a time trend is already included as a separate variable in the regression, this would make the explanatory variables collinear in large samples. Describing the asymptotic distribution of the estimates therefore requires not just a rescaling of variables but also a rotation of the kind introduced in Section 16.3.

Note that the regression model of [17.4.48] can equivalently be written as

$$\begin{aligned} y_t &= (1 - \rho)\alpha + \rho[y_{t-1} - \alpha(t - 1)] + (\delta + \rho\alpha)t + u_t \\ &\equiv \alpha^* + \rho^*\xi_{t-1} + \delta^* t + u_t, \end{aligned} \qquad [17.4.49]$$

where $\alpha^* \equiv (1 - \rho)\alpha$, $\rho^* \equiv \rho$, $\delta^* \equiv (\delta + \rho\alpha)$, and $\xi_t \equiv y_t - \alpha t$. Moreover, under the null hypothesis that $\rho = 1$ and $\delta = 0$,

$$\xi_t = y_0 + u_1 + u_2 + \cdots + u_t;$$

that is, $\xi_t$ is the random walk described in Proposition 17.1. Consider, as in Section 16.3, a hypothetical regression of $y_t$ on a constant, $\xi_{t-1}$, and a time trend, producing the *OLS* estimates

$$\begin{bmatrix} \hat{\alpha}_T^* \\ \hat{\rho}_T^* \\ \hat{\delta}_T^* \end{bmatrix} = \begin{bmatrix} T & \Sigma\xi_{t-1} & \Sigma t \\ \Sigma\xi_{t-1} & \Sigma\xi_{t-1}^2 & \Sigma\xi_{t-1}t \\ \Sigma t & \Sigma t\xi_{t-1} & \Sigma t^2 \end{bmatrix}^{-1} \begin{bmatrix} \Sigma y_t \\ \Sigma\xi_{t-1}y_t \\ \Sigma t y_t \end{bmatrix}. \qquad [17.4.50]$$

The maintained hypothesis is that $\alpha = \alpha_0$, $\rho = 1$, and $\delta = 0$, which in the transformed system would mean $\alpha^* = 0$, $\rho^* = 1$, and $\delta^* = \alpha_0$. The deviations of the *OLS* estimates from these true values are given by

$$\begin{bmatrix} \hat{\alpha}_T^* \\ \hat{\rho}_T^* - 1 \\ \hat{\delta}_T^* - \alpha_0 \end{bmatrix} = \begin{bmatrix} T & \Sigma\xi_{t-1} & \Sigma t \\ \Sigma\xi_{t-1} & \Sigma\xi_{t-1}^2 & \Sigma\xi_{t-1}t \\ \Sigma t & \Sigma t\xi_{t-1} & \Sigma t^2 \end{bmatrix}^{-1} \begin{bmatrix} \Sigma u_t \\ \Sigma\xi_{t-1}u_t \\ \Sigma t u_t \end{bmatrix}. \qquad [17.4.51]$$

Consulting the rates of convergence in Proposition 17.1, in this case the scaling matrix should be

$$\mathbf{Y}_T = \begin{bmatrix} T^{1/2} & 0 & 0 \\ 0 & T & 0 \\ 0 & 0 & T^{3/2} \end{bmatrix},$$

and [17.4.20] would be

$$\begin{aligned} &\begin{bmatrix} T^{1/2} & 0 & 0 \\ 0 & T & 0 \\ 0 & 0 & T^{3/2} \end{bmatrix} \begin{bmatrix} \hat{\alpha}_T^* \\ \hat{\rho}_T^* - 1 \\ \hat{\delta}_T^* - \alpha_0 \end{bmatrix} \\ &= \left\{ \begin{bmatrix} T^{-1/2} & 0 & 0 \\ 0 & T^{-1} & 0 \\ 0 & 0 & T^{-3/2} \end{bmatrix} \begin{bmatrix} T & \Sigma\xi_{t-1} & \Sigma t \\ \Sigma\xi_{t-1} & \Sigma\xi_{t-1}^2 & \Sigma\xi_{t-1}t \\ \Sigma t & \Sigma t\xi_{t-1} & \Sigma t^2 \end{bmatrix} \right. \\ &\qquad \left. \times \begin{bmatrix} T^{-1/2} & 0 & 0 \\ 0 & T^{-1} & 0 \\ 0 & 0 & T^{-3/2} \end{bmatrix} \right\}^{-1} \\ &\qquad \times \left\{ \begin{bmatrix} T^{-1/2} & 0 & 0 \\ 0 & T^{-1} & 0 \\ 0 & 0 & T^{-3/2} \end{bmatrix} \begin{bmatrix} \Sigma u_t \\ \Sigma\xi_{t-1}u_t \\ \Sigma t u_t \end{bmatrix} \right\} \end{aligned}$$

or

$$\begin{bmatrix} T^{1/2}\hat{\alpha}_T^* \\ T(\hat{\rho}_T^* - 1) \\ T^{3/2}(\hat{\delta}_T^* - \alpha_0) \end{bmatrix} = \begin{bmatrix} 1 & T^{-3/2}\Sigma\xi_{t-1} & T^{-2}\Sigma t \\ T^{-3/2}\Sigma\xi_{t-1} & T^{-2}\Sigma\xi_{t-1}^2 & T^{-5/2}\Sigma\xi_{t-1}t \\ T^{-2}\Sigma t & T^{-5/2}\Sigma t\xi_{t-1} & T^{-3}\Sigma t^2 \end{bmatrix}^{-1} \times \begin{bmatrix} T^{-1/2}\Sigma u_t \\ T^{-1}\Sigma\xi_{t-1}u_t \\ T^{-3/2}\Sigma t u_t \end{bmatrix} \qquad [17.4.52]$$

The asymptotic distribution can then be found from Proposition 17.1:

$$\begin{bmatrix} T^{1/2}\hat{\alpha}_T^* \\ T(\hat{\rho}_T^* - 1) \\ T^{3/2}(\hat{\delta}_T^* - \alpha_0) \end{bmatrix}$$

$$\xrightarrow{L} \begin{bmatrix} 1 & \sigma\cdot\int W(r)\,dr & \frac{1}{2} \\ \sigma\cdot\int W(r)\,dr & \sigma^2\cdot\int [W(r)]^2\,dr & \sigma\cdot\int rW(r)\,dr \\ \frac{1}{2} & \sigma\cdot\int rW(r)\,dr & \frac{1}{3} \end{bmatrix}^{-1}$$

$$\times \begin{bmatrix} \sigma\cdot W(1) \\ \frac{1}{2}\sigma^2\{[W(1)]^2 - 1\} \\ \sigma\cdot\{W(1) - \int W(r)\,dr\} \end{bmatrix}$$

$$= \sigma\begin{bmatrix} 1 & 0 & 0 \\ 0 & \sigma & 0 \\ 0 & 0 & 1 \end{bmatrix}^{-1} \begin{bmatrix} 1 & \int W(r)\,dr & \frac{1}{2} \\ \int W(r)\,dr & \int [W(r)]^2\,dr & \int rW(r)\,dr \\ \frac{1}{2} & \int rW(r)\,dr & \frac{1}{3} \end{bmatrix}^{-1} \qquad [17.4.53]$$

$$\times \begin{bmatrix} 1 & 0 & 0 \\ 0 & \sigma & 0 \\ 0 & 0 & 1 \end{bmatrix}^{-1} \begin{bmatrix} 1 & 0 & 0 \\ 0 & \sigma & 0 \\ 0 & 0 & 1 \end{bmatrix} \begin{bmatrix} W(1) \\ \frac{1}{2}\{[W(1)]^2 - 1\} \\ W(1) - \int W(r)\,dr \end{bmatrix}$$

$$= \begin{bmatrix} \sigma & 0 & 0 \\ 0 & 1 & 0 \\ 0 & 0 & \sigma \end{bmatrix} \begin{bmatrix} 1 & \int W(r)\,dr & \frac{1}{2} \\ \int W(r)\,dr & \int [W(r)]^2\,dr & \int rW(r)\,dr \\ \frac{1}{2} & \int rW(r)\,dr & \frac{1}{3} \end{bmatrix}^{-1}$$

$$\times \begin{bmatrix} W(1) \\ \frac{1}{2}\{[W(1)]^2 - 1\} \\ W(1) - \int W(r)\,dr \end{bmatrix}.$$

Note that $\hat{\rho}_T^*$, the *OLS* estimate of $\rho$ based on [17.4.49], is identical to $\hat{\rho}_T$, the *OLS* estimate of $\rho$ based on [17.4.48]. Thus, the asymptotic distribution of $T(\hat{\rho}_T - 1)$ is given by the middle row of [17.4.53]. Note that this distribution does not depend on either $\sigma$ or $\alpha$; in particular, it does not matter whether or not the true value of $\alpha$ is zero.

The asymptotic distribution of $\hat{\sigma}_{\hat{\rho}_T}$, the *OLS* standard error for $\hat{\rho}_T$, can be found using similar calculations to those in [17.4.31] and [17.4.32]. Notice that

$$\begin{aligned}
T^2 \cdot \hat{\sigma}^2_{\hat{\rho}_T} &= T^2 \cdot s_T^2 [0 \quad 1 \quad 0] \begin{bmatrix} T & \Sigma\xi_{t-1} & \Sigma t \\ \Sigma\xi_{t-1} & \Sigma\xi_{t-1}^2 & \Sigma\xi_{t-1}t \\ \Sigma t & \Sigma t\xi_{t-1} & \Sigma t^2 \end{bmatrix}^{-1} \begin{bmatrix} 0 \\ 1 \\ 0 \end{bmatrix} \\
&= s_T^2 [0 \quad 1 \quad 0] \begin{bmatrix} T^{1/2} & 0 & 0 \\ 0 & T & 0 \\ 0 & 0 & T^{3/2} \end{bmatrix} \\
&\quad \times \begin{bmatrix} T & \Sigma\xi_{t-1} & \Sigma t \\ \Sigma\xi_{t-1} & \Sigma\xi_{t-1}^2 & \Sigma\xi_{t-1}t \\ \Sigma t & \Sigma t\xi_{t-1} & \Sigma t^2 \end{bmatrix}^{-1} \begin{bmatrix} T^{1/2} & 0 & 0 \\ 0 & T & 0 \\ 0 & 0 & T^{3/2} \end{bmatrix} \begin{bmatrix} 0 \\ 1 \\ 0 \end{bmatrix} \\
&= s_T^2 [0 \quad 1 \quad 0] \\
&\quad \times \begin{bmatrix} 1 & T^{-3/2}\Sigma\xi_{t-1} & T^{-2}\Sigma t \\ T^{-3/2}\Sigma\xi_{t-1} & T^{-2}\Sigma\xi_{t-1}^2 & T^{-5/2}\Sigma\xi_{t-1}t \\ T^{-2}\Sigma t & T^{-5/2}\Sigma t\xi_{t-1} & T^{-3}\Sigma t^2 \end{bmatrix}^{-1} \begin{bmatrix} 0 \\ 1 \\ 0 \end{bmatrix} \\
&\xrightarrow{L} \sigma^2 [0 \quad 1 \quad 0] \begin{bmatrix} 1 & 0 & 0 \\ 0 & \sigma & 0 \\ 0 & 0 & 1 \end{bmatrix}^{-1} \\
&\quad \times \begin{bmatrix} 1 & \int W(r)\,dr & \frac{1}{2} \\ \int W(r)\,dr & \int [W(r)]^2\,dr & \int rW(r)\,dr \\ \frac{1}{2} & \int rW(r)\,dr & \frac{1}{3} \end{bmatrix}^{-1} \begin{bmatrix} 1 & 0 & 0 \\ 0 & \sigma & 0 \\ 0 & 0 & 1 \end{bmatrix}^{-1} \begin{bmatrix} 0 \\ 1 \\ 0 \end{bmatrix} \\
&= [0 \quad 1 \quad 0] \begin{bmatrix} 1 & \int W(r)\,dr & \frac{1}{2} \\ \int W(r)\,dr & \int [W(r)]^2\,dr & \int rW(r)\,dr \\ \frac{1}{2} & \int rW(r)\,dr & \frac{1}{3} \end{bmatrix}^{-1} \begin{bmatrix} 0 \\ 1 \\ 0 \end{bmatrix} \\
&\equiv Q.
\end{aligned} \tag{17.4.54}$$

From this result it follows that the asymptotic distribution of the *OLS* $t$ test of the hypothesis that $\rho = 1$ is given by

$$t_T = T(\hat{\rho}_T - 1) \div (T^2 \cdot \hat{\sigma}^2_{\hat{\rho}_T})^{1/2} \xrightarrow{p} T(\hat{\rho}_T - 1) \div \sqrt{Q}. \tag{17.4.55}$$

Again, this distribution does not depend on $\alpha$ or $\sigma$. The small-sample distribution of the *OLS* $t$ statistic under the assumption of Gaussian disturbances is presented under case 4 in Table B.6. If this distribution were truly $t$, then a value below $-2.0$ would be sufficient to reject the null hypothesis. However, Table B.6 reveals that, because of the nonstandard distribution, the $t$ statistic must be below $-3.4$ before the null hypothesis of a unit root could be rejected.

The assumption that the true value of $\delta$ is equal to zero is again an auxiliary hypothesis upon which the asymptotic properties of the test depend. Thus, as in case 2, it is natural to consider the *OLS F* test of the joint null hypothesis that $\delta = 0$ and $\rho = 1$. Though this $F$ test is calculated in the usual way, its asymptotic distribution is nonstandard, and the calculated $F$ statistic should be compared with the value under case 4 in Table B.7.

## *Summary of Dickey-Fuller Tests in the Absence of Serial Correlation*

We have seen that the asymptotic properties of the *OLS* estimate $\hat{\rho}_T$ when the true value of $\rho$ is unity depend on whether or not a constant term or a time trend is included in the regression that is estimated and on whether or not the random walk that describes the true process for $y_t$ includes a drift term. These results are summarized in Table 17.1.

Which is the "correct" case to use to test the null hypothesis of a unit root? The answer depends on why we are interested in testing for a unit root. If the analyst has a specific null hypothesis about the process that generated the data, then obviously this would guide the choice of test. In the absence of such guidance, one general principle would be to fit a specification that is a plausible description of the data under both the null hypothesis and the alternative. This principle would suggest using the case 4 test for a series with an obvious trend and the case 2 test for series without a significant trend.

For example, Figure 17.2 plots the nominal interest rate series used in the examples in this section. Although this series has tended upward over this sample period, there is nothing in economic theory to suggest that nominal interest rates should exhibit a deterministic time trend, and so a natural null hypothesis is that the true process is a random walk without trend. In terms of framing a plausible alternative, it is difficult to maintain that these data could have been generated by $i_t = \rho i_{t-1} + u_t$ with $|\rho|$ significantly less than 1. If these data were to be described by a stationary process, surely the process would have a positive mean. This argues for including a constant term in the estimated regression, even though under the null hypothesis the true process does not contain a constant term. Thus, case 2 is a sensible approach for these data, as analyzed in Examples 17.4 and 17.5.

As a second example, Figure 17.3 plots quarterly real GNP for the United States from 1947:I to 1989:I. Given a growing population and technological improvements, such a series would certainly be expected to exhibit a persistent upward trend, and this trend is unmistakable in the figure. The question is whether this trend arises from the positive drift term of a random walk:

$$H_0\colon y_t = \alpha + y_{t-1} + u_t \qquad \alpha > 0,$$

or from a deterministic time trend added to a stationary $AR(1)$:

$$H_A\colon y_t = \alpha + \delta t + \rho y_{t-1} + u_t \qquad |\rho| < 1.$$

Thus, the recommended test statistics for this case are those described in case 4.

The following model for 100 times the log of real GNP (denoted $y_t$) was estimated by *OLS* regression:

$$y_t = \underset{(13.53)}{27.24} + \underset{(0.019304)}{0.96252}\, y_{t-1} + \underset{(0.01521)}{0.02753}\, t. \qquad [17.4.56]$$

(standard errors in parentheses). The sample size is $T = 168$. The Dickey-Fuller

$\rho$ test is

$$T(\hat{\rho} - 1) = 168(0.96252 - 1.0) = -6.3.$$

Since $-6.3 > -21.0$, the null hypothesis that GNP is characterized by a random walk with possible drift is accepted at the 5% level. The Dickey-Fuller $t$ test,

$$t = \frac{0.96252 - 1.0}{0.019304} = -1.94,$$

exceeds the 5% critical value of $-3.44$, so that the null hypothesis of a unit root is accepted by this test as well. Finally, the $F$ test of the joint null hypothesis that $\delta = 0$ and $\rho = 1$ is 2.44. Since this is less than the 5% critical value of 6.42 from Table B.7, this null hypothesis is again accepted.

**TABLE 17.1**
**Summary of Dickey-Fuller Tests for Unit Roots in the Absence of Serial Correlation**

---

*Case 1:*

Estimated regression: $y_t = \rho y_{t-1} + u_t$
True process: $y_t = y_{t-1} + u_t \qquad u_t \sim \text{i.i.d. } N(0, \sigma^2)$
$T(\hat{\rho}_T - 1)$ has the distribution described under the heading Case 1 in Table B.5.
$(\hat{\rho}_T - 1)/\hat{\sigma}_{\hat{\rho}_T}$ has the distribution described under Case 1 in Table B.6.

*Case 2:*

Estimated regression: $y_t = \alpha + \rho y_{t-1} + u_t$
True process: $y_t = y_{t-1} + u_t \qquad u_t \sim \text{i.i.d. } N(0, \sigma^2)$
$T(\hat{\rho}_T - 1)$ has the distribution described under Case 2 in Table B.5.
$(\hat{\rho}_T - 1)/\hat{\sigma}_{\hat{\rho}_T}$ has the distribution described under Case 2 in Table B.6.
*OLS F* test of joint hypothesis that $\alpha = 0$ and $\rho = 1$ has the distribution described under Case 2 in Table B.7.

*Case 3:*

Estimated regression: $y_t = \alpha + \rho y_{t-1} + u_t$
True process: $y_t = \alpha + y_{t-1} + u_t \qquad \alpha \neq 0,\ u_t \sim \text{i.i.d. } (0, \sigma^2)$
$(\hat{\rho}_T - 1)/\hat{\sigma}_{\hat{\rho}_T} \xrightarrow{L} N(0, 1)$

*Case 4:*

Estimated regression: $y_t = \alpha + \rho y_{t-1} + \delta t + u_t$
True process: $y_t = \alpha + y_{t-1} + u_t \qquad \alpha \text{ any},\ u_t \sim \text{i.i.d. } N(0, \sigma^2)$
$T(\hat{\rho}_T - 1)$ has the distribution described under Case 4 in Table B.5.
$(\hat{\rho}_T - 1)/\hat{\sigma}_{\hat{\rho}_T}$ has the distribution described under Case 4 in Table B.6.
*OLS F* test of joint hypothesis that $\rho = 1$ and $\delta = 0$ has the distribution described under Case 4 in Table B.7.

---

*Notes to Table 17.1*

*Estimated regression* indicates the form in which the regression is estimated, using observations $t = 1, 2, \ldots, T$ and conditioning on observation $t = 0$.

*True process* describes the null hypothesis under which the distribution is calculated.

$\hat{\rho}_T$ is the *OLS* estimate of $\rho$ from the indicated regression based on a sample of size $T$.

$(\hat{\rho}_T - 1)/\hat{\sigma}_{\hat{\rho}_T}$ is the *OLS t* test of $\rho = 1$.

*OLS F test* of a hypothesis involving two restrictions is given by expression [17.7.39].

If $u_t \sim \text{i.i.d. } N(0, \sigma^2)$, then Tables B.5 through B.7 give Monte Carlo estimates of the exact small-sample distribution. The tables are also valid for large $T$ when $u_t$ is non-Gaussian i.i.d. as well as for certain heterogeneously distributed serially uncorrelated processes. For serially correlated $u_t$, see Table 17.2 or 17.3.

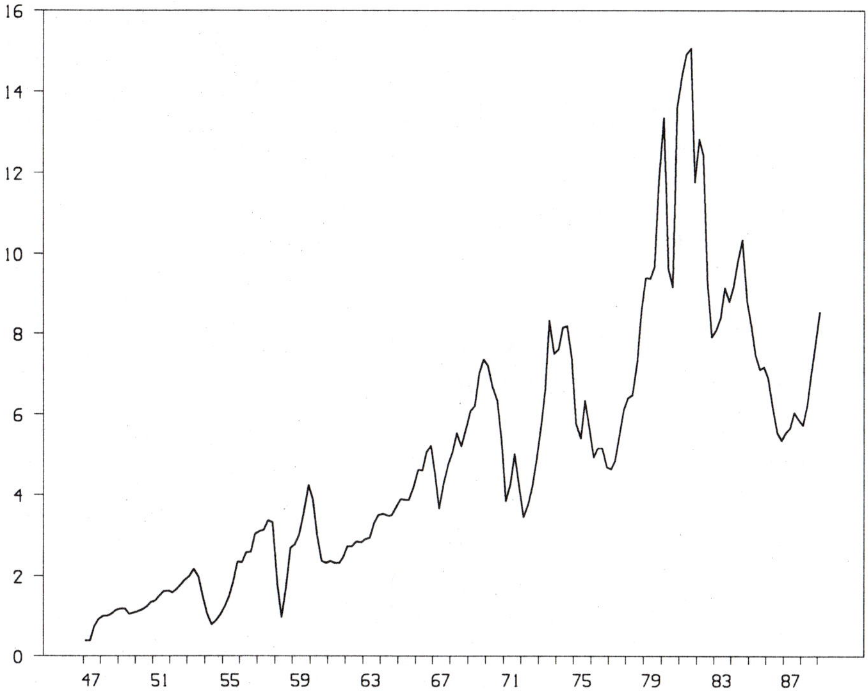


**FIGURE 17.2** U.S. nominal interest rate on 3-month Treasury bills, data sampled quarterly but quoted at an annual rate, 1947:I to 1989:I.

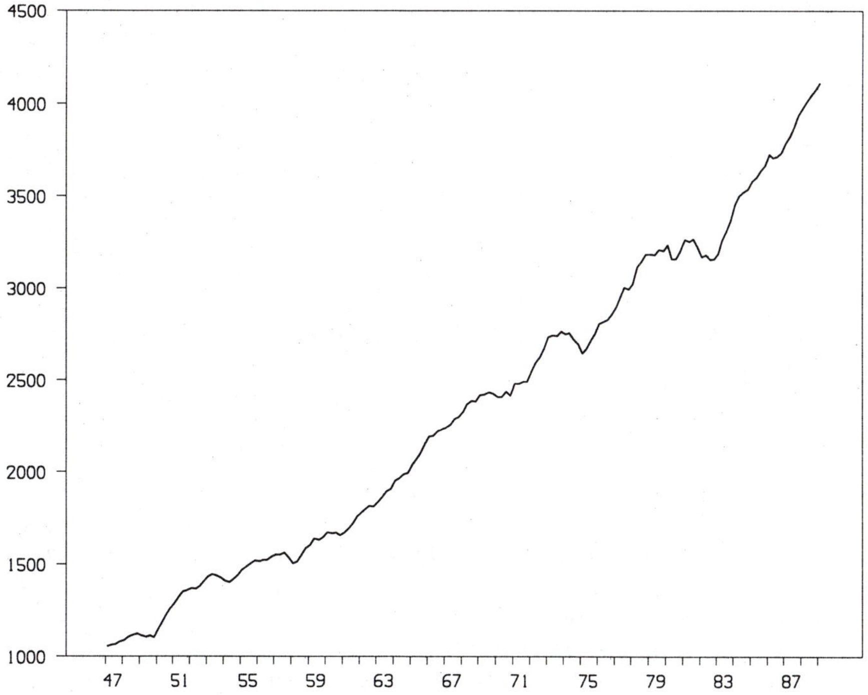


**FIGURE 17.3** U.S. real GNP, data sampled quarterly but quoted at an annual rate in billions of 1982 dollars, 1947:I to 1989:I.

Of the tests discussed so far, those developed for case 2 seem appropriate for the interest rate data and the tests developed for case 4 seem best for the GNP data. However, more general tests presented in Sections 17.6 and 17.7 are to be preferred for describing either of these series. This is because the maintained assumption throughout this section has been that the disturbance term $u_t$ in the regression is i.i.d. There is no strong reason to expect this for either of these time series. The next section develops results that can be used to test for unit roots in serially correlated processes.

## 17.5. *Asymptotic Results for Unit Root Processes with General Serial Correlation*

This section generalizes Proposition 17.1 to allow for serial correlation. The following preliminary result is quite helpful.

***Proposition 17.2:*** *Let*

$$u_t = \psi(L)\varepsilon_t = \sum_{j=0}^{\infty} \psi_j \varepsilon_{t-j}, \qquad [17.5.1]$$

*where*

$$E(\varepsilon_t) = 0$$

$$E(\varepsilon_t \varepsilon_\tau) = \begin{cases} \sigma^2 & \text{for } t = \tau \\ 0 & \text{otherwise} \end{cases}$$

$$\sum_{j=0}^{\infty} j \cdot |\psi_j| < \infty. \qquad [17.5.2]$$

*Then*

$$u_1 + u_2 + \cdots + u_t = \psi(1) \cdot (\varepsilon_1 + \varepsilon_2 + \cdots + \varepsilon_t) + \eta_t - \eta_0, \qquad [17.5.3]$$

*where* $\psi(1) \equiv \Sigma_{j=0}^{\infty} \psi_j$, $\eta_t = \Sigma_{j=0}^{\infty} \alpha_j \varepsilon_{t-j}$, $\alpha_j = -(\psi_{j+1} + \psi_{j+2} + \psi_{j+3} + \cdots)$, *and* $\Sigma_{j=0}^{\infty} |\alpha_j| < \infty$.

The condition in [17.5.2] is slightly stronger than absolute summability, though it is satisfied by any stationary *ARMA* process.

Notice that if $y_t$ is an $I(1)$ process $y_t$ whose first difference is given by $u_t$, or

$$\Delta y_t = u_t,$$

then

$$y_t = u_1 + u_2 + \cdots + u_t + y_0 = \psi(1) \cdot (\varepsilon_1 + \varepsilon_2 + \cdots + \varepsilon_t) + \eta_t - \eta_0 + y_0.$$

Proposition 17.2 thus states that any $I(1)$ process whose first difference satisfies [17.5.1] and [17.5.2] can be written as the sum of a random walk ($\psi(1) \cdot (\varepsilon_1 + \varepsilon_2 + \cdots + \varepsilon_t)$), initial conditions ($y_0 - \eta_0$), and a stationary process ($\eta_t$). This observation was first made by Beveridge and Nelson (1981), and [17.5.3] is sometimes referred to as the *Beveridge-Nelson decomposition*.

Notice that $\eta_t$ is a stationary process. An important implication of this is that if [17.5.3] is divided by $\sqrt{t}$, only the first term $(1/\sqrt{t})\psi(1) \cdot (\varepsilon_1 + \varepsilon_2 + \cdots + \varepsilon_t)$ should matter for the distribution of $(1/\sqrt{t}) \cdot (u_1 + u_2 + \cdots + u_t)$ as $t \to \infty$.

As an example of how this result can be used, suppose that $X_T(r)$ is defined as in [17.3.2]:

$$X_T(r) \equiv (1/T) \sum_{t=1}^{[Tr]^*} u_t, \qquad [17.5.4]$$

where $u_t$ satisfies the conditions of Proposition 17.2 with $\varepsilon_t$ i.i.d. and $E(\varepsilon_t^4) < \infty$. Then the continuous-time process $\sqrt{T}\cdot X_T(r)$ converges to $\sigma\cdot\psi(1)$ times standard Brownian motion:

$$\sqrt{T}\cdot X_T(\cdot) \xrightarrow{L} \sigma\cdot\psi(1)\cdot W(\cdot). \qquad [17.5.5]$$

To derive [17.5.5], note from Proposition 17.2 that

$$\begin{aligned} \sqrt{T}\cdot X_T(r) &= (1/\sqrt{T})\cdot \sum_{t=1}^{[Tr]^*} u_t \\ &= \psi(1)\cdot(1/\sqrt{T})\cdot \sum_{t=1}^{[Tr]^*} \varepsilon_t + (1/\sqrt{T})\cdot(\eta_{[Tr]^*} - \eta_0) \qquad [17.5.6] \\ &\equiv \psi(1)\cdot(1/\sqrt{T})\cdot \sum_{t=1}^{[Tr]^*} \varepsilon_t + S_T(r), \end{aligned}$$

where we have defined $S_T(r) \equiv (1/\sqrt{T})\cdot(\eta_{[Tr]^*} - \eta_0)$. Notice as in Example 17.2 that

$$S_T(\cdot) \xrightarrow{p} 0 \qquad [17.5.7]$$

as $T \to \infty$. Furthermore, from [17.3.8],

$$(1/\sqrt{T})\cdot \sum_{t=1}^{[Tr]^*} \varepsilon_t \xrightarrow{L} \sigma\cdot W(r). \qquad [17.5.8]$$

Substituting [17.5.7] and [17.5.8] into [17.5.6] produces [17.5.5].

Another implication is found by evaluating the functions in [17.5.5] at $r = 1$:

$$(1/\sqrt{T}) \sum_{t=1}^{T} u_t \xrightarrow{L} \sigma\cdot\psi(1)\cdot W(1). \qquad [17.5.9]$$

Since $W(1)$ is distributed $N(0, 1)$, result [17.5.9] states that

$$(1/\sqrt{T}) \sum_{t=1}^{T} u_t \xrightarrow{L} N(0, \sigma^2[\psi(1)]^2),$$

which is the usual central limit theorem of Proposition 7.11.

The following proposition uses this basic idea to generalize the other results from Proposition 17.1; for details on the proofs, see Appendix 17.A.

***Proposition 17.3:*** *Let $u_t = \psi(L)\varepsilon_t = \Sigma_{j=0}^{\infty} \psi_j\varepsilon_{t-j}$, where $\Sigma_{j=0}^{\infty} j\cdot|\psi_j| < \infty$ and $\{\varepsilon_t\}$ is an i.i.d. sequence with mean zero, variance $\sigma^2$, and finite fourth moment. Define*

$$\gamma_j \equiv E(u_t u_{t-j}) = \sigma^2 \sum_{s=0}^{\infty} \psi_s\psi_{s+j} \qquad \textit{for } j = 0, 1, 2, \ldots \qquad [17.5.10]$$

$$\lambda \equiv \sigma \sum_{j=0}^{\infty} \psi_j = \sigma\cdot\psi(1)$$

$$\xi_t \equiv u_1 + u_2 + \cdots + u_t \qquad \textit{for } t = 1, 2, \ldots, T \qquad [17.5.11]$$

*with $\xi_0 \equiv 0$. Then*

$$(a)\quad T^{-1/2}\sum_{t=1}^{T} u_t \xrightarrow{L} \lambda\cdot W(1);$$

$$(b)\quad T^{-1/2}\sum_{t=1}^{T} u_{t-j}\varepsilon_t \xrightarrow{L} N(0,\sigma^2\gamma_0) \qquad \textit{for } j = 1, 2, \ldots;$$

$$(c)\quad T^{-1}\sum_{t=1}^{T} u_t u_{t-j} \xrightarrow{p} \gamma_j \qquad \textit{for } j = 0, 1, 2, \ldots;$$

$$(d)\quad T^{-1}\sum_{t=1}^{T} \xi_{t-1}\varepsilon_t \xrightarrow{L} (1/2)\sigma\cdot\lambda\cdot\{[W(1)]^2 - 1\};$$

$$(e)\quad T^{-1}\sum_{t=1}^{T} \xi_{t-1}u_{t-j}$$

$$\xrightarrow{L} \begin{cases} (1/2)\{\lambda^2\cdot[W(1)]^2 - \gamma_0\} & \textit{for } j = 0 \\ (1/2)\{\lambda^2\cdot[W(1)]^2 - \gamma_0\} + \gamma_0 + \gamma_1 + \gamma_2 + \cdots + \gamma_{j-1} & \\ & \textit{for } j = 1, 2, \ldots; \end{cases}$$

$$(f)\quad T^{-3/2}\sum_{t=1}^{T} \xi_{t-1} \xrightarrow{L} \lambda\cdot\int_0^1 W(r)\,dr;$$

$$(g)\quad T^{-3/2}\sum_{t=1}^{T} tu_{t-j} \xrightarrow{L} \lambda\cdot\left\{W(1) - \int_0^1 W(r)\,dr\right\} \qquad \textit{for } j = 0, 1, 2, \ldots;$$

$$(h)\quad T^{-2}\sum_{t=1}^{T} \xi_{t-1}^2 \xrightarrow{L} \lambda^2\cdot\int_0^1 [W(r)]^2\,dr;$$

$$(i)\quad T^{-5/2}\sum_{t=1}^{T} t\xi_{t-1} \xrightarrow{L} \lambda\cdot\int_0^1 rW(r)\,dr;$$

$$(j)\quad T^{-3}\sum_{t=1}^{T} t\xi_{t-1}^2 \xrightarrow{L} \lambda^2\cdot\int_0^1 r\cdot[W(r)]^2\,dr;$$

$$(k)\quad T^{-(v+1)}\sum_{t=1}^{T} t^v \rightarrow 1/(v+1) \qquad \textit{for } v = 0, 1, \ldots.$$

Again, there are simpler ways to describe individual results; for example, (a) is a $N(0, \lambda^2)$ distribution, (d) is $(1/2)\sigma\lambda\cdot[\chi^2(1) - 1]$, and (f) and (g) are both $N(0, \lambda^2/3)$ distributions.

These results can be used to construct unit root tests for serially correlated observations in two ways. One approach, due to Phillips (1987) and Phillips and Perron (1988), is to continue to estimate the regressions in exactly the form indicated in Table 17.1, but to adjust the test statistics to take account of serial correlation and potential heteroskedasticity in the disturbances. This approach is described in Section 17.6. The second approach, due to Dickey and Fuller (1979), is to add lagged changes of $y$ as explanatory variables in the regressions in Table 17.1. This is described in Section 17.7.

## 17.6. *Phillips-Perron Tests for Unit Roots*

### *Asymptotic Distribution for Case 2 Assumptions with Serially Correlated Disturbances*

To illustrate the basic idea behind the Phillips (1987) and Phillips and Perron (1988) tests for unit roots, we will discuss in detail the treatment they propose for the analog of case 2 of Section 17.4. After this case has been reviewed, similar results will be stated for case 1 and case 4, with details developed in exercises at the end of the chapter.

Case 2 of Section 17.4 considered *OLS* estimation of $\alpha$ and $\rho$ in the regression model

$$y_t = \alpha + \rho y_{t-1} + u_t \qquad [17.6.1]$$

under the assumption that the true $\alpha = 0, \rho = 1$, and $u_t$ is i.i.d. Phillips and Perron (1988) generalized these results to the case when $u_t$ is serially correlated and possibly heteroskedastic as well. For now we will assume that the true process is

$$y_t - y_{t-1} = u_t = \psi(L)\varepsilon_t,$$

where $\psi(L)$ and $\varepsilon_t$ satisfy the conditions of Proposition 17.3. More general conditions under which the same techniques are valid will be discussed at the end of this section.

If [17.6.1] were a stationary autoregression with $|\rho| < 1$, the *OLS* estimate $\hat{\rho}_T$ in [17.4.15] would not give a consistent estimate of $\rho$ when $u_t$ is serially correlated. However, if $\rho$ is equal to 1, the rate $T$ convergence of $\hat{\rho}_T$ turns out to ensure that $\hat{\rho}_T \xrightarrow{p} 1$ even when $u_t$ is serially correlated. Phillips and Perron (1988) therefore proposed estimating [17.6.1] by *OLS* even when $u_t$ is serially correlated and then modifying the statistics in Section 17.4 to take account of the serial correlation.

Let $\hat{\alpha}_T$ and $\hat{\rho}_T$ be the *OLS* estimates based on [17.6.1] without any correction for serial correlation; that is, $\hat{\alpha}_T$ and $\hat{\rho}_T$ are the magnitudes defined in [17.4.15]. If the true values are $\alpha = 0$ and $\rho = 1$, then, as in [17.4.22],

$$\begin{bmatrix} T^{1/2}\hat{\alpha}_T \\ T(\hat{\rho}_T - 1) \end{bmatrix} = \begin{bmatrix} 1 & T^{-3/2}\Sigma y_{t-1} \\ T^{-3/2}\Sigma y_{t-1} & T^{-2}\Sigma y_{t-1}^2 \end{bmatrix}^{-1} \begin{bmatrix} T^{-1/2}\Sigma u_t \\ T^{-1}\Sigma y_{t-1}u_t \end{bmatrix}, \qquad [17.6.2]$$

where $\Sigma$ denotes summation over $t$ from 1 to $T$. Also, under the null hypothesis that $\alpha = 0$ and $\rho = 1$, it follows as in [17.4.4] that

$$y_t = y_0 + u_1 + u_2 + \cdots + u_t.$$

If $u_t = \psi(L)\varepsilon_t$ as in Proposition 17.3, then $y_t$ is the variable labeled $\xi_t$ in Proposition 17.3, plus the inconsequential value $y_0$. Using results (f) and (h) of that proposition,

$$\begin{aligned} &\begin{bmatrix} 1 & T^{-3/2}\Sigma y_{t-1} \\ T^{-3/2}\Sigma y_{t-1} & T^{-2}\Sigma y_{t-1}^2 \end{bmatrix}^{-1} \\ &\xrightarrow{L} \begin{bmatrix} 1 & \lambda\cdot\int W(r)\,dr \\ \lambda\cdot\int W(r)\,dr & \lambda^2\cdot\int [W(r)]^2\,dr \end{bmatrix}^{-1} \qquad [17.6.3] \\ &= \begin{bmatrix} 1 & 0 \\ 0 & \lambda \end{bmatrix}^{-1} \begin{bmatrix} 1 & \int W(r)\,dr \\ \int W(r)\,dr & \int [W(r)]^2\,dr \end{bmatrix}^{-1} \begin{bmatrix} 1 & 0 \\ 0 & \lambda \end{bmatrix}^{-1}, \end{aligned}$$

where the integral sign denotes integration over $r$ from 0 to 1. Similarly, results (a) and (e) of Proposition 17.3 give

$$\begin{aligned} \begin{bmatrix} T^{-1/2}\Sigma u_t \\ T^{-1}\Sigma y_{t-1}u_t \end{bmatrix} &\xrightarrow{L} \begin{bmatrix} \lambda\cdot W(1) \\ \frac{1}{2}\{\lambda^2[W(1)]^2 - \gamma_0\} \end{bmatrix} \\ &= \begin{bmatrix} \lambda\cdot W(1) \\ \frac{1}{2}\lambda^2\{[W(1)]^2 - 1\} \end{bmatrix} + \begin{bmatrix} 0 \\ \frac{1}{2}\{\lambda^2 - \gamma_0\} \end{bmatrix} \qquad [17.6.4] \\ &= \lambda\begin{bmatrix} 1 & 0 \\ 0 & \lambda \end{bmatrix} \begin{bmatrix} W(1) \\ \frac{1}{2}\{[W(1)]^2 - 1\} \end{bmatrix} + \begin{bmatrix} 0 \\ \frac{1}{2}\{\lambda^2 - \gamma_0\} \end{bmatrix}. \end{aligned}$$

Substituting [17.6.3] and [17.6.4] into [17.6.2] produces

$$\begin{bmatrix} T^{1/2}\hat{\alpha}_T \\ T(\hat{\rho}_T - 1) \end{bmatrix} \xrightarrow{L} \begin{bmatrix} 1 & 0 \\ 0 & \lambda \end{bmatrix}^{-1} \begin{bmatrix} 1 & \int W(r)\,dr \\ \int W(r)\,dr & \int [W(r)]^2\,dr \end{bmatrix}^{-1}$$

$$\times \begin{bmatrix} 1 & 0 \\ 0 & \lambda \end{bmatrix}^{-1} \left\{ \lambda \begin{bmatrix} 1 & 0 \\ 0 & \lambda \end{bmatrix} \begin{bmatrix} W(1) \\ \frac{1}{2}\{[W(1)]^2 - 1\} \end{bmatrix} + \begin{bmatrix} 0 \\ \frac{1}{2}\{\lambda^2 - \gamma_0\} \end{bmatrix} \right\}$$

$$= \begin{bmatrix} \lambda & 0 \\ 0 & 1 \end{bmatrix} \begin{bmatrix} 1 & \int W(r)\,dr \\ \int W(r)\,dr & \int [W(r)]^2\,dr \end{bmatrix}^{-1} \begin{bmatrix} W(1) \\ \frac{1}{2}\{[W(1)]^2 - 1\} \end{bmatrix}$$

$$+ \left\{ \begin{bmatrix} 1 & 0 \\ 0 & \lambda^{-1} \end{bmatrix} \begin{bmatrix} 1 & \int W(r)\,dr \\ \int W(r)\,dr & \int [W(r)]^2\,dr \end{bmatrix}^{-1} \begin{bmatrix} 0 \\ \frac{1}{2}\{\lambda^2 - \gamma_0\}/\lambda \end{bmatrix} \right\}. \qquad [17.6.5]$$

The second element of this vector states that

$$T(\hat{\rho}_T - 1)$$

$$\xrightarrow{L} [0 \quad 1] \begin{bmatrix} 1 & \int W(r)\,dr \\ \int W(r)\,dr & \int [W(r)]^2\,dr \end{bmatrix}^{-1} \begin{bmatrix} W(1) \\ \frac{1}{2}\{[W(1)]^2 - 1\} \end{bmatrix}$$

$$+ (1/2)\frac{\{\lambda^2 - \gamma_0\}}{\lambda^2} [0 \quad 1] \begin{bmatrix} 1 & \int W(r)\,dr \\ \int W(r)\,dr & \int [W(r)]^2\,dr \end{bmatrix}^{-1} \begin{bmatrix} 0 \\ 1 \end{bmatrix} \qquad [17.6.6]$$

$$= \frac{\frac{1}{2}\{[W(1)]^2 - 1\} - W(1)\int W(r)\,dr}{\int [W(r)]^2\,dr - \left[\int W(r)\,dr\right]^2} + \frac{(1/2)\cdot(\lambda^2 - \gamma_0)}{\lambda^2\left\{\int [W(r)]^2\,dr - \left[\int W(r)\,dr\right]^2\right\}}.$$

The first term of the last equality in [17.6.6] is the same as [17.4.28], which described the asymptotic distribution that $T(\hat{\rho}_T - 1)$ would have if $u_t$ were i.i.d. The final term in [17.6.6] is a correction for serial correlation. Notice that if $u_t$ is serially uncorrelated, then $\psi_0 = 1$ and $\psi_j = 0$ for $j = 1, 2, \ldots$. Thus, if $u_t$ is serially uncorrelated, then $\lambda^2 = \sigma^2\cdot[\psi(1)]^2 = \sigma^2$ and $\gamma_0 = E(u_t^2) = \sigma^2$. Hence [17.6.6] includes the earlier result [17.4.28] as a special case when $u_t$ is serially uncorrelated.

It is easy to use $\hat{\sigma}_{\hat{\rho}_T}$, the *OLS* standard error for $\hat{\rho}_T$, to construct a sample statistic that can be used to estimate the correction for serial correlation. Let $\mathbf{Y}_T$ be the matrix defined in [17.4.21], and let $s_T^2$ be the *OLS* estimate of the variance of $u_t$:

$$s_T^2 = (T - 2)^{-1} \sum_{t=1}^{T} (y_t - \hat{\alpha}_T - \hat{\rho}_T y_{t-1})^2.$$

Then the asymptotic distribution of $T^2\cdot\hat{\sigma}^2_{\hat{\rho}_T}$ can be found using the same approach as in [17.4.31] through [17.4.33]:

$$T^2 \cdot \hat{\sigma}^2_{\hat{\rho}_T}$$

$$= s_T^2 [0 \quad 1] \mathbf{Y}_T \begin{bmatrix} T & \Sigma y_{t-1} \\ \Sigma y_{t-1} & \Sigma y_{t-1}^2 \end{bmatrix}^{-1} \mathbf{Y}_T \begin{bmatrix} 0 \\ 1 \end{bmatrix}$$

$$\xrightarrow{p} s_T^2 [0 \quad 1] \begin{bmatrix} 1 & 0 \\ 0 & \lambda \end{bmatrix}^{-1} \begin{bmatrix} 1 & \int W(r)\,dr \\ \int W(r)\,dr & \int [W(r)]^2\,dr \end{bmatrix}^{-1} \begin{bmatrix} 1 & 0 \\ 0 & \lambda \end{bmatrix}^{-1} \begin{bmatrix} 0 \\ 1 \end{bmatrix} \qquad [17.6.7]$$

$$= (s_T^2/\lambda^2)[0 \quad 1] \begin{bmatrix} 1 & \int W(r)\,dr \\ \int W(r)\,dr & \int [W(r)]^2\,dr \end{bmatrix}^{-1} \begin{bmatrix} 0 \\ 1 \end{bmatrix}$$

$$= (s_T^2/\lambda^2) \frac{1}{\int [W(r)]^2\,dr - \left[\int W(r)\,dr\right]^2}.$$

It follows from [17.6.6] that

$$T(\hat{\rho}_T - 1) - \tfrac{1}{2}(T^2 \cdot \hat{\sigma}^2_{\hat{\rho}_T} \div s_T^2)(\lambda^2 - \gamma_0)$$

$$\xrightarrow{p} T(\hat{\rho}_T - 1) - \frac{1}{2}\left(\frac{1}{\lambda^2}\right) \frac{1}{\int [W(r)]^2\,dr - \left[\int W(r)\,dr\right]^2} (\lambda^2 - \gamma_0) \qquad [17.6.8]$$

$$\xrightarrow{L} \frac{\tfrac{1}{2}\{[W(1)]^2 - 1\} - W(1)\int W(r)\,dr}{\int [W(r)]^2\,dr - \left[\int W(r)\,dr\right]^2}.$$

Thus, the statistic in [17.6.8] has the same asymptotic distribution [17.4.28] as the variable tabulated under the heading Case 2 in Table B.5.

Result [17.6.8] can also be used to find the asymptotic distribution of the *OLS* $t$ test of $\rho = 1$:

$$t_T = \frac{(\hat{\rho}_T - 1)}{\hat{\sigma}_{\hat{\rho}_T}}$$

$$= \frac{T(\hat{\rho}_T - 1)}{\{T^2 \cdot \hat{\sigma}^2_{\hat{\rho}_T}\}^{1/2}}$$

$$\xrightarrow{p} \left\{ \frac{\tfrac{1}{2}\{[W(1)]^2 - 1\} - W(1)\int W(r)\,dr}{\int [W(r)]^2\,dr - \left[\int W(r)\,dr\right]^2} + \tfrac{1}{2}(T^2 \cdot \hat{\sigma}^2_{\hat{\rho}_T}/s_T^2)\cdot(\lambda^2 - \gamma_0) \right\}$$

$$\div \{T^2 \cdot \hat{\sigma}^2_{\hat{\rho}_T}\}^{1/2}$$

$$= \frac{\tfrac{1}{2}\{[W(1)]^2 - 1\} - W(1)\int W(r)\,dr}{\int [W(r)]^2\,dr - \left[\int W(r)\,dr\right]^2} \div \{T^2 \cdot \hat{\sigma}^2_{\hat{\rho}_T}\}^{1/2}$$

$$+ \{(1/2)(1/s_T)(\lambda^2 - \gamma_0)\} \times \{T^2 \cdot \hat{\sigma}^2_{\hat{\rho}_T} \div s_T^2\}^{1/2}$$

$$\xrightarrow{p} \left\{ \frac{\frac{1}{2}\{[W(1)]^2 - 1\} - W(1) \int W(r)\, dr}{\int [W(r)]^2\, dr - \left[\int W(r)\, dr\right]^2} \right\} \left( \frac{\lambda^2}{s_T^2} \right)^{1/2}$$

$$\times \left\{ \int [W(r)]^2\, dr - \left[ \int W(r)\, dr \right]^2 \right\}^{1/2}$$

$$+ \{(1/2)(1/s_T)(\lambda^2 - \gamma_0)\} \times \{T^2 \cdot \hat{\sigma}^2_{\hat{\rho}_T} \div s_T^2\}^{1/2} \qquad [17.6.9]$$

with the last convergence following from [17.6.7]. Moreover,

$$s_T^2 = (T-2)^{-1} \sum_{t=1}^{T} (y_t - \hat{\alpha}_T - \hat{\rho}_T y_{t-1})^2 \xrightarrow{p} E(u_t^2) = \gamma_0. \qquad [17.6.10]$$

Hence, [17.6.9] implies that

$$(\gamma_0/\lambda^2)^{1/2} \cdot t_T \xrightarrow{p} \frac{\frac{1}{2}\{[W(1)]^2 - 1\} - W(1) \int W(r)\, dr}{\left\{ \int [W(r)]^2\, dr - \left[ \int W(r)\, dr \right]^2 \right\}^{1/2}}$$

$$+ \{\tfrac{1}{2}(\lambda^2 - \gamma_0)/\lambda\} \times \{T \cdot \hat{\sigma}_{\hat{\rho}_T} \div s_T\}. \qquad [17.6.11]$$

Thus,

$$(\gamma_0/\lambda^2)^{1/2} \cdot t_T - \{\tfrac{1}{2}(\lambda^2 - \gamma_0)/\lambda\} \times \{T \cdot \hat{\sigma}_{\hat{\rho}_T} \div s_T\}$$

$$\xrightarrow{L} \frac{\frac{1}{2}\{[W(1)]^2 - 1\} - W(1) \int W(r)\, dr}{\left\{ \int [W(r)]^2\, dr - \left[ \int W(r)\, dr \right]^2 \right\}^{1/2}}, \qquad [17.6.12]$$

which is the same limiting distribution [17.4.36] obtained for the random variable tabulated for case 2 in Table B.6.

The statistics in [17.6.8] and [17.6.12] require knowledge of the population parameters $\gamma_0$ and $\lambda^2$. Although these moments are unknown, they are easy to estimate consistently. Since $\gamma_0 = E(u_t^2)$, one consistent estimate is given by

$$\hat{\gamma}_0 = T^{-1} \sum_{t=1}^{T} \hat{u}_t^2, \qquad [17.6.13]$$

where $\hat{u}_t = y_t - \hat{\alpha}_T - \hat{\rho}_T y_{t-1}$ is the *OLS* sample residual. Phillips and Perron (1988) instead used the standard *OLS* estimate $\hat{\gamma}_0 = (T-2)^{-1}\Sigma \hat{u}_t^2 = s_T^2$. Similarly, from result (a) of Proposition 17.3, $\lambda^2$ is the asymptotic variance of the sample mean of $u$:

$$\sqrt{T} \cdot \bar{u} = T^{-1/2} \sum_{t=1}^{T} u_t \xrightarrow{L} N(0, \lambda^2). \qquad [17.6.14]$$

Recalling the discussion of the variance of the sample mean in Sections 7.2 and 10.5, this magnitude can equivalently be described as

$$\lambda^2 = \sigma^2 \cdot [\psi(1)]^2 = \gamma_0 + 2 \sum_{j=1}^{\infty} \gamma_j = 2\pi s_u(0), \qquad [17.6.15]$$

where $\gamma_j$ is the $j$th autocovariance of $u_t$ and $s_u(0)$ is the population spectrum of $u_t$ at frequency zero. Thus, any of the estimates of this magnitude proposed in Section

10.5 might be used. For example, if only the first $q$ autocovariances are deemed relevant, the Newey-West estimator could be used:

$$\hat{\lambda}^2 = \hat{\gamma}_0 + 2\sum_{j=1}^{q}[1 - j/(q + 1)]\hat{\gamma}_j, \qquad [17.6.16]$$

where

$$\hat{\gamma}_j = T^{-1}\sum_{t=j+1}^{T}\hat{u}_t\hat{u}_{t-j} \qquad [17.6.17]$$

and $\hat{u}_t = y_t - \hat{\alpha}_T - \hat{\rho}_T y_{t-1}$.

To summarize, under the null hypothesis that the first difference of $y_t$ is a zero-mean covariance-stationary process, the Phillips and Perron[9] approach is to estimate equation [17.6.1] by *OLS* and use the standard *OLS* formulas to calculate $\hat{\rho}$ and its standard error $\hat{\sigma}_{\hat{\rho}}$ along with the standard error of the regression $s$. The $j$th autocovariance of $\hat{u}_t = y_t - \hat{\alpha} - \hat{\rho}y_{t-1}$ is then calculated from [17.6.17]. The resulting estimates $\hat{\gamma}_0$ and $\hat{\lambda}^2$ are then used in [17.6.8] to construct a statistic that has the same asymptotic distribution as does the variable tabulated in the case 2 section of Table B.5. The analogous adjustments to the standard *OLS* $t$ test of $\rho = 1$ described in [17.6.12] produce a statistic that can be compared with the case 2 section of Table B.6

### *Example 17.6*

Let $\hat{u}_t$ denote the *OLS* sample residual for the interest rate regression [17.4.37] of Example 17.4:

$$\hat{u}_t \equiv i_t - \underset{(0.112)}{0.211} - \underset{(0.019133)}{0.96691}\, i_{t-1} \qquad \text{for } t = 1, 2, \ldots, 168.$$

The estimated autocovariances of these *OLS* residuals are

$$\hat{\gamma}_0 = (1/T)\sum_{t=1}^{T}\hat{u}_t^2 = 0.630 \qquad \hat{\gamma}_1 = (1/T)\sum_{t=2}^{T}\hat{u}_t\hat{u}_{t-1} = 0.114$$

$$\hat{\gamma}_2 = (1/T)\sum_{t=3}^{T}\hat{u}_t\hat{u}_{t-2} = -0.162 \qquad \hat{\gamma}_3 = (1/T)\sum_{t=4}^{T}\hat{u}_t\hat{u}_{t-3} = 0.064$$

$$\hat{\gamma}_4 = (1/T)\sum_{t=5}^{T}\hat{u}_t\hat{u}_{t-4} = 0.047.$$

[9]The procedure recommended by Phillips and Perron differs slightly from that in the text. To see the relation, write the first line of [17.6.7] as

$$T^2\cdot\hat{\sigma}^2_{\hat{\rho}_T} \div s_T^2 = [0 \quad 1]\begin{bmatrix} 1 & T^{-3/2}\Sigma y_{t-1} \\ T^{-3/2}\Sigma y_{t-1} & T^{-2}\Sigma y_{t-1}^2 \end{bmatrix}^{-1}\begin{bmatrix} 0 \\ 1 \end{bmatrix}$$

$$= \frac{1}{T^{-2}\Sigma y_{t-1}^2 - T^{-3}(\Sigma y_{t-1})^2} = \frac{1}{T^{-1}[T^{-1}\Sigma y_{t-1}^2 - (T^{-1}\Sigma y_{t-1})^2]}$$

$$= \frac{1}{T^{-1}[T^{-1}\Sigma(y_{t-1} - \bar{y}_{-1})^2]},$$

where $\bar{y}_{-1} \equiv T^{-1}\Sigma y_{t-1}$ and the last equality follows from [4.A.5]. Instead of this expression, Phillips and Perron used

$$\frac{1}{T^{-2}\Sigma(y_t - \bar{y})^2}.$$

The advantage of the formula in the text is that it is trivial to calculate from the output produced by standard regression packages and the identical formula can be used for cases 1, 2, and 4.

Thus, if the serial correlation of $u_t$ is to be described with $q = 4$ autocovariances,

$$\begin{aligned}\hat{\lambda}^2 &= 0.630 + 2(\tfrac{4}{5})(0.114) + 2(\tfrac{3}{5})(-0.162) + 2(\tfrac{2}{5})(0.064) + 2(\tfrac{1}{5})(0.047) \\ &= 0.688.\end{aligned}$$

The usual *OLS* formula for the variance of the residuals from this regression is

$$s^2 = (T - 2)^{-1} \sum_{t=1}^{T} \hat{u}_t^2 = 0.63760.$$

Hence, the Phillips-Perron $\rho$ statistic is

$$\begin{aligned}&T(\hat{\rho} - 1) - (1/2)\cdot(T^2\cdot\hat{\sigma}_{\hat{\rho}}^2/s^2)\cdot(\hat{\lambda}^2 - \hat{\gamma}_0) \\ &\quad = 168(0.96691 - 1) - \tfrac{1}{2}\{[(168)(0.019133)]^2/(0.63760)\}(0.688 - 0.630) \\ &\quad = -6.03.\end{aligned}$$

Comparing this with the 5% critical value for case 2 of Table B.5, we see that $-6.03 > -13.8$. We thus accept the null hypothesis that the interest rate data could plausibly have been generated by a simple unit root process.

Similarly, the adjustment to the $t$ statistic from Example 17.4 described in [17.6.12] is

$$\begin{aligned}&(\hat{\gamma}_0/\hat{\lambda}^2)^{1/2}t - \{\tfrac{1}{2}(\hat{\lambda}^2 - \hat{\gamma}_0)(T\cdot\hat{\sigma}_{\hat{\rho}}/s) \div \hat{\lambda}\} \\ &\quad = \{(0.630)/(0.688)\}^{1/2}(0.96691 - 1)/0.019133 \\ &\qquad -\{(1/2)(0.688 - 0.630)[[(168)(0.019133)/\sqrt{(0.63760)}] \div \sqrt{(0.688)}\} \\ &\quad = -1.80.\end{aligned}$$

Since $-1.80 > -2.89$, the null hypothesis of a unit root is again accepted at the 5% level.

## *Phillips-Perron Tests for Cases 1 and 4*

The asymptotic distributions in [17.6.8] and [17.6.12] were derived under the assumption that the true process for the first difference of $y_t$ is serially correlated with mean zero. Even though the true unit root process exhibited no drift, it was assumed that the estimated *OLS* regression included a constant term as in case 2 of Section 17.4.

The same ideas can be used to generalize case 1 or case 4 of Section 17.4, and the statistics [17.6.8] and [17.6.12] can be compared in each case with the corresponding values in Tables B.5 and B.6. These results are summarized in Table 17.2. The reader is invited to confirm these claims in exercises at the end of the chapter.

***Example 17.7***

The residuals from the GNP regression [17.4.56] have the following estimated autocovariances:

$$\begin{aligned}&\hat{\gamma}_0 = 1.136 \quad && \hat{\gamma}_1 = 0.424 \quad && \hat{\gamma}_2 = 0.285 \\ &\hat{\gamma}_3 = 0.006 && \hat{\gamma}_4 = -0.110,\end{aligned}$$

from which

$$\hat{\lambda}^2 = 1.136 + 2\{\tfrac{4}{5}(0.424) + \tfrac{3}{5}(0.285) + \tfrac{2}{5}(0.006) - \tfrac{1}{5}(0.110)\} = 2.117.$$

Also, $s^2 = 1.15627$. Thus, for these data the Phillips-Perron $\rho$ test is

$$\begin{aligned}
&T(\hat{\rho} - 1) - \tfrac{1}{2}(T^2 \cdot \hat{\sigma}_{\hat{\rho}}^2/s^2)(\hat{\lambda}^2 - \hat{\gamma}_0) \\
&\quad = 168(0.96252 - 1) - \tfrac{1}{2}\left\{\frac{[(168)(0.019304)]^2}{1.15627}\right\}(2.117 - 1.136) \\
&\quad = -10.76.
\end{aligned}$$

Since $-10.76 > -21.0$, the null hypothesis that log GNP follows a unit root process with or without drift is accepted at the 5% level.

The Phillips-Perron $t$ test is

$$\begin{aligned}
&(\hat{\gamma}_0/\hat{\lambda}^2)^{1/2} t - \{\tfrac{1}{2}(\hat{\lambda}^2 - \hat{\gamma}_0)(T \cdot \hat{\sigma}_{\hat{\rho}}/s) \div \hat{\lambda}\} \\
&\quad = \{(1.136)/(2.117)\}^{1/2}(0.96252 - 1)/0.019304 \\
&\quad\quad - \{\tfrac{1}{2}(2.117 - 1.136)[[(168)(0.019304)]/\sqrt{1.15627})] \div \sqrt{(2.117)}\} \\
&\quad = -2.44.
\end{aligned}$$

Since $-2.44 > -3.44$, the null hypothesis of a unit root is again accepted.

## *More General Processes for* $u_t$

The Newey-West estimator $\hat{\lambda}^2$ in [17.6.16] can provide a consistent estimate of $\lambda^2$ for an $MA(\infty)$ process, provided that $q$, the lag truncation parameter, goes to infinity as the sample size $T$ grows, and provided that $q$ grows sufficiently slowly relative to $T$. Phillips (1987) established such consistency assuming that $q_T \rightarrow \infty$ and $q_T/T^{1/4} \rightarrow 0$; for example, $q_T = A \cdot T^{1/5}$ satisfies this requirement. Phillips's results warrant using a larger value of $q$ with a larger data set, though they do not tell us exactly how large to choose $q$ in practice. Monte Carlo investigations have been provided by Phillips and Perron (1988), Schwert (1989), and Kim and Schmidt (1990), though no simple rule emerges from these studies. Andrews's (1991) procedures might be used in this context.

Asymptotic results can also be obtained under weaker assumptions about $u_t$ than those in Proposition 17.3. For example, the reader may note from the proof of result 17.3(e) that the parameter $\gamma_0$ appears because it is the plim of $T^{-1} \times \Sigma_{t=1}^T u_t^2$. Under the conditions of the proposition, the law of large numbers ensures that this plim is just the expected value of $u_t^2$, which expected value was denoted $\gamma_0$. However, even if the data are heterogeneously distributed with $E(u_t^2) = \gamma_{0,t}$, it may still be the case that $T^{-1}\Sigma_{t=1}^T \gamma_{0,t}$ converges to some constant. If $T^{-1}\Sigma_{t=1}^T u_t^2$ also converges to this constant, then this constant plays the role of $\gamma_0$ in a generalization of result 17.3(e).

Similarly, let $\bar{u}_T$ denote the sample mean from some heterogeneously distributed process with population mean zero:

$$\bar{u}_T \equiv T^{-1} \sum_{t=1}^{T} u_t;$$

and let $\lambda_T^2$ denote $T$ times the variance of $\bar{u}_T$:

$$\lambda_T^2 \equiv T \cdot \text{Var}(\bar{u}_T) = T^{-1} \cdot E(u_1 + u_2 + \cdots + u_T)^2.$$

The sample mean $\bar{u}_T$ may still satisfy the central limit theorem:

$$T^{-1/2} \sum_{t=1}^{T} u_t \xrightarrow{L} N(0, \lambda^2)$$

**TABLE 17.2**
**Summary of Phillips-Perron Tests for Unit Roots**

*Case 1:*

Estimated regression: $y_t = \rho y_{t-1} + u_t$
True process: $y_t = y_{t-1} + u_t$
$Z_\rho$ has the same asymptotic distribution as the variable described under the heading Case 1 in Table B.5.
$Z_t$ has the same asymptotic distribution as the variable described under Case 1 in Table B.6.

*Case 2:*

Estimated regression: $y_t = \alpha + \rho y_{t-1} + u_t$
True process: $y_t = y_{t-1} + u_t$
$Z_\rho$ has the same asymptotic distribution as the variable described under Case 2 in Table B.5.
$Z_t$ has the same asymptotic distribution as the variable described under Case 2 in Table B.6.

*Case 4:*

Estimated regression: $y_t = \alpha + \rho y_{t-1} + \delta t + u_t$
True process: $y_t = \alpha + y_{t-1} + u_t$ $\quad\alpha$ any
$Z_\rho$ has the same asymptotic distribution as the variable described under Case 4 in Table B.5.
$Z_t$ has the same asymptotic distribution as the variable described under Case 4 in Table B.6.

*Notes to Table 17.2*

*Estimated regression* indicates the form in which the regression is estimated, using observations $t = 1, 2, \ldots, T$ and conditioning on observation $t = 0$.

*True process* describes the null hypothesis under which the distribution is calculated. In each case, $u_t$ is assumed to have mean zero but can be heterogeneously distributed and serially correlated with

$$\lim_{T\to\infty} T^{-1}\sum_{t=1}^{T} E(u_t^2) = \gamma_0$$

$$\lim_{T\to\infty} T^{-1}E(u_1 + u_2 + \cdots + u_T)^2 = \lambda^2.$$

$Z_\rho$ is the following statistic:

$$Z_\rho \equiv T(\hat{\rho}_T - 1) - (1/2)\{T^2\cdot\hat{\sigma}^2_{\hat{\rho}_T} \div s_T^2\}(\hat{\lambda}_T^2 - \hat{\gamma}_{0,T}),$$

where

$$\hat{\gamma}_{j,T} = T^{-1}\sum_{t=j+1}^{T}\hat{u}_t\hat{u}_{t-j}$$

$\hat{u}_t$ = *OLS* sample residual from the estimated regression

$$\hat{\lambda}_T^2 = \hat{\gamma}_{0,T} + 2\cdot\sum_{j=1}^{q}[1 - j/(q+1)]\hat{\gamma}_{j,T}$$

$$s_T^2 = (T-k)^{-1}\sum_{t=1}^{T}\hat{u}_t^2$$

$k$ = number of parameters in estimated regression

$\hat{\sigma}_{\hat{\rho}_T}$ = *OLS* standard error for $\hat{\rho}$.

$Z_t$ is the following statistic:

$$Z_t \equiv (\hat{\gamma}_{0,T}/\hat{\lambda}_T^2)^{1/2}\cdot(\hat{\rho}_T - 1)/\hat{\sigma}_{\hat{\rho}_T} - (1/2)(\hat{\lambda}_T^2 - \hat{\gamma}_{0,T})(1/\hat{\lambda}_T)\{T\cdot\hat{\sigma}_{\hat{\rho}_T} \div s_T\}.$$

or

$$T^{-1/2}\sum_{t=1}^{T} u_t \xrightarrow{L} \lambda\cdot W(1),$$

where

$$\lambda^2 \equiv \lim_{T\to\infty} \lambda_T^2, \qquad [17.6.18]$$

providing a basis for generalizing result 17.3(a).

If $u_t$ were a covariance-stationary process with absolutely summable autocovariances, then Proposition 7.5(b) would imply that $\lim_{T\to\infty} \lambda_T^2 = \Sigma_{j=-\infty}^{\infty}\gamma_j$. Recalling [7.2.8], expression [17.6.18] would in this case just be another way to describe the parameter $\lambda^2$ in Proposition 17.3.

Thus, the parameters $\gamma_0$ and $\lambda^2$ in [17.6.8] and [17.6.12] can more generally be defined as

$$\gamma_0 \equiv \lim_{T\to\infty} T^{-1}\sum_{t=1}^{T} E(u_t^2) \qquad [17.6.19]$$

$$\lambda^2 \equiv \lim_{T\to\infty} T^{-1}\cdot E(u_1 + u_2 + \cdots + u_T)^2. \qquad [17.6.20]$$

Phillips (1987) and Perron and Phillips (1988) derived [17.6.8] and [17.6.12] assuming that $u_t$ is a zero-mean but otherwise heterogeneously distributed process satisfying certain restrictions on the serial dependence and higher moments. From this perspective, expressions [17.6.19] and [17.6.20] can be used as the definitions of the parameters $\gamma_0$ and $\lambda^2$. Clearly, the estimators [17.6.13] and [17.6.16] continue to be appropriate for this alternative interpretation.

## *On the Observational Equivalence of Unit Root and Covariance-Stationary Processes*

We saw in Section 15.4 that given any $I(0)$ process for $y_t$ and any finite sample size $T$, there exists an $I(1)$ process that will be impossible to distinguish from the $I(0)$ representation on the basis of the first and second sample moments of $y$. Yet the Phillips and Perron procedures seem to offer a way to test the null hypothesis that the sample was generated from an arbitrary $I(1)$ process. What does it mean if the test leads us to reject the null hypothesis that $y_t$ is $I(1)$ when we know that there exists an $I(1)$ process that describes the sample arbitrarily well?

Some insight into this question can be gained by considering the example in equation [15.4.8],

$$(1 - L)y_t = (1 + \theta L)\varepsilon_t, \qquad [17.6.21]$$

where $\theta$ is slightly larger than $-1$ and $\varepsilon_t$ is i.i.d. with mean zero and variance $\sigma^2$. The model [17.6.21] implies that

$$\begin{aligned} y_t &= (\varepsilon_t + \theta\varepsilon_{t-1}) + (\varepsilon_{t-1} + \theta\varepsilon_{t-2}) + \cdots + (\varepsilon_1 + \theta\varepsilon_0) + y_0 \\ &= \varepsilon_t + (1+\theta)\varepsilon_{t-1} + (1+\theta)\varepsilon_{t-2} + \cdots + (1+\theta)\varepsilon_1 + \theta\varepsilon_0 + y_0 \\ &= \varepsilon_t + (1+\theta)\xi_{t-1} + \theta\varepsilon_0 + y_0, \end{aligned}$$

where

$$\xi_{t-1} \equiv \varepsilon_1 + \varepsilon_2 + \cdots + \varepsilon_{t-1}.$$

For large $t$, the variable $y_t$ is dominated by the unit root component, $(1 + \theta)\xi_{t-1}$, and the asymptotic results are all governed by this term. However, if $\theta$ is close to $-1$, then in a finite sample $y_t$ would behave essentially like the white noise series $\varepsilon_t$ plus a constant $(\theta\varepsilon_0 + y_0)$. In such a case the Phillips-Perron test is likely to reject the null hypothesis of a unit root in finite samples even though it is true.[10] For example, Schwert (1989) generated Monte Carlo samples of size $T = 1{,}000$ according to the unit root model [17.6.21] with $\theta = -0.8$. The Phillips-Perron test that is supposed to reject only 5% of the time actually rejected the null hypothesis in virtually every sample, even though the null hypothesis is true! Similar results were reported by Phillips and Perron (1988) and Kim and Schmidt (1990).

Campbell and Perron (1991) argued that such false rejections are not necessarily a bad thing. If $\theta$ is near $-1$, then for many purposes an $I(0)$ model may provide a more useful description of the process in [17.6.21] than does the true $I(1)$ model. In support of this claim, they generated samples from the process [17.6.21] and estimated by *OLS* both an autoregressive process in levels,

$$y_t = c + \phi_1 y_{t-1} + \phi_2 y_{t-2} + \cdots + \phi_p y_{t-p} + \varepsilon_t,$$

and an autoregressive process in differences,

$$\Delta y_t = \alpha + \zeta_1 \Delta y_{t-1} + \zeta_2 \Delta y_{t-2} + \cdots + \zeta_p \Delta y_{t-p} + \varepsilon_t.$$

They found that for $\theta$ close to $-1$, forecasts based on the levels $y_t$ tended to perform better than those based on the differences $\Delta y_t$, even though the true data-generating process was $I(1)$.

A related issue, of course, arises with false acceptances. Clearly, if the true model is

$$y_t = \rho y_{t-1} + \varepsilon_t \qquad [17.6.22]$$

with $\rho$ slightly below 1, then the null hypothesis that $\rho = 1$ is likely to be accepted in small samples, even though it is false. The value of accepting a false null hypothesis in this case is that imposing the condition $\rho = 1$ may produce a better forecast than one based on an estimated $\hat{\rho}_T$, particularly given the small-sample downward bias of $\hat{\rho}_T$. Furthermore, when $\rho$ is close to 1, the values in Table B.6 might give a better small-sample approximation to the distribution of $(\hat{\rho}_T - 1) \div \hat{\sigma}_{\hat{\rho}_T}$ than the traditional $t$ tables.[11]

This discussion underscores that the goal of unit root tests is to find a parsimonious representation that gives a reasonable approximation to the true process, as opposed to determining whether or not the true process is literally $I(1)$.

## 17.7. *Asymptotic Properties of a* pth-*Order Autoregression and the Augmented Dickey-Fuller Tests for Unit Roots*

The Phillips-Perron tests were based on simple *OLS* regressions of $y_t$ on its own lagged value and possibly a constant or time trend as well. Corrections for serial correlation were then made to the standard *OLS* coefficient and $t$ statistics. This section discusses an alternative approach, due to Dickey and Fuller (1979), which controls for serial correlation by including higher-order autoregressive terms in the regression.

[10]For more detailed discussion, see Phillips and Perron (1988, p. 344).

[11]See Evans and Savin (1981, 1984) for a description of the small-sample distributions.

### *An Alternative Representation of an* AR(p) *Process*

Suppose that the data were really generated from an $AR(p)$ process,

$$(1 - \phi_1 L - \phi_2 L^2 - \cdots - \phi_p L^p)y_t = \varepsilon_t, \qquad [17.7.1]$$

where $\{\varepsilon_t\}$ is an i.i.d. sequence with mean zero, variance $\sigma^2$, and finite fourth moment. It is helpful to write the autoregression [17.7.1] in a slightly different form. To do so, define

$$\rho \equiv \phi_1 + \phi_2 + \cdots + \phi_p \qquad [17.7.2]$$

$$\zeta_j \equiv -[\phi_{j+1} + \phi_{j+2} + \cdots + \phi_p] \quad \text{for } j = 1, 2, \ldots, p-1. \qquad [17.7.3]$$

Notice that for any values of $\phi_1, \phi_2, \ldots, \phi_p$, the following polynomials in $L$ are equivalent:

$$\begin{aligned}
&(1 - \rho L) - (\zeta_1 L + \zeta_2 L^2 + \cdots + \zeta_{p-1}L^{p-1})(1 - L)\\
&= 1 - \rho L - \zeta_1 L + \zeta_1 L^2 - \zeta_2 L^2 + \zeta_2 L^3 - \cdots - \zeta_{p-1}L^{p-1} + \zeta_{p-1}L^p\\
&= 1 - (\rho + \zeta_1)L - (\zeta_2 - \zeta_1)L^2 - (\zeta_3 - \zeta_2)L^3 - \cdots\\
&\quad - (\zeta_{p-1} - \zeta_{p-2})L^{p-1} - (-\zeta_{p-1})L^p\\
&= 1 - [(\phi_1 + \phi_2 + \cdots + \phi_p) - (\phi_2 + \phi_3 + \cdots + \phi_p)]L\\
&\quad - [-(\phi_3 + \phi_4 + \cdots + \phi_p) + (\phi_2 + \phi_3 + \cdots + \phi_p)]L^2 - \cdots\\
&\quad - [-(\phi_p) + (\phi_{p-1} + \phi_p)]L^{p-1} - (\phi_p)L^p\\
&= 1 - \phi_1 L - \phi_2 L^2 - \cdots - \phi_{p-1}L^{p-1} - \phi_p L^p.
\end{aligned} \qquad [17.7.4]$$

Thus, the autoregression [17.7.1] can equivalently be written

$$\{(1 - \rho L) - (\zeta_1 L + \zeta_2 L^2 + \cdots + \zeta_{p-1}L^{p-1})(1 - L)\}y_t = \varepsilon_t \qquad [17.7.5]$$

or

$$y_t = \rho y_{t-1} + \zeta_1 \Delta y_{t-1} + \zeta_2 \Delta y_{t-2} + \cdots + \zeta_{p-1}\Delta y_{t-p+1} + \varepsilon_t. \qquad [17.7.6]$$

Suppose that the process that generated $y_t$ contains a single unit root; that is, suppose one root of

$$(1 - \phi_1 z - \phi_2 z^2 - \cdots - \phi_p z^p) = 0 \qquad [17.7.7]$$

is unity,

$$1 - \phi_1 - \phi_2 - \cdots - \phi_p = 0, \qquad [17.7.8]$$

and all other roots of [17.7.7] are outside the unit circle. Notice that [17.7.8] implies that the coefficient $\rho$ in [17.7.2] is unity. Moreover, when $\rho = 1$, expression [17.7.4] would imply

$$\begin{aligned}
&(1 - \phi_1 z - \phi_2 z^2 - \cdots - \phi_p z^p)\\
&\qquad = (1 - \zeta_1 z - \zeta_2 z^2 - \cdots - \zeta_{p-1}z^{p-1})(1 - z).
\end{aligned} \qquad [17.7.9]$$

Of the $p$ values of $z$ that make the left side of [17.7.9] zero, one is $z = 1$ and all other roots are presumed to be outside the unit circle. The same must be true of the right side as well, meaning that all roots of

$$(1 - \zeta_1 z - \zeta_2 z^2 - \cdots - \zeta_{p-1}z^{p-1}) = 0$$

lie outside the unit circle. Under the null hypothesis that $\rho = 1$, expression [17.7.5] could then be written as

$$(1 - \zeta_1 L - \zeta_2 L^2 - \cdots - \zeta_{p-1} L^{p-1})\, \Delta y_t = \varepsilon_t$$

or

$$\Delta y_t = u_t, \qquad [17.7.10]$$

where

$$u_t = (1 - \zeta_1 L - \zeta_2 L^2 - \cdots - \zeta_{p-1} L^{p-1})^{-1} \varepsilon_t.$$

Equation [17.7.10] indicates that $y_t$ behaves like the variable $\xi_t$ described in Proposition 17.3, with

$$\psi(L) = (1 - \zeta_1 L - \zeta_2 L^2 - \cdots - \zeta_{p-1} L^{p-1})^{-1}.$$

One of the advantages of writing the autoregression of [17.7.1] in the equivalent form of [17.7.6] is that only one of the regressors in [17.7.6], namely, $y_{t-1}$, is $I(1)$, whereas all of the other regressors $(\Delta y_{t-1}, \Delta y_{t-2}, \ldots, \Delta y_{t-p+1})$ are stationary. Thus, [17.7.6] is the Sims, Stock, and Watson (1990) canonical form, originally proposed for this problem by Fuller (1976). Since no knowledge of any population parameters is needed to write the model in this canonical form, in this case it is convenient to estimate the parameters by direct *OLS* estimation of [17.7.6].

Results generalizing those for case 1 in Section 17.4 are obtained when the regression is estimated as written in [17.7.6] without a constant term. Cases 2 and 3 are generalized by including a constant term in [17.7.6], while case 4 is generalized by including a constant term and a time trend in [17.7.6]. For illustration, the case 2 regression is discussed in detail. Comparable results for case 1, case 3, and case 4 will be summarized in Table 17.3 later in this section, with details developed in exercises at the end of the chapter.

### *Case 2. The Estimated Autoregression Includes a Constant Term, but the Data Were Really Generated by a Unit Root Autoregression with No Drift*

Following the usual notational convention for *OLS* estimation of autoregressions, we assume that the initial sample is of size $T + p$, with observations numbered $\{y_{-p+1}, y_{-p+2}, \ldots, y_T\}$, and condition on the first $p$ observations. We are interested in the properties of *OLS* estimation of

$$\begin{aligned} y_t &= \zeta_1 \Delta y_{t-1} + \zeta_2 \Delta y_{t-2} + \cdots + \zeta_{p-1} \Delta y_{t-p+1} + \alpha + \rho y_{t-1} + \varepsilon_t \\ &\equiv \mathbf{x}_t' \boldsymbol{\beta} + \varepsilon_t, \end{aligned} \qquad [17.7.11]$$

where $\boldsymbol{\beta} \equiv (\zeta_1, \zeta_2, \ldots, \zeta_{p-1}, \alpha, \rho)'$ and $\mathbf{x}_t \equiv (\Delta y_{t-1}, \Delta y_{t-2}, \ldots, \Delta y_{t-p+1}, 1, y_{t-1})'$. The deviation of the *OLS* estimate $\mathbf{b}_T$ from the true value $\boldsymbol{\beta}$ is given by

$$\mathbf{b}_T - \boldsymbol{\beta} = \left[ \sum_{t=1}^{T} \mathbf{x}_t \mathbf{x}_t' \right]^{-1} \left[ \sum_{t=1}^{T} \mathbf{x}_t \varepsilon_t \right]. \qquad [17.7.12]$$

Letting $u_t \equiv y_t - y_{t-1}$, the individual terms in [17.7.12] are

$$\sum_{t=1}^{T} \mathbf{x}_t\mathbf{x}_t' = \qquad [17.7.13]$$

$$\begin{bmatrix} \Sigma u_{t-1}^2 & \Sigma u_{t-1}u_{t-2} & \cdots & \Sigma u_{t-1}u_{t-p+1} & \Sigma u_{t-1} & \Sigma u_{t-1}y_{t-1} \\ \Sigma u_{t-2}u_{t-1} & \Sigma u_{t-2}^2 & \cdots & \Sigma u_{t-1}u_{t-p+1} & \Sigma u_{t-2} & \Sigma u_{t-2}y_{t-1} \\ \vdots & \vdots & \cdots & \vdots & \vdots & \vdots \\ \Sigma u_{t-p+1}u_{t-1} & \Sigma u_{t-p+1}u_{t-2} & \cdots & \Sigma u_{t-p+1}^2 & \Sigma u_{t-p+1} & \Sigma u_{t-p+1}y_{t-1} \\ \Sigma u_{t-1} & \Sigma u_{t-2} & \cdots & \Sigma u_{t-p+1} & T & \Sigma y_{t-1} \\ \Sigma y_{t-1}u_{t-1} & \Sigma y_{t-1}u_{t-2} & \cdots & \Sigma y_{t-1}u_{t-p+1} & \Sigma y_{t-1} & \Sigma y_{t-1}^2 \end{bmatrix}$$

$$\sum_{t=1}^{T} \mathbf{x}_t\varepsilon_t = \begin{bmatrix} \Sigma u_{t-1}\varepsilon_t \\ \Sigma u_{t-2}\varepsilon_t \\ \vdots \\ \Sigma u_{t-p+1}\varepsilon_t \\ \Sigma \varepsilon_t \\ \Sigma y_{t-1}\varepsilon_t \end{bmatrix} \qquad [17.7.14]$$

with $\Sigma$ denoting summation over $t = 1, 2, \ldots, T$.

Under the null hypothesis that $\alpha = 0$ and $\rho = 1$, we saw in [17.7.10] that $y_t$ behaves like $\xi_t = u_1 + u_2 + \cdots + u_t$ in Proposition 17.3. Consulting the rates of convergence in Proposition 17.3, for this case the scaling matrix should be

$$\underset{(p+1 \times p+1)}{\mathbf{Y}_T} \equiv \begin{bmatrix} \sqrt{T} & 0 & \cdots & 0 & 0 \\ 0 & \sqrt{T} & \cdots & 0 & 0 \\ \vdots & \vdots & \cdots & \vdots & \vdots \\ 0 & 0 & \cdots & \sqrt{T} & 0 \\ 0 & 0 & \cdots & 0 & T \end{bmatrix}. \qquad [17.7.15]$$

Premultiplying [17.7.12] by $\mathbf{Y}_T$ as in [17.4.20] results in

$$\mathbf{Y}_T(\mathbf{b}_T - \boldsymbol{\beta}) = \left\{\mathbf{Y}_T^{-1}\left[\sum_{t=1}^{T} \mathbf{x}_t\mathbf{x}_t'\right]\mathbf{Y}_T^{-1}\right\}^{-1}\left\{\mathbf{Y}_T^{-1}\left[\sum_{t=1}^{T} \mathbf{x}_t\varepsilon_t\right]\right\}. \qquad [17.7.16]$$

Consider the matrix $\mathbf{Y}_T^{-1}\Sigma\mathbf{x}_t\mathbf{x}_t'\mathbf{Y}_T^{-1}$. Elements in the upper left $(p \times p)$ block of $\Sigma\mathbf{x}_t\mathbf{x}_t'$ are divided by $T$, the first $p$ elements of the $(p + 1)$th row or $(p + 1)$th column are divided by $T^{3/2}$, and the row $(p + 1)$, column $(p + 1)$ element of $\Sigma\mathbf{x}_t\mathbf{x}_t'$ is divided by $T^2$. Moreover,

$$T^{-1}\Sigma u_{t-i}u_{t-j} \xrightarrow{p} \gamma_{|i-j|} \qquad \text{from result (c) of Proposition 17.3}$$

$$T^{-1}\Sigma u_{t-j} \xrightarrow{p} E(u_{t-j}) = 0 \qquad \text{from the law of large numbers}$$

$$T^{-3/2}\Sigma y_{t-1}u_{t-j} \xrightarrow{p} 0 \qquad \text{from Proposition 17.3(e)}$$

$$T^{-3/2}\Sigma y_{t-1} \xrightarrow{L} \lambda \cdot \int W(r)\,dr \qquad \text{from Proposition 17.3(f)}$$

$$T^{-2}\Sigma y_{t-1}^2 \xrightarrow{L} \lambda^2 \cdot \int [W(r)]^2\,dr \qquad \text{from Proposition 17.3(h),}$$

where

$$\begin{aligned} \gamma_j &= E\{(\Delta y_t)(\Delta y_{t-j})\} \\ \lambda &\equiv \sigma \cdot \psi(1) = \sigma/(1 - \zeta_1 - \zeta_2 - \cdots - \zeta_{p-1}) \qquad [17.7.17] \\ \sigma^2 &= E(\varepsilon_t^2) \end{aligned}$$

and the integral sign denotes integration over $r$ from 0 to 1. Thus,

$$\mathbf{Y}_T^{-1}[\Sigma \mathbf{x}_t \mathbf{x}_t']\mathbf{Y}_T^{-1}$$

$$\xrightarrow{L} \begin{bmatrix} \gamma_0 & \gamma_1 & \cdots & \gamma_{p-2} & 0 & 0 \\ \gamma_1 & \gamma_0 & \cdots & \gamma_{p-3} & 0 & 0 \\ \vdots & \vdots & \cdots & \vdots & \vdots & \vdots \\ \gamma_{p-2} & \gamma_{p-3} & \cdots & \gamma_0 & 0 & 0 \\ 0 & 0 & \cdots & 0 & 1 & \lambda \cdot \int W(r)\, dr \\ 0 & 0 & \cdots & 0 & \lambda \cdot \int W(r)\, dr & \lambda^2 \cdot \int [W(r)]^2\, dr \end{bmatrix}$$

$$\equiv \begin{bmatrix} \mathbf{V} & \mathbf{0} \\ \mathbf{0} & \mathbf{Q} \end{bmatrix}, \qquad [17.7.18]$$

where

$$\mathbf{V} \equiv \begin{bmatrix} \gamma_0 & \gamma_1 & \cdots & \gamma_{p-2} \\ \gamma_1 & \gamma_0 & \cdots & \gamma_{p-3} \\ \vdots & \vdots & \cdots & \vdots \\ \gamma_{p-2} & \gamma_{p-3} & \cdots & \gamma_0 \end{bmatrix} \qquad [17.7.19]$$

$$\mathbf{Q} \equiv \begin{bmatrix} 1 & \lambda \cdot \int W(r)\, dr \\ \lambda \cdot \int W(r)\, dr & \lambda^2 \cdot \int [W(r)]^2\, dr \end{bmatrix}. \qquad [17.7.20]$$

Next, consider the second term in [17.7.16],

$$\mathbf{Y}_T^{-1}[\Sigma \mathbf{x}_t \varepsilon_t] = \begin{bmatrix} T^{-1/2}\Sigma u_{t-1}\varepsilon_t \\ T^{-1/2}\Sigma u_{t-2}\varepsilon_t \\ \vdots \\ T^{-1/2}\Sigma u_{t-p+1}\varepsilon_t \\ T^{-1/2}\Sigma \varepsilon_t \\ T^{-1}\Sigma y_{t-1}\varepsilon_t \end{bmatrix} \qquad [17.7.21]$$

The first $p - 1$ elements of this vector are $\sqrt{T}$ times the sample mean of a martingale difference sequence whose variance-covariance matrix is

$$E\begin{bmatrix} u_{t-1}\varepsilon_t \\ u_{t-2}\varepsilon_t \\ \vdots \\ u_{t-p+1}\varepsilon_t \end{bmatrix} [u_{t-1}\varepsilon_t \quad u_{t-2}\varepsilon_t \quad \cdots \quad u_{t-p+1}\varepsilon_t]$$

$$= \sigma^2 \begin{bmatrix} \gamma_0 & \gamma_1 & \cdots & \gamma_{p-2} \\ \gamma_1 & \gamma_0 & \cdots & \gamma_{p-3} \\ \vdots & \vdots & \cdots & \vdots \\ \gamma_{p-2} & \gamma_{p-3} & \cdots & \gamma_0 \end{bmatrix} \qquad [17.7.22]$$

$$= \sigma^2 \mathbf{V}.$$

Thus, the first $p - 1$ terms in [17.7.21] satisfy the usual central limit theorem,

$$\begin{bmatrix} T^{-1/2}\Sigma u_{t-1}\varepsilon_t \\ T^{-1/2}\Sigma u_{t-2}\varepsilon_t \\ \vdots \\ T^{-1/2}\Sigma u_{t-p+1}\varepsilon_t \end{bmatrix} \xrightarrow{L} \mathbf{h}_1 \sim N(\mathbf{0}, \sigma^2\mathbf{V}). \qquad [17.7.23]$$

The distribution of the last two elements in [17.7.21] can be obtained from results (a) and (d) of Proposition 17.3:

$$\begin{bmatrix} T^{-1/2}\Sigma\varepsilon_t \\ T^{-1}\Sigma y_{t-1}\varepsilon_t \end{bmatrix} \xrightarrow{L} \mathbf{h}_2 \sim \begin{bmatrix} \sigma\cdot W(1) \\ \frac{1}{2}\sigma\lambda\cdot\{[W(1)]^2 - 1\} \end{bmatrix}. \qquad [17.7.24]$$

Substituting [17.7.18] through [17.7.24] into [17.7.16] results in

$$\mathbf{Y}_T(\mathbf{b}_T - \boldsymbol{\beta}) \xrightarrow{L} \begin{bmatrix} \mathbf{V} & \mathbf{0} \\ \mathbf{0} & \mathbf{Q} \end{bmatrix}^{-1} \begin{bmatrix} \mathbf{h}_1 \\ \mathbf{h}_2 \end{bmatrix} = \begin{bmatrix} \mathbf{V}^{-1}\mathbf{h}_1 \\ \mathbf{Q}^{-1}\mathbf{h}_2 \end{bmatrix}. \qquad [17.7.25]$$

### *Coefficients on* $\Delta y_{t-j}$

The first $p - 1$ elements of $\boldsymbol{\beta}$ are $\zeta_1, \zeta_2, \ldots, \zeta_{p-1}$, which are the coefficients on zero-mean stationary regressors $(\Delta y_{t-1}, \Delta y_{t-2}, \ldots, \Delta y_{t-p+1})$. The block consisting of the first $p - 1$ elements in [17.7.25] states that

$$\sqrt{T}\begin{bmatrix} \hat{\zeta}_{1,T} - \zeta_1 \\ \hat{\zeta}_{2,T} - \zeta_2 \\ \vdots \\ \hat{\zeta}_{p-1,T} - \zeta_{p-1} \end{bmatrix} \xrightarrow{L} \mathbf{V}^{-1}\mathbf{h}_1. \qquad [17.7.26]$$

Recalling from [17.7.23] that $\mathbf{h}_1 \sim N(\mathbf{0}, \sigma^2\mathbf{V})$, it follows that $\mathbf{V}^{-1}\mathbf{h}_1 \sim N(\mathbf{0}, \sigma^2\mathbf{V}^{-1})$, or

$$\sqrt{T}\begin{bmatrix} \hat{\zeta}_{1,T} - \zeta_1 \\ \hat{\zeta}_{2,T} - \zeta_2 \\ \vdots \\ \hat{\zeta}_{p-1,T} - \zeta_{p-1} \end{bmatrix} \xrightarrow{L} N\left(\begin{bmatrix} 0 \\ 0 \\ \vdots \\ 0 \end{bmatrix}, \sigma^2\begin{bmatrix} \gamma_0 & \gamma_1 & \cdots & \gamma_{p-2} \\ \gamma_1 & \gamma_0 & \cdots & \gamma_{p-3} \\ \vdots & \vdots & \cdots & \vdots \\ \gamma_{p-2} & \gamma_{p-3} & \cdots & \gamma_0 \end{bmatrix}^{-1}\right), \qquad [17.7.27]$$

where $\gamma_j = E\{(\Delta y_t)(\Delta y_{t-j})\}$.

This means that a null hypothesis involving the coefficients on the stationary regressors $(\zeta_1, \zeta_2, \ldots, \zeta_{p-1})$ in [17.7.11] can be tested in the usual way, with the standard $t$ and $F$ statistics asymptotically valid. To see this, suppose that the null hypothesis is $H_0$: $\mathbf{R}\boldsymbol{\beta} = \mathbf{r}$ for $\mathbf{R}$ a known $[m \times (p + 1)]$ matrix where $m$ is the number of restrictions. The Wald form of the *OLS* $\chi^2$ test [8.2.23] is given by

$$\begin{aligned} \chi_T^2 &= (\mathbf{R}\mathbf{b}_T - \mathbf{r})'\left\{s_T^2\mathbf{R}\left[\sum_{t=1}^{T}\mathbf{x}_t\mathbf{x}_t'\right]^{-1}\mathbf{R}'\right\}^{-1}(\mathbf{R}\mathbf{b}_T - \mathbf{r}) \\ &= [\mathbf{R}\sqrt{T}(\mathbf{b}_T - \boldsymbol{\beta})]'\left\{s_T^2\mathbf{R}\cdot\sqrt{T}\left[\sum_{t=1}^{T}\mathbf{x}_t\mathbf{x}_t'\right]^{-1}\sqrt{T}\cdot\mathbf{R}'\right\}^{-1} \qquad [17.7.28] \\ &\quad \times [\mathbf{R}\cdot\sqrt{T}(\mathbf{b}_T - \boldsymbol{\beta})], \end{aligned}$$

where

$$\begin{aligned} s_T^2 = [T - (p + 1)]^{-1} \sum_{t=1}^{T} (y_t - \hat{\zeta}_{1,T}\Delta y_{t-1} - \hat{\zeta}_{2,T}\Delta y_{t-2} - \cdots \\ - \hat{\zeta}_{p-1,T}\Delta y_{t-p+1} - \hat{\alpha}_T - \hat{\rho}_T y_{t-1})^2 \\ \xrightarrow{p} E(\varepsilon_t^2) = \sigma^2. \end{aligned} \qquad [17.7.29]$$

If none of the restrictions involves $\alpha$ or $\rho$, then the last two columns of $\mathbf{R}$ contain all zeros:

$$\underset{[m\times(p+1)]}{\mathbf{R}} = \begin{bmatrix} \underset{[m\times(p-1)]}{\mathbf{R}_1} & \underset{(m\times 2)}{\mathbf{0}} \end{bmatrix}. \qquad [17.7.30]$$

In this case, $\mathbf{R}\sqrt{T} = \mathbf{R}\mathbf{Y}_T$ for $\mathbf{Y}_T$ the matrix in [17.7.15], so that [17.7.28] can be written as

$$\chi_T^2 = [\mathbf{R}\mathbf{Y}_T(\mathbf{b}_T - \boldsymbol{\beta})]' \left\{ s_T^2 \mathbf{R}\mathbf{Y}_T \left[ \sum_{t=1}^{T} \mathbf{x}_t \mathbf{x}_t' \right]^{-1} \mathbf{Y}_T \mathbf{R}' \right\}^{-1} [\mathbf{R}\mathbf{Y}_T(\mathbf{b}_T - \boldsymbol{\beta})].$$

From [17.7.18], [17.7.25], [17.7.29], and [17.7.30], this converges to

$$\begin{aligned} \chi_T^2 \xrightarrow{L} & \left\{ [\mathbf{R}_1 \;\; \mathbf{0}] \begin{bmatrix} \mathbf{V}^{-1}\mathbf{h}_1 \\ \mathbf{Q}^{-1}\mathbf{h}_2 \end{bmatrix} \right\}' \\ & \times \left\{ \sigma^2 [\mathbf{R}_1 \;\; \mathbf{0}] \begin{bmatrix} \mathbf{V} & \mathbf{0} \\ \mathbf{0} & \mathbf{Q} \end{bmatrix}^{-1} \begin{bmatrix} \mathbf{R}_1' \\ \mathbf{0} \end{bmatrix} \right\}^{-1} \left\{ [\mathbf{R}_1 \;\; \mathbf{0}] \begin{bmatrix} \mathbf{V}^{-1}\mathbf{h}_1 \\ \mathbf{Q}^{-1}\mathbf{h}_2 \end{bmatrix} \right\} \\ & = [\mathbf{R}_1\mathbf{V}^{-1}\mathbf{h}_1]'[\sigma^2\mathbf{R}_1\mathbf{V}^{-1}\mathbf{R}_1']^{-1}[\mathbf{R}_1\mathbf{V}^{-1}\mathbf{h}_1]. \end{aligned} \qquad [17.7.31]$$

But since $\mathbf{h}_1 \sim N(\mathbf{0}, \sigma^2\mathbf{V})$, it follows that the $(m \times 1)$ vector $[\mathbf{R}_1\mathbf{V}^{-1}\mathbf{h}_1]$ is distributed $N(\mathbf{0}, [\sigma^2\mathbf{R}_1\mathbf{V}^{-1}\mathbf{R}_1'])$. Hence, expression [17.7.31] is a quadratic form in a Gaussian vector that satisfies the conditions of Proposition 8.1:

$$\chi_T^2 \xrightarrow{L} \chi^2(m).$$

This verifies that the usual $t$ or $F$ tests applied to any subset of the coefficients $\hat{\zeta}_1, \hat{\zeta}_2, \ldots, \hat{\zeta}_{p-1}$ have the standard limiting distributions.

Note, moreover, that [17.7.27] is exactly the same asymptotic distribution that would be obtained if the data were differenced before estimating the autoregression:

$$\Delta y_t = \zeta_1 \Delta y_{t-1} + \zeta_2 \Delta y_{t-2} + \cdots + \zeta_{p-1}\Delta y_{t-p+1} + \alpha + \varepsilon_t.$$

Thus, if the goal is to estimate $\zeta_1, \zeta_2, \ldots, \zeta_{p-1}$ or test hypotheses about these coefficients, there is no need based on asymptotic distribution theory for differencing the data before estimating the autoregression. Many researchers do recommend differencing the data first, but the reason is to reduce the small-sample bias and small-sample mean squared errors of the estimates, not to change the asymptotic distribution.

### *Coefficients on Constant Term and* $y_{t-1}$

The last two elements of $\boldsymbol{\beta}$ are $\alpha$ and $\rho$, which are coefficients on the constant term and the $I(1)$ regressor, $y_{t-1}$. From [17.7.25], [17.7.20], and [17.7.24], their limiting distribution is given by

$$\begin{bmatrix} T^{1/2} & 0 \\ 0 & T \end{bmatrix} \begin{bmatrix} \hat{\alpha}_T \\ \hat{\rho}_T - 1 \end{bmatrix}$$

$$\xrightarrow{L} \begin{bmatrix} 1 & \lambda \cdot \int W(r)\,dr \\ \lambda \cdot \int W(r)\,dr & \lambda^2 \cdot \int [W(r)]^2\,dr \end{bmatrix}^{-1} \begin{bmatrix} \sigma \cdot W(1) \\ \frac{1}{2}\sigma\lambda \cdot \{[W(1)]^2 - 1\} \end{bmatrix}$$

$$= \sigma \begin{bmatrix} 1 & 0 \\ 0 & \lambda \end{bmatrix}^{-1} \begin{bmatrix} 1 & \int W(r)\,dr \\ \int W(r)\,dr & \int [W(r)]^2\,dr \end{bmatrix}^{-1} \begin{bmatrix} 1 & 0 \\ 0 & \lambda \end{bmatrix}^{-1} \qquad [17.7.32]$$

$$\times \begin{bmatrix} 1 & 0 \\ 0 & \lambda \end{bmatrix} \begin{bmatrix} W(1) \\ \frac{1}{2}\{[W(1)]^2 - 1\} \end{bmatrix}$$

$$= \begin{bmatrix} \sigma & 0 \\ 0 & \sigma/\lambda \end{bmatrix} \begin{bmatrix} 1 & \int W(r)\,dr \\ \int W(r)\,dr & \int [W(r)]^2\,dr \end{bmatrix}^{-1} \begin{bmatrix} W(1) \\ \frac{1}{2}\{[W(1)]^2 - 1\} \end{bmatrix}.$$

The second element of this vector implies that $(\lambda/\sigma)$ times $T(\hat{\rho}_T - 1)$ has the same asymptotic distribution as [17.4.28], which described the estimate of $\rho$ in a regression without lagged $\Delta y$ and with serially uncorrelated disturbances:

$$T \cdot (\lambda/\sigma) \cdot (\hat{\rho}_T - 1) \xrightarrow{L} \frac{\frac{1}{2}\{[W(1)]^2 - 1\} - W(1) \cdot \int W(r)\,dr}{\left\{ \int [W(r)]^2\,dr - \left[ \int W(r)\,dr \right]^2 \right\}}. \qquad [17.7.33]$$

Recall from [17.7.17] that

$$\lambda/\sigma = (1 - \zeta_1 - \zeta_2 - \cdots - \zeta_{p-1})^{-1}. \qquad [17.7.34]$$

This magnitude is clearly estimated consistently by

$$(1 - \hat{\zeta}_{1,T} - \hat{\zeta}_{2,T} - \cdots - \hat{\zeta}_{p-1,T})^{-1},$$

where $\hat{\zeta}_{j,T}$ denotes the estimate of $\zeta_j$ based on the *OLS* regression [17.7.11]. Thus, the generalization of the Dickey-Fuller $\rho$ test when lagged changes in $y$ are included in the regression is

$$\frac{T \cdot (\hat{\rho}_T - 1)}{1 - \hat{\zeta}_{1,T} - \hat{\zeta}_{2,T} - \cdots - \hat{\zeta}_{p-1,T}} \xrightarrow{L} \frac{\frac{1}{2}\{[W(1)]^2 - 1\} - W(1) \cdot \int W(r)\,dr}{\int [W(r)]^2\,dr - \left[ \int W(r)\,dr \right]^2}. \qquad [17.7.35]$$

This is to be compared with the case 2 section of Table B.5.

Consider next an *OLS* $t$ test of the null hypothesis that $\rho = 1$:

$$t_T = \frac{(\hat{\rho}_T - 1)}{\{s_T^2 \cdot \mathbf{e}'_{p+1} \cdot (\Sigma \mathbf{x}_t \mathbf{x}'_t)^{-1} \cdot \mathbf{e}_{p+1}\}^{1/2}}, \qquad [17.7.36]$$

where $\mathbf{e}_{p+1}$ denotes a $[(p + 1) \times 1]$ vector with unity in the last position and zeros elsewhere. Multiplying the numerator and denominator of [17.7.36] by $T$ results in

$$t_T = \frac{T(\hat{\rho}_T - 1)}{\left\{s_T^2 \cdot \mathbf{e}'_{p+1}\mathbf{Y}_T(\Sigma \mathbf{x}_t\mathbf{x}'_t)^{-1}\mathbf{Y}_T\mathbf{e}_{p+1}\right\}^{1/2}}. \qquad [17.7.37]$$

But

$$\begin{aligned}
\mathbf{e}'_{p+1}\mathbf{Y}_T(\Sigma \mathbf{x}_t\mathbf{x}'_t)^{-1}\mathbf{Y}_T\mathbf{e}_{p+1} &= \mathbf{e}'_{p+1}\left\{\mathbf{Y}_T^{-1}(\Sigma \mathbf{x}_t\mathbf{x}'_t)\mathbf{Y}_T^{-1}\right\}^{-1}\mathbf{e}_{p+1} \\
&\xrightarrow{L} \mathbf{e}'_{p+1}\begin{bmatrix} \mathbf{V}^{-1} & \mathbf{0} \\ \mathbf{0} & \mathbf{Q}^{-1} \end{bmatrix}\mathbf{e}_{p+1} \\
&= \frac{1}{\lambda^2 \cdot \left\{\int [W(r)]^2\, dr - \left[\int W(r)\, dr\right]^2\right\}}
\end{aligned}$$

by virtue of [17.7.18] and [17.7.20]. Hence, from [17.7.37] and [17.7.33],

$$\begin{aligned}
t_T &\xrightarrow{L} (\sigma/\lambda)\frac{\frac{1}{2}\{[W(1)]^2 - 1\} - W(1)\cdot\int W(r)\, dr}{\int [W(r)]^2\, dr - \left[\int W(r)\, dr\right]^2} \\
&\quad \div \left\{\frac{\sigma^2}{\lambda^2\left\{\int [W(r)]^2\, dr - \left[\int W(r)\, dr\right]^2\right\}}\right\}^{1/2} \qquad [17.7.38] \\
&= \frac{\frac{1}{2}\{[W(1)]^2 - 1\} - W(1)\cdot\int W(r)\, dr}{\left\{\int [W(r)]^2\, dr - \left[\int W(r)\, dr\right]^2\right\}^{1/2}}.
\end{aligned}$$

This is the same distribution as in [17.4.36]. Thus, the usual $t$ test of $\rho = 1$ for *OLS* estimation of [17.7.11] can be compared with the case 2 section of Table B.6 without any corrections for the fact that lagged values of $\Delta y$ are included in the regression.

A similar result applies to the Dickey-Fuller $F$ test of the joint hypothesis that $\alpha = 0$ and $\rho = 1$. This null hypothesis can be represented as $\mathbf{R}\boldsymbol{\beta} = \mathbf{r}$, where

$$\underset{[2\times(p+1)]}{\mathbf{R}} = \begin{bmatrix} \underset{[2\times(p-1)]}{\mathbf{0}} & \underset{(2\times 2)}{\mathbf{I}_2} \end{bmatrix}$$

and $\mathbf{r} = (0, 1)'$. The $F$ test is then

$$F_T = (\mathbf{b}_T - \boldsymbol{\beta})'\mathbf{R}'\left\{s_T^2 \cdot \mathbf{R}(\Sigma \mathbf{x}_t\mathbf{x}'_t)^{-1}\mathbf{R}'\right\}^{-1}\mathbf{R}(\mathbf{b}_T - \boldsymbol{\beta})/2. \qquad [17.7.39]$$

Define $\tilde{\mathbf{Y}}_T$ to be the following $(2 \times 2)$ matrix:

$$\tilde{\mathbf{Y}}_T \equiv \begin{bmatrix} T^{1/2} & 0 \\ 0 & T \end{bmatrix}. \qquad [17.7.40]$$

Notice that [17.7.39] can be written

$$F_T = (\mathbf{b}_T - \boldsymbol{\beta})'\mathbf{R}'\tilde{\mathbf{Y}}_T\left\{s_T^2\cdot\tilde{\mathbf{Y}}_T\mathbf{R}(\Sigma\mathbf{x}_t\mathbf{x}_t')^{-1}\mathbf{R}'\tilde{\mathbf{Y}}_T\right\}^{-1} \times \tilde{\mathbf{Y}}_T\mathbf{R}(\mathbf{b}_T - \boldsymbol{\beta})/2. \qquad [17.7.41]$$

The matrix in [17.7.40] has the property that

$$\tilde{\mathbf{Y}}_T\mathbf{R} = \mathbf{R}\mathbf{Y}_T$$

for $\mathbf{R} = [\mathbf{0} \quad \mathbf{I}_2]$ and $\mathbf{Y}_T$ the $(p + 1) \times (p + 1)$ matrix in [17.7.15]. From [17.7.25], $\mathbf{R}\mathbf{Y}_T(\mathbf{b}_T - \boldsymbol{\beta}) \xrightarrow{L} \mathbf{Q}^{-1}\mathbf{h}_2$. Thus, [17.7.41] implies that

$$\begin{aligned}
F_T &= (\mathbf{b}_T - \boldsymbol{\beta})'(\mathbf{R}\mathbf{Y}_T)'\left\{s_T^2\cdot\mathbf{R}\mathbf{Y}_T(\Sigma\mathbf{x}_t\mathbf{x}_t')^{-1}\mathbf{Y}_T\mathbf{R}'\right\}^{-1}\mathbf{R}\mathbf{Y}_T(\mathbf{b}_T - \boldsymbol{\beta})/2 \\
&\xrightarrow{L} (\mathbf{Q}^{-1}\mathbf{h}_2)'\{\sigma^2\mathbf{Q}^{-1}\}^{-1}(\mathbf{Q}^{-1}\mathbf{h}_2)/2 \\
&= \mathbf{h}_2'\mathbf{Q}^{-1}\mathbf{h}_2/(2\sigma^2) \\
&= [1/(2\sigma^2)]\begin{bmatrix}\sigma\cdot W(1) & \tfrac{1}{2}\sigma\lambda\{[W(1)]^2 - 1\}\end{bmatrix} \\
&\quad \times \begin{bmatrix} 1 & \lambda\cdot\int W(r)\,dr \\ \lambda\cdot\int W(r)\,dr & \lambda^2\cdot\int [W(r)]^2\,dr\end{bmatrix}^{-1}\begin{bmatrix}\sigma\cdot W(1) \\ \tfrac{1}{2}\sigma\lambda\{[W(1)]^2 - 1\}\end{bmatrix} \\
&= \left(\frac{1}{2\sigma^2}\right)\sigma^2\begin{bmatrix}W(1) & \dfrac{1}{2}\{[W(1)]^2 - 1\}\end{bmatrix}\begin{bmatrix}1 & 0 \\ 0 & \lambda\end{bmatrix} \\
&\quad \times \begin{bmatrix}1 & 0 \\ 0 & \lambda\end{bmatrix}^{-1}\begin{bmatrix} 1 & \int W(r)\,dr \\ \int W(r)\,dr & \int [W(r)]^2\,dr\end{bmatrix}^{-1}\begin{bmatrix}1 & 0 \\ 0 & \lambda\end{bmatrix}^{-1} \\
&\quad \times \begin{bmatrix}1 & 0 \\ 0 & \lambda\end{bmatrix}\begin{bmatrix}W(1) \\ \tfrac{1}{2}\{[W(1)]^2 - 1\}\end{bmatrix} \\
&= \tfrac{1}{2}\begin{bmatrix}W(1) & \tfrac{1}{2}\{[W(1)]^2 - 1\}\end{bmatrix} \\
&\quad \times \begin{bmatrix} 1 & \int W(r)\,dr \\ \int W(r)\,dr & \int [W(r)]^2\,dr\end{bmatrix}^{-1}\begin{bmatrix}W(1) \\ \tfrac{1}{2}\{[W(1)]^2 - 1\}\end{bmatrix}.
\end{aligned} \qquad [17.7.42]$$

This is identical to the asymptotic distribution of the $F$ test when the regression does not include lagged $\Delta y$ and the disturbances are i.i.d. Thus, the $F$ statistic in [17.7.41] based on *OLS* estimation of [17.7.11] can be compared with the case 2 section of Table B.7 without corrections.

Finally, consider a hypothesis test involving a restriction[12] across $\zeta_1, \zeta_2, \ldots, \zeta_{p-1}$ and $\rho$,

$$H_0\text{: } r_1\zeta_1 + r_2\zeta_2 + \cdots + r_{p-1}\zeta_{p-1} + 0\cdot\alpha + r_{p+1}\rho = r$$

[12]Since the maintained assumption is that $\rho = 1$, this is a slightly unnatural way to write a hypothesis. Nevertheless, framing the hypothesis this way will shortly prove useful in deriving the asymptotic distribution of an autoregression estimated in the usual form without the Dickey-Fuller transformation.

or

$$\mathbf{r}'\boldsymbol{\beta} = r. \qquad [17.7.43]$$

The distribution of the $t$ test of this hypothesis will be dominated asymptotically by the parameters with the slowest rate of convergence, namely, $\zeta_1, \zeta_2, \ldots, \zeta_{p-1}$. Since these are asymptotically Gaussian, the test statistic is asymptotically Gaussian and so can be compared with the usual $t$ tables. To demonstrate this formally, note that the usual $t$ statistic for testing this hypothesis is

$$t_T = \frac{\mathbf{r}'\mathbf{b}_T - r}{\left\{s_T^2\mathbf{r}'(\Sigma\mathbf{x}_t\mathbf{x}_t')^{-1}\mathbf{r}\right\}^{1/2}} = \frac{T^{1/2}(\mathbf{r}'\mathbf{b}_T - r)}{\left\{s_T^2 T^{1/2}\mathbf{r}'(\Sigma\mathbf{x}_t\mathbf{x}_t')^{-1}\mathbf{r}T^{1/2}\right\}^{1/2}}. \qquad [17.7.44]$$

Define $\tilde{\mathbf{r}}_T$ to be the vector that results when the last element of $\mathbf{r}$ is replaced by $r_{p+1}/\sqrt{T}$,

$$\tilde{\mathbf{r}}_T' \equiv [r_1 \quad r_2 \quad \cdots \quad r_{p-1} \quad 0 \quad r_{p+1}/\sqrt{T}], \qquad [17.7.45]$$

and notice that

$$T^{1/2}\mathbf{r} = \mathbf{Y}_T\tilde{\mathbf{r}}_T \qquad [17.7.46]$$

for $\mathbf{Y}_T$ the matrix in [17.7.15]. Using [17.7.46] and the null hypothesis that $r = \mathbf{r}'\boldsymbol{\beta}$, expression [17.7.44] can be written

$$t_T = \frac{\tilde{\mathbf{r}}_T'\mathbf{Y}_T(\mathbf{b}_T - \boldsymbol{\beta})}{\left\{s_T^2\tilde{\mathbf{r}}_T'\mathbf{Y}_T(\Sigma\mathbf{x}_t\mathbf{x}_t')^{-1}\mathbf{Y}_T\tilde{\mathbf{r}}_T\right\}^{1/2}}. \qquad [17.7.47]$$

Notice from [17.7.45] that

$$\tilde{\mathbf{r}}_T \to \tilde{\mathbf{r}},$$

where

$$\tilde{\mathbf{r}}' \equiv [r_1 \quad r_2 \quad \cdots \quad r_{p-1} \quad 0 \quad 0].$$

Using this result along with [17.7.18] and [17.7.25] in [17.7.47] produces

$$t_T \xrightarrow{L} \frac{\tilde{\mathbf{r}}'\begin{bmatrix}\mathbf{V}^{-1}\mathbf{h}_1 \\ \mathbf{Q}^{-1}\mathbf{h}_2\end{bmatrix}}{\left\{\sigma^2\tilde{\mathbf{r}}'\begin{bmatrix}\mathbf{V}^{-1} & \mathbf{0} \\ \mathbf{0} & \mathbf{Q}^{-1}\end{bmatrix}\tilde{\mathbf{r}}\right\}^{1/2}}$$
$$= \frac{[r_1 \quad r_2 \quad \cdots \quad r_{p-1}]\mathbf{V}^{-1}\mathbf{h}_1}{\{\sigma^2[r_1 \quad r_2 \quad \cdots \quad r_{p-1}]\mathbf{V}^{-1}[r_1 \quad r_2 \quad \cdots \quad r_{p-1}]'\}^{1/2}}. \qquad [17.7.48]$$

Since $\mathbf{h}_1 \sim N(\mathbf{0}, \sigma^2\mathbf{V})$, it follows that

$$[r_1 \quad r_2 \quad \cdots \quad r_{p-1}]\mathbf{V}^{-1}\mathbf{h}_1 \sim N(0, h),$$

where

$$h = \sigma^2[r_1 \quad r_2 \quad \cdots \quad r_{p-1}]\mathbf{V}^{-1}[r_1 \quad r_2 \quad \cdots \quad r_{p-1}]'.$$

Thus, the limiting distribution in [17.7.48] is that of a Gaussian scalar divided by its standard deviation and is therefore $N(0, 1)$. This confirms the claim that the $t$ test of $\mathbf{r}'\boldsymbol{\beta} = r$ can be compared with the usual $t$ tables.

One interesting implication of this last result concerns the asymptotic properties of the estimated coefficients if the autoregression is estimated in the usual levels form rather than the transformed regression [17.7.11]. Thus, suppose that the following specification is estimated by *OLS*:

$$y_t = \alpha + \phi_1 y_{t-1} + \phi_2 y_{t-2} + \cdots + \phi_p y_{t-p} + \varepsilon_t \qquad [17.7.49]$$

for some $p \geq 2$. Recalling [17.7.2] and [17.7.3], the relation between the estimates $(\hat{\zeta}_1, \hat{\zeta}_2, \ldots, \hat{\zeta}_{p-1}, \hat{\rho})$ investigated previously and estimates $(\hat{\phi}_1, \hat{\phi}_2, \ldots, \hat{\phi}_p)$ based on *OLS* estimation of [17.7.49] is

$$\begin{aligned} \hat{\phi}_p &= -\hat{\zeta}_{p-1} \\ \hat{\phi}_j &= \hat{\zeta}_j - \hat{\zeta}_{j-1} \qquad \text{for } j = 2, 3, \ldots, p-1 \\ \hat{\phi}_1 &= \hat{\rho} + \hat{\zeta}_1. \end{aligned}$$

Thus, each of the coefficients $\hat{\phi}_1, \hat{\phi}_2, \ldots, \hat{\phi}_p$ is a linear combination of the elements of $(\hat{\zeta}_1, \hat{\zeta}_2, \ldots, \hat{\zeta}_{p-1}, \hat{\rho})$. The analysis of [17.7.43] establishes that any individual estimate $\hat{\phi}_j$ converges at rate $\sqrt{T}$ to a Gaussian random variable. Recalling the discussion of [16.3.20] and [16.3.21], an *OLS* $t$ or $F$ test based on [17.7.49] is numerically identical to the equivalent $t$ or $F$ test expressed in terms of the representation in [17.7.11]. Thus, the usual $t$ tests associated with hypotheses about any individual coefficients $\hat{\phi}_1, \hat{\phi}_2, \ldots, \hat{\phi}_p$ in [17.7.49] can be compared with standard $t$ or $N(0, 1)$ tables. Indeed, any hypothesis about linear combinations of the $\phi$'s other than the sum $\phi_1 + \phi_2 + \cdots + \phi_p$ satisfies the standard conditions. The sum $\hat{\phi}_1 + \hat{\phi}_2 + \cdots + \hat{\phi}_p$, of course, has the nonstandard distribution of the estimate $\hat{\rho}$ described in [17.7.33].

## *Summary of Asymptotic Results for an Estimated Autoregression That Includes a Constant Term*

The preceding analysis applies to *OLS* estimation of

$$y_t = \zeta_1 \Delta y_{t-1} + \zeta_2 \Delta y_{t-2} + \cdots + \zeta_{p-1} \Delta y_{t-p+1} + \alpha + \rho y_{t-1} + \varepsilon_t$$

under the assumption that the true value of $\alpha$ is zero and the true value of $\rho$ is 1. The other maintained assumptions were that $\varepsilon_t$ is i.i.d. with mean zero, variance $\sigma^2$, and finite fourth moment and that roots of

$$(1 - \zeta_1 z - \zeta_2 z^2 - \cdots - \zeta_{p-1} z^{p-1}) = 0$$

are outside the unit circle. It was seen that the estimates $\hat{\zeta}_1, \hat{\zeta}_2, \ldots, \hat{\zeta}_{p-1}$ converge at rate $\sqrt{T}$ to Gaussian variates, and standard $t$ or $F$ tests for hypotheses about these coefficients have the usual limiting Gaussian or $\chi^2$ distributions. The estimates $\hat{\alpha}$ and $\hat{\rho}$ converge at rates $\sqrt{T}$ and $T$, respectively, to nonstandard distributions. If the difference between the *OLS* estimate $\hat{\rho}$ and the hypothesized true value of unity is multiplied by the sample size and divided by $(1 - \hat{\zeta}_1 - \hat{\zeta}_2 - \cdots - \hat{\zeta}_{p-1})$, the resulting statistic has the same asymptotic distribution as the variable tabulated in the case 2 section of Table B.5. The usual $t$ statistic of the hypothesis $\rho = 1$ does not need to be adjusted for sample size or serial correlation and has the same asymptotic distribution as the variable tabulated in the case 2 section of Table B.6. The usual $F$ statistic of the joint hypothesis $\alpha = 0$ and $\rho = 1$ likewise does not have to be adjusted for sample size or serial correlation and has the same distribution as the variable tabulated in the case 2 section of Table B.7.

When the autoregression includes lagged changes as here, tests for a unit root based on the value of $\rho$, $t$ tests, or $F$ tests are described as *augmented Dickey-Fuller tests*.

*Example 17.8*

The following model was estimated by *OLS* for the interest rate data described in Example 17.3 (standard errors in parentheses):

$$
\begin{aligned}
i_t = \underset{(0.0788)}{0.335}\, \Delta i_{t-1} - \underset{(0.0808)}{0.388}\, \Delta i_{t-2} + \underset{(0.0800)}{0.276}\, \Delta i_{t-3} \\
- \underset{(0.0794)}{0.107}\, \Delta i_{t-4} + \underset{(0.109)}{0.195} + \underset{(0.018604)}{0.96904}\, i_{t-1}.
\end{aligned}
$$

Dates $t$ = 1948:II through 1989:I were used for estimation, so in this case the sample size is $T = 164$. For these estimates, the augmented Dickey-Fuller $\rho$ test [17.7.35] would be

$$\frac{164}{1 - 0.335 + 0.388 - 0.276 + 0.107}(0.96904 - 1) = -5.74.$$

Since $-5.74 > -13.8$, the null hypothesis that the Treasury bill rate follows a fifth-order autoregression with no constant term, and a single unit root, is accepted at the 5% level. The *OLS* $t$ test for this same hypothesis is

$$(0.96904 - 1)/(0.018604) = -1.66.$$

Since $-1.66 > -2.89$, the null hypothesis of a unit root is accepted by the augmented Dickey-Fuller $t$ test as well. Finally, the *OLS* $F$ test of the joint null hypothesis that $\rho = 1$ and $\alpha = 0$ is 1.65. Since this is less than 4.68, the null hypothesis is again accepted.

The null hypothesis that the autoregression in levels requires only four lags is based on the *OLS* $t$ test of $\zeta_4 = 0$:

$$-0.107/0.0794 = -1.35.$$

From Table B.3, the 5% two-sided critical value for a $t$ variable with 158 degrees of freedom is $-1.98$. Since $-1.35 > -1.98$, the null hypothesis that only four lags are needed for the autoregression in levels is accepted.

## *Asymptotic Results for Other Autoregressions*

Up to this point in this section, we have considered an autoregression that is a generalization of case 2 of Section 17.4—a constant is included in the estimated regression, though the population process is presumed to exhibit no drift. Parallel generalizations for cases 1, 3, and 4 can be obtained in the same fashion. The reader is invited to derive these generalizations in exercises at the end of the chapter. The key results are summarized in Table 17.3.

**TABLE 17.3**
**Summary of Asymptotic Results for Autoregressions Containing a Unit Root**

*Case 1:*

Estimated regression:

$$y_t = \zeta_1 \Delta y_{t-1} + \zeta_2 \Delta y_{t-2} + \cdots + \zeta_{p-1} \Delta y_{t-p+1} + \rho y_{t-1} + \varepsilon_t$$

True process: same specification as estimated regression with $\rho = 1$

Any $t$ or $F$ test involving $\zeta_1, \zeta_2, \ldots, \zeta_{p-1}$ can be compared with the usual $t$ or $F$ tables for an asymptotically valid test.

**TABLE 17.3 (continued)**

$Z_{DF}$ has the same asymptotic distribution as the variable described under the heading Case 1 in Table B.5.

*OLS t* test of $\rho = 1$ has the same asymptotic distribution as the variable described under Case 1 in Table B.6.

***Case 2:***

Estimated regression:

$$y_t = \zeta_1 \Delta y_{t-1} + \zeta_2 \Delta y_{t-2} + \cdots + \zeta_{p-1} \Delta y_{t-p+1} + \alpha + \rho y_{t-1} + \varepsilon_t$$

True process: same specification as estimated regression with $\alpha = 0$ and $\rho = 1$

Any $t$ or $F$ test involving $\zeta_1, \zeta_2, \ldots, \zeta_{p-1}$ can be compared with the usual $t$ or $F$ tables for an asymptotically valid test.

$Z_{DF}$ has the same asymptotic distribution as the variable described under Case 2 in Table B.5.

*OLS t* test of $\rho = 1$ has the same asymptotic distribution as the variable described under Case 2 in Table B.6.

*OLS F* test of joint hypothesis that $\alpha = 0$ and $\rho = 1$ has the same asymptotic distribution as the variable described under Case 2 in Table B.7.

***Case 3:***

Estimated regression:

$$y_t = \zeta_1 \Delta y_{t-1} + \zeta_2 \Delta y_{t-2} + \cdots + \zeta_{p-1} \Delta y_{t-p+1} + \alpha + \rho y_{t-1} + \varepsilon_t$$

True process: same specification as estimated regression with $\alpha \neq 0$ and $\rho = 1$

$\hat{\rho}_T$ converges at rate $T^{3/2}$ to a Gaussian variable; all other estimated coefficients converge at rate $T^{1/2}$ to Gaussian variables.

Any $t$ or $F$ test involving any coefficients from the regression can be compared with the usual $t$ or $F$ tables for an asymptotically valid test.

***Case 4:***

Estimated regression:

$$y_t = \zeta_1 \Delta y_{t-1} + \zeta_2 \Delta y_{t-2} + \cdots + \zeta_{p-1} \Delta y_{t-p+1} + \alpha + \rho y_{t-1} + \delta t + \varepsilon_t$$

True process: same specification as estimated regression with $\alpha$ any value, $\rho = 1$, and $\delta = 0$

Any $t$ or $F$ test involving $\zeta_1, \zeta_2, \ldots, \zeta_{p-1}$ can be compared with the usual $t$ or $F$ tables for an asymptotically valid test.

$Z_{DF}$ has the same asymptotic distribution as the variable described under Case 4 in Table B.5.

*OLS t* test of $\rho = 1$ has the same asymptotic distribution as the variable described under Case 4 in Table B.6.

*OLS F* test of joint hypothesis that $\rho = 1$ and $\delta = 0$ has the same asymptotic distribution as the variable described under Case 4 in Table B.7.

*Notes to Table 17.3*

*Estimated regression* indicates the form in which the regression is estimated, using observations $t = 1, 2, \ldots, T$ and conditioning on observations $t = 0, -1, \ldots, -p + 1$.

*True process* describes the null hypothesis under which the distribution is calculated. In each case it is assumed that roots of

$$(1 - \zeta_1 z - \zeta_2 z^2 - \cdots - \zeta_{p-1} z^{p-1}) = 0$$

are all outside the unit circle and that $\varepsilon_t$ is i.i.d. with mean zero, variance $\sigma^2$, and finite fourth moment.

$Z_{DF}$ in each case is the following statistic:

$$Z_{DF} \equiv T(\hat{\rho}_T - 1)/(1 - \hat{\zeta}_{1,T} - \hat{\zeta}_{2,T} - \cdots - \hat{\zeta}_{p-1,T}),$$

where $\hat{\rho}_T, \hat{\zeta}_{1,T}, \hat{\zeta}_{2,T}, \ldots, \hat{\zeta}_{p-1,T}$ are the *OLS* estimates from the indicated regression.

*OLS t test of* $\rho = 1$ is $(\hat{\rho}_T - 1)/\hat{\sigma}_{\hat{\rho}_T}$, where $\hat{\sigma}_{\hat{\rho}_T}$ is the *OLS* standard error of $\hat{\rho}_T$.

*OLS F test* of a hypothesis involving two restrictions is given by expression [17.7.39].

***Example 17.9***

The following autoregression was estimated by *OLS* for the GNP data in Figure 17.3 (standard errors in parentheses):

$$\begin{aligned} y_t = {} & \underset{(0.0777)}{0.329}\, \Delta y_{t-1} + \underset{(0.0813)}{0.209}\, \Delta y_{t-2} - \underset{(0.0818)}{0.084}\, \Delta y_{t-3} \\ & - \underset{(0.0788)}{0.075}\, \Delta y_{t-4} + \underset{(13.57)}{35.92} + \underset{(0.019386)}{0.94969}\, y_{t-1} + \underset{(0.0152)}{0.0378}\, t. \end{aligned}$$

Here, $T = 164$ and the augmented Dickey-Fuller $\rho$ test is

$$\frac{164}{1 - 0.329 - 0.209 + 0.084 + 0.075}(0.94969 - 1) = -13.3.$$

Since $-13.3 > -21.0$, the null hypothesis that the log of GNP is $ARIMA(4, 1, 0)$ with possible drift is accepted at the 5% level. The augmented Dickey-Fuller $t$ test also accepts this hypothesis:

$$(0.94969 - 1)/(0.019386) = -2.60 > -3.44.$$

The *OLS F* test of the joint null hypothesis that $\rho = 1$ and $\delta = 0$ is $3.74 < 6.42$, and so the augmented Dickey-Fuller $F$ test is also consistent with the unit root specification.

## *Unit Root* AR(p) *Processes with* p *Unknown*

Various suggestions have been proposed for how to proceed when the process is regarded as $ARIMA(p, 1, 0)$ with $p$ unknown but finite. One simple approach is to estimate [17.7.11] with $p$ taken to be some prespecified upper bound $\bar{p}$. The *OLS t* test of $\zeta_{\bar{p}-1} = 0$ can then be compared with the usual critical value for a $t$ statistic from Table B.3. If the null hypothesis is accepted, the *OLS F* test of the joint null hypothesis that both $\zeta_{\bar{p}-1} = 0$ and $\zeta_{\bar{p}-2} = 0$ can be compared with the usual $F(2, T - k)$ distribution in Table B.4. The procedure continues sequentially until the joint null hypothesis that $\zeta_{\bar{p}-1} = 0, \zeta_{\bar{p}-2} = 0, \ldots, \zeta_{\bar{p}-\ell} = 0$ is rejected for some $\ell$. The recommended regression is then

$$y_t = \zeta_1 \Delta y_{t-1} + \zeta_2 \Delta y_{t-2} + \cdots + \zeta_{\bar{p}-\ell} \Delta y_{t-\bar{p}+\ell} + \alpha + \rho y_{t-1} + \delta t.$$

If no value of $\ell$ leads to rejection, the simple Dickey-Fuller test of Table 17.1 is used. Hall (1991) discussed a variety of alternative strategies for estimating $p$.

Just as in the Phillips-Perron consideration of the $MA(\infty)$ case, the researcher might want to choose bigger values for $p$, the autoregressive lag length, the larger is the sample size $T$. Said and Dickey (1984) showed that as long as $p$ goes to infinity sufficiently slowly relative to $T$, then the *OLS t* test of $\rho = 1$ can continue to be compared with the Dickey-Fuller values in Table B.6.

Again, it is worthwhile to keep in mind that there always exists a $p$ such that an $ARIMA(p, 1, 0)$ representation can describe a stationary process arbitrarily well for a given sample. The Said-Dickey test of $\rho = 1$ might therefore best be viewed as follows. For a given fixed $p$, we can certainly ask whether an $ARIMA(p - 1, 1, 0)$ describes the data nearly as well as an $ARIMA(p, 0, 0)$. Imposing $\rho = 1$ when the true value of $\rho$ is close to unity may improve forecasts and small-sample estimates of the other parameters. The Said-Dickey result permits the researcher to use a larger value of $p$ on which to base this comparison the larger is the sample size $T$.

## 17.8. *Other Approaches to Testing for Unit Roots*

This section briefly describes some alternative approaches to testing for unit roots.

### *Variance Ratio Tests*

Let

$$\Delta y_t = \alpha + u_t,$$

where

$$u_t = \sum_{j=0}^{\infty} \psi_j \varepsilon_{t-j} \equiv \psi(L)\varepsilon_t$$

for $\varepsilon_t$ a white noise sequence with variance $\sigma^2$. Recall from expression [15.3.10] that the permanent effect of $\varepsilon_t$ on the level of $y_{t+s}$ is given by

$$\lim_{s\to\infty} \frac{\partial y_{t+s}}{\partial \varepsilon_t} = \psi(1).$$

If $y_t$ is stationary or stationary around a deterministic time trend, an innovation $\varepsilon_t$ has no permanent effect on $y$, requiring $\psi(1) = 0$.

Cochrane (1988) and Lo and MacKinlay (1988) proposed a test for unit roots that exploits this property. Consider the change in $y$ over $s$ periods,

$$y_{t+s} - y_t = \alpha s + u_{t+s} + u_{t+s-1} + \cdots + u_{t+1}, \qquad [17.8.1]$$

and notice that

$$(y_{t+s} - y_t)/s = \alpha + s^{-1}(u_{t+s} + u_{t+s-1} + \cdots + u_{t+1}). \qquad [17.8.2]$$

The second term in [17.8.2] could be viewed as the sample mean of $s$ observations drawn from the process followed by $u$. Thus, Proposition 7.5(b) and result [7.2.8] imply that

$$\lim_{s\to\infty} s\cdot \text{Var}[s^{-1}(u_{t+s} + u_{t+s-1} + \cdots + u_{t+1})] = \sigma^2\cdot[\psi(1)]^2. \qquad [17.8.3]$$

Let $\hat{\alpha}_T$ denote the average change in $y$ in a sample of $T$ observations:

$$\hat{\alpha}_T = T^{-1} \sum_{t=1}^{T} (y_t - y_{t-1}).$$

Consider the following estimate of the variance of the change in $y$ over its value $s$ periods earlier:

$$\hat{J}_T(s) = T^{-1} \sum_{t=0}^{T-s} (y_{t+s} - y_t - \hat{\alpha}_T s)^2. \qquad [17.8.4]$$

This should converge in probability to

$$J(s) = E(y_{t+s} - y_t - \alpha s)^2 = E(u_{t+s} + u_{t+s-1} + \cdots + u_{t+1})^2 \qquad [17.8.5]$$

as the sample size $T$ becomes large. Comparing this expression with [17.8.3],

$$\lim_{s\to\infty} s^{-1}\cdot J(s) = \sigma^2\cdot[\psi(1)]^2.$$

Cochrane (1988) therefore proposed calculating [17.8.4] as a function of $s$. If the true process for $y_t$ is stationary or stationary around a deterministic time trend, this statistic should go to zero for large $s$. If the true process for $y_t$ is $I(1)$, this statistic gives a measure of the quantitative importance of permanent effects of $\varepsilon$ as reflected in the long-run multiplier $\psi(1)$. However, the statistic in [17.8.4] is not reliable unless $s$ is much smaller than $T$.

If the data truly followed a random walk so that $\psi(L) = 1$, then $J(s)$ in [17.8.5] would equal $s \cdot \sigma^2$ for any $s$, where $\sigma^2$ is the variance of $u_t$. Lo and MacKinlay (1988) exploited this property to suggest tests of the random walk hypothesis based on alternative values of $s$. See Lo and MacKinlay (1989) and Cecchetti and Lam (1991) for evidence on the small-sample properties of these tests.

### *Other Tests for Unit Roots*

The Phillips-Perron approach was based on an $MA(\infty)$ representation for $\Delta y_t$, while the Said-Dickey approach was based on an $AR(\infty)$ representation. Tests based on a finite $ARMA(p, q)$ representation for $\Delta y_t$ have been explored by Said and Dickey (1985), Hall (1989), Said (1991), and Pantula and Hall (1991).

A number of other approaches to testing for unit roots have been proposed, including Sargan and Bhargava (1983), Solo (1984), Bhargava (1986), Dickey and Pantula (1987), Park and Choi (1988), Schmidt and Phillips (1992), Stock (1991), and Kwiatkowski, Phillips, Schmidt, and Shin (1992). See Stock (1993) for an excellent survey. Asymptotic inference for processes with near unit root behavior has been discussed by Chan and Wei (1987), Phillips (1988), and Sowell (1990).

## 17.9. *Bayesian Analysis and Unit Roots*

Up to this point in the chapter we have adopted a classical statistical perspective, calculating the distribution of $\hat{\rho}$ conditional on a particular value of $\rho$ such as $\rho = 1$. This section considers the Bayesian perspective, in which the true value of $\rho$ is regarded as a random variable and the goal is to describe the distribution of this random variable conditional on the data.

Recall from Proposition 12.3 that if the prior density for the vector of unknown coefficients $\boldsymbol{\beta}$ and innovation precision $\sigma^{-2}$ is of the Normal-gamma form of [12.1.19] and [12.1.20], then the posterior distribution of $\boldsymbol{\beta}$ conditional on the data is multivariate $t$. This result holds exactly for any finite sample and holds regardless of whether the process is stationary. Thus, in the case of the diffuse prior distribution represented by $N = \lambda = 0$ and $\mathbf{M}^{-1} = \mathbf{0}$, a Bayesian would essentially use the usual $t$ and $F$ statistics in the standard way.

How can the classical distribution of $\hat{\rho}$ be strongly skewed while the Bayesian distribution of $\rho$ is that of a symmetric $t$ variable? Sims (1988) and Sims and Uhlig (1991) provided a detailed discussion of this question. The classical test of the null hypothesis $\rho = 1$ is based only on the distribution of $\hat{\rho}$ when the true value of $\rho$ is unity. By contrast, the Bayesian inference is based on the distribution of $\hat{\rho}|\rho$ for all the possible values of $\rho$, with the distribution of $\hat{\rho}|\rho$ weighted according to the prior probability for $\rho$. If the distribution of $\hat{\rho}|\rho$ had the same skew and dispersion for every $\rho$ as it does at $\rho = 1$, then we would conclude that, having observed any particular $\hat{\rho}$, the true value of $\rho$ is probably somewhat higher. However, the distribution of $\hat{\rho}|\rho$ changes with $\rho$—the lower the true value of $\rho$, the smaller the skew and the greater the dispersion, since from [17.1.3] the variance of $\sqrt{T}(\hat{\rho} - \rho)$ is approximately $(1 - \rho^2)$. Because lower values of $\rho$ imply greater dispersion for $\hat{\rho}$, in the absence of skew we would suspect that a given observation $\hat{\rho} = 0.95$ was more likely to have been generated by a distribution centered at $\rho = 0.90$ with large dispersion than by a distribution centered at $\rho = 1$ with small dispersion. The effects of skew and dispersion turn out to cancel, so that with a uniform prior distribution for the value of $\rho$, having observed $\hat{\rho} = 0.95$, it is just as likely that the true value of $\rho$ is greater than 0.95 as that the true value of $\rho$ is less than 0.95.

### *Example 17.10*

For the GNP regression in Example 17.9, the probability that $\rho \geq 1$ conditional on the data is the probability that a $t$ variable with $T = 164$ degrees of freedom[13] exceeds $(1 - 0.94969)/0.019386 = 2.60$. From Table B.3, this probability is around 0.005. Hence, although the value of $\rho$ must be large, it is unlikely to be as big as unity.

The contrast between the Bayesian inference in Example 17.10 and the classical inference in Example 17.9 is one of the reasons given by Sims (1988) and Sims and Uhlig (1991) for preferring Bayesian methods. Note that the probability calculated in Example 17.10 will be less than 0.025 if and only if a classical 95% confidence interval around the point estimate $\hat{\rho}$ does not contain unity. Thus, an alternative way of describing the finding of Example 17.10 is that the standard asymptotic classical confidence region around $\hat{\rho}$ does not include $\rho = 1$. Even so, Example 17.9 showed that the null hypothesis of a unit root is accepted by the augmented Dickey-Fuller test. The classical asymptotic confidence region centered at $\rho = \hat{\rho}$ seems inconsistent with a unit root, while the classical asymptotic confidence region centered at $\rho = 1$ supports a unit root. Such disconnected confidence regions resulting from the classical approach may seem somewhat troublesome and counterintuitive.[14] By contrast, the Bayesian has a single, consistent summary of the plausibility of different values of $\rho$, which is that implied by the posterior distribution of $\rho$ conditional on the data.

One could, of course, use a prior distribution that reflected more confidence in the prior information about the value of $\rho$. As long as the prior distribution was in the Normal-gamma class, this would cause us to shift the point estimate 0.94969 in the direction of the prior mean and reduce the standard error and increase the degrees of freedom as warranted by the prior information, but a $t$ distribution would still be used to interpret the resulting statistic.

Although the Normal-gamma class is convenient to work with, it might not be sufficiently flexible to reflect the researcher's true prior beliefs. Sims (1988, p. 470) discussed Bayesian inference in which a point mass with positive probability is placed on the possibility that $\rho = 1$. DeJong and Whiteman (1991) used numerical methods to calculate posterior distributions under a range of prior distributions defined numerically and concluded that the evidence for unit roots in many key economic time series is quite weak.

Phillips (1991a) noted that there is a prior distribution for which the Bayesian inference mimics the classical approach. He argued that the diffuse prior distribution of Proposition 12.3 is actually highly informative in a time series regression and suggested instead a prior distribution due to Jeffreys (1946). Although this prior distribution has some theoretical arguments on its behalf, it has the unusual property in this application that the prior distribution is a function of the sample size $T$—Phillips would propose using a different prior distribution for $f(\rho)$ when

[13] Recall from Proposition 12.3(b) that the degrees of freedom are given by $N^* = N + T$. Thus, the Bayesian interpretation is not quite identical to the classical $t$ statistic, whose degrees of freedom would be $T - k$.

[14] Stock (1991) has recently proposed a solution to this problem from the classical perspective. Another approach is to rely on the exact small-sample distribution, as advocated by Andrews (1993).

the analyst is going to obtain a sample of size 50 than when the analyst is going to obtain a sample of size 100. This would not be appropriate if the prior distribution is intended to represent the actual information available to the analyst before seeing the data. Phillips (1991b, pp. 468–69) argued that, in order to be truly uninformative, a prior distribution in this context would have this property, since the larger the true value of $\rho$, the more rapidly information about $\rho$ contained in the sample $\{y_1, y_2, \ldots, y_T\}$ is going to accumulate with the sample size $T$. Certainly the concept of what it means for a prior distribution to be "uninformative" can be difficult and controversial.[15]

The potential difficulty in persuading others of the validity of one's prior beliefs has always been the key weakness of Bayesian statistics, and it seems unavoidable here. The best a Bayesian can do may be to take an explicit stand on the nature and strength of prior information and defend it as best as possible. If the nature of the prior information is that all values of $\rho$ are equally likely, then it is satisfactory to use the standard $OLS$ $t$ and $F$ tests in the usual way. If one is unwilling to take such a stand, then Sims and Uhlig urged that investigators report both the classical hypothesis test of $\rho = 1$ and the classical confidence region around $\hat{\rho}$ and let the reader interpret the results as he or she sees fit.

## APPENDIX 17.A. *Proofs of Chapter 17 Propositions*

■ **Proof of Proposition 17.2.** Observe that

$$\begin{aligned}
\sum_{s=1}^{t} u_s &= \sum_{s=1}^{t}\sum_{j=0}^{\infty} \psi_j \varepsilon_{s-j} \\
&= \{\psi_0\varepsilon_t + \psi_1\varepsilon_{t-1} + \psi_2\varepsilon_{t-2} + \cdots + \psi_t\varepsilon_0 + \psi_{t+1}\varepsilon_{-1} + \cdots\} \\
&\quad + \{\psi_0\varepsilon_{t-1} + \psi_1\varepsilon_{t-2} + \psi_2\varepsilon_{t-3} + \cdots + \psi_{t-1}\varepsilon_0 + \psi_t\varepsilon_{-1} + \cdots\} \\
&\quad + \{\psi_0\varepsilon_{t-2} + \psi_1\varepsilon_{t-3} + \psi_2\varepsilon_{t-4} + \cdots + \psi_{t-2}\varepsilon_0 + \psi_{t-1}\varepsilon_{-1} + \cdots\} \\
&\quad + \cdots + \{\psi_0\varepsilon_1 + \psi_1\varepsilon_0 + \psi_2\varepsilon_{-1} + \cdots\} \\
&= \psi_0\varepsilon_t + (\psi_0 + \psi_1)\varepsilon_{t-1} + (\psi_0 + \psi_1 + \psi_2)\varepsilon_{t-2} + \cdots \\
&\quad + (\psi_0 + \psi_1 + \psi_2 + \cdots + \psi_{t-1})\varepsilon_1 + (\psi_1 + \psi_2 + \cdots + \psi_t)\varepsilon_0 \\
&\quad + (\psi_2 + \psi_3 + \cdots + \psi_{t+1})\varepsilon_{-1} + \cdots \\
&= (\psi_0 + \psi_1 + \psi_2 + \cdots)\varepsilon_t - (\psi_1 + \psi_2 + \psi_3 + \cdots)\varepsilon_t \\
&\quad + (\psi_0 + \psi_1 + \psi_2 + \cdots)\varepsilon_{t-1} - (\psi_2 + \psi_3 + \cdots)\varepsilon_{t-1} \\
&\quad + (\psi_0 + \psi_1 + \psi_2 + \cdots)\varepsilon_{t-2} - (\psi_3 + \psi_4 + \cdots)\varepsilon_{t-2} + \cdots \\
&\quad + (\psi_0 + \psi_1 + \psi_2 + \cdots)\varepsilon_1 - (\psi_t + \psi_{t+1} + \cdots)\varepsilon_1 \\
&\quad + (\psi_1 + \psi_2 + \psi_3 + \cdots)\varepsilon_0 - (\psi_{t+1} + \psi_{t+2} + \cdots)\varepsilon_0 \\
&\quad + (\psi_2 + \psi_3 + \psi_4 + \cdots)\varepsilon_{-1} - (\psi_{t+2} + \psi_{t+3} + \cdots)\varepsilon_{-1} + \cdots
\end{aligned}$$

or

$$\sum_{s=1}^{t} u_s = \psi(1)\cdot\sum_{s=1}^{t} \varepsilon_s + \eta_t - \eta_0, \qquad [17.A.1]$$

where

$$\begin{aligned}
\eta_t &\equiv -(\psi_1 + \psi_2 + \psi_3 + \cdots)\varepsilon_t - (\psi_2 + \psi_3 + \psi_4 + \cdots)\varepsilon_{t-1} \\
&\quad - (\psi_3 + \psi_4 + \psi_5 + \cdots)\varepsilon_{t-2} - \cdots \\
\eta_0 &= -(\psi_1 + \psi_2 + \psi_3 + \cdots)\varepsilon_0 - (\psi_2 + \psi_3 + \psi_4 + \cdots)\varepsilon_{-1} \\
&\quad - (\psi_3 + \psi_4 + \psi_5 + \cdots)\varepsilon_{-2} - \cdots.
\end{aligned}$$

[15]See the many comments accompanying Phillips (1991a).

Notice that $\eta_t = \Sigma_{j=0}^{\infty}\alpha_j\varepsilon_{t-j}$, where $\alpha_j = -(\psi_{j+1} + \psi_{j+2} + \cdots)$, with $\{\alpha_j\}_{j=0}^{\infty}$ absolutely summable:

$$\begin{aligned}\sum_{j=0}^{\infty}|\alpha_j| &= |\psi_1 + \psi_2 + \psi_3 + \cdots| + |\psi_2 + \psi_3 + \psi_4 + \cdots| + |\psi_3 + \psi_4 + \psi_5 + \cdots| + \cdots \\ &\le \{|\psi_1| + |\psi_2| + |\psi_3| + \cdots\} + \{|\psi_2| + |\psi_3| + |\psi_4| + \cdots\} \\ &\quad + \{|\psi_3| + |\psi_4| + |\psi_5| + \cdots\} + \cdots \\ &= |\psi_1| + 2|\psi_2| + 3|\psi_3| + \cdots \\ &= \sum_{j=0}^{\infty} j\cdot|\psi_j|,\end{aligned}$$

which is bounded by the assumptions in Proposition 17.2. ∎

■ **Proof of Proposition 17.3.**

(a) This was shown in [17.5.9].

(b) This follows from [7.2.17] and the fact that $E(u_t^2) = \gamma_0$.

(c) This is implied by [7.2.14].

(d) Since $\xi_t = \Sigma_{s=1}^{t}u_s$, Proposition 17.2 asserts that

$$\xi_t = \psi(1)\sum_{s=1}^{t}\varepsilon_s + \eta_t - \eta_0. \tag{17.A.2}$$

Hence,

$$\begin{aligned}T^{-1}\sum_{t=1}^{T}\xi_{t-1}\varepsilon_t &= T^{-1}\sum_{t=2}^{T}\left(\psi(1)\sum_{s=1}^{t-1}\varepsilon_s + \eta_{t-1} - \eta_0\right)\varepsilon_t \\ &= \psi(1)\cdot T^{-1}\sum_{t=2}^{T}(\varepsilon_1 + \varepsilon_2 + \cdots + \varepsilon_{t-1})\varepsilon_t \\ &\quad + T^{-1}\sum_{t=2}^{T}(\eta_{t-1} - \eta_0)\varepsilon_t.\end{aligned} \tag{17.A.3}$$

But [17.3.26] established that

$$T^{-1}\sum_{t=2}^{T}(\varepsilon_1 + \varepsilon_2 + \cdots + \varepsilon_{t-1})\varepsilon_t \xrightarrow{L} (1/2)\sigma^2\cdot\{[W(1)]^2 - 1\}. \tag{17.A.4}$$

Furthermore, Proposition 17.2 ensures that $\{(\eta_{t-1} - \eta_0)\varepsilon_t\}_{t=1}^{\infty}$ is a martingale difference sequence with finite variance, and so, from Example 7.11,

$$T^{-1}\sum_{t=2}^{T}(\eta_{t-1} - \eta_0)\varepsilon_t \xrightarrow{p} 0. \tag{17.A.5}$$

Substituting [17.A.4] and [17.A.5] into [17.A.3] yields

$$T^{-1}\sum_{t=1}^{T}\xi_{t-1}\varepsilon_t \xrightarrow{L} (1/2)\sigma^2\cdot[\psi(1)]\cdot\{[W(1)]^2 - 1\}, \tag{17.A.6}$$

as claimed in (d).

(e) For $j = 0$ we have from [17.1.11] that

$$T^{-1}\sum_{t=1}^{T}\xi_{t-1}u_t = (1/2)T^{-1}\xi_T^2 - (1/2)T^{-1}(u_1^2 + u_2^2 + \cdots + u_T^2). \tag{17.A.7}$$

But

$$T^{-1}\xi_T^2 = [T^{-1/2}(u_1 + u_2 + \cdots + u_T)]^2 \xrightarrow{L} \lambda^2\cdot[W(1)]^2 \tag{17.A.8}$$

from result (a). Also,

$$T^{-1}(u_1^2 + u_2^2 + \cdots + u_T^2) \xrightarrow{p} \gamma_0$$

from result (c). Thus, [17.A.7] converges to

$$T^{-1}\sum_{t=1}^{T}\xi_{t-1}u_t \xrightarrow{L} (1/2)\{\lambda^2\cdot[W(1)]^2 - \gamma_0\}, \qquad [17.A.9]$$

which establishes result (e) for $j = 0$.

For $j > 0$, observe that

$$\xi_{t-1} = \xi_{t-j-1} + u_{t-j} + u_{t-j+1} + \cdots + u_{t-1},$$

implying that

$$\begin{aligned} T^{-1}\sum_{t=j+1}^{T}\xi_{t-1}u_{t-j} &= T^{-1}\sum_{t=j+1}^{T}(\xi_{t-j-1} + u_{t-j} + u_{t-j+1} + \cdots + u_{t-1})u_{t-j} \\ &= T^{-1}\sum_{t=j+1}^{T}\xi_{t-j-1}u_{t-j} \qquad [17.A.10] \\ &\quad + T^{-1}\sum_{t=j+1}^{T}(u_{t-j} + u_{t-j+1} + \cdots + u_{t-1})u_{t-j}. \end{aligned}$$

But

$$T^{-1}\sum_{t=j+1}^{T}\xi_{t-j-1}u_{t-j} = [(T - j)/T]\cdot(T - j)^{-1}\sum_{t=1}^{T-j}\xi_{t-1}u_t \xrightarrow{L} (1/2)\{\lambda^2\cdot[W(1)]^2 - \gamma_0\},$$

as in [17.A.9]. Also,

$$T^{-1}\sum_{t=j+1}^{T}(u_{t-j} + u_{t-j+1} + \cdots + u_{t-1})u_{t-j} \xrightarrow{p} \gamma_0 + \gamma_1 + \gamma_2 + \cdots + \gamma_{j-1},$$

from result (c). This, [17.A.10] converges to

$$T^{-1}\sum_{t=j+1}^{T}\xi_{t-1}u_{t-j} \xrightarrow{L} (1/2)\{\lambda^2\cdot[W(1)]^2 - \gamma_0\} + \{\gamma_0 + \gamma_1 + \gamma_2 + \cdots + \gamma_{j-1}\}.$$

Clearly, $T^{-1}\sum_{t=1}^{T}\xi_{t-1}u_{t-j}$ has the same asymptotic distribution, since

$$T^{-1}\sum_{t=1}^{j}\xi_{t-1}u_{t-j} \xrightarrow{p} 0.$$

(f) From the definition of $\xi_t$ in [17.5.11] and $X_T(r)$ in [17.5.4], it follows as in [17.3.15] that

$$\int_0^1 \sqrt{T}\cdot X_T(r)\,dr = T^{-3/2}\sum_{t=1}^{T}\xi_{t-1}.$$

Result (f) then follows immediately from [17.5.5].

(g) First notice that

$$T^{-3/2}\sum_{t=1}^{T}tu_{t-j} = T^{-3/2}\sum_{t=1}^{T}(t - j + j)u_{t-j},$$

where $j\cdot T^{-3/2}\sum_{t=1}^{T}u_{t-j} \xrightarrow{p} 0$. Hence,

$$T^{-3/2}\sum_{t=1}^{T}tu_{t-j} \xrightarrow{p} T^{-3/2}\sum_{t=1}^{T}(t - j)u_{t-j} \xrightarrow{p} T^{-3/2}\sum_{t=1}^{T}tu_t.$$

But from [17.3.19],

$$T^{-3/2}\sum_{t=1}^{T}tu_t = T^{-1/2}\sum_{t=1}^{T}u_t - T^{-3/2}\sum_{t=1}^{T}\xi_{t-1} \xrightarrow{L} \lambda\cdot W(1) - \lambda\cdot\int_0^1 W(r)\,dr,$$

by virtue of (a) and (f).

(h) Using the same analysis as in [17.3.20] through [17.3.22], for $\xi_t$ defined in [17.5.11] and $X_T(r)$ defined in [17.5.4], we have

$$T^{-1}\{\xi_1^2/T + \xi_2^2/T + \cdots + \xi_{T-1}^2/T\} = \int_0^1 [\sqrt{T}\cdot X_T(r)]^2\, dr \xrightarrow{L} [\sigma\cdot\psi(1)]^2\cdot\int_0^1 [W(r)]^2\, dr,$$

by virtue of [17.5.5].

(i) As in [17.3.23],

$$\begin{aligned} T^{-5/2}\sum_{t=1}^{T} t\xi_{t-1} &= T^{1/2}\sum_{t=1}^{T}(t/T)\cdot(\xi_{t-1}/T^2) \\ &= T^{1/2}\int_0^1 \{([Tr]^* + 1)/T\}\cdot\{(u_1 + u_2 + \cdots + u_{[Tr]^*})/T\}\, dr \\ &= T^{1/2}\int_0^1 \{([Tr]^* + 1)/T\}\cdot X_T(r)\, dr \\ &\xrightarrow{L} \sigma\cdot\psi(1)\cdot\int_0^1 rW(r)\, dr, \end{aligned}$$

from [17.5.5] and the continuous mapping theorem.

(j) From the same argument as in (i),

$$\begin{aligned} T^{-3}\sum_{t=1}^{T} t\xi_{t-1}^2 &= \sum_{t=1}^{T}(t/T)(\xi_{t-1}^2/T^2) \\ &= T\int_0^1 \{([Tr]^* + 1)/T\}\cdot\{(u_1 + u_2 + \cdots + u_{[Tr]^*})/T\}^2\, dr \\ &= T\int_0^1 \{([Tr]^* + 1)/T\}\cdot[X_T(r)]^2\, dr \\ &\xrightarrow{L} [\sigma\cdot\psi(1)]^2\cdot\int_0^1 r[W(r)]^2\, dr. \end{aligned}$$

(k) This is identical to result (h) from Proposition 17.1, repeated in this proposition for the reader's convenience. ■

## *Chapter 17 Exercises*

17.1. Let $\{u_t\}$ be an i.i.d. sequence with mean zero and variance $\sigma^2$, and let $y_t = u_1 + u_2 + \cdots + u_t$ with $y_0 = 0$. Deduce from [17.3.17] and [17.3.18] that

$$\begin{bmatrix} T^{-1/2}\Sigma u_t \\ T^{-3/2}\Sigma y_{t-1}\end{bmatrix} \xrightarrow{L} N\left(\begin{bmatrix}0\\0\end{bmatrix}, \sigma^2\begin{bmatrix}1 & \frac{1}{2}\\ \frac{1}{2} & \frac{1}{3}\end{bmatrix}\right),$$

where $\Sigma$ indicates summation over $t$ from 1 to $T$. Comparing this result with Proposition 17.1, argue that

$$\begin{bmatrix} W(1) \\ \int W(r)\, dr\end{bmatrix} \sim N\left(\begin{bmatrix}0\\0\end{bmatrix}, \begin{bmatrix}1 & \frac{1}{2}\\ \frac{1}{2} & \frac{1}{3}\end{bmatrix}\right),$$

where the integral sign denotes integration over $r$ from 0 to 1.

17.2. *Phillips (1987) generalization of case 1.* Suppose that data are generated from the process $y_t = y_{t-1} + u_t$, where $u_t = \psi(L)\varepsilon_t$, $\Sigma_{j=0}^{\infty} j\cdot|\psi_j| < \infty$, and $\varepsilon_t$ is i.i.d. with mean zero, variance $\sigma^2$, and finite fourth moment. Consider *OLS* estimation of the autoregression $y_t = \rho y_{t-1} + u_t$. Let $\hat{\rho}_T = (\Sigma y_{t-1}^2)^{-1}(\Sigma y_{t-1}y_t)$ be the *OLS* estimate of $\rho$, $s_T^2 = (T - 1)^{-1} \times \Sigma\hat{u}_t^2$ the *OLS* estimate of the variance of the regression error, $\hat{\sigma}_{\hat{\rho}_T}^2 = s_T^2\cdot(\Sigma y_{t-1}^2)^{-1}$ the *OLS* estimate of the variance of $\hat{\rho}_T$, and $t_T = (\hat{\rho}_T - 1)/\hat{\sigma}_{\hat{\rho}_T}$ the *OLS* $t$ test of $\rho = 1$, and define

$\lambda \equiv \sigma\cdot\psi(1)$. Use Proposition 17.3 to show that

(a) $$T(\hat{\rho}_T - 1) \xrightarrow{L} \frac{\frac{1}{2}\{\lambda^2\cdot[W(1)]^2 - \gamma_0\}}{\lambda^2\cdot\int [W(r)]^2\,dr};$$

(b) $$T^2\cdot\hat{\sigma}^2_{\hat{\rho}_T} \xrightarrow{L} \frac{\gamma_0}{\lambda^2\cdot\int [W(r)]^2\,dr};$$

(c) $$t_T \xrightarrow{L} (\lambda^2/\gamma_0)^{1/2}\left\{\frac{\frac{1}{2}\{[W(1)]^2 - 1\}}{\left\{\int [W(r)]^2\,dr\right\}^{1/2}} + \frac{\frac{1}{2}(\lambda^2 - \gamma_0)}{\lambda^2\left\{\int [W(r)]^2\,dr\right\}^{1/2}}\right\};$$

(d) $$T(\hat{\rho}_T - 1) - \tfrac{1}{2}(T^2\cdot\hat{\sigma}^2_{\hat{\rho}_T} \div s_T^2)(\lambda^2 - \gamma_0) \xrightarrow{L} \frac{\frac{1}{2}\{[W(1)]^2 - 1\}}{\int [W(r)]^2\,dr};$$

(e) $$(\gamma_0/\lambda^2)^{1/2}\cdot t_T - \{\tfrac{1}{2}(\lambda^2 - \gamma_0)/\lambda\} \times \{T\cdot\hat{\sigma}_{\hat{\rho}_T} \div s_T\} \xrightarrow{L} \frac{\frac{1}{2}\{[W(1)]^2 - 1\}}{\left\{\int [W(r)]^2\,dr\right\}^{1/2}}.$$

Suggest estimates of $\gamma_0$ and $\lambda^2$ that could be used to construct the statistics in (d) and (e), and indicate where one could find critical values for these statistics.

17.3. *Phillips and Perron (1988) generalization of case 4.* Suppose that data are generated from the process $y_t = \alpha + y_{t-1} + u_t$, where $u_t = \psi(L)\varepsilon_t$, $\sum_{j=0}^{\infty} j\cdot|\psi_j| < \infty$, and $\varepsilon_t$ is i.i.d. with mean zero, variance $\sigma^2$, and finite fourth moment, and where $\alpha$ can be any value, including zero. Consider *OLS* estimation of

$$y_t = \alpha + \rho y_{t-1} + \delta t + u_t.$$

As in [17.4.49], note that the fitted values and estimate of $\rho$ from this regression are identical to those from an *OLS* regression of $y_t$ on a constant, time trend, and $\xi_{t-1} \equiv y_{t-1} - \alpha(t-1)$:

$$y_t = \alpha^* + \rho^*\xi_{t-1} + \delta^* t + u_t,$$

where, under the assumed data-generating process, $\xi_t$ satisfies the assumptions of Proposition 17.3. Let $(\hat{\alpha}_T^*, \hat{\rho}_T^*, \hat{\delta}_T^*)'$ be the *OLS* estimates given by equation [17.4.50], $s_T^2 = (T-3)^{-1} \times \sum\hat{u}_t^2$ the *OLS* estimate of the variance of the regression error, $\hat{\sigma}^2_{\hat{\rho}_T^*}$ the *OLS* estimate of the variance of $\hat{\rho}_T^*$ given in [17.4.54], and $t_T^* = (\hat{\rho}_T^* - 1)/\hat{\sigma}_{\hat{\rho}_T^*}$ the *OLS* $t$ test of $\rho = 1$. Recall further that $\hat{\rho}_T^*$, $\hat{\sigma}^2_{\hat{\rho}_T^*}$, and $t_T^*$ are numerically identical to the analogous magnitudes for the original regression, $\hat{\rho}_T$, $\hat{\sigma}^2_{\hat{\rho}_T}$, and $t_T$. Finally, define $\lambda \equiv \sigma\cdot\psi(1)$. Use Proposition 17.3 to show that

(a) $$\begin{bmatrix} 1 & T^{-3/2}\sum\xi_{t-1} & T^{-2}\sum t \\ T^{-3/2}\sum\xi_{t-1} & T^{-2}\sum\xi_{t-1}^2 & T^{-5/2}\sum\xi_{t-1}t \\ T^{-2}\sum t & T^{-5/2}\sum t\xi_{t-1} & T^{-3}\sum t^2 \end{bmatrix}$$

$$\xrightarrow{L} \begin{bmatrix} 1 & 0 & 0 \\ 0 & \lambda & 0 \\ 0 & 0 & 1 \end{bmatrix} \begin{bmatrix} 1 & \int W(r)\,dr & 1/2 \\ \int W(r)\,dr & \int [W(r)]^2\,dr & \int rW(r)\,dr \\ 1/2 & \int rW(r)\,dr & 1/3 \end{bmatrix} \begin{bmatrix} 1 & 0 & 0 \\ 0 & \lambda & 0 \\ 0 & 0 & 1 \end{bmatrix};$$

(b) $$\begin{bmatrix} T^{-1/2}\sum u_t \\ T^{-1}\sum\xi_{t-1}u_t \\ T^{-3/2}\sum tu_t \end{bmatrix} \xrightarrow{L} \lambda \begin{bmatrix} 1 & 0 & 0 \\ 0 & \lambda & 0 \\ 0 & 0 & 1 \end{bmatrix} \begin{bmatrix} W(1) \\ \frac{1}{2}\{[W(1)]^2 - [\gamma_0/\lambda^2]\} \\ W(1) - \int W(r)\,dr \end{bmatrix};$$

(c) $$\begin{bmatrix} T^{1/2}\hat{\alpha}_T^* \\ T(\hat{\rho}_T^* - 1) \\ T^{3/2}(\hat{\delta}_T^* - \alpha_0) \end{bmatrix} \xrightarrow{L} \begin{bmatrix} \lambda & 0 & 0 \\ 0 & 1 & 0 \\ 0 & 0 & \lambda \end{bmatrix} \begin{bmatrix} 1 & \int W(r)\,dr & 1/2 \\ \int W(r)\,dr & \int [W(r)]^2\,dr & \int rW(r)\,dr \\ 1/2 & \int rW(r)\,dr & 1/3 \end{bmatrix}^{-1}$$
$$\times \begin{bmatrix} W(1) \\ \tfrac{1}{2}\{[W(1)]^2 - [\gamma_0/\lambda^2]\} \\ \left\{W(1) - \int W(r)\,dr\right\} \end{bmatrix};$$

(d) $$T^2\cdot\hat{\sigma}^2_{\hat{\rho}_T} \xrightarrow{p} (s_T^2/\lambda^2)[0 \quad 1 \quad 0] \begin{bmatrix} 1 & \int W(r)\,dr & 1/2 \\ \int W(r)\,dr & \int [W(r)]^2\,dr & \int rW(r)\,dr \\ 1/2 & \int rW(r)\,dr & 1/3 \end{bmatrix}^{-1} \begin{bmatrix} 0 \\ 1 \\ 0 \end{bmatrix}$$
$$\equiv (s_T^2/\lambda^2)\cdot Q;$$

(e) $t_T \xrightarrow{p} (\lambda^2/\gamma_0)^{1/2}\cdot T(\hat{\rho}_T - 1)/\sqrt{Q}$;

(f) $$T(\hat{\rho}_T - 1) - \tfrac{1}{2}(T^2\cdot\hat{\sigma}^2_{\hat{\rho}_T} \div s_T^2)(\lambda^2 - \gamma_0)$$
$$\xrightarrow{L} [0 \quad 1 \quad 0] \begin{bmatrix} 1 & \int W(r)\,dr & 1/2 \\ \int W(r)\,dr & \int [W(r)]^2\,dr & \int rW(r)\,dr \\ 1/2 & \int rW(r)\,dr & 1/3 \end{bmatrix}^{-1}$$
$$\times \begin{bmatrix} W(1) \\ \tfrac{1}{2}\{[W(1)]^2 - 1\} \\ W(1) - \int W(r)\,dr \end{bmatrix}$$
$$\equiv V;$$

(g) $(\gamma_0/\lambda^2)^{1/2}\cdot t_T - \{\tfrac{1}{2}(\lambda^2 - \gamma_0)/\lambda\} \times \{T\cdot\hat{\sigma}_{\hat{\rho}_T} \div s_T\} \xrightarrow{L} V \div \sqrt{Q}$.

Suggest estimates of $\gamma_0$ and $\lambda^2$ that could be used to construct the statistics in (f) and (g), and indicate where one could find critical values for these statistics.

17.4. *Generalization of case 1 for autoregression.* Consider *OLS* estimation of
$$y_t = \zeta_1\Delta y_{t-1} + \zeta_2\Delta y_{t-2} + \cdots + \zeta_{p-1}\Delta y_{t-p+1} + \rho y_{t-1} + \varepsilon_t,$$
where $\varepsilon_t$ is i.i.d. with mean zero, variance $\sigma^2$, and finite fourth moment and the roots of $(1 - \zeta_1 z - \zeta_2 z^2 - \cdots - \zeta_{p-1}z^{p-1}) = 0$ are outside the unit circle. Define $\lambda \equiv \sigma/(1 - \zeta_1 - \zeta_2 - \cdots - \zeta_{p-1})$ and $\gamma_j = E\{(\Delta y_t)(\Delta y_{t-j})\}$. Let $\hat{\boldsymbol{\zeta}}_T \equiv (\hat{\zeta}_{1,T}, \hat{\zeta}_{2,T}, \ldots, \hat{\zeta}_{p-1,T})'$ be the $(p - 1) \times 1$ vector of estimated *OLS* coefficients on the lagged changes in $y$, and let $\boldsymbol{\zeta}$ be the corresponding true value. Show that if the true value of $\rho$ is unity, then
$$\begin{bmatrix} T^{1/2}(\hat{\boldsymbol{\zeta}}_T - \boldsymbol{\zeta}) \\ T(\hat{\rho}_T - 1) \end{bmatrix} \xrightarrow{L} \begin{bmatrix} \mathbf{V} & \mathbf{0} \\ \mathbf{0}' & \lambda^2\cdot\int [W(r)]^2\,dr \end{bmatrix}^{-1} \begin{bmatrix} \mathbf{h}_1 \\ \tfrac{1}{2}\sigma\lambda\{[W(1)]^2 - 1\} \end{bmatrix},$$
where $\mathbf{V}$ is the $[(p - 1) \times (p - 1)]$ matrix defined in [17.7.19] and $\mathbf{h}_1 \sim N(\mathbf{0}, \sigma^2\mathbf{V})$. Deduce from this that

(a) $T^{1/2}(\hat{\boldsymbol{\zeta}}_T - \boldsymbol{\zeta}) \xrightarrow{L} N(\mathbf{0}, \sigma^2\mathbf{V}^{-1})$;

(b) $$T(\hat{\rho}_T - 1)/(1 - \hat{\zeta}_{1,T} - \hat{\zeta}_{2,T} - \cdots - \hat{\zeta}_{p-1,T}) \xrightarrow{L} \frac{\tfrac{1}{2}\{[W(1)]^2 - 1\}}{\int [W(r)]^2\,dr};$$

(c) $(\hat{\rho}_T - 1)/\hat{\sigma}_{\hat{\rho}_T} \xrightarrow{L} \dfrac{\frac{1}{2}\{[W(1)]^2 - 1\}}{\left\{\int [W(r)]^2\,dr\right\}^{1/2}}.$

Where could you find critical values for the statistics in (b) and (c)?

17.5. *Generalization of case 3 for autoregression*. Consider *OLS* estimation of

$$y_t = \zeta_1 \Delta y_{t-1} + \zeta_2 \Delta y_{t-2} + \cdots + \zeta_{p-1} \Delta y_{t-p+1} + \alpha + \rho y_{t-1} + \varepsilon_t,$$

where $\varepsilon_t$ is i.i.d. with mean zero, variance $\sigma^2$, and finite fourth moment and the roots of $(1 - \zeta_1 z - \zeta_2 z^2 - \cdots - \zeta_{p-1} z^{p-1}) = 0$ are outside the unit circle.

(a) Show that the fitted values for this regression are identical to those for the following transformed specification:

$$y_t = \zeta_1 u_{t-1} + \zeta_2 u_{t-2} + \cdots + \zeta_{p-1} u_{t-p+1} + \mu + \rho y_{t-1} + \varepsilon_t,$$

where $u_t \equiv \Delta y_t - \mu$ and $\mu \equiv \alpha/(1 - \zeta_1 - \zeta_2 - \cdots - \zeta_{p-1})$.

(b) Suppose that the true value of $\rho$ is 1 and the true value of $\alpha$ is nonzero. Show that under these assumptions,

$$u_t = [1/(1 - \zeta_1 L - \zeta_2 L^2 - \cdots - \zeta_{p-1} L^{p-1})]\varepsilon_t$$
$$y_{t-1} = \mu(t - 1) + \xi_{t-1},$$

where

$$\xi_{t-1} \equiv y_0 + u_1 + u_2 + \cdots + u_{t-1}.$$

Conclude that for fixed $y_0$, the variables $u_t$ and $\xi_t$ satisfy the assumptions of Proposition 17.3 and that $y_t$ is dominated asymptotically by a time trend.

(c) Let $\gamma_j \equiv E(u_t u_{t-j})$, and let $\hat{\boldsymbol{\zeta}}_T \equiv (\hat{\zeta}_{1,T}, \hat{\zeta}_{2,T}, \ldots, \hat{\zeta}_{p-1,T})'$ be the $(p - 1) \times 1$ vector of estimated *OLS* coefficients on $(u_{t-1}, u_{t-2}, \ldots, u_{t-p+1})$; these, of course, are identical to the coefficients on $(\Delta y_{t-1}, \Delta y_{t-2}, \ldots, \Delta y_{t-p+1})$ in the original regression. Show that if $\rho = 1$ and $\alpha \neq 0$,

$$\begin{bmatrix} T^{1/2}(\hat{\boldsymbol{\zeta}}_T - \boldsymbol{\zeta}) \\ T^{1/2}(\hat{\mu}_T - \mu) \\ T^{3/2}(\hat{\rho}_T - 1) \end{bmatrix} \xrightarrow{L} \begin{bmatrix} \mathbf{V} & \mathbf{0} & \mathbf{0} \\ \mathbf{0}' & 1 & \mu/2 \\ \mathbf{0}' & \mu/2 & \mu^2/3 \end{bmatrix}^{-1} \begin{bmatrix} \mathbf{h}_1 \\ h_2 \\ h_3 \end{bmatrix},$$

where

$$\begin{bmatrix} \mathbf{h}_1 \\ h_2 \\ h_3 \end{bmatrix} \sim N\left( \begin{bmatrix} \mathbf{0} \\ 0 \\ 0 \end{bmatrix}, \sigma^2 \begin{bmatrix} \mathbf{V} & \mathbf{0} & \mathbf{0} \\ \mathbf{0}' & 1 & \mu/2 \\ \mathbf{0}' & \mu/2 & \mu^2/3 \end{bmatrix} \right)$$

and $\mathbf{V}$ is the matrix in [17.7.19]. Conclude as in the analysis of Section 16.3 that any *OLS* $t$ or $F$ test on the original regression can be compared with the standard $t$ and $F$ tables to give an asymptotically valid inference.

17.6. *Generalization of case 4 for autoregression*. Consider *OLS* estimation of

$$y_t = \zeta_1 \Delta y_{t-1} + \zeta_2 \Delta y_{t-2} + \cdots + \zeta_{p-1} \Delta y_{t-p+1} + \alpha + \rho y_{t-1} + \delta t + \varepsilon_t,$$

where $\varepsilon_t$ is i.i.d. with mean zero, variance $\sigma^2$, and finite fourth moment and then roots of $(1 - \zeta_1 z - \zeta_2 z^2 - \cdots - \zeta_{p-1} z^{p-1}) = 0$ are outside the unit circle.

(a) Show that the fitted values of this regression are numerically identical to those of the following specification:

$$y_t = \zeta_1 u_{t-1} + \zeta_2 u_{t-2} + \cdots + \zeta_{p-1} u_{t-p+1} + \mu^* + \rho \xi_{t-1} + \delta^* t + \varepsilon_t,$$

where $u_t \equiv \Delta y_t - \mu$, $\mu \equiv \alpha/(1 - \zeta_1 - \zeta_2 - \cdots - \zeta_{p-1})$, $\mu^* \equiv (1 - \rho)\mu$, $\xi_{t-1} \equiv y_{t-1} - \mu(t - 1)$, and $\delta^* \equiv \delta + \rho\mu$. Note that the estimated coefficients $\hat{\boldsymbol{\zeta}}_T$ and $\hat{\rho}_T$ and their standard errors will be identical for the two regressions.

(b) Suppose that the true value of $\rho$ is 1 and the true value of $\delta$ is 0. Show that under these assumptions,

$$u_t = [1/(1 - \zeta_1 L - \zeta_2 L^2 - \cdots - \zeta_{p-1} L^{p-1})]\varepsilon_t$$
$$\xi_{t-1} = y_0 + u_1 + u_2 + \cdots + u_{t-1}.$$

Conclude that for fixed $y_0$, the variables $u_t$ and $\xi_t$ satisfy the assumptions of Proposition 17.3.

(c) Again let $\rho = 1$ and $\delta = 0$, and define $\gamma_j \equiv E(u_t u_{t-j})$ and

$$\lambda \equiv \sigma/(1 - \zeta_1 - \zeta_2 - \cdots - \zeta_{p-1}).$$

Show that

$$\begin{bmatrix} T^{1/2}(\hat{\boldsymbol{\zeta}}_T - \boldsymbol{\zeta}) \\ T^{1/2}\hat{\mu}_T^* \\ T(\hat{\rho}_T - 1) \\ T^{3/2}(\hat{\delta}_T^* - \delta^*) \end{bmatrix} \xrightarrow{L} \begin{bmatrix} \mathbf{V} & \mathbf{0} & \mathbf{0} & \mathbf{0} \\ \mathbf{0}' & 1 & \lambda\cdot\int W(r)\,dr & 1/2 \\ \mathbf{0}' & \lambda\cdot\int W(r)\,dr & \lambda^2\cdot\int [W(r)]^2\,dr & \lambda\cdot\int rW(r)\,dr \\ \mathbf{0}' & 1/2 & \lambda\cdot\int rW(r)\,dr & 1/3 \end{bmatrix}^{-1}$$

$$\times \begin{bmatrix} \mathbf{h}_1 \\ \sigma\cdot W(1) \\ \tfrac{1}{2}\sigma\lambda\{[W(1)]^2 - 1\} \\ \sigma\cdot\left\{W(1) - \int W(r)\,dr\right\} \end{bmatrix}$$

where $\mathbf{h}_1 \sim N(\mathbf{0}, \sigma^2\mathbf{V})$ and $\mathbf{V}$ is as defined in [17.7.19].

(d) Deduce from answer (c) that

$T^{1/2}(\hat{\boldsymbol{\zeta}}_T - \boldsymbol{\zeta}) \xrightarrow{L} N(\mathbf{0}, \sigma^2\mathbf{V}^{-1})$;

$T(\hat{\rho}_T - 1)/(1 - \hat{\zeta}_{1,T} - \hat{\zeta}_{2,T} - \cdots - \hat{\zeta}_{p-1,T})$

$$\xrightarrow{L} [0 \quad 1 \quad 0] \begin{bmatrix} 1 & \int W(r)\,dr & 1/2 \\ \int W(r)\,dr & \int [W(r)]^2\,dr & \int rW(r)\,dr \\ 1/2 & \int rW(r)\,dr & 1/3 \end{bmatrix}^{-1} \begin{bmatrix} W(1) \\ \tfrac{1}{2}\{[W(1)]^2 - 1\} \\ W(1) - \int W(r)\,dr \end{bmatrix}$$

$\equiv V$;

$(\hat{\rho}_T - 1)/\hat{\sigma}_{\hat{\rho}_T} \xrightarrow{L} V \div \sqrt{Q}$,

where

$$Q \equiv [0 \quad 1 \quad 0] \begin{bmatrix} 1 & \int W(r)\,dr & 1/2 \\ \int W(r)\,dr & \int [W(r)]^2\,dr & \int rW(r)\,dr \\ 1/2 & \int rW(r)\,dr & 1/3 \end{bmatrix}^{-1} \begin{bmatrix} 0 \\ 1 \\ 0 \end{bmatrix}$$

Notice that the distribution of $V$ is the same as the asymptotic distribution of the variable tabulated for case 4 in Table B.5, while the distribution of $V/\sqrt{Q}$ is the same as the asymptotic distribution of the variable tabulated for case 4 in Table B.6.

## *Chapter 17 References*


Andrews, Donald W. K. 1991. "Heteroskedasticity and Autocorrelation Consistent Covariance Matrix Estimation." *Econometrica* 59:817–58.

———. 1993. "Exactly Median-Unbiased Estimation of First Order Autoregressive/Unit Root Models." *Econometrica* 61:139–65.

Beveridge, Stephen, and Charles R. Nelson. 1981. "A New Approcah to Decomposition of Economic Time Series into Permanent and Transitory Components with Particular Attention to Measurement of the 'Business Cycle.'" *Journal of Monetary Economics* 7:151–74.

Bhargava, Alok. 1986. "On the Theory of Testing for Unit Roots in Observed Time Series." *Review of Economic Studies* 53:369–84.

Billingsley, Patrick. 1968. *Convergence of Probability Measures*. New York: Wiley.

Campbell, John Y., and Pierre Perron. 1991. "Pitfalls and Opportunities: What Macroeconomists Should Know about Unit Roots." *NBER Macroeconomics Annual*. Cambridge, Mass.: MIT Press.

Cecchetti, Stephen G., and Pok-sang Lam. 1991. "What Do We Learn from Variance Ratio Statistics? A Study of Stationary and Nonstationary Models with Breaking Trends." Department of Economics, Ohio State University. Mimeo.

Chan, N. H., and C. Z. Wei. 1987. "Asymptotic Inference for Nearly Nonstationary AR(1) Processes." *Annals of Statistics* 15:1050–63.

——— and ———. 1988. "Limiting Distributions of Least Squares Estimates of Unstable Autoregressive Processes." *Annals of Statistics* 16:367–401.

Cochrane, John H. 1988. "How Big Is the Random Walk in GNP?" *Journal of Political Economy* 96:893–920.

DeJong, David N., and Charles H. Whiteman. 1991. "Reconsidering 'Trends and Random Walks in Macroeconomic Time Series.'" *Journal of Monetary Economics* 28:221–54.

Dickey, David A., and Wayne A. Fuller. 1979. "Distribution of the Estimators for Autoregressive Time Series with a Unit Root." *Journal of the American Statistical Association* 74:427–31.

——— and ———. 1981. "Likelihood Ratio Statistics for Autoregressive Time Series with a Unit Root." *Econometrica* 49:1057–72.

——— and S. G. Pantula. 1987. "Determining the Order of Differencing in Autoregressive Processes." *Journal of Business and Economic Statistics* 5:455–61.

Evans, G. B. A., and N. E. Savin. 1981. "Testing for Unit Roots: 1." *Econometrica* 49:753–79.

——— and ———. 1984. "Testing for Unit Roots: 2." *Econometrica* 52:1241–69.

Fuller, Wayne A. 1976. *Introduction to Statistical Time Series*. New York: Wiley.

Hall, Alastair. 1989. "Testing for a Unit Root in the Presence of Moving Average Errors." *Biometrika* 76:49–56.

———. 1991. "Testing for a Unit Root in Time Series with Pretest Data Based Model Selection." Department of Economics, North Carolina State University. Mimeo.

Hall, P., and C. C. Heyde. 1980. *Martingale Limit Theory and Its Application*. New York: Academic Press.

Hansen, Bruce E. 1992. "Consistent Covariance Matrix Estimation for Dependent Heterogeneous Processes." *Econometrica* 60:967–72.

Jeffreys, H. 1946. "An Invariant Form for the Prior Probability in Estimation Problems." *Proceedings of the Royal Society of London* Series A, 186:453–61.

Kim, Kiwhan, and Peter Schmidt. 1990. "Some Evidence on the Accuracy of Phillips-Perron Tests Using Alternative Estimates of Nuisance Parameters." *Economics Letters* 34:345–50.

Kwiatkowski, Denis, Peter C. B. Phillips, Peter Schmidt, and Yongcheol Shin. 1992. "Testing the Null Hypothesis of Stationarity against the Alternative of a Unit Root: How Sure Are We That Economic Time Series Have a Unit Root?" *Journal of Econometrics* 54:159–78.

Lo, Andrew W., and A. Craig MacKinlay. 1988. "Stock Prices Do Not Follow Random Walks: Evidence from a Simple Specification Test." *Review of Financial Studies* 1:41–66.

——— and ———. 1989. "The Size and Power of the Variance Ratio Test in Finite Samples: A Monte Carlo Investigation." *Journal of Econometrics* 40:203–38.

Malliaris, A. G., and W. A. Brock. 1982. *Stochastic Methods in Economics and Finance*. Amsterdam: North-Holland.

Pantula, Sastry G., and Alastair Hall. 1991. "Testing for Unit Roots in Autoregressive Moving Average Models: An Instrumental Variable Approach." *Journal of Econometrics* 48:325–53.

Park, Joon Y., and B. Choi. 1988. "A New Approach to Testing for a Unit Root." Cornell University. Mimeo.

Park, Joon Y., and Peter C. B. Phillips. 1988. "Statistical Inference in Regressions with Integrated Processes: Part 1." *Econometric Theory* 4:468–97.

——— and ———. 1989. "Statistical Inference in Regressions with Integrated Processes: Part 2." *Econometric Theory* 5:95–131.

Phillips, P. C. B. 1986. "Understanding Spurious Regressions in Econometrics." *Journal of Econometrics* 33:311–40.

———. 1987. "Time Series Regression with a Unit Root." *Econometrica* 55:277–301.

———. 1988. "Regression Theory for Near-Integrated Time Series." *Econometrica* 56:1021–43.

———. 1991a. "To Criticize the Critics: An Objective Bayesian Analysis of Stochastic Trends." *Journal of Applied Econometrics* 6:333–64.

———. 1991b. "Bayesian Routes and Unit Roots: De Rebus Prioribus Semper Est Disputandum." *Journal of Applied Econometrics* 6:435–73.

——— and Pierre Perron. 1988. "Testing for a Unit Root in Time Series Regression." *Biometrika* 75:335–46.

——— and Victor Solo. 1992. "Asymptotics for Linear Processes." *Annals of Statistics* 20:971–1001.

Said, Said E. 1991. "Unit-Root Tests for Time-Series Data with a Linear Time Trend." *Journal of Econometrics* 47:285–303.

——— and David A. Dickey. 1984. "Testing for Unit Roots in Autoregressive-Moving Average Models of Unknown Order." *Biometrika* 71:599–607.

——— and ———. 1985. "Hypothesis Testing in ARIMA($p$, 1, $q$) Models." *Journal of the American Statistical Association* 80:369–74.

Sargan, J. D., and Alok Bhargava. 1983. "Testing Residuals from Least Squares Regression for Being Generated by the Gaussian Random Walk." *Econometrica* 51:153–74.

Schmidt, Peter, and Peter C. B. Phillips. 1992. "LM Tests for a Unit Root in the Presence of Deterministic Trends." *Oxford Bulletin of Economics and Statistics* 54:257–87.

Schwert, G. William. 1989. "Tests for Unit Roots: A Monte Carlo Investigation." *Journal of Business and Economic Statistics* 7:147–59.

Sims, Christopher A. 1988. "Bayesian Skepticism on Unit Root Econometrics." *Journal of Economic Dynamics and Control* 12:463–74.

———, James H. Stock, and Mark W. Watson. 1990. "Inference in Linear Time Series Models with Some Unit Roots." *Econometrica* 58:113–44.

——— and Harald Uhlig. 1991. "Understanding Unit Rooters: A Helicopter Tour." *Econometrica* 59:1591–99.

Solo, V. 1984. "The Order of Differencing in ARIMA Models." *Journal of the American Statistical Association* 79:916–21.

Sowell, Fallaw. 1990. "The Fractional Unit Root Distribution." *Econometrica* 58:495–505.

Stinchcombe, Maxwell, and Halbert White. 1993. "An Approach to Consistent Specification Testing Using Duality and Banach Limit Theory." University of California, San Diego. Mimeo.

Stock, James H. 1991. "Confidence Intervals for the Largest Autoregressive Root in U.S. Macroeconomic Time Series." *Journal of Monetary Economics* 28:435–59.

———. 1993. "Unit Roots and Trend Breaks," in Robert Engle and Daniel McFadden, eds., *Handbook of Econometrics*, Vol. 4. Amsterdam: North-Holland.

White, J. S. 1958. "The Limiting Distribution of the Serial Correlation Coefficient in the Explosive Case." *Annals of Mathematical Statistics* 29:1188–97.

# 18 Unit Roots in Multivariate Time Series

The previous chapter investigated statistical inference for univariate processes containing unit roots. This chapter develops comparable results for vector processes. The first section develops a vector version of the functional central limit theorem. Section 18.2 uses these results to generalize the analysis of Section 17.7 to vector autoregressions. Section 18.3 discusses an important problem, known as *spurious regression*, that can arise if the error term in a regression is $I(1)$. One should be concerned about the possibility of a spurious regression whenever all the variables in a regression are $I(1)$ and no lags of the dependent variable are included in the regression.

## 18.1. *Asymptotic Results for Nonstationary Vector Processes*

Section 17.2 described univariate standard Brownian motion $W(r)$ as a scalar continuous-time process ($W: r \in [0, 1] \rightarrow \mathbb{R}^1$). The variable $W(r)$ has a $N(0, r)$ distribution across realizations, and for any given realization, $W(r)$ is a continuous function of the date $r$ with independent increments. If a set of $n$ such independent processes, denoted $W_1(r), W_2(r), \ldots, W_n(r)$, are collected in an $(n \times 1)$ vector $\mathbf{W}(r)$, the result is *n-dimensional standard Brownian motion*.

***Definition:*** *n-dimensional standard Brownian motion* $\mathbf{W}(\cdot)$ *is a continuous-time process associating each date* $r \in [0, 1]$ *with the* $(n \times 1)$ *vector* $\mathbf{W}(r)$ *satisfying the following:*

(*a*) $\mathbf{W}(0) = \mathbf{0}$;

(*b*) *For any dates* $0 \leq r_1 < r_2 < \cdots < r_k \leq 1$, *the changes* $[\mathbf{W}(r_2) - \mathbf{W}(r_1)]$, $[\mathbf{W}(r_3) - \mathbf{W}(r_2)], \ldots, [\mathbf{W}(r_k) - \mathbf{W}(r_{k-1})]$ *are independent multivariate Gaussian with* $[\mathbf{W}(s) - \mathbf{W}(r)] \sim N(\mathbf{0}, (s - r)\cdot\mathbf{I}_n)$;

(*c*) *For any given realization,* $\mathbf{W}(r)$ *is continuous in* $r$ *with probability* 1.

Suppose that $\{v_t\}_{t=1}^{\infty}$ is a univariate i.i.d. discrete-time process with mean zero and unit variance, and let

$$\tilde{X}_T^*(r) \equiv T^{-1}(v_1 + v_2 + \cdots + v_{[Tr]^*}),$$

where $[Tr]^*$ denotes the largest integer that is less than or equal to $Tr$. The functional central limit theorem states that as $T \to \infty$,

$$\sqrt{T}\cdot\tilde{X}_T^*(\cdot) \xrightarrow{L} W(\cdot).$$

This readily generalizes. Suppose that $\{\mathbf{v}_t\}_{t=1}^{\infty}$ is an $n$-dimensional i.i.d. vector process with $E(\mathbf{v}_t) = \mathbf{0}$ and $E(\mathbf{v}_t\mathbf{v}_t') = \mathbf{I}_n$, and let

$$\tilde{\mathbf{X}}_T^*(r) \equiv T^{-1}(\mathbf{v}_1 + \mathbf{v}_2 + \cdots + \mathbf{v}_{[Tr]^*}).$$

Then

$$\sqrt{T}\cdot\tilde{\mathbf{X}}_T^*(\cdot) \xrightarrow{L} \mathbf{W}(\cdot). \qquad [18.1.1]$$

Next, consider an i.i.d. $n$-dimensional process $\{\boldsymbol{\varepsilon}_t\}_{t=1}^{\infty}$ with mean zero and variance-covariance matrix given by $\boldsymbol{\Omega}$. Let $\mathbf{P}$ be any matrix such that

$$\boldsymbol{\Omega} = \mathbf{PP}'; \qquad [18.1.2]$$

for example, $\mathbf{P}$ might be the Cholesky factor of $\boldsymbol{\Omega}$. We could think of $\boldsymbol{\varepsilon}_t$ as having been generated from

$$\boldsymbol{\varepsilon}_t = \mathbf{P}\mathbf{v}_t, \qquad [18.1.3]$$

for $\mathbf{v}_t$ i.i.d. with mean zero and variance $\mathbf{I}_n$. To see why, notice that [18.1.3] implies that $\boldsymbol{\varepsilon}_t$ is i.i.d. with mean zero and variance given by

$$E(\boldsymbol{\varepsilon}_t\boldsymbol{\varepsilon}_t') = \mathbf{P}\cdot E(\mathbf{v}_t\mathbf{v}_t')\cdot\mathbf{P}' = \mathbf{P}\cdot\mathbf{I}_n\cdot\mathbf{P}' = \boldsymbol{\Omega}.$$

Let

$$\begin{aligned}\mathbf{X}_T^*(r) &\equiv T^{-1}(\boldsymbol{\varepsilon}_1 + \boldsymbol{\varepsilon}_2 + \cdots + \boldsymbol{\varepsilon}_{[Tr]^*})\\ &= \mathbf{P}\cdot T^{-1}(\mathbf{v}_1 + \mathbf{v}_2 + \cdots + \mathbf{v}_{[Tr]^*})\\ &= \mathbf{P}\cdot\tilde{\mathbf{X}}_T^*(r).\end{aligned}$$

It then follows from [18.1.1] and the continuous mapping theorem that

$$\sqrt{T}\cdot\mathbf{X}_T^*(\cdot) \xrightarrow{L} \mathbf{P}\cdot\mathbf{W}(\cdot). \qquad [18.1.4]$$

For given $r$, the variable $\mathbf{P}\cdot\mathbf{W}(r)$ represents $\mathbf{P}$ times a $N(\mathbf{0}, r\cdot\mathbf{I}_n)$ vector and so has a $N(\mathbf{0}, r\cdot\mathbf{PP}') = N(\mathbf{0}, r\cdot\boldsymbol{\Omega})$ distribution. The process $\mathbf{P}\cdot\mathbf{W}(r)$ is described as $n$-dimensional Brownian motion with variance matrix $\boldsymbol{\Omega}$.

The functional central limit theorem can also be applied to serially dependent vector processes using a generalization of Proposition 17.2.[1] Suppose that

$$\mathbf{u}_t = \sum_{s=0}^{\infty} \boldsymbol{\Psi}_s\boldsymbol{\varepsilon}_{t-s}, \qquad [18.1.5]$$

where if $\psi_{ij}^{(s)}$ denotes the row $i$, column $j$ element of $\boldsymbol{\Psi}_s$,

$$\sum_{s=0}^{\infty} s\cdot|\psi_{ij}^{(s)}| < \infty$$

for each $i, j = 1, 2, \ldots, n$. Then algebra virtually identical to that in Proposition 17.2 can be used to show that

$$\sum_{s=1}^{t} \mathbf{u}_s = \boldsymbol{\Psi}(1)\cdot\sum_{s=1}^{t} \boldsymbol{\varepsilon}_s + \boldsymbol{\eta}_t - \boldsymbol{\eta}_0, \qquad [18.1.6]$$

where $\boldsymbol{\Psi}(1) \equiv (\boldsymbol{\Psi}_0 + \boldsymbol{\Psi}_1 + \boldsymbol{\Psi}_2 + \cdots)$ and $\boldsymbol{\eta}_t = \Sigma_{s=0}^{\infty}\, \boldsymbol{\alpha}_s\boldsymbol{\varepsilon}_{t-s}$ for $\boldsymbol{\alpha}_s =$

[1]This is the approach used by Phillips and Solo (1992).

$-(\boldsymbol{\Psi}_{s+1} + \boldsymbol{\Psi}_{s+2} + \boldsymbol{\Psi}_{s+3} + \cdots)$, and $\{\boldsymbol{\alpha}_s\}_{s=0}^{\infty}$ is absolutely summable. Expression [18.1.6] provides a multivariate generalization of the Beveridge-Nelson decomposition.

If $\mathbf{u}_t$ satisfies [18.1.5] where $\boldsymbol{\varepsilon}_t$ is i.i.d. with mean zero, variance given by $\boldsymbol{\Omega} = \mathbf{PP}'$, and finite fourth moments, then it is straightforward to generalize to vector process the statements in Proposition 17.3 about univariate processes. For example, if we define

$$\mathbf{X}_T(r) \equiv (1/T) \sum_{s=1}^{[Tr]^*} \mathbf{u}_s, \qquad [18.1.7]$$

then it follows from [18.1.6] that

$$\sqrt{T}\cdot\mathbf{X}_T(r) = T^{-1/2}\left(\boldsymbol{\Psi}(1) \sum_{s=1}^{[Tr]^*} \boldsymbol{\varepsilon}_s + \boldsymbol{\eta}_{[Tr]^*} - \boldsymbol{\eta}_0\right).$$

As in Example 17.2, one can show that

$$\sup_{\substack{r\in[0,1] \\ i=1,2,\ldots,n}} T^{-1/2}|\eta_{i,[Tr]^*} - \eta_{i,0}| \xrightarrow{p} 0.$$

It then follows from [18.1.4] that

$$\sqrt{T}\cdot\mathbf{X}_T(\cdot) \xrightarrow{p} \boldsymbol{\Psi}(1)\cdot\mathbf{P}\cdot\sqrt{T}\cdot\tilde{\mathbf{X}}_T^*(\cdot) \xrightarrow{L} \boldsymbol{\Psi}(1)\cdot\mathbf{P}\cdot\mathbf{W}(\cdot), \qquad [18.1.8]$$

where $\boldsymbol{\Psi}(1)\cdot\mathbf{P}\cdot\mathbf{W}(r)$ is distributed $N(\mathbf{0}, r[\boldsymbol{\Psi}(1)]\cdot\boldsymbol{\Omega}\cdot[\boldsymbol{\Psi}(1)]')$ across realizations. Furthermore, for $\boldsymbol{\xi}_t \equiv \mathbf{u}_1 + \mathbf{u}_2 + \cdots + \mathbf{u}_t$, we have as in [17.3.15] that

$$T^{-3/2} \sum_{t=1}^{T} \boldsymbol{\xi}_{t-1} = \int_0^1 \sqrt{T}\cdot\mathbf{X}_T(r)\,dr \xrightarrow{L} \boldsymbol{\Psi}(1)\cdot\mathbf{P}\cdot\int_0^1 \mathbf{W}(r)\,dr, \qquad [18.1.9]$$

which generalizes result (f) of Proposition 17.3.

Generalizing result (e) of Proposition 17.3 requires a little more care. Consider for illustration the simplest case, where $\mathbf{v}_t$ is an i.i.d. $(n \times 1)$ vector with mean zero and $E(\mathbf{v}_t\mathbf{v}_t') = \mathbf{I}_n$. Define

$$\boldsymbol{\xi}_t^* \equiv \begin{cases} \mathbf{v}_1 + \mathbf{v}_2 + \cdots + \mathbf{v}_t & \text{for } t = 1, 2, \ldots, T \\ \mathbf{0} & \text{for } t = 0; \end{cases}$$

we use the symbols $\mathbf{v}_t$ and $\boldsymbol{\xi}_t^*$ here in place of $\mathbf{u}_t$ and $\boldsymbol{\xi}_t$ to emphasize that $\mathbf{v}_t$ is i.i.d. with variance matrix given by $\mathbf{I}_n$. For the scalar i.i.d. unit variance case ($n = 1$, $\lambda = \gamma_0 = 1$), result (e) of Proposition 17.3 stated that

$$T^{-1} \sum_{t=1}^{T} \xi_{t-1}^* v_t \xrightarrow{L} \tfrac{1}{2}\{[W(1)]^2 - 1\}. \qquad [18.1.10]$$

The corresponding generalization for the i.i.d. unit variance vector case ($n > 1$) turns out to be

$$T^{-1} \sum_{t=1}^{T} \{\boldsymbol{\xi}_{t-1}^*\mathbf{v}_t' + \mathbf{v}_t\boldsymbol{\xi}_{t-1}^{*\prime}\} \xrightarrow{L} [\mathbf{W}(1)]\cdot[\mathbf{W}(1)]' - \mathbf{I}_n; \qquad [18.1.11]$$

see result (d) of Proposition 18.1, to follow. Expression [18.1.11] generalizes the scalar result [18.1.10] to an $(n \times n)$ matrix. The row $i$, column $i$ diagonal element of this matrix expression states that

$$T^{-1} \sum_{t=1}^{T} \{\xi_{i,t-1}^* v_{it} + v_{it}\xi_{i,t-1}^*\} \xrightarrow{L} [W_i(1)]^2 - 1, \qquad [18.1.12]$$

where $\xi_{it}^*$, $v_{it}$, and $W_i(r)$ denote the $i$th elements of the vectors $\boldsymbol{\xi}_t^*$, $\mathbf{v}_t$, and $\mathbf{W}(r)$, respectively. The row $i$, column $j$ off-diagonal element of [18.1.11] asserts that

$$T^{-1}\sum_{t=1}^{T}\{\xi_{i,t-1}^{*}v_{jt}+v_{it}\xi_{j,t-1}^{*}\}\xrightarrow{L}[W_i(1)]\cdot[W_j(1)] \qquad \text{for } i\neq j. \qquad [18.1.13]$$

Thus, the sum of the random variables $T^{-1}\Sigma_{t=1}^{T}\xi_{i,t-1}^{*}v_{jt}$ and $T^{-1}\Sigma_{t=1}^{T}v_{it}\xi_{j,t-1}^{*}$ converges in distribution to the product of two independent standard Normal variables.

It is sometimes convenient to describe the asymptotic distribution of $T^{-1}\Sigma_{t=1}^{T}\xi_{i,t-1}^{*}v_{jt}$ alone. It turns out that

$$T^{-1}\sum_{t=1}^{T}\xi_{i,t-1}^{*}v_{jt}\xrightarrow{L}\int_0^1 W_i(r)\,dW_j(r). \qquad [18.1.14]$$

This expression makes use of the differential of Brownian motion, denoted $dW_j(r)$. A formal definition of the differential $dW_j(r)$ and derivation of [18.1.14] are somewhat involved—see Phillips (1988) for details. For our purposes, we will simply regard the right side of [18.1.14] as a compact notation for indicating the limiting distribution of the sequence represented by the left side. In practice, this distribution is constructed by Monte Carlo generation of the statistic on the left side of [18.1.14] for suitably large $T$.

It is evident from [18.1.13] and [18.1.14] that

$$\int_0^1 W_i(r)\,dW_j(r)+\int_0^1 W_j(r)\,dW_i(r)=W_i(1)\cdot W_j(1) \qquad \text{for } i\neq j,$$

whereas comparing [18.1.14] with [18.1.12] reveals that

$$\int_0^1 W_i(r)\,dW_i(r)=\tfrac{1}{2}\{[W_i(1)]^2-1\}. \qquad [18.1.15]$$

The expressions in [18.1.14] can be collected for $i, j = 1, 2, \ldots, n$ in an $(n \times n)$ matrix:

$$T^{-1}\sum_{t=1}^{T}\boldsymbol{\xi}_{t-1}^{*}\mathbf{v}_t'\xrightarrow{L}\int_0^1[\mathbf{W}(r)]\,[d\mathbf{W}(r)]'. \qquad [18.1.16]$$

The following proposition summarizes the multivariate convergence results that will be used in this chapter.[2]

***Proposition 18.1:*** *Let $\mathbf{u}_t$ be an $(n \times 1)$ vector with*

$$\mathbf{u}_t=\boldsymbol{\Psi}(L)\boldsymbol{\varepsilon}_t=\sum_{s=0}^{\infty}\boldsymbol{\Psi}_s\boldsymbol{\varepsilon}_{t-s},$$

*where $\{s\cdot\boldsymbol{\Psi}_s\}_{s=0}^{*}$ is absolutely summable, that is, $\Sigma_{s=0}^{\infty}s\cdot|\psi_{ij}^{(s)}|<\infty$ for each $i, j = 1, 2, \ldots, n$ for $\psi_{ij}^{(s)}$ the row $i$, column $j$ element of $\boldsymbol{\Psi}_s$. Suppose that $\{\boldsymbol{\varepsilon}_t\}$ is an i.i.d. sequence with mean zero, finite fourth moments, and $E(\boldsymbol{\varepsilon}_t\boldsymbol{\varepsilon}_t')=\boldsymbol{\Omega}$ a positive definite matrix. Let $\boldsymbol{\Omega}=\mathbf{PP}'$ denote the Cholesky factorization of $\boldsymbol{\Omega}$, and define*

$$\sigma_{ij}\equiv E(\varepsilon_{it}\varepsilon_{jt})=\text{row } i\text{, column } j \text{ element of } \boldsymbol{\Omega}$$

$$\underset{(n\times n)}{\boldsymbol{\Gamma}_s}\equiv E(\mathbf{u}_t\mathbf{u}_{t-s}')=\sum_{v=0}^{\infty}\boldsymbol{\Psi}_{s+v}\boldsymbol{\Omega}\boldsymbol{\Psi}_v' \qquad \text{for } s=0,1,2,\ldots$$

$$\underset{(nv\times 1)}{\mathbf{z}_t}\equiv\begin{bmatrix}\mathbf{u}_{t-1}\\ \mathbf{u}_{t-2}\\ \vdots\\ \mathbf{u}_{t-v}\end{bmatrix} \qquad \text{for arbitrary } v\geq 1 \qquad [18.1.17]$$

[2]These or similar results were derived by Phillips and Durlauf (1986), Park and Phillips (1988, 1989), Sims, Stock, and Watson (1990), and Phillips and Solo (1992).

$$\underset{(nv \times nv)}{\mathbf{V}} \equiv E(\mathbf{z}_t\mathbf{z}_t') = \begin{bmatrix} \mathbf{\Gamma}_0 & \mathbf{\Gamma}_1 & \cdots & \mathbf{\Gamma}_{v-1} \\ \mathbf{\Gamma}_{-1} & \mathbf{\Gamma}_0 & \cdots & \mathbf{\Gamma}_{v-2} \\ \vdots & \vdots & \cdots & \vdots \\ \mathbf{\Gamma}_{-v+1} & \mathbf{\Gamma}_{-v+2} & \cdots & \mathbf{\Gamma}_0 \end{bmatrix}$$

$$\underset{(n \times n)}{\mathbf{\Lambda}} \equiv \mathbf{\Psi}(1)\cdot\mathbf{P} = (\mathbf{\Psi}_0 + \mathbf{\Psi}_1 + \mathbf{\Psi}_2 + \cdots)\cdot\mathbf{P} \qquad [18.1.18]$$

$$\underset{(n \times 1)}{\boldsymbol{\xi}_t} \equiv \mathbf{u}_1 + \mathbf{u}_2 + \cdots + \mathbf{u}_t \qquad \text{for } t = 1, 2, \ldots, T \qquad [18.1.19]$$

*with* $\boldsymbol{\xi}_0 \equiv \mathbf{0}$. *Then*

(*a*) $T^{-1/2} \sum_{t=1}^{T} \mathbf{u}_t \xrightarrow{L} \mathbf{\Lambda}\cdot\mathbf{W}(1);$

(*b*) $T^{-1/2} \sum_{t=1}^{T} \mathbf{z}_t\varepsilon_{it} \xrightarrow{L} N(\mathbf{0}, \sigma_{ii}\cdot\mathbf{V}) \qquad \text{for } i = 1, 2, \ldots, n;$

(*c*) $T^{-1} \sum_{t=1}^{T} \mathbf{u}_t\mathbf{u}_{t-s}' \xrightarrow{p} \mathbf{\Gamma}_s \qquad \text{for } s = 0, 1, 2, \ldots;$

(*d*) $T^{-1} \sum_{t=1}^{T} (\boldsymbol{\xi}_{t-1}\mathbf{u}_{t-s}' + \mathbf{u}_{t-s}\boldsymbol{\xi}_{t-1}')$

$$\xrightarrow{L} \begin{cases} \mathbf{\Lambda}\cdot[\mathbf{W}(1)]\cdot[\mathbf{W}(1)]'\cdot\mathbf{\Lambda}' - \mathbf{\Gamma}_0 & \text{for } s = 0 \\ \mathbf{\Lambda}\cdot[\mathbf{W}(1)]\cdot[\mathbf{W}(1)]'\cdot\mathbf{\Lambda}' + \sum_{v=-s+1}^{s-1} \mathbf{\Gamma}_v & \text{for } s = 1, 2, \ldots; \end{cases}$$

(*e*) $T^{-1} \sum_{t=1}^{T} \boldsymbol{\xi}_{t-1}\mathbf{u}_t' \xrightarrow{L} \mathbf{\Lambda}\cdot\left\{\int_0^1 [\mathbf{W}(r)]\,[d\mathbf{W}(r)]'\right\}\cdot\mathbf{\Lambda}' + \sum_{v=1}^{\infty} \mathbf{\Gamma}_v';$

(*f*) $T^{-1} \sum_{t=1}^{T} \boldsymbol{\xi}_{t-1}\boldsymbol{\varepsilon}_t' \xrightarrow{L} \mathbf{\Lambda}\cdot\left\{\int_0^1 [\mathbf{W}(r)]\,[d\mathbf{W}(r)]'\right\}\cdot\mathbf{P}';$

(*g*) $T^{-3/2} \sum_{t=1}^{T} \boldsymbol{\xi}_{t-1} \xrightarrow{L} \mathbf{\Lambda}\cdot\int_0^1 \mathbf{W}(r)\,dr;$

(*h*) $T^{-3/2} \sum_{t=1}^{T} t\mathbf{u}_{t-s} \xrightarrow{L} \mathbf{\Lambda}\cdot\left\{\mathbf{W}(1) - \int_0^1 \mathbf{W}(r)\,dr\right\} \qquad \text{for } s = 0, 1, 2, \ldots;$

(*i*) $T^{-2} \sum_{t=1}^{T} \boldsymbol{\xi}_{t-1}\boldsymbol{\xi}_{t-1}' \xrightarrow{L} \mathbf{\Lambda}\cdot\left\{\int_0^1 [\mathbf{W}(r)]\cdot[\mathbf{W}(r)]'\,dr\right\}\cdot\mathbf{\Lambda}';$

(*j*) $T^{-5/2} \sum_{t=1}^{T} t\boldsymbol{\xi}_{t-1} \xrightarrow{L} \mathbf{\Lambda}\cdot\int_0^1 r\mathbf{W}(r)\,dr;$

(*k*) $T^{-3} \sum_{t=1}^{T} t\boldsymbol{\xi}_{t-1}\boldsymbol{\xi}_{t-1}' \xrightarrow{L} \mathbf{\Lambda}\cdot\left\{\int_0^1 r[\mathbf{W}(r)]\cdot[\mathbf{W}(r)]'\,dr\right\}\cdot\mathbf{\Lambda}';$

(*l*) $T^{-(v+1)} \sum_{t=1}^{T} t^v \to 1/(v + 1) \qquad \text{for } v = 0, 1, 2, \ldots.$

## 18.2. *Vector Autoregressions Containing Unit Roots*

Suppose that a vector $\mathbf{y}_t$ could be described by a vector autoregression in the differences $\Delta\mathbf{y}_t$. This section presents results developed by Park and Phillips (1988, 1989) and Sims, Stock, and Watson (1990) for the consequences of estimating the *VAR* in levels. We begin by generalizing the Dickey-Fuller variable transformation that was used in analyzing a univariate autoregression.

### *An Alternative Representation of a* VAR(p) *Process*

Let $\mathbf{y}_t$ be an $(n \times 1)$ vector satisfying

$$(\mathbf{I}_n - \boldsymbol{\Phi}_1 L - \boldsymbol{\Phi}_2 L^2 - \cdots - \boldsymbol{\Phi}_p L^p)\mathbf{y}_t = \boldsymbol{\alpha} + \boldsymbol{\varepsilon}_t, \qquad [18.2.1]$$

where $\boldsymbol{\Phi}_s$ denotes an $(n \times n)$ matrix for $s = 1, 2, \ldots, p$ and $\boldsymbol{\alpha}$ and $\boldsymbol{\varepsilon}_t$ are $(n \times 1)$ vectors. The scalar algebra in [17.7.4] works perfectly well for matrices, establishing that for any values of $\boldsymbol{\Phi}_1, \boldsymbol{\Phi}_2, \ldots, \boldsymbol{\Phi}_p$, the following polynomials are equivalent:

$$\begin{aligned}(\mathbf{I}_n &- \boldsymbol{\Phi}_1 L - \boldsymbol{\Phi}_2 L^2 - \cdots - \boldsymbol{\Phi}_p L^p) \\ &= (\mathbf{I}_n - \boldsymbol{\rho} L) - (\boldsymbol{\zeta}_1 L + \boldsymbol{\zeta}_2 L^2 + \cdots + \boldsymbol{\zeta}_{p-1} L^{p-1})(1 - L),\end{aligned} \qquad [18.2.2]$$

where

$$\boldsymbol{\rho} \equiv \boldsymbol{\Phi}_1 + \boldsymbol{\Phi}_2 + \cdots + \boldsymbol{\Phi}_p \qquad [18.2.3]$$

$$\boldsymbol{\zeta}_s \equiv -[\boldsymbol{\Phi}_{s+1} + \boldsymbol{\Phi}_{s+2} + \cdots + \boldsymbol{\Phi}_p] \quad \text{for } s = 1, 2, \ldots, p - 1. \qquad [18.2.4]$$

It follows that any *VAR*$(p)$ process [18.2.1] can always be written in the form

$$(\mathbf{I}_n - \boldsymbol{\rho} L)\mathbf{y}_t - (\boldsymbol{\zeta}_1 L + \boldsymbol{\zeta}_2 L^2 + \cdots + \boldsymbol{\zeta}_{p-1} L^{p-1})(1 - L)\mathbf{y}_t = \boldsymbol{\alpha} + \boldsymbol{\varepsilon}_t$$

or

$$\mathbf{y}_t = \boldsymbol{\zeta}_1 \Delta\mathbf{y}_{t-1} + \boldsymbol{\zeta}_2 \Delta\mathbf{y}_{t-2} + \cdots + \boldsymbol{\zeta}_{p-1} \Delta\mathbf{y}_{t-p+1} + \boldsymbol{\alpha} + \boldsymbol{\rho}\mathbf{y}_{t-1} + \boldsymbol{\varepsilon}_t. \qquad [18.2.5]$$

The null hypothesis considered throughout this section is that the first difference of $\mathbf{y}$ follows a *VAR*$(p - 1)$ process;

$$\Delta\mathbf{y}_t = \boldsymbol{\zeta}_1 \Delta\mathbf{y}_{t-1} + \boldsymbol{\zeta}_2 \Delta\mathbf{y}_{t-2} + \cdots + \boldsymbol{\zeta}_{p-1} \Delta\mathbf{y}_{t-p+1} + \boldsymbol{\alpha} + \boldsymbol{\varepsilon}_t, \qquad [18.2.6]$$

requiring from [18.2.5] that

$$\boldsymbol{\rho} = \mathbf{I}_n \qquad [18.2.7]$$

or, from [18.2.3],

$$\boldsymbol{\Phi}_1 + \boldsymbol{\Phi}_2 + \cdots + \boldsymbol{\Phi}_p = \mathbf{I}_n. \qquad [18.2.8]$$

Recalling Proposition 10.1, the vector autoregression [18.2.1] will be said to contain at least one unit root if the following determinant is zero:

$$|\mathbf{I}_n - \boldsymbol{\Phi}_1 - \boldsymbol{\Phi}_2 - \cdots - \boldsymbol{\Phi}_p| = 0. \qquad [18.2.9]$$

Note that [18.2.8] implies [18.2.9] but [18.2.9] does not imply [18.2.8]. Thus, this section is considering only a subset of the class of vector autoregressions containing a unit root, namely, the class described by [18.2.8]. Vector autoregressions for which [18.2.9] holds but [18.2.8] does not will be considered in Chapter 19.

This section begins with a vector generalization of case 2 from Chapter 17.

### *A Vector Autoregression with No Drift in Any of the Variables*

Here we assume that the *VAR* [18.2.1] satisfies [18.2.8] along with $\boldsymbol{\alpha} = \mathbf{0}$ and consider the consequences of estimating each equation in levels by *OLS* using observations $t = 1, 2, \ldots, T$ and conditioning on $\mathbf{y}_0, \mathbf{y}_{-1}, \ldots, \mathbf{y}_{-p+1}$. A constant term is assumed to be included in each regression. Under the maintained hypothesis [18.2.8], the data-generating process can be described as

$$(\mathbf{I}_n - \boldsymbol{\zeta}_1 L - \boldsymbol{\zeta}_2 L^2 - \cdots - \boldsymbol{\zeta}_{p-1} L^{p-1})\Delta \mathbf{y}_t = \boldsymbol{\varepsilon}_t. \qquad [18.2.10]$$

Assuming that all values of $z$ satisfying

$$|\mathbf{I}_n - \boldsymbol{\zeta}_1 z - \boldsymbol{\zeta}_2 z^2 - \cdots - \boldsymbol{\zeta}_{p-1} z^{p-1}| = 0$$

lie outside the unit circle, [18.2.10] implies that

$$\Delta \mathbf{y}_t = \mathbf{u}_t, \qquad [18.2.11]$$

where

$$\mathbf{u}_t = (\mathbf{I}_n - \boldsymbol{\zeta}_1 L - \boldsymbol{\zeta}_2 L^2 - \cdots - \boldsymbol{\zeta}_{p-1} L^{p-1})^{-1}\boldsymbol{\varepsilon}_t.$$

If $\boldsymbol{\varepsilon}_t$ is i.i.d. with mean zero, positive definite variance-covariance matrix $\boldsymbol{\Omega} = \mathbf{PP}'$, and finite fourth moments, then $\mathbf{u}_t$ satisfies the conditions of Proposition 18.1 with

$$\boldsymbol{\Psi}(L) = (\mathbf{I}_n - \boldsymbol{\zeta}_1 L - \boldsymbol{\zeta}_2 L^2 - \cdots - \boldsymbol{\zeta}_{p-1} L^{p-1})^{-1}. \qquad [18.2.12]$$

Also from [18.2.11], we have

$$\mathbf{y}_t = \mathbf{y}_0 + \mathbf{u}_1 + \mathbf{u}_2 + \cdots + \mathbf{u}_t,$$

so that $\mathbf{y}_t$ will have the same asymptotic behavior as $\boldsymbol{\xi}_t$ in Proposition 18.1.

Recall that the fitted values of a *VAR* estimated in levels [18.2.1] are identical to the fitted values for a *VAR* estimated in the form of [18.2.5]. Consider the $i$th equation in [18.2.5], which we write as

$$y_{it} = \boldsymbol{\zeta}'_{i1}\mathbf{u}_{t-1} + \boldsymbol{\zeta}'_{i2}\mathbf{u}_{t-2} + \cdots + \boldsymbol{\zeta}'_{i,p-1}\mathbf{u}_{t-p+1} + \alpha_i + \boldsymbol{\rho}'_i \mathbf{y}_{t-1} + \varepsilon_{it}, \qquad [18.2.13]$$

where $\mathbf{u}_t = \Delta\mathbf{y}_t$ and $\boldsymbol{\zeta}'_{is}$ denotes the $i$th row of $\boldsymbol{\zeta}_s$ for $s = 1, 2, \ldots, p - 1$. Similarly, $\boldsymbol{\rho}'_i$ denotes the $i$th row of $\boldsymbol{\rho}$. Under the null hypothesis [18.2.7], $\boldsymbol{\rho}'_i = \mathbf{e}'_i$, where $\mathbf{e}'_i$ is the $i$th row of the $(n \times n)$ identity matrix. Recall the usual expression [8.2.3] for the deviation of the *OLS* estimate $\mathbf{b}_T$ from its hypothesized true value:

$$\mathbf{b}_T - \boldsymbol{\beta} = (\Sigma \mathbf{x}_t \mathbf{x}'_t)^{-1}(\Sigma \mathbf{x}_t \varepsilon_t), \qquad [18.2.14]$$

where $\Sigma$ denotes summation over $t = 1$ through $T$. In the case of *OLS* estimation of [18.2.13],

$$\mathbf{b}_T - \boldsymbol{\beta} = \begin{bmatrix} \hat{\boldsymbol{\zeta}}_{i1} - \boldsymbol{\zeta}_{i1} \\ \hat{\boldsymbol{\zeta}}_{i2} - \boldsymbol{\zeta}_{i2} \\ \vdots \\ \hat{\boldsymbol{\zeta}}_{i,p-1} - \boldsymbol{\zeta}_{i,p-1} \\ \hat{\alpha}_i \\ \hat{\boldsymbol{\rho}}_i - \mathbf{e}_i \end{bmatrix} \qquad [18.2.15]$$

$\Sigma \mathbf{x}_t \mathbf{x}_t'$

$$= \begin{bmatrix} \Sigma \mathbf{u}_{t-1}\mathbf{u}_{t-1}' & \Sigma \mathbf{u}_{t-1}\mathbf{u}_{t-2}' & \cdots & \Sigma \mathbf{u}_{t-1}\mathbf{u}_{t-p+1}' & \Sigma \mathbf{u}_{t-1} & \Sigma \mathbf{u}_{t-1}\mathbf{y}_{t-1}' \\ \Sigma \mathbf{u}_{t-2}\mathbf{u}_{t-1}' & \Sigma \mathbf{u}_{t-2}\mathbf{u}_{t-2}' & \cdots & \Sigma \mathbf{u}_{t-2}\mathbf{u}_{t-p+1}' & \Sigma \mathbf{u}_{t-2} & \Sigma \mathbf{u}_{t-2}\mathbf{y}_{t-1}' \\ \vdots & \vdots & \cdots & \vdots & \vdots & \vdots \\ \Sigma \mathbf{u}_{t-p+1}\mathbf{u}_{t-1}' & \Sigma \mathbf{u}_{t-p+1}\mathbf{u}_{t-2}' & \cdots & \Sigma \mathbf{u}_{t-p+1}\mathbf{u}_{t-p+1}' & \Sigma \mathbf{u}_{t-p+1} & \Sigma \mathbf{u}_{t-p+1}\mathbf{y}_{t-1}' \\ \Sigma \mathbf{u}_{t-1}' & \Sigma \mathbf{u}_{t-2}' & \cdots & \Sigma \mathbf{u}_{t-p+1}' & T & \Sigma \mathbf{y}_{t-1}' \\ \Sigma \mathbf{y}_{t-1}\mathbf{u}_{t-1}' & \Sigma \mathbf{y}_{t-1}\mathbf{u}_{t-2}' & \cdots & \Sigma \mathbf{y}_{t-1}\mathbf{u}_{t-p+1}' & \Sigma \mathbf{y}_{t-1} & \Sigma \mathbf{y}_{t-1}\mathbf{y}_{t-1}' \end{bmatrix} \qquad [18.2.16]$$

$$\Sigma \mathbf{x}_t \varepsilon_t = \begin{bmatrix} \Sigma \mathbf{u}_{t-1}\varepsilon_{it} \\ \Sigma \mathbf{u}_{t-2}\varepsilon_{it} \\ \vdots \\ \Sigma \mathbf{u}_{t-p+1}\varepsilon_{it} \\ \Sigma \varepsilon_{it} \\ \Sigma \mathbf{y}_{t-1}\varepsilon_{it} \end{bmatrix}. \qquad [18.2.17]$$

Our earlier convention would append a subscript $T$ to the estimated coefficients $\hat{\boldsymbol{\zeta}}_{is}$ in [18.2.15]. For this discussion, the subscript $T$ will be suppressed to avoid excessively cumbersome notation.

Define $\boldsymbol{\Upsilon}_T$ to be the following matrix:

$$\underset{(np+1)\times(np+1)}{\boldsymbol{\Upsilon}_T} \equiv \begin{bmatrix} T^{1/2}\cdot \mathbf{I}_{n(p-1)} & \mathbf{0} & \mathbf{0} \\ \mathbf{0}' & T^{1/2} & \mathbf{0}' \\ \mathbf{0} & \mathbf{0} & T\cdot \mathbf{I}_n \end{bmatrix}. \qquad [18.2.18]$$

Premultiplying [18.2.14] by $\boldsymbol{\Upsilon}_T$ and rearranging as in [17.4.20] results in

$$\boldsymbol{\Upsilon}_T(\mathbf{b}_T - \boldsymbol{\beta}) = (\boldsymbol{\Upsilon}_T^{-1}\Sigma \mathbf{x}_t\mathbf{x}_t'\boldsymbol{\Upsilon}_T^{-1})^{-1}(\boldsymbol{\Upsilon}_T^{-1}\Sigma \mathbf{x}_t\varepsilon_t). \qquad [18.2.19]$$

Using results (a), (c), (d), (g), and (i) of Proposition 18.1, we find

$$(\boldsymbol{\Upsilon}_T^{-1}\Sigma \mathbf{x}_t\mathbf{x}_t'\boldsymbol{\Upsilon}_T^{-1}) = \begin{bmatrix} T^{-1}\Sigma \mathbf{u}_{t-1}\mathbf{u}_{t-1}' & T^{-1}\Sigma \mathbf{u}_{t-1}\mathbf{u}_{t-2}' & \cdots \\ T^{-1}\Sigma \mathbf{u}_{t-2}\mathbf{u}_{t-1}' & T^{-1}\Sigma \mathbf{u}_{t-2}\mathbf{u}_{t-2}' & \cdots \\ \vdots & \vdots & \cdots \\ T^{-1}\Sigma \mathbf{u}_{t-p+1}\mathbf{u}_{t-1}' & T^{-1}\Sigma \mathbf{u}_{t-p+1}\mathbf{u}_{t-2}' & \cdots \\ T^{-1}\Sigma \mathbf{u}_{t-1}' & T^{-1}\Sigma \mathbf{u}_{t-2}' & \cdots \\ T^{-3/2}\Sigma \mathbf{y}_{t-1}\mathbf{u}_{t-1}' & T^{-3/2}\Sigma \mathbf{y}_{t-1}\mathbf{u}_{t-2}' & \cdots \end{bmatrix.}$$

$$\begin{matrix} T^{-1}\Sigma \mathbf{u}_{t-1}\mathbf{u}_{t-p+1}' & T^{-1}\Sigma \mathbf{u}_{t-1} & T^{-3/2}\Sigma \mathbf{u}_{t-1}\mathbf{y}_{t-1}' \\ T^{-1}\Sigma \mathbf{u}_{t-2}\mathbf{u}_{t-p+1}' & T^{-1}\Sigma \mathbf{u}_{t-2} & T^{-3/2}\Sigma \mathbf{u}_{t-2}\mathbf{y}_{t-1}' \\ \vdots & \vdots & \vdots \\ T^{-1}\Sigma \mathbf{u}_{t-p+1}\mathbf{u}_{t-p+1}' & T^{-1}\Sigma \mathbf{u}_{t-p+1} & T^{-3/2}\Sigma \mathbf{u}_{t-p+1}\mathbf{y}_{t-1}' \\ T^{-1}\Sigma \mathbf{u}_{t-p+1}' & 1 & T^{-3/2}\Sigma \mathbf{y}_{t-1}' \\ T^{-3/2}\Sigma \mathbf{y}_{t-1}\mathbf{u}_{t-p+1}' & T^{-3/2}\Sigma \mathbf{y}_{t-1} & T^{-2}\Sigma \mathbf{y}_{t-1}\mathbf{y}_{t-1}' \end{matrix}$$

$$\xrightarrow{L} \begin{bmatrix} \mathbf{V} & \mathbf{0} \\ \mathbf{0} & \mathbf{Q} \end{bmatrix}, \qquad [18.2.20]$$

where

$$\underset{[n(p-1)\times n(p-1)]}{\mathbf{V}} \equiv \begin{bmatrix} \mathbf{\Gamma}_0 & \mathbf{\Gamma}_1 & \cdots & \mathbf{\Gamma}_{p-2} \\ \mathbf{\Gamma}_{-1} & \mathbf{\Gamma}_0 & \cdots & \mathbf{\Gamma}_{p-3} \\ \vdots & \vdots & \cdots & \vdots \\ \mathbf{\Gamma}_{-p+2} & \mathbf{\Gamma}_{-p+3} & \cdots & \mathbf{\Gamma}_0 \end{bmatrix} \qquad [18.2.21]$$

$$\mathbf{\Gamma}_s \equiv E(\Delta\mathbf{y}_t)(\Delta\mathbf{y}_{t-s})'$$

$$\underset{(n+1)\times(n+1)}{\mathbf{Q}} \equiv \begin{bmatrix} 1 & \left[\int \mathbf{W}(r)\,dr\right]'\cdot\mathbf{\Lambda}' \\ \mathbf{\Lambda}\cdot\int \mathbf{W}(r)\,dr & \mathbf{\Lambda}\cdot\left\{\int [\mathbf{W}(r)]\cdot[\mathbf{W}(r)]'\,dr\right\}\cdot\mathbf{\Lambda}' \end{bmatrix}. \qquad [18.2.22]$$

Also, the integral sign denotes integration over $r$ from 0 to 1, and

$$\mathbf{\Lambda} \equiv (\mathbf{I}_n - \boldsymbol{\zeta}_1 - \boldsymbol{\zeta}_2 - \cdots - \boldsymbol{\zeta}_{p-1})^{-1}\mathbf{P} \qquad [18.2.23]$$

with $E(\boldsymbol{\varepsilon}_t\boldsymbol{\varepsilon}_t') = \mathbf{PP}'$. Similarly, applying results (a), (b), and (f) from Proposition 18.1 to the second term in [18.2.19] reveals

$$(\mathbf{Y}_T^{-1}\Sigma\mathbf{x}_t\varepsilon_t) = \begin{bmatrix} T^{-1/2}\Sigma\mathbf{u}_{t-1}\varepsilon_{it} \\ T^{-1/2}\Sigma\mathbf{u}_{t-2}\varepsilon_{it} \\ \vdots \\ T^{-1/2}\Sigma\mathbf{u}_{t-p+1}\varepsilon_{it} \\ T^{-1/2}\Sigma\varepsilon_{it} \\ T^{-1}\Sigma\mathbf{y}_{t-1}\varepsilon_{it} \end{bmatrix} \xrightarrow{L} \begin{bmatrix} \mathbf{h}_1 \\ \mathbf{h}_2 \end{bmatrix}, \qquad [18.2.24]$$

where

$$\underset{[n(p-1)\times 1]}{\mathbf{h}_1} \sim N(\mathbf{0}, \sigma_{ii}\mathbf{V})$$

$$\sigma_{ii} = E(\varepsilon_{it}^2)$$

$$\underset{[(n+1)\times 1]}{\mathbf{h}_2} = \begin{bmatrix} \mathbf{e}_i'\mathbf{PW}(1) \\ \mathbf{\Lambda}\cdot\left\{\int [\mathbf{W}(r)]\,[d\mathbf{W}(r)]'\right\}\cdot\mathbf{P}'\mathbf{e}_i \end{bmatrix}$$

for $\mathbf{e}_i$ the $i$th column of $\mathbf{I}_n$. Results [18.2.19], [18.2.20], and [18.2.24] establish that

$$\mathbf{Y}_T(\mathbf{b}_T - \boldsymbol{\beta}) \xrightarrow{L} \begin{bmatrix} \mathbf{V}^{-1}\mathbf{h}_1 \\ \mathbf{Q}^{-1}\mathbf{h}_2 \end{bmatrix}. \qquad [18.2.25]$$

The first $n(p-1)$ elements of [18.2.25] imply that the coefficients on $\Delta\mathbf{y}_{t-1}$, $\Delta\mathbf{y}_{t-2}, \ldots, \Delta\mathbf{y}_{t-p+1}$ converge at rate $\sqrt{T}$ to Gaussian variables:

$$\sqrt{T}\begin{bmatrix} \hat{\zeta}_{i1} - \zeta_{i1} \\ \hat{\zeta}_{i2} - \zeta_{i2} \\ \vdots \\ \hat{\zeta}_{i,p-1} - \zeta_{i,p-1} \end{bmatrix} \xrightarrow{L} \mathbf{V}^{-1}\mathbf{h}_1 \sim N(\mathbf{0}, \sigma_{ii}\cdot\mathbf{V}^{-1}). \qquad [18.2.26]$$

This means that the Wald form of the *OLS* $\chi^2$ test of any linear hypothesis that involves only the coefficients on $\Delta\mathbf{y}_{t-s}$ has the usual asymptotic $\chi^2$ distribution, as the reader is invited to confirm in Exercise 18.1.

Notice that [18.2.26] is identical to the asymptotic distribution that would characterize the estimates if the $VAR$ were estimated in differences:

$$\Delta y_{it} = \alpha_i + \zeta_{i1}' \Delta \mathbf{y}_{t-1} + \zeta_{i2}' \Delta \mathbf{y}_{t-2} + \cdots + \zeta_{i,p-1}' \Delta \mathbf{y}_{t-p+1} + \varepsilon_{it}. \quad [18.2.27]$$

Thus, as in the case of a univariate autoregression, if the goal is to estimate the parameters $\zeta_{i1}, \zeta_{i2}, \ldots, \zeta_{i,p-1}$ or test hypotheses about these coefficients, there is no need based on the asymptotic distributions for estimating the $VAR$ in the difference form [18.2.27] rather than in the levels form,

$$\begin{aligned} y_{it} = {} & \zeta_{i1}' \Delta \mathbf{y}_{t-1} + \zeta_{i2}' \Delta \mathbf{y}_{t-2} + \cdots + \zeta_{i,p-1}' \Delta \mathbf{y}_{t-p+1} \\ & + \alpha_i + \boldsymbol{\rho}_i' \mathbf{y}_{t-1} + \varepsilon_{it}. \end{aligned} \quad [18.2.28]$$

Nevertheless, the small-sample distributions may well be improved by estimating the $VAR$ in differences, assuming that the restriction [18.2.8] is valid.

Although the asymptotic distribution of the coefficient on $\mathbf{y}_{t-1}$ is non-Gaussian, the fact that this estimate converges at rate $T$ means that a hypothesis test involving a single linear combination of $\boldsymbol{\rho}_i$ and $\zeta_{i1}, \zeta_{i2}, \ldots, \zeta_{i,p-1}$ will be dominated asymptotically by the coefficients with the slower rate of convergence, namely, $\zeta_{i1}, \zeta_{i2}, \ldots, \zeta_{i,p-1}$, and indeed will have the same asymptotic distribution as if the true value of $\boldsymbol{\rho} = \mathbf{I}_n$ were used. For example, if the $VAR$ is estimated in levels form [18.2.1], the individual coefficient matrices $\boldsymbol{\Phi}_s$ are related to the coefficients for the transformed $VAR$ [18.2.5] by

$$\hat{\boldsymbol{\Phi}}_p = -\hat{\zeta}_{p-1} \quad [18.2.29]$$

$$\hat{\boldsymbol{\Phi}}_s = \hat{\zeta}_s - \hat{\zeta}_{s-1} \qquad \text{for } s = 2, 3, \ldots, p-1 \quad [18.2.30]$$

$$\hat{\boldsymbol{\Phi}}_1 = \hat{\boldsymbol{\rho}} + \hat{\zeta}_1. \quad [18.2.31]$$

Since $\sqrt{T}(\hat{\zeta}_s - \zeta_s)$ is asymptotically Gaussian and since $\hat{\boldsymbol{\rho}}$ is $O_p(T^{-1})$, it follows that $\sqrt{T}(\hat{\boldsymbol{\Phi}}_s - \boldsymbol{\Phi}_s)$ is asymptotically Gaussian for $s = 1, 2, \ldots, p$ assuming that $p \geq 2$. This means that if the $VAR$ is estimated in levels in the standard way, any individual autoregressive coefficient converges at rate $\sqrt{T}$ to a Gaussian variable and the usual $t$ test of a hypothesis involving that coefficient is asymptotically valid. Moreover, an $F$ test involving a linear combination other than $\boldsymbol{\Phi}_1 + \boldsymbol{\Phi}_2 + \cdots + \boldsymbol{\Phi}_p$ has the usual asymptotic distribution.

Another important example is testing the null hypothesis that the data follow a $VAR(p_0)$ with $p_0 \geq 1$ against the alternative of a $VAR(p)$ with $p > p_0$. Consider $OLS$ estimation of the $i$th equation of the $VAR$ as represented in levels,

$$y_{it} = \alpha_i + \boldsymbol{\Phi}_{i1}' \mathbf{y}_{t-1} + \boldsymbol{\Phi}_{i2}' \mathbf{y}_{t-2} + \cdots + \boldsymbol{\Phi}_{ip}' \mathbf{y}_{t-p} + \varepsilon_{it}, \quad [18.2.32]$$

where $\boldsymbol{\Phi}_{is}'$ denotes the $i$th row of $\boldsymbol{\Phi}_s$. Consider the null hypothesis

$$H_0\colon \boldsymbol{\Phi}_{i,p_0+1} = \boldsymbol{\Phi}_{i,p_0+2} = \cdots = \boldsymbol{\Phi}_{ip} = \mathbf{0}. \quad [18.2.33]$$

The Wald form of the $OLS$ $\chi^2$ test of this hypothesis will be numerically identical to the test of

$$H_0\colon \zeta_{i,p_0} = \zeta_{i,p_0+1} = \cdots = \zeta_{i,p-1} = \mathbf{0} \quad [18.2.34]$$

for $OLS$ estimation of

$$\begin{aligned} y_{it} = {} & \zeta_{i1}' \Delta \mathbf{y}_{t-1} + \zeta_{i2}' \Delta \mathbf{y}_{t-2} + \cdots + \zeta_{i,p-1}' \Delta \mathbf{y}_{t-p+1} \\ & + \alpha_i + \boldsymbol{\rho}_i' \mathbf{y}_{t-1} + \varepsilon_{it}. \end{aligned} \quad [18.2.35]$$

Since we have seen that the usual $F$ test of [18.2.34] is asymptotically valid and since a test of [18.2.33] is based on the identical test statistic, it follows that the usual Wald test for assessing the number of lags to include in the regression is perfectly appropriate when the regression is estimated in levels form as in [18.2.32].

Of course, some hypothesis tests based on a *VAR* estimated in levels will not have the usual asymptotic distribution. An important example is a Granger-causality test of the null hypothesis that some of the variables in $\mathbf{y}_t$ do not appear in the regression explaining $y_{it}$. Partition $\mathbf{y}_t = (\mathbf{y}_{1t}', \mathbf{y}_{2t}')'$, where $\mathbf{y}_{2t}$ denotes the subset of variables that do not affect $y_{it}$ under the null hypothesis. Write the regression in levels as

$$\begin{aligned} y_{it} = {} & \boldsymbol{\omega}_1'\mathbf{y}_{1,t-1} + \boldsymbol{\lambda}_1'\mathbf{y}_{2,t-1} + \boldsymbol{\omega}_2'\mathbf{y}_{1,t-2} + \boldsymbol{\lambda}_2'\mathbf{y}_{2,t-2} + \cdots \\ & + \boldsymbol{\omega}_p'\mathbf{y}_{1,t-p} + \boldsymbol{\lambda}_p'\mathbf{y}_{2,t-p} + \alpha_i + \varepsilon_{it} \end{aligned} \qquad [18.2.36]$$

and the transformed regression as

$$\begin{aligned} y_{it} = {} & \boldsymbol{\beta}_1'\Delta\mathbf{y}_{1,t-1} + \boldsymbol{\gamma}_1'\Delta\mathbf{y}_{2,t-1} + \boldsymbol{\beta}_2'\Delta\mathbf{y}_{1,t-2} + \boldsymbol{\gamma}_2'\Delta\mathbf{y}_{2,t-2} + \cdots \\ & + \boldsymbol{\beta}_{p-1}'\Delta\mathbf{y}_{1,t-p+1} + \boldsymbol{\gamma}_{p-1}'\Delta\mathbf{y}_{2,t-p+1} + \alpha_i + \boldsymbol{\eta}'\mathbf{y}_{1,t-1} \\ & + \boldsymbol{\delta}'\mathbf{y}_{2,t-1} + \varepsilon_{it}. \end{aligned} \qquad [18.2.37]$$

The $F$ test of the null hypothesis $\boldsymbol{\lambda}_1 = \boldsymbol{\lambda}_2 = \cdots = \boldsymbol{\lambda}_p = \mathbf{0}$ based on *OLS* estimation of [18.2.36] is numerically identical to the $F$ test of the null hypothesis $\boldsymbol{\gamma}_1 = \boldsymbol{\gamma}_2 = \cdots = \boldsymbol{\gamma}_{p-1} = \boldsymbol{\delta} = \mathbf{0}$ based on *OLS* estimation of [18.2.37]. Since $\hat{\boldsymbol{\delta}}$ has a nonstandard limiting distribution, a test for Granger-causality based on a *VAR* estimated in levels typically does not have the usual limiting $\chi^2$ distribution (see Exercise 18.2 and Toda and Phillips, 1993b, for further discussion). Monte Carlo simulations by Ohanian (1988), for example, found that if an independent random walk is added to a vector autoregression, the random walk might spuriously appear to Granger-cause the other variables in 20% of the samples if the 5% critical value for a $\chi^2$ variable is mistakenly used to interpret the test statistic. Toda and Phillips (1993a) have an analytical treatment of this issue.

## *A Vector Autoregression with Drift in Some of the Variables*

Here we again consider estimation of a *VAR* written in the form

$$\mathbf{y}_t = \boldsymbol{\zeta}_1\Delta\mathbf{y}_{t-1} + \boldsymbol{\zeta}_2\Delta\mathbf{y}_{t-2} + \cdots + \boldsymbol{\zeta}_{p-1}\Delta\mathbf{y}_{t-p+1} + \boldsymbol{\alpha} + \boldsymbol{\rho}\mathbf{y}_{t-1} + \boldsymbol{\varepsilon}_t. \qquad [18.2.38]$$

As before, it is assumed that roots of

$$|\mathbf{I}_n - \boldsymbol{\zeta}_1 z - \boldsymbol{\zeta}_2 z^2 - \cdots - \boldsymbol{\zeta}_{p-1} z^{p-1}| = 0$$

are outside the unit circle, that $\boldsymbol{\varepsilon}_t$ is i.i.d. with mean zero, positive definite variance $\boldsymbol{\Omega}$, and finite fourth moments, and that the true value of $\boldsymbol{\rho}$ is the $(n \times n)$ identity matrix. These assumptions imply that

$$\Delta\mathbf{y}_t = \boldsymbol{\delta} + \mathbf{u}_t \qquad [18.2.39]$$

where

$$\boldsymbol{\delta} \equiv (\mathbf{I}_n - \boldsymbol{\zeta}_1 - \boldsymbol{\zeta}_2 - \cdots - \boldsymbol{\zeta}_{p-1})^{-1}\boldsymbol{\alpha} \qquad [18.2.40]$$

$$\mathbf{u}_t \equiv \boldsymbol{\Psi}(L)\boldsymbol{\varepsilon}_t \qquad [18.2.41]$$

$$\boldsymbol{\Psi}(L) \equiv (\mathbf{I}_n - \boldsymbol{\zeta}_1 L - \boldsymbol{\zeta}_2 L^2 - \cdots - \boldsymbol{\zeta}_{p-1}L^{p-1})^{-1}.$$

In contrast to the previous case, in which it was assumed that $\boldsymbol{\delta} = \mathbf{0}$, here we suppose that at least one and possibly all of the elements of $\boldsymbol{\delta}$ are nonzero.

Since this is a vector generalization of case 3 for the univariate autoregression considered in Chapter 17, one's first thought might be that, because of the nonzero drift in the $I(1)$ regressors, if all of the elements of $\boldsymbol{\delta}$ are nonzero, then all the coefficients will have the usual Gaussian limiting distribution. However, this turns out not to be the case. Any individual element $y_{jt}$ of the vector $\mathbf{y}_t$ is dominated by a deterministic time trend, and if $y_{jt}$ appeared alone in the regression, the asymptotic results would be the same as if $y_{jt}$ were replaced by the time trend $t$. Indeed, as noted by West (1988), in a regression in which there is a single $I(1)$ regressor with nonzero drift and in which all other regressors are $I(0)$, all of the coefficients would be asymptotically Gaussian and $F$ tests would have their usual limiting distribution. This can be shown using essentially the same algebra as in the univariate autoregression analyzed in case 3 in Chapter 17. However, as noted by Sims, Stock, and Watson (1990), in [18.2.38] there are $n$ different $I(1)$ regressors (the $n$ elements of $\mathbf{y}_{t-1}$), and if each of these were replaced by $\delta_i(t-1)$, the resulting regressors would be perfectly collinear. *OLS* will fit $n$ separate linear combinations of $\mathbf{y}_t$ so as to try to minimize the sum of squared residuals, and while one of these will indeed pick up the deterministic time trend $t$, the other linear combinations correspond to $I(1)$ driftless variables.

To develop the correct asymptotic distribution, it is convenient to work with a transformation of [18.2.38] that isolates these different linear combinations. Note that the difference equation [18.2.39] implies that

$$\mathbf{y}_t = \mathbf{y}_0 + \boldsymbol{\delta}\cdot t + \mathbf{u}_1 + \mathbf{u}_2 + \cdots + \mathbf{u}_t. \qquad [18.2.42]$$

Suppose for illustration that the $n$th variable in the system exhibits nonzero drift ($\delta_n \neq 0$); whether in addition $\delta_i \neq 0$ for $i = 1, 2, \ldots, n-1$ then turns out to be irrelevant, assuming that [18.2.8] holds. Define

$$\begin{aligned} y_{1t}^* &\equiv y_{1t} - (\delta_1/\delta_n)y_{nt} \\ y_{2t}^* &\equiv y_{2t} - (\delta_2/\delta_n)y_{nt} \\ &\vdots \\ y_{n-1,t}^* &\equiv y_{n-1,t} - (\delta_{n-1}/\delta_n)y_{nt} \\ y_{nt}^* &\equiv y_{nt}. \end{aligned}$$

Thus, for $i = 1, 2, \ldots, n-1$,

$$\begin{aligned} y_{it}^* &= [y_{i0} + \delta_i t + u_{i1} + u_{i2} + \cdots + u_{it}] \\ &\quad - (\delta_i/\delta_n)[y_{n0} + \delta_n t + u_{n1} + u_{n2} + \cdots + u_{nt}] \\ &\equiv y_{i0}^* + \xi_{it}^*, \end{aligned}$$

where we have defined

$$\begin{aligned} y_{i0}^* &\equiv [y_{i0} - (\delta_i/\delta_n)y_{n0}] \\ \xi_{it}^* &\equiv u_{i1}^* + u_{i2}^* + \cdots + u_{it}^* \\ u_{it}^* &\equiv u_{it} - (\delta_i/\delta_n)u_{nt}. \end{aligned}$$

Collecting $u_{1t}^*, u_{2t}^*, \ldots, u_{n-1,t}^*$ in an $[(n-1) \times 1]$ vector $\mathbf{u}_t^*$, it follows from [18.2.41] that

$$\mathbf{u}_t^* = \boldsymbol{\Psi}^*(L)\boldsymbol{\varepsilon}_t,$$

where $\boldsymbol{\Psi}^*(L)$ denotes the following $[(n-1) \times n]$ matrix polynomial:

$$\boldsymbol{\Psi}^*(L) \equiv \mathbf{H}\cdot\boldsymbol{\Psi}(L)$$

for

$$\underset{[(n-1)\times n]}{\mathbf{H}} \equiv \begin{bmatrix} 1 & 0 & 0 & \cdots & 0 & -(\delta_1/\delta_n) \\ 0 & 1 & 0 & \cdots & 0 & -(\delta_2/\delta_n) \\ \vdots & \vdots & \vdots & \cdots & \vdots & \vdots \\ 0 & 0 & 0 & \cdots & 1 & -(\delta_{n-1}/\delta_n) \end{bmatrix}.$$

Since $\{s \cdot \Psi_s\}_{s=0}^{\infty}$ is absolutely summable, so is $\{s \cdot \Psi_s^*\}_{s=0}^{\infty}$. Hence, the $[(n-1) \times 1]$ vector $\mathbf{y}_t^* \equiv (y_{1t}^*, y_{2t}^*, \ldots, y_{n-1,t}^*)'$ has the same asymptotic properties as the vector $\boldsymbol{\xi}_t$ in Proposition 18.1 with the matrix $\Psi(1)$ in Proposition 18.1 replaced by $\Psi^*(1)$.

If we had direct observations on $\mathbf{y}_t^*$ and $\mathbf{u}_t$, the fitted values of the *VAR* as estimated from [18.2.38] would clearly be identical to those from estimation of

$$\begin{aligned} \mathbf{y}_t = \boldsymbol{\zeta}_1\mathbf{u}_{t-1} + \boldsymbol{\zeta}_2\mathbf{u}_{t-2} + \cdots + \boldsymbol{\zeta}_{p-1}\mathbf{u}_{t-p+1} + \boldsymbol{\alpha}^* \\ + \boldsymbol{\rho}^*\mathbf{y}_{t-1}^* + \boldsymbol{\gamma} \cdot y_{n,t-1} + \boldsymbol{\varepsilon}_t, \end{aligned} \qquad [18.2.43]$$

where $\boldsymbol{\rho}^*$ denotes an $[n \times (n-1)]$ matrix of coefficients while $\boldsymbol{\gamma}$ is an $(n \times 1)$ vector of coefficients. This representation separates the zero-mean stationary regressors ($\mathbf{u}_{t-s} = \Delta\mathbf{y}_{t-s} - \boldsymbol{\delta}$), the constant term ($\boldsymbol{\alpha}^*$), the driftless $I(0)$ regressors ($\mathbf{y}_{t-1}^*$), and a term dominated asymptotically by a time trend ($y_{n,t-1}$). As in Section 16.3, once the hypothetical *VAR* [18.2.43] is analyzed, we can infer the properties of the *VAR* as actually estimated ([18.2.38] or [18.2.1]) from the relation between the fitted values for the different representations.

Consider the $i$th equation in [18.2.43],

$$\begin{aligned} y_{it} = \boldsymbol{\zeta}_{i1}'\mathbf{u}_{t-1} + \boldsymbol{\zeta}_{i2}'\mathbf{u}_{t-2} + \cdots + \boldsymbol{\zeta}_{i,p-1}'\mathbf{u}_{t-p+1} + \alpha_i^* \\ + \boldsymbol{\rho}_i^{*\prime}\mathbf{y}_{t-1}^* + \gamma_i y_{n,t-1} + \varepsilon_{it}, \end{aligned} \qquad [18.2.44]$$

where $\boldsymbol{\zeta}_{is}'$ denotes the $i$th row of $\boldsymbol{\zeta}_s$ and $\boldsymbol{\rho}_i^{*\prime}$ is the $i$th row of $\boldsymbol{\rho}^*$. Define

$$\underset{[(np+1)\times 1]}{\mathbf{x}_t^*} \equiv (\mathbf{u}_{t-1}', \mathbf{u}_{t-2}', \ldots, \mathbf{u}_{t-p+1}', 1, \mathbf{y}_{t-1}^{*\prime}, y_{n,t-1})'$$

$$\underset{[(np+1)\times(np+1)]}{\mathbf{Y}_T} \equiv \begin{bmatrix} T^{1/2}\cdot\mathbf{I}_{n(p-1)} & \mathbf{0} & \mathbf{0} & \mathbf{0} \\ \mathbf{0}' & T^{1/2} & \mathbf{0}' & 0 \\ \mathbf{0} & \mathbf{0} & T\cdot\mathbf{I}_{n-1} & \mathbf{0} \\ \mathbf{0}' & 0 & \mathbf{0}' & T^{3/2} \end{bmatrix} \qquad [18.2.45]$$

$$\underset{[(n-1)\times n]}{\boldsymbol{\Lambda}^*} \equiv \Psi^*(1)\cdot\mathbf{P},$$

where $E(\boldsymbol{\varepsilon}_t\boldsymbol{\varepsilon}_t') = \mathbf{PP}'$. Then, from Proposition 18.1,

$$\left(\mathbf{Y}_T^{-1} \sum_{t=1}^{T} (\mathbf{x}_t^*)(\mathbf{x}_t^{*\prime})\mathbf{Y}_T^{-1}\right) \qquad [18.2.46]$$

$$\xrightarrow{L} \begin{bmatrix} \mathbf{V} & \mathbf{0} & \mathbf{0} & \mathbf{0} \\ \mathbf{0}' & 1 & \left[\int \mathbf{W}(r)\,dr\right]'\cdot\boldsymbol{\Lambda}^{*\prime} & \delta_n/2 \\ \mathbf{0} & \boldsymbol{\Lambda}^*\cdot\int \mathbf{W}(r)\,dr & \boldsymbol{\Lambda}^*\cdot\left\{\int [\mathbf{W}(r)]\cdot[\mathbf{W}(r)]'\,dr\right\}\cdot\boldsymbol{\Lambda}^{*\prime} & \delta_n\cdot\boldsymbol{\Lambda}^*\cdot\int r\mathbf{W}(r)\,dr \\ \mathbf{0}' & \delta_n/2 & \delta_n\cdot\left[\int r\mathbf{W}(r)\,dr\right]'\cdot\boldsymbol{\Lambda}^{*\prime} & \delta_n^2/3 \end{bmatrix},$$

where

$$\underset{[n(p-1)\times n(p-1)]}{\mathbf{V}} \equiv \begin{bmatrix} \boldsymbol{\Gamma}_0 & \boldsymbol{\Gamma}_1 & \cdots & \boldsymbol{\Gamma}_{p-2} \\ \boldsymbol{\Gamma}_{-1} & \boldsymbol{\Gamma}_0 & \cdots & \boldsymbol{\Gamma}_{p-3} \\ \vdots & \vdots & \cdots & \vdots \\ \boldsymbol{\Gamma}_{-p+2} & \boldsymbol{\Gamma}_{-p+3} & \cdots & \boldsymbol{\Gamma}_0 \end{bmatrix} \qquad [18.2.47]$$

and $\mathbf{W}(r)$ denotes $n$-dimensional standard Brownian motion while the integral sign indicates integration over $r$ from 0 to 1. Similarly,

$$\mathbf{Y}_T^{-1} \sum_{t=1}^{T} \mathbf{x}_t^* \varepsilon_{it} \xrightarrow{L} \begin{bmatrix} \mathbf{h}_1 \\ h_2 \\ \mathbf{h}_3 \\ h_4 \end{bmatrix}, \qquad [18.2.48]$$

where $\mathbf{h}_1 \sim N(\mathbf{0}, \sigma_{ii}\mathbf{V})$. The variables $h_2$ and $h_4$ are also Gaussian, though $\mathbf{h}_3$ is non-Gaussian. If we define $\boldsymbol{\omega}$ to be the vector of coefficients on lagged $\Delta\mathbf{y}$,

$$\boldsymbol{\omega} \equiv (\boldsymbol{\zeta}_{i1}', \boldsymbol{\zeta}_{i2}', \ldots, \boldsymbol{\zeta}_{i,n-1}')',$$

then the preceding results imply that

$$\mathbf{Y}_T(\mathbf{b}_T^* - \boldsymbol{\beta}^*) = \begin{bmatrix} T^{1/2}(\hat{\boldsymbol{\omega}}_T - \boldsymbol{\omega}) \\ T^{1/2}(\hat{\boldsymbol{\alpha}}_{i,T}^* - \boldsymbol{\alpha}_i^*) \\ T(\hat{\boldsymbol{\rho}}_{i,T}^* - \boldsymbol{\rho}_i^*) \\ T^{3/2}(\hat{\gamma}_{i,T} - \gamma_i) \end{bmatrix} \xrightarrow{L} \begin{bmatrix} \mathbf{V}^{-1}\mathbf{h}_1 \\ \mathbf{Q}^{-1}\boldsymbol{\eta} \end{bmatrix}, \qquad [18.2.49]$$

where $\boldsymbol{\eta} \equiv (h_2, \mathbf{h}_3', h_4)'$ and $\mathbf{Q}$ is the $[(n + 1) \times (n + 1)]$ lower right block of the matrix in [18.2.46]. Thus, as usual, the coefficients on $\mathbf{u}_{t-s}$ in [18.2.43] are asymptotically Gaussian:

$$\sqrt{T}(\hat{\boldsymbol{\omega}}_{i,T} - \boldsymbol{\omega}_i) \xrightarrow{L} N(\mathbf{0}, \sigma_{ii}\mathbf{V}^{-1}).$$

These coefficients are, of course, numerically identical to the coefficients on $\Delta\mathbf{y}_{t-s}$ in [18.2.38]. Any $F$ tests involving just these coefficients are also identical for the two parameterizations. Hence, an $F$ test about $\boldsymbol{\zeta}_1, \boldsymbol{\zeta}_2, \ldots, \boldsymbol{\zeta}_{p-1}$ in [18.2.38] has the usual limiting $\chi^2$ distribution. This is the same asymptotic distribution as if [18.2.38] were estimated with $\boldsymbol{\rho} = \mathbf{I}_n$ imposed; that is, it is the same asymptotic distribution whether the regression is estimated in levels or in differences.

Since $\hat{\boldsymbol{\rho}}_T^*$ and $\hat{\boldsymbol{\gamma}}_T$ converge at a faster rate than $\hat{\boldsymbol{\omega}}_T$, the asymptotic distribution of a linear combination of $\hat{\boldsymbol{\omega}}_T$, $\hat{\boldsymbol{\rho}}_T^*$, and $\hat{\boldsymbol{\gamma}}_T$ that puts nonzero weight on $\hat{\boldsymbol{\omega}}_T$ has the same asymptotic distribution as a linear combination that uses the true values for $\boldsymbol{\rho}$ and $\boldsymbol{\gamma}$. This means, for example, that the original coefficients $\hat{\boldsymbol{\Phi}}_s$ of the *VAR* estimated in levels as in [18.2.1] are all individually Gaussian and can be interpreted using the usual $t$ tests. A Wald test of the null hypothesis of $p_0 \geq 1$ lag against the alternative of $p > p_0$ lags again has the usual $\chi^2$ distribution. However, Granger-causality tests typically have nonstandard distributions.

## 18.3. *Spurious Regressions*

Consider a regression of the form

$$y_t = \mathbf{x}_t'\boldsymbol{\beta} + u_t,$$

for which elements of $y_t$ and $\mathbf{x}_t$ might be nonstationary. If there does not exist some population value for $\boldsymbol{\beta}$ for which the residual $u_t = y_t - \mathbf{x}_t'\boldsymbol{\beta}$ is $I(0)$, then *OLS* is quite likely to produce spurious results. This phenomenon was first discovered in Monte Carlo experimentation by Granger and Newbold (1974) and later explained theoretically by Phillips (1986).

A general statement of the spurious regression problem can be made as follows. Let $\mathbf{y}_t$ be an $(n \times 1)$ vector of $I(1)$ variables. Define $g \equiv (n - 1)$, and partition $\mathbf{y}_t$ as

$$\mathbf{y}_t = \begin{bmatrix} y_{1t} \\ \mathbf{y}_{2t} \end{bmatrix},$$

where $\mathbf{y}_{2t}$ denotes a $(g \times 1)$ vector. Consider the consequences of an *OLS* regression of the first variable on the others and a constant,

$$y_{1t} = \alpha + \boldsymbol{\gamma}'\mathbf{y}_{2t} + u_t. \qquad [18.3.1]$$

The *OLS* coefficient estimates for a sample of size $T$ are given by

$$\begin{bmatrix} \hat{\alpha}_T \\ \hat{\boldsymbol{\gamma}}_T \end{bmatrix} = \begin{bmatrix} T & \Sigma\mathbf{y}'_{2t} \\ \Sigma\mathbf{y}_{2t} & \Sigma\mathbf{y}_{2t}\mathbf{y}'_{2t} \end{bmatrix}^{-1} \begin{bmatrix} \Sigma y_{1t} \\ \Sigma\mathbf{y}_{2t}y_{1t} \end{bmatrix}, \qquad [18.3.2]$$

where $\Sigma$ indicates summation over $t$ from 1 to $T$. It turns out that even if $y_{1t}$ is completely unrelated to $\mathbf{y}_{2t}$, the estimated value of $\boldsymbol{\gamma}$ is likely to appear to be statistically significantly different from zero. Indeed, consider any null hypothesis of the form $H_0$: $\mathbf{R}\boldsymbol{\gamma} = \mathbf{r}$ where $\mathbf{R}$ is a known $(m \times g)$ matrix representing $m$ separate hypotheses involving $\boldsymbol{\gamma}$ and $\mathbf{r}$ is a known $(m \times 1)$ vector. The *OLS F* test of this null hypothesis is

$$F_T = \{\mathbf{R}\hat{\boldsymbol{\gamma}}_T - \mathbf{r}\}'\left\{s_T^2\cdot[\mathbf{0} \quad \mathbf{R}]\begin{bmatrix} T & \Sigma\mathbf{y}'_{2t} \\ \Sigma\mathbf{y}_{2t} & \Sigma\mathbf{y}_{2t}\mathbf{y}'_{2t} \end{bmatrix}^{-1}\begin{bmatrix} \mathbf{0}' \\ \mathbf{R}' \end{bmatrix}\right\}^{-1} \times \{\mathbf{R}\hat{\boldsymbol{\gamma}}_T - \mathbf{r}\} \div m, \qquad [18.3.3]$$

where

$$s_T^2 \equiv (T - n)^{-1} \sum_{t=1}^{T} \hat{u}_t^2. \qquad [18.3.4]$$

Unless there is some value for $\boldsymbol{\gamma}$ such that $y_{1t} - \boldsymbol{\gamma}'\mathbf{y}_{2t}$ is stationary, the *OLS* estimate $\hat{\boldsymbol{\gamma}}_T$ will appear to be spuriously precise in the sense that the $F$ test is virtually certain to reject any null hypothesis if the sample size is sufficiently large, even though $\hat{\boldsymbol{\gamma}}_T$ does not provide a consistent estimate of any well-defined population constant!

The following proposition, adapted from Phillips (1986), provides the formal basis for these statements.

***Proposition 18.2:*** *Consider an $(n \times 1)$ vector $\mathbf{y}_t$ whose first difference is described by*

$$\Delta\mathbf{y}_t = \boldsymbol{\Psi}(L)\boldsymbol{\varepsilon}_t = \sum_{s=0}^{\infty} \boldsymbol{\Psi}_s\boldsymbol{\varepsilon}_{t-s}$$

*for $\boldsymbol{\varepsilon}_t$ an i.i.d. $(n \times 1)$ vector with mean zero, variance $E(\boldsymbol{\varepsilon}_t\boldsymbol{\varepsilon}_t') = \mathbf{PP}'$, and finite fourth moments and where $\{s\cdot\boldsymbol{\Psi}_s\}_{s=0}^{\infty}$ is absolutely summable. Let $g \equiv (n - 1)$ and $\boldsymbol{\Lambda} \equiv \boldsymbol{\Psi}(1)\cdot\mathbf{P}$. Partition $\mathbf{y}_t$ as $\mathbf{y}_t = (y_{1t}, \mathbf{y}'_{2t})'$, and partition $\boldsymbol{\Lambda\Lambda}'$ as*

$$\underset{(n\times n)}{\boldsymbol{\Lambda\Lambda}'} = \begin{bmatrix} \underset{(1\times 1)}{\Sigma_{11}} & \underset{(1\times g)}{\boldsymbol{\Sigma}'_{21}} \\ \underset{(g\times 1)}{\boldsymbol{\Sigma}_{21}} & \underset{(g\times g)}{\boldsymbol{\Sigma}_{22}} \end{bmatrix}. \qquad [18.3.5]$$

*Suppose that $\boldsymbol{\Lambda\Lambda}'$ is nonsingular, and define*

$$(\sigma_1^*)^2 \equiv (\Sigma_{11} - \boldsymbol{\Sigma}'_{21}\boldsymbol{\Sigma}_{22}^{-1}\boldsymbol{\Sigma}_{21}). \qquad [18.3.6]$$

*Let $\mathbf{L}_{22}$ denote the Cholesky factor of $\boldsymbol{\Sigma}_{22}^{-1}$; that is, $\mathbf{L}_{22}$ is the lower triangular matrix* *satisfying*

$$\boldsymbol{\Sigma}_{22}^{-1} = \mathbf{L}_{22}\mathbf{L}_{22}'. \qquad [18.3.7]$$

*Then the following hold.*

(*a*) *The OLS estimates* $\hat{\alpha}_T$ *and* $\hat{\boldsymbol{\gamma}}_T$ *in* [18.3.2] *are characterized by*

$$\begin{bmatrix} T^{-1/2}\hat{\alpha}_T \\ \hat{\boldsymbol{\gamma}}_T - \boldsymbol{\Sigma}_{22}^{-1}\boldsymbol{\Sigma}_{21} \end{bmatrix} \xrightarrow{L} \begin{bmatrix} \sigma_1^* h_1 \\ \sigma_1^* \mathbf{L}_{22}\mathbf{h}_2 \end{bmatrix}, \qquad [18.3.8]$$

*where*

$$\begin{bmatrix} h_1 \\ \mathbf{h}_2 \end{bmatrix} \equiv \begin{bmatrix} 1 & \int [\mathbf{W}_2^*(r)]'\,dr \\ \int \mathbf{W}_2^*(r)\,dr & \int [\mathbf{W}_2^*(r)]\cdot[\mathbf{W}_2^*(r)]'\,dr \end{bmatrix}^{-1} \times \begin{bmatrix} \int W_1^*(r)\,dr \\ \int \mathbf{W}_2^*(r)\cdot W_1^*(r)\,dr \end{bmatrix} \qquad [18.3.9]$$

*and the integral sign indicates integration over r from* 0 *to* 1, $W_1^*(r)$ *denotes scalar standard Brownian motion, and* $\mathbf{W}_2^*(r)$ *denotes g-dimensional standard Brownian motion with* $\mathbf{W}_2^*(r)$ *independent of* $W_1^*(r)$.

(*b*) *The sum of squared residuals* $RSS_T$ *from OLS estimation of* [18.3.1] *satisfies*

$$T^{-2}\cdot RSS_T \xrightarrow{L} (\sigma_1^*)^2\cdot H, \qquad [18.3.10]$$

*where*

$$H \equiv \int [W_1^*(r)]^2\,dr - \left\{ \begin{bmatrix} \int W_1^*(r)\,dr & \int [W_1^*(r)]\cdot[\mathbf{W}_2^*(r)]'\,dr \end{bmatrix} \times \begin{bmatrix} 1 & \int [\mathbf{W}_2^*(r)]'\,dr \\ \int \mathbf{W}_2^*(r)\,dr & \int [\mathbf{W}_2^*(r)]\cdot[\mathbf{W}_2^*(r)]'\,dr \end{bmatrix}^{-1} \begin{bmatrix} \int W_1^*(r)\,dr \\ \int [\mathbf{W}_2^*(r)]\cdot[W_1^*(r)]\,dr \end{bmatrix} \right\}. \qquad [18.3.11]$$

(*c*) *The OLS F test* [18.3.3] *satisfies*

$$\mathrm{T}^{-1}\cdot F_T \xrightarrow{L} \{\sigma_1^*\cdot\mathbf{R}^*\mathbf{h}_2 - \mathbf{r}^*\}' \times \left\{ (\sigma_1^*)^2\cdot H[\mathbf{0} \quad \mathbf{R}^*] \times \begin{bmatrix} 1 & \int [\mathbf{W}_2^*(r)]'\,dr \\ \int \mathbf{W}_2^*(r)\,dr & \int [\mathbf{W}_2^*(r)]\cdot[\mathbf{W}_2^*(r)]'\,dr \end{bmatrix}^{-1} \begin{bmatrix} \mathbf{0}' \\ \mathbf{R}^{*\prime} \end{bmatrix} \right\}^{-1} \times \{\sigma_1^*\cdot\mathbf{R}^*\mathbf{h}_2 - \mathbf{r}^*\} \div m, \qquad [18.3.12]$$

*where*

$$\mathbf{R}^* \equiv \mathbf{R}\cdot\mathbf{L}_{22}$$
$$\mathbf{r}^* \equiv \mathbf{r} - \mathbf{R}\boldsymbol{\Sigma}_{22}^{-1}\boldsymbol{\Sigma}_{21}.$$

The simplest illustration of Proposition 18.2 is provided when $y_{1t}$ and $y_{2t}$ are scalars following totally unrelated random walks:

$$y_{1t} = y_{1,t-1} + \varepsilon_{1t} \qquad [18.3.13]$$

$$y_{2t} = y_{2,t-1} + \varepsilon_{2t}, \qquad [18.3.14]$$

where $\varepsilon_{1t}$ is i.i.d. with mean zero and variance $\sigma_1^2$, $\varepsilon_{2t}$ is i.i.d. with mean zero and variance $\sigma_2^2$, and $\varepsilon_{1t}$ is independent of $\varepsilon_{2\tau}$ for all $t$ and $\tau$. For $\mathbf{y}_t = (y_{1t}, y_{2t})'$, this specification implies

$$\mathbf{P} = \begin{bmatrix} \sigma_1 & 0 \\ 0 & \sigma_2 \end{bmatrix}$$

$$\boldsymbol{\Psi}(1) = \mathbf{I}_2$$

$$\begin{bmatrix} \Sigma_{11} & \Sigma_{21} \\ \Sigma_{21} & \Sigma_{22} \end{bmatrix} = \boldsymbol{\Psi}(1)\cdot\mathbf{P}\cdot\mathbf{P}'\cdot[\boldsymbol{\Psi}(1)]' = \begin{bmatrix} \sigma_1^2 & 0 \\ 0 & \sigma_2^2 \end{bmatrix}$$

$$\sigma_1^* = \sigma_1$$

$$L_{22} = 1/\sigma_2.$$

Result (a) then claims that an *OLS* regression of $y_{1t}$ on $y_{2t}$ and a constant,

$$y_{1t} = \alpha + \gamma y_{2t} + u_t, \qquad [18.3.15]$$

produces estimates $\hat{\alpha}_T$ and $\hat{\gamma}_T$ characterized by

$$\begin{bmatrix} T^{-1/2}\hat{\alpha}_T \\ \hat{\gamma}_T \end{bmatrix} \xrightarrow{L} \begin{bmatrix} \sigma_1\cdot h_1 \\ (\sigma_1/\sigma_2)\cdot h_2 \end{bmatrix}.$$

Note the contrast between this result and any previous asymptotic distribution analyzed. Usually, the *OLS* estimates are consistent with $\mathbf{b}_T \xrightarrow{p} \mathbf{0}$ and must be multiplied by some increasing function of $T$ in order to obtain a nondegenerate asymptotic distribution. Here, however, neither estimate is consistent—different arbitrarily large samples will have randomly differing estimates $\hat{\gamma}_T$. Indeed, the estimate of the constant term $\hat{\alpha}_T$ actually *diverges*, and must be *divided* by $T^{1/2}$ to obtain a random variable with a well-specified distribution—the estimate $\hat{\alpha}_T$ itself is likely to get farther and farther from the true value of zero as the sample size $T$ increases.

Result (b) implies that the usual *OLS* estimate of the variance of $u_t$,

$$s_T^2 = (T - n)^{-1}\cdot RSS_T,$$

again diverges as $T \to \infty$. To obtain an estimate that does not grow with the sample size, the residual sum of squares has to be divided by $T^2$ rather than $T$. In this respect, the residuals $\hat{u}_t$ from a spurious regression behave like a unit root process; if $\xi_t$ is a scalar $I(1)$ series, then $T^{-1}\Sigma\xi_t^2$ diverges and $T^{-2}\Sigma\xi_t^2$ converges. To see why $\hat{u}_t$ behaves like an $I(1)$ series, notice that the *OLS* residual is given by

$$\hat{u}_t = y_{1t} - \hat{\alpha}_T - \hat{\boldsymbol{\gamma}}_T'\mathbf{y}_{2t},$$

from which

$$\Delta\hat{u}_t = \Delta y_{1t} - \hat{\boldsymbol{\gamma}}_T'\cdot\Delta\mathbf{y}_{2t} = \begin{bmatrix} 1 & -\hat{\boldsymbol{\gamma}}_T' \end{bmatrix}\begin{bmatrix} \Delta y_{1t} \\ \Delta\mathbf{y}_{2t} \end{bmatrix} \xrightarrow{L} \begin{bmatrix} 1 & -\mathbf{h}_2^{*\prime} \end{bmatrix}\Delta\mathbf{y}_t, \qquad [18.3.16]$$

where $\mathbf{h}_2^* \equiv \boldsymbol{\Sigma}_{22}^{-1}\boldsymbol{\Sigma}_{21} + \sigma_1^*\mathbf{L}_{22}\mathbf{h}_2$. This is a random vector $[1 \quad -\mathbf{h}_2^{*\prime}]$ times the $I(0)$ vector $\Delta\mathbf{y}_t$.

Result (c) means that any $OLS$ $t$ or $F$ test based on the spurious regression [18.3.1] also diverges; the $OLS$ $F$ statistic [18.3.3] must be divided by $T$ to obtain a variable that does not grow with the sample size. Since an $F$ test of a single restriction is the square of the corresponding $t$ test, any $t$ statistic would have to be divided by $T^{1/2}$ to obtain a convergent variable. Thus, as the sample size $T$ becomes larger, it becomes increasingly likely that the absolute value of an $OLS$ $t$ test will exceed any arbitrary finite value (such as the usual critical value of $t = 2$). For example, in the regression of [18.3.15], it will appear that $y_{1t}$ and $y_{2t}$ are significantly related whereas in reality they are completely independent.

In more general regressions of the form of [18.3.1], $\Delta y_{1t}$ and $\Delta \mathbf{y}_{2t}$ may be dynamically related through nonzero off-diagonal elements of $\mathbf{P}$ and $\mathbf{\Psi}(L)$. While such correlations will influence the values of the nuisance parameters $\sigma_1^*$, $\mathbf{\Sigma}_{21}$, and $\mathbf{\Sigma}_{22}$, provided that the conditions of Proposition 18.2 are satisfied, these correlations do not affect the overall nature of the results or rates of convergence for any of the statistics. Note that since $W_1^*(r)$ and $\mathbf{W}_2^*(r)$ are standard Brownian motion, the distributions of $h_1$, $\mathbf{h}_2$, and $H$ in Proposition 18.2 depend only on the number of variables in the regression and not on their dynamic relations.

The condition in Proposition 18.2 that $\mathbf{\Lambda}\cdot\mathbf{\Lambda}'$ is nonsingular might appear innocuous but is actually quite important. In the case of a single variable ($\mathbf{y}_t = y_{1t}$ with $\Delta y_{1t} = \psi(L)\varepsilon_{1t}$), the matrix $\mathbf{\Lambda}\cdot\mathbf{\Lambda}'$ would just be the scalar $[\psi(1)\cdot\sigma_1]^2$ and the condition that $\mathbf{\Lambda}\cdot\mathbf{\Lambda}'$ is nonsingular would come down to the requirement that $\psi(1)$ be nonzero. To understand what this means, suppose that $y_{1t}$ were actually stationary with Wold representation:

$$y_{1t} = \varepsilon_{1t} + C_1\varepsilon_{1,t-1} + C_2\varepsilon_{1,t-2} + \cdots = C(L)\varepsilon_{1t}.$$

Then the first difference $\Delta y_{1t}$ would be described by

$$\Delta y_{1t} = (1 - L)C(L)\varepsilon_{1t} \equiv \psi(L)\varepsilon_{1t},$$

where $\psi(L) \equiv (1 - L)C(L)$, meaning $\psi(1) = (1 - 1)\cdot C(1) = 0$. Thus, if $y_{1t}$ were actually $I(0)$ rather than $I(1)$, the condition that $\mathbf{\Lambda}\cdot\mathbf{\Lambda}'$ is nonsingular would not be satisfied.

For the more general case in which $\mathbf{y}_t$ is an $(n \times 1)$ vector, the condition that $\mathbf{\Lambda}\cdot\mathbf{\Lambda}'$ is nonsingular will not be satisfied if some explanatory variable $y_{it}$ is $I(0)$ or if some linear combination of the elements of $\mathbf{y}_t$ is $I(0)$. If $\mathbf{y}_t$ is an $I(1)$ vector but some linear combination of $\mathbf{y}_t$ is $I(0)$, then the elements of $\mathbf{y}_t$ are said to be *cointegrated*. Thus, Proposition 18.2 describes the consequences of $OLS$ estimation of [18.3.1] only when all of the elements of $\mathbf{y}_t$ are $I(1)$ with zero drift and when the vector $\mathbf{y}_t$ is not cointegrated. A regression is spurious only when the residual $u_t$ is nonstationary for all possible values of the coefficient vector.

## *Cures for Spurious Regressions*

There are three ways in which the problems associated with spurious regressions can be avoided. The first approach is to include lagged values of both the dependent and independent variable in the regression. For example, consider the following model as an alternative to [18.3.15]:

$$y_{1t} = \alpha + \phi y_{1,t-1} + \gamma y_{2t} + \delta y_{2,t-1} + u_t. \qquad [18.3.17]$$

This regression does not satisfy the conditions of Proposition 18.1, because there exist values for the coefficients, specifically $\phi = 1$ and $\gamma = \delta = 0$, for which the error term $u_t$ is $I(0)$. It can be shown that $OLS$ estimation of [18.3.17] yields consistent estimates of all of the parameters. The coefficients $\hat{\gamma}_T$ and $\hat{\delta}_T$ each individually converge at rate $\sqrt{T}$ to a Gaussian distribution, and the $t$ test of the hypothesis that $\gamma = 0$ is asymptotically $N(0, 1)$, as is the $t$ test of the hypothesis that $\delta = 0$. However, an $F$ test of the joint null hypothesis that $\gamma$ and $\delta$ are both zero has a nonstandard limiting distribution; see Exercise 18.3. Hence, including lagged values in the regression is sufficient to solve many of the problems associated with spurious regressions, although tests of some hypotheses will still involve nonstandard distributions.

A second approach is to difference the data before estimating the relation, as in

$$\Delta y_{1t} = \alpha + \gamma \Delta y_{2t} + u_t. \qquad [18.3.18]$$

Clearly, since the regressors and error term $u_t$ are all $I(0)$ for this regression under the null hypothesis, $\hat{\alpha}_T$ and $\hat{\gamma}_T$ both converge at rate $\sqrt{T}$ to Gaussian variables. Any $t$ or $F$ test based on [18.3.18] has the usual limiting Gaussian or $\chi^2$ distribution.

A third approach, analyzed by Blough (1992), is to estimate [18.3.15] with Cochrane-Orcutt adjustment for first-order serial correlation of the residuals. We will see in Proposition 19.4 in the following chapter that if $\hat{u}_t$ denotes the sample residual from *OLS* estimation of [18.3.15], then the estimated autoregressive coefficient $\hat{\rho}_T$ from an *OLS* regression of $\hat{u}_t$ on $\hat{u}_{t-1}$ converges in probability to unity. Blough showed that the Cochrane-Orcutt *GLS* regression is then asymptotically equivalent to the differenced regression [18.3.18].

Because the specification [18.3.18] avoids the spurious regression problem as well as the nonstandard distributions for certain hypotheses associated with the levels regression [18.3.15], many researchers recommend routinely differencing apparently nonstationary variables before estimating regressions. While this is the ideal cure for the problem discussed in this section, there are two different situations in which it might be inappropriate. First, if the data are really stationary (for example, if the true value of $\phi$ in [18.3.17] is 0.9 rather than than unity), then differencing the data can result in a misspecified regression. Second, even if both $y_{1t}$ and $y_{2t}$ are truly $I(1)$ processes, there is an interesting class of models for which the bivariate dynamic relation between $y_1$ and $y_2$ will be misspecified if the researcher simply differences both $y_1$ and $y_2$. This class of models, known as *cointegrated processes*, is discussed in the following chapter.

## APPENDIX 18.A. *Proofs of Chapter 18 Propositions*

■ **Proof of Proposition 18.1.**

(a) This follows from [18.1.7] and [18.1.8] with $r = 1$.

(b) The derivation is identical to that in [11.A.3].

(c) This follows from Proposition 10.2(d).

(d) Note first in a generalization of [17.1.10] and [17.1.11] that

$$\sum_{t=1}^{T} \boldsymbol{\xi}_t\boldsymbol{\xi}_t' = \sum_{t=1}^{T} (\boldsymbol{\xi}_{t-1} + \mathbf{u}_t)(\boldsymbol{\xi}_{t-1} + \mathbf{u}_t)' = \sum_{t=1}^{T} (\boldsymbol{\xi}_{t-1}\boldsymbol{\xi}_{t-1}' + \boldsymbol{\xi}_{t-1}\mathbf{u}_t' + \mathbf{u}_t\boldsymbol{\xi}_{t-1}' + \mathbf{u}_t\mathbf{u}_t'),$$

so that

$$\begin{aligned}\sum_{t=1}^{T} (\boldsymbol{\xi}_{t-1}\mathbf{u}_t' + \mathbf{u}_t\boldsymbol{\xi}_{t-1}') &= \sum_{t=1}^{T} \boldsymbol{\xi}_t\boldsymbol{\xi}_t' - \sum_{t=1}^{T} (\boldsymbol{\xi}_{t-1}\boldsymbol{\xi}_{t-1}') - \sum_{t=1}^{T} (\mathbf{u}_t\mathbf{u}_t') \\ &= \boldsymbol{\xi}_T\boldsymbol{\xi}_T' - \boldsymbol{\xi}_0\boldsymbol{\xi}_0' - \sum_{t=1}^{T} (\mathbf{u}_t\mathbf{u}_t') \qquad [18.A.1] \\ &= \boldsymbol{\xi}_T\boldsymbol{\xi}_T' - \sum_{t=1}^{T} (\mathbf{u}_t\mathbf{u}_t').\end{aligned}$$

Dividing by $T$,

$$T^{-1}\sum_{t=1}^{T}(\boldsymbol{\xi}_{t-1}\mathbf{u}_t' + \mathbf{u}_t\boldsymbol{\xi}_{t-1}') = T^{-1}\boldsymbol{\xi}_T\boldsymbol{\xi}_T' - T^{-1}\sum_{t=1}^{T}\mathbf{u}_t\mathbf{u}_t'. \qquad [18.A.2]$$

But from [18.1.7], $\boldsymbol{\xi}_T = T\cdot\mathbf{X}_T(1)$. Hence, from [18.1.8] and the continuous mapping theorem,

$$T^{-1}\boldsymbol{\xi}_T\boldsymbol{\xi}_T' = [\sqrt{T}\cdot\mathbf{X}_T(1)]\,[\sqrt{T}\cdot\mathbf{X}_T(1)]' \xrightarrow{L} \boldsymbol{\Lambda}\cdot[\mathbf{W}(1)]\cdot[\mathbf{W}(1)]'\cdot\boldsymbol{\Lambda}'. \qquad [18.A.3]$$

Substituting this along with result (c) into [18.A.2] produces

$$T^{-1}\sum_{t=1}^{T}(\boldsymbol{\xi}_{t-1}\mathbf{u}_t' + \mathbf{u}_t\boldsymbol{\xi}_{t-1}') \xrightarrow{L} \boldsymbol{\Lambda}\cdot[\mathbf{W}(1)]\cdot[\mathbf{W}(1)]'\cdot\boldsymbol{\Lambda}' - \boldsymbol{\Gamma}_0, \qquad [18.A.4]$$

which establishes result (d) for $s = 0$.

For $s > 0$, we have

$$\begin{aligned}
T^{-1}&\sum_{t=s+1}^{T}(\boldsymbol{\xi}_{t-1}\mathbf{u}_{t-s}' + \mathbf{u}_{t-s}\boldsymbol{\xi}_{t-1}')\\
&= T^{-1}\sum_{t=s+1}^{T}[(\boldsymbol{\xi}_{t-s-1} + \mathbf{u}_{t-s} + \mathbf{u}_{t-s+1} + \cdots + \mathbf{u}_{t-1})\mathbf{u}_{t-s}'\\
&\quad + \mathbf{u}_{t-s}(\boldsymbol{\xi}_{t-s-1}' + \mathbf{u}_{t-s}' + \mathbf{u}_{t-s+1}' + \cdots + \mathbf{u}_{t-1}')]\\
&= T^{-1}\sum_{t=s+1}^{T}(\boldsymbol{\xi}_{t-s-1}\mathbf{u}_{t-s}' + \mathbf{u}_{t-s}\boldsymbol{\xi}_{t-s-1}')\\
&\quad + T^{-1}\sum_{t=s+1}^{T}[(\mathbf{u}_{t-s}\mathbf{u}_{t-s}') + (\mathbf{u}_{t-s+1}\mathbf{u}_{t-s}') + \cdots + (\mathbf{u}_{t-1}\mathbf{u}_{t-s}')\\
&\quad + (\mathbf{u}_{t-s}\mathbf{u}_{t-s}') + (\mathbf{u}_{t-s}\mathbf{u}_{t-s+1}') + \cdots + (\mathbf{u}_{t-s}\mathbf{u}_{t-1}')]\\
&\xrightarrow{L} \boldsymbol{\Lambda}\cdot[\mathbf{W}(1)]\cdot[\mathbf{W}(1)]'\cdot\boldsymbol{\Lambda}' - \boldsymbol{\Gamma}_0\\
&\quad + [\boldsymbol{\Gamma}_0 + \boldsymbol{\Gamma}_1 + \cdots + \boldsymbol{\Gamma}_{s-1} + \boldsymbol{\Gamma}_0 + \boldsymbol{\Gamma}_{-1} + \cdots + \boldsymbol{\Gamma}_{-s+1}],
\end{aligned}$$

by virtue of [18.A.4] and result (c).

(e) See Phillips (1988).

(f) Define $\boldsymbol{\xi}_t^* \equiv \boldsymbol{\varepsilon}_1 + \boldsymbol{\varepsilon}_2 + \cdots + \boldsymbol{\varepsilon}_t$ and $E(\boldsymbol{\varepsilon}_t\boldsymbol{\varepsilon}_t') = \mathbf{PP}'$. Notice that result (e) implies that

$$T^{-1}\sum_{t=1}^{T}\boldsymbol{\xi}_{t-1}^*\boldsymbol{\varepsilon}_t' \xrightarrow{L} \mathbf{P}\cdot\left\{\int_0^1 [\mathbf{W}(r)]\,[d\mathbf{W}(r)]'\right\}\cdot\mathbf{P}'. \qquad [18.A.5]$$

For $\boldsymbol{\xi}_t \equiv \mathbf{u}_1 + \mathbf{u}_2 + \cdots + \mathbf{u}_t$, equation [18.1.6] establishes that

$$\begin{aligned}
T^{-1}\sum_{t=1}^{T}\boldsymbol{\xi}_{t-1}\boldsymbol{\varepsilon}_t' &= T^{-1}\sum_{t=1}^{T}\{\boldsymbol{\Psi}(1)\cdot\boldsymbol{\xi}_{t-1}^* + \boldsymbol{\eta}_{t-1} - \boldsymbol{\eta}_0\}\cdot\boldsymbol{\varepsilon}_t'\\
&= \boldsymbol{\Psi}(1)\cdot T^{-1}\sum_{t=1}^{T}\boldsymbol{\xi}_{t-1}^*\boldsymbol{\varepsilon}_t' + T^{-1}\sum_{t=1}^{T}(\boldsymbol{\eta}_{t-1} - \boldsymbol{\eta}_0)\cdot\boldsymbol{\varepsilon}_t'.
\end{aligned} \qquad [18.A.6]$$

But each column of $\{(\boldsymbol{\eta}_{t-1} - \boldsymbol{\eta}_0)\cdot\boldsymbol{\varepsilon}_t'\}_{t=1}^T$ is a martingale difference sequence with finite variance, and so, from Example 7.11 of Chapter 7,

$$T^{-1}\sum_{t=1}^{T}(\boldsymbol{\eta}_{t-1} - \boldsymbol{\eta}_0)\cdot\boldsymbol{\varepsilon}_t' \xrightarrow{p} \mathbf{0}. \qquad [18.A.7]$$

Substituting [18.A.5] and [18.A.7] into [18.A.6] produces

$$T^{-1}\sum_{t=1}^{T}\boldsymbol{\xi}_{t-1}\boldsymbol{\varepsilon}_t' \xrightarrow{L} \boldsymbol{\Psi}(1)\cdot\mathbf{P}\cdot\left\{\int_0^1 [\mathbf{W}(r)]\,[d\mathbf{W}(r)]'\right\}\cdot\mathbf{P}',$$

as claimed.

(g) This was shown in [18.1.9].

(h) As in [17.3.17], we have

$$T^{-3/2}\sum_{t=1}^{T}\boldsymbol{\xi}_{t-1} = T^{-1/2}\sum_{t=1}^{T}\mathbf{u}_t - T^{-3/2}\sum_{t=1}^{T}t\mathbf{u}_t$$

or

$$T^{-3/2}\sum_{t=1}^{T} t\mathbf{u}_t = T^{-1/2}\sum_{t=1}^{T}\mathbf{u}_t - T^{-3/2}\sum_{t=1}^{T}\boldsymbol{\xi}_{t-1} \xrightarrow{L} \boldsymbol{\Lambda}\cdot\mathbf{W}(1) - \boldsymbol{\Lambda}\cdot\int_0^1 \mathbf{W}(r)\,dr, \qquad [18.A.8]$$

from results (a) and (g). This establishes result (h) for $s = 0$. The asymptotic distribution is the same for any $s$, from simple adaptation of the proof of Proposition 17.3(g).

(i) As in [17.3.22],

$$T^{-2}\sum_{t=1}^{T}\boldsymbol{\xi}_{t-1}\boldsymbol{\xi}_{t-1}' = \int_0^1 [\sqrt{T}\cdot\mathbf{X}_T(r)]\cdot[\sqrt{T}\cdot\mathbf{X}_T(r)]'\,dr$$

$$\xrightarrow{L} \boldsymbol{\Lambda}\cdot\left\{\int_0^1 [\mathbf{W}(r)]\cdot[\mathbf{W}(r)]'\,dr\right\}\cdot\boldsymbol{\Lambda}'.$$

(j), (k), and (l) parallel Proposition 17.3(i), (j), and (k). ■

■ **Proof of Proposition 18.2.** The asymptotic distributions are easier to calculate if we work with the following transformed variables:

$$y_{1t}^* \equiv y_{1t} - \boldsymbol{\Sigma}_{21}'\boldsymbol{\Sigma}_{22}^{-1}\mathbf{y}_{2t} \qquad [18.A.9]$$

$$\mathbf{y}_{2t}^* \equiv \mathbf{L}_{22}'\mathbf{y}_{2t}. \qquad [18.A.10]$$

Note that the inverses $\boldsymbol{\Sigma}_{22}^{-1}$, $(\sigma_1^*)^{-1}$, and $\mathbf{L}_{22}^{-1}$ all exist, since $\boldsymbol{\Lambda}\boldsymbol{\Lambda}'$ is symmetric positive definite. An *OLS* regression of $y_{1t}^*$ on a constant and $\mathbf{y}_{2t}^*$,

$$y_{1t}^* = \alpha^* + \boldsymbol{\gamma}^{*\prime}\mathbf{y}_{2t}^* + u_t^*, \qquad [18.A.11]$$

would yield estimates

$$\begin{bmatrix}\hat{\alpha}_T^*\\ \hat{\boldsymbol{\gamma}}_T^*\end{bmatrix} = \begin{bmatrix} T & \Sigma\mathbf{y}_{2t}^{*\prime}\\ \Sigma\mathbf{y}_{2t}^* & \Sigma\mathbf{y}_{2t}^*\mathbf{y}_{2t}^{*\prime}\end{bmatrix}^{-1}\begin{bmatrix}\Sigma y_{1t}^*\\ \Sigma\mathbf{y}_{2t}^* y_{1t}^*\end{bmatrix}. \qquad [18.A.12]$$

Clearly, the residuals from *OLS* estimation of [18.A.11] are identical to those from *OLS* estimation of [18.3.1]:

$$\begin{aligned} y_{1t} - \hat{\alpha}_T - \hat{\boldsymbol{\gamma}}_T'\mathbf{y}_{2t} &= y_{1t}^* - \hat{\alpha}_T^* - \hat{\boldsymbol{\gamma}}_T^{*\prime}\mathbf{y}_{2t}^*\\ &= (y_{1t} - \boldsymbol{\Sigma}_{21}'\boldsymbol{\Sigma}_{22}^{-1}\mathbf{y}_{2t}) - \hat{\alpha}_T^* - \hat{\boldsymbol{\gamma}}_T^{*\prime}(\mathbf{L}_{22}'\mathbf{y}_{2t})\\ &= y_{1t} - \hat{\alpha}_T^* - \{\hat{\boldsymbol{\gamma}}_T^{*\prime}\mathbf{L}_{22}' + \boldsymbol{\Sigma}_{21}'\boldsymbol{\Sigma}_{22}^{-1}\}\mathbf{y}_{2t}.\end{aligned}$$

The *OLS* estimates for the transformed regression [18.A.11] are thus related to those of the original regression [18.3.1] by

$$\begin{aligned}\hat{\alpha}_T &= \hat{\alpha}_T^*\\ \hat{\boldsymbol{\gamma}}_T &= \mathbf{L}_{22}\hat{\boldsymbol{\gamma}}_T^* + \boldsymbol{\Sigma}_{22}^{-1}\boldsymbol{\Sigma}_{21},\end{aligned} \qquad [18.A.13]$$

implying that

$$\begin{aligned}\hat{\boldsymbol{\gamma}}_T^* &= \mathbf{L}_{22}^{-1}\hat{\boldsymbol{\gamma}}_T - \mathbf{L}_{22}^{-1}\boldsymbol{\Sigma}_{22}^{-1}\boldsymbol{\Sigma}_{21}\\ &= \mathbf{L}_{22}^{-1}\hat{\boldsymbol{\gamma}}_T - \mathbf{L}_{22}^{-1}(\mathbf{L}_{22}\mathbf{L}_{22}')\boldsymbol{\Sigma}_{21}\\ &= \mathbf{L}_{22}^{-1}\hat{\boldsymbol{\gamma}}_T - \mathbf{L}_{22}'\boldsymbol{\Sigma}_{21}.\end{aligned} \qquad [18.A.14]$$

The usefulness of this transformation is as follows. Notice that

$$\begin{bmatrix} y_{1t}^*/\sigma_1^*\\ \mathbf{y}_{2t}^*\end{bmatrix} = \begin{bmatrix}(1/\sigma_1^*) & (-1/\sigma_1^*)\cdot\boldsymbol{\Sigma}_{21}'\boldsymbol{\Sigma}_{22}^{-1}\\ \mathbf{0} & \mathbf{L}_{22}'\end{bmatrix}\begin{bmatrix} y_{1t}\\ \mathbf{y}_{2t}\end{bmatrix} \equiv \mathbf{L}'\mathbf{y}_t$$

for

$$\mathbf{L}' \equiv \begin{bmatrix}(1/\sigma_1^*) & (-1/\sigma_1^*)\cdot\boldsymbol{\Sigma}_{21}'\boldsymbol{\Sigma}_{22}^{-1}\\ \mathbf{0} & \mathbf{L}_{22}'\end{bmatrix}.$$

Moreover,

$$\mathbf{L}'\boldsymbol{\Lambda}\boldsymbol{\Lambda}'\mathbf{L} = \begin{bmatrix} (1/\sigma_1^*) & (-1/\sigma_1^*)\cdot\boldsymbol{\Sigma}_{21}'\boldsymbol{\Sigma}_{22}^{-1} \\ \mathbf{0} & \mathbf{L}_{22}' \end{bmatrix} \begin{bmatrix} \Sigma_{11} & \boldsymbol{\Sigma}_{21}' \\ \boldsymbol{\Sigma}_{21} & \boldsymbol{\Sigma}_{22} \end{bmatrix} \begin{bmatrix} (1/\sigma_1^*) & \mathbf{0}' \\ (-1/\sigma_1^*)\cdot\boldsymbol{\Sigma}_{22}^{-1}\boldsymbol{\Sigma}_{21} & \mathbf{L}_{22} \end{bmatrix}$$
$$= \begin{bmatrix} (1/\sigma_1^*)\cdot(\Sigma_{11} - \boldsymbol{\Sigma}_{21}'\boldsymbol{\Sigma}_{22}^{-1}\boldsymbol{\Sigma}_{21}) & \mathbf{0}' \\ \mathbf{L}_{22}'\boldsymbol{\Sigma}_{21} & \mathbf{L}_{22}'\boldsymbol{\Sigma}_{22} \end{bmatrix} \begin{bmatrix} (1/\sigma_1^*) & \mathbf{0}' \\ (-1/\sigma_1^*)\cdot\boldsymbol{\Sigma}_{22}^{-1}\boldsymbol{\Sigma}_{21} & \mathbf{L}_{22} \end{bmatrix}$$
$$= \begin{bmatrix} (\Sigma_{11} - \boldsymbol{\Sigma}_{21}'\boldsymbol{\Sigma}_{22}^{-1}\boldsymbol{\Sigma}_{21})/(\sigma_1^*)^2 & \mathbf{0}' \\ \mathbf{0} & \mathbf{L}_{22}'\boldsymbol{\Sigma}_{22}\mathbf{L}_{22} \end{bmatrix}. \qquad [18.A.15]$$

But [18.3.7] implies that

$$\boldsymbol{\Sigma}_{22} = (\mathbf{L}_{22}\mathbf{L}_{22}')^{-1} = (\mathbf{L}_{22}')^{-1}\mathbf{L}_{22}^{-1},$$

from which

$$\mathbf{L}_{22}'\boldsymbol{\Sigma}_{22}\mathbf{L}_{22} = \mathbf{L}_{22}'\{(\mathbf{L}_{22}')^{-1}\mathbf{L}_{22}^{-1}\}\mathbf{L}_{22} = \mathbf{I}_g.$$

Substituting this and [18.3.6] into [18.A.15] results in

$$\mathbf{L}'\boldsymbol{\Lambda}\boldsymbol{\Lambda}'\mathbf{L} = \mathbf{I}_n. \qquad [18.A.16]$$

One of the implications is that if $\mathbf{W}(r)$ is $n$-dimensional standard Brownian motion, then the $n$-dimensional process $\mathbf{W}^*(r)$ defined by

$$\mathbf{W}^*(r) \equiv \mathbf{L}'\boldsymbol{\Lambda}\cdot\mathbf{W}(r) \qquad [18.A.17]$$

is Brownian motion with variance matrix $\mathbf{L}'\boldsymbol{\Lambda}\boldsymbol{\Lambda}'\mathbf{L} = \mathbf{I}_n$. In other words, $\mathbf{W}^*(r)$ could also be described as standard Brownian motion. Since result (g) of Proposition 18.1 implies that

$$T^{-3/2}\sum_{t=1}^{T}\mathbf{y}_t \xrightarrow{L} \boldsymbol{\Lambda}\cdot\int_0^1 \mathbf{W}(r)\,dr,$$

it follows that

$$\begin{bmatrix} T^{-3/2}\Sigma y_{1t}^*/\sigma_1^* \\ T^{-3/2}\Sigma\mathbf{y}_{2t}^* \end{bmatrix} = T^{-3/2}\sum_{t=1}^{T}\mathbf{L}'\mathbf{y}_t \xrightarrow{L} \mathbf{L}'\boldsymbol{\Lambda}\cdot\int_0^1 \mathbf{W}(r)\,dr = \int_0^1 \mathbf{W}^*(r)\,dr. \qquad [18.A.18]$$

Similarly, result (i) of Proposition 18.1 gives

$$\begin{bmatrix} T^{-2}\Sigma(y_{1t}^*)^2/(\sigma_1^*)^2 & T^{-2}\Sigma y_{1t}^*\mathbf{y}_{2t}^{*\prime}/\sigma_1^* \\ T^{-2}\Sigma\mathbf{y}_{2t}^*y_{1t}^*/\sigma_1^* & T^{-2}\Sigma\mathbf{y}_{2t}^*\mathbf{y}_{2t}^{*\prime} \end{bmatrix}$$
$$= \mathbf{L}'\cdot T^{-2}\sum_{t=1}^{T}\mathbf{y}_t\mathbf{y}_t'\cdot\mathbf{L}$$
$$\xrightarrow{L} \mathbf{L}'\boldsymbol{\Lambda}\cdot\left\{\int_0^1 [\mathbf{W}(r)]\cdot[\mathbf{W}(r)]'\,dr\right\}\cdot\boldsymbol{\Lambda}'\mathbf{L} \qquad [18.A.19]$$
$$= \int_0^1 [\mathbf{W}^*(r)]\cdot[\mathbf{W}^*(r)]'\,dr.$$

It is now straightforward to prove the claims in Proposition 18.2.

**Proof of (a).** If [18.A.12] is divided by $\sigma_1^*$ and premultiplied by the matrix

$$\begin{bmatrix} T^{-1/2} & \mathbf{0}' \\ \mathbf{0} & \mathbf{I}_g \end{bmatrix},$$

the result is

$$\begin{bmatrix} T^{-1/2} & \mathbf{0}' \\ \mathbf{0} & \mathbf{I}_g \end{bmatrix} \begin{bmatrix} \hat{\alpha}_T^*/\sigma_1^* \\ \hat{\boldsymbol{\gamma}}_T^*/\sigma_1^* \end{bmatrix}$$

$$= \begin{bmatrix} T^{-1/2} & \mathbf{0}' \\ \mathbf{0} & \mathbf{I}_g \end{bmatrix} \begin{bmatrix} T & \Sigma \mathbf{y}_{2t}^{*\prime} \\ \Sigma \mathbf{y}_{2t}^* & \Sigma \mathbf{y}_{2t}^* \mathbf{y}_{2t}^{*\prime} \end{bmatrix}^{-1} \begin{bmatrix} T^{-3/2} & \mathbf{0}' \\ \mathbf{0} & T^{-2}\mathbf{I}_g \end{bmatrix}^{-1} \begin{bmatrix} T^{-3/2} & \mathbf{0}' \\ \mathbf{0} & T^{-2}\mathbf{I}_g \end{bmatrix} \begin{bmatrix} \Sigma y_{1t}^*/\sigma_1^* \\ \Sigma \mathbf{y}_{2t}^* y_{1t}^*/\sigma_1^* \end{bmatrix}$$

$$= \left( \begin{bmatrix} T^{-3/2} & \mathbf{0}' \\ \mathbf{0} & T^{-2}\mathbf{I}_g \end{bmatrix} \begin{bmatrix} T & \Sigma \mathbf{y}_{2t}^{*\prime} \\ \Sigma \mathbf{y}_{2t}^* & \Sigma \mathbf{y}_{2t}^* \mathbf{y}_{2t}^{*\prime} \end{bmatrix} \begin{bmatrix} T^{1/2} & \mathbf{0}' \\ \mathbf{0} & \mathbf{I}_g \end{bmatrix} \right)^{-1} \left( \begin{bmatrix} T^{-3/2} & \mathbf{0}' \\ \mathbf{0} & T^{-2}\mathbf{I}_g \end{bmatrix} \begin{bmatrix} \Sigma y_{1t}^*/\sigma_1^* \\ \Sigma \mathbf{y}_{2t}^* y_{1t}^*/\sigma_1^* \end{bmatrix} \right)$$

or

$$\begin{bmatrix} T^{-1/2}\hat{\alpha}_T^*/\sigma_1^* \\ \hat{\boldsymbol{\gamma}}_T^*/\sigma_1^* \end{bmatrix} = \begin{bmatrix} 1 & T^{-3/2}\Sigma \mathbf{y}_{2t}^{*\prime} \\ T^{-3/2}\Sigma \mathbf{y}_{2t}^* & T^{-2}\Sigma \mathbf{y}_{2t}^* \mathbf{y}_{2t}^{*\prime} \end{bmatrix}^{-1} \begin{bmatrix} T^{-3/2}\Sigma y_{1t}^*/\sigma_1^* \\ T^{-2}\Sigma \mathbf{y}_{2t}^* y_{1t}^*/\sigma_1^* \end{bmatrix}. \qquad [18.A.20]$$

Partition $\mathbf{W}^*(r)$ as

$$\underset{(n\times 1)}{\mathbf{W}^*(r)} = \begin{bmatrix} \underset{(1\times 1)}{W_1^*(r)} \\ \underset{(g\times 1)}{\mathbf{W}_2^*(r)} \end{bmatrix}.$$

Applying [18.A.18] and [18.A.19] to [18.A.20] results in

$$\begin{bmatrix} T^{-1/2}\hat{\alpha}_T^*/\sigma_1^* \\ \hat{\boldsymbol{\gamma}}_T^*/\sigma_1^* \end{bmatrix} \xrightarrow{L} \begin{bmatrix} 1 & \int [\mathbf{W}_2^*(r)]'\,dr \\ \int \mathbf{W}_2^*(r)\,dr & \int [\mathbf{W}_2^*(r)]\cdot[\mathbf{W}_2^*(r)]'\,dr \end{bmatrix}^{-1} \begin{bmatrix} \int W_1^*(r)\,dr \\ \int \mathbf{W}_2^*(r)\cdot W_1^*(r)\,dr \end{bmatrix} \qquad [18.A.21]$$

$$\equiv \begin{bmatrix} h_1 \\ \mathbf{h}_2 \end{bmatrix}.$$

Recalling the relation between the transformed estimates and the original estimates given in [18.A.14], this establishes that

$$\begin{bmatrix} T^{-1/2}\hat{\alpha}_T/\sigma_1^* \\ (1/\sigma_1^*)\cdot[\mathbf{L}_{22}^{-1}\hat{\boldsymbol{\gamma}}_T - \mathbf{L}_{22}'\boldsymbol{\Sigma}_{21}] \end{bmatrix} \xrightarrow{L} \begin{bmatrix} h_1 \\ \mathbf{h}_2 \end{bmatrix}.$$

Premultiplying by

$$\begin{bmatrix} \sigma_1^* & \mathbf{0}' \\ \mathbf{0} & \sigma_1^*\mathbf{L}_{22} \end{bmatrix}$$

and recalling [18.3.7] produces [18.3.8].

**Proof of (b).** Again we exploit the fact that *OLS* estimation of [18.A.11] would produce the identical residuals that would result from *OLS* estimation of [18.3.1]. Recall the expression for the residual sum of squares in [4.A.6]:

$$RSS_T = \Sigma(y_{1t}^*)^2 - \left\{ [\Sigma y_{1t}^* \quad \Sigma y_{1t}^* \mathbf{y}_{2t}^{*\prime}] \begin{bmatrix} T & \Sigma \mathbf{y}_{2t}^{*\prime} \\ \Sigma \mathbf{y}_{2t}^* & \Sigma \mathbf{y}_{2t}^* \mathbf{y}_{2t}^{*\prime} \end{bmatrix}^{-1} \begin{bmatrix} \Sigma y_{1t}^* \\ \Sigma y_{1t}^* \mathbf{y}_{2t}^* \end{bmatrix} \right\}$$

$$= \Sigma(y_{1t}^*)^2 - \left\{ [\Sigma y_{1t}^* \quad \Sigma y_{1t}^* \mathbf{y}_{2t}^{*\prime}] \begin{bmatrix} T^{1/2} & \mathbf{0}' \\ \mathbf{0} & \mathbf{I}_g \end{bmatrix} \right.$$

$$\left. \times \left( \begin{bmatrix} T^{-3/2} & \mathbf{0}' \\ \mathbf{0} & T^{-2}\mathbf{I}_g \end{bmatrix} \begin{bmatrix} T & \Sigma \mathbf{y}_{2t}^{*\prime} \\ \Sigma \mathbf{y}_{2t}^* & \Sigma \mathbf{y}_{2t}^* \mathbf{y}_{2t}^{*\prime} \end{bmatrix} \begin{bmatrix} T^{1/2} & \mathbf{0}' \\ \mathbf{0} & \mathbf{I}_g \end{bmatrix} \right)^{-1} \begin{bmatrix} T^{-3/2} & \mathbf{0}' \\ \mathbf{0} & T^{-2}\mathbf{I}_g \end{bmatrix} \begin{bmatrix} \Sigma y_{1t}^* \\ \Sigma y_{1t}^* \mathbf{y}_{2t}^* \end{bmatrix} \right\}.$$

[18.A.22]

If both sides of [18.A.22] are divided by $(T\cdot\sigma_1^*)^2$, the result is

$$T^{-2}\cdot RSS_T/(\sigma_1^*)^2$$

$$= T^{-2}\Sigma(y_{1t}^*/\sigma_1^*)^2 - \left\{[T^{-3/2}\Sigma(y_{1t}^*/\sigma_1^*) \quad T^{-2}\Sigma(y_{1t}^*/\sigma_1^*)\mathbf{y}_{2t}^{*\prime}]\right.$$

$$\left.\times \begin{bmatrix} 1 & T^{-3/2}\Sigma\mathbf{y}_{2t}^{*\prime} \\ T^{-3/2}\Sigma\mathbf{y}_{2t}^* & T^{-2}\Sigma\mathbf{y}_{2t}^*\mathbf{y}_{2t}^{*\prime} \end{bmatrix}^{-1} \begin{bmatrix} T^{-3/2}\Sigma y_{1t}^*/\sigma_1^* \\ T^{-2}\Sigma\mathbf{y}_{2t}^* y_{1t}/\sigma_1^* \end{bmatrix}\right\}$$

$$\xrightarrow{L} \int [W_1^*(r)]^2\,dr - \left\{\left[\int W_1^*(r)\,dr \quad \int [W_1^*(r)]\cdot[\mathbf{W}_2^*(r)]'\,dr\right]\right.$$

$$\left.\times \begin{bmatrix} 1 & \int [\mathbf{W}_2^*(r)]'\,dr \\ \int \mathbf{W}_2^*(r)\,dr & \int [\mathbf{W}_2^*(r)]\cdot[\mathbf{W}_2^*(r)]'\,dr \end{bmatrix}^{-1} \begin{bmatrix} \int W_1^*(r)\,dr \\ \int [\mathbf{W}_2^*(r)]\cdot[W_1^*(r)]\,dr \end{bmatrix}\right\}.$$

**Proof of (c).** Note that an $F$ test of the hypothesis $H_0$: $\mathbf{R}\boldsymbol{\gamma} = \mathbf{r}$ for the original regression [18.3.1] would produce exactly the same value as an $F$ test of $\mathbf{R}^*\boldsymbol{\gamma}^* = \mathbf{r}^*$ for $OLS$ estimation of [18.A.11], where, from [18.A.13],

$$\mathbf{R}\boldsymbol{\gamma} - \mathbf{r} = \mathbf{R}\{\mathbf{L}_{22}\boldsymbol{\gamma}^* + \boldsymbol{\Sigma}_{22}^{-1}\boldsymbol{\Sigma}_{21}\} - \mathbf{r} = \mathbf{R}^*\boldsymbol{\gamma}^* - \mathbf{r}^*$$

for

$$\mathbf{R}^* \equiv \mathbf{R}\cdot\mathbf{L}_{22} \qquad [18.A.23]$$

$$\mathbf{r}^* \equiv \mathbf{r} - \mathbf{R}\boldsymbol{\Sigma}_{22}^{-1}\boldsymbol{\Sigma}_{21}. \qquad [18.A.24]$$

The $OLS$ $F$ test of $\mathbf{R}^*\boldsymbol{\gamma}^* = \mathbf{r}^*$ is given by

$$F_T = \{\mathbf{R}^*\hat{\boldsymbol{\gamma}}_T^* - \mathbf{r}^*\}'$$

$$\times \left\{[s_T^*]^2\cdot[\mathbf{0} \quad \mathbf{R}^*]\begin{bmatrix} T & \Sigma\mathbf{y}_{2t}^{*\prime} \\ \Sigma\mathbf{y}_{2t}^* & \Sigma\mathbf{y}_{2t}^*\mathbf{y}_{2t}^{*\prime} \end{bmatrix}^{-1}\begin{bmatrix} \mathbf{0}' \\ \mathbf{R}^{*\prime} \end{bmatrix}\right\}^{-1} \{\mathbf{R}^*\hat{\boldsymbol{\gamma}}_T^* - \mathbf{r}^*\} \div m,$$

from which

$$T^{-1}\cdot F_T = \{\mathbf{R}^*\hat{\boldsymbol{\gamma}}_T^* - \mathbf{r}^*\}'$$

$$\times \left\{T^{-1}\cdot[s_T^*]^2\cdot[\mathbf{0} \quad \mathbf{R}^*]\begin{bmatrix} T^{1/2} & \mathbf{0}' \\ \mathbf{0} & T\cdot\mathbf{I}_g \end{bmatrix}\begin{bmatrix} T & \Sigma\mathbf{y}_{2t}^{*\prime} \\ \Sigma\mathbf{y}_{2t}^* & \Sigma\mathbf{y}_{2t}^*\mathbf{y}_{2t}^{*\prime} \end{bmatrix}^{-1}\right.$$

$$\left.\times \begin{bmatrix} T^{1/2} & \mathbf{0}' \\ \mathbf{0} & T\cdot\mathbf{I}_g \end{bmatrix}\begin{bmatrix} \mathbf{0}' \\ \mathbf{R}^{*\prime} \end{bmatrix}\right\}^{-1} \{\mathbf{R}^*\hat{\boldsymbol{\gamma}}_T^* - \mathbf{r}^*\} \div m \qquad [18.A.25]$$

$$= \{\mathbf{R}^*\hat{\boldsymbol{\gamma}}_T^* - \mathbf{r}^*\}'\left\{T^{-1}\cdot[s_T^*]^2\cdot[\mathbf{0} \quad \mathbf{R}^*]\right.$$

$$\left.\times \begin{bmatrix} 1 & T^{-3/2}\Sigma\mathbf{y}_{2t}^{*\prime} \\ T^{-3/2}\Sigma\mathbf{y}_{2t}^* & T^{-2}\Sigma\mathbf{y}_{2t}^*\mathbf{y}_{2t}^{*\prime} \end{bmatrix}^{-1}\begin{bmatrix} \mathbf{0}' \\ \mathbf{R}^{*\prime} \end{bmatrix}\right\}^{-1} \{\mathbf{R}^*\hat{\boldsymbol{\gamma}}_T^* - \mathbf{r}^*\} \div m.$$

But

$$[s_T^*]^2 = (T - n)^{-1}\sum_{t=1}^{T}(\hat{u}_t^*)^2 = (T - n)^{-1}\sum_{t=1}^{T}\hat{u}_t^2,$$

and so, from result (b),

$$T^{-1}\cdot[s_T^*]^2 = [T/(T-n)]\cdot T^{-2}\cdot RSS_T \xrightarrow{L} (\sigma_1^*)^2\cdot H. \qquad [18.A.26]$$

Moreover, [18.A.18] and [18.A.19] imply that

$$\begin{bmatrix} 1 & T^{-3/2}\Sigma \mathbf{y}_{2t}^{*\prime} \\ T^{-3/2}\Sigma \mathbf{y}_{2t}^* & T^{-2}\Sigma \mathbf{y}_{2t}^*\mathbf{y}_{2t}^{*\prime} \end{bmatrix}^{-1} \xrightarrow{L} \begin{bmatrix} 1 & \int [\mathbf{W}_2^*(r)]'\,dr \\ \int \mathbf{W}_2^*(r)\,dr & \int [\mathbf{W}_2^*(r)]\cdot[\mathbf{W}_2^*(r)]'\,dr \end{bmatrix}^{-1}, \qquad [18.A.27]$$

while from [18.A.21],

$$\hat{\boldsymbol{\gamma}}_T^* \xrightarrow{L} \sigma_1^*\cdot\mathbf{h}_2. \qquad [18.A.28]$$

Substituting [18.A.26] through [18.A.28] into [18.A.25], we conclude that

$$T^{-1}\cdot F_T \xrightarrow{L} \{\sigma_1^*\cdot\mathbf{R}^*\mathbf{h}_2 - \mathbf{r}^*\}' \times \Biggl\{(\sigma_1^*)^2\cdot H[\mathbf{0} \quad \mathbf{R}^*]$$

$$\times \begin{bmatrix} 1 & \int [\mathbf{W}_2^*(r)]'\,dr \\ \int \mathbf{W}_2^*(r)\,dr & \int [\mathbf{W}_2^*(r)]\cdot[\mathbf{W}_2^*(r)]'\,dr \end{bmatrix}^{-1} \begin{bmatrix} \mathbf{0}' \\ \mathbf{R}^{*\prime} \end{bmatrix}\Biggr\}^{-1} \{\sigma_1^*\cdot\mathbf{R}^*\mathbf{h}_2 - \mathbf{r}^*\} \div m. \quad \blacksquare$$

## Chapter 18 Exercises

18.1. Consider *OLS* estimation of

$$y_{it} = \boldsymbol{\zeta}_{i1}'\Delta\mathbf{y}_{t-1} + \boldsymbol{\zeta}_{i2}'\Delta\mathbf{y}_{t-2} + \cdots + \boldsymbol{\zeta}_{i,p-1}'\Delta\mathbf{y}_{t-p+1} + \alpha_i + \boldsymbol{\rho}_i'\mathbf{y}_{t-1} + \varepsilon_{it},$$

where $y_{it}$ is the $i$th element of the $(n \times 1)$ vector $\mathbf{y}_t$ and $\varepsilon_{it}$ is the $i$th element of the $(n \times 1)$ vector $\boldsymbol{\varepsilon}_t$. Assume that $\boldsymbol{\varepsilon}_t$ is i.i.d. with mean zero, positive definite variance $\boldsymbol{\Omega}$, and finite fourth moments and that $\Delta\mathbf{y}_t = \boldsymbol{\Psi}(L)\boldsymbol{\varepsilon}_t$, where the sequence of $(n \times n)$ matrices $\{s\cdot\boldsymbol{\Psi}_s\}_{s=0}^{\infty}$ is asolutely summable and $\boldsymbol{\Psi}(1)$ is nonsingular. Let $k = np + 1$ denote the number of regressors, and define

$$\mathbf{x}_t \equiv (\Delta\mathbf{y}_{t-1}', \Delta\mathbf{y}_{t-2}', \ldots, \Delta\mathbf{y}_{t-p+1}', 1, \mathbf{y}_{t-1}')'.$$

Let $\mathbf{b}_T$ denote the $(k \times 1)$ vector of estimated coefficients:

$$\mathbf{b}_T = (\Sigma\mathbf{x}_t\mathbf{x}_t')^{-1}(\Sigma\mathbf{x}_t y_{it}),$$

where $\Sigma$ denotes summation over $t$ from 1 to $T$. Consider any null hypothesis $H_0$: $\mathbf{R}\boldsymbol{\beta} = \mathbf{r}$ that involves only the coefficients on $\Delta\mathbf{y}_{t-s}$—that is, $\mathbf{R}$ is of the form

$$\underset{(m\times k)}{\mathbf{R}} = \begin{bmatrix} \underset{[m\times n(p-1)]}{\mathbf{R}_1} & \underset{[m\times(1+n)]}{\mathbf{0}} \end{bmatrix}.$$

Let $\chi_T^2$ be the Wald form of the *OLS* $\chi^2$ test of $H_0$:

$$\chi_T^2 \equiv (\mathbf{R}\mathbf{b}_T - \mathbf{r})'[s_T^2\mathbf{R}(\Sigma\mathbf{x}_t\mathbf{x}_t')^{-1}\mathbf{R}']^{-1}(\mathbf{R}\mathbf{b}_T - \mathbf{r}),$$

where

$$s_T^2 \equiv (T-k)^{-1}\Sigma(y_{it} - \mathbf{b}_T'\mathbf{x}_t)^2.$$

Under the maintained hypothesis that $\alpha_i = 0$ and $\boldsymbol{\rho}_i' = \mathbf{e}_i'$ (where $\mathbf{e}_i'$ denotes the $i$th row of $\mathbf{I}_n$), show that $\chi_T^2 \xrightarrow{L} \chi^2(m)$.

18.2. Suppose that the regression model

$$y_{it} = \boldsymbol{\zeta}_{i1}'\Delta\mathbf{y}_{t-1} + \boldsymbol{\zeta}_{i2}'\Delta\mathbf{y}_{t-2} + \cdots + \boldsymbol{\zeta}_{i,p-1}'\Delta\mathbf{y}_{t-p+1} + \alpha_i + \boldsymbol{\rho}_i'\mathbf{y}_{t-1} + \varepsilon_{it}$$

satisfies the conditions of Exercise 18.1. Partition this regression as in [18.2.37]:

$$\begin{aligned} y_{it} &= \boldsymbol{\beta}_1'\Delta\mathbf{y}_{1,t-1} + \boldsymbol{\gamma}_1'\Delta\mathbf{y}_{2,t-1} + \boldsymbol{\beta}_2'\Delta\mathbf{y}_{1,t-2} + \boldsymbol{\gamma}_2'\Delta\mathbf{y}_{2,t-2} + \cdots \\ &+ \boldsymbol{\beta}_{p-1}'\Delta\mathbf{y}_{1,t-p+1} + \boldsymbol{\gamma}_{p-1}'\Delta\mathbf{y}_{2,t-p+1} + \alpha_i + \boldsymbol{\eta}'\mathbf{y}_{1,t-1} \\ &+ \boldsymbol{\delta}'\mathbf{y}_{2,t-1} + \varepsilon_{it}, \end{aligned}$$

where $\mathbf{y}_{1t}$ is an $(n_1 \times 1)$ vector and $\mathbf{y}_{2t}$ is an $(n_2 \times 1)$ vector with $n_1 + n_2 = n$. Consider the null hypothesis $\boldsymbol{\gamma}_1 = \boldsymbol{\gamma}_2 = \cdots = \boldsymbol{\gamma}_{p-1} = \boldsymbol{\delta} = \mathbf{0}$. Describe the asymptotic distribution of the Wald form of the *OLS* $\chi^2$ test of this null hypothesis.

18.3. Consider *OLS* estimation of

$$y_{1t} = \gamma\Delta y_{2t} + \alpha + \phi y_{1,t-1} + \eta y_{2,t-1} + u_t,$$

where $y_{1t}$ and $y_{2t}$ are independent random walks as specified in [18.3.13] and [18.3.14]. Note that the fitted values of this regression are identical to those for [18.3.17] with $\hat{\alpha}_T$, $\hat{\gamma}_T$, and $\hat{\phi}_T$ the same for both regressions and $\hat{\delta}_T = \hat{\eta}_T - \hat{\gamma}_T$.

(a) Show that

$$\begin{bmatrix} T^{1/2}\hat{\gamma}_T \\ T^{1/2}\hat{\alpha}_T \\ T(\hat{\phi}_T - 1) \\ T\hat{\eta}_T \end{bmatrix} \xrightarrow{L} \begin{bmatrix} v_1 \\ v_2 \\ v_3 \\ v_4 \end{bmatrix},$$

where $v_1 \sim N(0, \sigma_1^2/\sigma_2^2)$ and $(v_2, v_3, v_4)'$ has a nonstandard limiting distribution. Conclude that $\hat{\gamma}_T$, $\hat{\alpha}_T$, $\hat{\phi}_T$, and $\hat{\eta}_T$ are consistent estimates of 0, 0, 1, and 0, respectively, meaning that all of the estimated coefficients in [18.3.17] are consistent.

(b) Show that the $t$ test of the null hypothesis that $\gamma = 0$ is asymptotically $N(0, 1)$.

(c) Show that the $t$ test of the null hypothesis that $\delta = 0$ in the regression model of [18.3.17] is also asymptotically $N(0, 1)$.

## *Chapter 18 References*


Blough, Stephen R. 1992. "Spurious Regressions, with AR(1) Correction and Unit Root Pretest." Johns Hopkins University. Mimeo.

Chan, N. H., and C. Z. Wei. 1988. "Limiting Distributions of Least Squares Estimates of Unstable Autoregressive Processes." *Annals of Statistics* 16:367–401.

Granger, C. W. J., and Paul Newbold. 1974. "Spurious Regressions in Econometrics." *Journal of Econometrics* 2:111–20.

Ohanian, Lee E. 1988. "The Spurious Effects of Unit Roots on Vector Autoregressions: A Monte Carlo Study." *Journal of Econometrics* 39:251–66.

Park, Joon Y., and Peter C. B. Phillips. 1988. "Statistical Inference in Regressions with Integrated Processes: Part 1." *Econometric Theory* 4:468–97.

——— and ———. 1989. "Statistical Inference in Regressions with Integrated Processes: Part 2." *Econometric Theory* 5:95–131.

Phillips, Peter C. B. 1986. "Understanding Spurious Regressions in Econometrics." *Journal of Econometrics* 33:311–40.

———. 1988. "Weak Convergence of Sample Covariance Matrices to Stochastic Integrals via Martingale Approximations." *Econometric Theory* 4:528–33.

——— and S. N. Durlauf. 1986. "Multiple Time Series Regression with Integrated Processes." *Review of Economic Studies* 53:473–95.

——— and Victor Solo. 1992. "Asymptotics for Linear Processes." *Annals of Statistics* 20:971–1001.

Sims, Christopher A., James H. Stock, and Mark W. Watson. 1990. "Inference in Linear Time Series Models with Some Unit Roots." *Econometrica* 58:113–44.

Toda, H. Y., and P. C. B. Phillips. 1993a. "The Spurious Effect of Unit Roots on Exogeneity

Tests in Vector Autoregressions: An Analytical Study." *Journal of Econometrics* 59:229–55.
——— and ———. 1993b. "Vector Autoregressions and Causality." *Econometrica* forthcoming.
West, Kenneth D. 1988. "Asymptotic Normality, When Regressors Have a Unit Root." *Econometrica* 56:1397–1417.

# 19 Cointegration

This chapter discusses a particular class of vector unit root processes known as *cointegrated* processes. Such specifications were implicit in the "error-correction" models advocated by Davidson, Hendry, Srba, and Yeo (1978). However, a formal development of the key concepts did not come until the work of Granger (1983) and Engle and Granger (1987).

Section 19.1 introduces the concept of cointegration and develops several alternative representations of a cointegrated system. Section 19.2 discusses tests of whether a vector process is cointegrated. These tests are summarized in Table 19.1. Single-equation methods for estimating a cointegrating vector and testing a hypothesis about its value are presented in Section 19.3. Full-information maximum likelihood estimation is discussed in Chapter 20.

## 19.1. *Introduction*

### *Description of Cointegration*

An $(n \times 1)$ vector time series $\mathbf{y}_t$ is said to be *cointegrated* if each of the series taken individually is $I(1)$, that is, nonstationary with a unit root, while some linear combination of the series $\mathbf{a}'\mathbf{y}_t$ is stationary, or $I(0)$, for some nonzero $(n \times 1)$ vector $\mathbf{a}$. A simple example of a cointegrated vector process is the following bivariate system:

$$y_{1t} = \gamma y_{2t} + u_{1t} \qquad [19.1.1]$$

$$y_{2t} = y_{2,t-1} + u_{2t}, \qquad [19.1.2]$$

with $u_{1t}$ and $u_{2t}$ uncorrelated white noise processes. The univariate representation for $y_{2t}$ is a random walk,

$$\Delta y_{2t} = u_{2t}, \qquad [19.1.3]$$

while differencing [19.1.1] results in

$$\Delta y_{1t} = \gamma \Delta y_{2t} + \Delta u_{1t} = \gamma u_{2t} + u_{1t} - u_{1,t-1}. \qquad [19.1.4]$$

Recall from Section 4.7 that the right side of [19.1.4] has an $MA(1)$ representation:

$$\Delta y_{1t} = v_t + \theta v_{t-1}, \qquad [19.1.5]$$

where $v_t$ is a white noise process and $\theta \neq -1$ as long as $\gamma \neq 0$ and $E(u_{2t}^2) > 0$. Thus, both $y_{1t}$ and $y_{2t}$ are $I(1)$ processes, though the linear combination

$(y_{1t} - \gamma y_{2t})$ is stationary. Hence, we would say that $\mathbf{y}_t = (y_{1t}, y_{2t})'$ is cointegrated with $\mathbf{a}' = (1, -\gamma)$.

Figure 19.1 plots a sample realization of [19.1.1] and [19.1.2] for $\gamma = 1$ and $u_{1t}$ and $u_{2t}$ independent $N(0, 1)$ variables. Note that either series ($y_{1t}$ or $y_{2t}$) will wander arbitrarily far from the starting value, though $y_{1t}$ should remain within a fixed distance of $\gamma y_{2t}$, with this distance determined by the standard deviation of $u_{1t}$.

Cointegration means that although many developments can cause permanent changes in the individual elements of $\mathbf{y}_t$, there is some long-run equilibrium relation tying the individual components together, represented by the linear combination $\mathbf{a}'\mathbf{y}_t$. An example of such a system is the model of consumption spending proposed by Davidson, Hendry, Srba, and Yeo (1978). Their results suggest that although both consumption and income exhibit a unit root, over the long run consumption tends to be a roughly constant proportion of income, so that the difference between the log of consumption and the log of income appears to be a stationary process.

Another example of an economic hypothesis that lends itself naturally to a cointegration interpretation is the theory of purchasing power parity. This theory holds that, apart from transportation costs, goods should sell for the same effective price in two countries. Let $P_t$ denote an index of the price level in the United States (in dollars per good), $P_t^*$ a price index for Italy (in lire per good), and $S_t$ the rate of exchange between the currencies (in dollars per lira). Then purchasing power parity holds that

$$P_t = S_t P_t^*,$$

or, taking logarithms,

$$p_t = s_t + p_t^*,$$

where $p_t \equiv \log P_t$, $s_t \equiv \log S_t$, and $p_t^* \equiv \log P_t^*$. In practice, errors in measuring prices, transportation costs, and differences in quality prevent purchasing power parity from holding exactly at every date $t$. A weaker version of the hypothesis is that the variable $z_t$ defined by

$$z_t \equiv p_t - s_t - p_t^* \qquad [19.1.6]$$

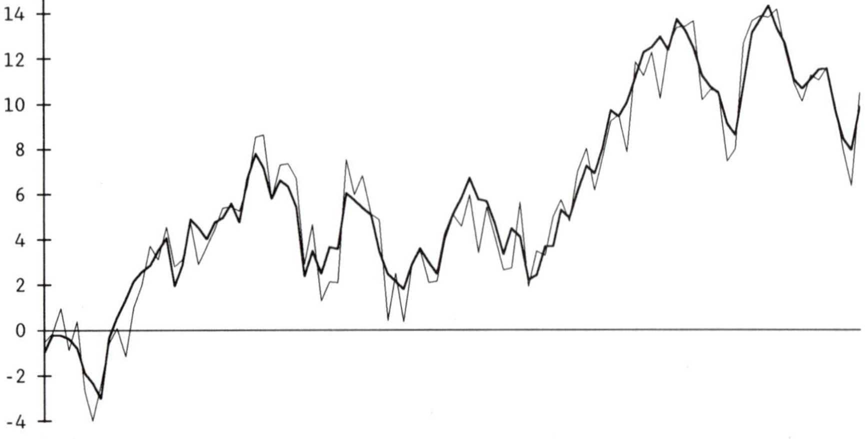


**FIGURE 19.1** Sample realization of cointegrated series.

is stationary, even though the individual elements ($p_t$, $s_t$, or $p_t^*$) are all $I(1)$. Empirical tests of this version of the puchasing power parity hypothesis have been explored by Baillie and Selover (1987) and Corbae and Ouliaris (1988).

Many other interesting applications of the idea of cointegration have been investigated. Kremers (1989) suggested that governments are forced politically to maintain their debt at a roughly constant multiple of GNP, so that log(debt) − log(GNP) is stationary even though each component individually is not. Campbell and Shiller (1988a, b) noted that if $y_{2t}$ is $I(1)$ and $y_{1t}$ is a rational forecast of future values of $y_2$, then $y_1$ and $y_2$ will be cointegrated. Other interesting applications include King, Plosser, Stock, and Watson (1991), Ogaki (1992), Ogaki and Park (1992), and Clarida (1991).

It was asserted in the previous chapter that if $\mathbf{y}_t$ is cointegrated, then it is not correct to fit a vector autoregression to the differenced data. We now verify this claim for the particular example of [19.1.1] and [19.1.2]. The issues will then be discussed in terms of a general cointegrated system involving $n$ different variables.

## *Discussion of the Example of [19.1.1] and [19.1.2]*

Returning to the example in [19.1.1] and [19.1.2], notice that $\varepsilon_{2t} \equiv u_{2t}$ is the error in forecasting $y_{2t}$ on the basis of lagged values of $y_1$ and $y_2$ while $\varepsilon_{1t} \equiv \gamma u_{2t} + u_{1t}$ is the error in forecasting $y_{1t}$. The right side of [19.1.4] can be written

$$(\gamma u_{2t} + u_{1t}) - u_{1,t-1} = \varepsilon_{1t} - (\varepsilon_{1,t-1} - \gamma\varepsilon_{2,t-1}) = (1 - L)\varepsilon_{1t} + \gamma L \varepsilon_{2t}.$$

Substituting this into [19.1.4] and stacking it in a vector system along with [19.1.3] produces the vector moving average representation for $(\Delta y_{1t}, \Delta y_{2t})'$,

$$\begin{bmatrix} \Delta y_{1t} \\ \Delta y_{2t} \end{bmatrix} = \boldsymbol{\Psi}(L)\begin{bmatrix} \varepsilon_{1t} \\ \varepsilon_{2t} \end{bmatrix}, \qquad [19.1.7]$$

where

$$\boldsymbol{\Psi}(L) \equiv \begin{bmatrix} 1 - L & \gamma L \\ 0 & 1 \end{bmatrix}. \qquad [19.1.8]$$

A *VAR* for the differenced data, if it existed, would take the form

$$\boldsymbol{\Phi}(L)\Delta\mathbf{y}_t = \boldsymbol{\varepsilon}_t,$$

where $\boldsymbol{\Phi}(L) = [\boldsymbol{\Psi}(L)]^{-1}$. But the matrix polynomial associated with the moving average operator for this process, $\boldsymbol{\Psi}(z)$, has a root at unity,

$$|\boldsymbol{\Psi}(1)| = \begin{vmatrix} (1 - 1) & \gamma \\ 0 & 1 \end{vmatrix} = 0.$$

Hence the matrix moving average operator is noninvertible, and no finite-order vector autoregression could describe $\Delta\mathbf{y}_t$.

The reason a finite-order *VAR* in differences affords a poor approximation to the cointegrated system of [19.1.1] and [19.1.2] is that the *level* of $y_2$ contains information that is useful for forecasting $y_1$ beyond that contained in a finite number of lagged *changes* in $y_2$ alone.

If we are willing to modify the *VAR* by including lagged levels along with lagged changes, a stationary representation similar to a *VAR* for $\Delta\mathbf{y}_t$ is easy to find. Recalling that $u_{1,t-1} = y_{1,t-1} - \gamma y_{2,t-1}$, notice that [19.1.4] and [19.1.3] can be written as

$$\begin{bmatrix} \Delta y_{1t} \\ \Delta y_{2t} \end{bmatrix} = \begin{bmatrix} -1 & \gamma \\ 0 & 0 \end{bmatrix}\begin{bmatrix} y_{1,t-1} \\ y_{2,t-1} \end{bmatrix} + \begin{bmatrix} \gamma u_{2t} + u_{1t} \\ u_{2t} \end{bmatrix}. \qquad [19.1.9]$$

The general principle of which [19.1.9] provides an illustration is that with a cointegrated system, one should include lagged levels along with lagged differences in a vector autoregression explaining $\Delta \mathbf{y}_t$. The lagged levels will appear in the form of those linear combinations of $\mathbf{y}$ that are stationary.

## *General Characterization of the Cointegrating Vector*

Recall that an $(n \times 1)$ vector $\mathbf{y}_t$ is said to be cointegrated if each of its elements individually is $I(1)$ and if there exists a nonzero $(n \times 1)$ vector $\mathbf{a}$ such that $\mathbf{a}'\mathbf{y}_t$ is stationary. When this is the case, $\mathbf{a}$ is called a *cointegrating vector*.

Clearly, the cointegrating vector $\mathbf{a}$ is not unique, for if $\mathbf{a}'\mathbf{y}_t$ is stationary, then so is $b\mathbf{a}'\mathbf{y}_t$ for any nonzero scalar $b$; if $\mathbf{a}$ is a cointegrating vector, then so is $b\mathbf{a}$. In speaking of the value of the cointegrating vector, an arbitrary normalization must be made, such as that the first element of $\mathbf{a}$ is unity.

If there are more than two variables contained in $\mathbf{y}_t$, then there may be two nonzero $(n \times 1)$ vectors $\mathbf{a}_1$ and $\mathbf{a}_2$ such that $\mathbf{a}_1'\mathbf{y}_t$ and $\mathbf{a}_2'\mathbf{y}_t$ are both stationary, where $\mathbf{a}_1$ and $\mathbf{a}_2$ are linearly independent (that is, there does not exist a scalar $b$ such that $\mathbf{a}_2 = b\mathbf{a}_1$). Indeed, there may be $h < n$ linearly independent $(n \times 1)$ vectors $(\mathbf{a}_1, \mathbf{a}_2, \ldots, \mathbf{a}_h)$ such that $\mathbf{A}'\mathbf{y}_t$ is a stationary $(h \times 1)$ vector, where $\mathbf{A}'$ is the following $(h \times n)$ matrix:[1]

$$\mathbf{A}' \equiv \begin{bmatrix} \mathbf{a}_1' \\ \mathbf{a}_2' \\ \vdots \\ \mathbf{a}_h' \end{bmatrix}. \qquad [19.1.10]$$

Again, the vectors $(\mathbf{a}_1, \mathbf{a}_2, \ldots, \mathbf{a}_h)$ are not unique; if $\mathbf{A}'\mathbf{y}_t$ is stationary, then for any nonzero $(1 \times h)$ vector $\mathbf{b}'$, the scalar $\mathbf{b}'\mathbf{A}'\mathbf{y}_t$ is also stationary. Then the $(n \times 1)$ vector $\boldsymbol{\pi}$ given by $\boldsymbol{\pi}' = \mathbf{b}'\mathbf{A}'$ could also be described as a cointegrating vector.

Suppose that there exists an $(h \times n)$ matrix $\mathbf{A}'$ whose rows are linearly independent such that $\mathbf{A}'\mathbf{y}_t$ is a stationary $(h \times 1)$ vector. Suppose further that if $\mathbf{c}'$ is any $(1 \times n)$ vector that is linearly independent of the rows of $\mathbf{A}'$, then $\mathbf{c}'\mathbf{y}_t$ is a nonstationary scalar. Then we say that there are exactly $h$ cointegrating relations among the elements of $\mathbf{y}_t$ and that $(\mathbf{a}_1, \mathbf{a}_2, \ldots, \mathbf{a}_h)$ form a *basis* for the space of cointegrating vectors.

## *Implications of Cointegration for the Vector Moving Average Representation*

We now discuss the general implications of cointegration for the moving average and vector autoregressive representations of a vector system.[2] Since it is assumed that $\Delta \mathbf{y}_t$ is stationary, let $\boldsymbol{\delta} \equiv E(\Delta \mathbf{y}_t)$ and define

$$\mathbf{u}_t \equiv \Delta \mathbf{y}_t - \boldsymbol{\delta}. \qquad [19.1.11]$$

Suppose that $\mathbf{u}_t$ has the Wold representation

$$\mathbf{u}_t = \boldsymbol{\varepsilon}_t + \boldsymbol{\Psi}_1 \boldsymbol{\varepsilon}_{t-1} + \boldsymbol{\Psi}_2 \boldsymbol{\varepsilon}_{t-2} + \cdots = \boldsymbol{\Psi}(L)\boldsymbol{\varepsilon}_t,$$

[1]If $h = n$ such linearly independent vectors existed, then $\mathbf{y}_t$ would itself be $I(0)$. This claim will become apparent in the triangular representation of a cointegrated system developed in [19.1.20] and [19.1.21].

[2]These results were first derived by Engle and Granger (1987).

where $E(\boldsymbol{\varepsilon}_t) = \mathbf{0}$ and

$$E(\boldsymbol{\varepsilon}_t\boldsymbol{\varepsilon}_\tau') = \begin{cases} \boldsymbol{\Omega} & \text{for } t = \tau \\ \mathbf{0} & \text{otherwise.} \end{cases}$$

Let $\boldsymbol{\Psi}(1)$ denote the $(n \times n)$ matrix polynomial $\boldsymbol{\Psi}(z)$ evaluated at $z = 1$; that is,

$$\boldsymbol{\Psi}(1) \equiv \mathbf{I}_n + \boldsymbol{\Psi}_1 + \boldsymbol{\Psi}_2 + \boldsymbol{\Psi}_3 + \cdots .$$

We first claim that if $\mathbf{A}'\mathbf{y}_t$ is stationary, then

$$\mathbf{A}'\boldsymbol{\Psi}(1) = \mathbf{0}. \qquad [19.1.12]$$

To verify this claim, note that as long as $\{s\cdot\boldsymbol{\Psi}_s\}_{s=0}^{\infty}$ is absolutely summable, the difference equation [19.1.11] implies that

$$\begin{aligned} \mathbf{y}_t &= \mathbf{y}_0 + \boldsymbol{\delta}\cdot t + \mathbf{u}_1 + \mathbf{u}_2 + \cdots + \mathbf{u}_t \\ &= \mathbf{y}_0 + \boldsymbol{\delta}\cdot t + \boldsymbol{\Psi}(1)\cdot(\boldsymbol{\varepsilon}_1 + \boldsymbol{\varepsilon}_2 + \cdots + \boldsymbol{\varepsilon}_t) + \boldsymbol{\eta}_t - \boldsymbol{\eta}_0, \end{aligned} \qquad [19.1.13]$$

where the last line follows from [18.1.6] for $\boldsymbol{\eta}_t$ a stationary process. Premultiplying [19.1.13] by $\mathbf{A}'$ results in

$$\mathbf{A}'\mathbf{y}_t = \mathbf{A}'(\mathbf{y}_0 - \boldsymbol{\eta}_0) + \mathbf{A}'\boldsymbol{\delta}\cdot t + \mathbf{A}'\boldsymbol{\Psi}(1)\cdot(\boldsymbol{\varepsilon}_1 + \boldsymbol{\varepsilon}_2 + \cdots + \boldsymbol{\varepsilon}_t) + \mathbf{A}'\boldsymbol{\eta}_t. \qquad [19.1.14]$$

If $E(\boldsymbol{\varepsilon}_t\boldsymbol{\varepsilon}_t')$ is nonsingular, then $\mathbf{c}'(\boldsymbol{\varepsilon}_1 + \boldsymbol{\varepsilon}_2 + \cdots + \boldsymbol{\varepsilon}_t)$ is $I(1)$ for every nonzero $(n \times 1)$ vector $\mathbf{c}$. However, in order for $\mathbf{y}_t$ to be cointegrated with cointegrating vectors given by the rows of $\mathbf{A}'$, expression [19.1.14] is required to be stationary. This could occur only if $\mathbf{A}'\boldsymbol{\Psi}(1) = \mathbf{0}$. Thus, [19.1.12] is a necessary condition for cointegration, as claimed.

As emphasized by Engle and Yoo (1987) and Ogaki and Park (1992), condition [19.1.12] is not by itself sufficient to ensure that $\mathbf{A}'\mathbf{y}_t$ is stationary. From [19.1.14], stationarity further requires that

$$\mathbf{A}'\boldsymbol{\delta} = \mathbf{0}. \qquad [19.1.15]$$

If some of the series exhibit nonzero drift ($\boldsymbol{\delta} \neq \mathbf{0}$), then unless the drift across series satisfies the restriction of [19.1.15], the linear combination $\mathbf{A}'\mathbf{y}_t$ will grow deterministically at rate $\mathbf{A}'\boldsymbol{\delta}$. Thus, if the underlying hypothesis suggesting the possibility of cointegration is that certain linear combinations of $\mathbf{y}_t$ are stable, this requires that both [19.1.12] and [19.1.15] hold.

Note that [19.1.12] implies that certain linear combinations of the rows of $\boldsymbol{\Psi}(1)$, such as $\mathbf{a}_1'\boldsymbol{\Psi}(1)$, are zero, meaning that the determinant $|\boldsymbol{\Psi}(z)| = 0$ at $z = 1$. This in turn means that the matrix operator $\boldsymbol{\Psi}(L)$ is noninvertible. Thus, a cointegrated system can never be represented by a finite-order vector autoregression in the differenced data $\Delta\mathbf{y}_t$.

For the example of [19.1.1] and [19.1.2], we saw in [19.1.7] and [19.1.8] that

$$\boldsymbol{\Psi}(z) = \begin{bmatrix} 1 - z & \gamma z \\ 0 & 1 \end{bmatrix}$$

and

$$\boldsymbol{\Psi}(1) = \begin{bmatrix} 0 & \gamma \\ 0 & 1 \end{bmatrix}.$$

This is a singular matrix with $\mathbf{A}'\boldsymbol{\Psi}(1) = \mathbf{0}$ for $\mathbf{A}' = [1 \quad -\gamma]$.

## *Phillips's Triangular Representation*

Another convenient representation for a cointegrated system was introduced by Phillips (1991). Suppose that the rows of the $(h \times n)$ matrix $\mathbf{A}'$ form a basis for the space of cointegrating vectors. If the (1, 1) element of $\mathbf{A}'$ is nonzero, we can conveniently normalize it to unity. If, instead, the (1, 1) element of $\mathbf{A}'$ is zero, we can reorder the elements of $\mathbf{y}_t$ so that $y_{1t}$ is included in the first cointegrating relation. Hence, without loss of generality, we take

$$\mathbf{A}' = \begin{bmatrix} \mathbf{a}_1' \\ \mathbf{a}_2' \\ \vdots \\ \mathbf{a}_h' \end{bmatrix} = \begin{bmatrix} 1 & a_{12} & a_{13} & \cdots & a_{1n} \\ a_{21} & a_{22} & a_{23} & \cdots & a_{2n} \\ \vdots & \vdots & \vdots & \cdots & \vdots \\ a_{h1} & a_{h2} & a_{h3} & \cdots & a_{hn} \end{bmatrix}.$$

If $a_{21}$ times the first row of $\mathbf{A}'$ is subtracted from the second row, the resulting row is a new cointegrating vector that is still linearly independent of $\mathbf{a}_1, \mathbf{a}_3, \ldots, \mathbf{a}_n$.[3] Similarly we can subtract $a_{31}$ times the first row of $\mathbf{A}'$ from the third row, and $a_{h1}$ times the first row from the $h$th row, to deduce that the rows of the following matrix also constitute a basis for the space of cointegrating vectors:

$$\mathbf{A}_1' = \begin{bmatrix} 1 & a_{12} & a_{13} & \cdots & a_{1n} \\ 0 & a_{22}^* & a_{23}^* & \cdots & a_{2n}^* \\ \vdots & \vdots & \vdots & \cdots & \vdots \\ 0 & a_{h2}^* & a_{h3}^* & \cdots & a_{hn}^* \end{bmatrix}.$$

Next, suppose that $a_{22}^*$ is nonzero; if $a_{22}^* = 0$, we can again switch $y_{2t}$ with some variable $y_{3t}, y_{4t}, \ldots, y_{nt}$ that does appear in the second cointegrating relation. Divide the second row of $\mathbf{A}_1'$ by $a_{22}^*$. The resulting row can then be multiplied by $a_{12}$ and subtracted from the first row. Similarly, $a_{32}^*$ times the second row of $\mathbf{A}_1'$ can be subtracted from the third row, and $a_{h2}^*$ times the second row can be subtracted from the $h$th. Thus, the space of cointegrating vectors can also be represented by

$$\mathbf{A}_2' = \begin{bmatrix} 1 & 0 & a_{13}^{**} & \cdots & a_{1n}^{**} \\ 0 & 1 & a_{23}^{**} & \cdots & a_{2n}^{**} \\ \vdots & \vdots & \vdots & \cdots & \vdots \\ 0 & 0 & a_{h3}^{**} & \cdots & a_{hn}^{**} \end{bmatrix}.$$

[3]Since the first and second moments of the $(h \times 1)$ vector

$$\begin{bmatrix} \mathbf{a}_1' \\ \mathbf{a}_2' \\ \vdots \\ \mathbf{a}_h' \end{bmatrix} \mathbf{y}_t$$

do not depend on time, neither will the first and second moments of

$$\begin{bmatrix} \mathbf{a}_1' \\ \mathbf{a}_2' - a_{21}\mathbf{a}_1' \\ \vdots \\ \mathbf{a}_h' \end{bmatrix} \mathbf{y}_t.$$

Furthermore, the assumption that $\mathbf{a}_1, \mathbf{a}_2, \ldots, \mathbf{a}_h$ are linearly independent means that no linear combination of $\mathbf{a}_1, \mathbf{a}_2, \ldots, \mathbf{a}_h$ is zero, and so no linear combination of $\mathbf{a}_1, \mathbf{a}_2 - a_{21}\mathbf{a}_1, \ldots, \mathbf{a}_h$ can be zero either. Hence $\mathbf{a}_1, \mathbf{a}_2 - a_{21}\mathbf{a}_1, \ldots, \mathbf{a}_h$ also constitute a basis for the space of cointegrating vectors.

Proceeding through each of the $h$ rows of $\mathbf{A}'$ in this fashion, it follows that given any $(n \times 1)$ vector $\mathbf{y}_t$ that is characterized by exactly $h$ cointegrating relations, it is possible to order the variables $(y_{1t}, y_{2t}, \ldots, y_{nt})$ in such a way that the cointegrating relations can be represented by an $(h \times n)$ matrix $\mathbf{A}'$ of the form

$$\mathbf{A}' = \begin{bmatrix} 1 & 0 & \cdots & 0 & -\gamma_{1,h+1} & -\gamma_{1,h+2} & \cdots & -\gamma_{1,n} \\ 0 & 1 & \cdots & 0 & -\gamma_{2,h+1} & -\gamma_{2,h+2} & \cdots & -\gamma_{2,n} \\ \vdots & \vdots & \cdots & \vdots & \vdots & \vdots & \cdots & \vdots \\ 0 & 0 & \cdots & 1 & -\gamma_{h,h+1} & -\gamma_{h,h+2} & \cdots & -\gamma_{h,n} \end{bmatrix} \qquad [19.1.16]$$

$$= [\mathbf{I}_h \quad -\mathbf{\Gamma}'],$$

where $\mathbf{\Gamma}'$ is an $(h \times g)$ matrix of coefficients for $g \equiv n - h$.

Let $\mathbf{z}_t$ denote the residuals associated with the set of cointegrating relations:

$$\underset{(h \times 1)}{\mathbf{z}_t} \equiv \mathbf{A}'\mathbf{y}_t. \qquad [19.1.17]$$

Since $\mathbf{z}_t$ is stationary, the mean $\boldsymbol{\mu}_1^* \equiv E(\mathbf{z}_t)$ exists, and we can define

$$\mathbf{z}_t^* \equiv \mathbf{z}_t - \boldsymbol{\mu}_1^*. \qquad [19.1.18]$$

Partition $\mathbf{y}_t$ as

$$\underset{(n \times 1)}{\mathbf{y}_t} = \begin{bmatrix} \underset{(h \times 1)}{\mathbf{y}_{1t}} \\ \underset{(g \times 1)}{\mathbf{y}_{2t}} \end{bmatrix}. \qquad [19.1.19]$$

Substituting [19.1.16], [19.1.18], and [19.1.19] into [19.1.17] results in

$$\mathbf{z}_t^* + \boldsymbol{\mu}_1^* = [\mathbf{I}_h \quad -\mathbf{\Gamma}'] \begin{bmatrix} \mathbf{y}_{1t} \\ \mathbf{y}_{2t} \end{bmatrix}$$

or

$$\underset{(h \times 1)}{\mathbf{y}_{1t}} = \underset{(h \times g)}{\mathbf{\Gamma}'} \cdot \underset{(g \times 1)}{\mathbf{y}_{2t}} + \underset{(h \times 1)}{\boldsymbol{\mu}_1^*} + \underset{(h \times 1)}{\mathbf{z}_t^*}. \qquad [19.1.20]$$

A representation for $\mathbf{y}_{2t}$ is given by the last $g$ rows of [19.1.11]:

$$\underset{(g \times 1)}{\Delta\mathbf{y}_{2t}} = \underset{(g \times 1)}{\boldsymbol{\delta}_2} + \underset{(g \times 1)}{\mathbf{u}_{2t}}, \qquad [19.1.21]$$

where $\boldsymbol{\delta}_2$ and $\mathbf{u}_{2t}$ represent the last $g$ elements of the $(n \times 1)$ vectors $\boldsymbol{\delta}$ and $\mathbf{u}_t$, respectively. Equations [19.1.20] and [19.1.21] constitute Phillips's (1991) triangular representation of a system with exactly $h$ cointegrating relations. Note that $\mathbf{z}_t^*$ and $\mathbf{u}_{2t}$ represent zero-mean stationary disturbances in this representation.

If a vector $\mathbf{y}_t$ is characterized by exactly $h$ cointegrating relations with the variables ordered so that [19.1.20] and [19.1.21] hold, then the $(g \times 1)$ vector $\mathbf{y}_{2t}$ is $I(1)$ with no cointegrating relations. To verify this last claim, notice that if some linear combination $\mathbf{c}'\mathbf{y}_{2t}$ were stationary, this would mean that $(\mathbf{0}', \mathbf{c}')\mathbf{y}_t$ would be stationary or that $(\mathbf{0}', \mathbf{c}')$ would be a cointegrating vector for $\mathbf{y}_t$. But $(\mathbf{0}', \mathbf{c}')$ is linearly independent of the rows of $\mathbf{A}'$ in [19.1.16], and by the assumption that the rows of $\mathbf{A}'$ constitute a basis for the space of cointegrating vectors, the linear combination $(\mathbf{0}', \mathbf{c}')\mathbf{y}_t$ cannot be stationary.

Expressions [19.1.1] and [19.1.2] are a simple example of a cointegrated system expressed in triangular form. For the purchasing power parity example

[19.1.6], the triangular representation would be

$$p_t = \gamma_1 s_t + \gamma_2 p_t^* + \mu_1^* + z_t^*$$

$$\Delta s_t = \delta_s + u_{st}$$

$$\Delta p_t^* = \delta_{p^*} + u_{p^*,t},$$

where the hypothesized values are $\gamma_1 = \gamma_2 = 1$.

## *The Stock-Watson Common Trends Representation*

Another useful representation for any cointegrated system was proposed by Stock and Watson (1988). Suppose that an $(n \times 1)$ vector $\mathbf{y}_t$ is characterized by exactly $h$ cointegrating relations with $g \equiv n - h$. We have seen that it is possible to order the elements of $\mathbf{y}_t$ in such a way that a triangular representation of the form of [19.1.20] and [19.1.21] exists with $(\mathbf{z}_t^{*\prime}, \mathbf{u}_{2t}^{\prime})^{\prime}$ a stationary $(n \times 1)$ vector with zero mean. Suppose that

$$\begin{bmatrix} \mathbf{z}_t^* \\ \mathbf{u}_{2t} \end{bmatrix} = \sum_{s=0}^{\infty} \begin{bmatrix} \mathbf{H}_s \boldsymbol{\varepsilon}_{t-s} \\ \mathbf{J}_s \boldsymbol{\varepsilon}_{t-s} \end{bmatrix}$$

for $\boldsymbol{\varepsilon}_t$ an $(n \times 1)$ white noise process, with $\{s \cdot \mathbf{H}_s\}_{s=0}^{\infty}$ and $\{s \cdot \mathbf{J}_s\}_{s=0}^{\infty}$ absolutely summable sequences of $(h \times n)$ and $(g \times n)$ matrices, respectively. Adapting the result in [18.1.6], equation [19.1.21] implies that

$$\begin{aligned} \mathbf{y}_{2t} &= \mathbf{y}_{2,0} + \boldsymbol{\delta}_2 \cdot t + \sum_{s=1}^{t} \mathbf{u}_{2s} \\ &= \mathbf{y}_{2,0} + \boldsymbol{\delta}_2 \cdot t + \mathbf{J}(1) \cdot (\boldsymbol{\varepsilon}_1 + \boldsymbol{\varepsilon}_2 + \cdots + \boldsymbol{\varepsilon}_t) + \boldsymbol{\eta}_{2t} - \boldsymbol{\eta}_{2,0}, \end{aligned} \qquad [19.1.22]$$

where $\mathbf{J}(1) \equiv (\mathbf{J}_0 + \mathbf{J}_1 + \mathbf{J}_2 + \cdots)$, $\boldsymbol{\eta}_{2t} \equiv \sum_{s=0}^{\infty} \boldsymbol{\alpha}_{2s} \boldsymbol{\varepsilon}_{t-s}$, and $\boldsymbol{\alpha}_{2s} \equiv -(\mathbf{J}_{s+1} + \mathbf{J}_{s+2} + \mathbf{J}_{s+3} + \cdots)$. Since the $(n \times 1)$ vector $\boldsymbol{\varepsilon}_t$ is white noise, the $(g \times 1)$ vector $\mathbf{J}(1) \cdot \boldsymbol{\varepsilon}_t$ is also white noise, implying that each element of the $(g \times 1)$ vector $\boldsymbol{\xi}_{2t}$ defined by

$$\boldsymbol{\xi}_{2t} \equiv \mathbf{J}(1) \cdot (\boldsymbol{\varepsilon}_1 + \boldsymbol{\varepsilon}_2 + \cdots + \boldsymbol{\varepsilon}_t) \qquad [19.1.23]$$

is described by a random walk.

Substituting [19.1.23] into [19.1.22] results in

$$\mathbf{y}_{2t} = \tilde{\boldsymbol{\mu}}_2 + \boldsymbol{\delta}_2 \cdot t + \boldsymbol{\xi}_{2t} + \boldsymbol{\eta}_{2t} \qquad [19.1.24]$$

for $\tilde{\boldsymbol{\mu}}_2 \equiv (\mathbf{y}_{2,0} - \boldsymbol{\eta}_{2,0})$. Substituting [19.1.24] into [19.1.20] produces

$$\mathbf{y}_{1t} = \tilde{\boldsymbol{\mu}}_1 + \boldsymbol{\Gamma}^{\prime}(\boldsymbol{\delta}_2 \cdot t + \boldsymbol{\xi}_{2t}) + \tilde{\boldsymbol{\eta}}_{1t} \qquad [19.1.25]$$

for $\tilde{\boldsymbol{\mu}}_1 \equiv \boldsymbol{\mu}_1^* + \boldsymbol{\Gamma}^{\prime} \tilde{\boldsymbol{\mu}}_2$ and $\tilde{\boldsymbol{\eta}}_{1t} \equiv \mathbf{z}_t^* + \boldsymbol{\Gamma}^{\prime} \boldsymbol{\eta}_{2t}$.

Equations [19.1.24] and [19.1.25] give Stock and Watson's (1988) common trends representation. These equations show that the vector $\mathbf{y}_t$ can be described as a stationary component,

$$\begin{bmatrix} \tilde{\boldsymbol{\mu}}_1 \\ \tilde{\boldsymbol{\mu}}_2 \end{bmatrix} + \begin{bmatrix} \tilde{\boldsymbol{\eta}}_{1t} \\ \boldsymbol{\eta}_{2t} \end{bmatrix},$$

plus linear combinations of up to $g$ common deterministic trends, as described by the $(g \times 1)$ vector $\boldsymbol{\delta}_2 \cdot t$, and linear combinations of $g$ common random walk variables as described by the $(g \times 1)$ vector $\boldsymbol{\xi}_{2t}$.

## *Implications of Cointegration for the Vector Autoregressive Representation*

Although a *VAR* in differences is not consistent with a cointegrated system, a *VAR* in levels could be. Suppose that the level of $\mathbf{y}_t$ can be represented as a nonstationary $p$th-order vector autoregression:

$$\mathbf{y}_t = \boldsymbol{\alpha} + \boldsymbol{\Phi}_1\mathbf{y}_{t-1} + \boldsymbol{\Phi}_2\mathbf{y}_{t-2} + \cdots + \boldsymbol{\Phi}_p\mathbf{y}_{t-p} + \boldsymbol{\varepsilon}_t, \qquad [19.1.26]$$

or

$$\boldsymbol{\Phi}(L)\mathbf{y}_t = \boldsymbol{\alpha} + \boldsymbol{\varepsilon}_t, \qquad [19.1.27]$$

where

$$\boldsymbol{\Phi}(L) \equiv \mathbf{I}_n - \boldsymbol{\Phi}_1 L - \boldsymbol{\Phi}_2 L^2 - \cdots - \boldsymbol{\Phi}_p L^p. \qquad [19.1.28]$$

Suppose that $\Delta\mathbf{y}_t$ has the Wold representation

$$(1 - L)\mathbf{y}_t = \boldsymbol{\delta} + \boldsymbol{\Psi}(L)\boldsymbol{\varepsilon}_t. \qquad [19.1.29]$$

Premultiplying [19.1.29] by $\boldsymbol{\Phi}(L)$ results in

$$(1 - L)\boldsymbol{\Phi}(L)\mathbf{y}_t = \boldsymbol{\Phi}(1)\boldsymbol{\delta} + \boldsymbol{\Phi}(L)\boldsymbol{\Psi}(L)\boldsymbol{\varepsilon}_t. \qquad [19.1.30]$$

Substituting [19.1.27] into [19.1.30], we have

$$(1 - L)\boldsymbol{\varepsilon}_t = \boldsymbol{\Phi}(1)\boldsymbol{\delta} + \boldsymbol{\Phi}(L)\boldsymbol{\Psi}(L)\boldsymbol{\varepsilon}_t, \qquad [19.1.31]$$

since $(1 - L)\boldsymbol{\alpha} = \mathbf{0}$. Now, equation [19.1.31] has to hold for all realizations of $\boldsymbol{\varepsilon}_t$, which requires that

$$\boldsymbol{\Phi}(1)\boldsymbol{\delta} = \mathbf{0} \qquad [19.1.32]$$

and that $(1 - L)\mathbf{I}_n$ and $\boldsymbol{\Phi}(L)\boldsymbol{\Psi}(L)$ represent the identical polynomials in $L$. This means that

$$(1 - z)\mathbf{I}_n = \boldsymbol{\Phi}(z)\boldsymbol{\Psi}(z) \qquad [19.1.33]$$

for all values of $z$. In particular, for $z = 1$, equation [19.1.33] implies that

$$\boldsymbol{\Phi}(1)\boldsymbol{\Psi}(1) = \mathbf{0}. \qquad [19.1.34]$$

Let $\boldsymbol{\pi}'$ denote any row of $\boldsymbol{\Phi}(1)$. Then [19.1.34] and [19.1.32] state that $\boldsymbol{\pi}'\boldsymbol{\Psi}(1) = \mathbf{0}'$ and $\boldsymbol{\pi}'\boldsymbol{\delta} = 0$. Recalling [19.1.12] and [19.1.15], this means that $\boldsymbol{\pi}$ is a cointegrating vector. If $\mathbf{a}_1, \mathbf{a}_2, \ldots, \mathbf{a}_h$ form a basis for the space of cointegrating vectors, then it must be possible to express $\boldsymbol{\pi}$ as a linear combination of $\mathbf{a}_1, \mathbf{a}_2, \ldots, \mathbf{a}_h$—that is, there exists an $(h \times 1)$ vector $\mathbf{b}$ such that

$$\boldsymbol{\pi} = [\mathbf{a}_1 \quad \mathbf{a}_2 \quad \cdots \quad \mathbf{a}_h]\mathbf{b}$$

or

$$\boldsymbol{\pi}' = \mathbf{b}'\mathbf{A}'$$

for $\mathbf{A}'$ the $(h \times n)$ matrix whose $i$th row is $\mathbf{a}_i'$. Applying this reasoning to each of the rows of $\boldsymbol{\Phi}(1)$, it follows that there exists an $(n \times h)$ matrix $\mathbf{B}$ such that

$$\boldsymbol{\Phi}(1) = \mathbf{B}\mathbf{A}'. \qquad [19.1.35]$$

Note that [19.1.34] implies that $\boldsymbol{\Phi}(1)$ is a singular $(n \times n)$ matrix—linear combinations of the columns of $\boldsymbol{\Phi}(1)$ of the form $\boldsymbol{\Phi}(1)\mathbf{x}$ are zero for $\mathbf{x}$ any column of $\boldsymbol{\Psi}(1)$. Thus, the determinant $|\boldsymbol{\Phi}(z)|$ contains a unit root:

$$|\mathbf{I}_n - \boldsymbol{\Phi}_1 z^1 - \boldsymbol{\Phi}_2 z^2 - \cdots - \boldsymbol{\Phi}_p z^p| = 0 \qquad \text{at } z = 1.$$

Indeed, in the light of the Stock-Watson common trends representation in [19.1.24] and [19.1.25], we could say that $\mathbf{\Phi}(z)$ contains $g = n - h$ unit roots.

### Error-Correction Representation

A final representation for a cointegrated system is obtained by recalling from equation [18.2.5] that any *VAR* in the form of [19.1.26] can equivalently be written as

$$\mathbf{y}_t = \boldsymbol{\zeta}_1 \Delta\mathbf{y}_{t-1} + \boldsymbol{\zeta}_2 \Delta\mathbf{y}_{t-2} + \cdots + \boldsymbol{\zeta}_{p-1} \Delta\mathbf{y}_{t-p+1} + \boldsymbol{\alpha} + \boldsymbol{\rho}\mathbf{y}_{t-1} + \boldsymbol{\varepsilon}_t, \quad [19.1.36]$$

where

$$\boldsymbol{\rho} \equiv \mathbf{\Phi}_1 + \mathbf{\Phi}_2 + \cdots + \mathbf{\Phi}_p \quad [19.1.37]$$

$$\boldsymbol{\zeta}_s \equiv -[\mathbf{\Phi}_{s+1} + \mathbf{\Phi}_{s+2} + \cdots + \mathbf{\Phi}_p] \quad \text{for } s = 1, 2, \ldots, p - 1. \quad [19.1.38]$$

Subtracting $\mathbf{y}_{t-1}$ from both sides of [19.1.36] produces

$$\Delta\mathbf{y}_t = \boldsymbol{\zeta}_1 \Delta\mathbf{y}_{t-1} + \boldsymbol{\zeta}_2 \Delta\mathbf{y}_{t-2} + \cdots + \boldsymbol{\zeta}_{p-1} \Delta\mathbf{y}_{t-p+1} + \boldsymbol{\alpha} + \boldsymbol{\zeta}_0\mathbf{y}_{t-1} + \boldsymbol{\varepsilon}_t, \quad [19.1.39]$$

where

$$\boldsymbol{\zeta}_0 \equiv \boldsymbol{\rho} - \mathbf{I}_n = -(\mathbf{I}_n - \mathbf{\Phi}_1 - \mathbf{\Phi}_2 - \cdots - \mathbf{\Phi}_p) = -\mathbf{\Phi}(1). \quad [19.1.40]$$

Note that if $\mathbf{y}_t$ has $h$ cointegrating relations, then substitution of [19.1.35] and [19.1.40] into [19.1.39] results in

$$\Delta\mathbf{y}_t = \boldsymbol{\zeta}_1 \Delta\mathbf{y}_{t-1} + \boldsymbol{\zeta}_2 \Delta\mathbf{y}_{t-2} + \cdots + \boldsymbol{\zeta}_{p-1} \Delta\mathbf{y}_{t-p+1} + \boldsymbol{\alpha} - \mathbf{B}\mathbf{A}'\mathbf{y}_{t-1} + \boldsymbol{\varepsilon}_t. \quad [19.1.41]$$

Define $\mathbf{z}_t \equiv \mathbf{A}'\mathbf{y}_t$, noticing that $\mathbf{z}_t$ is a stationary $(h \times 1)$ vector. Then [19.1.41] can be written

$$\Delta\mathbf{y}_t = \boldsymbol{\zeta}_1 \Delta\mathbf{y}_{t-1} + \boldsymbol{\zeta}_2 \Delta\mathbf{y}_{t-2} + \cdots + \boldsymbol{\zeta}_{p-1} \Delta\mathbf{y}_{t-p+1} + \boldsymbol{\alpha} - \mathbf{B}\mathbf{z}_{t-1} + \boldsymbol{\varepsilon}_t. \quad [19.1.42]$$

Expression [19.1.42] is known as the *error-correction* representation of the cointegrated system. For example, the first equation takes the form

$$\begin{aligned}\Delta y_{1t} = {} & \zeta_{11}^{(1)}\Delta y_{1,t-1} + \zeta_{12}^{(1)}\Delta y_{2,t-1} + \cdots + \zeta_{1n}^{(1)}\Delta y_{n,t-1} \\ & + \zeta_{11}^{(2)}\Delta y_{1,t-2} + \zeta_{12}^{(2)}\Delta y_{2,t-2} + \cdots + \zeta_{1n}^{(2)}\Delta y_{n,t-2} + \cdots \\ & + \zeta_{11}^{(p-1)}\Delta y_{1,t-p+1} + \zeta_{12}^{(p-1)}\Delta y_{2,t-p+1} + \cdots + \zeta_{1n}^{(p-1)}\Delta y_{n,t-p+1} \\ & + \alpha_1 - b_{11}z_{1,t-1} - b_{12}z_{2,t-1} - \cdots - b_{1h}z_{h,t-1} + \varepsilon_{1t},\end{aligned}$$

where $\zeta_{ij}^{(s)}$ indicates the row $i$, column $j$ element of the matrix $\boldsymbol{\zeta}_s$, $b_{ij}$ indicates the row $i$, column $j$ element of the matrix $\mathbf{B}$, and $z_{it}$ represents the $i$th element of $\mathbf{z}_t$. Thus, in the error-correction form, changes in each variable are regressed on a constant, $(p - 1)$ lags of the variable's own changes, $(p - 1)$ lags of changes in each of the other variables, and the levels of each of the $h$ elements of $\mathbf{z}_{t-1}$.

For example, recall from [19.1.9] that the system of [19.1.1] and [19.1.2] can be written in the form

$$\begin{bmatrix}\Delta y_{1t} \\ \Delta y_{2t}\end{bmatrix} = \begin{bmatrix}-1 & \gamma \\ 0 & 0\end{bmatrix}\begin{bmatrix}y_{1,t-1} \\ y_{2,t-1}\end{bmatrix} + \begin{bmatrix}\gamma u_{2t} + u_{1t} \\ u_{2t}\end{bmatrix}.$$

Note that this is a special case of [19.1.39] with $p = 1$,

$$\boldsymbol{\zeta}_0 = \begin{bmatrix}-1 & \gamma \\ 0 & 0\end{bmatrix},$$

$\varepsilon_{1t} = \gamma u_{2t} + u_{1t}$, $\varepsilon_{2t} = u_{2t}$, and all other parameters in [19.1.39] equal to zero.

The error-correction form is

$$\begin{bmatrix} \Delta y_{1t} \\ \Delta y_{2t} \end{bmatrix} = \begin{bmatrix} -1 \\ 0 \end{bmatrix} z_{t-1} + \begin{bmatrix} \varepsilon_{1t} \\ \varepsilon_{2t} \end{bmatrix},$$

where $z_t \equiv y_{1t} - \gamma y_{2t}$.

An economic interpretation of an error-correction representation was proposed by Davidson, Hendry, Srba, and Yeo (1978), who examined a relation between the log of consumption spending (denoted $c_t$) and the log of income ($y_t$) of the form

$$(1 - L^4)c_t = \beta_1(1 - L^4)y_t + \beta_2(1 - L^4)y_{t-1} + \beta_3(c_{t-4} - y_{t-4}) + u_t. \quad [19.1.43]$$

This equation was fitted to quarterly data, so that $(1 - L^4)c_t$ denotes the percentage change in consumption over its value in the comparable quarter of the preceding year. The authors argued that seasonal differences $(1 - L^4)$ provided a better description of the data than would simple quarterly differences $(1 - L)$. Their claim was that seasonally differenced consumption $(1 - L^4)c_t$ could not be described using only its own lags or those of seasonally differenced income. In addition to these factors, [19.1.43] includes the "error-correction" term $\beta_3(c_{t-4} - y_{t-4})$. One could argue that there is a long run, historical average ratio of consumption to income, in which case the difference between the logs of consumption and income, $c_t - y_t$, would be a stationary random variable, even though log consumption or log income viewed by itself exhibits a unit root. For $\beta_3 < 0$, equation [19.1.43] asserts that if consumption had previously been a larger-than-normal share of income (so that $c_{t-4} - y_{t-4}$ is larger than normal), then that causes $c_t$ to be lower for any given values of the other explanatory variables. The term $(c_{t-4} - y_{t-4})$ is viewed as the "error" from the long-run equilibrium relation, and $\beta_3$ gives the "correction" to $c_t$ caused by this error.

## *Restrictions on the Constant Term in the* VAR *Representation*

Notice that all the variables appearing in the error-correction representation [19.1.42] are stationary. Taking expectations of both sides of that equation results in

$$(\mathbf{I}_n - \boldsymbol{\zeta}_1 - \boldsymbol{\zeta}_2 - \cdots - \boldsymbol{\zeta}_{p-1})\boldsymbol{\delta} = \boldsymbol{\alpha} - \mathbf{B}\boldsymbol{\mu}_1^*, \quad [19.1.44]$$

where $\boldsymbol{\delta} = E(\Delta\mathbf{y}_t)$ and $\boldsymbol{\mu}_1^* = E(\mathbf{z}_t)$. Assuming that the roots of

$$|\mathbf{I}_n - \boldsymbol{\zeta}_1 z - \boldsymbol{\zeta}_2 z^2 - \cdots - \boldsymbol{\zeta}_{p-1} z^{p-1}| = 0$$

are all outside the unit circle, the matrix $(\mathbf{I}_n - \boldsymbol{\zeta}_1 - \boldsymbol{\zeta}_2 - \cdots - \boldsymbol{\zeta}_{p-1})$ is nonsingular. Thus, in order to represent a system in which there is no drift in any of the variables ($\boldsymbol{\delta} = \mathbf{0}$), we would have to impose the restriction

$$\boldsymbol{\alpha} = \mathbf{B}\boldsymbol{\mu}_1^*. \quad [19.1.45]$$

In the absence of any restriction on $\boldsymbol{\alpha}$, the system of [19.1.42] implies that there are $g$ separate time trends that account for the trend in $\mathbf{y}_t$.

## *Granger Representation Theorem*

For convenience, some of the preceding results are now summarized in the form of a proposition.

***Proposition 19.1:*** *(Granger representation theorem). Consider an* $(n \times 1)$ *vector* $\mathbf{y}_t$ *where* $\Delta\mathbf{y}_t$ *satisfies [19.1.29] for* $\boldsymbol{\varepsilon}_t$ *white noise with positive definite variance-covariance matrix and* $\{s \cdot \boldsymbol{\Psi}_s\}_{s=0}^{\infty}$ *absolutely summable. Suppose that there are exactly* $h$ *cointegrating relations among the elements of* $\mathbf{y}_t$. *Then there exists an* $(h \times n)$ *matrix* $\mathbf{A}'$ *whose rows are linearly independent such that the* $(h \times 1)$ *vector* $\mathbf{z}_t$ *defined by*

$$\mathbf{z}_t \equiv \mathbf{A}'\mathbf{y}_t$$

*is stationary. The matrix* $\mathbf{A}'$ *has the property that*

$$\mathbf{A}'\boldsymbol{\Psi}(1) = \mathbf{0}.$$

*If, moreover, the process can be represented as the pth-order VAR in levels as in equation [19.1.26], then there exists an* $(n \times h)$ *matrix* $\mathbf{B}$ *such that*

$$\boldsymbol{\Phi}(1) = \mathbf{B}\mathbf{A}',$$

*and there further exist* $(n \times n)$ *matrices* $\boldsymbol{\zeta}_1, \boldsymbol{\zeta}_2, \ldots, \boldsymbol{\zeta}_{p-1}$ *such that*

$$\Delta\mathbf{y}_t = \boldsymbol{\zeta}_1\Delta\mathbf{y}_{t-1} + \boldsymbol{\zeta}_2\Delta\mathbf{y}_{t-2} + \cdots + \boldsymbol{\zeta}_{p-1}\Delta\mathbf{y}_{t-p+1} + \boldsymbol{\alpha} - \mathbf{B}\mathbf{z}_{t-1} + \boldsymbol{\varepsilon}_t.$$

## 19.2. *Testing the Null Hypothesis of No Cointegration*

This section discusses tests for cointegration. The approach will be to test the null hypothesis that there is no cointegration among the elements of an $(n \times 1)$ vector $\mathbf{y}_t$; rejection of the null is then taken as evidence of cointegration.

### *Testing for Cointegration When the Cointegrating Vector Is Known*

Often when theoretical considerations suggest that certain variables will be cointegrated, or that $\mathbf{a}'\mathbf{y}_t$ is stationary for some $(n \times 1)$ cointegrating vector $\mathbf{a}$, the theory is based on a particular known value for $\mathbf{a}$. In the purchasing power parity example [19.1.6], $\mathbf{a} = (1, -1, -1)'$. The Davidson, Hendry, Srba, and Yeo hypothesis (1978) that consumption is a stable fraction of income implies a cointegrating vector of $\mathbf{a} = (1, -1)'$, as did Kremers's assertion (1989) that government debt is a stable multiple of GNP.

If the interest in cointegration is motivated by the possibility of a particular known cointegrating vector $\mathbf{a}$, then by far the best method is to use this value directly to construct a test for cointegration. To implement this approach, we first test whether each of the elements of $\mathbf{y}_t$ is individually $I(1)$. This can be done using any of the tests discussed in Chapter 17. Assuming that the null hypothesis of a unit root in each series individually is accepted, we next construct the scalar $z_t = \mathbf{a}'\mathbf{y}_t$. Notice that if $\mathbf{a}$ is truly a cointegrating vector, then $\mathbf{a}'\mathbf{y}_t$ will be $I(0)$. If $\mathbf{a}$ is not a cointegrating vector, then $\mathbf{a}'\mathbf{y}_t$ will be $I(1)$. Thus, a test of the null hypothesis that $z_t$ is $I(1)$ is equivalent to a test of the null hypothesis that $\mathbf{y}_t$ is not cointegrated. If the null hypothesis that $z_t$ is $I(1)$ is rejected, we would conclude that $z_t = \mathbf{a}'\mathbf{y}_t$ is stationary, or that $\mathbf{y}_t$ is cointegrated with cointegrating vector $\mathbf{a}$. The null hypothesis that $z_t$ is $I(1)$ can also be tested using any of the approaches in Chapter 17.

For example, Figure 19.2 plots monthly data from 1973:1 to 1989:10 for the consumer price indexes for the United States ($p_t$) and Italy ($p_t^*$), along with the

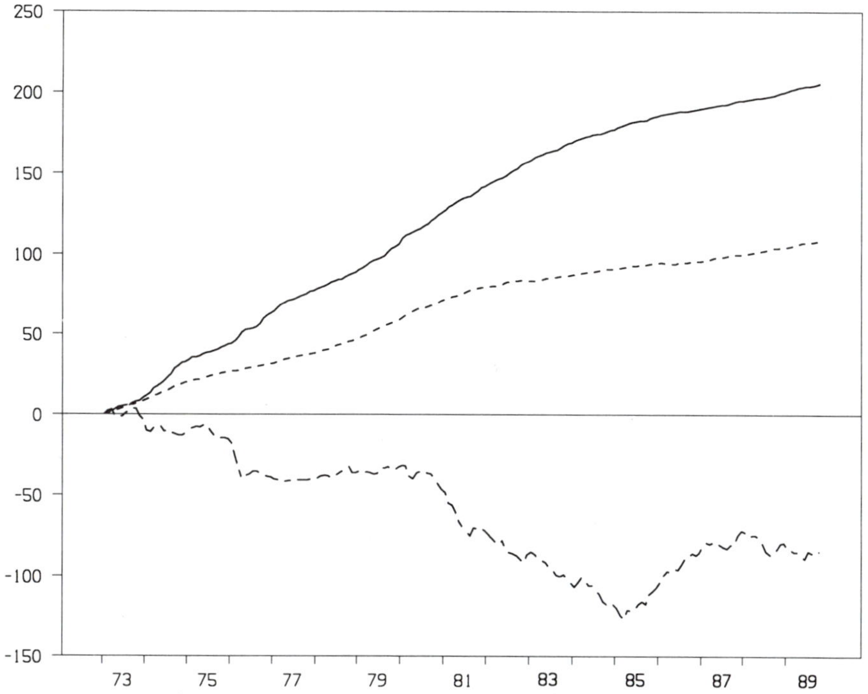


**FIGURE 19.2** One hundred times the log of the price level in the United States ($p_t$), the dollar-lira exchange rate ($s_t$), and the price level in Italy ($p_t^*$), monthly, 1973–89. Key: ---- $p_t$; ——— $s_t$; ——— $p_t^*$.

exchange rate ($s_t$), where $s_t$ is in terms of the number of U.S. dollars needed to purchase an Italian lira. Natural logs of the raw data were taken and multiplied by 100, and the initial value for 1973:1 was then subtracted, as in

$$p_t = 100 \cdot [\log(P_t) - \log(P_{1973:1})].$$

The purpose of subtracting the constant $\log(P_{1973:1})$ from each observation is to normalize each series to be zero for 1973:1 so that the graph is easier to read. Multiplying the log by 100 means that $p_t$ is approximately the percentage difference between $P_t$ and its starting value $P_{1973:1}$. The graph shows that Italy experienced about twice the average inflation rate of the United States over this period and that the lira dropped in value relative to the dollar (that is, $s_t$ fell) by roughly this same proportion.

Figure 19.3 plots the real exchange rate,

$$z_t \equiv p_t - s_t - p_t^*.$$

It appears that the trends are eliminated by this transformation, though deviations of the real exchange rate from its historical mean can persist for several years.

To test for cointegration, we first verify that $p_t$, $p_t^*$, and $s_t$ are each individually $I(1)$. Certainly, we anticipate the average inflation rate to be positive ($E(\Delta p_t) > 0$), so that the natural null hypothesis is that $p_t$ is a unit root process with positive drift, while the alternative is that $p_t$ is stationary around a deterministic time trend. With monthly data it is a good idea to include at least twelve lags in the regression. Thus, the following model was estimated by *OLS* for the U.S. data for $t$ = 1974:2

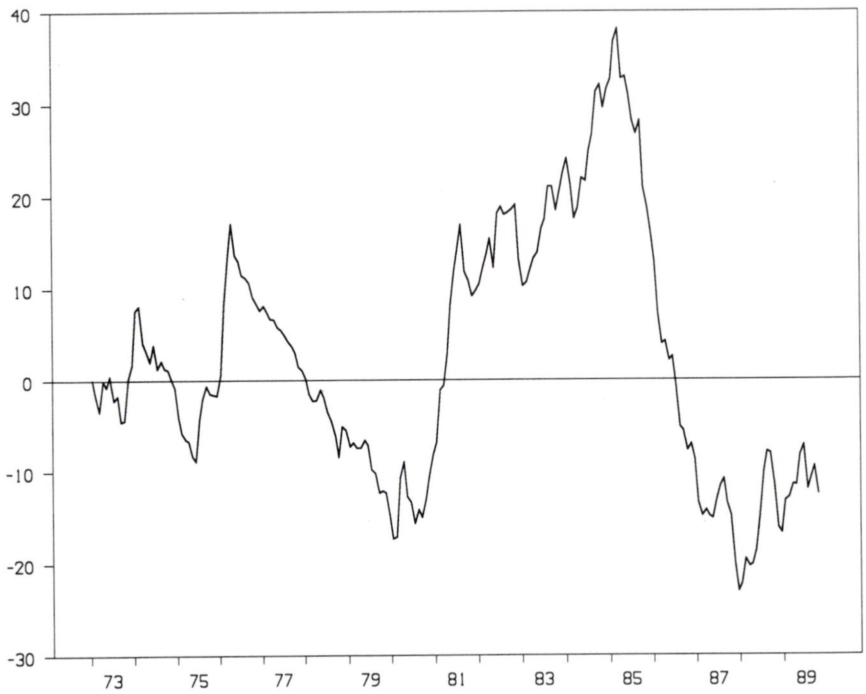


**FIGURE 19.3** The real dollar-lira exchange rate, monthly, 1973–89.

through 1989:10 (standard errors in parentheses):

$$\begin{aligned} p_t = {} & \underset{(0.08)}{0.55}\ \Delta p_{t-1} - \underset{(0.09)}{0.06}\ \Delta p_{t-2} + \underset{(0.08)}{0.07}\ \Delta p_{t-3} + \underset{(0.08)}{0.06}\ \Delta p_{t-4} \\ & - \underset{(0.08)}{0.08}\ \Delta p_{t-5} - \underset{(0.07)}{0.05}\ \Delta p_{t-6} + \underset{(0.07)}{0.17}\ \Delta p_{t-7} - \underset{(0.07)}{0.07}\ \Delta p_{t-8} \\ & + \underset{(0.07)}{0.24}\ \Delta p_{t-9} - \underset{(0.07)}{0.11}\ \Delta p_{t-10} + \underset{(0.07)}{0.12}\ \Delta p_{t-11} + \underset{(0.07)}{0.05}\ \Delta p_{t-12} \\ & + \underset{(0.09)}{0.14} + \underset{(0.00307)}{0.99400}\ p_{t-1} + \underset{(0.0018)}{0.0029}\ t. \end{aligned} \qquad [19.2.1]$$

The $t$ statistic for testing the null hypothesis that $\rho$ (the coefficient on $p_{t-1}$) is unity is

$$t = (0.99400 - 1.0)/(0.00307) = -1.95.$$

Comparing this with the 5% crtical value from the case 4 section of Table B.6 for a sample of size $T = 189$, we see that $-1.95 > -3.44$. Thus, the null hypothesis of a unit root is accepted. The $F$ test of the joint null hypothesis that $\rho = 1$ and $\delta = 0$ (for $\rho$ the coefficient on $p_{t-1}$ and $\delta$ the coefficient on the time trend) is 2.41. Comparing this with the critical value of 6.40 from the case 4 section of Table B.7, the null hypothesis is again accepted, further confirming the impression that U.S. prices follow a unit root process with drift.

If $p_t$ in [19.2.1] is replaced by $p_t^*$, the augmented Dickey-Fuller $t$ and $F$ tests are calculated to be $-0.13$ and 4.25, respectively, so that the null hypothesis that the Italian price level follows an $I(1)$ process is again accepted. When $p_t$ in [19.2.1] is replaced by $s_t$, the $t$ and $F$ tests are $-1.58$ and 1.49, so that the exchange rate likewise admits an $ARIMA(12, 1, 0)$ representation. Thus, each of the three series individually could reasonably be described as a unit root process with drift.

The next step is to test whether $z_t = p_t - s_t - p_t^*$ is stationary. According to the theory, there should not be any trend in $z_t$, and none appears evident in Figure 19.3. Thus, the augmented Dickey-Fuller test without trend might be used. The following estimates were obtained by *OLS*:

$$\begin{aligned} z_t = {} & \underset{(0.07)}{0.32}\, \Delta z_{t-1} - \underset{(0.08)}{0.01}\, \Delta z_{t-2} + \underset{(0.08)}{0.01}\, \Delta z_{t-3} + \underset{(0.08)}{0.02}\, \Delta z_{t-4} \\ & + \underset{(0.08)}{0.08}\, \Delta z_{t-5} - \underset{(0.08)}{0.00}\, \Delta z_{t-6} + \underset{(0.08)}{0.03}\, \Delta z_{t-7} + \underset{(0.08)}{0.08}\, \Delta z_{t-8} \\ & - \underset{(0.08)}{0.05}\, \Delta z_{t-9} + \underset{(0.08)}{0.08}\, \Delta z_{t-10} + \underset{(0.08)}{0.05}\, \Delta z_{t-11} - \underset{(0.08)}{0.01}\, \Delta z_{t-12} \\ & + \underset{(0.18)}{0.00} + \underset{(0.01410)}{0.97124}\, z_{t-1}. \end{aligned} \qquad [19.2.2]$$

Here the augmented Dickey-Fuller $t$ test is

$$t = (0.97124 - 1.0)/(0.01410) = -2.04.$$

Comparing this with the 5% critical value for case 2 of Table B.6, we see that $-2.04 > -2.88$, and so the null hypothesis of a unit root is accepted. The $F$ test of the joint null hypothesis that $\rho = 1$ and that the constant term is zero is 2.19 $< 4.66$, which is again accepted. Thus, we could accept the null hypothesis that the series are not cointegrated.

Alternatively, the null hypothesis that $z_t$ is nonstationary could be tested using the Phillips-Perron tests. *OLS* estimation gives

$$z_t = \underset{(0.178)}{-0.030} + \underset{(0.01275)}{0.98654}\, z_{t-1} + \hat{u}_t$$

with

$$\begin{aligned} s^2 &= (T-2)^{-1} \sum_{t=1}^{T} \hat{u}_t^2 = (2.49116)^2 \\ \hat{c}_j &= T^{-1} \sum_{t=j+1}^{T} \hat{u}_t \hat{u}_{t-j} \\ \hat{c}_0 &= 6.144 \\ \hat{\lambda}^2 &= \hat{c}_0 + 2 \cdot \sum_{j=1}^{12} [1 - (j/13)]\hat{c}_j = 13.031. \end{aligned}$$

The Phillips-Perron $Z_\rho$ test is then

$$\begin{aligned} Z_\rho &= T(\hat{\rho} - 1) - \tfrac{1}{2}\{T \cdot \hat{\sigma}_{\hat{\rho}} \div s\}^2(\hat{\lambda}^2 - \hat{c}_0) \\ &= (201)(0.98654 - 1) \\ &\quad - \tfrac{1}{2}\{(201)(0.01275) \div (2.49116)\}^2(13.031 - 6.144) \\ &= -6.35. \end{aligned}$$

Since $-6.35 > -13.9$, the null hypothesis of no cointegration is again accepted. Similarly, the Phillips-Perron $Z_t$ test is

$$\begin{aligned} Z_t &= (\hat{c}_0/\hat{\lambda}^2)^{1/2}(\hat{\rho} - 1)/\hat{\sigma}_{\hat{\rho}} - \tfrac{1}{2}\{T \cdot \hat{\sigma}_{\hat{\rho}} \div s\}(\hat{\lambda}^2 - \hat{c}_0)/\hat{\lambda} \\ &= (6.144/13.031)^{1/2}(0.98654 - 1)/(0.01275) \\ &\quad - \tfrac{1}{2}\{(201)(0.01275) \div (2.49116)\}(13.031 - 6.144)/(13.031)^{1/2} \\ &= -1.71, \end{aligned}$$

which, since $-1.71 > -2.88$, gives the same conclusion as the other tests.

Clearly, the comments about the observational equivalence of $I(0)$ and $I(1)$ processes are also applicable to testing for cointegration. There exist both $I(0)$ and $I(1)$ representations that are perfectly capable of describing the observed data for $z_t$ plotted in Figure 19.3. Another way of describing the results is to calculate how long a deviation from purchasing power parity is likely to persist. The regression of [19.2.2] implies an autoregression in levels of the form

$$z_t = \alpha + \phi_1 z_{t-1} + \phi_2 z_{t-2} + \cdots + \phi_{13} z_{t-13} + \varepsilon_t,$$

for which the impulse-response function,

$$\psi_j = \frac{\partial z_{t+j}}{\partial \varepsilon_t},$$

can be calculated using the methods described in Chapter 1. Figure 19.4 plots the estimated impulse-response coefficients as a function of $j$. An unanticipated increase in $z_t$ would cause us to revise upward our forecast of $z_{t+j}$ by 25% even 3 years into the future ($\psi_{36} = 0.27$). Hence, any forces that restore $z_t$ to its historical value must operate relatively slowly. The same conclusion might have been gleaned from Figure 19.3 directly, in that it is clear that deviations of $z_t$ from its historical norm can persist for a number of years.

## *Estimating the Cointegrating Vector*

If the theoretical model of the system dynamics does not suggest a particular value for the cointegrating vector **a**, then one approach to testing for cointegration is first to estimate **a** by *OLS*. To see why this produces a reasonable initial estimate,

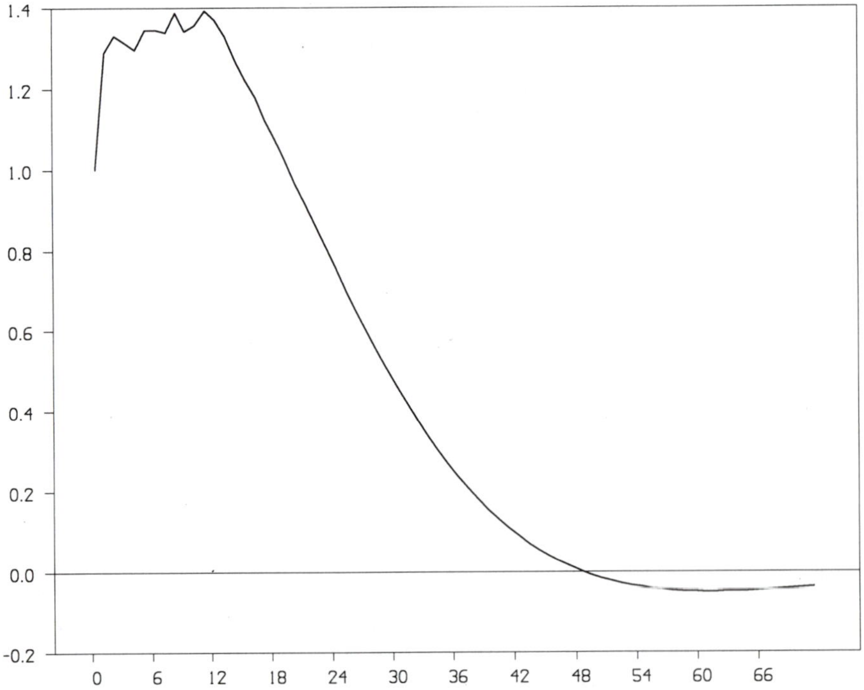


**FIGURE 19.4** Impulse-response function for the real dollar-lira exchange rate. Graph shows $\psi_j = \partial(p_{t+j} - s_{t+j} - p^*_{t+j})/\varepsilon_t$ as a function of $j$.

note that if $z_t = \mathbf{a}'\mathbf{y}_t$ is stationary and ergodic for second moments, then

$$T^{-1} \sum_{t=1}^{T} z_t^2 = T^{-1} \sum_{t=1}^{T} (\mathbf{a}'\mathbf{y}_t)^2 \xrightarrow{p} E(z_t^2). \qquad [19.2.3]$$

By contrast, if $\mathbf{a}$ is not a cointegrating vector, then $z_t = \mathbf{a}'\mathbf{y}_t$ is $I(1)$, and so, from result (h) of Proposition 17.3,

$$T^{-2} \sum_{t=1}^{T} (\mathbf{a}'\mathbf{y}_t)^2 \xrightarrow{L} \lambda^2 \cdot \int_0^1 [W(r)]^2 \, dr, \qquad [19.2.4]$$

where $W(r)$ is standard Brownian motion and $\lambda$ is a parameter determined by the autocovariances of $(1 - L)z_t$. Hence, if $\mathbf{a}$ is not a cointegrating vector, the statistic in [19.2.3] would diverge to $+\infty$.

This suggests that we can obtain a consistent estimate of a cointegrating vector by choosing $\mathbf{a}$ so as to minimize [19.2.3] subject to some normalization condition on $\mathbf{a}$. Indeed, such an estimator turns out to be superconsistent, converging at rate $T$ rather than $T^{1/2}$.

If it is known for certain that the cointegrating vector has a nonzero coefficient for the first element of $\mathbf{y}_t$ $(a_1 \neq 0)$, then a particularly convenient normalization is to set $a_1 = 1$ and represent subsequent entries of $\mathbf{a}$ $(a_2, a_3, \ldots, a_n)$ as the negatives of a set of unknown parameters $(\gamma_2, \gamma_3, \ldots, \gamma_n)$:

$$\begin{bmatrix} a_1 \\ a_2 \\ a_3 \\ \vdots \\ a_n \end{bmatrix} = \begin{bmatrix} 1 \\ -\gamma_2 \\ -\gamma_3 \\ \vdots \\ -\gamma_n \end{bmatrix}. \qquad [19.2.5]$$

In this case, the objective is to choose $(\gamma_2, \gamma_3, \ldots, \gamma_n)$ so as to minimize

$$T^{-1} \sum_{t=1}^{T} (\mathbf{a}'\mathbf{y}_t)^2 = T^{-1} \sum_{t=1}^{T} (y_{1t} - \gamma_2 y_{2t} - \gamma_3 y_{3t} - \cdots - \gamma_n y_{nt})^2. \qquad [19.2.6]$$

This minimization is, of course, achieved by an *OLS* regression of the first element of $\mathbf{y}_t$ on all of the others:

$$y_{1t} = \gamma_2 y_{2t} + \gamma_3 y_{3t} + \cdots + \gamma_n y_{nt} + u_t. \qquad [19.2.7]$$

Consistent estimates of $\gamma_2, \gamma_3, \ldots, \gamma_n$ are also obtained when a constant term is included in [19.2.7], as in

$$y_{1t} = \alpha + \gamma_2 y_{2t} + \gamma_3 y_{3t} + \cdots + \gamma_n y_{nt} + u_t \qquad [19.2.8]$$

or

$$y_{1t} = \alpha + \boldsymbol{\gamma}'\mathbf{y}_{2t} + u_t,$$

where $\boldsymbol{\gamma}' \equiv (\gamma_2, \gamma_3, \ldots, \gamma_n)$ and $\mathbf{y}_{2t} \equiv (y_{2t}, y_{3t}, \ldots, y_{nt})'$.

These points were first analyzed by Phillips and Durlauf (1986) and Stock (1987) and are formally summarized in the following proposition.

***Proposition 19.2:*** *Let $y_{1t}$ be a scalar and $\mathbf{y}_{2t}$ be a $(g \times 1)$ vector. Let $n \equiv g + 1$, and suppose that the $(n \times 1)$ vector $(y_{1t}, \mathbf{y}_{2t}')'$ is characterized by exactly one cointegrating relation ($h = 1$) that has a nonzero coefficient on $y_{1t}$. Let the triangular* *representation for the system be*

$$y_{1t} = \alpha + \boldsymbol{\gamma}'\mathbf{y}_{2t} + z_t^* \qquad [19.2.9]$$

$$\Delta\mathbf{y}_{2t} = \mathbf{u}_{2t}. \qquad [19.2.10]$$

*Suppose that*

$$\begin{bmatrix} z_t^* \\ \mathbf{u}_{2t} \end{bmatrix} = \boldsymbol{\Psi}^*(L)\boldsymbol{\varepsilon}_t, \qquad [19.2.11]$$

*where* $\boldsymbol{\varepsilon}_t$ *is an* $(n \times 1)$ *i.i.d. vector with mean zero, finite fourth moments, and positive definite variance-covariance matrix* $E(\boldsymbol{\varepsilon}_t\boldsymbol{\varepsilon}_t') = \mathbf{PP}'$. *Suppose further that the sequence of* $(n \times n)$ *matrices* $\{s \cdot \boldsymbol{\Psi}_s^*\}_{s=0}^{\infty}$ *is absolutely summable and that the rows of* $\boldsymbol{\Psi}^*(1)$ *are linearly independent. Let* $\hat{\alpha}_T$ *and* $\hat{\boldsymbol{\gamma}}_T$ *be estimates based on OLS estimation of [19.2.9],*

$$\begin{bmatrix} \hat{\alpha}_T \\ \hat{\boldsymbol{\gamma}}_T \end{bmatrix} = \begin{bmatrix} T & \Sigma\mathbf{y}_{2t}' \\ \Sigma\mathbf{y}_{2t} & \Sigma\mathbf{y}_{2t}\mathbf{y}_{2t}' \end{bmatrix}^{-1} \begin{bmatrix} \Sigma y_{1t} \\ \Sigma\mathbf{y}_{2t}y_{1t} \end{bmatrix}, \qquad [19.2.12]$$

*where* $\Sigma$ *indicates summation over t from* 1 *to T. Partition* $\boldsymbol{\Psi}^*(1)\cdot\mathbf{P}$ *as*

$$\underset{(n \times n)}{\boldsymbol{\Psi}^*(1)\cdot\mathbf{P}} = \begin{bmatrix} \underset{(1 \times n)}{\boldsymbol{\lambda}_1^{*\prime}} \\ \underset{(g \times n)}{\boldsymbol{\Lambda}_2^*} \end{bmatrix}.$$

*Then*

$$\begin{bmatrix} T^{1/2}(\hat{\alpha}_T - \alpha) \\ T(\hat{\boldsymbol{\gamma}}_T - \boldsymbol{\gamma}) \end{bmatrix} \xrightarrow{L} \begin{bmatrix} 1 & \left\{\int [\mathbf{W}(r)]'\,dr\right\}\cdot\boldsymbol{\Lambda}_2^{*\prime} \\ \boldsymbol{\Lambda}_2^*\cdot\int \mathbf{W}(r)\,dr & \boldsymbol{\Lambda}_2^*\cdot\left\{\int [\mathbf{W}(r)]\cdot[\mathbf{W}(r)]'\,dr\right\}\cdot\boldsymbol{\Lambda}_2^{*\prime} \end{bmatrix}^{-1} \begin{bmatrix} h_1 \\ \mathbf{h}_2 \end{bmatrix}, \qquad [19.2.13]$$

*where* $\mathbf{W}(r)$ *is n-dimensional standard Brownian motion, the integral sign denotes integration over r from* 0 *to* 1, *and*

$$h_1 \equiv \boldsymbol{\lambda}_1^{*\prime}\cdot\mathbf{W}(1)$$

$$\mathbf{h}_2 \equiv \boldsymbol{\Lambda}_2^*\cdot\left\{\int_0^1 [\mathbf{W}(r)]\,[d\mathbf{W}(r)]'\right\}\cdot\boldsymbol{\lambda}_1^* + \sum_{v=0}^{\infty} E(\mathbf{u}_{2t}z_{t+v}^*).$$

Note that the *OLS* estimate of the cointegrating vector is consistent even though the error term $u_t$ in [19.2.8] may be serially correlated and correlated with $\Delta y_{2t}, \Delta y_{3t}, \ldots, \Delta y_{nt}$. The latter correlation would contribute a bias in the limiting distribution of $T(\hat{\boldsymbol{\gamma}}_T - \boldsymbol{\gamma})$, for then the random variable $\mathbf{h}_2$ would not have mean zero. However, the bias in $\hat{\boldsymbol{\gamma}}_T$ is $O_p(T^{-1})$.

Since the *OLS* estimates are consistent, the average squared sample residual converges to

$$T^{-1}\sum_{t=1}^{T} \hat{u}_{t,T}^2 \xrightarrow{p} E(u_t^2),$$

whereas the sample variance of $y_{1t}$,

$$T^{-1}\sum_{t=1}^{T} (y_{1t} - \bar{y}_1)^2,$$

diverges to $+\infty$. Hence, the $R^2$ for the regression of [19.2.8] will converge to unity as the sample size grows.

Cointegration can be viewed as a structural assumption under which certain behavioral relations of interest can be estimated from the data by *OLS*. Consider the supply-and-demand example in equations [9.1.2] and [9.1.1]:

$$q_t^s = \gamma p_t + \varepsilon_t^s \qquad [19.2.14]$$

$$q_t^d = \beta p_t + \varepsilon_t^d. \qquad [19.2.15]$$

We noted in equation [9.1.6] that if $\varepsilon_t^d$ and $\varepsilon_t^s$ are i.i.d. with $\text{Var}(\varepsilon_t^s)$ finite, then as the variance of $\varepsilon_t^d$ goes to infinity, *OLS* estimation of [19.2.14] produces a consistent estimate of the supply elasticity $\gamma$ despite the potential simultaneous equations bias. This is because the large shifts in the demand curve effectively trace out the supply curve in the sample; see Figure 9.3. More generally, if $\varepsilon_t^s$ is $I(0)$ and $\varepsilon_t^d$ is $I(1)$, then [19.2.14] and [19.2.15] imply that $(q_t, p_t)'$ is cointegrated with cointegrating vector $(1, -\gamma)'$. In this case the cointegrating vector can be consistently estimated by *OLS* for essentially the same reason as in Figure 9.3. The hypothesis that a certain structural relation involving $I(1)$ variables is characterized by an $I(0)$ disturbance amounts to a structural assumption that can help identify the parameters of the structural relation.

Although the estimates based on [19.2.8] are consistent, there often exist alternative estimates that are superior. These will be discussed in Section 19.3. *OLS* estimation of [19.2.8] is proposed only as a quick way to obtain an initial estimate of the cointegrating vector.

It was assumed in Proposition 19.2 that $\Delta\mathbf{y}_{2t}$ had mean zero. If, instead, $E(\Delta\mathbf{y}_{2t}) = \boldsymbol{\delta}_2$, it is straightforward to generalize Proposition 19.2 using a rotation of variables as in [18.2.43]; for details, see Hansen (1992). As long as there is no time trend in the true cointegrating relation [19.2.9], the estimate $\hat{\boldsymbol{\gamma}}_T$ based on *OLS* estimation of [19.2.8] will be superconsistent regardless of whether the $I(1)$ vector $\mathbf{y}_{2t}$ includes a deterministic time trend or not.

## *The Role of Normalization*

The *OLS* estimate of the cointegrating vector was obtained by normalizing the first element of the cointegrating vector $\mathbf{a}$ to be unity. The proposal was then to regress the first element of $\mathbf{y}_t$ on the others. For example, with $n = 2$, we would regress $y_{1t}$ on $y_{2t}$:

$$y_{1t} = \alpha + \gamma y_{2t} + u_t.$$

Obviously, we might equally well have normalized $a_2 = 1$ and used the same argument to suggest a regression of $y_{2t}$ on $y_{1t}$:

$$y_{2t} = \theta + \aleph y_{1t} + v_t.$$

The *OLS* estimate $\hat{\aleph}$ is not simply the inverse of $\hat{\gamma}$, meaning that these two regressions will give different estimates of the cointegrating vector:

$$\begin{bmatrix} 1 \\ -\hat{\gamma} \end{bmatrix} \neq -\hat{\gamma}\begin{bmatrix} -\hat{\aleph} \\ 1 \end{bmatrix}.$$

Only in the limiting case where the $R^2$ is 1 would the two estimates coincide.

Thus, choosing which variable to call $y_1$ and which to call $y_2$ might end up making a material difference for the estimate of $\mathbf{a}$ as well as for the evidence one finds for cointegration among the series. One approach that avoids this normalization problem is the full-information maximum likelihood estimate proposed by Johansen (1988, 1991). This will be discussed in detail in Chapter 20.

### *What Is the Regression Estimating When There Is More Than One Cointegrating Relation?*

The limiting distribution of the *OLS* estimate in Proposition 19.2 was derived under the assumption that there is just one cointegrating relation ($h = 1$). In the more general case with $h > 1$, *OLS* estimation of [19.2.8] should still provide a consistent estimate of a cointegrating vector by virtue of the argument given in [19.2.3] and [19.2.4]. But which cointegrating vector is it?

Consider the general triangular representation for a vector with $h$ cointegrating relations given in [19.1.20] and [19.1.21]:

$$\mathbf{y}_{1t} = \boldsymbol{\mu}_1^* + \boldsymbol{\Gamma}'\mathbf{y}_{2t} + \mathbf{z}_t^* \qquad [19.2.16]$$

$$\Delta\mathbf{y}_{2t} = \boldsymbol{\delta}_2 + \mathbf{u}_{2t}, \qquad [19.2.17]$$

where the $(h \times 1)$ vector $\mathbf{y}_{1t}$ contains the first $h$ elements of $\mathbf{y}_t$ and $\mathbf{y}_{2t}$ contains the remaining $g$ elements. Since $\mathbf{z}_t^* \equiv (\mathbf{z}_{1t}^*, \mathbf{z}_{2t}^*, \ldots, \mathbf{z}_{ht}^*)'$ is covariance-stationary with mean zero, we can define $\beta_2, \beta_3, \ldots, \beta_h$ to be the population coefficients associated with a linear projection of $z_{1t}^*$ on $z_{2t}^*, z_{3t}^*, \ldots, z_{ht}^*$:

$$z_{1t}^* = \beta_2 z_{2t}^* + \beta_3 z_{3t}^* + \cdots + \beta_h z_{ht}^* + u_t, \qquad [19.2.18]$$

where $u_t$ by construction has mean zero and is uncorrelated with $z_{2t}^*, z_{3t}^*, \ldots, z_{ht}^*$.

The following proposition, adapted from Wooldridge (1991), shows that the sample residual $\hat{u}_t$ resulting from *OLS* estimation of [19.2.8] converges in probability to the population residual $u_t$ associated with the linear projection in [19.2.18]. In other words, among the set of possible cointegrating relations, *OLS* estimation of [19.2.8] selects the relation whose residuals are uncorrelated with any other $I(1)$ linear combinations of $(y_{2t}, y_{3t}, \ldots, y_{nt})$.

***Proposition 19.3:*** *Let $\mathbf{y}_t = (\mathbf{y}_{1t}', \mathbf{y}_{2t}')'$ satisfy [19.2.16] and [19.2.17] with $\mathbf{y}_{1t}$ an $(h \times 1)$ vector with $h > 1$, and let $\beta_2, \beta_3, \ldots, \beta_h$ denote the linear projection coefficients in [19.2.18]. Suppose that*

$$\begin{bmatrix} \mathbf{z}_t^* \\ \mathbf{u}_{2t} \end{bmatrix} = \sum_{s=0}^{\infty} \boldsymbol{\Psi}_s^* \boldsymbol{\varepsilon}_{t-s},$$

*where $\{s \cdot \boldsymbol{\Psi}_s^*\}_{s=0}^{\infty}$ is absolutely summable and $\boldsymbol{\varepsilon}_t$ is an i.i.d. $(n \times 1)$ vector with mean zero, variance $\mathbf{PP}'$, and finite fourth moments. Suppose further that the rows of $\boldsymbol{\Psi}^*(1) \cdot \mathbf{P}$ are linearly independent. Then the coefficient estimates associated with OLS estimation of*

$$y_{1t} = \alpha + \gamma_2 y_{2t} + \gamma_3 y_{3t} + \cdots + \gamma_n y_{nt} + u_t \qquad [19.2.19]$$

*converge in probability to*

$$\hat{\alpha}_T \xrightarrow{p} [1 \quad -\boldsymbol{\beta}']\boldsymbol{\mu}_1^*, \qquad [19.2.20]$$

*where*

$$\underset{(h-1)\times 1}{\boldsymbol{\beta}} \equiv (\beta_2, \beta_3, \ldots, \beta_h)'$$

*and*

$$\begin{bmatrix} \hat{\gamma}_{2,T} \\ \hat{\gamma}_{3,T} \\ \vdots \\ \hat{\gamma}_{n,T} \end{bmatrix} \xrightarrow{p} \begin{bmatrix} \boldsymbol{\beta} \\ \boldsymbol{\gamma}_2 \end{bmatrix} \qquad [19.2.21]$$

*where*

$$\underset{(g\times 1)}{\boldsymbol{\gamma}_2} \equiv \boldsymbol{\Gamma}\begin{bmatrix} 1 \\ -\boldsymbol{\beta} \end{bmatrix}.$$

Proposition 19.3 establishes that the sample residuals associated with *OLS* estimation of [19.2.19] converge in probability to

$$\begin{aligned} &y_{1t} - \hat{\alpha}_T - \hat{\gamma}_{2,T}y_{2t} - \hat{\gamma}_{3,T}y_{3t} - \cdots - \hat{\gamma}_{n,T}y_{nt} \\ &\quad \xrightarrow{p} y_{1t} - [1 \quad -\boldsymbol{\beta}']\boldsymbol{\mu}_1^* - \boldsymbol{\beta}'\begin{bmatrix} y_{2t} \\ y_{3t} \\ \vdots \\ y_{ht} \end{bmatrix} - [1 \quad -\boldsymbol{\beta}']\boldsymbol{\Gamma}'\begin{bmatrix} y_{h+1,t} \\ y_{h+2,t} \\ \vdots \\ y_{nt} \end{bmatrix} \\ &\quad = [1 \quad -\boldsymbol{\beta}']\cdot\{\mathbf{y}_{1t} - \boldsymbol{\mu}_1^* - \boldsymbol{\Gamma}'\mathbf{y}_{2t}\} \\ &\quad = [1 \quad -\boldsymbol{\beta}']\cdot\mathbf{z}_t^*, \end{aligned}$$

with the last equality following from [19.2.16]. But from [19.2.18] these are the same as the population residuals associated with the linear projection of $z_{1t}^*$ on $z_{2t}^*, z_{3t}^*, \ldots, z_{ht}^*$.

This is an illustration of a general property observed by Wooldridge (1991). Consider a regression model of the form

$$y_t = \alpha + \mathbf{x}_t'\boldsymbol{\beta} + u_t. \qquad [19.2.22]$$

If $y_t$ and $\mathbf{x}_t$ are $I(0)$, then $\alpha + \mathbf{x}_t'\boldsymbol{\beta}$ was said to be the linear projection of $y_t$ on $\mathbf{x}_t$ and a constant if the population residual $u_t = y_t - \alpha - \mathbf{x}_t'\boldsymbol{\beta}$ has mean zero and is uncorrelated with $\mathbf{x}_t$. We saw that in such a case *OLS* estimation of [19.2.22] would typically yield consistent estimates of these linear projection coefficients. In the more general case where $y_t$ can be $I(0)$ or $I(1)$ and elements of $\mathbf{x}_t$ can be $I(0)$ or $I(1)$, the analogous condition is that the residual $u_t = y_t - \alpha - \mathbf{x}_t'\boldsymbol{\beta}$ is a zero-mean stationary process that is uncorrelated with all $I(0)$ linear combinations of $\mathbf{x}_t$. Then $\alpha + \mathbf{x}_t'\boldsymbol{\beta}$ can be viewed as the $I(1)$ generalization of a population linear projection of $y_t$ on a constant and $\mathbf{x}_t$. As long as there is some value for $\boldsymbol{\beta}$ such that $y_t - \mathbf{x}_t'\boldsymbol{\beta}$ is $I(0)$, such a linear projection $\alpha + \mathbf{x}_t'\boldsymbol{\beta}$ exists, and *OLS* estimation of [19.2.22] should give a consistent estimate of this projection.

### *What Is the Regression Estimating When There Is No Cointegrating Relation?*

We have seen that if there is at least one cointegrating relation involving $y_{1t}$, then *OLS* estimation of [19.2.19] gives a consistent estimate of a cointegrating vector. Let us now consider the properties of *OLS* estimation when there is no cointegrating relation. Then [19.2.19] is a regression of an $I(1)$ variable on a set of $(n - 1)$ $I(1)$ variables for which no coefficients produce an $I(0)$ error term. The regression is therefore subject to the spurious regression problem described in Section 18.3. The coefficients $\hat{\alpha}_T$ and $\hat{\boldsymbol{\gamma}}_T$ do not provide consistent estimates of any population parameters, and the *OLS* sample residuals $\hat{u}_t$ will be nonstationary. However, this last property can be exploited to test for cointegration. If there is no cointegration, then a regression of $\hat{u}_t$ on $\hat{u}_{t-1}$ should yield a unit coefficient. If there is cointegration, then a regression of $\hat{u}_t$ on $\hat{u}_{t-1}$ should yield a coefficient that is less than 1.

The proposal is thus to estimate [19.2.19] by *OLS* and then construct one of the standard unit root tests on the estimated residuals, such as the augmented Dickey-Fuller $t$ test or the Phillips $Z_\rho$ or $Z_t$ test. Although these test statistics are constructed in the same way as when they are applied to an individual series $y_t$, when the tests are applied to the residuals $\hat{u}_t$ from a spurious regression, the critical values that are used to interpret the test statistics are different from those employed in Chapter 17.

Specifically, let $\mathbf{y}_t$ be an $(n \times 1)$ vector partitioned as

$$\underset{(n\times 1)}{\mathbf{y}_t} = \begin{bmatrix} \underset{(1\times 1)}{y_{1t}} \\ \underset{(g\times 1)}{\mathbf{y}_{2t}} \end{bmatrix} \qquad [19.2.23]$$

for $g \equiv (n - 1)$. Consider the regression

$$y_{1t} = \alpha + \boldsymbol{\gamma}'\mathbf{y}_{2t} + u_t. \qquad [19.2.24]$$

Let $\hat{u}_t$ be the sample residual associated with *OLS* estimation of [19.2.24] in a sample of size $T$:

$$\hat{u}_t = y_{1t} - \hat{\alpha}_T - \hat{\boldsymbol{\gamma}}_T'\mathbf{y}_{2t} \qquad \text{for } t = 1, 2, \ldots, T, \qquad [19.2.25]$$

where

$$\begin{bmatrix} \hat{\alpha}_T \\ \hat{\boldsymbol{\gamma}}_T \end{bmatrix} = \begin{bmatrix} T & \Sigma\mathbf{y}_{2t}' \\ \Sigma\mathbf{y}_{2t} & \Sigma\mathbf{y}_{2t}\mathbf{y}_{2t}' \end{bmatrix}^{-1} \begin{bmatrix} \Sigma y_{1t} \\ \Sigma\mathbf{y}_{2t}y_{1t} \end{bmatrix}$$

and where $\Sigma$ indicates summation over $t$ from 1 to $T$. The residual $\hat{u}_t$ can then be regressed on its own lagged value $\hat{u}_{t-1}$ without a constant term:

$$\hat{u}_t = \rho\hat{u}_{t-1} + e_t \qquad \text{for } t = 2, 3, \ldots, T, \qquad [19.2.26]$$

yielding the estimate

$$\hat{\rho}_T = \frac{\sum_{t=2}^{T} \hat{u}_{t-1}\hat{u}_t}{\sum_{t=2}^{T} \hat{u}_{t-1}^2}. \qquad [19.2.27]$$

Let $s_T^2$ be the *OLS* estimate of the variance of $e_t$ for the regression of [19.2.26]:

$$s_T^2 = (T - 2)^{-1} \sum_{t=2}^{T} (\hat{u}_t - \hat{\rho}_T\hat{u}_{t-1})^2, \qquad [19.2.28]$$

and let $\hat{\sigma}_{\hat{\rho}_T}$ be the standard error of $\hat{\rho}_T$ as calculated by the usual *OLS* formula:

$$\hat{\sigma}_{\hat{\rho}_T}^2 = s_T^2 \div \left\{\sum_{t=2}^{T} \hat{u}_{t-1}^2\right\}. \qquad [19.2.29]$$

Finally, let $\hat{c}_{j,T}$ be the $j$th sample autocovariance of the estimated residuals associated with [19.2.26]:

$$\hat{c}_{j,T} = (T - 1)^{-1} \sum_{t=j+2}^{T} \hat{e}_t \hat{e}_{t-j} \qquad \text{for } j = 0, 1, 2, \ldots, T - 2 \qquad [19.2.30]$$

for $\hat{e}_t \equiv \hat{u}_t - \hat{\rho}_T \hat{u}_{t-1}$; and let the square of $\hat{\lambda}_T$ be given by

$$\hat{\lambda}_T^2 = \hat{c}_{0,T} + 2 \cdot \sum_{j=1}^{q} [1 - j/(q + 1)] \hat{c}_{j,T}, \qquad [19.2.31]$$

where $q$ is the number of autocovariances to be used. Phillips's $Z_\rho$ statistic (1987) can be calculated just as in [17.6.8]:

$$Z_{\rho,T} = (T - 1)(\hat{\rho}_T - 1) - (1/2) \cdot \{(T - 1)^2 \cdot \hat{\sigma}_{\hat{\rho}_T}^2 \div s_T^2\} \cdot \{\hat{\lambda}_T^2 - \hat{c}_{0,T}\}. \qquad [19.2.32]$$

However, the asymptotic distribution of this statistic is not the expression in [17.6.8] but instead is a distribution that will be described in Proposition 19.4.

If the vector $\mathbf{y}_t$ is not cointegrated, then [19.2.24] will be a spurious regression and $\hat{\rho}_T$ should be near 1. On the other hand, if we find that $\hat{\rho}_T$ is well below 1—that is, if calculation of [19.2.32] yields a negative number that is sufficiently large in absolute value—then the null hypothesis that [19.2.24] is a spurious regression should be rejected, and we would conclude that the variables are cointegrated.

Similarly, Phillips's $Z_t$ statistic associated with the residual autoregression [19.2.26] would be

$$Z_{t,T} = (\hat{c}_{0,T}/\hat{\lambda}_T^2)^{1/2} \cdot t_T - (1/2) \cdot \{(T - 1) \cdot \hat{\sigma}_{\hat{\rho}_T} \div s_T\} \cdot \{\hat{\lambda}_T^2 - \hat{c}_{0,T}\}/\hat{\lambda}_T \qquad [19.2.33]$$

for $t_T$ the usual *OLS* $t$ statistic for testing the hypothesis $\rho = 1$:

$$t_T = (\hat{\rho}_T - 1)/\hat{\sigma}_{\hat{\rho}_T}.$$

Alternatively, lagged changes in the residuals could be added to the regression of [19.2.26] as in the augmented Dickey-Fuller test with no constant term:

$$\hat{u}_t = \zeta_1 \Delta\hat{u}_{t-1} + \zeta_2 \Delta\hat{u}_{t-2} + \cdots + \zeta_{p-1} \Delta\hat{u}_{t-p+1} + \rho\hat{u}_{t-1} + e_t. \qquad [19.2.34]$$

Again, this is estimated by *OLS* for $t = p + 1, p + 2, \ldots, T$, and the *OLS* $t$ test of $\rho = 1$ is calculated using the standard *OLS* formula [8.1.26]. If this $t$ statistic or the $Z_t$ statistic in [19.2.33] is negative and sufficiently large in absolute value, this again casts doubt on the null hypothesis of no cointegration.

The following proposition, adapted from Phillips and Ouliaris (1990), provides a formal statement of the asymptotic distributions of these three test statistics.

***Proposition 19.4:*** *Consider an* $(n \times 1)$ *vector* $\mathbf{y}_t$ *such that*

$$\Delta \mathbf{y}_t = \sum_{s=0}^{\infty} \mathbf{\Psi}_s \boldsymbol{\varepsilon}_{t-s}$$

*for* $\boldsymbol{\varepsilon}_t$ *an i.i.d. sequence with mean zero, variance* $E(\boldsymbol{\varepsilon}_t \boldsymbol{\varepsilon}_t') = \mathbf{PP}'$, *and finite fourth moments, and where* $\{s \cdot \mathbf{\Psi}_s\}_{s=0}^{\infty}$ *is absolutely summable. Let* $g \equiv n - 1$ *and* $\mathbf{\Lambda} \equiv \mathbf{\Psi}(1) \cdot \mathbf{P}$. *Suppose that the* $(n \times n)$ *matrix* $\mathbf{\Lambda\Lambda}'$ *is nonsingular, and let* $\mathbf{L}$ *denote the Cholesky factor of* $(\mathbf{\Lambda\Lambda}')^{-1}$:

$$(\mathbf{\Lambda\Lambda}')^{-1} = \mathbf{LL}'. \qquad [19.2.35]$$

*Then the following hold:*

(*a*) *The statistic* $\hat{\rho}_T$ *defined in* [*19.2.27*] *satisfies*

$$(T-1)(\hat{\rho}_T-1) \xrightarrow{L} \left\{\frac{1}{2}\left\{[1 \quad -\mathbf{h}_2']\cdot[\mathbf{W}^*(1)]\cdot[\mathbf{W}^*(1)]'\begin{bmatrix}1\\-\mathbf{h}_2\end{bmatrix}\right\} - h_1[\mathbf{W}^*(1)]'\begin{bmatrix}1\\-\mathbf{h}_2\end{bmatrix} - \frac{1}{2}[1 \quad -\mathbf{h}_2']\mathbf{L}'\{E(\Delta\mathbf{y}_t)(\Delta\mathbf{y}_t')\}\mathbf{L}\begin{bmatrix}1\\-\mathbf{h}_2\end{bmatrix}\right\} \div H_n. \qquad [19.2.36]$$

*Here,* $\mathbf{W}^*(r)$ *denotes n-dimensional standard Brownian motion partitioned as*

$$\underset{(n\times 1)}{\mathbf{W}^*(r)} = \begin{bmatrix}\underset{(1\times 1)}{W_1^*(r)}\\ \underset{(g\times 1)}{\mathbf{W}_2^*(r)}\end{bmatrix};$$

$h_1$ *is a scalar and* $\mathbf{h}_2$ *a* $(g \times 1)$ *vector given by*

$$\begin{bmatrix}h_1\\ \mathbf{h}_2\end{bmatrix} \equiv \begin{bmatrix}1 & \int [\mathbf{W}_2^*(r)]'\,dr\\ \int \mathbf{W}_2^*(r)\,dr & \int [\mathbf{W}_2^*(r)]\cdot[\mathbf{W}_2^*(r)]'\,dr\end{bmatrix}^{-1}\begin{bmatrix}\int W_1^*(r)\,dr\\ \int \mathbf{W}_2^*(r)\cdot W_1^*(r)\,dr\end{bmatrix},$$

*where the integral sign indicates integration over r from* 0 *to* 1; *and*

$$H_n \equiv \int [W_1^*(r)]^2\,dr - \left[\int W_1^*(r)\,dr \quad \int [W_1^*(r)]\cdot[\mathbf{W}_2^*(r)]'\,dr\right]\begin{bmatrix}h_1\\ \mathbf{h}_2\end{bmatrix}.$$

(*b*) *If* $q \to \infty$ *as* $T \to \infty$ *but* $q/T \to 0$, *then the statistic* $Z_{\rho,T}$ *in* [19.2.32] *satisfies*

$$Z_{\rho,T} \xrightarrow{L} Z_n, \qquad [19.2.37]$$

*where*

$$Z_n \equiv \left\{\frac{1}{2}\left\{[1 \quad -\mathbf{h}_2']\cdot[\mathbf{W}^*(1)]\cdot[\mathbf{W}^*(1)]'\begin{bmatrix}1\\-\mathbf{h}_2\end{bmatrix}\right\} - h_1[\mathbf{W}^*(1)]'\begin{bmatrix}1\\-\mathbf{h}_2\end{bmatrix} - \frac{1}{2}(1+\mathbf{h}_2'\mathbf{h}_2)\right\} \div H_n. \qquad [19.2.38]$$

(*c*) *If* $q \to \infty$ *as* $T \to \infty$ *but* $q/T \to 0$, *then the statistic* $Z_{t,T}$ *in* [*19.2.33*] *satisfies*

$$Z_{t,T} \xrightarrow{L} Z_n \cdot \sqrt{H_n} \div (1+\mathbf{h}_2'\mathbf{h}_2)^{1/2}. \qquad [19.2.39]$$

(*d*) *If, in addition to the preceding assumptions,* $\Delta\mathbf{y}_t$ *follows a zero-mean stationary vector ARMA process and if* $p \to \infty$ *as* $T \to \infty$ *but* $p/T^{1/3} \to 0$, *then the augmented Dickey-Fuller t test associated with* [19.2.34] *has the same limiting distribution* $Z_n$ *as the test statistic* $Z_{\rho,T}$ *described in* [*19.2.37*].

Result (a) implies that $\hat{\rho}_T \xrightarrow{p} 1$. Hence, when the estimated "cointegrating" regression [19.2.24] is spurious, the estimated residuals from this regression behave like a unit root process in the sense that if $\hat{u}_t$ is regressed on $\hat{u}_{t-1}$, the estimated coefficient should tend to unity as the sample size grows. No linear combination of $\mathbf{y}_t$ is stationary, and so the residuals from the spurious regression cannot be stationary.

Note that since $W_1^*(r)$ and $\mathbf{W}_2^*(r)$ are standard Brownian motion, the distributions of the terms $h_1$, $\mathbf{h}_2$, $H_n$, and $Z_n$ in Proposition 19.4 depend only on the number of stochastic explanatory variables included in the cointegrating regression $(n - 1)$ and on whether a constant term appears in that regression but are not affected by the variances, correlations, and dynamics of $\Delta\mathbf{y}_t$.

In the special case when $\Delta\mathbf{y}_t$ is i.i.d., then $\boldsymbol{\Psi}(L) = \mathbf{I}_n$ and the matrix $\boldsymbol{\Lambda}\boldsymbol{\Lambda}' = E[(\Delta\mathbf{y}_t)(\Delta\mathbf{y}_t')]$. Since $\mathbf{L}\mathbf{L}' = (\boldsymbol{\Lambda}\boldsymbol{\Lambda}')^{-1}$, it follows that $(\boldsymbol{\Lambda}\boldsymbol{\Lambda}') = (\mathbf{L}')^{-1}(\mathbf{L})^{-1}$. Hence, for this special case,

$$\mathbf{L}'\{E[(\Delta\mathbf{y}_t)(\Delta\mathbf{y}_t')]\}\mathbf{L} = \mathbf{L}'(\boldsymbol{\Lambda}\boldsymbol{\Lambda}')\mathbf{L} = \mathbf{L}'\{(\mathbf{L}')^{-1}(\mathbf{L})^{-1}\}\mathbf{L} = \mathbf{I}_n. \qquad [19.2.40]$$

If [19.2.40] is substituted into [19.2.36], the result is that when $\Delta\mathbf{y}_t$ is i.i.d.,

$$(T - 1)(\hat{\rho}_T - 1) \xrightarrow{L} Z_n$$

for $Z_n$ defined in [19.2.38].

In the more general case when $\Delta\mathbf{y}_t$ is serially correlated, the limiting distribution of $T(\hat{\rho}_T - 1)$ depends on the nature of this correlation as captured by the elements of $\mathbf{L}$. However, the corrections for autocorrelation implicit in Phillips's $Z_\rho$ and $Z_t$ statistics or the augmented Dickey-Fuller $t$ test turn out to generate variables whose distributions do not depend on any nuisance parameters.

Although the distributions of $Z_\rho$, $Z_t$, and the augmented Dickey-Fuller $t$ test do not depend on nuisance parameters, the distributions when these statistics are calculated from the residuals $\hat{u}_t$ are not the same as the distributions these statistics would have if calculated from the raw data $\mathbf{y}_t$. Moreover, different values for $n - 1$ (the number of stochastic explanatory variables in the cointegrating regression of [19.2.24]) imply different characterizations of the limiting statistics $h_1$, $\mathbf{h}_2$, $H_n$, and $Z_n$, meaning that a different critical value must be used to interpret $Z_\rho$ for each value of $n - 1$. Similarly, the asymptotic distributions of $\mathbf{h}_2$, $H_n$, and $Z_n$ are different depending on whether a constant term is included in the cointegrating regression [19.2.24].

The section labeled Case 1 in Table B.8 refers to the case when the cointegrating regression is estimated without a constant term:

$$y_{1t} = \gamma_2 y_{2t} + \gamma_3 y_{3t} + \cdots + \gamma_n y_{nt} + u_t. \qquad [19.2.41]$$

The table reports Monte Carlo estimates of the critical values for the test statistic $Z_\rho$ described in [19.2.32], for $\hat{u}_t$ the date $t$ residual from *OLS* estimation of [19.2.41]. The values were calculated by generating a sample of size $T = 500$ for $y_{1t}$, $y_{2t}$, $\ldots$, $y_{nt}$ independent Gaussian random walks, estimating [19.2.41] and [19.2.26] by *OLS*, and tabulating the distribution of $(T - 1)(\hat{\rho}_T - 1)$. For example, the table indicates that if we were to regress a random walk $y_{1t}$ on three other random walks ($y_{2t}$, $y_{3t}$, and $y_{4t}$), then in 95% of the samples, $(T - 1)(\hat{\rho}_T - 1)$ would be greater than $-27.9$, that is, $\hat{\rho}_T$ should exceed 0.94 in a sample of size $T = 500$. If the estimate $\hat{\rho}_T$ is below 0.94, then this might be taken as evidence that the series are cointegrated.

The section labeled Case 2 in Table B.8 gives critical values for $Z_{\rho,T}$ when a constant term is included in the cointegrating regression:

$$y_{1t} = \alpha + \gamma_2 y_{2t} + \gamma_3 y_{3t} + \cdots + \gamma_n y_{nt} + u_t. \qquad [19.2.42]$$

For this case, [19.2.26] is estimated with $\hat{u}_t$ now interpreted as the residual from

*OLS* estimation of [19.2.42]. Note that the different cases (1 and 2) refer to whether a constant term is included in the cointegrating regression [19.2.42] and not to whether a constant term is included in the residual regression [19.2.26]. In each case, the autoregression for the residuals is estimated in the form of [19.2.26] with no constant term.

Critical values for the $Z_t$ statistic or the augmented Dickey-Fuller $t$ statistic are reported in Table B.9. Again, if no constant term is included in the cointegrating regression as in [19.2.41], the case 1 entries are appropriate, whereas if a constant term is included in the cointegrating regression as in [19.2.42], the case 2 entries should be used. If the value for the $Z_t$ or augmented Dickey-Fuller $t$ statistic is negative and large in absolute value, this is evidence against the null hypothesis that $\mathbf{y}_t$ is not cointegrated.

When the corrections for serial correlation implicit in the $Z_\rho$, $Z_t$, or augmented Dickey-Fuller test are used, the justification for using the critical values in Table B.8 or B.9 is asymptotic, and accordingly these tables describe only the large-sample distribution. Small-sample critical values tabulated by Engle and Yoo (1987) and Haug (1992) can differ somewhat from the large-sample critical values.

## *Testing for Cointegration Among Trending Series*

It was assumed in Proposition 19.4 that $E(\Delta\mathbf{y}_t) = \mathbf{0}$, in which case none of the series would exhibit nonzero drift. Bruce Hansen (1992) described how the results change if instead $E(\Delta\mathbf{y}_t)$ contains one or more nonzero elements.

Consider first the case $n = 2$, a regression of one scalar on another:

$$y_{1t} = \alpha + \gamma y_{2t} + u_t. \qquad [19.2.43]$$

Suppose that

$$\Delta y_{2t} = \delta_2 + u_{2t}$$

with $\delta_2 \neq 0$. Then

$$y_{2t} = y_{2,0} + \delta_2 \cdot t + \sum_{s=1}^{t} u_{2s},$$

which is asymptotically dominated by the deterministic time trend $\delta_2 \cdot t$. Thus, estimates $\hat{\alpha}_T$ and $\hat{\gamma}_T$ based on *OLS* estimation of [19.2.43] have the same asymptotic distribution as the coefficients in a regression of an $I(1)$ series on a constant and a time trend. If

$$\Delta y_{1t} = \delta_1 + u_{1t}$$

(where $\delta_1$ may be zero), then the *OLS* estimate $\hat{\gamma}_T$ based on [19.2.43] gives a consistent estimate of $(\delta_1/\delta_2)$, and the first difference of the residuals from that regression converges to $u_{1t} - (\delta_1/\delta_2)u_{2t}$; see Exercise 19.1.

If, in fact, [19.2.43] were a simple time trend regression of the form

$$y_{1t} = \alpha + \gamma t + u_t,$$

then an augmented Dickey-Fuller test on the residuals,

$$\hat{u}_t = \zeta_1 \Delta\hat{u}_{t-1} + \zeta_2 \Delta\hat{u}_{t-2} + \cdots + \zeta_{p-1}\Delta\hat{u}_{t-p+1} + \rho\hat{u}_{t-1} + e_t, \qquad [19.2.44]$$

would be asymptotically equivalent to an augmented Dickey-Fuller test on the original series $y_{1t}$ that included a constant term and a time trend:

$$\begin{aligned} y_{1t} = {} & \zeta_1 \Delta y_{1,t-1} + \zeta_2 \Delta y_{1,t-2} + \cdots + \zeta_{p-1}\Delta y_{1,t-p+1} \\ & + \alpha + \rho y_{1,t-1} + \delta t + u_t. \end{aligned} \qquad [19.2.45]$$

Since the residuals from *OLS* estimation of [19.2.43] behave like the residuals from a regression of $[y_{1t} - (\delta_1/\delta_2)y_{2t}]$ on a time trend, Hansen (1992) showed that when $y_{2t}$ has a nonzero trend, the $t$ test of $\rho = 1$ in [19.2.44] for $\hat{u}_t$ the residual from *OLS* estimation of [19.2.43] has the same asymptotic distribution as the usual augmented Dickey-Fuller $t$ test for a regression of the form of [19.2.45] with $y_{1t}$ replaced by $[y_{1t} - (\delta_1/\delta_2)y_{2t}]$. Thus, if the cointegrating regression involves a single variable $y_{2t}$ with nonzero drift, we estimate the regression [19.2.43] and calculate the $Z_t$ or augmented Dickey-Fuller $t$ statistic in exactly the same manner that was specified in equation [19.2.33] or [19.2.34]. However, rather than compare these statistics with the $(n - 1) = 1$ entry for case 2 from Table B.9, we instead compare these statistics with the case 4 section of Table B.6.

For convenience, the values for a sample of size $T = 500$ for the univariate case 4 section of Table B.6 are reproduced in the $(n - 1) = 1$ row of the section labeled Case 3 in Table B.9. This is described as case 3 in the multivariate tabulations for the following reason. In the univariate analysis, "case 3" referred to a regression in which the single variable $y_t$ had a nonzero trend but no trend term was included in the regression. The multivariate generalization obtains when the explanatory variable $y_{2t}$ has a nonzero trend but no trend is included in the regression [19.2.43]. The asymptotic distribution that describes the residuals from that regression is the same as that for a univariate regression in which a trend is included.

Similarly, if $y_{2t}$ has a nonzero trend, we can estimate [19.2.43] by *OLS* and construct Phillips's $Z_\rho$ statistic exactly as in equation [19.2.32] and compare this with the values tabulated in the case 4 portion of Table B.5. These numbers are reproduced in row $(n - 1) = 1$ of the case 3 section of Table B.8.

More generally, consider a regression involving $n - 1$ stochastic explanatory variables of the form of [19.2.42]. Let $\delta_i$ denote the trend in the $i$th variable:

$$E(\Delta y_{it}) = \delta_i.$$

Suppose that at least one of the explanatory variables has a nonzero trend component; for illustration, call this the $n$th variable:

$$\delta_n \neq 0.$$

Whether or not other explanatory variables or the dependent variable also have nonzero trends turns out not to matter for the asymptotic distribution; that is, the values of $\delta_1, \delta_2, \ldots, \delta_{n-1}$ are irrelevant given that $\delta_n \neq 0$.

Note that the fitted values of [19.2.42] are identical to the fitted values from *OLS* estimation of

$$y_{1t}^* = \alpha^* + \gamma_2^* y_{2t}^* + \gamma_3^* y_{3t}^* + \cdots + \gamma_{n-1}^* y_{n-1,t}^* + \gamma_n^* y_{nt} + u_t, \qquad [19.2.46]$$

where

$$y_{it}^* \equiv y_{it} - (\delta_i/\delta_n)y_{nt} \qquad \text{for } i = 1, 2, \ldots, n - 1.$$

As in the analysis of [18.2.44], moments involving $y_{nt}$ are dominated by the time trend $\delta_n t$, while the $y_{it}^*$ are driftless $I(1)$ variables for $i = 1, 2, \ldots, n - 1$. Thus, the residuals from [19.2.46] have the same asymptotic properties as the residuals from *OLS* estimation of

$$y_{1t}^* = \alpha^* + \gamma_2^* y_{2t}^* + \gamma_3^* y_{3t}^* + \cdots + \gamma_{n-1}^* y_{n-1,t}^* + \gamma_n^* \delta_n t + u_t. \qquad [19.2.47]$$

The appropriate critical values for statistics constructed when $\hat{u}_t$ denotes the residual from *OLS* estimation of [19.2.42] can therefore be calculated from those for an *OLS* regression of an $I(1)$ variable on a constant, $(n - 2)$ other $I(1)$ variables, and a time trend. The appropriate critical values are tabulated under the heading Case 3 in Tables B.8 and B.9.

Of course, we could instead imagine including a time trend directly in the regression, as in

$$y_{1t} = \alpha + \gamma_2 y_{2t} + \gamma_3 y_{3t} + \cdots + \gamma_n y_{nt} + \delta t + u_t. \qquad [19.2.48]$$

Since [19.2.48] is in the same form as the regression of [19.2.47], critical values for such a regression could be found by treating this as if it were a regression involving $(n + 1)$ variables and looking in the case 3 section of Table B.8 or B.9 for the critical values that would be appropriate if we actually had $(n + 1)$ rather than $n$ total variables. Clearly, the specification in [19.2.42] has more power to reject a false null hypothesis than [19.2.48], since we would use the same table of critical values for [19.2.42] or [19.2.48] with one more degree of freedom used up by [19.2.48]. Conceivably, we might still want to estimate the regression in the form of [19.2.48] to cover the case when we are not sure whether any of the elements of $\mathbf{y}_t$ have a nonzero trend or not.

## *Summary of Residual-Based Tests for Cointegration*

The Phillips-Ouliaris-Hansen procedure for testing for cointegration is summarized in Table 19.1.

To illustrate this approach, consider again the purchasing power parity example where $p_t$ is the log of the U.S. price level, $s_t$ is the log of the dollar-lira exchange rate, and $p_t^*$ is the log of the Italian price level. We have already seen that the vector $\mathbf{a} = (1, -1, -1)'$ does not appear to be a cointegrating vector for $\mathbf{y}_t = (p_t, s_t, p_t^*)'$. Let us now ask whether there is any cointegrating relation among these variables.

The following regression was estimated by *OLS* for $t$ = 1973:1 to 1989:10 (standard errors in parentheses):

$$p_t = \underset{(0.37)}{2.71} + \underset{(0.012)}{0.051}\, s_t + \underset{(0.0067)}{0.5300}\, p_t^* + \hat{u}_t. \qquad [19.2.49]$$

The number of observations used to estimate [19.2.49] is $T = 202$. When the sample residuals $\hat{u}_t$ are regressed on their own lagged values, the result is

$$\hat{u}_t = \underset{(0.01172)}{0.98331}\, \hat{u}_{t-1} + \hat{e}_t$$

$$s^2 = (T - 2)^{-1} \sum_{t=2}^{T} \hat{e}_t^2 = (0.40374)^2$$

$$\hat{c}_0 = 0.1622$$

$$\hat{c}_j = (T - 1)^{-1} \sum_{t=j+2}^{T} \hat{e}_t \hat{e}_{t-j}$$

$$\hat{\lambda}^2 = \hat{c}_0 + 2 \cdot \sum_{j=1}^{12} [1 - (j/13)]\hat{c}_j = 0.4082.$$

The Phillips-Ouliaris $Z_\rho$ test is

$$\begin{aligned} Z_\rho &= (T - 1)(\hat{\rho} - 1) - (1/2)\{(T - 1) \cdot \hat{\sigma}_{\hat{\rho}} \div s\}^2(\hat{\lambda}^2 - \hat{c}_0) \\ &= (201)(0.98331 - 1) \\ &\quad - \tfrac{1}{2}\{(201)(0.01172) \div (0.40374)\}^2(0.4082 - 0.1622) \\ &= -7.54. \end{aligned}$$

Given the evidence of nonzero drift in the explanatory variables, this is to be compared with the case 3 section of Table B.8. For $(n - 1) = 2$, the 5% critical

**TABLE 19.1**
**Summary of Phillips-Ouliaris-Hansen Tests for Cointegration**

***Case 1:***

Estimated cointegrating regression:

$$y_{1t} = \gamma_2 y_{2t} + \gamma_3 y_{3t} + \cdots + \gamma_n y_{nt} + u_t$$

True process for $\mathbf{y}_t = (y_{1t}, y_{2t}, \ldots, y_{nt})'$:

$$\Delta \mathbf{y}_t = \sum_{s=0}^{\infty} \boldsymbol{\Psi}_s \boldsymbol{\varepsilon}_{t-s}$$

$Z_\rho$ has the same asymptotic distribution as the variable described under the heading Case 1 in Table B.8.

$Z_t$ and the augmented Dickey-Fuller $t$ test have the same asymptotic distribution as the variable described under Case 1 in Table B.9.

***Case 2:***

Estimated cointegrating regression:

$$y_{1t} = \alpha + \gamma_2 y_{2t} + \gamma_3 y_{3t} + \cdots + \gamma_n y_{nt} + u_t$$

True process for $\mathbf{y}_t = (y_{1t}, y_{2t}, \ldots, y_{nt})'$:

$$\Delta \mathbf{y}_t = \sum_{s=0}^{\infty} \boldsymbol{\Psi}_s \boldsymbol{\varepsilon}_{t-s}$$

$Z_\rho$ has the same asymptotic distribution as the variable described under Case 2 in Table B.8.

$Z_t$ and the augmented Dickey-Fuller $t$ test have the same asymptotic distribution as the variable described under Case 2 in Table B.9.

***Case 3:***

Estimated cointegrating regression:

$$y_{1t} = \alpha + \gamma_2 y_{2t} + \gamma_3 y_{3t} + \cdots + \gamma_n y_{nt} + u_t$$

True process for $\mathbf{y}_t = (y_{1t}, y_{2t}, \ldots, y_{nt})'$:

$$\Delta \mathbf{y}_t = \boldsymbol{\delta} + \sum_{s=0}^{\infty} \boldsymbol{\Psi}_s \boldsymbol{\varepsilon}_{t-s}$$

with at least one element of $\delta_2, \delta_3, \ldots, \delta_n$ nonzero.

$Z_\rho$ has the same asymptotic distribution as the variable described under Case 3 in Table B.8.

$Z_t$ and the augmented Dickey-Fuller $t$ test have the same asymptotic distribution as the variable described under Case 3 in Table B.9.

*Notes to Table 19.1*

*Estimated cointegrating regression* indicates the form in which the regression that could describe the cointegrating relation is estimated, using observations $t = 1, 2, \ldots, T$.

*True process* describes the null hypothesis under which the distribution is calculated. In each case, $\boldsymbol{\varepsilon}_t$ is assumed to be i.i.d. with mean zero, positive definite variance-covariance matrix, and finite fourth moments, and the sequence $\{s \cdot \boldsymbol{\Psi}_s\}_{s=0}^{\infty}$ is absolutely summable. The matrix $\boldsymbol{\Psi}(1)$ is assumed to be nonsingular, meaning that the vector $\mathbf{y}_t$ is not cointegrated under the null hypothesis. If the test statistic is below the indicated critical value (that is, if $Z_\rho$, $Z_t$, or $t$ is negative and sufficiently large in absolute value), then the null hypothesis of no cointegration is rejected.

$Z_\rho$ is the following statistic,

$$Z_\rho \equiv (T-1)(\hat{\rho}_T - 1) - (1/2)\{(T-1)^2 \cdot \hat{\sigma}^2_{\hat{\rho}_T} \div s_T^2\}(\hat{\lambda}_T^2 - \hat{c}_{0,T}),$$

where $\hat{\rho}_T$ is the estimate of $\rho$ based on $OLS$ estimation of $\hat{u}_t = \rho \hat{u}_{t-1} + e_t$ for $\hat{u}_t$ the $OLS$ sample residual

value for $Z_\rho$ is $-27.1$. Since $-7.54 > -27.1$, the null hypothesis of no cointegration is accepted. Similarly, the Phillips-Ouliaris $Z_t$ statistic is

$$\begin{aligned} Z_t &= (\hat{c}_0/\hat{\lambda}^2)^{1/2}(\hat{\rho} - 1)/\hat{\sigma}_{\hat{\rho}} - (1/2)\{(T - 1)\cdot\hat{\sigma}_{\hat{\rho}} \div s\}(\hat{\lambda}^2 - \hat{c}_0)/\hat{\lambda} \\ &= \{(0.1622)/(0.4082)\}^{1/2}(0.98331 - 1)/(0.01172) \\ &\quad - \tfrac{1}{2}\{(201)(0.01172) \div (0.40374)\}(0.4082 - 0.1622)/(0.4082)^{1/2} \\ &= -2.02. \end{aligned}$$

Comparing this with the case 3 section of Table B.9, we see that $-2.02 > -3.80$, so that the null hypothesis of no cointegration is also accepted by this test. An *OLS* regression of $\hat{u}_t$ on $\hat{u}_{t-1}$ and twelve lags of $\Delta\hat{u}_{t-j}$ produces an *OLS* $t$ test of $\rho = 1$ of $-2.73$, which is again above $-3.80$. We thus find little evidence that $p_t$, $s_t$, and $p_t^*$ are cointegrated. Indeed, the regression [19.2.49] displays the classic symptoms of a spurious regression—the estimated standard errors are small relative to the coefficient estimates, and the estimated first-order autocorrelation of the residuals is near unity.

As a second example, Figure 19.5 plots 100 times the logs of real quarterly aggregate personal disposable income ($y_t$) and personal consumption expenditures ($c_t$) for the United States over 1947:I to 1989:III. In a regression of $y_t$ on a constant, a time trend, $y_{t-1}$, and $\Delta y_{t-j}$ for $j = 1, 2, \ldots, 6$, the *OLS* $t$ test that the coefficient on $y_{t-1}$ is unity is $-1.28$. Similarly, in a regression of $c_t$ on a constant, a time trend, $c_{t-1}$, and $\Delta c_{t-j}$ for $j = 1, 2, \ldots, 6$, the *OLS* $t$ test that the coefficient on $c_{t-1}$ is unity is $-1.88$. Thus, both processes might well be described as $I(1)$ with positive drift.

The *OLS* estimate of the cointegrating relation is

$$c_t = \underset{(2.35)}{0.67} + \underset{(0.0032)}{0.9865}\, y_t + u_t. \qquad [19.2.50]$$

A first-order autoregression fitted to the residuals produces

$$\hat{u}_t = \underset{(0.048)}{0.782}\, \hat{u}_{t-1} + \hat{e}_t,$$

---

*Notes to Table 19.1 (continued).*

from the estimated regression. Here,

$$s_T^2 = (T - 2)^{-1} \sum_{t=2}^{T} \hat{e}_t^2,$$

where $\hat{e}_t = \hat{u}_t - \hat{\rho}_T\hat{u}_{t-1}$ is the sample residual from the autoregression describing $\hat{u}_t$ and $\hat{\sigma}_{\hat{\rho}_T}$ is the standard error for $\hat{\rho}_T$ as calculated by the usual *OLS* formula:

$$\hat{\sigma}_{\hat{\rho}_T}^2 = s_T^2 \div \sum_{t=2}^{T} \hat{u}_{t-1}^2.$$

Also,

$$\hat{c}_{j,T} = (T - 1)^{-1} \sum_{t=j+2}^{T} \hat{e}_t\hat{e}_{t-j}$$

$$\hat{\lambda}_T^2 = \hat{c}_{0,T} + 2\cdot\sum_{j=1}^{q} [1 - j/(q + 1)]\hat{c}_{j,T}.$$

$Z_t$ is the following statistic:

$$Z_t \equiv (\hat{c}_{0,T}/\hat{\lambda}_T^2)^{1/2}\cdot(\hat{\rho}_T - 1)/\hat{\sigma}_{\hat{\rho}_T} - (1/2)(\hat{\lambda}_T^2 - \hat{c}_{0,T})(1/\hat{\lambda}_T)\{(T - 1)\cdot\hat{\sigma}_{\hat{\rho}_T} \div s_T\}.$$

*Augmented Dickey-Fuller t statistic* is the *OLS* $t$ test of the null hypothesis that $\rho = 1$ in the regression

$$\hat{u}_t = \zeta_1\Delta\hat{u}_{t-1} + \zeta_2\Delta\hat{u}_{t-2} + \cdots + \zeta_{p-1}\Delta\hat{u}_{t-p+1} + \rho\hat{u}_{t-1} + e_t.$$

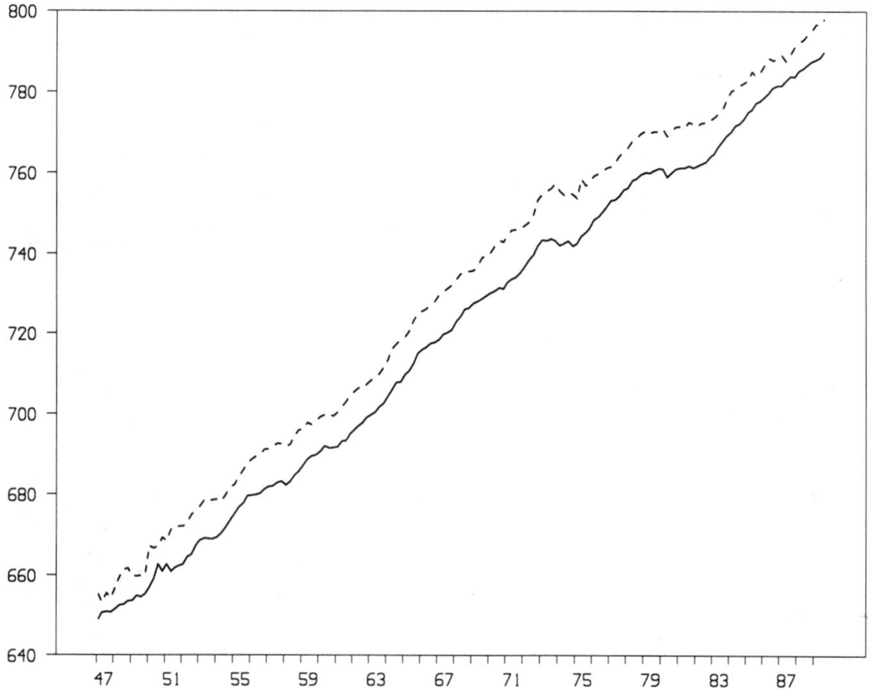


**FIGURE 19.5** One hundred times the log of personal consumption expenditures ($c_t$) and personal disposable income ($y_t$) for the United States in billions of 1982 dollars, quarterly, 1947–89. Key: ——— $c_t$; - - - - $y_t$.

for which the corresponding $Z_\rho$ and $Z_t$ statistics for $q = 6$ are $-32.0$ and $-4.28$. Since there is again ample evidence that $y_t$ has positive drift, these are to be compared with the case 3 sections of Tables B.8 and B.9, respectively. Since $-32.0 < -21.5$ and $-4.28 < -3.42$, in each case the null hypothesis of no cointegration is rejected at the 5% level. Thus consumption and income appear to be cointegrated.

### *Other Tests for Cointegration*

The tests that have been discussed in this section are based on the residuals from an *OLS* regression of $y_{1t}$ on $(y_{2t}, y_{3t}, \ldots, y_{nt})$. Since these are not the same as the residuals from a regression of $y_{2t}$ on $(y_{1t}, y_{3t}, \ldots, y_{nt})$, the tests can give different answers depending on which variable is labeled $y_1$. Important tests for cointegration that are invariant to the ordering of variables are the full-information maximum likelihood test of Johansen (1988, 1991) and the related tests of Stock and Watson (1988) and Ahn and Reinsel (1990). These will be discussed in Chapter 20. Other useful tests for cointegration have been proposed by Phillips and Ouliaris (1990), Park, Ouliaris, and Choi (1988), Stock (1990), and Hansen (1990).

## 19.3. *Testing Hypotheses About the Cointegrating Vector*

The previous section described some ways to test whether a vector $\mathbf{y}_t$ is cointegrated. It was noted that if $\mathbf{y}_t$ is cointegrated, then a consistent estimate of the cointegrating vector can be obtained by *OLS*. This section explores further the distribution theory of this estimate and proposes several alternative estimates that simplify hypothesis testing.

## *Distribution of the* OLS *Estimate for a Special Case*

Let $y_{1t}$ be a scalar and $\mathbf{y}_{2t}$ be a $(g \times 1)$ vector satisfying

$$y_{1t} = \alpha + \boldsymbol{\gamma}'\mathbf{y}_{2t} + z_t^* \quad [19.3.1]$$

$$\mathbf{y}_{2t} = \mathbf{y}_{2,t-1} + \mathbf{u}_{2t}. \quad [19.3.2]$$

If $y_{1t}$ and $\mathbf{y}_{2t}$ are both $I(1)$ but $z_t^*$ and $\mathbf{u}_{2t}$ are $I(0)$, then, for $n \equiv (g + 1)$, the $n$-dimensional vector $(y_{1t}, \mathbf{y}'_{2t})'$ is cointegrated with cointegrating relation [19.3.1].

Consider the special case of a Gaussian system for which $\mathbf{y}_{2t}$ follows a random walk and for which $z_t^*$ is white noise and uncorrelated with $\mathbf{u}_{2\tau}$ for all $t$ and $\tau$:

$$\begin{bmatrix} z_t^* \\ \mathbf{u}_{2t} \end{bmatrix} \sim \text{i.i.d. } N\left(\begin{bmatrix} 0 \\ \mathbf{0} \end{bmatrix}, \begin{bmatrix} \sigma_1^2 & \mathbf{0}' \\ \mathbf{0} & \boldsymbol{\Omega}_{22} \end{bmatrix}\right). \quad [19.3.3]$$

Then [19.3.1] describes a regression in which the explanatory variables ($\mathbf{y}_{2t}$) are independent of the error term ($z_\tau^*$) for all $t$ and $\tau$. The regression thus satisfies Assumption 8.2 in Chapter 8. There it was seen that *conditional* on $(\mathbf{y}_{21}, \mathbf{y}_{22}, \ldots, \mathbf{y}_{2T})$, the *OLS* estimates have a Gaussian distribution:

$$\begin{aligned} \left[\begin{matrix} (\hat{\alpha}_T - \alpha) \\ (\hat{\boldsymbol{\gamma}}_T - \boldsymbol{\gamma}) \end{matrix} \middle| (\mathbf{y}_{21}, \mathbf{y}_{22}, \ldots, \mathbf{y}_{2T}) \right] &= \begin{bmatrix} T & \Sigma\mathbf{y}'_{2t} \\ \Sigma\mathbf{y}_{2t} & \Sigma\mathbf{y}_{2t}\mathbf{y}'_{2t} \end{bmatrix}^{-1} \begin{bmatrix} \Sigma z_t^* \\ \Sigma\mathbf{y}_{2t}z_t^* \end{bmatrix} \\ &\sim N\left(\begin{bmatrix} 0 \\ \mathbf{0} \end{bmatrix}, \sigma_1^2 \begin{bmatrix} T & \Sigma\mathbf{y}'_{2t} \\ \Sigma\mathbf{y}_{2t} & \Sigma\mathbf{y}_{2t}\mathbf{y}'_{2t} \end{bmatrix}^{-1}\right), \end{aligned} \quad [19.3.4]$$

where $\Sigma$ indicates summation over $t$ from 1 to $T$.

Recall further from Chapter 8 that this conditional Gaussian distribution is all that is needed to justify small-sample application of the usual *OLS* $t$ or $F$ tests. Consider a hypothesis test involving $m$ restrictions on $\alpha$ and $\boldsymbol{\gamma}$ of the form

$$\mathbf{R}_\alpha \alpha + \mathbf{R}_\gamma \boldsymbol{\gamma} = \mathbf{r},$$

where $\mathbf{R}_\alpha$ and $\mathbf{r}$ are known $(m \times 1)$ vectors and $\mathbf{R}_\gamma$ is a known $(m \times g)$ matrix describing the restrictions. The Wald form of the *OLS F* test of the null hypothesis is

$$\begin{aligned} (\mathbf{R}_\alpha\hat{\alpha}_T + \mathbf{R}_\gamma\hat{\boldsymbol{\gamma}}_T - \mathbf{r})' &\left\{ s_T^2 [\mathbf{R}_\alpha \quad \mathbf{R}_\gamma] \begin{bmatrix} T & \Sigma\mathbf{y}'_{2t} \\ \Sigma\mathbf{y}_{2t} & \Sigma\mathbf{y}_{2t}\mathbf{y}'_{2t} \end{bmatrix}^{-1} \begin{bmatrix} \mathbf{R}'_\alpha \\ \mathbf{R}'_\gamma \end{bmatrix} \right\}^{-1} \\ &\times (\mathbf{R}_\alpha\hat{\alpha}_T + \mathbf{R}_\gamma\hat{\boldsymbol{\gamma}}_T - \mathbf{r}) \div m, \end{aligned} \quad [19.3.5]$$

where

$$s_T^2 = (T - n)^{-1} \sum_{t=1}^{T} (y_{1t} - \hat{\alpha}_T - \hat{\boldsymbol{\gamma}}'_T\mathbf{y}_{2t})^2.$$

Result [19.3.4] implies that conditional on $(\mathbf{y}_{21}, \mathbf{y}_{22}, \ldots, \mathbf{y}_{2T})$, under the null hypothesis the vector $(\mathbf{R}_\alpha\hat{\alpha}_T + \mathbf{R}_\gamma\hat{\boldsymbol{\gamma}}_T - \mathbf{r})$ has a Gaussian distribution with mean $\mathbf{0}$ and variance

$$\sigma_1^2 [\mathbf{R}_\alpha \quad \mathbf{R}_\gamma] \begin{bmatrix} T & \Sigma\mathbf{y}'_{2t} \\ \Sigma\mathbf{y}_{2t} & \Sigma\mathbf{y}_{2t}\mathbf{y}'_{2t} \end{bmatrix}^{-1} \begin{bmatrix} \mathbf{R}'_\alpha \\ \mathbf{R}'_\gamma \end{bmatrix}.$$

It follows that conditional on $(\mathbf{y}_{21}, \mathbf{y}_{22}, \ldots, \mathbf{y}_{2T})$, the term

$$(\mathbf{R}_\alpha \hat{\alpha}_T + \mathbf{R}_\gamma \hat{\boldsymbol{\gamma}}_T - \mathbf{r})' \left\{ \sigma_1^2 [\mathbf{R}_\alpha \quad \mathbf{R}_\gamma] \begin{bmatrix} T & \Sigma \mathbf{y}'_{2t} \\ \Sigma \mathbf{y}_{2t} & \Sigma \mathbf{y}_{2t}\mathbf{y}'_{2t} \end{bmatrix}^{-1} \begin{bmatrix} \mathbf{R}'_\alpha \\ \mathbf{R}'_\gamma \end{bmatrix} \right\}^{-1} \times (\mathbf{R}_\alpha \hat{\alpha}_T + \mathbf{R}_\gamma \hat{\boldsymbol{\gamma}}_T - \mathbf{r}) \qquad [19.3.6]$$

is a quadratic form in a Gaussian vector. Proposition 8.1 establishes that conditional on $(\mathbf{y}_{21}, \mathbf{y}_{22}, \ldots, \mathbf{y}_{2T})$, the magnitude in [19.3.6] has a $\chi^2(m)$ distribution. Thus, conditional on $(\mathbf{y}_{21}, \mathbf{y}_{22}, \ldots, \mathbf{y}_{2T})$, the *OLS F* test [19.3.5] could be viewed as the ratio of a $\chi^2(m)$ variable to the independent $\chi^2(T - n)$ variable $(T - n)s_T^2/\sigma_1^2$, with numerator and denominator each divided by its degree of freedom. The *OLS* *F* test thus has an exact $F(m, T - n)$ conditional distribution. Since this is the same distribution for all realizations of $(\mathbf{y}_{21}, \mathbf{y}_{22}, \ldots, \mathbf{y}_{2T})$, it follows that [19.3.5] has an unconditional $F(m, T - n)$ distribution as well. Hence, despite the $I(1)$ regressors and complications of cointegration, the correct approach for this example would be to estimate [19.3.1] by *OLS* and use standard $t$ or $F$ statistics to test any hypotheses about the cointegrating vector. No special procedures are needed to estimate the cointegrating vector, and no unusual critical values need be consulted to test a hypothesis about its value.

We now seek to make an analogous statement in terms of the corresponding asymptotic distributions. To do so it will be helpful to rescale the results in [19.3.4] and [19.3.5] so that they define sequences of statistics with nondegenerate asymptotic distributions. If [19.3.4] is premultiplied by the matrix

$$\begin{bmatrix} T^{1/2} & \mathbf{0}' \\ \mathbf{0} & T \cdot \mathbf{I}_g \end{bmatrix},$$

the implication is that the distribution of the *OLS* estimates conditional on $(\mathbf{y}_{21}, \mathbf{y}_{22}, \ldots, \mathbf{y}_{2T})$ is given by

$$\left[ \begin{matrix} T^{1/2}(\hat{\alpha}_T - \alpha) \\ T(\hat{\boldsymbol{\gamma}}_T - \boldsymbol{\gamma}) \end{matrix} \middle| (\mathbf{y}_{21}, \mathbf{y}_{22}, \ldots, \mathbf{y}_{2T}) \right]$$

$$\sim N\left( \begin{bmatrix} 0 \\ \mathbf{0} \end{bmatrix}, \sigma_1^2 \left\{ \begin{bmatrix} T^{1/2} & \mathbf{0}' \\ \mathbf{0} & T \cdot \mathbf{I}_g \end{bmatrix} \begin{bmatrix} T & \Sigma \mathbf{y}'_{2t} \\ \Sigma \mathbf{y}_{2t} & \Sigma \mathbf{y}_{2t}\mathbf{y}'_{2t} \end{bmatrix}^{-1} \begin{bmatrix} T^{1/2} & \mathbf{0}' \\ \mathbf{0} & T \cdot \mathbf{I}_g \end{bmatrix} \right\} \right) \qquad [19.3.7]$$

$$= N\left( \begin{bmatrix} 0 \\ \mathbf{0} \end{bmatrix}, \sigma_1^2 \begin{bmatrix} 1 & T^{-3/2}\Sigma \mathbf{y}'_{2t} \\ T^{-3/2}\Sigma \mathbf{y}_{2t} & T^{-2}\Sigma \mathbf{y}_{2t}\mathbf{y}'_{2t} \end{bmatrix}^{-1} \right).$$

To analyze the asymptotic distribution, notice that [19.3.1] through [19.3.3] are a special case of the system analyzed in Proposition 19.2 with $\boldsymbol{\Psi}^*(L) = \mathbf{I}_n$ and

$$\mathbf{P} = \begin{bmatrix} \sigma_1 & \mathbf{0}' \\ \mathbf{0} & \mathbf{P}_{22} \end{bmatrix},$$

where $\mathbf{P}_{22}$ is the Cholesky factor of $\boldsymbol{\Omega}_{22}$:

$$\boldsymbol{\Omega}_{22} = \mathbf{P}_{22}\mathbf{P}'_{22}.$$

For this special case,

$$\boldsymbol{\Psi}^*(1) \cdot \mathbf{P} = \begin{bmatrix} \sigma_1 & \mathbf{0}' \\ \mathbf{0} & \mathbf{P}_{22} \end{bmatrix}. \qquad [19.3.8]$$

The terms $\boldsymbol{\lambda}_1^{*\prime}$ and $\boldsymbol{\Lambda}_2^*$ referred to in Proposition 19.2 would then be given by

$$\underset{(1\times n)}{\boldsymbol{\lambda}_1^{*\prime}} = \begin{bmatrix} \underset{(1\times 1)}{\sigma_1} & \underset{(1\times g)}{\mathbf{0}'} \end{bmatrix}$$

$$\underset{(g\times n)}{\boldsymbol{\Lambda}_2^{*}} = \begin{bmatrix} \underset{(g\times 1)}{\mathbf{0}} & \underset{(g\times g)}{\mathbf{P}_{22}} \end{bmatrix}.$$

Thus, result [19.2.13] of Proposition 19.2 establishes that

$$\begin{bmatrix} T^{1/2}(\hat{\alpha}_T - \alpha) \\ T(\hat{\boldsymbol{\gamma}}_T - \boldsymbol{\gamma}) \end{bmatrix} = \begin{bmatrix} 1 & T^{-3/2}\Sigma\mathbf{y}_{2t}' \\ T^{-3/2}\Sigma\mathbf{y}_{2t} & T^{-2}\Sigma\mathbf{y}_{2t}\mathbf{y}_{2t}' \end{bmatrix}^{-1} \begin{bmatrix} T^{-1/2}\Sigma z_t^* \\ T^{-1}\Sigma\mathbf{y}_{2t}z_t^* \end{bmatrix}$$

$$\xrightarrow{L} \begin{bmatrix} 1 & \left\{\int [\mathbf{W}(r)]'\,dr\right\}\begin{bmatrix} \mathbf{0}' \\ \mathbf{P}_{22}' \end{bmatrix} \\ [\mathbf{0} \quad \mathbf{P}_{22}]\int \mathbf{W}(r)\,dr & [\mathbf{0} \quad \mathbf{P}_{22}]\left\{\int [\mathbf{W}(r)]\cdot[\mathbf{W}(r)]'\,dr\right\}\begin{bmatrix} \mathbf{0}' \\ \mathbf{P}_{22}' \end{bmatrix} \end{bmatrix}^{-1}$$

$$\times \begin{bmatrix} [\sigma_1 \quad \mathbf{0}']\mathbf{W}(1) \\ [\mathbf{0} \quad \mathbf{P}_{22}]\left\{\int [\mathbf{W}(r)]\,[d\mathbf{W}(r)]'\right\}\begin{bmatrix} \sigma_1 \\ \mathbf{0} \end{bmatrix} \end{bmatrix}, \qquad [19.3.9]$$

where the integral sign indicates integration over $r$ from 0 to 1. If the $n$-dimensional standard Brownian motion $\mathbf{W}(r)$ is partitioned as

$$\underset{(n\times 1)}{\mathbf{W}(r)} = \begin{bmatrix} \underset{(1\times 1)}{W_1(r)} \\ \underset{(g\times 1)}{\mathbf{W}_2(r)} \end{bmatrix},$$

then [19.3.9] can be written

$$\begin{bmatrix} T^{1/2}(\hat{\alpha}_T - \alpha) \\ T(\hat{\boldsymbol{\gamma}}_T - \boldsymbol{\gamma}) \end{bmatrix}$$

$$\xrightarrow{L} \begin{bmatrix} 1 & \left\{\int [\mathbf{W}_2(r)]'\,dr\right\}\mathbf{P}_{22}' \\ \mathbf{P}_{22}\int \mathbf{W}_2(r)\,dr & \mathbf{P}_{22}\left\{\int [\mathbf{W}_2(r)]\cdot[\mathbf{W}_2(r)]'\,dr\right\}\mathbf{P}_{22}' \end{bmatrix}^{-1} \qquad [19.3.10]$$

$$\times \begin{bmatrix} \sigma_1 W_1(1) \\ \mathbf{P}_{22}\left\{\int [\mathbf{W}_2(r)]\,dW_1(r)\right\}\sigma_1 \end{bmatrix}$$

$$\equiv \sigma_1\begin{bmatrix} \nu_1 \\ \boldsymbol{\nu}_2 \end{bmatrix},$$

where

$$\begin{bmatrix} \nu_1 \\ \boldsymbol{\nu}_2 \end{bmatrix} \equiv \begin{bmatrix} 1 & \left\{\int [\mathbf{W}_2(r)]'\,dr\right\}\mathbf{P}_{22}' \\ \mathbf{P}_{22}\int \mathbf{W}_2(r)\,dr & \mathbf{P}_{22}\left\{\int [\mathbf{W}_2(r)]\cdot[\mathbf{W}_2(r)]'\,dr\right\}\mathbf{P}_{22}' \end{bmatrix}^{-1} \qquad [19.3.11]$$

$$\times \begin{bmatrix} W_1(1) \\ \mathbf{P}_{22}\left\{\int [\mathbf{W}_2(r)]\,dW_1(r)\right\} \end{bmatrix}.$$

Since $W_1(\cdot)$ is independent of $\mathbf{W}_2(\cdot)$, the distribution of $(\nu_1, \boldsymbol{\nu}_2')'$ conditional on $\mathbf{W}_2(\cdot)$ is found by treating $\mathbf{W}_2(r)$ as a deterministic function of $r$ and leaving the process $W_1(\cdot)$ unaffected. Then $\int[\mathbf{W}_2(r)]\,dW_1(r)$ has a simple Gaussian distribution, and [19.3.11] describes a Gaussian vector. In particular, the exact finite-sample result for Gaussian disturbances [19.3.7] implied that

$$\left[\begin{matrix} T^{1/2}(\hat{\alpha}_T - \alpha) \\ T(\hat{\boldsymbol{\gamma}}_T - \boldsymbol{\gamma}) \end{matrix} \middle| (\mathbf{y}_{21}, \mathbf{y}_{22}, \ldots, \mathbf{y}_{2T}) \right] = \begin{bmatrix} 1 & T^{-3/2}\Sigma\mathbf{y}_{2t}' \\ T^{-3/2}\Sigma\mathbf{y}_{2t} & T^{-2}\Sigma\mathbf{y}_{2t}\mathbf{y}_{2t}' \end{bmatrix}^{-1} \begin{bmatrix} T^{-1/2}\Sigma z_t^* \\ T^{-1}\Sigma\mathbf{y}_{2t}z_t^* \end{bmatrix}$$

$$\sim N\left(\begin{bmatrix} 0 \\ \mathbf{0} \end{bmatrix}, \sigma_1^2 \begin{bmatrix} 1 & T^{-3/2}\Sigma\mathbf{y}_{2t}' \\ T^{-3/2}\Sigma\mathbf{y}_{2t} & T^{-2}\Sigma\mathbf{y}_{2t}\mathbf{y}_{2t}' \end{bmatrix}^{-1}\right).$$

Comparing this with the limiting distribution [19.3.10], it appears that the vector $(\nu_1, \boldsymbol{\nu}_2')'$ has distribution conditional on $\mathbf{W}_2(\cdot)$ that could be described as

$$\left[\begin{matrix} \nu_1 \\ \boldsymbol{\nu}_2 \end{matrix} \middle| \mathbf{W}_2(\cdot) \right]$$

$$\sim N\left(\begin{bmatrix} 0 \\ \mathbf{0} \end{bmatrix}, \begin{bmatrix} 1 & \left\{\int [\mathbf{W}_2(r)]'\,dr\right\}\mathbf{P}_{22}' \\ \mathbf{P}_{22}\int \mathbf{W}_2(r)\,dr & \mathbf{P}_{22}\left\{\int [\mathbf{W}_2(r)]\cdot[\mathbf{W}_2(r)]'\,dr\right\}\mathbf{P}_{22}' \end{bmatrix}^{-1}\right). \qquad [19.3.12]$$

Expression [19.3.12] allows the argument that was used to motivate the usual *OLS t* and *F* tests on the system of [19.3.1] and [19.3.2] with Gaussian disturbances satisfying [19.3.3] to give an asymptotic justification for these same tests in a system with non-Gaussian disturbances whose means and autocovariances are as assumed in [19.3.3]. Consider for illustration a hypothesis that involves only the cointegrating vector, so that $\mathbf{R}_\alpha = \mathbf{0}$. Then, under the null hypothesis, $m$ times the $F$ test in [19.3.5] becomes

$$m \cdot F_T = [\mathbf{R}_\gamma(\hat{\boldsymbol{\gamma}}_T - \boldsymbol{\gamma})]' \left\{ s_T^2 [\mathbf{0} \;\; \mathbf{R}_\gamma] \begin{bmatrix} T & \Sigma\mathbf{y}_{2t}' \\ \Sigma\mathbf{y}_{2t} & \Sigma\mathbf{y}_{2t}\mathbf{y}_{2t}' \end{bmatrix}^{-1} \begin{bmatrix} \mathbf{0}' \\ \mathbf{R}_\gamma' \end{bmatrix} \right\}^{-1} [\mathbf{R}_\gamma(\hat{\boldsymbol{\gamma}}_T - \boldsymbol{\gamma})]$$

$$= [\mathbf{R}_\gamma \cdot T(\hat{\boldsymbol{\gamma}}_T - \boldsymbol{\gamma})]' \left\{ s_T^2 [\mathbf{0} \;\; \mathbf{R}_\gamma \cdot T] \begin{bmatrix} T & \Sigma\mathbf{y}_{2t}' \\ \Sigma\mathbf{y}_{2t} & \Sigma\mathbf{y}_{2t}\mathbf{y}_{2t}' \end{bmatrix}^{-1} \begin{bmatrix} \mathbf{0}' \\ T \cdot \mathbf{R}_\gamma' \end{bmatrix} \right\}^{-1}$$
$$\times [\mathbf{R}_\gamma \cdot T(\hat{\boldsymbol{\gamma}}_T - \boldsymbol{\gamma})]$$

$$= [\mathbf{R}_\gamma \cdot T(\hat{\boldsymbol{\gamma}}_T - \boldsymbol{\gamma})]'(s_T^2)^{-1} \left\{ [\mathbf{0} \;\; \mathbf{R}_\gamma] \left( \begin{bmatrix} T^{1/2} & \mathbf{0}' \\ \mathbf{0} & T \cdot \mathbf{I}_g \end{bmatrix}^{-1} \right.\right.$$
$$\left.\left. \times \begin{bmatrix} T & \Sigma\mathbf{y}_{2t}' \\ \Sigma\mathbf{y}_{2t} & \Sigma\mathbf{y}_{2t}\mathbf{y}_{2t}' \end{bmatrix} \begin{bmatrix} T^{1/2} & \mathbf{0}' \\ \mathbf{0} & T \cdot \mathbf{I}_g \end{bmatrix}^{-1} \right)^{-1} \begin{bmatrix} \mathbf{0}' \\ \mathbf{R}_\gamma' \end{bmatrix} \right\}^{-1} [\mathbf{R}_\gamma \cdot T(\hat{\boldsymbol{\gamma}}_T - \boldsymbol{\gamma})]$$

$$\xrightarrow{p} [\mathbf{R}_\gamma \sigma_1 \boldsymbol{\nu}_2]'(s_T^2)^{-1} \left\{ [\mathbf{0} \;\; \mathbf{R}_\gamma] \right.$$
$$\left. \times \begin{bmatrix} 1 & \left\{\int [\mathbf{W}_2(r)]'\,dr\right\}\mathbf{P}_{22}' \\ \mathbf{P}_{22}\int \mathbf{W}_2(r)\,dr & \mathbf{P}_{22}\left\{\int [\mathbf{W}_2(r)]\cdot[\mathbf{W}_2(r)]'\,dr\right\}\mathbf{P}_{22}' \end{bmatrix}^{-1} \begin{bmatrix} \mathbf{0}' \\ \mathbf{R}_\gamma' \end{bmatrix} \right\}^{-1} [\mathbf{R}_\gamma \sigma_1 \boldsymbol{\nu}_2]$$

$$= (\sigma_1^2/s_T^2)[\mathbf{R}_\gamma \boldsymbol{\nu}_2]' \left\{ [\mathbf{0} \quad \mathbf{R}_\gamma] \right.$$

$$\left. \times \begin{bmatrix} 1 & \left\{ \int [\mathbf{W}_2(r)]' \, dr \right\} \mathbf{P}_{22}' \\ \mathbf{P}_{22} \int \mathbf{W}_2(r) \, dr & \mathbf{P}_{22} \left\{ \int [\mathbf{W}_2(r)] \cdot [\mathbf{W}_2(r)]' \, dr \right\} \mathbf{P}_{22}' \end{bmatrix}^{-1} \begin{bmatrix} \mathbf{0}' \\ \mathbf{R}_\gamma' \end{bmatrix} \right\}^{-1} [\mathbf{R}_\gamma \boldsymbol{\nu}_2]. \tag{19.3.13}$$

Result [19.3.12] implies that conditional on $\mathbf{W}_2(\cdot)$, the vector $\mathbf{R}_\gamma \boldsymbol{\nu}_2$ has a Gaussian distribution with mean $\mathbf{0}$ and variance

$$[\mathbf{0} \quad \mathbf{R}_\gamma] \begin{bmatrix} 1 & \left\{ \int [\mathbf{W}_2(r)]' \, dr \right\} \mathbf{P}_{22}' \\ \mathbf{P}_{22} \int \mathbf{W}_2(r) \, dr & \mathbf{P}_{22} \left\{ \int [\mathbf{W}_2(r)] \cdot [\mathbf{W}_2(r)]' \, dr \right\} \mathbf{P}_{22}' \end{bmatrix}^{-1} \begin{bmatrix} \mathbf{0}' \\ \mathbf{R}_\gamma' \end{bmatrix}.$$

Since $s_T^2$ provides a consistent estimate of $\sigma_1^2$, the limiting distribution of $m \cdot F_T$ conditional on $\mathbf{W}_2(\cdot)$ is thus $\chi^2(m)$, and so the unconditional distribution is $\chi^2(m)$ as well. This means that *OLS* $t$ or $F$ tests involving the cointegrating vector have their standard asymptotic Gaussian or $\chi^2$ distributions.

It is also straightforward to adapt the methods in Section 16.3 to show that the *OLS* $\chi^2$ test of a hypothesis involving just $\alpha$, or that for a joint hypothesis involving both $\alpha$ and $\boldsymbol{\gamma}$, also has a limiting $\chi^2$ distribution.

The analysis to this point applies in the special case when $y_{1t}$ and $\mathbf{y}_{2t}$ follow random walks. The analysis is easily extended to allow for serial correlation in $z_t^*$ or $\mathbf{u}_{2t}$, as long as the critical condition that $z_t^*$ is uncorrelated with $\mathbf{u}_{2\tau}$ for all $t$ and $\tau$ is maintained. In particular, suppose that the dynamic process for $(z_t^*, \mathbf{u}_{2t}')'$ is given by

$$\begin{bmatrix} z_t^* \\ \mathbf{u}_{2t} \end{bmatrix} = \boldsymbol{\Psi}^*(L)\boldsymbol{\varepsilon}_t,$$

with $\{s \cdot \boldsymbol{\Psi}_s^*\}_{s=0}^{\infty}$ absolutely summable, $E(\boldsymbol{\varepsilon}_t) = \mathbf{0}$, $E(\boldsymbol{\varepsilon}_t \boldsymbol{\varepsilon}_\tau') = \mathbf{PP}'$ if $t = \tau$ and $\mathbf{0}$ otherwise, and fourth moments of $\boldsymbol{\varepsilon}_t$ finite. In order for $z_t^*$ to be uncorrelated with $\mathbf{u}_{2\tau}$ for all $t$ and $\tau$, both $\boldsymbol{\Psi}^*(L)$ and $\mathbf{P}$ must be block-diagonal:

$$\boldsymbol{\Psi}^*(L) = \begin{bmatrix} \psi_{11}^*(L) & \mathbf{0}' \\ \mathbf{0} & \boldsymbol{\Psi}_{22}^*(L) \end{bmatrix}$$

$$\mathbf{P} = \begin{bmatrix} \sigma_1 & \mathbf{0}' \\ \mathbf{0} & \mathbf{P}_{22} \end{bmatrix},$$

implying that the matrix $\boldsymbol{\Psi}^*(1) \cdot \mathbf{P}$ is also block-diagonal:

$$\begin{aligned} \boldsymbol{\Psi}^*(1) \cdot \mathbf{P} &= \begin{bmatrix} \sigma_1 \psi_{11}^*(1) & \mathbf{0}' \\ \mathbf{0} & \boldsymbol{\Psi}_{22}^*(1) \cdot \mathbf{P}_{22} \end{bmatrix} \\ &\equiv \begin{bmatrix} \lambda_1^* & \mathbf{0}' \\ \mathbf{0} & \boldsymbol{\Lambda}_{22}^* \end{bmatrix}. \end{aligned} \tag{19.3.14}$$

Noting the parallel between [19.3.14] and [19.3.8], it is easy to confirm that if $\lambda_1^* \neq 0$ and the rows of $\mathbf{\Lambda}_{22}^*$ are linearly independent, then the analysis of [19.3.10] continues to hold, with $\sigma_1$ replaced by $\lambda_1^*$ and $\mathbf{P}_{22}$ replaced by $\mathbf{\Lambda}_{22}^*$:

$$\begin{bmatrix} T^{1/2}(\hat{\alpha}_T - \alpha) \\ T(\hat{\boldsymbol{\gamma}}_T - \boldsymbol{\gamma}) \end{bmatrix} \xrightarrow{L} \begin{bmatrix} 1 & \left\{\int [\mathbf{W}_2(r)]'\,dr\right\}\mathbf{\Lambda}_{22}^{*\prime} \\ \mathbf{\Lambda}_{22}^*\int \mathbf{W}_2(r)\,dr & \mathbf{\Lambda}_{22}^*\left\{\int [\mathbf{W}_2(r)]\cdot[\mathbf{W}_2(r)]'\,dr\right\}\mathbf{\Lambda}_{22}^{*\prime} \end{bmatrix}^{-1} \times \begin{bmatrix} \lambda_1^* W_1(1) \\ \mathbf{\Lambda}_{22}^*\left\{\int [\mathbf{W}_2(r)]\,dW_1(r)\right\}\lambda_1^* \end{bmatrix}. \quad [19.3.15]$$

Conditional on $\mathbf{W}_2(\cdot)$, this again describes a Gaussian vector with mean zero and variance

$$(\lambda_1^*)^2\begin{bmatrix} 1 & \left\{\int [\mathbf{W}_2(r)]'\,dr\right\}\mathbf{\Lambda}_{22}^{*\prime} \\ \mathbf{\Lambda}_{22}^*\int \mathbf{W}_2(r)\,dr & \mathbf{\Lambda}_{22}^*\left\{\int [\mathbf{W}_2(r)]\cdot[\mathbf{W}_2(r)]'\,dr\right\}\mathbf{\Lambda}_{22}^{*\prime} \end{bmatrix}^{-1}$$

The same calculations as in [19.3.13] further indicate that $m$ times the *OLS F* test of $m$ restrictions involving $\alpha$ or $\boldsymbol{\gamma}$ converges to $(\lambda_1^*)^2/s_T^2$ times a variable that is $\chi^2(m)$ conditional on $\mathbf{W}_2(\cdot)$. Since this distribution does not depend on $\mathbf{W}_2(\cdot)$, the unconditional distribution is also $[(\lambda_1^*)^2/s_T^2]\cdot\chi^2(m)$.

Note that the *OLS* estimate $s_T^2$ provides a consistent estimate of the variance of $z_t^*$:

$$s_T^2 \equiv (T - n)^{-1}\sum_{t=1}^{T}(y_{1t} - \hat{\alpha}_T - \hat{\boldsymbol{\gamma}}_T'\mathbf{y}_{2t})^2 \xrightarrow{p} E(z_t^*)^2.$$

However, if $z_t^*$ is serially correlated, this is not the same magnitude as $(\lambda_1^*)^2$. Fortunately, this is simple to correct for. For example, $s_T^2$ in the usual formula for the $F$ test [19.3.5] could be replaced with

$$(\hat{\lambda}_{1,T}^*)^2 = \hat{c}_{0,T} + 2\cdot\sum_{j=1}^{q}[1 - j/(q + 1)]\hat{c}_{j,T} \quad [19.3.16]$$

for

$$\hat{c}_{j,T} \equiv T^{-1}\sum_{t=j+1}^{T}\hat{u}_t\hat{u}_{t-j} \quad [19.3.17]$$

with $\hat{u}_t = (y_{1t} - \hat{\alpha}_T - \hat{\boldsymbol{\gamma}}_T'\mathbf{y}_{2t})$ the sample residual resulting from *OLS* estimation of [19.3.1]. If $q \to \infty$ but $q/T \to 0$, then $\hat{\lambda}_{1,T}^* \xrightarrow{p} \lambda_1^*$. It then follows that the test statistic given by

$$(\mathbf{R}_\alpha\hat{\alpha}_T + \mathbf{R}_\gamma\hat{\boldsymbol{\gamma}}_T - \mathbf{r})'\left\{(\hat{\lambda}_{1,T}^*)^2[\mathbf{R}_\alpha \;\; \mathbf{R}_\gamma]\begin{bmatrix} T & \Sigma\mathbf{y}_{2t}' \\ \Sigma\mathbf{y}_{2t} & \Sigma\mathbf{y}_{2t}\mathbf{y}_{2t}' \end{bmatrix}^{-1}\begin{bmatrix} \mathbf{R}_\alpha' \\ \mathbf{R}_\gamma' \end{bmatrix}\right\}^{-1} \times (\mathbf{R}_\alpha\hat{\alpha}_T + \mathbf{R}_\gamma\hat{\boldsymbol{\gamma}}_T - \mathbf{r}) \quad [19.3.18]$$

has an asymptotic $\chi^2(m)$ distribution.

The difficulties with nonstandard distributions for hypothesis tests about the cointegrating vector are thus due to the possibility of nonzero correlations between $z_t^*$ and $\mathbf{u}_{2\tau}$. The basic approach to constructing hypothesis tests will therefore be to transform the regression or the estimates so as to eliminate the effects of this correlation.

## *Correcting for Correlation by Adding Leads and Lags of* $\Delta\mathbf{y}_2$

One correction for the correlation between $z_t^*$ and $\mathbf{u}_{2\tau}$, suggested by Saikkonen (1991), Phillips and Loretan (1991), Stock and Watson (1993), and Wooldridge (1991), is to augment [19.3.1] with leads and lags of $\Delta\mathbf{y}_{2t}$. Specifically, since $z_t^*$ and $\mathbf{u}_{2t}$ are stationary, we can define $\tilde{z}_t$ to be the residual from a linear projection of $z_t^*$ on $\{\mathbf{u}_{2,t-p}, \mathbf{u}_{2,t-p+1}, \ldots, \mathbf{u}_{2,t-1}, \mathbf{u}_{2t}, \mathbf{u}_{2,t+1}, \ldots, \mathbf{u}_{2,t+p}\}$:

$$z_t^* = \sum_{s=-p}^{p} \boldsymbol{\beta}_s' \mathbf{u}_{2,t-s} + \tilde{z}_t,$$

where $\tilde{z}_t$ by construction is uncorrelated with $\mathbf{u}_{2,t-s}$ for $s = -p, -p+1, \ldots, p$. Recalling from [19.3.2] that $\mathbf{u}_{2t} = \Delta\mathbf{y}_{2t}$, equation [19.3.1] then can be written

$$y_{1t} = \alpha + \boldsymbol{\gamma}'\mathbf{y}_{2t} + \sum_{s=-p}^{p} \boldsymbol{\beta}_s'\Delta\mathbf{y}_{2,t-s} + \tilde{z}_t. \qquad [19.3.19]$$

If we are willing to assume that the correlation between $z_t^*$ and $\mathbf{u}_{2,t-s}$ is zero for $|s| > p$, then an $F$ test about the true value of $\boldsymbol{\gamma}$ that has an asymptotic $\chi^2$ distribution is easy to construct using the same approach adopted in [19.3.18].

For a more formal statement, let $y_{1t}$ and $\mathbf{y}_{2t}$ satisfy [19.3.19] and [19.3.2] with

$$\begin{bmatrix} \tilde{z}_t \\ \mathbf{u}_{2t} \end{bmatrix} = \sum_{s=0}^{\infty} \tilde{\boldsymbol{\Psi}}_s \boldsymbol{\varepsilon}_{t-s},$$

where $\{s \cdot \tilde{\boldsymbol{\Psi}}_s\}_{s=0}^{\infty}$ is an absolutely summable sequence of $(n \times n)$ matrices and $\{\boldsymbol{\varepsilon}_t\}_{t=-\infty}^{\infty}$ is an i.i.d. sequence of $(n \times 1)$ vectors with mean zero, variance $\mathbf{PP}'$, and finite fourth moments and with $\tilde{\boldsymbol{\Psi}}(1)\cdot\mathbf{P}$ nonsingular. Suppose that $\tilde{z}_t$ is uncorrelated with $\mathbf{u}_{2\tau}$ for all $t$ and $\tau$, so that

$$\mathbf{P} = \begin{bmatrix} \sigma_1 & \mathbf{0}' \\ \mathbf{0} & \mathbf{P}_{22} \end{bmatrix} \qquad [19.3.20]$$

$$\tilde{\boldsymbol{\Psi}}(L) = \begin{bmatrix} \tilde{\psi}_{11}(L) & \mathbf{0}' \\ \mathbf{0} & \tilde{\boldsymbol{\Psi}}_{22}(L) \end{bmatrix}, \qquad [19.3.21]$$

where $\mathbf{P}_{22}$ and $\tilde{\boldsymbol{\Psi}}_{22}(L)$ are $(g \times g)$ matrices for $g \equiv n - 1$. Define

$$\mathbf{w}_t \equiv (\mathbf{u}_{2,t-p}', \mathbf{u}_{2,t-p+1}', \ldots, \mathbf{u}_{2,t-1}', \mathbf{u}_{2t}', \mathbf{u}_{2,t+1}', \ldots, \mathbf{u}_{2,t+p}')'$$
$$\boldsymbol{\beta} \equiv (\boldsymbol{\beta}_p', \boldsymbol{\beta}_{p-1}', \ldots, \boldsymbol{\beta}_{-p}')',$$

so that the regression model [19.3.19] can be written

$$y_{1t} = \boldsymbol{\beta}'\mathbf{w}_t + \alpha + \boldsymbol{\gamma}'\mathbf{y}_{2t} + \tilde{z}_t. \qquad [19.3.22]$$

The reader is invited to confirm in Exercise 19.2 that the *OLS* estimates of [19.3.22] satisfy

$$\begin{bmatrix} T^{1/2}(\hat{\boldsymbol\beta}_T - \boldsymbol\beta) \\ T^{1/2}(\hat{\alpha}_T - \alpha) \\ T(\hat{\boldsymbol\gamma}_T - \boldsymbol\gamma) \end{bmatrix} \xrightarrow{L} \begin{bmatrix} \mathbf{Q}^{-1}\mathbf{h}_1 \\ \tilde{\lambda}_{11}\nu_1 \\ \tilde{\lambda}_{11}\boldsymbol\nu_2 \end{bmatrix}, \qquad [19.3.23]$$

where $\mathbf{Q} \equiv E(\mathbf{w}_t\mathbf{w}_t')$, $T^{-1/2}\Sigma\mathbf{w}_t\tilde{z}_t \xrightarrow{L} \mathbf{h}_1$, $\tilde{\lambda}_{11} \equiv \sigma_1 \cdot \tilde{\psi}_{11}(1)$, and

$$\begin{bmatrix} \nu_1 \\ \boldsymbol\nu_2 \end{bmatrix} = \begin{bmatrix} 1 & \left\{\int [\mathbf{W}_2(r)]'\,dr\right\}\tilde{\boldsymbol\Lambda}_{22}' \\ \tilde{\boldsymbol\Lambda}_{22}\int \mathbf{W}_2(r)\,dr & \tilde{\boldsymbol\Lambda}_{22}\left\{\int [\mathbf{W}_2(r)]\cdot[\mathbf{W}_2(r)]'\,dr\right\}\tilde{\boldsymbol\Lambda}_{22}' \end{bmatrix}^{-1} \times \begin{bmatrix} W_1(1) \\ \tilde{\boldsymbol\Lambda}_{22}\left\{\int [\mathbf{W}_2(r)]\,dW_1(r)\right\} \end{bmatrix}.$$

Here $\tilde{\boldsymbol\Lambda}_{22} \equiv \tilde{\boldsymbol\Psi}_{22}(1)\cdot\mathbf{P}_{22}$, $W_1(r)$ is univariate standard Brownian motion, $\mathbf{W}_2(r)$ is $g$-dimensional standard Brownian motion that is independent of $W_1(\cdot)$, and the integral sign denotes integration over $r$ from 0 to 1. Hence, as in [19.3.12],

$$\left[\begin{matrix} \nu_1 \\ \boldsymbol\nu_2 \end{matrix}\,\middle|\, \mathbf{W}_2(\cdot)\right] \sim N\left(\begin{bmatrix} 0 \\ \mathbf{0} \end{bmatrix}, \begin{bmatrix} 1 & \left\{\int [\mathbf{W}_2(r)]'\,dr\right\}\tilde{\boldsymbol\Lambda}_{22}' \\ \tilde{\boldsymbol\Lambda}_{22}\int \mathbf{W}_2(r)\,dr & \tilde{\boldsymbol\Lambda}_{22}\left\{\int [\mathbf{W}_2(r)]\cdot[\mathbf{W}_2(r)]'\,dr\right\}\tilde{\boldsymbol\Lambda}_{22}' \end{bmatrix}^{-1}\right). \qquad [19.3.24]$$

Moreover, the Wald form of the *OLS* $\chi^2$ test of the null hypothesis $\mathbf{R}_\gamma\boldsymbol\gamma = \mathbf{r}$, where $\mathbf{R}_\gamma$ is an $(m \times g)$ matrix and $\mathbf{r}$ is an $(m \times 1)$ vector, can be shown to satisfy

$$\chi_T^2 = \{\mathbf{R}_\gamma\hat{\boldsymbol\gamma}_T - \mathbf{r}\}'\left\{s_T^2[\mathbf{0} \quad 0 \quad \mathbf{R}_\gamma]\begin{bmatrix} \Sigma\mathbf{w}_t\mathbf{w}_t' & \Sigma\mathbf{w}_t & \Sigma\mathbf{w}_t\mathbf{y}_{2t}' \\ \Sigma\mathbf{w}_t' & T & \Sigma\mathbf{y}_{2t}' \\ \Sigma\mathbf{y}_{2t}\mathbf{w}_t' & \Sigma\mathbf{y}_{2t} & \Sigma\mathbf{y}_{2t}\mathbf{y}_{2t}' \end{bmatrix}^{-1}\begin{bmatrix} \mathbf{0} \\ \mathbf{0}' \\ \mathbf{R}_\gamma' \end{bmatrix}\right\}^{-1} \times \{\mathbf{R}_\gamma\hat{\boldsymbol\gamma}_T - \mathbf{r}\}$$

$$\xrightarrow{p} (\tilde{\lambda}_{11}^2/s_T^2)[\mathbf{R}_\gamma\boldsymbol\nu_2]'\left\{[\mathbf{0} \quad \mathbf{R}_\gamma] \times \begin{bmatrix} 1 & \left\{\int [\mathbf{W}_2(r)]'\,dr\right\}\tilde{\boldsymbol\Lambda}_{22}' \\ \tilde{\boldsymbol\Lambda}_{22}\int \mathbf{W}_2(r)\,dr & \tilde{\boldsymbol\Lambda}_{22}\left\{\int [\mathbf{W}_2(r)]\cdot[\mathbf{W}_2(r)]'\,dr\right\}\tilde{\boldsymbol\Lambda}_{22}' \end{bmatrix}^{-1}\begin{bmatrix} \mathbf{0}' \\ \mathbf{R}_\gamma' \end{bmatrix}\right\}^{-1}[\mathbf{R}_\gamma\boldsymbol\nu_2]; \qquad [19.3.25]$$

see Exercise 19.3. But result [19.3.24] implies that conditional on $\mathbf{W}_2(\cdot)$, the expression in [19.3.25] is $(\tilde{\lambda}_{11}^2/s_T^2)$ times a $\chi^2(m)$ variable. Since this distribution is the same for all $\mathbf{W}_2(\cdot)$, it follows that the unconditional distribution also satisfies

$$\chi_T^2 \xrightarrow{p} (\tilde{\lambda}_{11}^2/s_T^2)\cdot\chi^2(m). \qquad [19.3.26]$$

Result [19.3.26] establishes that in order to test a hypothesis about the value of the cointegrating vector $\boldsymbol{\gamma}$, we can estimate [19.3.19] by *OLS* and calculate a standard $F$ test of the hypothesis that $\mathbf{R}_\gamma\boldsymbol{\gamma} = \mathbf{r}$ using the usual formula. We need only to multiply the *OLS* $F$ statistic by a consistent estimate of $(s_T^2/\tilde{\lambda}_{11}^2)$, and the $F$ statistic can be compared with the usual $F(m, T - k)$ tables for $k$ the number of parameters estimated in [19.3.19] for an asymptotically valid test. Similarly, the *OLS* $t$ statistic could be multiplied by $(s_T^2/\tilde{\lambda}_{11}^2)^{1/2}$ and compared with the standard $t$ tables.

A consistent estimate of $\tilde{\lambda}_{11}^2$ is easy to obtain. Recall that $\tilde{\lambda}_{11} = \sigma_1\cdot\tilde{\psi}_{11}(1)$, where $\tilde{z}_t = \tilde{\psi}_{11}(L)\varepsilon_{1t}$ and $E(\varepsilon_{1t}^2) = \sigma_1^2$. Suppose we approximate $\tilde{\psi}_{11}(L)$ by an $AR(p)$ process, and let $\hat{u}_t$ denote the sample residual resulting from *OLS* estimation of [19.3.19]. If $\hat{u}_t$ is regressed on $p$ of its own lags:

$$\hat{u}_t = \phi_1\hat{u}_{t-1} + \phi_2\hat{u}_{t-2} + \cdots + \phi_p\hat{u}_{t-p} + e_t,$$

then a natural estimate of $\tilde{\lambda}_{11}$ is

$$\hat{\tilde{\lambda}}_{11} = \hat{\sigma}_1/(1 - \hat{\phi}_1 - \hat{\phi}_2 - \cdots - \hat{\phi}_p), \qquad [19.3.27]$$

where

$$\hat{\sigma}_1^2 = (T - p)^{-1}\sum_{t=p+1}^{T}\hat{e}_t^2$$

and where $T$ indicates the number of observations actually used to estimate [19.3.19]. Alternatively, if the dynamics implied by $\tilde{\psi}_{11}(L)$ were to be approximated on the basis of $q$ autocovariances, the Newey-West estimator could be used:

$$\hat{\tilde{\lambda}}_{11}^2 = \hat{c}_0 + 2\cdot\sum_{j=1}^{q}[1 - j/(q + 1)]\hat{c}_j, \qquad [19.3.28]$$

where

$$\hat{c}_j = T^{-1}\sum_{t=j+1}^{T}\hat{u}_t\hat{u}_{t-j}.$$

These results were derived under the assumption that there were no drift terms in any of the elements of $\mathbf{y}_{2t}$. However, it is not hard to show that the same procedure works in exactly the same way when some or all of the elements of $\mathbf{y}_{2t}$ involve deterministic time trends. In addition, there is no problem with adding a time trend to the regression of [19.3.19] and testing a hypothesis about its value using this same factor applied to the usual $F$ test. This allows testing separately the hypotheses that (1) $y_{1t} - \boldsymbol{\gamma}'\mathbf{y}_{2t}$ has no time trend and (2) $y_{1t} - \boldsymbol{\gamma}'\mathbf{y}_{2t}$ is $I(0)$, that is, testing separately the restrictions [19.1.15] and [19.1.12]. The reader is invited to verify these claims in Exercises 19.4 and 19.5.

### *Illustration—Testing Hypotheses About the Cointegrating Relation Between Consumption and Income*

As an illustration of this approach, consider again the relation between consumption $c_t$ and income $y_t$, for which evidence of cointegration was found earlier.

The following regression was estimated for $t$ = 1948:II to 1988:III by *OLS*, with the usual *OLS* formulas for standard deviations given in parentheses:

$$
\begin{aligned}
c_t = {} & \underset{(2.34)}{-4.52} + \underset{(0.00306)}{0.99216}\, y_t + \underset{(0.12)}{0.15}\, \Delta y_{t+4} + \underset{(0.12)}{0.29}\, \Delta y_{t+3} + \underset{(0.11)}{0.26}\, \Delta y_{t+2} \\
& + \underset{(0.12)}{0.49}\, \Delta y_{t+1} - \underset{(0.12)}{0.24}\, \Delta y_t - \underset{(0.11)}{0.01}\, \Delta y_{t-1} + \underset{(0.11)}{0.07}\, \Delta y_{t-2} \\
& + \underset{(0.11)}{0.04}\, \Delta y_{t-3} + \underset{(0.11)}{0.02}\, \Delta y_{t-4} + \hat{u}_t
\end{aligned}
\qquad [19.3.29]
$$

$$s^2 = (T - 11)^{-1} \sum_{t=1}^{T} \hat{u}_t^2 = (1.516)^2.$$

Here $T$, the number of observations actually used to estimate [19.3.29], is 162. To test the null hypothesis that the cointegrating vector is $\mathbf{a} = (1, -1)'$, we start with the usual *OLS* $t$ test of this hypothesis,

$$t = (0.99216 - 1)/0.00306 = -2.562.$$

A second-order autoregression fitted to the residuals of [19.3.29] by *OLS* produced

$$\hat{u}_t = 0.7180\, \hat{u}_{t-1} + 0.2057\, \hat{u}_{t-2} + \hat{e}_t, \qquad [19.3.30]$$

where

$$\hat{\sigma}_1^2 = (T - 2)^{-1} \sum_{t=3}^{T} \hat{e}_t^2 = 0.38092.$$

Thus, the estimate of $\tilde{\lambda}_{11}$ suggested in [19.3.27] is

$$\hat{\tilde{\lambda}}_{11} = (0.38092)^{1/2}/(1 - 0.7180 - 0.2057) = 8.089.$$

Hence, a test of the null hypothesis that $\mathbf{a} = (1, -1)'$ can be based on

$$t \cdot (s/\hat{\tilde{\lambda}}_{11}) = (-2.562)(1.516)/(8.089) = -0.48.$$

Since $-0.48$ is above the 5% critical value of $-1.96$ for a $N(0, 1)$ variable, we accept the null hypothesis that $\mathbf{a} = (1, -1)'$.

To test the restrictions implied by cointegration for the time trend and stochastic component separately, the regression of [19.3.29] was reestimated with a time trend included:

$$
\begin{aligned}
c_t = {} & \underset{(15.0)}{198.9} + \underset{(0.0229)}{0.6812}\, y_t + \underset{(0.0197)}{0.2690}\, t + \underset{(0.08)}{0.03}\, \Delta y_{t+4} + \underset{(0.08)}{0.17}\, \Delta y_{t+3} \\
& + \underset{(0.08)}{0.15}\, \Delta y_{t+2} + \underset{(0.08)}{0.40}\, \Delta y_{t+1} - \underset{(0.08)}{0.05}\, \Delta y_t + \underset{(0.08)}{0.13}\, \Delta y_{t-1} \\
& + \underset{(0.08)}{0.23}\, \Delta y_{t-2} + \underset{(0.08)}{0.20}\, \Delta y_{t-3} + \underset{(0.07)}{0.19}\, \Delta y_{t-4} + \hat{u}_t
\end{aligned}
\qquad [19.3.31]
$$

$$s^2 = (T - 12)^{-1} \sum_{t=1}^{T} \hat{u}_t^2 = (1.017)^2.$$

A second-order autoregression fitted to the residuals of [19.3.31] produced

$$\hat{u}_t = 0.6872\, \hat{u}_{t-1} + 0.1292\, \hat{u}_{t-2} + \hat{e}_t,$$

where

$$\hat{\sigma}_1^2 = (T - 2)^{-1} \sum_{t=3}^{T} \hat{e}_t^2 = 0.34395$$

and

$$\hat{\tilde{\lambda}}_{11} = (0.34395)^{1/2}/(1 - 0.6872 - 0.1292) = 3.194.$$

A test of the hypothesis that the time trend does not contribute to [19.3.31] is thus given by

$$[(0.2690)/(0.0197)]\cdot[(1.017)/(3.194)] = 4.35.$$

Since $4.35 > 1.96$, we reject the null hypothesis that the coefficient on the time trend is zero.

The *OLS* results in [19.3.29] are certainly consistent with the hypothesis that consumption and income are cointegrated with cointegrating vector $\mathbf{a} = (1, -1)'$. However, [19.3.31] indicates that this result is dominated by the deterministic time trend common to $c_t$ and $y_t$. It appears that while $\mathbf{a} = (1, -1)'$ is sufficient to eliminate the trend components of $c_t$ and $y_t$, the residual $c_t - y_t$ contains a stochastic component that could be viewed as $I(1)$. Figure 19.6 provides a plot of $c_t - y_t$. It is indeed the case that this transformation seems to have eliminated the trend, though stochastic shocks to $c_t - y_t$ do not appear to die out within a period as short as 2 years.

## *Further Remarks and Extensions*

It was assumed throughout the derivations in this section that $\tilde{z}_t$ is $I(0)$, so that $\mathbf{y}_t$ is cointegrated with the cointegrating vector having a nonzero coefficient on $y_{1t}$. If $\mathbf{y}_t$ were not cointegrated, then [19.3.19] would be a spurious regression and the tests that were described would not be valid. For this reason estimation of [19.3.19] would usually be undertaken after an initial investigation suggested the presence of a cointegrating relation.

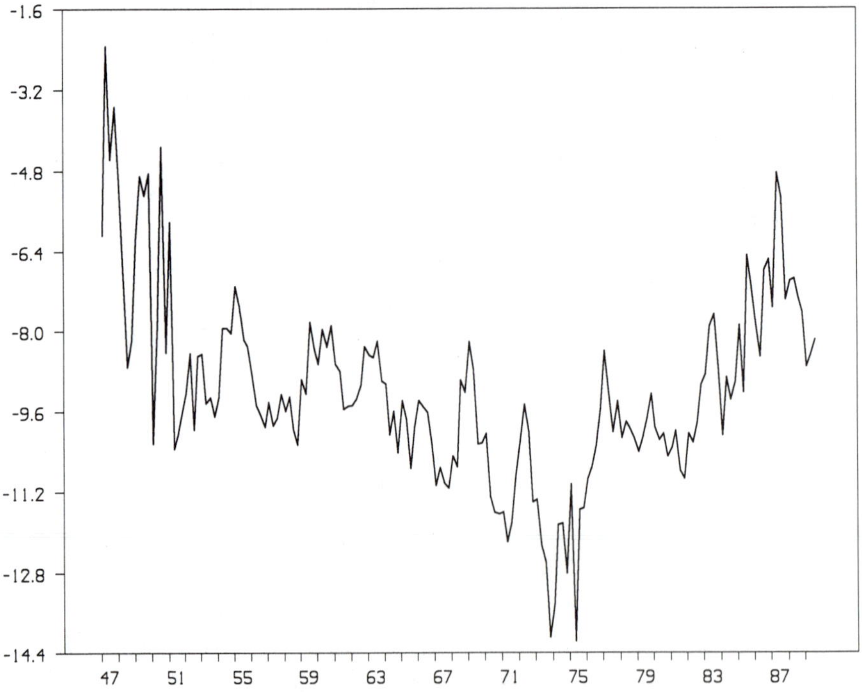


**FIGURE 19.6** One hundred times the difference between the log of personal consumption expenditures ($c_t$) and the log of personal disposable income ($y_t$) for the United States, quarterly, 1947–89.

It was also assumed that $\mathbf{\Lambda}_{22}$ is nonsingular, meaning that there are no cointegrating relations among the variables in $\mathbf{y}_{2t}$. Suppose instead that we are interested in estimating $h > 1$ different cointegrating vectors, as represented by a system of the form

$$\underset{(h\times 1)}{\mathbf{y}_{1t}} = \underset{(h\times g)}{\mathbf{\Gamma}'} \cdot \underset{(g\times 1)}{\mathbf{y}_{2t}} + \underset{(h\times 1)}{\boldsymbol{\mu}_1^*} + \underset{(h\times 1)}{\mathbf{z}_t^*} \qquad [19.3.32]$$

$$\underset{(g\times 1)}{\Delta\mathbf{y}_{2t}} = \underset{(g\times 1)}{\boldsymbol{\delta}_2} + \underset{(g\times 1)}{\mathbf{u}_{2t}} \qquad [19.3.33]$$

with

$$\begin{bmatrix} \mathbf{z}_t^* \\ \mathbf{u}_{2t} \end{bmatrix} = \mathbf{\Psi}^*(L)\boldsymbol{\varepsilon}_t$$

and $\mathbf{\Psi}^*(1)$ nonsingular. Here the generalization of the previous approach would be to augment [19.3.32] with leads and lags of $\Delta\mathbf{y}_{2t}$:

$$\mathbf{y}_{1t} = \boldsymbol{\mu}_1^* + \mathbf{\Gamma}'\mathbf{y}_{2t} + \sum_{s=-p}^{p} \mathbf{B}_s'\Delta\mathbf{y}_{2,t-s} + \tilde{\mathbf{z}}_t, \qquad [19.3.34]$$

where $\mathbf{B}_s'$ denotes an $(h \times g)$ matrix of coefficients and it is assumed that $\tilde{\mathbf{z}}_t$ is uncorrelated with $\mathbf{u}_{2\tau}$ for all $t$ and $\tau$. Expression [19.3.34] describes a set of $h$ equations. The $i$th equation regresses $y_{it}$ on a constant, on the current value of all the elements of $\mathbf{y}_{2t}$, and on past, present, and future changes of all the elements of $\mathbf{y}_{2t}$. This equation could be estimated by *OLS*, with the usual $F$ statistics multiplied by $[s_T^{(i)}/\hat{\lambda}_{11}^{(i)}]^2$, where $s_T^{(i)}$ is the standard error of the regression and $\hat{\lambda}_{11}^{(i)}$ could be estimated from the autocovariances of the residuals $\hat{\tilde{z}}_{it}$ for the regression.

The approach just described estimated the relation in [19.3.19] by *OLS* and made adjustments to the usual $t$ or $F$ statistics so that they could be compared with the standard $t$ and $F$ tables. Stock and Watson (1993) also suggested the more efficient approach of first estimating [19.3.19] by *OLS*, then using the residuals to construct a consistent estimate of the autocorrelation of $u_t$ as in [19.3.27] or [19.3.28], and finally reestimating the equation by generalized least squares. The resulting *GLS* standard errors could be used to construct asymptotically $\chi^2$ hypothesis tests.

Phillips and Loretan (1991, p. 424) suggested that instead autocorrelation of the residuals of [19.3.19] could be handled by including lagged values of the residual of the cointegrating relation in the form of

$$y_{1t} = \alpha + \boldsymbol{\gamma}'\mathbf{y}_{2t} + \sum_{s=-p}^{p} \boldsymbol{\beta}_s'\Delta\mathbf{y}_{2,t-s} + \sum_{s=1}^{p} \phi_s(y_{1,t-s} - \boldsymbol{\gamma}'\mathbf{y}_{2,t-s}) + \varepsilon_{1t}. \qquad [19.3.35]$$

Their proposal was to estimate the parameters in [19.3.35] by numerical minimization of the sum of squared residuals.

### *Phillips and Hansen's Fully Modified* OLS *Estimates*

A related approach was suggested by Phillips and Hansen (1990). Consider again a system with a single cointegrating relation written in the form

$$y_{1t} = \alpha + \boldsymbol{\gamma}'\mathbf{y}_{2t} + z_t^* \qquad [19.3.36]$$

$$\Delta\mathbf{y}_{2t} = \mathbf{u}_{2t} \qquad [19.3.37]$$

$$\begin{bmatrix} z_t^* \\ \mathbf{u}_{2t} \end{bmatrix} = \mathbf{\Psi}^*(L)\boldsymbol{\varepsilon}_t$$

$$E(\boldsymbol{\varepsilon}_t\boldsymbol{\varepsilon}_t') = \mathbf{PP}',$$

where $\mathbf{y}_{2t}$ is a $(g \times 1)$ vector and $\boldsymbol{\varepsilon}_t$ is an $(n \times 1)$ i.i.d. zero-mean vector for $n \equiv (g + 1)$. Define

$$\boldsymbol{\Lambda}^* \equiv \boldsymbol{\Psi}^*(1)\cdot\mathbf{P}$$

$$\underset{(n\times n)}{\boldsymbol{\Sigma}^*} \equiv \boldsymbol{\Lambda}^*\cdot[\boldsymbol{\Lambda}^*]' \equiv \begin{bmatrix} \underset{(1\times 1)}{\Sigma_{11}^*} & \underset{(1\times g)}{\boldsymbol{\Sigma}_{21}^{*\prime}} \\ \underset{(g\times 1)}{\boldsymbol{\Sigma}_{21}^*} & \underset{(g\times g)}{\boldsymbol{\Sigma}_{22}^*} \end{bmatrix}, \qquad [19.3.38]$$

with $\boldsymbol{\Lambda}^*$ as always assumed to be a nonsingular matrix.

Recall from equation [10.3.4] that the autocovariance-generating function for $(z_t^*, \mathbf{u}_{2t}')'$ is given by

$$\begin{aligned} \mathbf{G}(z) &\equiv \sum_{v=-\infty}^{\infty} z^v \begin{bmatrix} E(z_t^* z_{t-v}^*) & E(z_t^* \mathbf{u}_{2,t-v}') \\ E(\mathbf{u}_{2t} z_{t-v}^*) & E(\mathbf{u}_{2t}\mathbf{u}_{2,t-v}') \end{bmatrix} \\ &= [\boldsymbol{\Psi}^*(z)]\cdot\mathbf{P}\mathbf{P}'[\boldsymbol{\Psi}^*(z^{-1})]'. \end{aligned}$$

Thus, $\boldsymbol{\Sigma}^*$ could alternatively be described as the autocovariance-generating function $\mathbf{G}(z)$ evaluated at $z = 1$:

$$\begin{bmatrix} \Sigma_{11}^* & \boldsymbol{\Sigma}_{21}^{*\prime} \\ \boldsymbol{\Sigma}_{21}^* & \boldsymbol{\Sigma}_{22}^* \end{bmatrix} = \sum_{v=-\infty}^{\infty} \begin{bmatrix} E(z_t^* z_{t-v}^*) & E(z_t^* \mathbf{u}_{2,t-v}') \\ E(\mathbf{u}_{2t} z_{t-v}^*) & E(\mathbf{u}_{2t}\mathbf{u}_{2,t-v}') \end{bmatrix}. \qquad [19.3.39]$$

The difference between the general distribution for the estimated cointegrating vector described in Proposition 19.2 and the convenient special case investigated in [19.3.15] is due to two factors. The first is the possibility of a nonzero value for $\boldsymbol{\Sigma}_{21}^*$, and the second is the constant term that might appear in the variable $\mathbf{h}_2$ described in Proposition 19.2 arising from a nonzero value for

$$\boldsymbol{\aleph} \equiv \sum_{v=0}^{\infty} E(\mathbf{u}_{2t} z_{t+v}^*). \qquad [19.3.40]$$

The first issue can be addressed by subtracting $\boldsymbol{\Sigma}_{21}^{*\prime}(\boldsymbol{\Sigma}_{22}^*)^{-1}\Delta\mathbf{y}_{2t}$ from both sides of [19.3.36], arriving at

$$y_{1t}^\dagger = \alpha + \boldsymbol{\gamma}'\mathbf{y}_{2t} + z_t^\dagger,$$

where

$$\begin{aligned} y_{1t}^\dagger &\equiv y_{1t} - \boldsymbol{\Sigma}_{21}^{*\prime}(\boldsymbol{\Sigma}_{22}^*)^{-1}\Delta\mathbf{y}_{2t} \qquad [19.3.41] \\ z_t^\dagger &\equiv z_t^* - \boldsymbol{\Sigma}_{21}^{*\prime}(\boldsymbol{\Sigma}_{22}^*)^{-1}\Delta\mathbf{y}_{2t}. \end{aligned}$$

Notice that since $\Delta\mathbf{y}_{2t} = \mathbf{u}_{2t}$, the vector $(z_t^\dagger, \mathbf{u}_{2t}')'$ can be written as

$$\begin{bmatrix} z_t^\dagger \\ \mathbf{u}_{2t} \end{bmatrix} = \mathbf{L}' \begin{bmatrix} z_t^* \\ \mathbf{u}_{2t} \end{bmatrix} \qquad [19.3.42]$$

for

$$\mathbf{L}' \equiv \begin{bmatrix} 1 & -\boldsymbol{\Sigma}_{21}^{*\prime}(\boldsymbol{\Sigma}_{22}^*)^{-1} \\ \mathbf{0} & \mathbf{I}_g \end{bmatrix} \equiv \begin{bmatrix} \underset{(1\times n)}{\boldsymbol{\ell}_1'} \\ \underset{(g\times n)}{\mathbf{L}_2'} \end{bmatrix}. \qquad [19.3.43]$$

Suppose we were to estimate $\alpha$ and $\boldsymbol{\gamma}$ with an *OLS* regression of $y_{1t}^\dagger$ on a constant and $\mathbf{y}_{2t}$:

$$\begin{bmatrix} \hat{\alpha}_T^\dagger \\ \hat{\boldsymbol{\gamma}}_T^\dagger \end{bmatrix} = \begin{bmatrix} T & \Sigma\mathbf{y}_{2t}' \\ \Sigma\mathbf{y}_{2t} & \Sigma\mathbf{y}_{2t}\mathbf{y}_{2t}' \end{bmatrix}^{-1} \begin{bmatrix} \Sigma y_{1t}^\dagger \\ \Sigma\mathbf{y}_{2t} y_{1t}^\dagger \end{bmatrix}. \qquad [19.3.44]$$

The distribution of the resulting estimates is readily found from Proposition 19.2. Note that the vector $\boldsymbol{\lambda}_1^{*\prime}$ used in Proposition 19.2 can be written as $\mathbf{e}_1'\boldsymbol{\Lambda}^*$ for $\mathbf{e}_1'$ the first row of $\mathbf{I}_n$, while the matrix $\boldsymbol{\Lambda}_2^*$ in Proposition 19.2 can be written as $\mathbf{L}_2'\boldsymbol{\Lambda}^*$ for $\mathbf{L}_2'$ the last $g$ rows of $\mathbf{L}'$. The asymptotic distribution of the estimates in [19.3.44] is found by writing $\boldsymbol{\Lambda}_2^*$ in [19.2.13] as $\mathbf{L}_2'\boldsymbol{\Lambda}^*$, replacing $\boldsymbol{\lambda}_1^{*\prime} = \mathbf{e}_1'\boldsymbol{\Lambda}^*$ in [19.2.13] with $\boldsymbol{\ell}_1'\boldsymbol{\Lambda}^*$, and replacing $E(\mathbf{u}_{2t}z_{t+v}^*)$ with $E(\mathbf{u}_{2t}z_{t+v}^\dagger)$:

$$\begin{bmatrix} T^{1/2}(\hat{\alpha}_T^\dagger - \alpha) \\ T(\hat{\boldsymbol{\gamma}}_T^\dagger - \boldsymbol{\gamma}) \end{bmatrix} = \begin{bmatrix} 1 & T^{-3/2}\Sigma\mathbf{y}_{2t}' \\ T^{-3/2}\Sigma\mathbf{y}_{2t} & T^{-2}\Sigma\mathbf{y}_{2t}\mathbf{y}_{2t}' \end{bmatrix}^{-1} \begin{bmatrix} T^{-1/2}\Sigma z_t^\dagger \\ T^{-1}\Sigma\mathbf{y}_{2t}z_t^\dagger \end{bmatrix}$$

$$\xrightarrow{L} \begin{bmatrix} 1 & \left\{\int [\mathbf{W}(r)]'\,dr\right\}\boldsymbol{\Lambda}^{*\prime}\mathbf{L}_2 \\ \mathbf{L}_2'\boldsymbol{\Lambda}^*\int \mathbf{W}(r)\,dr & \mathbf{L}_2'\boldsymbol{\Lambda}^*\left\{\int [\mathbf{W}(r)]\cdot[\mathbf{W}(r)]'\,dr\right\}\boldsymbol{\Lambda}^{*\prime}\mathbf{L}_2 \end{bmatrix}^{-1}$$
$$\times \begin{bmatrix} \boldsymbol{\ell}_1'\boldsymbol{\Lambda}^*\mathbf{W}(1) \\ \mathbf{L}_2'\boldsymbol{\Lambda}^*\left\{\int [\mathbf{W}(r)]\,[d\mathbf{W}(r)]'\right\}\boldsymbol{\Lambda}^{*\prime}\boldsymbol{\ell}_1 + \boldsymbol{\aleph}^\dagger \end{bmatrix}, \qquad [19.3.45]$$

where $\mathbf{W}(r)$ denotes $n$-dimensional standard Brownian motion and

$$\begin{aligned} \boldsymbol{\aleph}^\dagger &\equiv \sum_{v=0}^{\infty} E(\mathbf{u}_{2t}z_{t+v}^\dagger) \\ &= \sum_{v=0}^{\infty} E\{\mathbf{u}_{2t}[z_{t+v}^* - \boldsymbol{\Sigma}_{21}^{*\prime}(\boldsymbol{\Sigma}_{22}^*)^{-1}\mathbf{u}_{2,t+v}]\} \\ &= \sum_{v=0}^{\infty} E\{\mathbf{u}_{2t}[z_{t+v}^* \quad \mathbf{u}_{2,t+v}']\}\begin{bmatrix} 1 \\ -(\boldsymbol{\Sigma}_{22}^*)^{-1}\boldsymbol{\Sigma}_{21}^* \end{bmatrix}. \end{aligned} \qquad [19.3.46]$$

Now, consider the $(n \times 1)$ vector process defined by

$$\mathbf{B}(r) \equiv \begin{bmatrix} \boldsymbol{\ell}_1' \\ \mathbf{L}_2' \end{bmatrix}\boldsymbol{\Lambda}^*\cdot\mathbf{W}(r). \qquad [19.3.47]$$

From [19.3.43] and [19.3.38], this is Brownian motion with variance matrix

$$\begin{aligned} E\{[\mathbf{B}(1)]\cdot[\mathbf{B}(1)]'\} &= \begin{bmatrix} \boldsymbol{\ell}_1' \\ \mathbf{L}_2' \end{bmatrix}\boldsymbol{\Lambda}^*\boldsymbol{\Lambda}^{*\prime}[\boldsymbol{\ell}_1 \quad \mathbf{L}_2] \\ &= \begin{bmatrix} 1 & -\boldsymbol{\Sigma}_{21}^{*\prime}(\boldsymbol{\Sigma}_{22}^*)^{-1} \\ \mathbf{0} & \mathbf{I}_g \end{bmatrix}\begin{bmatrix} \Sigma_{11}^* & \boldsymbol{\Sigma}_{21}^{*\prime} \\ \boldsymbol{\Sigma}_{21}^* & \boldsymbol{\Sigma}_{22}^* \end{bmatrix}\begin{bmatrix} 1 & \mathbf{0}' \\ -(\boldsymbol{\Sigma}_{22}^*)^{-1}\boldsymbol{\Sigma}_{21}^* & \mathbf{I}_g \end{bmatrix} \\ &= \begin{bmatrix} (\sigma_1^\dagger)^2 & \mathbf{0}' \\ \mathbf{0} & \boldsymbol{\Sigma}_{22}^* \end{bmatrix}, \end{aligned} \qquad [19.3.48]$$

where

$$(\sigma_1^\dagger)^2 \equiv \Sigma_{11}^* - \boldsymbol{\Sigma}_{21}^{*\prime}(\boldsymbol{\Sigma}_{22}^*)^{-1}\boldsymbol{\Sigma}_{21}^*. \qquad [19.3.49]$$

Partition $\mathbf{B}(r)$ as

$$\underset{(n\times 1)}{\mathbf{B}(r)} = \begin{bmatrix} \underset{(1\times 1)}{B_1(r)} \\ \underset{(g\times 1)}{\mathbf{B}_2(r)} \end{bmatrix} = \begin{bmatrix} \boldsymbol{\ell}_1'\boldsymbol{\Lambda}^*\mathbf{W}(r) \\ \mathbf{L}_2'\boldsymbol{\Lambda}^*\mathbf{W}(r) \end{bmatrix}.$$

Then [19.3.48] implies that $B_1(r)$ is scalar Brownian motion with variance $(\sigma_1^\dagger)^2$ while $\mathbf{B}_2(r)$ is $g$-dimensional Brownian motion with variance matrix $\mathbf{\Sigma}_{22}^*$, with $B_1(\cdot)$ independent of $\mathbf{B}_2(\cdot)$. The process $\mathbf{B}(r)$ in turn can be viewed as generated by a different standard Brownian motion $\mathbf{W}^\dagger(r)$, where

$$\begin{bmatrix} B_1(r) \\ \mathbf{B}_2(r) \end{bmatrix} = \begin{bmatrix} \sigma_1^\dagger & \mathbf{0}' \\ \mathbf{0} & \mathbf{P}_{22}^* \end{bmatrix} \begin{bmatrix} W_1^\dagger(r) \\ \mathbf{W}_2^\dagger(r) \end{bmatrix}$$

for $\mathbf{P}_{22}^*\mathbf{P}_{22}^{*\prime} = \mathbf{\Sigma}_{22}^*$ the Cholesky factorization of $\mathbf{\Sigma}_{22}^*$. The result [19.3.45] can then equivalently be expressed as

$$\begin{bmatrix} T^{1/2}(\hat{\alpha}_T^\dagger - \alpha) \\ T(\hat{\boldsymbol{\gamma}}_T^\dagger - \boldsymbol{\gamma}) \end{bmatrix} \xrightarrow{L} \begin{bmatrix} 1 & \left\{\int [\mathbf{W}_2^\dagger(r)]'\,dr\right\}\mathbf{P}_{22}^{*\prime} \\ \mathbf{P}_{22}^*\int \mathbf{W}_2^\dagger(r)\,dr & \mathbf{P}_{22}^*\left\{\int [\mathbf{W}_2^\dagger(r)]\cdot[\mathbf{W}_2^\dagger(r)]'\,dr\right\}\mathbf{P}_{22}^{*\prime} \end{bmatrix}^{-1} \times \begin{bmatrix} \sigma_1^\dagger\cdot W_1^\dagger(1) \\ \mathbf{P}_{22}^*\left\{\int \mathbf{W}_2^\dagger(r)\,dW_1^\dagger(r)\right\}\sigma_1^\dagger + \boldsymbol{\aleph}^\dagger \end{bmatrix}. \qquad [19.3.50]$$

If it were not for the presence of the constant $\boldsymbol{\aleph}^\dagger$, the distribution in [19.3.50] would be of the form of [19.3.11], from which it would follow that conditional on $\mathbf{W}_2^\dagger(\cdot)$, the variable in [19.3.50] would be Gaussian and test statistics that are asymptotically $\chi^2$ could be generated as before.

Recalling [19.3.39], one might propose to estimate $\mathbf{\Sigma}^*$ by

$$\begin{bmatrix} \hat{\Sigma}_{11}^* & \hat{\mathbf{\Sigma}}_{21}^{*\prime} \\ \hat{\mathbf{\Sigma}}_{21}^* & \hat{\mathbf{\Sigma}}_{22}^* \end{bmatrix} = \hat{\mathbf{\Gamma}}_0 + \sum_{v=1}^{q}\{1 - [v/(q+1)]\}(\hat{\mathbf{\Gamma}}_v + \hat{\mathbf{\Gamma}}_v'), \qquad [19.3.51]$$

where

$$\begin{aligned} \hat{\mathbf{\Gamma}}_v &= T^{-1}\sum_{t=v+1}^{T}\begin{bmatrix} (\hat{z}_t^*\hat{z}_{t-v}^*) & (\hat{z}_t^*\hat{\mathbf{u}}_{2,t-v}') \\ (\hat{\mathbf{u}}_{2t}\hat{z}_{t-v}^*) & (\hat{\mathbf{u}}_{2t}\hat{\mathbf{u}}_{2,t-v}') \end{bmatrix} \\ &\equiv \begin{bmatrix} \hat{\Gamma}_{11}^{(v)} & \hat{\mathbf{\Gamma}}_{12}^{(v)} \\ \hat{\mathbf{\Gamma}}_{21}^{(v)} & \hat{\mathbf{\Gamma}}_{22}^{(v)} \end{bmatrix} \end{aligned} \qquad [19.3.52]$$

for $\hat{z}_t^*$ the sample residual resulting from estimation of [19.3.36] by *OLS* and $\hat{\mathbf{u}}_{2t} = \Delta\mathbf{y}_{2t}$. To arrive at a similar estimate of $\boldsymbol{\aleph}^\dagger$, note that [19.3.46] can be written

$$\begin{aligned} \boldsymbol{\aleph}^\dagger &= \sum_{v=0}^{\infty} E\{\mathbf{u}_{2,t-v}[z_t^* \quad \mathbf{u}_{2t}']\}\begin{bmatrix} 1 \\ -(\mathbf{\Sigma}_{22}^*)^{-1}\mathbf{\Sigma}_{21}^* \end{bmatrix} \\ &= \sum_{v=0}^{\infty} E\left\{\begin{bmatrix} z_t^*\mathbf{u}_{2,t-v}' \\ \mathbf{u}_{2t}\mathbf{u}_{2,t-v}' \end{bmatrix}'\right\}\begin{bmatrix} 1 \\ -(\mathbf{\Sigma}_{22}^*)^{-1}\mathbf{\Sigma}_{21}^* \end{bmatrix} \\ &= \sum_{v=0}^{\infty}\begin{bmatrix} \mathbf{\Gamma}_{12}^{(v)} \\ \mathbf{\Gamma}_{22}^{(v)} \end{bmatrix}'\begin{bmatrix} 1 \\ -(\mathbf{\Sigma}_{22}^*)^{-1}\mathbf{\Sigma}_{21}^* \end{bmatrix}. \end{aligned}$$

This suggests the estimator

$$\hat{\boldsymbol{\aleph}}_T^\dagger = \sum_{v=0}^{q}\left\{1 - [v/(q+1)]\right\}\left\{\begin{bmatrix} [\hat{\mathbf{\Gamma}}_{12}^{(v)}]' & [\hat{\mathbf{\Gamma}}_{22}^{(v)}]' \end{bmatrix}\right\}\begin{bmatrix} 1 \\ -(\hat{\mathbf{\Sigma}}_{22}^*)^{-1}\hat{\mathbf{\Sigma}}_{21}^* \end{bmatrix}. \qquad [19.3.53]$$

The fully modified $OLS$ estimator proposed by Phillips and Hansen (1990) is then

$$\begin{bmatrix} \hat{\alpha}_T^{\dagger\dagger} \\ \hat{\boldsymbol{\gamma}}_T^{\dagger\dagger} \end{bmatrix} = \begin{bmatrix} T & \Sigma \mathbf{y}_{2t}' \\ \Sigma \mathbf{y}_{2t} & \Sigma \mathbf{y}_{2t}\mathbf{y}_{2t}' \end{bmatrix}^{-1} \begin{bmatrix} \Sigma \hat{y}_{1t}^{\dagger} \\ \{\Sigma \mathbf{y}_{2t}\hat{y}_{1t}^{\dagger} - T\hat{\boldsymbol{\aleph}}_T^{\dagger}\} \end{bmatrix}$$

for $\hat{y}_{1t}^{\dagger} \equiv y_{1t} - \hat{\boldsymbol{\Sigma}}_{21}^{*\prime}(\hat{\boldsymbol{\Sigma}}_{22}^{*})^{-1}\Delta\mathbf{y}_{2t}$. This analysis implies that

$$\begin{bmatrix} T^{1/2}(\hat{\alpha}_T^{\dagger\dagger} - \alpha) \\ T(\hat{\boldsymbol{\gamma}}_T^{\dagger\dagger} - \boldsymbol{\gamma}) \end{bmatrix} = \begin{bmatrix} 1 & T^{-3/2}\Sigma \mathbf{y}_{2t}' \\ T^{-3/2}\Sigma \mathbf{y}_{2t} & T^{-2}\Sigma \mathbf{y}_{2t}\mathbf{y}_{2t}' \end{bmatrix}^{-1} \begin{bmatrix} T^{-1/2}\Sigma \hat{z}_t^{\dagger} \\ T^{-1}\Sigma \mathbf{y}_{2t}\hat{z}_t^{\dagger} - \hat{\boldsymbol{\aleph}}_T \end{bmatrix}$$

$$\xrightarrow{L} \sigma_1^{\dagger}\begin{bmatrix} \nu_1 \\ \boldsymbol{\nu}_2 \end{bmatrix},$$

where

$$\begin{bmatrix} \nu_1 \\ \boldsymbol{\nu}_2 \end{bmatrix} \equiv \begin{bmatrix} 1 & \left\{\int [\mathbf{W}_2^{\dagger}(r)]'\,dr\right\}\mathbf{P}_{22}^{*\prime} \\ \mathbf{P}_{22}^{*}\int \mathbf{W}_2^{\dagger}(r)\,dr & \mathbf{P}_{22}^{*}\left\{\int [\mathbf{W}_2^{\dagger}(r)]\cdot[\mathbf{W}_2^{\dagger}(r)]'\,dr\right\}\mathbf{P}_{22}^{*\prime} \end{bmatrix}^{-1}$$

$$\times \begin{bmatrix} W_1^{\dagger}(1) \\ \mathbf{P}_{22}^{*}\left\{\int \mathbf{W}_2^{\dagger}(r)\,dW_1^{\dagger}(r)\right\} \end{bmatrix}.$$

It follows as in [19.3.12] that

$$\left[\begin{matrix} \nu_1 \\ \boldsymbol{\nu}_2 \end{matrix}\middle|\, \mathbf{W}_2^{\dagger}(\cdot)\right] \sim N\left(\begin{bmatrix} 0 \\ \mathbf{0} \end{bmatrix}, \mathbf{H}^{-1}\right)$$

for

$$\mathbf{H} \equiv \begin{bmatrix} 1 & \left\{\int [\mathbf{W}_2^{\dagger}(r)]'\,dr\right\}\mathbf{P}_{22}^{*\prime} \\ \mathbf{P}_{22}^{*}\int \mathbf{W}_2^{\dagger}(r)\,dr & \mathbf{P}_{22}^{*}\left\{\int [\mathbf{W}_2^{\dagger}(r)]\cdot[\mathbf{W}_2^{\dagger}(r)]'\,dr\right\}\mathbf{P}_{22}^{*\prime} \end{bmatrix}.$$

Furthermore, [19.3.49] suggests that a consistent estimate of $(\sigma_1^{\dagger})^2$ is provided by

$$(\hat{\sigma}_1^{\dagger})^2 = \hat{\Sigma}_{11}^{*} - \hat{\boldsymbol{\Sigma}}_{21}^{*\prime}(\hat{\boldsymbol{\Sigma}}_{22}^{*})^{-1}\hat{\boldsymbol{\Sigma}}_{21}^{*},$$

with $\hat{\boldsymbol{\Sigma}}_{ij}^{*}$ given by [19.3.51]. Thus, if we multiply the usual Wald form of the $\chi^2$ test of $m$ restrictions of the form $\mathbf{R}\boldsymbol{\gamma} = \mathbf{r}$ by $(s_T/\hat{\sigma}_1^{\dagger})^2$, the result is an asymptotically $\chi^2(m)$ statistic under the null hypothesis:

$$(s_T/\hat{\sigma}_1^{\dagger})^2\cdot\chi_T^2 = \{\mathbf{R}\hat{\boldsymbol{\gamma}}_T^{\dagger\dagger} - \mathbf{r}\}'\left\{(\hat{\sigma}_1^{\dagger})^2[\mathbf{0} \quad \mathbf{R}]\begin{bmatrix} T & \Sigma \mathbf{y}_{2t}' \\ \Sigma \mathbf{y}_{2t} & \Sigma \mathbf{y}_{2t}\mathbf{y}_{2t}' \end{bmatrix}^{-1}\begin{bmatrix} \mathbf{0}' \\ \mathbf{R}' \end{bmatrix}\right\}^{-1}\{\mathbf{R}\hat{\boldsymbol{\gamma}}_T^{\dagger\dagger} - \mathbf{r}\}$$

$$= \{\mathbf{R}\cdot T(\hat{\boldsymbol{\gamma}}_T^{\dagger\dagger} - \boldsymbol{\gamma})\}'\left\{(\hat{\sigma}_1^{\dagger})^2[\mathbf{0} \quad \mathbf{R}]\right.$$

$$\left.\times \begin{bmatrix} 1 & T^{-3/2}\Sigma \mathbf{y}_{2t}' \\ T^{-3/2}\Sigma \mathbf{y}_{2t} & T^{-2}\Sigma \mathbf{y}_{2t}\mathbf{y}_{2t}' \end{bmatrix}^{-1}\begin{bmatrix} \mathbf{0}' \\ \mathbf{R}' \end{bmatrix}\right\}^{-1}\{\mathbf{R}\cdot T(\hat{\boldsymbol{\gamma}}_T^{\dagger\dagger} - \boldsymbol{\gamma})\}$$

$$\xrightarrow{L} (\sigma_1^{\dagger})^2(\mathbf{R}\boldsymbol{\nu}_2)'\left\{(\sigma_1^{\dagger})^2[\mathbf{0} \quad \mathbf{R}]\mathbf{H}^{-1}\begin{bmatrix} \mathbf{0}' \\ \mathbf{R}' \end{bmatrix}\right\}^{-1}(\mathbf{R}\boldsymbol{\nu}_2)$$

$$\sim \chi^2(m).$$

This description has assumed that there was no drift in any elements of the system. Hansen (1992) showed that the procedure is easily modified if $E(\Delta\mathbf{y}_{2t}) = \boldsymbol{\delta}_2 \neq \mathbf{0}$, simply by replacing $\hat{\mathbf{u}}_{2t} = \Delta\mathbf{y}_{2t}$ in [19.3.52] with

$$\hat{\mathbf{u}}_{2t} = \Delta\mathbf{y}_{2t} - \hat{\boldsymbol{\delta}}_2,$$

where

$$\hat{\boldsymbol{\delta}}_2 = T^{-1}\sum_{t=1}^{T}\Delta\mathbf{y}_{2t}.$$

Hansen also showed that a time trend could be added to the cointegrating relation, as in

$$y_{1t} = \alpha + \boldsymbol{\gamma}'\mathbf{y}_{2t} + \delta t + z_t^*,$$

for which the fully modified estimator is

$$\begin{bmatrix} \hat{\alpha}_T^{\dagger\dagger} \\ \hat{\boldsymbol{\gamma}}_T^{\dagger\dagger} \\ \hat{\delta}_T^{\dagger\dagger} \end{bmatrix} = \begin{bmatrix} T & \Sigma\mathbf{y}_{2t}' & \Sigma t \\ \Sigma\mathbf{y}_{2t} & \Sigma\mathbf{y}_{2t}\mathbf{y}_{2t}' & \Sigma\mathbf{y}_{2t}t \\ \Sigma t & \Sigma t\mathbf{y}_{2t}' & \Sigma t^2 \end{bmatrix}^{-1} \begin{bmatrix} \Sigma\hat{y}_{1t}^{\dagger} \\ \Sigma\mathbf{y}_{2t}\hat{y}_{1t}^{\dagger} - T\hat{\boldsymbol{\aleph}}_T^{\dagger} \\ \Sigma t\hat{y}_{1t}^{\dagger} \end{bmatrix}.$$

Collecting these estimates in a vector $\mathbf{b}_T^{\dagger\dagger} = (\hat{\alpha}_T^{\dagger\dagger}, [\hat{\boldsymbol{\gamma}}_T^{\dagger\dagger}]', \hat{\delta}_T^{\dagger\dagger})'$, a hypothesis involving $m$ restrictions on $\boldsymbol{\beta}$ of the form $\mathbf{R}\boldsymbol{\beta} = \mathbf{r}$ can be tested by

$$\{\mathbf{R}\mathbf{b}_T^{\dagger\dagger} - \mathbf{r}\}'\left\{(\hat{\sigma}_1^{\dagger})^2\mathbf{R}\begin{bmatrix} T & \Sigma\mathbf{y}_{2t}' & \Sigma t \\ \Sigma\mathbf{y}_{2t} & \Sigma\mathbf{y}_{2t}\mathbf{y}_{2t}' & \Sigma\mathbf{y}_{2t}t \\ \Sigma t & \Sigma t\mathbf{y}_{2t}' & \Sigma t^2 \end{bmatrix}^{-1}\mathbf{R}'\right\}^{-1}\{\mathbf{R}\mathbf{b}_T^{\dagger\dagger} - \mathbf{r}\} \xrightarrow{L} \chi^2(m).$$

### *Park's Canonical Cointegrating Regressions*

A closely related idea has been suggested by Park (1992). In Park's procedure, both the dependent and explanatory variables in [19.3.36] are transformed, and the resulting transformed regression can then be estimated by *OLS* and tested using standard procedures. Park and Ogaki (1991) explored the use of the *VAR* prewhitening technique of Andrews and Monahan (1992) to replace the Bartlett estimate in expressions such as [19.3.51].

## APPENDIX 19.A. *Proofs of Chapter 19 Propositions*

■ **Proof of Proposition 19.2.** Define $\tilde{y}_{1t} \equiv z_1^* + z_2^* + \cdots + z_t^*$ for $t = 1, 2, \ldots, T$ and $\tilde{y}_{1,0} \equiv 0$. Then

$$\begin{bmatrix} \tilde{y}_{1t} \\ \mathbf{y}_{2t} \end{bmatrix} = \begin{bmatrix} 0 \\ \mathbf{y}_{2,0} \end{bmatrix} + \boldsymbol{\xi}_t^*,$$

where

$$\boldsymbol{\xi}_t^* \equiv \sum_{s=1}^{t}\begin{bmatrix} z_s^* \\ \mathbf{u}_{2s} \end{bmatrix}.$$

Hence, result (e) of Proposition 18.1 establishes that

$$T^{-1}\sum_{t=1}^{T}\begin{bmatrix} \tilde{y}_{1,t-1} \\ \mathbf{y}_{2,t-1} \end{bmatrix}[z_t^* \quad \mathbf{u}_{2t}'] \xrightarrow{L} \boldsymbol{\Lambda}^*\cdot\left\{\int_0^1 [\mathbf{W}(r)]\,[d\mathbf{W}(r)]'\right\}\cdot\boldsymbol{\Lambda}^{*\prime} + \sum_{v=1}^{\infty}\boldsymbol{\Gamma}_v^{*\prime} \qquad [19.A.1]$$

for

$$\mathbf{\Lambda}^* \equiv \mathbf{\Psi}^*(1)\cdot \mathbf{P}$$
$$\mathbf{\Gamma}_v^{*\prime} \equiv E\begin{bmatrix} z_t^* \\ \mathbf{u}_{2t} \end{bmatrix}[z_{t+v}^* \quad \mathbf{u}_{2,t+v}'].$$

It follows from [19.A.1] that

$$\begin{aligned} T^{-1}\sum_{t=1}^{T}\begin{bmatrix} \tilde{y}_{1t} \\ \mathbf{y}_{2t} \end{bmatrix}[z_t^* \quad \mathbf{u}_{2t}'] &= T^{-1}\sum_{t=1}^{T}\begin{bmatrix} \tilde{y}_{1,t-1} \\ \mathbf{y}_{2,t-1} \end{bmatrix}[z_t^* \quad \mathbf{u}_{2t}'] + T^{-1}\sum_{t=1}^{T}\begin{bmatrix} z_t^* \\ \mathbf{u}_{2t} \end{bmatrix}[z_t^* \quad \mathbf{u}_{2t}'] \\ &\xrightarrow{L} \mathbf{\Lambda}^*\cdot\left\{\int_0^1 [\mathbf{W}(r)]\,[d\mathbf{W}(r)]'\right\}\cdot\mathbf{\Lambda}^{*\prime} + \sum_{v=0}^{\infty}\mathbf{\Gamma}_v^{*\prime}. \end{aligned} \qquad [19.A.2]$$

Similarly, results (a), (g), and (i) of Proposition 18.1 imply

$$T^{-1/2}\sum_{t=1}^{T}\begin{bmatrix} z_t^* \\ \mathbf{u}_{2t} \end{bmatrix} \xrightarrow{L} \mathbf{\Lambda}^*\cdot\mathbf{W}(1) \qquad [19.A.3]$$

$$T^{-3/2}\sum_{t=1}^{T}\begin{bmatrix} \tilde{y}_{1t} \\ \mathbf{y}_{2t} \end{bmatrix} \xrightarrow{L} \mathbf{\Lambda}^*\cdot\int_0^1 \mathbf{W}(r)\,dr \qquad [19.A.4]$$

$$T^{-2}\sum_{t=1}^{T}\begin{bmatrix} \tilde{y}_{1t} \\ \mathbf{y}_{2t} \end{bmatrix}[\tilde{y}_{1t} \quad \mathbf{y}_{2t}'] \xrightarrow{L} \mathbf{\Lambda}^*\cdot\left\{\int_0^1 [\mathbf{W}(r)]\cdot[\mathbf{W}(r)]'\,dr\right\}\cdot\mathbf{\Lambda}^{*\prime}. \qquad [19.A.5]$$

Observe that the deviations of the *OLS* estimates in [19.2.12] from the population values $\alpha$ and $\boldsymbol{\gamma}$ that describe the cointegrating relation [19.2.9] are given by

$$\begin{bmatrix} \hat{\alpha}_T - \alpha \\ \hat{\boldsymbol{\gamma}}_T - \boldsymbol{\gamma} \end{bmatrix} = \begin{bmatrix} T & \Sigma\mathbf{y}_{2t}' \\ \Sigma\mathbf{y}_{2t} & \Sigma\mathbf{y}_{2t}\mathbf{y}_{2t}' \end{bmatrix}^{-1}\begin{bmatrix} \Sigma z_t^* \\ \Sigma\mathbf{y}_{2t}z_t^* \end{bmatrix},$$

from which

$$\begin{aligned} \begin{bmatrix} T^{1/2}(\hat{\alpha}_T - \alpha) \\ T(\hat{\boldsymbol{\gamma}}_T - \boldsymbol{\gamma}) \end{bmatrix} &= \left\{\begin{bmatrix} T^{-1/2} & \mathbf{0}' \\ \mathbf{0} & T^{-1}\cdot\mathbf{I}_g \end{bmatrix}\begin{bmatrix} T & \Sigma\mathbf{y}_{2t}' \\ \Sigma\mathbf{y}_{2t} & \Sigma\mathbf{y}_{2t}\mathbf{y}_{2t}' \end{bmatrix}\right. \\ &\quad \times \left.\begin{bmatrix} T^{-1/2} & \mathbf{0}' \\ \mathbf{0} & T^{-1}\cdot\mathbf{I}_g \end{bmatrix}\right\}^{-1}\left\{\begin{bmatrix} T^{-1/2} & \mathbf{0}' \\ \mathbf{0} & T^{-1}\cdot\mathbf{I}_g \end{bmatrix}\begin{bmatrix} \Sigma z_t^* \\ \Sigma\mathbf{y}_{2t}z_t^* \end{bmatrix}\right\} \\ &= \begin{bmatrix} 1 & T^{-3/2}\Sigma\mathbf{y}_{2t}' \\ T^{-3/2}\Sigma\mathbf{y}_{2t} & T^{-2}\Sigma\mathbf{y}_{2t}\mathbf{y}_{2t}' \end{bmatrix}^{-1}\begin{bmatrix} T^{-1/2}\Sigma z_t^* \\ T^{-1}\Sigma\mathbf{y}_{2t}z_t^* \end{bmatrix}. \end{aligned} \qquad [19.A.6]$$

But from [19.A.2],

$$\begin{aligned} T^{-1}\Sigma\mathbf{y}_{2t}z_t^* &= [\mathbf{0} \quad \mathbf{I}_g]T^{-1}\sum_{t=1}^{T}\begin{bmatrix} \tilde{y}_{1t} \\ \mathbf{y}_{2t} \end{bmatrix}[z_t^* \quad \mathbf{u}_{2t}']\begin{bmatrix} 1 \\ \mathbf{0} \end{bmatrix} \\ &\xrightarrow{L} [\mathbf{0} \quad \mathbf{I}_g]\mathbf{\Lambda}^*\cdot\left\{\int_0^1 [\mathbf{W}(r)]\,[d\mathbf{W}(r)]'\right\}\cdot\mathbf{\Lambda}^{*\prime}\begin{bmatrix} 1 \\ \mathbf{0} \end{bmatrix} \\ &\quad + [\mathbf{0} \quad \mathbf{I}_g]\sum_{v=0}^{\infty}\mathbf{\Gamma}_v^{*\prime}\begin{bmatrix} 1 \\ \mathbf{0} \end{bmatrix} \\ &= \mathbf{\Lambda}_2^*\cdot\left\{\int_0^1 [\mathbf{W}(r)]\,[d\mathbf{W}(r)]'\right\}\cdot\boldsymbol{\lambda}_1^* + \sum_{v=0}^{\infty}E(\mathbf{u}_{2t}z_{t+v}^*). \end{aligned} \qquad [19.A.7]$$

Similar use of [19.A.3] to [19.A.5] in [19.A.6] produces [19.2.13]. ■

■ **Proof of Proposition 19.3.** For simplicity of exposition, the discussion is restricted to the case when $E(\Delta\mathbf{y}_{2t}) = \mathbf{0}$, though it is straightforward to develop analogous results using a rescaling and rotation of variables similar to that in [18.2.43].

Consider first what the results would be from an *OLS* regression of $z_{1t}^*$ on $\mathbf{z}_{2t}^* \equiv (z_{2t}^*, z_{3t}^*, \ldots, z_{ht}^*)'$, a constant, and $\mathbf{y}_{2t}$:

$$z_{1t}^* = \boldsymbol{\beta}'\mathbf{z}_{2t}^* + \alpha^* + \boldsymbol{\aleph}^{*\prime}\mathbf{y}_{2t} + u_t. \qquad [19.A.8]$$

If this regression is evaluated at the true values $\alpha^* = 0$, $\boldsymbol{\aleph}^* = \mathbf{0}$, and $\boldsymbol{\beta} \equiv (\beta_2, \beta_3, \ldots, \beta_h)'$ the vector of population projection coefficients in [19.2.18], then the disturbance $u_t$ will be the residual defined in [19.2.18]. This residual had mean zero and was uncorrelated with $\mathbf{z}_{2t}^*$. The *OLS* estimates based on [19.A.8] would be

$$\begin{bmatrix} \hat{\boldsymbol{\beta}}_T \\ \hat{\alpha}_T^* \\ \hat{\boldsymbol{\aleph}}_T^* \end{bmatrix} = \begin{bmatrix} \Sigma\mathbf{z}_{2t}^*\mathbf{z}_{2t}^{*\prime} & \Sigma\mathbf{z}_{2t}^* & \Sigma\mathbf{z}_{2t}^*\mathbf{y}_{2t}' \\ \Sigma\mathbf{z}_{2t}^{*\prime} & T & \Sigma\mathbf{y}_{2t}' \\ \Sigma\mathbf{y}_{2t}\mathbf{z}_{2t}^{*\prime} & \Sigma\mathbf{y}_{2t} & \Sigma\mathbf{y}_{2t}\mathbf{y}_{2t}' \end{bmatrix}^{-1} \begin{bmatrix} \Sigma\mathbf{z}_{2t}^* z_{1t}^* \\ \Sigma z_{1t}^* \\ \Sigma\mathbf{y}_{2t} z_{1t}^* \end{bmatrix}. \qquad [19.A.9]$$

The deviations of these estimates from the corresponding population values satisfy

$$\begin{aligned}
\begin{bmatrix} \hat{\boldsymbol{\beta}}_T - \boldsymbol{\beta} \\ \hat{\alpha}_T^* \\ T^{1/2}\hat{\boldsymbol{\aleph}}_T^* \end{bmatrix} &= \begin{bmatrix} \mathbf{I}_{h-1} & \mathbf{0} & \mathbf{0} \\ \mathbf{0}' & 1 & \mathbf{0}' \\ \mathbf{0} & \mathbf{0} & T^{1/2}\mathbf{I}_g \end{bmatrix} \begin{bmatrix} \Sigma\mathbf{z}_{2t}^*\mathbf{z}_{2t}^{*\prime} & \Sigma\mathbf{z}_{2t}^* & \Sigma\mathbf{z}_{2t}^*\mathbf{y}_{2t}' \\ \Sigma\mathbf{z}_{2t}^{*\prime} & T & \Sigma\mathbf{y}_{2t}' \\ \Sigma\mathbf{y}_{2t}\mathbf{z}_{2t}^{*\prime} & \Sigma\mathbf{y}_{2t} & \Sigma\mathbf{y}_{2t}\mathbf{y}_{2t}' \end{bmatrix}^{-1} \\
&\quad \times \begin{bmatrix} T\cdot\mathbf{I}_{h-1} & \mathbf{0} & \mathbf{0} \\ \mathbf{0}' & T & \mathbf{0}' \\ \mathbf{0} & \mathbf{0} & T^{3/2}\mathbf{I}_g \end{bmatrix} \begin{bmatrix} T\cdot\mathbf{I}_{h-1} & \mathbf{0} & \mathbf{0} \\ \mathbf{0}' & T & \mathbf{0}' \\ \mathbf{0} & \mathbf{0} & T^{3/2}\mathbf{I}_g \end{bmatrix}^{-1} \begin{bmatrix} \Sigma\mathbf{z}_{2t}^* u_t \\ \Sigma u_t \\ \Sigma\mathbf{y}_{2t} u_t \end{bmatrix} \\
&= \begin{bmatrix} T^{-1}\Sigma\mathbf{z}_{2t}^*\mathbf{z}_{2t}^{*\prime} & T^{-1}\Sigma\mathbf{z}_{2t}^* & T^{-3/2}\Sigma\mathbf{z}_{2t}^*\mathbf{y}_{2t}' \\ T^{-1}\Sigma\mathbf{z}_{2t}^{*\prime} & 1 & T^{-3/2}\Sigma\mathbf{y}_{2t}' \\ T^{-3/2}\Sigma\mathbf{y}_{2t}\mathbf{z}_{2t}^{*\prime} & T^{-3/2}\Sigma\mathbf{y}_{2t} & T^{-2}\Sigma\mathbf{y}_{2t}\mathbf{y}_{2t}' \end{bmatrix}^{-1} \begin{bmatrix} T^{-1}\Sigma\mathbf{z}_{2t}^* u_t \\ T^{-1}\Sigma u_t \\ T^{-3/2}\Sigma\mathbf{y}_{2t} u_t \end{bmatrix}.
\end{aligned}$$

[19.A.10]

Recalling that $E(\mathbf{z}_{2t}^* u_t) = \mathbf{0}$, one can show that $T^{-1}\Sigma\mathbf{z}_{2t}^* u_t \xrightarrow{p} \mathbf{0}$ and $T^{-1}\Sigma u_t \xrightarrow{p} 0$ by the law of large numbers. Also, $T^{-3/2}\Sigma\mathbf{y}_{2t}u_t \xrightarrow{p} \mathbf{0}$, from the argument given in [19.A.7]. Furthermore,

$$\begin{bmatrix} T^{-1}\Sigma\mathbf{z}_{2t}^*\mathbf{z}_{2t}^{*\prime} & T^{-1}\Sigma\mathbf{z}_{2t}^* & T^{-3/2}\Sigma\mathbf{z}_{2t}^*\mathbf{y}_{2t}' \\ T^{-1}\Sigma\mathbf{z}_{2t}^{*\prime} & 1 & T^{-3/2}\Sigma\mathbf{y}_{2t}' \\ T^{-3/2}\Sigma\mathbf{y}_{2t}\mathbf{z}_{2t}^{*\prime} & T^{-3/2}\Sigma\mathbf{y}_{2t} & T^{-2}\Sigma\mathbf{y}_{2t}\mathbf{y}_{2t}' \end{bmatrix}$$

$$\xrightarrow{L} \begin{bmatrix} E(\mathbf{z}_{2t}^*\mathbf{z}_{2t}^{*\prime}) & \mathbf{0} & \mathbf{0} \\ \mathbf{0}' & 1 & \left\{\int [\mathbf{W}(r)]'\,dr\right\}\boldsymbol{\Lambda}_2^{*\prime} \\ \mathbf{0} & \boldsymbol{\Lambda}_2^*\int \mathbf{W}(r)\,dr & \boldsymbol{\Lambda}_2^*\left\{\int [\mathbf{W}(r)]\cdot[\mathbf{W}(r)]'\,dr\right\}\boldsymbol{\Lambda}_2^{*\prime} \end{bmatrix}, \qquad [19.A.11]$$

where $\mathbf{W}(r)$ is $n$-dimensional standard Brownian motion and $\boldsymbol{\Lambda}_2^*$ is a $(g \times n)$ matrix constructed from the last $g$ rows of $\boldsymbol{\Psi}^*(1)\cdot\mathbf{P}$. Notice that the matrix in [19.A.11] is almost surely nonsingular. Substituting these results into [19.A.10] establishes that

$$\begin{bmatrix} \hat{\boldsymbol{\beta}}_T - \boldsymbol{\beta} \\ \hat{\alpha}_T^* \\ T^{1/2}\hat{\boldsymbol{\aleph}}_T^* \end{bmatrix} \xrightarrow{p} \begin{bmatrix} \mathbf{0} \\ 0 \\ \mathbf{0} \end{bmatrix},$$

so that *OLS* estimation of [19.A.8] would produce consistent estimates of the parameters of the population linear projection [19.2.18].

An *OLS* regression of $y_{1t}$ on a constant and the other elements of $\mathbf{y}_t$ is a simple transformation of the regression in [19.A.8]. To see this, notice that [19.A.8] can be written as

$$[1 \quad -\boldsymbol{\beta}']\mathbf{z}_t^* = \alpha^* + \boldsymbol{\aleph}^{*\prime}\mathbf{y}_{2t} + u_t. \qquad [19.A.12]$$

Solving [19.2.16] for $\mathbf{z}_t^*$ and substituting the result into [19.A.12] gives

$$[1 \quad -\boldsymbol{\beta}'](\mathbf{y}_{1t} - \boldsymbol{\mu}_1^* - \boldsymbol{\Gamma}'\mathbf{y}_{2t}) = \alpha^* + \boldsymbol{\aleph}^{*\prime}\mathbf{y}_{2t} + u_t,$$

or, since $\mathbf{y}_{1t} = (y_{1t}, y_{2t}, \ldots, y_{ht})'$, we have

$$y_{1t} = \beta_2 y_{2t} + \beta_3 y_{3t} + \cdots + \beta_h y_{ht} + \alpha + \boldsymbol{\aleph}'\mathbf{y}_{2t} + u_t, \qquad [19.A.13]$$

where $\alpha \equiv \alpha^* + [1 \quad -\boldsymbol{\beta}']\boldsymbol{\mu}_1^*$ and $\boldsymbol{\aleph}' \equiv \boldsymbol{\aleph}^{*\prime} + [1 \quad -\boldsymbol{\beta}']\boldsymbol{\Gamma}'$.

*OLS* estimation of [19.A.8] will produce identical fitted values to those resulting from *OLS* estimation of [19.A.13], with the relations between the estimated coefficients as just given. Since *OLS* estimation of [19.A.8] yields consistent estimates of [19.2.18], *OLS* estimation of [19.A.13] yields consistent estimates of the corresponding transformed parameters, as claimed by the proposition. ■

■ **Proof of Proposition 19.4.** As in Proposition 18.2, partition $\boldsymbol{\Lambda\Lambda}'$ as

$$\underset{(n\times n)}{\boldsymbol{\Lambda\Lambda}'} \equiv \begin{bmatrix} \underset{(1\times 1)}{\Sigma_{11}} & \underset{(1\times g)}{\boldsymbol{\Sigma}_{21}'} \\ \underset{(g\times 1)}{\boldsymbol{\Sigma}_{21}} & \underset{(g\times g)}{\boldsymbol{\Sigma}_{22}} \end{bmatrix}, \qquad [19.A.14]$$

and define

$$\mathbf{L}' \equiv \begin{bmatrix} (1/\sigma_1^*) & (-1/\sigma_1^*)\cdot\boldsymbol{\Sigma}_{21}'\boldsymbol{\Sigma}_{22}^{-1} \\ \mathbf{0} & \mathbf{L}_{22}' \end{bmatrix}, \qquad [19.A.15]$$

where

$$(\sigma_1^*)^2 \equiv (\Sigma_{11} - \boldsymbol{\Sigma}_{21}'\boldsymbol{\Sigma}_{22}^{-1}\boldsymbol{\Sigma}_{21}) \qquad [19.A.16]$$

and $\mathbf{L}_{22}$ is the Cholesky factor of $\boldsymbol{\Sigma}_{22}^{-1}$:

$$\boldsymbol{\Sigma}_{22}^{-1} = \mathbf{L}_{22}\mathbf{L}_{22}'. \qquad [19.A.17]$$

Recall from expression [18.A.16] that

$$\mathbf{L}'\boldsymbol{\Lambda\Lambda}'\mathbf{L} = \mathbf{I}_n, \qquad [19.A.18]$$

implying that $\boldsymbol{\Lambda\Lambda}' = (\mathbf{L}')^{-1}(\mathbf{L})^{-1}$ and $(\boldsymbol{\Lambda\Lambda}')^{-1} = \mathbf{LL}'$; thus, $\mathbf{L}$ is the Cholesky factor of $(\boldsymbol{\Lambda\Lambda}')^{-1}$ referred to in Proposition 19.4.

Note further that the residuals from *OLS* estimation of [19.2.24] are identical to the residuals from *OLS* estimation of

$$y_{1t}^* = \alpha^* + \boldsymbol{\gamma}^{*\prime}\mathbf{y}_{2t}^* + u_t^* \qquad [19.A.19]$$

for $y_{1t}^* \equiv y_{1t} - \boldsymbol{\Sigma}_{21}'\boldsymbol{\Sigma}_{22}^{-1}\mathbf{y}_{2t}$ and $\mathbf{y}_{2t}^* \equiv \mathbf{L}_{22}'\mathbf{y}_{2t}$. Recall from equation [18.A.21] that

$$\begin{bmatrix} T^{-1/2}\hat{\alpha}_T^*/\sigma_1^* \\ \hat{\boldsymbol{\gamma}}_T^*/\sigma_1^* \end{bmatrix} \xrightarrow{L} \begin{bmatrix} h_1 \\ \mathbf{h}_2 \end{bmatrix}. \qquad [19.A.20]$$

Finally, for the derivations that are to follow,

$$T^* \equiv T - 1.$$

**Proof of (a).** Since the sample residuals $\hat{u}_t^*$ for *OLS* estimation of [19.A.19] are identical to those for *OLS* estimation of [19.2.24], we have that

$$\begin{aligned} T^*(\hat{\rho}_T - 1) &= T^*\left\{\frac{\sum_{t=2}^{T}\hat{u}_{t-1}^*\hat{u}_t^*}{\sum_{t=2}^{T}(\hat{u}_{t-1}^*)^2} - 1\right\} \\ &= \frac{(T^*)^{-1}\sum_{t=2}^{T}\hat{u}_{t-1}^*(\hat{u}_t^* - \hat{u}_{t-1}^*)}{(T^*)^{-2}\sum_{t=2}^{T}(\hat{u}_{t-1}^*)^2}. \end{aligned} \qquad [19.A.21]$$

But

$$\begin{aligned}\hat{u}_t^* &= \sigma_1^* \cdot \{(y_{1t}^*/\sigma_1^*) - (1/\sigma_1^*) \cdot \hat{\boldsymbol{\gamma}}_T^{*\prime} \mathbf{y}_{2t}^* - (\hat{\alpha}_T^*/\sigma_1^*)\} \\ &\equiv \sigma_1^* \cdot \{[1 \quad -\hat{\boldsymbol{\gamma}}_T^{*\prime}/\sigma_1^*] \boldsymbol{\xi}_t^* - (\hat{\alpha}_T^*/\sigma_1^*)\}\end{aligned} \qquad [19.A.22]$$

for

$$\boldsymbol{\xi}_t^* \equiv \begin{bmatrix} y_{1t}^*/\sigma_1^* \\ \mathbf{y}_{2t}^* \end{bmatrix} = \mathbf{L}'\mathbf{y}_t. \qquad [19.A.23]$$

Differencing [19.A.22] results in

$$(\hat{u}_t^* - \hat{u}_{t-1}^*) = \sigma_1^* \cdot [1 \quad -\hat{\boldsymbol{\gamma}}_T^{*\prime}/\sigma_1^*] \Delta \boldsymbol{\xi}_t^*. \qquad [19.A.24]$$

Using [19.A.22] and [19.A.24], the numerator of [19.A.21] can be written

$$\begin{aligned}(T^*)^{-1} \sum_{t=2}^{T} \hat{u}_{t-1}^* (\hat{u}_t^* - \hat{u}_{t-1}^*) \\ &= (\sigma_1^*)^2 \cdot (T^*)^{-1} \sum_{t=2}^{T} \left\{ [1 \quad -\hat{\boldsymbol{\gamma}}_T^{*\prime}/\sigma_1^*] \boldsymbol{\xi}_{t-1}^* - (\hat{\alpha}_T^*/\sigma_1^*) \right\} \left\{ (\Delta \boldsymbol{\xi}_t^{*\prime}) \begin{bmatrix} 1 \\ -\hat{\boldsymbol{\gamma}}_T^*/\sigma_1^* \end{bmatrix} \right\} \\ &= (\sigma_1^*)^2 \cdot [1 \quad -\hat{\boldsymbol{\gamma}}_T^{*\prime}/\sigma_1^*] \cdot \left\{ (T^*)^{-1} \sum_{t=2}^{T} \boldsymbol{\xi}_{t-1}^* (\Delta \boldsymbol{\xi}_t^{*\prime}) \right\} \begin{bmatrix} 1 \\ -\hat{\boldsymbol{\gamma}}_T^*/\sigma_1^* \end{bmatrix} \\ &\quad - (\sigma_1^*)^2 \cdot (T^*)^{-1/2} (\hat{\alpha}_T^*/\sigma_1^*) \cdot \left\{ (T^*)^{-1/2} \sum_{t=2}^{T} (\Delta \boldsymbol{\xi}_t^{*\prime}) \right\} \begin{bmatrix} 1 \\ -\hat{\boldsymbol{\gamma}}_T^*/\sigma_1^* \end{bmatrix}.\end{aligned} \qquad [19.A.25]$$

Notice that the expression

$$[1 \quad -\hat{\boldsymbol{\gamma}}_T^{*\prime}/\sigma_1^*] \cdot \left\{ (T^*)^{-1} \sum_{t=2}^{T} \boldsymbol{\xi}_{t-1}^* (\Delta \boldsymbol{\xi}_t^{*\prime}) \right\} \begin{bmatrix} 1 \\ -\hat{\boldsymbol{\gamma}}_T^*/\sigma_1^* \end{bmatrix}$$

is a scalar and accordingly equals its own transpose:

$$\begin{aligned}[1 \quad -\hat{\boldsymbol{\gamma}}_T^{*\prime}/\sigma_1^*] \cdot \left\{ (T^*)^{-1} \sum_{t=2}^{T} \boldsymbol{\xi}_{t-1}^* (\Delta \boldsymbol{\xi}_t^{*\prime}) \right\} \begin{bmatrix} 1 \\ -\hat{\boldsymbol{\gamma}}_T^*/\sigma_1^* \end{bmatrix} \\ &= (1/2) \left\{ [1 \quad -\hat{\boldsymbol{\gamma}}_T^{*\prime}/\sigma_1^*] \cdot \left\{ (T^*)^{-1} \sum_{t=2}^{T} \boldsymbol{\xi}_{t-1}^* (\Delta \boldsymbol{\xi}_t^{*\prime}) \right\} \begin{bmatrix} 1 \\ -\hat{\boldsymbol{\gamma}}_T^*/\sigma_1^* \end{bmatrix} \right. \\ &\quad \left. + [1 \quad -\hat{\boldsymbol{\gamma}}_T^{*\prime}/\sigma_1^*] \cdot \left\{ (T^*)^{-1} \sum_{t=2}^{T} (\Delta \boldsymbol{\xi}_t^*)(\boldsymbol{\xi}_{t-1}^{*\prime}) \right\} \begin{bmatrix} 1 \\ -\hat{\boldsymbol{\gamma}}_T^*/\sigma_1^* \end{bmatrix} \right\} \\ &= (1/2) \left\{ [1 \quad -\hat{\boldsymbol{\gamma}}_T^{*\prime}/\sigma_1^*] \left\{ (T^*)^{-1} \sum_{t=2}^{T} \left( \boldsymbol{\xi}_{t-1}^* (\Delta \boldsymbol{\xi}_t^{*\prime}) + (\Delta \boldsymbol{\xi}_t^*)(\boldsymbol{\xi}_{t-1}^{*\prime}) \right) \right\} \begin{bmatrix} 1 \\ -\hat{\boldsymbol{\gamma}}_T^*/\sigma_1^* \end{bmatrix} \right\}.\end{aligned} \qquad [19.A.26]$$

But from result (d) of Proposition 18.1,

$$\begin{aligned}(T^*)^{-1} \sum_{t=2}^{T} \left( \boldsymbol{\xi}_{t-1}^* (\Delta \boldsymbol{\xi}_t^{*\prime}) + (\Delta \boldsymbol{\xi}_t^*)(\boldsymbol{\xi}_{t-1}^{*\prime}) \right) \\ &= \mathbf{L}' \cdot \left\{ (T^*)^{-1} \sum_{t=2}^{T} \left( \mathbf{y}_{t-1}(\Delta \mathbf{y}_t') + (\Delta \mathbf{y}_t)(\mathbf{y}_{t-1}') \right) \right\} \cdot \mathbf{L} \qquad [19.A.27] \\ &\xrightarrow{L} \mathbf{L}' \cdot \{\boldsymbol{\Lambda} \cdot [\mathbf{W}(1)] \cdot [\mathbf{W}(1)]' \cdot \boldsymbol{\Lambda}' - E[(\Delta \mathbf{y}_t)(\Delta \mathbf{y}_t')]\} \cdot \mathbf{L} \\ &\equiv [\mathbf{W}^*(1)] \cdot [\mathbf{W}^*(1)]' - E[(\Delta \boldsymbol{\xi}_t^*)(\Delta \boldsymbol{\xi}_t^{*\prime})]\end{aligned}$$

for $\mathbf{W}^*(r) \equiv \mathbf{L}'\boldsymbol{\Lambda}\cdot\mathbf{W}(r)$ the $n$-dimensional standard Brownian motion discussed in equation [18.A.17]. Substituting [19.A.27] and [19.A.20] into [19.A.26] produces

$$[1 \quad -\hat{\boldsymbol{\gamma}}_T^{*\prime}/\sigma_1^*]\cdot\left\{(T^*)^{-1}\sum_{t=2}^{T}\boldsymbol{\xi}_{t-1}^*(\Delta\boldsymbol{\xi}_t^{*\prime})\right\}\begin{bmatrix}1\\ -\hat{\boldsymbol{\gamma}}_T^*/\sigma_1^*\end{bmatrix} \xrightarrow{L} (1/2)[1 \quad -\mathbf{h}_2']\{[\mathbf{W}^*(1)]\cdot[\mathbf{W}^*(1)]' - E[(\Delta\boldsymbol{\xi}_t^*)(\Delta\boldsymbol{\xi}_t^{*\prime})]\}\begin{bmatrix}1\\ -\mathbf{h}_2\end{bmatrix}. \qquad [19.A.28]$$

Similar analysis of the second term in [19.A.25] using result (a) of Proposition 18.1 reveals that

$$(T^*)^{-1/2}(\hat{\alpha}_T^*/\sigma_1^*)\cdot\left\{(T^*)^{-1/2}\sum_{t=2}^{T}(\Delta\boldsymbol{\xi}_t^{*\prime})\right\}\begin{bmatrix}1\\ -\hat{\boldsymbol{\gamma}}_T^*/\sigma_1^*\end{bmatrix} \xrightarrow{L} h_1\cdot[\mathbf{W}^*(1)]'\begin{bmatrix}1\\ -\mathbf{h}_2\end{bmatrix}. \qquad [19.A.29]$$

Substituting [19.A.28] and [19.A.29] into [19.A.25], we conclude that

$$\begin{aligned}(T^*)^{-1}\sum_{t=2}^{T}\hat{u}_{t-1}^*(\hat{u}_t^* - \hat{u}_{t-1}^*)&\\ \xrightarrow{L} (\sigma_1^*)^2\cdot\Bigg\{\frac{1}{2}\bigg\{[1 \quad -\mathbf{h}_2']\cdot[\mathbf{W}^*(1)]\cdot[\mathbf{W}^*(1)]'\cdot\begin{bmatrix}1\\ -\mathbf{h}_2\end{bmatrix}\bigg\} &- h_1\cdot[\mathbf{W}^*(1)]'\cdot\begin{bmatrix}1\\ -\mathbf{h}_2\end{bmatrix}\\ - (1/2)\cdot[1 \quad -\mathbf{h}_2']\cdot\{E[(\Delta\boldsymbol{\xi}_t^*)(\Delta\boldsymbol{\xi}_t^{*\prime})]\}\cdot\begin{bmatrix}1\\ -\mathbf{h}_2\end{bmatrix}\Bigg\}.\end{aligned} \qquad [19.A.30]$$

The limiting distribution for the denominator of [19.A.21] was obtained in result (b) of Proposition 18.2:

$$(T^*)^{-2}\sum_{t=2}^{T}\hat{u}_{t-1}^2 \xrightarrow{L} (\sigma_1^*)^2\cdot H_n. \qquad [19.A.31]$$

Substituting [19.A.30] and [19.A.31] into [19.A.21] produces [19.2.36].

**Proof of (b).** Notice that

$$\begin{aligned}\hat{c}_{j,T} &= (T^*)^{-1}\sum_{t=j+2}^{T}\hat{e}_t\hat{e}_{t-j}\\ &= (T^*)^{-1}\sum_{t=j+2}^{T}(\hat{u}_t^* - \hat{\rho}_T\hat{u}_{t-1}^*)(\hat{u}_{t-j}^* - \hat{\rho}_T\hat{u}_{t-j-1}^*)\\ &= (T^*)^{-1}\sum_{t=j+2}^{T}\{\Delta\hat{u}_t^* - (\hat{\rho}_T - 1)\hat{u}_{t-1}^*\}\cdot\{\Delta\hat{u}_{t-j}^* - (\hat{\rho}_T - 1)\hat{u}_{t-j-1}^*\}.\end{aligned} \qquad [19.A.32]$$

But [19.A.22] and [19.A.24] can be used to write

$$\begin{aligned}(T^*)^{-1}&\sum_{t=j+2}^{T}(\hat{\rho}_T - 1)\hat{u}_{t-1}^*\Delta\hat{u}_{t-j}^*\\ &= (\sigma_1^*)^2\cdot(\hat{\rho}_T - 1)\cdot(T^*)^{-1}\sum_{t=j+2}^{T}\left\{[1 \quad -\hat{\boldsymbol{\gamma}}_T^{*\prime}/\sigma_1^*]\boldsymbol{\xi}_{t-1}^* - (\hat{\alpha}_T^*/\sigma_1^*)\right\}(\Delta\boldsymbol{\xi}_{t-j}^{*\prime})\begin{bmatrix}1\\ -\hat{\boldsymbol{\gamma}}_T^*/\sigma_1^*\end{bmatrix}\\ &= \left\{(\sigma_1^*)^2\cdot[(T^*)^{1/2}(\hat{\rho}_T - 1)]\cdot[1 \quad -\hat{\boldsymbol{\gamma}}_T^{*\prime}/\sigma_1^*]\cdot(T^*)^{-3/2}\sum_{t=j+2}^{T}\boldsymbol{\xi}_{t-1}^*(\Delta\boldsymbol{\xi}_{t-j}^{*\prime})\begin{bmatrix}1\\ -\hat{\boldsymbol{\gamma}}_T^*/\sigma_1^*\end{bmatrix}\right\}\\ &\quad - \left\{(\sigma_1^*)^2\cdot[(T^*)^{1/2}(\hat{\rho}_T - 1)]\cdot[(T^*)^{-1/2}(\hat{\alpha}_T^*/\sigma_1^*)](T^*)^{-1}\sum_{t=j+2}^{T}(\Delta\boldsymbol{\xi}_{t-j}^{*\prime})\begin{bmatrix}1\\ -\hat{\boldsymbol{\gamma}}_T^*/\sigma_1^*\end{bmatrix}\right\}.\end{aligned} \qquad [19.A.33]$$

But result (a) implies that $(T^*)^{1/2}(\hat{\rho}_T - 1) \xrightarrow{p} 0$, while the other terms in [19.A.33] have convergent distributions in the light of [19.A.20] and results (a) and (e) of Proposition 18.1.

Hence,

$$(T^*)^{-1} \sum_{t=j+2}^{T} (\hat{\rho}_T - 1)\hat{u}^*_{t-1}\Delta\hat{u}^*_{t-j} \xrightarrow{p} 0. \qquad [19.A.34]$$

Similarly,

$$\begin{aligned}
&(T^*)^{-1} \sum_{t=j+2}^{T} (\hat{\rho}_T - 1)^2 \hat{u}^*_{t-1}\hat{u}^*_{t-j-1} \\
&= (\sigma_1^*)^2 \cdot (T^*)^{-1} \sum_{t=j+2}^{T} (\hat{\rho}_T - 1)^2 \Big\{[1 \quad -\hat{\boldsymbol{\gamma}}_T^{*\prime}/\sigma_1^*]\boldsymbol{\xi}^*_{t-1} - (\hat{\alpha}_T^*/\sigma_1^*)\Big\} \\
&\quad \times \Big\{[1 \quad -\hat{\boldsymbol{\gamma}}_T^{*\prime}/\sigma_1^*]\boldsymbol{\xi}^*_{t-j-1} - (\hat{\alpha}_T^*/\sigma_1^*)\Big\} \\
&= (\sigma_1^*)^2 \cdot (T^*)^{-1} \sum_{t=j+2}^{T} (\hat{\rho}_T - 1)^2 \begin{bmatrix} 1 & -\hat{\boldsymbol{\gamma}}_T^{*\prime}/\sigma_1^* & -(T^*)^{-1/2}\hat{\alpha}_T^*/\sigma_1^* \end{bmatrix} \begin{bmatrix} \boldsymbol{\xi}^*_{t-1} \\ (T^*)^{1/2} \end{bmatrix} \\
&\quad \times [\boldsymbol{\xi}^{*\prime}_{t-j-1} \quad (T^*)^{1/2}]\,[1 \quad -\hat{\boldsymbol{\gamma}}_T^{*\prime}/\sigma_1^* \quad -(T^*)^{-1/2}\hat{\alpha}_T^*/\sigma_1^*]' \qquad [19.A.35] \\
&= (\sigma_1^*)^2 \cdot [(T^*)^{1/2}(\hat{\rho}_T - 1)]^2 \cdot [1 \quad -\hat{\boldsymbol{\gamma}}_T^{*\prime}/\sigma_1^* \quad -(T^*)^{-1/2}\hat{\alpha}_T^*/\sigma_1^*] \\
&\quad \times \left\{(T^*)^{-2} \sum_{t=j+2}^{T} \begin{bmatrix} \boldsymbol{\xi}^*_{t-1}\boldsymbol{\xi}^{*\prime}_{t-j-1} & (T^*)^{1/2}\boldsymbol{\xi}^*_{t-1} \\ (T^*)^{1/2}\boldsymbol{\xi}^{*\prime}_{t-j-1} & T^* \end{bmatrix}\right\} \\
&\quad \times [1 \quad -\hat{\boldsymbol{\gamma}}_T^{*\prime}/\sigma_1^* \quad -(T^*)^{-1/2}\hat{\alpha}_T^*/\sigma_1^*]' \\
&\xrightarrow{p} 0,
\end{aligned}$$

given that $(T^*)^{-2}\Sigma_{t=j+2}^{T}\boldsymbol{\xi}^*_{t-1}\cdot\boldsymbol{\xi}^{*\prime}_{t-j-1}$ and $(T^*)^{-3/2}\Sigma\boldsymbol{\xi}^*_{t-s}$ are $O_p(1)$ by results (i) and (g) of Proposition 18.1. Substituting [19.A.34], [19.A.35], and then [19.A.24] into [19.A.32] gives

$$\begin{aligned}
\hat{c}_{j,T} &\xrightarrow{p} (T^*)^{-1} \sum_{t=j+2}^{T} (\Delta\hat{u}_t^*)\cdot(\Delta\hat{u}^*_{t-j}) \\
&= (\sigma_1^*)^2 \cdot [1 \quad -\hat{\boldsymbol{\gamma}}_T^{*\prime}/\sigma_1^*](T^*)^{-1} \sum_{t=j+2}^{T} (\Delta\boldsymbol{\xi}_t^*)\cdot(\Delta\boldsymbol{\xi}^{*\prime}_{t-j}) \begin{bmatrix} 1 \\ -\hat{\boldsymbol{\gamma}}_T^*/\sigma_1^* \end{bmatrix} \\
&\xrightarrow{L} (\sigma_1^*)^2 \cdot [1 \quad -\mathbf{h}_2'] \cdot E\{(\Delta\boldsymbol{\xi}_t^*)\cdot(\Delta\boldsymbol{\xi}^{*\prime}_{t-j})\} \begin{bmatrix} 1 \\ -\mathbf{h}_2 \end{bmatrix} \qquad [19.A.36] \\
&= (\sigma_1^*)^2 \cdot [1 \quad -\mathbf{h}_2'] \cdot \mathbf{L}' \cdot E\{(\Delta\mathbf{y}_t)\cdot(\Delta\mathbf{y}'_{t-j})\} \cdot \mathbf{L} \begin{bmatrix} 1 \\ -\mathbf{h}_2 \end{bmatrix}.
\end{aligned}$$

It follows that for given $q$,

$$\begin{aligned}
\hat{\lambda}_T^2 &= \hat{c}_{0,T} + 2\cdot \sum_{j=1}^{q} [1 - j/(q+1)]\hat{c}_{j,T} \\
&\xrightarrow{L} (\sigma_1^*)^2 \cdot [1 \quad -\mathbf{h}_2'] \cdot \mathbf{L}' \left\{ \sum_{j=-q}^{q} [1 - |j|/(q+1)] \cdot E[(\Delta\mathbf{y}_t)\cdot(\Delta\mathbf{y}'_{t-j})] \right\} \cdot \mathbf{L} \cdot \begin{bmatrix} 1 \\ -\mathbf{h}_2 \end{bmatrix}.
\end{aligned}$$

Thus, if $q \to \infty$ with $q/T \to 0$,

$$\begin{aligned}
\hat{\lambda}_T^2 &\xrightarrow{L} (\sigma_1^*)^2 \cdot [1 \quad -\mathbf{h}_2'] \cdot \mathbf{L}' \cdot \left\{ \sum_{j=-\infty}^{\infty} E[(\Delta\mathbf{y}_t)\cdot(\Delta\mathbf{y}'_{t-j})] \right\} \cdot \mathbf{L} \cdot \begin{bmatrix} 1 \\ -\mathbf{h}_2 \end{bmatrix} \\
&= (\sigma_1^*)^2 \cdot [1 \quad -\mathbf{h}_2'] \cdot \mathbf{L}' \boldsymbol{\Psi}(1)\mathbf{P}\mathbf{P}'[\boldsymbol{\Psi}(1)]'\mathbf{L} \cdot \begin{bmatrix} 1 \\ -\mathbf{h}_2 \end{bmatrix} \qquad [19.A.37] \\
&= (\sigma_1^*)^2 \cdot [1 \quad -\mathbf{h}_2'] \cdot \mathbf{I}_n \cdot \begin{bmatrix} 1 \\ -\mathbf{h}_2 \end{bmatrix},
\end{aligned}$$

by virtue of [19.A.18].

But from [19.2.29] and [19.A.31],

$$(T^*)^2 \cdot \hat{\sigma}^2_{\hat{\rho}_T} \div s_T^2 = \frac{1}{(T^*)^{-2} \sum_{t=2}^{T} \hat{u}_{t-1}^2} \xrightarrow{L} \frac{1}{(\sigma_1^*)^2 \cdot H_n}. \qquad [19.A.38]$$

It then follows from [19.A.36] and [19.A.37] that

$$\{(T^*)^2 \cdot \hat{\sigma}^2_{\hat{\rho}_T} \div s_T^2\} \cdot \{\hat{\lambda}_T^2 - \hat{c}_{0,T}\} \xrightarrow{L} [1 \quad -\mathbf{h}_2'] \cdot \{\mathbf{I}_n - (\mathbf{L}' \cdot E[(\Delta \mathbf{y}_t) \cdot (\Delta \mathbf{y}_t')] \cdot \mathbf{L})\} \cdot \begin{bmatrix} 1 \\ -\mathbf{h}_2 \end{bmatrix} \div H_n. \qquad [19.A.39]$$

Subtracting $\frac{1}{2}$ times [19.A.39] from [19.2.36] yields [19.2.37].

**Proof of (c).** Notice from [19.2.33] that

$$\begin{aligned} Z_{t,T} &= (1/\hat{\lambda}_T) \cdot \left\{ (\hat{c}_{0,T}/s_T^2)^{1/2} \frac{\hat{\rho}_T - 1}{\hat{\sigma}_{\hat{\rho}_T} \div s_T} - (1/2) \cdot \{T^* \cdot \hat{\sigma}_{\hat{\rho}_T} \div s_T\} \cdot \{\hat{\lambda}_T^2 - \hat{c}_{0,T}\} \right\} \\ &= (1/\hat{\lambda}_T) \frac{1}{T^* \cdot \hat{\sigma}_{\hat{\rho}_T} \div s_T} \left\{ (\hat{c}_{0,T}/s_T^2)^{1/2} T^* (\hat{\rho}_T - 1) - (1/2) \cdot \{(T^*)^2 \cdot \hat{\sigma}^2_{\hat{\rho}_T} \div s_T^2\} \cdot \{\hat{\lambda}_T^2 - \hat{c}_{0,T}\} \right\}. \end{aligned} \qquad [19.A.40]$$

But since

$$(\hat{c}_{0,T}/s_T^2) = (T - 2)/(T - 1) \to 1,$$

it follows that

$$\begin{aligned} Z_{t,T} &\xrightarrow{p} (1/\hat{\lambda}_T) \frac{1}{T^* \cdot \hat{\sigma}_{\hat{\rho}_T} \div s_T} Z_{\rho,T} \\ &\xrightarrow{L} \frac{1}{\sigma_1^* \cdot (1 + \mathbf{h}_2'\mathbf{h}_2)^{1/2}} (\sigma_1^* \cdot \sqrt{H_n}) Z_n, \end{aligned} \qquad [19.A.41]$$

with the last line following from [19.A.37], [19.A.38], and [19.2.37].

**Proof of (d).** See Phillips and Ouliaris (1990). ■

## *Chapter 19 Exercises*

19.1. Let

$$\begin{bmatrix} \Delta y_{1t} \\ \Delta y_{2t} \end{bmatrix} = \begin{bmatrix} \delta_1 \\ \delta_2 \end{bmatrix} + \begin{bmatrix} u_{1t} \\ u_{2t} \end{bmatrix},$$

where $\delta_2 \neq 0$ and $\delta_1$ may or may not be zero. Let $\mathbf{u}_t \equiv (u_{1t}, u_{2t})'$, and suppose that $\mathbf{u}_t = \boldsymbol{\Psi}(L)\boldsymbol{\varepsilon}_t$ for $\boldsymbol{\varepsilon}_t$ an i.i.d. $(2 \times 1)$ vector with mean zero, variance $\mathbf{PP}'$, and finite fourth moments. Assume further that $\{s \cdot \boldsymbol{\Psi}_s\}_{s=0}^{\infty}$ is absolutely summable and that $\boldsymbol{\Psi}(1) \cdot \mathbf{P}$ is nonsingular. Define $\xi_{1t} \equiv \Sigma_{s=1}^{t} u_{1s}$, $\xi_{2t} \equiv \Sigma_{s=1}^{t} u_{2s}$, and $\gamma_0 \equiv \delta_1/\delta_2$.

(a) Show that the *OLS* estimates of

$$y_{1t} = \alpha + \gamma y_{2t} + u_t$$

satisfy

$$\begin{bmatrix} T^{-1/2}\hat{\alpha}_T \\ T^{1/2}(\hat{\gamma}_T - \gamma_0) \end{bmatrix} \xrightarrow{p} \begin{bmatrix} 1 & \delta_2/2 \\ \delta_2/2 & \delta_2^2/3 \end{bmatrix}^{-1} \begin{bmatrix} T^{-3/2}\Sigma(\xi_{1t} - \gamma_0\xi_{2t}) \\ T^{-5/2}\Sigma\delta_2 t(\xi_{1t} - \gamma_0\xi_{2t}) \end{bmatrix}.$$

Conclude that $\hat{\alpha}_T$ and $\hat{\gamma}_T$ have the same asymptotic distribution as the coefficients from a regression of $(\xi_{1t} - \gamma_0\xi_{2t})$ on a constant and $\delta_2$ times a time trend.:

$$(\xi_{1t} - \gamma_0\xi_{2t}) = \alpha + \gamma\cdot\delta_2 t + u_t.$$

(b) Show that first differences of the OLS residuals converge to

$$\Delta\hat{u}_t \xrightarrow{p} u_{1t} - \gamma_0 u_{2t}.$$

19.2. Verify [19.3.23].

19.3. Verify [19.3.25].

19.4. Consider the regression model

$$y_{1t} = \boldsymbol{\beta}'\mathbf{w}_t + \alpha + \boldsymbol{\gamma}'\mathbf{y}_{2t} + \delta t + u_t,$$

where

$$\mathbf{w}_t = (\Delta\mathbf{y}'_{2,t-p}, \Delta\mathbf{y}'_{2,t-p+1}, \ldots, \Delta\mathbf{y}'_{2,t-1}, \Delta\mathbf{y}'_{2t}, \Delta\mathbf{y}'_{2,t+1}, \ldots, \Delta\mathbf{y}'_{2,t+p})'.$$

Let $\Delta\mathbf{y}_{2t} = \mathbf{u}_{2t}$, where

$$\begin{bmatrix} u_t \\ \mathbf{u}_{2t} \end{bmatrix} = \tilde{\boldsymbol{\Psi}}(L)\boldsymbol{\varepsilon}_t = \begin{bmatrix} \tilde{\psi}_{11}(L) & \mathbf{0}' \\ \mathbf{0} & \tilde{\boldsymbol{\Psi}}_{22}(L) \end{bmatrix} \begin{bmatrix} \varepsilon_{1t} \\ \boldsymbol{\varepsilon}_{2t} \end{bmatrix}$$

and where $\boldsymbol{\varepsilon}_t$ is i.i.d. with mean zero, finite fourth moments, and variance

$$E(\boldsymbol{\varepsilon}_t\boldsymbol{\varepsilon}_t') = \begin{bmatrix} \sigma_1 & \mathbf{0}' \\ \mathbf{0} & \mathbf{P}_{22} \end{bmatrix} \begin{bmatrix} \sigma_1 & \mathbf{0}' \\ \mathbf{0} & \mathbf{P}'_{22} \end{bmatrix}.$$

Suppose that $\{s\cdot\tilde{\boldsymbol{\Psi}}_s\}_{s=0}^{\infty}$ is absolutely summable, $\tilde{\lambda}_{11} \equiv \sigma_1\cdot\tilde{\psi}_{11}(1) \neq 0$, and $\tilde{\boldsymbol{\Lambda}}_{22} \equiv \tilde{\boldsymbol{\Psi}}_{22}(1)\cdot\mathbf{P}_{22}$ is nonsingular. Show that the *OLS* estimates satisfy

$$\begin{bmatrix} T^{1/2}(\hat{\boldsymbol{\beta}}_T - \boldsymbol{\beta}) \\ T^{1/2}(\hat{\alpha}_T - \alpha) \\ T(\hat{\boldsymbol{\gamma}}_T - \boldsymbol{\gamma}) \\ T^{3/2}(\hat{\delta}_T - \delta) \end{bmatrix} \xrightarrow{L} \begin{bmatrix} \mathbf{Q}^{-1}\mathbf{h}_1 \\ \tilde{\lambda}_{11}\cdot\nu_1 \\ \tilde{\lambda}_{11}\cdot\boldsymbol{\nu}_2 \\ \tilde{\lambda}_{11}\cdot\nu_3 \end{bmatrix},$$

where $\mathbf{Q} = \text{plim } T^{-1}\Sigma\mathbf{w}_t\mathbf{w}_t'$, $T^{-1/2}\Sigma\mathbf{w}_t u_t \xrightarrow{L} \mathbf{h}_1$, and

$$\begin{bmatrix} \nu_1 \\ \boldsymbol{\nu}_2 \\ \nu_3 \end{bmatrix} \equiv \mathbf{H}^{-1} \begin{bmatrix} W_1(1) \\ \tilde{\boldsymbol{\Lambda}}_{22}\cdot\left\{\int [\mathbf{W}_2(r)]\, dW_1(r)\right\} \\ \left\{W_1(1) - \int W_1(r)\, dr\right\} \end{bmatrix}$$

$$\mathbf{H} \equiv \begin{bmatrix} 1 & \left\{\int [\mathbf{W}_2(r)]'\, dr\right\}\tilde{\boldsymbol{\Lambda}}'_{22} & 1/2 \\ \tilde{\boldsymbol{\Lambda}}_{22}\int \mathbf{W}_2(r)\, dr & \tilde{\boldsymbol{\Lambda}}_{22}\left\{\int [\mathbf{W}_2(r)]\cdot[\mathbf{W}_2(r)]'\, dr\right\}\tilde{\boldsymbol{\Lambda}}'_{22} & \tilde{\boldsymbol{\Lambda}}_{22}\int r\mathbf{W}_2(r)\, dr \\ 1/2 & \left\{\int r[\mathbf{W}_2(r)]'\, dr\right\}\tilde{\boldsymbol{\Lambda}}'_{22} & 1/3 \end{bmatrix}.$$

Reason as in [19.3.12] that conditional on $\mathbf{W}_2(\cdot)$, the vector $(\nu_1, \boldsymbol{\nu}_2', \nu_3)'$ is Gaussian with mean zero and variance $\mathbf{H}^{-1}$. Use this to show that the Wald form of the *OLS* $\chi^2$ test of any $m$ restrictions involving $\alpha$, $\boldsymbol{\gamma}$, or $\delta$ converges to $(\tilde{\lambda}_{11}^2/s_T^2)$ times a $\chi^2(m)$ variable.

19.5. Consider the regression model

$$y_{1t} = \boldsymbol{\beta}'\mathbf{w}_t + \alpha + \boldsymbol{\gamma}'\mathbf{y}_{2t} + u_t,$$

where

$$\mathbf{w}_t = (\Delta\mathbf{y}'_{2,t-p}, \Delta\mathbf{y}'_{2,t-p+1}, \ldots, \Delta\mathbf{y}'_{2,t-1}, \Delta\mathbf{y}'_{2t}, \Delta\mathbf{y}'_{2,t+1}, \ldots, \Delta\mathbf{y}'_{2,t+p})'.$$

Suppose that

$$\Delta\mathbf{y}_{2t} = \boldsymbol{\delta}_2 + \mathbf{u}_{2t},$$

where at least one of the elements of $\boldsymbol{\delta}_2$ is nonzero. Let $u_t$ and $\mathbf{u}_{2t}$ satisfy the same conditions as in Exercise 19.4.

Let $\mathbf{y}_{2t} = (y_{2t}, y_{3t}, \ldots, y_{nt})'$ and $\boldsymbol{\delta}_2 = (\delta_2, \delta_3, \ldots, \delta_n)'$, and suppose that the elements of $\mathbf{y}_{2t}$ are ordered so that $E(\Delta y_{nt}) = \delta_n \neq 0$. Notice that the fitted values for the regression are identical to those of

$$y_{1t} = \boldsymbol{\beta}'\mathbf{w}^*_t + \alpha^* + \boldsymbol{\gamma}^{*\prime}\mathbf{y}^*_{2t} + \delta^* y_{nt} + u_t,$$

where

$$\mathbf{w}^*_t = [(\Delta\mathbf{y}_{2,t-p} - \boldsymbol{\delta}_2)', (\Delta\mathbf{y}_{2,t-p+1} - \boldsymbol{\delta}_2)', \ldots, (\Delta\mathbf{y}_{2,t+p} = \boldsymbol{\delta}_2)']'$$

$$\underset{[(g-1)\times 1]}{\mathbf{y}^*_{2t}} \equiv \begin{bmatrix} y_{2t} - (\delta_2/\delta_n)y_{nt} \\ y_{3t} - (\delta_3/\delta_n)y_{nt} \\ \vdots \\ y_{n-1,t} - (\delta_{n-1}/\delta_n)y_{nt} \end{bmatrix}$$

$$\boldsymbol{\gamma}^* \equiv \begin{bmatrix} \gamma_2 \\ \gamma_3 \\ \vdots \\ \gamma_{n-1} \end{bmatrix}$$

$$\delta^* = \gamma_n + \gamma_2(\delta_2/\delta_n) + \gamma_3(\delta_3/\delta_n) + \cdots + \gamma_{n-1}(\delta_{n-1}/\delta_n)$$

$$\alpha^* = \alpha + \boldsymbol{\beta}'(\mathbf{1} \otimes \boldsymbol{\delta}_2),$$

with $\mathbf{1}$ a $[(2p + 1) \times 1]$ column of 1s.

Show that the asymptotic properties of the transformed regression are identical to those of the time trend regression in Exercise 19.4. Conclude that any $F$ test involving $\boldsymbol{\gamma}$ in the original regression can be multiplied by $(s_T^2/\hat{\lambda}_{11}^2)$ and compared with the usual $F$ tables for an asymptotically valid test.

## *Chapter 19 References*


Ahn, S. K., and G. C. Reinsel. 1990. "Estimation for Partially Nonstationary Multivariate Autoregressive Models." *Journal of the American Statistical Association* 85:813–23.

Anderson, T. W. 1958. *An Introduction to Multivariate Statistical Analysis*. New York: Wiley.

Andrews, Donald W. K., and J. Christopher Monahan. 1992. "An Improved Heteroskedasticity and Autocorrelation Consistent Covariance Matrix Estimator." *Econometrica* 60:953–66.

Baillie, Richard T., and David D. Selover. 1987. "Cointegration and Models of Exchange Rate Determination." *International Journal of Forecasting* 3:43–51.

Campbell, John Y., and Robert J. Shiller. 1988a. "Interpreting Cointegrated Models." *Journal of Economic Dynamics and Control* 12:505–22.

——— and ———. 1988b. "The Dividend-Price Ratio and Expectations of Future Dividends and Discount Factors." *Review of Financial Studies* 1:195–228.

Clarida, Richard. 1991. "Co-Integration, Aggregate Consumption, and the Demand for Imports: A Structural Econometric Investigation." Columbia University. Mimeo.

Corbae, Dean, and Sam Ouliaris. 1988. "Cointegration and Tests of Purchasing Power Parity." *Review of Economics and Statistics* 70:508–11.

Davidson, James E. H., David F. Hendry, Frank Srba, and Stephen Yeo. 1978. "Econometric Modelling of the Aggregate Time-Series Relationship between Consumers' Expenditure and Income in the United Kingdom." *Economic Journal* 88:661–92.

Engle, Robert F., and C. W. J. Granger. 1987. "Co-Integration and Error Correction: Representation, Estimation, and Testing." *Econometrica* 55:251–76.

——— and Byung Sam Yoo. 1987. "Forecasting and Testing in Co-Integrated Systems." *Journal of Econometrics* 35:143–59.

Granger, C. W. J. 1983. "Co-Integrated Variables and Error-Correcting Models." Unpublished University of California, San Diego, Discussion Paper 83-13.

——— and Paul Newbold. 1974. "Spurious Regressions in Econometrics." *Journal of Econometrics* 2:111–20.

Hansen, Bruce E. 1990. "A Powerful, Simple Test for Cointegration Using Cochrane-Orcutt." University of Rochester. Mimeo.

———. 1992. "Efficient Estimation and Testing of Cointegrating Vectors in the Presence of Deterministic Trends." *Journal of Econometrics* 53:87–121.

Haug, Alfred A. 1992. "Critical Values for the $\hat{Z}_\alpha$-Phillips-Ouliaris Test for Cointegration." *Oxford Bulletin of Economics and Statistics* 54:473–80.

Johansen, Søren. 1988. "Statistical Analysis of Cointegration Vectors." *Journal of Economic Dynamics and Control* 12:231–54.

———. 1991. "Estimation and Hypothesis Testing of Cointegration Vectors in Gaussian Vector Autoregressive Models." *Econometrica* 59:1551–80.

King, Robert G., Charles I. Plosser, James H. Stock, and Mark W. Watson. 1991. "Stochastic Trends and Economic Fluctuations." *American Economic Review* 81:819–40.

Kremers, Jeroen J. M. 1989. "U.S. Federal Indebtedness and the Conduct of Fiscal Policy." *Journal of Monetary Economics* 23:219–38.

Mosconi, Rocco, and Carlo Giannini. 1992. "Non-Causality in Cointegrated Systems: Representation, Estimation and Testing." *Oxford Bulletin of Economics and Statistics* 54:399–417.

Ogaki, Masao. 1992. "Engel's Law and Cointegration." *Journal of Political Economy* 100:1027–46.

——— and Joon Y. Park. 1992. "A Cointegration Approach to Estimating Preference Parameters." Department of Economics, University of Rochester. Mimeo.

Park, Joon Y. 1992. "Canonical Cointegrating Regressions." *Econometrica* 60:119–43.

——— and Masao Ogaki. 1991. "Inference in Cointegrated Models Using VAR Prewhitening to Estimate Shortrun Dynamics." University of Rochester. Mimeo.

———, S. Ouliaris, and B. Choi. 1988. "Spurious Regressions and Tests for Cointegration." Cornell University. Mimeo.

Phillips, Peter C. B. 1987. "Time Series Regression with a Unit Root." *Econometrica* 55:277–301.

———. 1991. "Optimal Inference in Cointegrated Systems." *Econometrica* 59:283–306.

——— and S. N. Durlauf. 1986. "Multiple Time Series Regression with Integrated Processes." *Review of Economic Studies* 53:473–95.

——— and Bruce E. Hansen. 1990. "Statistical Inference in Instrumental Variables Regression with I(1) Processes." *Review of Economic Studies* 57:99–125.

——— and Mico Loretan. 1991. "Estimating Long-Run Economic Equilibria." *Review of Economic Studies* 58:407–36.

——— and S. Ouliaris. 1990. "Asymptotic Properties of Residual Based Tests for Cointegration." *Econometrica* 58:165–93.

Saikkonen, Pentti. 1991. "Asymptotically Efficient Estimation of Cointegration Regressions." *Econometric Theory* 7:1–21.

Sims, Christopher A., James H. Stock, and Mark W. Watson. 1990. "Inference in Linear Time Series Models with Some Unit Roots." *Econometrica* 58:113–44.

Stock, James H. 1987. "Asymptotic Properties of Least Squares Estimators of Cointegrating Vectors." *Econometrica* 55:1035–56.

———. 1990. "A Class of Tests for Integration and Cointegration." Harvard University. Mimeo.

Stock, James H., and Mark W. Watson. 1988. "Testing for Common Trends." *Journal of the American Statistical Association* 83:1097–1107.

——— and ———. 1993. "A Simple Estimator of Cointegrating Vectors in Higher Order Integrated Systems." *Econometrica* 61:783–820.

Wooldridge, Jeffrey M. 1991. "Notes on Regression with Difference-Stationary Data." Michigan State University. Mimeo.

# 20 Full-Information Maximum Likelihood Analysis of Cointegrated Systems

An $(n \times 1)$ vector $\mathbf{y}_t$ was said to exhibit $h$ cointegrating relations if there exist $h$ linearly independent vectors $\mathbf{a}_1, \mathbf{a}_2, \ldots, \mathbf{a}_h$ such that $\mathbf{a}_i'\mathbf{y}_t$ is stationary. If such vectors exist, their values are not uniquely defined, since any linear combinations of $\mathbf{a}_1, \mathbf{a}_2, \ldots, \mathbf{a}_h$ would also be described as cointegrating vectors. The approaches described in the previous chapter sidestepped this problem by imposing normalization conditions such as $a_{11} = 1$. For this normalization we would put $y_{1t}$ on the left side of a regression and the other elements of $\mathbf{y}_t$ on the right side. We might equally well have normalized $a_{12} = 1$ instead, in which case $y_{2t}$ would be the variable that belongs on the left side of the regression. The results obtained in practice can thus depend on an essentially arbitrary assumption. Furthermore, if the first variable does not appear in the cointegrating relation at all ($a_{11} = 0$), then setting $a_{11} = 1$ is not a harmless normalization but instead results in a fundamentally misspecified model.

For these reasons there is some value in using full-information maximum likelihood (*FIML*) to estimate the linear space spanned by the cointegrating vectors $\mathbf{a}_1, \mathbf{a}_2, \ldots, \mathbf{a}_h$. This chapter describes the solution to this problem developed by Johansen (1988, 1991), whose work is closely related to that of Ahn and Reinsel (1990), and more distantly to that of Stock and Watson (1988). Another advantage of *FIML* is that it allows us to test for the number of cointegrating relations. The approach of Phillips and Ouliaris (1990) described in Chapter 19 tested the null hypothesis that there are no cointegrating relations. This chapter presents more general tests of the null hypothesis that there are $h_0$ cointegrating relations, where $h_0$ could be $0, 1, \ldots,$ or $n - 1$.

To develop these ideas, Section 20.1 begins with a discussion of canonical correlation analysis. Section 20.2 then develops the *FIML* estimates, while Section 20.3 describes hypothesis testing in cointegrated systems. Section 20.4 offers a brief overview of unit roots in time series analysis.

## 20.1. *Canonical Correlation*

### *Population Canonical Correlations*

Let the $(n_1 \times 1)$ vector $\mathbf{y}_t$ and the $(n_2 \times 1)$ vector $\mathbf{x}_t$ denote stationary random variables. Typically, $\mathbf{y}_t$ and $\mathbf{x}_t$ are measured as deviations from their population means, so that $E(\mathbf{y}_t\mathbf{y}_t')$ represents the variance-covariance matrix of $\mathbf{y}_t$. In general, there might be complicated correlations among the elements of $\mathbf{y}_t$ and $\mathbf{x}_t$, summarized by the joint variance-covariance matrix

$$\begin{bmatrix} \underset{(n_1\times n_1)}{E(\mathbf{y}_t\mathbf{y}_t')} & \underset{(n_1\times n_2)}{E(\mathbf{y}_t\mathbf{x}_t')} \\ \underset{(n_2\times n_1)}{E(\mathbf{x}_t\mathbf{y}_t')} & \underset{(n_2\times n_2)}{E(\mathbf{x}_t\mathbf{x}_t')} \end{bmatrix} = \begin{bmatrix} \underset{(n_1\times n_1)}{\boldsymbol{\Sigma}_{\mathbf{YY}}} & \underset{(n_1\times n_2)}{\boldsymbol{\Sigma}_{\mathbf{YX}}} \\ \underset{(n_2\times n_1)}{\boldsymbol{\Sigma}_{\mathbf{XY}}} & \underset{(n_2\times n_2)}{\boldsymbol{\Sigma}_{\mathbf{XX}}} \end{bmatrix}.$$

We can often gain some insight into the nature of these correlations by defining two new $(n \times 1)$ random vectors, $\boldsymbol{\eta}_t$ and $\boldsymbol{\xi}_t$, where $n$ is the smaller of $n_1$ and $n_2$. These vectors are linear combinations of $\mathbf{y}_t$ and $\mathbf{x}_t$, respectively:

$$\boldsymbol{\eta}_t \equiv \mathcal{K}'\mathbf{y}_t \qquad [20.1.1]$$

$$\boldsymbol{\xi}_t \equiv \mathcal{A}'\mathbf{x}_t. \qquad [20.1.2]$$

Here $\mathcal{K}'$and $\mathcal{A}'$ are $(n \times n_1)$ and $(n \times n_2)$ matrices, respectively. The matrices $\mathcal{K}'$ and $\mathcal{A}'$ are chosen so that the following conditions hold.

(1) The individual elements of $\boldsymbol{\eta}_t$ have unit variance and are uncorrelated with one another:

$$E(\boldsymbol{\eta}_t\boldsymbol{\eta}_t') = \mathcal{K}'\boldsymbol{\Sigma}_{\mathbf{YY}}\mathcal{K} = \mathbf{I}_n. \qquad [20.1.3]$$

(2) The individual elements of $\boldsymbol{\xi}_t$ have unit variance and are uncorrelated with one another:

$$E(\boldsymbol{\xi}_t\boldsymbol{\xi}_t') = \mathcal{A}'\boldsymbol{\Sigma}_{\mathbf{XX}}\mathcal{A} = \mathbf{I}_n. \qquad [20.1.4]$$

(3) The $i$th element of $\boldsymbol{\eta}_t$ is uncorrelated with the $j$th element of $\boldsymbol{\xi}_t$ for $i \neq j$; for $i = j$, the correlation is positive and is given by $r_i$:

$$E(\boldsymbol{\xi}_t\boldsymbol{\eta}_t') = \mathcal{A}'\boldsymbol{\Sigma}_{\mathbf{XY}}\mathcal{K} = \mathbf{R}, \qquad [20.1.5]$$

where

$$\mathbf{R} = \begin{bmatrix} r_1 & 0 & \cdots & 0 \\ 0 & r_2 & \cdots & 0 \\ \vdots & \vdots & \cdots & \vdots \\ 0 & 0 & \cdots & r_n \end{bmatrix}. \qquad [20.1.6]$$

(4) The elements of $\boldsymbol{\eta}_t$ and $\boldsymbol{\xi}_t$ are ordered in such a way that

$$(1 \geq r_1 \geq r_2 \geq \cdots \geq r_n \geq 0). \qquad [20.1.7]$$

The correlation $r_i$ is known as the $i$th *population canonical correlation* between $\mathbf{y}_t$ and $\mathbf{x}_t$.

The population canonical correlations and the values of $\mathcal{K}$ and $\mathcal{A}$ can be calculated from $\boldsymbol{\Sigma}_{\mathbf{YY}}$, $\boldsymbol{\Sigma}_{\mathbf{XX}}$, and $\boldsymbol{\Sigma}_{\mathbf{XY}}$ using any computer program that generates eigenvalues and eigenvectors, as we now describe.

Let $(\lambda_1, \lambda_2, \ldots, \lambda_{n_1})$ denote the eigenvalues of the $(n_1 \times n_1)$ matrix

$$\boldsymbol{\Sigma}_{\mathbf{YY}}^{-1}\boldsymbol{\Sigma}_{\mathbf{YX}}\boldsymbol{\Sigma}_{\mathbf{XX}}^{-1}\boldsymbol{\Sigma}_{\mathbf{XY}}, \qquad [20.1.8]$$

ordered as

$$(\lambda_1 \geq \lambda_2 \geq \cdots \geq \lambda_{n_1}), \qquad [20.1.9]$$

with associated eigenvectors $(\tilde{\mathbf{k}}_1, \tilde{\mathbf{k}}_2, \ldots, \tilde{\mathbf{k}}_{n_1})$. Recall that the eigenvalue-eigenvector pair $(\lambda_i, \tilde{\mathbf{k}}_i)$ satisfies

$$\boldsymbol{\Sigma}_{\mathbf{YY}}^{-1}\boldsymbol{\Sigma}_{\mathbf{YX}}\boldsymbol{\Sigma}_{\mathbf{XX}}^{-1}\boldsymbol{\Sigma}_{\mathbf{XY}}\tilde{\mathbf{k}}_i = \lambda_i\tilde{\mathbf{k}}_i. \qquad [20.1.10]$$

Notice that if $\tilde{\mathbf{k}}_i$ satisfies [20.1.10], then so does $c\tilde{\mathbf{k}}_i$ for any value of $c$. The usual normalization convention for choosing $c$ and thus for determining "the" eigenvector $\tilde{\mathbf{k}}_i$ to associate with $\lambda_i$ is to set $\tilde{\mathbf{k}}_i'\tilde{\mathbf{k}}_i = 1$. For canonical correlation analysis, however, it is more convenient to choose $c$ so as to ensure that

$$\mathbf{k}_i'\mathbf{\Sigma}_{\mathbf{YY}}\mathbf{k}_i = 1 \qquad \text{for } i = 1, 2, \ldots, n_1. \tag{20.1.11}$$

If a computer program has calculated eigenvectors $(\tilde{\mathbf{k}}_1, \tilde{\mathbf{k}}_2, \ldots, \tilde{\mathbf{k}}_{n_1})$ of the matrix in [20.1.8] normalized by $(\tilde{\mathbf{k}}_i'\tilde{\mathbf{k}}_i) = 1$, it is trivial to change these to eigenvectors $(\mathbf{k}_1, \mathbf{k}_2, \ldots, \mathbf{k}_{n_1})$ normalized by the condition [20.1.11] by setting

$$\mathbf{k}_i = \tilde{\mathbf{k}}_i \div \sqrt{\tilde{\mathbf{k}}_i'\mathbf{\Sigma}_{\mathbf{YY}}\tilde{\mathbf{k}}_i}.$$

We further may multiply $\mathbf{k}_i$ by $-1$ so as to satisfy a certain sign convention to be detailed in the paragraphs following the next proposition.

The canonical correlations $(r_1, r_2, \ldots, r_n)$ turn out to be given by the square roots of the corresponding first $n$ eigenvalues $(\lambda_1, \lambda_2, \ldots, \lambda_n)$ of [20.1.8]. The associated $(n_1 \times 1)$ eigenvectors $\mathbf{k}_1, \mathbf{k}_2, \ldots, \mathbf{k}_n$, when normalized by [20.1.11] and a sign convention, turn out to make up the rows of the $(n \times n_1)$ matrix $\mathcal{K}'$ appearing in [20.1.1]. The matrix $\mathcal{A}'$ in [20.1.2] can be obtained from the normalized eigenvectors of a matrix closely related to [20.1.8]. These results are developed in the following proposition, proved in Appendix 20.A at the end of this chapter.

***Proposition 20.1:*** *Let*

$$\underset{(n_1+n_2)\times(n_1+n_2)}{\mathbf{\Sigma}} \equiv \begin{bmatrix} \underset{(n_1\times n_1)}{\mathbf{\Sigma}_{\mathbf{YY}}} & \underset{(n_1\times n_2)}{\mathbf{\Sigma}_{\mathbf{YX}}} \\ \underset{(n_2\times n_1)}{\mathbf{\Sigma}_{\mathbf{XY}}} & \underset{(n_2\times n_2)}{\mathbf{\Sigma}_{\mathbf{XX}}} \end{bmatrix}$$

*be a positive definite symmetric matrix and let $(\lambda_1, \lambda_2, \ldots, \lambda_{n_1})$ be the eigenvalues of the matrix in [20.1.8], ordered $\lambda_1 \geq \lambda_2 \geq \cdots \geq \lambda_{n_1}$. Let $(\mathbf{k}_1, \mathbf{k}_2, \ldots, \mathbf{k}_{n_1})$ be the associated $(n_1 \times 1)$ eigenvectors as normalized by [20.1.11]. Let $(\mu_1, \mu_2, \ldots, \mu_{n_2})$ be the eigenvalues of the $(n_2 \times n_2)$ matrix*

$$\mathbf{\Sigma}_{\mathbf{XX}}^{-1}\mathbf{\Sigma}_{\mathbf{XY}}\mathbf{\Sigma}_{\mathbf{YY}}^{-1}\mathbf{\Sigma}_{\mathbf{YX}}, \tag{20.1.12}$$

*ordered $\mu_1 \geq \mu_2 \geq \cdots \geq \mu_{n_2}$. Let $(\mathbf{a}_1, \mathbf{a}_2, \ldots, \mathbf{a}_{n_2})$ be the eigenvectors of [20.1.12]:*

$$\mathbf{\Sigma}_{\mathbf{XX}}^{-1}\mathbf{\Sigma}_{\mathbf{XY}}\mathbf{\Sigma}_{\mathbf{YY}}^{-1}\mathbf{\Sigma}_{\mathbf{YX}}\mathbf{a}_i = \mu_i\mathbf{a}_i, \tag{20.1.13}$$

*normalized by*

$$\mathbf{a}_i'\mathbf{\Sigma}_{\mathbf{XX}}\mathbf{a}_i = 1 \qquad \text{for } i = 1, 2, \ldots, n_2. \tag{20.1.14}$$

*Let $n$ be the smaller of $n_1$ and $n_2$, and collect the first $n$ vectors $\mathbf{k}_i$ and the first $n$ vectors $\mathbf{a}_j$ in matrices*

$$\underset{(n_1\times n)}{\mathcal{K}} = [\mathbf{k}_1 \quad \mathbf{k}_2 \quad \cdots \quad \mathbf{k}_n]$$

$$\underset{(n_2\times n)}{\mathcal{A}} = [\mathbf{a}_1 \quad \mathbf{a}_2 \quad \cdots \quad \mathbf{a}_n].$$

*Assuming that $\lambda_1, \lambda_2, \ldots, \lambda_n$ are distinct, then*

(a) $0 \leq \lambda_i < 1$ *for* $i = 1, 2, \ldots, n_1$ *and* $0 \leq \mu_j < 1$ *for* $j = 1, 2, \ldots, n_2$;
(b) $\lambda_i = \mu_i$ *for* $i = 1, 2, \ldots, n$;
(c) $\mathcal{K}'\mathbf{\Sigma}_{\mathbf{YY}}\mathcal{K} = \mathbf{I}_n$ *and* $\mathcal{A}'\mathbf{\Sigma}_{\mathbf{XX}}\mathcal{A} = \mathbf{I}_n$:
(d) $\mathcal{A}'\mathbf{\Sigma}_{\mathbf{XY}}\mathcal{K} = \mathbf{R}$,

*where $\mathbf{R}$ is a diagonal matrix whose squared diagonal elements correspond to the* *eigenvalues of* [20.1.8]:

$$\mathbf{R}^2 = \begin{bmatrix} \lambda_1 & 0 & \cdots & 0 \\ 0 & \lambda_2 & \cdots & 0 \\ \vdots & \vdots & \cdots & \vdots \\ 0 & 0 & \cdots & \lambda_n \end{bmatrix}.$$

If $\mathbf{\Sigma}$ denotes the variance-covariance matrix of the vector $(\mathbf{y}_t', \mathbf{x}_t')'$, then results (c) and (d) are the characterization of the canonical correlations given in [20.1.3] through [20.1.5]. Thus, the proposition establishes that the squares of the canonical correlations $(r_1^2, r_2^2, \ldots, r_n^2)$ can be found from the first $n$ eigenvalues of the matrix in [20.1.8]. Result (b) states that these are the same as the first $n$ eigenvalues of the matrix in [20.1.12]. The matrices $\mathcal{K}$ and $\mathcal{A}$ that characterize the canonical variates in [20.1.1] and [20.1.2] can be found from the normalized eigenvectors of these matrices.

The magnitude $\mathbf{a}_i'\mathbf{\Sigma}_{\mathbf{XY}}\mathbf{k}_i$ calculated by the algorithm described in Proposition 20.1 need not be positive—the proposition only ensures that its square is equal to the square of the corresponding canonical correlation. If $\mathbf{a}_i'\mathbf{\Sigma}_{\mathbf{XY}}\mathbf{k}_i < 0$ for some $i$, one can replace $\mathbf{k}_i$ as calculated with $-\mathbf{k}_i$, so that the $i$th diagonal element of $\mathbf{R}$ will correspond to the positive square root of $\lambda_i$.

As an illustration, suppose that $\mathbf{y}_t$ consists of a single variable ($n_1 = n = 1$). In this case, the matrix [20.1.8] is just a scalar, a $(1 \times 1)$ "matrix" that is equal to its own eigenvalue. Thus, the squared population canonical correlation between a scalar $y_t$ and a set of $n_2$ explanatory variables $\mathbf{x}_t$ is given by

$$r_1^2 = \frac{\Sigma_{Y\mathbf{X}}\mathbf{\Sigma}_{\mathbf{XX}}^{-1}\mathbf{\Sigma}_{\mathbf{X}Y}}{\Sigma_{YY}}.$$

To interpret this expression, recall from equation [4.1.15] that the mean squared error of a linear projection of $y_t$ on $\mathbf{x}_t$ is given by

$$MSE = \Sigma_{YY} - \Sigma_{Y\mathbf{X}}\mathbf{\Sigma}_{\mathbf{XX}}^{-1}\mathbf{\Sigma}_{\mathbf{X}Y},$$

and so

$$1 - r_1^2 = \frac{\Sigma_{YY}}{\Sigma_{YY}} - \frac{\Sigma_{Y\mathbf{X}}\mathbf{\Sigma}_{\mathbf{XX}}^{-1}\mathbf{\Sigma}_{\mathbf{X}Y}}{\Sigma_{YY}} = \frac{MSE}{\Sigma_{YY}}. \qquad [20.1.15]$$

Thus, for this simple case, $r_1^2$ is the fraction of the population variance that is explained by the linear projection; that is, $r_1^2$ is the population squared multiple correlation coefficient, commonly denoted $R^2$.

Another interpretation of canonical correlations is also sometimes helpful. The first canonical variates $\eta_{1t}$ and $\xi_{1t}$ can be interpreted as those linear combinations of $\mathbf{y}_t$ and $\mathbf{x}_t$, respectively, such that the correlation between $\eta_{1t}$ and $\xi_{1t}$ is as large as possible (see Exercise 20.1). The variates $\eta_{2t}$ and $\xi_{2t}$ give those linear combinations of $\mathbf{y}_t$ and $\mathbf{x}_t$ that are uncorrelated with $\eta_{1t}$ and $\xi_{1t}$ and yet yield the largest remaining correlation between $\eta_{2t}$ and $\xi_{2t}$, and so on.

## *Sample Canonical Correlations*

The canonical correlations $r_i$ calculated by the procedure just described are population parameters—they are functions of the population moments $\mathbf{\Sigma}_{\mathbf{YY}}$, $\mathbf{\Sigma}_{\mathbf{YX}}$, and $\mathbf{\Sigma}_{\mathbf{XX}}$. Here we describe their sample analogs, to be denoted $\hat{r}_i$.

Suppose we have a sample of $T$ observations on the $(n_1 \times 1)$ vector $\mathbf{y}_t$ and the $(n_2 \times 1)$ vector $\mathbf{x}_t$, whose sample moments are given by

$$\hat{\mathbf{\Sigma}}_{\mathbf{YY}} = (1/T) \sum_{t=1}^{T} \mathbf{y}_t \mathbf{y}_t' \qquad [20.1.16]$$

$$\hat{\mathbf{\Sigma}}_{\mathbf{YX}} = (1/T) \sum_{t=1}^{T} \mathbf{y}_t \mathbf{x}_t' \qquad [20.1.17]$$

$$\hat{\mathbf{\Sigma}}_{\mathbf{XX}} = (1/T) \sum_{t=1}^{T} \mathbf{x}_t \mathbf{x}_t'. \qquad [20.1.18]$$

Again, in many applications, $\mathbf{y}_t$ and $\mathbf{x}_t$ would be measured in deviations from their sample means.

To calculate sample canonical correlations, the objective is to generate a set of $T$ observations on a new $(n \times 1)$ vector $\hat{\boldsymbol{\eta}}_t$, where $n$ is the smaller of $n_1$ and $n_2$. The vector $\hat{\boldsymbol{\eta}}_t$ is a linear combination of the observed value of $\mathbf{y}_t$:

$$\hat{\boldsymbol{\eta}}_t = \hat{\mathcal{K}}'\mathbf{y}_t, \qquad [20.1.19]$$

for $\hat{\mathcal{K}}$ an $(n_1 \times n)$ matrix to be estimated from the data. The task will be to choose $\hat{\mathcal{K}}$ so that the $i$th generated series $(\hat{\eta}_{it})$ has unit sample variance and is orthogonal to the $j$th generated series:

$$(1/T) \sum_{t=1}^{T} \hat{\boldsymbol{\eta}}_t \hat{\boldsymbol{\eta}}_t' = \mathbf{I}_n. \qquad [20.1.20]$$

Similarly, we will generate an $(n \times 1)$ vector $\hat{\boldsymbol{\xi}}_t$ from the elements of $\mathbf{x}_t$:

$$\hat{\boldsymbol{\xi}}_t = \hat{\mathcal{A}}'\mathbf{x}_t. \qquad [20.1.21]$$

Each of the variables $\hat{\xi}_{it}$ has unit sample variance and is orthogonal to $\hat{\xi}_{jt}$ for $i \neq j$:

$$(1/T) \sum_{t=1}^{T} \hat{\boldsymbol{\xi}}_t \hat{\boldsymbol{\xi}}_t' = \mathbf{I}_n. \qquad [20.1.22]$$

Finally, $\hat{\eta}_{it}$ is orthogonal to $\hat{\xi}_{jt}$ for $i \neq j$, while the sample correlation between $\hat{\eta}_{it}$ and $\hat{\xi}_{it}$ is called the *sample canonical correlation coefficient*:

$$(1/T) \sum_{t=1}^{T} \hat{\boldsymbol{\xi}}_t \hat{\boldsymbol{\eta}}_t' = \hat{\mathbf{R}} \qquad [20.1.23]$$

for

$$\hat{\mathbf{R}} = \begin{bmatrix} \hat{r}_1 & 0 & \cdots & 0 \\ 0 & \hat{r}_2 & \cdots & 0 \\ \vdots & \vdots & \cdots & \vdots \\ 0 & 0 & \cdots & \hat{r}_n \end{bmatrix}. \qquad [20.1.24]$$

Finding matrices $\hat{\mathcal{K}}$, $\hat{\mathcal{A}}$, and $\hat{\mathbf{R}}$ satisfying [20.1.20], [20.1.22], and [20.1.23] involves exactly the same calculations as did finding matrices $\mathcal{K}$, $\mathcal{A}$, and $\mathbf{R}$ satisfying [20.1.3] through [20.1.5]. For example, [20.1.19] allows us to write [20.1.20] as

$$\mathbf{I}_n = (1/T) \sum_{t=1}^{T} \hat{\boldsymbol{\eta}}_t \hat{\boldsymbol{\eta}}_t' = \hat{\mathcal{K}}'(1/T) \sum_{t=1}^{T} \mathbf{y}_t \mathbf{y}_t' \hat{\mathcal{K}} = \hat{\mathcal{K}}'\hat{\mathbf{\Sigma}}_{\mathbf{YY}}\hat{\mathcal{K}}, \qquad [20.1.25]$$

where the last line follows from [20.1.16]. Expression [20.1.25] is identical to

[20.1.3] with hats placed over the variables. Similarly, substituting [20.1.21] into [20.1.22] gives $\hat{\mathscr{A}}'\hat{\Sigma}_{\mathbf{XX}}\hat{\mathscr{A}} = \mathbf{I}_n$, which corresponds to [20.1.4]. Equation [20.1.23] becomes $\hat{\mathscr{A}}'\hat{\Sigma}_{\mathbf{XY}}\hat{\mathscr{K}} = \hat{\mathbf{R}}$, as in [20.1.5]. Again, we can replace $\hat{\mathbf{k}}_i$ with $-\hat{\mathbf{k}}_i$ if any of the elements of $\hat{\mathbf{R}}$ should turn out negative.

Thus, to calculate the sample canonical correlations, the procedure described in Proposition 20.1 is simply applied to the sample moments ($\hat{\Sigma}_{\mathbf{YY}}$, $\hat{\Sigma}_{\mathbf{YX}}$, and $\hat{\Sigma}_{\mathbf{XX}}$) rather than to the population moments. In particular, the square of the $i$th sample canonical correlation ($\hat{r}_i^2$) is given by the $i$th largest eigenvalue of the matrix

$$\hat{\Sigma}_{\mathbf{YY}}^{-1}\hat{\Sigma}_{\mathbf{YX}}\hat{\Sigma}_{\mathbf{XX}}^{-1}\hat{\Sigma}_{\mathbf{XY}} = \left\{(1/T)\sum_{t=1}^{T}\mathbf{y}_t\mathbf{y}_t'\right\}^{-1}\left\{(1/T)\sum_{t=1}^{T}\mathbf{y}_t\mathbf{x}_t'\right\} \times \left\{(1/T)\sum_{t=1}^{T}\mathbf{x}_t\mathbf{x}_t'\right\}^{-1}\left\{(1/T)\sum_{t=1}^{T}\mathbf{x}_t\mathbf{y}_t'\right\}. \qquad [20.1.26]$$

The $i$th column of $\hat{\mathscr{K}}$ is given by the eigenvector associated with this $i$th eigenvalue, normalized so that

$$\hat{\mathbf{k}}_i'\left\{(1/T)\sum_{t=1}^{T}\mathbf{y}_t\mathbf{y}_t'\right\}\hat{\mathbf{k}}_i = 1.$$

The $i$th column of $\hat{\mathscr{A}}$ is given by the eigenvector associated with the eigenvalue $\hat{\lambda}_i$ for the matrix $\hat{\Sigma}_{\mathbf{XX}}^{-1}\hat{\Sigma}_{\mathbf{XY}}\hat{\Sigma}_{\mathbf{YY}}^{-1}\hat{\Sigma}_{\mathbf{YX}}$ normalized by the condition that $\hat{\mathbf{a}}_i'\hat{\Sigma}_{\mathbf{XX}}\hat{\mathbf{a}}_i = 1$.

For example, suppose that $\mathbf{y}_t$ is a scalar ($n = n_1 = 1$). Then [20.1.26] is a scalar equal to its own eigenvalue. Hence, the sample squared canonical correlation between the scalar $\mathbf{y}_t$ and a set of $n_2$ explanatory variables $\mathbf{x}_t$ is given by

$$\hat{r}_1^2 = \frac{\{T^{-1}\Sigma y_t\mathbf{x}_t'\}\{T^{-1}\Sigma\mathbf{x}_t\mathbf{x}_t'\}^{-1}\{T^{-1}\Sigma\mathbf{x}_t y_t\}}{\{T^{-1}\Sigma y_t^2\}} = \frac{\{\Sigma y_t\mathbf{x}_t'\}\{\Sigma\mathbf{x}_t\mathbf{x}_t'\}^{-1}\{\Sigma\mathbf{x}_t y_t\}}{\{\Sigma y_t^2\}},$$

which is just the squared sample multiple correlation coefficient $R^2$.

## 20.2. *Maximum Likelihood Estimation*

We are now in a position to describe Johansen's approach (1988, 1991) to full-information maximum likelihood estimation of a system characterized by exactly $h$ cointegrating relations.

Let $\mathbf{y}_t$ denote an ($n \times 1$) vector. The maintained hypothesis is that $\mathbf{y}_t$ follows a $VAR(p)$ in levels. Recall from equation [19.1.39] that any $p$th-order $VAR$ can be written in the form

$$\Delta\mathbf{y}_t = \boldsymbol{\zeta}_1\Delta\mathbf{y}_{t-1} + \boldsymbol{\zeta}_2\Delta\mathbf{y}_{t-2} + \cdots + \boldsymbol{\zeta}_{p-1}\Delta\mathbf{y}_{t-p+1} + \boldsymbol{\alpha} + \boldsymbol{\zeta}_0\mathbf{y}_{t-1} + \boldsymbol{\varepsilon}_t, \qquad [20.2.1]$$

with

$$E(\boldsymbol{\varepsilon}_t) = \mathbf{0}$$

$$E(\boldsymbol{\varepsilon}_t\boldsymbol{\varepsilon}_\tau') = \begin{cases}\boldsymbol{\Omega} & \text{for } t = \tau\\ \mathbf{0} & \text{otherwise.}\end{cases}$$

Suppose that each individual variable $y_{it}$ is $I(1)$, although $h$ linear combinations of $\mathbf{y}_t$ are stationary. We saw in equations [19.1.35] and [19.1.40] that this implies that $\boldsymbol{\zeta}_0$ can be written in the form

$$\boldsymbol{\zeta}_0 = -\mathbf{BA}' \qquad [20.2.2]$$

for $\mathbf{B}$ an $(n \times h)$ matrix and $\mathbf{A}'$ an $(h \times n)$ matrix. That is, under the hypothesis of $h$ cointegrating relations, only $h$ separate linear combinations of the level of $\mathbf{y}_{t-1}$ (the $h$ elements of $\mathbf{z}_{t-1} = \mathbf{A}'\mathbf{y}_{t-1}$) appear in [20.2.1].

Consider a sample of $T + p$ observations on $\mathbf{y}$, denoted $(\mathbf{y}_{-p+1}, \mathbf{y}_{-p+2}, \ldots, \mathbf{y}_T)$. If the disturbances $\boldsymbol{\varepsilon}_t$ are Gaussian, then the log likelihood of $(\mathbf{y}_1, \mathbf{y}_2, \ldots, \mathbf{y}_T)$ conditional on $(\mathbf{y}_{-p+1}, \mathbf{y}_{-p+2}, \ldots, \mathbf{y}_0)$ is given by

$$\begin{aligned}
&\mathscr{L}(\boldsymbol{\Omega}, \boldsymbol{\zeta}_1, \boldsymbol{\zeta}_2, \ldots, \boldsymbol{\zeta}_{p-1}, \boldsymbol{\alpha}, \boldsymbol{\zeta}_0) \\
&\quad = (-Tn/2)\log(2\pi) - (T/2)\log|\boldsymbol{\Omega}| \\
&\quad\quad - (1/2)\sum_{t=1}^{T}\Big[(\Delta\mathbf{y}_t - \boldsymbol{\zeta}_1\Delta\mathbf{y}_{t-1} - \boldsymbol{\zeta}_2\Delta\mathbf{y}_{t-2} - \cdots - \boldsymbol{\zeta}_{p-1}\Delta\mathbf{y}_{t-p+1} - \boldsymbol{\alpha} - \boldsymbol{\zeta}_0\mathbf{y}_{t-1})' \\
&\quad\quad \times \boldsymbol{\Omega}^{-1}(\Delta\mathbf{y}_t - \boldsymbol{\zeta}_1\Delta\mathbf{y}_{t-1} - \boldsymbol{\zeta}_2\Delta\mathbf{y}_{t-2} - \cdots - \boldsymbol{\zeta}_{p-1}\Delta\mathbf{y}_{t-p+1} - \boldsymbol{\alpha} - \boldsymbol{\zeta}_0\mathbf{y}_{t-1})\Big].
\end{aligned} \qquad [20.2.3]$$

The goal is to chose $(\boldsymbol{\Omega}, \boldsymbol{\zeta}_1, \boldsymbol{\zeta}_2, \ldots, \boldsymbol{\zeta}_{p-1}, \boldsymbol{\alpha}, \boldsymbol{\zeta}_0)$ so as to maximize [20.2.3] subject to the constraint that $\boldsymbol{\zeta}_0$ can be written in the form of [20.2.2].

We will first summarize Johansen's algorithm, and then verify that it indeed calculates the maximum likelihood estimates.

### *Step 1: Calculate Auxiliary Regressions*

The first step is to estimate a $(p-1)$th-order *VAR* for $\Delta\mathbf{y}_t$; that is, regress the scalar $\Delta y_{it}$ on a constant and all the elements of the vectors $\Delta\mathbf{y}_{t-1}, \Delta\mathbf{y}_{t-2}, \ldots, \Delta\mathbf{y}_{t-p+1}$ by *OLS*. Collect the $i = 1, 2, \ldots, n$ *OLS* regressions in vector form as

$$\Delta\mathbf{y}_t = \hat{\boldsymbol{\pi}}_0 + \hat{\boldsymbol{\Pi}}_1\Delta\mathbf{y}_{t-1} + \hat{\boldsymbol{\Pi}}_2\Delta\mathbf{y}_{t-2} + \cdots + \hat{\boldsymbol{\Pi}}_{p-1}\Delta\mathbf{y}_{t-p+1} + \hat{\mathbf{u}}_t, \qquad [20.2.4]$$

where $\hat{\boldsymbol{\Pi}}_i$ denotes an $(n \times n)$ matrix of *OLS* coefficient estimates and $\hat{\mathbf{u}}_t$ denotes the $(n \times 1)$ vector of *OLS* residuals. We also estimate a second battery of regressions, regressing the scalar $y_{i,t-1}$ on a constant and $\Delta\mathbf{y}_{t-1}, \Delta\mathbf{y}_{t-2}, \ldots, \Delta\mathbf{y}_{t-p+1}$ for $i = 1, 2, \ldots, n$. Write this second set of *OLS* regressions as[1]

$$\mathbf{y}_{t-1} = \hat{\boldsymbol{\theta}} + \hat{\boldsymbol{\aleph}}_1\Delta\mathbf{y}_{t-1} + \hat{\boldsymbol{\aleph}}_2\Delta\mathbf{y}_{t-2} + \cdots + \hat{\boldsymbol{\aleph}}_{p-1}\Delta\mathbf{y}_{t-p+1} + \hat{\mathbf{v}}_t, \qquad [20.2.5]$$

with $\hat{\mathbf{v}}_t$ the $(n \times 1)$ vector of residuals from this second battery of regressions.

[1]Johansen (1991) described his procedure as calculating $\dot{\mathbf{v}}_t$ in place of $\hat{\mathbf{v}}_t$, where $\dot{\mathbf{v}}_t$ is the *OLS* residual from a regression of $\mathbf{y}_{t-p}$ on a constant and $\Delta\mathbf{y}_{t-1}, \Delta\mathbf{y}_{t-2}, \ldots, \Delta\mathbf{y}_{t-p+1}$. Since $\mathbf{y}_{t-p} = \mathbf{y}_{t-1} - \Delta\mathbf{y}_{t-1} - \Delta\mathbf{y}_{t-2} - \cdots - \Delta\mathbf{y}_{t-p+1}$, the residual $\dot{\mathbf{v}}_t$ is numerically identical to $\hat{\mathbf{v}}_t$ described in the text.

## *Step 2: Calculate Canonical Correlations*

Next calculate the sample variance-covariance matrices of the *OLS* residuals $\hat{\mathbf{u}}_t$ and $\hat{\mathbf{v}}_t$:

$$\hat{\mathbf{\Sigma}}_{\mathbf{VV}} \equiv (1/T) \sum_{t=1}^{T} \hat{\mathbf{v}}_t \hat{\mathbf{v}}_t' \qquad [20.2.6]$$

$$\hat{\mathbf{\Sigma}}_{\mathbf{UU}} \equiv (1/T) \sum_{t=1}^{T} \hat{\mathbf{u}}_t \hat{\mathbf{u}}_t' \qquad [20.2.7]$$

$$\hat{\mathbf{\Sigma}}_{\mathbf{UV}} \equiv (1/T) \sum_{t=1}^{T} \hat{\mathbf{u}}_t \hat{\mathbf{v}}_t' \qquad [20.2.8]$$

$$\hat{\mathbf{\Sigma}}_{\mathbf{VU}} \equiv \hat{\mathbf{\Sigma}}_{\mathbf{UV}}'.$$

From these, find the eigenvalues of the matrix

$$\hat{\mathbf{\Sigma}}_{\mathbf{VV}}^{-1} \hat{\mathbf{\Sigma}}_{\mathbf{VU}} \hat{\mathbf{\Sigma}}_{\mathbf{UU}}^{-1} \hat{\mathbf{\Sigma}}_{\mathbf{UV}} \qquad [20.2.9]$$

with the eigenvalues ordered $\hat{\lambda}_1 > \hat{\lambda}_2 > \cdots > \hat{\lambda}_n$. The maximum value attained by the log likelihood function subject to the constraint that there are $h$ cointegrating relations is given by

$$\begin{aligned} \mathscr{L}^* = &-(Tn/2)\log(2\pi) - (Tn/2) - (T/2)\log|\hat{\mathbf{\Sigma}}_{\mathbf{UU}}| \\ &- (T/2)\sum_{i=1}^{h} \log(1 - \hat{\lambda}_i). \end{aligned} \qquad [20.2.10]$$

## *Step 3: Calculate Maximum Likelihood Estimates of Parameters*

If we are interested only in a likelihood ratio test of the number of cointegrating relations, step 2 provides all the information needed. If maximum likelihood estimates of parameters are also desired, these can be calculated as follows. Let $\hat{\mathbf{a}}_1, \hat{\mathbf{a}}_2, \ldots, \hat{\mathbf{a}}_h$ denote the $(n \times 1)$ eigenvectors of [20.2.9] associated with the $h$ largest eigenvalues. These provide a basis for the space of cointegrating relations; that is, the maximum likelihood estimate is that any cointegrating vector can be written in the form

$$\mathbf{a} = b_1\hat{\mathbf{a}}_1 + b_2\hat{\mathbf{a}}_2 + \cdots + b_h\hat{\mathbf{a}}_h$$

for some choice of scalars $(b_1, b_2, \ldots, b_h)$. Johansen suggested normalizing these vectors $\hat{\mathbf{a}}_i$ so that $\hat{\mathbf{a}}_i'\hat{\mathbf{\Sigma}}_{\mathbf{VV}}\hat{\mathbf{a}}_i = 1$. For example, if the eigenvectors $\tilde{\mathbf{a}}_i$ of [20.2.9] are calculated from a standard computer program that normalizes $\tilde{\mathbf{a}}_i'\tilde{\mathbf{a}}_i = 1$, Johansen's estimate is $\hat{\mathbf{a}}_i = \tilde{\mathbf{a}}_i \div \sqrt{\tilde{\mathbf{a}}_i'\hat{\mathbf{\Sigma}}_{\mathbf{VV}}\tilde{\mathbf{a}}_i}$. Collect the first $h$ normalized vectors in an $(n \times h)$ matrix $\hat{\mathbf{A}}$:

$$\hat{\mathbf{A}} \equiv [\hat{\mathbf{a}}_1 \quad \hat{\mathbf{a}}_2 \quad \cdots \quad \hat{\mathbf{a}}_h]. \qquad [20.2.11]$$

Then the *MLE* of $\boldsymbol{\zeta}_0$ is given by

$$\hat{\boldsymbol{\zeta}}_0 = \hat{\mathbf{\Sigma}}_{\mathbf{UV}}\hat{\mathbf{A}}\hat{\mathbf{A}}'. \qquad [20.2.12]$$

The *MLE* of $\boldsymbol{\zeta}_i$ for $i = 1, 2, \ldots, p - 1$ is

$$\hat{\boldsymbol{\zeta}}_i = \hat{\mathbf{\Pi}}_i - \hat{\boldsymbol{\zeta}}_0\hat{\boldsymbol{\aleph}}_i, \qquad [20.2.13]$$

and the *MLE* of $\boldsymbol{\alpha}$ is

$$\hat{\boldsymbol{\alpha}} = \hat{\boldsymbol{\pi}}_0 - \hat{\boldsymbol{\zeta}}_0\hat{\boldsymbol{\theta}}. \qquad [20.2.14]$$

The *MLE* of $\boldsymbol{\Omega}$ is

$$\hat{\boldsymbol{\Omega}} = (1/T) \sum_{t=1}^{T} [(\hat{\mathbf{u}}_t - \hat{\boldsymbol{\zeta}}_0 \hat{\mathbf{v}}_t)(\hat{\mathbf{u}}_t - \hat{\boldsymbol{\zeta}}_0 \hat{\mathbf{v}}_t)']. \qquad [20.2.15]$$

We now review the logic behind each of these steps in turn.

## *Motivation for Auxiliary Regressions*

The first step involves *concentrating* the likelihood function.[2] This means taking $\boldsymbol{\Omega}$ and $\boldsymbol{\zeta}_0$ as given and maximizing [20.2.3] with respect to $(\boldsymbol{\alpha}, \boldsymbol{\zeta}_1, \boldsymbol{\zeta}_2, \ldots, \boldsymbol{\zeta}_{p-1})$. This restricted maximization problem takes the form of seemingly unrelated regressions of the elements of the $(n \times 1)$ vector $\Delta\mathbf{y}_t - \boldsymbol{\zeta}_0\mathbf{y}_{t-1}$ on a constant and the explanatory variables $(\Delta\mathbf{y}_{t-1}, \Delta\mathbf{y}_{t-2}, \ldots, \Delta\mathbf{y}_{t-p+1})$. Since each of the $n$ regressions in this system has the identical explanatory variables, the estimates of $(\boldsymbol{\alpha}, \boldsymbol{\zeta}_1, \boldsymbol{\zeta}_2, \ldots, \boldsymbol{\zeta}_{p-1})$ would come from *OLS* regressions of each of the elements of $\Delta\mathbf{y}_t - \boldsymbol{\zeta}_0\mathbf{y}_{t-1}$ on a constant and $(\Delta\mathbf{y}_{t-1}, \Delta\mathbf{y}_{t-2}, \ldots, \Delta\mathbf{y}_{t-p+1})$. Denote the values of $(\boldsymbol{\alpha}, \boldsymbol{\zeta}_1, \boldsymbol{\zeta}_2, \ldots, \boldsymbol{\zeta}_{p-1})$ that maximize [20.2.3] for a given value of $\boldsymbol{\zeta}_0$ by

$$[\hat{\boldsymbol{\alpha}}^*(\boldsymbol{\zeta}_0), \hat{\boldsymbol{\zeta}}_1^*(\boldsymbol{\zeta}_0), \hat{\boldsymbol{\zeta}}_2^*(\boldsymbol{\zeta}_0), \ldots, \hat{\boldsymbol{\zeta}}_{p-1}^*(\boldsymbol{\zeta}_0)].$$

These values are characterized by the condition that the following residual vector must have sample mean zero and be orthogonal to $\Delta\mathbf{y}_{t-1}, \Delta\mathbf{y}_{t-2}, \ldots, \Delta\mathbf{y}_{t-p+1}$:

$$\begin{aligned}[][\Delta\mathbf{y}_t - \boldsymbol{\zeta}_0\mathbf{y}_{t-1}] - \{\hat{\boldsymbol{\alpha}}^*(\boldsymbol{\zeta}_0) + \hat{\boldsymbol{\zeta}}_1^*(\boldsymbol{\zeta}_0)\Delta\mathbf{y}_{t-1} + \hat{\boldsymbol{\zeta}}_2^*(\boldsymbol{\zeta}_0)\Delta\mathbf{y}_{t-2} \\ + \cdots + \hat{\boldsymbol{\zeta}}_{p-1}^*(\boldsymbol{\zeta}_0)\Delta\mathbf{y}_{t-p+1}\}.\end{aligned} \qquad [20.2.16]$$

But notice that the *OLS* residuals $\hat{\mathbf{u}}_t$ in [20.2.4] and $\hat{\mathbf{v}}_t$ in [20.2.5] each satisfy this orthogonality requirement, and therefore the vector $\hat{\mathbf{u}}_t - \boldsymbol{\zeta}_0\hat{\mathbf{v}}_t$ also has sample mean zero and is orthogonal to $\Delta\mathbf{y}_{t-1}, \Delta\mathbf{y}_{t-2}, \ldots, \Delta\mathbf{y}_{t-p+1}$. Moreover, $\hat{\mathbf{u}}_t - \boldsymbol{\zeta}_0\hat{\mathbf{v}}_t$ is of the form of expression [20.2.16],

$$\begin{aligned}\hat{\mathbf{u}}_t - \boldsymbol{\zeta}_0\hat{\mathbf{v}}_t = (\Delta\mathbf{y}_t - \hat{\boldsymbol{\pi}}_0 - \hat{\boldsymbol{\Pi}}_1\Delta\mathbf{y}_{t-1} - \hat{\boldsymbol{\Pi}}_2\Delta\mathbf{y}_{t-2} - \cdots - \hat{\boldsymbol{\Pi}}_{p-1}\Delta\mathbf{y}_{t-p+1}) \\ - \boldsymbol{\zeta}_0(\mathbf{y}_{t-1} - \hat{\boldsymbol{\theta}} - \hat{\boldsymbol{\aleph}}_1\Delta\mathbf{y}_{t-1} - \hat{\boldsymbol{\aleph}}_2\Delta\mathbf{y}_{t-2} - \cdots - \hat{\boldsymbol{\aleph}}_{p-1}\Delta\mathbf{y}_{t-p+1}),\end{aligned}$$

with

$$\hat{\boldsymbol{\alpha}}^*(\boldsymbol{\zeta}_0) = \hat{\boldsymbol{\pi}}_0 - \boldsymbol{\zeta}_0\hat{\boldsymbol{\theta}} \qquad [20.2.17]$$

$$\hat{\boldsymbol{\zeta}}_i^*(\boldsymbol{\zeta}_0) = \hat{\boldsymbol{\Pi}}_i - \boldsymbol{\zeta}_0\hat{\boldsymbol{\aleph}}_i \qquad \text{for } i = 1, 2, \ldots, p-1. \qquad [20.2.18]$$

Thus, the vector in [20.2.16] is given by $\hat{\mathbf{u}}_t - \boldsymbol{\zeta}_0\hat{\mathbf{v}}_t$.

The concentrated log likelihood function (to be denoted $\mathcal{M}$) is found by replacing $(\boldsymbol{\alpha}, \boldsymbol{\zeta}_1, \boldsymbol{\zeta}_2, \ldots, \boldsymbol{\zeta}_{p-1})$ in [20.2.3] with $[\hat{\boldsymbol{\alpha}}^*(\boldsymbol{\zeta}_0), \hat{\boldsymbol{\zeta}}_1^*(\boldsymbol{\zeta}_0), \hat{\boldsymbol{\zeta}}_2^*(\boldsymbol{\zeta}_0), \ldots, \hat{\boldsymbol{\zeta}}_{p-1}^*(\boldsymbol{\zeta}_0)]$:

$$\begin{aligned}\mathcal{M}(\boldsymbol{\Omega}, \boldsymbol{\zeta}_0) &\equiv \mathcal{L}\{\boldsymbol{\Omega}, \hat{\boldsymbol{\zeta}}_1^*(\boldsymbol{\zeta}_0), \hat{\boldsymbol{\zeta}}_2^*(\boldsymbol{\zeta}_0), \ldots, \hat{\boldsymbol{\zeta}}_{p-1}^*(\boldsymbol{\zeta}_0), \hat{\boldsymbol{\alpha}}^*(\boldsymbol{\zeta}_0), \boldsymbol{\zeta}_0\} \\ &= -(Tn/2)\log(2\pi) - (T/2)\log|\boldsymbol{\Omega}| \\ &\quad - (1/2)\sum_{t=1}^{T}[(\hat{\mathbf{u}}_t - \boldsymbol{\zeta}_0\hat{\mathbf{v}}_t)'\boldsymbol{\Omega}^{-1}(\hat{\mathbf{u}}_t - \boldsymbol{\zeta}_0\hat{\mathbf{v}}_t)].\end{aligned} \qquad [20.2.19]$$

The idea behind concentrating the likelihood function in this way is that if we can find the values of $\hat{\boldsymbol{\Omega}}$ and $\hat{\boldsymbol{\zeta}}_0$ for which $\mathcal{M}$ is maximized, then these same values (along with $\hat{\boldsymbol{\alpha}}^*(\hat{\boldsymbol{\zeta}}_0)$ and $\hat{\boldsymbol{\zeta}}_i^*(\hat{\boldsymbol{\zeta}}_0)$) will maximize [20.2.3].

[2]See Koopmans and Hood (1953, pp. 156–58) for more background on concentration of likelihood functions.

Continuing the concentration one step further, recall from the analysis of [11.1.25] that the value of $\boldsymbol{\Omega}$ that maximizes [20.2.19] (still regarding $\boldsymbol{\zeta}_0$ as fixed) is given by

$$\hat{\boldsymbol{\Omega}}^*(\boldsymbol{\zeta}_0) = (1/T)\sum_{t=1}^{T} [(\hat{\mathbf{u}}_t - \boldsymbol{\zeta}_0\hat{\mathbf{v}}_t)(\hat{\mathbf{u}}_t - \boldsymbol{\zeta}_0\hat{\mathbf{v}}_t)']. \qquad [20.2.20]$$

As in expression [11.1.32], the value obtained for [20.2.19] when evaluated at [20.2.20] is then

$$\begin{aligned}\mathcal{N}(\boldsymbol{\zeta}_0) &\equiv \mathcal{M}\{\hat{\boldsymbol{\Omega}}^*(\boldsymbol{\zeta}_0), \boldsymbol{\zeta}_0\} \\ &= -(Tn/2)\log(2\pi) - (T/2)\log|\hat{\boldsymbol{\Omega}}^*(\boldsymbol{\zeta}_0)| - (Tn/2) \\ &= -(Tn/2)\log(2\pi) - (Tn/2) \\ &\quad - (T/2)\log\left|(1/T)\sum_{t=1}^{T}[(\hat{\mathbf{u}}_t - \boldsymbol{\zeta}_0\hat{\mathbf{v}}_t)(\hat{\mathbf{u}}_t - \boldsymbol{\zeta}_0\hat{\mathbf{v}}_t)']\right|.\end{aligned} \qquad [20.2.21]$$

Expression [20.2.21] represents the biggest value one can achieve for the log likelihood for any given value of $\boldsymbol{\zeta}_0$. Maximizing the likelihood function thus comes down to choosing $\boldsymbol{\zeta}_0$ so as to minimize

$$\left|(1/T)\sum_{t=1}^{T}[(\hat{\mathbf{u}}_t - \boldsymbol{\zeta}_0\hat{\mathbf{v}}_t)(\hat{\mathbf{u}}_t - \boldsymbol{\zeta}_0\hat{\mathbf{v}}_t)']\right| \qquad [20.2.22]$$

subject to the constraint of [20.2.2].

## *Motivation for Canonical Correlation Analysis*

To see the motivation for calculating canonical correlations, consider first a simpler problem. Suppose that by an astounding coincidence, $\hat{\mathbf{u}}_t$ and $\hat{\mathbf{v}}_t$ were already in canonical form,

$$\hat{\mathbf{u}}_t = \hat{\boldsymbol{\eta}}_t$$
$$\hat{\mathbf{v}}_t = \hat{\boldsymbol{\xi}}_t,$$

with

$$(1/T)\sum_{t=1}^{T}\hat{\boldsymbol{\eta}}_t\hat{\boldsymbol{\eta}}_t' = \mathbf{I}_n \qquad [20.2.23]$$

$$(1/T)\sum_{t=1}^{T}\hat{\boldsymbol{\xi}}_t\hat{\boldsymbol{\xi}}_t' = \mathbf{I}_n \qquad [20.2.24]$$

$$(1/T)\sum_{t=1}^{T}\hat{\boldsymbol{\xi}}_t\hat{\boldsymbol{\eta}}_t' = \hat{\mathbf{R}} \qquad [20.2.25]$$

$$\hat{\mathbf{R}} = \begin{bmatrix} \hat{r}_1 & 0 & \cdots & 0 \\ 0 & \hat{r}_2 & \cdots & 0 \\ \vdots & \vdots & \cdots & \vdots \\ 0 & 0 & \cdots & \hat{r}_n \end{bmatrix}. \qquad [20.2.26]$$

Suppose that for these canonical data we were asked to choose $\boldsymbol{\zeta}_0$ so as to minimize

$$\left|(1/T)\sum_{t=1}^{T}\left[(\hat{\boldsymbol{\eta}}_t - \boldsymbol{\zeta}_0\hat{\boldsymbol{\xi}}_t)(\hat{\boldsymbol{\eta}}_t - \boldsymbol{\zeta}_0\hat{\boldsymbol{\xi}}_t)'\right]\right| \qquad [20.2.27]$$

subject to the constraint that $\boldsymbol{\zeta}_0\hat{\boldsymbol{\xi}}_t$ could make use of only $h$ linear combinations of $\hat{\boldsymbol{\xi}}_t$. If there were no restrictions on $\boldsymbol{\zeta}_0$ (so that $h = n$), then expression [20.2.27] would be minimized by $OLS$ regressions of $\hat{\eta}_{it}$ on $\hat{\boldsymbol{\xi}}_t$ for $i = 1, 2, \ldots, n$. Conditions [20.2.24] and [20.2.25] establish that the $i$th regression would have an estimated coefficient vector of

$$\left\{(1/T)\sum_{t=1}^{T}\hat{\boldsymbol{\xi}}_t\hat{\boldsymbol{\xi}}_t'\right\}^{-1}\left\{(1/T)\sum_{t=1}^{T}\hat{\boldsymbol{\xi}}_t\hat{\eta}_{it}\right\} = \hat{r}_i\cdot\mathbf{e}_i,$$

where $\mathbf{e}_i$ denotes the $i$th column of $\mathbf{I}_n$. Thus, even if all $n$ elements of $\hat{\boldsymbol{\xi}}_t$ appeared in the regression, only the $i$th element $\hat{\xi}_{it}$ would have a nonzero coefficient in the regression used to explain $\hat{\eta}_{it}$. The average squared residual for this regression would be

$$\begin{aligned}\left\{(1/T)\sum_{t=1}^{T}(\hat{\eta}_{it})^2\right\} - \left\{(1/T)\sum_{t=1}^{T}(\hat{\eta}_{it}\hat{\boldsymbol{\xi}}_t')\right\}&\left\{(1/T)\sum_{t=1}^{T}(\hat{\boldsymbol{\xi}}_t\hat{\boldsymbol{\xi}}_t')\right\}^{-1}\left\{(1/T)\sum_{t=1}^{T}(\hat{\boldsymbol{\xi}}_t\hat{\eta}_{it})\right\}\\ &= 1 - \hat{r}_i\cdot\mathbf{e}_i'\cdot\mathbf{I}_n\cdot\mathbf{e}_i\cdot\hat{r}_i\\ &= 1 - \hat{r}_i^2.\end{aligned}$$

Moreover, conditions [20.2.23] through [20.2.25] imply that the residual for the $i$th regression, $\hat{\eta}_{it} - \hat{r}_i\hat{\xi}_{it}$, would be orthogonal to the residual from the $j$th regression, $\hat{\eta}_{jt} - \hat{r}_j\hat{\xi}_{jt}$, for $i \neq j$. Thus, if $\boldsymbol{\zeta}_0$ were unrestricted, the optimal value for the matrix in [20.2.27] would be a diagonal matrix with $(1 - \hat{r}_i^2)$ in the row $i$, column $i$ position and zero elsewhere.

Now suppose that we are restricted to use only $h$ linear combinations of $\hat{\boldsymbol{\xi}}_t$ as regressors. From the preceding analysis, we might guess that the best we can do is use the $h$ elements of $\hat{\boldsymbol{\xi}}_t$ that have the highest correlations with elements of $\hat{\boldsymbol{\eta}}_t$, that is, choose $(\hat{\xi}_{1t}, \hat{\xi}_{2t}, \ldots, \hat{\xi}_{ht})$ as regressors.[3] When this set of regressors is used to explain $\hat{\eta}_{it}$ for $i \leq h$, the average squared residual will be $(1 - \hat{r}_i^2)$, as before. When this set of regressors is used to explain $\hat{\eta}_{it}$ for $i > h$, all of the regressors are orthogonal to $\hat{\eta}_{it}$ and would receive regression coefficients of zero. The average squared residual for the latter regression is simply $(1/T)\Sigma_{t=1}^{T}\hat{\eta}_{it}^2 = 1$ for $i = h + 1, h + 2, \ldots, n$. Thus, if we are restricted to using only $h$ linear combinations of $\hat{\boldsymbol{\xi}}_t$, the optimized value of [20.2.27] will be

$$\begin{aligned}&\left|(1/T)\sum_{t=1}^{T}[(\hat{\boldsymbol{\eta}}_t - \boldsymbol{\zeta}_0^*\hat{\boldsymbol{\xi}}_t)(\hat{\boldsymbol{\eta}}_t - \boldsymbol{\zeta}_0^*\hat{\boldsymbol{\xi}}_t)']\right|\\ &= \begin{vmatrix} 1-\hat{r}_1^2 & 0 & \cdots & 0 & 0 & \cdots & 0\\ 0 & 1-\hat{r}_2^2 & \cdots & 0 & 0 & \cdots & 0\\ \vdots & \vdots & \cdots & \vdots & \vdots & \cdots & \vdots\\ 0 & 0 & \cdots & 1-\hat{r}_h^2 & 0 & \cdots & 0\\ 0 & 0 & \cdots & 0 & 1 & \cdots & 0\\ \vdots & \vdots & \cdots & \vdots & \vdots & \cdots & \vdots\\ 0 & 0 & \cdots & 0 & 0 & \cdots & 1 \end{vmatrix} \qquad [20.2.28]\\ &= \prod_{i=1}^{h}(1 - \hat{r}_i^2).\end{aligned}$$

[3]See Johansen (1988) for a more formal demonstration of this claim.

Of course, the actual data $\hat{\mathbf{u}}_t$ and $\hat{\mathbf{v}}_t$ will not be in exact canonical form. However, the previous section described how to find $(n \times n)$ matrices $\hat{\mathcal{K}}$ and $\hat{\mathcal{A}}$ such that

$$\hat{\boldsymbol{\eta}}_t = \hat{\mathcal{K}}'\hat{\mathbf{u}}_t \qquad [20.2.29]$$

$$\hat{\boldsymbol{\xi}}_t = \hat{\mathcal{A}}'\hat{\mathbf{v}}_t. \qquad [20.2.30]$$

The columns of $\hat{\mathcal{A}}$ are given by the eigenvectors of the matrix in [20.2.9], normalized by the condition $\hat{\mathcal{A}}'\hat{\boldsymbol{\Sigma}}_{\mathbf{VV}}\hat{\mathcal{A}} = \mathbf{I}_n$. The eigenvalues of [20.2.9] give the squares of the canonical correlations:

$$\hat{\lambda}_i = \hat{r}_i^2. \qquad [20.2.31]$$

The columns of $\hat{\mathcal{K}}$ correspond to the normalized eigenvectors of the matrix $\hat{\boldsymbol{\Sigma}}_{\mathbf{UU}}^{-1}\hat{\boldsymbol{\Sigma}}_{\mathbf{UV}}\hat{\boldsymbol{\Sigma}}_{\mathbf{VV}}^{-1}\hat{\boldsymbol{\Sigma}}_{\mathbf{VU}}$, though it turns out that $\hat{\mathcal{K}}$ does not actually have to be calculated in order to use the following results. Assuming that $\hat{\mathcal{K}}$ and $\hat{\mathcal{A}}$ are nonsingular, [20.2.29] and [20.2.30] allow [20.2.22] to be written

$$\begin{aligned}
&\left|(1/T)\sum_{t=1}^{T}\left[(\hat{\mathbf{u}}_t - \boldsymbol{\zeta}_0\hat{\mathbf{v}}_t)(\hat{\mathbf{u}}_t - \boldsymbol{\zeta}_0\hat{\mathbf{v}}_t)'\right]\right| \\
&\quad = \left|(1/T)\sum_{t=1}^{T}\left[[(\hat{\mathcal{K}}')^{-1}\hat{\boldsymbol{\eta}}_t - \boldsymbol{\zeta}_0(\hat{\mathcal{A}}')^{-1}\hat{\boldsymbol{\xi}}_t][(\hat{\mathcal{K}}')^{-1}\hat{\boldsymbol{\eta}}_t - \boldsymbol{\zeta}_0(\hat{\mathcal{A}}')^{-1}\hat{\boldsymbol{\xi}}_t]'\right]\right| \\
&\quad = \left|(\hat{\mathcal{K}}')^{-1}(1/T)\sum_{t=1}^{T}\left[[\hat{\boldsymbol{\eta}}_t - \hat{\mathcal{K}}'\boldsymbol{\zeta}_0(\hat{\mathcal{A}}')^{-1}\hat{\boldsymbol{\xi}}_t][\hat{\boldsymbol{\eta}}_t - \hat{\mathcal{K}}'\boldsymbol{\zeta}_0(\hat{\mathcal{A}}')^{-1}\hat{\boldsymbol{\xi}}_t]'\right](\hat{\mathcal{K}})^{-1}\right| \\
&\quad = |(\hat{\mathcal{K}}')^{-1}|\left|(1/T)\sum_{t=1}^{T}\left[[\hat{\boldsymbol{\eta}}_t - \hat{\boldsymbol{\Pi}}\hat{\boldsymbol{\xi}}_t][\hat{\boldsymbol{\eta}}_t - \hat{\boldsymbol{\Pi}}\hat{\boldsymbol{\xi}}_t]'\right]\right||(\hat{\mathcal{K}})^{-1}| \\
&\quad = \left|(1/T)\sum_{t=1}^{T}\left[[\hat{\boldsymbol{\eta}}_t - \hat{\boldsymbol{\Pi}}\hat{\boldsymbol{\xi}}_t][\hat{\boldsymbol{\eta}}_t - \hat{\boldsymbol{\Pi}}\hat{\boldsymbol{\xi}}_t]'\right]\right| \div |\hat{\mathcal{K}}|^2,
\end{aligned}$$

$$[20.2.32]$$

where

$$\hat{\boldsymbol{\Pi}} \equiv \hat{\mathcal{K}}'\boldsymbol{\zeta}_0(\hat{\mathcal{A}}')^{-1}. \qquad [20.2.33]$$

Recall that maximizing the concentrated log likelihood function for the actual data [20.2.21] is equivalent to choosing $\boldsymbol{\zeta}_0$ so as to minimize the expression in [20.2.32] subject to the requirement that $\boldsymbol{\zeta}_0$ can be written as $\mathbf{BA}'$ for some $(n \times h)$ matrices $\mathbf{B}$ and $\mathbf{A}$. But $\boldsymbol{\zeta}_0$ can be written in this form if and only if $\hat{\boldsymbol{\Pi}}$ in [20.2.33] can be written in the form $\boldsymbol{\beta\gamma}'$ for some $(n \times h)$ matrices $\boldsymbol{\beta}$ and $\boldsymbol{\gamma}$. Thus, the task can be described as choosing $\hat{\boldsymbol{\Pi}}$ so as to minimize [20.2.32] subject to this condition. But this is precisely the problem solved in [20.2.28]—the solution is to use as regressors the first $h$ elements of $\hat{\boldsymbol{\xi}}_t$. The value of [20.2.32] at the optimum is given by

$$\prod_{i=1}^{h}(1 - \hat{r}_i^2) \div |\hat{\mathcal{K}}|^2. \qquad [20.2.34]$$

Moreover, the matrix $\hat{\mathcal{K}}$ satisfies

$$\mathbf{I}_n = (1/T)\sum_{t=1}^{T}\hat{\boldsymbol{\eta}}_t\hat{\boldsymbol{\eta}}_t' = (1/T)\sum_{t=1}^{T}\hat{\mathcal{K}}'\hat{\mathbf{u}}_t\hat{\mathbf{u}}_t'\hat{\mathcal{K}} = \hat{\mathcal{K}}'\hat{\boldsymbol{\Sigma}}_{\mathbf{UU}}\hat{\mathcal{K}}. \qquad [20.2.35]$$

Taking determinants of both sides of [20.2.35] establishes

$$1 = |\hat{\mathcal{K}}'|\,|\hat{\Sigma}_{UU}|\,|\hat{\mathcal{K}}|$$

or

$$1/|\hat{\mathcal{K}}|^2 = |\hat{\Sigma}_{UU}|.$$

Substituting this back into [20.2.34], it appears that the optimized value of [20.2.32] is equal to

$$|\hat{\Sigma}_{UU}| \times \prod_{i=1}^{h} (1 - \hat{r}_i^2).$$

Comparing [20.2.32] with [20.2.21], it follows that the maximum value achieved for the log likelihood function is given by

$$\mathcal{L}^* = \mathcal{N}(\hat{\zeta}_0) = -(Tn/2)\log(2\pi) - (Tn/2) - (T/2)\log\left\{|\hat{\Sigma}_{UU}| \times \prod_{i=1}^{h}(1 - \hat{r}_i^2)\right\},$$

as claimed in [20.2.10].

## *Motivation for Maximum Likelihood Estimates of Parameters*

We have seen that the concentrated log likelihood function [20.2.21] is maximized by selecting as regressors the first $h$ elements of $\hat{\boldsymbol{\xi}}_t$. Since $\hat{\boldsymbol{\xi}}_t = \hat{\mathcal{A}}'\hat{\mathbf{v}}_t$, this means using $\hat{\mathbf{A}}'\hat{\mathbf{v}}_t$ as regressors, where the $(n \times h)$ matrix $\hat{\mathbf{A}}$ denotes the first $h$ columns of the $(n \times n)$ matrix $\hat{\mathcal{A}}$. Thus,

$$\boldsymbol{\zeta}_0\hat{\mathbf{v}}_t = -\mathbf{B}\hat{\mathbf{A}}'\hat{\mathbf{v}}_t \qquad [20.2.36]$$

for some $(n \times h)$ matrix $\mathbf{B}$. This verifies the claim that $\hat{\mathbf{A}}$ is the maximum likelihood estimate of a basis for the space of cointegrating vectors.

Given that we want to choose $\hat{\mathbf{w}}_t \equiv \hat{\mathbf{A}}'\hat{\mathbf{v}}_t$ as regressors, the value of $\mathbf{B}$ for which the concentrated likelihood function will be maximized is obtained from *OLS* regressions of $\hat{\mathbf{u}}_t$ on $\hat{\mathbf{w}}_t$:

$$\hat{\mathbf{B}} = -\left[(1/T)\sum_{t=1}^{T}\hat{\mathbf{u}}_t\hat{\mathbf{w}}_t'\right]\left[(1/T)\sum_{t=1}^{T}\hat{\mathbf{w}}_t\hat{\mathbf{w}}_t'\right]^{-1}. \qquad [20.2.37]$$

But $\hat{\mathbf{w}}_t$ is composed of $h$ canonical variates, meaning that

$$\left[(1/T)\sum_{t=1}^{T}\hat{\mathbf{w}}_t\hat{\mathbf{w}}_t'\right] = \mathbf{I}_h. \qquad [20.2.38]$$

Moreover,

$$\left[(1/T)\sum_{t=1}^{T}\hat{\mathbf{u}}_t\hat{\mathbf{w}}_t'\right] = \left[(1/T)\sum_{t=1}^{T}\hat{\mathbf{u}}_t\hat{\mathbf{v}}_t'\hat{\mathbf{A}}\right] = \hat{\Sigma}_{UV}\hat{\mathbf{A}}. \qquad [20.2.39]$$

Substituting [20.2.39] and [20.2.38] into [20.2.37],

$$\hat{\mathbf{B}} = -\hat{\Sigma}_{UV}\hat{\mathbf{A}},$$

and so, from [20.2.2], the maximum likelihood estimate of $\boldsymbol{\zeta}_0$ is given by

$$\hat{\boldsymbol{\zeta}}_0 = \hat{\Sigma}_{UV}\hat{\mathbf{A}}\hat{\mathbf{A}}'$$

as claimed in [20.2.12].

Expressions [20.2.17] and [20.2.18] gave the values of $\boldsymbol{\alpha}$ and $\boldsymbol{\zeta}_i$ that maximized the likelihood function for any given value of $\boldsymbol{\zeta}_0$. Since the likelihood function is maximized with respect to $\boldsymbol{\zeta}_0$ by choosing $\hat{\boldsymbol{\zeta}}_0$ according to [20.2.12], it is maximized with respect to $\boldsymbol{\alpha}$ and $\boldsymbol{\zeta}_i$ by substituting $\hat{\boldsymbol{\zeta}}_0$ into [20.2.17] and [20.2.18], as claimed in [20.2.14] and [20.2.13]. Finally, substituting $\hat{\boldsymbol{\zeta}}_0$ into [20.2.20] verifies [20.2.15].

### *Maximum Likelihood Estimation in the Absence of Deterministic Time Trends*

The preceding analysis assumed that $\boldsymbol{\alpha}$, the $(n \times 1)$ vector of constant terms in the *VAR*, was unrestricted. The value of $\boldsymbol{\alpha}$ contributes $h$ constant terms for the $h$ cointegrating relations, along with $g \equiv n - h$ deterministic time trends that are common to each of the $n$ elements of $\mathbf{y}_t$. In some applications it might be of interest to allow constant terms in the cointegrating relations but to rule out deterministic time trends for any of the variables. We saw in equation [19.1.45] that this would require

$$\boldsymbol{\alpha} = \mathbf{B}\boldsymbol{\mu}_1^*, \qquad [20.2.40]$$

where $\mathbf{B}$ is the $(n \times h)$ matrix appearing in [20.2.2] while $\boldsymbol{\mu}_1^*$ is an $(h \times 1)$ vector corresponding to the unconditional mean of $\mathbf{z}_t = \mathbf{A}'\mathbf{y}_t$. Thus, for this restricted case, we want to estimate only the $h$ elements of $\boldsymbol{\mu}_1^*$ rather than all $n$ elements of $\boldsymbol{\alpha}$.

To maximize the likelihood function subject to the restrictions that there are $h$ cointegrating relations and no deterministic time trends in any of the series, Johansen's (1991) first step was to concentrate out $\boldsymbol{\zeta}_1, \boldsymbol{\zeta}_2, \ldots,$ and $\boldsymbol{\zeta}_{p-1}$ (but not $\boldsymbol{\alpha}$). For given $\boldsymbol{\alpha}$ and $\boldsymbol{\zeta}_0$, this is achieved by *OLS* regression of $(\Delta\mathbf{y}_t - \boldsymbol{\alpha} - \boldsymbol{\zeta}_0\mathbf{y}_{t-1})$ on $(\Delta\mathbf{y}_{t-1}, \Delta\mathbf{y}_{t-2}, \ldots, \Delta\mathbf{y}_{t-p+1})$. The residuals from this regression are related to the residuals from three separate regressions:

(1) A regression of $\Delta\mathbf{y}_t$ on $(\Delta\mathbf{y}_{t-1}, \Delta\mathbf{y}_{t-2}, \ldots, \Delta\mathbf{y}_{t-p+1})$ with no constant term,

$$\Delta\mathbf{y}_t = \tilde{\boldsymbol{\Pi}}_1\Delta\mathbf{y}_{t-1} + \tilde{\boldsymbol{\Pi}}_2\Delta\mathbf{y}_{t-2} + \cdots + \tilde{\boldsymbol{\Pi}}_{p-1}\Delta\mathbf{y}_{t-p+1} + \tilde{\mathbf{u}}_t; \qquad [20.2.41]$$

(2) A regression of a constant term on $(\Delta\mathbf{y}_{t-1}, \Delta\mathbf{y}_{t-2}, \ldots, \Delta\mathbf{y}_{t-p+1})$,

$$1 = \tilde{\boldsymbol{\omega}}_1'\Delta\mathbf{y}_{t-1} + \tilde{\boldsymbol{\omega}}_2'\Delta\mathbf{y}_{t-2} + \cdots + \tilde{\boldsymbol{\omega}}_{p-1}'\Delta\mathbf{y}_{t-p+1} + \tilde{w}_t; \qquad [20.2.42]$$

(3) A regression of $\mathbf{y}_{t-1}$ on $(\Delta\mathbf{y}_{t-1}, \Delta\mathbf{y}_{t-2}, \ldots, \Delta\mathbf{y}_{t-p+1})$ with no constant term,

$$\mathbf{y}_{t-1} = \tilde{\boldsymbol{\aleph}}_1\Delta\mathbf{y}_{t-1} + \tilde{\boldsymbol{\aleph}}_2\Delta\mathbf{y}_{t-2} + \cdots + \tilde{\boldsymbol{\aleph}}_{p-1}\Delta\mathbf{y}_{t-p+1} + \tilde{\mathbf{v}}_t. \qquad [20.2.43]$$

The concentrated log likelihood function is then

$$\begin{aligned}\tilde{\mathcal{M}}(\boldsymbol{\Omega}, \boldsymbol{\alpha}, \boldsymbol{\zeta}_0) &= -(Tn/2)\log(2\pi) - (T/2)\log|\boldsymbol{\Omega}| \\ &\quad - (1/2)\sum_{t=1}^{T}[(\tilde{\mathbf{u}}_t - \boldsymbol{\alpha}\tilde{w}_t - \boldsymbol{\zeta}_0\tilde{\mathbf{v}}_t)'\boldsymbol{\Omega}^{-1}(\tilde{\mathbf{u}}_t - \boldsymbol{\alpha}\tilde{w}_t - \boldsymbol{\zeta}_0\tilde{\mathbf{v}}_t)].\end{aligned}$$

Further concentrating out $\boldsymbol{\Omega}$ results in

$$\begin{aligned}&\tilde{\mathcal{N}}(\boldsymbol{\alpha}, \boldsymbol{\zeta}_0) \\ &\quad = -(Tn/2)\log(2\pi) - (Tn/2) \qquad [20.2.44] \\ &\qquad - (T/2)\log\left|\sum_{t=1}^{T}(1/T)\left\{(\tilde{\mathbf{u}}_t - \boldsymbol{\alpha}\tilde{w}_t - \boldsymbol{\zeta}_0\tilde{\mathbf{v}}_t)(\tilde{\mathbf{u}}_t - \boldsymbol{\alpha}\tilde{w}_t - \boldsymbol{\zeta}_0\tilde{\mathbf{v}}_t)'\right\}\right|.\end{aligned}$$

Imposing the constraints $\boldsymbol{\alpha} = \mathbf{B}\boldsymbol{\mu}_1^*$ and $\boldsymbol{\zeta}_0 = -\mathbf{B}\mathbf{A}'$, the magnitude in [20.2.44] can be written

$$\tilde{\mathcal{N}}(\boldsymbol{\alpha}, \boldsymbol{\zeta}_0) = -(Tn/2)\log(2\pi) - (Tn/2) - (T/2)\log\left|\sum_{t=1}^{T}(1/T)\{(\tilde{\mathbf{u}}_t + \mathbf{B}\tilde{\mathbf{A}}'\tilde{\mathbf{w}}_t)(\tilde{\mathbf{u}}_t + \mathbf{B}\tilde{\mathbf{A}}'\tilde{\mathbf{w}}_t)'\}\right|, \qquad [20.2.45]$$

where

$$\underset{(n+1)\times 1}{\tilde{\mathbf{w}}_t} \equiv \begin{bmatrix} \tilde{w}_t \\ \tilde{\mathbf{v}}_t \end{bmatrix}$$

$$\underset{h\times(n+1)}{\tilde{\mathbf{A}}'} \equiv [-\boldsymbol{\mu}_1^* \quad \mathbf{A}']. \qquad [20.2.46]$$

But setting $\boldsymbol{\zeta}_0 = -\mathbf{B}\mathbf{A}'$ in [20.2.21] produces an expression of exactly the same form as [20.2.45], with $\mathbf{A}$ in [20.2.21] replaced by $\tilde{\mathbf{A}}$ and $\hat{\mathbf{v}}_t$ replaced by $\tilde{\mathbf{w}}_t$. Thus, the restricted log likelihood is maximized simply by replacing $\hat{\mathbf{v}}_t$ in the analysis of [20.2.21] with $\tilde{\mathbf{w}}_t$.

To summarize, construct

$$\tilde{\boldsymbol{\Sigma}}_{\mathbf{WW}} = (1/T)\sum_{t=1}^{T}\tilde{\mathbf{w}}_t\tilde{\mathbf{w}}_t'$$

$$\tilde{\boldsymbol{\Sigma}}_{\mathbf{UU}} = (1/T)\sum_{t=1}^{T}\tilde{\mathbf{u}}_t\tilde{\mathbf{u}}_t'$$

$$\tilde{\boldsymbol{\Sigma}}_{\mathbf{UW}} = (1/T)\sum_{t=1}^{T}\tilde{\mathbf{u}}_t\tilde{\mathbf{w}}_t'$$

and find the eigenvalues of the $(n + 1) \times (n + 1)$ matrix

$$\tilde{\boldsymbol{\Sigma}}_{\mathbf{WW}}^{-1}\tilde{\boldsymbol{\Sigma}}_{\mathbf{WU}}\tilde{\boldsymbol{\Sigma}}_{\mathbf{UU}}^{-1}\tilde{\boldsymbol{\Sigma}}_{\mathbf{UW}}, \qquad [20.2.47]$$

ordered $\tilde{\lambda}_1 > \tilde{\lambda}_2 > \cdots > \tilde{\lambda}_{n+1}$. The maximum value achieved for the log likelihood function subject to the constraint that there are $h$ cointegrating relations and no deterministic time trends is

$$\tilde{\mathcal{L}}_h = -(Tn/2)\log(2\pi) - (Tn/2) - (T/2)\log|\tilde{\boldsymbol{\Sigma}}_{\mathbf{UU}}| - (T/2)\sum_{i=1}^{h}\log(1 - \tilde{\lambda}_i). \qquad [20.2.48]$$

Let $\tilde{\mathbf{a}}_1, \tilde{\mathbf{a}}_2, \ldots, \tilde{\mathbf{a}}_{n+1}$ denote the eigenvectors of [20.2.47] normalized by $\tilde{\mathbf{a}}_i'\tilde{\boldsymbol{\Sigma}}_{\mathbf{WW}}\tilde{\mathbf{a}}_i = 1$. Then the maximum likelihood estimate of $\tilde{\mathbf{A}}$ is given by the matrix $[\tilde{\mathbf{a}}_1 \quad \tilde{\mathbf{a}}_2 \quad \cdots \quad \tilde{\mathbf{a}}_h]$. The maximum likelihood estimate of $\mathbf{B}\tilde{\mathbf{A}}'$ is

$$\tilde{\mathbf{B}}\tilde{\mathbf{A}}' = -\tilde{\boldsymbol{\Sigma}}_{\mathbf{UW}}\tilde{\mathbf{A}}\tilde{\mathbf{A}}'. \qquad [20.2.49]$$

Recall from [20.2.46] that

$$\begin{aligned}\mathbf{B}\tilde{\mathbf{A}}' &= [-\mathbf{B}\boldsymbol{\mu}_1^* \quad \mathbf{B}\mathbf{A}'] \\ &= [-\boldsymbol{\alpha} \quad -\boldsymbol{\zeta}_0].\end{aligned} \qquad [20.2.50]$$

Thus, [20.2.49] implies that the maximum likelihood estimates of $\boldsymbol{\alpha}$ and $\boldsymbol{\zeta}_0$ are given by

$$[\tilde{\boldsymbol{\alpha}} \quad \tilde{\boldsymbol{\zeta}}_0] = \tilde{\boldsymbol{\Sigma}}_{\mathbf{UW}}\tilde{\mathbf{A}}\tilde{\mathbf{A}}'.$$

The *MLE* of $\boldsymbol{\zeta}_i$ is

$$\tilde{\boldsymbol{\zeta}}_i = \tilde{\boldsymbol{\Pi}}_i - \tilde{\boldsymbol{\alpha}}\tilde{\boldsymbol{\omega}}_i' - \tilde{\boldsymbol{\zeta}}_0\tilde{\boldsymbol{\aleph}}_i \qquad \text{for } i = 1, 2, \ldots, p - 1,$$

while the *MLE* of $\mathbf{\Omega}$ is

$$\tilde{\mathbf{\Omega}} = (1/T) \sum_{t=1}^{T} [(\tilde{\mathbf{u}}_t - \tilde{\boldsymbol{\alpha}}\tilde{w}_t - \tilde{\boldsymbol{\zeta}}_0\tilde{\mathbf{v}}_t)(\tilde{\mathbf{u}}_t - \tilde{\boldsymbol{\alpha}}\tilde{w}_t - \tilde{\boldsymbol{\zeta}}_0\tilde{\mathbf{v}}_t)'].$$

## 20.3. *Hypothesis Testing*

We saw in the previous chapter that tests of the null hypothesis of no cointegration typically involve nonstandard asymptotic distributions, while tests about the value of the cointegrating vector under the maintained hypothesis that cointegration is present will have asymptotic $\chi^2$ distributions, provided that suitable allowance is made for the serial correlation in the data. These results generalize to *FIML* analysis. The asymptotic distribution of a test of the number of cointegrating relations is nonstandard, but tests about the cointegrating vector are often $\chi^2$.

### *Testing the Null Hypothesis of* h *Cointegrating Relations*

Suppose that an $(n \times 1)$ vector $\mathbf{y}_t$ can be characterized by a $VAR(p)$ in levels, which we write in the form of [20.2.1]:

$$\Delta\mathbf{y}_t = \boldsymbol{\zeta}_1\Delta\mathbf{y}_{t-1} + \boldsymbol{\zeta}_2\Delta\mathbf{y}_{t-2} + \cdots + \boldsymbol{\zeta}_{p-1}\Delta\mathbf{y}_{t-p+1} + \boldsymbol{\alpha} + \boldsymbol{\zeta}_0\mathbf{y}_{t-1} + \boldsymbol{\varepsilon}_t. \qquad [20.3.1]$$

Under the null hypothesis $H_0$ that there are exactly $h$ cointegrating relations among the elements of $\mathbf{y}_t$, this *VAR* is restricted by the requirement that $\boldsymbol{\zeta}_0$ can be written in the form $\boldsymbol{\zeta}_0 = -\mathbf{BA}'$, for $\mathbf{B}$ an $(n \times h)$ matrix and $\mathbf{A}'$ an $(h \times n)$ matrix. Another way of describing this restriction is that only $h$ linear combinations of the levels of $\mathbf{y}_{t-1}$ can be used in the regressions in [20.3.1]. The largest value that can be achieved for the log likelihood function under this constraint was given by [20.2.10]:

$$\begin{aligned} \mathscr{L}_0^* = &-(Tn/2)\log(2\pi) - (Tn/2) - (T/2)\log|\hat{\mathbf{\Sigma}}_{\mathbf{UU}}| \\ &- (T/2)\sum_{i=1}^{h}\log(1 - \hat{\lambda}_i). \end{aligned} \qquad [20.3.2]$$

Consider the alternative hypothesis $H_A$ that there are $n$ cointegrating relations, where $n$ is the number of elements of $\mathbf{y}_t$. This amounts to the claim that *every* linear combination of $\mathbf{y}_t$ is stationary, in which case $\mathbf{y}_{t-1}$ would appear in [20.3.1] without constraints and no restrictions are imposed on $\boldsymbol{\zeta}_0$. The value for the log likelihood function in the absence of constraints is given by

$$\begin{aligned} \mathscr{L}_A^* = &-(Tn/2)\log(2\pi) - (Tn/2) - (T/2)\log|\hat{\mathbf{\Sigma}}_{\mathbf{UU}}| \\ &- (T/2)\sum_{i=1}^{n}\log(1 - \hat{\lambda}_i). \end{aligned} \qquad [20.3.3]$$

A likelihood ratio test of $H_0$ against $H_A$ can be based on

$$\mathscr{L}_A^* - \mathscr{L}_0^* = -(T/2)\sum_{i=h+1}^{n}\log(1 - \hat{\lambda}_i).$$

If the hypothesis involved just $I(0)$ variables, we would expect twice the log likelihood ratio,

$$2(\mathscr{L}_A^* - \mathscr{L}_0^*) = -T\sum_{i=h+1}^{n}\log(1 - \hat{\lambda}_i), \qquad [20.3.4]$$

to be asymptotically distributed as $\chi^2$. In the case of $H_0$, however, the hypothesis involves the coefficient on $\mathbf{y}_{t-1}$, which, from the Stock-Watson common trends representation, depends on the value of $g \equiv (n - h)$ separate random walks. Let $\mathbf{W}(r)$ be $g$-dimensional standard Brownian motion. Suppose that the true value of the constant term $\boldsymbol{\alpha}$ in [20.3.1] is zero, meaning that there is no intercept in any of the cointegrating relations and no deterministic time trend in any of the elements of $\mathbf{y}_t$. Suppose further that no constant term is included in the auxiliary regressions [20.2.4] and [20.2.5] that were used to construct $\hat{\mathbf{u}}_t$ and $\hat{\mathbf{v}}_t$. Johansen (1988) showed that under these conditions the asymptotic distribution of the statistic in [20.3.4] is the same as that of the trace of the following matrix:

$$\mathbf{Q} \equiv \left[\int_0^1 \mathbf{W}(r)\, d\mathbf{W}(r)'\right]' \left[\int_0^1 \mathbf{W}(r)\mathbf{W}(r)'\, dr\right]^{-1} \left[\int_0^1 \mathbf{W}(r)\, d\mathbf{W}(r)'\right]. \qquad [20.3.5]$$

Percentiles for the trace of the matrix in [20.3.5] are reported in the case 1 portion of Table B.10. These are based on Monte Carlo simulations.

If the number of cointegrating relations ($h$) is 1 less than the number of variables ($n$), then $g = 1$ and [20.3.5] describes the following scalar:

$$Q = \frac{\left\{\int_0^1 W(r)\, dW(r)\right\}^2}{\left\{\int_0^1 [W(r)]^2\, dr\right\}} = \frac{(1/2)^2\left\{[W(1)]^2 - 1\right\}^2}{\left\{\int_0^1 [W(r)]^2\, dr\right\}}, \qquad [20.3.6]$$

where the second equality follows from [18.1.15]. Expression [20.3.6] will be recognized as the square of the statistic [17.4.12] that described the asymptotic distribution of the Dickey-Fuller test based on the *OLS t* statistic. For example, if we are considering an autoregression involving a single variable ($n = 1$), the null hypothesis of no cointegrating relations ($h = 0$) amounts to the claim that $\zeta_0 = 0$ in [20.3.1] or that $\Delta y_t$ follows an $AR(p - 1)$ process. Thus, Johansen's procedure provides an alternative approach to testing for unit roots in univariate series, an idea explored further in Exercise 20.4.

Another approach would be to test the null hypothesis of $h$ cointegrating relations against the alternative of $h + 1$ cointegrating relations. Twice the log likelihood ratio for this case is given by

$$2(\mathcal{L}_A^* - \mathcal{L}_0^*) = -T \log(1 - \hat{\lambda}_{h+1}). \qquad [20.3.7]$$

Again, under the assumption that the true value of $\boldsymbol{\alpha} = \mathbf{0}$ and that no constant term is included in [20.2.4] or [20.2.5], the asymptotic distribution of the statistic in [20.3.7] is the same as that of the largest eigenvalue of the matrix $\mathbf{Q}$ defined in [20.3.5]. Monte Carlo estimates of this distribution are reported in the case 1 section of Table B.11.

Note that if $g = 1$, then $n = h + 1$. In this case the statistics [20.3.4] and [20.3.7] are identical. For this reason, the first row in Table B.10 is the same as the first row of Table B.11.

Typically, the cointegrating relations could include nonzero intercepts, in which case we would want to include constants in the auxiliary regressions [20.2.4] and [20.2.5]. As one might guess from the analysis in Chapter 18, the asymptotic distribution in this case depends on whether or not any of the series exhibit deterministic time trends. Suppose that the true value of $\boldsymbol{\alpha}$ is such that there are no deterministic trends in any of the series, so that the true $\boldsymbol{\alpha}$ satisfies $\boldsymbol{\alpha} = \mathbf{B}\boldsymbol{\mu}_1^*$ as in [20.2.40]. Assuming that no restrictions are imposed on the constant term in the estimation of the auxiliary regressions [20.2.4] and [20.2.5], then the asymptotic distribution of [20.3.4] is given in the case 2 section of Table B.10, while the asymptotic distribution of [20.3.7] is given in the case 2 panel of Table B.11. By contrast, if any of the variables exhibit deterministic time trends (one or more elements of $\boldsymbol{\alpha} - \mathbf{B}\boldsymbol{\mu}_1^*$ are nonzero), then the asymptotic distribution of [20.3.4] is that of the variable in the case 3 section of Table B.10, while the asymptotic distribution of [20.3.7] is given in the case 3 section of Table B.11.

When $g = 1$ and $\boldsymbol{\alpha} \neq \mathbf{B}\boldsymbol{\mu}_1^*$, the single random walk that is common to $\mathbf{y}_t$ is dominated by a deterministic time trend. In this situation, Johansen and Juselius (1990, p. 180) noted that the case 3 analog of [20.3.6] has a $\chi^2(1)$ distribution, for reasons similar to those noted by West (1988) and discussed in Chapter 18. The modest differences between the first row of the case 3 part of Table B.10 or B.11 and the first row of Table B.2 are presumably due to sampling error implicit in the Monte Carlo procedure used to generate the values in Tables B.10 and B.11.

## *Application to Exchange Rate Data*

Consider for illustration the monthly data for Italy and the United States plotted in Figure 19.2. The systems of equations in [20.2.4] and [20.2.5] were estimated by *OLS* for $\mathbf{y}_t = (p_t, s_t, p_t^*)'$, where $p_t$ is 100 times the log of the U.S. price level, $s_t$ is 100 times the log of the dollar-lira exchange rate, and $p_t^*$ is 100 times the log of the Italian price level. The regressions were estimated over $t =$ 1974:2 through 1989:10 (so that the number of observations used for estimation was $T = 189$); $p = 12$ lags were assumed for the *VAR* in levels.

The sample variance-covariance matrices for the residuals $\hat{\mathbf{u}}_t$ and $\hat{\mathbf{v}}_t$ were calculated from [20.2.6] through [20.2.8] to be

$$\hat{\boldsymbol{\Sigma}}_{\mathbf{UU}} = \begin{bmatrix} 0.0435114 & -0.0316283 & 0.0154297 \\ -0.0316283 & 4.68650 & 0.0319877 \\ 0.0154297 & 0.0319877 & 0.179927 \end{bmatrix}$$

$$\hat{\boldsymbol{\Sigma}}_{\mathbf{VV}} = \begin{bmatrix} 427.366 & -370.699 & 805.812 \\ -370.699 & 424.083 & -709.036 \\ 805.812 & -709.036 & 1525.45 \end{bmatrix}$$

$$\hat{\boldsymbol{\Sigma}}_{\mathbf{UV}} = \begin{bmatrix} -0.484857 & 0.498758 & -0.837701 \\ -1.81401 & -2.95927 & -2.46896 \\ -1.80836 & 1.46897 & -3.58991 \end{bmatrix}.$$

The eigenvalues of the matrix in [20.2.9] are then[4]

$$\hat{\lambda}_1 = 0.1105$$
$$\hat{\lambda}_2 = 0.05603$$
$$\hat{\lambda}_3 = 0.03039$$

with

$$T\log(1 - \hat{\lambda}_1) = -22.12$$
$$T\log(1 - \hat{\lambda}_2) = -10.90$$
$$T\log(1 - \hat{\lambda}_3) = -5.83.$$

[4]Calculations were based on more significant digits than reported, and so the reader may find slight discrepancies in trying to reproduce these results from the figures reported.

The likelihood ratio test of the null hypothesis of $h = 0$ cointegrating relations against the alternative of $h = 3$ cointegrating relations is then calculated from [20.3.4] to be

$$2(\mathcal{L}_A^* - \mathcal{L}_0^*) = 22.12 + 10.90 + 5.83 = 38.85. \qquad [20.3.8]$$

Here the number of unit roots under the null hypothesis is $g = n - h = 3$. Given the evidence of deterministic time trends, the magnitude in [20.3.8] is to be compared with the case 3 section of Table B.10. Since $38.85 > 29.5$, the null hypothesis of no cointegration is rejected at the 5% level. Similarly, the likelihood ratio test [20.3.7] of the null hypothesis of no cointegrating relations ($h = 0$) against the alternative of a single cointegrating relation ($h = 1$) is given by 22.12. Comparing this with the case 3 section of Table B.11, we see that $22.12 > 20.8$, so that the null hypothesis of no cointegration is also rejected by this test.

This differs from the conclusion of the Phillips-Ouliaris test for no cointegration between these series, on the basis of which the null hypothesis of no cointegration for these variables was found to be accepted in Chapter 19.

Searching for evidence of a possible second cointegrating relation, consider the likelihood ratio test of the null hypothesis of $h = 1$ cointegrating relation against the alternative of $h = 3$ cointegrating relations:

$$2(\mathcal{L}_A^* - \mathcal{L}_0^*) = 10.90 + 5.83 = 16.73.$$

For this test, $g = 2$. Since $16.73 > 15.2$, the null hypothesis of a single cointegrating relation is rejected at the 5% level. The likelihood ratio test of the null hypothesis of $h = 1$ cointegrating relation against the alternative of $h = 2$ relations is $10.90 < 14.0$; hence, the two tests offer conflicting evidence as to the presence of a second cointegrating relation.

The eigenvector $\hat{\mathbf{a}}_1$ of the matrix in [20.2.9] associated with $\hat{\lambda}_1$, normalized so that $\hat{\mathbf{a}}_1'\hat{\Sigma}_{VV}\hat{\mathbf{a}}_1 = 1$, is given by

$$\hat{\mathbf{a}}_1' = [-0.7579 \quad 0.02801 \quad 0.4220]. \qquad [20.3.9]$$

It is natural to renormalize this by taking the first element to be unity:

$$\tilde{\mathbf{a}}_1' = [1.00 \quad -0.04 \quad -0.56].$$

This is virtually identical to the estimate of the cointegrating vector based on *OLS* from [19.2.49].

## *Likelihood Ratio Tests About the Cointegrating Vector*

Consider a system of $n$ variables that is assumed (under both the null and the alternative) to be characterized by $h$ cointegrating relations. We might then want to test a restriction on these cointegrating vectors, such as that only $q$ of the variables are involved in the cointegrating relations. For example, we might be interested in whether the middle coefficient in [20.3.9] is zero, that is, in whether the cointegrating relation involves solely the U.S. and Italian price levels. For this example $h = 1$, $q = 2$, and $n = 3$. In general it must be the case that $h \leq q \leq n$. Since $h$ linear combinations of the $q$ variables included in the cointegrating relations are stationary, if $q = h$, then all $q$ of the included variables would have to be stationary in levels. If $q = n$, then the null hypothesis places no restrictions on the cointegrating relations.

Consider the general restriction that there is a known $(q \times n)$ matrix $\mathbf{D}'$ such that the cointegrating relations involve only $\mathbf{D}'\mathbf{y}_t$. For the preceding example,

$$\mathbf{D}' = \begin{bmatrix} 1 & 0 & 0 \\ 0 & 0 & 1 \end{bmatrix}. \qquad [20.3.10]$$

Hence, the error-correction term in [20.3.1] will take the form

$$\boldsymbol{\zeta}_0 \mathbf{y}_{t-1} = -\mathbf{B}\mathbf{A}'\mathbf{D}'\mathbf{y}_{t-1},$$

where $\mathbf{B}$ is now an $(n \times h)$ matrix and $\mathbf{A}'$ is an $(h \times q)$ matrix. Maximum likelihood estimation proceeds exactly as in the previous section, where $\hat{\mathbf{v}}_t$ in [20.2.5] is replaced by the *OLS* residuals from regressions of $\mathbf{D}'\mathbf{y}_{t-1}$ on a constant and $\Delta\mathbf{y}_{t-1}$, $\Delta\mathbf{y}_{t-2}, \ldots, \Delta\mathbf{y}_{t-p+1}$. This is equivalent to replacing $\hat{\mathbf{\Sigma}}_{\mathbf{VV}}$ in [20.2.6] and $\hat{\mathbf{\Sigma}}_{\mathbf{UV}}$ in [20.2.8] with

$$\tilde{\mathbf{\Sigma}}_{\mathbf{VV}} \equiv \mathbf{D}'\hat{\mathbf{\Sigma}}_{\mathbf{VV}}\mathbf{D} \qquad [20.3.11]$$

$$\tilde{\mathbf{\Sigma}}_{\mathbf{UV}} \equiv \hat{\mathbf{\Sigma}}_{\mathbf{UV}}\mathbf{D}. \qquad [20.3.12]$$

Let $\tilde{\lambda}_i$ denote the $i$th largest eigenvalue of

$$\tilde{\mathbf{\Sigma}}_{\mathbf{VV}}^{-1}\tilde{\mathbf{\Sigma}}_{\mathbf{VU}}\hat{\mathbf{\Sigma}}_{\mathbf{UU}}^{-1}\tilde{\mathbf{\Sigma}}_{\mathbf{UV}}. \qquad [20.3.13]$$

The maximized value for the restricted log likelihood is then

$$\mathscr{L}_0^* = -(Tn/2)\log(2\pi) - (Tn/2) - (T/2)\log|\hat{\mathbf{\Sigma}}_{\mathbf{UU}}| - (T/2)\sum_{i=1}^{h}\log(1 - \tilde{\lambda}_i).$$

A likelihood ratio test of the null hypothesis that the $h$ cointegrating relations only involve $\mathbf{D}'\mathbf{y}_t$ against the alternative hypothesis that the $h$ cointegrating relations could involve any elements of $\mathbf{y}_t$ would then be

$$2(\mathscr{L}_A^* - \mathscr{L}_0^*) = -T\sum_{i=1}^{h}\log(1 - \hat{\lambda}_i) + T\sum_{i=1}^{h}\log(1 - \tilde{\lambda}_i). \qquad [20.3.14]$$

In this case, the null hypothesis involves only coefficients on $I(0)$ variables (the error-correction terms $\mathbf{z}_t = \mathbf{A}'\mathbf{y}_t$), and standard asymptotic distribution theory turns out to apply. Johansen (1988, 1991) showed that the likelihood ratio statistic [20.3.14] has an asymptotic $\chi^2$ distribution with $h\cdot(n - q)$ degrees of freedom.

For illustration, consider the restriction represented by [20.3.10] that the exchange rate has a coefficient of zero in the cointegrating vector [20.3.9]. From [20.3.11] and [20.3.12], we calculate

$$\tilde{\mathbf{\Sigma}}_{\mathbf{VV}} = \begin{bmatrix} 427.366 & 805.812 \\ 805.812 & 1525.45 \end{bmatrix}$$

$$\tilde{\mathbf{\Sigma}}_{\mathbf{UV}} = \begin{bmatrix} -0.484857 & -0.837701 \\ -1.81401 & -2.46896 \\ -1.80836 & -3.58991 \end{bmatrix}.$$

The eigenvalues for the matrix in [20.3.13] are then

$$\tilde{\lambda}_1 = 0.1059 \qquad \tilde{\lambda}_2 = 0.04681,$$

with

$$T\log(1 - \tilde{\lambda}_1) = -21.15 \qquad T\log(1 - \tilde{\lambda}_2) = -9.06.$$

The likelihood ratio statistic [20.3.14] is

$$2(\mathcal{L}_A^* - \mathcal{L}_0^*) = 22.12 - 21.15$$
$$= 0.97.$$

The degrees of freedom for this statistic are

$$h \cdot (n - q) = 1 \cdot (3 - 2) = 1;$$

the null hypothesis imposes a single restriction on the cointegrating vector. The 5% critical value for a $\chi^2(1)$ variable is seen from Table B.2 to be 3.84. Since $0.97 < 3.84$, the null hypothesis that the exchange rate does not appear in the cointegrating relation is accepted. The restricted cointegrating vector (normalized with the coefficient on the U.S. price level to be unity) is

$$\tilde{\mathbf{a}}_1' = [1.00 \quad 0.00 \quad -0.54].$$

As a second example, consider the hypothesis that originally suggested interest in a possible cointegrating relation between these three variables. This was the hypothesis that the real exchange rate is stationary, or that the cointegrating vector is proportional to $(1, -1, -1)'$. For this hypothesis, $\mathbf{D}' = (1, -1, -1)$ and

$$\tilde{\Sigma}_{VV} = 88.5977$$

$$\tilde{\boldsymbol{\Sigma}}_{UV} = \begin{bmatrix} -0.145914 \\ 3.61422 \\ 0.312582 \end{bmatrix}.$$

In this case, the matrix [20.3.13] is the scalar 0.0424498, and so $\tilde{\lambda}_1 = 0.0424498$ and $T \log(1 - \tilde{\lambda}_1) = -8.20$. Thus, the likelihood ratio test of the null hypothesis that the cointegrating vector is proportional to $(1, -1, -1)'$ is

$$2(\mathcal{L}_A^* - \mathcal{L}_0^*) = 22.12 - 8.20$$
$$= 13.92.$$

In this case, the degrees of freedom are

$$h \cdot (n - q) = 1 \cdot (3 - 1) = 2.$$

The 5% critical value for a $\chi^2(2)$ variable is 5.99. Since $13.92 > 5.99$, the null hypothesis that the cointegrating vector is proportional to $(1, -1, -1)'$ is rejected.

## *Other Hypothesis Tests*

A number of other hypotheses can be tested in this framework. For example, Johansen (1991) showed that the null hypothesis that there are no deterministic time trends in any of the series can be tested by taking twice the difference between [20.2.10] and [20.2.48]. Under the null hypothesis, this likelihood ratio statistic is asymptotically $\chi^2$ with $g = n - h$ degrees of freedom. Johansen also discussed construction of Wald-type tests of hypotheses involving the cointegrating vectors.

Not all hypothesis tests about the coefficients in Johansen's framework are asymptotically $\chi^2$. Consider an error-correction *VAR* of the form of [20.2.1] where $\boldsymbol{\zeta}_0 = -\mathbf{BA}'$. Suppose we are interested in the null hypothesis that the last $n_3$ elements of $\mathbf{y}_t$ fail to Granger-cause the first $n_1$ elements of $\mathbf{y}_t$. Toda and Phillips (forthcoming) showed that a Wald test of this null hypothesis can have a nonstandard distribution. See Mosconi and Giannini (1992) for further discussion.

### *Comparison Between* FIML *and Other Approaches*

Johansen's *FIML* estimation represents the short-run dynamics of a system in terms of a vector autoregression in differences with the error-correction vector $\mathbf{z}_{t-1}$ added. Short-run dynamics can also be modeled with what are sometimes called nonparametric methods, such as the Bartlett window used to construct the fully modified Phillips-Hansen (1990) estimator in equation [19.3.53]. Related nonparametric estimators have been proposed by Phillips (1990, 1991a), Park (1992), and Park and Ogaki (1991). Park (1990) established the asymptotic equivalence of the parametric and nonparametric approaches, and Phillips (1991a) discussed the sense in which any *FIML* estimator is asymptotically efficient. Johansen (1992) provided a further discussion of the relation between limited-information and full-information estimation strategies.

In practice, the parametric and nonparametric approaches differ not just in their treatment of short-run dynamics but also in the normalizations employed. The fact that Johansen's method seeks to estimate the *space* of cointegrating relations rather than a particular set of coefficients can be both an asset and a liability. It is an asset if the researcher has no prior information about which variables appear in the cointegrating relations and is concerned about inadvertently normalizing $a_{11} = 1$ when the true value of $a_{11} = 0$. On the other hand, Phillips (1991b) has stressed that if the researcher wants to make structural interpretations of the separate cointegrating relations, this logically requires imposing further restrictions on the matrix $\mathbf{A}'$.

For example, let $r_t$ denote the nominal interest rate on 3-month corporate debt, $i_t$ the nominal interest rate on 3-month government debt, and $\pi_t$ the 3-month inflation rate. Suppose that these three variables appear to be $I(1)$ and exhibit two cointegrating relations. A natural view is that these cointegrating relations represent two stabilizing relations. The first reflects forces that keep the risk premium stationary, so that

$$r_t = \mu_{11}^* + \gamma_1 i_t + z_{1t}^*, \qquad [20.3.15]$$

with $z_{1t}^* \sim I(0)$. A second force is the Fisher effect, which tends to keep the real interest rate stationary:

$$\pi_t = \mu_{21}^* + \gamma_2 i_t + z_{2t}^*, \qquad [20.3.16]$$

with $z_{2t}^* \sim I(0)$. The system of [20.3.15] and [20.3.16] will be recognized as an example of Phillips's (1991a) triangular representation [19.1.20] for the vector $\mathbf{y}_t = (r_t, \pi_t, i_t)'$. Thus, in this example theoretical considerations suggest a natural ordering of variables for which the normalization used by Phillips would be of particular interest for structural inference—the coefficients $\mu_{11}^*$ and $\gamma_1$ tell us about the risk premium, and the coefficients $\mu_{21}^*$ and $\gamma_2$ tell us about the Fisher effect.

## 20.4. *Overview of Unit Roots—To Difference or Not to Difference?*

The preceding chapters have explored a number of issues in the statistical analysis of unit roots. This section attempts to summarize what all this means in practice.

Consider a vector of variables $\mathbf{y}_t$ whose dynamics we would like to describe and some of whose elements may be nonstationary. For concreteness, let us assume that the goal is to characterize these dynamics in terms of a vector autoregression.

One option is to ignore the nonstationarity altogether and simply estimate the *VAR* in levels, relying on standard $t$ and $F$ distributions for testing any hypotheses. This strategy has the following features to recommend it. (1) The parameters that describe the system's dynamics are estimated consistently. (2) Even if the true model is a *VAR* in differences, certain functions of the parameters and hypothesis tests based on a *VAR* in levels have the same asymptotic distribution as would estimates based on differenced data. (3) A Bayesian motivation can be given for the usual $t$ or $F$ distributions for test statistics even when the classical asymptotic theory for these statistics is nonstandard.

A second option is routinely to difference any apparently nonstationary variables before estimating the *VAR*. If the true process is a *VAR* in differences, then differencing should improve the small-sample performance of all of the estimates and eliminate altogether the nonstandad asymptotic distributions associated with certain hypothesis tests. The drawback to this approach is that the true process may not be a *VAR* in differences. Some of the series may in fact have been stationary, or perhaps some linear combinations of the series are stationary, as in a cointegrated *VAR*. In such circumstances a *VAR* in differenced form is misspecified.

Yet a third approach is to investigate carefully the nature of the nonstationarity, testing each series individually for unit roots and then testing for possible cointegration among the series. Once the nature of the nonstationarity is understood, a stationary representation for the system can be estimated. For example, suppose that in a four-variable system we determine that the first variable $y_{1t}$ is stationary while the other variables ($y_{2t}$, $y_{3t}$, and $y_{4t}$) are each individually $I(1)$. Suppose we further conclude that $y_{2t}$, $y_{3t}$, and $y_{4t}$ are characterized by a single cointegrating relation. For $\mathbf{y}_{2t} \equiv (y_{2t}, y_{3t}, y_{4t})'$, this implies a vector error-correction representation of the form

$$\begin{bmatrix} y_{1t} \\ \Delta\mathbf{y}_{2t} \end{bmatrix} = \begin{bmatrix} \alpha_1 \\ \boldsymbol{\alpha}_2 \end{bmatrix} + \begin{bmatrix} \zeta_{11}^{(1)} & \zeta_{12}^{(1)} \\ \zeta_{21}^{(1)} & \zeta_{22}^{(1)} \end{bmatrix} \begin{bmatrix} y_{1,t-1} \\ \Delta\mathbf{y}_{2,t-1} \end{bmatrix} + \begin{bmatrix} \zeta_{11}^{(2)} & \zeta_{12}^{(2)} \\ \zeta_{21}^{(2)} & \zeta_{22}^{(2)} \end{bmatrix} \begin{bmatrix} y_{1,t-2} \\ \Delta\mathbf{y}_{2,t-2} \end{bmatrix} + \cdots$$
$$+ \begin{bmatrix} \zeta_{11}^{(p-1)} & \zeta_{12}^{(p-1)} \\ \zeta_{21}^{(p-1)} & \zeta_{22}^{(p-1)} \end{bmatrix} \begin{bmatrix} y_{1,t-p+1} \\ \Delta\mathbf{y}_{2,t-p+1} \end{bmatrix} + \begin{bmatrix} \zeta_1^{(0)} \\ \boldsymbol{\zeta}_2^{(0)} \end{bmatrix} \mathbf{y}_{2,t-1} + \begin{bmatrix} \varepsilon_{1t} \\ \boldsymbol{\varepsilon}_{2t} \end{bmatrix},$$

where the $(4 \times 3)$ matrix $\begin{bmatrix} \zeta_1^{(0)} \\ \boldsymbol{\zeta}_2^{(0)} \end{bmatrix}$ is restricted to be of the form $\mathbf{ba}'$ where $\mathbf{b}$ is $(4 \times 1)$ and $\mathbf{a}'$ is $(1 \times 3)$. Such a system can then be estimated by adapting the methods described in Section 20.2, and most hypothesis tests on this system should be asymptotically $\chi^2$.

The disadvantage of the third approach is that, despite the care one exercises, the restrictions imposed may still be invalid—the investigator may have accepted a null hypothesis even though it is false, or rejected a null hypothesis that is actually true. Moreover, alternative tests for unit roots and cointegration can produce conflicting results, and the investigator may be unsure as to which should be followed.

Experts differ in the advice offered for applied work. One practical solution is to employ parts of all three approaches. This eclectic strategy would begin by estimating the *VAR* in levels without restrictions. The next step is to make a quick assessment as to which series are likely nonstationary. This assessment could be based on graphs of the data, prior information about the series and their likely cointegrating relations, or any of the more formal tests discussed in Chapter 17. Any nonstationary series can then be differenced or expressed in error-correction form and a stationary *VAR* could then be estimated. For example, to estimate a *VAR* that includes the log of income ($y_t$) and the log of consumption ($c_t$), these two variables might be included in a stationary *VAR* as $\Delta y_t$ and $(c_t - y_t)$. If the *VAR* for the data in levels form yields similar inferences to those for the *VAR* in stationary form, then the researcher might be satisfied that the results were not governed by the assumptions made about unit roots. If the answers differ, then some attempt to reconcile the results should be made. Careful efforts along the lines of the third strategy described in this section might convince the investigator that the stationary formulation was misspecified, or alternatively that the levels results can be explained by the appropriate asymptotic theory. A nice example of how asymptotic theory could be used to reconcile conflicting findings was provided by Stock and Watson (1989). Alternatively, Christiano and Ljungqvist (1988) proposed simulating data from the estimated levels model, and seeing whether incorrectly fitting such simulated data with the stationary specification would spuriously produce the results found when the stationary specification was fitted to the actual data. Similarly, data could be simulated from the stationary model to see if it could account for the finding of the levels specification. If we find that a single specification can account for both the levels and the stationary results, then our confidence in that specification increases.

## APPENDIX 20.A. *Proof of Chapter 20 Proposition*

■ **Proof of Proposition 20.1.**

(a) First we show that $\lambda_i < 1$ for $i = 1, 2, \ldots, n_1$. Any eigenvalue $\lambda$ of [20.1.8] satisfies

$$|\boldsymbol{\Sigma}_{\mathbf{YY}}^{-1}\boldsymbol{\Sigma}_{\mathbf{YX}}\boldsymbol{\Sigma}_{\mathbf{XX}}^{-1}\boldsymbol{\Sigma}_{\mathbf{XY}} - \lambda\mathbf{I}_{n_1}| = 0.$$

Since $\boldsymbol{\Sigma}_{\mathbf{YY}}$ is positive definite, this will be true if and only if

$$|\lambda\boldsymbol{\Sigma}_{\mathbf{YY}} - \boldsymbol{\Sigma}_{\mathbf{YX}}\boldsymbol{\Sigma}_{\mathbf{XX}}^{-1}\boldsymbol{\Sigma}_{\mathbf{XY}}| = 0. \qquad [20.A.1]$$

But from the triangular factorization of $\boldsymbol{\Sigma}$ in equation [4.5.26], the matrix

$$\boldsymbol{\Sigma}_{\mathbf{YY}} - \boldsymbol{\Sigma}_{\mathbf{YX}}\boldsymbol{\Sigma}_{\mathbf{XX}}^{-1}\boldsymbol{\Sigma}_{\mathbf{XY}} \qquad [20.A.2]$$

is positive definite. Hence, the determinant in [20.A.1] could not be zero at $\lambda = 1$. Note further that

$$\lambda\boldsymbol{\Sigma}_{\mathbf{YY}} - \boldsymbol{\Sigma}_{\mathbf{YX}}\boldsymbol{\Sigma}_{\mathbf{XX}}^{-1}\boldsymbol{\Sigma}_{\mathbf{XY}} = (\lambda - 1)\boldsymbol{\Sigma}_{\mathbf{YY}} + [\boldsymbol{\Sigma}_{\mathbf{YY}} - \boldsymbol{\Sigma}_{\mathbf{YX}}\boldsymbol{\Sigma}_{\mathbf{XX}}^{-1}\boldsymbol{\Sigma}_{\mathbf{XY}}]. \qquad [20.A.3]$$

If $\lambda > 1$, then the right side of expression [20.A.3] would be the sum of two positive definite matrices and so would be positive definite. The left side of [20.A.3] would then be positive definite, implying that the determinant in [20.A.1] could not be zero for $\lambda > 1$. Hence, $\lambda \geq 1$ is not consistent with [20.A.1].

To see that $\lambda_i \geq 0$, notice that if $\lambda$ were less than zero, then $\lambda\boldsymbol{\Sigma}_{\mathbf{YY}}$ would be a negative number times a positive definite matrix so that $\lambda\boldsymbol{\Sigma}_{\mathbf{YY}} - \boldsymbol{\Sigma}_{\mathbf{YX}}\boldsymbol{\Sigma}_{\mathbf{XX}}^{-1}\boldsymbol{\Sigma}_{\mathbf{XY}}$ would also be a negative number times a positive definite matrix. Hence, the determinant in [20.A.1] could not be zero for any value of $\lambda < 0$.

Parallel arguments establish that $0 \leq \mu_j < 1$ for $j = 1, 2, \ldots, n_2$.

(b) Let $\mathbf{k}_i$ be an eigenvector associated with a nonzero eigenvalue $\lambda_i$ of [20.1.8]:

$$\boldsymbol{\Sigma}_{\mathbf{YY}}^{-1}\boldsymbol{\Sigma}_{\mathbf{YX}}\boldsymbol{\Sigma}_{\mathbf{XX}}^{-1}\boldsymbol{\Sigma}_{\mathbf{XY}}\mathbf{k}_i = \lambda_i\mathbf{k}_i. \qquad [20.A.4]$$

Premultiplying both sides of [20.A.4] by $\boldsymbol{\Sigma}_{\mathbf{XY}}$ results in

$$[\boldsymbol{\Sigma}_{\mathbf{XY}}\boldsymbol{\Sigma}_{\mathbf{YY}}^{-1}\boldsymbol{\Sigma}_{\mathbf{YX}}\boldsymbol{\Sigma}_{\mathbf{XX}}^{-1}][\boldsymbol{\Sigma}_{\mathbf{XY}}\mathbf{k}_i] = \lambda_i[\boldsymbol{\Sigma}_{\mathbf{XY}}\mathbf{k}_i]. \qquad [20.A.5]$$

But $[\boldsymbol{\Sigma}_{\mathbf{XY}}\mathbf{k}_i]$ cannot be zero, for if $[\boldsymbol{\Sigma}_{\mathbf{XY}}\mathbf{k}_i]$ did equal zero, then the left side of [20.A.4] would be zero, implying that $\lambda_i = 0$. Thus, [20.A.5] implies that $\lambda_i$ is also an eigenvalue of the matrix $[\boldsymbol{\Sigma}_{\mathbf{XY}}\boldsymbol{\Sigma}_{\mathbf{YY}}^{-1}\boldsymbol{\Sigma}_{\mathbf{YX}}\boldsymbol{\Sigma}_{\mathbf{XX}}^{-1}]$ associated with the eigenvector $[\boldsymbol{\Sigma}_{\mathbf{XY}}\mathbf{k}_i]$. Recall further that eigenvalues are unchanged by transposition of a matrix:

$$[\boldsymbol{\Sigma}_{\mathbf{XY}}\boldsymbol{\Sigma}_{\mathbf{YY}}^{-1}\boldsymbol{\Sigma}_{\mathbf{YX}}\boldsymbol{\Sigma}_{\mathbf{XX}}^{-1}]' = \boldsymbol{\Sigma}_{\mathbf{XX}}^{-1}\boldsymbol{\Sigma}_{\mathbf{XY}}\boldsymbol{\Sigma}_{\mathbf{YY}}^{-1}\boldsymbol{\Sigma}_{\mathbf{YX}},$$

which is the matrix [20.1.12]. This proves that if $\lambda_i$ is a nonzero eigenvalue of [20.1.8], then it is also an eigenvalue of [20.1.12]. Exactly parallel calculations show that if $\mu_i$ is a nonzero eigenvalue of [20.1.12], then it is also an eigenvalue of [20.1.8].

(c) Premultiply [20.1.10] by $\mathbf{k}_j'\mathbf{\Sigma}_{\mathbf{YY}}$:

$$\mathbf{k}_j'\mathbf{\Sigma}_{\mathbf{YX}}\mathbf{\Sigma}_{\mathbf{XX}}^{-1}\mathbf{\Sigma}_{\mathbf{XY}}\mathbf{k}_i = \lambda_i\mathbf{k}_j'\mathbf{\Sigma}_{\mathbf{YY}}\mathbf{k}_i. \qquad [20.A.6]$$

Similarly, replace $i$ with $j$ in [20.1.10]:

$$\mathbf{\Sigma}_{\mathbf{YY}}^{-1}\mathbf{\Sigma}_{\mathbf{YX}}\mathbf{\Sigma}_{\mathbf{XX}}^{-1}\mathbf{\Sigma}_{\mathbf{XY}}\mathbf{k}_j = \lambda_j\mathbf{k}_j, \qquad [20.A.7]$$

and premultiply by $\mathbf{k}_i'\mathbf{\Sigma}_{\mathbf{YY}}$;

$$\mathbf{k}_i'\mathbf{\Sigma}_{\mathbf{YX}}\mathbf{\Sigma}_{\mathbf{XX}}^{-1}\mathbf{\Sigma}_{\mathbf{XY}}\mathbf{k}_j = \lambda_j\mathbf{k}_i'\mathbf{\Sigma}_{\mathbf{YY}}\mathbf{k}_j. \qquad [20.A.8]$$

Subtracting [20.A.8] from [20.A.6], we see that

$$0 = (\lambda_i - \lambda_j)\mathbf{k}_j'\mathbf{\Sigma}_{\mathbf{YY}}\mathbf{k}_i. \qquad [20.A.9]$$

If $i \neq j$, then $\lambda_i \neq \lambda_j$ and [20.A.9] establishes that $\mathbf{k}_j'\mathbf{\Sigma}_{\mathbf{YY}}\mathbf{k}_i = 0$ for $i \neq j$. For $i = j$, we normalized $\mathbf{k}_i'\mathbf{\Sigma}_{\mathbf{YY}}\mathbf{k}_i = 1$ in [20.1.11]. Thus we have established condition [20.1.3] for the case of distinct eigenvalues.

Virtually identical calculations show that [20.1.13] and [20.1.14] imply [20.1.4].

(d) Transpose [20.1.13] and postmultiply by $\mathbf{\Sigma}_{\mathbf{XY}}\mathbf{k}_j$:

$$\mathbf{a}_i'\mathbf{\Sigma}_{\mathbf{XY}}\mathbf{\Sigma}_{\mathbf{YY}}^{-1}\mathbf{\Sigma}_{\mathbf{YX}}\mathbf{\Sigma}_{\mathbf{XX}}^{-1}\mathbf{\Sigma}_{\mathbf{XY}}\mathbf{k}_j = \lambda_i\mathbf{a}_i'\mathbf{\Sigma}_{\mathbf{XY}}\mathbf{k}_j. \qquad [20.A.10]$$

Similarly, premultiply [20.A.7] by $\mathbf{a}_i'\mathbf{\Sigma}_{\mathbf{XY}}$:

$$\mathbf{a}_i'\mathbf{\Sigma}_{\mathbf{XY}}\mathbf{\Sigma}_{\mathbf{YY}}^{-1}\mathbf{\Sigma}_{\mathbf{YX}}\mathbf{\Sigma}_{\mathbf{XX}}^{-1}\mathbf{\Sigma}_{\mathbf{XY}}\mathbf{k}_j = \lambda_j\mathbf{a}_i'\mathbf{\Sigma}_{\mathbf{XY}}\mathbf{k}_j. \qquad [20.A.11]$$

Subtracting [20.A.11] from [20.A.10] results in

$$0 = (\lambda_i - \lambda_j)\mathbf{a}_i'\mathbf{\Sigma}_{\mathbf{XY}}\mathbf{k}_j.$$

This shows that $\mathbf{a}_i'\mathbf{\Sigma}_{\mathbf{XY}}\mathbf{k}_j = 0$ for $\lambda_i \neq \lambda_j$, as required by [20.1.5].

To find the value of $\mathbf{a}_i'\mathbf{\Sigma}_{\mathbf{XY}}\mathbf{k}_j$ for $i = j$, premultiply [20.1.13] by $\mathbf{a}_i'\mathbf{\Sigma}_{\mathbf{XX}}$, making use of [20.1.14]:

$$\mathbf{a}_i'\mathbf{\Sigma}_{\mathbf{XY}}\mathbf{\Sigma}_{\mathbf{YY}}^{-1}\mathbf{\Sigma}_{\mathbf{YX}}\mathbf{a}_i = \lambda_i. \qquad [20.A.12]$$

Let us suppose for illustration that $n_1$ is the smaller of $n_1$ and $n_2$; that is, $n = n_1$.[5] Then the matrix of eigenvectors $\mathcal{K}$ is $(n \times n)$ and nonsingular. In this case, [20.1.3] implies that

$$\mathbf{\Sigma}_{\mathbf{YY}} = [\mathcal{K}']^{-1}\mathcal{K}^{-1},$$

or, taking inverses,

$$\mathbf{\Sigma}_{\mathbf{YY}}^{-1} = \mathcal{K}\mathcal{K}'. \qquad [20.A.13]$$

Substituting [20.A.13] into [20.A.12], we find that

$$\mathbf{a}_i'\mathbf{\Sigma}_{\mathbf{XY}}\mathcal{K}\mathcal{K}'\mathbf{\Sigma}_{\mathbf{YX}}\mathbf{a}_i = \lambda_i. \qquad [20.A.14]$$

Now,

$$\begin{aligned}\mathbf{a}_i'\mathbf{\Sigma}_{\mathbf{XY}}\mathcal{K} &= \mathbf{a}_i'\mathbf{\Sigma}_{\mathbf{XY}}[\mathbf{k}_1 \quad \mathbf{k}_2 \quad \cdots \quad \mathbf{k}_n] \\ &= [\mathbf{a}_i'\mathbf{\Sigma}_{\mathbf{XY}}\mathbf{k}_1 \quad \mathbf{a}_i'\mathbf{\Sigma}_{\mathbf{XY}}\mathbf{k}_2 \quad \cdots \quad \mathbf{a}_i'\mathbf{\Sigma}_{\mathbf{XY}}\mathbf{k}_i \quad \cdots \quad \mathbf{a}_i'\mathbf{\Sigma}_{\mathbf{XY}}\mathbf{k}_n] \\ &= [0 \quad 0 \quad \cdots \quad \mathbf{a}_i'\mathbf{\Sigma}_{\mathbf{XY}}\mathbf{k}_i \quad \cdots \quad 0].\end{aligned} \qquad [20.A.15]$$

Substituting [20.A.15] into [20.A.14], it follows that

$$(\mathbf{a}_i'\mathbf{\Sigma}_{\mathbf{XY}}\mathbf{k}_i)^2 = \lambda_i.$$

Thus, the $i$th canonical correlation,

$$r_i \equiv \mathbf{a}_i'\mathbf{\Sigma}_{\mathbf{XY}}\mathbf{k}_i,$$

is given by the square root of the eigenvalue $\lambda_i$, as claimed:

$$r_i^2 = \lambda_i. \quad \blacksquare$$

[5] In the converse case when $n = n_2$, a parallel argument can be constructed using the fact that

$$\mathbf{k}_i'\mathbf{\Sigma}_{\mathbf{YX}}\mathbf{\Sigma}_{\mathbf{XX}}^{-1}\mathbf{\Sigma}_{\mathbf{XY}}\mathbf{k}_i = \lambda_i.$$

## Chapter 20 Exercises

20.1. In this problem you are asked to verify the claim in the text that the first canonical variates $\eta_{1t}$ and $\xi_{1t}$ represent the linear combinations of $\mathbf{y}_t$ and $\mathbf{x}_t$ with maximum possible correlation. Consider the following maximization problem:

$$\max_{\{\mathbf{k}_1,\mathbf{a}_1\}} E(\mathbf{k}_1'\mathbf{y}_t\mathbf{x}_t'\mathbf{a}_1)$$

subject to

$$E(\mathbf{k}_1'\mathbf{y}_t\mathbf{y}_t'\mathbf{k}_1) = 1$$
$$E(\mathbf{a}_1'\mathbf{x}_t\mathbf{x}_t'\mathbf{a}_1) = 1.$$

Show that the maximum value achieved for this problem is given by the square root of the largest eigenvalue of the matrix $\boldsymbol{\Sigma}_{\mathbf{XX}}^{-1}\boldsymbol{\Sigma}_{\mathbf{XY}}\boldsymbol{\Sigma}_{\mathbf{YY}}^{-1}\boldsymbol{\Sigma}_{\mathbf{YX}}$, and that $\mathbf{a}_1$ is the associated eigenvector normalized as stated. Show that $\mathbf{k}_1$ is the normalized eigenvector of $\boldsymbol{\Sigma}_{\mathbf{YY}}^{-1}\boldsymbol{\Sigma}_{\mathbf{YX}}\boldsymbol{\Sigma}_{\mathbf{XX}}^{-1}\boldsymbol{\Sigma}_{\mathbf{XY}}$, associated with this same eigenvalue.

20.2. It was claimed in the text that the maximized log likelihood function under the null hypothesis of $h$ cointegrating relations was given by [20.3.2]. What is the nature of the restriction on the $VAR$ in [20.3.1] when $h = 0$? Show that the value of [20.3.2] for this case is the same as the log likelihood for a $VAR(p - 1)$ process fitted to the differenced data $\Delta\mathbf{y}_t$.

20.3. It was claimed in the text that the maximized log likelihood function under the alternative hypothesis of $n$ cointegrating relations was given by [20.3.3]. This case involves regressing $\Delta\mathbf{y}_t$ on a constant, $\mathbf{y}_{t-1}$, and $\Delta\mathbf{y}_{t-1}, \Delta\mathbf{y}_{t-2}, \ldots, \Delta\mathbf{y}_{t-p+1}$ without restrictions. Let $\hat{\mathbf{g}}_t$ denote the residuals from this unrestricted regression, with $\hat{\boldsymbol{\Sigma}}_{\mathbf{GG}} = (1/T)\Sigma_{t=1}^{T} \hat{\mathbf{g}}_t\hat{\mathbf{g}}_t'$. Equation [11.1.32] would then assert that the maximized log likelihood function should be given by

$$\mathscr{L}_A^* = -(Tn/2)\log(2\pi) - (T/2)\log|\hat{\boldsymbol{\Sigma}}_{\mathbf{GG}}| - (Tn/2).$$

Show that this number is the same as that given by formula [20.3.3].

20.4. Consider applying Johansen's likelihood ratio test to univariate data ($n = 1$). Show that the test of the null hypothesis that $y_t$ is nonstationary ($h = 0$) against the alternative that $y_t$ is stationary ($h = 1$) can be written

$$T[\log(\hat{\sigma}_0^2) - \log(\hat{\sigma}_1^2)],$$

where $\hat{\sigma}_0^2$ is the average squared residual from a regression of $\Delta y_t$ on a constant and $\Delta y_{t-1}$, $\Delta y_{t-2}, \ldots, \Delta y_{t-p+1}$ while $\hat{\sigma}_1^2$ is the average squared residual when $y_{t-1}$ is added as an explanatory variable to this regression.

## Chapter 20 References


Ahn, S. K., and G. C. Reinsel. 1990. "Estimation for Partially Nonstationary Multivariate Autoregressive Models." *Journal of the American Statistical Association* 85:813–23.

Christiano, Lawrence J., and Lars Ljungqvist. 1988. "Money Does Granger-Cause Output in the Bivariate Money-Output Relation." *Journal of Monetary Economics* 22:217–35.

Johansen, Søren. 1988. "Statistical Analysis of Cointegration Vectors." *Journal of Economic Dynamics and Control* 12:231–54.

———. 1991. "Estimation and Hypothesis Testing of Cointegration Vectors in Gaussian Vector Autoregressive Models." *Econometrica* 59:1551–80.

———. 1992. "Cointegration in Partial Systems and the Efficiency of Single-Equation Analysis." *Journal of Econometrics* 52:389–402.

——— and Katarina Juselius. 1990. "Maximum Likelihood Estimation and Inference on Cointegration—with Applications to the Demand for Money." *Oxford Bulletin of Economics and Statistics* 52:169–210.

Koopmans, Tjalling C., and William C. Hood. 1953. "The Estimation of Simultaneous Linear Economic Relationships," in William C. Hood and Tjalling C. Koopmans, eds., *Studies in Econometric Method.* New York: Wiley.

Mosconi, Rocco, and Carlo Giannini. 1992. "Non-Causality in Cointegrated Systems: Representation, Estimation and Testing," *Oxford Bulletin of Economics and Statistics*. 54:399–417.

Park, Joon Y. 1990. "Maximum Likelihood Estimation of Simultaneous Cointegrated Models." University of Aarhus. Mimeo.

———. 1992. "Canonical Cointegrating Regressions." *Econometrica* 60:119–43.

——— and Masao Ogaki. 1991. "Inference in Cointegrated Models Using VAR Prewhitening to Estimate Shortrun Dynamics." University of Rochester. Mimeo.

Phillips, Peter C. B. 1990. "Spectral Regression for Cointegrated Time Series," in William Barnett, James Powell, and George Tauchen, eds., *Nonparametric and Semiparametric Methods in Economics and Statistics*. New York: Cambridge University Press.

———. 1991a. "Optimal Inference in Cointegrated Systems." *Econometrica* 59:283–306.

———. 1991b. "Unidentified Components in Reduced Rank Regression Estimation of ECM's." Yale University. Mimeo.

——— and Bruce E. Hansen. 1990. "Statistical Inference in Instrumental Variables Regression with I(1) Processes." *Review of Economic Studies* 57:99–125.

——— and S. Ouliaris. 1990. "Asymptotic Properties of Residual Based Tests for Cointegration." *Econometrica* 58:165–93.

Stock, James H., and Mark W. Watson. 1988. "Testing for Common Trends." *Journal of the American Statistical Association* 83:1097–1107.

——— and ———. 1989. "Interpreting the Evidence on Money-Income Causality." *Journal of Econometrics* 40:161–81.

Toda, H. Y., and Peter C. B. Phillips. Forthcoming. "Vector Autoregression and Causality." *Econometrica*.

West, Kenneth D. 1988. "Asymptotic Normality, When Regressors Have a Unit Root." *Econometrica* 56:1397–1417.

# 21 Time Series Models of Heteroskedasticity

## 21.1. *Autoregressive Conditional Heteroskedasticity* (ARCH)

An autoregressive process of order $p$ (denoted $AR(p)$) for an observed variable $y_t$ takes the form

$$y_t = c + \phi_1 y_{t-1} + \phi_2 y_{t-2} + \cdots + \phi_p y_{t-p} + u_t, \qquad [21.1.1]$$

where $u_t$ is white noise:

$$E(u_t) = 0 \qquad [21.1.2]$$

$$E(u_t u_\tau) = \begin{cases} \sigma^2 & \text{for } t = \tau \\ 0 & \text{otherwise.} \end{cases} \qquad [21.1.3]$$

The process is covariance-stationary provided that the roots of

$$1 - \phi_1 z - \phi_2 z^2 - \cdots - \phi_p z^p = 0$$

are outside the unit circle. The optimal linear forecast of the level of $y_t$ for an $AR(p)$ process is

$$\hat{E}(y_t | y_{t-1}, y_{t-2}, \ldots) = c + \phi_1 y_{t-1} + \phi_2 y_{t-2} + \cdots + \phi_p y_{t-p}, \qquad [21.1.4]$$

where $\hat{E}(y_t | y_{t-1}, y_{t-2}, \ldots)$ denotes the linear projection of $y_t$ on a constant and $(y_{t-1}, y_{t-2}, \ldots)$. While the conditional mean of $y_t$ changes over time according to [21.1.4], provided that the process is covariance-stationary, the unconditional mean of $y_t$ is constant:

$$E(y_t) = c/(1 - \phi_1 - \phi_2 - \cdots - \phi_p).$$

Sometimes we might be interested in forecasting not only the level of the series $y_t$ but also its variance. For example, Figure 21.1 plots the federal funds rate, which is an interest rate charged on overnight loans from one bank to another. This interest rate has been much more volatile at some times than at others. Changes in the variance are quite important for understanding financial markets, since investors require higher expected returns as compensation for holding riskier assets. A variance that changes over time also has implications for the validity and efficiency of statistical inference about the parameters $(c, \phi_1, \phi_2, \ldots, \phi_p)$ that describe the dynamics of the level of $y_t$.

Although [21.1.3] implies that the unconditional variance of $u_t$ is the constant $\sigma^2$, the conditional variance of $u_t$ could change over time. One approach is to

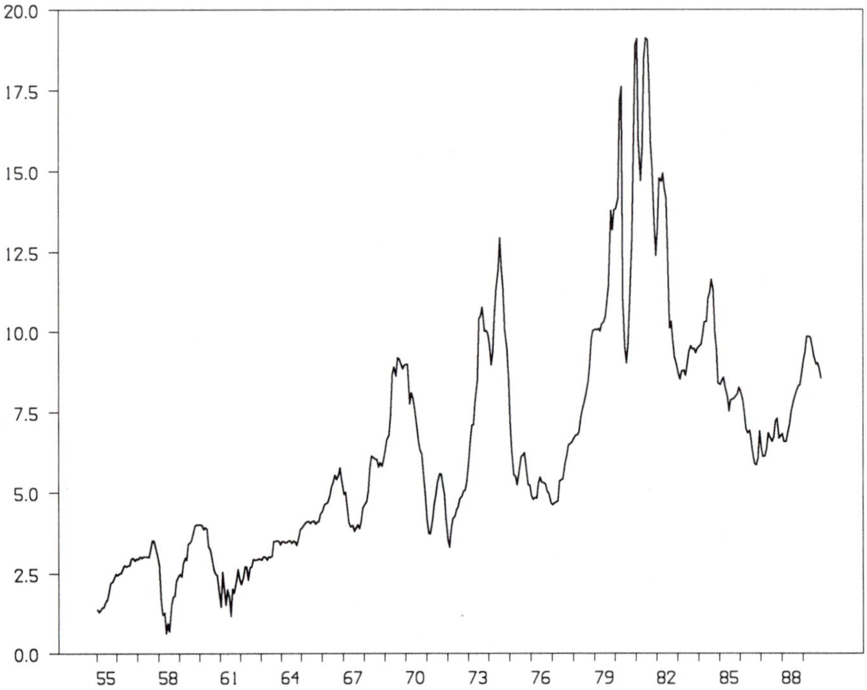


**FIGURE 21.1** U.S. federal funds rate (monthly averages quoted at an annual rate), 1955–89.

describe the square of $u_t$ as itself following an $AR(m)$ process:

$$u_t^2 = \zeta + \alpha_1 u_{t-1}^2 + \alpha_2 u_{t-2}^2 + \cdots + \alpha_m u_{t-m}^2 + w_t, \qquad [21.1.5]$$

where $w_t$ is a new white noise process:

$$E(w_t) = 0$$

$$E(w_t w_\tau) = \begin{cases} \lambda^2 & \text{for } t = \tau \\ 0 & \text{otherwise.} \end{cases}$$

Since $u_t$ is the error in forecasting $y_t$, expression [21.1.5] implies that the linear projection of the squared error of a forecast of $y_t$ on the previous $m$ squared forecast errors is given by

$$\hat{E}(u_t^2 | u_{t-1}^2, u_{t-2}^2, \ldots) = \zeta + \alpha_1 u_{t-1}^2 + \alpha_2 u_{t-2}^2 + \cdots + \alpha_m u_{t-m}^2. \qquad [21.1.6]$$

A white noise process $u_t$ satisfying [21.1.5] is described as an *autoregressive conditional heteroskedastic* process of order $m$, denoted $u_t \sim ARCH(m)$. This class of processes was introduced by Engle (1982).[1]

Since $u_t$ is random and $u_t^2$ cannot be negative, this can be a sensible representation only if [21.1.6] is positive and [21.1.5] is nonnegative for all realizations of $\{u_t\}$. This can be ensured if $w_t$ is bounded from below by $-\zeta$ with $\zeta > 0$ and if $\alpha_j \geq 0$ for $j = 1, 2, \ldots, m$. In order for $u_t^2$ to be covariance-stationary, we further require that the roots of

$$1 - \alpha_1 z - \alpha_2 z^2 - \cdots - \alpha_m z^m = 0$$

[1]A nice survey of *ARCH*-related models was provided by Bollerslev, Chou, and Kroner (1992).

lie outside the unit circle. If the $\alpha_j$ are all nonnegative, this is equivalent to the requirement that

$$\alpha_1 + \alpha_2 + \cdots + \alpha_m < 1. \qquad [21.1.7]$$

When these conditions are satisfied, the unconditional variance of $u_t$ is given by

$$\sigma^2 = E(u_t^2) = \zeta/(1 - \alpha_1 - \alpha_2 - \cdots - \alpha_m). \qquad [21.1.8]$$

Let $\hat{u}^2_{t+s|t}$ denote an $s$-period-ahead linear forecast:

$$\hat{u}^2_{t+s|t} = \hat{E}(u^2_{t+s}|u_t^2, u_{t-1}^2, \ldots).$$

This can be calculated as in [4.2.27] by iterating on

$$(\hat{u}^2_{t+j|t} - \sigma^2) = \alpha_1(\hat{u}^2_{t+j-1|t} - \sigma^2) + \alpha_2(\hat{u}^2_{t+j-2|t} - \sigma^2) + \cdots + \alpha_m(\hat{u}^2_{t+j-m|t} - \sigma^2)$$

for $j = 1, 2, \ldots, s$ where

$$\hat{u}^2_{\tau|t} = u_\tau^2 \qquad \text{for } \tau \leq t.$$

The $s$-period-ahead forecast $\hat{u}^2_{t+s|t}$ converges in probability to $\sigma^2$ as $s \to \infty$, assuming that $w_t$ has finite variance and that [21.1.7] is satisfied.

It is often convenient to use an alternative representation for an *ARCH*($m$) process that imposes slightly stronger assumptions about the serial dependence of $u_t$. Suppose that

$$u_t = \sqrt{h_t} \cdot v_t, \qquad [21.1.9]$$

where $\{v_t\}$ is an i.i.d. sequence with zero mean and unit variance:

$$E(v_t) = 0 \qquad E(v_t^2) = 1.$$

If $h_t$ evolves according to

$$h_t = \zeta + \alpha_1 u_{t-1}^2 + \alpha_2 u_{t-2}^2 + \cdots + \alpha_m u_{t-m}^2, \qquad [21.1.10]$$

then [21.1.9] implies that

$$E(u_t^2|u_{t-1}, u_{t-2}, \ldots) = \zeta + \alpha_1 u_{t-1}^2 + \alpha_2 u_{t-2}^2 + \cdots + \alpha_m u_{t-m}^2. \qquad [21.1.11]$$

Hence, if $u_t$ is generated by [21.1.9] and [21.1.10], then $u_t$ follows an *ARCH*($m$) process in which the linear projection [21.1.6] is also the conditional expectation.

Notice further that when [21.1.9] and [21.1.10] are substituted into [21.1.5], the result is

$$h_t \cdot v_t^2 = h_t + w_t.$$

Hence, under the specification in [21.1.9], the innovation $w_t$ in the *AR*($m$) representation for $u_t^2$ in [21.1.5] can be expressed as

$$w_t = h_t \cdot (v_t^2 - 1). \qquad [21.1.12]$$

Note from [21.1.12] that although the unconditional variance of $w_t$ was assumed to be constant,

$$E(w_t^2) = \lambda^2, \qquad [21.1.13]$$

the conditional variance of $w_t$ changes over time.

The unconditional variance of $w_t$ reflects the fourth moment of $u_t$, and this fourth moment does not exist for all stationary *ARCH* models. One can see this by squaring [21.1.12] and calculating the unconditional expectation of both sides:

$$E(w_t^2) = E(h_t^2) \cdot E(v_t^2 - 1)^2. \qquad [21.1.14]$$

Taking the $ARCH(1)$ specification for illustration, we find with a little manipulation of the formulas for the mean and variance of an $AR(1)$ process that

$$\begin{aligned} E(h_t^2) &= E(\zeta + \alpha_1 u_{t-1}^2)^2 \\ &= E\{(\alpha_1^2 \cdot u_{t-1}^4) + (2\alpha_1 \zeta \cdot u_{t-1}^2) + \zeta^2\} \\ &= \alpha_1^2 \cdot [\text{Var}(u_{t-1}^2) + [E(u_{t-1}^2)]^2] + 2\alpha_1 \zeta \cdot E(u_{t-1}^2) + \zeta^2 \qquad [21.1.15] \\ &= \alpha_1^2 \cdot \left[\frac{\lambda^2}{1 - \alpha_1^2} + \frac{\zeta^2}{(1 - \alpha_1)^2}\right] + \frac{2\alpha_1 \zeta^2}{1 - \alpha_1} + \zeta^2 \\ &= \frac{\alpha_1^2 \lambda^2}{1 - \alpha_1^2} + \frac{\zeta^2}{(1 - \alpha_1)^2}. \end{aligned}$$

Substituting [21.1.15] and [21.1.13] into [21.1.14], we conclude that $\lambda^2$ (the unconditional variance of $w_t$) must satisfy

$$\lambda^2 = \left[\frac{\alpha_1^2 \lambda^2}{1 - \alpha_1^2} + \frac{\zeta^2}{(1 - \alpha_1)^2}\right] \times E(v_t^2 - 1)^2. \qquad [21.1.16]$$

Even when $|\alpha_1| < 1$, equation [21.1.16] may not have any real solution for $\lambda$. For example, if $v_t \sim N(0, 1)$, then $E(v_t^2 - 1)^2 = 2$ and [21.1.16] requires that

$$\frac{(1 - 3\alpha_1^2)\lambda^2}{1 - \alpha_1^2} = \frac{2\zeta^2}{(1 - \alpha_1)^2}.$$

This equation has no real solution for $\lambda$ whenever $\alpha_1^2 \geq \frac{1}{3}$. Thus, if $u_t \sim ARCH(1)$ with the innovations $v_t$ in [21.1.9] coming from a Gaussian distribution, then the second moment of $w_t$ (or the fourth moment of $u_t$) does not exist unless $\alpha_1^2 < \frac{1}{3}$.

## *Maximum Likelihood Estimation with Gaussian* $v_t$

Suppose that we are interested in estimating the parameters of a regression model with $ARCH$ disturbances. Let the regression equation be

$$y_t = \mathbf{x}_t' \boldsymbol{\beta} + u_t. \qquad [21.1.17]$$

Here $\mathbf{x}_t$ denotes a vector of predetermined explanatory variables, which could include lagged values of $y$. The disturbance term $u_t$ is assumed to satisfy [21.1.9] and [21.1.10]. It is convenient to condition on the first $m$ observations ($t = -m + 1, -m + 2, \ldots, 0$) and to use observations $t = 1, 2, \ldots, T$ for estimation. Let $\mathcal{Y}_t$ denote the vector of observations obtained through date $t$:

$$\mathcal{Y}_t = (y_t, y_{t-1}, \ldots, y_1, y_0, \ldots, y_{-m+1}, \mathbf{x}_t', \mathbf{x}_{t-1}', \ldots, \mathbf{x}_1', \mathbf{x}_0', \ldots, \mathbf{x}_{-m+1}')'.$$

If $v_t \sim$ i.i.d. $N(0, 1)$ with $v_t$ independent of both $\mathbf{x}_t$ and $\mathcal{Y}_{t-1}$, then the conditional distribution of $y_t$ is Gaussian with mean $\mathbf{x}_t' \boldsymbol{\beta}$ and variance $h_t$:

$$f(y_t | \mathbf{x}_t, \mathcal{Y}_{t-1}) = \frac{1}{\sqrt{2\pi h_t}} \exp\left(\frac{-(y_t - \mathbf{x}_t' \boldsymbol{\beta})^2}{2h_t}\right), \qquad [21.1.18]$$

where

$$\begin{aligned} h_t &= \zeta + \alpha_1 (y_{t-1} - \mathbf{x}_{t-1}' \boldsymbol{\beta})^2 + \alpha_2 (y_{t-2} - \mathbf{x}_{t-2}' \boldsymbol{\beta})^2 + \cdots \\ &\quad + \alpha_m (y_{t-m} - \mathbf{x}_{t-m}' \boldsymbol{\beta})^2 \qquad [21.1.19] \\ &\equiv [\mathbf{z}_t(\boldsymbol{\beta})]' \boldsymbol{\delta} \end{aligned}$$

for

$$\boldsymbol{\delta} \equiv (\zeta, \alpha_1, \alpha_2, \ldots, \alpha_m)'$$
$$[\mathbf{z}_t(\boldsymbol{\beta})]' \equiv [1, (y_{t-1} - \mathbf{x}'_{t-1}\boldsymbol{\beta})^2, (y_{t-2} - \mathbf{x}'_{t-2}\boldsymbol{\beta})^2, \ldots, (y_{t-m} - \mathbf{x}'_{t-m}\boldsymbol{\beta})^2].$$

Collect the unknown parameters to be estimated in an $(a \times 1)$ vector $\boldsymbol{\theta}$:

$$\boldsymbol{\theta} \equiv (\boldsymbol{\beta}', \boldsymbol{\delta}')'.$$

The sample log likelihood conditional on the first $m$ observations is then

$$\begin{aligned}\mathcal{L}(\boldsymbol{\theta}) &= \sum_{t=1}^{T} \log f(y_t|\mathbf{x}_t, \mathcal{Y}_{t-1}; \boldsymbol{\theta}) \\ &= -(T/2)\log(2\pi) - (1/2)\sum_{t=1}^{T}\log(h_t) \\ &\quad - (1/2)\sum_{t=1}^{T}(y_t - \mathbf{x}_t'\boldsymbol{\beta})^2/h_t.\end{aligned} \qquad [21.1.20]$$

For a given numerical value for the parameter vector $\boldsymbol{\theta}$, the sequence of conditional variances can be calculated from [21.1.19] and used to evaluate the log likelihood function [21.1.20]. This can then be maximized numerically using the methods described in Section 5.7. The derivative of the log of the conditional likelihood of the $t$th observation with respect to the parameter vector $\boldsymbol{\theta}$, known as the $t$th score, is shown in Appendix 21.A to be given by

$$\begin{aligned}\underset{(a\times 1)}{\mathbf{s}_t(\boldsymbol{\theta})} &= \frac{\partial \log f(y_t|\mathbf{x}_t, \mathcal{Y}_{t-1}; \boldsymbol{\theta})}{\partial \boldsymbol{\theta}} \\ &= \{(u_t^2 - h_t)/(2h_t^2)\}\begin{bmatrix}\sum_{j=1}^{m} -2\alpha_j u_{t-j}\mathbf{x}_{t-j} \\ \mathbf{z}_t(\boldsymbol{\beta})\end{bmatrix} + \begin{bmatrix}(\mathbf{x}_t u_t)/h_t \\ \mathbf{0}\end{bmatrix}.\end{aligned} \qquad [21.1.21]$$

The likelihood function can be maximized using the method of scoring as in Engle (1982, p. 997) or using the Berndt, Hall, Hall, and Hausman (1974) algorithm as in Bollerslev (1986, p. 317). Alternatively, the gradient of the log likelihood function can be calculated analytically from the sum of the scores,

$$\nabla\mathcal{L}(\boldsymbol{\theta}) = \sum_{t=1}^{T} s_t(\boldsymbol{\theta}),$$

or numerically by numerical differentiation of the log likelihood [21.1.20]. The analytically or numerically evaluated gradient could then be used with any of the numerical optimization procedures described in Section 5.7.

Imposing the stationarity condition $(\Sigma_{j=1}^{m}\alpha_j < 1)$ and the nonnegativity condition $(\alpha_j \geq 0$ for all $j)$ can be difficult in practice. Typically, either the value of $m$ is very small or else some ad hoc structure is imposed on the sequence $\{\alpha_j\}_{j=1}^{m}$ as in Engle (1982, equation (38)).

## *Maximum Likelihood Estimation with Non-Gaussian* $v_t$

The preceding formulation of the likelihood function assumed that $v_t$ has a Gaussian distribution. However, the unconditional distribution of many financial time series seems to have fatter tails than allowed by the Gaussian family. Some of this can be explained by the presence of *ARCH*; that is, even if $v_t$ in [21.1.9] has a Gaussian distribution, the unconditional distribution of $u_t$ is non-Gaussian with heavier tails than a Gaussian distribution (see Milhøj, 1985, or Bollerslev, 1986, p. 313. Even so, there is a fair amount of evidence that the conditional distribution of $u_t$ is often non-Gaussian as well.

The same basic approach can be used with non-Gaussian distributions. For example, Bollerslev (1987) proposed that $v_t$ in [21.1.9] might be drawn from a $t$ distribution with $\nu$ degrees of freedom, where $\nu$ is regarded as a parameter to be estimated by maximum likelihood. If conditional on $M_t$, the term $u_t$ has a $t$ distribution with $\nu$ degrees of freedom and scale parameter $M_t$, then its density is given by

$$f(u_t|M_t) = \frac{\Gamma[(\nu + 1)/2]}{(\pi\nu)^{1/2}\Gamma(\nu/2)} M_t^{-1/2}\left[1 + \frac{u_t^2}{M_t\nu}\right]^{-(\nu+1)/2}, \qquad [21.1.22]$$

where $\Gamma(\cdot)$ is the gamma function described in the discussion following equation [12.1.18]. If $\nu > 2$, then $v_t$ has mean zero and variance[2]

$$E(u_t^2) = M_t\nu/(\nu - 2).$$

Hence, a $t$ variable with $\nu$ degrees of freedom and variance $h_t$ is obtained by taking the scale parameter $M_t$ to be

$$M_t = h_t(\nu - 2)/\nu,$$

for which the density [21.1.22] becomes

$$f(u_t|h_t) = \frac{\Gamma[(\nu + 1)/2]}{\pi^{1/2}\Gamma(\nu/2)} (\nu - 2)^{-1/2}h_t^{-1/2}\left[1 + \frac{u_t^2}{h_t(\nu - 2)}\right]^{-(\nu+1)/2}. \qquad [21.1.23]$$

This density can be used in place of the Gaussian specification [21.1.18] along with the same specification of the conditional mean and conditional variance used in [21.1.17] and [21.1.19]. The sample log likelihood conditional on the first $m$ observations then becomes

$$\begin{aligned}\sum_{t=1}^{T} \log f(y_t|\mathbf{x}_t, \mathcal{Y}_{t-1}; \boldsymbol{\theta}) &= T \log\left\{\frac{\Gamma[(\nu + 1)/2]}{\pi^{1/2}\Gamma(\nu/2)} (\nu - 2)^{-1/2}\right\} - (1/2)\sum_{t=1}^{T} \log(h_t) \\ &\quad - [(\nu + 1)/2]\sum_{t=1}^{T} \log\left[1 + \frac{(y_t - \mathbf{x}_t'\boldsymbol{\beta})^2}{h_t(\nu - 2)}\right],\end{aligned} \qquad [21.1.24]$$

where

$$\begin{aligned}h_t &= \zeta + \alpha_1(y_{t-1} - \mathbf{x}_{t-1}'\boldsymbol{\beta})^2 + \alpha_2(y_{t-2} - \mathbf{x}_{t-2}'\boldsymbol{\beta})^2 + \cdots + \alpha_m(y_{t-m} - \mathbf{x}_{t-m}'\boldsymbol{\beta})^2 \\ &= [\mathbf{z}_t(\boldsymbol{\beta})]'\boldsymbol{\delta}.\end{aligned}$$

The log likelihood [21.1.24] is then maximized numerically with respect to $\nu$, $\boldsymbol{\beta}$, and $\boldsymbol{\delta}$ subject to the constraint $\nu > 2$.

The same approach can be used with other distributions for $v_t$. Other distributions that have been employed with *ARCH*-related models include a Normal-Poisson mixture distribution (Jorion, 1988), power exponential distribution (Baillie and Bollerslev, 1989), Normal–log normal mixture (Hsieh, 1989), generalized exponential distribution (Nelson, 1991), and serially dependent mixture of Normals (Cai, forthcoming) or $t$ variables (Hamilton and Susmel, forthcoming).

[2]See, for example, DeGroot (1970, p. 42).

## *Quasi-Maximum Likelihood Estimation*

Even if the assumption that $v_t$ is i.i.d. $N(0, 1)$ is invalid, we saw in [21.1.6] that the *ARCH* specification can still offer a reasonable model on which to base a linear forecast of the squared value of $v_t$. As shown in Weiss (1984, 1986), Bollerslev and Wooldridge (1992), and Glosten, Jagannathan, and Runkle (1989), maximization of the Gaussian log likelihood function [21.1.20] can provide consistent estimates of the parameters $\zeta, \alpha_1, \alpha_2, \ldots, \alpha_m$ of this linear representation even when the distribution of $u_t$ is non-Gaussian, provided that $v_t$ in [21.1.9] satisfies

$$E(v_t|\mathbf{x}_t, \mathcal{Y}_{t-1}) = 0$$

and

$$E(v_t^2|\mathbf{x}_t, \mathcal{Y}_{t-1}) = 1.$$

However, the standard errors have to be adjusted. Let $\hat{\boldsymbol{\theta}}_T$ be the estimate that maximizes the Gaussian log likelihood [21.1.20], and let $\boldsymbol{\theta}$ be the true value that characterizes the linear representations [21.1.9], [21.1.17], and [21.1.19]. Then even when $v_t$ is actually non-Gaussian, under certain regularity conditions

$$\sqrt{T}(\hat{\boldsymbol{\theta}}_T - \boldsymbol{\theta}) \xrightarrow{L} N(\mathbf{0}, \mathbf{D}^{-1}\mathbf{S}\mathbf{D}^{-1}),$$

where

$$\mathbf{S} = \operatorname*{plim}_{T\to\infty} T^{-1} \sum_{t=1}^{T} [\mathbf{s}_t(\boldsymbol{\theta})]\cdot[\mathbf{s}_t(\boldsymbol{\theta})]'$$

for $\mathbf{s}_t(\boldsymbol{\theta})$ the score vector as calculated in [21.1.21], and where

$$\begin{aligned} \mathbf{D} &= \operatorname*{plim}_{T\to\infty} T^{-1} \sum_{t=1}^{T} -E\left\{\frac{\partial \mathbf{s}_t(\boldsymbol{\theta})}{\partial \boldsymbol{\theta}'}\middle| \mathbf{x}_t, \mathcal{Y}_{t-1}\right\} \\ &= \operatorname*{plim}_{T\to\infty} T^{-1} \sum_{t=1}^{T} \left\{[1/(2h_t^2)]\begin{bmatrix} \sum_{j=1}^{m} -2\alpha_j u_{t-j}\mathbf{x}_{t-j} \\ \mathbf{z}_t(\boldsymbol{\beta}) \end{bmatrix} \right. \\ &\quad \times \left. \begin{bmatrix} \sum_{j=1}^{m} -2\alpha_j u_{t-j}\mathbf{x}'_{t-j} & [\mathbf{z}_t(\boldsymbol{\beta})]' \end{bmatrix} + (1/h_t)\begin{bmatrix} \mathbf{x}_t\mathbf{x}_t' & \mathbf{0} \\ \mathbf{0} & \mathbf{0} \end{bmatrix}\right\}, \end{aligned} \qquad [21.1.25]$$

where

$$\mathcal{Y}_t = (y_t, y_{t-1}, \ldots, y_1, y_0, \ldots, y_{-m+1}, \mathbf{x}_t', \mathbf{x}_{t-1}', \ldots, \mathbf{x}_1', \mathbf{x}_0', \ldots, \mathbf{x}'_{-m+1})'.$$

The second equality in [21.1.25] is established in Appendix 21.A. The matrix $\mathbf{S}$ can be consistently estimated by

$$\hat{\mathbf{S}}_T = T^{-1} \sum_{t=1}^{T} [\mathbf{s}_t(\hat{\boldsymbol{\theta}}_T)]\cdot[\mathbf{s}_t(\hat{\boldsymbol{\theta}}_T)]',$$

where $\mathbf{s}_t(\hat{\boldsymbol{\theta}}_T)$ indicates the vector given in [21.1.21] evaluated at $\hat{\boldsymbol{\theta}}_T$. Similarly, the matrix $\mathbf{D}$ can be consistently estimated by

$$\begin{aligned} \hat{\mathbf{D}}_T &= T^{-1} \sum_{t=1}^{T} \left\{[1/(2\hat{h}_t^2)]\begin{bmatrix} \sum_{j=1}^{m} -2\hat{\alpha}_j \hat{u}_{t-j}\mathbf{x}_{t-j} \\ \mathbf{z}_t(\hat{\boldsymbol{\beta}}) \end{bmatrix} \right. \\ &\quad \times \left. \begin{bmatrix} \sum_{j=1}^{m} -2\hat{\alpha}_j \hat{u}_{t-j}\mathbf{x}'_{t-j} & [\mathbf{z}_t(\hat{\boldsymbol{\beta}})]' \end{bmatrix} + (1/\hat{h}_t)\begin{bmatrix} \mathbf{x}_t\mathbf{x}_t' & \mathbf{0} \\ \mathbf{0} & \mathbf{0} \end{bmatrix}\right\}. \end{aligned}$$

Standard errors for $\hat{\boldsymbol{\theta}}_T$ that are robust to misspecification of the family of densities can thus be obtained from the square root of diagonal elements of

$$T^{-1}\hat{\mathbf{D}}_T^{-1}\hat{\mathbf{S}}_T\hat{\mathbf{D}}_T^{-1}.$$

Recall that if the model is correctly specified so that the data were really generated by a Gaussian model, then $\mathbf{S} = \mathbf{D}$, and this simplifies to the usual asymptotic variance matrix for maximum likelihood estimation.

## *Estimation by Generalized Method of Moments*

The *ARCH* regression model of [21.1.17] and [21.1.19] can be characterized by the assumptions that the residual in the regression equation is uncorrelated with the explanatory variables,

$$E[(y_t - \mathbf{x}_t'\boldsymbol{\beta})\mathbf{x}_t] = \mathbf{0},$$

and that the implicit error in forecasting the squared residual is uncorrelated with lagged squared residuals,

$$E[(u_t^2 - h_t)\mathbf{z}_t] = \mathbf{0}.$$

As noted by Bates and White (1988), Mark (1988), Ferson (1989), Simon (1989), or Rich, Raymond, and Butler (1991), this means that the parameters of an *ARCH* model could be estimated by generalized method of moments,[3] choosing $\boldsymbol{\theta} = (\boldsymbol{\beta}', \boldsymbol{\delta}')'$ so as to minimize

$$[\mathbf{g}(\boldsymbol{\theta}; \mathcal{Y}_T)]'\hat{\mathbf{S}}_T[\mathbf{g}(\boldsymbol{\theta}; \mathcal{Y}_T)],$$

where

$$\mathbf{g}(\boldsymbol{\theta}; \mathcal{Y}_T) = \begin{bmatrix} T^{-1}\sum_{t=1}^{T}(y_t - \mathbf{x}_t'\boldsymbol{\beta})\mathbf{x}_t \\ T^{-1}\sum_{t=1}^{T}\{(y_t - \mathbf{x}_t'\boldsymbol{\beta})^2 - [\mathbf{z}_t(\boldsymbol{\beta})]'\boldsymbol{\delta}\}\mathbf{z}_t(\boldsymbol{\beta}) \end{bmatrix}.$$

The matrix $\hat{\mathbf{S}}_T$, standard errors for parameter estimates, and tests of the model can be constructed using the methods described in Chapter 14. Any other variables believed to be uncorrelated with $u_t$ or with $(u_t^2 - h_t)$ could be used as additional instruments.

## *Testing for* ARCH

Fortunately, it is simple to test whether the residuals $u_t$ from a regression model exhibit time-varying heteroskedasticity without actually having to estimate the *ARCH* parameters. Engle (1982, p. 1000) derived the following test based on the Lagrange multiplier principle. First the regression of [21.1.17] is estimated by *OLS* for observations $t = -m + 1, -m + 2, \ldots, T$ and the *OLS* sample residuals $\hat{u}_t$ are saved. Next, $\hat{u}_t^2$ is regressed on a constant and $m$ of its own lagged values:

$$\hat{u}_t^2 = \zeta + \alpha_1\hat{u}_{t-1}^2 + \alpha_2\hat{u}_{t-2}^2 + \cdots + \alpha_m\hat{u}_{t-m}^2 + e_t, \qquad [21.1.26]$$

for $t = 1, 2, \ldots, T$. The sample size $T$ times the centered $R_u^2$ from the regression

[3]As noted in Section 14.4, maximum likelihood estimation can itself be viewed as estimation by *GMM* in which the orthogonality condition is that the expected score is zero.

of [21.1.26] then converges in distribution to a $\chi^2$ variable with $m$ degrees of freedom under the null hypothesis that $u_t$ is actually i.i.d. $N(0, \sigma^2)$.

Recalling that the $ARCH(m)$ specification can be regarded as an $AR(m)$ process for $u_t^2$, another approach developed by Bollerslev (1988) is to use the Box-Jenkins methods described in Section 4.8 to analyze the autocorrelations of $u_t^2$. Other tests for $ARCH$ are described in Bollerslev, Chou, and Kroner (1992, p. 8).

## 21.2. *Extensions*

### *Generalized Autoregressive Conditional Heteroskedasticity* (GARCH)

Equations [21.1.9] and [21.1.10] described an $ARCH(m)$ process ($u_t$) characterized by

$$u_t = \sqrt{h_t}\cdot v_t,$$

where $v_t$ is i.i.d. with zero mean and unit variance and where $h_t$ evolves according to

$$h_t = \zeta + \alpha_1 u_{t-1}^2 + \alpha_2 u_{t-2}^2 + \cdots + \alpha_m u_{t-m}^2.$$

More generally, we can imagine a process for which the conditional variance depends on an infinite number of lags of $u_{t-j}^2$,

$$h_t = \zeta + \pi(L)u_t^2, \qquad [21.2.1]$$

where

$$\pi(L) = \sum_{j=1}^{\infty} \pi_j L^j.$$

A natural idea is to parameterize $\pi(L)$ as the ratio of two finite-order polynomials:

$$\pi(L) = \frac{\alpha(L)}{1 - \delta(L)} = \frac{\alpha_1 L^1 + \alpha_2 L^2 + \cdots + \alpha_m L^m}{1 - \delta_1 L^1 - \delta_2 L^2 - \cdots - \delta_r L^r}, \qquad [21.2.2]$$

where for now we assume that the roots of $1 - \delta(z) = 0$ are outside the unit circle. If [21.2.1] is multiplied by $1 - \delta(L)$, the result is

$$[1 - \delta(L)]h_t = [1 - \delta(1)]\zeta + \alpha(L)u_t^2$$

or

$$\begin{aligned} h_t = \kappa &+ \delta_1 h_{t-1} + \delta_2 h_{t-2} + \cdots + \delta_r h_{t-r} \\ &+ \alpha_1 u_{t-1}^2 + \alpha_2 u_{t-2}^2 + \cdots + \alpha_m u_{t-m}^2 \end{aligned} \qquad [21.2.3]$$

for $\kappa \equiv [1 - \delta_1 - \delta_2 - \cdots - \delta_r]\zeta$. Expression [21.2.3] is the *generalized autoregressive conditional heteroskedasticity* model, denoted $u_t \sim GARCH(r, m)$, proposed by Bollerslev (1986).

One's first guess from expressions [21.2.2] and [21.2.3] might be that $\delta(L)$ describes the "autoregressive" terms for the variance while $\alpha(L)$ captures the "moving average" terms. However, this is not the case. The easiest way to see why is to add $u_t^2$ to both sides of [21.2.3] and rewrite the resulting expression as

$$\begin{aligned} h_t + u_t^2 = \kappa &- \delta_1(u_{t-1}^2 - h_{t-1}) - \delta_2(u_{t-2}^2 - h_{t-2}) - \cdots \\ &- \delta_r(u_{t-r}^2 - h_{t-r}) + \delta_1 u_{t-1}^2 + \delta_2 u_{t-2}^2 + \cdots \\ &+ \delta_r u_{t-r}^2 + \alpha_1 u_{t-1}^2 + \alpha_2 u_{t-2}^2 + \cdots + \alpha_m u_{t-m}^2 + u_t^2 \end{aligned}$$

or

$$u_t^2 = \kappa + (\delta_1 + \alpha_1)u_{t-1}^2 + (\delta_2 + \alpha_2)u_{t-2}^2 + \cdots + (\delta_p + \alpha_p)u_{t-p}^2 + w_t - \delta_1 w_{t-1} - \delta_2 w_{t-2} - \cdots - \delta_r w_{t-r}, \quad [21.2.4]$$

where $w_t \equiv u_t^2 - h_t$ and $p \equiv \max\{m, r\}$. We have further defined $\delta_j \equiv 0$ for $j > r$ and $\alpha_j \equiv 0$ for $j > m$. Notice that $h_t$ is the forecast of $u_t^2$ based on its own lagged values and thus $w_t \equiv u_t^2 - h_t$ is the error associated with this forecast. Thus, $w_t$ is a white noise process that is fundamental for $u_t^2$. Expression [21.2.4] will then be recognized as an $ARMA(p, r)$ process for $u_t^2$, in which the $j$th autoregressive coefficient is the sum of $\delta_j$ plus $\alpha_j$ while the $j$th moving average coefficient is the negative of $\delta_j$. If $u_t$ is described by a $GARCH(r, m)$ process, then $u_t^2$ follows an $ARMA(p, r)$ process, where $p$ is the larger of $r$ and $m$.

The nonnegativity requirement is satisfied if $\kappa > 0$ and $\alpha_j \geq 0$, $\delta_j \geq 0$ for $j = 1, 2, \ldots, p$. From our analysis of $ARMA$ processes, it then follows that $u_t^2$ is covariance-stationary provided that $w_t$ has finite variance and that the roots of

$$1 - (\delta_1 + \alpha_1)z - (\delta_2 + \alpha_2)z^2 - \cdots - (\delta_p + \alpha_p)z^p = 0$$

are outside the unit circle. Given the nonnegativity restriction, this means that $u_t^2$ is covariance-stationary if

$$(\delta_1 + \alpha_1) + (\delta_2 + \alpha_2) + \cdots + (\delta_p + \alpha_p) < 1.$$

Assuming that this condition holds, the unconditional mean of $u_t^2$ is

$$E(u_t^2) = \sigma^2 = \kappa/[1 - (\delta_1 + \alpha_1) - (\delta_2 + \alpha_2) - \cdots - (\delta_p + \alpha_p)].$$

Nelson and Cao (1992) noted that the conditions $\alpha_j \geq 0$ and $\delta_j \geq 0$ are sufficient but not necessary to ensure nonnegativity of $h_t$. For example, for a $GARCH(1, 2)$ process, the $\pi(L)$ operator implied by [21.2.2] is given by

$$\begin{aligned}\pi(L) &= (1 - \delta_1 L)^{-1}(\alpha_1 L + \alpha_2 L^2) \\ &= (1 + \delta_1 L + \delta_1^2 L^2 + \delta_1^3 L^3 + \cdots)(\alpha_1 L + \alpha_2 L^2) \\ &= \alpha_1 L + (\delta_1\alpha_1 + \alpha_2)L^2 + \delta_1(\delta_1\alpha_1 + \alpha_2)L^3 \\ &\quad + \delta_1^2(\delta_1\alpha_1 + \alpha_2)L^4 + \cdots.\end{aligned}$$

The $\pi_j$ coefficients are all nonnegative provided that $0 \leq \delta_1 < 1$, $\alpha_1 \geq 0$, and $(\delta_1\alpha_1 + \alpha_2) \geq 0$. Hence, $\alpha_2$ could be negative as long as $-\alpha_2$ is less than $\delta_1\alpha_1$.

The forecast of $u_{t+s}^2$ based on $u_t^2, u_{t-1}^2, \ldots$, denoted $\hat{u}_{t+s|t}^2$, can be calculated as in [4.2.45] by iterating on

$$\hat{u}_{t+s|t}^2 - \sigma^2 = \begin{cases} (\delta_1 + \alpha_1)(\hat{u}_{t+s-1|t}^2 - \sigma^2) + (\delta_2 + \alpha_2)(\hat{u}_{t+s-2|t}^2 - \sigma^2) \\ \quad + \cdots + (\delta_p + \alpha_p)(\hat{u}_{t+s-p|t}^2 - \sigma^2) - \delta_s \hat{w}_t - \delta_{s+1}\hat{w}_{t-1} \\ \quad - \cdots - \delta_r \hat{w}_{t+s-r} \qquad \text{for } s = 1, 2, \ldots, r \\ (\delta_1 + \alpha_1)(\hat{u}_{t+s-1|t}^2 - \sigma^2) + (\delta_2 + \alpha_2)(\hat{u}_{t+s-2|t}^2 - \sigma^2) \\ \quad + \cdots + (\delta_p + \alpha_p)(\hat{u}_{t+s-p|t}^2 - \sigma^2) \qquad \text{for } s = r + 1, r + 2, \ldots, \end{cases}$$

$$\begin{aligned}\hat{u}_{\tau|t}^2 &= u_\tau^2 && \text{for } \tau \leq t \\ \hat{w}_\tau &= u_\tau^2 - \hat{u}_{\tau|\tau-1}^2 && \text{for } \tau = t, t - 1, \ldots, t - r + 1.\end{aligned}$$

See Baillie and Bollerslev (1992) for further discussion of forecasts and mean squared errors for $GARCH$ processes.

Calculation of the sequence of conditional variances $\{h_t\}_{t=1}^T$ from [21.2.3] requires presample values for $h_{-p+1}, \ldots, h_0$ and $u_{-p+1}^2, \ldots, u_0^2$. If we have observations on $y_t$ and $\mathbf{x}_t$ for $t = 1, 2, \ldots, T$, Bollerslev (1986, p. 316) suggested setting

$$h_j = u_j^2 = \hat{\sigma}^2 \qquad \text{for } j = -p + 1, \ldots, 0,$$

where

$$\hat{\sigma}^2 = T^{-1} \sum_{t=1}^{T} (y_t - \mathbf{x}_t'\boldsymbol{\beta})^2.$$

The sequence $\{h_t\}_{t=1}^T$ can be used to evaluate the log likelihood from the expression given in [21.1.20]. This can then be maximized numerically with respect to $\boldsymbol{\beta}$ and the parameters $\kappa, \delta_1, \ldots, \delta_r, \alpha_1, \ldots, \alpha_m$ of the *GARCH* process; for details, see Bollerslev (1986).

## *Integrated* GARCH

Suppose that $u_t = \sqrt{h_t} \cdot v_t$, where $v_t$ is i.i.d. with zero mean and unit variance and where $h_t$ obeys the $GARCH(r, m)$ specification

$$h_t = \kappa + \delta_1 h_{t-1} + \delta_2 h_{t-2} + \cdots + \delta_r h_{t-r} + \alpha_1 u_{t-1}^2 + \alpha_2 u_{t-2}^2 + \cdots + \alpha_m u_{t-m}^2.$$

We saw in [21.2.4] that this implies an *ARMA* process for $u_t^2$ where the $j$th autoregressive coefficient is given by $(\delta_j + \alpha_j)$. This *ARMA* process for $u_t^2$ would have a unit root if

$$\sum_{j=1}^{r} \delta_j + \sum_{j=1}^{m} \alpha_j = 1. \qquad [21.2.5]$$

Engle and Bollerslev (1986) referred to a model satisfying [21.2.5] as an *integrated GARCH* process, denoted *IGARCH*.

If $u_t$ follows an *IGARCH* process, then the unconditional variance of $u_t$ is infinite, so neither $u_t$ nor $u_t^2$ satisfies the definition of a covariance-stationary process. However, it is still possible for $u_t$ to come from a strictly stationary process in the sense that the unconditional density of $u_t$ is the same for all $t$; see Nelson (1990).

## *The* ARCH-*in-Mean Specification*

Finance theory suggests that an asset with a higher perceived risk would pay a higher return on average. For example, let $r_t$ denote the ex post rate of return on some asset minus the return on a safe alternative asset. Suppose that $r_t$ is decomposed into a component anticipated by investors at date $t - 1$ (denoted $\mu_t$) and a component that was unanticipated (denoted $u_t$):

$$r_t = \mu_t + u_t.$$

Then the theory suggests that the mean return ($\mu_t$) would be related to the variance of the return ($h_t$). In general, the *ARCH*-in-mean, or *ARCH-M*, regression model introduced by Engle, Lilien, and Robins (1987) is characterized by

$$y_t = \mathbf{x}_t'\boldsymbol{\beta} + \delta h_t + u_t$$
$$u_t = \sqrt{h_t} \cdot v_t$$
$$h_t = \zeta + \alpha_1 u_{t-1}^2 + \alpha_2 u_{t-2}^2 + \cdots + \alpha_m u_{t-m}^2$$

for $v_t$ i.i.d. with zero mean and unit variance. The effect that higher perceived variability of $u_t$ has on the level of $y_t$ is captured by the parameter $\delta$.

### *Exponential* GARCH

As before, let $u_t = \sqrt{h_t} \cdot v_t$ where $v_t$ is i.i.d. with zero mean and unit variance. Nelson (1991) proposed the following model for the evolution of the conditional variance of $u_t$:

$$\log h_t = \zeta + \sum_{j=1}^{\infty} \pi_j \cdot \{|v_{t-j}| - E|v_{t-j}| + \aleph v_{t-j}\}. \qquad [21.2.6]$$

Nelson's model is sometimes referred to as *exponential GARCH*, or *EGARCH*. If $\pi_j > 0$, Nelson's model implies that a deviation of $|v_{t-j}|$ from its expected value causes the variance of $u_t$ to be larger than otherwise, an effect similar to the idea behind the *GARCH* specification.

The $\aleph$ parameter allows this effect to be asymmetric. If $\aleph = 0$, then a positive surprise ($v_{t-j} > 0$) has the same effect on volatility as a negative surprise of the same magnitude. If $-1 < \aleph < 0$, a positive surprise increases volatility less than a negative surprise. If $\aleph < -1$, a positive surprise actually reduces volatility while a negative surprise increases volatility. A number of researchers have found evidence of asymmetry in stock price behavior—negative surprises seem to increase volatility more than positive surprises.[4] Since a lower stock price reduces the value of equity relative to corporate debt, a sharp decline in stock prices increases corporate leverage and could thus increase the risk of holding stocks. For this reason, the apparent finding that $\aleph < 0$ is sometimes described as the *leverage effect*.

One of the key advantages of Nelson's specification is that since [21.2.6] describes the log of $h_t$, the variance itself ($h_t$) will be positive regardless of whether the $\pi_j$ coefficients are positive. Thus, in contrast to the *GARCH* model, no restrictions need to be imposed on [21.2.6] for estimation. This makes numerical optimization simpler and allows a more flexible class of possible dynamic models for the variance. Nelson (1991, p. 351) showed that [21.2.6] implies that $\log h_t$, $h_t$, and $u_t$ are all strictly stationary provided that $\Sigma_{j=1}^{\infty} \pi_j^2 < \infty$.

A natural parameterization is to model $\pi(L)$ as the ratio of two finite-order polynomials as in the *GARCH(r, m)* specification:

$$\begin{aligned} \log h_t = \kappa &+ \delta_1 \log h_{t-1} + \delta_2 \log h_{t-2} + \cdots \\ &+ \delta_r \log h_{t-r} + \alpha_1\{|v_{t-1}| - E|v_{t-1}| + \aleph v_{t-1}\} \\ &+ \alpha_2\{|v_{t-2}| - E|v_{t-2}| + \aleph v_{t-2}\} + \cdots \\ &+ \alpha_m\{|v_{t-m}| - E|v_{t-m}| + \aleph v_{t-m}\}. \end{aligned} \qquad [21.2.7]$$

The *EGARCH* model can be estimated by maximum likelihood by specifying a density for $v_t$. Nelson proposed using the *generalized error distribution*, normalized to have zero mean and unit variance:

$$f(v_t) = \frac{\nu \exp[-(1/2)|v_t/\lambda|^{\nu}]}{\lambda \cdot 2^{[(\nu+1)/\nu]}\Gamma(1/\nu)}. \qquad [21.2.8]$$

Here $\Gamma(\cdot)$ is the gamma function, $\lambda$ is a constant given by

$$\lambda = \left\{\frac{2^{(-2/\nu)}\Gamma(1/\nu)}{\Gamma(3/\nu)}\right\}^{1/2},$$

[4]See Pagan and Schwert (1990), Engle and Ng (1991), and the studies cited in Bollerslev, Chou, and Kroner (1992, p. 24).

and $\nu$ is a positive parameter governing the thickness of the tails. For $\nu = 2$, the constant $\lambda = 1$ and expression [21.2.8] is just the standard Normal density. If $\nu < 2$, the density has thicker tails than the Normal, whereas for $\nu > 2$ it has thinner tails. The expected absolute value of a variable drawn from this distribution is

$$E|v_t| = \frac{\lambda \cdot 2^{1/\nu}\Gamma(2/\nu)}{\Gamma(1/\nu)}.$$

For the standard Normal case ($\nu = 2$), this becomes

$$E|v_t| = \sqrt{2/\pi}.$$

As an illustration of how this model might be used, consider Nelson's analysis of stock return data. For $r_t$ the daily return on stocks minus the daily interest rate on Treasury bills, Nelson estimated a regression model of the form

$$r_t = a + br_{t-1} + \delta h_t + u_t.$$

The residual $u_t$ was modeled as $\sqrt{h_t} \cdot v_t$, where $v_t$ is i.i.d. with density [21.2.8] and where $h_t$ evolves according to

$$\begin{aligned} \log h_t - \zeta_t = {} & \delta_1(\log h_{t-1} - \zeta_{t-1}) + \delta_2(\log h_{t-2} - \zeta_{t-2}) \\ & + \alpha_1\{|v_{t-1}| - E|v_{t-1}| + \aleph v_{t-1}\} \\ & + \alpha_2\{|v_{t-2}| - E|v_{t-2}| + \aleph v_{t-2}\}. \end{aligned} \qquad [21.2.9]$$

Nelson allowed $\zeta_t$, the unconditional mean of $\log h_t$, to be a function of time:

$$\zeta_t = \zeta + \log(1 + \rho N_t),$$

where $N_t$ denotes the number of nontrading days between dates $t - 1$ and $t$ and $\zeta$ and $\rho$ are parameters to be estimated by maximum likelihood. The sample log likelihood is then

$$\begin{aligned} \mathcal{L} = {} & T\{\log(\nu/\lambda) - (1 + \nu^{-1})\log(2) - \log[\Gamma(1/\nu)]\} \\ & - (1/2)\sum_{t=1}^{T} |(r_t - a - br_{t-1} - \delta h_t)/(\lambda \cdot \sqrt{h_t})|^{\nu} - (1/2)\sum_{t=1}^{T} \log(h_t). \end{aligned}$$

The sequence $\{h_t\}_{t=1}^{T}$ is obtained by iterating on [21.2.7] with

$$v_t = (r_t - a - br_{t-1} - \delta h_t)/\sqrt{h_t}$$

and with presample values of $\log h_t$ set to their unconditional expectations $\zeta_t$.

## *Other Nonlinear* ARCH *Specifications*

Asymmetric consequences of positive and negative innovations can also be captured with a simple modification of the linear *GARCH* framework. Glosten, Jagannathan, and Runkle (1989) proposed modeling $u_t = \sqrt{h_t} \cdot v_t$, where $v_t$ is i.i.d. with zero mean and unit variance and

$$h_t = \kappa + \delta_1 h_{t-1} + \alpha_1 u_{t-1}^2 + \aleph u_{t-1}^2 \cdot I_{t-1}. \qquad [21.2.10]$$

Here, $I_{t-1} = 1$ if $u_{t-1} \geq 0$ and $I_{t-1} = 0$ if $u_{t-1} < 0$. Again, if the leverage effect holds, we expect to find $\aleph < 0$. The nonnegativity condition is satisfied provided that $\delta_1 \geq 0$ and $\alpha_1 + \aleph \geq 0$.

A variety of other nonlinear functional forms relating $h_t$ to $\{u_{t-1}, u_{t-2}, \ldots\}$ have been proposed. Geweke (1986), Pantula (1986), and Milhøj (1987) suggested a specification in which the log of $h_t$ depends linearly on past logs of the squared residuals. Higgins and Bera (1992) proposed a power transformation of the form

$$h_t = [\zeta^\delta + \alpha_1(u_{t-1}^2)^\delta + \alpha_2(u_{t-2}^2)^\delta + \cdots + \alpha_m(u_{t-m}^2)^\delta]^{1/\delta},$$

with $\zeta > 0$, $\delta > 0$, and $\alpha_i \geq 0$ for $i = 1, 2, \ldots, m$. Gourieroux and Monfort (1992) used a Markov chain to model the conditional variance as a general stepwise function of past realizations.

## *Multivariate* GARCH *Models*

The preceding ideas can also be extended to an $(n \times 1)$ vector $\mathbf{y}_t$. Consider a system of $n$ regression equations of the form

$$\underset{(n\times 1)}{\mathbf{y}_t} = \underset{(n\times k)}{\mathbf{\Pi}'} \cdot \underset{(k\times 1)}{\mathbf{x}_t} + \underset{(n\times 1)}{\mathbf{u}_t},$$

where $\mathbf{x}_t$ is a vector of explanatory variables and $\mathbf{u}_t$ is a vector of white noise residuals. Let $\mathbf{H}_t$ denote the $(n \times n)$ conditional variance-covariance matrix of the residuals:

$$\mathbf{H}_t = E(\mathbf{u}_t\mathbf{u}_t' | \mathbf{y}_{t-1}, \mathbf{y}_{t-2}, \ldots, \mathbf{x}_t, \mathbf{x}_{t-1}, \ldots).$$

Engle and Kroner (1993) proposed the following vector generalization of a *GARCH*$(r, m)$ specification:

$$\mathbf{H}_t = \mathbf{K} + \mathbf{\Delta}_1\mathbf{H}_{t-1}\mathbf{\Delta}_1' + \mathbf{\Delta}_2\mathbf{H}_{t-2}\mathbf{\Delta}_2' + \cdots + \mathbf{\Delta}_r\mathbf{H}_{t-r}\mathbf{\Delta}_r' + \mathbf{A}_1\mathbf{u}_{t-1}\mathbf{u}_{t-1}'\mathbf{A}_1'$$
$$+ \mathbf{A}_2\mathbf{u}_{t-2}\mathbf{u}_{t-2}'\mathbf{A}_2' + \cdots + \mathbf{A}_m\mathbf{u}_{t-m}\mathbf{u}_{t-m}'\mathbf{A}_m'.$$

Here $\mathbf{K}$, $\mathbf{\Delta}_s$, and $\mathbf{A}_s$ for $s = 1, 2, \ldots$ denote $(n \times n)$ matrices of parameters. An advantage of this parameterization is that $\mathbf{H}_t$ is guaranteed to be positive definite as long as $\mathbf{K}$ is positive definite, which can be ensured numerically by parameterizing $\mathbf{K}$ as $\mathbf{PP}'$, where $\mathbf{P}$ is a lower triangular matrix.

In practice, for reasonably sized $n$ it is necessary to restrict the specification for $\mathbf{H}_t$ further to obtain a numerically tractable formulation. One useful special case restricts $\mathbf{\Delta}_s$ and $\mathbf{A}_s$ to be diagonal matrices for $s = 1, 2, \ldots$. In such a model, the conditional covariance between $u_{it}$ and $u_{jt}$ depends only on past values of $u_{i,t-s} \cdot u_{j,t-s}$, and not on the products or squares of other residuals.

Another popular approach introduced by Bollerslev (1990) assumes that the conditional correlations among the elements of $\mathbf{u}_t$ are constant over time. Let $h_{ii}^{(t)}$ denote the row $i$, column $i$ element of $\mathbf{H}_t$. Thus, $h_{ii}^{(t)}$ represents the conditional variance of the $i$th element of $\mathbf{u}_t$:

$$h_{ii}^{(t)} = E(u_{it}^2 | \mathbf{y}_{t-1}, \mathbf{y}_{t-2}, \ldots, \mathbf{x}_t, \mathbf{x}_{t-1}, \ldots).$$

This conditional variance might be modeled with a univariate *GARCH*$(1, 1)$ process driven by the lagged innovation in variable $i$:

$$h_{ii}^{(t)} = \kappa_i + \delta_i h_{ii}^{(t-1)} + \alpha_i u_{i,t-1}^2.$$

We might postulate $n$ such *GARCH* specifications $(i = 1, 2, \ldots, n)$, one for each element of $\mathbf{u}_t$. The conditional covariance between $u_{it}$ and $u_{jt}$, or the row $i$, column $j$ element of $\mathbf{H}_t$, is then taken to be a constant correlation $\rho_{ij}$ times the conditional standard deviations of $u_{it}$ and $u_{jt}$:

$$h_{ij}^{(t)} = E(u_{it}u_{jt} | \mathbf{y}_{t-1}, \mathbf{y}_{t-2}, \ldots, \mathbf{x}_t, \mathbf{x}_{t-1}, \ldots) = \rho_{ij} \cdot \sqrt{h_{ii}^{(t)}} \cdot \sqrt{h_{jj}^{(t)}}.$$

Maximum likelihood estimation of this specification turns out to be quite tractable; see Bollerslev (1990) for details.

Other multivariate models include a formulation for vech($\mathbf{H}_t$) proposed by Bollerslev, Engle, and Wooldridge (1988) and the factor *ARCH* specifications of Diebold and Nerlove (1989) and Engle, Ng, and Rothschild (1990).

## *Nonparametric Estimates*

Pagan and Hong (1990) explored a nonparametric kernel estimate of the expected value of $u_t^2$. The estimate is based on an average value of those $u_\tau^2$ whose preceding values of $u_{\tau-1}, u_{\tau-2}, \ldots, u_{\tau-m}$ were "close" to the values that preceded $u_t^2$:

$$h_t = \sum_{\substack{\tau=1 \\ \tau \neq t}}^{T} w_\tau(t) \cdot u_\tau^2.$$

The weights $\{w_\tau(t)\}_{\tau=1,\tau\neq t}^{T}$ are a set of $(T - 1)$ numbers that sum to unity. If the values of $u_{\tau-1}, u_{\tau-2}, \ldots, u_{\tau-m}$ that preceded $u_\tau$ were similar to the values $u_{t-1}, u_{t-2}, \ldots, u_{t-m}$ that preceded $u_t$, then $u_\tau^2$ is viewed as giving useful information about $h_t = E(u_t^2 | u_{t-1}, u_{t-2}, \ldots, u_{t-m})$. In this case, the weight $w_\tau(t)$ would be large. If the values that preceded $u_\tau$ are quite different from those that preceded $u_t$, then $u_\tau^2$ is viewed as giving little information about $h_t$ and so $w_\tau(t)$ is small. One popular specification for the weight $w_\tau(t)$ is to use a Gaussian kernel:

$$\kappa_\tau(t) = \prod_{j=1}^{m} (2\pi)^{-1/2} \lambda_j^{-1} \exp[-(u_{\tau-j} - u_{t-j})^2/(2\lambda_j^2)].$$

The positive parameter $\lambda_j$ is known as the *bandwidth*. The bandwidth calibrates the distance between $u_{\tau-j}$ and $u_{t-j}$—the smaller is $\lambda_j$, the closer $u_{\tau-j}$ must be to $u_{t-j}$ before giving the value of $u_\tau^2$ much weight in estimating $h_t$. To ensure that the weights $w_\tau(t)$ sum to unity, we take

$$w_\tau(t) = \frac{\kappa_\tau(t)}{\displaystyle\sum_{\substack{\tau=1 \\ \tau \neq t}}^{T} \kappa_\tau(t)}.$$

The key difficulty with constructing this estimate is in choosing the bandwidth parameter $\lambda_j$. One approach is known as *cross-validation*. To illustrate this approach, suppose that the same bandwidth is selected for each lag ($\lambda_j = \lambda$ for $j = 1, 2, \ldots, m$). Then the nonparametric estimate of $h_t$ is implicitly a function of the bandwidth parameter imposed, and accordingly could be denoted $h_t(\lambda)$. We might then choose $\lambda$ so as to minimize

$$\sum_{t=1}^{T} [u_t^2 - h_t(\lambda)]^2.$$

## *Semiparametric Estimates*

Other approaches to describing the conditional variance of $u_t$ include general series expansions for the function $h_t = h(u_{t-1}, u_{t-2}, \ldots)$ as in Pagan and Schwert (1990, p. 278) or for the density $f(v_t)$ itself as in Gallant and Tauchen (1989) and Gallant, Hsieh, and Tauchen (1989). Engle and Gonzalez-Rivera (1991) combined a parametric specification for $h_t$ with a nonparametric estimate of the density of $v_t$ in [21.1.9].

### *Comparison of Alternative Models of Stock Market Volatility*

A number of approaches have been suggested for comparing alternative *ARCH* specifications. One appealing measure is to see how well different models of heteroskedasticity forecast the value of $u_t^2$. Pagan and Schwert (1990) fitted a number of different models to monthly U.S. stock returns from 1834 to 1925. They found that the semiparametric and nonparametric methods did a good job in sample, though the parametric models yielded superior out-of-sample forecasts. Nelson's *EGARCH* specification was one of the best in overall performance from this comparison. Pagan and Schwert concluded that some benefits emerge from using parametric and nonparametric methods together.

Another approach is to calculate various specification tests of the fitted model. Tests can be constructed from the Lagrange mutiplier principle as in Engle, Lilien, and Robins (1987) or Higgins and Bera (1992), on moment tests and analysis of outliers as in Nelson (1991), or on the information matrix equality as in Bera and Zuo (1991). Related robust diagnostics were developed by Bollerslev and Wooldridge (1992). Other diagnostics are illustrated in Hsieh (1989). Engle and Ng (1991) suggested some particularly simple tests of the functional form of $h_t$ related to Lagrange multiplier tests, from which they concluded that Nelson's *EGARCH* specification or Glosten, Jagannathan, and Runkle's modification of *GARCH* described in [21.2.10] best describes the asymmetry in the conditional volatility of Japanese stock returns.

Engle and Mustafa (1992) proposed another approach to assessing the usefulness of a given specification of the conditional variance based on the observed prices for security options. These financial instruments give an investor the right to buy or sell the security at some date in the future at a price agreed upon today. The value of such an option increases with the perceived variability of the security. If the term for which the option applies is sufficiently short that stock prices can be approximated by Brownian motion with constant variance, a well-known formula developed by Black and Scholes (1973) relates the price of the option to investors' perception of the variance of the stock price. The observed option prices can then be used to construct the market's implicit perception of $h_t$, which can be compared with the specification implied by a given time series model. The results of such comparisons are quite favorable to simple *GARCH* and *EGARCH* specifications. Studies by Day and Lewis (1992) and Lamoureux and Lastrapes (1993) suggest that *GARCH*(1, 1) or *EGARCH*(1, 1) models can improve on the market's implicit assessment of $h_t$. Related evidence in support of the *GARCH*(1, 1) formulation was provided by Engle, Hong, Kane, and Noh (1991) and West, Edison, and Cho (1993).

## APPENDIX 21.A. *Derivation of Selected Equations for Chapter 21*

This appendix provides the details behind several of the assertions in the text.

■ **Derivation of [21.1.21].** Observe that

$$\frac{\partial \log f(y_t|\mathbf{x}_t, \mathcal{Y}_{t-1}; \boldsymbol{\theta})}{\partial \boldsymbol{\theta}} = -\frac{1}{2}\frac{\partial \log h_t}{\partial \boldsymbol{\theta}} - \frac{1}{2}\left\{\frac{1}{h_t}\frac{\partial (y_t - \mathbf{x}_t'\boldsymbol{\beta})^2}{\partial \boldsymbol{\theta}} - \frac{(y_t - \mathbf{x}_t'\boldsymbol{\beta})^2}{h_t^2}\frac{\partial h_t}{\partial \boldsymbol{\theta}}\right\}. \quad [21.A.1]$$

But

$$\frac{\partial(y_t - \mathbf{x}_t'\boldsymbol{\beta})^2}{\partial\boldsymbol{\theta}} = \begin{bmatrix} -2\mathbf{x}_t u_t \\ \mathbf{0} \end{bmatrix} \qquad [21.A.2]$$

and

$$\begin{aligned} \frac{\partial h_t}{\partial\boldsymbol{\theta}} &= \frac{\partial\left(\zeta + \sum_{j=1}^{m} \alpha_j u_{t-j}^2\right)}{\partial\boldsymbol{\theta}} \\ &= \partial\zeta/\partial\boldsymbol{\theta} + \sum_{j=1}^{m} (\partial\alpha_j/\partial\boldsymbol{\theta})\cdot u_{t-j}^2 + \sum_{j=1}^{m} \alpha_j \cdot (\partial u_{t-j}^2/\partial\boldsymbol{\theta}) \\ &= \begin{bmatrix} \mathbf{0} \\ 1 \\ 0 \\ \vdots \\ 0 \end{bmatrix} + \begin{bmatrix} \mathbf{0} \\ 0 \\ u_{t-1}^2 \\ \vdots \\ 0 \end{bmatrix} + \cdots + \begin{bmatrix} \mathbf{0} \\ 0 \\ 0 \\ \vdots \\ u_{t-m}^2 \end{bmatrix} + \sum_{j=1}^{m} \alpha_j \begin{bmatrix} -2u_{t-j}\mathbf{x}_{t-j} \\ 0 \\ 0 \\ \vdots \\ 0 \end{bmatrix} \\ &= \begin{bmatrix} \sum_{j=1}^{m} -2\alpha_j u_{t-j}\mathbf{x}_{t-j} \\ \mathbf{z}_t(\boldsymbol{\beta}) \end{bmatrix}. \end{aligned} \qquad [21.A.3]$$

Substituting [21.A.2] and [21.A.3] into [21.A.1] produces

$$\frac{\partial \log f(y_t|\mathbf{x}_t, \mathcal{Y}_{t-1}; \boldsymbol{\theta})}{\partial\boldsymbol{\theta}} = -\left\{\frac{1}{2h_t} - \frac{u_t^2}{2h_t^2}\right\}\begin{bmatrix} \sum_{j=1}^{m} -2\alpha_j u_{t-j}\mathbf{x}_{t-j} \\ \mathbf{z}_t(\boldsymbol{\beta}) \end{bmatrix} + \begin{bmatrix} (\mathbf{x}_t u_t)/h_t \\ \mathbf{0} \end{bmatrix},$$

as claimed. ■

■ **Derivation of [21.1.25].** Expression [21.A.1] can be written

$$\mathbf{s}_t(\boldsymbol{\theta}) = \frac{1}{2}\left\{\frac{u_t^2}{h_t} - 1\right\}\frac{\partial \log h_t}{\partial\boldsymbol{\theta}} - \frac{1}{2h_t}\frac{\partial u_t^2}{\partial\boldsymbol{\theta}},$$

from which

$$\begin{aligned} \frac{\partial \mathbf{s}_t(\boldsymbol{\theta})}{\partial\boldsymbol{\theta}'} &= \frac{1}{2}\frac{\partial \log h_t}{\partial\boldsymbol{\theta}}\left\{\frac{1}{h_t}\frac{\partial u_t^2}{\partial\boldsymbol{\theta}'} - \frac{u_t^2}{h_t^2}\frac{\partial h_t}{\partial\boldsymbol{\theta}'}\right\} + \frac{1}{2}\left\{\frac{u_t^2}{h_t} - 1\right\}\frac{\partial^2 \log h_t}{\partial\boldsymbol{\theta}\,\partial\boldsymbol{\theta}'} \\ &\quad - \frac{1}{2h_t}\frac{\partial^2 u_t^2}{\partial\boldsymbol{\theta}\,\partial\boldsymbol{\theta}'} + \frac{\partial u_t^2}{\partial\boldsymbol{\theta}}\frac{1}{2h_t^2}\frac{\partial h_t}{\partial\boldsymbol{\theta}'}. \end{aligned} \qquad [21.A.4]$$

From expression [21.A.2],

$$\begin{aligned} \frac{\partial^2 u_t^2}{\partial\boldsymbol{\theta}\,\partial\boldsymbol{\theta}'} &= \begin{bmatrix} -2\mathbf{x}_t \\ \mathbf{0} \end{bmatrix}\frac{\partial u_t}{\partial\boldsymbol{\theta}'} \\ &= \begin{bmatrix} 2\mathbf{x}_t\mathbf{x}_t' & \mathbf{0} \\ \mathbf{0} & \mathbf{0} \end{bmatrix}. \end{aligned}$$

Substituting this and [21.A.2] into [21.A.4] results in

$$\begin{aligned} \frac{\partial \mathbf{s}_t(\boldsymbol{\theta})}{\partial\boldsymbol{\theta}'} &= \frac{1}{2}\frac{\partial \log h_t}{\partial\boldsymbol{\theta}}\left\{\frac{1}{h_t}[-2u_t\mathbf{x}_t' \quad \mathbf{0}'] - \frac{u_t^2}{h_t^2}\frac{\partial h_t}{\partial\boldsymbol{\theta}'}\right\} + \frac{1}{2}\left\{\frac{u_t^2}{h_t} - 1\right\}\frac{\partial^2 \log h_t}{\partial\boldsymbol{\theta}\,\partial\boldsymbol{\theta}'} \\ &\quad - \frac{1}{2h_t}\begin{bmatrix} 2\mathbf{x}_t\mathbf{x}_t' & \mathbf{0} \\ \mathbf{0} & \mathbf{0} \end{bmatrix} + \begin{bmatrix} -2\mathbf{x}_t u_t \\ \mathbf{0} \end{bmatrix}\frac{1}{2h_t^2}\frac{\partial h_t}{\partial\boldsymbol{\theta}'}. \end{aligned} \qquad [21.A.5]$$

Recall that conditional on $\mathbf{x}_t$ and on $\mathcal{Y}_{t-1}$, the magnitudes $h_t$ and $\mathbf{x}_t$ are nonstochastic and

$$E(u_t|\mathbf{x}_t, \mathcal{Y}_{t-1}) = 0$$
$$E(u_t^2|\mathbf{x}_t, \mathcal{Y}_{t-1}) = h_t.$$

Thus, taking expectations of [21.A.5] conditional on $\mathbf{x}_t$ and $\mathcal{Y}_{t-1}$ results in

$$E\left\{\frac{\partial \mathbf{s}_t(\boldsymbol{\theta})}{\partial \boldsymbol{\theta}'}\,\middle|\,\mathbf{x}_t, \mathcal{Y}_{t-1}\right\} = -\frac{1}{2}\frac{\partial \log h_t}{\partial \boldsymbol{\theta}}\frac{\partial \log h_t}{\partial \boldsymbol{\theta}'} - \frac{1}{h_t}\begin{bmatrix} \mathbf{x}_t\mathbf{x}_t' & \mathbf{0} \\ \mathbf{0} & \mathbf{0} \end{bmatrix}$$

$$= -\frac{1}{2h_t^2}\begin{bmatrix} \sum_{j=1}^{m} -2\alpha_j u_{t-j}\mathbf{x}_{t-j} \\ \mathbf{z}_t(\boldsymbol{\beta}) \end{bmatrix}\begin{bmatrix} \sum_{j=1}^{m} -2\alpha_j u_{t-j}\mathbf{x}_{t-j}' & [\mathbf{z}_t(\boldsymbol{\beta})]' \end{bmatrix} - \frac{1}{h_t}\begin{bmatrix} \mathbf{x}_t\mathbf{x}_t' & \mathbf{0} \\ \mathbf{0} & \mathbf{0} \end{bmatrix},$$

where the last equality follows from [21.A.3]. ■

## Chapter 21 References


Baillie, Richard T., and Tim Bollerslev. 1989. "The Message in Daily Exchange Rates: A Conditional Variance Tale." *Journal of Business and Economic Statistics* 7:297–305.

——— and ———. 1992. "Prediction in Dynamic Models with Time-Dependent Conditional Variances." *Journal of Econometrics* 52:91–113.

Bates, Charles, and Halbert White. 1988. "Efficient Instrumental Variables Estimation of Systems of Implicit Heterogeneous Nonlinear Dynamic Equations with Nonspherical Errors," in William A. Barnett, Ernst R. Berndt, and Halbert White, eds., *Dynamic Econometric Modeling*. Cambridge, England: Cambridge University Press.

Bera, Anil K., and X. Zuo. 1991. "Specification Test for a Linear Regression Model with ARCH Process." University of Illinois at Champaign-Urbana. Mimeo.

Berndt, E. K., B. H. Hall, R. E. Hall, and J. A. Hausman. 1974. "Estimation and Inference in Nonlinear Structural Models." *Annals of Economic and Social Measurement* 3:653–65.

Black, Fischer, and Myron Scholes. 1973. "The Pricing of Options and Corporate Liabilities." *Journal of Political Economy* 81:637–54.

Bollerslev, Tim. 1986. "Generalized Autoregressive Conditional Heteroskedasticity." *Journal of Econometrics* 31:307–27.

———. 1987. "A Conditionally Heteroskedastic Time Series Model for Speculative Prices and Rates of Return." *Review of Economics and Statistics* 69:542–47.

———. 1988. "On the Correlation Structure for the Generalized Autoregressive Conditional Heteroskedastic Process." *Journal of Time Series Analysis* 9:121–31.

———. 1990. "Modelling the Coherence in Short-Run Nominal Exchange Rates: A Multivariate Generalized ARCH Model." *Review of Economics and Statistics* 72:498–505.

———, Ray Y. Chou, and Kenneth F. Kroner. 1992. "ARCH Modeling in Finance: A Review of the Theory and Empirical Evidence." *Journal of Econometrics* 52:5–59.

———, Robert F. Engle, and Jeffrey M. Wooldridge. 1988. "A Capital Asset Pricing Model with Time Varying Covariances." *Journal of Political Economy* 96:116–31.

——— and Jeffrey M. Wooldridge. 1992. "Quasi-Maximum Likelihood Estimation and Inference in Dynamic Models with Time Varying Covariances." *Econometric Reviews* 11:143–72.

Cai, Jun. Forthcoming. "A Markov Model of Unconditional Variance in ARCH." *Journal of Business and Economic Statistics*.

Day, Theodore E., and Craig M. Lewis. 1992. "Stock Market Volatility and the Information Content of Stock Index Options." *Journal of Econometrics* 52:267–87.

DeGroot, Morris H. 1970. *Optimal Statistical Decisions*. New York: McGraw-Hill.

Diebold, Francis X., and Mark Nerlove. 1989. "The Dynamics of Exchange Rate Volatility: A Multivariate Latent Factor ARCH Model." *Journal of Applied Econometrics* 4:1–21.

Engle, Robert F. 1982. "Autoregressive Conditional Heteroscedasticity with Estimates of the Variance of United Kingdom Inflation." *Econometrica* 50:987–1007.

——— and Tim Bollerslev. 1986. "Modelling the Persistence of Conditional Variances." *Econometric Reviews* 5:1–50.

——— and Gloria Gonzalez-Rivera. 1991. "Semiparametric ARCH Models." *Journal of Business and Economic Statistics* 9:345–59.

———, Ted Hong, Alex Kane, and Jaesun Noh. 1991. "Arbitration Valuation of Variance Forecasts Using Simulated Options Markets." *Advances in Futures and Options Research* forthcoming.

——— and Kenneth F. Kroner. 1993. "Multivariate Simultaneous Generalized ARCH." UCSD. Mimeo.

———, David M. Lilien, and Russell P. Robins. 1987. "Estimating Time Varying Risk Premia in the Term Structure: The ARCH-M Model." *Econometrica* 55:391–407.

——— and Chowdhury Mustafa. 1992. "Implied ARCH Models from Options Prices." *Journal of Econometrics* 52:289–311.

——— and Victor K. Ng. 1991. "Measuring and Testing the Impact of News on Volatility." University of California, San Diego. Mimeo.

———, Victor K. Ng, and Michael Rothschild. 1990. "Asset Pricing with a FACTOR-ARCH Covariance Structure: Empirical Estimates for Treasury Bills." *Journal of Econometrics* 45:213–37.

Ferson, Wayne E. 1989. "Changes in Expected Security Returns, Risk, and the Level of Interest Rates." *Journal of Finance* 44:1191–1218.

Gallant, A. Ronald, David A. Hsieh, and George Tauchen. 1989. "On Fitting a Recalcitrant Series: The Pound/Dollar Exchange Rate 1974–83." Duke University. Mimeo.

——— and George Tauchen. 1989. "Semi Non-Parametric Estimation of Conditionally Constrained Heterogeneous Processes: Asset Pricing Applications." *Econometrica* 57:1091–1120.

Geweke, John. 1986. "Modeling the Persistence of Conditional Variances: A Comment." *Econometric Reviews* 5:57–61.

Glosten, Lawrence R., Ravi Jagannathan, and David Runkle. 1989. "Relationship between the Expected Value and the Volatility of the Nominal Excess Return on Stocks." Northwestern University. Mimeo.

Gourieroux, Christian, and Alain Monfort. 1992. "Qualitative Threshold ARCH Models." *Journal of Econometrics* 52:159–99.

Hamilton, James D., and Raul Susmel. Forthcoming. "Autoregressive Conditional Heteroskedasticity and Changes in Regime." *Journal of Econometrics*.

Higgins, M. L., and A. K. Bera. 1992. "A Class of Nonlinear ARCH Models." *International Economic Review* 33:137–58.

Hsieh, David A. 1989. "Modeling Heteroscedasticity in Daily Foreign-Exchange Rates." *Journal of Business and Economic Statistics* 7:307–17.

Jorion, Philippe. 1988. "On Jump Processes in the Foreign Exchange and Stock Markets." *Review of Financial Studies* 1:427–45.

Lamoureux, Christopher G., and William D. Lastrapes. 1993. "Forecasting Stock Return Variance: Toward an Understanding of Stochastic Implied Volatilities." *Review of Financial Studies* 5:293–326.

Mark, Nelson. 1988. "Time Varying Betas and Risk Premia in the Pricing of Forward Foreign Exchange Contracts." *Journal of Financial Economics* 22:335–54.

Milhøj, Anders. 1985. "The Moment Structure of ARCH Processes." *Scandinavian Journal of Statistics* 12:281–92.

———. 1987. "A Multiplicative Parameterization of ARCH Models." Department of Statistics, University of Copenhagen. Mimeo.

Nelson, Daniel B. 1990. "Stationarity and Persistence in the GARCH(1, 1) Model." *Econometric Theory* 6:318–34.

———. 1991. "Conditional Heteroskedasticity in Asset Returns: A New Approach." *Econometrica* 59:347–70.

——— and Charles Q. Cao. 1992. "Inequality Constraints in the Univariate GARCH Model." *Journal of Business and Economic Statistics* 10:229–35.

Pagan, Adrian R., and Y. S. Hong. 1990. "Non-Parametric Estimation and the Risk Premium," in W. Barnett, J. Powell, and G. Tauchen, eds., *Semiparametric and Nonparametric Methods in Econometrics and Statistics*. Cambridge, England: Cambridge University Press.

Pagan, Adrian R., and G. William Schwert. 1990. "Alternative Models for Conditional Stock Volatility." *Journal of Econometrics* 45:267–90.

Pagan, Adrian R., and Aman Ullah. 1988. "The Econometric Analysis of Models with Risk Terms." *Journal of Applied Econometrics* 3:87–105.

Pantula, Sastry G. 1986. "Modeling the Persistence of Conditional Variances: A Comment." *Econometric Reviews* 5:71–74.

Rich, Robert W., Jennie Raymond, and J. S. Butler. 1991. "Generalized Instrumental Variables Estimation of Autoregressive Conditional Heteroskedastic Models." *Economics Letters* 35:179–85.

Simon, David P. 1989. "Expectations and Risk in the Treasury Bill Market: An Instrumental Variables Approach." *Journal of Financial and Quantitative Analysis* 24:357–66.

Weiss, Andrew A. 1984. "ARMA Models with ARCH Errors." *Journal of Time Series Analysis* 5:129–43.

———. 1986. "Asymptotic Theory for ARCH Models: Estimation and Testing." *Econometric Theory* 2:107–31.

West, Kenneth D., Hali J. Edison, and Dongchul Cho. 1993. "A Utility Based Comparison of Some Models of Foreign Exchange Volatility." *Journal of International Economics*, forthcoming.

# 22 Modeling Time Series with Changes in Regime

## 22.1. *Introduction*

Many variables undergo episodes in which the behavior of the series seems to change quite dramatically. A striking example is provided by Figure 22.1, which is taken from Rogers's (1992) study of the volume of dollar-denominated accounts held in Mexican banks. The Mexican government adopted various measures in 1982 to try to discourage the use of such accounts, and the effects are quite dramatic in a plot of the series.

Similar dramatic breaks will be seen if one follows almost any macroeconomic or financial time series for a sufficiently long period. Such apparent changes in the time series process can result from events such as wars, financial panics, or significant changes in government policies.

How should we model a change in the process followed by a particular time series? For the data plotted in Figure 22.1, one simple idea would be that the constant term for the autoregression changed in 1982. For data prior to 1982 we might use a model such as

$$y_t - \mu_1 = \phi(y_{t-1} - \mu_1) + \varepsilon_t, \qquad [22.1.1]$$

while data after 1982 might be described by

$$y_t - \mu_2 = \phi(y_{t-1} - \mu_2) + \varepsilon_t, \qquad [22.1.2]$$

where $\mu_2 < \mu_1$.

The specification in [22.1.1] and [22.1.2] seems a plausible description of the data in Figure 22.1, but it is not altogether satisfactory as a time series model. For example, how are we to forecast a series that is described by [22.1.1] and [22.1.2]? If the process has changed in the past, clearly it could also change again in the future, and this prospect should be taken into account in forming a forecast. Moreover, the change in regime surely should not be regarded as the outcome of a perfectly foreseeable, deterministic event. Rather, the change in regime is itself a random variable. A complete time series model would therefore include a description of the probability law governing the change from $\mu_1$ to $\mu_2$.

These observations suggest that we might consider the process to be influenced by an unobserved random variable $s_t^*$, which will be called the *state* or *regime* that the process was in at date $t$. If $s_t^* = 1$, then the process is in regime 1, while $s_t^* = 2$ means that the process is in regime 2. Equations [22.1.1] and [22.1.2] can then equivalently be written as

$$y_t - \mu_{s_t^*} = \phi(y_{t-1} - \mu_{s_{t-1}^*}) + \varepsilon_t, \qquad [22.1.3]$$

where $\mu_{s_t^*}$ indicates $\mu_1$ when $s_t^* = 1$ and indicates $\mu_2$ when $s_t^* = 2$.

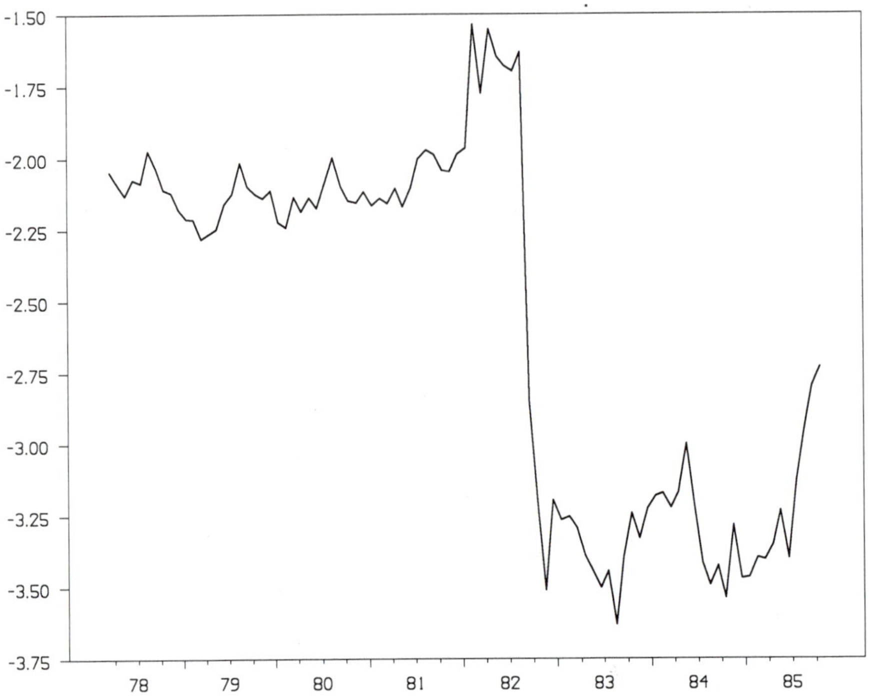


**FIGURE 22.1** Log of the ratio of the peso value of dollar-denominated bank accounts in Mexico to the peso value of peso-denominated bank accounts in Mexico, monthly, 1978–85. (Rogers, 1992).

We then need a description of the time series process for the unobserved variable $s_t^*$. Since $s_t^*$ takes on only discrete values (in this case, $s_t^*$ is either 1 or 2), this will be a slightly different time series model from those for continuous-valued random variables considered elsewhere in this book.

The simplest time series model for a discrete-valued random variable is a *Markov chain*. The theory of Markov chains is reviewed in Section 22.2. In Section 22.4 this theory will be combined with a conventional time series model such as an autoregression that is assumed to characterize any given regime. Prior to doing so, however, it will be helpful to consider a special case of such processes, namely, that for which $\phi = 0$ in [22.1.3] and $s_t^*$ is an i.i.d. discrete-valued random variable. Such a specification describes $y_t$ as a simple mixture of different distributions, the statistical theory for which is reviewed in Section 22.3.

## 22.2. *Markov Chains*

Let $s_t$ be a random variable that can assume only an integer value $\{1, 2, \ldots, N\}$. Suppose that the probability that $s_t$ equals some particular value $j$ depends on the past only through the most recent value $s_{t-1}$:

$$P\{s_t = j | s_{t-1} = i, s_{t-2} = k, \ldots\} = P\{s_t = j | s_{t-1} = i\} = p_{ij}. \quad [22.2.1]$$

Such a process is described as an $N$-state *Markov chain* with transition probabilities $\{p_{ij}\}_{i,j=1,2,\ldots,N}$. The transition probability $p_{ij}$ gives the probability that state $i$ will be followed by state $j$. Note that

$$p_{i1} + p_{i2} + \cdots + p_{iN} = 1. \quad [22.2.2]$$

It is often convenient to collect the transition probabilities in an $(N \times N)$ matrix $\mathbf{P}$ known as the *transition matrix*:

$$\mathbf{P} = \begin{bmatrix} p_{11} & p_{21} & \cdots & p_{N1} \\ p_{12} & p_{22} & \cdots & p_{N2} \\ \vdots & \vdots & \cdots & \vdots \\ p_{1N} & p_{2N} & \cdots & p_{NN} \end{bmatrix}. \qquad [22.2.3]$$

The row $j$, column $i$ element of $\mathbf{P}$ is the transition probability $p_{ij}$; for example, the row 2, column 1 element gives the probability that state 1 will be followed by state 2.

## *Representing a Markov Chain with a Vector Autoregression*

A useful representation for a Markov chain is obtained by letting $\boldsymbol{\xi}_t$ denote a random $(N \times 1)$ vector whose $j$th element is equal to unity if $s_t = j$ and whose $j$th element equals zero otherwise. Thus, when $s_t = 1$, the vector $\boldsymbol{\xi}_t$ is equal to the first column of $\mathbf{I}_N$ (the $N \times N$ identity matrix); when $s_t = 2$, the vector $\boldsymbol{\xi}_t$ is the second column of $\mathbf{I}_N$; and so on:

$$\boldsymbol{\xi}_t = \begin{cases} (1, 0, 0, \ldots, 0)' & \text{when } s_t = 1 \\ (0, 1, 0, \ldots, 0)' & \text{when } s_t = 2 \\ \quad\vdots & \quad\vdots \\ (0, 0, 0, \ldots, 1)' & \text{when } s_t = N. \end{cases}$$

If $s_t = i$, then the $j$th element of $\boldsymbol{\xi}_{t+1}$ is a random variable that takes on the value unity with probability $p_{ij}$ and takes on the value zero otherwise. Such a random variable has expectation $p_{ij}$. Thus, the conditional expectation of $\boldsymbol{\xi}_{t+1}$ given $s_t = i$ is given by

$$E(\boldsymbol{\xi}_{t+1} | s_t = i) = \begin{bmatrix} p_{i1} \\ p_{i2} \\ \vdots \\ p_{iN} \end{bmatrix}. \qquad [22.2.4]$$

This vector is simply the $i$th column of the matrix $\mathbf{P}$ in [22.2.3]. Moreover, when $s_t = i$, the vector $\boldsymbol{\xi}_t$ corresponds to the $i$th column of $\mathbf{I}_N$, in which case the vector in [22.2.4] could be described as $\mathbf{P}\boldsymbol{\xi}_t$. Hence, expression [22.2.4] implies that

$$E(\boldsymbol{\xi}_{t+1} | \boldsymbol{\xi}_t) = \mathbf{P}\boldsymbol{\xi}_t,$$

and indeed, from the Markov property [22.2.1], it follows further that

$$E(\boldsymbol{\xi}_{t+1} | \boldsymbol{\xi}_t, \boldsymbol{\xi}_{t-1}, \ldots) = \mathbf{P}\boldsymbol{\xi}_t. \qquad [22.2.5]$$

Result [22.2.5] implies that it is possible to express a Markov chain in the form

$$\boldsymbol{\xi}_{t+1} = \mathbf{P}\boldsymbol{\xi}_t + \mathbf{v}_{t+1}, \qquad [22.2.6]$$

where

$$\mathbf{v}_{t+1} \equiv \boldsymbol{\xi}_{t+1} - E(\boldsymbol{\xi}_{t+1} | \boldsymbol{\xi}_t, \boldsymbol{\xi}_{t-1}, \ldots). \qquad [22.2.7]$$

Expression [22.2.6] has the form of a first-order vector autoregression for $\boldsymbol{\xi}_t$; note that [22.2.7] implies that the innovation $\mathbf{v}_t$ is a martingale difference sequence. Although the vector $\mathbf{v}_t$ can take on only a finite set of values, on average $\mathbf{v}_t$ is zero. Moreover, the value of $\mathbf{v}_t$ is impossible to forecast on the basis of previous states of the process.

## *Forecasts for a Markov Chain*

Expression [22.2.6] implies that

$$\boldsymbol{\xi}_{t+m} = \mathbf{v}_{t+m} + \mathbf{P}\mathbf{v}_{t+m-1} + \mathbf{P}^2\mathbf{v}_{t+m-2} + \cdots + \mathbf{P}^{m-1}\mathbf{v}_{t+1} + \mathbf{P}^m\boldsymbol{\xi}_t, \qquad [22.2.8]$$

where $\mathbf{P}^m$ indicates the transition matrix multiplied by itself $m$ times. It follows from [22.2.8] that $m$-period-ahead forecasts for a Markov chain can be calculated from

$$E(\boldsymbol{\xi}_{t+m}|\boldsymbol{\xi}_t, \boldsymbol{\xi}_{t-1}, \ldots) = \mathbf{P}^m\boldsymbol{\xi}_t. \qquad [22.2.9]$$

Again, since the $j$th element of $\boldsymbol{\xi}_{t+m}$ will be unity if $s_{t+m} = j$ and zero otherwise, the $j$th element of the $(N \times 1)$ vector $E(\boldsymbol{\xi}_{t+m}|\boldsymbol{\xi}_t, \boldsymbol{\xi}_{t-1}, \ldots)$ indicates the probability that $s_{t+m}$ takes on the value $j$, conditional on the state of the system at date $t$. For example, if the process is in state $i$ at date $t$, then [22.2.9] asserts that

$$\begin{bmatrix} P\{s_{t+m} = 1|s_t = i\} \\ P\{s_{t+m} = 2|s_t = i\} \\ \vdots \\ P\{s_{t+m} = N|s_t = i\} \end{bmatrix} = \mathbf{P}^m \cdot \mathbf{e}_i, \qquad [22.2.10]$$

where $\mathbf{e}_i$ denotes the $i$th column of $\mathbf{I}_N$. Expression [22.2.10] indicates that the $m$-period-ahead transition probabilities for a Markov chain can be calculated by multiplying the matrix $\mathbf{P}$ by itself $m$ times. Specifically, the probability that an observation from regime $i$ will be followed $m$ periods later by an observation from regime $j$, $P\{s_{t+m} = j|s_t = i\}$, is given by the row $j$, column $i$ element of the matrix $\mathbf{P}^m$.

## *Reducible Markov Chains*

For a two-state Markov chain, the transition matrix is

$$\mathbf{P} = \begin{bmatrix} p_{11} & 1 - p_{22} \\ 1 - p_{11} & p_{22} \end{bmatrix}. \qquad [22.2.11]$$

Suppose that $p_{11} = 1$, so that the matrix $\mathbf{P}$ is upper triangular. Then, once the process enters state 1, there is no possibility of ever returning to state 2. In such a case we would say that state 1 is an *absorbing state* and that the Markov chain is *reducible*.

More generally, an $N$-state Markov chain is said to be reducible if there exists a way to label the states (that is, a way to choose which state to call state 1, which to call state 2, and so on) such that the transition matrix can be written in the form

$$\mathbf{P} = \begin{bmatrix} \mathbf{B} & \mathbf{C} \\ \mathbf{0} & \mathbf{D} \end{bmatrix},$$

where $\mathbf{B}$ denotes a $(K \times K)$ matrix for some $1 \leq K < N$. If $\mathbf{P}$ is upper block-triangular, then so is $\mathbf{P}^m$ for any $m$. Hence, once such a process enters a state $j$ such that $j \leq K$, there is no possibility of ever returning to one of the states $K + 1, K + 2, \ldots, N$.

A Markov chain that is not reducible is said to be *irreducible*. For example, a two-state chain is irreducible if $p_{11} < 1$ and $p_{22} < 1$.

## *Ergodic Markov Chains*

Equation [22.2.2] requires that every column of **P** sum to unity, or

$$\mathbf{P}'\mathbf{1} = \mathbf{1}, \qquad [22.2.12]$$

where **1** denotes an $(N \times 1)$ vector of 1s. Expression [22.2.12] implies that unity is an eigenvalue of the matrix **P**′ and that **1** is the associated eigenvector. Since a matrix and its transpose share the same eigenvalues, it follows that unity is an eigenvalue of the transition matrix **P** for any Markov chain.

Consider an $N$-state irreducible Markov chain with transition matrix **P**. Suppose that one of the eigenvalues of **P** is unity and that all other eigenvalues of **P** are inside the unit circle. Then the Markov chain is said to be *ergodic*. The $(N \times 1)$ vector of *ergodic probabilities* for an ergodic chain is denoted $\boldsymbol{\pi}$. This vector $\boldsymbol{\pi}$ is defined as the eigenvector of **P** associated with the unit eigenvalue; that is, the vector of ergodic probabilities $\boldsymbol{\pi}$ satisfies

$$\mathbf{P}\boldsymbol{\pi} = \boldsymbol{\pi}. \qquad [22.2.13]$$

The eigenvector $\boldsymbol{\pi}$ is normalized so that its elements sum to unity $(\mathbf{1}'\boldsymbol{\pi} = 1)$. It can be shown that if **P** is the transition matrix for an ergodic Markov chain, then

$$\lim_{m\to\infty} \mathbf{P}^m = \boldsymbol{\pi}\cdot\mathbf{1}'. \qquad [22.2.14]$$

We establish [22.2.14] here for the case when all the eigenvalues of **P** are distinct; a related argument based on the Jordan decomposition that is valid for ergodic chains with repeated eigenvalues is developed in Cox and Miller (1965, pp. 120–23). For the case of distinct eigenvalues, we know from [A.4.24] that **P** can always be written in the form

$$\mathbf{P} = \mathbf{T}\boldsymbol{\Lambda}\mathbf{T}^{-1}, \qquad [22.2.15]$$

where **T** is an $(N \times N)$ matrix whose columns are the eigenvectors of **P** while $\boldsymbol{\Lambda}$ is a diagonal matrix whose diagonal contains the corresponding eigenvalues of **P**. It follows as in [1.2.19] that

$$\mathbf{P}^m = \mathbf{T}\boldsymbol{\Lambda}^m\mathbf{T}^{-1}. \qquad [22.2.16]$$

Since the (1, 1) element of $\boldsymbol{\Lambda}$ is unity and all other elements of $\boldsymbol{\Lambda}$ are inside the unit circle, $\boldsymbol{\Lambda}^m$ converges to a matrix with unity in the (1, 1) position and zeros elsewhere. Hence,

$$\lim_{m\to\infty} \mathbf{P}^m = \mathbf{x}\cdot\mathbf{y}', \qquad [22.2.17]$$

where **x** is the first column of **T** and **y**′ is the first row of $\mathbf{T}^{-1}$.

The first column of **T** is the eigenvector of **P** corresponding to the unit eigenvalue, which eigenvector was denoted $\boldsymbol{\pi}$ in [22.2.13]:

$$\mathbf{x} = \boldsymbol{\pi}. \qquad [22.2.18]$$

Moreover, the first row of $\mathbf{T}^{-1}$, when expressed as a column vector, corresponds to the eigenvector of **P**′ associated with the unit eigenvalue, which eigenvector was seen to be proportional to the vector **1** in [22.2.12]:

$$\mathbf{y} = \alpha\cdot\mathbf{1}. \qquad [22.2.19]$$

To verify [22.2.19], note from [22.2.15] that the matrix of eigenvectors **T** of the matrix **P** is characterized by

$$\mathbf{P}\mathbf{T} = \mathbf{T}\boldsymbol{\Lambda}. \qquad [22.2.20]$$

Transposing [22.2.15] results in

$$\mathbf{P}' = (\mathbf{T}^{-1})'\mathbf{\Lambda}\mathbf{T}',$$

and postmultiplying by $(\mathbf{T}^{-1})'$ yields

$$\mathbf{P}'(\mathbf{T}^{-1})' = (\mathbf{T}^{-1})'\mathbf{\Lambda}. \qquad [22.2.21]$$

Comparing [22.2.21] with [22.2.20] confirms that the columns of $(\mathbf{T}^{-1})'$ correspond to eigenvectors of $\mathbf{P}'$. In particular, then, the first column of $(\mathbf{T}^{-1})'$ is proportional to the eigenvector of $\mathbf{P}'$ associated with the unit eigenvalue, which eigenvector was seen to be given by $\mathbf{1}$ in equation [22.2.12]. Since $\mathbf{y}$ was defined as the first column of $(\mathbf{T}^{-1})'$, this establishes the claim made in equation [22.2.19].

Substituting [22.2.18] and [22.2.19] into [22.2.17], it follows that

$$\lim_{m\to\infty} \mathbf{P}^m = \boldsymbol{\pi}\cdot\alpha\mathbf{1}'.$$

Since $\mathbf{P}^m$ can be interpreted as a matrix of transition probabilities, each column must sum to unity. Thus, since the vector of ergodic probabilities $\boldsymbol{\pi}$ was normalized by the condition that $\mathbf{1}'\boldsymbol{\pi} = 1$, it follows that the normalizing constant $\alpha$ must be unity, establishing the claim made in [22.2.14].

Result [22.2.14] implies that the long-run forecast for an ergodic Markov chain is independent of the current state, since, from [22.2.9],

$$E(\boldsymbol{\xi}_{t+m}|\boldsymbol{\xi}_t, \boldsymbol{\xi}_{t-1}, \ldots) = \mathbf{P}^m\boldsymbol{\xi}_t \xrightarrow{p} \boldsymbol{\pi}\cdot\mathbf{1}'\boldsymbol{\xi}_t = \boldsymbol{\pi},$$

where the final equality follows from the observation that $\mathbf{1}'\boldsymbol{\xi}_t = 1$ regardless of the value of $\boldsymbol{\xi}_t$. The long-run forecast of $\boldsymbol{\xi}_{t+m}$ is given by the vector of ergodic probabilities $\boldsymbol{\pi}$ regardless of the current value of $\boldsymbol{\xi}_t$.

The vector of ergodic probabilities can also be viewed as indicating the unconditional probability of each of the $N$ different states. To see this, suppose that we had used the symbol $\pi_j$ to indicate the unconditional probability $P\{s_t = j\}$. Then the vector $\boldsymbol{\pi} \equiv (\pi_1, \pi_2, \ldots, \pi_N)'$ could be described as the unconditional expectation of $\boldsymbol{\xi}_t$:

$$\boldsymbol{\pi} = E(\boldsymbol{\xi}_t). \qquad [22.2.22]$$

If one takes unconditional expectations of [22.2.6], the result is

$$E(\boldsymbol{\xi}_{t+1}) = \mathbf{P}\cdot E(\boldsymbol{\xi}_t).$$

Assuming stationarity and using the definition [22.2.22], this becomes

$$\boldsymbol{\pi} = \mathbf{P}\cdot\boldsymbol{\pi},$$

which is identical to equation [22.2.13] characterizing $\boldsymbol{\pi}$ as the eigenvector of $\mathbf{P}$ associated with the unit eigenvalue. For an ergodic Markov chain, this eigenvector is unique, and so the vector of ergodic probabilities $\boldsymbol{\pi}$ can be interpreted as the vector of unconditional probabilities.

An ergodic Markov chain is a covariance-stationary process. Yet [22.2.6] takes the form of a *VAR* with a unit root, since one of the eigenvalues of $\mathbf{P}$ is unity. This *VAR* is stationary despite the unit root because the variance-covariance matrix of $\mathbf{v}_t$ is singular. In particular, since $\mathbf{1}'\boldsymbol{\xi}_t = 1$ for all $t$ and since $\mathbf{1}'\mathbf{P} = \mathbf{1}'$, equation [22.2.6] implies that $\mathbf{1}'\mathbf{v}_t = 0$ for all $t$. Thus, from [22.2.19], the first element of the $(N \times 1)$ vector $\mathbf{T}^{-1}\mathbf{v}_t$ is always zero, meaning that from [22.2.16] the unit eigenvalue in $\mathbf{P}^m\mathbf{v}_t$ always has a coefficient of zero.

## *Further Discussion of Two-State Markov Chains*

The eigenvalues of the transition matrix $\mathbf{P}$ for any $N$-state Markov chain are found from the solutions to $|\mathbf{P} - \lambda\mathbf{I}_N| = 0$. For the two-state Markov chain, the eigenvalues satisfy

$$\begin{aligned} 0 &= \begin{vmatrix} p_{11} - \lambda & 1 - p_{22} \\ 1 - p_{11} & p_{22} - \lambda \end{vmatrix} \\ &= (p_{11} - \lambda)(p_{22} - \lambda) - (1 - p_{11})(1 - p_{22}) \\ &= p_{11}p_{22} - (p_{11} + p_{22})\lambda + \lambda^2 - 1 + p_{11} + p_{22} - p_{11}p_{22} \\ &= \lambda^2 - (p_{11} + p_{22})\lambda - 1 + p_{11} + p_{22} \\ &= (\lambda - 1)(\lambda + 1 - p_{11} - p_{22}). \end{aligned}$$

Thus, the eigenvalues for a two-state chain are given by $\lambda_1 = 1$ and $\lambda_2 = -1 + p_{11} + p_{22}$. The second eigenvalue, $\lambda_2$, will be inside the unit circle as long as $0 < p_{11} + p_{22} < 2$. We saw earlier that this chain is irreducible as long as $p_{11} < 1$ and $p_{22} < 1$. Thus, a two-state Markov chain is ergodic provided that $p_{11} < 1$, $p_{22} < 1$, and $p_{11} + p_{22} > 0$.

The eigenvector associated with $\lambda_1$ for the two-state chain turns out to be

$$\boldsymbol{\pi} = \begin{bmatrix} (1 - p_{22})/(2 - p_{11} - p_{22}) \\ (1 - p_{11})/(2 - p_{11} - p_{22}) \end{bmatrix}$$

(the reader is invited to confirm this and the claims that follow in Exercise 22.1). Thus, the unconditional probability that the process will be in regime 1 at any given date is given by

$$P\{s_t = 1\} = \frac{1 - p_{22}}{2 - p_{11} - p_{22}}.$$

The unconditional probability that the process will be in regime 2, the second element of $\boldsymbol{\pi}$, is readily seen to be 1 minus this magnitude. The eigenvector associated with $\lambda_2$ is

$$\begin{bmatrix} -1 \\ 1 \end{bmatrix}.$$

Thus, from [22.2.16], the matrix of $m$-period-ahead transition probabilities for an ergodic two-state Markov chain is given by

$$\begin{aligned} \mathbf{P}^m &= \begin{bmatrix} \dfrac{1 - p_{22}}{2 - p_{11} - p_{22}} & -1 \\ \dfrac{1 - p_{11}}{2 - p_{11} - p_{22}} & 1 \end{bmatrix} \begin{bmatrix} 1 & 0 \\ 0 & \lambda_2^m \end{bmatrix} \begin{bmatrix} 1 & 1 \\ \dfrac{-(1 - p_{11})}{2 - p_{11} - p_{22}} & \dfrac{1 - p_{22}}{2 - p_{11} - p_{22}} \end{bmatrix} \\ &= \begin{bmatrix} \dfrac{(1 - p_{22}) + \lambda_2^m(1 - p_{11})}{2 - p_{11} - p_{22}} & \dfrac{(1 - p_{22}) - \lambda_2^m(1 - p_{22})}{(2 - p_{11} - p_{22})} \\ \dfrac{(1 - p_{11}) - \lambda_2^m(1 - p_{11})}{2 - p_{11} - p_{22}} & \dfrac{(1 - p_{11}) + \lambda_2^m(1 - p_{22})}{2 - p_{11} - p_{22}} \end{bmatrix}. \end{aligned}$$

Thus, for example if the process is currently in state 1, the probability that $m$ periods later it will be in state 2 is given by

$$P\{s_{t+m} = 2|s_t = 1\} = \frac{(1 - p_{11}) - \lambda_2^m(1 - p_{11})}{2 - p_{11} - p_{22}},$$

where $\lambda_2 = -1 + p_{11} + p_{22}$.

A two-state Markov chain can also be represented by a simple scalar $AR(1)$ process, as follows. Let $\xi_{1t}$ denote the first element of the vector $\boldsymbol{\xi}_t$; that is, $\xi_{1t}$ is a random variable that is equal to unity when $s_t = 1$ and equal to zero otherwise. For the two-state chain, the second element of $\boldsymbol{\xi}_t$ is then $1 - \xi_{1t}$. Hence, [22.2.6] can be written

$$\begin{bmatrix} \xi_{1,t+1} \\ 1 - \xi_{1,t+1} \end{bmatrix} = \begin{bmatrix} p_{11} & 1 - p_{22} \\ 1 - p_{11} & p_{22} \end{bmatrix} \begin{bmatrix} \xi_{1t} \\ 1 - \xi_{1t} \end{bmatrix} + \begin{bmatrix} v_{1,t+1} \\ v_{2,t+1} \end{bmatrix}. \qquad [22.2.23]$$

The first row of [22.2.23] states that

$$\xi_{1,t+1} = (1 - p_{22}) + (-1 + p_{11} + p_{22})\xi_{1t} + v_{1,t+1}. \qquad [22.2.24]$$

Expression [22.2.24] will be recognized as an $AR(1)$ process with constant term $(1 - p_{22})$ and autoregressive coefficient equal to $(-1 + p_{11} + p_{22})$. Note that this autoregressive coefficient turns out to be the second eigenvalue $\lambda_2$ of $\mathbf{P}$ calculated previously. When $p_{11} + p_{22} > 1$, the process is likely to persist in its current state and the variable $\xi_{1t}$ would be positively serially correlated, whereas when $p_{11} + p_{22} < 1$, the process is more likely to switch out of a state than stay in it, producing negative serial correlation. Recall further from equation [3.4.3] that the mean of a first-order autoregression is given by $c/(1 - \phi)$. Hence, the representation [22.2.24] implies that

$$E(\xi_{1t}) = \frac{1 - p_{22}}{2 - p_{11} - p_{22}},$$

which reproduces the earlier calculation of the value for the ergodic probability $\pi_1$.

### *Calculating Ergodic Probabilities for an N-state Markov Chain*

For a general ergodic $N$-state process, the vector of unconditional probabilities represents a vector $\boldsymbol{\pi}$ with the properties that $\mathbf{P}\boldsymbol{\pi} = \boldsymbol{\pi}$ and $\mathbf{1}'\boldsymbol{\pi} = 1$, where $\mathbf{1}$ denotes an $(N \times 1)$ vector of 1s. We thus seek a vector $\boldsymbol{\pi}$ satisfying

$$\mathbf{A}\boldsymbol{\pi} = \mathbf{e}_{N+1}. \qquad [22.2.25]$$

where $\mathbf{e}_{N+1}$ denotes the $(N + 1)$th column of $\mathbf{I}_{N+1}$ and where

$$\underset{(N+1)\times N}{\mathbf{A}} = \begin{bmatrix} \mathbf{I}_N - \mathbf{P} \\ \mathbf{1}' \end{bmatrix}.$$

Such a solution can be found by premultiplying [22.2.25] by $(\mathbf{A}'\mathbf{A})^{-1}\mathbf{A}'$:

$$\boldsymbol{\pi} = (\mathbf{A}'\mathbf{A})^{-1}\mathbf{A}'\mathbf{e}_{N+1}. \qquad [22.2.26]$$

In other words, $\boldsymbol{\pi}$ is the $(N + 1)$th column of the matrix $(\mathbf{A}'\mathbf{A})^{-1}\mathbf{A}'$.

### *Periodic Markov Chains*

If a Markov chain is irreducible, then there is one and only one eigenvalue equal to unity. However, there may be more than one eigenvalue on the unit circle, meaning that not all irreducible Markov chains are ergodic. For example, consider a two-state Markov chain in which $p_{11} = p_{22} = 0$:

$$\mathbf{P} = \begin{bmatrix} 0 & 1 \\ 1 & 0 \end{bmatrix}.$$

The eigenvalues of this transition matrix are $\lambda_1 = 1$ and $\lambda_2 = -1$, both of which are on the unit circle. Thus, the matrix $\mathbf{P}^m$ does not converge to any fixed limit of the form $\boldsymbol{\pi}\cdot\mathbf{1}'$ for this case. Instead, if the process is in state 1 at date $t$, then it is certain to be there again for dates $t + 2, t + 4, t + 6, \ldots$, with no tendency to converge as $m \to \infty$. Such a Markov chain is said to be *periodic* with period 2.

In general, it is possible to show that for any irreducible $N$-state Markov chain, all the eigenvalues of the transition matrix will be on or inside the unit circle. If there are $K$ eigenvalues strictly on the unit circle with $K > 1$, then the chain is said to be periodic with period $K$. Such chains have the property that the states can be classified into $K$ distinct classes, such that if the state at date $t$ is from class $\alpha$, then the state at date $t + 1$ is certain to be from class $\alpha + 1$ (where class $\alpha + 1$ for $\alpha = K$ is interpreted to be class 1). Thus, there is a zero probability of returning to the original state $s_t$, and indeed zero probability of returning to any member of the original class $\alpha$, except at horizons that are integer multiples of the period (such as dates $t + K$, $t + 2K$, $t + 3K$, and so on). For further discussion of periodic Markov chains, see Cox and Miller (1965).

## 22.3. *Statistical Analysis of i.i.d. Mixture Distributions*

In Section 22.4, we will consider autoregressive processes in which the parameters of the autoregression can change as the result of a regime-shift variable. The regime itself will be described as the outcome of an unobserved Markov chain. Before analyzing such processes, it is instructive first to consider a special case of these processes known as i.i.d. *mixture distributions*.

Let the regime that a given process is in at date $t$ be indexed by an unobserved random variable $s_t$, where there are $N$ possible regimes ($s_t = 1, 2, \ldots$, or $N$). When the process is in regime 1, the observed variable $y_t$ is presumed to have been drawn from a $N(\mu_1, \sigma_1^2)$ distribution. If the process is in regime 2, then $y_t$ is drawn from a $N(\mu_2, \sigma_2^2)$ distribution, and so on. Hence, the density of $y_t$ conditional on the random variable $s_t$ taking on the value $j$ is

$$f(y_t|s_t = j; \boldsymbol{\theta}) = \frac{1}{\sqrt{2\pi}\sigma_j} \exp\left\{\frac{-(y_t - \mu_j)^2}{2\sigma_j^2}\right\} \qquad [22.3.1]$$

for $j = 1, 2, \ldots, N$. Here $\boldsymbol{\theta}$ is a vector of population parameters that includes $\mu_1, \ldots, \mu_N$ and $\sigma_1^2, \ldots, \sigma_N^2$.

The unobserved regime $\{s_t\}$ is presumed to have been generated by some probability distribution, for which the unconditional probability that $s_t$ takes on the value $j$ is denoted $\pi_j$:

$$P\{s_t = j; \boldsymbol{\theta}\} = \pi_j \qquad \text{for } j = 1, 2, \ldots, N. \qquad [22.3.2]$$

The probabilities $\pi_1, \ldots, \pi_N$ are also included in $\boldsymbol{\theta}$; that is, $\boldsymbol{\theta}$ is given by

$$\boldsymbol{\theta} \equiv (\mu_1, \ldots, \mu_N, \sigma_1^2, \ldots, \sigma_N^2, \pi_1, \ldots, \pi_N)'.$$

Recall that for any events $A$ and $B$, the conditional probability of $A$ given $B$ is defined as

$$P\{A|B\} = \frac{P\{A \text{ and } B\}}{P\{B\}},$$

assuming that the probability that event $B$ occurs is not zero. This expression implies that the joint probability of $A$ and $B$ occurring together can be calculated as

$$P\{A \text{ and } B\} = P\{A|B\} \cdot P\{B\}.$$

For example, if we were interested in the probability of the joint event that $s_t = j$ and that $y_t$ falls within some interval $[c, d]$, this could be found by integrating

$$p(y_t, s_t = j; \boldsymbol{\theta}) = f(y_t|s_t = j; \boldsymbol{\theta}) \cdot P\{s_t = j; \boldsymbol{\theta}\} \qquad [22.3.3]$$

over all values of $y_t$ between $c$ and $d$. Expression [22.3.3] will be called the *joint density-distribution function* of $y_t$ and $s_t$. From [22.3.1] and [22.3.2], this function is given by

$$p(y_t, s_t = j; \boldsymbol{\theta}) = \frac{\pi_j}{\sqrt{2\pi}\sigma_j} \exp\left\{\frac{-(y_t - \mu_j)^2}{2\sigma_j^2}\right\}. \qquad [22.3.4]$$

The unconditional density of $y_t$ can be found by summing [22.3.4] over all possible values for $j$:

$$\begin{aligned} f(y_t; \boldsymbol{\theta}) &= \sum_{j=1}^{N} p(y_t, s_t = j; \boldsymbol{\theta}) \\ &= \frac{\pi_1}{\sqrt{2\pi}\sigma_1} \exp\left\{\frac{-(y_t - \mu_1)^2}{2\sigma_1^2}\right\} \\ &\quad + \frac{\pi_2}{\sqrt{2\pi}\sigma_2} \exp\left\{\frac{-(y_t - \mu_2)^2}{2\sigma_2^2}\right\} + \cdots \\ &\quad + \frac{\pi_N}{\sqrt{2\pi}\sigma_N} \exp\left\{\frac{-(y_t - \mu_N)^2}{2\sigma_N^2}\right\}. \end{aligned} \qquad [22.3.5]$$

Since the regime $s_t$ is unobserved, expression [22.3.5] is the relevant density describing the actually observed data $y_t$. If the regime variable $s_t$ is distributed i.i.d. across different dates $t$, then the log likelihood for the observed data can be calculated from [22.3.5] as

$$\mathcal{L}(\boldsymbol{\theta}) = \sum_{t=1}^{T} \log f(y_t; \boldsymbol{\theta}). \qquad [22.3.6]$$

The maximum likelihood estimate of $\boldsymbol{\theta}$ is obtained by maximizing [22.3.6] subject to the constraints that $\pi_1 + \pi_2 + \cdots + \pi_N = 1$ and $\pi_j \geq 0$ for $j = 1, 2, \ldots, N$. This can be achieved using the numerical methods described in Section 5.7, or using the *EM* algorithm developed later in this section.

Functions of the form of [22.3.5] can be used to represent a broad class of different densities. Figure 22.2 gives an example for $N = 2$. The joint density-distribution $p(y_t, s_t = 1; \boldsymbol{\theta})$ is $\pi_1$ times a $N(\mu_1, \sigma_1^2)$ density, while $p(y_t, s_t = 2; \boldsymbol{\theta})$ is $\pi_2$ times a $N(\mu_2, \sigma_2^2)$ density. The unconditional density for the observed variable $f(y_t; \boldsymbol{\theta})$ is the sum of these two magnitudes.

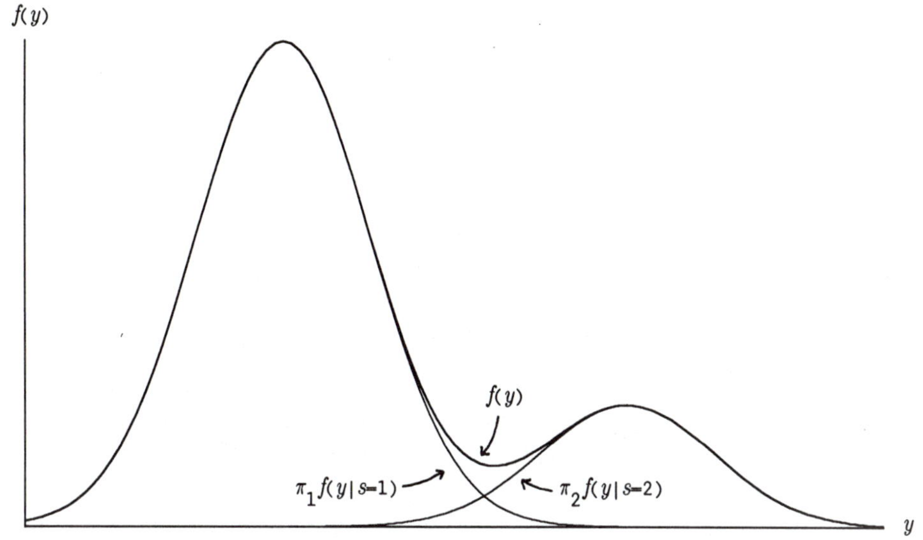


**FIGURE 22.2** Density of mixture of two Gaussian distributions with $y_t|s_t = 1 \sim N(0, 1)$, $y_t|s_t = 2 \sim N(4, 1)$, and $P\{s_t = 1\} = 0.8$.

A mixture of two Gaussian variables need not have the bimodal appearance of Figure 22.2. Gaussian mixtures can also produce a unimodal density, allowing skew or kurtosis different from that of a single Gaussian variable, as in Figure 22.3.

### *Inference About the Unobserved Regime*

Once one has obtained estimates of $\boldsymbol{\theta}$, it is possible to make an inference about which regime was more likely to have been responsible for producing the

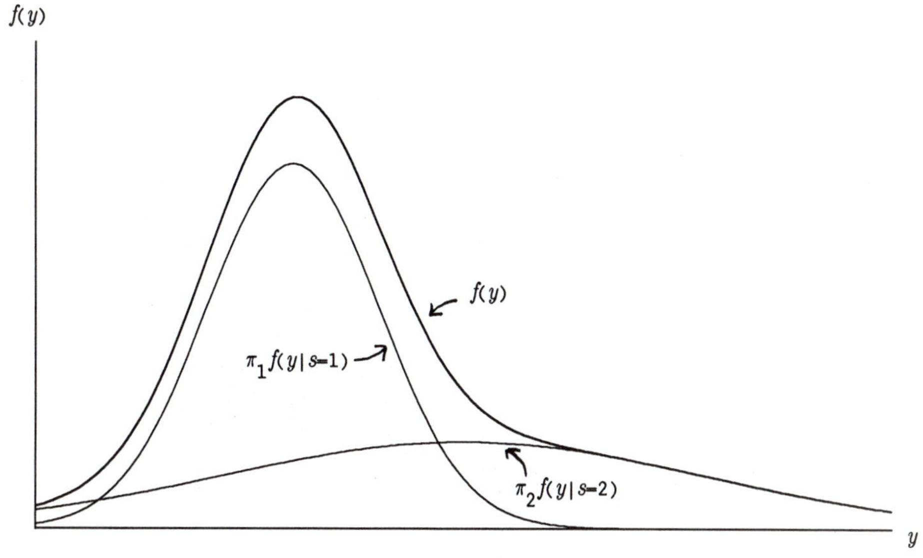


**FIGURE 22.3** Density of mixture of two Gaussian distributions with $y_t|s_t = 1 \sim N(0, 1)$, $y_t|s_t = 2 \sim N(2, 8)$, and $P\{s_t = 1\} = 0.6$.

date $t$ observation of $y_t$. Again, from the definition of a conditional probability, it follows that

$$P\{s_t = j|y_t; \boldsymbol{\theta}\} = \frac{p(y_t, s_t = j; \boldsymbol{\theta})}{f(y_t; \boldsymbol{\theta})} = \frac{\pi_j \cdot f(y_t|s_t = j; \boldsymbol{\theta})}{f(y_t; \boldsymbol{\theta})}. \qquad [22.3.7]$$

Given knowledge of the population parameters $\boldsymbol{\theta}$, it would be possible to use [22.3.1] and [22.3.5] to calculate the magnitude in [22.3.7] for each observation $y_t$ in the sample. This number represents the probability, given the observed data, that the unobserved regime responsible for observation $t$ was regime $j$. For example, for the mixture represented in Figure 22.2, if an observation $y_t$ were equal to zero, one could be virtually certain that the observation had come from a $N(0, 1)$ distribution rather than a $N(4, 1)$ distribution, so that $P\{s_t = 1|y_t; \boldsymbol{\theta}\}$ for that date would be near unity. If instead $y_t$ were around 2.3, it is equally likely that the observation might have come from either regime, so that $P\{s_t = 1|y_t; \boldsymbol{\theta}\}$ for such an observation would be close to 0.5.

## *Maximum Likelihood Estimates and the* EM *Algorithm*

It is instructive to characterize analytically the maximum likelihood estimates of the population parameter $\boldsymbol{\theta}$. Appendix 22.A demonstrates that the maximum likelihood estimate $\hat{\boldsymbol{\theta}}$ represents a solution to the following system of nonlinear equations:

$$\hat{\mu}_j = \frac{\sum_{t=1}^{T} y_t \cdot P\{s_t = j|y_t; \hat{\boldsymbol{\theta}}\}}{\sum_{t=1}^{T} P\{s_t = j|y_t; \hat{\boldsymbol{\theta}}\}} \qquad \text{for } j = 1, 2, \ldots, N \qquad [22.3.8]$$

$$\hat{\sigma}_j^2 = \frac{\sum_{t=1}^{T} (y_t - \hat{\mu}_j)^2 \cdot P\{s_t = j|y_t; \hat{\boldsymbol{\theta}}\}}{\sum_{t=1}^{T} P\{s_t = j|y_t; \hat{\boldsymbol{\theta}}\}} \qquad \text{for } j = 1, 2, \ldots, N \qquad [22.3.9]$$

$$\hat{\pi}_j = T^{-1} \sum_{t=1}^{T} P\{s_t = j|y_t; \hat{\boldsymbol{\theta}}\} \qquad \text{for } j = 1, 2, \ldots, N. \qquad [22.3.10]$$

Suppose we were virtually certain which observations came from regime $j$ and which did not, so that $P\{s_t = j|y_t; \boldsymbol{\theta}\}$ equaled unity for those observations that came from regime $j$ and equaled zero for those observations that came from other regimes. Then the estimate of the mean for regime $j$ in [22.3.8] would simply be the average value of $y_t$ for those observations known to have come from regime $j$. In the more general case where $P\{s_t = j|y_t; \boldsymbol{\theta}\}$ is between 0 and 1 for some observations, the estimate $\hat{\mu}_j$ is a weighted average of all the observations in the sample, where the weight for observation $y_t$ is proportional to the probability that date $t$'s observation was generated by regime $j$. The more likely an observation is to have come from regime $j$, the bigger the weight given that observation in estimating $\mu_j$. Similarly, $\hat{\sigma}_j^2$ is a weighted average of the squared deviations of $y_t$ from $\hat{\mu}_j$, while $\hat{\pi}_j$ is essentially the fraction of observations that appear to have come from regime $j$.

Because equations [22.3.8] to [22.3.10] are nonlinear, it is not possible to solve them analytically for $\hat{\boldsymbol{\theta}}$ as a function of $\{y_1, y_2, \ldots, y_T\}$. However, these equations do suggest an appealing iterative algorithm for finding the maximum likelihood estimate. Starting from an arbitrary initial guess for the value of $\boldsymbol{\theta}$, denoted $\boldsymbol{\theta}^{(0)}$, one could calculate $P\{s_t = j|y_t; \boldsymbol{\theta}^{(0)}\}$ from [22.3.7]. One could then calculate the magnitudes on the right sides of [22.3.8] through [22.3.10] with $\boldsymbol{\theta}^{(0)}$ in place of $\hat{\boldsymbol{\theta}}$. The left sides of [22.3.8] through [22.3.10] would then produce a new estimate $\boldsymbol{\theta}^{(1)}$. This estimate $\boldsymbol{\theta}^{(1)}$ could be used to reevaluate $P\{s_t = j|y_t; \boldsymbol{\theta}^{(1)}\}$ and recalculate the expressions on the right sides of [22.3.8] through [22.3.10]. The left sides of [22.3.8] through [22.3.10] then can produce a new estimate $\boldsymbol{\theta}^{(2)}$. One continues iterating in this fashion until the change between $\boldsymbol{\theta}^{(m+1)}$ and $\boldsymbol{\theta}^{(m)}$ is smaller than some specified convergence criterion.

This algorithm turns out to be a special case of the *EM* principle developed by Dempster, Laird, and Rubin (1977). One can show that each iteration on this algorithm increases the value of the likelihood function. Clearly, if the iterations reach a point such that $\boldsymbol{\theta}^{(m)} = \boldsymbol{\theta}^{(m+1)}$, the algorithm has found the maximum likelihood estimate $\hat{\boldsymbol{\theta}}$.

## *Further Discussion*

The mixture density [22.3.5] has the property that a global maximum of the log likelihood [22.3.6] does not exist. A singularity arises whenever one of the distributions is imputed to have a mean exactly equal to one of the observations ($\mu_1 = y_1$, say) with no variance ($\sigma_1^2 \to 0$). At such a point the log likelihood becomes infinite.

Such singularities do not pose a major problem in practice, since numerical maximization procedures typically converge to a reasonable local maximum rather than a singularity. The largest local maximum with $\sigma_j > 0$ for all $j$ is described as the *maximum likelihood estimate*. Kiefer (1978) showed that there exists a bounded local maximum of [22.3.6] that yields a consistent, asymptotically Gaussian estimate of $\boldsymbol{\theta}$ for which standard errors can be constructed using the usual formulas such as expression [5.8.3]. Hence, if a numerical maximization algorithm becomes stuck at a singularity, one satisfactory solution is simply to ignore the singularity and try again with different starting values.

Another approach is to maximize a slightly different objective function such as

$$\begin{aligned} Q(\boldsymbol{\theta}) = \mathscr{L}(\boldsymbol{\theta}) &- \sum_{j=1}^{N} (a_j/2)\log(\sigma_j^2) - \sum_{j=1}^{N} b_j/(2\sigma_j^2) \\ &- \sum_{j=1}^{N} c_j(m_j - \mu_j)^2/(2\sigma_j^2), \end{aligned} \qquad [22.3.11]$$

where $\mathscr{L}(\boldsymbol{\theta})$ is the log likelihood function described in [22.3.6]. If $a_j = c_j$, then expression [22.3.11] is the form the log likelihood would take if, in addition to the data, the analyst had $a_j$ observations from regime $j$ whose sample mean was $m_j$ and whose sample variance was $b_j/a_j$. Thus, $m_j$ represents the analyst's prior expectation of the value of $\mu_j$, and $b_j/a_j$ represents the analyst's prior expectation of the value of $\sigma_j^2$. The parameters $a_j$ and $c_j$ represent the strength of these priors, measured in terms of the confidence one would have if the priors were based on $a_j$ or $c_j$ direct observations of data known to have come from regime $j$. See Hamilton (1991) for further discussion of this approach.

Nice surveys of i.i.d. mixture distributions have been provided by Everitt and Hand (1981) and Titterington, Smith, and Makov (1985).

## 22.4. Time Series Models of Changes in Regime

### Description of the Process

We now return to the objective of developing a model that allows a given variable to follow a different time series process over different subsamples. As an illustration, consider a first-order autoregression in which both the constant term and the autoregressive coefficient might be different for different subsamples:

$$y_t = c_{s_t} + \phi_{s_t} y_{t-1} + \varepsilon_t, \qquad [22.4.1]$$

where $\varepsilon_t \sim$ i.i.d. $N(0, \sigma^2)$. The proposal will be to model the regime $s_t$ as the outcome of an unobserved $N$-state Markov chain with $s_t$ independent of $\varepsilon_\tau$ for all $t$ and $\tau$.

Why might a Markov chain be a useful description of the process generating changes in regime? One's first thought could be that a change in regime such as that in Figure 22.1 is a permanent event. Such a permanent regime change could be modeled with a two-state Markov chain in which state 2 is an absorbing state. The advantage of using a Markov chain over a deterministic specification for such a process is that it allows one to generate meaningful forecasts prior to the change that take into account the possibility of the change from regime 1 to regime 2.

We might also want a time series model of changes in regime to account for unusual short-lived events such as World War II. Again, it is possible to choose parameters for a Markov chain such that, given 100 years of data, it is quite likely that we would have observed a single episode of regime 2 lasting for about 5 years. A Markov chain specification, of course, implies that given another 100 years we could well see another such event. One might argue that this is a sensible property to build into a model. The essence of the scientific method is the presumption that the future will in some sense be like the past.

While the Markov chain can describe such examples of changes in regime, a further advantage is its flexibility. There seems some value in specifying a probability law consistent with a broad range of different outcomes, and choosing particular parameters within that class on the basis of the data alone.

In any case, the approach described here readily generalizes to processes in which the probability that $s_t = j$ depends not only on the value of $s_{t-1}$ but also on a vector of other observed variables—see Filardo (1992) and Diebold, Lee, and Weinbach (forthcoming).

The general model investigated in this section is as follows. Let $\mathbf{y}_t$ be an $(n \times 1)$ vector of observed endogenous variables and $\mathbf{x}_t$ a $(k \times 1)$ vector of observed exogenous variables. Let $\mathcal{Y}_t = (\mathbf{y}'_t, \mathbf{y}'_{t-1}, \ldots, \mathbf{y}'_{-m}, \mathbf{x}'_t, \mathbf{x}'_{t-1}, \ldots, \mathbf{x}'_{-m})'$ be a vector containing all observations obtained through date $t$. If the process is governed by regime $s_t = j$ at date $t$, then the conditional density of $\mathbf{y}_t$ is assumed to be given by

$$f(\mathbf{y}_t | s_t = j, \mathbf{x}_t, \mathcal{Y}_{t-1}; \boldsymbol{\alpha}), \qquad [22.4.2]$$

where $\boldsymbol{\alpha}$ is a vector of parameters characterizing the conditional density. If there are $N$ different regimes, then there are $N$ different densities represented by [22.4.2] for $j = 1, 2, \ldots, N$. These densities will be collected in an $(N \times 1)$ vector denoted $\boldsymbol{\eta}_t$.

For the example of [22.4.1], $y_t$ is a scalar ($n = 1$), the exogenous variables consist only of a constant term ($\mathbf{x}_t = 1$), and the unknown parameters in $\boldsymbol{\alpha}$ consist of $c_1, \ldots, c_N, \phi_1, \ldots, \phi_N$, and $\sigma^2$. With $N = 2$ regimes the two densities represented by [22.4.2] are

$$\boldsymbol{\eta}_t = \begin{bmatrix} f(y_t|s_t = 1, y_{t-1}; \boldsymbol{\alpha}) \\ f(y_t|s_t = 2, y_{t-1}; \boldsymbol{\alpha}) \end{bmatrix} = \begin{bmatrix} \dfrac{1}{\sqrt{2\pi}\sigma} \exp\left\{\dfrac{-(y_t - c_1 - \phi_1 y_{t-1})^2}{2\sigma^2}\right\} \\ \dfrac{1}{\sqrt{2\pi}\sigma} \exp\left\{\dfrac{-(y_t - c_2 - \phi_2 y_{t-1})^2}{2\sigma^2}\right\} \end{bmatrix}.$$

It is assumed in [22.4.2] that the conditional density depends only on the current regime $s_t$ and not on past regimes:

$$f(\mathbf{y}_t|\mathbf{x}_t, \mathcal{Y}_{t-1}, s_t = j; \boldsymbol{\alpha}) = f(\mathbf{y}_t|\mathbf{x}_t, \mathcal{Y}_{t-1}, s_t = j, s_{t-1} = i, s_{t-2} = k, \ldots; \boldsymbol{\alpha}), \qquad [22.4.3]$$

though this is not really restrictive. Consider, for example, the specification in [22.1.3], where the conditional density of $y_t$ depends on both $s_t^*$ and $s_{t-1}^*$ and where $s_t^*$ is described by a two-state Markov chain. One can define a new variable $s_t$ that characterizes the regime for date $t$ in a way consistent with [22.4.2] as follows:

$$\begin{aligned} s_t &= 1 \quad \text{if } s_t^* = 1 \text{ and } s_{t-1}^* = 1 \\ s_t &= 2 \quad \text{if } s_t^* = 2 \text{ and } s_{t-1}^* = 1 \\ s_t &= 3 \quad \text{if } s_t^* = 1 \text{ and } s_{t-1}^* = 2 \\ s_t &= 4 \quad \text{if } s_t^* = 2 \text{ and } s_{t-1}^* = 2. \end{aligned}$$

If $p_{ij}^*$ denotes $P\{s_t^* = j|s_{t-1}^* = i\}$, then $s_t$ follows a four-state Markov chain with transition matrix

$$\mathbf{P} = \begin{bmatrix} p_{11}^* & 0 & p_{11}^* & 0 \\ p_{12}^* & 0 & p_{12}^* & 0 \\ 0 & p_{21}^* & 0 & p_{21}^* \\ 0 & p_{22}^* & 0 & p_{22}^* \end{bmatrix}.$$

Hence, [22.1.3] could be represented as a special case of this framework with $N = 4$, $\boldsymbol{\alpha} = (\mu_1, \mu_2, \phi, \sigma^2)'$ and with [22.4.2] representing the four densities

$$f(y_t|y_{t-1}, s_t = 1; \boldsymbol{\alpha}) = \frac{1}{\sqrt{2\pi}\sigma} \exp\left\{\frac{-[(y_t - \mu_1) - \phi(y_{t-1} - \mu_1)]^2}{2\sigma^2}\right\}$$

$$f(y_t|y_{t-1}, s_t = 2; \boldsymbol{\alpha}) = \frac{1}{\sqrt{2\pi}\sigma} \exp\left\{\frac{-[(y_t - \mu_2) - \phi(y_{t-1} - \mu_1)]^2}{2\sigma^2}\right\}$$

$$f(y_t|y_{t-1}, s_t = 3; \boldsymbol{\alpha}) = \frac{1}{\sqrt{2\pi}\sigma} \exp\left\{\frac{-[(y_t - \mu_1) - \phi(y_{t-1} - \mu_2)]^2}{2\sigma^2}\right\}$$

$$f(y_t|y_{t-1}, s_t = 4; \boldsymbol{\alpha}) = \frac{1}{\sqrt{2\pi}\sigma} \exp\left\{\frac{-[(y_t - \mu_2) - \phi(y_{t-1} - \mu_2)]^2}{2\sigma^2}\right\}.$$

It is assumed that $s_t$ evolves according to a Markov chain that is independent of past observations on $\mathbf{y}_t$ or current or past $\mathbf{x}_t$:

$$P\{s_t = j|s_{t-1} = i, s_{t-2} = k, \ldots, \mathbf{x}_t, \mathcal{Y}_{t-1}\} = P\{s_t = j|s_{t-1} = i\} = p_{ij}. \qquad [22.4.4]$$

For generalizations of this assumption, see Lam (1990), Durland and McCurdy (1992), Filardo (1992), and Diebold, Lee, and Weinbach (forthcoming).

## *Optimal Inference About Regimes and Evaluation of the Likelihood Function*

The population parameters that describe a time series governed by [22.4.2] and [22.4.4] consist of $\boldsymbol{\alpha}$ and the various transition probabilities $p_{ij}$. Collect these parameters in a vector $\boldsymbol{\theta}$. One important objective will be to estimate the value of $\boldsymbol{\theta}$ based on observation of $\mathcal{Y}_T$. Let us nevertheless put this objective on hold for the moment and suppose that the value of $\boldsymbol{\theta}$ is somehow known with certainty to the analyst. Even if we know the value of $\boldsymbol{\theta}$, we will not know which regime the process was in at every date in the sample. Instead the best we can do is to form a probabilistic inference that is a generalization of [22.3.7]. In the i.i.d. case, the analyst's inference about the value of $s_t$ depends only on the value of $y_t$. In the more general class of time series models described here the inference typically depends on all the observations available.

Let $P\{s_t = j|\mathcal{Y}_t; \boldsymbol{\theta}\}$ denote the analyst's inference about the value of $s_t$ based on data obtained through date $t$ and based on knowledge of the population parameters $\boldsymbol{\theta}$. This inference takes the form of a conditional probability that the analyst assigns to the possibility that the $t$th observation was generated by regime $j$. Collect these conditional probabilities $P\{s_t = j|\mathcal{Y}_t; \boldsymbol{\theta}\}$ for $j = 1, 2, \ldots, N$ in an $(N \times 1)$ vector denoted $\hat{\boldsymbol{\xi}}_{t|t}$.

One could also imagine forming forecasts of how likely the process is to be in regime $j$ in period $t + 1$ given observations obtained through date $t$. Collect these forecasts in an $(N \times 1)$ vector $\hat{\boldsymbol{\xi}}_{t+1|t}$, which is a vector whose $j$th element represents $P\{s_{t+1} = j|\mathcal{Y}_t; \boldsymbol{\theta}\}$.

The optimal inference and forecast for each date $t$ in the sample can be found by iterating on the following pair of equations:

$$\hat{\boldsymbol{\xi}}_{t|t} = \frac{(\hat{\boldsymbol{\xi}}_{t|t-1} \odot \boldsymbol{\eta}_t)}{\mathbf{1}'(\hat{\boldsymbol{\xi}}_{t|t-1} \odot \boldsymbol{\eta}_t)} \qquad [22.4.5]$$

$$\hat{\boldsymbol{\xi}}_{t+1|t} = \mathbf{P} \cdot \hat{\boldsymbol{\xi}}_{t|t}. \qquad [22.4.6]$$

Here $\boldsymbol{\eta}_t$ represents the $(N \times 1)$ vector whose $j$th element is the conditional density in [22.4.2], $\mathbf{P}$ represents the $(N \times N)$ transition matrix defined in [22.2.3], $\mathbf{1}$ represents an $(N \times 1)$ vector of 1s, and the symbol $\odot$ denotes element-by-element multiplication. Given a starting value $\hat{\boldsymbol{\xi}}_{1|0}$ and an assumed value for the population parameter vector $\boldsymbol{\theta}$, one can iterate on [22.4.5] and [22.4.6] for $t = 1, 2, \ldots, T$ to calculate the values of $\hat{\boldsymbol{\xi}}_{t|t}$ and $\hat{\boldsymbol{\xi}}_{t+1|t}$ for each date $t$ in the sample. The log likelihood function $\mathcal{L}(\boldsymbol{\theta})$ for the observed data $\mathcal{Y}_T$ evaluated at the value of $\boldsymbol{\theta}$ that was used to perform the iterations can also be calculated as a by-product of this algorithm from

$$\mathcal{L}(\boldsymbol{\theta}) = \sum_{t=1}^{T} \log f(\mathbf{y}_t|\mathbf{x}_t, \mathcal{Y}_{t-1}; \boldsymbol{\theta}), \qquad [22.4.7]$$

where

$$f(\mathbf{y}_t|\mathbf{x}_t, \mathcal{Y}_{t-1}; \boldsymbol{\theta}) = \mathbf{1}'(\hat{\boldsymbol{\xi}}_{t|t-1} \odot \boldsymbol{\eta}_t). \qquad [22.4.8]$$

We now explain why this algorithm works.

## *Derivation of Equations [22.4.5] Through [22.4.8]*

To see the basis for the algorithm just described, note that we have assumed that $\mathbf{x}_t$ is exogenous, by which we mean that $\mathbf{x}_t$ contains no information about $s_t$

beyond that contained in $\mathcal{Y}_{t-1}$. Hence, the $j$th element of $\hat{\boldsymbol{\xi}}_{t|t-1}$ could also be described as $P\{s_t = j|\mathbf{x}_t, \mathcal{Y}_{t-1}; \boldsymbol{\theta}\}$. The $j$th element of $\boldsymbol{\eta}_t$ is $f(\mathbf{y}_t|s_t = j, \mathbf{x}_t, \mathcal{Y}_{t-1}; \boldsymbol{\theta})$. The $j$th element of the $(N \times 1)$ vector $(\hat{\boldsymbol{\xi}}_{t|t-1} \odot \boldsymbol{\eta}_t)$ is the product of these two magnitudes, which product can be interpreted as the conditional joint density-distribution of $\mathbf{y}_t$ and $s_t$:

$$\begin{aligned} P\{s_t = j|\mathbf{x}_t, \mathcal{Y}_{t-1}; \boldsymbol{\theta}\} &\times f(\mathbf{y}_t|s_t = j, \mathbf{x}_t, \mathcal{Y}_{t-1}; \boldsymbol{\theta}) \\ &= p(\mathbf{y}_t, s_t = j|\mathbf{x}_t, \mathcal{Y}_{t-1}; \boldsymbol{\theta}). \end{aligned} \qquad [22.4.9]$$

The density of the observed vector $\mathbf{y}_t$ conditioned on past observables is the sum of the $N$ magnitudes in [22.4.9] for $j = 1, 2, \ldots, N$. This sum can be written in vector notation as

$$f(\mathbf{y}_t|\mathbf{x}_t, \mathcal{Y}_{t-1}; \boldsymbol{\theta}) = \mathbf{1}'(\hat{\boldsymbol{\xi}}_{t|t-1} \odot \boldsymbol{\eta}_t),$$

as claimed in [22.4.8]. If the joint density-distribution in [22.4.9] is divided by the density of $\mathbf{y}_t$ in [22.4.8], the result is the conditional distribution of $s_t$:

$$\begin{aligned} \frac{p(\mathbf{y}_t, s_t = j|\mathbf{x}_t, \mathcal{Y}_{t-1}; \boldsymbol{\theta})}{f(\mathbf{y}_t|\mathbf{x}_t, \mathcal{Y}_{t-1}; \boldsymbol{\theta})} &= P\{s_t = j|\mathbf{y}_t, \mathbf{x}_t, \mathcal{Y}_{t-1}; \boldsymbol{\theta}\} \\ &= P\{s_t = j|\mathcal{Y}_t; \boldsymbol{\theta}\}. \end{aligned}$$

Hence, from [22.4.8],

$$P\{s_t = j|\mathcal{Y}_t; \boldsymbol{\theta}\} = \frac{p(\mathbf{y}_t, s_t = j|\mathbf{x}_t, \mathcal{Y}_{t-1}; \boldsymbol{\theta})}{\mathbf{1}'(\hat{\boldsymbol{\xi}}_{t|t-1} \odot \boldsymbol{\eta}_t)}. \qquad [22.4.10]$$

But recall from [22.4.9] that the numerator in the expression on the right side of [22.4.10] is the $j$th element of the vector $(\hat{\boldsymbol{\xi}}_{t|t-1} \odot \boldsymbol{\eta}_t)$, while the left side of [22.4.10] is the $j$th element of the vector $\hat{\boldsymbol{\xi}}_{t|t}$. Thus, collecting the equations in [22.4.10] for $j = 1, 2, \ldots, N$ into an $(N \times 1)$ vector produces

$$\hat{\boldsymbol{\xi}}_{t|t} = \frac{(\hat{\boldsymbol{\xi}}_{t|t-1} \odot \boldsymbol{\eta}_t)}{\mathbf{1}'(\hat{\boldsymbol{\xi}}_{t|t-1} \odot \boldsymbol{\eta}_t)},$$

as claimed in [22.4.5].

To see the basis for [22.4.6], take expectations of [22.2.6] conditional on $\mathcal{Y}_t$:

$$E(\boldsymbol{\xi}_{t+1}|\mathcal{Y}_t) = \mathbf{P}\cdot E(\boldsymbol{\xi}_t|\mathcal{Y}_t) + E(\mathbf{v}_{t+1}|\mathcal{Y}_t). \qquad [22.4.11]$$

Note that $\mathbf{v}_{t+1}$ is a martingale difference sequence with respect to $\mathcal{Y}_t$, so that [22.4.11] becomes

$$\hat{\boldsymbol{\xi}}_{t+1|t} = \mathbf{P}\cdot\hat{\boldsymbol{\xi}}_{t|t},$$

as claimed in [22.4.6].

## *Starting the Algorithm*

Given a starting value $\hat{\boldsymbol{\xi}}_{1|0}$, one can use [22.4.5] and [22.4.6] to calculate $\hat{\boldsymbol{\xi}}_{t|t}$ for any $t$. Several options are available for choosing the starting value. One approach is to set $\hat{\boldsymbol{\xi}}_{1|0}$ equal to the vector of unconditional probabilities $\boldsymbol{\pi}$ described in equation [22.2.26]. Another option is to set

$$\hat{\boldsymbol{\xi}}_{1|0} = \boldsymbol{\rho}, \qquad [22.4.12]$$

where $\boldsymbol{\rho}$ is a fixed $(N \times 1)$ vector of nonnegative constants summing to unity, such as $\boldsymbol{\rho} = N^{-1}\cdot\mathbf{1}$. Alternatively, $\boldsymbol{\rho}$ could be estimated by maximum likelihood along with $\boldsymbol{\theta}$ subject to the constraint that $\mathbf{1}'\boldsymbol{\rho} = 1$ and $\rho_j \geq 0$ for $j = 1, 2, \ldots, N$.

## *Forecasts and Smoothed Inferences for the Regime*

Generalizing the earlier notation, let $\hat{\boldsymbol{\xi}}_{t|\tau}$ represent the $(N \times 1)$ vector whose $j$th element is $P\{s_t = j|\mathcal{Y}_\tau; \boldsymbol{\theta}\}$. For $t > \tau$, this represents a forecast about the regime for some future period, whereas for $t < \tau$ it represents the *smoothed inference* about the regime the process was in at date $t$ based on data obtained through some later date $\tau$.

The optimal $m$-period-ahead forecast of $\boldsymbol{\xi}_{t+m}$ can be found by taking expectations of both sides of [22.2.8] conditional on information available at date $t$:

$$E(\boldsymbol{\xi}_{t+m}|\mathcal{Y}_t) = \mathbf{P}^m\cdot E(\boldsymbol{\xi}_t|\mathcal{Y}_t)$$

or

$$\hat{\boldsymbol{\xi}}_{t+m|t} = \mathbf{P}^m\cdot\hat{\boldsymbol{\xi}}_{t|t}, \qquad [22.4.13]$$

where $\hat{\boldsymbol{\xi}}_{t|t}$ is calculated from [22.4.5].

Smoothed inferences can be calculated using an algorithm developed by Kim (1993). In vector form, this algorithm can be written as

$$\hat{\boldsymbol{\xi}}_{t|T} = \hat{\boldsymbol{\xi}}_{t|t} \odot \{\mathbf{P}'\cdot[\hat{\boldsymbol{\xi}}_{t+1|T} \,(\div)\, \hat{\boldsymbol{\xi}}_{t+1|t}]\}, \qquad [22.4.14]$$

where the sign $(\div)$ denotes element-by-element division. The smoothed probabilities $\hat{\boldsymbol{\xi}}_{t|T}$ are found by iterating on [22.4.14] backward for $t = T-1, T-2, \ldots, 1$. This iteration is started with $\hat{\boldsymbol{\xi}}_{T|T}$, which is obtained from [22.4.5] for $t = T$. This algorithm is valid only when $s_t$ follows a first-order Markov chain as in [22.4.4], when the conditional density [22.4.2] depends on $s_t, s_{t-1}, \ldots$ only through the current state $s_t$, and when $\mathbf{x}_t$, the vector of explanatory variables other than the lagged values of $\mathbf{y}$, is strictly exogenous, meaning that $\mathbf{x}_t$ is independent of $s_\tau$ for all $t$ and $\tau$. The basis for Kim's algorithm is explained in Appendix 22.A at the end of the chapter.

## *Forecasts for the Observed Variables*

From the conditional density [22.4.2] it is straightforward to forecast $\mathbf{y}_{t+1}$ conditional on knowing $\mathcal{Y}_t$, $\mathbf{x}_{t+1}$, and $s_{t+1}$. For example, for the $AR(1)$ specification $y_{t+1} = c_{s_{t+1}} + \phi_{s_{t+1}}y_t + \varepsilon_{t+1}$, such a forecast is given by

$$E(y_{t+1}|s_{t+1} = j, \mathcal{Y}_t; \boldsymbol{\theta}) = c_j + \phi_j y_t. \qquad [22.4.15]$$

There are $N$ different conditional forecasts associated with the $N$ possible values for $s_{t+1}$. Note that the unconditional forecast based on actual observable variables is related to these conditional forecasts by

$$\begin{aligned} &E(\mathbf{y}_{t+1}|\mathbf{x}_{t+1}, \mathcal{Y}_t; \boldsymbol{\theta}) \\ &\quad = \int \mathbf{y}_{t+1}\cdot f(\mathbf{y}_{t+1}|\mathbf{x}_{t+1}, \mathcal{Y}_t; \boldsymbol{\theta})\, d\mathbf{y}_{t+1} \\ &\quad = \int \mathbf{y}_{t+1}\left\{\sum_{j=1}^{N} p(\mathbf{y}_{t+1}, s_{t+1} = j|\mathbf{x}_{t+1}, \mathcal{Y}_t; \boldsymbol{\theta})\right\} d\mathbf{y}_{t+1} \end{aligned}$$

$$= \int \mathbf{y}_{t+1} \left\{ \sum_{j=1}^{N} [f(\mathbf{y}_{t+1}|s_{t+1} = j, \mathbf{x}_{t+1}, \mathcal{Y}_t; \boldsymbol{\theta}) P\{s_{t+1} = j|\mathbf{x}_{t+1}, \mathcal{Y}_t; \boldsymbol{\theta}\}] \right\} d\mathbf{y}_{t+1}$$

$$= \sum_{j=1}^{N} P\{s_{t+1} = j|\mathbf{x}_{t+1}, \mathcal{Y}_t; \boldsymbol{\theta}\} \int \mathbf{y}_{t+1} \cdot f(\mathbf{y}_{t+1}|s_{t+1} = j, \mathbf{x}_{t+1}, \mathcal{Y}_t; \boldsymbol{\theta})\, d\mathbf{y}_{t+1}$$

$$= \sum_{j=1}^{N} P\{s_{t+1} = j|\mathcal{Y}_t; \boldsymbol{\theta}\} E(\mathbf{y}_{t+1}|s_{t+1} = j, \mathbf{x}_{t+1}, \mathcal{Y}_t; \boldsymbol{\theta}).$$

Thus, the forecast appropriate for the $j$th regime is simply multiplied by the probability that the process will be in the $j$th regime, and the resulting $N$ different products are added together. For example, if the $j = 1, 2, \ldots, N$ forecasts in [22.4.15] are collected in a $(1 \times N)$ vector $\mathbf{h}_t'$, then

$$E(y_{t+1}|\mathcal{Y}_t; \boldsymbol{\theta}) = \mathbf{h}_t' \hat{\boldsymbol{\xi}}_{t+1|t}.$$

Note that although the Markov chain itself admits the linear representation [22.2.6], the optimal forecast of $\mathbf{y}_{t+1}$ is a nonlinear function of observables, since the inference $\hat{\boldsymbol{\xi}}_{t|t}$ in [22.4.5] depends nonlinearly on $\mathcal{Y}_t$. Although one may use a linear model to form forecasts within a given regime, if an observation seems unlikely to have been generated by the same regime as preceding observations, the appearance of the outlier causes the analyst to switch to a new rule for forming future linear forecasts.

The Markov chain is clearly well suited for forming multiperiod forecasts as well. See Hamilton (1989, 1993b, 1993c) for further discussion.

## *Maximum Likelihood Estimation of Parameters*

In the iteration on [22.4.5] and [22.4.6], the parameter vector $\boldsymbol{\theta}$ was taken to be a fixed, known vector. Once the iteration has been completed for $t = 1, 2, \ldots, T$ for a given fixed $\boldsymbol{\theta}$, the value of the log likelihood implied by that value of $\boldsymbol{\theta}$ is then known from [22.4.7]. The value of $\boldsymbol{\theta}$ that maximizes the log likelihood can be found numerically using the methods described in Section 5.7.

If the transition probabilities are restricted only by the conditions that $p_{ij} \geq 0$ and $(p_{i1} + p_{i2} + \cdots + p_{iN}) = 1$ for all $i$ and $j$, and if the initial probability $\hat{\boldsymbol{\xi}}_{1|0}$ is taken to be a fixed value $\boldsymbol{\rho}$ unrelated to the other parameters, then it is shown in Hamilton (1990) that the maximum likelihood estimates for the transition probabilities satisfy

$$\hat{p}_{ij} = \frac{\sum_{t=2}^{T} P\{s_t = j, s_{t-1} = i|\mathcal{Y}_T; \hat{\boldsymbol{\theta}}\}}{\sum_{t=2}^{T} P\{s_{t-1} = i|\mathcal{Y}_T; \hat{\boldsymbol{\theta}}\}}, \qquad [22.4.16]$$

where $\hat{\boldsymbol{\theta}}$ denotes the full vector of maximum likelihood estimates. Thus, the estimated transition probability $\hat{p}_{ij}$ is essentially the number of times state $i$ seems to have been followed by state $j$ divided by the number of times the process was in state $i$. These counts are estimated on the basis of the smoothed probabilities.

If the vector of initial probabilities $\boldsymbol{\rho}$ is regarded as a separate vector of parameters constrained only by $\mathbf{1}'\boldsymbol{\rho} = 1$ and $\boldsymbol{\rho} \geq \mathbf{0}$, the maximum likelihood estimate of $\boldsymbol{\rho}$ turns out to be the smoothed inference about the initial state:

$$\hat{\boldsymbol{\rho}} = \hat{\boldsymbol{\xi}}_{1|T}. \qquad [22.4.17]$$

The maximum likelihood estimate of the vector $\boldsymbol{\alpha}$ that governs the conditional density [22.4.2] is characterized by

$$\sum_{t=1}^{T} \left( \frac{\partial \log \boldsymbol{\eta}_t}{\partial \boldsymbol{\alpha}'} \right)' \hat{\boldsymbol{\xi}}_{t|T} = \mathbf{0}. \qquad [22.4.18]$$

Here $\boldsymbol{\eta}_t$ is the $(N \times 1)$ vector obtained by vertically stacking the densities in [22.4.2] for $j = 1, 2, \ldots, N$ and $(\partial \log \boldsymbol{\eta}_t)/\partial \boldsymbol{\alpha}'$ is the $(N \times k)$ matrix of derivatives of the logs of these densities, where $k$ represents the number of parameters in $\boldsymbol{\alpha}$. For example, consider a Markov-switching regression model of the form

$$y_t = \mathbf{z}_t' \boldsymbol{\beta}_{s_t} + \varepsilon_t, \qquad [22.4.19]$$

where $\varepsilon_t \sim$ i.i.d. $N(0, \sigma^2)$ and where $\mathbf{z}_t$ is a vector of explanatory variables that could include lagged values of $y$. The coefficient vector for this regression is $\boldsymbol{\beta}_1$ when the process is in regime 1, $\boldsymbol{\beta}_2$ when the process is in regime 2, and so on. For this example, the vector $\boldsymbol{\eta}_t$ would be

$$\boldsymbol{\eta}_t = \begin{bmatrix} \dfrac{1}{\sqrt{2\pi}\sigma} \exp\left\{ \dfrac{-(y_t - \mathbf{z}_t'\boldsymbol{\beta}_1)^2}{2\sigma^2} \right\} \\ \vdots \\ \dfrac{1}{\sqrt{2\pi}\sigma} \exp\left\{ \dfrac{-(y_t - \mathbf{z}_t'\boldsymbol{\beta}_N)^2}{2\sigma^2} \right\} \end{bmatrix},$$

and for $\boldsymbol{\alpha} = (\boldsymbol{\beta}_1', \boldsymbol{\beta}_2', \ldots, \boldsymbol{\beta}_N', \sigma^2)'$, condition [22.4.18] becomes

$$\sum_{t=1}^{T} (y_t - \mathbf{z}_t'\hat{\boldsymbol{\beta}}_j)\mathbf{z}_t \cdot P\{s_t = j | \mathcal{Y}_T; \hat{\boldsymbol{\theta}}\} = \mathbf{0} \qquad \text{for } j = 1, 2, \ldots, N \qquad [22.4.20]$$

$$\hat{\sigma}^2 = T^{-1} \sum_{t=1}^{T} \sum_{j=1}^{N} (y_t - \mathbf{z}_t'\hat{\boldsymbol{\beta}}_j)^2 \cdot P\{s_t = j | \mathcal{Y}_T; \hat{\boldsymbol{\theta}}\}. \qquad [22.4.21]$$

Equation [22.4.20] describes $\hat{\boldsymbol{\beta}}_j$ as satisfying a weighted *OLS* orthogonality condition where each observation is weighted by the probability that it came from regime $j$. In particular, the estimate $\hat{\boldsymbol{\beta}}_j$ can be found from an *OLS* regression of $\tilde{y}_t(j)$ on $\tilde{\mathbf{z}}_t(j)$:

$$\hat{\boldsymbol{\beta}}_j = \left[ \sum_{t=1}^{T} [\tilde{\mathbf{z}}_t(j)][\tilde{\mathbf{z}}_t(j)]' \right]^{-1} \left[ \sum_{t=1}^{T} [\tilde{\mathbf{z}}_t(j)]\tilde{y}_t(j) \right], \qquad [22.4.22]$$

where

$$\begin{aligned} \tilde{y}_t(j) &= y_t \cdot \sqrt{P\{s_t = j | \mathcal{Y}_T; \hat{\boldsymbol{\theta}}\}} \\ \tilde{\mathbf{z}}_t(j) &= z_t \cdot \sqrt{P\{s_t = j | \mathcal{Y}_T; \hat{\boldsymbol{\theta}}\}}. \end{aligned} \qquad [22.4.23]$$

The estimate of $\sigma^2$ in [22.4.21] is just $(1/T)$ times the combined sum of the squared residuals from these $N$ different regressions.

Again, this suggests an appealing algorithm for finding maximum likelihood estimates. For the case when $\boldsymbol{\rho}$ is fixed a priori, given an initial guess for the parameter vector $\boldsymbol{\theta}^{(0)}$ one could evaluate [22.4.16], [22.4.22], and [22.4.21] to generate a new estimate $\boldsymbol{\theta}^{(1)}$. One then iterates in the same fashion described in equations [22.3.8] through [22.3.10] to calculate $\boldsymbol{\theta}^{(2)}, \boldsymbol{\theta}^{(3)}, \ldots$. This again turns out to be an application of the *EM* algorithm. Alternatively, if $\boldsymbol{\rho}$ is to be estimated by maximum likelihood, equation [22.4.17] would be added to the equations that are reevaluated with each iteration. See Hamilton (1990) for details.

## *Illustration: The Behavior of U.S. Real GNP*

As an illustration of this method, consider the data on U.S. real GNP growth analyzed in Hamilton (1989). These data are plotted in the bottom panel of Figure 22.4. The following switching model was fitted to these data by maximum likelihood:

$$\begin{aligned} y_t - \mu_{s_t^*} = \phi_1(y_{t-1} - \mu_{s_{t-1}^*}) + \phi_2(y_{t-2} - \mu_{s_{t-2}^*}) \\ + \phi_3(y_{t-3} - \mu_{s_{t-3}^*}) + \phi_4(y_{t-4} - \mu_{s_{t-4}^*}) + \varepsilon_t, \end{aligned} \qquad [22.4.24]$$

with $\varepsilon_t \sim$ i.i.d. $N(0, \sigma^2)$ and with $s_t^*$ presumed to follow a two-state Markov chain with transition probabilities $p_{ij}^*$. Maximum likelihood estimates of parameters are reported in Table 22.1. In the regime represented by $s_t^* = 1$, the average growth rate is $\mu_1 = 1.2\%$ per quarter, while when $s_t^* = 2$, the average growth rate is $\mu_2 = -0.4\%$. Each regime is highly persistent. The probability that expansion will be followed by another quarter of expansion is $p_{11}^* = 0.9$, so that this regime will persist on average for $1/(1 - p_{11}^*) = 10$ quarters. The probability that a contraction will be followed by contraction is $p_{22}^* = 0.75$, which episodes will typically persist for $1/(1 - p_{22}^*) = 4$ quarters.

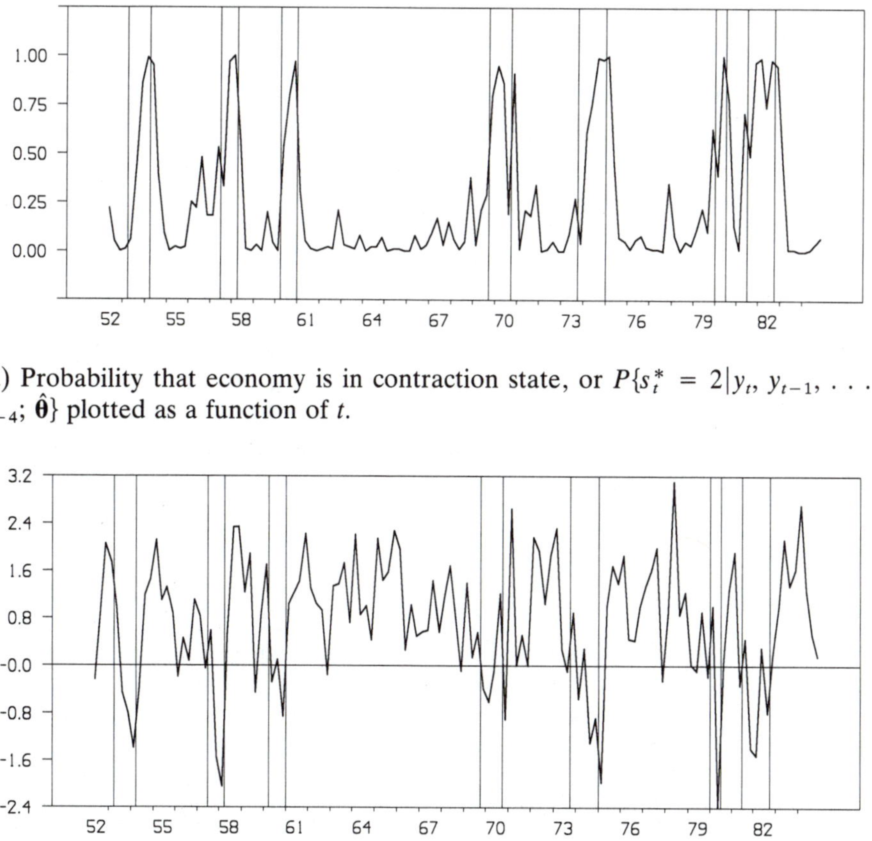


(a) Probability that economy is in contraction state, or $P\{s_t^* = 2 | y_t, y_{t-1}, \ldots, y_{-4}; \hat{\boldsymbol{\theta}}\}$ plotted as a function of $t$.



(b) Quarterly rate of growth of U.S. real GNP, 1952–84.

**FIGURE 22.4** Output growth and recession probabilities.

**TABLE 22.1**
**Maximum Likelihood Estimates of Parameters for Markov-Switching Model of U.S. GNP (Standard Errors in Parentheses)**

| | | | | |
|---|---|---|---|---|
| $\hat{\mu}_1 = 1.16$ (0.07) | $\hat{\mu}_2 = -0.36$ (0.26) | $\hat{p}^*_{11} = 0.90$ (0.04) | $\hat{p}^*_{22} = 0.75$ (0.10) | $\hat{\sigma}^2 = 0.59$ (0.10) |
| $\hat{\phi}_1 = 0.01$ (0.12) | $\hat{\phi}_2 = -0.06$ (0.14) | $\hat{\phi}_3 = -0.25$ (0.11) | $\hat{\phi}_4 = -0.21$ (0.11) | |

In order to write [22.4.24] in a form where $y_t$ depends only on the current value of the regime, a variable $s_t$ was defined that takes on one of 32 different values representing the 32 possible combinations for $s_t^*, s_{t-1}^*, \ldots, s_{t-4}^*$. For example, $s_t = 1$ when $s_t^*, s_{t-1}^*, \ldots$, and $s_{t-4}^*$ all equal 1, $s_t = 2$ when $s_t^* = 2$ and $s_{t-1}^* = \cdots = s_{t-4}^* = 1$, and so on. The vector $\hat{\boldsymbol{\xi}}_{t|t}$ calculated from [22.4.5] is thus a $(32 \times 1)$ vector that contains the probabilities of each of these 32 joint events conditional on data observed through date $t$.

The inference about the value of $s_t^*$ for a single date $t$ is obtained by summing together the relevant joint probabilities. For example, the inference

$$\begin{aligned} P\{s_t^* &= 2|y_t, y_{t-1}, \ldots, y_{-4}; \hat{\boldsymbol{\theta}}\} \\ &= \sum_{i_1=1}^{2}\sum_{i_2=1}^{2}\sum_{i_3=1}^{2}\sum_{i_4=1}^{2} P\{s_t^* = 2, s_{t-1}^* = i_1, s_{t-2}^* = i_2, s_{t-3}^* = i_3, s_{t-4}^* = i_4|y_t, \\ &\qquad y_{t-1}, \ldots, y_{-4}; \hat{\boldsymbol{\theta}}\} \end{aligned} \qquad [22.4.25]$$

is obtained by iterating on [22.4.5] and [22.4.6] with $\boldsymbol{\theta}$ equal to the maximum likelihood estimate $\hat{\boldsymbol{\theta}}$. One then sums together the elements in the even-numbered rows of $\hat{\boldsymbol{\xi}}_{t|t}$ to obtain $P\{s_t^* = 2|y_t, y_{t-1}, \ldots, y_{-4}; \hat{\boldsymbol{\theta}}\}$.

A probabilistic inference in the form of [22.4.25] can be calculated for each date $t$ in the sample. The resulting series is plotted as a function of $t$ in panel (a) of Figure 22.4. The vertical lines in the figure indicate the dates at which economic recessions were determined to begin and end according to the National Bureau of Economic Research. These determinations are made informally on the basis of a large number of time series and are usually made some time after the event. Although these business cycle dates were not used in any way to estimate parameters or form inferences about $s_t^*$, it is interesting that the traditional business cycle dates correspond fairly closely to the expansion and contraction phases as described by the model in [22.4.24].

## *Determining the Number of States*

One of the most important hypotheses that one would want to test for such models concerns the number of different regimes $N$ that characterize the data. Unfortunately, this hypothesis cannot be tested using the usual likelihood ratio test. One of the regularity conditions for the likelihood ratio test to have an asymptotic $\chi^2$ distribution is that the information matrix $\mathcal{J}$ be nonsingular. This condition fails to hold if the analyst tries to fit an $N$-state model when the true process has $N - 1$ states, since under the null hypothesis the parameters that describe the $N$th state are unidentified. Tests that get around the problems with the regularity conditions have been proposed by Davies (1977), Hansen (1993), Andrews and Ploberger (1992), and Stinchcombe and White (1993). Another approach is to take the $(N - 1)$-state model as the null and conduct a variety of tests of the validity of that specification as one way of seeing whether an $N$-state model is needed; Hamilton (1993a) proposed a number of such tests. Studies that illustrate the use of such tests include Engel and Hamilton (1990), Hansen (1992), and Goodwin (1993).

## APPENDIX 22.A. *Derivation of Selected Equations for Chapter 22*

■ **Derivation of [22.3.8] through [22.3.10].** The maximum likelihood estimates are obtained by forming the Lagrangean

$$J(\boldsymbol{\theta}) = \mathcal{L}(\boldsymbol{\theta}) + \lambda(1 - \pi_1 - \pi_2 - \cdots - \pi_N) \qquad [22.A.1]$$

and setting the derivative with respect to $\boldsymbol{\theta}$ equal to zero. From [22.3.6], the derivative of the log likelihood is given by

$$\frac{\partial \mathcal{L}(\boldsymbol{\theta})}{\partial \boldsymbol{\theta}} = \sum_{t=1}^{T} \frac{1}{f(y_t; \boldsymbol{\theta})} \times \frac{\partial f(y_t; \boldsymbol{\theta})}{\partial \boldsymbol{\theta}}. \qquad [22.A.2]$$

Observe from [22.3.5] that

$$\begin{aligned} \frac{\partial f(y_t; \boldsymbol{\theta})}{\partial \pi_j} &= \frac{1}{\sqrt{2\pi}\sigma_j} \exp\left\{\frac{-(y_t - \mu_j)^2}{2\sigma_j^2}\right\} \\ &= f(y_t|s_t = j; \boldsymbol{\theta}), \end{aligned} \qquad [22.A.3]$$

while

$$\frac{\partial f(y_t; \boldsymbol{\theta})}{\partial \mu_j} = \frac{y_t - \mu_j}{\sigma_j^2} \times p(y_t, s_t = j; \boldsymbol{\theta}) \qquad [22.A.4]$$

and

$$\frac{\partial f(y_t; \boldsymbol{\theta})}{\partial \sigma_j^2} = \left\{-\frac{1}{2}\sigma_j^{-2} + \frac{(y_t - \mu_j)^2}{2\sigma_j^4}\right\} \times p(y_t, s_t = j; \boldsymbol{\theta}). \qquad [22.A.5]$$

Thus, [22.A.2] becomes

$$\frac{\partial \mathcal{L}(\boldsymbol{\theta})}{\partial \pi_j} = \sum_{t=1}^{T} \frac{1}{f(y_t; \boldsymbol{\theta})} f(y_t|s_t = j; \boldsymbol{\theta}) \qquad [22.A.6]$$

$$\frac{\partial \mathcal{L}(\boldsymbol{\theta})}{\partial \mu_j} = \sum_{t=1}^{T} \frac{1}{f(y_t; \boldsymbol{\theta})} \times \frac{y_t - \mu_j}{\sigma_j^2} p(y_t, s_t = j; \boldsymbol{\theta}) \qquad [22.A.7]$$

$$\frac{\partial \mathcal{L}(\boldsymbol{\theta})}{\partial \sigma_j^2} = \sum_{t=1}^{T} \frac{1}{f(y_t; \boldsymbol{\theta})} \left\{-\frac{1}{2}\sigma_j^{-2} + \frac{(y_t - \mu_j)^2}{2\sigma_j^4}\right\} p(y_t, s_t = j; \boldsymbol{\theta}). \qquad [22.A.8]$$

Recalling [22.3.7], the derivatives in [22.A.6] through [22.A.8] can be written

$$\frac{\partial \mathcal{L}(\boldsymbol{\theta})}{\partial \pi_j} = \pi_j^{-1} \sum_{t=1}^{T} P\{s_t = j|y_t; \boldsymbol{\theta}\} \qquad [22.A.9]$$

$$\frac{\partial \mathcal{L}(\boldsymbol{\theta})}{\partial \mu_j} = \sum_{t=1}^{T} \frac{y_t - \mu_j}{\sigma_j^2} P\{s_t = j|y_t; \boldsymbol{\theta}\} \qquad [22.A.10]$$

$$\frac{\partial \mathcal{L}(\boldsymbol{\theta})}{\partial \sigma_j^2} = \sum_{t=1}^{T} \left\{-\frac{1}{2}\sigma_j^{-2} + \frac{(y_t - \mu_j)^2}{2\sigma_j^4}\right\} P\{s_t = j|y_t; \boldsymbol{\theta}\}. \qquad [22.A.11]$$

Setting the derivative of the Lagrangean in [22.A.1] with respect to $\mu_j$ equal to zero means setting [22.A.10] equal to zero, from which

$$\sum_{t=1}^{T} y_t \cdot P\{s_t = j|y_t; \boldsymbol{\theta}\} = \mu_j \sum_{t=1}^{T} P\{s_t = j|y_t; \boldsymbol{\theta}\}.$$

Equation [22.3.8] follows immediately from this condition. Similarly, the first-order conditions for maximization with respect to $\sigma_j^2$ are found by setting [22.A.11] equal to zero:

$$\sum_{t=1}^{T} \{-\sigma_j^2 + (y_t - \mu_j)^2\} P\{s_t = j | y_t; \boldsymbol{\theta}\} = 0,$$

from which [22.3.9] follows. Finally, from [22.A.9], the derivative of [22.A.1] with respect to $\pi_j$ is given by

$$\frac{\partial J(\boldsymbol{\theta})}{\partial \pi_j} = \pi_j^{-1} \sum_{t=1}^{T} P\{s_t = j | y_t; \boldsymbol{\theta}\} - \lambda = 0,$$

from which

$$\sum_{t=1}^{T} P\{s_t = j | y_t; \boldsymbol{\theta}\} = \lambda \pi_j. \qquad [22.A.12]$$

Summing [22.A.12] over $j = 1, 2, \ldots, N$ produces

$$\sum_{t=1}^{T} \left[ P\{s_t = 1 | y_t; \boldsymbol{\theta}\} + \cdots + P\{s_t = N | y_t; \boldsymbol{\theta}\} \right] = \lambda(\pi_1 + \pi_2 + \cdots + \pi_N)$$

or

$$\sum_{t=1}^{T} \{1\} = \lambda \cdot (1),$$

implying that $T = \lambda$. Replacing $\lambda$ with $T$ in [22.A.12] produces [22.3.10]. ■

■ **Derivation of [22.4.14].** Recall first that under the maintained assumptions, the regime $s_t$ depends on past observations $\mathcal{Y}_{t-1}$ only through the value of $s_{t-1}$. Similarly, $s_t$ depends on future observations only through the value of $s_{t+1}$:

$$P\{s_t = j | s_{t+1} = i, \mathcal{Y}_T; \boldsymbol{\theta}\} = P\{s_t = j | s_{t+1} = i, \mathcal{Y}_t; \boldsymbol{\theta}\}. \qquad [22.A.13]$$

The validity of [22.A.13] is formally established as follows (the implicit dependence on $\boldsymbol{\theta}$ will be suppressed to simplify the notation). Observe that

$$\begin{aligned} &P\{s_t = j | s_{t+1} = i, \mathcal{Y}_{t+1}\} \\ &= P\{s_t = j | s_{t+1} = i, \mathbf{y}_{t+1}, \mathbf{x}_{t+1}, \mathcal{Y}_t\} \\ &= \frac{p(\mathbf{y}_{t+1}, s_t = j | s_{t+1} = i, \mathbf{x}_{t+1}, \mathcal{Y}_t)}{f(\mathbf{y}_{t+1} | s_{t+1} = i, \mathbf{x}_{t+1}, \mathcal{Y}_t)} \\ &= \frac{f(\mathbf{y}_{t+1} | s_t = j, s_{t+1} = i, \mathbf{x}_{t+1}, \mathcal{Y}_t) \cdot P\{s_t = j | s_{t+1} = i, \mathbf{x}_{t+1}, \mathcal{Y}_t\}}{f(\mathbf{y}_{t+1} | s_{t+1} = i, \mathbf{x}_{t+1}, \mathcal{Y}_t)}, \end{aligned} \qquad [22.A.14]$$

which simplifies to

$$P\{s_t = j | s_{t+1} = i, \mathcal{Y}_{t+1}\} = P\{s_t = j | s_{t+1} = i, \mathbf{x}_{t+1}, \mathcal{Y}_t\}, \qquad [22.A.15]$$

provided that

$$f(\mathbf{y}_{t+1} | s_t = j, s_{t+1} = i, \mathbf{x}_{t+1}, \mathcal{Y}_t) = f(\mathbf{y}_{t+1} | s_{t+1} = i, \mathbf{x}_{t+1}, \mathcal{Y}_t), \qquad [22.A.16]$$

which is indeed the case, since the specification assumes that $\mathbf{y}_{t+1}$ depends on $\{s_{t+1}, s_t, \ldots\}$ only through the current value $s_{t+1}$. Since $\mathbf{x}$ is exogenous, [22.A.15] further implies that

$$P\{s_t = j | s_{t+1} = i, \mathcal{Y}_{t+1}\} = P\{s_t = j | s_{t+1} = i, \mathcal{Y}_t\}. \qquad [22.A.17]$$

By similar reasoning, it must be the case that

$$\begin{aligned} &P\{s_t = j | s_{t+1} = i, \mathcal{Y}_{t+2}\} \\ &= P\{s_t = j | s_{t+1} = i, \mathbf{y}_{t+2}, \mathbf{x}_{t+2}, \mathcal{Y}_{t+1}\} \\ &= \frac{p(\mathbf{y}_{t+2}, s_t = j | s_{t+1} = i, \mathbf{x}_{t+2}, \mathcal{Y}_{t+1})}{f(\mathbf{y}_{t+2} | s_{t+1} = i, \mathbf{x}_{t+2}, \mathcal{Y}_{t+1})} \\ &= \frac{f(\mathbf{y}_{t+2} | s_t = j, s_{t+1} = i, \mathbf{x}_{t+2}, \mathcal{Y}_{t+1}) \cdot P\{s_t = j | s_{t+1} = i, \mathbf{x}_{t+2}, \mathcal{Y}_{t+1}\}}{f(\mathbf{y}_{t+2} | s_{t+1} = i, \mathbf{x}_{t+2}, \mathcal{Y}_{t+1})}, \end{aligned}$$

which simplifies to

$$P\{s_t = j|s_{t+1} = i, \mathcal{Y}_{t+2}\} = P\{s_t = j|s_{t+1} = i, \mathbf{x}_{t+2}, \mathcal{Y}_{t+1}\}, \qquad [22.A.18]$$

provided that

$$f(\mathbf{y}_{t+2}|s_t = j, s_{t+1} = i, \mathbf{x}_{t+2}, \mathcal{Y}_{t+1}) = f(\mathbf{y}_{t+2}|s_{t+1} = i, \mathbf{x}_{t+2}, \mathcal{Y}_{t+1}). \qquad [22.A.19]$$

In this case, [22.A.19] is established from the fact that

$$\begin{aligned}
&f(\mathbf{y}_{t+2}|s_t = j, s_{t+1} = i, \mathbf{x}_{t+2}, \mathcal{Y}_{t+1}) \\
&= \sum_{k=1}^{N} p(\mathbf{y}_{t+2}, s_{t+2} = k|s_t = j, s_{t+1} = i, \mathbf{x}_{t+2}, \mathcal{Y}_{t+1}) \\
&= \sum_{k=1}^{N} [f(\mathbf{y}_{t+2}|s_{t+2} = k, s_t = j, s_{t+1} = i, \mathbf{x}_{t+2}, \mathcal{Y}_{t+1}) \\
&\quad \times P\{s_{t+2} = k|s_t = j, s_{t+1} = i, \mathbf{x}_{t+2}, \mathcal{Y}_{t+1}\}] \\
&= \sum_{k=1}^{N} [f(\mathbf{y}_{t+2}|s_{t+2} = k, s_{t+1} = i, \mathbf{x}_{t+2}, \mathcal{Y}_{t+1}) \\
&\quad \times P\{s_{t+2} = k|s_{t+1} = i, \mathbf{x}_{t+2}, \mathcal{Y}_{t+1}\}] \\
&= f(\mathbf{y}_{t+2}|s_{t+1} = i, \mathbf{x}_{t+2}, \mathcal{Y}_{t+1}).
\end{aligned}$$

Again, exogeneity of $\mathbf{x}$ means that [22.A.18] can be written

$$P\{s_t = j|s_{t+1} = i, \mathcal{Y}_{t+2}\} = P\{s_t = j|s_{t+1} = i, \mathcal{Y}_{t+1}\} = P\{s_t = j|s_{t+1} = i, \mathcal{Y}_t\},$$

where the last equality follows from [22.A.17].

Proceeding inductively, the same argument can be used to establish that

$$P\{s_t = j|s_{t+1} = i, \mathcal{Y}_{t+m}\} = P\{s_t = j|s_{t+1} = i, \mathcal{Y}_t\}$$

for $m = 1, 2, \ldots$, from which [22.A.13] follows.

Note next that

$$\begin{aligned}
P\{s_t = j|s_{t+1} = i, \mathcal{Y}_t\} &= \frac{P\{s_t = j, s_{t+1} = i|\mathcal{Y}_t\}}{P\{s_{t+1} = i|\mathcal{Y}_t\}} \\
&= \frac{P\{s_t = j|\mathcal{Y}_t\}\cdot P\{s_{t+1} = i|s_t = j\}}{P\{s_{t+1} = i|\mathcal{Y}_t\}} \\
&= \frac{p_{ji}\cdot P\{s_t = j|\mathcal{Y}_t\}}{P\{s_{t+1} = i|\mathcal{Y}_t\}}.
\end{aligned} \qquad [22.A.20]$$

It is therefore the case that

$$\begin{aligned}
P\{s_t = j, s_{t+1} = i|\mathcal{Y}_T\} &= P\{s_{t+1} = i|\mathcal{Y}_T\}\cdot P\{s_t = j|s_{t+1} = i, \mathcal{Y}_T\} \\
&= P\{s_{t+1} = i|\mathcal{Y}_T\}\cdot P\{s_t = j|s_{t+1} = i, \mathcal{Y}_t\} \\
&= P\{s_{t+1} = i|\mathcal{Y}_T\}\frac{p_{ji}\cdot P\{s_t = j|\mathcal{Y}_t\}}{P\{s_{t+1} = i|\mathcal{Y}_t\}},
\end{aligned} \qquad [22.A.21]$$

where the second equality follows from [22.A.13] and the third follows from [22.A.20].

The smoothed inference for date $t$ is the sum of [22.A.21] over $i = 1, 2, \ldots, N$:

$$\begin{aligned}
P\{s_t = j|\mathcal{Y}_T\} &= \sum_{i=1}^{N} P\{s_t = j, s_{t+1} = i|\mathcal{Y}_T\} \\
&= \sum_{i=1}^{N} P\{s_{t+1} = i|\mathcal{Y}_T\}\frac{p_{ji}\cdot P\{s_t = j|\mathcal{Y}_t\}}{P\{s_{t+1} = i|\mathcal{Y}_t\}} \\
&= P\{s_t = j|\mathcal{Y}_t\}\sum_{i=1}^{N}\frac{p_{ji}\cdot P\{s_{t+1} = i|\mathcal{Y}_T\}}{P\{s_{t+1} = i|\mathcal{Y}_t\}} \\
&= P\{s_t = j|\mathcal{Y}_t\}[p_{j1} \;\; p_{j2} \;\; \cdots \;\; p_{jN}] \\
&\quad \times \begin{bmatrix} P\{s_{t+1} = 1|\mathcal{Y}_T\}/P\{s_{t+1} = 1|\mathcal{Y}_t\} \\ P\{s_{t+1} = 2|\mathcal{Y}_T\}/P\{s_{t+1} = 2|\mathcal{Y}_t\} \\ \vdots \\ P\{s_{t+1} = N|\mathcal{Y}_T\}/P\{s_{t+1} = N|\mathcal{Y}_t\} \end{bmatrix} \\
&= P\{s_t = j|\mathcal{Y}_t\}\mathbf{p}_j'(\hat{\boldsymbol{\xi}}_{t+1|T} \,(\div)\, \hat{\boldsymbol{\xi}}_{t+1|t}),
\end{aligned} \qquad [22.A.22]$$

where the $(1 \times N)$ vector $\mathbf{p}_j'$ denotes the $j$th row of the matrix $\mathbf{P}'$ and the sign $(\div)$ indicates element-by-element division. When the equations represented by [22.A.22] for $j = 1, 2, \ldots, N$ are collected in an $(N \times 1)$ vector, the result is

$$\hat{\boldsymbol{\xi}}_{t|T} = \hat{\boldsymbol{\xi}}_{t|t} \odot \{\mathbf{P}'(\hat{\boldsymbol{\xi}}_{t+1|T} (\div) \hat{\boldsymbol{\xi}}_{t+1|t})\},$$

as claimed. ■

## Chapter 22 Exercise

22.1. Let $s_t$ be described by an ergodic two-state Markov chain with transition matrix $\mathbf{P}$ given by [22.2.11]. Verify that the matrix of eigenvectors of this matrix is given by

$$\mathbf{T} = \begin{bmatrix} (1 - p_{22})/(2 - p_{11} - p_{22}) & -1 \\ (1 - p_{11})/(2 - p_{11} - p_{22}) & 1 \end{bmatrix}$$

with inverse

$$\mathbf{T}^{-1} = \begin{bmatrix} 1 & 1 \\ -(1 - p_{11})/(2 - p_{11} - p_{22}) & (1 - p_{22})/(2 - p_{11} - p_{22}) \end{bmatrix}.$$

## Chapter 22 References


Andrews, Donald W. K., and Werner Ploberger. 1992. "Optimal Tests When a Nuisance Parameter Is Present Only under the Alternative." Yale University. Mimeo.

Cox, D. R., and H. D. Miller. 1965. *The Theory of Stochastic Processes*. London: Methuen.

Davies, R. B. 1977. "Hypothesis Testing When a Nuisance Parameter Is Present Only under the Alternative." *Biometrika* 64:247–54.

Dempster, A. P., N. M. Laird, and D. B. Rubin. 1977. "Maximum Likelihood from Incomplete Data via the EM Algorithm." *Journal of the Royal Statistical Society* Series B, 39:1–38.

Diebold, Francis X., Joon-Haeng Lee, and Gretchen C. Weinbach. Forthcoming. "Regime Switching with Time-Varying Transition Probabilities," in C. Hargreaves, ed., *Nonstationary Time Series Analysis and Cointegration*. Oxford: Oxford University Press.

Durland, J. Michael, and Thomas H. McCurdy. 1992. "Modelling Duration Dependence in Cyclical Data Using a Restricted Semi-Markov Process." Queen's University, Kingston, Ontario. Mimeo.

Engel, Charles, and James D. Hamilton. 1990. "Long Swings in the Dollar: Are They in the Data and Do Markets Know It?" *American Economic Review* 80:689–713.

Everitt, B. S., and D. J. Hand. 1981. *Finite Mixture Distributions*. London: Chapman and Hall.

Filardo, Andrew J. 1992. "Business Cycle Phases and Their Transitional Dynamics." Federal Reserve Bank of Kansas City. Mimeo.

Goodwin, Thomas H. 1993. "Business Cycle Analysis with a Markov-Switching-Model." *Journal of Business and Economic Statistics* 11:331–39.

Hamilton, James D. 1989. "A New Approach to the Economic Analysis of Nonstationary Time Series and the Business Cycle." *Econometrica* 57:357–84.

———. 1990. "Analysis of Time Series Subject to Changes in Regime." *Journal of Econometrics* 45:39–70.

———. 1991. "A Quasi-Bayesian Approach to Estimating Parameters for Mixtures of Normal Distributions." *Journal of Business and Economic Statistics* 9:27–39.

———. 1993a. "Specification Testing in Markov-Switching Time Series Models." University of California, San Diego. Mimeo.

———. 1993b. "Estimation, Inference, and Forecasting of Time Series Subject to Changes in Regime," in G. S. Maddala, C. R. Rao, and H. D. Vinod, eds., *Handbook of Statistics*, Vol. 11. New York: North-Holland.

———. 1993c. "State-Space Models," in Robert Engle and Daniel McFadden, eds., *Handbook of Econometrics*, Vol. 4. New York: North-Holland.

Hansen, Bruce E. 1992. "The Likelihood Ratio Test under Non-Standard Conditions: Testing the Markov Switching Model of GNP." *Journal of Applied Econometrics* 7:S61–82.

———. 1993. "Inference When a Nuisance Parameter Is Not Identified under the Null Hypothesis." University of Rochester. Mimeo.

Kiefer, Nicholas M. 1978. "Discrete Parameter Variation: Efficient Estimation of a Switching Regression Model." *Econometrica* 46:427–34.

Kim, Chang-Jin. 1993. "Dynamic Linear Models with Markov-Switching." *Journal of Econometrics*, forthcoming.

Lam, Pok-sang. 1990. "The Hamilton Model with a General Autoregressive Component: Estimation and Comparison with Other Models of Economic Time Series." *Journal of Monetary Economics* 26:409–32.

Rogers, John H. 1992. "The Currency Substitution Hypothesis and Relative Money Demand in Mexico and Canada." *Journal of Money, Credit, and Banking* 24:300–18.

Stinchcombe, Maxwell, and Halbert White. 1993. "An Approach to Consistent Specification Testing Using Duality and Banach Limit Theory." University of California, San Diego. Mimeo.

Titterington, D. M., A. F. M. Smith, and U. E. Makov. 1985. *Statistical Analysis of Finite Mixture Distributions*. New York: Wiley.

# A Mathematical Review

This book assumes some familiarity with elementary trigonometry, complex numbers, calculus, matrix algebra, and probability. Introductions to the first three topics by Chiang (1974) or Thomas (1972) are adequate; Marsden (1974) treated these issues in more depth. No matrix algebra is required beyond the level of standard econometrics texts such as Theil (1971) or Johnston (1984); for more detailed treatments, see O'Nan (1976), Strang (1976), and Magnus and Neudecker (1988). The concepts of probability and statistics from standard econometrics texts are also sufficient for getting through this book; for more complete introductions, see Lindgren (1976) or Hoel, Port, and Stone (1971).

This appendix reviews the necessary mathematical concepts and results. The reader familiar with these topics is invited to skip this material, or consult subheadings for desired coverage.

## A.1. *Trigonometry*

### *Definitions*

Figure A.1 displays a circle with unit radius centered at the origin in $(x, y)$-space. Let $(x_0, y_0)$ denote some point on this unit circle, and consider the angle $\theta$ between this point and the $x$-axis. The *sine* of $\theta$ is defined as the $y$-coordinate of the point, and the *cosine* is the $x$-coordinate:

$$\sin(\theta) = y_0 \qquad \text{[A.1.1]}$$

$$\cos(\theta) = x_0. \qquad \text{[A.1.2]}$$

This text always measures angles in *radians*. The radian measure of the angle $\theta$ is defined as the distance traveled counterclockwise along the unit circle starting at the $x$-axis before reaching $(x_0, y_0)$. The circumference of a circle with unit radius is $2\pi$. A rotation one-quarter of the way around the unit circle would therefore correspond to radian measure of $\theta = \frac{1}{4}(2\pi) = \pi/2$. An angle whose radian measure is $\pi/2$ is more commonly described as a right angle or a 90° angle. A 45° angle has radian measure of $\pi/4$, a 180° angle has radian measure of $\pi$, and so on.

### *Polar Coordinates*

Consider a smaller triangle—say, the triangle with vertex $(x_1, y_1)$ shown in Figure A.1—that shares the same angle $\theta$ as the original triangle with vertex

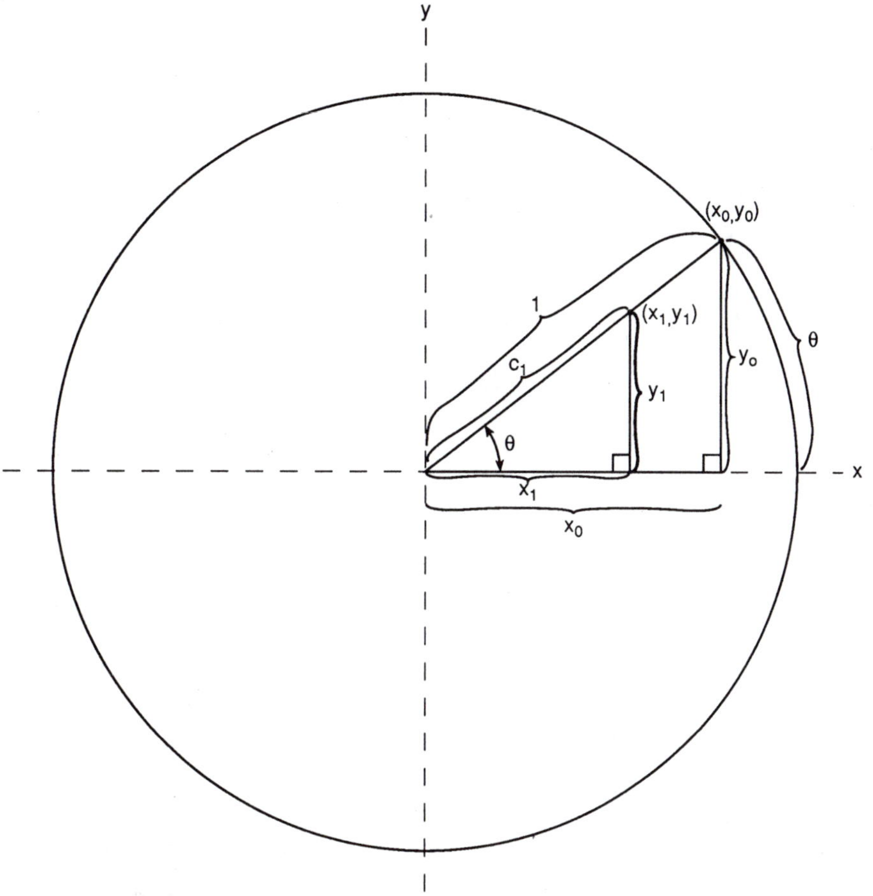


**FIGURE A.1** Trigonometric functions as distances in $(x, y)$-space.

$(x_0, y_0)$. The ratio of any two sides of such a smaller triangle will be the same as that for the larger triangle:

$$y_1/c_1 = y_0/1 \qquad [A.1.3]$$

$$x_1/c_1 = x_0/1. \qquad [A.1.4]$$

Comparing [A.1.3] with [A.1.1], the $y$-coordinate of any point such as $(x_1, y_1)$ in $(x, y)$-space may be expressed as

$$y_1 = c_1 \cdot \sin(\theta), \qquad [A.1.5]$$

where $c_1$ is the distance from the origin to $(x_1, y_1)$ and $\theta$ is the angle that the point $(x_1, y_1)$ makes with the $x$-axis. Comparing [A.1.4] with [A.1.2], the $x$-coordinate of $(x_1, y_1)$ can be expressed as

$$x_1 = c_1 \cdot \cos(\theta). \qquad [A.1.6]$$

Recall further that the magnitude $c_1$, which represents the distance from the origin to the point $(x_1, y_1)$, is given by the formula

$$c_1 = \sqrt{x_1^2 + y_1^2}. \qquad [A.1.7]$$

Taking a point in $(x, y)$-space and writing it as $(c \cdot \cos(\theta), c \cdot \sin(\theta))$ is called describing the point in terms of its *polar coordinates* $c$ and $\theta$.

## *Properties of Sine and Cosine Functions*

The functions $\sin(\theta)$ and $\cos(\theta)$ are called *trigonometric* or *sinusoidal* functions. Viewed as a function of $\theta$, the sine function starts out at zero:

$$\sin(0) = 0.$$

The sine function rises to 1 as $\theta$ increases to $\pi/2$ and then falls back to zero as $\theta$ increases further to $\pi$; see panel (a) of Figure A.2. The function reaches its minimum value of $-1$ at $\theta = 3\pi/2$ and then begins climbing back up.

If we travel a distance of $2\pi$ radians around the unit circle, we are right back where we started, and the function repeats itself:

$$\sin(2\pi + \theta) = \sin(\theta).$$

The function would again repeat itself if we made two full revolutions around the unit circle. Indeed for any integer $j$,

$$\sin(2\pi j + \theta) = \sin(\theta). \qquad \text{[A.1.8]}$$

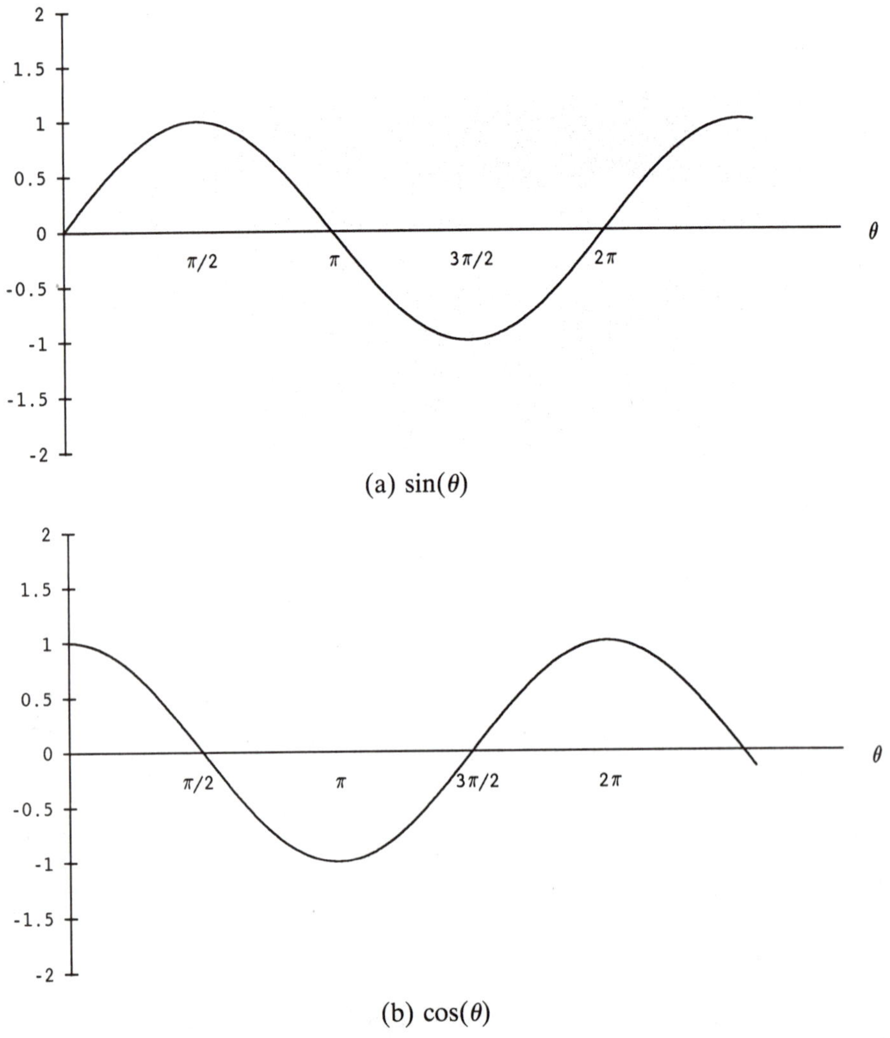


**FIGURE A.2** Sine and cosine functions.

The sine function is thus *periodic* and is for this reason often useful for describing a time series that repeats itself in a particular cycle.

The cosine function starts out at unity and falls to zero as $\theta$ increases to $\pi/2$; see panel (b) of Figure A.2. It turns out simply to be a horizontal shift of the sine function:

$$\cos(\theta) = \sin\left(\theta + \frac{\pi}{2}\right). \qquad [A.1.9]$$

The sine or cosine function can also be evaluated for negative values of $\theta$, defined as a clockwise rotation around the unit circle from the $x$-axis. Clearly,

$$\sin(-\theta) = -\sin(\theta) \qquad [A.1.10]$$

$$\cos(-\theta) = \cos(\theta). \qquad [A.1.11]$$

For $(x_0, y_0)$ a point on the unit circle, [A.1.7] implies that

$$1 = \sqrt{x_0^2 + y_0^2},$$

or, squaring both sides and using [A.1.1] and [A.1.2],

$$1 = [\cos(\theta)]^2 + [\sin(\theta)]^2. \qquad [A.1.12]$$

## *Using Trigonometric Functions to Represent Cycles*

Suppose we construct the function $g(\theta)$ by first multiplying $\theta$ by 2 and then evaluating the sine of the product:

$$g(\theta) = \sin(2\theta).$$

This doubles the frequency at which the function cycles. When $\theta$ goes from 0 to $\pi$, $2\theta$ goes from 0 to $2\pi$, and so $g(\theta)$ is back to its original value (see Figure A.3). In general, the function $\sin(k\theta)$ would go through $k$ cycles in the time it takes $\sin(\theta)$ to complete a single cycle.

We will sometimes describe the value a variable $y$ takes on at date $t$ as a function of sines or cosines, such as

$$y_t = R \cdot \cos(\omega t + \alpha). \qquad [A.1.13]$$

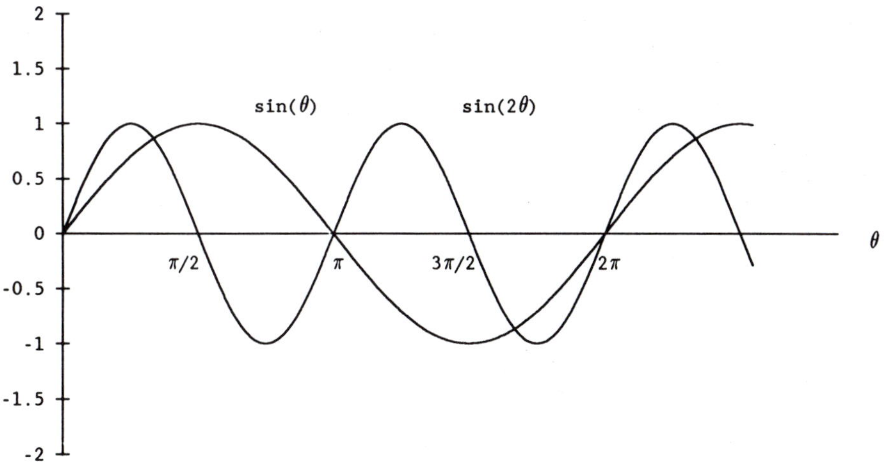


**FIGURE A.3** Effect of changing frequency of a periodic function.

The parameter $R$ gives the *amplitude* of [A.1.13]. The variable $y_t$ will attain a maximum value of $+R$ and a minimum value of $-R$. The parameter $\alpha$ is the *phase*. The phase determines where in the cycle $y_t$ would be at $t = 0$. The parameter $\omega$ governs how quickly the variable cycles, which can be summarized by either of two measures. The *period* is the length of time required for the process to repeat a full cycle. The period of [A.1.13] is $2\pi/\omega$. For example, if $\omega = 1$ then $y$ repeats itself every $2\pi$ periods, whereas if $\omega = 2$ the process repeats itself every $\pi$ periods. The *frequency* summarizes how frequently the process cycles compared with the simple function $\cos(t)$; thus, it measures the number of cycles completed during $2\pi$ periods. The frequency of $\cos(t)$ is unity, and the frequency of [A.1.13] is $\omega$. For example, if $\omega = 2$, the cycles are completed twice as quickly as those for $\cos(t)$. There is a simple relation between these two measures of the speed of cycles—the period is equal to $2\pi$ divided by the frequency.

## A.2. *Complex Numbers*

### *Definitions*

Consider the following expression:

$$x^2 = 1. \qquad [A.2.1]$$

There are two values of $x$ that satisfy [A.2.1], namely, $x = 1$ and $x = -1$.

Suppose instead that we were given the following equation:

$$x^2 = -1. \qquad [A.2.2]$$

No real number satisfies [A.2.2]. However, let us consider an imaginary number (denoted $i$) that does:

$$i^2 = -1. \qquad [A.2.3]$$

We assume that $i$ can be multiplied by a real number and manipulated using standard rules of algebra. For example,

$$2i + 3i = 5i$$

and

$$(2i)\cdot(3i) = (6)i^2 = -6.$$

This last property implies that a second solution to [A.2.2] is given by $x = -i$:

$$(-i)^2 = (-1)^2(i)^2 = -1.$$

Thus, [A.2.1] has two real roots ($+1$ and $-1$), whereas [A.2.2] has two imaginary roots ($i$ and $-i$).

For any real numbers $a$ and $b$, we can construct the expression

$$a + bi. \qquad [A.2.4]$$

If $b = 0$, then [A.2.4] is a *real* number; whereas if $a = 0$ and $b$ is nonzero, then [A.2.4] is an *imaginary* number. A number written in the general form of [A.2.4] is called a *complex* number.

### *Rules for Manipulating Complex Numbers*

Complex numbers are manipulated using standard rules of algebra. Two complex numbers are added as follows:

$$(a_1 + b_1 i) + (a_2 + b_2 i) = (a_1 + a_2) + (b_1 + b_2)i.$$

Complex numbers are multiplied this way:

$$(a_1 + b_1 i)\cdot(a_2 + b_2 i) = a_1 a_2 + a_1 b_2 i + b_1 a_2 i + b_1 b_2 i^2$$
$$= (a_1 a_2 - b_1 b_2) + (a_1 b_2 + b_1 a_2)i.$$

Note that the resulting expressions are always simplified by separating the real component (such as $[a_1 a_2 - b_1 b_2]$) from the imaginary component (such as $[a_1 b_2 + b_1 a_2]i$).

## *Graphical Representation of Complex Numbers*

A complex number $(a + bi)$ is sometimes represented graphically in an *Argand diagram* as in Figure A.4. The value of the real component ($a$) is plotted on the horizontal axis, and the imaginary component ($b$) is plotted on the vertical axis. The size, or *modulus*, of a complex number is measured the same way as the distance from the origin of a real element in $(x, y)$-space (see equation [A.1.7]):

$$|a + bi| \equiv \sqrt{a^2 + b^2}. \qquad \text{[A.2.5]}$$

The *complex unit circle* is the set of all complex numbers whose modulus is 1. For example, the real number +1 is on the complex unit circle (represented by

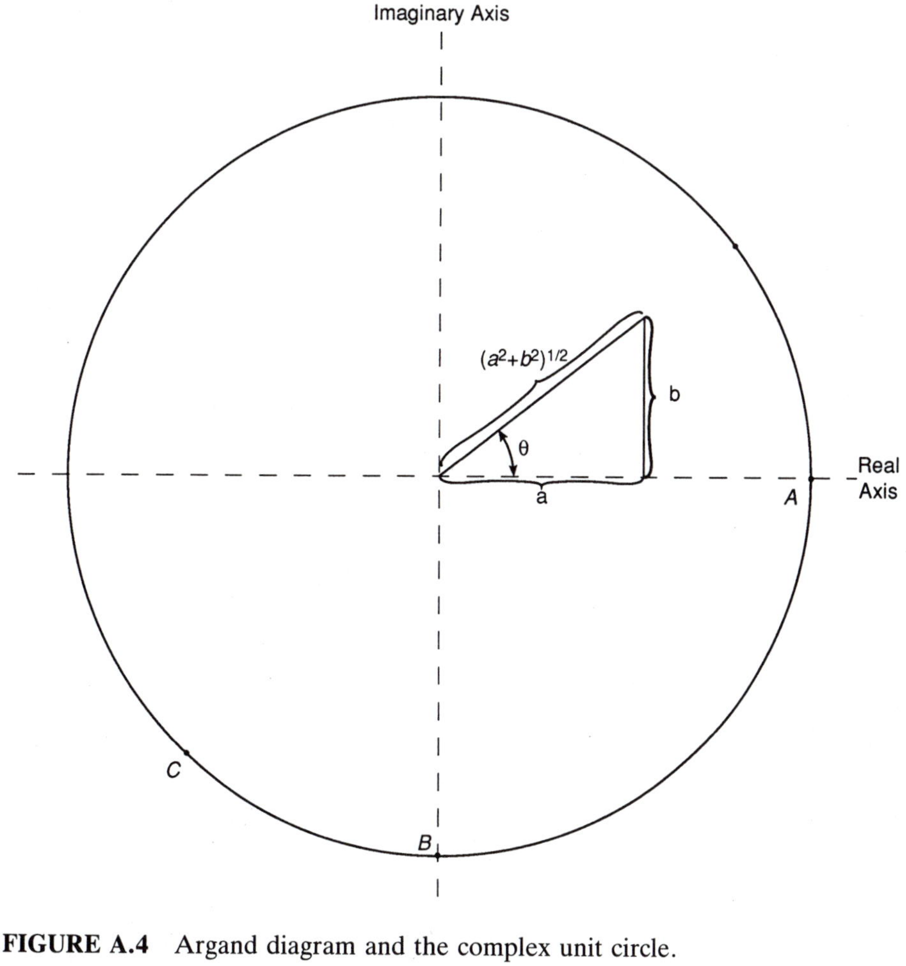


**FIGURE A.4** Argand diagram and the complex unit circle.

the point $A$ in Figure A.4). So are the imaginary number $-i$ (point $B$) and the complex number $(-0.6 - 0.8i)$ (point $C$).

We will often be interested in whether a complex number is less than 1 in modulus, in which case the number is said to be inside the unit circle. For example, $(-0.3 + 0.4i)$ has modulus 0.5, so it lies inside the unit circle, whereas $(3 + 4i)$, with modulus 5, lies outside the unit circle.

## *Polar Coordinates*

Just as a point in $(x, y)$-space can be represented by its distance $c$ from the origin and its angle $\theta$ with the $x$-axis, the complex number $a + bi$ can be represented by the distance of $(a, b)$ from the origin (the modulus of the complex number),

$$R = \sqrt{a^2 + b^2},$$

and by the angle $\theta$ that the point $(a, b)$ makes with the real axis, characterized by

$$\cos(\theta) = a/R$$
$$\sin(\theta) = b/R.$$

Thus, the complex number $a + bi$ is written in polar coordinate form as

$$[R \cdot \cos(\theta) + i \cdot R \cdot \sin(\theta)] = R[\cos(\theta) + i \cdot \sin(\theta)]. \qquad \text{[A.2.6]}$$

## *Complex Conjugates*

The *complex conjugate* of $(a + bi)$ is given by $(a - bi)$. The numbers $(a + bi)$ and $(a - bi)$ are described as a *conjugate pair*. Notice that adding a conjugate pair produces a real result:

$$(a + bi) + (a - bi) = 2a.$$

The product of a conjugate pair is also real:

$$(a + bi) \cdot (a - bi) = a^2 + b^2. \qquad \text{[A.2.7]}$$

Comparing this with [A.2.5], we see that the modulus of a complex number $(a + bi)$ can be thought of as the square root of the product of the number with its complex conjugate:

$$|a + bi| = \sqrt{(a + bi)(a - bi)}. \qquad \text{[A.2.8]}$$

## *Quadratic Equations*

A *quadratic equation*

$$\alpha x^2 + \beta x + \gamma = 0 \qquad \text{[A.2.9]}$$

with $\alpha \neq 0$ has two solutions:

$$x_1 = \frac{-\beta + (\beta^2 - 4\alpha\gamma)^{1/2}}{2\alpha} \qquad \text{[A.2.10]}$$

$$x_2 = \frac{-\beta - (\beta^2 - 4\alpha\gamma)^{1/2}}{2\alpha}. \qquad \text{[A.2.11]}$$

When $(\beta^2 - 4\alpha\gamma) \geq 0$, both these roots are real, whereas when $(\beta^2 - 4\alpha\gamma) < 0$, the roots are complex. Notice that when the roots are complex they appear as a conjugate pair:

$$x_1 = \{-\beta/[2\alpha]\} + \{(1/[2\alpha])(4\alpha\gamma - \beta^2)^{1/2}\}i$$
$$x_2 = \{-\beta/[2\alpha]\} - \{(1/[2\alpha])(4\alpha\gamma - \beta^2)^{1/2}\}i.$$

## A.3. *Calculus*

### *Continuity*

A function $f(x)$ is said to be *continuous* at $x = c$ if $f(c)$ is finite and if for every $\varepsilon > 0$ there is a $\delta > 0$ such that $|f(x) - f(c)| < \varepsilon$ whenever $|x - c| < \delta$.

### *Derivatives of Some Simple Functions*

The *derivative* of $f(\cdot)$ with respect to $x$ is defined by

$$\frac{df}{dx} = \lim_{\Delta \to 0} \frac{f(x + \Delta) - f(x)}{\Delta},$$

provided that this limit exists.

If $f(\cdot)$ is linear in $x$, or

$$f(x) = \alpha + \beta x,$$

then the derivative is just the coefficient on $x$:

$$\frac{df}{dx} = \lim_{\Delta \to 0} \frac{[\alpha + \beta(x + \Delta)] - [\alpha + \beta x]}{\Delta} = \lim_{\Delta \to 0} \frac{\beta\Delta}{\Delta} = \beta.$$

For a quadratic function

$$f(x) = x^2,$$

the derivative is

$$\begin{aligned} \frac{df}{dx} &= \lim_{\Delta \to 0} \frac{[x + \Delta]^2 - x^2}{\Delta} \\ &= \lim_{\Delta \to 0} \frac{[x^2 + 2x\Delta + \Delta^2] - x^2}{\Delta} \\ &= \lim_{\Delta \to 0} \{2x + \Delta\} \\ &= 2x, \end{aligned}$$

and in general,

$$\frac{dx^k}{dx} = kx^{k-1}. \qquad \text{[A.3.1]}$$

For the trigonometric functions, it can be shown that when $x$ is measured in radians,

$$\frac{d\sin(x)}{dx} = \cos(x) \qquad \text{[A.3.2]}$$

$$\frac{d\cos(x)}{dx} = -\sin(x). \qquad \text{[A.3.3]}$$

The derivative $df(x)/dx$ is itself a function of $x$. Often we want to specify the point at which the derivative should be evaluated, say, $c$. This is indicated by

$$\left.\frac{df(x)}{dx}\right|_{x=c}.$$

For example,

$$\left.\frac{dx^2}{dx}\right|_{x=3} = 2x|_{x=3} = 6.$$

Note that this notation refers to taking the derivative first and then evaluating the derivative at a particular point such as $x = 3$.

## *Chain Rule*

The *chain rule* states that for composite functions such as

$$g(x) = f(u(x)),$$

the derivative is

$$\frac{dg(x)}{dx} = \frac{df}{du}\cdot\frac{du}{dx}. \qquad [A.3.4]$$

For example, to evaluate

$$\frac{d(\alpha + \beta x)^k}{dx},$$

we let $f(u) = u^k$ and $u(x) = \alpha + \beta x$. Then

$$\frac{df}{du}\cdot\frac{du}{dx} = ku^{k-1}\cdot\beta.$$

Thus,

$$\frac{d(\alpha + \beta x)^k}{dx} = \beta k(\alpha + \beta x)^{k-1}.$$

## *Higher-Order Derivatives*

The *second derivative* is defined by

$$\frac{d^2f(x)}{dx^2} = \frac{d}{dx}\left[\frac{df(x)}{dx}\right].$$

For example,

$$\frac{d^2x^k}{dx^2} = \frac{d[kx^{k-1}]}{dx} = k(k-1)x^{k-2}$$

and

$$\frac{d^2\sin(x)}{dx^2} = \frac{d\cos(x)}{dx} = -\sin(x). \qquad [A.3.5]$$

In general, the $j$th-order derivative is the derivative of the $(j-1)$th-order derivative.

## Geometric Series

Consider the sum

$$s_T = 1 + \phi + \phi^2 + \phi^3 + \cdots + \phi^T. \qquad [A.3.6]$$

Multiplying both sides of [A.3.6] by $\phi$,

$$\phi s_T = \phi + \phi^2 + \phi^3 + \cdots + \phi^T + \phi^{T+1}. \qquad [A.3.7]$$

Subtracting [A.3.7] from [A.3.6] produces

$$(1 - \phi)s_T = 1 - \phi^{T+1}. \qquad [A.3.8]$$

For any $\phi \neq 1$, both sides of [A.3.8] can be divided by $(1 - \phi)$. Hence, the sum in [A.3.6] is equal to

$$s_T = \begin{cases} \dfrac{1 - \phi^{T+1}}{1 - \phi} & \phi \neq 1 \\ T + 1 & \phi = 1. \end{cases} \qquad [A.3.9]$$

From [A.3.9],

$$\lim_{T \to \infty} s_T = \frac{1}{1 - \phi} \qquad |\phi| < 1,$$

and so

$$(1 + \phi + \phi^2 + \phi^3 + \cdots) = \frac{1}{1 - \phi} \qquad |\phi| < 1. \qquad [A.3.10]$$

## Taylor Series Approximations

Suppose that the first through the $(r + 1)$th derivatives of a function $f(x)$ exist and are continuous in a neighborhood of $c$. *Taylor's theorem* states that the value of $f(x)$ at $x = c + \Delta$ is given by

$$\begin{aligned} f(c + \Delta) = f(c) &+ \left.\frac{df}{dx}\right|_{x=c} \cdot \Delta + \frac{1}{2!}\left.\frac{d^2f}{dx^2}\right|_{x=c} \cdot \Delta^2 \\ &+ \frac{1}{3!}\left.\frac{d^3f}{dx^3}\right|_{x=c} \cdot \Delta^3 + \cdots + \frac{1}{r!}\left.\frac{d^rf}{dx^r}\right|_{x=c} \cdot \Delta^r + R_r(c, x), \end{aligned} \qquad [A.3.11]$$

where $r!$ denotes *r factorial*:

$$r! \equiv r(r - 1)\cdot(r - 2)\cdots 2\cdot 1.$$

The remainder $R_r(c, x)$ is given by

$$R_r(c, x) = \frac{1}{(r + 1)!}\cdot\left.\frac{d^{r+1}f}{dx^{r+1}}\right|_{x=\delta} \cdot \Delta^{r+1},$$

where $\delta$ is a number between $c$ and $x$. Notice that the remainder vanishes for small $\Delta$:

$$\lim_{\Delta \to 0} \frac{R_r(c, x)}{\Delta^r} = 0.$$

Setting $R_r(c, x) = 0$ and $x = c + \Delta$ in [A.3.11] produces an *rth-order Taylor series approximation* to the function $f(x)$ in the neighborhood of $x = c$:

$$f(x) \cong f(c) + \left.\frac{df}{dx}\right|_{x=c} \cdot (x - c) + \frac{1}{2!}\left.\frac{d^2f}{dx^2}\right|_{x=c} \cdot (x - c)^2 + \cdots + \frac{1}{r!}\left.\frac{d^rf}{dx^r}\right|_{x=c} \cdot (x - c)^r. \qquad [A.3.12]$$

## *Power Series*

If the remainder $R_r(c, x)$ in [A.3.11] converges to zero for all $x$ as $r \to \infty$, a power series can be used to characterize the function $f(x)$. To find a power series, we choose a particular value $c$ around which to center the expansion, such as $c = 0$. We then use [A.3.12] with $r \to \infty$. For example, consider the sine function. The first two derivatives are given by [A.3.2] and [A.3.5], with the following higher-order derivatives:

$$\frac{d^3 \sin(x)}{dx^3} = -\cos(x)$$

$$\frac{d^4 \sin(x)}{dx^4} = \sin(x)$$

$$\frac{d^5 \sin(x)}{dx^5} = \cos(x),$$

and so on. Evaluated at $x = 0$, we have

$$f(0) = \sin(0) = 0$$

$$\left.\frac{df}{dx}\right|_{x=0} = \cos(0) = 1$$

$$\left.\frac{d^2f}{dx^2}\right|_{x=0} = -\sin(0) = 0$$

$$\left.\frac{d^3f}{dx^3}\right|_{x=0} = -\cos(0) = -1$$

$$\left.\frac{d^4f}{dx^4}\right|_{x=0} = \sin(0) = 0$$

$$\left.\frac{d^5f}{dx^5}\right|_{x=0} = \cos(0) = 1.$$

Substituting into [A.3.12] with $c = 0$ and letting $r \to \infty$ produces a power series for the sine function:

$$\sin(x) = x - \frac{1}{3!}x^3 + \frac{1}{5!}x^5 - \frac{1}{7!}x^7 + \cdots. \qquad [A.3.13]$$

Similar calculations give a power series for the cosine function:

$$\cos(x) = 1 - \frac{1}{2!}x^2 + \frac{1}{4!}x^4 - \frac{1}{6!}x^6 + \cdots. \qquad [A.3.14]$$

## *Exponential Functions*

A number $\gamma$ raised to the power $x$,

$$f(x) = \gamma^x,$$

is called an *exponential function* of $x$. The number $\gamma$ is called the *base* of this function, and $x$ is called the *exponent*. To multiply two exponential functions that share the same base, the exponents are added:

$$(\gamma^x)\cdot(\gamma^y) = \gamma^{(x+y)}. \qquad [A.3.15]$$

For example,

$$(\gamma^2)\cdot(\gamma^3) = (\gamma\cdot\gamma)\cdot(\gamma\cdot\gamma\cdot\gamma) = \gamma^5.$$

To raise an exponential function to the power $k$, the exponents are multiplied:

$$[\gamma^x]^k = \gamma^{xk}. \qquad [A.3.16]$$

For example,

$$[\gamma^2]^3 = [\gamma^2]\cdot[\gamma^2]\cdot[\gamma^2] = \gamma^6.$$

Exponentiation is distributive over multiplication:

$$(\alpha\cdot\beta)^x = (\alpha^x)\cdot(\beta^x). \qquad [A.3.17]$$

Negative exponents denote reciprocals:

$$\gamma^{-k} = (1/\gamma^k).$$

Any number raised to the power 0 is taken to be equal to unity:

$$\gamma^0 = 1. \qquad [A.3.18]$$

This convention is sensible, since if $y = -x$ in [A.3.15],

$$(\gamma^x)(\gamma^{-x}) = \gamma^0$$

and

$$(\gamma^x)(\gamma^{-x}) = \frac{\gamma^x}{\gamma^x} = 1.$$

## *The Number* e

The base for the natural logarithms is denoted $e$. The number $e$ has the property that an exponential function with base $e$ equals its own derivative:

$$\frac{de^x}{dx} = e^x. \qquad [A.3.19]$$

Clearly, all the higher-order derivatives of $e^x$ are equal to $e^x$ as well:

$$\frac{d^re^x}{dx^r} = e^x. \qquad [A.3.20]$$

We sometimes use the expression "exp[$x$]" to represent "$e$ raised to the power $x$":

$$\exp[x] \equiv e^x.$$

If $u(x)$ denotes a separate function of $x$, the derivative of the compound function $e^{u(x)}$ can be evaluated using the chain rule:

$$\frac{de^{u(x)}}{dx} = \frac{de^u}{du}\cdot\frac{du}{dx} = e^{u(x)}\frac{du}{dx}. \qquad [A.3.21]$$

To find a power series for the function $f(x) = e^x$, notice from [A.3.20] that

$$\frac{d^r f}{dx^r} = e^x,$$

and so, from [A.3.18],

$$\left.\frac{d^r f}{dx^r}\right|_{x=0} = e^0 = 1 \qquad \text{[A.3.22]}$$

for all $r$. Substituting [A.3.22] into [A.3.12] with $c = 0$ yields a power series for the function $f(x) = e^x$:

$$e^x = 1 + x + \frac{x^2}{2!} + \frac{x^3}{3!} + \frac{x^4}{4!} + \cdots . \qquad \text{[A.3.23]}$$

Setting $x = 1$ in [A.3.23] gives a numerical procedure for calculating the value of $e$:

$$e = 1 + 1 + \frac{1}{2!} + \frac{1}{3!} + \frac{1}{4!} + \cdots = 2.71828 \ldots .$$

## *Euler Relations and De Moivre's Theorem*

Suppose we evaluate the power series [A.3.23] at the imaginary number $x = i\theta$, where $i = \sqrt{-1}$ and $\theta$ is some real angle measured in radians:

$$\begin{aligned} e^{i\theta} &= 1 + (i\theta) + \frac{(i\theta)^2}{2!} + \frac{(i\theta)^3}{3!} + \frac{(i\theta)^4}{4!} + \frac{(i\theta)^5}{5!} + \cdots \\ &= \left\{1 - \frac{\theta^2}{2!} + \frac{\theta^4}{4!} - \cdots\right\} + i\cdot\left\{\theta - \frac{\theta^3}{3!} + \frac{\theta^5}{5!} - \cdots\right\}. \end{aligned} \qquad \text{[A.3.24]}$$

Reflecting on [A.3.13] and [A.3.14] gives another interpretation of [A.3.24]:

$$e^{i\theta} = \cos(\theta) + i\cdot\sin(\theta). \qquad \text{[A.3.25]}$$

Similarly,

$$\begin{aligned} e^{-i\theta} &= 1 + (-i\theta) + \frac{(-i\theta)^2}{2!} + \frac{(-i\theta)^3}{3!} + \frac{(-i\theta)^4}{4!} + \frac{(-i\theta)^5}{5!} + \cdots \\ &= \left\{1 - \frac{\theta^2}{2!} + \frac{\theta^4}{4!} - \cdots\right\} - i\cdot\left\{\theta - \frac{\theta^3}{3!} + \frac{\theta^5}{5!} - \cdots\right\} \\ &= \cos(\theta) - i\cdot\sin(\theta). \end{aligned} \qquad \text{[A.3.26]}$$

To raise a complex number $(a + bi)$ to the $k$th power, the complex number is written in polar coordinate form as in [A.2.6]:

$$a + bi = R[\cos(\theta) + i\cdot\sin(\theta)].$$

Using [A.3.25], this can then be treated as an exponential function of $\theta$:

$$a + bi = R\cdot e^{i\theta}. \qquad \text{[A.3.27]}$$

Now raise both sides of [A.3.27] to the $k$th power, recalling [A.3.17] and [A.3.16]:

$$(a + bi)^k = R^k\cdot[e^{i\theta}]^k = R^k\cdot e^{i\theta k}. \qquad \text{[A.3.28]}$$

Finally, use [A.3.25] in reverse,

$$e^{i(\theta k)} = \cos(\theta k) + i\cdot\sin(\theta k),$$

to deduce that [A.3.28] can be written

$$(a + bi)^k = R^k \cdot [\cos(\theta k) + i \cdot \sin(\theta k)]. \qquad \text{[A.3.29]}$$

### *Definition of Natural Logarithm*

The *natural logarithm* (denoted throughout the text simply by "log") is the inverse of the function $e^x$:

$$\log(e^x) \equiv x.$$

Notice from [A.3.18] that $e^0 = 1$ and therefore $\log(1) = 0$.

### *Properties of Logarithms*

For any $x > 0$, it is also the case that

$$x = e^{\log(x)}. \qquad \text{[A.3.30]}$$

From [A.3.30] and [A.3.15], we see that the log of the product of two numbers is equal to the sum of the logs:

$$\log(a \cdot b) = \log[(e^{\log(a)}) \cdot (e^{\log(b)})] = \log[e^{(\log(a) + \log(b))}] = \log(a) + \log(b).$$

Also, use [A.3.16] to write

$$x^a = [e^{\log(x)}]^a = e^{a \cdot \log(x)}. \qquad \text{[A.3.31]}$$

Taking logs of both sides of [A.3.31] reveals that the log of a number raised to the $a$ power is equal to $a$ times the log of the number:

$$\log(x^a) = a \cdot \log(x).$$

### *Derivatives of Natural Logarithms*

Let $u(x) = \log(x)$, and write the right side of [A.3.30] as $e^{u(x)}$. Differentiating both sides of [A.3.30] using [A.3.21] reveals that

$$\frac{dx}{dx} = e^{\log(x)} \cdot \frac{d \log(x)}{dx}$$

or

$$1 = x \frac{d \log(x)}{dx}.$$

Thus,

$$\frac{d \log(x)}{dx} = \frac{1}{x}. \qquad \text{[A.3.32]}$$

### *Logarithms and Elasticities*

It is sometimes also useful to differentiate a function $f(x)$ with respect to the variable $\log(x)$. To do so, write $f(x)$ as $f(u(x))$, where

$$u(x) = \exp[\log(x)].$$

Now use the chain rule to differentiate:

$$\frac{df(x)}{d\log(x)} = \frac{df}{du} \cdot \frac{du}{d\log(x)}. \qquad \text{[A.3.33]}$$

But from [A.3.21],

$$\frac{du}{d\log(x)} = \exp[\log(x)]\frac{d\log(x)}{d\log(x)} = x. \qquad \text{[A.3.34]}$$

Substituting [A.3.34] into [A.3.33] gives

$$\frac{df(x)}{d\log(x)} = x\frac{df}{dx}.$$

It follows from [A.3.32] that

$$\frac{d\log f(x)}{d\log(x)} = \frac{1}{f}x\frac{df}{dx} \cong \frac{[f(x+\Delta) - f(x)]/f(x)}{[(x+\Delta) - x]/x},$$

which has the interpretation as the *elasticity* of $f$ with respect to $x$, or the percent change in $f$ resulting from a 1% increase in $x$.

## *Logarithms and Percent*

An approximation to the natural log function is obtained from a first-order Taylor series around $c = 1$:

$$\log(1+\Delta) \cong \log(1) + \left.\frac{d\log(x)}{dx}\right|_{x=1} \cdot \Delta. \qquad \text{[A.3.35]}$$

But $\log(1) = 0$, and

$$\left.\frac{d\log(x)}{dx}\right|_{x=1} = \left.\frac{1}{x}\right|_{x=1} = 1.$$

Thus, for $\Delta$ close to zero, an excellent approximation is provided by

$$\log(1+\Delta) \cong \Delta. \qquad \text{[A.3.36]}$$

An implication of [A.3.36] is the following. Let $r$ denote the net interest rate measured as a fraction of 1; for example, $r = 0.05$ corresponds to a 5% interest rate. Then $(1 + r)$ denotes the gross interest rate (principal plus net interest). Equation [A.3.36] says that the log of the gross interest rate $(1 + r)$ is essentially the same number as the net interest rate $(r)$.

## *Definition of Indefinite Integral*

*Integration* (indicated by $\int dx$) is the inverse operation from differentiation. For example,

$$\int x\,dx = x^2/2, \qquad \text{[A.3.37]}$$

because

$$\frac{d(x^2/2)}{dx} = x. \qquad [A.3.38]$$

The function $x^2/2$ is not the only function satisfying [A.3.38]; the function

$$(x^2/2) + C$$

also works for any constant $C$. The term $C$ is referred to as the *constant of integration*.

## *Some Useful Indefinite Integrals*

The following integrals can be confirmed from [A.3.1], [A.3.32], [A.3.2], [A.3.3], and [A.3.21]:

$$\int x^k \, dx = \frac{x^{k+1}}{k+1} + C \qquad k \neq -1 \qquad [A.3.39]$$

$$\int x^{-1} \, dx = \begin{cases} \log(x) + C & x > 0 \\ \log(-x) + C & x < 0 \end{cases} \qquad [A.3.40]$$

$$\int \cos(x) \, dx = \sin(x) + C \qquad [A.3.41]$$

$$\int \sin(x) \, dx = -\cos(x) + C \qquad [A.3.42]$$

$$\int e^{ax} \, dx = (1/a) \cdot e^{ax} + C. \qquad [A.3.43]$$

It is also straightforward to demonstrate that for constants $a$ and $b$ not depending on $x$,

$$\int [a \cdot f(x) + b \cdot g(x)] \, dx = a \int f(x) \, dx + b \int g(x) \, dx + C.$$

## *Definite Integrals*

Consider the continuous function $f(x)$ plotted in Figure A.5. Define the function $A(x; a)$ to be the area under $f(x)$ between $a$ and $x$, viewed as a function of $x$. Thus, $A(b; a)$ would be the area between $a$ and $b$. Suppose we increase $b$ by a small amount $\Delta$. This is approximately the same as adding a rectangle of height $f(b)$ and width $\Delta$ to the area $A(b; a)$:

$$A(b + \Delta; a) \cong A(b; a) + f(b) \cdot \Delta,$$

or

$$\frac{A(b + \Delta; a) - A(b; a)}{\Delta} \cong f(b).$$

In the limit as $\Delta \to 0$,

$$\left. \frac{dA(x; a)}{dx} \right|_{x=b} = f(b). \qquad [A.3.44]$$

Now, [A.3.44] has to hold for any value of $b > a$ that we might have chosen,

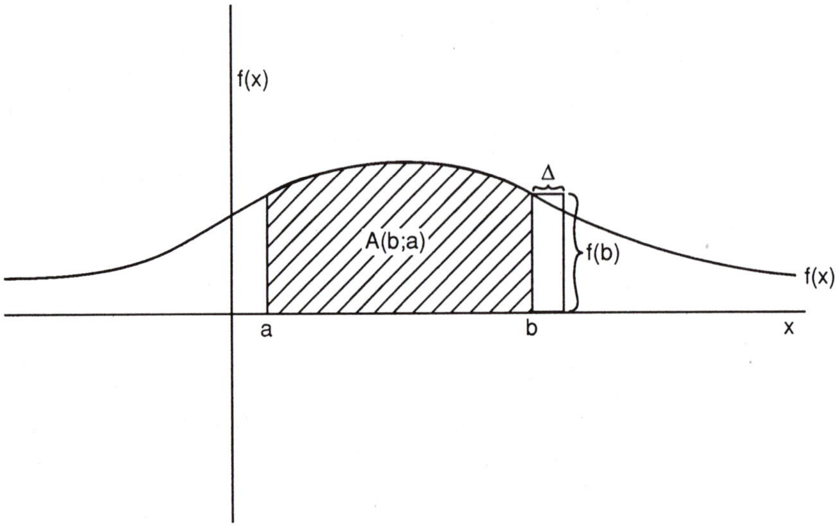


**FIGURE A.5** The definite integral as the area under a function.

implying that the area function $A(x; a)$ is the inverse of differentiation:

$$A(x; a) = F(x) + C, \qquad [A.3.45]$$

where

$$\frac{dF(x)}{dx} = f(x).$$

To find the value of $C$, notice that $A(a; a)$ in [A.3.45] should be equal to zero:

$$A(a; a) = 0 = F(a) + C.$$

For this to be true,

$$C = -F(a). \qquad [A.3.46]$$

Evaluating [A.3.45] at $x = b$, the area between $a$ and $b$ is given by

$$A(b; a) = F(b) + C;$$

or using [A.3.46],

$$A(b; a) = F(b) - F(a), \qquad [A.3.47]$$

where $F(x)$ satisfies $dF/dx = f(x)$:

$$F(x) = \int f(x)\, dx.$$

Equation [A.3.47] is known as the *fundamental theorem of calculus*.

The operation in [A.3.47] is known as calculating a *definite integral*:

$$\int_a^b f(x)\, dx \equiv \left[\int f(x)\, dx\right]\Bigg|_{x=b} - \left[\int f(x)\, dx\right]\Bigg|_{x=a}.$$

For example, to find the area under the sine function between $\theta = 0$ and $\theta = \pi/2$, we use [A.3.42]:

$$\int_0^{\pi/2} \sin(x)\,dx = [-\cos(x)]|_{x=\pi/2} - [-\cos(x)]|_{x=0}$$
$$= [-\cos(\pi/2)] + [\cos(0)]$$
$$= 0 + 1$$
$$= 1.$$

To find the area between 0 and $2\pi$, we take

$$\int_0^{2\pi} \sin(x)\,dx = [-\cos(2\pi)] + \cos(0)$$
$$= -1 + 1$$
$$= 0.$$

The positive values for $\sin(x)$ between 0 and $\pi$ exactly cancel out the negative values between $\pi$ and $2\pi$.

# A.4. *Matrix Algebra*

## *Definitions*

An $(m \times n)$ matrix is an array of numbers ordered into $m$ rows and $n$ columns:

$$\underset{(m\times n)}{\mathbf{A}} = \begin{bmatrix} a_{11} & a_{12} & \cdots & a_{1n} \\ a_{21} & a_{22} & \cdots & a_{2n} \\ \vdots & \vdots & \cdots & \vdots \\ a_{m1} & a_{m2} & \cdots & a_{mn} \end{bmatrix}.$$

If there is only one column ($n = 1$), then **A** is described as a *column vector*, whereas with only one row ($m = 1$), **A** is called a *row vector*. A single number ($n = 1$ and $m = 1$) is called a *scalar*.

If the number of rows equals the number of columns ($m = n$), the matrix is said to be *square*. The diagonal running through $(a_{11}, a_{22}, \ldots, a_{nn})$ in a square matrix is called the *principal diagonal*. If all elements off the principal diagonal are zero, the matrix is said to be *diagonal*.

A matrix is sometimes specified by describing the element in row $i$, column $j$:

$$\mathbf{A} = [a_{ij}].$$

## *Summation and Multiplication*

Two $(m \times n)$ matrices are added element by element:

$$\begin{bmatrix} a_{11} & a_{12} & \cdots & a_{1n} \\ a_{21} & a_{22} & \cdots & a_{2n} \\ \vdots & \vdots & \cdots & \vdots \\ a_{m1} & a_{m2} & \cdots & a_{mn} \end{bmatrix} + \begin{bmatrix} b_{11} & b_{12} & \cdots & b_{1n} \\ b_{21} & b_{22} & \cdots & b_{2n} \\ \vdots & \vdots & \cdots & \vdots \\ b_{m1} & b_{m2} & \cdots & b_{mn} \end{bmatrix}$$
$$= \begin{bmatrix} a_{11} + b_{11} & a_{12} + b_{12} & \cdots & a_{1n} + b_{1n} \\ a_{21} + b_{21} & a_{22} + b_{22} & \cdots & a_{2n} + b_{2n} \\ \vdots & \vdots & \cdots & \vdots \\ a_{m1} + b_{m1} & a_{m2} + b_{m2} & \cdots & a_{mn} + b_{mn} \end{bmatrix};$$

or, more compactly,

$$\underset{(m\times n)}{\mathbf{A}} + \underset{(m\times n)}{\mathbf{B}} = [a_{ij} + b_{ij}].$$

The product of an $(m \times n)$ matrix and an $(n \times q)$ matrix is an $(m \times q)$ matrix:

$$\underset{(m\times n)}{\mathbf{A}} \times \underset{(n\times q)}{\mathbf{B}} = \underset{(m\times q)}{\mathbf{C}},$$

where the row $i$, column $j$ element of $\mathbf{C}$ is given by $\Sigma_{k=1}^{n} a_{ik}b_{kj}$. Notice that multiplication requires that the number of columns of $\mathbf{A}$ be the same as the number of rows of $\mathbf{B}$.

To multiply $\mathbf{A}$ by a scalar $\alpha$, each element of $\mathbf{A}$ is multiplied by $\alpha$:

$$\underset{(1\times 1)}{\alpha} \times \underset{(m\times n)}{\mathbf{A}} = \underset{(m\times n)}{\mathbf{C}},$$

with

$$\mathbf{C} = [\alpha a_{ij}].$$

It is easy to show that addition is commutative:

$$\mathbf{A} + \mathbf{B} = \mathbf{B} + \mathbf{A};$$

whereas multiplication is not:

$$\mathbf{AB} \neq \mathbf{BA}.$$

Indeed, the product $\mathbf{BA}$ will not exist unless $m = q$, and even where it exists, $\mathbf{AB}$ would be equal to $\mathbf{BA}$ only in rather special cases.

Both addition and multiplication are associative:

$$(\mathbf{A} + \mathbf{B}) + \mathbf{C} = \mathbf{A} + (\mathbf{B} + \mathbf{C})$$
$$(\mathbf{AB})\mathbf{C} = \mathbf{A}(\mathbf{BC}).$$

## *Identity Matrix*

The *identity matrix* of order $n$ (denoted $\mathbf{I}_n$) is an $(n \times n)$ matrix with 1s along the principal diagonal and 0s elsewhere:

$$\mathbf{I}_n = \begin{bmatrix} 1 & 0 & \cdots & 0 \\ 0 & 1 & \cdots & 0 \\ \vdots & \vdots & \cdots & \vdots \\ 0 & 0 & \cdots & 1 \end{bmatrix}.$$

For any $(m \times n)$ matrix $\mathbf{A}$,

$$\mathbf{A} \times \mathbf{I}_n = \mathbf{A}$$

and also

$$\mathbf{I}_m \times \mathbf{A} = \mathbf{A}.$$

## *Powers of Matrices*

For an $(n \times n)$ matrix $\mathbf{A}$, the expression $\mathbf{A}^2$ denotes $\mathbf{A}\cdot\mathbf{A}$. The expression $\mathbf{A}^k$ indicates the matrix $\mathbf{A}$ multiplied by itself $k$ times, with $\mathbf{A}^0$ interpreted as the $(n \times n)$ identity matrix.

## *Transposition*

Let $a_{ij}$ denote the row $i$, column $j$ element of a matrix $\mathbf{A}$:

$$\mathbf{A} = [a_{ij}].$$

The *transpose* of $\mathbf{A}$ (denoted $\mathbf{A}'$) is given by

$$\mathbf{A}' = [a_{ji}].$$

For example, the transpose of

$$\begin{bmatrix} 2 & 4 & 6 \\ 3 & 5 & 7 \\ 1 & 2 & 3 \end{bmatrix}$$

is

$$\begin{bmatrix} 2 & 3 & 1 \\ 4 & 5 & 2 \\ 6 & 7 & 3 \end{bmatrix}.$$

The transpose of a row vector is a column vector.

It is easy to verify the following:

$$(\mathbf{A}')' = \mathbf{A} \quad \text{[A.4.1]}$$

$$(\mathbf{A} + \mathbf{B})' = \mathbf{A}' + \mathbf{B}' \quad \text{[A.4.2]}$$

$$(\mathbf{AB})' = \mathbf{B}'\mathbf{A}'. \quad \text{[A.4.3]}$$

## *Symmetric Matrices*

A square matrix satisfying $\mathbf{A} = \mathbf{A}'$ is said to be *symmetric*.

## *Trace of a Matrix*

The *trace* of an $(n \times n)$ matrix is defined as the sum of the elements along the principal diagonal:

$$\text{trace}(\mathbf{A}) \equiv a_{11} + a_{22} + \cdots + a_{nn}.$$

If $\mathbf{A}$ is an $(m \times n)$ matrix and $\mathbf{B}$ is an $(n \times m)$ matrix, then $\mathbf{AB}$ is an $(m \times m)$ matrix whose trace is

$$\text{trace}(\mathbf{AB}) = \sum_{j=1}^{n} a_{1j}b_{j1} + \sum_{j=1}^{n} a_{2j}b_{j2} + \cdots + \sum_{j=1}^{n} a_{mj}b_{jm} = \sum_{k=1}^{m}\sum_{j=1}^{n} a_{kj}b_{jk}.$$

The product $\mathbf{BA}$ is an $(n \times n)$ matrix whose trace is

$$\text{trace}(\mathbf{BA}) = \sum_{k=1}^{m} b_{1k}a_{k1} + \sum_{k=1}^{m} b_{2k}a_{k2} + \cdots + \sum_{k=1}^{m} b_{nk}a_{kn} = \sum_{j=1}^{n}\sum_{k=1}^{m} b_{jk}a_{kj}.$$

Thus,

$$\text{trace}(\mathbf{AB}) = \text{trace}(\mathbf{BA}).$$

If $\mathbf{A}$ and $\mathbf{B}$ are both $(n \times n)$ matrices, then

$$\text{trace}(\mathbf{A} + \mathbf{B}) = \text{trace}(\mathbf{A}) + \text{trace}(\mathbf{B}).$$

If $\mathbf{A}$ is an $(n \times n)$ matrix and $\lambda$ is a scalar, then

$$\text{trace}(\lambda\mathbf{A}) = \sum_{i=1}^{n} \lambda a_{ii} = \lambda \cdot \sum_{i=1}^{n} a_{ii} = \lambda \cdot \text{trace}(\mathbf{A}).$$

## *Partitioned Matrices*

A *partitioned matrix* is a matrix whose individual elements are themselves matrices. For example, the $(3 \times 4)$ matrix

$$\mathbf{A} = \begin{bmatrix} a_{11} & a_{12} & a_{13} & a_{14} \\ a_{21} & a_{22} & a_{23} & a_{24} \\ a_{31} & a_{32} & a_{33} & a_{34} \end{bmatrix}$$

could be written as

$$\mathbf{A} = \begin{bmatrix} \mathbf{A}_1 & \mathbf{A}_2 \\ \mathbf{a}_1' & \mathbf{a}_2' \end{bmatrix}$$

where

$$\mathbf{A}_1 \equiv \begin{bmatrix} a_{11} & a_{12} \\ a_{21} & a_{22} \end{bmatrix} \qquad \mathbf{A}_2 \equiv \begin{bmatrix} a_{13} & a_{14} \\ a_{23} & a_{24} \end{bmatrix}$$

$$\mathbf{a}_1' \equiv \begin{bmatrix} a_{31} & a_{32} \end{bmatrix} \qquad \mathbf{a}_2' \equiv \begin{bmatrix} a_{33} & a_{34} \end{bmatrix}.$$

Partitioned matrices are added or multiplied as if the individual elements were scalars, provided that the row and column dimensions permit the appropriate matrix operations. For example.

$$\begin{bmatrix} \underset{(m_1 \times n_1)}{\mathbf{A}_1} & \underset{(m_1 \times n_2)}{\mathbf{A}_2} \\ \underset{(m_2 \times n_1)}{\mathbf{A}_3} & \underset{(m_2 \times n_2)}{\mathbf{A}_4} \end{bmatrix} + \begin{bmatrix} \underset{(m_1 \times n_1)}{\mathbf{B}_1} & \underset{(m_1 \times n_2)}{\mathbf{B}_2} \\ \underset{(m_2 \times n_1)}{\mathbf{B}_3} & \underset{(m_2 \times n_2)}{\mathbf{B}_4} \end{bmatrix} = \begin{bmatrix} \underset{(m_1 \times n_1)}{\mathbf{A}_1 + \mathbf{B}_1} & \underset{(m_1 \times n_2)}{\mathbf{A}_2 + \mathbf{B}_2} \\ \underset{(m_2 \times n_1)}{\mathbf{A}_3 + \mathbf{B}_3} & \underset{(m_2 \times n_2)}{\mathbf{A}_4 + \mathbf{B}_4} \end{bmatrix}.$$

Similarly,

$$\begin{bmatrix} \underset{(m_1 \times n_1)}{\mathbf{A}_1} & \underset{(m_1 \times n_2)}{\mathbf{A}_2} \\ \underset{(m_2 \times n_1)}{\mathbf{A}_3} & \underset{(m_2 \times n_2)}{\mathbf{A}_4} \end{bmatrix} \times \begin{bmatrix} \underset{(n_1 \times q_1)}{\mathbf{B}_1} & \underset{(n_1 \times q_2)}{\mathbf{B}_2} \\ \underset{(n_2 \times q_1)}{\mathbf{B}_3} & \underset{(n_2 \times q_2)}{\mathbf{B}_4} \end{bmatrix} = \begin{bmatrix} \underset{(m_1 \times q_1)}{\mathbf{A}_1\mathbf{B}_1 + \mathbf{A}_2\mathbf{B}_3} & \underset{(m_1 \times q_2)}{\mathbf{A}_1\mathbf{B}_2 + \mathbf{A}_2\mathbf{B}_4} \\ \underset{(m_2 \times q_1)}{\mathbf{A}_3\mathbf{B}_1 + \mathbf{A}_4\mathbf{B}_3} & \underset{(m_2 \times q_2)}{\mathbf{A}_3\mathbf{B}_2 + \mathbf{A}_4\mathbf{B}_4} \end{bmatrix}.$$

## *Definition of Determinant*

The *determinant* of a $2 \times 2$ matrix is given by the following scalar:

$$|\mathbf{A}| = a_{11}a_{22} - a_{12}a_{21}. \qquad \text{[A.4.4]}$$

The determinant of an $n \times n$ matrix can be defined recursively. Let $\mathbf{A}_{ij}$ denote the $(n-1) \times (n-1)$ matrix formed by deleting row $i$ and column $j$ from $\mathbf{A}$. The determinant of $\mathbf{A}$ is given by

$$|\mathbf{A}| = \sum_{j=1}^{n} (-1)^{j+1} a_{1j} |\mathbf{A}_{1j}|. \qquad \text{[A.4.5]}$$

For example, the determinant of a $3 \times 3$ matrix is

$$\begin{vmatrix} a_{11} & a_{12} & a_{13} \\ a_{21} & a_{22} & a_{23} \\ a_{31} & a_{32} & a_{33} \end{vmatrix} = a_{11}\begin{vmatrix} a_{22} & a_{23} \\ a_{32} & a_{33} \end{vmatrix} - a_{12}\begin{vmatrix} a_{21} & a_{23} \\ a_{31} & a_{33} \end{vmatrix} + a_{13}\begin{vmatrix} a_{21} & a_{22} \\ a_{31} & a_{32} \end{vmatrix}.$$

## *Properties of Determinants*

A square matrix is said to be *lower triangular* if all the elements above the principal diagonal are zero ($a_{ij} = 0$ for $j > i$):

$$\mathbf{A} = \begin{bmatrix} a_{11} & 0 & 0 & \cdots & 0 \\ a_{21} & a_{22} & 0 & \cdots & 0 \\ \vdots & \vdots & \vdots & \cdots & \vdots \\ a_{n1} & a_{n2} & a_{n3} & \cdots & a_{nn} \end{bmatrix}.$$

The determinant of a lower triangular matrix is simply the product of the terms along the principal diagonal:

$$|\mathbf{A}| = a_{11}a_{22} \cdots a_{nn}. \qquad \text{[A.4.6]}$$

That [A.4.6] holds for $n = 2$ follows immediately from [A.4.4] Given that it holds for a matrix of order $n - 1$, equation [A.4.5] implies that it holds for $n$:

$$|\mathbf{A}| = a_{11} \begin{vmatrix} a_{22} & 0 & 0 & \cdots & 0 \\ a_{32} & a_{33} & 0 & \cdots & 0 \\ \vdots & \vdots & \vdots & \cdots & \vdots \\ a_{n2} & a_{n3} & a_{n4} & \cdots & a_{nn} \end{vmatrix} + 0 \cdot |\mathbf{A}_{12}| + \cdots + 0 \cdot |\mathbf{A}_{1n}|.$$

An immediate implication of [A.4.6] is that the determinant of the identity matrix is unity:

$$|\mathbf{I}_n| = 1. \qquad \text{[A.4.7]}$$

Another useful fact about determinants is that if an $n \times n$ matrix **A** is multiplied by a scalar $\alpha$, the effect is to multiply the determinant by $\alpha^n$:

$$|\alpha\mathbf{A}| = \alpha^n |\mathbf{A}|. \qquad \text{[A.4.8]}$$

Again, [A.4.8] is immediately apparent for the $n = 2$ case from [A.4.4]:

$$\begin{aligned} |\alpha\mathbf{A}| &= \begin{vmatrix} \alpha a_{11} & \alpha a_{12} \\ \alpha a_{21} & \alpha a_{22} \end{vmatrix} \\ &= (\alpha a_{11} \alpha a_{22}) - (\alpha a_{12} \alpha a_{21}) \\ &= \alpha^2 (a_{11}a_{22} - a_{12}a_{21}) \\ &= \alpha^2 |\mathbf{A}|. \end{aligned}$$

Given that it holds for $n - 1$, it is simple to verify for $n$ using [A.4.5].

By contrast, if a single row of **A** is multiplied by the constant $\alpha$ (as opposed to multiplying the entire matrix by $\alpha$), then the determinant is multiplied by $\alpha$. If the row that is multiplied by $\alpha$ is the first row, then this result is immediately apparent from [A.4.5]. If only the $i$th row of **A** is multiplied by $\alpha$, the result can be shown by recursively applying [A.4.5] until the elements of the $i$th row appear explicitly in the formula.

Suppose that some constant $c$ times the second row of a $2 \times 2$ matrix is added to the first row. This operation has no effect on the determinant:

$$\begin{aligned} \begin{vmatrix} a_{11} + ca_{21} & a_{12} + ca_{22} \\ a_{21} & a_{22} \end{vmatrix} &= (a_{11} + ca_{21})a_{22} - (a_{12} + ca_{22})a_{21} \\ &= a_{11}a_{22} - a_{12}a_{21}. \end{aligned}$$

Similarly, if some constant $c$ times the third row of a $3 \times 3$ matrix is added to the second row, the determinant will again be unchanged:

$$\begin{vmatrix} a_{11} & a_{12} & a_{13} \\ a_{21} + ca_{31} & a_{22} + ca_{32} & a_{23} + ca_{33} \\ a_{31} & a_{32} & a_{33} \end{vmatrix}$$

$$= a_{11}\begin{vmatrix} a_{22} + ca_{32} & a_{23} + ca_{33} \\ a_{32} & a_{33} \end{vmatrix} - a_{12}\begin{vmatrix} a_{21} + ca_{31} & a_{23} + ca_{33} \\ a_{31} & a_{33} \end{vmatrix}$$

$$+ a_{13}\begin{vmatrix} a_{21} + ca_{31} & a_{22} + ca_{32} \\ a_{31} & a_{32} \end{vmatrix}$$

$$= a_{11}\begin{vmatrix} a_{22} & a_{23} \\ a_{32} & a_{33} \end{vmatrix} - a_{12}\begin{vmatrix} a_{21} & a_{23} \\ a_{31} & a_{33} \end{vmatrix} + a_{13}\begin{vmatrix} a_{21} & a_{22} \\ a_{31} & a_{32} \end{vmatrix}.$$

In general, if any row of an $n \times n$ matrix is multiplied by $c$ and added to another row, the new matrix will have the same determinant as the original. Similarly, multiplying any column by $c$ and adding the result to another column will not change the determinant.

This can be viewed as a special case of the following result. If $\mathbf{A}$ and $\mathbf{B}$ are both $n \times n$ matrices, then

$$|\mathbf{AB}| = |\mathbf{A}| \cdot |\mathbf{B}|. \qquad \text{[A.4.9]}$$

Adding $c$ times the second column of a $2 \times 2$ matrix $\mathbf{A}$ to the first column can be thought of as postmultiplying $\mathbf{A}$ by the following matrix:

$$\mathbf{B} = \begin{bmatrix} 1 & 0 \\ c & 1 \end{bmatrix}.$$

Since $\mathbf{B}$ is lower triangular with 1s along the principal diagonal, its determinant is unity, and so, from [A.4.9],

$$|\mathbf{AB}| = |\mathbf{A}|.$$

Thus, the fact that adding a multiple of one column to another does not alter the determinant can be viewed as an implication of [A.4.9].

If two rows of a matrix are switched, the determinant changes signs. To switch the $i$th row with the $j$th, multiply the $i$th row by $-1$; this changes the sign of the determinant. Then subtract row $i$ from row $j$, add the new $j$ back to $i$, and subtract $i$ from $j$ once again. These last operations complete the switch and do not affect the determinant further. For example, let $\mathbf{A}$ be a $(4 \times 4)$ matrix written in partitioned form as

$$\mathbf{A} = \begin{bmatrix} \mathbf{a}_1' \\ \mathbf{a}_2' \\ \mathbf{a}_3' \\ \mathbf{a}_4' \end{bmatrix},$$

where the $(1 \times 4)$ vector $\mathbf{a}_i'$ represents the $i$th row of $\mathbf{A}$. The determinant when rows 1 and 4 are switched can be calculated from

$$\begin{vmatrix} \mathbf{a}_1' \\ \mathbf{a}_2' \\ \mathbf{a}_3' \\ \mathbf{a}_4' \end{vmatrix} = -\begin{vmatrix} -\mathbf{a}_1' \\ \mathbf{a}_2' \\ \mathbf{a}_3' \\ \mathbf{a}_4' \end{vmatrix} = -\begin{vmatrix} -\mathbf{a}_1' \\ \mathbf{a}_2' \\ \mathbf{a}_3' \\ \mathbf{a}_1' + \mathbf{a}_4' \end{vmatrix} = -\begin{vmatrix} \mathbf{a}_4' \\ \mathbf{a}_2' \\ \mathbf{a}_3' \\ \mathbf{a}_1' + \mathbf{a}_4' \end{vmatrix} = -\begin{vmatrix} \mathbf{a}_4' \\ \mathbf{a}_2' \\ \mathbf{a}_3' \\ \mathbf{a}_1' \end{vmatrix}.$$

This result permits calculation of the determinant of **A** in reference to any row of an $(n \times n)$ matrix **A**:

$$|\mathbf{A}| = \sum_{j=1}^{n} (-1)^{i+j} a_{ij} |\mathbf{A}_{ij}|. \qquad [A.4.10]$$

To derive [A.4.10], define $\mathbf{A}^*$ as

$$\mathbf{A}^* \equiv \begin{bmatrix} \mathbf{a}_i' \\ \mathbf{a}_1' \\ \mathbf{a}_2' \\ \vdots \\ \mathbf{a}_{i-1}' \\ \mathbf{a}_{i+1}' \\ \vdots \\ \mathbf{a}_n' \end{bmatrix}.$$

Then, from [A.4.5],

$$|\mathbf{A}^*| = \sum_{j=1}^{n} (-1)^{j+1} a_{1j}^* |\mathbf{A}_{1j}^*| = \sum_{j=1}^{n} (-1)^{j+1} a_{ij} |\mathbf{A}_{ij}|.$$

Moreover, $\mathbf{A}^*$ is obtained from **A** by $(i - 1)$ row switches, such as switching $i$ with $i - 1$, $i - 1$ with $i - 2$, . . . , and 2 with 1. Hence,

$$|\mathbf{A}| = (-1)^{i-1} |\mathbf{A}^*| = (-1)^{i-1} \sum_{j=1}^{n} (-1)^{j+1} a_{ij} |\mathbf{A}_{ij}|,$$

as claimed in [A.4.10].

An immediate implication of [A.4.10] is that if any row of a matrix contains all zeros, then the determinant of the matrix is zero.

It can also be shown that the transpose of a matrix has the same determinant as the original matrix:

$$|\mathbf{A}'| = |\mathbf{A}|. \qquad [A.4.11]$$

This means, for example, that if the $k$th column of a matrix consists entirely of zeros, then the determinant of the matrix is zero. It also implies that the determinant of an *upper triangular matrix* (one for which $a_{ij} = 0$ for all $j < i$) is the product of the terms on the principal diagonal.

## *Adjoint of a Matrix*

Let **A** denote an $(n \times n)$ matrix, and as before let $\mathbf{A}_{ji}$ denote the $[(n - 1) \times (n - 1)]$ matrix that results from deleting row $j$ and column $i$ of **A**. The *adjoint* of **A** is the $(n \times n)$ matrix whose row $i$, column $j$ element is given by $(-1)^{i+j}|\mathbf{A}_{ji}|$.

## *Inverse of a Matrix*

If the determinant of an $n \times n$ matrix **A** is not equal to zero, its *inverse* (an $n \times n$ matrix denoted $\mathbf{A}^{-1}$) exists and is found by dividing the adjoint by the determinant:

$$\mathbf{A}^{-1} = (1/|\mathbf{A}|) \cdot [(-1)^{i+j} |\mathbf{A}_{ji}|]. \qquad [A.4.12]$$

For example, for $n = 2$,

$$\begin{bmatrix} a_{11} & a_{12} \\ a_{21} & a_{22} \end{bmatrix}^{-1} = (1/[a_{11}a_{22} - a_{12}a_{21}]) \cdot \begin{bmatrix} a_{22} & -a_{12} \\ -a_{21} & a_{11} \end{bmatrix}. \qquad [A.4.13]$$

A matrix whose inverse exists is said to be *nonsingular*. A matrix whose determinant is zero is *singular* and has no inverse.

When an inverse exists,

$$\mathbf{A} \times \mathbf{A}^{-1} = \mathbf{I}_n. \qquad [A.4.14]$$

Taking determinants of both sides of [A.4.14] and using [A.4.9] and [A.4.7],

$$|\mathbf{A}| \cdot |\mathbf{A}^{-1}| = 1,$$

so

$$|\mathbf{A}^{-1}| = 1/|\mathbf{A}|. \qquad [A.4.15]$$

Alternatively, taking the transpose of both sides of [A.4.14] and recalling [A.4.3],

$$(\mathbf{A}^{-1})'\mathbf{A}' = \mathbf{I}_n,$$

which means that $(\mathbf{A}^{-1})'$ is the inverse of $\mathbf{A}'$:

$$(\mathbf{A}^{-1})' = (\mathbf{A}')^{-1}.$$

For $\alpha$ a nonzero scalar and $\mathbf{A}$ a nonsingular matrix,

$$[\alpha\mathbf{A}]^{-1} = \alpha^{-1}\mathbf{A}^{-1}.$$

Also, for $\mathbf{A}$, $\mathbf{B}$, and $\mathbf{C}$ all nonsingular $(n \times n)$ matrices,

$$[\mathbf{AB}]^{-1} = \mathbf{B}^{-1}\mathbf{A}^{-1}$$

and

$$[\mathbf{ABC}]^{-1} = \mathbf{C}^{-1}\mathbf{B}^{-1}\mathbf{A}^{-1}.$$

## *Linear Dependence*

Let $\mathbf{x}_1, \mathbf{x}_2, \ldots, \mathbf{x}_k$ be a set of $k$ different $(n \times 1)$ vectors. The vectors are said to be *linearly dependent* if there exists a set of $k$ scalars $(c_1, c_2, \ldots, c_k)$, not all of which are zero, such that

$$c_1\mathbf{x}_1 + c_2\mathbf{x}_2 + \cdots + c_k\mathbf{x}_k = \mathbf{0}.$$

If no such set of nonzero numbers $(c_1, c_2, \ldots, c_k)$ exists, then the vectors $(\mathbf{x}_1, \mathbf{x}_2, \ldots, \mathbf{x}_k)$ are said to be *linearly independent*.

Suppose the vectors $(\mathbf{x}_1, \mathbf{x}_2, \ldots, \mathbf{x}_k)$ are collected in an $(n \times k)$ matrix $\mathbf{T}$, written in partitioned form as

$$\mathbf{T} = [\mathbf{x}_1 \quad \mathbf{x}_2 \quad \cdots \quad \mathbf{x}_k].$$

If the number of vectors $(k)$ is equal to the dimension of each vector $(n)$, then there is a simple relation between the notion of linear dependence and the determinant of the $(n \times n)$ matrix $\mathbf{T}$; specifically, if $(\mathbf{x}_1, \mathbf{x}_2, \ldots, \mathbf{x}_n)$ are linearly dependent, then $|\mathbf{T}| = 0$. To see this, suppose that $\mathbf{x}_1$ is one of the vectors that have a nonzero value of $c_i$. Then linear dependence means that

$$\mathbf{x}_1 = -(c_2/c_1)\mathbf{x}_2 - (c_3/c_1)\mathbf{x}_3 - \cdots - (c_n/c_1)\mathbf{x}_n.$$

Then the determinant of $\mathbf{T}$ is equal to

$$|\mathbf{T}| = |[-(c_2/c_1)\mathbf{x}_2 - (c_3/c_1)\mathbf{x}_3 - \cdots - (c_n/c_1)\mathbf{x}_n] \quad \mathbf{x}_2 \quad \cdots \quad \mathbf{x}_n|.$$

But if we add $(c_n/c_1)$ times the $n$th column to the first column, $(c_{n-1}/c_1)$ times the $(n - 1)$th column to the first column, . . . , and $(c_2/c_1)$ times the second column to the first column, the result is

$$\begin{aligned} |\mathbf{T}| &= |\mathbf{0} \quad \mathbf{x}_2 \quad \cdots \quad \mathbf{x}_n| \\ &= 0. \end{aligned}$$

The converse can also be shown to be true: if $|\mathbf{T}| = 0$, then $(\mathbf{x}_1, \mathbf{x}_2, \ldots, \mathbf{x}_n)$ are linearly dependent.

## *Eigenvalues and Eigenvectors*

Suppose that an $n \times n$ matrix $\mathbf{A}$, a nonzero $n \times 1$ vector $\mathbf{x}$, and a scalar $\lambda$ are related by

$$\mathbf{Ax} = \lambda\mathbf{x}. \qquad \text{[A.4.16]}$$

Then $\mathbf{x}$ is called an *eigenvector* of $\mathbf{A}$ and $\lambda$ the associated *eigenvalue*. Equation [A.4.16] can be written

$$\mathbf{Ax} - \lambda\mathbf{I}_n\mathbf{x} = \mathbf{0}$$

or

$$(\mathbf{A} - \lambda\mathbf{I}_n)\mathbf{x} = \mathbf{0}. \qquad \text{[A.4.17]}$$

Suppose that the matrix $(\mathbf{A} - \lambda\mathbf{I}_n)$ were nonsingular. Then $(\mathbf{A} - \lambda\mathbf{I}_n)^{-1}$ would exist and we could premultiply [A.4.17] by $(\mathbf{A} - \lambda\mathbf{I}_n)^{-1}$ to deduce that

$$\mathbf{x} = \mathbf{0}.$$

Thus, if a nonzero vector $\mathbf{x}$ exists that satisfies [A.4.16], then it must be associated with a value of $\lambda$ such that $(\mathbf{A} - \lambda\mathbf{I}_n)$ is singular. An eigenvalue of the matrix $\mathbf{A}$ is therefore a number $\lambda$ such that

$$|\mathbf{A} - \lambda\mathbf{I}_n| = 0. \qquad \text{[A.4.18]}$$

## *Eigenvalues of Triangular Matrices*

Notice that if $\mathbf{A}$ is upper triangular or lower triangular, then $\mathbf{A} - \lambda\mathbf{I}_n$ is as well, and its determinant is just the product of terms along the principal diagonal:

$$|\mathbf{A} - \lambda\mathbf{I}_n| = (a_{11} - \lambda)(a_{22} - \lambda) \cdots (a_{nn} - \lambda).$$

Thus, for a triangular matrix, the eigenvalues (the values of $\lambda$ for which this expression equals zero) are just the values of $\mathbf{A}$ along the principal diagonal.

## *Linear Independence of Eigenvectors*

A useful result is that if the eigenvalues $(\lambda_1, \lambda_2, \ldots, \lambda_n)$ are all distinct, then the associated eigenvectors $(\mathbf{x}_1, \mathbf{x}_2, \ldots, \mathbf{x}_n)$ are linearly independent. To see this for the case $n = 2$, consider any numbers $c_1$ and $c_2$ such that

$$c_1\mathbf{x}_1 + c_2\mathbf{x}_2 = \mathbf{0}. \qquad \text{[A.4.19]}$$

Premultiplying both sides of [A.4.19] by $\mathbf{A}$ produces

$$c_1\mathbf{A}\mathbf{x}_1 + c_2\mathbf{A}\mathbf{x}_2 = c_1\lambda_1\mathbf{x}_1 + c_2\lambda_2\mathbf{x}_2 = \mathbf{0}. \qquad [A.4.20]$$

If [A.4.19] is multiplied by $\lambda_1$ and subtracted from [A.4.20], the result is

$$c_2(\lambda_2 - \lambda_1)\mathbf{x}_2 = \mathbf{0}. \qquad [A.4.21]$$

But $\mathbf{x}_2$ is an eigenvector of $\mathbf{A}$, and so it cannot be the zero vector. Also, $\lambda_2 - \lambda_1$ cannot be zero, since $\lambda_2 \neq \lambda_1$. Equation [A.4.21] therefore implies that $c_2 = 0$. A parallel set of calculations show that $c_1 = 0$. Thus, the only values of $c_1$ and $c_2$ consistent with [A.4.19] are $c_1 = 0$ and $c_2 = 0$, which means that $\mathbf{x}_1$ and $\mathbf{x}_2$ are linearly independent. A similar argument for $n > 2$ can be made by induction.

## *A Useful Decomposition*

Suppose an $n \times n$ matrix $\mathbf{A}$ has $n$ distinct eigenvalues $(\lambda_1, \lambda_2, \ldots, \lambda_n)$. Collect these in a diagonal matrix $\mathbf{\Lambda}$:

$$\mathbf{\Lambda} = \begin{bmatrix} \lambda_1 & 0 & \cdots & 0 \\ 0 & \lambda_2 & \cdots & 0 \\ \vdots & \vdots & \cdots & \vdots \\ 0 & 0 & \cdots & \lambda_n \end{bmatrix}.$$

Collect the eigenvectors $(\mathbf{x}_1, \mathbf{x}_2, \ldots, \mathbf{x}_n)$ in an $(n \times n)$ matrix $\mathbf{T}$:

$$\mathbf{T} = [\mathbf{x}_1 \quad \mathbf{x}_2 \quad \cdots \quad \mathbf{x}_n].$$

Applying the formula for multiplying partitioned matrices,

$$\mathbf{AT} = [\mathbf{A}\mathbf{x}_1 \quad \mathbf{A}\mathbf{x}_2 \quad \cdots \quad \mathbf{A}\mathbf{x}_n].$$

But since $(\mathbf{x}_1, \mathbf{x}_2, \ldots, \mathbf{x}_n)$ are eigenvectors, equation [A.4.16] implies that

$$\mathbf{AT} = [\lambda_1\mathbf{x}_1 \quad \lambda_2\mathbf{x}_2 \quad \cdots \quad \lambda_n\mathbf{x}_n]. \qquad [A.4.22]$$

A second application of the formula for multiplying partitioned matrices shows that the right side of [A.4.22] is in turn equal to

$$\begin{aligned} &[\lambda_1\mathbf{x}_1 \quad \lambda_2\mathbf{x}_2 \quad \cdots \quad \lambda_n\mathbf{x}_n] \\ &\quad = [\mathbf{x}_1 \quad \mathbf{x}_2 \quad \cdots \quad \mathbf{x}_n]\begin{bmatrix} \lambda_1 & 0 & \cdots & 0 \\ 0 & \lambda_2 & \cdots & 0 \\ \vdots & \vdots & \cdots & \vdots \\ 0 & 0 & \cdots & \lambda_n \end{bmatrix} \\ &\quad = \mathbf{T\Lambda}. \end{aligned}$$

Thus, [A.4.22] can be written

$$\mathbf{AT} = \mathbf{T\Lambda}. \qquad [A.4.23]$$

Now, since the eigenvalues $(\lambda_1, \lambda_2, \ldots, \lambda_n)$ are taken to be distinct, the eigenvectors $(\mathbf{x}_1, \mathbf{x}_2, \ldots, \mathbf{x}_n)$ are known to be linearly independent. Thus, $|\mathbf{T}| \neq 0$ and $\mathbf{T}^{-1}$ exists. Postmultiplying [A.4.23] by $\mathbf{T}^{-1}$ reveals a useful decomposition of $\mathbf{A}$:

$$\mathbf{A} = \mathbf{T\Lambda T}^{-1}. \qquad [A.4.24]$$

## *The Jordan Decomposition*

The decomposition in [A.4.24] required the $(n \times n)$ matrix $\mathbf{A}$ to have $n$ linearly independent eigenvectors. This will be true whenever $\mathbf{A}$ has $n$ distinct eigenvalues, and could still be true even if $\mathbf{A}$ has some repeated eigenvalues. In the completely general case when $\mathbf{A}$ has $s \leq n$ linearly independent eigenvectors, there always exists a decomposition similar to [A.4.24], known as the *Jordan decomposition*. Specifically, for such a matrix $\mathbf{A}$ there exists a nonsingular $(n \times n)$ matrix $\mathbf{M}$ such that

$$\mathbf{A} = \mathbf{MJM}^{-1}, \qquad \text{[A.4.25]}$$

where the $(n \times n)$ matrix $\mathbf{J}$ takes the form

$$\mathbf{J} = \begin{bmatrix} \mathbf{J}_1 & \mathbf{0} & \cdots & \mathbf{0} \\ \mathbf{0} & \mathbf{J}_2 & \cdots & \mathbf{0} \\ \vdots & \vdots & \cdots & \vdots \\ \mathbf{0} & \mathbf{0} & \cdots & \mathbf{J}_s \end{bmatrix} \qquad \text{[A.4.26]}$$

with

$$\mathbf{J}_i = \begin{bmatrix} \lambda_i & 1 & 0 & \cdots & 0 \\ 0 & \lambda_i & 1 & \cdots & 0 \\ 0 & 0 & \lambda_i & \cdots & 0 \\ \vdots & \vdots & \vdots & \cdots & \vdots \\ 0 & 0 & 0 & \cdots & \lambda_i \end{bmatrix}. \qquad \text{[A.4.27]}$$

Thus, $\mathbf{J}_i$ has the eigenvalue $\lambda_i$ repeated along the principal diagonal and has unity repeated along the diagonal above the principal diagonal. The same eigenvalue $\lambda_i$ can appear in two different Jordan blocks $\mathbf{J}_i$ and $\mathbf{J}_k$ if it corresponds to several linearly independent eigenvectors.

## *Some Further Results on Eigenvalues*

Suppose that $\lambda$ is an eigenvalue of the $(n \times n)$ matrix $\mathbf{A}$. Then $\lambda$ is also an eigenvalue of $\mathbf{SAS}^{-1}$ for any nonsingular $(n \times n)$ matrix $\mathbf{S}$. To see this, note that

$$(\mathbf{A} - \lambda\mathbf{I}_n)\mathbf{x} = \mathbf{0}$$

implies that

$$\mathbf{S}(\mathbf{A} - \lambda\mathbf{I}_n)\mathbf{S}^{-1}\mathbf{Sx} = \mathbf{0}$$

or

$$(\mathbf{SAS}^{-1} - \lambda\mathbf{I}_n)\mathbf{x}^* = \mathbf{0} \qquad \text{[A.4.28]}$$

for $\mathbf{x}^* \equiv \mathbf{Sx}$. Thus, $\lambda$ is an eigenvalue of $\mathbf{SAS}^{-1}$ associated with the eigenvector $\mathbf{x}^*$.

From [A.4.25], this implies that the determinant of any $(n \times n)$ matrix $\mathbf{A}$ is the same as the determinant of its Jordan matrix $\mathbf{J}$ defined in [A.4.26]. Since $\mathbf{J}$ is upper triangular, its determinant is the product of terms along the principal diagonal, which were just the eigenvalues of $\mathbf{A}$. Thus, the determinant of any matrix $\mathbf{A}$ is given by the product of its eigenvalues.

It is also clear that the eigenvalues of $\mathbf{A}$ are the same as those of $\mathbf{A}'$. Taking the transpose of [A.4.25],

$$\mathbf{A}' = (\mathbf{M}')^{-1}\mathbf{J}'\mathbf{M}',$$

we see that the eigenvalues of $\mathbf{A}'$ are the eigenvalues of $\mathbf{J}'$. Since $\mathbf{J}'$ is lower triangular, its eigenvalues are the elements on its principal diagonal. But $\mathbf{J}'$ and $\mathbf{J}$ have the same principal diagonal, meaning that $\mathbf{A}'$ and $\mathbf{A}$ have the same eigenvalues.

## *Matrix Geometric Series*

The results of [A.3.6] through [A.3.10] generalize readily to geometric series involving square matrices. Consider the sum

$$\mathbf{S}_T = \mathbf{I}_n + \mathbf{A} + \mathbf{A}^2 + \mathbf{A}^3 + \cdots + \mathbf{A}^T \qquad [A.4.29]$$

for $\mathbf{A}$ an $(n \times n)$ matrix. Premultiplying both sides of [A.4.29] by $\mathbf{A}$, we see that

$$\mathbf{A}\mathbf{S}_T = \mathbf{A} + \mathbf{A}^2 + \mathbf{A}^3 + \cdots + \mathbf{A}^T + \mathbf{A}^{T+1}. \qquad [A.4.30]$$

Subtracting [A.4.30] from [A.4.29], we find that

$$(\mathbf{I}_n - \mathbf{A})\mathbf{S}_T = \mathbf{I}_n - \mathbf{A}^{T+1}. \qquad [A.4.31]$$

Notice from [A.4.18] that if $|\mathbf{I}_n - \mathbf{A}| = 0$, then $\lambda = 1$ would be an eigenvalue of $\mathbf{A}$. Assuming that none of the eigenvalues of $\mathbf{A}$ is equal to unity, the matrix $(\mathbf{I}_n - \mathbf{A})$ is nonsingular and [A.4.31] implies that

$$\mathbf{S}_T = (\mathbf{I}_n - \mathbf{A})^{-1}(\mathbf{I}_n - \mathbf{A}^{T+1}) \qquad [A.4.32]$$

if no eigenvalue of $\mathbf{A}$ equals 1. If all the eigenvalues of $\mathbf{A}$ are strictly less than 1 in modulus, it can be shown that $\mathbf{A}^{T+1} \to \mathbf{0}$ as $T \to \infty$, implying that

$$(\mathbf{I}_n + \mathbf{A} + \mathbf{A}^2 + \mathbf{A}^3 + \cdots) = (\mathbf{I}_n - \mathbf{A})^{-1} \qquad [A.4.33]$$

assuming that the eigenvalues of $\mathbf{A}$ are all inside unit circle.

## *Kronecker Products*

For $\mathbf{A}$ an $(m \times n)$ matrix and $\mathbf{B}$ a $(p \times q)$ matrix, the *Kronecker product* of $\mathbf{A}$ and $\mathbf{B}$ is defined as the following $(mp) \times (nq)$ matrix:

$$\mathbf{A} \otimes \mathbf{B} = \begin{bmatrix} a_{11}\mathbf{B} & a_{12}\mathbf{B} & \cdots & a_{1n}\mathbf{B} \\ a_{21}\mathbf{B} & a_{22}\mathbf{B} & \cdots & a_{2n}\mathbf{B} \\ \vdots & \vdots & \cdots & \vdots \\ a_{m1}\mathbf{B} & a_{m2}\mathbf{B} & \cdots & a_{mn}\mathbf{B} \end{bmatrix}.$$

The following properties of the Kronecker product are readily verified. For any matrices $\mathbf{A}$, $\mathbf{B}$, and $\mathbf{C}$,

$$(\mathbf{A} \otimes \mathbf{B})' = \mathbf{A}' \otimes \mathbf{B}' \qquad [A.4.34]$$

$$(\mathbf{A} \otimes \mathbf{B}) \otimes \mathbf{C} = \mathbf{A} \otimes (\mathbf{B} \otimes \mathbf{C}). \qquad [A.4.35]$$

Also, for $\mathbf{A}$ and $\mathbf{B}$ both $(m \times n)$ matrices and $\mathbf{C}$ any matrix,

$$(\mathbf{A} + \mathbf{B}) \otimes \mathbf{C} = (\mathbf{A} \otimes \mathbf{C}) + (\mathbf{B} \otimes \mathbf{C}) \qquad [A.4.36]$$

$$\mathbf{C} \otimes (\mathbf{A} + \mathbf{B}) = (\mathbf{C} \otimes \mathbf{A}) + (\mathbf{C} \otimes \mathbf{B}). \qquad [A.4.37]$$

Let $\mathbf{A}$ be $(m \times n)$, $\mathbf{B}$ be $(p \times q)$, $\mathbf{C}$ be $(n \times k)$, and $\mathbf{D}$ be $(q \times r)$. Then

$$(\mathbf{A} \otimes \mathbf{B})(\mathbf{C} \otimes \mathbf{D}) = (\mathbf{AC}) \otimes (\mathbf{BD}); \qquad [A.4.38]$$

that is,

$$\begin{bmatrix} a_{11}\mathbf{B} & a_{12}\mathbf{B} & \cdots & a_{1n}\mathbf{B} \\ a_{21}\mathbf{B} & a_{22}\mathbf{B} & \cdots & a_{2n}\mathbf{B} \\ \vdots & \vdots & \cdots & \vdots \\ a_{m1}\mathbf{B} & a_{m2}\mathbf{B} & \cdots & a_{mn}\mathbf{B} \end{bmatrix} \begin{bmatrix} c_{11}\mathbf{D} & c_{12}\mathbf{D} & \cdots & c_{1k}\mathbf{D} \\ c_{21}\mathbf{D} & c_{22}\mathbf{D} & \cdots & c_{2k}\mathbf{D} \\ \vdots & \vdots & \cdots & \vdots \\ c_{n1}\mathbf{D} & c_{n2}\mathbf{D} & \cdots & c_{nk}\mathbf{D} \end{bmatrix}$$

$$= \begin{bmatrix} \sum a_{1j}c_{j1}\mathbf{BD} & \sum a_{1j}c_{j2}\mathbf{BD} & \cdots & \sum a_{1j}c_{jk}\mathbf{BD} \\ \sum a_{2j}c_{j1}\mathbf{BD} & \sum a_{2j}c_{j2}\mathbf{BD} & \cdots & \sum a_{2j}c_{jk}\mathbf{BD} \\ \vdots & \vdots & \cdots & \vdots \\ \sum a_{mj}c_{j1}\mathbf{BD} & \sum a_{mj}c_{j2}\mathbf{BD} & \cdots & \sum a_{mj}c_{jk}\mathbf{BD} \end{bmatrix}.$$

For $\mathbf{A}$ $(n \times n)$ and $\mathbf{B}$ $(p \times p)$ both nonsingular matrices we can set $\mathbf{C} = \mathbf{A}^{-1}$ and $\mathbf{D} = \mathbf{B}^{-1}$ in [A.4.38] to deduce that

$$(\mathbf{A} \otimes \mathbf{B})(\mathbf{A}^{-1} \otimes \mathbf{B}^{-1}) = (\mathbf{AA}^{-1}) \otimes (\mathbf{BB}^{-1}) = \mathbf{I}_n \otimes \mathbf{I}_p = \mathbf{I}_{np}.$$

Thus,

$$(\mathbf{A} \otimes \mathbf{B})^{-1} = (\mathbf{A}^{-1} \otimes \mathbf{B}^{-1}). \qquad \text{[A.4.39]}$$

## *Eigenvalues of a Kronecker Product*

For $\mathbf{A}$ an $(n \times n)$ matrix with (possibly nondistinct) eigenvalues $(\lambda_1, \lambda_2, \ldots, \lambda_n)$ and $\mathbf{B}$ $(p \times p)$ with eigenvalues $(\mu_1, \mu_2, \ldots, \mu_p)$, then the $(np)$ eigenvalues of $\mathbf{A} \otimes \mathbf{B}$ are given by $\lambda_i\mu_j$ for $i = 1, 2, \ldots, n$ and $j = 1, 2, \ldots, p$. To see this, write $\mathbf{A}$ and $\mathbf{B}$ in Jordan form as

$$\mathbf{A} = \mathbf{M}_A\mathbf{J}_A\mathbf{M}_A^{-1}$$
$$\mathbf{B} = \mathbf{M}_B\mathbf{J}_B\mathbf{M}_B^{-1}.$$

Then $(\mathbf{M}_A \otimes \mathbf{M}_B)$ has inverse given by $(\mathbf{M}_A^{-1} \otimes \mathbf{M}_B^{-1})$. Moreover, we know from [A.4.28] that the eigenvalues of $(\mathbf{A} \otimes \mathbf{B})$ are the same as the eigenvalues of

$$\begin{aligned}(\mathbf{M}_A^{-1} \otimes \mathbf{M}_B^{-1})(\mathbf{A} \otimes \mathbf{B})(\mathbf{M}_A \otimes \mathbf{M}_B) &= (\mathbf{M}_A^{-1}\mathbf{AM}_A) \otimes (\mathbf{M}_B^{-1}\mathbf{BM}_B) \\ &= \mathbf{J}_A \otimes \mathbf{J}_B.\end{aligned}$$

But $\mathbf{J}_A$ and $\mathbf{J}_B$ are both upper triangular, meaning that $(\mathbf{J}_A \otimes \mathbf{J}_B)$ is upper triangular as well. The eigenvalues of $(\mathbf{A} \otimes \mathbf{B})$ are thus just the terms on the principal diagonal of $(\mathbf{J}_A \otimes \mathbf{J}_B)$, which are given by $\lambda_i\mu_j$.

## *Positive Definite Matrices*

An $(n \times n)$ real symmetric matrix $\mathbf{A}$ is said to be *positive semidefinite* if for any real $(n \times 1)$ vector $\mathbf{x}$,

$$\mathbf{x}'\mathbf{Ax} \geq 0.$$

We make the stronger statement that a real symmetric matrix $\mathbf{A}$ is *positive definite* if for any real nonzero $(n \times 1)$ vector $\mathbf{x}$,

$$\mathbf{x}'\mathbf{Ax} > 0;$$

hence, any positive definite matrix could also be said to be positive semidefinite.

Let $\lambda$ be an eigenvalue of $\mathbf{A}$ associated with the eigenvector $\mathbf{x}$:

$$\mathbf{Ax} = \lambda\mathbf{x}.$$

Premultiplying this equation by $\mathbf{x}'$ results in

$$\mathbf{x}'\mathbf{Ax} = \lambda\mathbf{x}'\mathbf{x}.$$

Since an eigenvector $\mathbf{x}$ cannot be the zero vector, $\mathbf{x}'\mathbf{x} > 0$. Thus, for a positive semidefinite matrix $\mathbf{A}$, any eigenvalue $\lambda$ of $\mathbf{A}$ must be greater than or equal to zero. For $\mathbf{A}$ positive definite, all eigenvalues are strictly greater than zero. Since the determinant of $\mathbf{A}$ is the product of the eigenvalues, the determinant of a positive definite matrix $\mathbf{A}$ is strictly positive.

Let $\mathbf{A}$ be a positive definite $(n \times n)$ matrix and let $\mathbf{B}$ denote a nonsingular $(n \times n)$ matrix. Then $\mathbf{B}'\mathbf{AB}$ is positive definite. To see this, let $\mathbf{x}$ be any nonzero vector. Define

$$\tilde{\mathbf{x}} \equiv \mathbf{Bx}.$$

Then $\tilde{\mathbf{x}}$ cannot be the zero vector, for if it were, this equation would state that there exists a nonzero vector $\mathbf{x}$ such that

$$\mathbf{Bx} = 0 \cdot \mathbf{x},$$

in which case zero would be an eigenvalue of $\mathbf{B}$ associated with the eigenvector $\mathbf{x}$. But since $\mathbf{B}$ is nonsingular, none of its eigenvalues can be zero. Thus, $\tilde{\mathbf{x}} = \mathbf{Bx}$ cannot be the zero vector, and

$$\mathbf{x}'\mathbf{B}'\mathbf{ABx} = \tilde{\mathbf{x}}'\mathbf{A}\tilde{\mathbf{x}} > 0,$$

establishing that the matrix $\mathbf{B}'\mathbf{AB}$ is positive definite.

A special case of this result is obtained by letting $\mathbf{A}$ be the identity matrix. Then the result implies that any matrix that can be written as $\mathbf{B}'\mathbf{B}$ for some nonsingular matrix $\mathbf{B}$ is positive definite. More generally, any matrix that can be written as $\mathbf{B}'\mathbf{B}$ for an arbitrary matrix $\mathbf{B}$ must be positive semidefinite:

$$\mathbf{x}'\mathbf{B}'\mathbf{Bx} = \tilde{\mathbf{x}}'\tilde{\mathbf{x}} = \tilde{x}_1^2 + \tilde{x}_2^2 + \cdots + \tilde{x}_n^2 \geq 0, \qquad \text{[A.4.40]}$$

where $\tilde{\mathbf{x}} \equiv \mathbf{Bx}$.

The converse propositions are also true: if $\mathbf{A}$ is positive semidefinite, then there exists a matrix $\mathbf{B}$ such that $\mathbf{A} = \mathbf{B}'\mathbf{B}$; if $\mathbf{A}$ is positive definite, then there exists a nonsingular matrix $\mathbf{B}$ such that $\mathbf{A} = \mathbf{B}'\mathbf{B}$. A proof of this claim and an algorithm for calculating $\mathbf{B}$ are provided in Section 4.4.

## *Conjugate Transposes*

Let $\mathbf{A}$ denote an $(m \times n)$ matrix of (possibly) complex numbers:

$$\mathbf{A} = \begin{bmatrix} a_{11} + b_{11}i & \cdots & a_{1n} + b_{1n}i \\ a_{21} + b_{21}i & \cdots & a_{2n} + b_{2n}i \\ \vdots & \cdots & \vdots \\ a_{m1} + b_{m1}i & \cdots & a_{mn} + b_{mn}i \end{bmatrix}.$$

The *conjugate transpose* of $\mathbf{A}$, denoted $\mathbf{A}^H$, is formed by transposing $\mathbf{A}$ and replacing each element with its complex conjugate:

$$\mathbf{A}^H = \begin{bmatrix} a_{11} - b_{11}i & \cdots & a_{m1} - b_{m1}i \\ a_{12} - b_{12}i & \cdots & a_{m2} - b_{m2}i \\ \vdots & \cdots & \vdots \\ a_{1n} - b_{1n}i & \cdots & a_{mn} - b_{mn}i \end{bmatrix}.$$

Thus, if $\mathbf{A}$ is real, then $\mathbf{A}^H$ and $\mathbf{A}'$ would denote the same matrix.

Notice that if an $(n \times 1)$ complex vector is premultiplied by its conjugate transpose, the result is a nonnegative real scalar:

$$\mathbf{x}^H\mathbf{x} = [(a_1 - b_1 i) \quad (a_2 - b_2 i) \quad \cdots \quad (a_n - b_n i)] \begin{bmatrix} a_1 + b_1 i \\ a_2 + b_2 i \\ \vdots \\ a_n + b_n i \end{bmatrix}$$

$$= \sum_{i=1}^{n} (a_i^2 + b_i^2) \geq 0.$$

For $\mathbf{B}$ a real $(m \times n)$ matrix and $\mathbf{x}$ a complex $(n \times 1)$ vector,

$$(\mathbf{Bx})^H = \mathbf{x}^H\mathbf{B}'.$$

More generally, if both $\mathbf{B}$ and $\mathbf{x}$ are complex,

$$(\mathbf{Bx})^H = \mathbf{x}^H\mathbf{B}^H.$$

Notice that if $\mathbf{A}$ is positive semidefinite, then

$$\mathbf{x}^H\mathbf{A}\mathbf{x} = \mathbf{x}^H\mathbf{B}'\mathbf{B}\mathbf{x} = \tilde{\mathbf{x}}^H\tilde{\mathbf{x}},$$

with $\tilde{\mathbf{x}} \equiv \mathbf{Bx}$. Thus, $\mathbf{x}^H\mathbf{A}\mathbf{x}$ is a nonnegative real scalar for any $\mathbf{x}$ when $\mathbf{A}$ is positive semidefinite. It is a positive real scalar for $\mathbf{A}$ positive definite.

## *Continuity of Functions of Vectors*

A function of more than one argument, such as

$$y = f(x_1, x_2, \ldots, x_n), \qquad [A.4.41]$$

is said to be *continuous* at $(c_1, c_2, \ldots, c_n)$ if $f(c_1, c_2, \ldots, c_n)$ is finite and for every $\varepsilon > 0$ there is a $\delta > 0$ such that

$$|f(x_1, x_2, \ldots, x_n) - f(c_1, c_2, \ldots, c_n)| < \varepsilon$$

whenever

$$(x_1 - c_1)^2 + (x_2 - c_2)^2 + \cdots + (x_n - c_n)^2 < \delta^2.$$

## *Partial Derivatives*

The *partial derivative* of $f$ with respect to $x_i$ is defined by

$$\frac{\partial f}{\partial x_i} = \lim_{\Delta \to 0} \Delta^{-1} \cdot \{f(x_1, x_2, \ldots, x_{i-1}, x_i + \Delta, x_{i+1}, \ldots, x_n) - f(x_1, x_2, \ldots, x_{i-1}, x_i, x_{i+1}, \ldots, x_n)\}. \qquad [A.4.42]$$

## *Gradient*

If we collect the $n$ partial derivatives in [A.4.42] in a vector, we obtain the *gradient* of the function $f$, denoted $\boldsymbol{\nabla}$:

$$\underset{(n \times 1)}{\boldsymbol{\nabla}} \equiv \begin{bmatrix} \partial f/\partial x_1 \\ \partial f/\partial x_2 \\ \vdots \\ \partial f \partial x_n \end{bmatrix}. \qquad [A.4.43]$$

For example, suppose $f$ is a linear function:

$$f(x_1, x_2, \ldots, x_n) = a_1x_1 + a_2x_2 + \cdots + a_nx_n. \qquad \text{[A.4.44]}$$

Define **a** and **x** to be the following $(n \times 1)$ vectors:

$$\mathbf{a} \equiv \begin{bmatrix} a_1 \\ a_2 \\ \vdots \\ a_n \end{bmatrix} \qquad \text{[A.4.45]}$$

$$\mathbf{x} \equiv \begin{bmatrix} x_1 \\ x_2 \\ \vdots \\ x_n \end{bmatrix}. \qquad \text{[A.4.46]}$$

Then [A.4.44] can be written

$$f(\mathbf{x}) = \mathbf{a}'\mathbf{x}.$$

The partial derivative of $f(\cdot)$ with respect to the $i$th argument is

$$\frac{\partial f}{\partial x_i} = a_i,$$

and the gradient is

$$\boldsymbol{\nabla} = \begin{bmatrix} a_1 \\ a_2 \\ \vdots \\ a_n \end{bmatrix} = \mathbf{a}.$$

## *Second-Order Derivatives*

A *second-order derivative* of [A.4.41] is given by

$$\frac{\partial^2 f(x_1, \ldots, x_n)}{\partial x_i \, \partial x_j} = \frac{\partial}{\partial x_i}\left[\frac{\partial f(x_1, \ldots, x_n)}{\partial x_j}\right].$$

Where second-order derivatives exist and are continuous for all $i$ and $j$, the order of differentiation is irrelevant:

$$\frac{\partial}{\partial x_i}\left[\frac{\partial f(x_1, \ldots, x_n)}{\partial x_j}\right] = \frac{\partial}{\partial x_j}\left[\frac{\partial f(x_1, \ldots, x_n)}{\partial x_i}\right].$$

Sometimes these second-order derivatives are collected in an $n \times n$ matrix **H** called the *Hessian matrix*:

$$\mathbf{H} = \left[\frac{\partial^2 f}{\partial x_i \, \partial x_j}\right].$$

We will also use the notation

$$\frac{\partial^2 f}{\partial \mathbf{x} \, \partial \mathbf{x}'}$$

to represent the matrix **H**.

## *Derivatives of Vector-Valued Functions*

Suppose we have a set of $m$ functions $f_1(\cdot), f_2(\cdot), \ldots, f_m(\cdot)$, each of which depends on the $n$ variables $(x_1, x_2, \ldots, x_n)$. We can collect the $m$ functions into a single vector-valued function:

$$\underset{(m\times 1)}{\mathbf{f}(\mathbf{x})} = \begin{bmatrix} f_1(\mathbf{x}) \\ f_2(\mathbf{x}) \\ \vdots \\ f_m(\mathbf{x}) \end{bmatrix}.$$

We sometimes write

$$\mathbf{f}: \mathbb{R}^n \to \mathbb{R}^m$$

to indicate that the function takes $n$ different real numbers (summarized by the vector $\mathbf{x}$, an element of $\mathbb{R}^n$) and calculates $m$ different new numbers (summarized by the value of $\mathbf{f}$, an element of $\mathbb{R}^m$). Suppose that each of the functions $f_1(\cdot)$, $f_2(\cdot), \ldots, f_m(\cdot)$ has derivatives with respect to each of the arguments $x_1, x_2, \ldots, x_n$. We can summarize these derivatives in an $(m \times n)$ matrix, called the *Jacobian matrix* of $\mathbf{f}$ and indicated by $\partial\mathbf{f}/\partial\mathbf{x}'$:

$$\underset{(m\times n)}{\frac{\partial\mathbf{f}}{\partial\mathbf{x}'}} \equiv \begin{bmatrix} \partial f_1/\partial x_1 & \partial f_1/\partial x_2 & \cdots & \partial f_1/\partial x_n \\ \partial f_2/\partial x_1 & \partial f_2/\partial x_2 & \cdots & \partial f_2/\partial x_n \\ \vdots & \vdots & \cdots & \vdots \\ \partial f_m/\partial x_1 & \partial f_m/\partial x_2 & \cdots & \partial f_m/\partial x_n \end{bmatrix}.$$

For example, suppose that each of the functions $f_i(\mathbf{x})$ is linear:

$$\begin{aligned} f_1(\mathbf{x}) &= a_{11}x_1 + a_{12}x_2 + \cdots + a_{1n}x_n \\ f_2(\mathbf{x}) &= a_{21}x_1 + a_{22}x_2 + \cdots + a_{2n}x_n \\ &\vdots \\ f_m(\mathbf{x}) &= a_{m1}\mathbf{x}_1 + a_{m2}x_2 + \cdots + a_{mn}x_n. \end{aligned}$$

We could write this system in matrix form as

$$\mathbf{f}(\mathbf{x}) = \mathbf{A}\mathbf{x},$$

where

$$\underset{(m\times n)}{\mathbf{A}} \equiv \begin{bmatrix} a_{11} & a_{12} & \cdots & a_{1n} \\ a_{21} & a_{22} & \cdots & a_{2n} \\ \vdots & \vdots & \cdots & \vdots \\ a_{m1} & a_{m2} & \cdots & a_{mn} \end{bmatrix}$$

and $\mathbf{x}$ is the $(n \times 1)$ vector defined in [A.4.46]. Then

$$\frac{\partial\mathbf{f}}{\partial\mathbf{x}'} = \mathbf{A}.$$

## *Taylor's Theorem with Multiple Arguments*

Let $f: \mathbb{R}^n \to \mathbb{R}^1$ as in [A.4.41], with continuous second derivatives. A first-order Taylor series expansion of $f(\mathbf{x})$ around $\mathbf{c}$ is given by

$$f(\mathbf{x}) = f(\mathbf{c}) + \left.\frac{\partial f}{\partial\mathbf{x}'}\right|_{\mathbf{x}=\mathbf{c}} \cdot(\mathbf{x} - \mathbf{c}) + R_1(\mathbf{c}, \mathbf{x}). \qquad \text{[A.4.47]}$$

Here $\partial f/\partial \mathbf{x}'$ denotes the $(1 \times n)$ vector that is the transpose of the gradient, and the remainder $R_1(\cdot)$ satisfies

$$R_1(\mathbf{c}, \mathbf{x}) = \frac{1}{2}\sum_{i=1}^{n}\sum_{j=1}^{n} \left.\frac{\partial^2 f}{\partial x_i\, \partial x_j}\right|_{\mathbf{x}=\boldsymbol{\delta}(i,j)} \cdot (x_i - c_i)(x_j - c_j)$$

for $\boldsymbol{\delta}(i, j)$ an $(n \times 1)$ vector, potentially different for each $i$ and $j$, with each $\boldsymbol{\delta}(i, j)$ between $\mathbf{c}$ and $\mathbf{x}$, that is, $\boldsymbol{\delta}(i, j) = \lambda(i, j)\mathbf{c} + [1 - \lambda(i, j)]\mathbf{x}$ for some $\lambda(i, j)$ between 0 and 1. Furthermore,

$$\lim_{\mathbf{x}\to\mathbf{c}} \frac{R_1(\mathbf{c}, \mathbf{x})}{[(\mathbf{x} - \mathbf{c})'(\mathbf{x} - \mathbf{c})]^{1/2}} = 0.$$

An implication of [A.4.47] is that if we wish to approximate the consequences for $f$ of simultaneously changing $x_1$ by $\Delta_1$, $x_2$ by $\Delta_2$, . . . , and $x_n$ by $\Delta_n$, we could use

$$f(x_1 + \Delta_1, x_2 + \Delta_2, \ldots, x_n + \Delta_n) - f(x_1, x_2, \ldots, x_n) \cong \frac{\partial f}{\partial x_1}\cdot\Delta_1 + \frac{\partial f}{\partial x_2}\cdot\Delta_2 + \cdots + \frac{\partial f}{\partial x_n}\cdot\Delta_n. \qquad [A.4.48]$$

If $f(\cdot)$ has continuous third derivatives, a second-order Taylor series expansion of $f(\mathbf{x})$ around $\mathbf{c}$ is given by

$$f(\mathbf{x}) = f(\mathbf{c}) + \left.\frac{\partial f}{\partial \mathbf{x}'}\right|_{\mathbf{x}=\mathbf{c}} \cdot (\mathbf{x} - \mathbf{c}) + \frac{1}{2}(\mathbf{x} - \mathbf{c})' \left.\frac{\partial^2 f}{\partial \mathbf{x}\, \partial \mathbf{x}'}\right|_{\mathbf{x}=\mathbf{c}} (\mathbf{x} - \mathbf{c}) + R_2(\mathbf{c}, \mathbf{x}), \qquad [A.4.49]$$

where

$$R_2(\mathbf{c}, \mathbf{x}) = \frac{1}{3!}\sum_{i=1}^{n}\sum_{j=1}^{n}\sum_{k=1}^{n} \left.\frac{\partial^3 f}{\partial x_i\, \partial x_j\, \partial x_k}\right|_{\mathbf{x}=\boldsymbol{\delta}(i,j,k)} \cdot (x_i - c_i)(x_j - c_j)(x_k - c_k)$$

with $\boldsymbol{\delta}(i, j, k)$ between $\mathbf{c}$ and $\mathbf{x}$ and

$$\lim_{\mathbf{x}\to\mathbf{c}} \frac{R_2(\mathbf{c}, \mathbf{x})}{(\mathbf{x} - \mathbf{c})'(\mathbf{x} - \mathbf{c})} = 0.$$

## *Multiple Integrals*

The notation

$$\int_a^b\!\!\int_c^d f(x, y)\, dy\, dx$$

indicates the following operation: first integrate

$$\int_c^d f(x, y)\, dy$$

with respect to $y$, with $x$ held fixed, and then integrate the resulting function with respect to $x$. For example,

$$\int_0^1\!\!\int_0^2 x^4 y\, dy\, dx = \int_0^1 x^4[(2^2/2) - (0^2/2)]\, dx = 2[1^5/5 - 0^5/5] = 2/5.$$

Provided that $f(x, y)$ is continuous, the order of integration can be reversed. For example,

$$\int_0^2\int_0^1 x^4 y\, dx\, dy = \int_0^2 (1^5/5)y\, dy = (1/5)\cdot(2^2/2) = 2/5.$$

## A.5. *Probability and Statistics*

### *Densities and Distributions*

A *stochastic* or *random* variable $X$ is said to be *discrete-valued* if it can take on only one of $K$ particular values; call these $x_1, x_2, \ldots, x_K$. Its *probability distribution* is a set of numbers that give the probability of each outcome:

$$P\{X = x_k\} \equiv \text{probability that } X \text{ takes on the value } x_k, \qquad k = 1, \ldots, K.$$

The probabilities sum to unity:

$$\sum_{k=1}^{K} P\{X = x_k\} = 1.$$

Assuming that the possible outcomes are ordered $x_1 < x_2 < \cdots < x_K$, the probability that $X$ takes on a value less than or equal to the value $x_j$ is given by

$$P\{X \le x_j\} = \sum_{k=1}^{j} P\{X = x_k\}.$$

If $X$ is equal to a constant $c$ with probability 1, then $X$ is *nonstochastic*.

The probability law for a *continuous-valued* random variable $X$ can often be described by the *density* function $f_X(x)$ with

$$\int_{-\infty}^{\infty} f_X(x)\, dx = 1. \qquad \text{[A.5.1]}$$

The subscript $X$ in $f_X(x)$ indicates that this is the density of the random variable $X$; the argument $x$ of $f_X(x)$ indexes the integration in [A.5.1]. The *cumulative distribution function* of $X$ (denoted $F_X(a)$) gives the probability that $X$ takes on a value less than or equal to $a$:

$$\begin{aligned} F_X(a) &\equiv P\{X \le a\} \\ &= \int_{-\infty}^{a} f_X(x)\, dx. \end{aligned} \qquad \text{[A.5.2]}$$

### *Population Moments*

The *population mean* $\mu$ of a continuous-valued random variable $X$ is given by

$$\mu = \int_{-\infty}^{\infty} x\cdot f_X(x)\, dx,$$

provided this integral exists. (In the formulas that follow, we assume for simplicity of exposition that the density functions are continuous and that the indicated integrals all exist.) The *population variance* is

$$\mathrm{Var}(X) = \int_{-\infty}^{\infty} (x - \mu)^2 \cdot f_X(x)\, dx.$$

The square root of the variance is called the *population standard deviation*.

In general, the $r$th *population moment* is given by

$$\int_{-\infty}^{\infty} x^r \cdot f_X(x)\, dx.$$

The population mean could thus be described as the first population moment.

## Expectation

The population mean $\mu$ is also called the *expectation* of $X$, denoted $E(X)$ or sometimes simply $EX$. In general, the expectation of a function $g(X)$ is given by

$$E(g(X)) = \int_{-\infty}^{\infty} g(x) \cdot f_X(x)\, dx, \qquad \text{[A.5.3]}$$

where $f_X(x)$ is the density of $X$. For example, the $r$th population moment of $X$ is the expectation of $X^r$.

Consider the random variable $a + bX$ for constants $a$ and $b$. Its expectation is

$$\begin{aligned} E(a + bX) &= \int_{-\infty}^{\infty} [a + bx] \cdot f_X(x)\, dx \\ &= a \int_{-\infty}^{\infty} f_X(x)\, dx + b \int_{-\infty}^{\infty} x \cdot f_X(x)\, dx \\ &= a + b \cdot E(X). \end{aligned}$$

The variance of $a + bX$ is

$$\begin{aligned} \mathrm{Var}(a + bX) &= \int_{-\infty}^{\infty} [(a + bx) - (a + b\mu)]^2 \cdot f_X(x)\, dx \\ &= b^2 \cdot \int_{-\infty}^{\infty} (x - \mu)^2 \cdot f_X(x)\, dx \qquad \text{[A.5.4]} \\ &= b^2 \cdot \mathrm{Var}(X). \end{aligned}$$

Another useful result is

$$\begin{aligned} E(X^2) &= E[(X - \mu + \mu)^2] \\ &= E[(X - \mu)^2 + 2\mu(X - \mu) + \mu^2] \\ &= E[(X - \mu)^2] + 2\mu \cdot [E(X) - \mu] + \mu^2 \\ &= \mathrm{Var}(X) + 0 + [E(X)]^2. \end{aligned}$$

To simplify the appearance of expressions, we adopt the convention that exponentiation and multiplication are carried out before the expectation operator. Thus, we will use $E(X - \mu + \mu)^2$ to indicate the same operation as $E[(X - \mu + \mu)^2]$. The square of $E(X - \mu + \mu)$ is indicated by using additional parentheses, as $[E(X - \mu + \mu)]^2$.

## Sample Moments

A *sample moment* is a particular estimate of a population moment based on an observed set of data, say, $\{x_1, x_2, \ldots, x_T\}$. The first sample moment is the sample mean,

$$\bar{x} \equiv (1/T)\cdot(x_1 + x_2 + \cdots + x_T),$$

which is a natural estimate of the population mean $\mu$. The sample variance,

$$s^2 \equiv (1/T)\cdot\sum_{t=1}^{T}(x_t - \bar{x})^2,$$

affords an estimate of the population variance $\sigma^2$. More generally, the $r$th sample moment is given by

$$(1/T)\cdot(x_1^r + x_2^r + \cdots + x_T^r),$$

where $x_t^r$ denotes $x_t$ raised to the $r$th power.

## *Bias and Efficiency*

Let $\hat{\boldsymbol{\theta}}$ be a sample estimate of a vector of population parameters $\boldsymbol{\theta}$. For example, $\hat{\boldsymbol{\theta}}$ could be the sample mean $\bar{x}$ and $\boldsymbol{\theta}$ the population mean $\mu$. The estimate is said to be *unbiased* if $E(\hat{\boldsymbol{\theta}}) = \boldsymbol{\theta}$.

Suppose that $\hat{\boldsymbol{\theta}}$ is an unbiased estimate of $\boldsymbol{\theta}$. The estimate $\hat{\boldsymbol{\theta}}$ is said to be *efficient* if it is the case that for any other unbiased estimate $\hat{\boldsymbol{\theta}}^*$, the following matrix is positive semidefinite:

$$\mathbf{P} \equiv E[(\hat{\boldsymbol{\theta}}^* - \boldsymbol{\theta})\cdot(\hat{\boldsymbol{\theta}}^* - \boldsymbol{\theta})'] - E[(\hat{\boldsymbol{\theta}} - \boldsymbol{\theta})\cdot(\hat{\boldsymbol{\theta}} - \boldsymbol{\theta})'].$$

## *Joint Distributions*

For two random variables $X$ and $Y$ with the joint density $f_{X,Y}(x, y)$, we calculate the probability of the joint event that both $X \leq a$ and $Y \leq b$ from

$$P\{X \leq a, Y \leq b\} = \int_{-\infty}^{a}\int_{-\infty}^{b} f_{X,Y}(x, y)\, dy\, dx.$$

This can be represented in terms of the joint cumulative distribution function:

$$F_{X,Y}(a, b) = P\{X \leq a, Y \leq b\}.$$

The probability that $X \leq a$ by itself can be calculated from

$$P\{X \leq a, Y \text{ any}\} = \int_{-\infty}^{a}\left[\int_{-\infty}^{\infty} f_{X,Y}(x, y)\, dy\right] dx. \qquad [A.5.5]$$

Comparison of [A.5.5] with [A.5.2] reveals that the *marginal* density $f_X(x)$ is obtained by integrating the joint density $f_{X,Y}(x, y)$ with respect to $y$:

$$f_X(x) = \left[\int_{-\infty}^{\infty} f_{X,Y}(x, y)\, dy\right]. \qquad [A.5.6]$$

## *Conditional Distributions*

The *conditional density* of $Y$ given $X$ is given by

$$f_{Y|X}(y|x) \equiv \begin{cases} \dfrac{f_{X,Y}(x, y)}{f_X(x)} & \text{if } f_X(x) > 0 \\ 0 & \text{otherwise.} \end{cases} \qquad [A.5.7]$$

Notice that this satisfies the requirement of a density [A.5.1]:

$$\int_{-\infty}^{\infty} f_{Y|X}(y|x)\,dy = \int_{-\infty}^{\infty} \frac{f_{X,Y}(x, y)}{f_X(x)}\,dy$$

$$= \frac{1}{f_X(x)} \int_{-\infty}^{\infty} f_{X,Y}(x, y)\,dy$$

$$= \frac{f_X(x)}{f_X(x)} = 1.$$

A further obvious implication of the definition in [A.5.7] is that a joint density can be written as the product of the marginal density and the conditional density:

$$f_{X,Y}(x, y) = f_{Y|X}(y|x)\cdot f_X(x). \qquad [A.5.8]$$

The *conditional expectation* of $Y$ given that the random variable $X$ takes on the particular value $x$ is

$$E(Y|X = x) = \int_{-\infty}^{\infty} y\cdot f_{Y|X}(y|x)\,dy. \qquad [A.5.9]$$

## *Law of Iterated Expectations*

Note that the conditional expectation is a function of the value of the random variable $X$. For different realizations of $X$, the conditional expectation will be a different number. Suppose we view $E(Y|X)$ as a random variable and take its expectation with respect to the distribution of $X$:

$$E_X[E_{Y|X}(Y|X)] = \int_{-\infty}^{\infty} \left[\int_{-\infty}^{\infty} y\cdot f_{Y|X}(y|x)\,dy\right] f_X(x)\,dx.$$

Results [A.5.8] and [A.5.6] can be used to express this expectation as

$$\int_{-\infty}^{\infty}\int_{-\infty}^{\infty} y\cdot f_{Y,X}(y, x)\,dy\,dx = \int_{-\infty}^{\infty} y\cdot f_Y(y)\,dy.$$

Thus,

$$E_X[E_{Y|X}(Y|X)] = E_Y(Y). \qquad [A.5.10]$$

In words, the random variable $E(Y|X)$ has the same expectation as the random variable $Y$. This is known as the *law of iterated expectations*.

## *Independence*

The variables $Y$ and $X$ are said to be *independent* if

$$f_{X,Y}(x, y) = f_X(x)\cdot f_Y(y). \qquad [A.5.11]$$

Comparing [A.5.11] with [A.5.8], if $Y$ and $X$ are independent, then

$$f_{Y|X}(y|x) = f_Y(y). \qquad [A.5.12]$$

## *Covariance*

Let $\mu_X$ denote $E(X)$ and $\mu_Y$ denote $E(Y)$. The *population covariance* between $X$ and $Y$ is given by

$$\text{Cov}(X, Y) \equiv \int_{-\infty}^{\infty}\int_{-\infty}^{\infty} (x - \mu_X)(y - \mu_Y)\cdot f_{X,Y}(x, y)\,dy\,dx. \qquad [A.5.13]$$

### Correlation

The *population correlation* between $X$ and $Y$ is given by

$$\text{Corr}(X, Y) \equiv \frac{\text{Cov}(X, Y)}{\sqrt{\text{Var}(X)} \cdot \sqrt{\text{Var}(Y)}}.$$

If the covariance (or correlation) between $X$ and $Y$ is zero, then $X$ and $Y$ are said to be *uncorrelated*.

### Relation Between Correlation and Independence

Note that if $X$ and $Y$ are independent, then they are uncorrelated:

$$\begin{aligned} \text{Cov}(X, Y) &= \int_{-\infty}^{\infty} \int_{-\infty}^{\infty} (x - \mu_X)(y - \mu_Y) \cdot f_X(x) \cdot f_Y(y) \, dy \, dx \\ &= \int_{-\infty}^{\infty} (x - \mu_X) \left[ \int_{-\infty}^{\infty} (y - \mu_Y) \cdot f_Y(y) \, dy \right] \cdot f_X(x) \, dx. \end{aligned}$$

Furthermore,

$$\begin{aligned} \left[ \int_{-\infty}^{\infty} (y - \mu_Y) \cdot f_Y(y) \, dy \right] &= \int_{-\infty}^{\infty} y \cdot f_Y(y) \, dy - \mu_Y \cdot \int_{-\infty}^{\infty} f_Y(y) \, dy \\ &= \mu_Y - \mu_Y \\ &= 0. \end{aligned}$$

Thus, if $X$ and $Y$ are independent, then $\text{Cov}(X, Y) = 0$, as claimed.

The converse proposition, however, is not true—the fact that $X$ and $Y$ are uncorrelated is not enough to deduce that they are independent. To construct a counterexample, suppose that $Z$ and $Y$ are independent random variables each with mean zero, and let $X \equiv Z \cdot Y$. Then

$$\begin{aligned} E(X - \mu_X)(Y - \mu_Y) &= E[(ZY) \cdot \text{Y}] \\ &= E(Z) \cdot E(Y^2) = 0, \end{aligned}$$

and so $X$ and $Y$ are uncorrelated. They are not, however, independent—the value of $ZY$ depends on $Y$.

### Orthogonality

Consider a sample of size $T$ on two random variables, $\{x_1, x_2, \ldots, x_T\}$ and $\{y_1, y_2, \ldots, y_T\}$. The two variables are said to be *orthogonal* if

$$\sum_{t=1}^{T} x_t y_t = 0.$$

Thus, orthogonality is the sample analog of absence of correlation.

For example, let $x_t = 1$ denote a sequence of constants and let $y_t = w_t - \overline{w}$, where $\overline{w} \equiv (1/T)\Sigma_{t=1}^{T} w_t$ is the sample mean of the variable $w$. Then $x$ and $y$ are orthogonal:

$$\sum_{t=1}^{T} 1 \cdot (w_t - \overline{w}) = \sum_{t=1}^{T} w_t - T \cdot \overline{w} = 0.$$

## Population Moments of Sums

Consider the random variable $aX + bY$. Its mean is given by

$$E(aX + bY) = \int_{-\infty}^{\infty}\int_{-\infty}^{\infty} (ax + by)\cdot f_{X,Y}(x, y)\, dy\, dx$$

$$= a\int_{-\infty}^{\infty}\int_{-\infty}^{\infty} x\cdot f_{X,Y}(x, y)\, dy\, dx + b\int_{-\infty}^{\infty}\int_{-\infty}^{\infty} y\cdot f_{X,Y}(x, y)\, dy\, dx$$

$$= a\int_{-\infty}^{\infty} x\cdot f_X(x)\, dx + b\int_{-\infty}^{\infty} y\cdot f_Y(y)\, dy,$$

and so

$$E(aX + bY) = a\cdot E(X) + b\cdot E(Y). \qquad \text{[A.5.14]}$$

The variance of $(aX + bY)$ is

$$\text{Var}(aX + bY) = \int_{-\infty}^{\infty}\int_{-\infty}^{\infty} [(ax + by) - (a\mu_X + b\mu_Y)]^2\cdot f_{X,Y}(x, y)\, dy\, dx$$

$$= \int_{-\infty}^{\infty}\int_{-\infty}^{\infty} [(ax - a\mu_X)^2 + 2(ax - a\mu_X)(by - b\mu_Y) + (by - b\mu_Y)^2]\cdot f_{X,Y}(x, y)\, dy\, dx$$

$$= a^2\int_{-\infty}^{\infty}\int_{-\infty}^{\infty} (x - \mu_X)^2\cdot f_{X,Y}(x, y)\, dy\, dx$$

$$+ 2ab\int_{-\infty}^{\infty}\int_{-\infty}^{\infty} (x - \mu_X)(y - \mu_Y)\cdot f_{X,Y}(x, y)\, dy\, dx$$

$$+ b^2\int_{-\infty}^{\infty}\int_{-\infty}^{\infty} (y - \mu_Y)^2\cdot f_{X,Y}(x, y)\, dy\, dx.$$

Thus,

$$\text{Var}(aX + bY) = a^2\cdot\text{Var}(X) + 2ab\cdot\text{Cov}(X, Y) + b^2\cdot\text{Var}(Y). \qquad \text{[A.5.15]}$$

When $X$ and $Y$ are uncorrelated,

$$\text{Var}(aX + bY) = a^2\cdot\text{Var}(X) + b^2\cdot\text{Var}(Y).$$

It is straightforward to generalize results [A.5.14] and [A.5.15]. If $\{X_1, X_2, \ldots, X_n\}$ denotes a collection of $n$ random variables, then

$$E(a_1X_1 + a_2X_2 + \cdots + a_nX_n) = a_1\cdot E(X_1) + a_2\cdot E(X_2) + \cdots + a_n\cdot E(X_n) \qquad \text{[A.5.16]}$$

$$\begin{aligned}\text{Var}(a_1X_1 + a_2X_2 + \cdots + a_nX_n) &= a_1^2\cdot\text{Var}(X_1) + a_2^2\cdot\text{Var}(X_2) + \cdots + a_n^2\cdot\text{Var}(X_n)\\ &+ 2a_1a_2\cdot\text{Cov}(X_1, X_2) + 2a_1a_3\cdot\text{Cov}(X_1, X_3) + \cdots\\ &+ 2a_1a_n\cdot\text{Cov}(X_1, X_n) + 2a_2a_3\cdot\text{Cov}(X_2, X_3) + 2a_2a_4\cdot\text{Cov}(X_2, X_4)\\ &+ \cdots + 2a_{n-1}a_n\cdot\text{Cov}(X_{n-1}, X_n).\end{aligned} \qquad \text{[A.5.17]}$$

If the $X$'s are uncorrelated, then [A.5.17] simplifies to

$$\begin{aligned}&\text{Var}(a_1X_1 + a_2X_2 + \cdots + a_nX_n)\\&\quad = a_1^2\cdot\text{Var}(X_1) + a_2^2\cdot\text{Var}(X_2) + \cdots + a_n^2\cdot\text{Var}(X_n).\end{aligned} \qquad \text{[A.5.18]}$$

## *Cauchy-Schwarz Inequality*

The *Cauchy-Schwarz inequality* states that for any random variables $X$ and $Y$ whose variances and covariance exist, the correlation is no greater than unity in absolute value:

$$-1 \leq \text{Corr}(X, Y) \leq 1. \qquad \text{[A.5.19]}$$

To establish the far right inequality in [A.5.19], consider the random variable

$$Z \equiv \frac{X - \mu_X}{\sqrt{\text{Var}(X)}} - \frac{Y - \mu_Y}{\sqrt{\text{Var}(Y)}}.$$

The square of this variable cannot take on negative values, so

$$E\left[\frac{(X - \mu_X)}{\sqrt{\text{Var}(X)}} - \frac{(Y - \mu_Y)}{\sqrt{\text{Var}(Y)}}\right]^2 \geq 0.$$

Recognizing that $\text{Var}(X)$ and $\text{Var}(Y)$ denote population moments (as opposed to random variables), equation [A.5.15] can be used to deduce

$$\frac{E(X - \mu_X)^2}{\text{Var}(X)} - 2\left[\frac{E[(X - \mu_X)(Y - \mu_Y)]}{\sqrt{\text{Var}(X)}\sqrt{\text{Var}(Y)}}\right] + \frac{E(Y - \mu_Y)^2}{\text{Var}(Y)} \geq 0.$$

Thus,

$$1 - 2\cdot\text{Corr}(X, Y) + 1 \geq 0,$$

meaning that

$$\text{Corr}(X, Y) \leq 1.$$

To establish the far left inequality in [A.5.19], notice that

$$E\left[\frac{(X - \mu_X)}{\sqrt{\text{Var}(X)}} + \frac{(Y - \mu_Y)}{\sqrt{\text{Var}(Y)}}\right]^2 \geq 0,$$

implying that

$$1 + 2\cdot\text{Corr}(X, Y) + 1 \geq 0,$$

so that

$$\text{Corr}(X, Y) \geq -1.$$

## *The Normal Distribution*

The variable $Y_t$ has a *Gaussian*, or *Normal*, distribution with mean $\mu$ and variance $\sigma^2$ if

$$f_{Y_t}(y_t) = \frac{1}{\sqrt{2\pi}\sigma}\cdot\exp\left[\frac{-(y_t - \mu)^2}{2\sigma^2}\right]. \qquad \text{[A.5.20]}$$

We write

$$Y_t \sim N(\mu, \sigma^2)$$

to indicate that the density of $Y_t$ is given by [A.5.20].

Centered odd-ordered population moments for a Gaussian variable are zero:

$$E(Y_t - \mu)^r = 0 \qquad \text{for } r = 1, 3, 5, \ldots .$$

The centered fourth moment is

$$E(Y_t - \mu)^4 = 3\sigma^4.$$

## *Skew and Kurtosis*

The skewness of a variable $Y_t$ with mean $\mu$ is represented by

$$\frac{E(Y_t - \mu)^3}{[\text{Var}(Y_t)]^{3/2}}.$$

A variable with a negative skew is more likely to be far below the mean than it is to be far above the mean. The *kurtosis* is

$$\frac{E(Y_t - \mu)^4}{[\text{Var}(Y_t)]^2}.$$

A distribution whose kurtosis exceeds 3 has more mass in the tails than a Gaussian distribution with the same variance.

## *Other Useful Univariate Distributions*

Let $(X_1, X_2, \ldots, X_n)$ be independent and identically distributed (i.i.d.) $N(0, 1)$ variables, and consider the sum of their squares:

$$Y = X_1^2 + X_2^2 + \cdots + X_n^2.$$

Then $Y$ is said to have a *chi-square* distribution with $n$ degrees of freedom, denoted

$$Y \sim \chi^2(n).$$

Let $X \sim N(0, 1)$ and $Y \sim \chi^2(n)$ with $X$ and $Y$ independent. Then

$$Z = \frac{X}{\sqrt{Y/n}}$$

is said to have a *t distribution* with $n$ degrees of freedom, denoted

$$Z \sim t(n).$$

Let $Y_1 \sim \chi^2(n_1)$ and $Y_2 \sim \chi^2(n_2)$ with $Y_1$ and $Y_2$ independent. Then

$$Z = \frac{Y_1/n_1}{Y_2/n_2}$$

is said to have an *F distribution* with $n_1$ numerator degrees of freedom and $n_2$ denominator degrees of freedom, denoted

$$Z \sim F(n_1, n_2).$$

Note that if $Z \sim t(n)$, then $Z^2 \sim F(1, n)$.

## *Likelihood Function*

Suppose we have observed a sample of size $T$ on some random variable $Y_t$. Let $f_{Y_1, Y_2, \ldots, Y_T}(y_1, y_2, \ldots, y_T; \boldsymbol{\theta})$ denote the joint density of $Y_1, Y_2, \ldots, Y_T$.

The notation emphasizes that this joint density is presumed to depend on a vector of population parameters $\boldsymbol{\theta}$. If we view this joint density as a function of $\boldsymbol{\theta}$ (given the data on $Y$), the result is called the *sample likelihood function*.

For example, consider a sample of $T$ i.i.d. variables drawn from a $N(\mu, \sigma^2)$ distribution. For this distribution, $\boldsymbol{\theta} = (\mu, \sigma^2)'$, and from [A.5.11] the joint density is the product of individual terms such as [A.5.20]:

$$f_{Y_1,Y_2,\ldots,Y_T}(y_1, y_2, \ldots, y_T; \mu, \sigma^2) = \prod_{t=1}^{T} f_{Y_t}(y_t; \mu, \sigma^2).$$

The log of the joint density is the sum of the logs of these terms:

$$\begin{aligned} &\log f_{Y_1,Y_2,\ldots,Y_T}(y_1, y_2, \ldots, y_T; \mu, \sigma^2) \\ &= \sum_{t=1}^{T} \log f_{Y_t}(y_t; \mu, \sigma^2) \qquad \text{[A.5.21]} \\ &= (-T/2)\log(2\pi) - (T/2)\log(\sigma^2) - \sum_{t=1}^{T} \frac{(y_t - \mu)^2}{2\sigma^2}. \end{aligned}$$

Thus, for a sample of $T$ Gaussian random variables with mean $\mu$ and variance $\sigma^2$, the sample log likelihood function, denoted $\mathcal{L}(\mu, \sigma^2; y_1, y_2, \ldots, y_T)$, is given by:

$$\mathcal{L}(\mu, \sigma^2; y_1, y_2, \ldots, y_T) = k - (T/2)\log(\sigma^2) - \sum_{t=1}^{T} \frac{(y_t - \mu)^2}{2\sigma^2}. \qquad \text{[A.5.22]}$$

In calculating the sample log likelihood function, any constant term that does not involve the parameter $\mu$ or $\sigma^2$ can be ignored for most purposes. In [A.5.22], this constant term is

$$k \equiv -(T/2)\log(2\pi).$$

## *Maximum Likelihood Estimation*

For a given sample of observations $(y_1, y_2, \ldots, y_T)$, the value of $\boldsymbol{\theta}$ that makes the sample likelihood as large as possible is called the *maximum likelihood estimate* (*MLE*) of $\boldsymbol{\theta}$. For example, the maximum likelihood estimate of the population mean $\mu$ for an i.i.d. sample of size $T$ from a $N(\mu, \sigma^2)$ distribution is found by setting the derivative of [A.5.22] with respect to $\mu$ equal to zero:

$$\frac{\partial \mathcal{L}}{\partial \mu} = \sum_{t=1}^{T} \frac{y_t - \mu}{\sigma^2} = 0,$$

or

$$\hat{\mu} = (1/T) \sum_{t=1}^{T} y_t. \qquad \text{[A.5.23]}$$

The *MLE* of $\sigma^2$ is characterized by

$$\frac{\partial \mathcal{L}}{\partial \sigma^2} = -\frac{T}{2\sigma^2} + \sum_{t=1}^{T} \frac{(y_t - \mu)^2}{2\sigma^4} = 0. \qquad \text{[A.5.24]}$$

Substituting [A.5.23] into [A.5.24] and solving for $\sigma^2$ gives

$$\hat{\sigma}^2 = (1/T) \sum_{t=1}^{T} (y_t - \hat{\mu})^2. \qquad \text{[A.5.25]}$$

Thus, the sample mean is the *MLE* of the population mean and the sample variance is the *MLE* of the population variance for an i.i.d. sample of Gaussian variables.

## *Multivariate Gaussian Distribution*

Let

$$\mathbf{Y} = (Y_1, Y_2, \ldots, Y_n)'$$

be a collection of $n$ random variables. The vector $\mathbf{Y}$ has a *multivariate Normal*, or *multivariate Gaussian*, distribution if its density takes the form

$$f_{\mathbf{Y}}(\mathbf{y}) = (2\pi)^{-n/2}|\boldsymbol{\Omega}|^{-1/2} \exp[(-1/2)(\mathbf{y} - \boldsymbol{\mu})'\boldsymbol{\Omega}^{-1}(\mathbf{y} - \boldsymbol{\mu})]. \quad \text{[A.5.26]}$$

The mean of $\mathbf{Y}$ is given by the vector $\boldsymbol{\mu}$:

$$E(\mathbf{Y}) = \boldsymbol{\mu};$$

and its variance-covariance matrix is $\boldsymbol{\Omega}$:

$$E(\mathbf{Y} - \boldsymbol{\mu})(\mathbf{Y} - \boldsymbol{\mu})' = \boldsymbol{\Omega}.$$

Note that $(\mathbf{Y} - \boldsymbol{\mu})(\mathbf{Y} - \boldsymbol{\mu})'$ is symmetric and positive semidefinite for any $\mathbf{Y}$, meaning that any variance-covariance matrix must be symmetric and positive semidefinite; the form of the likelihood in [A.5.26] assumes that $\boldsymbol{\Omega}$ is positive definite.

Result [A.4.15] is sometimes used to write the multivariate Gaussian density in an equivalent form:

$$f_{\mathbf{Y}}(\mathbf{y}) = (2\pi)^{-n/2}|\boldsymbol{\Omega}^{-1}|^{1/2} \exp[(-1/2)(\mathbf{y} - \boldsymbol{\mu})'\boldsymbol{\Omega}^{-1}(\mathbf{y} - \boldsymbol{\mu})].$$

If $\mathbf{Y} \sim N(\boldsymbol{\mu}, \boldsymbol{\Omega})$, then for any nonstochastic $(r \times n)$ matrix $\mathbf{H}'$ and $(r \times 1)$ vector $\mathbf{b}$,

$$\mathbf{H}'\mathbf{Y} + \mathbf{b} \sim N\big((\mathbf{H}'\boldsymbol{\mu} + \mathbf{b}), \mathbf{H}'\boldsymbol{\Omega}\mathbf{H}\big).$$

## *Correlation and Independence for Multivariate Gaussian Variates*

If $\mathbf{Y}$ has a multivariate Gaussian distribution, then absence of correlation implies independence. To see this, note that if the elements of $\mathbf{Y}$ are uncorrelated, then $E[(Y_i - \mu)(Y_j - \mu)] = 0$ for $i \neq j$ and the off-diagonal elements of $\boldsymbol{\Omega}$ are zero:

$$\boldsymbol{\Omega} = \begin{bmatrix} \sigma_1^2 & 0 & \cdots & 0 \\ 0 & \sigma_2^2 & \cdots & 0 \\ \vdots & \vdots & \cdots & \vdots \\ 0 & 0 & \cdots & \sigma_n^2 \end{bmatrix}.$$

For such a diagonal matrix $\boldsymbol{\Omega}$,

$$|\boldsymbol{\Omega}| = \sigma_1^2\sigma_2^2 \cdots \sigma_n^2 \quad \text{[A.5.27]}$$

$$\boldsymbol{\Omega}^{-1} = \begin{bmatrix} 1/\sigma_1^2 & 0 & \cdots & 0 \\ 0 & 1/\sigma_2^2 & \cdots & 0 \\ \vdots & \vdots & \cdots & \vdots \\ 0 & 0 & \cdots & 1/\sigma_n^2 \end{bmatrix}. \quad \text{[A.5.28]}$$

Substituting [A.5.27] and [A.5.28] into [A.5.26] produces

$$\begin{aligned} f_{\mathbf{Y}}(\mathbf{y}) &= (2\pi)^{-n/2}[\sigma_1^2\sigma_2^2 \cdots \sigma_n^2]^{-1/2} \\ &\quad \times \exp[(-1/2)\{(y_1 - \mu_1)^2/\sigma_1^2 + (y_2 - \mu_2)^2/\sigma_2^2 + \cdots \\ &\quad + (y_n - \mu_n)^2/\sigma_n^2\}] \\ &= \prod_{i=1}^{n} (2\pi)^{-1/2}[\sigma_i^2]^{-1/2} \exp[(-1/2)\{(y_i - \mu_i)^2/\sigma_i^2\}], \end{aligned}$$

which is the product of $n$ univariate Gaussian densities. Since the joint density is the product of the individual densities, the random variables $(Y_1, Y_2, \ldots, Y_n)$ are independent.

## *Probability Limit*

Let $\{X_1, X_2, \ldots, X_T\}$ denote a sequence of random variables. Often we are interested in what happens to this sequence as $T$ becomes large. For example, $X_T$ might denote the sample mean of $T$ observations:

$$X_T = (1/T)\cdot(Y_1 + Y_2 + \cdots + Y_T), \quad \text{[A.5.29]}$$

in which case we might want to know the properties of the sample mean as the size of the sample $T$ grows large.

The sequence $\{X_1, X_2, \ldots, X_T\}$ is said to *converge in probability* to $c$ if for every $\varepsilon > 0$ and $\delta > 0$ there exists a value $N$ such that, for all $T \geq N$,

$$P\{|X_T - c| > \delta\} < \varepsilon. \quad \text{[A.5.30]}$$

When [A.5.30] is satisfied, the number $c$ is called the *probability limit*, or *plim*, of the sequence $\{X_1, X_2, \ldots, X_T\}$. This is sometimes indicated as

$$X_T \xrightarrow{p} c.$$

## *Law of Large Numbers*

Under fairly general conditions detailed in Chapter 7, the sample mean [A.5.29] converges in probability to the population mean:

$$(1/T)(Y_1 + Y_2 + \cdots + Y_T) \xrightarrow{p} E(Y_t). \quad \text{[A.5.31]}$$

When [A.5.31] holds, we say that the sample mean gives a *consistent* estimate of the population mean.

## *Convergence in Mean Square*

A stronger condition than convergence in probability is *mean square convergence*. The sequence $\{X_1, X_2, \ldots, X_T\}$ is said to converge in mean square if for every $\varepsilon > 0$ there exists a value $N$ such that, for all $T \geq N$,

$$E(X_T - c)^2 < \varepsilon. \quad \text{[A.5.32]}$$

We indicate that the sequence converges to $c$ in mean square as follows:

$$X_T \xrightarrow{m.s.} c.$$

Convergence in mean square implies convergence in probability, but convergence in probability does not imply convergence in mean square.

## *Appendix A References*


Chiang, Alpha C. 1974. *Fundamental Methods of Mathematical Economics*, 2d ed. New York: McGraw-Hill.

Hoel, Paul G., Sidney C. Port, and Charles J. Stone. 1971. *Introduction to Probability Theory*. Boston: Houghton Mifflin.

Johnston, J. 1984. *Econometric Methods*, 3d ed. New York: McGraw-Hill.

Lindgren, Bernard W. 1976. *Statistical Theory*, 3d ed. New York: Macmillan.

Magnus, Jan R., and Heinz Neudecker. 1988. *Matrix Differential Calculus with Applications in Statistics and Econometrics*. New York: Wiley.

Marsden, Jerrold E. 1974. *Elementary Classical Analysis*. San Francisco: Freeman.

O'Nan, Michael. 1976. *Linear Algebra*, 2d ed. New York: Harcourt Brace Jovanovich.

Strang, Gilbert. 1976. *Linear Algebra and Its Applications*. New York: Academic Press.

Theil, Henri. 1971. *Principles of Econometrics*. New York: Wiley.

Thomas, George B., Jr. 1972. *Calculus and Analytic Geometry*, alternate ed. Reading, Mass.: Addison-Wesley Publishing Company, Inc.

# B

# *Statistical Tables*

**TABLE B.1**
**Standard Normal Distribution**

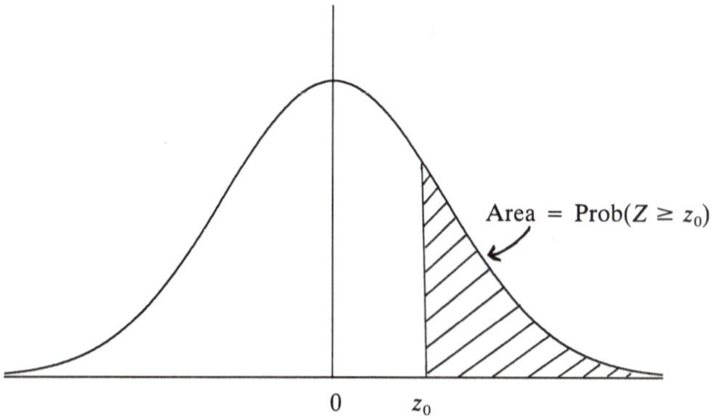


| → ↓ $z_0$ | Second decimal place of $z_0$ .00 | .01 | .02 | .03 | .04 | .05 | .06 | .07 | .08 | .09 |
|---|---|---|---|---|---|---|---|---|---|---|
| 0.0 | .5000 | .4960 | .4920 | .4880 | .4840 | .4801 | .4761 | .4721 | .4681 | .4641 |
| 0.1 | .4602 | .4562 | .4522 | .4483 | .4443 | .4404 | .4364 | .4325 | .4286 | .4247 |
| 0.2 | .4207 | .4168 | .4129 | .4090 | .4052 | .4013 | .3974 | .3936 | .3897 | .3859 |
| 0.3 | .3821 | .3783 | .3745 | .3707 | .3669 | .3632 | .3594 | .3557 | .3520 | .3483 |
| 0.4 | .3446 | .3409 | .3372 | .3336 | .3300 | .3264 | .3228 | .3192 | .3156 | .3121 |
| 0.5 | .3085 | .3050 | .3015 | .2981 | .2946 | .2912 | .2877 | .2843 | .2810 | .2776 |
| 0.6 | .2743 | .2709 | .2676 | .2643 | .2611 | .2578 | .2546 | .2514 | .2483 | .2451 |
| 0.7 | .2420 | .2389 | .2358 | .2327 | .2296 | .2266 | .2236 | .2206 | .2177 | .2148 |
| 0.8 | .2119 | .2090 | .2061 | .2033 | .2005 | .1977 | .1949 | .1922 | .1894 | .1867 |
| 0.9 | .1841 | .1814 | .1788 | .1762 | .1736 | .1711 | .1685 | .1660 | .1635 | .1611 |
| 1.0 | .1587 | .1562 | .1539 | .1515 | .1492 | .1469 | .1446 | .1423 | .1401 | .1379 |
| 1.1 | .1357 | .1335 | .1314 | .1292 | .1271 | .1251 | .1230 | .1210 | .1190 | .1170 |
| 1.2 | .1151 | .1131 | .1112 | .1093 | .1075 | .1056 | .1038 | .1020 | .1003 | .0985 |
| 1.3 | .0968 | .0951 | .0934 | .0918 | .0901 | .0885 | .0869 | .0853 | .0838 | .0823 |
| 1.4 | .0808 | .0793 | .0778 | .0764 | .0749 | .0735 | .0722 | .0708 | .0694 | .0681 |

*(continued on next page)*

**TABLE B.1 (continued)**

| → ↓ $z_0$ | Second decimal place of $z_0$ | | | | | | | | | |
|---|---|---|---|---|---|---|---|---|---|---|
| | *.00* | *.01* | *.02* | *.03* | *.04* | *.05* | *.06* | *.07* | *.08* | *.09* |
| 1.5 | .0668 | .0655 | .0643 | .0630 | .0618 | .0606 | .0594 | .0582 | .0571 | .0559 |
| 1.6 | .0548 | .0537 | .0526 | .0516 | .0505 | .0495 | .0485 | .0475 | .0465 | .0455 |
| 1.7 | .0446 | .0436 | .0427 | .0418 | .0409 | .0401 | .0392 | .0384 | .0375 | .0367 |
| 1.8 | .0359 | .0352 | .0344 | .0336 | .0329 | .0322 | .0314 | .0307 | .0301 | .0294 |
| 1.9 | .0287 | .0281 | .0274 | .0268 | .0262 | .0256 | .0250 | .0244 | .0239 | .0233 |
| 2.0 | .0228 | .0222 | .0217 | .0212 | .0207 | .0202 | .0197 | .0192 | .0188 | .0183 |
| 2.1 | .0179 | .0174 | .0170 | .0166 | .0162 | .0158 | .0154 | .0150 | .0146 | .0143 |
| 2.2 | .0139 | .0136 | .0132 | .0129 | .0125 | .0122 | .0119 | .0116 | .0113 | .0110 |
| 2.3 | .0107 | .0104 | .0102 | .0099 | .0096 | .0094 | .0091 | .0089 | .0087 | .0084 |
| 2.4 | .0082 | .0080 | .0078 | .0075 | .0073 | .0071 | .0069 | .0068 | .0066 | .0064 |
| 2.5 | .0062 | .0060 | .0059 | .0057 | .0055 | .0054 | .0052 | .0051 | .0049 | .0048 |
| 2.6 | .0047 | .0045 | .0044 | .0043 | .0041 | .0040 | .0039 | .0038 | .0037 | .0036 |
| 2.7 | .0035 | .0034 | .0033 | .0032 | .0031 | .0030 | .0029 | .0028 | .0027 | .0026 |
| 2.8 | .0026 | .0025 | .0024 | .0023 | .0023 | .0022 | .0021 | .0021 | .0020 | .0019 |
| 2.9 | .0019 | .0018 | .0017 | .0017 | .0016 | .0016 | .0015 | .0015 | .0014 | .0014 |
| 3.0 | .00135 | | | | | | | | | |
| 3.5 | .000 233 | | | | | | | | | |
| 4.0 | .000 031 7 | | | | | | | | | |
| 4.5 | .000 003 40 | | | | | | | | | |
| 5.0 | .000 000 287 | | | | | | | | | |

Table entries give the probability that a $N(0, 1)$ variable takes on a value greater than or equal to $z_0$. For example, if $Z \sim N(0, 1)$, the probability that $Z > 1.96 = 0.0250$. By symmetry, the table entries could also be interpreted as the probability that a $N(0, 1)$ variable takes a value less than or equal to $-z_0$.

*Source:* Thomas H. Wonnacott and Ronald J. Wonnacott, *Introductory Statistics*, 2d ed., p. 480. Copyright © 1972 by John Wiley & Sons, Inc., New York. Reprinted by permission of John Wiley & Sons, Inc.

**TABLE B.2**
**The $\chi^2$ Distribution**

| *Degrees of freedom (m)* | *Probability that $\chi^2(m)$ is greater than entry* | | | | | | |
|---|---|---|---|---|---|---|---|
| | *0.995* | *0.990* | *0.975* | *0.950* | *0.900* | *0.750* | *0.500* |
| 1 | $4 \times 10^{-5}$ | $2 \times 10^{-4}$ | 0.001 | 0.004 | 0.016 | 0.102 | 0.455 |
| 2 | 0.010 | 0.020 | 0.051 | 0.103 | 0.211 | 0.575 | 1.39 |
| 3 | 0.072 | 0.115 | 0.216 | 0.352 | 0.584 | 1.21 | 2.37 |
| 4 | 0.207 | 0.297 | 0.484 | 0.711 | 1.06 | 1.92 | 3.36 |
| 5 | 0.412 | 0.554 | 0.831 | 1.15 | 1.61 | 2.67 | 4.35 |
| 6 | 0.676 | 0.872 | 1.24 | 1.64 | 2.20 | 3.45 | 5.35 |
| 7 | 0.989 | 1.24 | 1.69 | 2.17 | 2.83 | 4.25 | 6.35 |
| 8 | 1.34 | 1.65 | 2.18 | 2.73 | 3.49 | 5.07 | 7.34 |
| 9 | 1.73 | 2.09 | 2.70 | 3.33 | 4.17 | 5.90 | 8.34 |
| 10 | 2.16 | 2.56 | 3.25 | 3.94 | 4.87 | 6.74 | 9.34 |
| 11 | 2.60 | 3.05 | 3.82 | 4.57 | 5.58 | 7.58 | 10.3 |
| 12 | 3.07 | 3.57 | 4.40 | 5.23 | 6.30 | 8.44 | 11.3 |
| 13 | 3.57 | 4.11 | 5.01 | 5.89 | 7.04 | 9.30 | 12.3 |
| 14 | 4.07 | 4.66 | 5.63 | 6.57 | 7.79 | 10.2 | 13.3 |
| 15 | 4.60 | 5.23 | 6.26 | 7.26 | 8.55 | 11.0 | 14.3 |
| 16 | 5.14 | 5.81 | 6.91 | 7.96 | 9.31 | 11.9 | 15.3 |
| 17 | 5.70 | 6.41 | 7.56 | 8.67 | 10.1 | 12.8 | 16.3 |
| 18 | 6.26 | 7.01 | 8.23 | 9.39 | 10.9 | 13.7 | 17.3 |
| 19 | 6.84 | 7.63 | 8.91 | 10.1 | 11.7 | 14.6 | 18.3 |
| 20 | 7.43 | 8.26 | 9.59 | 10.9 | 12.4 | 15.5 | 19.3 |
| 21 | 8.03 | 8.90 | 10.3 | 11.6 | 13.2 | 16.3 | 20.3 |
| 22 | 8.64 | 9.54 | 11.0 | 12.3 | 14.0 | 17.2 | 21.3 |
| 23 | 9.26 | 10.2 | 11.7 | 13.1 | 14.8 | 18.1 | 22.3 |
| 24 | 9.89 | 10.9 | 12.4 | 13.8 | 15.7 | 19.0 | 23.3 |
| 25 | 10.5 | 11.5 | 13.1 | 14.6 | 16.5 | 19.9 | 24.3 |
| 26 | 11.2 | 12.2 | 13.8 | 15.4 | 17.3 | 20.8 | 25.3 |
| 27 | 11.8 | 12.9 | 14.6 | 16.2 | 18.1 | 21.7 | 26.3 |
| 28 | 12.5 | 13.6 | 15.3 | 16.9 | 18.9 | 22.7 | 27.3 |
| 29 | 13.1 | 14.3 | 16.0 | 17.7 | 19.8 | 23.6 | 28.3 |
| 30 | 13.8 | 15.0 | 16.8 | 18.5 | 20.6 | 24.5 | 29.3 |
| 40 | 20.7 | 22.2 | 24.4 | 26.5 | 29.1 | 33.7 | 39.3 |
| 50 | 28.0 | 29.7 | 32.4 | 34.8 | 37.7 | 42.9 | 49.3 |
| 60 | 35.5 | 37.5 | 40.5 | 43.2 | 46.5 | 52.3 | 59.3 |
| 70 | 43.3 | 45.4 | 48.8 | 51.7 | 55.3 | 61.7 | 69.3 |
| 80 | 51.2 | 53.5 | 57.2 | 60.4 | 64.3 | 71.1 | 79.3 |
| 90 | 59.2 | 61.8 | 65.6 | 69.1 | 73.3 | 80.6 | 89.3 |
| 100 | 67.3 | 70.1 | 74.2 | 77.9 | 82.4 | 90.1 | 99.3 |

(*continued on next page*)

**TABLE B.2 (continued)**

| Degrees of freedom (*m*) | Probability that $\chi^2(m)$ is greater than entry | | | | | | |
|---|---|---|---|---|---|---|---|
| | *0.250* | *0.100* | *0.050* | *0.025* | *0.010* | *0.005* | *0.001* |
| 1 | 1.32 | 2.71 | 3.84 | 5.02 | 6.63 | 7.88 | 10.8 |
| 2 | 2.77 | 4.61 | 5.99 | 7.38 | 9.21 | 10.6 | 13.8 |
| 3 | 4.11 | 6.25 | 7.81 | 9.35 | 11.3 | 12.8 | 16.3 |
| 4 | 5.39 | 7.78 | 9.49 | 11.1 | 13.3 | 14.9 | 18.5 |
| 5 | 6.63 | 9.24 | 11.1 | 12.8 | 15.1 | 16.7 | 20.5 |
| 6 | 7.84 | 10.6 | 12.6 | 14.4 | 16.8 | 18.5 | 22.5 |
| 7 | 9.04 | 12.0 | 14.1 | 16.0 | 18.5 | 20.3 | 24.3 |
| 8 | 10.2 | 13.4 | 15.5 | 17.5 | 20.1 | 22.0 | 26.1 |
| 9 | 11.4 | 14.7 | 16.9 | 19.0 | 21.7 | 23.6 | 27.9 |
| 10 | 12.5 | 16.0 | 18.3 | 20.5 | 23.2 | 25.2 | 29.6 |
| 11 | 13.7 | 17.3 | 19.7 | 21.9 | 24.7 | 26.8 | 31.3 |
| 12 | 14.8 | 18.5 | 21.0 | 23.3 | 26.2 | 28.3 | 32.9 |
| 13 | 16.0 | 19.8 | 22.4 | 24.7 | 27.7 | 29.8 | 34.5 |
| 14 | 17.1 | 21.1 | 23.7 | 26.1 | 29.1 | 31.3 | 36.1 |
| 15 | 18.2 | 22.3 | 25.0 | 27.5 | 30.6 | 32.8 | 37.7 |
| 16 | 19.4 | 23.5 | 26.3 | 28.8 | 32.0 | 34.3 | 39.3 |
| 17 | 20.5 | 24.8 | 27.6 | 30.2 | 33.4 | 35.7 | 40.8 |
| 18 | 21.6 | 26.0 | 28.9 | 31.5 | 34.8 | 37.2 | 42.3 |
| 19 | 22.7 | 27.2 | 30.1 | 32.9 | 36.2 | 38.6 | 43.8 |
| 20 | 23.8 | 28.4 | 31.4 | 34.2 | 37.6 | 40.0 | 45.3 |
| 21 | 24.9 | 29.6 | 32.7 | 35.5 | 38.9 | 41.4 | 46.8 |
| 22 | 26.0 | 30.8 | 33.9 | 36.8 | 40.3 | 42.8 | 48.3 |
| 23 | 27.1 | 32.0 | 35.2 | 38.1 | 41.6 | 44.2 | 49.7 |
| 24 | 28.2 | 33.2 | 36.4 | 39.4 | 43.0 | 45.6 | 51.2 |
| 25 | 29.3 | 34.4 | 37.7 | 40.6 | 44.3 | 46.9 | 52.6 |
| 26 | 30.4 | 35.6 | 38.9 | 41.9 | 45.6 | 48.3 | 54.1 |
| 27 | 31.5 | 36.7 | 40.1 | 43.2 | 47.0 | 49.6 | 55.5 |
| 28 | 32.6 | 37.9 | 41.3 | 44.5 | 48.3 | 51.0 | 56.9 |
| 29 | 33.7 | 39.1 | 42.6 | 45.7 | 49.6 | 52.3 | 58.3 |
| 30 | 34.8 | 40.3 | 43.8 | 47.0 | 50.9 | 53.7 | 59.7 |
| 40 | 45.6 | 51.8 | 55.8 | 59.3 | 63.7 | 66.8 | 73.4 |
| 50 | 56.3 | 63.2 | 67.5 | 71.4 | 76.2 | 79.5 | 86.7 |
| 60 | 67.0 | 74.4 | 79.1 | 83.3 | 88.4 | 92.0 | 99.6 |
| 70 | 77.6 | 85.5 | 90.5 | 95.0 | 100 | 104 | 112 |
| 80 | 88.1 | 96.6 | 102 | 107 | 112 | 116 | 125 |
| 90 | 98.6 | 108 | 113 | 118 | 124 | 128 | 137 |
| 100 | 109 | 118 | 124 | 130 | 136 | 140 | 149 |

The probability shown at the head of the column is the area in the right-hand tail. For example, there is a 10% probability that a $\chi^2$ variable with 2 degrees of freedom would be greater than 4.61.

*Source:* Adapted from Henri Theil, *Principles of Econometrics*, pp. 718–19. Copyright © 1971 by John Wiley & Sons, Inc., New York. Also Thomas H. Wonnacott and Ronald J. Wonnacott, *Introductory Statistics*, 2d ed., p. 482. Copyright © 1972 by John Wiley & Sons, Inc., New York. Reprinted by permission of John Wiley & Sons, Inc.

**TABLE B.3**
**The *t* Distribution**

| *Degrees of freedom* (*m*) | *Probability that t(m) is greater than entry* | | | | | | |
|---|---|---|---|---|---|---|---|
| | *0.25* | *0.10* | *0.05* | *0.025* | *0.010* | *0.005* | *0.001* |
| 1 | 1.000 | 3.078 | 6.314 | 12.706 | 31.821 | 63.657 | 318.31 |
| 2 | .816 | 1.886 | 2.920 | 4.303 | 6.965 | 9.925 | 22.326 |
| 3 | .765 | 1.638 | 2.353 | 3.182 | 4.541 | 5.841 | 10.213 |
| 4 | .741 | 1.533 | 2.132 | 2.776 | 3.747 | 4.604 | 7.173 |
| 5 | .727 | 1.476 | 2.015 | 2.571 | 3.365 | 4.032 | 5.893 |
| 6 | .718 | 1.440 | 1.943 | 2.447 | 3.143 | 3.707 | 5.208 |
| 7 | .711 | 1.415 | 1.895 | 2.365 | 2.998 | 3.499 | 4.785 |
| 8 | .706 | 1.397 | 1.860 | 2.306 | 2.896 | 3.355 | 4.501 |
| 9 | .703 | 1.383 | 1.833 | 2.262 | 2.821 | 3.250 | 4.297 |
| 10 | .700 | 1.372 | 1.812 | 2.228 | 2.764 | 3.169 | 4.144 |
| 11 | .697 | 1.363 | 1.796 | 2.201 | 2.718 | 3.106 | 4.025 |
| 12 | .695 | 1.356 | 1.782 | 2.179 | 2.681 | 3.055 | 3.930 |
| 13 | .694 | 1.350 | 1.771 | 2.160 | 2.650 | 3.012 | 3.852 |
| 14 | .692 | 1.345 | 1.761 | 2.145 | 2.624 | 2.977 | 3.787 |
| 15 | .691 | 1.341 | 1.753 | 2.131 | 2.602 | 2.947 | 3.733 |
| 16 | .690 | 1.337 | 1.746 | 2.120 | 2.583 | 2.921 | 3.686 |
| 17 | .689 | 1.333 | 1.740 | 2.110 | 2.567 | 2.898 | 3.646 |
| 18 | .688 | 1.330 | 1.734 | 2.101 | 2.552 | 2.878 | 3.610 |
| 19 | .688 | 1.328 | 1.729 | 2.093 | 2.539 | 2.861 | 3.579 |
| 20 | .687 | 1.325 | 1.725 | 2.086 | 2.528 | 2.845 | 3.552 |
| 21 | .686 | 1.323 | 1.721 | 2.080 | 2.518 | 2.831 | 3.527 |
| 22 | .686 | 1.321 | 1.717 | 2.074 | 2.508 | 2.819 | 3.505 |
| 23 | .685 | 1.319 | 1.714 | 2.069 | 2.500 | 2.807 | 3.485 |
| 24 | .685 | 1.318 | 1.711 | 2.064 | 2.492 | 2.797 | 3.467 |
| 25 | .684 | 1.316 | 1.708 | 2.060 | 2.485 | 2.787 | 3.450 |
| 26 | .684 | 1.315 | 1.706 | 2.056 | 2.479 | 2.779 | 3.435 |
| 27 | .684 | 1.314 | 1.703 | 2.052 | 2.473 | 2.771 | 3.421 |
| 28 | .683 | 1.313 | 1.701 | 2.048 | 2.467 | 2.763 | 3.408 |
| 29 | .683 | 1.311 | 1.699 | 2.045 | 2.462 | 2.756 | 3.396 |
| 30 | .683 | 1.310 | 1.697 | 2.042 | 2.457 | 2.750 | 3.385 |
| 40 | .681 | 1.303 | 1.684 | 2.021 | 2.423 | 2.704 | 3.307 |
| 60 | .679 | 1.296 | 1.671 | 2.000 | 2.390 | 2.660 | 3.232 |
| 120 | .677 | 1.289 | 1.658 | 1.980 | 2.358 | 2.617 | 3.160 |
| ∞ | .674 | 1.282 | 1.645 | 1.960 | 2.326 | 2.576 | 3.090 |

The probability shown at the head of the column is the area in the right-hand tail. For example, there is a 10% probability that a *t* variable with 20 degrees of freedom would be greater than 1.325. By symmetry, there is also a 10% probability that a *t* variable with 20 degrees of freedom would be less than −1.325.

*Source:* Thomas H. Wonnacott and Ronald J. Wonnacott, *Introductory Statistics*, 2d ed., p. 481. Copyright © 1972 by John Wiley & Sons, Inc., New York. Reprinted by permission of John Wiley & Sons, Inc.

## TABLE B.4
## The *F* Distribution

| *Denominator degrees of freedom* ($m_2$) | *Numerator degrees of freedom* ($m_1$) | | | | | | | | | |
|---|---|---|---|---|---|---|---|---|---|---|
| | *1* | *2* | *3* | *4* | *5* | *6* | *7* | *8* | *9* | *10* |
| **1** | 161 | 200 | 216 | 225 | 230 | 234 | 237 | 239 | 241 | 242 |
| | **4052** | **4999** | **5403** | **5625** | **5764** | **5859** | **5928** | **5981** | **6022** | **6056** |
| **2** | 18.51 | 19.00 | 19.16 | 19.25 | 19.30 | 19.33 | 19.36 | 19.37 | 19.38 | 19.39 |
| | **98.49** | **99.00** | **99.17** | **99.25** | **99.30** | **99.33** | **99.34** | **99.36** | **99.38** | **99.40** |
| **3** | 10.13 | 9.55 | 9.28 | 9.12 | 9.01 | 8.94 | 8.88 | 8.84 | 8.81 | 8.78 |
| | **34.12** | **30.82** | **29.46** | **28.71** | **28.24** | **27.91** | **27.67** | **27.49** | **27.34** | **27.23** |
| **4** | 7.71 | 6.94 | 6.59 | 6.39 | 6.26 | 6.16 | 6.09 | 6.04 | 6.00 | 5.96 |
| | **21.20** | **18.00** | **16.69** | **15.98** | **15.52** | **15.21** | **14.98** | **14.80** | **14.66** | **14.54** |
| **5** | 6.61 | 5.79 | 5.41 | 5.19 | 5.05 | 4.95 | 4.88 | 4.82 | 4.78 | 4.74 |
| | **16.26** | **13.27** | **12.06** | **11.39** | **10.97** | **10.67** | **10.45** | **10.27** | **10.15** | **10.05** |
| **6** | 5.99 | 5.14 | 4.76 | 4.53 | 4.39 | 4.28 | 4.21 | 4.15 | 4.10 | 4.06 |
| | **13.74** | **10.92** | **9.78** | **9.15** | **8.75** | **8.47** | **8.26** | **8.10** | **7.98** | **7.87** |
| **7** | 5.59 | 4.74 | 4.35 | 4.12 | 3.97 | 3.87 | 3.79 | 3.73 | 3.68 | 3.63 |
| | **12.25** | **9.55** | **8.45** | **7.85** | **7.46** | **7.19** | **7.00** | **6.84** | **6.71** | **6.62** |
| **8** | 5.32 | 4.46 | 4.07 | 3.84 | 3.69 | 3.58 | 3.50 | 3.44 | 3.39 | 3.34 |
| | **11.26** | **8.65** | **7.59** | **7.01** | **6.63** | **6.37** | **6.19** | **6.03** | **5.91** | **5.82** |
| **9** | 5.12 | 4.26 | 3.86 | 3.63 | 3.48 | 3.37 | 3.29 | 3.23 | 3.18 | 3.13 |
| | **10.56** | **8.02** | **6.99** | **6.42** | **6.06** | **5.80** | **5.62** | **5.47** | **5.35** | **5.26** |
| **10** | 4.96 | 4.10 | 3.71 | 3.48 | 3.33 | 3.22 | 3.14 | 3.07 | 3.02 | 2.97 |
| | **10.04** | **7.56** | **6.55** | **5.99** | **5.64** | **5.39** | **5.21** | **5.06** | **4.95** | **4.85** |
| **11** | 4.84 | 3.98 | 3.59 | 3.36 | 3.20 | 3.09 | 3.01 | 2.95 | 2.90 | 2.86 |
| | **9.65** | **7.20** | **6.22** | **5.67** | **5.32** | **5.07** | **4.88** | **4.74** | **4.63** | **4.54** |
| **12** | 4.75 | 3.88 | 3.49 | 3.26 | 3.11 | 3.00 | 2.92 | 2.85 | 2.80 | 2.76 |
| | **9.33** | **6.93** | **5.95** | **5.41** | **5.06** | **4.82** | **4.65** | **4.50** | **4.39** | **4.30** |
| **13** | 4.67 | 3.80 | 3.41 | 3.18 | 3.02 | 2.92 | 2.84 | 2.77 | 2.72 | 2.67 |
| | **9.07** | **6.70** | **5.74** | **5.20** | **4.86** | **4.62** | **4.44** | **4.30** | **4.19** | **4.10** |
| **14** | 4.60 | 3.74 | 3.34 | 3.11 | 2.96 | 2.85 | 2.77 | 2.70 | 2.65 | 2.60 |
| | **8.86** | **6.51** | **5.56** | **5.03** | **4.69** | **4.46** | **4.28** | **4.14** | **4.03** | **3.94** |
| **15** | 4.54 | 3.68 | 3.29 | 3.06 | 2.90 | 2.79 | 2.70 | 2.64 | 2.59 | 2.55 |
| | **8.68** | **6.36** | **5.42** | **4.89** | **4.56** | **4.32** | **4.14** | **4.00** | **3.89** | **3.80** |
| **16** | 4.49 | 3.63 | 3.24 | 3.01 | 2.85 | 2.74 | 2.66 | 2.59 | 2.54 | 2.49 |
| | **8.53** | **6.23** | **5.29** | **4.77** | **4.44** | **4.20** | **4.03** | **3.89** | **3.78** | **3.69** |
| **17** | 4.45 | 3.59 | 3.20 | 2.96 | 2.81 | 2.70 | 2.62 | 2.55 | 2.50 | 2.45 |
| | **8.40** | **6.11** | **5.18** | **4.67** | **4.34** | **4.10** | **3.93** | **3.79** | **3.68** | **3.59** |
| **18** | 4.41 | 3.55 | 3.16 | 2.93 | 2.77 | 2.66 | 2.58 | 2.51 | 2.46 | 2.41 |
| | **8.28** | **6.01** | **5.09** | **4.58** | **4.25** | **4.01** | **3.85** | **3.71** | **3.60** | **3.51** |
| **19** | 4.38 | 3.52 | 3.13 | 2.90 | 2.74 | 2.63 | 2.55 | 2.48 | 2.43 | 2.38 |
| | **8.18** | **5.93** | **5.01** | **4.50** | **4.17** | **3.94** | **3.77** | **3.63** | **3.52** | **3.43** |

*(continued on page 758)*

| *11* | *12* | *14* | *16* | *20* | *24* | *30* | *40* | *50* | *75* | *100* | *200* | *500* | ∞ |
|---|---|---|---|---|---|---|---|---|---|---|---|---|---|
| 243 | 244 | 245 | 246 | 248 | 249 | 250 | 251 | 252 | 253 | 253 | 254 | 254 | 254 |
| **6082** | **6106** | **6142** | **6169** | **6203** | **6234** | **6258** | **6286** | **6302** | **6323** | **6334** | **6352** | **6361** | **6366** |
| 19.40 | 19.41 | 19.42 | 19.43 | 19.44 | 19.45 | 19.46 | 19.47 | 19.47 | 19.48 | 19.49 | 19.49 | 19.50 | 19.50 |
| **99.41** | **99.42** | **99.43** | **99.44** | **99.45** | **99.46** | **99.47** | **99.48** | **99.48** | **99.49** | **99.49** | **99.49** | **99.50** | **99.50** |
| 8.76 | 8.74 | 8.71 | 8.69 | 8.66 | 8.64 | 8.62 | 8.60 | 8.58 | 8.57 | 8.56 | 8.54 | 8.54 | 8.53 |
| **27.13** | **27.05** | **26.92** | **26.83** | **26.69** | **26.60** | **26.50** | **26.41** | **26.35** | **26.27** | **26.23** | **26.18** | **26.14** | **26.12** |
| 5.93 | 5.91 | 5.87 | 5.84 | 5.80 | 5.77 | 5.74 | 5.71 | 5.70 | 5.68 | 5.66 | 5.65 | 5.64 | 5.63 |
| **14.45** | **14.37** | **14.24** | **14.15** | **14.02** | **13.93** | **13.83** | **13.74** | **13.69** | **13.61** | **13.57** | **13.52** | **13.48** | **13.46** |
| 4.70 | 4.68 | 4.64 | 4.60 | 4.56 | 4.53 | 4.50 | 4.46 | 4.44 | 4.42 | 4.40 | 4.38 | 4.37 | 4.36 |
| **9.96** | **9.89** | **9.77** | **9.68** | **9.55** | **9.47** | **9.38** | **9.29** | **9.24** | **9.17** | **9.13** | **9.07** | **9.04** | **9.02** |
| 4.03 | 4.00 | 3.96 | 3.92 | 3.87 | 3.84 | 3.81 | 3.77 | 3.75 | 3.72 | 3.71 | 3.69 | 3.68 | 3.67 |
| **7.79** | **7.72** | **7.60** | **7.52** | **7.39** | **7.31** | **7.23** | **7.14** | **7.09** | **7.02** | **6.99** | **6.94** | **6.90** | **6.88** |
| 3.60 | 3.57 | 3.52 | 3.49 | 3.44 | 3.41 | 3.38 | 3.34 | 3.32 | 3.29 | 3.28 | 3.25 | 3.24 | 3.23 |
| **6.54** | **6.47** | **6.35** | **6.27** | **6.15** | **6.07** | **5.98** | **5.90** | **5.85** | **5.78** | **5.75** | **5.70** | **5.67** | **5.65** |
| 3.31 | 3.28 | 3.23 | 3.20 | 3.15 | 3.12 | 3.08 | 3.05 | 3.03 | 3.00 | 2.98 | 2.96 | 2.94 | 2.93 |
| **5.74** | **5.67** | **5.56** | **5.48** | **5.36** | **5.28** | **5.20** | **5.11** | **5.06** | **5.00** | **4.96** | **4.91** | **4.88** | **4.86** |
| 3.10 | 3.07 | 3.02 | 2.98 | 2.93 | 2.90 | 2.86 | 2.82 | 2.80 | 2.77 | 2.76 | 2.73 | 2.72 | 2.71 |
| **5.18** | **5.11** | **5.00** | **4.92** | **4.80** | **4.73** | **4.64** | **4.56** | **4.51** | **4.45** | **4.41** | **4.36** | **4.33** | **4.31** |
| 2.94 | 2.91 | 2.86 | 2.82 | 2.77 | 2.74 | 2.70 | 2.67 | 2.64 | 2.61 | 2.59 | 2.56 | 2.55 | 2.54 |
| **4.78** | **4.71** | **4.60** | **4.52** | **4.41** | **4.33** | **4.25** | **4.17** | **4.12** | **4.05** | **4.01** | **3.96** | **3.93** | **3.91** |
| 2.82 | 2.79 | 2.74 | 2.70 | 2.65 | 2.61 | 2.57 | 2.53 | 2.50 | 2.47 | 2.45 | 2.42 | 2.41 | 2.40 |
| **4.46** | **4.40** | **4.29** | **4.21** | **4.10** | **4.02** | **3.94** | **3.86** | **3.80** | **3.74** | **3.70** | **3.66** | **3.62** | **3.60** |
| 2.72 | 2.69 | 2.64 | 2.60 | 2.54 | 2.50 | 2.46 | 2.42 | 2.40 | 2.36 | 2.35 | 2.32 | 2.31 | 2.30 |
| **4.22** | **4.16** | **4.05** | **3.93** | **3.86** | **3.78** | **3.70** | **3.61** | **3.56** | **3.49** | **3.46** | **3.41** | **3.38** | **3.36** |
| 2.63 | 2.60 | 2.55 | 2.51 | 2.46 | 2.42 | 2.38 | 2.34 | 2.32 | 2.28 | 2.26 | 2.24 | 2.22 | 2.21 |
| **4.02** | **3.96** | **3.85** | **3.78** | **3.67** | **3.59** | **3.51** | **3.42** | **3.37** | **3.30** | **3.27** | **3.21** | **3.18** | **3.16** |
| 2.56 | 2.53 | 2.48 | 2.44 | 2.39 | 2.35 | 2.31 | 2.27 | 2.24 | 2.21 | 2.19 | 2.16 | 2.14 | 2.13 |
| **3.86** | **3.80** | **3.70** | **3.62** | **3.51** | **3.43** | **3.34** | **3.26** | **3.21** | **3.14** | **3.11** | **3.06** | **3.02** | **3.00** |
| 2.51 | 2.48 | 2.43 | 2.39 | 2.33 | 2.29 | 2.25 | 2.21 | 2.18 | 2.15 | 2.12 | 2.10 | 2.08 | 2.07 |
| **3.73** | **3.67** | **3.56** | **3.48** | **3.36** | **3.29** | **3.20** | **3.12** | **3.07** | **3.00** | **2.97** | **2.92** | **2.89** | **2.87** |
| 2.45 | 2.42 | 2.37 | 2.33 | 2.28 | 2.24 | 2.20 | 2.16 | 2.13 | 2.09 | 2.07 | 2.04 | 2.02 | 2.01 |
| **3.61** | **3.55** | **3.45** | **3.37** | **3.25** | **3.18** | **3.10** | **3.01** | **2.96** | **2.89** | **2.86** | **2.80** | **2.77** | **2.75** |
| 2.41 | 2.38 | 2.33 | 2.29 | 2.23 | 2.19 | 2.15 | 2.11 | 2.08 | 2.04 | 2.02 | 1.99 | 1.97 | 1.96 |
| **3.52** | **3.45** | **3.35** | **3.27** | **3.16** | **3.08** | **3.00** | **2.92** | **2.86** | **2.79** | **2.76** | **2.70** | **2.67** | **2.65** |
| 2.37 | 2.34 | 2.29 | 2.25 | 2.19 | 2.15 | 2.11 | 2.07 | 2.04 | 2.00 | 1.98 | 1.95 | 1.93 | 1.92 |
| **3.44** | **3.37** | **3.27** | **3.19** | **3.07** | **3.00** | **2.91** | **2.83** | **2.78** | **2.71** | **2.68** | **2.62** | **2.59** | **2.57** |
| 2.34 | 2.31 | 2.26 | 2.21 | 2.15 | 2.11 | 2.07 | 2.02 | 2.00 | 1.96 | 1.94 | 1.91 | 1.90 | 1.88 |
| **3.36** | **3.30** | **3.19** | **3.12** | **3.00** | **2.92** | **2.84** | **2.76** | **2.70** | **2.63** | **2.60** | **2.54** | **2.51** | **2.49** |

## TABLE B.4 (continued)

| *Denominator degrees of freedom* ($m_2$) | *Numerator degrees of freedom* ($m_1$) | | | | | | | | | |
|---|---|---|---|---|---|---|---|---|---|---|
| | *1* | *2* | *3* | *4* | *5* | *6* | *7* | *8* | *9* | *10* |
| **20** | 4.35 | 3.49 | 3.10 | 2.87 | 2.71 | 2.60 | 2.52 | 2.45 | 2.40 | 2.35 |
| | **8.10** | **5.85** | **4.94** | **4.43** | **4.10** | **3.87** | **3.71** | **3.56** | **3.45** | **3.37** |
| **21** | 4.32 | 3.47 | 3.07 | 2.84 | 2.68 | 2.57 | 2.49 | 2.42 | 2.37 | 2.32 |
| | **8.02** | **5.78** | **4.87** | **4.37** | **4.04** | **3.81** | **3.65** | **3.51** | **3.40** | **3.31** |
| **22** | 4.30 | 3.44 | 3.05 | 2.82 | 2.66 | 2.55 | 2.47 | 2.40 | 2.35 | 2.30 |
| | **7.94** | **5.72** | **4.82** | **4.31** | **3.99** | **3.76** | **3.59** | **3.45** | **3.35** | **3.26** |
| **23** | 4.28 | 3.42 | 3.03 | 2.80 | 2.64 | 2.53 | 2.45 | 2.38 | 2.32 | 2.28 |
| | **7.88** | **5.66** | **4.76** | **4.26** | **3.94** | **3.71** | **3.54** | **3.41** | **3.30** | **3.21** |
| **24** | 4.26 | 3.40 | 3.01 | 2.78 | 2.62 | 2.51 | 2.43 | 2.36 | 2.30 | 2.26 |
| | **7.82** | **5.61** | **4.72** | **4.22** | **3.90** | **3.67** | **3.50** | **3.36** | **3.25** | **3.17** |
| **25** | 4.24 | 3.38 | 2.99 | 2.76 | 2.60 | 2.49 | 2.41 | 2.34 | 2.28 | 2.24 |
| | **7.77** | **5.57** | **4.68** | **4.18** | **3.86** | **3.63** | **3.46** | **3.32** | **3.21** | **3.13** |
| **26** | 4.22 | 3.37 | 2.98 | 2.74 | 2.59 | 2.47 | 2.39 | 2.32 | 2.27 | 2.22 |
| | **7.72** | **5.53** | **4.64** | **4.14** | **3.82** | **3.59** | **3.42** | **3.29** | **3.17** | **3.09** |
| **27** | 4.21 | 3.35 | 2.96 | 2.73 | 2.57 | 2.46 | 2.37 | 2.30 | 2.25 | 2.20 |
| | **7.68** | **5.49** | **4.60** | **4.11** | **3.79** | **3.56** | **3.39** | **3.26** | **3.14** | **3.06** |
| **28** | 4.20 | 3.34 | 2.95 | 2.71 | 2.56 | 2.44 | 2.36 | 2.29 | 2.24 | 2.19 |
| | **7.64** | **5.45** | **4.57** | **4.07** | **3.76** | **3.53** | **3.36** | **3.23** | **3.11** | **3.03** |
| **29** | 4.18 | 3.33 | 2.93 | 2.70 | 2.54 | 2.43 | 2.35 | 2.28 | 2.22 | 2.18 |
| | **7.60** | **5.42** | **4.54** | **4.04** | **3.73** | **3.50** | **3.33** | **3.20** | **3.08** | **3.00** |
| **30** | 4.17 | 3.32 | 2.92 | 2.69 | 2.53 | 2.42 | 2.34 | 2.27 | 2.21 | 2.16 |
| | **7.56** | **5.39** | **4.51** | **4.02** | **3.70** | **3.47** | **3.30** | **3.17** | **3.06** | **2.98** |
| **32** | 4.15 | 3.30 | 2.90 | 2.67 | 2.51 | 2.40 | 2.32 | 2.25 | 2.19 | 2.14 |
| | **7.50** | **5.34** | **4.46** | **3.97** | **3.66** | **3.42** | **3.25** | **3.12** | **3.01** | **2.94** |
| **34** | 4.13 | 3.28 | 2.88 | 2.65 | 2.49 | 2.38 | 2.30 | 2.23 | 2.17 | 2.12 |
| | **7.44** | **5.29** | **4.42** | **3.93** | **3.61** | **3.38** | **3.21** | **3.08** | **2.97** | **2.89** |
| **36** | 4.11 | 3.26 | 2.86 | 2.63 | 2.48 | 2.36 | 2.28 | 2.21 | 2.15 | 2.10 |
| | **7.39** | **5.25** | **4.38** | **3.89** | **3.58** | **3.35** | **3.18** | **3.04** | **2.94** | **2.86** |
| **38** | 4.10 | 3.25 | 2.85 | 2.62 | 2.46 | 2.35 | 2.26 | 2.19 | 2.14 | 2.09 |
| | **7.35** | **5.21** | **4.34** | **3.86** | **3.54** | **3.32** | **3.15** | **3.02** | **2.91** | **2.82** |
| **40** | 4.08 | 3.23 | 2.84 | 2.61 | 2.45 | 2.34 | 2.25 | 2.18 | 2.12 | 2.07 |
| | **7.31** | **5.18** | **4.31** | **3.83** | **3.51** | **3.29** | **3.12** | **2.99** | **2.88** | **2.80** |
| **42** | 4.07 | 3.22 | 2.83 | 2.59 | 2.44 | 2.32 | 2.24 | 2.17 | 2.11 | 2.06 |
| | **7.27** | **5.15** | **4.29** | **3.80** | **3.49** | **3.26** | **3.10** | **2.96** | **2.86** | **2.77** |
| **44** | 4.06 | 3.21 | 2.82 | 2.58 | 2.43 | 2.31 | 2.23 | 2.16 | 2.10 | 2.05 |
| | **7.24** | **5.12** | **4.26** | **3.78** | **3.46** | **3.24** | **3.07** | **2.94** | **2.84** | **2.75** |
| **46** | 4.05 | 3.20 | 2.81 | 2.57 | 2.42 | 2.30 | 2.22 | 2.14 | 2.09 | 2.04 |
| | **7.21** | **5.10** | **4.24** | **3.76** | **3.44** | **3.22** | **3.05** | **2.92** | **2.82** | **2.73** |
| **48** | 4.04 | 3.19 | 2.80 | 2.56 | 2.41 | 2.30 | 2.21 | 2.14 | 2.08 | 2.03 |
| | **7.19** | **5.08** | **4.22** | **3.74** | **3.42** | **3.20** | **3.04** | **2.90** | **2.80** | **2.71** |
| **50** | 4.03 | 3.18 | 2.79 | 2.56 | 2.40 | 2.29 | 2.20 | 2.13 | 2.07 | 2.02 |
| | **7.17** | **5.06** | **4.20** | **3.72** | **3.41** | **3.18** | **3.02** | **2.88** | **2.78** | **2.70** |
| **55** | 4.02 | 3.17 | 2.78 | 2.54 | 2.38 | 2.27 | 2.18 | 2.11 | 2.05 | 2.00 |
| | **7.12** | **5.01** | **4.16** | **3.68** | **3.37** | **3.15** | **2.98** | **2.85** | **2.75** | **2.66** |

*(continued on page 760)*

| *11* | *12* | *14* | *16* | *20* | *24* | *30* | *40* | *50* | *75* | *100* | *200* | *500* | ∞ |
|---|---|---|---|---|---|---|---|---|---|---|---|---|---|
| 2.31 | 2.28 | 2.23 | 2.18 | 2.12 | 2.08 | 2.04 | 1.99 | 1.96 | 1.92 | 1.90 | 1.87 | 1.85 | 1.84 |
| **3.30** | **3.23** | **3.13** | **3.05** | **2.94** | **2.86** | **2.77** | **2.69** | **2.63** | **2.56** | **2.53** | **2.47** | **2.44** | **2.42** |
| 2.28 | 2.25 | 2.20 | 2.15 | 2.09 | 2.05 | 2.00 | 1.96 | 1.93 | 1.89 | 1.87 | 1.84 | 1.82 | 1.81 |
| **3.24** | **3.17** | **3.07** | **2.99** | **2.88** | **2.80** | **2.72** | **2.63** | **2.58** | **2.51** | **2.47** | **2.42** | **2.38** | **2.36** |
| 2.26 | 2.23 | 2.18 | 2.13 | 2.07 | 2.03 | 1.98 | 1.93 | 1.91 | 1.87 | 1.84 | 1.81 | 1.80 | 1.78 |
| **3.18** | **3.12** | **3.02** | **2.94** | **2.83** | **2.75** | **2.67** | **2.58** | **2.53** | **2.46** | **2.42** | **2.37** | **2.33** | **2.31** |
| 2.24 | 2.20 | 2.14 | 2.10 | 2.04 | 2.00 | 1.96 | 1.91 | 1.88 | 1.84 | 1.82 | 1.79 | 1.77 | 1.76 |
| **3.14** | **3.07** | **2.97** | **2.89** | **2.78** | **2.70** | **2.62** | **2.53** | **2.48** | **2.41** | **2.37** | **2.32** | **2.28** | **2.26** |
| 2.22 | 2.18 | 2.13 | 2.09 | 2.02 | 1.98 | 1.94 | 1.89 | 1.86 | 1.82 | 1.80 | 1.76 | 1.74 | 1.73 |
| **3.09** | **3.03** | **2.93** | **2.85** | **2.74** | **2.66** | **2.58** | **2.49** | **2.44** | **2.36** | **2.33** | **2.27** | **2.23** | **2.21** |
| 2.20 | 2.16 | 2.11 | 2.06 | 2.00 | 1.96 | 1.92 | 1.87 | 1.84 | 1.80 | 1.77 | 1.74 | 1.72 | 1.71 |
| **3.05** | **2.99** | **2.89** | **2.81** | **2.70** | **2.62** | **2.54** | **2.45** | **2.40** | **2.32** | **2.29** | **2.23** | **2.19** | **2.17** |
| 2.18 | 2.15 | 2.10 | 2.05 | 1.99 | 1.95 | 1.90 | 1.85 | 1.82 | 1.78 | 1.76 | 1.72 | 1.70 | 1.69 |
| **3.02** | **2.96** | **2.86** | **2.77** | **2.66** | **2.58** | **2.50** | **2.41** | **2.36** | **2.28** | **2.25** | **2.19** | **2.15** | **2.13** |
| 2.16 | 2.13 | 2.08 | 2.03 | 1.97 | 1.93 | 1.88 | 1.84 | 1.80 | 1.76 | 1.74 | 1.71 | 1.68 | 1.67 |
| **2.98** | **2.93** | **2.83** | **2.74** | **2.63** | **2.55** | **2.47** | **2.38** | **2.33** | **2.25** | **2.21** | **2.16** | **2.12** | **2.10** |
| 2.15 | 2.12 | 2.06 | 2.02 | 1.96 | 1.91 | 1.87 | 1.81 | 1.78 | 1.75 | 1.72 | 1.69 | 1.67 | 1.65 |
| **2.95** | **2.90** | **2.80** | **2.71** | **2.60** | **2.52** | **2.44** | **2.35** | **2.30** | **2.22** | **2.18** | **2.13** | **2.09** | **2.06** |
| 2.14 | 2.10 | 2.05 | 2.00 | 1.94 | 1.90 | 1.85 | 1.80 | 1.77 | 1.73 | 1.71 | 1.68 | 1.65 | 1.64 |
| **2.92** | **2.87** | **2.77** | **2.68** | **2.57** | **2.49** | **2.41** | **2.32** | **2.27** | **2.19** | **2.15** | **2.10** | **2.06** | **2.03** |
| 2.12 | 2.09 | 2.04 | 1.99 | 1.93 | 1.89 | 1.84 | 1.79 | 1.76 | 1.72 | 1.69 | 1.66 | 1.64 | 1.62 |
| **2.90** | **2.84** | **2.74** | **2.66** | **2.55** | **2.47** | **2.38** | **2.29** | **2.24** | **2.16** | **2.13** | **2.07** | **2.03** | **2.01** |
| 2.10 | 2.07 | 2.02 | 1.97 | 1.91 | 1.86 | 1.82 | 1.76 | 1.74 | 1.69 | 1.67 | 1.64 | 1.61 | 1.59 |
| **2.86** | **2.80** | **2.70** | **2.62** | **2.51** | **2.42** | **2.34** | **2.25** | **2.20** | **2.12** | **2.08** | **2.02** | **1.98** | **1.96** |
| 2.08 | 2.05 | 2.00 | 1.95 | 1.89 | 1.84 | 1.80 | 1.74 | 1.71 | 1.67 | 1.64 | 1.61 | 1.59 | 1.57 |
| **2.82** | **2.76** | **2.66** | **2.58** | **2.47** | **2.38** | **2.30** | **2.21** | **2.15** | **2.08** | **2.04** | **1.98** | **1.94** | **1.91** |
| 2.06 | 2.03 | 1.98 | 1.93 | 1.87 | 1.82 | 1.78 | 1.72 | 1.69 | 1.65 | 1.62 | 1.59 | 1.56 | 1.55 |
| **2.78** | **2.72** | **2.62** | **2.54** | **2.43** | **2.35** | **2.26** | **2.17** | **2.12** | **2.04** | **2.00** | **1.94** | **1.90** | **1.87** |
| 2.05 | 2.02 | 1.96 | 1.92 | 1.85 | 1.80 | 1.76 | 1.71 | 1.67 | 1.63 | 1.60 | 1.57 | 1.54 | 1.53 |
| **2.75** | **2.69** | **2.59** | **2.51** | **2.40** | **2.32** | **2.22** | **2.14** | **2.08** | **2.00** | **1.97** | **1.90** | **1.86** | **1.84** |
| 2.04 | 2.00 | 1.95 | 1.90 | 1.84 | 1.79 | 1.74 | 1.69 | 1.66 | 1.61 | 1.59 | 1.55 | 1.53 | 1.51 |
| **2.73** | **2.66** | **2.56** | **2.49** | **2.37** | **2.29** | **2.20** | **2.11** | **2.05** | **1.97** | **1.94** | **1.88** | **1.84** | **1.81** |
| 2.02 | 1.99 | 1.94 | 1.89 | 1.82 | 1.78 | 1.73 | 1.68 | 1.64 | 1.60 | 1.57 | 1.54 | 1.51 | 1.49 |
| **2.70** | **2.64** | **2.54** | **2.46** | **2.35** | **2.26** | **2.17** | **2.08** | **2.02** | **1.94** | **1.91** | **1.85** | **1.80** | **1.78** |
| 2.01 | 1.98 | 1.92 | 1.88 | 1.81 | 1.76 | 1.72 | 1.66 | 1.63 | 1.58 | 1.56 | 1.52 | 1.50 | 1.48 |
| **2.68** | **2.62** | **2.52** | **2.44** | **2.32** | **2.24** | **2.15** | **2.06** | **2.00** | **1.92** | **1.88** | **1.82** | **1.78** | **1.75** |
| 2.00 | 1.97 | 1.91 | 1.87 | 1.80 | 1.75 | 1.71 | 1.65 | 1.62 | 1.57 | 1.54 | 1.51 | 1.48 | 1.46 |
| **2.66** | **2.60** | **2.50** | **2.42** | **2.30** | **2.22** | **2.13** | **2.04** | **1.98** | **1.90** | **1.86** | **1.80** | **1.76** | **1.72** |
| 1.99 | 1.96 | 1.90 | 1.86 | 1.79 | 1.74 | 1.70 | 1.64 | 1.61 | 1.56 | 1.53 | 1.50 | 1.47 | 1.45 |
| **2.64** | **2.58** | **2.48** | **2.40** | **2.28** | **2.20** | **2.11** | **2.02** | **1.96** | **1.88** | **1.84** | **1.78** | **1.73** | **1.70** |
| 1.98 | 1.95 | 1.90 | 1.85 | 1.78 | 1.74 | 1.69 | 1.63 | 1.60 | 1.55 | 1.52 | 1.48 | 1.46 | 1.44 |
| **2.62** | **2.56** | **2.46** | **2.39** | **2.26** | **2.18** | **2.10** | **2.00** | **1.94** | **1.86** | **1.82** | **1.76** | **1.71** | **1.68** |
| 1.97 | 1.93 | 1.88 | 1.83 | 1.76 | 1.72 | 1.67 | 1.61 | 1.58 | 1.52 | 1.50 | 1.46 | 1.43 | 1.41 |
| **2.59** | **2.53** | **2.43** | **2.35** | **2.23** | **2.15** | **2.06** | **1.96** | **1.90** | **1.82** | **1.78** | **1.71** | **1.66** | **1.64** |

**TABLE B.4 (continued)**

| *Denominator degrees of freedom* | *Numerator degrees of freedom* ($m_1$) | | | | | | | | | |
|---|---|---|---|---|---|---|---|---|---|---|
| ($m_2$) | *1* | *2* | *3* | *4* | *5* | *6* | *7* | *8* | *9* | *10* |
| **60** | 4.00 | 3.15 | 2.76 | 2.52 | 2.37 | 2.25 | 2.17 | 2.10 | 2.04 | 1.99 |
| | **7.08** | **4.98** | **4.13** | **3.65** | **3.34** | **3.12** | **2.95** | **2.82** | **2.72** | **2.63** |
| **65** | 3.99 | 3.14 | 2.75 | 2.51 | 2.36 | 2.24 | 2.15 | 2.08 | 2.02 | 1.98 |
| | **7.04** | **4.95** | **4.10** | **3.62** | **3.31** | **3.09** | **2.93** | **2.79** | **2.70** | **2.61** |
| **70** | 3.98 | 3.13 | 2.74 | 2.50 | 2.35 | 2.23 | 2.14 | 2.07 | 2.01 | 1.97 |
| | **7.01** | **4.92** | **4.08** | **3.60** | **3.29** | **3.07** | **2.91** | **2.77** | **2.67** | **2.59** |
| **80** | 3.96 | 3.11 | 2.72 | 2.48 | 2.33 | 2.21 | 2.12 | 2.05 | 1.99 | 1.95 |
| | **6.96** | **4.88** | **4.04** | **3.56** | **3.25** | **3.04** | **2.87** | **2.74** | **2.64** | **2.55** |
| **100** | 3.94 | 3.09 | 2.70 | 2.46 | 2.30 | 2.19 | 2.10 | 2.03 | 1.97 | 1.92 |
| | **6.90** | **4.82** | **3.98** | **3.51** | **3.20** | **2.99** | **2.82** | **2.69** | **2.59** | **2.51** |
| **125** | 3.92 | 3.07 | 2.68 | 2.44 | 2.29 | 2.17 | 2.08 | 2.01 | 1.95 | 1.90 |
| | **6.84** | **4.78** | **3.94** | **3.47** | **3.17** | **2.95** | **2.79** | **2.65** | **2.56** | **2.47** |
| **150** | 3.91 | 3.06 | 2.67 | 2.43 | 2.27 | 2.16 | 2.07 | 2.00 | 1.94 | 1.89 |
| | **6.81** | **4.75** | **3.91** | **3.44** | **3.14** | **2.92** | **2.76** | **2.62** | **2.53** | **2.44** |
| **200** | 3.89 | 3.04 | 2.65 | 2.41 | 2.26 | 2.14 | 2.05 | 1.98 | 1.92 | 1.87 |
| | **6.76** | **4.71** | **3.88** | **3.41** | **3.11** | **2.90** | **2.73** | **2.60** | **2.50** | **2.41** |
| **400** | 3.86 | 3.02 | 2.62 | 2.39 | 2.23 | 2.12 | 2.03 | 1.96 | 1.90 | 1.85 |
| | **6.70** | **4.66** | **3.83** | **3.36** | **3.06** | **2.85** | **2.69** | **2.55** | **2.46** | **2.37** |
| **1000** | 3.85 | 3.00 | 2.61 | 2.38 | 2.22 | 2.10 | 2.02 | 1.95 | 1.89 | 1.84 |
| | **6.66** | **4.62** | **3.80** | **3.34** | **3.04** | **2.82** | **2.66** | **2.53** | **2.43** | **2.34** |
| $\infty$ | 3.84 | 2.99 | 2.60 | 2.37 | 2.21 | 2.09 | 2.01 | 1.94 | 1.88 | 1.83 |
| | **6.64** | **4.60** | **3.78** | **3.32** | **3.02** | **2.80** | **2.64** | **2.51** | **2.41** | **2.32** |

The table describes the distribution of an $F$ variable with $m_1$ numerator and $m_2$ denominator degrees of freedom. Entries in the standard typeface give the 5% critical value, and boldface entries give the 1% critical value for the distribution. For example, there is a 5% probability that an $F$ variable with 2 numerator and 50 denominator degrees of freedom would exceed 3.18; there is only a 1% probability that it would exceed 5.06.

*Source:* George W. Snedecor and William G. Cochran, *Statistical Methods*, 8th ed. Copyright 1989 by Iowa State University Press. Reprinted by permission of Iowa State University Press.

| *11* | *12* | *14* | *16* | *20* | *24* | *30* | *40* | *50* | *75* | *100* | *200* | *500* | ∞ |
|---|---|---|---|---|---|---|---|---|---|---|---|---|---|
| 1.95 | 1.92 | 1.86 | 1.81 | 1.75 | 1.70 | 1.65 | 1.59 | 1.56 | 1.50 | 1.48 | 1.44 | 1.41 | 1.39 |
| **2.56** | **2.50** | **2.40** | **2.32** | **2.20** | **2.12** | **2.03** | **1.93** | **1.87** | **1.79** | **1.74** | **1.68** | **1.63** | **1.60** |
| 1.94 | 1.90 | 1.85 | 1.80 | 1.73 | 1.68 | 1.63 | 1.57 | 1.54 | 1.49 | 1.46 | 1.42 | 1.39 | 1.37 |
| **2.54** | **2.47** | **2.37** | **2.30** | **2.18** | **2.09** | **2.00** | **1.90** | **1.84** | **1.76** | **1.71** | **1.64** | **1.60** | **1.56** |
| 1.93 | 1.89 | 1.84 | 1.79 | 1.72 | 1.67 | 1.62 | 1.56 | 1.53 | 1.47 | 1.45 | 1.40 | 1.37 | 1.35 |
| **2.51** | **2.45** | **2.35** | **2.28** | **2.15** | **2.07** | **1.98** | **1.88** | **1.82** | **1.74** | **1.69** | **1.62** | **1.56** | **1.53** |
| 1.91 | 1.88 | 1.82 | 1.77 | 1.70 | 1.65 | 1.60 | 1.54 | 1.51 | 1.45 | 1.42 | 1.38 | 1.35 | 1.32 |
| **2.48** | **2.41** | **2.32** | **2.24** | **2.11** | **2.03** | **1.94** | **1.84** | **1.78** | **1.70** | **1.65** | **1.57** | **1.52** | **1.49** |
| 1.88 | 1.85 | 1.79 | 1.75 | 1.68 | 1.63 | 1.57 | 1.51 | 1.48 | 1.42 | 1.39 | 1.34 | 1.30 | 1.28 |
| **2.43** | **2.36** | **2.26** | **2.19** | **2.06** | **1.98** | **1.89** | **1.79** | **1.73** | **1.64** | **1.59** | **1.51** | **1.46** | **1.43** |
| 1.86 | 1.83 | 1.77 | 1.72 | 1.65 | 1.60 | 1.55 | 1.49 | 1.45 | 1.39 | 1.36 | 1.31 | 1.27 | 1.25 |
| **2.40** | **2.33** | **2.23** | **2.15** | **2.03** | **1.94** | **1.85** | **1.75** | **1.68** | **1.59** | **1.54** | **1.46** | **1.40** | **1.37** |
| 1.85 | 1.82 | 1.76 | 1.71 | 1.64 | 1.59 | 1.54 | 1.47 | 1.44 | 1.37 | 1.34 | 1.29 | 1.25 | 1.22 |
| **2.37** | **2.30** | **2.20** | **2.12** | **2.00** | **1.91** | **1.83** | **1.72** | **1.66** | **1.56** | **1.51** | **1.43** | **1.37** | **1.33** |
| 1.83 | 1.80 | 1.74 | 1.69 | 1.62 | 1.57 | 1.52 | 1.45 | 1.42 | 1.35 | 1.32 | 1.26 | 1.22 | 1.19 |
| **2.34** | **2.28** | **2.17** | **2.09** | **1.97** | **1.88** | **1.79** | **1.69** | **1.62** | **1.53** | **1.48** | **1.39** | **1.33** | **1.28** |
| 1.81 | 1.78 | 1.72 | 1.67 | 1.60 | 1.54 | 1.49 | 1.42 | 1.38 | 1.32 | 1.28 | 1.22 | 1.16 | 1.13 |
| **2.29** | **2.23** | **2.12** | **2.04** | **1.92** | **1.84** | **1.74** | **1.64** | **1.57** | **1.47** | **1.42** | **1.32** | **1.24** | **1.19** |
| 1.80 | 1.76 | 1.70 | 1.65 | 1.58 | 1.53 | 1.47 | 1.41 | 1.36 | 1.30 | 1.26 | 1.19 | 1.13 | 1.08 |
| **2.26** | **2.20** | **2.09** | **2.01** | **1.89** | **1.81** | **1.71** | **1.61** | **1.54** | **1.44** | **1.38** | **1.28** | **1.19** | **1.11** |
| 1.79 | 1.75 | 1.69 | 1.64 | 1.57 | 1.52 | 1.46 | 1.40 | 1.35 | 1.28 | 1.24 | 1.17 | 1.11 | 1.00 |
| **2.24** | **2.18** | **2.07** | **1.99** | **1.87** | **1.79** | **1.69** | **1.59** | **1.52** | **1.41** | **1.36** | **1.25** | **1.15** | **1.00** |

**TABLE B.5**
**Critical Values for the Phillips-Perron $Z_\rho$ Test and for the Dickey-Fuller Test Based on Estimated *OLS* Autoregressive Coefficient**

| *Sample size T* | *Probability that $T(\hat{\rho} - 1)$ is less than entry* | | | | | | | |
|---|---|---|---|---|---|---|---|---|
| | *0.01* | *0.025* | *0.05* | *0.10* | *0.90* | *0.95* | *0.975* | *0.99* |
| | | | | *Case 1* | | | | |
| 25 | −11.9 | −9.3 | −7.3 | −5.3 | 1.01 | 1.40 | 1.79 | 2.28 |
| 50 | −12.9 | −9.9 | −7.7 | −5.5 | 0.97 | 1.35 | 1.70 | 2.16 |
| 100 | −13.3 | −10.2 | −7.9 | −5.6 | 0.95 | 1.31 | 1.65 | 2.09 |
| 250 | −13.6 | −10.3 | −8.0 | −5.7 | 0.93 | 1.28 | 1.62 | 2.04 |
| 500 | −13.7 | −10.4 | −8.0 | −5.7 | 0.93 | 1.28 | 1.61 | 2.04 |
| ∞ | −13.8 | −10.5 | −8.1 | −5.7 | 0.93 | 1.28 | 1.60 | 2.03 |
| | | | | *Case 2* | | | | |
| 25 | −17.2 | −14.6 | −12.5 | −10.2 | −0.76 | 0.01 | 0.65 | 1.40 |
| 50 | −18.9 | −15.7 | −13.3 | −10.7 | −0.81 | −0.07 | 0.53 | 1.22 |
| 100 | −19.8 | −16.3 | −13.7 | −11.0 | −0.83 | −0.10 | 0.47 | 1.14 |
| 250 | −20.3 | −16.6 | −14.0 | −11.2 | −0.84 | −0.12 | 0.43 | 1.09 |
| 500 | −20.5 | −16.8 | −14.0 | −11.2 | −0.84 | −0.13 | 0.42 | 1.06 |
| ∞ | −20.7 | −16.9 | −14.1 | −11.3 | −0.85 | −0.13 | 0.41 | 1.04 |
| | | | | *Case 4* | | | | |
| 25 | −22.5 | −19.9 | −17.9 | −15.6 | −3.66 | −2.51 | −1.53 | −0.43 |
| 50 | −25.7 | −22.4 | −19.8 | −16.8 | −3.71 | −2.60 | −1.66 | −0.65 |
| 100 | −27.4 | −23.6 | −20.7 | −17.5 | −3.74 | −2.62 | −1.73 | −0.75 |
| 250 | −28.4 | −24.4 | −21.3 | −18.0 | −3.75 | −2.64 | −1.78 | −0.82 |
| 500 | −28.9 | −24.8 | −21.5 | −18.1 | −3.76 | −2.65 | −1.78 | −0.84 |
| ∞ | −29.5 | −25.1 | −21.8 | −18.3 | −3.77 | −2.66 | −1.79 | −0.87 |

The probability shown at the head of the column is the area in the left-hand tail.

*Source:* Wayne A. Fuller, *Introduction to Statistical Time Series*, Wiley, New York, 1976, p. 371.

**TABLE B.6**
**Critical Values for the Phillips-Perron $Z_t$ Test and for the Dickey-Fuller Test Based on Estimated *OLS* $t$ Statistic**

| *Sample size T* | *Probability that $(\hat{\rho} - 1)/\hat{\sigma}_{\hat{\rho}}$ is less than entry* | | | | | | | |
|---|---|---|---|---|---|---|---|---|
| | *0.01* | *0.025* | *0.05* | *0.10* | *0.90* | *0.95* | *0.975* | *0.99* |
| | | | | *Case 1* | | | | |
| 25 | −2.66 | −2.26 | −1.95 | −1.60 | 0.92 | 1.33 | 1.70 | 2.16 |
| 50 | −2.62 | −2.25 | −1.95 | −1.61 | 0.91 | 1.31 | 1.66 | 2.08 |
| 100 | −2.60 | −2.24 | −1.95 | −1.61 | 0.90 | 1.29 | 1.64 | 2.03 |
| 250 | −2.58 | −2.23 | −1.95 | −1.62 | 0.89 | 1.29 | 1.63 | 2.01 |
| 500 | −2.58 | −2.23 | −1.95 | −1.62 | 0.89 | 1.28 | 1.62 | 2.00 |
| ∞ | −2.58 | −2.23 | −1.95 | −1.62 | 0.89 | 1.28 | 1.62 | 2.00 |
| | | | | *Case 2* | | | | |
| 25 | −3.75 | −3.33 | −3.00 | −2.63 | −0.37 | 0.00 | 0.34 | 0.72 |
| 50 | −3.58 | −3.22 | −2.93 | −2.60 | −0.40 | −0.03 | 0.29 | 0.66 |
| 100 | −3.51 | −3.17 | −2.89 | −2.58 | −0.42 | −0.05 | 0.26 | 0.63 |
| 250 | −3.46 | −3.14 | −2.88 | −2.57 | −0.42 | −0.06 | 0.24 | 0.62 |
| 500 | −3.44 | −3.13 | −2.87 | −2.57 | −0.43 | −0.07 | 0.24 | 0.61 |
| ∞ | −3.43 | −3.12 | −2.86 | −2.57 | −0.44 | −0.07 | 0.23 | 0.60 |
| | | | | *Case 4* | | | | |
| 25 | −4.38 | −3.95 | −3.60 | −3.24 | −1.14 | −0.80 | −0.50 | −0.15 |
| 50 | −4.15 | −3.80 | −3.50 | −3.18 | −1.19 | −0.87 | −0.58 | −0.24 |
| 100 | −4.04 | −3.73 | −3.45 | −3.15 | −1.22 | −0.90 | −0.62 | −0.28 |
| 250 | −3.99 | −3.69 | −3.43 | −3.13 | −1.23 | −0.92 | −0.64 | −0.31 |
| 500 | −3.98 | −3.68 | −3.42 | −3.13 | −1.24 | −0.93 | −0.65 | −0.32 |
| ∞ | −3.96 | −3.66 | −3.41 | −3.12 | −1.25 | −0.94 | −0.66 | −0.33 |

The probability shown at the head of the column is the area in the left-hand tail.

*Source:* Wayne A. Fuller, *Introduction to Statistical Time Series*, Wiley, New York, 1976, p. 373.

**TABLE B.7**
**Critical Values for the Dickey-Fuller Test Based on the *OLS F* Statistic**

| *Sample size T* | *Probability that F test is greater than entry* | | | | | | | |
|---|---|---|---|---|---|---|---|---|
| | *0.99* | *0.975* | *0.95* | *0.90* | *0.10* | *0.05* | *0.025* | *0.01* |
| | | | | *Case 2* | | | | |
| | ($F$ test of $\alpha = 0$, $\rho = 1$ in regression $y_t = \alpha + \rho y_{t-1} + u_t$) | | | | | | | |
| 25 | 0.29 | 0.38 | 0.49 | 0.65 | 4.12 | 5.18 | 6.30 | 7.88 |
| 50 | 0.29 | 0.39 | 0.50 | 0.66 | 3.94 | 4.86 | 5.80 | 7.06 |
| 100 | 0.29 | 0.39 | 0.50 | 0.67 | 3.86 | 4.71 | 5.57 | 6.70 |
| 250 | 0.30 | 0.39 | 0.51 | 0.67 | 3.81 | 4.63 | 5.45 | 6.52 |
| 500 | 0.30 | 0.39 | 0.51 | 0.67 | 3.79 | 4.61 | 5.41 | 6.47 |
| ∞ | 0.30 | 0.40 | 0.51 | 0.67 | 3.78 | 4.59 | 5.38 | 6.43 |
| | | | | *Case 4* | | | | |
| | ($F$ test of $\delta = 0$, $\rho = 1$ in regression $y_t = \alpha + \delta t + \rho y_{t-1} + u_t$) | | | | | | | |
| 25 | 0.74 | 0.90 | 1.08 | 1.33 | 5.91 | 7.24 | 8.65 | 10.61 |
| 50 | 0.76 | 0.93 | 1.11 | 1.37 | 5.61 | 6.73 | 7.81 | 9.31 |
| 100 | 0.76 | 0.94 | 1.12 | 1.38 | 5.47 | 6.49 | 7.44 | 8.73 |
| 250 | 0.76 | 0.94 | 1.13 | 1.39 | 5.39 | 6.34 | 7.25 | 8.43 |
| 500 | 0.76 | 0.94 | 1.13 | 1.39 | 5.36 | 6.30 | 7.20 | 8.34 |
| ∞ | 0.77 | 0.94 | 1.13 | 1.39 | 5.34 | 6.25 | 7.16 | 8.27 |

The probability shown at the head of the column is the area in the right-hand tail.

*Source:* David A. Dickey and Wayne A. Fuller, "Likelihood Ratio Statistics for Autoregressive Time Series with a Unit Root," *Econometrica* 49 (1981), p. 1063.

**TABLE B.8**
**Critical Values for the Phillips $Z_\rho$ Statistic When Applied to Residuals from Spurious Cointegrating Regression**

| *Number of right-hand variables in regression, excluding trend or constant* $(n - 1)$ | *Sample size* $(T)$ | *Probability that* $(T - 1)(\hat{\rho} - 1)$ *is less than entry* | | | | | | |
|---|---|---|---|---|---|---|---|---|
| | | *0.010* | *0.025* | *0.050* | *0.075* | *0.100* | *0.125* | *0.150* |
| | | | | | *Case 1* | | | |
| 1 | 500 | −22.8 | −18.9 | −15.6 | −13.8 | −12.5 | −11.6 | −10.7 |
| 2 | 500 | −29.3 | −25.2 | −21.5 | −19.6 | −18.2 | −17.0 | −16.0 |
| 3 | 500 | −36.2 | −31.5 | −27.9 | −25.5 | −23.9 | −22.6 | −21.5 |
| 4 | 500 | −42.9 | −37.5 | −33.5 | −30.9 | −28.9 | −27.4 | −26.2 |
| 5 | 500 | −48.5 | −42.5 | −38.1 | −35.5 | −33.8 | −32.3 | −30.9 |
| | | | | | *Case 2* | | | |
| 1 | 500 | −28.3 | −23.8 | −20.5 | −18.5 | −17.0 | −15.9 | −14.9 |
| 2 | 500 | −34.2 | −29.7 | −26.1 | −23.9 | −22.2 | −21.0 | −19.9 |
| 3 | 500 | −41.1 | −35.7 | −32.1 | −29.5 | −27.6 | −26.2 | −25.1 |
| 4 | 500 | −47.5 | −41.6 | −37.2 | −34.7 | −32.7 | −31.2 | −29.9 |
| 5 | 500 | −52.2 | −46.5 | −41.9 | −39.1 | −37.0 | −35.5 | −34.2 |
| | | | | | *Case 3* | | | |
| 1 | 500 | −28.9 | −24.8 | −21.5 | — | −18.1 | — | — |
| 2 | 500 | −35.4 | −30.8 | −27.1 | −24.8 | −23.2 | −21.8 | −20.8 |
| 3 | 500 | −40.3 | −36.1 | −32.2 | −29.7 | −27.8 | −26.5 | −25.3 |
| 4 | 500 | −47.4 | −42.6 | −37.7 | −35.0 | −33.2 | −31.7 | −30.3 |
| 5 | 500 | −53.6 | −47.1 | −42.5 | −39.7 | −37.7 | −36.0 | −34.6 |

The probability shown at the head of the column is the area in the left-hand tail.

*Source:* P. C. B. Phillips and S. Ouliaris, "Asymptotic Properties of Residual Based Tests for Cointegration," *Econometrica* 58 (1990), pp. 189–90. Also Wayne A. Fuller, *Introduction to Statistical Time Series*, Wiley, New York, 1976, p. 371.

**TABLE B.9**
**Critical Values for the Phillips $Z_t$ Statistic or the Dickey-Fuller $t$ Statistic When Applied to Residuals from Spurious Cointegrating Regression**

| *Number of right-hand variables in regression, excluding trend or constant* $(n-1)$ | *Sample size* $(T)$ | *Probability that* $(\hat{\rho}-1)/\hat{\sigma}_{\hat{\rho}}$ *is less than entry* | | | | | | |
|---|---|---|---|---|---|---|---|---|
| | | *0.010* | *0.025* | *0.050* | *0.075* | *0.100* | *0.125* | *0.150* |
| | | | | | *Case 1* | | | |
| 1 | 500 | −3.39 | −3.05 | −2.76 | −2.58 | −2.45 | −2.35 | −2.26 |
| 2 | 500 | −3.84 | −3.55 | −3.27 | −3.11 | −2.99 | −2.88 | −2.79 |
| 3 | 500 | −4.30 | −3.99 | −3.74 | −3.57 | −3.44 | −3.35 | −3.26 |
| 4 | 500 | −4.67 | −4.38 | −4.13 | −3.95 | −3.81 | −3.71 | −3.61 |
| 5 | 500 | −4.99 | −4.67 | −4.40 | −4.25 | −4.14 | −4.04 | −3.94 |
| | | | | | *Case 2* | | | |
| 1 | 500 | −3.96 | −3.64 | −3.37 | −3.20 | −3.07 | −2.96 | −2.86 |
| 2 | 500 | −4.31 | −4.02 | −3.77 | −3.58 | −3.45 | −3.35 | −3.26 |
| 3 | 500 | −4.73 | −4.37 | −4.11 | −3.96 | −3.83 | −3.73 | −3.65 |
| 4 | 500 | −5.07 | −4.71 | −4.45 | −4.29 | −4.16 | −4.05 | −3.96 |
| 5 | 500 | −5.28 | −4.98 | −4.71 | −4.56 | −4.43 | −4.33 | −4.24 |
| | | | | | *Case 3* | | | |
| 1 | 500 | −3.98 | −3.68 | −3.42 | — | −3.13 | — | — |
| 2 | 500 | −4.36 | −4.07 | −3.80 | −3.65 | −3.52 | −3.42 | −3.33 |
| 3 | 500 | −4.65 | −4.39 | −4.16 | −3.98 | −3.84 | −3.74 | −3.66 |
| 4 | 500 | −5.04 | −4.77 | −4.49 | −4.32 | −4.20 | −4.08 | −4.00 |
| 5 | 500 | −5.36 | −5.02 | −4.74 | −4.58 | −4.46 | −4.36 | −4.28 |

The probability shown at the head of the column is the area in the left-hand tail.

*Source:* P. C. B. Phillips and S. Ouliaris, "Asymptotic Properties of Residual Based Tests for Cointegration," *Econometrica* 58 (1990), p. 190. Also Wayne A. Fuller, *Introduction to Statistical Time Series*, Wiley, New York, 1976, p. 373.

**TABLE B.10**
**Critical Values for Johansen's Likelihood Ratio Test of the Null Hypothesis of $h$ Cointegrating Relations Against the Alternative of No Restrictions**

| *Number of random walks* $(g = n - h)$ $(g)$ | *Sample size* $(T)$ | *Probability that* $2(\mathcal{L}_A - \mathcal{L}_0)$ *is greater than entry* | | | | | |
|---|---|---|---|---|---|---|---|
| | | *0.500* | *0.200* | *0.100* | *0.050* | *0.025* | *0.010* |
| | | | | *Case 1* | | | |
| 1 | 400 | 0.58 | 1.82 | 2.86 | 3.84 | 4.93 | 6.51 |
| 2 | 400 | 5.42 | 8.45 | 10.47 | 12.53 | 14.43 | 16.31 |
| 3 | 400 | 14.30 | 18.83 | 21.63 | 24.31 | 26.64 | 29.75 |
| 4 | 400 | 27.10 | 33.16 | 36.58 | 39.89 | 42.30 | 45.58 |
| 5 | 400 | 43.79 | 51.13 | 55.44 | 59.46 | 62.91 | 66.52 |
| | | | | *Case 2* | | | |
| 1 | 400 | 2.415 | 4.905 | 6.691 | 8.083 | 9.658 | 11.576 |
| 2 | 400 | 9.335 | 13.038 | 15.583 | 17.844 | 19.611 | 21.962 |
| 3 | 400 | 20.188 | 25.445 | 28.436 | 31.256 | 34.062 | 37.291 |
| 4 | 400 | 34.873 | 41.623 | 45.248 | 48.419 | 51.801 | 55.551 |
| 5 | 400 | 53.373 | 61.566 | 65.956 | 69.977 | 73.031 | 77.911 |
| | | | | *Case 3* | | | |
| 1 | 400 | 0.447 | 1.699 | 2.816 | 3.962 | 5.332 | 6.936 |
| 2 | 400 | 7.638 | 11.164 | 13.338 | 15.197 | 17.299 | 19.310 |
| 3 | 400 | 18.759 | 23.868 | 26.791 | 29.509 | 32.313 | 35.397 |
| 4 | 400 | 33.672 | 40.250 | 43.964 | 47.181 | 50.424 | 53.792 |
| 5 | 400 | 52.588 | 60.215 | 65.063 | 68.905 | 72.140 | 76.955 |

The probability shown at the head of the column is the area in the right-hand tail. The number of random walks under the null hypothesis ($g$) is given by the number of variables described by the vector autoregression ($n$) minus the number of cointegrating relations under the null hypothesis ($h$). In each case the alternative is that $g = 0$.

*Source:* Michael Osterwald-Lenum, "A Note with Quantiles of the Asymptotic Distribution of the Maximum Likelihood Cointegration Rank Test Statistics," *Oxford Bulletin of Economics and Statistics* 54 (1992), p. 462; and Søren Johansen and Katarina Juselius, "Maximum Likelihood Estimation and Inference on Cointegration—with Applications to the Demand for Money," *Oxford Bulletin of Economics and Statistics* 52 (1990), p. 208.

**TABLE B.11**
**Critical Values for Johansen's Likelihood Ratio Test of the Null Hypothesis of $h$ Cointegrating Relations Against the Alternative of $h + 1$ Relations**

| *Number of random walks* $(g = n - h)$ $(g)$ | *Sample size* $(T)$ | *Probability that* $2(\mathcal{L}_A - \mathcal{L}_0)$ *is greater than entry* | | | | | |
|---|---|---|---|---|---|---|---|
| | | *0.500* | *0.200* | *0.100* | *0.050* | *0.025* | *0.010* |
| | | | | *Case 1* | | | |
| 1 | 400 | 0.58 | 1.82 | 2.86 | 3.84 | 4.93 | 6.51 |
| 2 | 400 | 4.83 | 7.58 | 9.52 | 11.44 | 13.27 | 15.69 |
| 3 | 400 | 9.71 | 13.31 | 15.59 | 17.89 | 20.02 | 22.99 |
| 4 | 400 | 14.94 | 18.97 | 21.58 | 23.80 | 26.14 | 28.82 |
| 5 | 400 | 20.16 | 24.83 | 27.62 | 30.04 | 32.51 | 35.17 |
| | | | | *Case 2* | | | |
| 1 | 400 | 2.415 | 4.905 | 6.691 | 8.083 | 9.658 | 11.576 |
| 2 | 400 | 7.474 | 10.666 | 12.783 | 14.595 | 16.403 | 18.782 |
| 3 | 400 | 12.707 | 16.521 | 18.959 | 21.279 | 23.362 | 26.154 |
| 4 | 400 | 17.875 | 22.341 | 24.917 | 27.341 | 29.599 | 32.616 |
| 5 | 400 | 23.132 | 27.953 | 30.818 | 33.262 | 35.700 | 38.858 |
| | | | | *Case 3* | | | |
| 1 | 400 | 0.447 | 1.699 | 2.816 | 3.962 | 5.332 | 6.936 |
| 2 | 400 | 6.852 | 10.125 | 12.099 | 14.036 | 15.810 | 17.936 |
| 3 | 400 | 12.381 | 16.324 | 18.697 | 20.778 | 23.002 | 25.521 |
| 4 | 400 | 17.719 | 22.113 | 24.712 | 27.169 | 29.335 | 31.943 |
| 5 | 400 | 23.211 | 27.899 | 30.774 | 33.178 | 35.546 | 38.341 |

The probability shown at the head of the column is the area in the right-hand tail. The number of random walks under the null hypothesis ($g$) is given by the number of variables described by the vector autoregression ($n$) minus the number of cointegrating relations under the null hypothesis ($h$). In each case the alternative is that there are $h + 1$ cointegrating relations.

*Source:* Michael Osterwald-Lenum, "A Note with Quantiles of the Asymptotic Distribution of the Maximum Likelihood Cointegration Rank Test Statistics," *Oxford Bulletin of Economics and Statistics* 54 (1992), p. 462; and Søren Johansen and Katarina Juselius, "Maximum Likelihood Estimation and Inference on Cointegration—with Applications to the Demand for Money," *Oxford Bulletin of Economics and Statistics* 52 (1990), p. 208.

# C Answers to Selected Exercises

## Chapter 3. Stationary ARMA Processes

3.1. Yes, any *MA* process is covariance-stationary. Autocovariances:

$$\gamma_0 = 7.4$$
$$\gamma_{\pm 1} = 4.32$$
$$\gamma_{\pm 2} = 0.8$$
$$\gamma_j = 0 \qquad \text{for } |j| > 2.$$

3.2. Yes, the process is covariance-stationary, since

$$(1 - 1.1z + 0.18z^2) = (1 - 0.9z)(1 - 0.2z);$$

the eigenvalues (0.9 and 0.2) are both inside the unit circle. The autocovariances are as follows:

$$\gamma_0 = 7.89$$
$$\gamma_1 = 7.35$$
$$\gamma_j = 1.1\gamma_{j-1} - 0.18\gamma_{j-2} \qquad \text{for } j = 2, 3, \ldots$$
$$\gamma_{-j} = \gamma_j.$$

3.3. Equating coefficients on:

$$\begin{aligned}
&L^0 \text{ gives } \psi_0 = 1\\
&L^1 \text{ gives } -\phi_1\psi_0 + \psi_1 = 0\\
&L^2 \text{ gives } -\phi_2\psi_0 - \phi_1\psi_1 + \psi_2 = 0\\
&\quad\vdots\\
&L^j \text{ gives } -\phi_p\psi_{j-p} - \phi_{p-1}\psi_{j-p+1} - \cdots - \phi_1\psi_{j-1} + \psi_j = 0,\\
&\qquad\qquad \text{for } j = p, p+1, \ldots.
\end{aligned}$$

These imply

$$\begin{aligned}
\psi_0 &= 1\\
\psi_1 &= \phi_1\\
\psi_2 &= \phi_1^2 + \phi_2\\
&\vdots\\
\psi_j &= \phi_1\psi_{j-1} + \phi_2\psi_{j-2} + \cdots + \phi_p\psi_{j-p} \qquad \text{for } j = p, p+1, \ldots.
\end{aligned}$$

Thus the values of $\psi_j$ are the solution to a $p$th-order difference equation with starting values $\psi_0 = 1$ and $\psi_{-1} = \psi_{-2} = \cdots = \psi_{-p+1} = 0$. Thus, from the results on difference equations,

$$\begin{bmatrix} \psi_j \\ \psi_{j-1} \\ \vdots \\ \psi_{j-p+1} \end{bmatrix} = \mathbf{F}^j \begin{bmatrix} 1 \\ 0 \\ \vdots \\ 0 \end{bmatrix};$$

that is

$$\psi_j = f_{11}^{(j)}.$$

3.4. From [2.1.6],

$$\psi(L)c = (\psi_0 + \psi_1 + \psi_2 + \psi_3 + \cdots)\cdot c.$$

But the sum $(\psi_0 + \psi_1 + \psi_2 + \psi_3 + \cdots)$ can be viewed as the polynomial $\psi(z)$ evaluated at $z = 1$:

$$\psi(L)c = \psi(1)\cdot c.$$

Moreover, from [3.4.19],

$$\psi(1) = 1/(1 - \phi_1 - \phi_2).$$

3.5. Let $\lambda_1$ and $\lambda_2$ satisfy $(1 - \phi_1 z - \phi_2 z^2) = (1 - \lambda_1 z)(1 - \lambda_2 z)$, noting that $\lambda_1$ and $\lambda_2$ are both inside the unit circle for a covariance-stationary $AR(2)$ process.

Consider first the case where $\lambda_1$ and $\lambda_2$ are real and distinct. Then from [1.2.29],

$$\begin{aligned}\sum_{j=0}^{\infty} |\psi_j| &= \sum_{j=0}^{\infty} |c_1\lambda_1^j + c_2\lambda_2^j| \\ &< \sum_{j=0}^{\infty} |c_1\lambda_1^j| + \sum_{j=0}^{\infty} |c_2\lambda_2^j| \\ &= |c_1|/(1 - |\lambda_1|) + |c_2|/(1 - |\lambda_2|) \\ &< \infty.\end{aligned}$$

Consider next the case where $\lambda_1$ and $\lambda_2$ are distinct complex conjugates. Let $R = |\lambda_i|$ denote the modulus of $\lambda_1$ or $\lambda_2$. Then $0 \leq R < 1$, and from [1.2.39],

$$\begin{aligned}\sum_{j=0}^{\infty} |\psi_j| &= \sum_{j=0}^{\infty} |c_1\lambda_1^j + c_2\lambda_2^j| \\ &= \sum_{j=0}^{\infty} |2\alpha R^j \cos(\theta j) - 2\beta R^j \sin(\theta j)| \\ &\leq |2\alpha| \sum_{j=0}^{\infty} R^j |\cos(\theta j)| + |2\beta| \sum_{j=0}^{\infty} R^j |\sin(\theta j)| \\ &\leq |2\alpha| \sum_{j=0}^{\infty} R^j + |2\beta| \sum_{j=0}^{\infty} R^j \\ &= 2(|\alpha| + |\beta|)/(1 - R) \\ &< \infty.\end{aligned}$$

Finally, for the case of a repeated real root $|\lambda| < 1$,

$$\sum_{j=0}^{\infty} |\psi_j| = \sum_{j=0}^{\infty} |k_1\lambda^j + k_2 j\lambda^{j-1}| \leq |k_1| \sum_{j=0}^{\infty} |\lambda|^j + |k_2| \sum_{j=0}^{\infty} |j\lambda^{j-1}|.$$

But

$$|k_1| \sum_{j=0}^{\infty} |\lambda|^j = |k_1|/(1 - |\lambda|) < \infty$$

and

$$\begin{aligned}\sum_{j=0}^{\infty} |j\lambda^{j-1}| &= 1 + 2|\lambda| + 3|\lambda|^2 + 4|\lambda|^3 + \cdots \\ &= 1 + (|\lambda| + |\lambda|) + (|\lambda|^2 + |\lambda|^2 + |\lambda|^2) \\ &\quad + (|\lambda|^3 + |\lambda|^3 + |\lambda|^3 + |\lambda|^3) + \cdots \\ &= (1 + |\lambda| + |\lambda|^2 + |\lambda|^3 + \cdots) + (|\lambda| + |\lambda|^2 + |\lambda|^3 + \cdots) \\ &\quad + (|\lambda|^2 + |\lambda|^3 + \cdots) \\ &= 1/(1 - |\lambda|) + |\lambda|/(1 - |\lambda|) + |\lambda|^2/(1 - |\lambda|) + \cdots \\ &= 1/(1 - |\lambda|)^2 \\ &< \infty.\end{aligned}$$

3.8. $(1 + 2.4z + 0.8z^2) = (1 + 0.4z)(1 + 2z)$.

The invertible operator is

$$(1 + 0.4z)(1 + 0.5z) = (1 + 0.9z + 0.2z^2),$$

so the invertible representation is

$$Y_t = (1 + 0.9L + 0.2L^2)\varepsilon_t$$
$$E(\varepsilon_t^2) = 4.$$

## Chapter 4. Forecasting

4.3. $$\begin{bmatrix} 1 & 0 & 0 \\ -2 & 1 & 0 \\ 3 & 1 & 1 \end{bmatrix} \begin{bmatrix} 1 & 0 & 0 \\ 0 & 2 & 0 \\ 0 & 0 & 1 \end{bmatrix} \begin{bmatrix} 1 & -2 & 3 \\ 0 & 1 & 1 \\ 0 & 0 & 1 \end{bmatrix}$$

4.4. No. The projection of $Y_4$ on $Y_3$, $Y_2$, and $Y_1$ can be calculated from

$$\hat{P}(Y_4|Y_3, Y_2, Y_1) = a_{41}Y_1 + a_{42}[Y_2 - \hat{P}(Y_2|Y_1)] + a_{43}[Y_3 - \hat{P}(Y_3|Y_2, Y_1)].$$

The projection $\hat{P}(Y_3|Y_2, Y_1)$, in turn, is given by

$$\hat{P}(Y_3|Y_2, Y_1) = a_{31}Y_1 + a_{32}[Y_2 - \hat{P}(Y_2|Y_1)].$$

The coefficient on $Y_2$ in $\hat{P}(Y_4|Y_3, Y_2, Y_1)$ is therefore given by $a_{42} - a_{43}a_{32}$.

## Chapter 5. Maximum Likelihood Estimation

5.2. The negative of the matrix of second derivatives is

$$\mathbf{H}(\boldsymbol{\theta}) = \begin{bmatrix} 3 & 0 \\ 0 & 4 \end{bmatrix},$$

so that [5.7.12] implies

$$\boldsymbol{\theta}^{(1)} = \begin{bmatrix} -1 \\ 1 \end{bmatrix} + \begin{bmatrix} 3 & 0 \\ 0 & 4 \end{bmatrix}^{-1} \begin{bmatrix} 3 \\ -4 \end{bmatrix} = \begin{bmatrix} 0 \\ 0 \end{bmatrix}.$$

## Chapter 7. Asymptotic Distribution Theory

7.1. By continuity, $|g(X_T, c_T) - g(\xi, c)| > \delta$ only if $|X_T - \xi| + |c_T - c| > \eta$ for some $\eta$. But $c_T \rightarrow c$ and $X_T \xrightarrow{p} \xi$ means that we can find an $N$ such that $|c_T - c| < \eta/2$ for all $T \geq N$ and such that $P\{|X_T - \xi| > \eta/2\} < \varepsilon$ for all $T \geq N$. Hence $P\{|X_T - \xi| + |c_T - c| > \eta\}$ is less than $\varepsilon$ for all $T \geq N$, implying that $P\{|g(X_T, c_T) - g(\xi, c)| > \delta\} < \varepsilon$.

7.2. (a) For an $AR(1)$ process, $\psi(z) = 1/(1 - \phi z)$ and $g_Y(z) = \sigma^2/(1 - \phi z)(1 - \phi z^{-1})$, with

$$g_Y(1) = \frac{\sigma^2}{(1 - \phi)(1 - \phi)} = \frac{1}{(1 - 0.8)^2} = 25.$$

Thus $\lim_{T\rightarrow\infty} T \cdot \text{Var}(\overline{Y}_T) = 25$.

(b) $T = 10{,}000$ ($\sqrt{25/10{,}000} = 0.05$).

7.3. No, the variance can be a function of time.

7.4. Yes, $\varepsilon_t$ has variance $\sigma^2$ for all $t$. Since $\varepsilon_t$ is a martingale difference sequence, it has mean zero and must be serially uncorrelated. Thus $\{\varepsilon_t\}$ is white noise and this is a covariance-stationary $MA(\infty)$ process.

7.7. From the results of Chapter 3, $Y_t$ can be written as $Y_t = \mu + \sum_{j=0}^{\infty}\psi_j\varepsilon_{t-j}$ with $\sum_{j=0}^{\infty}|\psi_j| < \infty$. Then (a) follows immediately from Proposition 7.5 and result [3.3.19]. For (b), notice that $E|\varepsilon_t|^r < \infty$ for $r = 4$, so that result [7.2.14] establishes that

$$[1/(T - k)] \sum_{t=k+1}^{T} \tilde{Y}_t\tilde{Y}_{t-k} \xrightarrow{p} E(\tilde{Y}_t\tilde{Y}_{t-k}),$$

where $\tilde{Y}_t \equiv Y_t - \mu$. But

$$[1/(T-k)] \sum_{t=k+1}^{T} Y_t Y_{t-k} = [1/(T-k)] \sum_{t=k+1}^{T} (\tilde{Y}_t + \mu)(\tilde{Y}_{t-k} + \mu)$$

$$= [1/(T-k)] \sum_{t=k+1}^{T} \tilde{Y}_t \tilde{Y}_{t-k} + \mu[1/(T-k)] \sum_{t=k+1}^{T} \tilde{Y}_{t-k}$$

$$+ \mu[1/(T-k)] \sum_{t=k+1}^{T} \tilde{Y}_t + \mu^2$$

$$\xrightarrow{p} E(\tilde{Y}_t \tilde{Y}_{t-k}) + 0 + 0 + \mu^2$$

$$= E(\tilde{Y}_t + \mu)(\tilde{Y}_{t-k} + \mu)$$

$$= E(Y_t Y_{t-k}).$$

## *Chapter 8. Linear Regression Models*

8.1. $$R_u^2 = \frac{\mathbf{y}'\mathbf{X}(\mathbf{X}'\mathbf{X})^{-1}\mathbf{X}'\mathbf{y}}{\mathbf{y}'\mathbf{y}}$$

$$= \frac{\mathbf{y}'\mathbf{y} - \mathbf{y}'[\mathbf{I}_T - \mathbf{X}(\mathbf{X}'\mathbf{X})^{-1}\mathbf{X}']\mathbf{y}}{\mathbf{y}'\mathbf{y}}$$

$$= 1 - [(\mathbf{y}'\mathbf{M_X}\mathbf{M_X}\mathbf{y})/(\mathbf{y}'\mathbf{y})]$$

$$= 1 - [(\hat{\mathbf{u}}'\hat{\mathbf{u}})/(\mathbf{y}'\mathbf{y})].$$

$$R_c^2 = \frac{\mathbf{y}'\mathbf{y} - \mathbf{y}'\mathbf{M_X}\mathbf{y} - T\bar{y}^2}{\mathbf{y}'\mathbf{y} - T\bar{y}^2}$$

$$= 1 - [(\hat{\mathbf{u}}'\hat{\mathbf{u}})/(\mathbf{y}'\mathbf{y} - T\bar{y}^2)]$$

and

$$\mathbf{y}'\mathbf{y} - T\bar{y}^2 = \sum_{t=1}^{T} y_t^2 - T\bar{y}^2 = \sum_{t=1}^{T} (y_t - \bar{y})^2.$$

8.2. The 5% critical value for a $\chi^2(2)$ variable is 5.99. An $F(2, N)$ variable will thus have a critical value that approaches $5.99/2 = 3.00$ as $N \to \infty$. One needs $N$ of around 300 observations before the critical value of an $F(2, N)$ variable reaches 3.03, or within 1% of the limiting value.

8.3. Fourth moments of $\mathbf{x}_t u_t$ are of the form $E(\varepsilon_t^4) \cdot E(y_{t-i} y_{t-j} y_{t-l} y_{t-m})$. The first term is bounded under Assumption 8.4, and the second term is bounded as in Example 7.14. Moreover, a typical element of $(1/T)\Sigma_{t=1}^{T} u_t^2 \mathbf{x}_t \mathbf{x}_t'$ is of the form

$$(1/T) \sum_{t=1}^{T} \varepsilon_t^2 y_{t-i} y_{t-j} = (1/T) \sum_{t=1}^{T} (\varepsilon_t^2 - \sigma^2) y_{t-i} y_{t-j} + \sigma^2 \cdot (1/T) \sum_{t=1}^{T} y_{t-i} y_{t-j}$$

$$\xrightarrow{p} 0 + \sigma^2 \cdot E(y_{t-i} y_{t-j}).$$

Hence, the conditions of Proposition 7.9 are satisfied.

8.4. Proposition 7.5 and result [7.2.14] establish

$$\begin{bmatrix} \hat{c}_T \\ \hat{\phi}_{1,T} \\ \vdots \\ \hat{\phi}_{p,T} \end{bmatrix} = \begin{bmatrix} 1 & (1/T)\Sigma y_{t-1} & \cdots & (1/T)\Sigma y_{t-p} \\ (1/T)\Sigma y_{t-1} & (1/T)\Sigma y_{t-1}^2 & \cdots & (1/T)\Sigma y_{t-1} y_{t-p} \\ \vdots & \vdots & \cdots & \vdots \\ (1/T)\Sigma y_{t-p} & (1/T)\Sigma y_{t-p} y_{t-1} & \cdots & (1/T)\Sigma y_{t-p}^2 \end{bmatrix}^{-1} \begin{bmatrix} (1/T)\Sigma y_t \\ (1/T)\Sigma y_{t-1} y_t \\ \vdots \\ (1/T)\Sigma y_{t-p} y_t \end{bmatrix}$$

$$\xrightarrow{p} \begin{bmatrix} 1 & \mu & \cdots & \mu \\ \mu & \gamma_0 + \mu^2 & \cdots & \gamma_{p-1} + \mu^2 \\ \vdots & \vdots & \cdots & \vdots \\ \mu & \gamma_{p-1} + \mu^2 & \cdots & \gamma_0 + \mu^2 \end{bmatrix}^{-1} \begin{bmatrix} \mu \\ \gamma_1 + \mu^2 \\ \vdots \\ \gamma_p + \mu^2 \end{bmatrix},$$

which equals $\boldsymbol{\alpha}^{(p)}$ given in [4.3.6].

## Chapter 10. Covariance-Stationary Vector Processes

10.2. (a) $$\Gamma_0 = \begin{bmatrix} (1+\theta^2)\sigma_\varepsilon^2 & h_1\theta\sigma_\varepsilon^2 \\ h_1\theta\sigma_\varepsilon^2 & \{h_1^2(1+\theta^2)\sigma_\varepsilon^2 + \sigma_u^2\} \end{bmatrix}$$

$$\Gamma_1 = \begin{bmatrix} \theta\sigma_\varepsilon^2 & 0 \\ h_1(1+\theta^2)\sigma_\varepsilon^2 & h_1^2\theta\sigma_\varepsilon^2 \end{bmatrix}$$

$$\Gamma_2 = \begin{bmatrix} 0 & 0 \\ h_1\theta\sigma_\varepsilon^2 & 0 \end{bmatrix}$$

$$\Gamma_{-1} = \Gamma_1' \qquad \Gamma_{-2} = \Gamma_2'$$

$$\Gamma_k = \mathbf{0} \qquad \text{for } k = \pm 3, \pm 4, \ldots .$$

(b) $$\mathbf{s_Y}(\omega) = (2\pi)^{-1}\begin{bmatrix} s_{11} & s_{12} \\ s_{21} & s_{22} \end{bmatrix}$$

$$s_{11} = (1+\theta^2)\sigma_\varepsilon^2 + \theta\sigma_\varepsilon^2 e^{-i\omega} + \theta\sigma_\varepsilon^2 e^{i\omega}$$

$$s_{12} = h_1\theta\sigma_\varepsilon^2 e^{2i\omega} + h_1(1+\theta^2)\sigma_\varepsilon^2 e^{i\omega} + h_1\theta\sigma_\varepsilon^2$$

$$s_{21} = h_1\theta\sigma_\varepsilon^2 e^{-2i\omega} + h_1(1+\theta^2)\sigma_\varepsilon^2 e^{-i\omega} + h_1\theta\sigma_\varepsilon^2$$

$$s_{22} = h_1^2(1+\theta^2)\sigma_\varepsilon^2 + \sigma_u^2 + h_1^2\theta\sigma_\varepsilon^2 e^{-i\omega} + h_1^2\theta\sigma_\varepsilon^2 e^{i\omega}$$

$$c_{YX}(\omega) = (2\pi)^{-1}h_1\sigma_\varepsilon^2\{\theta\cdot\cos(2\omega) + (1+\theta^2)\cdot\cos(\omega) + \theta\}$$

$$q_{YX}(\omega) = -(2\pi)^{-1}h_1\sigma_\varepsilon^2\{\theta\cdot\sin(2\omega) + (1+\theta^2)\cdot\sin(\omega)\}.$$

(c) The variable $X_t$ follows an $MA(1)$ process, for which the spectrum is indeed $s_{11}$. The term $s_{21}$ is $s_{11}$ times $h(e^{-i\omega}) = h_1\cdot e^{-i\omega}$. Multiplying $s_{21}$ in turn by $h(e^{i\omega}) = h_1\cdot e^{i\omega}$ and adding $\sigma_u^2$ produces $s_{22}$.

(d) $$(2\pi)^{-1}\int_{-\pi}^{\pi}\frac{s_{YX}(\omega)}{s_{XX}(\omega)}e^{i\omega k}\,d\omega = (2\pi)^{-1}\int_{-\pi}^{\pi} h_1\cdot e^{-i\omega}e^{i\omega k}\,d\omega.$$

When $k = 1$, this is simply

$$(2\pi)^{-1}\int_{-\pi}^{\pi} h_1\,d\omega = h_1,$$

as desired. When $k \neq 1$, the integral is

$$\begin{aligned}
&(2\pi)^{-1}\int_{-\pi}^{\pi} h_1\cdot e^{(k-1)i\omega}\,d\omega \\
&= (2\pi)^{-1}\int_{-\pi}^{\pi} h_1\cdot\cos[(k-1)\omega]\,d\omega + i\cdot(2\pi)^{-1}\int_{-\pi}^{\pi} h_1\cdot\sin[(k-1)\omega]\,d\omega \\
&= [(k-1)2\pi]^{-1}h_1\Big[\sin[(k-1)\omega]\Big]_{\omega=-\pi}^{\pi} - [(k-1)2\pi]^{-1}h_1\Big[\cos[(k-1)\omega]\Big]_{\omega=-\pi}^{\pi} \\
&= 0.
\end{aligned}$$

## Chapter 11. Vector Autoregressions

11.1. A typical element of [11.A.2] states that

$$(1/T)\sum_{t=1}^{T}\varepsilon_{i_1,t}y_{j_1,t-l_1}\varepsilon_{i_2,t}y_{j_2,t-l_2} \xrightarrow{p} E(\varepsilon_{i_1,t}\varepsilon_{i_2,t})\cdot E(y_{j_1,t-l_1}y_{j_2,t-l_2}).$$

But

$$(1/T)\sum_{t=1}^{T}\varepsilon_{i_1,t}y_{j_1,t-l_1}\varepsilon_{i_2,t}y_{j_2,t-l_2} = (1/T)\sum_{t=1}^{T}z_t + E(\varepsilon_{i_1,t}\varepsilon_{i_2,t})\cdot(1/T)\sum_{t=1}^{T}y_{j_1,t-l_1}y_{j_2,t-l_2},$$

where

$$z_t \equiv \{\varepsilon_{i_1,t}\varepsilon_{i_2,t} - E(\varepsilon_{i_1,t}\varepsilon_{i_2,t})\}y_{j_1,t-l_1}y_{j_2,t-l_2}.$$

Notice that $z_t$ is a martingale difference sequence whose variance is finite by virtue of

Proposition 7.10. Hence, $(1/T)\Sigma_{t=1}^{T} z_t \xrightarrow{p} 0$. Moreover,

$$(1/T) \sum_{t=1}^{T} y_{j_1,t-l_1} y_{j_2,t-l_2} \xrightarrow{p} E(y_{j_1,t-l_1} y_{j_2,t-l_2}),$$

by virtue of Proposition 10.2(d).

11.2. (a) No. (b) Yes. (c) No.

11.3.
$$\begin{aligned}
\alpha_j &= \zeta_j && \text{for } j = 1, 2, \ldots, p \\
\beta_j &= \eta_j && \text{for } j = 1, 2, \ldots, p \\
\lambda_0 &= \Omega_{21}\Omega_{11}^{-1} \\
\lambda_j &= \gamma_j - \Omega_{21}\Omega_{11}^{-1}\alpha_j && \text{for } j = 1, 2, \ldots, p \\
\xi_j &= \delta_j - \Omega_{21}\Omega_{11}^{-1}\beta_j && \text{for } j = 1, 2, \ldots, p \\
\sigma_1^2 &= \Omega_{11} \\
\sigma_2^2 &= \Omega_{22} - \Omega_{21}\Omega_{11}^{-1}\Omega_{12} \\
u_{1t} &= \varepsilon_{1t} \\
u_{2t} &= \varepsilon_{2t} - \Omega_{21}\Omega_{11}^{-1}\varepsilon_{1t}
\end{aligned}$$

11.4. Premultiplying by $\mathbf{A}^*(L)$ results in

$$\begin{aligned}
\begin{bmatrix} |\mathbf{A}(L)| & 0 \\ 0 & |\mathbf{A}(L)| \end{bmatrix} \begin{bmatrix} y_{1t} \\ y_{2t} \end{bmatrix} &= \begin{bmatrix} 1 - \xi(L) & \eta(L) \\ \lambda_0 + \lambda(L) & 1 - \zeta(L) \end{bmatrix} \begin{bmatrix} u_{1t} \\ u_{2t} \end{bmatrix} \\
&= \begin{bmatrix} [1 - \xi(L)]u_{1t} + \eta(L)u_{2t} \\ [\lambda_0 + \lambda(L)]u_{1t} + [1 - \zeta(L)]u_{2t} \end{bmatrix} \\
&= \begin{bmatrix} v_{1t} \\ v_{2t} \end{bmatrix}.
\end{aligned}$$

Thus,

$$\begin{aligned}
|\mathbf{A}(L)|y_{1t} &= v_{1t} \\
|\mathbf{A}(L)|y_{2t} &= v_{2t}.
\end{aligned}$$

Now the determinant $|\mathbf{A}(L)|$ is the following polynomial in the lag operator:

$$|\mathbf{A}(L)| = [1 - \xi(L)][1 - \zeta(L)] - [\eta(L)][\lambda_0 + \lambda(L)].$$

The coefficient on $L^0$ in this polynomial is unity, and the highest power of $L$ is $L^{2p}$, which has coefficient $(\xi_p\zeta_p - \eta_p\lambda_p)$:

$$|\mathbf{A}(L)| = 1 + a_1 L + a_2 L^2 + \cdots + a_{2p} L^{2p}.$$

Furthermore, $v_{1t}$ is the sum of two mutually uncorrelated $MA(p)$ processes, and so $v_{1t}$ is itself $MA(p)$. Hence, $y_{1t}$ follows an $ARMA(2p, p)$ process; a similar argument shows that $y_{2t}$ follows an $ARMA(2p, p)$ process with the same autoregressive coefficients but different moving average coefficients.

In general, consider an $n$-variable $VAR$ of the form

$$\mathbf{\Phi}(L)\mathbf{y}_t = \boldsymbol{\varepsilon}_t$$

with

$$E(\boldsymbol{\varepsilon}_t\boldsymbol{\varepsilon}_\tau') = \begin{cases} \mathbf{\Omega} & \text{if } t = \tau \\ \mathbf{0} & \text{otherwise.} \end{cases}$$

Find the triangular factorization of $\mathbf{\Omega} = \mathbf{ADA}'$ and premultiply the system by $\mathbf{A}^{-1}$, yielding

$$\mathbf{A}(L)\mathbf{y}_t = \mathbf{u}_t,$$

where

$$\begin{aligned}
\mathbf{A}(L) &= \mathbf{A}^{-1}\mathbf{\Phi}(L) \\
\mathbf{u}_t &= \mathbf{A}^{-1}\boldsymbol{\varepsilon}_t \\
E(\mathbf{u}_t\mathbf{u}_t') &= \mathbf{D}.
\end{aligned}$$

Thus, the elements of $\mathbf{u}_t$ are mutually uncorrelated and $\mathbf{A}(0)$ has 1s along its principal diagonal. The adjoint matrix $\mathbf{A}^*(L)$ has the property

$$\mathbf{A}^*(L)\cdot\mathbf{A}(L) = |\mathbf{A}(L)|\cdot\mathbf{I}_n.$$

Premultiplying the system by $\mathbf{A}^*(L)$,

$$|\mathbf{A}(L)|\cdot\mathbf{y}_t = \mathbf{A}^*(L)\mathbf{u}_t.$$

The determinant $|\mathbf{A}(L)|$ is a scalar polynomial containing terms up to order $L^{np}$, while elements of $\mathbf{A}^*(L)$ contain terms up to order $L^{(n-1)p}$. Hence, the $i$th row of the system takes the form

$$|\mathbf{A}(L)|\cdot y_{it} = v_{it},$$

where $v_{it}$ is the sum of $n$ mutually uncorrelated $MA[(n-1)p]$ processes and is therefore itself $MA[(n-1)p]$. Hence, $y_{it} \sim ARMA[np, (n-1)p]$.

11.5. (a) $$\begin{aligned}|\mathbf{I}_2 - \mathbf{\Phi}_1 z| &= (1 - 0.3z)(1 - 0.4z) - (0.8z)(0.9z)\\ &= 1 - 0.7z - 0.6z^2\\ &= (1 - 1.2z)(1 + 0.5z).\end{aligned}$$

Since $z^* = 1/1.2$ is inside the unit circle, the system is nonstationary.

(b) $$\mathbf{\Psi}_0 = \begin{bmatrix}1 & 0\\ 0 & 1\end{bmatrix} \qquad \mathbf{\Psi}_1 = \begin{bmatrix}0.3 & 0.8\\ 0.9 & 0.4\end{bmatrix} \qquad \mathbf{\Psi}_2 = \begin{bmatrix}0.81 & 0.56\\ 0.63 & 0.88\end{bmatrix}$$

$\mathbf{\Psi}_s$ diverges as $s \to \infty$.

(c) $$\begin{aligned}y_{1,t+2} - \hat{E}(y_{1,t+2}|\mathbf{y}_t, \mathbf{y}_{t-1}, \ldots) &= \varepsilon_{1,t+2} + 0.3\varepsilon_{1,t+1} + 0.8\varepsilon_{2,t+1}\\ MSE &= 1 + (0.3)^2 + (0.8)^2(2) = 2.37.\end{aligned}$$

The fraction due to $\varepsilon_1 = 1.09/2.37 = 0.46$.

## Chapter 12. Bayesian Analysis

12.1. Take $k = 1$, $\mathbf{X} = \mathbf{1}$, $\boldsymbol{\beta} = \mu$, and $\mathbf{M} = 1/\nu$, and notice that $\mathbf{1}'\mathbf{1} = T$ and $\mathbf{1}'\mathbf{y} = T\bar{y}$.

## Chapter 13. The Kalman Filter

13.3. No, because $\mathbf{v}_t$ is not white noise.

13.5. Notice that

$$\begin{aligned}\tilde{\sigma}^2 + \tilde{\theta}^2\tilde{p}_{t+1} &= \frac{\tilde{\sigma}^2(1 + \tilde{\theta}^2 + \tilde{\theta}^4 + \cdots + \tilde{\theta}^{2[t+1]})}{1 + \tilde{\theta}^2 + \tilde{\theta}^4 + \cdots + \tilde{\theta}^{2t}}\\ &= \frac{\tilde{\sigma}^2(1 - \tilde{\theta}^{2[t+2]})}{1 - \tilde{\theta}^{2[t+1]}}\\ &= \frac{\theta^2\sigma^2(1 - \theta^{-2[t+2]})}{1 - \theta^{-2[t+1]}}\\ &= \frac{\theta^2\sigma^2(\theta^{2[t+2]} - 1)}{\theta^{2[t+2]} - \theta^2}\\ &= \frac{\sigma^2(1 - \theta^{2[t+2]})}{1 - \theta^{2[t+1]}}\\ &= \sigma^2 + \theta^2 p_{t+1}.\end{aligned}$$

Furthermore, from [13.3.19],

$$\begin{aligned}\tilde{\theta}\tilde{\varepsilon}_{t|t} &= \{\tilde{\theta}\tilde{\sigma}^2/[\tilde{\sigma}^2 + \tilde{\theta}^2\tilde{p}_t]\}\cdot\{y_t - \mu - \tilde{\theta}\tilde{\varepsilon}_{t-1|t-1}\}\\ &= \{\theta^{-1}\theta^2\sigma^2/[\sigma^2 + \theta^2 p_t]\}\cdot\{y_t - \mu - \tilde{\theta}\tilde{\varepsilon}_{t-1|t-1}\}\\ &= \{\theta\sigma^2/[\sigma^2 + \theta^2 p_t]\}\cdot\{y_t - \mu - \tilde{\theta}\tilde{\varepsilon}_{t-1|t-1}\},\end{aligned}$$

which is the same difference equation that generates $\{\theta\hat{\varepsilon}_{t|t}\}$, with both sequences, of course, beginning with $\theta\hat{\varepsilon}_{0|0} = \tilde{\theta}\tilde{\varepsilon}_{0|0} = 0$. With the sequences $(\mathbf{H}'\mathbf{P}_{t+1|t}\mathbf{H} + \mathbf{R})$ and $\mathbf{A}'\mathbf{x}_{t+1} + \mathbf{H}'\hat{\boldsymbol{\xi}}_{t+1|t}$ identical for the two representations, the likelihood in [13.4.1] to [13.4.3] must be identical.

13.6. The innovation $\varepsilon_t$ in [13.5.22] will be fundamental when $|\phi - K| < 1$. From [13.5.25], we see that

$$\phi - K = \phi\sigma_W^2/(\sigma_W^2 + P).$$

Since $P$ is a variance, it follows that $P \geq 0$, and so $|\phi - K| \leq |\phi|$, which is specified to be less than unity. This arises as a consequence of the general result in Proposition 13.2 that the eigenvalues of $\mathbf{F} - \mathbf{KH}'$ lie inside the unit circle.

From [13.5.23] and the preceding expression for $\phi - K$,

$$-(\phi - K)E(\varepsilon_t^2) = -(\phi - K)(\sigma_W^2 + P) = -\phi\sigma_W^2,$$

as claimed. Furthermore,

$$\begin{aligned}[1 + (\phi - K)^2]E(\varepsilon_t^2) &= (\sigma_W^2 + P) + (\phi - K)\phi\sigma_W^2\\ &= (1 + \phi^2)\sigma_W^2 + P - K\phi\sigma_W^2.\end{aligned}$$

But from [13.5.24] and [13.5.25],

$$P = K\phi\sigma_W^2 + \sigma_V^2,$$

and so

$$[1 + (\phi - K)^2]E(\varepsilon_t^2) = (1 + \phi^2)\sigma_W^2 + \sigma_V^2.$$

To understand these formulas from the perspective of the formulas in Chapter 4, note that the model adds an $AR(1)$ process to white noise, producing an $ARMA(1, 1)$ process:

$$(1 - \phi L)y_{t+1} = v_{t+1} + (1 - \phi L)w_{t+1}.$$

The first autocovariance of the $MA(1)$ process on the right side of this expression is $-\phi\sigma_W^2$, while the variance is $(1 + \phi^2)\sigma_W^2 + \sigma_V^2$.

## *Chapter 16. Processes with Deterministic Time Trends*

16.1. $$E\left((1/T)\sum_{t=1}^{T}[\lambda_1 + \lambda_2(t/T)]^2\varepsilon_t^2 - (1/T)\sum_{t=1}^{T}\sigma^2[\lambda_1^2 + 2\lambda_1\lambda_2(t/T) + \lambda_2^2(t/T)^2]\right)^2$$
$$= (1/T^2)\sum_{t=1}^{T}[\lambda_1^2 + 2\lambda_1\lambda_2(t/T) + \lambda_2^2(t/T)^2]^2\cdot E(\varepsilon_t^2 - \sigma^2)^2.$$

But

$$(1/T)\sum_{t=1}^{T}[\lambda_1^2 + 2\lambda_1\lambda_2(t/T) + \lambda_2^2(t/T)^2]^2 \to M < \infty,$$

and thus

$$T\cdot E\left((1/T)\sum_{t=1}^{T}[\lambda_1 + \lambda_2(t/T)]^2\varepsilon_t^2 - (1/T)\sum_{t=1}^{T}\sigma^2[\lambda_1^2 + 2\lambda_1\lambda_2(t/T) + \lambda_2^2(t/T)^2]\right)^2$$
$$\to M\cdot E(\varepsilon_t^2 - \sigma^2)^2 < \infty.$$

Thus

$$\begin{aligned}&(1/T)\sum_{t=1}^{T}[\lambda_1 + \lambda_2(t/T)]^2\varepsilon_t^2\\ &\xrightarrow{m.s.} (1/T)\sum_{t=1}^{T}\sigma^2[\lambda_1^2 + 2\lambda_1\lambda_2(t/T) + \lambda_2^2(t/T)^2]\\ &\to \sigma^2\,\boldsymbol{\lambda}'\mathbf{Q}\boldsymbol{\lambda}.\end{aligned}$$

16.2. Recall that the variance of $\mathbf{b}_T$ is given by

$$E(\mathbf{b}_T - \boldsymbol{\beta})(\mathbf{b}_T - \boldsymbol{\beta})' = \sigma^2\left(\sum_{t=1}^{T} \mathbf{x}_t\mathbf{x}_t'\right)^{-1}$$
$$= \sigma^2\begin{bmatrix} T & T(T+1)/2 \\ T(T+1)/2 & T(T+1)(2T+1)/6 \end{bmatrix}^{-1}.$$

Pre- and postmultiplying by $\mathbf{Y}_T$ results in

$$E[\mathbf{Y}_T(\mathbf{b}_T - \boldsymbol{\beta})(\mathbf{b}_T - \boldsymbol{\beta})'\mathbf{Y}_T]$$
$$= \sigma^2\mathbf{Y}_T\begin{bmatrix} T & T(T+1)/2 \\ T(T+1)/2 & T(T+1)(2T+1)/6 \end{bmatrix}^{-1}\mathbf{Y}_T$$
$$= \sigma^2\cdot\left\{\mathbf{Y}_T^{-1}\begin{bmatrix} T & T(T+1)/2 \\ T(T+1)/2 & T(T+1)(2T+1)/6 \end{bmatrix}\mathbf{Y}_T^{-1}\right\}^{-1}$$
$$\to \sigma^2\begin{bmatrix} 1 & \frac{1}{2} \\ \frac{1}{2} & \frac{1}{3} \end{bmatrix}^{-1}.$$

The (2, 2) element of this matrix expression holds that

$$E[T^{3/2}(\hat{\delta}_T - \delta)]^2 \to 12\sigma^2,$$

and so

$$T(\hat{\delta}_T - \delta) \overset{m.s.}{\to} 0.$$

16.3. Notice that

$$\left[T^{-1}\sum_{t=1}^{T}(t/T)y_t\right]^2 = T^{-2}[(1/T)y_1 + (2/T)y_2 + \cdots + (T/T)y_T]$$
$$\times [(1/T)y_1 + (2/T)y_2 + \cdots + (T/T)y_T],$$

which has expectation

$$E\left[T^{-1}\sum_{t=1}^{T}(t/T)y_t\right]^2$$
$$= T^{-2}\{[(1/T)^2 + (2/T)^2 + \cdots + (T/T)^2]\gamma_0$$
$$+ [(1/T)(2/T) + (2/T)(3/T) + \cdots + [(T-1)/T](T/T)]2\gamma_1$$
$$+ [(1/T)(3/T) + (2/T)(4/T) + \cdots + [(T-2)/T](T/T)]2\gamma_2$$
$$+ \cdots + [(1/T)(T/T)]2\gamma_{T-1}\}$$
$$\leq T^{-1}\{|\gamma_0| + 2|\gamma_1| + 2|\gamma_2| + \cdots + 2|\gamma_{T-1}|\}$$
$$\to 0.$$

## *Chapter 17. Univariate Processes with Unit Roots*

17.2. (a) $$T(\hat{\rho}_T - 1) = \frac{T^{-1}\Sigma y_{t-1}u_t}{T^{-2}\Sigma y_{t-1}^2} \overset{L}{\to} \frac{\frac{1}{2}\{\lambda^2\cdot[W(1)]^2 - \gamma_0\}}{\lambda^2\cdot\int [W(r)]^2\,dr}$$

from Proposition 17.3(e) and (h).

(b) $$T^2\cdot\hat{\sigma}_{\hat{\rho}_T}^2 = T^2\cdot s_T^2 \div (\Sigma y_{T-1}^2)$$
$$= s_T^2 \div (T^{-2}\Sigma y_{t-1}^2)$$
$$\overset{L}{\to} \gamma_0 \div \left(\lambda^2\cdot\int [W(r)]^2\,dr\right),$$

from Proposition 17.3(h) and [17.6.10].

(c) $$t_T = T(\hat{\rho}_T - 1) \div (T^2\cdot\hat{\sigma}_{\hat{\rho}_T}^2)^{1/2}$$
$$\overset{L}{\to} \frac{\frac{1}{2}\{\lambda^2\cdot[W(1)]^2 - \gamma_0\}}{\lambda^2\cdot\int [W(r)]^2\,dr} \times \left(\lambda^2\cdot\int [W(r)]^2\,dr\right)^{1/2} \div (\gamma_0)^{1/2},$$

from answers (a) and (b). This, in turn, can be written

$$(\lambda^2/\gamma_0)^{1/2}\frac{\frac{1}{2}\{\lambda^2\cdot[W(1)]^2-\gamma_0\}}{\lambda^2\left\{\int[W(r)]^2\,dr\right\}^{1/2}}=(\lambda^2/\gamma_0)^{1/2}\left\{\frac{\frac{1}{2}\{[W(1)]^2-1\}}{\left\{\int[W(r)]^2\,dr\right\}^{1/2}}+\frac{\frac{1}{2}(\lambda^2-\gamma_0)}{\lambda^2\left\{\int[W(r)]^2\,dr\right\}^{1/2}}\right\}.$$

$$\text{(d)}\quad (T^2\cdot\hat{\sigma}^2_{\hat{\rho}_T}\div s_T^2)=1/(T^{-2}\Sigma y^2_{t-1})\xrightarrow{L}1\Big/\left(\lambda^2\cdot\int[W(r)]^2\,dr\right),$$

from Proposition 17.3(h). Thus,

$$\begin{aligned}T(\hat{\rho}_T-1)&-\tfrac{1}{2}(T^2\cdot\hat{\sigma}^2_{\hat{\rho}_T}\div s_T^2)(\lambda^2-\gamma_0)\\&\xrightarrow{p}T(\hat{\rho}_T-1)-\frac{\frac{1}{2}(\lambda^2-\gamma_0)}{\lambda^2\cdot\int[W(r)]^2\,dr}\\&\xrightarrow{L}\frac{\frac{1}{2}\{\lambda^2\cdot[W(1)]^2-\gamma_0\}}{\lambda^2\cdot\int[W(r)]^2\,dr}-\frac{\frac{1}{2}(\lambda^2-\gamma_0)}{\lambda^2\cdot\int[W(r)]^2\,dr}\\&=\frac{\frac{1}{2}\{[W(1)]^2-1\}}{\int[W(r)]^2\,dr},\end{aligned}$$

with the next-to-last line following from answer (a).

$$\begin{aligned}\text{(e)}\quad &(\gamma_0/\lambda^2)^{1/2}\cdot t_T-\{\tfrac{1}{2}(\lambda^2-\gamma_0)/\lambda\}\times\{T\cdot\hat{\sigma}_{\hat{\rho}_T}\div s_T\}\\&\xrightarrow{L}\left\{\frac{\frac{1}{2}\{[W(1)]^2-1\}}{\left\{\int[W(r)]^2\,dr\right\}^{1/2}}+\frac{\frac{1}{2}(\lambda^2-\gamma_0)}{\lambda^2\left\{\int[W(r)]^2\,dr\right\}^{1/2}}\right\}\\&\quad-\left\{\{(1/2)(\lambda^2-\gamma_0)/\lambda\}\div\left(\lambda^2\cdot\int[W(r)]^2\,dr\right)^{1/2}\right\},\end{aligned}$$

from answers (c) and (b). Adding these terms produces the desired result.

To estimate $\gamma_0$ and $\lambda$, one could use

$$\hat{\gamma}_j=T^{-1}\sum_{t=j+1}^{T}\hat{u}_t\hat{u}_{t-j}\qquad\text{for } j=0,1,\ldots,q$$

$$\hat{\lambda}^2=\hat{\gamma}_0+2\sum_{j=1}^{q}[1-j/(q+1)]\hat{\gamma}_j,$$

where $\hat{u}_t$ is the *OLS* sample residual and $q$ is the number of autocovariances used to represent the serial correlation of $\psi(L)\varepsilon_t$. The statistic in (d) can then be compared with the case 1 entries of Table B.5, while the statistic in (e) can be compared with the case 1 entries of Table B.6.

17.3. (a)

$$\begin{bmatrix}1 & T^{-3/2}\Sigma\xi_{t-1} & T^{-2}\Sigma t\\ T^{-3/2}\Sigma\xi_{t-1} & T^{-2}\Sigma\xi^2_{t-1} & T^{-5/2}\Sigma\xi_{t-1}t\\ T^{-2}\Sigma t & T^{-5/2}\Sigma t\xi_{t-1} & T^{-3}\Sigma t^2\end{bmatrix}$$

$$\xrightarrow{L}\begin{bmatrix}1 & \lambda\cdot\int W(r)\,dr & 1/2\\ \lambda\cdot\int W(r)\,dr & \lambda^2\cdot\int[W(r)]^2\,dr & \lambda\cdot\int rW(r)\,dr\\ 1/2 & \lambda\cdot\int rW(r)\,dr & 1/3\end{bmatrix}.$$

$$\text{(b)}\quad \begin{bmatrix} T^{-1/2}\Sigma u_t \\ T^{-1}\Sigma \xi_{t-1} u_t \\ T^{-3/2}\Sigma t u_t \end{bmatrix} \xrightarrow{L} \begin{bmatrix} \lambda \cdot W(1) \\ (1/2)\{\lambda^2 \cdot [W(1)]^2 - \gamma_0\} \\ \lambda \cdot \{W(1) - \int W(r)\, dr\} \end{bmatrix}.$$

(c) This follows from expression [17.4.52] and answers (a) and (b).

(d) The calculations are virtually identical to those in [17.4.54].

(e) $t_T = T(\hat{\rho}_T - 1) \div \{T^2 \cdot \hat{\sigma}^2_{\hat{\rho}_T}\}^{1/2} \xrightarrow{p} T(\hat{\rho}_T - 1) \div \{(s_T^2/\lambda^2) \cdot Q\}^{1/2}$.

(f) Answer (c) establishes that

$$T(\hat{\rho}_T - 1)$$

$$\xrightarrow{L} \left\{ [0 \quad 1 \quad 0] \begin{bmatrix} 1 & \int W(r)\, dr & 1/2 \\ \int W(r)\, dr & \int [W(r)]^2\, dr & \int rW(r)\, dr \\ 1/2 & \int rW(r)\, dr & 1/3 \end{bmatrix}^{-1} \begin{bmatrix} W(1) \\ \frac{1}{2}\{[W(1)]^2 - 1\} \\ W(1) - \int W(r)\, dr \end{bmatrix} \right\}$$

$$+ \tfrac{1}{2}\{1 - (\gamma_0/\lambda^2)\}[0 \quad 1 \quad 0] \begin{bmatrix} 1 & \int W(r)\, dr & 1/2 \\ \int W(r)\, dr & \int [W(r)]^2\, dr & \int rW(r)\, dr \\ 1/2 & \int rW(r)\, dr & 1/3 \end{bmatrix}^{-1} \begin{bmatrix} 0 \\ 1 \\ 0 \end{bmatrix}$$

$$= V + \tfrac{1}{2}\{1 - (\gamma_0/\lambda^2)\}Q.$$

Moreover, answer (d) implies that

$$\begin{aligned} \tfrac{1}{2}(T^2 \cdot \hat{\sigma}^2_{\hat{\rho}_T} \div s_T^2) \cdot (\lambda^2 - \gamma_0) &\xrightarrow{L} \tfrac{1}{2}(Q/\lambda^2)(\lambda^2 - \gamma_0) \\ &= \tfrac{1}{2}\{1 - (\gamma_0/\lambda^2)\}Q. \end{aligned}$$

(g) From answers (d) and (e),

$$\begin{aligned} &(\gamma_0/\lambda^2)^{1/2} \cdot t_T - \{\tfrac{1}{2}(\lambda^2 - \gamma_0)\lambda\} \times \{T \cdot \hat{\sigma}_{\hat{\rho}_T} \div s_T\} \\ &\xrightarrow{p} T(\hat{\rho}_T - 1)/\sqrt{Q} - \{\tfrac{1}{2}(\lambda^2 - \gamma_0)/\lambda\} \times \sqrt{Q}/\lambda \\ &= \{T(\hat{\rho}_T - 1) - \tfrac{1}{2}(Q/\lambda^2)\,(\lambda^2 - \gamma_0)\} \div \sqrt{Q} \\ &\xrightarrow{L} V \div \sqrt{Q}, \end{aligned}$$

from the analysis of (f).

To estimate $\gamma_0$ and $\lambda$, one could use

$$\hat{\gamma}_j = T^{-1} \sum_{t=j+1}^{T} \hat{u}_t \hat{u}_{t-j} \qquad \text{for } j = 0, 1, \ldots, q$$

$$\hat{\lambda}^2 = \hat{\gamma}_0 + 2 \sum_{j=1}^{q} [1 - j/(q+1)]\hat{\gamma}_j,$$

where $\hat{u}_t$ is the *OLS* sample residual and $q$ is the number of autocovariances used to approximate the dynamics of $\psi(L)\varepsilon_t$. The statistic in (f) can then be compared with the case 4 entries of Table B.5, while the statistic in (g) can be compared with the case 4 entries of Table B.6.

17.4. (b) Case 1 of Table B.5 is appropriate asymptotically. (c) Case 1 of Table B.6 is appropriate asymptotically.

## *Chapter 18. Unit Roots in Multivariate Time Series*

18.1. Under the null hypothesis $\mathbf{R\beta} = \mathbf{r}$, we have

$$\begin{aligned} \chi_T^2 &= [\mathbf{R}(\mathbf{b}_T - \boldsymbol{\beta})]'\left[s_T^2 \mathbf{R}(\Sigma \mathbf{x}_t \mathbf{x}_t')^{-1}\mathbf{R}'\right]^{-1}[\mathbf{R}(\mathbf{b}_T - \boldsymbol{\beta})] \\ &= [\sqrt{T} \cdot \mathbf{R}(\mathbf{b}_T - \boldsymbol{\beta})]'\left[s_T^2 \sqrt{T} \cdot \mathbf{R}(\Sigma \mathbf{x}_t \mathbf{x}_t')^{-1}\sqrt{T} \cdot \mathbf{R}'\right]^{-1}[\sqrt{T} \cdot \mathbf{R}(\mathbf{b}_T - \boldsymbol{\beta})]. \end{aligned}$$

For $\mathbf{Y}_T$ the $(k \times k)$ matrix defined in [18.2.18] and $\mathbf{R}$ of the specified form, observe that $\sqrt{T}\cdot\mathbf{R} = \mathbf{R}\mathbf{Y}_T$. Thus,

$$\begin{aligned}
\chi_T^2 &= [\mathbf{R}\mathbf{Y}_T(\mathbf{b}_T - \boldsymbol{\beta})]'\left[s_T^2\mathbf{R}\mathbf{Y}_T(\Sigma\mathbf{x}_t\mathbf{x}_t')^{-1}\mathbf{Y}_T\mathbf{R}'\right]^{-1}[\mathbf{R}\mathbf{Y}_T(\mathbf{b}_T - \boldsymbol{\beta})] \\
&= [\mathbf{R}\mathbf{Y}_T(\mathbf{b}_T - \boldsymbol{\beta})]'\left[s_T^2\mathbf{R}(\mathbf{Y}_T^{-1}\Sigma\mathbf{x}_t\mathbf{x}_t'\mathbf{Y}_T^{-1})^{-1}\mathbf{R}'\right]^{-1}[\mathbf{R}\mathbf{Y}_T(\mathbf{b}_T - \boldsymbol{\beta})] \\
&\xrightarrow{L} \left(\mathbf{R}\begin{bmatrix}\mathbf{V}^{-1}\mathbf{h}_1 \\ \mathbf{Q}^{-1}\mathbf{h}_2\end{bmatrix}\right)'\left(\sigma_{ii}\mathbf{R}\begin{bmatrix}\mathbf{V}^{-1} & \mathbf{0} \\ \mathbf{0} & \mathbf{Q}^{-1}\end{bmatrix}\mathbf{R}'\right)^{-1}\left(\mathbf{R}\begin{bmatrix}\mathbf{V}^{-1}\mathbf{h}_1 \\ \mathbf{Q}^{-1}\mathbf{h}_2\end{bmatrix}\right) \\
&= (\mathbf{R}_1\mathbf{V}^{-1}\mathbf{h}_1)'(\sigma_{ii}\mathbf{R}_1\mathbf{V}^{-1}\mathbf{R}_1')^{-1}(\mathbf{R}_1\mathbf{V}^{-1}\mathbf{h}_1),
\end{aligned}$$

where the indicated convergence follows from [18.2.25], [18.2.20], and consistency of $s_T^2$. Since $\mathbf{h}_1 \sim N(\mathbf{0}, \sigma_{ii}\mathbf{V})$, it follows that

$$\mathbf{R}_1\mathbf{V}^{-1}\mathbf{h}_1 \sim N(\mathbf{0}, \sigma_{ii}\mathbf{R}_1\mathbf{V}^{-1}\mathbf{R}_1').$$

Hence, from Proposition 8.1, the asymptotic distribution of $\chi_T^2$ is $\chi^2(m)$.

18.2. Here

$$\chi_T^2 \equiv (\mathbf{R}\mathbf{b}_T)'\left[s_T^2\mathbf{R}(\Sigma\mathbf{x}_t\mathbf{x}_t')^{-1}\mathbf{R}'\right]^{-1}(\mathbf{R}\mathbf{b}_T),$$

where $\mathbf{x}_t$ is as defined in Exercise 18.1 and

$$\underset{(n_2p\times k)}{\mathbf{R}} = \begin{bmatrix} \underset{[n_2(p-1)\times n(p-1)]}{(\mathbf{I}_{p-1}\otimes\mathbf{R}_1)} & \underset{[n_2(p-1)\times(n+1)]}{\mathbf{0}} \\ \underset{[n_2\times n(p-1)]}{\mathbf{0}} & \underset{[n_2\times(n+1)]}{\mathbf{R}_2} \end{bmatrix}$$

$$\underset{(n_2\times n)}{\mathbf{R}_1} = \begin{bmatrix} \underset{(n_2\times n_1)}{\mathbf{0}} & \underset{(n_2\times n_2)}{\mathbf{I}_{n_2}} \end{bmatrix}$$

$$\underset{[n_2\times(n+1)]}{\mathbf{R}_2} = \begin{bmatrix} \underset{(n_2\times 1)}{\mathbf{0}} & \underset{(n_2\times n)}{\mathbf{R}_1} \end{bmatrix}.$$

From the results of Exercise 18.1,

$$\begin{aligned}
\chi_T^2 &\xrightarrow{L} \left(\mathbf{R}\begin{bmatrix}\mathbf{V}^{-1}\mathbf{h}_1 \\ \mathbf{Q}^{-1}\mathbf{h}_2\end{bmatrix}\right)'\left(\sigma_{ii}\mathbf{R}\begin{bmatrix}\mathbf{V}^{-1} & \mathbf{0} \\ \mathbf{0} & \mathbf{Q}^{-1}\end{bmatrix}\mathbf{R}'\right)^{-1}\left(\mathbf{R}\begin{bmatrix}\mathbf{V}^{-1}\mathbf{h}_1 \\ \mathbf{Q}^{-1}\mathbf{h}_2\end{bmatrix}\right) \\
&= \begin{bmatrix}(\mathbf{I}_{p-1}\otimes\mathbf{R}_1)\mathbf{V}^{-1}\mathbf{h}_1 \\ \mathbf{R}_2\mathbf{Q}^{-1}\mathbf{h}_2\end{bmatrix}'\sigma_{ii}^{-1}\cdot\begin{bmatrix}(\mathbf{I}_{p-1}\otimes\mathbf{R}_1)\mathbf{V}^{-1}(\mathbf{I}_{p-1}\otimes\mathbf{R}_1') & \mathbf{0} \\ \mathbf{0} & \mathbf{R}_2\mathbf{Q}^{-1}\mathbf{R}_2'\end{bmatrix}^{-1} \\
&\quad\times\begin{bmatrix}(\mathbf{I}_{p-1}\otimes\mathbf{R}_1)\mathbf{V}^{-1}\mathbf{h}_1 \\ \mathbf{R}_2\mathbf{Q}^{-1}\mathbf{h}_2\end{bmatrix}.
\end{aligned}$$

18.3. (a) The null hypothesis is that $\phi = 1$ and $\gamma = \alpha = \eta = 0$, in which case $\Delta y_{2t} = \varepsilon_{2t}$ and $u_t = \varepsilon_{1t}$. Let $\mathbf{x}_t \equiv (\varepsilon_{2t}, 1, y_{1,t-1}, y_{2,t-1})'$ and

$$\mathbf{Y}_T \equiv \begin{bmatrix} T^{1/2} & 0 & 0 & 0 \\ 0 & T^{1/2} & 0 & 0 \\ 0 & 0 & T & 0 \\ 0 & 0 & 0 & T \end{bmatrix}.$$

Then

$$\begin{aligned}
&\mathbf{Y}_T^{-1}\Sigma\mathbf{x}_t\mathbf{x}_t'\mathbf{Y}_T^{-1} \\
&= \begin{bmatrix} T^{-1}\Sigma\varepsilon_{2t}^2 & T^{-1}\Sigma\varepsilon_{2t} & T^{-3/2}\Sigma\varepsilon_{2t}y_{1,t-1} & T^{-3/2}\Sigma\varepsilon_{2t}y_{2,t-1} \\ T^{-1}\Sigma\varepsilon_{2t} & 1 & T^{-3/2}\Sigma y_{1,t-1} & T^{-3/2}\Sigma y_{2,t-1} \\ T^{-3/2}\Sigma y_{1,t-1}\varepsilon_{2t} & T^{-3/2}\Sigma y_{1,t-1} & T^{-2}\Sigma y_{1,t-1}^2 & T^{-2}\Sigma y_{1,t-1}y_{2,t-1} \\ T^{-3/2}\Sigma y_{2,t-1}\varepsilon_{2t} & T^{-3/2}\Sigma y_{2,t-1} & T^{-2}\Sigma y_{2,t-1}y_{1,t-1} & T^{-2}\Sigma y_{2,t-1}^2 \end{bmatrix} \\
&\xrightarrow{L} \begin{bmatrix} \sigma_2^2 & \mathbf{0}' \\ \mathbf{0} & \mathbf{Q} \end{bmatrix},
\end{aligned}$$

where

$$\mathbf{Q} \equiv \begin{bmatrix} 1 & \sigma_1 \cdot \int W_1(r)\,dr & \sigma_2 \cdot \int W_2(r)\,dr \\ \sigma_1 \cdot \int W_1(r)\,dr & \sigma_1^2 \cdot \int [W_1(r)]^2\,dr & \sigma_1\sigma_2 \cdot \int [W_1(r)]\cdot[W_2(r)]\,dr \\ \sigma_2 \cdot \int W_2(r)\,dr & \sigma_2\sigma_1 \cdot \int [W_2(r)]\cdot[W_1(r)]\,dr & \sigma_2^2 \cdot \int [W_2(r)]^2\,dr \end{bmatrix}$$

and

$$\mathbf{Y}_T^{-1}\Sigma\mathbf{x}_t u_t = \begin{bmatrix} T^{-1/2}\Sigma\varepsilon_{2t}\varepsilon_{1t} \\ T^{-1/2}\Sigma\varepsilon_{1t} \\ T^{-1}\Sigma y_{1,t-1}\varepsilon_{1t} \\ T^{-1}\Sigma y_{2,t-1}\varepsilon_{1t} \end{bmatrix} \xrightarrow{L} \begin{bmatrix} h_1 \\ \mathbf{h}_2 \end{bmatrix},$$

and where $h_1 \sim N(0, \sigma_1^2\sigma_2^2)$ and the second and third elements of the $(3 \times 1)$ vector $\mathbf{h}_2$ have a nonstandard distribution. Hence,

$$\begin{aligned} \mathbf{Y}_T(\mathbf{b}_T - \boldsymbol{\beta}) &= (\mathbf{Y}_T^{-1}\Sigma\mathbf{x}_t\mathbf{x}_t'\mathbf{Y}_T^{-1})^{-1}(\mathbf{Y}_T^{-1}\Sigma\mathbf{x}_t u_t) \\ &\xrightarrow{L} \begin{bmatrix} \sigma_2^2 & \mathbf{0}' \\ \mathbf{0} & \mathbf{Q} \end{bmatrix}^{-1} \begin{bmatrix} h_1 \\ \mathbf{h}_2 \end{bmatrix} \\ &= \begin{bmatrix} \sigma_2^{-2}h_1 \\ \mathbf{Q}^{-1}\mathbf{h}_2 \end{bmatrix}. \end{aligned}$$

(b) Let $\mathbf{e}_1$ denote the first column of the $(4 \times 4)$ identity matrix. Then

$$\begin{aligned} t_T &= \hat{\gamma}_T \div \left\{s_T^2\,\mathbf{e}_1'(\Sigma\mathbf{x}_t\mathbf{x}_t')^{-1}\mathbf{e}_1\right\}^{1/2} \\ &= T^{1/2}\hat{\gamma}_T \div \left\{s_T^2\mathbf{e}_1'\mathbf{Y}_T(\Sigma\mathbf{x}_t\mathbf{x}_t')^{-1}\mathbf{Y}_T\mathbf{e}_1\right\}^{1/2} \\ &= T^{1/2}\hat{\gamma}_T \div \left\{s_T^2\mathbf{e}_1'(\mathbf{Y}_T^{-1}\Sigma\mathbf{x}_t\mathbf{x}_t'\mathbf{Y}_T^{-1})^{-1}\mathbf{e}_1\right\}^{1/2} \\ &\xrightarrow{L} \sigma_2^{-2}h_1 \div \left\{\sigma_1^2\mathbf{e}_1'\begin{bmatrix} \sigma_2^2 & \mathbf{0}' \\ \mathbf{0} & \mathbf{Q} \end{bmatrix}^{-1}\mathbf{e}_1\right\}^{1/2} \\ &= h_1/(\sigma_1\sigma_2) \sim N(0, 1). \end{aligned}$$

(c) Recall that $\hat{\delta}_T = \hat{\eta}_T - \hat{\gamma}_T$, where $\hat{\eta}_T$ is $O_p(T^{-1})$ and $\hat{\gamma}_T$ is $O_p(T^{-1/2})$. Under the null hypothesis, all three values are zero; hence,

$$T^{1/2}\hat{\delta}_T \xrightarrow{p} -T^{1/2}\hat{\gamma}_T,$$

which is asymptotically Gaussian. The $t$ test of $\delta = 0$ is asymptotically equivalent to the $t$ test of $\gamma = 0$.

## *Chapter 19. Cointegration*

19.1. (a) The *OLS* estimates are given by

$$\begin{bmatrix} \hat{\alpha}_T \\ \hat{\gamma}_T \end{bmatrix} = \begin{bmatrix} T & \Sigma y_{2t} \\ \Sigma y_{2t} & \Sigma y_{2t}^2 \end{bmatrix}^{-1} \begin{bmatrix} \Sigma y_{1t} \\ \Sigma y_{2t}y_{1t} \end{bmatrix},$$

from which

$$\begin{aligned} \begin{bmatrix} \hat{\alpha}_T \\ \hat{\gamma}_T - \gamma_0 \end{bmatrix} &= \begin{bmatrix} T & \Sigma y_{2t} \\ \Sigma y_{2t} & \Sigma y_{2t}^2 \end{bmatrix}^{-1} \left\{ \begin{bmatrix} \Sigma y_{1t} \\ \Sigma y_{2t}y_{1t} \end{bmatrix} - \gamma_0 \begin{bmatrix} \Sigma y_{2t} \\ \Sigma y_{2t}^2 \end{bmatrix} \right\} \\ &= \begin{bmatrix} T & \Sigma y_{2t} \\ \Sigma y_{2t} & \Sigma y_{2t}^2 \end{bmatrix}^{-1} \begin{bmatrix} \Sigma(y_{1t} - \gamma_0 y_{2t}) \\ \Sigma y_{2t}(y_{1t} - \gamma_0 y_{2t}) \end{bmatrix} \end{aligned}$$

and

$$\begin{bmatrix} T^{-1/2} & 0 \\ 0 & T^{1/2} \end{bmatrix}\begin{bmatrix} \hat{\alpha}_T \\ \hat{\gamma}_T - \gamma_0 \end{bmatrix} = \begin{bmatrix} T^{-1/2} & 0 \\ 0 & T^{1/2} \end{bmatrix}\begin{bmatrix} T & \Sigma y_{2t} \\ \Sigma y_{2t} & \Sigma y_{2t}^2 \end{bmatrix}^{-1}\begin{bmatrix} T^{-3/2} & 0 \\ 0 & T^{-5/2} \end{bmatrix}^{-1}$$

$$\times \begin{bmatrix} T^{-3/2} & 0 \\ 0 & T^{-5/2} \end{bmatrix}\begin{bmatrix} \Sigma(y_{1t} - \gamma_0 y_{2t}) \\ \Sigma y_{2t}(y_{1t} - \gamma_0 y_{2t}) \end{bmatrix}$$

$$= \left\{\begin{bmatrix} T^{-3/2} & 0 \\ 0 & T^{-5/2} \end{bmatrix}\begin{bmatrix} T & \Sigma y_{2t} \\ \Sigma y_{2t} & \Sigma y_{2t}^2 \end{bmatrix}\begin{bmatrix} T^{1/2} & 0 \\ 0 & T^{-1/2} \end{bmatrix}\right\}^{-1}$$

$$\times \begin{bmatrix} T^{-3/2} & 0 \\ 0 & T^{-5/2} \end{bmatrix}\begin{bmatrix} \Sigma(y_{1t} - \gamma_0 y_{2t}) \\ \Sigma y_{2t}(y_{1t} - \gamma_0 y_{2t}) \end{bmatrix}$$

$$= \begin{bmatrix} 1 & T^{-2}\Sigma y_{2t} \\ T^{-2}\Sigma y_{2t} & T^{-3}\Sigma y_{2t}^2 \end{bmatrix}^{-1}\begin{bmatrix} T^{-3/2}\Sigma(y_{1t} - \gamma_0 y_{2t}) \\ T^{-5/2}\Sigma y_{2t}(y_{1t} - \gamma_0 y_{2t}) \end{bmatrix}.$$

But

$$\Sigma y_{2t} = \underbrace{Ty_{2,0}}_{O_p(T)} + \underbrace{\delta_2 \cdot \Sigma t}_{O_p(T^2)} + \underbrace{\Sigma \xi_{2t}}_{O_p(T^{3/2})},$$

and thus $T^{-2}\Sigma y_{2t} \xrightarrow{p} T^{-2}\delta_2 \cdot \Sigma t \to \delta_2/2$. Similarly, $T^{-3}\Sigma y_{2t}^2 \xrightarrow{p} T^{-3}\delta_2^2 \cdot \Sigma t^2 \to \delta_2^2/3$. Furthermore,

$$\Sigma(y_{1t} - \gamma_0 y_{2t}) = \underbrace{T(y_{1,0} - \gamma_0 y_{2,0})}_{O_p(T)} + \underbrace{\Sigma(\xi_{1t} - \gamma_0 \xi_{2t})}_{O_p(T^{3/2})},$$

establishing that $T^{-3/2}\Sigma(y_{1t} - \gamma_0 y_{2t}) \xrightarrow{p} T^{-3/2}\Sigma(\xi_{1t} - \gamma_0 \xi_{2t})$. Similarly,

$$\Sigma y_{2t}(y_{1t} - \gamma_0 y_{2t}) = \Sigma(y_{2,0} + \delta_2 t + \xi_{2t})(y_{1,0} + \xi_{1t} - \gamma_0 y_{2,0} - \gamma_0 \xi_{2t})$$

and $T^{-5/2}\Sigma y_{2t}(y_{1t} - \gamma_0 y_{2t}) \xrightarrow{p} T^{-5/2}\Sigma \delta_2 t(\xi_{1t} - \gamma_0 \xi_{2t})$.

(b) $$\begin{aligned} \Delta \hat{u}_t &= (y_{1t} - \hat{\alpha}_T - \hat{\gamma}_T y_{2t}) - (y_{1,t-1} - \hat{\alpha}_T - \hat{\gamma}_T y_{2,t-1}) \\ &= \Delta y_{1t} - \hat{\gamma}_T \Delta y_{2t} \\ &\xrightarrow{p} \Delta y_{1t} - \gamma_0 \Delta y_{2t}, \end{aligned}$$

since $\hat{\gamma}_T \xrightarrow{p} \gamma_0$.

19.2. Proposition 18.1 is used to show that

$$\begin{bmatrix} T^{1/2}(\hat{\boldsymbol{\beta}}_T - \boldsymbol{\beta}) \\ T^{1/2}(\hat{\alpha}_T - \alpha) \\ T(\hat{\boldsymbol{\gamma}}_T - \boldsymbol{\gamma}) \end{bmatrix} = \begin{bmatrix} T^{-1}\Sigma \mathbf{w}_t \mathbf{w}_t' & T^{-1}\Sigma \mathbf{w}_t & T^{-3/2}\Sigma \mathbf{w}_t \mathbf{y}_{2t}' \\ T^{-1}\Sigma \mathbf{w}_t' & 1 & T^{-3/2}\Sigma \mathbf{y}_{2t}' \\ T^{-3/2}\Sigma \mathbf{y}_{2t}\mathbf{w}_t' & T^{-3/2}\Sigma \mathbf{y}_{2t} & T^{-2}\Sigma \mathbf{y}_{2t}\mathbf{y}_{2t}' \end{bmatrix}^{-1}\begin{bmatrix} T^{-1/2}\Sigma \mathbf{w}_t \tilde{z}_t \\ T^{-1/2}\Sigma \tilde{z}_t \\ T^{-1}\Sigma \mathbf{y}_{2t}\tilde{z}_t \end{bmatrix}$$

$$\xrightarrow{L} \begin{bmatrix} \mathbf{Q} & \mathbf{0} & \mathbf{0} \\ \mathbf{0}' & 1 & \left\{\int [\mathbf{W}_2(r)]'\, dr\right\}\tilde{\boldsymbol{\Lambda}}_{22}' \\ \mathbf{0} & \tilde{\boldsymbol{\Lambda}}_{22}\int \mathbf{W}_2(r)\, dr & \tilde{\boldsymbol{\Lambda}}_{22}\left\{\int [\mathbf{W}_2(r)]\cdot[\mathbf{W}_2(r)]'\, dr\right\}\tilde{\boldsymbol{\Lambda}}_{22}' \end{bmatrix}^{-1}$$

$$\times \begin{bmatrix} \mathbf{h}_1 \\ \tilde{\lambda}_{11}\cdot W_1(1) \\ \tilde{\boldsymbol{\Lambda}}_{22}\cdot\left\{\int [\mathbf{W}_2(r)]\, dW_1(r)\right\}\cdot\tilde{\lambda}_{11} \end{bmatrix},$$

as claimed.

19.3. Notice as in [19.3.13] that under the null hypothesis,

$$\chi_T^2 = \{\mathbf{R}_\gamma \cdot T(\hat{\boldsymbol{\gamma}}_T - \boldsymbol{\gamma})\}' \left\{ s_T^2 [\mathbf{0} \quad \mathbf{0} \quad \mathbf{R}_\gamma] \right.$$

$$\left. \times \begin{bmatrix} T^{-1}\Sigma \mathbf{w}_t \mathbf{w}_t' & T^{-1}\Sigma \mathbf{w}_t & T^{-3/2}\Sigma \mathbf{w}_t \mathbf{y}_{2t}' \\ T^{-1}\Sigma \mathbf{w}_t' & 1 & T^{-3/2}\Sigma \mathbf{y}_{2t}' \\ T^{-3/2}\Sigma \mathbf{y}_{2t}\mathbf{w}_t' & T^{-3/2}\Sigma \mathbf{y}_{2t} & T^{-2}\Sigma \mathbf{y}_{2t}\mathbf{y}_{2t}' \end{bmatrix}^{-1} \begin{bmatrix} \mathbf{0} \\ \mathbf{0}' \\ \mathbf{R}_\gamma' \end{bmatrix} \right\}^{-1} \{\mathbf{R}_\gamma \cdot T(\hat{\boldsymbol{\gamma}}_T - \boldsymbol{\gamma})\}$$

$$\xrightarrow{p} [\mathbf{R}_\gamma \tilde{\lambda}_{11} \boldsymbol{\nu}_2]' \left\{ s_T^2 [\mathbf{0} \quad \mathbf{0} \quad \mathbf{R}_\gamma] \right.$$

$$\left. \times \begin{bmatrix} \mathbf{Q} & \mathbf{0} & \mathbf{0} \\ \mathbf{0}' & 1 & \left\{ \int [\mathbf{W}_2(r)]'\, dr \right\} \tilde{\boldsymbol{\Lambda}}_{22}' \\ \mathbf{0} & \tilde{\boldsymbol{\Lambda}}_{22} \int \mathbf{W}_2(r)\, dr & \tilde{\boldsymbol{\Lambda}}_{22} \left\{ \int [\mathbf{W}_2(r)] \cdot [\mathbf{W}_2(r)]'\, dr \right\} \tilde{\boldsymbol{\Lambda}}_{22}' \end{bmatrix}^{-1} \begin{bmatrix} \mathbf{0} \\ \mathbf{0}' \\ \mathbf{R}_\gamma' \end{bmatrix} \right\}^{-1} [\mathbf{R}_\gamma \tilde{\lambda}_{11} \boldsymbol{\nu}_2],$$

from which [19.3.25] follows immediately.

19.4.

$$\begin{bmatrix} T^{1/2}(\hat{\boldsymbol{\beta}}_T - \boldsymbol{\beta}) \\ T^{1/2}(\hat{\alpha}_T - \alpha) \\ T(\hat{\boldsymbol{\gamma}}_T - \boldsymbol{\gamma}) \\ T^{3/2}(\hat{\delta}_T - \delta) \end{bmatrix} = \begin{bmatrix} T^{-1}\Sigma \mathbf{w}_t \mathbf{w}_t' & T^{-1}\Sigma \mathbf{w}_t & T^{-3/2}\Sigma \mathbf{w}_t \mathbf{y}_{2t}' & T^{-2}\Sigma \mathbf{w}_t t \\ T^{-1}\Sigma \mathbf{w}_t' & 1 & T^{-3/2}\Sigma \mathbf{y}_{2t}' & T^{-2}\Sigma t \\ T^{-3/2}\Sigma \mathbf{y}_{2t}\mathbf{w}_t' & T^{-3/2}\Sigma \mathbf{y}_{2t} & T^{-2}\Sigma \mathbf{y}_{2t}\mathbf{y}_{2t}' & T^{-5/2}\Sigma \mathbf{y}_{2t} t \\ T^{-2}\Sigma t \mathbf{w}_t' & T^{-2}\Sigma t & T^{-5/2}\Sigma t \mathbf{y}_{2t}' & T^{-3}\Sigma t^2 \end{bmatrix}^{-1}$$

$$\times \begin{bmatrix} T^{-1/2}\Sigma \mathbf{w}_t u_t \\ T^{-1/2}\Sigma u_t \\ T^{-1}\Sigma \mathbf{y}_{2t} u_t \\ T^{-3/2}\Sigma t u_t \end{bmatrix}$$

$$\xrightarrow{L} \begin{bmatrix} \mathbf{Q} & \mathbf{0} & \mathbf{0} & \mathbf{0} \\ \mathbf{0}' & 1 & \left\{ \int [\mathbf{W}_2(r)]'\, dr \right\} \tilde{\boldsymbol{\Lambda}}_{22}' & 1/2 \\ \mathbf{0} & \tilde{\boldsymbol{\Lambda}}_{22} \int \mathbf{W}_2(r)\, dr & \tilde{\boldsymbol{\Lambda}}_{22} \left\{ \int [\mathbf{W}_2(r)] \cdot [\mathbf{W}_2(r)]'\, dr \right\} \tilde{\boldsymbol{\Lambda}}_{22}' & \tilde{\boldsymbol{\Lambda}}_{22} \int r \mathbf{W}_2(r)\, dr \\ \mathbf{0}' & 1/2 & \left\{ \int r [\mathbf{W}_2(r)]'\, dr \right\} \tilde{\boldsymbol{\Lambda}}_{22}' & 1/3 \end{bmatrix}^{-1}$$

$$\times \begin{bmatrix} \mathbf{h}_1 \\ \tilde{\lambda}_{11} W_1(1) \\ \tilde{\boldsymbol{\Lambda}}_{22} \left\{ \int [\mathbf{W}_2(r)]\, dW_1(r) \right\} \tilde{\lambda}_{11} \\ \tilde{\lambda}_{11} \left\{ W_1(1) - \int W_1(r)\, dr \right\} \end{bmatrix},$$

as claimed.

## *Chapter 20. Full-Information Maximum Likelihood Analysis of Cointegrated Systems*

20.1. Form the Lagrangean

$$\mathbf{k}_1' \boldsymbol{\Sigma}_{\mathbf{YX}} \mathbf{a}_1 + \mu_k (1 - \mathbf{k}_1' \boldsymbol{\Sigma}_{\mathbf{YY}} \mathbf{k}_1) + \mu_a (1 - \mathbf{a}_1' \boldsymbol{\Sigma}_{\mathbf{XX}} \mathbf{a}_1),$$

with $\mu_k$ and $\mu_a$ Lagrange multipliers. First-order conditions are

$$\text{(a)}\quad \mathbf{\Sigma_{YX}a}_1 = 2\mu_k\mathbf{\Sigma_{YY}k}_1$$

$$\text{(b)}\quad \mathbf{\Sigma_{XY}k}_1 = 2\mu_a\mathbf{\Sigma_{XX}a}_1.$$

Premultiply (a) by $\mathbf{k}_1'$ and (b) by $\mathbf{a}_1'$ to deduce that

$$2\mu_k = 2\mu_a \equiv r_1.$$

Next, premultiply (a) by $r_1^{-1}\mathbf{\Sigma_{YY}^{-1}}$ and substitute the result into (b):

$$\mathbf{\Sigma_{XY}\Sigma_{YY}^{-1}\Sigma_{YX}a}_1 = r_1^2\mathbf{\Sigma_{XX}a}_1$$

or

$$\mathbf{\Sigma_{XX}^{-1}\Sigma_{XY}\Sigma_{YY}^{-1}\Sigma_{YX}a}_1 = r_1^2\mathbf{a}_1.$$

Thus, $r_1^2$ is an eigenvalue of $\mathbf{\Sigma_{XX}^{-1}\Sigma_{XY}\Sigma_{YY}^{-1}\Sigma_{YX}}$ with $\mathbf{a}_1$ the associated eigenvector, as claimed.

Similarly, premultiplying (b) by $r_1^{-1}\mathbf{\Sigma_{XX}^{-1}}$ and substituting the result into (a) reveals that

$$\mathbf{\Sigma_{YY}^{-1}\Sigma_{YX}\Sigma_{XX}^{-1}\Sigma_{XY}k}_1 = r_1^2\mathbf{k}_1.$$

20.2. The restriction when $h = 0$ is that $\boldsymbol{\zeta}_0 = \mathbf{0}$. In this case, [20.3.2] would be

$$\mathcal{L}_0^* = -(Tn/2)\log(2\pi) - (Tn/2) - (T/2)\log|\hat{\mathbf{\Sigma}}_{\mathbf{UU}}|,$$

where $\hat{\mathbf{\Sigma}}_{\mathbf{UU}}$ is the variance-covariance matrix for the residuals of [20.2.4]. This will be recognized from expression [11.1.32] as the maximum value attained for the log likelihood for the model

$$\Delta\mathbf{y}_t = \boldsymbol{\pi}_0 + \mathbf{\Pi}_1\Delta\mathbf{y}_{t-1} + \mathbf{\Pi}_2\Delta\mathbf{y}_{t-2} + \cdots + \mathbf{\Pi}_{p-1}\Delta\mathbf{y}_{t-p+1} + \mathbf{u}_t,$$

as claimed.

20.3. The residuals $\hat{\mathbf{g}}_t$ are the same as the residuals from an unrestricted regression of $\hat{\mathbf{u}}_t$ on $\hat{\mathbf{v}}_t$. The *MSE* matrix for the latter regression is given by $\hat{\mathbf{\Sigma}}_{\mathbf{UU}} - \hat{\mathbf{\Sigma}}_{\mathbf{UV}}\hat{\mathbf{\Sigma}}_{\mathbf{VV}}^{-1}\hat{\mathbf{\Sigma}}_{\mathbf{VU}}$. Thus,

$$\begin{aligned}|\hat{\mathbf{\Sigma}}_{\mathbf{GG}}| &= |\hat{\mathbf{\Sigma}}_{\mathbf{UU}} - \hat{\mathbf{\Sigma}}_{\mathbf{UV}}\hat{\mathbf{\Sigma}}_{\mathbf{VV}}^{-1}\hat{\mathbf{\Sigma}}_{\mathbf{VU}}| \\ &= |\hat{\mathbf{\Sigma}}_{\mathbf{UU}}|\cdot|\mathbf{I}_n - \hat{\mathbf{\Sigma}}_{\mathbf{UU}}^{-1}\hat{\mathbf{\Sigma}}_{\mathbf{UV}}\hat{\mathbf{\Sigma}}_{\mathbf{VV}}^{-1}\hat{\mathbf{\Sigma}}_{\mathbf{VU}}| \\ &= |\hat{\mathbf{\Sigma}}_{\mathbf{UU}}|\cdot\prod_{i=1}^{n}\theta_i,\end{aligned}$$

where $\theta_i$ denotes the $i$th eigenvalue of $\mathbf{I}_n - \hat{\mathbf{\Sigma}}_{\mathbf{UU}}^{-1}\hat{\mathbf{\Sigma}}_{\mathbf{UV}}\hat{\mathbf{\Sigma}}_{\mathbf{VV}}^{-1}\hat{\mathbf{\Sigma}}_{\mathbf{VU}}$. Recalling that $\lambda_i$ is an eigenvalue of $\hat{\mathbf{\Sigma}}_{\mathbf{UU}}^{-1}\hat{\mathbf{\Sigma}}_{\mathbf{UV}}\hat{\mathbf{\Sigma}}_{\mathbf{VV}}^{-1}\hat{\mathbf{\Sigma}}_{\mathbf{VU}}$ associated with the eigenvector $\mathbf{k}_i$, we have that

$$\left[\mathbf{I}_n - \hat{\mathbf{\Sigma}}_{\mathbf{UU}}^{-1}\hat{\mathbf{\Sigma}}_{\mathbf{UV}}\hat{\mathbf{\Sigma}}_{\mathbf{VV}}^{-1}\hat{\mathbf{\Sigma}}_{\mathbf{VU}}\right]\mathbf{k}_i = (1 - \lambda_i)\mathbf{k}_i,$$

so that $\theta_i = (1 - \lambda_i)$ is an eigenvalue of $\mathbf{I}_n - \hat{\mathbf{\Sigma}}_{\mathbf{UU}}^{-1}\hat{\mathbf{\Sigma}}_{\mathbf{UV}}\hat{\mathbf{\Sigma}}_{\mathbf{VV}}^{-1}\hat{\mathbf{\Sigma}}_{\mathbf{VU}}$ and

$$|\hat{\mathbf{\Sigma}}_{\mathbf{GG}}| = |\hat{\mathbf{\Sigma}}_{\mathbf{UU}}|\cdot\prod_{i=1}^{n}(1 - \lambda_i).$$

Hence, the two expressions are equivalent.

20.4. Here, $\hat{\lambda}_1$ is the scalar

$$\hat{\lambda}_1 = \hat{\Sigma}_{VV}^{-1}\hat{\Sigma}_{VU}\hat{\Sigma}_{UU}^{-1}\hat{\Sigma}_{UV}$$

and the test statistic is

$$-T\log(1 - \hat{\lambda}_1) = -T\log[(\hat{\Sigma}_{UU}^{-1})\cdot(\hat{\Sigma}_{UU} - \hat{\Sigma}_{UV}\hat{\Sigma}_{VV}^{-1}\hat{\Sigma}_{VU})].$$

But $\hat{u}_t$ is the residual from a regression of $\Delta y_t$ on a constant and $\Delta y_{t-1}, \Delta y_{t-2}, \ldots, \Delta y_{t-p+1}$, meaning that $\hat{\Sigma}_{UU} = \hat{\sigma}_0^2$. Likewise, $\hat{v}_t$ is the residual from a regression of $y_{t-1}$ on $\Delta y_{t-1}$, $\Delta y_{t-2}, \ldots, \Delta y_{t-p+1}$. The residual from a regression of $\hat{u}_t$ on $\hat{v}_t$, whose average squared value is given by $(\hat{\Sigma}_{UU} - \hat{\Sigma}_{UV}\hat{\Sigma}_{VV}^{-1}\hat{\Sigma}_{VU})$, is the same as the residual from a regression of $y_t$ on a constant, $y_{t-1}$, and $\Delta y_{t-1}, \Delta y_{t-2}, \ldots, \Delta y_{t-p+1}$, whose average squared value is denoted $\hat{\sigma}_1^2$:

$$(\hat{\Sigma}_{UU} - \hat{\Sigma}_{UV}\hat{\Sigma}_{VV}^{-1}\hat{\Sigma}_{VU}) = \hat{\sigma}_1^2.$$

Hence, the test statistic is equivalent to $T[\log(\hat{\sigma}_0^2) - \log(\hat{\sigma}_1^2)]$, as claimed.

## Chapter 22. Modeling Time Series with Changes in Regime

22.1. $$\mathbf{PT} = \begin{bmatrix} p_{11} & 1 - p_{22} \\ 1 - p_{11} & p_{22} \end{bmatrix} \times \begin{bmatrix} (1 - p_{22})/(2 - p_{11} - p_{22}) & -1 \\ (1 - p_{11})/(2 - p_{11} - p_{22}) & 1 \end{bmatrix}$$

$$= \begin{bmatrix} (1 - p_{22})\left(\dfrac{p_{11}}{2 - p_{11} - p_{22}} + \dfrac{1 - p_{11}}{2 - p_{11} - p_{22}}\right) & 1 - p_{11} - p_{22} \\ (1 - p_{11})\left(\dfrac{1 - p_{22}}{2 - p_{11} - p_{22}} + \dfrac{p_{22}}{2 - p_{11} - p_{22}}\right) & -1 + p_{11} + p_{22} \end{bmatrix}$$

$$= \begin{bmatrix} (1 - p_{22})/(2 - p_{11} - p_{22}) & -\lambda_2 \\ (1 - p_{11})/(2 - p_{11} - p_{22}) & \lambda_2 \end{bmatrix}$$

$$= \mathbf{T\Lambda}.$$

# D

# *Greek Letters and Mathematical Symbols Used in the Text*

**Greek letters and common interpretation**

| | | |
|---|---|---|
| alpha | $\alpha$ | population linear projection coefficient (page 74) |
| beta | $\boldsymbol{\beta}$ | population regression coefficient (page 200) |
| gamma | $\boldsymbol{\Gamma}$ | autocovariance matrix for vector process (page 261) |
| | $\gamma$ | autocovariance for scalar process (page 45) |
| delta | $\Delta$ | change in value of variable (page 436) |
| | $\delta$ | small number;<br>coefficient on time trend (page 435) |
| epsilon | $\varepsilon$ | a white noise variable (page 47) |
| zeta | $\zeta$ | constant term in *ARCH* specification (page 658) |
| eta | $\eta$ | $AR(\infty)$ coefficient (page 79) |
| theta | $\boldsymbol{\Theta}$ | matrix of moving average coefficients (page 262) |
| | $\boldsymbol{\theta}$ | vector of population parameters (page 747) |
| | $\theta$ | scalar $MA(q)$ coefficient (page 50) |
| kappa | $\kappa$ | kernel (page 165) |
| lambda | $\boldsymbol{\Lambda}$ | matrix of eigenvalues (page 730) |
| | $\lambda$ | individual eigenvalue (page 729)<br>Lagrange multiplier (page 135) |
| mu | $\mu$ | population mean (page 739) |
| nu | $\nu$ | degrees of freedom (page 409) |
| xi | $\boldsymbol{\Xi}$ | matrix of derivatives (page 339) |
| | $\boldsymbol{\xi}$ | state vector (pages 7 and 372) |
| pi | $\Pi$ | product (page 747) |
| | $\pi$ | the number 3.14159.... |
| rho | $\rho$ | autocorrelation (page 49)<br>autoregressive coefficient (page 517) |
| sigma | $\sum$ | summation |
| | $\boldsymbol{\Sigma}$ | long-run variance-covariance matrix (page 614) |
| | $\sigma$ | population standard deviation (page 745) |
| tau | $\tau$ | time index |
| upsilon | $\boldsymbol{\Upsilon}$ | scaling matrix to calculate asymptotic distributions (page 457) |
| phi | $\boldsymbol{\Phi}$ | matrix of autoregressive coefficients (page 257) |
| | $\phi$ | scalar autoregressive coefficient (page 53) |
| chi | $\chi$ | a variable with a chi-square distribution (page 746) |
| psi | $\boldsymbol{\Psi}$ | matrix of moving average coefficients for vector $MA(\infty)$ process (page 262) |
| | $\psi$ | moving average coefficient for scalar $MA(\infty)$ process (page 52) |
| omega | $\boldsymbol{\Omega}$ | variance-covariance matrix (page 748) |
| | $\omega$ | frequency (page 153) |

## Common uses of other letters

| | |
|---|---|
| $a$ | number of elements of unknown parameter vector (page 135) |
| $\mathbf{b}$ or $\mathbf{b}_T$ | estimated *OLS* regression coefficient based on sample of size $T$ (page 75) |
| $\mathbf{c}$ | vector of constant terms for vector autoregression (page 257) |
| $c$ | constant term in univariate autoregression (page 53) |
| $\mathbf{e}_i$ | the $i$th column of the identity matrix |
| $e$ | the base for the natural logarithms (page 715) |
| $\mathbf{I}_n$ | the $(n \times n)$ identity matrix (page 722) |
| $i$ | the square root of negative one (page 708) |
| $J$ | value of Lagrangean (page 135) |
| $k$ | the number of explanatory variables in a regression |
| $L$ | the lag operator (page 26) |
| $\mathscr{L}$ | value of log likelihood function (page 747) |
| $n$ | number of variables observed at date $t$ in a vector system (page 257) |
| $O_p(T)$ | order $T$ in probability (page 460) |
| $\mathbf{P}_{\tau\|t}$ | *MSE* matrix for inference about state vector (page 378) |
| $p$ | the order of an autoregressive process (page 58) |
| $\mathbf{Q}$ | limiting value of $(\mathbf{X}'\mathbf{X}/T)$ for $\mathbf{X}$ the $(T \times k)$ matrix of explanatory variables for an *OLS* regression (page 208); variance-covariance matrix of disturbances in state equation (page 373) |
| $q$ | the order of a moving average process (page 50); number of autocovariances used in Newey-West estimate (page 281) |
| $\mathbf{R}$ | variance-covariance matrix of disturbances in observation equation (page 373) |
| $\mathbb{R}^n$ | the set consisting of all real $n$-dimensional vectors (page 737) |
| $r$ | number of variables in state equation (page 372); index of date for a continuous-time process |
| $s^2$ or $s_T^2$ | unbiased estimate of residual variance for an *OLS* regression with sample of size $T$ (page 203) |
| $s_t$ | state at date $t$ for a Markov chain |
| $T$ | the number of dates included in a sample |
| $\mathbf{X}$ | $(T \times k)$ matrix of explanatory variables for an *OLS* regression (page 201) |
| $\mathcal{Y}_t$ | history of observations through date $t$ (page 143) |
| $z$ | argument of autocovariance generating function (page 61) |

## Mathematical symbols

| | |
|---|---|
| $\aleph$ | aleph (first letter of the Hebrew alphabet), used for matrix of regression coefficients (page 636) |
| $\exp(x)$ | the number $e$ (the base for natural logarithms) raised to the $x$ power (page 715) |
| $\log(x)$ | natural logarithm of $x$ (page 717) |
| $x!$ | $x$ factorial (page 713) |
| $[x(L)]_+$ | annihilation operator (page 78) |
| $[x]^*$ | greatest integer less than or equal to $x$ |
| $\|x\|$ | absolute value of a real scalar or modulus of a complex scalar $x$ (page 709) |
| $\|\mathbf{X}\|$ | determinant of a square matrix $\mathbf{X}$ (page 724) |
| $\mathbf{X}'$ | transpose of the matrix $\mathbf{X}$ (page 723) |
| $\mathbf{0}_{nm}$ | an $(n \times m)$ matrix of zeros |
| $\mathbf{0}'$ | a $(1 \times n)$ row vector of zeros |
| $\nabla$ | gradient vector (page 735) |
| $\otimes$ | Kronecker product (page 732) |

| | |
|---|---|
| $\odot$ | element-by-element multiplication (page 692) |
| $y \cong x$ | $y$ is approximately equal to $x$ |
| $y \equiv x$ | $y$ is defined to be the value represented by $x$ |
| $\max\{y,x\}$ | the value given by the larger of $y$ or $x$ |
| $y = \sup_{r \in [0,1]} f(r)$ | $y$ is the smallest number such that $y \geq f(r)$ for all $r$ in [0,1] (page 481) |
| $x \in A$ | $x$ is an element of $A$ |
| $A \subset B$ | $A$ is a subset of $B$ (page 189) |
| $P\{\text{A}\}$ | probability that event $A$ occurs (page 739) |
| $f_Y(y)$ | probability density of the random variable $Y$ (page 739) |
| $Y \sim N(\mu,\sigma^2)$ | $Y$ has a $N(\mu,\sigma^2)$ distribution (page 745) |
| $Y \approx N(\mu,\sigma^2$ | $Y$ has a distribution that is approximately $N(\mu,\sigma^2)$ (page 210) |
| $E(X)$ | expectation of $X$ (page 740) |
| $\text{Var}(X)$ | variance of $X$ (page 740) |
| $\text{Cov}(X,Y)$ | covariance between $X$ and $Y$ (page 742) |
| $\text{Corr}(X,Y)$ | correlation between $X$ and $Y$ (page 743) |
| $Y\|X$ | $Y$ conditional on $X$ (page 741) |
| $\hat{P}(Y\|X)$ | linear projection of $Y$ on $X$ (pages 74–75) |
| $\hat{E}(Y\|X)$ | linear projection of $Y$ on $X$ and a constant (pages 74–75) |
| $\hat{y}_{t+s\|t}$ | linear projection of $y_{t+s}$ on a constant and a set of variables observed at date $t$ (page 74) |
| $x_T \rightarrow y$ | $\lim_{T\to\infty} x_T = y$ (page 180) |
| $x_T \xrightarrow{p} y$ | $x_T$ converges in probability to $y$ (pages 181, 749) |
| $x_T \xrightarrow{m.s.} y$ | $x_T$ converges in mean square to $y$ (pages 182, 749) |
| $x_T \xrightarrow{L} y$ | $x_T$ converges in distribution to $y$ (page 184) |
| $x_T(\cdot) \xrightarrow{p} x(\cdot)$ | the sequence of functions whose value at $r$ is $x_T(r)$ converges in probability to the function whose value at $r$ is $x(r)$ (page 481) |
| $x_T(\cdot) \xrightarrow{L} x(\cdot)$ | the sequence of functions whose value at $r$ is $x_T(r)$ converges in probability law to the function whose value at $r$ is $x(r)$ (page 481) |

# Author Index

# Subject Index

## *C*



## *D*

## *H*



## *I*



## *J*



## *K*



## *L*

## *M*